THE YEARBOOK OF WORLD SOCCER

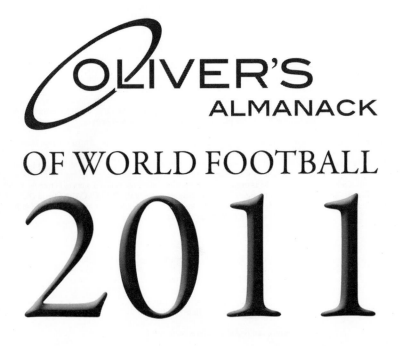

OLIVER'S ALMANACK
OF WORLD FOOTBALL
2011

GUY OLIVER

HARPASTUM PUBLISHING

OLIVERSALMANACK.COM

First published in 2011
by HARPASTUM PUBLISHING LIMITED

1

Front cover photographs: (left) Fans with vuvuzelas at the FIFA World Cup in South Africa - *Action Images*;
(centre left) Lionel Messi, winner of the 2010 FIFA Ballon d'Or, playing for Barcelona - *Action Images*;
(centre right) Internazionale are crowned kings of Europe after beating Bayern in the 2010 UEFA Champions
League final - *Action Images*; (right) Diego Forlan playing for Uruguay at the FIFA World Cup where he won
the Golden Ball as the player of the tournament - *Action Images*

Spine photograph: Spain celebrate winning the 2010 FIFA World Cup in South Africa - *Action Images*

Back cover photographs: (left) Internacional celebrate winning the 2010 Copa Libertadores after beating
Mexico's Guadalajara in the final - *Action Images*;
(centre left) Korea DPR's Jong Tae Se is overcome with emotion during the national anthem before the match
with Brazil - *Action Images*; (centre right) Tanzania celebrate winning the 2010 CECAFA Cup in Dar es
Salaam in December - *CECAFA*; (right) Spain's Andres Iniesta and Wesley Sneijder in action during the 2010
FIFA World Cup final in Johannesburg - *Action Images*

A CIP catalogue record for this title is available from the British Library

ISBN 978-0-9564909-1-9

Design and layout: Guy Oliver
Cover design: Helen Williams

Printed and bound in India at Nutech Print Services

The data within the Almanack of World Football has been obtained from a variety of sources, official
and unofficial. The Author cannot vouch for the accuracy of the data in all cases.

HARPASTUM PUBLISHING LIMITED
Vatcher's Farm, Thorney Hill
Christchurch, Dorset
United Kingdom, BH23 8DF

CONTENTS

PART ONE – FIFA AND WORLD FOOTBALL

PART TWO – THE NATIONS OF THE WORLD

PART THREE – THE CONTINENTAL CONFEDERATIONS

ASIA

AFRICA

CENTRAL AMERICA, NORTH AMERICA & THE CARIBBEAN

SOUTH AMERICA

OCEANIA

EUROPE

ALPHABETICAL LISTING OF THE NATIONS OF THE WORLD

Where a name appears in brackets, it is not an official name for the country in question and is only referred to as such in order that the correct name can be easily identified.

COUNTRY		PAGE	COUNTRY		PAGE
Kyrgyzstan	KGZ	516	Rwanda	RWA	699
Laos	LAO	530	Samoa	SAM	702
Latvia	LVA	552	San Marino	SMR	728
Lebanon	LIB	541	São Tomé e Príncipe	STP	742
Lesotho	LES	539	Saudi Arabia	KSA	524
Liberia	LBR	532	Scotland	SCO	704
Libya	LBY	534	Senegal	SEN	711
Liechtenstein	LIE	544	Serbia	SRB	735
Lithuania	LTU	546	Seychelles	SEY	714
Luxembourg	LUX	549	Sierra Leone	SLE	723
Macau	MAC	555	Singapore	SIN	717
Macedonia FYR	MKD	579	Slovakia	SVK	753
Madagascar	MAD	557	Slovenia	SVN	757
Malawi	MWI	601	Solomon Islands	SOL	731
Malaysia	MAS	563	Somalia	SOM	733
Maldives	MDV	570	South Africa	RSA	683
Mali	MLI	582	(South Korea) Korea Republic	KOR	519
Malta	MLT	585	Spain	ESP	347
Mauritania	MTN	599	Sri Lanka	SRI	739
Mauritius	MRI	594	St Kitts and Nevis	SKN	720
Mexico	MEX	573	St Lucia	LCA	537
Moldova	MDA	567	St Vincent and the Grenadines	VIN	846
Mongolia	MGL	577	Sudan	SUD	744
Montenegro	MNE	588	Surinam	SUR	751
Montserrat	MSR	597	Swaziland	SWZ	765
Morocco	MAR	560	Sweden	SWE	761
Mozambique	MOZ	591	Switzerland	SUI	747
Myanmar (Burma)	MYA	604	Syria	SYR	768
Namibia	NAM	606	Tahiti (French Polynesia)	TAH	771
Nepal	NEP	620	(Taiwan) Chinese Taipei	TPE	793
Netherlands (Holland)	NED	615	Tajikistan	TJK	783
Netherlands Antilles	ANT	136	Tanzania	TAN	774
New Caledonia	NCL	612	Thailand	THA	780
New Zealand	NZL	635	Timor-Leste (East Timor)	TLS	789
Nicaragua	NCA	609	Togo	TOG	791
Niger	NIG	625	Tonga	TGA	778
Nigeria	NGA	622	Trinidad and Tobago	TRI	795
Northern Ireland	NIR	627	Tunisia	TUN	798
(North Korea) Korea DPR	PRK	668	Turkey	TUR	802
Norway	NOR	631	Turkmenistan	TKM	786
Oman	OMA	638	Turks and Caicos Islands	TCA	776
Pakistan	PAK	641	Uganda	UGA	809
Palestine	PLE	655	Ukraine	UKR	812
Panama	PAN	644	United Arab Emirates	UAE	806
Papua New Guinea	PNG	657	United States of America	USA	820
Paraguay	PAR	647	Uruguay	URU	816
Peru	PER	650	US Virgin Islands	VIR	848
Philippines	PHI	653	Uzbekistan	UZB	832
Poland	POL	659	Vanuatu	VAN	835
Portugal	POR	663	Venezuela	VEN	837
Puerto Rico	PUR	670	Vietnam	VIE	843
Qatar	QAT	672	Wales	WAL	850
Republic of Ireland	IRL	463	Yemen	YEM	854
Romania	ROU	679	Zambia	ZAM	857
Russia	RUS	687	Zimbabwe	ZIM	860

ACKNOWLEDGEMENTS

In 1963 journalist Gordon Jeffrey wrote a groundbreaking book called European International Football in which he compiled a list of all the international matches played by the 32 countries in Europe. His introduction is illuminating, describing the seemingly impossible task of gathering together the information relying on nothing more than letters delivered by the postman from his contacts abroad. How things have changed in the past 48 years. I trust Oliver's Almanack of World Football is a worthy successor to Jeffrey's pioneering work but thankfully I have the internet and email to help me so my first debt of gratitude goes to the thousands of people who contribute their knowledge and time to make the internet such a wonderful resource for football fans worldwide. FIFA.com is at the cutting edge of this and I am proud to produce Oliver's Almanack in association with them. One click of a button takes you through to a list of all the international matches played by the 208 countries affiliated to FIFA whilst FIFA's World Match Centre has up to date results and tables from 187 leagues around the world with 59 of them covered live. And that is just a fraction of what they have to offer... I have also relied heavily on the websites of the six continental confederations as well as numerous other sites including the RSSSF, Soccerway, World Football Net, ESPN Soccernet and Wikipedia, which although it has its detractors is actually a very useful resource. I do have a number of individuals whom I would like to thank including Marius Schneider and his Content Management Service team at FIFA, Matt Stone and his team at FIFA.com, Steve Torres at CONCACAF who has again been invaluable, Mark Gleeson for his inside knowledge of all things Africa, Michael Church for his insight into Asia and to Jerome Champagne. My thanks once again to Marion Greenleaves for her work on the stats side and to my wife Sharyn who has also made an invaluable contribution on that front this year - a great team. Thanks also to my father Michael Oliver for his editing skills and to Ally and Archie for just being you.

Guy Oliver, The New Forest, March 2011 (guyoliver@harpastumpublishing.com)

HOW TO USE OLIVER'S ALMANACK

Oliver's Almanack of World Football contains many traditional techniques used across the world to present information, most of which will be familiar to the seasoned football fan. This guide serves a tool for those who are, perhaps, less familiar. We have tried to be as international in our language as possible - hence, for example, our referring to Red Star Belgrade as Crvena Zvezda Beograd except in written reviews. This may not be to everyone's taste but to see Bayern München and FC København written is becoming much more commonplace. Another tricky area is accents and this year we have taken the decision to remove them from players names but to keep them for the names of teams and stadia. Inconsistent maybe, but Peñarol just doesn't look right as Penarol. Many players by contrast don't use accents on their names and where do you draw the line with some of the more obsure languages of the world.

A major innovation this year has been the introduction of the football field graphics for all of the FIFA World Cup matches and for the finals of all of the continental club competitions. Again, they should be self explanatory. Each player is located on the pitch in his position at the start of the match. The two following examples from the Brazil - Côte d'Ivoire World Cup match show that Kaka played in the number 10 shirt, was booked in the 85th and 88th minutes and sent-off in the 88th minute. The other box shows that Salomon Kalou was substituted by Kader Keita after 68 minutes and that Keita was then booked in the 75th minute.

THE LEAGUE TABLE

② ↓

BRAZIL 2009

③→ SERIE A   ⑤
⤹ ↓ ⤵

		Pl	W	D	L	F	A	Pts	Flamengo	Internacional	São Paulo	Cruzeiro	Palmeiras
①→	**Flamengo**	38	19	10	9	58	44	**67**		4-0	2-1	1-2	1-2
	Internacional	38	19	8	11	65	44	**65**	0-0		2-2	2-3	2-0
	São Paulo FC	38	18	11	9	57	42	**65**	2-2	1-0		3-0	0-0
	Cruzeiro	38	18	8	12	58	53	**62**	2-0	1-1	1-2		1-2	←④
	Palmeiras	38	17	11	10	58	45	**62**	0-2	2-1	0-0	3-1	

① The club in bold at the top of the league ladder are the league champions. If the club is not in bold it means that there was a further stage to be played. The relegated teams are also listed in bold at the foot of the table

② This refers to the season in which the league campaign was played. In this instance the Brazilian championship was played through the course of 2009. Other leagues overlap the end of the year - 2008–09 for instance

③ The league in Brazil is known as Serie A. Sponsors names are also included where applicable whilst (2) after the name means that the league is at the second level. (3) would mean the third level and so on

④ The scoreline of 1-2 indicated in the box refers to the match between Cruzeiro at home against Palmeiras who were the visiting team. The first number (1) refers to the number of goals the home team Cruzeiro scored, the second (2) to the goals scored by Palmeiras, the away team. So in this instance Cruzeiro lost 1-2 at home to Palmeiras

⑤ These columns refer to the number of games played during the season (Pl), games won (W), games drawn (D), games lost (L), goals scored (F), goals conceded (A) and the number of points obtained (Pts) during the course of the season by the team listed in each row. Different languages uses the annotations listed in the table below

English	Pl	W	D	L	F	A	Pts
French	J	G	N	P	Bp	Bc	Pts
German	Sp	G	U	V	Tore		Pkte
Italian	G	V	N	P	RF	RS	Pt
Portuguese	J	V	E	D	Gp	Gc	Pt
Spanish	J	G	E	P	Gf	Gc	Pts

② ↓   FIFA WORLD CUP RECORD   ③ ↓

① ⤵ **1930** DNE **1934** 4 SF **1938** Qualified but did not take part **1950** DNE **1954** 3 SF **1958** 15 r1 **1962** DNE ④ ⤵
1966-1974 DNQ **1978** 7 r2 **1982** 7 r2 **1986** DNQ **1990** 18 r1 **1994** DNQ **1998** 23 r1 **2002-2010** DNQ ←⑤

① The first World Cup was held in 1930 and has been held every four years since then with the exception of 1942 and 1946

② When the year is in larger type it means that the nation in question qualified for the final tournament. In this case it indicates that Austria qualified for the finals in 1934

③ When a nation has qualified for the finals, their performance is indicated by their final placing and the round that they reached. In this case, Austria finished third at the 1954 finals and reached the semi-finals. **r1** means that the team got no further than the first round group stage. In 1934 and 1938 there was no group stage so **r1** refers to the first knock-out round. **r2** indicates that the team qualified from the first round group stage but were knocked out in the round of 16. In 1950, 1974 1978 and 1982 there was a second group stage. **r2** refers to this. **QF** indicates that the team reached the quarter-finals. **SF** indicates the team reached the semi-finals. Finalist and winners is self explanatory

④ **DNE** indicates that the nation in question did not enter that particular World Cup

⑤ **DNQ** indicates that the nation in question did not qualify for that particular World Cup. In this case Austria did not qualify for the 2002, 2006 or 2010 World Cups

CUP BRACKETS

SAA SUPA 8 CUP 2008

First Round		Semi–finals		Final	
Kaiser Chiefs *	4				
Santos	0	Kaiser Chiefs *	2 0		
Ajax Cape Town	3	Swallows	0 1		
Swallows *	4			Kaiser Chiefs	0 4p
SuperSport Utd	2			Sundowns	0 3p
Orlando Pirates*	1	SuperSport Utd	1 3		
Free State Stars	0	Sundowns *	2 2		
Sundowns *	1	* Home team/Home team in the 1st leg			

 (pointing to Kaiser Chiefs/Santos)

←③ (at SuperSport Utd / Sundowns semi-final)

←④ (at Kaiser Chiefs / Sundowns final)

① The name of the Cup tournament and the year in which it was played. In this case the tournament is South Africa's SAA Supa 8 Cup that was played in 2008

② This shows that Kaiser Chiefs played Santos at home in the first round winning 4-0. The brackets are constructed so that the Cup winners always feature as the top bracket in each round with the beaten finalists as the bottom bracket. The winners of each tie are indicated in bold

③ This bracket shows that Sundowns played SuperSport United in the semi-final over two legs. The asterisk indicates that Sundowns played the first leg at home and won 2-0. In the second leg, played away from home, Sundowns lost 2-3. When a tie finishes level on aggregate, as this tie did, away goals are used to determine the winners unless stated. With two goals scored away from home as opposed to the one goal scored away from home by SuperSport United, Sundowns qualified for the final

④ This bracket indicates that the final of the 2008 Supa 8 Cup was between Kaiser Chiefs and Sundowns. The match finished 0-0 but Chiefs won the Cup after winning the penalty shoot-out 4-3

COUNTRY INFORMATION

①

FEDERATA SHQIPTARE E FUTBOLIT (FSHF)

Rruga Labinoti,
✉ Pallati perballe Shkolles, Tirana
☎ +355 43 46605
📠 +355 43 46 609
✉ fshf@fshf.org.al
🖥 www.fshf.org
FA 1930 CON 1954 FIFA 1932
P Armand Duka
GS Eduard Prodani

Most of the items on the front page for each country should be self explanatory. The FIFA Big Count 2006 was a survey conducted by FIFA in 2006 of all of the member associations and followed a similar survey carried out in 2000. The information for the box at the bottom of each page is sourced from the CIA Factbook whilst the population figures for cities and towns are sourced from the World gazetteer

① This box with information about the football association in each country is divided into the name of the association and its abbreviation • ✉ Address • ☎ Phone • 📠 Fax • ✉ Email address • 🖥 Website address - along with the year the FA was formed (FA), the year it joined its continental confederation (CON) and the year it joined FIFA. The names indicted beside 'P' are the president of the FA and the general-secretary 'GS'

② The name of the country is given in its local form first and then English form. The figures in brackets are the countries world ranking according to the CIA Factbook. Therefore Albania's population of 3,639,453 (a 2009 estimate) is the 129th largest (out of 228) in the world

②

REPUBLIKA E SHQIPERISE • REPUBLIC OF ALBANIA

Capital	Tirana	Population	3 639 453 (129)	% in cities	47%
GDP per capita	$6000 (132)	Area km²	28 748 km² (144)	GMT + / -	+1
Neighbours (km)	Greece 282, Macedonia 151, Montenegro 172, Kosovo 112 • Coast 362				

MATCH BOXES

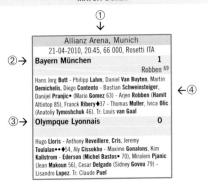

① This match was played at the Allianz Arena in Munich on the 21st April, 2010. Kick-off was at 20:45 in the evening and there were 66,000 fans in the stadium. The match referee was Italy's Rosetti

② Bayern Munich were the home side and scored one goal. The goalscorer was Arjen Robben in the 69th minute. Had the goal been scored from a penalty the time indicator would have read ⁶⁹ᵖ. A + after the minute of the goal indicates that it was scored in injury-time. Thus 93+ means a goal was scored in the third minute of stoppage time. 93 on the other hand would mean that the goal was scored in the 93rd minute - ie the third minute of extra-time

③ Olympique Lyonnais were the away team. They did not score and lost the match 0-1

④ This box indicates the line-up of the Bayern Munich team. Each team is divided by three hyphens into Goalkeepers - Defenders - Midfielders - Forwards where it is possible to gather this information. For the major tournaments we have also listed the players from right to left across the field. Thus in this UEFA Champions League semi-final Philipp Lahm played at right back with Van Buyten and Demichelis in the central defensive positions and Diego Contento at left back. If a player has • after his name it indicates that he was booked. If a player has ♦37 as in the case of Frank Ribery, it means he was sent off in the 37th minute. Jeremy Toulalan on the other hand has ••♦54 after his name indicating that he was sent off in the 54th minute after receiving two yellow cards.

The exact composition of match boxes varies from tournament to tournament - in some tournaments players are listed with shirt numbers for example - but the principles remain the same

PART ONE

FIFA AND WORLD FOOTBALL

FIFA

Fédération Internationale de Football Association

2010 will be remembered as the year when South Africa put on a fantastic show as the first-ever African World Cup hosts and as the year when Spain finally conquered the world. The 2010 FIFA World Cup in South Africa left a lasting legacy both on and off the pitch, despite the fact that the tournament started slowly and that the hosts failed to progress beyond the group stage. Unlike some previous tournaments in which fatigue had been a major factor in the latter stages after an entertaining group stage, the opposite was true in South Africa. Played during winter, the weather was never a factor and from the last round of group games onwards, the football improved as did the number of goals - up to 39 in the knockout rounds from the 26 scored four years previously in Germany. Surprisingly, just four of those were scored by Spain who proved to be the masters of the 1-0 victory on the way to their first title. Yet has there ever been a more deserving world champion? In 55 international matches from 2007 up to the final, the Spanish won 50 and drew three, comfortably the most successful run in the history of international football. The team also succeeded in uniting a nation where regional identities are paramount and expressed through club football. The sight of fans celebrating in the streets of Barcelona after the final was extraordinary

THE FIFA BIG COUNT OF 2006

	Male	Female		Total
Number of players	238 557 000	25 995 000	Referees and Assistant Referees	843 000
Professionals	113 000		Admin, Coaches, Technical, Medical	4 214 000
Amateurs 18+	15 481 000		Number of clubs	301 000
Youth under 18	21 548 000		Number of teams	1 752 000
Unregistered	226 265 000		Clubs with women's teams	26 000
Total players	264 552 000		Players as % of population	4.13%

but with six Barcelona players and five Catalans in the team which beat the Netherlands 1-0 in Johannesburg, it was as much their triumph as the rest of Spain's. There can be little doubt that the FIFA World Cup remains the most prized trophy in world sport and the race to host the 2018 and 2022 tournaments brought FIFA even more firmly into the limelight. The process was made more difficult by newspaper allegations involving FIFA Executive Committee members Amos Adamu and Reynald Temarii, entrapped by journalists looking to buy their votes, though it appeared to be more a case of entrapment that 'caused' a crime rather than entrapment that 'exposed' a crime. Both were removed from the ExCo which took the bold decision to broaden the frontiers of football by awarding the 2018 finals to Russia and the 2022 finals to Qatar. FIFA organised three other tournaments in 2010 with Korea Republic beating rivals Japan on penalties in an all-Asian final of the FIFA U-17 Women's World Cup in Trinidad; Germany beating Nigeria on home soil in the final of the FIFA U-20 Women's World Cup, whilst Italy's Internazionale beat surprise finalists TP Mazembe from Congo in the final of the FIFA Club World Cup in Abu Dhabi. In the semi-finals Mazembe had caused the shock of the year by beating Brazil's Internacional 2-0.

Fédération Internationale de Football Association (FIFA)
FIFA-Strasse 20, PO Box, 8044 Zürich, Switzerland
Tel +41 43 222 7777   Fax +41 43 222 7878
contact@fifa.org
www.fifa.com
President: Joseph S. Blatter
Secretary General: Jérôme Valcke
Deputy Secretary General: Markus Kattner

MAP OF FIFA CONFEDERATIONS

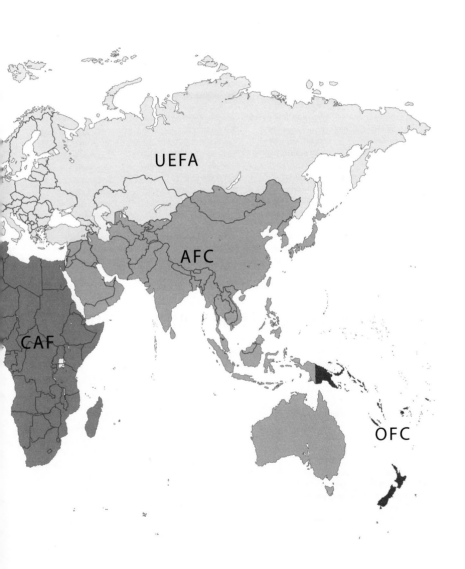

FIFA EXECUTIVE COMMITTEE

President: Joseph S. Blatter SUI	Senior Vice-President: Julio H. Grondona ARG	Vice-President: Issa Hayatou CMR
Vice-President: Chung Mong Joon KOR	Vice-President: Jack A. Warner TRI	Vice-President: Angel María Villar Llona ESP
Vice-President: Michel Platini FRA	Vice-President: Geoff Thompson ENG	Vice-President: David Chung PNG

ORDINARY MEMBERS OF THE EXECUTIVE COMMITTEE

Michel D'Hooghe BEL	Ricardo Terra Teixeira BRA	Mohamed Bin Hammam QAT
Senes Erzik TUR	Chuck Blazer USA	Worawi Makudi THA
Nicolás Leoz PAR	Junji Ogura JPN	Marios Lefkaritis CYP
Jacques Anouma CIV	Franz Beckenbauer GER	Rafael Salguero GUA
Hany Abo Rida EGY	Vitaliy Mutko RUS	Mohamed Raouraoua ALG
	Secretary General: Jérôme Valcke	

OTHER FIFA COMMITTEES

	Chairman	Organising Committee for...	Chairman
Emergency Committee	Joseph S. Blatter SUI	The FIFA World Cup	Issa Hayatou CMR
Finance Committee	Julio H. Grondona ARG	The FIFA Confederations Cup	TBD
Internal Audit Committee	Franco Carraro ITA	The Olympic Football Tournaments	Chung Mong Joon KOR
Referees' Committee	Angel María Villar Llona ESP	The FIFA U-20 World Cup	Jack A. Warner TRI
Technical & Development Committee	Reynald Temarii TAH	The FIFA U-17 World Cup	Jack A. Warner TRI
Medical Committee	Michel D'Hooghe BEL	Women's Football and FIFA Women's World Cup	Worawi Makudi THA
Players' Status Committee	Geoff Thompson ENG	The U-20 and U-17 Women's World Cups	Franz Beckenbauer GER
Legal Committee	Angel María Villar Llona ESP	Futsal and Beach Soccer Committee	Ricardo Terra Teixeira BRA
Fair Play and Social Responsibility	Senes Erzik TUR	The FIFA Club World Cup	Chuck Blazer USA
Media Committee	Marios Lefkaritis CYP	Associations Committee	Geoff Thompson ENG
Football Committee	Franz Beckenbauer GER	Strategic Committee	Joseph S. Blatter SUI
Marketing & TV Advisory Board	Julio H. Grondona ARG	Goal Bureau	Mohamed Bin Hammam QAT
Committe for Club Football	Michel Platini FRA	FIFA Medical Assessment and Research Centre	Michel D'Hooghe BEL
Doping Control Sub-Committee	Michel D'Hooghe BEL	Stadium and Security Committee	Junji Ogura JPN
Disciplinary Committee	Marcel Mathier SUI	Appeal Committee	Larry Mussenden BER
Ethics Committee	Claudio Sulser SUI	Dispute Resolution Chamber	Slim Aloulou TUN

FIFA NATIONAL TEAM TOURNAMENTS

FIFA WORLD CUP

Year	Host Country	Winners	Score	Runners-up	Venue
1930	Uruguay	Uruguay	4-2	Argentina	Centenario, Montevideo
1934	Italy	Italy	2-1	Czechoslovakia	PNF, Rome
1938	France	Italy	4-2	Hungary	Colombes, Paris
1950	Brazil	Uruguay	2-1	Brazil	Maracana, Rio de Janeiro
1954	Switzerland	Germany FR	3-2	Hungary	Wankdorf, Berne
1958	Sweden	Brazil	5-2	Sweden	Råsunda, Stockholm
1962	Chile	Brazil	3-1	Czechoslovakia	Estadio Nacional, Santiago
1966	England	England	4-2	Germany FR	Wembley, London
1970	Mexico	Brazil	4-1	Italy	Azteca, Mexico City
1974	Germany FR	Germany FR	2-1	Netherlands	Olympiastadion, Munich
1978	Argentina	Argentina	3-1	Netherlands	Monumental, Buenos Aires
1982	Spain	Italy	3-1	Germany FR	Bernabeu, Madrid
1986	Mexico	Argentina	3-2	Germany FR	Azteca, Mexico City
1990	Italy	Germany FR	1-0	Argentina	Olimpico, Rome
1994	USA	Brazil	0-0 3-2p	Italy	Rose Bowl, Pasadena
1998	France	France	3-0	Brazil	Stade de France, Paris
2002	Korea Rep/Japan	Brazil	2-0	Germany	International Stadium, Yokohama
2006	Germany	Italy	1-1 5-3p	France	Olympiastadion, Berlin
2010	South Africa	Spain	1-0	Netherlands	Soccer City, Johannesburg
2014	Brazil				Maracana, Rio de Janeiro

FIFA WORLD CUP MEDALS TABLE

Country	G	S	B	F	SF
Brazil	5	2	2	7	7
Italy	4	2	1	6	7
Germany	3	4	4	7	11
Argentina	2	2		4	3
Uruguay	2			2	4
France	1	1	2	2	5
England	1			1	2
Spain	1			1	1
Netherlands		3		3	2
Czechoslovakia		2		2	2
Hungary		2		2	2
Sweden		1	2	1	3
Poland			2		1
Austria			1		2
Portugal			1		2
Yugoslavia			1		2
Chile			1		1
Croatia			1		1
Turkey			1		1
USA			1		1
Belgium					1
Bulgaria					1
Korea Republic					1
Soviet Union					1
	19	19	20	38	64

This table represents the Gold (winners), Silver (runners-up) and Bronze (3rd place) winners of nations in the FIFA World Cup, along with the number of appearances in the final and semi-finals

FIFA CONFEDERATIONS CUP

Year	Host Country	Winners	Score	Runners-up	Venue
1992	Saudi Arabia †	Argentina	3-1	Saudi Arabia	King Fahd, Riyadh
1995	Saudi Arabia †	Denmark	2-0	Argentina	King Fahd, Riyadh
1997	Saudi Arabia	Brazil	6-0	Australia	King Fahd, Riyadh
1999	Mexico	Mexico	4-3	Brazil	Azteca, Mexico City
2001	Korea/Japan	France	1-0	Japan	International Stadium, Yokohama
2003	France	France	1-0	Cameroon	Stade de France, Paris
2005	Germany	Brazil	4-1	Argentina	Waldstadion, Frankfurt
2009	South Africa	Brazil	3-2	USA	Ellis Park, Johannesburg

† Intercontinental Champions Cup

MEN'S OLYMPIC FOOTBALL TOURNAMENT

Year	Host City	Winners	Score	Runners-up	Venue
1896	Athens ‡	No tournament took place			
1900	Paris ‡	Great Britain	4-0	France	Vélodrome Municipal, Paris
1904	St Louis ‡	Canada	4-0	USA	Francis Field, St Louis
1906	Athens ‡	Denmark	9-0	Greece	Podilatodromino, Athens
1908	London	England (as GBR)	2-0	Denmark	White City, London
1912	Stockholm	England (as GBR)	4-2	Denmark	Stockholms Stadion, Stockholm
1916	Berlin	Games cancelled			
1920	Antwerp	Belgium	2-0	Czechoslovakia	Olympisch Stadion, Antwerp
1924	Paris	Uruguay	3-0	Switzerland	Colombes, Paris
1928	Amsterdam	Uruguay	1-1 2-1	Argentina	Olympisch Stadion, Amsterdam
1932	Los Angeles	No football tournament played			
1936	Berlin	Italy	2-1	Austria	Olympiastadion, Berlin
1940	Tokyo/Helsinki	Games cancelled			
1944	London	Games cancelled			

MEN'S OLYMPIC FOOTBALL TOURNAMENT (CONT'D)

Year	Host City	Winners	Score	Runners-up	Venue
1948	London	Sweden	3-1	Yugoslavia	Wembley, London
1952	Helsinki	Hungary	2-0	Yugoslavia	Olympiastadion, Helsinki
1956	Melbourne	Soviet Union	1-0	Yugoslavia	Melbourne Cricket Ground
1960	Rome	Yugoslavia	3-1	Denmark	Flaminio, Rome
1964	Tokyo	Hungary	2-1	Czechoslovakia	National Stadium, Tokyo
1968	Mexico City	Hungary	4-1	Bulgaria	Azteca, Mexico City
1972	Munich	Poland	2-1	Hungary	Olympiastadion, Munich
1976	Montreal	German DR	3-1	Poland	Olympic Stadium, Montreal
1980	Moscow	Czechoslovakia	1-0	German DR	Centralny, Moscow
1984	Los Angeles	France	2-0	Brazil	Rose Bowl, Pasadena
1988	Seoul	Soviet Union	2-1	Brazil	Olympic Stadium, Seoul
1992	Barcelona	Spain	3-2	Poland	Camp Nou, Barcelona
1996	Atlanta	Nigeria	3-2	Argentina	Sanford Stadium, Athens
2000	Sydney	Cameroon	2-2 5-4p	Spain	Olympic Stadium, Sydney
2004	Athens	Argentina	1-0	Paraguay	Olympic Stadium, Athens
2008	Beijing	Argentina	1-0	Nigeria	Bird's Nest, Beijing

‡ Unofficial tournament

FIFA CLUB TOURNAMENTS

FIFA CLUB WORLD CUP

Year	Host Country	Winners		Score		Runners-up		Venue
2000	Brazil	Corinthians	BRA	0-0 4-3p	BRA	Vasco da Gama		Maracana, Rio de Janeiro
2005	Japan	São Paulo FC	BRA	1-0	ENG	Liverpool		International, Yokohama
2006	Japan	Internacional	BRA	1-0	ESP	Barcelona		International, Yokohama
2007	Japan	Milan	ITA	4-2	ARG	Boca Juniors		International, Yokohama
2008	Japan	Manchester United	ENG	1-0	ECU	LDU Quito		International, Yokohama
2009	UAE	Barcelona	ESP	2-1	ARG	Estudiantes LP		Zayed SC, Abu Dhabi
2010	UAE	Internazionale	ITA	3-0	COD	TP Mazembe		Zayed SC, Abu Dhabi

FIFA YOUTH TOURNAMENTS

FIFA U–20 WORLD CUP

Year	Host Country	Winners	Score	Runners-up	Final Venue
1977	Tunisia	Soviet Union	2-2 9-8p	Mexico	El Menzah, Tunis
1979	Japan	Argentina	3-1	Soviet Union	National Stadium, Tokyo
1981	Australia	Germany FR	4-0	Qatar	Sydney Cricket Ground
1983	Mexico	Brazil	1-0	Argentina	Azteca, Mexico City
1985	Soviet Union	Brazil	1-0	Spain	Centralny, Moscow
1987	Chile	Yugoslavia	1-1 5-4p	Germany FR	Estadio Nacional, Santiago
1989	Saudi Arabia	Portugal	2-0	Nigeria	King Fahd, Riyadh
1991	Portugal	Portugal	0-0 4-2p	Brazil	Da Luz, Lisbon
1993	Australia	Brazil	2-1	Ghana	Sydney Football Stadium, Sydney
1995	Qatar	Argentina	2-0	Brazil	Khalifa, Doha
1997	Malaysia	Argentina	2-1	Uruguay	Shahalam Stadium, Shah Alam
1999	Nigeria	Spain	4-0	Japan	Surulere, Lagos
2001	Argentina	Argentina	3-0	Ghana	Jose Amalfitani, Buenos Aires
2003	UAE	Brazil	1-0	Spain	Zayed Sports City, Abu Dhabi
2005	Netherlands	Argentina	2-1	Nigeria	Galgenwaard, Utrecht
2007	Canada	Argentina	2-1	Czech Republic	National Soccer Stadium, Toronto
2009	Egypt	Ghana	0-0 4-3p	Brazil	International, Cairo

FIFA U–17 WORLD CHAMPIONSHIP

Year	Host Country	Winners	Score	Runners-up	Final Venue
1985	China	Nigeria	2-0	Germany FR	Workers' Stadium, Beijing
1987	Canada	Soviet Union	1-1 3-1p	Nigeria	Varsity Stadium, Toronto
1989	Scotland	Saudi Arabia	2-2 5-4p	Scotland	Hampden Park, Glasgow
1991	Italy	Ghana	1-0	Spain	Comunale, Florence
1993	Japan	Nigeria	2-1	Ghana	National Stadium, Tokyo
1995	Ecuador	Ghana	3-2	Brazil	Monumental, Guayaquil
1997	Egypt	Brazil	2-1	Ghana	National Stadium, Cairo
1999	New Zealand	Brazil	0-0 8-7p	Australia	North Harbour, Auckland
2001	Trinidad & Tobago	France	3-0	Nigeria	Hasely Crawford, Port of Spain
2003	Finland	Brazil	1-0	Spain	Töölö, Helsinki
2005	Peru	Mexico	3-0	Brazil	Estadio Nacional, Lima
2007	Korea Republic	Nigeria	0-0 3-0p	Spain	World Cup Stadium, Seoul
2009	Nigeria	Switzerland	1-0	Nigeria	National Stadium, Abuja

FIFA WOMEN'S TOURNAMENTS

FIFA WOMEN'S WORLD CUP

Year	Host Country	Winners	Score	Runners-up	Venue
1991	China PR	USA	2-1	Norway	Tianhe, Guangzhou
1995	Sweden	Norway	2-0	Germany	Råsunda, Stockholm
1999	USA	USA	0-0 5-4p	China PR	Rose Bowl, Pasadena
2003	USA	Germany	2-1	Sweden	Home Depot Centre, Carson
2007	China PR	Germany	2-0	Brazil	Hongkou, Shanghai

FIFA WOMEN'S WORLD CUP MEDALS TABLE

	Country	G	S	B	F	SF
1	Germany	2	1		3	4
2	USA	2		3	2	5
3	Norway	1	1		2	4
4	Brazil		1	1	1	2
	Sweden		1	1	1	2
6	China PR		1		1	2
7	Canada					1
		5	5	5	10	20

This table represents the Gold (winners), Silver (runners-up) and Bronze (3rd place) winners of nations in the FIFA Women's World Cup, along with the number of appearances in the final and semi-finals

WOMEN'S OLYMPIC FOOTBALL TOURNAMENT

Year	Host City	Winners	Score	Runners-up	Venue
1996	Atlanta	USA	2-1	China	Sanford Stadium, Athens
2000	Sydney	Norway	3-2	USA	Sydney Football Stadium, Sydney
2004	Athens	USA	2-1	Brazil	Karaiskaki, Piraeus
2008	Beijing	USA	1-0	Brazil	Worker's Stadium, Beijing

FIFA U–20 WOMEN'S WORLD CUP

Year	Host Country	Winners	Score	Runners-up	Final Venue
2002	Canada	USA	1-0	Canada	Commonwealth, Edmonton
2004	Thailand	Germany	2-0	China PR	Rajamangala National, Bangkok
2006	Russia	Korea DPR	5-0	China PR	Lokomotiv, Moscow
2008	Chile	USA	2-1	Korea DPR	Municipal, La Florida, Santiago
2010	Germany	Germany	2-0	Nigeria	Schüco Arena, Bielefeld

FIFA U–17 WOMEN'S WORLD CUP

Year	Host Country	Winners	Score	Runners-up	Final Venue
2008	New Zealand	Korea DPR	2-1	USA	North Harbour, Auckland
2010	Trinidad & Tobago	Korea Republic	3-3 5-4p	Japan	Hasely Crawford, Port of Spain

FIFA BALLON D'OR 2010

The Ballon d'Or was awarded by France Football magazine from 1956 until 2009. Until 1994 it was open only to Europeans. From 1995 until 2006 it was open to any player signed to a European club but in the final three years it was open to any player in the world. In 2010 the Ballon d'Or and FIFA's World Player of the Year award combined to form the FIFA Ballon d'Or.

FIFA BALON D'OR 2010

Rank	Player	Club	Nat	Total %
1	Lionel Messi	Barcelona	ARG	22.65
2	Andres Iniesta	Barcelona	ESP	17.36
3	Xavi	Barcelona	ESP	16.48
4	Wesley Sneijder	Internazionale	NED	14.48
5	Diego Forlan	Atlético Madrid	URU	7.61
6	Cristiano Ronaldo	Real Madrid	POR	3.92
7	Iker Casillas	Real Madrid	ESP	2.90
8	David Villa	Valencia/Barcelona	ESP	2.25
9	Didier Drogba	Chelsea	CIV	1.68
10	Xabi Alonso	Real Madrid	ESP	1.52
11	Carles Puyol	Barcelona	ESP	1.43
12	Samuel Eto'o	Internazionale	CMR	1.37
13	Mesut Ozil	Werder Bremen/Real Madrid	GER	1.21
14	Arjen Robben	Bayern München	NED	1.16
15	Thomas Muller	Bayern München	GER	0.91
16	Bastian Schweinsteiger	Bayern München	GER	0.75
17	Maicon	Internazionale	BRA	0.57
18	Asamoah Gyan	Rennes/Sunderland	GHA	0.46
19	Cesc Fabregas	Arsenal	ESP	0.22
	JJulio Cesar	Internazionale	BRA	0.22
21	Miroslav Klose	Bayern München	GER	0.19
22	Dani Alves	Barcelona	BRA	0.05
	Philipp Lahm	Bayern München	GER	0.05

FIFA WOMEN'S WORLD PLAYER 2010

Rank	Player	Club	Nat	Total %
1	Marta	Santos/FC Gold Pride	BRA	38.20
2	Birgit Prinz	1.FFC Frankfurt	GER	15.18
3	Fatmire Bajramaj	Turbine Potsdam	GER	9.96
4	Kelly Smith	Boston Breakers	ENG	9.29
5	Abby Wambach	Washington Freedom	USA	6.25
6	Ji So Yun	Hanyang Women's College	KOR	5.24
7	Christine Sinclair	FC Gold Pride	CAN	4.42
8	Hope Solo	Atlanta Beat	USA	3.85
9	Caroline Seger	Philadelphia Independence	SWE	3.64
10	Camille Abily	FC Gold Pride/Olymp Lyonnais	FRA	3.38

FIFA WORLD COACH MEN'S FOOTBALL 2010

Rank	Coach	Team	Nat	Total %
1	Jose Mourinho	Internazionale/Real Madrid	POR	35.92
2	Vicente Del Bosque	Spain	ESP	33.08
3	Josep Guardiola	Barcelona	ESP	8.45
4	Joachim Low	Germany	GER	5.12
5	Carlos Ancelotti	Chelsea	ITA	3.78
6	Alex Ferguson	Manchester United	SCO	3.66
7	Oscar Tabarez	Uruguay	URU	2.95
8	Bert van Marwijk	Netherlands	NED	2.69
9	Arsene Wenger	Arsenal	FRA	2.25
10	Louis van Gaal	Bayern München	NED	1.89

FIFA WORLD COACH WOMEN'S FOOTBALL 2010

Rank	Coach	Team	Nat	Total %
1	Silvia Neid	Germany	GER	24.06
2	Maren Meinert	Germany U-20	GER	18.26
3	Pia Sundhage	USA	SWE	11.68
4	Hope Powell	England	ENG	10.54
5	Choi In Cheul	Korea Republic	KOR	9.26
6	Bernd Schroder	Turbine Potsdam	GER	6.81
7	Bruno Bini	France	FRA	6.62
8	Albertin Montoya	FC Gold Pride	USA	5.49
9	Beatrice Von Siebenthal	Switzerland	SUI	3.67
10	Norio Sasaki	Japan	JPN	3.39

BALLON D'OR WINNERS

Year	Player	Club	Nat
1956	Stanley Matthews	Blackpool	ENG
1957	Alfredo Di Stefano	Real Madrid	ESP
1958	Raymond Kopa	Real Madrid	FRA
1959	Alfredo Di Stefano	Real Madrid	ESP
1960	Luis Suarez	Barcelona	ESP
1961	Omar Sivori	Juventus	ITA
1962	Josef Masopust	Dukla Praha	CZE
1963	Lev Yashin	Dyn. Moskva	URS
1964	Denis Law	Man United	SCO
1965	Eusebio	Benfica	POR
1966	Bobby Charlton	Man United	ENG
1967	Florian Albert	Ferencvaros	HUN
1968	George Best	Man United	NIR
1969	Gianni Rivera	Milan	ITA
1970	Gerd Müller	Bay. München	GER
1971	Johan Cruijff	Barcelona	NED
1972	Franz Beckenbauer	Bay. München	GER
1973	Johan Cruijff	Barcelona	NED
1974	Johan Cruijff	Barcelona	NED
1975	Oleg Blokhin	Dynamo Kyiv	URS
1976	Franz Beckenbauer	Bay. München	GER
1977	Alan Simonsen	B. M'gladbach	DEN
1978	Kevin Keegan	Hamburger SV	ENG
1979	Kevin Keegan	Hamburger SV	ENG
1980	K-H Rummenigge	Bay. München	GER
1981	K-H Rummenigge	Bay. München	GER
1982	Paolo Rossi	Juventus	ITA
1983	Michel Platini	Juventus	FRA
1984	Michel Platini	Juventus	FRA
1985	Michel Platini	Juventus	FRA
1986	Igor Belanov	Dynamo Kyiv	URS
1987	Ruud Gullit	Milan	NED
1988	Marco Van Basten	Milan	NED
1989	Marco Van Basten	Milan	NED
1990	Lothar Matthäus	Internazionale	GER
1991	Jean-Pierre Papin	Oly. Marseille	FRA
1992	Marco Van Basten	Milan	NED
1993	Roberto Baggio	Juventus	ITA
1994	Hristo Stoitchkov	Barcelona	BUL
1995	George Weah	Milan	LBR
1996	Matthias Sammer	Bor. Dortmund	GER
1997	Ronaldo	Internazionale	BRA
1998	Zinedine Zidane	Juventus	FRA
1999	Rivaldo	Barcelona	BRA
2000	Luis Figo	Real Madrid	POR
2001	Michael Owen	Liverpool	ENG
2002	Ronaldo	Real Madrid	BRA
2003	Pavel Nedved	Juventus	CZE
2004	Andriy Shevchenko	Milan	UKR
2005	Ronaldinho	Barcelona	BRA
2006	Fabio Cannavaro	Real Madrid	ITA
2007	Kaká	Milan	BRA
2008	Cristiano Ronaldo	Man United	POR
2009	Lionel Messi	Barcelona	ARG

FIFA WORLD PLAYER WINNERS

	Men			Women	
1st	2nd	3rd	1st	2nd	3rd
1991 Lothar Matthäus	Jean-Pierre Papin	Gary Lineker			
1992 Marco van Basten	Hristo Stoichkov	Thomas Hässler			
1993 Roberto Baggio	Romario	Dennis Bergkamp			
1994 Romario	Hristo Stoichkov	Roberto Baggio			
1995 George Weah	Paolo Maldini	Jürgen Klinsmann			
1996 Ronaldo	George Weah	Alan Shearer			
1997 Ronaldo	Roberto Carlos	Bergkamp/Zidane			
1998 Zinedine Zidane	Ronaldo	Davor Suker			
1999 Rivaldo	David Beckham	Gabriel Batistuta			
2000 Zinedine Zidane	Luis Figo	Rivaldo			
2001 Luis Figo	David Beckham	Raúl	Mia Hamm	Sun Wen	Tiffeny Milbrett
2002 Ronaldo	Oliver Kahn	Zinedine Zidane	Mia Hamm	Birgit Prinz	Sun Wen
2003 Zinedine Zidane	Thierry Henry	Ronaldo	Birgit Prinz	Mia Hamm	Hanna Ljungberg
2004 Ronaldinho	Thierry Henry	Andriy Shevchenko	Birgit Prinz	Mia Hamm	Marta
2005 Ronaldinho	Frank Lampard	Samuel Eto'o	Birgit Prinz	Marta	Shannon Boxx
2006 Fabio Cannavaro	Zinedine Zidane	Ronaldinho	Marta	Kristine Lilly	Renate Lingor
2007 Kaka	Lionel Messi	Cristiano Ronaldo	Marta	Birgit Prinz	Cristiane
2008 Cristiano Ronaldo	Lionel Messi	Fernando Torres	Marta	Birgit Prinz	Cristiane
2009 Lionel Messi	Cristiano Ronaldo	Xavi	Marta	Birgit Prinz	Kelly Smith

2010 FIFA WORLD CUP SOUTH AFRICA

2010 FIFA WORLD CUP SOUTH AFRICA

First round groups

GROUP A	PL	W	D	L	F	A	GD	PTS	URU	MEX	RSA	FRA
1 Uruguay	3	2	1	0	4	0	+4	7		1-0	3-0	0-0
2 Mexico	3	1	1	1	3	2	+1	4			1-1	2-0
3 South Africa	3	1	1	1	3	5	-2	4				2-1
4 France	3	0	1	2	1	4	-3	1				

GROUP B	PL	W	D	L	F	A	GD	PTS	ARG	KOR	GRE	NGA
1 Argentina	3	3	0	0	7	1	+6	9		4-1	2-0	1-0
2 Korea Republic	3	1	1	1	5	6	-1	4			2-0	2-2
3 Greece	3	1	0	2	2	5	-3	3				2-1
4 Nigeria	3	0	1	2	3	5	-2	1				

GROUP C	PL	W	D	L	F	A	GD	PTS	USA	ENG	SVN	ALG
1 USA	3	1	2	0	4	3	+1	5		1-1	2-2	1-0
2 England	3	1	2	0	2	1	+1	5			1-0	0-0
3 Slovenia	3	1	1	1	3	3	0	4				1-0
4 Algeria	3	0	1	2	0	2	-2	1				

GROUP D	PL	W	D	L	F	A	GD	PTS	GER	GHA	AUS	SRB
1 Germany	3	2	0	1	5	1	+4	6		1-0	4-0	0-1
2 Ghana	3	1	1	1	2	2	0	4			1-1	1-0
3 Australia	3	1	1	1	3	6	-3	4				2-1
4 Serbia	3	1	0	2	2	3	-1	3				

GROUP E	PL	W	D	L	F	A	GD	PTS	NED	JPN	DEN	CMR
1 Netherlands	3	3	0	0	5	1	+4	9		1-0	2-0	2-1
2 Japan	3	2	0	1	4	2	+2	6			3-1	1-0
3 Denmark	3	1	0	2	3	6	-3	3				2-1
4 Cameroon	3	0	0	3	2	5	-3	0				

GROUP F	PL	W	D	L	F	A	GD	PTS	PAR	SVK	NZL	ITA
1 Paraguay	3	1	2	0	3	1	+2	5		2-0	0-0	1-1
2 Slovakia	3	1	1	1	4	5	-1	4			1-1	3-2
3 New Zealand	3	0	3	0	2	2	0	3				1-1
4 Italy	3	0	2	1	4	5	-1	2				

GROUP G	PL	W	D	L	F	A	GD	PTS	BRA	POR	CIV	PRK
1 Brazil	3	2	1	0	5	2	+3	7		0-0	3-1	2-1
2 Portugal	3	1	2	0	7	0	+7	5			0-0	7-0
3 Côte d'Ivoire	3	1	1	1	4	3	+1	4				3-0
4 Korea DPR	3	0	0	3	1	12	-11	0				

GROUP H	PL	W	D	L	F	A	GD	PTS	ESP	CHI	SUI	HON
1 Spain	3	2	0	1	4	2	+2	6		2-1	0-1	2-0
2 Chile	3	2	0	1	3	2	+1	6			1-0	1-0
3 Switzerland	3	1	1	1	1	1	0	4				0-0
4 Honduras	3	0	1	2	0	3	-3	1				

2010 FIFA WORLD CUP SOUTH AFRICA

Round of Sixteen	Quarter-finals	Semi-finals	Final

Spain 1
Portugal 0

| Spain | 1 |
| Paraguay | 0 |

Japan 0 3p
Paraguay 0 5p

| Spain | 1 |
| Germany | 0 |

Argentina 3
Mexico 1

| Argentina | 0 |
| **Germany** | 4 |

England 1
Germany 4

| Spain | 1 |
| Netherlands | 0 |

Uruguay 2
Korea Republic 1

| **Uruguay** | 1 4p |
| Ghana | 1 2p |

USA 1
Ghana 2

| Uruguay | 2 |
| **Netherlands** | 3 |

Brazil 3
Chile 0

| Brazil | 1 |
| **Netherlands** | 2 |

Top scorers: **5** - Thomas Muller GER • **5** - David Villa ESP • **5** - Wesley
Sneijder NED • **5** - Diego Forland URU • **4** - Gonzalo Higuain ARG •
4 - Robert Vittek SVK • **4** - Miroslav Klose GER
Thomas Muller won the Golden Boot as he had three assists to one
apiece for Villa and Sneijder

Slovakia 1
Netherlands 2

Third Place Play-off

| **Germany** | 3 |
| Uruguay | 2 |

First Round Group A	Soccer City Johannesburg	Friday 11-06-2010
Kick-off: 16:00	Sunny 14°	Attendance: 84 490

SOUTH AFRICA   1   1   MEXICO

Siphiwe Tshabalala [55]   Rafael Marquez [79]

SOUTH AFRICA
Gold shirts, Green shorts, Gold socks
Tr: Carlos Alberto Parreira

16 Itumeleng Khune

2 Siboniso Gaxa   4 Aaron Mokoena (c)   20 Bongani Khumalo   [46] 15 Lucas Thwala
3 Tsepo Masilela [70]

12 Reneilwe Letsholonyane   13 Kagisho Dikgacoi [27]
11 Teko Modise   8 Siphiwe Tshabalala †

[83] 10 Steven Pienaar
17 Bernard Parker

9 Katlego Mphela

[73] 9 Guillermo Franco
14 Javier Hernandez

[69] 11 Carlos Vela   17 Giovani Dos Santos
10 Cuauhtemoc Blanco

6 Gerardo Torrado (c) [57]   16 Efrain Juarez [18]

4 Rafael Marquez

3 Carlos Salcido   [55] 12 Paul Aguilar
                                              18 Andres Guardado
2 Francisco Rodriguez   5 Ricardo Osorio

1 Oscar Perez

Tr: Javier Aguirre
Dark Green shirts, Dark green shorts, Dark green socks

MEXICO

MATCH STATS

RSA		MEX
9	Shots	14
5	Shots on Goal	5
17	Fouls Committed	13
4	Corner Kicks	5
3	Caught offside	6
335	Passes	561
209	Completed Passes	447
62%	Passes Success	80%
118	Km Covered	116
22	Av. Top Speed km/h	22
42%	Possession	58%

MATCH OFFICIALS
REFEREE
Ravshan Irmatov UZB
ASSISTANTS
Rafael Ilyasov UZB
Bakhadyr Kochkarov KGZ
4TH OFFICIAL
Subkhiddin Mohd Salleh MAS

(C) Captain † Man of the Match

TABLE

	PL	GD	Pts
RSA	1	0	1
MEX	1	0	1
URU	0	0	0
FRA	0	0	0

Considering it was the Opening Match, this is a good result for us. The pressure got to the boys to begin with but then they started to play the ball around and took control. This is going to be a tight group and anyone who gets four points will go through.
Carlos Alberto Parreira

Apart from the first 20 minutes I think we did well. This is the first World Cup for many of us and we should be pleased with ourselves.
Siphiwe Tshabalala

I'm not happy with our performance today. We played really badly after their goal and we had to work extremely hard to get back into it. That was the key factor to my mind.
Javier Aguirre

It was a fair result and the two halves were very different. We were the better side in the first and created chances, but in the second they were more organised and made life hard for us.
Carlos Salcido

First Round Group A	Green Point Cape Town	Friday 11-06-2010
Kick-off: 20:30		Attendance: 64 100

URUGUAY   0 0   FRANCE

URUGUAY

Sky Blue shirts, Back shorts, Black socks

Tr: Oscar Tabarez

1 Fernando Muslera

6 Mauricio Victorino 59   3 Diego Godin

16 Maximiliano Pereira   2 Diego Lugano (c) 93+   11 Alvaro Pereira

15 Diego Perez   17 Egidio Arevalo   18 Ignacio Gonzalez
87 8 Sebastian Eguren   63 14 Nicolas Lodeiro 65 81 81

9 Luis Suarez   10 Diego Forlan †
74 13 Sebastian Abreu

21 Nicolas Anelka
72 12 Thierry Henry

7 Franck Ribery 19   10 Sidney Govou
85 11 Andre Pierre Gignac

19 Abou Diaby   8 Yoann Gourcuff
75 15 Florent Malouda

14 Jeremy Toulalan 68

13 Patrice Evra (c) 12   3 Eric Abidal   5 William Gallas   2 Bakari Sagna

1 Hugo Lloris

Tr: Raymond Domenech

White shirts, White shorts, White socks

FRANCE

MATCH STATS

URU		FRA
7	Shots	18
3	Shots on Goal	3
13	Fouls Committed	20
0	Corner Kicks	4
5	Caught Offside	4
434	Passes	531
277	Completed Passes	369
64%	Passes Success	69%
101	Km Covered	101
22	Av. Top Speed km/h	22
47%	Possession	53%

MATCH OFFICIALS

REFEREE
Yuichi Nishimura JPN

ASSISTANTS
Toru Sagara JPN
Jeong Hae Sang KOR

4TH OFFICIAL
Joel Aguilar SLV

(C) Captain † Man of the Match

TABLE

	PL	GD	Pts
RSA	1	0	1
MEX	1	0	1
URU	1	0	1
FRA	1	0	1

It was a hard match and we expected that. We're more or less content with the result but not with our play. We didn't have enough of the ball. Ribery played very well and Diaby brought lots of balance. He was very effective in the centre of the park and changed the midfield in a way. I don't want to say that France deserved to win, though, as we kept them quiet in front of our goal.

Oscar Tabarez

It's frustrating when it goes like that, when we push and push and say to ourselves, 'It has to go in'. It was very irritating but the players who came on nonetheless made things happen with those already out there and they imposed a certain rhythm. Our opponents were solid, as you'll see in the coming matches. We succeeded in stopping them from building almost any moves. As a team, we performed very well.

Raymond Domenech

First Round Group A	Loftus Versfeld Tshwane/Pretoria	Wednesday 16-06-2010
Kick-off: 20:30	Cloudy Night 10°	Attendance: 42 658

SOUTH AFRICA   0   3   URUGUAY

Diego Forlan 2 [24] [80p], **Alvaro Pereira** [95+]

SOUTH AFRICA

Gold shirts, Green shorts, Gold socks

Tr: Carlos Alberto Parreira

16 Itumeleng Khune [76]

2 Siboniso Gaxa   4 Aaron Mokoena (c)   20 Bongani Khumalo   3 Tsepo Masilela

13 Kagisho Dikgacoi [42]   [57] 12 Reneilwe Letsholonyane
19 Surprise Moriri

11 Teko Modise   8 Siphiwe Tshabalala

[79] 10 Steven Pienaar [6]
1 Moneeb Josephs (GK)

9 Katlego Mphela

10 Diego Forlan †   9 Luis Suarez   [89] 7 Edinson Cavani
21 Sebastian Fernandez

11 Alvaro Pereira   [90] 15 Diego Perez   17 Egidio Arevalo
5 Walter Gargano

[71] 4 Jorge Fucile   3 Diego Godin   2 Diego Lugano (c)   16 Maximiliano Pereira
20 Alvaro Fernandez

1 Fernando Muslera

Tr: Oscar Tabarez

White shirts, White shorts, White socks

URUGUAY

MATCH STATS

RSA		URU
10	Shots	19
3	Shots on Goal	6
14	Fouls Committed	10
3	Corner Kicks	4
3	Caught Offside	2
596	Passes	448
468	Completed Passes	322
79%	Passes Success	72%
95	Km Covered	101
20	Av. Top Speed km/h	21
51%	Possession	49%

MATCH OFFICIALS
REFEREE
Massimo Busacca SUI
ASSISTANTS
Matthias Arnet SUI
Francesco Buragina SUI
4TH OFFICIAL
Wolfgang Stark GER

(C) Captain † Man of the Match

TABLE

	PL	GD	Pts
URU	2	+3	4
MEX	1	0	1
FRA	1	0	1
RSA	2	-3	1

The 3-0 doesn't reflect the game. Their experience told at important moments. Our hopes are not over. We need to beat France, but we will have to be more aggressive. Everyone is very sad, but I told them it's not yet finished. I always said everything would be decided in the last round. I don't think we can stay behind the ball, wait for one mistake and hit on the break.

Carlos Alberto Parreira

Winning this victory over the home team, the national squad, with all the fans behind them, this was not easy. This result has us happy and satisfied. The group is not over, but today we took an important step. I think that in the first half we could have done things better about the ball possession. In the second half we made better plays, and we control the game defensively: South Africa did not create a single goal situation because of our defensive system.

Oscar Tabarez

First Round Group A	Peter Mokaba Polokwane	Thursday 17-06-2010
Kick-off: 20:30	Partly Cloudy 5°	Attendance: 35 370

FRANCE   0 2   MEXICO

Javier Hernandez [64], Cuauhtemoc Blanco [79p]

FRANCE
Blue shirts, Blue shorts, Blue socks
Tr: Raymond Domenech

MATCH STATS

FRA		MEX
13	Shots	12
4	Shots on Goal	5
23	Fouls Committed	25
7	Corner Kicks	1
2	Caught Offside	4
482	Passes	434
326	Completed Passes	286
68%	Passes Success	66%
101	Km Covered	108
23	Av. Top Speed km/h	22
53%	Possession	47%

MATCH OFFICIALS

REFEREE
Khalil Al Ghamdi KSA

ASSISTANTS
Hassan Kamranifar IRN
Saleh Al Marzouqi UAE

4TH OFFICIAL
Peter O'Leary NZL

(C) Captain † Man of the Match

TABLE

	PL	GD	Pts
URU	2	+3	4
MEX	2	+2	4
FRA	2	-2	1
RSA	2	-3	1

1 Hugo Lloris

2 Bakari Sagna   5 William Gallas   3 Eric Abidal [78]   13 Patrice Evra

19 Abou Diaby   14 Jeremy Toulalan [45]

[69] 10 Sidney Govou   7 Franck Ribery   15 Florent Malouda
20 Mathieu Valbuena

[46] 21 Nicolas Anelka
11 Andre Pierre Gignac

[31] 11 Carlos Vela   [62] 9 Guillermo Franco [4]   17 Giovani Dos Santos
7 Pablo Barrera   10 Cuauhtemoc Blanco

6 Gerardo Torrado   [55] 16 Efrain Juarez [48]
14 Javier Hernandez †

4 Rafael Marquez (c)

3 Carlos Salcido   15 Hector Moreno [49]   2 Francisco Rodriguez [82]   5 Ricardo Osorio

1 Oscar Perez

Tr: Javier Aguirre
Green shirts, White shorts, White socks

MEXICO

I don't know what to say - it's a real disappointment. The match turned on a stroke of bad luck and we never managed to get back on track. We showed good intentions and desire, but there's still something not quite right. For the moment, I don't know what I'm going to say to my players. We've got one match to play and to at least show that we have pride. I definitely blame myself for certain things, but for now I'm keeping them to myself.

Raymond Domenech

It was a very even game in which the first team to score was probably going to win. The French pressed us from the start of the match and the first half was very tough. Things got easier in the second half. We've been together for three months now, this team is well-oiled, and with our potential going forward we always try to trouble our opponents. We now have 90 minutes against Uruguay to reach our first goal, which is to qualify for the Round of 16.

Javier Aguirre

First Round Group A	Royal Bafokeng Rustenburg	Tuesday 22-06-2010
Kick-off: 16:00	Sunny 19°	Attendance: 33 425

MEXICO   0   1   URUGUAY

Luis Suarez 43

MEXICO

Green shirts, White shorts, White socks
Tr: Javier Aguirre

1 Oscar Perez

5 Ricardo Osorio   2 Francisco Rodriguez   57 15 Hector Moreno   3 Carlos Salcido
8 Israel Castro 86

4 Rafael Marquez

6 Gerardo Torrado   46 18 Andres Guardado
7 Pablo Barrera

17 Giovani Dos Santos   9 Guillermo Franco   10 Cuauhtemoc Blanco (c)
63 14 Javier Hernandez 77

10 Diego Forlan   85 9 Luis Suarez †   7 Edinson Cavani
20 Alvaro Fernandez

77 11 Alvaro Pereira   17 Egidio Arevalo   15 Diego Perez
19 Andres Scotti

4 Jorge Fucile   6 Mauricio Victorino   2 Diego Lugano (c)   16 Maximiliano Pereira

1 Fernando Muslera

Tr: Oscar Tabarez
Sky blue shirts, Black shorts, Black socks

URUGUAY

MATCH STATS		
MEX		URU
11	Shots	15
2	Shots on Goal	5
20	Fouls Committed	13
6	Corner Kicks	7
2	Caught Offside	0
595	Passes	315
476	Completed Passes	188
80%	Passes Success	60%
106	Km Covered	102
22	Av. Top Speed km/h	21
59%	Possession	41%

MATCH OFFICIALS
REFEREE
Viktor Kassai HUN
ASSISTANTS
Gabor Eros HUN
Tibor Vamos HUN
4TH OFFICIAL
Martin Hansson SWE

(C) Captain † Man of the Match

TABLE			
	PL	GD	Pts
URU	3	+4	7
MEX	3	+1	4
RSA	3	-2	4
FRA	3	-3	1

The team were a bit tense when they took the field today. I don't know why, but we have to work on that. We weren't looking for the draw, we were trying to win the game. But then they scored and we couldn't quite get ourselves going.
Javier Aguirre

We're left with a sour taste in our mouths. It's true we've qualified and that's the most important thing, but we need to go over all the errors we made today.
Rafael Marquez

If look at what Uruguayan national teams have done at recent World Cups, we can't be anything but totally satisfied. It was clear over the course of the first phase that we're tough opponents for anybody.
Oscar Tabarez

Mexico keep the ball well and they made life very difficult for us today. Fortunately we struck at the right time, just before the interval, and that gave us the composure we needed to see out the game.
Diego Forlan

First Round Group A	Free State Stadium Mangaung/Bloemfontein	Tuesday 22-06-2010
Kick-off: 16:00	Sunny 15°	Attendance: 39 415

FRANCE   1   2   SOUTH AFRICA

Florent Malouda 70   **Bongani Khumalo** 20, **Katlego Mphela** 37

FRANCE
Blue shirts, White shorts, Red socks
Tr: Raymond Domenech

1 Hugo Lloris

2 Bakari Sagna   17 Sebastien Squillaci   5 William Gallas   22 Gael Clichy

82 18 Alou Diarra (c)   19 Abou Diaby 71
    10 Sidney Govou

46 11 Andre Pierre Gignac   8 Yoann Gourcuff 25   7 Franck Ribery
    15 Florent Malouda

55 9 Djibril Cisse
    12 Thierry Henry

9 Katlego Mphela †

68 17 Bernard Parker
    18 Siyabonga Nomvethe

8 Siphiwe Tshabalala   23 Thanduyise Khuboni 6 MacBeth Sibaya   10 Steven Pienaar
                       78 11 Teko Modise

3 Tsepo Masilela   20 Bongani Khumalo   4 Aaron Mokoena (c)   55 5 Anele Ngcongca
                                                                  2 Siboniso Gaxa

1 Moneeb Josephs

Tr: Carlos Alberto Parreira
Gold shirts, Green shorts, Gold socks

SOUTH AFRICA

MATCH STATS

FRA		RSA
10	Shots	21
4	Shots on Goal	10
10	Fouls Committed	12
3	Corner Kicks	5
6	Caught Offside	3
428	Passes	491
309	Completed Passes	381
72%	Passes Success	78%
98	Km Covered	106
23	Av. Top Speed km/h	22
50%	Possession	50%

MATCH OFFICIALS
REFEREE
Oscar Ruiz COL
ASSISTANTS
Abraham Gonzalez COL
Humberto Clavijo COL
4TH OFFICIAL
Hector Baldassi ARG

(C) Captain † Man of the Match

TABLE

	PL	GD	Pts
URU	3	+4	7
MEX	3	+1	4
RSA	3	-2	4
FRA	3	-3	1

We're sad and disappointed, even if I saw what I wanted to see in this match: selflessness, heart and solidarity. When things aren't going well for you, they really don't go well. We tried to muster some energy. This team has real potential. I wish my successor and the France team good luck. I've enjoyed being coach and I cared deeply about this France team. This isn't the end because the France team never dies. The players still want to achieve something.
Raymond Domenech

We had chances. I'm very proud of the players and the way in which they played right from the start and for the whole 90 minutes. We didn't fall too far short of qualifying. Even though I think at 2-0 we should have killed the game off by scoring a third goal, I'm happy to have seen my players make progress. They've made the whole country proud. The foundations are there and I'm very confident about the future of South African football.
Carlos Alberto Parreira

First Round Group B	Port Elizabeth Stadium Nelson Mandela Bay/Port Elizabeth	Saturday 12-06-2010
Kick-off: 13:30	19°	Attendance: 31 513

KOREA REPUBLIC   2   0   GREECE

Lee Jung Soo [7], Park Ji Sung [52]

KOREA REPUBLIC

Red shirts, White shorts, Red socks

Tr: Huh Jung Moo

18 Jung Sung Ryong

22 Cha Du Ri   4 Cho Yong Hyung   14 Lee Jung Soo   12 Lee Young Pyo

91+ 17 Lee Chung Yong   8 Kim Jung Woo   74 16 Ki Sung Yueng   7 Park Ji Sung†(c)
13 Kim Jae Sung   5 Kim Nam Il

19 Yeom Ki Hun   87 10 Park Chu Young
11 Lee Seung Yeoul

59 7 Georgios Samaras   17 Theofanis Gekas   61 9 Angelos Charisteas
14 Dimitrios Salpingidis   20 Pantelis Kapetanos

46 10 Georgios Karagounis (c)   6 Alexandros Tziolis   21 Konstantinos Katsouranis
3 Christos Patsatzoglou

15 Vasileios Torosidis 56   2 Giourkas Seitaridis

8 Avraam Papadopoulos   11 Loukas Vyntra

12 Alexandros Tzorvas

Tr: Otto Rehhagel (GER)

Blue shirts, Blue shorts, Blue socks

GREECE

MATCH STATS

KOR		GRE
18	Shots	6
7	Shots on Goal	2
14	Fouls Committed	12
6	Corner Kicks	11
1	Caught Offside	4
499	Passes	500
333	Completed Passes	340
67%	Passes Success	68%
108	Km Covered	105
23	Av. Top Speed km/h	23
50%	Possession	50%

MATCH OFFICIALS

REFEREE

Michael Hester NZL

ASSISTANTS

Jan Hendrik Hintz NZL

Tevita Makasini TGA

4TH OFFICIAL

Martin Vazquez URU

(C) Captain † Man of the Match

TABLE

	PL	GD	Pts
KOR	1	+2	3
ARG	0	0	0
NGA	0	0	0
GRE	1	-2	0

We were determined to do well. We rehearsed lots of set-pieces in particular, and looked to put them under pressure down the left. It wasn't a perfect performance but we met the expectations placed on us. We knew Greece would drop back even further if they went ahead, so scoring first was so important. Another key factor was that we carried on attacking in an attempt to add a second.

Huh Jung Moo

Neither team knew exactly where they stood going into the match. We had the first chance but we were unable to take it. We were caught napping on the first goal and never really got into the match after that. We just didn't have that bit of luck you need. South Korea were worth their win because they took their chances and we didn't. We didn't tackle well and Korea played themselves into a frenzy.

Otto Rehhagel

First Round Group B	Ellis Park Johannesburg	Saturday 12-06-2010
Kick-off: 16:00	16°	Attendance: 55 686

ARGENTINA   1   0   NIGERIA

Gabriel Heinze 6

ARGENTINA
Sky-blue and white striped shirts, Black shorts, White socks
Tr: Diego Maradona

MATCH STATS

ARG		NGA
24	Shots	11
7	Shots on Goal	1
7	Fouls Committed	8
10	Corner Kicks	4
0	Caught Offside	0
597	Passes	367
446	Completed Passes	231
75%	Passes Success	63%
95	Km Covered	93
23	Av. Top Speed km/h	22
58%	Possession	42%

MATCH OFFICIALS
REFEREE
Wolfgang Stark GER
ASSISTANTS
Jan-Hendrik Salver GER
Mike Pickel GER
4TH OFFICIAL
Khalil Al Ghamdi KSA

(C) Captain † Man of the Match

TABLE

	PL	GD	Pts
KOR	1	+2	3
ARG	1	+1	3
NGA	1	-1	0
GRE	1	-2	0

22 Sergio Romero

17 Jonas Gutierrez 41   2 Martin Demichelis   13 Walter Samuel   6 Gabriel Heinze

74 8 Juan Veron   14 Javier Mascherano (c)
    20 Maxi Rodriguez

11 Carlos Tevez   10 Lionel Messi   7 Angel Di Maria
                                      85 4 Nicolas Burdisso

79 9 Gonzalo Higuain
    19 Diego Milito

8 Yakubu Ayegbeni   18 Victor Obinna
                     52 9 Obafemi Martins

60 19 Chinedu Ogbuke Obasi 20 Dickson Etuhu 15 Lukman Haruna 77 14 Sani Kaita
    11 Peter Odemwingie

75 3 Taye Taiwo   6 Danny Shittu   2 Joseph Yobo (c)   17 Chidi Odiah
    12 Kalu Uche

1 Vincent Enyeama †

Tr: Lars Lagerback (SWE)
Green shirts, Green shorts, Green socks

NIGERIA

That was an important step for us today but we need to make a whole lot of improvements if we want to reach the Final. The game played out just as I thought it would, and if we'd converted the chances we made then we'd be talking right now about a fantastic Argentina performance. However, we were very wasteful and that's something we need to sort out.
Diego Maradona

I am a little disappointed with the result although I am proud at how my players performed. Unfortunately we made an error that led to the corner they scored from, and at this level if you lose your concentration for a second you pay for it. That's exactly what happened. If we hadn't made that mistake, we might have come away with a draw.
Lars Lagerback

First Round Group B	Soccer City Johannesburg	Thursday 17-06-2010
Kick-off: 13:30	Sunny 7°	Attendance: 82 174

ARGENTINA   4   1   KOREA REPUBLIC

Park Chu Young OG [17], Gonzalo Higuain 3 [33 76 80]   Lee Chung Yong [45]

ARGENTINA

Sky-blue and white striped shirts, Black shorts, White socks

Tr: Diego Maradona

22 Sergio Romero

17 Jonas Gutierrez [54]   2 Martin Demichelis [23] 13 Walter Samuel   6 Gabriel Heinze [74]
4 Nicolas Burdisso

14 Javier Mascherano (c) [55]

20 Maxi Rodriguez   7 Angel Di Maria

10 Lionel Messi

[82] 9 Gonzalo Higuain †   [75] 11 Carlos Tevez
5 Mario Bolatti   16 Sergio Aguero

[81] 10 Park Chu Young
20 Lee Dong Gook

19 Yeom Ki Hun [10]   7 Park Ji Sung (c)   17 Lee Chung Yong [34]

[46] 16 Ki Sung Yueng   8 Kim Jung Woo
5 Kim Nam Il

12 Lee Young Pyo   14 Lee Jung Soo   4 Cho Yong Hyung   2 Oh Beom Seok

18 Jung Sung Ryong

Tr: Huh Jung Moo

Red shirts, White shorts, Red socks

KOREA REPUBLIC

MATCH STATS

ARG		KOR
22	Shots	13
11	Shots on Goal	2
19	Fouls Committed	19
6	Corner Kicks	2
4	Caught Offside	0
484	Passes	336
360	Completed Passes	207
74%	Passes Success	62%
97	Km Covered	103
23	Av. Top Speed km/h	21
57%	Possession	43%

MATCH OFFICIALS

REFEREE

Frank De Bleeckere BEL

ASSISTANTS

Peter Hermans BEL

Walter Vromans BEL

4TH OFFICIAL

Jerome Damon RSA

(C) Captain † Man of the Match

TABLE

	PL	GD	Pts
ARG	2	+4	6
KOR	2	-1	3
NGA	1	-1	0
GRE	1	-2	0

I want to congratulate my players for having perfectly executed our game plan. We deserved a win like this because we'd already threatened this kind of result against Nigeria. Except from the [Martin] Demichelis error, we had all the play and did what we wanted with the ball. Korea [Republic] never managed to get behind us, they never had the ball and, aside from one counter-attack in the second period, I can hardly remember them having a shot on goal.

Diego Maradona

I didn't expect us to lose by such a large margin. We didn't play well and Argentina did. They got a slice of luck with their first goal whereas we weren't able to take our chances.

Huh Jung Moo

Our strategy was to stay tight at the back and then take any available opportunities to hit them on the break. But we conceded the first goal very early and that upset our game plan.

Oh Beom Seok

First Round Group B	Free State Stadium Mangaung/Bloemfontein	Thursday 17-06-2010
Kick-off: 16:00	Sunny 10°	Attendance: 31 593

GREECE   2   1   NIGERIA

Dimitrios Salpingidis 44, Vasileios Torosidis 71   Kalu Uche 16

GREECE

White shirts, White shorts, White socks

Tr: Otto Rehhagel (GER)

12 Alexandros Tzorvas

19 Sokratis Papastathopoulos 15 8 Avraam Papadopoulos 16 Sotirios Kyrgiakos
37
7 Georgios Samaras 88

11 Loukas Vyntra   15 Vasileios Torosidis

6 Alexandros Tziolis 59   21 Konstantinos Katsouranis

14 Dimitrios Salpingidis   17 Theofanis Gekas   10 Georgios Karagounis (c)
79
18 Sotiris Ninis

8 Yakubu Ayegbeni   11 Peter Odemwingie
46
19 Chinedu Ogbuke Obasi 89

12 Kalu Uche   15 Lukman Haruna   20 Dickson Etuhu   14 Sani Kaita 33

3 Taye Taiwo   6 Danny Shittu   2 Joseph Yobo (c)   17 Chidi Odiah
55
21 Uwa Echiejile
77
5 Rabiu Afolabi

1 Vincent Enyeama †

Tr: Lars Lagerback (SWE)

Green shirts, Green shorts, Green socks

NIGERIA

MATCH STATS

GRE		NGA
27	Shots	10
11	Shots on Goal	4
13	Fouls Committed	15
11	Corner Kicks	3
3	Caught Offside	1
462	Passes	375
357	Completed Passes	267
77%	Passes Success	71%
96	Km Covered	85
25	Av. Top Speed km/h	22
56%	Possession	44%

MATCH OFFICIALS

REFEREE
Oscar Ruiz COL

ASSISTANTS
Abraham Gonzalez COL
Humberto Clavijo COL

4TH OFFICIAL
Joel Aguilar SLV

(C) Captain † Man of the Match

TABLE

	PL	GD	Pts
ARG	2	+4	6
KOR	2	-1	3
GRE	2	-1	3
NGA	2	-2	0

Unfortunately, the game started just like the last one and we went a goal down. My team needed quite some time to recover. We were dominant after the red card, but there are plenty of examples where the team with the extra man goes on to lose. However, we reacted well to conceding the first goal, showed tremendous passion and belief, and turned the game around.

Otto Rehhagel

The positive thing is that we still have a chance of qualifying, although we need a helping hand from Argentina. We need a fresh start, and we'll do that by beating Korea Republic. We were comfortably in control, but we had problems reorganising after the sending-off. I'm pleased with my players' attitude in the circumstances. We played well in the second half and managed to create a couple of decent chances.

Lars Lagerback

First Round Group B	Durban Stadium Durban		Tuesday 22-06-2010
Kick-off: 20:30	Partly Cloudy	18°	Attendance: 61 874

NIGERIA   2   2   KOREA REPUBLIC

Kalu Uche 12, Yakubu Ayegbeni 69p   Lee Jung Soo 38, Park Chu Young 49

NIGERIA

Green shirts, Green shorts, Green socks

Tr: Lars Lagerback (SWE)

1 Vincent Enyeama 31

17 Chidi Odiah   2 Joseph Yobo   6 Danny Shittu   5 Rabiu Afolabi
                   46 21 Uwa Echiejile

      4 Nwankwo Kanu(c)   20 Dickson Etuhu   13 Yussuf Ayila 42 12 Kalu Uche
  57 9 Obafemi Martins

19 Chinedu Ogbuke Obasi 37   8 Yakubu Ayegbeni
                              70 18 Victor Obinna

      19 Yeom Ki Hun   10 Park Chu Young
  64 5 Kim Nam Il 68   93+ 15 Kim Dong Jin

7 Park Ji Sung(c)†   16 Ki Sung Yueng   8 Kim Jung Woo   17 Lee Chung Yong
                 87 13 Kim Jae Sung

12 Lee Young Pyo   14 Lee Jung Soo   4 Cho Yong Hyung   22 Cha Du Ri

18 Jung Sung Ryong

Tr: Huh Jung Moo

White shirts, Blue shorts, White socks

KOREA REPUBLIC

MATCH STATS

NGA		KOR
11	Shots	16
4	Shots on Goal	8
22	Fouls Committed	12
1	Corner Kicks	7
1	Caught Offside	2
438	Passes	490
301	Completed Passes	364
69%	Passes Success	74%
99	Km Covered	107
21	Av. Top Speed km/h	22
46%	Possession	54%

MATCH OFFICIALS
REFEREE
Olegario Benquerenca POR
ASSISTANTS
Jose Cardinal POR
Bertino Miranda POR
4TH OFFICIAL
Marco Rodriguez MEX

(C)Captain †Man of the Match

TABLE

	PL	GD	Pts
ARG	3	+6	9
KOR	3	-1	4
GRE	3	-3	3
NGA	3	-2	1

We went down fighting. I think they players did really well today. They showed a big heart for Nigeria and I think we deserved to win.

Lars Lagerback

It's like we have let down a whole lot of people. I would just like to apologise for letting the whole country down, the whole continent down. We have ourselves to blame and are at fault.

Vincent Enyeama

I knew it would be difficult if we conceded an early goal, but the players reacted very well. And the penalty made it more difficult for us mentally as well. Asian football is on the up. But there's still a gap between us and the rest of the world.

Huh Jung Moo

I recognise how difficult it is to reach the Round of 16, and I could see how much Korean football has progressed to see the team overcoming the pressure.

Park Ji Sung

First Round Group B	Peter Mokaba Polokwane	Tuesday 22-06-2010
Kick-off: 20:30	Clear Night 8°	Attendance: 38 891

GREECE   0   2   ARGENTINA

Martin Demichelis 77, **Martin Palermo** 89

GREECE

White shirts, White shorts, White socks
Tr: Otto Rehhagel (GER)

MATCH STATS

GRE		ARG
7	Shots	22
3	Shots on Goal	12
15	Fouls Committed	8
1	Corner Kicks	10
0	Caught Offside	2
277	Passes	800
145	Completed Passes	662
52%	Passes Success	83%
98	Km Covered	99
22	Av. Top Speed km/h	22
33%	Possession	67%

MATCH OFFICIALS

REFEREE
Ravshan Irmatov UZB

ASSISTANTS
Rafael Ilyasov UZB
Bakhadyr Kochkarov KGZ

4TH OFFICIAL
Peter O'Leary NZL

(C) Captain † Man of the Match

TABLE

	PL	GD	Pts
ARG	3	+6	9
KOR	3	-1	4
GRE	3	-3	3
NGA	3	-2	1

12 Alexandros Tzorvas

8 Avraam Papadopoulos   5 Vangelis Moras   16 Sotirios Kyrgiakos

11 Loukas Vyntra

55   15 Vasileios Torosidis
3 Christos Patsatzoglou

19 Sokratis Papastathopoulos

21 Konstantinos Katsouranis 30   10 Georgios Karagounis (c)   6 Alexandros Tziolis
54   18 Sotiris Ninis   46   4 Nikos Spiropoulos

7 Georgios Samaras

77   16 Sergio Aguero   80   19 Diego Milito
23 Javier Pastore   18 Martin Palermo

10 Lionel Messi (c) †

8 Juan Veron   5 Mario Bolatti 76   20 Maxi Rodriguez
63   7 Angel Di Maria

3 Clemente Rodriguez   4 Nicolas Burdisso   2 Martin Demichelis   15 Nicolas Otamendi

22 Sergio Romero

Tr: Diego Maradona
Blue shirts, Blue shorts, Blue socks

ARGENTINA

To get knocked out is really hard to take and we should be focusing our thoughts on the game right now. We paid dearly for losing the first match to Korea Republic. We'd gone into that game with high expectations. All the same, we've shown real character in these three matches, and you have to remember that there are a lot of good sides here who haven't played their best football. And there are some other good sides that didn't even make it.

Otto Rehhagel

The team did a fantastic job. Every single one of my players did exactly what I wanted them to do. We knew we had to be careful at set-pieces and with shots from distance but we also knew that if we put pressure on them we'd force them to make mistakes. Things worked out perfectly for us. I was sorry [Lionel] Messi didn't get a goal. I dived on the ground when his shot hit the post and if there'd been a swimming pool around I'd have jumped in head first.

Diego Maradona

First Round Group C	Royal Bafokeng Rustenburg	Saturday 12-06-2010
Kick-off: 20:30	14°	Attendance: 38 646

ENGLAND   1 1   USA

Steven Gerrard [4]   Clint Dempsey [40]

ENGLAND

White shirts, White shorts, White socks
Tr: Fabio Capello (ITA)

12 Robert Green

2 Glen Johnson   20 Ledley King   6 John Terry   3 Ashley Cole
                 [46] 18 Jamie Carragher [60]

              4 Steven Gerrard (c) [61]   8 Frank Lampard

7 Aaron Lennon   16 James Milner [26]
                                    [31] 17 Shaun Wright-Phillips

              21 Emile Heskey
         [79] 9 Peter Crouch   10 Wayne Rooney

         17 Jozy Altidore   20 Robbie Findley [74]
    [86] 11 Stuart Holden [77] 14 Edson Buddle

8 Clint Dempsey   13 Ricardo Clark   4 Michael Bradley   10 Landon Donovan

3 Carlos Bocanegra (c) 5 Oguchi Onyewu 15 Jay DeMerit [47] 6 Steve Cherundolo [39]

              1 Tim Howard †

Tr: Bob Bradley
Dark blue shirts with a white sash, Dark blue shorts, Dark blue socks

USA

MATCH STATS

ENG		USA
18	Shots	13
8	Shots on Goal	4
12	Fouls Committed	14
8	Corner Kicks	4
5	Caught Offside	2
487	Passes	376
339	Completed Passes	218
70%	Passes Success	58%
108	Km Covered	107
23	Av. Top Speed km/h	23
54%	Possession	46%

MATCH OFFICIALS
REFEREE
Carlos Simon BRA
ASSISTANTS
Altemir Hausmann BRA
Roberto Braatz BRA
4TH OFFICIAL
Luis Chiriboga ECU

(C) Captain † Man of the Match

TABLE

	PL	GD	Pts
USA	1	0	1
ENG	1	0	1
SVN	0	0	0
ALG	0	0	0

We need to get behind Robert (Green) and support him. I'm sure he will play a big part for us further down the line and he might make an important save that wins us a match so we are all behind him. When you go in front, a team like us and the way we defend, we expect to go on and win the match. It was a bit of a shock (conceding the goal) and took us a while to get over it but I thought we went on to finish the game stronger.

Steven Gerrard

Our first game is still about getting something, but when you go behind early, I thought the response was good. I think after the goal, we started to put some plays together and built up confidence.

Bob Bradley

You always see people scoring like that and think 'hey how come that never happens to me'. Finally, it's a goal that the keeper probably should have made a save on but they all count the same if they go in.

Clint Dempsey

First Round Group C	Peter Mokaba Polokwane	Sunday 13-06-2010

Kick-off: 13:30	Sunny	19°	Attendance: 30 325

ALGERIA 0 1 SLOVENIA

Robert Koren [79]

ALGERIA

White shirts, White shorts, White socks
Tr: Rabah Saadane

MATCH STATS

ALG		SVN
11	Shots	7
2	Shots on Goal	4
17	Fouls Committed	10
4	Corner Kicks	3
2	Caught Offside	3
480	Passes	538
343	Completed Passes	398
71%	Passes Success	74%
99	Km Covered	106
22	Av. Top Speed km/h	21
48%	Possession	52%

MATCH OFFICIALS

REFEREE
Carlos Batres GUA

ASSISTANTS
Leonel Leal CRC
Carlos Pastrana HON

4TH OFFICIAL
Peter O'Leary NZL

(C) Captain † Man of the Match

TABLE

	PL	GD	Pts
SVN	1	+1	3
USA	1	0	1
ENG	1	0	1
ALG	1	-1	0

16 Faouzi Chaouchi

2 Madjid Bougherra   5 Rafik Halliche   4 Anther Yahia(c)

82 21 Foued Kadir   3 Nadir Belhadj
    17 Adlane Guedioura

19 Hassan Yebda 95+   8 Medhi Lacen

81 13 Karim Matmour   15 Karim Ziani
    10 Rafik Saifi

58 11 Rafik Djebbour
    9 Abdelkader Ghezzal 59 73 73

53 14 Zlatko Dedic   11 Milivoje Novakovic
    9 Zlatan Ljubijankic

84 10 Valter Birsa   17 Andraz Kirm
    7 Nejc Pecnik

8 Robert Koren(c)†   87 18 Aleksandar Radosavljevic 35
                          20 Andrej Komac 93+

13 Bojan Jokic   5 Bostjan Cesar   4 Marko Suler   2 Miso Brecko

1 Samir Handanovic

Tr: Matjaz Kek
Dark green shirts, Dark green shorts, Dark green socks

SLOVENIA

It was between Slovenia and us for second place and we missed our chance. We're going to find it very difficult in our next two games now. Mistakes are part and parcel of the game and I'm not going to criticise Faouzi Chaouchi and Abdelkader Ghezzal.
Rabah Saadane

I expected a lot more from what was a good performance from us. We were hoping to take at least a point from this game but it wasn't to be.
Rafik Halliche

We deserved to win and I think we outplayed Algeria. We scored a goal and that's what counts in football. Maybe we pushed a bit harder for the win and wanted it more. It's Slovenia's first World Cup victory!
Matjaz Kek

This win can only increase our confidence. We made a few changes after their red card. I pushed forward a bit more and we made an opening, though I have to say there was a touch of good fortune about my goal.
Robert Koren

First Round Group C	Ellis Park Johannesburg	Friday 18-06-2010
Kick-off: 16:00	Sunny 14°	Attendance: 45 573

SLOVENIA   2   2   USA

Valter Birsa [13], **Zlatan Ljubijankic** [42]

Landon Donovan [48], **Michael Bradley** [82]

SLOVENIA
White shirts, White shorts, White socks
Tr: Matjaz Kek

1 Samir Handanovic

2 Miso Brecko   4 Marko Suler [69]   5 Bostjan Cesar [35]   13 Bojan Jokic [75]

[87] 10 Valter Birsa   18 Aleksandar Radosavljevic   8 Robert Koren(c)   17 Andraz Kirm [72]
14 Zlatko Dedic

9 Zlatan Ljubijankic
[74] 7 Nejc Pecnik   11 Milivoje Novakovic
[94+] 20 Andrej Komac

[46] 20 Robbie Findley [40]   17 Jozy Altidore
22 Benny Feilhaber

10 Landon Donovan† [46] 16 Francisco Torres   4 Michael Bradley   8 Clint Dempsey
19 Maurice Edu

3 Carlos Bocanegra(c) [80] 5 Oguchi Onyewu   15 Jay DeMerit   6 Steve Cherundolo
9 Herculez Gomez

1 Tim Howard

Tr: Bob Bradley
Dark blue shirts with a white sash, Dark blue shorts, Dark blue socks

USA

MATCH STATS

SVN		USA
7	Shots	14
4	Shots on Goal	6
15	Fouls Committed	18
2	Corner Kicks	4
3	Caught Offside	0
406	Passes	428
276	Completed Passes	303
68%	Passes Success	71%
106	Km Covered	107
21	Av. Top Speed km/h	21
49%	Possession	51%

MATCH OFFICIALS
REFEREE
Koman Coulibaly MLI
ASSISTANTS
Redouane Achik MAR
Inacio Candido ANG
4TH OFFICIAL
Subkhiddin Mohd Salleh MAS

(C) Captain †Man of the Match

TABLE

	PL	GD	Pts
SVN	2	+1	4
USA	2	0	2
ENG	1	0	1
ALG	1	-1	0

It was a great match but it shouldn't have happened that we made such dumb mistakes in the second half. It was a really tough match and my team showed they were of high quality. We gained a point today and we are in a very good position. Now we need to recover to prepare for England.

Matjaz Kek

In an early play Birsa slipped in the gap and hit a great shot. Then we were already pushing for a goal and they hit us for a well-timed counter. This team still understands how to fight for 90 minutes.

Bob Bradley

I don't know that there are many teams that would have responded in that way to going two goals down. We said at half-time if we don't believe we can do it, then let's not go back out.

Landon Donovan

First Round Group C	Greenpoint Cape Town	Friday 18-06-2010
Kick-off: 20:30	Clear Night 17°	Attendance: 64 100

ENGLAND   0   0   ALGERIA

ENGLAND

White shirts, white shorts, white socks

Tr: Fabio Capello (ITA)

1 David James

2 Glen Johnson   18 Jamie Carragher 58   6 John Terry   3 Ashley Cole †

7 Aaron Lennon   8 Frank Lampard   14 Gareth Barry   4 Steven Gerrard (c)
63 17 Shaun Wright-Phillips   84 9 Peter Crouch

74 21 Emile Heskey   10 Wayne Rooney
19 Jermain Defoe

13 Karim Matmour

81 15 Karim Ziani   74 7 Ryad Boudebouz
17 Adlane Guedioura   22 Djamel Abdoun

3 Nadir Belhadj   8 Medhi Lacen 85   88 19 Hassan Yebda   21 Foued Kadir
20 Djamel Mesbah

4 Anther Yahia   5 Rafik Halliche   2 Madjid Bougherra

23 Rais M'Bolhi

Tr: Rabah Saadane

Green shirts, Green shorts, Green socks

ALGERIA

MATCH STATS

ENG		ALG
15	Shots	11
6	Shots on Goal	1
13	Fouls Committed	13
10	Corner Kicks	3
1	Caught Offside	3
606	Passes	533
463	Completed Passes	384
76%	Passes Success	72%
111	Km Covered	106
23	Av. Top Speed km/h	23
48%	Possession	52%

MATCH OFFICIALS

REFEREE
Ravshan Irmatov UZB

ASSISTANTS
Rafael Ilyasov UZB
Bakhadyr Kochkarov KGZ

4TH OFFICIAL
Michael Hester NZL

(C) Captain † Man of the Match

TABLE

	PL	GD	Pts
SVN	2	+1	4
USA	2	0	2
ENG	2	0	2
ALG	2	-1	1

This is not the team I recognise from training or from qualifying. We missed too many passes, lost too many balls. It was not a good game. We have to do better. We have another game to play. It's our last chance to continue in the tournament. The players know what they have to do. We need to get to the ball quicker. It's not just a question of one player. It's the team. We can change the tactics if we have to, but we have to do better.

Fabio Capello

We could have won and so could they. Both teams had opportunities. I think it was a match where everyone tried as much as they could and it's a pity it was a draw and a goalless draw at that.

Rabah Saadane

We are pleased with the draw as the English underestimated us in the media over recent days. We were determined to show them we were not just here for the ride and that we have a decent team.

Ryad Boudebouz

First Round Group C	Port Elizabeth Stadium Nelson Mandela Bay/Port Elizabeth	Wednesday 23-06-2010
Kick-off: 16:00	Sunny 19°	Attendance: 36 893

SLOVENIA 0 1 ENGLAND

Jermain Defoe [23]

SLOVENIA
White shirts, White shorts, White socks
Tr: Matjaz Kek

1 Samir Handanovic

2 Miso Brecko   4 Marko Suler   5 Bostjan Cesar   13 Bojan Jokic [40]

10 Valter Birsa [79]   18 Aleksandar Radosavljevic   8 Robert Koren(c) [79]   17 Andraz Kirm   23 Tim Matavz

[62] 9 Zlatan Ljubijankic   11 Milivoje Novakovic
14 Zlatko Dedic [81]

[72] 10 Wayne Rooney   [86] 19 Jermain Defoe †
11 Joe Cole   21 Emile Heskey

4 Steven Gerrard(c)   14 Gareth Barry   8 Frank Lampard   16 James Milner

3 Ashley Cole   15 Matthew Upson   6 John Terry   2 Glen Johnson [48]

1 David James

Tr: Fabio Capello (ITA)
Red shirts, Red shorts, Red socks

ENGLAND

MATCH STATS

SVN		ENG
13	Shots	13
6	Shots on Goal	8
19	Fouls Committed	20
2	Corner Kicks	11
1	Caught Offside	1
391	Passes	575
241	Completed Passes	419
62%	Passes Success	73%
106	Km Covered	106
22	Av. Top Speed km/h	22
46%	Possession	54%

MATCH OFFICIALS
REFEREE
Wolfgang Stark GER
ASSISTANTS
Jan-Hendrik Salver GER
Mike Pickel GER
4TH OFFICIAL
Joel Aguilar SLV

(C) Captain † Man of the Match

TABLE

	PL	GD	Pts
USA	3	+1	5
ENG	3	+1	5
SVN	3	0	4
ALG	3	-2	1

It's an indescribable feeling, but this is sport. Of course we are disappointed but I hope in time my players can focus on what they've achieved. I congratulate my team and England. England played well but at the end we could have got a draw, but sport is like that, very unpredictable. I hope these players will be role models for those who might play for Slovenia in the future. They are maturing a lot and they will come to a point where they will play their best.
Matjaz Kek

This was the team that I know. We played together with spirit; we fought together and I am really, really happy with the result. I'm also happy that I re-found the team that I knew from the qualifiers. This team can go forward now. All the team the coaches; our minds are free. We can go forward without fear, without everything. I'm happy for the fans.
Fabio Capello

First Round Group C	Loftus Versfeld Tshwane/Pretoria	Wednesday 23-06-2010
Kick-off: 16:00	Sunny 19°	Attendance: 35 827

USA   1   0   ALGERIA

Landon Donovan 91+

USA
White shirts, White shorts, White socks
Tr: Bob Bradley

MATCH STATS		
USA		ALG
22	Shots	19
10	Shots on Goal	4
11	Fouls Committed	21
4	Corner Kicks	6
1	Caught Offside	4
470	Passes	447
350	Completed Passes	331
74%	Passes Success	74%
110	Km Covered	104
24	Av. Top Speed km/h	24
52%	Possession	48%

MATCH OFFICIALS
REFEREE
Frank De Bleeckere BEL
ASSISTANTS
Peter Hermans BEL
Walter Vromans BEL
4TH OFFICIAL
Subkhiddin Mohd Salleh MAS

(C) Captain † Man of the Match

TABLE			
	PL	GD	Pts
USA	3	+1	5
ENG	3	+1	5
SVN	3	0	4
ALG	3	-2	1

1 Tim Howard

6 Steve Cherundolo   15 Jay DeMerit   3 Carlos Bocanegra (c)   12 Jonathan Bornstein 80
7 DaMarcus Beasley 90

10 Landon Donovan †   4 Michael Bradley   19 Maurice Edu 64   8 Clint Dempsey
14 Edson Buddle

9 Herculez Gomez   17 Jozy Altidore 62
46 22 Benny Feilhaber

11 Rafik Djebbour   13 Karim Matmour
65 9 Abdelkader Ghezzal   85 10 Rafik Saifi

15 Karim Ziani
69 17 Adlane Guedioura

3 Nadir Belhadj   8 Medhi Lacen 83   19 Hassan Yebda 12   21 Foued Kadir

4 Anther Yahia 76 93+ 93+   5 Rafik Halliche   2 Madjid Bougherra

23 Rais M'Bolhi

Tr: Rabah Saadane
Green shirts, Green shorts, Green socks

ALGERIA

These guys never give up and they showed that again today.
Bob Bradley
We should have and could have scored earlier, which would have spared us that dramatic ending. In the end, though, it's a good thing that it happened that way, so quickly. I didn't even have time to think what I was going to do. Being in the right place and putting the ball in the net just came naturally.
Landon Donovan

I think it was a very good match from us. We played well - in fact, both teams did. There were a lot of chances at both ends. We were unlucky. The altitude played a role in the physical side of things and some players struggled in the second half.
Rabah Saadane
We're sorry for the people of Algeria, but they need to know that we gave everything. We never gave up. We had chances but conceded on the break. That's football.
Karim Ziani

First Round Group D	Loftus Versfeld Tshwane/Pretoria	Sunday 13-06-2010
Kick-off: 16:00	Sunny 21°	Attendance: 38833

SERBIA   0 1   GHANA

Asamoah Gyan [85p]

SERBIA

Red shirts with an off centre white cross, Blue shorts, Red socks

Tr: Radomir Antic

1 Vladimir Stojkovic

5 Nemanja Vidic 13 Aleksandar Lukovic [54] [74] [74]

6 Branislav Ivanovic   3 Aleksandar Kolarov

11 Nenad Milijas [62]
10 Dejan Stankovic(c)   22 Zdravko Kuzmanovic [83]

17 Milos Krasic   14 Milan Jovanovic [76]
                                          20 Neven Subotic

9 Marko Pantelic   15 Nikola Zigic [19]
[69]   8 Danko Lazovic

3 Asamoah Gyan † [93+]
20 Quincy Owusu-Abeyie

21 Kwadwo Asamoah [73]
10 Stephen Appiah

13 Andre Ayew   23 Kevin Prince Boateng 6 Anthony Annan 12 Prince Tagoe [89]
[91+]   19 Lee Addy

2 Hans Sarpei   15 Isaac Vorsah 5 John Mensah(c)   4 John Pantsil

22 Richard Kingson

Tr: Milovan Rajevac (SRB)

White shirts, White shorts, White socks

GHANA

MATCH STATS

SRB		GHA
13	Shots	16
2	Shots on Goal	3
10	Fouls Committed	15
4	Corner Kicks	4
2	Caught Offside	0
458	Passes	467
328	Completed Passes	340
72%	Passes Success	73%
94	Km Covered	97
21	Av. Top Speed km/h	22
52%	Possession	48%

MATCH OFFICIALS

REFEREE
Hector Baldassi ARG

ASSISTANTS
Ricardo Casas ARG
Hernan Maidana ARG

4TH OFFICIAL
Subkhiddin Mohd Salleh MAS

(C)Captain † Man of the Match

TABLE

	PL	GD	Pts
GHA	1	+1	3
AUS	0	0	0
GER	0	0	0
SRB	1	-1	0

Of course this is a big blow for us. We were nervous from the start and made a lot of mistakes. We have two more games, so we must now be positive and regain our energy.

Radomir Antic

I've apologised to my team-mates. It was a foolish mistake to make. I tried to head the ball and when I realised that I was going to miss it, my arm went out - it was a reflex action.

Zdravko Kuzmanovic

This is a great victory but I'm sorry for the Serbian team. I know many of their players and I could see how saddened they were but I tried to concentrate on my job and perform my duties in a professional manner. Maybe we got lucky, they're a very good team.

Milovan Rajevac

We showed a lot of experience and we were better today. I have to say thank you to the crowd. Every African is behind us.

Asamoah Gyan

First Round Group D	Durban Stadium Durban	Sunday 13-06-2010
Kick-off: 20:30	Partly Cloudy 19°	Attendance: 62 660

GERMANY   4   0   AUSTRALIA

Lukas Podolski [8], **Miroslav Klose** [26],
Thomas Müller [68], **Cacau** [70]

GERMANY

White shirts, Black shorts, White socks
Tr: Joachim Löw

MATCH STATS

GER		AUS
16	Shots	10
10	Shots on Goal	2
10	Fouls Committed	19
4	Corner Kicks	7
7	Caught Offside	1
618	Passes	530
474	Completed Passes	384
77%	Passes Success	72%
112	Km Covered	113
21	Av. Top Speed km/h	21
55%	Possession	45%

MATCH OFFICIALS

REFEREE
Marco Rodriguez MEX

ASSISTANTS
Jose Luis Camargo MEX
Alberto Morin MEX

4TH OFFICIAL
Martin Hansson SWE

(C) Captain † Man of the Match

TABLE

	PL	GD	Pts
GER	1	+4	3
GHA	1	+1	3
SRB	1	-1	0
AUS	1	-4	0

1 Manuel Neuer

16 Philipp Lahm (c)   17 Per Mertesacker   3 Arne Friedrich   14 Holger Badstuber

7 Bastian Schweinsteiger   6 Sami Khedira

74 8 Mesut Ozil 12
23 Mario Gomez

13 Thomas Müller

81 10 Lukas Podolski †
21 Marko Marin

68 11 Miroslav Klose
19 Cacau 92+

64 19 Richard Garcia
17 Nikita Rukavytsya

5 Jason Culina

74 7 Brett Emerton
15 Mile Jedinak

4 Tim Cahill 56

46 13 Vince Grella
14 Brett Holman

16 Carl Valeri 58

11 Scott Chipperfield   3 Craig Moore 24   2 Lucas Neill (c) 46   8 Luke Wilkshire

1 Mark Schwarzer

Tr: Pim Verbeek (NED)
Dark blue shirts with blue sleeves, Dark blue shorts, Dark blue socks

AUSTRALIA

We did our homework on Australia and we knew where they have problems. It was fun watching the team in lots of situations. The win was important for us as it will give us confidence.
Joachim Löw

You saw there that we're still a young team. This side has lots and lots of quality in it and we created a string of chances. We should have gone further ahead earlier than we did.
Philipp Lahm

It was tough for us after the sending-off. It was tough enough before that. Germany were better and we have to win the next two games now. We need to learn from this. We didn't play as a team and after the first goal we had to do a bit more going forward.
Pim Verbeek

The Germans are a very good team but we made it easy for them by conceding early. It was very difficult for us when we were 2-0 down with only ten men.
Lucas Neill

First Round Group D	Port Elizabeth Stadium Nelson Mandela Bay/Port Elizabeth	Friday 18-06-2010
Kick-off: 13:30	Sunny 15°	Attendance: 38 294

GERMANY   0   1   SERBIA

Penalty miss: Lukas Podolski [60]   Milan Jovanovic [38]

GERMANY

White shirts, Black shorts, White socks

Tr: Joachim Löw

1 Manuel Neuer

16 Philipp Lahm(c) [32]   17 Per Mertesacker   3 Arne Friedrich   [77] 14 Holger Badstuber   23 Mario Gomez

6 Sami Khedira [22]   7 Bastian Schweinsteiger [73]

[70] 13 Thomas Müller   [70] 8 Mesut Ozil   10 Lukas Podolski
21 Marko Marin   19 Cacau

11 Miroslav Klose [12] [37] [37]

15 Nikola Zigic

[79] 14 Milan Jovanovic   17 Milos Krasic
8 Danko Lazovic

[70] 18 Milos Ninkovic   [75] 22 Zdravko Kuzmanovic
4 Gojko Kacar   19 Radosav Petrovic

10 Dejan Stankovic (c)

3 Aleksandar Kolarov [19]   6 Branislav Ivanovic [18]

20 Neven Subotic [57]   5 Nemanja Vidic [59]

1 Vladimir Stojkovic †

Tr: Radomir Antic

Red shirts with an off centre white cross, Red shorts, Red socks

SERBIA

MATCH STATS

GER		SRB
15	Shots	10
4	Shots on Goal	3
19	Fouls Committed	10
7	Corner Kicks	1
3	Caught Offside	3
570	Passes	448
459	Completed Passes	328
81%	Passes Success	73%
102	Km Covered	111
22	Av. Top Speed km/h	21
51%	Possession	49%

MATCH OFFICIALS
REFEREE
Alberto Undiano ESP
ASSISTANTS
Fermin Martinez ESP
Juan Carlos Yuste Jimenez ESP
4TH OFFICIAL
Martin Vazquez URU

(C) Captain † Man of the Match

TABLE

	PL	GD	Pts
GER	2	+3	3
GHA	1	+1	3
SRB	2	0	3
AUS	1	-4	0

We definitely had a few problems getting going in the first half. It was a big setback, going a man down and then letting in the goal straight afterwards. In the second half, my team tried everything and put in an unbelievable amount of work.

Joachim Löw

The sending-off was a big blow, and then I've missed a penalty. I'm normally good from the penalty spot, but the keeper guessed correctly and that was that.

Lukas Podolski

We played very well in the first half, and we set out to protect the lead after half-time. We ended up playing very defensively. We actually intended to get forward more than that, but they put us under all kinds of pressure.

Radomir Antic

We desperately needed the win. I had no idea which way Podolski was going to shoot, it was just a guess, but I'm thrilled with the save.

Vladimir Stojkovic

First Round Group D	Royal Bafokeng Rustenburg	Saturday 19-06-2010
Kick-off: 16:00	Sunny 13°	Attendance: 34 812

GHANA   1   1   AUSTRALIA

Asamoah Gyan 25p   Brett Holman 11

GHANA

White shirts, White shorts, White socks
Tr: Milovan Rajevac (SRB)

MATCH STATS

GHA		AUS
22	Shots	8
6	Shots on Goal	5
22	Fouls Committed	18
6	Corner Kicks	1
2	Caught Offside	2
501	Passes	476
388	Completed Passes	340
77%	Passes Success	71%
101	Km Covered	102
22	Av. Top Speed km/h	22
50%	Possession	50%

MATCH OFFICIALS

REFEREE
Roberto Rosetti ITA

ASSISTANTS
Paolo Calcagno ITA
Stefano Ayroldi ITA

4TH OFFICIAL
Carlos Simon BRA

(C) Captain † Man of the Match

TABLE

	PL	GD	Pts
GHA	2	+1	4
GER	2	+3	3
SRB	2	0	3
AUS	2	-4	1

22 Richard Kingson (c)

4 John Pantsil   8 Jonathan Mensah 79   19 Lee Addy 40   2 Hans Sarpei

6 Anthony Annan 84   23 Kevin Prince Boateng
                      87   14 Matthew Amoah

12 Prince Tagoe 56   21 Kwadwo Asamoah   13 Andre Ayew
20 Quincy Owusu-Abeyie   77 11 Sulley Muntari

3 Asamoah Gyan †

10 Harry Kewell 24

23 Marco Bresciano 66   14 Brett Holman 68   7 Brett Emerton
11 Scott Chipperfield   9 Joshua Kennedy

16 Carl Valeri   5 Jason Culina

21 David Carney   3 Craig Moore 85   2 Lucas Neill (c)   8 Luke Wilkshire
                                    84 17 Nikita Rukavytsya

1 Mark Schwarzer

Tr: Pim Verbeek (NED)
Yellow shirts with green sleeves, Green shorts, Yellow socks

AUSTRALIA

The match was quite difficult because we had youngsters in the team, but they started to fight for the result. We tried to score a second but could not convert our chances. All my players had a good game and we have four points now.

Milovan Rajevac

We were playing ten against 11 for a long time and when it's in a competition like this, you have to do better. We should have capitalised.

Andre Ayew

We went ahead and it was going well. Once we went down to ten men we had to work very hard, and I think that's what they did. I'm proud of the players – playing with a man less for that long is not easy.

Pim Verbeek

You would think Ghana should roll over the top of us with ten men but we dug in and fought for each other, and that is a complement to our boys.

Brett Holman

First Round Group D	Soccer City Johannesburg	Wednesday 23-06-2010
Kick-off: 20:30	Clear Night 11°	Attendance: 83 391

GHANA   0   1   GERMANY

Mesut Özil 60

GHANA

White shirts, White shorts, White socks

Tr: Milovan Rajevac (SRB)

22 Richard Kingson

4 John Pantsil   8 Jonathan Mensah   5 John Mensah   2 Hans Sarpei

6 Anthony Annan   23 Kevin Prince Boateng

64 12 Prince Tagoe   21 Kwadwo Asamoah   92+ 13 Andre Ayew 40
11 Sulley Muntari   18 Dominic Adiyiah

82 3 Asamoah Gyan
14 Matthew Amoah

19 Cacau

10 Lukas Podolski   8 Mesut Özil †   67 13 Thomas Müller 43
                                          15 Piotr Trochowski

81 7 Bastian Schweinsteiger   6 Sami Khedira
18 Toni Kroos

73 20 Jerome Boateng   3 Arne Friedrich   17 Per Mertesacker   16 Philipp Lahm (c)
2 Marcell Jansen

1 Manuel Neuer

Tr: Joachim Löw

Black shirts, Black shorts, Black socks

GERMANY

MATCH STATS

GHA		GER
17	Shots	13
5	Shots on Goal	6
11	Fouls Committed	5
4	Corner Kicks	7
3	Caught Offside	4
460	Passes	640
325	Completed Passes	491
71%	Passes Success	77%
106	Km Covered	108
22	Av. Top Speed km/h	22
46%	Possession	54%

MATCH OFFICIALS

REFEREE

Carlos Simon BRA

ASSISTANTS

Altemir Hausmann BRA

Roberto Braatz BRA

4TH OFFICIAL

Martin Vazquez URU

(C) Captain † Man of the Match

TABLE

	PL	GD	Pts
GER	3	+4	6
GHA	3	0	4
AUS	3	-3	4
SRB	3	-1	3

Germany are an excellent team, but at the end of the day, we deserve to be in the next round. We were tactically very disciplined, but we can't be conceding a goal like that. They're a good team, and they took advantage of the situation, but at the end of the day, it's worked out well for us. I hope we'll have the support of most of the South African people now. I hope we'll benefit from the tremendous support here in South Africa. I hope we start scoring goals!

Milovan Rajevac

It was an unbelievably hard-fought game. A number of our tactics didn't really come off, but at the end of the day, we're through to the next stage. Manuel Neuer made two or three outstanding saves in a terrific display. You could see our young team struggling to cope with the pressure, but these are the games you have to win. We've done it, and I'm delighted. It's a mark of Mesut Özil's class that he brilliantly took his second chance of the game.

Joachim Löw

First Round Group D	Royal Bafokeng Rustenburg	Wednesday 23-06-2010
Kick-off: 20:30	Clear Night 15°	Attendance: 37 836

AUSTRALIA   2   1   SERBIA

Tim Cahill [69], Brett Holman [73]   Marko Pantelic [84]

AUSTRALIA

Yellow shirts with green sleeves, Green shorts, Yellow socks
Tr: Pim Verbeek (NED)

1 Mark Schwarzer

8 Luke Wilkshire [50] **6 Michael Beauchamp** [49] **2 Lucas Neill** (c) **21 David Carney**
[82] **19 Richard Garcia**

7 Brett Emerton [67] **5 Jason Culina** [66] **16 Carl Valeri** [66] **23 Marco Bresciano**
14 Brett Holman **11 Scott Chipperfield**

4 Tim Cahill †

9 Joshua Kennedy

---

15 Nikola Zigic
14 Milan Jovanovic [67] **9 Marko Pantelic** [62] **17 Milos Krasic**
7 Zoran Tosic

18 Milos Ninkovic [59] **10 Dejan Stankovic** (c) [77] **22 Zdravko Kuzmanovic**
8 Danko Lazovic

16 Ivan Obradovic **13 Aleksandar Lukovic** [18] **5 Nemanja Vidic** **6 Branislav Ivanovic**

1 Vladimir Stojkovic

Tr: Radomir Antic
Red shirts with an off centre white cross, Blue shorts, White socks

SERBIA

MATCH STATS

AUS		SRB
17	Shots	23
7	Shots on Goal	6
25	Fouls Committed	10
5	Corner Kicks	6
1	Caught Offside	7
481	Passes	579
321	Completed Passes	418
67%	Passes Success	72%
121	Km Covered	117
22	Av. Top Speed km/h	24
46%	Possession	54%

MATCH OFFICIALS
REFEREE
Jorge Larrionda URU
ASSISTANTS
Pablo Fandino URU
Mauricio Espinosa URU
4TH OFFICIAL
Carlos Batres GUA

(C) Captain † Man of the Match

TABLE

	PL	GD	Pts
GER	3	+4	6
GHA	3	0	4
AUS	3	-3	4
SRB	3	-1	3

I am disappointed, but we were not good enough in the end. We gave away some chances, and it was those that hurt us. At half-time, I told the boys that we had another 45 minutes to get a result - that it was an all or nothing situation. We needed that extra bit of luck at 2-0, to go up 3-0. The boys were fantastic. I'm just disappointed. We earned four points in the tournament, but the Germany game killed us.
Pim Verbeek

It is a very sombre atmosphere in the dressing room because we played a very good first half, the best since beating Romania 5-0 in the qualifiers. Australia were more aggressive in the second and we ran out of steam after they started pounding us with long balls and sharp crosses into our penalty box. We are very disappointed because we expected to reach the knockout stage, especially after beating Germany and giving ourselves a good chance of progressing.
Radomir Antic

First Round Group E	Soccer City Johannesburg	Monday 14-06-2010
Kick-off: 13:30	Sunny 16°	Attendance: 83 465

NETHERLANDS   2   0   DENMARK

Daniel Agger OG [46], **Dirk Kuyt** [85]

NETHERLANDS
Orange shirts, Black shorts, Orange socks
Tr: Bert van Marwijk

1 Maarten Stekelenburg

2 Gregory Van der Wiel   3 John Heitinga   4 Joris Mathijsen   5 Gio Van Bronckhorst (c)

6 Mark Van Bommel   88   8 Nigel De Jong 44   14 Demy De Zeeuw

7 Dirk Kuyt   10 Wesley Sneijder †   67   23 Rafael Van der Vaart   17 Eljero Elia

77   9 Robin Van Persie 49   20 Ibrahim Afellay

62   11 Nicklas Bendtner   17 Mikkel Beckmann

56   20 Thomas Enevoldsen   8 Jesper Gronkjaer   19 Dennis Rommedahl

10 Martin Jorgensen (c)   73   12 Thomas Kahlenberg   21 Christian Eriksen

2 Christian Poulsen

15 Simon Poulsen   4 Daniel Agger   3 Simon Kjaer 63   6 Lars Jacobsen

1 Thomas Sorensen

Tr: Morten Olsen
White shirts, Red shorts, White socks

DENMARK

MATCH STATS

NED		DAN
18	Shots	10
7	Shots on Goal	3
13	Fouls Committed	20
6	Corner Kicks	2
4	Caught Offside	2
576	Passes	374
460	Completed Passes	252
80%	Passes Success	67%
99	Km Covered	101
22	Av. Top Speed km/h	23
58%	Possession	42%

MATCH OFFICIALS
REFEREE
Stephane Lannoy FRA
ASSISTANTS
Eric Dansault FRA
Laurent Ugo FRA
4TH OFFICIAL
Roberto Rosetti ITA

(C) Captain † Man of the Match

TABLE

	PL	GD	Pts
NED	1	+2	3
CMR	0	0	0
JPN	0	0	0
DEN	1	-2	0

The Danes are very strong defensively. The final period of the first half was the worst for us, but when things aren't working you have to be patient, and we did that well. Scoring just a minute after the restart was perfect. Then the Danes had to come out and attack, which gave us more space. From then on we controlled the game and hardly gave them anything. By the end we had shown everyone that we can play good football.

Bert van Marwijk

To start with the game went according to plan, but then we let in an unbelievable goal. That settled the game. But for that goal we would have got at least a point.

Morten Olsen

Right at the start of the second half I put through my own goal. I was looking to head the cross well clear, but unfortunately it skidded away from me and was deflected off Daniel Agger's back. That goal completely changed the game.

Simon Poulsen

First Round Group E	Free State Stadium Mangaung/Bloemfontein	Monday 14-06-2010
Kick-off: 16:00	Sunny 13°	Attendance: 30 620

JAPAN   1   0   CAMEROON

Keisuke Honda [39]

JAPAN
Blue shirts, White shorts, Blue socks
Tr: Takeshi Okada

21 Eiji Kawashima

3 Yuichi Komano   22 Yuji Nakazawa   4 Marcus Tulio Tanaka   5 Yuto Nagatomo

2 Yuki Abe [91+]

69 8 Daisuke Matsui   88 17 Makoto Hasebe(c)   7 Yasuhito Endo
    9 Shinji Okazaki   20 Junichi Inamoto

18 Keisuke Honda†   82 16 Yoshito Okubo
                          12 Kisho Yano

15 Pierre Webo

75 13 Eric Choupo Moting   9 Samuel Eto'o(c)
    8 Geremi

18 Eyong Enoh   75 11 Jean Makoun
                         17 Mohamadou Idrissou

21 Joel Matip
63 10 Achille Emana

2 Benoit Assou-Ekotto   5 Sebastien Bassong   3 Nicolas Nkoulou [72] 19 Stephane Mbia

16 Hamidou Souleymanou

Tr: Paul Le Guen (FRA)
Yellow shirts, Green shorts, Green socks

CAMEROON

MATCH STATS
JPN		CMR
5	Shots	11
5	Shots on Goal	4
20	Fouls Committed	29
0	Corner Kicks	3
4	Caught Offside	2
389	Passes	481
230	Completed Passes	341
59%	Passes Success	71%
109	Km Covered	102
24	Av. Top Speed km/h	23
45%	Possession	55%

MATCH OFFICIALS
REFEREE
Olegario Benquerenca POR
ASSISTANTS
Jose Cardinal POR
Bertino Miranda POR
4TH OFFICIAL
Oscar Ruiz COL

(C) Captain † Man of the Match

TABLE
	PL	GD	Pts
NED	1	+2	3
JPN	1	+1	3
CMR	1	-1	0
DEN	1	-2	0

We were prepared for a very tough game. I told the players they couldn't just be defensive and they had to alternate between attacking spells and defensive ones. In the first half, we had a few difficult moments, but we put lots of pressure on them and were able to score. After that, they attacked us, but our defence did a good job. I think we'll need to be more aggressive in the future, though.
Takeshi Okada

My regret is that my players weren't able to play at the level they can. I think they were too nervous in the first half. They fought well afterwards but in an unorganised manner. We missed an incalculable number of easy balls. This is my biggest disappointment. It's very frustrating to see your team play at a level that's beneath them.
Paul Le Guen

First Round Group E	Durban Stadium Durban		Saturday 19-06-2010
Kick-off: 13:30	Sunny	22°	Attendance: 62 010

NETHERLANDS   1   0   JAPAN

Wesley Sneijder 53

NETHERLANDS
Orange shirts, Black shorts, Orange socks
Tr: Bert van Marwijk

1 Maarten Stekelenburg

3 John Heitinga   4 Joris Mathijsen

2 Gregory Van der Wiel 36   5 Giovanni Van Bronckhorst(c)

6 Mark Van Bommel   8 Nigel De Jong

7 Dirk Kuyt   83 10 Wesley Sneijder†   72 23 Rafael Van der Vaart
                     20 Ibrahim Afellay   17 Eljero Elia

88 9 Robin Van Persie
    21 Klaas Jan Huntelaar

18 Keisuke Honda

77 16 Yoshito Okubo   8 Daisuke Matsui 64
    11 Keiji Tamada   10 Shunsuke Nakamura

7 Yasuhito Endo   77 17 Makoto Hasebe(c)
                      9 Shinji Okazaki

2 Yuki Abe

5 Yuto Nagatomo   4 Marcus Tulio Tanaka   22 Yuji Nakazawa   3 Yuichi Komano

21 Eiji Kawashima

Tr: Takeshi Okada
White shirts, Blue shorts, White socks

JAPAN

MATCH STATS

NED		JPN
9	Shots	10
5	Shots on Goal	3
18	Fouls Committed	11
4	Corner Kicks	5
2	Caught Offside	1
668	Passes	406
517	Completed Passes	259
77%	Passes Success	64%
104	Km Covered	108
21	Av. Top Speed km/h	21
61%	Possession	39%

MATCH OFFICIALS
REFEREE
Hector Baldassi ARG
ASSISTANTS
Ricardo Casas ARG
Hernan Maidana ARG
4TH OFFICIAL
Martin Hansson SWE

(C) Captain †Man of the Match

TABLE

	PL	GD	Pts
NED	2	+3	6
JPN	2	0	3
CMR	1	-1	0
DEN	1	-2	0

You've got to be happy about winning your first two games. But we can play better than that, and we'll have to. We'll be taking a good look at ourselves and keeping our feet on the ground.

Bert van Marwijk

We passed well in the first half. We kept it up in the second half, we started creating chances, and we took one of them. I hit it well and the ball certainly wobbled in the air.

Wesley Sneijder

Our players tried everything they could, but we've been unable to beat the Netherlands. I'm really sorry for our supporters.

Takeshi Okada

First Round Group E	Loftus Versfeld Tshwana/Pretoria	Saturday 19-06-2010
Kick-off: 20:30	Clear Night 10°	Attendance: 38 074

CAMEROON   1   2   DENMARK

Samuel Eto'o [10]   Nicklas Bendtner [33], Dennis Rommedahl [61]

CAMEROON

Green shirts, Red shorts, Yellow socks
Tr: Paul Le Guen (FRA)

MATCH STATS

CMR		DEN
23	Shots	13
8	Shots on Goal	6
9	Fouls Committed	12
7	Corner Kicks	2
1	Caught Offside	1
559	Passes	445
429	Completed Passes	320
77%	Passes Success	72%
99	Km Covered	106
22	Av. Top Speed km/h	22
54%	Possession	46%

MATCH OFFICIALS

REFEREE
Jorge Larrionda URU

ASSISTANTS
Pablo Fandino URU
Mauricio Espinosa URU

4TH OFFICIAL
Peter O'Leary NZL

(C) Captain † Man of the Match

TABLE

	PL	GD	Pts
NED	2	+3	6
JPN	2	0	3
DEN	2	-1	3
CMR	2	-2	0

16 Hamidou Souleymanou

3 Nicolas Nkoulou   5 Sebastien Bassong 49
              72   17 Mohamadou Idrissou
19 Stephane Mbia 75   2 Benoit Assou-Ekotto

6 Alexandre Song   18 Eyong Enoh
              46   11 Jean Makoun
8 Geremi
10 Achille Emana

9 Samuel Eto'o (c)   15 Pierre Webo
              78   23 Vincent Aboubakar

11 Nicklas Bendtner

8 Jesper Gronkjaer   9 Jon Dahl Tomasson (c)   19 Dennis Rommedahl
67 12 Thomas Kahlenberg 86 14 Jakob Poulsen

2 Christian Poulsen   10 Martin Jorgensen
              46   7 Daniel Jensen

15 Simon Poulsen   4 Daniel Agger †   3 Simon Kjaer 87   6 Lars Jacobsen

1 Thomas Sorensen 86

Tr: Morten Olsen
White shirts, White shorts, White socks

DENMARK

What I think what we lacked was efficiency in front of goal. We had an enormous amount of very clear chances and we failed to put them away. We were clumsy with our finishing, but I feel that we gave everything we could tonight. We did what we could on the pitch. I have regrets after these two matches and that's understandable given the quality of the match we played tonight. Honestly, we came very close and we just didn't make it.

Paul Le Guen

We didn't start well and we made a mistake that Cameroon pounced on. We demonstrated that we had desire and a good attitude. We made mistakes that we just can't repeat in this tournament and Cameroon could have punished us even more heavily than they did. It was hard for us to get the ball back. We were surprised by their tactical set-up, but we reacted well. I was angry when I left the pitch because we made too many straightforward errors.

Morten Olsen

First Round Group E	Royal Bafokeng Rustenburg	Thursday 24-06-2010
Kick-off: 20:30	Clear Night 12°	Attendance: 27 967

DENMARK   1   3   JAPAN

Jon Dahl Tomasson [81p]   Keisuke Honda [17], Yasuhito Endo [30], Shinji Okazaki [87]

DENMARK
Red shirts, White shorts, Red socks
Tr: Morten Olsen

1 Thomas Sorensen

6 Lars Jacobsen   4 Daniel Agger   13 Per Kroldrup [29]   15 Simon Poulsen
[56]   18 Soren Larsen

[34] 10 Martin Jorgensen   2 Christian Poulsen [48]   12 Thomas Kahlenberg
14 Jakob Poulsen   [63]   21 Christian Eriksen

19 Dennis Rommedahl   9 Jon Dahl Tomasson (c)

11 Nicklas Bendtner [66]

18 Keisuke Honda †

[88] 16 Yoshito Okubo   8 Daisuke Matsui
15 Yasuyuki Konno   [74] 9 Shinji Okazaki

7 Yasuhito Endo [12]   17 Makoto Hasebe (c)
[91+] 20 Junichi Inamoto

2 Yuki Abe

5 Yuto Nagatomo [26] 4 Marcus Tulio Tanaka 22 Yuji Nakazawa 3 Yuichi Komano

21 Eiji Kawashima

Tr: Takeshi Okada
Blue shirts, Blue shorts, Blue socks

JAPAN

MATCH STATS

DEN		JPN
19	Shots	15
7	Shots on Goal	10
23	Fouls Committed	10
7	Corner Kicks	2
0	Caught Offside	5
592	Passes	348
464	Completed Passes	220
78%	Passes Success	63%
107	Km Covered	112
22	Av. Top Speed km/h	21
57%	Possession	43%

MATCH OFFICIALS
REFEREE
Jerome Damon RSA
ASSISTANTS
Celestin Ntagungira RWA
Enock Molefe RSA
4TH OFFICIAL
Martin Hansson SWE

(C) Captain † Man of the Match

TABLE

	PL	GD	Pts
NED	3	+4	9
JPN	3	+2	6
DEN	3	-3	3
CMR	3	-3	0

The way the whole match progressed was decided on the two set pieces when they scored the two goals. We knew which two players were going to take the free-kicks. We prepared, but it didn't help. They took their chances, we didn't take ours and it became an uphill struggle for us. The way the whole match evolved was decided by the two free-kicks in the first half.

Morten Olsen

Our team has a strength that others don't have. We are truly united. We wanted to demonstrate that football is a team sport. The players kept going until the end without losing their focus.

Takeshi Okada

Prior to the match, the coach said we shouldn't concentrate on the defence and that we should attack. It was really effective and led to this wonderful result.

Keisuke Honda

First Round Group E	Green Point Cape Town	Thursday 24-06-2010
Kick-off: 20:30	Clear Night 15°	Attendance: 63 093

CAMEROON 1 2 NETHERLANDS

Samuel Eto'o 65p   Robin Van Persie 36, Klaas Jan Huntelaar 83

CAMEROON

Green shirts, Red shorts, Yellow socks
Tr: Paul Le Guen (FRA)

16 Hamidou Souleymanou

8 Geremi   19 Stephane Mbia 81   3 Nicolas Nkoulou 25   2 Benoit Assou-Ekotto
73   4 Rigobert Song

14 Aurelien Chedjou   11 Jean Makoun

7 Landry Nguemo   12 Gaetan Bong
                               56   23 Vincent Aboubakar

72   13 Eric Choupo Moting   9 Samuel Eto'o(c)
     17 Mohamadou Idrissou

59   9 Robin Van Persie †
     21 Klaas Jan Huntelaar

73   23 Rafael Van der Vaart 65   10 Wesley Sneijder   66   7 Dirk Kuyt 17
     11 Arjen Robben   17 Eljero Elia

8 Nigel De Jong   6 Mark Van Bommel

5 Gio Van Bronckhorst(c) 70   12 Khalid Boulahrouz

4 Joris Mathijsen   3 John Heitinga

1 Maarten Stekelenburg

Tr: Bert van Marwijk
White shirts, Blue shorts, White socks

NETHERLANDS

MATCH STATS

CMR		NED
15	Shots	15
3	Shots on Goal	8
18	Fouls Committed	15
6	Corner Kicks	1
3	Caught Offside	6
616	Passes	563
431	Completed Passes	369
70%	Passes Success	66%
102	Km Covered	104
20	Av. Top Speed km/h	21
51%	Possession	49%

MATCH OFFICIALS

REFEREE
Pablo Pozo CHI

ASSISTANTS
Patricio Basualto CHI
Francisco Mondria CHI

4TH OFFICIAL
Khalil Al Ghamdi KSA

(C) Captain † Man of the Match

TABLE

	PL	GD	Pts
NED	3	+4	9
JPN	3	+2	6
DEN	3	-3	3
CMR	3	-3	0

It's not like we waited until the second half this evening to start playing decent football. I think we played some good football in our previous matches too but we weren't able to come up with enough to beat the Netherlands today. They're stronger than us. We've given it our best shot, we've stood up to them and tried to beat them, especially towards the end. Our record of three defeats is a crushing blow. I've not succeeded in turning the team into a unit.

Paul Le Guen

Winning three times in a row at a World Cup obviously looks good at first sight, but I'm not really satisfied with our performance today. It was good enough in the first half, but we started very poorly after half-time. We spent too much time on the back foot and gave Cameroon far too much space. We were more in control in the other group games, but we could easily have lost today.

Bert van Marwijk

First Round Group F	Green Point Cape Town		Monday 14-06-2010
Kick-off: 20:30	Rain	8°	Attendance: 62 869

ITALY 1 1 PARAGUAY

Daniele De Rossi 63   Antolin Alcaraz 39

ITALY

Blue shirts, White shorts, Blue socks
Tr: Marcello Lippi

MATCH STATS		
ITA		PAR
10	Shots	8
5	Shots on Goal	1
15	Fouls Committed	15
8	Corner Kicks	4
3	Caught Offside	4
611	Passes	475
427	Completed Passes	300
70%	Passes Success	63%
107	Km Covered	108
21	Av. Top Speed km/h	23
52%	Possession	48%

MATCH OFFICIALS
REFEREE
Benito Archundia MEX
ASSISTANTS
Hector Vergara CAN
Marvin Torrentera MEX
4TH OFFICIAL
Joel Aguilar SLV

(C)Captain †Man of the Match

TABLE			
	PL	GD	Pts
PAR	1	0	1
ITA	1	0	1
NZL	0	0	0
SVK	0	0	0

Italy lineup:
- 1 Gianluigi Buffon **46**
- 12 Federico Marchetti
- 19 Gianluca Zambrotta   5 Fabio Cannavaro(c)   4 Giorgio Chiellini   3 Domenico Criscito
- 6 Daniele De Rossi   22 Riccardo Montolivo
- 15 Claudio Marchisio **59**
- 16 Mauro Camoranesi **70**
- 7 Simone Pepe   9 Vincenzo Iaquinta
- 11 Alberto Gilardino **72**
- 10 Antonio Di Natale

Paraguay lineup:
- 18 Nelson Valdez **68**   19 Lucas Barrios **76**
- 9 Roque Santa Cruz   7 Oscar Cardozo
- 17 Aureliano Torres **60**   16 Cristian Riveros   13 Enrique Vera
- 11 Jonathan Santana
- 15 Victor Caceres **60**
- 3 Claudio Morel   21 Antolin Alcaraz†   14 Paulo Da Silva   6 Carlos Bonet
- 1 Justo Villar(c)

Tr: Gerardo Martino (ARG)
Red and white striped shirts, Blue shorts, Red and white hooped socks

PARAGUAY

I'm happy because we played as a team, but it's a shame not to have won because we deserved to. By the end our opponents had handed us control and they didn't create any danger in the second period, we didn't even let them have a single shot on goal. We still have to improve, however.

Marcello Lippi

We're really pleased to have gone toe-to-toe with the reigning world champions and, above and beyond the result, we're very satisfied with our performance, particularly as it's the start of the World Cup. We couldn't move the ball around accurately because of the way our opponents play, but we also made life difficult for them. The fact the goals came from set pieces says a lot.

Gerardo Martino

First Round Group F	Royal Bafokeng Rustenburg	Tuesday 15-06-2010
Kick-off: 13:30	Sunny 6°	Attendance: 23 871

NEW ZEALAND   1   1   SLOVAKIA

Winston Reid 93+   Robert Vittek 50

NEW ZEALAND

White shirts, White shorts, White socks

Tr: Ricki Herbert

MATCH STATS

NZL		SVK
8	Shots	13
2	Shots on Goal	3
17	Fouls Committed	15
3	Corner Kicks	10
0	Caught Offside	1
421	Passes	407
286	Completed Passes	248
68%	Passes Success	61%
107	Km Covered	105
23	Av. Top Speed km/h	21
52%	Possession	48%

1 Mark Paston

4 Winston Reid 93+   6 Ryan Nelsen (c)   19 Tommy Smith

11 Leo Bertos   5 Ivan Vicelich   7 Simon Elliott   3 Tony Lochhead 42
            78   21 Jeremy Christie

        10 Chris Killen   14 Rory Fallon   9 Shane Smeltz
    72   20 Chris Wood

        9 Stanislav Sestak   11 Robert Vittek †
    81   13 Filip Holosko   84   15 Miroslav Stoch

18 Erik Jendrisek   7 Vladimir Weiss
                              91+   19 Juraj Kucka

        17 Marek Hamsik (c)   6 Zdenko Strba

4 Marek Cech   16 Jan Durica   3 Martin Skrtel   5 Radoslav Zabavnik

                1 Jan Mucha

Tr: Vladimir Weiss

Blue shirts, Blue shorts, Blue socks

SLOVAKIA

MATCH OFFICIALS

REFEREE

Jerome Damon RSA

ASSISTANTS

Celestin Ntagungira RWA

Enock Molefe RSA

4TH OFFICIAL

Ravshan Irmatov UZB

(C) Captain † Man of the Match

TABLE

	PL	GD	Pts
PAR	1	0	1
ITA	1	0	1
NZL	1	0	1
SVK	1	0	1

It's terrific. Over the last five years, I've never stopped believing in this team. Playing at a World Cup was a dream come true, but this is even better. We came to South Africa with the intention of making a difference, and we certainly did that against a highly-rated team. We're very, very proud. You would have to say this is our best-ever result. We've never picked up a point in a World Cup before. I thought it was an extremely well-deserved result

Ricki Herbert

That's a minor sporting tragedy for us. We were the better team throughout the match. It's incredibly frustrating, the way we failed to take our chances and then conceded a last-minute equaliser. But it's simple: we let our opponents play far too much football.

Vladimir Weiss

I think we deserved all three points. We've put ourselves in an extremely difficult position, but we need to forget about the points we've dropped today.

Robert Vittek

First Round Group F	Free State Mangaung/Bloemfontein	Sunday 20-06-2010
Kick-off: 13:30	Sunny 15°	Attendance: 26 643

SLOVAKIA   0 2   PARAGUAY

Enrique Vera ²⁷, Cristian Riveros ⁸⁶

SLOVAKIA

White shirts, White shorts, White socks

Tr: Vladimir Weiss

MATCH STATS

SVK		PAR
6	Shots	11
1	Shots on Goal	5
14	Fouls Committed	18
3	Corner Kicks	1
3	Caught Offside	0
472	Passes	463
330	Completed Passes	312
70%	Passes Success	67%
99	Km Covered	99
22	Av. Top Speed km/h	22
51%	Possession	49%

MATCH OFFICIALS
REFEREE
Eddy Maillet SEY
ASSISTANTS
Evarist Menkouande CMR
Bechir Hassani TUN
4TH OFFICIAL
Joel Aguilar SLV

(C) Captain † Man of the Match

TABLE

	PL	GD	Pts
PAR	2	+2	4
ITA	1	0	1
NZL	1	0	1
SVK	2	-2	1

Tr: Gerardo Martino (ARG)

Red and white striped shirts, Blue shorts, Blue socks

PARAGUAY

They were better than us in what was a very important match. We made two mistakes and they took full toll by scoring both their goals. Paraguay played some excellent football and they were always looking for the win. We gave it our all but this is a sport that shows you what you are actually capable of.
Vladimir Weiss
We didn't play badly but we couldn't take our chances and they took theirs. That was the difference.
Marek Hamsik

We were deserved winners. We played better today and we've come through a very difficult and decisive match. It's difficult to control a World Cup game all the way through but that's what we did. The movement of our three strikers was great and we pressed them a lot, though there were times in the second half when we didn't build up play from defence and just hit hopeful long balls. Even so we still managed to work some openings.
Gerardo Martino

First Round Group F	Mbombela Nelspruit	Sunday 20-06-2010
Kick-off: 16:00	Sunny 20°	Attendance: 38 229

ITALY   1   1   NEW ZEALAND

Vincenzo Iaquinta 29p   Shane Smeltz 7

ITALY

Blue shirts, Blue shorts, Blue socks

Tr: Marcello Lippi

12 Federico Marchetti

19 Gianluca Zambrotta 5 Fabio Cannavaro(c) 4 Giorgio Chiellini 3 Domenico Criscito

6 Daniele De Rossi †

46 7 Simone Pepe
    16 Mauro Camoranesi   22 Riccardo Montolivo   61 15 Claudio Marchisio
                                                              20 Giampaolo Pazzini

9 Vincenzo Iaquinta   46 11 Alberto Gilardino
                              10 Antonio Di Natale

63 14 Rory Fallon 14   93+ 10 Chris Killen
    20 Chris Wood   13 Andy Barron

9 Shane Smeltz

3 Tony Lochhead 81 5 Ivan Vicelich   7 Simon Elliott   11 Leo Bertos
                     21 Jeremy Christie

19 Tommy Smith 28   6 Ryan Nelsen(c) 87   4 Winston Reid

1 Mark Paston

Tr: Ricki Herbert

White shirts, White shorts, White socks

NEW ZEALAND

MATCH STATS

ITA		NZL
23	Shots	3
7	Shots on Goal	1
11	Fouls Committed	25
15	Corner Kicks	0
1	Caught Offside	1
571	Passes	310
426	Completed Passes	162
75%	Passes Success	52%
105	Km Covered	104
24	Av. Top Speed km/h	22
57%	Possession	43%

MATCH OFFICIALS
REFEREE
Carlos Batres GUA
ASSISTANTS
Leonel Leal CRC
Carlos Pastrana HON
4TH OFFICIAL
Koman Coulibaly MLI

(C) Captain † Man of the Match

TABLE

	PL	GD	Pts
PAR	2	+2	4
ITA	2	0	2
NZL	2	0	2
SVK	2	-2	1

We didn't get a lot of luck but we didn't create much either. This is the second time that our opponents have put a ball in the box and we've conceded a goal. After that happened, we pulled ourselves together and put everything into attacking. The players didn't lack desire, just clear-headedness.

Marcello Lippi

We have a lot of regrets because our opponents never came close to our area aside from their two chances.

Fabbio Cannavaro

I think our entire country, which numbers four million inhabitants, came to a stop to watch our performance. It's an incredible result for football in New Zealand. It's historic and greater than anything else we've ever achieved when you consider the standing of our opponents.

Ricki Herbert

It leaves me speechless when I think about what we've accomplished thanks to everyone's dedication.

Ryan Nelsen

First Round Group F	Ellis Park Johannesburg		Thursday 24-06-2010
Kick-off: 16:00	Sunny	17°	Attendance: 53 412

SLOVAKIA   3 2   ITALY

Robert Vittek 2 25 73, **Kamil Kopunek** 89   **Antonio Di Natale** 81, **Fabio Quagliarella** 92+

SLOVAKIA

White shirts, White shorts, White socks

Tr: Vladimir Weiss

1 Jan Mucha 82

2 Peter Pekarik 50   3 Martin Skrtel   16 Jan Durica   5 Radoslav Zabavnik

19 Juraj Kucka   6 Zdenko Strba 16   87   20 Kamil Kopunek

15 Miroslav Stoch   17 Marek Hamsik (c)   94+   18 Erik Jendrisek   22 Martin Petras

92+   11 Robert Vittek † 40   9 Stanislav Sestak

10 Antonio Di Natale   9 Vincenzo Iaquinta   7 Simone Pepe 76

46   8 Gennaro Gattuso   6 Daniele De Rossi   56   22 Riccardo Montolivo   21 Andrea Pirlo
18 Fabio Quagliarella 83

46   3 Domenico Criscito   19 Gianluca Zambrotta
2 Christian Maggio

4 Giorgio Chiellini 67   5 Fabio Cannavaro (c) 31

12 Federico Marchetti

Tr: Marcello Lippi

Blue shirts, Blue shorts, Blue socks

ITALY

MATCH STATS

SVK		ITA
10	Shots	16
4	Shots on Goal	6
20	Fouls Committed	17
6	Corner Kicks	3
1	Caught Offside	3
422	Passes	487
292	Completed Passes	367
69%	Passes Success	75%
106	Km Covered	104
22	Av. Top Speed km/h	23
51%	Possession	49%

MATCH OFFICIALS
REFEREE
Howard Webb ENG
ASSISTANTS
Darren Cann ENG
Michael Mullarkey ENG
4TH OFFICIAL
Stephane Lannoy FRA

(C) Captain † Man of the Match

TABLE

	PL	GD	Pts
PAR	3	+2	5
SVK	3	-1	4
NZL	3	0	3
ITA	3	-1	2

We prepared for this match perfectly. I'm proud of my players. They put in a performance of the very highest level and played a fantastic game.

Vladimir Weiss

Italy were undoubtedly surprised by how we performed and what we were able to do. This is a huge win. We've pushed the boundaries of Slovakian football. We never would have dared dream of this. We proved that we're capable of great things.

Robert Vittek

I assume complete responsibility for this failure. I was convinced this squad could do a lot better than that - not win the World Cup, but do a lot better. When a team goes into a match as important as this with fear in the stomachs and paralysis in their legs, it's because the coach hasn't prepared them well enough mentally, physically and tactically, but above all mentally. I offer my apologies to Italian sport, the players, the football association - everyone.

Marcello Lippi

First Round Group F	Peter Mokaba Polokwane	Thursday 24-06-2010
Kick-off: 16:00	Partly Cloudy 16°	Attendance: 34 850

PARAGUAY   0 0   NEW ZEALAND

PARAGUAY

Red and white striped shirts, Blue shorts, Red and white hooped socks

Tr: Gerardo Martino (ARG)

MATCH STATS

PAR		NZL
17	Shots	4
5	Shots on Goal	0
13	Fouls Committed	19
2	Corner Kicks	0
0	Caught Offside	2
580	Passes	362
439	Completed Passes	215
76%	Passes Success	59%
102	Km Covered	97
23	Av. Top Speed km/h	22
58%	Possession	42%

MATCH OFFICIALS

REFEREE

Yuichi Nishimura JPN

ASSISTANTS

Toru Sagara JPN

Jeong Hae Sang KOR

4TH OFFICIAL

Koman Coulibaly MLI

(C) Captain † Man of the Match

TABLE

	PL	GD	Pts
PAR	3	+2	5
SVK	3	-1	4
NZL	3	0	3
ITA	3	-1	2

1 Justo Villar

4 Denis Caniza(c)   5 Julio Cesar Caceres   14 Paulo Da Silva   3 Claudio Morel

15 Victor Caceres   16 Cristian Riveros

13 Enrique Vera   67 18 Nelson Valdez
                                            10 Edgar Benitez

                    66 7 Oscar Cardozo   9 Roque Santa Cruz †
                       19 Lucas Barrios

              69 14 Rory Fallon   79 10 Chris Killen
                 20 Chris Wood   22 Jeremy Brockie

                       9 Shane Smeltz

3 Tony Lochhead   5 Ivan Vicelich   7 Simon Elliott   11 Leo Bertos

      19 Tommy Smith   6 Ryan Nelsen(c)   4 Winston Reid

                       1 Mark Paston

Tr: Ricki Herbert

Black shirts, Black shorts, Black socks

NEW ZEALAND

We were poor in the first half, but we played better after the break. We wanted to try and win the game but without leaving ourselves exposed because a one-goal defeat would send us out. I'm not happy with the way we played, but I'm pleased we made it through.

Gerardo Martino

The game got a bit monotonous because they defended so much, but I don't think we were ever in danger of not getting at least a draw.

Roque Santa Cruz

For us it was important to try and stay in the game as long as possible. We made a more concerted effort to win the match towards the end by putting on fresher forwards, but it wasn't enough. Despite the fact we didn't reach the last 16, this has been a great experience for New Zealand. I feel a little disappointed but I'm very proud of what this team's achieved. I'd never have dreamed we'd be going home unbeaten. I'm delighted with what my players have done.

Ricki Herbert

First Round Group G	Port Elizabeth Stadium Nelson Mandela Bay/Port Elizabeth	Tuesday 15-06-2010
Kick-off: 16:00	Sunny 12°	Attendance: 37 034

COTE D'IVOIRE   0   0   PORTUGAL

COTE D'IVOIRE

Orange shirts, Orange shorts, Orange socks
Tr: Sven-Goran Eriksson (SWE)

1 Boubacar Barry

20 Guy Demel 21   4 Kolo Toure (c)   5 Didier Zokora 7   17 Siaka Tiene

19 Yaya Toure

89 21 Emmanuel Eboue
13 Romaric   9 Ismael Tiote

15 Aruna Dindane   66 8 Salomon Kalou
82 10 Gervinho   11 Didier Drogba
18 Kader Keita

9 Liedson

55 10 Danny   7 Cristiano Ronaldo (c) † 21
11 Simao

62 20 Deco
19 Tiago

8 Pedro Mendes   85 16 Raul Meireles
17 Ruben Amorim

23 Fabio Coentrao   2 Bruno Alves   6 Ricardo Carvalho   3 Paulo Ferreira

1 Eduardo

Tr: Carlos Queiroz
White shirts with a thin green and red central stripe, Green shorts, White socks

PORTUGAL

MATCH STATS

CIV		POR
5	Shots	7
1	Shots on Goal	2
18	Fouls Committed	13
6	Corner Kicks	4
2	Caught Offside	1
458	Passes	543
350	Completed Passes	430
76%	Passes Success	79%
105	Km Covered	109
21	Av. Top Speed km/h	21
50%	Possession	50%

MATCH OFFICIALS
REFEREE
Jorge Larrionda URU
ASSISTANTS
Pablo Fandino URU
Mauricio Espinosa URU
4TH OFFICIAL
Martin Vazquez URU

(C) Captain † Man of the Match

TABLE

	PL	GD	Pts
CIV	1	0	1
POR	1	0	1
BRA	0	0	0
PRK	0	0	0

It was a very tense match, but I think that if one team was going to win it, it should have been us as we had more chances. I'm satisfied with our performance, our discipline and our organisation throughout the 90 minutes. I would have preferred to take three points, but Portugal are a great team and holding them to a draw is satisfying in itself. As for Drogba, yesterday he told me that he'd prefer to stay on the bench, but that if I needed him I could count on him.

Sven-Goran Eriksson

How could anyone be frustrated with that result? Everyone saw that it was a match between two of the favourites. Côte d'Ivoire waited for us to attack them and we tried to build moves and were able to dominate, but it's difficult to come by chances against a team that's set up to defend. We'll need to take more risks in our next match. What we need to take out of this is that we've collected a point against one of the favourites in the group.

Carlos Queiroz

First Round Group G	Ellis Park Johannesburg	Tuesday 15-06-2010
Kick-off: 20:30	Clear Night 3°	Attendance: 54 331

BRAZIL   2   1   KOREA DPR

Maicon [55], **Elano** [72]   **Ji Yun Nam** [89]

BRAZIL

Yellow shirts, Blue shorts, White socks

Tr: Carlos Dunga

1 Julio Cesar

2 Maicon†   3 Lucio(c)   4 Juan   6 Michel Bastos

8 Gilberto Silva   84 5 Felipe Melo / 18 Ramires 88

78 10 Kaka / 21 Nilmar   11 Robinho

73 7 Elano / 13 Dani Alves

9 Luis Fabiano

10 Hong Yong Jo(c)   9 Jong Tae Se

4 Pak Nam Chol   17 An Yong Hak   80 11 Mun In Guk / 6 Kim Kum Il

8 Ji Yun Nam   5 Ri Kwang Chon   3 Ri Jun Il   13 Pak Chol Jin   2 Cha Jong Hyok

1 Ri Myong Guk

Tr: Kim Jong Hun

Red shirts, Red shorts, Red socks

KOREA DPR

MATCH STATS

BRA		PRK
26	Shots	11
10	Shots on Goal	3
9	Fouls Committed	10
7	Corner Kicks	3
3	Caught Offside	1
715	Passes	362
595	Completed Passes	239
83%	Passes Success	66%
103	Km Covered	103
24	Av. Top Speed km/h	22
63%	Possession	37%

MATCH OFFICIALS

REFEREE
Viktor Kassai HUN

ASSISTANTS
Gabor Eros HUN
Tibor Vamos HUN

4TH OFFICIAL
Subkhiddin Mohd Salleh MAS

(C) Captain † Man of the Match

TABLE

	PL	GD	Pts
BRA	1	+1	3
CIV	1	0	1
POR	1	0	1
PRK	1	-1	0

Every team has to play efficiently, in attack and in defence. Overall we played well, especially in the second half, because in the first we didn't get our game together and didn't manage to pass the ball quickly.

Carlos Dunga

The cold weather wasn't as much of a problem as the way they played, with everybody behind the ball. You have to be patient. When we scored, things got easier.

Robinho

Throughout the match the players followed our game-plan and defended well. We were very well prepared and we got some good shots in on goal.

Kim Jong Hung

We played well in the first half, we defended really well and didn't let Brazil create any chances. But in the second half we had two lapses in concentration and they scored their two goals one after the other.

Ji Yun Nam

First Round Group G	Soccer City Johannesburg	Sunday 20-06-2010
Kick-off: 20:30	Clear Night 12°	Attendance: 84 445

BRAZIL   3   1   COTE D'IVOIRE

Luis Fabiano 2 25 50, Elano 62   Didier Drogba 79

BRAZIL

Yellow shirts, Blue shorts, Blue socks

Tr: Carlos Dunga

1 Julio Cesar

2 Maicon   3 Lucio (c)   4 Juan   6 Michel Bastos

5 Felipe Melo   8 Gilberto Silva

10 Kaka 85 88 88

7 Elano
67
13 Dani Alves

11 Robinho
93+
18 Ramires

9 Luis Fabiano †

11 Didier Drogba

8 Salomon Kalou
68
18 Kader Keita 75

15 Aruna Dindane
54
10 Gervinho

9 Ismael Tiote 86   19 Yaya Toure

21 Emmanuel Eboue
72
13 Romaric

17 Siaka Tiene 31   5 Didier Zokora   4 Kolo Toure (c)   20 Guy Demel

1 Boubacar Barry

Tr: Sven-Goran Eriksson (SWE)

Green and white hooped shirts, White shorts, White socks

COTE D'IVOIRE

MATCH STATS

BRA		CIV
12	Shots	10
6	Shots on Goal	4
17	Fouls Committed	23
4	Corner Kicks	3
0	Caught Offside	2
545	Passes	400
456	Completed Passes	305
84%	Passes Success	76%
97	Km Covered	95
25	Av. Top Speed km/h	23
56%	Possession	44%

MATCH OFFICIALS

REFEREE

Stephane Lannoy FRA

ASSISTANTS

Eric Dansault FRA

Laurent Ugo FRA

4TH OFFICIAL

Subkhiddin Mohd Salleh MAS

(C) Captain † Man of the Match

TABLE

	PL	GD	Pts
BRA	2	+3	6
POR	1	0	1
CIV	2	-2	1
PRK	1	-1	0

We had to be totally focused in this game because Côte d'Ivoire's main strength is their speed. Against Portugal they sat back and tried to take advantage of mistakes before hitting them on the break. But we were patient and moved the ball around a bit more.

Carlos Dunga

We were a bit nervous in our opening game. Anxiety had taken hold, but I knew that we'd play better today and that's why we've come off the pitch happy.

Julio Cesar

I'm not sad, just a little disappointed. Our team has made progress since the last World Cup, but we could have been a bit more ambitious and tried to go for the game a bit more.

Didier Drogba

They took the first chance they had and that changed everything. After the goal we changed the way we'd been playing. We can't afford to waste counter-attacks like we did today, it's unforgivable.

Kolo Toure

First Round Group G	Green Point Cape Town	Tuesday 15-06-2010
Kick-off: 13:30	Cloudy 12°	Attendance: 63 644

PORTUGAL   7 0   KOREA DPR

Raul Meireles 29, **Simão** 53, **Hugo Almeida** 56
Tiago 2 60 89, **Liedson** 81, **Cristiano Ronaldo** 87

PORTUGAL

Red shirts, Red shorts, Red socks
Tr: Carlos Queiroz

MATCH STATS

POR		PRK
26	Shots	15
13	Shots on Goal	4
18	Fouls Committed	3
5	Corner Kicks	1
2	Caught Offside	3
586	Passes	461
440	Completed Passes	323
75%	Passes Success	70%
109	Km Covered	106
21	Av. Top Speed km/h	22
55%	Possession	45%

MATCH OFFICIALS
REFEREE
Pablo Pozo CHI
ASSISTANTS
Patricio Basualto CHI
Francisco Mondria CHI
4TH OFFICIAL
Jerome Damon RSA

(C) Captain † Man of the Match

TABLE

	PL	GD	Pts
BRA	2	+3	6
POR	2	+7	4
CIV	2	-2	1
PRK	2	-8	0

1 Eduardo

13 Miguel   6 Ricardo Carvalho   2 Bruno Alves   23 Fabio Coentrao

19 Tiago   8 Pedro Mendes 38   70 16 Raul Meireles
                                    14 Miguel Veloso

74 11 Simao   77 18 Hugo Almeida   7 Cristiano Ronaldo(c)†
   5 Duda   9 Liedson

9 Jong Tae Se   10 Hong Yong Jo(c) 47

58 4 Pak Nam Chol   17 An Yong Hak   58 11 Mun In Guk
   6 Kim Kum Il   15 Kim Yong Jun

8 Ji Yun Nam 5 Ri Kwang Chon 3 Ri Jun Il 13 Pak Chol Jin 32 75 2 Cha Jong Hyok
                                                                  16 Nam Song Chol

1 Ri Myong Guk

Tr: Kim Jong Hun
White shirts, White shorts, White socks

KOREA DPR

It was a great display with good goals and the right attitude. We needed a game like this, but we have to remember that we've not won anything yet. The most important thing is to secure qualification. We'd seen some North Korean matches, like the one against Brazil, and we felt that we should make a few changes. So we decided to put our faith in these players. We proved that all our players are ready to play their part.

Carlos Queiroz

Our players did all they could, but we tactically collapsed and, all of a sudden, we were no longer able to stop the Portuguese. As head coach of the team, I feel like this is my fault, as I wasn't able to pass the proper strategy on to the players. The Portuguese simply became more and more aggressive as the match went on and after we conceded the first goal we lost the balance between our defence and offense. Our players started to panic.

Kim Jong Hung

First Round Group G	Durban Stadium Durban	Friday 25-06-2010
Kick-off: 16:00	Sunny 25°	Attendance: 62 712

PORTUGAL   0   0   BRAZIL

PORTUGAL

Red shirts with a green band on chest, White shorts, Green socks

Tr: Carlos Queiroz

1 Eduardo

21 Ricardo Costa   6 Ricardo Carvalho   2 Bruno Alves   23 Fabio Coentrao 64

19 Tiago 31   64 15 Pepe 40   84 16 Raul Meireles   54 5 Duda 25
8 Pedro Mendes   14 Miguel Veloso   11 Simao

10 Danny   7 Cristiano Ronaldo (c) †

85 9 Luis Fabiano 15
21 Nilmar   23 Grafite   13 Dani Alves

82 19 Julio Baptista
18 Ramires

8 Gilberto Silva   44 5 Felipe Melo 43
17 Josue

6 Michel Bastos   4 Juan 25   3 Lucio (c)   2 Maicon

1 Julio Cesar

Tr: Carlos Dunga

Yellow shirts, blue shorts, White socks

BRAZIL

MATCH STATS

POR		BRA
13	Shots	19
3	Shots on Goal	5
11	Fouls Committed	18
4	Corner Kicks	7
2	Caught Offside	0
398	Passes	712
275	Completed Passes	596
69%	Passes Success	84%
108	Km Covered	102
22	Av. Top Speed km/h	22
40%	Possession	60%

MATCH OFFICIALS

REFEREE
Benito Archundia MEX

ASSISTANTS
Hector Vergara CAN
Marvin Torrentera MEX

4TH OFFICIAL
Peter O'Leary NZL

(C) Captain † Man of the Match

TABLE

	PL	GD	Pts
BRA	3	+3	7
POR	3	+7	5
CIV	3	+1	4
PRK	3	-11	0

It was a good game and the attitude of the Portugal team was superb. I thought all the players went about their work brilliantly. We are in the second round and things are going to be different from now on. I have to say it was a tricky game for us and for Brazil too. We had to put our overalls on to begin with because Brazil started very strongly, but by the end we were wearing our dinner jackets. It was a great footballing spectacle and a draw was the right result in my view.

Carlos Queiroz

Portugal put a lot of people behind the ball. We kept trying right till the end and we even had two or three chances. I can't say I'm happy. Brazil always plays attacking football and always try to win. We had a lot of possession today and we tried to keep hold of the ball to tire the opposition and keep things tight. I think we've played pretty consistently so far and we've got the results we needed to get. The team has kept its shape and overall I'm happy with them.

Carlos Dunga

First Round Group G	Mbombela Nelspruit	Friday 25-06-2010
Kick-off: 16:00	Sunny 22°	Attendance: 34 763

KOREA DPR   0   3   COTE D'IVOIRE

Yaya Toure [14], Romaric [20], Salomon Kalou [82]

KOREA DPR

Red shirts, Red shorts, Red socks

Tr: Kim Jong Hun

1 Ri Myong Guk

2 Cha Jong Hyok   13 Pak Chol Jin   3 Ri Jun Il   5 Ri Kwang Chon   8 Ji Yun Nam

11 Mun In Guk   17 An Yong Hak   10 Hong Yong Jo(c)   4 Pak Nam Chol
67 12 Choe Kum Chol

9 Jong Tae Se

11 Didier Drogba

64 10 Gervinho   18 Kader Keita
   15 Aruna Dindane   64 8 Salomon Kalou

79 13 Romaric   9 Ismael Tiote   19 Yaya Toure
   7 Seydou Doumbia

3 Arthur Boka   5 Didier Zokora   4 Kolo Toure(c)   21 Emmanuel Eboue

1 Boubacar Barry

Tr: Sven-Goran Eriksson (SWE)

Green and white hooped shirts, White shorts, White socks

COTE D'IVOIRE

MATCH STATS

PRK		CIV
8	Shots	28
4	Shots on Goal	15
13	Fouls Committed	16
0	Corner Kicks	7
2	Caught Offside	4
414	Passes	622
242	Completed Passes	470
58%	Passes Success	76%
104	Km Covered	105
22	Av. Top Speed km/h	22
40%	Possession	60%

MATCH OFFICIALS
REFEREE
Alberto Undiano ESP
ASSISTANTS
Fermin Martinez ESP
Juan Carlos Yuste Jimenez ESP
4TH OFFICIAL
Massimo Busacca SUI

(C) Captain † Man of the Match

TABLE

	PL	GD	Pts
BRA	3	+3	7
POR	3	+7	5
CIV	3	+1	4
PRK	3	-11	0

I think this experience has been positive, and despite the three defeats we put in at least two good performances. This competition can help us lay foundations that we'll be able to build on to improve and return. This World Cup has been very useful to us. My players didn't stop working hard until the last minute of the final match.

Kim Jong Hung

We did everything we could to get out of the group, but the FIFA rankings were respected in the end. We had a hugely difficult group back in 2006 and it was the same this year. We're disappointed. We have very good players in this squad and we showed in our matches that we can compete with the best teams. I have a few regrets, particularly about our game against Portugal; we could have scored. I'm happy to have contested my second consecutive World Cup.

Sven-Goran Eriksson

First Round Group H	Mbombela Nelspruit	Wednesday 16-06-2010
Kick-off: 13:30	Sunny 17°	Attendance: 32 664

HONDURAS   0   1   CHILE

Jean Beausejour 34

HONDURAS

White shirts, White shorts, White socks

Tr: Reinaldo Rueda (COL)

18 Noel Valladares

23 Sergio Mendoza   2 Osman Chavez   3 Maynor Figueroa   21 Emilio Izaguirre

66 20 Amado Guevarra (c)   8 Wilson Palacios 33
6 Hendry Thomas

78 7 Ramon Nunez
15 Walter Martinez

17 Edgar Alvarez   13 Roger Espinoza

60 9 Carlos Pavon
12 George Welcome

15 Jean Beausejour †   87 10 Jorge Valdivia   7 Alexis Sanchez
11 Mark Gonzalez

14 Matias Fernandez   52 20 Rodrigo Millar
18 Gonzalo Jara

6 Carlos Carmona

81 8 Arturo Vidal   3 Waldo Ponce   17 Gary Medel   4 Mauricio Isla
5 Pablo Contreras

1 Claudio Bravo (c)

Tr: Marcelo Bielsa (ARG)

Red shirts, Blue shorts, Blue socks

CHILE

MATCH STATS

HON		CHI
7	Shots	20
2	Shots on Goal	5
15	Fouls Committed	21
4	Corner Kicks	6
2	Caught Offside	4
348	Passes	526
201	Completed Passes	383
58%	Passes Success	73%
100	Km Covered	86
23	Av. Top Speed km/h	21
44%	Possession	56%

MATCH OFFICIALS

REFEREE

Eddy Maillet SEY

ASSISTANTS

Evariste Menkouande CMR

Bechir Hassani TUN

4TH OFFICIAL

Yuichi Nishimura JPN

(C) Captain † Man of the Match

TABLE

	PL	GD	Pts
CHI	1	+1	3
ESP	0	0	0
SUI	0	0	0
HON	1	-1	0

I feel bad about the goal because I didn't clear the ball away. I don't think it's a fair result because their goal had a touch of fortune about it. They didn't make any more chances after that and though we had some important players out we never let our heads drop. We are mentally strong and we are ready for our next two opponents. They are tough teams but it's not impossible for us.

Sergio Mendoza

I think it was the right result. We played well, we never sat on our lead and they didn't make us suffer. We attacked well although we could have had a few more goals, and that might work against us in the final reckoning. Honduras have had a lot of problems with the availability of some of their key players and they weren't able to play the way they would have wanted to.

Marcelo Bielsa

First Round Group H	Durban Stadium Durban	Wednesday 16-06-2010
Kick-off: 16:00	Sunny 20°	Attendance: 62453

SPAIN   0   1   SWITZERLAND

Gelson Fernandes 52

SPAIN

Red shirts, Blue shorts, Red socks
Tr: Vicente Del Bosque

MATCH STATS

ESP		SUI
24	Shots	8
8	Shots on Goal	3
8	Fouls Committed	21
12	Corner Kicks	3
2	Caught Offside	1
683	Passes	318
527	Completed Passes	182
77%	Passes Success	57%
104	Km Covered	119
19	Av. Top Speed km/h	20
63%	Possession	37%

MATCH OFFICIALS

REFEREE
Howard Webb ENG

ASSISTANTS
Darren Cann ENG
Michael Mullarkey ENG

4TH OFFICIAL
Martin Hansson SWE

(C) Captain † Man of the Match

TABLE

	PL	GD	Pts
CHI	1	+1	3
SUI	1	+1	3
HON	1	-1	0
ESP	1	-1	0

1 Iker Casillas(c)

15 Sergio Ramos   3 Gerard Pique   5 Carles Puyol   11 Joan Capdevila

61   16 Sergio Busquets   14 Xabi Alonso
9 Fernando Torres

62   21 David Silva   8 Xavi   77   6 Andres Iniesta
22 Jesus Navas   18 Pedro

7 David Villa

10 Blaise Nkufo   79   19 Eren Derdiyok
15 Hakan Yakin 94+

16 Gelson Fernandes† 8 Gokhan Inler(c) 6 Benjamin Huggel 92+ 7 Tranquillo Barnetta
22 Mario Eggimann

17 Reto Ziegler 73   2 Stephan Lichtsteiner

13 Stephane Grichting 30   36   4 Philippe Senderos
5 Steve Von Bergen

1 Diego Benaglio 91+

Tr: Ottmar Hitzfeld (GER)
White shirts, Red shorts, White socks

SWITZERLAND

There's always a chance you can lose, and their football didn't deserve such a big reward. We fought hard for the win but it wasn't to be. I want to avenge this defeat and I'm up for the challenge, and that's the way we all need to feel. This is no time for feeling sorry for ourselves and cursing our bad luck.
Vicente Del Bosque

I think the way we play the game will bring us rewards. We can turn this around.
Iker Casillas

I'm well aware we made history. We've never beaten Spain before and I've always said there would be a first time. I could see they were getting nervous because they were the favourites, and we are absolutely thrilled with these three wholly unexpected three points. We really concentrated on the job and we closed down space in the midfield. But we still haven't achieved anything yet and we have to improve if we want to beat Chile.
Ottmar Hitzfeld

First Round Group H	Port Elizabeth Stadium Nelson Mandela Bay/Port Elizabeth	Monday 21-06-2010
Kick-off: 16:00	Sunny 18°	Attendance: 34 872

CHILE 1 0 SWITZERLAND

Mark Gonzalez 75

CHILE

Red shirts, Blue shorts, White socks

Tr: Marcelo Bielsa (ARG)

1 Claudio Bravo (c)

4 Mauricio Isla   17 Gary Medel 61   3 Waldo Ponce 25   18 Gonzalo Jara

6 Carlos Carmona 22

14 Matias Fernandez 60 65   8 Arturo Vidal 46
22 Esteban Paredes   11 Mark Gonzalez †

7 Alexis Sanchez   9 Humberto Suazo 2 46   15 Jean Beausejour
10 Jorge Valdivia 92+

10 Blaise Nkufo 18 68   9 Alexander Frei (c) 42
19 Eren Derdiyok   7 Tranquillo Barnetta 48

16 Gelson Fernandes 8 Gokhan Inler 60 6 Benjamin Huggel 11 Valon Behrami 31
77 18 Albert Bunjaku

17 Reto Ziegler   13 Stephane Grichting   5 Steve Von Bergen   2 Stephan Lichtsteiner

1 Diego Benaglio

Tr: Ottmar Hitzfeld (GER)

White shirts, Red shorts, Red socks

SWITZERLAND

MATCH STATS

CHI		SUI
20	Shots	7
7	Shots on Goal	1
19	Fouls Committed	26
5	Corner Kicks	3
9	Caught Offside	0
570	Passes	296
437	Completed Passes	165
77%	Passes Success	56%
111	Km Covered	103
22	Av. Top Speed km/h	21
58%	Possession	42%

MATCH OFFICIALS

REFEREE

Khalil Al Ghamdi KSA

ASSISTANTS

Hassan Kamranifar IRN

Saleh Al Marzouqi UAE

4TH OFFICIAL

Martin Vazquez URU

(C) Captain † Man of the Match

TABLE

	PL	GD	Pts
CHI	2	+2	6
SUI	2	0	3
HON	1	-1	0
ESP	1	-1	0

Taking the game as a whole, we had a lot more possession than them. We created all kinds of chances, but we've only scored once. That should be a warning to us, because it could easily have ended in a draw, when you consider Switzerland's huge chance just before the end. But I think we deserved to win. After they had a man sent off, we could safely send on more forwards, and that was enough to earn us the victory.

Marcelo Bielsa

It was unbelievably difficult against such hard-running opponents once we'd gone a man down after just 30 minutes. We were well aware that the Chileans would be more skilful than us. After Valon Behrami was sent off, we just concentrated on keeping it tight at the back. We nearly made it through to the final whistle, and we even came close to an equaliser from Eren Derdiyok just before the end. However, despite this setback, I'm upbeat about our meeting with Honduras.

Ottmar Hitzfeld

First Round Group H	Ellis Park Johannesburg	Monday 21-06-2010
Kick-off: 20:30	Clear Night 13°	Attendance: 54 386

SPAIN   2   0   HONDURAS

David Villa 2 [17] [51]
Penalty miss: David Villa [62]

SPAIN

Red shirts, Blue shorts, Red socks
Tr: Vicente Del Bosque

MATCH STATS

ESP		HON
22	Shots	9
8	Shots on Goal	0
9	Fouls Committed	19
12	Corner Kicks	2
1	Caught Offside	7
632	Passes	429
486	Completed Passes	293
77%	Passes Success	68%
105	Km Covered	104
23	Av. Top Speed km/h	22
57%	Possession	43%

MATCH OFFICIALS
REFEREE
Yuichi Nishimura JPN
ASSISTANTS
Toru Sagara JPN
Jeong Hae Sang KOR
4TH OFFICIAL
Subkhiddin Mohd Salleh MAS

(C) Captain † Man of the Match

TABLE

	PL	GD	Pts
CHI	2	+2	6
ESP	2	+1	3
SUI	2	0	3
HON	2	-3	0

1 Iker Casillas (c)

77 15 Sergio Ramos / 17 Alvaro Arbeloa   3 Gerard Pique   5 Carles Puyol   11 Joan Capdevila

16 Sergio Busquets   14 Xabi Alonso

66 8 Xavi / 10 Cesc Fabregas

22 Jesus Navas   7 David Villa †

70 9 Fernando Torres / 13 Juan Manuel Mata

84 11 David Suazo / 10 Jerry Palacios

46 13 Roger Espinoza / 12 George Welcome   63 19 Danilo Turcios 8 / 7 Ramon Nunez   15 Walter Martinez

8 Wilson Palacios   20 Amado Guevarra (c)

21 Emilio Izaguirre 38   3 Maynor Figueroa   2 Osman Chavez   23 Sergio Mendoza

18 Noel Valladares

Tr: Reinaldo Rueda (COL)
White shirts, White shorts, White socks

HONDURAS

We've paved the way for us to take on Chile for a place in the next round, though I don't think that we've had a good game. Yes, we created a lot of goalscoring situations and we ought to have won by more goals, but I'm not totally happy - once again our finishing was off. I felt that we were too open and very vulnerable, and if we play like that against Chile we could suffer. Why? Because they're a very active and aggressive team who are very difficult to get at.
Vicente Del Bosque

The idea was to get the ball off Spain and try and feed our forwards, and we had two or three chances but we weren't clinical enough to score.
Reinaldo Rueda

We managed to keep Spain at bay for a while, but they were able to dictate the tempo of the game and put away their chances. We worked hard and tried to catch them on the counter-attack, but in football you have to score to win the game.
David Suazo

First Round Group H	Loftus Versfeld Tshwane/Pretoria	Friday 25-06-2010
Kick-off: 20:30	Clear Night 13°	Attendance: 41 958

CHILE 1 2 SPAIN

Rodrigo Millar [47]

David Villa [24], Andres Iniesta [37]

CHILE
Red shirts, Blue shorts, Blue socks
Tr: Marcelo Bielsa (ARG)

1 Claudio Bravo (c)

17 Gary Medel [15]   3 Waldo Ponce [19]   18 Gonzalo Jara   8 Arturo Vidal

4 Mauricio Isla

15 Jean Beausejour

13 Marco Estrada [21] [37] [37]

[46] 11 Mark Gonzalez
22 Esteban Paredes

[65] 7 Alexis Sanchez   [46] 10 Jorge Valdivia
16 Fabian Orellana   20 Rodrigo Millar

7 David Villa   [55] 9 Fernando Torres
10 Cesc Fabregas

6 Andres Iniesta †   8 Xavi

[73] 14 Xabi Alonso   16 Sergio Busquets
20 Javier Martinez

11 Joan Capdevila   5 Carles Puyol   3 Gerard Pique   15 Sergio Ramos

1 Iker Casillas (c)

Tr: Vicente Del Bosque
Navy blue shirts, White shorts, White socks

SPAIN

MATCH STATS		
CHI		ESP
9	Shots	9
4	Shots on Goal	3
21	Fouls Committed	13
3	Corner Kicks	4
3	Caught Offside	1
406	Passes	734
292	Completed Passes	617
72%	Passes Success	84%
100	Km Covered	103
22	Av. Top Speed km/h	22
42%	Possession	58%

MATCH OFFICIALS
REFEREE
Marco Rodriguez MEX
ASSISTANTS
Jose Luis Camargo MEX
Alberto Morin MEX
4TH OFFICIAL
Subkhiddin Mohd Salleh MAS

(C) Captain † Man of the Match

TABLE			
	PL	GD	Pts
ESP	3	+2	6
CHI	3	+1	6
SUI	3	0	4
HON	3	-3	1

The game was well-balanced until the sending-off, thanks to the effort we put in. After that it was an uphill struggle. Our numerical disadvantage became more obvious in the second half, but despite the fact they had the ball all the time, they didn't create many opportunities - though neither did we. It was one game before the red card and a different one afterwards. You feel a bit ambivalent when you lose but still qualify, which is why we didn't celebrate.

Marcelo Bielsa

We had the game under control until they scored, but we let it affect us too much. It was an intense game against opponents who deserve plenty of praise for putting in a performance of incredible energy. I give a lot of credit to the Chileans, who've done a great job, and I wish them all the best. We were having difficulties but were able to respond via a goal from David Villa, which helped us relax. Emotionally speaking, we responded well to the defeat by Switzerland.

Vicente Del Bosque

First Round Group H	Ellis Park Johannesburg	Friday 25-06-2010
Kick-off: 20:30	Clear Night 6°	Attendance: 28 042

SWITZERLAND   0   0   HONDURAS

SWITZERLAND

Red shirts, white shorts, Red socks

Tr: Ottmar Hitzfeld (GER)

MATCH STATS

SUI		HON
17	Shots	8
5	Shots on Goal	2
12	Fouls Committed	18
5	Corner Kicks	3
2	Caught Offside	9
611	Passes	401
485	Completed Passes	263
79%	Passes Success	66%
104	Km Covered	94
23	Av. Top Speed km/h	22
57%	Possession	43%

MATCH OFFICIALS

REFEREE
Hector Baldassi ARG

ASSISTANTS
Ricardo Vasas ARG
Hernan Maidana ARG

4TH OFFICIAL
Olegario Benquerenca POR

(C) Captain † Man of the Match

TABLE

	PL	GD	Pts
ESP	3	+2	6
CHI	3	+1	6
SUI	3	0	4
HON	3	-3	1

1 Diego Benaglio

2 Stephan Lichtsteiner   5 Steve Von Bergen   13 Stephane Grichting   17 Reto Ziegler

8 Gokhan Inler (c)   6 Benjamin Huggel   78
23 Xherdan Shaqiri

7 Tranquillo Barnetta   16 Gelson Fernandes 34   46
15 Hakan Yakin

19 Eren Derdiyok   69   10 Blaise Nkufo
9 Alexander Frei

11 David Suazo 58   87
19 Danilo Turcios

7 Ramon Nunez   67   10 Jerry Palacios   78   17 Edgar Alvarez
15 Walter Martinez   12 George Welcome

6 Hendry Thomas 4   8 Wilson Palacios 89

3 Maynor Figueroa   5 Victor Bernardez   2 Osman Chavez 64   16 Mauricio Sabillon

18 Noel Valladares (c)†

Tr: Reinaldo Rueda (COL)

Blue shirts, Blue shorts, Blue socks

HONDURAS

We were fired up for this one, but we didn't start at all well. Our challenges were a little timid and we couldn't get the final ball away in attack. We built up a head of steam in the second half, but that handed our opponents chances on the break, so it was end-to-end stuff for a time. But to score, you also need a little luck, and we were out of luck today. And overall, we have to be honest and say we've not performed at a level which would justify a place in the last 16.

Ottmar Hitzfeld

It was a very exciting match. We could have come away with more than a point, but we only got going once it was too late. We failed to make the most of our chances. On the one hand, that's due to the inexperience of some of my players, and on the other hand, we tried to do things on our own at times when it would have been better to look for a team-mate. I'm very disappointed, but we can still be proud of that performance.

Reinaldo Rueda

Round of 16	Port Elizabeth Stadium Nelson Mandela Bay/Port Elizabeth	Saturday 26-06-2010
Kick-off: 16:00	Sunny 18°	Attendance: 30 597

URUGUAY   2 1   KOREA REPUBLIC

Luis Suarez 2 [8] [80]   Lee Chung Yong [68]

URUGUAY

Sky blue shirts, Black shorts, Black socks

Tr: Oscar Tabarez

1 Fernando Muslera

16 Maximiliano Pereira   2 Diego Lugano (c)   [46] 3 Diego Godin   4 Jorge Fucile
                                                6 Mauricio Victorino

15 Diego Perez   17 Egidio Arevalo   [74] 11 Alvaro Pereira
                                             14 Nicolas Lodeiro

7 Edinson Cavani   [84] 9 Luis Suarez †   10 Diego Forlan
                        20 Alvaro Fernandez

10 Park Chu Young

7 Park Ji Sung (c)   [61] 13 Kim Jae Sung   17 Lee Chung Yong
                           20 Lee Dong Gook

[85] 16 Ki Sung Yueng   8 Kim Jung Woo [38]
     19 Yeom Ki Hun

12 Lee Young Pyo   14 Lee Jung Soo   4 Cho Yong Hyung [83]   22 Cha Du Ri [69]

18 Jung Sung Ryong

Tr: Huh Jung Moo

White shirts, White shorts, White socks

KOREA REPUBLIC

MATCH STATS

URU		KOR
14	Shots	15
8	Shots on Goal	5
12	Fouls Committed	12
3	Corner Kicks	3
1	Caught Offside	0
434	Passes	596
268	Completed Passes	424
62%	Passes Success	71%
106	Km Covered	108
22	Av. Top Speed km/h	22
46%	Possession	54%

MATCH OFFICIALS

REFEREE

Wolfgang Stark GER

ASSISTANTS

Jan-Hendrik Salver GER

Mike Pickel GER

4TH OFFICIAL

Joel Aguilar SLV

(C) Captain † Man of the Match

That was a demonstration of temperament, maturity and class. We played better towards the end and fortunately Suarez was able to score that spectacular winning goal. Korea played a great game, but that slice of luck went our way not theirs this time - that's football. It was a very hard-fought victory. The team's solidity and cohesion really came to the fore late on and, without getting carried away, I think that is a great quality to have whatever team you're up against.

Oscar Tabarez

There are some things we need to improve to compete at international level. It's good to play against opponents from other continents and take part in tournaments on foreign soil. Uruguay have some very good individuals. The result didn't go the way we wanted but my players gave their all. Uruguay were just fortunate enough to get those goals. We played very well but we ought to have played a bit more intelligently. Our players never gave in.

Huh Jung Moo

Round of 16	Royal Bafokeng Rustenburg	Saturday 26-06-2010
Kick-off: 20:30	Clear Night 14°	Attendance: 34 976

USA   1   2   GHANA

Landon Donovan 62p

Kevin Prince Boateng 5, **Asamoah Gyan** 93

USA

White shirts, White shorts, White socks

Tr: Bob Bradley

MATCH STATS

USA		GHA
20	Shots	16
6	Shots on Goal	6
11	Fouls Committed	19
5	Corner Kicks	4
1	Caught Offside	4
632	Passes	711
381	Completed Passes	451
60%	Passes Success	63%
148	Km Covered	140
23	Av. Top Speed km/h	23
51%	Possession	49%

MATCH OFFICIALS

REFEREE
Viktor Kassai HUN

ASSISTANTS
Gabor Eros HUN
Tibor Vamos HUN

4TH OFFICIAL
Michael Hester NZL

(C) Captain † Man of the Match

1 Tim Howard

15 Jay DeMerit   3 Carlos Bocanegra (c) 68

6 Steve Cherundolo 18   12 Jonathan Bornstein

4 Michael Bradley   31   13 Ricardo Clark 7
                          19 Maurice Edu

10 Landon Donovan   8 Clint Dempsey

46   20 Robbie Findley   91   17 Jozy Altidore
      22 Benny Feilhaber   9 Herculez Gomez

3 Asamoah Gyan

13 Andre Ayew†   113   7 Samuel Inkoom
                                               11 Sulley Muntari

78   23 Kevin Prince Boateng   21 Kwadwo Asamoah
      10 Stephen Appiah

6 Anthony Annan

73   2 Hans Sarpei   5 John Mensah (c)   8 Jonathan Mensah 61   4 John Pantsil
      19 Lee Addy

22 Richard Kingson

Tr: Milovan Rajevac

Red and yellow striped shirts, Red shorts, Red socks

GHANA

We have gone down a goal early one too many times. There were some chances for us but early in the overtime we went down again, and at that point, with everything we had put in physically we just didn't have enough after that. At the moment it is just a stinging tough defeat. We felt that as we went through the first round, that we were ready to go deep into this tournament. We knew Ghana were a good team but tonight we didn't get the job done.

Bob Bradley

We have done this before, we did it in 2006, but now we have advanced one step higher. I'm the happiest man in the world. We have made everybody proud, not Ghana alone, but the whole of Africa.

Asamoah Gyan

We're very disappointed there were no African teams with us. We must fight, not just for us, but for the other teams. We feel we have the whole of Africa behind us and that's given us a lot more energy.

Andre Ayew

Round of 16	Free State Mangaung/Bloemfontein	Sunday 27-06-2010
Kick-off: 16:00	Sunny 19°	Attendance: 40 510

GERMANY 4 1 ENGLAND

Miroslav Klose [20], Lukas Podolski [32],
Thomas Müller 2 [67 70]

Matthew Upson [37]

GERMANY

White shirts, Black shorts, White socks

Tr: Joachim Löw

1 Manuel Neuer

16 Philipp Lahm(c)   17 Per Mertesacker   3 Arne Friedrich [47]   20 Jerome Boateng

6 Sami Khedira   7 Bastian Schweinsteiger

8 Mesut Özil [83]
13 Thomas Müller† [72]   9 Stefan Kiessling   10 Lukas Podolski
15 Piotr Trochowski

11 Miroslav Klose [72]
23 Mario Gomez

10 Wayne Rooney   19 Jermain Defoe [71]
21 Emile Heskey

4 Steven Gerrard(c)   14 Gareth Barry   8 Frank Lampard   16 James Milner [64]
11 Joe Cole

3 Ashley Cole   15 Matthew Upson   6 John Terry [87]   2 Glen Johnson [81]
17 Shaun Wright-Phillips

1 David James

Tr: Fabio Capello

Red shirts, Red shorts, Red socks

ENGLAND

MATCH STATS		
GER		ENG
17	Shots	19
7	Shots on Goal	9
7	Fouls Committed	6
4	Corner Kicks	6
4	Caught Offside	2
411	Passes	508
273	Completed Passes	357
66%	Passes Success	70%
108	Km Covered	106
23	Av. Top Speed km/h	23
49%	Possession	51%

MATCH OFFICIALS

REFEREE
Jorge Larrionda URU
ASSISTANTS
Pablo Fandino URU
Mauricio Espinosa URU
4TH OFFICIAL
Martin Vazquez URU

(C)Captain †Man of the Match

We are very satisfied. It was a fantastic performance against a very experienced England team. I'm sure it was a fun game to watch for the fans. We definitely played with lot of confidence, and the first goals were good for our morale. I said to my team at the half-time break, we need to try and score the third goal. We knew we could hit England on the counter-attack because they were open. Our players carried it off brilliantly.

Joachim Löw

We made some mistakes when they played the counter-attack. The little things always decide the results. After we lost the third goal, we played I think a little bit disappointing.

Fabio Capello

Germany are a fantastic team and they deserved their win. At 2-1, though, we had a good goal disallowed. At this level the small details dictate games and that would have been a key goal for us.

Steven Gerrard

Round of 16	Soccer City Johannesburg	Sunday 27-06-2010
Kick-off: 20:30	Clear Night 14°	Attendance: 84 377

ARGENTINA   3   1   MEXICO

Carlos Tevez 2 [26] [52], **Gonzalo Higuain** [33]   **Javier Hernandez** [71]

ARGENTINA

Sky-blue and white striped shirts, Dark blue shorts, Dark blue socks

Tr: Diego Maradona

22 Sergio Romero

15 Nicolas Otamendi   2 Martin Demichelis   4 Nicolas Burdisso   6 Gabriel Heinze

14 Javier Mascherano (c)

20 Maxi Rodriguez [87]   [79] **7 Angel Di Maria**
23 Javier Pastore   **17 Jonas Gutierrez**

10 Lionel Messi

[69] **11 Carlos Tevez †**
9 Gonzalo Higuain   **8 Juan Veron**

14 Javier Hernandez

18 Andres Guardado [61]   **21 Adolfo Bautista** [46]   **17 Giovani Dos Santos**
9 Guillermo Franco   **7 Pablo Barrera**

6 Gerardo Torrado   4 Rafael Marquez [28]

3 Carlos Salcido   2 Francisco Rodriguez   5 Ricardo Osorio   16 Efrain Juarez

1 Oscar Perez

Tr: Javier Aguirre

Green shirts, White shorts, White socks

MEXICO

MATCH STATS

ARG		MEX
11	Shots	16
6	Shots on Goal	6
11	Fouls Committed	26
2	Corner Kicks	5
1	Caught Offside	2
522	Passes	522
380	Completed Passes	389
73%	Passes Success	75%
101	Km Covered	108
21	Av. Top Speed km/h	22
52%	Possession	48%

MATCH OFFICIALS

REFEREE
Roberto Rosetti ITA

ASSISTANTS
Paolo Calcagno ITA
Stefano Ayroldi ITA

4TH OFFICIAL
Jerome Damon RSA

(C) Captain † Man of the Match

It was a strange and tense match. We know each other well but we also knew that if we could attack certain areas, then we'd get something out of it. I think Argentina were the better side over the 90 minutes and we didn't have any real scares. All I can do is congratulate the players because they're doing things well, playing the ball around and enjoying themselves. The team looked comfortable out there, despite the quality of the opposition.

Diego Maradona

We were stronger up until the first goal. After the referee gave that offside goal we lost our concentration. Just as we were trying to come back from that they scored another. That changed the course of the game, though the team played with a lot of dignity and tried hard to come back. We almost made it to 3-2 but there's not much else you can say really. We need to keep working because we've got a generation of very good players here.

Javier Aguirre

Round of 16	Durban Stadium Durban	Monday 28-06-2010
Kick-off: 16:00	Sunny 23°	Attendance: 61 962

NETHERLANDS   2   1   SLOVAKIA

Arjen Robben ¹⁸, Wesley Sneijder ⁸⁴   Robert Vittek ⁹⁴⁺ᵖ

NETHERLANDS

Orange shirts, Black shorts, Orange socks

Tr: Bert van Marwijk

1 Maarten Stekelenburg 93+

3 John Heitinga   4 Joris Mathijsen

2 Gregory Van der Wiel   5 Giovanni Van Bronckhorst(c)

6 Mark Van Bommel   8 Nigel De Jong

71 11 Arjen Robben† 31   92+ 10 Wesley Sneijder   7 Dirk Kuyt
    17 Eljero Elia   20 Ibrahim Afellay

80 9 Robin Van Persie
    21 Klaas Jan Huntelaar

11 Robert Vittek

7 Vladimir Weiss   15 Miroslav Stoch

87 17 Marek Hamsik(c)   71 18 Erik Jendrisek
    10 Marek Sapara   20 Kamil Kopunek 72

19 Juraj Kucka 40

88 5 Radoslav Zabavnik   16 Jan Durica   3 Martin Skrtel 84   2 Peter Pekarik
    14 Martin Jakubko

1 Jan Mucha

Tr: Vladimir Weiss

White shirts, White shorts, White socks

SLOVAKIA

MATCH STATS

NED		SVK
16	Shots	12
9	Shots on Goal	3
17	Fouls Committed	19
5	Corner Kicks	2
2	Caught Offside	3
527	Passes	504
391	Completed Passes	366
74%	Passes Success	73%
103	Km Covered	105
22	Av. Top Speed km/h	22
52%	Possession	48%

MATCH OFFICIALS
REFEREE
Alberto Undiano ESP
ASSISTANTS
Fermin Martinez ESP
Juan Carlos Yuste Jimenez ESP
4TH OFFICIAL
Stephane Lannoy FRA

(C) Captain † Man of the Match

We played well for the first half-hour. We were good at the start of the second half too. Maarten Stekelenburg then saved us twice at a very important time. It's obviously fantastic to have Robben come back after injury and show that he's already fit enough to be scoring that kind of goal.
Bert van Marwijk
Winning was the most important thing. We've yet to turn in anything close to a perfect performance.
Arjen Robben

The Netherlands were tough opponents. We were courageous and we threw our hearts into it. We're proud we made it into the last sixteen, but the better team is through to the next round. The penalty at the end will lighten the mood a little on the plane home.
Vladimir Weiss
We're going home proud and with our heads held high. We're winners to the people of Slovakia.
Robert Vittek

Round of 16	Ellis Park Johannesburg	Monday 28-06-2010
Kick-off: 20:30	Partly Cloudy 12°	Attendance: 54 096

BRAZIL   3 0   CHILE

Juan 35, **Luis Fabiano** 38, **Robinho** 59

BRAZIL

Yellow shirts, Blue shorts, Blue socks

Tr: Carlos Dunga

1 Julio Cesar

2 Maicon   3 Lucio (c)   4 Juan   6 Michel Bastos

8 Gilberto Silva

13 Dani Alves   18 Ramires 72

81 10 Kaka 30   85 11 Robinho †
    20 Kleberson   16 Gilberto Melo

76 9 Luis Fabiano
    21 Nilmar

MATCH STATS

BRA		CHI
17	Shots	15
6	Shots on Goal	3
14	Fouls Committed	18
8	Corner Kicks	6
1	Caught Offside	1
451	Passes	507
282	Completed Passes	329
63%	Passes Success	65%
100	Km Covered	108
22	Av. Top Speed km/h	23
51%	Possession	49%

MATCH OFFICIALS

REFEREE
Howard Webb ENG

ASSISTANTS
Darren Cann ENG
Michael Mullarkey ENG

4TH OFFICIAL
Martin Hansson SWE

(C) Captain † Man of the Match

9 Humberto Suazo

46 11 Mark Gonzalez   7 Alexis Sanchez
    21 Rodrigo Tello

15 Jean Beausejour   62 4 Mauricio Isla
                                20 Rodrigo Millar 80

6 Carlos Carmona

2 Ismael Fuentes 68

46 5 Pablo Contreras   8 Arturo Vidal 30   18 Gonzalo Jara
    10 Jorge Valdivia

1 Claudio Bravo (c)

Tr: Marcelo Bielsa

White shirts, White shorts, White socks

CHILE

Today's was a nice game to watch, because Chile like to attack too. They're difficult opponents to mark, because their players never stop moving, but Brazil were able to hold firm and play a balanced match. When we had the ball, we were able to use it quickly. The quality Brazilian players have makes that easier and this team now has an ingrained playing style, even if there are personnel changes.

Carlos Dunga

We deserved to reach this stage but we also deserved to go out. Perhaps the margin of victory was a bit excessive but, overall, it was clear just how superior our opponents were. Brazil had the patience to take advantage of any spaces we gave them, and it's always dangerous when you concede the first goal against them. We did a good job despite being one of the youngest sides in the competition. With the benefit of experience, we can continue to progress in the future.

Marcelo Bielsa

Round of 16	Loftus Versfeld Tshwane/Pretoria	Tuesday 29-06-2010
Kick-off: 16:00	Cloudy 17°	Attendance: 36 742

PARAGUAY   0 0   JAPAN

5 ᵖˢₒ 3

PARAGUAY
Red and white striped shirts, white shorts, Red and white hooped socks
Tr: Gerardo Martino

1 Justo Villar (c)

6 Carlos Bonet   14 Paulo Da Silva   21 Antolin Alcaraz   3 Claudio Morel

13 Enrique Vera   75 20 Nestor Ortigoza   16 Cristian Riveros 118
                       8 Edgar Barreto

94 9 Roque Santa Cruz   19 Lucas Barrios   60 10 Edgar Benitez
    7 Oscar Cardozo   18 Nelson Valdez

18 Keisuke Honda † 93+

106 16 Yoshito Okubo   8 Daisuke Matsui 58
     11 Keiji Tamada   65 9 Shinji Okazaki

7 Yasuhito Endo 113   17 Makoto Hasebe (c)

81 2 Yuki Abe
    14 Kengo Nakamura

5 Yuto Nagatomo 72 4 Marcus Tulio Tanaka 22 Yuji Nakazawa 3 Yuichi Komano

21 Eiji Kawashima

Tr: Takeshi Okada
Blue shirts, Blue shorts, Blue socks

JAPAN

MATCH STATS		
PAR		JPN
18	Shots	16
6	Shots on Goal	6
26	Fouls Committed	29
6	Corner Kicks	5
1	Caught Offside	1
615	Passes	428
368	Completed Passes	225
60%	Passes Success	53%
134	Km Covered	133
23	Av. Top Speed km/h	23
58%	Possession	42%

MATCH OFFICIALS
REFEREE
Frank De Bleeckere BEL
ASSISTANTS
Peter Hermans BEL
Walter Vromans BEL
4TH OFFICIAL
Peter O'Leary NZL

(C) Captain † Man of the Match

PENALTIES		
PAR		JPN
✓	Barreto	
	Endo	✓
✓	Barrios	
	Hasebe	✓
✓	Riveros	
	Komano	✗¹
✓	Valdez	
	Honda	✓
✓	Cardozo	

¹ Hit crossbar

It was a very tight game, though I think we had a slight edge on our opponents. We showed more heart than football and, in a game like this, that's enough. Other teams need to play more football to win. That said, we're not going to understate the value of being among the top eight teams in the world. The Japanese also worked really hard but luck was on our side. Let's hope we can recover quickly and keep making history.

Gerardo Martino

Everything we've done during the tournament makes me feel really happy. This team has done Japan and all Asia proud. But, as far as today's defeat is concerned, I feel as we should have done more. Honda was very isolated and that was my fault. If you want to win you have to score goals.

Takeshi Okada

Despite the defeat, we've shown the world just what Japanese football is about.

Makoto Hasebe

Round of 16	Green Point Cape Town	Tuesday 29-06-2010
Kick-off: 20:30	Partly Cloudy 13°	Attendance: 62 955

SPAIN   1   0   PORTUGAL

David Villa 63

SPAIN

Red shirts, Blue shorts, Red socks

Tr: Vicente Del Bosque

1 Iker Casillas (c)

15 Sergio Ramos   3 Gerard Pique   5 Carles Puyol   11 Joan Capdevila

16 Sergio Busquets   93+ 14 Xabi Alonso 74
                            4 Carlos Marchena

6 Andres Iniesta   8 Xavi †   88 7 David Villa
                                            18 Pedro

58 9 Fernando Torres
    19 Fernando Llorente

72 11 Simao   58 18 Hugo Almeida   7 Cristiano Ronaldo (c)
    9 Liedson   10 Danny

16 Raul Meireles   19 Tiago 80

72 15 Pepe
    8 Pedro Mendes

23 Fabio Coentrao   2 Bruno Alves   6 Ricardo Carvalho   21 Ricardo Costa 89

1 Eduardo

Tr: Carlos Queiroz

White shirts with a green and red front panel, Green shorts, white socks

PORTUGAL

MATCH STATS

ESP		POR
19	Shots	9
10	Shots on Goal	3
13	Fouls Committed	18
6	Corner Kicks	3
0	Caught Offside	3
754	Passes	453
635	Completed Passes	315
84%	Passes Success	70%
107	Km Covered	112
21	Av. Top Speed km/h	22
61%	Possession	39%

MATCH OFFICIALS
REFEREE
Hector Baldassi ARG
ASSISTANTS
Ricardo Casas ARG
Hernan Maidana ARG
4TH OFFICIAL
Carlos Batres GUA

(C) Captain † Man of the Match

We looked comfortable out there today. We played well and we were vigilant in defence and when we were on the ball we created a lot of good chances. When we're in that form it's difficult to stop us. The players who came on did a good job for us. Fernando Torres did what he had to do and we all felt pretty comfortable with how we played. This is a team that wants to make history and we'll just have to wait and see if luck's on our side.

Vicente Del Bosque

Spain had more possession and it was no surprise they dominated play. It was a fair result when you consider the possession they had and the chances they created. We had a few chances of our own but we failed to take them, which was a shame. If we'd put them away, things could have been a lot tighter. We can feel proud of our performance because we went on the attack and the players fought to the end. They're pretty pleased with how they played.

Carlos Queiroz

Quarter-finals	Port Elizabeth Stadium Nelson Mandela Bay/Port Elizabeth	Friday 2-07-2010
Kick-off: 16:00	Sunny 24°	Attendance: 40 186

NETHERLANDS   2   1   BRAZIL

Wesley Sneijder 2 53 68   **Robinho** 10

NETHERLANDS
Orange shirts, Black shorts, Orange socks
Tr: Bert van Marwijk

1 Maarten Stekelenburg

3 John Heitinga 14   13 Andre Ooijer 76

2 Gregory Van der Wiel 47   5 Giovanni Van Bronckhorst(c)

6 Mark Van Bommel   8 Nigel De Jong 64

11 Arjen Robben   10 Wesley Sneijder   7 Dirk Kuyt

85 9 Robin Van Persie
21 Klaas Jan Huntelaar

77 9 Luis Fabiano
21 Nilmar

11 Robinho   10 Kaka   13 Dani Alves

5 Felipe Melo 73   8 Gilberto Silva

62 6 Michel Bastos 37   4 Juan   3 Lucio(c)   2 Maicon
16 Gilberto Melo

1 Julio Cesar

Tr: Carlos Dunga
Blue shirts, White shorts, Blue socks

BRAZIL

MATCH STATS

NED		BRA
11	Shots	15
5	Shots on Goal	4
19	Fouls Committed	20
4	Corner Kicks	8
3	Caught Offside	0
422	Passes	435
307	Completed Passes	325
73%	Passes Success	75%
97	Km Covered	96
22	Av. Top Speed km/h	22
51%	Possession	49%

MATCH OFFICIALS
REFEREE
Yuichi Nishimura JPN
ASSISTANTS
Toru Sagara JPN
Jeong Hae Sang KOR
4TH OFFICIAL
Khalil Al Ghamdi KSA

(C) Captain † Man of the Match

It took us about 25 minutes of today's game to deal with our nerves, and I was pleased to be only 1-0 down at the interval. During the break I told them to play their usual game during the second half. Once we scored our first goal we played much better and proved that we've got a very strong squad.
Bert van Marwijk
Finally we beat them. We gave it our all for 45 minutes and we were rewarded.
Wesley Sneijder

There's no doubt we're all down because, even though we knew this would be a very tough game, we weren't expecting this. After the interval we weren't able to play with the same style or level of concentration as we had in the first half.
Carlos Dunga
They deserved it in the second half. Their first goal hit us hard. I went for the ball and got caught up with Felipe Melo. I missed the ball and it clipped his head.
Julio Cesar

Quarter-finals	Soccer City Johannesburg	Friday 2-07-2010
Kick-off: 20:30	Partly Cloudy 13°	Attendance: 84 017

URUGUAY 1 1 GHANA

Diego Forlan 55

4 $^P_{S_O}$ 2

Sulley Muntari 45
Penalty miss: Asamoah Gyan 122+

URUGUAY

Sky blue shirts, Black shorts, Black socks
Tr: Oscar Tabarez

MATCH STATS

URU		GHA
14	Shots	26
7	Shots on Goal	10
23	Fouls Committed	23
12	Corner Kicks	8
6	Caught Offside	1
493	Passes	615
254	Completed Passes	350
52%	Passes Success	57%
135	Km Covered	131
23	Av. Top Speed km/h	22
48%	Possession	52%

MATCH OFFICIALS

REFEREE
Olegario Benquerenca POR

ASSISTANTS
Jose Cardinal POR
Bertino Miranda POR

4TH OFFICIAL
Alberto Undiano ESP

(C) Captain † Man of the Match

PENALTIES

URU		GHA
✓	Forlan	
	Gyan	✓
✓	Victorino	
	Appiah	✓
✓	Scotti	
	John Mensah	✗¹
✗²	Max Pereira	
	Adiyah	✗¹
✓	Abreu	

¹ Saved, ² Missed

1 Fernando Muslera

16 Maximiliano Pereira 38 2 Diego Lugano(c) 6 Mauricio Victorino 4 Jorge Fucile 38
19 Andres Scotti

20 Alvaro Fernandez 46 14 Nicolas Lodeiro 15 Diego Perez 59 17 Egidio Arevalo 48

9 Luis Suarez 121+ 10 Diego Forlan 7 Edinson Cavani 76 13 Sebastian Abreu

3 Asamoah Gyan

11 Sulley Muntari 88 18 Dominic Adiyiah 23 Kevin Prince Boateng 7 Samuel Inkoom 74 10 Stephen Appiah

21 Kwadwo Asamoah 6 Anthony Annan

2 Hans Sarpei 77 5 John Mensah(c) 93 15 Isaac Vorsah 4 John Pantsil 54

22 Richard Kingson

Tr: Milovan Rajevac
Red and yellow striped shirts, Red shorts, Red socks

GHANA

People who believe in destiny might explain it otherwise. But I don't have an explanation for what happened today. It really was a hard match, we didn't play well but we survived very difficult circumstances. We conceded a goal at the end of the first half and we had a penalty against us in the last second. Maybe we didn't play that well but we had the guts to do it.
Oscar Tabarez

The Hand of God now belongs to me!
Luis Suarez

All I can say is this is football. It was a very difficult game for us because in the previous game we also played for 120 minutes and in the end we had the historic opportunity to reach the semi-final and we had the penalty. We have to be proud of what we have achieved. This is sport and justice. Today Uruguay were the lucky ones.
Milovan Rajevac

Quarter-finals	Green Point Cape Town	Saturday 3-07-2010
Kick-off: 16:00	Sunny　　　　　16°	Attendance: 64 100

ARGENTINA　　0　4　GERMANY

Thomas Müller 3, Miroslav Klose 2 68 89,
Arne Friedrich 74

ARGENTINA

Sky blue and white striped shirts, Black shorts, White socks

Tr: Diego Maradona

22 Sergio Romero

70 15 Nicolas Otamendi 11　2 Martin Demichelis　4 Nicolas Burdisso　6 Gabriel Heinze
23 Javier Pastore

14 Javier Mascherano (c) †

75 7 Angel Di Maria
16 Sergio Aguero　　　　　　　　　20 Maxi Rodriguez

10 Lionel Messi
11 Carlos Tevez

9 Gonzalo Higuain

11 Miroslav Klose

10 Lukas Podolski　　8 Mesut Ozil　　84 13 Thomas Müller 84
15 Piotr Trochowski

7 Bastian Schweinsteiger †　77 6 Sami Khedira
18 Toni Kroos

72 20 Jerome Boateng　3 Arne Friedrich　17 Per Mertesacker　16 Philipp Lahm (c)
2 Marcell Jansen

1 Manuel Neuer

Tr: Joachim Löw

Black shirts, Black shorts, Black socks

GERMANY

MATCH STATS		
ARG		GER
20	Shots	18
7	Shots on Goal	6
20	Fouls Committed	14
5	Corner Kicks	4
5	Caught Offside	0
623	Passes	529
446	Completed Passes	334
72%	Passes Success	63%
100	Km Covered	106
24	Av. Top Speed km/h	23
53%	Possession	47%

MATCH OFFICIALS

REFEREE
Ravsham Irmatov UZB

ASSISTANTS
Rafael Ilyasov UZB
Bakhadyr Kochkarov KGZ

4TH OFFICIAL
Jerome Damon RSA

(C) Captain † Man of the Match

We were appalling today. Sometimes you fail to live up to your own expectations. I really don't now why this has happened. They totally dominated us, and we never had enough possession. On top of that, our counter-attacking play was atrocious.

Carlos Tevez

This is a real kick in the face. I have no more energy for anything. Have I felt hurt like this before? The day I quit football but this sadness is really tough.

Diego Maradona

The football we played in the second half was top class. My team showed the desire and commitment of champions. I never imagined we'd win by this margin. We talked about many things, and my team did so many of them to perfection, it was terrific. The way we fought our way out of adversity in the second half was top drawer. There was enormous speed in our game. We were brave enough to go on the attack and put them under pressure and win every one-to-one.

Joachim Löw

Quarter-finals	Ellis Park Johannesburg	Saturday 3-07-2010
Kick-off: 20:30	Partly Cloudy 13°	Attendance: 55 359

PARAGUAY　　　0　1　　　SPAIN

Penalty miss: Oscar Cardozo [59]

David Villa [83]
Penalty miss: Xabi Alonso [62]

PARAGUAY

Red and white striped shirts, white shorts, Red and white hooped socks

Tr: Gerardo Martino

1 Justo Villar (c)

2 Dario Veron　　21 Antolin Alcaraz [59]　14 Paulo Da Silva　3 Claudio Morel [71]

8 Edgar Barreto [64]　15 Victor Caceres [59]　16 Cristian Riveros
13 Enrique Vera [84]　19 Lucas Barrios

11 Jonathan Santana [88]

7 Oscar Cardozo　　18 Nelson Valdez [72]
9 Roque Santa Cruz

MATCH STATS

PAR		ESP
9	Shots	16
4	Shots on Goal	6
25	Fouls Committed	12
1	Corner Kicks	7
2	Caught Offside	1
347	Passes	672
190	Completed Passes	532
55%	Passes Success	79%
105	Km Covered	101
23	Av. Top Speed km/h	23
40%	Possession	60%

MATCH OFFICIALS

REFEREE
Carlos Batres GUA

ASSISTANTS
Leonel Leal CRC
Carlos Pastrana HON

4TH OFFICIAL
Benito Archundia MEX

(C) Captain † Man of the Match

7 David Villa　　9 Fernando Torres [56]
10 Cesc Fabregas

8 Xavi　　6 Andres Iniesta †

14 Xabi Alonso [75]　16 Sergio Busquets [63]
18 Pedro

11 Joan Capdevila　　5 Carles Puyol [84]　3 Gerard Pique [57]　15 Sergio Ramos
4 Carlos Marchena

1 Iker Casillas (c)

Tr: Vicente Del Bosque

Navy blue shirts, Navy blue shorts, Navy blue socks

SPAIN

I thought we gave everything we had to give. We had our chances but unfortunately Spain went through and not Paraguay. That's football. Chances were created and one side took one of the few that came along. I'd like to thank the players for their commitment. They gave their all.

Gerardo Martino

Spain weren't better than us, anything but, and we had our chances during the course of the game.

Roque Santa Cruz

We didn't play well and we never looked comfortable, but that was partly down to Paraguay. Even so, I think we deserved to go through and the best thing about the game was the result.

Vicente Del Bosque

We knew it wasn't going to be easy. It wasn't exactly our greatest game ever, and they ran hard. You have to congratulate Paraguay for what they've done.

Iker Casillas

Semi-finals	Green Point Cape Town	Tuesday 6-07-2010
Kick-off: 20:30	Clear Night 11°	Attendance: 62 479

URUGUAY   2   3   NETHERLANDS

Diego Forlan [41], Maximiliano Pereira [92+]

Giovanni van Bronckhorst [18], Wesley Sneijder [70],
Arjen Robben [73]

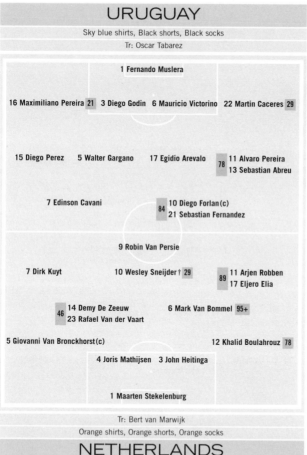

URUGUAY

Sky blue shirts, Black shorts, Black socks

Tr: Oscar Tabarez

1 Fernando Muslera

16 Maximiliano Pereira [21]   3 Diego Godin   6 Mauricio Victorino   22 Martin Caceres [29]

15 Diego Perez   5 Walter Gargano   17 Egidio Arevalo   [78] 11 Alvaro Pereira / 13 Sebastian Abreu

7 Edinson Cavani   [84] 10 Diego Forlan (c) / 21 Sebastian Fernandez

9 Robin Van Persie

7 Dirk Kuyt   10 Wesley Sneijder † [29]   [89] 11 Arjen Robben / 17 Eljero Elia

[46] 14 Demy De Zeeuw / 23 Rafael Van der Vaart   6 Mark Van Bommel [95+]

5 Giovanni Van Bronckhorst (c)   12 Khalid Boulahrouz [78]

4 Joris Mathijsen   3 John Heitinga

1 Maarten Stekelenburg

Tr: Bert van Marwijk

Orange shirts, Orange shorts, Orange socks

NETHERLANDS

MATCH STATS

URU		NED
12	Shots	11
6	Shots on Goal	7
15	Fouls Committed	16
4	Corner Kicks	5
4	Caught Offside	5
565	Passes	610
326	Completed Passes	390
58%	Passes Success	64%
110	Km Covered	108
23	Av. Top Speed km/h	23
47%	Possession	53%

MATCH OFFICIALS
REFEREE
Ravshan Irmatov UZB
ASSISTANTS
Rafael Ilyasov UZB
Bakhadyr Kochkarov KGZ
4TH OFFICIAL
Yuichi Nishimura JPN

(C)Captain †Man of the Match

It was a match worthy of the World Cup semi-finals. I'm proud of my players. We're disappointed, but we've shown everyone who wrote us off beforehand that we're not very far off the top. We gave it our best shot, but it wasn't quite enough. I'm still completely satisfied with my team. They reacted well to going a goal down, they fought back and equalised, and they battled right to the end. I can't ask for more than that, nor can the players, and nor can our country.

Oscar Tabarez

When I took this job two years ago, I said to the players, 'We're on a mission, and we just have to believe in ourselves'. We're only a small country but we're through to the Final, that's just unbelievable. I love beautiful football, but I also want to win. In the second half, we proved we're a decent footballing side. We took control of the match. We actually should have made it 4-1, but it was a close-run thing at the end.

Bert van Marwijk

Semi-finals	Durban Stadium Durban	Wednesday 7-07-2010
Kick-off: 20:30	Cloudy Night 18°	Attendance: 60 960

GERMANY   0   1   SPAIN

Carles Puyol 73

GERMANY

White shirts, Black shorts, White socks

Tr: Joachim Löw

1 Manuel Neuer

16 Philipp Lahm (c)   17 Per Mertesacker   3 Arne Friedrich   52 20 Jerome Boateng
2 Marcell Jansen

81 6 Sami Khedira   7 Bastian Schweinsteiger
23 Mario Gomez

62 15 Piotr Trochowski   8 Mesut Ozil   10 Lukas Podolski
18 Toni Kroos

11 Miroslav Klose

81 7 David Villa
9 Fernando Torres

6 Andres Iniesta   8 Xavi †   86 18 Pedro
21 David Silva

93+ 14 Xabi Alonso   16 Sergio Busquets
4 Carlos Marchena

11 Joan Capdevila   5 Carles Puyol   3 Gerard Pique   15 Sergio Ramos

1 Iker Casillas (c)

Tr: Vicente Del Bosque

Red shirts, Blue shorts, Red socks

SPAIN

MATCH STATS

GER		ESP
5	Shots	13
2	Shots on Goal	5
9	Fouls Committed	7
6	Corner Kicks	7
2	Caught Offside	1
589	Passes	731
441	Completed Passes	590
75%	Passes Success	81%
111	Km Covered	109
22	Av. Top Speed km/h	21
49%	Possession	51%

MATCH OFFICIALS
REFEREE
Viktor Kassai HUN
ASSISTANTS
Gabor Eros HUN
Tibor Vamos HUN
4TH OFFICIAL
Frank De Bleeckere BEL

(C) Captain † Man of the Match

They stifled us in certain areas, and we weren't able to break free. Their passing game is so good, you spend practically all your time just chasing the ball. We were unable to win possession in the key areas which would have allowed us to switch from defence to attack at speed. Overall, my young team has had a magnificent tournament, but it's not worked out the way we wanted it today. It's a shame, we're sad, and we're disappointed, but at the end of the day, Spain were terrific.
Joachim Löw

We're delighted about the win, which we deserved. The team did a great job, we put our stamp on the game, we dominated Germany, especially in the second half. We felt good out there and controlled the ball. Added to that, we were lucky enough to get the goal from the corner for Puyol.
Xavi
This was the best we've played so far this tournament. The bigger the challenge, the better we get.
David Villa

Third Place Play-off	Port Elizabeth Stadium Nelson Mandela Bay/Port Elizabeth	Saturday 10-07-2010
Kick-off: 20:30	Rain 14°	Attendance: 36 254

URUGUAY   2   3   GERMANY

Edinson Cavani [28], Diego Forlan [51]   Thomas Müller [19], Marcell Jansen [56], Sami Khedira [82]

URUGUAY
Sky blue shirts, Sky blue shorts, Sky blue socks
Tr: Oscar Tabarez

1 Fernando Muslera

4 Jorge Fucile   2 Diego Lugano (c)   3 Diego Godin   22 Martin Caceres

15 Diego Perez [61]   17 Egidio Arevalo
[77] 5 Walter Gargano

16 Maximiliano Pereira

7 Edinson Cavani
[88] 13 Sebastian Abreu

9 Luis Suarez   10 Diego Forlan

19 Cacau [7]
[73] 9 Stefan Kiessling

2 Marcell Jansen   8 Mesut Ozil   13 Thomas Müller †
[81] 18 Toni Kroos   [91+] 5 Serdar Tasci

7 Bastian Schweinsteiger (c)   6 Sami Khedira

4 Dennis Aogo [5] 3 Arne Friedrich [92+] 17 Per Mertesacker   20 Jerome Boateng

22 Hans-Jörg Butt

Tr: Joachim Löw
Black shirts, Black shorts, Black socks

GERMANY

MATCH STATS
URU		GER
16	Shots	18
7	Shots on Goal	7
13	Fouls Committed	11
6	Corner Kicks	12
2	Caught Offside	3
485	Passes	591
303	Completed Passes	393
62%	Passes Success	66%
105	Km Covered	107
23	Av. Top Speed km/h	22
47%	Possession	53%

MATCH OFFICIALS
REFEREE
Benito Archundia MEX
ASSISTANTS
Hector Vergara CAN
Marvin Torrentera MEX
4TH OFFICIAL
Marco Rodriguez MEX

(C) Captain † Man of the Match

We've proved we can hold our own against any side in the world. These teams are the best around and Germany have played as well as anyone at this tournament. Sadly we made a lot of mistakes in both areas today and you pay for that in football. That said, I thought we dominated the match at various times tonight. After all, we couldn't just come here and play defensively. We took risks and we lost but we gave a really good account of ourselves in doing so.

Oscar Tabarez

After tonight, we're not going home empty-handed. My team deserved to win, based on the second half alone. We played well and fought hard. Taking the tournament as a whole, my team has been magnificent. Just looking at the way they've put a bitter defeat to Spain behind them, their performance as a whole at the finals, and the number of goals they've scored, you have to be delighted. We can go home now feeling justifiably proud.

Joachim Löw

Final	Soccer City Johannesburg		Sunday 11-07-2010
Kick-off: 20:30	Partly cloudy	14°	Attendance: 84 490

NETHERLANDS   0   1   SPAIN

Andres Iniesta [116]

NETHERLANDS

Orange shirts, Orange shorts, Orange socks
Tr: Bert van Marwijk

MATCH STATS

NED		ESP
13	Shots	18
5	Shots on Goal	6
28	Fouls Committed	19
6	Corner Kicks	8
7	Caught Offside	6
475	Passes	715
294	Completed Passes	542
62%	Passes Success	76%
134	Km Covered	136
25	Av. Top Speed km/h	24
43%	Possession	57%

MATCH OFFICIALS

REFEREE
Howard Webb ENG

ASSISTANTS
Darren Cann ENG
Michael Mullarkey ENG

4TH OFFICIAL
Yuichi Nishimura JPN

(C) Captain † Man of the Match

1 Maarten Stekelenburg

3 John Heitinga 57 109 **109**   4 Joris Mathijsen 117

2 Gregory Van der Wiel 111   5 Giovanni Van Bronckhorst(c) 54   105   15 Edson Braafheid

6 Mark Van Bommel 22   99   8 Nigel De Jong 28   23 Rafael Van der Vaart

11 Arjen Robben 84   10 Wesley Sneijder   7 Dirk Kuyt   71   17 Eljero Elia

9 Robin Van Persie 15

7 David Villa   106   9 Fernando Torres

6 Andres Iniesta † 118   8 Xavi 121+   18 Pedro   60   22 Jesus Navas

14 Xabi Alonso   87   16 Sergio Busquets   10 Cesc Fabregas

11 Joan Capdevila 67   5 Carles Puyol 16   3 Gerard Pique   15 Sergio Ramos 23

1 Iker Casillas(c)

Tr: Vicente Del Bosque
Navy blue shirts, Navy blue shorts, Navy blue socks

SPAIN

Obviously, we're devastated by the result. We were down to ten men but almost made it to penalties. You have to say the better team won, but losing the World Cup Final is hard to take. Spain created far more chances, but Arjen Robben twice came within inches of scoring for us. If he had, I think we'd have been world champions.

Bert van Marwijk

This is an unforgettable moment. There's a great sense of happiness in the dressing room right now. It's hard to put it all into words and the way the players feel goes way beyond words. The satisfaction people feel goes way beyond sport and this is a reward that's richly deserved. I'd like to thank the Spain fans for all their support. They're enjoying this as much as the players.

Vicente Del Bosque

ALG – ALGERIA SQUAD 2010 FIFA WORLD CUP

No	Pos	Name	Shirt Name	DoB	Club	Cms	Kg	Games	Mins	Goals	Y	R	Cap	Gls
1	GK	Lounes GAOUAOUI	GAOUAOUI	28-09-1977	ASO Chlef	188	87	0	0				48	0
2	DF	Madjid BOUGHERRA	BOUGHERRA	7-10-1982	Rangers SCO	190	91	3	270				44	3
3	DF	Nadir BELHADJ	BELHADJ	18-06-1982	Portsmouth ENG	180	75	3	270				48	4
4	DF	Anther YAHIA	YAHIA	21-03-1982	Bochum GER	185	80	3	269		1		47	5
5	DF	Rafik HALLICHE	HALLICHE	2-09-1986	Nacional POR	187	84	3	270				20	1
6	MF	Yazid MANSOURI	MANSOURI	25-02-1978	Lorient FRA	175	72	0	0				67	0
7	MF	Ryad BOUDEBOUZ	BOUDEBOUZ	19-02-1990	Sochaux FRA	178	80	1	74				3	0
8	MF	Medhi LACEN	LACEN	15-03-1984	RacingSantanderESP	178	82	3	270		2		6	0
9	FW	Abdelkader GHEZZAL	GHEZZAL	5-12-1984	Siena ITA	186	85	2	40		1		21	3
10	FW	Rafik SAIFI	SAIFI	7-02-1975	Istres FRA	178	75	2	14				62	18
11	MF	Rafik DJEBBOUR	DJEBBOUR	8-03-1984	AEK Athens GRE	185	80	2	123				18	3
12	DF	Habib BELLAID	BELLAID	28-03-1986	Boulogne FRA	189	88	0	0				1	0
13	MF	Karim MATMOUR	MATMOUR	25-06-1985	B Mön'gladbach GER	181	78	3	256				26	2
14	DF	Abdelkader LAIFAOUI	LAIFAOUI	29-07-1981	Entente Setif	177	72	0	0				7	0
15	MF	Karim ZIANI	ZIANI	17-08-1982	Wolfsburg GER	168	68	3	240				58	5
16	GK	Faouzi CHAOUCHI	CHAOUCHI	5-12-1984	Entente Setif	180	85	1	90				11	0
17	MF	Adlane GUEDIOURA	GUEDIOURA	12-111985	Wolverhampton ENG	183	80	3	38				5	0
18	DF	Carl MEDJANI	MEDJANI	15 -05-1985	Ajaccio FRA	184	82	0	0				0	0
19	MF	Hassan YEBDA	YEBDA	14-05-1984	Portsmouth ENG	188	82	3	268		2		12	0
20	DF	Djamel MESBAH	MESBAH	9-10-1984	Lecce ITA	180	65	1	2				2	0
21	MF	Foued KADIR	KADIR	5-12-1983	Valenciennes FRA	180	78	3	262				5	0
22	MF	Djamal ABDOUN	ABDOUN	14-02-1986	Nantes FRA	180	71	1	16				8	0
23	GK	Rais M'BOLHI	MBOLHI	25-04-1986	Slavia Sofia BUL	190	88	2	180				3	0

ARG – ARGENTINA SQUAD 2010 FIFA WORLD CUP

No	Pos	Name	Shirt Name	DoB	Club	Cms	Kg	Games	Mins	Goals	Y	R	Cap	Gls
1	GK	Diego POZO	POZO	16-02-1978	Colón Santa Fe	183	80	0	0				3	0
2	DF	Martin DEMICHELIS	DEMICHELIS	20-12-1980	Bayern München GER	184	80	5	450	1			30	2
3	DF	Clemente RODRIGUEZ	RODRIGUEZ C	31-07-1981	Estudiantes La Plata	166	66	1	90				13	0
4	DF	Nicolas BURDISSO	BURDISSO	12-04-1981	Roma ITA	174	77	5	342				34	2
5	MF	Mario BOLATTI	BOLATTI	17-02-1985	Fiorentina ITA	189	84	2	98		1		7	1
6	DF	Gabriel HEINZE	HEINZE	19-04-1978	Olymp. Marseille FRA	178	78	4	360	1	1		68	3
7	MF	Angel DI MARIA	DI MARIA	14-02-1988	Benfica POR	180	55	5	356				13	1
8	MF	Juan VERON	VERON	9-03-1975	Estudiantes La Plata	183	81	3	185				73	9
9	FW	Gonzalo HIGUAIN	HIGUAIN	10-12-1987	Real Madrid ESP	182	76	4	341	4			9	6
10	FW	Lionel MESSI	MESSI	24-06-1987	Barcelona ESP	170	65	5	450				50	13
11	FW	Carlos TEVEZ	CARLITOS	5-02-1984	Manchester City ENG	173	75	4	324	2			58	11
12	DF	Ariel GARCE	GARCE	14-07-1979	Colón Santa Fe	175	76	0	0				4	0
13	DF	Walter SAMUEL	SAMUEL	23-03-1978	Inter ITA	182	83	2	113				56	4
14	MF	Javier MASCHERANO	MASCHERANO	8-06-1984	Liverpool ENG	171	66	4	360		2		61	2
15	DF	Nicolas OTAMENDI	OTAMENDI	12-02-1988	Velez Sarsfield	171	74	3	250		1		10	0
16	FW	Sergio AGUERO	KUN AGUERO	2-06-1988	Atletico Madrid ESP	170	69	3	107				25	8
17	MF	Jonas GUTIERREZ	JONAS	5-07-1983	Newcastle Utd ENG	182	70	3	191		2		19	1
18	FW	Martin PALERMO	PALERMO	7-11-1973	Boca Juniors	188	84	1	10	1			15	9
19	FW	Diego MILITO	MILITO D	12-06-1979	Inter ITA	177	75	2	91				23	4
20	MF	Maxi RODRIGUEZ	RODRIGUEZ M	2-01-1981	Liverpool ENG	173	73	5	346				41	12
21	GK	Mariano ANDUJAR	ANDUJAR	30-07-1983	Catania ITA	180	86	0	0				4	0
22	GK	Sergio ROMERO	ROMERO	22-02-1987	AZ Alkmaar NED	191	86	5	450				11	0
23	MF	Javier PASTORE	PASTORE	20-06-1989	Palermo ITA	173	71	3	36				4	0

AUS – AUSTRALIA SQUAD 2010 FIFA WORLD CUP

No	Pos	Name	Shirt Name	DoB	Club	Cms	Kg	Games	Mins	Goals	Y	R	Cap	Gls
1	GK	Mark SCHWARZER	SCHWARZER	6-10-1972	Fulham ENG	196	86	3	270				78	0
2	DF	Lucas NEILL	NEILL	9-03-1978	Galatasaray TUR	185	80	3	270		1		59	0
3	DF	Craig MOORE	MOORE	12-12-1975	No club	186	80	2	180		2		52	3
4	FW	Tim CAHILL	CAHILL	6-12-1979	Everton ENG	180	76	2	146	1	1		42	21
5	MF	Jason CULINA	CULINA	5-08-1980	Gold Coast United	175	75	3	270				52	1
6	DF	Michael BEAUCHAMP	BEAUCHAMP	8-03-1981	Al Jazira UAE	191	85	1	90				22	1
7	MF	Brett EMERTON	EMERTON	22-02-1979	Blackburn Rov ENG	185	85	3	254		1		75	17
8	DF	Luke WILKSHIRE	WILKSHIRE	2-10-1981	Dynamo Moscow RUS	177	80	3	256		1		45	2
9	FW	Joshua KENNEDY	KENNEDY	20-08-1982	Nagoya Grampus JPN	192	82	2	112				22	7
10	FW	Harry KEWELL	KEWELL	22-09-1978	Galatasaray TUR	183	85	1	24	1	1		46	13
11	DF	Scott CHIPPERFIELD	CHIPPERFIELD	30-12-1975	Basel SUI	180	70	3	138				68	12
12	GK	Adam FEDERICI	FEDERICI	31-01-1985	Reading ENG	188	90	0	0				1	0
13	MF	Vince GRELLA	GRELLA	5-10-1979	Blackburn Rov ENG	183	79	1	45				46	0
14	FW	Brett HOLMAN	HOLMAN	27-03-1984	AZ Alkmaar NED	176	73	3	137	2			34	4
15	MF	Mile JEDINAK	JEDINAK	3-08-1984	Antalyaspor TUR	188	78	1	16				12	0
16	MF	Carl VALERI	VALERI	14-08-1984	Sassuolo ITA	180	76	3	246		1		25	0
17	FW	Nikita RUKAVYTSYA	RUKAVYTSYA	22-06-1987	Twente Enschede NED	183	77	2	32				6	0
18	GK	Eugene GALEKOVIC	GALEKOVIC	12-06-1981	Adelaide Utd	186	91	0	0				4	0
19	FW	Richard GARCIA	GARCIA	4-09-1981	Hull City ENG	180	72	2	72				9	0
20	DF	Mark MILLIGAN	MILLIGAN	4-08-1985	JEF United JPN	178	78	0	0				10	1
21	DF	David CARNEY	CARNEY	30-11-1983	FC Twente NED	181	78	2	180				28	3
22	MF	Dario VIDOSIC	VIDOSIC	8-04-1987	MSV Duisburg GER	185	75	0	0				7	1
23	FW	Marco BRESCIANO	BRESCIANO	11-02-1980	Palermo ITA	182	73	2	132				57	11

BRA – BRAZIL SQUAD 2010 FIFA WORLD CUP

No	Pos	Name	Shirt Name	DoB	Club	Cms	Kg	Games	Mins	Goals	Y	R	Cap	Gls
1	GK	JULIO CESAR	JULIO CESAR	3-09-1979	Internazionale ITA	186	84	5	450				53	0
2	DF	MAICON	MAICON	26-07-1981	Internazionale ITA	186	91	5	450	1			63	6
3	DF	LUCIO	LÚCIO	8-05-1978	Internazionale ITA	188	87	5	450				96	4
4	DF	JUAN	JUAN	1-02-1979	Roma ITA	182	80	5	450	1	1		79	7
5	MF	FELIPE MELO	FELIPE MELO	26-06-1983	Juventus ITA	183	85	4	291		1	1	22	2
6	DF	MICHEL BASTOS	M- BASTOS	2-08-1983	Lyon FRA	179	71	5	422		1		10	1
7	MF	ELANO	ELANO	14-06-1981	Galatasaray TUR	174	72	2	140	2			45	9
8	MF	GILBERTO SILVA	G- SILVA	7-10-1976	Panathinaikos GRE	184	80	5	450				93	3
9	FW	LUIS FABIANO	L- FABIANO	8-11-1980	Sevilla ESP	186	86	5	418	3	1		43	28
10	MF	KAKA	KAKÁ	22-04-1982	Real Madrid ESP	186	82	4	337		1	1	82	27
11	FW	ROBINHO	ROBINHO	25-01-1984	Santos BRA	175	69	4	354	2			79	25
12	GK	GOMES	GOMES	15-02-1981	Tottenham H'pur ENG	191	88	0	0				11	0
13	DF	DANI ALVES	D- ALVES	6-05-1983	Barcelona ESP	173	68	5	310				40	3
14	DF	LUISAO	LUISÃO	13-02-1981	Benfica POR	193	95	0	0				42	3
15	DF	THIAGO SILVA	T- SILVA	22-09-1984	Milan ITA	183	79	0	0				7	0
16	DF	GILBERTO MELO	GILBERTO	25-04-1976	Cruzeiro BRA	180	81	2	33				35	1
17	MF	JOSUE	JOSUÉ	19-07-1979	Wolfsburg GER	169	66	1	46				28	1
18	MF	RAMIRES	RAMIRES	24-03-1987	Benfica POR	179	63	4	105		2		16	2
19	MF	JULIO BAPTISTA	J- BAPTISTA	1-10-1981	Roma ITA	185	88	1	82				47	5
20	MF	KLEBERSON	KLEBERSON	19-06-1979	Flamengo BRA	175	66	1	9				32	2
21	FW	NILMAR	NILMAR	14-07-1984	Villarreal ESP	180	69	4	129				21	8
22	GK	DONI	DONI	22-10-1979	Roma ITA	194	93	0	0				10	0
23	FW	GRAFITE	GRAFITE	2-04-1979	Wolfsburg GER	189	83	1	5				4	1

CHI – CHILE SQUAD 2010 FIFA WORLD CUP

No	Pos	Name	Shirt Name	DoB	Club	Cms	Kg	Games	Mins	Goals	Y	R	Cap	Gls
1	GK	Claudio BRAVO	BRAVO	13-04-1983	Real Sociedad ESP	183	85	4	360				47	0
2	DF	Ismael FUENTES	FUENTES	4-08-1981	Universidad Catolica	181	78	1	90		1		30	1
3	DF	Waldo PONCE	PONCE	4-12-1982	Universidad Catolica	183	82	3	270		2		28	2
4	DF	Mauricio ISLA	ISLA	12-06-1988	Udinese ITA	177	76	4	332				16	0
5	DF	Pablo CONTRERAS	CONTRERAS	11-09-1978	PAOK GRE	178	73	2	54				53	1
6	MF	Carlos CARMONA	CARMONA	21-02-1987	Reggina ITA	179	77	3	270		2		23	0
7	FW	Alexis SANCHEZ	SANCHEZ	19-12-1988	Udinese ITA	168	70	4	335				33	11
8	MF	Arturo VIDAL	VIDAL	22-05-1987	B. Leverkusen GER	178	74	4	306		1		27	1
9	FW	Humberto SUAZO	SUAZO	10-05-1981	Real Zaragoza ESP	171	80	2	135		1		44	18
10	MF	Jorge VALDIVIA	VALDIVIA	19-10-1983	Al Ain UAE	173	71	4	222		1		43	4
11	FW	Mark GONZALEZ	M- GONZALEZ	14-07-1984	CSKA Moskva RUS	175	74	4	138	1			43	4
12	GK	Miguel PINTO	PINTO	4-07-1983	Universidad de Chile	180	80	0	0				14	0
13	MF	Marco ESTRADA	ESTRADA	28-05-1983	Universidad de Chile	174	78	1	37			1	23	1
14	MF	Matias FERNANDEZ	FERNANDEZ	15-05-1986	Sporting CP POR	176	74	2	155		2		39	7
15	FW	Jean BEAUSEJOUR	BEAUSEJOUR	1-06-1984	America MEX	178	80	4	360	1			31	2
16	FW	Fabian ORELLANA	ORELLANA	27-01-1986	Xerez ESP	168	59	1	25				17	2
17	DF	Gary MEDEL	MEDEL	3-08-1987	Boca Juniors ARG	171	75	3	270		2		27	3
18	DF	Gonzalo JARA	JARA	29-08-1985	West Brom Alb ENG	177	74	4	308				38	3
19	MF	Gonzalo FIERRO	FIERRO	21-03-1983	Flamengo BRA	171	70	0	0				18	1
20	MF	Rodrigo MILLAR	MILLAR	3-11-1981	Colo Colo	182	76	3	125	1	1		24	2
21	MF	Rodrigo TELLO	TELLO	14-10-1979	Besiktas TUR	171	77	1	45				35	3
22	FW	Esteban PAREDES	PAREDES	1-08-1980	Colo Colo	179	82	2	70				16	6
23	GK	Luis MARIN	MARIN	18-05-1983	Union Espanola	186	88	0	0				3	0

CIV – COTE D'IVOIRE SQUAD 2010 FIFA WORLD CUP

No	Pos	Name	Shirt Name	DoB	Club	Cms	Kg	Games	Mins	Goals	Y	R	Cap	Gls
1	GK	Boubacar BARRY	BARRY	30-12-1979	Lokeren BEL	180	69	3	270				48	0
2	DF	Brou ANGOUA	ANGOUA	28-11-1986	Valenciennes FRA	178	69	0	0				7	1
3	DF	Arthur BOKA	BOKA	02-04-1983	VfB Stuttgart GER	166	67	1	90				55	1
4	DF	Kolo TOURE	TOURE KOLO	19-03-1981	Manchester City ENG	183	76	3	270				84	3
5	MF	Didier ZOKORA	ZOKORA	14-12-1980	Sevilla ESP	183	78	3	270				89	1
6	DF	Steve GOHOURI	GOHOURI	08-02-1981	Wigan Ath ENG	187		0	0				8	3
7	FW	Seydou DOUMBIA	DOUMBIA	31-12-1987	Young Boys SUI	183		1	11				8	1
8	FW	Salomon KALOU	KALOU	05-08-1985	Chelsea ENG	175	72	3	160	1			35	11
9	MF	Ismael TIOTE	TIOTE	21-06-1986	Twente Enschede NED	175		3	270		1		13	0
10	FW	GERVINHO	GERVINHO	27-05-1987	Lille OSC FRA	179	80	3	182				19	3
11	FW	Didier DROGBA	DROGBA	11-03-1978	Chelsea ENG	180	84	3	204	1			71	42
12	MF	Jean Jacques GOSSO	GOSSO	15-03-1983	Monaco FRA	177	73	0	0				4	0
13	MF	ROMARIC	ROMARIC	04-06-1983	Sevilla ESP	187	88	3	98	1			32	3
14	MF	Emmanuel KONE	KOUAMATIEN	31-12-1986	International ROU	177	65	0	0				12	0
15	FW	Aruna DINDANE	DINDANE	26-11-1980	Portsmouth ENG	174	76	3	170				61	18
16	GK	Aristide ZOGBO	ZOGBO	30-12-1981	Maccabi Netanya ISR	183		0	0				6	0
17	DF	Siaka TIENE	TIENE	22-02-1982	Valenciennes FRA	176	72	2	180			1	59	2
18	FW	Kader KEITA	KEITA	06-08-1981	Galatasaray TUR	184	78	3	94		1		58	11
19	MF	Yaya TOURE	TOURE YAYA	13-05-1983	Barcelona ESP	189	79	3	270	1			53	6
20	DF	Guy DEMEL	DEMEL	13-06-1981	Hamburger SV GER	191	83	2	180		1		27	0
21	DF	Emmanuel EBOUE	EBOUE	04-06-1983	Arsenal ENG	178	72	3	251				45	1
22	DF	Souleymane BAMBA	BAMBA	13-01-1985	Hibernian SCO	190	88	0	0				16	2
23	GK	Daniel YEBOAH	YEBOAH	13-11-1984	ASEC Mimosas CIV	187	80	0	0				4	0

CMR – CAMEROON SQUAD 2010 FIFA WORLD CUP

No	Pos	Name	Shirt Name	DoB	Club	Cms	Kg	Games	Mins	Goals	Y	R	Cap	Gls
1	GK	Idriss KAMENI	KAMENI	18-02-1984	Espanyol ESP	185	79	0	0				55	0
2	DF	Benoit ASSOU-EKOTTO	ASSOU EKOTTO	24-03-1984	Tottenham H'pur ENG	178		3	270				12	0
3	DF	Nicolas NKOULOU	NKOULOU	27-03-1990	Monaco FRA	185	79	3	253		2		20	0
4	DF	Rigobert SONG	SONG	1-07-1976	Trabzonspor TUR	185	77	1	17				137	4
5	DF	Sebastien BASSONG	BASSONG	9-07-1986	Tottenham H'pur ENG	187		2	162		1		9	0
6	MF	Alexandre SONG	A. SONG	9-09-1987	Arsenal ENG	183	70	1	90				24	0
7	MF	Landry NGUEMO	NGUEMO	28-11-1985	Celtic SCO	172	70	1	90				21	2
8	DF	GEREMI	NJITAP	20-12-1978	Ankaragucu TUR	177	78	3	195				118	13
9	FW	Samuel ETOO	ETO'O	10-03-1981	Internazionale ITA	178	79	3	270	2			95	44
10	FW	Achille EMANA	EMANA	5-06-1982	Betis ESP	180	77	2	117				37	5
11	MF	Jean MAKOUN	MAKOUN	29-05-1983	Lyon FRA	170		3	210				54	3
12	DF	Gaetan BONG	BONG	25-04-1988	Valenciennes FRA	183	80	1	56				3	0
13	FW	Eric CHOUPO MOTING	CHOUPO MOTING	23-03-1989	1.FC Nurnberg GER	190		2	147				4	1
14	DF	Aurelien CHEDJOU	CHEDJOU	20-06-1985	Lille OSC FRA	185	81	1	90				10	0
15	FW	Pierre WEBO	WEBO	20-01-1982	Mallorca ESP	180		2	168				44	17
16	GK	Hamidou SOULEYMANOU	SOULEYMANOU	22-11-1973	Kayserispor TUR	187		3	270				25	0
17	FW	Mohamadou IDRISSOU	IDRISSOU	8-03-1980	Freiburg GER	190	82	3	51				34	6
18	MF	Eyong ENOH	EYONG	23-03-1986	Ajax NED	180		2	135				14	1
19	DF	Stephane MBIA	MBIA	20-05-1986	Marseille FRA	190	75	3	270		2		34	3
20	MF	Georges MANDJECK	MANDJECK	9-12-1988	Kaiserslautern GER	181	64	0	0				7	0
21	MF	Joel MATIP	MATIP	8-08-1991	Schalke GER	194		1	63				5	0
22	GK	Guy NDY	NDY ASSEMBE	28-02-1986	Valenciennes FRA	185		0	0				1	0
23	FW	Vincent ABOUBAKAR	ABOUBAKAR	22-01-1992	Cotonsport	176		2	46				4	0

DEN – DENMARK SQUAD 2010 FIFA WORLD CUP

No	Pos	Name	Shirt Name	DoB	Club	Cms	Kg	Games	Mins	Goals	Y	R	Cap	Gls
1	GK	Thomas SORENSEN	SØRENSEN	12-06-1976	Stoke City ENG	185	78	3	270		1		89	0
2	MF	Christian POULSEN	C. POULSEN	28-02-1980	Juventus ITA	182	76	3	270		1		77	6
3	DF	Simon KJAER	KJÆR	26-03-1989	Palermo ITA	191		2	180		2		11	0
4	DF	Daniel AGGER	AGGER	12-12-1984	Liverpool ENG	188		3	270				35	3
5	MF	William KVIST	KVIST	24-02-1985	FC København	185		0	0				14	0
6	DF	Lars JACOBSEN	L. JACOBSEN	20-09-1979	Blackburn Rov ENG	184		3	270				34	0
7	MF	Daniel JENSEN	JENSEN	25-06-1979	Werder Bremen GER	180		1	45				50	3
8	FW	Jesper GRONKJAER	GRØNKJÆR	12-08-1977	FC København	187	82	2	101				80	5
9	FW	Jon Dahl TOMASSON	TOMASSON	29-08-1976	Feyenoord NED	182	74	2	176	1			112	52
10	MF	Martin JORGENSEN	JØRGENSEN	6-10-1975	AGF Aarhus DEN	180	76	3	169				99	12
11	FW	Nicklas BENDTNER	BENDTNER	16-01-1988	Arsenal ENG	194		3	242	1	1		35	12
12	MF	Thomas KAHLENBERG	KAHLENBERG	20-03-1983	Wolfsburg GER	185		3	159				34	3
13	DF	Per KROLDRUP	KRØLDRUP	31-07-1979	Fiorentina ITA	194		1	56		1		31	0
14	MF	Jakob POULSEN	J. POULSEN	7-07-1983	AGF Aarhus	185		2	60				15	1
15	DF	Simon POULSEN	S.B. POULSEN	7-04-1984	AZ Alkmaar NED	187		3	270				8	0
16	GK	Stephan ANDERSEN	ANDERSEN	26-11-1981	Brøndby	188		0	0				7	0
17	FW	Mikkel BECKMANN	BECKMANN	24-10-1983	Randers	178		1	28				6	0
18	FW	Soren LARSEN	LARSEN	6-09-1981	MSV Duisburg GER	194		1	34				20	11
19	FW	Dennis ROMMEDAHL	ROMMEDAHL	22-07-1978	Ajax NED	178	68	3	270	1			99	17
20	MF	Thomas ENEVOLDSEN	ENEVOLDSEN	27-07-1987	Groningen NED	182		1	56				7	1
21	MF	Christian ERIKSEN	ERIKSEN	14-02-1992	Ajax NED	181		2	44				5	0
22	GK	Jesper CHRISTIANSEN	CHRISTIANSEN	24-04-1978	FC København	192	86	0	0				11	0
23	DF	Patrick MTILIGA	MTILIGA	28-01-1981	Malaga ESP	170		0	0				4	0

ENG – ENGLAND SQUAD 2010 FIFA WORLD CUP

No	Pos	Name	Shirt Name	DoB	Club	Cms	Kg	Games	Mins	Goals	Y	R	Cap	Gls
1	GK	David JAMES	JAMES	1-08-1970	Portsmouth	196	91	3	270				53	0
2	DF	Glen JOHNSON	JOHNSON	23-08-1984	Liverpool	178	72	4	357		2		26	1
3	DF	Ashley COLE	A COLE	20-12-1980	Chelsea	173	69	4	360				82	0
4	MF	Steven GERRARD	GERRARD	30-05-1980	Liverpool	185	80	4	360	1	1		84	17
5	DF	Michael DAWSON	DAWSON	18-11-1983	Tottenham Hotspur	188	76	0	0				0	0
6	DF	John TERRY	TERRY	7-12-1980	Chelsea	188	79	4	360				64	6
7	MF	Aaron LENNON	LENNON	16-04-1987	Tottenham Hotspur	165	63	2	153				19	0
8	MF	Frank LAMPARD	LAMPARD	20-06-1978	Chelsea	183	79	4	360				82	20
9	FW	Peter CROUCH	CROUCH	30-01-1981	Tottenham Hotspur	201	71	2	17				40	21
10	FW	Wayne ROONEY	ROONEY	24-10-1985	Manchester Utd	178	79	4	342				64	25
11	MF	Joe COLE	J COLE	8-11-1981	Chelsea	175	70	2	44				56	10
12	GK	Robert GREEN	GREEN	18-01-1980	West Ham Utd	187	77	1	90				11	0
13	DF	Stephen WARNOCK	WARNOCK	12-12-1981	Aston Villa	175	77	0	0				1	0
14	MF	Gareth BARRY	BARRY	23-02-1981	Manchester City	180	81	3	264				39	2
15	DF	Matt UPSON	UPSON	18-04-1979	West Ham Utd	185	72	2	180	1			21	2
16	MF	James MILNER	MILNER	4-01-1986	Aston Villa	170	69	3	185		1		11	0
17	MF	Shaun WRIGHT-PHILLIPS	WRIGHTPHILLIPS	25-10-1981	Manchester City	168	64	3	89				34	6
18	DF	Jamie CARRAGHER	CARRAGHER	28-01-1978	Liverpool	185	77	2	135		2		38	0
19	FW	Jermain DEFOE	DEFOE	7-10-1982	Tottenham Hotspur	170	66	3	173	1			43	12
20	DF	Ledley KING	KING	12-10-1980	Tottenham Hotspur	188	88	1	45				21	2
21	FW	Emile HESKEY	HESKEY	11-01-1978	Aston Villa	188	84	4	176				62	7
22	MF	Michael CARRICK	CARRICK	28-07-1981	Manchester Utd	183	71	0	0				22	0
23	GK	Joe HART	HART	19-04-1987	Birmingham City	191	82	0	0				3	0

ESP – SPAIN SQUAD 2010 FIFA WORLD CUP

No	Pos	Name	Shirt Name	DoB	Club	Cms	Kg	Games	Mins	Goals	Y	R	Cap	Gls
1	GK	Iker CASILLAS	CASILLAS	20-05-1981	Real Madrid	184	80	7	660				111	0
2	DF	Raul ALBIOL	R.ALBIOL	04-09-1985	Real Madrid	187	77	0	0				23	0
3	DF	Gerard PIQUE	PIQUÉ	02-02-1987	Barcelona	192	85	7	660		1		23	4
4	DF	Carlos MARCHENA	C.MARCHENA	31-07-1979	Valencia	182	75	3	8				62	2
5	DF	Carles PUYOL	PUYOL	13-04-1978	Barcelona	178	80	7	654	1	1		90	3
6	MF	Andres INIESTA	A.INIESTA	11-05-1984	Barcelona	170	85	6	557	2	1		49	8
7	FW	David VILLA	DAVID VILLA	03-12-1981	Valencia	175	69	7	634	5			65	43
8	MF	XAVI	XAVI	25-01-1980	Barcelona	170	69	7	636		1		94	8
9	FW	Fernando TORRES	TORRES	20-03-1984	Liverpool ENG	181	78	7	292				80	24
10	MF	Cesc FABREGAS	FABREGAS	04-05-1987	Arsenal ENG	175	70	4	126				54	6
11	DF	Joan CAPDEVILA	CAPDEVILA	03-02-1978	Villarreal	182	78	7	660		1		52	4
12	GK	Victor VALDES	V.VALDES	14-01-1982	Barcelona	183	78	0	0				1	0
13	FW	Juan Manuel MATA	MATA	28-04-1988	Valencia	174	65	1	20				9	3
14	MF	XABI ALONSO	ALONSO	25-11-1981	Real Madrid	183	75	7	593		1		76	9
15	DF	SERGIO RAMOS	RAMOS	30-03-1986	Real Madrid	183	73	7	647		1		67	5
16	MF	Sergio BUSQUETS	SERGIO	16-07-1988	Barcelona	189	77	7	631		1		20	0
17	DF	Alvaro ARBELOA	ARBELOA	17-01-1983	Real Madrid	184	79	1	13				16	0
18	FW	PEDRO	PEDRO	28-07-1987	Barcelona	169	64	5	176				8	1
19	FW	Fernando LLORENTE	LLORENTE	26-02-1985	Athletic Bilbao	194	88	1	32				8	3
20	MF	Javier MARTINEZ	J.MARTINEZ	02-09-1988	Athletic Bilbao	190	81	1	17				3	0
21	MF	DAVID SILVA	SILVA	08-01-1986	Valencia	177	76	2	66				38	7
22	FW	Jesus NAVAS	J.NAVAS	21-11-1985	Sevilla	172	65	3	178				9	1
23	GK	Pepe REINA	REINA	31-08-1982	Liverpool ENG	187	85	0	0				20	0

FRA – FRANCE SQUAD 2010 FIFA WORLD CUP

No	Pos	Name	Shirt Name	DoB	Club	Cms	Kg	Games	Mins	Goals	Y	R	Cap	Gls
1	GK	Hugo LLORIS	LLORIS	26-12-1986	Lyon	188	78	3	270				14	0
2	DF	Bakari SAGNA	SAGNA	14-02-1983	Arsenal ENG	175	72	3	270				23	0
3	DF	Eric ABIDAL	ABIDAL	11-09-1979	Barcelona ESP	180	75	2	180		1		50	0
4	DF	Anthony REVEILLERE	REVEILLERE	10-11-1979	Lyon	181	76	0	0				6	0
5	DF	William GALLAS	GALLAS	17-08-1977	Arsenal ENG	181	72	3	270				84	5
6	DF	Marc PLANUS	PLANUS	7-03-1982	Bordeaux	183	76	0	0				1	0
7	FW	Franck RIBERY	RIBERY	7-04-1983	Bayern München GER	175	72	3	270		1		48	7
8	MF	Yoann GOURCUFF	GOURCUFF	11-07-1986	Bordeaux	185	79	2	100		1	1	22	1
9	FW	Djibril CISSE	CISSE	12-08-1981	Panathinaikos GRE	182	78	1	55				40	9
10	FW	Sidney GOVOU	GOVOU	27-07-1979	Lyon	175	72	3	162				49	10
11	FW	Andre Pierre GIGNAC	GIGNAC	5-12-1985	Toulouse	187	84	3	95				16	4
12	FW	Thierry HENRY	HENRY	17-08-1977	Barcelona ESP	188	83	2	53				123	51
13	DF	Patrice EVRA	EVRA	15-05-1981	Manchester Utd ENG	171	67	2	180		1		32	0
14	MF	Jeremy TOULALAN	TOULALAN	10-09-1983	Lyon	183	77	2	180		2		36	0
15	MF	Florent MALOUDA	MALOUDA	13-06-1980	Chelsea ENG	184	73	3	150	1			57	4
16	GK	Steve MANDANDA	MANDANDA	28-03-1985	Marseille	185	82	0	0				13	0
17	DF	Sebastien SQUILLACI	SQUILLACI	11-08-1980	Sevilla ESP	184	79	1	90				21	0
18	MF	Alou DIARRA	A. DIARRA	15-07-1981	Bordeaux	190	79	1	82				26	0
19	MF	Abou DIABY	DIABY	11-05-1986	Arsenal ENG	188	78	3	270		1		8	0
20	FW	Mathieu VALBUENA	VALBUENA	28-09-1984	Marseille	167	58	1	21				3	1
21	FW	Nicolas ANELKA	ANELKA	14-03-1979	Chelsea ENG	185	82	2	117				69	14
22	DF	Gael CLICHY	CLICHY	26-07-1985	Arsenal ENG	181	72	1	90				5	0
23	GK	Cedric CARRASSO	CARRASSO	30-12-1981	Bordeaux	187	87	0	0				0	0

GER – GERMANY SQUAD 2010 FIFA WORLD CUP

No	Pos	Name	Shirt Name	DoB	Club	Cms	Kg	Games	Mins	Goals	Y	R	Cap	Gls
1	GK	Manuel NEUER	NEUER	27-03-1986	Schalke 04	190	85	6	540				11	0
2	MF	Marcell JANSEN	JANSEN	4-11-1985	Hamburger SV	190	88	4	154	1			35	3
3	DF	Arne FRIEDRICH	FRIEDRICH	29-05-1979	Hertha Berlin	185	78	7	630	1	2		79	1
4	DF	Dennis AOGO	AOGO	14-01-1987	Hamburger SV	184		1	90		1		3	0
5	DF	Serdar TASCI	TASCI	24-04-1987	VfB Stuttgart	186		1	1				13	0
6	MF	Sami KHEDIRA	KHEDIRA	4-04-1987	VfB Stuttgart	189		7	608	1	1		12	1
7	MF	Bastian SCHWEINSTEIGER	SCHWEINSTEIGER	1-08-1984	Bayern München	180	76	7	621		1		81	21
8	MF	Mesut OZIL	OZIL	15-10-1988	Werder Bremen	182		7	586	1	1		17	2
9	FW	Stefan KIESSLING	KIEßLING	25-01-1984	Bayer Leverkusen	191		2	24				6	0
10	FW	Lukas PODOLSKI	PODOLSKI	4-06-1985	1.FC Köln	180	81	6	531	2			79	40
11	FW	Miroslav KLOSE	KLOSE	9-06-1978	Bayern München	182	74	5	357	4		1	101	52
12	GK	Tim WIESE	WIESE	17-12-1981	Werder Bremen	193	91	0	0				2	0
13	MF	Thomas MUELLER	MÜLLER	13-09-1989	Bayern München	186		6	473	5	2		8	5
14	DF	Holger BADSTUBER	BADSTUBER	13-03-1989	Bayern München	190		2	167				4	0
15	MF	Piotr TROCHOWSKI	TROCHOWSKI	22-03-1984	Hamburger SV	168	68	4	109				35	2
16	DF	Philipp LAHM	LAHM	11-11-1983	Bayern München	170	62	6	540		1		71	4
17	DF	Per MERTESACKER	MERTESACKER	29-09-1984	Werder Bremen	196	85	7	630				69	1
18	MF	Toni KROOS	KROOS	4-01-1990	Bayer Leverkusen	180	68	4	59				8	0
19	FW	CACAU	CACAU	27-03-1981	VfB Stuttgart	180		4	205	1	2		12	4
20	DF	Jerome BOATENG	BOATENG	3-09-1988	Hamburger SV	192		5	377				10	0
21	MF	Marko MARIN	MARIN	13-03-1989	Werder Bremen	169		2	29				11	1
22	GK	Hans Jörg BUTT	BUTT	28-05-1974	Bayern München	191	91	1	90				4	0
23	FW	Mario GOMEZ	GOMEZ	10-07-1985	Bayern München	189	82	4	56				38	12

GHA – GHANA SQUAD 2010 FIFA WORLD CUP

No	Pos	Name	Shirt Name	DoB	Club	Cms	Kg	Games	Mins	Goals	Y	R	Cap	Gls
1	GK	Daniel AGYEI	AGYEI	10-11-1989	Liberty	186	60	0	0				3	0
2	DF	Hans SARPEI	SARPEI	28-06-1976	B. Leverkusen GER	178	68	5	463		1		34	0
3	FW	Asamoah GYAN	A. GYAN	22-11-1985	Rennes Fra	186	77	5	501	3			44	22
4	DF	John PANTSIL	PANTSIL	15-06-1981	Fulham ENG	178	80	5	510		1		60	0
5	DF	John MENSAH	MENSAH	29-11-1982	Sunderland ENG	177	72	4	420		1		67	0
6	MF	Anthony ANNAN	ANNAN	21-07-1986	Rosenborg NOR	171	74	5	510		1		37	0
7	DF	Samuel INKOOM	INKOOM	1-06-1989	Basel SUI	179	58	2	187				18	0
8	DF	Jonathan MENSAH	JONATHAN	13-07-1990	Free State Stars RSA	182		3	300		2		8	0
9	MF	Derek BOATENG	D. BOATENG	2-05-1983	Getafe ESP	185	78	0	0				22	3
10	MF	Stephen APPIAH	S. APPIAH	24-12-1980	Bologna ITA	178	77	3	105				68	16
11	MF	Sulley MUNTARI	MUNTARI	27-08-1984	Internazionale ITA	180	76	4	134	1			56	17
12	FW	Prince TAGOE	TAGOE	9-11-1986	Hoffenheim GER	179	80	3	210		1		21	3
13	MF	Andre AYEW	A. AYEW	17-12-1989	Arles-Avignon FRA	175	66	4	389		2		25	1
14	FW	Matthew AMOAH	AMOAH	24-10-1980	NAC Breda NED	175	66	2	11				44	11
15	DF	Isaac VORSAH	VORSAH	21-06-1988	Hoffenheim GER	180	80	2	210		1		16	0
16	GK	Stephen AHORLU	AHORLU	5-09-1988	Heart of Lions	179	80	0	0				0	0
17	DF	Ibrahim AYEW	I. AYEW	16-04-1988	Zamalek EGY	176	81	0	0				6	0
18	FW	Dominic ADIYIAH	ADIYIAH	29-11-1989	Milan ITA	170	75	2	33				8	0
19	DF	Lee ADDY	ADDY	7-07-1990	Bechem Chelsea	178	80	3	138		1		13	0
20	FW	Quincy OWUSU-ABEYIE	OWUSU ABEYIE	15-04-1986	Al Sadd QAT	180	74	2	35				15	1
21	MF	Kwadwo ASAMOAH	K. ASAMOAH	9-12-1988	Udinese ITA	168	76	5	480				20	1
22	GK	Richard KINGSON	KINGSON	13-06-1978	Wigan Ath ENG	182	83	5	510				83	1
23	FW	Kevin Prince BOATENG	PRINCE	6-03-1987	Portsmouth ENG	182	81	5	464	1			6	1

GRE – GREECE SQUAD 2010 FIFA WORLD CUP

No	Pos	Name	Shirt Name	DoB	Club	Cms	Kg	Games	Mins	Goals	Y	R	Cap	Gls
1	GK	Konstantinos CHALKIAS	CHALKIAS	30-05-1974	PAOK	198	97	0	0				26	0
2	DF	Giourkas SEITARIDIS	SEITARIDIS	4-06-1981	Panathinaikos	185	79	1	90				70	1
3	DF	Christos PATSATZOGLOU	PATSA	19-03-1979	Omonia CYP	183	78	2	80				44	1
4	DF	Nikos SPIROPOULOS	SPYROPOULOS	10-10-1983	Panathinaikos	171	70	1	45				19	0
5	DF	Vangelis MORAS	MORAS	26-08-1981	Bologna ITA	193	82	1	90				12	0
6	MF	Alexandros TZIOLIS	TZIOLIS	13-02-1985	Siena ITA	190	90	3	270		1		21	0
7	FW	Georgios SAMARAS	SAMARAS	21-02-1985	Celtic SCO	192	90	3	202		1		36	5
8	DF	Avraam PAPADOPOULOS	PAPADOPOULOS	3-12-1984	Olympiacos	186	85	3	270				16	0
9	FW	Angelos CHARISTEAS	CHARISTEAS	9-02-1980	1.FC Nürnberg GER	191	82	1	61				85	24
10	MF	Georgios KARAGOUNIS	KARAGOUNIS	6-03-1977	Panathinaikos	176	79	3	180				96	6
11	DF	Loukas VYNTRA	VYNTRA	5-02-1981	Panathinaikos	184	80	3	270				31	0
12	GK	Alexandros TZORVAS	TZORVAS	12-08-1982	Panathinaikos	190	82	3	270				11	0
13	GK	Michail SIFAKIS	SIFAKIS	9-09-1984	Aris Thessaloniki	186	85	0	0				2	0
14	FW	Dimitrios SALPINGIDIS	SALPINGIDIS	18-08-1981	Panathinaikos	171	78	2	121	1			37	3
15	DF	Vasileios TOROSIDIS	TOROSIDIS	10-06-1985	Olympiacos	185	82	3	235	1	1		29	3
16	DF	Sotirios KYRGIAKOS	KYRGIAKOS	23-07-1979	Liverpool ENG	192	92	2	180				60	4
17	FW	Theofanis GEKAS	GEKAS	23-05-1980	Hertha Berlin GER	179	76	2	169				49	20
18	MF	Sotiris NINIS	NINIS	3-04-1990	Panathinaikos	173	70	2	47				6	1
19	DF	Sokratis PAPASTATHOPOULOS	SOKRATIS	9-06-1988	Genoa ITA	186	83	2	127		1		11	0
20	FW	Pantelis KAPETANOS	KAPETANOS	8-06-1983	Steaua ROU	190	80	1	29				4	0
21	MF	Konstantinos KATSOURANIS	KATSOURANIS	21-06-1979	Panathinaikos	183	83	3	234		1		72	8
22	DF	Stelios MALEZAS	MALEZAS	11-03-1985	PAOK	192	80	0	0				0	0
23	MF	Athanasios PRITTAS	PRITTAS	9-01-1979	Aris Thessaloniki	185		0	0				0	0

HON – HONDURAS SQUAD 2010 FIFA WORLD CUP

No	Pos	Name	Shirt Name	DoB	Club	Cms	Kg	Games	Mins	Goals	Y	R	Cap	Gls
1	GK	Ricardo CANALES	CANALES	30-05-1982	Motagua	180	77	0	0				3	0
2	DF	Osman CHAVEZ	CHAVEZ	29-07-1984	Platense	187	91	3	270		1		31	0
3	DF	Maynor FIGUEROA	FIGUEROA	2-05-1983	Wigan Ath ENG	182	81	3	270				72	2
4	DF	Jhony PALACIOS	J. PALACIOS	20-12-1986	Olimpia	182	80	0	0				6	0
5	DF	Victor BERNARDEZ	BERNARDEZ	24-05-1982	Anderlecht BEL	187	89	1	90				42	1
6	MF	Hendry THOMAS	THOMAS	23-02-1985	Wigan Ath ENG	180	80	2	114		1		43	2
7	MF	Ramon NUNEZ	NUNEZ	14-11-1985	Olimpia Tegucigalpa	169	68	3	172				32	3
8	MF	Wilson PALACIOS	W. PALACIOS	29-07-1984	Tottenham H'pur ENG	176	80	3	270		2		73	4
9	FW	Carlos PAVON	PAVON	9-10-1973	Real Espana	180	85	1	60				100	56
10	MF	Jerry PALACIOS	J.N. PALACIOS	13-05-1982	Guangzhou CHN	183	75	2	84				14	4
11	FW	David SUAZO	SUAZO	5-11-1979	Genoa ITA	183	81	2	171		1		54	16
12	FW	Georgie WELCOME	WELCOME	9-03-1985	Motagua	192	83	3	87				16	2
13	FW	Roger ESPINOZA	ESPINOZA	25-10-1986	Kansas City W USA	178	77	2	135				14	3
14	DF	Oscar GARCIA	GARCIA	4-09-1984	Olimpia	176	69	0	0				43	0
15	FW	Walter MARTINEZ	MARTINEZ	24-03-1982	Marathon	166	70	3	125				40	9
16	DF	Mauricio SABILLON	SABILLON	11-11-1978	Guangzhou CHN	180	74	1	90				26	0
17	MF	Edgar ALVAREZ	ALVAREZ	18-01-1980	Bari ITA	170	73	2	180				48	3
18	GK	Noel VALLADARES	VALLADARES	3-05-1977	Olimpia	179	82	3	270				75	0
19	MF	Danilo TURCIOS	TURCIOS	8-05-1978	Olimpia	166	64	2	66		1		86	7
20	MF	Amado GUEVARA	GUEVARA	2-05-1976	Motagua	176	74	2	156				137	27
21	DF	Emilio IZAGUIRRE	IZAGUIRRE	10-05-1986	Motagua	178	79	2	180		1		42	1
22	GK	Donis ESCOBER	ESCOBER	3-02-1981	Olimpia	180	75	0	0				12	0
23	DF	Sergio MENDOZA	MENDOZA	23-05-1981	Motagua	177	78	2	180				50	1

ITA – ITALY SQUAD 2010 FIFA WORLD CUP

No	Pos	Name	Shirt Name	DoB	Club	Cms	Kg	Games	Mins	Goals	Y	R	Cap	Gls
1	GK	Gianluigi BUFFON	BUFFON	28-01-1978	Juventus	190	83	1	45				102	0
2	DF	Christian MAGGIO	MAGGIO	11-02-1982	Napoli	184	79	1	45				6	0
3	DF	Domenico CRISCITO	CRISCITO	30-12-1986	Genoa	175	74	3	225				10	0
4	DF	Giorgio CHIELLINI	CHIELLINI	14-08-1984	Juventus	192	84	3	270		1		32	2
5	DF	Fabio CANNAVARO	CANNAVARO	13-09-1973	Juventus	175	72	3	270		1		136	2
6	MF	Daniele DE ROSSI	DE ROSSI	24-07-1983	Roma	182	80	3	270	1			57	9
7	MF	Simone PEPE	PEPE	30-08-1983	Udinese	179	76	3	225		1		18	0
8	MF	Gennaro GATTUSO	GATTUSO	9-01-1978	Milan	177	77	1	45				73	1
9	FW	Vincenzo IAQUINTA	IAQUINTA	21-11-1979	Juventus	186	77	3	270	1			40	6
10	FW	Antonio DI NATALE	DI NATALE	13-10-1977	Udinese	170	68	3	153	1			36	10
11	FW	Alberto GILARDINO	GILARDINO	5-07-1982	Fiorentina	184	79	2	117				43	16
12	GK	Federico MARCHETTI	MARCHETTI	7-02-1983	Cagliari	188	82	3	225				8	0
13	DF	Salvatore BOCCHETTI	BOCCHETTI	30-11-1986	Genoa	178	77	0	0				5	0
14	GK	Morgan DE SANCTIS	DE SANCTIS	26-03-1977	Napoli	190	80	0	0				3	0
15	MF	Claudio MARCHISIO	MARCHISIO	19-01-1986	Juventus	179	66	2	120				6	0
16	MF	Mauro CAMORANESI	CAMORANESI	4-10-1976	Juventus	174	70	2	76		1		55	4
17	MF	Angelo PALOMBO	PALOMBO	25-09-1981	Sampdoria	177	77	0	0				17	0
18	FW	Fabio QUAGLIARELLA	QUAGLIARELLA	31-01-1983	Napoli	180	79	1	45	1	1		21	5
19	DF	Gianluca ZAMBROTTA	ZAMBROTTA	19-02-1977	Milan	181	76	3	270				97	2
20	FW	Giampaolo PAZZINI	PAZZINI	2-08-1984	Sampdoria	180	77	1	29				9	1
21	MF	Andrea PIRLO	PIRLO	19-05-1979	Milan	177	68	1	34				67	8
22	MF	Riccardo MONTOLIVO	MONTOLIVO	18-01-1985	Fiorentina	181	73	3	236				16	0
23	DF	Leonardo BONUCCI	BONUCCI	1-05-1987	Bari	190	82	0	0				2	1

JPN – JAPAN SQUAD 2010 FIFA WORLD CUP

No	Pos	Name	Shirt Name	DoB	Club	Cms	Kg	Games	Mins	Goals	Y	R	Cap	Gls
1	GK	Seigo NARAZAKI	NARAZAKI	15-04-1976	Nagoya G'pus Eight	187	80	0	0				76	0
2	MF	Yuki ABE	ABE	6-09-1981	Urawa Reds	177	77	4	351		1		48	3
3	DF	Yuichi KOMANO	KOMANO	25-07-1981	Jubilo Iwata	172	76	4	390				57	0
4	DF	Marcus Tulio TANAKA	TULIO	24-04-1981	Nagoya G'pus Eight	185	82	4	390				43	8
5	DF	Yuto NAGATOMO	NAGATOMO	12-09-1986	FC Tokyo	170	68	4	390		2		30	3
6	DF	Atsuto UCHIDA	UCHIDA	27-03-1988	Kashima Antlers	176	62	0	0				31	1
7	MF	Yasuhito ENDO	ENDO	28-01-1980	Gamba Osaka	178	75	4	389	1	2		98	9
8	MF	Daisuke MATSUI	MATSUI	11-05-1981	Grenoble FRA	175	64	4	272		1		28	1
9	FW	Shinji OKAZAKI	OKAZAKI	16-04-1986	Shimizu S-Pulse	174	76	4	105	1			32	17
10	MF	Shunsuke NAKAMURA	NAKAMURA	24-06-1978	Yokohama F Marinos	178	70	1	26				98	24
11	FW	Keiji TAMADA	TAMADA	11-04-1980	Nagoya G'pus Eight	173	67	2	28				72	16
12	FW	Kisho YANO	YANO	5-04-1984	Albirex Niigata	185	76	1	8				19	2
13	DF	Daiki IWAMASA	IWAMASA	30-01-1982	Kashima Antlers	187	85	0	0				2	0
14	MF	Kengo NAKAMURA	K. NAKAMURA	31-10-1980	Kawasaki Frontale	175	67	1	39				48	5
15	MF	Yasuyuki KONNO	KONNO	25-01-1983	FC Tokyo	178	73	1	2				38	0
16	FW	Yoshito OKUBO	OKUBO	9-06-1982	Vissel Kobe	170	73	4	352				54	5
17	MF	Makoto HASEBE	HASEBE	18-01-1984	Wolfsburg GER	177	66	4	375				35	1
18	MF	Keisuke HONDA	HONDA	13-06-1986	CSKA Moskva RUS	182	74	4	390	2	1		19	6
19	FW	Takayuki MORIMOTO	MORIMOTO	7-05-1988	Catania ITA	180	73	0	0				6	1
20	MF	Junichi INAMOTO	INAMOTO	18-09-1979	Kawasaki Frontale	181	75	2	3				82	5
21	GK	Eiji KAWASHIMA	KAWASHIMA	20-03-1983	Kawasaki Frontale	185	80	4	390				14	0
22	DF	Yuji NAKAZAWA	NAKAZAWA	25-02-1978	Yokohama F Marinos	187	78	4	390				109	17
23	GK	Yoshikatsu KAWAGUCHI	KAWAGUCHI	15-08-1975	Jubilo Iwata	180	77	0	0				117	0

KOR – KOREA REPUBLIC SQUAD 2010 FIFA WORLD CUP

No	Pos	Name	Shirt Name	DoB	Club	Cms	Kg	Games	Mins	Goals	Y	R	Cap	Gls
1	GK	LEE Woon Jae	WOONJAE	26-04-1973	Suwon Bluewings	182	90	0	0				130	0
2	DF	OH Beom Seok	BEOMSEOK	29-07-1984	Ulsan Hyundai	181	77	1	90				39	2
3	DF	KIM Hyung Il	HYUNGIL	27-04-1984	Pohang Steelers	187	83	0	0				2	0
4	DF	CHO Yong Hyung	YONGHYUNG	3-11-1983	Jeju Utd	182	71	4	360		1		36	0
5	MF	KIM Nam Il	NAMIL	14-03-1977	Tom Tomsk RUS	180	75	3	87		1		96	2
6	MF	KIM Bo Kyung	BOKYUNG	6-10-1989	Oita Trinita JPN	178	73	0	0				6	0
7	MF	PARK Ji Sung	JISUNG	25-02-1981	Manchester Utd ENG	178	73	4	360	1			92	13
8	MF	KIM Jung Woo	JUNGWOO	9-05-1982	Gwangju Sangmu	183	70	4	360		1		61	4
9	FW	AHN Jung Hwan	JUNGHWAN	27-01-1976	Dalian Shide CHN	177	73	0	0				71	17
10	FW	PARK Chu Young	CHUYOUNG	10-07-1985	Monaco FRA	183	76	4	347	1			45	15
11	FW	LEE Seung Yeoul	SEUNGYEOUL	6-03-1989	FC Seoul	183	73	1	3				9	3
12	DF	LEE Young Pyo	YOUNGPYO	23-04-1977	Al Hilal KSA	177	67	4	360				117	5
13	MF	KIM Jae Sung	JAESUNG	3-10-1983	Pohang Steelers	180	70	3	65				11	2
14	DF	LEE Jung Soo	JUNGSOO	8-01-1980	Kashima Antlers JPN	185	76	4	360	2			29	4
15	DF	KIM Dong Jin	DONGJIN	29-01-1982	Ulsan Hyundai	184	78	1	1				62	2
16	MF	KI Sung Yueng	SUNGYUENG	24-01-1989	Celtic SCO	187	75	4	291				26	4
17	MF	LEE Chung Yong	CHUNGYONG	2-07-1988	Bolton Wand. ENG	180	69	4	359	2	1		28	5
18	GK	JUNG Sung Ryong	SUNGRYONG	4-01-1985	Seongnam I. Chunma	190	88	4	360				20	0
19	MF	YEOM Ki Hun	KIHUN	30-03-1983	Suwon Bluewings	182	80	4	249		1		39	3
20	FW	LEE Dong Gook	DONGGOOK	29-04-1979	Jeonbuk Motors	187	83	2	38				85	25
21	GK	KIM Young Kwang	YOUNGKWANG	28-06-1983	Ulsan Hyundai	184	80	0	0				14	0
22	DF	CHA Du Ri	DURI	25-07-1980	SC Freiburg GER	181	79	3	270		1		50	4
23	DF	KANG Min Soo	MINSOO	14-02-1986	Suwon Bluewings	186	76	0	0				31	0

MEX – MEXICO SQUAD 2010 FIFA WORLD CUP

No	Pos	Name	Shirt Name	DoB	Club	Cms	Kg	Games	Mins	Goals	Y	R	Cap	Gls
1	GK	Oscar PEREZ	O PEREZ	1-02-1973	Jaguares	174	75	4	360				56	0
2	DF	Francisco RODRIGUEZ	F RODRIGUEZ	20-10-1981	PSV Eindhoven NED	191	82	4	360		1		52	1
3	DF	Carlos SALCIDO	C SALCIDO	2-04-1980	PSV Eindhoven NED	176	74	4	360				77	6
4	DF	Rafael MARQUEZ	R MARQUEZ	13-02-1979	Barcelona ESP	182	77	4	360	1	1		94	11
5	DF	Ricardo OSORIO	R OSORIO	30-03-1980	VfB Stuttgart GER	173	73	4	360				80	1
6	MF	Gerardo TORRADO	G TORRADO	30-04-1979	Cruz Azul	174	74	4	360		1		115	5
7	FW	Pablo BARRERA	P BARRERA	21-06-1987	Pumas UNAM	172	71	3	149				24	3
8	MF	Israel CASTRO	I CASTRO	20-12-1980	Pumas UNAM	175	70	1	33		1		30	1
9	FW	Guillermo FRANCO	G FRANCO	3-11-1976	West Ham Utd ENG	182	78	4	254		1		25	7
10	FW	Cuauhtemoc BLANCO	C BLANCO	17-01-1973	Veracruz	177	77	3	112	1			118	39
11	FW	Carlos VELA	C VELA	1-03-1989	Arsenal ENG	179	75	2	100				30	9
12	DF	Paul AGUILAR	P AGUILAR	6-03-1986	Pachuca	178	68	1	55				11	2
13	GK	Guillermo OCHOA	G OCHOA	13-07-1985	America	183	80	0	0				37	0
14	FW	Javier HERNANDEZ	J HERNANDEZ	1-06-1988	Chivas	175	74	4	169	2	1		16	9
15	DF	Hector MORENO	H MORENO	17-01-1988	AZ Alkmaar NED	184	82	2	147		1		12	0
16	DF	Efrain JUAREZ	E JUAREZ	22-02-1988	Pumas UNAM	175	71	3	235		2		22	0
17	FW	Giovani DOS SANTOS	G DOS SANTOS	11-05-1989	Galatasaray TUR	175	76	4	360				30	5
18	MF	Andres GUARDADO	A GUARDADO	28-09-1986	Deportivo LC ESP	169	67	3	141				59	8
19	DF	Jonny MAGALLON	J MAGALLON	21-11-1981	Chivas	178	76	0	0				52	3
20	MF	Jorge TORRES	J TORRES	16-01-1988	Atlas	182	76	0	0				8	0
21	FW	Adolfo BAUTISTA	A BAUTISTA	15-05-1979	Chivas	185	82	1	45				38	11
22	FW	Alberto MEDINA	A MEDINA	29-05-1983	Chivas	172	67	0	0				56	6
23	GK	Luis MICHEL	L MICHEL	21-07-1979	Chivas	183	79	0	0				4	0

NED – NETHERLANDS SQUAD 2010 FIFA WORLD CUP

No	Pos	Name	Shirt Name	DoB	Club	Cms	Kg	Games	Mins	Goals	Y	R	Cap	Gls
1	GK	Maarten STEKELENBURG	STEKELENBURG	22-09-1982	Ajax	197	92	7	660		1		34	0
2	DF	Gregory VAN DER WIEL	VAN DER WIEL	3-02-1988	Ajax	180	69	5	480		3		15	0
3	DF	John HEITINGA	HEITINGA	15-11-1983	Everton ENG	182	77	7	649		1	1	61	6
4	DF	Joris MATHIJSEN	MATHIJSEN	5-04-1980	Hamburger SV GER	182	84	6	570		1		62	3
5	DF	Gio VAN BRONCKHORST	V. BRONCKHORST	5-02-1975	Feyenoord	176	73	7	644	1	2		106	6
6	MF	Mark VAN BOMMEL	V. BOMMEL	22-04-1977	Bayern München GER	187	87	7	660		2		63	10
7	FW	Dirk KUYT	KUYT	22-07-1980	Liverpool ENG	183	84	7	587	1	1		70	16
8	MF	Nigel DE JONG	DE JONG	30-11-1984	Manchester City ENG	174	79	6	547		3		48	1
9	FW	Robin VAN PERSIE	V. PERSIE	6-08-1983	Arsenal ENG	184	76	7	599	1	2		51	19
10	MF	Wesley SNEIJDER	SNEIJDER	9-06-1984	Internazionale ITA	170	73	7	652	5	1		68	19
11	FW	Arjen ROBBEN	ROBBEN	23-01-1984	Bayern München GER	180	80	5	387	2	2		52	15
12	DF	Khalid BOULAHROUZ	BOULAHROUZ	28-12-1981	VfB Stuttgart GER	184	87	2	180		1		31	0
13	DF	Andre OOIJER	OOIJER	11-07-1974	PSV Eindhoven	184	82	1	90		1		55	3
14	MF	Demy DE ZEEUW	DE ZEEUW	26-05-1983	Ajax	174	71	2	47				27	0
15	DF	Edson BRAAFHEID	BRAAFHEID	8-04-1983	Celtic SCO	174	76	1	16				8	0
16	GK	Michel VORM	VORM	20-10-1983	Utrecht	182	86	0	0				4	0
17	FW	Eljero ELIA	ELIA	13-02-1987	Hamburger SV GER	177	77	6	134				15	2
18	MF	Stijn SCHAARS	SCHAARS	11-01-1984	AZ Alkmaar	178	75	0	0				12	0
19	FW	Ryan BABEL	BABEL	19-12-1986	Liverpool ENG	185	86	0	0				39	5
20	MF	Ibrahim AFELLAY	AFELLAY	2-04-1986	PSV Eindhoven	184	76	3	21				26	0
21	FW	Klaas Jan HUNTELAAR	HUNTELAAR	12-08-1983	Milan ITA	185	80	4	48	1			36	16
22	GK	Sander BOSCHKER	BOSCHKER	20-10-1970	Twente Enschede	185	86	0	0				1	0
23	MF	Rafael VAN DER VAART	VAN DER VAART	11-02-1983	Real Madrid ESP	178	75	5	278		1		83	16

NGA – NIGERIA SQUAD 2010 FIFA WORLD CUP

No	Pos	Name	Shirt Name	DoB	Club	Cms	Kg	Games	Mins	Goals	Y	R	Cap	Gls
1	GK	Vincent ENYEAMA	ENYEAMA	29-08-1982	Hapoel Tel-Aviv ISR	185	80	3	270		1		58	0
2	DF	Joseph YOBO	YOBO	6-09-1980	Everton ENG	185	76	3	225				70	3
3	DF	Taye TAIWO	TAIWO	16-04-1985	Marseille FRA	188	84	2	130				44	4
4	MF	Nwankwo KANU	KANU	1-08-1976	Portsmouth ENG	197	80	1	57				86	13
5	DF	Rabiu AFOLABI	AFOLABI	18-04-1980	RB Salzburg AUT	183	75	2	103				18	0
6	DF	Danny SHITTU	SHITTU	2-09-1980	Bolton Wand ENG	190	89	3	270				30	0
7	FW	John UTAKA	UTAKA	8-01-1982	Portsmouth ENG	179	82	0	0				44	5
8	FW	Yakubu AYEGBENI	YAKUBU	22-11-1982	Everton ENG	188	89	3	250	1			53	21
9	FW	Obafemi MARTINS	MARTINS	28-10-1984	Wolfsburg GER	170	70	2	71				36	17
10	FW	Brown IDEYE	IDEYE	10-10-1988	Sochaux FRA	180	70	0	0				0	0
11	FW	Peter ODEMWINGIE	ODEMWINGIE	15-07-1981	Lokomotiv Moskva RUS	181	72	2	75				51	8
12	MF	Kalu UCHE	UCHE	15-11-1982	Almeria ESP	171	72	3	195	2			26	4
13	MF	Yussuf AYILA	AYILA	4-11-1984	Dynamo Kyiv UKR	179	75	1	90		1		28	2
14	MF	Sani KAITA	KAITA	2-05-1986	Alania Vlad'kaz RUS	180	76	2	123			1	24	0
15	MF	Lukman HARUNA	HARUNA	4-12-1990	Monaco FRA	177	75	2	180		1		7	1
16	GK	Austin EJIDE	EJIDE	8-04-1984	Hapoel PT ISR	186	87	0	0				19	0
17	DF	Chidi ODIAH	ODIAH	17-12-1983	CSKA Moskva RUS	181	73	3	270				29	1
18	FW	Victor OBINNA	OBINNA	25-03-1987	Malaga ESP	178	71	2	72				35	9
19	FW	Chinedu OGBUKE OBASI	OBASI	1-06-1986	Hoffenheim GER	181	78	3	195		2		16	1
20	MF	Dickson ETUHU	ETUHU	8-06-1982	Fulham ENG	191	80	3	270				17	0
21	FW	Uwa ECHIEJILE	ECHIEJILE	20-01-1988	Rennes FRA	198	60	2	67				14	0
22	DF	Dele ADELEYE	ADELEYE	25-12-1988	Sparta Rotterdam NED	189	72	0	0				6	0
23	GK	Dele AIYENUGBA	AIYENUGBA	20-11-1983	Bnei Yehuda ISR	186	81	0	0				8	0

NZL – NEW ZEALAND SQUAD 2010 FIFA WORLD CUP

No	Pos	Name	Shirt Name	DoB	Club	Cms	Kg	Games	Mins	Goals	Y	R	Cap	Gls
1	GK	Mark PASTON	PASTON	13-12-1976	Wellington Phoenix	195	86	3	270				26	0
2	DF	Ben SIGMUND	SIGMUND	3-02-1981	Wellington Phoenix	187	88	0	0				14	1
3	DF	Tony LOCHHEAD	LOCHHEAD	12-01-1982	Wellington Phoenix	183	74	3	270			1	33	0
4	DF	Winston REID	REID	3-07-1988	Midtjylland DEN	190	88	3	270	1	1		6	1
5	DF	Ivan VICELICH	VICELICH	3-09-1976	Auckland City	193	84	3	249				69	6
6	DF	Ryan NELSEN	NELSEN	18-10-1977	Blackburn Rov ENG	185	84	3	270			2	44	6
7	MF	Simon ELLIOTT	ELLIOTT	10-06-1974	no club	180	80	3	270				66	6
8	MF	Tim BROWN	BROWN	6-03-1981	Wellington Phoenix	185	83	0	0				25	0
9	FW	Shane SMELTZ	SMELTZ	29-09-1981	Gold Coast Utd AUS	184	78	3	270	1			33	17
10	FW	Chris KILLEN	KILLEN	8-10-1981	Middlesbrough ENG	188	86	3	240				34	11
11	MF	Leo BERTOS	BERTOS	20-12-1981	Wellington Phoenix	177	80	3	270				37	0
12	GK	Glen MOSS	MOSS	19-01-1983	Melbourne Victory AUS	188	83	0	0				15	0
13	MF	Andy BARRON	BARRON	24-12-1980	Team Wellington	178	75	1	1				12	1
14	FW	Rory FALLON	FALLON	20-03-1982	Plymouth Argyle ENG	191	88	3	222		1		10	3
15	MF	Michael McGLINCHEY	MC GLINCHEY	7-01-1987	Motherwell SCO	173	65	0	0				5	0
16	MF	Aaron CLAPHAM	CLAPHAM	15-01-1987	Canterbury Utd	172	63	0	0				0	0
17	MF	Dave MULLIGAN	MULLIGAN	24-03-1982	no club	173	66	0	0				25	3
18	DF	Andy BOYENS	BOYENS	18-09-1983	New York RB USA	192	85	0	0				15	0
19	DF	Tommy SMITH	SMITH	31-03-1990	Ipswich Town ENG	187	78	3	270			1	7	0
20	FW	Chris WOOD	WOOD	7-12-1991	West Brom Alb ENG	191	90	3	66				12	0
21	MF	Jeremy CHRISTIE	CHRISTIE	22-05-1983	Tampa Bay USA	180	75	2	21				24	1
22	FW	Jeremy BROCKIE	BROCKIE	7-10-1987	North Q'land Fury AUS	182	82	1	11				19	0
23	GK	James BANNATYNE	BANNATYNE	30-06-1975	Team Wellington	195	95	0	0				3	0

PAR – PARAGUAY SQUAD 2010 FIFA WORLD CUP

No	Pos	Name	Shirt Name	DoB	Club	Cms	Kg	Games	Mins	Goals	Y	R	Cap	Gls
1	GK	Justo VILLAR	J. VILLAR	30-06-1977	Valladolid ESP	180	83	5	480				78	0
2	DF	Dario VERON	VERON	26-07-1979	Pumas UNAM MEX	181	80	1	90				30	0
3	DF	Claudio MOREL	MOREL R.	2-02-1978	Boca Juniors ARG	175	78	5	480		1		33	0
4	DF	Denis CANIZA	CANIZA	29-08-1974	Leon MEX	174	73	1	90				99	1
5	DF	Julio Cesar CACERES	J. CACERES	5-10-1979	Atletico Mineiro BRA	181	77	1	90				63	2
6	MF	Carlos BONET	BONET	2-10-1977	Olimpia	176	76	3	300				67	1
7	FW	Oscar CARDOZO	CARDOZO	20-05-1983	Benfica POR	192	91	5	204				34	4
8	MF	Edgar BARRETO	E. BARRETO	15-07-1984	Atalanta ITA	178	81	3	111				51	2
9	FW	Roque SANTA CRUZ	SANTA CRUZ	16-08-1981	Manchester City ENG	191	86	5	314		1		75	21
10	FW	Edgar BENITEZ	BENITEZ	8-11-1987	Pachuca MEX	176	71	2	83				15	1
11	MF	Jonathan SANTANA	SANTANA	19-10-1981	Wolfsburg GER	181	80	2	120		1		24	0
12	GK	Diego BARRETO	D. BARRETO	16-07-1981	Cerro Porteno	182	76	0	0				4	0
13	MF	Enrique VERA	VERA	10-03-1979	LDU Quito	178	68	5	414	1	1		34	3
14	DF	Paulo DA SILVA	DA SILVA	1-02-1980	Sunderland ENG	184	83	5	480				76	2
15	MF	Victor CACERES	V. CACERES	25-03-1985	Libertad	186	77	4	354		3		31	0
16	MF	Cristian RIVEROS	RIVEROS	16-10-1982	Cruz Azul MEX	179	77	5	480	1	1		54	9
17	DF	Aureliano TORRES	TORRES	16-06-1982	San Lorenzo ARG	178	69	2	82				30	2
18	FW	Nelson VALDEZ	H. VALDEZ	28-11-1983	Bor. Dortmund GER	178	71	5	335				43	9
19	FW	Lucas BARRIOS	LUCAS	13-11-1984	Bor. Dortmund GER	187	83	5	308				8	3
20	MF	Nestor ORTIGOZA	ORTIGOZA	7-10-1984	Argentinos Jun ARG	180	79	1	75				7	0
21	DF	Antolin ALCARAZ	ALCARAZ	30-07-1982	Club Brugge BEL	184	80	4	390	1	1		10	1
22	GK	Aldo BOBADILLA	BOBADILLA	20-04-1976	Indep. Medellin COL	192	88	0	0				19	0
23	FW	Rodolfo GAMARRA	GAMARRA	10-12-1988	Libertad	168	66	0	0				3	0

POR – PORTUGAL SQUAD 2010 FIFA WORLD CUP

No	Pos	Name	Shirt Name	DoB	Club	Cms	Kg	Games	Mins	Goals	Y	R	Cap	Gls
1	GK	EDUARDO	EDUARDO	19-09-1982	Braga	187	84	4	360				19	0
2	DF	BRUNO ALVES	B. ALVES	27-11-1981	Porto	187	83	4	360				35	5
3	DF	PAULO FERREIRA	P. FERREIRA	18-01-1979	Chelsea ENG	181	76	1	90				62	0
4	DF	ROLANDO	ROLANDO	31-08-1985	Porto	189	77	0	0				8	0
5	DF	DUDA	DUDA	27-06-1980	Malaga ESP	175	72	2	70		1		18	1
6	DF	RICARDO CARVALHO	R. CARVALHO	18-05-1978	Chelsea ENG	183	79	4	360				67	4
7	FW	CRISTIANO RONALDO	RONALDO	5-02-1985	Real Madrid ESP	185	78	4	360	1	1		76	23
8	MF	PEDRO MENDES	P. MENDES	26-02-1979	Sporting CP	177	78	4	224		1		12	0
9	FW	LIEDSON	LIEDSON	17-12-1977	Sporting CP	173	63	3	121	1			13	4
10	FW	DANNY	DANNY	7-08-1983	Zenit RUS	179	68	3	177				14	2
11	FW	SIMAO	SIMÃO	31-10-1979	Atletico Madrid ESP	170	64	4	217	1			85	22
12	GK	BETO	BETO	1-05-1982	Porto	183	79	0	0				1	0
13	DF	MIGUEL	MIGUEL	4-01-1980	Valencia ESP	175	64	1	90				58	1
14	MF	MIGUEL VELOSO	M. VELOSO	11-05-1986	Sporting CP	181	85	2	26				14	1
15	MF	PEPE	PEPE	26-02-1983	Real Madrid ESP	186	72	2	136		1		27	2
16	MF	RAUL MEIRELES	R. MEIRELES	17-03-1983	Porto	179	66	4	329	1			38	6
17	MF	RUBEN AMORIM	R. AMORIM	27-01-1985	Benfica	180	77	1	5				1	0
18	FW	HUGO ALMEIDA	H. ALMEIDA	23-05-1984	Werder Bremen GER	193	82	3	135	1	1		28	10
19	MF	TIAGO	TIAGO	2-05-1981	Atletico Madrid ESP	183	79	4	298	2	2		55	3
20	MF	DECO	DECO	27-08-1977	Chelsea ENG	175	74	1	62				75	5
21	DF	RICARDO COSTA	R. COSTA	16-05-1981	Lille FRA	183	80	2	179			1	10	0
22	GK	DANIEL FERNANDES	D. FERNANDES	25-09-1983	Iraklis GRE	194	93	0	0				2	0
23	DF	FABIO COENTRAO	F. COENTRÃO	11-03-1988	Benfica	181	70	4	360			1	8	0

PRK – KOREA DPR SQUAD 2010 FIFA WORLD CUP

No	Pos	Name	Shirt Name	DoB	Club	Cms	Kg	Games	Mins	Goals	Y	R	Cap	Gls
1	GK	RI Myong Guk	R. MYONG GUK	9-09-1986	Pyongyang City	187	76	3	270	0		0	37	0
2	DF	CHA Jong Hyok	C. JONG HYOK	25-09-1985	Amrokgang	178	77	3	255	0		0	37	0
3	DF	RI Jun Il	R. JUN IL	24-08-1987	Sobaeksu	178	73	3	270	0		0	30	0
4	MF	PAK Nam Chol	P. NAM CHOL	2-07-1985	April 25	172	72	3	238	0		0	35	10
5	DF	RI Kwang Chon	R. KWANG CHON	4-09-1985	April 25	183	77	3	270	0		0	41	0
6	MF	KIM Kum Il	K. KUM IL	10-10-1987	April 25	170	68	2	42	0		0	14	2
7	FW	AN Chol Hyok	A. CHOL HYOK	27-06-1987	Rimyongsu	178	75	0	0	0		0	38	7
8	DF	JI Yun Nam	J. YUN NAM	20-11-1976	April 25	172	64	3	270	1		0	32	4
9	FW	JONG Tae Se	J. TAE SE	2-03-1984	Kawasaki Frontale JPN	181	80	3	270	0		0	27	16
10	FW	HONG Yong Jo	H. YONG JO	22-05-1982	FK Rostov RUS	174	73	3	270	0		1	69	22
11	MF	MUN In Guk	M. IN GUK	29-09-1978	April 25	167	63	3	205	0		0	45	10
12	FW	CHOE Kum Chol	C. KUM CHOL	9-02-1987	April 25	178	75	1	23	0		0	23	3
13	DF	PAK Chol Jin	P. CHOL JIN	5-09-1985	Amrokgang	184	77	3	270	0		1	36	0
14	DF	PAK Nam Chol	NAM CHOL	3-10-1988	Amrokgang	183	80	0	0	0		0	6	0
15	MF	KIM Yong Jun	K. YONG JUN	19-07-1983	Pyongyang City	182	75	1	32	0		0	86	11
16	DF	NAM Song Chol	N. SONG CHOL	7-05-1982	April 25	178	73	1	15	0		0	53	2
17	MF	AN Yong Hak	A. YONG HAK	25-10-1978	Omiya Ardija JPN	182	75	3	270	0		0	30	2
18	GK	KIM Myong Gil	K. MYONG GIL	16-10-1984	Amrokgang	181	70	0	0	0		0	31	0
19	MF	RI Chol Myong	R. CHOL MYONG	18-02-1988	Pyongyang City	173	68	0	0	0		0	5	0
20	GK	KIM Myong Won	K. MYONG WON	15-07-1983	Amrokgang	180	72	0	0	0		0	10	0
21	DF	RI Kwang Hyok	R. KWANG HYOK	17-08-1987	Kyonggongpo	178	72	0	0	0		0	5	0
22	MF	KIM Kyong Il	K. KYONG IL	11-12-1988	Rimyongsu	174	67	0	0	0		0	3	0
23	MF	PAK Sung Hyok	P. SUNG HYOK	30-05-1990	Sobaeksu	175	70	0	0	0		0	3	0

RSA – SOUTH AFRICA SQUAD 2010 FIFA WORLD CUP

No	Pos	Name	Shirt Name	DoB	Club	Cms	Kg	Games	Mins	Goals	Y	R	Cap	Gls
1	GK	Moneeb JOSEPHS	JOSEPHS	19-05-1980	Orlando Pirates	184	79	2	101				19	0
2	DF	Siboniso GAXA	GAXA	6-04-1984	Mamelodi Sundowns	178	68	3	215				40	0
3	DF	Tsepo MASILELA	MASILELA	5-05-1985	Maccabi Haifa ISR	174	72	3	225		1		34	0
4	DF	Aaron MOKOENA	MOKOENA	25-11-1980	Portsmouth ENG	183	81	3	270				104	1
5	DF	Anele NGCONGCA	NGCONGCA	20-10-1987	RC Genk BEL	177	67	1	55				6	0
6	MF	MacBeth SIBAYA	SIBAYA	25-11-1977	Rubin Kazan RUS	176	77	1	90				59	0
7	MF	Lance DAVIDS	DAVIDS	11-04-1985	Ajax Cape Town	171	80	0	0				22	0
8	MF	Siphiwe TSHABALALA	TSHABALALA	25-09-1984	Kaizer Chiefs	170	67	3	270	1			52	6
9	FW	Katlego MPHELA	MPHELA	29-11-1984	Mamelodi Sundowns	180	77	3	270	1			34	14
10	MF	Steven PIENAAR	PIENAAR	17-03-1982	Everton ENG	173	73	3	252		1		53	2
11	MF	Teko MODISE	MODISE	22-12-1982	Orlando Pirates	172	66	3	192				55	10
12	MF	Reneilwe LETSHOLONYANE	LETSHOLONYANE	9-06-1982	Kaizer Chiefs	173	66	2	147				15	1
13	MF	Kagisho DIKGACOI	DIKGACOI	24-11-1984	Fulham ENG	180	86	2	180		2		39	2
14	DF	Matthew BOOTH	BOOTH	14-03-1977	Mamelodi Sundowns	198	95	0	0				27	1
15	DF	Lucas THWALA	THWALA	19-10-1981	Orlando Pirates	170	74	1	45				25	1
16	GK	Itumeleng KHUNE	KHUNE	20-06-1987	Kaizer Chiefs	180	81	2	166			1	29	0
17	FW	Bernard PARKER	PARKER	16-03-1986	Twente Enschede NED	172	68	2	75				30	8
18	FW	Siyabonga NOMVETHE	NOMVETHE	2-12-1977	Moroka Swallows	173	70	1	22				77	16
19	MF	Surprise MORIRI	MORIRI	20-03-1980	Mamelodi Sundowns	173	72	1	33				35	5
20	DF	Bongani KHUMALO	KHUMALO	6-01-1987	SuperSport Utd	184	78	3	270	1			17	1
21	DF	Siyabonga SANGWENI	SANGWENI	29-09-1981	Golden Arrows	182	78	0	0				8	1
22	GK	Shu-Aib WALTERS	WALTERS	26-12-1981	Maritzburg Utd	188	87	0	0				0	0
23	MF	Thanduyise KHUBONI	KHUBONI	23-05-1986	Golden Arrows	181	71	1	78				10	0

SRB – SERBIA SQUAD 2010 FIFA WORLD CUP

No	Pos	Name	Shirt Name	DoB	Club	Cms	Kg	Games	Mins	Goals	Y	R	Cap	Gls
1	GK	Vladimir STOJKOVIC	STOJKOVIC	28-07-1983	Wigan ENG	195	92	3	270	0			36	0
2	DF	Antonio RUKAVINA	RUKAVINA	26-01-1984	München 1860 GER	177	71	0	0	0			20	0
3	DF	Aleksandar KOLAROV	KOLAROV	10-11-1985	Lazio ITA	187	83	2	180	0	1		15	0
4	MF	Gojko KACAR	KACAR	26-01-1987	Hertha Berlin GER	185	83	1	20	0			18	0
5	DF	Nemanja VIDIC	VIDIC	21-10-1981	Manchester Utd ENG	185	84	3	270	0	1		48	2
6	DF	Branislav IVANOVIC	IVANOVIC	22-02-1984	Chelsea ENG	188	84	3	270	0	1		34	4
7	MF	Zoran TOSIC	TOSIC	28-04-1987	1.FC Köln GER	171	69	1	28	0			22	3
8	FW	Danko LAZOVIC	LAZOVIC	17-05-1983	Zenit RUS	185	79	3	45	0			40	10
9	FW	Marko PANTELIC	PANTELIC	15-09-1978	Ajax NED	181	75	2	113	1			34	7
10	MF	Dejan STANKOVIC	STANKOVIC	11-09-1978	Internazionale ITA	181	75	3	270	0			91	14
11	MF	Nenad MILIJAS	MILIJAS	30-04-1983	Wolves ENG	182	78	1	62	0			18	4
12	GK	Bojan ISAILOVIC	ISAILOVIC	25-03-1980	Zaglebie Lubin POL	192	86	0	0	0			4	0
13	DF	Aleksandar LUKOVIC	LUKOVIC	23-10-1982	Udinese ITA	184	73	2	164	0	1	1	23	0
14	MF	Milan JOVANOVIC	JOVANOVIC	18-04-1981	Standard CL BEL	183	76	3	245	1			29	10
15	FW	Nikola ZIGIC	ZIGIC	25-09-1980	Valencia ESP	202	96	3	226	0	1		48	16
16	DF	Ivan OBRADOVIC	OBRADOVIC	25-07-1988	Real Zaragoza ESP	181	74	1	90	0			13	1
17	MF	Milos KRASIC	KRASIC	01-11-1984	CSKA Moskva RUS	185	76	3	242	0			34	3
18	MF	Milos NINKOVIC	NINKOVIC	25-12-1984	Dynamo Kyiv UKR	179	75	2	160	0	1		11	0
19	MF	Radosav PETROVIC	PETROVIC	08-03-1989	Partizan	193	84	1	15	0			10	0
20	DF	Neven SUBOTIC	SUBOTIC	10-12-1988	Bor Dortmund GER	193	79	2	104	0	1		15	1
21	FW	Dragan MRDJA	MRDJA	23-01-1984	Vojvodina Novi Sad	187	77	0	0	0			6	2
22	MF	Zdravko KUZMANOVIC	KUZMANOVIC	22-09-1987	VfB Stuttgart GER	187	81	3	180	0	1		30	4
23	GK	Andjelko DJURICIC	DURICIC	21-11-1980	Leiria POR	194	83	0	0	0			1	0

SVK – SLOVAKIA SQUAD 2010 FIFA WORLD CUP

No	Pos	Name	Shirt Name	DoB	Club	Cms	Kg	Games	Mins	Goals	Y	R	Cap	Gls
1	GK	Jan MUCHA	MUCHA	5-12-1982	Legia Warsaw POL	189	88	4	360		1		19	0
2	DF	Peter PEKARIK	PEKARIK	30-10-1986	Wolfsburg GER	176	70	3	270		1		24	1
3	DF	Martin SKRTEL	SKRTEL	15-12-1984	Liverpool ENG	188	84	4	360		1		43	5
4	DF	Marek CECH	CECH	26-01-1983	West Brom ENG	181	75	1	90				41	5
5	DF	Radoslav ZABAVNIK	ZABAVNIK	16-09-1980	Mainz 05 GER	180	78	3	268				47	1
6	MF	Zdenko STRBA	STRBA	9-06-1976	Xanthi	187	81	3	267		2		24	0
7	MF	Vladimir WEISS	WEISS	30-11-1989	Manchester City ENG	176	70	3	269		1		12	0
8	MF	Jan KOZAK	KOZAK	22-04-1980	Timisoara ROU	192	86	1	90				25	2
9	FW	Stanislav SESTAK	SESTAK	16-12-1982	Bochum GER	178	72	3	152		1		36	11
10	MF	Marek SAPARA	SAPARA	31-07-1982	Ankaragucu TUR	176	73	1	3				26	2
11	FW	Robert VITTEK	VITTEK	1-04-1982	Ankaragucu TUR	188	84	4	353	4	1		74	23
12	GK	Dusan PERNIS	PERNIS	28-11-1984	Dundee Utd SCO	190	96	0	0				3	0
13	FW	Filip HOLOSKO	HOLOSKO	17-01-1984	Besiktas TUR	186	85	2	29				40	5
14	FW	Martin JAKUBKO	JAKUBKO	26-02-1980	FC Moskva RUS	193	95	1	2				25	4
15	MF	Miroslav STOCH	STOCH	19-10-1989	Twente Enschede NED	168	64	4	193				16	1
16	DF	Jan DURICA	DURICA	10-12-1981	Hannover 96 GER	187	86	4	360		1		43	1
17	MF	Marek HAMSIK	HAMSIK	27-07-1987	Napoli ITA	184	78	4	357				36	8
18	FW	Erik JENDRISEK	JENDRISEK	26-10-1986	Kaiserslautern GER	176	75	3	250				18	2
19	MF	Juraj KUCKA	KUCKA	26-02-1987	Sparta Praha CZE	186	85	3	181		1		9	0
20	MF	Kamil KOPUNEK	KOPUNEK	18-05-1984	Spartak Trnava	180	70	2	22	1	1		11	2
21	DF	Kornel SALATA	SALATA	24-01-1985	Slovan Bratislava	190	87	1	83				5	0
22	DF	Martin PETRAS	PETRAS	2-11-1979	Cesena ITA	187	82	1	1				39	1
23	GK	Dusan KUCIAK	KUCIAK	21-05-1985	Vaslui ROU	195	90	0	0				3	0

SVN – SLOVENIA SQUAD 2010 FIFA WORLD CUP

No	Pos	Name	Shirt Name	DoB	Club	Cms	Kg	Games	Mins	Goals	Y	R	Cap	Gls
1	GK	Samir HANDANOVIC	HANDANOVIC S.	14-07-1984	Udinese	193		3	270				42	0
2	DF	Miso BRECKO	BRECKO	1-05-1984	1.FC Köln GER	172		3	270				34	0
3	DF	Elvedin DZINIC	DZINIC	25-08-1985	Maribor	189		0	0				0	0
4	DF	Marko SULER	SULER	9-03-1983	KAA Gent BEL	187		3	270	1			20	2
5	DF	Bostjan CESAR	CESAR	9-07-1982	Grenoble FRA	190		3	270	1			45	3
6	DF	Branko ILIC	ILIC	6-02-1983	Lokomotiv Moskva RUS	186		0	0				37	0
7	FW	Nejc PECNIK	PECNIK	3-01-1986	Nacional POR	187		2	21				10	2
8	MF	Robert KOREN	KOREN	20-09-1980	West Brom ENG	173		3	270	1			49	5
9	FW	Zlatan LJUBIJANKIC	LJUBIJANKIC	15-12-1983	KAA Gent BEL	185		3	173	1			20	5
10	MF	Valter BIRSA	BIRSA	7-08-1986	Auxerre FRA	180		3	261	1	1		37	3
11	FW	Milivoje NOVAKOVIC	NOVAKOVIC	18-05-1979	1.FC Köln GER	191		3	270				41	16
12	GK	Jasmin HANDANOVIC	HANDANOVIC J.	28-01-1978	Mantova ITA	197		0	0				3	0
13	DF	Bojan JOKIC	JOKIC	17-05-1986	Chievo ITA	171		3	270		2		37	1
14	FW	Zlatko DEDIC	DEDIC	5-10-1984	Bochum GER	172		3	84		1		27	3
15	MF	Rene KRHIN	KRHIN	21-05-1990	Internazionale ITA	184		0	0				4	0
16	GK	Aleksander SELIGA	SELIGA	1-02-1980	Sparta Rotterdam NED	187		0	0				1	0
17	MF	Andraz KIRM	KIRM	6-09-1984	Wisla Krakow POL	185		3	259		1		29	3
18	MF	Aleksandar RADOSAVLJEVIC	RADOSAVLJEVIC	25-04-1979	Larissa GRE	181		3	267		1		18	1
19	DF	Suad FILEKOVIC	FILEKOVIC	16-09-1978	Maribor	190		0	0				13	0
20	MF	Andrej KOMAC	KOMAC	4-12-1979	Maccabi Tel-Aviv ISR	170		2	4		1		43	0
21	MF	Dalibor STEVANOVIC	STEVANOVIC	27-09-1984	Vitesse Arnhem NED	183		0	0				15	1
22	DF	Matej MAVRIC	MAVRIC	29-01-1979	TuS Koblenz GER	186		0	0				32	1
23	FW	Tim MATAVZ	MATAVZ	13-01-1989	Groningen NED	190		1	11				2	0

SUI – SWITZERLAND SQUAD 2010 FIFA WORLD CUP

No	Pos	Name	Shirt Name	DoB	Club	Cms	Kg	Games	Mins	Goals	Y	R	Cap	Gls
1	GK	Diego BENAGLIO	BENAGLIO	8-09-1983	Wolfsburg GER	193	83	3	270		1		30	0
2	DF	Stephan LICHTSTEINER	LICHTSTEINER	16-01-1984	Lazio ITA	180	75	3	270				31	0
3	DF	Ludovic MAGNIN	MAGNIN	20-04-1979	FC Zurich	186	79	0	0				62	3
4	DF	Philippe SENDEROS	SENDEROS	14-02-1985	Everton ENG	190	87	1	36				41	5
5	DF	Steve VON BERGEN	VON BERGEN	10-06-1983	Hertha Berlin GER	183	77	3	234				14	0
6	MF	Benjamin HUGGEL	HUGGEL	7-07-1977	Basel	190	90	3	258				41	2
7	MF	Tranquillo BARNETTA	BARNETTA	22-05-1985	B. Leverkusen GER	178	70	3	227		1		55	6
8	MF	Gokhan INLER	INLER	27-06-1984	Udinese ITA	183	79	3	270		1		39	3
9	FW	Alexander FREI	FREI	15-07-1979	Basel	180	73	2	63				77	40
10	FW	Blaise NKUFO	NKUFO	25-05-1975	Twente Enschede NED	186	84	3	227		1		34	7
11	MF	Valon BEHRAMI	BEHRAMI	19-04-1985	West Ham Utd ENG	184	71	1	31			1	28	2
12	GK	Marco WOELFLI	WÖLFLI	22-08-1982	Young Boys	185	83	0	0				5	0
13	DF	Stephane GRICHTING	GRICHTING	30-03-1979	Auxerre FRA	186	80	3	270		1		38	1
14	MF	Marco PADALINO	PADALINO	8-12-1983	Sampdoria ITA	177	72	0	0				8	1
15	MF	Hakan YAKIN	YAKIN	22-02-1977	Lucerne	180	79	2	56		1		83	20
16	MF	Gelson FERNANDES	FERNANDES	2-09-1986	Saint-Etienne FRA	183	70	3	212	1	1		27	2
17	DF	Reto ZIEGLER	ZIEGLER	16-01-1986	Sampdoria ITA	183	86	3	270		1		15	1
18	FW	Albert BUNJAKU	BUNJAKU	29-11-1983	1.FC Nürnberg GER	178	76	1	13				4	0
19	FW	Eren DERDIYOK	DERDIYOK	12-06-1988	B. Leverkusen GER	190	83	3	191				24	2
20	MF	Pirmin SCHWEGLER	SCHWEGLER	9-03-1987	Eint. Frankfurt GER	178	74	0	0				4	0
21	GK	Johnny LEONI	LEONI	30-06-1984	FC Zurich	189	80	0	0				0	0
22	DF	Mario EGGIMANN	EGGIMANN	24-01-1981	Hannover 96 GER	184	79	1	1				9	0
23	MF	Xherdan SHAQIRI	SHAQIRI	10-10-1991	Basel	169	70	1	12				4	0

URU – URUGUAY SQUAD 2010 FIFA WORLD CUP

No	Pos	Name	Shirt Name	DoB	Club	Cms	Kg	Games	Mins	Goals	Y	R	Cap	Gls
1	GK	Fernando MUSLERA	MUSLERA	16-06-1986	Lazio ITA	190	74	7	660				13	0
2	DF	Diego LUGANO	LUGANO	2-11-1980	Fenerbahce TUR	188	87	6	488				48	4
3	DF	Diego GODIN	GODIN	16-02-1986	Villarreal ESP	185	73	5	405		1		43	3
4	DF	Jorge FUCILE	FUCILE	19-11-1984	FC Porto POR	177	73	5	461		2		29	0
5	MF	Walter GARGANO	GARGANO	23-07-1984	Napoli ITA	168	65	3	104				31	0
6	DF	Mauricio VICTORINO	VICTORINO	11-10-1982	Univ. de Chile CHI	182	78	5	435		1		9	0
7	FW	Edinson CAVANI	CAVANI	14-02-1987	Palermo ITA	188	78	6	523	1			20	3
8	MF	Sebastian EGUREN	EGUREN	8-01-1981	AIK Stockholm SWE	186	84	1	3				28	5
9	FW	Luis SUAREZ	SUAREZ	24-01-1987	Ajax NED	181	81	6	542	3		1	36	13
10	FW	Diego FORLAN	FORLAN	19-05-1979	Atlético Madrid ESP	181	75	7	654	5			69	29
11	MF	Alvaro PEREIRA	A.PEREIRA	28-11-1985	FC Porto POR	182	75	5	409	1			20	3
12	GK	Juan CASTILLO	CASTILLO	17-04-1978	Deportivo Cali COL	181	77	0	0				11	0
13	FW	Sebastian ABREU	W.S.ABREU.G	17-10-1976	Botafogo BRA	193	84	4	74				60	26
14	MF	Nicolas LODEIRO	LODEIRO	21-03-1989	Ajax NED	173	71	3	109		1		7	0
15	MF	Diego PEREZ	PEREZ	18-05-1980	Monaco FRA	176	75	7	643		2		57	0
16	DF	Maximiliano PEREIRA	M.PEREIRA	8-06-1984	Benfica POR	173	73	7	660	1	1		44	1
17	MF	Egidio AREVALO	AREVALO RIOS	1-01-1982	Penarol	168	72	7	660		1		13	0
18	MF	Ignacio GONZALEZ	I.GONZALEZ	14-05-1982	Valencia ESP	180	73	1	63				18	1
19	DF	Andres SCOTTI	SCOTTI	14-12-1975	Colo Colo CHI	183	80	2	95				28	1
20	MF	Alvaro FERNANDEZ	A. FERNANDEZ	11-10-1985	Univ. de Chile CHI	185	72	4	75				11	0
21	FW	Sebastian FERNANDEZ	S.FERNANDEZ	23-05-1985	Banfield ARG	167	65	2	7				8	0
22	DF	Martin CACERES	CACERES	7-04-1987	Juventus ITA	178	75	2	180		1		21	0
23	GK	Martin SILVA	SILVA	25-03-1983	Defensor Sporting	187	82	0	0				1	0

USA – USA SQUAD 2010 FIFA WORLD CUP

No	Pos	Name	Shirt Name	DoB	Club	Cms	Kg	Games	Mins	Goals	Y	R	Cap	Gls
1	GK	Tim HOWARD	HOWARD	6-03-1979	Everton ENG	187	90	4	390				55	0
2	DF	Jonathan SPECTOR	SPECTOR	1-03-1986	West Ham Utd ENG	183	79	0	0				25	0
3	DF	Carlos BOCANEGRA	BOCANEGRA	25-05-1979	Rennes FRA	184	77	4	390		1		83	12
4	MF	Michael BRADLEY	BRADLEY	31-07-1987	Mönchengladbach GER	185	74	4	390	1			47	8
5	DF	Oguchi ONYEWU	ONYEWU	13-05-1982	Milan ITA	192	91	2	170				56	5
6	DF	Steve CHERUNDOLO	CHERUNDOLO	19-02-1979	Hannover 96 GER	168	66	4	390		2		64	2
7	MF	DaMarcus BEASLEY	BEASLEY	24-05-1982	Rangers SCO	170	64	1	10		1		93	17
8	MF	Clint DEMPSEY	DEMPSEY	9-03-1983	Fulham ENG	185	77	4	390	1			66	19
9	FW	Herculez GOMEZ	GOMEZ	6-04-1982	Puebla MEX	178	75	3	84				7	2
10	MF	Landon DONOVAN	DONOVAN	4-03-1982	LA Galaxy	173	67	4	390	3			126	45
11	MF	Stuart HOLDEN	HOLDEN	1-08-1985	Bolton Wand. ENG	178	73	1	4				15	2
12	DF	Jonathan BORNSTEIN	BORNSTEIN	7-11-1984	Chivas USA	175	66	2	200				34	2
13	MF	Ricardo CLARK	CLARK	10-02-1983	Eint. Frankfurt GER	178	75	2	121		1		31	2
14	FW	Edson BUDDLE	BUDDLE	21-05-1981	LA Galaxy	185	77	2	39				4	2
15	DF	Jay DeMERIT	DEMERIT	4-12-1979	Watford ENG	180	82	4	390		1		23	0
16	MF	Francisco TORRES	TORRES	29-10-1987	Pachuca MEX	168	62	1	45				11	0
17	FW	Jozy ALTIDORE	ALTIDORE	6-11-1989	Hull City ENG	185	91	4	357		1		29	9
18	GK	Brad GUZAN	GUZAN	9-09-1984	Aston Villa ENG	193	95	0	0				16	0
19	MF	Maurice EDU	EDU	18-04-1986	Rangers SCO	183	77	3	198				16	1
20	FW	Robbie FINDLEY	FINDLEY	4-08-1985	Real Salt Lake	175	75	3	167		2		9	0
21	DF	Clarence GOODSON	GOODSON	17-05-1982	IK Start NOR	193	77	0	0				14	2
22	MF	Benny FEILHABER	FEILHABER	19-01-1985	AGF Aarhus DEN	175	68	3	165				35	2
23	GK	Marcus HAHNEMANN	HAHNEMANN	15-06-1972	Wolves ENG	192	99	0	0				8	0

KEY

No = Shirt number • Pos = position (GK = goalkeeper • DF = defender • MF = midfielder • FW = forward) • Shirt name = the name that appears on the players shirt • DoB = date of birth • Club = player's club • Cms = height of the player in centimetres • Kg = weight of the player in kilogrammes • Games = games played during the 2010 FIFA World Cup finals • Mins = minutes played during the finals • Goals = goals scored during the finals • Y = Yellow cards received during the finals • R = red cards received during the finals (the award of two yellows in a match is considered as one red. A straight red ard is indicated in bold) • Cap = number of appearances made by the player in all international matches before the kick-off of the 2010 FIFA World Cup • Gls = number of goals scored by the player in all international matches before the kick-off of the 2010 FIFA World Cup.

FIFA U-20 WOMEN'S WORLD CUP GERMANY 2010

FIFA U-20 WOMEN'S WORLD CUP GERMANY 2010

First round groups	Pts	Quarter-finals		Semi-finals		Final	
Germany	9						
Colombia	4	**Germany**	2				
France	4	Korea DPR	0				
Costa Rica	0						
				Germany	5		
	Pts			Korea Republic	1		
Sweden	7						
Korea DPR	6	Mexico	1				
Brazil	4	**Korea Republic**	3				
New Zealand	0						
						Germany	2
	Pts					Nigeria	0
Mexico	5						
Nigeria	5	**Colombia**	2				
Japan	4	Sweden	0				
England	1						
				Colombia	0		
	Pts			**Nigeria**	1		
USA	7					**3rd Place Play-off**	
Korea Republic	6	USA	1 2p			**Korea Republic**	1
Ghana	4	**Nigeria**	1 4p			Colombia	0
Switzerland	0						

Top scorers: **10** - Alexandra Popp GER • **8** - Ji So Yun KOR • **5** - Sydney Leroux USA • **4** - Antonia Goransson SWE • **3** - Elizabeth Cudjoe GHA; Marina Makanza FRA & Lee Hyun Young KOR

GROUP A	PL	W	D	L	F	A	PTS		COL	FRA	CRC
1 Germany	3	3	0	0	11	4	9		3-1	4-1	4-2
2 Colombia	3	1	1	1	5	4	4			1-1	3-0
3 France	3	1	1	1	4	5	4				2-0
4 Costa Rica	3	0	0	3	2	9	0				

GROUP B	PL	W	D	L	F	A	PTS		PRK	BRA	NZL
1 Sweden	3	2	1	0	6	4	7		3-2	1-1	2-1
2 Korea DPR	3	2	0	1	5	4	6			1-0	2-1
3 Brazil	3	1	1	1	5	3	4				4-1
4 New Zealand	3	0	0	3	3	8	0				

GROUP C	PL	W	D	L	F	A	PTS		NGA	JPN	ENG
1 Mexico	3	1	2	0	5	4	5		1-1	3-3	1-0
2 Nigeria	3	1	2	0	4	3	5			2-1	1-1
3 Japan	3	1	1	1	7	6	4				3-1
4 England	3	0	1	2	2	5	1				

GROUP D	PL	W	D	L	F	A	PTS		KOR	GHA	SUI
1 USA	3	2	1	0	7	1	7		1-0	1-1	5-0
2 Korea Republic	3	2	0	1	8	3	6			4-2	4-0
3 Ghana	3	1	1	1	5	5	4				2-0
4 Switzerland	3	0	0	3	0	11	0				

GROUP A

Bochum
13-07-2010, 11:30, 23 995, Hong Eun Ah KOR

Germany   **4**

Huth [2], Popp 2 [16 53], Hegering [57]

Almuth **Schult** - Tabea **Kemme** (Stefanie **Mirlach** 21), Marith **Priessen**, Kristina **Gessat**, Marina **Hegering** (c), Svenja **Huth** (Inka **Wesely** 74), Alexandra **Popp**, Sylvia **Arnold**, Turid **Knaak** (Jessica **Wich** 62), Kim **Kulig•**, Bianca **Schmidt♦71**. Tr: Maren **Meinert**

Costa Rica   **2**

Venegas [45], Katherine Alvarado [72p]

Priscilla **Tapia** - Mariela **Campos** (Paola **Alvarado** 46), Daniela **Cruz•**, Carolina **Venegas**, Katherine **Alvarado•** (c), Raquel **Rodriguez Cedeno**, Raquel **Rodriguez Vasquez•**, Yocxelin **Rodriguez•** (Monica **Vargas** 61), Ana **Aguilar** (Maria **Moreira** 84), Fabiola **Sanchez**, Hazel **Quiros•**. Tr: Randall **Chacon**

Bochum
16-07-2010, 15:00, 15 545, Damkova CZE

Costa Rica   **0**

Priscilla **Tapia** - Mariela **Campos** (Paola **Alvarado** 73), Daniela **Cruz**, Carolina **Venegas**, Katherine **Alvarado•** (c), Raquel **Rodriguez Cedeno**, Raquel **Rodriguez Vasquez**, Yocxelin **Rodriguez**, Ana **Aguilar** (Monica **Vargas** 65), Fabiola **Sanchez** (Maria **Moreira** 83), Hazel **Quiros**. Tr: Randall **Chacon**

France   **2**

Makanza 2 [67 83]

Laetitia **Philippe** - Annaig **Butel**, Kelly **Gadea** (c), Adeline **Rousseau** (Solene **Barbance** 46), Pauline **Crammer**, Fanny **Tenret** (Ines **Jaurena** 46), Caroline **La Villa•**, Alexandra **Plantive**, Aude **Moreau**, Amelie **Barbetta**, Camilla **Catala** (Marina **Makanza** 61). Tr: Jean Michel **Degrange**

Bochum
13-07-2010, 14:30, 2500, Fukando JPN

Colombia   **1**

Andrade [86]

Paula **Forero** - Natalia **Gaitan** (c), Natalia **Ariza**, Ingrid **Vidal** (Katerin **Castro** 74), Paola **Sanchez** (Ana Maria **Montoya** 67), Yorely **Rincon**, Liana **Salazar**, Yulieht **Dominguez**, (Lina **Taborda** 61), Tatiana **Ariza**, Lady **Andrade•**, Carolina **Arias**. Tr: Ricardo **Rozo**

France   **1**

Makanza [16]

Laetitia **Philippe**, Charlotte **Bilbault** (Annaig **Butel** 66), Kelly **Gadea**, Lea **Rubio**, Marina **Makanza**, Audrey **Fevrier** (c), Solene **Barbance** (Camille **Catala** 66), Caroline **La Villa**, Ines **Jaurena**, Rose **Lavaud** (Pauline **Crammer** 58), Marion **Torrent**. Tr: Jean Michel **Degrange**

Augsburg
20-07-2010, 11:30, 26 273, Ihringova ENG

France   **1**

Crammer [49]

Laetitia **Philippe** - Charlotte **Bilbauly** (c), Kelly **Gadea**, Adeline **Rousseau**, Lea **Rubio**, Audrey **Fevrier** (Annaig **Butel** 46), Solene **Barbance**, Fanny **Tenret** (Marina **Makanza** 46), Alexandra **Plantive** (Pauline **Crammer** 46), Ines **Jaurena**, Amelie **Barbetta•**. Tr: Jean Michel **Degrange**

Germany   **4**

Popp 3 [10 35 60], Marozsan [73]

Desiree **Schumann** - Stefanie **Mirlach**, Marith **Priessen•**, Kristina **Gessat**, Marina **Hegering** (c) (Kim **Kulig** 46), Selina **Wagner**, Svenja **Huth** (Anne **Bartke** 76), Dzsenifer **Marozsan**, Alexandra **Popp**, Turid **Knaak** (Jessica **Wich** 46), Bianca **Schmidt**. Tr: Maren **Meinert**

Bochum
16-07-2010, 18:00, 15 545, Chenard CAN

Germany   **3**

Popp [21], Arnold [50], Hegering [55]

Almuth **Schult** - Stefanie **Mirlach**, Marith **Priessen**, Kristina **Gessat**, Marina **Hegering** (c), Svenja **Huth** (Selina **Wagner** 62), Dzsenifer **Marozsan**, Alexandra **Popp**, Sylvia **Arnold** (Turid **Knaak** 67), Inka **Wesely**, Kim **Kulig** (Marie-Louise **Bagehorn** 75). Tr: Maren **Meinert**

Colombia   **1**

Ortiz [81]

Paula **Forero** - Natalia **Gaitan** (c), Natalia **Ariza**, Katerin **Castro** (Melissa **Ortiz** 59), Yorely **Rincon**, Liana **Salazar** (Vanessa **Aponte** 75), Yulieht **Dominguez•**, Tatiana **Ariza** (Daniela **Montoya** 82), Lady **Andrade**, Carolina **Arias**, Ana Maria **Montoya**. Tr: Ricardo **Rozo**

Dresden
20-07-2010, 11:30, 12 863, Dorcioman ROU

Costa Rica   **0**

Priscilla **Tapia** - Mariela **Campos** (Daniela **Vega** 64), Paola **Alvarado**, Daniela **Cruz**, Carolina **Venegas**, Katherine **Alvarado•** (c), Raquel **Rodriguez Cedeno**, Raquel **Rodriguez Vasquez**, Yocxelin **Rodriguez**, Fabiola **Sanchez** (Maria **Moreira** 17). Tr: Randall **Chacon**

Colombia   **3**

Montoya 2 [24 40], Rincon [93+p]

Paula **Forero** - Lina **Taborda**, Natalia **Gaitan•** (c), Daniela **Montoya**, Ingrid **Vidal** (Karerin **Castro** 77), Paola **Sanchez**, Yorely **Rincon•**, Lady **Andrade**, Carolina **Arias**, Vanessa **Aponte** (Liana **Salazar** 61), Melissa **Ortiz** (Tatiana **Ariza** 49). Tr: Ricardo **Rozo**

GROUP B

Bielefeld
13-07-2010, 11:30, 10 065, Ihringova ENG

Brazil 0

Aline - Juliana **Cardozo**, Estergiane (c), Bruna, **Rafaelle**, Ketlen (Rafaela 66), Camila (**Thaynara** 57), Lanna, **Andressa**, Aline Fernanda, Poliana (**Leah** 60). Tr: Marcos Gaspar

Korea DPR 1
Ho Un Byol [69]

Hong Myong Hui - **Hyon** Un Hui, **Yun** Song Mi, **Won** Un Ha, **Choe** Un Ju, **Choe** Mi Gyong, **Kim** Myong Gum (**Kim** Un Hyang 58), **Kim** Chung Sim (c), **Yun** Hyon Hi (**Ho** Un Byol 49), **Jon** Myong Hwa (**Kim** Un Ju 89), **Sin** Sol Ryon. Tr: **Choe** Kwang Sok

Bielefeld
16-07-2010, 18:00, 6630, Tagoe GHA

Korea DPR 2
Yun Hyon Hi [12], Kim Un Hyang [65p]

Hong Myong Hui - **Hyon** Un Hui, **Yun** Song Mi, **Won** Un Ha, **Choe** Un Ju, **Choe** Mi Gyong (**Kim** Un Ju 84), **Kim** Myong Gum, **Kim** Chung Sim (c) (**Kim** Un Hyang 60), **Yun** Hyon Hi (**Ho** Un Byol 48), **Jon** Myong Hwa, **Sin** Sol Ryon. Tr: **Choe** Kwang Sok

New Zealand 1
Armstrong [90]

Erin **Nayler** - Anna **Green** (c), Briony **Fisher**, Bridgette **Armstrong**, Hannah **Wilkinson**•, Betsy **Hassett**, Hannah **Wall**, Annalie **Longo** (Terri Amber Carlson 85), Rosie **White**, Nadia **Pearl** (Claudia Crasborn 77), Renee **Leota**. Tr: Tony **Readings**

Bielefeld
13-07-2010, 14:30, 10 065, Chenard CAN

Sweden 2
Goransson 2 [56] [67]

Hilda **Carlen** - Catrine **Johansson**, Emma **Kullberg**, Elin **Borg**, Mia **Karlsson**, Emilia **Appelqvist** (c), Sofia **Jakobsson**, Tilda **Heimersson**, Olivia **Schough** (Kristin **Karlsson** 68), Antonia **Goransson** (Amanda Wegerman 75), Jennifer **Egelryd** (Josefine Alfsson 59). Tr: Calle **Barrling**

New Zealand 1
Wilkinson [33]

Erin **Nayler** - Anna **Green** (c), Chelsey **Wood** (Nadia **Pearl** 72), Briony **Fisher**, Bridgette **Armstrong**, Hannah **Wilkinson** (Sarah McLaughlin 72), Betsy **Hassett**•, Hannah **Wall**, Annalie **Longo** (Claudia Crasborn 84), Rosie **White**, Renee **Leota**. Tr: Tony **Readings**

Dresden
20-07-2010, 14:30, 12 863, Damkova CZE

New Zealand 1
White [89]

Erin **Nayler** - Elizabeth **Milne** (Hannah **Wilkinson** 46), Anna **Green** (c), Briony **Fisher**•, Bridgette **Armstrong**, Betsy **Hassett**, Hannah **Wall**, Annalie **Longo**, Rosie **White**, Nadia **Pearl** (Sarah McLaughlin 46), Renee **Leota** (Chelsey **Wood** 72). Tr: Tony **Readings**

Brazil 4
Ludmila [25], Leah [59], Debora 2 [87] [90]

Aline - **Leah**, Juliana **Cardozo**, Estergiane (c), **Rafaelle**, Camila, Alanna, **Andressa** (**Edna** 41), Aline Fernanda, **Thaynara**, **Ludmila** (**Debora** 74). Tr: Marcos Gaspar

Bielefeld
16-07-2010, 15:00, 6630, Hong Eun Ah KOR

Brazil 1
Rafaelle [53p]

Aline - **Leah**, Juliana **Cardozo**•, Estergiane (c), **Rafaelle**, Ketlen (Ludmila 46), Camila, Alanna (Rafaela 80), **Andressa** (Edna 63), Aline Fernanda, **Thaynara**. Tr: Marcos Gaspar

Sweden 1
Goransson [36]

Hilda **Carlen**• - Catrine **Johansson**, Emma **Kullberg**, Elin **Borg** (Amanda **Ilestedt** 34), Mia **Karlsson**, Emilia **Appelqvist** (c), Josefine **Alfsson**•, Sofia **Jakobsson** (Amanda **Wegerman** 82), Tilda **Heimersson**, Olivia **Schough** (Kristin **Karlsson** 50), Antonia **Goransson**. Tr: Calle **Barrling**

Augsburg
20-07-2010, 14:30, 26 273, Chenard CAN

Korea DPR 2
Kim Myong Gum [26], Jon Myong Hwa [62]

Hong Myong Hui - **Hyon** Un Hui, **Yun** Song Mi, **Won** Un Ha, **Choe** Un Ju, **Choe** Mi Gyong (**Kim** Un Ju 60), **Kim** Myong Gum (**Kim** Un Hyang 81), **Kim** Chung Sim (c), **Yun** Hyon Hi (**Ho** Un Byol 55), **Jon** Myong Hwa, **Sin** Sol Ryon. Tr: **Choe** Kwang Sok

Sweden 3
Jakobsson [43], Goransson [52], Hyon UH OG [75]

Hilda **Carlen** - Emma **Kullberg**, Elin **Borg**, Mia **Karlsson**, Emilia **Appelqvist** (c), Josefine **Alfsson**, Sofia **Jakobsson** (Emilie **Lovgren** 91), Tilda **Heimersson** (Sarah **Stork** 83), Amanda **Ilestedt**, Antonia **Goransson**, Kristin **Karlsson** (Jessica **Samuelsson** 89). Tr: Calle **Barrling**

GROUP C

Augsburg
14-07-2010, 11:30, 2400, Palmqvist SWE

England 1
Harrop [45]

Rebecca **Spencer** - Chelsea **Weston**, Jade **Moore**, Kerys **Harrop**, Jessica **Holbrook** (Lucy **Stanforth** 6), Jordan **Nobbs**, Toni **Duggan**, Michelle **Hinnigan** (c) (Danielle **Carter** 63), Lyndsey **Cunningham**, Lucy **Bronze**, Isobel **Christiansen** (Demi **Stokes** 75). Tr: Mo **Marley**

Nigeria 1
Oparanozie [60]

Alaba **Jonathan** - Martina **Ohadugha**, Esther **Sunday**, Ebere **Orji** (Charity **Adule** 69), Desire **Oparanozie**, Rebecca **Kalu**, Glory **Iroka** (Amarachi **Okoronkwo** 51), Soo **Adekwagh**, Joy **Jegede** (c), Helen **Ukaonu**, Osinachi **Ohale** (Blessing **Edoho** 48).Tr: Ndem **Egan**

Augsburg
14-07-2010, 14:30, 2400, Steinhaus GER

Mexico 3
Cuellar [31], Corral [41], Rangel [45]

Cecilia **Santiago** - Alina **Garciamendez**, Valeria **Miranda**, Kenti **Robles** (Bianca **Sierra** 87), Nayeli **Rangel** (c), Mirelle **Arciniega** (Angelica **Figueroa** 41), Stephany **Mayor**•, Charlyn **Corral** (Olivia **Jimenez** 72), Renae **Cuellar**, Monica **Alvarado**, Natalie **Garcia**. Tr: Roberto **Medina**

Japan 3
Takase [19], Cuellar OG [64], Iwabuchi [88]

Erina **Yamane** - Natsuki **Kishikawa**, Saki **Kumagai** (c), Yuria **Obara** (Sawako **Yasumoto** 63), Nozomi **Fujita**, Megumi **Takase**, Mana **Iwabuchi**, Emi **Nakajima**, Yuka **Kado**, Ayano **Dozono** (Yuika **Sugasawa** 72), Shoko **Yamada**. Tr: Norio **Sasaki**

Augsburg
17-07-2010, 18:00, 3100, Reyes PER

England 0

Rebecca **Spencer** - Chelsea **Weston**, Gilly **Flaherty**, Jade **Moore**, Kerys **Harrop**, Jordan **Nobbs**, Toni **Duggan**, Michelle **Hinnigan** (c) (Rebecca **Jane** 86), Demi **Stokes** (Lucy **Stanforth** 64), Lucy **Bronze**, Isobel **Christiansen** (Danielle **Carter** 78). Tr: Mo **Marley**

Mexico 1
Cuellar [62]

Cecilia **Santiago** - Bianca **Sierra**, Alina **Garciamendez**, Kenti **Robles**, Nayeli **Rangel** (c), Stephany **Mayor**, Charlyn **Corral** (Natalia Gomez **Junco** 88), Renae **Cuellar** (Ashley **Kotero** 90), Monica **Alvarado** (Olivia **Jimenez** 26), Natalie **Garcia**, Mar **Rodriguez**. Tr: Roberto **Medina**

Augsburg
17-07-2010, 15:00, 3100, Dorcioman ROU

Nigeria 2
Okoronkwo [6], Oparanozie [17]

Alaba **Jonathan** - Martina **Ohadugha**, Esther **Sunday** (Charity **Adule** 71), Ebere **Orji**, Desire **Oparanozie**, Rebecca **Kalu**, Soo **Adekwagh** (Cecelia **Nku** 66), Joy **Jegede** (c), Amarachi **Okoronkwo**, Helen **Ukaonu**, Osinachi **Ohale**. Tr: Ndem **Egan**

Japan 1
Iwabuchi [62]

Erina **Yamane** - Natsuki **Kishikawa**, Saki **Kumagai** (c), Yuria **Obara** (Yuika **Sugasawa** 46), Nozomi **Fujita**, Megumi **Takase**•, Mana **Iwabuchi**, Emi **Nakajima**, Yuka **Kado**, Ayano **Dozono** (Michi **Goto** 63), Shoko **Yamada**. Tr: Norio **Sasaki**

Bielefeld
21-07-2010, 15:00, 5420, Tagoe GHA

Japan 3
Nakajima [20], Kishikawa 2 [74] [78]

Erina **Yamane** - Misaki **Kobayashi**, Natsuki **Kishika** (Shiori **Kinoshita** 90), Saki **Kumagai** (c), Yuria **Obara** (Yuko **Takeyama** 91), Nozomi **Fujita**, Megumi **Takase**, Mana **Iwabuchi** (Nanami **Seguchi** 89), Emi **Nakajima**, Yuka **Kado**•, Akane **Saito**•. Tr: Norio **Sasaki**

England 1
Duggan [83p]

Rebecca **Spencer** - Chelsea **Weston**, Gilly **Flaherty** (Rebecca **Jane** 76), Jade **Moore**, Kerys **Harrop**, Jordan **Nobbs**, Toni **Duggan**, Michelle **Hinnigan** (c) (Danielle **Carter** 52), Demi **Stokes**, Lucy **Bronze**, Isobel **Christiansen** (Lucy **Stanforth** 63). Tr: Mo **Marley**

Bochum
21-07-2010, 15:00, 2450, Pedersen NOR

Nigeria 1
Orji [16]

Alaba **Jonathan** - Martina **Ohadugha** (Charity **Adule** 88), Cecilia **Nku**, Esther **Sunday**, Ebere **Orji** (Ngozi **Ebere** 46) (Uchechi **Sunday** 68), Desire **Oparanozie**, Rebecca **Kalu**, Joy **Jegede** (c), Amarachi **Okoronkwo**, Helen **Ukaonu**, Osinachi **Ohale**. Tr: Ndem **Egan**

Mexico 1
Garciamendez [77]

Cecilia **Santiago** - Bianca **Sierra**, Alina **Garciamendez**, Kenti **Robles**, Nayeli **Rangel** (c), Stephany **Mayor**, Charlyn **Corral** (Olivia **Jimenez** 46), Renae **Cuellar**, Angelica **Figueroa** (Natalia Gomez **Junco** 59), Natalie **Garcia**, Mar **Rodriguez** (Ana **Cruz** 74). Tr: Roberto **Medina**

GROUP D

Dresden
14-07-2010, 18:00, 9430, Damkova CZE

USA	**1**
	Leroux [70]

Bianca **Henninger** - Toni **Pressley**, Rachel **Quon**, Crystal **Dunn**, Kendall **Johnson**, Vicki **DiMartino** (Maya **Hayes** 46), Kristie **Mewis**, Christine **Nairn** (Teresa **Noyola** 54), Zakiya **Bywaters** (Courtney **Verloo** 77), Sydney **Leroux** (c), Amber **Brooks**. Tr: Jill **Ellis**

Ghana	**1**
	Cudjoe [7]

Patricia **Mantey** - Janet **Egyir**, Rosemary **Ampem**, Elizabeth **Cudjoe** (Samira **Suleman** 67), Florence **Dadson**, Deborah **Afriyie**, Mantenn **Kobblah**, Mercy **Myles** (c) (Elizabeth **Addo** 35), Juliet **Acheampong**, Faiza **Ibrahim**• (Janet **Owusu** 83), Edem **Atovor**. Tr: James **Dadzie**

Dresden
14-07-2010, 15:00, 9430, Reyes PER

Switzerland	**0**

Nathalie **Schwery** - Sarah **Sreinmann**, Danique **Stein** (c), Selina **Kuster**, Chantal **Fimian**, Ana **Crnogorcevic** (Nadine **Baker** 77), Ramona **Bachmann**•, Samira **Susuri**, Michelle **Probst** (Lara **Keller** 57), Lia **Waeltu**, Jehona **Mehmeti** (Cinzia **Joerg** 69). Tr: Yannick **Schwery**

Korea Republic	**4**
	Ji So Sun 3 [34 52 64], Lee Hyun Young [42]

Moon So Ri - **Seo** Hyun Sook, **Lim** Seon Joo, **Jeong** Yeonga, **Kim Narae** (**Kwon** Eun Som 78), **Jung** Hae In (**Kang** Yumi 66), **Ji** So Yun, **Lee** Hyun Young (**Jeoun** Eun Ha 74), **Lee** Min A, **Kim** Jin Young, **Kim** Hye Ri (c). Tr: **Choi** In Cheul

Dresden
17-07-2010, 18:00, 17 234, Fukano JPN

USA	**5**
	Mewis [4], Leroux 3 [23 52 76], Bywaters [25]

Bianca **Henninger** - Toni **Pressley**, Rachel **Quon**, Crystal **Dunn**, Kendall **Johnson**, Kristie **Mewis**, Christine **Nairn** (c), Zakiya **Bywaters** (Mollie **Pathman** 70), Maya **Hayes** (Meg **Morris**• 78), Sydney **Leroux** (Sam **Mewis** 81), Amber **Brooks**. Tr: Jill **Ellis**

Switzerland	**0**

Nathalie **Schwery** - Sarah **Steinmann**, Muriel **Bouakaz** (Cinzia **Joerg** 46), Danique **Stein** (c), Selina **Kuster**, Lara **Keller**, Chantal **Fimian**, Ana **Crnogorcevic**, Ramona **Bachmann** (Cora **Canetta** 74), Lia **Waelti**, Jehona **Mehmeti** (Rahel **Kiwic** 46). Tr: Yannick **Schwery**

Dresden
17-07-2010, 15:00, 17 234, Pedersen NOR

Ghana	**2**
	Afriye [28], Cudjoe [56]

Patricia **Mantey** - Janet **Egyir**, Rosemary **Ampem**, Elizabeth **Cudjoe** (Samira **Suleman** 91), Elizabeth **Addo**, Florence **Dadson**, Deborah **Afriyie** (Faiza **Ibrahim** 89), Mantenn **Kobblah**, Mercy **Myles** (c) (Priscilla **Saahene** 76), Juliet **Acheampong**, Edem **Atovor**. Tr: James **Dadzie**

Korea Republic	**4**
Ji So Yun 2 [41 87], Kim Narae [62], Kim Jin Young [70]	

Moon So Ri - **Seo** Hyun Sook, **Lim** Seon Joo, **Jeong** Yeonga, **Kim Narae**•, **Jung** Hae In (**Lee** Young Ju• 82), **Ji** So Yun, **Lee** Hyun Young (**Jeoun** Eun Ha 64), **Lee** Min A (**Kwon** Eun Som 73), **Kim** Jin Young, **Kim** Hye Ri (c). Tr: **Choi** In Cheul

Bielefeld
21-07-2010, 18:00, 5420, Steinhaus GER

Korea Republic	**0**

Moon So Ri - **Seo** Hyun Sook, **Lim** Seon Joo, **Jeong** Yeonga, **Kwon** Eun Som, **Jung** Hae In, **Lee** Hyun Young (**Ji** So Yun 46), **Lee** Young Ju (**Lee** Min A 64), **Kang** Yumi, **Jeoun** Eun Ha (**Kim** Jin Young 56), **Kim** Hye Ri (c). Tr: **Choi** In Cheul

USA	**1**
	Leroux [21]

Bianca **Henninger** - Toni **Pressley**, Rachel **Quon**, Crystal **Dunn**, Kendall **Johnson**, Kristie **Mewis**, Christine **Nairn**, Zakiya **Bywaters** (Courtney **Verloo** 69), Maya **Hayes** (Teresa **Noyola** 57), Sydney **Leroux** (c) (Meg **Morris** 86), Amber **Brooks**. Tr: Jill **Ellis**

Bochum
21-07-2010, 18:00, 2450, Guillemin FRA

Ghana	**2**
	Addo [31], Cudjoe [42]

Patricia **Mantey** - Janet **Egyir** (Cynthia **Adobia** 25), Rosemary **Ampem**, Elizabeth **Cudjoe** (Mercy **Myles** 76), Elizabeth **Addo** (c), Florence **Dadson**, Deborah **Afriyie** (Samira **Suleman** 58), Mantenn **Kobblah**, Juliet **Acheampong**, Edem **Atovor**, Janet **Owusu**. Tr: James **Dadie**

Switzerland	**0**

Pascale **Kueffer** - Carolyn **Mallaun** (Cora **Canetta** 46), Sarah **Steinmann**, Muriel **Bouakaz** (c), Lara **Keller**, Chantal **Fimian** (Nadine **Baker** 83), Ana **Crnogorcevic**, Samira **Susuri**, Michelle **Probst**, Lia **Waelti** (Cinzia **Joerg** 60), Vanessa **Pittet**. Tr: Yannick **Schwery**

QUARTER-FINALS

Bochum
24-07-2010, 18:00, 16 946, Reyes PER

Germany	**2**
	Popp [43], Arnold [69]

Almuth **Schult** - Tabea **Kemme**, Marith **Priessen**, Kristina **Gessat**, Marina **Hegering** (c), Svenja **Huth** (Selina **Wagner** 86), Dzsenifer **Marozsan**•, Alexandra **Popp**, Sylvia **Arnold** (Turid **Knaak** 80), Kim **Kulig**, Bianca **Schmidt**. Tr: Maren **Meinert**

Korea DPR	**0**

Hong Myong Hui - **Hyon** Un Hui•, **Jo** Myong Hui, **Yun** Song Mi, **Choe** Un Ju, **Choe** Mi Gyong••◆53, Kim Myong Gum (**Ho** Un Byol• 72), **Kim** Chung Sim (c), **Yun** Hyon Hi, **Jon** Myong Hwa (**Kim** Un Hyang 80), **Sin** Sol Ryon. Tr: **Choe** Kwang Sok

Dresden
25-07-2010, 18:30, 21 146, Damkova CZE

Mexico	**1**
	Gomez Junco [83]

Cecilia **Santiago** - Bianca **Sierra** (Ashley **Kotero** 78), Alina **Garciamendez**, Kenti **Robles**, Nayeli **Rangel**, Stephany **Mayor**, Charlyn **Corral**, Renae **Cuellar**, Monica **Alvarado** (Olivia **Jimenez** 88), Natalie **Garcia**, Mar **Rodriguez** (Natalia Gomez **Junco** 52). Tr: Roberto **Medina**

Korea Republic	**3**
	Lee Hyun Young 2 [14 67], Ji So Yun [28]

Moom So Ri - **Seo** Hyun Sook, **Lim** Seon Joo (**Koh** Kyung Yeon 84), **Jeong** Yeonga, **Kim** Narae, **Jung** Hae In, **Ji** So Yun, **Lee** Hyun Young (**Jeoun** Eun Ha 76), **Lee** Min A (**Kwon** Eun Som 56), **Kim** Jin Young, **Kim** Hye Ri (c). Tr: **Choi** In Cheul

Bielefeld
24-07-2010, 11:30, 4735, Hong Eun Ah KOR

Sweden	**0**

Hilda **Carlen** - Emma **Kullberg**, Elin **Borg** (Cartine **Johansson** 26), Mia **Karlsson**, Emilia **Appelqvist** (c), Josefine **Alfsson** (Sarah **Stork**• 78), Sofia **Jakobsson**, Tilda **Heimersson**, Amanda **Ilestedt**, Antonia **Goransson**, Kristin **Karlsson** (Olivia **Schough** 55). Tr: Calle **Barrling**

Colombia	**2**
	Rincon [11], Ariza [22]

Paula **Forero** - Natalia **Gaitan** (c), Natalia **Ariza**, Daniela **Montoya** (Melissa **Ortiz** 83), Paola **Sanchez** (Ana Maria **Montoya** 88), Yorely **Rincon**, Liana **Salazar**, Yulieth **Dominguez**, Tatiana **Ariza**, Lady **Andrade**• (Ingrid **Vidal** 93+), Carolina **Arias**. Tr: Ricardo **Rozo**

Augsburg
25-07-2010, 11:30, 7135, Ihrinova ENG

USA	**1 2p**
	Brooks [9]

Bianca **Henninger** - Toni **Pressley**, Rachel **Quon**, Crystal **Dunn**, Kendall **Johnson**, Kristie **Mewis**, Christine **Nairn** (c), Zakiya **Bywaters** (Maya **Hayes** 70) (Meg **Morris** 106), Casey **Short** (Mollie **Pathman** 66), Sydney **Leroux**, Amber **Brooks**. Tr: Jill **Ellis**

Nigeria	**1 4p**
	Ukaonu [79]

Alaba **Jonathan** - Cecilia **Nku**, Ebere **Orji** (Ngozi **Ebere** 114), Desire **Oparanozie**•, Rebecca **Kalu**, Glory **Iroka**, Joy **Jegede** (c), Amarachi **Okoronkwo**• (Esther **Sunday** 68), Helen **Ukaonu**, Charity **Adule**•, Osinachi **Ohale**•. Tr: Ndem **Egan**

SEMI-FINALS

Bochum
29-07-2010, 15:30, 18 217, Reyes PER

Germany   **5**

Huth [13], Kulig 2 [26 53], Popp 2 [50 67p]

Almuth **Schult** - Tabea **Kemme**, Marith **Priessen**, Kristina **Gessat**, Marina **Hegering** (c) (Stefanie **Mirlach** 70), Svenja **Huth**, Dzsenifer **Marozsan**, Alexandra **Popp** (Selina **Wagner** 76), Sylvia **Arnold**, Kim **Kulig** (Valeria **Kleiner**• 80), Bianca **Schmidt**. Tr: Maren Meinert

Korea Republic   **1**

Ji So Yun [64]

Moon So Ri - **Seo** Hyun Sook, **Lim** Seon Joo (**Kwon** Eun Som 57), **Jeong** Yeonga, **Kim** Narae, **Jung** Hae In (**Jeoun** Eun Ha• 62), **Ji** So Yun, **Lee** Hyun Young, **Lee** Min A, **Kim** Jin Young (**Lee** Young Ju 81), **Kim** Hye Ri (c). Tr: **Choi** In Cheul

Bielefeld
29-07-2010, 18:30, 7 040, Pedersen NOR

Colombia   **0**

Paula **Forero** - Natalia **Gaitan**• (c), Natalia **Ariza**, Daniela **Montoya** (Katerin **Castro** 43), Ingrid **Vidal**, Paola **Sanchez** (Ana Maria **Montoya** 57), Yorely **Rincon**, Liana **Salazar**, Yulieht **Dominguez**, Tatiana **Ariza**, Carolina **Arias** (Melissa **Ortiz** 86). Tr: Ricardo Rozo

Nigeria   **1**

Orji [2]

Alaba **Jonathan** - Cecilia **Nku**, Esther **Sunday** (Charity **Adule** 38), Ebere **Orji**•, Desire **Oparanozie**, Rebecca **Kalu**, Glory **Iroka**, Joy **Jegede** (c), Amarachi **Okoronkwo**• (Soo **Adekwagh** 67), Helen **Ukaonu**•, Osinachi **Ohale**. Tr: Ndem Egan

3RD PLACE PLAY-OFF

Bochum
1-08-2010, 12:00, 24 633, Steinhaus GER

Korea Republic   **1**

Ji So Yun [49]

Moon So Ri - **Seo** Hyun Sook, **Lim** Seon Joo, **Jeong** Yeonga, **Kwon** Eun Som, **Kim** Narae, **Ji** So Yun, **Lee** Hyun Young (**Park** Hee Young 83), **Lee** Min A (**Jung** Hae In 61), **Kim** Jin Young (**Jeoun** Eun Ha 46), **Kim** Hye Ri (c). Tr: **Choi** In Cheul

Colombia   **0**

Paula **Forero** - Natalia **Gaitan** (c), Natalia **Ariza**•, Daniela **Montoya**, Yorely **Rincon**, Liana **Salazar**•, Yulieht **Dominguez**•, Tatiana **Ariza** (Katerin **Castro** 46), Lady **Andrade** (Melissa **Ortiz** 76), Carolina **Arias**, Ana Maria **Montoya** (Lina **Taborda** 78). Tr: Ricardo Rozo

FINAL

Bochum
1-08-2010, 15:00, 24 633, Chenard CAN

Germany   **2**

Popp [8], Ohale OG [92+]

Almuth **Schult** - Tabea **Kemme**, Marith **Priessen**, Kristina **Gessat**, Marina **Hegering** (c), Svenja **Huth** (Turid **Knaak** 82), Dzsenifer **Marozsan** (Stefanie **Mirlach** 79), Alexandra **Popp**, Sylvia **Arnold** (Selina **Wagner** 88), Kim **Kulig**, Bianca **Schmidt**. Tr: Maren Meinert

Nigeria   **0**

Alaba **Jonathan** - Gloria **Ofoegbu** (Amarachi **Okoronkwo** 55), Cecilia **Nku**, Esther **Sunday**, Ebere **Orji**, Desire **Oparanozie**, Rebecca **Kalu**•, Glory **Iroka**, Joy **Jegede** (c), Helen **Ukaonu**, Osinachi **Ohale**. Tr: Ndem **Egan**

FIFA U-17 WOMEN'S WORLD CUP
TRINIDAD AND TOBAGO 2010

FIFA U-17 WOMEN'S WORLD CUP TRINIDAD AND TOBAGO 2010

First round groups	Pts	Quarter-finals		Semi-finals		Final		
Nigeria	9							
Korea DPR	6	**Korea Republic**	6					
Trinidad and Tobago	3	Nigeria	5					
Chile	0							
				Korea Republic	2			
	Pts			Spain	1			
Germany	9							
Korea Republic	6	Brazil	1					
Mexico	3	**Spain**	2					
South Africa	0							
						Korea Republic	3	5p
	Pts					Japan	3	4p
Spain	9							
Japan	6	**Korea DPR**	1					
Venezuela	3	Germany	0					
New Zealand	0							
				Korea DPR	1			
	Pts			**Japan**	2			
Republic of Ireland	6							
Brazil	6	Republic of Ireland	1			**3rd Place Play-off**		
Canada	3	**Japan**	2			**Spain**	1	
Ghana	3					Korea DPR	0	

Top scorers: **8** - Yeo Min Ji KOR • **7** - Kyra Malinowski GER • **6** - Kumi Yokoyama & Loveth Ayila NGA • **5** - Lena Petermann GER; Ngozi Okobi & Kim Kum Jong PRK • **4** - Lena Lotzen GER & Yoko Tanaka JPN • **3** - Francisca Ordega NGA; Paloma Lazaro ESP; Raquel Pinel ESP & Mai Kyokawa JPN

GROUP A	PL	W	D	L	F	A	PTS	PRK	TRI	CHI
1 Nigeria	3	3	0	0	10	3	9	3-2	2-1	5-0
2 Korea DPR	3	2	0	1	6	3	6		1-0	3-0
3 Trinidad and Tobago	3	1	0	2	3	4	3			2-1
4 Chile	3	0	0	3	1	10	0			

GROUP B	PL	W	D	L	F	A	PTS	KOR	MEX	RSA
1 Germany	3	3	0	0	22	1	9	3-0	9-0	10-1
2 Korea Republic	3	2	0	1	7	5	6		4-1	3-1
3 Mexico	3	1	0	2	5	13	3			4-0
4 South Africa	3	0	0	3	2	17	0			

GROUP C	PL	W	D	L	F	A	PTS	JPN	VEN	NZL
1 Spain	3	3	0	0	9	3	9	4-1	2-1	3-1
2 Japan	3	2	0	1	13	4	6		6-0	6-0
3 Venezuela	3	1	0	2	3	9	3			2-1
4 New Zealand	3	0	0	3	2	11	0			

GROUP D	PL	W	D	L	F	A	PTS	BRA	CAN	GHA
1 Republic of Ireland	3	2	0	1	5	2	6	1-2	1-0	3-0
2 Brazil	3	2	0	1	4	2	6		2-0	0-1
3 Canada	3	1	0	2	1	3	3			1-0
4 Ghana	3	1	0	2	1	4	3			

GROUP A

Hasely Crawford, Port of Spain
5-09-2010, 18:00, 13 646, Gaal HUN

Trinidad and Tobago 2
Simmons 9, Hinds 80

Linfah **Jones** - Rose **Bahadursingh**, Diarra **Simmons** (Jo Marie Lewis 64), Patrice **Vincent**, Lauren **Schmidt** (c), Khadisha **Debesette**, Brianna **Ryce** (Khadidra **Debesette** 73), Victoria **Swift**, Liana **Hinds**, Kayla **Taylor** (Anique **Walker** 91), Emma **Abdul**. Tr: Even **Pellerud**

Chile 1
Rothfield 83

Veronica **Saez** - Yocelyn **Cisternas**, Nicole **Cornejo**, Camila **Saez**, Leticia **Torres** (c), Yorky **Arriagada**, Yanara **Aedo**, Barbara **Santibanez** (Iona **Rothfeld** 70), Francisca **Moroso**, Maria **Urrutia** (Jetzabeth **Zepeda** 87), Claudia **Soto** (Yudith **Rojas** 62). Tr: Ronnie **Radonich**

Manny Ramjohn, Marabella
8-09-2010, 16:00, 10 000, Vulivuli FIJ

Korea DPR 3
Kim Kum Jong 2 44 72, Pong Son Hwa 85p

Choe Kyong Im - **Song** Im, **Ri** Un Gyong, **Pong** Son Hwa, **O** Hui Sun• (c), **Kim** Kum Jong, **Kim** Su Gyong (**Kim** Yun Mi 52) (**Ri** Yong Mi 79), **Choe** Jong Hwa, **Kim** Nam Hui• (**Pak** Kyong Mi 83), **Kim** Un Ha, **Kang** Ok Gum. Tr: **Ri** Song Gun

Chile 0

Veronica **Saez** - Yocelyn **Cisternas**, Nicole **Cornejo**••♦70, Camila **Saez**, Leticia **Torres** (c), Yorky **Arriagada**, Yanara **Aedo**, Barbara **Santibanez** (Francisca **Moroso** 46), Iona **Rothfield** (Rocio **Soto** 64), Claudia **Soto** (Melissa **Espina** 46), Yudith **Rojas**. Tr: Ronnie **Radonich**

Hasely Crawford, Port of Spain
5-09-2010, 15:00, 13 646, Heikkinen FIN

Nigeria 3
Okobi 2 3 79, Ordega 77

Amina **Abu** - Sarah **Nnodim**•, Oluchi **Ofoegbu** (c), Ugo **Njoku**, Francisca **Ordega** (Jane **David** 83), Ngozi **Okobi**, Kemi **Abiodun**, Halimatu **Ayinde** (Winifred **Eyebhoria** 62), Victoria **Aidelomon**, Omolade **Akinbiyi**, Yetunde **Aluko**. Tr: Peter **Dedevbo**

Korea DPR 2
Kim Su Gyong 28, Kim Kum Jong 58

Choe Kyong Im - **Song** Im, **Ri** Un Gyong, **O** Hui Sun (c) (**Han** Hyang Suk 72), **Kim** Kum Jong, **Kim** Su Gyong, **Choe** Jong Hwa, **Kim** Nam Hui, **Kim** Un Ha, **Kang** Ok Gum (**Kim** Yun Mi 31), **Pak** Kyong Mi. Tr: **Ri** Song Gun

Ato Boldon, Couva
12-09-2010, 18:00, 8500, Mitsi GRE

Korea DPR 1
Kim Su Gyong 3

Choe Kyong Im - **Song** Im, **Ri** Un Gyong, **Pong** Son Hwa, **O** Hui Sun (c), **Kim** Kum Jong, **Kim** Su Gyong (**Han** Hyang Suk 86), **Choe** Jong Hwa (**Kim** Yun Mi 65), **Kim** Nam Hui, **Kim** Un Ha, **Kang** Ok Gum•. Tr: **Ri** Song Gun

Trinidad and Tobago 0

Linfah **Jones** - Rose **Bahadursingh**, Diarra **Simmons** (Jasmine **Sampson** 81), Patrice **Vincent**, Lauren **Schmidt** (c), Khadisha **Debesette**, Brianna **Ryce** (Jo Marie **Lewis** 46), Victoria **Swift**, Liana **Hinds** (Nykosi **Simmons** 73), Khadidra **Debesette**, Kayla **Taylor**. Tr: Even **Pellerud**

Manny Ramjohn, Marabella
8-09-2010, 19:00, 10 000, Schett AUT

Trinidad and Tobago 1
Hinds 36

Linfah **Jones** - Rose **Bahadursingh**, Diarra **Simmons** (Brianna **Ryce** 84), Patrice **Vincent** (Jonelle **Warrick** 72), Lauren **Schmidt** (c), Khadisha **Debesette**, Victoria **Swift**•, Liana **Hinds**, Khadidra **Debesette**, Kayla **Taylor**, Emma **Abdul** (Jo Marie **Lewis** 46). Tr: Even **Pellerud**

Nigeria 2
Ordega 28, Ayila 86

Amina **Abu** - Sarah **Nnodim**•, Oluchi **Ofoegbu** (c), Ugo **Njoku**•, Loveth **Ayila**, Francisca **Ordega**, Ngozi **Okobi**, Kemi **Abiodun**, Halimatu **Ayinde** (Winifred **Eyebhoria** 44), Victoria **Aidelomon**•, Omolade **Akinbiyi**. Tr: Peter **Dedevbo**

Larry Gomes, Arima
12-09-2010, 18:00, 2335, Pye CAN

Chile 0

Veronica **Saez** - Yocelyn **Cisternas**, Camila **Saez**, Leticia **Torres** (c), Yorky **Arriagada**, Yanara **Aedo**, Francisca **Moroso** (Michelle **Bernstein** 46), Maria **Urrutia**, Isadora **Cubillos** (Jetzabeth **Zepeda** 72), Fernanda **Pinilla** (Yudith **Rojas** 46), Melissa **Espina**. Tr: Ronnie **Radonich**

Nigeria 5
Ordega 15, Ayila 3 41 51 72, Okobi 91+

Ibijoke **Sangonuga** - Oluchi **Ofoegbu** (c), Chioma **Alimba**• (Gladys **Abasi** 90), Loveth **Ayila**, Francisca **Ordega** (Yetunde **Aluko** 59), Ngozi **Okobi**, Winifred **Eyebhoria**, Kemi **Abiodun** (Christiana **Osundele** 67), Victoria **Aidelomon**, Omolade **Akinbiyi**, Ebere **Okoye**. Tr: Peter **Dedevbo**

GROUP B

Dwight Yorke, Scarborough
5-09-2010, 16:00, 2961, Yamagishi JPN

Germany 9
Lotzen 2 4 35, Peterman 3 12 13 72, Malinowski 3 42 55 66, Demann 47

Lena Nuding - Luisa Wensing, Kristin Demann (c), Jennifer Cramer (Anne Rheinheimer 46), Isabella Schmid (Karoline Heinze 57), Lina Magull, Kyra Malinowski, Lena Lotzen, Melanie Leupolz (Annabel Jaeger 67), Lena Petermann, Sarah Romert. Tr: Ralf Peter

Mexico 0

Rosa Merida - Amber Hernandez (Paola Lopez 27), Alejandra Amador, Alexandra Duran, Paulina Bueno, Amanda Perez, Diana Gonzalez (c) (Daniela Solis 28), Christina Murillo (Adrianna Nunez 73), Andrea Sanchez, Cristina Ferral•, Cintia Sandoval. Tr: Saul Resendiz

---

Dwight Yorke, Scarborough
5-09-2010, 19:00, 2961, Schett AUT

South Africa 1
Seoposenwe 53

Kaylin Swart - Mapula Kgoale (Octovia Nogwanya 68), Jabulile Mazibuko, Meagan Newman, Maphuti Manamela, Rachel Sebati (c) (Alice Khosa 87), Robyn Moodaly, Christelene Jantjies, Kelso Peskin (Tshegofatso Makinta 23), Jermaine Seoposenwe•, Manthipu Mabote•. Tr: Solomon Luvhengo

Korea Republic 3
Yeo Min Ji 2 37 56, Shin Damyeong 77

Kim Minah - Jang Selgi, Oh Dahye•, Shin Damyeong, Lee Jungeun (Lee So Dam 88), Kim Nari (Lee Yoo Na 65), Kim Areum (c), Kim Dahye, Lee Geum Min, Baek Eunmi, Lee Yoo Na (Yeo Min Ji 27). Tr: Choi Duck Joo

---

Dwight Yorke, Scarborough
8-09-2010, 16:00, 1830, Pye CAN

Germany 10
Lotzen 12, Malinowski 4 19 29 36 57, Leupolz 2 24 25, Petermann 2 35 37, OG 45

Friederike Abt - Luisa Wensing, Kristin Demann (c), Jennifer Cramer, Isabella Schmid, Lina Magull, Kyra Malinowski, Lena Lotzen (Claire Savin 55), Melanie Leupolz (Silvana Chojnowski 61), Lena Petermann, Sarah Romert (Natalie Moik 55). Tr: Ralf Peter

South Africa 0
Seoposenwe 31

Kaylin Swart - Mapula Kgoale (Khosi Mnyakeni 60), Jabulile Mazibuko (Octovia Nogwanya 46), Meagan Newman, Maphuti Manamela, Rachel Sebati (c), Robyn Moodaly•, Christelene Jantjies (Presocious Matabologa 52), Tshegofatso Makinta, Jermaine Seoposenwe, Manthipu Mabote. Tr: Soloman Luvhengo

---

Dwight Yorke, Scarborough
8-09-2010, 19:00, 1830, Alvarez ARG

Korea Republic 4
Kim Nari 27, Yeo Min Ji 40, Kim Dahye 76, Lee Yoo Na 90

Kim Minah - Jang Selgi, Oh Dahye, Shin Damyeong, Lee Jungeun, Kim Nari (Lee Yoo Na 61), Kim Areum (c), Kim Dahye (Lee So Dam 89), Yeo Min Ji, Lee Geum Min (Joo Soojin 80), Baek Eunmi. Tr: Choi Duck Joo

Mexico 1

Rosa Merida - Alexandra Duran, Paulina Bueno, Amanda Perez• (Diana Gonzalez 74), Tanya Samarzich (Fabiola Ibarra 55), Christina Murillo (c), Andrea Sanchez, Cristina Ferral, Cintia Sandoval, Fernanda Pina (Paola Lopez 77), Daniela Solis. Tr: Saul Resendiz

---

Larry Gomes, Arima
12-09-2010, 15:00, 2335, De Silva TRI

Korea Republic 0

Kim Minah - Jang Selgi, Shin Damyeong (Kim Bichna 61), Lee Jungeun, Kim Nari, Kim Areum (c), Lee Geum Min, Joo Soojin (Lee So Dam 74), Baek Eunmi, Jeon Hanwool (Yeo Min Ji 46), Lim Hayoung. Tr: Choi Duck Joo

Germany 3
Schmid 72, Lotzen 76, Chojnowski 93+

Lena Nuding - Luisa Wensing, Kristin Demann (c), Jennifer Cramer, Isabella Schmid, Lina Magull (Clara Schoene 79), Kyra Malinowski• (Annabel Jaeger 59), Lena Lotzen, Melanie Leupolz (Silvana Chojnowski 59), Lena Petermann, Sarah Romert. Tr: Ralf Peter

---

Ato Boldon, Couva
12-09-2010, 15:00, 8500, Staubli SUI

Mexico 4
Solis 21, Sanchez 52, Murillo 68, Pina 78

Rosa Merida - Amber Hernandez, Alexandra Duran, Amanda Perez (Anakaren Llamas 82), Diana Gonzalez (c) (Adrianna Nunez 72), Christina Murillo, Andrea Sanchez, Cristina Ferral, Mariel Gutierrez, Fernanda Pina• (Daniela Solis (Tanya Samarzich 76). Tr: Saul Resendiz

South Africa 0

Kaylin Swart - Mapula Kgoale (Tshegofatso Makinta 26), Jabulile Mazibuko, Meagan Newman, Maphuti Manamela, Rachel Sebati (c), Robyn Moodaly•, Christelene Jantjies (Caytlin Fryer 59), Kelso Peskin (Aviwe Kalolo 81), Jermaine Seoposenwe, Lindiwe Mkhize. Tr: Soloman Luvhengo

---

GROUP C

Ato Boldon, Couva
6-09-2010, 19:00, 1364, Mitsi GRE

New Zealand 1
Loye 10

Chloe-May Geurts - Rachel Head (Hannah Wong 84), Tessa McPherson, Olivia Chance (Megan Lee 84), Evie Millynn, Holly Patterson, Kate Loye, Stephanie Skilton (Brittany Dudley Smith 70), Katie Bowen (c), Sivitha Boyce, Rebecca Burrows. Tr: Dave Edmondson

Venezuela 2
Viso 2 24 67

Maleike Pacheco - Genesis Moreno, Yaribeth Ulacio, Soleidys Rengel, Yurimar Toledo, Maria Rodriguez• (Paola Villamizar 87), Maria Carrero (Natasha Rosas 46), Ysaura Viso, Marialba Zambrano (c), Michelle Clemente (Joemar Guarecuco 75), Maryeling Martinez. Tr: Kennith Zseremeta

---

Ato Boldon, Couva
6-09-2010, 16:00, 1364, Alvarado MEX

Spain 4
Perez 26, Putellas 28, Gutierrez 41, Pinel 55

Dolores Gallardo - Ana Maria Catala• (Paula Nicart 59), Ivana Andres, Laura Gutierrez, Marina Garcia, Amanda Sampedro (c) (Nerea Perez 79), Alexia Putellas, Iraia Perez (Nagore Calderon 69), Sara Merida, Raquel Pinel, Paula Lopez•. Tr: Jorge Vilda

Japan 1
Yokoyama 56

Eri Hirao - Serina Kashimoto (c), Mami Kanazawa, Naoko Wada (Hikari Takagi 75), Ayu Nakada (Mai Kyokawa 46), Hikaru Naomoto, Yoko Tanaka, Haruna Kawashima, Mina Tanaka (Kumi Yokoyama 35), Tomoko Muramatsu, Chika Kato. Tr: Hiroshi Yoshida

---

Ato Boldon, Couva
9-09-2010, 16:00, 1758, Cha Sung Mi KOR

New Zealand 1
Loye 15

Chloe-May Geurts - Rachel Head, Tessa McPherson (Michelle Windsor 73), Olivia Chance, Evie Millynn (Grace Parkinson 84), Holly Patterson (Brittany Dudley Smith 75), Kate Loye, Stephanie Skilton, Katie Bowen (c), Sivitha Boyce, Rebecca Burrows. Tr: Dave Edmondson

Spain 3
Gili 4, Merida 48, Lazaro 86

Dolores Gallardo - Ana Maria Catala, Ivana Andres, Laura Gutierrez, Nagore Calderon, Gema Gili, Amanda Sampedro (c) (Marina Garcia 83), Alexia Putellas (Isara Tazo 78), Arene Altonaga, Sara Merida•, Raquel Pinel (Paloma Lazaro 72). Tr: Jorge Vilda

---

Ato Boldon, Couva
9-09-2010, 19:00, 1758, Alvarado MEX

Japan 6
Kyokawa 3 10 32p 59, Yoko Tanaka 27, Yokoyama 70, Nagashima 92+

Eri Hirao - Serina Kashimoto (Ami Goto 68), Yume Nagasawa, Naoko Wada, Ayu Nakada, Hikaru Naomoto, Yoko Tanaka, Haruna Kawashima, Mai Kyokawa•, Hikari Takagi (Hikari Nagashima 80), Chika Kato (Kumi Yokoyama• 53). Tr: Hiroshi Yoshida

Venezuela 0

Maleike Pacheco - Genesis Moreno, Yaribeth Ulacio, Soleidys Rengel, Yurimar Toledo (Joemar Guarecuco 63), Maria Rodriguez• (Paola Villamizar 73), Natasha Rosas 25), Ysaura Viso, Marialba Zambrano (c), Michelle Clemente (Jessyca Montes 73), Maryeling Martinez. Tr: Kenneth Zseremeta

---

Dwight Yorke, Scarborough
13-09-2010, 16:00, 2140, Heikkinen FIN

Japan 6
Yokoyama 2 24 58, Yoko Tanaka 2 59 89, Mina Tanaka 74, Honda 91+

Eri Hirao (c) - Mami Kanazawa, Yume Nagasawa, Hikaru Naomoto (Naoko Wada 63), Yoko Tanaka, Haruna Kawashima, Mai Kyokawa (Chika Kato 63), Mina Tanaka, Tomoko Muramatsu, Haruka Hamada, Kumi Yokoyama (Yuka Honda 78). Tr: Hiroshi Yoshida

New Zealand 0

Jess Reddaway - Rachel Head, Tessa McPherson, Olivia Chance (Megan Lee 76), Holly Patterson, Kate Loye, Hannah Carlsen (Jessie Mathews 63), Hannah Wong (Kate Carlton 50), Katie Bowen (c), Sivitha Boyce, Rebecca Burrows. Tr: Dave Edmondson

---

Manny Ramjohn, Marabella
13-09-2010, 16:00, 2579, Sagno GUI

Venezuela 1
Alvarado 74

Maleike Pacheco - Genesis Moreno, Yaribeth Ulacio, Soleidys Rengel, Yurimar Toledo•, Ysaura Viso, Marialba Zambrano (c), Michelle Clemente (Arena Alvarado 63), Natasha Rosas, Maryeling Martinez•, Jessyca Montes (Joemar Guarecuco 46). Tr: Kenneth Zseremeta

Spain 2
Lazaro 2 28 83

Dolores Gallardo - Ivana Andres (Arene Altonaga 58), Laura Gutierrez (Nerea Perez 78), Nagore Calderon, Gema Gili, Marina Garcia, Paloma Lazaro, Amanda Sampedro (c), Iraia Perez (Sara Tazo 46), Paula Nicart, Paula Lopez. Tr: Jorge Vilda

GROUP D

Larry Gomes, Arima
6-09-2010, 16:00, 1881, Wang Jia CHN

Republic of Ireland 1
Killeen [58]

Grace Moloney - Ciara O'Brien, Megan Campbell, Jessica Gleeson, Jennifer Byrne, Ciara Grant•, Aileen Gilroy (Clare Shine 74), Dora Gorman (c), Denise O'Sullivan, Siobhan Killeen (Rebecca Kearney 91), Stacie Donnelly (Rianna Jarrett 74). Tr: Noel King

Brazil 2
Glaucia 2 [4 61]

Danele - Ingrid, Caroline, Lucimara, Roberta• (Tainara 81), Andressa, Beatriz, Thais• (c), Glaucia, Jucinara, Luana (Paula 66). Tr: Edvaldo Erlacher

Larry Gomes, Arima
6-09-2010, 19:00, 1881, Cha Sung Mi KOR

Canada 1
Cantave [54]

Sabrina D'Angelo - Chantale Campbell, Kylie Davis (Jade Kovacevic 46), Diamond Simpson, Vanessa Kovacs (Charlene Achille 74), Alison Clarke, Nicole Setterlund (c), Kinley McNicoll, Haisha Cantave (Ashley Lawrence 83), Alexandra Courtnall, Abigail Raymer. Tr: Bryan Rosenfeld

Ghana 0

Margaret Otoo - Cynthia Yiadom (Grace Adams 65), Linda Addai, Ellen Coleman, Felicia Djabaah (Rasheda Abdul-Rahman 74), Sherifatu Sumaila, Rita Okyere, Beatrice Sesu (c), Alice Danso, Mary Essiful (Kesewa Antwi 64), Regina Antwi. Tr: Abrahams Allotey

Larry Gomes, Arima
9-09-2010, 16:00, 2293, Yamagishi JPN

Republic of Ireland 1
Killeen [76]

Grace Moloney - Ciara O'Brien, Megan Campbell, Jessica Gleeson, Jennifer Byrne, Ciara Grant, Aileen Gilroy, Dora Gorman (c), Denise O'Sullivan, Siobhan Killeen (Harriet Scott 89), Stacie Donnelly. Tr: Noel King

Canada 0

Sabrina D'Angelo - Chantale Campbell, Diamond Simpson, Nour Ghoneim (Jade Kovacevic 46), Vanessa Kovacs, Alison Clarke, Nicole Setterlund (c), Kinley McNicoll (Abigail Raymer 70), Haisha Cantave, Charlene Achille (Alexandra Courtnall 46), Caroline Beaulne. Tr: Bryan Rosenfeld

Larry Gomes, Arima
9-09-2010, 19:00, 2293, Staubli SUI

Ghana 1
Danso [22]

Margaret Otoo• - Linda Addai, Ellen Coleman, Felicia Djabaah, Sherifatu Sumaila•, Rita Okyere•, Beatrice Sesu• (c), Alice Danso• (Kasira Malik-Jebdon 94), Regina Antwi, Kesewa Antwi (Jennifer Cudjoe 64), Rebecca Asante. Tr: Abrahams Allotey

Brazil 0

Daniele - Ingrid•, Caroline, Lucimara, Roberta, Andressa (Tatiane 67), Beatriz (Luana 67), Thais (c), Glaucia, Jucinara, Bianca (Paula 86). Tr: Edvaldo Erlacher

Dwight Yorke, Scarborough
13-09-2010, 19:00, 2140, Alvarez ARG

Ghana 0

Margaret Otoo - Cynthia Yiadom• (Ivy Kolli• 68), Linda Addai, Ellen Coleman (Rebecca Asante 21), Sherifatu Sumaila, Rita Okyere, Beatrice Sesu (c), Alice Danso, Mary Essiful, Regina Antwi, Rasheda Abdul-Rahman (Felici Djabaah 52). Tr: Abrahams Allotey

Republic of Ireland 3
Campbell [5], Donnelly [36], Gilroy [77]

Grace Moloney - Ciara O'Brien, Megan Campbell, Jessica Gleeson, Jennifer Byrne, Ciara Grant, Aileen Gilroy (Emma Hansberry 87), Dora Gorman (c), Denise O'Sullivan, Siobhan Killeen (Harriet Scott 75), Stacie Donnelly (Rianna Jarrett 69). Tr: Noel King

Dwight Yorke, Scarborough
13-09-2010, 19:00, 2579, Gaal HUN

Brazil 2
Paula [20], Thais [51]

Daniele - Ingrid, Caroline, Lucimara, Roberta, Andressa, Paula (Luana 67), Beatriz•, Thais (c) (Tatiane 92), Glaucia (Bianca 85), Jucinara. Tr: Edvaldo Erlacher

Canada 0

Sabrina D'Angelo - Jade Kovacevic (Ashley Lawrence 68), Chantale Campbell, Yazmin Ongtengco, Diamond Simpson, Alison Clarke•, Nicole Setterlund (c), Zakiya McIntosh (Charlene Achille 46), Haisha Cantave, Alexandra Courtnall, Caroline Beaulne (Abigail Raymer 46). Tr: Bryan Rosenfeld

QUARTER-FINALS

Manny Ramjohn, Marabella
16-09-2010, 16:00, 4034, Mitsi GRE

Nigeria 5
Ayila 2 [2 105], Eyebhoria [3], Okobi 2 [37 91+]

Amina Abu - Sarah Nnodim• (Ugo Njoku 61), Oluchi Ofoegbu (c), Chioma Alimba, Loveth Ayila, Francisca Ordega (Yetunde Aluko 80), Ngozi Okobi, Winifred Eyebhoria, Kemi Abiodun, Victoria Aidelomon, Ebere Okoye•. Tr: Peter Dedevbo

Korea Republic 6
Lee Geum Min [15], Yeo Min Ji 4 [23 70p 89 98], Kim Areum [94]

Kim Minah - Jang Selgi, Oh Dahye, Shin Damyeong, Lee Jungeun, Kim Nari (Lee So Dam 74), Kim Areum (c), Yeo Min Ji, Lee Geum Min (Jeon Hanwool 120), Joo Soojin (Kim Bichna• 60), Baek Eunmi. Tr: Choi Duck Joo

Manny Ramjohn, Marabella
16-09-2010, 19:00, 4034, Alvarado MEX

Germany 0

Lena Nuding - Luisa Wensing, Kristin Demann (c), Jennifer Cramer, Isabella Schmid, Lina Magull, Kyra Malinowski (Silvana Chojnowski 57), Lena Lotzen, Melanie Leupolz (Annabel Jaeger 78), Lena Petermann, Sarah Romert. Tr: Ralf Peter

Korea DPR 1
Kim Kum Jong [44]

Choe Kyong Im - Song Im (Pak Kyong Mi 31), Ri Un Gyong, Pong Son Hwa, O Hui Sun (c), Kim Kum Jong (Ri Yong Mi 90), Kim Su Gyong, Choe Jong Hwa, Kim Nam Hui (Kim Yun Mi 57), Kim Un Ha, Kang Ok Gum. Tr: Ri Song Gun

Ato Boldon, Couva
17-09-2010, 16:00, 1265, Yamagishi JPN

Spain 2
Pinel [35], Calderon [65]

Dolores Gallardo - Ana Maria Catala, Ivana Andres•, Laura Gutierrez, Nagore Calderon, Gema Gili, Amanda Sampedro (c), Alexia Putellas, Sara Merida, Raquel Pinel (Paloma Lazaro 78), Paula Lopez. Tr: Jorge Vilda

Brazil 1
Andres OG [76]

Daniele - Ingrid, Caroline, Lucimara, Roberta, Andressa, Paula (Tatiane 86), Beatriz•, Thais (c), Glaucia (Luana 63), Jucinara (Tainara 68). Tr: Edvaldo Erlacher

Larry Gomes, Arima
17-09-2010, 19:00, 1427, Pye CAN

Republic of Ireland 1
O'Sullivan [53]

Grace Moloney - Ciara O'Brien, Megan Campbell, Jessica Gleeson, Jennifer Byrne, Ciara Grant, Aileen Gilroy (Rianna Jarrett 71), Dora Gorman (c), Denise O'Sullivan, Siobhan Killeen (Harriet Scott 89), Stacie Donnelly (Harriet Scott 89). Tr: Noel King

Japan 2
Naomoto [34p], Yokoyama [66]

Eri Hirao (c) - Naoko Wada, Ayu Nakada (Mai Kyokawa 46), Hikaru Naomoto, Yoko Tanaka, Haruna Kawashima, Tomoko Muramatsu, Haruka Hamada, Hikari Takagi (Serina Kashimoto 94), Chika Kato, Kumi Yokoyama. Tr: Hiroshi Yoshida

SEMI-FINALS

Ato Boldon, Couva
21-09-2010, 16:00, 3428, Pye CAN

Korea Republic   **2**
Yeo Min Ji [25], Joo Soojin [39]

Kim Minah - Kim Bichna, Jang Selgi, Shin Damyeong, Lee Jungeun, Kim Nari (Kim Soobin 80), Kim Areum (c), Yeo Min Ji, Lee Geum Min (Kim In Ji 92), Joo Soojin (Lee So Dam 73), Lim Hayoung•. Tr: Choi Duck Joo

Spain   **1**
Sampedro [23]

Dolores Gallardo - Ana Maria Catala (Paloma Lazaro 80), Ivana Andres, Laura Gutierrez, Nagore Calderon, Gema Gili, Amanda Sampedro (c), Alexia Putellas, Sara Merida, Raquel Pinel, Paula Lopez. Tr: Jorge Vilda

Ato Boldon, Couva
21-09-2010, 19:00, 3428, Gaal HUN

Korea DPR   **1**
Kim Kum Jong [59]

Choe Kyong Im - Ri Un Gyong, Pong Son Hwa (Jo Jong Sim 42), O Hui Sun (c), Kim Kum Jong, Kim Su Gyong (Ri Yong Mi 84), Choe Jong Hwa (Kim Yun Mi 53), Kim Nam Hui, Kim Un Ha, Kang Ok Gum, Pak Kyong Mi. Tr: Ri Song Gun

Japan   **2**
Takagi [69], Yokoyama [70]

Eri Hirao (c) - Naoko Wada, Ayu Nakada (Kumi Yokoyama 32), Hikaru Naomoto, Yoko Tanaka, Haruna Kawashima (Yume Nagasawa 68), Mai Kyokawa, Tomoko Muramatsu, Haruka Hamada, Hikari Takagi•, Chika Kato. Tr: Hiroshi Yoshida

3RD PLACE PLAY-OFF

Hasely Crawford, Port of Spain
25-09-2010, 15:00, 12 983, Alvarado MEX

Spain   **1**
Pinel [56]

Dolores Gallardo• - Ana Maria Catala, Ivana Andres, Laura Gutierrez, Nagore Calderon (Iraia Perez 88), Gema Gili (Marina Garcia 67), Amanda Sampedro (c), Alexia Putellas, Sara Merida, Raquel Pinel (Paloma Lazaro 56), Paula Lopez. Tr: Jorge Vilda

Korea DPR   **0**

Choe Kyong Im - Song Im, Ri Un Gyong, Han Hyang Suk, Pong Son Hwa (Pak Kyong Mi 78), O Hui Sun (c), Kim Kum Jong, Kim Su Gyong (Kim Yun Mi 59), Kim Nam Hui (Choe Jong Hwa 74), Kim Un Ha, Kang Ok Gum•. Tr: Ri Song Gun

FINAL

Hasely Crawford, Port of Spain
25-09-2010, 18:00, 12 983, Heikkinen FIN

Korea Republic   **3 5p**
Lee Jungeun [6], Kim Areum [45], Lee So Dam [79]

Kim Minah - Kim Bichna, Jang Selgi, Shin Damyeong, Lee Jungeun, Kim Nari (Lee So Dam 78), Kim Areum (c), Yeo Min Ji, Lee Geum Min (Baek Eunmi 36), Joo Soojin (Kim Dahye 46), Lim Hayoung. Tr: Choi Duck Joo

Japan   **3 4p**
Naomoto [11], Yoko Tanaka [17], Kato [57]

Eri Hirao (c) - Naoko Wada, Hikaru Naomoto, Yoko Tanaka, Haruna Kawashima (Yume Nagasawa 50), Mai Kyokawa (Ayu Nakada 87), Tomoko Muramatsu, Haruka Hamada, Hikari Takagi, Chika Kato, Kumi Yokoyama (Mina Tanaka 104). Tr: Hiroshi Yoshida

PENALTIES		
JPN		KOR
✓	Yoko Tanaka	
	Lee Jungeun	✗[1]
✗[2]	Naoko Wada	
	Yeo Min Ji	✓
✓	Ayu Nakada	
	Lee So Dam	✓
✓	Haruka Hamada	
	Kim Dahye	✓
✓	Hikaru Naomoto	
	Kim Areum	✓
✗[3]	Tomoko Muramatsu	
	Jang Selgi	✓

[1] Saved [2] Missed [3] Hit crossbar

FIFA CLUB WORLD CUP UAE 2010

FIFA CLUB WORLD CUP UAE 2010

Quarter-finals			Semi-finals		Final	
Internazionale	ITA	Bye				
			Internazionale	3		
			Seongnam Ilhwa Chunma	0		
Al Wahda	UAE	1				
Seongnam I. Chunma	KOR	4				
					Internazionale	3
					TP Mazembe	0
Internacional	BRA	Bye				
			Internacional	0		
			TP Mazembe	2		
Pachuca	MEX	0				
TP Mazembe	COD	1				

Preliminary Round			Fifth Place Play–off			Third Place Play–off		
Al Wahda	UAE	3	**Pachuca**	2	4p	**Internacional**		4
Hekari United	PNG	0	Al Wahda	2	2p	Seongnam Ilhwa Chunma		2

PRELIMINARY ROUNDS

Preliminary Round
Mohammad Bin Zayed, Abu Dhabi
8-12-2010, 20:00, 23 895, Bennett RSA
Al Wahda 3
Hugo [40], Fernando [44], Jumaa [71]
Adel **Al Hosani** - Eisa Ahmed, Hamdan **Al Kamali**, Basheer **Saeed**, Haidar **Ali** (c) - **Magrao**, **Hugo•** - Fahed **Masoud** (Abdulraheem **Jumaa** 63), Mahmoud Khamis **Al Hammadi** - **Fernando** Baiano (Modibi **Diarra** 72), Ismaeil **Matar** (Amer **Bazuhair** 83). Tr: Josef **Hickersberger**
Hekari United 0
Simione **Tamanisau** - Pita **Bolatoga**, Gideon **Omokirio**, Alvin **Singh**, Koriak **Upaiga** - Abraham **Iniga•** (Niel **Hans** 79), David **Muta** (c) - Henry **Faarodo**, Malakai **Tiwa**, Kema **Jack**, Osea **Vakatalesau**. Tr: Tommy **Mana**

First Round
Mohammad Bin Zayed, Abu Dhabi
10-12-2010, 20:00, 17 960, Nishimura JPN
TP Mazembe 1
Bedi [21]
Robert Muteba **Kidiaba** - Joel **Kimwaki**, Jean Kiritcho **Kasusula**, Pamphile Kazembe **Mihayo** (c)•, Eric Miala **Nkulukuta** - Narcisse Amia **Ekanga** (Ngandu **Kasongo•** 46), Hugues Mbenza **Bedi•**, Stopila **Sunzu••♦**81 - Given **Singuluma**, Alain Dioko **Kaluyituka** (Deo Mukok **Kanda** 91+), Patou Mulota **Kabangu** (Mukinayi **Tshani** 85). Tr: Lamine **N'Diaye**
Pachuca 0
Miguel **Calero** (c) - Paul **Aguilar**, Leobardo **Lopez**, Javier **Munoz**, Braulio **Luna** (Herculez **Gomez** 74) - Carlos Alberto **Pena** (Edgar **Benitez** 58), Raul **Martinez**, Francisco **Torres** (Edy **Brambila** 73) - Alejandro **Manso**, Dario **Cvitanich**, Franco **Arizala**. Tr: Pablo **Marini**

First Round
Zayed Sports City, Abu Dhabi
11-12-2010, 20:00, 30 625, Carrillo PER
Al Wahda 1
Fernando [27]
Adel **Al Hosani** - Eisa **Ahmed**, Hamdan **Al Kamali**, Basheer **Saeed•**, Haidar **Ali** (c) (Mohamed **Al Shehhi** 54) - **Magrao** (Khalid **Jalal** 90), **Hugo•** - Fahed **Masoud** (Saeed **Al Kathiri** 64), Mahmoud Khamis **Al Hammadi** - **Fernando** Baiano, Ismaeil **Matar**. Tr: Josef **Hickersberger**
Seongnam Ilhwa Chunma 4
Molina [4], Ognenovski [30], Choi Sung Kuk [71], Cho Dong Geon [81]
Jung Sung Ryong - **Ko** Jae Sung, **Cho** Byung Kuk, Sasa **Ognenovski•** (c), **Hong** Chul - **Kim** Sung Hwan, **Cheon** Kwang Jin (**Jo** Jae Cheol• 45) - **Cho** Dong Geon, **Choi** Sung Kuk, Mauricio **Molina** (**Kim** Jin Ryong 84) - Dzenan **Radoncic** (**Song** Ho Young 69). Tr: **Shin** Tae Yong

SEMI-FINALS

Semi-final
Mohammad Bin Zayed, Abu Dhabi
14-12-2010, 20:00, 22 131, Kuipers NED
TP Mazembe 2
Kabangu [53], Kaluyituka [85]
Robert **Kidiaba** - Joel **Kimwaki**, Jean **Kasusula•**, Pamphile **Mihayo** (c), Eric **Nkulukuta•** - Narcisse **Ekanga**, Hugues **Bedi**, Ngandu **Kasongo** - Given **Singuluma**, Alain **Kaluyituka**, Patou **Kabangu** (Deo **Kanda** 85). Tr: Lamine **N'Diaye**
Internacional 0
Renan - **Nei**, **Bolivar** (c), **Indio•**, **Kleber** - Wilson **Matias**, Pablo **Guinazu** - Andres **D'Alessandro**, **Tinga** (**Giuliano** 63), Rafael **Sobis** (**Oscar** 76) - **Alecsandro** (**Leandro Damiao** 63). Tr: Celso **Roth**

Semi-final
Zayed Sports City, Abu Dhabi
15-12-2010, 21:00, 35 995, Moreno PAN
Seongnam Ilhwa Chunma 0
Jung Sung Ryong - **Ko** Jae Sung, **Cho** Byung Kuk, Sasa **Ognenovski•** (c), **Hong** Chul - **Kim** Sung Hwan - **Cho** Dong Geon, **Choi** Sung Kuk (**Song** Ho Young 67), **Jo** Jae Cheol (**Cheon** Kwang Jin 68), Mauricio **Molina** - Dzenan **Radoncic** (**Kim** Jin Ryong 87). Tr: **Shin** Tae Yong
Internazionale 3
Stankovic [3], Zanetti [32], Milito [73]
Julio Cesar - Javier **Zanetti** (c), **Lucio**, Ivan **Cordoba**, Cristian **Chivu** (Davide **Santon** 79) - Dejan **Stankovic**, Esteban **Cambiasso** - Goran **Pandev**, Wesley **Sneijder** (**Thiago Motta** 4), Samuel **Eto'o** - Diego **Milito**. Tr: Rafael **Benitez**

PLAY-OFFS

5th place play-off
Zayed Sports City, Abu Dhabi
15-12-2010, 18:00, 10 908, Bennett RSA
Pachuca 2 4p
Cvitanich 2 [82 89]
Miguel **Calero** (c) - Paul **Aguilar•** (Juan Carlos **Rojas** 62), Leobardo **Lopez**, Javier **Munoz**, Braulio **Luna** - Raul **Martinez** (Dario **Cvitanich** 77), Francisco **Torres** - Franco **Arizala**, Alejandro **Manso**, Luis Montes - Herculez Gomez (Edgar **Benitez** 62). Tr: Pablo **Marini**
Al Wahda 2 2p
Ismaeil Matar [44], Al Hammadi [77]
Adel **Al Hosani** -Eisa **Ahmed**, Hamdan **Al Kamali••♦**72, Basheer **Saeed•**, Mahmoud Khamis **Al Hammadi** - Abdelrahim **Jumaa**, Yaqoub **Al Hosani** - Fahed **Masoud•** (Mohamed **Al Shehhi•** 64), Ismaeil **Matar** (Omar **Ahmed** 75), **Hugo** - Saeed **Al Kathiri** (Modibi **Diarra** 46). Tr: Josef **Hickersberger**

3rd place play-off
Zayed Sports City, Abu Dhabi
18-12-2010, 18:00, 16 563, Hester NZL
Internacional 4
Tinga [15], Alecsandro 2 [27 71], D'Alessandro [52]
Renan (Roberto **Abbondanzieri** 74) - **Nei**, **Bolivar** (c), **Indio•**, **Kleber** - Wilson **Matias** (**Andrezinho** 81), Pablo **Guinazu** - Rafael **Sobis** (**Giuliano** 62), **Tinga**, Andres **D'Alessandro** - **Alecsandro**. Tr: Celso **Roth**
Seongnam Ilhwa Chunma 2
Molina 2 [84 93+]
Jung Sung Ryong - **Jang** Suk Won••♦34, **Yun** Young Sun, **Hong** Chul - **Kim** Sung Hwan (c) - **Jo** Jae Cheol, **Choi** Sung Kuk - Song Ho Young (Dzenan **Radoncic** 28) (**Kim** Jin Ryong 43) (**Cheon** Kwang Jin 78), **Cho** Dong Geon, Mauricio **Molina**. Tr: **Shin** Tae Yong

FIFA Club World Cup Final	Zayed Sports City Abu Dhabi	Saturday 18-12-2010
Kick-off: 21:00		Attendance: 42 174

TP MAZEMBE 0 3 INTERNAZIONALE

Pandev [13], Eto'o [17], Biabiany [85]

TP MAZEMBE

White shirts with black stripes, White shorts, White socks
Tr: Lamine N'Diaye SEN

Robert Kidiaba

Joel Kimwaki   Jean Kasusula 84 Pamphile Mihayo (c)   Eric Nkulukuta

Hugues Bedi 43   Narcisse Ekanga 33

46 Ngandu Kasongo
   Deo Kanda

Given Singulama   Patou Kabangu

90 Alain Kaluyituka 12
   Mianga Ndonga

70 Diego Milito
Samuel Eto'o   Jonathan Biabiany   Goran Pandev

Esteban Cambiasso   87 Thiago Motta 79   Javier Zanetti (c)
                       McDonald Mariaga

54 Cristian Chivu   Ivan Cordoba   Lucio   Maicon
   Dejan Stankovic

12 Julio Cesar

Tr: Rafael Benitez ESP
Black and blue striped shirts, Black shorts, Black and blue hooped socks

INTERNAZIONALE

MATCH STATS

COD		ITA
16	Shots	9
5	Shots on Goal	6
21	Fouls Committed	9
4	Corner Kicks	5
4	Caught Offside	1
44%	Possession	56%

MATCH OFFICIALS

REFEREE
Yuichi Nishimura JPN

ASSISTANTS
Toru Sagara JPN
Toshiyuki Nagi JPN

4TH OFFICIAL
Victor Carrillo PER

We hoped to give a better performance but we committed a lot of tactical mistakes early in the match and paid for that by losing two goals. From a physical point of view, my players were very tired because the Pachuca and Inter matches were both very difficult. But I must say that Inter were better than us and deserved to win.

Lamine N'Diaye

We had to be very focused from the beginning. We controlled the ball, dominated midfield and ultimately controlled the game because of that. The game had to be about control of the ball and we made sure it was not easy for Mazembe tactically. I chose a strong defence because I knew our oppoents were very dangerous, especially their number 15 Kaluyituka.

Rafa Benitez

PART TWO

THE
NATIONS OF
THE WORLD

AFG – AFGHANISTAN

FIFA/COCA-COLA WORLD RANKING

1993	1994	1995	1996	1997	1998	1999	2000	2001	2002	2003	2004	2005	2006	2007	2008	2009	2010
-	-	-	-	-	-	-	-	-	-	196	200	189	180	191	183	193	195

	2010												Hi/Lo
	Jan	Feb	Mar	Mar	Apr	May	Jul	Aug	Sep	Oct	Nov	Dec	**173**
	193	194	194	191	193	189	193	195	194	196	195	195	**204**

The Afghanistan under-23 team wrote the major story in Afghan football in 2010 by reaching the final of the South Asian Federation Games which were held in Bangladesh in February. Although not the most illustrious tournament in the international football calendar it still represented a significant step forward for Afghanistan who won all three of their first round group games in Dhaka before defeating the Maldives in the semi-finals. That set up a final against the hosts who ran out comfortable 4-0 winners but despite coming away with the silver medal the team wasn't entered into the football tournament of the Asian Games, which is also run as an under-23 event. The full national team played just one match in 2010 - a friendly against neighbours Tajikistan at the end of the year - and their involvement at international level remains confined largely to a cycle of FIFA World Cup qualifiers, regional South Asian tournaments and the biennial AFC Challenge Cup. In the latter, Afghanistan were drawn against Bhutan in a preliminary round play-off for the 2012 tournament but with the security situation in Afghanistan still preventing the national team playing matches in Kabul, both legs of the tie were scheduled to be played in neutral India at the Tau Devi Lal Stadium in Guragon.

FIFA WORLD CUP RECORD
1930-2002 DNE 2006-2010 DNQ

AFGHANISTAN FOOTBALL FEDERATION (AFF)

PO Box 128, Kabul

☎ +93 75 2023770
📠 +93 75 2023770
✉ aff.kabul@gmail.com
🖥 www.aff.com
FA 1933 CON 1954 FIFA 1948
P Keramuddin Karim
GS Mukhtar Rustami

FIFA BIG COUNT 2006

Total players	526 781
% of population	1.70%
Male	526 441
Female	340
Amateurs 18+	4928
Youth under 18	13 188
Unregistered	4000
Professionals	0
Referees	100
Admin & coaches	45
Number of clubs	224
Number of teams	500

MAJOR CITIES/TOWNS

		Population
1	Kabul	2 413 032
2	Herat	395 877
3	Kandahar	358 845
4	Mazar-e-Sharif	277 302
5	Jalabad	143 525
6	Kunduz	113 746
7	Balkh	89 782
8	Baglan	76 968
9	Meymaneh	58 801
10	Gurian	52 573
11	Ghazni	50 535
12	Khanabad	49 701
13	Taluqan	44 658
14	Pagman	44 072
15	Sibargan	39 412
16	Charikar	38 850
17	Aqcah	38 734
18	Pil-e Humri	378 374
19	Tash Gozar	29 875

AFGHANESTAN • AFGHANISTAN

Capital	Kabul	Population	28 396 000 (43)	% in cities	24%
GDP per capita	$700 (219)	Area km²	652 230 km² (41)	GMT +/-	+4.5
Neighbours (km)	China 76, Iran 936, Pakistan 2430, Tajikistan 1206, Turkmenistan 744, Uzbekistan 137				

RECENT INTERNATIONALS PLAYED BY AFGHANISTAN

2005	Opponents	Score		Venue	Comp	Scorers	Att	Referee
9-11	Tajikistan	L	0-4	Dushanbe	Fr			
7-12	Maldives	L	1-9	Karachi	SAFr1	Sayed Maqsood [39]		
9-12	Pakistan	L	0-1	Karachi	SAFr1			
11-12	Sri Lanka	W	2-1	Karachi	SAFr1	Hafizullah Qadami [35], Abdul Maroof Gullistani [41]		
2006								
1-04	India	L	0-2	Chittagong	CCr1		2 500	Al Ghatrifi OMA
3-04	Chinese Taipei	D	2-2	Chittagong	CCr1	Hafizullah Qadami 2 [20 23]	2 500	Lee Gi Young KOR
5-04	Philippines	D	1-1	Chittagong	CCr1	Sayed Maqsood [26]	3 000	Mujghef JOR
2007								
8-10	Syria	L	0-3	Damascus	WCq		3 000	Al Ghamdi KSA
26-10	Syria	L	1-2	Dushanbe	WCq	Obaidullah Karimi [15]	2 000	Irmatov UZB
2008								
5-05	Bangladesh	D	0-0	Bishkek	CCq		3 000	Al Senan UAE
7-05	Kyrgyzstan	W	1-0	Bishkek	CCq	Ata Yamrali [38]	7 000	Shaharul MAS
4-06	Sri Lanka	D	2-2	Colombo	SAFr1	Harez-Arian Habib 2 [7 49]		
6-06	Bangladesh	D	2-2	Colombo	SAFr1	Ata Yamrali [7], Mustafa Hadid [24]		
8-06	Bhutan	L	1-3	Colombo	SAFr1	Harez-Arian Habib [87]		
30-07	India	L	0-1	Hyderabad	CCr1		300	Iemoto JPN
1-08	Turkmenistan	L	0-5	Hyderabad	CCr1		350	Shamsuzzaman BAN
3-08	Tajikistan	L	0-4	Hyderabad	CCr1		150	Vo Minh Tri VIE
17-10	Nepal	D	2-2	Petaling Jaya	Fr	Hashmatullah Barekzai 2 [62 72]		
20-10	Malaysia	L	0-6	Petaling Jaya	Fr			
2009								
5-12	India †	L	0-1	Dhaka	SAFr1			
7-12	Maldives	L	1-3	Dhaka	SAFr1	Hashmatullah Barekzai [30]		
9-12	Nepal	L	0-3	Dhaka	SAFr1			
2010								
17-11	Tajikistan	L	0-1	Dushanbe	Fr			

SAF = South Asian Football Federation Cup • AC = Asian Cup • CC = AFC Challenge Cup • WC = FIFA World Cup
q = qualifier • r1 = first round group • † Not a full international

AIA – ANGUILLA

FIFA/COCA-COLA WORLD RANKING

1993	1994	1995	1996	1997	1998	1999	2000	2001	2002	2003	2004	2005	2006	2007	2008	2009	2010
-	-	-	-	190	197	202	197	194	196	198	197	198	196	198	201	203	203

2010												Hi/Lo
Jan	Feb	Mar	Mar	Apr	May	Jul	Aug	Sep	Oct	Nov	Dec	**189**
203	203	203	202	202	202	202	202	203	203	203	203	**205**

A 2-1 victory over close neighbours Saint Martin in the 2010 Digicel Caribbean Cup was a cause for celebration on the tiny island of Anguilla although the win will not go down in the record books as Saint Martin is not a member of FIFA and has only associate membership status of the regional governing body CONCACAF. Nevertheless it represented a first win for nine years for the national team and only their third overall. The timing could not have been better, coming the week after the official opening of the Anguilla Football Association Technical Centre. This latest Goal Project also provides football on the island with a floodlit pitch, stands, dressing rooms and new offices for the AFA. Described by the AFA as the "first proper football facilities" in the country, the hope is that they will help the national team to make progress up the FIFA/Coca-Cola World Ranking. With the win over Saint Martin not contributing to the ranking, Anguilla once again found itself at the bottom at the end of the year, level with San Marino, Montserrat, American Samoa and Papua New Guinea. The facilities should also help the club game to develop. In 2010, Roaring Lions completed the double by winning their first league title since 2006 and then beat Attackers - double winners in 2008 and 2009 - 3-1 in the Cup Final at Webster Park.

FIFA WORLD CUP RECORD
1930-1998 DNE 2002-2010 DNQ

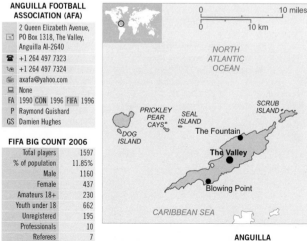

ANGUILLA FOOTBALL ASSOCIATION (AFA)

✉	2 Queen Elizabeth Avenue, PO Box 1318, The Valley, Anguilla AI-2640
☎	+1 264 497 7323
📠	+1 264 497 7324
✉	axafa@yahoo.com
🖳	None
FA	1990 CON 1996 FIFA 1996
P	Raymond Guishard
GS	Damien Hughes

FIFA BIG COUNT 2006

Total players	1597
% of population	11.85%
Male	1160
Female	437
Amateurs 18+	230
Youth under 18	662
Unregistered	195
Professionals	10
Referees	7
Admin & coaches	63
Number of clubs	11
Number of teams	16

MAJOR CITIES/TOWNS

		Population
1	The Valley	1767
2	The Quarter	1500
3	Stoney Ground	1435
4	Island Harbour	1048
5	George Hill	1040
6	The Farrington	977
7	West End	940
8	Blowing Point	911
9	Sandy Hill	872
10	East End	689
11	North Hill	507
12	Sandy Ground	425

ANGUILLA

Capital	The Valley	Population	14 436 (221)	% in cities	100%
GDP per capita	$8800 (113)	Area km²	91 km² (226)	GMT + / -	-4
Neighbours (km)	Coast 61				

RECENT INTERNATIONALS PLAYED BY ANGUILLA

2004	Opponents	Score		Venue	Comp	Scorers	Att	Referee
19-03	Dominican Republic	D	0-0	Santo Domingo	WCq		400	Mattus CRC
21-03	Dominican Republic	L	0-6	Santo Domingo	WCq		850	Porras CRC
2005								
No international matches played in 2005								
2006								
20-09	Antigua and Barbuda	L	3-5	St John's	CCq	Gaekwad St Hillaire [13], Kapil Assent [51], Richard O'Connor [90]	300	Wijngaarde SUR
22-09	St Kitts and Nevis	L	1-6	St John's	CCq	Richard O'Connor [22]	500	Phillips GRN
24-09	Barbados	L	1-7	St John's	CCq	Girdon Connor [48]	2 800	Wijngaarde SUR
2007								
No international matches played in 2007								
2008								
6-02	El Salvador	L	0-12	San Salvador	WCq		15 000	Jauregui ANT
26-03	El Salvador	L	0-4	Washington DC	WCq		22 670	Bedeau GRN
17-09	St Vincent/Grenadines	L	1-3	Fort de France	CCq	Troy Jeffers OG [38]	100	Fanus LCA
19-09	Martinique †	L	1-3	Fort de France	CCq	Kapil Battice [83]	500	George LCA
2009								
No international matches played in 2009								
2010								
18-09	British Virgin Islands	L	1-2	Saint Martin	Fr			
2-10	Puerto Rico	L	1-3	Bayamon	CCq	Walwyn Benjamin [54p]	2 050	Thomas JAM
4-10	Cayman Islands	L	1-4	Bayamon	CCq	Javille Brooks [32]	500	Davis TRI
6-10	Saint Martin †	W	2-1	Bayamon	CCq	Javille Brooks [19], Terrence Rogers [38]	500	Davis TRI

Fr = Friendly match • WC = FIFA World Cup • CC = Digicel Caribbean Cup • q = qualifier • † Not a full international

CCCAFA CUP 2010
RWP Annexe, The Valley, 25-04-2010
Roaring Lions 3-1 Attackers

ALB – ALBANIA

FIFA/COCA-COLA WORLD RANKING

1993	1994	1995	1996	1997	1998	1999	2000	2001	2002	2003	2004	2005	2006	2007	2008	2009	2010
92	100	91	116	116	106	83	72	96	93	89	86	82	87	80	81	96	65

						2010							Hi/Lo
Jan	Feb	Mar	Mar	Apr	May	Jul	Aug	Sep	Oct	Nov	Dec		**58**
96	97	96	83	80	79	71	70	67	65	58	65		**124**

In stark contrast to the final day dramas of recent seasons, the destination of the 2010 championship was never in question as Dinamo Tirana secured their 18th title at a canter. Indeed, they could afford to lose eight of their last 10 matches - including seven in a row - and still finish eight points clear of Besa in second place. Dinamo's collapse of form in the spring was remarkable and they finished with the third worst defensive record in the league, but having won 17 and drawn three of their first 21 games - thanks largely to the goals of Elis Bakaj and Fatjon Sefa - it didn't matter. Their hopes of a first double since 1990 fell by the wayside during their spring collapse and it was Besa who won an exciting final against Vllaznia. Besa equalised with just five minutes remaining before an injury-time winner from Paulin Dhembi secured Besa a second cup triumph in four seasons. The appointment of Josip Kuze as national team coach in mid-2009 had a galvanising effect as the Croat steered his team to a run of eight games without defeat, double the previous record. With the run also including a record equalling four consecutive wins, not to mention the record 6-1 victory over Cyprus and the solid start to the qualifiers for Euro 2012, it saw Albania climb to their highest ever position of 58th in the FIFA/Coca-Cola World Ranking.

FIFA WORLD CUP RECORD

1930-1962 DNE 1966 DNQ 1970 DNE 1974 DNQ 1978 DNE 1982-2010 DNQ

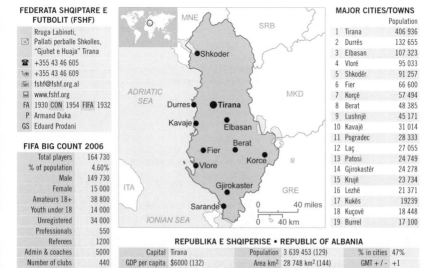

FEDERATA SHQIPTARE E FUTBOLIT (FSHF)

Rruga Labinoti,
Pallati perballe Shkolles,
"Gjuhet e Huaja" Tirana

☎ +355 43 46 605
📠 +355 43 46 609
📧 fshf@fshf.org.al
🖥 www.fshf.org
FA 1930 CON 1954 FIFA 1932
P Armand Duka
GS Eduard Prodani

FIFA BIG COUNT 2006

Total players	164 730
% of population	4.60%
Male	149 730
Female	15 000
Amateurs 18+	38 800
Youth under 18	14 000
Unregistered	34 000
Professionals	550
Referees	1200
Admin & coaches	5000
Number of clubs	440
Number of teams	574

MAJOR CITIES/TOWNS

		Population
1	Tirana	406 936
2	Durrës	132 655
3	Elbasan	107 323
4	Vlorë	95 033
5	Shkodër	91 257
6	Fier	66 600
7	Korçë	57 494
8	Berat	48 385
9	Lushnjë	45 171
10	Kavajë	31 014
11	Pogradec	28 333
12	Laç	27 055
13	Patosi	24 749
14	Gjirokastër	24 278
15	Krujë	23 734
16	Lezhë	21 371
17	Kukës	19239
18	Kuçovë	18 448
19	Burrel	17 100

REPUBLIKA E SHQIPERISE • REPUBLIC OF ALBANIA

Capital	Tirana	Population	3 639 453 (129)	% in cities	47%
GDP per capita	$6000 (132)	Area km²	28 748 km² (144)	GMT +/-	+1
Neighbours (km)	Greece 282, Macedonia 151, Montenegro 172, Kosovo 112 • Coast 362		

RECENT INTERNATIONALS PLAYED BY ALBANIA

2007	Opponents	Score		Venue	Comp	Scorers	Att	Referee
7-02	FYR Macedonia	L	0-1	Tirana	Fr		8 000	Bertini ITA
24-03	Slovenia	D	0-0	Shkoder	ECq		7 000	Attard MLT
28-03	Bulgaria	D	0-0	Sofia	ECq		19 800	Eriksson SWE
2-06	Luxembourg	W	2-0	Tirana	ECq	Kapllani [38], Haxhi [57]	3 000	Silgava GEO
6-06	Luxembourg	W	3-0	Luxembourg	ECq	Skela [25], Kapllani 2 [36 72]	4 325	Malzinskas LTU
22-08	Malta	W	3-0	Tirana	Fr	Salihi [34], Berisha [46], Duro [60]		
12-09	Netherlands	L	0-1	Tirana	ECq		15 000	Riley ENG
13-10	Slovenia	D	0-0	Celje	ECq		3 700	Gomes POR
17-10	Bulgaria	D	1-1	Tirana	ECq	Duro.K [25]	3 000	Stuchlik AUT
17-11	Belarus	L	2-4	Tirana	ECq	Bogdani [43], Kapllani [44]	2 064	Demirlek TUR
21-11	Romania	L	1-6	Bucharest	ECq	Kapllani [64]	23 427	Trivkovic CRO
2008								
27-05	Poland	L	0-1	Reutlingen	Fr		2 200	Kircher GER
20-08	Liechtenstein	W	2-0	Tirana	Fr	Hyka [1], Kapllani [18]	1 500	Vlk SVK
6-09	Sweden	D	0-0	Tirana	WVq		13 522	Undiano ESP
10-09	Malta	W	3-0	Tirana	WCq	Bogdani [45], Duro [84], Dallku [90]	7 400	Schoergenhofer AUT
11-10	Hungary	L	0-2	Budapest	WCq		18 000	Circhetta SUI
15-10	Portugal	D	0-0	Braga	WCq		29 500	Kircher GER
19-11	Azerbaijan	D	1-1	Baku	Fr	Skela [12]	10 000	Silagava GEO
2009								
11-02	Malta	D	0-0	Ta'Qali	WCq		2041	Deaconu ROU
28-03	Hungary	L	0-1	Tirana	WCq		12 000	Kuipers NED
1-04	Denmark	L	0-3	Copenhagen	WCq		24 320	Skomina SVN
6-06	Portugal	L	1-2	Tirana	WCq	Bogdani [29]	13 320	Meyer GER
10-06	Georgia	D	1-1	Tirana	Fr	Agolli [58]	2 000	Stavrev MKD
12-08	Cyprus	W	6-1	Tirana	Fr	Skela 2 [25p 44p], Bogdani [65], OG [67], Agolli [71], Vila [75]		Yildrim TUR
9-09	Denmark	D	1-1	Tirana	WCq	Bogdani [51]	8 000	Cakir TUR
14-10	Sweden	L	1-4	Stockholm	WCq	Salihi [57]	25 342	Ivanov.N RUS
14-11	Estonia	D	0-0	Tallinn	Fr		2 110	Kancleris LTU
2010								
3-03	Northern Ireland	W	1-0	Tirana	Fr	Skela [25]	7 500	Pilav BIH
25-05	Montenegro	W	1-0	Podgorica	Fr	Salihi [79]	7 000	Strahonja CRO
2-06	Andorra	W	1-0	Tirana	Fr	Salihi [44]	3 000	Meckarovski MKD
11-08	Uzbekistan	W	1-0	Durres	Fr	Salihi [14]	8 000	Radovanovic MNE
3-09	Romania	D	1-1	Piatra-Neamt	ECq	Muzaka [87]	13 000	Schorgenhofer AUT
7-09	Luxembourg	W	1-0	Shkoder	ECq	Salihi [37]	11 800	Trutz SVK
8-10	Bosnia-Herzegovina	D	1-1	Tirana	ECq	Duro [45]	11 300	Jakobsson ISL
12-10	Belarus	L	0-2	Minsk	ECq		7 000	Rasmussen DEN
17-11	Macedonia FYR	D	0-0	Korce	Fr		12 000	Gocek TUR

Fr = Friendly match • EC = UEFA EURO 2008/2012 • WC = FIFA World Cup • q = qualifier

ALBANIA NATIONAL TEAM HISTORICAL RECORDS

Caps
73 - Foto Strakosha 1990-2004 • **71** - Altin Lala 1998- • **68** - Igli Tare 1997-2007 • **67** - Alban Bushi 1995-2007 • **66** - Altin Haxhi 1995-2009 & Ervin Skela 2000- • **63** - Altin Rraklli 1992-2005 • **62** - Klodian Duro 2000- • **59** - Rudi Vata 1990-2000 • **54** - Erjon Bogdani 1996-

Goals
14 - Alban Bushi 1995-2007 • **13** - Ervin Skela 2000- • **12** - Erjon Bogdani 1996- • **11** - Altin Rraklli 1992-2005 • **10** - Sokol Kushta 1987-96, Igli Tare 1997-2007 • **8** - Adrian Aliaj 2002-06 • **6** - Loro Borici 1946-58, Edmond Kapllani 2004-08, Bledar Kola 1994-2001 & Hamdi Salihi 2006-

Past Coaches
Ljubisa Brocic YUG 1946 • Adem Karapici 1947 • Sllave Llambi 1948-50 • Miklos Vadas HUN 1953 • Zyber Konci 1963-65 • Loro Borici 1965-72 • Myslym Alla 1972-73 • Ilia Shuke 1973 • Zyber Konci 1980 • Loro Borici 1981 • Shyqyri Rreli 1982-85 • Agron Sulaj 1985-88 • Shyqyri Rreli 1988-90 • Agron Sulaj 1990 • Bejkush Birce 1990-94 • Neptun Bajko 1994-96 • Astrit Hafizi 1996-99 • Medin Zhega 2000-01 • Sulejman Demollari 2001-02 • Giuseppe Dossena ITA 2002 • Hans-Peter Briegel GER 2002-06 • Otto Baric CRO 2006-07 • Slavko Kovacic 2007 • Arie Haan NED 2008-09 • Josip Kuze CRO 2009-

ALBANIA 2009-10

KATEGORIA SUPERIORE

	Pl	W	D	L	F	A	Pts	Dinamo	Besa	Tirana	Laçi	Flamurtari	Vllaznia	Shkumbini	Teuta	Kastrioti	Skënd'beu	Apolonia	Gramozi
Dinamo Tiranë †	33	19	4	10	56	42	61		1-0 4-3	2-1	1-1 2-4	1-0	4-2	2-1	1-0 1-2	2-0 1-1	3-0	3-2	4-0 1-0
Besa Kavajë ‡	33	15	8	10	42	33	53	0-1		1-1 1-1	1-0	1-0 1-2	2-0 1-2	2-0 2-0	1-1	1-0	1-0 1-2	0-0 2-0 1-0	6-4
KF Tirana ‡	33	15	7	11	38	32	52	1-2 3-2	0-0		1-0 1-2	1-3	0-1 1-2	2-0	2-0 2-1	1-1 0-1	1-0	4-1	1-1 1-0
Laçi ‡	33	14	9	10	35	28	51	0-1	0-0 0-1	1-0		3-2 3-1	3-1	1-0 0-0	0-0	1-0	0-0 1-0	3-2 2-0 1-1	1-0
Flamurtari Vlorë	33	13	8	12	42	39	47	0-3 2-1	3-0	0-2 3-1	0-0		2-0	1-1 3-2	0-3	2-0 3-0	1-1	2-0 1-0	2-0
Vllaznia Shkodër	33	13	7	13	34	39	46	0-0	2-3 2-0	0-1	1-2 1-0	2-2 1-1		2-0	2-1 0-2	1-0	3-2 0-2	1-0	1-0
Shkumbini Peqin	33	13	6	14	33	33	45	4-0 1-0	1-2	1-0 0-1	1-0	2-1	2-1 0-0		4-1 1-0	1-0 2-0	1-0	3-0	1-1 2-1
Teuta Durrës	33	13	6	14	33	40	45	1-3	1-1 3-2	0-1	2-1 0-0	1-0 3-1	1-0	1-0		2-1	2-0 0-0 0-2	1-1 2-0 0-2	
Kastrioti Krujë §3	33	13	6	14	33	35	42	1-3	1-0 3-2	0-1	0-0 1-0	1-1	1-0 2-0	4-1	1-2 3-0		2-1 1-2	1-1	1-0
Skënderbeu Korçë	33	11	9	13	41	41	42	1-1 4-3	0-2	1-1 2-2	4-3	1-0 0-1	1-1	1-0 3-1	3-0	0-1		2-3 1-1	4-1
Apolonia Fier	33	10	8	15	36	43	38	3-0 2-1	0-2	2-0 1-2	2-0	1-1	1-1 0-1	1-0 0-0	2-0	2-3 2-1	1-1		3-0
Gramozi Ersekë	33	6	8	19	25	43	26	0-1	0-0	0-1	1-2	2-0 1-1	1-1 1-2	0-0		2-0	0-0 0-1 2-0	0-2 1-0	3-0

23/08/2009 - 19/05/2010 • † Qualified for the UEFA Champions League • ‡ Qualified for the Europa League • § = points deducted • Matches in bold awarded • Relegation play-offs: **Skënderbeu** 1-0 Kamëz • **Kastrioti** 1-0 Lushnja • Top scorers: **18** - Daniel Xhafaj, Besa • **15** - Elis Bakaj, Dinamo; Mladen Brkic SRB, Apolonia & Migen Memelli, Flamurtari • **13** - Fatjon Sefa, Dinamo • **11** - Milaim Guerrib CRO, Skënderbeu

ALBANIA 2009-10
KATEGORIA E PARE (2)

	Pl	W	D	L	F	A	Pts
Bylis Ballshi	30	22	3	5	57	26	69
KF Elbasani	30	19	5	6	56	25	62
Dajti Kamëz	30	19	5	6	50	21	62
KS Lushnja	30	17	9	4	59	10	60
Partizani Tiranë	30	17	6	7	49	35	57
Pogradeci	30	14	6	10	40	39	48
Ada Velipojë	30	13	3	14	46	34	42
Besëlidhja Lezhë	30	10	7	13	32	39	37
Luftëtari Gjirokastër	30	10	6	14	38	45	36
Gramshi	30	8	8	14	23	34	32
Bilisht Sport	30	9	5	16	30	49	32
Burreli	30	7	10	13	26	41	31
Skrapari	30	9	4	17	29	56	31
Memaliaj	30	7	8	15	23	37	29
Turbina Cërrik	30	7	6	17	34	53	27
Sopoti Librazhd	30	5	3	22	14	62	18

29/08/2009 - 15/05/2010 • § = points deducted • Relegation play-offs: Memaliaj 0-1 **Tomori** • Skrapari 0-1 **Tërbuni**

MEDALS TABLE

		Overall			League			Cup	
		G	S	B	G	S	B	G	S
1	KF Tiranë	36	21	12	24	13	12	12	8
2	Partizani Tiranë	30	27	8	15	19	8	15	8
3	Dinamo Tiranë	31	14	11	18	9	11	13	5
4	Vllaznia Shkodër	15	18	14	9	11	14	6	7
5	Teuta Durrës	4	11	5	1	5	5	3	6
6	SK Elbasani	4	2	1	2	1	1	2	1
7	Flamurtari Vlorë	4	14	3	1	6	3	3	8
8	Besa Kavajë	2	8	10		2	10	2	6
9	Skënderbeu Korçë	1	6	2	1	3	2		3
10	Apollonia Fier	1						1	
11	Lushnja		3						3
12	Tomori Berat		2			1			1
13	Albpetrol Patosi		1						1
	Luftëtari Gjirokastër	1			1				
15	Bylis Ballshi			1			1		

KUPA E SHQIPERISE 2009-10

Round of 16		Quarter-finals			Semi-finals			Final	
Besa Kavajë	1	1							
Laçi *	0	1	**Besa Kavajë** *	2	2				
KS Lushnja *	2	1	KF Tirana	0	4				
KF Tirana	2	2				**Besa Kavajë** *	1	1	
Dinamo Tiranë	0	3				Shkumbini Peqin	1	0	
Bylis Ballshi *	1	1	Dinamo Tiranë	1	0				
Kastrioti Krujë *	1	0	**Shkumbini Peqin** *	2	1				
Shkumbini Peqin	1	1						**Besa Kavajë** ‡	2
Teuta Durrës	1	2						Vllaznia Shkodër	1
Partizani Tiranë *	1	0	**Teuta Durrës**	1	0				
Flamurtari Vlorë	0	1	Gramozi Ersekë *	1	0			**CUP FINAL**	
Gramozi Ersekë *	1	1				Teuta Durrës *	1	0	Qemal Stafa, Tirana
Skënderbeu Korçë *	1	1				**Vllaznia Shkodër**	0	2	9-05-2010, Ref: Ceferin SVN
Apolonia Fier	0	2	Skënderbeu Korçë *	0	0				Scorers - Renato Arapi [85], Paulin
Dajti Kamëz *	1	2	**Vllaznia Shkodër**	0	4				Dhembi [97] for Besa; Bekim Bala [63]
Vllaznia Shkodër	3	2				* Home team in the first leg • ‡ Qualified for the Europa League			for Vllaznia

Cup Final line-ups: **Besa** - Shehi, Dragusha, Vrapi, Fagu, Mihani, Poçi (Babamusta 120), Sinani (Hasalla 79), Xhafa, Mançaku (Dhëmbi 67), Arapi, Shkëmbi. Tr: Shpetim Duro • **Vllaznia** - Grima, Smajli, Kraja, Osja (Hadzibulic 90), Phoenix (Djepaxhija 95), Shtupina, Belisha, Rajovic, Bala, Nallbani, Doçi (Alikaj 100). Tr: Edi Martini

ALG – ALGERIA

FIFA/COCA-COLA WORLD RANKING

1993	1994	1995	1996	1997	1998	1999	2000	2001	2002	2003	2004	2005	2006	2007	2008	2009	2010
35	57	48	49	59	71	86	82	75	68	62	73	80	80	79	64	26	35

2010												Hi/Lo
Jan	Feb	Mar	Mar	Apr	May	Jul	Aug	Sep	Oct	Nov	Dec	26
26	31	32	27	31	30	33	33	35	33	34	35	103

A single match at the FIFA World Cup finals rescued a disastrous year for Algeria's national team, glossing over a record of just three wins and seven goals scored in 16 matches. The 0-0 draw with England in Cape Town proved a massive highlight for Algeria, whose dramatic qualification for the tournament in November 2009 and semi-final place at the 2010 African Nations Cup finals held out high hopes of a repeat of their giant killing feat at the 1982 World Cup. But coach Rabah Saadane showed little faith in his squad and just weeks before the World Cup was still looking for players with Algerian roots among the large North African Diaspora in Europe. He took several new additions to South Africa, dropped long-standing captain Karim Matmour and, in the end, engendered some feisty performances albeit without scoring a single goal. Saadane departed three months later after a home draw with Tanzania at the start of the 2012 Nations Cup qualifying campaign, replaced by Abdelhak Benchikha, who suffered the ignominy of defeat by the Central African Republic in his October debut. JS Kabylie reached the semi-final of the CAF Champions League, winning their group in the league phase but then being beaten 3-1 by eventual winners TP Mazembe in the final four whilst Mouloudia Alger won the league and Entente Setif the cup.

FIFA WORLD CUP RECORD
1930-1966 DNE 1970-1978 DNQ **1982** 13 r1 **1986** 22 r1 1990-2006 DNQ **2010** 28 r1

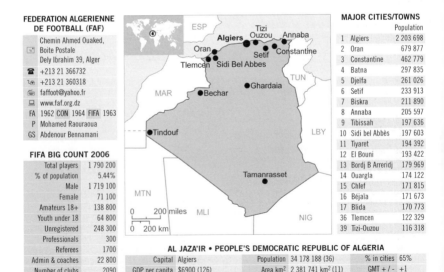

FEDERATION ALGERIENNE DE FOOTBALL (FAF)

Chemin Ahmed Ouaked,
Boite Postale
Dely Ibrahim 39, Alger
☎ +213 21 366732
📠 +213 21 360318
📧 faffoot@yahoo.fr
🖥 www.faf.org.dz
FA 1962 CON 1964 FIFA 1963
P Mohamed Raouraoua
GS Abdenour Bennamani

FIFA BIG COUNT 2006

Total players	1 790 200
% of population	5.44%
Male	1 719 100
Female	71 100
Amateurs 18+	138 800
Youth under 18	64 800
Unregistered	248 300
Professionals	300
Referees	1700
Admin & coaches	22 800
Number of clubs	2090
Number of teams	2560

MAJOR CITIES/TOWNS

		Population
1	Algiers	2 203 698
2	Oran	679 877
3	Constantine	462 779
4	Batna	297 835
5	Djelfa	261 026
6	Setif	233 913
7	Biskra	211 890
8	Annaba	205 597
9	Tibissah	197 636
10	Sidi bel Abbès	197 603
11	Tiyaret	194 392
12	El Bouni	193 422
13	Bordj B Arreridj	179 969
14	Ouargla	174 122
15	Chlef	171 815
16	Béjaïa	171 673
17	Blida	170 773
36	Tlemcen	122 329
39	Tizi-Ouzou	116 318

AL JAZA'IR • PEOPLE'S DEMOCRATIC REPUBLIC OF ALGERIA

Capital	Algiers	Population	34 178 188 (36)	% in cities	65%
GDP per capita	$6900 (126)	Area km²	2 381 741 km² (11)	GMT +/-	+1
Neighbours (km)	Libya 982, Mali 1376, Mauritania 463, Morocco 1559, Niger 956, Tunisia 965 • Coast 998		

RECENT INTERNATIONALS PLAYED BY ALGERIA

2008	Opponents	Score		Venue	Comp	Scorers	Att	Referee
26-03	Congo DR	D	1-1	Goussainville	Fr	Ghilas 89p		Rouinsard FRA
31-05	Senegal	L	0-1	Dakar	WCq		50 000	Kotey GHA
6-06	Liberia	W	3-0	Blida	WCq	Djebbour 15, Ziani 2 20 48p	40 000	Lemghambodj MTN
14-06	Gambia	L	0-1	Banjul	WCq		18 000	Coulibaly MLI
20-06	Gambia	W	1-0	Blida	WCq	Yahia 33	25 000	Ndume GAB
20-08	UAE	W	1-0	Le Touquet	Fr	Bezzaz 7	1 000	Gauthier FRA
5-09	Senegal	W	3-2	Blida	WCq	OG 60, Saifi 66, Yahia 72	35 000	Maillet SEY
11-10	Liberia	D	0-0	Monrovia	WCq		2 000	Auda EGY
18-11	Mali	D	1-1	Rouen	Fr	Abdesslam 90		
2009								
11-02	Benin	W	2-1	Blida	Fr	Ghezzal 35, Ghilas 45		
28-03	Rwanda	D	0-0	Kigali	WCq		22 000	Codjia BEN
7-06	Egypt	W	3-1	Blida	WCq	Matmour 60, Ghezzal 64, Djebbour 77	26 500	Bennett RSA
20-06	Zambia	W	2-0	Chililabombwe	WCq	Bougherra 21, Saifi 66	9 000	Evehe CMR
12-08	Uruguay	W	1-0	Algiers	Fr	Djebbour 79	20 000	Harzi TUN
6-09	Zambia	W	1-0	Blida	WCq	Saifi 59	30 000	Seechurn MRI
11-10	Rwanda	W	3-1	Blida	WCq	Ghezzal 22, Belhadj 45, Ziani 95+p	22 000	Keita GUI
14-11	Egypt	L	0-2	Cairo	WCq		75 000	Damon RSA
18-11	Egypt	W	1-0	Omdurman	WCpo	Yahia 40	35 000	Maillet SEY
2010								
11-01	Malawi	L	0-3	Luanda	CNr1		1 000	Diatta SEN
14-01	Mali	W	1-0	Luanda	CNr1	Halliche 43	4 000	Ssegonga UGA
18-01	Angola	D	0-0	Luanda	CNr1		40 000	Damon RSA
24-01	Côte d'Ivoire	W	3-2	Cabinda	CNqf	Matmour 39, Bougherra 92+, Bouazza 92	10 000	Maillet SEY
28-01	Egypt	L	0-4	Benguela	CNsf		30 000	Codjia BEN
30-01	Nigeria	L	0-1	Benguela	CN3p		12 000	Diatta SEN
3-03	Algeria	L	0-3	Algiers	Fr		65 000	Diatta SEN
28-05	Republic of Ireland	L	0-3	Dublin	Fr		16 800	Braamhaar NED
5-06	UAE	W	1-0	Fürth	Fr	Ziani 51p	12 500	Grafe GER
13-06	Slovenia	L	0-1	Polokwane	WCr1		30 325	Batres GUA
18-06	England	D	0-0	Cape Town	WCr1		64 100	Irmatov UZB
23-06	USA	L	0-1	Pretoria	WCr1		35 827	De Bleeckere BEL
11-08	Gabon	L	1-2	Algiers	Fr	Djebbour 85	55 000	Rouaissi MAR
3-09	Tanzania	D	1-1	Blida	CNq	Guedioura 44	30 000	Djaoupe TOG
8-10	Central African Rep	L	0-2	Bangui	CNq		25 000	Carvalho ANG
17-11	Luxembourg	D	0-0	Luxembourg	Fr		7 033	Sippel GER

Fr = Friendly match • CN = CAF African Cup of Nations • WC = FIFA World Cup • q = qualifier • r1 = first round group • qf = quarter-final

ALGERIA NATIONAL TEAM HISTORICAL RECORDS

Caps
107 - Mahieddine Meftah 1989-2002 • **89** - Lakhdar Belloumi 1978-89 • **88** - Abdelhafid Tasfaout 1991-2002 • **87** - Billel Dziri 1992-2005 • **83** - Rabah Madjer 1978-92 • **80** - Djamel Menad 1980-95 • **73** - Fodil Megharia 1984-92 • **71** - Mahmoud Guendouz 1977-86 • **67** - Salah Assad 1977-89 • Yazid Mansouri 2001-

Goals
35 - Abdelhafid Tasfaout 1990-2002 • **34** - Lakhdar Belloumi 1978-89 • **29** - Rabah Madjer 1978-92 • **24** - Djamel Menad 1982-95 • **22** - Tedj Bensaoula 1979-86 • **18** - Rafik Saifi 1999- • **13** - Salah Assad 1978-88 • **12** - Hacene Lalmas 1964-74 • **10** - Ali Mecabih 1995-2003 • **9** - Billel Dziri 1993-2002

Past Coaches
Kader Firoud 1963 • Smail Khabatou 1963-64 • Abderrahmane Ibrir 1964-65 • Smail Khabatou 1965-66 • Lucien Leduc FRA 1966-69 • Said Amara 1969 • Hamid Zouba & Abdelaziz Ben Tifour 1969-70 • Hamid Zouba 1970-71 • Rachid Mekloufi 1971-72 • Mohamed El Kenz & Abdulhamid Sellal 1972-73 • Said Amara 1973 • Valentin Makkri ROU 1974-75 • Rachid Mekloufi 1975-79 • Mahieddine Khalef 1979 • Mahieddine Khalef & Zdravko Rajkov YUG 1979-80 • Zdravko Rajkov YUG 1980-81 • Evgeni Rogov URS, Mohamed Maouche & Rabah Saadane 1981-82 • Mahieddine Khalef 1982 • Hamid Zouba 1982-84 • Mahieddine Khalef 1984 • Rabah Saadane 1984-86 • Evgeni Rogov 1986-88 • Kamel Lemoui 1988-89 • Abdelhamid Kermali & Ali Fergani 1989-92 • Meziane Ighil 1992-93 • Rabah Madjer 1993-95 • Ali Fergani & Mourad Abdelouahab 1995-96 • Hamid Zouba & Abdelhamid Kermali 1996-97 • Abderrahmane Mehdaoui 1997-98 • Meziane Ighil & Marcel Pigulea ROU 1998-99 • Boualem Charef & Rabah Saadane 1999 • Nacer Sandjak 1999-2000 • Abdelghani Djaadaoui 2000-01 • Hamid Zouba & Abdelhamid Kermali 2001 • Rabah Madjer 2001-02 • Hamid Zouba 2002-03 • Rachid Bouaratta 2003 • George Leekens BEL 2003 • Rabah Saadane 2003-04 • Robert Waseige BEL 2004 • Ali Fergani & Lakhdar Belloumi 2004-05 • Meziane Ighil 2005-06 • Jean-Michel Cavalli FRA 2006-07 • Rabah Saadane 2007-10 • Abdelhak Benchikha 2010-

ALGERIA 2009–10

CHAMPIONNAT NATIONAL DIVISION 1

Team	Pl	W	D	L	F	A	Pts	MCA	ESS	JSK	USMA	USMH	JSMB	USMAn	WAT	CABBA	ASK	ASOC	CRB	MCEE	USMB	MCO	CAB	MSPB	NAHD
MC Alger †	34	18	12	4	50	23	66		1-1	1-0	0-0	2-1	1-1	4-0	1-0	3-1	1-1	1-0	4-2	3-1	1-0	4-1	2-1	4-0	2-0
ES Sétif †	34	17	12	5	51	32	63	2-1		2-0	2-2	1-1	1-0	1-0	0-1	2-0	4-1	1-1	1-1	0-0	2-1	3-2	2-1	4-1	3-0
JS Kabylie ‡	34	15	9	10	39	27	54	1-1	1-1		2-2	1-0	1-1	4-0	3-1	2-0	3-0	1-0	2-1	1-0	3-1	0-0	3-1	2-1	2-0
USM Alger	34	14	11	9	47	33	53	1-2	2-0	1-1		0-0	1-0	2-1	1-2	2-1	1-1	5-0	1-0	2-1	1-0	1-1	6-0	3-1	2-1
USM El Harrach	34	13	13	8	47	35	52	0-0	0-1	2-1	0-1		1-2	1-0	1-0	3-2	5-0	1-0	0-0	1-0	2-1	5-2	1-1	3-1	0-0
JSM Béjaïa	34	13	13	8	38	28	52	1-1	2-2	1-0	1-0	2-2		2-2	4-2	2-1	3-2	0-1	1-1	1-1	2-3	2-0	5-1	0-0	2-1
USM Annaba	34	12	13	9	40	35	49	2-0	0-0	3-0	1-0	1-1	3-1		4-2	3-3	0-0	1-0	3-0	1-1	1-2	0-0	1-0	3-0	1-1
WA Tlemcen	34	13	10	11	44	42	49	2-1	2-1	1-1	2-2	2-0	1-1	0-0		3-1	1-1	2-1	2-3	1-0	1-1	2-2	2-0	3-2	2-0
CA Bordj Bou Arréridj	34	13	10	11	41	45	46	**1-0**	2-0	1-0	1-1	1-1	1-1	3-2	0-2		1-4	1-0	1-0	1-1	1-0	3-1	2-1	3-2	1-0
AS Khroub	34	12	9	13	37	45	45	0-2	1-1	1-0	1-0	1-0	2-1	1-1	1-1	2-0		4-1	1-1	2-1	3-2	2-1	0-1	1-1	1-0
ASO Chlef	34	12	7	15	38	41	43	0-2	3-3	0-1	2-0	2-3	0-1	1-1	1-0	1-1	1-0		5-0	2-1	2-0	3-1	1-0	3-2	0-0
CR Bélouizdad	34	11	10	13	36	39	43	0-0	0-1	1-0	2-1	1-1	1-0	0-0	1-0	1-2	1-0	2-0		3-0	1-0	2-0	0-1	4-0	3-1
MC El Eulma	34	11	10	13	33	36	43	1-1	3-2	1-0	1-0	1-1	0-1	3-0	2-0	3-3	2-0	1-1	2-1		0-0	0-0	1-0	0-1	2-0
USM Blida	34	11	10	13	29	33	43	1-1	1-2	1-1	2-1	1-1	0-2	0-0	1-1	1-0	1-0	2-0	0-0	2-0		2-1	1-0	1-0	0-0
MC Oran	34	10	11	13	33	42	41	0-0	1-1	0-1	1-1	2-1	1-1	0-0	0-2	1-0	0-0	2-0	1-0	1-2	2-2		0-0	2-0	2-1
CA Batna	34	10	7	17	27	40	37	1-2	0-1	0-1	2-0	2-3	0-0	2-1	3-1	0-0	1-0	0-0	1-0	2-0	0-0	2-0		0-0	2-1
MSP Batna	34	5	9	20	23	53	24	1-1	0-1	1-0	0-1	0-0	0-3	0-1	1-1	0-1	1-0	2-3	1-1	0-1	0-2	1-0	1-0		1-1
NA Hussein Dey	34	3	10	21	22	49	19	0-1	0-2	1-1	1-2	1-4	1-1	0-1	1-0	1-1	1-2	0-1	1-2	1-2	2-0	1-1	2-1	1-1	

6/08/2009 - 31/05/2010 • † Qualified for the CAF Champions League • ‡ Qualified for the CAF Confederation Cup • Match in bold was awarded as a defeat for both teams • Top scorer:

ALGERIA 2009–10 CHAMPIONNAT NATIONAL DIVISION 2

Team	Pl	W	D	L	F	A	Pts
MC Saïda	34	16	12	6	45	22	60
ASM Oran	34	15	11	8	36	29	56
ES Mostaganem	34	14	12	8	53	39	54
AB Mérouana	34	15	8	11	42	40	53
USM Bel Abbès	34	13	12	9	38	28	51
CR Témouchent	34	14	8	12	26	21	50
CS Constantine	34	13	11	10	30	29	50
Paradou AC	34	12	11	11	32	33	47
USM Sétif	34	12	8	14	31	36	44
SA Mohamadia	34	11	11	12	27	33	44
JSM Skikda	34	11	9	14	40	45	42
USMM Hadjout	34	9	14	11	28	34	41
WR Bentalha	34	10	11	13	30	35	41
RC Kouba	34	11	7	16	37	39	40
MO Constantine	34	10	10	14	35	40	40
US Biskra	34	10	8	16	34	38	38
OM Arzew	34	10	8	16	39	50	38
MO Béjaïa	34	9	11	14	24	36	38

14/08/2009 - 14/05/2010

MEDALS TABLE

	Club		Overall			League			Cup		Africa		
			G	S	B	G	S	B	G	S	G	S	B
1	JS Kabylie	JSK	24	14	6	14	10	4	4	4	6		2
2	MC Alger	MCA	14	2	4	7	2	4	6		1		
3	USM Alger	USMA	12	13	3	5	4	1	7	9			2
4	CR Belouizdad	CRB	12	5	3	6	3	2	6	2			1
5	ES Sétif	ESS	12	4	5	4	3	4	7		1	1	1
6	MC Oran	MCO	8	12	4	4	9	3	4	2		1	1
7	USM El Harrach	USMH	3	2		1	2		2				
8	NA Hussein Dey	NAHD	2	8	5	1	4	4	1	3		1	1
9	WA Tlemcen	WAT	2	3	3					3	2		3
10	USM Annaba	USMAn	2			1			1				
11	MO Constantine	MOC	1	4	2	1	1	2		3			
12	RC Kouba	RCK	1	3	2	1	2	2		1			
13	ASO Chlef	ASO	1	2	3		1	3	1	1			
14	CS Constantine	CSC	1	2		1	1			1			
15	USM Bel Abbés	USMBA	1	2					1	2			
16	US Chaouia	USC	1	1					1	1			
17	JSM Béjaïa	JSMB	1	1					1	1			
18	DNC Alger	DNCA	1						1				
	GC Mascara	GCM	1			1							
	MC Ouargla	MCOu	1						1				
	MC Saida	MCS	1						1				
22	ASM Oran	ASMO		2	2					2			2
23	USM Blida	USMB		2	1		1	1		1			
24	AS Ain Mlila	ASAM		2			1			1			
	CA Batna	CAB		2						2			
	MSP Batna	MSPB		2			1			1			
	ES Mostaganem	ESM		2						2			
28	JS Bordj Menaiel	JSBM		1	1					1			1
	WFK Collo	WFKC		1	1					1			1
	ES Guelma	ESG		1	1		1	1					
31	CA Bordj Bou Arréridj	CABBA			1								1

COUPE D'ALGERIE 2009–10

Round of 32			Round of 16			Quarter-finals		Semi-finals		Final	
ES Sétif *	1		ES Sétif	1	4p	ES Sétif *	1	ES Sétif *	3	ES Sétif	3
MC Saïda	0		WA Tlemcen *	1	2p	USM Bel Abbès	0	ASO Chlef	1	CA Batna ‡	0
WR Bentalha	1										
WA Tlemcen *	3										
USM Khenchela	1	5p	USM Khenchela *	1							
JSH El Djabel *	1	4p	USM Bel Abbès	3							
JSM Chéraga	1										
USM Bel Abbès *	3										
ICS Tlemcen *	2		ICS Tlemcen	1		ICS Tlemcen	0				
Hamra Annaba	1		WA Mostaganem *	0		ASO Chlef *	1				
IB Mouzaia	0										
WA Mostaganem *	1										
ES Sour El Ghoziane *	0		ES Sour El Ghoziane	0							
MO Béjaïa	0		ASO Chlef *	1							
NA Hussein Dey *	2										
ASO Chlef	3										
JS Kabylie *	4		JS Kabylie	1		JS Kabylie	1	JS Kabylie	0	5p	
ASA Prot. Civile	0		CR Bélouizdad *	0		USM Annaba *	0	CA Batna *	0	6p	
JS Djijel	1										
CR Bélouizdad	2										
CA Bordj Bou Arréridj *	4		CA Bordj Bou Arréridj	1							
ES Mostaganem	2		USM Annaba *	3							
MC El Eulma	0										
USM Annaba *	1										
MC Alger	3		MC Alger	3		MC Alger	0				
SC Aïn Merane *	0		USM Alger *	0		CA Batna *	1				
US Chaouia *	1										
USM Alger	3										
USM Blida *	2	3p	USM Blida	0	3p						
JSM Béjaïa	2	2p	CA Batna *	0	4p						
CS Hamma Loulou *	1										
CA Batna	2										

CUP FINAL

Stade de 5 Juillet, Alger
1-05-2010, At: 50 000. Ref: Djamel Haimoudi
Scorers - Metref 2 ^{36} ^{72}, Chebana OG ^{68}

ESS - Fawzi Chaouchi - Slimane Raho (c), Abdelkader Laifaoui, Farouk Belkaid, Mohamed Yekhlef (Smain Diss 76) - Mourad Delhoum, Khaled Lemmouchia, Francis Ambane (Bouazza Feham 79), Hocine Metref•, Lazhar Hadj Aïssa - Nabil Hemani• (Lamouri Djediat 81). Tr: Noureddine Zekri

CAB - Yacine Babouche - Nacerdine Bensaci•, Salim Aribi (c), Saber Chebana, Samir Soualah - Ali Daira, Abdellah Rassmal (Toufik Bettoumi 77), Amine Fezzani, Lazar Benhacene - Abdelhak Bourahli (Ahmed Messadia 57), Amine Boukhlouf. Tr: Mustapha Biskri

* Home team • ‡ Qualified for the CAF Confederation Cup

AND – ANDORRA

FIFA/COCA-COLA WORLD RANKING

1993	1994	1995	1996	1997	1998	1999	2000	2001	2002	2003	2004	2005	2006	2007	2008	2009	2010
-	-	-	187	185	171	145	145	140	137	147	138	125	164	175	194	202	202

2010												Hi/Lo
Jan	Feb	Mar	Mar	Apr	May	Jul	Aug	Sep	Oct	Nov	Dec	**125**
202	202	202	201	201	201	201	201	202	202	202	202	**202**

After 11 years as coach of the Andorra national team, David Rodrigo's long reign came to an end in 2010 when he was replaced at the helm by Koldo Alvarez. Koldo, the former national team goalkeeper who made his debut in 1998, the year before Rodrigo became coach, inherited a team on a 21-game losing streak and by the end of the year that had been extended to 28. Rivals San Marino may have broken Luxembourg's long-standing record of 36 consecutive defeats in 2010 but with the Andorrans playing more matches per season a world record could be a possibility down the line. In club football Santa Coloma went the league season unbeaten but still only managed to secure the title on the last day, finishing just three points ahead of their village rivals UE Santa Coloma in a three way race that also included defending champions Sant Julia. Having as often in the past finished as runners-up in the league and as losing cup finalists, Sant Julia confirmed their growing status by winning the Copa Constitucio for the second time in three years, with a 1-0 victory over UE Santa Coloma. They also progressed through a round of the UEFA Champions League after beating San Marino's Tre Fiori on penalties but then lost 9-0 on aggregate to Bulgaria's Levski Sofia.

FIFA WORLD CUP RECORD
1930-1998 DNE 2002-2010 DNQ

FEDERACIO ANDORRANA DE FUTBOL (FAF)

Avinguda Carlemany 67,
3° pis, Apartado postal 65,
AD Escaldes-Engordany
☎ +376 805830
🖷 +376 862006
✉ administracio@fedanfut.com
🖳 www.fedanfut.com
FA 1994 CON 1996 FIFA 1996
P Antoni Giribet Fiter
GS Victor Dos Santos

FIFA BIG COUNT 2006

Total players	5037
% of population	7.07%
Male	4681
Female	356
Amateurs 18+	804
Youth under 18	1366
Unregistered	700
Professionals	0
Referees	52
Admin & coaches	116
Number of clubs	26
Number of teams	34

MAJOR CITIES/TOWNS

		Population
1	Andorra la Vella	25 608
2	Les Escaldes	16 285
3	Encamp	15 416
4	La Massana	10 480
5	Sant Julià de L'oria	10 305
6	Canillo	6 542
7	Ordino	4 179

PRINCIPAT D'ANDORRA • ANDORRA

			% in cities	89%
Capital	Andorra La Vella	Population	83 888 (199)	
GDP per capita	$42 500 (15)	Area km²	468 km² (195)	GMT +/- +1
Neighbours (km)	France 56, Spain 63			

RECENT INTERNATIONALS PLAYED BY ANDORRA

2004	Opponents		Score	Venue	Comp	Scorers	Att	Referee
13-10	FYR Macedonia	W	1-0	Andorra la Vella	WCq	Bernaus [60]	350	Podeschi SMR
17-11	Netherlands	L	0-3	Andorra la Vella	WCq		2 000	Yefet ISR
2005								
9-02	FYR Macedonia	D	0-0	Skopje	WCq		5 000	Verbist BEL
26-03	Armenia	L	1-2	Yerevan	WCq	Silva [56]	2 100	Attard MLT
30-03	Czech Republic	L	0-4	Andorra la Vella	WCq		900	Messner AUT
4-06	Czech Republic	L	1-8	Liberec	WCq	Riera [36]	9 520	Dereli TUR
17-08	Romania	L	0-2	Constanta	WCq		8 200	Jakov ISR
3-09	Finland	D	0-0	Andorra la Vella	WCq		860	Ver Eecke BEL
7-09	Netherlands	L	0-4	Eindhoven	WCq		34 000	Hanacsek HUN
12-10	Armenia	L	0-3	Andorra la Vella	WCq		430	Stokes IRL
2006								
16-08	Belarus	L	0-3	Minsk	Fr			
2-09	England	L	0-5	Manchester	ECq		56 290	Brugger AUT
6-09	Israel	L	1-4	Nijmegan	ECq	Fernández [84]	400	Zrnic BIH
7-10	Croatia	L	0-7	Zagreb	ECq		17 618	Zammit MLT
11-10	FYR Macedonia	L	0-3	Andorra la Vella	ECq		300	Silagava GEO
2007								
7-02	Armenia	D	0-0	Andorra la Vella	Fr			
28-03	England	L	0-3	Barcelona	ECq		12 800	Duarte Paixao POR
2-06	Russia	L	0-4	St Petersburg	ECq		21 520	Skjerven NOR
6-06	Israel	L	0-2	Andorra la Vella	ECq		680	Stokes IRL
22-08	Estonia	L	1-2	Tallinn	ECq	Silva [82]	7 500	McCourt NIR
12-09	Croatia	L	0-6	Andorra la Vella	ECq		925	Thual FRA
17-10	FYR Macedonia	L	0-3	Skopje	ECq		17 500	Malzinskas LTU
17-11	Estonia	L	0-2	Andorra la Vella	ECq		700	Collum SCO
21-11	Russia	L	0-1	Andorra la Vella	ECq		780	Hauge NOR
2008								
26-03	Latvia	L	0-3	Andorra la Vella	Fr			Perez ESP
4-06	Azerbaijan	L	1-2	Andorra la Vella	Fr	Lima.I [71]		Gomes POR
20-08	Kazakhstan	L	0-3	Almaty	WCq		7 700	Banari MDA
6-09	England	L	0-2	Barcelona	WCq		10 300	Cakir TUR
10-09	Belarus	L	1-3	Andorra la Vella	WCq	Pujol [67p]	600	Evans WAL
15-10	Croatia	L	0-4	Zagreb	WCq		14 441	Vad HUN
2009								
11-02	Lithuania	L	1-3	Albufeira	Fr	Lima.I [78p]		Xistra POR
1-04	Croatia	L	0-2	Andorra la Vella	WCq		1 100	Trattou CYP
6-06	Belarus	L	1-5	Grodno	WCq	Lima.I [93+p]	8 500	Kranjc SVN
10-06	England	L	0-6	London	WCq		57 897	Nijhuis NED
5-09	Ukraine	L	0-5	Kyiv	WCq		14 870	Sipailo LVA
9-09	Kazakhstan	L	1-3	Andorra la Vella	WCq	Sonejee [70]	510	Toussaint LUX
14-10	Ukraine	L	0-6	Andorra la Vella	WCq		820	Thomson SCO
2010								
29-05	Iceland	L	0-4	Reykjavik	Fr		2 567	Reinert FRO
2-06	Albania	L	0-1	Tirana	Fr		3 000	Meckarovski MKD
11-08	Cyprus	L	0-1	Larnaca	Fr		1 700	Spathas GRE
3-09	Russia	L	0-2	Andorra la Vella	ECq		1 100	Borg MLT
7-09	Republic of Ireland	L	1-3	Dublin	ECq	Martinez [45]	40 283	Trattou CYP
8-10	FYR Macedonia	L	0-2	Andorra La Vella	ECq		550	Mazeika LTU
12-10	Armenia	L	0-4	Yerevan	ECq		12 000	Mikulski POL

Fr = Friendly match • EC = UEFA EURO 2008/2012 • WC = FIFA World Cup • q = qualifier

ANDORRA NATIONAL TEAM HISTORICAL RECORDS

App 85 - Oscar Sonejee 1997- • **78** - Koldo 1998-2009 • **75** - Manolo Jimenez 1998- • **71** - Josep Txema 1997- • **67** - Ildefons Lima 1997-
• **65** - Justo Ruiz 1996-2008 & Jordi Escura 1998-

G 7 - Ildefons Lima 1997- • **3** - Oscar Sonejee 1997-, Fernando Silva 2002-, Jesus Julian Lucendo 1996-2003

Tr Isidrea Codina 1996 • Manuel Miloie 1997-99, David Rodrigo 1999-2010 • Koldo Alvarez 2010-

ANDORRA 2009–10

LLIGA ANDORRANA PRIMERA DIVISIO	Pl	W	D	L	F	A	Pts	S'ta Coloma	UE Coloma	St Julià	Lusitans	Principat	Inter	Encamp	Engordany
Santa Coloma †	20	13	7	0	46	14	46		2-2 1-1	0-0 1-1	2-1 4-1	6-1	4-0	3-0	5-1
UE Santa Coloma ‡	20	13	4	3	50	26	43	2-2 1-2		3-2 1-1	0-2 2-0	5-3	1-0	5-0	5-0
Sant Julià ‡	20	12	5	3	69	18	41	1-2 0-0	3-1 1-2		0-0 4-0	6-0	4-0	6-2	4-0
Lusitans ‡	20	7	3	10	34	32	24	1-3 0-0	1-2 1-2	2-3 2-3		0-2	5-2	5-1	4-0
Principat	20	8	2	10	42	50	26	0-1	1-4	1-3	0-2		3-0 2-3	4-0 5-5	2-0 1-2
Inter Escaldes	20	6	1	13	25	49	19	0-4	1-2	0-7	1-1	1-2 2-3		2-3 1-0	1-0 2-1
Encamp	20	4	3	13	31	67	15	0-2	2-5	1-10	0-3	2-4 3-3	2-0 1-3		1-1 1-4
Engordany	20	4	1	15	22	63	13	1-2	1-4	0-10	1-3	3-4 2-1	3-2 1-4	0-5 1-2	

20/09/2009 - 28/03/2010 • † Qualified for the UEFA Champions League • ‡ Qualified for the Europa League
Relegation play-off: **Encamp** 2-1 3-1 Extremenya • Top scorers: **19** - Gabriel Riera, Sant Julia • **16** - Luis Miguel POR, UE Santa Coloma • **12** - Alejandro Romero ARG, Sant Julia & Norberto Urbani ARG, Santa Coloma • **11** - Pedro Reis POR, Lusitans & Victor Hugo, Sant Julia

ANDORRA 2009–10 SEGONA DIVISIO (2)

	Pl	W	D	L	F	A	Pts
Casa del Benfica	20	13	3	4	47	25	42
Lusitans B	20	13	1	6	49	19	40
Extremenya ‡	20	12	3	5	45	24	39
Jenlai	20	10	6	4	52	28	36
Ranger's	14	5	3	6	28	22	18
Athlètic Escaldes §3	14	2	3	9	13	37	6
Penya Encarnada	14	1	0	13	13	57	3
Principat B §6	14	1	3	10	17	52	0

19/09/2009 - 27/03/2010 • ‡ Qualified for play-off
(Lusitans B ineligible) • § = points deducted

MEDALS TABLE

		Overall			League			Cup	
		G	S	B	G	S	B	G	S
1	Santa Coloma	13	8	4	5	5	4	8	3
2	Principat	9	1	1	3	1	1	6	
3	Sant Julià	4	11	3	2	5	3	2	6
4	Encamp	2	2	3	2	1	3		1
5	Ranger's	2	2	2	2	1	2		1
6	Constelacio	2			1			1	
7	UE Santa Coloma		2			1			1
8	Inter Escaldes		1	2				2	1
9	Veterans		1			1			

COPA CONSTITUCIO 2009–10

Round of 16		Quarter–finals		Semi–finals		Final
Sant Julià	Bye					
		Sant Julià	5 8			
Jenlai	1	Engordany *	0 0			
Engordany	2			**Sant Julià** *	1 2	
Santa Coloma	Bye			Lusitans	0 0	
		Santa Coloma	0 1			
Lusitans B	0	**Lusitans** *	6 1			
Lusitans	4					**Sant Julià ‡** 1
Principat	Bye					UE Santa Coloma 0
		Principat	2 3			
Encamp	1	Extremenya *	0 0			**CUP FINAL**
Extremenya	2			Principat	1 3	
Inter Escaldes	2			**UE Santa Coloma** *	3 2	Aixovall, Andorra La Vella
Casa del Benfica	0	Inter Escaldes *	3 0			16-05-2010, Ref: Sanchez
						Scorer - Sebas Gomez [82]
		UE Santa Coloma	0 4			
UE Santa Coloma	Bye	* Home team in the first leg • ‡ Qualified for the Europa League				

Cup Final line-ups: **Sant Julia**: Guilermo Burgos - Walter Wagner, Yael Fontan, Josep Matamala, Christian Xinos, Vitor Pinto (Juan Bernales 92+), Alejandro Romero, Carlos Peppe, Sebas Gomez, Luciano Nastri, Sebastian Varela. Tr: Patricio Gonzalez
UE Santa Coloma: Josep Rivas - Nieto, Alex Martinez, Carles Sirvan, Gerard Aloy, Rodriguez.V, Lafoz, Rodriguez.X, Bernat, Luis Miguel, Jordi Rubio. Tr: Lluis Aloy

ANG – ANGOLA

FIFA/COCA-COLA WORLD RANKING

1993	1994	1995	1996	1997	1998	1999	2000	2001	2002	2003	2004	2005	2006	2007	2008	2009	2010
102	106	80	70	58	50	52	55	55	76	83	72	61	55	73	70	95	88

2010												Hi/Lo
Jan	Feb	Mar	Mar	Apr	May	Jul	Aug	Sep	Oct	Nov	Dec	45
95	88	86	86	85	88	86	87	93	92	92	88	124

The investment of an estimated US$1-billion in infrastructure and organisation costs for the hosting of the 2010 African Nations Cup finals did not deliver the desired outcome on the pitch but it has left Angola with impressive football facilities. Four new stadiums across the country have since been transformed into regular venues for the country's various representatives teams and for leading clubs competing in the GiraBola, the league which is amongst the best funded on the continent. Oil riches have elevated Angola's economy into a roaring tiger and the impact on football is evidenced by the liberal hiring of foreign coaches by almost all of the top-flight clubs, most of them from Portugal, the former colonial power. The national side sought expatriate leadership too after the 'Palancas Negras' were knocked out in the quarter-finals of the Nations Cup but Frenchman Herve Renard was ousted within six months after a 3-0 loss in Uganda at the start of the 2012 Nations Cup qualifiers. His replacement was Zeca Amaral, but he too was replaced at the turn of the year by former Angolan international Lito Vidigal, who was previously in charge of Portuguese club Uniao Leiria. Police team InterClube won the 2010 Girabola on goal difference from Recreativo Caala but lost in the Cup Final on post-match penalties to Atletico Aviacao.

FIFA WORLD CUP RECORD
1930-1978 DNE   1982-2002 DNQ   **2006** 23 r1   **2010** DNQ

FEDERACAO ANGOLANA DE FUTEBOL (FAF)

Senado de Camara,
✉ Compl. da Cidadela Desportiva, Luanda - 3449,
☎ +244 222 264948
📠 +244 222 260566
📧 sgeral@fafutebol.ebonet.net
🖥 www.fafutebol-angola.og.ao
FA 1979 CON 1996 FIFA 1980
P Justino Fernandes
GS Augusto Pereira Da Silva

FIFA BIG COUNT 2006

Total players	664 690
% of population	5.48%
Male	634 090
Female	30 600
Amateurs 18+	5240
Youth under 18	10 800
Unregistered	36 250
Professionals	0
Referees	259
Admin & coaches	1800
Number of clubs	100
Number of teams	500

MAJOR CITIES/TOWNS

		Population
1	Luanda	2 583 981
2	Cabinda	377 931
3	Huambo	333 387
4	Lubango	250 921
5	Kuito	180 764
6	Malanje	156 829
7	Lobito	145 652
8	Benguela	131 281
9	Uige	116 751
10	Namibe	89 442
11	Luena	84 619
12	Saurimo	78 417
13	Soyo	75 224
14	Sumbe	50 458
15	N'Dalatando	45 295
16	Caála	41 181
17	Cubal	41 142
18	Dundo	40 055
19	Negage	37 622

REPUBLICA DE ANGOLA • REPUBLIC OF ANGOLA

Capital	Luanda	Population 12 799 293 (69)	% in cities 57%
GDP per capita	$8800 (112)	Area km² 1 246 700 km² (23)	GMT +/- +1
Neighbours (km)	Congo DR 2511, Congo 201, Namibia 1376, Zambia 1110 • Coast 1600		

RECENT INTERNATIONALS PLAYED BY ANGOLA

2007 Opponents		Score	Venue	Comp	Scorers	Att	Referee
22-08 Congo DR	L	1-3	Kinshasa	Fr	Flavio [33]		
8-09 Kenya	L	1-2	Bairobi	CNq	Manucho [35]		Katjimune NAM
17-11 Côte d'Ivoire	W	2-1	Melun	Fr	Andre [13], Flavio [39]		
20-11 Guinea	L	0-3	Melun	Fr			
2008							
13-01 Egypt	D	3-3	AlvercaDoRibatejo	Fr	Figueiredo [22], Flavio [36], Manucho [47]		
16-01 Morocco	L	1-2	Rabat	Fr	Flavio [17]		
23-01 South Africa	D	1-1	Tamale	CNr1	Manucho [30]		Coulibaly MLI
27-01 Senegal	W	3-1	Tamale	CNr1	Manucho 2 [50 67], Flavio [78]		Haimoudi ALG
31-01 Tunisia	D	0-0	Tamale	CNr1			Codjia BEN
4-02 Egypt	L	1-2	Kumasi	CNqf	Manucho [27]		Nichimura JPN
1-06 Benin	W	3-0	Luanda	WCq	Flavio [62], Job [81], Mendonca [86]	6 000	Damon RSA
8-06 Niger	W	2-1	Niamey	WCq	Flavio [30], Yamba Asha [71]	23 000	Jedidi TUN
14-06 Uganda	L	1-3	Kampala	WCq	Mantorras [91+]	20 000	Mailett SEY
23-06 Uganda	D	0-0	Luanda	WCq		16 000	Mana NGA
20-08 Tunisia	D	1-1	Monastir	Fr	Santana [90]		
7-09 Benin	L	2-3	Cotonou	WCq	Flavio [12], Loco [84]	30 000	Benouza ALG
12-10 Niger	W	3-1	Luanda	WCq	Daouda OG [53], Gilberto [66], Ze Kalanga [70]	3 200	Gasingwa RWA
19-11 Venezuela	D	0-0	Barinas	Fr		15 000	Argote VEN
2009							
11-02 Mali	L	0-4	Bois-Guillaume	Fr			
25-03 Cape Verde Islands	L	0-1	Olhao	Fr			
31-03 Morocco	L	0-2	Lisbon	Fr			
4-04 Namibia	D	0-0	Dundo	Fr			
14-06 Guinea	D	0-0	Amadora	Fr			
12-08 Togo	W	2-0	Lisbon	Fr	Flavio [55], Mateus [73]	700	Proença POR
5-09 Senegal	D	1-1	Portimao	Fr	Mangane OG [66]	300	Paixao POR
9-09 Cape Verde Islands	D	1-1	Faro	Fr	Gilberto [23p]		
10-10 Malta	W	2-1	Vila Real	Fr	Djalma [37], Andre Makanga [64]		Almeida POR
14-10 Cameroon	D	0-0	Olhao	Fr			
14-11 Congo	D	1-1	Luanda	Fr	Flavio [2]		
18-11 Ghana	D	0-0	Luanda	Fr			
30-12 Estonia	L	0-1	Vila Real	Fr		200	Almeida POR
2010							
3-01 Gambia	D	1-1	Vila Real	Fr	Manucho [29]		
10-01 Mali	D	4-4	Luanda	CNr1	Flávio 2 [36 42], Gilberto [67p], Manucho [74p]	45 000	Abd El Fatah EGY
14-01 Malawi	W	2-0	Luanda	CNr1	Flávio [49], Manucho [55]	48 500	Doue CIV
18-01 Algeria	D	0-0	Luanda	CNr1		40 000	Damon RSA
24-01 Ghana	L	0-1	Luanda	CNqf		50 000	Benouza ALG
13-05 Mexico	L	0-1	Houston	Fr		70 099	Toledo USA
11-08 Uruguay	L	0-2	Lisbon	Fr		1 000	Hugo Miguel POR
4-09 Uganda	L	0-3	Kampala	CNq			Osman EGY
9-10 Guinea-Bissau	W	1-0	Luanda	CNq	Gilberto [22p]		Coulibaly MLI
12-10 UAE	W	2-0	Abu Dhabi	Fr	Rasca [23], Vado [89]		

Fr = Friendly match • CN = CAF African Cup of Nations • CC = COSAFA Castle Cup • WC = FIFA World Cup
q = qualifier • r1 = first round group • qf = quarter-final • sf = semi-final • f = final

ANGOLA 2010

CAMPEONATO NACIONAL
XXXII GIRABOLA 1° DIVISAO

	Pl	W	D	L	F	A	Pts	Inter	Caála	1° Agosto	Petro At.	Libolo	ASA	Onze Bravos	Kabuscorp	Académica	Benfica L'da	Cabinda	Sagrada	Santos	Huíla	Sp Cabinda	Benfica L'go
InterClube †	30	17	4	9	45	20	55		1-0	0-1	0-1	1-1	5-1	0-1	2-1	1-0	2-1	2-0	2-0	0-1	5-0	1-0	6-2
Recreativo Caála †	30	16	7	7	40	25	55	1-0		0-0	2-0	1-0	1-0	1-2	0-1	2-2	1-0	4-0	2-1	2-0	2-2	1-0	2-0
Primeiro de Agosto ‡	30	14	9	7	43	26	51	2-0	2-1		1-1	2-0	4-1	1-1	0-1	2-0	0-0	3-0	3-0	0-1	3-2	1-0	0-1
Petro Atlético	30	14	8	8	36	21	50	0-1	0-1	0-1		1-2	1-3	0-0	0-0	3-2	0-0	0-1	1-0	0-0	3-0	1-0	4-0
Recreativo Libolo	30	13	9	8	38	29	48	0-1	1-2	2-2	1-4		0-0	0-0	3-0	0-0	2-0	1-0	1-2	1-0	3-1	2-1	1-0
Atlético Aviação ‡	30	13	7	10	29	30	46	1-0	1-2	1-0	0-1	2-0		1-0	0-0	0-2	0-1	1-1	1-0	0-0	3-1	2-0	4-0
Onze Bravos Maqui	30	12	9	9	38	33	45	1-0	0-1	2-1	1-2	1-1	0-1		1-2	2-1	3-2	2-3	2-0	4-1	1-1	1-1	2-0
Kabuscorp Palanca	30	11	10	9	39	33	43	1-0	2-1	1-1	1-2	2-1	0-0	3-4		1-2	0-0	2-0	1-2	4-0	2-2	3-1	3-3
Académica Soyo	30	11	9	10	39	35	42	0-3	1-2	0-0	1-1	0-1	1-1	1-2	1-0		2-1	1-0	1-1	2-0	1-0	3-2	4-0
Benfica Luanda	30	11	6	13	34	39	39	1-4	3-1	1-4	1-2	0-0	5-0	0-0	1-1	1-3		1-3	2-1	2-1	1-0	1-0	2-1
FC Cabinda	30	9	9	12	30	39	36	1-2	0-2	4-2	0-0	0-1	1-1	3-0	2-1	1-1	1-2		0-0	1-0	1-0	1-2	2-1
Sagrada Esperança	30	8	11	11	28	35	35	1-1	1-1	0-2	1-3	2-2	2-0	1-0	0-0	2-2	2-0	1-1		1-2	1-0	2-0	2-1
Santos	30	8	9	13	27	42	33	1-1	1-1	1-1	1-0	2-5	0-1	2-2	0-2	2-1	2-1	1-1	0-0		1-1	1-0	1-0
Desportivo Huíla	30	8	8	14	31	42	32	0-0	0-0	3-1	0-2	0-0	1-0	0-1	2-1	1-1	1-2	3-0	2-0	5-4		1-0	2-1
Sporting Cabinda	30	7	4	19	19	36	25	0-1	2-1	1-1	0-3	0-1	0-1	1-0	2-3	2-1	0-1	1-1	0-0	1-0	1-0		1-0
Benfica Lubango	30	5	7	18	28	59	22	0-3	2-2	1-2	0-0	2-5	1-2	2-2	0-0	1-2	2-1	1-1	2-2	2-1	1-0	1-0	

19/02/2010 - 31/10/2010 • † Qualified for CAF Champions League • ‡ Qualified for CAF Confederation Cup
Progresso Sambizanga won Serie A of the national stage of the second division and were promoted along with Primeiro do Maio, winners of Serie B.

MEDALS TABLE

		Overall			League			Cup		Africa			City
		G	S	B	G	S	B	G	S	G	S	B	
1	Petro Atlético	23	6	5	15	3	5	8	2		1		Luanda
2	Primeiro de Agosto	14	8	4	9	3	4	5	4		1		Luanda
3	Atlético Sport Aviação	6	7	2	3	5	1	3	2			1	Luanda
4	Primeiro de Maio	5	8		2	5		3	2		1		Benguela
5	Inter Clube	4	7	4	2	1	4	2	5		1		Luanda
6	Sagrada Esperança	3	5		1	3		2	2				Dundo
7	Ferroviário Huíla	2	1	1				2	1				Lubango
8	Atlético Petróleas Namibe	2						2					Namibe
9	Progresso Sambiganza	1						1					Luanda
	Santos	1						1					Viana
11	Petro Huambo		2	3		1	3		1				Huambo
12	SL Benfica Luanda		2	1		1			2				Luanda
	Independente		2	1		1			2				Tombwa
	Recreativo Libolo		2	1		1	1		1				Calulo
15	Nacional Benguela		1	1		1	1						Benguela

TACA NACIONAL 2010

Round of 16		Quarter–finals		Semi–finals		Final	
Atlético Aviação *	4						
Domant Bengo	1	Atlético Aviação *	w-0				
Petro Atlético *	1	Benfica Lubango					
Benfica Lubango	2			Atlético Aviação	2		
Santos	0 4p			Sagrada Esperança	1		
Sporting Cabinda *	0 3p	Santos	1 5p				
Progresso Sambizanga	1	Sagrada Esperança *	1 6p			Atlético Aviação ‡	0 4p
Sagrada Esperança *	2					InterClube	0 3p
Recreativo Libolo	1						
Kabuscorp Palanca *	0	Recreativo Libolo	0 5p				
Recreativo Caála	1	Académica Soyo *	0 4p			**CUP FINAL**	
Académica Soyo *	2			Recreativo Libolo	0		
Primeiro de Agosto *	2			InterClube	3		
Onze Bravos Maqui	1	Primeiro de Agosto	0 3p			Cidadela, Luanda	
Desportivo Huíla *	1 4p	InterClube *	0 5p			11-11-2010. Ref: Helder Martins	
InterClube	1 5p						

* Home team • ‡ Qualified for CAF Confederation Cup

ANT – NETHERLANDS ANTILLES

FIFA/COCA-COLA WORLD RANKING

1993	1994	1995	1996	1997	1998	1999	2000	2001	2002	2003	2004	2005	2006	2007	2008	2009	2010
128	152	125	142	156	156	167	175	183	177	188	163	168	177	183	152	168	151

2010												Hi/Lo
Jan	Feb	Mar	Mar	Apr	May	Jul	Aug	Sep	Oct	Nov	Dec	**98**
168	169	166	162	157	154	150	165	166	170	153	151	**188**

After a history spanning 56 years, the Netherlands Antilles finally ceased to exist as a country in October 2010. Founded in 1954 in an attempt to give the Dutch islands of Curaçao, Sint Maarten, Bonaire, Saba, Sint Eustatius and Aruba a unified structure, it had never been an entirely happy arrangement. Aruba was the first to break away in 1986 and they will now be joined by Curaçao and Sint Maarten as autonomous countries within the Kingdom of the Netherlands. Bonaire, Saba and Sint Eustatius on the other hand will become more closely integrated within the Netherlands and are being referred to as the Caribbean Netherlands. Three days after the formal dissolution the national team took part in a Digicel Caribbean Cup qualifying group in Suriname. With FIFA yet to ratify any change in status the team competed under the old name although for the ABCS Football Tournament, staged on home soil in Willemstad at the end of the month, the team was referred to as Curaçao. In September what is likely to be the last edition of the Kopa Antiano was played in Bonaire. Taking part in the four-team tournament were Curaçao champions Hubentut Fortuna and Bonaire champions Juventus, although it was the runners-up in both leagues who qualified for the final, with Curaçao's Centro Barber beating Real Rincon 2-0.

FIFA WORLD CUP RECORD
1930-1954 DNE 1958-2010 DNQ

NEDERLANDS ANTILLIAANSE VOETBAL UNIE (NAVU)

Bonamweg 49, PO Box 341, Willemstad, Curaçao
☎ +599 97365040
📠 +599 97365047
📧 navusoccer@interneeds.net
🖥 www.navusoccer.org
FA 1921 CON 1961 FIFA 1932
P Rignaal Francisca
GS Hubert Isenia

FIFA BIG COUNT 2006

Total players	4220
% of population	1.90%
Male	3940
Female	280
Amateurs 18+	780
Youth under 18	980
Unregistered	2400
Professionals	0
Referees	42
Admin & coaches	320
Number of clubs	40
Number of teams	75

MAJOR CITIES/TOWNS

		Population
1	**Willemstad**	101 096
2	*Princess Quarter*	16 081
3	*Cul De Sac*	10 435
4	*Cole Bay*	8 006
5	**Sint Michiel**	5 323
6	**Montaña Abou**	4 390
7	**Tera Cora**	3 797
8	**Montaña Rey**	3 699
9	**Souax**	3 618
10	Kralendijk	3 265
11	Antriol	3 157
12	*Little Bay*	2 881
13	**Groot Piscadera**	2 669
14	**Barber**	2 511
15	**Labadera**	2 441
16	**Soto**	2 059

Bold = Curaçao
Italic = Sint Maarten
Underlined = Bonaire

NEDERLANDSE ANTILLEN • NETHERLANDS ANTILLES

Capital Willemstad	Population 227 049 (182)	% in cities 93%
GDP per capita $16 000 (74)	Area km² 800 km² (187)	GMT + / - -4
Neighbours (km) Saint Martin 15 • Coast 364 (includes Bonaire, Curacao, Saba, Sint Eustatius & Sint Maarten)		

RECENT INTERNATIONALS PLAYED BY NETHERLANDS ANTILLES

2008	Opponents	Score		Venue	Comp	Scorers	Att	Referee
17-07	Trinidad and Tobago	L	0-2	Macoya	Fr		2 100	Hospedales TRI
27-07	Aruba	D	0-0	Willemstad	CCq		995	Hospedales TRI
31-07	Grenada	W	2-0	Willemstad	CCq	John Bacuna [79], Joshua Bicintini [81]	800	Hospedales TRI
23-10	Cuba	L	1-7	Havana	CCq	Ashar Bernandus [61p]	1 000	Whittaker CAY
25-10	Suriname	L	1-2	Havana	CCq	Demy Rosario [81]	1 000	Holder CAY
27-10	Barbados	L	1-2	Havana	CCq	Joshua Bicintini [45]	1 000	Morrison JAM
2009								
28-10	French Guiana ‡	L	1-4	Paramaribo	Fr	Riangelo Rodriguez [41]	500	Wijngaarde SUR
30-10	Guyana	L	0-1	Paramaribo	Fr		500	Pinas SUR
1-11	Suriname	D	1-1	Paramaribo	Fr	Lisandro Trenidad [28]	2 500	
2010								
13-10	Suriname	L	1-2	Paramaribo	CCq	Lacey Pauletta [81]	800	Willet ATG
15-10	Guyana	L	2-3	Paramaribo	CCq	Hujoybert Delando [74p], Kenneth Kunst [84]	750	Matthew SKN
17-10	St Lucia	D	2-2	Paramaribo	CCq	Lisandro Trenidad [30], Bryan Anastatia [89p]	2 800	Willet ATG
29-10	Aruba	W	3-0	Willemstad	Fr	Everon Espacia, Lisandro Trenidad, Giandro Steba		Dimie ANT
31-10	Suriname	D	2-2	Willemstad	Fr	Everon Espacia, Vilyson Lake. L 5-6p		

Fr = Friendly match • CC = Digicel Caribbean Cup • WC = FIFA World Cup • q = qualifier • ‡ Not a full international

CURACAO 2009-10

SEKSHON PAGA FIRST STAGE	Pl	W	D	L	F	A	Pts	VESTA	Centro Dom	Fortuna	Sithoc	C. Barber	Victory Boys	J. Holland	SUBT	Undeba	J. Colombia	Buena Vista
VESTA †	20	13	2	5	37	22	41		2-3	1-4	1-0	2-0	2-3	3-0	1-0	2-0	1-2	2-0
Centro Dominguito §3 †	19	13	4	2	49	17	40	4-2		0-2	2-1	2-1	4-0	3-1	1-1	3-2	5-0	1-0
Hubentut Fortuna †	20	12	3	5	39	18	39	1-3	1-1		2-0	0-1	1-1	0-1	3-1	5-0	5-3	2-0
Sithoc †	20	11	5	4	34	22	38	2-2	1-0	1-0		1-1	3-1	3-2	5-2	1-0	3-1	3-0
Centro Barber †	19	11	4	4	43	12	37	0-2	0-1	1-0	3-0		1-1	1-2	3-0	1-1	10-0	2-0
Victory Boys †	20	6	6	8	33	27	24	0-1	2-2	2-3	0-0	0-2		0-1	7-0	0-3	1-0	0-0
Jong Holland	20	7	3	10	27	31	24	2-3	0-0	0-1	1-2	1-3	1-2		0-0	1-3	4-2	6-2
SUBT	20	5	5	10	22	43	20	0-1	1-7	1-1	0-0	0-3	2-1	1-0		3-3	2-1	0-2
Undeba	20	4	5	11	28	35	17	1-2	1-2	1-2	1-3	0-0	1-1	0-1	1-3		6-0	1-1
Jong Colombia	20	4	3	13	20	55	15	0-0	0-4	0-1	1-1	1-2	0-2	2-2	0-4	3-1		3-1
Real Buena Vista	20	2	2	16	12	62	8	0-4	0-6	0-5	2-4	0-9	0-9	0-1	3-1	1-2	0-1	

6/12/2009 - 27/06/2010 • † Qualified for the Kaya 6 • § = points deducted • Match in bold annulled and not replayed
Relegation play-off: **Jong Colombia** 1-0 4-1 Didi Skerpene

PLAY-OFF KAYA 6

	Pl	W	D	L	F	A	Pts	HF	Si	CB	VE	VB
Centro Dominguito †	5	3	2	0	8	5	11	3-2	1-1	1-0	2-1	1-1
Hubentut Fortuna †	5	3	1	1	14	7	10		2-2	2-1	5-0	3-1
Sithoc †	5	2	2	1	9	6	8			0-2	2-1	4-0
Centro Barber †	5	2	1	2	8	6	7				2-2	3-1
VESTA	5	1	1	3	7	11	4					3-0
Victory Boys	5	0	1	4	3	14	1					

30/06/2010 - 23/07/2010 • † Qualified for the Kaya 4

PLAY-OFF KAYA 4

	Pl	W	D	L	F	A	Pts	HF	CD	Si
Centro Barber †	3	3	0	0	3	0	9	1-0	1-0	1-0
Hubentut Fortuna †	3	1	1	1	5	4	4		2-2	1-0
Centro Dominguito	3	0	2	1	3	4	2			1-1
Sithoc	3	0	1	2	1	5	1			

27/07/2010 - 11/08/2010 • † Qualified for the final

CURACAO FINAL	KOPA ANTIANO FINAL
Stadion Ergilio Hato, Willemstad, 15-08-2010, Att: 10 000	Bonaire, 19-09-2010
Hubentut Fortuna 1-0 Centro Barber	Real Rincon 0-2 **Centro Barber**
Scorer: Tyrone Maria [64]	Scorer - Oscar Molina 2

ARG – ARGENTINA

FIFA/COCA-COLA WORLD RANKING

1993	1994	1995	1996	1997	1998	1999	2000	2001	2002	2003	2004	2005	2006	2007	2008	2009	2010
8	10	7	22	17	5	6	3	2	5	5	3	4	3	1	6	8	5

	2010											Hi/Lo
Jan	Feb	Mar	Mar	Apr	May	Jul	Aug	Sep	Oct	Nov	Dec	1
8	8	9	9	7	7	5	5	5	5	5	5	24

The stage was all set for Lionel Messi to conquer the world in South Africa but the Argentine striker, who turned 23 during the World Cup finals, will have to wait until Brazil in 2014 to try and elevate his status to that of Pele and Diego Maradona by winning the ultimate prize in football. It could be argued that he is already playing at the level of those two after another sensational year with his club side Barcelona but in South Africa he was disappointing, as were an Argentine side coached by the erratic Maradona. There was never a dull moment with Maradona in the Argentina Camp and their form going into the finals had been excellent, but a lack of focus told in the 4-0 quarter-final defeat at the hands of Germany. There was a morale boosting 4-1 victory over world champions Spain in Buenos Aires after the finals, a result that saw caretaker coach Sergio Batista get the job full-time. At club level, Independiente added the Copa Sudamericana to their trophy collection after beating Goiás on penalties in the final - their first international trophy since 1995 but a record tenth overall in South America. At home the small clubs continued to flourish with Argentinos Juniors winning the 2010 Clausura, their first title since the mid-1980s when they built a successful team on the proceeds from selling Diego Maradona to Boca Juniors.

FIFA WORLD CUP RECORD

1930 2 Finalists **1934** 9 r1 **1938-1954** DNE **1958** 13 r1 **1962** 10 r1 **1966** 5 QF **1970** DNQ **1974** 8 r2 **1978** (hosts) 1 Winners
1982 11 r2 **1986** 1 Winners **1990** 2 Finalists **1994** 10 r2 **1998** 6 QF **2002** 18 r1 **2006** 6 QF **2010** 5 QF

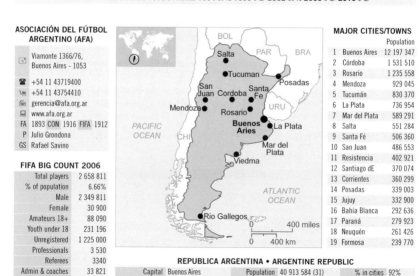

ASOCIACIÓN DEL FÚTBOL ARGENTINO (AFA)

Viamonte 1366/76,
Buenos Aires - 1053

☎ +54 11 43719400
📠 +54 11 43754410
📧 gerencia@afa.org.ar
🖥 www.afa.org.ar
FA 1893 CON 1916 FIFA 1912
P Julio Grondona
GS Rafael Savino

FIFA BIG COUNT 2006

Total players	2 658 811
% of population	6.66%
Male	2 349 811
Female	30 900
Amateurs 18+	88 090
Youth under 18	231 196
Unregistered	1 225 000
Professionals	3 530
Referees	3340
Admin & coaches	33 821
Number of clubs	3348
Number of teams	23 623

MAJOR CITIES/TOWNS

		Population
1	Buenos Aires	12 197 347
2	Córdoba	1 531 510
3	Rosario	1 235 558
4	Mendoza	929 045
5	Tucumán	830 370
6	La Plata	736 954
7	Mar del Plata	589 291
8	Salta	551 284
9	Santa Fé	506 360
10	San Juan	486 553
11	Resistencia	402 921
12	Santiago dE	370 074
13	Corrientes	360 299
14	Posadas	339 003
15	Jujuy	332 900
16	Bahía Blanca	292 636
17	Paraná	279 923
18	Neuquén	261 426
19	Formosa	239 770

REPUBLICA ARGENTINA • ARGENTINE REPUBLIC

Capital	Buenos Aires	Population	40 913 584 (31)	% in cities	92%
GDP per capita	$14 200 (80)	Area km²	2 780 400 km² (8)	GMT + / -	-3
Neighbours (km)	Bolivia 832, Brazil 1261, Chile 5308, Paraguay 1880, Uruguay 580 • Coast 4989				

RECENT INTERNATIONAL MATCHES PLAYED BY ARGENTINA

2008	Opponents	Score	Venue	Comp	Scorers	Att	Referee
26-03	Egypt	W 2-0	Cairo	Fr	Aguero [65], Burdisso [84]		Haimoudi ALG
4-06	Mexico	W 4-1	San Diego	Fr	Burdisso [10], Messi [17], Rodriguez.M [29], Aguero [70]	68 498	Navarro CAN
8-06	USA	D 0-0	New York	Fr		78 682	Aguilar SLV
15-06	Ecuador	D 1-1	Buenos Aires	WCq	Palacio [89]	41 167	Ortube BOL
18-06	Brazil	D 0-0	Belo Horizonte	WCq		65 000	Ruiz COL
20-08	Belarus	D 0-0	Minsk	Fr			Sukhina RUS
6-09	Paraguay	D 1-1	Buenos Aires	WCq	Aguero [60]	46 250	Simon BRA
10-09	Peru	D 1-1	Lima	WCq	Cambiasso [82]	40 000	Amarilla PAR
11-10	Uruguay	W 2-1	Buenos Aires	WCq	Messi [5], Aguero [12]	42 421	Torres PAR
15-10	Chile	L 0-1	Santiago	WCq		65 000	Ruiz COL
19-11	Scotland	W 1-0	Glasgow	Fr	Rodriguez.M [8]	32 492	Brych GER
2009							
11-02	France	W 2-0	Marseille	Fr	Gutierrez [41], Messi [83]	60 000	Eriksson SWE
28-03	Venezuela	W 4-0	Buenos Aires	WCq	Messi [25], Tevez [47], Rodriguez.M [51], Aguero [72]	46 085	Rivera PER
1-04	Bolivia	L 1-6	La Paz	WCq	Gonzalez [25]	30 487	Vazquez URU
20-05	Panama	W 3-1	Santa Fe	Fr	De Federico [27], Bergessio 2 [40 85]	20 000	Antequera BOL
6-06	Colombia	W 1-0	Buenos Aires	WCq	Diaz [55]	55 000	Ortube BOL
10-06	Ecuador	L 0-2	Quito	WCq		36 359	Chandia CHI
12-08	Russia	W 3-2	Moscow	Fr	Aguero [45], Lopez [46], Datalo [59]	28 800	De Bleeckere BEL
5-09	Brazil	L 1-3	Rosario	WCq		37 000	Ruiz COL
9-09	Paraguay	L 0-1	Asuncion	WCq		38 000	Fagundes BRA
30-09	Ghana	W 2-0	Cordoba	Fr	Palermo 2 [29 40]		Osses CHI
10-10	Peru	W 2-1	Buenos Aires	WCq	Higuain [48], Palermo [92+]	38 019	Ortube BOL
14-10	Uruguay	W 1-0	Montevideo	WCq	Bolatti [84]	50 000	Amarilla PAR
14-11	Spain	L 1-2	Madrid	Fr	Messi [61p]	54 000	Kelly IRL
2010							
26-01	Costa Rica	W 3-2	San Juan	Fr	Sosa [12], Burdisso [38], Jara [79]	19 000	Amarilla PAR
10-02	Jamaica	W 2-1	Mar del Plata	Fr	Palermo [77], Canuto [93+]	20 000	Rivera PER
3-03	Germany	W 1-0	Munich	Fr	Higuain [45]	65 152	Atkinson ENG
5-05	Haiti	W 4-0	Cutral Co	Fr	Bertoglio 2 [33 56], Palermo [42], Blanco [50]	16 500	Osses CHI
24-05	Canada	W 5-0	Buenos Aires	Fr	Maxi Rodriguez 2 [15 31], Di Maria [36], Tevez [62], Aguero [74]	60 000	Rivera PER
12-06	Nigeria	W 1-0	Johannesburg	WCr1	Heinze [6]	55 686	Stark GER
17-06	Korea Republic	W 4-1	Johannesburg	WCr1	Park Chu Young OG [17], Higuain 3 [33 76 80]	82 174	De Bleeckere BEL
22-06	Greece	W 2-0	Polokwane	WCr1	Demichelis [77], Palermo [89]	38 891	Irmatov UZB
27-06	Mexico	W 3-1	Johannesburg	WCr2	Tevez 2 [26 52], Higuain [33]	84 377	Rosetti ITA
3-07	Germany	L 0-4	Cape Town	WCqf		64 100	Irmatov UZB
11-08	Republic of Ireland	W 1-0	Dublin	Fr	Di Maria [20]	49 500	Rasmussen DEN
7-09	Spain	W 4-1	Buenos Aires	Fr	Messi [10], Higuain [13], Tevez [34], Aguero [90]	53 000	Ruiz COL
8-10	Japan	L 0-1	Saitama	Fr		57 735	Gil POL
17-11	Brazil	W 1-0	Doha	Fr	Messi [92+]	40 000	Balideh QAT

Fr = Friendly match • CA = Copa América • WC = FIFA World Cup

q = qualifier • r1 = 1st round group stage • r2 = first knockout round • qf = quarter-final • sf = semi-final • f = final

ARGENTINA NATIONAL TEAM HISTORICAL RECORDS

Caps

137 - Javier Zanetti 1994- • **115** - Roberto Ayala 1994-2007 • **106** - Diego Simeone 1988-2002 • **97** - Oscar Ruggeri 1983-94 • **91** - Diego Maradona 1977-94 • **87** - Ariel Ortega 1993-2010 • **78** - Gabriel Batistuta 1991-2002 • **76** - Juan Pablo Sorín 1995-2006 • **73** - Américo Gallego 1975-82 & Juan Sebastián Verón 1996- • **70** - Gabriel Heinze 2003- & Juan Pablo Sorín

Goals

56 - Gabriel Batistuta 1991-2002 • **35** - Hernán Crespo 1995-2007 • **34** - Diego Maradona 1977-94 • **24** - Luis Artime 1961-67 • **22** - Leopoldo Luque 1975-81 & Daniel Passarella 1976-86 • **21** - José Sanfilippo 1956-62 & Herminio Masantonio 1935-42 • **20** - Mario Kempes 1973-82 • **19** - Norberto Méndez 1945-56, José Manuel Moreno 1936-50 & René Pontoni 1942-47

Past Coaches

Angel Vázquez 1924-25 • José Lago Millán 1927-28 • Francisco Olazar 1928-29 • Francisco Olazar & Juan Jose Tramutola 1929-30 • Felipe Pascucci 1934 • Manuel Seoane 1934-37 • Angel Roca 1937-39 • Guillermo Stábile 1939-60 • Victorio Spinetto 1960-61 • José D'Amico 1961 • Juan Carlos Lorenzo 1962-63 • Alejandro Galán 1963 • Horacio Torres 1963-64 • José María Minella 1964-68 • Renato Cesarini 1968 • Humberto Maschio 1968-69 • Adolfo Pedernera 1969-69 • Juan José Pizzuti 1969-72 • Enrique Sívori 1972-74 • Vladislao Cap & José Varacka 1974 • César Luis Menotti 1974-83 • Carlos Bilardo 1983-90 • Alfio Basile 1990-94 • Daniel Passarella 1994-98 • Marcelo Bielsa 1998-2004 • José Pekerman 2004-06 • Alfio Basile 2006-08 • Diego Maradona 2008-10 • Sergio Batista 2010-

ARGENTINA 2009-10 PRIMERA A APERTURA

	Pl	W	D	L	F	A	Pts
Banfield †	19	12	5	2	25	11	41
Newell's Old Boys	19	12	3	4	26	15	39
Colón Santa Fe	19	10	4	5	27	16	34
Independiente	19	10	4	5	30	20	34
Vélez Sarsfield	19	10	4	5	29	21	34
Argentinos Juniors	19	8	8	3	29	20	32
San Lorenzo	19	9	5	5	28	20	32
Estudiantes LP	19	9	4	6	28	19	31
Lanús	19	8	7	4	26	17	31
Rosario Central	19	8	7	4	21	14	31
Boca Juniors	19	7	6	6	28	24	27
Arsenal	19	7	6	6	20	24	27
Atlético Tucumán	19	6	4	9	24	32	22
River Plate	19	5	6	8	23	26	21
Chacarita Juniors	19	5	4	10	18	25	19
Racing Club	19	4	5	10	17	26	17
Godoy Cruz	19	3	7	9	18	28	16
Gimnasia y Esg LP	19	3	4	12	16	29	13
Huracán	19	2	5	12	12	34	11
Tigre	19	2	2	15	18	42	8

21/08/2009 - 14/12/2009 • † Qualified for Copa Libertadores
Top scorers: 14 - Santiago Silva URU, Banfield • 12 - Federico Nieto, Colón • 11 - Antonio Boghossian URU, Newell's • 10 - Dario Gandin, Independiente & Gabriel Hauche, Argentinos Juniors • 9 - Mauro Boselli, Estudiantes LP

ARGENTINA 2009-10 PRIMERA A CLAUSURA

	Pl	W	D	L	F	A	Pts
Argentinos Juniors †	19	12	5	2	35	23	41
Estudiantes LP	19	12	4	3	33	14	40
Godoy Cruz	19	11	4	4	28	14	37
Independiente	19	10	4	5	25	18	34
Banfield	19	9	5	5	24	16	32
Newell's Old Boys	19	8	6	5	32	18	30
Lanús	19	8	5	6	25	23	29
Racing Club	19	9	2	8	21	22	29
Vélez Sarsfield	19	7	6	6	25	20	27
Huracán	19	7	5	7	21	22	26
Tigre	19	7	3	9	28	26	24
Gimnasia y Esg LP	19	6	6	7	21	29	24
River Plate	19	6	4	9	16	21	22
Colón Santa Fe	19	4	9	6	20	32	21
San Lorenzo	19	6	2	11	16	21	20
Boca Juniors	19	5	5	9	28	35	20
Rosario Central	19	3	10	6	12	19	19
Arsenal	19	5	4	10	19	33	19
Chacarita Juniors	19	4	1	14	22	33	13
Atlético Tucumán	19	1	10	8	14	26	13

29/01/2010 - 16/05/2010 • † Qualified for Copa Libertadores
Top scorers: 13 - Mauro Boselli, Estudiantes • 10 - Martin Palermo, Boca & Ruben Ramirez, Banfield & Marco Perez COL, Gimnasia • 9 - Carlos Luna, Tigre & Ismael Sosa, Argentinos Juniors 9

ARGENTINA 2009-10 PRIMERA A APERTURA & CLAUSURA RESULTS AND RELEGATION TABLE

	07-08	08-09	09-10	Pts	Pl	RA	Est	Lan	Vél	SLo	Boc	New	Ban	Arg	Ind	Col	God	Riv	Tig	Hur	Ars	Rac	RosC	Gim	AtlT	Cha
Estudiantes LP ‡	69	57	71	197	114	1.728		1-1	3-0	2-0	2-1	2-0	1-1	0-1	2-1	0-1	2-1	1-0	3-1	2-0	3-0	4-0	0-0	3-0	1-0	0-0
Lanús	56	75	60	191	114	1.675	0-0		1-1	3-2	1-2	0-2	1-2	3-6	0-0	3-0	1-0	1-0	4-0	3-2	4-1	1-0	0-0	2-0	3-0	0-3
Vélez Sarsfield‡	59	66	61	186	114	1.632	0-1	1-0		0-0	4-4	1-2	0-1	0-3	0-1	1-0	2-0	3-1	4-2	1-2	2-1	1-0	4-1			
San Lorenzo	64	63	52	179	114	1.57	2-2	0-1	0-0		3-0	2-1	0-1	1-2	0-3	2-2	0-1	2-1	1-0	3-0	3-2	0-1	0-0	1-0	3-1	3-1
Boca Juniors	70	61	47	178	114	1.561	1-1	3-1	3-2	2-0		1-1	2-0	2-2	1-2	0-0	2-3	2-0	2-1	1-2	4-0	1-2	1-2	4-0	0-0	3-0
Newell's Old Boys ‡	56	52	69	177	114	1.553	2-1	1-1	1-1	0-2	4-2		2-1	0-1	0-5	0-2	1-0	2-1	1-0	1-2	1-0	2-2	6-0	0-3	3-0	
Banfield ‡	54	46	73	173	114	1.518	2-1	2-0	3-0	2-0	3-0	2-1		3-0	1-3	3-1	3-0	2-0	1-0	1-0	0-0	1-0	0-0	3-2	1-1	1-0
Argentinos Juniors‡	61	38	73	172	114	1.509	1-0	0-0	1-0	2-1	2-1	1-1	1-1		4-3	3-1	1-2	1-2	1-1	5-1	1-1	2-0	1-1	3-1	2-1	2-1
Independiente ‡	59	39	68	166	114	1.456	3-2	1-0	2-2	0-1	2-3	0-1	1-2	1-1		3-2	2-0	2-0	2-0	2-0	1-0	1-0	2-0	1-0	3-1	1-1
Colón Santa Fe †	45	57	55	157	114	1.377	1-4	1-0	1-0	2-1	3-0	0-0	2-0	1-2	0-1		1-0	1-0	5-3	0-4	4-1	2-1	1-1	1-0	0-3	1-1
Godoy Cruz	0	49	53	102	76	1.342	1-2	2-1	2-0	1-1	1-1	1-2	0-2	4-0	0-3	0-0		1-1	6-2	1-1	0-0	3-1	1-1	1-0	2-1	1-0
River Plate	66	41	43	150	114	1.316	1-1	0-1	2-1	1-0	1-0	1-0	0-1	0-1	1-3	0-0	2-1		1-5	2-0	1-1	2-0	0-0	2-2	3-1	4-3
Tigre	56	62	32	150	114	1.316	1-2	0-1	0-3	2-3	3-0	1-2	1-2	1-1	0-1	2-2	2-0	0-2		2-2	1-2	1-2	1-2	1-1	3-1	0-2
Huracán	52	58	37	147	114	1.289	1-4	1-2	3-2	2-0	2-0	2-1	0-1	1-2	0-0	0-0	0-0	2-3	1-1		3-1	0-3	3-1	1-0	2-1	1-0
Arsenal	51	46	46	143	114	1.254	0-2	2-5	0-3	1-0	1-2	1-1	2-1	1-0	3-0	1-2	1-0	0-2	0-1	3-1		0-0	1-0	1-0	2-0	0-3
Racing Club	40	52	46	138	114	1.211	1-0	1-1	3-1	1-0	1-2	1-0	2-0	0-1	1-2	1-1	0-0	0-3	1-0	1-1	2-4		3-0	1-1	4-0	0-2
Rosario Central ‡‡	41	40	50	131	114	1.149	3-0	0-0	0-1	0-1	2-1	1-1	0-0	0-1	2-0	0-1	1-0	2-1	0-1	0-2	2-3	1-0		1-1	1-1	1-1
Gimnasia LP ‡‡	36	55	37	128	114	1.123	3-1	0-0	1-2	2-1	1-0	2-0	1-2	2-1	1-2	0-2	1-1	2-0	4-1	0-2	1-0	1-1	3-3			2-0
Atlético Tucumán	0	0	35	38	38	0.921	1-3	2-2	1-2	0-1	2-1	1-1	0-0	0-1	0-1	1-1	2-4	2-0	1-1	0-4	2-0	0-1	1-0	1-1		2-1
Chacarita Juniors	0	0	32	32	38	0.842	1-2	1-2	0-0	0-2	4-1	0-1	2-1	2-2	0-1	1-2	2-1	2-3	1-2	1-0	1-0	0-1	0-1	1-2		

† Qualified for the Copa Libertadores • ‡ Qualified for the Copa Sudamericana • Apertura results are in the shaded boxes • RA = Relegation average based on the average number of points per game over the past three seasons • ‡‡ play-off against Primera B Nacional team
Relegation play-offs: Rosario Central 1-1 0-3 **All Boys** • Gimnasia y Esgrima LP 0-1 3-1 Atletico de Rafaela

ARGENTINA 2009–10
PRIMERA B
NACIONAL (2)

	Pl	W	D	L	F	A	Pts
Olimpo B. Blanca	38	19	14	5	50	24	71
Quilmes	38	17	13	8	39	31	64
Atlético Rafaela †	38	18	9	11	53	35	63
All Boys †	38	19	6	13	45	37	63
Instituto Córdoba	38	16	12	10	39	29	60
Belgrano Córdoba	38	15	12	11	47	41	57
San Martín San Juan	38	14	14	10	48	39	56
Gimnasia y Esg Jujuy	38	14	12	12	34	37	54
Unión Santa Fé	38	14	11	13	54	49	53
Defensa y Justicia	38	14	10	14	54	53	52
San Martín Tucumán	38	12	14	12	39	41	50
Ferro Carril Oeste	38	12	13	13	36	39	49
Boca Unidos	38	11	15	12	42	48	48
Platense	38	11	14	13	39	40	47
Independiente R'davia	38	12	11	15	47	58	47
Deportivo Merlo ‡	38	12	10	16	35	44	46
Tiro Federal	38	12	8	18	52	53	44
CAI ‡	38	11	10	17	47	52	43
Aldosivi	38	12	6	20	44	54	42
Sportivo Italiano	38	6	4	28	34	74	22

21/08/2009 - 17/05/2010
† Promotion play-off (see Primera A) • ‡ Relegation play-off
Platense and Sportivo Italiano relegated over three season
record • Top scorer: Diego Armani, Tiro Federal 19

RELEGATION PLAY-OFFS
Sarmiento 0-1 0-1 **Deportivo Merlo** • Santamarina 2-2 0-5 **CAI**

ARGENTINA 2009–10
PRIMERA DIVISION B
METROPOLITANA (3)

	Pl	W	D	L	F	A	Pts
Almirante Brown	40	22	11	7	49	30	77
Sarmiento Junín †	40	20	15	5	56	26	75
Tristán Suárez †	40	14	20	6	40	32	62
Estudiantes BA †	40	16	13	11	52	40	61
Colegiales †	40	16	13	11	44	40	61
Los Andes	40	15	15	10	41	35	60
Atlanta	40	15	13	12	38	27	58
Temperley	40	14	14	12	36	31	56
Acassuso	40	12	19	9	44	37	55
Defensores de Belgrano	40	12	19	9	41	35	55
San Telmo	40	13	15	12	31	25	54
Brown Adrogué	40	14	12	14	45	46	54
Nueva Chicago	40	13	12	15	34	35	51
Villa San Carlos	40	11	15	14	43	49	48
Deportivo Morón	40	10	17	13	36	34	47
Flandria	40	12	11	17	48	55	47
Social Español	40	11	11	18	36	47	44
Almagro ‡	40	10	14	16	29	42	44
Deportivo Armenio	40	7	17	16	29	44	38
Comunicaciones	40	9	8	23	34	54	35
Central Córdoba	40	6	12	22	22	64	30

22/08/2009 - 8/05/2010
† Promotion play-offs (for final see Primera B Nacional)
Central Córdoba relegated on three season average
‡ Relegation play-off • Talleres RE 0-3 0-1 **Almagro**

PROMOTION PLAY-OFFS
Semi-finals: Tristán Suárez 1-0 Estudiantes
Sarmiento 2-1 Colegiales
Final: Sarmiento 0-0 Tristán Suárez (Sarmiento qualified to meet Deportivo Merlo due to better season record

Beneath the top two divisions the AFA operates two different league structures - one for the metropolitan area centered on Buenos Aires and the other for the rest of the country (the interior). There is promotion to the Primera B Nacional from both the metropolitan and interior tournaments. Drawn ties in the promotion and relegation play-offs are decided by the overall season record

ARGENTINA 2009–10
TORNEO ARGENTINA A
APERTURA
FASE FINAL INTERIOR (3)

Group A	Pl	W	D	L	F	A	Pts
Unión de Sunchales †	4	3	0	1	8	4	9
Crucero de Norte	4	2	0	2	9	9	6
Patronato	4	2	0	2	5	7	6
Juventud Antoniana	4	1	1	2	8	8	4
Libertad	4	1	1	2	5	7	4

Group B	Pl	W	D	L	F	A	Pts
Cipolletti †	4	2	2	0	3	1	8
Huracán Tres Arroyos	4	1	2	1	5	4	5
Central Córdoba	4	1	2	1	3	4	5
Rivadavia	4	1	1	2	4	4	4
Deportivo Maipu	4	1	1	2	1	3	4

5/12/2009 - 20/12/2009 • † Qualified for the play-offs

ARGENTINA 2009–10
TORNEO ARGENTINA A
CLAUSURA
FASE FINAL INTERIOR (3)

Group A	Pl	W	D	L	F	A	Pts
Deportivo Santamarina †	4	3	1	0	11	6	10
Huracán Tres Arroyos	4	3	0	1	6	6	9
Talleres Córdoba	4	0	3	1	4	5	3
Estudiantes Rio Cuarto	4	0	2	2	5	7	2
Sportivo Desamparados	4	0	2	2	4	6	2

Group B	Pl	W	D	L	F	A	Pts
Patronato †	4	3	0	1	8	4	9
Guillermo Brown	4	2	1	1	10	11	7
Crucero de Norte	4	2	0	2	10	9	6
Juventud Antoniana	3	1	1	1	6	5	4
Gimnasia Concepción	3	0	0	3	2	7	0

21/04/2010 - 19/05/2010 • † Qualified for the play-offs

INTERIOR (3) PLAY-OFFS

Semi-finals

Patronato	1 3 3p
Cipolletti	3 1 2p

Unión de Sunchales	1 3 2p
Deportivo Santamarina	2 2 4p

Finals

Patronato	2 2
Deportivo Santamarina	1 0

Patronato promoted to Primera B Nacional •
Deportivo Santamarina qualified to meet CIA
Relegated: Ben Hur de Rafaela and Juventud
Pergamino

ARGENTINA 2009–10
PRIMERA DIVISION C
METROPOLITANA (4)

	Pl	W	D	L	F	A	Pts
Barracas Central	38	21	10	7	55	24	73
Excursionistas †	38	21	10	7	57	28	73
Defensores Unidos †	38	19	8	11	59	43	65
Sacachispas †	38	16	10	12	52	52	58
Talleres R de Escalada †	38	15	12	11	46	40	57
Justo Jose de Urquiza †	38	15	10	13	45	41	55
Argentino Rosario ‡	38	16	6	16	50	42	54
El Porvenir †	38	13	14	11	39	43	53
F.C. Midland †	38	12	17	9	27	32	53
San Miguel †	38	14	10	14	36	37	52
Deportivo Laferrere	38	13	11	14	41	38	50
Berazategui	38	13	9	16	34	38	48
Defensores Cambaceres	38	12	12	14	40	54	48
Leandro N. Alem	38	9	19	10	38	42	46
Fénix	38	12	10	16	45	50	46
General Lamadrid	38	11	10	17	41	52	43
Argentino Merlo	38	10	12	16	30	40	42
Villa Dálmine	38	10	10	18	27	39	40
Luján	38	9	10	19	35	45	37
Sp. Barracas Bolívar	38	9	10	19	27	44	37

22/08/2009 - 8/05/2010 • † Promotion play-offs
Championship play-off: Barracas Central 1-0 Excursionistas
Bolivar relegated on three season average • ‡ relegation play-off • **Liniers** 3-1 0-1 Argentino Rosario

PLAY-OFFS
Quarter-finals: **Sacachispas** 0-0 El Porvenir • **Talleres** 2-0 Justo José • Defensores 0-1 **Midland** • **Excursionistas** 2-0 San Miguel
Semi-finals: **Talleres** 1-0 2-1 Sacachispas •
Midland 2-2 0-2 **Excursionistas**
Final: **Talleres** 1-1 1-0 Excursionistas

ARGENTINA 2009–10
PRIMERA DIVISION D
METROPOLITANA (5)

	Pl	W	D	L	F	A	Pts
UAI-Urquiza	34	18	12	4	58	23	66
San Martín Burzaco †	34	18	10	6	53	23	64
Yupanqui †	34	18	7	9	44	31	61
Liniers †	34	15	12	7	57	38	57
Argentino Quilmes †	34	16	8	10	46	26	56
Sportivo Dock Sud †	34	16	8	10	46	35	56
Cañuelas †	34	12	15	7	30	22	51
Atlas †	34	13	11	10	49	40	50
Victoriano Arenas †	34	14	7	13	49	38	49
Ituzaingó	34	13	10	11	36	36	49
Centro Español	34	14	7	13	36	41	49
Deportivo Riestra	34	12	9	13	39	33	45
Claypole	34	12	8	14	46	49	44
Central Ballester	34	8	13	13	34	48	37
Juventud Unida	34	9	5	20	27	54	32
Deportivo Paraguayo	34	7	8	19	34	59	29
Atlético Lugano	34	7	7	20	27	52	28
Muñiz	34	3	5	26	14	77	14

22/08/2009 - 20/04/2010 • † Qualified for the play-offs
Muñiz relegated on three season average

PLAY-OFFS
Quarter-finals: San Martin 2-0 Victoriano • Argentino Quilmes 1-1 Dock Sud • Liniers 2-1 Cañuelas • Yupanqui 0-1 **Atlas**
Semi-finals: Argentino Quilmes 1-2 1-2 **Liniers** •
Atlas 1-1 1-2 **San Martin**
Final: **Liniers** 3-1 0-1 San Martin

ARGENTINA 2009–10
TORNEO ARGENTINA B
FASE FINAL INTERIOR (4)

Group A	Pl	W	D	L	F	A	Pts
Douglas Haig	4	2	1	1	9	6	7
La Emilia ‡	4	2	1	1	7	5	7
Sp. Biblioteca Atenas	4	2	1	1	7	6	7
Sportivo Las Parejas	4	2	0	2	7	7	6
Hirácan Com. Rivadavia	4	0	1	3	4	10	1

Group B	Pl	W	D	L	F	A	Pts
Central Norte Salta	4	3	0	1	8	4	9
At. Unión Villa Krause ‡	4	2	1	1	4	2	7
General Paz Juniors	4	2	1	1	6	5	7
Gimnasia y Tiro Salta	4	2	0	2	3	3	6
Guaraní Posadas	4	0	0	4	1	8	0

15/05/2010 - 2/06/2010 • ‡ Qualified for the play-offs
Relegated: La Florida, Atlético Argentino, Real Arroyo Seco,
Defensores de Salto & Luján de Cuyo

ARGENTINA 2009–10
TORNEO DEL INTERIOR
FASE FINAL (5)

Semi-finals		Finals	
Teniente Origone	1 2		
Deportivo Rivadavia	1 1	**Teniente Origone**	2 0 3p
Atlas Salta	1 0	Altos Hornos Zapla	1 1 2p
Altos Hornos Zapla	2 2		
Sarmiento	0 2		
Resistencia Central	0 0	**Sarmiento**	1 1 4p
General Rojo	1 0	Atlético Paraná	2 0 3p
Atlético Paraná	0 2		
Atlético Argentino	1 3		
Deportivo Coreano	2 1	**Atlético Argentino**	0 1 4p
Jorge Newberry	2 1 5p	FC Oeste General Pico	0 1 3p
FC Oeste General Pico	1 2 6p		

Atlético Paraná and Altos Hornos Zapla promoted via play-offs

MEDALS TABLE

#	Team	Overall			League			Amateur			Pro			National			Metro			AP/CL			South Am		
		G	S	B	G	S	B	G	S	B	G	S	B	G	S	B	G	S	B	G	S	B	G	S	B
1	Boca Juniors	38	25	21	29	21	17	6	3	5	10	8	5	3			2	2	3	8	8	4	9	4	4
2	River Plate	37	34	29	34	30	14	1	5	4	14	11	5	3	7		4	2		12	5	5	3	4	15
3	Independiente	26	17	14	16	16	9	2	2	3	6	8	6	3	1		3	2		2	3		10	1	5
4	Racing Club	18	8	14	16	7	12	9	1	1	6	3	7			1		2		1	1	3	2	1	2
5	San Lorenzo	15	13	22	13	13	16	3	2	2	3	7	5	2	1	3	2	1	2	3	2	4	2		6
6	Alumni	10	2		10	2		10	2																
7	Estudiantes La Plata	9	9	11	5	7	9	1	3	2			3	1	2		2	1	2	1	1	2	4	2	2
8	Velez Sarsfield	9	8	10	7	8	8		1			1	1	1	1	2		2	1	6	3	4	2		2
9	Huracán	5	6	8	5	6	7	4	2	3			3				1	2	1		2				1
10	Rosario Central	5	5	5	4	4	2						1	3	2				1	1	2		1	1	3
11	Newell's Old Boys	5	5	3	5	3	3				2	2	1				1		1	2	1	1		2	
12	Lomas Athletic	5	2	3	5	2	3	5	2	3															
13	Argentinos Juniors	4	2	4	3	2	1					1	1	1			1	1		1			1		3
14	Belgrano Athletic	3	3	3	3	3	3	3	3	3															
15	Lanús	2	4	5	1	3	5			1		1								1	2	4	1	1	
16	Ferro Carril Oeste	2	3	1	2	3	1								2	1	2	1							
17	CA Porteño	2	2		2	2		2	2																
18	Quilmes	2	1	3	2	1	3	1		3					1		1								
19	Estudantil Porteño	2			2			2																	
20	Gimnasia y Esgrima LP	1	6	4	1	6	3	1	1				1								5	2			1
21	Banfield	1	4	4	1	4	4		2	2		1								1	1	2			
22	Talleres Córdoba	1	1	2		1	2								1				1			1	1		
23	Lomas Academy	1	1		1	1		1	1																
24	Chacarita Juniors	1		1	1		1										1		1						
	Sportivo Barracas	1		1	1		1	1		1															
	Sportivo Doc Sud	1		1	1		1	1		1															
27	Arsenal Sarandi	1																					1		
	St Andrews	1			1			1																	
	Old Caledonians	1			1			1																	
30	San Isidro		3	3		3	3		3	3															
31	Estudiantes BA		2	2		2	2		2	2															
32	Flores AC		2	1		2	1		2	1															
33	Lobos AC		2			2			2																
	Nueva Chicago		2			2			2																
	Tigre		2			2															2				
36	Platense		1	4		1	4		1	3			1												
37	Colón Santa Fe		1	3		1	2														1	2			1
38	Unión Santa Fe		1	1		1	1								1				1						
	Barracas AC		1	1		1	1		1	1															
40	Almagro		1			1			1																
	Barracas Central		1			1			1																
	Colegiales		1			1			1																
	Del Plata		1			1			1																
	Gimnasia y Esgrima BA		1			1			1																
	Lanus AC		1			1			1																
	Racing Cordoba		1			1									1										
	Rosario AC		1			1			1																
	Sportivo Palermo		1			1			1																
	Temperley		1			1			1																
50	Deportivo Español			3			2									2									1
51	Atlanta			2			2			1						1									
	Argentino Quilmes			2			2			2															
	Quilmes Rowers			2			2			2															
54	Belgrano A			1			1			1															
	El Porvenir			1			1			1															
	Defensores Belgrano			1			1			1															
	Godoy Cruz			1																					1
	Old Boys			1			1			1															
	Rosario Railway			1			1			1															
	Sporting Almagro			1			1			1															
	Sportivo Buenos Aires			1			1			1															
		208	188	201	172	172	156	55	55	56	42	42	41	19	19	7	18	18	14	38	38	38	36	16	45

Amateur = Amateur Championship 1891-1934 • Pro = Professional Championship 1931-66 & 1986-91 • National = National Championship 1967-85 • Metro = Metropoltian Championship 1967-84 • AP/CL = Apertura and Clausura tournaments 1991- • League column is a combination of all

CLUB BY CLUB GUIDE TO 2010 IN ARGENTINA

ARGENTINA 2009–10 PRIMERA A CLAUSURA	Pl	W	D	L	F	A	Pts
Argentinos Juniors †	19	12	5	2	35	23	41
Estudiantes LP	19	12	4	3	33	14	40
Godoy Cruz	19	11	4	4	28	14	37
Independiente	19	10	4	5	25	18	34
Banfield	19	9	5	5	24	16	32
Newell's Old Boys	19	8	6	5	32	18	30
Lanús	19	8	5	6	25	23	29
Racing Club	19	9	2	8	21	22	29
Vélez Sarsfield	19	7	6	6	25	20	27
Huracán	19	7	5	7	21	22	26
Tigre	19	7	3	9	28	26	24
Gimnasia y Esg LP	19	6	6	7	21	29	24
River Plate	19	6	4	9	16	21	22
Colón Santa Fe	19	4	9	6	20	32	21
San Lorenzo	19	6	2	11	16	21	20
Boca Juniors	19	5	5	9	28	35	20
Rosario Central	19	3	10	6	12	19	19
Arsenal	19	5	4	10	19	33	19
Chacarita Juniors	19	4	1	14	22	33	13
Atlético Tucumán	19	1	10	8	14	26	13

29/01/2010 - 16/05/2010 • † Qualified for Copa Libertadores

ARGENTINA 2010–11 PRIMERA A APERTURA	Pl	W	D	L	F	A	Pts
Estudiantes LP †	19	14	3	2	32	8	45
Vélez Sarsfield	19	13	4	2	33	9	43
Arsenal	19	9	5	5	22	19	32
River Plate	19	8	7	4	21	18	31
Godoy Cruz	19	7	8	4	32	25	29
Racing Club	19	8	5	6	25	18	29
Lanús	19	8	4	7	20	25	28
All Boys	19	7	5	7	24	23	26
Newell's Old Boys	19	6	8	5	13	12	26
Colón Santa Fe	19	7	5	7	21	29	26
Boca Juniors	19	7	4	8	20	20	25
Tigre	19	7	4	8	24	24	25
Argentinos Juniors	19	6	6	7	22	21	24
San Lorenzo	19	6	6	7	18	20	24
Banfield	19	4	8	7	20	19	20
Quilmes	19	4	7	8	14	23	19
Olimpo	19	5	3	11	18	26	18
Huracán	19	4	4	11	16	33	16
Gimnasia La Plata	19	3	6	10	13	23	15
Independiente	19	2	8	9	13	26	14

6/08/2010 - 6/02/2011 • † Qualified for Copa Libertadores

The following guide covers the two league tournaments staged during the course of 2010 although the Argentine season technically runs from August to May. The tables from those two campaigns are listed above for ease of reference • Cl = Clausura • Ap = Apertura • CL = Copa Libertadores • CS = Copa Sudamericana • RSA = Recopa Sudamericana • g1 = group 1 etc • r1 = first round etc • qf = quarter-final • sf = semi-final • f = final Appearances and goals for the 2009-10 Clausura are marked in **bold** • Appearances and goals for the 2010-11 Apertura are in *italics* The figures consist of three elements - matches started+appearances as a substitute/goals scored

ALL BOYS 2010

May	19	Rosario C	D	1-1	Clpo	Matos [14]	17 000
	23	Rosario C	W	3-0	Clpo	Vieytes [7], Camp'co [43], Vella [65]	32 000
	7	Racing	L	0-1	Ap		40 000
Aug	15	Velez	L	1-2	Ap	Sanchez [78]	12 000
	22	Boca Jun	W	2-0	Ap	Matos [30p], Dominguez [40]	30 000
	28	S. Lorenzo	L	1-3	Ap	Matos [70p]	29 000
Sep	4	Olimpo	W	1-0	Ap	Perez Garcia [39]	15 000
	10	Colon	D	1-1	Ap	Matos [7p]	17 000
	19	Estudiantes	W	2-1	Ap	Dominguez [29], Grazzini [50]	14 000
	25	Lanus	L	0-1	Ap		11 000
	2	Tigre	D	3-3	Ap	Grazzini 2 [32 66], Matos [81]	15 000
	9	Huracan	D	1-1	Ap	Ferrari [76]	15 000
Oct	16	Indep'iente	W	3-1	Ap	Ferrari [5], Rodriguez [14], Casteglione [48]	16 000
	23	Arg Juniors	L	0-1	Ap		16 000
	7	River Plate	W	1-0	Ap	Rodriguez [53]	20 000
Nov	13	Arsenal	D	0-0	Ap		9 000
	20	Newells OB	W	2-0	Ap	Matos [36], Perea [67]	22 000
	27	Quilmes	L	1-2	Ap	Matos [12]	10 000
	3	Banfield	W	2-1	Ap	OG [11], Matos [31]	12 000
Dec	7	Gimnasia	L	1-3	Ap	Barrientos [49]	12 000
	11	Godoy Cruz	D	2-2	Ap	Perez Garcia [29], Matos [90p]	12 000

ATLETICO TUCUMAN 2010

Jan	30	S. Lorenzo	L	0-1	Cl		24 000
	4	Indep'iente	L	1-3	Cl	Escobar [28]	30 000
	8	Huracan	D	0-0	Cl		15 000
Feb	14	Boca Jun	D	0-0	Cl		40 000
	21	Arg Juniors	D	1-1	Cl	Sarria [2]	16 000
	28	Lanus	L	0-3	Cl		8 000
	4	Newells OB	D	1-1	Cl	Pereyra [89]	15 000
	7	Banfield	D	0-0	Cl		17 000
Mar	12	Godoy Cruz	L	1-2	Cl	Paez [61]	10 000
	19	Estudiantes	L	1-3	Cl	Azconzabal [45]	16 000
	28	Velez	L	0-1	Cl		17 000
	6	Tigre	L	1-3	Cl	Escobar [86]	12 000
	11	River Plate	D	0-0	Cl		27 000
Apr	17	Charcarita	W	2-1	Cl	Gigliotti [67], Blanes [77]	7 000
	21	Racing	L	0-1	Cl		20 000
	25	Rosario C	D	2-2	Cl	Rodriguez 2 [3 51]	19 000
	2	Colon	D	0-0	Cl		14 000
May	9	Arsenal	D	1-1	Cl	Pereyra [54]	15 000
	15	Gimnasia	D	3-3	Cl	Gigliotti [62], Montiglio [79], Barone [81]	7 000

Atlético Tucuman were relegated at the end of the 2009-10 Clausura

ALL BOYS LEAGUE APPEARANCES/GOALS 2010
Goalkeepers Nicolas Cambiasso *18* • Matias Giordano *1+1*
Defenders Mariano Brau *0+1/0* • Carlos Casteglione *14/1* • Eduardo Dominguez *18/2* • Jonathan Ferrari *9+3/2* • Carlos Madeo *1/0* • Armando Panceri *3/0* • Matias Rudler *0+1/0* • Carlos Soto *16/0* • Cristian Vella *15/0*
Midfield Hugo Barrientos *18/1* • Sebastien Grazzini *7+3/0* • Emanuel Perea *11+1/1* • Matias Perez Garcia *9+6/2* • Victor David Lopez *0+1/0* • Lucas Rimoldi *5+6/0* • Juan Pablo Rodriguez URU *13+4/2* • Fernando Sanchez *16+1/1* • Marcelo Vieytes *0+2/0* • Ariel Zarate *1+6/0*
Forwards Sebastian Ereros *13+4/0* • Cristian Fabbiani *1+7/0* • Mauro Matos *19/8* • Matias Saad *0+1/0* • Agustin Torassa *1+7/0*
Coach Jose Santos

TUCUMAN LEAGUE APPEARANCES/GOALS 2010
Goalkeepers Esteban Dei Rossi **2** • Lucas Ischuk **17**
Defenders Juan Azconzabal **8/1** • Deivis Barone URU **16+2/1** • Andres Bressan **7/0** • Rodrigo Herrera **3/0** • Juan Martinez **1+1/0** • Cesar More **4+1/0** • Ricardo Moreira **10+1/0** • Javier Paez **14/1** • Raul Saavedra **8/0**
Midfield Santiago del Conte **0+2/0** • David Drocco **5+2/0** • Diego Erroz **12+2/0** • Matias Escobar **1+1/0** • Martin Granero **10+2/0** • Sebastian Longo **9+5/0** • Cesar Montiglio **12+2/1** • Damian Musto **9+3/0** • Claudio Sarria **3+5/1** • Claudio Vargas PAR **10+3/0**
Forwards Johnatan Blanes URU **1+1/1** • Fabio Escobar PAR **5+6/2** • Emanuel Gigliotti **13+6/2** • Juan Pereyra **11+2/2** • Luis Rodriguez **10+2/2** • Jose Saavedra **3+2/0**
Coach Osvaldo Sosa • Mario Gomez (8-03-2010)

ARGENTINOS JUNIORS 2010

	Date	Opponent		Score		Scorers	Att
Jan	31	Boca Jun	D	2-2	Cl	OG 81, Sosa 90	20 000
	6	Lanus	W	6-3	Cl	OG 23, Pavlovich 2 43 55, Sosa 62, Ortigoza 68p, Hernández 79	25 000
Feb	21	A. Tucuman	D	1-1	Cl	OG 28	16 000
	24	Banfield	L	0-3	Cl		10 000
	28	Godoy Cruz	L	1-2	Cl	Gentiletti 32	7 000
	3	Estudiantes	W	1-0	Cl	Calderon 33	8 000
	7	Velez	W	1-0	Cl	OG 85	15 000
Mar	14	Racing	W	1-0	Cl	Pavlovich 78	30 000
	17	Newells OB	D	1-1	Cl	Sosa 73. First 66' on 15/02	7 000
	20	Tigre	D	1-1	Cl	Pavlovich 15	11 000
	29	River Plate	W	1-0	Cl	Sosa 21	25 000
	3	Charcarita	W	2-1	Cl	Coria 2 19 21	15 000
	8	Rosario C	W	1-0	Cl	Sosa 59	30 000
Apr	12	Colon	W	3-1	Cl	Ortigoza 32, Calderon 45, Sosa 89	12 000
	19	Arsenal	D	2-2	Cl	Calderon 9, Coria 89	8 000
	25	Gimnasia	W	3-1	Cl	Ortigoza 26p, Sosa 70, Raymonda 87	12 000
May	2	S. Lorenzo	W	2-1	Cl	Sosa 2 60 90	20 000
	9	Indep'iente	W	4-3	Cl	Pavlovich 2 27 73, Sabia 89, Caruzzo 90	20 000
	16	Huracan	W	2-1	Cl	Mercier 24, Coria 77	36 000
	7	Huracan	L	1-2	Ap	Vargas 40	15 000
	16	Indep'iente	D	1-1	Ap	Prosperi 16	25 000
Aug	21	Velez	L	0-2	Ap		25 000
	26	Indep'iente	L	0-1	CSr1		
	29	River Plate	D	0-0	Ap		15 000
	4	Arsenal	L	0-1	Ap		5 000
	9	Indep'iente	D	1-1	CSr1	Ortigoza 34p	19 000
Sep	12	Newells OB	L	1-2	Ap	Vargas 64	8 000
	18	Quilmes	D	2-2	Ap	Sabia 49, Berardo 90	9 000
	25	Banfield	W	1-0	Ap	Vargas 77	8 000
	2	Gimnasia	W	4-2	Ap	Vargas 18, Mercier 22, Hernandez 30, Niell 71	14 000
Oct	9	Godoy Cruz	D	0-0	Ap		8 000
	17	Racing	L	1-2	Ap	Niell 28	22 000
	23	All Boys	W	1-0	Ap	Niell 82	16 000
	6	Boca Jun	W	2-0	Ap	Gentiletti 87, Rius 88	35 000
Nov	14	S. Lorenzo	W	1-0	Ap	Blandi 23	12 000
	22	Olimpo	D	1-1	Ap	Niell 81	10 000
	29	Colon	W	3-0	Ap	Niell 51, Blandi 78, Hernandez 81	6 500
	4	Estudiantes	L	1-3	Ap	Rius 30	22 000
Dec	9	Lanus	L	1-2	Ap	OG 43	
	13	Tigre	D	1-1	Ap	Ruis 62	13 000

ARSENAL 2010

	Date	Opponent		Score		Scorers	Att
Jan	29	Estudiantes	L	0-3	Cl		18 000
	2	Velez	L	0-3	Cl		13 000
	7	Racing	W	4-2	Cl	Jara 25, Galvan 73, Obolo 2 86 89	55 000
Feb	12	Tigre	L	0-2	Cl		10 000
	21	River Plate	D	1-1	Cl	Sena 40	35 000
	26	Charcarita	L	0-3	Cl		5 000
	2	Rosario C	W	3-2	Cl	Yucuzzi 17, Obolo 21, Sena 61	27 000
	8	Colon	W	3-0	Cl	Obolo 2 32 46, Alvarez 90	3 000
Mar	13	Banfield	D	0-0	Cl		5 000
	21	Gimnasia	W	2-0	Cl	Leguizamon 32, Obolo 79	16 000
	28	S. Lorenzo	W	1-0	Cl	Aguirre 17	5 500
	3	Indep'iente	L	0-1	Cl		30 000
	6	Huracan	L	0-1	Cl		3 000
Apr	12	Boca Jun	L	0-4	Cl		25 000
	19	Arg Juniors	D	2-2	Cl	Leguizamon 2 35 50p	8 000
	24	Lanus	L	1-4	Cl	Leguizamon 62	5 000
	29	Newells OB	L	0-2	Cl		8 000
May	9	A. Tucuman	D	1-1	Cl	Leguizamon 19	15 000
	14	Godoy Cruz	L	1-2	Cl	Alvarez 53	2 500
	6	Lanus	L	1-2	Ap	Obolo 53	9 000
Aug	14	Tigre	W	2-1	Ap	Leguizamon 2 11 16	14 000
	22	Huracan	W	2-0	Ap	Obolo 17, Leguizamon 63p	6 000
	29	Indep'iente	W	2-1	Ap	Sena 60, Choy 78	22 000
	4	Arg Juniors	W	1-0	Ap	Obolo 39	5 000
Sep	12	River Plate	L	0-1	Ap		50 000
	18	Velez	D	0-0	Ap		8 000
	26	Newells OB	D	0-0	Ap		9 000
	1	Quilmes	W	1-0	Ap	Aguilar 83	8 000
	8	Banfield	W	1-0	Ap	Obolo 90	6 000
Oct	16	Gimnasia	W	3-2	Ap	Leguizamon 29, Obolo 49, Aguilar 88	13 000
	22	Godoy Cruz	L	1-3	Ap	Leguizamon 34p	3 000
	6	Racing	D	2-2	Ap	Obolo 19, Alvarez 78	25 000
Nov	13	All Boys	D	0-0	Ap		9 000
	21	Boca Jun	L	1-2	Ap	Lopez 48	20 000
	26	S. Lorenzo	W	2-1	Ap	Obolo 62, Mosca 90	5 000
	1	Olimpo	D	1-1	Ap	Alustiza 11p	8 000
Dec	7	Colon	W	2-1	Ap	Mosca 39, Alustiza 67p	3 000
	12	Estudiantes	L	0-2	Ap		20 000

ARGENTINOS LEAGUE APPEARANCES/GOALS 2010
Goalkeepers Nicolas Navarro 19/0 • Luis Ojeda 3+2 • Nicolas Peric CHI 16
Defenders Ignacio Canuto 8+5/0 • Matias Caruzzo 19/1 • Federico Dominguez 7+7/0 - 2+4/0 • Sergio Escudero 17/0 • Santiago Gentiletti 15+1/1 - 16/1 • Federico Pistone 1/0 • Gonzalo Prosperi 17+1/0 - 19/1 • Lucas Rodriguez 1/0 • Juan Sabia 14/1 - 18/1 • Miguel Torren 11/0
Midfield German Basualdo 3+5/0 - 12+10/0 • Nicolas Berardo 5+1/1 • Mauro Bogado 12+5/0 • Emilio Hernandez CHI 1+11/1 - 6+4/2 • Juan Mercier 18/1 - 18/1 • Gustavo Oberman 14+2/0 - 3+3/0 • Dario Ocampo 1+3/0 • Nestor Ortigoza 17/3 - 13/0 • Santiago Raymonda 3+6/1 • Carlos Recalde PAR 0+2/0 • Ciro Rius 6+4/3 • Andres Romero 0+2/0 - 2+5/0
Forwards Leandro Barrera 0+2/0 • Nicolas Blandi 11+4/2 • Jose Calderon 17/3 • Facundo Coria 16/4 • Fabio Escobar PAR 0+4/0 • Franco Niell 14+1/5 • Nicolas Pavlovich 9+8/6 • Gabriel Perez Tarifa 0+1/0 • Victor Sosa 12+5/9 • Gonzalo Vargas URU 11+6/4
Coach Claudio Borghi • Pedro Troglio (1-06-2010)

ARSENAL LEAGUE APPEARANCES/GOALS 2010
Goalkeepers Christian Campestrini 18 - 19 • Catriel Orcellet 1
Defenders Pablo Aguilar PAR 18/2 • Cristian Alvarez 9+8/2 - 5+2/1 • Ignacio Boggino 1/0 • Dario Espinola 12+2/0 • Juan Krupoviesa 12/0 • Lisandro Lopez 18/1 • Anibal Matellan 8/3 • Hugo Nervo 12+1/0 - 17/0 • Franco Peppino 13+1/0 • Matias Perez URU 5+1/0 • Gustavo Toranzo 0+1/0 • Cristian Tula 14/0 • Javier Yacuzzi 7+2/1
Midfield Nicolas Aguirre 5+1/1 • Gonzalo Choy 12+6/1 • Nicolas Domingo 3/0 • Gaston Esmerado 0+4/0 • Andres Franzoia 3+10/0 • Diego Galvan 5+4/1 • Adrian Gonzalez 4+8/0 • Franco Jara 9+8/1 • Cristian Leiva 17/0 • Ivan Marcone 13+1/0 - 7/0 • Leonardo Morales • Jorge Ortiz 15+2/0 • Damian Perez 4+1/0 - 7/0 • Facundo Perez 6+2/0 • Federico Poggi 14+3/0 • Sergio Sena 18/2 - 11+2/1 • Matias Sierra 0+1/0 • Facundo Silva 0+6/0 - 1+4/0
Forwards Matias Alustiza 2+13/2 • Luciano Leguizamon 13+4/5 - 16/5 • Jonathan Lopez 0+1/0 • Gonzalo Menendez 1+4/0 • Claudio Mosca 5+3/0 - 5+4/2 • Ivan Obolo 16+3/6 - 19/7
Coach Jorge Burruchaga • Carlos Ruiz (2-05-2010) • Gustavo Alfaro (12-07-2010)

BANFIELD 2010

Jan	31	River Plate	W	1-0	CI	Fernandez [74]	35 000
	7	Charcarita	L	1-2	CI	Garcia [10]	8 000
	10	Morelia	W	2-1	CLg6	Rodriguez [55], Battion [79]	5 804
	13	Lanus	W	2-0	CI	Battion [58], Rodriguez [90]	25 000
Feb	17	Cuenca	W	4-1	CLg6	Erviti [35], Fernandez 2 [38 60], Rodriguez [71]	11 345
	21	Rosario C	D	0-0	CI		11 000
	24	Arg Juniors	W	3-0	CI	Fernandez [16], Quinteros [29], Ramirez [50]	10 000
	28	Newells OB	L	1-2	CI	Ramirez [77]	31 000
	4	Colon	W	3-1	CI	Ramirez 2 [14 90], Garcia [32]	12 000
	7	A. Tucuman	D	0-0	CI		17 000
	10	Nacional	D	2-2	CLg6	Rodriguez 2 [18 37p]	34 468
Mar	13	Arsenal	D	0-0	CI		5 000
	16	Nacional	L	0-2	CLg6		9 507
	21	Godoy Cruz	L	0-2	CI		15 000
	27	Gimnasia	W	3-2	CI	Ramirez 2 [46 66], Fernandez [73]	12 000
	31	Morelia	D	1-1	CLg6	Laso [92+]	16 516
	4	Estudiantes	D	1-1	CI	Quinteros [41]	17 000
	7	S. Lorenzo	W	2-0	CI	Battion [12], Ramirez [44p]	16 000
	11	Velez	D	0-0	CI		14 000
Apr	17	Indep'iente	L	1-3	CI	Ramirez [36]	18 000
	21	Cuenca	W	4-1	CLg6	Ramirez 2 [48 68], Erviti [87], Lucchetti [90p]	5 486
	25	Racing	L	0-2	CI		30 000
	28	Inter	W	3-1	CLr2	Rodriguez [47], Battion [59], Fernandez [81]	6 794
	2	Huracan	W	1-0	CI	Laso [59]	10 000
May	6	Inter	L	0-2	CLr2		34 643
	9	Tigre	W	2-1	CI	Ramirez [47p], Battion [66]	10 000
	14	Boca Jun	W	3-0	CI	Bustamente [41], OG [67], Ramirez [83]	25 000
	8	Olimpo	W	2-1	Ap	Erviti [27p], Garcia [35]	15 000
Aug	13	Colon	W	1-0	Ap	Garcia [80]	20 000
	20	Estudiantes	D	0-0	Ap		13 000
	28	Lanus	D	0-0	Ap		30 000
	2	Velez	W	1-0	CSr2	Garcia [30]	
	5	Tigre	D	1-1	Ap	Romero [87]	12 000
	11	Huracan	D	2-2	Ap	Carrusca [17], Zelaya [62]	13 000
Sep	15	Velez	D	1-1	CSr2	Cristaldo [90]	12 000
	19	Indep'iente	W	4-0	Ap	Ramirez 2 [3 50], Romero [21], Zelaya [82]	13 000
	25	Arg Juniors	L	0-1	Ap		8 000
	29	Tolima	W	2-0	CSr3	Lopez [14], Zelaya [24]	19 000
	3	River Plate	D	2-2	Ap	Ramirez [4], Victor Lopez [68]	22 000
	8	Arsenal	L	0-1	Ap		6 000
Oct	12	Tolima	L	0-3	CSr3		15 000
	16	Newells OB	D	0-0	Ap		20 000
	23	Quilmes	W	2-0	Ap	Mendez [16], Ramirez [53]	12 000
	7	Velez	L	2-3	Ap	Mendez [20], Bustamente [59]	15 000
Nov	12	Gimnasia	D	0-0	Ap		10 000
	19	Godoy Cruz	L	1-2	Ap	Mendez [90]	10 000
	27	Racing	L	1-2	Ap	Carrusca [25]	15 000
	3	All Boys	L	1-2	Ap	Mendez [68]	12 000
Dec	9	Boca Jun	D	0-0	Ap		27 000
	12	S. Lorenzo	L	1-2	Ap	Erviti [38]	10 000

BANFIELD LEAGUE APPEARANCES/GOALS 2010

Goalkeepers Enrique Bologna 7 - 19 • Sebastian Lopez 1 • Cristian Lucchetti 12
Defenders Julio Barraza 7/0 - 3/0 • Marcelo Bustamente 12/1 - 17/1 • Alejandro Delfino 1/0 - 1+1/0 • Mauro Dos Santos 6+3/0 - 17/0 • Santiago Ladino 10+3/0 - 13+2/0 • Victor Lopez 13/0 - 16/1 • Jonatan Maidana 13/0 • Favio Segovia 6+1/0 - 3+1/0 • Jose Shaffer 6/0 • Gustavo Toledo 5+2/0 • Pablo Vergara 2+2/0
Midfield Roberto Battion 13/3 • Maximiliano Bustos 1/0 • Mathias Cardaccio URU 5+8/0 • Marcelo Carrusca 11+3/2 • Guido Di Vanni 1+5/0 • Walter Erviti 13/0 - 19/2 • Cristian Garcia 6+5/2 - 2+8/2 • Maximiliano Laso 4+7/1 • Julio Marchant 5+5/0 • Gabriel Mendez 5+9/4 • Heran Pereyra 0+1/0 • Emmanuel Pio 6+7/0 - 2+4/0 • Marcelo Quinteros 12/2 - 16+1/0 • Sebastian Romero 11+6/2 • Javier Rosada 10/0 • Federico Sardella 6/0 - 7+1/0 • Nahuel Yeri 0+2/0 - 0+2/0
Forwards Jeronimo Barrales 3+11/0 • Sebastian Fernandez URU 12/3 • Facundo Ferreyra 2+1/0 • Ruben Ramirez 12/10 - 16/4 • James Rodriguez COL 12/1 • Luis Salmeron 5+6/0 • Emilio Zelaya 9+1/2
Coach Julio Falcioni • Sebastian Mendez (21-12-2010)

BOCA JUNIORS 2010

Jan	31	Arg Juniors	D	2-2	CI	Palermo [44], Riquelme [86]	20 000
	3	Lanus	W	3-1	CI	Medel [15], Palermo [47], Erbes [55]	22 000
	6	Newells OB	L	2-4	CI	Palermo [35p], Viatri [86]	32 000
Feb	14	A. Tucuman	D	0-0	CI		40 000
	21	Godoy Cruz	D	1-1	CI	Palermo [70]	40 000
	26	Estudiantes	D	1-1	CI	Palermo [25p]	35 000
	2	Velez	D	4-4	CI	Monzon [36], Palermo [39], Gaitan [56], Medel [88]	35 000
	6	Racing	L	1-2	CI	Gaitan [14]	33 000
Mar	14	Tigre	L	0-3	CI		20 000
	25	River Plate	W	2-0	CI	Medel 2 [14 44]	40 000
	28	Charcarita	L	1-4	CI	Gimenez [29]	20 000
	4	Rosario C	L	1-2	CI	Gaitan [61]	30 000
	8	Colon	L	0-3	CI		25 000
Apr	12	Arsenal	W	4-0	CI	Palermo 2 [10 62], Chavez [11], Riquelme [47]	25 000
	18	Gimnasia	L	0-1	CI		20 000
	25	S. Lorenzo	W	2-0	CI	Gimenez [3], Palermo [69]	37 000
	2	Indep'iente	W	3-2	CI	Monzon [33], Palermo [39], Mouche [88]	35 000
May	9	Huracan	L	1-2	CI	Paletta [50]	40 000
	14	Banfield	L	0-3	CI		25 000
	8	Godoy Cruz	D	1-1	Ap	Viatri [21]	30 000
Aug	14	Racing	L	1-2	Ap	Viatri [10]	40 000
	22	All Boys	L	0-2	Ap		30 000
	29	Velez	W	2-1	Ap	Battaglia [37], Viatri [67]	40 000
	4	S. Lorenzo	L	1-2	Ap	Palermo [90]	35 000
Sep	12	Olimpo	W	3-1	Ap	Viatri [15], Palermo [59], Insaurralde [59]	15 000
	19	Colon	W	3-1	Ap	Palermo 3 [45 50 85]	38 000
	25	Estudiantes	L	0-1	Ap		35 000
	3	Lanus	L	1-2	Ap	Insaurralde [35]	35 000
Oct	10	Tigre	W	2-1	Ap	Gimenez [24], Chavez [85]	25 000
	17	Huracan	W	2-0	Ap	Palermo [44], Viatri [66]	38 000
	24	Indep'iente	D	0-0	Ap		30 000
	6	Arg Juniors	L	0-2	Ap		35 000
Nov	16	River Plate	L	0-1	Ap		60 000
	21	Arsenal	W	2-1	Ap	Araujo [28], Battaglia [76]	20 000
	28	Newells OB	L	0-1	Ap		40 000
	5	Quilmes	W	1-0	Ap	Erbes [73]	32 000
Dec	9	Banfield	D	0-0	Ap		27 000
	13	Gimnasia	D	1-1	Ap	Palermo [4]	25 000

BOCA LEAGUE APPEARANCES/GOALS 2010

Goalkeepers Roberto Abbondanzieri 3 • Josue Ayala 1 • Javier Garcia 15 - 6 • Cristian Lucchetti 13
Defenders David Achucarro 1/1 • Julio Barroso 5+1/0 • Breiner Bonilla COL 2/0 • Matias Caruzzo 16/0 • Christian Cellay 11/0 • Hugo Ibarra 9/0 • Juan Insaurralde 18/2 • Juan Krupoviesa 1/0 • Luiz Alberto BRA 7/0 • Lucas Marin 0+1/0 - 2/0 • Breyner Montano COL 1/0 • Luciano Monzon 13/2 - 3+5/0 • Claudio Morel PAR 12/0 • Ezequiel Munoz 14+1/0 • Gabriel Paletta 5+2/1 • Clemente Rodriguez 12/0 • Enzo Ruiz 2+1/0 • Gaston Sauro 0+2/0 • Santiago Villafane 3/0
Midfield Joel Acosta 0+1/0 • Sebastian Battaglia 14/2 • Marcelo Canete 3+4/0 • Cristian Chavez 11+6/1 - 12+5/1 • Nicolas Colazo 0+1/0 - 0+1/0 • Cristian Erbes 11+6/1 - 8+1/1 • Damian Escudero 7+6/0 • Nicolas Gaitan 15/3 • Orlando Gaona PAR 0+1/0 - 3+1/0 • Matias Gimenez 8/2 - 13/1 • Federico Insua 4+9/0 • Guillermo Marino 0+4/0 • Gary Medel CHI 15/4 - 17/0 • Jesus Mendez 10/0 - 8+4/0 • Leandro Paredes 0+1/0 • Sebastian Prediger 3/0 • Juan Roman Riquelme 16/2 - 2/0 • Javier Rosada 2+2/0 • Juan Sanchez Mino 1+2/0
Forwards Sergio Araujo – 4+4/1 • Pablo Mouche 2+8/1 - 2+11/0 • Ricardo Noir 0+1/0 • Martin Palermo 19/10 - 19/7 • Lucas Viatri 1+11/1 - 13+2/5
Coach Abel Alves • Roberto Pompei (9-04-2010) • Claudio Borghi (20-05-2010) • Roberto Pompei (17-11-2010)

CHACARITA JUNIORS 2010

Jan	30	Tigre	W	2-0	Cl	Echeverria 2 [12 53]	15 000
	4	River Plate	L	2-3	Cl	Grabinski [76], Parra [89]	18 000
	7	Banfield	W	2-1	Cl	Lopez [49], Parra [55]	8 000
Feb	12	Rosario C	D	1-1	Cl	Lopez [87]	34 000
	19	Colon	L	1-2	Cl	Parra [61]	8 000
	26	Arsenal	W	3-0	Cl	Morales 2 [31 50], Parra [82]	5 000
	4	Gimnasia	L	0-1	Cl		15 000
	8	S. Lorenzo	L	1-3	Cl	Parra [43]	14 000
Mar	13	Indep'iente	L	0-1	Cl		13 000
	19	Huracan	L	0-2	Cl		10 000
	28	Boca Jun	W	4-1	Cl	Parra 2 [47 81], Ramirez [57], Sciorilli [88]	20 000
	3	Arg Juniors	L	1-2	Cl	Zarif [71]	15 000
	7	Lanus	L	1-2	Cl	Vismara [59]	8 000
Apr	10	Newells OB	L	0-3	Cl		26 000
	17	A. Tucuman	L	1-2	Cl	Avalos [87]	7 000
	23	Godoy Cruz	L	0-1	Cl		18 000
	2	Estudiantes	L	1-2	Cl	Zarif [19]	20 000
May	8	Velez	L	1-4	Cl	Parra [19]	15 000
	15	Racing	L	1-2	Cl	D'Angelo [79]	15 000

Chacarita Juniors were relegated at the end of the 2009-10 Clausura

COLON SANTA FE 2010

Jan	26	U Catolica	W	3-2	CLpr	Nieto [5], Fuertes [66], Bertoglio [69]	14 902
	30	Velez	D	1-1	Cl	Acosta [79]	18 000
	2	Racing	W	2-1	Cl	Fuertes [38], Lucero [49]	22 000
	6	Tigre	D	2-2	Cl	Rios.D [3], Pellerano [49]	12 000
	9	U Catolica	L	2-3	CLpr	Moreno y Fabianesi [53], Fuertes [55p]	12 272
Feb	14	River Plate	W	1-0	Cl	Fuertes [43p]	28 000
	19	Chacarita	W	2-1	Cl	Rivarola [15], Nieto [90]	8 000
	27	Rosario C	D	1-1	Cl	Rivarola [36]	28 000
	4	Banfield	L	1-3	Cl	Fuertes [87]	12 000
	8	Arsenal	L	0-3	Cl		3 000
Mar	13	Gimnasia	D	1-1	Cl	Goux [42]	20 000
	20	S. Lorenzo	D	2-2	Cl	Bertoglio [5], Coudet [45]	12 000
	28	Indep'iente	D	1-1	Cl	Fuertes [19]	20 000
	2	Huracan	D	0-0	Cl		14 000
	8	Boca Jun	W	3-0	Cl	Fuertes [15], Bertoglio 2 [35 51]	25 000
Apr	12	Arg Juniors	L	1-3	Cl	Bauman [90]	12 000
	19	Lanus	D	1-1	Cl	Fuertes [49p]	20 000
	24	Newells OB	L	0-5	Cl		26 000
	2	A. Tucuman	D	0-0	Cl		14 000
May	10	Godoy Cruz	L	0-3	Cl		20 000
	16	Estudiantes	L	1-4	Cl	Curuchet [76]	14 000
	7	Quilmes	D	1-1	Ap	Fuertes [41]	16 000
Aug	13	Banfield	L	0-1	Ap		20 000
	22	Gimnasia	D	0-0	Ap		16 000
	28	Godoy Cruz	L	1-3	Ap	Diaz [31]	18 000
	3	Racing	W	2-1	Ap	Fuertes [5], Larrivey [41]	18 000
Sep	10	All Boys	D	1-1	Ap	Fuertes [54]	17 000
	19	Boca Jun	L	1-3	Ap	Moreno y Fabienesi [42]	38 000
	25	S. Lorenzo	W	2-0	Ap	Diaz [36], Larrivey [90]	15 000
	3	Olimpo	W	3-2	Ap	Higuain 2 [16 45], Moreno y Fab [25]	12 000
Oct	10	Velez	L	0-6	Ap		18 000
	16	Estudiantes	D	1-1	Ap	Fuertes [4]	18 000
	23	Lanus	W	2-1	Ap	Larrivey [42], Diaz [51]	12 000
	7	Tigre	W	1-0	Ap	Bellone [7]	18 000
Nov	12	Huracan	W	2-1	Ap	Larrivey [34], Goux [85]	11 000
	22	Indep'iente	D	1-1	Ap	Fuertes [74]	22 000
	29	Arg Juniors	L	0-3	Ap		6 500
	4	River Plate	L	1-2	Ap	Moreno y Fabianesi [42]	28 000
Dec	7	Arsenal	L	1-2	Ap	Goux [49]	3 000
	12	Newells OB	W	1-0	Ap	Acosta [82]	18 000

CHACARITA LEAGUE APPEARANCES/GOALS 2010

Goalkeepers Sebastian Cejas **10** • Nicolas Tauber **9**
Defenders Franco Coria **4/0** • Diego Crosa **3+2/0** • Fernando Crosa **3+2/0** • Mariano Echeverria **14/2** • Rodrigo Espindola **4/0** • Cristian Grabinski **15/1** • Lisandro Lopez **14/2** • Jorge Nunez **6/0** • Maximiliano Paredes **3/0**
Midfield Claudio Cebasco **0+1/0** • Emanuel Centurion **15/0** • Claudio Cevasco **1/0** • Mauren Franco **1+9/0** • Alejandro Frezzotti **15/0** • Daniel Pereira **6+1/0** • Matias Pisano **0+6/0** • Sergio Ponce **2+4/0** • Sebastian Sciorilli **1+4/1** • Federico Vismara **13/1** • Omar Zarif **18+1/2** • Bernardo Zeballos **2+2/0**
Forwards Erwin Avalos **2+2/1** • German Cano **1+6/0** • Federico Chiocarello **4/0** • Jose D'Angelo **3/1** • Diego Morales **12+2/2** • Facundo Parra **19/8** • Nicolas Ramirez **10+2/1** • Leandro Serapio **0+1/0**
Coach Fernando Gamboa • Mauro Navas (22-03-2010) • Luis Marabotto (21-04-2010)

COLON LEAGUE APPEARANCES/GOALS 2010

Goalkeepers Marcos Diaz *1+2* • Diego Pozo **19** - *18*
Defenders Maximiliano Caire **12/0** - *0+2/0* • Salustiano Candia PAR **16/0** - *8/0* • Pablo De Miranda **4+3/0** • Ariel Garce **12/0** - *16/0* • Marcelo Goux **10/1** - *15+1/2* • Mauricio Mansilla **0+1/0** • Omar Merlo **3/0** • Josimar Mosquera COL **2/0** • Ismael Quilez **2+2/0** - *17/0* • Juan Quiroga *17/0* • Ronald Raldes BOL *15/0* • German Rivarola **12/2** - *2+3/0*
Midfield Lucas Acosta **5+2/1** - *0+1/1* • Mauro Bellone **0+1/0** - *12+1/1* • Facundo Bertoglio **15+2/3** • Alejandro Capurro **8+2/0** • Eduardo Coudet **3+2/1** • Damian Diaz *15+2/3* • Ricardo Gomez **10+6/0** - *2+5/0* • Federico Higuain *13+4/2* • Cristian Ledesma *8+1/0* • Ivan Moreno y Fabianesi ESP **12+4/0** - *15+3/3* • Lucas Mugni **0+1/0** - *0+1/0* • Cristian Pellerano **11+1/1** • Alfredo Ramirez **1+5/0** - *3+8/0* • Facundo Sanchez **0+1/0** - *0+1/0* • Santiago Soto **3+2/0** - *0+6/0* • Nicolas Torres **13+1/0**
Forwards Jonathan Bauman **3+3/1** • Rodrigo Canario **1/0** • Facundo Curuchet **0+1/1** - *3+6/0* • Esteban Fuertes **14/6** - *15/5* • Joaquin Larrivey *13+3/4* • German Lessman *1+3/0* • Juan Lucero **6+7/1** - *0+2/0* • Federico Nieto **7+5/1** • Daniel Rios **5+4/1**
Coach Antonio Mohamed MEX • Mario Sciacqua (25-09-2010) • Fernando Gamboa (27-09-2010)

ESTUDIANTES LA PLATA

Mon	Day	Opponent	Res	Score	Comp	Scorers	Att
Jan	29	Arsenal	W	3-0	Cl	Carrusca 41, Boselli 2 66 69p	18 000
	3	Gimnasia	L	1-3	Cl	Veron 89	19 000
	7	S. Lorenzo	W	2-0	Cl	Boselli 2, Veron 44	18 000
	11	Juan Aurich	W	5-1	CLg3	Boselli 3 6p 59 72, Re 43, Gonzalez 89	10 704
Feb	14	Indep'iente	L	2-3	Cl	Nunez 59, Morales 72	29 000
	18	Alianza	L	1-4	CLg3	Sosa 1	16 310
	22	Huracan	W	2-0	Cl	Boseli 30, Veron 61	7 000
	26	Boca Jun	D	1-1	Cl	Gonzalez 90	35 000
	3	Arg Juniors	L	0-1	Cl		8 000
	6	Lanus	D	0-0	Cl		15 000
	9	Bolivar	D	0-0	CLg3		7 887
Mar	13	Newells OB	W	2-0	Cl	OG 45, Boselli 58	13 000
	19	A. Tucuman	W	3-1	Cl	Boselli 2 2p 75, Sosa 47	16 000
	23	Bolivar	W	2-0	CLg3	Sosa 51, Boselli 79	8 907
	26	Godoy Cruz	W	2-1	Cl	Boselli 14, Fernandez 36	15 000
	30	Juan Aurich	W	2-0	CLg3	Fernandez 52, Brana 68	19 904
	4	Banfield	D	1-1	Cl	Boselli 15	17 000
	8	Velez	W	1-0	Cl	Fernandez 4	15 000
	12	Racing	W	4-0	Cl	Sosa 10, Rodriguez 31, Gonzalez 2 35 65	18 000
Apr	17	Tigre	W	2-1	Cl	Desabato 8, Sosa 27	15 000
	20	Alianza	W	1-0	CLg3	Fernandez 6	14 982
	24	River Plate	W	1-0	Cl	OG 21	18 000
	27	San Luis	W	1-0	CLr2	Gonzalez 25	5 666
	2	Chacarita	W	2-1	Cl	Boselli 32p, Cellay 35	20 000
	5	San Luis	W	3-1	CLr2	Gonzalez 4, Benitez 2 50 55	9 359
	9	Rosario C	D	0-0	Cl		30 000
May	13	Inter	L	0-1	CLqf		40 115
	16	Colon	W	4-1	Cl	Boselli 3 11 22 49, Perez 54	14 000
	20	Inter	W	2-1	CLqf	Gonzalez 19, Perez 21	14 500
	7	Newells	W	1-0	Ap	Veron 71p	30 000
Aug	15	Quilmes	W	2-0	Ap	Brana 82, Lopez 90p	22 000
	20	Banfield	D	0-0	Ap		13 000
	25	LDU Quito	L	1-2	RSA	Rojo 12	
	3	Godoy Cruz	W	2-1	Ap	OG 20, Gonzalez 90	12 000
	8	LDU Quito	D	0-0	RSA		
	11	Racing	W	2-0	Ap		18 000
Sep	16	Newell's OB	L	0-1	CSr1		23 000
	19	All Boys	L	1-2	Ap	Brana 45	14 000
	22	Newell's OB	D	1-1	CSr1	Fernandez 12	22 000
	25	Boca Jun	W	1-0	Ap	Rojo 2	35 000
	29	Gimnasia	W	2-0	Ap	Fernandez 37, Veron 45p	21 000
	3	San Lorenzo	W	1-0	Ap	Fernandez 26	35 000
Oct	8	Olimpo	W	2-0	Ap	Fernandez 43p, Lopez 86p	17 000
	16	Colon	D	1-1	Ap	Fernandez 29p	18 000
	22	Velez	D	0-0	Ap		28 000
	5	Lanus	W	3-0	Ap	Fernandez 53, Hoyos 63, Perez 85	18 000
Nov	13	Tigre	L	1-2	Ap	Benitez 51	9 000
	20	Huracan	W	2-0	Ap	Mercado 8, Perez 57	18 000
	28	Indep'iente	W	2-1	Ap	Pereyra 11, Fernandez 86	25 000
	4	Arg Juniors	W	3-1	Ap	Fernandez 35, Nunez 58, Mercado 75	22 000
Dec	8	River	W	4-0	Ap	Desabato 2, Sanchez 45, Rojo 47, Mercado 57	50 000
	12	Arsenal	W	2-0	Ap	Lopez 2 74 87	20 000

GIMNASIA LA PLATA 2010

Mon	Day	Opponent	Res	Score	Comp	Scorers	Att
Jan	29	Godoy Cruz	L	0-1	Cl		7 000
	3	Estudiantes	W	3-1	Cl	Stracqualursi 2 43 81, Cuevas 90	19 000
	6	Velez	L	1-2	Cl	Perez 40	20 000
Feb	13	Racing	W	1-0	Cl	Perez 31	19 000
	20	Tigre	D	1-1	Cl	Stracqualursi 13	12 000
	28	River Plate	D	1-1	Cl	Perez 8	23 000
	4	Chacarita	W	1-0	Cl	Encina 86	15 000
	8	Rosario C	D	1-1	Cl	OG 23	20 000
Mar	13	Colon	D	1-1	Cl	Perez 25	20 000
	21	Arsenal	L	0-2	Cl		16 000
	27	Banfield	L	2-3	Cl	Stracqualursi 21, Perez 69	12 000
	3	S. Lorenzo	W	1-0	Cl	Romero 6	15 000
	7	Indep'iente	W	2-1	Cl	Perez 2 21 68	19 000
Apr	10	Huracan	L	1-3	Cl	Aguero 54	20 000
	18	Boca Jun	W	1-0	Cl	Perez 59	20 000
	25	Arg Juniors	L	1-3	Cl	Castro 68	12 000
	30	Lanus	D	0-0	Cl		15 000
May	9	Newells OB	L	0-6	Cl		28 000
	16	A. Tucuman	D	3-3	Cl	Casas 10, Navarro 19, Gonzalez 35	7 000
Aug	8	S. Lorenzo	D	0-0	Ap		15 000
	15	Olimpo	L	0-1	Ap		14 000
	22	Colon	D	0-0	Ap		16 000
	5	Lanus	L	0-2	Ap		17 000
	10	Tigre	L	0-2	Ap		8 000
Sep	17	Huracan	W	3-0	Ap	Navarro 33, Encina 2 82 90	14 000
	24	Indep'iente	L	0-1	Ap		10 000
	29	Estudiates	L	0-2	Ap		21 000
	2	Arg Juniors	L	2-4	Ap	Cordoba 2 16 60	14 000
Oct	11	River Plate	D	0-0	Ap		52 000
	16	Arsenal	L	2-3	Ap	Cordoba 2 1 46	13 000
	24	Newells OB	L	0-1	Ap		35 000
	6	Quilmes	W	1-0	Ap	Aguero 69	14 000
Nov	12	Banfield	D	0-0	Ap		10 000
	21	Gimnasia	D	0-0	Ap		18 000
	26	Godoy Cruz	L	1-3	Ap	Rojano 33	12 000
	3	Racing	L	0-2	Ap		32 000
Dec	7	All Boys	W	3-1	Ap	OG 2, Neira 63, Casas 85	12 000
	13	Boca Jun	D	1-1	Ap	Neira 70	25 000

ESTUDIANTES LEAGUE APPEARANCES/GOALS 2010

Goalkeepers Damian Albil 2 • Agustin Orion 17 - 17 • Cesar Taborda 2+2

Defenders Marcos Angeleri 11+1/0 • Christian Cellay 15/1 • Leandro Desabato 16/1 - 17/1 • Federico Fernandez 5+1/1 - 14+1/1 • Raul Iberbia 2/0 - 0+4/0 • Gabriel Mercado 16/4 • German Re 13/0 - 14/0 • Clemente Rodriguez 10+2/1 • Faustino Rojo 6+5/0 - 18+1/2 • Facundo Roncaglia 8+2/0

Midfield Carlos Auzqui 3+2/0 • Leandro Benitez 11+4/0 - 12+7/1 • Rodrigo Brana 11/0 - 18/2 • Ramon Fernandez 3/0 • Cristian Gaitan 0+2/0 • Michael Hoyos USA 2+3/0 - 4+3/1 • Maximiliano Nunez 9+6/1 - 2+2/1 • Gabriel Penalba 3+6/0 • Enzo Perez 12+3/1 - 17/3 • Matias Sanchez 4+5/0 - 1+7/1 • Jose Sosa 15+2/3 • Dario Stefanatto 2+4/0 - 1+3/0 • Juan Veron 13/3 - 15/2

Forwards Mauricio Carrasco 4+1/1 • Mauro Boselli 13+1/13 • Gaston Fernandez 9+1/1 - 12+2/6 • Leandro Gonzalez 6+4/3 - 6+2/1 • Hernan Lopez 0+7/4 • Jeronimo Morales 1+5/1

Coach Alejandro Sabella

GIMNASIA LEAGUE APPEARANCES/GOALS 2010

Goalkeepers Pablo Bangardino 1+1 • Fernando Monetti 1 • Gaston Sessa 18 - 18

Defenders Ariel Aguero 17/1 - 16/1 • Oliver Benitez 0+2/0 • Ignacio Fernandez 0+1/0 • Pablo Fontanello 13/0 • Patricio Graff 10/0 • Facundo Imboden 3+4/0 • Hugo Iriarte 9+1/0 - 8+1/0 • Lucas Landa 2+3/0 • Lisandro Magallan 1/0 • Ruben Maldonado PAR 17/0 • Abel Masuero 17/0 • Ricardo Moreira 9/0 • Alvaro Ormeno CHI 17/0 • Cristian Piarrou 3/0 • Leandro Sapetti 7/0

Midfield Luciano Aued 15/0 - 11+1/0 • Alejandro Capurro 8/0 • Milton Casco 2/0 - 10+1/0 • Lucas Castro 3+13/1 - 3+12/0 • Juan Cuevas 1+5/1 • Hernan Encina 17/1 - 14+2/2 • Alejandro Frezzotti 9+2/0 • Esteban Gonzalez 5+4/1 • Walter Jimenez 3+6/0 • Emiliano Mendez 0+1/0 - 0+1/0 • Mariano Messera 1+4/0 • Fabian Rinaudo 16/0 - 14/0 • Sebastian Romero 14+1/1 • Diego Villar 4+5/0

Forwards Gaston Casas 2+5/1 - 0+3/1 • Jorge Cordoba 9+7/4 • Claudio Graf 7+5/0 • Alvaro Navarro URU 1+4/1 - 7+2/1 • Juan Neira 0+1/0 - 10+2/2 • Marco Perez COL 15+2/8 • Antonio Rojano 8+1/1 • Joaquin Romea 0+1 • Roberto Sosa 0+1/0 • Gonzalo Sotomayor PER 1/0 • Denis Stracqualursi 18/4 • Jose Vizcarra 2+4/0

Coach Diego Cocca • Pablo Javier Morant (30-09-2010) • Angel Cappa (21-12-2010)

GODOY CRUZ 2010

Mon	Date	Opponent		Score		Scorers	Att
Jan	29	Gimnasia	W	1-0	Cl	Higuain [81]	7 000
	4	S. Lorenzo	W	1-0	Cl	Carranza [36]	15 000
	8	Indep'iente	D	0-0	Cl		27 000
Feb	13	Huracan	D	0-0	Cl		13 000
	21	Boca Jun	D	1-1	Cl	Higuain [23]	40 000
	28	Arg Juniors	W	2-1	Cl	Higuain [6], Sanchez [20]	7 000
Mar	3	Lanus	W	2-1	Cl	Castillo [36], Sanchez [74]	12 000
	7	Newells OB	L	1-2	Cl	Castillo [33]	28 000
	12	A. Tucuman	W	2-1	Cl	Higuain 2 [34 90]	10 000
	21	Banfield	W	2-0	Cl	Sigali [18], Ramirez [74]	15 000
	26	Estudiantes	L	1-2	Cl	Carranza [85]	15 000
	3	Velez	W	2-0	Cl	Salinas [72], Carranza [74]	15 000
	7	Racing	D	0-0	Cl		22 000
Apr	12	Tigre	W	6-2	Cl	Dutari [12], Salinas 3 [46 69 84], OG [57], Vega [50]	12 000
	21	River Plate	L	1-2	Cl	Higuain [32]	37 000
	26	Chacarita	W	1-0	Cl	Ramirez [19]	18 000
	30	Rosario C	L	0-1	Cl		32 000
May	9	Colon	W	3-0	Cl	Higuain [69], Castillo [79], Martinez [86]	20 000
	16	Arsenal	W	2-1	Cl	Sigali [68], Salinas [71]	2 500
Aug	8	Boca Jun	D	1-1	Ap	Russo [14]	30 000
	14	S. Lorenzo	D	2-2	Ap	Ramirez 2 [42 46]	22 000
	21	Olimpo	W	1-0	Ap	Rojas [41]	13 000
	28	Colon	W	3-1	Ap	Castillo [68], Ramirez [72], Salinas [77]	18 000
	3	Estudiantes	L	1-2	Ap	Villar [8]	12 000
Sep	11	Lanus	W	4-1	Ap	Ramirez [11], Rojas [61], Castillo [77], Villar [82]	15 000
	18	Tigre	L	1-2	Ap	Ramirez [18]	15 000
	26	Huracan	D	1-1	Ap	Castillo [43]	15 000
Oct	2	Indep'iente	W	4-1	Ap	Castillo [20], Salinas [28], Sanchez [37], Curbelo [47]	20 000
	9	Arg Juniors	D	0-0	Ap		8 000
	17	River Plate	D	2-2	Ap	Ramirez [53], Carranza [78]	43 000
	22	Arsenal	W	3-1	Ap	Rojas [57], OG [59], Carranza [90p]	3 000
Nov	6	Newells OB	D	0-0	Ap		15 000
	14	Quilmes	L	1-2	Ap	Castillo [33]	BCD
	19	Banfield	W	2-1	Ap	Ramirez [10], Sanchez [16]	10 000
	26	Gimnasia	W	3-1	Ap	Sanchez [12], Ramirez [67p], OG [72]	12 000
Dec	5	Velez	L	0-4	Ap		26 000
	8	Racing	D	1-1	Ap	Castillo [7]	25 000
	11	All Boys	D	2-2	Ap	Rojas [1], Donda [7]	12 000

HURACAN 2010

Mon	Date	Opponent		Score		Scorers	Att
Jan	31	Lanus	L	2-3	Cl	Toranzo [19], Machin [24]	12 000
	3	Newells OB	W	2-1	Cl	Goltz [28p], Balvorin [82]	11 000
	8	A. Tucuman	D	0-0	Cl		15 000
Feb	13	Godoy Cruz	D	0-0	Cl		13 000
	22	Estudiantes	L	0-2	Cl		7 000
	27	Velez	W	3-2	Cl	Balvorin [49p], Toranzo [79p], Laurito [80]	22 000
	2	Racing	D	1-1	Cl	Dominguez [89]	22 000
	7	Tigre	L	2-3	Cl	Dominguez [28], Esmerado [54]	20 000
Mar	14	River Plate	L	0-2	Cl		40 000
	19	Chacarita	W	2-0	Cl	Clara [56], Goltz [88]	10 000
	26	Rosario C	W	2-0	Cl	Peralta [80], Venegas [90]	37 000
	2	Colon	D	0-0	Cl		14 000
	6	Arsenal	W	1-0	Cl	Clara [61]	3 000
Apr	10	Gimnasia	W	3-1	Cl	Franzoia [47], Rodriguez [53], Balvorin [90]	20 000
	18	S. Lorenzo	L	0-3	Cl		35 000
	24	Indep'iente	D	0-0	Cl		18 000
	2	Banfield	L	0-1	Cl		10 000
May	9	Boca Jun	W	2-1	Cl	Peralta [45], Machin [79]	40 000
	16	Arg Juniors	L	1-2	Cl	Sanchez [88]	36 000
	7	Arg Juniors	W	2-1	Ap	Martinez [68], Montiglio [70]	15 000
Aug	15	River Plate	L	0-1	Ap		25 000
	22	Arsenal	L	0-2	Ap		6 000
	27	Newells OB	D	1-1	Ap	Zarate [20]	15 000
	5	Quilmes	W	2-1	Ap	Quintana [45], Nieto [74]	10 000
Sep	11	Banfield	D	2-2	Ap	Zarate 2 [10p 56]	13 000
	17	Gimnasia	L	0-3	Ap		14 000
	26	Godoy Cruz	D	1-1	Ap	Machin [45]	15 000
	2	Racing	L	0-3	Ap		28 000
Oct	9	All Boys	D	1-1	Ap	Soplan [90]	15 000
	17	Boca Jun	L	0-2	Ap		38 000
	24	S. Lorenzo	W	3-0	Ap	Quintana [17], Quiroga [51], Rodriguez [72p]	25 000
	5	Olimpo	L	0-4	Ap		9 000
Nov	12	Colon	L	1-2	Ap	OG [54]	11 000
	20	Estudiantes	L	0-2	Ap		18 000
	29	Lanus	L	1-2	Ap	Filippetto [26]	9 000
	5	Tigre	L	1-3	Ap	Zarate [29p]	8 000
Dec	8	Velez	L	0-2	Ap		30 000
	13	Indep'iente	W	1-0	Ap	Roffes [47]	10 000

GODOY CRUZ LEAGUE APPEARANCES/GOALS 2010

Goalkeepers Nelson Ibanez 19 - 8 • Jose Ramirez 1 • Sebastian Torrico 11
Defenders Lucas Ceballos - 2/0 • Jorge Curbelo URU 18/0 - 10/1 • Francisco Dutari 6+2/1 - 1+3/0 • Lautaro Formica 8/0 • Zelmar Garcia 7+2/0 - 17/0 • Sebastian Martinez URU 15/1 • Roberto Russo 7+9/1 • Nicolas Sanchez 8+3/1 • Leonardo Sigali 17/3 - 19/0
Midfield Martin Aguirre 4+2/0 • Alejandro Camargo 4+2/0 - 1/0 • Cesar Carranza 14+3/3 - 13+4/2 • Israel Damonte 2+7/0 • Mariano Donda 1+2/1 • Federico Higuain 16+2/7 • Nicolas Olmedo 18/0 - 16/0 • David Ramirez 13+3/2 - 15/8 • Ariel Rojas 19/0 - 18/4 • Carlos Sanchez URU 15+1/2 - 14+1/2 • Sergio Sanchez 2+9/0 - 1+1/0 • Adrian Torres 2+1/0 • Leandro Torres 1+3/0 • Diego Villar 17/2
Forwards Jairo Castillo COL 9+5/3 - 12+4/6 • Cristian Chavez 0+6/0 • Pablo Miranda 0+4/0 • Fabricio Nunez URU 0+7/0 • Jorge Pinero 0+4/0 • Rodrigo Salinas 2+14/5 - 12+5/2 • Daniel Vega 2+3/1 • Jesus Vera 1+2/0
Coach Omar Asad • Jorge da Silva (15-12-2010)

HURACAN LEAGUE APPEARANCES/GOALS 2010

Goalkeepers Lucas Calvino 3+1/0 • Gaston Monzon 19 - 16
Defenders David Alcides Angeloff 0+1/0 • Kevin Cura 0+2/0 - 4/0 • Eduardo Dominguez 18/2 • Ezequiel Filippetto 11+3/0 - 10+1/1 • Lautaro Formica 2+3/0 • Gonzalo Garcia 5/0 • Paolo Goltz 18/2 • Jonathan Herenu 1/0 • Pablo Jerez 10+1/0 • Rodrigo Lemos 8+1/0 • Luciano Ospina 1+1/0 • Agustin Pena URU 8+2/0 • Carlos Quintana 17+1/2 • Facundo Quiroga 16/1 • Diego Rodriguez URU 14+1/1 - 13/1 • Leonardo Villan 1+1/0 - 3+2/0
Midfield Rodrigo Battaglia 11/0 • Leandro Benegas 2+2/0 • Marcos Britez Ojeda 6+1/0 • Franco Chivilo 1/0 • Leandro Diaz 7+2/0 • Gaston Esmerado 15+1/1 • Andres Franzoia 14+2/1 • Gaston Machin 15+1/2 - 12/1 • Cesar Montiglio 16+1/1 • Angel Morales 13+2/0 • Luciano Nieto 2+9/0 - 11+5/1 • Harrison Otalvaro 2+3/0 • Nahuel Oviedo 1/0 • Adrian Peralta 15/2 • Alejandro Quintana 0+1/0 • Guillermo Roffes 2/1 • Alan Sanchez 0+3/1 • Dario Soplan 8+3/1 • Patricio Toranzo 19/2 • Mariano Torres 1+3/0 • Nicolas Velez 0+1/0
Forwards Gustavo Balvorin 9+8/3 • Julian Bottaro 0+1/0 - 2+4/0 • Gino Clara 11/2 • Federico Laurito 2+5/1 • Emiliano Lencina 0+8/0 • Mariano Martinez 6+4/1 • Muriel Orlando 0+4/0 • Federico Ortiz 0+2/0 • Leandro Venegas 1+8/1 • Rolando Zarate 16+2/4
Coach Hector Rivoira • Miguel Brindisi (22-09-2010)

INDEPENDIENTE 2010

Month	Date	Opponent	Res	Score	Comp	Scorers	Att
Jan	31	Newells OB	D	0-0	Cl		32 000
	4	A. Tucuman	W	3-1	Cl	Silvera 3 20 57 58	30 000
	8	Godoy Cruz	D	0-0	Cl		27 000
Feb	14	Estudiantes	W	3-2	Cl	Silvera 43, Gandin 57, Piatti 78	29 000
	19	Velez	L	0-3	Cl		20 000
	27	Racing	W	1-0	Cl	Gandin 41p	35 000
Mar	3	Tigre	W	1-0	Cl	Silvera 57	20 000
	7	River Plate	W	2-0	Cl	Gandin 43, Silvera 61	32 000
	13	Chacarita	W	1-0	Cl	Tuzzio 5	13 000
	21	Rosario C	W	2-0	Cl	Mareque 77, Nunez 85	25 000
	28	Colon	D	1-1	Cl	Nunez 9	20 000
	3	Arsenal	W	1-0	Cl	Nunez 30	30 000
	7	Gimnasia	L	1-2	Cl	Mancuello 40	19 000
Apr	10	S. Lorenzo	L	0-1	Cl		30 000
	17	Banfield	W	3-1	Cl	Silvera 22, Gracian 36, Nunez 90	18 000
	24	Huracan	D	0-0	Cl		18 000
	2	Boca Jun	L	2-3	Cl	Piatti 30, Nunez 90p	35 000
May	9	Arg Juniors	L	3-4	Cl	Nunez 2 28 67, Gandin 48	20 000
	15	Lanus	W	1-0	Cl	Piatti 87	18 000
	8	Velez	L	0-1	Ap		25 000
	16	Arg Juniors	D	1-1	Ap	Mancuello 17	25 000
Aug	22	River Plate	L	2-3	Ap	Silvera 18, OG 89	60 000
	26	Arg Juniors	W	1-0	CSr2	Galeano 9	
	29	Arsenal	L	1-2	Ap	Galeano 89	22 000
	4	Newells OB	D	1-1	Ap	Silvera 24	32 000
	9	Arg Juniors	D	1-1	CSr2	Ortigoza 34p	19 000
Sep	12	Quilmes	D	0-0	Ap		20 000
	19	Banfield	L	0-4	Ap		13 000
	24	Gimnasia	W	1-0	Ap	Galeano 28	10 000
	28	Defensor	L	0-1	CSr3		
	2	Godoy Cruz	L	1-4	Ap	Silvera 8	20 000
	10	Racing	W	1-0	Ap	Baez 45	35 000
Oct	16	All Boys	L	1-3	Ap	Parra 45	16 000
	19	Defensor	W	4-2	CSr3	Silvera 15, Fredes 19, Cabrera 28, Martinez 75	24 000
	24	Boca Jun	D	0-0	Ap		30 000
	3	Tolima	D	2-2	CSqf	Silvera 30p, Velazquez 78	20 000
	7	San Lorenzo	D	1-1	Ap	Pacheco 54	22 000
	11	Tolima	D	0-0	CSqf		
Nov	14	Olimpo	D	1-1	Ap	Matheu 58	19 000
	18	LDU Quito	L	2-3	CSsf	Silvera 58, Mareque 63	20 000
	22	Colon	D	1-1	Ap	Velazquez 23	22 000
	25	LDU Quito	W	2-1	CSsf	Silvera 58, Mareque 63	20 000
	28	Estudiantes	L	1-2	Ap	Martinez 46	25 000
	1	Goias	L	0-2	CSf		35 500
Dec	5	Lanus	D	0-0	Ap		12 000
	8	Goias	W	3-1	CSf	Velazquez 19, Parra 2 27 35, W 5-3p	40 000
	13	Huracan	L	0-1	Ap		10 000
Fb	6	Tigre	L	0-1	Ap		

LANUS 2010

Month	Date	Opponent	Res	Score	Comp	Scorers	Att
Jan	31	Huracan	W	3-2	Cl	Castillejos 2 74 90, Velazquez 86p	12 000
	3	Boca Jun	L	1-3	Cl	Castillejos 43	22 000
	6	Arg Juniors	L	3-6	Cl	Aguirre 9, Salcedo 12, Diaz 80	25 000
	9	Libertad	L	0-2	CLg4		4 220
	13	Banfield	L	0-2	Cl		25 000
Feb	17	Univer'tario	L	0-2	CLg4		12 507
	20	Newell's OB	D	1-1	Cl	Salcedo 83	30 000
	25	Blooming	W	4-1	CLg4	Blanco 24, Salcedo 39, Lagos 2 60 76	3 709
	28	A. Tucuman	W	3-0	Cl	Blanco 39, Lagos 52, Salcedo 67	8 000
	3	Godoy Cruz	L	1-2	Cl	Salcedo 57	12 000
	6	Estudiantes	D	0-0	Cl		15 000
	12	Velez	L	0-1	Cl		18 000
Mar	20	Racing	W	1-0	Cl	Blanco 74	15 000
	24	Blooming	W	1-0	CLg4	Salcedo 17p	4 271
	27	Tigre	W	1-0	Cl	Aguirre 81	18 000
	30	Libertad	D	1-1	CLg4	Velazquez 84	902
	4	River Plate	W	1-0	Cl	Blanco 41	15 000
	7	Chacarita	W	2-1	Cl	Castillejos 2 88 90	8 000
	11	Rosario C	D	0-0	Cl		12 000
Apr	15	Univer'tario	D	0-0	CLg4		4 198
	19	Colon	D	1-1	Cl	Pizarro 87	20 000
	24	Arsenal	W	4-1	Cl	Hoyos 12, Salcedo 45, Diaz 50, Carrasco 81	5 000
	30	Gimnasia	D	0-0	Cl		15 000
May	10	S. Lorenzo	W	3-2	Cl	Castillejos 66, Salcedo 81, Velazquez 87	12 000
	15	Indep'iente	L	0-1	Cl		18 000
	6	Arsenal	W	2-1	Ap	Aguirre 26, Pizarro 74	9 000
Aug	14	Newells OB	D	1-1	Ap	Salcedo 14	10 000
	21	Quilmes	D	1-1	Ap	Salcedo 13	17 000
	28	Banfield	D	0-0	Ap		30 000
	5	Gimnasia	W	2-0	Ap	Regueiro 48, Romero 70	17 000
Sep	11	Godoy Cruz	L	1-4	Ap	Regueiro 28p	15 000
	17	Racing	L	0-4	Ap		20 000
	25	All Boys	W	1-0	Ap	Hoyos 44	11 000
	3	Boca Jun	W	2-1	Ap	Blanco 8, Pelletieri 90p	35 000
Oct	9	S. Lorenzo	W	2-0	Ap	Castillejos 54, Romero 61p	19 000
	17	Olimpo	L	0-1	Ap		9 000
	23	Colon	L	1-2	Ap	Romero 67	12 000
	5	Estudiantes	L	0-3	Ap		18 000
Nov	14	Velez	L	0-1	Ap		30 000
	22	Tigre	W	2-0	Ap	Regueiro 2 27 58	20 000
	29	Huracan	W	2-1	Ap	Goltz 6, Castillejos 82	9 000
	5	Indep'iente	D	0-0	Ap		12 000
Dec	9	Arg Juniors	W	2-1	Ap	Castillejos 2 9 16	10 000
	13	River Plate	L	1-4	Ap	Romero 31p	

INDEPENDIENTE LEAGUE APPEARANCES/GOALS 2010

Goalkeepers Adrian Gabbarini 19 - 11 • Hilario Navarro 8+1
Defenders Cristian Baez 5/1 • Ignacio Barcia 4/0 • Samuel Caceres 2+1/0 • Leonel Galeano 16/0 - 11+2/2 • Lucas Kruspzky 0+1/0 • Lucas Mareque 19/1 - 10+1/0 • Carlos Matheu 8/1 • Eduardo Tuzzio 18/1 - 12/0 • Gabriel Valles 3+7/0 - 9+1/0 • Julian Velazquez 5+2/0 - 12/0 • Maximiliano Velazquez 12+1/1 • Luciano Vella 14/0
Midfield Walter Acevedo 17/0 • Roberto Battion 7/0 • Walter Busse 7/0 • Nicolas Cabrera 7+2/0 • Nicolas Delmonte 0+3/0 • Hernan Fredes 11+3/0 - 5+3/0 • Fernando Godoy 9+3/0 • Sebastian Godoy 0+1/0 • Leandro Gracian 4+8/1 - 13+1/0 • Mariano Herron 1+1/0 • Federico Mancuello 14/1 - 8+4/1 • Nicolas Martinez 4+6/1 • Cristian Pellerano 8/0 • Jorge Perez 3+2/0 • Ignacio Piatti 17+1/3 • Patricio Rodriguez 0+13/0 - 6+6/0 • Jonathan Ezequiel Suarez 0+1/0 • Sergio Vittor 2+10/0
Forwards Dario Gandin 14+3/4 • Martin Gomez 2+4/0 • Federico Gonzalez 2+4/0 • Nicolas Mazzola 0+1/0 • Brian Nieva 2+4/0 • Leonel Nunez 8+3/7 • German Pacheco 1+1/0 • Facundo Parra 7+6/1 • Andres Silvera 18/7 - 13+2/3 • Lucas Villafanez 1/0
Coach Americo Gallego • Daniel Garnero (20-05-2010) • Ricardo Pavoni URU (24-09-2010) • Antonio Mohamed MEX (5-10-2010)

LANUS LEAGUE APPEARANCES/GOALS 2010

Goalkeepers Mauricio Caranta 3 - 7 • Agustin Marchesin 16 - 12
Defenders Carlos Arce 10/0 - 6+1/0 • Luciano Balbi 1/0 - 10/0 • Rodrigo Erramuspe 11/0 - 11+2/0 • Emir Faccioli 1/0 • Paolo Goltz 15/1 • Hernan Grana 5+2/0 - 14+2/0 • Santiago Hoyos 16+1/1 - 18/1 • Carlos Izquierdoz 0+1/0 • Jadson BRA 15/0 • Hernan Lopes 1/0 • Maximiliano Lugo 6/0 - 9+4/0 • Carlos Quintana 3/0 • Maximiliano Velazquez 12/2
Midfield Marcos Aguirre 10+6/2 - 9+1/1 • Sebastian Blanco 15+1/3 - 10+4/1 • Javier Carrasco 1+6/1 - 1+3/0 • Matias Fritzler 10+3/0 • Diego Gonzalez 1/0 • Eduardo Ledesma PAR 4+8/0 - 9+6/0 • Cristian Menendez 3+4/0 • Agustin Pelletieri 12/0 - 14/1 • Adrian Peralta 0+3/0 • Guido Pizarro 16/1 - 19/1 • Mario Regueiro URU 15+1/4 • Mario Zaninovich 0+1/0
Forwards Eric Aparicio 0+7/0 - 0+2/0 • German Cano 0+1/0 • Gonzalo Castillejos 4+13/6 - 5+10/4 • Leandro Diaz 9+3/2 • Diego Lagos 7+2/1 - 0+2/0 • Nicolas Ramirez 2+6/0 • Silvio Romero 15+2/4 • Santiago Salcedo PAR 15+1/6 - 8+3/2
Coach Luis Zubeldia • Gabriel Schurrer (15-11-2010)

NEWELL'S OLD BOYS 2010

Jan	27	Emelec	D	0-0	CLpr	15 292
	31	Indep'iente	D	0-0	Cl	32 000
	3	Huracan	L	1-2	Cl	Nunez [68]	11 000
Feb	6	Boca Jun	W	4-2	Cl	Insaurralde [2], Achucarro [16], Formica [18], Bernardi [90]	32 000
	10	Emelec	L	1-2	CLpr	Barrientos [52]	14 634
	20	Lanus	D	1-1	Cl	Achucarro [54]	30 000
	28	Banfield	W	2-1	Cl	Nunez [65], Boghossian [75]	31 000
Mar	4	A. Tucuman	D	1-1	Cl	Sperdutti [63]	15 000
	7	Godoy Cruz	W	2-1	Cl	Boghossian 2 [39p 50]	28 000
	13	Estudiantes	L	0-2	Cl		13 000
	17	Arg Juniors	D	1-1	Cl	Achucarro [84], First 66' on 15/02	7 000
	20	Velez	D	1-1	Cl	Schiavi [62p]	18 000
	27	Racing	L	0-1	Cl		30 000
	3	Tigre	L	0-2	Cl		26 000
	7	River Plate	W	1-0	Cl	Achucarro [51]	25 000
	10	Chacarita	W	3-0	Cl	Nunez 2 [38 70], OG [87]	26 000
Apr	18	Rosario C	D	1-1	Cl	Schiavi [17p]	40 000
	24	Colon	W	5-0	Cl	Boghossian 2 [17 57], Sperdutti [24], Formica [32], Achucarro [42]	26 000
	29	Arsenal	W	2-0	Cl	Alayes [12], Schiavi [31]	8 000
May	8	Gimnasia	W	6-0	Cl	Boghossian [14p], Formica 2 [15 59], Bernardi [34], Insaurralde [57], Schiavi [63p]	28 000
	14	S. Lorenzo	L	1-2	Cl	Schiavi [63p]	12 000
Aug	7	Estudiantes	L	0-1	Ap		30 000
	14	Lanus	D	1-1	Ap	Sperdutti [40]	10 000
	20	Tigre	W	2-0	Ap	Schiavi [45], Rodriguez [88]	28 000
	27	Huracan	D	1-1	Ap	Sperdutti [50]	15 000
Sep	4	Indep'iente	D	1-1	Ap	Formica [76]	32 000
	12	Arg Juniors	W	2-1	Ap	Cichero [78], Rodriguez [84]	8 000
	16	Estudiantes	W	1-0	CSr2	Formica [90p]	23 000
	19	River Plate	W	1-0	Ap	Borghello [11]	36 000
	22	Estudiantes	D	1-1	CSr2	Borghello [43]	22 000
	26	Arsenal	D	0-0	Ap		9 000
Oct	1	Velez	W	2-0	Ap	Sperdutti [42], Schiavi [48p]	30 000
	6	San Jose	W	6-0	CSr3	Schiavi 2 [5 34], Formica 2 [26 62], Estigarribia [60], Salvatierra [90]	28 000
	9	Quilmes	D	1-1	Ap	Formica [30]	32 000
	16	Banfield	D	0-0	Ap		20 000
	21	San Jose	L	0-2	CSr3		18 000
	24	Gimnasia	W	1-0	Ap	Sperdutti [12]	35 000
Nov	2	LDU Quito	D	0-0	CSqf		
	6	Godoy Cruz	D	0-0	Ap		15 000
	2	LDU Quito	L	0-1	CSqf		32 000
	14	Racing	L	0-2	Ap		38 000
	20	All Boys	L	0-2	Ap		22 000
	28	Boca Jun	W	1-0	Ap	Rodriguez [86]	40 000
Dec	5	S. Lorenzo	D	0-0	Ap		15 000
	9	Olimpo	L	0-1	Ap		18 000
	12	Colon	L	0-1	Ap		18 000

NEWELL'S LEAGUE APPEARANCES/GOALS 2010

Goalkeepers Nahuel Guzman 1 - *1* • Sebastian Peratta 18 - *18*
Defenders Agustin Alayes 17/1 - *17/0* • Gabriel Cichero VEN 15/1 • Cristian Diaz *1+2/0* • Ignacio Fideleff 3/0 - *4+2/0* • Juan Insaurralde 16/2 • Christian Lema -*1+1/0* • Alexis Machuca 2+1/0 - *3+1/0* • Juan Quiroga 4+5/0 • Nahuel Roselli 7+2/0 • Rolando Schiavi 17/5 - *18/2* • Luciano Vella *14+2/0*
Midfield Hugo Barrientos 5+6/0 • Lucas Bernardi 16/2 - *11/0* • Cristian Diaz 2+1/0 • Franco Dolci 5+4/0 - *4+4/0* • Federico Dominguez *0+2/0* • Marcelo Estigarribia PAR 10+5/0 - *13+4/0* • Mauro Formica 17/4 - *16+1/2* • Diego Mateo 8/0 - *18/0* • Cristian Sanchez 2+5/0 • Mauricio Sperdutti 8+5/2 - *17+1/4* • Carlos Vaca *1/0* • Leonel Vangioni 11/0 - *3+2/0* • Leandro Velazquez *3+7/0* • Raul Villalba 2/0 - *5/0*
Forwards Jorge Achucarro PAR 14+1/5 • Joaquin Boghossian URU 14+2/6 • Ivan Borghello *13+5/1* • Emanuel Dening 1+4/0 • Cristian Nunez 6+9/4 • Luis Rodriguez *6+6/3* • Daniel Salvatierra *2+11/0* • Sebastian Taborda URU *5+5/0* • Diego Torres 3+6/0
Coach Roberto Sensini

OLIMPO 2010

Aug	8	Banfield	L	1-2	Ap	Delorte [1]	15 000
	15	Gimnasia	W	1-0	Ap	Mosset [23]	14 000
	21	Godoy Cruz	L	0-1	Ap		13 000
	29	Racing	W	1-0	Ap	Bareiro [38]	15 000
	4	All Boys	L	0-1	Ap		15 000
Sep	12	Boca Jun	L	1-3	Ap	Cobo [18]	15 000
	18	S. Lorenzo	L	1-3	Ap	Vega [13]	18 000
	24	Velez	L	0-3	Ap		18 000
	3	Colon	L	2-3	Ap	Tejera [63], Galvan [90]	12 000
	8	Estudiantes	L	0-2	Ap		17 000
Oct	17	Lanus	W	1-0	Ap	OG [48]	9 000
	24	Tigre	L	2-3	Ap	Furch [33], Bareiro [60]	9 000
	5	Huracan	W	4-0	Ap	Galvan [9], Brum [26], Bareiro [33], Vega [55]	9 000
Nov	14	Indep'iente	D	1-1	Ap	Salom [90]	19 000
	22	Arg Juniors	D	1-1	Ap	Aguirre [62]	10 000
	28	River Plate	L	0-1	Ap		40 000
Dec	1	Arsenal	D	1-1	Ap	Bareiro [28]	8 000
	9	Newells OB	W	1-0	Ap	Villanueva [39]	18 000
	13	Quilmes	L	0-1	Ap		9 000

OLIMPO LEAGUE APPEARANCES/GOALS 2010

Goalkeepers Laureano Tombolini *19*
Defenders Nicolas Bianchi Arce 15/0 • Eduardo Casais *16/0* • Pablo Jerez 3/0 • Julio Mosset *14/1* • Diego Reynoso *5+1/0* • Juan Tejera URU *5+3/1* • Cristian Villanueva *10/1*
Midfield Martin Aguirre *3+7/1* • Roberto Brum URU *15+2/1* • Juan Cobo *15+3/1* • Diego Galvan *14/2* • Sebastian Longo *6+2/0* • Martin Rolle *7+8/0* • Juan Schefer *6+2/0* • David Vega *17/2*
Forwards Nestor Bareiro PAR *15+3/4* • Facundo Castillon *6+6/0* • Alejandro Delorte *8+4/1* • Julio Furch *9+3/1* • Marcos Litre *0+3/0* • Emerson Panigutti *0+1/0* • Carlos Salom *1+7/1*
Coach Omar De Felippe

QUILMES 2010

Aug	7	Colon	D	1-1	Ap	Morales [89]	16 000
	15	Estudiantes	L	0-2	Ap		22 000
	21	Lanus	D	1-1	Ap	Morales [8]	17 000
	28	Tigre	L	0-3	Ap		17 000
Sep	5	Huracan	L	1-2	Ap	Hirsig [1]	10 000
	12	Indep'iente	D	0-0	Ap		20 000
	18	Arg Juniors	D	2-2	Ap	Torres [63], Morales [78]	9 000
	26	River Plate	D	1-1	Ap	Caneo [90]	45 000
Oct	1	Arsenal	L	0-1	Ap		8 000
	9	Newells OB	D	1-1	Ap	Gerlo [60]	32 000
	15	Velez	L	0-2	Ap		15 000
	23	Banfield	L	0-2	Ap		12 000
	6	Gimnasia	L	0-1	Ap		14 000
Nov	14	Godoy Cruz	W	2-1	Ap	Raymonda [2], Caneo [90]	BCD
	21	Racing	D	1-1	Ap	Cerro [69]	30 000
	27	All Boys	W	2-1	Ap	Morales [74], Romeo [79]	10 000
Dec	5	Boca Jun	L	0-1	Ap		32 000
	9	S. Lorenzo	W	1-0	Ap	Morales [17]	10 000
	13	Olimpo	W	1-0	Ap	Gerlo [2]	9 000

QUILMES LEAGUE APPEARANCES/GOALS 2010

Goalkeepers Hernan Galindez *6* • Emanuel Tripodi *13*
Defenders Ariel Broggi *11+1/0* • Fabricio Fontanini *19* • Danilo Gerlo *16/2* • Leandro Gioda *9/0* • Sebastian Martinez URU *4/0* • Martin Quiles *7/0* • Nahuel Roselli *2+2/0*
Midfield Charles Aranguiz CHI *13+1/0* • Miguel Caneo *3+10/2* • Francisco Cerro *7+2/1* • Leandro Coronel *4+3/0* • Pablo Garnier *8+1/0* • Damian Gomez *0+2/0* • Santiago Hirsig *9+2/1* • Enzo Kalinski *12+1/0* • Oscar Morales URU *5+1/0* • Gervasio Nunez *12+1/0* • Santiago Raymonda *17+2/1* • Gustavo Varela URU *7+7/0*
Forwards Juan Morales *16/5* • Enrique Narvay *0+2/1* • Bernardo Romeo *1+6/1* • Diego Torres *7+9/1*
Coach Hugo Tocalli • Leonardo Madelon (18-10-2010)

RACING CLUB 2010

Mo	Date	Opponent	Res	Score	Comp	Scorers	Att
Jan	30	Rosario C	W	3-0	Cl	Luguercio 39, Martinez 43, Bieler 77	38 000
	2	Colon	L	1-2	Cl	Falcon 13	22 000
	7	Arsenal	L	2-4	Cl	Cahais 9, Hauche 61	55 000
Feb	13	Gimnasia	L	0-1	Cl		19 000
	20	S. Lorenzo	W	1-0	Cl	Hauche 83	35 000
	27	Indep'iente	L	0-1	Cl		35 000
	2	Huracan	D	1-1	Cl	Bieler 16	22 000
	6	Boca Jun	W	2-1	Cl	Lluy 16, Hauche 45	33 000
Mar	14	Arg Juniors	L	0-1	Cl		30 000
	20	Lanus	L	0-1	Cl		15 000
	27	Newells OB	W	1-0	Cl	Martinez 77	30 000
	8	Godoy Cruz	D	0-0	Cl		22 000
	12	Estudiantes	L	0-4			18 000
Apr	18	Velez	W	3-1	Cl	Luguercio 75, Yacob 77, Bieler 80	25 000
	21	A. Tucuman	W	1-0	Cl	Grazzini 46	20 000
	25	Banfield	W	2-0	Cl	Martinez 74, Bieler 81	30 000
	30	Tigre	W	2-1	Cl	Bieler 22, Aveldano 32	12 000
May	8	River Plate	L	0-3	Cl		35 000
	15	Chacarita	W	2-1	Cl	Fernandez 40, Bieler 63p	15 000
	7	All Boys	W	1-0	Ap	Aveldano 62	40 000
	14	Boca Jun	W	2-1	Ap	Yacob 33, Caceres 50	40 000
Aug	21	S. Lorenzo	L	1-2	Ap	Luguercio 56	35 000
	29	Olimpo	L	0-1	Ap		15 000
	3	Colon	L	1-2	Ap	Bieler 31	18 000
	11	Estudiantes	L	0-2	Ap		18 000
Sep	17	Lanus	W	4-0	Ap	Martinez 44, Moreno 64p, Cahais 72, Hauche 90	20 000
	26	Tigre	D	0-0	Ap		16 000
	2	Huracan	W	3-0	Ap	Hauche 14, Fernandez 24, Moreno 78	28 000
Oct	10	Indep'iente	L	0-1	Ap		35 000
	17	Arg Juniors	W	2-1	Ap	Moreno 2 60 74	22 000
	23	River Plate	D	1-1	Ap	Moreno 35	45 000
	6	Banfield	D	2-2	Ap	Luguercio 73, Aveldano 86	25 000
Nov	14	Newells OB	W	2-0	Ap	Hauche 90, Luguerico 90	38 000
	21	Quilmes	D	1-1	Ap	Hauche 72	30 000
	27	Banfield	W	2-1	Ap	Hauche 22, Bieler 26	15 000
	3	Gimnasia	W	2-0	Ap	Hauche 20, Toranzo 61	32 000
Dec	8	Godoy Cruz	D	1-1	Ap	Pillud 42	25 000
	12	Velez	L	0-2	Ap		40 000

RIVER PLATE 2010

Mo	Date	Opponent	Res	Score	Comp	Scorers	Att
Jan	31	Banfield	L	0-1	Cl		35 000
	3	Chacarita	W	3-2	Cl	Ferrari 2 21 28, Bou 81	18 000
	6	Rosario C	D	0-0	Cl		30 000
Feb	14	Colon	L	0-1	Cl		28 000
	21	Arsenal	D	1-1	Cl	Gallardo 51	35 000
	26	Gimnasia	D	1-1	Cl	Canales 90	23 000
	3	S. Lorenzo	W	1-0	Cl	Affranchino 74	42 000
	7	Indep'iente	L	0-2	Cl		32 000
Mar	14	Huracan	W	2-0	Cl	OG 2, Canales 76	40 000
	20	Boca Jun	L	0-2	Cl		40 000
	29	Arg Juniors	L	0-1	Cl		25 000
	3	Lanus	L	0-1	Cl		15 000
	8	Newells OB	L	0-1	Cl		25 000
Apr	12	A. Tucuman	D	0-0	Cl		27 000
	19	Godoy Cruz	W	2-1	Cl	Ortega 69, Ferrari 70	37 000
	25	Estudiantes	L	0-1	Cl		18 000
	2	Velez	W	2-1	Cl	Ferrari 45, Buonanotte 82	30 000
May	9	Racing	W	3-0	Cl	Funes 3 3 17 24	35 000
	16	Tigre	L	1-5	Cl	Funes 51	45 000
	8	Tigre	W	1-0	Ap	Funes 90	55 000
Aug	15	Huracan	W	1-0	Ap	Affranchino 12	25 000
	22	Indep'iente	W	3-2	Ap	Funes 2 9 19, Ferrari 25	60 000
	29	Arg Juniors	D	0-0	Ap		15 000
	5	Velez	L	1-2	Ap	Buonanotte 41	30 000
Sep	12	Arsenal	W	1-0	Ap	Funes 75	50 000
	19	Newells OB	L	0-1	Ap		36 000
	26	Quilmes	D	1-1	Ap	Pavone 47	45 000
	3	Banfield	D	2-2	Ap	Ortega 63, Roman 87	22 000
Oct	11	Gimnasia	D	0-0	Ap		52 000
	17	Godoy Cruz	D	2-2	Ap	OG 41, Carranza 78	43 000
	23	Racing	D	1-1	Ap	Buonanotte 46	45 000
	7	All Boys	L	0-1	Ap		20 000
Nov	16	Boca Jun	W	1-0	Ap	Maidana 54	60 000
	21	S. Lorenzo	D	0-0	Ap		36 000
	28	Olimpo	W	1-0	Ap	Roman 32	40 000
	4	Colon	W	2-1	Ap	Lamela 56, Pavone 90	28 000
Dec	8	Estudiantes	L	0-4	Ap		50 000
	13	Lanus	W	4-1	Ap	Lamela 28, Roman 51, Pavone 2 53 76	10 000

RACING LEAGUE APPEARANCES/GOALS 2010

Goalkeepers Jorge De Olivera 19 - *14* • Roberto Fernandez URU 5

Defenders Lucas Aveldano 18/1 - *18/2* • Roberto Ayala 7+3/0 - *3+3/0* • Marcos Caceres PAR *13/1* • Matias Cahais 15+1/1 - *18/1* • Gonzalo Garcia *0+1/0* • Damian Ledesma 0+3/0 • Lucas Licht 4+1/0 - *6+5/0* • Braian Lluy 12/1 - *5+4/0* • Matias Martinez 13/3 - *18/1* • Gabriel Mercado 15/0 • Ivan Pillud *3+1/1* • Nicolas Sainz 2/0 • Cristian Tavio *0+1/0*

Midfield Marcos Britez Ojeda 0+1/0 • Lucas Castroman 6+10/0 - *0+7/0* • Juan Falcon 7+1/1 • Jose Fernandez 9/1 - *15+4/1* • Sebastien Grazzini 5+7/1 • Adrian Lucero 6+1/0 • Lorenzo Mayorga 3+1/0 • Giovanni Moreno COL *10/5* • Sebastian Rosano URU 3+1/0 • Patricio Toranzo *18/1* • Martin Wagner 4+1/0 • Claudio Yacob 15/1 - *12/1* • Bruno Zuculini 5+2/0 - *5/0*

Forwards Luis Benitez 0+1/0 • Claudio Bieler 17+2/6 - *14+3/2* • Ignacio Colombini 0+1/0 • Luis Farina 0+3/0 - *1/0* • Gabriel Hauche 12+6/3 - *12+5/6* • Pablo Luguercio 15+3/2 - *11+7/3* • Damian Steinert 0+4/0 • Valentin Viola 0+2/0

Coach Claudio Vivas • Miguel Russo (17-02-2010)

RIVER LEAGUE APPEARANCES/GOALS 2010

Goalkeepers Juan Carrizo 19 • Juan Ojeda 1+1 • Daniel Vega 18

Defenders Carlos Arano 14+2/0 • Gustavo Cabral 3+1/0 • Maximiliano Coronel 1+1/0 - *1+1/0* • Juan Diaz URU 11/0 - *0+2/0* • Paulo Ferrari 16/4 - *18/1* • Alexis Ferrero 18/0 - *13+1/0* • Jonatan Maidana *18/1* • Adalberto Roman PAR *12/3* • Facundo Quiroga 10/0 • Nicolas Sanchez 9+1/0 • Cristian Villagra 7/0

Midfield Matias Abelairas 9+1/0 • Walter Acevedo 10+1/0 • Facundo Affranchino 8+5/1 - *6+3/1* • Oscar Ahumada 6+1/0 • Matias Almeyda 15/0 - *13/0* • Josepmir Ballon PER 5+5/0 • Diego Barrado 4+2/0 • Diego Buonanotte 0+5/1 - *7+8/2* • Adrian Cirigliano 2+2/0 - *1+1/0* • Mauro Diaz 7+4/0 - *1+3/0* • Marcelo Gallardo 6+3/1 • Manuel Lanzini *4+4/0* • Roberto Pereyra 8+2/0 - *14+1/0* • Rodrigo Rojas PAR 10+3/0 - *3+3/0*

Forwards Juan Antonio 0+2/0 • Gustavo Bou 1+3/1 • Gustavo Canales 10+4/2 • Leandro Caruso 1+6/0 • Rogelio Funes 11+5/4 - *12+6/4* • Erik Lamela *12+1/2* • Gonzalo Luduena 1+1/0 • Ariel Ortega 9/1 - *13+3/1* • Hugo Pavone *12+3/5* • Mauro Rosales 1+2/0 • Daniel Villalva 7+6/0

Coach Leonardo Astrada • Angel Cappa (12-04-2010) • Juan Jose Lopez (10-11-2010)

ROSARIO CENTRAL 2010

Jan	31	Racing	L	0-3	Cl		38 000
	6	Tigre	L	0-1	Cl		28 000
	15	River Plate	D	0-0	Cl		30 000
Feb	21	Chacarita	D	1-1	Cl	Zelaya [45]	34 000
	24	Banfield	D	0-0	Cl		11 000
	28	Colon	D	1-1	Cl	Figueroa [58]	28 000
	3	Arsenal	L	2-3	Cl	Caraglio [10], Figueroa [78]	27 000
	7	Gimnasia	D	1-1	Cl	Nunez [59]	20 000
Mar	14	S. Lorenzo	W	1-0	Cl	Caraglio [88]	33 000
	20	Indep'iente	L	0-2	Cl		25 000
	29	Huracan	L	0-2	Cl		37 000
	3	Boca Jun	W	2-1	Cl	De Leon [43], Caraglio [87]	30 000
	8	Arg Juniors	L	0-1	Cl		30 000
Apr	12	Lanus	D	0-0	Cl		12 000
	19	Newells OB	D	1-1	Cl	Braghieri [3]	40 000
	25	A. Tucuman	D	2-2	Cl	Zelaya [21], Caraglio [58]	19 000
	2	Godoy Cruz	W	1-0	Cl	Chitzoff [90]	32 000
	9	Estudiantes	D	0-0	Cl		30 000
May	16	Velez	D	0-0	Cl		23 000
	19	All Boys	D	1-1	Clpo	Burdisso [90]	17 000
	23	All Boys	L	0-3	Clpo		32 000

Rosario Central were relegated at the end of the 2009-10 Clausura

ROSARIO LEAGUE APPEARANCES/GOALS 2010

Goalkeepers Jorge Bava 1 • Hernan Galindez 18
Defenders Paul Ambrosi 9/0 • Matias Ballini 9+5/0 • Ignacio Boggino 3+2/0 • Diego Braghieri 11/1 • Guillermo Burdisso 13/0 • Diego Chitzoff 18/1 • Alexis Danelon 3+7/0 • Martin Garcia 3/0 • Santiago Garcia 10/0 • Cristian Godoy 0+1/0 • Nahuel Valentini 11+4/0 • Mario Vallejo 1/0
Midfield Martin Astudillo 4+1/0 • Federico Carrizo 1+1/0 • Adrian de Leon 7+7/1 • Leandro Gurrieri 0+3/0 • Lucas Moya 1+1/0 • Gervasio Nunez 15+2/1 • Dario Ocampo 0+1/0 • Mario Paglialunga 16/0 • Martin Rivero 3+5/0 • Milton Zarate 4+1/0
Forwards Milton Caraglio 12+4/4 • Fernando Coniglio 0+1/0 • Luciano Figueroa 7+3/2 • Jonatan Gomez 16/0 • Emilio Zelaya 13+4/2
Coach Cuffaro Russo • Leonardo Madelon (29-03-2010)

SAN LORENZO 2010

Jan	31	A. Tucuman	W	1-0	Cl	Bordagaray [25]	24 000
	3	Godoy Cruz	L	0-1	Cl		15 000
	6	Estudiantes	L	0-2	Cl		18 000
Feb	14	Velez	D	0-0	Cl		25 000
	21	Racing	L	0-1	Cl		35 000
	26	Tigre	W	1-0	Cl	Alfaro [83]	26 000
	3	River	L	0-1	Cl		42 000
	7	Chacarita	W	3-1	Cl	Romeo 2 [11 66], Gonzalez [69]	14 000
Mar	14	Rosario C	L	0-1	Cl		33 000
	20	Colon	D	2-2	Cl	Gomez 2 [12 90]	12 000
	29	Arsenal	L	0-1	Cl		5 500
	3	Gimnasia	L	0-1	Cl		15 000
	8	Banfield	L	0-2	Cl		16 000
Apr	12	Indep'iente	W	1-0	Cl	Benitez [8]	30 000
	19	Huracan	W	3-0	Cl	Gomez [22], Bordagaray [70], Leiva [73]	35 000
	25	Boca Jun	L	0-2	Cl		37 000
	2	Arg Juniors	L	1-2	Cl	Alfaro [40]	20 000
May	9	Lanus	L	2-3	Cl	Romeo [26], Gomez [88]	12 000
	16	Newells OB	W	2-1	Cl	Romeo [46], Benitez [70]	12 000
	8	Gimnasia	D	0-0	Ap		15 000
Aug	14	Godoy Cruz	D	2-2	Ap	Tula [20], Rivero [77]	22 000
	21	Racing	W	2-1	Ap	Pereyra [19], Balsas [85]	35 000
	28	All Boys	W	3-1	Ap	Menseguez [55], Pereyra [68], Tula [82]	29 000
	4	Boca Jun	W	2-1	Ap	Balsas [52], Menseguez [88]	35 000
Sep	11	Velez	D	0-0	Ap		32 000
	18	Olimpo	W	3-1	Ap	Tula [32], Bottinelli [63], Rivero [80]	18 000
	25	Colon	L	0-2	Ap		15 000
	3	Estudiantes	L	0-1	Ap		35 000
Oct	9	Lanus	L	0-2	Ap		19 000
	15	Tigre	W	2-0	Ap	Menseguez [4], Balsas [77]	15 000
	24	Huracan	L	0-3	Ap		25 000
	7	Indep'iente	D	1-1	Ap	Tula [46]	22 000
Nov	14	Arg Juniors	L	0-1	Ap		12 000
	21	River Plate	D	0-0	Ap		36 000
	26	Arsenal	L	1-2	Ap	Rovira [37]	5 000
	5	Newells OB	D	0-0	Ap		15 000
Dec	9	Quilmes	L	0-1	Ap		10 000
	12	Banfield	W	2-1	Ap	Bottinelli [47], Menseguez [85]	10 000

SAN LORENZO LEAGUE APPEARANCES/GOALS 2010

Goalkeepers Damian Albil *8* • Pablo Migliore **19** - *11*
Defenders Gaston Aguirre 6/0 - *2/0* • Nelson Benitez 11+3/2 - *4+1/0* • Jonathan Bottinelli 11/0 - *19/2* • Diego Herner 4+1/0 • Nahuel Iribarren 2+1/0 • Walter Kannemann 1/0 • Sebastian Luna 4/0 - *7+5/0* • Damian Martinez 4/0 • Fernando Meza 15+1/0 - *12/0* • Jose Palomino 4/0 - *4/0* • Diego Placente *10+1/0* • Jose San Roman 4+1/0 • Cristian Tula *14+1/4* • German Voboril 3/0 - *1/0*
Midfield Pablo Alvarado *0+1/0* • Gonzalo Ismael Bazan 1/0 - *1/0* • Miguel Bertocchi 1+2/0 • Nahuel De Vico 0+1/0 • Alejandro Gomez 13+3/4 • Kily Gonzalez 15+1/0 • Sebastian Gonzalez 3+7/1 - *2+5/0* • Fernando Gutierrez *1/0* • Axel Juarez 0+1/0 • Cristian Leiva 13/1 • Leonardo Lopez COL 4+2/0 • Guillermo Pereyra *13+2/2* • Pablo Pintos URU 13+3/0 • Salvador Reynoso 4+5/0 - *4+3/0* • Diego Rivero 11/0 - *8+5/2* • Leandro Romagnoli 5+3/0 - *14+1/0* • Sebastian Rusculleda 1+3/0 - *0+3/0* • Aureliano Torres PAR 10/0 - *8+5/0* • Juan Torres 10/0 - *17/0*
Forwards Emiliano Alfaro URU 10+5/2 - *2+1/0* • Sebastian Balsas URU *9+7/3* • Nahuel Benitez 0+1/0 - *1+2/0* • Fabian Bordagaray 14+4/2 - *4+5/0* • Juan Menseguez 3+8/0 - *16+2/4* • Bernardo Romeo 8+3/4 • Gonzalo Rovira *6+1/1*
Coach Diego Simone • Sebastian Mendez (4-04-2010) • Ramon Diaz (25-05-2010)

TIGRE 2010

	Day	Opponent	Res	Score	Comp	Scorers	Att
Jan	30	Chacarita	L	0-2	Cl		15 000
	2	Rosario C	W	1-0	Cl	Luna 59	28 000
	6	Colon	D	2-2	Cl	Ayala 2 18 63p	12 000
Feb	12	Arsenal	W	2-0	Cl	Ayala 10, Luna 57p	10 000
	20	Gimnasia	D	1-1	Cl	Fontanello 20	12 000
	28	S. Lorenzo	L	0-1	Cl		26 000
	3	Indep'iente	L	0-1	Cl		20 000
	7	Huracan	W	3-2	Cl	OG 14, Luna 45, Perez 67	20 000
Mar	14	Boca Jun	W	3-0	Cl	Luna 3 10 44 78	20 000
	20	Arg Juniors	D	1-1	Cl	Luna 78	11 000
	27	Lanus	L	0-1	Cl		18 000
	3	Newells OB	W	2-0	Cl	Garat 4, Rodriguez 71	26 000
	6	A. Tucuman	W	3-1	Cl	Fondacaro 22, Luna 2 42p 79	12 000
Apr	12	Godoy Cruz	L	2-6	Cl	Lazzaro 55, OG 57	12 000
	17	Estudiantes	L	1-2	Cl	OG 40	15 000
	23	Velez	L	0-1	Cl		15 000
	30	Racing	L	1-2	Cl	Castano 26	12 000
	9	Banfield	L	1-2	Cl	Rodriguez 90	10 000
May	15	River	W	5-1	Cl	Perez 11, San Roman 12, Fontanello 17, Pasini 37, Lazzaro 44	45 000
	8	River Plate	L	0-1	Ap		55 000
	14	Arsenal	L	1-2	Ap	Stracqualursi 70	14 000
Aug	20	Newells OB	L	0-2	Ap		28 000
	28	Quilmes	W	3-0	Ap	Echeverria 9, Morales 76, Stracqualursi 77	17 000
	5	Banfield	D	1-1	Ap	Leone 82	12 000
Sep	10	Gimnasia	W	2-0	Ap	Castano 30, Telechea 47	8 000
	18	Godoy Cruz	W	2-1	Ap	Stracqualursi 47, Perez 75	15 000
	26	Racing	D	0-0	Ap		16 000
	2	All Boys	D	3-3	Ap	Gonzalez 2 22 60, Stracqualursi 74	15 000
Oct	10	Boca Jun	L	1-2	Ap	Stracqualursi 37	25 000
	15	S. Lorenzo	L	0-2	Ap		15 000
	24	Olimpo	W	3-2	Ap	Stracqualursi 4, Galmarini 17, Castano 87	9 000
	7	Colon	L	0-1	Ap		18 000
Nov	13	Estudiantes	W	2-1	Ap	Morales 24, Stracqualursi 73	9 000
	22	Lanus	L	0-2	Ap		20 000
	30	Velez	L	1-2	Ap	Castano 90	25 000
Dec	5	Huracan	W	3-1	Ap	Stracqualursi 2 6 31, Altobelli 38	8 000
	14	Arg Juniors	D	1-1	Ap	Stracqualursi 45p	13 000
Feb	6	Indep'iente	W	1-0	Ap	Stracqualursi 80	

VELEZ SARSFIELD 2010

	Day	Opponent	Res	Score	Comp	Scorers	Att
Jan	30	Colon	D	1-1	Cl	Silva 35	18 000
	2	Arsenal	W	3-0	Cl	Lopez 2 49 89, Moralez 58	13 000
	6	Gimnasia	W	2-1	Cl	OG 7, Tobio 25	20 000
	10	Cruzeiro	W	2-0	CLg7	Silva 5, Martinez 77	11 100
Feb	14	S. Lorenzo	D	0-0	Cl		25 000
	19	Indep'iente	W	3-0	Cl	Martinez 45, Moralez 65p, Silva 89	20 000
	23	Dep. Italia	W	1-0	CLg7	Lopez 54	1 351
	27	Huracan	L	2-3	Cl	Zarate 42, Silva 87	22 000
	2	Boca Jun	D	4-4	Cl	Zapata 13, Silva 2 62 82, Martinez 74	35 000
	7	Arg Juniors	L	0-1	Cl		15 000
	12	Lanus	W	1-0	Cl	Zarate 7	18 000
Mar	16	Colo Colo	D	1-1	CLg7	Silva 92+	11 204
	20	Newells OB	D	1-1	Cl	Lima 86	18 000
	25	Colo Colo	W	2-1	CLg7	Lopez 14, Silva 30	9 325
	28	A. Tucuman	W	1-0	Cl	Torsiglieri 16	17 000
	31	Cruzeiro	L	0-3	CLg7		43 374
	4	Godoy Cruz	L	0-2	Cl		15 000
	8	Estudiantes	L	0-1	Cl		15 000
	11	Banfield	D	0-0	Cl		14 000
Apr	15	Dep. Italia	W	4-0	CLg7	Zapata 42, Lopez 2 48p 83, Papa 73	5 408
	18	Racing	L	1-3	Cl	Tobio 40	25 000
	23	Tigre	W	1-0	Cl	Zarate 90	15 000
	27	Guadalajara	L	0-3	CLr2		8 322
	30	River	L	1-2	Cl	Alvarez 9	30 000
	4	Guadalajara	W	2-0	CLr2	Silva 3, Zarate 88	10 055
May	8	Chacarita	W	4-1	Cl	Lopez 4 7 13 28 81p	15 000
	15	Rosario C	D	0-0	Cl		23 000
	8	Indep'iente	W	1-0	Ap	Silva 34	25 000
Aug	15	All Boys	W	2-1	Ap	Moralez 37, Martinez 44	12 000
	21	Arg Juniors	W	2-0	Ap	Somoza 70p, Silva 75	25 000
	29	Boca Jun	L	1-2	Ap	Silva 85	40 000
	2	Banfield	L	0-1	CSr1		30 000
	5	River	W	2-1	Ap	Martinez 33, Silva 59p	30 000
	11	S. Lorenzo	D	0-0	Ap		32 000
Sep	15	Banfield	D	1-1	CSr1	Cristaldo 90	12 000
	18	Arsenal	D	0-0	Ap		8 000
	24	Olimpo	W	3-0	Ap	Martinez 22, Moralez 28, Dominguez 73	18 000
	1	Newells OB	L	0-2	Ap		30 000
Oct	10	Colon	W	6-0	Ap	Silva 2 44p 58p, Martinez 3 55 60 69, Cristaldo 85	18 000
	15	Quilmes	W	2-0	Ap	Martinez 39, Silva 84	15 000
	22	Estudiantes	D	0-0	Ap		28 000
	7	Banfield	W	3-2	Ap	Silva 6, Martinez 22, Cristaldo 72	15 000
Nov	14	Lanus	W	1-0	Ap	Alvarez 59	30 000
	21	Gimnasia	D	0-0	Ap		18 000
	30	Tigre	W	2-1	Ap	Silva 11, Martinez 62p	25 000
	5	Godoy Cruz	W	4-0	Ap	Silva 2 32 52, Moralez 55, Cristaldo 83	26 000
Dec	8	Huracan	W	2-0	Ap	Cristaldo 2 52 84	30 000
	12	Racing	W	2-0	Ap	Martinez 24, Moralez 57	40 000

TIGRE LEAGUE APPEARANCES/GOALS 2010
Goalkeepers Luis Ardente 2 - 8 • Daniel Islas 17 - 11
Defenders Alberto Alarcon 0+2/0 • Rodolfo Arruabarrena 16/0 • Juan Blengio 7/0 • Pablo Caceres URU 5+2/0 • Pablo De Miranda - 0+2/0 • Mariano Echeverria 19/1 • Carlos Fondacaro 6/1 • Pablo Fontanello 19/2 • Juan Garat 8/1 • Damian Leyes 13+1/0 • Daniel Mustafa 0+2/0 • Maximiliano Oliva 4+3/0 • Claudio Perez 12/2 - 16/1 • Jose San Roman 3+2/1 • Walter Sanchez 4/0 • Cristian Trombetta 11+2/0 • Renzo Vera 6+1/0
Midfield Jonathan Blanco 11+4/0 - 2+1/0 • Ruben Botta 5+4/0 - 1+9/0 • Diego Castano 18/1 - 18/3 • Gonzalo Choy URU 5+4/0 • Angel Diaz 3+1/0 • Martin Galmarini 17/1• Esteban Gonzalez 5+5/2 • Ramiro Leone 10+1/0 - 19/1 • Roman Martinez 10/0 • Martin Morel 6+4/0 • Lucas Oviedo 0+3/0 • Mariano Pasini 1+8/1 - 2+2/0 • Ribair Rodriguez URU 11+2/0 - 7+1/0 • Fernando Telechea 6+8/1
Forwards Victor Altobelli 7+1/1 • Nestor Ayala PAR 4+5/3 • Pablo Caballero 2+4/0 • Leandro Lazzaro 12+6/2 • Carlos Luna 18/9 • Diego Morales 8+9/2• Braian Rodriguez URU 4+8/2 • Lucas Simon 1+3/0 • Denis Stracqualursi 19+1/11
Coach Ricardo Caruso • Rodolfo Arruabarrena (5-01-2011)

VELEZ LEAGUE APPEARANCES/GOALS 2010
Goalkeepers Marcelo Barovero 10+1 - 16 • German Montoya 9 - 3
Defenders Mariano Bittolo 1+3/0 - 0+1/0 • Gaston Diaz 10+1/0 - 5+6/0 • Sebastian Dominguez 9/0 - 19/1 • Pablo Lima URU 12/1 • Emanuel Olivera 5/0 • Fernando Ortiz 9/0 • Nicolas Otamendi 6/0 - 2/0 • Fernando Tobio 9+1/2 - 8/0 • Marco Torsiglieri 13/1
Midfield Ivan Bella 1+4/0 - 8+5/0 • Alejandro Cabral 8+4/0 • Nicolas Cabrera 11/0 • Hector Canteros 0+4/0 - 1+5/0• Luciano Cigno 1/0 • Leandro Coronel 6+2/0 • Fabian Cubero 7/0 - 16/0 • Augusto Fernandez 12/0 • Maximiliano Moralez 8+2/2 - 17/4 • Emiliano Papa 6+1/0 - 16/0 • Franco Razzotti 8+3/0 - 3+5/0 • Leandro Somoza 8/0 - 17/1 • Leandro Velazquez 9+1/0 • Victor Zapata 10/1 - 16/0
Forwards Ricardo Alvarez 4+7/1 - 2+13/1 • Eduardo Beron 0+1/0 • Leandro Caruso 4+3/0 • Matias Conti 1+2/0 • Jonathan Cristaldo 0+4/0 - 1+17/5 • Hernan Lopez 7+1/6 • Juan Martinez 9+4/2 - 19/10 • Leonardo Piris 1+1/0 • Ezequiel Rescaldani 0+2/0 • Tanque Silva URU 6+3/5 - 19/11 • Rolando Zarate 9+2/3
Coach Ricardo Gareca

ARM – ARMENIA

FIFA/COCA-COLA WORLD RANKING

1993	1994	1995	1996	1997	1998	1999	2000	2001	2002	2003	2004	2005	2006	2007	2008	2009	2010
-	141	113	106	105	100	85	90	95	107	113	119	108	123	93	113	100	60

2010												Hi/Lo
Jan	Feb	Mar	Mar	Apr	May	Jul	Aug	Sep	Oct	Nov	Dec	59
100	102	103	106	99	100	96	96	105	60	59	60	159

Pyunik Yerevan started the new decade exactly as they had finished the previous one - by winning the double. In the process they achieved the milestone of a tenth consecutive championship and equalled Ararat's total of five Armenian Cups, but it was a close run thing in the league. With three rounds to go, rivals Banants held a two-point lead over Pyunik going into a crunch match between the two. A draw would almost certainly have won Banants the title with straightforward games against the bottom two to follow. Deep into injury-time it looked as if they had achieved their aim but following a long hopeful ball into the penalty area, Karlen Mkrtchian got on the end of the knockdown and beat three defenders to score a sensational winner for Pyunik. It was a bitterly disappointing end to the year for Banants having earlier also lost to Pyunik in the Cup Final. For Pyunik coach Vardan Minasyan the celebrations didn't stop at club level. In his dual role as national team coach he steered Armenia to a bright start in the Euro 2012 qualifiers, most notably with a victory over World Cup finalists Slovakia. The country has made good progress at youth level and it is hoped that this will provide a good foundation for the game to regain the status that it previously enjoyed during Soviet times.

FIFA WORLD CUP RECORD
1930-1994 DNE 1998-2010 DNQ

FOOTBALL FEDERATION OF ARMENIA (FFA)

Khanjyan Street 27,
Yerevan 0010

☎ +374 10 568883
📠 +374 10 547173
✉ ffarm@arminco.com
🖥 www.ffa.am
FA 1992 CON 1993 FIFA 1992
P Ruben Hayrapetyan
GS Armen Minasyan

FIFA BIG COUNT 2006

Total players	151 353
% of population	5.09%
Male	136 212
Female	15 141
Amateurs 18+	37 228
Youth under 18	2 915
Unregistered	37 900
Professionals	656
Referees	134
Admin & coaches	4 810
Number of clubs	80
Number of teams	178

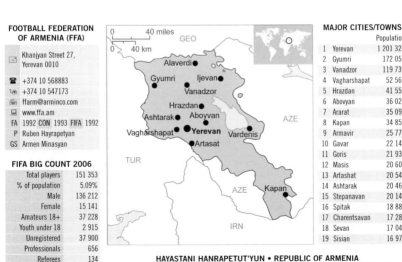

MAJOR CITIES/TOWNS

		Population
1	Yerevan	1 201 322
2	Gyumri	172 053
3	Vanadzor	119 739
4	Vagharshapat	52 567
5	Hrazdan	41 557
6	Abovyan	36 021
7	Ararat	35 093
8	Kapan	34 857
9	Armavir	25 777
10	Gavar	22 143
11	Goris	21 932
12	Masis	20 609
13	Artashat	20 544
14	Ashtarak	20 465
15	Stepanavan	20 143
16	Spitak	18 885
17	Charentsavan	17 287
18	Sevan	17 042
19	Sisian	16 976

HAYASTANI HANRAPETUT'YUN • REPUBLIC OF ARMENIA

Capital	Yerevan	Population	2 967 004 (137)	% in cities	64%
GDP per capita	$6300 (128)	Area km²	29 743 km² (142)	GMT +/-	+4
Neighbours (km)	Azerbaijan 787, Georgia 164, Iran 35, Turkey 268				

RECENT INTERNATIONALS PLAYED BY ARMENIA

2007	Opponents	Score		Venue	Comp	Scorers	Att	Referee
14-01	Panama	D	1-1	Monterey Park	Fr	Ara Hakopyan [p]		
7-02	Andorra	D	0-0	Andorra la Vella	Fr			
28-03	Poland	L	0-1	Kielce	ECq		13 450	Undiano ESP
2-06	Kazakhstan	W	2-1	Almaty	ECq	Arzumanyan [31], Hovsepyan [39p]	17 100	Kralovec CZE
6-06	Poland	W	1-0	Yerevan	ECq	Hamlet Mkhitaryan [66]	9 800	Balaj ROU
22-08	Portugal	D	1-1	Yerevan	ECq	Arzumanyan [11]	14 935	Larsen DEN
8-09	Cyprus	L	1-3	Larnaca	Fr	Arzumanyan [35]		Trattos CYP
12-09	Malta	W	1-0	Ta'Qali	Fr	Voskanyan [29]		Richmond SCO
13-10	Serbia	D	0-0	Yerevan	ECq		7 150	Johannesson SWE
17-10	Belgium	L	0-3	Brussels	ECq		14 812	Valgeirsson ISL
17-11	Portugal	L	0-1	Leiria	ECq		22 048	Riley ENG
21-11	Kazakhstan	L	0-1	Yerevan	ECq		3 100	Fautrel FRA
2008								
2-02	Malta	W	1-0	Ta'Qali	Fr	Ara Hakopyan [69]		Porisson ISL
4-02	Belarus	W	2-1	Ta'Qali	Fr	Arakelyan [18], Ara Hakopyan [76]		Zammit MLT
6-02	Iceland	L	0-2	Ta'Qali	Fr			Attard MLT
26-03	Kazakhstan	W	1-0	Pernis	Fr	Manucharyan [62]		Vink NED
28-05	Moldova	D	2-2	Tiraspol	Fr	Pizzelli [25], Pachajyan [54]		Ishchenko UKR
1-06	Greece	D	0-0	Offenbach/Main	Fr		8 032	Rafati GER
6-09	Turkey	L	0-2	Yerevan	WCq		30 000	Ovrebo NOR
10-09	Spain	L	0-4	Albacete	WCq		16 996	Asumaa FIN
11-10	Belgium	L	0-2	Brussels	WCq		20 949	Rasmussen DEN
15-10	Bosnia-Herzegovina	L	1-4	Zenica	WCq	Minasyan [85]	13 000	Kenan ISR
2009								
11-02	Latvia	D	0-0	Limassol	Fr		150	
28-03	Estonia	D	2-2	Yerevan	WCq	Henrikh Mkhitaryan [33], Ghazaryan [87]	3 000	Wilmes LUX
1-04	Estonia	L	0-1	Tallinn	WCq		5 200	Zimmermann SUI
12-08	Moldova	L	1-4	Yerevan	Fr	Arakelyan [75]	1 000	Silagava GEO
5-09	Bosnia-Herzegovina	L	0-2	Yerevan	WCq		1 800	Braamhaar NED
9-09	Belgium	W	2-1	Yerevan	WCq	Goharyan [23], Hovsepyan [50]	2 300	Stavrev MKD
10-10	Spain	L	1-2	Yerevan	WCq	Arzumanyan [58]	10 500	Jech CZE
14-10	Turkey	L	0-2	Bursa	WCq		16 200	Hansson SWE
2010								
3-03	Belarus	L	1-3	Antalya	Fr	Pachajyan [59]	BCD	
25-05	Uzbekistan	W	3-1	Yerevan	Fr	Henrikh Mkhitaryan [7], Manucharyan 2 [18p 27]	20 000	Kvaratskhelia GEO
11-08	Iran	L	1-3	Yerevan	Fr	Mkrtchyan [37]	3 000	Kvaratskhelia GEO
3-09	Republic of Ireland	L	0-1	Yerevan	ECq		8 600	Szabo HUN
7-09	Macedonia FYR	D	2-2	Skopje	ECq	Movsisyan [41], Manucharyan [91+]	9 000	Berntsen NOR
8-10	Slovakia	W	3-1	Yerevan	ECq	Movsisyan [23], Ghazaryan [50], Henrikh Mkhitaryan [89]	8 500	Orsato ITA
12-10	Andorra	W	4-0	Yerevan	ECq	Ghazaryan [4], Henrikh Mkhitaryan [16], Movsisyan [33], Pizzelli [33]	12 000	Undiano ESP

Fr = Friendly match • EC = UEFA EURO 2008/2012 • WC = FIFA World Cup • q = qualifier

ARMENIA NATIONAL TEAM HISTORICAL RECORDS

Caps — 115 - Sargis Hovsepyan 1992- • 69 - Arthur Petrosyan 1992-2005 • 62 - Roman Berezovsky 1996- & Harutyun Vardanyan 1994-2004 • 57 - Hamlet Mkhitaryan 1994-2008 • 55 - Romik Khachatryan 1997-2008 • 54 - Arthur Voskanyan 1999- • 53 - Armen Shahgeldyan 1992-2007 • 48 - Karen Dokhoyan 1999-2008 & Artavazd Karamyan 2000- • 47 - Arman Karamyan 2000-

Goals — 11 - Arthur Petrosyan 1992-2005 • 7 - Ara Hakobyan 1998-2008 • 6 - Armen Shahgeldyan 1992-2007 • 5 - Edgar Manucharyan 2000- & Arman Karamyan 2000- • 4 - Henrikh Mkhitaryan 2007-, Robert Arzumanyan 2005- & Tigran Yesayan 1996-99

Past Coaches — Eduard Markarov 1992-1994 • Samvel Darbinyan 1995-1996 • Khoren Hovhannisyan 1996-1997 • Souren Barseghyan 1998-1999 • Varuzhan Sukiasyan 2000-2001 • Andranik Adamyan 2002 • Oscar Lopez ARG 2002 • Andranik Adamyan 2003 • Mihai Stoichita ROU 2003-2004 • Bernard Casoni FRA 2004-2005 • Henk Wisman NED 2005-2006 • Ian Porterfield SCO 2006-2007 • Vardan Minasyan & Tom Jones ENG 2007 • Jan Poulsen DEN 2008-2009 • Vardan Minasyan 2009-

ARMENIA 2010

PREMIER LEAGUE

	Pl	W	D	L	F	A	Pts	Pyunik	Banants	Ulysses	Mika	Impuls	Gandzasar	Kilikia	Shirak
Pyunik Yerevan †	28	20	5	3	73	22	65		2-3 1-0	1-0 5-1	4-2 2-0	3-0 3-3	0-1 3-0	4-2 5-0	4-1 5-0
Banants Yerevan	28	20	4	4	58	24	64	1-1 2-2		2-0 0-2	2-0 2-1	5-2 6-1	3-0 5-0	2-0 1-0	5-1 1-1
Ulysses Yerevan	28	17	4	7	44	23	55	3-1 0-1	2-2 1-0		0-0 1-2	2-0 1-2	1-0 2-1	2-0 0-0	4-0 1-1
Mika Ashtarak	28	14	4	10	47	31	46	0-2 1-3	4-0 0-1	0-1 2-3		1-0 2-0	2-0 1-0	2-0 4-1	6-1 5-1
Impuls Dilijan	28	10	7	11	29	43	37	0-0 1-1	0-1 0-1	0-3 2-1	2-2 2-1		1-0 1-1	0-3 2-0	2-1 2-2
Gandzasar Kapan	28	8	3	17	24	45	27	1-6 0-3	1-2 0-1	0-1 0-3	1-1 0-1	1-2 1-0		3-0 3-0	1-0 3-3
Kilikia Yerevan	28	4	3	21	19	60	15	0-3 0-1	0-3 1-2	1-3 0-3	1-1 1-4	0-1 0-0	3-1 0-2		3-1 2-1
Shirak Gyumri	28	2	4	22	22	68	10	0-3 0-4	0-3 1-2	0-2 0-1	0-1 0-1	0-1 1-2	0-1 0-2	4-1 2-0	

27/03/2010 - 14/11/2010 • † Qualified for the UEFA Champions League • ‡ Qualified for the Europa League
Top scorers: 16 - Marcos Pizzelli, Pyunik & Gevorg Ghazaryan, Pyunik • 11 - Eduardo Du Bala BRA, Banants • 10 - Ednei BRA, Mika

ARMENIA 2010
SECOND DIVISION

	Pl	W	D	L	F	A	Pts
Ararat Yerevan	24	17	4	3	50	19	55
Banants-2 Yerevan	24	16	2	6	59	35	50
Pyunik-2 Yerevan	24	16	2	6	52	20	50
Gandzasar-2 Kapan	24	13	5	6	37	20	44
Shengavit Yerevan	24	8	7	9	42	41	31
Mika-2 Ashtarak	24	7	5	12	28	44	26
Impuls-2 Dilijan	24	5	4	15	22	41	19
Pyunik-3 Yerevan	24	5	3	16	22	53	18
Shirak-2 Gyumri	24	4	2	18	18	57	14

9/04/2010 - 13/11/2010

MEDALS TABLE

		Overall			League			Cup	
		G	S	B	G	S	B	G	S
1	Pyunik Yerevan	16	4		13	1		5	3
2	Ararat Yerevan	6	6	1	1	4	1	5	2
3	Mika Ashtarak	5	3	2		3	2	5	
4	Shirak Gyumri	3	8	2	3	5	2		3
5	Tsement Yerevan	3		1	1		1	2	
6	Banants Yerevan	2	9	3		4	3	2	5
7	FK Yerevan	1	1	3	1		3		1
8	Araks Ararat	1			1				
9	Zvartnots Yerevan		3			1			2
10	Kotayk Abovyan		2	2			2		2
11	Kilikia Yerevan		1						1
12	Ulysses Yerevan			2			2		
13	Gandzasar Kapan			1			1		
	Homenmen Yerevan			1			1		
	Spartak Yerevan			1			1		

ARMENIAN CLUBS IN THE SOVIET UNION

		Overall			League			Cup	
8	Ararat Yerevan	3	4		1	2		2	2

FFA CUP 2010

1st Round			Semi-finals			Final		
Pyunik Yerevan *	1	1						
Impuls Dilijan	0	0	Pyunik Yerevan	2	1			
Gandzasar Kapan *	1	0	Ulysses Yerevan *	0	0			
Ulysses Yerevan	1	2				Pyunik Yerevan	4	
Mika Ashtarak *	3	1				Banants Yerevan ‡	0	
Kilikia Yerevan	0	0	Mika Ashtarak	1	0			
Shirak Gyumri *	0	0	Banants Yerevan *	1	2			
Banants Yerevan	1	3	* Home team in the first leg • ‡ Qualified for the Europa League					

CUP FINAL 2010

Hanrapetakan, Yerevan, 10-05-2010, Att: 8000, Ref: Chagharian. Scorers - Manoyan [14], Marcos Pizeli [41], Ghazarian 2 [45 70]
Pyunik - Artur Lesko - Sargis Hovsepyan, Artur Yuzbashyan, Vahagn Minasyan• (Varazdat Haroyan 85), Artak Yedigaryan, Karlen Mkrtchyan, Davit Manoyan, Edgar Malakyan (Kamo Hovhannesian 80), Gevorg Ghazaryan, Marcos Pizelsi, Albert Tadevosyan. Tr: Vardan Minasyan;
Banants - Stepan Ghazarian - Hovhannes Hambardzumyan, Nikola Nikolov, Darko Lovric, Gagik Daghbashyan, Artur Voskanyan (Norayr Giozalian 69), Vebert Miguel da Silva Beto (Noah Kasule 80), Sargis Karapetyan, Samvel Melkonyan, Ortega Deniran (Ararat Arakelyan 52), Du Bala. Tr: Stevica Kuzmanoski

ARU – ARUBA

FIFA/COCA-COLA WORLD RANKING

1993	1994	1995	1996	1997	1998	1999	2000	2001	2002	2003	2004	2005	2006	2007	2008	2009	2010
165	173	171	181	177	180	191	184	185	189	195	198	200	198	201	193	198	199

2010												Hi/Lo
Jan	Feb	Mar	Mar	Apr	May	Jul	Aug	Sep	Oct	Nov	Dec	**160**
198	198	198	198	197	198	197	198	199	199	199	199	**202**

SV Britannia from the village of Piedra Plat continued their quest to establish themselves in the top echelons of football in Aruba with yet another impressive year in 2010. In January they beat La Fama in the final of the Copa Betico Croes to win the cup for the third consecutive season, while in June they beat Estrella in the league final to complete the double for the second year running. Since winning their first national title in 2005, Britannia have now won six trophies in five years. They didn't, however, take part in the 2010 CFU Caribbean Club Champions Cup, despite having twice entered in the past and there was a similar absence for the national team from the 2010 Digicel Caribbean Cup. In the two internationals that Aruba did play, both saw 3-0 defeats. The first came against Venezuela in Oranjestad, the first time their huge southern neighbours have made the journey over the short stretch of Caribbean Sea that separates the two countries. The second defeat came at the hands of local rivals Netherlands Antilles, a match that may well be the last between the two. With Curaçao and Sint Maarten breaking away from the union of Dutch territories - as Aruba did in 1986 - the Netherlands Antilles is no longer. The break up should, however, mean more scope for internationals between all of the former members of the union.

FIFA WORLD CUP RECORD
1930-1994 DNE 1998-2010 DNQ

ARUBAANSE VOETBAL BOND (AVB)

⌖	Technical Centre "Angel Botta", Shaba 24, PO Box 376 Noord
☎	+297 5877357
📠	+297 5876496
✉	avbaruba@setarnet.aw
🖥	www.avbaruba.aw
FA	1932 CON 1961 FIFA 1988
P	Rufo Kelly
GS	Egbert Lacle

FIFA BIG COUNT 2006

Total players	10 700
% of population	14.88%
Male	9 900
Female	800
Amateurs 18+	2 400
Youth under 18	3 500
Unregistered	1 000
Professionals	0
Referees	26
Admin & coaches	100
Number of clubs	60
Number of teams	140

MAJOR CITIES/TOWNS

		Population
1	Oranjestad	33 575
2	San Nicolas	18 395
3	Noord	16 944
4	Santa Cruz	12 326
5	Savaneta	9 996
6	Paradera	9 037

ARUBA

Capital	Oranjestad	Population	103 065 (193)	% in cities	47%
GDP per capita	$21 800 (57)	Area km²	180 km² (217)	GMT + / -	-5
Neighbours (km)	Coast 68				

RECENT INTERNATIONALS PLAYED BY ARUBA

2008	Opponents		Score	Venue	Comp	Scorers	Att	Referee
6-02	Antigua and Barbuda	L	0-3	Oranjestad	WCq		250	Delgado CUB
26-03	Antigua and Barbuda	L	0-1	St John's	WCq		1 000	Campbell JAM
27-07	Netherlands Antilles	D	0-0	Willemstad	CCq		995	Hospedales TRI
29-07	Grenada	L	1-3	Willemstad	CCq	Theric Ruiz [50]	450	Jordan TRI
2009								
No international matches played in 2009								
2010								
20-05	Venezuela	L	0-3	Oranjestad	Fr		3 500	Jauregui ANT
29-10	Netherlands Antilles	L	0-3	Willemstad	Fr			

Fr = Friendly match • CC = Digicel Caribbean Cup • WCq = FIFA World Cup • q = qualifier

ARUBA 2009-10

DIVISION DI HONOR FIRST STAGE

	Pl	W	D	L	F	A	Pts	Britannia	La Fama	Estrella	Bubali	Nacional	Racing	Riverplate	Brazil Jun	Sportboys	Dakota
Britannia †	18	11	4	3	49	17	37		2-0	6-1	2-2	1-0	0-0	4-0	7-0	5-0	3-2
La Fama †	18	10	3	5	31	18	33	1-1		0-1	4-0	6-4	1-0	1-0	1-2	2-0	2-0
Estrella †	18	10	1	7	26	22	31	1-2	1-2		2-0	2-1	0-3	1-0	0-1	0-2	5-1
Bubali †	18	9	3	6	33	25	29	2-1	1-1	0-2		1-3	4-1	2-0	3-1	1-2	4-0
Nacional	18	8	4	6	34	18	28	0-0	2-0	0-1	0-0		0-1	5-0	1-0	0-0	1-1
Racing Club Aruba	18	7	6	5	25	17	27	2-1	1-1	0-2	3-0	2-3		2-1	1-1	4-0	0-0
Riverplate	18	5	3	10	18	33	18	1-3	2-1	2-1	0-3	1-0	1-1		1-1	2-2	2-1
Brazil Juniors	18	5	3	10	18	38	18	1-6	0-1	0-3	1-3	1-2	2-1	2-1		2-1	2-4
Sportboys	18	4	4	10	15	43	16	1-0	0-5	2-3	2-3	0-9	0-3	2-1	1-1		0-2
Dakota	18	3	5	10	18	36	14	3-5	1-2	0-0	0-4	1-3	0-0	1-3	1-0	0-0	

4/09/2009 - 18/04/2010 • † Qualified for the championship play-off

DIVISION DI HONOR CHAMPIONSHIP PLAY-OFF

	Pl	W	D	L	F	A	Pts	Br	Es	Bu	LF
Britannia †	6	3	3	0	10	5	12		2-1	0-0	0-0
Estrella †	6	3	0	3	8	9	9	1-3		1-2	2-0
Bubali	6	2	2	2	6	6	8	0-0	0-1		0-3
La Fama	6	1	1	4	8	13	1	3-5	1-2	1-4	

24/05/2010 - 9/06/2010 • † Qualified for the final

FINAL

1st leg. 12-06-2010 , 2nd leg. 12-06-2010
3rd leg. 12-06-2010
Britannia 0-1 2-0 2-0 Estrella

MEDALS TABLE

		All	Lge	Cp	Town
		G	G	G	
1	Dakota	16	15	1	Oranjestad
2	Estrella	12	12		Santa Cruz
3	Racing Club	11	11		Oranjestad
4	Britannia	6	3	3	Paradera
5	Nacional	4	4		Noord
6	Riverplate	2	2		Oranjestad
7	Bubali	1	1		Noord
	Estudiantes	1		1	Oranjestad
	San Luis	1	1		Savaneta
	Sportboys	1		1	Santa Cruz

COPA BETICO CROES 2009-10

Round of 16		Quarter-finals		Semi-finals		Final	
Britannia	2						
San Luis	0	**Britannia**	3				
Brazil Juniors	1 2p	Bubali	2				
Bubali	1 3p			**Britannia**	7		
Juventud	1			Unistars	0		
Sporting	0	Juventud	0				
Sportboys	2	**Unistars**	5			**Britannia**	2
Unistars	7					La Fama	0
Nacional	2						
Racing Club Aruba	1	**Nacional**	7				
Trupial	1	Arsenal	0				
Arsenal	2			Nacional	0 2p		
San Nicolas	5			**La Fama**	0 4p	CUP FINAL	
Riverplate	1	San Nicolas	2			Frans Figaroa, Onranjestad	
Dakota	0 3p	**La Fama**	8			25-01-2010	
La Fama	0 5p					Scorer - Jonathan Lake 2 [6] [70]	

ASA – AMERICAN SAMOA

FIFA/COCA-COLA WORLD RANKING

1993	1994	1995	1996	1997	1998	1999	2000	2001	2002	2003	2004	2005	2006	2007	2008	2009	2010
-	-	-	-	-	193	199	203	201	201	202	204	205	198	201	201	203	203

2010												Hi/Lo
Jan	Feb	Mar	Mar	Apr	May	Jul	Aug	Sep	Oct	Nov	Dec	**192**
203	203	203	202	202	202	202	202	203	203	203	203	**205**

In a sign of just how far the game has developed in American Samoa, the football federation made sure that the 2010 season was played to the full, despite the Tsunami of the previous September. Indeed, a new cup competition - the FFAS President's Cup - was introduced and played in addition to the FFAS Senior League. The inaugural winners were Vailoatai Youth Soccer Club who beat Lion Heart 3-2 in the final. With Pago Park undergoing extensive renovation and upgrading in the wake of the Tsunami, the final was held at the Kananafou Theological Centre. With the score 1-1 at full-time it was left to Petaia to score the winner in the last minute of extra-time. Having only just joined the FFAS, it was a fantastic end to their first season for Vailoatai having also reached the semi-finals of the senior league. There they lost to Pago Youth who then beat defending champions Black Roses in the final with a convincing 6-2 victory to win the championship. Pago Youth won all ten matches they played to win back the title they had won two years previously. Once again there were no senior international fixtures with the next matches expected to be amongst the first of the qualifiers for the 2014 FIFA World Cup in Brazil, although the federation continued to focus much of its effort on youth and women's football during the course of 2010.

FIFA WORLD CUP RECORD
1930-1998 DNE 2002-2010 DNQ

FOOTBALL FEDERATION AMERICAN SAMOA (FFAS)

Pago Park,
PO Box 999413,
Pago Pago 96799

☎ +684 6447104
📠 +689 6447102
✉ ffas@blueskynet.as
🖥 www.ffas.as

FA	1984	CON	1994	FIFA	1998

P Alex Godinet
GS Tavita Taumua

FIFA BIG COUNT 2006

Total players	3 248
% of population	5.62%
Male	2 406
Female	842
Amateurs 18+	810
Youth under 18	1 000
Unregistered	410
Professionals	0
Referees	102
Admin & coaches	135
Number of clubs	27
Number of teams	33

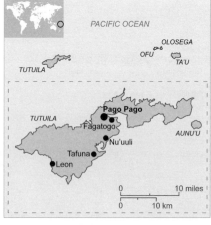

MAJOR CITIES/TOWNS

		Population
1	Tafuna	14 221
2	Nu'uuli	5 934
3	Faleniu	4 778
4	Leone	4 639
5	Pago Pago	4 533
6	Ili'ili	3 791
7	Pava'ia'i	3 107
8	Mapusagafou	2 547
9	Aua	2 264
10	Fagatogo	1 835
11	Vaitogi	1 560
12	Malaeimi	1 493
13	Vailoatai	1 331
14	Aoloau	1 194
15	Faga'alu	1 104
16	Fagasa	997
17	Lauli'i	963
18	Taputimu	863
19	Futiga	834

AMERICAN SAMOA

Capital	Pago Pago	Population	65 628 (204)	% in cities	92%
GDP per capita	$8000 (120)	Area km²	199 km² (215)	GMT +/-	-10
Neighbours (km)	Coast 116		

RECENT INTERNATIONALS PLAYED BY AMERICAN SAMOA

2006	Opponents	Score	Venue	Comp	Scorers	Att	Referee
\ No international matches played in 2006							
2007							
25-08	Solomon Islands	L 1-12	Apia	WCq	Ott [55p]	300	Sosongan PNG
27-08	Samoa	L 0-7	Apia	WCq		2 800	Minan PNG
29-08	Vanuatu	L 0-15	Apia	WCq		200	Hester NZL
1-09	Tonga	L 0-4	Apia	WCq		200	Minan PNG
2008							
No international matches played in 2008							
2009							
No international matches played in 2009							
2010							
No international matches played in 2010							

WC = FIFA World Cup • q = qualifier

AMERICAN SAMOA 2010

FFAS SENIOR LEAGUE

GROUP A

	Pl	W	D	L	F	A	Pts	Vailoatai Youth	FC SKBC	Lion Heart	Pansa	Laulii	Green Bay	Tafuna Jets B
Pago Youth †	7	7	0	0	23	6	21	3-2	3-2	3-1	5-0	2-0	4-1	3-0
Vailoatai Youth †	7	5	1	1	42	9	16		1-1	2-0	2-1	10-2	10-1	15-1
FC SKBC ‡	7	4	2	1	27	7	14			0-0	2-1	2-1	10-1	10-0
Lion Heart ‡	6	3	1	2	18	9	10				2-1	n/p	5-1	10-2
Pansa ‡	6	2	0	4	14	12	6					4-0	7-1	n/p
Laulii ‡	6	2	0	4	11	21	6						4-3	4-0
Green Bay	7	1	0	6	14	40	3							6-0
Tafuna Jets B	6	0	0	6	3	48	0							

GROUP B

	Pl	W	D	L	F	A	Pts	Fagasa Youth	Kiwi Soccers	Utulei Youth	Tafuna Jets	Ilaoa & T'mata	Pago Youth B
Black Roses †	5	4	1	0	31	8	13	1-1	9-0	5-3	n/p	7-2	9-2
Fagasa Youth †	6	2	4	0	14	11	10		3-3	2-1	2-1	5-3	1-1
Kiwi Soccers ‡	6	3	1	2	18	25	10			6-3	3-2	1-5	5-3
Utulei Youth ‡	6	3	0	3	19	16	9				3-1	4-0	5-2
Tafuna Jets ‡	5	2	1	2	9	10	7					1-0	3-2
Ilaoa & Toomata ‡	6	2	0	4	12	19	6						2-1
Pago Youth B	6	0	1	5	11	25	1						

25/09/2010 - 13/11/2010 • † Qualified for the quarter-finals • ‡ Qualified for the quarter-final play-offs

FFAS SENIOR LEAGUE PLAY-OFFS

Quarter-finals Play-offs		Quarter-finals		Semi-finals		Final	
Lions Heart	3	**Pago Youth**	2				
Pansa	0	Lion Heart	1	**Pago Youth**	4		
Laulii	1	FC SKBC	3	Vailoatai Youth	1		
FC SKBC	2	**Vailoatai Youth**	4			**Pago Youth**	6
Kiwi Soccers	1	**Fagasa Youth**	3			Black Roses	2
Ilaoa & Toomata	0	Kiwi Soccers	0	Fagasa Youth	0	Kananafou Theological Centre	
Tafuna Jets	1	Utulei Youth	1	**Black Roses**	1	11-12-2010	
Utulei Youth	3	**Black Roses**	2				

3rd place: Vailoatai Youth 2-1 Fagasa Youth

ATG – ANTIGUA AND BARBUDA

FIFA/COCA-COLA WORLD RANKING

1993	1994	1995	1996	1997	1998	1999	2000	2001	2002	2003	2004	2005	2006	2007	2008	2009	2010
117	136	137	145	159	137	147	144	157	155	170	153	154	132	151	128	130	106

2010												Hi/Lo
Jan	Feb	Mar	Mar	Apr	May	Jul	Aug	Sep	Oct	Nov	Dec	**106**
130	127	123	120	119	119	129	129	123	131	115	106	**170**

Having qualified for the finals of the 2008 Digicel Caribbean Cup, Antigua were given the benefit of a bye into the second round of qualifiers for the 2010 tournament and there they made home advantage count to qualify for the final tournament in Martinique. A creditable 2-1 win over Suriname in the opening match of a qualifying group played in St John's, ultimately sealed their place in Martinique, although they still needed a draw in their final match against Cuba to ensure qualification. Antigua opened the finals with a 3-1 defeat at the hands of favourites Jamaica but gave themselves hope of a semi-final place and qualification for the 2011 CONCACAF Gold Cup in the USA thanks to a 1-0 victory over Guyana courtesy of a long range effort from Gayson Gregory. Their hopes, however, were dashed at the hands of Guadeloupe in the final match, who won 1-0 and qualified instead. At home, 2010 was a good year for Bassa who won the Premier Division and then the FA Cup, although it took post-match penalties in the latter to beat Goldsmitty after the final had finished 1-1. They missed out on a treble though, having earlier lost to Old Road in the final of the Super Eight Championship. It was Gayson Gregory who denied Bassa, scoring what proved to be the winner in a 2-1 victory for Old Road.

FIFA WORLD CUP RECORD
1930-1970 DNE 1974 DNQ 1978-1982 DNE 1986-2010 DNQ

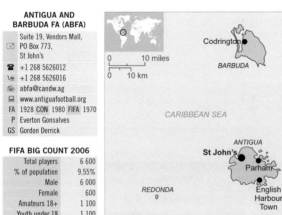

ANTIGUA AND BARBUDA FA (ABFA)

Suite 19, Vendors Mall,
PO Box 773,
St John's
☎ +1 268 5626012
📠 +1 268 5626016
✉ abfa@candw.ag
🖥 www.antiguafootball.org
FA 1928 CON 1980 FIFA 1970
P Everton Gonsalves
GS Gordon Derrick

FIFA BIG COUNT 2006

Total players	6 600
% of population	9.55%
Male	6 000
Female	600
Amateurs 18+	1 100
Youth under 18	1 100
Unregistered	800
Professionals	0
Referees	33
Admin & coaches	100
Number of clubs	20
Number of teams	60

MAJOR CITIES/TOWNS

		Population
1	St John's	21 969
2	All Saints	4 602
3	Liberta	2 986
4	Potters Village	2 933
5	Bolands	2 056
6	Seaview Farm	1 881
7	Swetes	1 775
8	Pigotts	1 726
9	Clare Hill	1 402
10	Carlisle	1 253
11	New Winthropes	1 189
12	Bendals	1 174
13	Willikies	1 145
14	Old Road	1 108
15	Jennings	1 005
16	Freemans Village	953
17	Cedar Grove	897
18	Urlings	869
19	Parham	821

ANTIGUA AND BARBUDA

Capital	St John's	Population	85 632 (198)	% in cities 30%
GDP per capita	$19 600 (64)	Area km²	442 km² (199)	GMT + / - -4.5
Neighbours (km)	Coast 153			

RECENT INTERNATIONALS PLAYED BY ANTIGUA AND BARBUDA

2008	Opponents		Score	Venue	Comp	Scorers	Att	Referee
4-12	Haiti	D	1-1	Montego Bay	CCr1	Peter Byers [72]	2 500	Forde BRB
6-12	Cuba	L	0-3	Trelawny	CCr1		1 000	Campbell JAM
8-12	Guadeloupe †	D	2-2	Montego Bay	CCr1	Peter Byers 2 [35 81]	1 500	Campbell JAM
2009								
3-06	Guyana	W	2-1	Paramaribo	Fr	Kelly Frederick [79], Quintin Griffith [90]	1 700	Wijngaarde SUR
28-06	Grenada	D	2-2	St George's	Fr	Gayson Gregory [33], Roy Gregory [90]	800	Phillip GRN
2010								
21-07	Trinidad and Tobago	L	1-4	Macoya	Fr	Tamarley Thomas [29]	1 700	Brizan TRI
28-08	St Kitts and Nevis	D	1-1	Basseterre	Fr	Akeem Thomas [43]	500	Matthew SKN
19-09	Trinidad and Tobago	L	0-1	St John's	Fr		500	Willett ATG
23-09	St Lucia	W	5-0	St John's	Fr	Randolph Burton 2 [17 55], Peter Byers 2 [45 67], Jamie Thomas 75	500	Willett ATG
10-11	Suriname	W	2-1	St John's	CCq	Randolph Burton [18], Justin Cochrane [64]	2 000	Morrison JAM
12-11	Dominica	D	0-0	St John's	CCq		400	Purser JAM
14-11	Cuba	D	0-0	St John's	CCq		500	Campbell JAM
27-11	Jamaica	L	1-3	Riviere-Pilote	CCr1	Gayson Gregory [49]	3 000	Wijngaarde SUR
29-11	Guyana	W	1-0	Riviere-Pilote	CCr1	Gayson Gregory [69]	3 000	Wijngaarde SUR
1-12	Guadeloupe †	L	0-1	Riviere-Pilote	CCr1		3 000	Lopez GUA

Fr = Friendly match • CC = Digicel Caribbean Cup • WC = FIFA World Cup • q = qualifier • † Not an official FIFA international

ANTIGUA AND BARBUDA 2009–10

DIGICEL, HADEED AND OBSERVER GROUP PREMIER DIVISION	Pl	W	D	L	F	A	Pts	Bassa	Old Road	All Saints	Hoppers	Goldsmitty	Sap	Parham	Villa Lions	Willikies	Potters
Bassa	18	13	3	2	43	16	42		2-0	1-0	4-3	0-2	1-0	6-1	2-0	3-1	5-0
Old Road	18	11	4	3	39	16	37	1-1		2-0	1-1	4-1	0-2	2-3	1-0	2-0	3-0
All Saints United	18	11	2	5	29	23	35	2-2	1-5		0-1	2-1	2-1	4-2	4-1	2-0	3-1
Hoppers	18	10	2	6	37	24	32	0-2	0-2	0-1		2-0	3-2	1-2	3-2	1-1	3-1
Goldsmitty	18	8	1	9	30	30	25	1-3	0-4	lt	1-3		2-5	3-1	1-4	4-0	5-0
Sap	18	5	6	7	29	33	21	3-1	0-0	2-4	1-6	0-2		1-1	2-2	3-1	1-1
Parham	18	6	2	10	29	42	20	0-2	3-4	3-1	0-4	0-2	1-1		1-3	3-0	0-4
Villa Lions	18	4	6	8	31	33	18	1-1	1-3	1-1	2-3	1-2	4-1	2-3		2-2	1-1
Willikies	18	4	3	11	12	36	15	0-4	0-4	0-1	1-0	1-1	0-2	2-1	1-3		1-0
Potters Tigers	18	1	5	12	14	40	8	1-3	1-1	0-1	1-3	0-2	2-2	3-1	1-1	0-1	

20/09/2009 - 24/01/2010 • Relegation play-offs: Freemansville 3-6 Villa Lions; Villa Lions 3-1 Bullets • Villa Lions remain in the Premier Division

FA CUP 2010

Quarter-finals		Semi-finals		Final	
Bassa	3				
Hoppers	1	Bassa	2		
Young Warriors	1	All Saints Utd	1		
All Saints Utd	3			Bassa	1 4p
Black Panthers	1			Goldsmitty	1 1p
Old Road	0	Black Panthers	1		
Guydadli	0	Goldsmitty	5		
Goldsmitty	2				

Recreation Ground
7-03-2010, Scorers - Schyan
Jeffers [34] for Bassa; Darren
Stevens [42] for Goldsmitty

SUPER EIGHT CHAMPIONSHIP 2010

Quarter-finals		Semi-finals		Final	
Old Road	2				
Sea View Farm	0	Old Road			
All Saints Utd	2	Sap			
Sap	3			Old Road	2
Goldsmitty	4			Bassa	1
Hoppers	2	Goldsmitty			
Bullets	1	Bassa			
Bassa	4				

31-01-2010, Scorers - Stephan
Smith [24], Gayson Gregory [39]
for Old Road; Randolph
Burton [70p] for Bassa

MEDALS TABLE

		Overall	Lge	Cup
		G	G	G
1	Empire	13	13	
2	Bassa	7	5	2
3	Sap	4	2	2
4	Lion Hill	4	4	
5	English Harbour	3	3	
6	Parham (incl J & J)	3	3	
7	Villa Lions	2	2	
8	Liberta	2	2	
9	Five Islands	1	1	
10	Golden Stars	1	1	
	Freemansville	1		1

AUS – AUSTRALIA

FIFA/COCA-COLA WORLD RANKING

1993	1994	1995	1996	1997	1998	1999	2000	2001	2002	2003	2004	2005	2006	2007	2008	2009	2010
49	58	51	50	35	39	89	73	48	50	82	58	48	39	48	28	21	26

	2010											Hi/Lo
Jan	Feb	Mar	Mar	Apr	May	Jul	Aug	Sep	Oct	Nov	Dec	14
21	23	23	19	20	20	20	20	24	21	20	26	92

Australia's hopes of capping a 12-month period spent consolidating their position as Asia's leading football nation fell short when Holger Osieck's side suffered a 1-0 defeat at the hands of Japan in the final of the AFC Asian Cup in Qatar in January 2011. The Socceroos reached the final for the first time in their second appearance at the finals, but will have to wait until they host the tournament in 2015 for another crack at becoming Asian champions for the first time. Osieck had replaced controversial Dutchman Pim Verbeek as coach after the 2010 FIFA World Cup finals in South Africa, where Australia just missed out on a place in the second round. A 4-0 defeat against Germany in their opening game had left the Australians playing catch-up and despite a draw with Ghana and a 2-1 win over Serbia they missed out on goal-difference to the Ghanaians. Verbeek's two-year spell in Australia had polarised opinion, especially after his dismissive comments about the A-League. Still only in its fifth year, Sydney won the 2010 A-League after they beat Melbourne Victory on post-match penalties in the Grand Final to take the title for the second time. 2010 was not a good year for Australian clubs in the AFC Champions League, however, with Melbourne falling at the group stage and Adelaide knocked out in the last 16 by Korea's Jeonbuk.

FIFA WORLD CUP RECORD
1930-1962 DNE 1966-1970 DNQ **1974** 14 r1 1978-2002 DNQ **2006** 16 r2 **2010** 21 r1

FOOTBALL FEDERATION AUSTRALIA (FFA)

Level 22, 1 Oxford Street, Darlinghurst, NSW 2010

☎ +61 2 80204000
🖷 +61 2 80204100
✉ info@footballaustralia.com.au
🖵 www.footballaustralia.com.au
FA 1961 CON 2006 FIFA 1963
P Frank Lowy
GS Ben Buckley

FIFA BIG COUNT 2006

Total players	970 728
% of population	4.79%
Male	781 246
Female	189 482
Amateurs 18+	107 013
Youth under 18	299 775
Unregistered	338 000
Professionals	200
Referees	8 650
Admin & coaches	58 982
Number of clubs	2 316
Number of teams	20 018

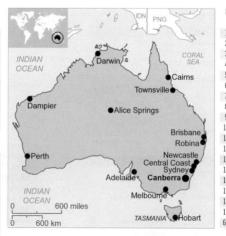

MAJOR CITIES/TOWNS

		Population
1	Melbourne	3 676 105
2	Sydney	3 653 646
3	Brisbane	1 855 083
4	Perth	1 272 193
5	Adelaide	1 040 987
6	Gold Coast	566 739
7	Canberra	331 755
8	Central Coast	302 341
9	Newcastle	292 516
10	Wollongong	232 310
11	Sunshine Coast	182 861
12	Geelong	134 145
13	Townsville	132 225
14	Hobart	125 305
15	Cairns	114 586
16	Toowoomba	99 767
17	Bunbury	94 163
18	Rockingham	83 584
66	Robina	19 182

COMMONWEALTH OF AUSTRALIA

Capital	Canberra	Population	21 262 641 (54)	% in cities	89%
GDP per capita	$38 100 (25)	Area km²	7 741 220 km² (6)	GMT + / -	+10
Neighbours (km)	Coast 25 760				

RECENT INTERNATIONALS PLAYED BY AUSTRALIA

2008	Opponents	Score		Venue	Comp	Scorers	Att	Referee
19-08	South Africa	D	2-2	London	Fr	Sterjovski [25], Kennedy [38]	10 000	Webb ENG
6-09	Netherlands	W	2-1	Eindhoven	Fr	Kewell [45p], Kennedy [76]	22 500	Atkinson ENG
10-09	Uzbekistan	W	1-0	Tashkent	WCq	Chipperfield [26]	34 000	Al Fadhli KUW
15-10	Qatar	W	4-0	Brisbane	WCq	Cahill [8], Emerton 2 [17p 58], Kennedy [76]	34 320	Al Ghamdi KSA
19-11	Bahrain	W	1-0	Manama	WCq	Bresciano [93+]	10 000	Moradi IRN
2009								
28-01	Indonesia	D	0-0	Jakarta	ACq		50 000	Abdul Bashir SIN
11-02	Japan	D	0-0	Yokohama	WCq		66 000	Basma SYR
5-03	Kuwait	L	0-1	Canberra	ACq		20 032	Moradi IRN
1-04	Uzbekistan	W	2-0	Sydney	WCq	Kennedy [66], Kewell [73p]	57 292	Albadwawi UAE
6-06	Qatar	D	0-0	Doha	WCq		7 000	Abdul Bashir SIN
10-06	Bahrain	W	2-0	Sydney	WCq	Sterjovski [55], Carney [88]	39 540	Al Hilali OMA
17-06	Japan	W	2-1	Melbourne	WCq	Cahill 2 [59 77]	69 238	Al Ghamdi KSA
12-08	Republic of Ireland	W	3-0	Limerick	Fr	Cahill 2 [38 44], Carney [90]	19 000	Perez ESP
5-09	Korea Republic	L	1-3	Seoul	Fr	Kisnorbo [33]	40 215	Mohd Salleh MAS
10-10	Netherlands	D	0-0	Sydney	Fr		40 537	Minoru JPN
14-10	Oman	W	1-0	Melbourne	ACq	Cahill [73]	20 595	Maasaki JPN
14-11	Oman	W	2-1	Muscat	ACq	Wilkshire [43], Emerton [83]	12 000	Sun Baojie CHN
2010								
6-01	Kuwait	D	2-2	Kuwait City	ACq	Wilkshire [3], Heffernan [5]	20 000	Irmatov UZB
3-03	Indonesia	W	1-0	Brisbane	ACq	Milligan [42]	20 422	Ogiya JPN
24-05	New Zealand	W	2-1	Melbourne	Fr	Vidosic [57], Holman [90]	55 659	Salazar USA
1-06	Denmark	W	1-0	Roodepoort	Fr	Kennedy [71]	5 000	Bennet RSA
5-06	USA	L	1-3	Roodepoort	Fr	Cahill [19]	6 000	Ebrahim RSA
13-06	Germany	L	0-4	Durban	WCr1		62 660	Rodriguez MEX
19-06	Ghana	D	1-1	Rustenburg	WCr1	Holman [11]	34 812	Rosetti ITA
23-06	Serbia	W	2-1	Nelspruit	WCr1	Cahill [69], Holman [73]	37 836	Larrionda URU
11-08	Slovenia	L	0-2	Ljubljana	Fr		16 135	Tagliavento ITA
3-09	Switzerland	D	0-0	St Gall	Fr		14 660	Einwaller AUT
7-09	Poland	W	2-1	Krakow	Fr	Holman [15], Wilkshire [26p]	17 000	Bebek CRO
9-10	Paraguay	W	1-0	Sydney	Fr	Carney [53]	25 210	Nishimura JPN
17-11	Egypt	L	0-3	Cairo	Fr			Genov BUL
2011								
5-01	UAE	D	0-0	Al Ain	Fr			Shaban KUW
10-01	India	W	4-0	Doha	ACr1	Cahill 2 [12 65], Kewell [25], Holman [45]	9 783	Albadwawi UAE
14-01	Korea Republic	D	1-1	Doha	ACr1	Jedinak [62]	15 526	Abdou QAT
18-01	Bahrain	W	1-0	Doha	ACr1	Jedinak [37]	3 919	Nishimura JPN
22-01	Iraq	W	1-0	Doha	ACqf	Kewell [118]	7 889	Abdou QAT
25-01	Uzbekistan	W	6-0	Doha	ACsf	Kewell [5], Ognenovski [35], Carney [65], Emerton [73], Valeri [82], Kruse [83]	24 826	Albadwawi UAE
29-01	Japan	L	0-1	Doha	ACf		37 174	Irmatov UZB

Fr = Friendly match • AC = AFC Asian Cup • WC = FIFA World Cup
q = qualifier • r1 = first round group • qf = quarter-final • sf = semi-final • f = final

AUSTRALIA NATIONAL TEAM HISTORICAL RECORDS

Caps
87 - Alex Tobin 1988-98 • 84 - Paul Wade 1986-96 • 82 - Mark Schwarzer 1993- • 77 - Brett Emerton 1998- • 76 - Tony Vidmar 1991-2006 • 68 - Scott Chipperfield 1998- 64 - Peter Wilson 1970-79 • 62 - Lucas Neill 1996- • 61 - Attila Abonyi 1967-77 • 60 - John Kosmina 1976-88 & Stan Lazaridis 1993-2006

Goals
29 - Damian Mori 1992-2002 • 27 - John Aloisi 1997-2008 • 25 - John Kosmina 1976-88 & Attila Abonyi 1967-77 • 21 - Archie Thompson 2001- & Tim Cahill 2004- • 20 - David Zdrilic 1997-2005 • 19 - Graham Arnold 1985-97 • 18 - Ray Baartz 1967-74 • 17 - Gary Cole 1978-82, Aurelio Vidmar 1991-2001 & Brett Emerton 1998-

Past Coaches
Tiko Jelisavcic YUG 1965 • Jozef Venglos CZE 1965-67 • Joe Vlatsis YUG 1967-69 • Rale Rasic YUG 1970-74 • Brian Green ENG 1976 • Jim Shoulder ENG 1976-78 • Rudi Gutendorf GER 1979-81 • Les Scheinflug 1981-83 • Frank Arok YUG 1983-89 • Eddie Thomson SCO 1990-96 • Raul Blanco 1996 • Terry Venables ENG 1997-98 • Raul Blanco 1998-99 • Frank Farina 1999-2005 • Guus Hiddink NED 2005-06 • Graham Arnold 2006-07 • Pim Verbeek NED 2007-10 • Holger Osieck GER 2010-

AUSTRALIA 2009–10

HYUNDAI A–LEAGUE

	Pl	W	D	L	F	A	Pts	Sydney	Melbourne	Gold Coast	Wellington	Perth	Newcastle	Queensland	Cent Coast	Brisbane	Adelaide
Sydney FC	27	15	3	9	35	23	48		2-0	0-1	2-0 3-1	3-2	2-1 1-3	0-1 4-1	1-0 1-0	2-1	1-0 1-0
Melbourne Victory	27	14	5	8	47	32	47	0-3 0-0		4-0	1-1 4-0	6-2	1-1	2-0	0-2 0-4	3-3 2-1	3-1 2-0
Gold Coast United	27	13	5	9	39	35	44	2-1 1-0	2-3 1-0		0-0 0-1	2-1 2-0	2-0	5-0 0-2	2-1	5-1	1-1
Wellington Phoenix	27	10	10	7	37	29	40	0-1	1-1	6-0		2-1 1-1	3-0	1-1 3-0	0-0 3-0	3-1	1-1 1-0
Perth Glory	27	11	6	10	40	34	39	2-0 0-0	2-1 1-2	2-2 3-1	2-0		2-0 4-0	1-1		1-1 2-0	1-0
Newcastle Jets	27	10	4	13	33	45	34	1-3	1-3 3-2	1-0 3-2	3-2 0-1	0-1		2-0 3-2	2-1	0-3	1-2 1-0
North Queensland Fury	27	8	8	11	29	46	32	2-3	0-1 1-0	2-1	1-1	2-1 1-0	2-1		1-5	1-1 1-1	0-2 2-1
Central Coast Mariners	27	7	9	11	32	29	30	0-0	0-3	3-0	0-2	2-1 0-0	1-1 3-0	1-1 1-1		2-3	0-0
Brisbane Roar	27	8	6	13	32	42	30	1-0 1-0	0-1	1-3 0-1	1-1 4-1	2-4	1-1 0-2	2-0	1-0 0-3		0-1
Adelaide United	27	7	8	12	24	33	29	2-1	0-2	0-2 1-1	1-1	1-0 2-3	1-1 0-2	3-3	1-0	0-2 2-0	

6/08/2009 - 14/02/2010 • † Qualified for the Major Semi-final • ‡ Qualified for the Minor Semi-final • Top scorers: **19** - Shane Smeltz NZL, Gold Coast • **13** - Sergio van Dijk IDN, Brisbane, Paul Ifill BRB, Wellington & Carlos Hernandez CRC, Melbourne • **11** - Archie Thompson, Melbourne
Melbourne Victory and Sydney FC qualified for the 2011 AFC Champions League

A–LEAGUE FINALS SERIES

First Round

Wellington Phoenix	1 4p
Perth Glory	1 2p

Gold Coast United	0 5p
Newcastle Jets	0 6p

Minor Semi–final

Wellington Phoenix	3
Newcastle Jets	1

Preliminary Final

Sydney FC	4
Wellington Phoenix	2

Major Semi–Final

Sydney FC	1 2
Melbourne Victory	2 2

Grand Final

Sydney FC	1 4p
Melbourne Victory	1 2p

20/02/2010 - 20/03/2010 • The loser of the Major Semi-final meets the winner of the Minor Semi-final in the Preliminary Final • The winners of the Major Semi-final and the Preliminary Final meet in the Grand Final

GRAND FINAL 2010

Etihad Stadium, Melbourne, 20-03-2010, 19:00, Att: 44 560, Ref: Delovski

Sydney FC	1 4p Bridge [63]
Melbourne Victory	1 2p Leijer [81]

Sydney - Clint Bolton - Sebastian Ryall•, Stephan Keller, Simon Colosimo•, Byun Sung Hwan - Karol Kisel•, Stuart Musialik (Hayden Foxe 105), Terry McFlynn (c) - Alex Brosque (Joey Gibbs 116), Chris Payne (Shannon Cole 75), Mark Bridge•.
Tr: Vitezslav Lavicka
Melbourne - Mitchell Langerak - Kevin Muscat• (c), Surat Sukha (Evan Berger• 71), Rodrigo Vargas, Adrian Leijer - Leigh Broxham, Carlos Hernandez, Nick Ward (Aziz Behich 76) - Grant Brebner, Archie Thompson (Marvin Angulo 16), Robbie Kruse.
Tr: Ernie Merrick

GRAND FINAL PENALTY SHOOT-OUT

Sydney		Melbourne	
✓	Colosimo		
		Muscat	✗ [1]
✗ [2]	Cole		
		Brebner	✓
✓	Foxe		
		Angulo	✗ [2]
✓	Kisel		
		Broxham	✓
✓	Byun		

1 = hit post • 2 = saved

MEDALS TABLE

		Overall			A-Lge			Asia			City/Town
		G	S	B	G	S	B	G	S	B	
1	Melbourne Victory	2	1		2	1					Melbourne
2	Sydney FC	2			2						Sydney
3	Newcastle Jets	1			1						Newcastle
4	Adelaide United			3			2			1	Adelaide
5	Central Coast Mariners			2			2				Gosford
6	Brisbane Roar										Brisbane
	Gold Coast United										Gold Coast
	Melbourne Heart										Melbourne
	North Queensland Fury										Townsville
	Perth Glory										Perth
	Wellington Phoenix										Wellington
		5	6		5	5			1		

MEDALS TABLE PRE A-LEAGUE

		Overall			League			Cup		CL	ST	City
		G	S	B	G	S	B	G	S	G	G	
1	Sydney City	7	4	1	4	3	1	3	1		5	Sydney
2	South Melbourne	7	3	2	4	2	2	2	1	1	7	Melbourne
3	Adelaide City	7	3		3	2		3	1	1	12	Adelaide
4	Marconi Stallions	5	6		4	3		1	3			Sydney
5	Sydney Olympic	4	6		2	4		2	2			Sydney
6	APIA Leichhardt Tigers	4	3		1			3	3		4	Sydney
7	Melbourne Knights	3	4		2	3		1	1		1	Melbourne
8	Wollongong City Wolves	3		1	2		1			1		Wollongong
9	Heidelberg United	2	6	1	2	1		2	4		1	Melbourne
10	Perth Glory	2	2		2	2						Perth
11	Parramatta Eagles	2	1					2	1			Sydney
	Brisbane City	2		1	1			2				Brisbane
13	Sydney United	1	4		3			1	1			Sydney
14	St George Saints	1	3	1	1	1	1	2			3	Sydney
15	West Adelaide	1	2		1			2			7	Adelaide

League = League championship 1977-2004 • Cup = Cup tournament 1962-77 • CL = OFC Champions Cup • ST = State Championship pre 1977

CLUB BY CLUB GUIDE TO THE 2009-10 SEASON IN AUSTRALIA

ADELAIDE UNITED 2009-10

Aug	7	Perth	W	1-0	AL	Dodd 31p	13 847
	16	Sydney	L	0-1	AL		14 942
	21	Gold Coast	L	0-2	AL		12 741
	28	NQ Fury	D	3-3	AL	Pantelis 2 23 90p, Owusu 33	10 773
Sep	4	Wellington	D	1-1	AL	Fyfe 41	7 578
	11	Cent. Coast	W	1-0	AL	Cassio 33	10 262
	18	Melbourne	L	0-2	AL		15 038
	27	NQ Fury	W	2-0	AL	Pantelis 60, Leckie 90	6 745
Oct	5	Newcastle	D	1-1	AL	Cassio 76	12 090
	9	Perth	L	0-1	AL		9 482
	16	Sydney	W	2-1	AL	Cristiano 2 29 54	10 791
	24	Melbourne	L	1-3	AL	Hughes 64	21 182
	31	Cent. Coast	D	0-0	AL		5 437
Nov	6	Brisbane	L	0-2	AL		11 209
	20	Gold Coast	D	1-1	AL	Leckie 90	9 578
	28	NQ Fury	L	1-2	AL	Cristiano 90	5 356
Dec	4	Newcastle	L	0-2	AL		8 502
	12	Brisbane	W	1-0	AL	Barbiero 78	5 801
	18	Wellington	D	1-1	AL	Alemao 57	9 070
	27	Sydney	L	0-1	AL		11 741
Jan	9	Gold Coast	D	1-1	AL	Dodd 20	4 505
	15	Cent. Coast	D	1-1	AL	Dodd 43	10 156
	19	Perth	L	2-3	AL	Pantelis 13, Dodd 53	8 904
	23	Melbourne	L	0-2	AL		20 361
	30	Wellington	L	0-1	AL		19 258
Feb	6	Brisbane	W	2-0	AL	Barbiero 7, Pantelis 51	8 244
	12	Newcastle	W	2-1	AL	Barbiero 8, Leckie 74	6 880
	24	Pohang	W	1-0	CLgH	Leckie 45	8 374
Mar	10	Shandong	W	2-0	CLgH	Van Dijk 27, Leckie 70	22 176
	24	Sanfrecce	W	3-2	CLgH	Dodd 12, Cornthwaite 79, Cassio 82	12 841
Apr	30	Sanfrecce	L	0-1	CLgH		12 094
	13	Pohang	D	0-0	CLgH		8 217
	27	Shandong	L	0-1	CLgH		10 313
	12	Jeonbuk	L	2-3	CLr2	Cornthwaite 78, Van Dijk 95+	12 015

ADELAIDE LEAGUE APPEARANCES/GOALS 2009-10
Goalkeepers Eugene Galekovic 27
Defenders Alemao BRA 14+2/1 • Cassio BRA 14+5/2 • Robert Cornthwaite 18+1 • Iain Fyfe 26/1 • Scott Jamieson 22+2/0 • Michael Marrone 13+3/0 • Daniel Mullen 12+1/0 • Mark Rudan 19/0
Midfield Fabian Barbiero 14+4/3 • Joe Costa 0+1/0 • Travis Dodd 21+2/4 • Marcos Flores ARG 1+1/0 • Adam Hughes 19+7/1 • Mathew Leckie 15+5/3 • Lucas Pantelis 20+3/5 • Paul Reid 8+0 • Kristian Sarkies 11/0 • Shin In Seob KOR 1/0
Forwards Cristiano BRA 13+11/3 • Evan Kostopoulos 0+1/0 • Francesco Monterosso 0+5/0 • Lloyd Owusu GHA 10+6/1
Coach Aurelio Vidmar

BRISBANE ROAR 2009-10

Aug	8	Gold Coast	L	1-3	AL	Van Dijk 90p	19 902
	15	Melbourne	D	3-3	AL	Tiatto 22, Van Dijk 24p, Henrique 37	18 603
	23	Wellington	D	1-1	AL	Van Dijk 10	7 084
	29	Cent. Coast	W	1-0	AL	Moore 11	6 433
Sep	5	NQ Fury	D	1-1	AL	Nichols 84	7 173
	12	Newcastle	W	3-0	AL	Henrique 23, Reinaldo 26, Miller 71	6 026
	20	Perth	L	2-4	AL	Henrique 50, OG 64	7 367
	27	Sydney	W	1-0	AL	Van Dijk 85	7 677
Oct	3	Melbourne	L	1-2	AL	Reinaldo 11	19 587
	1	Gold Coast	L	0-1	AL		8 882
	17	Cent. Coast	L	0-3	AL		7 434
	25	Sydney	L	1-2	AL	Cernak 72	8 456
	30	Newcastle	D	1-1	AL	Van Dijk 36p	7 509
Nov	6	Adelaide	W	2-0	AL	Van Dijk 2 35p 51	11 209
	21	Melbourne	L	0-1	AL		9 904
	29	Wellington	W	4-1	AL	Reinaldo 2 17 56, Van Dijk 79, Dodd 90	6 307
Dec	6	Perth	D	1-1	AL	DeVere 52	7 217
	12	Adelaide	L	0-1	AL		5 801
	16	NQ Fury	W	2-0	AL	Van Dijk 2 20 42	11 530
	19	Cent. Coast	W	3-2	AL	Oar 10, Van Dijk 22, McKay 90	5 684
	26	Gold Coast	L	1-5	AL	McKay 7	10 024
	9	Wellington	L	1-3	AL	Van Dijk 88	8 125
Jan	16	Newcastle	L	0-2	AL		6 680
	23	NQ Fury	D	1-1	AL	DeVere 48	7 610
	30	Sydney	W	1-0	AL	Van Dijk 87	8 613
Feb	6	Adelaide	L	0-2	AL		8 244
	12	Perth	L	0-2	AL		8 054

BRISBANE LEAGUE APPEARANCES/GOALS 2009-10
Goalkeepers Matthew Ham 5 • Griffin McMaster 12 • Liam Reddy 10
Defenders Pieter Collen BEL 5/0 • Luke DeVere 22+2/2 • Ivan Franjic 19/0 • Josh McCloughlan 11+7/0 • Bob Malcolm SCO 11/0 • Craig Moore 19/1 • Matt Mundy 6+2/0 • Calum O'Connell 1/0 • Andrew Packer 7+3/0 • Danny Tiatto 12+2/1
Midfield Luke Brattan 0+1/0 • David Dodd 9+6/1 • Isaka Cernak 2+9/1 • Mario Karlovic 2+4/0 • Robbie Kruse 5/0 • Matt McKay 19/2 • Charlie Miller SCO 9+2/1 • Massimo Murdocca 7+2/0 • Mitch Nichols 10+10/1 • Adam Sarota 10+3/0 • Michael Zullo 10+3/0
Forwards Henrique BRA 16+2/3 • Tommy Oar 14+4/1 • Reinaldo BRA 15+3/4 • Tim Smits 0+5/0 • Sergio van Dijk IDN 27/13
Coach Frank Farina • Ange Postecoglou (16-10-2009)

CENTRAL COAST MARINERS 2009–10

Mon	Day	Opponent	Res	Score	Comp	Scorers	Att
Aug	6	Melbourne	W	2-0	AL	Simon 10, McGlinchey 15	18 855
Aug	14	Newcastle	D	1-1	AL	Boogaard 50	9 573
Aug	22	Sydney	D	0-0	AL		10 029
Aug	29	Brisbane	L	0-1	AL		6 433
Sep	4	Perth	W	2-1	AL	Wilkinson 42, Simon 89	5 139
Sep	11	Adelaide	L	0-1	AL		10 262
Sep	19	Gold Coast	W	3-0	AL	Travis 26, Simon 54, Hutchinson 70	7 943
Sep	27	Wellington	D	0-0	AL		6 769
Oct	5	Sydney	L	0-1	AL		13 887
Oct	11	NQ Fury	D	1-1	AL	Simon 1	8 043
Oct	17	Brisbane	W	3-0	AL	Travis 4, Hutchinson 18, Bojic 70	7 434
Oct	23	Newcastle	L	1-2	AL	Kwasnik 19	6 118
Oct	31	Adelaide	D	0-0	AL		5 437
Nov	7	Melbourne	W	4-0	AL	Kwasnik 15, Simon 75, Heffernan 81, Mrdja 83	18 531
Nov	21	NQ Fury	W	5-1	AL	Bojic 22, Mrdja 2 35 59, Elrich 61, Hutchinson 82	7 578
Nov	27	Perth	D	0-0	AL		7 875
Dec	5	Gold Coast	L	1-2	AL	Simon 39	4 117
Dec	12	Melbourne	L	0-3	AL		7 571
Dec	19	Brisbane	L	2-3	AL	Travis 34, Macallister 76	5 684
Dec	23	Sydney	L	0-1	AL		12 689
Dec	31	Wellington	L	0-2	AL		11 137
Jan	9	NQ Fury	D	1-1	AL	Mrdja 3	6 556
Jan	15	Adelaide	D	1-1	AL	Mrdja 39p	10 156
Jan	22	Gold Coast	D	1-1	AL	Mrdja 68p	5 724
Jan	31	Perth	L	1-3	AL	Kwasnik 49	8 160
Feb	8	Newcastle	W	3-0	AL	Boogaard 17, Kwasnik 50, Simon 72	5 842
Feb	12	Wellington	L	0-3	AL		14 327

GOLD COAST UNITED 2009–10

Mon	Day	Opponent	Res	Score	Comp	Scorers	Att
Aug	8	Brisbane	W	3-1	AL	Smeltz 18, Culina 58, Robson 90	19 902
Aug	15	NQ Fury	W	5-0	AL	Smeltz 4 29 54p 62 63, Minniecon 80	7 526
Aug	21	Adelaide	W	2-0	AL	Smeltz 12, Fitzsimmons 50	12 741
Aug	30	Newcastle	L	0-1	AL		6 390
Sep	5	Sydney	W	2-1	AL	Smeltz 2 45 56	6 406
Sep	13	Perth	D	2-2	AL	Van den Brink 52, Smeltz 90	9 408
Sep	19	Cent. Coast	L	0-3	AL		7 943
Sep	26	Melbourne	L	2-3	AL	Culina 18p, Porter 44	5 603
Oct	2	Wellington	D	0-0	AL		4 209
Oct	11	Brisbane	W	1-0	AL	Porter 31	8 882
Oct	18	Perth	W	2-1	AL	OG 12, Smeltz 56	4 905
Oct	25	Wellington	L	0-6	AL		6 571
Oct	31	NQ Fury	L	0-2	AL		2 616
Nov	7	Sydney	W	1-0	AL	Smeltz 36	5 364
Nov	20	Adelaide	D	1-1	AL	Fitzsimmons 64	9 578
Nov	28	Newcastle	L	0-4	AL		20 537
Dec	5	Cent. Coast	W	2-1	AL	Smeltz 68, Barisic 76	4 117
Dec	13	Newcastle	L	2-3	AL	Smeltz 2 44p 84	5 254
Dec	20	Perth	W	2-0	AL	Smeltz 4, Miller 76	4 310
Dec	26	Brisbane	W	5-1	AL	Smeltz 50p 61 77, Rees 2 45 53	10 024
Jan	9	Adelaide	D	1-1	AL	Smeltz 90	4 505
Jan	13	Newcastle	W	2-0	AL	Culina 33, Brown 38	4 853
Jan	17	Sydney	W	1-0	AL	Porter 19	14 941
Jan	22	Cent. Coast	D	1-1	AL	Porter 66	5 724
Jan	29	Melbourne	W	1-0	AL	Caravella 76	7 249
Feb	7	Wellington	L	0-1	AL		4 202
Feb	13	NQ Fury	L	1-2	AL	Porter 62	8 517
Feb	20	Newcastle	D	0-0	ALpo L 5-6		4 109

MARINERS LEAGUE APPEARANCES/GOALS 2009-10

Goalkeepers Andrew Redmayne 1 • Danny Vukovic 26
Defenders Pedj Bojic 23+2/2 • Nigel Boogaard 25/2 • Andrew Clark 9+8/0 • Chris Doig SCO 13/0 • Dean Heffernan 19+1/1 • Panagiotis Nikas 2+1/0 • Alex Wilkinson 27+1
Midfield Matty Crowell WAL 9+4/0 • David D'Apuzzo 1+1/0 • Ahmad Elrich 3+9/1 • Shane Huke 3/0 • John Hutchinson MLT 23/3 • Matthew Lewis 4+2/0 • Michael McGlinchey NZL 18+3/1 • Mitchell Mallia 0+1/0 • Bradley Porter 21+4/0
Forwards Bernie Ibini-Isei 0+1/0 • Adam Kwasnik 15+8/4 • Dylan Macallister 5+12/1 • Nik Mrdja 11+6/6 • Matt Simon 24+1/7 • Brady Smith 1+1/0 • Nicky Travis ENG 14+6/3
Coach Lawrie McKinna

GOLD COAST LEAGUE APPEARANCES/GOALS 2009-10

Goalkeepers Scott Higgins 10+1 • Jess Vanstrattan 18
Defenders Anderson BRA 20+7/0 • Zachary Anderson 1+1/0 • Mark Byrnes 0+1/0 • Dino Djulbic 5+3/0 • Adam Griffiths 1/0 • Daniel Piorkowski 2/0 • Kristian Rees 25+1/2 • Michael Thwaite 28/0 • Adama Traoré CIV 11/0 • Bas van den Brink NED 27/1 • Ben Wearing 1/0
Midfield Mitchell Bevan 0+1/0 • James Brown 2+7/1 • Zenon Caravella 21+3/1 • Jason Culina 26/3 • Steve Fitzsimmons 10+9/2 • Jefferson BRA 1/0 • Steve Lustica 1+1/0 • Charlie Miller SCO 8+2/1 • Matt Osman 5+10/0 • Steven Pantelidis 17+3/0 • Robson BRA 9+2/1
Forwards Andrew Barisic 1+5/1 • Gol Gol Mebrahtu 2+4/0 • Milson BRA 1+8/0 • Tahj Minniecon 7+10/1 • Joel Porter 22+2/5 • Shane Smeltz NZL 26/19
Coach Miron Bleiberg ISR

MELBOURNE VICTORY 2009–10

Aug	6	Cent. Coast	L	0-2	AL		18 855
	15	Brisbane	D	3-3	AL	Hernandez 2 [33 70], Allsopp [63]	18 603
	22	NQ Fury	W	1-0	AL	Thompson [45]	6 514
	28	Perth	L	1-2	AL	Thompson [9]	8 057
Sep	3	Newcastle	D	1-1	AL	Thompson [42]	15 168
	13	Wellington	D	1-1	AL	Hernandez [4]	17 644
	18	Adelaide	W	2-0	AL	Ward [7], Brebner [89]	15 038
	26	Gold Coast	W	3-2	AL	Hernandez [22], Thompson [43], Muscat [86p]	5 603
Oct	3	Brisbane	W	2-1	AL	Fabiano [4], Leijer [73]	19 587
	9	Sydney	L	0-3	AL		30 668
	18	Newcastle	W	3-1	AL	Thompson [62], Pondeljak [79], Hernandez [84]	6 029
	24	Adelaide	W	3-1	AL	Dugandzic 2 [18 56], Leijer [89]	21 182
Nov	1	Perth	W	2-1	AL	OG [6], Hernandez [68]	10 035
	6	Cent. Coast	L	0-4	AL		18 531
	20	Brisbane	W	1-0	AL	Thompson [8]	9 904
	28	Gold Coast	W	4-0	AL	Kruse [28], Ward [45], Thompson 2 [54 68]	20 537
Dec	4	Wellington	D	1-1	AL	Vargas [86]	8 200
	12	Cent. Coast	W	3-0	AL	Hernandez [57], Kemp [70], OG [77]	7 571
	19	Sydney	D	0-0	AL		27 344
	27	NQ Fury	L	0-1	AL		7 031
Jan	10	Newcastle	L	2-3	AL	Muscat [35p], Hernandez [90]	6 979
	16	Perth	W	6-2	AL	Thompson [4], Kruse 3 [12 26 39], Muscat [81p], Hernandez [83]	20 448
	23	Adelaide	W	2-0	AL	Pondeljak [1], Muscat [90p]	20 361
	26	Wellington	W	4-0	AL	OG [16], Thompson [50], Hernandez [65], Kemp [87]	18 819
	29	Gold Coast	L	0-1	AL		7 249
Feb	5	NQ Fury	W	2-0	AL	Hernandez 2 [35 66]	27 726
	14	Sydney	L	0-2	AL		25 407
	18	Sydney	W	2-1	ALsf	Mrdja [16], Hernandez [40]	18 453
	23	Beijing	L	0-1	CLgE		31 000
Mar	7	Sydney	D	2-2	ALsf	Kruse [15], Thompson [114]	23 818
	9	Seongnam	L	0-2	CLgE		7 899
	20	Sydney	D	1-1	ALf	Leijer [81]. L 2-4p	44 560
	23	Kawasaki	L	0-4	CLgE		9 728
	31	Kawasaki	W	1-0	CLgE	Muscat [60p]	6 011
Apr	14	Beijing	D	0-0	CLgE		6 394
	28	Seongnam	L	2-3	CLgE	Dugandzic [46], Pondeljak [77]	502

NEWCASTLE JETS 2009–10

Aug	9	Wellington	W	3-2	AL	Hoffman 2 [12 20], Naidovski [84]	6 654
	14	Cent. Coast	D	1-1	AL	Jin [47]	9 573
	23	Perth	L	0-2	AL		9 973
	30	Gold Coast	W	1-0	AL	Rooney [40]	6 390
Sep	3	Melbourne	D	1-1	AL	Haliti [87]	15 168
	12	Brisbane	L	0-3	AL		6 026
	20	Sydney	L	1-2	AL	Thompson [37]	10 357
	25	Perth	L	0-1	AL		4 738
Oct	5	Adelaide	D	1-1	AL	Jin [6]	12 090
	18	Melbourne	L	1-3	AL	Haliti [22]	6 029
	23	Cent. Coast	W	2-1	AL	Bridges [8], Haliti [14]	6 118
	30	Brisbane	D	1-1	AL	Haliti [32]	7 509
Nov	4	Wellington	L	0-3	AL		4 100
	8	NQ Fury	W	2-0	AL	Thompson [55], Bridges [85p]	6 127
	22	Wellington	L	0-1	AL		4 239
	29	Sydney	W	3-1	AL	Bridges 2 [24 51], Thompson [58]	10 114
Dec	4	Adelaide	W	2-0	AL	Thompson [45], Jin [81p]	8 502
	13	Gold Coast	W	3-2	AL	Wheelhouse [6], Rooney [70], Petrovski [81]	5 254
	20	NQ Fury	W	3-2	AL	OG [25], Jin [38], Petrovski [83]	7 026
	26	Perth	L	0-4	AL		9 418
Jan	10	Melbourne	W	3-2	AL	Thompson [26], Bridges [45], Haliti [56]	6 979
	13	Gold Coast	L	0-2	AL		4 853
	16	Brisbane	W	2-0	AL	Thompson [50], Bridges [55p]	6 680
	24	Sydney	L	1-3	AL	Wheelhouse [32]	9 892
Feb	2	NQ Fury	L	1-2	AL	Thompson [19]	4 156
	8	Cent. Coast	L	0-3	AL		5 842
	12	Adelaide	L	1-2	AL	Abbas [40]	6 880
	20	Gold Coast	D	0-0	ALpo	W 6-5p	4 109
	7	Wellington	L	1-3	ALsf	Thompson [20]	32 792

VICTORY LEAGUE APPEARANCES/GOALS 2009-10
Goalkeepers Mitchell Langerak 16 • Glen Moss NZL 14
Defenders Evan Berger 5+7/0 • Matthew Foschini 1+10/0 • Matthew Kemp 21+1/2 • Adrian Leijer 28/3 • Kevin Muscat 23/4 • Luke Pilkington 0+1/0 • Surat Sukha THA 15+3/0 • Rodrigo Vargas 29/1
Midfield Marvin Angulo CRC 5+5/0 • Aziz Behich 0+5/0 • Grant Brebner SCO 18+9/1 • Leigh Broxham 26+3/0 • Billy Celeski 3+2/0 • Mate Dugandzic 3+7/2 • Carlos Hernandez CRC 28/13 • Tom Pondeljak 19+4/2 • Nick Ward 17+5/2
Forwards Danny Allsopp 4/1 • Nathan Elasi 0+7/0 • Ney Fabiano BRA 7+7/1 • Robbie Kruse 17+3/5 • Nik Mrdja 2+1/1 • Sutee Suksomkit THA 4+5/0 • Archie Thompson 25+1/11
Coach Ernie Merrick

NEWCASTLE LEAGUE APPEARANCES/GOALS 2009-10
Goalkeepers Ben Kennedy 20+1 • Neil Young 9
Defenders Adam D'Apuzzo 25+2/0 • Angelo Costanzo 6+11/2 • Tarek Elrich 29/0 • Ljubo Milicevic 26/0 • Shaun Ontong 1/0 •
Midfield Ali Abbas IRQ 6+11/1 • Scott Balderson 0+1/0 • Labinot Haliti SRB 19+4/5 • Ben Kantarovski 15+1/0 • Kaz Patafta 7+13/0 • Song Jin Hyung KOR 28/4 • Chris Triantis 3/0 • Fabio Vignaroli ITA 14+1/0 • Jobe Wheelhouse 14+4/2
Forwards Michael Bridges ENG 15/6 • Donny de Groot NED 1+3/0 • Jason Hoffman 6+3/2 • Jason Naidovski 0+5/1 • Mirjan Pavlovic 1+2/0 • Sasho Petrovski 6+13/2 • Sean Rooney 11+7/2
Coach Branko Culina

NORTH QUEENSLAND FURY 2009–10

	Date	Opp	Res	Score		Scorers	Att
Aug	8	Sydney	L	2-3	AL	Griffiths [41], Fowler [60p]	8 897
	15	Gold Coast	L	0-5	AL		7 526
	22	Melbourne	L	0-1	AL		6 514
	28	Adelaide	D	3-3	AL	Fowler [5], Daal [83], McBreen [87]	10 773
Sep	5	Brisbane	D	1-1	AL	Fowler [7]	7 173
	12	Sydney	W	1-0	AL	Fowler [54]	16 699
	20	Wellington	D	1-1	AL	Grossman [90]	9 713
	27	Adelaide	L	0-2	AL		6 745
Oct	3	Perth	D	1-1	AL	Tambouras [71]	12 872
	11	Cent. Coast	D	1-1	AL	McBreen [75]	8 043
	17	Wellington	D	1-1	AL	Fowler [84]	6 191
	24	Perth	W	2-1	AL	Fowler [65], Daal [71]	6 332
	31	Gold Coast	W	2-0	AL	Fowler 2 [64 75p]	2 616
Nov	8	Newcastle	L	0-2	AL		6 127
	21	Cent. Coast	L	1-5	AL	Griffiths [68]	7 578
	28	Adelaide	W	2-1	AL	McBreen [39], Fowler [66]	5 356
Dec	5	Sydney	L	1-4	AL	Cooke [60]	11 871
	11	Perth	W	1-0	AL	Williams [33]	5 287
	16	Brisbane	L	0-2	AL		11 530
	20	Newcastle	L	2-3	AL	Daal 2 [44 61]	7 026
	27	Melbourne	W	1-0	AL	Daal [31]	7 031
Jan	9	Cent. Coast	D	1-1	AL	Brockie [19]	6 556
	15	Wellington	L	0-3	AL		7 727
	23	Brisbane	D	1-1	AL	Williams [55]	7 610
Feb	2	Newcastle	W	2-1	AL	Grossman [39], Tadrosse [80]	4 156
	5	Melbourne	L	0-2	AL		27 726
	13	Gold Coast	W	2-1	AL	Williams [8], Cooke [83]	8 517

PERTH GLORY 2009–10

	Date	Opp	Res	Score		Scorers	Att
Aug	7	Adelaide	L	0-1	AL		13 847
	16	Wellington	L	1-2	AL	Sikora [4]	10 024
	23	Newcastle	W	2-0	AL	Srhoj [23], Pelegrino [73]	9 973
	28	Melbourne	W	2-1	AL	Jelic 2 [4 54]	8 057
	4	Cent. Coast	L	1-2	AL	Sterjovski [82]	5 139
Sep	13	Gold Coast	D	2-2	AL	Jelic [14], Sikora [16]	9 408
	20	Brisbane	W	4-2	AL	OG [2], Srhoj [40], Jelic [60], Pelegrino [75]	7 367
	25	Newcastle	W	1-0	AL	Sterjovski [81p]	4 738
Oct	3	NQ Fury	D	1-1	AL	Sterjovski [49p]	12 872
	9	Adelaide	W	1-0	AL	Sikora [80]	9 482
	18	Gold Coast	L	1-2	AL	Howarth [55]	4 905
	24	NQ Fury	L	1-2	AL	Sikora [25]	6 332
Nov	1	Melbourne	L	1-2	AL	Sterjovski [19]	10 035
	8	Wellington	D	1-1	AL	Srhoj [69]	6 930
	22	Sydney	W	2-0	AL	Bulloch [57], Jelic [88]	8 932
	27	Cent. Coast	D	0-0	AL		7 875
Dec	6	Brisbane	D	1-1	AL	Harnwell [78]	7 217
	11	NQ Fury	L	0-1	AL		5 287
	20	Gold Coast	L	0-2	AL		4 310
	26	Newcastle	W	4-0	AL	Sekulovski [19], Harnwell 2 [24 69], Sterjovski [36]	9 418
	10	Sydney	D	0-0	AL		9 319
Jan	16	Melbourne	L	2-6	AL	OG [20], Sterjovski [53]	20 448
	19	Adelaide	W	3-2	AL	Burns 2 [63 69], McBreen [77]	8 904
	22	Wellington	W	2-0	AL	McBreen [22], Howarth [41]	9 638
	31	Cent. Coast	W	3-1	AL	McBreen 2 [1 13], Jukic [45]	8 160
Feb	7	Sydney	L	2-3	AL	Srhoj [45], McBreen [79]	8 359
	13	Brisbane	W	2-0	AL	Neville [9], Bulloch [73]	8 054
	21	Wellington	D	1-1	ALpo	Neville [67]. L 2-4	24 278

FURY LEAGUE APPEARANCES/GOALS 2009-10

Goalkeepers Paul Henderson 14 • Justin Pasfield 13
Defenders Beau Busch 8/0 • Karl Dodd 8/0 • Jimmy Downey 4/0 • Jack Hingert 6+1/0 • Kojiro Kaimoto 1+1/0 • Robbie Middleby 21/0 • Matt Smith 11/0 • Shane Stefanutto 7/0 • John Tambouras 16/1 • Scott Wilson SCO 3+1/0
Midfield Fred Agius 2+3/0 • Jeremy Brockie NZL 9+5/1 • Terry Cooke ENG 4+6/2 • Rostyn Griffiths 21+2/2 • Chris Grossman 13+9/2 • Paul Kohler 10+11/0 • Osama Malik 4+2/0 • James Robinson ENG 12+1/0 • Grant Smith SCO 4+1/0 • Jason Spagnuolo 8+11/0 • Chris Tadrosse 23/1 • Ufuk Talay 11/0
Forwards Dyron Daal ANT 8+14/5 • Robbie Fowler ENG 26/9 • Daniel McBreen 16+5/3 • David Williams 14+7/3
Coach Ian Ferguson SCO

PERTH GLORY LEAGUE APPEARANCES/GOALS 2009-10

Goalkeepers Tando Velaphi 25 • Alex Vrteski 3
Defenders Chris Coyne 25/0 • Jamie Coyne 23/0 • Jimmy Downey 0+3/0 • Jamie Harnwell 6+6/3 • Scott Neville 20+5/2 • Naum Sekulovski 27/1 • Andy Todd ENG 26/0
Midfield Amaral BRA 0+2/0 • Scott Bulloch 1+13/2 • Jacob Burns 24/2 • Todd Howarth 17+9/2 • Andrija Jukic 3+13/1 • Steven McGarry SCO 6/0 • Adriano Pellegrino 25+2/2 • Wayne Srhoj 19+2/4
Forwards Tommy Amphlett 0+5/0 • Ludovic Boi 0+1/0 • Eugene Dadi CIV 3+3/0 • Branko Jelic SRB 14+4/5 • Daniel McBreen 6+1/5 • Matthew Mayora 0+4/0 • Victor Sikora NED 15+2/4 • Mile Sterjovski 20+3/6
Coach David Mitchell

SYDNEY FC 2009–10

Aug	8	NQ Fury	W	3-2	AL	Aloisi 2 [4 73p], Danning [28]	8 897
	16	Adelaide	W	1-0	AL	Bridge [77]	14 942
	22	Cent. Coast	D	0-0	AL		10 029
	30	Wellington	W	2-0	AL	Gan [77], Aloisi [81]	11 718
Sep	5	Gold Coast	L	1-2	AL	Corica [75]	6 406
	12	NQ Fury	L	0-1	AL		16 699
	20	Newcastle	W	2-1	AL	Bridge [26], Corica [55p]	10 357
	27	Brisbane	L	0-1	AL		7 677
Oct	5	Cent. Coast	W	1-0	AL	McFlynn [21]	13 887
	9	Melbourne	W	3-0	AL	Brosque [15], Bridge [16 19]	30 668
	16	Adelaide	L	1-2	AL	Aloisi [78]	10 291
	25	Brisbane	W	2-1	AL	Brosque [54], Kisel [69]	8 456
Nov	1	Wellington	W	3-1	AL	Bridge 2 [15 35], Corica [31]	10 653
	7	Gold Coast	L	0-1	AL		5 364
	22	Perth	L	0-2	AL		8 932
	29	Newcastle	L	1-3	AL	Brosque [75]	10 114
Dec	5	NQ Fury	W	4-1	AL	Aloisi [14], Brosque 2 [19 58], Corica [64]	11 871
	12	Wellington	W	1-0	AL	Corica [16p]	6 936
	19	Melbourne	D	0-0	AL		27 344
	23	Cent. Coast	W	1-0	AL	Brosque [34]	12 689
	27	Adelaide	W	1-0	AL	Corica [49]	11 741
Jan	10	Perth	D	0-0	AL		9 319
	17	Gold Coast	L	0-1	AL		14 941
	24	Newcastle	W	3-1	AL	Aloisi [45], Musialik [50], Payne [90]	9 892
	30	Brisbane	L	0-1	AL		8 613
Feb	7	Perth	W	3-2	AL	Corica [24p], Aloisi 2 [50 87]	8 359
	14	Melbourne	W	2-0	AL	Kisel [34], Aloisi [49]	25 407
	18	Melbourne	L	1-2	ALsf	Aloisi [42]	18 453
Mar	7	Melbourne	D	2-2	ALsf	Kisel [36p], Bridge [54]	23 818
	13	Wellington	W	4-2	ALsf	Payne 2 [21 30], Brosque [62], Bridge [71]	13 196
	20	Melbourne	D	1-1	ALf	Bridge [63]. W 4-2p	44 560

WELLINGTON PHOENIX 2009–10

Aug	9	Newcastle	L	2-3	AL	Sigmund [26], Greenacre [43]	6 654
	16	Perth	W	2-1	AL	Ifill [25], Bertos [88]	10 024
	23	Brisbane	D	1-1	AL	Greenacre [85]	7 084
	30	Sydney	L	0-2	AL		11 718
Sep	4	Adelaide	D	1-1	AL	Ifill [34]	7 578
	13	Melbourne	D	1-1	AL	Hernandez [4]	17 644
	20	NQ Fury	D	1-1	AL	Bertos [6]	9 713
	27	Cent. Coast	D	0-0	AL		6 769
Oct	2	Gold Coast	D	0-0	AL		4 209
	17	NQ Fury	D	1-1	AL	Brown [6]	6 191
	25	Gold Coast	W	6-0	AL	Daniel 2 [28 52], Brown [48], Greenacre [53], Ifill [60], Hearfield [82]	6 571
Nov	1	Sydney	L	1-3	AL	Barbarouses [81]	10 653
	4	Newcastle	W	3-0	AL	Brown [27], Greenacre [55], Ifill [90]	4 100
	8	Perth	D	1-1	AL	Ifill [82]	6 930
	22	Newcastle	W	1-0	AL	Ifill [13]	4 239
	29	Brisbane	L	1-4	AL	Greenacre [27]	6 307
	4	Melbourne	D	1-1	AL	Brown [57]	8 200
Dec	12	Sydney	L	0-1	AL		6 936
	18	Adelaide	D	1-1	AL	Caceres [77]	9 070
	31	Cent. Coast	W	2-0	AL	Ifill 2 [47p 80]	11 137
Jan	9	Brisbane	W	3-1	AL	Brown [26], Dadi 2 [55 61]	8 125
	15	NQ Fury	W	3-0	AL	Dadi [47], Ifill [78], McKain [90]	7 727
	22	Perth	L	0-2	AL		9 638
	26	Melbourne	L	0-4	AL		18 819
	30	Adelaide	W	1-0	AL	McKain [21]	19 258
Feb	7	Gold Coast	W	1-0	AL	Ifill [45p]	4 202
	12	Cent. Coast	W	3-0	AL	Brown [14], Ifill 2 [79 80]	14 327
	21	Perth	D	1-1	ALpo	Greenacre [37]. W 4-2p	24 278
Mar	7	Newcastle	W	3-1	ALsf	Brown [33], Ifill [105], Dadi [115]	32 792
	13	Sydney	L	2-4	ALsf	Durante [25], Dadi [80]	13 196

SYDNEY LEAGUE APPEARANCES/GOALS 2009-10
Goalkeepers Clint Bolton **31**
Defenders Byun Sung Hwan KOR **31/0** • Shannon Cole **26+3/0** • Simon Colosimo **29/0** • Hayden Foxe **0+9/0** • Anthony Golec **1+2/0** • Rhyan Grant **3+6/0** • Matthew Jurman **0+7/0** • Stephan Keller SUI **24+1/0** • Sebastian Ryall **13+5/0**
Midfield Adam Casey **1+2/0** • Steve Corica **23+3/7** • Brendan Gan **4+15/1** • Karol Kisel SVK **29/3** • Terry McFlynn NIR **27/1** • Stuart Musialik **25/1** • Iain Ramsay **0+1/0**
Forwards John Aloisi **16+8/10** • Mark Bridge **20+3/9** • Alex Brosque **29/7** • Kofi Danning **4+3/1** • Joe Gibbs **0+1/0** • Chris Payne **2+12/3**
Coach Vitezslav Lavicka CZE

WELLINGTON LEAGUE APPEARANCES/GOALS 2009-10
Goalkeepers Reece Crowther USA **5+1** • Mark Paston NZL **13** • Liam Reddy AUS **12**
Defenders Andrew Durante AUS **30/1** • Tony Lochhead NZL **28/0** • Jon McKain AUS **18+1/2** • Manny Muscat MLT **25+1/0** • Ben Sigmund NZL **19/2**
Midfield Leo Bertos NZL **25+5/2** • Tim Brown NZL **27/8** • Adrian Caceres ARG **6+13/1** • Daniel BRA **14+8/2** • Diego BRA **5+7/0** • Michael Ferrante **3+3/0** • Troy Hearfield AUS **16+13/1** • Vince Lia AUS **23+3/0** • Marco Rojas NZL **0+4/0**
Forwards Kosta Barbarouses NZL **3+10/1** • Chen Jiang CHN **0+2/0** • Eugène Dadi CIV **5+5/5** • Chris Greenacre ENG **23+1/6** • Paul Ifill BRB **30/13**
Coach Ricki Herbert NZL

AUT – AUSTRIA

FIFA/COCA-COLA WORLD RANKING

1993	1994	1995	1996	1997	1998	1999	2000	2001	2002	2003	2004	2005	2006	2007	2008	2009	2010
36	49	39	34	25	22	28	44	56	65	67	83	69	65	94	92	61	46

						2010						Hi/Lo
Jan	Feb	Mar	Mar	Apr	May	Jul	Aug	Sep	Oct	Nov	Dec	17
61	61	56	55	64	68	60	60	61	49	49	46	105

The 2010 Bundesliga went right down to the wire with Salzburg, FK Austria and Rapid all in with a chance going into the final round of matches. Salzburg had lost two and drawn two of their five previous matches - including a last minute 1-0 defeat at home to FK Austria four days earlier - to throw the race wide open again, but they held their nerve to win a tricky match away to Sturm Graz 2-0 and claim their sixth title - their third in the five years since the club was bought by Red Bull owner Dietrich Mateschitz. Having won the title, coach Huub Stevens immediately stated that qualification for the UEFA Champions League group stage was the priority, but once again Salzburg fell short in the 2010-11 tournament, losing to Israeli opposition for the second year running in the play-off round. With the drive and energy of a company like Red Bull behind them, Salzburg's time is sure to come, although they still don't have it all their way at home. They have yet to win the Austrian Cup which was won in 2010 by Sturm Graz, 1-0 victors over Wiener Neustadt in the final. The national team continues to find its feet under coach Dietmar Constantini who has placed the emphasis on bringing younger players into the team. Showing a new fighting spirit, four of the nine goals in their opening three Euro 2012 matches were scored in injury-time.

FIFA WORLD CUP RECORD

1930 DNE **1934** 4 SF **1938** Qualified but did not take part 1950 DNE **1954** 3 SF **1958** 15 r1 1962 DNE
1966-1974 DNQ **1978** 7 r2 **1982** 7 r2 1986 DNQ **1990** 18 r1 1994 DNQ **1998** 23 r1 2002-2010 DNQ

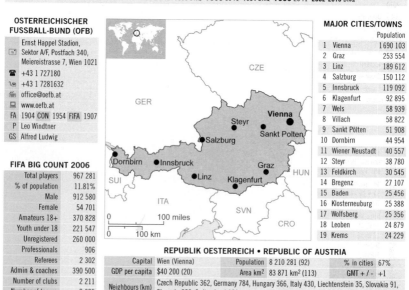

OSTERREICHISCHER
FUSSBALL-BUND (OFB)

Ernst Happel Stadion,
Sektor A/F, Postfach 340,
Meiereistrasse 7, Wien 1021
☎ +43 1 727180
📠 +43 1 7281632
✉ office@oefb.at
🖥 www.oefb.at
FA 1904 CON 1954 FIFA 1907
P Leo Windtner
GS Alfred Ludwig

FIFA BIG COUNT 2006

Total players	967 281
% of population	11.81%
Male	912 580
Female	54 701
Amateurs 18+	370 828
Youth under 18	221 547
Unregistered	260 000
Professionals	906
Referees	2 302
Admin & coaches	390 500
Number of clubs	2 211
Number of teams	9 685

MAJOR CITIES/TOWNS

		Population
1	Vienna	1 690 103
2	Graz	253 554
3	Linz	189 612
4	Salzburg	150 112
5	Innsbruck	119 092
6	Klagenfurt	92 895
7	Wels	58 939
8	Villach	58 822
9	Sankt Pölten	51 908
10	Dornbirn	44 954
11	Wiener Neustadt	40 557
12	Steyr	38 780
13	Feldkirch	30 545
14	Bregenz	27 107
15	Baden	25 456
16	Klosterneuburg	25 388
17	Wolfsberg	25 356
18	Leoben	24 879
19	Krems	24 229

REPUBLIK OESTERREICH • REPUBLIC OF AUSTRIA

Capital	Wien (Vienna)	Population	8 210 281 (92)	% in cities	67%
GDP per capita	$40 200 (20)	Area km²	83 871 km² (113)	GMT +/-	+1
Neighbours (km)	Czech Republic 362, Germany 784, Hungary 366, Italy 430, Liechtenstein 35, Slovakia 91, Slovenia 330, Switzerland 164				

RECENT INTERNATIONALS PLAYED BY AUSTRIA

2007	Opponents	Score		Venue	Comp	Scorers	Att	Referee
22-08	Czech Republic	D	1-1	Vienna	Fr	Harnik [78]	24 500	Mejuto Gonzalez ESP
7-09	Japan	D	0-0	Klagenfurt	Fr	W 4-3p	26 142	Merk GER
11-09	Chile	L	0-2	Vienna	Fr			Granat POL
13-10	Switzerland	L	1-3	Zürich	Fr	Aufhauser [11]	22 500	Hamer LUX
17-10	Côte d'Ivoire	W	3-2	Innsbruck	Fr	Kuljic [30p], Ivanschitz [64p], Standfest [74]	30 000	Kuipers NED
16-11	England	L	0-1	Vienna	Fr		39 432	Vollquartz DEN
21-11	Tunisia	D	0-0	Vienna	Fr		13 800	Olsiak SVK
2008								
6-02	Germany	L	0-3	Vienna	Fr		48 500	Dondarini ITA
26-03	Netherlands	L	3-4	Vienna	Fr	Ivanschitz [6], Prodl 2 [18 35]	40 500	Hansson SWE
27-05	Nigeria	D	1-1	Graz	Fr	Kienast [12]	15 000	Gumienny BEL
30-05	Malta	W	5-1	Graz	Fr	Aufhauser [8], Linz 2 [11 67p], Vastic [77], Harnik [90]	14 200	Krajnc SVN
8-06	Croatia	L	0-1	Vienna	ECr1		51 428	Vink NED
12-06	Poland	D	1-1	Vienna	ECr1	Vastic [93+]	51 428	Webb ENG
16-06	Germany	L	0-1	Vienna	ECr1		51 428	Mejuto Gonzalez ESP
20-08	Italy	D	2-2	Nice	Fr	Pogatetz [15], Janko [39]	14 000	Coue FRA
6-09	France	W	3-1	Vienna	WCq	Janko [8], Aufhauser [41], Ivanschitz [72p]	48 000	Larsen DEN
10-09	Lithuania	L	0-2	Marijampole	WCq		4 500	Tagliavento ITA
11-10	Faroe Islands	D	1-1	Torshavn	WCq	Stranzl [49]	1 890	Ceferin SVN
15-10	Serbia	L	1-3	Vienna	WCq	Janko [80]	47 998	Riley ENG
19-11	Turkey	L	2-4	Vienna	Fr	Holzl 2 [28 53]	23 100	Grafe GER
2009								
11-02	Sweden	L	0-2	Graz	Fr		11 800	Kassai HUN
1-04	Romania	W	2-1	Klagenfurt	WCq	Hoffer 2 [26 44]	23 000	Thomas SCO
6-06	Serbia	L	0-1	Belgrade	WCq		41 000	Vink NED
12-08	Cameroon	L	0-2	Klagenfurt	Fr		28 800	Olsiak SVK
5-09	Faroe Islands	W	3-1	Graz	WCq	Maierhofer [1], Janko 2 [15 58p]	12 300	Borg MLT
9-09	Romania	D	1-1	Bucharest	WCq	Schiemer [83]	7 505	Atkinson ENG
10-10	Lithuania	W	2-1	Innsbruck	WCq	Janko [16], Wallner [80p]	14 200	Gumienny BEL
14-10	France	L	1-3	Paris	WCq	Janko [49]	78 099	Proença POR
18-11	Spain	L	1-5	Vienna	Fr	Jantscher [8]	32 000	Meyer GER
2010								
3-03	Denmark	W	2-1	Vienna	Fr	Schiemer [11], Wallner [37]	13 500	Kralovec CZE
19-05	Croatia	L	0-1	Klagenfurt	Fr		20 000	Blom NED
11-08	Switzerland	L	0-1	Klagenfurt	Fr		18 000	Rubinos ESP
7-09	Kazakhstan	W	2-0	Salzburg	ECq	Linz [91+], Hoffer [92+]	22 500	Strahonja CRO
8-10	Azerbaijan	W	3-0	Vienna	ECq	Prodl [3], Arnautovic 2 [53 92+]	26 500	Vollquartz DEN
12-10	Belgium	D	4-4	Brussels	ECq	Schiemer 2 [14 62], Arnautovic [29], Harnik [93+]	24 231	Dean ENG
17-11	Greece	L	1-2	Vienna	Fr	Fuchs [67]	16 200	Kever SUI

Fr = Friendly match • EC = UEFA EURO 2008/2012 • WC = FIFA World Cup • q = qualifier • r1 = first round group

AUSTRIA NATIONAL TEAM HISTORICAL RECORDS

Caps
103 - Andreas Herzog 1988-2003 • 95 - Anton Polster 1982-2000 • 93 - Gerhard Hanappi 1948-62 • 86 - Karl Koller 1952-65 • 84 - Friedl Koncilia 1970-85 & Bruno Pezzey 1975-90 • 83 - Herbert Prohaska 1974-89 • 69 - Hans Krankl 1973-85 • 68 - Heribert Weber 1976-89 • 65 - Peter Stöger 1988-99 • 64 - Walter Schachner 1976-94 • 63 - Andreas Ogris 1986-97, Anton Pfeffer 1988-99 & Peter Schöttel

Goals
44 - Anton Polster 1982-2000 • 34 - Hans Krankl 1973-85 • 29 - Hans Horvath 1924-34 • 28 - Eric Hof 1957-69 • 27 - Anton Schall 1927-34 • 26 - Matthias Sindelar 1926-37 & Andreas Herzog 1988-2003 • 24 - Karl Zischek 1931-45 • 23 - Walter Schachner 1976-94 • 22 - Theodor Wagner 1946-57 • 19 - Karl Decker 1945-52 • 18 - Erich Probst 1951-60, Ferdinand Swatosch 1914-25 & Jan Studnicka 1902-18

Past Coaches
Hugo Meisl 1912-1914 • Heinrich Retschury 1914-19 • Hugo Meisl 1919-37 • Heinrich Retschury 1937 • Karl Zankl 1945 • Edi Bauer 1945-48 • Eduard Frühwirth 1948 • Walter Nausch 1948-54 (1954 World Cup) • Hans Kaulich 1954-55 • Josef Molzer 1955 • Karl Geyer 1955-56 • Josef Argauer & Josef Molzer 1956-58 (1958 World Cup) • Alfred Frey, Franz Putzendopler, Egon Selzer & Josef Molzer 1958 • Karl Decker 1958-64 • Josef Walter & Bela Guttmann HUN 1964 • Eduard Frühwirth 1964-67 • Erwin Alge & Hans Pesser 1967-68 • Leopold Stasny CZE 1968-75 • Branko Elsner YUG 1975 • Helmut Senekowitsch 1976-78 (1978 World Cup) • Karl Stotz 1978-81 • Georg Schmidt & Felix Latzke 1982 (1982 World Cup) • Erich Hof 1982-84 • Branko Elsner YUG 1985-87 • Josef Hickersberger 1988-90 (1990 World Cup) • Alfred Riedl 1990-91 • Dietmar Constantini 1991 • Ernst Happel 1992 • Dietmar Constantini 1992 • Herbert Prohaska 1993-99 (1998 World Cup) • Otto Bari 1999-2001 • Hans Krankl 2002-05 • Willibald Ruttensteiner, Andreas Herzog & Slavko Kovacic 2005 • Josef Hickersberger 2006-08 (Euro 2008) • Karel Bruckner CZE 2008-09 • Dietmar Constantini 2009-

AUSTRIA 2009-10

TIPP 3 BUNDESLIGA POWERED BY T-MOBILE

	Pl	W	D	L	F	A	Pts	Salzburg	FK Austria	Rapid	Sturm	W Neustadt	Mattersburg	LASK	Reid	Kapfenburg	Kärnten
RB Austria Salzburg †	36	22	10	4	68	27	76		2-1 0-1	0-0 1-1	4-2 3-0	1-1 4-2	2-0 2-0	3-2 3-0	1-1 2-0	4-0 1-0	7-1 1-0
FK Austria Wien ‡	36	23	6	7	60	34	75	1-0 1-1		1-1 1-0	1-0 1-0	2-1 1-0	1-0 5-1	3-0 0-1	1-1 2-0	3-0 4-3	1-0 4-1
SK Rapid Wien ‡	36	21	10	5	80	38	73	2-2 0-1	4-1 2-0		2-1 4-1	3-1 3-0	4-0 3-1	4-1 0-0	1-0 2-1	3-1 5-5	5-1 1-0
SK Sturm Graz ‡	36	16	10	10	50	36	58	0-0 0-2	0-1 2-2	1-0 1-1		3-0 1-0	2-0 4-0	3-3 0-1	0-2 1-0	0-1 1-1	4-0 3-2
SCM Wiener Neustadt	36	13	8	15	54	58	47	1-1 2-3	4-3 0-1	0-4 2-2	0-0 0-0		3-0 2-1	4-1 4-0	2-1 2-0	2-3 3-1	3-1 2-1
SV Mattersburg	36	12	5	19	45	71	41	2-3 1-6	1-3 1-1	2-1 1-1	3-0 2-0	0-1 3-1		3-2 2-1	3-0 3-1	4-1 3-1	4-1 1-1
LASK Linz	36	9	13	14	59	70	40	0-0 0-0	4-5 0-1	3-3 4-2	2-2 1-2	4-2 1-1	4-0 2-0		2-2 3-0	4-0 1-1	3-1 0-0
SV Ried	36	10	8	18	39	47	38	0-1 0-2	0-2 0-1	1-1 1-3	1-2 1-2	3-0 0-1	0-0 3-0	5-2 2-2		3-0 2-1	1-0 3-1
SV Kapfenberg	36	8	9	19	44	67	33	0-2 2-0	1-0 1-1	0-1 2-2	0-1 0-3	3-1 2-3	0-1 2-2	7-2 2-0	0-1 1-1		3-2 0-0
SK Austria Kärnten	36	2	9	25	29	80	15	1-2 0-2	2-1 0-2	1-3 2-4	1-3 0-3	0-0 2-2	0-3 2-4	1-1 2-2	0-0 1-0	1-1 0-1	

17/07/2009 - 13/05/2010 • † Qualified for the UEFA Champions League • ‡ Qualified for the Europa League • Kärnten relegated to the third level
Top scorers: **20** - Steffen Hofmann GER, Rapid • **19** - Roman Wallner, Lask/Salzburg • **18** - Marc Janko, Salzburg & Nikica Jelavic CRO, Rapid • **17** - Hamdi Salihi ALB, Rapid • **14** - Robert Waltner HUN, Mattersburg • **11** - Daniel Beichler, Sturm

AUSTRIA 2009-10

ADEG ERSTE LIGA (2)

	Pl	W	D	L	F	A	Pts	Wacker	Admira	Rheindorf	Sankt Pölten	SC Lustenau	RB Salzburg	Gratkorn	FC Lustenau	Hartberg	FK Austria	First Vienna	Dornbirn
FC Wacker Innsbruck	33	21	6	6	67	26	69		0-1 1-0	2-1	2-2 2-1	5-0	2-1	0-0	2-1 1-0	6-0 1-0	2-0	3-0	7-0 2-0
FCT Admira	33	20	7	6	68	22	67	0-0		2-2 2-0	0-0 1-0	2-1	3-0 1-0	3-0	0-1 3-4	0-1	1-1 2-1	2-0 3-0	4-0
SC Rheindorf Altach	33	20	6	7	60	27	66	4-1 3-0	0-0		0-3	1-2 2-0	3-1 2-0	4-2	1-1 4-1	4-0	3-1 1-2	3-0 0-0	2-0
SKN Sankt Pölten	33	14	9	10	44	42	51	1-0	1-0 2-4	1-0 0-2		0-4 1-1 2-2	2-0	3-2	2-0 3-0	2-0	0-3	1-1 0-2	2-0
SC Austria Lustenau	33	15	5	13	43	46	50	2-2 2-2	1-0	0-2	1-0		2-1	2-1	0-2 4-1 1-2	0-3 3-3	0-1 0-2	2-1	3-0 1-0
RB Salzburg Amateure	33	13	5	15	58	49	44	3-3 1-5	1-3	1-2	3-3	4-0 3-0		3-3 1-2	1-3	7-0	1-1 2-0	2-1 5-1	4-2
FC Gratkorn	33	11	10	12	57	51	43	0-3	0-1 2-3	1-1	2-4 1-1	1-1	2-2		1-2	3-2	0-0 1-2	4-0 1-1	1-2 5-0
FC Lustenau	33	12	5	16	42	52	41	0-1	0-3	0-1	0-0	1-2	0-2 0-2	3-3 0-1		2-2 3-1	3-0 3-1	2-0 1-0	1-2 0-1 2-0
TSV Hartberg	33	11	5	17	36	68	38	0-2	0-3 0-4	0-2	1-0 1-1	1-2	2-0	2-1 2-1	0-3		1-0	2-2	1-5 5-3 2-0
FK Austria Amateure	33	9	8	16	42	57	35	0-5 2-1	2-2	0-1	4-1 1-3	0-0	1-0	0-0 2-3	3-0 1-2	2-3 3-2		1-4	1-1 2-1
First Vienna FC	33	8	6	19	37	57	30	1-3 0-1	0-4	0-0	0-2 1-0	0-2 1-0	1-2 4-2	1-1 1-3	2-0 1-2	0-1	2-2 2-2		2-0
FC Dornbirn 1913	33	6	4	23	24	81	22	0-3	0-4 1-8	0-2	0-4 0-3	0-0	3-2	0-1 0-2	1-2	2-0	1-1	2-1 2-1 2-1	

13/07/2009 - 28/05/2010 • Both RB Salzburg and FK Austria's reserve teams were relegated

MEDALS TABLE

		Overall			League			Cup		Europe			
		G	S	B	G	S	B	G	S	G	S	B	
1	FK Austria Wien	52	28	17	23	18	13	27	9	2	1	4	
2	SK Rapid Wien	47	39	22	32	23	20	14	12	1	4	2	
3	FC Wacker Tirol	17	11	7	10	5	6	7	6				
4	Admira Wien	13	6	6	8	5	5	5			1	1	1905-71
5	First Vienna FC	10	12	13	6	6	11	3	6	1		2	
6	RB Austria Salzburg	6	10	1	6	5	1		4		1		
7	SK Sturm Graz	6	9	4	2	5	4	4	4				
8	Grazer AK	5	4	6	1	2	6	4	2				
9	Wiener Sport-Club	4	14	5	3	7	5	1	7				
10	Wiener AC	4	5	6	1	1	6	3	3		1		
11	Wacker Wien	2	8	3	1	7	3	1	1				1908-71
12	Linzer ASK	2	5	4	1	1	4	1	4				
13	Wiener AF	2	2	3	1	2	3	1					1912-35
14	FC Linz	1	4	1	1	2	1		2				1949-97
15	Floridsdorfer AC	1	3	1	1	3	1						
16	FC Kärnten	1	1					1	1				
	Hakoah Wien	1	1		1	1							1901-39
	SV Ried	1	1					1					
19	Kremser SC	1						1					
	SV Stockerau	1						1					

European medals include those won in the Mitropa Cup 1927-1939

OFB POKAL 2009-10

Second Round

SK Sturm Graz	1	
WSG Wattens *	0	
SV Grödig *	0	
RB Austria Salzburg	1	
FC Gratkorn	2	5p
RB Salzburg Amateure *	2	3p
SAK Klagenfurt *	1	
FCT Admira	3	
SC Austria Lustenau	3	
SVL Flavia Solva *	1	
SPG Reichenau *	1	
FC Wacker Innsbruck	4	
FC Dornbirn 1913 *	3	
TSV Hartberg	1	
SK Sturm Graz Amateure *	1	
SV Ried	2	
SK Austria Kärnten	2	
USV Allerheiligen *	1	
FCT Admira Amateure *	0	
First Vienna FC	2	
Blau Weiß Linz *	2	5p
FK Austria Amateure	2	4p
FC Sankt Veit *	1	
SK Rapid Wien	7	
LASK Linz	3	
ASK Kottingbrunn *	1	
FAC Team für Wien *	0	
FK Austria Wien	6	
FC Lustenau	2	
Grazer AK *	0	
FC Superfund Pasching *	2	2p
SCM Wiener Neustadt	2	4p

Round of 16

SK Sturm Graz *	2	
RB Austria Salzburg	0	
FC Gratkorn	0	2p
FCT Admira *	0	4p
SC Austria Lustenau	1	
FC Wacker Innsbruck *	0	
FC Dornbirn 1913 *	0	
SV Ried	2	
SK Austria Kärnten *	3	
First Vienna FC	2	
Blau Weiß Linz *	1	
SK Rapid Wien	2	
LASK Linz *	1	
FK Austria Wien	0	
FC Lustenau *	1	
SCM Wiener Neustadt	3	

Quarter-finals

SK Sturm Graz *	1	
FCT Admira	0	
SC Austria Lustenau	1	2p
SV Ried *	1	4p
SK Austria Kärnten *	3	
SK Rapid Wien	2	
LASK Linz	1	
SCM Wiener Neustadt *	2	

Semi-finals

SK Sturm Graz	1
SV Ried *	0
SK Austria Kärnten *	0
SCM Wiener Neustadt	4

Final

SK Sturm Graz ‡	1
SCM Wiener Neustadt	0

CUP FINAL

Hypo-Arena, Klagenfurt, 16-05-2010, 16:30
Att: 28 000, Ref: Gerhard Grobelnik
Scorers – Lavric 81 for Sturm
Sturm – Christian Gratzei - Fabian Lamotte, Mario Sonnleitner, Ilia Kandelaki, Gordon Schildenfeld, Manuel Weber, Jakob Jantscher (Mario Haas 78), Mario Kienzl, Klaus Salmutter (Daniel Beichler 56), Roman Kienast (Samir Muratovic 74), Klemen Lavric. Tr: Franco Foda
Wiener Neustadt – Saso Fornezzi - Pavel Kostal●, Ronald Gercaliu, Petr Johana● (Mario Reiter 51), Christian Ramsebner, Michael Stanislaw, Alexander Grünwald●, Tomas Simkovic, Patrick Wolf (Vaclav Koloušek 83), Mirnel Sadovic (Diego Viana 60), Hannes Aigner. Tr: Peter Schöttel

* Home team ● ‡ Qualified for the Europa League

AZE – AZERBAIJAN

FIFA/COCA-COLA WORLD RANKING

1993	1994	1995	1996	1997	1998	1999	2000	2001	2002	2003	2004	2005	2006	2007	2008	2009	2010
-	147	141	125	123	99	97	115	113	113	119	113	114	125	115	134	114	98

2010												Hi/Lo
Jan	Feb	Mar	Mar	Apr	May	Jul	Aug	Sep	Oct	Nov	Dec	90
114	114	109	110	110	109	106	105	102	91	90	98	170

Although Azerbaijan's spectacular 1-0 victory over Turkey in the qualifiers for Euro 2012 is unlikely to see them launch a successful bid to reach the finals in Poland and Ukraine, it was nevertheless one of the finest results in the short history of the Azeri national team. Masterminded by the veteran Berti Vogts, it came, however, hot on the heels of two heavy defeats away to Germany and to Austria in one of the more difficult groups in the qualifiers. The hope is that results like this, and the draw at home to Russia 12 months earlier, can be used as a springboard to realise the undoubted potential that exists in the country and with a booming economy there are the resources to back up the federation's development plans. At club level Inter Baku reclaimed the league title from rivals FK Baku but it was an extraordinarily tight climax to the season with just one point separating the top four going into the final round of fixtures. Khazar Lenkoran saw their title hopes go up in smoke after losing 1-0 at home to FK Baku, while Inter beat Gabala 4-1 to secure their second title in three years. A week later there was more misery for Khazar in the Cup Final and again it was FK Baku who were responsible, beating them 2-1 in a match that went into extra-time. It was FK Baku's second cup triumph and their first since 2005.

FIFA WORLD CUP RECORD
1930-1994 DNE **1998-2010** DNQ

ASSOCIATION OF FOOTBALL FEDERATIONS OF AZERBAIJAN (AFFA)

2208 Nobel prospekti, Baku AZ-1025
☎ +994 12 4908721
📠 +994 12 4908722
📧 info@affa.az
🖥 www.affa.az
FA 1992 CON 1994 FIFA 1994
P Rovnag Abdullayev
GS Elkhan Mammadov

FIFA BIG COUNT 2006

Total players	306 370
% of population	3.85%
Male	267 900
Female	38 470
Amateurs 18+	3 150
Youth under 18	14 120
Unregistered	82 700
Professionals	400
Referees	100
Admin & coaches	12 900
Number of clubs	80
Number of teams	320

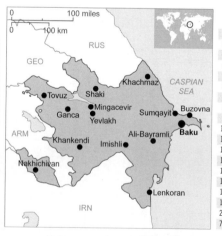

MAJOR CITIES/TOWNS

		Population
1	Baku	1 194 524
2	Gãncã	323 760
3	Sumqayit	282 280
4	Mingãçevir	100 778
5	Qaraçuxur	78 730
6	Ali Bayramli	76 648
7	Naxçivan	75 972
8	Bakikhanov	71 836
9	Shãki	65 616
10	Yevlakh	57 449
11	Xankãndi	55 282
12	Lenkoran	50 534
13	Rãsulzadã	48 716
14	Bilãcãri	45 678
15	Mastaga	42 635
16	Agdam	42 587
17	Barda	40 741
22	Shamkir	38 331
70	Tovuz	13 612

AZARBAYCAN RESPUBLIKASI • REPUBLIC OF AZERBAIJAN

Capital	Baku	Population	8 238 672 (91)	% in cities	52%
GDP per capita	$9 500 (107)	Area km²	86 600 km² (112)	GMT + / -	+5
Neighbours (km)	Armenia 787, Georgia 322, Iran 611, Russia 284, Turkey 9 • Coast 713 (Caspian Sea)				

RECENT INTERNATIONALS PLAYED BY AZERBAIJAN

2007	Opponents	Score		Venue	Comp	Scorers	Att	Referee
22-08	Tajikistan	W	3-2	Dushanbe	Fr	Aliyev.S 2 [25] [29], Branimir Subasic [43]		
12-09	Georgia	D	1-1	Baku	Fr	Branimir Subasic [44]	10 000	Kovalenko UZB
13-10	Portugal	L	0-2	Baku	ECq		25 000	Bebek CRO
17-10	Serbia	L	1-6	Baku	ECq	Aliyev.S [26]	3 100	Einwaller AUT
17-11	Finland	L	1-2	Helsinki	ECq	Makhmud Gurbanov [63]	10 325	Hamer LUX
21-11	Belgium	L	0-1	Baku	ECq		7 000	Kenan ISR
2008								
3-02	Kazakhstan	D	0-0	Antalya	Fr			
26-03	Lithuania	L	0-1	Vilnius	Fr		1 500	Satchi MDA
1-06	Bosnia-Herzegovina	L	0-1	Zenica	Fr			
4-06	Andorra	W	2-1	Andorra la Vella	Fr	Fabio Ramin [17], Branimir Subasic [43]		
20-08	Iceland	D	1-1	Reykjavik	Fr	Fabio Ramin [48]	5 133	Evans WAL
27-08	Iran	L	0-1	Tehran	Fr		10 000	Mombini IRN
6-09	Wales	L	0-1	Cardiff	WCq		17 106	Stavrev MKD
10-09	Liechtenstein	D	0-0	Baku	WCq		25 000	Georgiev BUL
11-10	Finland	L	0-1	Helsinki	WCq		22 124	Collum SCO
15-10	Bahrain	W	2-1	Manama	Fr	Zeynal Zeynalov [45], Elvin Mammadov [65]		Al Mirdas KSA
19-11	Albania	D	1-1	Baku	Fr	Branimir Subasic [4]	10 000	Silagava GEO
2009								
1-02	Uzbekistan	D	1-1	Dubai	Fr	Fabio Ramin [63p]		Albadwawi UAE
11-02	Kuwait	D	1-1	Kuwait City	Fr	Vagif Javadov [1]		Al Mirdas KSA
28-03	Russia	L	0-2	Moscow	WCq		62 000	Gumienny BEL
2-06	Turkey	L	0-2	Kayseri	Fr			Vlk SVK
6-06	Wales	L	0-1	Baku	WCq		25 000	Strombersson SWE
9-06	Spain	L	0-6	Baku	Fr		20 000	Ischenko UKR
12-08	Germany	L	0-2	Baku	WCq		22 500	Kelly IRL
5-09	Finland	L	1-2	Lenkoran	WCq	Elvin Mammadov [49]	12 000	Trifonos CYP
9-09	Germany	L	0-4	Hanover	WCq		35 369	Kakos GRE
10-10	Liechtenstein	W	2-0	Vaduz	WCq	Vagif Javadov [55], Elvin Mammadov [82]	1 635	Radovanovic MNE
14-10	Russia	D	1-1	Baku	WCq	Vagif Javadov [53]	17 000	Webb ENG
15-11	Iraq	L	0-1	Al Ain	Fr			
18-11	Czech Republic	W	2-0	Al Ain	Fr	Vagif Javadov [24], Samir Abasov [89]		Al Marzouqi UAE
2010								
25-02	Jordan	W	2-0	Amman	Fr	Fabio Ramin [1], Afran Ismaylov [31]		Shaaban EGY
3-03	Luxembourg	W	2-1	Luxembourg	Fr	Farid Guliyev [28], Elvin Mammadov [37]	874	Kari FIN
26-05	Moldova	D	1-1	Seekirchen	Fr	Elvin Mammadov [21]	200	Lechner AUT
29-05	FYR Macedonia	L	1-3	Villach	Fr	Elvin Mammadov [89]	100	Drabek AUT
2-06	Honduras	D	0-0	Zell Am See	Fr		500	Brandner AUT
11-08	Kuwait	D	1-1	Baku	Fr	Elvin Mammadov [42]	9 000	Karasev RUS
7-09	Germany	L	1-6	Cologne	ECq	Vagif Javadov [57]	43 751	Strombergsson SWE
8-10	Austria	L	0-3	Vienna	ECq		26 500	Vollquartz DEN
12-10	Turkey	W	1-0	Baku	ECq	Rashad F. Sadygov [38]	29 500	Deaconu ROU
17-11	Montenegro	L	0-2	Podgorica	Fr		3 000	Stavrev MKD

Fr = Friendly match • EC = UEFA EURO 2008/2012 • WCq = FIFA World Cup • q = qualifier

AZERBAIJAN NATIONAL TEAM HISTORICAL RECORDS

Caps
75 - Aslan Kerimov 1994-2007 • **73** - Tarlan Akhmedov 1992-2005 • **69** - Makhmud Gurbanov 1994-2008 • **65** - Emin Agaev 1994-2005 & Gurban Gurbanov 1992-2005 • **64** - Rashad F. Sadygov 2001- • **49** - Emin Guliyev 2000-08 • **46** - Kamal Guliyev 2000-05 • **45** - Vyacheslav Lichkin 1995-2001 • **44** - Emin Imamaliev 2000-07

Goals
12 - Gurban Gurbanov 1992-2005 • **7** - Elvin Mammadov 2008- & Branimir Subasic 2007-09 • **6** - Vagif Javadov 2006- & Zaur Tagizade 1997-2005 • **5** - Farrukh Ismayilov 1998-2006, Vidadi Rzayev 1992-2001 & Nazim Suleymanov 1992-98

Past Coaches
Alakbar Mammadov 1992-1993 • Kazbek Tuayev 1993-1994 • Agaselim Mirjavadov 1994-1995 • Kazbek Tuayev 1995-1997 • Vagif Sadygov 1997-1998 • Ahmad Alaskarov 1998-2000 • Igor Ponomaryov 2000-2001 • Vagif Sadygov 2002 • Asgar Abdullayev 2003-2004 • Carlos Alberto Torres BRA 2004-2005 • Vagif Sadygov 2005 • Shahin Diniyev 2005-2007 • Gjoko Hadzievski MKD 2007-2008 • Berti Vogts GER 2008-

AZERBAIJAN 2009-10

PREMYER LIGA (1)

	Pl	W	D	L	F	A	Pts	Inter Baku	FK Baku	Karabakh	Khazar	Neftchi	Gabala	Olimpik	Simurq	Turan	Mugan	Standard	Karvan
Inter Baku †	20	7	8	5	22	19	29		1-0 1-2	1-0 1-1	1-1 0-1	0-1 1-3	2-4 1-0	2-2	2-1	3-1	1-0	4-2	1-0
FK Baku ‡	20	7	7	6	19	15	28	2-0 0-0		0-1 2-0	0-3 1-0	0-2 1-1	2-0 1-1	0-0	1-2	2-1	0-0	0-0	1-0
Karabakh Agdam ‡	20	6	9	5	16	18	27	1-1 1-0	0-1 1-4		1-0 2-1	1-0 2-0	0-0 1-1	1-0	0-0	2-1	2-1	1-0	3-2
Khazar Lenkoran ‡	20	6	9	5	19	14	27	1-0 2-2	1-1 0-1	0-0 2-1		0-0 0-1	0-4 2-1	3-0	1-1	2-0	3-0	1-1	2-0
Neftchi Baku	20	4	11	5	11	12	23	2-1 1-0	1-1 1-0	0-0 0-0	0-0 0-0		1-1 1-2	0-0	0-1	2-0	0-2	2-0	1-0
FK Gabala	20	4	8	8	18	27	20	0-1 1-1	0-2 1-0	1-0 1-3	1-1 1-1	2-1 0-0		2-1	2-1	1-0	3-0	2-1	1-0
Olimpik Baku	20	10	6	4	27	15	36	0-1	0-1	1-1	1-0	0-1	0-2		0-3 0-3	3-4 1-0	0-2 0-2	0-1 2-4	0-0
Simurq Zaqatala	20	8	7	5	21	21	31	1-1	1-2	1-0	1-2	1-1	2-1	2-0 0-3		1-0 1-2	3-1 1-2	1-0 4-2	0-0 0-0
Turan Tovuz	20	7	8	5	27	22	29	1-0	0-1	1-2	1-2	2-3	0-1	0-0 0-1	2-0 0-0		1-0 1-2	3-0 0-0	2-1 2-0
Mugan Salyan	20	7	6	7	17	16	27	1-6	0-1	0-1	1-2	2-2	0-0	0-1 2-0	0-3 1-2	3-0 0-0		1-0 1-0	1-0 2-3
Standard Baku	20	7	4	9	26	23	25	0-1	3-4	0-1	1-2	1-2	2-1	0-1 0-1	1-2 3-1	1-2 1-3	1-0 0-2		1-0 6-0
Karvan Yevlakh	20	2	7	11	14	35	13	0-2	1-1	1-1	0-2	0-1	4-1	1-3 0-1	3-2 0-0	0-0 1-4	1-0 0-2	2-2 1-2	

14/08/2009 - 16/05/2010 • † Qualified for the UEFA Champions League • ‡ Qualified for the Europa League • After a first round of home and away matches, the league splits into a championship group and a relegation group with only the record against group opponents carried forward
Top scorers: **16** - Farid Guliev, Standard • **12** - Anatoli Doros MDA, Olimpik & Robertas Poskus LTU, Inter • **11** - Adrian Neaga ROU, Neftchi

AZERBAIJAN 2009-10 BIRINCI DASTA (2)

	Pl	W	D	L	F	A	Pts
FK Gança	22	14	5	3	51	15	47
MOIK Baku	22	15	2	5	48	25	47
Bakili Baku	22	14	1	7	41	19	43
Neftchi ISM Baku	22	12	3	7	38	26	39
MTK-Araz Imishli	22	11	5	6	41	29	38
Ravan Baku	22	11	4	7	32	28	37
ABN Barda	22	11	3	8	31	23	36
Shahdag Khusar	22	8	8	6	33	24	32
ANSAD-Petrol Neftçala	22	5	2	15	25	61	17
Energetik Mingacevir	22	3	6	13	24	51	15
Adliyya Baku	22	3	5	14	16	40	14
Geyazan Gazakh	22	1	4	17	16	55	7

5/09/2009 - 16/05/2010 • No teams promoted

MEDALS TABLE

		Overall			League			Cup	
		G	S	B	G	S	B	G	S
1	Neftchi Baku	10	3	4	5	2	4	5	1
2	FK Gança	7	1	2	3	1	2	4	
3	Karabakh Agdam	4	6	2	1	3	2	3	3
4	FK Baku	4	1	1	2	1	1	2	
5	Khazar Lenkoran	3	3		1	1		2	2
6	FK Shamkir	2	4	1	2	1	1		3
7	Inter Baku	2	4		2	1			3
8	Turan Tovuz	1	1	1	1	1	1		
9	Inshaatchi Baku	1							1
	Shafa Baku	1							1
11	Karvan Yevlakh		2	1		1	1		1
	Khazri Buznova		2	1		1	1		1
13	Khazar Sumgayit		2			2			
	Kur-Nur Mingäçevir		2						2
15	Dinamo Baku	1	1		1	1			
16	Inshaatchi Sabirabad	1							1
	MTK-Araz Imishli	1							1
	Olimpik Baku	1			1				
19	Simurq Zaqatala		1						1

AZERBAIJAN KUBOKU 2009-10

First Round			Quarter-finals			Semi-finals			Final		
FK Baku *	6	0									
Bakili Baku	0	0	**FK Baku** *	1	3						
Turan Tovuz	1	0	Standard Baku	1	1						
Standard Baku *	3	0				**FK Baku** *	0	3			
Neftchi Baku *	5	2				Inter Baku	1	1			
Neftchi ISM Baku	0	0	Neftchi Baku *	0	1						
Karvan Yevlakh	0	2	**Inter Baku**	3	2						
Inter Baku *	4	3							**FK Baku** ‡		2
Olimpik Baku *	2	0							Khazar Lenkoran		1
FK Gabala	0	1	**Olimpik Baku**	0	4						
FK Gança	0	0	Simurq Zaqatala *	0	2						
Simurq Zaqatala *	2	1				Olimpik Baku *	1	1			
Karabakh Agdam *	4	0				**Khazar Lenkoran**	1	2			
Shahdag Khusar	0	0	**Karabakh Agdam** *	2	0						
Mugan Salyan	1	0	**Khazar Lenkoran**	1	1						
Khazar Lenkoran *	3	1									

* Home team in the first leg • ‡ Qualified for the Europa League

CUP FINAL
Tofik Bakramov, Baku
22-05-2010, 26 000
Scorers - Veaceslav Sofroni [93], Aleksandar Solic [103] for Baku; Elvin Beqiri [120] for Khazar

Preliminary Round: ANSAD-Petrol 1-1 2-3 **Shahdag** • MTK-Arz 1-3 1-2 **Bakili** • **FK Gança** 1-1 2-0 Ravan • MOIK 2-1 0-2 **Neftçhi ISM**

BAH – BAHAMAS

FIFA/COCA-COLA WORLD RANKING

1993	1994	1995	1996	1997	1998	1999	2000	2001	2002	2003	2004	2005	2006	2007	2008	2009	2010
167	-	-	-	-	-	189	178	184	187	193	192	193	146	174	170	180	194

	2010											Hi/Lo
	Jan	Feb	Mar	Mar	Apr	May	Jul	Aug	Sep	Oct	Nov	Dec	**138**
	180	176	175	182	181	181	179	177	194	194	193	194	**197**

Bears once again proved their credentials as the powerhouse of football in the Bahamas when they ran riot in the BFA Senior League, dropping just two points in the entire campaign, and they then finished the season by completing the double of league and FA Cup. For good measure they also won both the President's Cup and the Charity Shield to complete a memorable year. It wasn't just the trophies, however, that made it such a landmark season. It was the manner in which they did it. In the league Bears averaged nearly seven goals a game, finishing with a total of 108 in just 16 matches with star striker Leslie St Fleur topping the scoring charts. Newly-promoted Lyford Cay were the only team to give Bears a run for their money, finishing a creditable 11 points behind the champions. They were also the only team to take points off Bears, thanks to a 1-1 draw in January 2010, and in June they reached the FA Cup final. Once again, however, Bears put their opponents to the sword in a 4-0 victory although it did take Bears 65 minutes to break down a determined Lyford Cay team. A notable feature of the season was the use of youth players during the league campaign with Youth Player of the Year Richard Munroe not only appearing for Baha Juniors but also for the Bahamas Under-14 team.

FIFA WORLD CUP RECORD
1930-1998 DNE 2002-2010 DNQ

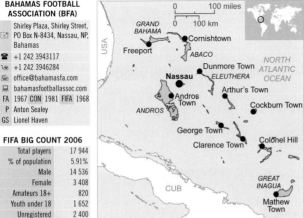

BAHAMAS FOOTBALL ASSOCIATION (BFA)

Shirley Plaza, Shirley Street,
PO Box N-8434, Nassau, NP,
Bahamas

☎ +1 242 3943117

📠 +1 242 3946284

✉ office@bahamasfa.com

🖥 bahamasfootballassoc.com

FA 1967 CON 1981 FIFA 1968

P Anton Sealey

GS Lionel Haven

FIFA BIG COUNT 2006

Total players	17 944
% of population	5.91%
Male	14 536
Female	3 408
Amateurs 18+	820
Youth under 18	1 652
Unregistered	2 400
Professionals	0
Referees	36
Admin & coaches	230
Number of clubs	34
Number of teams	111

MAJOR CITIES/TOWNS

		Population
1	Nassau	238 132
2	Freeport	47 085
3	West End	13 004
4	Coopers Town	9 069
5	Marsh Harbour	5 728
6	Freetown	4 222
7	High Rock	3 827
8	Andros Town	2 318
9	Spanish Wells	1 805
10	Clarence Town	1 705
11	Dunmore Town	1 578
12	Rock Sound	1 447
13	Arthur's Town	1 216
14	Cockburn Town	1 045
15	George Town	1 038
16	Alice Town	936
17	Sweeting Cay	494
18	Matthew Town	435
19	Snug Corner	402

THE BAHAMAS

Capital Nassau	Population 309 156 (176)	% in cities 84%
GDP per capita $29 600 (46)	Area km² 13 880 km² (160)	GMT +/- -5
Neighbours (km) Coast 3542		

RECENT INTERNATIONAL MATCHES PLAYED BY BAHAMAS

2006	Opponents	Score		Venue	Comp	Scorers	Att	Referee
2-09	Cayman Islands	W	3-1	Havana	CCq	OG [5], Moseley [36], Thompson [86]	200	Stewart JAM
4-09	Cuba	L	0-6	Havana	CCq		100	Prendergast JAM
6-09	Turks & Caicos Isl	W	3-2	Havana	CCq	Nassies [59], Hall [63], Jean [87]	120	Campbell JAM
19-11	Barbados	L	1-2	Bridgetown	CCq	Jean [76p]	4 500	Jauregui ANT
21-11	Bermuda	L	0-4	Bridgetown	CCq		3 500	Angela URU
23-11	St Vincent/Grenadines	L	2-3	Bridgetown	CCq	Christie [55], Moseley [65]	4 000	Angela URU
2007								
No international matches played in 2007								
2008								
26-03	British Virgin Islands	D	1-1	Nassau	WCq	St Fleur [47]	450	Moreno PAN
30-03	British Virgin Islands	D	2-2	Nassau	WCq	Bethel [41], Mitchell [57]	940	Suazo DOM
15-06	Jamaica	L	0-7	Kingston	WCq		20 000	Navarro CAN
18-06	Jamaica	L	0-6	Greenfield-Tr'wny	WCq		10 500	Archundia MEX
2009								
No international matches played in 2009								
2010								
No international matches played in 2010								

Fr = Friendly match • CC = Digicel Caribbean Cup • WC = FIFA World Cup • q = qualifier

BAHAMAS 2009–10
BFA SENIOR LEAGUE

	Pl	W	D	L	F	A	Pts
Bears	16	15	1	0	108	12	**46**
Lyford Cay	16	11	2	3	48	21	**35**
Dynamos	16	9	3	4	45	27	**30**
Cavalier	16	6	3	7	28	48	**21**
College of Bahamas	16	6	2	8	34	33	**20**
United	16	6	2	8	30	47	**20**
Sharks	16	4	1	11	20	47	**13**
Baha Juniors	16	4	0	12	19	55	**12**
Nassau	16	4	0	12	21	63	**12**

25/10/2009 - 19/04/2010

BFA KNOCK-OUT CUP FINAL 2010
27-06-2010

Bears   4-0   Lyford Cay

MEDALS TABLE

		Overall	Lge	Cup
		G	G	G
1	Bears	10	6	4
2	Cavalier	6	4	2
3	Britam United	4	4	
4	Caledonia Celtic	3	2	1
5	Abacom United	1	1	
	Freeport	1	1	
	JJ Johnson	1		1

BAN – BANGLADESH

FIFA/COCA-COLA WORLD RANKING

1993	1994	1995	1996	1997	1998	1999	2000	2001	2002	2003	2004	2005	2006	2007	2008	2009	2010
116	130	138	136	141	157	130	151	146	159	151	167	160	144	168	174	149	159

	2010											Hi/Lo
	Jan	Feb	Mar	Mar	Apr	May	Jul	Aug	Sep	Oct	Nov	Dec	**110**
	149	150	158	158	160	157	153	152	145	150	151	159	**183**

The national team played only three matches in 2010, all of them at the AFC Challenge Cup in Sri Lanka where they got their campaign off to a great start with a 2-1 victory over Tajikistan. Their Serbian coach Zoran Dordevic had come to the job from a successful spell in India with Churchill Brothers who he had taken to the I-League title in 2009, but he was unable to inspire Bangladesh to any further magic with his side losing their remaining two games against Myanmar and the hosts Sri Lanka and he was replaced after the tournament with local coach Saiful Bari Titu. Earlier in the year Dordevic had led the under-23 side to victory in the football tournament of the South Asian Games in Dhaka and as a result they were entered into the Asian Games football tournament in Guangzhou. For the competition Titu was replaced by Croatian Robert Rubcic but all three games - against Hong Kong, Uzbekistan and the United Arab Emirates - were lost. At home the B-League was renamed the Bangladesh League to rid it of any inference that it was a second rate tournament and in 2010 it was won by Abahani from the capital Dhaka. Four months later at the Federation Cup in Kamalapur they completed the double. In an entertaining final against Sheikh Jamal they won the trophy after a winning 5-3 with two late goals in extra-time.

FIFA WORLD CUP RECORD
1930-1982 DNE **1986-2010** DNQ

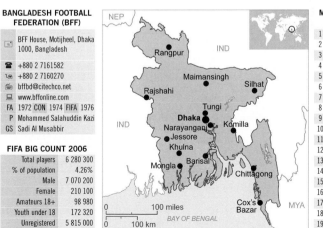

BANGLADESH FOOTBALL FEDERATION (BFF)

- BFF House, Motijheel, Dhaka 1000, Bangladesh
- ☎ +880 2 7161582
- 🖷 +880 2 7160270
- ✉ bffbd@citechco.net
- 🖳 www.bffonline.com
- FA 1972 CON 1974 FIFA 1976
- P Mohammed Salahuddin Kazi
- GS Sadi Al Musabbir

FIFA BIG COUNT 2006

Total players	6 280 300
% of population	4.26%
Male	7 070 200
Female	210 100
Amateurs 18+	98 980
Youth under 18	172 320
Unregistered	5 815 000
Professionals	0
Referees	4 304
Admin & coaches	71 300
Number of clubs	4 100
Number of teams	8 200

MAJOR CITIES/TOWNS

		Population
1	Dhaka	10 468 510
2	Chittagong	3 761 337
3	Narayanganj	1 448 975
4	Khulna	1 406 963
5	Gazipur	1 159 557
6	Rajshahi	791 051
7	Tungi	417 507
8	Silhat	399 381
9	Maimansingh	388 598
10	Narsingdi	351 538
11	Komilla	337 854
12	Rangpur	323 001
13	Barisal	267 423
14	Jessor	255 716
15	Bogra	254 635
16	Pabna	180 400
17	Dinajpur	180 301
18	Nawabganj	175 363
19	Brahman	157 089

BANLADESH • BANGLADESH

Capital	Dhaka	Population	156 050 883 (7)	% in cities	27%
GDP per capita	$1500 (196)	Area km²	143 998 km² (94)	GMT +/-	+6
Neighbours (km)	Myanmar 193, India 4053 • Coast 580				

RECENT INTERNATIONAL MATCHES PLAYED BY BANGLADESH

2006	Opponents	Score		Venue	Comp	Scorers	Att	Referee
16-08	Qatar	L	1-4	Chittagong	ACq	Mohamad Arman [23]	7 000	Al Yarimi YEM
6-09	Qatar	L	0-3	Doha	ACq		500	Najm LIB
11-10	Uzbekistan	L	0-4	Dhaka	ACq		120	Tan Hai CHN
15-11	Hong Kong	L	0-2	Hong Kong	ACq		1 273	Kim Dong Jin KOR
2007								
18-08	Syria	L	0-2	New Delhi	Fr			
20-08	India	L	0-1	New Delhi	Fr			
22-08	Cambodia	D	1-1	New Delhi	Fr	Abdul Hossain [30]		
24-08	Kyrgyzstan	L	0-3	New Delhi	Fr			
8-10	Tajikistan	D	1-1	Dhaka	WCq	Zumratul Hossain Mithu [50]	700	Al Hilali OMA
28-10	Tajikistan	L	0-5	Dushanbe	WCq		10 000	Chynybekov KGZ
2008								
5-05	Afghanistan	D	0-0	Bishkek	CCq		3 000	Al Senan UAE
9-05	Kyrgyzstan	L	1-2	Bishkek	CCq		5 000	Al Enezi KUW
4-06	Bhutan	D	1-1	Colombo	SAFr1	Arup Baidya [26]		
6-06	Afghanistan	D	2-2	Colombo	SAFr1	Hasan Ameli [52], Mamunul Islam Mamun [76]		
8-06	Sri Lanka	L	0-1	Colombo	SAFr1			
18-10	Myanmar	L	0-1	Kuala Lumpur	Fr			
11-11	Myanmar	D	0-0	Yangon	Fr			
13-11	Indonesia	L	0-2	Yangon	Fr			
2009								
26-04	Cambodia	W	1-0	Dhaka	CCq	Anamul Hoque [73]	8 060	Yazdi IRN
28-04	Myanmar	L	1-2	Dhaka	CCq	Anamul Hoque [12]	14 000	Matsuo JPN
30-04	Macau	W	3-0	Dhaka	CCq	Mamunul Islam Mamun [38], Zahid Hossain 2 [68 71]	8 700	Mashentsev KGZ
4-12	Bhutan	W	4-1	Dhaka	SAFr1	Das [11], Anamul Hoque 2 [22 51], Ameli [72]		
6-12	Pakistan	D	0-0	Dhaka	SAFr1			
8-12	Sri Lanka	W	2-1	Dhaka	SAFr1	Anamul Hoque 2 [8 64]		
11-12	India †	L	0-1	Dhaka	SAFsf			
2010								
16-02	Tajikistan	W	2-1	Colombo	CCr1	Anamul Hoque [67], Atiqur Meshu [74]	1 000	Matsuo JPN
18-02	Myanmar	L	1-2	Colombo	CCr1	Mohammed Hossain [49]	500	Al Yarimi YEM
20-02	Sri Lanka	L	0-3	Colombo	CCr1		600	Mahapab THA

SAF = South Asian Football Federation Cup • AC = AFC Asian Cup • CC = AFC Challenge Cup • WCq = FIFA World Cup
q = qualifier • r1 = first round group • sf = semi-final • f = final

BANGLADESH NATIONAL TEAM HISTORICAL RECORDS

Past Coaches Hamzah Hussain Wahid 1992-95 • Otto Pfister GER 1996-97 • Mark Harrison ENG 2000 • Aurel Ticleanu ROU 2002 • Gyorgy Kottan AUT 2002-03 • Andres Cruciani ARG 2005-07 • Sayeed Hassan Kanan 2007-08 • Abu Yusuf Mohammad Bilal 2008 • Shafiq Islam Malik 2008 • Dido BRA 2009 • Rizwan Ali Jahed 2009 • Zoran Djordjevic SRB 2010 • Saiful Bari Titu 2010 • Robert Rupcic CRO 2010-

BANGLADESH 2009-10

BANGLADESH LEAGUE

	Pl	W	D	L	F	A	Pts	Abahani D	Moham'dan	Sh. Russell	Feni	Arambagh	Muktijoddha	Brothers Un	Rahmatganj	Moham'dan	Farashganj	Abahani C	Shukhtara	Biyanibazar
Abahani Dhaka †	24	22	1	1	63	8	67		1-2	2-1	2-0	4-0	5-0	1-0	3-1	4-0	1-0	6-2	3-0	3-1
Mohammedan	24	19	5	0	63	12	62	0-0		0-0	3-0	7-0	4-0	3-0	3-1	1-1	1-0	3-0	7-0	4-1
Sheikh Russell	24	15	5	4	49	19	50	0-2	1-2		4-1	2-2	3-0	0-2	1-0	4-1	2-0	3-1	2-0	2-0
Feni	24	7	9	8	16	22	30	0-1	1-4	0-0		1-1	0-1	1-1	2-1	0-0	0-1	1-0	0-0	1-1
Arambagh	24	6	9	9	30	43	27	0-3	1-2	1-6	0-0		2-3	0-0	0-1	0-1	2-2	4-3	0-2	0-0
Muktijoddha Sangsad	24	8	3	13	26	46	27	0-1	0-3	1-3	1-2	1-2		3-1	1-5	2-1	1-5	1-2	0-0	1-1
Brothers Union	24	5	11	8	20	26	26	0-4	0-2	0-1	0-0	0-0	1-0		2-3	0-0	1-0	2-2	0-0	4-0
Rahmatganj	24	7	5	12	28	36	26	1-5	0-1	1-1	0-0	1-2	1-4	0-0		0-0	0-2	5-1	2-1	2-0
Mohammedan Ch'gong	24	5	11	8	21	33	26	0-2	1-4	2-2	0-2	1-6	1-0	1-1	2-0		0-0	1-1	5-1	1-1
Farashganj	24	4	11	9	20	25	23	0-4	2-2	1-2	0-1	0-0	0-1	2-2	0-1	0-0		0-0	1-1	1-1
Abahani Chittagong	24	5	6	13	24	43	21	0-1	1-3	0-2	1-0	1-4	1-1	1-1	1-0	1-0	1-1		0-1	4-1
Narayanganj Shukhtara	24	4	8	12	12	35	20	0-1	0-1	0-4	0-2	0-1	0-1	0-1	2-2	1-1	0-0	1-0		0-0
Beanibazar	24	3	8	13	19	43	17	0-4	1-1	0-3	0-1	2-2	2-3	2-1	2-0	0-1	1-2	1-0	1-2	

25/10/2009 - 5/06/2010 • † Qualified for the AFC President's Cup

MEDALS TABLE

		Overall G	Overall S	Nat G	Nat B	Cup G	Cup S	Dhaka G	City
1	Mohammedan SC	31	9	2	5	10	4	19	Dhaka
2	Abahani Ltd	23	9	4	2	8	7	11	Dhaka
3	Dhaka Wanderers	7	1				1	7	Dhaka
4	Muktijoddha SKC	6	4	1	1	3	3	2	Dhaka
5	Brothers Union	6	2	1		3	2	2	Dhaka
6	Bangladesh IDC	4						4	Dhaka
7	Victoria SC	3						3	Dhaka
8	Azad	1						1	Dhaka
9	Bangladesh Jute Mill Corp.	1						1	Dhaka
10	Bengal Government Press	1						1	Dhaka
11	East Pakistan Gymkhana	1						1	Dhaka
12	Fakirerpool Young Men's Club	1						1	Dhaka
13	Arambagh KS		1				1		Dhaka
	Sheikh Jamal Dhanmondi		1				1		

FEDERATION CUP 2010

Second round

Sheikh Jamal	2
Arambagh	0

Rahmatganj	2 4p
Abahani Chittagong	2 3p

Muktijoddha Sangsad	3
Farashganj	0

Brothers Union	1
Mohammedan Ch'gong	0

Quarter-final Groups

Group A	Pts
Abahani Dhaka	5
Sheikh Jamal	5
Sheikh Russell	3
Rahmatganj	1

Group B	Pts
Muktijoddha Sangsad	7
Brothers Union	6
Mohammedan	2
Feni	1

Semi-finals

Abahani Dhaka	1
Brothers Union	0

Muktijoddha Sangsad	0
Sheikh Jamal	1

Final

Abahani Dhaka	5
Sheikh Jamal	3

CUP FINAL

Birsreshtha Kamal, Kamalapur
30-10-2010
Scorers - Awudu 3 [32 80 118],
Frank [50p], Yusuf [112] for Abahani;
Enamul 2 [31 48], Mamum [86] for Sheikh
Jamal

First round: **Abahani Chittagong** 2-1 Bangladesh Police • **Mohammedan Chittagong** 1-0 Victoria •
Muktijoddha Sangsad 8-1 Bangladesh Navy • **Farashganj** 1-0 Bangladesh Air Force • Arambagh 0-0 3-0p BKSP
• Sheikh Jamal 3-0 Young Men's Club

The top four teams from the 2009-10 league season received byes to the quarter-final group stage
Tournament held in Kamalapur from 8-10-2010 to 30-10-2010

BDI – BURUNDI

FIFA/COCA-COLA WORLD RANKING

1993	1994	1995	1996	1997	1998	1999	2000	2001	2002	2003	2004	2005	2006	2007	2008	2009	2010
101	126	146	137	152	141	133	126	139	135	145	152	147	117	109	136	126	128

	2010											Hi/Lo
Jan	Feb	Mar	Mar	Apr	May	Jul	Aug	Sep	Oct	Nov	Dec	96
126	147	147	145	145	144	141	142	122	136	136	128	160

The Burundi national team spent the first eight months of the year in international isolation, 'Les Hirondelles' going without a game before getting their African Nations Cup qualifying campaign for 2012 underway with a morale-boosting draw away to Benin in September. Coached by Algerian-Belgian Adel Amrouche, they then turned in a credible performance at home to group favourites Côte d'Ivoire but still lost by a single goal, a result that almost certainly ended any aspirations of a first-ever Nations Cup finals appearance. There was further disappointment at the end of the year in the CECAFA Cup in Tanzania where a defeat at the hands of the hosts saw Burundi knocked out after the first round group stage despite having beaten Somalia and drawn with group winners Zambia. Vital'O won Burundi's Ligue A for the fourth time in five years with an 11-point advantage over perennial rivals Inter Star. It was their 21st championship success and yet another triumph for long-standing coach Jean Gilbert Kanyankore. In the African Champions League, Vital'O held Tiko United of Cameroon to a 4-4 aggregate draw over two legs in the first round, only to be eliminated on post-match penalties. Vital'O did reach the quarter-finals of the regional CECAFA Inter-Club Cup in neighbouring Rwanda only to lose to local side ATRACO.

FIFA WORLD CUP RECORD
1930-1990 DNE 1994 DNQ 1998 Withdrew 2002 DNE 2006- 2010 DNQ

FEDERATION DE FOOTBALL DU BURUNDI (FFB)

Avenue Muyinga, Boite postale 3426, Bujumbura, Burundi

☎ +257 79 928762
📠 +257 22 242892
📧 lydiansekera@yahoo.fr

FA 1948 CON 1972 FIFA 1972
P Lydia Nsekera
GS Jeremie Manirakiza

FIFA BIG COUNT 2006

Total players	352 334
% of population	4.36%
Male	335 284
Female	17 050
Amateurs 18+	5 612
Youth under 18	6 289
Unregistered	17 400
Professionals	3
Referees	412
Admin & coaches	9 220
Number of clubs	165
Number of teams	189

MAJOR CITIES/TOWNS
Population

1	Bujumbura	367 544
2	Muyinga	95 840
3	Ruyigi	44 854
4	Makamba	25 231
5	Gitega	24 794
6	Rutana	24 150
7	Ngozi	23 779
8	Bururi	21 862
9	Muramvya	21 287
10	Kayanza	20 647
11	Cibitoke	17 142
12	Bubanza	14 945
13	Karuzi	12 729
14	Cankuzo	7 498
15	Kirundo	7 034
16	Rumonge	6 727
17	Mwaro	5 270

REPUBLIKA Y'U BURUNDI • REPUBLIC OF BURUNDI

Capital	Bujumbura	Population	8 988 091 (89)	% in cities	10%
GDP per capita	$400 (227)	Area km²	27 830 km² (146)	GMT + / -	+2
Neighbours (km)	Congo DR 233, Rwanda 290, Tanzania 451				

RECENT INTERNATIONAL MATCHES PLAYED BY BURUNDI

2007	Opponents	Score		Venue	Comp	Scorers	Att	Referee
25-03	Botswana	L	0-1	Gaborone	CNq			Marange ZIM
27-05	Rwanda	L	0-1	Kigali	Fr			
2-06	Botswana	W	1-0	Kigali	CNq	Abdul Ndayishimiye [80]		Ssegonga UGA
9-09	Egypt	D	0-0	Bujumbura	CNq			Louzaya CGO
13-10	Mauritania	L	1-2	Nouakchott	CNq	Irambona [85]		Aboubacar CIV
10-12	Somalia	W	3-0	Dar es Salaam	CCr1	Nzohabonayo [18], Ndikumana 2 [77 82]		
12-12	Kenya	W	1-0	Dar es Salaam	CCr1	Mbazumutima [33]		
15-12	Tanzania	D	0-0	Dar es Salaam	CCr1			
17-12	Eritrea	W	2-1	Dar es Salaam	CCqf	Mbazumutima [69], Nzohabonayo [81]		
19-12	Sudan	L	1-2	Dar es Salaam	CCsf	Nahimana [12]		
22-12	Uganda	L	0-2	Dar es Salaam	CC3p			
2008								
6-02	Rwanda	D	0-0	Bujumbura	Fr			
1-06	Seychelles	W	1-0	Bujumbura	WCq	Ndikumana [81]	4 000	Imiere NGA
7-06	Burkina Faso	L	0-2	Ouagadougou	WCq		0	Ndume GAB
15-06	Tunisia	L	0-1	Bujumbura	WCq		7 000	Damon RSA
21-06	Tunisia	L	1-2	Rades	WCq	Mbazumutima [45]	6 000	Younis EGY
6-09	Seychelles	W	2-1	Victoria	WCq	Mbazumutima [28], Nahimana [58]	3 000	Djaoupe TOG
12-10	Burkina Faso	L	1-3	Bujumbura	WCq	Nahimana [43p]	10 000	Ssegonga UGA
2009								
2-01	Djibouti	W	4-0	Jinja	CCr1	Gatoto 2, Nahimana 2		
4-01	Zambia	D	1-1	Jinja	CCr1	Nahimana [90]		
6-01	Sudan	W	1-0	Jinja	CCr1	Gatoto [8]		
8-01	Kenya	L	0-1	Kampala	CCr1			
11-01	Uganda	L	0-5	Kampala	CCsf			
13-01	Tanzania	L	2-3	Kampala	CC3p	Irambona [5p], Jumapili [41]		
29-11	Zanzibar †	L	0-4	Mumias	CCr1			
2-12	Uganda	L	0-2	Mumias	CCr1			
4-12	Tanzania	L	0-1	Mumias	CCr1			
2010								
5-09	Benin	D	1-1	Cotonou	CNq	Kavumbagu [86]		Bennett RSA
9-10	Côte d'Ivoire	L	0-1	Bujumbura	CNq			El Raay LBY
28-11	Somalia	W	2-0	Dar Es Salaam	CCr1	Nahimana [18], Habarugira [72]		
30-11	Zambia	D	0-0	Dar Es Salaam	CCr1			
4-12	Tanzania	L	0-2	Dar Es Salaam	CCr1			

Fr = Friendly match • CN = CAF African Cup of Nations qualifier • CC = CECAFA Cup • WCq = FIFA World Cup
q = qualifier • r1 = 1st round • † Not a full international

BURUNDI 2010

LIGUE A	Pl	W	D	L	F	A	Pts	Vital'O	Inter Star	A. Olympique	LLB Académic	Tchité	Prince Louis	Muzinga	Espoir	Flamengo	Un. Sporting	Wazee	Delta Star
Vital'O †	22	18	2	2	57	16	56		2-0	1-0	2-4	1-0	3-1	1-1	6-2	6-0	4-1	1-0	1-0
Inter Star ‡	22	13	6	3	41	18	45	2-1		0-1	2-1	1-1	0-0	2-1	2-1	1-1	2-1	6-0	2-0
Atlético Olympique	22	13	5	4	47	21	44	2-3	1-2		1-0	1-1	3-2	3-0	1-1	3-0	7-1	4-1	1-0
LLB Académic	22	10	5	7	46	23	35	1-2	0-1	1-2		1-1	2-3	0-0	0-0	0-1	3-1	5-1	2-1
Académie Tchité	22	8	9	5	29	22	33	1-1	0-0	1-2	1-3		0-0	2-0	2-2	2-1	2-0	1-1	6-0
Prince Louis	22	8	8	6	26	27	32	0-1	2-1	0-3	0-0	2-1		1-1	2-0	2-1	3-3	1-2	1-1
Muzinga	22	6	9	7	27	25	27	0-2	2-2	1-1	1-1	0-1	1-1		5-0	3-2	1-2	4-1	2-0
Espoir	22	5	7	10	22	40	22	0-4	0-2	0-0	2-7	4-0	2-0	1-1		2-1	1-1	1-0	1-1
Flamengo de Ngagara	22	5	6	11	24	39	21	0-3	1-3	4-2	1-2	1-3	0-1	0-0	2-1		2-2	0-0	2-1
Union Sporting	22	4	8	10	23	44	20	1-2	0-6	2-2	0-3	0-1	1-1	0-1	2-0	1-1		1-0	2-1
Wazee Rumonge	22	4	7	11	16	37	19	0-5	2-2	0-1	0-1	0-0	0-1	2-0	1-0	1-1	0-0		1-1
Delta Star	22	0	4	18	10	56	4	0-5	0-2	0-6	0-9	1-2	1-2	0-2	0-1	0-2	1-1	1-3	

24/12/2009 - 29/05/2010 • † Qualified for the CAF Champions League • ‡ Qualified for the CAF Confederation Cup

BEL – BELGIUM

FIFA/COCA-COLA WORLD RANKING

1993	1994	1995	1996	1997	1998	1999	2000	2001	2002	2003	2004	2005	2006	2007	2008	2009	2010
25	24	24	42	41	35	33	27	20	17	16	45	55	53	49	54	66	57

	2010											Hi/Lo
Jan	Feb	Mar	Mar	Apr	May	Jul	Aug	Sep	Oct	Nov	Dec	**16**
66	66	68	66	62	59	48	48	62	62	62	57	**71**

It was back to winning ways for Anderlecht as they cruised to a landmark 30th league title in an overly fussy new championship format which saw the introduction of a play-off round once all 16 teams had played each other home and away. Anderlecht won 22 of their 28 games in the regular season but even with their points total halved for the play-offs they still managed to finish 18 points ahead of Gent in second place. In the cup Michel Preud'homme enhanced his reputation as one of the best Belgian coaches of his generation by steering Gent to a 3-0 final triumph over Cercle Brugge before taking over at Twente Enschede in Holland. It was Gent's first trophy since last winning the cup in 1984 and only their third title overall. The 2009-10 European tournaments saw a measure of Belgian success for a change with both Anderlecht and Standard reaching the latter stages of the UEFA Europa League, albeit after disappointing campaigns in the Champions League. Anderlecht made it to the last 16 with Standard going one round further to the quarter-finals, but the hopes of both clubs were ended by Hamburg. It was a different story in the 2010-11 tournaments with no Belgian presence in the Champions League group stage at all, whilst Anderlecht were the only club to make it through to the knockout stage of the Europa League.

FIFA WORLD CUP RECORD

1930 11 r1 **1934** 15 r1 **1938** 13 r1 **1950** DNE **1954** 12 r1 **1958-1966** DNQ **1970** 10 r1 **1974-1978** DNQ
1982 10 r2 **1986** 4 SF **1990** 11 r2 **1994** 11 r2 **1998** 19 r1 **2002** 14 r2 **2006-2010** DNQ

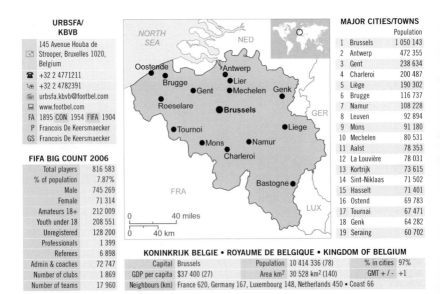

URBSFA/ KBVB

145 Avenue Houba de
Strooper, Bruxelles 1020,
Belgium
☎ +32 2 4771211
📠 +32 2 4782391
📧 urbsfa.kbvb@footbel.com
🖥 www.footbel.com
FA 1895 CON 1954 FIFA 1904
P Francois De Keersmaecker
GS Francois De Keersmaecker

FIFA BIG COUNT 2006

Total players	816 583
% of population	7.87%
Male	745 269
Female	71 314
Amateurs 18+	212 009
Youth under 18	208 551
Unregistered	128 200
Professionals	1 399
Referees	6 898
Admin & coaches	72 747
Number of clubs	1 869
Number of teams	17 960

MAJOR CITIES/TOWNS

		Population
1	Brussels	1 050 143
2	Antwerp	472 355
3	Gent	238 634
4	Charleroi	200 487
5	Liège	190 302
6	Brugge	116 737
7	Namur	108 228
8	Leuven	92 594
9	Mons	91 180
10	Mechelen	80 531
11	Aalst	78 353
12	La Louvière	78 031
13	Kortrijk	73 615
14	Sint-Niklaas	71 502
15	Hasselt	71 401
16	Ostend	69 783
17	Tournai	67 471
18	Genk	64 282
19	Seraing	60 702

KONINKRIJK BELGIE • ROYAUME DE BELGIQUE • KINGDOM OF BELGIUM

Capital	Brussels	Population	10 414 336 (78)	% in cities	97%
GDP per capita	$37 400 (27)	Area km²	30 528 km² (140)	GMT +/-	+1
Neighbours (km)	France 620, Germany 167, Luxembourg 148, Netherlands 450 • Coast 66				

RECENT INTERNATIONAL MATCHES PLAYED BY BELGIUM

2007	Opponents	Score		Venue	Comp	Scorers	Att	Referee
7-02	Czech Republic	L	0-2	Brussels	Fr		12 000	Granat POL
24-03	Portugal	L	0-4	Lisbon	ECq		47 009	Vassaras GRE
2-06	Portugal	L	1-2	Brussels	ECq	Fellaini [55]	45 383	Hansson SWE
6-06	Finland	L	0-2	Helsinki	ECq		34 818	Riley ENG
22-08	Serbia	W	3-2	Brussels	ECq	Dembélé 2 [10 88], Mirallas [30]	19 202	Hauge NOR
12-09	Kazakhstan	D	2-2	Almaty	ECq	Geraerts [13], Mirallas [24]	18 100	Tudor ROU
13-10	Finland	D	0-0	Brussels	ECq		21 393	Kapitanis CYP
17-10	Armenia	W	3-0	Brussels	ECq	Sonck [63], Dembélé [69], Geraerts [76]	14 812	Valgeirsson ISL
17-11	Poland	L	0-2	Chorzow	ECq		41 450	Larsen DEN
21-11	Azerbaijan	W	1-0	Baku	ECq	Pieroni [52]	7 000	Kenan ISR
2008								
26-03	Morocco	L	1-4	Brussels	Fr	Witsel [50]	24 000	Nijhuis NED
30-05	Italy	L	1-3	Florence	Fr	Sonck [92+]	12 500	Atkinson ENG
20-08	Germany	L	0-2	Nuremberg	Fr		34 117	Vejlgaard DEN
6-09	Estonia	W	3-2	Liege	WCq	Sonck 2 [39 81], Delfour [75]	17 992	Dean ENG
10-09	Turkey	D	1-1	Istanbul	WCq	Sonck [32]	34 097	Lannoy FRA
11-10	Armenia	W	2-0	Brussels	WCq	Sonck [21], Fellaini [37]	20 949	Ramussen DEN
15-10	Spain	L	1-2	Brussels	WCq	Sonck [7]	45 888	Ovrebo NOR
19-11	Luxembourg	D	1-1	Luxembourg	Fr	Mirallas [21]	4 172	Riley ENG
2009								
11-02	Slovenia	W	2-0	Genk	Fr	Van Buyten 2 [21 86]	13 135	Kever SUI
28-03	Bosnia-Herzegovina	L	2-4	Genk	WCq	Dembele [66], Sonck [85p]	20 041	Ivanov.N RUS
1-04	Bosnia-Herzegovina	L	1-2	Zenica	WCq	Swerts [88]	13 800	Hrinak SVK
29-05	Chile	D	1-1	Chiba	Fr	Roelandts [15]	9 700	Tojo JPN
31-05	Japan	L	0-4	Chiba	Fr		42 520	Styles ENG
12-08	Czech Republic	L	1-3	Teplice	Fr	Vertonghen [12]	13 890	Sippel GER
5-09	Spain	L	0-5	La Coruña	WCq		30 441	Layec FRA
9-09	Armenia	L	1-2	Yerevan	WCq	Van Buyten [92+]	2 300	Stavrev MKD
10-10	Turkey	W	2-0	Brussels	WCq	Mpenza.E 2 [7 84]	30 131	Trefolini ITA
14-10	Estonia	L	0-2	Tallinn	WCq		4 680	Vollquartz DEN
14-11	Hungary	W	3-0	Gent	Fr	Fellaini [39], Vermaelen [55], Mirallas [61p]	8 000	Picirillo FRA
17-11	Qatar	W	2-0	Sedan	Fr	Witsel [20], Sonck [54]	3 000	Buquet FRA
2010								
19-05	Bulgaria	W	2-1	Brussels	Fr	Lepoint [89], Kompany [91+]	15 000	Weiner GER
11-08	Finland	L	0-1	Turku	Fr		7 451	Hamer LUX
3-09	Germany	L	0-1	Brussels	ECq		41 126	Hauge NOR
7-09	Turkey	L	2-3	Istanbul	ECq	Van Buyten 2 [28 69]	43 538	Skomina SVN
8-10	Kazakhstan	W	2-0	Astana	ECq	Ogunjimi 2 [52 70]	8 500	Borski POL
12-10	Austria	D	4-4	Brussels	ECq	Vossen [11], Fellaini [47], Ogunjimi [87], Lombaerts [90]	24 231	Dean ENG
17-11	Russia	W	2-0	Voronezh	Fr	Lukaku 2 [2 73]	31 743	Kaasik EST

Fr = Friendly match • EC = UEFA EURO 2008/12 • WCq = FIFA World Cup • q = qualifier

BELGIUM NATIONAL TEAM HISTORICAL RECORDS

Caps
96 - Jan Ceulemans 1977-91 • **86** - Eric Gerets 1975-91 & Franky Van der Elst 1984-98 • **84** - Enzo Scifo 1984-99 • **81** - Paul Van Himst 1960-74 • **79** - Timmy Simons 2001- • **78** - Bart Goor 1999-2008 • **77** - Georges Grun 1984-95 • **70** - Lorenzo Staelens 1990-2000 & Marc Wilmots 1990-2002 • **68** - Victor Mees 1949-60 • **67** - Georges Heylens 1961-73 • **64** - Joseph Jurion 1955-67 & Jean-Marie Pfaff 1976-87 • **63** - Franky Vercauteren 1977-8 & Marc Degryse 1984-2002 • **63** - Bernard Voorhoof 1928-40

Goals
30 - Bernard Voorhoof 1928-40 & Paul van Himst 1960-74 • **28** - Marc Wilmots 1990-2002 • **27** - Joseph Mermans 1945-56 • **26** - Robert de Veen 1906-13 & Raymond Braine 1925-39 • **24** - Wesley Sonck 2001- • **23** - Marc Degryse 1984-96 & Jan Ceulemans 1976-91 • **21** - Henri 'Rik' Coppens 1949-59 • **20** - Leopold Anoul 1947-54 & Erwin Vandenbergh 1979-91

Past Coaches
William Maxwell SCO 1910-13 • Charles Bunyan ENG 1914 • William Maxwell SCO 1920-28 • Victor Lowenfelt 1928-30 •Hector Goetinck 1930-34 • Jules Turnauer 1935 • Jack Butler ENG 1935-40 • François Demol 1944-46 • Bill Gormlie ENG 1947-53 • Dougall Livingstone SCO 1953-54 • Andre Vandeweyer 1955-57 • Louis Nicolay 1957 • Geza Toldi HUN 1957-58 • Constant Vanden Stock 1958-68 • Raymond Goethals 1968-76 • Guy Thys 1976-89 • Walter Meeuws 1989-90 • Guy Thys 1990-91 • Paul Van Himst 1991-96 • Wilfried Van Moer 1996 • Georges Leekens 1997-99 • Robert Waseige 1999-2002 • Aime Anthuenis 2002-05 • Rene Vandereycken 2006-09 • Franky Vercauteren 2009 • Dick Advocaat NED 2009-10 • Georges Leekens 2010-

BELGIUM 2009-10

JUPILER PRO LEAGUE FIRST ROUND

	Pl	W	D	L	F	A	Pts	Anderlecht	Brugge	Gent	Kortrijk	St-Truiden	Z-Waregem	Mechelen	Standard	Cercle	Beerschot	Genk	Westerlo	Charleroi	Lokeren	Roeselare	Mouscron
RSC Anderlecht †	28	22	3	3	62	20	69		3-2	1-1	1-0	1-2	2-1	2-0	1-1	3-2	1-0	2-0	3-0	2-0	2-0	3-1	
Club Brugge †	28	17	6	5	52	33	57	4-2		1-0	2-2	1-0	3-1	1-1	2-1	2-1	1-2	1-1	2-1	1-0	2-0	1-0	
KAA Gent †	28	14	7	7	49	30	49	2-2	1-1		2-2	0-1	0-2	2-1	2-1	3-1	0-1	2-1	1-2	2-1	4-1	5-1	1-1
KV Kortrijk †	28	12	9	7	39	30	45	0-2	1-4	1-0		0-1	1-0	2-0	0-2	3-1	3-0	2-1	1-1	2-1	3-1	2-0	2-2
Sint-Truiden VV †	28	12	6	10	35	35	42	2-1	1-1	1-2	0-2		1-2	5-2	2-0	1-1	2-0	2-4	0-1	0-0	2-1	2-1	
Zulte-Waregem	28	10	11	7	39	32	41	0-2	1-1	3-1	0-2	2-0		4-1	1-1	1-0	4-0	2-2	1-0	2-2	1-0	1-1	3-1
KV Mechelen ‡	28	12	3	13	36	46	39	0-2	2-1	2-5	1-1	0-2	2-1		0-0	1-2	1-0	2-1	4-1	1-0	2-0	3-2	0-1
Standard Club Liège ‡	28	10	9	9	38	34	39	0-4	3-1	0-2	3-1	2-2	1-1	3-0		1-1	2-2	1-0	1-0	1-1	2-0	0-1	
Cercle Brugge ‡	28	11	5	12	45	40	38	1-3	2-3	1-3	1-1	3-1	2-2	1-1	2-0		1-2	1-0	2-1	1-0	4-0	2-0	5-0
Germinal Beerschot ‡	28	9	8	11	30	43	35	0-5	1-4	1-1	1-0	4-1	1-1	1-3	1-1	1-4		1-0	3-1	0-0	2-1	3-0	3-2
KRC Genk ‡	28	8	10	10	33	31	34	0-2	2-0	1-1	0-1	0-0	2-2	1-2	1-0	2-0	1-1		0-0	1-2	3-1	1-1	1-2
KVC Westerlo ‡	28	8	8	12	28	34	32	0-2	1-4	0-0	1-1	2-0	1-2	2-0	2-0	2-1	1-1	0-1		4-0	1-0	2-2	
RSC Charleroi ‡	28	5	8	15	28	45	23	0-2	1-2	0-2	3-3	0-0	0-0	1-2	2-3	0-4	1-0	1-3	1-1		4-1	3-0	
KSC Lokeren ‡	28	5	3	20	22	54	18	0-4	0-1	0-1	0-0	1-2	1-1	2-1	1-3	1-1	2-0	0-2	1-0	4-1		1-4	4-1
KSV Roeselare ‡‡	28	4	6	18	29	58	18	1-2	2-3	0-4	0-2	1-2	2-0	1-2	1-5	3-2	1-1	1-1	0-0	1-3	1-2		1-2
Excelsior Mouscron	20	6	5	9	22	37	23	1-2	1-1		0-5	2-1		0-0	0-1		2-0	0-1	4-1	0-5	0-0		

31/07/2009 - 21/03/2010 • † Qualified for the Championship round • ‡ Qualified for the Play-off II round • ‡‡ Relegation play-off
Mouscron excluded after 20 games. Their results were annulled • Points totals were halved and rounded up for the second round
Top scorers (all rounds): **16** - Dorge Kouemaha CMR, Brugge • **15** - Romelu Lukaku, Anderlecht & Ibrahim Sidibe SEN, Sint-Truiden

JUPILER PRO LEAGUE PLAY-OFFS

Championship	Pl	W	D	L	F	A	Pts	An	Ge	CB	ST	Ko	ZW
RSC Anderlecht †	10	7	3	0	24	9	59		2-2	2-1	4-2	1-0	6-0
KAA Gent †	10	4	4	2	20	13	41	1-3		6-2	0-0	0-0	5-0
Club Brugge ‡	10	3	3	4	14	15	41	1-2	1-1		2-0	3-0	3-0
Sint-Truiden VV	10	3	4	3	9	10	34	1-1	1-1	0-0		1-0	1-2
KV Kortrijk	10	3	1	6	9	13	33	1-3	1-2	2-0	1-2		2-0
Zulte-Waregem	10	2	1	7	7	23	28	0-0	1-2	2-0	1-2	1-2	

Play-off 2 Group A	Pl	W	D	L	F	A	Pts	We	Me	CB	Lo
KVC Westerlo ‡‡	6	3	1	2	12	9	10		0-2	4-1	2-0
KV Mechelen	6	3	1	2	10	8	10	1-3		1-0	3-1
Cercle Brugge	6	2	1	3	9	12	7	2-0	2-1		1-1
KSC Lokeren	6	1	3	2	12	14	6	3-3	2-2	5-3	

Play-off 2 Group B	Pl	W	D	L	F	A	Pts	Ge	SL	CB	Ch
KRC Genk ‡‡	6	5	1	0	12	3	16		1-0	2-0	3-0
Standard C Liège	6	2	2	2	8	5	8	1-1		3-0	2-0
G'nal Beerschot	6	1	2	3	6	12	5	1-3	2-2		2-2
RSC Charleroi	6	1	1	4	4	10	4	1-2	1-0	0-1	

27/03/2010 - 8/05/2010 • † Qualified for the UEFA Champions League •
‡ Qualified for the Europa League • ‡‡ Qualified for Play-off 2 final
Final: **Genk** 2-2 3-0 KVC Westerlo. Genk qualify for Europa League play-off
Europa League play-off: **Genk** 2-1 3-2 St-Truiden

MEDALS TABLE

	Overall			League			Cup			Europe		
	G	S	B	G	S	B	G	S	B	G	S	B
1 RSC Anderlecht	42	27	9	30	20	7	9	3		3	4	2
2 Club Brugge	23	25	15	13	17	13	10	6			2	2
3 Standard Liège	15	20	21	10	10	19	5	9			1	2
4 Union St Gilloise	13	8	8	11	8	7	2					1
5 Beerschot VAV	9	8	5	7	7	5	2	1				
6 Racing CB	7	5	3	6	5	3	1					
7 Royal Antwerp	6	14	7	4	12	7	2	1			1	
8 KV Mechelen	6	9	4	4	5	3	1	4				1
9 Royal FC Liègeois	6	4	5	5	3	4	1	1				1
10 Lierse SK	6	3	2	4	2	2	2	1				
11 Daring CB	5	5	4	5	4	4	1					
12 Cercle Brugge	5	4	6	3		6	2	4				
13 KRC Genk	5	2		2	2		3					
14 SK Beveren	4	3	1	2			2	3				1
15 KAA Gent	3	3	6		2	6	3	1				

BELGIUM 2009-10 TWEEDE CLASSE (2)

	Pl	W	D	L	F	A	Pts
Lierse SK	36	21	12	3	75	32	75
KVSK United ‡	36	20	10	6	55	27	70
RAEC Mons ‡	36	19	9	8	56	32	66
AS Eupen ‡	36	16	12	8	56	37	60
Boussu Dour Borinage	36	13	14	9	46	43	53
Red Star Waasland	36	13	10	13	46	49	52
KV Oostende	36	12	15	9	49	45	51
Royal Antwerp	36	10	17	9	55	53	47
Oud-Heverlee Leuven	36	11	12	13	50	66	45
Standaard Wetteren	36	12	8	16	48	59	44
RFC Tournai	36	11	11	14	50	51	44
KVK Tienen	36	11	10	15	44	58	43
Verbroedering Dender	36	10	13	13	45	49	43
FC Brussels	36	11	9	16	50	57	42
AFC Tubize	36	9	15	12	41	41	42
KV Turnhout	36	10	11	15	50	57	41
KSK Ronse	36	10	9	17	51	57	39
KSK Beveren	36	8	12	16	37	55	36
RFC Liège	36	5	8	23	23	60	23

19/08/2009 - 2/05/2010 • ‡ Qualified for promotion play-off

PROMOTION/RELEGATION PLAY-OFFS

	Pl	W	D	L	F	A	Pts	Eu	Mo	KU	Ro
AS Eupen	6	4	1	1	9	4	13		2-1	1-0	3-0
RAEC Mons	6	2	2	2	8	8	8	3-2		2-1	2-2
KVSK United	6	2	0	4	7	7	6	0-1	1-0		4-1
KSV Roeselare	6	1	3	2	5	10	6	0-0	0-0	2-1	

9/05/2010 - 27/05/2010 • Eupen promoted, Roeselare relegated

COUPE DE BELGIQUE/BEKER VAN BELGIE 2009-10

Round of 32

Team	Score
KAA Gent *	3
White Star Woluwe	1
KMSK Deinze	0
Germinal Beerschot *	3
KSC Lokeren *	2
AFC Tubize	0
VW Hamme	0
Club Brugge *	5
KVC Westerlo *	3
Eendracht Aalst	2
Excelsior Mouscron	1
RAEC Mons *	2
RSC Charleroi	2
Standaard Wetteren *	1
Spouwen-Mopertingen	0
KV Mechelen *	2
KSV Roeselare *	2
KSK Beveren	1
Sint-Truiden VV *	0
KRC Genk	1
Standard Club Liège *	2
Lierse SK	1
Excelsior Virton *	0
KV Kortrijk	1
RSC Anderlecht *	2
RSC Verviers	0
Royal Antwerp *	0
Verbroedering Dender	1
Zulte-Waregem *	3
KSK Ronse	0
Oud-Heverlee Leuven	0
Cercle Brugge *	2

Round of 16

Team	Score
KAA Gent *	1
Germinal Beerschot	0
KSC Lokeren	1
Club Brugge *	2
KVC Westerlo *	3
RAEC Mons	1
RSC Charleroi *	2
KV Mechelen	5
KSV Roeselare	2
KRC Genk *	1
Standard Club Liège *	1
KV Kortrijk	2
RSC Anderlecht *	3
Verbroedering Dender	0
Zulte-Waregem *	1
Cercle Brugge	3

Quarter-finals

Team	Leg 1	Leg 2
KAA Gent	4	1
Club Brugge *	1	0
KVC Westerlo	3	0
KV Mechelen *	2	0
KSV Roeselare	2	1
KV Kortrijk *	3	0
RSC Anderlecht *	2	0
Cercle Brugge	1	1

Semi-finals

Team	Leg 1	Leg 2
KAA Gent	2	1
KV Mechelen *	2	0
KSV Roeselare	0	3
Cercle Brugge *	3	1

Final

Team	Score
KAA Gent	3
Cercle Brugge ‡	0

CUP FINAL

Roi Baudouin, Brussels
15-05-2010, Att: 50 000, Ref: Paul Allaerts
Scorers - Coulibaly 35, Leye 85, Grondin 93+
Gent - Bojan Jorgacevic - Roberto Rosales, Marko Suler, Stef Wils, Kenny Thompson• - Bernd Thijs (c), Christophe Lepoint•, Yassine El Ghanassy• (Zlatan Ljubijankic 72) - Mbaye Leye, Elimane Coulibaly (Stijn De Smet 90), Randall Azofeifa (Christophe Grondin 83).
Tr: Michel Preud'Homme
Mechelen - Bram Verbist - Denis Viane (c) (Anthony Portier 34), Dejan Kelhar, Hans Cornelis, Bernt Evens - Frederik Boi (Reynaldo 46), Tony Sergeant (Lukas Van Eenoo 64), Jelle Vossen, Sergiy Serebrennikov - Oleg Iachtchouk•, Dominic Foley. Tr: Glen De Boeck

* Home team/home team in 1st leg • ‡ Qualified for the Europa League

BEN – BENIN

FIFA/COCA-COLA WORLD RANKING

1993	1994	1995	1996	1997	1998	1999	2000	2001	2002	2003	2004	2005	2006	2007	2008	2009	2010
130	143	161	143	137	127	140	148	152	146	121	122	113	114	97	101	59	71

	2010											Hi/Lo
	Jan	Feb	Mar	Mar	Apr	May	Jul	Aug	Sep	Oct	Nov	Dec	59
	59	67	65	61	59	60	61	61	69	68	72	71	165

Benin equalled their all-time high of 59th in the FIFA/Coca-Cola World Ranking in April 2010, not long after their return from the African Nations Cup finals in Angola where they had been eliminated early after picking up just a single point in the first round group. That lead to the departure of coach Michel Dussuyer and an on-going crisis in the administration of the game that continued to rage through the rest of the year. The appointment and then hasty departure of two successive coaches in Brazilian Paolo Rubim and Jean-Marc Nobilo of France reflected the instability that had resulted from of a clash of personalities at government and federation level. With the government controlling the purse strings that provide the backing for the national team, they argued that they should be able to more than just influence the major decisions, leading to several impasses. It took months before Denis Goavec was confirmed as the new coach of 'Les Ecureuils', who, despite the problems started their qualifying campaign for the 2012 African Nations Cup finals with four points from a possible six. At home L'Association Sportive du Port Autonome de Cotonou (ASPAC) were crowned champions, led by the 40-year old Swiss-born Alain Gaspoz, whose mother hails from Benin. Gaspoz first played for Benin in 2003 and returned to coach there in 2009.

FIFA WORLD CUP RECORD
1930-1970 DNE **1974** DNQ **1978-1982** DNE **1986** DNQ **1990** DNE **1994** DNQ **1998** DNE **2002-2010** DNQ

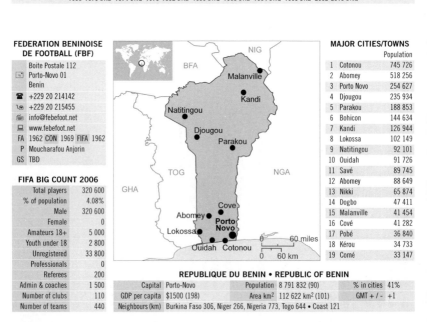

**FEDERATION BENINOISE
DE FOOTBALL (FBF)**

	Boite Postale 112
✉	Porto-Novo 01
	Benin
☎	+229 20 214142
📠	+229 20 215455
@	info@febefoot.net
🖥	www.febefoot.net
FA	1962 CON 1969 FIFA 1962
P	Moucharafou Anjorin
GS	TBD

FIFA BIG COUNT 2006

Total players	320 600
% of population	4.08%
Male	320 600
Female	0
Amateurs 18+	5 000
Youth under 18	2 800
Unregistered	33 800
Professionals	0
Referees	200
Admin & coaches	1 500
Number of clubs	110
Number of teams	440

MAJOR CITIES/TOWNS
Population

1	Cotonou	745 726
2	Abomey	518 256
3	Porto Novo	254 627
4	Djougou	235 934
5	Parakou	188 853
6	Bohicon	144 634
7	Kandi	126 944
8	Lokossa	102 149
9	Natitingou	92 101
10	Ouidah	91 726
11	Savé	89 745
12	Abomey	88 649
13	Nikki	65 874
14	Dogbo	47 411
15	Malanville	41 454
16	Cové	41 282
17	Pobé	36 840
18	Kérou	34 733
19	Comé	33 147

REPUBLIQUE DU BENIN • REPUBLIC OF BENIN

Capital	Porto-Novo	Population	8 791 832 (90)	% in cities	41%
GDP per capita	$1500 (198)	Area km²	112 622 km² (101)	GMT +/-	+1
Neighbours (km)	Burkina Faso 306, Niger 266, Nigeria 773, Togo 644 • Coast 121				

RECENT INTERNATIONAL MATCHES PLAYED BY BENIN

2008	Opponents	Score		Venue	Comp	Scorers	Att	Referee
1-06	Angola	L	0-3	Luanda	WCq		6 000	Damon RSA
8-06	Uganda	W	4-1	Cotonou	WCq	Omotoyossi 2 [16 87], Tchomogo.O [21], Sessegnon [70]	10 200	Karembe MLI
14-06	Niger	W	2-0	Niamey	WCq	Tchomogo.S [54], Omotoyossi [70]	5 000	Haimoudi ALG
22-06	Niger	W	2-0	Cotonou	WCq	Ahoueya [45]	25 000	Niyongabo BDI
20-08	Morocco	L	1-3	Rabat	Fr	Omotoyossi [36]		
7-09	Angola	W	3-2	Cotonou	WCq	Adenon [1], Omotoyossi 2 [52 65]	30 000	Benouza ALG
12-10	Uganda	L	1-2	Kampala	WCq	Omotoyossi [30]	2 913	Abd El Fatah
19-11	Egypt	L	1-5	Cairo	Fr	Omotoyossi [85]		
2009								
11-02	Algeria	L	1-2	Blida	Fr	Boco [85]		
29-03	Ghana	L	0-1	Kumasi	WCq		39 000	Bennett RSA
7-06	Sudan	W	1-0	Cotonou	WCq	Omotoyossi [22]	26 000	Marange ZIM
21-06	Mali	L	1-3	Bamako	WCq	Tchomogo.S [15]	40 000	Abd El Fatah EGY
11-08	Gabon	D	1-1	Dieppe	Fr	Maiga [10]		
6-09	Mali	D	1-1	Cotonou	WCq	Aoudou [87]	33 000	Damon RSA
11-10	Ghana	W	1-0	Cotonou	WCq	Aoudou [89]	20 000	Lwanja MWI
14-11	Sudan	W	2-1	Omdurman	WCq	Omotoyossi [34p], Koukou [62]	600	Jedidi TUN
2010								
6-01	Libya	W	1-0	Cotonou	Fr	Sessegnon [19]		
12-01	Mozambique	D	2-2	Benguela	CNr1	Omotoyossi [14p], Khan OG [20]	15 000	Abdel Rahman SUD
16-01	Nigeria	L	0-1	Benguela	CNr1		8 000	Carvalho ANG
20-01	Egypt	L	0-2	Benguela	CNr1		12 500	Bennett RSA
11-08	Niger	D	0-0	Porto Novo	Fr			
5-09	Burundi	D	1-1	Cotonou	CNq	Pote [2]		Bennett RSA
9-10	Rwanda	W	3-0	Kigali	CNq	Tchomogo [68], Omotoyossi [81], Sessegnon [88]		Haimoudi ALG

Fr = Friendly match • CN = CAF African Cup of Nations • WCq = FIFA World Cup • q = qualifier • r1 = first round group

MEDALS TABLE

		Overall			Lge	Cup	Africa			City/Town
		G	S	B	G	G	G	S	B	
1	Dragons de l'Ouémé	17	1		12	5			1	Porto-Novo
2	Mogas 90	12			3	9				Porto-Novo
3	Requins de l'Atlantique	8			3	5				Cotonou
4	Buffles de Borgou	5			2	3				Parakou
5	AS Porto Novo	3			3					Porto-Novo
6	ASPAC	2			1	1				Cotonou
7	Etoile Sportive	2			1	1				Porto-Novo
8	Univ National de Benin	2				2				Porto-Novo

BENIN 2009–10

PREMIERE DIVISION	Pl	W	D	L	F	A	Pts	ASPAC	Buffles	USS Kraké	Tonnerre	Dragons	Requins	Mambas	Panthères	Avrankou	Mogas 90	Abomey	Soleil	Parakou	Espoir
ASPAC †	26	12	9	5	40	19	45		0-1	1-1	2-1	2-2	1-1	0-0	4-0	3-1	4-1	2-0	2-0	1-1	3-0
Buffles Borgou	26	12	8	6	28	19	44	0-0		2-0	0-1	0-1	3-1	1-0	1-0	0-2	1-0	1-0	3-1	2-1	1-1
USS Kraké ‡	26	12	7	7	27	22	43	0-1	1-0		0-0	2-0	3-1	1-1	1-1	2-1	2-2	0-0	2-1	2-0	0-2
Tonnerre	26	8	14	4	23	14	38	0-0	2-1	0-1		1-1	1-1	2-0	1-0	0-0	0-0	0-0	1-1	0-0	0-0
Dragons de l'Ouémé	26	9	11	6	32	25	38	1-1	1-2	3-2	0-0		1-0	2-2	0-0	1-0	2-6	4-0	0-0	5-0	0-0
Requins de l'Atlantique	26	10	5	11	43	41	35	1-1	0-2	2-1	0-3	3-2		0-1	3-1	3-0	0-4	3-0	2-3	4-3	7-2
Mambas Noirs	26	9	8	9	23	27	35	0-5	1-2	0-1	2-2	2-0	1-1		1-1	1-0	1-0	1-0	1-3	0-0	1-0
Panthères Djougou	26	8	10	8	22	21	34	2-0	0-0	0-1	0-0	1-0	1-1	0-0		2-1	1-0	0-0	2-1	2-0	2-0
Avrankou Omnisport	26	9	6	11	21	26	33	1-0	1-1	0-1	0-1	0-1	3-1	2-1	1-0		0-0	0-0	1-0	2-1	2-2
Mogas 90	26	8	8	10	27	26	32	1-3	1-1	2-0	2-2	0-1	0-1	0-1	1-1	0-1		0-0	2-1	1-0	2-1
Dynamo Abomey	26	5	13	8	14	24	28	1-0	1-1	0-1	1-1	0-0	3-2	2-1	0-3	1-1	0-0		1-0	0-0	1-1
Soleil FC	26	8	4	14	23	35	28	0-2	1-0	0-1	0-2	0-3	0-4	2-1	1-1	0-1	1-0	2-1		2-0	0-0
Dynamo Parakou	26	6	8	12	17	28	26	3-1	1-1	1-0	0-1	0-0	1-0	0-1	1-0	2-0	0-1	0-0	2-1		0-0
Espoir Savalou	26	5	11	10	20	33	26	0-1	1-1	1-1	2-1	1-1	0-1	0-2	2-1	2-0	1-1	0-2	0-2	1-0	

3/10/2009 - 30/05/2010 • † Qualified for the CAF Champions League • ‡ Qualified for the CAF Confederations Cup

BER – BERMUDA

FIFA/COCA-COLA WORLD RANKING

1993	1994	1995	1996	1997	1998	1999	2000	2001	2002	2003	2004	2005	2006	2007	2008	2009	2010
84	102	140	167	176	185	163	153	166	172	183	157	161	107	147	124	142	175

	2010											Hi/Lo
	Jan	Feb	Mar	Mar	Apr	May	Jul	Aug	Sep	Oct	Nov	Dec	**58**
	142	135	136	136	134	134	159	158	163	170	173	175	**185**

There was a first-ever foray for Bermuda into Caribbean club competition when Devonshire Cougars entered the 2010 CFU club championship. At a first round group staged in St Vincent, the 2009 league champions got off to an encouraging start with a 2-2 draw against hosts Avenue United. The next two games, however, showed the gulf in standards between Bermuda and the bigger Caribbean nations with a 5-2 defeat at the hands of Suriname's Leo Victor and an 8-2 thrashing by Trinidad's Joe Public. There was consolation at home for Cougars when they won the FA Cup for the first time, beating Somerset Eagles on penalties in the final. Cougars failed to retain their league title in 2010 which went instead to Dandy Town who finished a point ahead of North Village in a very tight race to the finish. Dandy Town also won the Martonmere Cup after beating Boulevard Blazers on penalties in the final although North Village did pick up the remaining two trophies on offer during the season - the 2009 Dudley Eve trophy and the 2010 Friendship Trophy. At national team level there were no internationals played for the second year running after the BFA declined to take part in the 2010 Digicel Caribbean Cup and as a result had slipped down the FIFA/Coca-Cola World Ranking to 175 - just 10 places off their worst position set in 1998.

FIFA WORLD CUP RECORD
1930-1966 DNE **1970** DNQ **1974-1990** DNE **1994** DNQ **1998** DNE **2002-2010** DNQ

BERMUDA FOOTBALL ASSOCIATION (BFA)

	48 Cedar Avenue, PO Box HM 745, Hamilton, Bermuda
☎	+1 441 2952199
	+1 441 2950773
	dsabir@bermudafootball.com
	www.bermudafa.com
FA	1928 CON 1966 FIFA 1966
P	Larry Mussenden
GS	David Sabir

FIFA BIG COUNT 2006

Total players	7 155
% of population	10.88%
Male	6 205
Female	950
Amateurs 18+	2 250
Youth under 18	1 600
Unregistered	800
Professionals	5
Referees	35
Admin & coaches	220
Number of clubs	50
Number of teams	100

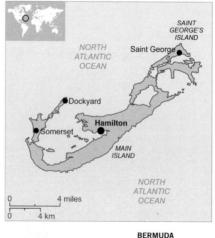

MAJOR CITIES/TOWNS

		Population
1	Saint George	1 648
2	Hamilton	1 100

BERMUDA

Capital	Hamilton	Population	67 837 (202)	% in cities	100%
GDP per capita	$69 900 (4)	Area km²	54 km² (231)	GMT +/-	-4
Neighbours (km)	Coast 103				

RECENT INTERNATIONAL MATCHES PLAYED BY BERMUDA

2008	Opponents	Score		Venue	Comp	Scorers	Att	Referee
16-01	Puerto Rico	L	0-2	Hamilton	Fr		500	Mauchette BER
18-01	Puerto Rico	L	0-1	Hamilton	Fr		325	Raynor BER
3-02	Cayman Islands	D	1-1	Hamilton	WCq	Burgess [18]	2 000	Navarro CAN
30-03	Cayman Islands	W	3-1	Georgetown	WCq	DeGraff 2 [19 23], Steede [53]	3 200	Marrufo USA
6-06	Barbados	W	2-1	Hamilton	Fr	Shakir [41], Ming [86]	2 000	Raynor BER
9-06	Barbados	W	3-0	Hamilton	Fr	Bean 2 [12 18], Nusum [45]	2 200	Francis BER
15-06	Trinidad and Tobago	W	2-1	Macoya	WCq	Nusum 2 [7 38]	4 585	Quesada CRC
22-06	Trinidad and Tobago	L	0-2	Prospect	WCq		5 000	Batres GUA
27-08	Antigua and Barbuda	L	0-4	Grand Cayman	CCq		300	Stennett JAM
30-08	Saint Martin †	W	7-0	Grand Cayman	CCq	Lambe 4 [23 45 60 85], Ming [26], Lowe [83], Castle [88]	350	Morisson JAM
31-08	Cayman Islands	D	0-0	Grand Cayman	CCq		350	Hospedales TRI
2009								

No international matches played in 2009

| 2010 | | | | | | | | |

No international matches played in 2010

Fr = Friendly match • CC = Digicel Caribbean Cup • WC = FIFA World Cup • q = qualifier • † Not a full international

BERMUDA 2009-10

CINGULAR WIRELESS PREMIER DIVISION

	Pl	W	D	L	F	A	Pts	Hornets	Rams	Zebras	Cougars	Blazers	Eagles	Rangers	Colts	Hamilton	Trojans
Dandy Town Hornets	18	13	1	4	55	31	40		1-3	5-3	6-2	2-0	4-2	5-3	2-1	3-4	3-1
North Village Rams	18	12	3	3	46	18	39	1-1		3-2	3-2	0-1	1-2	3-1	1-0	3-0	6-0
PHC Zebras	18	9	4	5	34	27	31	1-3	1-1		2-1	1-0	2-1	2-1	1-1	2-1	2-2
Devonshire Cougars	18	9	3	6	43	29	30	1-0	1-0	1-4		1-3	1-1	3-2	4-0	1-1	2-1
Boulevard Blazers	18	9	2	7	37	30	29	3-5	2-4	2-2	0-1		3-2	2-1	6-2	1-2	1-0
Somerset Eagles	18	8	3	7	29	29	27	3-2	0-2	1-2	3-2	2-2		0-0	2-1	3-2	2-0
Southampton Rangers	18	5	3	10	20	30	18	0-5	1-1	1-0	1-1	2-0	0-1		2-0	2-1	2-1
Devonshire Colts	18	5	2	11	26	39	17	1-4	1-4	2-1	1-2	1-4	3-2	3-1		3-0	0-2
Hamilton Parish	18	4	2	12	20	58	14	1-2	1-8	0-3	1-16	1-3	0-1	1-0	0-5		1-1
Somerset Trojans	18	3	3	12	17	36	12	1-2	1-2	1-3	0-1	1-4	2-1	1-0	1-1	1-3	

4/10/2009 - 4/04/2010

MEDALS TABLE

		Overall			Lge		Cup		FT		M'mere		DE		CON'CAF		
		G	S	B	G	S	G	S	G	S	G	S	G	S	G	S	B
1	North Village Rams	41	22		7	10	10	2	9	2	8	5	7	3			
2	PHC Zebras	38	26	1	9	4	10	8	10	5	3	6	6	3		1	
3	Somerset Trojans	37	25		9	9	9	3	9	3	7	4	3	6			
4	Dandy Town Hornets	19	25		5	8	1	8	4	4	6	2	3	3			
5	Devonshire Colts	17	33		3	4	5	10	4	11	2	6	3	2			
6	Vasco da Gama	16	9		3	1	5	2	1	3	3	2	4	1			
7	Boulevard Blazers	12	8		2	2	5	1	1	1	3	3	1	1			
8	Devonshire Cougars	9	13		3	2	1	2	1	4	3	3	1	2			
9	Hotels International	7	6		2	2	1		2	2	2	2					
10	YMSC	6	5		3	1	3	1		2		1					
11	Southampton Rangers	5	10		1		1	4	3	3		3		1			
12	Wolves	2	2					1			1	1	1				
13	Dock Hill Rangers	1	4			1	1	3									
14	BAA Wanderers	1	1				1	1									
	Casuals SC	1	1			1	1										
	St George's Colts	1	1						1	1							
	Wellington Rovers	1	1			1				1							
18	Somerset Eagles		3					1		2							
19	Pembroke Juniors		2					2									
	WWC		2					1		1							

BERMUDA 2009–10
SECOND DIVISION (2)

	Pl	W	D	L	F	A	Pts
St David's	20	15	4	1	73	12	49
St George's Colts	20	14	5	1	51	11	47
Robin Hood	20	13	3	4	38	12	42
X'roads Warriors	20	12	5	3	46	18	41
MR Onions	20	9	4	7	42	29	31
Wolves	20	9	2	9	31	43	29
YMSC	20	6	3	11	23	34	21
Prospect United	20	6	2	12	30	47	20
Ireland Rangers	20	3	4	13	35	52	13
BAA Wanderers	20	3	3	14	24	76	12
Paget Lions	20	1	3	16	12	71	6

4/10/2009 - 4/04/2010

MARTONMERE CUP 2009–10

Semi-finals		Final
Dandy Town Hornets		
St David's		
		Dandy Town Hornets	1 5p
		Boulevard Blazers	1 4p
Devonshire Cougars	1	
Boulevard Blazers	2	19-04-2010

FRIENDSHIP TROPHY 2009–10

First Round		Semi-finals		Final	
North Village Rams	1				
Devonshire Cougars	0	North Village Rams	3		
Somerset Eagles	0	Somerset Trojans	1		
Somerset Trojans	1			North Village Rams	3
PHC Zebras	2			Southampton Rangers	2
Devonshire Colts	1	PHC Zebras	1 7p		
Boulevard Blazers	0	Southampton Rangers	1 8p	11-04-2010	
Southampton Rangers	1				

DUDLEY EVE TROPHY 2009

First Round Group Stage

Group A	Pl	W	D	L	F	A	Pts	DC	HP
Dandy Town Hornets	2	1	0	1	4	1	3	0-1	4-0
Devonshire Cougars	2	1	0	1	1	1	3	0-1	
Hamilton Parish	2	1	0	1	1	4	3		

Semi-finals		Final	
North Village Rams	2		
Devonshire Cougars	0		
		North Village Rams	1 2p
		PHC Zebras	1 1p

Group B	Pl	W	D	L	F	A	Pts	PZ	BB
North Village Rams	2	1	1	0	6	5	4	3-3	3-2
PHC Zebras	2	0	2	0	4	4	2	1-1	
Boulevard Blazers	2	0	1	1	3	4	1		

Dandy Town Hornets	1
PHC Zebras	2

11-11-2009

FA CUP 2009–10

First Round		Quarter–finals		Semi–finals		Final	
Devonshire Cougars	W-0						
BAA Wanderers		Devonshire Cougars	7				
X'roads Warriors	0	YMSC	1				
YMSC	2			Devonshire Cougars	2 4p		
Robin Hood	2			North Village Rams	2 1p		
Southampton Rangers	0	Robin Hood	0 0				
Dandy Town Hornets	0	North Village Rams	0 1				
North Village Rams	1					Devonshire Cougars	2 5p
Hamilton Parish	1					Somerset Eagles	2 3p
St David's	0	Hamilton Parish	1				
Wolves	1	Boulevard Blazers	0				
Boulevard Blazers	6			Hamilton Parish	2		
PHC Zebras	6			Somerset Eagles	3		
MR Onions	0	PHC Zebras	2				
Ireland Rangers	0	Somerset Eagles	3				
Somerset Eagles	5						

CUP FINAL

18-04-2010
Scorers - Kwame Steede, Darius
Cox [90] for Cougars; Keishan Bean [42],
Troy Tucker [45] for Eagles

Elimination round: **X'road Warriors** 6-2 Prospect United; Somerset Trojans 1-2 **Southampton Rangers**;
Devonshire Colts 0-2 **Dandy Town Hornets**; **YMSC** 6-1 Paget lions; **Robin Hood** 2-1 St George's Colts

BFA – BURKINA FASO

FIFA/COCA-COLA WORLD RANKING

1993	1994	1995	1996	1997	1998	1999	2000	2001	2002	2003	2004	2005	2006	2007	2008	2009	2010
127	97	101	107	106	75	71	69	78	75	78	84	87	61	113	62	49	41

2010												Hi/Lo
Jan	Feb	Mar	Mar	Apr	May	Jul	Aug	Sep	Oct	Nov	Dec	37
49	51	51	52	52	48	45	45	39	37	41	41	127

In the past decade the Burkina Faso national team has established itself as one of the heavyweights in African football and at the African Nations Cup at the start of the year a draw with Cote d'Ivoire held out the promise of a finals to remember. It wasn't to be, however, after a defeat at the hands of Ghana saw them go home early but the performance saw Portuguese coach Paulo Duarte offered a chance to stay on for the 2012 Nations Cup qualifiers. After the withdrawal of Mauritania, Burkina Faso were left with only three teams in their qualifying group, leaving them to finish ahead of Gambia and Namibia to book a place at the next finals in Gabon and Equatorial Guinea. They started their campaign with a 3-1 home win over the Gambians and will be heavily fancied to reach a seventh finals in the last nine editions. At home ASFA Yennenga won the Premier Division for a second successive year but their bid for significant progress in the CAF Champions League came unstuck in the second round of the preliminaries where they were soundly beaten by Esperance of Tunisia. In the CAF Confederation Cup, army club USFA went out at the first hurdle but after beating Racing Club from Bobo-Dioulasso 1-0 in the 2010 Cup Final it meant that the soldiers would be back again for another crack in the 2011 edition.

FIFA WORLD CUP RECORD
1930-1974 DNE 1978 DNQ 1982-1986 DNE 1990 DNQ 1994 DNE 1998- 2010 DNQ

FEDERATION BURKINABE DE FOOT-BALL (FBF)
Centre Technique National, Ouaga 2000, Boite Postale 57, Ouagadougou 01
☎ +226 50 396864
📠 +226 50 396866
✉ febefoo@fasonet.bf
🖥 www.fasofoot.com
FA 1960 CON 1964 FIFA 1964
P Theodore Sawadogo
GS Emmanuel Zombre

FIFA BIG COUNT 2006

Total players	605 100
% of population	4.35%
Male	576 800
Female	28 300
Amateurs 18+	13 000
Youth under 18	10 200
Unregistered	45 900
Professionals	0
Referees	700
Admin & coaches	2 400
Number of clubs	100
Number of teams	850

MAJOR CITIES/TOWNS

		Population
1	Ouagadougou	1 351 245
2	Bobo Dioulasso	471 426
3	Koudougou	85 157
4	Banfora	80 491
5	Ouahigouya	76 392
6	Pouytenga	71 278
7	Kaya	57 295
8	Garango	55 851
9	Fada N'gourma	44 629
10	Tenkodogo	43 447
11	Houndé	39 575
12	Dédougou	39 187
13	Tanghin-D'ouri	37 477
14	Kindi	31 614
15	Léo	28 541
16	Réo	28 401
17	Kongoussi	27 155
18	Gaoua	26 835
19	Gourcy	26 527

BURKINA FASO

Capital	Ouagadougou	Population	15 746 232 (61)	% in cities	20%
GDP per capita	$1200 (208)	Area km²	274 200 km² (74)	GMT +/-	0
Neighbours (km)	Benin 306, Cote d'Ivoire 584, Ghana 549, Mali 1000, Niger 628, Togo 126				

RECENT INTERNATIONAL MATCHES PLAYED BY BURKINA FASO

2006 Opponents	Score		Venue	Comp	Scorers	Att	Referee
28-02 Algeria	D	0-0	Rouen	Fr		2 000	Duhamel FRA
16-08 Morocco	L	0-1	Rabat	Fr			
29-08 Uganda	D	0-0	Kampala	Fr			
2-09 Tanzania	L	1-2	Dar es Salaam	CNq	Abdoulaye Cisse 39		Ndinya KEN
7-10 Senegal	W	1-0	Ouagadougou	CNq	Yameogo 59p		Guezzaz MAR
15-11 Algeria	W	2-1	Aix-en-Provence	Fr	Yameogo 60p, Koffi 82	700	Falcone FRA
2007							
24-03 Mozambique	D	1-1	Ouagadougou	CNq	Pitroipa 26		Imiere NGA
29-05 Zimbabwe	D	1-1	Masvingo	Fr	Kabore 71	12 000	
3-06 Mozambique	L	1-3	Maputo	CNq	Sanou 38		Raolimanana MAD
9-06 Mali	L	0-1	Ouagadougou	Fr			
16-06 Tanzania	L	0-1	Ouagadougou	CNq			Coulibaly MLI
22-08 Mali	L	2-3	Paris	Fr	Sanou, Coulibaly		
8-09 Senegal	L	1-5	Dakar	CNq	Alain Traore 34		Haimoudi ALG
2008							
24-05 Cape Verde Islands	L	0-1	Alcochete	Fr			
1-06 Tunisia	W	2-1	Rades	WCq	Yssouf Kone 2 85 87	15 000	Ambaya LBY
7-06 Burundi	W	2-0	Ouagadougou	WCq	Dagano 2 23p 44p		Ndume GAB
14-06 Seychelles	W	3-2	Victoria	WCq	Dagano 3 25 57 78	1 000	Seechurn MRI
21-06 Seychelles	W	4-1	Ouagadougou	WCq	Kabore 21, Kere 28, Ouattara 54, Yssouf Kone 89	12 500	Lamptey GHA
20-08 Bahrain	L	1-3	Manama	Fr	Minoungou 64		
6-09 Tunisia	D	0-0	Ouagadougou	WCq		10 000	Katjimune NAM
12-10 Burundi	W	3-1	Bujumbura	WCq	Bance 15, Dagano 2 60 80	10 000	Ssegonga UGA
2009							
11-02 Togo	D	1-1	Le Petit-Quevilly	Fr	Pitroipa 32		
28-03 Guinea	W	4-2	Ouagadougou	WCQ	Kere 23, Alain Traore 30, Dagano 2 55p 71	30 000	Benouza ALG
6-06 Malawi	W	1-0	Blantyre	WCQ	Dagano 68	25 000	Bennaceur TUN
20-06 Côte d'Ivoire	L	2-3	Ouagadougou	WCQ	Pitroipa 27, Bance 78	33 056	Damon RSA
12-08 Mali	L	0-3	Le Petit-Quevilly	Fr			
5-09 Côte d'Ivoire	L	0-5	Abidjan	WCQ		28 209	Maillet SEY
11-10 Guinea	W	2-1	Accra	WCQ	Dagano 37, Bamogo 59	5 000	Ambaya LBY
14-11 Malawi	W	1-0	Ouagadougou	WCQ	Dagano 47	20 000	Abd El Fatah EGY
2010							
11-01 Côte d'Ivoire	D	0-0	Cabinda	CNr1		5 000	Bennaceur TUN
19-01 Ghana	L	0-1	Luanda	CNr1		8 000	Maillet SEY
11-08 Congo	W	3-0	Senlis	Fr	Dagano 17, Panandetiguiri 30, Alain Traore 81		
6-09 Gabon	D	1-1	Cannes	Fr	Alain Traore 87p		
9-10 Gambia	W	3-1	Ouagadougou	CNq	Dagano 16, Balima 57, Kabore 69		Osman EGY
17-11 Guinea	W	2-1	Mantes-La-Ville	Fr	Pitroipa 35, Balima 84		

Fr = Friendly match • CN = CAF African Cup of Nations • WC = FIFA World Cup • q = qualifier, r1 = first round group

BURKINA FASO 2009–10

PREMIERE DIVISION

	Pl	W	D	L	F	A	Pts	ASFA/Y	EFO	USFA	ASS	RCK	RCB	BPFC	Bobo Sport	USCO	Koupèla	USY	ASMB	Sourou	Sama
ASFA/Yennenga †	26	18	7	1	39	9	61		4-1	2-2	1-1	1-0	1-1	1-1	5-1	4-1	1-0	1-0	2-0	2-0	3-0
Etoile Filante	26	14	7	5	44	19	49	0-1		1-1	2-0	2-1	1-1	1-0	5-0	2-0	2-1	4-1	3-0	1-1	5-0
US Forces Armées	26	13	9	4	41	17	48	0-2	1-4		1-2	0-0	1-0	5-1	2-0	1-0	4-0	7-1	0-1	1-0	5-0
AS SONABEL	26	12	9	5	31	21	45	0-3	0-0	1-4		2-2	0-0	1-0	0-0	3-0	0-0	3-1	1-0	1-0	5-0
Rail Club Kadiogo	26	11	10	5	40	21	43	0-0	0-0	0-1	1-1		1-1	2-1	1-1	2-0	1-0	2-1	0-1	5-2	6-0
Racing Club B-D	26	7	14	5	26	21	35	1-0	1-0	1-1	1-2	2-1		1-1	1-1	2-0	0-0	2-1	0-0	1-0	4-1
Bouloumpokou FC	26	8	11	7	26	24	35	0-2	0-1	0-0	1-1	1-4	1-1		2-1	0-0	0-0	1-1	1-0	3-0	2-0
Bobo Sport	26	7	10	9	21	28	31	0-0	0-0	0-0	1-2	0-1	2-1	1-3		2-0	0-0	0-1	1-1	3-0	2-0
US Comoé	26	8	7	11	17	27	31	0-2	2-0	0-0	0-0	0-0	2-0	0-1	1-0		0-1	2-1	0-0	3-1	1-0
AS Koupèla	26	5	14	7	10	15	29	0-0	1-0	1-1	0-0	1-0	1-1	0-0	1-1	0-0		0-1	0-0	0-0	1-0
US Yatenga	26	8	5	13	27	37	29	0-1	2-1	0-0	1-0	2-4	1-1	0-2	0-1	2-0	0-0		0-1	2-0	5-1
AS Maya B-D	26	5	11	10	11	22	26	0-1	0-2	1-1	0-2	0-0	1-1	0-0	1-1	0-1	1-1	1-2		0-1	1-0
Sourou Sport	26	3	8	15	16	37	17	0-0	1-3	0-1	1-2	1-2	1-1	1-1	0-1	2-2	1-0	2-1	0-1		0-0
Sama Sport	26	0	4	22	7	58	4	0-1	1-3	0-1	0-1	0-3	0-2	0-3	0-1	1-2	1-2	0-0	1-1	1-1	

26/12/2009 - 17/06/2010 • † Qualified for the CAF Champions League • Matches in bold were awarded • Rail Club Kadiogo also relegated as the worst club from Ougadougou after a play-off with USO, the best placed club from Ouagadougou in the second division
Play-off: USO 3-1 2-1 Rail Club Kadiogo

MEDALS TABLE

				Overall			Lge	Cup	Africa		
				G	S	B	G	G	G	S	B
1	Etoile Filante	EFO	Ougadougou	32			12	20			
2	ASFA/Yennega (ex Jeanne d'Arc)	ASFA-Y	Ougadougou	13			10	3			
3	Union Sportive des Forces Armées	USFA	Ougadougou	10			7	3			
4	Silures (folded in 1982)		Bobo-Dioulasso	8			7	1			
5	Racing Club de Bobo	RCB	Bobo-Dioulasso	8			3	5			
6	Union Sportive du Foyer de la Regie Abidjan-Niger	USFRAN	Bobo-Dioulasso	8			3	5			
7	Association Sportive des Fonctionnaires de Bobo	ASFB	Bobo-Dioulasso	7			2	5			
8	Union Sportive Ouagadougou	USO		3			2	1			
9	Rail Club Kadiogo	RCK	Kadiogo	2	2		1	1			2
10	Commune	CFO	Ougadougou	2			1	1			

COUPE NATIONALE DU FASO 2009–10

Round of 16

US Forces Armées	3
Rail Club Kadiogo	1
Bobo Sport	0
AS Maya B-D	1
Centre Formation Bobo	1 8p
Sourou Sport	1 7p
Black Stars	0
US Yatenga	3
US Ouagadougou	2
Bouloumpokou FC	1
Commune FC	2
USFRAN *	1
ASFA/Yennenga	4
US Comoé	0
Etoile Filante	0
Racing Club B-D	1

Quarter–finals

US Forces Armées	2
AS Maya B-D	0
Centre Formation Bobo	0
US Yatenga	1
US Ouagadougou	1
USFRAN	0
ASFA/Yennenga	0 7p
Racing Club B-D	0 8p

Semi–finals

US Forces Armées	1
US Yatenga	0
US Ouagadougou	0
Racing Club B-D	1

Final

US Forces Armées ‡	1
Racing Club B-D	0

CUP FINAL

Stade di 4-août, Ouagadougou
5-08-2010
Scorer - Aziz Djelebéogo [27] for USFA

* Awarded to USFRAN • ‡ Qualified for the CAF Confederation Cup

3rd Place Play-off: US Ouagadougou 4-0 US Yatenga

BHR – BAHRAIN

FIFA/COCA-COLA WORLD RANKING

1993	1994	1995	1996	1997	1998	1999	2000	2001	2002	2003	2004	2005	2006	2007	2008	2009	2010
78	73	99	118	121	119	136	138	110	105	64	49	52	97	102	80	60	93

2010												Hi/Lo
	Jan	Feb	Mar	Mar	Apr	May	Jul	Aug	Sep	Oct	Nov	Dec	**44**
	60	60	63	67	69	69	69	68	75	84	87	93	**139**

Bahrain's status as one of the strongest national teams in the Middle East has been on the wane since the agonizing failure to qualify for the World Cup finals in South Africa. 2010 saw former Austria coach Josef Hickersberger take over but he didn't last long in the hot seat, resigning after Bahrain's poor performance with a youthful squad at the West Asian Championship in September. Local coach Salman Sharida had no better luck at the Gulf Cup in Yemen in November, in which Bahrain were also eliminated in the first round and as a result the Bahrainis went to the 2011 AFC Asian Cup in January with low expectations despite their relatively lofty ranking within the confederation. After an opening loss against South Korea, they flattered to deceive in their 5-2 victory over India while an improved performance against Australia in a must-win encounter almost revitalized their hopes, but a solitary goal by Mile Jedinak ended Bahrain's participation in the tournament at the group stage for the second Asian Cup in a row. In club football local giants Muharraq followed up their incredible five-trophy haul in the 2008-09 season by failing to win any at all the following season. Instead, the league title went to Al Ahli - their first since 1996 - while an Ismaeel Latif inspired Riffa won the 2010 King's Cup final against Busaiteen.

FIFA WORLD CUP RECORD
1930-1974 DNE 1978-1986 DNQ 1990 DNE 1994-2010 DNQ

BAHRAIN FOOTBALL ASSOCIATION (BFA)

✉	Bahrain National Stadium, PO Box 5464, Manama, Bahrain
☎	+973 17 689569
📠	+973 17 781188
✉	bhrfa@batelco.com.bh
🖥	www.bahrainfootball.org
FA	1957 CON 1970 FIFA 1966
P	Shk. Salman Al Khalifa
GS	Abdulrahman Sayyar

FIFA BIG COUNT 2006

Total players	18 278
% of population	2.62%
Male	16 828
Female	1 450
Amateurs 18+	730
Youth under 18	2 800
Unregistered	2 400
Professionals	66
Referees	90
Admin & coaches	620
Number of clubs	48
Number of teams	150

MAJOR CITIES/TOWNS

		Population
1	Manama	156 872
2	ar-Rifa'a	116 568
3	Muharraq	108 180
4	Madinat Hamad	84 709
5	Ali	66 113
6	Sitra	42 223
7	Isa Town	40 637
8	al-Budayyi	38 438
9	Jidhaf	34 757
10	al-Malikiyah	16 116
11	al-Hidd	14 703

MAMLAKAT AL BAHRAYN • KINGDOM OF BAHRAIN

Capital	Manama	Population	727 785 (162)	% in cities	89%
GDP per capita	$37 300 (28)	Area km²	741 km² (190)	GMT +/-	+3
Neighbours (km)	Coast 161				

RECENT INTERNATIONAL MATCHES PLAYED BY BAHRAIN

2009	Opponents	Score	Venue	Comp	Scorers	Att	Referee
4-01	Iraq	W 3-1	Muscat	GCr1	Abdulla Omar 28, Sayed Mohamed 69, Al Dakeel 90		
7-01	Kuwait	L 0-1	Muscat	GCr1			
10-01	Oman	L 0-2	Muscat	GCr1			
21-01	Hong Kong	W 3-1	Hong Kong	ACq	Ismaeel Latif 10, Abdulla Fatadi 37, Salman Isa 87	6 013	Vo Minh Tri VIE
28-01	Japan	W 1-0	Manama	ACq	Salman Isa 24	11 200	Irmatov UZB
4-02	Korea Republic	D 2-2	Dubai	Fr	Fouzi Aaish 62p, Abdulrahman 83		
11-02	Uzbekistan	W 1-0	Tashkent	WCq	Abdulrahman 94+	30 000	Mohd Salleh MAS
23-03	Zimbabwe	W 5-2	Manama	Fr	Mohamed Salmeen 27, Fouzi Aaish 36, Jaycee Okunwanne 54, Abdulla Fatati 64, Abdulrahman 76		
28-03	Japan	L 0-1	Saitama	WCq		57 276	Kim Dong Jin KOR
1-04	Qatar	W 1-0	Manama	WCq	Fouzi Aaish 52	20 000	Sun Baojie CHN
31-05	Congo	W 3-1	Manama	Fr	Ahmed Hassan 7, Fouzi Aaish 44, Salman Isa 71		
3-06	Jordan	W 4-0	Manama	Fr	Mohamed Salmeen 15, Abdulla Omar 54, Latif 2 66 74		
10-06	Australia	L 0-2	Sydney	WCq		39 540	Al Hilali OMA
17-06	Uzbekistan	W 1-0	Manama	WCq	Abdulrahman 73	14 100	Moradi IRN
26-08	Kenya	W 2-1	Manama	Fr	Husain Ahmed 2 25 44		
31-08	Iran	W 4-2	Manama	Fr	Abdulrahman 12, Latif 30, Isa 54, Sayed Mohamed 54		
5-09	Saudi Arabia	D 0-0	Manama	WCpo		16 000	Nishimura JPN
9-09	Saudi Arabia	D 2-2	Riyadh	WCpo	Jaycee Okunwanne 42, Ismaeel Latif 93+	50 000	Irmatov UZB
10-10	New Zealand	D 0-0	Manama	WCpo		37 000	Kassai HUN
6-11	Togo	W 5-1	Manama	Fr	Abdulla Fatadi 2 39 90, Latif 2 40 57, Hussain Ali 86p		
14-11	New Zealand	L 0-1	Wellington	WCpo		36 500	Larrionda URU
18-11	Yemen	W 4-0	Manama	ACq	Ismaeel Latif 20, Abdulla Fatadi 28, Habib 64, OG 75	1 000	Basma SYR
2010							
6-01	Hong Kong	W 4-0	Manama	ACq	Ismaeel Latif 3 34 40 43, Abdulla Al Dakeel 79	1 550	Balideh QAT
20-01	Yemen	L 0-3	Sana'a	ACq		7 000	Torky IRN
25-02	Kuwait	L 1-4	Al Ain City	Fr	Abdulrahman 19		
3-03	Japan	L 0-2	Toyota	ACq		38 042	Abdul Bashir SIN
11-08	China PR	D 1-1	Nanning	Fr	Ismaeel Latif 17		
3-09	Qatar	D 1-1	Doha	Fr	Faouzi Aaish 21		
19-09	Jordan	L 0-2	Zarqa	Fr			
24-09	Iran	L 0-3	Amman	WАr1		8 000	Darwish JOR
26-09	Oman	W 2-0	Amman	WАr1	Ismaeel Latif 2 63 67	500	
8-10	Kuwait	W 3-1	Kuwait City	Fr	Ismaeel Latif 9, Faouzi Aaish 47, Salman Isa 51	10 000	
12-10	Uzbekistan	L 2-4	Manama	Fr	Faouzi Aaish 30, Hussein Salman 53		
10-11	Uganda	D 0-0	Manama	Fr			
14-11	Syria	L 0-2	Manama	Fr			
23-11	Oman	D 1-1	Aden	GCr1	Ebrahim Moshkhas 67		Al Enezi KUW
26-11	Iraq	L 2-3	Aden	GCr1	Faouzi Aaish 44, Ismaeel Latif 96+p		Allabany YEM
29-11	UAE	L 1-3	Aden	GCr1	Abdulla Fatadi 35		Al Marry BHR
28-12	Jordan	W 2-1	Dubai	Fr	Faouzi Aaish 32p, Ismaeel Latif 69		
31-12	Saudi Arabia	L 0-1	Riffa	Fr			
2011							
4-01	Korea DPR	L 0-1	Riffa	Fr			
10-01	Korea Republic	L 1-2	Doha	ACr1	Faouzi Aaish 86p	6 669	Al Hilali OMA
14-01	India	W 5-2	Doha	ACr1	Faouzi Aaish 8p, Ismaeel Latif 4 16 20 35 77	11 032	Mohd Salleh MAS
18-01	Australia	L 0-1	Doha	ACr1		3 919	Nishimura JPN

Fr = Friendly match • AC = AFC Asian Cup • GC = Gulf Cup • WA = West Asian Championship • WC = FIFA World Cup
q = qualifier • r1 = first round group • qf = quarter-final • sf = semi-final • f = final • 3p = third place play-off • po = play-off

BAHRAIN NATIONAL TEAM HISTORICAL RECORDS

Past Coaches (Since 2003) Wolfgang Sidka GER • Yves Herbet FRA • Srecko Juricic CRO • Wolfgang Sidka GER • Luka Peruzovic CRO • Riyadh Al Thawadi BHR 2006 • Hans-Peter Briegel GER 2006-07 • Milan Macala CZE 2007-10 • Josef Hickersberger AUT 2010 • Salman Sharida 2010-

BAHRAIN 2009–10

PREMIER LEAGUE

	Pl	W	D	L	F	A	Pts	Al Ahli	Muharraq	Riffa	Al Najma	Busaiteen	Manama	Al Shabab	Al Hala	Malikiya	East Riffa
Al Ahli	18	13	2	3	26	17	41		2-6	1-0	1-0	2-0	3-1	1-1	1-0	1-0	2-0
Muharraq	18	13	1	4	38	20	40	0-1		2-1	0-1	1-0	7-3	3-2	3-0	1-1	1-0
Riffa	18	12	2	4	36	18	38	0-1	2-0		0-1	3-2	0-0	3-0	4-3	4-1	4-0
Al Najma	18	10	2	6	27	18	32	4-0	1-2	1-2		2-1	1-1	1-0	2-1	3-1	3-1
Busaiteen	18	6	5	7	29	23	23	1-2	2-1	1-1	1-1		1-1	1-3	1-0	1-1	4-0
Manama	18	4	6	8	23	33	18	0-2	2-3	2-1	0-1			3-2	2-1	1-2	1-1
Al Shabab	18	5	2	11	18	35	17	1-2	1-3	0-2	0-1	0-6	1-1		1-4	2-1	1-0
Al Hala	18	4	4	10	27	30	16	1-2	1-2	1-2	2-1	1-1	2-1	0-1		2-2	3-3
Malikiya	18	4	4	10	18	31	16	0-0	1-2	1-2	1-0	1-4	2-0	1-2	0-3		0-3
East Riffa	18	3	4	11	21	38	13	0-3	1-2	1-3	2-3	3-1	2-2	2-1	2-2	0-2	

24/09/2009 - 17/05/2010 • † Qualified for the AFC Cup
9th place play-off: Malikiya 2-3 **Al Hala** • Relegation play-off: **Malikiya** 2-3 2-1 6-5p Setra. Malikiya remain in the Premier League

BAHRAIN 2009–10 FIRST DIVISION

	Pl	W	D	L	F	A	Pts
Al Hadd	16	14	0	2	47	10	42
Setra ‡	16	13	1	2	42	17	40
Bahrain Club	16	13	1	2	54	16	40
Al Ittihad	16	9	2	5	42	24	29
Budaia	16	7	2	7	28	39	23
Essa Town	16	3	3	10	23	33	12
Qalali	16	3	2	11	24	50	11
Al Ittifaq	16	2	3	11	16	44	9
Al Tadamun	16	0	2	14	8	51	2

27/09/2009 - 10/05/2010 • ‡ Play-off (see Premier League)

MEDALS TABLE

		All	Lge	KC	FAC	CPC	Asia		
		G	G	G			G	S	B
1	Muharraq	65	31	27	2	5		2	
2	Riffa	21	9	5	3	4			
3	Al Ahli	14	5	8	1				
4	Bahrain Club	7	5	2					
5	Al Hala	4	1	3					
6	East Riffa	3	1	2					
	Al Wahda	3		3					
8	Al Arabi	2	1	1					
	Al Najma	2		2					
10	Al Shabab	1		1					
	Busaiteen	1			1				
	Al Nasr	1	1						

KINGS CUP 2009–10

First Round

Riffa	4
Bahrain Club	1
Qalali	2
Al Shabab	3
Al Hadd	2
East Riffa	0
Al Hala	1
Manama	3
Muharraq	2
Al Ittifaq	0
Budaia	0
Malikiya	3
Setra	3
Al Najma	2
Al Ittihad	1
Busaiteen	2

Quarter–finals

Riffa	5
Al Shabab	1
Al Hadd	0
Manama	3
Muharraq	3
Malikiya	0
Setra	0
Busaiteen	4

Semi–finals

Riffa	2
Manama	1
Muharraq	1
Busaiteen	2

Final

Riffa	4
Busaiteen	0

CUP FINAL

National Stadium, Manama
11-02-2010
Scorers - OG [5], Ismaeel Latif 2 [46] [55], Sayyed Issa [66] for Riffa

Preliminary Round: **Al Ittifaq** 3-0 Al Tadamun; **Qalali** 1-0 Essa Town

BHU – BHUTAN

FIFA/COCA-COLA WORLD RANKING

1993	1994	1995	1996	1997	1998	1999	2000	2001	2002	2003	2004	2005	2006	2007	2008	2009	2010
-	-	-	-	-	-	-	201	202	199	187	187	190	192	198	187	196	197

2010												Hi/Lo
Jan	Feb	Mar	Mar	Apr	May	Jul	Aug	Sep	Oct	Nov	Dec	**187**
196	197	197	196	197	196	198	197	198	198	197	197	**202**

Bhutan maintained their status as one of the minnows of Asian football with the tiny Himalayan country absent from international competition at every level bar one during the course of 2010. The federation withdrew the under-19 team from a qualifying group for the Asian U-19 Championship which was staged in the United Arab Emirates but they did let the under-16 side take part in the Asian U-16 Championship. The team travelled to Yemen to take part in a six-team qualifying group made up of opponents from the Middle-East but it wasn't the best experience for the youngsters who shipped 30 goals in losing all five matches including a 10-0 defeat at the hands of group winners Syria. Club side Druk Star, who won the domestic title in 2009, took part in the 2010 AFC President's Cup in Myanmar, but struggled in the group stages and suffered a pair of heavy defeats. An 8-0 loss at the hands of HTTU Ashgabat of Turkmenistan was followed by an 11-0 thrashing by eventual champions Yadanabon of Myanmar, leaving the Bhutanese in last place in their three-team group. At home, Druk Star relinquished their grip on the domestic title as they finished fourth in the seven-team competition. Yeedzin claimed the title, finishing nine points clear of second-placed Drukpol over the championship's 12 matches.

FIFA WORLD CUP RECORD
1930-2010 DNE

BHUTAN FOOTBALL FEDERATION (BFF)

PO Box 365, Thimphu

☎ +975 2 322350
🖷 +975 2 321131
✉ mindubff_05@yahoo.com
💻
FA 1983 CON 1993 FIFA 2000
P Ugen Tsechup Dorji
GS Ugyen Wangchhuk

FIFA BIG COUNT 2006

Total players	17 100
% of population	0.75%
Male	17 100
Female	0
Amateurs 18+	600
Youth under 18	600
Unregistered	2 900
Professionals	0
Referees	100
Admin & coaches	100
Number of clubs	10
Number of teams	70

MAJOR CITIES/TOWNS

		Population
1	Thimphu	90 300
2	Phuentsholing	22 467
3	Geylegphug	9 901
4	Wangdue	7 174
5	Samdrup Jongkhar	6 389
6	Samtse	5 272
7	Gedu	4 691
8	Bumthang	4 507
9	Gomtu	4 503
10	Monggar	3 722
11	Chhukha	3 123
12	Trashiyangtse	2 900
13	Trongsa	2 866
14	Deothang	2 838
15	Sarpang	2 819
16	Ha	2 657
17	Tsimalakha	2 583
18	Trashigang	2 513
19	Tshongdue	2 477

DRUK GYALKHAP • KINGDOM OF BHUTAN

Capital	Thimphu	Population	691 141 (163)	% in cities	35%
GDP per capita	$5200 (138)	Area km²	38 394 km² (136)	GMT + / -	+6
Neighbours (km)	China 470, India 605				

RECENT INTERNATIONAL MATCHES PLAYED BY BHUTAN

2003	Opponents	Score		Venue	Comp	Scorers	Att	Referee
6-10	Indonesia	L	0-2	Jeddah	ACq			
8-10	Saudi Arabia	L	0-6	Jeddah	ACq			
10-10	Yemen	L	0-8	Jeddah	ACq			
13-10	Indonesia	L	0-2	Jeddah	ACq			
15-10	Saudi Arabia	L	0-4	Jeddah	ACq			
17-10	Yemen	L	0-4	Jeddah	ACq			
2004								
No international matches played in 2004								
2005								
8-12	Bangladesh	L	0-3	Karachi	SAFr1			
10-12	India	L	0-3	Karachi	SAFr1			
12-12	Nepal	L	1-3	Karachi	SAFr1	Pradhan [47]		
2006								
2-04	Nepal	L	0-2	Chittagong	CCr1		3 500	Gosh BAN
4-04	Sri Lanka	L	0-1	Chittagong	CCr1			Saidov UZB
6-04	Brunei Darussalam	D	0-0	Chittagong	CCr1		2 000	Al Ghatrifi OMA
2007								
No international matches played in 2007								
2008								
13-05	Tajikistan	L	1-3	Barotac	CCq	Pasang Tshering [69]	5 000	Ng Chiu Kok HGK
15-05	Brunei Darussalam	D	1-1	Barotac	CCq	Nawang Dendup [12]	4 000	Mahapab THA
17-05	Philippines	L	0-3	Barotac	CCq		7 000	Saleem MDV
4-06	Bangladesh	D	1-1	Colombo	SAFr1	Nima Sanghe [79]		
6-06	Sri Lanka	L	0-2	Colombo	SAFr1			
8-06	Afghanistan	W	3-1	Colombo	SAFr1	Kinlay Dorji [13], Gyeltshen 2 [31 80]		
11-06	India	L	1-2	Male	SAFsf	Kinlay Dorji [18]		
2009								
14-04	Philippines	L	0-1	Male	CCq		200	Lazeem IRQ
16-04	Turkmenistan	L	0-7	Male	CCq		300	Perera SRI
18-04	Maldives	L	0-5	Male	CCq		9 000	Lazeem IRQ
29-11	Nepal	L	1-2	Calcutta	Fr	Pasang Tshering [59p]		
4-12	Bangaldesh	L	1-4	Dhaka	SAFr1	Nawang Dendup [42p]		
6-12	Sri Lanka	L	0-6	Dhaka	SAFr1			
8-12	Pakistan	L	0-7	Dhaka	SAFr1			
2010								
No international matches played in 2010								

SAF = South Asian Football Federation Cup • AC = AFC Asian Cup • CC = AFC Challenge Cup • q = qualifier • r1 = first round group

BHUTAN 2010

10TH NATIONAL LEAGUE A-DIVISION	Pl	W	D	L	F	A	Pts	Yeedzin	Drukpol	Transport U	Drukstar	Choden	Druk Ath'tic	Nangpa
Yeedzin †	12	11	1	0	48	11	34		0-0	1-0	3-1	2-1	2-1	9-1
Drukpol	12	8	1	3	46	15	25	2-3		4-2	2-0	8-0	7-1	9-1
Transport United	12	8	1	3	33	19	25	2-4	3-2		5-3	3-1	6-0	4-2
Drukstar	12	7	1	4	38	20	22	0-5	2-1	0-0		2-0	12-1	2-0
Choden	12	3	0	9	17	39	9	0-6	2-3	1-2	1-5		1-2	4-2
Druk Athletic	12	2	1	9	15	56	7	1-4	0-5	1-4	1-8	3-4		3-2
Nangpa	12	0	1	11	14	51	1	2-9	1-3	0-2	1-3	1-2	1-1	

26/06/2010 - 17/08/2010 • † Qualified for the AFC President's Cup

BIH – BOSNIA-HERZEGOVINA

FIFA/COCA-COLA WORLD RANKING

1993	1994	1995	1996	1997	1998	1999	2000	2001	2002	2003	2004	2005	2006	2007	2008	2009	2010
-	-	-	152	99	96	75	78	69	87	59	79	65	59	51	61	51	

	2010											Hi/Lo
Jan	Feb	Mar	Mar	Apr	May	Jul	Aug	Sep	Oct	Nov	Dec	**25**
51	48	49	47	51	51	57	57	59	53	51	44	**173**

A great FIFA World Cup qualifying campaign which ended in heartbreak at the hands of Portugal in the play-offs, gave football a huge boost in this still fractured country. The task of maintaining the momentum may prove to be more difficult, especially after an indifferent start to the qualifiers for Euro 2012, but Bosnian players continue to be in high demand around Europe, especially star striker Edin Dzeko, who joined big spending Manchester City for £27m in January 2011 after another prolific season for Wolfsburg in the Bundesliga in which he finished as the league's top scorer yet again. At home Dzeko's first club, Zeljeznicar, won a first league title for eight years, inspired by the return of coach Amar Osim, the man who lead them to their two previous titles in 2001 and 2002. He couldn't, however, repeat his Cup triumph of 2003 with the club although Zeljeznicar came agonizingly close. Unbeaten going into the two-legged final, they finished their campaign unbeaten - but without the trophy after losing on away goals to Borac after both games ended in draws. For Borac, from the city of Banja Luka - the capital of the Serb territories in Bosnia-Herzegovina - winning the cup ended a trophy drought stretching back to 1988, the year they beat Red Star in the Yugoslav Cup Final in what was their only previous honour.

FIFA WORLD CUP RECORD
1930-1994 DNE 1998-2010 DNQ

FOOTBALL FEDERATION OF BOSNIA-HERZEGOVINA (FFBH/NSBIH)

Ferhadija 30,
Sarajevo - 71000
☎ +387 33 276660
📠 +387 33 444332
✉ nsbih@bih.net.ba
🖥 www.nfsbih.ba
FA 1992 CON 1996 FIFA 1996
P Sulejman Colakovic
GS Jasmin Bakovic

FIFA BIG COUNT 2006

Total players	200 240
% of population	4.45%
Male	181 640
Female	18 600
Amateurs 18+	40 370
Youth under 18	26 570
Unregistered	36 200
Professionals	430
Referees	1 720
Admin & coaches	10 100
Number of clubs	763
Number of teams	1 000

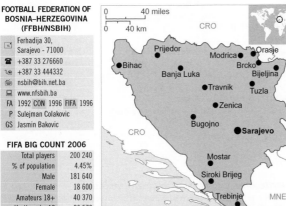

MAJOR CITIES/TOWNS

		Population
1	Banja Luka	221 686
2	Sarajevo	192 264
3	Samac	110 246
4	Tuzla	97 038
5	Zenica	93 043
6	Bijeljina	70 528
7	Mostar	70 270
8	Gradiska	42 262
9	Prijedor	41 938
10	Bihac	39 683
11	Brcko	36 483
12	Pale	34 617
13	Teslic	34 556
33	Zepce	12 504
44	Banovici	10 619
58	Modrica	8 763
60	Siroki Brijeg	8 434
117	Posusje	4 137
188	Orasje	3 088

BOSNA I HERCEGOVINA • BOSNIA AND HERZEGOVINA

Capital	Sarajevo	Population	4 613 414 (119)	% in cities	47%
GDP per capita	$6500 (127)	Area km²	51 197 km² (128)	GMT +/-	+1
Neighbours (km)	Croatia 932, Montenegro 249, Serbia 357 • Coast 20				

RECENT INTERNATIONAL MATCHES PLAYED BY BOSNIA–HERZEGOVINA

2007	Opponents	Score		Venue	Comp	Scorers	Att	Referee
24-03	Norway	W	2-1	Oslo	ECq	Misimovic [18], Muslimovic [33]	16 987	Riley ENG
2-06	Turkey	W	3-2	Sarajevo	ECq	Muslimovic [27], Dzeko [47], Custovic [90]	13 800	Fröjdfeldt SWE
6-06	Malta	W	1-0	Sarajevo	ECq	Muslimovic [6]	15 000	Richards WAL
22-08	Croatia	L	3-5	Sarajevo	Fr	Muslimovic 3 [37 70 77]	8 000	Skomina SVN
8-09	Hungary	L	0-1	Szekesfehervar	ECq		10 773	Trefoloni ITA
12-09	Moldova	L	0-1	Sarajevo	ECq		2 000	Hyytia FIN
13-10	Greece	L	2-3	Athens	ECq	Hrgovic.M [54], Ibisevic [92+]	30 250	Gilewski POL
17-10	Norway	L	0-2	Sarajevo	ECq		1 500	Lannoy FRA
21-11	Turkey	L	0-1	Istanbul	ECq		20 106	Braamhaar NED
2008								
30-01	Japan	L	0-3	Tokyo	Fr		26 971	Kim Eui Soo KOR
26-03	FYR Macedonia	D	2-2	Zenica	Fr	Damjanovic 2 [17 20]		Svilokos CRO
1-06	Azerbaijan	W	1-0	Zenica	Fr	Nokolic [72]	800	Radovanovic MNE
20-08	Bulgaria	L	1-2	Zenica	Fr	Ibricic [59]	7 000	Stankovic SRB
6-09	Spain	L	0-1	Murcia	WCq		29 152	Thomson SCO
10-09	Estonia	W	7-0	Zenica	WCq	Misimovic 3 [24 30p 56], Muslimovic [59], Dzeko 2 [60 72], Ibricic [88]	12 500	Balaj ROU
11-10	Turkey	L	1-2	Istanbul	WCq	Dzeko [26]	23 628	Kassai HUN
15-10	Armenia	W	4-1	Zenica	WCq	Spahic [31], Dzeko [39], Muslimovic 2 [56 89]	13 000	Kenan ISR
19-11	Slovenia	W	4-3	Maribor	Fr	Ibisevic 2 [2 62], Misimovic [11p], Dzeko [53]	10 000	Kari FIN
2009								
28-03	Belgium	W	4-2	Genk	WCq	Dzeko [7], Jahic [75], Bajramovic [77], Misimovic [81]	20 041	Ivanov.N RUS
1-04	Belgium	W	2-1	Zenica	WCq	Dzeko 2 [12 14]	13 800	Hrinak SVK
1-06	Uzbekistan	D	0-0	Tashkent	Fr		15 000	Kovalenko UZB
9-06	Oman	W	2-1	Cannes	Fr	Dzeko [14], Salihovic [85]		
12-08	Iran	L	2-3	Sarajevo	Fr	Dzeko 2 [52 69]		
5-09	Armenia	W	2-0	Yerevan	WCq	Ibricic [6], Muslimovic [74]	1 800	Braamhaar NED
9-09	Turkey	D	1-1	Zenica	WCq	Salihovic [25]	14 000	Benquerença POR
10-10	Estonia	W	2-0	Tallinn	WCq	Dzeko [30], Ibisevic [64]	6 450	Rizzoli ITA
14-10	Spain	L	2-5	Zenica	WCq	Dzeko [90], Misimovic [92+]	13 500	Plautz AUT
14-11	Portugal	L	0-1	Lisbon	WCpo		60 588	Atkinson ENG
18-11	Portugal	L	0-1	Zenica	WCpo		15 000	Rosetti ITA
2010								
3-03	Ghana	W	2-1	Sarajevo	Fr	Ibisevic [40], Pjanic [65]	10 000	Batinic CRO
29-05	Sweden	L	2-4	Stockholm	Fr	Salihovic [47], Zec [90]	22 589	Grafe GER
3-06	Germany	L	1-3	Frankfurt	Fr	Dzeko [15]	48 000	Rizzoli ITA
10-08	Qatar	D	1-1	Sarajevo	Fr	Ibisevic [9]	18 000	Vuckov CRO
3-09	Luxembourg	W	3-1	Luxembourg	ECq	Ibricic [6], Pjanic [12], Dzeko [16]	7 327	Banari MDA
7-09	France	L	0-2	Sarajevo	ECq		28 000	Brych GER
8-10	Albania	D	1-1	Tirana	ECq	Ibisevic [21]	14 220	Jakobsson ISL
17-11	Slovakia	W	3-2	Bratislava	Fr	Medunjanin [28], Pjanic [50], Dzeko [60]	7 822	Mikulski POL
10-12	Poland	D	2-2	Antalya	Fr	Subasic [23], Misimovic [56p]	100	Ogretmenoglu TUR

Fr = Friendly match • EC = UEFA EURO 2008/2012 • WC = FIFA World Cup • q = qualifier • po = play-off

BOSNIA-HERZEGOVINA NATIONAL TEAM HISTORICAL RECORDS

Caps — 55 - Zvjezdan Misimovic 2004- • **51** - Elvir Bolic 1996-2006 • **47** - Sergej Barbarez 1998-2006 • **45** - Vedin Music 1995-2007, Emir Spahic 2003- & Hasan Salihamidzic 1996-2006 • **39** - Elvir Baljic 1996-2005 • **38** - Muhamed Konjic 1995-2004 • **37** - Kenan Hasagic 2002- • **36** - Mirsad Hibic 1997-2004 • **35** - Zlatan Bajramovic 2002-

Goals — 22 - Elvir Bolic 1996-2006 • 17 - Sergej Barbarez 1998-2006, Zvjezdan Misimovic 2004- & Edin Dzeko 2007- • 14 - Elvir Baljic 1996-2005 • 11 - Zlatan Muslimovic 2006- • 6 - Hasan Salihamidzic 1996-2006

Past Coaches — Mirsad Fazlagi 1992-1993 • Fuad Muzurovi 1993-1998 • Faruk Hadzibegic 1999 • Miso Smajlovi 1999-2002 • Blaz Sliskovi 2002-2006 • Fuad Muzurovi 2006-2007 • Meho Kodro 2008-2008 • Miroslav Blazevi 2008-2009 • Safet Susi 2009-

BOSNIA-HERZEGOVINA 2009-10

PREMIJER LIGA

	Pl	W	D	L	F	A	Pts	Zeljeznicar	Siroki	Borac	Zrinjski	Sarajevo	Olimpik	Velez	Sloboda	Travnik	Rudar	Leotar	Zvijezda	Celik	Slavija	Laktasi	Modrica
Zeljeznicar Sarajevo †	30	18	7	5	52	22	61	—	1-0	4-2	1-1	1-2	2-0	1-0	4-1	2-0	1-1	3-1	2-0	4-1	2-0	4-1	3-0
Siroki Brijeg ‡	30	16	7	7	46	27	55	0-2	—	0-0	2-1	2-0	2-2	2-0	2-0	1-0	1-0	4-1	5-0	2-1	0-0	3-0	2-0
Borac Banja Luka ‡	30	17	2	11	37	29	53	2-0	3-2	—	3-0	0-1	0-2	2-0	1-0	1-0	1-0	2-0	2-0	2-1	3-1	1-0	4-0
Zrinjski Mostar ‡	30	15	6	9	46	33	51	1-1	4-1	3-0	—	1-1	3-0	2-1	2-0	2-0	3-1	3-0	0-1	2-0	0-0	2-1	4-0
Sarajevo	30	14	8	8	43	25	50	0-0	1-1	3-0	3-0	—	2-1	1-1	1-1	2-1	3-0	3-0	1-0	3-1	2-0	3-1	2-0
Olimpik Sarajevo	30	12	8	10	30	34	44	0-2	0-1	1-2	1-0	1-1	—	1-0	1-0	1-0	3-1	1-0	1-0	0-0	3-0	0-0	2-2
Velez Mostar	30	13	4	13	42	33	43	0-2	1-0	2-0	0-0	1-0	4-1	—	1-0	5-0	1-0	6-2	4-0	0-0	4-2	4-1	1-0
Sloboda Tuzla	30	13	3	14	30	34	42	1-0	1-0	2-0	2-0	1-0	0-0	2-0	—	2-1	1-0	1-0	1-0	2-1	1-0	2-4	1-2
Travnik	30	11	6	13	40	41	39	0-0	1-2	2-0	3-3	1-0	1-0	2-1	4-0	—	1-0	2-2	4-1	2-1	3-0	2-2	6-5
Rudar Prijedor	30	11	5	14	27	32	38	0-2	1-1	1-0	2-0	2-2	3-1	2-0	1-0	2-0	—	0-0	3-0	1-1	1-0	2-0	1-0
Leotar Trebinje	30	11	5	14	32	48	38	3-3	0-1	2-1	2-3	1-0	0-0	0-1	1-0	2-0	1-0	—	1-1	2-1	2-1	3-1	3-1
Zvijezda Gradacac	30	11	4	15	35	47	37	2-1	1-1	1-1	2-0	2-1	3-4	2-1	2-2	1-0	1-0	5-0	—	1-0	2-3	4-1	0-1
Celik Zenica	30	10	5	15	33	37	35	0-1	0-0	0-1	4-1	0-0	1-2	2-1	2-1	2-1	3-0	0-1	4-2	—	3-1	2-1	1-0
Slavija Sarajevo	30	10	5	15	32	46	35	1-1	3-2	0-1	0-2	0-4	0-0	2-0	2-1	1-1	2-0	2-0	0-1	1-0	—	3-1	4-1
Laktasi	30	10	4	16	38	46	34	0-1	1-2	0-2	0-1	2-1	4-0	3-1	2-0	0-0	0-1	1-0	2-0	4-1		—	1-1
Modrica Maksima	30	7	3	20	28	57	24	2-1	2-4	1-0	1-2	3-0	0-1	1-1	0-4	0-2	1-2	2-1	0-1	0-1	2-0	0-2	—

1/08/2009 - 26/05/2010 • † Qualified for the UEFA Champions League • ‡ Qualified for the Europa League
Top scorers: **16** - Feda Dudic, Travnik • **15** - Samir Bekric, Zeljeznicar • **14** - Juan Manuel Varea ARG, Siroki

BOSNIA 2009-10
PRVA LIGA NS FBIH (2)

	Pl	W	D	L	F	A	Pts
Buducnost Banovici	30	22	2	6	57	19	68
Orasje	30	18	0	12	51	34	54
Iskra Bugojno	30	16	5	9	56	26	53
Rudar Kakanj	30	16	5	9	47	29	53
Napredak Sarajevo	30	15	3	12	50	39	48
GOSK Gabela	30	15	1	14	42	31	46
Slaven Zivinice	30	14	4	12	37	40	46
Bosna Visoko	30	14	3	13	49	40	45
Igman Konjic	30	13	5	12	43	36	44
Omladinac Mionica	30	14	2	14	43	49	44
Krajisnik	30	13	5	12	41	50	44
Vitez	30	13	3	14	42	42	42
Jedinstvo Bihac	30	12	5	13	36	47	41
Gorazde	30	12	4	14	32	40	40
Zepce Limorad	30	4	3	23	23	64	15
Posusje	30	2	4	24	8	71	10

14/08/2009 - 5/06/2010 • Posusje withdrew after 10 games.
All their remaining games awarded 3-0 to their opponents

BOSNIA 2009-10
PRVA LIGA FS RS (2)

	Pl	W	D	L	F	A	Pts
Drina Zvornik	26	12	11	3	39	18	47
Radnik Bijeljina	26	12	7	7	47	32	43
BSK Banja Luka	26	11	6	9	34	26	39
Proleter Teslic	26	9	10	7	27	22	37
Kozara Gradiska	26	9	9	8	36	23	36
Sutjeska Foca	26	9	9	8	31	30	36
Sloga Doboj	26	9	8	9	27	25	35
Sloboda Novi Grad	26	9	8	9	29	28	35
Famos Vojkovici	26	10	5	11	29	34	35
Mladost Gacko	26	10	5	11	31	43	35
Drina Visegrad	26	8	10	8	28	31	34
Romanije Pale	26	8	8	10	32	33	32
Ljubic Prnjavor	26	6	7	13	26	52	25
Sloga Trn	26	4	9	13	25	44	21

15/08/2009 - 29/05/2010

MEDALS TABLE

		Overall			League			Cup		Europe		
		G	S	B	G	S	B	G	S	G	S	B
1	Zeljeznicar Sarajevo	7	6		4	3		3	3			
2	FK Sarajevo	5	6	3	1	4	3	4	2			
3	Celik Zenica	5		1	3		1	2				
4	NK Siroki Brijeg	3	5	1	2	3	1	1	2			
5	Zrinjski Mostar	3	1	1	2	1	1	1				
6	FK Modrica Maxima	2			1			1				
7	Slavija Sarajevo	1	2	1				1	1	1	1	
8	Borac Banja Luka	1	1	1				1		1	1	
	Brotnjo Citluk	1	1	1	1	1	1					
10	Leotar Trebinje	1	1		1			1				
11	Bosna Visoko	1		2				2		1		
12	NK Orase	1						1				
13	Sloboda Tuzla		5	2					2	5		
14	Buducnost Banovici	1						1				
	Radniki Lukavac	1						1				

BOSNIAN CLUBS IN YUGOSLAV FOOTBALL

		Overall			League			Cup		Europe		
7	Velez Mostar	2	5	4		3	4	2	2			
9	FK Sarajevo	2	4		2	2		2				
13	Zeljeznicar Sarajevo	1	2	2	1	1	2	1				1
14	Borac Banja Luka	1	1					1	1			
21	Slavia		1	1				1	1			
21	Sloboda Tuzla	1	1					1		1		
23	SASK Sarajevo	1										

KUP BIH 2009-10

First Round

	W-O
Borac Banja Luka *	
Posusje	
Kozara Gradiska *	0
Siroki Brijeg	4
Olimpik Sarajevo *	4
Radnik Lipnica	2
Proleter Teslic *	2
Leotar Trebinje	3
Sloboda Tuzla	2
Rudar Kakanj *	0
Jedinstvo Bihac	1
Travnik *	2
Celik Zenica *	4
Krajina Cazin	2
Turbina Jablanica	
Slavija Sarajevo *	2
Zrinjski Mostar *	4
Mladost Donji Svilaj	0
Radnik Hadzici	0
Sarajevo *	4
Modrica Maksima *	7
Sloboda Novi Grad	1
Laktasi *	0
Sloga Doboj	2
Rudar Prijedor *	4
Sutjeska Foca	1
Zvijezda Gradacac	2 5p
Sloga Uskoplje *	2 6p
Velez Mostar *	4
BSK Banja Luka	0
Bosna Sarajevo	0
Zeljeznicar Sarajevo *	1

Round of 16

Borac Banja Luka *	2	1
Siroki Brijeg	0	1
Olimpik Sarajevo	0	0
Leotar Trebinje *	3	1
Sloboda Tuzla	1	2
Travnik *	1	0
Celik Zenica *	1	0
Slavija Sarajevo	0	3
Zrinjski Mostar *	1	0
Sarajevo *	1	0
Modrica Maksima *	1	1
Sloga Doboj	2	1
Rudar Prijedor *	2	1
Sloga Uskoplje *	1	0
Velez Mostar *	0	1
Zeljeznicar Sarajevo *	0	2

Quarter-finals

Borac Banja Luka *	3	1
Leotar Trebinje *	0	0
Sloboda Tuzla	0	1
Slavija Sarajevo *	2	0
Zrinjski Mostar	2	1
Sloga Doboj *	0	0
Rudar Prijedor	0	0
Zeljeznicar Sarajevo *	3	0

Semi-finals

Borac Banja Luka	2	1
Slavija Sarajevo *	2	0
Zrinjski Mostar	1	1
Zeljeznicar Sarajevo *	3	1

Final

CUP FINAL 1ST LEG

First leg. Gradski, Banja Luka
5-05-2010. Att: 11 000, Ref: Edin Jakupovic
Scorers - Vukelja [11] for Borac; Visca [83] for Zeljeznicar

Borac - Marko Susac - Milan Stupar, Vule Trivunovic, Leonid Coric, Drasko Zaric - Dusko Sakan, Perica Stanceski, Miroslav Stevanovic, Oliver Jandric (Dragomir Vukobratovic 65), Sasa Kajkut (Aleksandar Petrovic 86) - Ljubisa Vukelja. Tr: Zoran Maric
Zeljeznicar - Ibrahim Sehic - Delimir Bajic, Mirko Radovanovic, Elvis Mesic, Semir Kerla, Milan Culum - Muamer Svraka (Edin Visca 46), Sead Bucan (Srdan Stanic 65), Samir Bekric, Mirsad Bestija (Goran Perak 86) - Lazar Popovic. Tr: Amar Osim

Borac Banja Luka * ‡	1	2
Zeljeznicar Sarajevo	1	2

CUP FINAL 2ND LEG

Second leg. Grbavica, Sarajevo
19-05-2010. Att: 14 000, Ref: Dragan Skakic
Scorers - Visca [49], Bestija [55] for Zeljeznicar; Stevanovic [6], Kajkut [26] for Borac

Zeljeznicar - Ibrahim Sehic - Predrag Simic (Damir Rovcanin 72), Mirko Radovanovic, Elvis Mesic, Delimir Bajic (Edin Visca 30) - Muamer Svraka, Milan Culum, Mirsad Bestija, Samir Bekric - Lazar Popovic (Alen Mesanovic 72), Sead Bucan. Tr: Amar Osim
Borac - Marko Knezevic - Milan Stupar, Drasko Zaric, Bojan Petric (Nemanja Damjanovic 17), Vule Trivunovic - Dusko Sakan, Oliver Jandric (Leonid Coric 90), Perica Stanceski - Miroslav Stevanovic, Ljubisa Vukelja, Sasa Kajkut (Dragomir Vukobratovic 83). Tr: Zoran Maric

Zrinjski Mostar	1	1
Zeljeznicar Sarajevo *	3	1

* Home team/Home team in the 1st leg • ‡ Qualified for the Europa League

BLR – BELARUS

FIFA/COCA-COLA WORLD RANKING

1993	1994	1995	1996	1997	1998	1999	2000	2001	2002	2003	2004	2005	2006	2007	2008	2009	2010
137	121	88	90	110	104	95	96	85	74	90	69	61	70	60	84	80	38

	2010											Hi/Lo
Jan	Feb	Mar	Mar	Apr	May	Jul	Aug	Sep	Oct	Nov	Dec	38
80	80	79	80	81	82	77	78	55	42	40	38	146

Nothing illustrated the inconsistent and erratic nature of the Belarus national team more succinctly than the first four fixtures they played in their Euro 2012 qualifying group. What better way to start your campaign than with an away victory against France in Paris... but the next two games undermined hopes fans in Belarus may have had of crossing the border into Poland or Ukraine to watch their team play in the finals, especially the draw away to lowly Luxembourg. The award of the 2018 FIFA World Cup to Russia offers a unique opportunity for football in Eastern Europe and Belarus will look to play its part. Certainly there is the potential, even at club level where BATE Borisov have done much to raise standards. In November 2010 they won a fifth consecutive league title having six months earlier won the Belarus cup by beating Torpedo Zhodino 5-0 in the final and they now stand just one trophy short of Dinamo Minsk's overall record of ten trophies. BATE then crowned a magnificent year by qualifying for the knockout rounds of the 2010-11 UEFA Europa League by finishing second in their group, a point behind Dynamo Kyiv but ahead of AZ Alkmaar and Sheriff Tiraspol - another important milestone having two years earlier been the first and so far only club from Belarus to qualify for the Champions League group stage.

FIFA WORLD CUP RECORD
1930-1994 DNE 1998-2010 DNQ

BELARUS FOOTBALL FEDERATION (BFF)

Prospekt Pobeditelei 20/3
Minsk 220 020

☎ +375 172 545600
📠 +375 172 544483
✉ info@bff.by
🖥 www.bff.by
FA 1989 CON 1993 FIFA 1992
P Gennady Nevyglas
GS Leonid Dmitranitsa

FIFA BIG COUNT 2006

Total players	373 810
% of population	3.63%
Male	326 390
Female	47 420
Amateurs 18+	4 530
Youth under 18	18 760
Unregistered	113 000
Professionals	1 370
Referees	527
Admin & coaches	948
Number of clubs	155
Number of teams	270

MAJOR CITIES/TOWNS

		Population
1	Minsk	1 758 453
2	Gomel	476 151
3	Mogilev	367 786
4	Vitebsk	341 713
5	Grodno	327 496
6	Brest	309 934
7	Bobruisk	218 294
8	Baranovici	169 390
9	Borisov	150 634
10	Pinsk	131 382
11	Orsja	125 947
12	Mozyr	112 318
13	Soligorsk	102 557
14	Molodechno	98 614
15	Novopolotsk	98 563
16	Lida	96 717
17	Polotsk	79 884
18	Zhlobin	73 525
19	Svetlogorsk	68 634

RESPUBLIKA BYELARUS • REPUBLIC OF BELARUS

Capital	Minsk	Population	9 648 533 (86)	% in cities	73%
GDP per capita	$11 800 (93)	Area km²	207 600 km² (85)	GMT +/-	+2
Neighbours (km)	Latvia 171, Lithuania 680, Poland 605, Russia 959, Ukraine 891				

RECENT INTERNATIONAL MATCHES PLAYED BY BELARUS

2007	Opponents	Score		Venue	Comp	Scorers	Att	Referee
7-02	Iran	D	2-2	Tehran	Fr	Hleb.V 2 [53] [59]	15 000	Al Fadhli KUW
24-03	Luxembourg	W	2-1	Luxembourg	ECq	Kalachev [25], Kutuzov [54]	2 021	Whitby WAL
2-06	Bulgaria	L	0-2	Minsk	ECq		29 000	Jara CZE
6-06	Bulgaria	L	1-2	Sofia	ECq	Vasilyuk [5p]	10 501	Jakobsson ISL
22-08	Israel	W	2-1	Minsk	Fr	Vasilyuk [2], Romaschenko [90p]	10 000	Malzinskas LTU
8-09	Romania	L	1-3	Minsk	ECq	Romaschenko [20]	19 320	Fröjdfeldt SWE
12-09	Slovenia	L	0-1	Celje	ECq		3 500	Banari MDA
13-10	Luxembourg	L	0-1	Gomel	ECq		14 000	Svendson DEN
17-10	Israel	L	1-2	Tel Aviv	Fr	Romaschenko [68]	4 362	Georgiev BUL
17-11	Albania	W	4-2	Tirana	ECq	Romaschenko 2 [32] [63p], Kutuzov 2 [45] [54]	2 064	Demirlek TUR
21-11	Netherlands	W	2-1	Minsk	ECq	Bulyga [49], Korythko [65]	11 900	Layec FRA
2008								
2-02	Iceland	W	2-0	Ta'Qali	Fr	Vasilyuk [33], Plaskonny [47]	100	Lautier MLT
4-02	Armenia	L	1-2	Ta'Qali	Fr	Hleb.V [5]	100	Zammit MLT
6-02	Malta	W	1-0	Ta'Qali	Fr	Romaschenko [89]	1 000	Tshagharyan ARM
26-03	Turkey	D	2-2	Minsk	Fr	Kutuzov [35], Hleb.V [64]	12 000	Malzinskas LTU
27-05	Germany	D	2-2	Kaiserslautern	Fr	Bulyga 2 [61] [88]	47 258	Ceferin SVN
2-06	Finland	D	1-1	Turku	Fr	Shitov [90]	6 474	Skomina SVN
20-08	Argentina	D	0-0	Minsk	Fr			Sukhina RUS
6-09	Ukraine	L	0-1	Lviv	WCq		24 000	Rizzoli ITA
10-09	Andorra	W	3-1	Andorra La Vella	WCq	Verkhovtsov [37], Rodionov [79], Hleb [90]	600	Evans WAL
15-10	England	L	1-3	Minsk	WCq	Sitko [28]	29 600	Hauge NOR
19-11	Cyprus	L	1-2	Nicosia	Fr	Kovel [55]	300	Kenan ISR
2009								
1-04	Kazakhstan	W	5-1	Almaty	WCq	Hleb.A [48], Kalachev 2 [54] [64], Stasevich [57], Rodionov [88]	19 000	Jech CZE
6-06	Andorra	W	5-1	Grodno	WCq	Blizniuk 2 [1] [76], Kalachev [44], Kornilenko 2 [50] [65]	8 500	Kranjc SVN
10-06	Moldova	D	2-2	Borisov	Fr	Rodionov [4], Bliznyuk [27]	2 000	Mazeika LTU
12-08	Croatia	L	1-3	Minsk	WCq	Verkhovtsov [81]	21 651	Brych GER
5-09	Croatia	L	0-1	Zagreb	WCq		25 628	Plautz AUT
9-09	Ukraine	D	0-0	Minsk	WCq		21 727	Kassai HUN
10-10	Kazakhstan	W	4-0	Brest	WCq	Bordachev [23], Kalachev 2 [69] [92+], Kovel [86]	9 530	Ennjimmi FRA
14-10	England	L	0-3	London	WCq		76 897	Batista POR
14-11	Saudi Arabia	D	1-1	Dammam	Fr	Bordachev [20]		
18-11	Montenegro	L	0-1	Podgorica	Fr		5 000	Stavrev MKD
2010								
3-03	Armenia	W	3-1	Antalya	Fr	Putsila [58], Hleb [73], Rodionov [86]	BCD	
27-05	Honduras	D	2-2	Villach	Fr	Putsila 2 [57] [60]	400	Eisner AUT
30-05	Korea Republic	W	1-0	Kufstein	Fr	Kislyak [53]	1 000	Brugger AUT
2-06	Sweden	L	0-1	Minsk	Fr		12 000	Nikolaev RUS
11-08	Lithuania	W	2-0	Kaunas	Fr	Hleb.V 2 [49] [90]	3 500	Satchi MDA
3-09	France	W	1-0	Paris	ECq	Kislyak [86]	76 395	Collum SCO
7-09	Romania	D	0-0	Minsk	ECq		26 354	Kralovec CZE
8-10	Luxembourg	D	0-0	Luxembourg	ECq		1 857	Stavrev MKD
12-10	Albania	W	2-0	Minsk	ECq	Rodionov [10], Krivets [77]	7 000	Rasmussen DEN
17-11	Oman	W	4-0	Muscat	Fr	Martynovich 2 [5] [11], Hleb.V [35], Rodionov [57p]	1 000	Al Amri KSA

Fr = Friendly match • EC = UEFA EURO 2008/2012 • WC = FIFA World Cup • q = qualifier

BELARUS NATIONAL TEAM HISTORICAL RECORDS

Caps — 88 - Aleksandr Kulchiy 1996- • 80 - Sergei Gurenko 1994-2006 • 71 - Sergei Shtanyuk 1995-2007 • 66 - Sergei Omelyanchuk 2002- • 64 - Maksim Romaschenko 1998-2008 • 56 - Valentin Byalkevich 1992-2005 • 54 - Aleksandr Hleb 2001- • 52 - Andrei Ostrovskiy 1994-2005- • 51 - Vitaly Kutuzov 2002-

Goals — 20 - Maksim Romaschenko 1998-2008 • 13 - Vitaly Kutuzov 2002- • 11 - Vyacheslav Hleb 2004- • 10 - Valentin Byalkevich 1992-2005 & Roman Vasilyuk 2000-08 • 9 - Sergei Kornilenko 2003- • 8 - Vitaly Bulyga 2003-08

Past Coaches — Mihail Verhejenka 1992-1994 • Siarhej Barouski 1994-1996 • Mihail Verhejenka 1997-1999 • Siarhej Barouski 1999-2000 • Eduard Malofeev 2000-2003 • Anatoly Baidachny RUS 2003-2005 • Yuri Puntus 2006-2007 • Bernd Stange GER 2007-

BELARUS 2010

VYSSHAYA LIGA

	Pl	W	D	L	F	A	Pts	BATE	Shakhter	FK Minsk	Dinamo M	Dinamo B	Belshina	Naftan	Dnepr	FK Vitebsk	Neman	Torpedo	Partizan
BATE Borisov †	33	21	9	3	64	18	72		2-0	1-2	1-2	2-1	1-3	4-0	1-0	2-0	2-0	1-1	1-0	3-0	4-0	0-0	1-0	6-0
Shakhter Soligorsk ‡	33	19	9	5	51	23	66	0-0		1-0	2-4	3-0	2-0	1-1	1-1	0-0	0-0	3-2	1-2	1-4	1-0	1	4-1	1-0	4-0
FK Minsk ‡	33	18	6	9	59	32	60	0-0	0-2	1-2		0-2	0-0	1-1	2-2	3-1	3-1	2-0	2-1	5-1	3-1	2-0	2-1	3-0
Dinamo Minsk	33	17	5	11	49	34	56	0-1	0-1	0-2		2-2	2-0	3-0	4-0	0-0	3-0	2-1	1-1	0-2	1-0	1-0	5-1	0-0	5-1
Dinamo Brest	33	12	10	11	48	40	46	1-4	1-1	2-1	1-2		1-1	2-0	0-0	2-3	5-2	2-0	4-0	2-1	3-2	3-1	1-1	4-0
Belshina Bobruisk	33	12	9	12	31	42	45	0-1	1-3	1-0	1-3	1-0	2-0	0-2		1-0	1-0	1-2	1-1	1-1	0-0	0-2	2-0	1-1	2-0
Naftan Novopolotsk	33	11	11	11	41	34	44	0-2	0-2	1-0	0-0	0-2	2-0	3-1	1-0	4-0		5-0	1-2	0-0	4-1	2-1	1-1	1-0	4-4
Dnepr Mogilev	33	11	7	15	40	53	40	0-2	2-3	0-2	1-5	3-0	1-0	2-1	1-1	1-3	1-0		0-0	0-0	1-0	3-1	0-1	3-0
FK Vitebsk	33	7	11	15	31	52	32	0-0	1-6	1-3	0-3	1-3	3-1	0-1	0-0	0-2	4-2	2-2	0-1	1-1	1		2-2	0-2	0-1	0-1
Neman Grodno	33	7	10	16	27	42	31	0-5	1-1	0-0	0-1	0-1	0-0	2-2	2-0	0-0	1-2	0-0	3-0		0-0	2-1	0-1	2-0
Torpedo Zhodino ‡	33	7	7	19	33	58	28	0-1	1-1	1-1	0-1	0-4	1-1	2-0	3-1	0-1	1-2	1-4	0-2	2-3	0-4	2-0		2-2
Partizan Minsk	33	5	8	20	24	70	23	1-1	1-1	0-2	1-4	1-3	0-2	0-3	1-2	0-0	1-1	1-0	4-3	0-2	0-1	0-4	2-3	1-0	

3/04/2010 - 21/11/2010 • † Qualified for the UEFA Champions League • ‡ Qualified for the Europa League

Relegation/promotion play-off: SKVICh Minsk 1-3 0-0 Torpedo Zhodino
Top scorers: **15** - Renan Bressan BRA, BATE • **12** - Dzmitry Kavalyonak, Neman
• **11** - Andrey Razin, FK Minsk

BELARUS 2010
PERSHAYA LIGA (2)

	Pl	W	D	L	F	A	Pts
FC Gomel	30	27	1	2	80	16	82
SKVICh Minsk	30	17	7	6	52	21	58
DSK Gomel	30	17	7	6	52	26	58
Granit Mikashevichi	30	16	8	6	52	23	56
FK Rudensk	30	12	7	11	37	39	43
FC Baranovichi	30	11	10	9	31	37	43
FC Polatsak	30	9	12	9	38	34	39
Khimik Svetlogorsk	30	10	7	13	37	44	37
Slavija Moazyr	30	10	7	13	33	44	37
Khvalya Pinsk	30	11	2	17	31	48	35
Veras Nesvizh	30	9	8	13	31	39	35
FC Smorgon	30	8	8	14	33	43	32
Dinamo Grodno	30	8	6	16	25	40	30
Vedrich-97 Rechitsa	30	8	6	16	29	46	30
Kommunalnik Slonim	30	5	13	12	23	48	28
FC Lida	30	4	7	19	23	59	19

17/04/2010 - 13/11/2010

MEDALS TABLE

		Overall			League			Cup		
		G	S	B	G	S	B	G	S	
1	Dinamo Minsk	10	8	2	7	6	2	3	2	
2	BATE Borisov	9	7	1	7	4	1	2	3	
3	Slavija Mozyr	4	4		2	2		2	2	
4	Belshina Bobruisk	4	2	2	1	1	2	3	1	
5	Shakhter Soligorsk	2	4	4	1	1	4	1	3	
6	FC Gomel	2	2	1	1	1	1	1	1	
7	Partizan Minsk (ex MTZ)	2		2				2	2	
8	Dinamo-93 Minsk	1	2	3		1	3	1	1	
	Lokomotiv Vitebsk	1	2	2		2	2	1		
10	Dnepr-Transmash	1	2		1	1				
11	Neman Grodno	1	1			1		1	1	
12	Dinamo Brest	1		1				1	1	
13	Naftan Novopolotsk	1						1		
14	Lokomotiv Minsk		1							1
	Torpedo Mogilev		1							1
	Torpedo-SKA Minsk		1							1
	Torpedo Zhodino		1							1
	Vedrich Rechitsa		1							1
19	Dnepr Mogilev			1			1			
	FK Minsk			1						

BELARUS CLUBS IN THE SOVIET ERA

14	Dinamo Minsk	1	1	3		1		3	1

KUBOK 2009–10

Round of 16			Quarter–finals			Semi–finals			Final	
BATE Borisov *	1	2								
FK Minsk	0	0	**BATE Borisov** *	7	0					
FC Polatsak	2	1	MTZ-RIPO Minsk	0	1					
MTZ-RIPO Minsk *	5	0				**BATE Borisov**	2	1		
Neman Grodno	1	1				Shakhter Soligorsk *	1	0		
Granit Mikashevichi *	0	0	Neman Grodno *	1	0					
Belshina Bobruisk *	0	2	**Shakhter Soligorsk**	2	2					
Shakhter Soligorsk	1	2							**BATE Borisov**	5
DSK Gomel	1	3							Torpedo Zhodino ‡	0
FC Gomel *	1	2	**DSK Gomel** *	0	3					
Dnepr Mogilev *	2	0	Dinamo Minsk	2	1					
Dinamo Minsk	4	3				**DSK Gomel** *	1	1		
Naftan Novopolotsk *	4	3				**Torpedo Zhodino**	2	0		
Slavija Moazyr	0	1	Naftan Novopolotsk *	0	1					
Veras Nesvizh	0	0	**Torpedo Zhodino**	2	3					
Torpedo Zhodino *	5	3								

CUP FINAL

Dinamo, Minsk
23-05-2010, Ref: Sakharevich
Scorers - Renan 2 [5] [64],
Rodionov 2 [22] [69], Kontsevoi [57]p for
BATE

* Home team in the 1st leg • ‡ Qualified for the Europa League

BLZ – BELIZE

FIFA/COCA-COLA WORLD RANKING

1993	1994	1995	1996	1997	1998	1999	2000	2001	2002	2003	2004	2005	2006	2007	2008	2009	2010
-	-	173	182	179	186	190	186	167	158	174	181	180	198	201	173	173	172

2010												Hi/Lo
Jan	Feb	Mar	Mar	Apr	May	Jul	Aug	Sep	Oct	Nov	Dec	157
173	186	182	182	181	179	182	180	168	174	175	172	201

Belize Defence Force, the club of the army, emerged as the best team of 2010 when they completed a hat trick of league championships. After ending 2009 with a 5-2 aggregate victory over FC Belize to clinch the 2009 fall title, Defence Force then comfortably led the league standings in the 2010 spring season before going into the play-offs. With six teams qualifying for the play-offs from the eight-team league, the first stage of the championship is almost an irrelevance with the only advantage for Defence Force being a bye to the semi-finals. In the final they met Georgetown Ibayani, a team that had finished the league campaign with almost half their points total but justice was done with a 4-1 aggregate victory. The final of the 2010 fall season was delayed until February 2011 because of the national team's participation in the 2011 Copa Centroamericana. Defence Force made it three finals in-a-row, this time facing Toledo Ambassadors and after being held to a 2-2 draw in Punda Gorda they won the return at the Norman Broaster Stadium in San Ignacio 2-0. In the Copa Centroamericana, Belize finished bottom of their first round group for the fourth tournament running but only missed out on the fifth place play-off - and a shot at qualifying for the CONCACAF Gold Cup - on goal difference to Nicaragua.

FIFA WORLD CUP RECORD
1930-1994 DNE 1998-2010 DNQ

FOOTBALL FEDERATION OF BELIZE (FFB)

26 Hummingbird Highway, Belmopan, PO Box 1742, Belize City

☎ +501 822 3410
📠 +501 822 3377
✉ belizefootball@gmail.com
🖥 www.belizefootball.bz
FA 1980 CON 1986 FIFA 1986
P Bertie Chimilio
GS Marguerite Hulse

FIFA BIG COUNT 2006

Total players	17 800
% of population	6.19%
Male	14 800
Female	3 000
Amateurs 18+	1 700
Youth under 18	1 300
Unregistered	3 650
Professionals	150
Referees	45
Admin & coaches	625
Number of clubs	32
Number of teams	140

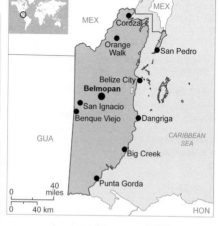

MAJOR CITIES/TOWNS

		Population
1	Belize City	68 170
2	San Ignacio	19 906
3	Belmopan	19 151
4	Orange Walk	16 530
5	San Pedro	12 535
6	Dangriga	12 431
7	Corozal	9 458
8	Benque Viejo	9 300
9	Punta Gorda	5 469

BELIZE

Capital	Belmopan	Population	307 899 (177)	% in cities	52%
GDP per capita	$8400 (116)	Area km²	22 966 km² (151)	GMT + / -	-6
Neighbours (km)	Guatemala 266, Mexico 250 • Coast 386				

RECENT INTERNATIONAL MATCHES PLAYED BY BELIZE

2009	Opponents	Score	Venue	Comp	Scorers	Att	Referee
22-01	Honduras	L 1-2	Tegucigalpa	UCr1	Lisby Castillo [86]	20 000	Moreno PAN
24-01	El Salvador	L 1-4	Tegucigalpa	UCr1	Jerome James [73]	20 000	Quesada CRC
26-01	Nicaragua	D 1-1	Tegucigalpa	UCr1	Bryon Usher [27]	8 000	Moncada HON
2010							
10-09	Trinidad and Tobago	D 0-0	Belmopan	Fr		5 000	Mejia SLV
9-10	Guatemala	L 2-4	San Jose	Fr	Harrison Roches [43], Elroy Kuylen [54]	5 500	Bermudez SLV
2011							
14-01	Panama	L 0-2	Panama City	UCr1		10 000	Pineda HON
16-01	El Salvador	L 2-5	Panama City	UCr1	Elroy Smith [45p], Orlando Jimenez [76]	1 500	Cerdas CRC
18-01	Nicaragua	D 1-1	Panama City	UCr1	Daniel Jimenez [81]	10 000	Brea CUB

UC = UNCAF Cup/Copa Centroamericana • WC = FIFA World Cup • q = qualifier

BELIZE 2009

PREMIER FOOTBALL LEAGUE CARIBBEAN MOTORS CUP FALL SEASON

	Pl	W	D	L	F	A	Pts	Hankook	Defence	San Pedro	FC Belize	Wagiya	Nizhee
Hankook Verdes Utd †	8	5	3	0	20	3	18		0-0	3-0	2-1	0-0	
Defence Force †	8	4	2	2	9	3	14	0-0		0-1	0-1	2-0	
San Pedro Dolphins †	8	3	1	4	7	11	10	2-2	0-1		1-0	1-2	
FC Belize †	8	3	0	5	9	11	9	0-1	0-4	2-0		4-1	0-2
Wagiya	8	2	0	6	7	24	6	**0-3**	1-2	1-2	2-1		
Nizhee Corozal	4	4	0	0	6	0	0	1-0	1-0			2-0	

30/08/2009 - 8/11/2009 • † Qualified for the play-offs • Ilagulei withdrew before the start of the season • Nizhee withdrew after four matches
Play-off semi-finals: **Defence Force** 4-1 1-1 San Pedro Dolphins • Hankook Verdes 1-0 0-1 2-4p **FC Belize**
Play-off final: **Defence Force** 1-2 4-0 FC Belize (played 29-11-2009 and 6-12-2009)

BELIZE 2010

PREMIER FOOTBALL LEAGUE CARIBBEAN MOTORS CUP SPRING SEASON

	Pl	W	D	L	F	A	Pts	Defence	Hankook	Fighters	FC Belize	San Pedro	Georgetown	BRC Blaze	Shanaiah
Defence Force †	14	10	2	2	31	10	32		0-0	2-1	2-1	1-0	2-2	3-1	8-0
Hankook Verdes Utd †	14	8	2	4	33	9	26	2-0		2-0	0-3	1-2	1-0	2-0	5-1
Freedom Fighters †	14	8	1	5	23	19	25	3-0	1-0		1-0	1-1	0-4	1-0	1-0
FC Belize †	14	7	3	4	24	14	24	0-3	1-0	3-0		2-1	5-0	**0-3**	1-1
San Pedro Sea Dogs †	13	5	4	4	17	10	19	0-2	0-0	5-1	1-1		n/p	0-0	2-0
Georgetown Ibayani †	13	5	2	6	18	20	17	0-3	1-2	1-2	1-1	0-3		2-0	**3-0**
BRC Blaze	14	3	1	10	9	24	10	0-3	0-3	0-1	0-3	1-0	1-3		2-1
Shanaiah Corozal	14	1	1	12	8	57	4	1-2	0-15	1-11	1-3	0-2	0-1	2-1	

13/02/2010 - 2/05/2010 • † Qualified for the play-offs • Play-off quarter-finals: **FC Belize** 1-1 4-3p San Pedro Sea Dogs • **Georgetown Ibayani** beat Freedom Fighters • Play-off semi-finals: **Defence Force** 1-0 **3-0** FC Belize • **Georgetown Ibayani** 2-1 2-2 Hankook Verdes
Play-off final: Georgetown Ibayani 1-2 0-2 **Defence Force** (played 23-05-2010 and 30-05-2010) • Matches in bold awarded

BELIZE 2010

PREMIER FOOTBALL LEAGUE CARIBBEAN MOTORS CUP FALL SEASON

	Pl	W	D	L	F	A	Pts	Defence	FC Belize	Toledo	Griga Utd	San Felipe	BRC Blaze	Hankook	San Pedro
Defence Force †	14	11	2	1	34	11	35		2-1	4-3	0-0	4-2	4-0	1-0	7-0
FC Belize †	14	9	2	3	35	19	29	1-2		3-4	1-0	3-2	4-2	2-0	3-1
Toledo Ambassadors †	14	7	3	4	24	16	24	0-3	0-0		2-0	0-1	2-0	1-1	3-0
Griga United †	14	6	4	4	18	13	22	0-2	1-2	2-1		1-1	3-0	1-1	3-2
San Felipe Barcelona †	14	6	3	5	22	21	21	2-1	1-3	1-1	1-3		2-0	2-1	3-2
BRC Blaze †	14	4	2	8	18	28	14	1-1	1-6	1-3	0-1	1-1		2-0	3-0
Hankook Verdes Utd	14	3	4	7	13	17	13	0-1	2-2	0-1	0-0	1-0	1-4		3-0
San Pedro Sea Dogs	14	0	0	14	7	46	0	1-2	1-4	0-3	0-3	0-3	0-3	0-3	

5/09/2010 - 23/12/2010 • † Qualified for the play-offs • Play-off quarter-finals: **Toledo** 0-0 4-2p Hankook • Griga 2-3 San Felipe
Play-off semi-finals: FC Belize 1-1 0-3 **Toledo** • San Felipe 1-2 2-6 **Defence Force**
Play-off final: Toledo Ambassadors 2-2 0-2 **Belize Defence Force** (played 6-02-2011 and 13-02-2011)

BOL – BOLIVIA

FIFA/COCA-COLA WORLD RANKING

1993	1994	1995	1996	1997	1998	1999	2000	2001	2002	2003	2004	2005	2006	2007	2008	2009	2010
58	44	53	39	24	61	61	65	70	92	99	94	96	101	108	58	56	97

	2010												Hi/Lo
	Jan	Feb	Mar	Mar	Apr	May	Jul	Aug	Sep	Oct	Nov	Dec	18
	56	55	58	51	67	65	53	50	50	100	99	97	114

Having succeeded Erwin Sanchez as coach of the Bolivian national team at the end of the World Cup qualifiers in November 2009, Eduardo Villegas saw just three games in charge before he was replaced by Gustavo Quinteros. With the Copa America in Argentina looming, the Argentine born Quinteros was a natural choice after his championship successes with Bolivar in 2009 and with Oriente Petrolero in 2010. The 45-year old, who first came to prominence as coach of Blooming with whom he won the title in 2005, faces a difficult Copa America group having been drawn with the hosts, Colombia and guest team Japan. As coach of Oriente Petrolero, Quinteros lead the club to their first title since 2001 by winning the 2010 Clausura. Oriente had been awarded the 2004 Clausura title and for five years were regarded as the champions but in 2009 The Strongest were given their title back following the resolution of the nationality of Marcelo Robledo, their goalkeeper at the time. The 2010 season threw up a bizarre curiosity in which Jorge Wilstermann won the Apertura title but then finished bottom of the Clausura. There was nothing novel in that but as relegation is calculated over two seasons Wilstermann were then relegated - surely the first team to be crowned champions and relegated in the same season based purely on performance.

FIFA WORLD CUP RECORD
1930 12 r1   **1934-1938** DNE   **1950** 15 r1   **1954-1958** DNE   **1962-1990** DNQ   **1994** 20 r1   **1998-2010** DNQ

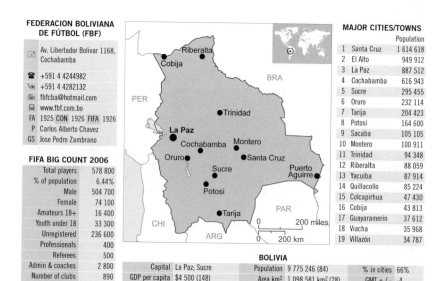

FEDERACION BOLIVIANA DE FÚTBOL (FBF)

🖷 Av. Libertador Bolivar 1168, Cochabamba

☎ +591 4 4244982
📠 +591 4 4282132
📧 fbfcba@hotmail.com
🖥 www.fbf.com.bo
FA 1925   CON 1926   FIFA 1926
P   Carlos Alberto Chavez
GS   Jose Pedro Zambrano

FIFA BIG COUNT 2006

Total players	578 800
% of population	6.44%
Male	504 700
Female	74 100
Amateurs 18+	16 400
Youth under 18	33 300
Unregistered	236 600
Professionals	400
Referees	500
Admin & coaches	2 800
Number of clubs	890
Number of teams	1 100

MAJOR CITIES/TOWNS

		Population
1	Santa Cruz	1 614 618
2	El Alto	949 912
3	La Paz	887 512
4	Cochabamba	616 943
5	Sucre	295 455
6	Oruro	232 114
7	Tarija	204 423
8	Potosí	164 600
9	Sacaba	105 105
10	Montero	100 911
11	Trinidad	94 348
12	Riberalta	88 059
13	Yacuiba	87 914
14	Quillacollo	85 224
15	Colcapirhua	47 430
16	Cobija	43 813
17	Guayaramerín	37 612
18	Viacha	35 968
19	Villazón	34 787

BOLIVIA

Capital	La Paz; Sucre	Population	9 775 246 (84)	% in cities 66%
GDP per capita	$4 500 (148)	Area km²	1 098 581 km² (28)	GMT + / - -4
Neighbours (km)	Argentina 832, Brazil 3423, Chile 860, Paraguay 750, Peru 1075		

RECENT INTERNATIONAL MATCHES PLAYED BY BOLIVIA

2007	Opponents	Score		Venue	Comp	Scorers	Att	Referee
26-06	Venezuela	D	2-2	San Cristobal	CArl	Moreno [38], Arce [84]	42 000	Reinoso ECU
30-08	Uruguay	L	0-1	San Cristobal	CArl		18 000	Toledo USA
3-07	Peru	D	2-2	Merida	CArl	Moreno [24], Campos [45]	35 000	Chandia CHI
22-08	Ecuador	L	0-1	Quito	Fr		20 000	Parra COL
12-09	Peru	L	0-2	Lima	Fr		15 000	Rivera PER
13-10	Uruguay	L	0-5	Montevideo	WCq		25 200	Selman CHI
17-10	Colombia	D	0-0	La Paz	WCq		19 469	Reinoso ECU
17-11	Argentina	L	0-3	Buenos Aires	WCq		43 308	Rivera PER
20-11	Venezuela	L	3-5	San Cristobal	WCq	Martins 2 [19 78], Arce [27]	18 632	Fagundes BRA
2008								
6-02	Peru	W	2-1	La Paz	Fr	Pedriel [65], Reyes.L [88]		
26-03	Venezuela	W	1-0	Puerto La Cruz	Fr	Cichero OG [79]	16 000	Buitrago COL
15-06	Chile	L	0-2	La Paz	WCq		27 722	Rivera PER
18-06	Paraguay	W	4-2	La Paz	WCq	Botero 2 [23 70], Garcia.R [25], Martins [76]	8 561	Gaciba BRA
6-08	Guatemala	L	0-3	Washington DC	Fr		18 000	Toledo USA
20-08	Panama	W	1-0	Santa Cruz	Fr	Cabrera [78]		Antequera BOL
6-09	Ecuador	L	1-3	Quito	WCq	Botero [40]	35 000	Pozo CHI
10-09	Brazil	D	0-0	Rio de Janeiro	WCq		31 422	Intriago ECU
11-10	Peru	W	3-0	La Paz	WCq	Botero 2 [3 16], Garcia.R [81]	23 147	Buitrago COL
14-10	Uruguay	D	2-2	La Paz	WCq	Martins 2 [15 41]	21 075	Baldassi ARG
22-10	El Salvador	L	0-2	Washington DC	Fr		20 000	Ward CAN
2009								
11-03	Mexico	L	1-5	Commerce City	Fr	Torrico [68]	20 000	Toledo USA
28-03	Colombia	L	0-2	Bogota	WCq		22 044	Intriago ECU
1-04	Argentina	W	6-1	La Paz	WCq	Martins [12], Botero 3 [34p 55 66], Da Rosa [45], Torrico [87]	30 487	Vazquez URU
6-06	Venezuela	L	0-1	La Paz	WCq		23 427	Vera ECU
10-06	Chile	L	0-4	Santiago	WCq		60 214	Silvera URU
5-09	Paraguay	L	0-1	Asuncion	WCq		25 094	Carrillo PER
9-09	Ecuador	L	1-3	La Paz	WCq	Yecerotte [85]	10 200	Baldassi ARG
11-10	Brazil	W	2-1	La Paz	WCq	Olivares [10], Martins [32]	16 557	Pozo CHI
14-10	Peru	L	0-1	Lima	WCq		4 373	Soto VEN
2010								
24-02	Mexico	L	0-5	San Francisco	Fr		34 244	Vaughn USA
11-08	Colombia	D	1-1	La Paz	Fr	Galindo [64]	4 000	Favale ARG
7-10	Venezuela	L	1-3	Santa Cruz	Fr	Moreno [53]	35 000	Chaibou NIG

Fr = Friendly match • CA = Copa América • WC = FIFA World Cup • q = qualifier • r1 = first round group

BOLIVIA NATIONAL TEAM HISTORICAL RECORDS

Caps
93 - Luis Hector Cristaldo 1989-2005 & Marco Antonio Sandy 1993-2003 • **89** - Jose Milton Melgar 1980-97 • **88** - Carlos Fernando Borja 1979-97 • **85** - Julio Cesar Baldivieso 1991-2005 & Juan Manuel Pena 1991-2009 • **80** - Miguel Angel Rimba 1989-2000 • **78** - Oscar Sanchez 1994-2006 • **75** - Jaime Moreno 1991-2008 • **71** - Marco Antonio Etcheverry 1989-2003

Goals
20 - Joaquin Botero 1999-2009 • **16** - Victor Agustin Ugarte 1947-63 • **15** - Carlos Aragones 1977-81, Julio Cesar Baldivieso 1991-2005 & Erwin Sanchez 1989-2005 • **13** - Marco Antonio Etcheverry 1989-2003 & Maximo Alcocer 1953-63 • **10** - Miguel Aguilar 1977-83 • **9** - Jaime Moreno 1991-2008 & William Ramallo 1989-97

Past Coaches
Jorge Luis Valderrama 1927 • Ulises Sauchedo 1930 • Julio Borelli 1938 & 1945 • Diogenes Lara 1946-47 • Felix Deheza 1948-49 • Mario Pretto ITA 1950 • Cesar Vicino 1953 • Vicente Arraya 1959 • Danilo Alvim BRA 1963 • Freddy Valda 1965 • Carlos Trigo 1967 • Freddy Valda 1969 & 1973 • Carlos Trigo 1973 • Freddy Valda 1975 • Wilfredo Camacho 1977 • Ramiro Blacutt 1979-81 • Jose Saldanha BRA 1981 • Wilfredo Camacho 1983 • Carlos Rodrigues ARG 1985 • Osvaldo Veiga ARG 1987 • Jorge Habbegger ARG 1989 • Ramiro Blacutt 1991 • Xabier Azkargorta ESP 1993-94 • Antoino Lopez ESP 1995 • Dusan Draskovic YUG 1996 • Antoino Lopez ESP 1996-97 • Hector Veira ARG 1999 • Carlos Aragones 2000-01 • Jorge Habbegger ARG 2001 • Carlos Trucco 2001-02 • Vladimir Soria 2002 • Walter Roque 2003 • Dalcio Giovagnoli 2003 • Nelson Acosta CHI 2003-04 • Ramiro Blacutt 2004 • Ovidio Messa 2004-06 • Erwin Sanchez 2006-09 • Eduardo Villegas 2009-10 • Gustavo Quinteros 2010-

BOLIVIA 2010

CAMPEONATO APERTURA — FIRST STAGE

Serie A

	Pl	W	D	L	F	A	Pts	Strongest	San José	Aurora	Universitario	Guabirá	Blooming	Bolívar	Petrolero	Wilstermann	Real Potosí	La Paz	Real Mamoré
The Strongest †	12	5	4	3	21	18	19		3-2	2-1	2-3	2-1	2-1	2-2					
San José †	12	5	3	4	24	19	18	2-2		0-1	0-0	3-0	3-1					4-2	
Aurora †	12	4	5	3	17	16	17	1-1	2-1		2-1	0-0	2-0				1-2		
Universitario Sucre ‡	12	5	1	6	21	18	16	1-3	2-3	3-2		4-1	2-1					5-0	
Guabirá ‡	12	3	3	6	15	24	12	2-1	1-1	3-3	2-0		3-1						1-2
Blooming ‡	12	3	2	7	13	20	11	1-1	1-3	1-1	1-0	4-1				1-0			

Serie B

	Pl	W	D	L	F	A	Pts	Strongest	San José	Aurora	Universitario	Guabirá	Blooming	Bolívar	Petrolero	Wilstermann	Real Potosí	La Paz	Real Mamoré
Bolívar †	12	9	1	2	23	11	28	1-0							1-0	1-2	2-1	1-0	6-1
Oriente Petrolero †	12	7	1	4	21	10	22				2-0			3-1		3-1	3-0	2-1	5-1
Jorge Wilstermann †	12	5	3	4	17	17	18						2-2	0-1	1-0		2-0	3-3	2-0
Real Potosí ‡	12	5	1	6	11	19	16			1-0				1-3	0-0	3-0		2-0	2-1
La Paz FC ‡	12	4	2	6	19	19	14		4-2					0-1	2-1	2-2	0-1		2-0
Real Mamoré ‡	12	4	0	8	15	25	12					3-0		1-3	1-2	1-0	3-0	1-2	

6/03/2010 - 6/05/2010 • † Qualified for the Winners Hexagonal • ‡ Qualified for the Losers Hexagonal
Top scorers (whole Apertura): 18 - Christian Diaz ARG, San José • 13 - Jair Reynoso COL, Aurora • 12 - Roberto Galindo, Universitario

APERTURA WINNERS HEXAGONAL

	Pl	W	D	L	F	A	Pts	JW	OP	Au	TS	Bo	SJ
Jorge Wilstermann †	10	6	2	2	15	11	20		1-3	2-1	2-1	2-0	3-1
Oriente Petrolero	10	6	1	3	18	11	19	1-1		1-2	2-1	2-0	4-0
Aurora	10	4	2	4	19	18	14	2-0	2-1		3-5	2-2	4-4
The Strongest	10	3	4	3	15	14	13	1-1	1-2	2-1		1-1	1-1
Bolívar	10	3	2	5	7	14	11	0-1	2-1	1-0	0-1		1-0
San José	10	1	3	6	13	24	6	1-2	0-1	0-3	1-1	4-3	

9/05/2010 - 9/06/2010 • † Qualified for the Copa Libertadores

APERTURA LOSERS HEXAGONAL

	Pl	W	D	L	F	A	Pts	US	Bl	RP	LP	RM	Gu
Universitario Sucre †	10	6	2	2	20	10	20		2-0	2-1	3-1	4-0	3-1
Blooming	10	6	1	3	21	15	19	2-1		5-2	4-3	3-0	2-0
Real Potosí	10	5	1	4	19	16	16	4-3	3-2		1-1	3-1	3-0
La Paz FC	10	3	2	5	17	17	11	0-0	2-0	0-2		3-0	5-1
Real Mamoré	10	3	2	5	10	20	11	1-1	2-2	1-0	2-1		1-0
Guabirá	10	3	0	7	10	19	9	0-1	0-1	1-0	3-1	3-2	

9/05/2010 - 9/06/2010 • † Qualified for the Copa Sudamericana

TORNEO DE INVIERNO

Quarter-finals

Oriente Petrolero	1 3
Real Mamoré *	1 0
Blooming	0 3 1p
Jorge Wilstermann *	2 0 4p
Bolívar	3 4 5p
Real Potosí *	5 1 3p
The Strongest	0 1
San Jose *	0 2

Semi-finals

Oriente Petrolero *	3 1
Jorge Wilstermann	1 0
Bolívar	0 5 1
San Jose *	1 1 2

Final

Oriente Petrolero †	0 5 1 6p
San Jose *	2 2 1 5p

* Home team in 1st leg • † Qualified for the Copa Sudamericana

BOLIVIA 2010 RELEGATION TABLE

	Pl	Pts	Av
Bolívar	68	129	1.897
Oriente Petrolero	68	116	1.706
Real Potosí	68	106	1.559
San José	68	102	1.5
The Strongest	68	101	1.485
Universitario Sucre	68	89	1.309
Guabirá	34	44	1.294
Aurora	68	88	1.294
Blooming	68	87	1.279
La Paz FC	68	82	1.206
Real Mamoré †	68	73	1.074
Jorge Wilstermann	68	72	1.059

† Relegation play-off
Nacional Potosí promoted after winning the Copa Simon Bolivar • Copa Simon Bolivar final: Nacional Potosí 2-0 1-0 Real América
Real América play-off against Real Marmoré
Real Marmoré 2-1 4-3 Real América

BOLIVIA 2010

CAMPEONATO CLAUSURA

	Pl	W	D	L	F	A	Pts	O. Petrolero	Bolívar	Aurora	San José	Guabirá	Blooming	Real Potosí	Strongest	Real Mamoré	La Paz FC	Universitario	Wilstermann
Oriente Petrolero †	22	12	4	6	38	26	**40**		2-4	2-2	2-1	1-0	1-0	3-1	4-0	2-0	1-0	3-1	3-1
Bolívar †	22	10	6	6	37	28	**36**	2-1		1-0	0-0	4-3	1-0	2-0	2-2	2-2	4-4	4-1	0-0
Aurora ‡	22	10	4	8	34	30	**34**	2-0	3-2		4-1	1-0	2-1	0-2	2-1	3-0	2-1	2-1	2-2
San José	22	10	4	8	40	37	**34**	0-3	0-1	3-3		5-1	2-0	2-3	3-2	1-0	1-0	2-1	2-0
Guabirá	22	9	5	8	22	28	**32**	1-1	1-0	1-0	3-1		0-0	2-0	2-1	0-0	1-0	1-0	2-1
Blooming	22	9	4	9	24	28	**31**	1-0	2-0	0-1	2-2	2-3		2-2	2-1	3-0	2-0	2-1	3-0
Real Potosí	22	8	5	9	38	35	**29**	1-2	1-1	2-1	1-3	4-0	3-0		3-2	4-0	2-3	1-1	2-1
The Strongest	22	10	2	10	37	36	**29**	1-1	3-2	4-2	1-2	1-0	2-1	4-2		3-0	1-3	3-0	2-1
Real Mamoré	22	7	7	8	21	30	**28**	3-2	2-1	2-1	3-0	0-0	1-1	2-1	1-0		2-2	2-0	0-0
La Paz FC	22	7	5	10	33	34	**26**	0-0	1-3	1-1	4-3	3-1	4-1	1-2	0-1	1-0		1-1	1-0
Universitario Sucre	22	5	7	10	24	33	**22**	1-2	1-0	2-0	2-2	2-0	0-2	1-1	1-0	1-1	3-1		1-1
Jorge Wilstermann	22	5	7	10	26	32	**22**	4-2	0-1	1-0	1-3	1-1	0-1	1-1	3-1	2-0	4-2	2-2	

24/07/2010 - 28/11/2010 • † Qualified for the Copa Libertadores • ‡ Qualified for the Copa Sudamericana
Top scorers: **14** - William Ferreira URU, Bolívar • **11** - Christian Ruiz ARG, Potosí; Jose Carlos Santos, Bolívar & Pablo Vasquez ARG, The Strongest

MEDALS TABLE

		Overall			Pro		Nat		LL		Sth Am			City
		G	S	B	G	S	G	S	G	S	G	S	B	
1	Bolívar	21	11	2	17	8	4	2	12	11		1	2	La Paz
2	Jorge Wilstermann	10	7	1	5	5	5	2	12	3			1	Cochabamba
3	The Strongest	7	8		6	6	1	2	18	10				La Paz
4	Oriente Petrolero	6	12		5	10	1	2	7	3				Santa Cruz
5	Blooming	5	3	1	5	3			1	2			1	Santa Cruz
6	San José	3	2		2	2	1		9	2				Oruro
7	Real Potosí	1	5		1	5								Potosí
8	Deportivo Municipal	1	4				1	4	4	3				La Paz
9	Always Ready	1	2				1	2	2	5				La Paz
	Guabirá	1	2			1	1	1	1	1				Montero
11	Aurora	1	1		1	1			3	8				Cochabamba
	Chaco Petrolero	1	1				1	1		1				La Paz
13	Litoral	1					1		4	1				La Paz
	Universitario	1					1		1	4				La Paz
	Universitario	1			1									Sucre
16	La Paz FC		2			2								La Paz
17	31 de Octubre		1					1	1	2				La Paz
	Deportivo Chaco		1					1	1					La Paz
19	Destroyers								2	1				Santa Cruz
	Real Santa Cruz													Santa Cruz
	Union Central													Tarija

Pro = the Professional League played since 1977 • Nat = the various national competitions played between 1954 and 1976 • LL = the local leagues played throughout the country until 1976 • The totals for the local leagues are not included in the overall totals

BOT – BOTSWANA

FIFA/COCA-COLA WORLD RANKING

1993	1994	1995	1996	1997	1998	1999	2000	2001	2002	2003	2004	2005	2006	2007	2008	2009	2010
140	145	155	161	162	155	165	150	153	136	112	102	101	108	103	117	118	53

	2010												Hi/Lo
	Jan	Feb	Mar	Mar	Apr	May	Jul	Aug	Sep	Oct	Nov	Dec	53
	118	119	119	116	116	116	93	93	82	79	67	53	165

2010 was without question the most outstanding year in the history of football in Botswana with the national team moving to within just one win of qualifying for a first-ever African Nations Cup finals appearance. The arid southern African country has traditionally been one of the continent's whipping boys but they now look set to finish top of their qualifying group for the 2012 finals which are being co-hosted by Equatorial Guinea and Gabon. The transformation began while the World Cup was being hosted in neighbouring South Africa when Botswana started the preliminaries with a shock 1-0 win in Tunisia. The impact of the result was overshadowed by the spectacle in South Africa but the momentum was not lost on the Zebras, who since then have beaten Tunisia again as well as Chad and Togo. Nine unbeaten matches in 2010, a record for the team, saw the Zebras end the year in 53rd place in the FIFA/Coca-Cola World Ranking, having broken through into the top 100 in July. The rise in the standards is being mirrored at club level too with a shock win for Gaborone United in the African Champions League over Orlando Pirates of South Africa getting 2010 off to a great start. In local football Township Rollers were the team of the season comfortably winning the league title and beating Centre Chiefs 2-1 in the Cup Final.

FIFA WORLD CUP RECORD
1930-1990 DNE   **1994** DNQ   **1998** DNE   **2002-2010** DNQ

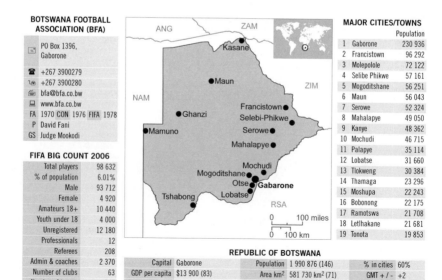

BOTSWANA FOOTBALL ASSOCIATION (BFA)

PO Box 1396, Gaborone

☎ +267 3900279
📠 +267 3900280
✉ bfa@bfa.co.bw
🖥 www.bfa.co.bw
FA 1970 CON 1976 FIFA 1978
P David Fani
GS Judge Mookodi

FIFA BIG COUNT 2006

Total players	98 632
% of population	6.01%
Male	93 712
Female	4 920
Amateurs 18+	10 440
Youth under 18	4 000
Unregistered	12 180
Professionals	12
Referees	208
Admin & coaches	2 370
Number of clubs	63
Number of teams	348

MAJOR CITIES/TOWNS

		Population
1	Gaborone	230 936
2	Francistown	96 292
3	Molepolole	72 122
4	Selibe Phikwe	57 161
5	Mogoditshane	56 251
6	Maun	56 043
7	Serowe	52 324
8	Mahalapye	49 050
9	Kanye	48 362
10	Mochudi	46 715
11	Palapye	35 114
12	Lobatse	31 660
13	Tlokweng	30 384
14	Thamaga	23 296
15	Moshupa	22 243
16	Bobonong	22 175
17	Ramotswa	21 708
18	Letlhakane	21 681
19	Tonota	19 853

REPUBLIC OF BOTSWANA

Capital	Gaborone	Population 1 990 876 (146)	% in cities 60%
GDP per capita	$13 900 (83)	Area km² 581 730 km² (71)	GMT +/- +2
Neighbours (km)	Namibia 1360, South Africa 1840, Zimbabwe 813		

RECENT INTERNATIONAL MATCHES PLAYED BY BOTSWANA

2006	Opponents		Score	Venue	Comp	Scorers	Att	Referee
28-07	Namibia	W	1-0	Gaborone	CCr1	Michael Mogaladi [19]		Lwanja MWI
29-07	Angola	D	0-0	Gaborone	CCr1	W 3-1p		
29-09	South Africa	L	0-1	Pretoria	CCsf			Marange ZIM
13-10	Egypt	L	0-1	Cairo	CNq			Imiere NGA
2008								
16-01	South Africa	L	1-2	Durban	Fr	Moemedi Moatlhaping [54]		
9-02	Swaziland	W	4-1	Mbabane	Fr	Jerome Ramatlhakwane 2 [21] [45], Moemedi Moatlhaping [54], Pontsho Moloi [73]		
26-03	Zimbabwe	L	0-1	Gaborone	Fr			
31-05	Madagascar	D	0-0	Gaborone	WCq		11 087	Kaoma ZAM
8-06	Mozambique	W	2-1	Maputo	WCq	Diphetogo Selolwane [30], Boitumelo Mafoko [82]	30 000	Fakudze SWZ
14-06	Côte d'Ivoire	D	1-1	Gaborone	WCq	Diphetogo Selolwane [25]	21 400	Ssegonga UGA
22-06	Côte d'Ivoire	L	0-4	Abidjan	WCq		15 000	Bennaceur TUN
27-07	Mozambique	L	0-2	Secunda	CCqf			Katjimune NAM
20-08	Zimbabwe	L	0-1	Harare	Fr			
30-08	Lesotho	W	1-0	Gaborone	Fr	Praxis Rabemananjara [18]		
7-09	Madagascar	L	0-1	Antananarivo	WCq		20 000	Seechurn MRI
11-10	Mozambique	L	0-1	Gaborone	WCq		2 000	Seck SEN
2009								
21-03	Namibia	D	0-0	Keetmanshoop	Fr			
1-04	Lesotho	D	0-0	Maseru	Fr			
6-06	New Zealand	D	0-0	Gaborone	Fr			
5-07	Iran	D	1-1	Gaborone	Fr	Mokgathi Mokgathi [30]		
30-09	China PR	L	1-4	Hohhot	Fr	Mokgathi Mokgathi [68]		
18-10	Comoros	D	0-0	Bulawayo	CCr1			Rachide MOZ
20-10	Swaziland	W	1-0	Bulawayo	CCr1	Malepa Bolelang [56]		Seechurn MRI
22-10	Seychelles	W	2-0	Bulawayo	CCr1	Pontsho Moloi [6], Malepa Bolelang [39]		Seechurn MRI
26-10	Zimbabwe	L	0-1	Bulawayo	CCqf			Carvalho ANG
2010								
3-03	Mozambique	W	1-0	Maputo	Fr	Michael Mogaladi [6p]		
21-03	Namibia	D	0-0	Windhoek	Fr			
1-07	Tunisia	W	1-0	Tunis	CNq	Jerome Ramatlhkwane [31]		Ditta SEN
9-07	Chad	W	1-0	Gaborone	CNq	Phenyo Mongala [49]		Seechurn MRI
4-08	Zimbabwe	W	2-0	Selibe-Phikwe	Fr	Mokgathi Mokgathi [9], Jerome Ramatlhkwane [14]		
11-08	Malawi	D	1-1	Blantyre	CNq	Jerome Ramatlhkwane [62]		Martins ANG
4-09	Togo	W	2-1	Gaborone	CNq	Joel Mogorosi [6], Jerome Ramatlhkwane [47]		Kagabo RWA
12-10	Equatorial Guinea	W	2-0	Malabo	Fr	Mogogi Gabonamong, Phenyo Mongala		
17-11	Tunisia	W	1-0	Gaborone	CNq	Jerome Ramatlhkwane [45]		

Fr = Friendly match • CN = CAF African Cup of Nations • CC = COSAFA Cup • WC = FIFA World Cup
q = qualifier • r1 = first round group • qf = quarter-final • sf = semi-final

MEDALS TABLE				
	Overall	Lge	Cup	
	G	G	G	City
1 Township Rollers	16	10	6	Gaborone
2 Gaborone United	12	6	6	Gaborone
3 Botswana Defence Force	10	7	3	Gaborone
4 Mogoditshane Fighters	7	4	3	Mogoditshane
5 Notwane FC	6	3	3	Gaborone
6 Extension Gunners	5	3	2	Lobatse
7 Centre Chiefs	3	1	2	Mochudi
Police XI	2	1	1	Otse
TASC (Tati Sporting Club)	2		2	Francistown
10 Botswana Meat Commission	1		1	Lobatse
ECCO City Greens	1	1		Francistown
Nico United	1		1	Selibe-Pikwe
TAFIC	1		1	Francistown
Uniao Flamengo Santos	1		1	Gabane

BOTSWANA 2009–10

PREMIER LEAGUE

	Pl	W	D	L	F	A	Pts	Rollers	Chiefs	Santos	Gunners	Greens	BDF	Gaborone Utd	Notwane	Nico Utd	TAFIC	Police	Motlakase	BMC	Giants	Comets	Young Fighters
Township Rollers †	30	25	3	2	83	23	78		2-3	0-1	2-0	3-0	1-0	1-1	2-0	2-1	1-1	2-0	3-0	2-1	6-0	1-0	5-0
Centre Chiefs	30	19	8	3	70	35	65	2-2		5-2	2-2	3-4	2-0	1-2	2-2	3-0	4-1	3-1	3-3	5-1	3-0	2-2	2-1
Uniao Flamengo Santos	30	19	3	8	74	48	60	2-3	2-3		3-1	3-2	1-2	1-2	2-0	4-0	0-0	3-1	4-1	2-2	1-3	4-2	4-4
Extension Gunners	30	17	7	6	56	31	58	0-2	1-2	4-1		3-0	3-1	2-1	3-1	3-1	2-0	1-0	4-1	0-0	3-1	6-1	3-0
ECCO City Greens	30	15	5	10	61	51	50	3-6	1-1	2-4	2-1		2-1	2-3	0-2	6-0	0-0	1-2	3-0	4-1	4-2	2-1	2-2
Defence Force	30	12	7	11	35	33	43	1-2	1-1	1-2	1-1	1-3		2-1	2-0	2-0	0-1	1-0	1-1	0-0	2-0	2-3	1-1
Gaborone United	30	11	9	10	43	44	42	1-4	0-2	1-3	1-2	1-1	2-1		2-3	2-1	2-1	2-1	2-1	0-0	0-2	1-1	6-2
Notwane FC	30	9	9	12	47	52	36	2-3	3-1	2-5	2-2	2-3	0-2	0-0		1-1	0-0	2-2	1-1	2-5	1-2	1-2	3-1
Nico United	30	10	3	17	34	50	33	1-2	0-2	1-0	0-1	0-1	1-2	1-1	2-0		1-0	1-0	1-2	1-0	2-1	2-0	4-1
TAFIC	30	8	8	14	32	47	32	2-5	1-2	0-4	0-2	3-1	1-0	1-1	0-4	1-0		1-1	2-0	1-1	1-1	4-0	5-4
Police	30	7	9	14	25	34	30	0-2	0-1	0-2	2-0	0-1	0-1	1-0	2-2	2-2	2-1		2-1	2-1	3-0	0-0	0-1
Motlakase	30	8	5	17	37	62	29	0-7	0-1	2-3	0-0	1-2	0-1	4-1	0-3	2-4	0-2	1-0		1-1	3-2	1-0	4-1
Bot. Meat Commission	30	6	10	14	36	46	28	1-2	1-4	1-2	2-2	2-0	2-3	1-1	3-4	4-1	1-0	0-0	2-1		1-2	0-1	1-2
Killer Giants ‡	30	7	7	16	31	59	28	0-2	0-2	0-4	1-1	1-6	0-0	0-3	0-1	2-1	2-1	1-1	1-2	0-0		4-0	1-3
Jwaneng Comets	30	6	9	15	31	54	27	0-3	0-0	2-3	1-2	1-1	0-1	2-2	0-1	2-4	3-1	0-0	4-2	1-0	1-1		1-1
Boteti Young Fighters	30	6	8	16	38	64	26	0-5	0-3	1-2	0-1	1-2	2-2	0-1	2-2	1-0	3-0	0-0	1-2	0-1	1-1	2-0	

18/09/2009 - 23/05/2010 • † Qualified for the CAF Champions League

‡ Relegation/promotion play-offs: Killer Giants 1-1 3-1 Letlapeng • TASC 1-1 4-1 Killer Giants • Letlapeng 1-1 1-3 TASC • TASC promoted, Killers Giants relegated, Letlapeng remain in the first division

BOTSWANA 2009–10 FIRST DIVISION NORTH (2)

	Pl	W	D	L	F	A	Pts
Miscellaneous Serowe	22	16	3	3	50	25	53
TASC ‡	22	14	4	4	53	17	46
Orapa Wanderers ‡	22	14	4	4	43	23	46
Great North Tigers	22	11	3	8	36	36	36
FC Satmos	22	11	2	9	50	37	35
Mahalapye Hotspurs	22	9	3	10	38	39	30
BR Highlanders	22	8	5	9	29	29	29
Maun Terrors	22	6	5	11	29	40	23
Sua Flamingoes	22	5	8	9	36	48	23
Ferry Wanderers	21	7	2	12	23	42	23
Orapa Bucs	21	6	4	11	37	51	22
Palapye United	22	2	1	19	24	61	7

26/09/2009 - 22/05/2010 • ‡ Qualified for the play-offs

BOTSWANA 2009–10 FIRST DIVISION SOUTH (2)

	Pl	W	D	L	F	A	Pts
Black Peril	19	9	7	3	25	15	34
Prisons	19	8	6	5	30	16	30
Letlapeng Ramotswa ‡	18	8	5	5	31	22	29
Masitaoka	19	7	6	6	34	26	27
Mogoditshane Fighters	18	5	10	3	20	17	25
Mathaithai	19	6	5	8	18	21	23
Mochudi Buffaloes	19	6	5	8	21	27	23
Tlokweng United	19	6	5	8	15	24	23
Naughty Boys	18	6	4	8	21	26	22
Mochudi Eastern Tigers	17	6	4	7	10	19	22
Southern Callies	19	4	9	6	16	23	21
Young Strikers	18	4	6	8	17	22	18

26/09/2009 - 22/05/2010 • ‡ Qualified for the play-offs (Last available table)

COCA-COLA CUP 2009–10

Round of 16

Township Rollers	2
Miscellaneous Serowe*	1
Prisons XI *	0
Un. Flamengo Santos	6
Gaborone United *	5
Great North Tigers	0
Police	1 3p
Mogod'shane Fighters *	1 4p
Extension Gunners *	3
Mathaithai	1
Defence Force	0
ECCO City Greens *	1
TAFIC *	2
Nico United	1
Letlapeng *	1
Centre Chiefs	5

Quarter–finals

Township Rollers *	2
Un. Flamengo Santos	0
Gaborone United *	1
Mogoditshane Fighters	2
Extension Gunners	2
ECCO City Greens *	0
TAFIC *	1
Centre Chiefs †	2

Semi–finals

Township Rollers ‡‡	5
Mogoditshane Fighters	0
Extension Gunners	0
Centre Chiefs ‡	4

Final

Township Rollers	3
Centre Chiefs	1

* Home Team

† Abandoned. Awarded 2-0

‡ Played at UB Stadium • ‡‡ Played at Molepolole Sports Complex

CUP FINAL

University of Botswana, Gaborone
15-05-2010

Scorers - Terrence Mandaza 2, Edwin Moalosi for Rollers; Sekhana Koko for Chiefs

BRA – BRAZIL

FIFA/COCA-COLA WORLD RANKING

1993	1994	1995	1996	1997	1998	1999	2000	2001	2002	2003	2004	2005	2006	2007	2008	2009	2010
3	1	1	1	1	1	1	1	1	3	1	1	1	1	2	5	2	4

2010												Hi/Lo
Jan	Feb	Mar	Mar	Apr	May	Jul	Aug	Sep	Oct	Nov	Dec	1
2	2	2	2	1	1	3	3	4	3	3	4	8

2010 turned out to be a crushing disappointment for a Brazilian nation fully expecting a sixth world title to come their way at the World Cup in South Africa. Brazil went into the tournament as favourites and in their first five games showed flashes which justified the tag. Defensive discipline, speed, technique and individual flair - hallmarks of the 1994 World Cup winning team of which coach Dunga was captain - saw Brazil through to a quarter-final against the Netherlands, but despite going ahead through Robinho and dominating the first half, their defensive discipline deserted them in the second and they lost to a doggedly determined Dutch team inspired by Wesley Sneijder. The Selecao finds itself in a difficult moment with four years to find a winning formula before Brazil hosts the World Cup in 2014, and fans will be aware that just one host nation has won the tournament since 1978. In club football Internacional confirmed their growing status by winning the Copa Libertadores for the second time in five years whilst at home Fluminense won Serie A on the final day of the season with a 1-0 win over Guarani - their first title for over a quarter of a century and only their second overall. A Neymar-inspired Santos won the Copa do Brasil for the first time since Pele played for them, with a 3-2 aggregate victory over Vitória in the final.

FIFA WORLD CUP RECORD

1930 6 r1 **1934** 14 r1 **1938** 3 SF **1950** 2 Finalists (hosts) **1954** 5 QF **1958** 1 Winners **1962** 1 Winners **1966** 11 r1 **1970** 1 Winners **1974** 4 r2 **1978** 3 r2 **1982** 5 r2 **1986** 5 QF **1990** 9 r2 **1994** 1 Winners **1998** 2 Finalists **2002** 1 Winners **2006** 5 QF **2010** 6 QF

CONFEDERACAO BRASILEIRA DE FUTEBOL (CBF)

Rua Victor Civita 66, Bloco
1 - Edificio 5 - 5 Andar, Barra
da Tijuca, Rio de Janeiro
☎ +55 21 35721900
📠 +55 21 35721989
✉ cbf@cbf.com.br
🖳 www.cbf.com.br
FA 1914 CON 1916 FIFA 1923
P Ricardo Teixeira
GS Marco Antonio Teixeira

FIFA BIG COUNT 2006

Total players	13 197 733
% of population	7.02%
Male	11 752 783
Female	1 444 950
Amateurs 18+	472 165
Youth under 18	1 347 100
Unregistered	6 080 000
Professionals	16 200
Referees	16 000
Admin & coaches	45 000
Number of clubs	28 970
Number of teams	86 910

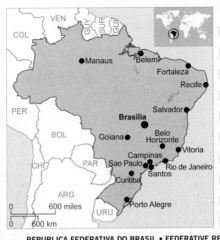

MAJOR CITIES/TOWNS

		Population
1	São Paulo	10 328 094
2	Rio de Janeiro	6 227 355
3	Salvador	2 949 222
4	Fortaleza	2 513 812
5	Belo Horizonte	2 506 025
6	Brasília	2 463 923
7	Curitiba	1 871 087
8	Manaus	1 817 778
9	Belém	1 554 295
10	Recife	1 542 678
11	Porto Alegre	1 421 272
12	Guarulhos	1 325 997
13	Goiânia	1 267 151
14	Campinas	1 111 854
15	Maceió	1 111 536
16	Nova Iguaçu	1 087 086
17	São Luís	1 007 604
18	São Gonçalo	998 325
19	Natal	821 794

REPUBLICA FEDERATIVA DO BRASIL • FEDERATIVE REPUBLIC OF BRAZIL

Capital	Brasilia	Population	198 739 269 (5)	% in cities	86%
GDP per capita	$10 200 (102)	Area km²	8 514 877 km² (5)	GMT +/-	-3
Neighbours (km)	Argentina 1261, Bolivia 3423, Colombia 1644, French Guiana 730, Guyana 1606, Paraguay 1365, Peru 2995, Suriname 593, Uruguay 1068, Venezuela 2200 • Coast 7491				

RECENT INTERNATIONAL MATCHES PLAYED BY BRAZIL

2008	Opponents	Score	Venue	Comp	Scorers	Att	Referee
7-09	Chile	W 3-0	Santiago	WCq	Luis Fabiano 2 [21] [83], Robinho [44]	60 239	Torres PAR
10-09	Bolivia	D 0-0	Rio de Janeiro	WCq		31 422	Intriago ECU
12-10	Venezuela	W 4-0	San Cristobal	WCq	Kaka [6], Robinho 2 [9] [66], Adriano [19]	38 000	Rivera PER
15-10	Colombia	D 0-0	Rio de Janeiro	WCq		54 910	Selman CHI
19-11	Portugal	W 6-2	Gama	Fr	Luis Fabiano 3 [8] [25] [57], Maicon [55], Elano [65], Adriano [91+]	19 157	Larrionda URU
2009							
10-02	Italy	W 2-0	London	Fr	Elano [13], Robinho [27]	60 077	Webb ENG
29-03	Ecuador	D 1-1	Quito	WCq	Julio Baptista [72]	40 000	Chandia CHI
1-04	Peru	W 3-0	Port Alegre	WCq	Luis Fabiano 2 [18p] [27], Felipe Melo [64]	55 000	Pezzotta ARG
6-06	Uruguay	W 4-0	Montevideo	WCq	Dani Alves [12], Juan [36], Luis Fabiano [52], Kaka [75p]	52 000	Laverni ARG
10-06	Paraguay	W 2-1	Recife	WCq	Robinho [40], Nilmar [50]	56 682	Ruiz COL
15-06	Egypt	W 4-3	Bloemfontein	CCr1	Kaka 2 [5] [90p], Luis Fabiano [12], Juan [37]	27 851	Webb ENG
18-06	USA	W 3-0	Pretoria	CCr1	Felipe Melo [7], Robinho [20], Maicon [62]	39 617	Busacca SUI
21-06	Italy	W 3-0	Pretoria	CCr1	Luis Fabiano 2 [37] [43], Dossena OG [45]	41 195	Archundia MEX
25-06	South Africa	W 1-0	Johannesburg	CCsf	Dani Alves [88]	48 049	Busacca SUI
28-06	USA	W 3-2	Johannesburg	CCf	Luis Fabiano 2 [46] [74], Lucio [84]	52 291	Hansson SWE
12-08	Estonia	W 1-0	Tallinn	Fr	Luis Fabiano [43]	8 550	Ingvarsson SWE
5-09	Argentina	W 3-1	Rosario	WCq	Luisao [23], Luis Fabiano 2 [30] [68]	37 000	Ruiz COL
9-09	Chile	W 4-2	Salvador	WCq	Nilmar 3 [31] [74] [76], Julio Baptista [40]	30 000	Larrionda URU
11-10	Bolivia	L 1-2	La Paz	WCq	Nilmar [70]	16 557	Pozo CHI
14-10	Venezuela	D 0-0	Campo Grande	WCq		30 000	Carrillo PER
14-11	England	W 1-0	Doha	Fr	Nilmar [47]	50 000	Abdou QAT
17-11	Oman	W 2-0	Muscat	Fr	Nilmar [4], Al Ghalani OG [60]	20 000	Braamhaar NED
2010							
2-03	Republic of Ireland	W 2-0	London	Fr	OG [44], Robinho [76]	40 082	Dean ENG
2-06	Zimbabwe	W 3-0	Harare	Fr	Michel Bastos [42], Robinho [43], Elano [57]	30 000	Martins ANG
7-06	Tanzania	W 5-1	Dar es Salaam	Fr	Robinho 2 [10] [33], Ramires 2 [53] [90], Kaka [75]	35 000	Ssegonga UGA
15-06	Korea DPR	W 2-1	Johannesburg	WCr1	Maicon [55], Elano [72]	54 331	Kassai HUN
20-06	Côte d'Ivoire	W 3-1	Johannesburg	WCr1	Luis Fabiano 2 [25] [50], Elano [62]	84 445	Lannoy FRA
25-06	Portugal	D 0-0	Durban	WCr1		62 712	Archundia MEX
28-06	Chile	W 3-0	Johannesburg	WCr2	Juan [35], Luis Fabiano [38], Robinho [59]	54 096	Webb ENG
2-07	Netherlands	L 1-2	Port Elizabeth	WCqf	Robinho [10]	40 186	Nishimura JPN
10-08	USA	W 2-0	New Jersey	Fr	Neymar [29], Pato [45]	77 223	Petrescu CAN
7-10	Iran	W 3-0	Abu Dhabi	Fr	Dani Alves [14], Pato [69], Nilmar [90]	49 000	Al Marzouqi UAE
11-10	Ukraine	W 2-0	Derby	Fr	Dani Alves [25], Pato [64]	13 088	Atkinson ENG
17-11	Argentina	L 0-1	Doha	Fr		50 000	Balideh QAT

Fr = Friendly match • CA = Copa America • CC = FIFA Confederations Cup • WC = FIFA World Cup
q = qualifier • r1 = 1st round group • r2 = second round • qf = quarter-final • sf = semi-final • f = final

BRAZIL NATIONAL TEAM HISTORICAL RECORDS

Caps

142 - Cafu 1990-2006 • 125 - Roberto Carlos 1992-2006 • 101 - Claudio Taffarel 1988-98 • 98 - Djalma Santos 1952-68 • 97 - Ronaldo 1994-2006 • 96 - Lucio 2000- • 94 - Gilmar 1953-69 • 93 - Gilberto Silva 2001- • 92 - Pele 1957-71 & Rivelino 1965-78 • 91 - Dunga 1987-98 & Dida 1995-2006 • 88 - Ronaldinho 1999- • 84 - Ze Roberto 1995-2006 • 83 - Ronaldinho 2003- • 82 - Kaka 2002- • 81 - Jairzinho 1964-82 & Aldair 1989-2000 • 80 - Emerson Leao 1970-86 • 79 - Juan 2001- • 75 - Bebeto 1985-98 & Nilton Santos 1949-62

Goals

77 - Pele 1957-71 • 62 - Ronaldo 1994-2006 • 55 - Romario 1987-2005 • 52 - Zico 1976-86 • 39 - Bebeto 1985-98 • 34 - Rivaldo 1993-2003 • 33 - Jairzinho 1964-82 • 32 - Ademir 1945-53, Tostao 1966-72 & Ronaldinho 1999- • 30 - Zizinho 1942-57 • 29 - Careca 1982-93 • 28 - Luis Fabiano 2003- • 27 - Adriano 2000- & Kaka 2002- • 26 - Rivelino 1965-78 • 25 - Robinho 2003- • 22 - Jair 1940-50 & Socrates 1979-86 • 21 - Leonidas 1932-46 • 20 - Didi 1952-62 & Roberto Dinamite 1975-84 • 16 - Baltazar 1950-56 & Pepe 1956-63

Past Coaches

Silvio Lagreca 1914-17 • Haroldo Domingues 1919 • Silvio Lagreca 1920 • Lais 1921-22 • Francisco Abatte 1922 • Almeda Rego 1923 • Joaquim Guimaraes 1925 • Pindaro de Carvalho Rodrigues 1930 • Luis Vinhaes 1931-34 • Carlito Rocha 1934 • Adhemar Pimenta 1936-38 • Carlos Nascimento 1939 • Armando Del Debbio 1940 • Jayme Barcelos 1940 • Adhemar Pimenta 1942 • Flavio Costa 1944-50 • Zeze Moreira 1952 • Aymore Moreira 1953 • Zeze Moreira 1954-55 • Vicente Feola 1955 • Flavio Costa 1955 • Osvaldo Brandao 1955-56 • Tete Duarte 1956 • Flavio Costa 1956 • Osvaldo Brandao 1957 • Silvio Pirillo 1957 • Pedrinho 1957 • Vicente Feola 1958-59 • Gentil Cardoso 1959 • Foguinho 1960 • Vicente Feola 1960 • Aymore Moreira 1961-63 • Vicente Feola 1964-65 • Aymore Ferreira 1965 • Carlos Froner 1966 • Vicente Feola 1966 • Aymore Ferreira 1967-68 • Antonio 1968 • Mario Zagallo 1968 • Aymore Ferreira 1968 • Dorival Yustrich 1968 • Joao Saldanha 1969-70 • Mario Zagallo 1970-74 • Osvaldo Brandao 1975-77 • Claudio Coutinho 1977-79 • Tele Santana 1980-82 • Carlos Alberto Parreira 1983 • Edu 1984 • Evaristo de Macedo 1985 • Tele Santana 1985-86 • Carlos Alberto Silva 1987-88 • Sebastiao Lazaroni 1989-90 • Paulo Roberto Falcao 1990-91 • Ernesto Paulo 1991 • Carlos Alberto Parreira 1991-94 • Mario Zagallo 1994-98 • Vanderlei Luxemburgo 1998-2000 • Candido 2000 •Emerson Leao 2000-01 • Luiz Felipe Scolari 2001-02 • Mario Zagallo 2002 • Carlos Alberto Parreira 2001-06 • Dunga 2006-10 • Mano Menezes 2010-

BRAZIL 2010

SERIE A

	Pl	W	D	L	F	A	Pts	Fluminense	Cruzeiro	Corinthians	Grêmio	Atlético PR	Botafogo	Internacional	Santos	São Paulo	Palmeiras	Vasco	Ceará	Atlético MG	Flamengo	Avaí	Atlético GO	Vitória	Guarani	Goiás	Grêmio Prud'te
Fluminense †	38	20	11	7	62	36	71		1-0	1-2	2-0	3-1	0-0	3-0	0-3	2-2	1-1	1-0	3-1	5-1	2-1	1-0	1-0	2-1	1-0	1-1	1-1
Cruzeiro †	38	20	9	9	53	38	69	1-0		1-0	2-2	0-0	1-0	1-0	0-0	0-2	2-1	3-1	2-0	3-4	1-0	2-2	3-0	0-1	4-2	1-0	0-0
Corinthians †	38	19	11	8	65	41	68	1-0	1-0		0-1	2-1	1-1	2-0	4-2	3-0	1-0	2-0	2-2	1-0	1-0	4-0	3-4	2-1	3-1	5-1	3-0
Grêmio †	38	17	12	9	68	43	63	1-2	2-1	1-2		3-1	3-0	2-2	1-2	4-2	1-2	1-1	5-1	2-1	2-2	3-0	2-0	1-1	1-0	2-0	4-0
Atlético Paranaense ‡	38	17	9	12	43	45	60	2-2	0-2	1-1	1-1		3-2	1-0	2-0	1-1	1-0	0-0	2-1	2-1	1-0	1-0	2-1	1-0	2-2	2-1	2-1
Botafogo ‡	38	14	17	7	54	42	59	1-1	2-2	2-2	2-2	1-1		1-2	3-3	2-0	0-0	1-1	0-3	0-1	1-1	0-3	2-1	0-1	1-3	0-3	3-1
Internacional †	38	16	10	12	48	41	58	0-0	1-2	3-2	0-0	4-1	1-0		1-1	0-2	1-1	1-1	0-1	1-1	0-3	1-1	1-1	3-0	0-0	2-0	
Santos †	38	15	11	12	63	50	56	0-1	4-1	2-3	0-0	2-0	0-1	1-0		1-0	1-4	0-1	4-0	1-1	2-0	0-0	2-1	4-2	1-1	3-1	2-0	2-3
São Paulo FC ‡	38	15	10	13	54	54	55	1-4	2-2	0-2	3-1	2-1	1-2	1-3	4-3		1-0	0-0	2-1	4-0	2-0	1-2	2-1	2-3	2-1	0-3	1-1
Palmeiras ‡	38	12	14	12	42	43	50	1-2	2-3	1-1	4-2	2-0	2-2	2-0	2-1	0-2		0-0	1-1	0-2	0-1	4-1	0-3	1-0	1-0	3-2	0-0
Vasco da Gama ‡	38	11	16	11	43	45	49	2-2	1-1	2-0	3-3	3-1	2-2	3-2	3-1	1-1	0-0		2-0	2-0	1-1	2-0	1-0	0-1	3-2	2-1	
Ceará ‡	38	10	17	11	35	44	47	1-0	1-0	0-0	2-1	1-1	2-2	1-0	2-1	2-0	0-0	0-2		0-0	2-2	2-0	0-0	1-0	2-0	1-2	1-2
Atlético Mineiro ‡	38	13	6	19	52	64	45	1-3	0-1	2-1	1-2	3-1	0-2	1-2	2-2	2-3	1-2	2-1	0-1		4-1	2-0	3-2	2-3	3-1	3-1	1-0
Flamengo ‡	38	9	17	12	41	44	44	3-3	1-2	1-1	1-1	0-1	1-0	3-0	0-0	1-1	1-3	0-0	1-0	0-0		1-1	2-0	2-2	2-1	1-2	3-1
Avaí	38	11	10	17	49	58	43	0-3	1-2	3-2	0-3	0-1	0-0	0-1	3-2	0-0	4-2	2-0	5-0	0-0	2-2		3-0	0-0	0-4	1-6	6-1
Atlético Goiâniense	38	11	9	18	51	57	42	2-1	2-1	3-1	0-0	1-2	0-2	2-2	1-2	1-1	3-0	2-0	1-1	2-3	0-1	2-2		4-1	1-1	1-3	3-0
Vitória	38	9	15	14	42	48	42	1-2	0-1	1-1	0-3	1-0	1-3	0-0	4-2	3-2	1-1	4-2	0-0	4-3	1-1	3-0	0-0		1-1	2-2	2-0
Guarani	38	8	13	17	33	53	37	2-1	1-2	2-0	0-0	3-1	0-1	1-0	3-0	0-0	0-0	1-0	1-1	0-2	1-4	1-0	1-1	1-1		1-0	1-0
Goiás	38	8	9	21	41	68	33	0-3	0-1	1-1	1-0	0-2	0-4	1-2	3-1	1-4	2-1	1-1	0-0	0-1	1-3	1-1	0-1	1-3	1-0	3-1	1-2
Grêmio Prudente §3	38	7	10	21	39	64	28	1-1	0-2	2-2	2-0	0-1	0-1	0-3	1-2	2-3	0-1	1-2	1-1	4-0	1-2	1-1	1-0	0-4	2-4	1-0	

8/05/2020 – 5/12/2010 • † Qualified for the Copa Libertadores • ‡ Qualified for the Copa Sudamericana • § = Points deducted
Top scorers: 23 – Jonas, Grêmio • 17 – Neymar, Santos • 14 – Bruno Cesar, Corinthians • 12 – Elias, Atlético GO & Obina, Atlético MG •
11 – Sebastian Abreu URU, Botafogo & Andre Lima, Grêmio • 10 – Alecsandro, Inter; Diego Tardelli, Atlético MG; Kleber, Palmeiras; Washington, Fluminense; Wesley Morais, Grêmio Prudente; Ze Eduardo, Santos

BRAZIL 2010

SERIE B

	Pl	W	D	L	F	A	Pts	Coritiba	Figueirense	Bahia	América MG	Portuguesa	Sport Recife	Paraná	Bragantino	ASA	São Caetano	Duque de Caxias	Icasa	Náutico	Ponte Preta	Guaratinguetá	Vila Nova	Brasiliense	Santo André	Ipatinga	América RN
Coritiba	38	21	8	9	69	49	71		2-1	2-0	1-1	2-0	2-1	0-0	0-0	2-0	1-2	0-2	3-0	3-1	2-1	2-3	5-1	2-1	3-2	3-0	5-1
Figueirense	38	19	10	9	68	37	67	2-0		1-0	0-1	2-1	0-0	4-2	0-0	6-0	1-0	0-0	5-1	1-2	4-2	2-2	2-0	1-0	2-2	5-0	4-0
Bahia	38	19	8	11	63	44	65	1-1	2-2		3-0	3-0	2-0	1-1	5-1	3-0	0-1	2-4	3-0	1-1	2-1	1-1	1-1	1-2	3-1	1-0
América Mineiro	38	19	6	13	56	42	63	1-1	1-0	0-1		2-3	2-1	1-0	0-0	1-3	2-0	2-2	1-0	3-1	3-1	2-0	2-1	4-1	4-0	4-1
Portuguesa	38	19	5	14	69	52	62	2-2	1-0	2-4	1-0		1-2	6-1	2-0	2-0	3-1	0-2	3-1	3-1	0-1	3-0	4-1	3-1	3-2	2-1	1-2
Sport Recife	38	15	11	12	54	42	56	3-2	2-1	1-2	1-0	1-2		1-0	2-0	2-0	4-1	1-2	1-2	1-1	1-1	1-0	0-3	0-1	1-0	1-0	3-0
Paraná	38	15	8	15	47	44	53	0-1	1-1	0-1	1-0	2-1	0-2		0-0	2-1	1-0	1-0	0-0	4-0	2-2	1-1	1-0	2-0	3-0	0-3	0-0
Bragantino	38	13	14	11	52	37	53	2-3	0-2	2-0	1-2	2-0	0-0	1-0		2-1	1-1	4-1	0-0	3-0	0-1	1-1	5-1	2-2	3-1	2-0	5-0
ASA Arapiraca	38	16	4	18	52	56	52	1-2	1-2	0-1	2-1	1-1	4-1	0-1	2-0		3-1	0-2	3-0	2-0	1-1	1-2	2-1	6-1	2-0	2-1	1-2
São Caetano	38	14	10	15	50	52	52	3-1	0-1	1-1	0-0	1-3	2-1	2-2	0-0	2-0		1-0	2-1	5-0	3-1	3-1	1-2	1-1	3-2	2-1	1-0
Duque de Caxias	38	15	5	18	46	56	50	2-1	1-0	1-0	1-5	2-1	1-1	1-1	1-0		1-0	1-2	3-2	1-2	1-0	3-0	3-2	1-0
Icasa	38	13	10	15	53	51	49	2-2	3-1	4-0	2-3	3-1	0-0	3-0	2-1	0-1	1-1	3-1		3-1	2-0	0-0	1-4	3-0	1-2	2-0	2-2
Náutico	38	14	6	18	41	60	48	3-1	1-1	3-2	2-1	1-0	1-1	1-4	1-1	2-1	1-2	2-0	1-0		1-1	0-1	4-1	0-0	1-0	2-0	2-2
Ponte Preta	38	12	12	14	49	48	48	2-2	1-2	1-2	0-0	0-2	3-1	1-0	0-1	0-0	1-2	1-0	0-1	2-0		1-1	2-2	2-0	2-0	1-1	3-0
Guaratinguetá	38	11	14	13	47	59	47	1-0	2-2	4-2	1-3	1-1	0-1	0-2	2-2	0-2	0-0	3-1	1-1	1-0	2-3		2-1	0-1	3-1	2-1	1-1
Vila Nova	38	13	7	18	50	69	46	0-1	3-1	0-4	2-4	2-1	1-1	2-2	3-2	1-3	2-1	1-1	0-2	1-1	1-0		4-0	0-3	2-2	2-1
Brasiliense	38	12	10	16	41	59	46	0-1	1-1	3-2	1-1	1-1	2-1	3-0	0-4	2-3	1-1	2-0	2-0	0-1	2-1	2-2	3-0		1-0	1-0	1-0
Santo André	38	11	10	17	53	61	43	1-3	0-2	1-0	3-0	3-4	2-2	3-1	1-3	3-0	1-0	4-1	1-1	1-0	2-0	1-1	0-0	1-1		2-2	1-1
Ipatinga	38	11	8	19	47	62	41	5-1	0-2	1-2	1-2	0-0	1-3	1-2	2-1	1-2	4-1	2-0	2-2	2-1	2-1	3-0	2-0	3-1	1-1		1-1
América Natal	38	11	8	19	40	68	41	1-2	1-3	0-2	0-2	1-3	0-5	1-0	0-0	1-0	3-3	2-1	2-0	2-1	1-1	5-2	1-2	1-2	2-0	0-1	

7/05/2010 – 17/11/2010 • Top scorers: 21 – Alessandro, Ipatinga • 19 – Fabio Junior, América MG • 17 – Eduardo, São Caetano

BRAZIL 2010
SERIE C FINAL ROUNDS

Quarter-finals		Semi-finals		Final	
ABC *	1 3				
Aguia Marabá	0 1	ABC	1 2		
Paysandu *	1 2	Salgueiro *	1 0		
Salgueiro	1 3			ABC	1 0
Criciúma *	2 2			Ituiutaba *	0 0
Macaé	3 0	Criciúma	4p		
Chapecoense	1 0	Ituiutaba * ‡	4p		
Ituiutaba *	1 0	* Home team in the 1st leg			

ABC, Ituiutaba, Criciúma & Salgueiro Promoted
‡ Both matches finished 2-2

BRAZIL 2010
SERIE D FINAL ROUNDS

Quarter-finals		Semi-finals		Final	
Guarany *	2 2				
Vila Aurora	0 1	Guarany *	2 0		
Uberaba	2p	Araguaína	2 0		
Araguaína * ‡	3p			Guarany	1 4
Madureira *	4 6			América AM *	1 1
Operário PR	2 2	Madureira *	2 0		
Joinville	1 1	América AM	1 2		
América AM	1 2	* Home team in the 1st leg			

Guarany, Madureira & Araguaína promoted • América Manaus refused promotion for fielding ineligible player against Joinville. Joinville promoted instead • ‡ Both matches finished 0-0

BRAZIL STATE CHAMPIONSHIPS 2010

State	Winners	Score	Runners-up	State	Winners	Score	Runners-up
Acre	Rio Branco	5-3 1-1	Náuas	Paraíba	Treze	†	Botafogo
Alagoas	Murici	2-0 2-1	ASA	Paraná	Coritiba	†	Atlético PR
Amapá	Trem	‡	Santana	Pernambuco	Sport Recife	2-3 1-0	Nautico
Amazonas	Peñarol	1-1 5-4p	São Raimundo	Piauí	Comercial PI	‡	
Bahia	Vitória	1-0 1-2	Bahia	Rio de Janeiro	Botafogo	‡	
Ceará	Fortaleza	1-0 1-2 3-1p	Ceará	Rio Grande Nor.	ABC	5-1 1-2	Corintians
Distrito Federal	Ceilândia	3-1 2-2	Brasiliense	Rio Grande Sul	Grêmio	2-0 0-1	Internacional
Espirito Santo	Rio Branco	1-0 0-0	Vitória ES	Rondônia	Vilhena	2-1 3-3	Ariquemes
Goiás	Atlético GO	4-0 3-1	Santa Helena	Roraima	Bare	‡	
Maranhão	Sampaio Corrêa		Moto Club	Santa Catarina	Avai	3-1 2-0	Joinville
Mato Grosso	União Rondonópolis	3-3 3-2	Operário MT	São Paulo	Santos	3-2 2-3	Santo André
Mato Grosso Sul	Comercial MS	2-1 1-0	Naviraiense	Sergipe	River Plate	‡	
Minas Gerais	Atlético MG	3-2 2-0	Ipatinga	Tocantins	Gurupi	0-1 3-1	Araguaia
Pará	Paysandu	0-1 3-1	Aguia				

‡ Won both stages so no final needed. † Played on a league basis

BRAZIL STATE CHAMPIONSHIPS 2010 – SÃO PAULO

CAMPEONATO PAULISTA
SERIE A1

	Pl	W	D	L	F	A	Pts	Santos	Santo André	Prudente	São Paulo	Corinthians	Portuguesa	Botafogo	S. Caetano	Oeste	Ponte Preta	Palmeiras	Mogi Mirim	Ituano	Mirassol	Paulista	Bragantino	Rio Claro	Monte Azul	Sertãozinho	Rio Branco
Santos ‡	19	15	2	2	61	24	47		5-0	2-1		2-0 1-1	3-4	9-1		6-3 2-1 5-0 4-2											
Santo André ‡	19	11	4	4	45	27	37	1-2		1-3	2-0 4-1	2-2 2-2			2-1 4-2 4-1	3-0											
Grêmio Prudente ‡	19	11	4	4	34	28	37		1-3		2-0	0-4 1-0		3-1 2-2 3-0			3-2 1-0		2-0								
São Paulo FC ‡	19	11	3	5	41	19	36	1-2	3-1		1-3 5-0 3-0		3-0		3-0	3-0 5-1		2-1									
Corinthians	19	10	5	4	32	18	35	2-1	4-3		1-1		1-0		1-1 0-1 2-1 5-1 1-1 4-0 0-0											
Portuguesa	19	9	4	6	29	20	31	1-1	1-2	1-1	1-2 1-0		0-1 2-3	2-1		3-1	2-0										
Botafogo RP	19	9	4	6	27	25	31	2-4		1-0 2-1 1-0 1-1 3-0 0-0					2-1 3-1											
São Caetano	19	8	3	8	30	25	27	1-3		0-1		2-2 2-0	1-0		2-0		2-2 5-1 1-2									
Oeste	19	6	8	5	27	26	26		1-1 0-0 1-2 1-2					2-0	2-2		2-2 2-1 3-1									
Ponte Preta	19	7	4	8	25	30	25	1-1	0-2 2-1 2-1		1-3			1-3		4-3 2-2 2-1 2-3										
Palmeiras	19	6	7	6	31	32	25	4-3 1-4	2-0	1-1	1-4 0-0 0-2		5-1 3-3 1-1		1-0	3-2 2-2										
Mogi Mirim	19	7	3	9	22	35	24	2-1 3-2	0-3		1-3 1-0		3-0	1-0 1-1			2-2									
Ituano	19	6	4	9	23	37	22	1-2 0-4 0-1 0-2		0-1	1-1		4-0 1-0		1-0											
Mirassol	19	5	7	7	24	27	22	1-2	2-2 1-1	0-1 1-1 0-3 1-1		1-0		3-0 1-2												
Paulista	19	6	2	11	23	32	20	2-3	1-2		1-0		0-1 3-1		0-2	2-2 2-1		1-0								
Bragantino	19	5	5	9	37	42	20		2-3 1-0	1-1 2-0 2-3 4-0		2-3	3-4			1-1	4-3									
Rio Claro	19	5	4	10	24	34	19	1-1		1-3 3-1 0-1	1-0 0-0 1-0		1-3			3-0										
Monte Azul	19	3	6	10	23	41	15		1-1 0-4	0-1 5-3 2-2 1-2 2-3		3-2	5-2												
Sertãozinho	19	3	5	11	24	41	14	2-3 1-1 2-2		2-3	2-1 3-2 1-1 1-1		0-0													
Rio Branco	19	2	6	11	17	36	12	0-4 1-4		0-2 1-0	1-2 2-2	1-2 2-2		0-0												

16/01/2010 - 7/04/2010 • ‡ Qualified for the semi-finals • Semi-finals: São Paulo 2-3 0-3 **Santos**; Grêmio Prudente 1-2 2-1 **Santo André**
Final: 1st leg. Pacaembú, São Paulo, 25-04-2010, Att: 33 354, Ref: Oliveira. **Santo Andre 2-3 Santos**. Scorers - Bruno Cesar [36], Rodriguinho [83] for Santo André; André [57], Wesley 2 [61 69] for Santos
Final: 2nd leg. Pacaembú, São Paulo, 2-05-2010, Att: 36 260, Ref: Fagundes. **Santos 2-3 Santo André**. Scorers - Neymar 2 [7 32] for Santos; Nunes [1], Alê [20], Branquinho [44] for Santo Andre
Santos are the 2010 São Paulo state champions due to their better season record

BRAZIL STATE CHAMPIONSHIPS 2010 – RIO DE JANEIRO

TAÇA GUANABARA

Group A	Pl	W	D	L	F	A	Pts
Flamengo †	7	6	1	0	21	13	17
Fluminense †	7	5	1	1	17	5	16
Olaria	7	3	3	1	12	8	12
Boavista	7	3	1	3	9	8	10
Bangu	7	3	0	4	8	11	9
Volta Redonda	7	2	2	3	11	10	8
Americano	7	1	0	6	7	20	3
Duque de Caxias	7	0	2	5	6	16	2

Group B	Pl	W	D	L	F	A	Pts
Vasco da Gama †	7	6	1	0	19	3	19
Botafogo †	7	6	0	1	18	13	18
Madureira	7	4	1	2	12	12	13
América	7	3	1	3	13	12	10
Friburgense	7	2	1	4	6	10	7
Resende	7	1	3	3	12	15	6
Macaé	7	1	1	5	10	17	4
Tigres do Brasil	7	1	0	6	7	16	3

16/01/2010 - 7/02/2010 • † Qualified for the semis

TAÇA RIO

Group A	Pl	W	D	L	F	A	Pts
Flamengo †	8	7	1	0	21	5	22
Fluminense †	8	6	1	1	19	8	19
Bangu	8	4	2	2	14	11	14
Boavista	8	4	0	4	14	13	12
Americano	8	3	2	3	11	12	11
Duque de Caxias	8	3	1	4	10	11	10
Olaria	8	3	0	5	6	11	9
Volta Redonda	8	2	1	5	8	11	7

Group B	Pl	W	D	L	F	A	Pts
Botafogo †	8	5	2	1	17	9	17
Vasco da Gama †	8	5	0	3	14	9	15
América	8	4	2	2	12	8	14
Macaé	8	3	1	4	13	15	10
Madureira	8	2	1	5	6	12	7
Tigres do Brasil	8	2	0	6	9	15	6
Resende	8	2	0	6	5	19	6
Friburgense	8	1	2	5	7	16	5

27/02/2010 - 4/04/2010 • † Qualified for the semis

GUANABARA PLAY-OFFS

Semi-finals

Botafogo	2
Flamengo	1
Fluminense	0 5p
Vasco da Gama	0 6p

Final

Botafogo	2
Vasco da Gama	0

Maracana, Rio, 21-02-2010, Att: 77 757, Ref: Lima.
Scorers - Fabio Ferreira 70, Sebastian Abreu 84p

TAÇA RIO PLAY-OFFS

Semi-finals

Botafogo	3
Fluminense	2
Vasco da Gama	1
Flamengo	2

Final

Botafogo	2
Flamengo	1

Maracana, Rio, 18-04-2010, Att: 57 093, Ref: Fonseca.
Scorers - German Herrera 23p, Sebastian Abreu 71p for Botafogo; Vágner Love 44 for Flamengo

BRAZIL STATE CHAMPIONSHIPS 2010 – RIO DE JANEIRO

CAMPEONATO CARIOCA 2010 RESULTS	Botafogo	Flamengo	Fluminense	Vasco	América	Bangu	Boavista	Olaria	Madureira	V. Redonda	Macaé	Americano	Duque de Caxias	Friburgense	Resende	Tigres
Botafogo		2-2		0-6	2-1	2-2		2-0						2-1	2-0	5-2
Flamengo				1-0	2-1				3-3	2-0		3-2	3-2			3-1
Fluminense	2-1	3-5				3-0	3-0							5-1	2-1	
Vasco da Gama			3-0				1-0		2-2	2-1	4-0	2-3				1-0
América			1-1	1-2			3-2				2-0	3-1			2-2	3-0
Bangu		1-2		0-2	1-1		0-3		2-1			2-0	3-0			2-1
Boavista	1-4	1-2						3-0			2-1	2-0	0-0	0-1	4-1	1-0
Olaria			0-0	1-0	0-1	2-0			1-2		2-2					1-0
Madureira	1-4		1-3		2-1			1-2		0-2			0-0	2-1		
Volta Redonda	0-1	1-3				1-2	3-0				0-2			1-1	4-0	
Macaé	2-3	1-4			2-3	2-1		3-1	1-2			2-2	0-1			
Americano	1-3		0-3					1-5	1-3		2-1			3-2	1-1	2-0
Duque de Caxias ‡			0-4	3-4	1-0			1-2	0-1	1-1						2-1
Friburgense ‡		0-3		0-3	1-2	2-3		1-2				0-1			0-0	3-1
Resende ‡		0-4		0-1	0-3			2-0	1-2		3-3	1-0				4-2
Tigres do Brasil	1-2		0-3		1-3			2-1	3-0	2-1						

Clubs listed according to overall position • Taça Guanabara results in shaded boxes • Taça Rio results in unshaded boxes • ‡ Relegation play-offs
Top scorers: 15 - Vágner Love, Flamengo • 11 - Dodô, Vasco; Adriano, Flamengo & Sebastian Abreu URU, Botafogo
Relegation play-offs: Duque 2-1 2-2 Resende; Resende 0-0 0-0 Friburgense; Friburgense 1-1 0-2 Duque. Friburgense relegated with fewest points

COPA DO BRASIL 2010

First Round

Santos	1	10
Naviraiense *	0	0
São Mateus *	1	1
Remo	2	4
Fortaleza	2	3
Tigres do Brasil *	2	2
Araguaína *	0	1
Guarani	1	2
Sport Recife	4	
Brasilia *	2	
Ceramica *	1	1
Paraná	1	6
Chapecoense *	3	1
Brasiliense	0	2
Juventus *	0	
Atlético Mineiro	7	
Fluminense	1	2
Confiança *	1	0
Londrina	0	0
Uberaba *	1	2
Ponte Preta	0	4
JV Lideral *	0	0
Atlético Roriama *	0	
Portuguesa	7	
Avai	3	
Ypiranga *	0	
Luverdense *	0	0
Coritiba	1	1
Votoraty *	4	1
Treze	0	2
Araguaia *	1	
Grêmio	3	
Atlético Goiâniense	3	
ASSU *	0	
Vitória ES *	0	
Bahia	2	
Botafogo	0	4
São Raimundo * ‡	1	3
América AM *	0	0
Santa Cruz	1	3
Atlético Paranaense	2	4
Vilhena *	2	0
São Domingos *	1	1
Sampaio Correa	1	2
Paysandu	0	3
Potyguar Seridoense *	0	1
Flamengo Teresina *	0	0
Palmeiras	1	4
Vasco da Gama	2	0
Sousa *	1	0
Nacional	0	2
ASA *	0	2
Ceará	5	
Picos *	0	
Juventude	0	0
Corinthians Paranaense *	1	1
Goiás	3	0
Ituiutaba *	2	0
América Natal	1	0
São José *	1	1
Náutico	1	3
Ivinhema *	1	1
Corinthians Alagoano *	3	0
Vitoria	1	4

Second Round

Santos	4	
Remo *	0	
Fortaleza *	2 0 3p	
Guarani	0 2 4p	
Sport Recife	1	1
Paraná *	1	0
Chapecoense *	1	0
Atlético Mineiro	0	6
Fluminense	2	
Uberaba *	0	
Ponte Preta *	1	1
Portuguesa	1	2
Avai *	1	1
Coritiba	1	0
Votoraty *	0	0
Grêmio	1	3
Atlético Goiâniense *	2	0
Bahia	0	1
Botafogo	1	2
Santa Cruz *	0	3
Atlético Paranaense	1	2
Sampaio Correa *	1	0
Paysandu *	1	0
Palmeiras	2	1
Vasco da Gama	1	3
ASA *	1	1
Ceará	1	1
Corinthians Paranaense *	2	1
Goiás	1	7
São José *	0	0
Náutico *	0	0
Vitoria	1	5

Third Round

Santos	8	2
Guarani *	1	3
Sport Recife *	0	0
Atlético Mineiro	1	2
Fluminense	1	3
Portuguesa *	0	2
Avai	1	3
Grêmio *	3	2
Atlético Goiâniense	2	2
Santa Cruz *	1	0
Atlético Paranaense	0	1
Palmeiras *	1	1
Vasco da Gama	1	2
Corinthians Paranaense *	0	1
Goiás	0	2
Vitoria *	4	2

‡ São Raimundo fielded ineligible player

If the away team wins the first leg by two goals in the first or second round no second leg is played

COPA DO BRASIL 2010

Quarter-finals	Semi-finals	Final

Santos	2	3
Atlético Mineiro *	3	1

Santos	3	3
Grêmio *	4	1

Fluminense *	2	0
Grêmio	3	2

Santos * †	2	1
Vitória	0	2

Atlético Goiâniense	1 0 2p
Palmeiras *	1 0 1p

Atlético Goiâniense *	1	0
Vitoria	0	4

Vasco da Gama	0	3
Vitoria *	2	1

COPA DO BRASIL FINAL

Vila Belmiro, Santos, 28-07-2010, 21:50, Att: 14 060, Ref: Leonardo Gaciba

Santos	2	Neymar [14], Marquinhos [83]
Vitória	0	

Santos - Rafael - Para●, Durval●, Alex Sandro, Bruno Aguiar● - Ganso (Ze Eduardo● 80), Wesley, Arouca - Andre (Marcel 65), Neymar, Robinho (Marquinhos 80). Tr: Dorival Junior
Vitória - Lee - Anderson Martins●, Egidio, Wallace, Ramon● (Renato 63) - Neto, Rafael Granja (Bida 23), Vanderson●, Fernando (Gabriel 75) - Elkeson, Schwenck●. Tr: Ricardo Silva

Barradão, Salvador, 4-08-2010, 21:50, Att: 28 978, Ref: Carlos Simon

Vitória	2	Wallace [57], Junior [77]
Santos	1	Edu Dracena [44]

Vitória - Viafara - Anderson Martins●, Egidio, Wallace●, Nino Paraiba (Gabriel 18) - Neto, Elkeson●, Bida● (Adailton 83), Ramon (Renato 67) - Junior, Schwenck. Tr: Ricardo Silva
Santos - Rafael● - Para●, Durval, Edu Dracena●, Alex Sandro - Ganso, Wesley, Arouca - Andre (Marquinhos 62), Neymar (Marcel 78), Robinho● (Rodriguinho 87). Tr: Dorival Junior

† Qualified for the Copa Libertadores
* Home team in the first leg

MEDALS TABLE

		Overall			Nat			Cup		TRGP			Rio-SP			SL		Sth Am			City
		G	S	B	G	S	B	G	S	G	S	B	G	S	B	G	S	G	S	B	
1	Santos	12	7	4	2	4		6	2	1			5	1		18	9	3	1	4	Santos
2	São Paulo FC	11	10	8	6	5	3		1				1	5	1	21	17	5	4	5	São Paulo
3	Palmeiras	11	9	3	4	2		3	1	2	1		5	1	3	22	23	2	5	3	São Paulo
4	Cruzeiro	10	11	5	1	4	1	5	1		1					36		4	5	4	Belo Horizonte
5	Flamengo	10	7	4	6	1		2	4				1	3	2	31	25	2	3	3	Rio de Janeiro
6	Grêmio	8	6	6	2	2	1	4	2							36		2	2	5	Porto Alegre
7	Internacional	7	10	3	3	5		1	2			2				39		3	1	3	Porto Alegre
8	Corinthians	7	5	6	4	3	1	3	2			2	5	3	2	26	18			3	São Paulo
9	Vasco da Gama	6	4	2	4	2			2		1		3	5	2	22	21	2	1		Rio de Janeiro
10	Atlético Mineiro	3	4	5	1	3					1					40		2	1	4	Belo Horizonte
11	Botafogo	3	4	2	1	2		1	2				4	3	1	18	15	1	2		Rio de Janeiro
12	Fluminense	4	4		2			1	2	1			2	1	1	30	20		2		Rio de Janeiro
13	EC Bahia	2	2		1			1	2							45					Salvador
14	Sport Recife	2	1		1			1	1							38					Recife
15	Guarani	1	2	1	1	2														1	Campinas
	Atlético Paranaense	1	2	1	1	1										22			1	1	Curitiba
17	Coritiba	1			1											34					Curitiba
	Criciúma	1						1								8					Criciúma
	Juventude	1						1								1					Caxias do Sul
	Paulista	1						1													Jundiai
	Santo André	1						1												1	Santo Andre
22	São Caetano		3			2										1	1		1		São Caetano
23	Goiãs AC		2	1					1							22			1	1	Goiânia
24	Fortaleza		2						2							39					Fortaleza
	Vitória		2			1			1							26					Salvador
26	Portuguesa		1			1							2	3		3	4				São Paulo
	Bangu		1			1								1		2	6				Rio de Janeiro
	Bragantino		1			1										1					Bragança Paul.
	Brasiliense		1						1							6					Taguatinga
	Ceará SC		1						1							39					Fortaleza
	CSA		1													37				1	Maceió
	Figueirense		1						1							15					Florianópolis
	Nautico		1						1							21					Recife
34	Sampaio Corrêa			1												28				1	São Luis
	São Raimundo			1												7				1	Manaus
		103	105	53	41	41	8	32	32	4	4	4						26	28	41	

Nat = the national championship played since 1971 • Cup = the Copa do Brasil played between 1959-68 and since 1989 • TRGP = Torneio Roberto Gomes Pedrosa played from 1967-70 • Rio-SP = Torneio Rio-São Paulo played in 1933, 1950-66, 1993 & 1997-2002 • SL = the state leagues played throughout the country • The totals for the Torneio Rio-São Paulo and the state leagues are not included in the overall totals as they are not national competitions

CLUB BY CLUB GUIDE TO 2010 IN BRAZIL

The following guide covers the state championships played in Brazil in the first half of the year along with Serie A in the second half of the year

SA = Serie A • CB = Copa do Brasil • CL = Copa Libertadores • CS = Copa Sudamericana • g1 = group 1 etc • r1 = first round etc • qf = quarter-final • sf = semi-final • f = final

State championship abbreviations

CG = Campeonato Goiano (Atlético GO & Goiás) • CM = Campeonato Mineiro (Atlético MG & Cruzeiro) • CP = Campeonato Paranaense (Atlético PR) • CC = Campeonato Catarinense (Avai) • TG = Taça Guanabara & Taça Rio (Botafogo, Flamengo, Fluminense & Vasco) • CC1 = Campeonato Cearense round 1 etc (Ceara) • CP = Campeonato Paulista (Corinthians, Grêmio Prudente, Palmeiras, Santos & São Paulo. Guarani played the 2010 season at the second) • CG = Campeonato Gaúcho (Grêmio & Internacional) • TB = Campeonato Baiano (Vitória)

ATLETICO GOIANIENSE 2010

Mon	Day	Opponent	Res	Score	Comp	Scorers	Att
Jan	17	Anapolina	D	0-0	CG		7 607
	20	Itumbiara	D	2-2	CG	Juninho 63, Brasao 90	3 531
	24	Goiás	W	2-1	CG	Juninho 51, Washington 58	4 453
	27	Canedense	W	4-1	CG	Pituca 2 28 56, Marcao 2 34 68	2 094
	31	CRAC	L	2-3	CG	Elias 67, Robston 76	5 881
Feb	3	Morrinhos	W	5-0	CG	Washington 40, Chiquinho 59, Elias 63p, Rodrigo Tiui 2 89 90	4 043
	6	Vila Nova	W	3-1	CG	Weslley 14, Elias 57, Marcio 77	4 088
	10	ASSU	W	3-0	CBr1	Robston 8, Rodrigo Tiui 46, Erandir 54	960
	13	Trindade	D	2-2	CG	Elias 86, Rodrigo Tiui 94+	3 680
	17	Sta Helena	L	1-2	CG	Rodrigo Tiui 2	2 899
	21	Sta Helena	W	4-2	CG	Elias 31, Juninho 2 55 72, Marcao 92+	3 872
	28	Goiás	L	1-2	CG	Elias 58	2 581
Mar	3	Canedense	W	8-1	CG	Marcao 2 8 26, Juninho 14, Marcio 32, Robston 3 40 84 87, Anailson 81	3 550
	6	Vila Nova	W	3-2	CG	Marcio 30, Washington 64, Anailson 76	3 499
	14	Morrinhos	D	2-2	CG	Marcao 20, Elias 43	2 753
	18	Bahia	W	2-0	CBr2	Rodrigo Tiui 6, Marcao 85	2 294
	21	CRAC	W	3-1	CG	Elias 22, Juninho 33, Robston 78	3 834
	24	Trindade	L	2-4	CG	Jairo 71, Robston 90	1 703
	27	Itumbiara	W	2-1	CG	Chiquinho 19, Elias 42	24 840
Apr	1	Bahia	L	0-1	CBr2		21 718
	4	Anapolina	L	0-3	CG		3 590
	10	Goiás	D	0-0	CGsf		23 373
	15	Santa Cruz	W	2-1	CBr3	Robston 2 43 70	39 279
	18	Goiás	W	4-2	CGsf	Rodrigo Tiui 45, Elias 63p, Marcio Gabriel 2 55 74	13 566
	22	Santa Cruz	W	2-0	CBr3	Robston 73, Marcao 87	4 805
	25	Sta Helena	W	4-0	CGf	Juninho 1, Elias 2 54 69p, Marcao 88	11 512
	29	Palmeiras	L	0-1	CBqf		23 892
May	2	Sta Helena	W	3-1	CGf	Rodrigo Tiui 11, Washington 68p, Agenor 75	5 170
	5	Palmeiras	W	1-0	CBqf	Marcao 71. W 2-1p	21 889
	8	Grêmio	D	0-0	SA		5 647
	13	Vitória	W	1-0	CBsf	Rodrigo Tiui 55	6 367
	15	Fluminense	L	0-1	SA		9 839
	20	Vitória	L	0-4	CBsf		32 891
	22	Santos	L	1-2	SA	Boka 87	4 669
	27	Atlético PR	L	1-2	SA	Elias 72p	10 631
	30	Goiás	L	1-3	SA	Elias 11p	5 213
Jun	2	Grêmio Pr.	L	0-1	SA		1 759
	6	Cruzeiro	W	2-1	SA	Rodrigo Tiui 29, Pedro Paulo 84	3 419
	15	Atlético MG	L	2-3	SA	Marcao 31, Rodrigo Tiui 60	3 179
	18	Flamengo	L	0-1	SA		18 544
Jul	21	Corinthians	W	3-1	SA	Robston 22p, Pedro Paulo 67, Marcao 79	17 445
	24	Vasco	L	0-2	SA		13 157
	31	Guarani	D	1-1	SA	Rodrigo Tiui 4	2 340
Aug	8	Ceará	D	0-0	SA		16 973
	14	Botafogo	L	0-2	SA		9 433
	22	Inter	D	1-1	SA	Ferraz 42	15 571
	26	Palmeiras	W	3-0	SA	Elias 3 26p 36 83	12 559
	29	Avai	D	2-2	SA	Elias 2 29 43	3 211
	2	São Paulo	L	1-2	SA	Juninho 50	9 364
	5	Vitoria	W	4-1	SA	Elias 2 45 80p, Juninho 2 54 85p	2 323
	8	Grêmio	L	0-2	SA		22 758
Sep	11	Fluminense	W	2-1	SA	William 29, Juninho 90	10 475
	15	Santos	L	2-4	SA	Josiel 13, William 47	3 873
	18	Atlético PR	L	1-2	SA	Diogo Galvao 59	2 500
	22	Goiás	W	3-1	SA	Elias 6, Gilson 49, Juninho 85	11 242
	25	Grêmio Pr.	W	3-0	SA	Agenor 25, Feltri 59, Marcao 61	2 641
	29	Cruzeiro	L	0-3	SA		10 869
	2	Atlético MG	L	2-3	SA	Robston 11, Juninho 40	3 183
	7	Flamengo	L	0-2	SA		7 772
Oct	10	Corinthians	W	4-3	SA	Juninho 19, Gilson 39, Marcao 2 45 66	23 459
	17	Vasco	W	2-0	SA	Anailson 80, Marcio 87p	14 175
	23	Guarani	W	1-0	SA	Marcao 62	2 986
	28	Ceará	D	1-1	SA	Marcao 26	3 840
	3	Botafogo	L	2-3	SA	Juninho 83, Robston 90	17 118
	6	Inter	D	2-2	SA	Juninho 12, Elias 22p	4 459
Nov	14	Palmeiras	W	3-0	SA	Gilson 31, Robston 2 55 64	8 472
	21	Avai	L	0-3	SA		17 252
	28	São Paulo	L	1-2	SA	Elias 65	27 938
Dc	5	Vitoria	D	0-0	SA		35 000

ATLETICO MINEIRO 2010

Mon	Day	Opponent	Res	Score	Comp	Scorers	Att
Jan	24	América	D	1-1	CM	Fabiano 54	39 123
	31	Tupi	W	3-2	CM	Diego Tardelli 42, Coelho 63, Muriqui 72	18 968
Feb	7	Ipatinga	D	1-1	CM	Muriqui 87	28 749
	13	Uberaba	D	2-2	CM	Obina 23, Muriqui 37	5 578
	20	Cruzeiro	L	1-3	CM	Jairo Campos 30	41 591
	25	Juventus	W	7-0	CBr1	Diego Tardelli 7, Marques 50, Obina 5 16 40 63 80 90	6 030
	28	Uberlândia	W	5-2	CM	Obina 3 21 23 48, Muriqui 27, Carlos Alberto 78	9 885
	3	América TO	D	2-2	CM	Coelho 25, OG 46	5 000
	6	Democrata	W	1-0	CM	Junior 64	11 548
Mar	13	Caldense	W	4-0	CM	Renan Oliveira 40, Fabiano 2 49 62, Obina 51	11 544
	17	Chapecoense	L	0-1	CBr2		5 020
	21	Villa Nova	W	3-1	CM	Obina 2 8 25, Renan Oliveira 54	3 019
	28	Ituiutaba	W	6-0	CM	Fabiano 2 10 15, Renan Oliveira 51, Diego Tardelli 3 29p 76 85	12 012
	1	Chapecoense	W	6-0	CBr2	Fabiano 2 9 60, Renan Oliveira 68, Diego Tardelli 2 46p 77, Junior 54	35 396
	4	América	D	3-3	CMqf	Fabiano 3 30 39 44	15 423
	7	América	D	2-2	CMqf	Zé Luis 50, Carlos Alberto 67	8 461
Apr	10	Democrata	W	2-1	CMsf	Diego Tardelli 15, Renan Oliveira 25	4 787
	15	Sport	W	1-0	CBr3	Fabiano 43	17 253
	17	Democrata	D	0-0	CMsf		15 114
	22	Sport	W	2-0	CBr3	Muriqui 20, Diego Tardelli 39	26 661
	25	Ipatinga	W	3-2	CMf	Diego Tardelli 29p, Muriqui 2 51 83	11 000
	29	Santos	W	3-2	CBqf	Diego Tardelli 3 2 40 47	46 239
	2	Ipatinga	W	2-0	CMf	Diego Tardelli 70, Marques 87	60 704
	6	Santos	L	1-3	CBqf	Corrêa 45	14 245
	9	Vasco	W	2-1	SA	Ricardinho 10, Muriqui 21	12 790
	15	Grêmio Pr.	L	0-4	SA		2 500
	23	Atlético PR	W	3-1	SA	Muriqui 57, Diego Tardelli 59, Ricardinho 73	13 464
	26	Vitória	L	3-4	SA	Muriqui 34, Ricardinho 68, Diego Tardelli 81	6 692
	30	Fluminense	L	1-3	SA	Muriqui 2	15 613
Jun	3	Grêmio	L	1-2	SA	Ricardinho 44	14 605
	6	Ceará	L	0-1	SA		26 659
	15	Atlético GO	W	3-2	SA	Diego Tardelli 2 17 35p, Bueno 43	3 179
Jul	18	Corinthians	L	0-1	SA		22 163
	21	Inter	L	1-2	SA	Diego Souza 12	4 713
	24	Avai	D	0-0	SA		9 733
	1	Cruzeiro	L	0-1	SA		12 340
	8	Botafogo Pr.	D	0-0	CSr2		2 576
	7	Botafogo	L	0-3	SA		27 576
Aug	11	Grêmio Pr.	W	1-0	CSr2	Ricardinho 90	3 658
	14	Guarani	W	3-1	SA	Diego Tardelli 2 63 69, Obina 75	5 748
	22	Santos	L	0-2	SA		10 220
	26	Flamengo	D	0-0	SA		9 566
	29	Palmeiras	L	1-2	SA	Neto Berola 51	11 120
	1	Goiás	W	3-1	SA	Obina 2 39p 80p, Diego Souza 74	3 312
	5	São Paulo	L	2-3	SA	Obina 2 16p 35p	11 120
	12	Vasco	W	1-0	SA	Obina 84	12 380
Sep	15	Atlético PR	L	1-2	SA	Obina 32	14 386
	19	Vitória	L	2-3	SA	Daniel Carvalho 41, Neto Berola 65	13 144
	23	Fluminense	L	1-5	SA	Daniel Carvalho 19	6 197
	26	Grêmio	L	1-2	SA	Diego Tardelli 29	12 262
	30	Ceará	D	0-0	SA		12 628
	2	Atlético GO	W	3-2	SA	Diego Souza 22, Rever 76, Bueno 90	3 183
	7	Corinthians	W	2-1	SA	Werley 60, Ze Luis 77	16 667
	10	Inter	L	0-1	SA		13 328
	14	Santa Fe	W	2-0	CSr3	Obinna 2 29 63	20 000
Oct	17	Avai	W	2-0	SA	Rafael Cruz 50, Neto Berola 67	16 824
	24	Cruzeiro	W	4-3	SA	Obina 3 6 23 30, Rever 62	18 732
	27	Palmeiras	D	1-1	CSqf	Obina 75p	11 542
	30	Botafogo	L	0-2	SA		17 012
	3	Guarani	D	0-0	SA		5 922
	6	Santos	D	2-2	SA	Diego Tardelli 24, Obina 60	16 771
	10	Palmeiras	L	0-2	CSqf		35 985
Nov	13	Flamengo	W	4-1	SA	Obina 35, Renan Oliveira 2 44 69, Diego Tardelli 67	16 465
	21	Palmeiras	W	2-0	SA	Diego Souza 29, Neto Berola 77	4 662
	28	Goiás	W	3-1	SA	Diego Souza 15, Renan Oliveira 45, Diego Tardelli 64	17 234
Dc	5	São Paulo	L	0-4	SA		9 782

ATLETICO PARANAENSE 2010

Month	Date	Opponent	Res	Score	Comp	Scorers	Att
Jan	17	Toledo	D	1-1	CP	Raul 13	3 178
	20	Operário	L	1-2	CP	Netinho 44	10 605
	23	Serrano	W	8-0	CP	Alan Bahia 2 5 24, Marcio Azevedo 30, Bruno Mineiro 2 38 70, Netinho 56p, Marcelo 66, Bruno 82	8 033
	27	Cascavel	D	0-0	CP		2 510
	30	Corinthians	W	2-0	CP	Alan Bahia 2 3 90	10 517
Feb	3	Cianorte	W	4-1	CP	Rodolfo 12, Manoel 28, Bruno Mineiro 42, Marcelo 55	11 404
	7	Paraná	W	1-0	CP	Bruno Mineiro 22	6 123
	10	Vilhena	D	2-2	CBr1	Rodolfo 25, Chico 34	1 528
	18	En. Beltrão	W	3-0	CP	Tartá 2 51 62, Alan Bahia 57	9 689
	21	Nacional	D	1-1	CP	Netinho 3	685
	24	Vilhena	W	4-0	CBr1	Alan Bahia 14p, Netinho 2 38 54, Patrick 79	9 484
	28	Rio Branco	W	2-1	CP	Bruno Mineiro 2 57 67	1 470
Mar	7	Coritiba	D	1-1	CP	Manoel 36	21 353
	14	Iraty	L	0-1	CP		2 733
	18	S. Corrêa	D	1-1	CBr2	Paulo Baier 21	14 598
	21	Paranavai	W	4-0	CP	Bruno Mineiro 41, Rodolfo 46, Netinho 57, Alan Bahia 73p	9 934
	24	Corinthians	W	4-1	CP	Rodolfo 18, Bruno Mineiro 2 51 75, Paulo Baier 86	6 069
	27	Cascavel	W	5-0	CP	Pepe Toledo 1, Bruno Mineiro 2 6 63, Raul 36, Rodolfo 43	11 565
Apr	1	S. Corrêa	W	2-0	CBr2	Marcio Azevedo 46, Bruno Mineiro 90	13 222
	4	Paraná	W	1-0	CP	Pepe Toledo 51	15 011
	7	Operário	W	3-2	CP	Alan Bahia 2 48p 59p, Patrick 64	7 604
	9	Paranavai	W	1-0	CP	Pepe Toledo 18	11 279
	15	Palmeiras	L	0-1	CBr3		20 269
	18	Coritiba	L	0-2	CP		27 449
	22	Palmeiras	D	1-1	CBr3	Alan Bahia 82	20 367
	25	Iraty	D	0-0	CP		2 916
May	9	Corinthians	L	1-2	SA	Wagner Diniz 45	9 232
	23	Atlético MG	L	1-3	SA	Bruno Mineiro 85	13 464
	27	Atlético GO	W	2-1	SA	Paulo Baier 21, Wagner Diniz 33	10 631
	30	Inter	L	1-4	SA	Manoel 80	11 058
Jun	2	Botafogo	W	3-2	SA	Paulo Baier 2 27 47, Alex Mineiro 58	12 356
	5	Vitória	L	0-1	SA		9 109
	14	Cruzeiro	L	0-2	SA		13 952
	17	Vasco	L	1-3	SA	Bruno Mineiro 45	5 976
Jul	21	Santos	W	2-0	SA	Bruno Costa 2, Bruno Mineiro 47	20 001
	25	Goiás	W	2-0	SA	Manoel 27, Maikon Leite 80	4 020
	31	Fluminense	L	1-3	SA	Bruno Mineiro 87	30 763
Aug	8	São Paulo	D	1-1	SA	Maikon Leite 68	21 789
	14	Palmeiras	L	0-2	SA		10 074
	22	Flamengo	W	1-0	SA	Manoel 81	21 734
	25	Grêmio Pr.	W	1-0	SA	Branquinho 58	2 419
	29	Grêmio	D	1-1	SA	Maikon Leite 36	18 771
Sep	2	Ceará	W	2-1	SA	Branquinho 62, Chico 74	11 096
	5	Avaí	W	1-0	SA	Maikon Leite 90	8 099
	9	Corinthians	D	1-1	SA	Bruno Mineiro 69p	23 362
	12	Guarani	L	0-1	SA		4 235
	15	Atlético MG	W	2-1	SA	Bruno Mineiro 3, Ivan Gonzalez 87	14 386
	18	Atlético GO	W	2-1	SA	Branquinho 2 7 15	2 500
	23	Inter	W	1-0	SA	Paulo Baier 44	9 877
	26	Botafogo	D	1-1	SA	Joffre Guerron 90	7 409
	29	Vitória	W	1-0	SA	Rhodolfo 37	15 791
Oct	2	Cruzeiro	D	0-0	SA		17 254
	7	Vasco	D	0-0	SA		16 161
	9	Santos	L	0-2	SA		8 417
	16	Goiás	W	2-1	SA	Branquinho 3, Ivan Gonzalez 69	14 128
	24	Fluminense	D	2-2	SA	OG 61, Wagner Diniz 83	22 132
	28	São Paulo	L	1-2	SA	Joffre Guerron 26	16 480
Nov	4	Palmeiras	W	1-0	SA	Federico Nieto 84	19 749
	7	Flamengo	W	1-0	SA	Paulo Baier 40p	6 585
	14	Grêmio Pr.	W	2-1	SA	Paulo Baier 2 21p 90	16 991
	20	Grêmio	L	1-3	SA	Paulo Baier 17p	27 044
	28	Ceará	D	1-1	SA	Rafael Santos 36	38 997
Dc	5	Avaí	W	1-0	SA	Paulo Baier 7	9 879

AVAI 2010

Month	Date	Opponent	Res	Score	Comp	Scorers	Att
Jan	16	Brusque	W	3-0	CC	Gabriel 2 25 47, Medina 33	3 541
	20	Juventus	D	1-1	CC	Gabriel 75	289
	23	Chapecoense	W	1-0	CC	Eltinho 89p	5 225
	27	Criciúma	D	2-2	CC	Emerson 2 16 29	2 676
Feb	1	Imbituba	W	4-2	CC	Rafael 7, Jandson 15, Medina 80, Roberto 93+	6 265
	4	Figueirense	D	2-2	CC	Rudinei 5, Leonardo 92+p	12 028
	7	Joinville	W	5-1	CC	Davi 14p, Patrick 24, Leonardo 2 34 53, Roberto 83	5 119
	10	H Aichinger	L	1-3	CC	Medina 93+	1 085
	13	Metrop'tano	W	1-0	CC	Leonardo 80	3 320
	18	H Aichinger	W	2-0	CCsf	Emerson 20, Leonardo 66p	5 943
	20	Joinville	D	1-1	CCf	Patrick 59	13 404
	25	Ypiranga	W	3-0	CBr1	Savio 2 47 90, Robson 56	1 938
	28	Brusque	W	2-0	CC	Savio 30, Batista 77	1 320
Mar	4	Juventus	W	3-1	CC	Leonardo 6, Medina 10, Roberto 92+	4 585
	6	Chapecoense	W	3-1	CC	Leonardo 19, Emerson 49, Roberto 91+	6 105
	13	Criciúma	W	1-0	CC	Clayton 65	5 695
	18	Coritiba	D	1-1	CBr2	Vandinho 88	6 595
	21	Imbituba	L	0-1	CC		2 704
	24	Figueirense	D	1-1	CC	Rafael 46	9 010
	28	Joinville	L	2-3	CC	Patrick 70, Batista 95+	6 076
Apr	1	Coritiba	W	1-0	CBr2	Caio 68	7 530
	4	H Aichinger	W	5-0	CC	Leonardo 29, Vandinho 3 37 43 72, Caio 78	6 333
	7	Metrop'tano	W	2-1	CC	Vandinho 2 40 92+	1 042
	10	Brusque	W	4-3	CCsf	Savio 5, Rudinei 13, Vandinho 2 54 77	6 754
	15	Grêmio	L	1-3	CBr3	Robson 57	16 628
	18	Figueirense	D	1-1	CCf	Davi 61	13 706
	22	Grêmio	D	3-2	CBr3	Roberto 44, Carrerinha 2 72 92+	11 856
	25	Joinville	W	3-1	CCpo	Davi 23, Rudinei 47, Roberto 83p	11 392
May	2	Joinville	W	2-0	CCpo	Roberto 12, Davi 32	16 416
	9	Grêmio Pr.	W	6-1	SA	Emerson 3 9 43 90, Roberto 53, Caio 2 66 72	6 868
	16	Cruzeiro	D	2-2	SA	Para 25, Roberto 45	8 115
	23	Vasco	W	2-0	SA	Roberto 27, Robinho 90	9 594
	26	Grêmio	L	0-3	SA		9 220
	29	Vitória	D	0-0	SA		6 178
Jun	2	Ceará	L	0-2	SA		26 084
	4	Fluminense	L	0-3	SA		8 458
	14	São Paulo	W	2-1	SA	Roberto 60, Vandinho 65	7 717
	18	Palmeiras	W	4-2	SA	Caio 2 24 90, Robinho 40, Roberto 90	7 851
Jul	21	Flamengo	D	1-1	SA	Gabriel 74	14 051
	24	Atlético MG	D	0-0	SA		9 733
Aug	1	Goiás	W	4-1	SA	Emerson 9, Davi 2 10 42, Robinho 76	7 973
	7	Guarani	L	1-4	SA	Robinho 13p	3 776
	13	Santos	W	3-1	CSr2	Rudinei 17, Vandinho 2 64 76	6 673
	15	Corinthians	W	3-2	SA	Davi 11, OG 46, Rafael 52	14 721
	19	Santos	L	0-1	CSr2		
	21	Botafogo	L	0-1	SA		30 664
	25	Inter	L	0-1	SA		10 501
	29	Atlético GO	D	2-2	SA	Vandinho 2 22 70	3 211
Sep	2	Santos	L	1-2	SA	Valber 87	7 141
	5	Atlético PR	L	0-1	SA		8 099
	9	Grêmio Pr.	D	1-1	SA	Rudnei 37	1 475
	12	Cruzeiro	L	1-2	SA	Laercio 79	5 962
	16	Vasco	D	1-1	SA	Caio 72	6 299
	19	Grêmio	L	0-3	SA		9 146
	23	Vitória	L	0-3	SA		11 184
	26	Ceará	W	5-0	SA	Rudnei 5, Davi 2 10p 59, Jeferson 2 18 33	4 160
	29	Fluminense	L	0-1	SA		8 923
Oct	2	São Paulo	D	0-0	SA		8 040
	7	Palmeiras	L	1-4	SA	Roberto 35	6 306
	10	Flamengo	D	2-2	SA	Emerson 53, Roberto 59	11 690
	14	Emelec	L	1-2	CSr3	Marcelinho 70	20 000
	17	Atlético MG	L	0-2	SA		16 824
	14	Emelec	W	3-1	CSr3	Roberto 48, Eltinho 51, Emerson 54	12 000
	24	Goiás	L	0-1	SA		4 663
	27	Goiás	D	2-2	CSqf	Davi 52p, Marcelinho 70	3 742
	30	Guarani	W	1-0	SA	Eltinho 26	10 873
Nov	3	Corinthians	L	0-4	SA		23 275
	7	Botafogo	D	0-0	SA		14 538
	11	Goiás	L	0-1	CSqf		9 752
	14	Inter	W	3-2	SA	Patric 1, Batista 39, Robinho 61	12 690
	21	Atlético GO	W	3-0	SA	Eltinho 40, Jeferson 2 85 89	17 252
	28	Santos	W	3-2	SA	Caio 3 40 45 81	17 136
Dc	5	Atlético PR	L	0-1	SA		9 879

BOTAFOGO 2010

Mon	Date	Opponent	Res	Score	Comp	Scorers	Att
Jan	16	Macaé	W	3-2	TG	Herrera 2, Lucio Flavio 36, Marcelo Cordeiro 43	2 908
	21	Frib'guense	W	2-0	TG	Renato Caja 73, Herrera 89p	7 474
	24	Vasco	L	0-6	TG		25 052
	27	Tigres	W	2-1	TG	Herrera 14, Antonio Carlos 51	
	30	América	W	2-1	TG	Abreu 35, Caio 87	5 816
Feb	4	Madureira	W	4-1	TG	Fabio Ferreira 39, Caio 76, Fahel 83, Abreu 85	9 808
	7	Resende	W	5-2	TG	Abreu 3 18 30 55, Marcelo Cordeiro 65, Wellington Junior 78	6 803
	11	S.Raimundo	L	0-1	CBr1		12 768
	13	Flamengo	W	2-1	TGsf	Marcelo Cordeiro 34, Caio 83	37 154
	21	Vasco	W	2-0	TGf	Fabio Ferreira 70, Abreu 84p	77 757
	27	Americano	W	3-1	TR	Marcelo Cordeiro 32, Caio 2 66 85	3 496
Mar	4	Caixas	W	2-1	TR	Herrera 2 38p 52p	2 784
	7	Fluminense	L	1-2	TR	Herrera 36p	15 465
	12	Botafogo	W	4-3	CBr1	Danny Morais 15, Sandro Silva 64, Abreu 2 73 83	2 841
	14	Olaria	W	2-0	TR	Antonio Carlos 19, Gabriel 49	3 393
	21	Flamengo	D	2-2	TR	Herrera 2 16p 54	9 074
	24	V. Redonda	W	1-0	TR	Caio 87	5 707
	29	Boavista	W	4-1	TR	Abreu 3 13 77 88, Marcelo Cordeiro 54	
Apr	4	Bangu	D	2-2	TR	Diguinho 2, Alessandro 38	1 368
	10	Fluminense	W	3-2	TRsf	Abreu 4, Fahel 60, Caio 70	20 971
	18	Flamengo	W	2-1	TRf	Herrera 23p, Abreu 71p	57 093
	8	Santos	D	3-3	SA	Antonio Carlos 2 8 45, Herrera 89	25 634
	16	São Paulo	W	2-1	SA	Jancarlos 28, Caio 86	11 622
May	22	Goiás	W	3-0	SA	Lucio Flavio 41, Somalia 42, Herrera 74	13 837
	26	Cruzeiro	L	0-1	SA		8 501
	30	Vasco	D	1-1	SA	Herrera 34p	16 368
Jun	2	Atlético PR	L	2-3	SA	Herrera 11, Lucio Flavio 24	12 356
	6	Corinthians	D	2-2	SA	Caio 47, Lucio Flavio 72	14 267
	14	Flamengo	L	0-1	SA		19 313
Jul	18	Guarani	D	1-1	SA	Danny Morais 45	5 522
	22	Palmeiras	D	2-2	SA	Jobson 69, Jancarlos 78	12 107
	25	Fluminense	D	1-1	SA	Edno 75	19 970
	1	Vitória	W	3-1	SA	Edno 81, Jobson 2 83 90	8 217
	7	Atlético MG	W	3-0	SA	Maicosuel 33, Somalia 41, Herrera 69p	27 576
Aug	14	Atlético GO	W	2-0	SA	Somalia 52, Jobson 83	9 433
	21	Avai	W	1-0	SA	Fabio Ferreira 32	30 664
	25	Ceará	W	1-0	SA	Jobson 50	16 460
	28	Inter	L	0-1	SA		16 580
	1	Grêmio Pr.	W	1-0	SA	Maicosuel 75	3 211
	4	Grêmio	D	2-2	SA	Antonio Carlos 16, Herrera 20	16 921
	9	Santos	W	1-0	SA	Abreu 90	15 472
	12	São Paulo	W	2-0	SA	Abreu 68, Edno 80	24 050
Sep	15	Goiás	L	1-4	SA	Abreu 43	12 480
	18	Cruzeiro	D	2-2	SA	Alessandro 5, Abreu 76p	14 128
	22	Vasco	D	2-2	SA	Herrera 54, Abreu 90p	16 736
	26	Atlético PR	D	1-1	SA	Edno 23	7 409
	30	Corinthians	D	1-1	SA	Abreu 27	24 001
	2	Flamengo	D	1-1	SA	Lucio Flavio 36	13 182
	6	Guarani	D	1-1	SA	Abreu 45	3 601
Oct	10	Palmeiras	D	0-0	SA		9 950
	17	Fluminense	D	0-0	SA		13 663
	23	Vitória	W	1-0	SA	Cordeiro 44	10 041
	30	Atlético MG	W	2-0	SA	Edno 78, Abreu 90	17 012
	3	Atlético GO	W	3-2	SA	Caio 43, Jobson 48, Abreu 65p	17 118
	7	Avai	D	0-0	SA		14 538
Nov	10	Ceará	D	2-2	SA	Abreu 2 12 57	16 330
	21	Inter	L	1-2	SA	Antonio Carlos 74	19 604
	28	Grêmio Pr.	W	3-1	SA	Antonio Carlos 30, Edno 44, Cordeiro 89p	4 932
Dc	5	Grêmio	L	0-3	SA		45 420

CEARA 2010

Mon	Date	Opponent	Res	Score	Comp	Scorers	Att
	10	Horizonte	W	1-0	CC1	Misael	4 417
	13	Itapipoca	L	1-2	CC1	Vagner Silva	2 209
	17	Guarani/J	W	4-1	CC1	Wellington 2, Rone Dias, Fabricio	3 093
	20	Maranguape	L	0-1	CC1		1 166
	24	Ferroviário	L	0-1	CC1		
	27	Boa Viagem	L	2-3	CC1	Misael, Vagner Silva	903
	31	Fortaleza	D	0-0	CC1		21 014
	4	Limoeiro	L	2-3	CC1	Jorge Henrique, Thiago Xavier	1 725
	7	Crato	W	2-0	CC1	Romulo, Wellington	982
Feb	10	Picos	W	5-0	CBr1	Esley 20, Leozinho 2 38p 64, Fabricio 56, Misael 90	729
	13	Quixada	W	5-1	CC1	Romulo, Anderson, Valdinei 3	1 881
	17	Guarani/S	L	1-2	CC1	Jorge Henrique	3 718
	27	Itapipoca	W	1-0	CC2	Esley	8 010
	2	Horizonte	D	1-1	CC2	Thiago Xavier	7 248
	7	Guarani/J	L	1-1	CC2	Leonardo Ferreira	1 089
	10	Maranguape	D	0-0	CC2		5 367
	14	Ferroviário	W	2-0	CC2	Erick Flores, Valdinei	11 866
Mar	17	C'thians PR	L	1-2	CBr2	Misael 7	
	19	Boa Viagem	W	2-0	CC2	Jonathan, Luizinho	6 323
	21	Fortaleza	W	3-1	CC2		28 119
	24	Limoeiro	W	4-0	CC2	Fabricio, Valdinei, Geraldo, Erick Flores	6 815
	28	Crato	W	4-0	CC2	Geraldo 2, Luizinho, Valdinei	2 407
	1	C'thians PR	D	1-1	CBr2	Geraldo 52p	18 361
	4	Quixada	W	4-0	CC2	Erick Flores, Diogo, Thyago 2	4 533
	7	Guarani/S	D	1-1	CC2	Valdinei	2 921
Apr	11	Crato	W	4-0	CCsf	Erick Flores 2 8 77, Luizinho 66, Geraldo 81	15 918
	18	Guarani/S	W	1-0	CCf	Joao Carlos OG 16	28 901
	25	Fortaleza	L	0-1	CCpo		24 916
	2	Fortaleza	W	2-1	CCpo	Misael 47, Geraldo 84. L 1-3p	52 766
	9	Fluminense	W	1-0	SA	Geraldo 34p	18 340
May	16	Santos	D	1-1	SA	Washington 7	8 998
	23	Vitória	W	1-0	SA	Washington 90	19 697
	27	Goiás	D	0-0	SA		2 309
	30	Cruzeiro	W	1-0	SA	Lopes 38	19 694
	2	Avai	W	2-0	SA	Misael 74, Lopes 90	26 084
Jun	6	Atlético MG	W	1-0	SA	Washington 55	26 659
	9	Corinthians	D	0-0	SA		44 500
	18	Inter	L	1-2	SA	Michel 62	6 483
	22	Guarani	D	1-1	SA	Ernandes 53	4 595
	25	Palmeiras	D	0-0	SA		24 935
	31	São Paulo	L	1-2	SA	Erick Flores 84	11 793
	8	Atlético GO	D	0-0	SA		16 973
	14	Flamengo	L	0-1	SA		20 696
Aug	21	Grêmio	W	2-1	SA	OG 1, Geraldo 89	14 981
	25	Botafogo	L	0-1	SA		16 460
	28	Grêmio Pr.	D	2-2	SA	Washington 11, Careca 82	11 867
	2	Atlético PR	L	1-2	SA	Magno Alves 88	11 096
	4	Vasco	L	0-2	SA		19 528
	8	Fluminense	L	1-3	SA	Geraldo 90	5 698
	12	Santos	W	2-1	SA	Magno Alves 28, Geraldo 69	23 374
Sep	16	Vitória	D	0-0	SA		9 082
	19	Goiás	D	1-1	SA	Oziel 17	19 417
	22	Cruzeiro	D	0-0	SA		16 914
	26	Avaí	L	0-5	SA		4 160
	30	Atlético MG	D	0-0	SA		12 628
	2	Corinthians	D	2-2	SA	Marcelo Nicacio 16, Magno Alves 65	31 495
	7	Inter	W	1-0	SA	Heleno 50	15 897
Oct	10	Guarani	W	2-0	SA	Geraldo 15, Boaideiro 44	18 544
	17	Palmeiras	D	1-1	SA	Geraldo 82p	8 257
	24	São Paulo	W	2-0	SA	Magno Alves 2 21 35	44 591
	28	Atlético GO	D	1-1	SA	Michel 76	3 840
	3	Flamengo	D	2-2	SA	Magno Alves 2 28 82	44 171
	6	Grêmio	L	1-5	SA	Magno Alves 77	20 789
Nov	10	Botafogo	D	2-2	SA	Magno Alves 23, Geraldo 35	16 330
	20	Grêmio Pr.	D	1-1	SA	Geraldo 85p	842
	28	Atlético PR	D	1-1	SA	OG 43	38 997
Dc	5	Vasco	L	0-2	SA		2 989

CORINTHIANS 2010

		Opponent		Score	Comp	Scorers	Att
Jan	17	Monte Azul	D	1-1	CP	Iarley [15]	25 294
	20	Bragantino	W	2-1	CP	Elias [58], Jorge Henrique [83]	32 179
	24	Oeste	W	2-1	CP	Paulo Andre [27], Boquita [35]	10 196
	27	Mirassol	D	1-1	CP	Ronaldo [44]	15 584
	31	Palmeiras	W	1-0	CP	Jorge Henrique [6]	28 587
	3	Ponte Preta	L	1-2	CP		11 535
	6	Sertãozinho	W	4-0	CP	Chicão [8], Jorge Henrique [43], Marcelo Mattos [60], Edno [83]	16 780
Feb	13	Portuguesa	D	1-1	CP	Elias [60]	8 753
	17	Mogi Mirim	W	3-0	CP	Souza 2 [33] [51], Chicao [75]	4 740
	20	Rio Branco	D	0-0	CP		10 193
	25	Racing URU	W	2-1	CLg1	Elias 2 [11] [71]	40 260
	28	Santos	L	1-2	CP	Dentinho [68]	9 029
	4	Botafogo	D	1-1	CP	Dentinho [70]	9 298
	7	S. Caetano	W	1-0	CP	Dentinho [85]	4 031
	11	I. Medellin	D	1-1	CLg1	Dentinho [85]	53 000
	14	S'to André	W	2-1	CP	Dentinho [3], Roberto Carlos [10]	7 845
Mar	18	C. Porteño	W	1-0	CLg1	Ronaldo [41]	3 000
	21	Grêmio Pr	L	0-2	CP		16 749
	24	Paulista	L	0-1	CP		6 514
	28	São Paulo	W	4-3	CP	Elias [17], Danilo [34], Roberto Carlos [52], Alex Silva [92+]	23 372
Apr	1	C. Porteño	W	2-1	CLg1	Ronaldo [37], Chicao [63]	40 260
	4	Ituano	W	2-0	CP	Jucilei [81], Ronaldo [84]	18 717
	10	Rio Claro	W	5-1	CP	Ronaldo [32], Dentinho 2 [48] [75], Iarley [52], Roberto Carlos [67]	12 013
	15	Racing URU	W	2-0	CLg1	Dentinho [18], Elias [87]	12 000
	23	I. Medellin	W	1-0	CLg1	OG [23]	30 507
May	29	Flamengo	L	0-1	CLr2		72 442
	6	Flamengo	W	2-1	CLr2	OG [29], Ronaldo [40]	35 561
	9	Atlético PR	W	2-1	SA	Souza [58], Ronaldo [83p]	9 232
	16	Grêmio	W	2-1	SA	Ralf [5], Souza [64]	17 119
	23	Fluminense	W	1-0	SA	Chicao [12]	28 196
	26	Grêmio Pr	D	2-2	SA	William [32], OG [74]	9 235
Jun	30	Santos	W	4-2	SA	Jorge Henrique [3], Bruno Cesar [55], Ralf [67], Paulinho [85]	30 103
	3	Inter	W	2-0	SA	Roberto Carlos [38p], Iarley [52]	33 361
	6	Botafogo	D	2-2	SA	Bruno Cesar [30], Paulo Andre [90]	14 267
	14	Ceará	D	0-0	SA		44 500
Jul	18	Atlético MG	W	1-0	SA	Bruno Cesar [78]	22 163
	21	Atlético GO	L	1-3	SA	Iarley [33]	17 445
	25	Guarani	W	3-1	SA	Jorge Henrique 2, Bruno Cesar 2 [78] [85]	27 700
Aug	1	Palmeiras	D	1-1	SA	Jorge Henrique [21]	24 491
	8	Flamengo	W	1-0	SA	Elias [39]	33 032
	15	Avai	L	2-3	SA	Bruno Cesar 2 [40] [75]	14 721
	22	São Paulo	W	3-0	SA	Elias 2 [22] [45], Jucilei [71]	28 159
	26	Cruzeiro	L	0-1	SA		37 377
	29	Vitória	W	2-1	SA	Iareley [10], Paulinho [44]	36 142
Sep	4	Goiás	W	5-1	SA	Bruno Cesar [42], Iarley 2 [55] [73p], Jorge Henrique [60], Boquita [84]	31 638
	9	Atlético PR	D	1-1	SA	Ronaldo [34p]	23 362
	11	Grêmio	L	0-1	SA		29 533
	16	Fluminense	W	2-1	SA	Jucilei [44], Iarley [65]	20 728
	18	Grêmio Pr	W	3-0	SA	Iarley [22], Jorge Henrique [48], Elias [82]	23 815
	23	Santos	L	3-2	SA	Iarley [8], Elias [42], Paulo Andre [70]	10 898
	26	Inter	L	2-3	SA	Jorge Henrique [68], Bruno Cesar [89p]	33 787
Oct	30	Botafogo	D	1-1	SA	Bruno Cesar [3]	24 001
	2	Ceará	D	2-2	SA	Paulinho [70], De Federico [83]	31 495
	7	Atlético MG	L	1-2	SA	Paulinho [44]	16 667
	10	Atlético GO	L	3-4	SA	Leandro Castan [3], William Morais [71], Thiago Heleno [86]	23 459
	14	Vasco	L	0-2	SA		9 285
	17	Guarani	D	0-0	SA		17 469
	24	Palmeiras	W	1-0	SA	Bruno Cesar [23]	32 391
	27	Flamengo	D	1-1	SA	Ronaldo [30]	9 782
Nov	3	Avai	W	4-0	SA	Bruno Cesar [20], Elias [64], Ronaldo 2 [83] [88p]	23 275
	7	São Paulo	W	2-0	SA	Elias [40], Dentinho [84]	42 667
	13	Cruzeiro	W	1-0	SA	Ronaldo [89p]	35 935
	21	Vitória	D	1-1	SA	Danilo [20]	37 468
	28	Vasco	W	2-0	SA	Bruno Cesar [40], Danilo [58]	33 487
Dc	5	Goiás	D	1-1	SA	Dentinho [30]	28 917

CRUZEIRO 2010

		Opponent		Score	Comp	Scorers	Att
Jan	20	Uberlândia	W	6-0	CM	Thiago Ribeiro [33], Kleber 3 [44] [63] [83], Claudio Caçapa [68], Diego Renan [85]	13 267
	27	Real Potosi	D	1-1	CLpr	Wellington Paulista [7]	7 064
	30	Ipatinga	L	0-3	CM		6 990
	3	Real Potosi	W	7-0	CLpr	W. Paulista [29], Thiago Ribeiro [30], Kleber [39], Jonathan [45], Eliandro [87], Bernardo [88], Guerrón [91+]	36 574
Feb	6	Villa Nova	W	4-2	CM	Wellington Paulista [6], Bernardo [28], Thiago Ribeiro [64], Jonathan [76]	8 960
	10	Velez	L	0-2	CLg7		30 000
	13	Caldense	W	2-0	CM	Wellington Paulista [4], Gilberto [54p]	5 638
	20	Atlético MG	W	3-1	CM	Gil [23], Leonardo Silva [82], Roger [82]	41 591
	24	Colo Colo	W	4-1	CLg7	Thiago Ribeiro [6], Kleber 2 [62p] [71p], Pedro Ken [69]	30 000
	27	Ituiutaba	W	1-0	CM	Fabinho [89]	1 800
Mar	3	Uberaba	W	5-0	CM	Eliandro [22], Bernardo [67], Thiago Ribeiro 2 [69] [76], Anderson Lessa [78]	
	7	Tupi	L	2-3	CM	Anderson Lessa [40], Pedro Ken [90]	7 844
	12	Dep. Italia	D	2-2	CLg7	Kleber 2 [27] [50]	20 000
	14	América	W	3-2	CM	Wellington Paulista [45], Kieza [69], Fabiano [86]	12 111
	20	América TO	W	2-1	CM	Roger [59], Kleber [81]	7 671
	25	Dep. Italia	W	2-0	CLg7	Fabinho [6], Pedro Ken [69]	30 000
	28	Democrata	L	1-3	CM	Kieza [5]	5 500
	31	Colo Colo	W	3-0	CLg7	Thiago Ribeiro [33], Kleber 2 [48] [54]	30 000
	3	Uberaba	D	2-2	CMqf	Kleber [28], Leonardo Silva [74]	11 618
Apr	7	Uberaba	W	3-0	CMqf	Leonardo Silva [6], Gilberto [62], Thiago Ribeiro [45]	6 357
	16	Colo Colo	D	1-1	CLg7	Thiago Ribeiro [57]	10 000
	11	Ipatinga	D	0-0	CMsf		11 000
	18	Ipatinga	L	1-3	CMsf	Wellington Paulista [89p]	17 396
	29	Nacional	W	3-1	CLr2	Thiago Ribeiro 3 [7] [22] [42]	32 254
	6	Nacional	W	3-0	CLr2	Thiago Ribeiro [31], Diego Renan [49], Gilberto [81]	22 000
May	9	Inter	W	2-1	SA	Kleber 2 [5p] [36]	14 177
	13	São Paulo	L	0-2	CLqf		48 602
	16	Avaí	D	2-2	SA	Wellington Paulista 2 [52] [62p]	
	20	São Paulo	L	0-2	CLqf		52 196
	23	Guarani	D	2-2	SA	Gil [51], Joffre Guerron [75]	8 589
	26	Botafogo	W	1-0	SA	Thiago Ribeiro [18]	8 501
	30	Ceará	L	0-1	SA		19 694
Jun	2	Santos	D	0-0	SA		15 708
	8	Atlético GO	L	1-2	SA	Wellington Paulista [42]	3 419
	14	Atlético PR	W	2-0	SA	Wellington Paulista [45], Robert [86]	13 952
	18	Goiás	W	1-0	SA	Gilberto [10]	3 579
Jul	22	Fluminense	L	0-1	SA		34 008
	25	Grêmio	D	2-2	SA	Henrique 2 [46] [86]	9 672
	1	Atlético MG	W	1-0	SA	Wellington Paulista [32]	12 340
	8	Grêmio Pr	D	0-0	SA		10 109
Aug	15	São Paulo	D	2-2	SA	Wellington Paulista [66], Thiago Ribeiro [82]	12 338
	22	Vitória	L	0-1	SA		10 195
	26	Corinthians	W	1-0	SA	Montillo [2]	37 377
	28	Vasco	D	1-1	SA	OG [45]	13 691
	2	Flamengo	W	1-0	SA	Robert [10]	29 414
	5	Palmeiras	W	3-2	SA	Roger [55], Montillo [59], Farias [80]	21 560
	8	Inter	W	1-0	SA	Everton [14]	13 677
	12	Avaí	W	2-1	SA	Roger [24p], Thiago Ribeiro [70]	5 962
Sep	15	Guarani	W	4-2	SA	Romulo [24], Wallyson [38], Fabinho [75], Farias [87]	14 428
	18	Botafogo	D	2-2	SA	Montillo 2 [57p] [72]	14 128
	22	Ceará	W	2-0	SA	Montillo [83p], Farias [90]	16 914
	25	Santos	L	1-4	SA	Thiago Robeiro [80]	9 542
	29	Atlético GO	W	3-0	SA	Cacapa [30], Montillo [44], Wallyson [44]	10 869
Oct	2	Atlético PR	D	0-0	SA		17 254
	7	Goiás	W	1-0	SA	OG [56]	6 170
	10	Fluminense	W	1-0	SA	Wellington Paulista [14]	24 338
	17	Grêmio	L	1-2	SA	Montillo [28]	41 435
	24	Atlético MG	L	3-4	SA	Gilberto [35], Thiago Ribeiro 2 [76] [76]	18 732
	30	Grêmio Pr	W	2-0	SA	Leo [20], Robert [41]	1 872
	3	São Paulo	L	0-2	SA		25 694
Nov	7	Vitória	W	1-0	SA	Thiago Ribeiro [35]	34 540
	13	Corinthians	L	0-1	SA		35 935
	21	Vasco	W	3-1	SA	Roger [14], Henrique [15], Edcarlos [15]	16 228
	28	Flamengo	W	2-1	SA	Roger [16], Thiago Ribeiro [68]	14 575
Dc	5	Palmeiras	W	2-1	SA	Henrique [63], Wallyson [89]	16 191

FLAMENGO 2010

Month	Date	Opponent	Res	Score	Comp	Scorers	Att
Jan	17	D. Caxias	W	3-2	TG	Kléberson 50, Fierro 52, Fernando 84	16 067
	20	V. Redonda	W	3-1	TG	Bruno Mezenga 2 36 42, Petkovic 72	8 580
	23	Bangu	W	2-1	TG	Vágner Love 2 18 45	17 576
	27	Americano	W	3-2	TG	Adriano 40, Fernando 45, Vagner Love 79	12 308
	31	Fluminense	W	5-3	TG	Adriano 3 42 81p 90, Vagner Love 51, Kleberson 53	51 233
Feb	3	Olaria	D	3-3	TG	Adriano 6, Vagner Love 2 56 82	6 554
	7	Boavista	W	2-1	TG	Bruno Mezenga 41, Kleberson 60	2 506
	17	Botafogo	L	1-2	TGsf	Vinicius Pacheco 24	37 154
	25	U. Católica	W	2-0	CLg8	Leo Moura 11, Adriano 59	
	27	Macaé	W	4-1	TR	Vagner Love 2 28p 66, Vinicius Pacheco 2 58 71	1 489
Mar	3	Mudureira	W	2-0	TR	Fernando 14, Vagner Love 89	4 326
	6	Resende	W	4-0	TR	Bruno Mezenga 37, Leo Moura 62, V'cius Pacheco 72, Vagner Love 78	1 217
	11	Caracas	W	3-1	CLg8	Vagner Love 2 36p 75, Rodrigo Alvim 92+	20 000
	14	Vasco	W	1-0	TR	Adriano 51p	34 707
	18	U. de Chile	L	1-2	CLg8	Rodrigo Alvim 51	47 017
	21	Botafogo	D	2-2	TR	Adriano 2 20 93+	9 074
	24	Tigres	W	3-1	TR	Adriano 2 37 77, Vagner Love 52	3 118
	28	América	W	2-1	TR	Adriano 69p, Vagner Love 81	4 819
Apr	4	Frib'guense	W	3-0	TR	Ronaldo Angelim 18, Denis Marques 33, Camacho 75	1 642
	8	U. de Chile	D	2-2	CLg8	Michael 68, Leo Moura 83	16 784
	11	Vasco	W	2-1	TRsf	Vagner Love 2 10 71p	29 382
	15	U. Católica	L	0-2	CLg8		12 000
	18	Botafogo	L	1-2	TRf	Vagner Love 44	57 093
	22	Caracas	W	3-2	CLg8	Ronaldo Angelim 16, Michael 18, David 76	34 106
May	29	Corinthians	W	1-0	CLr2	Adriano 65p	72 442
	6	Corinthians	L	1-2	CLr2	Vagner Love 49	35 561
	9	São Paulo	D	1-1	SA	Denis Marques 51	11 195
	12	U. de Chile	L	2-3	CLqf	Adriano 39, Juan 90	72 442
	15	Vitória	D	1-1	SA	Vagner Love 3	14 862
	21	U. de Chile	W	2-1	CLqf	Vagner Love 45, Adriano 79	20 000
	23	Grêmio Pr.	W	3-1	SA	Vagner Love 2 45p 90p, Juan 87	3 978
	26	Fluminense	L	1-2	SA	Bruno 90	14 496
	29	Grêmio	D	1-1	SA	Petkovic 8	10 983
Jun	2	Palmeiras	W	1-0	SA	Vagner Love 87	8 618
	5	Goiás	L	1-2	SA	Toro 50	11 855
Jul	14	Botafogo	W	1-0	SA	Paulo Sergio 69	19 313
	18	Atlético GO	W	1-0	SA	Petkovic 36p	18 544
	21	Avai	D	1-1	SA	Diego Mauricio 10	14 051
	25	Inter	L	0-1	SA		25 002
Aug	1	Vasco	D	0-0	SA		50 447
	8	Corinthians	L	0-1	SA		33 032
	14	Ceará	W	1-0	SA	Petkovic 45p	20 696
	22	Atlético PR	L	0-1	SA		21 734
	26	Atlético MG	D	0-0	SA		9 566
	29	Guarani	L	1-2	SA	Jean 45	10 317
	2	Cruzeiro	L	0-1	SA		29 414
Sep	5	Santos	D	0-0	SA		34 897
	9	São Paulo	L	0-2	SA		14 389
	11	Vitória	D	2-2	SA	Kleberson 2 76 82	3 895
	16	Grêmio Pr.	W	2-1	SA	Diego Mauricio 86, Toro 90	3 815
	19	Fluminense	D	3-3	SA	Deivid 23, David 40, Renato 66	18 911
	23	Grêmio	D	2-2	SA	Kleberson 33, Petkovic 86	24 968
	25	Palmeiras	L	1-3	SA	Petkovic 80p	9 894
	28	Goiás	D	1-1	SA	Deivid 89	12 403
Oct	2	Botafogo	D	1-1	SA	Leo Moura 76	13 182
	7	Atlético GO	W	2-0	SA	Val Baiano 75, Diego Mauricio 86	7 772
	10	Avai	D	2-2	SA	Val Baiano 2 14 17	11 690
	16	Inter	W	3-0	SA	Deivid 2 14p 47, Renato 39	9 479
	24	Vasco	D	0-0	SA	Renato 81	21 519
	27	Corinthians	D	1-1	SA	Diogo 47	9 782
	3	Ceará	D	2-2	SA	Wellinton Souza 2, Ronaldo Angelim 68	44 171
Nov	7	Atlético PR	L	0-1	SA		6 585
	13	Atlético MG	L	1-4	SA	Marquinhos 74	16 465
	20	Guarani	W	2-1	SA	Renato 2, Diego Mauricio 33	34 932
	28	Cruzeiro	L	1-2	SA	Diego Mauricio 9	14 575
Dc	5	Santos	D	0-0	SA		9 086

FLUMINENSE 2010

Month	Date	Opponent	Res	Score	Comp	Scorers	Att
Jan	17	Americano	W	3-0	TG	Ewerton 23, Maicon 45, Julio Cesar 56	4 781
	20	Bangu	W	3-0	TG	Fred 2 19p 69p, Alan 94+	11 706
	24	V. Redonda	W	1-0	TG	Euzebio 5	11 862
	27	D. Caxias	W	4-0	TG	Maicon 4, Julio Cesar 23, Marquinho 2 70 85	3 543
	31	Flamengo	L	3-5	TG	Alan 13, Conca 40p, Cassio 45	51 233
Feb	3	Boavista	W	3-0	TG	Conca 14p, Thiaguinho 2 84 86	9 808
	7	Olaria	D	0-0	TG		6 803
	13	Vasco	D	0-0	TGsf	L 5-6p	36 481
	25	Confiança	D	1-1	CBr1	Gum 24	8 563
	28	Frib'guense	W	5-1	TR	Fred 19, Wellington Silva 20, Andre Lima 87, Ewerton 65, Conca 70	5 981
Mar	4	Tigres	W	3-0	TR	Fred 23, Ewerton 40, Conca 87	2 784
	7	Botafogo	W	2-1	TR	Fred 61, Marinho 83	15 465
	10	Confiança	W	2-0	CBr1	Fred 2 61 88	4 883
	13	América	D	1-1	TR	Marquinho 34	3 123
	14	Uberaba	W	2-0	CBr2	Alan 2 30 50	9 300
	21	Resende	W	2-1	TR	Andre Lima 2 35 44	2 715
	24	Mudureira	W	3-1	TR	Mariano 2, Andre Lima 16, Conca 41	1 488
	28	Vasco	L	0-3	TR		17 469
	4	Macaé	W	3-1	TR	Alan 2 29 75, Ewerton 39	5 485
Apr	10	Botafogo	L	2-3	TRsf	Fred 2 27 32	20 971
	14	Portuguesa	W	1-0	CBr3	Fred 61	2 728
	23	Portuguesa	W	3-2	CBr3	Fred 3 2 17p 21	11 242
	30	Grêmio	L	2-3	CBqf	Andre Lima 12, Gonzalez 77	20 489
	6	Grêmio	L	0-2	CBqf		23 356
May	9	Ceará	L	0-1	SA		18 340
	15	Atlético GO	W	1-0	SA	Marquinho 68	9 839
	23	Corinthians	L	0-1	SA		28 196
	26	Flamengo	W	2-1	SA	Rodriguinho 10, Conca 56	14 496
	30	Atlético MG	W	3-1	SA	Gum 60, Alan 63, Fred 90	15 613
Jun	2	Vitória	W	2-1	SA	Fred 20, Alan 87	25 430
	3	Avai	W	3-0	SA	Euzebio 43, Fred 48, Alan 56	8 458
	15	Grêmio Pr.	D	1-1	SA	Fred 16	24 335
	18	Santos	W	1-0	SA	Alan 77	9 193
Jul	22	Cruzeiro	W	1-0	SA	Euzebio 54	34 008
	25	Botafogo	D	1-1	SA	Emerson 61	19 970
	31	Atlético PR	W	3-1	SA	Washington 2 21 69, Emerson 54	30 763
	8	Grêmio	W	2-1	SA	Mariano 16, Emerson 18	12 001
Aug	15	Inter	W	3-0	SA	Mariano 20, Washington 22, Emerson 59	49 471
	22	Vasco	D	2-2	SA	Gum 6, Julio Cesar 59	66 757
	25	Goiás	W	3-0	SA	Washington 65, Emerson 74, Marquinho 90	10 147
	29	São Paulo	D	2-2	SA	Deco 9, Euzebio 59	25 518
Sep	2	Palmeiras	D	1-1	SA	Emerson 14	18 356
	5	Guarani	L	1-2	SA	Emerson 12	9 962
	8	Ceará	W	3-1	SA	Mariano 6, Washington 2 22 30	5 698
	11	Atlético GO	L	1-2	SA	Washington 22	10 475
	16	Corinthians	L	1-2	SA	Washington 70	20 728
	19	Flamengo	D	3-3	SA	Euzebio 9, Rodriguinho 2 64 73	18 911
	23	Atlético MG	W	5-1	SA	Euzebio 11, Carlinhos 2 36 76, Gum 64, Marquinho 90	6 197
Oct	26	Vitória	W	2-1	SA	Conca 55p, Rodriguinho 64	11 187
	29	Avai	W	1-0	SA	Conca 82	8 923
	2	Grêmio Pr.	D	1-1	SA	Rodriguinho 33	2 781
	6	Santos	L	0-3	SA		14 385
	10	Cruzeiro	L	0-1	SA		24 338
	17	Botafogo	D	0-0	SA		13 663
	24	Atlético PR	D	2-2	SA	Marquinho 69, Conca 87p	22 132
	28	Grêmio	W	2-0	SA	Conca 2 19 81	16 467
Nov	3	Inter	D	0-0	SA		21 069
	7	Vasco	W	1-0	SA	Tarta 4	16 263
	14	Goiás	D	1-1	SA	Conca 83p	30 897
	21	São Paulo	W	4-1	SA	Gum 34, Conca 2 74 87, Fred 77	14 410
	28	Palmeiras	W	2-1	SA	Carlinhos 19, Tarta 58	11 291
Dc	5	Guarani	W	1-0	SA	Emerson 62	40 905

GOIAS 2010

Mo	Date	Opponent	Res	Score	Comp	Scorers	Att
Jan	17	CRAC	L	0-1	CG		5 873
	20	Anapolina	L	2-5	CG	Rafael Toloi 15, Felipe 45	4 423
	24	Atlético GO	L	1-2	CG	Joao Paulo 19	4 453
	27	Trindade	D	1-1	CG	Amaral 19	3 912
	30	Vila Nova	W	2-0	CG	Fernandao 38, Felipe 71	2 364
Feb	3	Itumbiara	D	1-1	CG	Felipe 20	23 410
	7	Sta Helena	W	2-0	CG	Marcus Vinicius 30, Rafael Toloi 33	3 910
	13	Morrinhos	W	2-1	CG	Felipe 26, Fernandao 77	3 098
	17	Canedense	D	2-2	CG	Fernandao 2 28 51	3 434
	20	Canedense	W	3-1	CG	Felipe 58, Raf Moura 63, Amaral 76	3 970
	25	Ituiutaba	W	3-2	CBr1	Felipe 1, Rafael Moura 56, Fernandao 59	806
	28	Atlético GO	W	2-1	CG	Felipe 65, Rafael Moura 72	2 581
Mar	3	Trindade	D	1-1	CG	Fernandao 83	2 274
	7	Anapolina	L	1-2	CG	Rafael Toloi 86	8 511
	11	Ituiutaba	D	0-0	CBr1		1 725
	14	Itumbiara	W	3-0	CG	Fernandao 9, Felipe 81, Romerito 90	3 948
	18	São José	W	1-0	CBr2	Rafael Moura 75	2 521
	22	Morrinhos	W	3-0	CG	Wellington Saci 28, David Sacconi 2 58 76	4 542
	25	Sta Helena	L	2-3	CG	OG 43, Fernandao 81	5 088
	28	Vila Nova	L	1-2	CG	OG 6	4 157
Apr	1	São José	W	7-0	CBr2	Rafael Moura 4 12 15 27 41, Romerito 2 50 82, Rithely 88	1 009
	4	CRAC	W	2-0	CG	Felipe 18, Deyvd Sacconi 31	5 710
	10	Atlético GO	D	0-0	CGsf		23 373
	16	Vitória	D	0-0	CBr3		8 746
	18	Atlético GO	L	2-4	CGsf	Romerito 42, Rafael Toloi 79	13 566
	22	Vitória	D	2-2	CBr3	Felipe 6p, Fernandao 32	2 107
May	9	Guarani	L	0-1	SA		6 205
	16	Inter	L	2-3	SA	Everton Santos 30, Amaral 42	3 731
	22	Botafogo	L	0-3	SA		13 837
	27	Ceará	D	0-0	SA		2 309
	30	Atlético GO	W	3-1	SA	Romerito 2 24 54, Bernardo 57	5 213
Jun	2	São Paulo	W	2-1	SA	Bernardo 38p, Jonilson 89	15 592
	5	Flamengo	W	2-1	SA	Hugo 85, Otacilio Neto 87	11 855
	14	Vasco	D	0-0	SA		11 000
	18	Cruzeiro	L	0-1	SA		3 579
Jul	21	Vitória	D	2-2	SA	Rafael Moura 31, Everton Santos 33	9 568
	25	Atlético PR	L	0-2	SA		4 020
	1	Avai	L	1-4	SA	Bernardo 68	7 973
	5	Grêmio	D	1-1	CSr2	Rafael Moura 77p	2 453
	8	Palmeiras	D	1-1	SA	Amaral 90	13 178
Aug	12	Grêmio	W	2-0	CSr2	Amaral 9, Everton Santos 90	
	15	Grêmio	L	0-2	SA		11 409
	21	Grêmio Pr.	L	1-2	SA	Everton Santos 55	
	25	Fluminense	L	0-3	SA		10 147
	28	Santos	L	0-2	SA		17 968
Sep	1	Atlético MG	L	1-3	SA	Bernardo 6p	3 312
	4	Corinthians	L	1-5	SA	Junior 7	31 638
	8	Guarani	W	3-1	SA	Felipe 2 20 68p, Rafael Moura 42p	2 019
	12	Inter	D	0-0	SA		8 495
	15	Botafogo	W	4-1	SA	Wellington Monteiro 15, Rafael Moura 2 31 80p, Bernardo 86	12 480
	19	Ceará	D	1-1	SA	Wellington Monteiro 85	19 417
	22	Atlético GO	L	1-3	SA	Amaral 26	11 242
	26	São Paulo	W	3-0	SA	C. Alberto 23, Rafael Moura 2 35 45	18 528
	28	Flamengo	D	1-1	SA	OG 46	12 403
Oct	3	Vasco	L	2-3	SA	Felipe 7, Jones 36	6 805
	7	Cruzeiro	L	0-1	SA		6 170
	10	Vitória	W	1-0	SA	Bernardo 77	1 806
	13	Peñarol	W	1-0	CSr3	Rafael Moura 23	
	16	Atlético PR	L	1-4	SA	Rafael Moura 83	14 128
	20	Peñarol	L	2-3	CSr3	Rafael Moura 17, Carlos Alberto 77	37 000
	24	Avaí	W	1-0	SA	Bernardo 43p	4 663
	27	Avaí	D	2-2	CSqf	Rafael Moura 2 29 90	3 742
	30	Palmeiras	L	2-3	SA	Carlos Alberto 82, Everton Santos 82	5 811
Nov	3	Grêmio	L	0-2	SA		2 235
	7	Grêmio Pr.	L	1-4	SA	Rafael Moura 8	674
	11	Avaí	W	1-0	CSqf	Rafael Moura 45	9 572
	14	Fluminense	D	1-1	SA	Rafael Moura 19	30 897
	17	Palmeiras	L	0-1	CSsf		14 128
	21	Santos	L	1-4	SA	Ernando 12	2 865
	24	Palmeiras	W	2-1	CSsf	Carlos Alberto 45, Ernando 82	36 410
	28	Atlético MG	L	1-3	SA	Everton Santos 38	17 234
Dc	1	Indepen'te	W	2-0	CSf	Rafael Moura 15, Otacilio Neto 21	35 500
	5	Corinthians	L	0-1	CSf	Felipe Amorim 19	28 917
	8	Indepen'te	L	1-3	CSf	Rafael Moura 22. L 3-5p	38 000

GREMIO 2010

Mo	Date	Opponent	Res	Score	Comp	Scorers	Att
Jan	17	Pelotas	W	3-2	CG	Jonas 54, Borges 80, Maylson 83	10 917
	21	Caxias	W	3-2	CG	Borges 27, OG 60, Jonas 68	13 431
	24	Veranópolis	D	1-1	CG	Jonas 64	9 638
	27	Santa Cruz	W	2-1	CG	Jonas 79, Borges 91+	2 170
	31	Inter	L	0-1	CG		16 388
Feb	3	São Luiz	D	1-1	CG	Borges 71	4 170
	7	Univ'sidade	W	5-1	CG	Borges 3 11 36 81, OG 54, Jonas 46	794
	10	Araguaia	W	3-1	CBr1	Borges 2 39 86, Rochemback 75	2 297
	13	São José	W	2-1	CG	Mithyue 54, Fabio Santos 61	3 332
	17	Veranópolis	W	4-2	CGqf	Jonas 9, Borges 36, Mario Fernandes 82, Hugo 88	6 517
	20	Inter SM	W	4-1	CGsf	Rafael Marques 34, Borges 36, Rochemback 41, Hugo 81	8 652
	28	NHamburgo	W	1-0	CGf	Ferdinando 19	30 252
Mar	3	Avenida	W	3-1	CG	Maylson 1, Edilson 13, Jonas 82	1 912
	6	Porto Alegre	W	1-0	CG	Willian 6	9 329
	14	Inter SM	W	3-0	CG	Maylson 2 40 74, Fernando 88	9 651
	17	Votoraty	W	1-0	CBr2	Jonas 51	5 238
	21	Ypiranga	W	3-1	CG	Jonas 2 68 91+, Maylson 74	5 730
	24	NHamburgo	W	2-1	CG	Maylson 5, Willian 17	9 702
	28	Esportivo	W	2-0	CG	Willian Magrao 12, Maylson 57	8 029
Apr	1	Votoraty	W	3-0	CBr2	Jonas 14, Maylson 18, Rodrigo 68	4 911
	4	Juventude	W	2-1	CG	Jonas 2 11 62	5 738
	8	Pelotas	L	1-2	CGqf	Maylson 47	11 724
	15	Avai	W	3-1	CBr3	Jonas 2 18 56, Borges 28	16 628
	22	Avai	L	2-3	CBr3	Jonas 55, Rochemback 77	11 856
	25	Inter	W	2-0	CGpo	Rodrigo 68, Borges 87	34 744
	30	Fluminense	W	3-2	CBqf	Douglas 2 20 72, Jonas 30	20 489
May	2	Inter	L	0-1	CGpo		
	6	Fluminense	W	2-0	CBqf	Hugo 61, Jonas 67	23 356
	8	Atlético GO	D	0-0	SA		5 647
	13	Santos	W	4-3	CBsf	Borges 3 58 64 75, Jonas 68	35 215
	16	Corinthians	L	1-2	SA	Maylson 75	17 119
	1	Santos	L	1-3	CBsf	Rafael Marques 74	13 896
	22	Palmeiras	L	2-4	SA	Jonas 31, Hugo 49	18 635
	26	Avai	W	3-0	SA	Jonas 2 11 26, Rochemback 90	9 220
	29	Flamengo	D	1-1	SA	Rodrigo 52	10 983
Jun	3	Atlético MG	W	2-1	SA	Hugo 2 37 60	14 605
	5	São Paulo	L	1-3	SA	Hugo 7	14 408
	14	Vitória	D	1-1	SA	OG 75	8 359
	18	Grêmio Pr	L	0-2	SA		4 163
	21	Vasco	D	1-1	SA	Jonas 9	4 820
	25	Cruzeiro	D	2-2	SA	Borges 45, Jonas 79	9 672
Jul	1	Inter	D	0-0	SA		36 240
	5	Goiás	D	1-1	CSr1	Hugo 35	
	8	Fluminense	L	1-2	SA	Andre Lima 88	12 001
	12	Goiás	L	0-2	CSr1		
Aug	15	Goiás	W	2-0	SA	Willian Magrao 2 33 71	11 409
	21	Ceará	L	1-2	SA	OG 25	14 981
	26	Santos	L	1-2	SA	Borges 6	12 379
	29	Atlético PR	D	1-1	SA	Vilson 60	18 771
	1	Guarani	W	1-0	SA	Jonas 23	26 419
Sep	4	Botafogo	D	2-2	SA	Jonas 2 53 85	16 921
	8	Atlético GO	W	2-0	SA	Douglas 6, Borges 82	22 758
	11	Corinthians	W	1-0	SA	Douglas 34	29 533
	15	Palmeiras	L	1-2	SA	Jonas 90	34 166
	19	Avai	W	3-0	SA	Jonas 2 36 72, Andre Lima 64	9 146
	23	Flamengo	D	2-2	SA	Douglas 6, Jonas 57	24 968
	26	Atlético MG	W	2-1	SA	Jonas 1 Gabriel 15	12 262
	30	São Paulo	W	4-2	SA	Andre Lima 2 29 39, Jonas 70p, Diego 75	25 322
Oct	2	Vitória	W	3-0	SA	Maylson 20, Diego 90, Edilson 90	10 998
	6	Grêmio Pr	W	4-0	SA	Andre Lima 1, Jonas 3 25 32 86p	18 198
	9	Vasco	D	3-3	SA	Jonas 2 41 72, Gabriel 89	13 651
	17	Cruzeiro	W	2-1	SA	Junior Vicosa 45, Jonas 73	41 435
	24	Inter	D	2-2	SA	Andre Lima 36, Fabio Santos 69	45 234
	28	Fluminense	L	0-2	SA		16 467
	3	Goiás	W	2-0	SA	Andre Lima 30, Diego 90	2 235
Nov	6	Ceará	W	5-1	SA	Andre Lima 2 24 61, Jonas 30, Rochemback 34, Douglas 56	20 789
	13	Santos	D	0-0	SA		7 421
	20	Atlético PR	W	3-1	SA	Neuton 12, Douglas 58p, Diego 89	27 044
	28	Guarani	W	3-0	SA	Andre Lima 23, Jonas 79p, Diego 89	5 725
Dc	5	Botafogo	W	3-0	SA	Andre Lima 21, Jonas 39, Douglas 89	45 420

GREMIO PRUDENTE 2010

Mon	Day	Opponent	Res	Score	Comp	Scorers	Att
Jan	17	Sertãozinho	D	1-1	CP	William [87]	2 054
	21	Palmeiras	D	2-2	CP	Flavinho [7], Tadeu [59]	10 031
	24	Mirassol	D	2-2	CP	Diego [34], Tadeu [87]	1 321
	27	Santos	L	0-5	CP		6 294
	30	Rio Claro	W	3-2	CP	Marcos Assuncao 2 [11] [60], Tadeu [36]	2 332
	3	Botafogo	L	0-4	CP		3 328
Feb	6	Ituano	W	4-0	CP	OG [34], Tadeu [59], Jefferson [72], Wesley [9]	398
	12	Monte Azul	W	1-0	CP	OG [45]	2 396
	18	São Paulo	L	1-3	CP	Marcos Assuncao [21]	5 945
	21	Santo André	L	1-3	CP	Wesley [48]	1 550
	28	Ponte Preta	W	3-1	CP	Wesley [10], Jefferson [42], Marcos Assuncao [68]	1 888
Mar	3	Rio Branco	W	2-0	CP	Tadeu [57], David [92+]	2 175
	6	Oeste	D	1-1	CP	Flavinho [92+]	1 940
	13	Paulista	W	2-1	CP	Tadeu [26], Flavinho [64]	852
	21	Corinthians	W	2-0	CP	Robson 2 [63] [94+]	16 749
	25	Mogi Mirim	W	3-0	CP	Araujo 3 [6] [39] [83]	2 450
	28	Portuguesa	W	2-1	CP	Tadeu [67], Henrique Dias [77]	3 306
Apr	4	Bragantino	W	3-2	CP	Marcelo Oliveira [34], Tadeu [49], Araujo [80]	3 290
	7	S. Caetano	W	1-0	CP	Wesley [23]	8 232
	11	Santo André	L	1-2	CPsf	Diego [41]	10 919
	18	Santo André	W	2-1	CPsf	Tadeu [16], Marcos Assuncao [43]	11 835
	9	Avai	L	1-6	SA	Willian [25]	6 868
May	15	Atlético MG	W	4-0	SA	Araujo [2], Flavinho [16], Henrique Dias [41p], Diego [45]	2 500
	23	Flamengo	L	1-3	SA	Wanderley [49]	3 978
	26	Corinthians	D	2-2	SA	Wanderley [18], Diego [44]	9 235
	29	Palmeiras	D	0-0	SA		4 016
Jun	2	Atlético GO	W	1-0	SA	Tadeu [32]	1 759
	6	Guarani	L	0-1	SA		5 685
	15	Fluminense	D	1-1	SA	Wesley [83]	24 335
	18	Grêmio	W	2-0	SA	Paulo Cesar [22], Wanderley [90]	4 163
Jul	21	São Paulo	D	1-1	SA	Anderson Luis [20]	9 646
	24	Vitória	D	0-0	SA		4 922
	1	Santos	L	1-2	SA	Robson [83]	15 890
	4	Atlético MG	D	0-0	CSr1		2 576
	8	Cruzeiro	D	0-0	SA		10 109
Aug	11	Atlético MG	L	0-1	CSr1		3 658
	15	Vasco	L	1-2	SA	Joao Vitor [58]	5 047
	21	Goiás	W	2-1	SA	Wanderley [51], Anderson Luis [78]	1 493
	25	Atlético PR	L	0-1	SA		2 419
	28	Ceará	D	2-2	SA	Wesley 2 [36] [41]	11 867
Sep	1	Botafogo	L	0-1	SA		3 211
	5	Inter	L	0-2	SA		17 811
	9	Avai	D	1-1	SA	Rafael Martins [86]	1 475
	12	Atlético MG	L	0-1	SA		12 380
	16	Flamengo	L	1-2	SA	Adriano Pimenta [45]	3 815
	18	Corinthians	L	0-3	SA		23 815
	22	Palmeiras	L	0-1	SA		11 127
	25	Atlético GO	L	0-3	SA		2 641
	29	Guarani	W	4-2	SA	Willian [23p], Wesley 2 [41] [62], Wanderley [74]	882
Oct	2	Fluminense	D	1-1	SA	Willian [71]	2 781
	6	Grêmio	L	0-4	SA		18 198
	9	São Paulo	L	2-3	SA	Wesley 2 [32] [90]	12 969
	17	Vitória	L	0-2	SA		27 199
	24	Santos	W	3-2	SA	Wesley 2 [46] [61], Gilmar [54p]	22 132
	30	Cruzeiro	L	0-2	SA		1 872
	4	Vasco	L	1-2	SA	Adriano Pimenta [8]	2 474
Nov	7	Goiás	W	4-1	SA	Joao Vitor [22], Willian [53], Wesley [67], Rhayner [89]	674
	14	Atlético PR	L	1-2	SA	Willian [32]	16 991
	20	Ceará	D	1-1	SA	Rhayner [28]	842
	28	Botafogo	L	1-3	SA	Henrique [68]	4 932
Dc	2	Inter	L	0-3	SA		1 246

GUARANI 2010

Mon	Day	Opponent	Res	Score	Comp	Scorers	Att
Jan	13	Osv'do Cruz	L	0-1	CP		1 075
	17	São Bento	W	3-1	CP	Ricardo Xavier 2 [49] [58], OG [65]	3 384
	20	Linense	D	0-0	CP		3 588
	24	Rio Preto	D	1-1	CP	Fabio Souza [32]	3 014
	27	Taquaritinga	W	6-3	CP	Leo Mineiro [6], Rodrigo Cesar [28], Ricardo Xavier 2 [38] [65], Fabio Souza [67], Cleber [84]	594
	30	São José	L	1-2	CP	Dannyu [88]	5 547
Feb	2	Noroeste	L	0-1	CP		3 361
	6	A. Sorocaba	D	1-1	CP	Helio [88]	2 562
	10	S. Bernardo	L	2-4	CP	Ricardo Xavier [18], Walter Junio [59]	4 732
	13	Flamengo	D	1-1	CP	Helio [44]	911
	17	GE Osasco	W	5-1	CP	Fabio Souza [28], Leo Mineiro [51], Ricardo Xavier 2 [62] [66], Da Silva [74]	2 389
	21	América	W	2-0	CP	Da Silva [36], Leonardo [89]	322
	25	Linense	W	1-0	CBr1	Anderson Costa [79]	1 848
	28	U. São João	L	0-2	CP		4 186
Mar	3	Marila	D	3-3	CP	Ricardo Xavier 2 [36] [44], Fabio Souza [53]	2 432
	7	Guarat'eta	L	0-3	CP		2 033
	11	Araguaina	W	2-1	CBr1	Fabio Souza 2 [6] [76]	1 437
	13	Votoraty	L	0-1	CP		1 874
	17	Fortaleza	L	0-2	CBr2		3 660
	21	PAEC	W	4-0	CP	Fabio Souza [34], Valdir Teodoro [50], OG [61], Ricardo Xavier [73]	1 336
	24	Barbarense	L	1-2	CP	Carlos Cesar Neves [47]	2 853
	28	Cata'vense	W	3-0	CP	Cleber [36], Fabio Souza [41], Ricardo Xavier [79]	1 773
Apr	1	Fortaleza	W	2-0	CBr2	Almeida [34], Marcinho [68]. W 4-3p	2 042
	15	Santos	L	1-8	CBr3	Moreno [73]	8 131
	21	Santos	W	3-2	CBr3	Da Silva [51], Richard Falcao 2 [83] [90]	8 481
	9	Goiás	W	1-0	SA	Mazola [9]	6 205
May	16	Atlético PR	D	2-2	SA	Roger 2 [35] [51p]	12 872
	23	Cruzeiro	D	2-2	SA	Roger 2 [11] [32]	8 589
	26	Santos	L	1-3	SA	Baiano [38]	5 146
	30	São Paulo	D	0-0	SA		14 528
Jun	3	Vasco	W	1-0	SA	Roger [90]	6 002
	6	Grêmio Pr	W	1-0	SA	Roger [90p]	5 685
	14	Inter	L	0-3	SA		2 193
Jul	18	Botafogo	D	1-1	SA	Ricardo Xavier [40]	5 522
	22	Ceará	D	1-1	SA	Ricardo Xavier [74]	4 595
	25	Corinthians	L	1-3	SA	Mazola [63]	27 700
	31	Atlético GO	D	1-1	SA	Mazola [16]	2 340
	7	Avai	W	4-1	SA	Renan [9], Ricardo Xavier [11], Mazola [36], Fabao [70]	3 776
Aug	14	Atlético MG	L	1-3	SA	Mazola [90]	5 748
	22	Palmeiras	D	0-0	SA		19 809
	26	Vitória	D	1-1	SA	Romulo [76p]	6 338
	29	Flamengo	W	2-1	SA	Alison [90], Reinaldo [90]	10 317
	1	Grêmio	L	0-1	SA		26 419
	5	Fluminense	W	2-1	SA	Baiano [35], Fabao [75]	9 962
	8	Goiás	L	1-3	SA	Mario Lucio [82]	2 019
	12	Atlético PR	W	1-0	SA	Mazola [84]	4 235
Sep	15	Cruzeiro	L	2-4	SA	Geovane [70], Paulo Roberto [74]	14 428
	19	Santos	D	0-0	SA		10 998
	22	São Paulo	L	1-2	SA	Baiano [45p]	10 264
	25	Vasco	W	1-0	SA	Baiano [81p]	4 294
	29	Grêmio Pr	L	2-4	SA	Mazola [77p], Reinaldo [78]	882
	2	Inter	L	0-3	SA		10 819
	6	Botafogo	D	1-1	SA	Barboza [27]	3 601
	10	Ceará	L	0-2	SA		18 544
Oct	17	Corinthians	D	0-0	SA		17 469
	23	Atlético GO	L	0-1	SA		2 986
	30	Avai	L	0-1	SA		10 873
	3	Atlético MG	D	0-0	SA		5 922
	7	Palmeiras	L	0-1	SA		3 154
Nov	14	Vitória	D	1-1	SA	Geovane [80]	6 051
	20	Flamengo	L	1-2	SA	Baiano [12]	34 932
	28	Grêmio	L	0-3	SA		5 725
Dc	5	Fluminense	L	0-1	SA		40 905

INTERNACIONAL 2010

Month	Day	Opponent	Res	Score	Comp	Scorers	Att
Jan	17	Ypiranga	W	4-2	CG	Leandro Damiao 2 [9] [52], Ytalo [38],	7 131
	20	Porto Alegre	W	1-0	CG	Leandro Damiao [27] Walter [41]	954
	24	Inter SM	D	1-1	CG	Daniel [47]	1 377
	27	Juventude	W	5-0	CG	Kleber [12], Bolivar [22], Taison [75], Alecsandro [72p], Giuliano [80]	16 624
	31	Grêmio	W	1-0	CG	Alecsandro [79]	16 388
Feb	3	NHamburgo	W	3-1	CG	Leandro Damiao [14], Sorondo [46], Thiago Humberto [86]	1 887
	7	Avenida	W	2-1	CG	Taison [30], Edu [48]	7 829
	13	Esportivo	W	2-1	CG	Kleber [6], Alecsandro [59]	1 243
	18	Juventude	W	2-0	CGqf	Alecsandro [4], Sorondo [66]	10 064
	20	NHamburgo	L	1-2	CGsf	Bruno Silva [53]	7 745
	26	Emelec	W	2-1	CLg5	Nei [51], Alecsandro [87]	39 304
Mar	3	Santa Cruz	W	4-1	CG	Kleber [15], Alecsandro 2 [43] [82p],	5 243
	7	São Luiz	W	1-0	CG	Eltinho [85] Giuliano [54]	1 529
	11	Dep Quito	D	1-1	CLg5	Giuliano [40]	4 088
	14	Veranópolis	D	1-1	CG	D'Alessandro [78]	1 177
	18	CA Cerro	D	0-0	CLg5		25 510
	21	Pelotas	D	2-2	CG	Fabiano Eller [30], D'Alessandro [72]	10 145
	24	São José	L	0-3	CG		822
	27	Caxias	L	0-2	CG		9 854
	31	CA Cerro	W	2-0	CLg5	OG [58], Alecsandro [72]	36 897
Apr	4	Univ'sidade	W	4-0	CG	Alecsandro 2 [68p] [77], Taison 2 [88] [90]	6 768
	7	NHamburgo	D	3-3	CGqf	Alecsandro 2 [7] [71], Walter [22]	1 406
	11	Ypiranga	W	2-0	CGsf	Walter 2 [30] [34]	19 942
	4	Emelec	D	0-0	CLg5		3 774
	6	Pelotas	W	3-2	CGf	Bolivar [42], Edu [74], D'Alessandro [81]	26 823
	22	Dep Quito	W	3-0	CLg5	Andrezinho 3, Bolivar [61], Giuliano [90]	31 360
	25	Grêmio	L	0-2	CGpo		34 744
	28	Banfield	L	1-0	CLr2	Kleber [50]	6 794
May	2	Grêmio	W	1-0	CGpo	Giuliano [10]	
	6	Banfield	W	2-0	CLr2	Alecsandro [42], Walter [57]	34 643
	9	Cruzeiro	L	1-2	SA	Taison [6]	14 177
	13	Estudiantes	W	1-0	CLqf	Sorondo [88]	40 115
	16	Goiás	W	3-2	SA	Walter 2 [60p] [74], Giuliano [80]	3 731
	20	Estudiantes	L	1-2	CLqf	Giuliano [88]	14 500
	23	São Paulo	L	0-2	SA		25 185
	27	Vasco	L	2-3	SA	Andrezinho 2 [40] [41]	4 081
	30	Atlético PR	W	4-1	SA	Alecsandro 2 [46] [72], Sorondo [48], ↓	11 058
Jun	3	Corinthians	L	0-2	SA	Andrezinho [52]	33 361
	6	Palmeiras	D	1-1	SA	Giuliano [66]	11 743
	14	Guarani	W	3-0	SA	Sandro [59], Alecsandro [71], Taison [90]	2 193
	18	Ceará	W	2-1	SA	Alecsandro [15p], Kleber [47]	6 483
Jul	21	Atlético MG	W	2-1	SA	Alecsandro 2 [13] [61]	4 713
	25	Flamengo	W	1-0	SA	Taison [4]	25 002
	28	São Paulo	W	1-0	CLsf	Giuliano [68]	48 166
	1	Grêmio	D	0-0	SA		36 240
	5	São Paulo	L	1-2	CLsf	Alecsandro [52]	62 129
	11	Guadalajara	W	2-1	CLf	Giuliano [73], Bolivar [77]	30 870
	15	Fluminense	L	0-3	SA		49 471
Aug	18	Guadalajara	W	3-2	CLf	Rafael Sobis [61], Leandro Damiao [75], Giuliano [88]	56 000
	22	Atlético GO	D	1-1	SA	Leandro Damiao [67]	15 571
	25	Avaí	W	1-0	SA	Indio [9]	10 501
	28	Botafogo	W	1-0	SA	Leandro Damiao [24]	16 580
	1	Vitória	D	0-0	SA		8 040
	5	Grêmio Pr.	W	2-0	SA	Rafael Sobis [51], Leandro Damiao [51]	17 811
	8	Cruzeiro	L	0-1	SA		13 677
	12	Goiás	D	0-0	SA		8 495
Sep	16	São Paulo	W	3-1	SA	Wilson Mathias [10], L. Damiao [39],	11 327
	19	Vasco	W	1-0	SA	Edu [46] Giuliano [62]	30 981
	23	Atlético PR	L	0-1	SA		9 877
	26	Corinthians	W	3-2	SA	Tinga [30], Alecsandro [76], ↓	33 787
	29	Palmeiras	L	0-2	SA	Andrezinho [90]	12 264
	2	Guarani	W	3-0	SA	Daniel [51], Glaydson [64], Giuliano [81]	10 819
	7	Ceará	L	0-1	SA		15 897
	10	Atlético MG	W	1-0	SA	Alecsandro [45]	13 328
Oct	14	Santos	L	0-1	SA		10 036
	16	Flamengo	L	0-3	SA		9 479
	24	Grêmio	D	2-2	SA	Alecsandro [66p], D'Alessandro [83]	45 234
	30	Santos	D	1-1	SA	Leandro Damiao [80]	29 565
	3	Fluminense	D	0-0	SA		21 069
		Atlético GO	D	2-2	SA	Leandro Damiao [54], Giuliano [70p]	4 459
Nov	14	Avaí	L	2-3	SA	L. Damiao [52], Rafael Sobis [58]	12 690
	21	Botafogo	W	2-1	SA	Andrezinho [63], Rafael Sobis [73]	19 604
	28	Vitória	D	1-1	SA	Rafael Sobis [62]	22 444
Dec	2	Grêmio Pr.	W	3-0	SA	Alecsandro [16], Tinga [23], Giuliano [81]	1 246
	14	Mazembe	L	0-2	CWsf		22 131
	18	Seongnam	W	4-2	CW3p	Tinga [15], Alecsandro 2 [27] [71], D'Alessandro [52]	16 563

PALMEIRAS 2010

Month	Day	Opponent	Res	Score	Comp	Scorers	Att
Jan	16	Mogi Mirim	W	5-1	CP	Diego Souza 2 [30] [68], Leo [43], Robert [61], Cleiton Xavier [76p]	17 051
	21	Grêmio Pr	D	2-2	CP	Deyvid Sacconi [28], Diego Souza [84]	10 031
	24	Ituano	D	3-3	CP	Diego Souza [31], Robert [56], Deyvid Sacconi [79]	9 684
	27	Monte Azul	W	1-0	CP	Cleiton Xavier [30p]	7 665
	30	Corinthians	L	0-1	CP		28 587
	4	Portuguesa	D	1-1	CP	Danilo [47]	6 533
	7	Bragantino	W	3-2	CP	Cleiton Xavier [6], Robert [50], Lenny [83]	4 913
Feb	10	Flamengo Pl	W	1-0	CBr1	Diego Souza [75]	33 117
	13	Botafogo	D	1-1	CP	Leo [73]	10 481
	17	S. Caetano	L	1-4	CP	Diego Souza [64]	3 324
	21	São Paulo	W	2-0	CP	Robert 2 [53] [69]	13 590
	25	Flamengo Pl	W	4-0	CBr1	Robert 2 [3p] [35], Leo [26], Edinho [74]	6 859
	28	Rio Claro	L	0-1	CP		5 307
	3	S'to André	L	1-3	CP	Robert [43]	3 840
	8	Sertãozinho	W	3-2	CP	Lenny [23], Cleiton Xavier 2 [83] [93+]	3 224
Mar	14	Santos	W	4-3	CP	Robert 3 [41] [43] [87], Diego Souza [55]	11 452
	17	Paysandu	W	2-1	CBr2	Lincoln [13], Ewerthon [48]	27 073
	20	Ponte Preta	L	0-2	CP		17 247
	24	Rio Branco	D	2-2	CP	Diego Souza [17], Ewerthon [33]	6 477
	27	Mirassol	D	1-1	CP	Robert [6]	3 764
	31	Paysandu	W	1-0	CBr2	Robert [60]	7 406
	3	Oeste	D	0-0	CP		3 560
	7	Paulista	L	1-3	CP	Lincoln [53]	3 220
Apr	15	Atlético PR	W	1-0	CBr3	Robert [14]	20 269
	21	Atlético PR	D	1-1	CBr3	Lincoln [88]	20 367
	29	Atlético GO	W	1-0	CBqf	Cleiton Xavier [94+p]	23 892
	5	Atlético GO	L	0-1	CBqf	L 1-2p	21 889
	8	Vitória	W	1-0	SA	Lincoln [79]	6 025
	16	Vasco	D	0-0	SA		8 765
May	22	Grêmio	W	4-1	SA	Ewerthon 2 [16] [30], Mauricio Ramos [61], Cleiton Xavier [70]	18 635
	26	São Paulo	L	0-1	SA		15 522
	29	Grêmio Pr	D	0-0	SA		4 016
	2	Flamengo	L	0-1	SA		8 618
Jun	6	Inter	D	1-1	SA	Lincoln [14]	11 743
	15	Santos	W	2-1	SA	Ewerthon [12], Tinga [67]	9 400
	18	Avaí	L	2-4	SA	Gabriel Silva [12], Kleber [54p]	7 851
Jul	22	Botafogo	D	2-2	SA	Marcos Assuncao [47], Kleber [57]	12 107
	25	Ceará	D	0-0	SA		24 935
	1	Corinthians	D	1-1	SA	Edinho [34]	24 491
	8	Goiás	D	1-1	SA	Ewerthon [13]	13 178
	11	Vitória	L	0-2	CSr2		
	14	Atlético PR	W	2-0	SA	Danilo [2], Ewerthon [76]	10 074
Aug	19	Vitória	W	3-0	CSr2		
	22	Guarani	D	0-0	SA		19 809
	26	Atlético GO	L	0-3	SA		12 559
	29	Atlético MG	W	2-1	SA	Marcos Assuncao [64], Kleber [75]	11 120
	2	Fluminense	D	1-1	SA	Ewerthon [90]	18 356
	5	Cruzeiro	L	2-3	SA	Kleber [35], Mauricio Ramos [38]	21 560
	9	Vitória	D	1-1	SA	Tadeu [73]	6 543
	12	Vasco	D	0-0	SA		15 313
Sep	15	Grêmio	W	2-1	SA	Marcos Assuncao [13], Ewerthon [48]	34 166
	19	São Paulo	L	0-2	SA		16 009
	22	Grêmio Pr	W	1-0	SA	Marcio Araujo [60]	11 127
	25	Flamengo	W	3-1	SA	Kleber 2 [19p] [30], Lincoln [90]	9 894
	29	Inter	W	2-0	SA	Marcos Assuncao 2 [31] [58]	12 264
	2	Santos	D	1-1	SA	Kleber [20]	8 900
	7	Avaí	W	4-1	SA	Jorge Valdivia 2 [10] [49], Kleber [57p], Gabriel Silva [69]	6 306
	10	Botafogo	D	0-0	SA		9 950
Oct	14	Ceará	W	1-0	CSr3	Marcos Assuncao [27]	
	17	Ceará	D	1-1	SA	Marcos Assuncao [45]	8 257
	20	Univ Sucre	W	1-0	CSr3	Kleber [12], Luan [28], Danilo [71]	10 741
	24	Corinthians	L	0-1	SA		32 391
	27	Atlético MG	D	1-1	CSqf	Kleber [55]	11 542
	30	Goiás	W	3-2	SA	Tinga [21], Marcio Araujo [80], Dinei [86]	5 911
	4	Atlético PR	L	0-1	SA		19 749
	7	Guarani	W	1-0	SA	Leandro Amaro [42]	3 154
	10	Atlético MG	W	2-0	CSqf	Marcos Assuncao [27], Luan [79]	35 985
Nov	14	Atlético GO	L	0-3	SA		8 472
	17	Goiás	W	1-0	CSsf	Marcos Assuncao [48]	14 128
	21	Atlético MG	L	0-2	SA		4 662
	24	Goiás	L	1-2	CSsf	Luan [34]	36 410
	28	Fluminense	L	1-2	SA	Dinei [4]	11 291
Dec	5	Cruzeiro	L	1-2	SA	Rivaldo [53]	16 191

SANTOS 2010

Mon	Date	Opponent		Result	Comp	Scorers	Att
Jan	17	Rio Branco	W	4-0	CP	Ganso 2 [2 65], Neymar 2 [19 45]	12 153
	20	Ponte Preta	D	1-1	CP	Andre [47]	10 676
	24	Mogi Mirim	L	1-2	CP	Ganso [30]	2 317
	27	Grêmio Pr	W	5-0	CP	Andre [33], Wesley [69], Ze Eduardo [73], Neymar 2 [78 87p]	5 294
	30	Oeste	W	2-0	CP	Andre [6], Neymar [92+]	10 393
Feb	4	S'to André	W	2-1	CP	Neymar [24], Ganso [63]	9 822
	7	São Paulo	W	2-1	CP	Neymar [37], Robinho [87]	14 519
	14	Rio Claro	W	2-1	CP	Andre [69], Giovanni [88]	32 001
	18	Bagantino	W	6-3	CP	Wesley [23], Robinho 2 [27 57], Andre 2 [41 46], Zé Roberto [90]	11 794
	21	Mirassol	W	2-1	CP	Wesley [26], Madson [58]	8 161
	24	Naviraiense	W	1-0	CBr1	Marquinhos [82]	7 062
	28	Corinthians	W	2-1	CP	Neymar [33], Andre [60]	9 029
Mar	4	Paulista	W	3-2	CP	Wesley [26], Ganso [52], Robinho [69]	8 033
	7	Portuguesa	D	1-1	CP	Ze Eduardo [89]	9 135
	10	Naviraiense	W	10-0	CBr1	Ganso [6], Andre 3 [27 37 59], Neymar 2 [28 54], Robinho [31], Marquinhos [45], Madson 2 [65 76]	11 336
	14	Palmeiras	L	3-4	CP	Para [9], Neymar [30], Madson [80]	11 452
	18	Remo	W	4-0	CBr2	Neymar [21 81p], Andre 2 [42 48], Andre 3 [14 39 90p], Ganso 2 [27 73],	19 445
	21	Ituano	W	9-1	CP	Ze Eduardo [40], Madson 2 [45 54], Maikon Leite [61]	10 053
	25	Botafogo	W	4-2	CP	Ganso [41], Marquinhos 2 [56 62], Ze Eduardo [89]	11 171
	28	Monte Azul	W	5-0	CP	Marquinhos 2 [12 64], Ganso 2 [34 58], Andre [27]	11 929
Apr	4	S. Caetano	W	3-1	CP	OG [2], Neymar [67], Robinho [79]	3 793
	7	Sertãozinho	W	4-2	CP	Germano [8], Alex Sandro [32], Ze Eduardo [38], Marcelo [94+p]	2 060
	11	São Paulo	W	3-2	CPsf	Junior Cesar [25], Andre [40], Durval [40]	35 695
	14	Guarani	W	8-1	CBr3	Neymar 5 [2p 29 38 81 84], Robinho [31 59], Marcel [56p]	8 131
	18	São Paulo	W	3-0	CPsf	Neymar 2 [59 82p], Ganso [87]	13 785
	21	Guarani	L	2-3	CBr3	Breitner [56], Alex Sandro [65]	8 481
	25	S'to André	W	3-2	CPf	Andre [57], Wesley 2 [61 69]	33 354
	28	Atlético MG	L	2-3	CBqf	Robinho [44], Edu Dracena [82]	46 239
May	2	S'to André	L	2-3	CPf	Neymar 2 [7 31]	36 260
	5	Atlético MG	W	3-1	CBqf	Andre [17], Neymar [44], Wesley [49]	14 245
	8	Botafogo	D	3-3	SA	Neymar [30], Andre [33], Ze Eduardo [81]	25 634
	12	Grêmio	L	3-4	CBsf	Andre 2 [15 20], Robinho [83]	35 215
	16	Ceará	D	1-1	SA	Neymar [38p]	8 998
	19	Grêmio	W	3-1	CBsf	Ganso [51], Robinho [69], Wesley [85]	13 896
	22	Atlético GO	W	2-1	SA	Wesley [65], Ze Eduardo [71]	4 669
	26	Guarani	W	3-1	SA	Neymar [3], Marcel [85], André [88]	5 146
	30	Corinthians	L	2-4	SA	Andre [53], Marcel [88]	30 103
Jun	2	Cruzeiro	D	0-0	SA		15 708
	6	Vasco	W	4-0	SA	Andre 2 [34p 62], Maranhao [51], ↓	8 585
	5	Palmeiras	L	1-2	SA	Marcel [82] Madson [73]	9 400
	18	Fluminense	L	0-1	SA		9 193
Jul	21	Atlético PR	L	0-2	SA		20 001
	25	São Paulo	W	1-0	SA	OG [60]	9 367
	28	Vitória	W	2-0	CBf	Neymar [14], Marquinhos [83]	14 060
	1	Grêmio Pr	W	2-1	SA	Danilo [6], Rodriguinho [66]	15 890
	4	Vitória	L	1-2	CBf	Edu Dracena [44]	28 978
Aug	12	Avai	L	1-3	CSr1	Ze Eduardo [69]	6 673
	15	Vitória	L	2-4	SA	Marcel [30], Ze Eduardo [67]	10 648
	18	Avai	W	1-0	CSr1	Ze Eduardo [24]	
	22	Atlético MG	W	2-0	SA	Neymar [55p], Danilo [77]	10 220
	26	Grêmio	W	2-1	SA	Neymar [66p], Rodriguinho [90]	12 379
	28	Goiás	W	2-0	SA	Ze Eduardo [75], Alan Patrick [81]	17 968
Sep	2	Avaí	W	2-1	SA	Neymar [1], Marcel [83]	7 141
	5	Flamengo	D	0-0	SA		34 897
	9	Botafogo	L	0-1	SA		15 472
	12	Ceará	L	1-2	SA	Keirrison [29]	23 374
	15	Atlético GO	W	4-2	SA	Edu Dracena [48], Madson [74],	3 873
	19	Guarani	D	0-0	SA	Alan Patrick [77], Marcel [80p]	10 998
	23	Corinthians	L	2-3	SA	Durval [2], Neymar [27]	10 898
	25	Cruzeiro	W	4-1	SA	Marcel [54], Edu Dracena [70], Alex	9 542
	28	Vasco	L	1-3	SA	Danilo [55], Sandro [88], Neymar [9]	2 819
Oct	2	Palmeiras	D	1-1	SA	Alan Patrick [52]	8 900
	6	Fluminense	W	3-0	SA	Ze Eduardo 3 [56 73 87]	14 385
	9	Atlético PR	W	2-0	SA	Maranhao [62], Ze Eduardo [65]	8 417
	14	Inter	W	1-0	SA	Neymar [27]	10 036
	17	São Paulo	L	3-4	SA	Alan Patrick [4], Ze Eduardo [20], Neymar [70p]	23 791
	24	Grêmio Pr	L	2-3	SA	Keirrison [19], Durval [35]	22 132
	30	Inter	D	1-1	SA	Ze Eduardo [75]	29 565

(cont'd on page 236)

SAO PAULO FC 2010

Mon	Date	Opponent		Result	Comp	Scorers	Att
Jan	17	Portuguesa	L	1-3	CP	Marcelinho Paraiba [39]	18 074
	20	Mirassol	D	1-1	CP	Richarlyson [89]	6 166
	23	Rio Claro	W	3-0	CP	Hernanes [38], Washington [55], Rogerio Ceni [89p]	8 384
	28	Paulista	W	3-0	CP	Dagoberto 2 [29 54], Andre Dias [65]	4 979
	31	Sertãozinho	D	2-2	CP	Leo Lima [56], Jorge Wagner [94+]	5 637
Feb	3	S. Caetano	W	3-0	CP	Washington [23], Dagoberto [36], Hernanes [89]	4 875
	7	Santos	L	1-2	CP	Roger [66]	14 519
	10	Monterrey	W	2-0	CLg2	Washington 2 [12 76]	34 501
	13	Ituano	W	1-0	CP	Rogerio Ceni [15p]	6 671
	18	Grêmio Pr	W	3-1	CP	Washington [23], Marcelinho Paraiba [44p], Henrique [92+]	5 945
	21	Palmeiras	L	0-2	CP		13 590
	25	Once Caldas	L	1-2	CLg2	Rogerio Ceni [32]	21 766
	28	Monte Azul	W	5-1	CP	Leo Lima [4], Fernandinho 4 [49 62 69 86]	4 362
Mar	3	Oeste	D	0-0	CP		7 610
	7	Ponte Preta	W	2-0	CP	Washington 2 [15 41]	9 487
	11	Nacional	W	2-0	CLg2	Washington 2 [59 89]	700
	14	Rio Branco	W	2-1	CP	Jorge Wagner [11], Andre Luis [91+]	9 370
	18	Nacional	W	3-0	CLg2	Dagoberto [30], Leo Lima [33], Washington [55]	31 411
	21	Mogi Mirim	W	3-0	CP	Rogerio Ceni [13p], Cleber Santana [40], Hernanes [92+]	9 763
	24	Bragantino	L	0-1	CP		4 248
	26	Corinthians	L	3-4	CP	Jean [43], Rodrigo Souto 2 [74 77]	23 372
	31	Monterrey	D	0-0	CLg2		28 472
Apr	4	Botafogo	W	5-0	CP	Marlos [45], Hernanes 2 [59 81], Rodrigo Souto [67], Junior Cesar [69]	8 774
	7	S'to André	W	3-1	CP	Washington [8], Dagoberto [20], Miranda [63]	12 908
	11	Santos	L	2-3	CPsf	Hernanes [52], Dagoberto [66]	35 695
	18	Santos	L	0-3	CPsf		13 785
	22	Once Caldas	W	1-0	CLg2	Fernandinho [40]	50 461
	28	Univ'sitario	D	0-0	CLr2		27 034
	4	Univ'sitario	D	0-0	CLr2	W 3-1p	43 838
May	9	Flamengo	D	1-1	SA	Washington [45]	11 195
	12	Cruzeiro	W	2-0	CLqf	Dagoberto [23], Hernanes [65]	48 602
	16	Botafogo	L	1-2	SA	Leo Lima [9]	11 622
	19	Cruzeiro	W	2-0	CLqf	Hernanes [23], Dagoberto [53]	52 196
	23	Inter	W	2-0	SA	Hernanes [37], Fernandao [62]	25 185
	26	Palmeiras	W	1-0	SA	Fernandao [55]	15 522
	30	Guarani	D	0-0	SA		14 528
Jun	2	Goiás	L	1-2	SA	Marcelinho [14]	15 592
	6	Grêmio	W	3-1	SA	Dagoberto 3 [17 65 69]	14 408
	14	Avai	L	1-2	SA	Hernanes [75]	7 717
	17	Vitória	L	2-3	SA	Jean [38], Fernandao [61]	11 915
Jul	21	Grêmio Pr	D	1-1	SA	Washington [1]	9 646
	25	Santos	L	0-1	SA		9 367
	28	Inter	L	0-1	CLsf		48 166
	31	Ceará	W	2-1	SA	Fernandao [66], Ricardo Oliveira [68]	11 793
	5	Inter	W	2-1	CLsf	Alex Silva [30], Ricardo Oliveira [54]	62 129
	8	Atlético PR	L	1-1	SA	Cleber Santana [63]	21 789
Aug	15	Cruzeiro	D	2-2	SA	Casimiro [41], Ricardo Oliveira [89]	12 338
	22	Corinthians	L	0-3	SA		28 159
	26	Vasco	D	0-0	SA		10 802
	29	Fluminense	D	2-2	SA	Rogerio Ceni [34], Fernandao [36]	25 518
	2	Atlético GO	W	2-1	SA	Xandao [24], Dagoberto [70]	9 364
	5	Atlético MG	W	3-2	SA	Casimiro [8], Lucas [55], Fernandao [60]	11 120
	9	Flamengo	W	2-0	SA	Marlos [8], Fernandao [42]	14 389
	12	Botafogo	L	0-2	SA		24 050
Sep	16	Inter	L	1-3	SA	Cleber Santana [20]	11 327
	19	Palmeiras	W	2-0	SA	Lucas [54], Fernandao [75]	16 009
	22	Guarani	W	2-1	SA	Marlos [14], Ricardo Oliveira [63]	10 264
	25	Goiás	L	0-3	SA		18 528
	30	Grêmio	L	2-4	SA	Rogerio Ceni [41p], Marlos [53]	25 322
Oct	2	Avaí	D	0-0	SA		8 040
	6	Vitória	W	2-0	SA	Dagoberto [17], Fernandinho [90]	14 364
	9	Grêmio Pr	W	3-2	SA	Ricardo Oliveira 3 [7 33 59]	12 969
	17	Santos	W	4-3	SA	Dagoberto 2 [7 16], OG [19], Jean [90]	23 791
	24	Ceará	L	0-2	SA		44 591
	28	Atlético PR	W	2-1	SA	Ricardo Oliveira [13], Miranda [51]	16 480
	3	Cruzeiro	W	2-0	SA	Lucas [53], Rogerio Ceni [80p]	25 694
	7	Corinthians	L	0-2	SA		42 667
Nov	14	Vasco	D	1-1	SA	Lucas Gaucho [70]	5 674
	21	Fluminense	L	1-4	SA	Lucas Gaucho [55]	14 410
	28	Atlético GO	D	1-1	SA	Rogerio Ceni [54p]	27 938
Dc	5	Atlético MG	W	4-0	SA	Ilsinho [27], Lucas [31], Marlos [42], Renato Silva [46]	9 782

VASCO DA GAMA 2010

Month	Date	Opponent	Res	Score	Comp	Scorers	Att
Jan	16	Tigres	W	1-0	TG	Fagner 38	13 433
	20	América	W	2-1	TG	Nilton 50, Carlos Alberto 81	4 244
	24	Botafogo	W	6-0	TG	Dodo 3 4 32 34, Leo Gago 55, Countinho 2 59 81	25 052
	28	Macaé	W	4-0	TG	Leo Gago 12, Rafael Coelho 31, Nilton 37, Magno Cruz 54	4 704
	31	Frib'guense	W	3-0	TG	Dodo 3 44 83 87	3 932
Feb	4	Resende	W	1-0	TG	Dodo 17p	4 974
	7	Mudureira	D	2-2	TG	Nilton 7, Thiago Martinelli 72	3 699
	10	Sousa	W	2-1	CBr1	Tiago 61p, Elton 91+	7 329
	13	Fluminense	D	0-0	TGsf	W 6-5p	36 481
	21	Botafogo	L	0-2	TGf		77 757
	24	Sousa	D	0-0	CBr1		1 294
	28	V Redonda	W	2-1	TR	Coutinho 39, Elton 75	1 967
Mar	3	Bangu	W	2-0	TR	Dodo 56, Fernando 91	1 471
	7	Boavista	W	1-0	TR	Carlos Alberto 70p	2 942
	14	Flamengo	L	0-1	TR		34 707
	17	ASA	D	1-1	CBr2	Coutinho 64p	3 087
	20	Olaria	L	0-1	TR		1 829
	24	Americano	L	2-3	TR	Elton 18, Leo Gago 43	1 543
	28	Fluminense	W	3-0	TR	Thiago Martinelli 58, Dodo 83, Fagner 90	17 469
	31	ASA	W	3-1	CBr2	Elton 2 18 67, Magno Cruz 71	2 204
Apr	4	Caxias	W	4-3	TR	Fagner 17, Elton 23, Dodo 2 50 82	2 206
	11	Flamengo	L	1-2	TRsf	Thiago Martinelli 30	29 382
	14	C'thians PR	W	1-0	CBr3	Leo Gago 67	1 462
	21	C'thians PR	W	2-1	CBr3	Elton 12, Carlos Alberto 87	11 798
	28	Vitória	L	0-2	CBqf		12 881
May	5	Vitória	W	3-1	CBqf	Magno Cruz 12, Ramon 58, Carlos Alberto 78p	14 221
	9	Atlético MG	L	1-2	SA	Elton 55	12 790
	16	Palmeiras	D	0-0	SA		8 765
	23	Avaí	L	0-2	SA		9 594
	27	Inter	W	3-2	SA	Elton 50, Coutinho 76p, Nilton 84	4 081
	30	Botafogo	D	1-1	SA	Ernani 26	16 368
Jun	3	Guarani	L	0-1	SA		6 002
	6	Santos	L	0-4	SA		8 585
	14	Goiás	D	0-0	SA		11 000
Jul	17	Atlético PR	W	3-1	SA	Jonathan 20, Nunes 25p, Leo Gago 62	5 976
	21	Grêmio	D	1-1	SA	Nunes 6	4 820
	24	Atlético GO	W	2-0	SA	Nilton 33, Fumagalli 53	13 157
Aug	1	Flamengo	D	0-0	SA		50 447
	8	Vitória	W	1-0	SA	Ze Roberto 22	14 062
	15	Grêmio Pr	W	2-1	SA	Eder Luis 5, Nilton 79p	5 047
	22	Fluminense	D	2-2	SA	Eder Luis 37, Fagner 48	66 757
	26	São Paulo	D	0-0	SA		10 802
	28	Cruzeiro	D	1-1	SA	Ze Roberto 44	13 691
Sep	4	Ceará	W	2-0	SA	Ze Roberto 7, Fellipe Bastos 80	19 528
	9	Atlético MG	D	1-1	SA	Eder Luis 37	6 536
	12	Palmeiras	D	0-0	SA		15 313
	16	Avaí	D	1-1	SA	Ramon 24	6 299
	19	Inter	L	0-1	SA		30 981
	22	Botafogo	D	2-2	SA	Ramon 14, Eder Luis 37	16 736
	25	Guarani	L	0-1	SA		4 294
	28	Santos	W	3-1	SA	Fagner 31, Felipe 37, Eder Luis 90	2 819
Oct	3	Goiás	W	3-2	SA	Eder Luis 26, Max 63, Ze Roberto 63	6 805
	7	Atlético PR	D	0-0	SA		16 161
	9	Grêmio	D	3-3	SA	Eder Luis 16, Cesinha 45, Fellipe Bastos 79	13 651
	14	Corinthians	W	2-0	SA	Ze Roberto 9, Eder Luis 21	9 285
	17	Atlético GO	L	0-2	SA		14 175
	24	Flamengo	D	1-1	SA	Cesinha 29	21 519
	30	Vitória	L	2-4	SA	Nunes 49, Fumagalli 90	31 449
Nov	4	Grêmio Pr	W	2-1	SA	Romulo 2 29 32	2 474
	7	Fluminense	L	0-1	SA		16 263
	14	São Paulo	D	1-1	SA	Eder Luis 61	5 674
	21	Cruzeiro	L	1-3	SA	Renato Augusto 44	16 228
	28	Corinthians	L	0-2	SA		33 487
Dec	5	Ceará	W	2-0	SA	Dede 32, OG 46	2 989

VITORIA 2010

Month	Date	Opponent	Res	Score	Comp	Scorers	Att
Jan	17	Camaçari	W	2-1	TB	Neto Berola 27, Edson 78	8 385
	20	Itabuna	L	0-1	TB		7 359
	24	Bahia	W	2-0	TB	Schwenck 50, Ramon 88	21 871
	27	Ipitanga	W	4-1	TB	Ramon 2 10p 44p, Indio 12, Schwenck 49	2 302
	31	Fluminense	D	2-2	TB	Ramon 67p, Bida 78	5 499
Feb	3	Feirense	W	1-0	TB	Wallace 69	4 998
	7	Feirense	W	3-0	TB	Ramon 2 5 31p, Adailton 89	2 293
	18	Fluminense	W	3-1	TB	Ueliton 45, Ramon 55p, Adailton 45	5 811
	21	Ipitanga	W	4-0	TB	Jose Junior 2 42 92+, Adailton 86, Elkeson 90	5 288
	24	C'thians AL	L	1-3	CBr1	Ramon 79	872
	28	Bahia	L	1-2	TB	Schwenck 27	21 744
Mar	3	Itabuna	W	1-0	TB	Ramon 61p	1 329
	7	Camaçari	W	3-0	TB	Jose Junior 2 55 79, Ueliton 90	1 841
	10	C'thians AL	W	4-0	CBr1	Jose Junior 44, Renato 72, Ueliton 78, Viafara 82	13 917
	14	Bahia Feira	L	0-2	TB		3 070
	17	Náutico	W	1-0	CBr2	Bida 83	3 854
	21	Atlético	W	4-0	TB	Jose Junior 4 20 23 27 67	6 818
	24	Conquista	W	3-0	TB	Jose Junior 61, Egidio 81, Viafara 81p	6 861
	28	Conquista	W	1-0	TB	Wallace 87	5 023
	31	Náutico	W	5-0	CBr2	Ramon 26, Jose Junior 36, Nino Paraiba 45, Elkeson 60, Renato 86	12 071
Apr	4	Atlético	D	1-1	TB	Marconi 39	4 787
	7	Bahia Feira	W	3-1	TB	Ramon 6, Jose Junior 18, Ueliton 26	5 501
	11	Camaçari	D	2-2	TBsf	Ramon 61, Wallace 84	2 991
	15	Goiás	W	4-0	CBr3	Ramon 68, Jose Junior 74, Bida 76, Schwenck 91+	8 746
	18	Camaçari	D	1-1	TBsf	Murilo 90	12 832
	22	Goiás	D	2-2	CBr3	Ueliton 16, Jose Junior 41	2 107
	25	Bahia	W	1-0	TBf	Jose Junior 79	33 883
	28	Vasco	W	2-0	CBqf	Renato 39, Neto Berola 84	12 881
May	2	Bahia	L	1-2	TBf	Elkeson 20	27 582
	5	Vasco	L	1-3	CBqf	Viafara 27p	14 221
	8	Palmeiras	L	0-1	SA		6 025
	12	Atlético GO	L	0-1	CBsf		6 367
	15	Flamengo	D	1-1	SA	Elkeson 86	14 862
	19	Atlético GO	W	4-0	CBsf	Ueliton 30, Junior 2 32 89, Viafara 90	32 891
	23	Ceará	L	0-1	SA		19 697
	26	Atlético MG	W	4-3	SA	Schwenck 3 12 40 73, Evandro 88	6 692
	29	Avaí	D	0-0	SA		6 178
Jun	2	Fluminense	L	1-2	SA	Jonas 84	25 430
	5	Atlético PR	W	1-0	SA	Schwenck 80	9 109
	9	Grêmio	D	1-1	SA	Wallace 33	8 359
	17	São Paulo	W	3-2	SA	Elkeson 13, Schwenck 46, Ramon 57	11 915
Jul	21	Goiás	D	2-2	SA	Ricardo Conceicao 45, Soares 89	9 568
	24	Grêmio Pr	D	0-0	SA		4 922
	28	Santos	L	0-2	CBf		14 060
Aug	1	Botafogo	L	1-3	SA	Jose Junior 82	8 217
	4	Santos	W	2-1	CBf	Wallace 57, Jose Junior 77	28 978
	8	Vasco	L	0-1	SA		14 062
	11	Palmeiras	W	2-0	CSr1	Ramon 48, Neto Coruja 88	
	15	Santos	W	4-2	SA	Henrique 2 20 45, Wallace 26, Schwenck 72p	10 648
	19	Palmeiras	L	0-3	CSr1		
	22	Cruzeiro	W	1-0	SA	Jose Junior 53	10 195
	26	Guarani	D	1-1	SA	Jose Junior 12	6 338
	29	Corinthians	L	1-2	SA	Kleber Pereira 82	36 142
Sep	1	Inter	D	0-0	SA		8 040
	5	Atlético GO	L	1-4	SA	Elkeson 70	2 323
	9	Palmeiras	D	1-1	SA	Elkeson 9	6 543
	11	Flamengo	D	2-2	SA	Jose Junior 68, Schwenck 81	3 895
	16	Ceará	D	0-0	SA		9 082
	19	Atlético MG	W	3-2	SA	Viafara 3p, Egidio 15, Henrique 74	13 144
	23	Avaí	W	3-0	SA	Jose Junior 2, Elkeson 57, Thiago Humberto 76	11 184
	26	Fluminense	L	1-2	SA	Henrique 61	11 187
	29	Atlético PR	L	0-1	SA		15 791
Oct	2	Grêmio	L	0-3	SA		10 998
	6	São Paulo	L	0-2	SA		14 364
	10	Goiás	L	0-1	SA		1 806
	17	Grêmio Pr	W	2-0	SA	Viafara 40p, Jose Junior 69	27 199
	23	Botafogo	L	0-1	SA		10 041
	30	Vasco	W	4-2	SA	Adailton 2, Elkeson 41, Neto Coruja 45, Jose Junior 54	31 449
Nov	3	Santos	D	1-1	SA	Neymar 33	4 643
	7	Cruzeiro	L	0-1	SA		34 540
	14	Guarani	D	1-1	SA	Adailton 78	6 051
	21	Corinthians	D	1-1	SA	Viafara 43p	37 468
	28	Inter	D	1-1	SA	Adailton 51	22 444
Dec	5	Atlético GO	D	0-0	SA		35 000

SANTOS 2010 (cont'd from page 235)

Month	Date	Opponent	Res	Score	Comp	Scorers	Att
Nov	3	Vitória	D	1-1	SA	Neymar 33	4 643
	6	Atlético MG	D	2-2	SA	Neymar 2 8 67	16 771
	13	Grêmio	D	0-0	SA		7 421
	20	Goiás	W	4-1	SA	Danilo 20, Neymar 3 76p 79 83	2 865
	28	Avaí	L	2-3	SA	Keirrison 9, Neymar 31	17 136
Dec	5	Flamengo	D	0-0	SA		9 086

BRB – BARBADOS

FIFA/COCA-COLA WORLD RANKING

1993	1994	1995	1996	1997	1998	1999	2000	2001	2002	2003	2004	2005	2006	2007	2008	2009	2010
114	107	103	110	113	121	113	104	107	99	124	121	115	98	128	122	129	131

					2010							Hi/Lo
Jan	Feb	Mar	Mar	Apr	May	Jul	Aug	Sep	Oct	Nov	Dec	**92**
129	128	141	137	135	135	128	127	121	107	120	131	**152**

Barbados went into their 2010 Digicel Caribbean Cup qualifying group on the back of two surprising home defeats in friendly matches at the hands of Dominica and while that may not have instilled confidence for the trip to Kingstown in St Vincent where the group was held, the Bajans were very unfortunate not to progress. Having drawn their opening match with St Kitts and Nevis, Barbados then thumped rank outsiders Montserrat 5-0. Their final match against the hosts in a packed Victoria Park, saw five players sent-off in a bad tempered game but although a 0-0 draw gave Barbados five points along with both St Kitts and St Vincent, they were the ones to lose out. With all matches between the three ending in draws, St Kitts qualified on the head-to-head rule having scored a goal more than Barbados and St Vincent. Goals difference was then used to divide the teams and thanks to their 7-0 win over Montserrat, the hosts made it through. At home, Notre Dame secured a second championship in three years although Brittons Hill put up a spirited defence of their title. Despite Notre Dame winning 11 of their first 13 matches it wasn't until they beat Brittons Hill 2-1 with four rounds to go that they could be sure of the title. Two months later a Kyle Gibson hat trick in a 4-0 Cup Final win against Ellerton secured the double for Notre Dame.

FIFA WORLD CUP RECORD
1930-1974 DNE 1978 DNQ 1982-1990 DNE 1994-2010 DNQ

BARBADOS FOOTBALL ASSOCIATION (BFA)

Richmond Welches,
✉ PO Box 1362, Bridgetown,
St Michael, BB 11000
☎ +1 246 2281707
📠 +1 246 2286484
📧 bdosfootball@caribsurf.com
🖥 www.barbadossoccer.com
FA 1910 CON 1968 FIFA 1968
P Ronald Jones
GS Charles Husbands

FIFA BIG COUNT 2006

Total players	37 550
% of population	13.41%
Male	33 590
Female	3 960
Amateurs 18+	7 095
Youth under 18	8 505
Unregistered	18 710
Professionals	0
Referees	86
Admin & coaches	1 240
Number of clubs	130
Number of teams	240

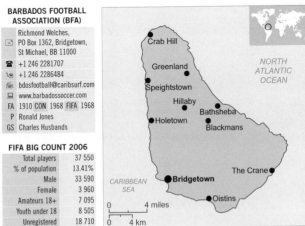

MAJOR CITIES/TOWNS

		Population
1	Bridgetown	93 312
2	Speightstown	2 402
3	Bathsheba	1 575
4	Holetown	1 494
5	Oistins	1 444
6	Bulkeley	1 115
7	Crane	1 016
8	Crab Hill	716
9	Blackmans	550
10	Greenland	524
11	Hillaby	509

BARBADOS

Capital	Bridgetown	Population	284 589 (180)	% in cities	40%
GDP per capita	$19 100 (66)	Area km²	430 km² (200)	GMT +/-	-4
Neighbours (km)	Coast 97				

RECENT INTERNATIONAL MATCHES PLAYED BY BARBADOS

2006	Opponents	Score		Venue	Comp	Scorers	Att	Referee
2-09	Guyana	L	0-1	Bridgetown	Fr		2 000	Forde BRB
10-09	St Vincent/Grenadines	D	1-1	Bridgetown	Fr	Parris 51		Small BRB
17-09	Dominica	W	5-0	Roseau	Fr	Lovell 2 27 57, Goodridge 42p, Williams 75, Marshall 80	900	Charles DMA
20-09	St Kitts and Nevis	D	1-1	St John's	CCq	Ifill 42	300	Campbell JAM
22-09	Antigua & Barbuda	W	3-1	St John's	CCq	Williams 44, McCammon 58, Lovell 90	2 500	Frederick VIR
24-09	Anguilla	W	7-1	St John's	CCq	McCammon 3 35 44 76, Ifill 3 40 58 83, Niblett 75	2 800	Wijngaarde SUR
5-11	Grenada	D	2-2	Black Rock	Fr	Parris 28, Goodridge 67p		
19-11	Bahamas	W	2-1	Bridgetown	CCq	Forde.N 38, Skinner 44	4 500	Jauregui ANT
21-11	St Vincent/Grenadines	W	3-0	Bridgetown	CCq	James 16, Forde.N 34, Ifill 60p	3 500	Jauregui ANT
23-11	Bermuda	D	1-1	Bridgetown	CCq	Ifill 4	4 000	Jauregui ANT
2007								
12-01	Trinidad and Tobago	D	1-1	Port of Spain	CCr1	Harvey 66		Moreno PAN
15-01	Haiti	L	0-2	Port of Spain	CCr1			Jauregua ANT
17-01	Martinique	L	2-3	Port of Spain	CCr1	Harvey 27, Soares 42		Jauregua ANT
25-03	Guatemala	D	0-0	Bridgetown	Fr		2 500	Forde BRB
2008								
13-01	Antigua & Barbuda	W	3-2	Black Rock	Fr	Vaughan 17, Straker 39, Lynch 63	2 700	Small BRB
6-02	Dominica	D	1-1	Roseau	WCq	Rashida Williams 43	4 200	Quesada CRC
13-03	St Vincent/Grenadines	W	2-0	Kingstown	Fr	Stanford 38, Norman Forde 87	1 050	Cambridge VIN
15-03	Grenada	D	1-1	St George's	Fr	Worrell 75	2 500	Phillip GRN
26-03	Dominica	W	1-0	Bridgetown	WCq	Stanford 80	4 150	Batres GUA
11-05	Trinidad and Tobago	L	0-3	Macoya	Fr		1 200	Brizan TRI
6-06	Bermuda	L	1-2	Hamilton	Fr	Norman Forde 44	2 000	Raynor BER
9-06	Bermuda	L	0-3	Hamilton	Fr		2 200	Francis BER
15-06	USA	L	0-8	Carson	WCq		11 500	Rodriguex MEX
22-06	USA	L	0-1	Bridgetown	WCq		2 000	Moreno PAN
26-09	British Virgin Isles	W	2-1	Basseterre	CCq	Rashida Williams 11, Norman Forde 53	150	Baptiste DMA
28-09	St Kitts and Nevis	W	3-1	Basseterre	CCq	Straker 35, Skeete 45, Rashida Williams 80	500	Charles DMA
23-10	Surinam	W	3-2	Havana	CCq	Norman Forde 3 62 65 70	100	Morrison JAM
25-10	Cuba	D	1-1	Havana	CCq	Doyle 66	1 000	Campbell JAM
27-10	Netherlands Antilles	W	2-1	Havana	CCq	Norman Forde 6p, Parris 20	1 000	Morrison JAM
3-12	Jamaica	L	1-2	Kingston	CCr1	Riviere Williams 45	20 000	Aguilar SLV
5-12	Trinidad and Tobago	L	1-2	Montego Bay	CCr1	Goodridge 17	2 000	Jauregui ANT
7-12	Grenada	L	2-4	Trelawny	CCr1	Riviere Williams 2 71 79	9 000	Aguilar SLV
2009								
8-02	Grenada	W	5-0	Bridgetown	Fr	Jeffrey Williams 2 35 68, Stanford 43, Harte 44, Chandler 88	3 000	Forde BRB
2010								
25-09	Dominica	L	0-2	Bridgetown	Fr		625	Taylor BRB
26-09	Dominica	L	1-3	Bridgetown	Fr	Harte 21	580	Skeete DMA
6-10	St Kitts and Nevis	D	1-1	Kingstown	CCq	Rashida Williams 14	250	Elskampr SUR
8-10	Montserrat	W	5-0	Kingstown	CCq	Norman Forde 2 19 83, Riviere Williams 36, Terry Adamson 53, Kadeem Atkins 90	350	Pinas SUR
10-10	St Vincent/Grenadines	D	0-0	Kingstown	CCq		5 420	Jauregui ANT

Fr = Friendly match • CC = Digicel Caribbean Cup • WC = FIFA World Cup • q = qualifier • r1 = first round group

BARBADOS 2010

DIGICEL PREMIER LEAGUE

	Pl	W	D	L	F	A	Pts	Notre Dame	Brittons Hill	Youth Milan	Weymouth W	Gall Hill	Paradise	Ellerton	Pinelands	Silver Sands	BDF
Notre Dame	17	13	2	2	32	11	41		0-1	4-0	0-0	1-0	1-1	0-2	2-1	1-0	3-0
Brittons Hill	17	11	2	4	28	12	35	1-2		0-1	2-1	0-0	1-0	4-1	2-1	3-0	2-0
Youth Milan	17	10	2	5	33	19	32	1-2	2-0		0-2	1-0	0-0	5-1	3-2	1-0	3-0
Weymouth Wales	17	8	4	5	25	15	28	1-2	2-1	0-1		1-2	1-1	3-1	4-0	1-1	3-0
Pride of Gall Hill	17	8	3	6	18	12	27	0-2	0-0	1-0	0-1		0-1	2-1	1-1	3-0	3-0
Paradise	17	3	8	6	14	16	17	0-2	1-3	3-1	1-2	0-1		0-1	0-0	1-1	3-0
Ellerton	17	3	7	7	20	31	16	2-3	1-3	1-1	1-1	1-3	1-1		0-0	1-0	1-1
Pinelands	17	3	5	9	16	30	14	1-2	0-2	2-4	1-0	1-0	0-0	1-1		1-2	3-0
Silver Sands	17	2	4	11	16	37	10	0-4	0-3	1-6	1-2	1-2	1-1	3-3	2-4		3-0
Bar'dos Defence Force	9	1	1	7	3	22	4	0-1	0-3	0-6	0-3	0-3	0-3	0-3	2-0	0-3	

14/02/2010 - 23/05/2010 • Barbados Defence Force withdrew at the halfway point. All their remaining matches were awarded as 3-0 defeats

BARBADOS 2010
DIVISION ONE

	Pl	W	D	L	F	A	Pts
Bagatelle	22	15	6	1	53	13	51
St John's Sonnets	22	15	6	1	37	12	51
Dayrells Road	22	15	4	3	39	10	49
Univ. of West Indies	22	12	2	8	36	22	38
St Peter's Cosmos	22	9	6	7	26	20	33
Clarkes Hill	22	8	7	7	26	15	31
Benfica	22	5	8	9	28	34	23
Haynesville	22	6	5	11	30	46	23
Maxwell	22	6	4	12	24	49	22
Technico	22	4	5	13	23	45	17
Eden Stars	22	4	5	13	26	49	17
Haggatt Hall	22	3	2	17	22	55	11

17/02/2010 - 23/05/2010

SUPER 8 TOURNAMENT

Quarter-finals		Semi-finals		Final	
Brittons Hill	7				
Empire	1	Brittons Hill			
L&R United	1	St John Sonnets			
St John Sonnets	4			Brittons Hill	0 3p
Deacons	4			Notre Dame	0 1p
Bagatelle	1	Deacons		13-06-2010	
Trents	0	Notre Dame			
Notre Dame	2	3rd Place: Sonnets 4-0 Deacons			

Played between the top two teams from the Premier League, Division One, Division Two and Division Three

FA CUP 2010

Round of 16		Quarter-finals		Semi-finals		Final	
Notre Dame	1						
Deacons	0	Notre Dame	3				
Paradise	2	Shawn Hope United	2				
Shawn Hope United	3			Notre Dame	1		
Carlton	3			Brittons Hill	0		
Belfield	0	Carlton	1				
Horse Hill	1	Brittons Hill	4			Notre Dame	4
Brittons Hill	2					Ellerton	0
Sunrise	6						
Villa United	1	Sunrise	8				
Univ. of West Indies	1 3p	Lodge Road	0				
Lodge Road	1 4p			Sunrise	3		
Silver Sands	2			Ellerton	4		
Pinelands	1	Silver Sands	1				
Gall Hill	0	Ellerton	2				
Ellerton	2						

CUP FINAL

National Stadium, Waterford
4-07-2010

Scorers - Kyle Gibson 3 [6] [51] [53], Ricky Barnes [26]

BRU – BRUNEI DARUSSALAM

FIFA/COCA-COLA WORLD RANKING

1993	1994	1995	1996	1997	1998	1999	2000	2001	2002	2003	2004	2005	2006	2007	2008	2009	2010
151	165	167	170	178	183	185	193	189	194	194	199	199	175	188	181	191	197

2010												Hi/Lo
Jan	Feb	Mar	Mar	Apr	May	Jul	Aug	Sep	Oct	Nov	Dec	**140**
191	191	191	189	193	189	187	187	185	186	197	197	**199**

Brunei's footballers continue to exist on the outside of the global game with the country still suspended by FIFA from taking part in any matches outside of Brunei Darussalam. The dispute had even threatened to lead to the expulsion of Brunei from FIFA at the Congress held in Johannesburg prior to the World Cup finals. The issue stems from the disbanding of the Football Association of Brunei Darussalam by the government and the establishment in its place of the Football Federation of Brunei Darussalam. The move ran contrary to FIFA's statutes and, as a result, Brunei's involvement in all football outside of the country has come to a halt. The BAFA has been deregistered and the FFBD is likely to apply for membership of FIFA, leading to the creation of a new entity that will serve as an associate member of FIFA for two years before gaining voting rights and full membership. The national side has not played since the qualifying rounds of the AFC Challenge Cup in April 2009 while the suspension also saw club side DPMM forced to withdraw from Singapore's S-League in late 2009. Domestically, however, the Brunei Premier League restarted after not being held in the 2008-09 season with QAF winning the title as they did on the last two previous occasions the tournament was held, finishing two points ahead of cup winners ABDB.

FIFA WORLD CUP RECORD

1930-1982 DNE   1986 DNQ   1990-1998 DNE   2002 DNQ   2006-2010 DNE

THE FOOTBALL ASSOCIATION OF BRUNEI DARUSSALAM (BAFA)

Stadium Negara Hassanal Bolkiah, PO Box 2010, Bandar Seri Begawan, BB 4313, Brunei

☎ +673 2 382761
📠 +673 2 456358
✉ bruneifasg@yahoo.com
🖥 www.bafa.org.bn
FA 1959 CON 1970 FIFA 1969
P TBD
GS TBD

FIFA BIG COUNT 2006

Total players	7 500
% of population	1.98%
Male	7 300
Female	200
Amateurs 18+	300
Professionals	0
Referees	33
Admin & coaches	100
Number of clubs	20
Number of teams	40

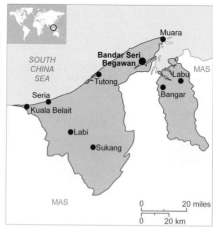

MAJOR CITIES/TOWNS

		Population
1	Bandar S Begawan	33 026
2	Kuala Belait	27 726
3	Seria	27 620
4	Tutong	20 962
5	Bangar	3 501

NEGARA BRUNEI DARUSSALAM • BRUNEI DARUSSALAM

Capital	Bandar Seri Begawan	Population	388 190 (175)	% in cities	75%
GDP per capita	$53 100 (8)	Area km²	5 765 km² (172)	GMT +/-	+8
Neighbours (km)	Malaysia 381 • Coast 161				

RECENT INTERNATIONAL MATCHES PLAYED BY BRUNEI DARUSSALAM

2006	Opponents	Score	Venue	Comp	Scorers	Att	Referee
12-11	Timor Leste	W 3-2	Bacolod	AFFq	Adie Mohammed Salleh 2 [11] [70], Hardi Bujang [66]		
16-11	Cambodia	D 1-1	Bacolod	AFFq	Hardi Bujang [90]		
18-11	Laos	L 1-4	Bacolod	AFFq	Riwandi Wahit [20]		
20-11	Philippines	L 1-4	Bacolod	AFFq	Kamarul Ariffin Ramlee [81]		
2007							
No international matches played in 2007							
2008							
13-05	Philippines	L 0-1	Iloilo City	CCq		3 500	Saleem MDV
15-05	Bhutan	D 1-1	Barotac	CCq	Muhammad Khayrun Bin Salleh [76]	4 000	Mahapab THA
17-05	Tajikistan	L 0-4	Iloilo City	CCq		450	Al Badwawi UAE
19-10	Philippines	D 1-1	Phnom Penh	AFFq	Shahraezn Said [17]	12 000	
21-10	Timor-Leste	W 4-1	Phnom Penh	AFFq	Shahraezn Said 2 [9] [26], Azwan Saleh [57], Sallehuddin Damit [76p]		
23-10	Laos	L 2-3	Phnom Penh	AFFq	Hardi Bujang [28], Abu Bakar Mahari [84]		
25-10	Cambodia	L 1-2	Phnom Penh	AFFq	Hardi Bujang [28],	15 000	
2009							
4-04	Sri Lanka	L 1-5	Colombo	CCq	Kamarul Ariffin Ramlee [82]	700	Zhao Liang CHN
6-04	Pakistan	L 0-6	Colombo	CCq		200	Orzuev TJK
8-04	Chinese Taipei	L 0-5	Colombo	CCq		1 000	Al Zahrani KSA
2010							
No international matches played in 2010							

CC = AFC Challenge Cup • AFF = ASEAN Championship • q = qualifier

BRUNEI DARUSSALAM 2009–10

DST GROUP PREMIER LEAGUE

	Pl	W	D	L	F	A	Pts	QAF	ABDB	Gunners	Jerudong	Majra	Indera	AH United	Wijaya	NBT	Brunei Shell
QAF	18	15	2	1	60	16	**47**		1-1	5-0	3-2	3-2	1-0	2-1	7-1	6-1	10-0
ABDB	18	14	3	1	57	13	**45**	3-1		2-0	1-1	4-0	2-1	7-0	3-0	5-1	1-0
AM Gunners	18	13	3	2	52	22	**42**	2-2	2-1		1-1	2-1	4-2	6-0	4-1	1-0	4-0
Jerudong	18	8	5	5	36	28	**29**	1-2	1-1	1-5		1-2	3-2	1-1	2-1	2-0	5-2
Majra	18	9	0	9	43	39	**27**	1-3	0-2	1-4	4-1		1-2	4-3	2-1	3-0	6-3
Indera	18	7	1	10	24	31	**22**	1-3	2-4	1-1	0-3	0-2		2-1	1-0	2-0	1-2
AH United	18	5	1	12	29	58	**16**	0-2	0-11	1-3	1-2	1-5	0-2		7-2	3-2	4-2
Wijaya	18	4	2	12	24	49	**14**	0-1	1-4	1-2	0-4	5-3	1-4	4-1		2-2	2-1
NBT ‡	18	2	3	13	19	54	**9**	0-6	0-2	1-6	1-4	2-5	3-0	1-4	0-0		4-2
Brunei Shell	18	2	2	14	20	54	**8**	0-2	2-3	1-5	1-1	2-1	0-1	0-1	1-2	1-1	

25/05/2009 - 28/02/2010 • ‡ Relegation play-off. NBT 1-5 Penjara. NBT relegated

FA CUP 2010

Round of 16		Quarter–finals		Semi–finals		Final	
ABDB	8						
Brunei Shell	1	**ABDB**	3				
Lun Bawang		Jerudong	2				
Jerudong				**ABDB**	2		
Indera	3			AM Gunners	1		
Penjara	2	Indera	1				
AH United	2	**AM Gunners**	2			**ABDB**	2
AM Gunners	5					QAF	1
NBT	1						
Penjara	0	**NBT**	4				
Perkasa	3	Kilanas	2			**CUP FINAL**	
Kilanas	4			NBT	1	National Stadium	
LLRC	2			**QAF**	7	17-04-2010	
Muara Vella	1	LLRC	0			Scorers - Amalul Ariffin [28], Rosmin Kamis [42] for ABDB; Vivan Francis Bayong [61] for QAF	
Wijaya	0	**QAF**	3				
QAF	5						

BUL – BULGARIA

FIFA/COCA-COLA WORLD RANKING

1993	1994	1995	1996	1997	1998	1999	2000	2001	2002	2003	2004	2005	2006	2007	2008	2009	2010
31	16	17	15	36	49	37	53	51	42	34	37	39	43	18	27	30	49

	2010											Hi/Lo
Jan	Feb	Mar	Mar	Apr	May	Jul	Aug	Sep	Oct	Nov	Dec	8
30	30	30	38	39	39	43	43	54	43	45	49	58

After the worst possible start to the qualifiers for Euro 2012 - a heavy defeat away to England followed by an embarrassing home defeat at the hands of Montenegro - Stanimir Stoilov was replaced as national team coach by Lothar Matthaus. Even with a victory over Wales in his first match in charge, the 1990 World Cup winning captain will have his work cut out to take the team to the finals in Poland and the Ukraine and he will also have to do it without star striker Dimitar Berbatov, who after becoming Bulgaria's leading all-time goalscorer decided to quit the national team just two goals shy of the half-century mark. At home, Litex Lovech comfortably won the championship for the third time in their history following their triumphs in 1998 and 1999, but what made the 2009-10 season so notable was the absence of trophies for clubs from the capital Sofia. Only once before in the history of Bulgarian football - in 2004 - had teams from Sofia failed to win a trophy. They were also absent from the Cup Final for the third year running which in 2010 was won by Beroe Stara Zagora, a team promoted to the top level only the season before. With just one previous honour to their name, Beroe completed a great year for the underdogs, an injury-time goal by Doncho Atanasov beating second division Chernomorets Pomorie.

FIFA WORLD CUP RECORD
1930-1938 DNQ 1950 DNE 1954-1958 DNQ **1962** 15 r1 **1966** 15 r1 **1970** 13 r1 **1974** 12 r1
1978-1982 DNQ **1986** 12 r2 1990 DNQ **1994** 4 SF **1998** 29 r1 2002-2010 DNQ

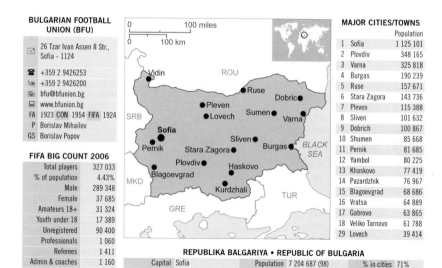

BULGARIAN FOOTBALL UNION (BFU)

26 Tzar Ivan Assen II Str., Sofia - 1124

☎ +359 2 9426253
📠 +359 2 9426200
✉ bfu@bfunion.bg
🖥 www.bfunion.bg
FA 1923 CON 1954 FIFA 1924
P Borislav Mihailov
GS Borislav Popov

FIFA BIG COUNT 2006

Total players	327 033
% of population	4.43%
Male	289 348
Female	37 685
Amateurs 18+	31 324
Youth under 18	17 389
Unregistered	90 400
Professionals	1 060
Referees	1 411
Admin & coaches	1 160
Number of clubs	559
Number of teams	1 301

MAJOR CITIES/TOWNS

		Population
1	Sofia	1 125 101
2	Plovdiv	348 165
3	Varna	325 818
4	Burgas	190 239
5	Ruse	157 671
6	Stara Zagora	143 736
7	Pleven	115 388
8	Sliven	101 632
9	Dobrich	100 867
10	Shumen	85 668
11	Pernik	81 685
12	Yambol	80 225
13	Khaskovo	77 419
14	Pazardzhik	76 967
15	Blagoevgrad	68 686
16	Vratsa	64 889
17	Gabrovo	63 865
18	Veliko Tarnovo	61 788
29	Lovech	39 414

REPUBLIKA BALGARIYA • REPUBLIC OF BULGARIA

Capital	Sofia	Population	7 204 687 (98)	% in cities	71%
GDP per capita	$12 900 (85)	Area km²	110 879 km² (104)	GMT +/-	+2
Neighbours (km)	Greece 494, Macedonia 148, Romania 608, Serbia 318, Turkey 240 • Coast 354				

RECENT INTERNATIONAL MATCHES PLAYED BY BULGARIA

2007	Opponents	Score		Venue	Comp	Scorers	Att	Referee
22-08	Wales	L	0-1	Burgas	Fr		15 000	Germanakos GRE
8-09	Netherlands	L	0-2	Amsterdam	ECq		49 500	Cantalejo ESP
12-09	Luxembourg	W	3-0	Sofia	ECq	Berbatov 2 [27 28], Petrov.M [54p]	4 674	Demirlek TUR
17-10	Albania	D	1-1	Tirana	ECq	Berbatov [87]	3 000	Stuchlik AUT
17-11	Romania	W	1-0	Sofia	ECq	Dimitrov.V [6]	6 000	Plautz AUT
21-11	Slovenia	W	2-0	Celje	ECq	Georgiev [82], Berbatov [84]	3 700	Webb ENG
2008								
6-02	Northern Ireland	W	1-0	Belfast	Fr	Evans OG [38]	11 000	McDonald SCO
26-03	Finland	W	2-1	Sofia	Fr	Lazarov [49], Guenchev [90]	2 500	Tudor ROU
20-08	Bosnia-Hercegovina	W	2-1	Zenica	Fr	Berbatov 2 [26 57]	7 000	Stankovic SRB
6-09	Montenegro	D	2-2	Podgorica	WCq	Petrov.S [11], Georgiev [92+]	9 000	Oriekhov UKR
11-10	Italy	D	0-0	Sofia	WCq		35 000	Lannoy FRA
15-10	Georgia	D	0-0	Tbilisi	WCq		35 250	Kuipers NED
19-11	Serbia	L	1-6	Belgrade	Fr	Georgiev [20]	6 000	Sippel GER
2009								
11-02	Switzerland	D	1-1	Geneva	Fr	Popov [34]	9 500	Duarte POR
28-03	Republic of Ireland	D	1-1	Dublin	WCq	Kilbane OG [74]	60 002	Bebek CRO
1-04	Cyprus	W	2-0	Sofia	WCq	Popov [8], Makriev [94+]	16 916	Ingvarsson SWE
6-06	Republic of Ireland	D	1-1	Sofia	WCq	Telkiyski [29]	38 000	Larsen DEN
12-08	Latvia	W	1-0	Sofia	Fr	Rangelov [54]	2 000	Pamporidis GRE
5-09	Montenegro	W	4-1	Sofia	WCq	Kishishev [45], Telkiyski [49], Berbatov [83], Domovchiyski [91+]	7 543	Asumaa FIN
9-09	Italy	L	0-2	Turin	WCq		26 122	Meyer GER
10-10	Cyprus	L	1-4	Larnaca	WCq	Berbatov [44]	3 700	Allaerts BEL
14-10	Georgia	W	6-2	Sofia	WCq	Berbatov 3 [6 23 35], Petrov.M 2 [14 44], Angelov [31]	700	Jakobsson ISL
18-11	Malta	W	4-1	Paola	Fr	Bozhinov [5], Berbabtov 2 [76 83], Georgiev [81]		Nijhuis NED
2010								
3-03	Poland	L	0-2	Warsaw	Fr		6 800	Kever SUI
19-05	Belgium	L	1-2	Brussels	Fr	Popov [31]	15 000	Weiner GER
24-05	South Africa	D	1-1	Johannesburg	Fr	Bojinov [31]	25 000	Fagla TOG
11-08	Russia	L	0-1	St. Petersburg	Fr		8 200	Rizzoli ITA
3-09	England	L	0-4	London	ECq		73 426	Kassai HUN
7-09	Montenegro	L	0-1	Sofia	ECq		9 470	Bezborodov RUS
8-10	Wales	W	1-0	Cardiff	ECq	Popov [48]	14 061	Eriksson SWE
12-10	Saudi Arabia	W	2-0	Istanbul	Fr	Rangelov [39], Domovchiyski [44]	100	Gocek TUR
17-11	Serbia	L	0-1	Sofia	Fr		1 500	Avram ROU

Fr = Friendly match • EC = UEFA EURO 2008/2012 • WC = FIFA World Cup • q = qualifier

BULGARIA NATIONAL TEAM HISTORICAL RECORDS

Caps
102 - Borislav Mihaylov 1983-98 • 98 - Stilian Petrov 1998- • 96 - Hristo Bonev 1967-79 • 92 - Krasimir Balakov 1988-2003 • 90 - Dimitar Penev 1965-74 • 87 - Martin Petrov 1999- • 83 - Hristo Stoichkov 1986-99 & Radostin Kishishev 1996-2009 • 80 - Zlatko Yankov 1989-99 • 79 - Anyo Sadkov 1981-91 • 78 - Dimitar Berbatov 1999- & Nasko Sirakov 1983-96 • 77 - Georgi Dimitrov 1978-87

Goals
48 - Dimitar Berbatov 1999- • 47 - Hristo Bonev 1967-79 • 37 - Hristo Stoichkov 1986-99 • 26 - Emil Kostadinov 1988-98 • 25 - Lyubomir Angelov 1931-40, Ivan Kolev 1950-63 & Petar Jekov 1963-72 • 23 - Nasko Sirakov 1983-96 • 20 - Dimitar Milanov 1948-59 • 19 - Georgi Asparukov 1962-70 & Dinko Dermendjiev 1966-77 • 18 - Martin Petrov 1999- • 16 - Krasimir Balakov 1988-2003 & Todor Diev 1955-65

Past Coaches
Leopold Nich AUT 1924 • Willibold Scheiscal AUT 1925 • Pavel Grozdanov 1927-30 • Carl Nemes 1930 AUT • Otto Feist GER 1931 • Pavel Grozdanov 1932-33 • Karoly Foggle HUN 1934-35 • Nikola Kalkandzhiev 1935 • Ivan Batandzhiev 1936 • Geno Mateev 1936 • Stanislav Toms CZE 1937-38 • Kostantin Maznikov 1938 • Ivan Radoev 1939 • Franz Koler AUT 1940-41 • Ivan Radoev 1942 • Ivan Batandzhiev 1943 • Todor Konov 1946 • Mihail Manov 1947 • Rezso Somlaly HUN • Ivan Radoev 1947 • Ivan Radoev 1947 • Lubomir Angelov 1948 • Andor Haidu HUN 1948-49 • Ivan Radoev 1950 • Lubomir Angelov 1950 • Andor Haidu HUN 1950 • Lubomir Angelov 1953 • Stoyan Ormandzhiev 1950-53 • Stoyan Ormandzhiev & Krum Milev 1954-60 • Georgi Pachedzhiev 1955-62 • Stoyan Ormandzhiev 1963 • Bella Volentik HUN 1963-64 • Rudolf Vytlacil CZE 1965-66 • Dobromir Tashkov 1966 • Stefan Bozhkov 1967-70 • Vasil Spasov 1970-72 • Hristo Mladenov 1972-74 • Stoyan Ormandzhiev 1974-77 • Cvetan Ilchev 1978-80 • Atanas Purzhelov 1980-82 • Ivan Vutsov 1982-86 • Hristo Mladenov 1986-87 • Boris Angelov 1988-89 • Ivan Vutsov 1989-91 • Krasimir Borisov 1991 • Dimitar Penev 1991-96 • Hristo Bonev 1996-98 • Dimitar Dimitrov 1998-99 • Stoycho Mladenov 2000-01 • Plamen Markov 2002-04 • Hristo Stoichkov 2004-07 • Stanimir Stoilov 2007 • Dimitar Penev 2007 • Plamen Markov 2008 • Stanimir Stoilov 2009-10 • Lothar Matthaus GER 2010-

BULGARIA 2009–10

'A' PFG

	Pl	W	D	L	F	A	Pts	Litex Lovech	CSKA Sofia	Levski Sofia	Lokomotiv S	Chernomorets	Slavia Sofia	Cherno More	Minyor Pernik	Pirin	Beroe	Montana	Lokomotiv Pl	Sliven	Lokomotiv M	Sportist	Botev Plovdiv
Litex Lovech †	30	22	4	4	59	17	**70**		2-0	3-0	2-0	2-0	1-0	4-0	1-0	0-1	3-0	3-0	5-0	1-0	3-0	2-0	2-1
CSKA Sofia ‡	30	16	10	4	51	25	**58**	1-0		2-0	5-1	0-0	2-0	2-2	0-3	1-1	3-0	1-1	3-2	1-0	4-0	4-1	3-0
Levski Sofia ‡	30	17	6	7	57	26	**57**	2-2	0-0		1-2	0-1	3-0	3-0	3-1	2-0	0-1	3-1	2-0	2-0	3-1	5-0	5-0
Lokomotiv Sofia	30	15	7	8	47	33	**52**	0-1	2-2	2-0		0-1	0-0	1-2	1-1	1-0	2-0	0-0	3-0	2-0	2-1	3-2	2-2
Chernomorets Burgas	30	15	6	9	44	29	**51**	1-2	2-0	1-1	0-2		2-2	2-1	3-1	2-1	0-2	1-1	2-1	2-0	3-0	3-0	2-0
Slavia Sofia	30	14	8	8	34	28	**50**	1-1	1-3	1-3	0-0	3-2		1-0	1-0	0-0	3-1	4-0	1-3	2-1	1-0	1-0	3-0
Cherno More Varna	30	13	9	8	40	28	**48**	0-0	0-0	1-1	4-2	2-0	1-1		1-0	1-1	0-0	2-1	3-2	4-0	2-0	3-0	3-0
Minyor Pernik	30	13	6	11	38	26	**45**	0-1	0-0	0-2	1-2	2-0	0-1	1-0		0-1	3-0	1-1	0-0	4-2	1-0	1-2	3-0
Pirin Blagoevgrad	30	11	10	9	34	32	**43**	4-1	0-0	0-2	1-1	1-3	1-0	1-0	0-1		2-2	2-0	0-0	2-0	3-1	2-0	3-0
Beroe Stara Zagora ‡	30	10	8	12	30	36	**38**	3-0	0-0	1-3	2-1	1-1	0-1	0-0	0-3	1-1		0-0	0-1	0-1	1-0	1-0	3-1
Montana	30	9	9	12	30	37	**36**	0-0	1-2	0-2	0-1	2-0	2-0	1-2	0-0	0-3	2-1		2-3	0-0	1-1	1-0	3-0
Lokomotiv Plovdiv	30	9	6	15	36	52	**33**	0-3	0-5	2-2	2-1	2-1	0-2	1-0	3-3	2-0	1-3	2-4		1-2	0-1	3-0	3-0
Sliven 2000	30	9	5	16	29	40	**32**	1-2	2-4	1-0	1-3	0-1	1-2	0-0	1-3	4-0	1-1	1-0	1-1		1-0	1-0	3-0
Lokomotiv Mezdra	30	7	6	17	30	48	**27**	0-5	**4-0**	1-1	1-2	0-5	0-0	1-2	0-1	4-0	2-1	0-2	0-0	1-1		2-1	2-2
Sportist Svoge	30	5	4	21	23	59	**19**	2-4	0-2	2-3	1-5	0-0	1-1	2-1	0-1	1-1	1-2	0-1	2-1	1-0	0-4		3-0
Botev Plovdiv	30	1	4	25	12	78	**7**	**0-3**	0-1	**0-3**	**0-3**	0-1	**0-3**	0-3	2-2	**0-3**	2-3	1-0	**0-3**	**0-3**	1-1		

7/08/2009 – 16/05/2010 • † Qualified for the UEFA Champions League • ‡ Qualified for the Europa League • Botev excluded after 15 games
Top scorers: **19** – Wilfried Niflore FRA, Litex • **16** – Martin Kamburov, Lokomotiv Sofia • **12** – Jose Junior BRA, Slavia • **11** – Hristo Yovov, Levski • **10** – Ismail Isa, Lokomotiv Mezdra & Deyan Hristov, Sliven • **9** – Georgu Andonov, Beroe; Miroslav Antonov, Sportist/Levski

BULGARIA 2009–10
WESTERN 'B' PFG (2)

	Pl	W	D	L	F	A	Pts
Vidima-Rakovski	30	19	3	8	53	32	**60**
Akademik 1947 Sofia †	30	18	5	7	49	37	**59**
Bansko 1951	30	17	8	5	50	22	**59**
Vihren Sandanski	30	16	8	6	45	24	**56**
Etar Veliko Tarnovo	30	13	8	9	47	38	**47**
Botev Vratsa	30	11	12	7	39	26	**45**
Septemvri Simitli	30	13	4	13	40	34	**43**
Chavdar Etropole	30	12	7	11	34	32	**43**
Balkan Botevgrad	30	9	14	7	35	28	**41**
Marek Dupnitsa	30	12	5	13	35	36	**41**
Pirin Gotse Delchev	30	11	7	12	35	38	**40**
Kom Minyor Berkovitsa	30	10	8	12	36	43	**38**
Botev Krivodol	30	8	7	15	21	40	**31**
Rilski sportist Samokov	30	8	6	16	32	49	**30**
Bdin Vidin	30	4	8	18	26	47	**20**
Belite orli Pleven	30	2	4	24	20	71	**10**

8/08/2009 – 15/05/2010 • † Play-off

BULGARIA 2009–10
EASTERN 'B' PFG (2)

	Pl	W	D	L	F	A	Pts
Kaliakra Kavarna	28	17	6	5	44	20	**57**
Nesebar †	28	17	6	5	56	24	**57**
Dunav Ruse	28	16	6	6	48	29	**54**
Spartak Plovdiv	28	13	8	7	36	24	**47**
Lyubimets	28	12	9	7	39	24	**45**
Brestnik Plovdiv	28	13	6	9	42	29	**45**
Chernomorets Pomorie	28	13	4	11	45	36	**43**
Chernomorets Balchik	28	12	6	10	37	30	**42**
Spartak Varna	28	11	4	13	33	41	**37**
Panayot Volov Shumen	28	9	6	13	37	39	**33**
Svetkavitsa Targovishte	28	8	8	12	28	31	**32**
Svilengrad	28	10	1	17	36	58	**31**
Dobrudzha Dobrich	28	8	6	14	27	39	**30**
Minyor Radnevo	28	8	6	14	34	46	**30**
Rodopa Smolyan	28	1	2	25	6	78	**5**

7/08/2009 – 15/05/2010 • † Play-off
Promotion play-off: Nesebar 1-2 **Akademik**

MEDALS TABLE

		Overall			League			Cup		SAC		Europe		
		G	S	B	G	S	B	G	S	G	S	G	S	B
1	Levski Sofia	51	39	8	26	30	8	12	5	13	4			
2	CSKA Sofia	49	32	6	31	20	3	9	6	9	6			3
3	Slavia Sofia	14	11	13	7	9	12	1		6	2			1
4	Lokomotiv Sofia	8	8	9	4	6	9	1		3	2			
5	Litexs Lovech	7	4	2	3	1	2	4	3					
6	Botev Plovdiv	4	10	11	2	2	11			4		2	4	
7	Cherno More Varna	4	8	3	4	6	3	2						
8	Spartak Sofia	3	4					2		2		1	2	
9	Beroe Stara Zagora	2	4	1	1		1	1		4				
10	Spartak Plovdiv	2	3		1	1				1	2			
11	AC 23 Sofia	2			1			1						
12	Lokomotiv Plovdiv	1	5	4	1	1	4			4				
13	Spartak Varna	1	4	1	1	2	1	1				1		

KUPA NA BULGARIYA 2009-10

Second Round

Beroe Stara Zagara	1	
Montana *	0	
Sportist Svoge	0	
Lokomotiv Mezdra *	3	
Litex Lovech	4	
Pirin Gotse Delchev *	0	
Svilengrad *	0	
CSKA Sofia	1	
Slavia Sofia	0	4p
Vihren Sandanski *	0	3p
Botev Plovdiv	1	
Lokomotiv Sofia *	2	
Maritsa Plovdiv *	3	
Minyor Radnevo	1	
Rilski sportist Samokov *	0	
Chavdar Etropole	2	
Kaliakra Kavarna *	2	
Lokomotiv Plovdiv	0	
Belite orli Pleven	0	
Marek Dupnitsa *	2	
Levski sofia	2	
Brestnik Plovdiv *	0	
Chernomorets Burgas *	0	
Cherno More Varna *	2	
Minyor Pernik *	0	5p
Septemvri Simitli *	0	4p
Pirin Blagoevgrad	0	
Sliven 2000 *	1	
Botev Vratsa *	2	
Chernomorets Balchik	0	
Dunav Ruse	0	
Chernomorets Pomories *	3	

Round of 16

Beroe Stara Zagara	3	
Lokomotiv Mezdra *	0	
Litex Lovech	0	
CSKA Sofia *	1	
Slavia Sofia	2	
Lokomotiv Sofia *	1	
Maritsa Plovdiv *	0	
Chavdar Etropole	1	
Kaliakra Kavarna	5	
Marek Dupnitsa *	1	
Levski sofia	1	
Cherno More Varna *	4	
Minyor Pernik *	1	
Sliven 2000	0	
Botev Vratsa	0	
Chernomorets Pomories *	1	

Quarter-finals

Beroe Stara Zagara *	1	
CSKA Sofia	0	
Slavia Sofia	0	2p
Chavdar Etropole *	0	4p
Kaliakra Kavarna *	0	3p
Cherno More Varna	0	2p
Minyor Pernik	0	
Chernomorets Pomories *	2	

Semi-finals

Beroe Stara Zagara	1	
Chavdar Etropole *	0	
Kaliakra Kavarna *	1	0p
Chernomorets Pomories	1	3p

Final

Beroe Stara Zagara ‡	1	
Chernomorets Pomories	0	

CUP FINAL

Gradski, Lovech

5-05-2010, 18:00, Att: 5250, Ref: Yordanov
Scorer - Doncho Atanasov 92+

Beroe - Boyan Peikov - Zdravko Iliev, Ivo Ivanov, Stanislav Bachev, Atanas Atanasov (Todor Todorov 46) - Petar Kostadinov, Dian Genchev (Nikolai Stankov 71), Iskren Pisarov, Slavi Zhekov - Doncho Atanasov, Georgi Andonov. Tr: Ilian Iliev

Chernomorets - Yanko Georgiev - Miroslav Koev, Plamen Dimov, Velkov, Orachev - Emanuil Manev, Georgi Kostadinov●, Georgi Chakarov (Galin Dimov 89), Tsvetan Filipov (Venelin Filipov) - Stanimir Mitev, Yani Pehlivanov. Tr: Petar Houbchev

'A' PFG teams enter at the second round ● * Home team ● ‡ Qualified for the Europa League

CAM – CAMBODIA

FIFA/COCA-COLA WORLD RANKING

1993	1994	1995	1996	1997	1998	1999	2000	2001	2002	2003	2004	2005	2006	2007	2008	2009	2010
-	-	180	186	170	162	168	169	169	176	178	184	188	174	183	178	175	

	2010												Hi/Lo
	Jan	Feb	Mar	Mar	Apr	May	Jul	Aug	Sep	Oct	Nov	Dec	**156**
	175	173	172	171	171	185	180	178	178	182	170	166	**188**

New coach Lee Tae Hoon from Korea Republic took over at the helm of the Cambodia national team from Australian Scott O'Donnell in 2010 but he was unable to steer his new charges into the final phase of the AFF Suzuki Cup. The Cambodians finished third in the four-team qualifying group that was staged in Vientiane, narrowly losing out to the Philippines and hosts Laos in their quest to appear at the finals of the regional competition. The Cambodians had made it through the qualifiers in 2008 but were denied a place in the 2010 finals on goal-difference. Scoreless draws in all three games between Cambodia, Laos and the Philippines meant it all came down to who scored the most goals against Timor-Leste. With the Philippines having won 5-0, Laos secured their passage to the finals with a 6-1 victory - significantly better than the 4-2 win the Cambodians had achieved. In club football Phnom Penh Crown regained their league title from Nagacorp, beating their rivals in the play-off semi-finals. In the final they then beat Preah Khan Reach in an exciting game with two late goals in a 4-3 victory. There was also an exciting climax to the Cup final with Crown looking to have forced extra-time against Defence Ministry with a last minute equaliser only to concede a goal deep into injury-time.

FIFA WORLD CUP RECORD
1930-1994 DNE 1998-2002 DNQ 2006 DNE 2010 DNQ

CAMBODIAN FOOTBALL FEDERATION (CFF)

National Football Centre, Road Kabsrov, Sangkat Samrongkrom, Khan Dangkor, Phnom Penh 2327 PPT3

☎ +855 23 364889
🖷 +855 23 223537
✉ info@the-ffc.com
🖵 ffcambodia.com

FA	1933	CON	1957	FIFA	1953
P	Sokha Sao				
GS	Sethycheat Ouk				

FIFA BIG COUNT 2006

Total players	229 511
% of population	1.65%
Male	229 411
Female	100
Amateurs 18+	1 600
Unregistered	6 000
Professionals	11
Referees	70
Admin & coaches	160
Number of clubs	65
Number of teams	420

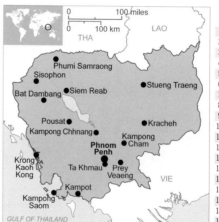

MAJOR CITIES/TOWNS

		Population
1	Phnom Penh	1 438 317
2	Bat Dâmbâng	182 574
3	Preah Sihanouk	148 139
4	Siem Reab	131 497
5	Kâmpóng Chhnang	86 876
6	Prey Veaeng	64 659
7	Kâmpóng Cham	61 814
8	Pousat	53 622
9	Phumi Takaev	52 422
10	Ta Khmau	49 443
11	Dong Tong	38 524
12	Phumi Sâmraông	34 494
13	Kâmpóng Spoeu	32 782
14	Stueng Traeng	29 665
15	Sisophon	26 364
16	Phumi Sâmraông	26 201
17	Tbeng Mean Chey	25 286
18	Svay Rieng	25 002
19	Kâmpôt	21 601

PREAHREACHEANACHAKR KAMPUCHEA • KINGDOM OF CAMBODIA

Capital	Phnom Penh	Population	14 494 293 (65)	% in cities	22%
GDP per capita	$2000 (187)	Area km²	181 035 km² (89)	GMT + / -	+7
Neighbours (km)	Laos 541, Thailand 803, Vietnam 1228 • Coast 443				

RECENT INTERNATIONAL MATCHES PLAYED BY CAMBODIA

2006	Opponents		Score	Venue	Comp	Scorers	Att	Referee
14-11	Laos	D	2-2	Bacolod	AFFq	Teab Vadhanak [50], Hem Samchay [75]		
16-11	Brunei Darussalam	D	1-1	Bacolod	AFFq	Samel Nasa [79]		
18-11	Philippines	L	0-1	Bacolod	AFFq			
20-11	Timor Leste	W	4-1	Bacolod	AFFq	Hem Samchay [37], Teab Vadhanak [58], Chan Rithy 2 [82 86]		
2007								
18-06	Malaysia	L	0-6	Kuala Lumpur	Fr			
17-08	India	L	0-6	New Delhi	Fr			
19-08	Kyrgyzstan	L	3-4	New Delhi	Fr	Hok Sotitya [34], Chan Rithy [40], Chin Chum [43]		
22-08	Bangladesh	D	1-1	New Delhi	Fr	Keo Kasal [90]		
25-08	Syria	L	1-5	New Delhi	Fr	Teab Vadhanak [69]		
11-10	Turkmenistan	L	0-1	Phnom Penh	WCq		3 000	Gosh BAN
28-10	Turkmenistan	L	1-4	Ashgabat	WCq	Samel Nasa [12]	5 000	Saidov UZB
2008								
26-05	Nepal	L	0-1	Phnom Penh	CCq		3 000	Torky IRN
28-05	Macau	W	3-1	Phnom Penh	CCq	Nuth Sinoun 2 [30 92+], Chan Rithy [67]	3 000	Kurbanov TKM
21-08	Indonesia	L	0-7	Jakarta	Fr			
22-08	Myanmar	L	1-7	Jakarta	Fr	Khim Borey [18p]		
17-10	Laos	W	3-2	Phnom Penh	AFFq	Khim Borey [24], Samel Nasa [45], Sun Sovannarith [55]		
19-10	Timor-Leste	D	2-2	Phnom Penh	AFFq	Khim Borey [78p], Sun Sovannarith [80]		
23-10	Philippines	L	2-3	Phnom Penh	AFFq	Samel Nasa 2 [14 44]		
25-10	Brunei Darussalam	W	2-1	Phnom Penh	AFFq	Samel Nasa [45], Khim Borey [73]		
5-12	Singapore	L	0-5	Jakarta	AFFr1		18 000	Mahapab THA
7-12	Indonesia	L	0-4	Jakarta	AFFr1		30 000	Abdul Wahab MAS
9-12	Myanmar	L	2-3	Bandung	AFFr1	Kouch Sokumpheak [40], Khim Borey [77]		Martinez PHI
2009								
26-04	Bangladesh	L	0-1	Dhaka	CCq		8 060	Yazdi IRN
28-04	Macau	W	2-1	Dhaka	CCq	Teab Vathanak [12], Keo Sokngon [66]	6 000	Saleem MDV
30-04	Myanmar	L	0-1	Dhaka	CCq		2 500	Yazdi IRN
2010								
22-10	Laos	D	0-0	Vientiane	AFFq			Abdul Wahab MAS
24-10	Timor-Leste	W	4-2	Vientiane	AFFq	Khim Borey 3 [26 29 40], Nuth Sinoun [75]		Phung VIE
26-10	Philippines	D	0-0	Vientiane	AFFq			Abdul Wahab MAS

Fr = Friendly match • AFF = ASEAN Football Federation Championship • CC = AFC Challenge Cup • WC = FIFA World Cup • r1 = first round group

CAMBODIA 2010

PREMIER LEAGUE FIRST STAGE

	Pl	W	D	L	F	A	Pts	Naga Corp	Build Bright	Preah Khan	PP Crown	Kirivon	Defence	Khemara Keila	Prek Pra Keila	Wat Phnom	Chhma Khmao
Naga Corp ‡	18	13	4	1	52	22	43		1-0	2-1	2-2	1-0	2-2	4-3	5-0	3-1	7-0
Build Bright United ‡	18	12	3	3	50	21	39	1-1		2-1	1-3	1-4	2-1	5-1	4-1	6-0	4-1
Preah Khan Reach ‡	18	12	2	4	54	26	38	2-2	2-2		3-1	1-0	3-1	2-3	3-1	3-2	6-0
Phnom Penh Crown ‡	18	10	6	2	56	22	36	4-0	1-1	3-1		2-3	1-1	1-1	2-1	8-1	9-1
Kirivon Sok Sen Chey	18	11	0	7	46	22	33	1-2	1-2	0-1	0-1		2-1	3-1	5-0	6-1	4-2
Defence Ministry	18	6	4	8	39	28	22	0-1	1-2	1-4	1-1	4-0		2-1	0-0	0-1	5-1
Khemara Keila	18	5	3	10	30	45	18	0-2	1-2	3-6	2-2	0-2	3-2		0-3	0-3	6-4
Prek Pra Keila	18	3	3	12	26	52	12	1-2	1-4	1-5	2-3	0-3	2-4	2-2		2-2	3-1
Wat Phnom	18	3	2	13	28	67	11	4-9	0-3	1-5	1-3	2-4	0-6	0-2	6-3		3-3
Chhma Khmao	18	1	1	16	18	94	4	0-6	0-8	1-5	0-9	0-8	2-7	0-1	1-3	1-0	

27/03/2010 – 8/08/2010 • ‡ Qualified for the championship play-offs

CHAMPIONSHIP PLAY–OFFS

Semi-finals			Finals	
Phnom Penh Crown	4			
Naga Corp	2		**Phnom Penh Crown** †	4
Build Bright United	1		Preah Khan Reach	3
Preah Khan Reach	2			

† Qualified for the AFC President's Cup
Final: National Olympic, Phnom Penh, 21-08-2010, Att: 10 000
Scorers - Keo Songan 2 [17] [88], Srey Veasna [53], Hong Makara [81] for Crown;
Khuon Laboravy [7], Tum Saray [33], Sam El Nasa [90] for Preah Khan
3rd place play-off: Build Bright United 2-2 5-3p Naga Corp

HUN SEN CUP 2010

Round of 16		Quarter–finals		Semi–finals		Final	
Defence Ministry	0 4p						
Koh Kong	0 3p	**Defence Ministry**	9				
Kirivon Sok Sen Chey	2	Rithy San	1				
Rithy Sen	4			**Defence Ministry**	1		
Khemara Keila	5			Preah Khan Reach	0		
Prek Pra Keila	0	Khemara Keila	0				
Oddar Meanchey	0	**Preah Khan Reach**	3				
Preah Khan Reach	5					**Defence Ministry**	3
Naga Corp	6					Phnom Penh Crown	2
Chhma Khmao	2	**Naga Corp**	6				
Prey Veng	0	Build Bright United	0				
Build Bright United	7			Naga Corp	3 3p		
Wat Phnom	10			**Phnom Penh Crown**	3 4p		
Mekong Kampuchea U	1	Wat Phnom	1				
Phuchung Neak	0	**Phnom Penh Crown**	5				
Phnom Penh Crown	1			Third place: Preah Khan Reach 3-2 Naga Corp			

CUP FINAL

Defence Ministry 3
Phnom Penh Crown 2

National Olympic, Phnom Penh,
7-03-2010
Scorers - Sin Dalin [26], Chhin
Chhoeun [65], Thong Oudom [93+] for
Defence; Heng Sok Ly [39],
Chan Rithy [89] for Crown

CAN – CANADA

FIFA/COCA-COLA WORLD RANKING

1993	1994	1995	1996	1997	1998	1999	2000	2001	2002	2003	2004	2005	2006	2007	2008	2009	2010
44	63	65	40	66	101	81	63	92	70	87	90	84	82	55	90	56	84

	2010												Hi/Lo
Jan	Feb	Mar	Mar	Apr	May	Jul	Aug	Sep	Oct	Nov	Dec		40
56	57	62	64	63	63	100	101	88	83	85	84		103

With Vancouver Whitecaps as the latest edition to Major League Soccer and with Montreal Impact set to join for the 2012 season, Canadian soccer looks on course to emulate the 1970s and 80s when Vancouver, Toronto and Montreal represented the country with distinction in the old NASL. Toronto have yet to qualify for the play-offs in their first four seasons in MLS but their fans have established themselves as amongst the most loyal in the league, with BMO Field filled to capacity for most games. 2010 also saw the club take part in the CONCACAF Champions League for the second year running and although they beat Motagua from Honduras in the qualifying round for the 2010-11 tournament, they narrowly failed to advance to the knockout rounds after finishing third behind Real Salt Lake and Cruz Azul in the group stage. Toronto had qualified by winning the three team Nutrilite Canadian Championship ahead of Vancouver and Montreal and although billed as the Canadian championship its role is primarily to choose the Canadian representatives for the CONCACAF Champions League. In preparation for the 2011 CONCACAF Gold Cup in the USA, Stephen Hart was given the role of national team coach after having held the position on an interim basis as the Canadians look to improve on their quarter-final finish in 2009.

FIFA WORLD CUP RECORD
1930-1954 DNE **1958** DNQ **1962-1966** DNE **1970-1982** DNQ **1986** 24 r1 **1990-2010** DNQ

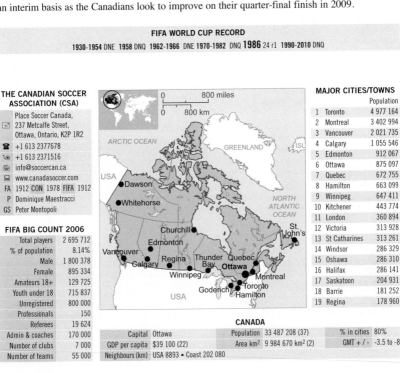

THE CANADIAN SOCCER ASSOCIATION (CSA)

Place Soccer Canada,
237 Metcalfe Street,
Ottawa, Ontario, K2P 1R2

☎ +1 613 2377678
📠 +1 613 2371516
✉ info@soccercan.ca
🖥 www.canadasoccer.com
FA 1912 CON 1978 FIFA 1912
P Dominique Maestracci
GS Peter Montopoli

FIFA BIG COUNT 2006

Total players	2 695 712
% of population	8.14%
Male	1 800 378
Female	895 334
Amateurs 18+	129 725
Youth under 18	715 837
Unregistered	800 000
Professionals	150
Referees	19 624
Admin & coaches	170 000
Number of clubs	7 000
Number of teams	55 000

MAJOR CITIES/TOWNS

		Population
1	Toronto	4 977 164
2	Montreal	3 402 994
3	Vancouver	2 021 735
4	Calgary	1 055 546
5	Edmonton	912 067
6	Ottawa	875 097
7	Quebec	672 755
8	Hamilton	663 099
9	Winnipeg	647 411
10	Kitchener	443 774
11	London	360 894
12	Victoria	313 928
13	St Catharines	313 261
14	Windsor	286 329
15	Oshawa	286 310
16	Halifax	286 141
17	Saskatoon	204 931
18	Barrie	181 252
19	Regina	178 960

CANADA

Capital	Ottawa	Population	33 487 208 (37)	% in cities	80%
GDP per capita	$39 100 (22)	Area km²	9 984 670 km² (2)	GMT +/-	-3.5 to -8
Neighbours (km)	USA 8893 • Coast 202 080		

RECENT INTERNATIONAL MATCHES PLAYED BY CANADA

2006	Opponents	Score		Venue	Comp	Scorers	Att	Referee
4-09	Jamaica	W	1-0	Montreal	Fr	Friend [41]	6 526	Quesada CRC
8-10	Jamaica	L	1-2	Kingston	Fr	Radzinski [8]	5 000	Brizan TRI
15-11	Hungary	L	0-1	Szekesfehervar	Fr		6 000	Weiner GER
2007								
25-03	Bermuda	W	3-0	Hamilton	Fr	Hutchinson [25], Radzinski [30], Stalteri [44]	2 500	Raynor BER
1-06	Venezuela	D	2-2	Maracaibo	Fr	De Rosario [5], Gerba [85]	20 000	Lopez COL
6-06	Costa Rica	W	2-1	Miami	GCr1	Deguzman 2 [57 73]	17 420	Wingaarde SUR
9-06	Guadeloupe †	L	1-2	Miami	GCr1	Gerba [35]	22 529	Brizan TRI
11-06	Haiti	W	2-0	Miami	GCr1	De Rosario 2 [32 35p]	15 892	Rodriguez MEX
16-06	Guatemala	W	3-0	Foxboro	GCqf	De Rosario [17], Gerba 2 [33 44]	22 412	Campbell JAM
21-06	USA	L	1-2	Chicago	GCsf	Hume [76]	50 760	Archundia MEX
22-08	Iceland	D	1-1	Reykjavík	Fr	Occean [75]	4 359	Asumaa FIN
12-09	Costa Rica	D	1-1	Toronto	Fr	De Rosario [53]	9 325	Marrufo USA
20-11	South Africa	L	0-2	Durban	Fr		23 000	Kalyoyo MWI
2008								
26-03	Estonia	L	0-2	Tallinn	Fr		1 600	Zuta LTU
31-05	Brazil	L	2-3	Seattle	Fr	Friend [10], De Guzman [56]	47 052	Stott USA
4-06	Panama	D	2-2	Sunrise	Fr	Peters [20], Jazic [82]	BCD	
15-06	St Vincent/Grenadines	W	3-0	Kingstown	WCq	Nakjima-Farran [29], Gerba 2 [29 89]	6 500	Batres GUA
22-06	St Vincent/Grenadines	W	4-1	Montreal	WCq	De Rosario 2 [29 50], Gerba 2 [38 63]	11 500	Aguilar SLV
20-08	Jamaica	D	1-1	Toronto	WCq	De Guzman [47]	22 000	Batres GUA
6-09	Honduras	L	1-2	Montreal	WCq	Serioux [5]	13 032	Quesada CRC
10-09	Mexico	L	1-2	Tuxtla Gutierrez	WCq	Gerba [78]	26 900	Brizan TRI
11-10	Honduras	L	1-3	San Pedro Sula	WCq	Hainault [52]	35 000	Marrufo USA
15-10	Mexico	D	2-2	Edmonton	WCq	Gerba [13], Radzinski [50]	14 145	Wijngaarde SUR
19-11	Jamaica	L	0-3	Kingston	WCq		28 000	Aguilar SLV
2009								
30-05	Cyprus	W	1-0	Larnaca	Fr	Jackson [53]	200	Kenan ISR
30-06	Guatemala	W	3-0	Oxnard	Fr	Gerba 2 [4 67p], Bernier [55]	200	Singh USA
3-07	Jamaica	W	1-0	Carson	GCr1	Gerba [75]	27 000	Vaughn USA
7-07	El Salvador	W	1-0	Columbus	GCr1	Gerba [32]	7 059	Garcia MEX
10-07	Costa Rica	D	2-2	Miami	GCr1	Bernier [25], De Jong [28]	17 269	Vaughn USA
18-07	Honduras	L	0-1	Philadelphia	GCqf		31 987	Aguilar SLV
14-11	Macedonia FYR	L	0-3	Strumica	Fr		6 000	Genov BUL
18-11	Poland	L	0-1	Bydgoszcz	Fr		10 400	Christoffersen DEN
2010								
31-01	Jamaica	L	0-1	Kingston	Fr		18 000	Hospedales TRI
24-05	Argentina	L	0-5	Buenos Aires	Fr		60 000	Rivera PER
29-05	Venezuela	D	1-1	Merida	Fr	McCallum [90]	20 000	Buitrago COL
4-09	Peru	L	0-2	Toronto	Fr		10 619	Jurisevic USA
7-09	Honduras	W	2-1	Montreal	Fr	Simpson [29], McKenna [42]	7 525	Geiger USA
8-10	Ukraine	D	2-2	Kyiv	Fr	Jackson [13], Hutchinson [29]	10 000	Mikulski POL

Fr = Friendly match • GC = CONCACAF Gold Cup • WC = FIFA World Cup • † Not a full international
q = qualifier • r1 = first round group • qf = quarter-final • sf = semi-final

CANADA NATIONAL TEAM HISTORICAL RECORDS

Caps

84 - Paul Staltieri 1997- • **82** - Randy Samuel 1983-97 • **77** - Mark Watson 1991-2004 • **66** - Lyndon Hooper 1986-97 • **64** - Alex Bunbury 1986-97 • **61** - Nick Dasovic 1992-2004, Colin Miller 1983-97 & Mike Sweeney 1980-93 • **59** - Carlo Corazzin 1994-2004 & Richard Hastings 1998- • **57** - Pat Onstad 1988- & Bruce Wilson 1974-86 • **55** - Dwayne DeRosario 2000-, Craig Forrest 1988-2001 & Dale Mitchell 1980-93 • **53** - Paul Peschisolido 1992-2004 • **52** - Paul Dolan 1984-97 & Frank Yallop 1990-97 • **51** - Dave Norman 1983-94

Goals

19 - John Catliff 1984-94 & Dale Mitchell 1980-93 • **16** - Alex Bunbury 1986-97 • **15** - Dwayne DeRosario 2000- & Ali Gerba 2005- • **12** - Igor Vrablic 1984-86 • **11** - Carlo Corazzin 1994-2004 & Paul Peschisolido 1992-2004 • **10** - Tomasz Radzinski 1995- & Kevin McKenna 2000-

Past Coaches

Don Petrie 1957 • Peter Dinsdale ENG 1968-70 • Frank Pike ENG 1970-73 • Bill McAllister 1973 • Eckhard Krautzun GER 1973-75 • Bill McAllister 1975 • Eckhard Krautzun GER 1975-77 • Barrie Clarke 1978-81 • Tony Waiters ENG 1981-86 • Bob Bearpark ENG 1986-87 • Tony Taylor SCO 1988-89 • Bob Lenarduzzi 1989-90 • Tony Waiters ENG 1990-91 • Bob Lenarduzzi 1992-97 • Bruce Twamley 1998 • Holger Osieck GER 1999-2003 • Colin Miller 2003 • Frank Yallop 2004-06 • Stephen Hart TRI 2006-07 • Dale Mitchell 2007-09 • Stephen Hart TRI 2009-

CANADA 2010

NUTRILITE CANADIAN CHAMPIONSHIP (1)

	Pl	W	D	L	F	A	Pts	Toronto	Whitecaps	Impact
Toronto FC †	4	2	2	0	3	0	**8**		0-0	2-0
Vancouver Whitecaps	4	0	4	0	2	2	**4**	0-0		1-1
Montreal Impact	4	0	2	2	2	5	**2**	0-1	1-1	

28/04/2010 - 2/06/2010 • † Qualified for the CONCACAF Champions League

CANADA 2010
CANADIAN SOCCER LEAGUE PLAY-OFFS

Quarter-finals

Brantford Galaxy	0 1
Serbian White Eagles	0 0
Milltown	0 2
Portugal FC	1 2
Toronto Croatia	2 1
York Region Shooters	0 1
Toronto FC Academy	1 0
Hamilton Croatia	2 1

Semi-finals

Brantford Galaxy	5
Portugal FC	3
Toronto Croatia	0
Hamilton Croatia	2

Final

Brantford Galaxy	3
Hamilton Croatia	0

Centennial, Etobicoke, 31-10-2010
Scorers - Haris Fazlagic 2 [22] [66], Ranko Golijanin [60] for Galaxy

TORONTO FC 2010

Apr	27	Columbus	L	0-2	MLS	13 536
	10	NE Revs	L	1-4	MLS De Rosario [29]	12 798
	15	Philadelphia	W	2-1	MLS De Rosario 2 [35] [81p]	21 978
	18	Colorado	L	1-3	MLS De Rosario [58p]	9 928
	25	Seattle	W	2-0	MLS De Rosario [58], White [76]	18 394
	28	Montreal	W	2-0	CC Harden [12], Barrett [61]	21 346
May	1	Salt Lake	L	1-2	MLS De Rosario [88p]	12 659
	8	Chicago	W	4-1	MLS LaBrocca [25], White [47], Barrett 2 [66] [69]	20 060
	12	Montreal	W	1-0	CC De Rosario [73]	10 737
	15	LA Galaxy	D	0-0	MLS	20 007
	19	Vancouver	D	0-0	CC	4 928
	22	NE Revs	W	1-0	MLS Barrett [52]	20 672
	29	San Jose	W	3-1	MLS Barrett [31], De Rosario 2 [66] [90]	10 214
Jun	2	Vancouver	D	0-0	CC	15 176
	5	Kansas City	D	0-0	MLS	21 583
	26	LA Galaxy	D	0-0	MLS	18 809
	1	Houston	D	1-1	MLS Gargan [84]	21 374
	10	Colorado	W	1-0	MLS Ibrahim [61]	21 836
Jul	17	Philadelphia	L	1-2	MLS Barrett [81]	17 251
	24	Dallas	D	1-1	MLS Maicon [61]	19 743
	27	Motagua	W	1-0	CLpr	
	31	Kansas City	L	0-1	MLS	10 385
	3	Motagua	D	2-2	CLpr	
	7	Chivas	W	2-1	MLS Attakora-Gyan [21], Barrett [32]	20 648
	11	New York	L	0-1	MLS	19 035
Aug	17	Cruz Azul	W	2-1	CLgA	
	21	New York	L	1-4	MLS De Rosario [49]	22 108
	24	Arabe Un	L	0-1	CLgA	
	28	Salt Lake	D	0-0	MLS	21 047
	4	Dallas	L	0-1	MLS	10 033
	8	Chicago	D	0-0	MLS	12 891
	11	DC United	L	0-1	MLS	20 395
Sep	15	Salt Lake	L	1-4	CLgA	
	18	Houston	W	2-1	MLS De Rosario 2 [60] [90]	16 435
	21	Cruz Azul	D	0-0	CLgA	
	25	San Jose	L	2-3	MLS De Rosario [66], Maicon [80]	20 064
	28	Salt Lake	D	1-1	CLgA	
	2	Seattle	L	2-3	MLS De Rosario [17], Barrett [88]	36 079
	9	Chivas	L	0-3	MLS	12 426
Oct	16	Columbus	D	2-2	MLS Maicon [29], Peterson [38]	18 084
	19	Arabe Un	W	1-0	CLgA	
	23	DC United	W	3-2	MLS Maicon [23], De Rosario 2 [48] [65]	18 071

CANADA 2009
CANADIAN SOCCER LEAGUE (2) FIRST ROUND

	Pl	W	D	L	F	A	Pts
York Region Shooters ‡	24	13	7	4	45	29	**46**
Serbian White Eagles ‡	24	12	9	3	40	16	**45**
Hamilton Croatia ‡	24	13	5	6	51	27	**44**
Milltown ‡	24	12	7	5	43	22	**43**
Portugal FC ‡	24	11	5	8	46	39	**38**
TFC Academy ‡	24	10	8	6	32	27	**38**
Brantford Galaxy ‡	24	9	5	10	45	51	**32**
Toronto Croatia ‡	24	7	9	8	36	38	**30**
Montreal Impact Acad.	24	7	7	10	34	31	**28**
Brampton Lions	24	7	7	10	33	37	**28**
London City	24	4	8	12	38	61	**20**
North York Astros	24	4	6	14	32	62	**18**
St Catherines Wolves	24	4	4	16	19	54	**16**

8/05/2010 - 9/10/2010 • ‡ Qualified for the play-offs

TORONTO MLS APPEARANCES/GOALS 2010

Goalkeepers Jon Conway USA 1 • Stefan Frei SUI 28 • Milos Kocic SRB 1+1

Defenders Nana Attakora-Gyan CAN 24+1/1 • Adrian Cann CAN 26/0 • Gabe Gala CAN 1+9/0 • Nick Garcia USA 20+3/0 • Ty Harden USA 10+2/0 • Doneil Henry CAN 0+1/0 • Raivis Hscanovics LVA 10+1/0 • Maksim Usanov RUS 13+1/0

Midfield Jim Brennan CAN 1/0 • Sam Cronin 4+2/0 • Julian de Guzman CAN 21+4/0 • Dan Gargan USA 25+2/1 • Nick LaBrocca USA 24+4/1 • Nicholas Lindsay CAN 2+2/0 • Joseph Nane CMR 8+3/0 • Jacob Peterson USA 15+9/1 • Amadou Sanyang GAM 12+1/0 • Martin Saric ARG 15+2/0

Forwards Chad Barrett USA 18+4/7 • Dwayne De Rosario CAN 24+3/15 • Fuad Ibrahim CAN 3+5/1 • Maicon BRA 10+3/4 • Mista ESP 5+4/0 • O'Brian White CAN 9+15/2

Coach Preki Radosavljevic USA

CAY – CAYMAN ISLANDS

FIFA/COCA-COLA WORLD RANKING

1993	1994	1995	1996	1997	1998	1999	2000	2001	2002	2003	2004	2005	2006	2007	2008	2009	2010
154	150	131	148	164	153	148	159	165	164	181	176	181	189	192	172	183	157

2010												Hi/Lo
Jan	Feb	Mar	Mar	Apr	May	Jul	Aug	Sep	Oct	Nov	Dec	**127**
183	179	178	177	174	173	173	173	181	158	160	157	**192**

Despite finishing as runners-up to Puerto Rico in their 2010 Digicel Caribbean Cup qualifying group, the Cayman Islands missed out on progressing to the second round after they failed to finish as one of the two best runners-up in the four first round groups. A 1-1 draw with Saint Martin in the opening match of the group, staged in Bayamon, Puerto Rico, ultimately proved costly. There was a handsome 4-1 win against minnows Anguilla but that was followed by a 2-0 defeat at the hands of a resurgent Puerto Rican side that is starting to pull its weight in Caribbean football. With CIFA enjoying the benefits of their newly opened headquarters and with a technical centre in the pipeline as part of the FIFA Goal initiative, coach Carl Brown will be aiming to take the Cayman Islands to a level where they can start to compete with some of the bigger Caribbean islands. At club level, 2009 champions Elite entered the CFU Club Championship in 2010 but then later withdrew. They also lost their league crown to Scholars who won their fourth title in five years. The CIFA Digicel Cayman Cup was won by George Town, 2-1 winners over Bodden Town in the final and three months later they completed a cup double after beating Tigers 1-0 in the CIFA FA Cup, the winner coming from Tex Whitelocke after just five minutes.

FIFA WORLD CUP RECORD
1930-1994 DNE **1998-2010** DNQ

CAYMAN ISLANDS FOOT BALL ASSOCIATION (CIFA)

Centre for Excellence
✉ Poindexter Road, PO Box 178
Grand Cayman KYI-1104
☎ +1 345 9495775
📠 +1 345 9457673
✉ cifa@candw.ky
🖥 www.cifa.ky
FA 1966 CON 1993 FIFA 1992
P Jeffrey Webb
GS Bruce Blake

FIFA BIG COUNT 2006

Total players	3 700
% of population	8.14%
Male	3 400
Female	300
Amateurs 18+	700
Youth under 18	600
Unregistered	1 100
Professionals	0
Referees	100
Admin & coaches	200
Number of clubs	10
Number of teams	50

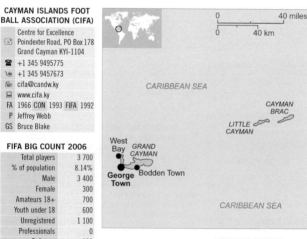

MAJOR CITIES/TOWNS

		Population
1	George Town	35 633
2	West Bay	12 620
3	Bodden Town	7 634
4	East End	1 619
5	North Side	1 313

CAYMAN ISLANDS

Capital	George Town	Population	49 035 (207)	% in cities	100%
GDP per capita	$43 800 (13)	Area km²	264 km² (210)	GMT +/-	-5
Neighbours (km)	Coast 160				

RECENT INTERNATIONAL MATCHES PLAYED BY THE CAYMAN ISLANDS

2006	Opponents		Score	Venue		Scorers	Att.	Referee
2-09	Bahamas	L	1-3	Havana	CCq	Leon Whittaker [76]	200	Stewart JAM
4-09	Turks & Caicos Isl	L	0-2	Havana	CCq		100	Stennett JAM
6-09	Cuba	L	0-7	Havana	CCq		120	Stewart JAM
2007								
No international matches played in 2007								
2008								
3-02	Bermuda	D	1-1	Hamilton	WCq	Allean Grant [87]	2 000	Navarro CAN
30-03	Bermuda	L	1-3	Georgetown	WCq	Marshall Forbes [64p]	3 200	Marrufo USA
27-08	Saint Martin †	W	3-0	Grand Cayman	CCq	Calvin Jefford [55], Jairo Sanchez [65], Nikolai Hill [90]	300	Thomas JAM
30-08	Antigua and Barbuda	D	1-1	Grand Cayman	CCq	O'Neil Taylor [67]	350	Hospedales
31-08	Bermuda	D	0-0	Grand Cayman	CCq		350	Hospedales
11-10	Guadeloupe †	L	1-7	Abymes	CCq	Carson Fagan [86]	4 200	McArthur GUY
13-10	Martinique †	L	0-1	Abymes	CCq		1 000	Matthew SKN
15-10	Grenada	L	2-4	Abymes	CCq	Erickson Brown 2 [32 83]	3 358	Willett ATG
9-11	Jamaica	L	0-2	Grand Cayman	Fr		500	Whittaker CAY
2009								
28-06	Jamaica	L	1-4	Grand Cayman	Fr	Rene Carter [40]	500	Holder CAY
2010								
2-10	Saint Martin †	D	1-1	Bayamon	CCq	Paul Brown [18p]	600	Campbell JAM
4-10	Anguilla	W	4-1	Bayamon	CCq	Mark Ebanks 2 [45p 49], Theron Wood [57], Paul Brwn [59]	500	Davis TRI
6-10	Puerto Rico	L	0-2	Bayamon	CCq		3 800	Campbell JAM

Fr = Friendly match • CC = Digicel Caribbean Cup • WC = FIFA World Cup • q = qualifier • † Not an official international

CAYMAN ISLANDS 2009–10

CIFA PREMIER LEAGUE

	Pl	W	D	L	F	A	Pts	Scholars	Bodden T	George Town	Tigers	Elite	Future	Roma	Sunset
Scholars International	21	12	4	5	52	30	40		4-0 4-4	4-1 1-1	**3-0** 1-2	4-3 2-3	3-1	2-0	0-1
Bodden Town	21	9	7	5	43	33	34	2-2		2-3 1-2	3-2 1-2	0-1 1-0	0-0 1-1	4-2	1-1 3-0
George Town	21	9	7	5	39	31	34	0-1	1-2		2-2 5-3	2-2 4-1	1-0 2-0	4-1	0-0
Tigers	21	10	2	9	41	40	32	**0-3**	**0-3**	0-3		4-2	3-0 2-2	3-1 4-0	1-2 3-1
Elite	21	7	6	8	37	39	27	1-4	2-2	2-2	2-1 0-1		2-3 4-1	1-0 3-0	2-2 2-2
Future	21	7	6	8	25	31	27	2-2 3-2	1-1	2-1	2-1	2-0		0-1	0-1
Roma	21	6	2	13	25	43	20	1-3 2-0	2-4 2-4	1-1 0-1	4-2	1-3	2-2 1-0		0-1
Sunset	21	4	6	11	22	37	18	3-4 0-3	1-4	1-2 2-2	1-2	1-1	0-1 1-2	1-2 0-2	

27/09/2009 - 25/04/2010 • Relegation play-off: Roma 3-2 Academy. Roma remain in the Premier League

CIFA FA CUP 2010

Quarter–finals		Semi–finals		Final	
George T	3				
Scholars	2	**George T**	2		
Sunset	0	Latinos	0		
Latinos	1			**George Town**	1
Elite	1			Tigers	0
Bodden T	0	Elite	4	
Roma	0	**Tigers**	6	Truman Bodden SC, 2-05-2010
Tigers	3			Scorer - Tex Whitelocke [5]

CIFA DIGICEL CAYMAN CUP 2010

First Round		Semi–finals		Final	
George T	3 4p				
Roma	3 2p	**George T**	1 1		
Future	2	Tigers ‡	1 5		
Tigers	3			**George Town**	2
Elite	2			Bodden Town	1
Sunset	0	Elite	1 0	TE McField SC, 17-02-2010
Scholars	1	**Bodden T**	3 0	Scorers - Justin Pierre [5], Ian
Bodden T	2			Lindo [26] for George Town;
				Theron Wood [60] for Bodden T

‡ 2nd leg awarded 3-0 to George Town. Tigers used ineligible players

CGO – CONGO

FIFA/COCA-COLA WORLD RANKING

1993	1994	1995	1996	1997	1998	1999	2000	2001	2002	2003	2004	2005	2006	2007	2008	2009	2010
103	114	119	100	101	112	94	86	94	97	108	117	110	89	91	68	101	121

2010												Hi/Lo
Jan	Feb	Mar	Mar	Apr	May	Jul	Aug	Sep	Oct	Nov	Dec	57
101	103	103	99	101	103	107	106	117	115	119	121	139

Congo kept a relatively low profile in 2010 with the 'Diables Rouges' not playing an international until August. The following month they got their 2012 African Nations Cup qualifiers underway but suffered a 2-0 defeat at the hands of Sudan in Khartoum before reviving their hopes of a first appearance at the finals since 2000 win a win over Swaziland. Veteran French coach Robert Corfu came in just days before the trip to Khartoum to take the team through the qualifiers, having previously worked in Cameroon. In September and October Brazzaville played host to the CEMAC Cup, a tournament no longer played at full international level, but nevertheless a Congo triumph still brought a huge sense of satisfaction. It was their second win in the regional event in the last four years, beating Cameroon 9-8 on post-match penalties after the final. Boukama Kaye had scored to give the home side the lead in the deciding game but Hermann Nkodia netted an own goal to level the scores. In club football St Michel de Ouenze won only their second-ever championship, beating AC Leopard Dolisie 3-2 in the final with two early goals from Lorry Nkolo and a late winner from Charvely Bitsindou. Leopard did reach the second round of the CAF Confederation Cup but lost on the away goals rule to Cameroon's highly rated Cotonsport.

FIFA WORLD CUP RECORD
1930-1970 DNE   1974-1978 DNQ   1982-1990 DNE   1994-2010 DNQ

FEDERATION CONGOLAISE DE FOOTBALL (FECOFOOT)

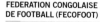

✉ PO Box 1423,
Brazzaville

☎ +242 811563
📠 +242 812524
✉ fecofoot@yahoo.fr
🖥
FA 1962 CON 1966 FIFA 1962
P Jean Michel Mbono
GS Wantete Badji-Mombo

FIFA BIG COUNT 2006

Total players	200 210
% of population	5.41%
Male	191 600
Female	8 610
Amateurs 18+	5 410
Youth under 18	3 650
Unregistered	35 150
Professionals	0
Referees	504
Admin & coaches	595
Number of clubs	90
Number of teams	320

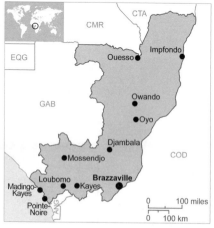

MAJOR CITIES/TOWNS

		Population
1	Brazzaville	1 158 513
2	Pointe Noire	634 995
3	Loubomo	130 080
4	Nkayi	58 559
5	Gamboma	29 357
6	Kinkala	29 248
7	Ouesso	27 142
8	Madingou	23 342
9	Impfondo	20 729
10	Mossendjo	20 414
11	Sibiti	20 096
12	Loandjili	18 488
13	Owando	15 871
14	Djambala	13 570
15	Ngamaba-Mfilou	11 389
16	Makoua	7 427
17	Matsanga	6 246
18	Ewo	5 859
19	Sembé	4 047

REPUBLIQUE DU CONGO • REPUBLIC OF THE CONGO

Capital	Brazzaville	Population 4 012 809 (127)	% in cities 61%
GDP per capita	$3900 (154)	Area km² 342 000 km² (63)	GMT +/- +1
Neighbours (km)	Angola 201, Cameroon 523, C. African Rep 467, Congo DR 2410, Gabon 1903 • Coast 169		

RECENT INTERNATIONAL MATCHES PLAYED BY CONGO

2006	Opponents		Score	Venue	Comp	Scorers	Att	Referee
2-09	South Africa	D	0-0	Joheannesburg	CNq			Aboubacar CIV
8-10	Chad	W	3-1	Brazzaville	CNq	Abdoulaye Bruce [17], Malonga [30], Nguessi [46]		Djaoupe TOG
14-11	Mali	L	0-1	La Courneuve	Fr			
2007								
5-03	Equatorial Guinea	W	2-1	N'Djamena	CMr1	Likibi [81], Ngoua [94+]		
7-03	Gabon	D	2-2	N'Djamena	CMr1	Lepaye 2 [27 44]		
12-03	Central African Rep	W	4-1	N'Djamena	CMsf	Lepaye [4], Likibi 2 [28 84], Beaulia [47]		
16-03	Gabon	W	1-0	N'Djamena	CMf	Papou [59]		
25-03	Zambia	D	0-0	Brazzaville	CNq			Coulibaly MLI
4-04	Angola	D	0-0	Cabinda	Fr			
28-05	Congo DR	W	2-1	Brazzaville	Fr	Minga [35], De Bouisson [55p]		
2-06	Zambia	L	0-3	Chililabombwe	CNq			Rahman SUD
17-06	South Africa	D	1-1	Pointe-Noire	CNq	Bantsimba [65]		Eyene CMR
9-09	Chad	D	1-1	N'Djamena	CNq	Mayembi [6]		Pare BFA
2008								
1-06	Mali	L	2-4	Bamoko	WCq	Mouithys 2 [5 74]	40 000	Bennaceur TUN
8-06	Sudan	W	1-0	Brazzaville	WCq	Endzanga [70]	25 000	Mana NGA
14-06	Chad	L	1-2	N'Djamena	WCq	Batota [42]	8 000	Doue CIV
22-06	Chad	W	2-0	Brazzaville	WCq	Mouithys [14], Ibara [64]	8 000	Diouf SEN
7-09	Mali	W	1-0	Brazzaville	WCq	Endzanga [87]	16 000	Haimoudi ALG
11-10	Sudan	L	0-2	Omdurman	WCq		27 000	Ambaya LBY
2009								
27-05	Jordan	D	1-1	Amman	Fr	Epako [47]		
31-05	Bahrain	L	1-3	Manama	Fr	Kapolongo [20]		
12-08	Morocco	D	1-1	Rabat	Fr	Moussilou [18]		
13-10	Korea DPR	D	0-0	Le Mans	Fr			
14-11	Angola	D	1-1	Luanda	Fr	Douniama [91+]		
2010								
11-08	Burkina Faso	L	0-3	Senlis	Fr			
4-09	Sudan	L	0-2	Khartoum	CNq			Kaoma ZAM
10-10	Swaziland	W	3-1	Brazzaville	CNq	Mouko [21p], Sembolo 2 [35 74]		Ssegonga UGA

Fr = Friendly match • CN = African Cup of Nations • CM = CEMAC Cup • WC = FIFA World Cup
q = qualifier • r1 = first round group • sf = semi-final • 3p = third place play-off

CONGO 2010
LINAFOOT

Final Stage

Group A

	Pl	W	D	L	F	A	Pts	DN	ACM	ICB
St Michel Ouenzé	3	1	2	0	5	1	5	1-1	0-0	4-0
Diables Noirs	3	1	2	0	4	2	5		1-1	2-0
ACM	3	1	2	0	3	2	5			2-1
Inter Club Brazzaville	3	0	0	3	1	8	0			

Group B

	Pl	W	D	L	F	A	Pts	VCM	NN	PV
AC Léopard Dolisie	3	2	1	0	8	1	7	1-1	3-0	4-0
V. Club Mokanda	3	1	1	1	4	3	4		3-0	0-2
Nico Nicoye	3	1	0	2	2	6	3			2-0
Pigeon Vert	3	1	0	2	2	6	3			

14/11/2010 to 23/11/2010 • ‡ Qualified for the CAF Champions League

Final

St Michel Ouenzé ‡	3
AC Léopard Dolisie	2

CUP FINAL

23-11-2010

CHA – CHAD

FIFA/COCA-COLA WORLD RANKING

1993	1994	1995	1996	1997	1998	1999	2000	2001	2002	2003	2004	2005	2006	2007	2008	2009	2010
166	175	180	188	184	178	166	163	176	173	152	168	159	142	141	119	145	141

2010												Hi/Lo
Jan	Feb	Mar	Mar	Apr	May	Jul	Aug	Sep	Oct	Nov	Dec	118
145	143	144	144	144	143	124	124	134	147	147	141	190

Club football provided a rare highlight for Chad in pan-African competition with the shock win for Gazelle in the African Champions League over Nigerian representatives Bayelsa United. A 1-0 home win in the first leg of the first round tie was followed by a 2-2 draw away in Yenagoa where Chadian international Cesar Madalngue scored a last minute goal to ensure a shock 3-2 aggregate triumph. Gazelle performed well in the next round as well, holding Sudan's El Merreikh to a 1-1 draw at home but lost the return in Omdurman 2-0 to go out. After almost 20 months without any international action, Chad's national side suddenly found themselves with a whirlwind programme in a five-team qualifying group for the 2012 African Nations Cup. Draws home and away with Togo represented their only profit after the first six months of competition but the 'Sao' showed signs of improvement under Egyptian coach Sherif Khashab. Chad also participated in the CEMAC Cup, although it is no longer recognised by FIFA at A international level. They finished fourth in Brazzaville with Ezechiel Ndouassel finishing as top scorer. Club side Foullah Edifice won the first trophy in their history by taking the N'Djamena League Cup while the 2010 N'Djamena League title was won by Tourbillon, four points ahead of defending champions Gazelle.

FIFA WORLD CUP RECORD
1930-1998 DNE 2002-2010 DNQ

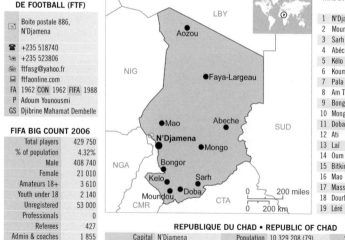

FEDERATION TCHADIENNE DE FOOTBALL (FTF)

Boite postale 886,
N'Djamena

☎ +235 518740
📠 +235 523806
✉ ftfasg@yahoo.fr
🖥 ftfaonline.com
FA 1962 CON 1962 FIFA 1988
P Adoum Younousmi
GS Djibrine Mahamat Dembelle

FIFA BIG COUNT 2006

Total players	429 750
% of population	4.32%
Male	408 740
Female	21 010
Amateurs 18+	3 610
Youth under 18	2 140
Unregistered	53 000
Professionals	0
Referees	427
Admin & coaches	1 855
Number of clubs	50
Number of teams	148

MAJOR CITIES/TOWNS

		Population
1	N'Djaména	776 126
2	Moundou	145 486
3	Sarh	110 355
4	Abéché	79 851
5	Kélo	45 780
6	Koumra	39 031
7	Pala	38 173
8	Am Timan	31 089
9	Bongor	29 889
10	Mongo	29 882
11	Doba	26 194
12	Ati	25 912
13	Laï	20 862
14	Oum Hadjer	20 742
15	Bitkine	19 907
16	Mao	19 407
17	Massaguet	19 273
18	Dourbali	19 032
19	Léré	18 440

REPUBLIQUE DU CHAD • REPUBLIC OF CHAD

Capital N'Djamena	Population 10 329 208 (79)	% in cities 27%
GDP per capita $1600 (192)	Area km² 1 284 000 km² (21)	GMT + / - +1
Neighbours (km) Cameroon 1094, C. African Rep 1197, Libya 1055, Niger 1175, Nigeria 87, Sudan 1360		

RECENT INTERNATIONAL MATCHES PLAYED BY CHAD

2005	Opponents		Score	Venue	Comp	Scorers	Att	Referee
8-02	Equatorial Guinea	D	0-0	Libreville	CMr1			
10-02	Gabon	W	3-2	Libreville	CMsf	Djenet [3], Doumbé [8], Nguembaye [56]		
22-05	Sudan	L	1-4	Khartoum	Fr			
27-05	Sudan	D	1-1	Khartoum	Fr			
2006								
6-03	Equatorial Guinea	D	1-1	Bata	CMr1			
8-03	Congo	D	0-0	Bata	CMr1			
11-03	Cameroon †	L	0-1	Bata	CMsf			
14-03	Gabon	D	2-2	Bata	CM3p	Mahamat [20p], Doumbé [52]		
3-09	Zambia	L	0-2	N'Djamena	CNq			Shelmani LBY
8-10	Congo	L	1-3	Brazzaville	CNq	Missdongarle Betolinga [89]		Djaoupe TOG
2007								
22-02	Benin	W	1-0	Cotonou	Fr	Mahamat [53]		
4-03	Cameroon	W	2-1	N'Djamena	CMr1			
6-03	Central African Rep	W	3-2	N'Djamena	CMr1	Ndouassel [60p], Missdongarle Betolinga [61], Mahamat [89]		
11-03	Gabon	L	1-2	N'Djamena	CMsf	Kedigui [70]		
16-03	Central African Rep	W	1-0	N'Djamena	CM3p	Medego [95]		
24-03	South Africa	L	0-3	N'Djamena	CNq			Aguidissou BEN
2-06	South Africa	L	0-4	Durban	CNq			Gasingwa RWA
16-06	Zambia	D	1-1	Chililabombwe	CNq	Kedigui [13]		Ssegonga UGA
9-09	Congo	D	1-1	N'Djamena	CNq	Djimenam [88]		Pare BFA
2008								
7-06	Mali	L	1-2	N'Djamena	WCq	Kedigui [37]	15 000	Aguidissou BEN
14-06	Congo	W	2-1	N'Djamena	WCq	Kedigui [44p], Syriakata Hassan [48]	8 000	Doue CIV
22-06	Congo	L	0-2	Brazzaville	WCq		8 000	Diouf SEN
24-08	Libya	L	0-3	Tripoli	Fr			
6-09	Sudan	W	2-1	Cairo	WCq	Mbaiam [29], Syriakata Hassan [81]	4 000	Trabelsi TUN
10-09	Sudan	L	1-3	Cairo	WCq	Djime [34]	10 000	Diatta SEN
11-10	Mali	L	1-2	Bamako	WCq	Misdongarde [64]	40 000	Keita GUI
2009								
No international matches played in 2009								
2010								
19-06	Niger	D	1-1	Niamey	Fr	Barthelemy [39]		
1-07	Togo	D	2-2	N'Djamena	CNq	Djimrangar [20], Mbaiam [28]		Benouza ALG
9-07	Botswana	L	0-1	Gaborone	CNq			Seechurn MRI
11-08	Tunisia	L	1-3	N'Djamena	CNq	N'Douassel [72]		Doue CIV
29-08	Ethiopia	L	0-1	Addis Abeba	Fr			
9-10	Malawi	L	2-6	Blantyre	CNq	N'Douassel [26], Mbaiam [81]		Kirwa KEN
17-11	Togo	D	0-0	Lome	CNq			Coulibaly MLI

Fr = Friendly match • CN = African Cup of Nations • CM = CEMAC Cup • WC = FIFA World Cup
q = qualifier • r1 = first round group • sf = semi-final • 3p = third place play-off • † Not an official international

CHAD 2010 LIGUE DE N'DJAMENA PREMIERE DIVISION	Pl	W	D	L	F	A	Pts
Tourbillon †	18						38
Gazelle	18						34
CotonTchad	18						31
Foullah Edifice	18						30
Rennaissance	18						26
Elect-Sport	18						24
Toumai	18						21
AS DGSSIE	18						19
Postel 2000	18						15
US Moursal	18						11

01/2010 - 10/2010 • † Qualified for CAF Champions League

COUPE DE LIGUE DE N'DJAMENA 2010

Quarter-finals		Semi-finals		Final	
Foullah Edifice	1				
Postel 2000	0	**Foullah Edifice**	2		
US Moursal	0	Gazelle	1		
Gazelle	3			**Foullah Edifice** ‡	2
CotonTchad	5			Rennaissance	1
Saccoger	1	CotonTchad	1		
Elect-Sport	0	**Rennaissance**	2	31-10-2010	
Rennaissance	1	‡ Qualified for CAF Confederation Cup			

Preliminary round: Gazelle beat Toumai; Elect-Sport beat Tourbillon

CHI – CHILE

FIFA/COCA-COLA WORLD RANKING

1993	1994	1995	1996	1997	1998	1999	2000	2001	2002	2003	2004	2005	2006	2007	2008	2009	2010
55	47	36	26	16	16	23	19	39	84	80	74	64	41	45	31	15	15

					2010							Hi/Lo
Jan	Feb	Mar	Mar	Apr	May	Jul	Aug	Sep	Oct	Nov	Dec	6
15	16	14	13	15	18	10	10	10	14	16	15	84

2010 was an extraordinary year for Chile, a year in which the country came to world attention in the aftermath of the huge earthquake in February and then during the 69-day saga that unfolded at the Copiapo mine. An estimated audience of one billion people watched the trapped miners emerge from their ordeal on October 13th, one of whom was Franklin Lobos, a retired footballer who had represented Chile in the qualifiers for the 1984 Olympic Games. Because of the earthquake, the football season was reorganised into a single round-robin tournament of 34 matches instead of the usual Apertura and Clausura and it was won by Universidad Católica for the tenth time in the club's history. The Copa Chile was won by Municipal Iquique who beat Deportes Concepción on penalties in the final of a tournament staged to celebrate the bicentennial of Chile's independence in 1810. The other big story of the year was Chile's appearance in the World Cup finals in South Africa where they qualified for the second round. Marcelo Bielsa's team played some attractive football throughout the year and impressed at the finals but drew Brazil in the second round where they lost 3-0. There was disappointment for fans in Chile when Bielsa decided to quit following the ousting of federation president Harold Mayne-Nicholls at the end of the year.

FIFA WORLD CUP RECORD

1930 5 r1 1934-1938 DNE **1950** 9 r1 1954 DNE 1958 DNQ **1962** 3 SF (hosts) **1966** 13 r1 1970 DNQ **1974** 11 r1
1978 DNQ **1982** 22 r1 1986-1990 DNQ 1994 DNE **1998** 16 r2 2002-2006 DNQ **2010** 10 r2

**FEDERACION DE FUTBOL
DE CHILE (FFCH)**

Av. Quilin No. 5635, Comuna
Peñalolén, Casilla No. 3733,
Santiago de Chile

☎ +56 2 8101800
📠 +56 2 2843510
✉ ffch@anfpchile.cl
🖥 www.anfp.cl
FA 1895 CON 1916 FIFA 1913
P Sergio Jadue
GS Nibaldo Jaque Zuniga

FIFA BIG COUNT 2006

Total players	2 608 337
% of population	16.17%
Male	2 469 837
Female	138 500
Amateurs 18+	138 200
Youth under 18	326 500
Unregistered	2 010 000
Professionals	637
Referees	5 204
Admin & coaches	21 170
Number of clubs	5 715
Number of teams	31 228

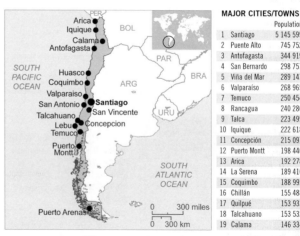

MAJOR CITIES/TOWNS

		Population
1	Santiago	5 145 599
2	Puente Alto	745 752
3	Antofagasta	344 919
4	San Bernardo	298 757
5	Viña del Mar	289 147
6	Valparaíso	268 965
7	Temuco	250 454
8	Rancagua	240 286
9	Talca	223 499
10	Iquique	222 618
11	Concepción	215 097
12	Puerto Montt	198 446
13	Arica	192 278
14	La Serena	189 416
15	Coquimbo	188 995
16	Chillán	155 488
17	Quilpué	153 933
18	Talcahuano	153 532
19	Calama	146 334

REPUBLICA DE CHILE • REPUBLIC OF CHILE

Capital Santiago	Population 16 601 707 (60)	% in cities 88%
GDP per capita $14 900 (77)	Area km² 576 102 km² (38)	GMT + / - -4
Neighbours (km) Argentina 5308, Bolivia 860, Peru 171 • Coast 6435		

RECENT INTERNATIONAL MATCHES PLAYED BY CHILE

2008	Opponents	Score		Venue	Comp	Scorers	Att	Referee
20-08	Turkey	L	0-1	Izmit	Fr			Kakos GRE
7-09	Brazil	L	0-3	Santiago	WCq		60 239	Torres PAR
10-09	Colombia	W	4-0	Santiago	WCq	Jara [26], Suazo [38], Fuentes [48], Fernandez [71]	47 459	Larrionda URU
24-09	Mexico	W	1-0	Los Angeles	Fr	Valenzuela OG [75]		Stott USA
12-10	Ecuador	L	0-1	Quito	WCq		33 079	Vazquez URU
15-10	Argentina	W	1-0	Santiago	WCq	Orellana [35]	65 000	Ruiz COL
19-11	Spain	L	0-3	Villarreal	Fr		30 000	Vadachkoria GEO
2009								
18-01	Honduras	L	0-2	Fort Lauderdale	Fr		12 282	Moody USA
11-02	South Africa	W	2-0	Polokwane	Fr	Valdivia [45], Sanchez [67]	16 300	Mpanisi ZAM
29-03	Peru	W	3-1	Lima	WCq	Sanchez [2], Suazo [32p], Fernandez [70]	48 700	Amarilla PAR
1-04	Uruguay	D	0-0	Santiago	WCq		55 000	Baldassi ARG
27-05	Japan	L	0-4	Osaka	Fr		43 531	Hermansen DEN
29-05	Belgium	D	1-1	Chiba	Fr	Medel [23]	9 700	Tojo JPN
6-06	Paraguay	W	2-0	Asuncion	WCq	Fernandez [13], Suazo [51]	34 000	Pezzotta ARG
10-06	Bolivia	W	4-0	Santiago	WCq	Beausejour [44], Estrada [74], Sanchez 2 [77 89]	60 214	Silvera URU
12-08	Denmark	W	2-1	Brondby	Fr	Paredes [61], Sanchez [69]	8 700	Jakobsen ISL
5-09	Venezuela	D	2-2	Santiago	WCq	Vidal [10], Millar [52]	44 000	Ortube BOL
9-09	Brazil	L	2-4	Salvador	WCq	Suazo 2 [45p 52]	30 000	Larrionda URU
10-10	Colombia	W	4-2	Medellin	WCq	Ponce [34], Suazo [35], Valdivia [71], Orellana [78]	18 000	Rivera PER
14-10	Ecuador	W	1-0	Santiago	WCq	Suazo [53]	47 000	Torres PAR
17-11	Slovakia	W	2-1	Zilina	Fr	Jara [9], Paredes [55]	11 072	Vad HUN
2010								
20-01	Panama	W	2-1	Coquimbo	Fr	Paredes 2 [51 53]	15 000	Vazquez URU
31-03	Venezuela	D	0-0	Temuco	Fr		20 000	Silvera URU
5-05	Trinidad and Tobago	W	2-0	Iquique	Fr	Morales [2], Toro [48]	10 000	Antequera BOL
16-05	Mexico	L	0-1	Mexico City	Fr		95 000	Geiger USA
26-05	Zambia	W	3-0	Calama	Fr	Sanchez 2 [54 85], Valdivia [87]	12 000	Favale ARG
30-05	Northern Ireland	W	1-0	Chillan	Fr	Paredes [30]	12 000	Prudente URU
30-05	Israel	W	3-0	Concepcion	Fr	Suazo [22], Sanchez [49], Tello [90]	25 000	Arias PAR
16-06	Honduras	W	1-0	Nelspruit	WCr1	Beausejour [34]	32 664	Maillet SEY
21-06	Switzerland	W	1-0	Port Elizabeth	WCr1	Gonzalez [75]	34 872	Al Ghamdi KSA
25-06	Spain	L	1-2	Pretoria	WCr1	Millar [47]	41 958	Rodriguez MEX
28-06	Brazil	L	0-3	Johannesburg	WCr2		54 096	Webb ENG
7-09	Ukraine	L	1-2	Kyiv	Fr	Isla [86]	10 000	Sevastsyanik BLR
9-10	UAE	W	2-0	Abu Dhabi	Fr	Cereceda [6p], Morales [37]	500	Al Ghamdi KSA
12-10	Oman	W	1-0	Muscat	Fr	Morales [21]	9 000	Blooshi KUW
17-11	Uruguay	W	2-0	Santiago	Fr	Sanchez [38], Vidal [74]	45 017	Torres PAR

Fr = Friendly match • CA = Copa América • WC = FIFA World Cup • q = qualifier • r1 = first round group

CHILE NATIONAL TEAM HISTORICAL RECORDS

Caps

84 - Leonel Sanchez 1955-68 • 73 - Nelson Tapia 1994-2005 • 70 - Alberto Fouilloux 1960-72 & Marcelo Salas 1994-2009 • 69 - Ivan Zamorano 1987-2001 & Fabian Estay 1990-2001 • 63 - Javier Margas 1990-2000 • 62 - Miguel Ramirez 1991-2003 • 61 - Clarence Acuna 1995-2004 • 57 - Juan Carlos Letelier 1979-89 • 55 - Pedro Reyes 1994-2001

Goals

37 - Marcelo Salas 1994-2009 • 34 - Ivan Zamorano 1987-2001 • 29 - Carlos Caszely 1969-85 • 23 - Leonel Sanchez 1955-68 • 22 - Jorge Aravena 1983-89 • 18 - Humberto Suazo 2005- & Juan Carlos Letelier 1979-89 • 17 - Enrique Hormazabal 1950-63 • 12 - Alexis Sanchez 2006- ; Hugo Eduardo Rubio 1983-91; Jaime Ramirez 1954-66 & Raul Toro 1936-41 • 11 - Pedro Araya 1964-71 & Julio Crisosto 1971-77

Past Coaches

Carlos Fanta 1916 • Julian Bertola URU 1917 • Hector Parra 1918-19 • Juan Carlos Bertone URU 1920-22 • Carlos Acuna 1924 • Jose Rosetti ITA 1926 • Frank Powell ITA 1928 • Gyorgy Orth HUN 1930 • Pedro Mazullo URU 1936-39 • Maximum Garay HUN 1941 • Franz Platko HUN 1941-45 • Luis Tirado 1946-56 • Jose Salerno ARG 1956-57 • Ladislao Pakozdi HUN 1957 • Fernando Riera 1958-62 • Francisco Hormazabal 1962-65 • Luis Alamos 1965-66 • Alejandro Scopelli ARG 1966-67 • Salvador Nocetti 1968-69 • Francisco Hormazabal 1970 • Fernando Riera 1970 • Luis Vera 1971 • Raul Pino 1971-72 • Rudi Gutendorf GER 1972 • Luis Alamos 1973-74 • Pedro Morales 1974-75 • Caupolican Pena 1976-77 • Luis Santibanez 1977-82 • Luis Ibarra 1983 • Isaac Carrasco 1984 • Vicente Cantatore ARG 1984 • Pedro Morales 1985 • Luis Ibarra 1986 • Orlando Aravena 1987 • Manuel Rodriguez 1987 • Orlando Aravena 1988-89 • Arturo Salah 1990-93 • Nelson Acosta 1993 • Mirko Jozic CRO 1994 • Xabier Azkargorta ESP 1995-96 • Nelson Acosta 1996-2000 • Pedro Garcia 2001 • Jorge Garces 2001 • Cesar Vaccia 2002 • Juvenal Olmos 2003-05 • Nelson Acosta 2005-07 • Marcelo Bielsa ARG 2007-10

CHILE 2010

PRIMERA DIVISION

	Pl	W	D	L	F	A	Pts	Univ Católica	Colo Colo	Audax	Univ de Chile	Unión	Huachipato	Wanderers	La Serena	U San Felipe	Cobresal	Palestino	O'Higgins	Nublense	Cobreloa	U Concepción	S'go Morning	Everton	San Luis
Universidad Católica †	34	23	5	6	77	39	74	–	0-0	2-3	4-2	2-0	2-0	3-1	2-1	2-1	0-2	2-1	4-1	4-2	2-1	1-0	4-0	5-0	4-1
Colo Colo † ‡	34	22	5	7	67	34	71	3-2	–	1-3	1-0	1-0	0-0	3-0	6-1	5-2	1-0	3-0	2-0	2-2	3-1	4-2	0-1	2-0	3-1
Audax Italiano	34	20	5	9	75	58	65	1-3	2-3	–	1-2	5-2	1-1	0-4	2-1	1-0	4-2	1-3	2-1	5-6	3-1	4-1	1-0	2-0	2-2
Universidad de Chile ‡	34	20	4	10	75	48	64	1-2	2-2	2-2	–	4-3	3-0	1-0	1-2	4-2	5-1	1-2	0-1	1-2	3-1	4-2	2-1	5-1	4-0
Unión Española †	34	14	10	10	58	50	52	2-1	1-0	2-2	2-1	–	5-0	3-0	1-1	1-2	2-0	3-2	1-1	1-3	3-1	3-0	2-2	3-2	2-1
Huachipato	34	12	12	10	44	40	48	1-3	1-2	1-2	1-2	1-2	–	3-2	0-0	1-1	4-3	0-0	2-1	1-1	2-0	3-0	1-0	1-1	2-1
Santiago Wanderers	34	12	9	13	48	52	45	2-4	0-1	1-0	3-3	1-1	0-0	–	5-0	2-1	0-4	2-0	1-1	2-2	2-1	1-0	1-1	2-0	0-2
Deportes La Serena	34	13	6	15	45	59	45	1-1	1-2	1-3	2-4	3-1	0-3	4-0	–	3-1	3-0	0-0	4-2	1-0	1-0	0-0	2-0	2-1	1-3
Unión San Felipe	34	12	7	15	38	47	43	1-3	3-2	1-2	1-2	2-4	1-1	1-1	1-0	–	1-0	1-1	2-0	3-1	1-0	0-0	1-0	1-3	3-0
Cobresal	34	12	6	16	47	52	42	3-1	2-5	2-1	1-2	1-0	2-1	1-0	0-2	0-0	–	2-1	1-2	0-0	0-1	3-1	3-0	1-2	4-2
Palestino	34	11	9	14	35	41	42	0-1	1-2	2-5	0-1	0-0	2-1	0-1	3-0	1-0	1-0	–	1-0	2-0	1-0	1-1	2-1	2-2	3-2
O'Higgins	34	10	11	13	46	44	41	1-0	2-1	5-1	3-3	0-0	0-0	2-2	4-0	1-2	0-1	4-1	–	2-2	2-2	1-2	1-0	0-0	0-0
Nublense	34	9	13	12	54	66	40	1-4	0-0	1-5	0-2	1-1	1-1	2-2	2-0	1-1	0-3			–	1-1	2-2	1-2	1-0	0-0
Cobreloa	34	10	9	15	45	47	39	2-3	2-1	1-1	0-2	3-1	1-1	2-1	4-0	0-0	2-1	0-0	1-1	3-2	–	1-1	2-1	4-0	5-0
Univ. de Concepción	34	9	11	14	39	50	38	2-2	0-1	1-3	2-0	3-3	0-2	1-2	1-0	0-1	1-1	1-0	2-1	4-1	3-0	–	0-0	2-1	1-1
Santiago Morning	34	9	9	16	34	45	36	0-2	0-2	0-1	1-2	1-1	0-3	2-1	2-3	1-0	1-1	2-1	2-1	4-1	0-0	2-0	–	3-0	2-0
Everton	34	8	10	16	38	58	34	2-1	2-2	1-1	1-0	2-1	1-1	1-1	0-0	1-1	0-3	2-2	1-1	1-0	2-3	2-1	1-1	–	1-1
San Luis	34	5	9	20	36	71	24	1-1	0-2	1-2	0-3	3-1	1-4	3-4	0-1	1-1	0-0	1-2	3-3	2-1	1-0	2-2	0-2		–

23/01/2010 - 5/12/2010 • † Qualified for Copa Libertadores • ‡ Qualified for Copa Sudamericana
Relegation play-offs: **Santiago Morning** 1-2 3-1 Antofagasta • **Universidad de Concepción** 2-0 3-2 Curicó Unido
Top scorers: **19** - Milovan Mirosevic, Católica • **18** - Mauro Olivi ARG, Audax • **17** - Carlos Munoz, Wanderers • **16** - Juan Manuel Olivera URU,
U de Chile & Diego Rivarola ARG, U de Chile • **14** - Roberto Gutierrez, Católica; Ezequiel Miralles ARG, Colo Colo & Gabriel Rodriguez ARG, Nublense

MEDALS TABLE

		Overall			League			Cup		Sth Am			City
		G	S	B	G	S	B	G	S	G	S	B	
1	Colo Colo	40	23	20	29	17	15	10	4	1	2	5	Santiago
2	Universidad de Chile	16	8	17	13	8	13	3				4	Santiago
3	Universidad Catolica	13	24	9	10	16	4	3	7		1	5	Santiago
4	Cobreloa	9	12	6	8	7	5	1	3		2	1	Calama
5	Unión Española	8	11	6	6	8	5	2	2		1	1	Santiago
6	Santiago Wanderers	5	5	2	3	3	2	2	2				Valparaíso
7	Everton	5	2		4	2		1					Viña del Mar
8	Audax Italiano	4	10	9	4	8	9		2				Santiago
9	Palestino	4	5	3	2	4	2	2	1			1	Santiago
10	Magallanes	4	4	2	4	4	2						Santiago
11	Deportes Iquique	2	1	1			1	2	1				Iquique
12	Union San Felipe	2			1			1					San Felipe
13	Santiago Morning	1	3	1	1	2	1		1				Santiago
14	Cobresal	1	2					2				1	El Salvador
15	Deportes La Serena	1	1	2			2	1	1				La Serena
16	Universidad Concepción	1	1		1			1					Concepción
17	Temuco	1		2	1		2						Temuco
18	Huachipato	1	1		1	1							Talcahuano
19	Luis Cruz Martinez	1					1						Curicó
20	Rangers		3	2		2	2	1					Talca
21	O'Higgins		2	3			3	2				1	Rancagua
22	Deportes Concepción		2	1		1		1				1	Concepción
23	Coquimbo Unido		2			2							Coquimbo
24	Fernandez Vial		1					1					Concepción
	Lota Schwager		1					1					Lota
	Deportes Ovalle		1					1					Ovalle
27	Provincial Curicó Unido			2			2						Curicó
	Santiago Juventus			2			1						

CHILE 2010
PRIMERA B REGIONAL STAGE (2)

North	Pl	W	D	L	F	A	Pts
Antofagasta ‡	24	13	6	5	37	22	45
Unión La Calera ‡	24	12	9	3	39	24	45
Municipal Iquique ‡	24	9	7	8	30	25	34
Prov. Curicó Unido ‡	24	9	6	9	34	29	33
San Marcos Arica	24	7	6	11	41	55	27
Coquimbo Unido	24	6	8	10	24	34	26
Deportes Copiapó	24	4	6	14	28	44	18

South	Pl	W	D	L	F	A	Pts
Puerto Montt ‡	24	12	9	3	34	22	45
Unión Temuco ‡	24	12	5	7	35	27	41
Deportes Concepción ‡	24	9	9	6	31	24	36
Lota Schwager ‡	24	9	7	8	31	29	34
Naval Talcahuano	24	8	5	11	27	26	29
Rangers Talca	24	8	4	12	26	33	28
Provincial Osorno	24	5	3	16	17	40	18

29/01/2010 - 12/09/2010 • ‡ Qualified for the final stage
Relegation play-off: **Dep. Copiapó** 2-0 0-1 Provincial Osorno
Provincial Osorno relegated

CHILE 2010
PRIMERA B FINAL STAGE (2)

	Pl	W	D	L	F	A	Pts
Municipal Iquique	14	9	3	2	22	9	31
Unión La Calera	14	6	6	2	19	11	26
Antofagasta †	14	6	3	5	17	15	24
Prov. Curicó Unido †	14	6	4	4	19	12	22
Unión Temuco	14	6	2	6	19	22	22
Deportes Concepción	14	4	3	7	14	18	16
Puerto Montt	14	3	3	8	13	22	15
Lota Schwager	14	3	2	9	13	27	11

17/09/2010 - 5/12/2010 • Bonus points in brackets
† Promotion play-off (see Primera Division)
4th place play-off: Unión Temuco 0-0 2-3p **Curicó Unido**

COPA CHILE 2008-09

Round of 16		Quarter-finals		Semi-finals		Final	
Univ. Concepción	1 4p						
Provincial Osorno	1 1p	**Univ. Concepción**	3				
Antofagasta	0 4p	Cobreloa	0				
Cobreloa	0 5p			**Univ. Concepción**	2		
Deportes Melipilla	2			Unión Española	1		
Rangers Talca	1	Deportes Melipilla	0				
Santiago Morning	3	**Unión Española**	1				
Unión Española	4					**Univ. Concepción**	2
Huachipato	2					Deportes Ovalle	1
O'Higgins	1	**Huachipato**	0 4p				
Audax Italiano	2 2p	Santiago Wanderers	0 2p				
Santiago Wanderers	2 4p			Huachipato	2 0p	CUP FINAL	
Colo Colo	3 5p			**Deportes Ovalle**	2 3p	Francisco Rumoroso, Coquimbo	
Unión La Calera	3 3p	Colo Colo	2 1p			17-02-2009, Att: 17 073, Ref: Osorio	
Cobresal	1 3p	**Deportes Ovalle**	2 4p			Scorers - Gabriel Vargas [10],	
Deportes Ovalle	1 4p			Semi-finals played at Bicentenario, La Florida		Fernando Solis [51] for Concepción;	
						Gonzalo Soto [5] for Ovalle	

COPA CHILE 2009

Round of 16		Quarter-finals		Semi-finals		Final	
Unión San Felipe							
Unión Española		**Unión San Felipe**	1 6p				
Lota Schwager	0	Colo Colo	1 5p				
Colo Colo	1			**Unión San Felipe** *	2		
Unión Temuco	2 5p			Univ. Concepción	0		
Provincial Osorno	2 4p	Unión Temuco	0 5p				
San Luis	1 3p	**Univ. Concepción**	0 6p				
Univ. Concepción	1 5p					**Unión San Felipe**	3
Santiago Morning	0 5p					Municipal Iquique	0
Santiago Wanderers	0 3p	**Santiago Morning**	3				
Deportes Melipilla	2	Prov. Curicó Unido	1				
Prov. Curicó Unido	4			Santiago Morning	1 2p	CUP FINAL	
Coquimbo Unido	1			**Municipal Iquique** *	1 4p	Chiledeportes, Valparaiso	
Cobresal	0	Coquimbo Unido	0			15-11-2009, Att: 5000, Ref: Chandia	
Antofagasta	0	**Municipal Iquique**	1			Scorers - Angel Vildozo 2 [21p 45],	
Municipal Iquique	1					Daniel Briceno [93+] for San Felipe	
				* Home team			

COPA CHILE BICENTENARIO 2010

Second Round

Municipal Iquique	1 1 4p
San Marcos Arica *	5 0 2p
Antofagasta *	0 0
Cobreloa	0 1
Linares Unido *	1 0 4p
O'Higgins	0 3 3p
Naval Talcahuano *	0 0
Nublense	2 2
Unión Española	8 6
Pudahuel Barrancas *	5 1
Deportes La Serena	1 1 7p
Coquimbo Unido *	1 1 8p
Universidad Católica	5 5
Deportes Temuco *	0 3
Provincial Osorno	0 3
Puerto Montt *	0 7
Palestino	6 2
Santiago Morning *	2 2
General Velasquez *	0
San Luis	6
Audax Italiano *	2 3
Cobresal	1 1
Rangers Talca *	1 0 2p
Curicó Unido	1 0 4p
Unión La Calera *	1 3
Everton	1 1
Unión San Felipe *	2 0 5p
Santiago Wanderers	1 3 6p
Huachipato	2 2
Lota Schwager *	1 2
Univ. de Concepción	0 1
Deportes Concepción *	1 2

Round of 16

Municipal Iquique *	2
Cobreloa	1
Linares Unido *	0
Nublense	4
Unión Española	3
Coquimbo Unido *	0
Universidad Católica	2
Puerto Montt *	4
Palestino *	3
San Luis	0
Audax Italiano	0
Curicó Unido *	1
Unión La Calera *	1
Santiago Wanderers	0
Huachipato	1 1p
Deportes Concepción *	1 4p

Quarter-finals

Municipal Iquique *	2
Nublense	0
Unión Española	1
Puerto Montt *	2
Palestino	2
Curicó Unido *	0
Unión La Calera	1
Deportes Concepción *	3

Semi-finals

Municipal Iquique	3
Puerto Montt *	2
Palestino	0 2p
Deportes Concepción *	0 4p

Final

Municipal Iquique	1 4p
Deportes Concepción	1 3p

PENALTIES

	MI	DC
Ayala	✓	✓
Ricard	✓	✓
Mas	✓	
Almendra		✗
Millape	✓	✓
Nasa		✓
Nunez	✓	
Figueroa		✓
Martel	✗	
Salazar		✗

CUP FINAL

Francisco Sanchez Rumoroso, Coquimbo 8-12-2010, Att: 2,124, Ref: Jorge Osorio

Scorers - Ramos 56 for Iquique; Ricard 33 for Concepción

Iquique - Rodrigo Naranjo (Cristian Limenza 46) - Frank Carilao, Luis Fuentes, Miguel Angel Ayala, Rodrigo Perez (Leonardo Mas 66) - Marco Millape, Nestor Contreras (Sebastian Marchant 74), Rodrigo Nunez, Fernando Martel - Marco Olea, Alvaro Ramos. Tr. Jose Cantillana

Concepción - Luis de Agustini - Alexis Salazar, Cristobal Gonzalez, Cesar Vergara - Hector Berrios (Manuel Simpertegui 84) - Patricio Almendra, Mauricio Lagos, Alejandro Figueroa - Nasa - Hamilton Ricard, David Llanos. Tr. Oscar del Solar

* Home Team/home team in the 1st leg

CHN – CHINA PR

FIFA/COCA-COLA WORLD RANKING

1993	1994	1995	1996	1997	1998	1999	2000	2001	2002	2003	2004	2005	2006	2007	2008	2009	2010
53	40	66	76	55	37	88	75	54	63	86	54	72	84	81	100	93	87

	2010												Hi/Lo
	Jan	Feb	Mar	Mar	Apr	May	Jul	Aug	Sep	Oct	Nov	Dec	37
	93	87	83	84	85	84	78	77	82	89	89	87	108

China's struggles at international level continued in 2010 despite occasional encouraging results, notably their triumph in the East Asian Championship in February 2010 and a friendly win over France prior to the World Cup finals. Their success against the Japanese and Korea Republic in the regional tournament had lifted hopes for a successful Asian Cup in Qatar in January 2011 but that optimism was unfounded as China crashed out in the group stages, just as they had done in four years earlier. The Chinese team in Qatar, however, was an experimental side with the majority under the age of 24, with coach Gao Hongbo declaring his intention to use the Asian Cup as part of his preparation for the qualifying rounds for the 2014 FIFA World Cup finals in Brazil. Chinese clubs also continue to struggle in continental competition although Beijing Guoan did become the first Chinese Super League side to reach the knockout phase of the AFC Champions League since 2006. Changchun, Henan and Shandong all fell at the first hurdle while Beijing were knocked out in the round of 16 by Korea's Suwon Bluewings. At home Shandong won the Super League title for the third time in five years, finishing comfortably ahead of the rest of the field and qualifying for the 2011 AFC Champions League along with Tianjin, Shanghai Shenhua and Hangzhou Greentown.

FIFA WORLD CUP RECORD

1930-1954 DNE **1958** DNQ **1962-1978** DNE **1982-1998** DNQ **2002** 31 r1 **2006-2010** DNQ

FOOTBALL ASSOCIATION OF THE PEOPLE'S REPUBLIC OF CHINA (CFA)

Building A, Dong Jiu Da Sha,
Xi Zhao Si Street, Chongwen
District, Beijing 100061
☎ +86 10 59291030
📠 +86 10 59290309
📧 info.footballchina@gmail.com
🖥 www.fa.org.cn
FA 1924 CON 1974 FIFA 1974
P Yuan Weimin
GS Wei Di

FIFA BIG COUNT 2006

Total players	26 166 335
% of population	1.99%
Male	24 266 330
Female	1 900 000
Amateurs 18+	325 992
Youth under 18	382 762
Unregistered	5 045 100
Professionals	2 239
Referees	21 6574
Admin & coaches	107 400
Number of clubs	1 621
Number of teams	11 347

MAJOR CITIES/TOWNS

		Population
1	Shanghai	15 968 867
2	Beijing	7 817 968
3	Chongqing	4 579 725
4	Xian	4 445 222
5	Wuhan	4 303 340
6	Chengdu	3 916 581
7	Tianjin	3 666 320
8	Shenyang	3 543 444
9	Harbin	3 363 096
10	Nanjing	3 320 712
11	Guangzhou	3 103 466
12	Taiyuan	2 786 596
13	Changchun	2 750 684
14	Shijiazhuang	2 319 694
15	Changsha	2 267 008
16	Jinan	2 191 110
17	Dalian	2 158 193
18	Jilin	2 150 510
19	Nanchang	2 092 603

ZHONGHUA RENMIN GONGHEGUO • PEOPLE'S REPUBLIC OF CHINA

Capital	Beijing	Population	1 338 612 968 (1)	% in cities	43%
GDP per capita	$6000 (133)	Area km²	9 596 961 km² (4)	GMT +/-	+8
Neighbours (km)	Afghanistan 76, Bhutan 470, Burma 2185, India 3380, Kazakhstan 1533, Korea DPR 1416, Kyrgyzstan 858, Laos 423, Mongolia 4677, Nepal 1236, Pakistan 523, Russia 3645, Tajikistan 414, Vietnam 1281 • Coast 14 500				

RECENT INTERNATIONAL MATCHES PLAYED BY CHINA PR

2009	Opponents	Score		Venue	Comp	Scorers	Att	Referee
9-01	Iran	L	1-3	Tehran	Fr	Huang Bowen 65	10 000	Yazdi IRN
14-01	Syria	L	2-3	Aleppo	ACq	Qu Bo 51, Liu Jian 94+	7 000	Torky IRN
21-01	Vietnam	W	6-1	Zhejiang	ACq		15 300	Kim Dong Jin KOR
29-05	Germany	D	1-1	Shanghai	Fr	Hao Junmin 5	25 000	Lee Dong Jun KOR
1-06	Iran	W	1-0	Qinhuangdao	Fr	Gao Lin 45		
4-06	Saudi Arabia	L	1-4	Tianjin	Fr	Jiang Ning 33		
18-07	Palestine	W	3-1	Tianjin	Fr	Qu Bo 11, Gao Lin 46, Yang Hao 59		
25-07	Kyrgyzstan	W	3-0	Tianjin	Fr	Han Peng 17, Hao Junmin 28, Yu Hai 46		
12-08	Singapore	D	1-1	Singapore	Fr	Yang Hao 27. W 4-3p		
15-08	Malaysia	D	0-0	Kuala Lumpur	Fr			
30-09	Botswana	W	4-1	Hohhot	Fr	Gao Lin 29, Qu Bo 52, Zhao Peng 54, Yu Hai 58		
8-11	Kuwait	D	2-2	Kuwait City	Fr	Zheng Long 55, Han Peng 59		
14-11	Lebanon	W	2-0	Beirut	ACq	Yu Hai 44, Qu Bo 72	2 000	Albadwawi UAE
22-11	Lebanon	W	1-0	Zhejiang	ACq	Du Wei 19	21 520	Breeze AUS
30-12	Jordan	D	2-2	Jinan	Fr	Zhang Linpeng 48, Han Peng 56		
2010								
6-01	Syria	D	0-0	Zhejiang	ACq		29 570	Toma JPN
17-01	Vietnam	W	2-1	Hanoi	ACq	Xu Yang 35, Zhang Linpeng 43	3 000	Abdul Bashir SIN
6-02	Japan	D	0-0	Tokyo	EAC		25 964	Delovski AUS
10-02	Korea Republic	W	3-0	Tokyo	EAC	Yu Hai 5, Gao Lin 27, Deng Zhuoxiang 60	3 629	Ng Kai Lam HKG
14-02	Hong Kong	W	2-0	Tokyo	EAC	Qu Bo 2 44 74p	16 439	Kim Jong Hyeok KOR
4-06	France	W	1-0	Saint-Pierre (REU)	Fr	Deng Zhuoxiang 68	10 043	Proenca POR
26-06	Tajikistan	W	4-0	Kunming	Fr	Yan Xiangchuang 10, Yu Hanchao 2 47 78, Qu Bo 78		
11-08	Bahrain	D	1-1	Nanning	Fr	Hai Yu 10		
3-09	Iran	L	0-2	Zhengzhou	Fr			
7-09	Paraguay	D	1-1	Nanjing	Fr	Gao Lin 33		
8-10	Syria	W	2-1	Kunming	Fr	Zhao Peng 38, Zhang Linpeng 50		
12-10	Uruguay	L	0-4	Wuhan	Fr		50 000	Lee Dong Jun KOR
17-11	Latvia	W	1-0	Kunming	Fr	Xu Yang 89	7 500	Ko Hyung Jin KOR
18-12	Estonia	W	3-0	Zhuhai	Fr	Du Wei 17, Yu Hai 20, Yang Xu 38	8 500	Ko Hyung Jin KOR
22-12	Macedonia FYR	W	1-0	Guangzhou	Fr	Deng Zhuoxiang 90	8 000	
2011								
8-01	Kuwait	W	2-0	Doha	ACr1	Zhang Linpeng 58, Deng Zhuoxiang 67	7 423	Williams AUS
12-01	Qatar	L	0-2	Doha	ACr1		30 778	Kim Dong Jin KOR
16-01	Uzbekistan	D	2-2	Doha	ACr1	Yu Hai 6, Hao Junmin 56	3 529	Al Hilali OMA

Fr = Friendly match • EAC = East Asian Championship • AC = AFC Asian Cup • WC = FIFA World Cup • q = qualifier

CHINA PR NATIONAL TEAM HISTORICAL RECORDS

Caps
141 - Li Ming 1991-2004 • 136 - Jia Xiuquan 1982-93 • 132 - Fan Zhiyi 1987-2002 • 120 - Xie Yuxin 1987-96 • 119 - Li Fusheng 1976-84 • 115 - Hao Haidong 1987-2004 • 113 - Lin Lefeng 1977-86 • 109 - Ou Chuliang 1990-2002 • 106 - Li Weifeng 1997- • (These figures include matches not classified as full 'A' international matches. Hao Haidong with 115, Fan Zhiyi with 108 and Li Weifeng with 106 are the only players included in the FIFA Men's Century Club)

Goals
41 - Hao Haidong 1987-2004 • 36 - Liu Haiguang 1983-90 • 33 - Ma Lin 1984-90 • 28 - Li Hui 1983-88 • 26 - Su Maozhen 1992-2002 • 23 - Zuo Shusheng 1979-85 • 19 - Zhao Dayu 1982-86; Fan Zhiyi 1987-2002 & Mai Chao 1986-92 • 17 - Qu Bo 2000-

Past Coaches
Li Fenglou 1951-52 • A Joseph HUN 1954-56 • Dai Linjing 1957 • Chen Chengda 1958-62 • Nian Weisi 1963 • Fang Renqiu 1964 • Nian Weisi 1965-73 • Nian Weisi & Ren Bin 1974-76 • Zhang Honggen 1977 • Nian Weisi 1978 • Zhang Honggen 1979 • Nian Weisi 1980 • Su Yongshun 1980-82 • Zhang Honggen 1982 • Zeng Xuelin 1983-85 • Nian Weisi 1985-86 • Gao Fengwen 1986-90 • Xu Genbao 1991-92 • Klaus Schlappner GER 1992-93 • Qi Wusheng 1994-97 • Bobby Houghton ENG 1997-99 • Jin Zhiyang 2000 • Bora Milutinovic SRB 2000-02 • Shen Xiangfu 2002 • Arie Haan NED 2002-04 • Zhu Guanghu 2005-07 • Vladimir Petrovic SRB & Ratomir Dujkovic SRB 2007-08 • Yin Tiesheng 2008-09 • Gao Hongbo 2009-

CHINA PR 2010

CSL (CHINESE SUPER LEAGUE)

	Pl	W	D	L	F	A	Pts	Shandong	Tianjin	Shanghai	Hangzhou	Beijing	Dalian	Liaoning	Henan	Changchun	Shaanxi	Jiangsu	Shenzhen	Nanchang	Qingdao	Chongqing	Changsha
Shandong Luneng †	30	18	9	3	59	34	**63**		1-0	5-2	4-2	1-0	2-1	2-0	2-2	2-2	1-0	3-0	3-2	1-0	1-1	3-0	4-1
Tianjin Teda †	30	13	11	6	37	29	**50**	1-1		0-2	0-0	0-0	3-4	2-1	2-1	1-2	3-1	2-1	1-0	1-0	1-3	1-1	3-2
Shanghai Shenhua †	30	14	6	10	44	41	**48**	1-2	1-0		2-1	3-2	3-3	1-0	3-2	1-0	1-0	1-3	0-0	1-3	0-0	1-2	2-1
Hangzhou Greentown †	30	13	9	8	38	30	**48**	2-1	0-0	1-1		1-2	1-0	2-1	2-0	1-1	2-0	2-1	2-1	1-1	1-2	0-0	1-1
Beijing Guoan	30	12	10	8	35	29	**46**	2-3	1-1	4-1	0-2		2-1	3-0	2-2	2-1	1-0	1-0	1-2	2-0	1-1	1-0	0-0
Dalian Shide	30	10	12	8	40	37	**42**	2-2	1-2	0-2	2-1	3-0		0-2	0-0	2-1	2-2	1-0	0-0	2-1	3-2	2-2	0-1
Liaoning Whowin	30	10	10	10	39	36	**40**	4-1	1-3	1-0	1-0	2-2	1-1		1-1	5-1	2-1	2-1	1-0	1-0	3-3	1-0	0-1
Henan Construction	30	9	13	8	31	31	**40**	1-1	0-1	2-1	1-0	1-1	0-1	0-2		3-2	1-0	0-2	1-0	1-0	2-2	2-0	2-0
Changchun Yatai	30	10	8	12	40	41	**38**	1-1	1-1	3-1	3-4	0-1	3-2	0-0	0-0		2-0	1-0	2-1	1-2	2-0	1-2	3-0
Shaanxi Chanba	30	9	10	11	33	36	**37**	1-0	0-0	2-1	0-2	0-0	1-1	1-0	1-1	1-0		1-1	3-2	0-3	1-0	2-2	5-0
Jiangsu Sainty	30	8	11	11	27	27	**35**	3-3	1-0	1-1	1-1	0-1	0-0	0-0	0-0	1-2	1-0		0-0	0-2	4-0	3-0	0-0
Shenzhen Ruby	30	8	8	14	34	41	**32**	0-1	1-2	0-4	0-1	1-0	0-0	4-4	1-1	2-1	1-3	0-0		1-0	3-4	3-1	0-0
Nanchang Hengyuan	30	8	8	14	33	35	**32**	1-1	2-2	1-2	3-2	0-1	1-1	0-0	1-1	2-0	1-1	0-1	0-1		2-0	2-5	0-0
Qingdao Jonoon	30	6	12	12	31	44	**30**	1-3	1-1	0-2	0-1	0-0	1-1	0-0	1-0	0-1	0-1	1-1	3-2	0-2		2-1	2-2
Chongqing Lifan	30	7	9	14	36	48	**30**	1-2	1-2	0-1	0-1	2-1	1-1	1-1	1-0	1-1	1-2	2-2	2-3	0-2	3-2		2-0
Changsha Ginde	30	6	12	12	24	42	**30**	0-2	0-0	2-0	1-1	1-0	2-3	1-0	1-2	2-2	1-1	0-0	0-0	2-1	0-2	2-2	

27/03/2010 - 6/11/2010 • † Qualified for the AFC Champions League • Top scorers: **20** - Duvier Riascos COL, Shanghai • **17** - Han Peng, Shandong • **14** - Luis Ramirez HON, Hangzhou • **11** - Leandro Neto BRA, Henan & Yang Xu, Liaoning

CHINA PR 2010

CHINA LEAGUE (2)

	Pl	W	D	L	F	A	Pts	Guangzhou	Chengdu	Yanbian	Shanghai	Hubei	Hunan	Shenyang	Beijing B	Anhui	Pudong	Guangdong	Beijing IT	Nanjing
Guangzhou Evergrande	24	17	6	1	61	21	**57**		2-2	2-1	1-1	2-1	3-1	2-3	3-1	1-0	3-1	2-1	3-1	10-0
Chengdu Blades	24	17	5	2	56	15	**56**	0-0		3-2	0-3	5-2	3-0	1-1	3-1	4-0	4-0	3-0	2-1	3-0
Yanbian	24	12	4	8	30	21	**40**	0-0	0-2		1-0	1-0	2-0	2-0	1-0	2-0	1-0	1-0	3-2	4-1
Shanghai East Asia	24	9	10	5	25	18	**37**	1-3	0-1	0-0		1-0	2-1	0-0	0-0	1-0	4-1	2-0	1-1	1-0
Hubei Orient	24	10	7	7	30	24	**37**	1-1	1-1	0-0	0-0		3-1	0-1	0-0	1-0	1-1	3-0	1-0	1-0
Hunan Billows	24	10	5	9	21	24	**35**	0-1	0-1	1-0	2-1	0-0		1-0	1-0	2-0	1-1	2-0	2-0	0-0
Shenyang Dongjin	24	6	12	6	23	23	**30**	0-2	0-0	1-1	3-1	0-2	0-1		0-1	0-0	1-1	2-2	0-1	3-1
Beijing Baxy §6	24	10	4	10	24	24	**28**	1-0	1-2	2-1	1-3	2-1	0-0	1-2		0-1	0-2	3-0	2-1	0-1
Anhui Jiufang	24	7	3	14	17	36	**24**	0-4	0-4	2-1	0-1	1-0	1-2	1-1	1-3		2-1	0-3	1-0	4-0
Pudong Zobon	24	5	8	11	22	37	**23**	3-3	1-0	1-2	0-0	1-1	1-1	1-1	0-1	1-1		1-0	3-1	1-0
Guangdong S'ray Cave	24	5	7	12	34	39	**22**	2-3	0-3	1-1	1-2	5-1	1-1	3-3	0-1	0-1	5-1		2-1	4-2
Beijing I. Technology	24	4	6	14	22	40	**18**	0-3	0-4	1-3	1-2	0-2	2-0	0-0	0-0	1-2	1-0	2-2		2-2
Nanjing Yoyo	24	3	5	16	19	62	**14**	0-5	0-4	1-0	2-2	2-6	2-1	0-1	1-3	1-0	1-2	2-2	0-2	

3/04/2010 - 30/10/2010 • § = points deducted • Top scorer: **20** - Gao Lin, Guangzhou

MEDALS TABLE

		Overall			League			Cup		Asia			City
		G	S	B	G	S	B	G	S	G	S	B	
1	Liaoning Whowin	11	9	5	8	6	4	2	2	1	1	1	Anshan & Fushun
2	Dalian Shide	11	6	6	8		5	3	4		2	1	Dalian
3	Beijing Guoan	10	6	13	6	3	12	4	3			1	Beijing
4	Shandong Luneng	8	5	2	4	3	2	4	2				Ji'nan
5	Shanghai Shenhua	7	13	5	4	11	5	3	2				Shanghai
6	August 1st	6	6	5	5	6	5	1					Liuzhou
7	Tianjin Teda	3	7	4	2	6	4	1	1				Tianjin
8	North East China	2	1		2	1							
9	Guangdong Hongyuan	1	5	1	1	1	1		4				Guiyang
10	Shenzhen Ruby	1	1	1	1	1						1	Shenzhen
11	Changchun Yatai	1	1		1	1							Changchun
12	Chongqing Lifan	1						1					Chongqing
	Qingdao Hailifeng	1						1					Qingdao

CIV – COTE D'IVOIRE

FIFA/COCA-COLA WORLD RANKING

1993	1994	1995	1996	1997	1998	1999	2000	2001	2002	2003	2004	2005	2006	2007	2008	2009	2010
33	25	20	51	52	44	53	51	44	64	70	40	42	18	37	29	16	21

2010												Hi/Lo
Jan	Feb	Mar	Mar	Apr	May	Jul	Aug	Sep	Oct	Nov	Dec	**16**
16	22	22	25	27	27	26	26	23	19	19	21	**75**

Cote d'Ivoire's surprise quarter-final elimination by Algeria at the African Nations Cup finals in Angola at the start of the year precipitated a tumultuous build-up to the FIFA World Cup finals, which saw Sven Goran Eriksson step in as a very late replacement for Valid Halilhodzic. With little preparation time the Swede departed after the tournament with minimal damage to his reputation but unable to take Côte d'Ivoire to the knockout rounds after they fell at the group stage for the second successive tournament. Star striker Didier Drogba, named in early 2010 as the African Footballer of the Year for 2009, had been in doubt for the tournament after breaking a hand in a warm-up match against Japan but played with a plastic cast and scored a consolation goal against Brazil at Soccer City in a 3-1 defeat. Having drawn with Portugal, the 3-0 victory over North Korea proved academic. Eriksson's flamboyant reputation contrasted with the low key appointment of Francois Zahoui as his replacement, the former international striker scoring a 1-0 win over former world champions Italy in a friendly at London's Upton Park in his debut game. At home ASEC Abidjan won the Ligue 1 title for the 17th time in the last 21 seasons while rivals Africa Sport won the cup with a 2-0 victory over Jeunesse Abidjan - surprise runners-up in both the league and cup.

FIFA WORLD CUP RECORD
1930-1970 DNE 1974-1978 DNQ 1982 DNE 1986-2002 DNQ **2006** 19 r1 **2010** 17 r1

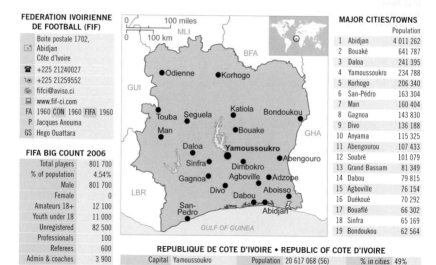

FEDERATION IVOIRIENNE DE FOOTBALL (FIF)

Boite postale 1702,
Abidjan
Côte d'Ivoire
☎ +225 21240027
📠 +225 21259552
✉ fifci@aviso.ci
🖥 www.fif-ci.com

FA	1960	CON	1960	FIFA	1960

P Jacques Anouma
GS Hego Ouattara

FIFA BIG COUNT 2006

Total players	801 700
% of population	4.54%
Male	801 700
Female	0
Amateurs 18+	12 100
Youth under 18	11 000
Unregistered	82 500
Professionals	100
Referees	600
Admin & coaches	3 900
Number of clubs	220
Number of teams	1320

MAJOR CITIES/TOWNS

		Population
1	Abidjan	4 011 262
2	Bouaké	641 787
3	Daloa	241 395
4	Yamoussoukro	234 788
5	Korhogo	206 340
6	San-Pédro	163 304
7	Man	160 404
8	Gagnoa	143 830
9	Divo	136 188
10	Anyama	115 325
11	Abengourou	107 433
12	Soubré	101 079
13	Grand Bassam	81 349
14	Dabou	79 815
15	Agboville	76 154
16	Duékoué	70 292
17	Bouaflé	66 302
18	Sinfra	65 169
19	Bondoukou	62 564

REPUBLIQUE DE COTE D'IVOIRE • REPUBLIC OF COTE D'IVOIRE

Capital	Yamoussoukro	Population	20 617 068 (56)	% in cities	49%
GDP per capita	$1700 (191)	Area km²	322 463 km² (68)	GMT + / -	0

Neighbours (km) Burkina Faso 584, Ghana 668, Guinea 610, Liberia 716, Mali 532 • Coast 515

RECENT INTERNATIONAL MATCHES PLAYED BY COTE D'IVOIRE

2008	Opponents		Score	Venue	Comp	Scorers	Att	Referee
8-06	Madagascar	D	0-0	Antananarivo	WCq			Labrosse SEY
14-06	Botswana	D	1-1	Gaborone	WCq	Meite 65	21 400	Ssegonga UGA
22-06	Botswana	W	4-0	Abidjan	WCq	Sanogo 16, Zokora 22, Sekou Cisse 2 46 70	15 000	Bennaceur TUN
20-08	Guinea	W	2-1	Chantilly	Fr	Bakary Kone 10, Sanogo 45		
7-09	Mozambique	D	1-1	Maputo	WCq	Kone 48	35 000	El Achiri MAR
11-10	Madagascar	W	3-0	Abidjan	WCq	Sanogo 2 41 55, Kalou 65	24 000	Benouza ALG
19-11	Israel	D	2-2	Tel Aviv	Fr	Strul OG 32, Sanogo 85	27 167	
2009								
11-02	Turkey	D	1-1	Izmir	Fr	Drogba 92+		Corpodean ROU
29-03	Malawi	W	5-0	Abidjan	WCq	Romaric 1, Drogba 2 6p 27, Kalou 59, Bakary Kone 70	34 000	Haimoudi ALG
7-06	Guinea	W	2-1	Conakry	WCq	Bakary Kone 43, Romaric 70	14 000	Abd El Fatah EGY
20-06	Burkina Faso	W	3-2	Ouagadougou	WCq	Yaya Toure 14, Tall OG 54, Drogba 70	33 056	Damon RSA
12-08	Tunisia	D	0-0	Sousse	Fr			
5-09	Burkina Faso	W	5-0	Abidjan	WCq	OG 9, Drogba 2 48 64, Yaya Toure 54, Keita 68	28 209	Maillet SEY
10-10	Malawi	D	1-1	Blantyre	WCq	Drogba 67	25 000	El Achiri MAR
14-11	Guinea	W	3-0	Abidjan	WCq	Gervinho 2 16 31, Tiene 67	28 000	Marange ZIM
18-11	Germany	D	2-2	Gelsenkirchen	Fr	Eboue 57, Doumbia 85	33 015	Kuipers NED
2010								
4-01	Tanzania	W	1-0	Dar es Salaam	Fr	Drogba 37	60 000	Mbaga TAN
7-01	Rwanda	W	2-0	Dar es Salaam	Fr	Bamba 85, Angoua 90	5 000	Waziri TAN
11-01	Burkina Faso	D	0-0	Cabinda	CNr1		5 000	Bennaceur TUN
15-01	Ghana	W	3-1	Cabinda	CNr1	Gervinho 23, Tiéné 66, Drogba 90	23 000	Damon RSA
24-01	Algeria	L	2-3	Cabinda	CNqf	Kalou 4, Keita 89	10 000	Maillet SEY
3-03	Korea Republic	L	0-2	London	Fr		6 000	Marriner ENG
30-05	Paraguay	D	2-2	Thonon-Les-Bains	Fr	Drogba 53, Bamba 73	2 000	Bien FRA
4-06	Japan	W	2-0	Sion	Fr	OG 13, Kolo Toure 80	4 919	Studer SUI
15-06	Portugal	D	0-0	Port Elizabeth	WCr1		34 850	Nishimura JPN
20-06	Brazil	L	1-3	Johannesburg	WCr1	Drogba 79	84 445	Lannoy FRA
25-06	Korea DPR	W	3-0	Nelspruit	WCr1	Yaya Toure 14, Romaric 20, Kalou 82	34 763	Undiano ESP
10-08	Italy	W	1-0	London	Fr	Kolo Toure 55	11 176	Atkinson ENG
4-09	Rwanda	W	3-0	Abidjan	CNq	Yaya Toure 10, Kalou 19, Eboue 39		Maillet SEY
9-10	Burundi	W	1-0	Bujumbura	CNq	Romaric 34		El Raay LBY
17-11	Poland	L	1-3	Poznan	Fr	Gervinho 45	42 000	Toma JPN

Fr = Friendly match • CN = African Cup of Nations • WC = FIFA World Cup
q = qualifier • r1 = first round group • qf = quarter-final • sf = semi-final • f = final

MEDALS TABLE

		Overall			Lge	Cup		Africa			
		G	S	B	G	G	S	G	S	B	City
1	ASEC Mimosas	41	5	6	24	16	4	1	1	6	Abidjan
2	Africa Sports National	33	10	2	16	15	7	2	3	2	Abidjan
3	Stade d'Abidjan	11	7	1	5	5	7	1		1	Abidjan
4	Stella Club d'Adjamé	6	6		3	2	5	1	1		Abidjan
5	Onze Freres	2			2						Grand-Bassam
6	Sporting Club de Gagnoa	1	7		1		7				Gagnoa
7	ASC Bouaké	1	2			1	2				Bouaké
	Jeunesse Club d'Abidjan	1	2			1	2				Abidjan
9	SCR Alliance Bouaké	1	1			1	1				Bouaké
	Réveil Club de Daloa	1	1			1	1				Daloa
	Société Omnisport de l'Armée	1	1			1	1				Abidjan
	Issia Wazi FC	1	1			1	1				Gagnoa
13	ASI Abengourou	1				1					Abengourou
	CO Bouaflé	1				1					Bouaflé
	ASC Espoir de Man	1				1					Man
16	Séwé Sport de San Pedro		2				2				San Pedro

COTE D'IVOIRE 2010

LIGUE 1 ORANGE

	Pl	W	D	L	F	A	Pts	ASEC	JCA	Séwé	SOA	Stella	AFAD	Issia	Africa Sports	Bassam	Denguélé	Ouragahio	Stade	Sabé	Hiré
ASEC Mimosas †	26	13	9	4	41	14	48		1-0	3-1	5-1	1-1	1-0	2-0	0-0	3-0	1-1	4-0	2-1	3-0	5-0
Jeunesse Abidjan †	26	11	8	7	30	20	41	0-0		0-0	1-1	0-1	2-0	2-0	1-0	1-2	2-1	1-1	3-0	0-0	2-2
Séwé San Pedro ‡	26	11	7	8	27	20	40	0-0	1-0		3-2	0-2	0-0	2-0	1-0	3-0	1-0	0-0	2-0	1-1	2-0
SO Armée	26	10	9	7	29	24	39	2-1	1-2	0-1		1-2	0-0	4-0	0-0	1-0	0-0	0-0	1-0	3-1	3-2
Stella Adjamé	26	10	8	8	26	25	38	0-1	0-0	2-1	0-2		1-1	2-1	1-1	0-1	0-1	2-1	0-2	2-0	0-0
Acad'y Amadou Diallo	26	8	12	6	21	18	36	2-1	1-0	1-1	0-0	0-0		1-1	0-1	1-0	1-0	0-0	1-0	2-0	3-1
Issia Wazi	26	9	9	8	27	31	36	1-1	2-1	0-0	1-0	2-0	1-1		1-1	1-0	0-0	2-1	1-1	1-2	0-2
Africa Sports ‡	26	9	8	9	16	17	35	0-0	1-3	0-1	0-0	1-0	1-0	3-1		0-1	0-1	1-0	0-0	1-0	0-0
USC Bassam	26	10	4	12	24	30	34	0-0	0-1	2-1	1-0	0-2	1-2	1-1	0-1		3-1	1-1	1-1	1-0	3-2
Denguélé Odienné	26	9	6	11	28	24	33	2-1	0-1	1-0	1-2	4-0	1-1	0-1	1-0	0-1		0-0	4-1	1-2	2-2
ASC Ouragahio	26	8	9	9	30	32	33	1-2	1-1	2-1	1-2	1-2	0-0	1-3	2-0	3-1	2-1		1-0	3-1	3-2
Stade Abidjan	26	9	5	12	20	32	32	1-0	0-2	1-0	0-0	1-4	1-1	1-2	2-1	1-0	0-3	2-1		0-1	2-1
Sabé Sports Bouna	26	8	5	13	29	38	29	0-0	2-3	2-1	1-1	1-1	2-1	1-3	0-1	3-0	2-1	3-4	0-1		3-1
FC Hiré	26	4	7	15	26	49	19	0-3	2-1	1-3	1-2	1-1	2-1	1-1	1-2	0-4	0-1	0-0	0-1	2-1	

16/01/2010 - 17/10/2010 • † Qualified for the CAF Champions League • ‡ Qualified for the CAF Confederation Cup

COTE D'IVOIRE 2010
2ÈME DIVISION (2) – ABIDJAN

	Pl	W	D	L	F	A	Pts
FC Adzopé	22	15	3	4	26	11	48
Entente Bingerville	22	14	5	3	31	8	47
Ecole Yéo Martial	22	11	7	4	30	15	40
RC Koumassi	22	9	4	9	22	17	31
CO Korhogo	22	8	7	7	14	17	31
C'tre Domoraud Cyrille	22	8	6	8	23	15	30
FC Moossou	22	8	6	8	22	28	30
Ahnéby Sport	22	7	6	9	16	18	27
Athletic Adjamé	22	5	10	7	18	17	25
Yopougon FC	22	6	6	10	19	33	24
N'Zi Dimbokro	22	2	8	12	14	35	14
Man FC	22	1	8	13	7	36	11

16/01/2010 - 17/10/2010

COTE D'IVOIRE 2010
2ÈME DIVISION (2) – INTERIOR

	Pl	W	D	L	F	A	Pts
AS Indenié	22	15	5	2	29	8	50
AS AGIR	22	12	5	5	30	13	41
CO Bouaflé	22	9	7	6	23	21	34
Sporting Gagnoa	22	9	6	7	23	23	33
IF Ehouman Richard	22	9	5	8	21	22	32
US Fermiers	22	6	9	7	14	16	27
Lagoké FC	22	7	5	10	22	23	26
San Pedro FC	22	6	7	9	16	21	25
RFC Daoukro	21	5	9	7	16	22	24
Ban Danané	21	5	7	9	10	21	22
Renaissance Bettié	22	5	6	11	20	29	21
Sirocco San Pedro	22	4	7	11	15	24	19

16/01/2010 - 17/10/2010

COUPE NATIONALE 2010

Round of 16

- Africa Sports
- Ecole Yéo Martial
- Stade Abidjan
- ASEC Mimosas
- Djékanou
- FC Hiré
- US Fermiers
- ASC Ouragahio
- Issia Wazi
- Renaissance Bettié
- Man FC
- USC Bassam
- Sabé Sports Bouna
- Denguélé Odienné
- Stella Adjamé
- Jeunesse Abidjan

Quarter-finals

Africa Sports	2
ASEC Mimosas	1
Djékanou	2 5p
ASC Ouragahio	2 6p
Issia Wazi	2
USC Bassam	0
Sabé Sports Bouna	1
Jeunesse Abidjan	3

Semi-finals

Africa Sports	3
ASC Ouragahio	0
Issia Wazi	1
Jeunesse Abidjan	4

Final

Africa Sports ‡	2
Jeunesse Abidjan	0

CUP FINAL

8-08-2010
Scorer - Christian Koffi 2 [30] [62]

* Home team in the 1st leg • ‡ Qualified for the CAF Confederation Cup

CMR – CAMEROON

FIFA/COCA-COLA WORLD RANKING

1993	1994	1995	1996	1997	1998	1999	2000	2001	2002	2003	2004	2005	2006	2007	2008	2009	2010
23	31	37	56	53	41	58	39	38	16	14	23	23	11	24	14	11	37

2010												Hi/Lo
Jan	Feb	Mar	Mar	Apr	May	Jul	Aug	Sep	Oct	Nov	Dec	11
11	20	20	20	19	19	40	40	37	38	38	37	62

Cameroon made an African record sixth appearance at the FIFA World Cup finals in South Africa but departed early after turning in a disappointing performance, their squad riven by divisive personality clashes and mired in a rut of poor form. Even though the Indomitable Lions went seven matches without a win before the finals, they arrived in South Africa with high hopes. An opening group match against Japan presented them with the chance to get off to a good start but they were stunned by a single goal defeat in Bloemfontein and were then beaten by Denmark and the Netherlands. The stark fact is that since the win over Colombia at Italia '90 that proved the genesis of their worldwide reputation, Cameroon have won just once in 13 matches at the finals. French coach Paul Le Guen departed after the finals and was replaced by Javier Clemente, the former Spain manager, who immediately ran into the same pressures and problems previous incumbents of the job have had to deal with. Samuel Eto'o finished the year as a deserved winner of the African Footballer of the Year award, more for his achievement at winning the treble with Inter than for anything in national colours. At home Cotonsport were back into their winning ways, winning a seventh championship in eight years while Fovu beat Les Astres 2-1 in the Cup Final.

FIFA WORLD CUP RECORD

1930-1966 DNE 1970-1978 DNQ **1982** 17 r1 **1986** DNQ **1990** 7 QF **1994** 22 r1 **1998** 25 r1 **2002** 20 r1 **2006** DNQ **2010** 31 r1

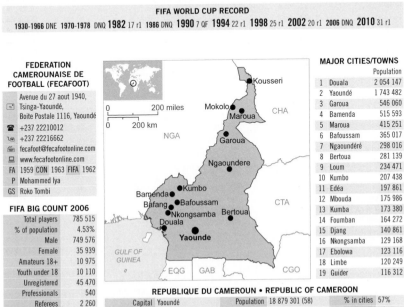

FEDERATION CAMEROUNAISE DE FOOTBALL (FECAFOOT)

Avenue du 27 aout 1940,
Tsinga-Yaoundé,
Boite Postale 1116, Yaoundé
☎ +237 22210012
📠 +237 22216662
✉ fecafoot@fecafootonline.com
🖥 www.fecafootonline.com

FA	1959	CON	1963	FIFA	1962

P Mohammed Iya
GS Roko Tombi

FIFA BIG COUNT 2006

Total players	785 515
% of population	4.53%
Male	749 576
Female	35 939
Amateurs 18+	10 975
Youth under 18	10 110
Unregistered	45 470
Professionals	540
Referees	2 260
Admin & coaches	5 516
Number of clubs	220
Number of teams	1 100

MAJOR CITIES/TOWNS

		Population
1	Douala	2 054 147
2	Yaoundé	1 743 482
3	Garoua	546 060
4	Bamenda	515 593
5	Maroua	415 251
6	Bafoussam	365 017
7	Ngaoundéré	298 016
8	Bertoua	281 139
9	Loum	234 471
10	Kumbo	207 438
11	Edéa	197 861
12	Mbouda	175 986
13	Kumba	173 380
14	Foumban	164 272
15	Djang	140 861
16	Nkongsamba	129 168
17	Ebolowa	123 116
18	Limbe	120 249
19	Guider	116 312

REPUBLIQUE DU CAMEROUN • REPUBLIC OF CAMEROON

Capital	Yaoundé	Population	18 879 301 (58)	% in cities	57%
GDP per capita	$2300 (177)	Area km²	475 440 km² (53)	GMT +/-	+1
Neighbours (km)	Central African Republic 797, Chad 1094, Congo 523, Equatorial Guinea 189, Gabon 298, Nigeria 1690 • Coast 402				

RECENT INTERNATIONAL MATCHES PLAYED BY CAMEROON

2007	Opponents		Score	Venue	Comp	Scorers	Att	Referee
7-02	Togo	D	2-2	Lome	Fr	Boya [65], Ngom Kome [90]		
24-03	Liberia	W	3-1	Yaoundé	CNq	Webo 2 [12 24], Idrissou [85]		Djaoupe TOG
3-06	Liberia	W	2-1	Monrovia	CNq	Mbia [9], Eto'o [54]		Coulibaly MLI
17-06	Rwanda	W	2-1	Garoua	CNq	Idrissou [33], Geremi [48]		Sowe GAM
22-08	Japan	L	0-2	Oita	Fr		37 240	Choi Myung Yong KOR
9-09	Equatorial Guinea	L	0-1	Malabo	CNq			Sidibe MLI
2008								
22-01	Egypt	L	2-4	Kumasi	CNr1	Eto'o 2 [51 89p]		Sowe GAM
26-01	Zambia	W	5-1	Kumasi	CNr1	Geremi [28], Job 2 [31 82], Emana [43], Eto'o [66p]		Nichimura JPN
30-01	Sudan	W	3-0	Tamale	CNr1	Eto'o 2 [27p 89], Ali Khider OG [33]		Djaoupe TOG
4-02	Tunisia	W	3-2	Tamale	CNqf	Mbia 2 [18 92], Geremi [27]		Coulibaly MLI
7-02	Ghana	W	1-0	Accra	CNsf	Nkong [72]		El Arjoun MAR
10-02	Egypt	L	0-1	Accra	CNf			Codjia BEN
31-05	Cape Verde Islands	W	2-0	Yaoundé	WCq	Rigobert Song [8], Eto'o [57p]	20 000	Djaoupe TOG
8-06	Mauritius	W	3-0	Curepipe	WCq	Bikey [11], Eto'o [27], Bebey [87]	2 400	Martins ANG
14-06	Tanzania	D	0-0	Dar es Salaam	WCq		55 000	Codjia BEN
21-06	Tanzania	W	2-1	Yaoundé	WCq	Eto'o 2 [65 89]	25 000	Mendy GAM
6-09	Cape Verde Islands	W	2-1	Praia	WCq	Emana [51], Somen [65]	5 000	Labrosse SEY
11-10	Mauritius	W	5-0	Yaoundé	WCq	Eto'o 2 [26 46p], Meyong Ze 2 [56 72], Makoun [70]	12 000	Lemhambodj MTN
19-11	South Africa	L	2-3	Rustenburg	Fr	Kome [27], Somen [34]	35 000	Mwanza ZAM
2009								
11-02	Guinea	W	3-1	Bondoufle	Fr	Geremi [31], Eto'o 2 [58 87]		
28-03	Togo	L	0-1	Accra	WCq		26 450	Abd El Fatah EGY
7-06	Morocco	D	0-0	Yaoundé	WCq		35 000	Seechurn MRI
12-08	Austria	W	2-0	Klagenfurt	Fr	Webo 2 [28 35]	28 800	Olsiak SVK
5-09	Gabon	W	2-0	Libreville	WCq	Emana [65], Eto'o [67]	10 000	Ndinya KEN
9-09	Gabon	W	2-1	Yaoundé	WCq	Makoun [25], Eto'o [64]	38 000	Bennaceur TUN
10-10	Togo	W	3-0	Yaoundé	WCq	Geremi [29], Makoun [46], Emana [54]	36 401	Kaoma ZAM
14-10	Angola	D	0-0	Olhao	Fr			
14-11	Morocco	W	2-0	Fes	WCq	Webo [19], Eto'o [52]	17 000	Bennett RSA
2010								
9-01	Kenya	W	3-1	Nairobi	Fr	Webo [36], Emana [56], Idrissou [58]	6 000	Amwayi KEN
13-01	Gabon	L	0-1	Lubango	CNr1		15 000	Bennett RSA
17-01	Zambia	W	3-2	Lubango	CNr1	Geremi [68], Eto'o [72], Idrissou [86]	15 000	Al Ghamdi KSA
21-01	Tunisia	D	2-2	Lubango	CNr1	Eto'o [47], N'Guemo [64]	19 000	Doue CIV
25-01	Egypt	L	1-3	Benguela	CNqf	Emana [25]	12 000	Damon RSA
3-03	Italy	D	0-0	Monte Carlo	Fr		10 752	Ennjimi FRA
25-05	Georgia	D	0-0	Linz	Fr		3 500	Brugger AUT
29-05	Slovakia	D	1-1	Klagenfurt	Fr	Enoh [84]	10 000	Lechner AUT
1-06	Portugal	L	1-3	Covilha	Fr	Webo [69]	6 125	Weiner GER
5-06	Serbia	L	3-4	Belgrade	Fr	Webo 2 [5 20], Choupo-Moting [67]	30 000	Trattou CYP
14-06	Japan	L	0-1	Bloemfontein	WCr1		30 620	Benquerenca POR
19-06	Denmark	L	1-2	Pretoria	WCr1	Eto'o [10]	38 074	Larrionda URU
24-06	Netherlands	L	1-2	Cape Town	WCr1	Eto'o [65p]	63 093	Pozo CHI
11-08	Poland	W	3-0	Szczecin	Fr	Eto'o 2 [30 52], Aboubakar [86]	17 000	Asumaa FIN
4-09	Mauritius	W	3-1	Bellevue	CNq	Eto'o 2 [39 47], Choupo-Moting [63p]		Damon RSA
9-10	Congo DR	D	1-1	Garoua	CNq	OG [54]		Maillet SEY

Fr = Friendly match • CN = Africa Cup of Nations • WC = FIFA World Cup • q = qualifier

CAMEROON NATIONAL TEAM HISTORICAL RECORDS

Valeri Nepomniachi RUS 1988-90 • Philippe Redon FRA 1991-92 • Jules Nyongha 1992-93 • Henri Michel FRA 1994 • Jules Nyongha 1994-96 • Henri Depireux BEL 1996-97 • Jean Manga Onguene 1997-98 • Claude Le Roy FRA 1998 • Pierre Lechantre FRA 1998-00 • Jean-Paul Akono 2000-01 • Pierre Lechantre FRA 2001 • Robert Corfu FRA 2001 • Winfried Schafer GER 2001-04 • Artur Jorge POR 2005-06 • Arie Haan NED 2006-07 • Jules Nyongha 2007 • Otto Pfister GER 2007-09 • Thomas Nkono 2009 • Paul Le Guen FRA 2009-10 • Javier Clemente ESP 2010-

CAMEROON 2009–10

DIVISION 1 MTN

	Pl	W	D	L	F	A	Pts	Cotonsport	Les Astres	Tiko United	Panthère	YOSA	Unisport	Union	Renaissance	Canon	Université	Sable	Fovu	Matelots	Roumdé
Cotonsport Garoua †	26	17	5	4	50	20	56	–	1-0*	2-0	4-1	2-1	4-2	2-1	2-1	1-1	2-0	2-1	5-2	5-0	3-0
Les Astres Douala †	26	14	7	5	37	21	49	1-3	–	2-0	3-2	0-0	2-1	1-1	3-0	2-1	2-1	4-0	2-0	5-2	1-1
Tiko United ‡	26	13	6	7	29	21	45	1-2	2-2	–	4-0	1-0	0-2	2-1	1-0	1-0	2-0	1-0	2-1	1-0	3-1
Panthère Bangangté	26	10	11	5	28	24	41	0-0	0-2	1-1	–	0-0	1-0	0-0	2-0	1-0	0-0	1-1	0-0	2-0	1-0
Young Sports Academy	26	8	12	6	26	17	36	0-1	2-0	1-0	1-1	–	1-0	1-1	1-1	1-1	0-0	0-0	0-0	2-0	2-1
Unisport Bafang	26	10	6	10	26	25	36	1-1	1-2	0-1	1-2	0-0	–	1-1	2-1	2-0	2-0	0-2	1-1	1-2	0-0
Union Douala	26	8	10	8	33	29	34	2-5	0-1	2-1	0-0	2-2	3-1	–	3-2	0-0	5-0	1-1	2-2	1-2	2-1
Renaissance Ngoumou	26	10	4	12	23	30	34	1-0	1-0	0-1	1-1	0-3	0-1	1-0	–	2-0	1-2	3-0	0-3	0-0	3-2
Canon Yaoundé	26	8	8	10	27	25	32	0-2	0-0	1-2	1-1	2-1	0-1	0-0	1-2	–	1-0	2-0	2-1	3-0	6-2
Université Ngaoundéré	26	8	8	10	18	25	32	1-0	0-0	1-0	0-1	1-0	0-1	2-1	0-0	0-0	–	2-0	1-1	1-1	3-1
Sable Batie	26	8	7	11	18	27	31	0-0	0-0	0-0	1-0	0-2	0-2	2-0*	1-2	1-1	0-1	–	1-0	1-0	1-0
Fovu Baham	26	7	9	10	23	26	30	2-0	2-1	0-0	0-2	0-0	1-1	0-1	2-1*	1-0	1-0	0-1	–	1-1	2-1
Matelots Douala	26	7	4	15	22	42	25	0-1	0-1	1-1	2-3	1-5	0-1	1-0	1-0	1-3	2-1	1-2	1-0	–	3-0
Roumdé Adjia	26	4	3	19	21	49	15	1-1	1-0	1-0	2-5	2-0	0-1	0-3	0-1	0-1	0-1	2-4	1-2	1-0	–

25/10/2009 – 6/06/2010 • † Qualified for the CAF Champions League • ‡ Qualified for the Confederation Cup • Matches in bold was awarded
* Matches were awarded as 0-0 wins to Les Astres, Union and Renaissance respectively

CAMEROON 2009–10 MTN ELITE TWO (2)

	Pl	W	D	L	F	A	Pts
Lausanne Yaoundé	26	14	9	3	27	9	51
Caïman Douala	26	14	8	4	51	26	50
Scorpion Bay	26	12	9	5	34	17	45
APEJES Mfou	26	11	10	5	41	18	43
Achille Yaoundé	26	8	12	6	28	22	36
Njala Quan Academy	26	9	9	8	22	21	36
Sahel Maroua	26	10	6	10	27	29	36
Tonnerre Kalara	26	10	5	11	18	22	35
Douala AC	26	8	10	8	27	23	34
Avenir Bertoua	26	8	9	9	23	23	33
Aigle Royal Dschang	26	7	8	11	21	30	29
Danay Yagoua	26	7	5	14	17	45	26
Renaissance Meiganga	26	4	8	14	18	39	20
Espérance Guider §3	26	4	4	18	15	45	13

31/10/2009 – 5/06/2010 • § = points deducted

MEDALS TABLE

		Overall			Lge	Cup			Africa			City
		G	S	B	G	G	S	B	G	S	B	
1	Canon	25	8	4	10	11	5		4	3	4	Yaoundé
2	Cotonsport	14	3	1	10	4	1			2	1	Garoua
3	Union	12	6	1	4	6	6		2		1	Douala
4	Tonnerre Kalara	10	5	1	5	4	3		1	2	1	Yaoundé
5	Oryx	9	1	1	5	3	1		1		1	Douala
6	Racing Club	5	3		4	1	3					Bafoussam
7	Diamant	4	4	1	1	3	4				1	Yaoundé
8	Lion Club	4				4						Yaoundé
9	Caïman	3	3			3				3		Douala
10	Fovu	3	1		1	2	1					Baham
11	Dynamo	3				3						Douala
12	Aigle Royal	2	2		2		2					Nkongsamba
13	Léopards	2	1	1	2		1			1		Douala
14	Olympique	2				2						Mvolyé
	Panthère	2				2						Bagante
16	Sable	1	2		1		2					Batié
	Unisport	1	2		1		2					Bafang
17	Dihep Nkam	1	1			1	1					Yabassi

COUPE DU CAMEROUN 2010

Round of 16

Fovu Baham *	3 3
Danay Yagoua	0 0
Fleuron *	0 1
Renaissance Ngoumou	2 5
Unisport Bafang	2 3
Titanic *	2 2
Sable Batie	0 1 2p
Racing Bafoussam *	1 0 4p
Cotonsport Garoua *	5 0
Panthère Bangangté	1 1
Univ'té Ngaoundéré	0 0
Tiko United *	3 3
Union Douala	2 5
Canon Yaoundé *	0 1
Lausanne Yaoundé	2 1
Les Astres Douala *	2 2

Quarter-finals

Fovu Baham	1 1
Renaissance Ng'mou *	1 0
Unisport Bafang *	0 0
Racing Bafoussam	0 3
Cotonsport Garoua	1 0
Tiko United *	1 0
Union Douala *	0 0 4p
Les Astres Douala	0 0 5p

Semi-finals

Fovu Baham *	0 1 5p
Racing Bafoussam	1 0 4p
Cotonsport Garoua	1 0
Les Astres Douala *	1 1

Final

Fovu Baham ‡	2
Les Astres Douala	1

* Home team in the 1st leg • ‡ Qualified for the CAF Confederation Cup

CUP FINAL

Ahmadou Ahidjo, Yaoundé
31-10-2010
Scorers – Romeo Mbelle [41], Tresor Owona Zoa [90] for Fovu; Ndemen Feuleu [71] for Astres

COD – CONGO DR

FIFA/COCA-COLA WORLD RANKING

1993	1994	1995	1996	1997	1998	1999	2000	2001	2002	2003	2004	2005	2006	2007	2008	2009	2010
71	68	68	66	76	62	59	70	77	65	56	78	77	66	74	91	107	130

2010												Hi/Lo
Jan	Feb	Mar	Mar	Apr	May	Jul	Aug	Sep	Oct	Nov	Dec	51
107	111	112	111	111	121	124	123	132	124	129	130	132

In 2010, for the second year running, the all powerful TP Mazembe Englebert were crowned African champions, the second time they had claimed consecutive continental titles having also won in 1967 and 1968. And it was done with some style by beating Esperance of Tunisia 6-1 on aggregate in the final, their 5-0 win in the first leg matching the record win for a final that they already held from 1968. But that was just the start of Mazembe's celebrations when the following month they became the first African side to reach the final of the FIFA Club World Cup, beating Copa Libertadores winners Internacional of Brazil 2-0 in the semi-finals before losing to Italy's Internazionale in the final. The achievement produced fulsome tributes across the continent, breaking down another barrier for the African game, particularly in a tournament where African sides have performed poorly in past years. The success at club level contrasted starkly with the form of the national team, the Leopards, who had a disappointing 2010, losing five out of their six internationals. The one highlight was a potentially vital point away to Cameroon in their 2012 African Nations Cup qualifier in October. Frenchman Robert Nouzaret's debut with the side had seen Congo lose 4-2 at home to Senegal in September in their opening match of campaign.

FIFA WORLD CUP RECORD
1930-1970 DNE **1974** 16 r1 1978-1982 DNQ 1986 DNE 1990-2010 DNQ

FEDERATION CONGOLAISE DE FOOTBALL-ASSOCIATION (FECOFA)

31 Avenue de la Justice, c/Gombe, Boite postale 1284, Kinshasa 1

☎ +243 81 9049788

✆ +243 81 3013527

✉ fecofa_sg@yahoo.fr

▯

FA 1919 CON 1973 FIFA 1962

P Selemani Omari

GS Gregoire Badi

FIFA BIG COUNT 2006

Total players	2 515 600
% of population	4.01%
Male	2 515 600
Female	0
Amateurs 18+	55 600
Youth under 18	22 000
Unregistered	165 000
Professionals	0
Referees	2 900
Admin & coaches	7 700
Number of clubs	770
Number of teams	3 300

MAJOR CITIES/TOWNS

		Population
1	Kinshasa	9 518 988
2	Lubumbashi	1 713 852
3	Mbuji-Mayi	1 546 705
4	Kolwezi	970 520
5	Kisangani	600 011
6	Boma	527 725
7	Likasi	521 341
8	Kananga	514 070
9	Tshikapa	317 830
10	Bukavu	241 690
11	Mwene-Ditu	218 782
12	Uvira	202 240
13	Kikwit	200 880
14	Mbandaka	199 333
15	Matadi	194 903
16	Gandajika	181 987
17	Kalemie	181 496
18	Butembo	180 721
19	Goma	164 348

REPUBLIQUE DEMOCRATIQUE DU CONGO • DEMOCRATIC REPUBLIC OF THE CONGO

Capital	Kinshasa	Population	68 692 542 (18)	% in cities	34%
GDP per capita	$300 (228)	Area km²	2 344 858 km² (12)	GMT +/-	+1
Neighbours (km)	Angola 2511, Burundi 233, Central African Republic 1577, Congo 2410, Rwanda 217, Sudan 628, Tanzania 459, Uganda 765, Zambia 1930 • Coast 37				

RECENT INTERNATIONAL MATCHES PLAYED BY CONGO DR

2006	Opponents	Score		Venue	Comp	Scorers	Att	Referee
3-09	Namibia	W	3-2	Kinshasa	CNq	Mbele [32], Kalulika [63], Kinkela [80]		Evehe CMR
7-10	Libya	D	1-1	Tripoli	CNq	Bageta [37]		Pare BFA
9-12	Tanzania	L	0-2	Dar es Salaam	Fr			
2007								
29-04	Ethiopia	W	2-0	Kinshasa	CNq	Mbutu [29], LuaLua [52p]		Bennett RSA
28-05	Congo	L	1-2	Brazzaville	Fr	Nkulukuta [72]		
1-06	Ethiopia	L	0-1	Addis Abeba	CNq			Hicuburundi BDI
16-06	Namibia	D	1-1	Windhoek	CNq	Matumona [25]		Mwanza ZAM
29-07	Madagascar	D	0-0	Antananarivo	Fr			
22-08	Angola	W	3-1	Kinshasa	Fr	Oneseke [6], Yemweni [52], Mputu [90]		
8-09	Libya	D	1-1	Kinshasa	CNq	Nonda [39p]		Djaopupe TOG
2008								
25-03	Gabon	D	0-0	Aubervilliers	Fr			
26-03	Algeria	D	1-1	Nanterre	Fr	Mbokani [25]		
1-06	Egypt	L	1-2	Cairo	WCq	Ilunga [43]	40 000	Seechurn MRI
8-06	Malawi	W	1-0	Kinshasa	WCq	Matumona [76]	35 000	Abdel Gadir SUD
13-06	Djibouti	W	6-0	Djibouti	WCq	Mbokani 2 [24 47], Nonda [30], Matumona 2 [39 51], Mputu [80]	3 000	Disang BOT
22-06	Djibouti	W	5-1	Kinshasa	WCq	Nonda 3 [10 45 52], Tshiolola [60], Mbokani [64]	15 000	Rouaissi MAR
20-08	Togo	W	2-1	Dreux	Fr	Makiadi [49], Lua Lua [68]		
7-09	Egypt	L	0-1	Kinshasa	WCq		80 000	Bennett RSA
11-10	Malawi	L	1-2	Blantyre	WCq	Lua Lua [13]	50 000	Codjia BEN
2009								
9-05	Tanzania	W	2-0	Dar es Salaam	Fr	Kaluyitukadioko 2 [5 49]		
6-06	Namibia	L	0-4	Windhoek	Fr			
12-08	Senegal	L	1-2	Blois	Fr	Makiadi [73]		
14-10	Qatar	D	2-2	Sannois St-Gratien	Fr	Mbayo 2 [35 72p]		
2010								
3-03	Nigeria	L	2-5	Abuja	Fr	Bedi 2 [43 71]	5 000	
21-05	Saudi Arabia	L	0-2	Innsbruck	Fr			
11-08	Egypt	L	3-6	Cairo	Fr	Ilunga [17], Matumona 2 [54 69p]		
5-09	Senegal	L	2-4	Kinshasa	CNq	Mihayo [42], Kabangu [71]		Haimoudi ALG
9-10	Cameroon	D	1-1	Garoua	CNq	Diba [37]		Maillet SEY
17-11	Mali	L	1-3	Evreux	Fr	Ilunga [16]		

Fr = Friendly match • CN = CAF African Cup of Nations • WC = FIFA World Cup • q = qualifier

COUPE DU CONGO 2010

Second Round Group Stage

Group A

Group A	Pl	W	D	L	F	A	Pts	ASVC	SMSB	OCBD
AS Ndoki a Ndombe	3	2	1	0	5	1	7	1-1	1-0	3-0
AS Veti Club	3	1	1	1	2	3	4		1-0	0-2
SM Sanga Balende	3	1	0	2	3	3	3			3-1
OC Bukavu Dawa	3	1	0	2	3	6	3			

Group B

Group B	Pl	W	D	L	F	A	Pts	ASD	TSM	ASN
DC Motema Pembe	3	2	1	0	8	1	7	0-0	6-1	2-0
AS Dragons	3	1	2	0	4	2	5		3-1	1-1
TS Malekesa	3	1	0	2	3	9	3			1-0
AS Nika	3	0	1	2	1	4	1			

Final

DC Motema Pembe ‡	3
AS Ndoki a Ndombe	0

Held in Lubumbashi from 19/08/2010 to 26/08/2010 • ‡ Qualified for the CAF Confederation Cup
Final: Stade de la Kenya, Lubumbashi, 26-08-2010. Scorers - Diavita [40], Nlandu Mankela [p], Isama Penko [85]

CONGO DR 2010
LIGUE NATIONAL DE FOOTBALL XV (LINAFOOT)

First Round Group Stage

Group A (Kinshasa)	Pl	W	D	L	F	A	Pts	Vita	Veti	TPM	CSMM
AS Vita Club	6	5	1	0	24	0	16		4-0	6-0	9-0
AS Veti Club	6	4	1	1	12	5	13	0-0		1-0	5-0
TP Molunge	6	2	0	4	5	13	6	0-2	1-3		2-0
CS Matiti Mabe	6	0	0	6	1	24	0	0-3	0-3	1-2	

Group B (Matadi)	Pl	W	D	L	F	A	Pts	TCE	DCMP	ASV	ASBS
TC Elima	6	6	0	0	11	2	18		2-0	2-1	1-0
DC Motema Pembe	6	4	0	2	13	6	12	0-3		3-0	2-0
AS Vutuka	6	2	0	4	7	11	6	0-1	1-3		3-1
AS Babeti ya Sika	6	0	0	6	3	15	0	1-2	0-5	1-2	

Group C (Mbuji-Mayi)	Pl	W	D	L	F	A	Pts	SMSB	ASNS	OCK	UST
SM Sanga Balende	6	4	1	1	7	3	13		1-0	1-2	2-0
AS New Soger	6	2	2	2	4	3	8	1-1		0-0	1-0
Olympic Kinshasa	6	2	2	2	4	5	8	0-1	0-2		1-1
US Tshinkunku	6	1	1	4	2	6	4	0-1	1-0	0-1	

Group D (Lubumbashi)	Pl	W	D	L	F	A	Pts	SEL	JSL	ASB
St Eloi Lupopo	4	4	0	0	13	0	12		1-0	5-0
JS Likasi	4	1	1	2	4	5	4	0-2		3-1
AS Bantous	4	0	1	3	2	14	1	0-5	1-1	
AS Saint-Luc				Disqualified						

Group E (Goma)	Pl	W	D	L	F	A	Pts	TSM	DCV	OCM
TS Malekesa	4	2	0	1	5	2	9		2-0	2-1
DC Virunga	4	3	1	1	3	3	7	1-0		1-0
OC Muungano	4	0	1	3	2	5	1	0-1	1-1	
TP CIOD Pangi				Disqualified						

Group F (Kisangani)	Pl	W	D	L	F	A	Pts	ASN	AB	ASK	ASN
AS Nika	6	6	0	0	20	5	18		2-0	2-1	4-2
Ajax Bukavu	6	3	1	2	17	7	10	2-3		5-1	8-0
AS Kabasha	6	2	0	4	15	13	6	0-3	1-2		7-1
AS Ndjadi	6	0	1	5	3	30	1	0-6	0-0	0-5	

MEDALS TABLE

		Overall			Lge	Cup	Africa		
		G	S	B	G	G	G	S	B
1	DC Motema Pembe	26		3	12	13	1		3
2	AS Vita Club	22	1	3	12	9	1	1	3
3	TP Mazembe	20	2	2	10	5	5	2	2
4	AS Dragons	9	2		4	5	2		
5	St Eloi Lupopo	8		1	6	2			1
6	AS Kalamu	4				4			
7	US Bilombe	2			1		1		
8	AC Sodigraf	1	1			1		1	
9	AS Bantous	1			1				
	OC Bukavu Dawa	1				1			
	CS Cilu	1				1			
	US Kenya	1				1			
	Lubumbashi Sport	1				1			
	Maniema Union	1				1			
	SCOM Mikishi	1			1				
	SM Sanga Balende	1	1		1				
	US Tshinkunku	1			1				
	AS Vita Kabasha	1					1		

LIGUE NATIONAL DE FOOTBALL XV (LINAFOOT)

Second Round Group Stage

Group A - Ouest	Pl	W	D	L	F	A	Pts	Vita	TCE	ASN	TSM
AS Vita Club	6	5	0	1	13	4	15		1-3	2-0	3-0
TC Elima	6	3	2	1	11	5	11	1-2		1-1	3-0
AS Nika	6	1	2	3	5	8	5	0-3	1-1		3-0
TS Malekesa	6	1	0	5	1	13	3	0-2	0-2	1-0	

Group B - Est	Pl	W	D	L	F	A	Pts	TPM	SEL	SMSB	ASVC
TP Mazembe	6	4	2	0	23	8	14		5-0	3-3	5-2
St Eloi Lupopo	6	3	1	2	8	15	10	1-7		1-0	4-3
SM Sanga Balende	6	0	5	1	6	7	5	0-0	0-0		1-1
AS Veti Club	6	0	2	4	10	17	2	2-3	0-2	2-2	

Final Stage

	Pl	W	D	L	F	A	Pts	Vita	TPM	SEL	TCE
AS Vita Club †	6	3	3	0	9	2	12		0-0	1-0	5-0
TP Mazembe †	6	3	3	0	7	3	12	1-1		1-0	2-1
St Eloi Lupopo ‡	6	1	1	4	5	6	4	0-1	0-0		3-0
TC Elima	6	1	1	4	6	16	4	1-1	1-3	3-2	

COK – COOK ISLANDS

FIFA/COCA-COLA WORLD RANKING

1993	1994	1995	1996	1997	1998	1999	2000	2001	2002	2003	2004	2005	2006	2007	2008	2009	2010
-	-	-	188	192	173	182	170	179	182	190	190	194	197	200	201	184	188

2010												Hi/Lo
Jan	Feb	Mar	Mar	Apr	May	Jul	Aug	Sep	Oct	Nov	Dec	169
184	184	182	182	181	181	193	193	190	190	189	188	202

With the completion of the 'House of Football' at Matavera in 2009 - the culmination of a seven-year project funded by the FIFA Goal Programme - footballers in the Cook Islands now have at their disposal excellent facilities. The football association had an active 2010 even though the national team didn't play any international matches. Instead the focus was on the domestic game and the seven clubs which cater for the sport at all age groups, both male and female. The most successful team of the season was Tupapa. They prevented Nikao Sokattak from winning a hat trick of league titles although it came down to goal difference in an expanded season which saw each team face each other twice. The Tupapa women's team were successful in both their league and cup tournaments although the club failed to make it a clean sweep after losing to Nikao in the men's CIFA Cup Final. In a dramatic game Tupapa went 2-0 up, but the introduction of Tuka Tisam changed the game for Nikao. A minute after coming on he was brought down in the box and Dawn Tare scored the resulting penalty and then with just minutes remaining and having dribbled for 30 metres up the field, he set up his brother Anonga to score the equaliser. The match ended 2-2 but Nikao then won the penalty shoot out to take the trophy.

FIFA WORLD CUP RECORD
1930-1994 DNE 1998-2010 DNQ

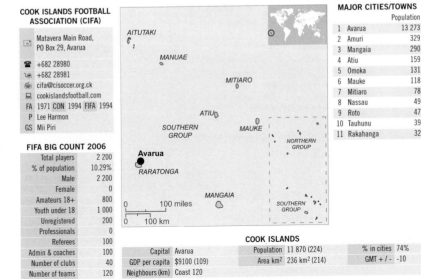

COOK ISLANDS FOOTBALL ASSOCIATION (CIFA)

Matavera Main Road,
PO Box 29, Avarua

☎ +682 28980
🖷 +682 28981
✉ cifa@cisoccer.org.ck
🖵 cookislandsfootball.com
FA 1971 CON 1994 FIFA 1994
P Lee Harmon
GS Mii Piri

FIFA BIG COUNT 2006

Total players	2 200
% of population	10.29%
Male	2 200
Female	0
Amateurs 18+	800
Youth under 18	1 000
Unregistered	200
Professionals	0
Referees	100
Admin & coaches	100
Number of clubs	40
Number of teams	120

MAJOR CITIES/TOWNS

		Population
1	Avarua	13 273
2	Amuri	329
3	Mangaia	290
4	Atiu	159
5	Omoka	131
6	Mauke	118
7	Mitiaro	78
8	Nassau	49
9	Roto	47
10	Tauhunu	39
11	Rakahanga	32

COOK ISLANDS

Capital	Avarua	Population	11 870 (224)	% in cities	74%
GDP per capita	$9100 (109)	Area km²	236 km² (214)	GMT + / -	-10
Neighbours (km)	Coast 120				

RECENT INTERNATIONAL MATCHES PLAYED BY COOK ISLANDS

2002	Opponents	Score		Venue	Comp	Scorers	Att	Referee
	No international matches played in 2002							
2003								
	No international matches played in 2003							
2004								
5-05	Samoa	D	0-0	Auckland	Fr			
10-05	Tahiti	L	0-2	Honiara	WCq		12 000	Singh FIJ
12-05	Solomon Islands	L	0-5	Honiara	WCq		14 000	Fred VAN
15-05	Tonga	L	1-2	Honiara	WCq	John Pareanga 59	15 000	Sosongan PNG
17-05	New Caledonia	L	0-8	Honiara	WCq		400	Singh FIJ
2005								
	No international matches played in 2005							
2006								
	No international matches played in 2006							
2007								
27-08	Fiji	L	0-4	Apia	WCq		400	Fred VAN
29-08	New Caledonia	L	0-3	Apia	WCq		200	Fox NZL
1-09	Tuvalu †	W	4-1	Apia	WCq	Teariki Mateariki 2 28 69, Tom Le Mouton 88, Kunda Tom 93+	200	Hester NZL
3-09	Tahiti	L	0-1	Apia	WCq		100	Aimaasu SAM
2008								
	No international matches played in 2008							
2009								
11-06	Tonga	D	1-1	Atele	Fr	Joseph Ngauora 29		
13-06	Tonga	W	2-1	Atele	Fr	Campbell Best 3, Joseph Ngauora 8	204	Cross NZL
2010								
	No international matches played in 2010							

Fr = Friendly match • WC = FIFA World Cup • q = qualifier • † Not an official international

CIFA CUP 2010

Quarter-finals		Semi-finals		Final	
Nikao Sokattak					
Arorangi		**Nikao Sokattak**	4		
Avatiu		Matavera	0		
Matavera				**Nikao Sokattak**	2 4p
Titikaveka				Tupapa	2 3p
Takuvaine		Titikaveka	0		
		Tupapa	4		
Tupapa	Bye				

Final: Matavera, 18-12-2010. Scorers - Dawn Tare 52p, Anonga Tisam 85 for Nikao; Campbel Best 2 5 50 for Tupapa

COOK ISLANDS 2010

RAROTONGA LEAGUE ROUND CUP	Pl	W	D	L	F	A	Pts	Tupapa	Nikao	Takuvaine	Avatiu	Titikaveka	Matavera	Arorangi
Tupapa	12	10	1	1	64	8	**31**		0-0	9-0	0-1	4-1	6-0	7-1
Nikao Sokattak	12	10	1	1	56	12	**31**	1-3		2-1	4-1	7-0	4-1	12-0
Takuvaine	12	5	2	5	27	44	**17**	1-11	2-3		1-1	3-2	3-2	3-1
Avatiu	12	4	3	5	31	31	15	1-5	2-4	1-4		4-0	2-2	1-7
Titikaveka	12	2	3	7	21	44	9	1-6	1-4	9-4	1-7		2-2	1-1
Matavera	12	1	5	6	17	32	8	0-5	1-3	2-2	2-2	1-1		3-0
Arorangi	12	2	1	9	16	61	7	1-8	0-12	1-3	1-8	1-2	2-1	

27/08/2010 - 27/11/2010 • Match in bold awarded

COL – COLOMBIA

FIFA/COCA-COLA WORLD RANKING

1993	1994	1995	1996	1997	1998	1999	2000	2001	2002	2003	2004	2005	2006	2007	2008	2009	2010
21	17	15	4	10	34	25	15	5	37	39	26	24	34	17	49	39	48

2010												Hi/Lo
Jan	Feb	Mar	Mar	Apr	May	Jul	Aug	Sep	Oct	Nov	Dec	4
39	39	38	39	34	35	39	36	40	46	47	48	51

The Colombian football federation appointed Hernan Dario Gomez as the national team coach in May 2010 in a bid to revive the fortunes of a team that has spent much of the past decade in the doldrums. Widely seen as a safe pair of hands, Gomez had previously taken Colombia to the 1998 World Cup and Ecuador to the 2002 finals. His first task after a year of friendly matches will be to lead Colombia in the 2011 Copa America in Argentina but the real target remains a place at the 2014 World Cup in Brazil after missing out on three consecutive tournaments. In club football, 2010 threw up three different winners and yet again none were from Bogota. La Equidad came close to breaking a barren spell in the league stretching back to 1988 for clubs from the capital but despite winning the first leg of the opening championship final at the end of May, they lost 3-0 to Atlético Junior in the return in Barraquilla to miss out on a first title. In the closing championship Once Caldas added to their growing reputation by beating Tolima 4-3 on aggregate in the final whilst Deportivo Cali won the Copa Postabon. Boasting one of the newest stadiums in South America, Cali beat second division champions Itagui in front of a full house as their 'Monumental' Palma Seca witnessed what fans hope will be the first of many trophies won at their new home.

FIFA WORLD CUP RECORD

1930-1954 DNE 1958 DNQ **1962** 14 r1 1966-1986 DNQ **1990** 14 r2 **1994** 19 r1 **1998** 21 r1 2002-2010 DNQ

FEDERACION COLOMBIANA DE FUTBOL (COLFUTBOL)

Avenida 32,
No. 16-22 Piso 5°,
Apdo Aéreo 17602, Bogotá

☎ +57 1 2889838
🖷 +57 1 2889793
🖳 info@colfutbol.org
🖳 www.colfutbol.org
FA 1924 CON 1940 FIFA 1936
P Luis Bedoya
GS Celina Sierra

FIFA BIG COUNT 2006

Total players	3 043 229
% of population	6.98%
Male	2 670 029
Female	364 200
Amateurs 18+	89 000
Youth under 18	166 000
Unregistered	1 440 000
Professionals	929
Referees	2 200
Admin & coaches	13 600
Number of clubs	2 750
Number of teams	7 700

MAJOR CITIES/TOWNS

		Population
1	Bogotá	7 240 836
2	Medellín	2 318 002
3	Cali	2 195 218
4	Barranquilla	1 145 015
5	Cartagena	900 111
6	Cúcuta	596 735
7	Soledad	546 854
8	Bucaramanga	519 207
9	Ibagué	494 669
10	Soacha	458 672
11	Santa Marta	429 670
12	Villavicencio	401 559
13	Pereira	387 796
14	Bello	383 740
15	Manizales	363 255
16	Valledupar	332 135
17	Pasto	330 423
18	Buenaventura	315 594
19	Neiva	314 693

REPUBLICA DE COLOMBIA • REPUBLIC OF COLOMBIA;

Capital	Bogotá	Population	45 644 023 (28)	% in cities 74%
GDP per capita	$8800 (114)	Area km²	1 138 914 km² (26)	GMT + / - -5
Neighbours (km)	Brazil 1644, Ecuador 590, Panama 225, Peru 1800, Venezuela • Coast 3208			

RECENT INTERNATIONAL MATCHES PLAYED BY COLOMBIA

2007	Opponents	Score		Venue	Comp	Scorers	Att	Referee
14-10	Brazil	D	0-0	Bogota	WCq		41 000	Amarilla PAR
17-10	Bolivia	D	0-0	La Paz	WCq		19 469	Reinoso ECU
17-11	Venezuela	W	1-0	Bogota	WCq	Bustos [82]	28 273	Selman CHI
20-11	Argentina	W	2-1	Bogota	WCq	Bustos [62], Moreno [83]	41 700	Larrionda URU
2008								
6-02	Uruguay	D	2-2	Montevideo	Fr	Edixon Perea 2 [23 73]		
26-03	Honduras	L	1-2	Fort Lauderdale	Fr	Renteria [55]	13 000	Griselich USA
30-04	Venezuela	W	5-2	Bucaramanga	Fr	Rodallega 2 [1 75], Polo [11], Hernandez [65], Luis Fernandes Mosquera [84p]	25 000	Carrillo PER
29-05	Republic of Ireland	L	0-1	London	Fr		15 000	Clattenburg ENG
3-06	France	L	0-1	Paris	Fr		79 727	Dean ENG
14-06	Peru	D	1-1	Lima	WCq	Rodallega [8]	25 000	Torres PAR
18-06	Ecuador	D	0-0	Quito	WCq		33 588	Baldassi ARG
20-08	Ecuador	L	0-1	New Jersey	Fr		32 439	Prus USA
6-09	Uruguay	L	0-1	Bogota	WCq		35 024	Gaciba BRA
10-09	Chile	L	0-4	Santiago	WCq		47 459	Larrionda URU
11-10	Paraguay	L	0-1	Bogota	WCq		26 000	Lunati ARG
15-10	Brazil	D	0-0	Rio de Janeiro	WCq		54 910	Selman CHI
19-11	Nigeria	W	1-0	Cali	Fr	Falcao Garcia [82]	10 000	Duarte COL
2009								
11-02	Haiti	W	2-0	Pereira	Fr	Marin [14], Torres [60]	20 000	Ruiz COL
28-03	Bolivia	W	2-0	Bogota	WCq	Torres [26], Renteria [88]	22 044	Intriago ECU
31-03	Venezuela	L	0-2	Puerto Ordaz	WCq		35 000	Pozo CHI
6-06	Argentina	L	0-1	Buenos Aires	WCq		55 000	Ortube BOL
10-06	Peru	W	1-0	Medellin	WCq	Falcao Garcia [25]	32 300	Simon BRA
7-08	El Salvador	W	2-1	Houston	Fr	Gutierrez [12], Mendoza [87]	20 418	Marrufo USA
12-08	Venezuela	L	1-2	New Jersey	Fr	Falcao Garcia [38]		Prus USA
5-09	Ecuador	W	2-0	Medellin	WCq	Martinez [82], Gutierrez [94+]	42 000	Pezzotta ARG
9-09	Uruguay	L	1-3	Montevideo	WCq	Martinez [63]	30 000	Torres PAR
30-09	Mexico	W	2-1	Dallas	Fr	Giovanni Moreno [44], Quintero [79]	50 000	Salazar USA
10-10	Chile	L	2-4	Medellin	WCq	Martinez [14], Giovanni Moreno [53]	18 000	Rivera PER
14-10	Paraguay	W	2-0	Asuncion	WCq	Ramos [61], Rodallega [80]	17 503	De Oliveira BRA
2010								
27-05	South Africa	L	1-2	Johannesburg	Fr	Giovanni Moreno [19p]	76 000	Kipngetich KEN
30-05	Nigeria	D	1-1	Milton Keynes	Fr	Valdez [19]	BCD	Atkinson ENG
11-08	Bolivia	D	1-1	La Paz	Fr	Bacca [40]	4 000	Favale ARG
3-09	Venezuela	W	2-0	Puerto La Cruz	Fr	Cuadrado [17], Dayro Moreno [66]	30 000	Moreno PAN
7-09	Mexico	L	0-1	Monterrey	Fr		43 000	Pineda HON
8-10	Ecuador	W	1-0	Harrison	Fr	Falcao Garcia [88]	25 000	Chapin USA
12-10	USA	D	0-0	Chester	Fr		8 823	Garcia MEX
17-11	Peru	D	1-1	Bogota	Fr	Luis Nunez [74]	6 900	Laverni ARG

Fr = Friendly match • CA = Copa America • WC = FIFA World Cup • q = qualifier

COLOMBIA NATIONAL TEAM HISTORICAL RECORDS

Caps
111 - Carlos Valderrama 1985-98 • 101 - Leonel Alvarez 1985-97 • 84 - Freddy Rincon 1990-2001 • 78 - Luis Carlos Perea 1987-94 • 73 - Ivan Cordoba 1997-, Mario Yepes 1999- & Oscar Cordoba 1993-2006 • 68 - Arnoldo Iguaran 1979-93 & Rene Higuita 1987-99 • 67 - Alexis Mendoza 1987-97 • 66 - Victor Aristizabal 1993-2003 • 61 - Luis Herrera 1987-96 • 57 - Faustino Asprilla 1993-2001

Goals
25 - Arnoldo Iguaran 1979-93 • 20 - Faustino Asprilla 1993-2001 • 17 - Freddy Rincon 1990-2001 • 15 - Victor Aristizabal 1993-2003 • 14 - Adolfo Valencia 1992-98 • 13 - Ivan Valenciano 1991-2000 & Anthony de Avila 1983-98 • 12 - Willington Ortiz 1973-85 • 11 - Carlos Valderrama 1985-98 • 9 - Juan Pablo Angel 1996-2006, Edixon Perea 2004-08 & Hernan Herrera 1979-85 • 8 - Hugo Rodallega 2005-

Past Coaches
Alfonso Novoa 1938 • Fernando Paternoster ARG 1938 • Roberto Melendez 1945 • Jose Arana Cruz PER 1946 • Lino Taioli ARG 1947 • Pedro Lopez 1957 • Rafael Orlandi ARG 1957 • Adolfo Pedernera ARG 1961-62 • Gabriel Ochoa Uribe 1963 • Efrain Sanchez 1963 • Antonio Julio De la Hoz 1965 • Cesar Lopez Fretes PAR 1966 • Francisco Zuluaga 1968 • Cesar Lopez Fretes PAR 1970 • Toza Veselinovic YUG 1972-73 • Efrain Sanchez 1975 • Blagoje Vidinic YUG 1976-79 • Carlos Bilardo ARG 1980-81 • Efrain Sanchez 1983-84 • Gabriel Ochoa Uribe 1985 • Francisco Maturana 1987-90 • Luis Garcia 1991 • Humberto Ortiz 1992 • Francisco Maturana 1993-94 • Hernan Dario Gomez 1995-98 • Javier Alvarez 1999 • Luis Garcia 2000-01 • Francisco Maturana 2001 • Reynaldo Rueda 2002 • Francisco Maturana 2002-03 • Reynaldo Rueda 2004-06 • Jorge Pinto 2007-08 • Eduardo Lara 2008-09 • Hernan Dario Gomez 2010-

COLOMBIA 2010
PRIMERA A COPA MUSTANG I

	Pl	W	D	L	F	A	Pts
Deportes Tolima †	18	10	4	4	36	22	34
Indep. Medellín †	18	9	6	3	29	17	33
Atlético Junior †	18	9	5	4	28	17	32
La Equidad Bogotá †	18	9	4	5	29	25	31
Deportivo Cali	18	9	3	6	28	20	30
Indep. Santa Fe	18	9	3	6	25	23	30
Boyacá Chico	18	8	5	5	25	24	29
At. Nacional Medellín	18	9	1	8	28	24	28
Real Cartagena	18	8	4	6	24	26	28
Once Caldas	18	7	4	7	32	28	25
Atlético Huila	18	6	6	6	30	26	24
Envigado	18	6	5	7	23	30	23
Cúcuta Deportivo	18	5	5	8	14	21	20
Millonarios	18	5	4	9	22	29	19
Deportivo Pereira	18	4	6	8	23	28	18
América Cali	18	4	4	10	18	28	16
Corporación Tuluá	18	4	3	11	19	32	15
Deportes Quindío	18	4	2	12	9	22	14

30/01/2010 - 16/05/2010 • † Qualified for the second stage
Top scorers (overall): **12** - Carlos Bacca, Junior & Carlos
Renteria, Equidad • **11** - Franco Arizala, Tolima; Giovanni
Moreno, At Nacional & Fernando Uribe, Once Caldas

COPA MUSTANG I SECOND STAGE

Semi-finals

Atlético Junior	3	0
Indep. Medellín	1	1

Deportes Tolima	2 1 1p	
La Equidad Bogotá	2 1 3p	

Finals

Atlético Junior †	0	3
La Equidad Bogotá	1	1

† Qualified for the Copa Libertadores

COPA MUSTANG I FINAL

1st leg. El Campin, Bogota, 26-05-2010, Att: 30 000, Ref: Machado
La Equidad   1   Sheput [12]
Atlético Junior   0
Equidad - Nelson Ramos - Jhon Cano• (Ariel Carreno 80), Edwin Rivas•, Marco
Canchila•, Jhon Viafara - Renzo Sheput (Oscar Martinez 87), Dager Palacios•,
Dahwling Leudo, David Castro• (Hugo Soto 60) - Sherman Cardenas, Carlos
Renteria. Tr: Alexis Garcia
Junior - Carlos Rodriguez - Roman Torres, John Valencia, Haider Palacio, Cesar
Fawcett - John Jaramillo, Vladimir Hernandez (Carlos Bacca 46), Jorge Casanova,
Giovanni Hernandez - Luis Ruiz, Martin Arzuaga (Victor Cortes• 46). Tr: Diego
Umana
2nd leg. Roberto Melendez, Barranquilla, 3-06-2010, Att: 49 600, Ref: Roldan
Atlético Junior   3   Bacca 2 [11][87], Cortes [17]
La Equidad   1   Castro [47]
Junior - Carlos Rodriguez - Roman Torres, John Valencia, Haider Palacio, Cesar
Fawcett - Jossymar Gomez, Jorge Casanova, Giovanni Hernandez (Vladimir
Hernandez 83), Carlos Bacca (Braynner Garcia 89) - Luis Ruiz•, Victor Cortes
(Martin Arzuaga 85). Tr: Diego Umana
Equidad - Nelson Ramos - Edwin Rivas, Hugo Soto• (Renzo Sheput 70), Jhon
Viafara•, Dager Palacios• - Dahwling Leudo, Jhersson Cordoba• (Jhon Cano 77),
Marco Canchila, Carlos Renteria (Herly Alcazar 83) - David Castro, Sherman
Cardenas. Tr: Alexis Garcia

COLOMBIA 2010 PRIMERA A REGULAR SEASON RESULTS

PRIMERA A	América	Cali	Cartagena	Chico	Cúcuta	Envigado	Huila	Junior	La Equidad	Medellín	Millonarios	Nacional	Once Caldas	Pereira	Quindío	Santa Fe	Tolima	Tuluá
América Cali		1-2 1-2	0-2	4-0	0-0	2-2	2-2	2-2	3-1	1-0	3-2	2-0	2-1	1-1	1-1	1-2	1-0	0-1
Deportivo Cali	1-1 6-3		3-1	3-0	1-1	1-0	0-0	2-2	0-0	0-0	4-1	3-1	5-3	1-1	2-0	0-1	1-1	5-3
Real Cartagena	1-0	0-1		0-0	0-2	1-1	2-1	1-0 1-1	1-4	1-1	1-0	1-2	4-3	1-0	1-1	2-2	1-4	1-0
Boyacá Chico	1-0	1-0	0-2		2-0	2-1	1-1	1-0	2-0 0-0	3-3	1-1	3-2	0-1	1-1	2-0	2-0	1-1	1-0
Cúcuta Deportivo	3-0	2-1	2-0	2-0		2-2 2-0	2-3	3-3	2-0	1-2	2-1	1-1	1-0	0-2	1-0	1-1	1-0	3-0
Envigado	1-3	2-2	2-1	1-0 1-0 1-1		0-1	2-2	1-2	1-7	1-2	2-1	1-2	2-1	2-0	1-1	2-3	2-0
Atlético Huila	1-1	1-0	2-1	4-0	4-1	2-2		0-0	4-1	1-1	1-1	3-2	3-2	1-0	3-0	1-3 3-1	1-1
Atlético Junior	0-2	3-0	0-3 1-1	3-1	2-0	2-0	1-1		2-0	1-1	2-0	4-2	2-2	2-1	0-2	2-0	1-1	3-2
La Equidad Bogotá	0-2	0-3	2-1	2-1 1-1	0-0	2-0	4-1	1-0		2-1	2-0	2-1	4-2	2-0	1-0	1-2	4-3	3-0
Indep. Medellín	1-0	2-1	1-1	0-0	3-0	2-2	3-2	1-1	1-1		3-2	2-1 1-2	0-0	1-1	1-0	0-0	1-0	2-1
Millonarios	2-0	1-0	4-0	2-3	2-0	2-1	1-2	1-1	1-1	3-1		2-1	1-2	2-1	0-0	2-1 0-0	2-2	0-2
At. Nacional Medellín	2-0	2-0	4-2	2-0	1-0	1-1	2-1	1-0	3-1	1-2 1-0	2-1		1-2	3-2	1-0	0-1	1-0	2-1
Once Caldas	3-1	0-3	2-1	3-3	1-0	3-1	2-1	1-0	2-3	2-1	3-1	2-3		5-1 1-0	4-2	1-2	1-3	2-1
Deportivo Pereira	1-0	1-3	3-0	2-2	1-2	1-1	1-3	2-2	2-2	1-2	1-1	0-0 1-1 0-0		0-0	0-1	1-2	0-0
Deportes Quindío	2-0	2-0	0-0	2-1	1-0	3-2	2-1	1-2	1-0	1-1	3-2	0-1	0-2	1-0		3-2	0-3	1-2 2-0
Indep. Santa Fe	2-0	1-1	2-2	2-3	2-0	1-0	3-0	2-0	0-1	2-0	2-1 2-0	3-0	1-1	0-2	2-1		3-2	3-0
Deportes Tolima	2-1	3-1	3-1	3-1	1-0	2-0	1-0 3-0	2-2	3-0	1-1	2-1	3-0	1-1	1-0	2-0	1-2		3-0
Corporación Tuluá	1-2	1-1	1-2	1-2	0-0	2-1	1-1	2-0	2-2	1-2	1-2	0-2	0-3	1-1	0-1 2-1	2-0	1-5	

Apertura 2010 results are shown in the shaded boxes • Local rivals play each other four times in the regular season. In this instance the Copa Mustang
I results are listed first • Matches in bold awarded • Corporación Tuluá relegated • Relegation play-off: **Envigado** 1-0 2-0 Deportivo Pasto

COLOMBIA 2010
PRIMERA A COPA MUSTANG II

	Pl	W	D	L	F	A	Pts
Deportes Tolima †	18	11	3	4	35	15	36
Once Caldas †	18	11	3	4	34	26	36
Indep. Santa Fe †	18	10	5	3	26	13	35
At. Nacional Medellín†	18	10	3	5	25	23	33
Deportes Quindío †	18	9	4	5	25	20	31
Atlético Huila †	18	8	6	4	28	24	30
Cúcuta Deportivo †	18	8	4	6	24	18	28
La Equidad Bogotá †	18	8	4	6	23	23	28
Deportivo Cali	18	6	8	4	31	23	26
América Cali	18	7	4	7	25	23	25
Indep. Medellín	18	5	9	4	22	22	24
Millonarios	18	6	4	8	25	25	22
Boyacá Chico	18	5	6	7	16	26	21
Atlético Junior	18	2	10	6	21	28	16
Real Cartagena	18	3	6	9	17	29	15
Corporación Tuluá	18	3	4	11	14	30	13
Deportivo Pereira	18	0	9	9	12	22	9
Envigado	18	1	6	11	19	32	9

17/07/2010 - 14/11/2010 • † Qualified for the second stage
Top scorers (overall): **12** - Wilder Medina, Tolima • **16** - Dayro Moreno, Once Caldas • **14** - Wilson Carpintero, Cúcuta • **13** - Fernando Uribe, Once Caldas

COPA MUSTANG II SECOND STAGE

Group A	Pl	W	D	L	F	A	Pts	DT	SF	AH	LE
Deportes Tolima †	6	3	2	1	11	9	11		2-2	4-3	1-1
Indep. Santa Fe	6	3	1	2	8	6	10	0-1		2-1	3-1
Atlético Huila	6	2	1	3	9	10	7	2-3	1-0		2-1
La Equidad Bogotá	6	1	2	3	4	7	5	1-0	0-1	0-0	

Group B	Pl	W	D	L	F	A	Pts	OC	CD	DQ	AN
Once Caldas †	6	4	1	1	14	7	13		0-0	4-1	3-2
Cúcuta Deportivo	6	2	3	1	7	6	9	2-1		1-0	2-2
Deportes Quindío	6	2	0	4	7	12	6	1-3	2-1		1-2
At. Nacional Medellín	6	1	2	3	9	12	5	1-3	1-1	1-2	

20/11/2010 - 12/12/2010 • † Qualified for the final

COPA MUSTANG II FINAL

1st leg. Manuel Toro, Ibague, 16-12-2010, Att: 30 000, Ref: Ruiz

Deportes Tolima	2	Henriquez OG [35], Marangoni [48p]
Once Caldas	1	Moreno [7p]

Tolima - Anthony Silva - Yesid Martinez•, Jair Arrechea, Gerardo Vallejo, Danny Aguilar - Gustavo Bolivar, Rodrigo Marangoni, Christian Marrugo (Fernando Cardenas 83), Yimmi Chara - Jorge Perlaza, Wilder Medina. Tr: Hernan Torres
Caldas - Luis Martinez - Alexis Henriquez, Oswaldo Vizcarrondo•, Jose Velez, Luis Nunez• - Harrison Henao (Felix Micolta 58), Jaime Castrillon, Diego Arias♦74, John Valencia• (Wilson Mena 68) - Fernando Uribe• (Diego Arango 76), Dayro Moreno•. Tr: Juan Carlos Osorio

2nd leg. Palogrande, Manizales, 19-12-2010, Att: 45 000, Ref: Roldan

Once Caldas	3	Castrillon [45], Uribe [53], Mena [76]
Deportes Tolima	1	Aguilar [86]

Caldas - Luis Martinez - Luis Nunez, Alexis Henriquez, Oswaldo Vizcarrondo, Jose Velez• - Felix Micolta• (Wilson Mena 71), Harison Henao, Jaime Castrillon•, John Valencia - Fernando Uribe (Diego Arango 84), Dayro Moreno. Tr: Juan Carlos Osorio
Tolima - Anthony Silva - Yesid Martinez, Jair Arrechea•, Gerardo Vallejo♦90, Danny Aguilar• - Gustavo Bolivar, Rodrigo Marangoni, Mike Campaz (Fernando Cardenas• 56), Christian Marrugo (Hugo Centurion 69) - Jorge Perlaza, Wilder Medina. Tr: Hernan Torres

Once Caldas qualified for the Copa Libertadores

COLOMBIA 2010
PRIMERA B PLAY-OFFS (2)

Semi-final Cuadrangular

Group A	Pl	W	D	L	F	A	Pts	ID	UM	RS	DR
Itagüi Ditaires †	6	5	0	1	13	3	15		3-0	2-0	4-0
Unión Magdalena	6	3	1	2	7	7	10	2-0		3-2	2-0
Real Santander	6	2	1	3	7	8	7	1-2	0-0		3-1
Deportivo Rionegro	6	1	0	5	3	12	3	0-2	2-0	0-1	

Group B	Pl	W	D	L	F	A	Pts	DP	Bo	Pa	AB
Deportivo Pasto †	6	4	1	1	12	9	13		2-2	0-1	2-1
Bogotá FC	6	3	2	1	12	9	11	2-3		1-1	1-0
Patriotas	6	3	1	2	9	8	10	1-2	2-3		1-0
At. Bucaramanga	6	0	0	6	6	13	0	2-3	1-3	2-3	

6/11/2010 to 26/08/2010 • † Qualified for the final

Final

Itagüi Ditaires	1	2
Deportivo Pasto	1	1

COPA COLOMBIA POSTOBON 2010

Round of 16		Quarter–finals		Semi–finals		Final	
Deportivo Cali	0 3 4p						
Atlético Junior *	1 2 2p	**Deportivo Cali**	1 3				
Real Cartagena	0 3 2p	Indep. Santa Fe *	0 1				
Indep. Santa Fe *	2 1 3p			**Deportivo Cali ***	2 5		
Deportivo Pereira	2 3			La Equidad Bogotá	0 3		
Deportivo Pasto *	1 0	Deportivo Pereira	0 1				
Atlético Huila *	2 0	**La Equidad Bogotá ***	2 2				
La Equidad Bogotá	1 2					**Deportivo Cali †**	1 2
Millonarios	2 1 2p					Itagui Ditaires *	0 0
At. Bucaramanga *	1 2 1p	**Millonarios ***	1 1				
Atético de la Sabana *	1 0	Cúcuta Deportivo	1 0				
Cúcuta Deportivo	0 4			Millonarios *	2 3 4p		
At. Nacional Medellín	2 2			**Itagui Ditaires**	3 2 5p		
Boyacá Chico *	2 1	At. Nacional Medellín	0 5 4p				
Deportes Tolima	0 2	**Itagui Ditaires ***	4 1 5p				
Itagui Ditaires *	1 2						

† Qualified for Copa Sudamericana • * Home team in the first leg

CUP FINAL

1st leg. 27-10-2010
2nd leg. 3-11-2010

For details see below

1st leg. Metropolitano, Itagui, Medellin, 27-10-2010. Att: 9000, Ref: Imer Machado. Scorer - Andres Escobar [59]
Itagui - Roberto Mosquera - Carlos Arboleda•, Felipe Correa•, Sergio Guzman, Fernando Monroy - Anderson Zapata (Gustavo Davila 66), Elkin Barrera, Mauricio Restrepo (Mauricio Gomez 76), Cleider Alzate - Jorge Aguirre (Jorge Aguirre 80), Luis Paez. Tr: Alvaro de Jesus Gomez
Cali - Juan Castillo - Elkin Calle, Camilo Ceballos, Edgar Zapata, Jarol Martinez• - Andres Perez, Diego Valdes• (Felipe Chara 53), Gustavo Cuellar, Martin Morel• (John Castillo 66) - Andres Escobar, Fabian Castillo (Diego Alvarez 53). Tr. Jaime De La Pava
2nd leg. Palma Seca, Cali, 3-11-2010, Att: 50 000, Ref: Albert Duarte. Scorers - Cesar Amaya [12]**, Andres Escobar** [54] **for Cali**
Cali - Juan Castillo - Elkin Calle, Camilo Ceballos, Edgar Zapata, Jarol Martinez - Andres Perez, Diego Valdes••♦36, Jonathan Alvarez (Martin Morel 67), Diego Alvarez•, Cesar Amaya (Fabian Castillo 75) - Andres Escobar (Gustavo Cuellar 83). Tr: Jaime de la Pava
Itagui - Jaime Gomez - John Zea (Felipe Correa 62), Sergio Guzman•, Anderson Zapata, Alvaro Manga - Emerson Chamorro (Carlos Arboleda 57), Mauricio Restrepo••♦14, Carlos Ortiz•, Cleider Alzate• - Luiz Peaz, Jorge Aguirre (John Castillo 83). Tr: Alvaro de Jesus Gomez

MEDALS TABLE

		Overall			League			Cup		Euro			City
		G	S	B	G	S	B	G	S	G	S	B	
1	América Cali	14	11	12	13	7	5			1	4	7	Cali
2	Millonarios	14	10	13	13	9	8			1	1	5	Bogotá
3	Atlético Nacional	13	11	10	10	9	5			3	2	5	Medellin
4	Deportivo Cali	9	15	8	8	12	6	1			3	2	Cali
5	Independiente Santa Fe	7	5	5	6	3	4	1			2	1	Bogotá
6	Atlético Junior	6	6	3	6	6	2					1	Barranquilla
7	Independiente Medellín	5	7	4	5	7	3					1	Medellin
8	Once Caldas	5	2	1	4	1	1	1	1				Manizales
9	Deportes Tolima	1	5	2	1	5	1						Ibagué
10	Deportes Quindío	1	2	1	1	2	1						Armenia
11	Deportivo Pasto	1	2		1	1		1					Pasto
	CD La Equidad	1	2			2		1					Bogotá
13	Cúcuta Deportivo	1	1	3	1	1	2					1	Cúcuta
14	Union Magdalena	1		1	1		1						Santa Marta
15	Boyacá Chico	1			1								Tunja
16	Boca Junior		2	2		2	2						Cali
17	Atlético Huila		2			2							Neiva
18	Atlético Bucaramanga		1	3		1	3						Bucaramanga
19	Real Cartagena		1			1							Cartagena
	Itagui Ditaires		1						1				Itagui, Medellin
21	Deportivo Pereira			4			4						Pereira

COM – COMOROS

FIFA/COCA-COLA WORLD RANKING

1993	1994	1995	1996	1997	1998	1999	2000	2001	2002	2003	2004	2005	2006	2007	2008	2009	2010
-	-	-	-	-	-	-	-	-	-	-	-	-	207	187	198	176	186

2010												Hi/Lo
Jan	Feb	Mar	Mar	Apr	May	Jul	Aug	Sep	Oct	Nov	Dec	171
176	176	175	174	172	171	172	172	174	181	186	186	207

Participation in a first-ever African Nations Cup qualifying campaign presents the Comoros Islands with a chance to improve their standing in the continental game. The country lost the first two of those qualifying matches for the 2012 finals but have displayed a much more competitive edge to their game as they learn the rigours of international football. The Comoros remain Africa's youngest footballing nation, only joining FIFA's ranks in 2005, and in the 14 matches played since, the 'Coelacanthes' have won twice and shown the ability to be competitive and in the last 12 months that has seen them rise to a high of 171 in the FIFA/Coca-Cola World Ranking. Against Mozambique they conceded the match winner in the last minute as coach Mohamed Chamite Abderemane used for the first time six expatriate players, including brothers Youssouf and Mohamed Mchangama from Nimes in France and Nadjim Abdou from Millwall in England. In club football Elan from Mitsudje were crowned champions in the three-club play-off for the title drawn from the island leagues. They were unbeaten in four games against AS Komorozin from Anjouan island and Fomboni Club. In the 2010 CAF Champions League, Apaches Mitsamiouli were soundly beaten 9-4 on aggregate in the first round by Mozambique's Ferroviario Maputo.

FIFA WORLD CUP RECORD
1930-2006 DNE 2010 DNQ

FEDERATION COMORIENNE DE FOOTBALL (FFC)

Boite Postale 798, Moroni

☎ +269 733179
📠 +269 733236
📧 fedcom_cenfoot@yahoo.fr

FA	1979	CON	1986	FIFA	2005
P	Tourqui Salim
GS	Mariyatta Abdou Chacour

FIFA BIG COUNT 2006

Total players	27 100
% of population	3.92%
Male	27 100
Female	0
Amateurs 18+	600
Youth under 18	500
Unregistered	0
Professionals	0
Referees	0
Admin & coaches	100
Number of clubs	10
Number of teams	30

Mitsamiouli
● Mbeni
GRANDE COMORE
● Moroni
Dembeni
  Mutsamudu ANJOUAN
Fomboni ●   ● Domoni
MOHELI Moya
Wanani

MAYOTTE
(French administration, claimed by COMOROS)

0   20 miles
0   20 km

MAJOR CITIES/TOWNS

		Population
1	Moroni	48 192
2	Mutsamudu	24 980
3	Fomboni	16 581
4	Domoni	15 363
5	Tsémbehou	12 232
6	Ongodjou	11 413
7	Sima	10 986
8	Adda Daouéni	10 858
9	Ouani	10 779
10	Mirontsi	10 767
11	Bazmini	8 952
12	Koni Djodjo	8 876
13	Iconi	8 250
14	Moya	8 242
15	Ounkazi	8 024
16	Dindri	7 816
17	Ngandzalé	7 484
18	Mbéni	7 229
19	Mitsamiouli	6 770

UDZIMA WA KOMORI • UNION DE COMORES • UNION OF THE COMOROS

Capital	Moroni	Population	752 438 (161)	% in cities	28%
GDP per capita	$1000 (211)	Area km²	2235 km² (179)	GMT +/-	+3
Neighbours (km)	Coast 340				

RECENT INTERNATIONAL MATCHES PLAYED BY COMOROS

2003	Opponents	Score		Venue	Comp	Scorers	Att	Referee
30-08	Reunion †	L	0-1	Flacq	IOr1		103	Labrosse SEY
2-09	Reunion †	L	0-4	Flacq	IOr1			
4-09	Mauritius †	L	0-5	Curepipe	IOsf		4 500	Labrosse SEY
6-09	Seychelles †	L	0-2	Curepipe	IO3p			
2004								
No international matches played in 2004								
2005								
No international matches played in 2005								
2006								
14-12	Yemen	L	0-2	Sana'a	ARq			
17-12	Djibouti	W	4-2	Sana'a	ARq	Meknesh Bin Daoud [5], Ahmed Seif 2 [33] [75], Mohamed Moni [70]		
2007								
14-08	Madagascar	L	0-3	Antananarivo	Fr			
14-10	Madagascar	L	2-6	Antananarivo	WCq	Daoud Midtadi [6], Ibor Bakar [53p]	7 754	Kaoma ZAM
17-11	Madagascar	L	0-4	Moroni	WCq		1 610	Damon RSA
2008								
20-07	Namibia	L	0-3	Secunda	CCr1			Labrosse SEY
22-07	Malawi	L	0-1	Secunda	CCr1			Marange ZIM
24-07	Lesotho	L	0-1	Secunda	CCr1			Labrosse SEY
2009								
18-10	Botswana	D	0-0	Bulawayo	CCr1			Rachide MOZ
20-10	Seychelles	W	2-1	Bulawayo	CCr1	Ahmed Ali [9], Mouigni Mohamed [64]		Rachide MOZ
22-10	Swaziland	L	0-3	Bulawayo	CCr1			Carvalho ANG
2010								
29-08	Madagascar	L	0-1	Mahajanga	Fr			
5-09	Zambia	L	0-4	Lusaka	CNq			Eyob Russom ERI
9-10	Mozambique	L	0-1	Moroni	CNq			Ibada TAN

IO = Indian Ocean Games • CC = COSAFA Castle Cup • AR = Arab Cup • q = qualifier
r1 = first round group • sf = semi-final • 3p = third place play-off
† Not regarded as a full international because Comoros was not yet a member of FIFA

COMOROS 2010

	Pl	W	D	L	F	A	Pts	EC	Ko	FC
Elan Club †	4	2	2	0	7	4	8		2-0	1-1
Komorozine	4	1	2	1	6	7	5	2-2		2-2
Fomboni Club	4	0	2	2	5	7	2	1-2	1-2	

31/10/2010 - 21/11/2010 • † Qualified for the CAF Champions League

CPV – CAPE VERDE ISLANDS

FIFA/COCA-COLA WORLD RANKING

1993	1994	1995	1996	1997	1998	1999	2000	2001	2002	2003	2004	2005	2006	2007	2008	2009	2010
147	161	144	155	171	167	177	156	159	154	143	129	118	78	111	107	97	75

2010												Hi/Lo
Jan	Feb	Mar	Mar	Apr	May	Jul	Aug	Sep	Oct	Nov	Dec	68
97	100	98	116	117	114	108	108	77	82	83	75	182

Growing access to quality players from the large Cape Verde community overseas saw the national team continue to punch well above its weight. In addition to the home-based population of under half a million, there are an estimated one million Cape Verdeans or people descended from island emigrants living around the world, with the large population groups in Portugal, the Netherlands, France and the USA providing a growing pool of players to pick from. Again the Cape Verde Islands are in with a credible chance of qualification for the African Nations Cup finals, beginning the 2012 preliminary campaign under youthful coach Luis Antunes with a home win over group favourites Mali and then drawing 0-0 away to Zimbabwe. A first-ever meeting with former colonial master Portugal produced a goalless draw in Covilha as the Cape Verdeans provided warm-up opposition for Carlos Queiroz's side just before they departed the World Cup finals in South Africa. Although a match of little importance, the result held great significance for Cape Verde because of the colonial links and because it showed proof of their potential. At home Boavista won the national championship with a 3-1 aggregate win in the final over Sporting Praia. It was their first league success in 15 years and it prevented their opponents from winning five titles in a row.

FIFA WORLD CUP RECORD
1930-1998 DNE 2002-2010 DNQ

FEDERACAO CABOVERDIANA DE FUTEBOL (FCF)

FCF CX, Case postale 234, Praia
☎ +238 2 600847
📠 +238 2 611362
📧 fcf@cvtelecom.cv
🖥 www.fcf.cv
FA 1982 CON 1986 FIFA 1986
P Mario Semedo
GS Jose João Rezende

FIFA BIG COUNT 2006

Total players	35 100
% of population	8.34%
Male	33 500
Female	1 600
Amateurs 18+	7 000
Youth under 18	4 500
Unregistered	4 200
Professionals	0
Referees	256
Admin & coaches	500
Number of clubs	82
Number of teams	180

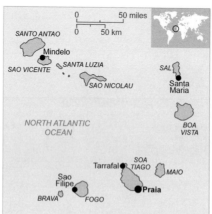

MAJOR CITIES/TOWNS

		Population
1	Praia	128 653
2	Mindelo	76 014
3	Santa Maria	21 195
4	Pedra Badejo	10 237
5	Assomada	8 553
6	São Filipe	8 212
7	Tarrafal	6 974
8	São Miguel	5 888
9	Porto Novo	5 523
10	Ribeira Brava	5 121
11	Ponta do Sol	4 023
12	Vila do Maio	3 264
13	São Domingos	3 220
14	Sal Rei	2 200
15	Pombas	1 799
16	Nova Sintra	1 793
17	Mosteiros	478

REPUBLICA DE CABO VERDE • REPUBLIC OF CAPE VERDE

Capital	Praia	Population	429 474 (171)	% in cities	60%
GDP per capita	$3800 (156)	Area km²	4033 km² (175)	GMT + / -	-1
Neighbours (km)	Coast 965				

RECENT INTERNATIONAL MATCHES PLAYED BY THE CAPE VERDE ISLANDS

2007 Opponents	Score	Venue	Comp	Scorers	Att	Referee
24-03 Algeria	L 0-2	Algiers	CNq			Abd El Fatah EGY
2-06 Algeria	D 2-2	Praia	CNq	Marco Soares 58, Hernani 89		Aboubacar CIV
16-06 Gambia	D 0-0	Praia	CNq			Aguidissou BEN
9-09 Guinea	L 0-4	Conakry	CNq			Trabelsi TUN
3-12 Gambia	D 0-0	Bissau	Fr			
7-12 Guinea-Bissau	D 1-1	Bissau	Fr	Babanco 10. W 3-2p		
2008						
24-05 Burkina Faso	W 1-0	Alcochete	Fr	Toy Adao		
27-05 Luxembourg	D 1-1	Luxembourg	Fr	Valter 83	2 051	Radovanovic MNE
31-05 Cameroon	L 0-2	Yaoundé	WCq		20 000	Djaoupe TOG
7-06 Tanzania	W 1-0	Praia	WCq	Babanco 73	6 000	El Achiri MAR
15-06 Mauritius	W 1-0	Curepipe	WCq	Dady 43p	1 480	Kaoma ZAM
22-06 Mauritius	W 3-1	Praia	WCq	Dady 2 45 58, Marco Soares 78	2 850	Coulibaly MLI
6-09 Cameroon	L 1-2	Praia	WCq	Lito 38	5 000	Labrosse SEY
11-10 Tanzania	L 1-3	Dar es Salaam	WCq	Semedo 35	10 000	Damon RSA
2009						
25-03 Angola	W 1-0	Olhao	Fr	Dady 33p		
28-03 Equatorial Guinea	W 5-0	Sal	Fr	Cadu 2 6 44, Dario 38p, Rodi 2 45 90		
4-09 Malta	W 2-0	Ta'Qali	Fr	Heldon Ramos 15p, Adilson Monteiro 40		
9-09 Angola	D 1-1	Faro	Fr	Dario 35p		
2010						
24-05 Portugal	D 0-0	Covilha	Fr		6 000	Gomez ESP
11-08 Senegal	L 0-1	Dakar	Fr			
4-09 Mali	W 1-0	Praia	CNq	Varela 44		Benouza ALG
10-10 Zimbabwe	D 0-0	Harare	CNq			Ndume GAB
16-11 Guinea-Bissau	W 2-1	Lisbon	Fr	Lito 6, Ronny Souto 24		

Fr = Friendly match • CN = CAF African Cup of Nations • WC = FIFA World Cup
q = qualifier • * Abandoned after 85 minutes when Mauritania were reduced to six players - the result stood

CAPE VERDE ISLANDS 2009-10
CAMPEONATO NACIONAL

First Round Group Stage

Group A	Pl	W	D	L	F	A	Pts	AB	Ma	Mo	Bo	So
Batuque	5	2	3	0	9	3	9	1-1	2-0	1-1	4-0	1-1
Boavista	5	2	2	1	15	8	8		3-4	0-0	4-2	7-1
Marítimo	5	2	1	2	7	9	7			1-0	2-2	0-2
Morabeza	5	1	3	1	5	4	6				1-1	3-1
Botafogo	5	1	2	2	8	13	5					3-2
Solpontense	5	1	1	3	7	14	4					

Semi-finals

Boavista	1	1
Batuque	0	1

Final

Boavista	2	1
Sporting da Praia	0	0

Group B	Pl	W	D	L	F	A	Pts	SP	SV	BV	RB	Ba
Académico do Sal	5	4	1	0	12	4	13	0-0	3-1	3-0	2-0	4-3
Sporting da Praia	5	3	2	0	16	6	11		3-1	1-1	7-2	5-2
Scorpion Vermelho	5	2	0	3	7	8	6			2-0	1-2	2-0
Boa Vista	5	1	2	2	4	8	5				2-2	1-0
Ribeira Brava	5	1	1	3	6	12	4					n/p*
Barreirense	5	0	0	5	5	12	0					

Académico do Sal	0	1
Sporting da Praia	0	1

1st leg. 3-07-2010
2nd leg. 10-07-2010

* Awarded as a loss to both teams

8/05/2010 -10/07/2010

CRC – COSTA RICA

FIFA/COCA-COLA WORLD RANKING

1993	1994	1995	1996	1997	1998	1999	2000	2001	2002	2003	2004	2005	2006	2007	2008	2009	2010
42	65	78	72	51	67	64	60	30	21	17	27	21	68	70	53	44	69

	2010												Hi/Lo
Jan	Feb	Mar	Mar	Apr	May	Jul	Aug	Sep	Oct	Nov	Dec		17
44	45	44	42	42	40	49	53	53	66	63	69		93

There were surprise first time champions in Costa Rica after Brujas, formed only in 2004, won the opening championship of the 2009-10 season. Based in Desamparados, the southern most suburb of the capital San Jose, Brujas hosted Puntarenas at their compact Jorge 'Cuty' Monge stadium in the second leg of the final having drawn the first leg 0-0 in Puntarenas. The match finished 1-1 with Brujas winning the penalty shoot-out 5-4 to secure the title. In a league usually dominated by the big three of Saprissa, Alajuelense and Herediano, it was a welcome triumph following as it did Liberia's first championship earlier in the year but it was back to business as usual in 2010. Saprissa saw off the challenge of minnows San Carlos in the first of the two championship finals whilst Alajuelense won the second, beating Herediano 4-3 on penalties. Following the disappointment of failing to qualify for the FIFA World Cup in South Africa, Argentine Ricardo La Volpe was appointed national team coach with his first assignment the 2011 Copa Centroamericana in Panama. It wasn't the success that La Volpe hoped for and although the Costa Ricans did reach the final, they were beaten 2-1 by Honduras, a team still relishing their World Cup experience in South Africa and looking to depose Costa Rica as the major power in Central America.

FIFA WORLD CUP RECORD

1930-1954 DNE 1958-1986 DNQ **1990** 13 r2 1994-1998 DNQ **2002** 19 r1 **2006** 31 r1 2010 DNQ

FEDERACION COSTARRICENSE DE FUTBOL (FEDEFUTBOL)

Radial Santa Ana Belen, 500 mts Este del cruce de la Panasonic, San José 670-1000

☎ +506 25891450
📠 +506 25891457
📧 ejecutivo@fedefutbol.com
🖥 www.fedefutbol.org
FA 1921 CON 1962 FIFA 1927
P Eduardo Li
GS Lidia Rojas

FIFA BIG COUNT 2006

Total players	1 084 588
% of population	26.61%
Male	1 050 120
Female	34 468
Amateurs 18+	17 500
Professionals	1 025
Referees	630
Admin & coaches	4 236
Number of clubs	248
Number of teams	1 391

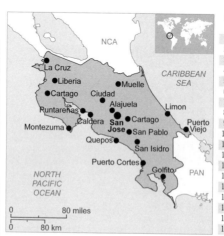

MAJOR CITIES/TOWNS

		Population
1	San José	345 447
2	San Francisco	70 200
3	Limón	66 620
4	Liberia	54 852
5	Alajuela	49 930
6	Paraíso	48 400
7	San Isidro	39 833
8	Desamparados	39 767
9	Curridabat	37 263
10	Puntarenas	37 080
11	San Vicente	35 624
12	San José	33 913
13	Purral	32 125
14	Turrialba	31 987
15	Mercedes	31 713
16	San Rafael Abajo	31 251
17	San Rafael	31 023
18	San Miguel	30 834
19	Aguacaliente	30 547

REPUBLICA DE COSTA RICA • REPUBLIC OF COSTA RICA

Capital	San José	Population	4 253 877 (123)	% in cities 63%
GDP per capita	$11 500 (95)	Area km²	51 100 km² (129)	GMT + / - -6
Neighbours (km)	Nicaragua 309, Panama 330 • Coast 1290			

RECENT INTERNATIONAL MATCHES PLAYED BY COSTA RICA

2009	Opponents	Score		Venue	Comp	Scorers	Att	Referee
23-01	Panama	W	3-0	Tegucigalpa	UCr1	Furtado 2 [8 15], Alvaro Sanchez [55]	2 000	Campbell JAM
25-01	Guatemala	W	3-1	Tegucigalpa	UCr1	Alvaro Sanchez [34], Herrera [59], Segura [61]	3 000	Rodriguez.M MEX
30-01	El Salvador	W	1-0	Tegucigalpa	UCsf	Furtado [18]	2 500	Moreno PAN
1-02	Panama	D	0-0	Tegucigalpa	UCf	L 3-5p	900	Batres GUA
11-02	Honduras	W	2-0	San Jose	WCq	Furtado 2 [48 59]	18 000	Aguilar SLV
28-03	Mexico	L	0-2	Mexico City	WCq		90 000	Vaughn USA
1-04	El Salvador	W	1-0	San Jose	WCq	Centeno [69]	19 200	Marrufo USA
13-05	Venezuela	D	1-1	San Cristobal	Fr	Warren Granados [28]	10 000	Escalante VEN
3-06	USA	W	3-1	San Jose	WCq	Saborio [2], Borges [13], Herrera [68]	19 200	Brizan TRI
6-06	Trinidad and Tobago	W	3-2	Bacolet	WCq	Saborio [40], Borges 2 [52 69]	8 000	Campbell JAM
27-06	Venezuela	W	1-0	San Jose	Fr	Saborio [38]	17 000	Zelaya HON
3-07	El Salvador	L	1-2	Carson	GCr1	Warren Granados [64]	27 000	Archundia MEX
7-07	Jamaica	W	1-0	Columbus	GCr1	Borges [62]	7 059	Marrufo USA
10-07	Canada	D	2-2	Miami	GCr1	Herron [23], Centeno [35]	17 269	Vaughn USA
19-07	Guadeloupe †	W	5-1	Arlington	GCqf	Borges [3], Saborio 2 [16 71], Herron [47], Herrera [89]	85 000	Pineda HON
23-07	Mexico	D	1-1	Chicago	GCsf	Ledezma [90]. L 3-5p	55 173	Moreno PAN
12-08	Honduras	L	0-4	San Pedro Sula	WCq		30 000	Rodriguez MEX
5-09	Mexico	L	0-3	San Jose	WCq		20 000	Brizan TRI
9-09	El Salvador	L	0-1	San Salvador	WCq		18 000	Archundia MEX
10-10	Trinidad and Tobago	W	4-0	San Jose	WCq	James OG [26], Centeno [51], Saborio 2 [61 64]	10 000	Marrufo USA
14-10	USA	D	2-2	Washington DC	WCq	Ruiz 2 [20 23]	26 243	Archundia MEX
14-11	Uruguay	L	0-1	San Jose	WCpo		19 500	Undiano ESP
18-11	Uruguay	D	1-1	Montevideo	WCpo	Centeno [74]	55 000	Busacca SUI
2010								
26-01	Argentina	L	2-3	San Juan	Fr	Barrantes [20], Madrigal [76]	22 000	Amarilla PAR
26-05	France	L	1-2	Lens	Fr	Hernandez [11]	40 000	Bezborodov RUS
1-06	Switzerland	W	1-0	Sion	Fr	Parks [57]	10 000	Buttimer IRL
5-06	Slovakia	L	0-3	Bratislava	Fr		12 000	Messner AUT
11-08	Paraguay	L	0-2	Asuncion	Fr		22 000	Beligoy ARG
3-09	Panama	D	2-2	Panama City	Fr	Barrantes [7], Saborio [52]	23 005	Delgadillo MEX
5-09	Jamaica	L	0-1	Kingston	Fr		15 000	Brizan TRI
8-10	Peru	L	0-2	Lima	Fr		15 000	Ponce ECU
12-10	El Salvador	W	2-1	Quesada	Fr	Jose Sanchez [10], Josue Martinez [87]	4 000	Rodriguez PAN
17-11	Jamaica	D	0-0	Fort Lauderdale	Fr		4 000	Renso USA
2011								
14-01	Honduras	D	1-1	Panama City	UCr1	Victor Nunez [42]	6 000	Garcia MEX
16-01	Guatemala	W	2-0	Panama City	UCr1	Marcos Urena 2 [48 81]	1 500	Moreno PAN
21-01	Panama	D	1-1	Panama City	UCsf	Celso Borges [67]. W 4-2p	10 000	Aguilar SLV
23-01	Honduras	L	1-2	Panama City	UCf	Marcos Urena [73]	2 000	Lopez GUA

Fr = Friendly match • UC = UNCAF Cup/Copa Centroamericana • GC = CONCACAF Gold Cup • WC = FIFA World Cup
q = qualifier • r1 = first round group • qf = quarter-finals • † not a full international

COSTA RICA NATIONAL TEAM HISTORICAL RECORDS

Caps
137 - Walter Centeno 1995-2009 • 128 - Luis Marin 1993-2006 • 110 - Mauricio Solis 1993-2006 • 109 - Rolando Fonseca 1992-2008 • 101 - Harold Wallace 1995-2009 • 91 - Ronald Gomez 1993-2008 • 89 - Hernan Medford 1987-2002 • 76 - Erick Lonnis 1992-2002 & Wilmer Lopez 1995-2003 • 75 - Oscar Ramirez 1985-97 • 73 - Jervis Drummond 1995-2008 & Paulo Wanchope 1996-2008

Goals
47 - Rolando Fonseca 1992-2008 • 45 - Paulo Wanchope 1996-2008 • 27 - Juan Ulloa • 24 - Walter Centeno 1995-2009 & Ronald Gomez 1993-2008 • 23 - Jorge Monge 1954-68 • 21 - Alvaro Saborio 2002- • 18 - Hernan Medford 1987-2002 • 15 - Rafael Madrigal • 14 - Rodolfo Herrera • 12 - Roy Saenz

Past Coaches
Randolph Galloway ENG 1946-48 • Otto Bumbel BRA 1950-56 • Luis Lucho Tirado CHI 1956-58 • Hugo Tassara Olivares CHI 1958-60 • Eduardo Toba ESP 1960-61 • Alfredo Piedra 1961-62 • Mario Cordero 1962-65 • Eduardo Viso Abella ESP 1965-71 • Humberto Maschio ARG 1971-75 • Jose Etchegoyen URU 1975-80 • Antonio Moyano Reyna ESP 1980-85 • Odir Jacques BRA 1985-87 • Gustavo de Simone URU 1987-89 • Marvin Rodriguez 1989-90 • Bora Milutinovic SRB 1990 • Rolando Villalobos 1991-92 • Hector Nunez URU 1992 • Juan Jose Gamez 1993 • Toribio Rojas 1993-95 • Ignacio Nunez 1995 • Valdeir Viera BRA 1996 • Horacio Cordero ARG 1997 • Juan Hernandez 1997 • Rolando Villalobos 1998 • Francisco Maturana COL 1999 • Marvin Rodriguez 1999-2000 • Gilson Siqueira Nunes BRA 2000 • Alexandre Guimaraes BRA 2001-02 • Rodrigo Kenton 2002 • Steve Sampson USA 2002-04 • Jorge Luis Pinto COL 2004-05 • Alexandre Guimaraes BRA 2005-06 • Hernan Medford 2006-08 • Rodrigo Kenton 2008-09 • Rene Simoes BRA 2009 • Ronald Gonzalez 2009-10 • Ricardo La Volpe ARG 2010-

COSTA RICA 2009–10

PRIMERA DIVISION
TORNEO CLAUSURA VERANO

Group 1

	Pl	W	D	L	F	A	Pts	Saprissa	Alajuelense	Santos	Cartaginés	P Zeledón	Liberia	San Carlos	Herediano	Puntarenas	Ramonense	UCR	Brujas
Deportivo Saprissa †	16	10	5	1	26	12	35		1-0	2-0	0-0	2-1	3-1	2-0	3-2				1-0
LD Alajuelense ‡	16	11	1	4	19	6	34	1-0		1-0	2-0	3-0	1-0	1-0					2-0
Santos de Guápiles ‡	16	6	2	8	18	19	20	0-2	1-3		2-1	1-0	1-1		4-0	1-1	2-1		
CS Cartaginés	16	4	8	4	14	15	20	2-2	1-0	1-0			1-1	0-0		1-1	2-2	1-0	
AD Pérez Zeledón	16	5	4	7	18	22	19	1-1	1-0	1-0	3-2		2-2			2-3	2-0	0-2	
Liberia Mia	16	3	6	7	19	24	15	2-3	1-2	2-3	0-1	5-1		1-1	2-1				0-2

Group 2

	Pl	W	D	L	F	A	Pts	Saprissa	Alajuelense	Santos	Cartaginés	P Zeledón	Liberia	San Carlos	Herediano	Puntarenas	Ramonense	UCR	Brujas
San Carlos †	16	8	5	3	16	12	29			2-1	1-0	1-0			0-0	1-0	1-0	1-1	1-0
CS Herediano ‡	16	5	5	6	20	22	20			1-0	0-0	1-3		2-1		0-0	3-3	2-1	2-0
Puntarenas FC ‡	16	3	8	5	14	21	17	2-2	1-0				0-1	2-2	2-2		2-1	0-2	0-0
AD Ramonense	16	2	10	4	15	18	16	0-0	0-2				1-1	0-0	1-0	3-1		0-0	1-1
Universidad Costa Rica	16	3	7	6	13	14	16	0-2	0-0				0-0	1-2	1-2	0-0	1-1		2-0
Brujas FC	16	2	7	7	11	18	13			0-2	1-1	0-0		1-2	4-2	0-0	1-1	1-1	

16/01/2010 - 15/05/2010 • † Qualified for the play-off semi-finals • ‡ Qualified for the play-off quarter-finals
Play-off quarter-finals: Herediano 1-2 1-1 **Santos** • **Alajuelense** 2-1 3-2 Puntarenas
Play-off semi-finals: **Saprissa** 1-0 0-0 Santos • **San Carlos** 1-1 2-1 Alajuelense
Play-off final: **Saprissa** 4-2 3-0 San Carlos. **Deportivo Saprissa** are the Verano champions • Liberia and Ramonense relegated

COSTA RICA 2010–11

PRIMERA DIVISION
TORNEO APERTURA INVIERNO

Group 1

	Pl	W	D	L	F	A	Pts	B. Mexico	Cartaginés	P. Zeledón	Puntarenas	Limon	Saprissa	Alajuelense	Herediano	San Carlos	Brujas	Santos	UCR
Barrio Mexico †	16	9	4	3	26	16	31		2-0	0-1	1-1	1-0	3-2		1-0	2-1		0-0	
CS Cartaginés †	16	6	5	5	22	20	23	0-0		1-0	3-1	2-1	1-1		0-0	0-0		7-1	
AD Pérez Zeledón †	16	6	3	7	18	22	21	1-1	1-2		1-0	2-1	4-3	0-1			0-2		2-1
Puntarenas FC	16	5	3	8	23	27	18	2-5	2-0	1-2		2-0	1-1	0-2			5-2		3-0
Limon FC	16	5	2	9	18	22	17	3-2	2-1	0-0	4-1		0-0		1-2	2-0		0-1	
Deportivo Saprissa	16	4	4	8	26	27	16	2-3	1-2	4-1	1-2	3-1		0-0			3-2		4-1

Group 2

	Pl	W	D	L	F	A	Pts	B. Mexico	Cartaginés	P. Zeledón	Puntarenas	Limon	Saprissa	Alajuelense	Herediano	San Carlos	Brujas	Santos	UCR
LD Alajuelense †	16	11	3	2	29	13	36	2-1	2-0			2-1			3-1	0-1	3-2	3-0	3-0
CS Herediano †	16	8	5	3	33	18	29			3-2	2-0		3-1	2-2		4-1	1-1	1-1	4-1
San Carlos †	16	7	4	5	19	18	25	1-0	2-1				1-0	3-1	0-3		4-1	2-3	2-0
Brujas FC †	16	6	3	7	33	29	21	0-1	3-3			3-1		2-4	2-1	0-0		5-0	0-1
Santos de Guápiles †	16	4	8	4	16	26	20	1-1	1-1					2-0	0-0	2-2	0-0		0-2
Universidad Costa Rica	16	2	2	12	13	38	8	1-3	3-0			0-1		0-1	0-4	1-1	2-6	2-2	

24/07/2010 - 19/12/2010 • † Qualified for the play-off quarter-finals
Quarter-finals: Pérez Zeledón 2-2 1-4 **Alajuelense** • **Santos** 3-0 3-0 Barrio Mexico • San Carlos 2-0 0-4 **Herediano** • Brujas 2-3 1-1 **Cartagines**
Play-off semi-finals: **Alajuelense** 2-1 3-0 Cartagines • Santos 1-0 0-1 **Herediano**. (Herediano advanced on better season record)
Play-off final: Herediano 0-0 1-1 3-4p **Alajuelense**. **LD Alajuelense** are the Invierno champions

MEDALS TABLE

		Overall			League			CON'CAF			City
		G	S	B	G	S	B	G	S	B	
1	Deportivo Saprissa	32	17	7	29	15	1	3	2	6	San José
2	Liga Deportiva Alajuelense	27	23	13	25	20	9	2	3	4	Alajuela
3	CS Herediano	21	14	12	21	14	11			1	Heredia
4	CS La Libertad	6	7	4	6	7	4				San José
5	CS Cartaginés	4	10	7	3	10	7	1			Cartago
6	Orión FC	2	6	7	2	6	7				
7	Municipal Puntarenas	1	3	1	1	3	1				Puntarenas
8	CS Uruguay	1	1		1	1					Coronado
9	Universidad de Costa Rica	1		3	1		3				San José
10	Brujas Escazú FC	1			1						San José
11	AD Carmelita	1			1						Alajuela
	Liberia Mia	1			1						Liberia

CRO – CROATIA

FIFA/COCA-COLA WORLD RANKING

1993	1994	1995	1996	1997	1998	1999	2000	2001	2002	2003	2004	2005	2006	2007	2008	2009	2010
122	62	41	24	19	4	9	18	19	32	20	23	20	15	10	7	10	10

	2010											Hi/Lo
Jan	Feb	Mar	Mar	Apr	May	Jul	Aug	Sep	Oct	Nov	Dec	**3**
10	11	11	10	9	10	15	14	11	9	9	10	**125**

Dinamo Zagreb made it five league titles in a row for the second time in the short history of the Croatian league and they will look to break new ground with a sixth in 2011. They were rarely troubled during the campaign despite finishing just four points ahead of fierce rivals Hajduk Split with two of their four defeats coming in their last four games. They sealed the title with a 0-0 draw at home to Hajduk but there was a huge consolation for the team from Split when they won the cup four days later. Dinamo's hopes of a fourth consecutive double had gone up in flames in the semi-final thanks to a 1-0 aggregate defeat at the hands of Hajduk, who then beat Sibenik 4-1 over two legs in the final to claim their first trophy for five years. There was embarrassment for Dinamo in the 2010-11 UEFA Champions League as they once again failed to make the group stage - this time losing in the third qualifying round to Moldova's Sheriff Tiraspol. Despite the failure of the national team to qualify for the World Cup in South Africa, Croatia's record of just four defeats since coach Slaven Bilic took over in July 2006 bears few comparisons. Bilic resisted the temptation to return to club football and fans were rewarded with a solid start in the qualifiers for Euro 2012 in Poland as they look to qualify for the finals for a fourth time in five tournaments.

FIFA WORLD CUP RECORD
1930-1994 DNE **1998** 3 SF **2002** 23 r1 **2006** 22 r1 **2010** DNQ

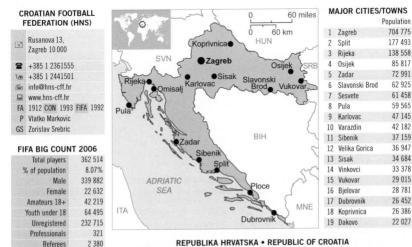

CROATIAN FOOTBALL FEDERATION (HNS)		**MAJOR CITIES/TOWNS**	Population
Rusanova 13, Zagreb 10 000		1 Zagreb	704 775
		2 Split	177 493
☎ +385 1 2361555		3 Rijeka	138 558
📠 +385 1 2441501		4 Osijek	85 817
✉ info@hns-cff.hr		5 Zadar	72 991
🖥 www.hns-cff.hr		6 Slavonski Brod	62 925
FA 1912 CON 1993 FIFA 1992		7 Sesvete	61 458
P Vlatko Markovic		8 Pula	59 565
GS Zorislav Srebric		9 Karlovac	47 145
		10 Varazdin	42 182
FIFA BIG COUNT 2006		11 Sibenik	37 159
Total players	362 514	12 Velika Gorica	36 947
% of population	8.07%	13 Sisak	34 684
Male	339 882	14 Vinkovci	33 378
Female	22 632	15 Vukovar	29 015
Amateurs 18+	42 219	16 Bjelovar	28 781
Youth under 18	64 495	17 Dubrovnik	26 452
Unregistered	232 715	18 Koprivnica	26 386
Professionals	321	19 Dakovo	22 027
Referees	2 380		
Admin & coaches	15 108		
Number of clubs	1 463		
Number of teams	3 353		

REPUBLIKA HRVATSKA • REPUBLIC OF CROATIA

Capital	Zagreb	Population	4 489 409 (121)	% in cities	57%
GDP per capita	$18 300 (67)	Area km²	56 594 km² (126)	GMT +/-	+1
Neighbours (km)	Bosnia-Herzegovina 932, Hungary 329, Serbia 241, Montenegro 25, Slovenia 455 • Coast 5835				

RECENT INTERNATIONAL MATCHES PLAYED BY CROATIA

2007	Opponents	Score		Venue	Comp	Scorers	Att	Referee
7-02	Norway	W	2-1	Rijeka	Fr	Petric 26, Modric 38	8 000	Kalt FRA
24-03	FYR Macedonia	W	2-1	Zagreb	ECq	Srna 58, Eduardo 88	29 969	Plautz AUT
2-06	Estonia	W	1-0	Tallinn	ECq	Eduardo 32	8 651	Kassai HUN
6-06	Russia	D	0-0	Zagreb	ECq		36 194	Michel SVK
22-08	Bosnia-Herzegovina	W	5-3	Sarajevo	Fr	Eduardo 18, Srna 2 35 74, Kovac.N 2 73 81	8 000	Skomina SVN
8-09	Estonia	W	2-0	Zagreb	ECq	Eduardo 2 39 45	15 102	Laperierre SUI
12-09	Andorra	W	6-0	Andorra la Vella	ECq	Srna 34, Petric 2 38 44, Kranjcar 49, Eduardo 55, Rakitic 64	925	Thual FRA
13-10	Israel	W	1-0	Zagreb	ECq	Eduardo 52	30 084	Stark GER
16-10	Slovakia	W	3-0	Rijeka	Fr	Olic 2 45 69, Vukojevic 48	5 000	Laperriere SUI
17-11	FYR Macedonia	L	0-2	Skopje	ECq		14 500	De Bleeckere BEL
21-11	England	W	3-2	London	ECq	Kranjcar 8, Olic 14, Petric 77	88 017	Fröjdfeldt SWE
2008								
6-02	Netherlands	L	0-3	Split	Fr		28 000	Fernandez ESP
26-03	Scotland	D	1-1	Glasgow	Fr	Kranjcar 10	28 821	Hauge NOR
24-05	Moldova	W	1-0	Rijeka	Fr	Kovac.N 30	7 000	Ceferin SVN
31-05	Hungary	D	1-1	Budapest	Fr	Kovac.N 24	10 000	Ledentu FRA
8-06	Austria	W	1-0	Vienna	ECr1	Modric 4p	51 428	Vink NED
12-06	Germany	W	2-1	Klagenfurt	ECr1	Srna 24, Olic 62	30 461	De Bleeckere BEL
16-06	Poland	W	1-0	Klagenfurt	ECr1	Klasnic 53	30 461	Vassaras GRE
20-06	Turkey	D	1-1	Vienna	ECqf	Klasnic 119	51 428	Rosetti ITA
20-08	Slovenia	W	3-2	Maribor	Fr	Rakitic 2 37 64, Srna 58p	11 500	Circhetta SUI
6-09	Kazakhstan	W	3-0	Zagreb	WCq	Kovac.N 13, Modric 36, Petric 81	17 424	Johannesson SWE
10-09	England	L	1-4	Zagreb	WCq	Mandzukic 78	35 218	Michel SVK
11-10	Ukraine	D	0-0	Kharkov	WCq		38 500	Braamhaar NED
15-10	Andorra	W	4-0	Zagreb	WCq	Rakitic 2 16 87p, Olic 32, Modric 75	14 441	Vad HUN
2009								
11-02	Romania	W	2-1	Bucharest	Fr	Rakitic 28, Kranjcar 75	9 000	Balaj ROU
1-04	Andorra	W	2-0	Andorra La Vella	WCq	Klasnic 15, Eduardo 36	1 100	Trattou CYP
6-06	Ukraine	D	2-2	Zagreb	WCq	Petric 2, Modric 68	32 073	Hauge NOR
12-08	Belarus	W	3-1	Minsk	WCq	Olic 2 22 83, Eduardo 69	21 651	Brych GER
5-09	Belarus	W	1-0	Zagreb	WCq	Rakitic 24	25 628	Plautz AUT
9-09	England	L	1-5	London	WCq	Eduardo 71	87 319	Undiano ESP
8-10	Qatar	W	3-2	Rijeka	Fr	Corluka 7, Klasnic 11, Jelavic 90	5 000	Balaj ROU
14-10	Kazakhstan	W	2-1	Astana	WCq	Vukojevic 10, Kranjcar 93+	10 250	Circhetta SUI
14-11	Liechtenstein	W	5-0	Vinkovci	Fr	Bilic 2 1 48, Srna 10, Eduardo 2 24 46	10 000	Fabian HUN
2010								
19-05	Austria	W	1-0	Klagenfurt	Fr	Bilic 86	20 000	Blom NED
23-05	Wales	W	2-0	Osijek	Fr	Rakitic 45, Gabric 81	15 000	Vincic SVN
26-05	Estonia	D	0-0	Tallinn	Fr		3 000	Svendsen DEN
11-08	Slovakia	D	1-1	Bratislava	Fr	Jelavic 54	6 366	Matejek CZE
3-09	Latvia	W	3-0	Riga	ECq	Petric 43, Olic 51, Srna 82	7 600	Kuipers NED
7-09	Greece	D	0-0	Zagreb	ECq		24 399	Larsen DEN
9-10	Israel	W	2-1	Tel Aviv	ECq	Kranjcar 2 36p 41	33 421	Stark GER
12-10	Norway	W	2-1	Zagreb	Fr	Mandzukic 35, Kranjcar 50	3 000	Skomina SVN
17-11	Malta	W	3-0	Zagreb	ECq	Kranjcar 2 18 42, Kalinic 81	9 000	Gomes POR

Fr = Friendly match • EC = UEFA EURO 2008/12 • WC = FIFA World Cup • q = qualifier • r1 = first round group • qf = quarter-final

CROATIA NATIONAL TEAM HISTORICAL RECORDS

Caps 100 - Dario Simic 1996-2008 • 84 - Robert Kovac 1999-2009 • 83 - Niko Kovac 1996-2008 & Josip Simunic 2001- • 81 - Robert Jarni 1990-2002 & Stipe Pletikosa 1999- • 79 - Darijo Srna 2002- • 73 - Ivica Olic 2002- • 69 - Davor Suker 1990-2002 • 62 - Aljosa Asanovic 1990-2000 • 61 - Niko Kranjcar 2004- & Zvonimir Soldo 1994-2002 • 59 - Drazen Ladic 1990-99 & Jerko Leko 2002-

Goals 45 - Davor Suker 1990-2002 • 19 - Darijo Srna 2002- • 18 - Eduardo da Silva 2004- • 15 - Goran Vlaovic 1992-2002 • 14 - Niko Kranjcar 2004- ; Niko Kovac 1996-2008 & Ivica Olic 2002- • 12 - Zvonimir Boban 1990-99; Ivan Klasnic 2004-; Mladen Petric 2001- & Franjo Wolfl 1940-44 • 10 - Bosko Balaban 2000-07; Alen Boksic 1993-2002 & Robert Prosinecki 1993-2002

Past Coaches Drazan Jerkovic 1990-91 • Stanko Poklepovic 1992 • Vlatko Markovic 1993 • Miroslav Blazevic 1994-2000 • Mirko Jozic 2000-02 • Otto Baric 2002-04 • Zlatko Kranjcar 2004-06 • Slaven Bilic 2006-

CROATIA 2009-10

PRVA HNL OZUJSKO (1)

	Pl	W	D	L	F	A	Pts	Dinamo	Hajduk	Cibalia	Sibenik	Osijek	Karlovac	Slaven	Lokomotiva	Rijeka	Varteks	Istra	Zadar	Inter	Zagreb	Medimurje	Croatia Ses'te
Dinamo Zagreb †	30	18	8	4	70	20	62		0-0	1-1	5-0	5-0	1-1	6-0	1-0	6-0	2-1	7-1	0-0	3-1	1-1	4-0	6-0
Hajduk Split ‡	30	17	7	6	50	21	58	2-1		2-1	0-1	1-0	1-0	5-0	1-0	1-1	2-0	1-0	0-1	2-2	2-0	4-1	6-0
Cibalia Vinkovci ‡	30	16	9	5	46	20	57	2-0	0-0		4-3	1-1	2-2	2-0	1-0	1-0	4-0	0-0	2-0	2-0	1-0	3-0	5-0
NK Sibenik ‡	30	14	8	8	34	37	50	2-1	0-1	0-2		2-2	1-0	0-0	0-0	1-0	2-1	1-1	1-1	0-0	3-1	1-0	2-0
NK Osijek	30	13	8	9	49	36	47	0-1	1-1	2-0	3-0		0-1	0-1	3-0	1-0	1-1	3-0	3-0	4-2	5-3	3-1	0-0
NK Karlovac	30	12	11	7	32	23	47	1-3	1-0	3-0	0-2	1-0		0-0	0-1	2-0	1-1	1-1	2-0	1-0	0-0	2-0	0-0
Slaven B. Koprivnica	30	11	10	9	44	45	43	0-1	2-1	1-1	2-2	5-2	1-3		1-0	1-1	2-3	3-0	2-1	5-2	2-0	3-2	4-0
Lokomotiva Zagreb	30	12	6	12	35	38	42	0-1	2-1	2-0	0-0	2-2	0-0	1-1		3-0	2-0	2-1	1-0	0-1	1-0	1-3	3-2
NK Rijeka	30	10	10	10	49	44	40	2-2	2-0	1-1	0-1	1-1	1-1	2-3	6-0		3-3	2-0	3-2	3-1	3-1	4-0	4-2
Varteks Varazdin	30	9	9	12	36	43	36	1-2	0-3	1-1	5-1	1-2	0-1	0-0	2-1	1-1		0-2	1-0	2-1	1-0	3-0	4-1
Istra Pula	30	9	8	13	31	40	35	0-0	0-1	0-0	1-2	1-3	2-0	2-0	3-1	2-0	0-1		2-0	2-0	2-1	1-2	1-0
NK Zadar	30	9	7	14	27	41	34	0-0	1-2	0-3	2-1	2-1	1-1	1-0	1-1	1-1	2-0	1-1		0-1	1-0	2-0	2-0
Inter Zapresic	30	10	3	17	36	50	33	0-1	0-3	1-0	0-1	0-3	0-1	2-0	4-2	3-0	1-1	1-0	4-3		1-3	2-1	1-2
NK Zagreb	30	9	6	15	43	49	33	1-0	1-1	0-1	0-2	1-0	4-2	3-3	2-4	1-1	3-0	1-1	4-0	0-3		2-1	4-2
Medimurje Cakovec	30	8	5	17	37	61	29	1-4	1-1	0-2	4-0	1-1	1-1	1-1	0-3	1-5	0-0	4-2	3-0	2-1	4-2		2-1
Croatia Sesvete	30	3	5	22	30	81	14	2-5	2-5	0-3	1-2	1-2	0-3	1-1	1-2	1-2	2-2	2-2	1-2	3-1	1-4	2-1	

24/07/2009 - 13/05/2010 • † Qualified for the UEFA Champions League • ‡ Qualified for the Europa League • Top scorers: **18** - Davor Vugrinec, NK Zagreb • **17** - Senijad Ibricic BIH, Hajduk • **15** - Asim Sehic BIH, Istra • **14** - Mario Mandzukic, Dinamo & Nino Bule, Lokomotiva

CROATIA 2009-10

DRUGA HNL (2)

	Pl	W	D	L	F	A	Pts	Radniki	Pomorac	Hrvatski	Lucko	Solin	Vinogradar	Rudes	Imotski	Junak	Mosor	Suhopolje	Vukovar	Moslavina	Segesta
Radniki Split	26	16	5	5	56	26	53		2-0	2-0	4-1	3-4	3-0	2-2	3-0	2-0	1-2	2-1	3-0	4-0	4-1
Pomorac Kostrena	26	14	5	7	39	22	47	4-2		1-1	0-1	2-0	3-1	2-0	4-1	1-0	3-0	1-0	0-1	3-0	2-1
Hrvatski Dragovoljac	26	11	9	6	33	21	42	0-1	0-0		1-2	0-0	1-0	1-0	5-0	1-1	2-0	2-1	4-1	4-1	1-0
NK Lucko	26	12	6	8	38	28	42	1-0	3-1	5-1		1-1	1-1	1-1	0-1	2-2	0-0	2-0	0-1	2-0	4-0
NK Solin	26	10	10	6	29	22	40	0-3	0-0	0-0	2-1		2-0	2-1	1-1	2-0	3-0	1-0	3-0	0-0	3-0
Vinogradar Lokosin Dol	26	11	4	11	38	37	37	1-4	3-1	1-0	3-1	0-0		3-1	1-3	2-0	3-2	2-1	3-3	1-2	3-1
Rudes Zagreb	26	10	7	9	38	38	37	1-1	0-3	0-0	1-3	2-0	2-6		6-2	2-0	1-0	1-0	1-1	1-0	3-0
NK Imotski	26	10	5	11	29	31	35	5-2	1-1	0-2	1-2	1-2	1-0	0-0		3-0	2-1	3-3	3-4	2-0	
Junak Sinj	26	10	4	12	40	49	34	1-1	0-1	1-2	1-0	2-0	1-0	3-1	2-0		2-0	1-2	2-1	3-0	3-0
Mosor Zrnovnica	26	9	6	11	26	34	33	1-1	0-2	0-2	3-0	1-1	0-1	3-3	0-2	1-1		1-1	2-1	2-1	1-0
NK Suhopolje	26	8	7	11	29	31	31	0-1	1-0	0-0	2-2	1-0	1-1	1-0	3-1	3-1	0-1		2-1	0-0	3-2
HNK Vukovar '91	26	7	10	9	31	39	31	1-1	1-1	1-1	1-0	0-0	2-1	2-1	1-2	3-2	0-1	0-0		0-0	2-1
Moslavina Kutina	26	6	6	14	25	44	24	0-3	3-1	2-2	0-2	0-0	0-1	1-3	0-1	1-1	1-2	3-2	3-1		2-0
Segesta Sisak	26	4	4	18	17	46	16	0-1	0-2	1-0	0-1	1-1	1-0	1-1	0-0	3-0	0-2	1-1	1-3	2-1	

22/08/2009 - 29/05/2010 • Pomorac ineligible for promotion
Top scorers: **17** - Romano Oblinovic, Imotski • **13** - Igor Raic, Rudes • **12** - Ante Zuzul, Radniki

MEDALS TABLE

	Overall			League			Cup		Europe			City
	G	S	B	G	S	B	G	S	G	S	B	
1 Dinamo Zagreb	22	7	2	12	3	2	10	4				Zagreb
2 Hajduk Split	11	14	1	6	10	1	5	4				Split
3 NK Rijeka	2	3	2		2	2	2	1				Rijeka
4 NK Zagreb	1	3	3	1	2	3		1				Zagreb
5 Inter Zapresic	1	1			1		1					Zapresic
6 NK Osijek	1		6			6	1					Osijek
7 Varteks Varazdin		5	3			3		5				Varazdin
8 Slaven Belupo			2			1		1				Koprivnica
9 Cibalia Vinkovci		1	1			1		1				Vinkovci
10 NK Pula		1						1				Pula
NK Sibenik		1						1				Sibenik
CROATIAN CLUBS IN YUGOSLAV FOOTBALL												
3 Hajduk Split	19	16	11	9	10	10	9	5	1	1	1	
4 Dinamo Zagreb	12	20	8	4	12	6	8	8			2	

HRVATSKOG NOGOMETNOG KUPA 2009-10

First Round		Round of 16		Quarter-finals			Semi-finals			Final
Hajduk Split	5	Hajduk Split *	5							
Lipik *	3	Moslavina Kutina	1	Hajduk Split	0	4				
Konavljanin *	0						Hajduk Split	0	1	
Moslavina Kutina	2	Segesta Sisak	1	NK Zagreb *	0	1				
Segesta Sisak	1	NK Zagreb *	3							
Nehaj *	0									
Orijent *	1	Pomorac Kostrena *	9							
NK Zagreb	2	Rudar Labin	0	Pomorac Kostrena *	0	2				
Pomorac Kostrena	5						Dinamo Zagreb *	0	0	
Slavonac Stari Perkovci *	2	Vinogradar Lokosin Dol	1	Dinamo Zagreb	2	3				
Cibalia Vinkovci	2	Dinamo Zagreb *	4							
Rudar Labin *	5									
Vinogradar Lokosin Dol	4	Varteks Varazdin *	2							
Medimurje Cakovec	1	NK Karlovac	1	Varteks Varazdin	4	2				
Plitvica *	0						Varteks Varazdin	0	0	
Dinamo Zagreb	4	Istra Pula *	0	Slaven B. Koprivnica *	1	0				
Varteks Varazdin	2	Slaven B. Koprivnica	1							
Velebit *	0									
HASK Zagreb	0	NK Osijek *	1							
NK Karlovac *	3	Inter Zapresic	0	NK Osijek *	1	0				
Istra Pula	1						NK Sibenik *	0	2	
Croatia Sesvete *	0	NK Rijeka	0	NK Sibenik	1	4				
Radnicki Split *	0	NK Sibenik	4							
Slaven B. Koprivnica	2									
NK Osijek	3									
Granicar *	1									
NK Suhopolje *	2 8p									
Inter Zapresic	2 9p									
NK Rijeka	2									
MV Croatia *	0									
NK Belisce *	0									
NK Sibenik	3									

Final

CUP FINAL 1ST LEG

Poljud, Split
21-04-2010, Att: 15 000, Ref: Drazenko Kovacic
Scorers – Ticinovic 62, Ibricic 88 for Hajduk;
Zec 65p for Sibenik

Hajduk - Danijel Subasic - Jurica Buljat, Mario Maloca, Mirko Oremus (Mario Ticinovic 61), Ivan Strinic, Josip Skoko, Marin Ljubicic●, Florin Cernat (Srdan Andric 70), Anas Sharbini (Marin Tomasov 83), Senijad Ibricic, Ante Vukusic●. Tr: Stanko Poklepovic
Sibenik - Goran Blazevic - Velimir Vidic, Igor Budisa●, Ante Bulat●, Ivan Elez●, Zeni Husman●, Arijan Ademi, Stipe Bacelic–Grgic (Sandro Bloudek 88), Mehmed Alispahic●, Ivan Fustar (Ivan Bozic 74) (Antonio Jakolis 90), Ermin Zec. Tr: Branko Karacic

Hajduk Split *	2	2
NK Sibenik	1	0

CUP FINAL 2ND LEG

Subicevac, Sibenik
5-05-2010, Att: 5 500, Ref: Domagoj Vuckov
Scorers – Vukusic 16, Ibricic 93+p

Sibenik - Goran Blazevic - Ante Bulat●, Velimir Vidic, Igor Budisa, Ivan Medvid, Sandro Bloudek● (Ivan Elez 62), Stipe Bacelic–Grgic, Arijan Ademi, Zeni Husmani (Antonio Jakolis 71), Jusuf Dajic (Ivan Fustar 46), Ermin Zec●. Tr: Branko Karacic
Hajduk - Danijel Subasic - Ivan Strinic, Mario Maloca, Jurica Buljat, Mirko Oremus (Marin Ljubicic 46), Srdan Andric, Josip Skoko● (Boris Pandza 79), Srdan Andric, Anas Sharbini (Mario Ticinovic 85), Senijad Ibricic, Ante Vukusic. Tr: Stanko Poklepovic

Varteks Varazdin	0	0
NK Sibenik *	0	2

* Home team/home team in the first leg

CTA – CENTRAL AFRICAN REPUBLIC

FIFA/COCA-COLA WORLD RANKING

1993	1994	1995	1996	1997	1998	1999	2000	2001	2002	2003	2004	2005	2006	2007	2008	2009	2010
157	174	180	183	188	192	175	176	182	179	177	180	183	179	182	199	200	111

2010												Hi/Lo
Jan	Feb	Mar	Mar	Apr	May	Jul	Aug	Sep	Oct	Nov	Dec	**111**
200	200	200	202	202	202	202	202	172	112	112	111	**202**

The Central African Republic created a major sensation in October 2010 with a shock 2-0 win over Algeria in the 2012 African Nations Cup qualifiers. 'Les Fauves de Bas-Oubangui' have only ever sporadically taken part in the Nations Cup and have entered the FIFA World Cup just once. Indeed, a 4-2 victory at home to Cote d'Ivoire in 1973 was their only competitive victory in an international before the Algeria match. Having surprised everyone with an equally extraordinary draw away to Morocco in September, they contrived to produce an even bigger shock with the triumph over a bewildered Algeria in Bangui. A side with just a handful of foreign-based players is coached by 73-year-old Frenchman Jules Accorsi and has provided a rare highlight for the game in a country where basketball far overshadows football for popularity and resources. Olympique Real de Bangui were runaway champions in the Ligue de Bangui, the de-facto national championship whose specificity to the capital reflects the poor sporting infrastructure around the country. The Coupe Barthelemy Boganda was won by Diplomate Football Club de 8eme Arrondissment (DFC8), who saw Moussa Liman score a 47th minute winner in a 1-0 victory over the more established Stade Centrafricain, losers in the final for a second successive year.

FIFA WORLD CUP RECORD
1930-1998 DNE **2002** DNQ **2006-2010** DNE

FEDERATION CENTRAFRICAINE DE FOOTBALL (RCA)

Avenue de Martyrs, Boite Postale 344, Bangui
☎ +236 70169828
📠 +236 21615660
✉ fedefoot60@yahoo.fr
💻
FA 1961 CON 1965 FIFA 1963
P Edouard Patrice Ngaissona
GS Elie Delphin Feidangamo

FIFA BIG COUNT 2006

Total players	192 404
% of population	4.47%
Male	183 004
Female	9 400
Amateurs 18+	5 200
Youth under 18	3 200
Unregistered	13 000
Professionals	4
Referees	360
Admin & coaches	3 250
Number of clubs	80
Number of teams	400

MAJOR CITIES/TOWNS

		Population
1	Bangui	563 383
2	Bimbo	164 208
3	Mbaiki	75 809
4	Berbérati	66 668
5	Kaga-Bandoro	58 353
6	Bozoum	47 187
7	Carnot	39 353
8	Sibut	38 643
9	Bambari	30 894
10	Nola	30 292
11	Bria	30 241
12	Bossangoa	26 259
13	Bouar	26 134
14	Bangassou	24 039
15	Damara	22 749
16	Mobaye	19 742
17	Paoua	19 282
18	Boda	17 719
19	Ippy	16 936

REPUBLIQUE CENTRAFRICAINE • CENTRAL AFRICAN REPUBLIC

Capital Bangui	Population 4 511 488 (120)	% in cities 39%
GDP per capita $700 (221)	Area km² 622 984 km² (44)	GMT +/- +1
Neighbours (km) Cameroon 797, Chad 1197, Congo DR 1577, Congo 467, Sudan 1165		

294 PART TWO – THE NATIONS OF THE WORLD

RECENT INTERNATIONAL MATCHES PLAYED BY THE CENTRAL AFRICAN REPUBLIC

2003	Opponents		Score	Venue	Comp	Scorers	Att	Referee
4-05	Congo	L	1-2	Brazzaville	CNq	Makita [84]		
8-06	Congo	D	0-0	Bangui	CNq			Hissene CHA
22-06	Mozambique	L	0-1	Maputo	CNq		15 000	
6-07	Burkina Faso	L	0-3	Bangui	CNq			
7-12	Cameroon	D	2-2	Brazzaville	CMr1	Oroko [10], Sandjo [30]		Mbera GAB
9-12	Cameroon	W	1-0	Brazzaville	CMr1	Sandjo [85]		Mandioukouta CGO
11-12	Gabon	W	2-0	Brazzaville	CMsf			
13-12	Cameroon	L	2-3	Brazzaville	CMf	Oroko [63], Destin [74]		Bansimba CGO
2004								
No international matches played in 2004								
2005								
3-02	Gabon	L	0-4	Libreville	CMr1			
5-02	Congo	L	0-1	Libreville	CMr1			
2006								
6-03	Cameroon	L	0-2	Malabo	CMr1			
8-03	Gabon	D	2-2	Malabo	CMr1			
2007								
6-03	Chad	L	2-3	N'Djamena	CMr1	Momi Hilaire [14], Greyanda Fiacre [34]		
8-03	Cameroon	D	0-0	N'Djamena	CMr1			
12-03	Congo	L	1-4	N'Djamena	CMsf	Zinda Romaric [15]		
16-03	Chad	L	0-1	N'Djamena	CM3p			
2008								
No international matches played in 2008								
2009								
No international matches played in 2009								
2010								
4-09	Morocco	D	0-0	Rabat	CNq			Coulibaly MLI
10-10	Algeria	W	2-0	Bangui	CNq	Charlie Dopekoulouyen [81], Momi Hilaire [85]		Carvalho ANG

CN = CAF African Cup of Nations • CM = CEMAC Cup
q = qualifier • r1 = first round group • sf = semi-final • 3p = third place play-off • f = final

CENTRAL AFRICAN REPUBLIC 2010
LIGUE DE BANGUI

	Pl	W	D	L	F	A	Pts
Olympique Réal	22	18	3	1	50	8	**57**
SCAF	22	13	7	2	44	18	**46**
AS Tempête Mocaf	22	13	4	5	39	13	**43**
DFC8	22	13	3	6	39	18	**42**
Anges de Fatima	22	10	3	9	38	31	**33**
Kpèténè Star	22	8	3	11	42	40	**27**
USCA	22	7	6	9	35	38	**27**
Anégrée	22	7	6	9	28	34	**27**
Sica Sport	22	6	6	10	28	45	**24**
Espérance	22	5	8	9	29	32	**23**
Castel Foot	22	5	2	15	15	47	**17**
Asset de Gobongo	22	0	3	19	13	76	**3**

28/03/2010 - 12/2010

COUPE BARTHELEMY BOGANDA FINAL
Bangui

DFC8	1-0	SCAF

Scorer - Moussa Limane [47]

CUB – CUBA

FIFA/COCA-COLA WORLD RANKING

1993	1994	1995	1996	1997	1998	1999	2000	2001	2002	2003	2004	2005	2006	2007	2008	2009	2010
159	175	96	68	88	107	77	77	76	71	75	76	75	46	71	79	119	62

2010												Hi/Lo
Jan	Feb	Mar	Mar	Apr	May	Jul	Aug	Sep	Oct	Nov	Dec	**46**
119	125	124	125	125	126	114	114	113	121	94	62	**175**

Cuba fell short once again in its quest for a first Caribbean title after losing a tight semi-final against Guadeloupe at the 2010 Digicel Caribbean Cup finals in Martinique - the third time in four tournaments that the Cubans had lost in the semi-finals. In front of a partisan crowd favouring their opponents, Cuba took the lead in the first half but a hotly disputed penalty ten minutes into the second half turned the game in favour of Guadeloupe who then sealed the game with a spectacular long range free-kick 12 minutes from the end. For the Cubans there was at least the consolation of a place at the 2011 CONCACAF Gold Cup finals and a victory in the third place play-off against Grenada. In club football, the Campeonato Nacional was won by Ciego de Avila who beat Camagüey 6-3 on aggregate in the final. It was the club's third title in the past nine seasons making them the most successful team of the past decade, and they did it without their talismanic former striker Lester More who defected to the USA in 2008. In Sander Fernandez, however, the club has found prolific replacement. Fernandez scored at the rate of nearly a goal a game including eight in the play-offs and four in the final, although he fell just short of the 32 scored by Lester More for Ciego de Avila in the 2003 season.

FIFA WORLD CUP RECORD

1930 DNE 1934 DNQ **1938** 8 QF 1950-1962 DNE 1966 DNQ 1970-1974 DNE 1978-1982 DNQ 1986 DNE 1990 DNQ 1994 DNE 1998-2010 DNQ

ASOCIACION DE FUTBOL DE CUBA (AFC)

Estadio Pedro Marrero,
Escuela Nacional de Futbol,
Mario Lopez Avenida 41, 44 y 46,
Municipio Playa La Habana

☎ +53 7 2076440
📠 +53 7 2043563
📧 futbol@inder.co.cu
FA 1924 CON 1961 FIFA 1932
P Luis Hernandez
GS Luis Yero

FIFA BIG COUNT 2006

Total players	1 141 825
% of population	10.03%
Male	1 045 900
Female	95 925
Amateurs 18+	27 375
Unregistered	1 012 400
Professionals	100
Referees	225
Admin & coaches	5 030
Number of clubs	338
Number of teams	1 500

MAJOR CITIES/TOWNS

		Population
1	Havana	2 133 920
2	Santiago de Cuba	443 585
3	Camagüey	309 818
4	Holguín	291 638
5	Guantánamo	221 373
6	Santa Clara	219 713
7	Las Tunas	165 601
8	Bayamo	162 747
9	Cienfuegos	160 060
10	Pinar del Rio	158 392
11	Matanzas	139 765
12	Ciego de Ávila	121 769
13	Sancti Spíritus	113 739
14	Manzanillo	103 209
15	Cárdenas	97 402
16	Palma Soriano	77 471
17	Mayarí	65 425
18	Moa	64 618
19	Nueva Gerona	60 579

REPUBLICA DE CUBA • REPUBLIC OF CUBA

Capital	Havana	Population	11 451 652 (72)	% in cities	76%
GDP per capita	$9500 (108)	Area km²	110 860 km² (105)	GMT + / -	-5
Neighbours (km)	Coast 3735				

RECENT INTERNATIONAL MATCHES PLAYED BY CUBA

2006	Opponents		Score	Venue	Comp	Scorers	Att	Referee
17-10	Haiti	D	0-0	Port-au-Prince	Fr		3 000	Grant HAI
19-10	Haiti	W	1-0	Cap Haitien	Fr	Villaurrutia 8p	1 500	
8-11	Haiti	W	2-1	Fort-de-France	CCq	Marquez 21, Moré 79	2 500	Stewart JAM
10-11	Suriname	W	3-1	Fort-de-France	CCq	Alvarez 2 4 26, Jaime Colome 41	3 200	Stennett JAM
12-11	Martinique †	D	0-0	Fort-de-France	CCq		2 500	Small BRB
2007								
14-01	Guadeloupe †	L	1-2	Marabella	CCr1	Alonso 69	3 000	Brizan TRI
16-01	St Vincent/Grenadines	W	3-0	Marabella	CCr1	Moré 2 27 59, Duarte 90	1 700	Angela ARU
18-01	Guyana	D	0-0	Marabella	CCr1		2 000	Moreno PAN
20-01	Trinidad and Tobago	L	1-3	Port of Spain	CCsf	Duarte 75	15 000	Campbell JAM
23-01	Guadeloupe †	W	2-1	Port of Spain	CC3p	Cervantes 2 24 48	6 000	Brizan TRI
24-03	Venezuela	L	1-3	Merida	Fr	Alcantara 47	12 000	Andarcia VEN
9-05	Chile	L	0-3	Osorno	Fr		1 800	Cabrera VEN
16-05	Chile	L	0-2	Temuco	Fr		3 500	Grance PAR
8-06	Mexico	L	1-2	New Jersey	GCr1	Alcantara 22	20 230	Aguilar SLV
10-06	Panama	D	2-2	New Jersey	GCr1	Jaime Colome 29, Alcantara 78	68 123	Davis TRI
13-06	Honduras	L	0-5	Houston	GCr1		68 417	Aguilar SLV
2008								
22-02	Guyana	L	1-2	Linden	Fr	Alvarez 12	1 000	Lancaster GUY
24-02	Guyana	D	0-0	Georgetown	Fr		2 500	James GUY
7-06	St Vincent/Grenadines	W	1-0	Havana	Fr		400	Duran CUB
17-06	Antigua and Barbuda	W	4-3	St John's	WCq	Jaime Colome 2 10 74, Linares 22, Duarte 85	4 500	Moreno PAN
22-06	Antigua and Barbuda	W	4-0	Havana	WCq	Linares 2 9 53, Gonsalves OG 45, Marquez 69	2 000	Quesada CRC
20-08	Trinidad and Tobago	L	1-3	Havana	WCq	Marquez 88	4 000	Archundia MEX
6-09	USA	L	0-1	Havana	WCq		12 000	Aguilar SLV
10-09	Guatemala	L	1-4	Guatemala City	WCq	Linares 25	19 750	Rodriguez MEX
11-10	USA	L	1-6	Washington DC	WCq	Munoz 31	20 249	Moreno PAN
15-10	Guatemala	W	2-1	Havana	WCq	Jaime Colome 45p, Urgelles 90	6 000	Campbell JAM
23-10	Netherlands Antilles	W	7-1	Havana	CCq	Duarte 2 21 45, Marquez 25, Linares 2 39 86, Jaime Colome 79, Clavelo 82	1 000	Whittaker CAY
25-10	Barbados	D	1-1	Havana	CCq	Clavelo 68	1 000	Campbell JAM
27-10	Suriname	W	6-0	Havana	CCq	Cervantes 2 11 38, Marquez 47, Linares 54, Duarte 64, Dranguet 76	1 000	Holder CAY
19-11	Trinidad and Tobago	L	0-3	Port of Spain	WCq		18 000	Wijngaarde SUR
4-12	Guadeloupe †	W	2-1	Montego Bay	CCr1	Fernandez 8, Linares 74	2 500	Brizan TRI
6-12	Antigua and Barbuda	W	3-0	Trelawny	CCr1	Marquez 7, Linares 21, Jaime Colome 35	1 000	Campbell JAM
8-12	Haiti	L	0-1	Montego Bay	CCr1		1 500	Brizan TRI
11-12	Grenada	D	2-2	Kingston	CCsf	Joel Colome 14, Linares 33. L 5-6p	10 000	Moreno PAN
14-12	Guadeloupe †	D	0-0	Kingston	CC3p	L 4-5p	9 000	Taylor BRB
2009								
No international matches played in 2009								
2010								
26-10	Panama	W	3-0	Pamama City	Fr	Marquez 44, Coroneaux 2 45 90	2 116	Moreno PAN
10-11	Dominica	W	4-2	St John's	CCq	Coroneaux 9, Fernandez 20, Joel Colome 27, Hernandez 35	500	Lancaster GUY
12-11	Suriname	D	3-3	St John's	CCq	Coroneaux 45, Cervantes 65, Ramos 87	400	Campbell JAM
14-11	Antigua and Barbuda	D	0-0	St John's	CCq		500	Campbell JAM
26-11	Trinidad and Tobago	W	2-0	Fort-de-France	CCr1	Jaime Colome 23, Linares 79	5 000	Lancaster GUY
28-11	Martinique †	W	1-0	Fort-de-France	CCr1	Marquez 29	500	Taylor BRB
30-11	Grenada	D	0-0	Fort-de-France	CCr1		2 000	Bogle JAM
3-12	Guadeloupe †	L	1-2	Fort-de-France	CCsf	Fernandez 35	2 001	Wijngaarde SUR
5-12	Grenada	W	1-0	Fort-de-France	CC3p	Linares 12	4 000	Lopez GUA

Fr = Friendly match • CC = Caribbean Championship • GC = CONCACAF Gold Cup • WC = FIFA World Cup • q = qualifier
r1 = first round group • sf = semi-final • 3p = third place play-off • † Not a full international

CUBA 2009-10

CAMPEONATO NACIONAL

Occidental Group A

	Pl	W	D	L	F	A	Pts	LH	CLH	PR	IJ	VC	Cf	Ind	Mat	CA	LT	Cam	SS	Gua	StC	Gra	Hol
La Habana †	30	14	6	10	38	38	48		1-2	1-0	1-0	0-0	2-1	4-0	2-1	1-1	1-0	1-1	0-2	1-2	3-0	0-5	2-1
Ciudad de La Habana †	30	13	8	9	38	20	47	0-1		0-0	2-3	1-0	3-0	2-2	7-0	0-2	1-1	2-0	0-0	0-0	0-1	0-0	2-0
Pinar del Río	30	7	9	14	27	47	30	0-1	1-0		2-1	1-4	0-1	2-1	3-0	0-5	0-4	0-2	2-1	1-2	1-4	2-1	0-0
Isla de la Juventud	29	5	5	19	30	53	20	4-1	0-2	4-1		3-3	0-1	3-0	3-0	0-2	0-2	0-1	n/p	0-1	2-3	0-5	0-0

Occidental Group B

	Pl	W	D	L	F	A	Pts	LH	CLH	PR	IJ	VC	Cf	Ind	Mat	CA	LT	Cam	SS	Gua	StC	Gra	Hol
Villa Clara †	30	18	7	5	49	23	61	2-1	2-1	1-1	3-0		2-1	3-0	2-0	0-1	1-0	2-2	1-1	3-0	1-0	1-0	1-1
Cienfuegos	30	14	4	12	34	29	46	4-1	0-2	1-0	2-1	0-1		0-0	3-0	1-1	0-1	2-1	3-1	2-1	0-1	1-1	1-0
Industriales	30	3	7	20	23	57	16	1-2	0-0	1-2	3-0	0-1	1-3		0-1	1-6	2-3	0-4	1-1	2-2	0-1	1-1	2-0
Matanzas	30	4	4	22	24	71	16	1-1	1-3	2-2	2-0	0-3	0-3	3-0		0-0	1-4	2-3	3-1	1-4	0-2	1-1	1-2

Oriental Group C

	Pl	W	D	L	F	A	Pts	LH	CLH	PR	IJ	VC	Cf	Ind	Mat	CA	LT	Cam	SS	Gua	StC	Gra	Hol
Ciego de Avila †	30	17	8	5	61	22	59	0-1	0-1	1-1	3-0	0-1	2-0	4-1	6-1		3-1	6-0	1-0	1-1	2-0	1-1	2-0
Las Tunas †	30	18	5	7	45	25	59	1-0	0-3	2-1	1-1	2-1	0-0	1-0	2-0	1-2		2-1	3-0	2-2	2-0	1-0	3-1
Camagüey †	30	14	9	7	40	31	51	1-1	1-0	2-2	1-0	0-0	1-0	0-0	4-0	2-2	1-0		1-2	0-2	2-0	2-2	0-0
Sancti Spíritus	29	7	11	11	21	30	32	2-2	1-1	0-0	2-1	1-0	0-2	1-0	1-0	0-0	1-2	0-3		0-1	0-0	0-0	0-1

Oriental Group D

	Pl	W	D	L	F	A	Pts	LH	CLH	PR	IJ	VC	Cf	Ind	Mat	CA	LT	Cam	SS	Gua	StC	Gra	Hol
Guantánamo †	30	14	10	6	40	29	52	2-1	1-0	1-0	2-2	1-2	3-0	5-3	1-0	2-1	0-2	0-1	0-0		0-0	2-1	0-1
Santiago de Cuba †	30	14	7	9	35	26	49	1-2	1-2	0-0	1-1	3-2	1-0	0-1	3-1	2-0	2-0	2-0	1-1	0-0		0-1	3-0
Granma	30	12	10	8	43	30	46	3-2	1-0	3-1	2-1	2-4	2-1	1-0	2-0	3-4	0-0	1-2	1-0	1-1	1-1		0-1
Holguín	30	7	6	17	19	36	27	0-1	0-1	1-1	4-0	0-2	0-1	1-0	3-2	0-2	0-2	0-1	0-2	1-1	1-2	0-1	

3/10/2009 - 6/03/2010 • † Qualified for the quarter-finals • Top scorer: **29** - Sander Fernandez, Ciego de Avila

CAMPEONATO NACIONAL PLAY-OFFS

Quarter-finals

Ciego de Avila	0 3
Santiago de Cuba *	2 0
Las Tunas *	1 1 2p
La Habana	1 1 3p
Villa Clara	1 0
Ciudad de La Habana*	1 0
Guantánamo *	0 1
Camagüey	1 1

Semi-finals

Ciego de Avila	1 3
La Habana *	1 0
Villa Clara	1 0
Camagüey *	2 2

Final

Ciego de Avila *	3 3
Camagüey	0 3

* at home in the first leg • 3rd place: La Habana 0-2 2-4 **Villa Clara**

CAMPEONATO NACIONAL FINAL

1st leg. 30-03-2010

Ciego de Avila 3-0 Camagüey

Scorers - Alain Cervantes [19], Leonel Duarte [29], Sander Fernández [78] for Ciego de Avila

CAMPEONATO NACIONAL FINAL

2nd leg. 4-04-2010

Camagüey 3-3 **Ciego de Avila**

Scorers - Armando Coroneaux [14], Keyler Garcia [42], Dagoberto Quesada [87] for Camagüey; Sander Fernandez 3 [31] [70] [88]

MEDALS TABLE

		Overall	Lge	CON'CAF			City/Town
		G	G	G	S	B	
1	Villa Clara	10	10				Santa Clara
2	DC Gallego	8	8				Havana
	Real Iberia	8	8				Havana
4	Pinar del Río	7	7	2			Pinar del Río
5	Ciudad de La Habana	6	6				Havana
	Dep. San Francisco	6	6				San Francisco
7	Granjeros	5	5				Granjeros
	Hispano America	5	5				Havana
9	Industriales	4	4				Havana
	La Habana	4	4				Havana
	Cienfuegos	4	4				Cienfuegos
	Ciego de Avila	4	4				Ciego de Avila

CYP – CYPRUS

FIFA/COCA-COLA WORLD RANKING

1993	1994	1995	1996	1997	1998	1999	2000	2001	2002	2003	2004	2005	2006	2007	2008	2009	2010
72	67	73	78	82	78	63	62	79	80	97	108	96	73	66	94	68	90

2010												Hi/Lo
Jan	Feb	Mar	Mar	Apr	May	Jul	Aug	Sep	Oct	Nov	Dec	**43**
68	68	66	70	68	67	63	63	43	88	93	90	**113**

With both Anorthosis and Apoel having qualified for the group stage of successive UEFA Champions Leagues, 2010 league champions Omonia missed out on making it a hat trick of appearances after losing to Red Bull Salzburg in the third qualifying round of the 2010-11 tournament, to the huge disappointment of their fans. That expectations were so high shows just how club football has developed in recent years, helped by the intense rivalry between the top five clubs - Omonia, APOEL, Anorthosis, Apollon and AEL. Apollon were the season's other winners, beating APOEL 2-1 in the Cup Final in Larnaca, their Ivorian striker Mustapha Bangora giving Apollon the lead after 45 seconds with the fastest goal in the history of the final. With the majority of players in the league now coming from abroad there are rumblings of concern over the impact on local talent and the effect that will have on the national team, especially with the established stars of the side nearing the end of their careers. The qualifiers for UEFA Euro 2012 got off to a bright start with a stunning 4-4 draw away to Portugal - a late Andreas Avraam goal earning a point for Cyprus after they had twice taken the lead in the match - but defeats at the hands of Norway and Denmark mean that a first appearance at a major finals remains an unlikely dream.

FIFA WORLD CUP RECORD
1930-1958 DNE 1962-2010 DNQ

CYPRUS FOOTBALL ASSOCIATION (CFA)

10 Achaion Street,
2413 Engomi, 25071
Nicosia 1306
☎ +357 22 352341
📠 +357 22 590544
✉ info@cfa.com.cy
🖥 www.cfa.com
FA 1934 CON 1962 FIFA 1948
P Costakis Koutsokoumnis
GS Phivos Vakis

FIFA BIG COUNT 2006

Total players	52 403
% of population	6.68%
Male	47 768
Female	4 635
Amateurs 18+	10 091
Youth under 18	6 644
Unregistered	20 200
Professionals	800
Referees	200
Admin & coaches	2 000
Number of clubs	100
Number of teams	328

MEDITERRANEAN SEA

Rizokarpaso

Kyrenia

Morphou   Nicosia   Famagusta

Polis

Larnaca

Paphos   Vasilikos

Limassol

MEDITERRANEAN SEA

0   20 miles
0   20 km

MAJOR CITIES/TOWNS

		Population
1	Nicosia	215 551
2	Limassol	169 507
3	Nicosia (T)	53 045
4	Larnaca	52 949
5	Paphos	42 296
6	Famagusta (T)	36 481
7	Girne (T)	29 723
8	Aradippou	16 155
9	Morphou (T)	13 324
10	Paralimni	13 052
11	Gönyeli	12 985
12	Geri	9 446
13	Ypsonas	8 715
14	Lefka (T)	8 456
15	Degirmenlik	8 114
16	Dali	7 008
17	Tseri	6 332
18	Lapta (T)	6 315

(T) = in Turkish controlled zone

KYPRIAKI DIMOKRATIA • REPUBLIC OF CYPRUS

Capital	Nicosia	Population	796 740 (159)	% in cities	70%
GDP per capita	$21 300 (58)	Area km²	9 251 km² (170)	GMT + / -	+2
Neighbours (km)	Coast 648				

RECENT INTERNATIONAL MATCHES PLAYED BY CYPRUS

2006	Opponents	Score		Venue	Comp	Scorers	Att	Referee
16-08	Romania	L	0-2	Constanta	Fr		10 000	Corpodean ROU
2-09	Slovakia	L	1-6	Bratislava	ECq	Yiasoumis [90]	4 723	Orekhov UKR
7-10	Republic of Ireland	W	5-2	Nicosia	ECq	Konstantinou.M 2 [10 50p], Garpozis [16], Charalambides 2 [60 75]	5 000	Batista OR
11-10	Wales	L	1-3	Cardiff	ECq	Okkas [83]	20 456	Granat POL
15-11	Germany	D	1-1	Nicosia	ECq	Okkas [43]	12 300	Fröjdfeldt SWE
2007								
6-02	Hungary	W	2-1	Limassol	Fr	Yiasoumis [18], Okkas [72]	500	Gerasimou CYP
7-02	Bulgaria	L	0-3	Nicosia	Fr		2 000	
24-03	Slovakia	L	1-3	Nicosia	ECq	Aloneftis [43]	2 696	Lehner AUT
28-03	Czech Republic	L	0-1	Liberec	ECq		9 310	Bebek CRO
22-08	San Marino	W	1-0	Serravalle	ECq	Okkas [54]	552	Janku ALB
8-09	Armenia	W	3-1	Larnaca	Fr	Michael [31], Okkas [42], Constantinou [52]		Trattos CYP
12-09	San Marino	W	3-0	Nicosia	ECq	Makridis [15], Aloneftis 2 [41 92+]	1 000	Kulbakov BLR
13-10	Wales	W	3-1	Nicosia	ECq	Okkas 2 [59 68], Charalampidis [79]	2 852	Bertolini SUI
17-10	Republic of Ireland	D	1-1	Dublin	ECq	Okkarides [80]	54 861	Vuorela FIN
17-11	Germany	L	0-4	Hanover	ECq		45 016	Rasmussen DEN
21-11	Czech Republic	L	0-2	Nicosia	ECq		5 866	Paniashvili GEO
2008								
6-02	Ukraine	D	1-1	Nicosia	Fr	Aloneftis [19p]	500	
19-05	Greece	L	0-2	Patras	Fr		16 216	MacDonald SCO
20-08	Switzerland	L	1-4	Geneva	Fr	Makridis [35]	14 500	Ceferin SVN
6-09	Italy	L	1-2	Larnaca	WCq	Aloneftis [28]	6 000	Vink NED
11-10	Georgia	D	1-1	Tbilisi	WCq	Konstantinou.M [67]	40 000	Matejak CZE
15-10	Republic of Ireland	L	0-1	Dublin	WCq		55 833	Tudor ROU
19-11	Belarus	W	2-1	Nicosia	Fr	Christofi [29], Avraam [48]		
2009								
10-02	Serbia	L	0-2	Nicosia	Fr			
11-02	Slovakia	W	3-2	Nicosia	Fr	Maragkos [32p], Nicolaou [74], Okkas [82]	300	
28-03	Georgia	W	2-1	Larnaca	WCq	Konstantinou.M [33], Christofi [56]	1 500	Fautrel FRA
1-04	Bulgaria	L	0-2	Sofia	WCq		16 916	Ingvarsson SWE
30-05	Canada	L	0-1	Larnaca	Fr			
6-06	Montenegro	D	2-2	Larnaca	WCq	Konstantinou.M [14], Michail [45p]	3 000	Velasco ESP
12-08	Albania	L	1-6	Tirana	Fr	Charalampidis		Yildirim TUR
5-09	Republic of Ireland	L	1-2	Nicosia	WCq	Ilia [30]	5 191	Einwaller AUT
9-09	Montenegro	D	1-1	Podgorica	WCq	Okkas [63]	4 000	Zimmermann SUI
10-10	Bulgaria	W	4-1	Larnaca	WCq	Charalampidis 2 [11 20], Konstantinou.M [58], Aloneftis [78]	3 700	Allaerts BEL
14-10	Italy	L	2-3	Parma	WCq	Makridis [12], Michail [48]	15 009	Yefet ISR
2010								
3-03	Iceland	D	0-0	Larnaca	Fr			Yordanov.N BUL
11-08	Andorra	W	1-0	Larnaca	Fr	Konstantinou [4]	1 700	Spathas GRE
3-09	Portugal	D	4-4	Guimaraes	ECq	Aloneftis [3], Konstantinou [11], Okkas [57], Avraam [89]	9 100	Clattenburg ENG
8-10	Norway	L	1-2	Larnaca	ECq	Okkas [58]	7 648	Gumienny BEL
12-10	Denmark	L	0-2	Copenhagen	ECq		15 544	Muniz ESP
16-11	Jordan	D	0-0	Amman	Fr		3 500	Ebrahim BHR

Fr = Friendly match • EC = UEFA EURO 2008/2012 • WC = FIFA World Cup • q = qualifier

CYPRUS NATIONAL TEAM HISTORICAL RECORDS

Caps
99 - Yiannis Okkas 1997- • **82** - Pambos Pittas 1987-99 • **78** - Nicos Panayiotou 1994-2006 • **75** - Michalis Konstantinou 1998- • **70** - Giorgos Theodotou 1996-2008 • **68** - Yiannis Yiangoudakis 1998-2008 • **64** - Chrysis Michail 2000- • **63** - Yiasemakis Yiasoumi 1998-2009 • **60** - Marios Charalambous 1991-2002 • **58** - Marinos Satsias 2000- • **54** - Kostas Charalambides 2003-

Goals
30 - Michalis Konstantinou 1998- • **25** - Yiannis Okkas 1997- • **11** - Kostas Charalambides 2003- • **10** - Marios Agathokleous 1994-2003 • **8** - Efstathios Aloneftis 2005- ; Andros Sotiriou 1991-99, Phivos Vrahimis 1977-82; Milenko Spoljaric 1997-2001 & Sinisa Gogic 1994-99

Past Coaches
Gyula Zsengeller HUN 1958-59 • Argyrios Gavalas GRE 1960-67 • Pambos Avraamidis 1968-69 • Ray Wood ENG 1969-71 • Sima Milovanov YUG 1972 • Pambos Avraamidis 1972-76 • Panikos Krystallis 1976-77 • Kostas Talianos GRE 1977-82 • Vassil Spasov BUL 1982-84 • Panikos Iakovou 1984-91 • Andreas Michaelides 1991-97 • Panikos Georgiou 1997-99 • Stavros Papadopoulos 1999-2001 • Momcilo Vukotic SRB 2001-04 • Angelos Anastasiadis GRE 2004-

CYPRUS 2009–10

MARFIN LAIKI A KATEGORIA (1)

	Pl	W	D	L	F	A	Pts	Omonia	APOEL	Anorthosis	Apollon	AEL	ENP	Ethnikos	APOP	Ermis	AEP	Doxa	Aris	Nea	APEP
Omonia Nicosia †	32	22	8	2	60	25	74		1-1	1-0	1-1	1-1	2-1	1-1	4-0	0-0	2-0	1-0	1-0	3-2	2-1	1-1	4-3
APOEL Nicosia ‡	32	19	8	5	53	24	65	1-2		0-1	2-0	1-0	1-1	3-2	1-0	3-1	2-0	3-1	1-0	0-0	3-0	5-0	0-0	3-1
Anorthosis Famagusta ‡	32	19	7	6	51	27	64	1-3	2-4		0-0	1-1	1-1	2-0	1-0	2-0	2-1	2-1	1-0	3-0	3-0	3-1	4-1	3-0
Apollon Limassol ‡	32	17	9	6	47	23	60	0-1	0-0	0-2		0-1	2-2	0-0	0-2	1-1	3-1	1-0	2-1	0-0	2-0	3-0	4-1	2-0
AEL Limassol	32	18	4	10	50	33	58	1-0	1-2	0-1	0-0		2-1	2-2	2-1	0-2	0-4	2-2	2-1	3-1	1-0	1-0	3-1	2-0
ENP Paralimni	32	10	10	12	40	42	40	0-4	1-1	1-2	0-3	1-2		1-3	1-2	1-3	1-4	0-2	0-0	5-1	1-1	1-0	1-1	2-0
Ethnikos Achnas	32	10	8	14	34	42	38	2-1	0-0	1-3	0-1	1-4	4-3		1-0	0-1	3-1	4-2	0-0	1-2	1-0	0-0	2-1	1-0
APOP/Kinyras	32	11	4	17	50	65	37	1-3	4-3	2-0	1-3	1-0	2-5	1-2		1-2	3-0	3-2		1-1	0-0	2-2	1-1	2-1	1-2
Ermis Aradippou	32	12	8	12	43	38	44	1-2	1-2	0-0	1-2	1-0	1-0	1-0	2-3		0-0	1-0	2-1	1-0	5-3	4-0	1-1	2-1
AEP Paphos	32	9	9	14	39	50	36	1-3	0-1	0-2	1-2	1-0	2-0	0-0	3-2	3-1		3-0		1-2	4-1	1-3	2-4	0-0	1-0
Doxa Katokopia	32	9	8	15	36	46	35	2-4	1-2	2-3	0-1	1-0	2-2	1-0	1-2	1-1	1-4	2-2	4-0		0-0	3-0	0-0	1-0
Aris Limassol	32	4	9	19	30	63	21	0-1	0-2	0-3	1-1	0-0	1-1	0-0	2-4	2-2	0-2	2-2	1-2	1-2	1-4		3-1	2-0
Nea Salamina	26	2	8	16	19	45	14	0-2	0-3	1-2	0-1	1-3	0-0	1-1	1-2	0-3	0-0	0-1	3-2			1-2
APEP §6	26	4	4	18	25	54	10	1-1	1-4	0-2	0-4	0-1	1-2	0-3	1-3	3-3	3-3	0-0	2-1	2-1		

29/08/2009 – 8/05/2010 • † Qualified for the UEFA Champions League • ‡ Qualified for the Europa League • § = points deducted
Top scorers: **22** - Jose Semedo CPV, APOP & Joeano BRA, Ermis • **13** - Gaston Sangoy ARG, Apollon • Matches in bold awarded

CYPRUS 2009–10 B KATEGORIA (2)

	Pl	W	D	L	F	A	Pts
Alki Larnaca	32	19	7	6	52	33	64
AEK Larnaca	32	17	6	9	49	27	57
Olympiakos Nicosia	32	14	9	9	55	43	51
Othellos Athienou	32	12	10	10	40	38	46
Atromitas	26	10	7	9	35	31	37
Omonia Aradippou	26	9	9	8	26	28	36
PAEEK	26	9	9	8	24	27	36
Digenis Morfu	26	9	9	8	35	33	36
ASIL	26	8	11	7	29	29	35
Onisilos Sotiras	26	9	6	11	30	31	33
Akritas Chloraka	26	7	11	8	25	26	32
Frenaros FC 2000	26	7	7	12	26	32	28
Ayia Napa	26	5	5	16	19	41	20
MEAP Nisou	26	2	8	16	19	45	14

19/09/2009 – 8/05/2010

MEDALS TABLE

		Overall			League			Cup	
		G	S	B	G	S	B	G	S
1	APOEL Nicosia	39	29	15	20	19	15	19	10
2	Omonia Nicosia	32	20	8	20	14	8	12	6
3	Anorthosis Famagusta	23	16	7	13	10	7	10	6
4	AEL Limassol	12	9	6	6	1	6	6	8
5	Apollon Limassol	9	10	4	3	4	4	6	6
6	EPA Larnaca	7	9	4	2	6	4	5	3
7	Olympiakos Nicosia	4	7	2	3	4	2	1	3
8	Trust AC	4	3		1	2		3	1
9	Pezoporikos Larnaca	3	15	14	2	8	14	1	7
10	Chetin Kaya	3	3	3	1	1	3	2	2
11	NEA Salamina	1	2	4			4	1	2
12	AEK Larnaca	1	2					1	2
13	APOP/Kinyras	1						1	
14	Union Paralimni (ENP)		5	2		1	2		4
15	Alki Larnaca	5	1				1		5
16	Digenis Morphou	2				1			1
17	Aris Limassol	1	1				1		1
18	Ethnikos Achnas	1							1

KYPELLO KYPROY 2009–10

Round of 16		Quarter-finals		Semi-finals		Final	
Apollon Limassol	0 2						
Nea Salamina *	1 0	Apollon Limassol *	3 3				
Ayia Napa	0 2	Anorthosis Famagusta	1 2				
Anorthosis Famagusta *	6 1			Apollon Limassol	1 1		
APEP *	1 1			AEL Limassol *	0 0		
Doxa Katokopia	1 0	APEP *	0 0				
Omonia Nicosia	1 0	AEL Limassol	0 2				
AEL Limassol *	0 2					Apollon Limassol ‡	2
Aris Limassol *	0 1					APOEL Nicosia	1
AEZ Zakakiou	0 0	Aris Limassol *	1 1				
AEP Paphos	1 4	APOP/Kinyras	1 0				
APOP/Kinyras *	4 2			Aris Limassol	0 0	CUP FINAL	
Ermis Aradippou *	4 0			APOEL Nicosia *	0 2	GSZ, Larnaca, 15-05-2010,	
ENP Paralimni	0 2	Ermis Aradippou	0 0			Att: 12 000, Ref: Rosetti ITA	
Ethnikos Achnas	2 0	APOEL Nicosia *	5 1			Scorers - Mustapha Bangura [1],	
APOEL Nicosia *	0 4	* Home team in the first leg • ‡ Qualified for the Europa League				Giorgos Merkis [71] for Apollon; Marcin Zewlakow [23] for APOEL	

CZE – CZECH REPUBLIC

FIFA/COCA-COLA WORLD RANKING

1993	1994	1995	1996	1997	1998	1999	2000	2001	2002	2003	2004	2005	2006	2007	2008	2009	2010
-	34	14	5	3	8	2	5	14	15	6	4	2	10	6	11	25	30

2010												Hi/Lo
Jan	Feb	Mar	Mar	Apr	May	Jul	Aug	Sep	Oct	Nov	Dec	2
25	25	25	30	29	33	31	31	37	31	31	30	67

As the most likely challengers to Spain in their Euro 2012 qualifying group, the Czech Republic got off to the worst possible start with a 1-0 home defeat to Lithuania in coach Michal Bilek's first competitive game in charge. Having qualified for all four European Championship finals since the split with Slovakia, Bilek has a lot to live up to but as the fifth coach in just two years, these are proving to be troubled times for a national team in need of fresh inspiration. At home, Sparta Praha got back into their winning ways in the league but although they went through the season undefeated, the fact that they drew almost half of their games meant that they didn't secure the title until the last match of the season against Teplice - leaders at the winter break. Level on points with Banik but with a better goal difference, Sparta needed to win to claim the title and thanks to a headed goal just after half-time from their captain Tomas Repka, they did just that. The cup saw Viktoria Plzen win their first silverware - a 2-1 victory condemning their opponents FK Jablonec to a second runners-up spot in the season. In Europe, Czech clubs have seen their UEFA Champions League representation fall to just one club and in the 2010-11 tournament Sparta were beaten in the preliminaries by Slovakia's Zilina to miss out on the group stage.

FIFA WORLD CUP RECORD
1930-1994 DNE (played as Czechoslovakia) **1998-2002** DNQ **2006** 20 r1 **2010** DNQ

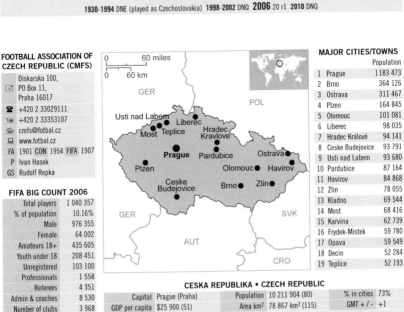

FOOTBALL ASSOCIATION OF CZECH REPUBLIC (CMFS)

Diskarska 100,
PO Box 11,
Praha 16017
☎ +420 2 33029111
📠 +420 2 33353107
📧 cmfs@fotbal.cz
🖥 www.fotbal.cz
FA 1901 CON 1954 FIFA 1907
P Ivan Hasek
GS Rudolf Repka

FIFA BIG COUNT 2006

Total players	1 040 357
% of population	10.16%
Male	976 355
Female	64 002
Amateurs 18+	435 605
Youth under 18	208 451
Unregistered	103 100
Professionals	1 558
Referees	4 351
Admin & coaches	8 530
Number of clubs	3 968
Number of teams	15 463

MAJOR CITIES/TOWNS

		Population
1	Prague	1 183 473
2	Brno	364 126
3	Ostrava	311 467
4	Plzen	164 845
5	Olomouc	101 081
6	Liberec	98 035
7	Hradec Králové	94 141
8	Ceske Budejovice	93 791
9	Usti nad Labem	93 680
10	Pardubice	87 164
11	Havirov	84 868
12	Zlin	78 055
13	Kladno	69 544
14	Most	68 416
15	Karvina	62 739
16	Frydek-Mistek	59 780
17	Opava	59 549
18	Decin	52 284
19	Teplice	52 193

CESKA REPUBLIKA • CZECH REPUBLIC

Capital	Prague (Praha)	Population	10 211 904 (80)	% in cities	73%
GDP per capita	$25 900 (51)	Area km²	78 867 km² (115)	GMT +/-	+1
Neighbours (km)	Austria 362, Germany 815, Poland 615, Slovakia 197				

RECENT INTERNATIONAL MATCHES PLAYED BY THE CZECH REPUBLIC

2007	Opponents	Score		Venue	Comp	Scorers	Att	Referee
7-02	Belgium	W	2-0	Brussels	Fr	Koller 6, Kulic 74	12 000	Granat POL
24-03	Germany	L	1-2	Prague	ECq	Baros 77	17 821	Rosetti ITA
28-03	Cyprus	W	1-0	Liberec	ECq	Kovác 22	9 310	Bebek CRO
2-06	Wales	D	0-0	Cardiff	ECq		30 174	Allaerts BEL
22-08	Austria	D	1-1	Vienna	Fr	Koller 33	24 500	Gonzalez ESP
8-09	San Marino	W	3-0	Serravalle	ECq	Rosicky 33, Jankulovski 75, Koller 93+	3 412	Filipovic SRB
12-09	Republic of Ireland	W	1-0	Prague	ECq	Jankulovski 15	16 648	Vassaras GRE
17-10	Germany	W	3-0	Munich	ECq	Sionko 2, Matejovski 23, Plasil 63	66 445	Webb ENG
17-11	Slovakia	W	3-1	Prague	ECq	Grygera 13, Kulic 76, Rosicky 83	15 651	Asumaa FIN
21-11	Cyprus	W	2-0	Nicosia	ECq	Pudil 11, Koller 74	5 866	Paniashvili GEO
2008								
6-02	Poland	L	0-2	Larnaca	Fr		1 500	Tryfonos CYP
26-03	Denmark	D	1-1	Herning	Fr	Koller 42	11 900	Mikulski POL
27-05	Lithuania	W	2-0	Prague	Fr	Koller 2 39 63	14 220	Hrinak SVK
30-05	Scotland	W	3-1	Prague	Fr	Sionko 2 60 90, Michal Kadlec 84	11 314	Braamhaar NED
7-06	Switzerland	W	1-0	Basel	ECr1	Sverkos 71	39 730	Rosetti ITA
11-06	Portugal	L	1-3	Geneva	ECr1	Sionko 17	29 016	Vassaras GRE
15-06	Turkey	L	2-3	Geneva	ECr1	Koller 34, Plasil 62	29 016	Fröjdfeldt SWE
20-08	England	D	2-2	London	Fr	Baros 22, Jankulovski 48	69 738	Hauge NOR
10-09	Northern Ireland	D	0-0	Belfast	WCq		12 882	Bebek CRO
11-10	Poland	L	1-2	Chorzow	WCq	Fenin 87	38 293	Stark GER
15-10	Slovenia	W	1-0	Teplice	WCq	Sionko 62	15 220	Atkinson ENG
19-11	San Marino	W	3-0	Serravalle	WCq	Kovac 47, Pospech 53, Necid 66	1 318	Kaasik EST
2009								
11-02	Morocco	D	0-0	Casablanca	Fr		38 000	Alakim TUN
28-03	Slovenia	D	0-0	Maribor	WCq		12 500	Proença POR
1-04	Slovakia	L	1-2	Prague	WCq	Jankulovski 30	14 956	Undiano ESP
5-06	Malta	W	1-0	Jablonec	Fr	Necid 77	6 019	Fautrel Fra
12-08	Belgium	W	3-1	Teplice	Fr	Hubnik 27, Baros 42p, Rozehnal 78	13 890	Sippel GER
5-09	Slovakia	D	2-2	Bratislava	WCq	Pudil 68, Baros 83	23 800	Ovrebo NOR
9-09	San Marino	W	7-0	Uherske Hradiste	WCq	Baros 4 28 44 45 66, Sverkos 2 47 94+, Necid 86	8 121	Amirkhanyan ARM
10-10	Poland	W	2-0	Prague	WCq	Necid 51, Plasil 72	14 010	Larsen DEN
14-10	Northern Ireland	D	0-0	Prague	WCq		8 002	Duhamel FRA
15-11	UAE	D	0-0	Al Ain	Fr	L 2-3p	5 000	Dalkam JOR
18-11	Azerbaijan	L	0-2	Al Ain	Fr			Al Marzouqi UAE
2010								
3-03	Scotland	L	0-1	Glasgow	Fr		26 530	Fautrel FRA
22-05	Turkey	L	1-2	Harrison	Fr	Cerny 81	16 371	Geiger USA
25-05	USA	W	4-2	East Hartford	Fr	Sivok 44, Polak 58, Fenin 77, Necid 90	36 218	Morales MEX
11-08	Latvia	W	4-1	Liberec	Fr	Bednar 49, Fenin 54, Pospech 74, Necid 77	7 456	Dankovsky UKR
7-09	Lithuania	L	0-1	Olomouc	ECq		12 038	Yefet ISR
8-10	Scotland	W	1-0	Prague	ECq	Hubnik 69	14 922	Bebek CRO
12-10	Liechtenstein	W	2-0	Vaduz	ECq	Necid 12, Vaclav Kadlec 29	2 555	Sukhina RUS
17-11	Denmark	D	0-0	Aarhus	Fr		9 184	Webb ENG

Fr = Friendly match • EC = UEFA EURO 2008/2012 • WC = FIFA World Cup • q = qualifier • r1 = first round group

CZECH REPUBLIC NATIONAL TEAM HISTORICAL RECORDS

Caps 118 - Karel Poborsky 1994-2006 • 91 - Jan Koller 1999-2009 & Pavel Nedved 1994-2006 • 81 - Vladimir Smicer 1993-2005 • 78 - Milan Baros 2001- & Tomas Ujfalusi 2001-09 • 77 - Petr Cech 2002- & Marek Jankulovski 2000-09 • 74 - Tomas Rosicky 2000- & Vratislav Lokvenc 1995-2006 • 69 - Tomas Galasek 1995-2008 • 64 (84) - Jiri Nemec 1994-2001 • 63 (87) - Pavel Kuka 1994-2001
Figures in brackets include overall total including matches played for Czechoslovakia

Goals 55 - Jan Koller 1999-2009 • 38 - Milan Baros 2001- • 27 - Vladimir Smicer 1993-2005 • 22 (29) - Pavel Kuka 1994-2001 • 19 - Tomas Rosicky 2000- • 18 - Patrick Berger 1994-2001 & Pavel Nedved 1994-2006 • 14 - Vratislav Lokvenc 1995-2006

Past Coaches Vaclav Jezek 1993 • Dusan Uhrin 1994-97 • Jozef Chovanec 1998-2001 • Karel Bruckner 2001-08 • Petr Rada 2008-09 • Frantisek Straka 2009 • Ivan Hasek 2009 • Michal Bilek 2009-

CZECH REPUBLIC 2009–10

I. GAMBRINUS LIGA

	Pl	W	D	L	F	A	Pts	Sparta	Jablonec	Baník	Teplice	Viktoria	Sigma	Slavia	Mladá	Slovan	Pribram	Brno	Bohemians	Budejovice	Slovácko	Kladno	Bohemians
Sparta Praha †	30	16	14	0	42	14	**62**		2-0	1-1	1-0	0-0	4-0	1-0	1-0	2-0	1-1	3-0	1-0	1-1	4-0	2-0	0-0
FK Jablonec ‡	30	18	7	5	42	24	**61**	0-0		2-1	0-0	0-1	3-1	1-1	1-0	2-1	0-0	1-0	1-0	2-0	3-2	1-0	3-0
Baník Ostrava ‡	30	17	9	4	47	25	**60**	1-1	4-1		2-2	1-0	2-0	3-1	2-2	1-0	2-1	1-1	1-0	0-1	3-2	2-0	3-1
FK Teplice	30	15	10	5	44	25	**55**	0-0	1-0	0-1		2-1	1-1	1-1	2-2	2-0	1-0	0-1	2-1	3-0	2-1	5-0	1-0
Viktoria Plzen ‡	30	12	12	6	42	33	**48**	2-2	1-1	0-0	2-2		1-0	4-2	2-1	2-3	3-1	1-1	3-2	0-0	2-2	1-0	3-0
Sigma Olomouc	30	14	5	11	49	36	**47**	1-1	0-1	0-0	6-2	1-0		3-1	1-2	2-0	3-1	5-0	3-0	2-0	1-0	1-2	1-1
Slavia Praha	30	11	8	11	37	35	**41**	0-1	0-3	3-1	0-0	0-0	1-2		1-1	0-2	3-0	3-1	3-1	3-2	3-0	0-0	3-0
Mladá Boleslav	30	11	6	13	47	41	**39**	1-2	1-2	3-1	0-1	4-0	2-2	0-1		4-1	2-0	0-0	4-2	0-1	3-2	0-1	0-1
Slovan Liberec	30	10	7	13	34	39	**37**	2-2	4-2	0-1	1-0	0-2	0-4	1-1	3-0		1-0	0-1	2-3	3-0	2-0	1-1	1-1
1.FK Pribram	30	10	6	14	35	41	**36**	1-1	1-2	1-1	0-3	1-0	2-1	1-0	2-2	1-1		3-1	3-2	3-1	2-0	3-2	2-0
1.FC Brno	30	9	8	13	31	40	**35**	1-1	0-1	1-1	2-3	2-2	1-2	2-0	2-3	1-0	2-1		0-0	0-3	1-0	3-0	1-2
Bohemians 1905 Praha	30	8	10	12	21	29	**34**	2-3	0-4	0-3	1-3	2-2	0-2	0-1	2-4	2-1	1-0	2-1		0-2	1-1	1-4	**3-0**
Ceské Budejovice	30	7	10	13	24	35	**31**	0-0	1-1	1-2	0-0	0-0	2-1	0-1	1-3	1-1	2-1	1-3	3-0		0-0	0-0	0-0
1.FC Slovácko	30	8	6	16	28	42	**30**	0-1	1-1	0-2	0-2	2-3	2-0	3-1	1-0	0-0	2-1	0-2	2-0	1-0		2-0	1-1
SK Kladno	30	7	4	19	24	50	**25**	0-1	1-2	0-3	0-2	1-3	2-3	0-2	1-3	1-2	0-2	1-0	3-2	2-1	1-0		1-2
Bohemians Praha §20	30	4	4	22	27	65	**-4**	0-2	0-1	0-1	1-1	0-1	2-0	1-1	2-0	0-1	1-0	0-0	3-0	2-0	0-1	0-0	

24/07/2009 - 15/05/2010 • † Qualified for the UEFA Champions League • ‡ Qualified for the Europa League • § = points deducted
Top scorers: **12** - Michal Ordos, Sigma • **11** - David Lafata, Jablonec & Marek Kulic, Mlada • **9** - Pavel Sultes, Sigma & Bony Wilfred CIV, Sparta

CZECH REPUBLIC 2009–10
DRUHA LIGA (2)

	Pl	W	D	L	F	A	Pts
Hradec Králové	30	20	8	2	47	18	**68**
Usti nad Labem	30	20	5	5	52	27	**65**
Tescoma Zlin	30	17	5	8	49	33	**56**
Vysocina Jihlava	30	15	7	8	57	37	**52**
Viktoria Zizkov	30	13	7	10	42	41	**46**
Dukla Praha	30	12	8	10	45	41	**44**
Graffin Vlasim	30	11	7	12	40	41	**40**
MFK Karviná	30	11	6	13	44	36	**39**
Trinec	30	10	8	12	34	38	**38**
Baník Sokolov	30	9	10	11	37	43	**37**
FK Most	30	8	12	10	35	38	**36**
Sparta Praha B	30	6	11	13	33	50	**29**
FC Hlucin	30	6	11	13	27	43	**29**
Zenit Cáslav	30	7	8	15	28	49	**29**
Slezsky Opava	30	6	11	13	30	37	**29**
FC Vitkovice	30	4	6	20	23	51	**18**

31/07/2009 - 5/06/2010

CZECH REPUBLIC MEDALS TABLE POST 1993

		Overall			League			Cup	
		G	S	B	G	S	B	G	S
1	Sparta Praha	16	7		11	4		5	3
2	Slavia Praha	6	9	2	3	9	2	3	
3	Slovan Liberec	3	2	1	2		1	1	2
4	Banik Ostrava	2	2	3	1		3	1	2
5	Viktoria Zizkov	2	1	2			2	2	1
6	FK Teplice	2	1	1		1	1	2	
7	FK Jablonec	1	4	2		1	2	1	3
8	FC Hradec Králové	1						1	
	Viktoria Plzen	1						1	
10	1.FK Drnovice		2	1		1			2
11	1.FC Slovácko		2						2
12	Sigma Olomouc		1	3	1	3			
	Mladá Boleslav		1	1	1	1			
	FK Marila Príbram		1						1
15	Banik Ratiskovice		1						1
	1.FC Brno			1		1			

CLUBS IN CZECHOSLOVAKIAN FOOTBALL 1925–1993

		Overall			League			Cup		Europe		
		G	S	B	G	S	B	G	S	G	S	B
1	Sparta Praha	27	21	8	19	16	7	8	5			1
2	Dukla Praha	19	9	5	11	7	3	8	2			2
4	Slavia Praha	9	11	8	9	9	7		2			1
6	Banik Ostrava	6	7	2	3	6	1	3	1			1
10	Bohemians Praha	1	2	12	1	1	11		1			1

CLUBS IN CZECH FOOTBALL 1896–1946

		Overall			League		Cup	
		G	S	B	G	S	B	G	S
1	Sparta Praha	25	15		11	3		14	12
2	Slavia Praha	25	13		10	7		15	6
3	Viktoria Zizkov	7	4	3	1	2		7	3

POHAR CMFS 2009-10

Third Round

Viktoria Plzen	4	
Dukla Praha *	1	
Breclav *	0	
SK Kladno	1	
Banik Ostrava	1	5p
Slezsky Opava *	1	3p
Varnsdorf *	0	
1.FK Pribram	1	
Slovan Liberec	1	3p
Tescoma Zlin *	1	1p
Trinec *	0	
Bohemians 1905 Praha	1	
1.SC Znojmo	1	
Trebic *	0	
Protivanov *	0	
Sigma Olomouc	5	
Slavia Praha	1	5p
Karlovy Vary *	1	4p
1.FC Brno	1	4p
MFK Karviná *	1	5p
Ceské Budejovice	1	
Viktoria Zizkov *	0	
Náchod-Destné *	0	
Sparta Praha	6	
FK Teplice	3	
FC Hlucin	1	
Bohemians Praha	1	
Hradec Králové *	2	
Sokol Zivanice *	1	
FC Vitkovice	0	
Plsek *	1	1p
FK Jablonec	1	4p

Round of 16

Viktoria Plzen	3	1
SK Kladno *	0	1
Banik Ostrava	0	0
1.FK Pribram *	2	0
Slovan Liberec	2	1
Bohemians 1905 Praha *	1	1
1.SC Znojmo	1	0
Sigma Olomouc	3	0
Slavia Praha	0	2
MFK Karviná *	1	0
Ceské Budejovice *	0	0
Sparta Praha	5	1
FK Teplice	2	2
Hradec Králové *	1	1
Sokol Zivanice *	3	1
FK Jablonec	6	5

Quarter-finals

Viktoria Plzen *	1	1
1.FK Pribram	0	1
Slovan Liberec *	0	0
Sigma Olomouc	2	1
Slavia Praha *	1	1
Sparta Praha	0	0
FK Teplice *	1	0
FK Jablonec	3	1

Semi-finals

Viktoria Plzen *	2	3
Sigma Olomouc	2	1
Slavia Praha	0	2
FK Jablonec *	1	1

Final

Viktoria Plzen ‡	2
FK Jablonec	1

* Home team in the first leg. ‡ Qualified for the Europa League

DEN – DENMARK

FIFA/COCA-COLA WORLD RANKING

1993	1994	1995	1996	1997	1998	1999	2000	2001	2002	2003	2004	2005	2006	2007	2008	2009	2010
6	14	9	6	8	19	11	22	18	12	13	14	13	21	31	37	28	28

2010												Hi/Lo
Jan	Feb	Mar	Mar	Apr	May	Jul	Aug	Sep	Oct	Nov	Dec	3
28	26	33	34	35	36	29	29	29	27	27	28	38

In 2010 FC København won their seventh championship in ten years and then confirmed their growing reputation by becoming the first Danish side to make it through the UEFA Champions League group stage and qualify for the last 16. Such has been their dominance at home that they are now the fourth most successful club in the history of Danish football, despite having only been formed in 1992 when KB - the most successful club in Danish football - and B1903 joined forces. København finished comfortably ahead of OB Odense in the league but they failed to retain the Cup which was won instead by FC Nordsjælland from the town of Farum, a short distance north of the capital - the club's first trophy since its formation in 1991. At international level, Denmark failed to set the world alight at the 2010 FIFA World Cup in South Africa although expectations of Morten Olsen's team amongst fans at home were not high. With both the Danes and Japan losing to Holland and beating Cameroon in their opening two matches, the final group game between the two was a winner-takes-all affair in which Denmark were outclassed by their Asian opponents. They never recovered from falling behind to two wonderful first half free-kicks, losing 3-1 in a match notable for Jon Dahl Tomasson equalling the Danish record of 52 international goals.

FIFA WORLD CUP RECORD

1930-1954 DNE 1958 DNQ 1962 DNE 1966-1982 DNQ **1986** 10 r2 1990-1994 DNQ **1998** 8 QF **2002** 10 r2 **2006** DNQ **2010** 24 r1

DANSK BOLDSPIL-UNION (DBU)

DBU Allé 1,
Brøndby 2605

☎ +45 43 262222
📠 +45 43 262245
✉ dbu@dbu.dk
🖳 www.dbu.dk

FA 1889 CON 1954 FIFA 1904
P Allan Hansen
GS Jim Stjerne Hansen

FIFA BIG COUNT 2006

Total players	511 333
% of population	9.38%
Male	420 258
Female	91 075
Amateurs 18+	111 757
Youth under 18	188 724
Unregistered	100 000
Professionals	852
Referees	2 992
Admin & coaches	54 000
Number of clubs	1 615
Number of teams	17 365

MAJOR CITIES/TOWNS

		Population
1	Copenhagen	1 081 788
2	Aarhus	228 723
3	Odense	159 162
4	Aalborg	100 601
5	Esbjerg	70 872
6	Randers	56 134
7	Kolding	55 147
8	Horsens	53 008
9	Vejle	49 901
10	Roskilde	48 219
11	Silkeborg	45 752
12	Herning	44 968
13	Næstved	42 091
14	Greve Strand	40 725
15	Fredericia	37 087
16	Køge	35 860
17	Viborg	35 517
18	Helsingør	35 149
19	Holstebro	32 161

KONGERIGET DANMARK • KINGDOM OF DENMARK

Capital	Copenhagen (København)	Population	5 500 510 (110)	% in cities	87%
GDP per capita	$37 200 (30)	Area km²	43 094 km² (133)	GMT +/-	+1
Neighbours (km)	Germany 68 • Coast 7314				

RECENT INTERNATIONAL MATCHES PLAYED BY DENMARK

2007	Opponents	Score		Venue	Comp	Scorers	Att	Referee
22-08	Republic of Ireland	L	0-4	Aarhus	Fr		30 000	Einwaller AUT
8-09	Sweden	D	0-0	Stockholm	ECq		33 082	De Bleeckere BEL
12-09	Liechtenstein	W	4-0	Aarhus	ECq	Nordstrand 2 [3 36], Laursen.M [12], Tomasson [18]	20 005	Clattenburg ENG
13-10	Spain	L	1-3	Aarhus	ECq	Tomasson [87]	19 849	Michel SVK
17-10	Latvia	W	3-1	Copenhagen	ECq	Tomasson [7p], Laursen.U [27], Rommedahl [90]	19 004	Cakir TUR
17-11	Northern Ireland	L	1-2	Belfast	ECq	Bendtner [51]	12 997	Vink NED
21-11	Iceland	W	3-0	Copenhagen	ECq	Bendtner [34], Tomasson [44], Kahlenberg [59]	15 393	Benquerenca POR
2008								
6-02	Slovenia	W	2-1	Nova Gorica	Fr	Tomasson [30p], Bendtner [62]	1 700	Kinhofer GER
26-03	Czech Republic	D	1-1	Herning	Fr	Bendtner [25]	11 900	Mikulski POL
29-05	Netherlands	D	1-1	Eindhoven	Fr	Poulsen [56]	35 000	Chapron FRA
1-06	Poland	D	1-1	Chorzow	Fr	Vingaard [29]	40 000	Kalt FRA
20-08	Spain	L	0-3	Copenhagen	Fr		26 155	Hansson SWE
6-09	Hungary	D	0-0	Budapest	WCq		18 984	Hamer LUX
10-09	Portugal	W	3-2	Lisbon	WCq	Bendtner [83], Christian Poulsen [88], Jensen [92+]	33 000	Webb ENG
11-10	Malta	W	3-0	Copenhagen	WCq	Larsen 2 [10 46], Daniel Agger [29p]	33 124	Paniashvili GEO
19-11	Wales	L	0-1	Brøndby	Fr		10 271	Weiner GER
2009								
11-02	Greece	D	1-1	Piraeus	Fr	Borring [49]		Undiano ESP
28-03	Malta	W	3-0	Ta'Qali	WCq	Larsen 2 [12 23], Nordstrand [89]	6 235	Mikulski POL
1-04	Albania	W	3-0	Copenhagen	WCq	Andreason [31], Larsen [37], Christian Poulsen [80]	24 320	Skomina SVN
6-06	Sweden	W	1-0	Stockholm	WCq	Kahlenberg [22]	33 619	Riley ENG
12-08	Chile	L	1-2	Brøndby	Fr	Schone [63]	8 700	Jakobsen ISL
5-09	Portugal	D	1-1	Copenhagen	WCq	Bendtner [43]	37 998	Busacca SUI
9-09	Albania	D	1-1	Tirana	WCq	Bendtner [40]	8 000	Cakir TUR
10-10	Sweden	W	1-0	Copenhagen	WCq	Jakob Poulsen [78]	37 800	Mejuto ESP
14-10	Hungary	L	0-1	Copenhagen	WCq		36 956	Meyer GER
14-11	Korea Republic	D	0-0	Esbjerg	Fr		15 789	Hansson SWE
18-11	USA	W	3-1	Aarhus	Fr	Absalonsen [47], Rieks [52], Bernburg [55]	15 172	Thomson SCO
2010								
3-03	Austria	L	1-2	Vienna	Fr	Bendtner [17]	13 500	Kralovec CZE
27-05	Senegal	W	2-0	Aalborg	Fr	Christian Poulsen [26], Enevoldsen [90]	14 112	Nijhuis NED
1-06	Australia	L	0-1	Roodepoort	Fr		6 000	Bennett RSA
5-06	South Africa	L	0-1	Atteridgeville	Fr		28 000	Mbaga TAN
14-06	Netherlands	L	0-2	Johannesburg	WCr1		83 465	Lannoy FRA
19-06	Cameroon	W	2-1	Pretoria	WCr1	Bendtner [33], Rommedahl [61]	38 074	Larrionda URU
24-06	Japan	L	1-3	Rustenburg	WCr1	Tomasson [81p]	27 967	Damon RSA
11-08	Germany	D	2-2	Copenhagen	Fr	Rommedahl [74], Junker [87]	19 071	Kelly IRL
7-09	Iceland	W	1-0	Copenhagen	ECq	Kahlenberg [91+]	18 908	McDonald SCO
8-10	Portugal	L	1-3	Porto	ECq	OG [79]	27 117	Braamhaar NED
12-10	Cyprus	W	2-0	Copenhagen	ECq	Morten Rasmussen [48], Lorentzen [81]	15 544	Muniz ESP
17-11	Czech Republic	D	0-0	Aarhus	Fr		9 184	Webb ENG

Fr = Friendly match • EC = UEFA EURO 2008/2012 • WC = FIFA World Cup • q = qualifier • r1 = first round group • qf = quarter-final

DENMARK NATIONAL TEAM HISTORICAL RECORDS

Caps

129 - Peter Schmeichel 1987-2001 • 112 - Jon Dahl Tomasson 1997-2010 • 108 - Thomas Helveg 1994-2008 • 104 - Michael Laudrup 1982-98 & Dennis Rommedahl 2000- • 102 - Morten Olsen 1970-89 • 100 - Martin Jorgensen 1998-2010 • 91 - Thomas Sorensen 1999- • 87 - John Sivebæk 1982-92 • 86 - Jan Heintze 198-2002 • 84 - Lars Olsen 1986-96 • 82 - Brian Laudrup 1987-98 • 80 - Jesper Gronkjær 1999- & Christian Poulsen 2001- • 77 - Kim Vilfort 1983-96 • 75 - Per Rontved 1970-82

Goals

52 - Poul Nielsen 1910-25 & Jon Dahl Tomasson 1997-2010 • 44 - Pauli Jorgensen 1925-39 • 42 - Ole Madsen 1958-69 • 38 - Preben Elkjær-Larsen 1977-88 • 37 - Michael Laudrup 1982-98 • 29 - Henning Enoksen 1958-66 • 22 - Michael Rohde 1915-31 & Ebbe Sand 1998-2004 • 21 - Brian Laudrup 1987-98, Flemming Povlsen 1987-94 & Allan Simonsen

Past Coaches

Charles Willims ENG 1908-10 • Axel Anderson Byrval 1913-5 & 1917-18 • Arne Sorensen 1956-61 • Poul Petersen 1962-66 • Erik Hansen 1967-69 • John Hansen 1969 • Rudi Strittich AUT 1970-75 • Kurt Nielsen 1976-79 • Sepp Piontek GER 1979-90 • Richard Moller Nielsen 1990-96 • Bo Johansson 1996-2000 • Morten Olsen 2000-

DENMARK 2009-10
SAS LIGAEN

	Pl	W	D	L	F	A	Pts	København	OB	Brøndby	Esbjerg	AaB	Midtjylland	Nordsjælland	Silkeborg	SønderjyskE	Randers	AGF	Herfølge
FC København †	33	21	5	7	61	22	68		2-0	1-1 2-0	2-1 3-2	2-0	2-0	0-2	1-1 1-0	3-1	3-0 2-0	0-1 5-0	7-1 4-0
OB Odense ‡	33	17	8	8	46	34	59	1-1 0-2		0-1	0-0	2-1 1-1	1-0 1-2	2-0 2-1	1-0	3-1 1-1	1-0 1-3	2-0	1-0
Brøndby IF ‡	33	15	7	11	57	50	52				0-2	2-2 1-3	2-4	0-2 2-0	3-1 1-1	6-3 0-1	2-2	1-1	1-1 1-0 1-0 6-1 1-3
Esbjerg FB ‡	33	13	11	9	48	43	50	0-0	1-2 1-2 1-1			2-0 1-1	2-1	3-3	4-0	2-0	0-0	3-2 0-4 3-2 2-1	
AaB Aalborg	33	13	9	11	36	30	48	1-2 1-0	1-0	1-2	0-0		1-0 3-2 1-0 2-1 0-1 1-0 1-0 1-0 1-1	1-1	0-0	0-0			
FC Midtjylland	33	14	5	14	45	48	47	1-4 3-2	2-2	2-4	0-0 3-0	2-0		0-2 1-0	3-0	0-2 0-0 4-1 2-1	1-0	2-1 2-1	
FC Nordsjælland ‡	33	12	7	14	40	41	43	2-0 0-3	0-2	0-1	0-4 1-0	1-1	3-0		3-0 0-1	3-1	2-2 1-1 0-2 0-1	1-1	
Silkeborg IF	33	12	7	14	47	51	43	2-0	3-1 0-1 4-1 3-0 2-3 2-2	1-1	4-0 0-2	1-4		1-1 1-2	1-3	1-4	3-0		
SønderjyskE	33	11	8	14	32	37	41	0-1 0-2	2-0	2-4 1-3 1-1 1-0	2-0	0-2	1-0 0-1 4-0	1-0 0-1	1-0	0-0			
Randers FC ‡(Fair play)	33	10	10	13	37	43	40	1-0	1-1	1-3 1-3 0-1 4-0 0-3 3-1	2-0	0-0	1-2 0-2	0-0		2-3 2-1 1-1 2-1			
AGF Aarhus	33	10	8	15	36	47	38	0-0	2-2 0-3	1-0	1-1 1-0 2-4 1-2 2-2 0-2	2-2 1-1 2-1 1-2	0-0		2-1 0-3				
Herfølge BK	33	4	7	22	30	69	19	0-2	1-3 1-2	1-2	1-2 0-5 0-3 1-0 1-1 1-2 1-1 1-4 1-0 1-2	1-2	1-1						

18/07/2009 - 16/05/2010 • † Qualified for the UEFA Champions League • ‡ Qualified for the Europa League
Top scorers: **18** - Peter Utaka NGR • **15** - Tim Janssen NED, Esbjerg • **14** - Dame N'Doye SEN, København • **14** - Rajko Lekic, Silkeborg • **13** - Morten Rasmussen, Brøndby • **11** - Christian Holst FRO, Silkeborg & Cesat Santin BRA, København

DENMARK 2009-10
VIASAT SPORT DIVISION (2)

	Pl	W	D	L	F	A	Pts
AC Horsens	30	21	3	6	67	27	**66**
Lyngby BK	30	19	5	6	59	39	**62**
FC Fredericia	30	18	5	7	56	22	**59**
Akademisk Boldclub	30	15	9	6	47	30	**54**
FC Vestsjælland	30	14	8	8	56	46	**50**
Næstved BK	30	13	5	12	44	34	**44**
Viborg FF	30	10	14	6	30	26	**44**
FC Fyn	30	12	6	12	42	51	**42**
Skive IK	30	13	2	15	44	52	**41**
Vejle BK	30	7	12	11	33	34	**33**
FC Roskilde	30	9	6	15	37	51	**33**
Hvidovre IF	30	7	11	12	37	43	**32**
Kolding FC	30	8	7	15	41	59	**31**
Thisted FC	30	8	6	16	33	57	**30**
Frem København	30	7	7	16	38	59	**28**
Braband IF	30	1	10	19	18	52	**13**

8/08/2009 - 20/06/2010 • § = points deducted

MEDALS TABLE

		Overall			League			Cup			Europe			City
		G	S	B	G	S	B	G	S	B	G	S	B	
1	KB København	16	19	8	15	15	8	1	4					Copenhagen
2	Brøndby IF	16	11	5	10	9	4	6	2			1		Copenhagen
3	AGF Aarhus	14	8	11	5	5	11	9	3					Aarhus
4	FC København	12	6	2	8	3	2	4	3					Copenhagen
5	B 93 København	11	5	9	10	5	9	1						Copenhagen
6	Vejle BK	11	4	2	5	3	2	6	1					Vejle
7	Akademisk København	10	14	11	9	11	11	1	3					Copenhagen
8	B 1903 København	9	10	8	7	8	8	2	2					Copenhagen
9	Frem København	8	15	9	6	12	9	2	3					Copenhagen
10	OB Odense	8	6	5	3	5	5	5	1					Odense
11	Esbjerg FB	7	9	2	5	3	2	2	6					Esbjerg
12	AaB Aalborg	5	8	3	3			3	2	8				Aalborg
13	Lyngby BK	5	5	3	2	3	3	3	2					Lyngby
14	B 1909 Odense	4	1	1	2			1			2	1		Odense
	Hvidovre IF	4	1	1	3	1	1	1						Copenhagen
16	Randers FC	4	1					1			4			Randers
17	Køge BK	2	3		2	1					2			Køge
18	Silkeborg IF	2	1	2	1	1	2	1						Silkeborg

DBU LANDSPOKAL 2009-10

Third Round		Round of 16		Quarter-finals		Semi-finals		Final	
FC Nordsjælland	4								
Akademisk Boldclub *	1	**FC Nordsjælland**	5						
Tarnby FF	4	AIK 65 Strøby *	1	**FC Nordsjælland**	3				
AIK 65 Strøby *	5			Silkeborg IF *	1				
Viborg FF	4								
Rishøj BK *	0	Viborg FF *	1						
Marstal/Rise *	1	**Silkeborg IF**	3			**FC Nordsjælland** *	2 2		
Silkeborg IF	3					Vejle BK	0 0		
SønderjyskE	4								
Hellerup IK *	2	**SønderjyskE** *	5						
Elite 3000 Helsingør *	1	FC København	0	SønderjyskE	1				
FC København	2			**Vejle BK** *	2				
Brøndby IF	2								
Blokhus FC *	0	Brøndby IF	0						
Frederiksberg BK *	0	**Vejle BK** *	1						
Vejle BK	4								
OB Odense	5								
FC Fredericia *	3	**OB Odense**	2						
Vejen SF *	0	Randers FC *	1	**OB Odense**	3				
Randers FC	9			Køge BK *	1				
Braband IF	4								
Aarhus Fremad *	3	Braband IF *	0						
Tved BK *	0	**Køge BK**	2			**OB Odense**	0 2		
Køge BK	2					**FC Midtjylland** *	2 2		
Hobro IK	2								
Allerød FK *	0	**Hobro IK** *	2						
Thisted FC *	0	AaB Aalborg	1	Hobro IK *	1				
AaB Aalborg	3			**FC Midtjylland**	2				
Esbjerg FB	2								
Lyngby BK *	1	Esbjerg FB *	0						
Brønshøj BK *	1	**FC Midtjylland**	5						
FC Midtjylland	3								

Final

FC Nordsjælland ‡	2
FC Midtjylland	0

CUP FINAL

Parken, Copenhagen

13-05-2010. Att: 18 856. Ref: Vollquartz

Scorers - Stokholm 97, Fetai 106

Nordsjælland - Jesper Hansen - Pierre Bengtsson, Michael Parkhurst•, Benjamin Kibebe, Henrik Kildentoft - Andreas Bjelland, Nikolai Stokholm, Matti Nielsen (Sibusiso Zuma 60), Tobias Mikkelsen (Andreas Laudrup 66) - Bajram Fetai, Nicki Bille Nielsen (Andreas Granskov-Hansen 99). Tr: Morten Wieghorst

Midtjylland - Jonas Lossl - Kolja Afriyie, Leon Jessen, Winston Reid•, Martin Albrechtsen - Mikkel Thygesen, Jonas Borring, Mads Albæk (Christian Sivebæk 100), Izunna Uzochukwu - Ken Ilso Larsen (Frank Kristensen 73), Baba Collins (Danny Olsen 73). Tr: Allan Kuhn

* Home team/home team in the first leg • ‡ Qualified for the Europa League

DJI – DJIBOUTI

FIFA/COCA-COLA WORLD RANKING

1993	1994	1995	1996	1997	1998	1999	2000	2001	2002	2003	2004	2005	2006	2007	2008	2009	2010
-	169	177	185	189	191	195	189	193	195	197	201	200	198	173	188	189	191

	2010												Hi/Lo
	Jan	Feb	Mar	Mar	Apr	May	Jul	Aug	Sep	Oct	Nov	Dec	169
	189	193	193	190	188	188	191	191	188	187	187	191	201

After competing in the East and Central African Senior Challenge Cup for five successive years, Djibouti failed to take part in the 2010 edition in Tanzania and having also declined to enter the qualifiers for the 2012 African Nations Cup, it left the team without any international action during the course of the year for the first time since 2004. The lack of action saw the team slip down the FIFA/Coca-Cola World Ranking with just the Seychelles and the unranked Sao Tome and Principe below them from Africa. Djibouti Telecom - also known as Ali Sabieh - did, however, play in the CECAFA Inter-Club Cup in Rwanda in May, where despite losing all three group games and conceding 17 goals in the process, they still won a quarter-final pace when TP Mazembe were disqualified. The last eight meeting with St George of Ethiopia predictably ended in defeat as their more experienced opponents ran out comfortable 5-0 winners. At home AS Port Taco had a fantastic 2010 as they swept all before them. They beat Guellah Batai, the team of the Republican Guard, 3-2 in the Cup Final in mid-year to complete the league and cup double with Mohamed Hassan the hero of their Cup Final success and they ended the year on a high too when they beat Guellah Batai 1-0 in the Super Cup in October.

FIFA WORLD CUP RECORD
1930-1998 DNE 2002 DNQ 2006 DNE 2010 DNQ

FEDERATION DJIBOUTIENNE DE FOOTBALL (FDF)

Centre Technique National, Boite postale 2694, Djibouti
☎ +253 353599
📠 +253 353588
✉ fdf-1979@yahoo.fr
FA 1979 CON 1986 FIFA 1994
P Fadoul Houssein
GS Ali Kamil Ali

FIFA BIG COUNT 2006

Total players	36 320
% of population	7.47%
Male	34 480
Female	1 840
Amateurs 18+	1 800
Youth under 18	720
Unregistered	2 800
Professionals	0
Referees	75
Admin & coaches	405
Number of clubs	6
Number of teams	84

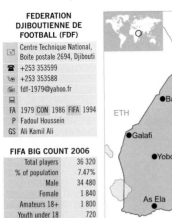

MAJOR CITIES/TOWNS

		Population
1	Djibouti	610 608
2	Ali Sabieh	22 999
3	Dikhil	16 721
4	Arta	11 635
5	Tadjoura	8 740
6	Obock	7 469
7	Ali Adde	5 419
8	Holhol	3 517
9	Yoboki	3 109
10	We'a	3 000
11	Airoli	2 577
12	Dorra	1 465

REPUBLIQUE DE DJIBOUTI • JUMHURIYAT JIBUTI • REPUBLIC OF DJIBOUTI

Capital	Djibouti	Population	516 055 (168)	% in cities	87%
GDP per capita	$2700 (170)	Area km²	23 200 km² (150)	GMT +/-	+3
Neighbours (km)	Eritrea 109, Ethiopia 349, Somalia 58 • Coast 314				

RECENT INTERNATIONAL MATCHES PLAYED BY DJIBOUTI

2005	Opponents		Score	Venue	Comp	Scorers	Att	Referee
27-11	Somalia	L	1-2	Kigali	CCr1	Abdoul Rahman Okishi		
30-11	Uganda	L	1-6	Kigali	CCr1	Abdirahman Okieh		
3-12	Ethiopia	L	0-6	Kigali	CCr1			
5-12	Sudan	L	0-4	Kigali	CCr1			
2006								
26-11	Malawi	L	0-3	Addis Abeba	CCr1			
28-11	Ethiopia	L	0-4	Addis Abeba	CCr1			
1-12	Tanzania	L	0-3	Addis Abeba	CCr1			
17-12	Comoros	L	2-4	Sana'a	ARq	Khaliff Hassan [45], Abdoul Rahman Okishi [92+]		
20-12	Yemen	L	1-4	Sana'a	ARq	Abdoul Rahman Okishi [7]		
2007								
16-11	Somalia	W	1-0	Djibouti	WCq	Hussein Yassin [84]	10 000	Abdel Rahman SUD
9-12	Uganda	L	0-7	Dar es Salaam	CCr1			
11-12	Eritrea	L	2-3	Dar es Salaam	CCr1	Ahmed Hassan Daher [45], Salim Kadar [84]		
13-12	Rwanda	L	0-9	Dar es Salaam	CCr1			
2008								
31-05	Malawi	L	1-8	Blantyre	WCq	Ahmed Hassan Daher [23]	35 000	Katjimune NAM
6-06	Egypt	L	0-4	Djibouti	WCq		6 000	Eyob ERI
13-06	Congo DR	L	0-6	Djibouti	WCq		3 000	Disang BOT
22-06	Congo DR	L	1-5	Kinshasa	WCq	Moussa Hirir [85]	15 000	Rouaissi MAR
5-09	Malawi	L	0-3	Djibouti	WCq		700	Carvalho ANG
12-10	Egypt	L	0-4	Cairo	WCq		10 000	Pare BFA
23-12	Somalia	L	2-3	Djibouti	Fr			
31-12	Zambia	L	0-3	Jinja	CCr1			
2009								
2-01	Burundi	L	0-4	Jinja	CCr1			
4-01	Sudan	D	1-1	Jinja	CCr1	Ahmed Hassan Daher [59]		
6-01	Kenya	L	1-5	Jinja	CCr1	Ahmed Hassan Daher [53]		
30-11	Ethiopia	L	0-5	Nairobi	CCr1			
2-12	Kenya	L	0-2	Nairobi	CCr1			
4-12	Zambia	L	0-6	Nairobi	CCr1			
2010								

No international matches played in 2010

CC = CECAFA Cup • AR = Arab Cup • WC = FIFA World Cup • q = qualifier • r1 = First round group

COUPE DU 27 JUIN FINAL		
18-06-2010		
AS Port	3-2	Guelleh Batal

DMA – DOMINICA

FIFA/COCA-COLA WORLD RANKING

1993	1994	1995	1996	1997	1998	1999	2000	2001	2002	2003	2004	2005	2006	2007	2008	2009	2010
-	-	158	138	139	133	149	152	161	174	185	165	172	181	189	191	197	129

	2010												Hi/Lo
	Jan	Feb	Mar	Mar	Apr	May	Jul	Aug	Sep	Oct	Nov	Dec	**128**
	197	182	185	185	184	183	180	178	178	132	128	129	**198**

In the period spanning over half a decade between March 2004 and December 2009, the Dominica national team managed to score just three goals in 16 international matches; and yet in the space of just six weeks in 2010 they managed to find the back of the net 18 times in just five matches. Add in the four scored against the British Virgin Islands at the end of 2009 and the stats read 22 goals in six games - 12 of them coming from striker Kurlson Benjamin. Dominica began their preparations for the 2010 Digicel Caribbean Cup with back-to-back victories in warm up games over Barbados - the first time the Dominicans had ever beaten Barbados. They then travelled to San Cristobal in the Dominican Republic for a first round group and got off to a flyer, scoring after just 26 seconds - the fastest goal in the history of the tournament - in a record 10-0 victory over the British Virgin Islands. With the Dominican Republic having dispatched the BVI with a tournament record 17-0 win, Dominica needed to beat their hosts to qualify for the next round - which they did with an impressive 1-0 victory - the first time they had ever progressed beyond the first round. That the step up in standards in the next round proved to be too much, couldn't put a damper on what had been a truly memorable year for Kurt Hector's team.

FIFA WORLD CUP RECORD
1930-1994 DNE 1998-2010 DNQ

DOMINICA FOOTBALL ASSOCIATION (DFA)

Patrick John Football House, Bath Estate, PO Box 372, Roseau

☎ +1 767 4487577
📠 +1 767 4487587
✉ domfootball@cwdom.dm
🖥

FA 1970 CON 1994 FIFA 1994
P Patrick John
GS Clifford Celaire

FIFA BIG COUNT 2006

Total players	4 500
% of population	6.53%
Male	3 900
Female	600
Amateurs 18+	500
Youth under 18	700
Unregistered	600
Professionals	0
Referees	39
Admin & coaches	100
Number of clubs	20
Number of teams	20

MAJOR CITIES/TOWNS

		Population
1	Roseau	13 623
2	Canefield	3 363
3	Portsmouth	3 277
4	Marigot	2 669
5	Salisbury	2 531
6	Atkinson	2 257
7	Berekua	2 061
8	Saint Joseph	1 919
9	Castle Bruce	1 870
10	Wesley	1 625
11	Soufrière	1 518
12	La Plaine	1 250
13	Pointe Michel	1 229
14	Mahaut	1 199
15	Woodford Hill	951
16	Calibishie	913
17	Rosalie	760
18	Petite Savane	742
19	Pont Cassé	702

DOMINICA

Capital Roseau	Population 72 660 (201)	% in cities 74%
GDP per capita $10 000 (106)	Area km² 751 km² (188)	GMT +/- -4
Neighbours (km) Coast 148		

RECENT INTERNATIONAL MATCHES PLAYED BY DOMINICA

2004	Opponents	Score		Venue	Comp	Scorers	Att	Referee
28-01	British Virgin Islands	W	1-0	Tortola	Fr	Elry Cuffy [34]	200	Matthew SKN
31-01	US Virgin Islands	W	5-0	St Thomas	Fr	OG [12], Shane Marshall [42], George Dangler [68], Vincent Casimir [87], Sherwin George [90]	550	Matthew SKN
1-02	British Virgin Islands	W	2-1	Tortola	Fr	Shane Marshall [44], Kelly Peters [70]	100	Charles DMA
12-03	Barbados	L	1-2	Bridgetown	Fr	Kelly Peters [88]	46	Small BRB
26-03	Bahamas	D	1-1	Nassau	WCq	Vincent Casimir [88]	800	Forde BRB
28-03	Bahamas	W	3-1	Nassau	WCq	Vincent Casimir 2 [39 86], Kelly Peters [85]	900	Pineda HON
19-06	Mexico	L	0-10	San Antonio, USA	WCq		36 451	Callender BRB
27-06	Mexico	L	0-8	Aguascalientes	WCq		17 000	Stott USA
10-11	Martinique †	L	1-5	Fort de France	CCq	Peltier [42]	1 110	Arthur LCA
12-11	Guadeloupe †	L	0-7	Rivière-Pilote	CCq		2 400	Arthur LCA
14-11	French Guyana †	L	0-4	Fort de France	CCq		5 800	Fenus LCA
2005								
30-09	Guyana	L	0-3	Linden	Fr		800	Lancaster GUY
2-10	Guyana	L	0-3	Georgetown	Fr		1 000	Kia SUR
2006								
3-09	Antigua and Barbuda	L	0-1	St John's	Fr		400	Willett ATG
17-09	Barbados	L	0-5	Roseau	Fr		900	Charles DMA
20-09	Martinique †	L	0-4	Abymes	CCq		1 000	Fanus LCA
22-09	Guadeloupe †	L	0-1	Abymes	CCq		1 100	Willett ATG
24-09	Saint Martin †	D	0-0	Abymes	CCq		500	Willett ATG
2007								
No international matches played in 2007								
2008								
6-02	Barbados	D	1-1	Roseau	WCq	Richard Pacquette [21]	4 200	Quesada CRC
26-03	Barbados	L	0-1	Bridgetown	WCq		4 150	Batres GUA
8-08	Guyana	L	0-3	Georgetown	CCq		3 000	Forde BRB
9-08	Surinam	L	1-3	Georgetown	CCq	Prince Austrie [7]	175	Taylor BRB
2009								
5-12	British Virgin Islands	W	4-0	Roseau	Fr	Prince Austrie [8], Kelly Peters [23], Kurlson Benjamin [25], Cheston Benjamin [85]	600	Baptiste DMA
2010								
25-09	Barbados	W	2-0	Bridgetown	Fr	Kurlson Benjamin [24], Mitchell Joseph [38]	625	Taylor BRB
26-09	Barbados	W	3-1	Bridgetown	Fr	Kurlson Benjamin 3 [35 45 74]	580	Skeete DMA
15-10	British Virgin Islands	W	10-0	San Cristobal	CCq	Mitchell Joseph 3 [1 12 13], Chad Bertrand [55], Kurlson Benjamin 5 [47 71 81 84 85], Donald Jervier [87]	200	Santos PUR
17-10	Dominican Republic	W	1-0	San Cristobal	CCq	Elmond Derrick [66]	600	Lebron PUR
10-11	Cuba	L	2-4	St John's	CCq	Kurlson Benjamin 2 [11 87]	500	Lancaster GUY
12-11	Antigua and Barbuda	D	0-0	St John's	CCq		400	Purser JAM
14-11	Suriname	L	0-5	St John's	CCq		500	Lancaster GUY

Fr = Friendly match • CC = Digicel Caribbean Cup • WC = FIFA World Cup • q = qualifier • † Not a full international

DOM – DOMINICAN REPUBLIC

FIFA/COCA-COLA WORLD RANKING

1993	1994	1995	1996	1997	1998	1999	2000	2001	2002	2003	2004	2005	2006	2007	2008	2009	2010
153	164	159	130	144	152	155	157	160	149	171	170	174	136	166	185	190	168

2010												Hi/Lo
Jan	Feb	Mar	Mar	Apr	May	Jul	Aug	Sep	Oct	Nov	Dec	**116**
190	190	190	188	187	187	185	184	181	162	162	168	**190**

October 14th, 2010 was an historic day for football in the Caribbean. At the Estadio Panamericano in San Cristobal, the Dominican Republic thrashed the British Virgin Islands 17-0 to write themselves into the record books. It was not just the biggest victory in the history of the Caribbean Cup but also for international football in the entire Americas. That it was achieved by a country with no football pedigree made the achievement all the more extraordinary. In front of just 200 fans in a country with a population of almost 10 million, Darly Batista got the ball rolling after four minutes with the first of his five goals. He was one of three players to score a hat trick but missing from the scoresheet was the team's star player Jonathan Fana Frias who was substituted after just 18 minutes with the score at 1-0. Needing just a draw against Dominica to progress to the next round of the 2010 Digicel Caribbean Cup but without the injured Fana Frias, the Dominican Republic then reverted to type losing by a solitary goal to exit the tournament. In club football, the Liga Mayor was played in consecutive years for the first time since 2003 and sixth edition since its inception in 2001 was won by Don Bosco from the town of Moca. With Batista and Domingo Peralta, another of the hat trick heroes against the BVI in the team, they finished five points ahead of Domingo Savio.

FIFA WORLD CUP RECORD
1930-1974 DNE 1978 DNQ 1982-1990 DNE 1994-2010 DNQ

FEDERACION DOMINICANA DE FUTBOL (FEDOFUTBOL)

Centro Olimpico, Ensanche
Miraflores, Apartado postal
1953, Santo Domingo
☎ +1 809 5426923
📠 +1 809 3812734
📧 fedofutbol.f@codetel.net.do
🖥 www.fedofutbol.org
FA 1953 CON 1964 FIFA 1958
P Osiris Guzman
GS Angel Miranda

FIFA BIG COUNT 2006

Total players	501 004
% of population	5.46%
Male	417 804
Female	83 200
Amateurs 18+	35 000
Youth under 18	12 000
Unregistered	106 000
Professionals	4
Referees	1 420
Admin & coaches	190
Number of clubs	250
Number of teams	600

MAJOR CITIES/TOWNS

		Population
1	Santo Domingo	2 491 547
2	Santiago	643 162
3	San Pedro	262 142
4	La Romana	240 235
5	San Cristóbal	183 890
6	Higüey	160 651
7	Puerto Plata	134 206
8	San Francisco	131 000
9	La Vega	110 276
10	Barahona	81 960
11	San Juan	80 560
12	Baní	75 621
13	Bonao	75 464
14	Bajos de Haina	73 199
15	Moca	67 171
16	Azua	64 229
17	Boca Chica	60 169
18	Mao	50 093
19	Villa Altagracia	45 930

REPUBLICA DOMINICANA • DOMINICAN REPUBLIC

Capital	Santo Domingo	Population 9 650 054 (85)	% in cities 69%
GDP per capita	$8200 (119)	Area km² 48 670 km² (131)	GMT + / - -4
Neighbours (km)	Haiti 360 • Coast 1288		

RECENT INTERNATIONAL MATCHES PLAYED BY THE DOMINICAN REPUBLIC

2004	Opponents		Score	Venue	Comp	Scorers	Att	Referee
19-03	Anguilla	D	0-0	Santo Domingo	WCq		400	Mattus CRC
21-03	Anguilla	W	6-0	Santo Domingo	WCq	Zapata [15], Severino 2 [38 61], Contrera 2 [57 90], Casquez [77]	850	Porras CRC
27-04	Netherlands Antilles	L	1-3	Willemstad	Fr	Zapata [9]	800	Faneijte ANT
13-06	Trinidad and Tobago	L	0-2	Santo Domingo	WCq		2 500	Moreno PAN
20-06	Trinidad and Tobago	L	0-4	Marabella	WCq		5 500	Pinas SUR
2005								
No international matches played in 2005								
2006								
15-09	Haiti	L	1-3	Saint-Marc	Fr	Perez.M [22]	600	
17-09	Haiti	L	1-2	Port-au-Prince	Fr	Perez.M [30p]	950	Grant HAI
29-09	Bermuda	L	1-3	Charlotte Amalie	CCq	Faña [85]	300	Martis ANT
1-10	US Virgin Islands	W	6-1	Charlotte Amalie	CCq	Corporan [14], Faña 4 [25 55 82 89], Rodriguez.K [87]	250	Davis TRI
24-11	Guadeloupe	L	0-3	Georgetown	CCq		5 000	Wijngaarde SUR
26-11	Antigua and Barbuda	W	2-0	Georgetown	CCq	Severino [70p], Batista [81]	5 000	Brizan TRI
28-11	Guyana	L	0-4	Georgetown	CCq		5 000	Brizan TRI
2007								
No international matches played in 2007								
2008								
27-02	Haiti	L	1-2	San Cristobal	Fr		1 300	Minyetty DOM
28-02	Haiti	L	0-2	San Cristobal	Fr		825	Minyetty DOM
26-03	Puerto Rico	L	0-1	Bayamon	WCq		8 000	Morales MEX
8-10	Trinidad and Tobago	L	0-9	Port of Spain	Fr		2 000	
2009								
No international matches played in 2009								
2010								
14-10	British Virgin Islands	W	17-0	San Cristobal	CCq	Darly Batista 5 [4 67 68 72 78], Domingo Peralta 3 [21 43 76], Inoel Navarro 3 [26 47 81], Manuel Reinoso 2 [60 73], Kerwin Severino [63], Erick Obuna 2 [83 90], Gonzalo Frechilla [90]	200	Lebron PUR
17-10	Dominica	L	0-1	San Cristobal	CCq		600	Lebron PUR

Fr = Friendly match • CC = Digicel Caribbean Cup • WC = FIFA World Cup • q = qualifier

DOMINICAN REPUBLIC 2010

LIGA MAYOR (VI)	Pl	W	D	L	F	A	Pts	Don Bosco	Domingo Savio	Jarabacoa	Pantoja	Barcelona	Bauger	San Cristobal	Universidad
Don Bosco	20	13	5	2	34	12	**44**		3-1	1-0 2-0	1-0 1-1	0-1 1-0	1-0	3-1 5-1	2-1
Domingo Savio	20	11	6	3	39	22	**39**	0-0 n/p		4-1	2-2 2-0	6-1	0-0 1-0	2-1	3-0
SDB Jarabacoa	20	10	3	7	31	15	**33**	1-1	0-0 4-0		1-0 1-2	2-1	1-0	2-1 0-1	7-0
Deportivo Pantoja	19	9	6	4	31	20	**33**	1-1	0-1	1-0		0-0 2-2	3-2	3-3 4-0	2-0 n/p
Barcelona	20	5	9	6	21	23	**24**	2-2	2-2 1-2	0-0 1-0	0-3		0-0 1-1	0-1	4-0 3-0
Bauger	19	6	5	8	19	18	**23**	0-1 0-3	3-1	0-2 n/p	0-1 n/p	0-0		2-1	1-0
San Cristobal	20	5	2	13	22	45	**17**	1-0	1-3 0-5	0-2	2-3	0-0 n/p	1-3 1-4		0-2 4-2
Universidad OyM	20	1	2	17	11	53	**5**	0-3 1-3	1-2 2-2	0-4 0-3	1-3	1-2	0-3 0-0	0-2	

23/05/2010 - 31/10/2010

ECU – ECUADOR

FIFA/COCA-COLA WORLD RANKING

1993	1994	1995	1996	1997	1998	1999	2000	2001	2002	2003	2004	2005	2006	2007	2008	2009	2010
48	55	55	33	28	63	65	54	37	31	37	39	37	30	56	36	37	53

	2010											Hi/Lo
	Jan	Feb	Mar	Mar	Apr	May	Jul	Aug	Sep	Oct	Nov	Dec	24
	37	35	37	36	36	44	58	58	72	67	61	53	76

LDU Quito reached the significant milestone of a tenth league title in December 2010 as they continued to cement their position as the top team in the country. In the mid-1990's the club was regarded as one of the smaller and less well supported teams in Ecuador but the completion of their 55,000 capacity Casa Blanca stadium in 1997 transformed the fortunes of the club. In 1998 they won the first of six league titles that would follow in the next 12 years, their latest coming once again thanks to a fantastic home record. In 23 matches played at La Casa Blanca, LDU won 18 and drew four, including a 2-0 victory over Emelec in the first leg of the 2010 championship final - Miller Bolanos scoring both goals. Emelec won the return in Guayaquil but the 1-0 victory was not enough to deny LDU the title. LDU failed, however, in their bid to win a continental title for the third year running when they were knocked out in the semi-finals of the 2010 Copa Sudamericana by Argentina's Independiente on away goals. That they came so close is testament to their growing status, not just in Ecuadorian football but also world football. In a slow year for the national team, Colombian Reinaldo Rueda was appointed coach in an attempt to revive fortunes, having successfully lead Honduras to the 2010 FIFA World Cup finals in South Africa.

FIFA WORLD CUP RECORD

1930-1958 DNE **1962-1998** DNQ **2002** 24 r1 **2006** 12 r2 **2010** DNQ

FEDERACION ECUATORIANA DE FUTBOL (FEF)

Avenida las Aguas y Calle, Alianza, PO Box 09-01-7447, Guayaquil 593
☎ +593 42 880610
📠 +593 42 880615
📧 fef@gye.satnet.net
💻 www.ecuafutbol.org
FA 1925 CON 1930 FIFA 1926
P Luis Chiriboga
GS Francisco Acosta

FIFA BIG COUNT 2006

Total players	1 029 655
% of population	7.60%
Male	918 800
Female	110 855
Amateurs 18+	12 855
Youth under 18	9 800
Unregistered	811 800
Professionals	700
Referees	405
Admin & coaches	4 050
Number of clubs	199
Number of teams	416

MAJOR CITIES/TOWNS

		Population
1	Guayaquil	2 248 800
2	Quito	1 621 817
3	Cuenca	322 955
4	Machala	247 290
5	Santo Domingo	232 207
6	Manta	210 712
7	Portoviejo	195 941
8	Eloy Alfaro	193 293
9	Ambato	180 048
10	Quevedo	140 945
11	Riobamba	139 778
12	Loja	128 578
13	Ibarra	128 288
14	Milagro	126 831
15	Esmeraldas	112 192
16	Babahoyo	90 016
17	La Libertad	87 417
18	El Carmen	80 270
19	Rosa Zárate	62 813

REPUBLICA DEL ECUADOR • REPUBLIC OF ECUADOR

Capital	Quito	Population	14 573 101 (64)	% in cities	66%
GDP per capita	$7500 (123)	Area km²	283 561 km² (73)	GMT + / -	-5
Neighbours (km)	Colombia 590, Peru 1420 • Coast 2237		

RECENT INTERNATIONAL MATCHES PLAYED BY ECUADOR

2007	Opponents	Score	Venue	Comp	Scorers	Att	Referee
27-06	Chile	L 2-3	Puerto Ordaz	CAr1	Valencia [16], Benítez [23]	35 000	Ruiz COL
1-07	Mexico	L 1-2	Maturin	CAr1	Méndez [84]	42 000	Ortube BOL
4-07	Brazil	L 0-1	Puerto La Cruz	CAr1		34 000	Pezzotta ARG
22-08	Bolivia	W 1-0	Quito	Fr	Urrutia [34p]	20 000	Parra COL
8-09	El Salvador	W 5-1	Quito	Fr	Lara [13], Benitez 2 [29 49], Caicedo.F [45], Urrutia [53p]		Carillo PER
12-09	Honduras	L 1-2	San Pedro Sula	Fr	Guagua [89]	25 000	Batres GUA
13-10	Venezuela	L 0-1	Quito	WCq		29 644	Ortube BOL
17-10	Brazil	L 0-5	Rio de Janeiro	WCq		87 000	Larrionda URU
17-11	Paraguay	L 1-5	Asuncion	WCq	Kaviedes [80]	25 433	Lopes BRA
21-11	Peru	W 5-1	Quito	WCq	Ayovi.W 2 [10 48], Kaviedes [24], Mendez 2 [44 62]	28 557	Chandia CHI
2008							
26-03	Haiti	W 3-1	Latacunga	Fr	Castillo 45, Ayovi.W 58, Tenorio.C 60p	10 000	
27-05	France	L 0-2	Grenoble	Fr		20 000	Allaerts BEL
15-06	Argentina	D 1-1	Buenos Aires	WCq	Urrutia [69]	41 167	Ortube BOL
18-06	Colombia	D 0-0	Quito	WCq		33 588	Baldassi ARG
20-08	Colombia	W 1-0	New Jersey	Fr	Benitez [40]	32 439	Prus USA
6-09	Bolivia	W 3-1	Quito	WCq	Caicedo [21], Mendez [51p], Benitez [72]	35 000	Pozo CHI
10-09	Uruguay	D 0-0	Montevideo	WCq		45 000	Ruiz COL
12-10	Chile	W 1-0	Quito	WCq	Benitez [70]	33 079	Vazquez URU
15-10	Venezuela	L 1-3	Puerto La Cruz	WCq	Mina [12]	10 581	Osses CHI
12-11	Mexico	L 1-2	Phoenix	Fr	Mina [7]		Prus USA
17-12	Iran	W 1-0	Muscat	Fr	Martinez [56]		
19-12	Oman	L 0-2	Muscat	Fr			
2009							
29-03	Brazil	D 1-1	Quito	WCq	Noboa [89]	40 000	Chandia CHI
1-04	Paraguay	D 1-1	Quito	WCq	Noboa [63]	36 853	Roldan COL
27-05	El Salvador	L 1-3	Los Angeles	Fr	Montero [9]		
7-06	Peru	W 2-1	Lima	WCq	Montero [38], Tenorio.C [58]	17 050	Torres PAR
10-06	Argentina	W 2-0	Quito	WCq	Ayovi [72], Palacios [83]	36 359	Chandia CHI
12-08	Jamaica	D 0-0	New Jersey	Fr			Marrufo USA
5-09	Colombia	L 0-2	Medellin	WCq		42 000	Pezzotta ARG
9-09	Bolivia	W 3-1	La Paz	WCq	Mendez [4], Valancia [46], Benitez [66]	10 200	Baldassi ARG
10-10	Uruguay	L 1-2	Quito	WCq	Valencia [68]	42 700	Fagundes BRA
14-10	Chile	L 0-1	Santiago	WCq		47 000	Torres PAR
2010							
7-05	Mexico	D 0-0	New York	Fr		77 507	Depiero CAN
16-05	Korea Republic	L 0-2	Seoul	Fr		62 209	Wongkamdee THA
4-09	Mexico	W 2-1	Guadalajara	Fr	Benitez [1], Ayovi [58]	43 800	Quesada CRC
7-09	Venezuela	L 0-1	Barquisimento	Fr		37 262	Torres PAN
8-10	Colombia	L 0-1	Harrison	Fr		25 000	Chapin USA
12-10	Poland	D 2-2	Montreal	Fr	Benitez 2 [31 78]	1 000	Navarro CAN
17-11	Venezuela	W 4-1	Quito	Fr	Benitez 2 [2 4], Ayovi 2 [45p 46]	9 000	Chaibou NGA

Fr = Friendly match • CA = Copa America • WC = FIFA World Cup • q = qualifier • r1 = first round group

ECUADOR NATIONAL TEAM HISTORICAL RECORDS

Caps — 168 - Ivan Hurtado 1992- • 109 - Alex Aguinaga 1987-2004 • 102 - Ulises de la Cruz 1995- • 100 - Luis Capurro 1985-2003 • 90 - Edison Mendez 2000- & Giovanny Espinoza 2000- • 89 - José Francisco Cevallos 1994- • 86 - Cleber Chala 1994-2004 • 78 - Edwin Tenorio 1998-2007 • 77 - Angel Fernandez 1991-2004

Goals — 31 - Agustin Delgado 1994-2006 • 26 - Eduardo Hurtado 1992-2000 • 23 - Alex Aguinaga 1987-2004 • 16 - Ivan Kaviedes 1998- & Raul Aviles 1987-2003 • 15 - Ariel Graziani 1997-2000, Edison Mendez 2000- & Christian Benitez 2005-

Past Coaches — Enrique Lamas CHI 1938 • Ramon Unamuno 1939 • Juan Parodi ARG 1941-42 • Rodolfo Orlandini ARG 1945 • Ramon Unamuno 1947 • Jose Planas ESP 1949 • Gregorio Esperon ARG 1953 • Jose Maria Diaz Granados 1955 • Eduardo Spandre ARG 1957 • Juan Lopez URU 1959-60 • Fausto Montalvan 1963 • Jose Maria Rodriguez URU 1965 • Fausto Montalvan 1966 • Jose Gomes Nogueira BRA 1969 • Ernesto Guerra 1970 • Jorge Lazo 1972 • Roberto Resquin ARG 1973 • Roque Maspoli URU 1975-77 • Hector Morales 1979 • Otto Vieira BRA 1981 • Juan Eduardo Hohberg URU 1981 • Ernesto Guerra 1984 • Antoninho Ferreira BRA 1984-85 • Luis Grimaldi URU 1986-87 • Dusan Draskovic YUG 1988-93 • Carlos Torres Garces 1994 • Carlos Ron 1994 • Francisco Maturana COL 1995-97 • Luis Fernando Suarez COL 1997 • Francisco Maturana COL 1997 • Polo Carrera 1998 • Carlos Sevilla 1999 • Hernan Dario Gomez COL 1999-2004 • Luis Fernando Suarez COL 2004-07 • Sixto Vizuete 2007-10 • Reinaldo Rueda COL 2010-

ECUADOR 2010

SERIE A COPA CREDIFE PRIMERA ETAPA	Pl	W	D	L	F	A	Pts	Emelec	LDU Quito	Barcelona	Dep Quito	Dep Cuenca	El Nacional	Ind Del Valle	Manta	Olmedo	Espoli	Un. Católica	Macará
Emelec ‡	22	14	4	4	36	21	46		1-0	3-0	1-1	4-0	1-0	1-1	3-3	4-1	4-0	1-0	2-0
LDU Quito	22	12	8	2	36	10	44	5-0		0-0	2-0	2-0	1-0	3-0	3-0	5-0	1-1	2-1	3-1
Barcelona	22	12	7	3	26	12	43	1-2	0-0		1-0	2-1	1-0	0-1	2-1	1-0	2-0	5-1	2-0
Deportivo Quito	22	10	4	8	27	23	34	1-0	0-1	0-1		1-1	1-3	3-2	2-1	2-0	2-0	2-0	2-0
Deportivo Cuenca	22	6	9	7	21	25	27	2-0	1-1	1-1	1-0		0-0	3-0	0-0	0-1	3-0	1-0	0-1
El Nacional	22	5	10	7	34	27	25	5-0	0-0	0-0	2-1	0-0		1-1	4-0	2-2	4-0	1-2	1-1
Indep. Del Valle	22	5	10	7	26	30	25	0-0	0-2	1-1	2-2	2-2	3-1		1-0	1-1	1-2	1-1	0-0
Manta	22	5	9	8	24	31	24	1-3	0-0	0-0	3-0	1-1	2-2	3-1		1-0	1-0	1-1	2-1
Olmedo	22	5	8	9	19	28	23	0-1	0-1	0-0	0-1	1-1	2-1	2-3	1-0		1-1	2-0	0-0
Espoli	22	6	4	12	22	41	22	0-3	2-1	0-1	0-3	3-0	5-3	0-4	2-0	2-2		0-1	0-1
Universidad Católica	22	4	8	10	21	32	20	0-1	1-1	0-3	1-1	3-1	1-1	2-0	1-1	0-0	2-3		2-3
Macará	22	3	9	10	22	34	18	1-2	2-2	1-2	1-2	1-2	3-3	1-1	2-2	0-2	1-1	1-1	

5/02/2010 - 4/07/2010 • ‡ Qualified for the Championship final

ECUADOR 2010

SERIE A COPA CREDIFE SEGUNDA ETAPA	Pl	W	D	L	F	A	Pts	LDU Quito	Emelec	Dep. Cuenca	Dep. Quito	Barcelona	El Nacional	Manta	Olmedo	Espoli	Macará	Un. Católica	José Terán
LDU Quito ‡	22	14	5	3	42	17	47		0-1	2-0	1-1	2-1	2-1	4-2	1-0	3-0	3-0	1-0	2-0
Emelec	22	13	7	2	29	12	46	1-1		0-1	2-1	0-0	2-0	0-0	1-0	3-1	2-0	2-0	2-1
Deportivo Cuenca	22	12	5	5	32	25	41	1-1	1-1		2-0	1-0	0-0	3-1	2-3	2-1	0-2	2-1	3-1
Deportivo Quito	22	11	4	7	35	22	37	1-1	1-0	1-2		4-0	1-0	4-0	1-0	2-0	0-0	5-0	1-1
Barcelona	22	8	6	8	25	24	30	1-1	0-0	1-2	1-0		1-2	1-2	0-0	0-3	2-1	5-1	3-0
El Nacional	22	8	5	9	23	23	29	2-3	0-0	0-0	1-3	0-1		4-0	3-1	0-0	2-1	0-1	3-0
Manta	22	7	6	9	23	33	27	1-0	1-2	2-0	1-2	1-0	1-0		3-0	0-0	1-0	2-2	0-2
Olmedo	22	6	5	11	20	33	23	0-3	0-1	0-0	3-2	0-1	1-1	2-2		3-2	0-1	1-1	2-1
Espoli	22	5	8	9	22	28	23	0-1	1-1	2-5	2-3	0-0	0-1	1-0	3-0		1-1	2-1	1-0
Macará	22	5	6	11	21	32	21	2-4	1-4	1-2	1-0	1-1	4-1	1-1	0-1	1-1		1-0	0-2
Universidad Católica	22	5	5	12	27	37	20	2-1	2-3	2-3	3-0	2-2	0-1	3-0	1-2	0-0	1-1		1-2
Indep. José Terán	22	5	4	13	23	36	19	0-4	0-1	3-0	1-2	1-2	0-1	2-2	1-1	1-1	3-1	1-3	

9/07/2010 - 27/11/2010 • ‡ Qualified for the Championship final • 3rd Place Play-off (overall) Deportivo Quito 2-0 1-3 Barcelona
Top scorers (all stages): 23 - Jaime Ayovi, Emelec • 22 - Hernan Barcos ARG, LDU & Julio Bevacqua ARG, Manta • Un. Católica & Macara relegated

CHAMPIONSHIP FINAL 2010 1ST LEG

Casa Blanca, Quito, 5-12-2010, Att: 27 506, Ref: Tomas Alarcon

LDU Quito   2   Bolanos 2 50 92+

Emelec   0

LDU - Jose Francisco Cevallos - Norberto Araujo, Diego Calderon●, Jorge Guagua - William Araujo, Miller Bolanos●, Ulises de la Cruz●, Marlon Ganchozo (Gonzalo Chila 72), Neicer Reasco● (c) - Carlos Luna (Walter Calderon 59), Juan Manuel Salgueiro (Jose Valencia 76). Tr: Edgardo Bauza

Emelec - Javier Klimowicz - Gabriel Achilier, Eduardo Morante, Carlos Andres Quinonez, Jose Luis Quinonez - Fernando Gaibor (Enner Valencia 46), Fernando Gimenez, Pedro Quinonez●, David Quiroz (c) - Jaime Ayovi, Joao Rojas (Leandro Torres 58). Tr: Jorge Sampaoli

CHAMPIONSHIP FINAL 2010 2ND LEG

George Capwell, Guayaquil, 12-12-2010, Att: 23 112, Ref: Carlos Vera

Emelec   1   Quiroz 60

LDU Quito   0

Emelec - Javier Klimowicz - Gabriel Achilier (Carlos Andres Quinonez 45), Marcelo Fleitas● (c), Eduardo Morante - Fernando Gaibor (Leandro Torres 45), Fernando Gimenez●, Pedro Quinonez●, David Quiroz, Joao Rojas (Santiago Biglieri 68) - Jaime Ayovi, Cristian Menendez. Tr: Jorge Sampaoli

LDU - Jose Francisco Cevallos●◆94+ - Norberto Araujo, Diego Calderon, Jorge Guagua● - William Araujo, Ulises de la Cruz, Marlon Ganchozo● (Jose Valencia 55), Neicer Reasco● (c), Patricio Urrutia - Carlos Luna (Walter Calderon 84), Juan Manuel Salgueiro (Miller Bolanos 64●◆91+). Tr: Edgardo Bauza

MEDALS TABLE

		Overall			League			Sth Am			City
		G	S	B	G	S	B	G	S	B	
1	Barcelona	13	13	10	13	11	5		2	5	Guayaquil
2	El Nacional	13	7	7	13	7	4			3	Quito
3	LDU Quito	12	3	10	10	3	6	2		4	Quito
4	Emelec	10	11	13	10	10	11		1	2	Guayaquil
5	Deportivo Quito	4	3	4	4	3	4				Quito
6	Deportivo Cuenca	1	5	1	1	5	1				Cuenca
7	Olmedo	1	1	2	1	1	2				Riobamba
8	Everest	1		1	1		1				Guayaquil

EGY – EGYPT

FIFA/COCA-COLA WORLD RANKING

1993	1994	1995	1996	1997	1998	1999	2000	2001	2002	2003	2004	2005	2006	2007	2008	2009	2010
26	22	23	28	32	28	38	33	41	39	32	34	32	27	39	16	24	9

2010												Hi/Lo
Jan	Feb	Mar	Mar	Apr	May	Jul	Aug	Sep	Oct	Nov	Dec	9
24	10	17	14	13	12	9	9	9	11	10	9	44

As the Egyptian team watched on from the sidelines during the 2010 FIFA World Cup finals while six other countries flew the flag for Africa, it would have not been too far off the mark to suggest that they would have willingly traded their third successive Nations Cup title, won earlier in the year in Angola, for a spot at the tournament in South Africa. The Egyptians were the highest ranked nation absent from the finals and a golden generation of players, including Ahmed Hassan, Mohamed Aboutrika, Essam Al Hadari and Wael Gomaa, will forever have the void of never having competed at the World Cup. Remarkably, a poor start to the 2012 Nations Cup qualifying campaign has put Egypt in danger of not being able to defend their African title in Gabon and Equatorial Guinea while the effects of the sweeping political changes in the country on a team which had always enjoyed closed links with the Mubarak regime remains to be seen. In club football both Al Ahly and Haras Al Hedod retained the trophies they won in 2009 but for Al Ahly winning the league was not enough to secure Hossam Al Badari his job as coach long-term. In June Al Ahly lost the Cup Final on penalties to Haras Al Hedod but at the end of the year he resigned after they were beaten on the away goals rule by Tunisia's Esperance in the Champions League semi-final.

FIFA WORLD CUP RECORD

1930 DNE **1934** 13 r1 1938-1950 DNE 1954 DNQ 1958-1970 DNE 1974-1986 DNQ **1990** 20 r1 1994- 2010 DNQ

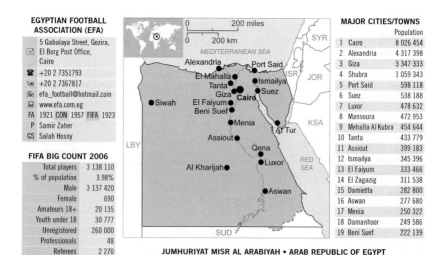

EGYPTIAN FOOTBALL ASSOCIATION (EFA)

5 Gabalaya Street, Gezira,
El Borg Post Office,
Cairo

☎ +20 2 7351793
📠 +20 2 7367817
✉ efa_football@hotmail.com
🖥 www.efa.com.eg
FA 1921 CON 1957 FIFA 1923
P Samir Zaher
GS Salah Hosny

FIFA BIG COUNT 2006

Total players	3 138 110
% of population	3.98%
Male	3 137 420
Female	690
Amateurs 18+	20 135
Youth under 18	30 777
Unregistered	260 000
Professionals	48
Referees	2 270
Admin & coaches	16 000
Number of clubs	590
Number of teams	6 495

MAJOR CITIES/TOWNS

		Population
1	Cairo	8 026 454
2	Alexandria	4 317 398
3	Giza	3 347 333
4	Shubra	1 059 343
5	Port Said	598 118
6	Suez	538 188
7	Luxor	478 632
8	Mansoura	472 953
9	Mehalla Al Kubra	454 644
10	Tanta	433 779
11	Assiout	399 183
12	Ismailya	345 396
13	El Faiyum	333 466
14	El Zagazig	311 538
15	Damietta	282 800
16	Aswan	277 680
17	Menia	250 322
18	Damanhoor	249 586
19	Beni Suef	222 139

JUMHURIYAT MISR AL ARABIYAH • ARAB REPUBLIC OF EGYPT

Capital	Cairo	Population	83 082 869 (15)	% in cities	43%
GDP per capita	$5800 (134)	Area km²	1 001 450 km² (30)	GMT +/-	+2
Neighbours (km)	Gaza Strip 11, Israel 266, Libya 1115, Sudan 1273 • Coast 2450				

RECENT INTERNATIONAL MATCHES PLAYED BY EGYPT

2008	Opponents	Score		Venue	Comp	Scorers	Att	Referee
1-06	Congo DR	W	2-1	Cairo	WCq	Amr Zaki [68], Ahmed Abdelmalk [80]	40 000	Seechurn MRI
6-06	Djibouti	W	4-0	Djibouti	WCq	Amr Zaki [40], Hosny Abd Rabo [46p], Ahmed Hassan [53], Ahmed Abdelmalk [64]	6 000	Eyob ERI
14-06	Malawi	L	0-1	Blantyre	WCq		40 000	Keita GUI
22-06	Malawi	W	2-0	Cairo	WCq	Moteab 2 [17 50]		Diatta SEN
20-08	Sudan	L	0-4	Omdurman	Fr			
7-09	Congo DR	W	1-0	Kinshasa	WCq	Aboutrika [30]	80 000	Bennett RSA
12-10	Djibouti	W	4-0	Cairo	WCq	Moteab [18], Ahmed Hassan [49], Aboutrika [65], OG [91+]	10 000	Pare BFA
19-11	Benin	W	5-1	Cairo	Fr	Hosny Abd Rabo [20p], Moteab 2 [27 41], Aboutrika 2 [43 41]		
2009								
23-01	Kenya	W	1-0	Cairo	Fr	Ahmed Hassan [26]		
11-02	Ghana	D	2-2	Cairo	Fr	Shawky [40], Moteab [83]		
29-03	Zambia	D	1-1	Cairo	WCq	Amr Zaki [27]	70 000	Coulibaly MLI
30-05	Oman	W	1-0	Muscat	Fr	Aboutrika [49]		
7-06	Algeria	L	1-3	Blida	WCq	Aboutrika [86]	26 500	Bennett RSA
15-06	Brazil	L	3-4	Bloemfontein	CCr1	Zidan 2 [9 55], Shawky [54]	27 851	Webb ENG
18-06	Italy	W	1-0	Johannesburg	CCr1	Homos [40]	52 150	Hansson SWE
21-06	USA	L	0-3	Rustenburg	CCr1		23 140	Hester NZL
5-07	Rwanda	W	3-0	Cairo	WCq	Aboutrika 2 [64 90], Hosny Abd Rabo [74p]	18 000	Imiere NGA
12-08	Guinea	D	3-3	Cairo	Fr	Hosny Abd Rabo 2 [3 31], Abdelmalek [90]		
5-09	Rwanda	W	1-0	Kigali	WCq	Ahmed Hassan [67]	20 000	Lamptey GHA
2-10	Mauritius	W	4-0	Cairo	Fr	Aboutrika 2 [7 83], Ahmed Hassan [17p], Amr Zaki [90p]		
10-10	Zambia	W	1-0	Chililabombwe	WCq	Hosny Abd Rabo [69]	10 000	Djaoupe TOG
5-11	Tanzania	W	5-1	Aswan	Fr	Moteab 2 [8 33], Amr Zaki [19], Barakat [42], Raouf [86]		
14-11	Algeria	W	2-0	Cairo	WCq	Amr Zaki [3], Moteab [95+]	75 000	Damon RSA
18-11	Algeria	L	0-1	Omdurman	WCpo		35 000	Maillet SEY
29-12	Malawi	D	1-1	Cairo	Fr	Hosny Abd Rabo [45p]		
2010								
4-01	Mali	W	1-0	Dubai	Fr	Geddo [65]		
12-01	Nigeria	W	3-1	Benguela	CNr1	Moteab [34], Ahmed Hassan [54], Geddo [87]	18 000	Seechurn MRI
16-01	Mozambique	W	2-0	Benguela	CNr1	Khan OG [47], Geddo [81]	16 000	Djaoupe TOG
20-01	Benin	W	2-0	Benguela	CNr1	Al Muhamadi [7], Moteab [23]	12 500	Bennett RSA
25-01	Cameroon	W	3-1	Benguela	CNqf	Ahmed Hassan 2 [37 103], Geddo [92]	12 000	Damon RSA
28-01	Algeria	W	4-0	Benguela	CNsf	Hosny Abd Rabo [39p], Zidan [65], Abdel Shafy [80], Geddo [92+]	25 000	Codjia BEN
31-01	Ghana	W	1-0	Luanda	CNf	Geddo [85]	50 000	Coulibaly MLI
3-03	England	L	1-3	London	Fr	Zidan [23]	80 602	Torres PAR
11-08	Congo DR	W	6-3	Cairo	Fr	Ahmed Ali Kamal 2 [3 34], Ahmed Fathy [41], Aboutrika [44], Ahmed Hassan [49], Geddo [67]		
5-09	Sierra Leone	D	1-1	Cairo	CNq	Mahmoud Fathallah [61]		Diatta SEN
10-10	Niger	L	0-1	Niamey	CNq			Doue CIV
17-11	Australia	W	3-0	Cairo	Fr	El Zaher [29], Geddo [60], Zidan [90p]		Genov BUL
16-12	Qatar	L	1-2	Doha	Fr	Walid Soliman [72]		

Fr = Friendly match • CN = CAF African Cup of Nations • CC = FIFA Confederations Cup • WC = FIFA World Cup

EGYPT NATIONAL TEAM HISTORICAL RECORDS

Caps

175 - Ahmed Hassan 1995- • **169** - Hossam Hassan 1985-2006 • **125** - Ibrahim Hassan 1985-2004 • **124** - Hany Ramzy 1988-2003 • **122** - Essam El Hadary • **110** - Nader El Sayed 1992-2005 & Abdel Zaher El Sakka 1997- • **97** - Ismail Youssef 1985-97 • **93** - Magdi Abdelghani 1980-90 & Wael Gomaa 2001-

Goals

69 - Hossam Hassan 1985-2006 • **39** - Mahmoud Al Khatib 1974-86 • **34** - Magdi Abdelghani 1980-90 • **32** - Ahmed Hassan 1995- • **31** - Emad Moteab 2005- • **28** - Amr Zaki 2004- • **25** - Mohamed Aboutrika 2004- • **19** - Ahmed Hossam 'Mido' 2001-

Past Coaches

Hussein Hegazi 1920-24 • James McRea SCO 1934-36 • Tawfik Abdullah 1940-44 • Eric Keen ENG 1947-48 • Edward Jones ENG 1949-52 • Committee 1953-54 • Ljubisa Brociaje YUG 1954-55 • Mohamed El-Guindy & Hanafy Bastan 1958 • Pal Titkos HUN 1959-61 • Mohamed El Guindy & Hanafy Bastan 1962 • Foad Sidqui 1963 • Vendler YUG 1964 • Kovae YUG 1965 • Mohamed Abdou Saleh El-Wahsh & Kamal El Sabagh 1969-70 • Dettmar Cramer GER 1971-74 • Burkhard Pape GER 1975-77 • Dusan Nenkovic YUG 1977-78 • Taha Ismail 1978 • Bundzsak Dezso HUN 1979 • Foad Sidqui 1980 • Abdel Monem El-Hajj 1980 • Hamada El-Sharqawy 1980 • Karl-Heinz Heddergott GER 1980-82 • Mohamed Abdou Saleh El-Wahsh & Ali Osman 1982-85 • Mike Smith WAL 1985-88 • Foad Sidqui 1988 • Mahmoud El Gohary 1988-90 • Dietrich Weise GER 1990-91 • Mahmoud El Gohary 1991-93 • Mohamed Sadiq "Shehta" 1993 • Mircea Radulescu ROU 1993-94 • Taha Ismail 1994 • Nol de Ruiter NED 1994-95 • Mohsen Saleh 1995 • Ruud Krul NED 1995-96 • Farouk Gaafar 1996-97 • Mahmoud El-Gohary 1997-99 • Anwar Salama 1999 • Gerard Gili FRA 1999-2000 • Mahmoud El-Gohary 2000 • Mohsen Saleh 2000-03 • Marco Tardelli ITA 2003-04 • Hassan Shehata 2004-

EGYPT 2009-10

PREMIER LEAGUE

	Pl	W	D	L	F	A	Pts	Ahly	Zamalek	Ismaily	Shorta	Petrojet	Haras	Intag Harby	ENPPI	Jaish	Ittihad	Mokawloon	Gouna	Masry	Ghazl	Mansoura	Assiout
Al Ahly †	30	18	11	1	47	23	65		0-0	1-1	4-2	2-1	1-1	1-0	2-0	2-2	1-0	2-0	1-0	2-0	2-0	3-0	1-0
Zamalek †	30	16	7	7	43	26	55	3-3		0-1	1-1	1-2	2-1	2-0	0-1	1-0	1-0	1-1	3-0	0-1	1-0		4-1
Ismaily ‡	30	11	15	4	34	25	48	1-1	0-0		1-0	1-3	0-0	2-1	2-3	1-1	3-0	1-0	1-2	1-1	2-0	2-1	0-0
Ittihad Al Shorta	30	12	11	7	35	24	47	1-2	2-0	0-0		0-0	2-1	2-0	0-0	2-0	2-0	1-1	1-0	1-1	4-0	1-0	2-1
Petrojet	30	13	8	9	42	37	47	0-1	2-3	1-1	2-1		1-4	2-2	0-0	2-1	3-1	0-3	3-1	0-0	1-0	1-0	1-1
Haras Al Hedod ‡	30	11	12	7	39	31	45	1-1	2-1	0-0	1-1	1-3		2-3	4-0	0-0	0-1		1-1	2-2	1-1	2-1	2-0
Intag Harby	30	11	8	11	36	32	41	0-1	2-3	1-0	1-1	3-1	0-2		3-1	1-2	2-0	3-1	2-0	2-0	0-0	0-0	
ENPPI	30	10	11	9	29	35	41	1-2	1-3	1-1	1-0	0-0	2-1	1-2		0-0	1-0	2-1	2-1	1-1	2-2	1-0	3-1
Al Jaish	30	9	13	8	42	38	40	2-4	0-1	1-1	2-2	3-2	2-3	1-1	2-0		0-1	2-1	1-2	3-1	0-0	3-1	3-1
Ittihad	30	9	8	13	27	36	35	1-1	1-2	0-1	1-1	1-0	1-0	1-0	1-1	1-3		1-1	2-0	1-1	1-0	1-1	4-0
Mokawloon	30	7	13	10	36	34	34	1-1	2-2	1-1	0-0	1-1	2-0	0-0	1-1	1-1	4-1		2-0	1-1	1-1	2-0	4-2
Al Gouna	30	8	10	12	26	32	34	0-0	0-1	2-2	0-1	1-0	2-0	2-0	0-1	1-1	2-1	3-2		0-0	0-2	1-1	0-1
Al Masry	30	6	16	8	28	35	34	1-1	1-3	1-2	1-3	0-1	1-1	2-1	0-0	2-2	1-1	0-0	1-1		1-0	0-0	2-1
Ghazl Al Mehalla	30	7	10	13	17	30	31	2-0	0-1	1-0	0-0	1-3	0-0	1-1	1-0	1-0	0-0	2-1	0-0	0-3		1-0	1-2
Al Mansoura	30	3	10	17	21	37	19	1-2	0-0	2-2	2-0	1-3	1-2	1-1	0-0	0-0	1-1	1-1	0-2	1-1	1-0		4-0
Assiout Petrol	30	4	7	19	29	56	19	1-2	0-2	1-2	1-2	2-3	0-1	0-1	1-1	3-3	4-2	0-1	1-1	1-2	0-0	3-2	

6/08/2009 - 17/05/2010 • † Qualified for the CAF Champions League • ‡ Qualified for the CAF Confederation Cup • Top scorers: **14** - Minusu Buba NGA, Shorta • **13** - Eric Bekoe GHA, Petrojet • **9** - Ahmed Abdel Ghani, Haras; Ahmed Gaafar, Zamalek; Talaat Moharam, Jaish & Emad Moteab, Ahly

EGYPT 2009-10 — SECOND DIVISION A (2)

	Pl	W	D	L	F	A	Pts
Misr Al Maqasah	30	19	8	3	56	27	65
Telefonad Beni Suef	30	17	9	4	49	17	60
Grand Hotel Hurghada	30	16	9	5	49	30	57
Aswan	30	16	8	6	50	25	56
Al Minya	30	14	9	7	37	25	51
Wadi Dakla Ibshawai	30	12	7	11	38	40	43
Sohaq	30	11	9	10	38	35	42
Shabab Al Waladeya	30	9	9	12	38	45	36
Aluminium N Hammadi	30	8	11	11	30	35	35
Al Fayoum	30	7	12	11	27	30	33
Sokar Al Hawamdia	30	8	9	13	29	37	33
Sukar Abu Qourqas	30	9	5	16	38	51	32
Al Wosta	30	7	9	14	23	43	30
Shoban Qenah	30	6	11	13	30	48	29
Wadi Al Gedid	30	7	5	18	32	51	26
Madina Al Monowara	30	6	6	18	32	57	24

23/09/2009 - 12/05/2010

EGYPT 2009-10 — SECOND DIVISION B (2)

	Pl	W	D	L	F	A	Pts
Wadi Degla	30	17	12	1	44	14	63
Gasco	30	15	13	2	44	18	58
Al Dakhleya	30	16	10	4	40	18	58
Itesalat Al Masry	30	15	10	5	41	23	55
Al Nasr Egypt	30	10	12	8	40	37	42
Al Sharkya	30	10	11	9	23	33	41
Al Tersana	30	10	9	11	26	30	39
Al Rabat we Al Anwar	30	9	9	12	25	31	36
Olympi Al Qanal	30	6	15	9	32	31	33
Al Shams	30	7	12	11	22	29	33
Montakhab Al Suweis	30	7	11	12	22	27	32
Al Mareekh	30	6	14	10	23	33	32
Gomhoreyat Shepin	30	6	11	13	27	36	29
Asmant Al Suweis	30	7	8	15	25	35	29
Banha	30	8	5	17	32	49	29
Al Seka Al Hadid	30	3	14	13	30	52	23

23/09/2009 - 12/05/2010

EGYPT 2009-10 — SECOND DIVISION C (2)

	Pl	W	D	L	F	A	Pts
Smouha	30	19	8	3	61	26	65
Al Koroum	30	13	14	3	42	20	53
Baladeyet Al Mahalla	30	15	6	9	38	32	51
Olympic	30	14	8	8	39	28	50
Ala'ab Damanhour	30	12	9	9	37	34	45
Tanta FC	30	9	13	8	31	25	40
Shabab Al Hamam	30	9	12	9	27	28	39
Abou Qair Semadis	30	9	10	11	36	40	37
Nabrouh	30	9	9	12	38	44	36
Samanod	30	8	11	11	31	38	35
Razja'h	30	7	14	9	29	36	35
Meyah Al Behairah	30	7	13	10	24	32	34
Maleyet Kafr Al Zayiat	30	5	18	7	29	32	33
Kafr Al Sheikh	30	8	7	15	31	43	31
Al Zarqa	30	5	14	11	31	41	29
Al Senbellawin	30	3	10	17	23	48	19

23/09/2009 - 12/05/2010

MEDALS TABLE

		Overall			League			Cup			Africa			City
		G	S	B	G	S	B	G	S	B	G	S	B	
1	Al Ahly	79	22	5	35	10	2	35	10		10	2	3	Cairo
2	Zamalek	38	40	10	11	29	6	21	10		6	1	4	Cairo
3	Al Tersana	7	8	7	1	4	7	6	4					Cairo
4	Mokawloon	7	3	2	1			3	3		3		1	Cairo
5	Ismaily	6	12	19	3	6	15	2		4	1	2	4	Ismailya
6	Al Ittihad	6	4	3				2	6	4			1	Alexandria
7	Olympic	3	3	1	1			2	3					Alexandria
8	Haras Al Hedod	2		1				1	2					Alexandria
9	Al Masry	1	9	7				5	1	9			2	Port Said
10	Ghazl Al Mehalla	1	7	6	1		5		6			1	1	Al Mehalla
11	ENPPI	1	3	2		1	1	1	2			1		Cairo
12	Suez	1	3	1				1	1	3				Suez
13	Al Teram	1						1						Alexandria
14	Sekka	6						6						Cairo
15	Mansoura	1	2					1				1		Mansoura

EGYPT CUP 2009-10

Second Round

Team	Score
Haras Al Hedod	1
Senbellawin *	0
Ittihad Al Shorta	0 3p
Razia'h *	0 5p
Al Masry *	2
Telefonad Beni Suef	0
Misr Al Maqasah	0
Mokawloon *	2
Ittihad *	1
Al Tersana	0
Al Mansoura	2 1p
Tanta *	2 4p
Al Jaish	2
Al Nasr Taadin *	0
Aluminium Nag Hammadi	0
Ismaily *	3
Intag Harby	2
Al Nasr Egypt *	1
Al Dakhleya	2 3p
Al Gouna	2 4p
Assiout Petrol *	5
Al Koroum	3
Gasco *	0
ENPPI	1
Petrojet	3
Olympi Al Qanal *	0
Ghazl Al Mehalla	2 3p
Al Rabat we Al Anwar *	2 4p
Zamalek	1
Al Fayoum *	0
Nabrouh *	0
Al Ahly	3

Third Round

Team	Score
Haras Al Hedod *	2
Razia'h *	1
Al Masry *	2
Mokawloon	3
Ittihad *	6
Tanta	1
Al Jaish	0
Ismaily *	4
Intag Harby *	2 4p
Al Gouna	2 2p
Assiout Petrol *	0
ENPPI *	5
Petrojet	2
Al Rabat we Al Anwar *	0
Zamalek	1
Al Ahly	3

Quarter-finals

Team	Score
Haras Al Hedod *	3
Mokawloon	1
Ittihad	1 3p
Ismaily *	1 5p
Intag Harby *	2
ENPPI	1
Petrojet	0
Al Ahly *	1

Semi-finals

Team	Score
Haras Al Hedod *	2
Ismaily	1
Intag Harby	1
Al Ahly *	2

Final

Team	Score
Haras Al Hedod ‡	1 5p
Al Ahly	1 4p

CUP FINAL

Cairo Stadium
7-06-2010, 20.30
Scorers - Salem Safi [45] for Haras; Barakat [82] for Ahly

Haras - Ali Farag - Islam Al Shater, Islam Ramadan, Ahmed Salem Safi, Ahmed Kamal - Abdul Rahman Mohie, Mohamed Halim, Mohamed Mekki - Ahmed Hassan Mekki, Ahmed Abdul Ghanie, Ahmed Eid. Tr: Tarek Al Ashri

Ahly - Sherif Ekrami - Ahmed Al Sayed, Sayed Moawad, Sherif Abdul-Fadil, Wael Gomaa - Ahmed Fathie, Hossam Ashour, Shebab Ahmed, Mohamed Aboutreika, Mohamed Barakat - Mohemed Fadl. Tr: Hossam Al Badri

* Home team ● ‡ Qualified for the CAF Confederation Cup

ENG – ENGLAND

FIFA/COCA-COLA WORLD RANKING

1993	1994	1995	1996	1997	1998	1999	2000	2001	2002	2003	2004	2005	2006	2007	2008	2009	2010
11	18	21	12	4	9	12	17	10	7	8	8	9	5	12	8	9	6

2010												Hi/Lo
Jan	Feb	Mar	Mar	Apr	May	Jul	Aug	Sep	Oct	Nov	Dec	**4**
9	9	8	7	8	8	7	7	6	6	6	6	**27**

2010 was not a vintage year for English football. The national team put in a feeble performance at the FIFA World Cup finals in South Africa, the FA failed in its bid to secure England the hosting of the 2018 finals whilst English clubs failed to progress beyond the quarter-finals in the UEFA Champions League for the first time since 2003. Despite huge public expectation, England only just reached the last 16 in South Africa before suffering their heaviest-ever defeat in the World Cup finals, a 4-1 thrashing at the hands of Germany. Not even a disallowed Frank Lampard goal against the Germans that was clearly over line with the score at 1-2, could paper over the gulf in class between England and the top teams at the finals. At home, Carlo Ancelotti enjoyed a season to remember as he led Chelsea to an historic first League and FA Cup double having taken over at the start of the season. In the League they became the first club since Spurs in 1961 to score more than 100 goals as they finished a point ahead of Manchester United, who failed in their quest to win four consecutive titles. The Old Trafford club had to be content with retaining the League Cup in a season during which their huge debt, Portsmouth's financial collapse and the indiscretions in the private lives of a number of high profile footballers were major talking points.

FIFA WORLD CUP RECORD

1930-1938 DNE **1950** 8 r1 **1954** 6 QF **1958** 11 r1 **1962** 8 QF **1966** 1 Winners (Hosts) **1970** 8 QF 1974-1978 DNQ **1982** 6 r2 **1986** 8 QF **1990** 4 SF 1994 DNQ **1998** 9 r2 **2002** 6 QF **2006** 7 QF **2010** 13 r2

THE FOOTBALL ASSOCIATION (FA)

Wembley Stadium,
PO Box 1966,
London SW1P 9EQ
☎ +44 844 9808200
🖷 +44 844 9808201
✉ communique@thefa.com
🖥 www.TheFA.com
FA 1863 CON 1954 FIFA 1905
P David Bernstein
GS Alex Horne

FIFA BIG COUNT 2006

Total players	4 164 110
% of population	8.47%
Male	3 829 000
Female	335 110
Amateurs 18+	656 800
Youth under 18	820 000
Unregistered	2 415 000
Professionals	6 110
Referees	33 186
Admin & coaches	135 000
Number of clubs	40 000
Number of teams	119 000

MAJOR CITIES/TOWNS

		Population
1	London	7 683 316
2	Birmingham	945 747
3	Liverpool	454 654
4	Leeds	441 108
5	Sheffield	417 666
6	Manchester	396 309
7	Bristol	374 037
8	Leicester	294 864
9	Bradford	280 407
10	Coventry	271 129
11	Hull	263 227
12	Plymouth	251 916
13	Stoke-on-Trent	248 276
14	Wolverhampton	246 754
15	Derby	244 663
16	Nottingham	237 567
17	Southampton	234 791
18	Portsmouth	201 808
19	Dudley	193 161

ENGLAND (PART OF THE UNITED KINGDOM)

Capital	London	Population	49 138 831 (23)	% in cities	90%
GDP per capita	$43 785 (20)	Area km²	130 439 km² (96)	GMT + / -	0
Neighbours (km)	Scotland 164, Wales 468 • Coast 3200				

RECENT INTERNATIONAL MATCHES PLAYED BY ENGLAND

2007	Opponents	Score	Venue	Comp	Scorers	Att	Referee
22-08	Germany	L 1-2	London	Fr	Lampard [9]	86 133	Busacca SUI
8-09	Israel	W 3-0	London	ECq	Wright-Phillips [20], Owen [49], Richards [66]	85 372	Vink NED
12-09	Russia	W 3-0	London	ECq	Owen 2 [7 31], Ferdinand [84]	86 106	Hansson SWE
13-10	Estonia	W 3-0	London	ECq	Wright-Phillips [11], Rooney [32], Rahm OG [33]	86 655	Vollquartz DEN
17-10	Russia	L 1-2	Moscow	ECq	Rooney [29]	84 700	Medina ESP
16-11	Austria	W 1-0	Vienna	Fr	Crouch [44]	39 432	Vollquartz DEN
21-11	Croatia	L 2-3	London	ECq	Lampard [56p], Crouch [65]	88 091	Frojdfeldt SWE
2008							
6-02	Switzerland	W 2-1	London	Fr	Jenas [40], Wright-Phillips [62]	86 857	Brych GER
26-03	France	L 0-1	Paris	Fr		78 500	Meyer GER
28-05	USA	W 2-0	London	Fr	Terry [38], Gerrard [59]	71 233	Vassaras GRE
1-06	Trinidad and Tobago	W 3-0	Port of Spain	Fr	Barry [12], Defoe 2 [15 49]	25 001	Wijngaarde SUR
20-08	Czech Republic	D 2-2	London	Fr	Brown [45], Cole.J [92+]	69 738	Hauge NOR
6-09	Andorra	W 2-0	Barcelona	WCq	Cole.J 2 [48 55]	10 300	Cakir TUR
10-09	Croatia	W 4-1	Zagreb	WCq	Walcott 3 [26 59 82], Rooney [63]	35 218	Michel SVK
11-10	Kazakhstan	W 5-1	London	WCq	Ferdinand [52], OG [64], Rooney 2 [76 86], Defoe [90]	89 107	Allarts BEL
15-10	Belarus	W 3-1	Minsk	WCq	Gerrard [1], Rooney 2 [50 74]	29 600	Hauge NOR
19-11	Germany	W 2-1	Berlin	Fr	Upson [23], Terry [84]	74 244	Busacca SUI
2009							
11-02	Spain	L 0-2	Seville	Fr		42 102	Lannoy FRA
28-03	Slovakia	W 4-0	London	Fr	Heskey [7], Rooney 2 [70 90], Lampard [82]	85 512	Hamer LUX
1-04	Ukraine	W 2-1	London	WCq	Crouch [29], Terry [85]	87 548	Larsen Den
6-06	Kazakhstan	W 4-0	Almaty	WCq	Barry [40], Heskey [45], Rooney [72], Lampard [77p]	24 000	Jakobsson ISL
10-06	Andorra	W 6-0	London	WCq	Rooney 2 [4 39], Lampard [29], Defoe 2 [73 75], Crouch [80]	57 897	Nijhuis NED
12-08	Netherlands	D 2-2	Amsterdam	Fr	Defoe 2 [49 77]	48 000	Rizzoli ITA
5-09	Slovenia	W 2-1	London	Fr	Lampard [31p], Defoe [63]	67 232	Eriksson SWE
9-09	Croatia	W 5-1	London	WCq	Lampard 2 [7p 59], Gerrard 2 [18 67], Rooney [77]	87 319	Undiano ESP
10-10	Ukraine	L 0-1	Dnepropetrovsk	WCq		31 000	Skomina SVN
14-10	Belarus	W 3-0	London	WCq	Crouch 2 [4 76], Wright-Phillips [60]	76 897	Batista POR
14-11	Brazil	L 0-1	Doha	Fr		50 000	Abdou QAT
2010							
3-03	Egypt	W 3-1	London	Fr	Crouch 2 [56 80], Wright-Phillips [75]	80 602	Torres PAR
24-05	Mexico	W 3-1	London	Fr	King [17], Crouch [34], Johnson [47]	88 638	Toma JPN
30-05	Japan	W 2-1	Graz	Fr	Tanaka.MT OG [72], Nakazawa OG [83]	15 326	Eisner AUT
12-06	USA	D 1-1	Rustenburg	WCr1	Gerrard [4]	38 646	Simon BRA
18-06	Algeria	D 0-0	Cape Town	WCr1		64 100	Irmatov UZB
23-06	Slovenia	W 1-0	Port Elizabeth	WCr1	Defoe [23]	36 893	Stark GER
27-06	Germany	L 1-4	Bloemfontein	WCr2	Upson [37]	40 510	Larrionda URU
11-08	Hungary	W 2-1	London	Fr	Gerrard 2 [69 73]	72 024	Lannoy FRA
3-09	Bulgaria	W 4-0	London	ECq	Defoe 3 [3 61 86], Johnson.A [83]	73 426	Kassai HUN
7-09	Switzerland	W 3-1	Basel	ECq	Rooney [10], Johnson.A [69], Bent [88]	37 500	Rizzoli ITA
12-10	Montenegro	D 0-0	London	ECq		73 451	Grafe GER
17-11	France	L 1-2	London	Fr	Crouch [86]	85 495	Larsen DEN

Fr = Friendly • EC = UEFA EURO 2008/2012 • WC = FIFA World Cup • q = qualifier

ENGLAND NATIONAL TEAM HISTORICAL RECORDS

Caps

125 - Peter Shilton 1970-90 • **115** - David Beckham 1996-2009 • **108** - Bobby Moore 1962-73 • **106** - Bobby Charlton 1958-70 • **105** - Billy Wright 1946-59 • **90** - Bryan Robson 1980-91 • **89** - Michael Owen 1998-2008 & Steven Gerrard 2000- • **86** - Ashley Cole 2001- • **85** - Gary Neville 1995-2007 • **84** - Ray Wilkins 1976-86 • **82** - Frank Lampard 1999- • **80** - Rio Ferdinand 1997- & Gary Lineker 1984-92 • **79** - John Barnes 1983-95 • **78** - Stuart Pearce 1987-99 • **77** - Terry Butcher 1980-90 • **76** - Tom Finney 1946-58 • **75** - David Seaman 1988-2002 • **73** - Gordon Banks 1963-72 & Sol Campbell 1996-2007 • **72** - Alan Ball 1965-75 • **68** - Wayne Rooney 2003-

Goals

49 - Bobby Charlton 1958-70 • **48** - Gary Lineker 1984-92 • **44** - Jimmy Greaves 1959-67 • **40** - Michael Owen 1998-2008 • **30** - Tom Finney 1946-58, Nat Lofthouse 1950-58 & Alan Shearer 1992-2000 • **29** - Vivian Woodward 1903-11 • **28** - Steve Bloomer 1895-1907 • **27** - David Platt 1986-96 • **26** - Bryan Robson 1980-91 • **25** - Wayne Rooney 2003- • **24** - Geoff Hurst 1966-72 • **23** - Stan Mortensen 1947-53 • **22** - Tommy Lawton 1938-48 & Peter Crouch 2005- • **21** - Mick Channon 1972-77 & Kevin Keegan 1972-82 • **20** - Martin Peters 1966-74 & Frank Lampard 1999- • **19** - Steven Gerrard 2000- • **18** - George Camsell 1929-36, Dixie Dean 1927-32, Roger Hunt 1962-69 & Johnny Haynes 1954-62 • **17** - David Beckham 1996-2009 • **16** - Tommy Taylor 1953-57 & Tony Woodcock 1978-86 • **15** - Jermain Defoe 2004-

Past Coaches

Walter Winterbottom 1946-63 • Alf Ramsey 1963-74 • Joe Mercer 1974 • Don Revie 1974-77 • Ron Greenwood 1977-82 • Bobby Robson 1982-90 • Graham Taylor 1990-93 • Terry Venables 1994-96 • Glenn Hoddle 1996-99 • Howard Wilkinson 1999 • Kevin Keegan 1999-2000 • Howard Wilkinson 2000 • Peter Taylor 2000 • Sven-Goran Eriksson SWE 2001-06 • Steve McLaren 2006-07 • Fabio Capello ITA 2008-

MEDALS TABLE

		Overall			League			Cup			LC			Europe		
		G	S	B	G	S	B	G	S	B	G	S	B	G	S	B
1	Liverpool	40	24	24	18	12	7	7	6	9	7	3	3	8	3	5
2	Manchester United	37	26	28	18	14	6	11	7	8	4	4	4	4	1	9
3	Arsenal	27	23	24	13	8	7	10	7	9	2	4	7	2	4	1
4	Aston Villa	20	16	17	7	10	2	7	3	10	5	3	5	1		
5	Tottenham Hotspur	17	9	27	2	4	9	8	1	9	4	3	6	3	1	3
6	Chelsea	16	10	25	4	3	5	6	4	9	4	2	4	2	1	7
7	Everton	15	17	20	9	7	7	5	8	11		2	2	1		
8	Newcastle United	11	10	8	4	2	4	6	7	3		1		1		1
9	Blackburn Rovers	10	3	18	3	1	3	6	2	10	1		5			
10	Wolverhampton Wanderers	9	10	14	3	5	6	4	4	6	2		1		1	1
11	Manchester City	9	8	5	2	3	3	4	4	2	2	1	3	1		1
12	Nottingham Forest	9	5	14	1	2	4	2	1	9	4	2		2		1
13	Sunderland	8	8	18	6	5	8	2	2	8		1	2			
14	Sheffield Wednesday	8	5	19	4	1	7	3	3	10	1	1	2			
15	Leeds United	7	12	13	3	5	2	1	3	4	1	1	3	2	3	4
16	West Bromwich Albion	7	9	12	1	2	1	5	5	10	1	2	1			
17	Sheffield United	5	4	8	1	2		4	2	7			1			
18	The Wanderers	5						5								
19	Preston North End	4	11	5	2	6	2	2	5	3						
20	Huddersfield Town	4	7	6	3	3	3	1	4	2			1			
21	Bolton Wanderers	4	5	11			3	4	3	6	2	2				
22	West Ham United	4	5	9			1	3	2	2		2	5	1	1	1
23	Portsmouth	4	3	3	2			2	3	2						
24	Leicester City	3	7	5		1	1		4	4	3	2				
25	Derby County	3	6	16	2	3	4	1	3	9			2			1
26	Burnley	3	4	14	2	2	5	1	2	5			4			
27	Ipswich Town	3	2	8	1	2	3	1		2			3	1		

ENGLAND 2009–10

BARCLAYS PREMIER LEAGUE

	Pl	W	D	L	F	A	Pts	Chelsea	Man Utd	Arsenal	Spurs	Man City	Aston Villa	Liverpool	Everton	B'ham City	Blackburn	Stoke City	Fulham	Sunderland	Bolton	Wolves	Wigan Ath	West Ham	Burnley	Hull City	Portsmouth
Chelsea †	38	27	5	6	103	32	86		1-0	2-0	3-0	2-4	7-1	2-0	3-3	3-0	5-0	7-0	2-1	7-2	1-0	4-0	8-0	4-1	3-0	2-1	2-1
Manchester United †	38	27	4	7	86	28	85	1-2		2-1	3-1	4-3	0-1	2-1	3-0	1-0	2-0	4-0	3-0	2-2	2-1	3-0	5-0	3-0	3-0	4-0	5-0
Arsenal †	38	23	6	9	83	41	75	0-3	1-3		3-0	0-0	3-0	1-0	2-2	3-1	6-2	2-0	4-0	2-0	4-2	1-0	4-0	2-0	3-1	3-0	4-1
Tottenham Hotspur †	38	21	7	10	67	41	70	2-1	1-3	2-1		3-0	0-0	2-1	2-1	2-1	3-1	0-1	2-0	2-0	1-0	0-1	9-1	2-0	5-0	0-0	2-0
Manchester City ‡	38	18	13	7	73	45	67	2-1	0-1	4-2	0-1		3-1	0-0	0-2	5-1	4-1	2-0	2-2	4-3	2-0	1-0	3-0	3-1	3-3	1-1	2-0
Aston Villa ‡	38	17	13	8	52	39	64	2-1	1-1	0-0	1-1	1-1		0-1	2-2	1-0	0-1	1-0	2-0	1-1	5-1	2-2	0-2	0-0	5-2	3-0	2-0
Liverpool ‡	38	18	9	11	61	35	63	0-2	2-0	1-2	2-0	2-2	1-3		1-0	2-2	2-1	4-0	0-0	3-0	2-0	2-0	2-1	3-0	4-0	6-1	4-1
Everton	38	16	13	9	60	49	61	2-1	3-1	1-6	2-2	2-0	1-1	0-2		1-1	3-0	1-1	2-1	2-0	2-0	1-1	2-1	2-2	2-0	5-1	1-0
Birmingham City	38	13	11	14	38	47	50	0-0	1-1	1-1	1-1	0-0	0-1	1-1	1-2		2-1	0-0	1-0	0-1	2-1	1-2	2-1	1-0	1-0	2-1	0-0	1-0
Blackburn Rovers	38	13	11	14	41	55	50	1-1	0-0	2-1	0-2	0-2	2-1	0-0	2-3	2-1		0-0	2-0	2-2	3-0	3-1	2-1	0-0	3-2	1-0	3-1
Stoke City	38	11	14	13	34	48	47	1-2	0-2	1-3	1-2	1-1	0-0	1-1	0-0	0-1	3-0		3-2	1-0	1-2	2-2	2-2	2-1	2-0	2-0	1-0
Fulham	38	12	10	16	39	46	46	0-2	3-0	0-1	0-0	1-2	0-2	3-1	2-1	2-1	3-0	0-1		1-0	1-1	0-0	2-1	3-2	3-0	2-0	1-0
Sunderland	38	11	11	16	48	56	44	1-3	0-1	1-0	3-1	1-1	0-2	1-0	1-1	3-1	2-1	0-0	0-0		4-0	5-2	1-1	2-2	2-1	4-1	1-1
Bolton Wanderers	38	10	9	19	42	67	39	0-4	0-4	0-2	2-2	3-3	0-1	2-3	3-2	2-1	0-2	1-1	0-0	0-1		1-0	4-0	3-1	1-0	2-2	2-2
Wolverhampton Wand	38	9	11	18	32	56	38	0-2	0-1	1-4	1-0	0-3	0-0	0-0	0-1	1-1	0-0	2-1	2-1	2-1		0-2	0-2	2-0	1-1	0-1	
Wigan Athletic	38	9	9	20	37	79	36	3-1	0-5	3-2	0-3	1-1	1-2	1-0	0-1	2-3	1-1	1-1	1-1	1-0	0-0	0-1		1-0	1-0	2-2	0-0
West Ham United	38	8	11	19	47	66	35	1-1	0-4	2-2	1-2	1-1	2-1	2-3	1-2	2-0	0-0	0-1	2-2	1-0	1-1	3-2		5-3	3-0	2-0
Burnley	38	8	6	24	42	82	30	1-2	1-0	1-1	4-2	1-6	1-1	0-4	1-0	2-1	0-1	1-1	1-1	3-1	1-1	1-1	2-1		2-0	1-2
Hull City	38	6	12	20	34	75	30	1-1	1-3	1-2	1-5	2-1	0-2	0-0	3-2	0-1	0-0	2-1	2-0	0-1	1-0	2-2	2-1	3-3	1-4		0-0
Portsmouth §9	38	7	7	24	34	66	19	0-5	1-4	1-4	1-2	0-1	1-2	2-0	0-1	1-2	0-0	1-2	0-1	1-1	2-3	3-1	4-0	1-1	2-0	3-2	

15/08/2009 - 9/05/2010 • † Qualified for the UEFA Champions League • ‡ Qualified for the Europa League • § = points deducted
Top scorers: **29** - Didier Drogba CIV, Chelsea • **26** - Wayne Rooney, Man Utd • **24** - Darren Bent, Sunderland • **23** - Carlos Tevez ARG, Man City •
22 - Frank Lampard, Chelsea • **18** - Jermain Defoe, Tottenham & Fernando Torres ESP, Liverpool • **15** - Cesc Fabregas ESP, Arsenal

ENGLAND 2009-10

COCA-COLA FOOTBALL LEAGUE CHAMPIONSHIP (2)

Team	Pl	W	D	L	F	A	Pts
Newcastle United	46	30	12	4	90	35	102
West Bromwich Alb	46	26	13	7	89	48	91
Nottingham Forest ‡	46	22	13	11	65	40	79
Cardiff City ‡	46	22	10	14	73	54	76
Leicester City ‡	46	21	13	12	61	45	76
Blackpool ‡	46	19	13	14	74	58	70
Swansea City	46	17	18	11	40	37	69
Sheffield United	46	17	14	15	62	55	65
Reading	46	17	12	17	68	63	63
Bristol City	46	15	18	13	56	65	63
Middlesbrough	46	16	14	16	58	50	62
Doncaster Rovers	46	15	15	16	59	58	60
Queens Park Rang's	46	14	15	17	58	65	57
Derby County	46	15	11	20	53	63	56
Ipswich Town	46	12	20	14	50	61	56
Watford	46	14	12	20	61	68	54
Preston North End	46	13	15	18	58	73	54
Barnsley	46	14	12	20	53	69	54
Coventry City	46	13	15	18	47	64	54
Scunthorpe United	46	14	10	22	62	84	52
Crystal Palace §10	46	14	17	15	50	53	49
Sheffield Wed'day	46	11	14	21	49	69	47
Plymouth Argyle	46	11	8	27	43	68	41
Peterborough Utd	46	8	10	28	46	80	34

7/08/2009 - 2/05/2010 • ‡ Qualified for the play-offs • § = points deducted • Top scorer: 22 - Peter Whittingham, Cardiff

Play-off semi-finals: **Blackpool** 2-1 4-3 Nottingham Forest • Leicester City 0-1 3-2 3-4p **Cardiff City**

Play-off final: **Blackpool** 3-2 Cardiff City, Wembley, 22-05-2010, Att: 82 244, Ref: Marriner. Scorers - Adam [13,] Taylor-Fletcher [41,] Ormerod [45] for Blackpool; Chopra [9,] Ledley [37] for Cardiff City

ENGLAND 2009-10

COCA-COLA FOOTBALL LEAGUE ONE (3)

Team	Pl	W	D	L	F	A	Pts
Norwich City	46	29	8	9	89	47	95
Leeds United	46	25	11	10	77	44	86
Millwall ‡	46	24	13	9	76	44	85
Charlton Athletic ‡	46	23	15	8	73	57	84
Swindon Town ‡	46	22	16	8	71	48	82
Huddersfield Town ‡	46	23	11	12	82	56	80
Southampton §10	46	23	14	9	85	47	73
Colchester United	46	20	12	14	64	52	72
Brentford	46	14	20	12	55	52	62
Walsall	46	16	14	16	60	63	62
Bristol Rovers	46	19	5	22	59	70	62
Milton Keynes Dons	46	17	9	20	60	68	60
Brighton & Hove Alb	46	15	14	17	56	60	59
Carlisle United	46	15	13	18	63	66	58
Yeovil Town	46	13	14	19	55	59	53
Oldham Athletic	46	13	13	20	39	57	52
Leyton Orient	46	13	12	21	53	63	51
Exeter City	46	11	18	17	48	60	51
Tranmere Rovers	46	14	9	23	45	72	51
Hartlepool §3	46	14	11	21	59	67	50
Gillingham	46	12	14	20	48	64	50
Wycombe Wanderers	46	10	15	21	56	76	45
Southend United	46	10	13	23	51	72	43
Stockport County	46	5	10	31	35	95	25

8/08/2009 - 8/05/2010 • ‡ Qualified for the play-offs • § = points deducted • Top scorer: 31 - Rickie Lambert, Southampton

Play-off semi-finals: Huddersfield 0-0 0-2 **Millwall** • **Swindon Town** 2-1 1-2 5-4p Charlton Athletic

Play-off final: Millwall 1-0 Swindon Town, Wembley, 29-05-2010, Att: 73 108, Ref: Webster. Scorer - Robinson [39] for Millwall

ENGLAND 2009–10

COCA-COLA FOOTBALL LEAGUE TWO (4)

	Pl	W	D	L	F	A	Pts
Notts County	46	27	12	7	96	31	**93**
Bournemouth	46	25	8	13	61	44	**83**
Rochdale	46	25	7	14	82	48	**82**
Morecambe ‡	46	20	13	13	73	64	**73**
Rotherham United ‡	46	21	10	15	55	52	**73**
Aldershot Town ‡	46	20	12	14	69	56	**72**
Dagenham & Red. ‡	46	20	12	14	69	58	**72**
Chesterfield	46	21	7	18	61	62	**70**
Bury	46	19	12	15	54	59	**69**
Port Vale	46	17	17	12	61	50	**68**
Northampton Town	46	18	13	15	62	53	**67**
Shrewsbury Town	46	17	12	17	55	54	**63**
Burton Albion	46	17	11	18	71	71	**62**
Bradford City	46	16	14	16	59	62	**62**
Accrington Stanley	46	18	7	21	62	74	**61**
Hereford United	46	17	8	21	54	65	**59**
Torquay United	46	14	15	17	64	55	**57**
Crewe Alexandra	46	15	10	21	68	73	**55**
Macclesfield Town	46	12	18	16	49	58	**54**
Lincoln City	46	13	11	22	42	65	**50**
Barnet	46	12	12	22	47	63	**48**
Cheltenham Town	46	10	18	18	54	71	**48**
Grimsby Town	46	9	17	20	45	71	**44**
Darlington	46	8	6	32	33	87	**30**

	Notts Co	B'mouth	Rochdale	M'cambe	Rotherham	Aldershot	Dagenham	Chesterfield	Bury	Port Vale	Northants	Shrewsbury	Burton Alb	Bradford C	Accrington	Hereford U	Torquay U	Crewe Alex	Macc'field	Lincoln C	Barnet	Cheltenham	Grimsby T	Darlington
Notts County		2-2	1-0	4-1	1-0	0-0	3-0	1-0	5-0	3-1	5-2	1-1	1-1	5-0	1-2	5-0	2-2	2-0	1-0	3-1	2-0	5-0	1-1	4-0
Bournemouth	2-1		0-4	1-0	1-0	1-0	0-0	1-2	1-2	4-0	0-2	1-0	1-0	1-0	2-0	2-1	2-1	1-0	1-1	3-1	3-0	0-0	3-1	2-0
Rochdale	2-1	0-0		4-1	4-0	1-0	3-1	2-3	3-0	0-0	1-0	4-0	1-2	1-3	1-2	4-1	2-1	2-0	3-0	1-1	2-1	0-1	4-1	0-1
Morecambe	2-1	5-0	3-3		2-0	1-0	1-0	0-1	3-0	1-0	2-4	1-1	3-2	0-0	1-2	2-2	2-0	4-3	2-2	3-1	2-1	1-0	1-1	2-0
Rotherham United	0-0	1-3	2-1	0-0		0-0	2-0	3-1	1-0	1-2	1-0	1-1	2-2	1-2	1-0	1-1	1-1	0-0	3-1	2-0	3-0	0-0	2-1	1-2
Aldershot Town	1-1	2-1	1-1	4-1	3-0		2-3	1-0	2-3	1-1	2-1	2-0	0-2	1-0	3-1	2-2	0-2	1-1	0-0	3-1	4-0	4-1	1-1	3-1
Dagenham & Red.	0-3	1-0	1-2	1-1	0-1	2-5		2-1	3-1	1-1	0-1	5-0	2-1	2-1	3-1	2-1	5-3	2-0	3-1	3-0	4-1	0-2	2-0	2-0
Chesterfield	2-1	2-1	2-0	1-1	0-1	0-1	2-2		1-0	0-5	1-0	0-1	5-2	1-1	1-0	1-2	1-0	2-3	4-1	2-1	1-0	1-0	3-2	5-2
Bury	3-3	0-3	1-0	0-0	2-1	1-2	0-0	2-1		1-1	2-2	1-0	3-0	2-1	0-2	1-0	0-3	3-0	2-1	2-0	2-0	0-1	0-1	1-1
Port Vale	2-1	0-0	1-1	0-2	1-2	1-1	3-1	1-2	0-1		1-3	1-1	3-1	2-1	2-2	2-0	2-2	0-1	0-0	4-0	0-2	1-1	4-0	1-0
Northampton Town	0-1	2-0	1-2	2-0	3-1	0-3	1-0	0-0	1-1	1-1		2-0	1-1	2-2	4-0	1-3	0-0	2-2	0-0	1-0	1-3	2-1	0-0	2-0
Shrewsbury Town	0-1	1-0	0-1	2-3	2-0	3-1	2-1	1-1	1-1	0-1	3-0		3-1	1-2	0-1	3-1	1-1	2-0	2-2	1-0	2-0	0-0	0-0	0-2
Burton Albion	1-4	0-2	1-0	5-2	0-1	6-1	0-1	2-2	0-0	1-0	3-2	1-1		1-1	0-2	3-2	0-2	1-2	1-1	1-0	2-0	5-6	3-0	1-2
Bradford City	0-0	1-1	0-3	2-0	2-4	2-1	3-3	3-0	0-1	0-0	2-0	1-3	1-1		1-1	1-0	2-0	2-3	1-2	0-2	2-1	1-1	0-0	1-0
Accrington Stanley	0-3	0-1	2-4	3-2	2-1	2-1	0-1	2-0	2-4	1-2	0-3	1-3	0-2	2-0		1-2	4-2	5-3	1-1	1-0	1-0	4-0	2-3	2-1
Hereford United	0-2	2-1	2-1	0-1	3-0	2-0	1-1	1-0	1-3	2-2	0-2	2-1	3-4	2-0	2-0		1-0	1-1	0-2	2-0	2-1	1-1	0-1	2-1
Torquay United	0-0	1-2	5-0	2-2	0-2	1-1	0-0	2-0	1-1	1-2	1-0	2-1	2-3	1-2	2-1	1-0		1-1	1-0	2-3	0-1	3-0	0-2	5-0
Crewe Alexandra	0-1	1-2	2-2	1-2	2-3	1-2	1-2	0-1	2-3	1-2	3-2	0-3	2-1	0-1	5-1	1-0	1-1		2-1	0-0	2-2	1-2	4-2	3-0
Macclesfield Town	0-4	1-2	0-1	2-2	1-3	1-1	2-2	2-0	2-0	2-0	0-2	0-1	1-1	2-2	0-0	3-1	2-1	4-1		0-1	1-1	1-0	0-0	0-2
Lincoln City	0-3	2-1	1-3	1-3	1-2	1-0	1-1	2-1	1-0	1-2	1-1	0-2	0-2	2-1	2-1	3-1	0-0	1-1	0-0		1-0	1-1	0-0	3-0
Barnet	1-0	1-1	1-0	2-0	0-1	3-0	2-0	3-1	0-0	0-0	0-0	2-2	1-1	2-2	1-2	0-0	1-1	1-2	1-2	1-2		1-1	3-0	3-0
Cheltenham Town	1-1	0-1	1-4	2-0	1-1	1-2	1-1	0-1	5-2	1-1	2-2	1-2	0-1	4-5	1-1	0-1	1-1	0-4	1-2	1-0	5-1		2-1	3-3
Grimsby Town	0-1	3-2	0-2	1-1	1-2	1-2	1-1	2-2	1-1	1-2	1-2	3-0	1-2	0-3	2-2	1-0	0-3	0-4	1-1	2-2	2-0	0-0		1-1
Darlington	0-5	0-2	0-2	0-4	2-0	1-2	0-2	2-3	0-1	1-3	1-2	2-1	1-0	0-1	0-0	0-1	1-3	0-1	0-1	1-1	1-2	1-1	0-2	

8/08/2009 - 8/05/2010 • ‡ Qualified for the play-offs • § = points deducted • Top scorer: **30** - Lee Hughes, Notts County

Play-off semi-finals: **Dagenham & Redbridge** 6-0 1-2 Morecambe • Aldershot 0-1 0-2 **Rotherham**

Play-off final: **Dagenham & Redbridge** 3-2 Rotherham, Wembley, 30-05-2010, Att: 32 054, Ref: Linington. Scorers - Benson [38], Green [56], Nurse [70] for Dagenham & Redbridge; Taylor 2 [39] [61] for Rotherham

ENGLAND 2009–10

FOOTBALL CONFERENCE BLUE SQUARE PREMIER (5)

	Pl	W	D	L	F	A	Pts
Stevenage Borough	44	30	9	5	79	24	**99**
Luton Town	44	26	10	8	84	40	**88**
Oxford United	44	25	11	8	64	31	**86**
Rushden & D'monds	44	22	13	9	77	39	**79**
York City	44	22	12	10	62	35	**78**
Kettering Town	44	18	12	14	51	41	**66**
Crawley Town	44	19	9	16	50	57	**66**
AFC Wimbledon	44	18	10	16	61	47	**64**
Mansfield Town	44	17	11	16	69	60	**62**
Cambridge United	44	15	14	15	65	53	**59**
Wrexham	44	15	13	16	45	39	**58**
Salisbury City §10	44	21	5	18	58	63	**58**
Kidderminster Har's	44	15	12	17	57	52	**57**
Altrincham	44	13	15	16	53	51	**54**
Barrow	44	13	13	18	50	67	**52**
Tamworth	44	11	16	17	42	52	**49**
Hayes & Yeading	44	12	12	20	59	85	**48**
Histon	44	11	13	20	44	67	**46**
Eastbourne Boro	44	11	13	20	42	72	**46**
Gateshead §1	44	13	7	24	46	69	**45**
Forest Green	44	12	9	23	50	76	**45**
Ebbsfleet United	44	12	8	24	50	82	**44**
Grays Athletic §2	44	5	13	26	35	91	**26**
Chester City §25	28	5	7	16	23	42	**-3**

	Stevenage	Luton Town	Oxford Utd	Rushden & D	York City	Kettering T	Crawley T	Wimbledon	Mansfield T	Cambridge U	Wrexham	Salisbury C	Kid'minster	Altrincham	Barrow	Tamworth	Hayes & Y	Histon	Eastbourne	Gateshead	ForestGreen	Ebbsfleet U	Grays Ath	Chester City
Stevenage Borough		0-1	1-0	2-1	1-0	2-0	2-0	0-0	3-1	4-1	0-0	3-1	2-0	1-1	4-0	1-1	4-0	1-0	2-0	5-3	2-0	3-0	1-1	2-0
Luton Town	0-1		2-1	0-2	1-1	0-1	3-0	1-2	4-1	2-2	1-0	4-0	3-1	0-0	1-0	2-1	8-0	6-3	4-1	2-1	2-1	2-3	6-0	0-0
Oxford United	2-1	2-0		1-0	2-1	1-1	3-1	2-0	2-0	0-0	1-0	1-0	0-0	1-0	1-0	0-1	1-2	2-0	4-0	2-1	0-0	4-2	5-0	4-0
Rushden & D'monds	1-0	1-1	1-1		0-1	0-0	1-1	0-1	1-0	1-1	0-0	0-2	2-1	0-1	4-1	3-2	2-1	2-1	2-0	8-0	4-2	2-0	5-4	
York City	1-1	0-0	1-1	0-0		2-0	2-0	5-0	3-0	2-2	2-1	1-2	3-2	2-1	3-0	1-1	4-1	3-1	0-1	1-0	2-0	1-0	1-1	3-2
Kettering Town	1-1	0-0	1-1	0-3	0-1		1-1	1-2	2-2	0-1	2-2	1-2	0-2	2-0	2-1	0-0	0-1	1-1	4-0	4-0	0-2	3-0	2-0	
Crawley Town	0-3	2-1	1-2	2-1	3-1	2-1		2-1	0-2	1-0	1-0	2-0	2-2	1-0	0-1	2-0	1-0	2-0	2-2	1-4	3-1	2-1	1-1	
AFC Wimbledon	0-3	1-1	0-1	0-1	0-1	1-2	1-1		2-0	0-0	1-1	4-0	0-1	1-1	0-2	0-1	5-0	4-0	2-0	2-0	2-0	3-0	0-2	
Mansfield Town	2-3	0-0	2-1	3-2	0-1	0-0	4-0	0-1		2-1	0-1	4-2	3-3	1-1	4-1	0-0	3-1	1-1	1-1	0-2	1-0	3-0	0-0	4-0
Cambridge United	1-3	3-4	1-1	2-2	0-1	0-2	0-1	2-2	3-2		2-0	3-1	2-0	0-0	0-2	2-0	4-1	2-1	0-1	3-0	7-0	4-0	3-0	1-0
Wrexham	0-1	3-0	0-1	0-1	1-0	1-2	2-0	1-0	2-1	2-2		1-2	2-2	1-1	0-0	0-0	0-2	3-0	3-0	0-0	1-0	1-1	2-1	0-0
Salisbury City	0-1	1-1	1-1	1-3	1-0	2-0	2-2	0-2	0-1	2-1	1-1		1-0	4-1	3-0	1-0	3-1	3-0	1-1	0-1	1-3	3-1	2-0	1-1
Kidderminster Har's	0-2	1-2	3-1	1-1	0-1	0-1	1-0	0-1	3-1	1-0	2-0	0-1		3-0	1-2	0-0	1-0	3-0	0-2	3-2	2-1	2-2	4-1	2-0
Altrincham	0-1	0-1	0-1	2-2	0-0	2-0	0-0	0-1	1-2	0-2	1-3	5-0	3-2		0-1	0-0	3-2	2-1	3-0	3-2	2-2	1-1	1-1	1-1
Barrow	0-0	0-1	1-1	1-6	0-0	0-2	4-1	2-2	3-1	0-1	2-1	0-1	1-0	0-3		1-0	1-1	0-0	3-2	3-3	1-1	2-0	2-2	
Tamworth	1-0	1-1	0-0	0-1	2-3	1-3	0-1	2-2	2-4	0-0	2-1	2-0	2-1	0-2	3-0		0-2	1-3	1-1	1-0	0-0	3-4	2-1	3-1
Hayes & Yeading	1-1	2-3	2-1	1-6	1-1	1-2	2-1	1-0	1-1	3-0	0-1	3-4	2-2	1-2	1-1	2-2		0-2	1-1	3-2	2-3	4-2	4-0	0-0
Histon	0-2	0-2	3-4	0-1	1-1	1-0	0-1	1-3	0-5	1-1	0-0	2-0	1-1	0-0	2-2	1-0	3-3		2-0	0-0	5-2	1-0	0-0	
Eastbourne Boro	0-6	0-1	1-0	1-1	3-1	0-1	0-2	1-0	1-2	2-2	2-1	0-1	0-0	2-2	2-1	1-1	3-1	1-1		2-1	1-0	1-2	2-2	1-1
Gateshead	0-1	0-1	0-1	0-0	1-2	0-2	2-1	1-0	1-3	2-0	1-0	2-1	0-2	1-0	2-1	1-1		0-3	3-0		3-1	1-3	3-0	0-1
Forest Green	0-1	0-1	0-1	1-0	2-1	1-2	1-0	2-5	1-4	1-1	0-2	3-1	1-1	4-3	1-0	3-4	0-0	2-0	1-1	1-0		0-0	2-1	
Ebbsfleet United	2-1	1-6	0-2	0-0	1-0	1-2	0-0	2-2	2-1	1-3	0-1	1-2	0-0	1-2	1-4	0-1	1-2	0-1	3-2	2-0	4-3		2-1	
Grays Athletic	1-2	0-2	0-4	0-3	0-4	0-0	2-3	2-4	1-1	2-0	0-2	0-2	1-3	0-3	3-3	1-0	0-0	0-1	1-0	0-0	2-1	0-3		1-3
Chester City	0-1	0-0		0-1				3-1	0-1	2-4		0-1		1-3		1-2		2-0		2-1	1-2	1-2		

8/08/2009 - 24/04/2010 • ‡ Qualified for the play-offs • § = points deducted • Chester City expelled on 26/02/2010 with all their games annulled

Top scorer: 27 - Matt Tubbs, Salisbury City. Richard Brodie of York City also scored 27, but the total included one scored in the play-offs

Play-off semi-finals: Rushden & Diamonds 1-1 0-2 **Oxford Utd** • **York City** 1-0 1-0 Luton Town

Play-off final: **Oxford Utd** 3-1 York, Wembley, 16-05-2010, Att: 42 669, Ref: Naylor. Scorers - Green [15], Constable [20], Potter [90] for Oxford; Clarke OG [42]

ENGLAND 2009–10
FOOTBALL CONFERENCE
BLUE SQUARE NORTH (6)

	Pl	W	D	L	F	A	Pts
Southport	40	25	11	4	91	45	86
Fleetwood Town ‡	40	26	7	7	86	44	85
Alfreton Town ‡	40	21	11	8	77	45	74
Workington ‡	40	20	10	10	46	37	70
Droylsden ‡	40	18	10	12	82	62	64
Corby Town	40	18	9	13	73	62	63
Hinckley United	40	16	14	10	60	52	62
Ilkeston Town	40	16	13	11	53	45	61
Stalybridge Celtic	40	16	7	17	71	64	55
Eastwood Town	40	15	9	16	50	55	54
AFC Telford United	40	14	9	17	52	55	51
Northwich Victoria	40	15	13	12	62	55	48
Blyth Spartans	40	13	9	18	67	72	48
Gainsborough Tr'ty	40	12	11	17	50	57	47
Hyde United	40	11	12	17	45	72	45
Stafford Rangers	40	10	14	16	59	70	44
Solihull Moors	40	11	9	20	47	58	42
Gloucester City	40	12	6	22	47	59	42
Redditch United	40	10	8	22	49	83	38
Vauxhall Motors	40	7	14	19	45	81	35
Harrogate Town	40	8	6	26	41	80	30
Farsley Celtic				Withdrew			

8/08/2009 - 24/04/2010 • ‡ Qualified for the play-offs
Play-off semis: Droylsden 2-0 1-3 **Fleetwood Town** •
Workington 0-1 1-3 **Alfreton Town**
Play-off final: **Fleetwood Town** 2-1 Alfreton Town

ENGLAND 2009–10
FOOTBALL CONFERENCE
BLUE SQUARE SOUTH (6)

	Pl	W	D	L	F	A	Pts
Newport County	42	32	7	3	93	26	103
Dover Athletic ‡	42	22	9	11	66	47	75
Chelmsford City ‡	42	22	9	11	62	48	75
Bath City ‡	42	20	12	10	66	46	72
Woking ‡	42	21	9	12	57	44	72
Havant & Wat'ville	42	19	14	9	65	44	71
Braintree Town	42	18	17	7	56	41	71
Staines Town	42	18	13	11	59	40	67
Welling United	42	18	9	15	66	51	63
Thurrock	42	16	13	13	66	60	61
Eastleigh	42	17	9	16	71	66	60
Bromley	42	15	10	17	68	64	55
St Albans City	42	15	10	17	45	55	55
Hampton & Rich'd	42	14	9	19	56	66	51
Basingstoke Town	42	13	10	19	49	68	49
Maidenhead United	42	12	12	18	52	59	48
Dorchester Town	42	13	9	20	56	74	48
Bishops Stortford	42	12	11	19	48	59	47
Lewes	42	9	15	18	49	63	42
Worcester City	42	10	10	22	48	60	40
Weston-Super-Mare	42	5	8	29	48	93	23
Weymouth	42	5	7	30	31	103	22

8/08/2009 - 24/04/2010 • ‡ Qualified for the play-offs
Play-off semis: **Woking** 2-1 0-0 Dover Athletic •
Bath City 2-0 1-0 Chelmsford
Play-off final: **Bath City** 1-0 Woking

ENGLAND 2009–10
ISTHMIAN LEAGUE
RYMAN PREMIER (7)

	Pl	W	D	L	F	A	Pts
Dartford	42	29	6	7	101	45	93
Sutton United ‡	42	22	9	11	65	45	75
Aveley ‡	42	21	7	14	83	62	70
Boreham Wood ‡	42	20	8	14	54	44	68
Kingstonian ‡	42	20	8	14	73	69	68
Wealdstone	42	17	14	11	65	65	65
Hastings United	42	18	9	15	68	56	63
Tonbridge Angels	42	18	8	16	69	67	62
AFC Hornchurch	42	16	13	13	51	47	61
Hendon	42	18	6	18	61	59	60
Horsham	42	16	8	18	65	67	56
Tooting &Mitcham	42	15	10	17	60	64	55
Billericay Town	42	14	12	16	44	42	54
Harrow Borough	42	13	14	15	66	63	53
Cray Wanderers	42	14	9	19	54	70	51
Canvey United	42	13	11	18	57	62	50
Carshalton Ath	42	12	13	17	58	64	49
Maidstone United	42	13	10	19	39	57	49
Margate	42	11	12	19	49	71	45
Ashford Town	42	11	11	20	62	80	44
Waltham Abbey	42	12	8	22	49	74	44
Bognor Regis T	42	9	14	19	45	65	41

15/08/2009 - 24/04/2010 • ‡ Play-offs
Play-off semis: Sutton Utd 2-4 **Kingstonian** •
Aveley 0-1 **Boreham Wood**
Play-off final: **Boreham Wood** 2-0 Kingstonian

ENGLAND 2009–10
SOUTHERN LEAGUE
BRITISH GAS PREMIER (7)

	Pl	W	D	L	F	A	Pts
Farnborough	42	28	9	5	100	44	93
Nuneaton Town ‡	42	26	10	6	91	37	88
Chippenham T ‡	42	21	11	10	67	43	74
Hednesford T ‡	42	20	13	9	79	51	73
Brackley Town ‡	42	21	9	12	83	61	72
Cambridge City	42	18	17	7	73	44	71
Bashley	42	20	11	11	79	61	71
Halesowen Town	42	21	7	4	84	53	70
Stourbridge	42	19	13	10	80	65	70
Leamington	42	19	8	15	84	75	65
Truro City	42	17	11	14	78	65	62
Banbury Utd	42	14	13	15	53	67	55
Oxford City	42	13	15	14	63	66	54
Swindon S'marine	42	10	14	18	48	76	44
Didcott Town	42	10	11	21	56	70	41
Evesham Utd	42	9	14	19	35	52	41
Merthyr Tydfil	42	12	11	19	62	72	37
Bedford Town	42	9	10	23	50	88	37
Tiverton Town	42	8	12	22	35	61	36
Hemel Hempstead	42	8	10	24	50	81	34
Clevedon Town	42	6	11	25	48	92	29
Rugby Town	42	4	8	30	41	114	20

15/08/2009 - 24/04/2010 • ‡ Play-offs
Play-off semis: **Nuneaton** 6-0 Brackley •
Chippenham 2-0 Hednesford
Play-off final: **Nuneaton** 2-1 Chippenham

ENGLAND 2009–10
NORTHERN LEAGUE
UNIBOND PREMIER (7)

	Pl	W	D	L	F	A	Pts
Guiseley	38	25	4	9	73	41	79
Bradford Park Av‡	38	24	6	8	94	51	78
Boston United ‡	38	23	8	7	90	34	77
North Ferriby Utd‡	38	22	9	7	70	38	75
Kendal Town ‡	38	21	8	9	75	47	71
Retford United	38	18	11	9	73	46	65
Matlock Town	38	17	9	12	72	49	60
Buxton	38	16	12	10	66	43	60
Marine	38	17	6	15	60	55	57
Nantwich Town	38	16	6	16	64	69	54
Stocksbridge PS	38	15	7	16	80	68	52
Ashton United	38	15	6	17	48	63	51
FC Utd Manchester	38	13	8	17	62	65	47
Whitby Town	38	12	10	16	56	62	46
Frickley Athletic	38	12	9	17	50	66	45
Burscough	38	13	5	20	55	65	44
Hucknall Town	38	12	8	18	65	81	44
Worksop Town	38	7	9	22	45	68	30
Ossett Town	38	6	7	25	46	92	25
Durham City	38	2	0	36	27	168	0
King's Lynn				Withdrew			
New'tle Blue Star				Withdrew			

15/08/2009 - 24/04/2010 • ‡ Play-offs
Play-off semis: **Bradford PA** 2-1 Kendal •
Boston 2-1 North Ferriby
Play-off final: Bradford PA 1-2 **Boston**

FA CUP (SPONSORED BY E.ON) 2009–10

Third Round

Chelsea *	5	
Watford	0	
Colchester United	0	
Preston North End *	7	
Leicester City *	2	
Swansea City	1	
Bristol City *	1	0
Cardiff City	1	1
Manchester City	1	
Middlesbrough *	0	
Barnsley	0	
Scunthorpe United *	1	
Arsenal	2	
West Ham United *	1	
York City	1	
Stoke City *	3	
Reading *	1	2
Liverpool	1	1
Milton Keynes Dons *	1	
Burnley	2	
Newcastle United	0	3
Plymouth Argyle *	0	0
Huddersfield Town *	0	
West Bromwich Albion	2	
Crystal Palace	2	
Sheffield Wednesday *	1	
Tranmere Rovers *	0	
Wolverhampton Wanderers	1	
Brighton & Hove Albion	1	
Torquay United *	0	
Blackburn Rovers	1	
Aston Villa *	3	
Tottenham Hotspur *	4	
Peterborough United	0	
Manchester United *	0	
Leeds United	1	
Sheffield United *	1	3
Queens Park Rangers	1	2
Lincoln City	0	
Bolton Wanderers *	4	
Notts County *	2	
Forest Green Rovers	1	
Hull City	1	
Wigan Athletic *	4	
Accrington Stanley *	1	
Gillingham	0	
Swindon Town	0	
Fulham *	1	
Birmingham City	0	1
Nottingham Forest *	0	0
Carlisle United	1	
Everton *	3	
Doncaster Rovers	1	
Brentford *	0	
Millwall *	1 1 3p	
Derby County	1 1 5p	
Southampton *	1	
Luton Town	0	
Blackpool *	1	
Ipswich Town	2	
Sunderland *	3	
Barrow	0	
Coventry City	1	1
Portsmouth *	1	2

Fourth Round

Chelsea	2	
Preston North End *	0	
Leicester City	2	
Cardiff City *	4	
Manchester City	4	
Scunthorpe United *	2	
Arsenal	1	
Stoke City *	3	
Reading *	1	
Burnley	0	
Newcastle United	2	
West Bromwich Albion *	4	
Crystal Palace	2	3
Wolverhampton Wanderers *	2	1
Brighton & Hove Albion	2	
Aston Villa *	3	
Tottenham Hotspur *	2	3
Leeds United	2	1
Sheffield United	0	
Bolton Wanderers *	2	
Notts County *	2	2
Wigan Athletic	2	0
Accrington Stanley *	1	
Fulham	3	
Birmingham City	2	
Everton *	1	
Doncaster Rovers	0	
Derby County *	1	
Southampton *	2	
Ipswich Town	1	
Sunderland	1	
Portsmouth *	2	

Fifth Round

Chelsea *	4	
Cardiff City	1	
Manchester City *	1	1
Stoke City	1	3
Reading *	2	3
West Bromwich Albion	2	2
Crystal Palace *	2	1
Aston Villa	2	3
Tottenham Hotspur	1	4
Bolton Wanderers *	1	0
Notts County	0	
Fulham *	4	
Birmingham City	2	
Derby County *	1	
Southampton *	1	
Portsmouth	4	

* Home team

FA CUP (SPONSORED BY E.ON) 2009–10

Quarter–finals   **Semi–finals**   Final

| **Chelsea** * | 2 |
| Stoke City | 0 |

| Chelsea | 3 |
| Aston Villa | 0 |

| Reading * | 2 |
| **Aston Villa** | 4 |

| Chelsea | 1 |
| Portsmouth | 0 |

| **Tottenham Hotspur** | 0 3 |
| Fulham * | 0 1 |

| Tottenham Hotspur | 0 |
| **Portsmouth** | 2 |

FA CUP FINAL 2010
Wembley Stadium, London, 15-05-2010, 15:00, Att: 88 335, Ref: Chris Foy

Chelsea   1   Drogba [59]

Portsmouth

| Birmingham City | 0 |
| **Portsmouth** * | 2 |

Chelsea - Petr Cech - Branislav Ivanovic, Alex, John Terry (c), Ashley Cole - Frank Lampard, Michael Ballack (Juliano Belletti 44), Florent Malouda - Salomon Kalou (Joe Cole 71), Didier Drogba, Nicolas Anelka (Daniel Sturridge 90). Tr: Carlo Ancelotti

Portsmouth - David James - Steve Finnan, Ricardo Rocha●, Aaron Mokoena, Hayden Mullins (Nadir Belhadj 81) - Aruna Dindane, Michael Brown, Papa Bouba Diop (Nwankwo Kanu 81), Kevin-Prince Boateng● (John Utaka 73) - Jamie O'Hara●, Frederic Piquionne. Tr: Avram Grant

Semi-finals played at Wembley Stadium, London

CARLING LEAGUE CUP 2009–10

Second Round

Manchester United	Bye
Swindon Town	0 5p
Wolverhampton Wanderers *	0 6p
Burnley	1
Hartlepool *	2
Reading *	1
Barnsley	2
Everton	Bye
Southend United	1
Hull City *	3
Preston North End *	2
Leicester City	1
Doncaster Rovers *	1
Tottenham Hotspur	5
Arsenal	Bye
Rotherham United	3
West Bromwich Albion *	4
Leeds United *	2
Watford	1
Liverpool	Bye
Scunthorpe United	2
Swansea City *	1
Sheffield Wednesday	0
Port Vale *	2
Fulham	Bye
Crystal Palace *	0
Manchester City	2
Blackburn Rovers	3
Gillingham *	1
Middlesbrough	1
Nottingham Forest *	2
Newcastle United *	4
Huddersfield Town	3
Ipswich Town	1
Peterborough United *	2
Bolton Wanderers	1
Tranmere Rovers *	0
Millwall	1
West Ham United *	3
Queens Park Rangers *	2
Accrington Stanley	1
Chelsea	Bye
Portsmouth *	4
Hereford United	1
Bristol City *	0
Carlisle United	2
Blackpool *	4
Wigan Athletic	1
Leyton Orient *	0
Stoke City	1
Sunderland	4
Norwich City *	1
Southampton *	1
Birmingham City	2
Cardiff City *	3
Bristol Rovers	1
Aston Villa	Bye

Third Round

Manchester United *	1
Wolverhampton Wanderers	0
Burnley	2
Barnsley *	3
Everton	4
Hull City *	0
Preston North End *	1
Tottenham Hotspur	5
Arsenal *	2
West Bromwich Albion	0
Leeds United *	0
Liverpool	1
Scunthorpe United *	2
Port Vale	0
Fulham	1
Manchester City *	2
Blackburn Rovers	1
Nottingham Forest *	0
Newcastle United	0
Peterborough United *	2
Bolton Wanderers *	3
West Ham United	1
Queens Park Rangers	0
Chelsea *	1
Portsmouth	3
Carlisle United *	1
Blackpool	3
Stoke City *	4
Sunderland *	2
Birmingham City	0
Cardiff City	0
Aston Villa *	1

Fourth Round

Manchester United	2
Barnsley *	0
Everton	0
Tottenham Hotspur *	2
Arsenal *	2
Liverpool	1
Scunthorpe United	1
Manchester City *	5
Blackburn Rovers *	5
Peterborough United	2
Bolton Wanderers	0
Chelsea *	4
Portsmouth *	4
Stoke City	0
Sunderland *	0 1p
Aston Villa	0 3p

* Home team/Home team in the first leg

CARLING LEAGUE CUP 2009–10

Quarter–finals   **Semi–finals**   **Final**

Manchester United *	2	
Tottenham Hotspur	0	

Manchester United	1	3
Manchester City *	2	1

Arsenal	0	
Manchester City *	3	

Manchester United	2	
Aston Villa	1	

Blackburn Rovers *	3	4p
Chelsea	3	3p

Blackburn Rovers *	0	4
Aston Villa	1	6

CARLING LEAGUE CUP FINAL 2010
Wembley Stadium, London, 28-02-2010, Att: 88 596, Ref: Phil Dowd

Manchester United	2	Owen [12], Rooney [74]
Aston Villa	1	Milner [5p]

Portsmouth *	2	
Aston Villa	4	

Man Utd - Tomasz Kuszczak - Rafael da Silva (Gary Neville 66), Nemanja Vidic•, Jonny Evans, Patrice Evra• - Luis Valencia, Darren Fletcher, Michael Carrick, Park Ji Sung (Darron Gibson 85) - Michael Owen (Wayne Rooney 42), Dimitar Berbatov. Tr: Alex Ferguson
Aston Villa - Brad Friedel - Carlos Cuellar (John Carew 80), James Collins•, Richard Dunne, Stephen Warnock - Ashley Young, James Milner, Stiliyan Petrov, Stewart Downing• - Emile Heskey, Gabriel Agbonlahor. Tr: Martin O'Neill

JOHNSTONE'S PAINT FOOTBALL LEAGUE TROPHY 2009-10

Second Round

Southampton *	2	5p
Torquay United	2	3p
Barnet	1	
Charlton Athletic *	4	
Swindon Town	1	4p
Exeter City *	1	3p
Gillingham *	0	
Norwich City	1	
Hereford United *	2	4p
Aldershot Town	2	3p
Brighton & Hove Albion	0	
Leyton Orient *	1	
Northampton Town *	2	
Bournemouth	1	
Southend United	0	
Milton Keynes Dons *	2	
Leeds United *	2	
Darlington	1	
Hartlepool United *	0	
Grimsby Town	2	
Bury *	2	
Tranmere Rovers	1	
Shrewsbury Town	0	
Accrington Stanley *	2	
Bradford City *	2	3p
Notts County	2	2p
Stockport County	1	
Port Vale *	3	
Chesterfield *	3	4p
Huddersfield Town	3	2p
Macclesfield Town	2	
Carlisle United *	4	

Third Round

Southampton *	2	
Charlton Athletic	1	
Swindon Town *	0	3p
Norwich City	0	5p
Hereford United	1	3p
Leyton Orient *	1	2p
Northampton Town	1	
Milton Keynes Dons *	3	
Leeds United *	3	
Grimsby Town	1	
Bury	2	
Accrington Stanley *	3	
Bradford City *	2	5p
Port Vale	2	4p
Chesterfield *	1	
Carlisle United	3	

Quarter-finals (regional semi-finals)

Southampton *	2	6p
Norwich City	2	5p
Hereford United *	1	
Milton Keynes Dons	4	
Leeds United *	2	
Accrington Stanley	0	
Bradford City	0	
Carlisle United *	3	

Semi-finals (regional finals)

Southampton	1	3	
Milton Keynes Dons *	0	1	
Leeds United *	1	3	5p
Carlisle United	2	2	6p

Final

Southampton	4
Carlisle United	1

TROPHY FINAL

Wembley Stadium, London
28-03-2010, Att: 73 476, Ref: Mathieson

Scorers - Lambert 15p, Lallana 44, Waigo 50, Antonio 60 for Southampton; Madine 84 for Carlisle

Saints - Davis - Harding, Jaidi (Perry 92+), Fonte, Mills - Wotton (Connolly 85), Hammond (c), Antonio, Lallana - Lambert, Waigo (Gillett 76). Tr: Pardew

Carlisle - Collin - Horwood, Murphy, Harte, Keogh - Bridge-Wilkinson (Anyinsah 61), Kavanagh (Madine 73), Robson, Thirlwell (c) (Taiwo 79), Clayton - Dobie. Tr: Abbott

* Home team/home team in the first leg

ARSENAL 2009-10

	Date	Opponent	Res	Score	Comp	Scorers	Att
Aug	15	Everton	W	6-1	PL	Denilson 26, Vermaelen 36, Galas 40, Fabregas 2 47 69, Eduardo 88	39 309
	18	Celtic	W	2-0	CLpo	Gallas 43, Caldwell OG 71	58 165
	22	Portsmouth	W	4-1	PL	Diaby 2 17 21, Gallas 50, Ramsey 68	60 049
	26	Celtic	W	3-1	CLpo	Eduardo 28p, Eboué 53, Arshavin 74	59 962
	29	Man Utd	L	1-2	PL	Arshavin 40	75 095
Sep	12	Man City	L	2-4	PL	Van Persie 62, Rosicky 87	47 339
	16	Standard	W	3-2	CLgH	Bendtner 45, Vermaelen 77, Eduardo 81	23 022
	19	Wigan	W	4-0	PL	Vermaelen 2 24 49, Eduardo 58, Fabregas 90	59 103
	22	West Brom	W	2-0	LCr3	Watt 68, Vela 76	56 592
	26	Fulham	W	1-0	PL	Van Persie 52	25 700
	29	Olympiacos	W	2-0	CLgH	Van Persie 78, Arshavin 86	59 884
Oct	4	Blackburn	W	6-2	PL	Vermaelen 17, V Persie 33, Arshavin 37, Fabregas 57, Walcott 75, Bendtner 89	59 431
	17	B'ham City	W	3-1	PL	Van Persie 16, Diaby 18, Arshavin 84	60 082
	20	AZ Alkmaar	D	1-1	CLgH	Fabregas 36	16 666
	25	West Ham	D	2-2	PL	Van Persie 16, Gallas 37	34 442
	28	Liverpool	W	2-1	LCr4	Merida 19, Bendtner 50	60 004
	31	Tottenham	W	3-0	PL	Van Persie 2 42 60, Fabregas 43	60 103
Nov	4	AZ Alkmaar	W	4-1	CLgH	Fabregas 2 25 52, Nasri 43, Diaby 72	59 345
	7	Wolves	W	4-1	PL	OG 2 28 35, Fabregas 45, Arshavin 66	28 937
	21	Sunderland	L	0-1	PL		44 918
	24	Standard	W	2-0	CLgH	Nasri 35, Denilson 45	59 941
	29	Chelsea	L	0-3	PL		60 067
Dec	2	Man City	L	0-3	LCqf		46 015
	5	Stoke	W	2-0	PL	Arshavin 26, Ramsey 79	60 048
	9	Olympiacos	L	0-1	CLgH		30 277
	13	Liverpool	W	2-1	PL	OG 50, Arshavin 58	43 853
	16	Burnley	D	1-1	PL	Fabregas 7	21 309
	19	Hull	W	3-0	PL	Denilson 45, Eduardo 59, Diaby 80	60 006
	26	Aston Villa	W	3-0	PL	Fabregas 2 65 81, Diaby 90	60 056
	30	Portsmouth	W	4-1	PL	OG 27, Nasri 42, Ramsey 69, Song 81	20 404
Jan	3	West Ham	W	2-1	FAr3	Ramsey 78, Eduardo 83	25 549
	9	Everton	D	2-2	PL	OG 28, Rosicky 90	60 053
	17	Bolton	W	2-0	PL	Fabregas 28, Merida 78	23 893
	20	Bolton	W	4-2	PL	Rosicky 43, Fabregas 52, Vermaelen 65, Arshavin 85	59 084
	24	Stoke	L	1-3	FAr4	Denilson 42	19 735
	27	Aston Villa	D	0-0	PL		39 601
	31	Man Utd	L	1-3	PL	Vermaelen 80	60 091
Feb	7	Chelsea	L	0-2	PL		41 794
	10	Liverpool	W	1-0	PL	Diaby 72	60 045
	17	Porto	L	1-2	CLr2	Campbell 18	40 717
	20	Sunderland	W	2-0	PL	Bendtner 27, Fabregas 90p	60 083
	27	Stoke	W	3-1	PL	Bendtner 32, Fabregas 89p, Vermaelen 90	27 011
Mar	6	Burnley	W	3-1	PL	Fabregas 34, Walcott 60, Arshavin 90	60 043
	9	Porto	W	5-0	CLr2	Bendtner 3 10 25 91+p, Nasri 63, Eboue 66	59 661
	13	Hull	W	2-1	PL	Arshavin 14, Bendtner 90	25 023
	14	West Ham	W	2-0	PL	Denilson 5, Fabregas 83p	60 077
	27	B'ham City	D	1-1	PL	Nasri 81	27 039
	31	Barcelona	D	2-2	CLqf	Walcott 69, Fabregas 85p	59 572
Apr	3	Wolves	W	1-0	PL	Bendtner 90	60 067
	6	Barcelona	L	1-4	CLqf	Bendtner 18	93 330
	14	Tottenham	L	1-2	PL	Bendtner 85	36 041
	18	Wigan	L	2-3	PL	Walcott 41, Silvestre 48	22 113
	24	Man City	D	0-0	PL		60 086
May	3	Blackburn	L	1-2	PL	Van Persie 13	26 138
	9	Fulham	W	4-0	PL	Arshavin 21, Van Persie 26, OG 37, Vela 84	60 039

ARSENAL LEAGUE APPEARANCES/GOALS 2009-10

Goalkeepers Manuel Almunia ESP 29 • Lukasz Fabianski POL 4 • Vito Mannone ITA 5

Defenders Sol Campbell 10+1/0 • Gael Clichy FRA 23+1/0 • Johan Djourou SUI 0+1/0 • Emmanuel Eboue CIV 17+8/1 • William Gallas FRA 26/3 • Kieran Gibbs 3/0 • Bacary Sagna FRA 31+4/0 • Mikael Silvestre FRA 9+3/1 • Armand Traore FRA 9/0 • Thomas Vermaelen BEL 33/7

Midfield Denilson BRA 19+1/4 • Abou Diaby FRA 26+3/6 • Craig Eastmond 2+2/0 • Cesc Fabregas ESP 26+1/15 • Fran Merida ESP 0+4/1 • Henri Lansbury 0+1/0 • Samir Nasri FRA 22+4/2 • Aaron Ramsey WAL 7+11/3 • Tomas Rosicky CZE 14+11/3 • Alex Song CMR 25+1/1 • Jack Wilshere 0+1/0

→ **Forwards** Andrei Arshavin RUS 25+5/10 • Nicklas Bendtner DEN 13+10/6 • Eduardo CRO 13+11/3 • Robin Van Persie NED 14+2/9 • Carlos Vela MEX 1+10/1 • Theo Walcott 12+11/3
Coach Arsene Wenger FRA

ASTON VILLA 2009-10

	Date	Opponent	Res	Score	Comp	Scorers	Att
Aug	15	Wigan Ath	L	0-2	PL		35 578
	20	SK Rapid	L	0-1	ELpo		17 800
	24	Liverpool	W	3-1	PL	OG 34, Davies 45, Young 75p	43 667
	27	SK Rapid	W	2-1	ELpo	Milner 38p, Carew 53	23 563
	30	Fulham	W	2-0	PL	OG 3, Agbonlahor 59	32 917
Sep	13	B'ham City	W	1-0	PL	Agbonlahor 85	25 196
	19	Portsmouth	W	2-0	PL	Milner 34p, Agbonlahor 43	35 979
	23	Cardiff City	W	1-0	LCr3	Agbonlahor 3	22 527
	26	Blackburn	L	1-2	PL	Agbonlahor 3	25 172
Oct	5	Man City	D	1-1	PL	Dunne 15	37 924
	17	Chelsea	W	2-1	PL	Dunne 32, Collins 52	39 047
	24	Wolves	D	1-1	PL	Agbonlahor 9	28 734
	27	Sunderland	D	0-0	LCr4	W 3-1p	27 666
	31	Everton	D	1-1	PL	Carew 46	36 648
	4	West Ham	L	1-2	PL	Young 52	30 024
Nov	7	Bolton	W	5-1	PL	Young 5, Agbonlahor 43, Carew 53, Milner 72, Cuellar 75	38 101
	21	Burnley	D	1-1	PL	Heskey 86	21 178
	28	Tottenham	D	1-1	PL	Agbonlahor 10	39 866
Dec	1	Portsmouth	W	4-2	LCqf	Heskey 12, Milner 27, Downing 74, Young 89	17 034
	5	Hull City	W	3-0	PL	Dunne 13, Milner 29, Carew 88p	39 748
	12	Man Utd	W	1-0	PL	Agbonlahor 21	75 130
	15	Sunderland	W	2-0	PL	Heskey 24, Milner 61	34 821
	19	Stoke	W	1-0	PL	Carew 61	35 852
	27	Arsenal	L	0-3	PL		60 056
	29	Liverpool	L	0-1	PL		42 788
Jan	2	Blackburn	W	3-1	FAr3	Delfouneso 12, Cuellar 37, Carew 91+p	25 453
	14	Blackburn	W	1-0	LCsf	Milner 23	18 595
	17	West Ham	D	0-0	PL		35 646
	20	Blackburn	W	6-4	LCsf	Warnock 30, Milner 40p, OG 53, Agbonlahor 58, Heskey 62, Young 93+	40 406
	23	Brighton	W	3-2	FAr4	Delfouneso 5, Young 48, Delph 63	39 725
	27	Arsenal	D	0-0	PL		39 601
	30	Fulham	W	2-0	PL	Agbonlahor 2 40 44	25 408
Feb	6	Tottenham	D	0-0	PL		35 899
	10	Man Utd	D	1-1	PL	Cuellar 19	42 788
	14	C Palace	D	2-2	FAr5	Collins 35, Petrov 87	20 486
	21	Burnley	W	5-2	PL	Young 32, Downing 2 56 58, Heskey 61, Agbonlahor 68	38 709
	24	C Palace	W	3-1	FAr5	Agbonlahor 42, Carew 2 81p 89p	31 874
	28	Man Utd	L	1-2	LCf	Milner 5p	88 596
Mar	7	Reading	W	4-2	FAqf	Young 47, Carew 3 51 57 93+p	23 175
	13	Stoke	D	0-0	PL		27 598
	16	Wigan Ath	W	2-1	PL	OG 25, Milner 63	16 186
	20	Wolves	D	2-2	PL	Carew 2 16 82	37 562
	24	Sunderland	D	1-1	PL	Carew 30	37 473
	27	Chelsea	L	1-7	PL	Carew 29	41 825
	3	Bolton	W	1-0	PL	Young 11	21 111
	10	Chelsea	L	0-3	FAsf		81 869
Apr	14	Everton	D	2-2	PL	Agbonlahor 72, OG 90	38 729
	18	Portsmouth	W	2-1	PL	Carew 16, Delfouneso 82	16 523
	21	Hull City	W	2-0	PL	Agbonlahor 13, Milner 76p	23 842
	25	B'ham City	W	1-0	PL	Milner 83p	42 788
May	1	Man City	L	1-3	PL	Carew 16	47 102
	9	Blackburn	L	0-1	PL		41 799

VILLA LEAGUE APPEARANCES/GOALS 2009-10

Goalkeepers Brad Friedel USA 38

Defenders Habib Beye SEN 5+1/0 • Cairan Clark 1/0 • James Collins WAL 26+1/1 • Carlos Cuellar ESP 36/2 • Curtis Davies 2/1 • Richard Dunne IRL 35/3 • Nicky Shorey 3/0 • Stephen Warnock 30/0 • Luke Young 14+2/0 •

Midfield Marc Albrighton 0+3/0 • Fabian Delph 4+4/0 • Stewart Downing 23+2/2 • Craig Gardner 0+4/0 • James Milner 37/7 • Stilian Petrov BUL 37/0 • Nigel Reo-Coker 6+4/0 • Steve Sidwell 12+13/0 • Ashley Young 37/5

Forwards Gabriel Agbonlahor 35+1/13 • John Carew NOR 22+11/10 • Nathan Delfouneso 0+9/1 • Emile Heskey 16+15/3
Coach Martin O'Neill NIR

BIRMINGHAM CITY 2009–10

Aug	16	Man Utd	L	0-1	PL		75 062
	19	Portsmouth	W	1-0	PL	McFadden 90p	19 922
	22	Stoke	D	0-0	PL		21 694
	25	S'thampton	W	2-1	LCr2	Bowyer 77, Carsley 80	11 753
	29	Tottenham	L	1-2	PL	Bowyer 75	35 318
Sep	13	Aston Villa	L	0-1	PL		25 196
	19	Hull	W	1-0	PL	O'Connor 75	23 759
	22	Sunderland	L	0-2	LCr3		20 576
	26	Bolton	L	1-2	PL	Phillips 84	28 671
Oct	3	Burnley	L	1-2	PL	Larsson 90	20 102
	17	Arsenal	L	1-3	PL	Bowyer 38	60 082
	24	Sunderland	W	2-1	PL	Ridgewell 37, McFadden 48	21 723
Nov	1	Man City	D	0-0	PL		21 462
	9	Liverpool	D	2-2	PL	Benitez 26, Jerome 45	42 560
	21	Fulham	W	1-0	PL	Bowyer 16	23 659
	29	Wolves	W	1-0	PL	Bowyer 3	26 668
Dec	5	Wigan	W	3-2	PL	Larsson 2 61 72, Benitez 66	18 797
	12	West Ham	W	1-0	PL	Bowyer 52	28 203
	15	Blackburn	W	2-1	PL	Jerome 2 12 48	23 187
	20	Everton	D	1-1	PL	Larsson 30	33 660
	26	Chelsea	D	0-0	PL		28 958
	28	Stoke	W	1-1	PL	Jerome 50	27 211
Jan	2	Nottm For	D	0-0	FAr3		20 975
	3	Man Utd	D	1-1	PL	Jerome 39	28 907
	12	Nottm For	W	1-0	FAr3	Ferguson 62	9 399
	23	Everton	W	2-1	FAr4	Benitez 7, Ferguson 40	30 875
	27	Chelsea	L	0-3	PL		41 293
	30	Tottenham	D	1-1	PL	Ridgewell 90	27 238
Feb	7	Wolves	W	2-1	PL	Phillips 2 80 85	24 165
	10	West Ham	L	0-2	PL		34 458
	13	Derby Co	W	2-1	FAr5	Dann 73, Ridgewell 93+	21 043
	21	Fulham	L	1-2	PL	OG 3	21 758
	27	Wigan	W	1-0	PL	McFadden 45p	25 921
Mar	6	Portsmouth	L	0-2	FAqf		20 456
	9	Portsmouth	W	2-1	PL	Jerome 2 16 42	18 465
	13	Everton	D	2-2	PL	Jerome 26, Gardner 51	24 579
	20	Sunderland	L	1-3	PL	Jerome 60	37 962
	24	Blackburn	L	1-2	PL	McFadden 55	23 856
	27	Arsenal	D	1-1	PL	Phillips 90	27 039
Apr	4	Liverpool	D	1-1	PL	Ridgewell 56	27 909
	11	Man City	L	1-5	PL	Jerome 42	45 209
	17	Hull	D	0-0	PL		26 669
	25	Aston Villa	L	0-1	PL		42 788
May	1	Burnley	W	2-1	PL	Jerome 29, Benitez 41	24 578
	9	Bolton	L	1-2	PL	McFadden 76	22 863

BLACKBURN ROVERS 2009–10

Aug	15	Man City	L	0-2	PL		29 584
	22	Sunderland	L	1-2	PL	Givet 21	37 106
	25	Gillingham	W	3-1	LCr2	Dunn 5, Hoilett 47, Pedersen 74	7 203
	29	West Ham	D	0-0	PL		23 421
Sep	12	Wolves	W	3-1	PL	Diouf 19, Roberts 56, Dunn 64	24 845
	20	Everton	L	0-3	PL		35 546
	22	Nottm For	W	1-0	LCr3	McCarthy 37	11 553
	26	Aston Villa	W	2-1	PL	Samba 24, Dunn 88p	25 172
Oct	4	Arsenal	L	2-6	PL	N'Zonzi 4, Dunn 30	59 431
	18	Burnley	W	3-2	PL	Dunn 9, Di Santo 21, Chimbonda 43	26 689
	24	Chelsea	L	0-5	PL		40 836
	27	Peter'boro	W	5-2	LCr4	Pedersen 4, Reid 45p, Salgado 57, McCarthy 72, Kalinic 74p	8 419
	31	Man Utd	L	0-2	PL		74 658
Nov	7	Portsmouth	W	3-1	PL	Roberts 2 53 86, Nelsen 73	23 110
	22	Bolton	W	2-0	PL	Dunn 32, OG 73	21 777
	25	Fulham	L	0-3	PL		21 414
	28	Stoke	D	0-0	PL		25 143
Dec	2	Chelsea	D	3-3	LCqf	Kalinic 9, Emerton 64, McCarthy 93p. W 4-3p	18 136
	5	Liverpool	D	0-0	PL		29 660
	12	Hull	D	0-0	PL		24 124
	15	B'ham City	L	1-2	PL	Nelsen 69	23 187
	19	Tottenham	L	0-2	PL		26 490
	26	Man City	D	1-1	PL	McCarthy 30	20 243
	28	Sunderland	D	2-2	PL	Pedersen 53, Diouf 77	25 656
Jan	2	Aston Villa	L	1-3	FAr3	Kalinic 55	25 453
	11	Man City	L	1-4	PL	Pedersen 71	40 292
	14	Aston Villa	L	0-1	LCsf		18 595
	17	Fulham	W	2-0	PL	Samba 25, Nelsen 54	21 287
	20	Aston Villa	L	4-6	LCsf	Kalinic 2 10 26, Olsson 63, Emerton 84	40 406
	27	Wigan	W	2-1	PL	Pedersen 20, Kalinic 76	22 190
	30	West Ham	D	0-0	PL		33 093
Feb	6	Stoke	L	0-3	PL		27 386
	10	Hull	W	1-0	PL	Olsson 16	23 518
	21	Bolton	W	3-0	PL	Kalinic 41, Roberts 73, Givet 84	23 888
	28	Liverpool	L	1-2	PL	Andrews 40p	42 795
Mar	13	Tottenham	L	1-3	PL	Samba 80	35 474
	21	Chelsea	D	1-1	PL	Diouf 70	25 554
	24	B'ham City	W	2-1	PL	Dunn 2 5 67	23 856
	28	Burnley	W	1-0	PL	Dunn 20p	21 546
Apr	3	Portsmouth	D	0-0	PL		16 207
	11	Man Utd	D	0-0	PL		29 912
	17	Everton	L	2-3	PL	N'Zonzi 69, Roberts 81	27 022
	24	Wolves	D	1-1	PL	Nelsen 28	28 967
May	3	Arsenal	W	2-1	PL	Dunn 43, Samba 68	26 138
	9	Aston Villa	W	1-0	PL	OG 84	41 799

BIRMINGHAM LEAGUE APPEARANCES/GOALS 2009-10
Goalkeepers Joe Hart 36 • Maik Taylor NIR 2
Defenders Stephen Carr IRL 35/0 • Scott Dann 30/0 • Roger Johnson 38/0 • Stuart Parnaby 6+2/0 • Franck Queudrue Fra 6/0 • Liam Ridgewell 30+1/3 • Gregory Vignal FRA 6+2/0
Midfield Lee Bowyer 34+1/5 • Lee Carsley IRL 3+4/0 • Keith Fahey 18+16/0 • Barry Ferguson 37/0 • Craig Gardner 10+3/1 • Damien Johnson NIR 0+1/0 • Sebastian Larsson SWE 26+7/4 • Gary McSheffrey 1+4/0 • Michel ESP 3+6/0 • Jay O'Shea IRL 0+1/0 • Teemu Taino 5+1/0
Forwards Cristian Benitez ECU 21+9/3 • Cameron Jerome 32/10 • James McFadden SCO 32+4/5 • Garry O'Connor SCO 5+5/1 • Kevin Phillips 2+17/4
Coach Alex McLeish SCO

BLACKBURN LEAGUE APPEARANCES/GOALS 2009-10
Goalkeepers Jason Brown WAL 3+1 • Paul Robinson 35
Defenders Pascal Chimbonda FRA 22+2/1 • Gael Givet FRA 33+1/2 • Grant Hanley SCO 1/0 • Lars Jacobsen DEN 11+2/0 • Phil Jones 7+2/0 • Michel Salgado ESP 16+5/0 • Ryan Nelson NZL 25+3/4 • Martin Olsson SWE 19+2/0 • Christopher Samba CGO 30/4 • Stephen Warnock 1/0
Midfield Keith Andrews NIR 22+10/1 • Yildiray Basturk TUR 1/0 • David Dunn 20+3/9 • Brett Emerton AUS 17+7/0 • Morten Gamst Pedersen NOR 27+6/3 • Vince Grella AUS 10+5/0 • Amine Linganze ALG 1/0 • Steven N'Zonzi FRA 33/2 • Steven Reid IRL 1+3/0
Forwards El Hadji Diouf SEN 24+2/3 • Franco Di Santo ARG 15+7/1 • Paul Gallagher SCO 0+1/0 • David Hoilett CAN 8+15/0 • Nikola Kalinic CRO 14+12/2 • Benni McCarthy RSA 7+7/1 • Jason Roberts GRN 15+14/5
Coach Sam Allardyce

KEY TO THE CLUB SECTION

CS = Community Shield • PL = FA Premier League (Barclays Premier League) • FA = FA Cup • LC = Carling League Cup • CL = UEFA Champions League • EL = Europa League • r1 = first round etc • p3 = third preliminary round • po = preliminary round play-off • gA = Group A etc • qf = quarter-final • sf = semi-final • f = final

Matches that are shaded were played at home; matches with no shading were played either away or on a neutral ground • The figures for the player appearances and goals consist of three elements - matches started+appearances as a substitute/goals scored

BOLTON WANDERERS 2009–10

	Date	Opponent	Res	Score	Comp	Scorers	Att
Aug	15	Sunderland	L	0-1	PL		22 247
	22	Hull	L	0-1	PL		22 999
	25	Tranmere	W	1-0	LCr2	Davies [41]	5 381
	29	Liverpool	L	2-3	PL	Davies [33], Cohen [47]	23 284
Sep	2	Portsmouth	W	3-2	PL	Cohen [13], Taylor [41p], Cahill [89]	17 564
	19	Stoke	D	1-1	PL	Taylor [89p]	20 265
	22	West Ham	W	3-1	LCr3	Davies [86], Cahill [96], Elmander [119]	8 050
	26	B'ham City	W	2-1	PL	Cohen [10], Lee [86]	28 671
Oct	3	Tottenham	D	2-2	PL	Gardner [3], Davies [69]	21 305
	17	Man Utd	L	1-2	PL	Taylor [75]	75 103
	25	Everton	W	3-2	PL	Lee [16], Cahill [27], Klasnic [86]	21 547
	28	Chelsea	L	0-4	LCr4		41 538
	31	Chelsea	L	0-4	PL		22 680
Nov	7	Aston Villa	L	1-5	PL	Elmander [44]	38 101
	22	Blackburn	L	0-2	PL		21 777
	28	Fulham	D	1-1	PL	Klasnic [35]	23 554
Dec	5	Wolves	L	1-2	PL	Elmander [79]	27 362
	12	Man City	D	3-3	PL	Klasnic 2 [11 53], Cahill [43]	22 735
	15	West Ham	W	3-1	PL	Lee [64], Klasnic [77], Cahill [88]	17 849
	26	Burnley	D	1-1	PL	Taylor [29]	21 761
	29	Hull	D	2-2	PL	Klasnic [20], Davies [61]	20 696
Jan	2	Lincoln	W	4-0	FAr3	OG [49], Lee [51], Cahill [83], Davies [90]	11 193
	17	Arsenal	L	0-2	PL		23 893
	20	Arsenal	L	2-4	PL	Cahill [7], Taylor [28p]	59 084
	23	Sheff Utd	W	2-0	FAr4	Steinsson [48], Elmander [84]	14 572
	26	Burnley	W	1-0	PL	Lee [35]	23 986
	30	Liverpool	L	0-2	PL		43 413
Feb	6	Fulham	D	0-0	PL		22 289
	9	Man City	L	0-2	PL		42 016
	14	Tottenham	D	1-1	FAr5	Davies [34]	13 596
	17	Wigan	D	0-0	PL		18 089
	21	Blackburn	L	0-3	PL		23 888
	24	Tottenham	L	0-4	FAr5		31 436
	27	Wolves	W	1-0	PL	Knight [45]	21 261
	6	West Ham	W	2-1	PL	Davies [10], Wilshere [16]	33 824
	9	Sunderland	L	0-4	PL		36 087
Mar	13	Wigan	W	4-0	PL	Elmander [10], Davies [48p], Muamba [53], Taylor [69]	20 053
	20	Everton	L	0-2	PL		36 503
	27	Man Utd	L	0-4	PL		25 370
	3	Aston Villa	L	0-1	PL		21 111
Apr	13	Chelsea	L	0-1	PL		40 539
	17	Stoke	W	2-1	PL	Taylor 2 [85 88]	27 250
	24	Portsmouth	D	2-2	PL	Klasnic [26], Davies [28]	20 526
May	1	Tottenham	L	0-1	PL		35 852
	9	B'ham City	W	2-1	PL	Davies [33], Klasnic [60]	22 863

BURNLEY 2009–10

	Date	Opponent	Res	Score	Comp	Scorers	Att
Aug	15	Stoke	L	0-2	PL		27 385
	19	Man Utd	W	1-0	PL	Blake [19]	20 872
	23	Everton	W	1-0	PL	Elliott [34]	19 983
	25	Hartlepool	W	2-1	LCr2	Fletcher 2 [84 108]	3 501
	29	Chelsea	L	0-3	PL		40 906
Sep	12	Liverpool	L	0-4	PL		43 817
	19	Sunderland	W	3-1	PL	Alexander [13p], Nugent 2 [67 86]	20 196
	22	Barnsley	L	2-3	LCr3	Fletcher [21], Eagles [52]	6 270
	26	Tottenham	L	0-5	PL		35 462
Oct	3	B'ham City	W	2-1	PL	Fletcher [53], Bikey [62]	20 102
	18	Blackburn	L	2-3	PL	Blake [5], Eagles [90]	26 689
	24	Wigan	L	1-3	PL	Fletcher [4]	19 430
	31	Hull	W	2-0	PL	Alexander 2 [20p 77]	20 219
Nov	7	Man City	D	3-3	PL	Alexander [19p], Fletcher [32], McDonald [87]	47 205
	21	Aston Villa	D	1-1	PL	Caldwell [9]	21 178
	28	West Ham	L	3-5	PL	Fletcher 2 [68 74], Eagles [90]	34 003
Dec	5	Portsmouth	L	0-2	PL		17 822
	12	Fulham	D	1-1	PL	Elliott [60]	18 397
	16	Arsenal	D	1-1	PL	Alexander [28p]	21 309
	20	Wolves	L	0-2	PL		27 410
	26	Bolton	D	1-1	PL	Nugent [56]	21 761
	28	Everton	L	0-2	PL		39 419
	2	MK Dons	W	2-1	FAr3	Alexander [23p], Fletcher [35]	11 816
	16	Man Utd	L	0-3	PL		75 120
Jan	23	Reading	L	0-1	FAr4		12 910
	26	Bolton	L	0-1	PL		23 986
	30	Chelsea	L	1-2	PL	Fletcher [50]	21 131
	6	West Ham	W	2-1	PL	Nugent [14], Fox [55]	21 001
	9	Fulham	L	0-3	PL		23 005
Feb	21	Aston Villa	L	2-5	PL	Fletcher [10], Paterson [90]	38 709
	27	Portsmouth	L	1-2	PL	Paterson [31]	19 714
	6	Arsenal	L	1-3	PL	Nugent [50]	60 043
	10	Stoke	D	1-1	PL	Nugent [52]	20 323
Mar	13	Wolves	L	1-2	PL	Thompson [73]	21 217
	20	Wigan	L	0-1	PL		18 498
	28	Blackburn	L	0-1	PL		21 546
	3	Man City	L	1-6	PL	Fletcher [71]	21 330
Apr	10	Hull	W	4-1	PL	Paterson [35], Alexander 2 [64p 70p], Elliott [90]	24 369
	17	Sunderland	L	1-2	PL	Thompson [82]	41 341
	25	Liverpool	L	0-4	PL		21 553
May	1	B'ham City	L	1-2	PL	Thompson [87]	24 578
	9	Tottenham	W	4-2	PL	Elliott [42], Cork [54], Paterson [71], Thompson [88]	21 161

BOLTON LEAGUE APPEARANCES/GOALS 2009-10

Goalkeepers Jussi Jaaskelainen FIN 38

Defenders Gary Cahil 29/5 • Zat Knight 35/1 • Andy O'Brien IRL 6/0 • Sam Ricketts WAL 25+2/0 • Paul Robinson 24+1/0 • Jlloyd Samuel 12+1/0 • Gretar Steinsson ISL 25+2/0

Midfield Chris Basham 2+6/0 • Tamir Cohen ISR 26+1/3 • Mark Davies 5+12/0 • Sean Davis 3/0 • Ricardo Gardner JAM 11+10/1 • Stuart Holden USA 1+1/0 • Lee Chung Yong KOR 27+7/4 • Gavin McCann 5+6/0 • Matthew Taylor 29+8/8 • Danny Ward 0+2/0 • Vladimir Weiss SVK 3+10/0 • Jack Wilshere 13+1/1

Forwards Kevin Davies 37/7 • Johan Elmander 15+10/3 • Ivan Klasnic CRO 12+15/8 • Mustapha Riga NED 0+1/0

Coach Gary Megson • Chris Evans & Steve Wigley (30/12/09) Owen Coyle IRL (8/01/10)

BURNLEY LEAGUE APPEARANCES/GOALS 2009-10

Goalkeepers Brian Jensen DEN 38 • Diego Penny PER 0+1

Defenders Andre Bikey CMR 26+2/1 • Stephen Caldwell SCO 12+1/1 • Clarke Carlisle 27/0 • Leon Cort 15/0 • Michael Duff NIR 10+1/0 • David Edgar CAN 2+2/0 • Danny Fox 13+1/1 • Stephen Jordan 23+2/0 • Christian Kalvenes NOR 3+3/0 • Tyrone Mears 38/0

Midfield Graham Alexander SCO 33/7 • Robbie Blake 20+11/2 • Jack Cork 8+3/1 • Chris Eagles 20+14/2 • Wade Elliott 34+4/4 • Joey Gudjonsson ISL 1+9/0 • Fernando Guerrero ECU 0+7/0 • Chris McCann IRL 7/0 • Kevin McDonald 15+11/1

Forwards Steven Fletcher SCO 35/8 • Frederic Nimani FRA 0+2/0 • David Nugent 20+10/6 • Martin Paterson NIR 17+6/4 • Steven Thompson SCO 1+19/4

Coach Owen Coyle NIR • Brian Laws (13/01/10)

CHELSEA 2009–10

Month	Date	Opponent	Res	Score	Comp	Scorers	Att
Aug	9	Man Utd	D	2-2	CS	Carvalho 52, Lampard 71, W 4-1p	85 896
	15	Hull City	W	2-1	PL	Drogba 2 37 90	41 597
	18	Sunderland	W	3-1	PL	Ballack 52, Lampard 61p, Deco 70	41 179
	23	Fulham	W	2-0	PL	Drogba 39, Anelka 76	25 404
	29	Burnley	W	3-0	PL	Anelka 45, Ballack 47, Cole.A 52	40 906
Sep	12	Stoke	W	2-1	PL	Drogba 45, Malouda 90	27 440
	15	Porto	W	1-0	CLgD	Anelka 48	39 436
	20	Tottenham	W	3-0	PL	Cole.A 32, Ballack 58, Drogba 63	41 623
	23	QPR	W	1-0	LCr3	Kalou 52	37 781
	26	Wigan	L	1-3	PL	Drogba 47	18 542
	30	APOEL	W	1-0	CLgD	Anelka 18	21 657
Oct	4	Liverpool	W	2-0	PL	Anelka 60, Malouda 90	41 732
	17	Aston Villa	L	1-2	PL	Drogba 15	39 047
	21	At. Madrid	W	4-0	CLgD	Kalou 2 41 52, Lampard 69, OG 91+	39 997
	24	Blackburn	W	5-0	PL	OG 20, Lampard 2 48 59p, Essien 52, Drogba 64	40 836
	28	Bolton	W	4-0	LCr4	Kalou 15, Malouda 26, Deco 67, Drogba 89	41 538
	31	Bolton	W	4-0	PL	Lampard 45p, Deco 61, Ivanovic 82, Drogba 90	22 680
Nov	3	At. Madrid	D	2-2	CLgD	Drogba 2 82 88	36 284
	8	Man Utd	W	1-0	PL	Terry 76	41 836
	21	Wolves	W	4-0	PL	Malouda 5, Essien 2 12 22, Cole.J 56	41 786
	25	Porto	W	1-0	CLgD	Anelka 69	38 410
	29	Arsenal	W	3-0	PL	Drogba 2 41 86, OG 45	60 067
Dec	2	Blackburn	D	3-3	LCqf	Drogba 48, Kalou 52, Ferreira 122+, L 3-4p	18 136
	5	Man City	L	1-2	PL	OG 8	47 348
	8	APOEL	D	2-2	CLgD	Essien 19, Drogba 26	40 917
	12	Everton	D	3-3	PL	Drogba 2 18 59, Anelka 23	41 579
	16	Portsmouth	W	2-1	PL	Anelka 23, Lampard 79p	40 137
	20	West Ham	D	1-1	PL	Lampard 61p	33 388
	26	B'ham City	D	0-0	PL		28 958
	28	Fulham	W	2-1	PL	Drogba 73, OG 75	41 805
Jan	3	Watford	W	5-0	FAr3	Sturridge 2 5 68, OG 15, Malouda 22, Lampard 64	40 912
	16	Sunderland	W	7-2	PL	Anelka 2 8 65, Malouda 17, Cole.A 22, Lampard 2 34 90, Ballack 52	41 776
	23	Preston NE	W	2-0	FAr4	Anelka 37, Sturridge 47	23 119
	27	B'ham City	W	3-0	PL	Malouda 5, Lampard 2 32 90	41 293
	30	Burnley	W	2-1	PL	Anelka 27, Terry 82	21 131
Feb	2	Hull	D	1-1	PL	Drogba 42	24 957
	7	Arsenal	W	2-0	PL	Drogba 2 8 23	41 794
	10	Everton	L	1-2	PL	Malouda 17	36 411
	13	Cardiff	W	4-1	FAr5	Drogba 2, Ballack 51, Sturridge 69, Kalou 86	40 827
	20	Wolves	W	2-0	PL	Drogba 2 40 67	28 978
	24	Inter	L	1-2	CLr2	Kalou 51	78 971
	27	Man City	L	2-4	PL	Lampard 2 42 90p	41 814
Mar	7	Stoke	W	2-0	FAqf	Lampard 35, Terry 67	41 322
	13	West Ham	W	4-1	PL	Alex 16, Drogba 2 56 90, Malouda 77	41 755
	16	Inter	L	0-1	CLr2		38 112
	21	Blackburn	D	1-1	PL	Drogba 6	25 554
	24	Portsmouth	W	5-0	PL	Drogba 2 32 77, Malouda 2 50 60, Lampard 90	18 753
	27	Aston Villa	W	7-1	PL	Lampard 4 15 44p 62p 90, Malouda 2 57 68, Kalou 83	41 825
Apr	3	Man Utd	W	2-1	PL	Cole.J 20, Drogba 79	75 217
	10	Aston Villa	W	3-0	FAsf	Drogba 68, Malouda 89, Lampard 95+	81 869
	13	Bolton	W	1-0	PL	Anelka 43	40 539
	17	Tottenham	L	1-2	PL	Lampard 90	35 814
	25	Stoke	W	7-0	PL	Kalou 3 24 31 68, Lampard 2 44p 81, Sturridge 87, Malouda 89	41 013
May	2	Liverpool	W	2-0	PL	Drogba 33, Lampard 54	44 375
	9	Wigan	W	8-0	PL	Anelka 2 6 56, Lampard 32p, Kalou 54, Drogba 3 63 68p 80, Cole.A 90	41 383
	15	Portsmouth	W	1-0	FAf	Drogba 59	88 335

CHELSEA LEAGUE APPEARANCES/GOALS 2009-10

Goalkeepers Petr Cech CZE 34 • Hilario POR 2+1 • Ross Turnbull 2
Defenders Alex BRA 13+3/1 • Belletti BRA 4+7/0 • Bosingwa POR 8/0 • Jeffrey Bruma NED 0+2/0 • Ashley Cole 25+2/4 • Sam Hutchinson 0+2/0 • Branislav Ivanovic SRB 25+3/0 • Paulo Ferreira POR 11+2/0 • Ricardo Carvalho POR 22/0 • John Terry 37/2 • Patrick van Aanholt NED 0+2/0
Midfield Michael Ballack GER 26+6/4 • Joe Cole 14+12/2 • Deco POR 14+5/2 • Michael Essien GHA 13+1/3 • Frank Lampard 36/22 • Florent Malouda FRA 26+7/12 • Nemanja Matic SRB 0+2/0 • John Mikel NGA 21+4/0 • Yuriy Zhirkov RUS 10+7/0
Forwards Nicolas Anelka FRA 31+2/11 • Fabio Borini ITA 0+4/0 • Didier Drogba CIV 31+1/29 • Gael Kakuta FRA 0+1/0 • Salomon Kalou CIV 11+12/5 • Andriy Shevchenko 0+1/0 • Daniel Sturridge 2+11/1
Coach Carlo Ancelotti

EVERTON 2009–10

Month	Date	Opponent	Res	Score	Comp	Scorers	Att
Aug	15	Arsenal	L	1-6	PL	Saha 90	39 309
	20	Sigma	W	4-0	ELpo	Saha 2 34 72, Rodwell 2 40 53	27 433
	23	Burnley	L	0-1	PL		19 983
	29	Sigma	D	1-1	ELpo	Pienaar 44	10 212
	30	Wigan	W	2-1	PL	Saha 62, Baines 90p	35 122
Sep	13	Fulham	L	1-2	PL	Cahill 33	24 191
	17	AEK Athens	W	4-0	ELgl	Yobo 10, Distin 17, Pienaar 37, Jo 82	26 747
	20	Blackburn	W	3-0	PL	Saha 2 22 54, Yobo 58	35 546
	23	Hull	W	4-0	LCr3	Yakubu 11, Jo 20, Gosling 24, Osman 57	13 558
	26	Portsmouth	W	1-0	PL	Saha 42	18 116
Oct	1	BATE	W	2-1	ELgl	Fellaini 68, Cahill 77	21 200
	4	Stoke	D	1-1	PL	Osman 55	36 753
	17	Wolves	D	1-1	PL	Bilyaletdinov 88	39 319
	22	Benfica	L	0-5	ELgl		44 534
	25	Bolton	L	2-3	PL	Saha 32, Fellaini 55	21 547
	27	Tottenham	L	0-2	LCr4		35 843
	31	Aston Villa	D	1-1	PL	Bilyaletdinov 45	36 648
Nov	5	Benfica	L	0-2	ELgl		30 790
	8	West Ham	W	2-1	PL	Saha 27, Gosling 64	32 466
	21	Man Utd	L	0-3	PL		75 169
	25	Hull	L	2-3	PL	OG 49, Saha 65p	24 685
	29	Liverpool	L	0-2	PL		39 652
Dec	2	AEK Athens	W	1-0	ELgl	Bilyaletdinov 6	15 000
	6	Tottenham	D	2-2	PL	Saha 78, Cahill 86	34 003
	12	Chelsea	D	3-3	PL	OG 12, Yakubu 45, Saha 63	41 579
	17	BATE	L	0-1	ELgl		18 242
	20	B'ham City	D	1-1	PL	Bilyaletdinov 5	33 660
	26	Sunderland	D	1-1	PL	Fellaini 85	46 990
	28	Burnley	W	2-0	PL	Vaughan 83, Pienaar 90	39 419
Jan	2	Carlisle	W	3-1	FAr3	Vaughan 12, Cahill 82, Baines 95+	31 196
	9	Arsenal	D	2-2	PL	Osman 12, Pienaar 81	60 053
	16	Man City	W	2-0	PL	Pienaar 36, Saha 45p	37 378
	23	B'ham City	L	1-2	FAr4	Osman 56	30 875
	27	Sunderland	W	2-0	PL	Cahill 6, Donovan 19	32 163
	30	Wigan	W	1-0	PL	Cahill 84	16 869
Feb	6	Liverpool	L	0-1	PL		44 316
	10	Chelsea	W	2-1	PL	Saha 2 33 75	36 411
	16	Sporting CL	W	2-1	ELr2	Pienaar 35, Distin 49	28 131
	20	Man Utd	W	3-1	PL	Bilyaletdinov 19, Gosling 76, Rodwell 90	39 448
	25	Sporting CL	L	0-3	ELr2		17 609
	28	Tottenham	L	1-2	PL	Yakubu 55	35 912
Mar	7	Hull	W	5-1	PL	Arteta 2 17 39, OG 51, Donovan 82, Rodwell 86	34 682
	13	B'ham City	D	2-2	PL	Anichebe 19, Yakubu 22	24 579
	20	Bolton	W	2-0	PL	Arteta 72, Pienaar 89	36 503
	24	Man City	W	2-0	PL	Cahill 33, Arteta 85	45 708
	27	Wolves	D	0-0	PL		28 995
Apr	4	West Ham	D	2-2	PL	Bilyaletdinov 24, Yakubu 85	37 451
	14	Aston Villa	D	2-2	PL	Cahill 2 23 74	38 729
	17	Blackburn	W	3-2	PL	Arteta 4p, Yakubu 79, Cahill 90	27 022
	25	Fulham	W	2-1	PL	OG 50, Arteta 90p	35 578
May	1	Stoke	D	0-0	PL		27 579
	9	Portsmouth	W	1-0	PL	Bilyaletdinov 90	38 730

EVERTON LEAGUE APPEARANCES/GOALS 2009-10

Goalkeepers Tim Howard USA 38
Defenders Leighton Baines 37/1 • Seamus Coleman IRL 0+3/0 • Sylvain Distin FRA 29/0 • Johnny Heitinga NED 29+2/0 • Tony Hibbert 17+3/0 • Phil Jagielka 11+1/0 • Joleon Lescott 1/0 • Lucas Neill AUS 10+2/0 • Phil Neville 22+1/0 • Philippe Senderos SUI 1+1/0 • Joseph Yobo NGA 14+3/1
Midfield Arteta ESP 11+2/6 • Diniyar Bilyaletdinov RUS 16+7/6 • Tim Cahill AUS 33/8 • Marouane Fellaini BEL 20+3/2 • Dan Gosling 3+8/2 • Leon Osman 25+1/2 • Steven Pienaar RSA 30/4 • Jack Rodwell 17+9/2
Forwards Kieran Agard 0+1/0 • Victor Anichebe NGA 6+5/1 • Yakubu Ayegbeni NGA • 9+16/5 • Jose Baxter 0+2/0 • Landon Donovan USA 7+3/2 • Jo BRA 6+9/0 • Louis Saha FRA 26+7/13 • James Vaughan 0+8/1
Coach David Moyes

FULHAM 2009-10

	Date	Opponent	Res	Score	Comp	Scorers	Att
Jly	30	Vetra	W	3-0	ELp3	Zamora 45, Murphy 57p, Seol 85	12 000
Aug	6	Vetra	W	3-0	ELp3	Etuhu 57, Johnson 2 80 84	15 016
	15	Portsmouth	W	1-0	PL	Zamora 13	17 510
	20	Amkar	W	3-1	ELp3	Johnson 4, Dempsey 51, Zamora 75	13 000
	23	Chelsea	L	0-2	PL		25 404
	27	Amkar	L	0-1	ELp3		20 000
	30	Aston Villa	L	0-2	PL		32 917
Sep	13	Everton	W	2-1	PL	Konchesky 57, Duff 79	24 191
	17	CSKA Sofia	D	1-1	ELgE	Kamara 65	28 000
	20	Wolves	L	1-2	PL	Murphy 66p	27 670
	23	Man City	L	1-2	LCr3	Gera 34	24 507
	26	Arsenal	L	0-1	PL		25 700
Oct	1	Basel	W	1-0	ELgE	Murphy 57	16 100
	4	West Ham	D	2-2	PL	Murphy 47p	32 612
	19	Hull	W	2-0	PL	Zamora 43, Kamara 64	22 943
	22	Roma	D	1-1	ELgE	Hangeland 24	23 561
	25	Man City	D	2-2	PL	Duff 62, Dempsey 68	44 906
	31	Liverpool	W	3-1	PL	Zamora 24, Nevland 73, Dempsey 87	25 700
Nov	.	Roma	L	1-2	ELgE	Kamara 19p	14 457
	8	Wigan	D	1-1	PL	Dempsey 39p	16 172
	21	B'ham City	L	0-1	PL		23 659
	25	Blackburn	W	3-0	PL	Nevland 43, Dempsey 2 67 88	21 414
	28	Bolton	D	1-1	PL	Duff 75	23 554
Dec	3	CSKA Sofia	W	1-0	ELgE	Gera 15	23 604
	6	Sunderland	W	1-0	PL	Zamora 7	23 168
	12	Burnley	D	1-1	PL	Zamora 52	18 397
	16	Basel	W	3-2	ELgE	Zamora 2 42 45, Gera 77	20 063
	19	Man Utd	L	3-0	PL	Murphy 22, Zamora 46, Duff 75	25 700
	26	Tottenham	D	0-0	PL		25 679
	28	Chelsea	L	1-2	PL	Gera 4	41 805
Jan	2	Swindon	W	1-0	FAr3	Zamora 16	19 623
	5	Stoke	L	2-3	PL	Duff 61, Dempsey 85	25 104
	17	Blackburn	L	0-2	PL		21 287
	23	Accrington	W	3-1	FAr4	Nevland 21, Duff 59, Gera 80	3 712
	26	Tottenham	L	0-2	PL		35 467
	30	Aston Villa	L	0-2	PL		25 408
Feb	3	Portsmouth	W	1-0	PL	Greening 74	21 934
	6	Bolton	D	0-0	PL		22 289
	9	Burnley	W	3-0	PL	Murphy 23, Elm 31, Zamora 54	23 005
	14	Notts Co	W	4-0	FAr5	Davies 22, Zamora 41, Duff 73, Okaka Chuka 79	16 132
	18	Shakhtar	W	2-1	ELr3	Gera 3, Zamora 63	21 832
	21	B'ham City	W	2-1	PL	Duff 59, Zamora 90	21 758
	25	Shakhtar	D	1-1	ELr3	Hangeland 33	47 509
	28	Sunderland	D	0-0	PL		40 192
Mar	6	Tottenham	D	0-0	FAqf		24 533
	11	Juventus	L	1-3	ELr3	Etuhu 36	11 406
	14	Man Utd	L	0-3	PL		75 207
	18	Juventus	W	4-1	ELr3	Zamora 9, Gera 2 39 48p, Dempsey 82	23 458
	21	Man City	L	1-2	PL	Murphy 75p	25 359
	24	Tottenham	L	1-3	FAqf	Zamora 17	35 432
	27	Hull	L	0-2	PL		24 361
Apr	1	Wolfsburg	W	2-1	ELqf	Zamora 59, Duff 63	22 307
	4	Wigan	W	2-1	PL	Okaka Chuka 47, Hangeland 58	22 730
	8	Wolfsburg	W	1-0	ELqf	Zamora 1	24 843
	11	Liverpool	D	0-0	PL		42 331
	17	Wolves	D	0-0	PL		25 597
	22	Hamburg	D	0-0	ELsf		49 171
	25	Everton	L	1-2	PL	Nevland 36	35 578
	29	Hamburg	W	2-1	ELsf	Davies 69, Gera 76	23 705
May	2	West Ham	W	3-2	PL	Dempsey 45, OG 58, Okaka Chuka 79	24 201
	5	Stoke	L	0-1	PL		20 831
	9	Arsenal	L	0-4	PL		60 039
	12	At. Madrid	L	1-2	ELf	Davies 37	49 000

FULHAM LEAGUE APPEARANCES/GOALS 2009-10

Goalkeepers Mark Schwarzer AUS **37** • David Stockdale **1**
Defenders Chris Baird NIR **29+3/0** • Brede Hangeland NOR **32/1** • Aaron Hughes NIR **34/0** • Toni Kallio FIN **0+1/0** • Stephen Kelly IRL **7+1/0** • Paul Konchesky **27/1** • John Paintsil GHA **22/0** • Nicky Shorey **9/0** • Chris Smalling **9+3/0** • Fredrik Stoor SWE **0+2/0**
Midfield Simon Davies WAL **12+5/0** • Clint Dempsey USA **27+2/7** • Kagisho Dikgacoi RSA **7+5/0** • Damien Duff IRL **30+2/6** • Dickson Etuhu NGA **14+6/0** • Zoltan Gera HUN **19+8/2** • Jonathan Greening **15+8/1** • Danny Murphy **25/5** • Bjorn Helge Riise NOR **5+7/0**
Forwards David Elm SWE **3+7/1** • Zoltan Gera HUN **19+8/2** • Andy Johnson **7+1/0** • Eddie Johnson USA **0+2/0** • Diomansy Kamara SEN **5+4/1** • Seol Ki Hyeon KOR **0+2/0** • Erik Nevland NOR **12+11/3** • Stefano Okaka ITA **3+8/2** • Bobby Zamora **27/8**
Coach Roy Hodgson

→

HULL CITY 2009-10

	Date	Opponent	Res	Score	Comp	Scorers	Att
Aug	15	Chelsea	L	1-2	PL	Hunt 28	41 597
	19	Tottenham	L	1-5	PL	Hunt 25	24 735
	22	Bolton	W	1-0	PL	Ghilas 61	22 999
	25	Southend	W	3-1	LCr2	Cairney 7, Altidore 42, Geovanni 75	7 994
	29	Wolves	D	1-1	PL	Geovanni 3	27 906
Sep	12	Sunderland	L	1-4	PL	Zayatte 43	38 997
	19	B'ham City	L	0-1	PL		23 759
	23	Everton	L	0-4	LCr3		13 558
	26	Liverpool	L	1-6	PL	Geovanni 15	44 392
Oct	3	Wigan	W	2-1	PL	Vennegoor 60, Geovanni 68	22 822
	19	Fulham	L	0-2	PL		22 943
	25	Portsmouth	D	0-0	PL		23 720
	31	Burnley	L	0-2	PL		20 219
Nov	8	Stoke	W	2-1	PL	Olofinjana 62, Vennegoor 90	24 516
	21	West Ham	D	3-3	PL	Bullard 2 27 45p, Zayatte 44	24 909
	25	Everton	W	3-2	PL	Hunt 9, Dawson 20, Marney 23	24 685
	28	Man City	D	1-1	PL	Bullard 82p	46 382
Dec	5	Aston Villa	L	0-3	PL		39 748
	12	Blackburn	D	0-0	PL		24 124
	19	Arsenal	L	0-3	PL		60 006
	27	Man Utd	L	1-3	PL	Fagan 59p	24 627
	29	Bolton	D	2-2	PL	Hunt 2 71 78	20 696
Jan	2	Wigan	L	1-4	FAr3	Geovanni 35	5 335
	16	Tottenham	D	0-0	PL		35 729
	23	Man Utd	L	0-4	PL		73 933
	30	Wolves	D	2-2	PL	Vennegoor 11, Hunt 52p	24 957
Feb	2	Chelsea	D	1-1	PL	Mouyokolo 30	24 957
	6	Man City	W	2-1	PL	Altidore 31, Boateng 54	24 959
	10	Blackburn	L	0-1	PL		23 518
	20	West Ham	L	0-3	PL		33 971
Mar	7	Everton	L	1-5	PL	Cairney 32	34 682
	13	Arsenal	L	1-2	PL	Bullard 28p	25 023
	20	Portsmouth	L	2-3	PL	Folan 2 27 73	16 513
	27	Fulham	W	2-0	PL	Bullard 16p, Fagan 48	24 361
Apr	3	Stoke	L	0-2	PL		27 604
	10	Burnley	L	1-4	PL	Kilbane 3	24 369
	17	B'ham City	D	0-0	PL		26 669
	24	Aston Villa	L	0-2	PL		23 842
	24	Sunderland	L	0-1	PL		25 012
May	3	Wigan	D	2-2	PL	Atkinson 42, Cullen 64	20 242
	9	Liverpool	D	0-0	PL		25 030

HULL LEAGUE APPEARANCES/GOALS 2009-10

Goalkeepers Matt Duke **11** • Boaz Myhill WAL **27**
Defenders Liam Cooper SCO **1+1/0** • Andrew Dawson **35/1** • Anthony Gardner **24/0** • Paul McShane IRL **26+1/0** • Bernard Mendy FRA **15+6/0** • Steven Mouyokolo FRA **19+2/1** • Ibrahima Sonko SEN **9/0** • Michael Turner **4/0** • Kamil Zayatte GUI **21+2/2**
Midfield Will Atkinson **2/1** • Nick Barmby **6+14/0** • George Boateng NED **26+3/1** • Jimmy Bullard **13+1/4** • Thomas Cairney **10+1/1** • Geovanni BRA **16+10/3** • Stephen Hunt IRL **27/6** • Kevin Kilbane IRL **15+6/1** • Dean Marney **15+1/1** • Seyi Olofinjana NGA **11+8/1** • Richard Garcia AUS **14+4/0**
Forwards Jozy Altidore USA **16+12/1** • Daniel Cousin GAB **1+2/0** • Mark Cullen **2+1/1** • Craig Fagan **20+5/2** • Caleb Folan IRL **7+1/2** • Kamel Ghilas ALG **6+7/1** • Jan Vennegoor NED **17+14/3** • Amr Zaki EGY **2+4/0**
Coach Phil Brown • Iain Dowie (17/03/10)

LIVERPOOL 2009–10

Mon	Date	Opponent	Res	Score	Comp	Scorers	Att
	16	Tottenham	L	1-2	PL	Gerrard 56p	35 935
Aug	19	Stoke	W	4-0	PL	Torres 4, Johnson 45, Kuyt 78, N'Gog 90	44 318
	24	Aston Villa	L	1-3	PL	Torres 72	43 667
	29	Bolton	W	3-2	PL	Johnson 41, Torres 56, Gerrard 83	23 284
	12	Burnley	W	4-0	PL	Benayoun 3 27 61 82, Kuyt 41	43 817
	16	Debreceni	W	1-0	CLgE	Kuyt 45	41 591
	19	West Ham	W	3-2	PL	Torres 2 20 75, Kuyt 41	34 658
Sep	22	Leeds Utd	W	1-0	LCr3	N'Gog 66	38 168
	26	Hull	W	6-1	PL	Torres 3 12 28 47, Gerrard 61, Babel 88 90	44 392
	29	Fiorentina	L	0-2	CLgE		33 426
	4	Chelsea	L	0-2	PL		41 732
	11	Sunderland	L	0-1	PL		47 327
	20	Lyon	L	1-2	CLgE	Benayoun 41	41 562
Oct	25	Man Utd	W	2-0	PL	Torres 65, N'Gog 90	44 188
	28	Arsenal	L	1-2	LCr4	Insua 26	60 004
	31	Fulham	L	1-3	PL	Torres 42	25 700
	4	Lyon	D	.1-1	CLgE	Babel 83	39 180
	9	B'ham City	D	2-2	PL	N'Gog 13, Gerrard 71p	42 560
	21	Man City	D	2-2	PL	Skrtel 50, Benayoun 77	44 164
	24	Debreceni	W	1-0	CLgE	N'Gog 4	41 500
Nov	29	Everton	W	2-0	PL	OG 12, Kuyt 80	39 652
	5	Blackburn	D	0-0	PL		40 900
	9	Fiorentina	L	1-2	CLgE	Benayoun 43	40 863
	13	Arsenal	L	1-2	PL	Kuyt 41	43 853
	16	Wigan	W	2-1	PL	N'Gog 9, Torres 79	41 116
	19	Portsmouth	L	0-2	PL		20 534
	26	Wolves	W	2-0	PL	Gerrard 62, Benayoun 70	41 956
Dec	29	Aston Villa	W	1-0	PL	Torres 90	42 788
	2	Reading	D	1-1	FAr3	Gerrard 36	23 656
	3	Reading	D	1-1	FAr3	OG 45	31 063
	16	Stoke City	D	1-1	PL	Kyrgiakos 57	27 247
	20	Tottenham	W	2-0	PL	Kuyt 2 6 90p	42 016
	26	Wolves	D	0-0	PL		28 763
Jan	30	Bolton	W	2-0	PL	Kuyt 37, OG 70	43 413
	6	Everton	W	1-0	PL	Kuyt 55	44 316
	10	Arsenal	L	0-1	PL		60 045
	18	Unirea	W	1-0	ELr2	N'Gog 81	40 450
	21	Man City	D	0-0	PL		47 203
Feb	25	Unirea	W	3-1	ELr2	Mascherano 30, Babel 41, Gerrard 57	17 632
	28	Blackburn	W	2-1	PL	Gerrard 20, Torres 44	42 795
	8	Wigan	L	0-1	PL		17 427
	11	Lille	L	0-1	ELr3		17 700
	15	Portsmouth	W	4-1	PL	Torres 2 26 77, Babel 28, Aquilani 32	40 316
	18	Lille	W	3-0	ELr3	Gerrard 9p, Torres 2 49 89	38 139
	21	Man Utd	L	1-2	PL	Torres 5	75 216
	28	Sunderland	W	3-0	PL	Torres 2 3 60, Johnson 32	43 121
	1	Benfica	L	1-2	ELqf	Agger 9	62 629
	4	B'ham City	D	1-1	PL	Gerrard 47	27 909
	8	Benfica	W	4-1	ELqf	Kuyt 27, Lucas 34, Torres 2 59 82	42 500
Apr	11	Fulham	D	0-0	PL		42 331
	19	West Ham	W	3-0	PL	Benayoun 19, N'Gog 29, OG 59	37 697
	22	At. Madrid	L	0-1	ELsf		47 042
	25	Burnley	W	4-0	PL	Gerrard 2 52 59, Rodriguez 74, Babel 90	21 553
	29	At. Madrid	W	2-1	ELsf	Aquilani 44, Benayoun 95	42 040
May	2	Chelsea	L	0-2	PL		44 375
	9	Hull	D	0-0	PL		25 030

MANCHESTER CITY 2009–10

Mon	Date	Opponent	Res	Score	Comp	Scorers	Att
	15	Blackburn	W	2-0	PL	Adebayor 3, Ireland 90	29 584
Aug	22	Wolves	W	1-0	PL	Adebayor 17	47 287
	27	C Palace	W	2-0	LCr2	W-Phillips 50, Tevez 71	14 725
	30	Portsmouth	W	1-0	PL	Adebayor 30	17 826
	12	Arsenal	W	4-2	PL	Richards 20, Bellamy 74, Adebayor 80, W-Phillips 84	47 339
Sep	20	Man Utd	L	3-4	PL	Barry 16, Bellamy 2 52 90	75 065
	13	Fulham	W	2-1	LCr3	Barry 52, Toure.K 111	24 507
	28	West Ham	W	3-1	PL	Tevez 2 5 61, Petrov 31	42 745
	5	Aston Villa	D	1-1	PL	Bellamy 67	37 924
	8	Wigan	D	1-1	PL	Petrov 47	20 005
Oct	25	Fulham	D	2-2	PL	Lescott 54, Petrov 60	44 906
	28	Scunthorpe	W	5-1	LCr4	Ireland 3, Santa Cruz 38, Lescott 56, Tevez 71, Johnson 77	36 358
	1	B'ham City	D	0-0	PL		21 462
	7	Burnley	D	3-3	PL	W-Phillips 43, Toure.K 55, Bellamy 58	47 205
Nov	21	Liverpool	D	2-2	PL	Adebayor 69, Ireland 76	44 164
	28	Hull	D	1-1	PL	W-Phillips 45	46 382
	2	Arsenal	W	3-0	LCqf	Tevez 50, W-Phillips 69, Weiss 89	46 015
	5	Chelsea	W	2-1	PL	Adebayor 37, Tevez 56	47 348
	12	Bolton	D	3-3	PL	Tevez 2 28 77, Richards 45	22 735
	16	Tottenham	L	0-3	PL		35 891
Dec	19	Sunderland	W	4-3	PL	Santa Cruz 2 4 69, Tevez 12p, Bellamy 35	44 735
	26	Stoke	W	2-0	PL	Petrov 28, Tevez 45	47 325
	28	Wolves	W	3-0	PL	Tevez 2 33 86, Garrido 69	28 957
	2	Midd'boro	W	1-0	FAr3	Mwaruwari 45	12 474
	11	Blackburn	W	4-1	PL	Tevez 3 7 49 90, Richards 39	40 292
	16	Everton	L	0-2	PL		37 378
Jan	19	Man Utd	W	2-1	LCsf	Tevez 2 42p 65	46 067
	24	Scunthorpe	W	4-2	FAr4	Petrov 3, Onuoha 45, Sylvinho 57, Robinho 84	8 861
	27	Man Utd	L	1-3	LCsf	Tevez 76	74 576
	31	Portsmouth	W	2-0	PL	Adebayor 40, Kompany 45	44 015
	6	Hull	L	1-2	PL	Adebayor 59	24 959
	9	Bolton	W	2-0	PL	Tevez 31p, Adebayor 73	42 016
	13	Stoke	D	1-1	FAr5	W-Phillips 11	28 019
Feb	16	Stoke	D	1-1	PL	Barry 85	26 778
	21	Liverpool	D	0-0	PL		47 203
	24	Stoke	L	1-3	FAr5	Bellamy 81	21 813
	27	Chelsea	W	4-2	PL	Tevez 2 45 76p, Bellamy 2 51 87	41 814
	14	Sunderland	D	1-1	PL	Johnson 90	41 398
	21	Fulham	W	2-1	PL	Santa Cruz 7, Tevez 36	25 359
Mar	24	Everton	L	0-2	PL		45 708
	29	Wigan	W	3-0	PL	Tevez 3 72 74 84	43 534
	3	Burnley	W	6-1	PL	Adebayor 2 4 45, Bellamy 5, Tevez 7, Vieira 20, Kompany 58	21 330
Apr	11	B'ham City	W	5-1	PL	Tevez 2 38p 40, Adebayor 2 43 88, Onuoha 74	45 209
	17	Man Utd	L	0-1	PL		47 019
	24	Arsenal	D	0-0	PL		60 086
	1	Aston Villa	W	3-1	PL	Tevez 41p, Adebayor 43, Bellamy 89	47 102
May	5	Tottenham	L	0-1	PL		47 370
	9	West Ham	D	1-1	PL	W-Phillips 21	34 989

LIVERPOOL LEAGUE APPEARANCES/GOALS 2009-10
Goalkeepers Pepe Reina ESP **38**
Defenders Daniel Agger DEN **23/0** • Jamie Carragher **37/0** • Fabio Aurelio BRA **8+6/0** • Stephen Darby **0+1/0** • Philipp Degen SUI **3+4/0** • Andrea Dossena ITA **1+1/0** • Emiliano Insua ARG **30+1/0** • Glen Johnson **24+1/3** • Martin Kelly **0+1/0** • Sotirios Kyrgiakos GRE **13+1/1** • Jack Robinson **0+1/0** • Daniel Sanchez Ayala **2+3/0** • Martin Skrtel SVK **16+3/1**
Midfield Alberto Aquilani ITA **9+9/1** • Yossi Benayoun ISR **19+11/6** • Steven Gerrard **32+1/9** • Lucas Leiva BRA **32+3/0** • Javier Mascherano **31+3/0** • Albert Riera **9+3/0** • Maxi Rodriguez ARG **14+3/1** • Jay Spearing **1+2/0**
Forwards Ryan Babel NED **9+16/4** • Nathan Eccleston **0+1/0** • Nabil El Zhar MAR **1+2/0** • Fernando Torres ESP **20+2/18** • Dirk Kuyt NED **35+2/9** • David N'Gog FRA **10+14/5** • Dani Pacheco ESP **0+4/0** • Andriy Voronin UKR **1+7/0**
Coach Rafa Benitez

MAN CITY LEAGUE APPEARANCES/GOALS 2009-10
Goalkeepers Marton Fulop HUN **3** • Shay Given IRL **35** • Gunnar Nielsen FRO **0+1**
Defenders Dedryk Boyata BEL **1+2/0** • Wayne Bridge **23/0** • Greg Cunningham IRL **0+2/0** • Richard Dunne IRL **2/0** • Garrido ESP **7+2/1** • Vincent Kompany BEL **21+4/2** • Joleon Lescott **17+1/1** • Nedum Onuoha **5+5/1** • Micah Richards **19+4/2** • Sylvinho BRA **6+4/0** • Kolo Toure CIV **31/1** • Pablo Zabaleta ARG **23+4/0**
Midfield Gareth Barry **34/2** • Nigel de Jong NED **30+4/0** • Abdisalam Ibrahim NOR **0+1/0** • Stephen Ireland IRL **16+6/2** • Adam Johnson **14+2/1** • Michael Johnson **0+1/0** • Martin Petrov BUL **8+8/4** • Patrick Vieira FRA **8+5/1** • Shaun Wright-Phillips **19+11/4** • Pablo Zabaleta ARG **23+4/0**
Forwards Emmanuel Adebayor TOG **25+1/14** • Craig Bellamy WAL **26+6/10** • Benjamin Benjani ZIM **1+1/0** • Alex Nimely-Tchuimeni **0+1/0** • Roque Santa Cruz PAR **6+13/3** • Carlos Tevez ARG **32+3/23**
Coach Mark Hughes WAL • Roberto Mancini ITA (19/12/09)

MANCHESTER UNITED 2009–10

Aug	9	Chelsea	D	2-2	CS	Nani [10], Rooney [90]. L 1-4p	85 896
	16	B'ham City	W	1-0	PL	Rooney [34]	75 062
	19	Burnley	L	0-1	PL		20 872
	22	Wigan	W	5-0	PL	Rooney 2 [56][65], Berbatov [58], Owen [85], Nani [90]	18 164
	29	Arsenal	W	2-1	PL	Rooney [59p], OG [64]	75 095
Sep	12	Tottenham	W	3-1	PL	Giggs [25], Anderson [41], Rooney [78]	35 785
	15	Besiktas	W	1-0	CLgB	Scholes [77]	26 448
	20	Man City	W	4-3	PL	Rooney 2, Fletcher 2 [49][80], Owen [90]	75 065
	23	Wolves	W	1-0	LCr3	Welbeck [66]	51 160
	26	Stoke	W	2-0	PL	Berbatov [62], O'Shea [77]	27 500
	30	Wolfsburg	W	2-1	CLgB	Giggs [59], Carrick [78]	74 037
Oct	3	Sunderland	D	2-2	PL	Berbatov [51], OG [90]	75 114
	17	Bolton	W	2-1	PL	OG [5], Valencia [33]	75 103
	21	CSKA	W	1-0	CLgB	Valencia [86]	51 250
	25	Liverpool	L	0-2	PL		44 188
	27	Barnsley	W	2-0	LCr4	Welbeck [6], Owen [59]	20 019
	31	Blackburn	W	2-0	PL	Berbatov [55], Rooney [87]	74 658
Nov	3	CSKA	D	3-3	CLgB	Owen [29], Scholes [84], Valencia [92+]	73 718
	8	Chelsea	L	0-1	PL		41 836
	21	Everton	W	3-0	PL	Fletcher [35], Carrick [67], Valencia [76]	75 169
	25	Besiktas	L	0-1	CLgB		74 242
	28	Portsmouth	W	4-1	PL	Rooney 3 [25p][48][54p], Giggs [87]	20 482
Dec	1	Tottenham	W	2-0	LCqf	Gibson 2 [16][38]	57 212
	5	West Ham	W	4-0	PL	Scholes [45], Gibson [61], Valencia [70], Rooney [72]	34 980
	8	Wolfsburg	W	3-1	CLgB	Owen 3 [44][83][91+]	26 490
	12	Aston Villa	L	0-1	PL		75 130
	15	Wolves	W	3-0	PL	Rooney [30p], Vidic [43], Valencia [66]	73 709
	19	Fulham	L	0-3	PL		25 700
	27	Hull	W	3-1	PL	Rooney [45], OG [73], Berbatov [82]	24 627
	30	Wigan	W	5-0	PL	Rooney [28], Carrick [32], Rafael [45], Berbatov [50], Valencia [75]	74 560
Jan	3	Leeds Utd	L	0-1	FAr3		74 526
	9	B'ham City	D	1-1	PL	OG [63]	28 907
	16	Burnley	W	3-0	PL	Berbatov [64], Rooney [69], Diouf [90]	75 120
	19	Man City	L	1-2	LCsf	Giggs [17]	46 067
	23	Hull	W	4-0	PL	Rooney 4 [8][82][86][90]	73 933
	27	Man City	W	3-1	LCsf	Scholes [52], Carrick [71], Rooney [92+]	74 576
	31	Arsenal	W	3-1	PL	Nani [33], Rooney [37], Park [52]	60 091
Feb	6	Portsmouth	W	5-0	PL	Rooney [40], OG [45], Carrick [59], Berbatov [62], OG [69]	74 684
	10	Aston Villa	D	1-1	PL	OG [23]	42 788
	16	Milan	W	3-2	CLr2	Scholes [36], Rooney 2 [66][74]	78 587
	20	Everton	L	1-3	PL	Berbatov [16]	39 448
	23	West Ham	W	3-0	PL	Rooney 2 [38][55], Owen [80]	73 797
	28	Aston Villa	W	2-1	LCf	Owen [12], Rooney [74]	88 596
Mar	6	Wolves	W	1-0	PL	Scholes [72]	28 883
	10	Milan	W	4-0	CLr2	Rooney 2 [13][46], Park [59], Fletcher [88]	74 595
	14	Fulham	W	3-0	PL	Rooney 2 [46][84], Berbatov [89]	75 207
	21	Liverpool	W	2-1	PL	Rooney [12], Park [60]	75 216
	27	Bolton	W	4-0	PL	OG [38], Berbatov 2 [69][78], Gibson [82]	25 370
	30	Bayern	L	1-2	CLqf	Rooney [1]	66 000
Apr	3	Chelsea	L	1-2	PL	Macheda [81]	75 217
	7	Bayern	W	3-2	CLqf	Gibson [3], Nani 2 [7][41]	74 482
	11	Blackburn	D	0-0	PL		29 912
	17	Man City	W	1-0	PL	Scholes [90]	47 019
	24	Tottenham	W	3-1	PL	Giggs 2 [58p][86p], Nani [81]	75 268
May	2	Sunderland	W	1-0	PL	Nani [28]	47 641
	9	Stoke	W	4-0	PL	Fletcher [31], Giggs [38], OG [54], Park [84]	75 316

MAN UTD LEAGUE APPEARANCES/GOALS 2009-10

Goalkeepers Ben Foster **9** • Tomasz Kuszczak POL **8** • Edwin van der Sar NED **21**

Defenders Wes Brown **18+1/0** • Ritchie De Laet BEL **2/0** • Jonny Evans NIR **18/0** • Patrice Evra FRA **37+1/0** • Fabio BRA **1+4/0** • Rio Ferdinand **15+2/0** • Gary Neville **15+2/0** • John O'Shea IRL **12+3/1** • Rafael BRA **8/1** • Nemanja Vidic SRB **24/1**

Midfield Anderson BRA **10+4/1** • Michael Carrick **22+8/2** • Darren Fletcher SCO **29+1/4** • Darron Gibson IRL **6+9/2** • Ryan Giggs WAL **20+5/5** • Owen Hargreaves **0+1/0** • Nani POR **19+4/3** • Park Ji Sung KOR **10+7/3** • Paul Scholes **24+4/3** • Luis Valencia ECU **29+5/5**

Forwards Dimitar Berbatov BUL **24+9/12** • Mame Diouf SEN **0+5/1** • Federico Macheda ITA **1+4/1** • Gabriel Obertan FRA **1+6/0** • Michael Owen **5+14/3** • Wayne Rooney **32/26** • Danny Welbeck **1+4/0**

Coach Alex Ferguson

PORTSMOUTH 2009–10

Aug	15	Fulham	L	0-1	PL		17 510
	19	B'ham City	L	0-1	PL		19 922
	22	Arsenal	L	1-4	PL	Kaboul [37]	60 049
	25	Hereford	W	4-1	LCr2	Piquionne [20], Utaka [23], Kranjcar [43], Hughes [56]	6 645
	30	Man City	L	0-1	PL		17 826
Sep	12	Bolton	L	2-3	PL	Kaboul [25], Boateng [63]	17 564
	19	Aston Villa	L	0-2	PL		35 979
	22	Carlisle	W	3-1	LCr3	Dindane [26], Webber [33], Vanden Borre [63]	7 042
	26	Everton	L	0-1	PL		18 116
Oct	3	Wolves	W	1-0	PL	Yebda [19]	29 023
	17	Tottenham	L	1-2	PL	Boateng [59]	20 821
	24	Hull	D	0-0	PL		23 720
	27	Stoke	W	4-0	LCr4	Piquionne 2 [17][59], Webber [55], Kanu [81]	11 251
	31	Wigan	W	4-0	PL	Dindane 3 [35][65][90p], Piquionne [45]	18 212
Nov	7	Blackburn	L	1-3	PL	O'Hara [15]	23 110
	22	Stoke	L	0-1	PL		27 069
	28	Man Utd	L	1-4	PL	Boateng [32p]	20 482
Dec	1	Aston Villa	L	2-4	LCqf	OG [10], Kanu [87]	17 034
	5	Burnley	W	2-0	PL	Hreidarsson [65], Dindane [84]	17 822
	12	Sunderland	D	1-1	PL	Kaboul [90]	37 578
	16	Chelsea	L	1-2	PL	Piquionne [51]	40 137
	19	Liverpool	W	2-0	PL	Belhadj [33], Piquionne [82]	20 534
	26	West Ham	L	0-2	PL		33 686
	30	Arsenal	L	1-4	PL	Belhadj [74]	20 404
Jan	2	Coventry	D	1-1	FAr3	Boateng [45]	11 214
	12	Coventry	W	2-1	FAr3	OG [90], Mokoena [121+]	7 097
	23	Sunderland	W	2-1	FAr4	Utaka 2 [42][57]	10 315
	26	West Ham	D	1-1	PL	Webber [76]	18 322
	31	Man City	L	0-2	PL		44 015
Feb	3	Fulham	L	0-1	PL		21 934
	6	Man Utd	L	0-5	PL		74 684
	9	Sunderland	D	1-1	PL	Dindane [90]	16 242
	13	S'hampton	W	4-1	FAr5	Owusu-Abeyie [66], Dindane [75], Belhadj [82], O'Hara [85]	31 385
	20	Stoke	L	1-2	PL	Piquionne [35]	17 208
	27	Burnley	W	2-1	PL	Piquionne [25], Yebda [76p]	19 714
Apr	6	B'ham City	W	2-0	FAqf	Piquionne 2 [67][70]	20 456
	9	B'ham City	L	1-2	PL	Kanu [90]	18 465
	15	Liverpool	L	1-4	PL	Belhadj [88]	40 316
	20	Hull	W	3-2	PL	Smith [37], O'Hara [88], Kanu [89]	16 513
	24	Chelsea	L	0-5	PL		18 753
	27	Tottenham	L	0-2	PL		35 870
	3	Blackburn	D	0-0	PL		16 207
	11	Tottenham	W	2-0	FAsf	Piquionne [99], Boateng [117p]	88 591
	14	Wigan	D	0-0	PL		14 323
	18	Aston Villa	L	1-2	PL	Brown [9]	16 523
	24	Bolton	D	2-2	PL	Dindane 2 [54][68]	20 526
May	1	Wolves	W	3-1	PL	Dindane [20], Utaka [39], Brown [67]	19 213
	9	Everton	L	0-1	PL		38 730
	15	Chelsea	L	0-1	FAf		88 335

PORTSMOUTH LEAGUE APPEARANCES/GOALS 2009-10

Goalkeepers Jamie Ashdown **5** • Asmir Begovic BIH **8+1/0** • David James **25**

Defenders Nadir Belhadj ALG **16+3/3** • Tal Ben Haim ISR **21+1/0** • Sylvain Distin FRA **3/0** • Steve Finnan IRL **20+1/0** • Hermann Hreioarsson ISL **17/1** • Younes Kaboul FRA **19/3** • Aaron Mokoena RSA **21+2/0** • Ricardo Rocha POR **10/0** • Lennard Sowah GER **3+2/0** • Anthony Vanden Borre BEL **15+4/0** • Joel Ward **1+2/0** • Marc Wilson IRL **28/0**

Midfield Angelos Basinas GRE **7+5/0** • Kevin Prince Boateng GHA **20+2/3** • Michael Brown **22+2/2** • Papa Bouba Diop SEN **9+3/0** • Richard Hughes SCO **9+1/0** • Niko Kranjcar CRO **4+0/0** • Hayden Mullins **15+3/0** • Jamie O'Hara **25+1/2** • Matt Ritchie **1+1/0** • Hassan Yebda ALG **15+3/2**

Forwards Aruna Dindane CIV **18+1/8** • Nwankwo Kanu NGA **6+17/2** • David Nugent **0+3/0** • Quincy Owusu-Abeyie GHA **3+7/0** • Frederic Piquionne FRA **26+8/5** • Tommy Smith **12+4/1** • John Utaka NGA **10+8/1** • Danny Webber **4+13/1**

Coach Paul Hart • Avram Grant (26/11/09)

STOKE CITY 2009–10

Month	Date	Opponent	Res	Score	Comp	Scorers	Att
Aug	15	Burnley	W	2-0	PL	Shawcross [19], OG [33]	27 385
	19	Liverpool	L	0-4	PL		44 318
	22	B'ham City	D	0-0	PL		21 694
	26	Orient	W	1-0	LCr2	Kitson [94]	2 742
	29	Sunderland	W	1-0	PL	Kitson [43]	27 091
Sep	12	Chelsea	L	1-2	PL	Diagne-Faye [32]	27 440
	19	Bolton	D	1-1	PL	Kitson [53]	20 265
	22	Blackpool	W	4-3	LCr3	Higginbotham [75], Etherington [78], Fuller [80], Griffin [96+]	13 957
	26	Man Utd	L	0-2	PL		27 500
Oct	4	Everton	D	1-1	PL	Huth [50]	36 753
	17	West Ham	W	2-1	PL	Beattie 2 [11p 69]	27 026
	24	Tottenham	W	1-0	PL	Whelan [86]	36 031
	27	Portsmouth	L	0-4	LCr4		11 251
	31	Wolves	D	2-2	PL	Beattie [17], Etherington [44]	27 500
Nov	8	Hull	L	1-2	PL	Etherington [29]	24 516
	22	Portsmouth	W	1-0	PL	Fuller [74]	27 069
	28	Blackburn	D	0-0	PL		25 143
Dec	5	Arsenal	L	0-2	PL		60 048
	12	Wigan	D	2-2	PL	Tuncay [37], Shawcross [74]	26 728
	19	Aston Villa	L	0-1	PL		35 852
	26	Man City	L	0-2	PL		47 325
	28	B'ham City	L	0-1	PL		27 211
Jan	2	York City	W	3-1	FAr3	OG [24], Fuller [25], Etherington [58]	15 586
	5	Fulham	W	3-2	PL	Tuncay [12], Diagne-Faye [34], Sidibe [37]	25 104
	16	Liverpool	D	1-1	PL	Huth [90]	27 247
	24	Arsenal	W	3-1	FAr4	Fuller 2 [2 78], Whitehead [86]	19 735
Feb	1	Sunderland	D	0-0	PL		35 078
	6	Blackburn	W	3-0	PL	Higginbotham [8], Sidibe [45], Etherington [67]	27 386
	9	Wigan	D	1-1	PL	Tuncay [74]	16 033
	13	Man City	D	1-1	FAr5	Fuller [57]	28 019
	16	Man City	D	1-1	PL	Whelan [72]	26 778
	20	Portsmouth	W	2-1	PL	Huth [50], Diao [90]	17 208
	24	Man City	W	3-1	FAr5	Kitson [79], Shawcross [95], Sanli [99]	21 813
	27	Arsenal	L	1-3	PL	Pugh [8]	27 011
Mar	7	Chelsea	L	0-2	FAqf		41 322
	10	Burnley	D	1-1	PL	Tuncay [23]	20 323
	13	Aston Villa	D	0-0	PL		27 598
	20	Tottenham	L	1-2	PL	Etherington [64p]	27 575
	27	West Ham	W	1-0	PL	Fuller [69]	34 564
Apr	3	Hull	W	2-0	PL	Fuller [6], Lawrence [90]	27 604
	11	Wolves	D	0-0	PL		28 455
	17	Bolton	L	1-2	PL	Kitson [13]	27 250
	25	Chelsea	L	0-7	PL		41 013
May	1	Everton	D	0-0	PL		27 579
	5	Fulham	W	1-0	PL	Etherington [83]	20 831
	9	Man Utd	L	0-4	PL		75 316

SUNDERLAND 2009–10

Month	Date	Opponent	Res	Score	Comp	Scorers	Att
Aug	15	Bolton	W	1-0	PL	Bent [5]	22 247
	18	Chelsea	L	1-3	PL	Bent [18]	41 179
	22	Blackburn	W	2-1	PL	Jones 2 [32 53]	37 106
	24	Norwich	W	4-1	LCr2	Tainio [26], Reid 2 [30 36], OG [67]	12 345
	29	Stoke	L	0-1	PL		27 091
Sep	12	Hull	W	4-1	PL	Bent 2 [13p 66], OG [75], Reid [49]	38 997
	19	Burnley	L	1-3	PL	Bent [39]	20 196
	22	B'ham City	W	2-0	LCr3	Henderson [4], Campbell [23]	20 576
	27	Wolves	W	5-2	PL	Bent [8p], Jones 2 [48p 70], Turner [73], OG [89]	37 566
Oct	3	Man Utd	D	2-2	PL	Bent [7], Jones [58]	75 114
	17	Liverpool	W	1-0	PL	Bent [5]	47 327
	24	B'ham City	L	1-2	PL	Turner [82]	21 723
		Aston Villa	D	0-0	LCr4		27 666
	31	West Ham	D	2-2	PL	Reid [39], Richardson [76]	39 033
Nov	7	Tottenham	L	0-2	PL		35 955
	21	Arsenal	W	1-0	PL	Bent [71]	44 918
	28	Wigan	L	0-1	PL		20 447
	6	Fulham	L	0-1	PL		23 168
Dec	12	Portsmouth	D	1-1	PL	Bent [23]	37 578
	15	Aston Villa	L	0-2	PL		34 821
	19	Man City	L	3-4	PL	Mensah [16], Henderson [24], Jones [62]	44 735
	26	Everton	D	1-1	PL	Bent [17]	46 990
	28	Blackburn	D	2-2	PL	Bent 2 [52 65]	25 656
Jan	2	Barrow	W	3-0	FAr3	Malbranque [17], Campbell 2 [52 58]	25 190
	16	Chelsea	L	2-7	PL	Zenden [56], Bent [90]	41 776
	23	Portsmouth	L	1-2	FAr4		10 315
	27	Everton	L	0-2	PL		32 163
Feb	1	Stoke	D	0-0	PL		35 078
	6	Wigan	D	1-1	PL	Jones [64]	38 350
	9	Portsmouth	D	1-1	PL	Bent [12p]	16 242
	20	Arsenal	L	0-1	PL		60 083
	28	Fulham	D	0-0	PL		40 192
Mar	6	Bolton	W	4-0	PL	Campbell [1], Bent 3 [64 74p 88]	36 087
	14	Man City	D	1-1	PL	Jones [9]	41 398
	20	B'ham City	W	3-1	PL	Bent 2 [5 11], Campbell [88]	37 962
	24	Aston Villa	D	1-1	PL	Campbell [22]	37 473
	28	Liverpool	L	0-3	PL		43 121
Apr	3	Tottenham	W	3-1	PL	Bent 2 [1 29p], Zenden [86]	43 184
	10	West Ham	L	0-1	PL		34 685
	17	Burnley	W	2-1	PL	Campbell [25], Bent [41p]	41 341
	24	Hull City	W	1-0	PL	Bent [7]	25 012
May	2	Man Utd	L	0-1	PL		47 641
	9	Wolves	L	1-2	PL	Jones [8]	28 971

STOKE LEAGUE APPEARANCES/GOALS 2009-10
Goalkeepers Asmir Begovic BIH 3+1 • Steve Simonsen 2 • Thomas Sorensen DEN 33
Defenders Danny Collins WAL 22+3/0 • Danny Higginbotham 23+1/1 • Robert Huth GER 30+2/3 • Ryan Shawcross 27+1/2 • Andrew Wilkinson 21+4/0
Midfield Rory Delap IRL 34+2/0 • Salif Diao 11+5/1 • Matthew Etherington 33+1/5 • Abdoulaye Faye SEN 30+1/2 • Liam Lawrence IRL 14+11/1 • Danny Pugh 1+6/1 • Glenn Whelan IRL 25+8/2 • Dean Whitehead 33+3/0
Forwards James Beattie 11+11/2 • Richard Cresswell 1+1/0 • Ricardo Fuller JAM 22+13/3 • Dave Kitson 10+8/3 • Louis Moult 0+1/0 • Mamady Sidibe MLI 19+5/2 • Tuncay Sanli TUR 13+17/4
Coach Tony Pulis

SUNDERLAND LEAGUE APPEARANCES/GOALS 2009-10
Goalkeepers Marton Fulop HUN 12+1 • Craig Gordon SCO 26
Defenders Phil Bardsley 18+8/0 • Danny Collins WAL 3/0 • Paulo da Silva PAR 12+4/0 • Anton Ferdinand 19+5/0 • Alan Hutton SCO 11/0 • Matthew Kilgallon 6+1/0 • George McCartney NIR 20+5/0 • John Mensah GHA 14+2/1 • Nyron Nosworthy JAM 7+3/0 • Michael Turner 29/1
Midfield Lorik Cana ALB 29+2/0 • Lee Cattermole 19+3/0 • Jack Colback 0+1/0 • Jordan Henderson 23+10/1 • Grant Leadbitter 0+1/0 • Steed Malbranque FRA 30+1/0 • David Meyler IRL 9+1/0 • Daryl Murphy IRL 2+1/0 • Andy Reid IRL 18+3/2 • Kieran Richardson 28+1/1 • Boudewijn Zenden NED 1+19/2
Forwards Benjani ZIM 1+7/0 • Darren Bent 38/24 • Frazier Campbell 19+12/4 • David Healy NIR 0+3/0 • Kenwyne Jones TRI 24+8/9
Coach Steve Bruce

TOTTENHAM HOTSPUR 2009-10

16 Liverpool	W	2-1	PL	Assou-Ekotto 44, Bassong 59	35 935
19 Hull	W	5-1	PL	Defoe 3 10 45 90, Palacios 14, Keane 78	24 735
23 West Ham	W	2-1	PL	Defoe 54, Lennon 79	33 095
26 Doncaster	W	5-1	LCr2	Crouch 37, Bentley 52, Huddlestone 9, O'Hara 11, Pavlyuchenko 69	12 923
29 B'ham City	W	2-1	PL	Crouch 72, Lennon 90	35 318
12 Man Utd	L	1-3	PL	Defoe 1	35 785
20 Chelsea	L	0-3	PL		41 623
23 Preston NE	W	5-1	LCr3	Crouch 3 14 77 92+, Defoe 37, Keane 87	16 533
26 Burnley	W	5-0	PL	Keane 4 18p 74 77 87, Jenas 33	35 462
3 Bolton	D	2-2	PL	Kranjcar 34, Corluka 73	21 305
17 Portsmouth	W	2-1	PL	King 29, Defoe 45	20 821
24 Stoke	L	0-1	PL		36 031
27 Everton	W	2-0	LCr4	Huddlestone 31, Keane 57	35 843
31 Arsenal	L	0-3	PL		60 103
7 Sunderland	W	2-0	PL	Keane 12, Huddlestone 68	35 955
22 Wigan	W	9-1	PL	Crouch 9, Defoe 5 51 54 58 69 87, Lennon 64, Bentley 88, Kranjcar 90	35 650
28 Aston Villa	D	1-1	PL	Dawson 77	39 866
1 Man Utd	L	0-2	LCqf		57 212
6 Everton	D	2-2	PL	Defoe 47, Dawson 59	34 003
12 Wolves	L	0-1	PL		36 012
16 Man City	W	3-0	PL	Kranjcar 2 37 90, Defoe 54	35 891
19 Blackburn	W	2-0	PL	Crouch 2 45 83	26 490
26 Fulham	D	0-0	PL		25 679
28 West Ham	W	2-0	PL	Modric 11, Defoe 81	35 994
2 Peter'boro	W	4-0	FAr3	Kranjcar 2 35 57, Defoe 70, Keane 95+p	35 862
16 Hull	D	0-0	PL		35 729
20 Liverpool	L	0-2	PL		42 016
23 Leeds Utd	D	2-2	FAr4	Crouch 42, Pavlyuchenko 75	35 750
26 Fulham	W	2-0	PL	Crouch 27, Bentley 60	35 467
30 B'ham City	D	1-1	PL	Defoe 69	27 238
3 Leeds Utd	W	3-1	FAr4	Defoe 3 37 73 90	37 704
6 Aston Villa	D	0-0	PL		35 899
10 Wolves	L	0-1	PL		27 992
14 Bolton	D	1-1	FAr5	Defoe 61	13 596
21 Wigan	W	3-0	PL	Defoe 27, Pavlyuchenko 2 84 90	16 165
24 Bolton	W	4-0	FAr5	Pavlyuchenko 2 23 87, OG 2 35 47	31 436
28 Everton	W	2-1	PL	Pavlyuchenko 11, Modric 28	35 912
6 Fulham	D	0-0	FAqf		24 533
13 Blackburn	W	3-1	PL	Defoe 45, Pavlyuchenko 2 55 85	35 474
20 Stoke	W	2-1	PL	Gujohnsen 46, Kranjcar 77	27 575
24 Fulham	W	3-1	FAqf	Bentley 47, Pavlyuchenko 60, Gudjohnsen 66	35 432
27 Portsmouth	W	2-0	PL	Crouch 27, Kranjcar 41	35 870
3 Sunderland	L	1-3	PL	Crouch 72	43 184
11 Portsmouth	L	0-2	FAsf		84 602
14 Arsenal	W	2-1	PL	Rose 10, Bale 47	36 041
17 Chelsea	W	2-1	PL	Defoe 15p, Bale 44	35 814
24 Man Utd	L	1-3	PL	King 70	75 268
1 Bolton	W	1-0	PL	Huddlestone 38	35 852
5 Man City	W	1-0	PL	Crouch 82	47 370
9 Burnley	L	2-4	PL	Bale 3, Modric 32	21 161

WEST HAM UNITED 2009-10

15 Wolves	W	2-0	PL	Noble 22, Upson 69	28 674
23 Tottenham	L	1-2	PL	Cole 49	33 095
25 Millwall	W	3-1	LCr2	Stanislas 2 87 98, Hines 100	24 492
29 Blackburn	D	0-0	PL		23 421
12 Wigan	L	0-1	PL		17 142
19 Liverpool	L	2-3	PL	Diamanti 29p, Cole 45	34 658
22 Bolton	L	1-3	LCr3	Ilunga 59	8 050
28 Man City	L	1-3	PL	Cole 24	42 745
4 Fulham	D	2-2	PL	Cole 16, Stanislas 90	32 612
17 Stoke	L	1-2	PL	Upson 34	27 026
25 Arsenal	D	2-2	PL	Cole 74, Diamanti 80p	34 442
1 Sunderland	D	2-2	PL	Franco 30, Cole 36	39 033
4 Aston Villa	W	2-1	PL	Noble 45p, Hines 90	30 024
8 Everton	L	1-2	PL	Stanislas 65	32 466
21 Hull	D	3-3	PL	Franco 5, Collison 11, Da Costa 69	24 909
28 Burnley	W	5-3	PL	Collison 18, Stanislas 33, Cole 43p, Franco 51, Jimenez 64p	34 003
5 Man Utd	L	0-4	PL		34 980
12 B'ham City	L	0-1	PL		28 203
15 Bolton	L	1-3	PL	Diamanti 69	17 849
20 Chelsea	D	1-1	PL	Diamanti 45p	33 388
26 Portsmouth	W	2-0	PL	Diamanti 43p, Kovac 89	33 686
28 Tottenham	L	0-2	PL		35 994
3 Arsenal	L	1-2	FAr3	Diamanti 45	25 549
17 Aston Villa	D	0-0	PL		35 646
26 Portsmouth	D	1-1	PL	Upson 52	18 322
30 Blackburn	D	0-0	PL		33 093
6 Burnley	L	1-2	PL	Ilan 81	21 001
10 B'ham City	W	2-0	PL	Diamanti 45, Cole 67	34 458
20 Hull	W	3-0	PL	Behrami 3, Cole 59, Faubert 90	33 971
23 Man Utd	L	0-3	PL		73 797
6 Bolton	L	1-2	PL	Diamanti 88	33 824
13 Chelsea	L	1-4	PL	Parker 30	41 755
20 Arsenal	L	0-2	PL		60 077
23 Wolves	L	1-3	PL	Franco 90	33 988
27 Stoke	L	0-1	PL		34 564
4 Everton	D	2-2	PL	Da Costa 60, Ilan 87	37 451
10 Sunderland	W	1-0	PL	Ilan 51	34 685
19 Liverpool	L	0-3	PL		37 697
24 Wigan	W	3-2	PL	Ilan 31, Kovac 45, Parker 77	33 057
2 Fulham	L	2-3	PL	Cole 61, Franco 90	24 201
9 Man City	D	1-1	PL	Boa Morte 17	34 989

SPURS LEAGUE APPEARANCES/GOALS 2009-10
Goalkeepers Ben Alnwick 1 • Carlo Cudicini ITA 6 • Gomes BRA 31
Defenders Benoit Assou-Ekotto CMR 29+1/1 • Gareth Bale WAL 18+5/3 • Sebastien Bassong CMR 25+3/1 • Vedran Corluka CRO 29/0 • Michael Dawson 25+4/2 • Alan Hutton 1+7/0 • Younes Kaboul FRA 8+2/0 • Ledley King 19+1/2 • Kyle Naughton 0+1/0 • Kyle Walker 2+0/0 • Jonathan Woodgate 3/0
Midfield David Bentley 11+4/1 • Giovani MEX 0+1/0 • Tom Huddlestone 33/2 • Jermaine Jenas 9+10/1 • Niko Kranjcar CRO 19+5/6 • Aaron Lennon 20+2/3 • Jake Livermore 0+1/0 • Luka Modric CRO 21+4/3 • Jamie O'Hara 0+2/0 • Wilson Palacios HON 29+4/1 • Danny Rose 1/1
Forwards Peter Crouch 21+17/8 • Jermain Defoe 31+3/18 • Eiour Guojohnsen ISL 3+8/1 • Robbie Keane IRL 15+5/6 • Roman Pavlyuchenko RUS 8+8/5
Coach Harry Redknapp

WEST HAM LEAGUE APPEARANCES/GOALS 2009-10
Goalkeepers Robert Green 38 • Peter Kurucz HUN 0+1/0
Defenders James Collins WAL 3/0 • Manuel Da Costa POR 12+3/2 • Fabio Daprela SUI 4+3/0 • Julien Faubert FRA 32+1/1 • Daniel Gabbidon WAL 8+2/0 • Herita Ilunga COD 16/0 • Radoslav Kovac CZE 27+4/2 • Jonathan Spector USA 22+5/0 • Jordan Spence 0+1/0 • James Tomkins 22+1/0 • Matthew Upson 33/3
Midfield Valon Behrami SUI 24+3/1 • Boa Morte POR 1/1 • Jack Collison WAL 19+3/2 • Kieron Dyer 4+6/0 • Luis Jimenez CHI 6+5/1 • Radoslav Kovac CZE 27+4/2 • Mark Noble 25+2/2 • Scott Parker 30+1/2 • Junior Stanislas 11+15/2
Forwards Carlton Cole 26+4/10 • Alessandro Diamanti 18+9/7 • Guillermo Franco MEX 16+7/5 • Zavon Hines JAM 5+8/1 • Ilan BRA 6+5/4 • Benny McCarthy RSA 2+3/0 • Mido EGY 5+4/0 • Frank Nouble 3+5/0 • Freddie Sears 0+1/0
Coach Gianfranco Zola

WIGAN ATHLETIC 2009–10

Month	Date	Opponent	Result	Comp	Scorers	Attendance
Aug	15	Aston Villa	W 2-0	PL	Rodallega 31, Koumas 56	35 578
	18	Wolves	L 0-1	PL		16 661
	22	Man Utd	L 0-5	PL		18 164
	26	Blackpool	L 1-4	LCr2	Amaya 94+	8 089
	30	Everton	L 1-2	PL	Scharner 57	35 122
Sep	12	West Ham	W 1-0	PL	Rodallega 55	17 142
	19	Arsenal	L 0-4	PL		59 103
	26	Chelsea	W 3-1	PL	Bramble 16, Rodallega 53p, Scharner 90	18 542
Oct	3	Hull	L 1-2	PL	Sinclair 87	22 822
	18	Man City	D 1-1	PL	N'Zogbia 45	20 005
	24	Burnley	W 3-1	PL	Rodallega 2 11 51, Boyce 76	19 430
	31	Portsmouth	L 0-4	PL		18 212
Nov	8	Fulham	D 1-1	PL	Boyce 13	16 172
	22	Tottenham	L 1-9	PL	Scharner 57	35 650
	28	Sunderland	W 1-0	PL	Rodallega 76	20 447
Dec	5	B'ham City	L 2-3	PL	N'Zogbia 33, Gomez 89	18 797
	12	Stoke	D 2-2	PL	Boyce 15, Figueroa 72	26 728
	16	Liverpool	L 1-2	PL	N'Zogbia 90	41 116
	26	Blackburn	D 1-1	PL	Rodallega 53	20 243
	30	Man Utd	L 0-5	PL		74 560
Jan	2	Hull	W 4-1	FAr3	N'Zogbia 2 47 66, McCarthy 63, Sinclair 91+	5 335
	16	Wolves	W 2-0	PL	McCarthy 60, N'Zogbia 73	27 604
	23	Notts Co	D 2-2	FAr4	Scotland 52, Watson 83	9 073
	27	Blackburn	L 1-2	PL	Caldwell 57	22 190
	30	Everton	L 0-1	PL		16 869
Feb	2	Notts Co	L 0-2	FAr4		5 519
	6	Sunderland	D 1-1	PL	Diame 20	38 350
	9	Stoke	D 1-1	PL	Scharner 14	16 033
	17	Bolton	D 0-0	PL		18 089
	21	Tottenham	L 0-3	PL		16 165
	27	B'ham City	L 0-1	PL		25 921
Mar	8	Liverpool	W 1-0	PL	Rodallega 35	17 427
	13	Bolton	L 0-4	PL		20 053
	16	Aston Villa	L 1-2	PL	Caldwell 27	16 186
	20	Burnley	W 1-0	PL	Rodallega 90	18 498
	29	Man City	L 0-3	PL		43 534
Apr	4	Fulham	L 1-2	PL	Scotland 34	22 730
	14	Portsmouth	D 0-0	PL		14 323
	18	Arsenal	W 3-2	PL	Watson 80, Bramble 89, N'Zogbia 90	22 113
	24	West Ham	L 2-3	PL	OG 4, Rodallega 52	33 057
May	3	Hull	D 2-2	PL	Moses 30, Gohouri 90	20 242
	9	Chelsea	L 0-8	PL		41 383

WOLVERHAMPTON WANDERERS 2009–10

Month	Date	Opponent	Result	Comp	Scorers	Attendance
Aug	15	West Ham	L 0-2	PL		28 674
	18	Wigan	W 1-0	PL	Keogh 6	16 661
	22	Man City	L 0-1	PL		47 287
	25	Swindon	D 0-0	LCr2	W 6-5p	11 416
	29	Hull	D 1-1	PL	Stearman 46	27 906
Sep	12	Blackburn	L 1-3	PL	Maierhofer 88	24 845
	20	Fulham	W 2-1	PL	Doyle 18, Edwards 50	27 670
	23	Man Utd	L 0-1	LCr3		51 160
	27	Sunderland	L 2-5	PL	OG 50, Doyle 55	37 566
Oct	3	Portsmouth	L 0-1	PL		29 023
	17	Everton	D 1-1	PL	Doyle 76	39 319
	24	Aston Villa	D 1-1	PL	Ebanks-Blake 83p	28 734
	27	Stoke	D 2-2	PL	Craddock 2 48 64	27 500
Nov	7	Arsenal	L 1-4	PL	Craddock 89	28 937
	21	Chelsea	L 0-4	PL		41 786
	29	B'ham City	L 0-1	PL		26 668
Dec	5	Bolton	W 2-1	PL	Craddock 3, Milijas 63	27 362
	12	Tottenham	W 1-0	PL	Doyle 3	36 012
	15	Man Utd	L 0-3	PL		73 709
	20	Burnley	W 2-0	PL	Milijas 15, Doyle 50	27 410
	26	Liverpool	L 0-2	PL		41 956
	28	Man City	L 0-3	PL		28 957
Jan	2	Tranmere	W 1-0	FAr3	Jarvis 77	7 476
	16	Wigan	L 0-2	PL		27 604
	23	C Palace	D 2-2	FAr4	Lee 3, Ambrose 49	14 449
	26	Liverpool	D 0-0	PL		28 763
	30	Hull	D 2-2	PL	OG 49, Jarvis 67	24 957
Feb	2	C Palace	L 1-3	FAr4	Henry 90	10 282
	7	B'ham City	L 1-2	PL	Doyle 42	24 165
	10	Tottenham	W 1-0	PL	Jones 27	27 992
	20	Chelsea	L 0-2	PL		28 978
	27	Bolton	L 0-1	PL		21 261
Mar	6	Man Utd	L 0-1	PL		28 883
	13	Burnley	W 2-1	PL	Jarvis 26, OG 47	21 217
	20	Aston Villa	D 2-2	PL	Craddock 23, OG 38	37 562
	23	West Ham	W 3-1	PL	Doyle 28, Zubar 58, Jarvis 61	33 988
	27	Everton	D 0-0	PL		28 995
Apr	3	Arsenal	L 0-1	PL		60 067
	11	Stoke	D 0-0	PL		28 455
	17	Fulham	D 0-0	PL		25 597
	24	Blackburn	D 1-1	PL	Ebanks-Blake 81	28 967
May	1	Portsmouth	L 1-3	PL	Doyle 35	19 213
	9	Sunderland	W 2-1	PL	Doyle 10p, Guedioura 78	28 971

WIGAN LEAGUE APPEARANCES/GOALS 2009-10
Goalkeepers Chris Kirkland 32 • Mike Pollitt 2 • Vladimir Stojkovic SRB 4
Defenders Emmerson Boyce 23+1/3 • Titus Bramble 35/2 • Gary Caldwell SCO 16/2 • Erik Edman SWE 2+1/0 • Maynor Figueroa HON 35/1 • Steve Gohouri CIV 4+1/1 • Mario Melchiot NED 32/0 • Paul Scharner AUT 30+8/4
Midfield Michael Brown 2/0 • Cho Won Hee KOR 1+3/0 • Mohamed Diame FRA 34/1 • Jordi Gomez ESP 11+12/1 • Olivier Kapo FRA 0+1/0 • Jason Koumas WAL 6+2/1 • James McCarthy SCO 19+1/1 • Charles N'Zogbia FRA 35+1/5 • Paul Scharner AUT 30+8/4 • Hendry Thomas HON 27+4/0 • Ben Watson 4+1/1
Forwards Marlon King JAM 0+3/0 • Marcelo Moreno BOL 9+3/0 • Victor Moses 2+12/1 • Hugo Rodallega COL 38/10 • Jason Scotland TRI 14+18/1 • Scott Sinclair 1+17/1
Coach Roberto Martinez ESP

WOLVES LEAGUE APPEARANCES/GOALS 2009-10
Goalkeepers Marcus Hahnemann USA 25 • Wayne Hennessey WAL 13
Defenders Christophe Berra SCO 32/0 • Jody Craddock 33/5 • George Elokobi CMR 17+5/0 • Kevin Foley IRL 23+2/0 • Greg Halford 12+3/0 • Matthew Hill 2/0 • Michael Mancienne 22+8/0 • Richard Stearman 12+4/1 • Stephen Ward IRL 18+4/0 • Ronald Zubar FRA 23/1
Midfield Segundo Castillo ECU 7+1/0 • David Edwards WAL 16+4/1 • George Friend 1/0 • Adlene Guedioura ALG 7+7/1 • Karl Henry 34/0 • Matthew Jarvis 30+4/3 • David Jones 16+4/1 • Michael Kightly 3+6/0 • Nenad Milijas SRB 12+7/2 • Geoffrey Mujangi Bia BEL 1+2/0 • Andrew Surman 3+4/0
Forwards Kevin Doyle IRL 33+1/9 • Sylvain Ebanks-Blake 12+11/2 • Chris Iwelumo SCO 2+13/0 • Andy Keogh IRL 8+5/1 • Stefan Maierhofer AUT 1+7/1 • Sam Vokes WAL 0+5/0
Coach Mick McCarthy

EQG – EQUATORIAL GUINEA

FIFA/COCA-COLA WORLD RANKING

1993	1994	1995	1996	1997	1998	1999	2000	2001	2002	2003	2004	2005	2006	2007	2008	2009	2010
-	-	-	-	-	195	188	187	190	192	160	171	171	109	85	123	135	165

2010												Hi/Lo
Jan	Feb	Mar	Apr	May	Jun	Jul	Aug	Sep	Oct	Nov	Dec	**64**
135	138	138	143	141	141	147	145	164	167	167	165	**195**

Equatorial Guinea qualified for a first appearance at a FIFA tournament when the women's national team finished as runners-up at the 2010 African Women's Championship in South Africa. A 4-2 defeat at the hands of Nigeria in the final meant that they failed to retain the trophy they won on home soil two years previously but it did ensure qualification for the 2011 FIFA Women's World Cup in Germany. An extra time victory over hosts South Africa in the semi-finals ensured their progress, although the liberal use of expatriate players granted nationality ensured a controversial cloud over their achievement. The women's game continued to overshadow that of the men, who are preparing to co-host the 2012 African Nations Cup finals along with neighbours Gabon. The Confederation of African Football, impressed with the new stadiums in Bata and Malabo, gave local organisers' preparations a hearty recommendation more than 12 months before the kick off. That contrasted with the scramble to get ready in Gabon but the form of the national side, 'Nzalang Nacional', remained a concern and after a defeat to Morocco in a friendly in August, the Paraguay-born coach Carlos Diarte was removed from the job. In December, the much-travelled former France manager Henri Michel was picked to prepare the side for the Nations Cup finals.

FIFA WORLD CUP RECORD
1930-1998 DNE 2002-2010 DNQ

FEDERACION ECUATOGUINEANA DE FUTBOL (FEGUIFUT)

Avenida de Hassan II,
Apartado postal 1017,
Malabo

☎ +240 222274048
📠 +240 333096565
✉ bonmanga@orange.gq
🖥 www.feguifut.net
FA 1960 CON 1986 FIFA 1986
P Bonifacio Manga Obiang
GS Mariano Ebang Anguesomo

FIFA BIG COUNT 2006

Total players	25 590
% of population	4.74%
Male	25 240
Female	350
Amateurs 18+	1 400
Unregistered	3 300
Professionals	230
Referees	50
Admin & coaches	65
Number of clubs	18
Number of teams	48

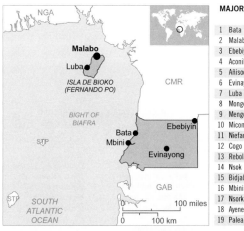

MAJOR CITIES/TOWNS

		Population
1	Bata	219 302
2	Malabo	175 365
3	Ebebiyin	31 827
4	Aconibe	14 182
5	Añisoc	13 657
6	Evinayong	8 924
7	Luba	8 042
8	Mongomo	6 979
9	Mengomeyen	6 700
10	Micomeseng	6 310
11	Niefang	5 495
12	Cogo	5 417
13	Rebola	5 354
14	Nsok	5 335
15	Bidjabidjan	4 837
16	Mbini	4 690
17	Nsork	4 246
18	Ayene	3 922
19	Palea	3 824

REPUBLICA DE GUINEA ECUATORIAL • REPUBLIC OF EQUATORIAL GUINEA

Capital	Malabo	Population	633 441 (165)	% in cities	39%
GDP per capita	$37 300 (29)	Area km²	28 051 km² (145)	GMT +/-	+1
Neighbours (km)	Cameroon 189, Gabon 350 • Coast 296				

RECENT INTERNATIONAL MATCHES PLAYED BY EQUATORIAL GUINEA

2006	Opponents		Score	Venue	Comp	Scorers	Att	Referee
3-09	Liberia	W	2-1	Malabo	CNq	Juan Epitie [24], Rodolfo Bodipo [88]		Agbenyega GHA
7-10	Cameroon	L	0-3	Yaounde	CNq			Daami TUN
2007								
5-03	Congo	L	1-2	N'Djamena	CMr1	Desire Pierre [18]		
9-03	Gabon	D	1-1	N'Djamena	CMr1	Ibrahima Toure [44p]		
25-03	Rwanda	W	3-1	Malabo	CNq	Andre Moreira [29], Juvenal Edjogo [75], Juan Epitie [81]		Louzaya CGO
2-06	Rwanda	L	0-2	Kigali	CNq			Auda EGY
17-06	Liberia	D	0-0	Monrovia	CNq			Diouf SEN
9-09	Cameroon	W	1-0	Malabo	CNq	Juvenal Edjogo [39]		Sidibe MLI
21-11	Niger	D	1-1	Malabo	Fr	Rodolfo Bodipo		
2008								
1-06	Sierra Leone	W	2-0	Malabo	WCq	Falcao Carolino [47], Juan Epitie [57]	13 000	Codjia BEN
7-06	South Africa	L	1-4	Atteridgeville	WCq	Juvenal Edjogo [78p]	10 000	Diouf SEN
15-06	Nigeria	L	0-1	Malabo	WCq		15 200	Mendy GAM
21-06	Nigeria	L	0-2	Abuja	WCq		20 000	Ambaya LBY
6-09	Sierra Leone	L	1-2	Freetown	WCq	Rodolfo Bodipo [83p]	22 000	Doue CIV
11-10	South Africa	L	0-1	Malabo	WCq		6 500	Djaoupe TOG
2009								
28-03	Cape Verde Islands	L	0-5	Sal	Fr			
25-04	Mali	L	0-3	Bamoko	Fr			
6-06	Estonia	L	0-3	Tallinn	Fr		2 150	Malzinskas LTU
2010								
11-08	Morocco	L	1-2	Rabat	Fr	Anselmo Eyegue [38]		
12-10	Botswana	L	0-2	Malabo	Fr			

Fr = Friendly match • CN = CAF African Cup of Nations • CM = CEMAC Cup • WC = FIFA World Cup
q = qualifier • r1 = first round group • sf = semi-final • f = final • † Not a full international

RECENT LEAGUE AND CUP RECORD

Year	Champions	Cup Winners
1997	Deportivo Mongomo	Union Vesper
1998	CD Ela Nguema	Union Vesper
1999	Akonangui	CD Unidad
2000	CD Ela Nguema	CD Unidad
2001	FC Akonangui	Atlético Malabo
2002	CD Ela Nguema	FC Akonangui
2003	Atlético Malabo	Deportivo Mongomo
2004	Renacimiento	CD Ela Nguema
2005	Renacimiento	
2006	Renacimiento	
2007	Renacimiento	FC Akonangui
2008	Akonangui	
2009	CD Ela Nguema	Dragon FC Bata
2010	Deportivo Mongomo	

ERI – ERITREA

FIFA/COCA-COLA WORLD RANKING

1993	1994	1995	1996	1997	1998	1999	2000	2001	2002	2003	2004	2005	2006	2007	2008	2009	2010
-	-	-	-	-	189	169	158	171	157	155	169	169	140	132	162	163	177

	2010											Hi/Lo
Jan	Feb	Mar	Apr	May	Jun	Jul	Aug	Sep	Oct	Nov	Dec	**121**
163	162	164	163	159	155	158	157	161	165	165	177	**189**

A spate of defections and asylum bids on foreign trips in recent years by footballers playing for both the national team and club sides led to a self-imposed exile for Eritrea in 2010. The Red Sea state did not allow travel abroad for any of its teams which meant the national side was absent from both the 2010 East and Central African Senior Challenge Cup in Tanzania as well as from the qualifiers for the 2012 African Nations Cup. It was the second Nations Cup in a row that they failed to enter having last competed in the preliminaries for the 2008 finals in Ghana, where they achieved a remarkable double triumph home and away over Kenya, drew both ties with Swaziland and held group winners Angola to a draw. In August 2007 the team reached a high of 121 in the FIFA/Coca-Cola World Ranking and since then have twice reached the quarter-finals of the East and Central African Senior Challenge Cup. The under-20 side was initially scheduled to take part in the 2011 African Youth Championship qualifiers but was withdrawn before the preliminaries started. Eritrea did enter one tournament in 2010 - the CECAFA U-20 tournament in August 2010 - but only because they hosted the event in Asmara. In a sign of the talent available, the Eritreans finished as runners-up to Uganda.

FIFA WORLD CUP RECORD
1930-1998 DNE 2002-2006 DNQ 2010 DNE

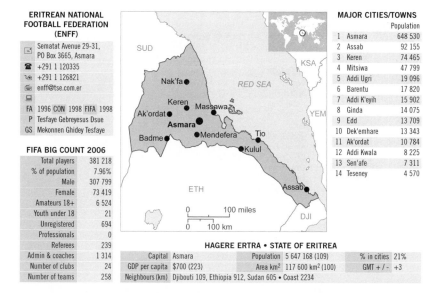

ERITREAN NATIONAL FOOTBALL FEDERATION (ENFF)

Sematat Avenue 29-31, PO Box 3665, Asmara
☎ +291 1 120335
📠 +291 1 126821
✉ enff@tse.com.er

FA	1996	CON	1998	FIFA	1998
P	Tesfaye Gebreyesus Dsue				
GS	Mekonnen Ghidey Tesfaye				

FIFA BIG COUNT 2006

Total players	381 218
% of population	7.96%
Male	307 799
Female	73 419
Amateurs 18+	6 524
Youth under 18	21
Unregistered	694
Professionals	0
Referees	239
Admin & coaches	1 314
Number of clubs	24
Number of teams	258

MAJOR CITIES/TOWNS

		Population
1	Asmara	648 530
2	Assab	92 155
3	Keren	74 465
4	Mitsiwa	47 799
5	Addi Ugri	19 096
6	Barentu	17 820
7	Addi K'eyih	15 902
8	Ginda	14 075
9	Edd	13 709
10	Dek'emhare	13 343
11	Ak'ordat	10 784
12	Addi Kwala	8 225
13	Sen'afe	7 311
14	Teseney	4 570

HAGERE ERTRA • STATE OF ERITREA

Capital	Asmara	Population	5 647 168 (109)	% in cities	21%
GDP per capita	$700 (223)	Area km²	117 600 km² (100)	GMT +/-	+3
Neighbours (km)	Djibouti 109, Ethiopia 912, Sudan 605 • Coast 2234				

RECENT INTERNATIONAL MATCHES PLAYED BY ERITREA

2005	Opponents	Score		Venue	Comp	Scorers	Att	Referee
28-11	Zanzibar †	L	0-3	Kigali	CCr1			
30-11	Rwanda	L	2-3	Kigali	CCr1	Suleiman Muhamoul 2		
2-12	Burundi	D	0-0	Kigali	CCr1			
4-12	Tanzania	L	0-1	Kigali	CCr1			
2006								
2-09	Kenya	W	2-1	Nairobi	CNq	Origi OG 15, Shimangus Yednekatchew 67		Lwanja MWI
7-10	Swaziland	D	0-0	Asmara	CNq			Gasingwa RWA
2007								
7-01	Yemen	L	1-4	Sana'a	Fr			
25-03	Angola	L	1-6	Luanda	CNq	Misgina Besirat 73		Evehe CMR
21-05	Sudan	W	1-0	Asmara	Fr	Shimangus Yednekatchew 46		
26-05	Sudan	D	1-1	Asmara	Fr			
2-06	Angola	D	1-1	Asmara	CNq	Hamiday Abdelkadir 15		Marange ZIM
16-06	Kenya	W	1-0	Asmara	CNq	Berhane Arega 80		Abdelrahman SUD
9-09	Swaziland	D	0-0	Manzini	CNq			Ssegonga UGA
30-11	Sudan	L	0-1	Omdurman	Fr			
3-12	Sudan	L	0-1	Omdurman	Fr			
9-12	Rwanda	L	1-2	Dar es Salaam	CCr1	Berhane Arega 38		
11-12	Djibouti	W	3-2	Dar es Salaam	CCr1	Berhane Arega 6, Shimangus Yednekatchew 42, Binam Fissehaye 68		
14-12	Uganda	W	3-2	Dar es Salaam	CCr1	Elmon Yeamekibron 2 53 64, Samuel Ghebrehine 82		
17-12	Burundi	L	1-2	Dar es Salaam	CCqf	Berhane Arega 20		
2008								
No international matches played in 2008								
2009								
1-12	Zimbabwe †	D	0-0	Nairobi	CCr1			
3-12	Rwanda	L	1-2	Nairobi	CCr1	Yosief Tzerezghi 83		
5-12	Somalia	W	3-1	Nairobi	CCr1	Isaias Andberhian 25p, Filmon Tseqay 27, OG 60		
8-12	Tanzania	L	0-4	Nairobi	CCqf			
2010								
No international matches played in 2010								

CN = CAF African Cup of Nations • CC = CECAFA Cup • WC = FIFA World Cup • q = qualifier • r1 = first round group • † Not a full international

ERITREA 2009 SUPER DIVISION A						
	Pl	W	D	L	F	A	Pts
Red Sea FC	20						43
Denden	20						38
Al Tahrir	20						35
Adulis Club	20						33
Maitemenai	20						31
Tesfa	20						24
Geza Banda	20						21
Asmara Berra	20						21
City Center	20						17
Edagahmus	20						16
Akria	20						15

Started 28/12/2008

ESP – SPAIN

FIFA/COCA-COLA WORLD RANKING

1993	1994	1995	1996	1997	1998	1999	2000	2001	2002	2003	2004	2005	2006	2007	2008	2009	2010
5	2	4	8	11	15	4	7	7	3	3	5	5	12	4	1	1	1

	2010											Hi/Lo
Jan	Feb	Mar	Apr	May	Jun	Jul	Aug	Sep	Oct	Nov	Dec	1
1	1	1	1	2	2	1	1	1	1	1	1	25

Victory against the Netherlands in the final of the 2010 FIFA World Cup in Johannesburg meant that Spain became only the eighth nation to be crowned world champions and the first Europeans to win the title outside Europe. But the achievements of this Spanish national team don't end there. From the start of 2007 until the final, they lost just twice in 55 games - a record unmatched in the history of international football. As champions of Europe and now as world champions, this Spanish team will surely go down in history as one of the greatest of all time - a match even for the legendary Brazilians of 1970. With five Catalans and six Barcelona based players in the team that beat the Netherlands, the Catalan capital witnessed jubilant scenes long into the night of the final - an extraordinary sight given that the city has only ever played host to two competitive international matches in the 90-year history of the Spanish national team - a 1969 World Cup qualifier in the Camp Nou and a 1975 European Championship qualifier in the old Sarria stadium. At club level it was also Barcelona's year in the championship as they and Real Madrid scored 200 league goals between them in a close race that left the rest of the field trailing in their wake. Sevilla won the Copa del Rey while Atlético Madrid beat Fulham 2-1 in the first Europa League final.

FIFA WORLD CUP RECORD

1930 DNE **1934** 5 QF 1938 DNE **1950** 4 2r 1954-1958 DNQ **1962** 12 r1 **1966** 10 r1 1970-1974 DNQ **1978** 10 r1 **1982** 12 r2 (hosts) **1986** 7 QF **1990** 10 r2 **1994** 8 QF **1998** 17 r1 **2002** 5 QF **2006** 9 r2 **2010** 1 Winners

REAL FEDERACION ESPANOLA DE FUTBOL (RFEF).

Ramon y Cajal
s/n Apartado postale 385, Las Rozas 28230, Madrid
☎ +34 91 4959800
📠 +34 91 4959801
📧 rfef@rfef.es
🖥 www.rfef.es
FA 1913 CON 1954 FIFA 1904
P Angel Maria Villar Llona
GS Jorge Perez

FIFA BIG COUNT 2006

Total players	2 834 190
% of population	7.02%
Male	2 536 103
Female	298 087
Amateurs 18+	136 132
Unregistered	1 915 000
Professionals	1 331
Referees	9 573
Admin & coaches	53 000
Number of clubs	18 092
Number of teams	39 811

MAJOR CITIES/TOWNS

		Population
1	Madrid	3 119 376
2	Barcelona	1 641 281
3	Valencia	890 020
4	Sevilla	706 146
5	Zaragoza	658 434
6	Málaga	570 055
7	Murcia	440 303
8	Palma	384 097
9	Las Palmas	378 356
10	Bilbao	354 726
11	Córdoba	327 809
12	Valladolid	317 149
13	Alacante	305 523
14	Vigo	294 682
15	Gijón	276 260
16	La Coruña	243 838
34	San Sebastian	184 790
124	Irun	62 743
159	Villarreal	45 214

REINO DE ESPANA • KINGDOM OF SPAIN

Capital Madrid	Population 40 525 002 (32)	% in cities 77%
GDP per capita $34 600 (36)	Area km² 505 370 km² (51)	GMT +/- +1
Neighbours (km) Andorra 63, France 623, Gibraltar 1, Portugal 1214, Morocco 16 • Coast 4964		

RECENT INTERNATIONAL MATCHES PLAYED BY SPAIN

2006	Opponents	Score		Venue	Comp	Scorers	Att	Referee
14-06	Ukraine	W	4-0	Leipzig	WCr1	Xabi Alonso [13], Villa 2 [17 48p], Fernando Torres [81]	43 000	Busacca SUI
19-06	Tunisia	W	3-1	Stuttgart	WCr1	Raul [71], Fernando Torres 2 [76 91+]	52 000	Simon BRA
23-06	Saudi Arabia	W	1-0	Kaiserslautern	WCr1	Juanito [36]	46 000	Codjia BEN
27-06	France	L	1-3	Hanover	WCr2	Villa [28p]	43 000	Rosetti ITA
15-08	Iceland	D	0-0	Reykjavik	Fr		12 327	Stokes IRL
2-09	Liechtenstein	W	4-0	Badajoz	ECq	Torres [20], Villa 2 [45 62], Luis Garcia [66]	13 876	Bozinovski MKD
6-09	Northern Ireland	L	2-3	Belfast	ECq	Xavi [14], Villa [52]	13 885	De Bleeckere BEL
7-10	Sweden	L	0-2	Stockholm	ECq		41 482	Bennett ENG
11-10	Argentina	W	2-1	Murcia	Fr	Xavi [33], Villa [64p]	31 000	Duhamel FRA
15-11	Romania	L	0-1	Cadiz	Fr		15 000	Messina ITA
2007								
7-02	England	W	1-0	Manchester	Fr	Iniesta [63]	58 247	Weiner GER
24-03	Denmark	W	2-1	Madrid	ECq	Morientes [34], Villa [46+]	73 575	Busacca SUI
28-03	Iceland	W	1-0	Palma	ECq	Iniesta [81]	18 326	Duhamel FRA
2-06	Latvia	W	2-0	Riga	ECq	Villa [45], Xavi [60]	10 000	Thomson SCO
6-06	Liechtenstein	W	2-0	Vaduz	ECq	Villa 2 [8 14]	5 739	Ivanov.N RUS
22-08	Greece	W	3-2	Thessaloniki	Fr	Marchena [37], Silva 2 [66 90]	15 000	Lannoy FRA
8-09	Iceland	D	1-1	Reykjavik	ECq	Iniesta [86]	9 483	Stark GER
12-09	Latvia	W	2-0	Oviedo	ECq	Xavi [13], Torres [85]	22 560	Yefet ISR
13-10	Denmark	W	3-1	Aarhus	ECq	Tamudo [14], Sergio Ramos [40], Riera [89]	19 849	Michel SVK
17-10	Finland	D	0-0	Helsinki	Fr		8 000	Bre FRA
17-11	Sweden	W	3-0	Madrid	ECq	Capdevila [14], Iniesta [39], Sergio Ramos [65]	67 055	Rosetti ITA
21-11	Northern Ireland	W	1-0	Las Palmas	ECq	Xavi [52]	30 339	Fandel GER
2008								
6-02	France	W	1-0	Malaga	Fr	Capdevila [80]	35 000	Asumaa FIN
26-03	Italy	W	1-0	Elche	Fr	Villa [78]	38 000	Stuchlik AUT
31-05	Peru	W	2-1	Huelva	Fr	Villa [38], Capdevila [90]	17 500	Meckarovski MKD
4-06	USA	W	1-0	Santander	Fr	Xavi [79]	14 232	Jareci ALB
10-06	Russia	W	4-1	Innsbruck	ECr1	Villa 3 [20 44 75], Fabregas [93+]	30 772	Plautz AUT
14-06	Sweden	W	2-1	Innsbruck	ECr1	Torres [15], Villa [92+]	30 772	Vink NED
18-06	Greece	W	2-1	Salzburg	ECr1	De la Red [61], Güiza [88]	30 883	Webb ENG
22-06	Italy	D	0-0	Vienna	ECqf	W 4-2p	48 000	Fandel GER
26-06	Russia	W	3-0	Vienna	ECsf	Xavi [8], Güiza [73], Silva [82]	51 428	De Bleeckere BEL
29-06	Germany	W	1-0	Vienna	ECf	Torres [33]	51 428	Rosetti ITA
20-08	Denmark	W	3-0	Copenhagen	Fr	Xabi Alonso 2 [50 90], Xavi [73]	26 155	Hansson SWE
6-09	Bosnia-Herzegovina	W	1-0	Murcia	WCq	Villa [58]	29 152	Thomson SCO
10-09	Armenia	W	4-0	Albacete	WCq	Capdevila [7], Villa 2 [16 79], Marcos Senna [83]	16 996	Asumaa FIN
11-10	Estonia	W	3-0	Tallinn	WCq	Juanito [34], Villa [38], Puyol [69]	9 200	Eriksson SWE
15-10	Belgium	W	2-1	Brussels	WCq	Iniesta [36], Villa [88]	45 888	Ovrebo NOR
19-11	Chile	W	3-0	Villarreal	Fr	Villa [37p], Torres [67], Cazorla [86]	30 000	Vadachkoria GEO
2009								
11-02	England	W	2-0	Seville	Fr	Villa [36], Llorente [82]	42 102	Lannoy FRA
28-03	Turkey	W	1-0	Madrid	WCq	Pique [61]	73 820	Busacca SUI
1-04	Turkey	W	2-1	Istanbul	WCq	Xabi Alonso [63p], Riera [92+]		Ischenko UKR
9-06	Azerbaijan	W	6-0	Baku	Fr	Villa 3 [34 38 45p], Riera [67], Guiza [74], Torres [87]	20 000	Codjia BEN
14-06	New Zealand	W	5-0	Rustenburg	CCr1	Torres 3 [6 14 17], Fabregas [24], Villa [48]	21 649	Breeze AUS
17-06	Iraq	W	1-0	Bloemfontein	CCr1	Villa [55]	30 512	Pozo CHI
20-06	South Africa	W	2-0	Bloemfontein	CCr1	Villa [52], Llorente [72]	38 212	Larrionda URU
24-06	USA	L	0-2	Bloemfontein	CCsf		35 369	Breeze AUS
28-06	South Africa	W	3-2	Rustenburg	CC3p	Guiza 2 [88 89], Xabi Alonso [107]	31 788	Vink NEN
12-08	Macedonia	W	3-2	Skopje	Fr	Torres [52], Pique [54], Riera [56]	25 000	Layec FRA
5-09	Belgium	W	5-0	La Coruña	WCq	David Silva 2 [41 67], Villa 2 [49 85], Pique [50]	30 441	Oriekhov UKR
9-09	Estonia	W	3-0	Merida	WCq	Fabregas [33], Cazorla [82], Mata [92+]	14 362	Jech CZE
10-10	Armenia	W	2-1	Yerevan	WCq	Fabregas [33], Mata [64]	10 500	Plautz AUT
14-10	Bosnia-Herzegovina	W	5-2	Zenica	WCq	Pique [13p], David Silva [14], Negredo 2 [50 55], Mata [81]	13 500	Kelly IRL
14-11	Argentina	W	2-1	Madrid	Fr	Xabi Alonso 2 [16 86p]	54 000	Meyer GER
18-11	Austria	W	5-1	Vienna	Fr	Fabregas [10], Villa 2 [20 45], Guiza [56], Hernandez [57]	32 000	

RECENT INTERNATIONAL MATCHES PLAYED BY SPAIN (CONT'D)

2010	Opponents	Score		Venue	Comp	Scorers	Att	Referee
3-03	France	W	2-0	Paris	Fr	Villa [21], Sergio Ramos [45]	79 021	Thomson SCO
29-05	Saudi Arabia	W	3-2	Innsbruck	Fr	Villa [31], Xabi Alonso [59], Llorente [90]	7 200	Einwaller AUT
3-06	Korea Republic	W	1-0	Innsbruck	Fr	Navas [85]	17 400	Schorgenhofer AUT
8-06	Poland	W	6-0	Murcia	Fr	Villa [12], Silva [14], Xabi Alonso [52], Fabregas [58], Torres [76], Pedro [81]	30 000	Koukoulakis GRE
16-06	Switzerland	L	0-1	Durban	WCr1		62 453	Webb ENG
21-06	Honduras	W	2-0	Johannesburg	WCr1	Villa 2 [17 51]	54 386	Nishimura JPN
25-06	Chile	W	2-1	Pretoria	WCr1	Villa [24], Iniesta [37]	41 958	Rodriguez MEX
29-06	Portugal	W	1-0	Cape Town	WCr2	Villa [63]	62 955	Baldassi ARG
3-07	Paraguay	W	1-0	Johannesburg	WCqf	Villa [83]	55 359	Batres GUA
7-07	Germany	W	1-0	Durban	WCsf	Puyol [73]	60 960	Kassai HUN
11-07	Netherlands	W	1-0	Johannesburg	WCf	Iniesta [116]	84 490	Webb ENG
11-08	Mexico	D	1-1	Mexico City	Fr	Silva [90]	105000	Moreno PAN
3-09	Liechtenstein	W	4-0	Vaduz	ECq	Torres 2 [18 54], Villa [26], Silva [62]	6 100	Yoldirim TUR
7-09	Argentina	L	1-4	Buenos Aires	Fr	Llorente [84]	65 600	Ruiz COL
8-10	Lithuania	W	3-1	Salamanca	ECq	Llorente 2 [47 56], Silva [79]	16 800	Rocchi ITA
12-10	Scotland	W	3-2	Glasgow	ECq	Villa [44p], Iniesta [55], Llorente [79]	51 322	Busacca SUI
17-11	Portugal	L	0-4	Lisbon	Fr		38 000	Gautier FRA

Fr = Friendly match • EC = UEFA EURO 2008/2012 • WC = FIFA World Cup
q = qualifier • r1 = first round group • r2 = second round • qf = quarter-final • sf = semi-final • f = final

SPAIN NATIONAL TEAM HISTORICAL RECORDS

Caps
126 - Andoni Zubizarreta 1985-98 • **113** - Iker Casillas 2000- • **102** - Raul 1996-2006 • **97** - Xavi 2000- • **91** - Carles Puyol 2000- • **89** - Fernando Hierro 1989-2002 • **81** - Jose Antonio Camacho 1975-88 • **79** - Xabi Alonso 2003- • **75** - Rafael Gordillo 1978-88 • **73** - Fernando Torres 2003- • **69** - Sergio Ramos 2005- & Emilio Butragueno 1984-92 • **68** - Luis Arconada 1977-85 • **67** - David Villa 2005- • **66** - Michel 1985-92 • **65** - Carlos Marchena 2002- • **62** - Luis Enrique 1991-2002 & Miguel Angel Nadal 1991-2002

Goals
44 - David Villa 2005- & Raul 1996-2006 • **29** - Fernando Hierro 1989-2002 • **27** - Fernando Morientes 1998-2007 • **26** - Fernando Torres 2003- & Emilio Butragueno 1984-92 • **23** - Alfredo di Stefano 1957-61 & Julio Salinas 1986-96 • **21** - Michel 1985-92 • **20** - Telmo Zarra 1945-71 • **17** - Isidro Langara 1932-36 • **16** - Pirri 1966-78 & Luis Regueiro 1927-36 • **15** - Santillana 1975-85

Past Coaches
Francisco Bru 1920 • Julian Ruete 1921-22 • Pedro Parages 1923-24 • Fernando Gutierrez Alzaga 1925 • Ricardo Cabot Montalt 1925 • Ezequiel Montero Roman 1926-27 • Fred Pentland 1929 • Jose Maria Mateos 1929-33 • Amadeo Garcia Salazar 1934-36 • Eduardo Teus Lopez 1941-42 • Jacinto Quincoces 1945 • Paulino Alcantara 1951 • Ricardo Zamora 1952 • Pedro Escartin Moran 1952-61 • Helenio Herrera 1959-62 • Jose Villalonga 1962-66 • Domingo Balmanya 1966-68 • Luis Molowny 1969 • Miguel Munoz 1969 • Ladislao Kubala 1969-80 • Jose Santamaria 1980-82 • Luis Suarez 1988-91 • Vicente Miera 1991-92 • Javier Clemente 1992-98 • Jose Antonio Camacho 1998-2002 • Inaki Saez 2002-04 • Luis Aragones 2004-08 • Vicente del Bosque 2008-

MEDALS TABLE

		Overall			League			Cup			Europe		
		G	S	B	G	S	B	G	S	B	G	S	B
1	Real Madrid	59	43	17	31	19	7	17	19		11	5	10
2	Barcelona	55	36	22	20	22	12	25	8		10	6	10
3	Athletic Bilbao	31	20	10	8	7	10	23	12			1	
4	Atlético Madrid	20	20	19	9	8	12	9	9		2	3	7
5	Valencia	17	18	8	6	6	8	7	9		4	3	
6	Real Zaragoza	8	7	6		1	4	6	5		2	1	2
7	Sevilla	8	6	4	1	4	4	5	2		2		
8	RCD Espanyol	4	7	4			4	4	5		2		
9	Real Sociedad	4	7	3	2	3	2	2	4				1
10	Deportivo La Coruña	3	5	6	1	5	4	2					2
11	Real Betis Balompié	3	2	2	1		2	2	2				
12	Real Union Irún	3	1					3	1				
13	RCD Mallorca	1	3	2			2	1	2		1		
14	Arenas Guecho Bilbao	1	3	1			1	1	3				
15	Racing Irún	1						1					
16	Sporting Gijón		3	1		1	1		2				
17	Celta Vigo		3						3				
18	Las Palmas		2	1		1	1		1				
19	Español Madrid		2						2				
	Getafe		2						2				
	Real Valladolid		2						2				
22	Villarreal		1	3		1	1						2
23	Racing Santander		1	1		1	1						

SPAIN 2009-10

PRIMERA DIVISION

Team	Pl	W	D	L	F	A	Pts
Barcelona †	38	31	6	1	98	24	99
Real Madrid †	38	31	3	4	102	35	96
Valencia †	38	21	8	9	59	40	71
Sevilla †	38	19	6	13	65	49	63
RCD Mallorca	38	18	8	12	59	44	62
Getafe ‡	38	17	7	14	58	48	58
Villarreal ‡	38	16	8	14	58	57	56
Athletic Bilbao	38	15	9	14	50	53	54
Atlético Madrid ‡	38	13	8	17	57	61	47
Deportivo La Coruña	38	13	8	17	35	49	47
RCD Espanyol	38	11	11	16	29	46	44
Osasuna	38	11	10	17	37	46	43
Almería	38	10	12	16	43	55	42
Real Zaragoza	38	10	11	17	46	64	41
Sporting Gijón	38	9	13	16	36	51	40
Racing Santander	38	9	12	17	42	59	39
Málaga	38	7	16	15	42	48	37
Real Valladolid	38	7	15	16	37	62	36
Tenerife	38	9	9	20	40	74	36
Xerez	38	8	10	20	38	66	34

Head-to-head results (home team in row, away team in column; order: Barcelona, Real Madrid, Valencia, Sevilla, Mallorca, Getafe, Villarreal, Ath. Bilbao, At. Madrid, Deportivo, Espanyol, Osasuna, Almería, Zaragoza, Sp. Gijón, Racing, Málaga, Valladolid, Tenerife, Xerez):

Team	Bar	RMa	Val	Sev	Mal	Get	Vil	Ath	AtM	Dep	Esp	Osa	Alm	Zar	Gij	Rac	Mál	Vld	Ten	Xer
Barcelona	–	1-0	3-0	4-0	4-2	2-1	1-1	4-1	5-2	3-0	1-0	2-0	1-0	6-1	3-0	4-0	2-1	4-0	4-1	3-1
Real Madrid	0-2	–	2-0	3-2	2-0	2-0	6-2	5-1	3-2	3-2	3-0	3-2	4-2	6-0	3-1	1-0	2-0	4-2	3-0	5-0
Valencia	0-0	2-3	–	2-0	1-1	2-1	4-1	2-0	2-2	1-0	1-0	3-0	2-0	3-1	2-2	0-0	1-0	2-0	1-0	3-1
Sevilla	2-3	2-1	2-1	–	2-0	0-3	1-1	1-0	1-0	1-0	4-1	3-0	1-2	2-2	1-1	3-0	1-2	2-1	1-1	3-1
RCD Mallorca	0-1	1-4	3-2	1-3	–	3-1	1-0	2-0	4-1	2-0	2-0	2-0	3-1	4-1	3-0	1-1	1-3	0-4	0-2	0-0
Getafe	0-2	2-4	3-1	4-3	3-0	–	3-0	2-0	1-0	0-2	1-1	2-1	2-2	0-2	1-1	0-0	2-1	1-0	2-1	5-1
Villarreal	1-4	0-2	2-0	3-0	1-1	3-2	–	2-1	2-1	1-0	0-0	0-2	1-1	4-2	1-0	2-0	2-1	3-1	5-0	2-0
Athletic Bilbao	1-1	1-0	1-2	0-4	1-3	2-2	3-2	–	1-0	2-0	1-0	2-0	4-1	0-0	1-2	4-3	1-1	2-0	4-1	3-2
Atlético Madrid	2-1	2-3	4-1	2-1	1-1	0-3	1-2	2-0	–	3-0	4-0	1-0	2-2	2-1	3-2	1-1	0-2	3-1	3-1	1-2
Deportivo La Coruña	1-3	1-3	0-0	1-0	1-0	1-3	1-0	3-1	2-1	–	2-3	1-0	0-0	0-1	1-1	1-1	1-0	0-2	3-1	2-1
RCD Espanyol	0-0	0-3	0-2	2-0	1-1	0-2	0-0	1-0	3-0	2-0	–	2-1	2-0	2-1	0-0	0-4	2-1	1-1	2-1	0-0
Osasuna	1-1	0-0	1-3	0-2	0-1	0-0	1-1	0-3	0-3	1-2	0-1	–	2-0	1-0	1-3	2-1	1-1	1-0	1-1	1-1
Almería	2-2	1-2	0-3	2-3	1-1	0-4	2-1	4-1	1-0	1-1	0-1	2-0	–	1-0	3-2	2-2	2-0	1-0	1-1	1-1
Real Zaragoza	2-4	1-2	3-0	2-1	1-1	3-0	3-3	1-2	1-1	0-0	1-0	0-1	2-1	–	1-3	2-2	2-0	1-2	1-0	0-0
Sporting Gijón	0-1	0-0	1-1	0-1	4-1	1-0	1-0	0-0	1-1	2-1	1-0	3-2	1-0	1-1	–	0-1	2-2	0-2	0-2	2-2
Racing Santander	1-4	0-2	0-1	1-5	2-1	1-0	4-1	2-0	2-1	1-0	1-3	1-1	1-0	2-0	0-2	–	0-3	1-1	2-0	0-2
Málaga	0-2	1-1	0-1	1-2	2-1	1-0	2-1	1-0	0-3	0-0	0-2	1-1	1-1	2-1	1-1	1-1	–	0-0	1-1	2-4
Real Valladolid	0-3	1-4	2-4	2-1	1-2	0-0	0-2	2-0	4-4	0-0	0-1	2-1	1-1	1-2	2-1	1-1	1-1	–	3-3	0-0
Tenerife	0-5	1-5	0-0	1-2	1-0	3-2	2-2	1-0	1-0	1-0	4-1	2-1	2-2	1-3	2-1	2-1	2-2	0-0	–	1-0
Xerez	0-2	0-3	1-3	0-2	2-1	0-1	2-1	0-1	0-2	0-3	1-1	1-2	2-1	3-2	0-0	2-2	1-1	3-0	2-1	–

29/08/2009 - 16/05/2010 • † Qualified for the UEFA Champions League • ‡ Qualified for the Europa Cup
Top scorers: **34** - Lionel Messi, Barcelona • **27** - Gonzalo Higuaín, Real Madrid • **26** - Cristiano Ronaldo, Real Madrid • **21** - David Villa, Valencia • **18** - Diego Forlan, At. Madrid • **16** - Roberto Soldado, Getafe & Zlatan Ibrahimovic, Barcelona • **15** - Luis Fabiano, Sevilla • **14** - Fernando Llorente, Ath. Bilbao & Nino, Tenerife

SPAIN 2009-10

SEGUNDA DIVISION A (2)

Team	Pl	W	D	L	F	A	Pts
Real Sociedad	42	20	14	8	53	37	74
Hércules	42	19	14	9	61	34	71
Levante	42	19	14	9	63	45	71
Real Betis	42	18	14	9	61	38	71
Cartagena	42	18	11	13	58	49	65
Elche	42	18	9	15	67	57	63
Villarreal B	42	16	13	13	60	56	61
Numancia	42	16	11	15	55	53	59
Recreativo Huelva	42	14	15	13	40	42	57
Córdoba	42	14	13	15	40	46	55
Rayo Vallecano	42	13	14	15	67	58	53
Celta Vigo	42	13	13	16	38	44	52
Huesca	42	12	16	14	36	40	52
Girona	42	13	13	16	45	59	52
Albacete	42	12	16	14	60	62	52
Salamanca	42	13	13	16	44	54	52
Las Palmas	42	12	15	15	49	49	51
Gimnàstic Tarragona	42	14	9	19	42	55	51
Cádiz	42	12	14	16	49	64	50
Real Murcia	42	11	17	14	49	51	50
Real Unión Irún	42	12	10	20	40	59	46
Castellón	42	7	12	23	37	62	33

Head-to-head results (home team in row, away team in column; order: Sociedad, Hércules, Levante, Real Betis, Cartagena, Elche, Villarreal B, Numancia, Recreativo, Córdoba, Vallecano, Celta Vigo, Huesca, Girona, Albacete, Salamanca, Las Palmas, Gimnàstic, Cádiz, Real Murcia, Real Unión, Castellón):

Team	Soc	Hér	Lev	Bet	Car	Elc	ViB	Num	Rec	Cór	Val	Cel	Hue	Gir	Alb	Sal	LPa	Gim	Cád	Mur	Uni	Cas
Real Sociedad	–	1-0	3-1	2-0	1-0	0-1	2-1	2-1	1-0	1-0	2-0	2-0	2-0	2-0	2-2	0-2	2-1	0-4	1-0	0-4	1-0	0-0
Hércules	5-1	–	2-1	3-2	2-0	3-0	4-2	1-0	2-0	4-0	2-1	1-0	2-0	2-0	5-1	4-0	0-1	0-1	1-0	1-1	0-1	1-2
Levante	1-0	2-1	–	1-0	1-2	2-1	3-1	1-1	0-0	2-1	1-0	1-1	3-2	1-2	0-1	1-6	1-1	1-2	2-1	0-3	1-1	0-1
Real Betis	1-0	1-1	4-0	–	0-0	3-4	0-2	0-3	0-3	1-1	1-1	0-1	0-1	0-1	0-3	0-4	0-4	3-0	4-0	1-1	1-2	0-1
Cartagena	1-1	0-3	5-1	2-0	–	2-0	0-0	2-1	1-1	0-4	1-0	4-3	4-4	1-0	4-3	4-4	1-3	2-1	0-2	1-0	2-1	2-0
Elche	4-1	2-0	0-0	3-0	1-0	–	2-3	0-1	3-2	3-0	2-1	0-0	2-4	0-2	1-2	2-2	5-2	2-1	1-1	2-2	1-2	0-0
Villarreal B	1-1	1-0	2-2	2-0	0-2	0-2	–	1-0	1-4	0-0	2-1	0-1	1-2	0-2	2-1	2-2	5-1	0-2	0-2	1-3	1-3	1-3
Numancia	1-6	1-0	1-1	5-5	1-0	1-3	0-2	–	1-1	2-1	1-0	0-1	0-3	1-1	1-1	1-1	3-1	1-1	3-1	1-1	3-1	1-0
Recreativo Huelva	2-0	0-0	1-1	1-0	2-1	1-1	2-1	1-3	–	0-0	2-1	0-2	2-0	2-0	0-0	2-2	0-0	2-2	0-0	2-0	2-0	0-0
Córdoba	2-0	1-2	1-0	1-1	2-2	0-3	1-2	1-1	0-0	–	0-1	1-0	1-2	2-2	0-1	0-1	1-1	0-0	1-4	0-0	1-4	0-0
Rayo Vallecano	3-3	4-0	0-2	2-2	3-0	1-0	2-4	1-4	0-3	2-0	–	1-2	4-1	0-3	3-0	0-0	3-2	2-3	2-2	2-2	0-2	3-0
Celta Vigo	1-0	1-1	1-1	1-1	0-2	1-2	1-1	1-0	0-2	1-2	1-1	–	0-0	0-1	2-1	2-1	1-1	0-3	1-2	1-1	0-2	0-2
Huesca	1-1	0-0	0-0	1-0	2-0	0-0	0-0	1-0	1-0	2-0	2-1	1-1	–	2-2	2-1	2-0	1-0	1-0	3-2	1-1	0-2	3-2
Girona	1-0	1-1	1-0	4-0	2-0	1-3	2-3	1-0	0-0	0-2	1-1	1-1	2-2	–	0-0	2-2	1-0	0-2	0-4	0-1	1-0	2-1
Albacete	0-0	1-2	1-0	1-3	0-0	2-2	1-1	2-1	3-1	2-3	3-3	0-2	0-2	0-3	–	0-3	2-1	3-2	1-1	0-1	3-2	1-0
Salamanca	0-0	0-0	0-3	2-1	1-1	0-0	1-2	4-1	3-1	2-1	0-0	1-1	2-1	0-1	3-2	–	0-1	1-0	1-0	2-3	3-0	1-1
Las Palmas	1-1	0-0	0-1	1-0	1-4	1-4	0-1	0-1	0-1	1-2	1-0	1-3	2-0	1-0	3-2	4-0	–	2-2	1-0	1-1	0-3	2-1
Gimnàstic Tarragona	1-2	1-1	0-0	1-3	2-3	1-2	1-0	1-1	2-1	0-2	0-1	1-1	3-1	2-2	1-0	0-2	2-3	–	1-2	2-2	1-2	1-1
Cádiz	1-3	2-2	4-2	2-1	3-2	1-3	2-1	0-0	4-2	1-0	0-0	1-1	3-1	0-0	2-0	4-3	0-1	0-0	0-1	–	1-0	2-1
Real Murcia	1-1	0-0	1-2	0-1	4-0	2-2	2-1	0-0	1-1	1-0	3-4	1-1	1-0	0-0	2-2	2-1	0-0	1-2	2-1	3-0	–	1-1
Real Unión Irún	0-0	0-2	2-1	1-3	1-0	3-0	1-4	3-0	1-2	3-2	1-2	0-1	1-1	1-2	1-1	1-0	0-1	0-0	0-2	0-0	–	3-1
Castellón	0-1	0-0	0-1	0-2	2-0	2-3	2-0	1-0	0-0	1-1	3-2	1-1	2-0	1-3	5-1	2-2	0-0	0-4	1-2	1-1	3-1	–

29/08/2009 - 19/06/2010 • Top scorer: **26** - Jorge Molina, Elche

SPAIN 2009-10
SEGUNDA DIVISION B (3)
GROUP 1

	Pl	W	D	L	F	A	Pts
Ponferradina †	38	21	12	5	44	21	75
Eibar ‡	38	19	9	10	45	34	66
Palencia ‡	38	16	17	5	46	27	65
Pontevedra ‡	38	18	9	11	48	37	63
Deportivo Alavés	38	16	14	8	45	31	62
Lemona	38	13	14	11	51	32	53
Lugo	38	13	14	11	49	41	53
Osasuna B	38	13	13	12	38	43	52
Celta B	38	15	6	17	53	61	51
Montañeros	38	13	10	15	47	49	49
Barakaldo	38	12	13	13	40	43	49
Cultural Leonesa	38	12	13	13	46	49	49
Mirandés	38	11	15	12	44	42	48
Zamora	38	12	10	16	39	51	46
Bilbao Athletic	38	12	10	16	35	42	46
Guijuelo ‡	38	10	15	13	38	36	45
Sestao River	38	11	11	16	32	40	41
Izarra	38	10	9	19	41	50	39
Racing Ferrol	38	7	16	15	31	43	37
Compostela	38	7	8	23	36	66	29

29/08/2009 - 9/05/2010 • † Championship playoff
‡ Play-offs

SPAIN 2009-10
SEGUNDA DIVISION B (3)
GROUP 2

	Pl	W	D	L	F	A	Pts
Alcorcón †	38	21	10	7	50	30	73
Oviedo ‡	38	19	11	8	58	36	68
Guadalajara ‡	38	17	13	8	53	36	64
Universidad LPGC ‡	38	18	10	10	59	51	64
Leganés	38	17	11	10	54	45	62
Puertollano	38	17	11	10	47	39	62
Atlético B	38	16	10	12	64	44	58
Real Madrid Castilla	38	15	11	12	68	51	56
Gimnástica Torrelavega	38	14	9	15	40	35	51
Conquense	38	12	14	12	50	45	50
Vecindario	38	12	13	13	45	56	49
Sporting de Gijón B	38	13	8	17	40	52	47
Alcalá	38	11	11	16	40	52	44
Cerro Reyes	38	10	14	14	42	53	44
Cacereño	38	10	14	14	43	45	44
Toledo ‡	38	12	7	19	40	57	43
Racing Santander B	38	10	11	17	36	49	41
Villanovense	38	9	11	18	45	54	41
Tenerife B	38	9	11	18	46	51	38
Lanzarote	38	10	4	24	46	85	34

29/08/2009 - 9/05/2010 • † Championship playoff
‡ Play-offs

SEGUNDA DIVISION B (3) CHAMPIONSHIP PLAY-OFFS

Semi-finals: **Granada** 2-0 0-1 Alcorcón • Sant Andreu 0-1 1-0 9-8p **Ponferradina**
Final: Ponferradina 0-1 0-0 **Granada** • Granada and Ponferradina promoted • Alcorcón and Sant Andreu join regular play-offs in the second round

SPAIN 2009-10
SEGUNDA DIVISION B (3)
GROUP 3

	Pl	W	D	L	F	A	Pts
Sant Andreu †	38	23	9	6	66	35	78
Barcelona B ‡	38	22	10	6	65	35	76
Ontinyent ‡	38	19	14	5	47	25	71
Alcoyano ‡	38	20	9	9	52	32	69
Dénia	38	17	13	8	48	35	64
Benidorm	38	18	10	10	68	51	64
Orihuela	38	15	10	13	37	42	55
Mallorca B	38	15	10	13	49	39	55
Logroñés	38	13	15	10	41	33	54
Sabadell	38	13	10	15	42	45	49
Lleida	38	12	13	13	45	44	49
Badalona	38	13	9	16	41	45	48
Alicante	38	11	13	14	38	42	46
Sporting Mahonés	38	10	15	13	36	43	45
Atlètica Gramenet	38	11	10	17	48	59	43
Español B ‡	38	8	17	13	38	45	41
Villajoyosa	38	7	13	18	41	52	34
Valencia Mestalla	38	6	12	20	30	49	30
Gavà	38	7	9	22	33	72	30
Terrassa	38	6	7	25	29	71	25

29/08/2009 - 9/05/2010 • † Championship playoff
‡ Play-offs

SPAIN 2009-10
SEGUNDA DIVISION B (3)
GROUP 4

	Pl	W	D	L	F	A	Pts
Granada †	38	23	7	8	74	37	76
Melilla ‡	38	22	10	6	55	37	76
Real Jaén ‡	38	20	9	9	58	32	69
Polideportivo Ejido ‡	38	19	8	11	47	28	65
Ceuta	38	17	10	11	56	44	61
Lucena	38	14	13	11	58	39	55
Atlético Ciudad	38	16	5	17	48	55	53
San Roque	38	15	8	15	54	47	53
Unión Estepona	38	14	10	14	48	50	52
Ecija	38	15	7	16	54	52	52
Caravaca	38	13	13	12	47	44	52
Sangonera Atlético	38	13	12	13	51	55	51
Real Murcia B	38	13	12	13	45	45	51
Real Betis B	38	13	12	13	39	37	51
Sevilla Atlético	38	15	6	17	41	42	51
Roquetas ‡	38	14	8	16	44	46	50
Moratalla	38	14	8	16	44	46	42
Jerez Industrial	38	10	12	16	36	48	35
Marbella	38	7	10	21	36	62	31
Aguilas	38	4	9	25	28	79	21

29/08/2009 - 9/05/2010 • † Championship playoff
‡ Play-offs

SEGUNDA DIVISION B (3) PLAY-OFFS

FIRST ROUND: Pontevedra 2-1 2-1 Real Oviedo • Alcoyano 0-0 0-2 **Eibar** • Universidad 1-0 3-0 Melilla • Ejido 3-3 1-1 **Barcelona B** •
Ontinyent 2-0 3-1 Guadalajara • **Real Jaén** 1-1 2-1 Palencia • **SECOND ROUND:** Real Jaén 0-0 0-3 **Barcelona B** • Pontevedra 0-0 0-3 **Alcorcón** •
Ontinyent 2-1 1-0 Eibar • Universidad 0-2 2-2 **Sant Andreu** • **THIRD ROUND:** Barcelona B 1-0 0-0 Sant Andreu • Ontinyent 1-1 2-3 **Alcorcón** •
Barcelona and Alcorcón promoted • Relegation play-offs: Espanyol B 2-2 0-1 **Guijuelo** • **Roquetas** 1-0 1-1 Toledo • Espanyol and Toledo relegated

COPA DEL REY 2009–10

Third Elimination Round | **Round of 32** | **Round of 16**

Round of 32

Sevilla	4	5
Atlético Ciudad *	2	1

Third Elimination Round

Poli Ejido	0	4p
Atlético Ciudad *	0	5p
Cultural Leonesa	0	5p
Ontinyent *	0	3p

Round of 16

Sevilla	2	0
Barcelona *	1	1

Round of 32

Cultural Leonesa *	0	0
Barcelona	2	5
Valencia	1	2
Alcoyano *	0	2

Third Elimination Round

Mérida *	1
Alcoyano	3

Round of 16

Valencia *	1	2
Deportivo La Coruña	2	2

Round of 32

Real Murcia *	0	0
Deportivo La Coruña	1	0
RCD Mallorca	1	1
Real Valladolid *	2	0

Round of 16

RCD Mallorca	1	3
Rayo Vallecano *	2	1

Round of 32

Athletic Bilbao	0	2
Rayo Vallecano *	2	2

Third Elimination Round

Córdoba *	0
Rayo Vallecano	1

Round of 32

Málaga	1	0
Real Zaragoza *	1	0

Round of 16

Málaga *	2	1
Getafe	1	5

Round of 32

RCD Espanyol	0	1
Getafe *	2	1
Racing Santander	0	4
Salamanca *	1	1

Third Elimination Round

Cartagena	0
Salamanca *	2

Round of 16

Racing Santander	3	0
Alcorcón *	2	0

Round of 32

Real Madrid	0	1
Alcorcón *	4	0

Third Elimination Round

Lagun Onak *	1
Alcorcón	2
Hercules *	2
Huesca	0

Round of 32

Hércules *	2	1
Almeria	1	0

Round of 16

Hércules *	2	0
Osasuna	1	1

Round of 32

Xerez *	1	0
Osasuna	2	1

Third Elimination Round

Celta Vigo	3
Girona *	1

Round of 32

Celta Vigo *	2	1
Tenerife	1	0

Round of 16

Celta Vigo *	1	1
Villarreal	1	0

Third Elimination Round

Puertollano *	2
Sant Andreu	1

Round of 32

Puertollano *	1	0
Villarreal	1	1

Third Elimination Round

Recreativo Huelva *	2
Las Palmas	1

Round of 32

Recreativo Huelva *	1	1	4p
Sporting Gijón	1	1	2p

Round of 16

Recreativo Huelva *	3	1
Atlético Madrid	0	5

Third Elimination Round

Marbella *	2
Alicante	1

Round of 32

Marbella *	0	0
Atlético Madrid	2	6

* Home team/home team in the first leg

COPA DEL REY 2009-10

Quarter–finals   **Semi–finals**   **Final**

Sevilla	3	0
Deportivo La Coruña *	0	1

Sevilla *	2	0
Getafe	0	1

RCD Mallorca *	1	1
Getafe	2	0

Sevilla	2	
Atlético Madrid	0	

Racing Santander *	2	3
Osasuna	1	0

Racing Santander	0	3
Atlético Madrid *	4	2

COPA DEL REY FINAL 2010

Camp Nou, Barcelona, 19-05-2010, 21:30, Att: 93 000, Ref: Manuel Mejuto Gonzalez

Sevilla	2	Capel [5], Jesus Navas [91+]
Atlético Madrid	0	

Celta Vigo	1	0
Atlético Madrid *	1	1

Sevilla - Andres Palop (c) - Abdoulay Konko, Sebastien Squillaci●, Julien Escude, Antonio Luna● - Jesus Navas, Renato●, Didier Zokora, Diego Capel (Diego Perotti 87) - Alvaro Negredo (Koffi Romaric 66), Frederic Kanoute●. Tr: Antonio Alvarez
At. Madrid - David de Gea - Tomas Ujfalusi●, Luis Perea, Alvaro Dominguez, Antonio Lopez (c) - Jose Antonio Reyes, Paulo Assuncao (Raul Garcia 59), Tiago Mendes, Simao Sabrosa (Jose Manuel Jurado 59) - Sergio Aguero, Diego Forlan. Tr: Quique Sanchez Flores

CLUB BY CLUB GUIDE TO THE 2009-10 SEASON IN SPAIN

ALMERIA 2009-10

Ag	30	Valladolid	D	0-0	PD	9 100
	13	Sp. Gijon	L	0-1	PD	25 000
Sep	20	Getafe	W	1-0	PD Michel [48]	9 000
	23	At. Madrid	D	2-2	PD Piatti 2 [26 90]	44 500
	27	Racing	D	2-2	PD Crusat [17], Uche [89]	13 200
	3	Barcelona	L	0-1	PD	74 177
Oct	18	Malaga	W	2-1	PD Cisma [39], Soriano [41]	21 000
	25	Valencia	L	0-3	PD	12 171
	28	Hercules	L	1-2	CRr4 Chico [39]	8 000
	1	Zaragoza	L	1-2	PD Ortiz [39]	24 000
	8	Osasuna	W	2-0	PD OG [2], Uche [90]	10 260
Nov	12	Hercules	L	0-1	CRr4	3 000
	22	Mallorca	L	1-3	PD Rodriguez [77]	11 000
	29	Ath. Bilbao	L	1-4	PD Uche [84p]	8 858
Dec	5	Real Madrid	L	2-4	PD Soriano [58], Uche [62]	77 000
	13	Deportivo	D	1-1	PD Uche [59]	9 360
	20	Espanyol	L	0-2	PD	22 275
	3	Xerez	W	1-0	PD Ortiz [89]	9 574
	9	Villarreal	D	1-1	PD Corona [67p]	18 000
Jan	17	Tenerife	D	1-1	PD Goitom [61]	17 732
	23	Sevilla	L	0-1	PD	32 000
	31	Valladolid	D	1-1	PD Crusat [12]	14 700
	7	Sp. Gijon	W	3-1	PD Crusat [15], Cisma [43], Guilherme [81]	11 000
Feb	14	Getafe	D	2-2	PD Piatti [47], Soriano [90]	11 000
	21	At. Madrid	W	1-0	PD Piatti [87]	14 000
	28	Racing	W	2-0	PD Soriano [29], Crusat [67]	15 486
	6	Barcelona	D	2-2	PD Cisma [12], OG [57]	14 758
	14	Malaga	W	1-0	PD Soriano [56]	10 000
Mar	21	Valencia	L	0-2	PD	33 000
	24	Zaragoza	W	1-0	PD Uche [61]	15 772
	28	Osasuna	L	0-1	PD	16 421
	4	Mallorca	D	1-1	PD Uche [4]	9 574
	11	Ath. Bilbao	L	1-4	PD Piatti [71]	36 600
Apr	15	Real Madrid	L	1-2	PD Crusat [14]	17 000
	18	Deportivo	D	0-0	PD	12 000
	25	Espanyol	L	0-1	PD	11 000
	1	Xerez	L	1-2	PD Soriano [34]	15 000
May	4	Villarreal	W	4-2	PD Crusat [13], Uche 2 [28 41], Piatti [90]	18 000
	8	Tenerife	D	2-2	PD Piatti [18], Crusat [81]	20 810
	15	Sevilla	L	2-3	PD Soriano [43], Ortiz [79]	18 194

ALMERIA LEAGUE APPEARANCES/GOALS 2009-10

Goalkeepers Diego BRA 37 • Esteban 1+1
Defenders Santiago Acasiete PER 31/0 • Chico 27/0 • Cisma 29+4/3 • Guilherme BRA 11+4/1 • Michel Macedo BRA 28/1 • Hernan Pellerano ARG 17+2/0
Midfield Alex Quillo 0+1/0 • Hernan Bernardello ARG 35/0 • Leonardo Borzani ARG 2+1/0 • Corona 13+9/1 • Albert Crusat 31+2/7 • Jose Ortiz 0+17/1 • Juanma Ortiz 24+11/2 • Modeste M'Bami CMR 28/0 • Nieto 3+11/0 • Fernando Soriano 33+2/7 • Fabian Vargas COL 6+4/0
Forwards David Rodriguez 2+7/1 • Henok Goitom SWE 11+10/1 • Pablo Piatti ARG 28+7/7 • Esteban Solari ARG 0+2/0 • Kalu Uche NGA 21+7/9
Coach Hugo Sanchez • Juanma Lillo (24/12/09)

KEY TO THE CLUB SECTION

SC = Supercopa • USC = UEFA Super Cup • PD = Primera Division • CR = Copa del Rey • CL = UEFA Champions League • EL = Europa League • r1 = first round etc • p3 = third preliminary round • po = preliminary round play-off • gA = Group A etc • qf = quarter-final • sf = semi-final • f = final

Matches that are shaded were played at home; matches with no shading were played either away or on a neutral ground

The figures for the player appearances and goals consist of three elements - matches started+appearances as a substitute/goals scored

ATHLETIC BILBAO 2009-10

Jul	30	Young Boys	L	0-1	ELp3	28 000
	6	Young Boys	W	2-1	ELp3 Llorente [26], Muniain [72]	21 277
	16	Barcelona	L	1-2	SC De Marcos [44]	35 000
Aug	20	Tromsø	W	3-2	ELpo Martinez [62p], De Marcos [86], Llorente [90]	25 000
	23	Barcelona	L	0-3	SC	61 083
	27	Tromsø	D	1-1	ELpo Martinez [56p]	6 000
	30	Espanyol	W	1-0	PD Toquero [78]	38 000
	13	Xerez	W	1-0	PD OG [32]	17 566
Sep	17	FK Austria	W	3-0	ELgL Llorente 2 [8p 24], Muniain [56]	26 000
	20	Villarreal	W	3-2	PD Llorente 2 [11 40], Martinez [59]	32 000
	23	Tenerife	L	0-1	PD	19 200
	26	Sevilla	L	0-4	PD	40 000
	1	W. Bremen	L	1-3	ELgL Llorente [91+]	24 305
	4	Valladolid	D	2-2	PD Susaeta [9], Muniain [77]	19 800
	18	Sp. Gijon	L	1-2	PD Toquero [81]	33 600
Oct	22	Nacional	W	2-1	ELgL Etxeberria [67], Llorente [86]	24 569
	25	Getafe	L	0-2	PD	12 000
	28	Vallecano	L	0-2	CRr4	13 000
	31	At. Madrid	W	1-0	PD Martinez [19]	39 000
	5	Nacional	D	1-1	ELgL Etxeberria [85p]	2 945
	8	Racing	W	2-0	PD Gurpegi [31], Iraola [75p]	14 412
Nov	11	Vallecano	D	2-2	CRr4 Llorente [42], Martinez [75]	39 000
	21	Barcelona	D	1-1	PD Toquero [63]	40 000
	29	Almeria	W	4-1	PD Martinez [37], Ustaritz [41], Llorente [59], De Marcos [77]	8 585
	3	FK Austria	W	3-0	ELgL Llorente 2 [19 84], San Jose [62]	11 500
	6	Valencia	L	1-2	PD Muniain [58]	40 000
Dec	12	Zaragoza	W	2-1	PD San Jose [61], Susaeta [81]	23 000
	16	W. Bremen	L	0-3	ELgL	27 500
	19	Osasuna	W	2-0	PD Yeste [1], Llorente [12]	38 000
	3	Mallorca	L	0-2	PD	12 800
	10	Malaga	D	1-1	PD Llorente [78p]	15 000
Jan	16	Real Madrid	W	1-0	PD Llorente [3]	40 000
	23	Deportivo	L	1-3	PD OG [80]	13 000
	30	Espanyol	L	0-1	PD	25 110
	7	Xerez	W	3-2	PD Muniain 2, Llorente 65 86	36 000
	13	Villarreal	L	1-2	PD Gabilondo [24]	12 000
	18	Anderlecht	D	1-1	ELr2 San Jose [58]	38 000
Feb	21	Tenerife	W	4-1	PD Llorente [18p], Toquero [23], Iraola [54], Gabilondo [63]	36 000
	25	Anderlecht	L	0-4	ELr2	19 858
	28	Sevilla	D	0-0	PD	35 000
	7	Valladolid	W	2-0	PD Toquero 2 [27 37]	37 000
	13	Sp. Gijon	D	0-0	PD	22 188
Mar	20	Getafe	D	2-2	PD Orbaiz [14], Llorente [78p]	35 000
	25	At. Madrid	L	0-2	PD	47 128
	29	Racing	W	4-3	PD Llorente 2 [13 78p], Toquero [18], Susaeta [88]	30 000
	3	Barcelona	L	1-4	PD Susaeta [77]	77 630
Apr	11	Almeria	W	4-1	PD Martinez 2 [13 49], Gabilondo [32], Llorente [51]	36 600
	15	Valencia	L	0-2	PD	41 250
	18	Zaragoza	D	0-0	PD	34 000
	26	Osasuna	D	0-0	PD	18 215
	2	Mallorca	L	1-3	PD Llorente [45]	35 000
May	5	Malaga	D	1-1	PD Toquero [4]	35 000
	8	Real Madrid	L	1-5	PD Yeste [41]	79 000
	15	Deportivo	W	2-0	PD Muniain [20], Martinez [77]	39 000

ATHLETIC LEAGUE APPEARANCES/GOALS 2009-10

Goalkeepers Armando 1 • Gorka Iraizoz 37
Defenders Aitor Ocio 3/0 • Fernando Amorebieta 34/0 • Eneko Boveda 0+1/0 • Andoni Iraola 37/2 • Koikili 20+1/0 • Mikel San Jose 24+1/1 • Ustaritz 15/1 • Xabi Castillo 18+1/0
Midfield Aketxe 0+1/0 • Xabier Etxeita 1+2/0 • David Lopez 7+10/0 • Igor Gabilondo 16+10/3 • Carlos Gurpegi 30+4/1 • Inigo Perez 0+3/0 • Ander Iturraspe 11+4/0 • Javi Martinez 34/6 • Inaki Munoz 0+1/0 • Pablo Orbaiz 17+3/1 • Markel Susaeta 23+12/4 • Francisco Yeste 13+9/2
Forwards Oscar de Marcos 9+10/1 • Diaz de Cerio 0+5/0 • Joseba Etxeberria 2+5/0 • Ion Velez 1+1/0 • Fernando Llorente 35+2/14 • Iker Muniain 4+22/4 • Gaizka Toquero 26+5/8
Coach Joaquin Caparros

ATLETICO MADRID 2009–10

		Opponent	Res	Score	Comp	Scorers	Att
Aug	19	P'thinaikos	W	3-2	CLpo	Rodriguez 36, Forlan 63, Aguero 70	50 540
	25	P'thinaikos	W	2-0	CLpo	OG 4, Aguero 83	29 910
	30	Malaga	L	0-3	PD		30 000
Sep	12	Racing	D	1-1	PD	Jurado 43	39 000
	15	APOEL	D	0-0	CLgD		30 628
	19	Barcelona	L	2-5	PD	Aguero 45, Forlan 84	95 739
	23	Almeria	D	2-2	PD	Cleber Santana 27, Forlan 55	44 500
	26	Valencia	D	2-2	PD	Aguero 7, Rodriguez 90	36 000
	30	Porto	L	0-2	CLgD		37 609
Oct	3	Zaragoza	W	2-1	PD	Jurado 2, Lopez 66	41 100
	18	Osasuna	L	0-3	PD		15 000
	21	Chelsea	L	0-4	CLgD		39 997
	24	Mallorca	D	1-1	PD	Forlan 51p	45 000
	27	Marbella	W	2-0	CRr4	OG 18, Rodriguez 82	4 000
	31	Ath. Bilbao	L	0-1	PD		39 000
Nov	3	Chelsea	D	2-2	CLgD	Aguero 2 66 91+	36 284
	7	Real Madrid	L	2-3	PD	Forlan 79, Aguero 81	55 000
	10	Marbella	W	6-0	CRr4	Jurado 11, Sinama-Pongolle 18, Rodriguez 4 22 31 47 63	15 000
	21	Deportivo	L	1-2	PD	Aguero 3	17 000
	25	APOEL	D	1-1	CLgD	Simão 62	21 178
	29	Espanyol	W	4-0	PD	Forlan 27, Aguero 2 62 85, Rodriguez 89	25 000
Dec	5	Xerez	W	2-0	PD	Forlan 29, Aguero 65	17 805
	8	Porto	L	0-3	CLgD		24 603
	13	Villarreal	L	1-2	PD	Simão 37	42 000
	20	Tenerife	D	1-1	PD	Jurado 22	21 414
	2	Sevilla	W	2-1	PD	OG 48, Lopez 90	35 000
	6	Recreativo	L	0-3	CRr5		2 310
	9	Valladolid	W	4-0	PD	Jurado 16, Forlan 32, Reyes 59, Aguero 90	16 200
Jan	14	Recreativo	W	5-1	CRr5	Simão 2 20 83, Aguero 2 23 61, Assunção 38	28 700
	17	Sp. Gijon	W	3-2	PD	Forlan 13, Assunção 53, Balde 66	50 000
	21	Celta Vigo	D	1-1	CRqf	Tiago 11	45 000
	24	Getafe	L	0-1	PD		14 000
	28	Celta Vigo	W	1-0	CRqf	Forlan 26	27 335
	31	Malaga	L	0-2	PD		40 000
Feb	4	Racing	W	4-0	CRsf	Simão 9, Reyes 41, Forlan 2 63p 72p	30 000
	7	Racing	D	1-1	PD	Forlan 24	15 430
	11	Racing	L	2-3	CRsf	OG 8, Jurado 51	20 000
	14	Barcelona	W	2-1	PD	Forlan 9, Simão 23	53 000
	18	Galatasaray	D	1-1	ELr2	Reyes 23	28 056
	21	Almeria	L	0-1	PD		14 000
	25	Galatasaray	W	2-1	ELr2	Simão 63, Forlan 90	22 747
	28	Valencia	W	4-1	PD	Forlan 2 30p 86, Aguero 78, Jurado 90	52 000
Mar	7	Zaragoza	D	1-1	PD	Balde 90	24 000
	11	Sporting CP	D	0-0	ELr3		34 540
	14	Osasuna	W	1-0	PD	Jurado 79	35 000
	18	Sporting CP	D	2-2	ELr3	Aguero 2 3 33	41 919
	21	Mallorca	L	1-4	PD	Forlan 26	13 000
	25	Ath. Bilbao	W	2-0	PD	Forlan 68, Aguero 86	47 128
	28	Real Madrid	L	2-3	PD	Reyes 10, Forlan 68p	80 000
Apr	1	Valencia	D	2-2	ELqf	Forlan 59, Lopez 72	46 310
	4	Deportivo	W	3-0	PD	Juanito 22, Forlan 57, Tiago 61	35 000
	8	Valencia	D	0-0	ELqf		49 907
	11	Espanyol	L	0-3	PD		32 620
	14	Xerez	L	1-2	PD	Forlan 12	20 000
	17	Villarreal	L	1-2	PD	Aguero 64	13 020
	22	Liverpool	W	1-0	ELsf	Forlan 9	47 042
	25	Tenerife	W	3-1	PD	Salvio 2 11 31, Aguero 78	52 060
	29	Liverpool	L	1-2	ELsf	Forlan 102	42 040
	2	Sevilla	L	1-3	PD	Tiago 8	40 000
May	5	Valladolid	W	3-1	PD	Juanito 43, Jurado 67, Forlan 73	25 000
	8	Sp. Gijon	D	1-1	PD	Balde 71	25 800
	12	Fulham	W	2-1	ELf	Forlan 2 32 116	49 000
	15	Getafe	L	0-3	PD		45 000
	19	Sevilla	L	0-2	CRf		93 000

See page 356 for the Atletico Madrid League appearances and goals

BARCELONA 2009–10

		Opponent	Res	Score	Comp	Scorers	Att
Aug	16	Ath. Bilbao	W	2-1	SC	Xavi 58, Pedro 68	35 000
	23	Ath. Bilbao	W	3-0	SC	Messi 2 50 68, Krkic 72	61 083
	28	Shakhtar	W	1-0	USC	Pedro 115	17 738
Sep	1	Sp. Gijon	W	3-0	PD	Krkic 18, Keita 42, Ibrahimovic 82	71 932
	12	Getafe	W	2-0	PD	Ibrahimovic 66, Messi 80	16 000
	16	Inter	D	0-0	CLgF		77 321
	19	At. Madrid	W	5-2	PD	Ibrahimovic 2, Messi 2 16 90, Alves 30, Keita 41	95 739
	22	Racing	W	4-1	PD	Ibrahimovic 20, Messi 2 24 63, Pique 27	24 500
	26	Malaga	W	2-0	PD	Ibrahimovic 39, Pique 59	27 150
	29	Dy. Kyiv	W	2-0	CLgF	Messi 26, Pedro 76	68 221
Oct	3	Almeria	W	1-0	PD	Pedro 31	74 177
	17	Valencia	D	0-0	PD		45 000
	20	Rubin	L	1-2	CLgF	Ibrahimovic 48	55 930
	25	Zaragoza	W	6-1	PD	Keita 3 24 41 86, Ibrahimovic 2 29 56, Messi 80	75 653
	28	Leonesa	W	2-0	CRr4	Pedro 2 40 63	12 500
	31	Osasuna	D	1-1	PD	Keita 72	18 891
Nov	4	Rubin	D	0-0	CLgF		24 600
	7	Mallorca	W	4-2	PD	Pedro 2 11 40, Henry 44, Messi 87p	77 491
	10	Leonesa	W	5-0	CRr4	Krkic 2 52 54, Pedro 64, Messi 66, Xavi 75	26 322
	18	Ath. Bilbao	D	1-1	PD	Alves 54	40 000
	24	Inter	W	2-0	CLgF	Pique 10, Pedro 26	93 524
	29	Real Madrid	W	1-0	PD	Ibrahimovic 56	95 000
Dec	2	Xerez	W	2-0	PD	Henry 47, Ibrahimovic 90	17 584
	5	Deportivo	W	3-1	PD	Messi 2 27 80, Ibrahimovic 87	34 000
	9	Dy. Kyiv	W	2-1	CLgF	Xavi 33, Messi 86	16 300
	12	Espanyol	W	1-0	PD	Ibrahimovic 39p	84 759
	16	Atlante	W	3-1	CWsf	Busquets 35, Messi 55, Pedro 67	40 955
	19	Estudiantes	W	2-1	CWf	Pedro 89, Messi 110	43 050
	2	Villarreal	D	1-1	PD	Pedro 7	77 622
	5	Sevilla	L	1-2	CRr5	Ibrahimovic 70	48 167
Jan	10	Tenerife	W	5-0	PD	Messi 3 36 45 75, Pedro 44, OG 85	22 510
	13	Sevilla	W	1-0	CRr5	Xavi 64	35 000
	16	Sevilla	W	4-0	PD	OG 49, Pedro 70, Messi 2 85 90	63 274
	23	Valladolid	W	3-0	PD	Xavi 20, Alves 22, Messi 57	24 200
	30	Sp. Gijon	W	1-0	PD	Pedro 29	24 500
Feb	6	Getafe	W	2-1	PD	Messi 7, Xavi 67	74 859
	14	At. Madrid	L	1-2	PD	Ibrahimovic 27	53 000
	20	Racing	W	4-0	PD	Iniesta 7, Henry 29, Marquez 34, Thiago 84	75 935
	23	Stuttgart	D	1-1	CLr2	Ibrahimovic 52	39 430
	27	Malaga	W	2-1	PD	Pedro 69, Messi 84	64 837
Mar	6	Almeria	D	2-2	PD	Messi 2 42 66	14 758
	14	Valencia	W	3-0	PD	Messi 3 56 81 83	87 601
	17	Stuttgart	W	4-0	CLr2	Messi 2 13 60, Pedro 22, Krkic 89	88 543
	21	Zaragoza	W	4-2	PD	Messi 3 5 66 78, Ibrahimovic 90p	
	24	Osasuna	W	2-0	PD	Ibrahimovic 73, Krkic 89	70 645
	27	Mallorca	W	1-0	PD	Ibrahimovic 63	
	31	Arsenal	D	2-2	CLqf	Ibrahimovic 2 46 59	59 572
Apr	3	Ath. Bilbao	W	4-1	PD	Jeffren 27, Krkic 2 40 59, Messi 67	77 630
	6	Arsenal	W	4-1	CLqf	Messi 4 21 37 42 89	93 330
	10	Real Madrid	W	2-0	PD	Messi 32, Pedro 56	80 000
	14	Deportivo	W	3-0	PD	Krkic 16, Pedro 69, Yaya Toure 72	75 897
	17	Espanyol	D	0-0	PD		39 263
	20	Inter	L	1-3	CLsf	Pedro 19	79 000
	24	Xerez	W	3-1	PD	Jeffren 14, Henry 24, Ibrahimovic 56	82 456
	28	Inter	W	1-0	CLsf	Pique 84	96 214
May	1	Villarreal	W	4-1	PD	Messi 2 18 88, Xavi 34, Krkic 42	21 700
	4	Tenerife	W	4-1	PD	Messi 2 17 90, Krkic 63, Pedro 77	57 401
	8	Sevilla	W	3-2	PD	Messi 5, Krkic 28, Pedro 62	45 000
	16	Valladolid	W	4-0	PD	OG 27, Pedro 31, Messi 2 62 76	98 772

BARCELONA LEAGUE APPEARANCES/GOALS 2009-10

Goalkeepers Victor Valdes 38

Defenders Eric Abidal FRA 15+2/0 • Marc Bartra 0+1/0 • Dmytro Chyhrynskiy UKR 10+2/0 • Dani Alves BRA 28+1/3 • Andreu Fontas 0+1/0 • Rafael Marquez MEX 7+8/1 • Maxwell BRA 25/0 Gabriel Milito ARG 9+2/0 • Gerard Pique 29+3/2 • Carles Puyol 31+1/1

Midfield Sergio Busquets 26+7/0 • Andres Iniesta 20+9/1 Jeffren 6+6/2 • Jonathan MEX 1+2/0 • Seydou Keita MLI 23+6/6 Thiago 0+1/1 • Yaya Toure CIV 18+5/1 • Xavi 31+3/3

Forwards Bojan Krkic 11+12/8 • Thierry Henry FRA 15+6/4 • Zlatan Ibrahimovic SWE 23+6/16 • Lionel Messi 30+5/34 • Pedro 22+12/12

Coach Josep Guardiola

DEPORTIVO LA CORUNA 2009–10

Month	Date	Opponent	Res	Score	Comp	Scorers	Att
Ag	29	RealMadrid	L	2-3	PD	Riki 30, Valeron 46	79 000
	13	Malaga	W	1-0	PD	Filipe 82	15 000
Sep	19	Espanyol	L	2-3	PD	Adrian 28, Lassad 76	32 524
	23	Xerez	W	3-0	PD	Juca 26, OG 71, Riki 78	17 200
	27	Villarreal	W	1-0	PD	Juca 8	22 220
	3	Tenerife	W	1-0	PD	Colotto 61	24 000
Oct	17	Sevilla	W	1-0	PD	Rodriguez 38	29 064
	25	Valladolid	L	0-4	PD		15 000
	28	Real Murcia	W	1-0	CRr4	Lopo 77	6 533
	1	Sp. Gijon	D	1-1	PD	Lassad 42	25 000
	7	Getafe	W	2-0	PD	Mista 13, Filipe 59	12 000
Nov	10	Real Murcia	D	0-0	CRr4		5 000
	21	At. Madrid	W	2-1	PD	Colotto 21, Guardado 90p	17 000
	29	Racing	W	1-0	PD	Lopo 76	12 000
	5	Barcelona	L	1-3	PD	Adrian 39	34 000
Dec	13	Almeria	D	1-1	PD	Alvarez 74	9 360
	20	Valencia	D	0-0	PD		26 988
	3	Zaragoza	D	0-0	PD		22 000
	6	Valencia	W	2-1	CRr5	Guardado 47, Alvarez 55	25 000
	10	Osasuna	W	1-0	PD	Rodriguez 49	12 000
	13	Valencia	D	2-2	CRr5	Filipe 49, Rodriguez 72	13 000
Jan	17	Mallorca	L	0-2	PD		14 000
	20	Sevilla	L	0-3	CRqf		14 000
	23	Ath. Bilbao	W	3-1	PD	Filipe 49, Juca 59, Alvarez 89	13 000
	27	Sevilla	W	1-0	CRqf	Bodipo 43	15 000
	30	RealMadrid	L	1-3	PD	Riki 86p	34 600
	7	Malaga	D	0-0	PD		25 000
Feb	14	Espanyol	L	0-2	PD		24 210
	20	Xerez	W	2-1	PD	Guardado 3, Riki 7	12 000
	28	Villarreal	L	0-1	PD		17 000
	6	Tenerife	W	3-1	PD	Rodriguez 33, Guardado 55, Colotto 67	12 000
Mar	13	Sevilla	D	1-1	PD	Adrian 24	38 675
	20	Valladolid	L	0-2	PD		27 000
	23	Sp. Gijon	L	1-2	PD	Adrian 65	18 000
	28	Getafe	L	1-3	PD	Riki 71	14 000
	4	At. Madrid	L	0-3	PD		35 000
	11	Racing	D	1-1	PD	Riki 1	22 000
Apr	14	Barcelona	L	0-3	PD		75 897
	18	Almeria	D	0-0	PD		12 000
	24	Valencia	L	0-1	PD		40 000
	1	Zaragoza	L	0-1	PD		17 000
May	5	Osasuna	L	1-3	PD	Riki 15	14 417
	8	Mallorca	W	1-0	PD	Riki 68	9 000
	15	Ath. Bilbao	L	0-2	PD		39 000

RCD ESPANYOL 2009–10

Month	Date	Opponent	Res	Score	Comp	Scorers	Att
Ag	30	Ath. Bilbao	L	0-1	PD		38 000
	12	RealMadrid	L	0-3	PD		39 170
Sep	19	Deportivo	W	3-2	PD	Callejon 20, Forlin 43, Verdu 54	32 524
	23	Malaga	W	2-1	PD	Ben Sahar 55, Alonso 81	37 200
	27	Xerez	D	0-0	PD		35 600
	4	Villarreal	D	0-0	PD		16 000
Oct	18	Tenerife	W	2-1	PD	Alonso 2 11 60	33 000
	24	Sevilla	D	0-0	PD		43 225
	28	Getafe	L	0-2	CRr4		8 000
	1	Valladolid	D	1-1	PD	Garcia 50	27 130
	8	Sp. Gijon	L	0-1	PD		17 000
Nov	11	Getafe	D	1-1	CRr4	Alonso 37	20 650
	22	Getafe	L	0-2	PD		29 280
	29	At. Madrid	L	0-4	PD		25 000
	6	Racing	L	0-4	PD		25 180
Dec	12	Barcelona	L	0-1	PD		84 759
	20	Almeria	W	2-0	PD	Marquez 45, Coro 80	22 275
	2	Valencia	L	0-1	PD		45 000
	10	Zaragoza	W	2-1	PD	Verdu 11, Marques 71	24 025
Jan	16	Osasuna	L	0-2	PD		16 926
	24	Mallorca	D	1-1	PD	Osvaldo 49	26 210
	30	Ath. Bilbao	W	1-0	PD	Garcia 58	25 110
	6	RealMadrid	L	0-3	PD		72 000
Feb	14	Deportivo	W	2-0	PD	Verdu 39, Callejon 59	24 210
	21	Malaga	L	1-2	PD	Ruiz 45	23 000
	28	Xerez	D	1-1	PD	Osvaldo 17	13 000
	7	Villarreal	D	0-0	PD		26 345
	14	Tenerife	L	1-4	PD	Verdu 70	16 000
Mar	20	Sevilla	W	2-0	PD	Osvaldo 2 8 60	24 112
	24	Valladolid	D	0-0	PD		16 000
	28	Sp. Gijon	D	0-0	PD		26 724
	4	Getafe	D	1-1	PD	Osvaldo 51	10 000
Apr	11	At. Madrid	W	3-0	PD	Ruiz 47, Osvaldo 67, Alonso 90	32 620
	14	Racing	L	1-3	PD	Alonso 33	14 171
	17	Barcelona	D	0-0	PD		39 263
	25	Almeria	W	1-0	PD	Garcia 55	11 000
	1	Valencia	L	0-2	PD		30 029
May	5	Zaragoza	L	0-1	PD		22 000
	8	Osasuna	W	2-1	PD	Forlin 50, Osvaldo 52	27 000
	15	Mallorca	L	0-2	PD		14 000

ESPANYOL LEAGUE APPEARANCES/GOALS 2009-10
Goalkeepers Cristian Alvarez ARG 7+1 • Carlos Kameni CMR 31/0
Defenders Francisco Chica 27+1/0 • David Garcia 21/0 • Didac Vila 11/0 • Juan Forlin ARG 23+1/2 • Jordi Amat 4+2/0 • Nicolas Pareja ARG 30/0 • Ivan Pillud ARG 6+3/0 • Facundo Roncaglia ARG 15+6/0 • Victor Ruiz 21+1/2
Midfield Mahamat Azrack CHA 0+2/0 • Jose Baena 11+8/0 • Ivan De la Pena 0+4/0 • Javi Lopez 0+1/0 • Fernando Marques 10+11/1 • Javier Marquez 12+3/1 • Moises Hurtado 30+1/0 • Shunsuke Nakamura JPN 6+7/0 • Joan Verdu 31+3/4
Forwards Jose Callejon 31+5/2 • Ferran Coro 11+12/1 • Ivan Alonso URU 19+15/5 • Luis Garcia 35+1/3 • Pablo Osvaldo ITA 17+3/7 • Marc Pedraza 0+1/0 • Ben Sahar ISR 5+17/1 • Raul Tamudo 4+2/0
Coach Mauricio Pochettino ARG

DEPORTIVO LEAGUE APPEARANCES/GOALS 2009-10
Goalkeepers Daniel Aranzubia 36 • Manu 2+1
Defenders Diego Colotto ARG 30/3 • David Rochela 3+1/0 • Filipe Luis BRA 20+1/3 • Laure 19+1/0 • Alberto Lopo 34/1 • Manuel Pablo 33/0 • Piscu 3/0 • Raul Garcia 4+1/0 • Diego Seoane 1/0 • Ze Castro POR 8+2/0
Midfield Antonio Tomas 28+2/0 • David Anon Gonzalez 1+2/0 • Andres Guardado MEX 23+3/3 • Ivan Perez 3+17/0 • Juan Dominguez 8+5/0 • Juan Rodriguez 34+1/3 • Juca BRA 14+2/3 • Lafita Castillo 0+1/0 • Pablo Alvarez 17+11/2 • Sergio 21+3/0 • Juan Carlos Valeron 12+12/1
Forwards Adrian Lopez 25+9/4 • Rodolfo Bodipo EQG 6+9/0 • Lassad TUN 10+9/2 • Mista 5+8/1 • Riki 18+8/8
Coach Miguel Angel Lotina

ATLETICO MADRID LEAGUE APPEARANCES/GOALS 2009-10 (FROM PAGE 355)
Goalkeepers Sergio Asenjo 15 • David De Gea 19 • Joel 1+1 • Roberto 3
Defenders Antonio Lopez 29+2/2 • Leandro Cabrera URU 4/0 • Alvaro Dominguez 26/0 • John Heitinga NED 1/0 • Juanito 15+2/2 • Pablo Ibanez 6+1/0 • Luis Perea COL 27+1/0 • Mariano Andres Pernia 1/0 • Tomas Ujfalusi CZE 26+1/0 • Juan Valera 19+4/0
Midfield Ignacio Camacho 6+6/0 • Cleber Santana BRA 8+6/1 • Jose Manuel Jurado 29+9/7 • Koke 1+3/0 • Raul Garcia 12+8/0 • Keko 0+1/0 • Paulo Assuncao BRA 29+1/1 • Jose Antonio Reyes 19+11/2 • Maxi Rodriguez ARG 9+5/2 • Ruben Perez 0+1/0 • Eduardo Salvio ARG 9+8/2 • Simao POR 30+4/2 • Tiago POR 16+2/2
Forwards Kun Agüero 24+7/12 • Ibrahima Balde SEN 5+13/3 • Borja 0+1/0 • Diego Forlan URU 30+3/18 • Jorge Molino 0+1/0 • Florent Sinama-Pongolle FRA 3+7/0
Coach Quique Flores

GETAFE 2009–10

Month	Date	Opponent	Res	Score	Comp	Scorers	Att
Ag	30	Racing	W	4-1	PD	Rafa 12, Soldado 3 28 33 55	16 121
Sep	12	Barcelona	L	0-2	PD		16 000
Sep	20	Almeria	L	0-1	PD		9 000
Sep	23	Valencia	W	3-1	PD	Del Moral 2 24 38, Leon 69	14 110
Sep	27	Zaragoza	L	0-3	PD		27 600
Oct	4	Osasuna	W	2-1	PD	Diaz 55, Leon 76	11 800
Oct	18	Mallorca	L	1-3	PD	Albin 79	16 000
Oct	25	Ath. Bilbao	W	2-0	PD	Soldado 60, Parejo 71p	12 000
Oct	28	Espanyol	W	2-0	CRr4	Albin 60, Gavilan 70	8 000
Oct	31	Real Madrid	L	0-2	PD		79 000
Nov	7	Deportivo	L	0-2	PD		12 000
Nov	11	Espanyol	D	1-1	CRr4	Soldado 21	20 650
Nov	22	Espanyol	W	2-0	PD	Casquero 79, Rios 90	29 280
Nov	29	Xerez	W	5-1	PD	Soldado 3 44 45p 58, Parejo 57, Casquero 61	11 000
Dec	6	Villarreal	L	2-3	PD	Leon 3, Soldado 51p	18 000
Dec	12	Tenerife	W	2-1	PD	Albin 2 37 68	11 000
Dec	19	Sevilla	W	2-1	PD	Soldado 2 12 33	40 000
Dec	3	Valladolid	W	1-0	PD	Casquero 84	9 000
Dec	7	Malaga	L	1-2	CRr5	OG 67	7 000
Dec	10	Sp. Gijon	L	0-1	PD		22 500
Jan	13	Malaga	W	5-1	CRr5	Soldado 2 15 49, Rafa 29, Leon 53, Parejo 78	2 000
Jan	17	Malaga	L	0-1	PD		21 000
Jan	20	Mallorca	W	2-1	CRqf	Del Moral 51, Miku 68	11 000
Jan	24	At. Madrid	W	1-0	PD	Del Moral 39	14 000
Jan	28	Mallorca	L	0-1	CRqf		1 500
Jan	31	Racing	D	0-0	PD		10 000
Feb	3	Sevilla	L	0-2	CRsf		28 000
Feb	6	Barcelona	L	1-2	PD	Soldado 90p	74 859
Feb	10	Sevilla	W	1-0	CRsf	Soldado 52	13 000
Feb	14	Almeria	D	2-2	PD	Piatti 47, Soriano 90	11 000
Feb	22	Valencia	L	1-2	PD	Del Moral 75	40 000
Feb	27	Zaragoza	L	0-2	PD		12 000
Mar	7	Osasuna	D	0-0	PD		16 348
Mar	13	Mallorca	W	3-0	PD	Parejo 31, Miku 80, Del Moral 85p	11 000
Mar	20	Ath. Bilbao	D	2-2	PD	Del Moral 32, Leon 86	35 000
Mar	25	RealMadrid	L	2-4	PD	Parejo 38, Leon 80	15 000
Mar	28	Deportivo	W	3-1	PD	Miku 2 21 57, OG 32	14 000
Apr	4	Espanyol	D	1-1	PD	Del Moral 28	10 000
Apr	10	Xerez	W	1-0	PD	Rafa 60	16 674
Apr	13	Villarreal	W	3-0	PD	Miku 2 56 86, OG 72	10 200
Apr	18	Tenerife	L	2-3	PD	Leon 11, Casquero 75	18 996
Apr	25	Sevilla	W	4-3	PD	Gonzalez 17, Leon 59, Del Moral 76, Parejo 90p	11 390
May	1	Valladolid	D	0-0	PD		24 798
May	4	Sp. Gijon	D	1-1	PD	Miguel 18	10 000
May	8	Malaga	W	2-1	PD	Soldado 26, Leon 56	10 000
May	15	At. Madrid	W	3-0	PD	Soldado 2 14 53, Parejo 87	45 000

MALAGA 2009–10

Month	Date	Opponent	Res	Score	Comp	Scorers	Att
Ag	30	At. Madrid	W	3-0	PD	Baha 33, Manu 62, Torres 89	30 000
Sep	13	Deportivo	L	0-1	PD		15 000
Sep	19	Racing	L	1-2	PD	Duda 72	20 604
Sep	23	Espanyol	L	1-2	PD	Fernando 28	37 200
Sep	26	Barcelona	L	0-2	PD		27 150
Oct	4	Xerez	D	1-1	PD	Obinna 83	17 430
Oct	18	Almeria	L	1-2	PD	Edinho 68	21 000
Oct	25	Villarreal	L	1-2	PD	Luque 45	15 000
Oct	28	Zaragoza	D	1-1	CRr4	Apono 76p	8 000
Nov	1	Valencia	L	0-1	PD		30 000
Nov	7	Tenerife	D	2-2	PD	Edinho 29, Lopez 77	16 800
Nov	11	Zaragoza	D	0-0	CRr4		10 000
Nov	22	Zaragoza	D	1-1	PD	Gonzalez 74	25 000
Nov	28	Sevilla	D	2-2	PD	Fernando 22, Duda 45	40 000
Dec	6	Osasuna	D	1-1	PD	Apono 83	25 000
Dec	13	Valladolid	D	1-1	PD	Duda 34	13 400
Dec	20	Mallorca	W	2-1	PD	Fernando 24, Forestieri 77	21 000
Jan	3	Sp. Gijon	D	2-2	PD	Duda 10, Weligton 60	19 800
Jan	7	Getafe	W	2-1	CRr5	Apono 10, Edinho 45	7 000
Jan	10	Ath. Bilbao	D	1-1	PD	Weligton 48	15 000
Jan	13	Getafe	L	1-5	CRr5	Juanmi 63	2 000
Jan	17	Getafe	W	1-0	PD	Baha 84	21 000
Jan	24	RealMadrid	L	0-2	PD		72 000
Jan	31	At. Madrid	W	2-0	PD	Duda 3, Lopez 70	40 000
Feb	7	Deportivo	D	0-0	PD		25 000
Feb	14	Racing	W	3-0	PD	Weligton 9, Caicedo 35, Obinna 66	13 296
Feb	21	Espanyol	W	2-1	PD	Fernando 13, Obinna 75	23 000
Feb	27	Barcelona	L	1-2	PD	Valdo 81	64 837
Mar	7	Xerez	L	2-4	PD	Duda 40, Valdo 55	23 000
Mar	14	Almeria	L	0-1	PD		10 000
Mar	21	Villarreal	W	2-0	PD	Baha 2 64 84	19 149
Mar	24	Valencia	L	0-1	PD		35 000
Mar	27	Tenerife	D	1-1	PD	Apono 66	25 000
Apr	3	Zaragoza	L	0-2	PD		22 000
Apr	10	Sevilla	L	1-2	PD	Caicedo 17	22 517
Apr	14	Osasuna	D	2-2	PD	Caicedo 31, Baha 76	15 532
Apr	18	Valladolid	D	0-0	PD		19 152
Apr	25	Mallorca	D	1-1	PD	Obinna 86	13 200
May	1	Sp. Gijon	D	1-1	PD	Caicedo 79	30 000
May	5	Ath. Bilbao	D	1-1	PD	Duda 19	35 000
May	8	Getafe	L	1-2	PD	Fernando 90	10 000
May	16	RealMadrid	D	1-1	PD	Duda 9	22 800

GETAFE LEAGUE APPEARANCES/GOALS 2009-10

Goalkeepers Jordi Codina 22 • Oscar Ustari ARG 16
Defenders David Belenguer 7+6/0 • Cosmin Contra ROU 0+3/0 • David Cortes 19+1/0 • Cata Diaz 30/1 • Mane 35/1 • Pedro Mario 12+1/0 • Miguel Torres 22+4/0 • Rafa Lopez 27/2
Midfield Adrian Gonzalez 19+6/1 • Derek Boateng GHA 26+3/0 • Francisco Casquero 23+9/5 • Fabio Celestini SUI 22+2/0 • Alberto Escasi 0+1/0 • Jaime Gavilan 16+11/0 • Daniel Parejo 16+12/6 • Pedro Leon 33+2/8 • Pedro Rios 4+14/1
Forwards Juan Albin 12+11/3 • Kepa 0+5/0 • Manu del Moral 21+15/8 • Miku VEN 11+5/5 • Roberto Soldado 25+1/16
Coach Michel

MALAGA LEAGUE APPEARANCES/GOALS 2009-10

Goalkeepers Gustavo Munua URU 38
Defenders Cuadrado 4/0 • Ivan Gonzalez 22+1/1 • Helder Rosario POR 3/0 • Jesus Gamez 32/0 • Manolo 13+2/0 • Manu Torres 15+2/1 • Patrick Mtiliga DEN 24/0 • Daniel Orozco 4/0 • Milan Stepanov SRB 12/0 • Weligton BRA 20+1/3
Midfield Apono 17+7/2 • Selim Ben Achour TUN 18+5/0 • Duda POR 33+1/8 • Edinho POR 2+8/2 • Edu Ramos 4/0 • Fernando 29+1/5 • Javi Lopez 9+2/2 • Juanito 25+5/0 • Pedrito 0+3/0 • Francisco Portillo 0+1/0 • Daniel Toribio 17+4/0 • Valdo 10+9/2 • Xavier Torres 10+1/1
Forwards Nabil Baha MAR 21+11/5 • Felipe Caicedo ECU 15+3/4 • Fernando Forestieri ITA 5+14/1 • Juanmi 0+5/0 • Alberto Luque 4+12/1 • Victor Obinna NGA 16+10/4
Coach Juan Ramon Lopez Muniz

RCD MALLORCA 2009–10

Aug	30	Xerez	W	2-0	PD	Aduriz [56], Tuni [60]	11 595
	13	Villarreal	D	1-1	PD	Borja [75]	18 000
Sep	19	Tenerife	W	4-0	PD	Mario [17], Aduriz [51], Alvarez [59], Webo [87p]	12 000
	22	Sevilla	L	0-2	PD		48 000
	27	Valladolid	W	3-0	PD	Nunes [4], Aduriz [70], Borja [72]	12 809
	4	Sp. Gijon	L	1-4	PD	Marti [12]	20 000
Oct	18	Getafe	W	3-1	PD	Alvarez [31], Aduriz 2 [53 70]	16 000
	24	At. Madrid	D	1-1	PD	Borja [90]	45 000
	29	Valladolid	L	1-2	CRr4	Marti [28p]	13 728
	1	Racing	W	1-0	PD	Webo [18]	12 600
	7	Barcelona	L	2-4	PD	Nunes [20], Keita [90]	77 491
Nov	11	Valladolid	W	1-0	CRr4	Keita [39]	9 300
	22	Almeria	W	3-1	PD	Castro 2 [48 90], Victor [89]	11 000
	28	Valencia	D	1-1	PD	Borja [85p]	40 000
Dec	6	Zaragoza	W	4-1	PD	Aduriz 2 [38 68], Mario [75], Keita [83]	12 600
	13	Osasuna	W	1-0	PD	Castro [61]	16 088
	20	Malaga	L	1-2	PD	Alvarez [56]	21 000
	3	Ath. Bilbao	W	2-0	PD	Alvarez [49], Aduriz [66]	12 800
	7	Vallecano	L	1-2	CRr5	Alvarez [21]	8 000
	10	Real Madrid	L	0-2	PD		57 000
Jan	14	Vallecano	W	3-1	CRr5	Victor 2 [50 60], Mario [89]	5 214
	17	Deportivo	W	2-0	PD	Mario [46], Castro [53]	14 000
	20	Getafe	L	1-2	CRqf	Castro [90]	11 000
	24	Espanyol	D	1-1	PD	Borja [80p]	26 210
	28	Getafe	W	1-0	CRqf	Aduriz [45]	1 500
	31	Xerez	L	1-2	PD	Webo [24]	14 764
Feb	7	Villarreal	W	1-0	PD	Nunes [81]	12 000
	15	Tenerife	L	0-1	PD		17 966
	20	Sevilla	L	1-3	PD	Mario [5]	11 100
	28	Valladolid	W	2-1	PD	Ruben [69], Alvarez [83]	16 500
	7	Sp. Gijon	W	3-0	PD	Alvarez [12], Victor [76], Webo [89]	12 700
	13	Getafe	L	0-3	PD		11 000
Mar	21	At. Madrid	W	4-1	PD	Victor [10], Aduriz [28], OG [86], Mattioni [90]	13 000
	24	Racing	D	0-0	PD		15 000
	27	Barcelona	L	0-1	PD		19 600
	4	Almeria	D	1-1	PD	Webo [88]	9 574
	11	Valencia	W	3-2	PD	Castro [7], Webo [22], OG [63]	14 000
Apr	14	Zaragoza	D	1-1	PD	Ruben [13]	25 000
	19	Osasuna	W	2-0	PD	Ruben [36], Keita [90]	11 380
	25	Malaga	D	1-1	PD	Aduriz [90]	13 200
	2	Ath. Bilbao	W	3-1	PD	Castro [43], Nunes [49], Aduriz [51]	35 000
May	5	Real Madrid	L	1-4	PD	Aduriz [16]	19 200
	8	Deportivo	L	0-1	PD		9 000
	15	Espanyol	W	2-0	PD	Victor [24], Mario [78]	14 000

OSASUNA 2009–10

Aug	30	Villarreal	D	1-1	PD	Pandiani [37]	17 135
	13	Tenerife	L	1-2	PD	Pandiani [52]	18 300
Sep	19	Sevilla	L	0-2	PD		16 670
	23	Valladolid	W	2-1	PD	Pandiani [25], Galan [72]	10 000
	27	Sp. Gijon	W	1-0	PD	Nekounam [56p]	15 840
	4	Getafe	L	1-2	PD	Aranda [62]	11 800
Oct	18	At. Madrid	W	3-0	PD	Pandiani 2 [4 27], Aranda [30]	15 000
	25	Racing	D	1-1	PD	Pandiani [51]	16 154
	28	Xerez	W	2-1	CRr4	Sergio [16], Dady [20]	4 588
	31	Barcelona	D	1-1	PD	OG [90]	18 891
	8	Almeria	L	0-2	PD		10 260
Nov	11	Xerez	W	1-0	CRr4	Dady [79]	10 015
	22	Valencia	L	1-3	PD	Shojaei [68]	17 401
	29	Zaragoza	W	1-0	PD	Nekounam [27]	24 000
	6	Malaga	D	1-1	PD	Shojaei [47]	25 000
Dec	13	Mallorca	L	0-1	PD		16 088
	19	Ath. Bilbao	L	0-2	PD		38 000
	3	Real Madrid	D	0-0	PD		18 810
	7	Hercules	L	1-2	CRr5	Galan [51]	4 500
	10	Deportivo	L	0-1	PD		12 000
Jan	13	Hercules	W	1-0	CRr5	Shojaei [48]	11 103
	16	Espanyol	W	2-0	PD		16 926
	20	Racing	L	1-2	CRqf	Pandiani [88]	12 600
	24	Xerez	W	2-1	PD	Monreal [10], Camunas [83]	14 909
	28	Racing	L	0-3	CRqf		13 126
	31	Villarreal	W	2-0	PD	Juanfran 2 [15 84]	17 000
Feb	7	Tenerife	W	1-0	PD	Aranda [48]	16 786
	14	Sevilla	L	0-1	PD		35 000
	21	Valladolid	D	1-1	PD	Camunas [86]	15 950
	28	Sp. Gijon	L	2-3	PD	Nekounam [39p], Vadocz [50]	22 000
	7	Getafe	D	0-0	PD		16 348
Mar	15	At. Madrid	L	0-1	PD		35 000
	21	Racing	L	1-3	PD	Flano [32]	16 614
	24	Barcelona	L	0-2	PD		70 645
	28	Almeria	W	1-0	PD	Pandiani [20]	16 421
	4	Valencia	L	0-3	PD		42 000
Apr	11	Zaragoza	W	2-0	PD	Aranda [1], Vadocz [90]	17 601
	14	Malaga	D	2-2	PD	Pandiani 2 [10 48]	15 532
	19	Mallorca	L	0-2	PD		11 380
	26	Ath. Bilbao	D	0-0	PD		18 215
	2	Real Madrid	L	2-3	PD	Aranda [7], Vadocz [42]	78 000
May	5	Deportivo	W	3-1	PD	Camunas [11], Pandiani [24], Juanfran [32]	14 417
	8	Espanyol	L	1-2	PD	Vadocz [5]	27 000
	16	Xerez	D	1-1	PD	Dady [55]	15 042

MALLORCA LEAGUE APPEARANCES/GOALS 2009-10
Goalkeepers Dudu Awat ISR 38 • German Lux ARG 0+1
Defenders Ayoze 33/0 • Enrique Corrales 5+2/0 • Felipe Mattioni BRA 14+6/1 • Josemi 26+2/0 • Jose Nunes POR 34/4 • Ivan Ramis 26/0 • Ruben Gonzalez 16+3/3
Midfield Borja Valero 32+1/6 • Bruno China POR 2+7/0 • Chori Castro URU 32+3/6 • Julio Alvarez VEN 21+5/6 • Mario Suarez 27+7/4 • Jose Luis Marti 27+9/1 • Paulo Pezzolano URU 1+11/0 • Tomas Pina 0+1/0 • Fernando Varela 10+5/0
Forwards Artiz Aduriz 33+1/12 • Alhassane Keita GUI 2+21/3 • Sergi 0+1/0 • Tuni 7+2/1 • Victor 20+7/4 • Pierre Webo CMR 12+19/6
Coach Gregorio Manzano

OSASUNA LEAGUE APPEARANCES/GOALS 2009-10
Goalkeepers Ricardo 36 • Roberto 2
Defenders Cesar Azpilicueta 33/0 • Jon Echaide 2/0 • Josetxo 18+1/0 • Miguel Flano 31+1/1 • Ignacio Monreal 31/1 • Oier 8+3/0 • Roversio BRA 3/0 • Sergio 24/0
Midfield Alan Baro 0+1/0 • Javier Calleja 6+16/0 • Javier Camunas 34+2/3 • Jokin Esparza 0+5/0 • Juanfran 32+1/4 • Javad Nekounam IRN 31/3 • Francisco Punal 27+6/0 • Ruper 11+16/0 • Masoud Shojaei IRN 18+18/2 • Krisztian Vadocz HUN 11+9/4
Forwards Carlos Aranda 28+1/5 • Dady CPV 4+6/1 • Jorge Galan 0+20/1 • Walter Pandiani URU 28+1/11 • Javier Portillo 0+2/0
Coach Jose Antonio Camacho

RACING SANTANDER 2009-10

Mo	Date	Opponent		Res	Comp	Scorers	Att
Ag	30	Getafe	L	1-4	PD	Lacen 43	16 121
	12	At. Madrid	D	1-1	PD	Serrano 45	39 000
Sp	19	Malaga	W	2-1	PD	Arana 37, Morris 80	20 604
	22	Barcelona	L	1-4	PD	Serrano 72	24 500
	27	Almeria	D	2-2	PD	Tchite 59, Lacen 71	13 200
	4	Valencia	L	0-1	PD		16 000
Oc	18	Zaragoza	D	2-2	PD	Pavon 22, Arizmendi 33	25 000
	25	Osasuna	D	1-1	PD	Arana 90	16 154
	29	Salamanca	L	0-1	CRr4		6 000
	1	Mallorca	L	0-1	PD		12 600
	8	Ath. Bilbao	L	0-2	PD		14 412
Nv	10	Salamanca	W	4-1	CRr4	Tchite 2 36 44p, OG 57, Xisco 74	11 859
	21	RealMadrid	L	0-1	PD		75 000
	29	Deportivo	L	0-1	PD		12 000
Dc	6	Espanyol	W	4-0	PD	Henrique 47, Canales 2 52 72, Tchite	25 180
	13	Xerez	W	3-2	PD	Lacen 26, Arana 49, Xisco 82	14 439
	20	Villarreal	L	0-2	PD		16 000
	3	Tenerife	W	2-0	PD	Colsa 72, Xisco 75	15 274
	6	Alcorcon	W	3-2	CRr5	Christian 31, Geijo 47, Moraton 62	3 000
	9	Sevilla	W	2-1	PD	Canales 2 26 38	40 000
Jan	13	Alcorcon	D	0-0	CRr5		12 627
	17	Valladolid	D	1-1	PD	Canales 60	16 402
	21	Osasuna	W	2-1	CRqf	Colsa 63, Diop 84	12 600
	24	Sp. Gijon	W	1-0	PD	Geijo 44	23 500
	27	Osasuna	W	3-0	CRqf	Xisco 6, Henrique 23, Canales 79	13 126
	31	Getafe	D	0-0	PD		10 000
	4	At. Madrid	L	0-4	CRsf		30 000
Feb	7	At. Madrid	D	1-1	PD	Colsa 36	15 430
	11	At. Madrid	W	3-2	CRsf	OG 3, Xisco 89, Tchite 90	20 000
	14	Malaga	L	0-3	PD		13 296
	20	Barcelona	L	0-4	PD		75 935
	28	Almeria	L	0-2	PD		15 486
Mar	8	Valencia	D	0-0	PD		35 000
	14	Zaragoza	D	0-0	PD		16 212
	21	Osasuna	W	3-1	PD	Colsa 35, Christian 51, Diop 89	16 614
	24	Mallorca	D	0-0	PD		15 000
	29	Ath. Bilbao	L	3-4	PD	Tchite 41, Bolado 2 81 90	30 000
	4	RealMadrid	L	0-2	PD		22 000
	11	Deportivo	D	1-1	PD	Moral 85	22 000
Apr	14	Espanyol	W	3-1	PD	Tchite 2 37 50, Arana 90	14 171
	18	Xerez	D	2-2	PD	Tchite 2 44 58p	18 000
	25	Villarreal	L	1-2	PD	Canales 39	16 781
	1	Tenerife	L	1-2	PD	Xisco 71	16 000
May	5	Sevilla	L	1-5	PD	Tchite 61	17 000
	8	Valladolid	L	1-2	PD	Christian 28	17 500
	16	Sp. Gijon	W	2-0	PD	Tchite 2 35 55	20 000

REAL MADRID 2009-10

Mo	Date	Opponent		Res	Comp	Scorers	Att
Ag	29	Deportivo	W	3-2	PD	Raul 27, Ronaldo 35p, Diarra 60	79 000
	12	Espanyol	W	3-0	PD	Granero 39, Guti 77, Ronaldo 90	39 170
	15	Zurich	W	5-2	CLgC	Ronaldo 2 27 89, Raul 34, Higuain 45, Guti 94+	24 424
Sp	20	Xerez	W	5-0	PD	Ronaldo 2 1 75, Guti 79, Benzema 82, Van Nistelrooy 89	72 000
	23	Villarreal	W	2-0	PD	Ronaldo 2, Kaka 73p	20 615
	26	Tenerife	W	3-0	PD	Benzema 2 47 58, Kaka 78	75 200
	30	Marseille	W	3-0	CLgC	Ronaldo 2 58 64, Kaka 61p	67 244
	4	Sevilla	L	1-2	PD	Pepe 49	45 000
	17	Valladolid	W	4-2	PD	Raul 2 13 18, Marcelo 45, Higuain 79	72 000
Oc	21	Milan	L	2-3	CLgC	Raul 19, Drenthe 76	71 569
	24	Sp. Gijon	D	0-0	PD		23 000
	27	Alcorcon	L	0-4	CRr4		7 000
	31	Getafe	W	2-0	PD	Higuain 2 53 56	79 000
	3	Milan	D	1-1	CLgC	Benzema 29	75 092
	7	At. Madrid	W	3-2	PD	Kaka 5, Marcelo 24, Higuain 64	55 000
Nv	10	Alcorcon	W	1-0	CRr4	Van der Vaart 81	79 500
	21	Racing	W	1-0	PD	Higuain 22	75 000
	25	Zurich	W	1-0	CLgC	Higuain 21	67 867
	29	Barcelona	L	0-1	PD		95 000
Dc	5	Almeria	W	4-2	PD	Ramos 31, Higuain 73, Benzema 82, Ronaldo 84	77 000
	8	Marseille	W	3-1	CLgC	Ronaldo 2 5 80, Albiol 60	55 722
	12	Valencia	W	3-2	PD	Higuain 2 54 65, Garay 83	50 000
	19	Zaragoza	W	6-0	PD	Higuain 2 3 34, Van der Vaart 2 26 28, Ronaldo 50, Benzema 71	60 000
	3	Osasuna	D	0-0	PD		18 810
	10	Mallorca	W	2-0	PD	Higuain 8, Granero 50	57 000
	16	Ath. Bilbao	L	0-1	PD		40 000
	24	Malaga	W	2-0	PD	Ronaldo 2 35 39	72 000
	30	Deportivo	W	3-1	PD	Granero 13, Benzema 2 40 90	34 600
	6	Espanyol	W	3-0	PD	Ramos 5, Kaka 30, Higuain 90	72 000
	9	Xerez	W	3-0	PD	Arbeloa 64, Ronaldo 2 69 71	20 398
	16	Lyon	L	0-1	CLr2		40 327
Feb	21	Villarreal	W	6-2	PD	Ronaldo 18, Kaka 2 20p 79, Higuain 2 54 71, Alonso 87p	78 000
	27	Tenerife	W	5-1	PD	Higuain 2 29 41, Kaka 48, Ronaldo 78p, Raul 90	22 123
	6	Sevilla	W	3-2	PD	Ronaldo 60, Ramos 64, Van der Vaart 90	79 000
	10	Lyon	D	1-1	CLr2	Ronaldo 6	71 569
	14	Valladolid	W	4-1	PD	Ronaldo 28, Higuain 3 45 52 65	22 000
Mar	20	Sp. Gijon	W	3-1	PD	Van der Vaart 55, Alonso 57, Higuain 68	78 000
	25	Getafe	W	4-2	PD	Ronaldo 2 13 37, Higuain 2 21 23	15 000
	28	At. Madrid	W	3-2	PD	Alonso 49, Arbeloa 55, Higuain 62	80 000
	4	Racing	W	2-0	PD	Ronaldo 23p, Higuain 76	22 000
	10	Barcelona	L	0-2	PD		80 000
Apr	15	Almeria	W	2-1	PD	Ronaldo 27, Van der Vaart 69	17 000
	18	Valencia	W	2-0	PD	Higuain 25, Ronaldo 78	80 000
	24	Zaragoza	W	2-1	PD	Raul 50, Kaka 82	32 775
	2	Osasuna	W	3-2	PD	Ronaldo 2 25 89, Marcelo 44	78 000
	5	Mallorca	W	4-1	PD	Ronaldo 3 26 57 72, Higuain 82	19 200
May	8	Ath. Bilbao	W	5-1	PD	Ronaldo 22p, Higuain 73, Ramos 80, Benzema 81, Marcelo 88	79 000
	16	Malaga	D	1-1	PD	Van der Vaart 49	22 800

RACING LEAGUE APPEARANCES/GOALS 2009-10
Goalkeepers Fabio Coltorti SUI 22+1 • Tono 16
Defenders Christian Fernandez 28+1/2 • Jose Crespo 13/0 • Henrique BRA 21+1/1 • Jose Moraton 10+1/0 • Nassif Morris RSA 12/1 • Oriol 15+4/0 • Osmar Barba 1/0 • Pablo Pinillos 22+1/0 • Marc Torrejon 27/0
Midfield Manuel Arana 17+14/4 • Sergio Canales 19+7/6 • Gonzalo Colsa 28+2/3 • Papa Kouli Diop SEN 21+2/1 • Edu Bedia 0+5/0 • Medhi Lacen ALG 28+5/3 • Luisma 0+1/0 • Mario Ortiz 0+2/0 • Laszlo Sepsi ROU 4+1/0 • Oscar Serrano 27+6/3 • Toni Moral 10+8/1
Forwards Alexandre Geijo SUI 8+11/1 • Ivan Bolado 3+9/2 • Luis Garcia 4+11/0 • Juanjo 0+1/0 • Pedro Munitis 27+2/0 • Mohamed Tchite COD 28+1/11 • Xisco 7+16/3
Coach Juan Carlos Mandia • Juan Jose Gonzalez (9/11/09) • Miguel Angel Portugal (19/11/09)

REAL LEAGUE APPEARANCES/GOALS 2009-10
Goalkeepers Iker Casillas 38
Defenders Raul Albiol 32+1/0 • Alvaro Arbeloa 30/2 • Royston Drenthe NED 3+5/0 • Ezequiel Garay ARG 19+1/1 • Marcelo BRA 34+1/4 • Marcos Alonso 0+1/0 • Christoph Metzelder GER 2/0 • Pepe POR 10/1 • Sergio Ramos 33/4
Midfield Lassana Diarra FRA 19+4/1 • Mahamadou Diarra MLI 4+11/0 • Fernando Gago 14+4/0 • Esteban Granero 21+10/3 • Guti 10+16/2 • Kaka BRA 21+4/8 • Pedro Mosquera 0+1/0 • Rafael van der Vaart NED 16+10/6 • Xabi Alonso 34/3
Forwards Karim Benzema FRA 14+13/8 • Cristiano Ronaldo POR 28+1/26 • Gonzalo Higuain ARG 28+4/27 • Juanfran 0+1/0 • Raul 8+22/5 • Ruud Van Nistelrooy NED 0+1/1
Coach Manuel Pellegrini

SEVILLA 2009–10

	Opponent		Score	Comp	Scorers	Att
Ag 30	Valencia	L	0-2	PD		46 000
12	Zaragoza	W	4-1	PD	Konko 8, Luis Fabiano 2 45 86, Perotti 57	42 000
16	Unirea	W	2-0	CLgG	Luis Fabiano 45, Renato 70	32 691
19	Osasuna	W	2-0	PD	Negredo 37, Kanoute 71	16 670
Sep 22	Mallorca	W	2-0	PD	Squillaci 17, Perotti 25	48 000
26	Ath. Bilbao	W	4-0	PD	Renato 5, Negredo 21, Kanoute 45, Navas 75	40 000
29	Rangers	W	4-1	CLgG	Konko 50, Adriano 64, Luis Fabiano 72, Kanoute 74	40 572
4	RealMadrid	W	2-1	PD	Navas 33, Renato 66	45 000
17	Deportivo	L	0-1	PD		29 064
20	Stuttgart	W	3-1	CLgG	Squillaci 2 23 72, Navas 55	37 000
Oct 24	Espanyol	D	0-0	PD		43 225
27	At. Ciudad	W	4-2	CRr4	Luis Fabiano 2 18 19, Navas 28, Capel 36	14 000
31	Xerez	W	2-0	PD	Negredo 42, Luis Fabiano 90	21 000
4	Stuttgart	D	1-1	CLgG	Navas 14	32 669
8	Villarreal	W	3-2	PD	Luis Fabiano 2 9 61, Kanoute 66	38 000
Nov 10	At. Ciudad	W	5-1	CRr4	Navas 51, Kanoute 59p, Luis Fabiano 63, Jose Carlos 2 65 88	15 000
21	Tenerife	L	2-1	PD	Perotti 32, Renato 48	20 551
24	Unirea	L	0-1	CLgG		10 007
28	Malaga	D	2-2	PD	Luis Fabiano 2 58 72	40 000
5	Valladolid	D	1-1	PD	Luis Fabiano 45p	40 000
Dec 9	Rangers	W	1-0	CLgG	Kanoute 8p	31 560
13	Sp. Gijon	W	1-0	PD	Kanoute 9	17 000
19	Getafe	L	1-2	PD	Negredo 51	40 000
2	At. Madrid	L	1-2	PD	Renato 44	35 000
5	Barcelona	W	2-1	CRr5	Capel 60, Negredo 75p	48 167
9	Racing	L	1-2	PD	Romaric 62	40 000
Jan 13	Barcelona	L	0-1	CRr5		35 000
16	Barcelona	L	0-4	PD		63 274
20	Deportivo	W	3-0	CRqf	Negredo 27, Renato 68, Navas 70	14 000
23	Almeria	W	1-0	PD	Negredo 9	32 000
27	Deportivo	L	0-1	CRqf		15 000
31	Valencia	W	2-1	PD	Negredo 2 21 69	42 000
3	Getafe	W	2-0	CRsf	Luis Fabiano 45, OG 80	28 000
7	Zaragoza	L	1-2	PD	Kanoute 34	23 000
10	Getafe	L	0-1	CRsf		13 000
Feb 14	Osasuna	W	1-0	PD	Luis Fabiano 35	35 000
20	Mallorca	W	3-1	PD	Navas 23, Dragutinovic 57, Perotti 62	11 100
24	CSKA	D	1-1	CLr2	Negredo 25	28 600
28	Ath. Bilbao	D	0-0	PD		35 000
6	RealMadrid	L	2-3	PD	OG 10, Dragutinovic 53	79 000
13	Deportivo	D	1-1	PD	Fazio 21	38 675
Mar 16	CSKA	L	1-2	CLr2	Perotti 41	29 666
20	Espanyol	L	0-2	PD		24 112
23	Xerez	D	1-1	PD	Kanoute 63p	40 000
28	Villarreal	L	0-3	PD		18 000
3	Tenerife	W	3-0	PD	Kanoute 22, Luis Fabiano 44, Jose Carlos 87	30 000
Apr 10	Malaga	W	2-1	PD	Cala 66, Lolo 85	22 517
13	Valladolid	L	1-2	PD	Cala 83	23 850
17	Sp. Gijon	W	3-0	PD	Kanoute 8, Luis Fabiano 53, Cala 80	25 480
25	Getafe	L	3-4	PD	Luis Fabiano 2 33 61, Kanoute 38	11 390
2	At. Madrid	W	3-1	PD	Luis Fabiano 6, Negredo 2 13p 40p	40 000
May 5	Racing	W	5-1	PD	Negredo 2 3 89, Kanoute 21p, Navas 46, Capel 48	17 000
8	Barcelona	L	2-3	PD	Kanoute 69, Luis Fabiano 71	45 000
15	Almeria	W	3-2	PD	Kanoute 16, OG 53, Rodri 90	18 194
19	At. Madrid	W	2-0	CRf	Capel 5, Navas 90	93 000

SPORTING GIJON 2009–10

	Opponent		Score	Comp	Scorers	Att
Ag 31	Barcelona	L	0-3	PD		71 932
13	Almeria	W	1-0	PD	Castro 6	25 000
Sep 20	Valencia	D	2-2	PD	Barral 5, Arnolin 86	40 000
24	Zaragoza	D	1-1	PD	Castro 29	18 000
27	Osasuna	L	0-1	PD		15 840
4	Mallorca	W	4-1	PD	Moran 59, Miguel 2 64 69, Bilic 83	20 000
Oct 18	Ath. Bilbao	W	2-1	PD	Miguel 2 65 77	33 600
24	RealMadrid	D	0-0	PD		23 000
27	Recreativo	D	1-1	CRr4	Bilic 47	4 956
1	Deportivo	D	1-1	PD	Castro 69	25 000
8	Espanyol	W	1-0	PD	Bilic 3	17 000
Nov 10	Recreativo	D	1-1	CRr4	Barral 2	7 000
22	Xerez	D	0-0	PD		16 000
28	Villarreal	W	1-0	PD	Bilic 75	17 000
6	Tenerife	L	1-2	PD	Castro 4	19 281
Dec 13	Sevilla	L	0-1	PD		17 000
20	Valladolid	L	1-2	PD	Moran 13	16 700
3	Malaga	D	2-2	PD	Arnolin 45, Canella 69	19 800
10	Getafe	W	1-0	PD	Castro 39	22 500
Jan 17	At. Madrid	L	2-3	PD	Castro 34p, Moran 90	50 000
24	Racing	L	0-1	PD		23 500
30	Barcelona	L	0-1	PD		24 500
7	Almeria	L	1-3	PD	Castro 13p	11 000
13	Valencia	D	1-1	PD	Castro 5	22 000
Feb 21	Zaragoza	W	3-1	PD	Bilic 38, Moran 63, Barral 90	28 000
28	Osasuna	W	3-2	PD	Miguel 18, Barral 71, Castro 81p	22 000
7	Mallorca	L	0-3	PD		12 700
13	Ath. Bilbao	D	0-0	PD		22 188
Mar 20	RealMadrid	L	1-3	PD	Barral 53	78 000
23	Deportivo	W	2-1	PD	Bilic 30, Castro 90p	18 000
28	Espanyol	D	0-0	PD		26 724
4	Xerez	D	2-2	PD	Rivera 12, Miguel 57	20 000
10	Villarreal	L	0-1	PD		19 530
Apr 13	Tenerife	L	0-2	PD		25 885
17	Sevilla	L	0-3	PD		25 480
25	Valladolid	L	0-2	PD		24 500
1	Malaga	D	1-1	PD	OG 43	30 000
May 4	Getafe	D	1-1	PD	Miguel 18	10 000
8	At. Madrid	D	1-1	PD	Miguel 57	25 800
16	Racing	L	0-2	PD		20 000

SPORTING LEAGUE APPEARANCES/GOALS 2009-10

Goalkeepers Juan Pablo 38
Defenders Gregory Arnolin FRA 35/2 • Alberto Botia 26/0 • Roberto Canella 28/1 • Gerard 8/0 • Ivan Hernandez 7+3/0 • Jose Angel 10+3/0 • Rafael Sastre 11+3/0
Midfield Sergio Alvarez 1/0 • Carmelo 11+16/0 • Diego Camacho 16+7/0 • Cristian Portilla 3+1/0 • Miguel De las Cuevas 32+5/8 • Diego Castro 31+4/10 • Kike Mateo 2+14/0 • Alberto Lora 31+1/0 • Marcos Landeira 1/0 • Sergio Matabuena 5+9/0 • Miguel 12+1/0 • Pedro 4+1/0 • Alberto Rivera 34/1 • Milan Smiljanic SRB 5+1/0
Forwards David Barral 23+10/4 • Mate Bilic CRO 17+14/5 • Juan Muniz 0+1/0 • Luis Moran 21+7/4 • Francisco Maldonado 6+9/0 • Borja Navarro 0+2/0
Coach Manolo Preciado

SEVILLA LEAGUE APPEARANCES/GOALS 2009-10

Goalkeepers Javi Varas 5 • Andres Palop 33
Defenders Adriano BRA 23+4/0 • Cala 5/3 • Ivica Dragutinovic SRB 20/2 • Julien Escude FRA 24/0 • Federico Fazio ARG 10/0 • Fernando Navarro 26+3/0 • Abdoulay Konko FRA 17+1/1 • Lolo 9+12/1 • Antonio Luna 1/0 • Marc Valiente 2+1/0 • Sergio Sanchez 6+1/0 • Sebastien Squillaci FRA 14+2/1 • Marius Stankevicius LTU 14+2/0
Midfield Lautaro Acosta ARG 1+5/0 • Aldo Duscher ARG 7+3/0 • Jesus Navas 32+2/4 • Jose Carlos 2+8/1 • Arouna Kone CIV 3+9/0 • Diego Perotti ARG 22+6/4 • Renato BRA 30+3/4 • Romaric CIV 10+9/1 • Didier Zokora CIV 25+1/0
Forwards Alvaro Negredo 25+10/11 • Enrique Carreno 0+1/0 • Ernesto Chevanton URU 0+1/0 • Diego Capel 14+15/1 • Frederic Kanoute MLI 20+7/12 • Luis Fabiano BRA 18+5/15 • Rodri 0+2/1
Coach Manuel Jimenez • Antonio Alvarez (24/03/2010)

TENERIFE 2009-10

Mon	Date	Opponent	Res	Score	Comp	Scorers	Att
Ag	29	Zaragoza	L	0-1	PD		17 000
	13	Osasuna	W	2-1	PD	Nino 48, Ricardo 63	18 300
Sep	19	Mallorca	L	0-4	PD		12 000
	23	Ath. Bilbao	W	1-0	PD	Mikel 87	19 200
	26	Real Madrid	L	0-3	PD		75 200
	3	Deportivo	L	0-1	PD		24 000
Oct	18	Espanyol	L	1-2	PD	Alfaro 15	33 000
	25	Xerez	W	1-0	PD	Alfaro 74	15 500
	28	Celta Vigo	L	1-2	CRr4	Richi 44	5 000
	1	Villarreal	L	0-5	PD		18 000
Nov	7	Malaga	D	2-2	PD	Martinez 18, Alfaro 27	16 800
	10	Celta Vigo	L	0-1	CRr4		13 328
	21	Sevilla	L	1-2	PD	Nino 75	20 551
	29	Valladolid	D	3-3	PD	Nino 62, Angel 73, Ayoze 85	12 700
Dec	6	Sp. Gijon	W	2-1	PD	Ricardo 55, Nino 66	19 281
	13	Getafe	L	1-2	PD	Hens 81	11 000
	20	At. Madrid	D	1-1	PD	Nino 3	21 414
Jan	3	Racing	L	0-2	PD		15 274
	10	Barcelona	L	0-5	PD		22 510
	17	Almeria	D	1-1	PD	Hens 2	17 732
	24	Valencia	D	0-0	PD		21 366
	31	Zaragoza	L	1-3	PD	Hens 48	19 198
Feb	7	Osasuna	L	0-1	PD		16 786
	15	Mallorca	W	1-0	PD	Nino 14	17 966
	21	Ath. Bilbao	L	1-4	PD	Alfaro 59	36 000
	27	Real Madrid	L	1-5	PD	Ayoze 46	22 123
Mar	6	Deportivo	L	1-3	PD	Hens 17	12 000
	14	Espanyol	W	4-1	PD	Richi 20, Nino 2 49 90, Alfaro 82	16 000
	20	Xerez	L	1-2	PD	Nino 49	16 668
	24	Villarreal	D	2-2	PD	Nino 60, Culebras 76	18 000
	27	Malaga	D	1-1	PD	Alfaro 85p	25 000
	3	Sevilla	L	0-3	PD		30 000
Apr	10	Valladolid	D	0-0	PD		15 801
	13	Sp. Gijon	W	2-0	PD	Martinez 71, Alfaro 89	25 885
	18	Getafe	W	3-2	PD	Nino 3 30 69 76	18 996
	25	At. Madrid	L	1-3	PD	Martinez 61	52 060
May	1	Racing	W	2-1	PD	Martinez 45, Ayoze 56p	16 000
	4	Barcelona	L	1-4	PD	Martinez 39	57 401
	8	Almeria	D	2-2	PD	Bertran 15, Nino 90	20 810
	16	Valencia	L	0-1	PD		50 000

VALENCIA 2009-10

Mon	Date	Opponent	Res	Score	Comp	Scorers	Att
Ag	20	Stabæk	W	3-0	ELpo	Hernandez 29, Villa 35, Joaquin 80	9 600
	27	Stabæk	W	4-1	ELpo	Miku 3 28 29 80, Zigic 77	15 000
	30	Sevilla	W	2-0	PD	Mata 47, Hernandez 80	46 000
Sep	13	Valladolid	W	4-2	PD	Silva 10, Villa 2 34 55, Mata 45	18 200
	17	Lille	D	1-1	ELgB	Mata 78	14 676
	20	Sp. Gijon	D	2-2	PD	Villa 2 22 60	40 000
	23	Getafe	L	1-3	PD	Villa 22	14 110
Oct	26	At. Madrid	D	2-2	PD	Hernandez 25, Villa 27	36 000
	1	Genoa	W	3-2	ELgB	Silva 52, Zigic 56, Villa 82p	21 333
	4	Racing	W	1-0	PD	Zigic 61	16 000
	17	Barcelona	D	0-0	PD		45 000
	22	Slavia	D	1-1	ELgB	Navarro 63	20 632
	25	Almeria	W	3-0	PD	Villa 54, Hernandez 74, Mata 87	12 171
	28	Alcoyano	W	1-0	CRr4	Joaquin 10	4 500
Nov	1	Malaga	W	1-0	PD	Navarro 69	30 000
	5	Slavia	D	2-2	ELgB	Joaquin 22p, Maduro 47	10 624
	8	Zaragoza	W	3-1	PD	Mata 17, Villa 40, Hernandez 41	35 000
	10	Alcoyano	D	2-2	CRr4	Marchena 4, Zigic 16	10 000
	22	Osasuna	W	3-1	PD	Villa 12, Albelda 20, Marchena 56	17 401
	28	Mallorca	D	1-1	PD	Villa 48	40 000
Dec	2	Lille	W	3-1	ELgB	Joaquin 2 3 32, Mata 52	26 193
	6	Ath. Bilbao	W	2-1	PD	Villa 61, Mathieu 83	40 000
	12	Real Madrid	L	2-3	PD	Villa 60, Joaquin 80	50 000
	17	Genoa	W	2-1	ELgB	Bruno 45, Villa 95+	23 480
	20	Deportivo	D	0-0	PD		26 988
Jan	2	Espanyol	W	1-0	PD	Zigic 90	45 000
	6	Deportivo	L	1-2	CRr5	Silva 73	25 000
	10	Xerez	W	3-1	PD	Mata 11, Silva 33, Marchena 76	12 000
	13	Deportivo	D	2-2	CRr5	Zigic 2 10 29	13 000
	17	Villarreal	W	4-1	PD	Banega 6, Villa 2 28p 90, Silva 56	40 000
	24	Tenerife	D	0-0	PD		21 366
	31	Sevilla	L	1-2	PD	Navarro 89	42 000
Feb	6	Valladolid	W	2-0	PD	Banega 8, Villa 29	50 000
	13	Sp. Gijon	D	1-1	PD	Mata 76	22 000
	18	Brugge	L	0-1	ELr2		21 657
	22	Getafe	W	2-1	PD	Villa 2 39 52	40 000
	25	Brugge	W	3-0	ELr2	Mata 1, Hernandez 2 96 117	45 297
	28	At. Madrid	L	1-4	PD	Silva 20	52 000
Mar	8	Racing	D	0-0	PD		35 000
	11	W. Bremen	D	1-1	ELr3	Mata 57	37 223
	14	Barcelona	L	0-3	PD		87 601
	21	Almeria	W	2-0	PD	Mata 63, Silva 70	33 000
	18	W. Bremen	D	4-4	ELr3	Villa 3 3 45 66, Mata 15	24 200
	24	Malaga	W	1-0	PD	Villa 13	35 000
	27	Zaragoza	L	0-3	PD		27 000
Apr	1	At. Madrid	D	2-2	ELqf	Fernandes 66, Villa 82	46 310
	4	Osasuna	W	3-0	PD	Joaquin 48, Villa 2 89 90p	42 000
	8	At. Madrid	D	0-0	ELqf		49 907
	11	Mallorca	L	2-3	PD	Alba 47, Hernandez 86	14 000
	15	Ath. Bilbao	W	2-0	PD	Silva 2 35 63	41 250
	18	Real Madrid	L	0-2	PD		80 000
	24	Deportivo	W	1-0	PD	Villa 34p	40 000
May	1	Espanyol	W	2-0	PD	Zigic 2 62 75	30 029
	4	Xerez	W	3-1	PD	Mata 2 45 58, Silva 68	36 850
	8	Villarreal	L	0-2	PD		24 000
	16	Tenerife	W	1-0	PD	Alexis 90	50 000

TENERIFE LEAGUE APPEARANCES/GOALS 2009-10

Goalkeepers Sergio Aragoneses 38
Defenders Aitor Nunez 4+1/0 • Ayoze 17+8/3 • Carlos Bellvis 15/0 • Marc Bertran 21/1 • Jose Culebras 16+2/1 • Ezequiel Luna ARG 22+1/0 • Hector Sanchez 11/0 • Manolo Martinez 26+4/0 • Pablo Sicilia 33+1/0
Midfield Alejandro Alfaro 36/7 • Juanlu Hens 31+1/4 • Roman Martinez ARG 18+5/5 • Mikel Alonso 21+7/21 • Julian Omar 7+16/0 • Ricardo 29/2 • Richi 16+6/1
Forwards Angel 0+24/1 • Dinei BRA 1+22/0 • Daniel Kome CMR 19+10/0 • Nino 37+1/14 • Gaizka Saizar 0+4/0
Coach Jose Luis Oltra

VALENCIA LEAGUE APPEARANCES/GOALS 2009-10

Goalkeepers Cesar Sanchez 30 • Miguel Angel Moya 8
Defenders Joel Alajarin 1/0 • Alexis 21+3/1 • Bruno 25+1/0 • David Navarro 19/2 • Angel Dealbert 22+2/0 • Jorge Alba 12+3/1 • Lillo 1/0 • Hedwiges Maduro NED 12+6/0 • Carlos Marchena 17+7/2 • Jeremy Mathieu FRA 14+3/1 • Luis Miguel POR 20+5/0
Midfield David Albelda 22+6/1 • Ruben Baraja 7+11/0 • David Silva 28+2/8 • Ever Banega ARG 33+3/2 • Joaquin 17+11/2 • Manuel Fernandes POR 8+7/0 • Michel 0+3/0 • Pablo Hernandez 25+8/5 • Vicente 5+6/0
Forwards David Villa 31+1/21 • Alejandro Dominguez ARG 4+9/0 • Juan Manuel Mata 30+5/9 • Miku VEN 1+1/0 • Nikola Zigic SRB 5+8/4
Coach Unai Emery

REAL VALLADOLID 2009–10

Month	Day	Opponent	Res	Score	Comp	Scorers	Att
Aug	30	Almeria	D	0-0	PD		9 100
Sep	13	Valencia	L	2-4	PD	Nauzet 30, Manucho 66	18 200
	20	Zaragoza	W	2-1	PD	Marquitos 4, Sisi 56	29 325
	23	Osasuna	L	1-2	PD	Costa 48	10 000
	27	Mallorca	L	0-3	PD		12 809
Oct	4	Ath. Bilbao	D	2-2	PD	Costa 60, Nivaldo 75	19 800
	17	Real Madrid	L	2-4	PD	Nauzet 28, Marquitos 52	72 000
	25	Deportivo	W	4-0	PD	Nauzet 2 19 47, Costa 78, Medunjanin 89	15 000
	29	Mallorca	L	2-1	CRr4	Arzo 3, Costa 78	13 728
Nov	1	Espanyol	D	1-1	PD	Medunjanin 90	27 130
	8	Xerez	D	0-0	PD		16 300
	11	Mallorca	L	0-1	CRr4		9 300
	22	Villarreal	L	1-3	PD	Costa 61	18 000
	29	Tenerife	D	3-3	PD	Costa 2 28 50, Canobbio 35p	12 700
Dec	5	Sevilla	D	1-1	PD	Manucho 33	40 000
	13	Malaga	D	1-1	PD	OG 69	13 400
	20	Sp. Gijon	W	2-1	PD	Nivaldo 29, Medunjanin 90	16 700
Jan	3	Getafe	L	0-1	PD		9 000
	9	At. Madrid	L	0-4	PD		16 200
	17	Racing	D	1-1	PD	OG 20	16 402
	23	Barcelona	L	0-3	PD		24 200
	31	Almeria	D	1-1	PD	Arzo 81	14 700
Feb	6	Valencia	L	0-2	PD		50 000
	14	Zaragoza	D	1-1	PD	Costa 23	15 700
	21	Osasuna	D	1-1	PD	Medunjanin 80	15 950
	28	Mallorca	L	1-2	PD	Bueno 49	16 500
Mar	7	Ath. Bilbao	L	0-2	PD		37 000
	14	Real Madrid	L	1-4	PD	OG 58	73 000
	20	Deportivo	W	2-0	PD	Nauzet 40, Medunjanin 90	27 000
	24	Espanyol	D	0-0	PD		16 000
	28	Xerez	L	0-3	PD		13 438
Apr	4	Villarreal	L	0-2	PD		13 000
	10	Tenerife	D	0-0	PD		15 801
	13	Sevilla	W	2-1	PD	Costa 42, Manucho 54	23 850
	18	Malaga	D	0-0	PD		19 152
	25	Sp. Gijon	W	2-0	PD	Manucho 80, Baraja 90	24 500
May	1	Getafe	D	0-0	PD		24 798
	4	At. Madrid	L	1-3	PD	Sesma 78	25 000
	8	Racing	W	2-1	PD	Baraja 57, Nauzet 77p	17 500
	16	Barcelona	L	0-4	PD		98 772

VILLARREAL 2009–10

Month	Day	Opponent	Res	Score	Comp	Scorers	Att
Aug	20	NAC Breda	W	3-1	ELpo	Rossi 14, Ibagaza 49, Llorente 92+	15 200
	27	NAC Breda	W	6-1	ELpo	Santi Cazorla 16, Rossi 2 23p 37p, Senna 46, Pereira 57, Kiko 61	15 200
	30	Osasuna	D	1-1	PD	Cazorla 32	17 135
Sep	13	Mallorca	D	1-1	PD	Rossi 54	18 000
	17	Levski	W	1-0	ELgG	Nilmar 72	5 244
	20	Ath. Bilbao	L	2-3	PD	Cani 49, Cazorla 85	32 000
	23	Real Madrid	L	0-2	PD		20 615
	27	Deportivo	L	0-1	PD		22 220
Oct	1	Salzburg	L	0-2	ELgG		18 800
	4	Espanyol	D	0-0	PD		16 000
	18	Xerez	L	1-2	PD	Pires 18	16 374
	22	Lazio	L	1-2	ELgG	Eguren 40	14 388
	25	Malaga	W	2-1	PD	Nilmar 27, Capdevila 54	15 000
	31	Puertollano	D	1-1	CRr4	Pires 65	6 000
Nov	1	Tenerife	W	5-0	PD	Llorente 2 16 53, Pires 47, Rossi 52, Cani 89	18 000
	5	Lazio	W	4-1	ELgG	Pires 2 15p, Cani 13, Rossi 83p	14 114
	8	Sevilla	L	2-3	PD	Pires 29, Fuster 60	38 000
	10	Puertollano	W	1-0	CRr4	Rossi 75	2 000
	22	Valladolid	W	3-1	PD	Nilmar 2 7 48, Rossi 57	18 000
	28	Sp. Gijon	L	0-1	PD		17 000
Dec	2	Levski	W	2-0	ELgG	Rossi 37, Senna 84	5 600
	6	Getafe	W	3-2	PD	Capdevila 2 17 87, Cazorla 67	18 000
	13	At. Madrid	W	2-1	PD	Fuster 49, Llorente 90	42 000
	17	Salzburg	L	0-1	ELgG		5 860
	20	Racing	W	2-0	PD	Llorente 50, Rossi 72	16 000
Jan	2	Barcelona	D	1-1	PD	Fuster 51	77 622
	6	Celta Vigo	D	1-1	CRr5	Rossi 12	9 437
	9	Almeria	D	1-1	PD	Nilmar 40	18 000
	12	Celta Vigo	L	0-1	CRr5		8 000
	17	Valencia	L	1-1	PD	Nilmar 61	40 000
	24	Zaragoza	W	4-2	PD	Capdevila 4, Nilmar 19, Rossi 25, Ibagaza 87	17 000
	31	Osasuna	L	0-2	PD		17 000
Feb	7	Mallorca	L	0-1	PD		12 000
	13	Ath. Bilbao	W	2-1	PD	Capdevila 5, Nilmar 45	12 000
	18	Wolfsburg	D	2-2	ELr2	Senna 43, Marco Ruben 85	11 384
	21	Real Madrid	L	2-6	PD	Senna 31, Nilmar 66	78 000
	25	Wolfsburg	L	1-4	ELr2	Capdevila 30	16 613
	28	Deportivo	W	1-0	PD	Llorente 36	17 000
Mar	7	Espanyol	D	0-0	PD		26 345
	14	Xerez	W	2-0	PD	Llorente 33, Escudero 90	17 000
	21	Malaga	L	0-2	PD		19 149
	24	Tenerife	D	2-2	PD	Nilmar 45, Rossi 88	18 000
	28	Sevilla	W	3-0	PD	Rossi 5, Llorente 18, Pires 90	18 000
Apr	4	Valladolid	W	2-0	PD	Angel 9, Nilmar 59	13 000
	10	Sp. Gijon	W	1-0	PD	Godin 16	19 530
	13	Getafe	L	0-3	PD		10 200
	17	At. Madrid	W	2-1	PD	Godin 21, Rossi 44	13 020
	25	Racing	W	2-1	PD	Godin 70, Nilmar 83	16 781
May	1	Barcelona	L	1-4	PD	Llorente 67	21 700
	4	Almeria	L	2-4	PD	Marcano 54, Ibagaza 66	18 000
	8	Valencia	W	2-0	PD	Rossi 11, Llorente 19	24 000
	15	Zaragoza	D	3-3	PD	Cazorla 2 40 56, Rossi 77	22 000

VALLADOLID LEAGUE APPEARANCES/GOALS 2009-10
Goalkeepers Fabricio 1 • Jacobo 14+1 • Justo Villar PAR 23
Defenders Alberto Marcos 17+4/0 • Cesar Arzo 17+5/1 • Javier Baraja 18+7/2 • Antonio Barragan 14+3/0 • Asier Del Horno 13/0 • Luis Prieto 19+1/0 • Nivaldo BRA 23+2/2 • Pedro Lopez 30+1/0 • Raul Navas 1/0 • Henrique Sereno POR 12/0 • Yuri 1/0
Midfield Alvaro Rubio 16/0 • Asier 1/0 • Borja 30+1/0 • Carlos Lazaro 6+2/0 • Hector Font 3+7/0 • Jonathan Sesma 14+3/1 • Keko 4+9/0 • Marquitos 18+8/2 • Haris Medunjanin BIH 9+15/5 • Nauzet Alemann 21+5/6 • Pele POR 17+6/0 • Sisi 3+2/1
Forwards Alberto Bueno 7+13/1 • Nestor Canobbio URU 21+3/1 • Diego Costa BRA 32+2/8 • Manucho ANG 20+8/4 • Sergio Garcia 0+1/0
Coach Jose Luis Mendilibar (1/02/10) • Javier Clemente (6/04/10)

VILLARREAL LEAGUE APPEARANCES/GOALS 2009-10
Goalkeepers Diego Lopez 38
Defenders Angel 22+2/1 • Joan Capevila 37/5 • Diego Godin URU 36/3 • Gonzalo Rodriguez ARG 19+2/0 • Javi Venta 16+2/0 • Kiko 2/0 • Ivan Marcano 15+1/1 • Mateo Musacchio ARG 5+2/0
Midfield Bruno 31+2/0 • Cani 27+8/2 • David Fuster 11+11/3 • Sebastian Eguren URU 9+5/0 • Damian Escudero ARG 3+10/1 • Ariel Ibagaza ARG 14+10/2 • Marcos Gullon 0+1/0 • Javier Matilla 2/0 • Robert Pires FRA 13+15/4 • Santi Cazorla 16+8/5 • Marcos Senna 26+4/1
Forwards Jonathan Pereira 0+6/0 • Joseba Llorente 20+9/9 • Marco Ruben ARG 1+3/0 • Nilmar BRA 28+5/11 • Giuseppe Rossi ITA 27+7/10
Coach Ernesto Valverde • Juan Carlos Garrido (1/02/10)

XEREZ 2009-10

Month	Day	Opponent		Score	Comp	Scorers	Att
Aug	30	Mallorca	L	0-2	PD		11 595
	13	Ath. Bilbao	L	0-1	PD		17 566
Sep	20	Real Madrid	L	0-5	PD		72 000
	23	Deportivo	L	0-3	PD		17 200
	27	Espanyol	D	0-0	PD		35 600
	4	Malaga	D	1-1	PD	Armenteros 47	17 430
	18	Villarreal	W	2-1	PD	Bermejo 42, Antonito 80	16 374
Oct	25	Tenerife	L	0-1	PD		15 500
	28	Osasuna	L	1-2	CRr4	Maldonado 67	4 588
	31	Sevilla	L	0-2	PD		21 000
	8	Valladolid	D	0-0	PD		16 300
Nov	10	Osasuna	L	0-1	CRr4		10 015
	22	Sp. Gijon	D	0-0	PD		16 000
	29	Getafe	L	1-5	PD	Aythami 33	11 000
	2	Barcelona	L	0-2	PD		17 584
Dec	5	At. Madrid	L	0-2	PD		17 805
	13	Racing	L	2-3	PD	Bermejo 3, Antonito 69	14 439
	3	Almeria	L	0-1	PD		9 574
	10	Valencia	L	1-3	PD	Calvo 25	12 000
Jan	17	Zaragoza	D	0-0	PD		23 000
	24	Osasuna	L	1-2	PD	Bermejo 22	14 909
	31	Mallorca	W	2-1	PD	Calvo 2 52 79	14 764
	7	Ath. Bilbao	L	2-3	PD	Moreno 10, Bermejo 41	36 000
Feb	13	Real Madrid	L	0-3	PD		20 398
	20	Deportivo	L	1-2	PD	Bermejo 38	12 000
	28	Espanyol	D	1-1	PD	Bermejo 76	13 000
	7	Malaga	W	4-2	PD	Momo 2 5p 72, Gioda 76, Orellana 90	23 000
Mar	14	Villarreal	L	0-2	PD		17 000
	20	Tenerife	W	2-1	PD	Bermejo 7, Aythami 15	16 668
	23	Sevilla	D	1-1	PD	Gioda 90	40 000
	28	Valladolid	W	3-0	PD	Sanchez 1, Michel 34, Bermejo 72p	13 438
	4	Sp. Gijon	D	2-2	PD	Bermejo 52, Alustiza 78	20 000
	10	Getafe	L	0-1	PD		16 674
Apr	14	At. Madrid	W	2-1	PD	Bermejo 9, Armenteros 72	20 000
	18	Racing	D	2-2	PD	Orellana 7, Sanchez 73	18 000
	24	Barcelona	L	1-3	PD	Bermejo 25	82 456
	1	Almeria	W	2-1	PD	Armenteros 28, Bermejo 90	15 000
May	4	Valencia	L	1-3	PD	Armenteros 37	36 850
	8	Zaragoza	W	3-2	PD	Francis 21, Michel 68, Calvo 73	12 000
	16	Osasuna	D	1-1	PD	Antonito 61	15 042

REAL ZARAGOZA 2009-10

Month	Day	Opponent		Score	Comp	Scorers	Att
Aug	29	Tenerife	W	1-0	PD	Arizmendi 74	17 000
	12	Sevilla	L	1-4	PD	Arizmendi 33	42 000
Sep	20	Valladolid	L	1-2	PD	Lopez 26	29 325
	24	Sp. Gijon	D	1-1	PD	Aguilar 54	18 000
	27	Getafe	W	3-0	PD	Pavon 17, Aguilar 2 24 81	27 600
	3	At. Madrid	L	1-2	PD	Ewerthon 71p	41 100
Oct	18	Racing	D	2-2	PD	Pavon 22, Arizmendi 33	25 000
	25	Barcelona	L	1-6	PD	Lopez 78	75 653
	28	Malaga	D	1-1	CRr4	Lafita 10	8 000
	1	Almeria	W	2-1	PD	Lafita 30, Pulido 35	24 000
	8	Valencia	L	1-3	PD	Aguilar 65	35 000
Nov	10	Malaga	D	0-0	CRr4		10 000
	22	Malaga	D	1-1	PD	Ewerthon 49	25 000
	29	Osasuna	L	0-1	PD		24 000
	6	Mallorca	L	1-4	PD	Herrera 86	12 600
Dec	12	Ath. Bilbao	L	1-2	PD	Diogo 90	23 000
	19	Real Madrid	L	0-6	PD		60 000
	3	Deportivo	D	0-0	PD		22 000
	10	Espanyol	L	1-2	PD	Arizmendi 39	24 025
Jan	17	Xerez	D	0-0	PD		23 000
	24	Villarreal	L	2-4	PD	Eliseu 74, Lafita 81	17 000
	31	Tenerife	W	3-1	PD	Suazo 76p, Colunga 79, Lafita 83	19 198
	7	Sevilla	W	2-1	PD	Contini 31, OG 42	23 000
Feb	14	Valladolid	D	1-1	PD	Suazo 39	15 700
	21	Sp. Gijon	L	1-3	PD	Arizmendi 90	28 000
	27	Getafe	W	2-0	PD	Suazo 2 3 20	12 000
	7	At. Madrid	D	1-1	PD	Jarosik 7	24 000
	14	Racing	D	0-0	PD		16 212
Mar	21	Barcelona	L	2-4	PD	Colunga 2 85 89	30 000
	24	Almeria	L	0-1	PD		15 772
	27	Valencia	W	3-0	PD	Diogo 41, Arizmendi 63, Jarosik 71	27 000
	3	Malaga	W	2-0	PD	Ponzio 45, Suazo 76	22 000
	11	Osasuna	L	0-2	PD		17 601
Apr	14	Mallorca	D	1-1	PD	Suazo 22	25 000
	18	Ath. Bilbao	D	0-0	PD		34 000
	24	Real Madrid	L	1-2	PD	Colunga 61	32 775
	1	Deportivo	W	1-0	PD	Colunga 50	17 000
May	5	Espanyol	W	1-0	PD	Colunga 78p	22 000
	8	Xerez	L	2-3	PD	Herrera 66, Gabi 75	12 000
	15	Villarreal	D	3-3	PD	Eliseu 4, Colunga 29, Pulido 35	22 000

XEREZ LEAGUE APPEARANCES/GOALS 2009-10

Goalkeepers Chema 3 • Renan BRA 35
Defenders Aythami 29+1/2 • Jose Casado 26+1/0 • David Prieto 20+1/0 • Leandro Gioda ARG 28+1/2 • Jesus Mendoza 12/0 • Juan Redondo 11+2/0
Midfield Abel Gomez 9+8 • Emiliano Armenteros ARG 16+9/3 • Alejandro Bergantinos 22+4/0 • Carlos Calvo 26+9/4 • Francis 25/1 • Sidi Keita MLI 24/0 • Momo 22+4/2 • Vicente Moreno 15+7/1 • Victor Sanchez 22+3/2 • Emilio Viqueira 4+13/0
Forwards Matias Alustiza ARG 1+10/1 • Antonito 2+23/3 • Mario Bermejo 33+1/12 • Giancarlo Maldonado VEN 6+3/0 • Michel 7+7/2 • Fabian Orellana CHI 20+6/2
Coach Jose Angel Ziganda • Antonio Poyatos (12/01/10) • Nestor Gorosito ARG (19/01/10)

ZARAGOZA LEAGUE APPEARANCES/GOALS 2009-10

Goalkeepers Juan Carrizo ARG 16 • Lopez Vallejo 7 • Roberto 15
Defenders Roberto Ayala ARG 13/0 • Matteo Contini ITA 15/1 • Carlos Diogo URU 13+2/2 • Edmilson BRA 14+3/0 • Raul Goni 6/0 • Victor Laguardia 3/0 • Ivan Obradovic SRB 6+3/0 • Pablo Amo 7+2/0 • Javier Paredes 18+2/0 • Francisco Pavon 11/2 • Ruben Pulido 20+2/2
Midfield Abel Aguilar COL 20+7/4 • Ander Herrera 23+7/2 • Marko Babic CRO 7+7/0 • Gabi 29+3/1 • Jiri Jarosik CZE 20/2 • Jorge Lopez 20+9/2 • Angel Lafita 17+7/3 • Jermaine Pennant ENG 13+12/0 • Leonardo Ponzio ARG 34/1 • Franck Songo'o CMR 0+5/0
Forwards Adrian Colunga 7+9/7 • Angel Arizmendi 25+6/5 • Braulio 0+2/0 • Eliseu 19+2/2 • Ewerthon BRA 1+9/2 • Kevin Lacruz 0+3/0 • Alex Sanchez 0+3/0 • Humberto Suazo CHI 17/6 • Ikechukwu Uche NGA 2+1/0
Coach Marcelino Garcia Toral • Jose Aurelio Gay (13/12/09)

EST – ESTONIA

FIFA/COCA-COLA WORLD RANKING

1993	1994	1995	1996	1997	1998	1999	2000	2001	2002	2003	2004	2005	2006	2007	2008	2009	2010
109	119	129	102	100	90	70	67	83	60	68	81	76	106	124	119	102	82

	2010												Hi/Lo
	Jan	Feb	Mar	Apr	May	Jun	Jul	Aug	Sep	Oct	Nov	Dec	60
	102	104	97	100	104	99	95	94	85	74	74	82	137

Flora Tallinn won an increasingly rare league title at the end of 2010 and in the process denied their cross-town rivals Levadia a fifth straight championship. Without a title since 2003, Flora turned to former player Martin Reim at the start of the season and despite his lack of coaching experience Estonia's record cap winner steered his side to a five point winning margin over Levadia. It wasn't plain sailing, however, especially when the majority of the squad went on strike in June after their wages weren't paid. Reim was forced to rely on youngsters with top scorer Sander Post the oldest at 26. Levadia didn't finish the season empty handed after they convincingly beat Flora 3-0 in the Cup Final in May. Of concern, however, were allegations against Trans Narva of match fixing picked up by UEFA's gambling monitoring with one online tipster accusing them of "rapidly becoming the most corrupt side in Eastern Europe." The national team had a solid start to its Euro 2012 qualifying campaign, notably a stunning 3-1 victory over Serbia in Belgrade, a win described by goalscorer Tarmo Kink as the most important result in the history of the national team. Unfortunately, Tarmo Ruutli's team then went and undid all the good work by losing 1-0 at home to Slovenia in the next game.

FIFA WORLD CUP RECORD
1930 DNE 1934-1938 DNQ 1950-1990 DNE 1994-2010 DNQ

ESTONIAN FOOTBALL ASSOCIATION (EFA)

A. Le Coq Arena,
Asula 4c,
Tallinn 11312
☎ +372 6 279960
📠 +372 6 279969
✉ efa@jalgpall.ee
🖥 www.jalgpall.ee
FA 1921 CON 1992 FIFA 1992
P Aivar Pohlak
GS Tonu Sirel

FIFA BIG COUNT 2006

Total players	57 024
% of population	4.31%
Male	49 725
Female	7 299
Amateurs 18+	3 922
Youth under 18	5 042
Unregistered	15 700
Professionals	140
Referees	182
Admin & coaches	480
Number of clubs	138
Number of teams	671

MAJOR CITIES/TOWNS

		Population
1	Tallinn	393 971
2	Tartu	102 285
3	Narva	66 028
4	Kohtla-Järve	44 657
5	Pärnu	43 429
6	Viljandi	20 046
7	Maardu	16 541
8	Rakvere	16 492
9	Sillamäe	16 200
10	Kuressaare	14 951
11	Voru	14 364
12	Valga	13 684
13	Haapsalu	11 605
14	Johvi	11 121
15	Paide	9 826
16	Keila	9 435
17	Kivioli	6 634
18	Polva	6 557
19	Tapa	6 410

ESTI VABARIIK • REPUBLIC OF ESTONIA

Capital	Tallinn	Population	1 299 371 (152)	% in cities	69%
GDP per capita	$21 400 (57)	Area km²	45 228 km² (132)	GMT +/-	+2
Neighbours (km)	Latvia 343, Russia 290 • Coast 3794				

RECENT INTERNATIONAL MATCHES PLAYED BY ESTONIA

2008	Opponents	Score		Venue	Comp	Scorers	Att	Referee
30-05	Latvia	L	0-1	Riga	BC		4 500	Zuta LTU
31-05	Lithuania	L	0-1	Jurmala	BC		1 300	Lajuks LVA
4-06	Faroe Islands	W	4-3	Tallinn	Fr	Zahovaiko 2 [9 14], Kink [28], Novikov [75]	2 300	Stalhammar SWE
20-08	Malta	W	2-1	Tallinn	Fr	Purje [21], Oper [52]	2 700	Gilewski POL
6-09	Belgium	L	2-3	Liege	WCq	Zenjov [57], Oper [92+]	17 992	Dean ENG
10-09	Bosnia-Herzegovina	L	0-7	Zenica	WCq		12 500	Balaj ROU
11-10	Spain	L	0-3	Tallinn	WCq		9 200	Eriksson SWE
15-10	Turkey	D	0-0	Tallinn	WCq		6 500	Malek POL
12-11	Latvia	D	1-1	Tallinn	Fr	Kink [52]	2 000	Sandmoen NOR
18-11	Moldova	W	1-0	Tallinn	Fr	Voskoboinikov [56]	1 500	Larsen DEN
22-11	Lithuania	D	1-1	Kuressaare	Fr	Puri [6]	1 000	Nieminen FIN
2009								
11-02	Kazakhstan	L	0-2	Antalya	Fr		200	Gocek TUR
28-03	Armenia	D	2-2	Yerevan	WCq	Vassiljev [38], Zenjov [67]	3 000	Wilmes LUX
1-04	Armenia	W	1-0	Tallinn	WCq	Puri [83]	5 200	Zimmermann SUI
29-05	Wales	L	0-1	Llanelli	Fr		4 071	Thorisson ISL
6-06	Equatorial Guinea	W	3-0	Tallinn	Fr	Vikmae [8], Voskoboinikov [35], Zenjov [90]	2 150	Malzinskas LTU
10-06	Portugal	D	0-0	Tallinn	Fr		6 350	Svendsen DEN
12-08	Brazil	L	0-1	Tallinn	Fr		8 550	Ingvarsson SWE
5-09	Turkey	L	2-4	Kayseri	WCq	Voskoboinikov [7], Vassiljev [52]	28 569	Skjerven NOR
9-09	Spain	L	0-3	Merida	WCq		14 362	Oriekhov UKR
10-10	Bosnia-Herzegovina	L	0-2	Tallinn	WCq		6 450	Rizzoli ITA
14-10	Belgium	W	2-0	Tallinn	WCq	Piiroja [30], Vassiljev [67]	4 680	Vollquartz DEN
14-11	Albania	D	0-0	Tallinn	Fr		2 110	Kancleris LTU
30-12	Angola	W	1-0	Vila Real	Fr	Saag [78]	200	Almeida POR
2010								
3-03	Georgia	L	1-2	Tbilisi	Fr	Purje [83]	40 000	Banari MDA
21-05	Finland	W	2-0	Tallinn	Fr	Oper [5], Post [55]	5 650	Vad HUN
26-05	Croatia	D	0-0	Tallinn	Fr		3 000	Svendsen DEN
19-06	Latvia	D	0-0	Kaunas	BC		300	Mazeika LTU
20-06	Lithuania	L	0-2	Kaunas	BC		600	Sipailo LVA
11-08	Faroe Islands	W	2-1	Tallinn	ECq	Saag [91+], Piiroja [93+]	5 470	Vucemilovic CRO
3-09	Italy	L	1-2	Tallinn	ECq	Zenjov [31]	8 600	Velasco ESP
7-09	Uzbekistan	D	3-3	Tallinn	Fr	Purje [25], Vassilijev 2 [62 71p]	2 055	Jones WAL
8-10	Serbia	W	3-1	Belgrade	ECq	Kink [63], Vassiljev [73], OG [91+]	12 000	Layushkin RUS
12-10	Slovenia	L	0-1	Tallinn	ECq		5 722	Skjerven NOR
17-11	Liechtenstein	D	1-1	Tallinn	Fr	Vassilijev [57p]	1 909	Gvardis RUS
18-12	China PR	L	0-3	Zhuhai	Fr		8 500	Ko Hyung Jin KOR
22-12	Qatar	L	0-2	Doha	Fr			

Fr = Friendly match • EC = UEFA EURO 2008/2012 • BC = Baltic Cup • WC = FIFA World Cup • q = qualifier

ESTONIA NATIONAL TEAM HISTORICAL RECORDS

Caps
157 - Martin Reim 1992-2007 • **143** - Marko Kristal 1992-2005 • **120** - Mart Poom 1992-2009 • **118** - Andres Oper 1995- • **114** - Kristen Viikmae 1997- • **103** - Indrek Zelinski 1994-2010 • **99** - Raio Piiroja 1998- • **94** - Marek Lemsalu 1992-2007 • **83** - Andrei Stepanov 1999- • **80** - Urmas Kirs 1991-2000 • **74** - Enar Jaager 2002- & Joel Lindpere 1999-

Goals
36 - Andres Oper 1995- • **27** - Indrek Zelinski 1994-2010 • **21** - Eduard Ellman-Eelma 1921-35 • **18** - Richard Kuremaa 1933-40 • **17** - Arnold Pihlak 1920-31 • **15** - Kristen Viikmae 1997- • **14** - Georg Siimenson 1932-39 & Martin Reim 1992-2007

Past Coaches
Ferenc Konya HUN 1924 • Ferenc Nagy HUN 1925 • Antal Mally HUN 1927 • Fritz Kerr AUT 1930 • Albert Vollrat 1932 • Bernhard Rein 1934 • Antal Mally HUN 1935 • Bernhard Rein 1936-38 • Elmar Saar 1939-40 • Uno Piir 1992-93 • Roman Ubakivi 1994-95 • Aavo Sarap 1995 • Teitur Thordarson ISL 1996-99 • Tarmo Ruutli 1999-2000 • Arno Pijpers NED 2000-04 • Jelle Goes NED 2004-07 • Viggo Jensen DEN 2007 • Tarmo Ruutli 2008-

ESTONIA 2010

MEISTRILIIGA

	Pl	W	D	L	F	A	Pts	Flora Tallinn	Levadia	Trans Narva	Nomme Kalju	Sillamäe	Tammeka	Tulevik	Paide	Kuressaare	Lootus
Flora Tallinn †	36	29	4	3	104	32	91		2-1 2-0	1-1 4-0	1-0 3-0	4-2 3-0	3-2 6-3	1-1 1-0	2-1 6-2	4-0 6-0	2-1 5-0
Levadia Tallinn ‡	36	26	8	2	100	16	86	2-1 2-2		3-0 1-1	0-0 1-1	3-1 2-0	2-0 6-0	2-0 3-0	6-0 4-0	1-1 4-0	5-1 5-0
Trans Narva ‡	36	23	7	6	67	31	76	1-0 1-2	1-2 0-3		2-2 1-0	2-2 2-1	0-0 1-1	2-0 2-0	4-1 **0-0**	3-0 5-1	0-1 4-1
Nomme Kalju	36	18	8	10	59	42	62	1-2 3-3	0-3 1-5	0-1 0-2		2-1 0-2	1-1 3-1	1-0 3-0	1-1 0-2	1-1 0-1	0-2 **0-0**
Kalev Sillamäe	36	18	5	13	79	52	59	1-2 2-5	1-1 0-4	1-2 1-3	2-2 4-1		4-0 2-0	2-1 5-2	4-0 0-0	**0-0** 2-0	3-1 4-0
Tammeka Tartu	36	11	7	18	50	66	40	0-1 2-1	0-0 0-0	1-2 0-1	2-3 0-1	1-4 2-3		2-0 2-2	0-0 1-2	2-0 0-2	1-0 5-1
Tulevik Viljandi	36	8	5	23	33	62	29	0-1 1-6	0-1 0-1	0-1 0-3	1-4 0-1	1-2 3-2	0-3 4-0		1-0 1-0	0-0 4-1	1-0 4-0
Paide Linnameeskond	36	6	7	23	30	79	25	0-2 1-4	0-4 1-4	0-4 1-1	0-3 0-1	0-1 1-8	1-3 3-4	2-0 1-1		1-2 3-0	1-0 1-1
FC Kuressaare	36	7	3	26	32	93	24	1-2 0-2	0-7 0-4	0-1 1-4	1-2 1-5	0-4 2-2	2-3 3-2	3-2 4-2	1-0 2-3		1-2 0-1
Lootus Kohtla-Järve	36	6	2	28	22	103	20	0-4 0-8	0-3 0-5	0-5 0-4	0-5 0-6	0-1 0-5	1-3 1-3	0-1 0-0	2-1 1-2	5-2 2-0	

9/03/2010 - 7/11/2010 • † Qualified for the UEFA Champions League • ‡ Qualified for the Europa Cup • Matches in bold awarded as 0-0 wins to Kuressaare and Trans Narva • Relegation play-off: Tamme Auto 2-1 0-2 FC Kuressaare • Top scorers: 24 - Sander Post, Flora • 21 - Juri Jevdokimov, Nomme Kalju • 20 - Tarmo Neemelo, Levadia • 16 - Vitali Leitan, Levadia • 14 - Deniss Malov, Levadia

ESTONIA 2010 ESILIIGA (2)

	Pl	W	D	L	F	A	Pts
Levadia Tallinn II	36	28	5	3	107	28	89
Flora Tallinn II	36	22	6	8	93	45	72
Ajax Lasnamäe	36	20	9	7	71	38	69
Tamme Auto	36	17	6	13	85	72	57
Kalev Tallinn §4	36	17	6	13	67	65	53
TJK Legion	36	11	6	19	57	81	39
Vaprus Pärnu	36	10	7	19	57	78	37
Warrior Valga	36	10	6	20	57	90	36
Flora Rakvere	36	10	3	23	45	95	31
Orbiit Johvi	36	6	4	26	35	82	22

10/03/2010 - 7/11/2010 • § = points deducted
Relegation play-off: Atletik Tallinn 3-1 0-0 Warrior Valga
Second teams of the major clubs ineligible for promotion

MEDALS TABLE

		Overall			League			Cup	
		G	S	B	G	S	B	G	S
1	Levadia Tallinn	13	4	2	7	3	2	6	1
2	Flora Tallinn	12	10	3	8	6	3	4	4
3	TVMK Tallinn	3	5	5	1	3	5	2	2
4	Lantana Tallinn	3	4	5	2	1	5	1	3
5	Norma Tallinn	3	2		2	1		1	1
6	Tallinna Sadam	2	2	1		2	1	2	
7	Trans Narva	1	3	4		1	4	1	2
8	Levadia II Tallinn	1					1		
9	Tulevik Viljandi		3			1			2
10	EP Johvi		2			1			1
11	Tammeka Tartu	1							1
	Nomme Kalju	1							1
	Kalev Sillamäe	1			1				

EESTI KARIKAS 2009-10

Round of sixteen

Levadia Tallinn	3
Trans Narva *	0
Piraaja Tallinn	0
Kalev Sillamäe *	3
Ganvix Türi *	4
Võru JK	2
Atletik Tallinn	0
Lootus Kohtla-Järve *	6
Tammeka Tartu *	4
Nomme United	0
Flora Tallinn II *	0
Warrior Valga	1
Nomme Kalju *	3
Kalev Tallinn	1
FC Kuressaare *	0
Flora Tallinn	4

Quarter-finals

Levadia Tallinn	1
Kalev Sillamäe *	0
Ganvix Türi	0
Lootus Kohtla-Järve *	5
Tammeka Tartu *	4
Warrior Valga	1
Nomme Kalju	0
Flora Tallinn *	2

Semi-finals

Levadia Tallinn *	2
Lootus Kohtla-Järve	0
Tammeka Tartu	1
Flora Tallinn *	4

Final

Levadia Tallinn ‡	3
Flora Tallinn	0

CUP FINAL

Kadriorg, Tallinn
11-05-2010, Att: 950, Ref: Kotter
Scorers - Andero Pebre [33], Vitali Leitan [61], Yaroslav Dmitriev [72] for Levadia

* Home team • ‡ Qualified for the Europa Cup

ETH – ETHIOPIA

FIFA/COCA-COLA WORLD RANKING

1993	1994	1995	1996	1997	1998	1999	2000	2001	2002	2003	2004	2005	2006	2007	2008	2009	2010
96	115	105	108	126	145	142	133	155	138	130	151	112	92	105	103	122	124

					2010							Hi/Lo
Jan	Feb	Mar	Mar	Apr	May	Jul	Aug	Sep	Oct	Nov	Dec	85
122	121	122	123	123	123	146	144	135	133	131	124	155

Anglo-Nigerian Iffy Onuora, who played at 10 different English league clubs during his career, was appointed as new national team coach in 2010 and took Ethiopia to a semi-final place at the East and Central African Senior Challenge Cup at the end of the year. They finished fourth after being beaten by a Cote d'Ivoire 'B' side in the semi-final and then by Uganda in a thrilling bronze medal match in Dar es Salaam. Ethiopia had made disastrous start to their bid to qualify for the 2012 African Nations Cup finals with a 4-1 home defeat by Guinea, but then surprised themselves by picking up the pieces within a month to beat Madagascar 1-0 away in Antananarivo although they face tough matches in 2011 against Nigeria, the other team in the group. In club football Saint George proved dominant at home with a runaway league triumph. Under coach Milutin Sredojevic they finished 24 points clear of Dedebit in second place and also finished as runner-up at the CECAFA Club Cup in Rwanda. After the season Sredojevic moved to Al Hilal in Sudan and was replaced by former Italy international Giuseppe Dossena - a former Ghana national team coach - as Saint George try to translate domestic form to the African Champions League. In 2010 they had been beaten in the first round by Sudan's Al Merreikh, the only low point of the season.

FIFA WORLD CUP RECORD
1930-1958 DNE **1962** DNQ **1966** DNE **1970-1986** DNQ **1990** DNE **1994** DNQ **1998** DNE **2002-2010** DNQ

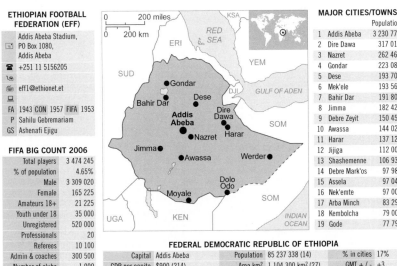

ETHIOPIAN FOOTBALL FEDERATION (EFF)

Addis Abeba Stadium,
PO Box 1080,
Addis Abeba
☎ +251 11 5156205
✆
✉ eff1@ethionet.et
🖳
FA 1943 CON 1957 FIFA 1953
P Sahilu Gebremariam
GS Ashenafi Ejigu

FIFA BIG COUNT 2006

Total players	3 474 245
% of population	4.65%
Male	3 309 020
Female	165 225
Amateurs 18+	21 225
Youth under 18	35 000
Unregistered	520 000
Professionals	20
Referees	10 100
Admin & coaches	300 500
Number of clubs	1 000
Number of teams	3 000

MAJOR CITIES/TOWNS

		Population
1	Addis Abeba	3 230 771
2	Dire Dawa	317 010
3	Nazret	262 462
4	Gondar	223 080
5	Dese	193 705
6	Mek'ele	193 567
7	Bahir Dar	191 804
8	Jimma	182 422
9	Debre Zeyit	150 454
10	Awassa	144 029
11	Harar	137 123
12	Jijiga	112 002
13	Shashemenne	106 938
14	Debre Mark'os	97 983
15	Assela	97 048
16	Nek'emte	97 005
17	Arba Minch	83 299
18	Kembolcha	79 002
19	Gode	77 792

FEDERAL DEMOCRATIC REPUBLIC OF ETHIOPIA

Capital	Addis Abeba	Population	85 237 338 (14)	% in cities	17%
GDP per capita	$900 (214)	Area km²	1 104 300 km² (27)	GMT +/-	+3
Neighbours (km)	Djibouti 349, Eritrea 912, Kenya 861, Somalia 1600, Sudan 1606				

RECENT INTERNATIONAL MATCHES PLAYED BY ETHIOPIA

2007	Opponents	Score		Venue	Comp	Scorers	Att	Referee
29-04	Congo DR	L	0-2	Kinshasa	CNq			Bennett RSA
1-06	Congo DR	W	1-0	Addis Abeba	CNq	Salhadin Said 30		Hicuburundi BDI
17-06	Libya	L	1-3	Tripoli	CNq	Fikru Tefera 58		Saadallah TUN
8-09	Namibia	L	2-3	Addis Abeba	CNq	Birhanu Bogale 44, Salhadin Said 66		Auda EGY
15-12	Sudan	D	0-0	Arusha	Fr			
2008								
31-05	Morocco	L	0-3	Casablanca	WCq		5 000	Diatta SEN
8-06	Rwanda	L	1-2	Addis Abeba	WCq	Tesfaye Tafese 44	18 000	Ndinya KEN
13-06	Mauritania	W	1-0	Nouakchott	WCq	Salhadin Said 93+	5 000	Ambaya LBY
22-06	Mauritania	W	6-1	Addis Abeba	WCq	Fikru Tefera 2 38p 89, Andualem Negussie 2 55 63, Mohamed Mesud 83, Girma Adane 90	13 000	Lwanja MWI
2009								
30-11	Djibouti	W	5-0	Nairobi	CCr1	Ayenew Aklilu 49, Aden Girma 53, Tafese Tesfaye 55, Umed Ukuri 2 70 89		
2-12	Zambia	L	0-1	Nairobi	CCr1			
5-12	Kenya	L	0-2	Nairobi	CCr1			
2010								
18-08	Kenya	L	0-3	Addis Abeba	Fr			
29-08	Chad	W	1-0	Addis Abeba	Fr			
5-09	Guinea	L	1-4	Addis Abeba	CNq	Umed Ukuri 29		Mnkantjo ZIM
10-10	Madagascar	W	1-0	Antananarivo	CNq	Fikru Tefera 56		Ngosi MWI
29-11	Uganda	L	1-2	Dar es Salaam	CCr1	Shimelis Bekele 24		
2-12	Kenya	W	2-1	Dar es Salaam	CCr1	Shimelis Bekele 2 25 44		
4-12	Malawi	D	1-1	Dar es Salaam	CCr1	Umed Ukuri 70		
7-12	Zambia	W	2-1	Dar es Salaam	CCqf	OG 17, Umed Ukuri 70		
12-12	Uganda	L	3-4	Dar es Salaam	CC3p	Umed Ukuri 2 2 33, Tesfaye Alebachew 67		

Fr = Friendly match • CN = CAF African Cup of Nations • CC = CECAFA Cup • WC = FIFA World Cup
q = qualifier • r1 = first round group • sf = semi-final • f = final • † Not an official International

ETHIOPIA 2009–10

PREMIER LEAGUE	Pl	W	D	L	F	A	Pts	Saint George	Dedebit	Eth. Coffee	Awassa City	Adama City	Defence	Muger Cem't	Sid'ma Coffee	Harar Beer	Sebeta City	Banks	Dire Dawa C	Trans Ethiopia	EEPCO	Insurance	S'thern Police	M'hara Sugar	Meta Abo
Saint George †	34	26	6	2	62	17	84		2-1	0-0	5-2	3-1	1-0	3-1	0-0	1-0	1-0	3-1	2-0	3-0	1-0	3-0	2-0	6-3
Dedebit ‡	34	17	9	8	48	29	60	0-0		1-0	1-2	1-2	2-2	1-1	5-2	1-1	0-0	2-2	3-1	1-0	2-0	1-2	3-0	3-1	1-0
Ethiopian Coffee	34	16	8	10	52	32	56	0-1	2-3		1-1	6-1	1-0	0-0	1-1	0-1	0-0	2-1	3-0	1-0	6-2	1-1	5-0	2-1	3-2
Awassa City	34	13	13	8	37	32	52	2-1	0-0	1-1		0-1	0-1	2-0	1-1	1-0	0-0	2-0	1-1	1-0	1-1	2-1	0-0	3-1	2-1
Adama City	34	13	10	11	39	35	49	1-2	0-1	0-0	2-2		2-1	1-1	2-0	1-1	2-0	4-1	1-1	1-2	1-0	0-1	1-1	3-1	1-0
Defence Mekelakeya	34	13	9	12	46	44	48	0-1	2-3	3-0	1-1	1-1		0-0	1-1	1-0	2-0	1-1	4-0	4-2	0-2	1-2	2-0	2-1	3-2
Muger Cement	34	11	14	9	29	26	47	0-2	1-0	0-1	1-0	1-1	1-2		1-0	0-0	3-0	2-1	0-0	2-1	1-1	0-0	1-0	1-1	2-0
Sidama Coffee	33	11	13	9	24	30	46	0-0	1-0	1-0	0-0	0-0	4-2	0-3		0-0	1-0	2-1	0-1	1-1	2-1	0-0	1-1	1-0	2-0
Harar Beer	33	9	17	7	28	24	44	1-1	0-3	1-0	0-0	1-1	1-1	0-0		2-1	0-1	1-1	0-0	2-1	0-0	1-0	1-1		1-1
Sebeta City	34	12	8	14	28	31	44	1-2	0-1	1-0	2-0	1-0	2-0	1-0	1-0	2-2		4-1	1-0	0-0	0-1	2-1	2-0	2-2	1-0
Banks	34	11	9	14	48	52	42	1-1	0-1	2-4	2-0	2-0	1-1	1-1	3-0	2-2	2-0		0-2	5-2	3-2	1-2	1-0	3-2	3-2
Dire Dawa City	34	10	12	12	30	42	42	0-4	1-0	0-2	2-0	0-2	2-3	0-0	0-0	0-1	1-0	1-1		1-0	2-2	1-0	3-0	2-2	1-0
Trans Ethiopia	34	9	14	11	27	36	41	0-2	1-1	0-1	0-0	1-0	2-2	0-0	0-0	0-0	1-0	2-1	0-0		1-0	1-1	1-0	0-0	1-1
EEPCO Mebrat Hail	34	10	10	14	39	43	40	0-2	0-0	0-1	2-3	0-3	4-0	0-1	2-0	1-1	3-0	0-1	2-2	2-2		2-3	1-1	2-1	1-0
Insurance	34	11	7	16	38	45	40	1-2	1-2	2-1	0-2	1-1	3-1	4-2	0-1	0-2	2-1	1-2	2-1	1-2	0-1		0-1	1-0	3-2
Southern Police	34	9	8	17	19	40	35	0-1	0-2	2-1	0-2	1-0	0-1	2-1	0-1	1-0	1-1	1-0	0-0	0-1	0-1	0-0		2-1	3-1
Metehara Sugar	34	8	10	16	38	49	34	1-0	2-1	1-3	2-2	1-0	0-0	0-1	3-0	2-1	0-2	1-1	1-1	4-1	1-0	1-1	2-2		2-1
Meta Abo Brewery	34	5	5	24	30	55	20	0-1	0-1	2-3	1-0	1-2	0-1	1-0	0-1	2-1	2-1	1-1	2-2	0-2	1-1	2-1	1-0	2-0	

7/11/2009 - 13/06/2010 • † Qualified for the CAF Champions League • ‡ Qualified for the CAF Confederations Cup

FIJ – FIJI

FIFA/COCA-COLA WORLD RANKING

1993	1994	1995	1996	1997	1998	1999	2000	2001	2002	2003	2004	2005	2006	2007	2008	2009	2010
107	120	139	157	146	124	135	141	123	140	149	135	135	150	131	106	132	152

	2010												Hi/Lo
	Jan	Feb	Mar	Mar	Apr	May	Jul	Aug	Sep	Oct	Nov	Dec	94
	132	129	130	131	130	132	130	130	127	143	143	152	170

With the Fiji national team out of action until the 2011 Pacific Games in New Caledonia, international attention in 2010 was focused on club football. National League champions Lautoka came within a whisker of qualifying for the 2010 OFC Champions League final but lost a crucial home match against eventual winners Hekari United from Papua New Guinea. A win would have taken Lautoka through to a first final and there was further disappointment when they failed to retain their league crown in 2010 after finishing a point behind rivals Ba. Lautoka had lodged a complaint - still unresolved - about a draw earlier in the season with Rewa, a result that they claim cost them the title and it was they and not Ba who lined up in the 2010-11 OFC Champions League which kicked-off a month after the National Football League finished. Of the three major cup tournaments, Ba won the first - the FA Cup Tournament - by beating Navua 1-0 at the end of May but both of the others were won by Rewa, who are based in the town of Nausori to the northeast of the capital Suva. They beat Navua 1-0 in the Battle of the Giants in August and then followed that up with a 3-1 win over Lautoka in the final of the Inter District Cup in October - the first trophies won by the club for six years.

FIFA WORLD CUP RECORD
1930-1978 DNE **1982** DNQ **1986** DNE **1990-2010** DNQ

FIJI FOOTBALL ASSOCIATION (FFA)

73 Knolly Street,
PO Box 2514,
Suva
☎ +679 3300453
📠 +679 3304642
📧 bobkumar@fijifootball.com.fj
🖥 www.fijifootball.com
FA 1938 CON 1966 FIFA 1963
P Muhammad Sahu Khan
GS Bob Kumar

FIFA BIG COUNT 2006

Total players	49 688
% of population	5.48%
Male	46 338
Female	3 350
Amateurs 18+	11 188
Youth under 18	17 300
Unregistered	8 200
Professionals	0
Referees	117
Admin & coaches	2 929
Number of clubs	400
Number of teams	2 000

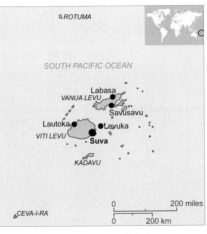

MAJOR CITIES/TOWNS

		Population
1	Nasinu	88 013
2	Suva	85 919
3	Lautoka	54 356
4	Nausori	52 451
5	Nadi	45 519
6	Labasa	28 083
7	Lami	20 461
8	Ba	16 040
9	Sigatoka	9 826
10	Savusavu	7 446
11	Vatukoula	5 616
12	Navua	5 151
13	Rakiraki	5 078
14	Levuka	4 394
15	Tavua	2 457
16	Deuba	1 881
17	Pacific Harbour	1 874
18	Seaqaqa	888
19	Navouvalu	557

MATANITU KO VITI • REPUBLIC OF THE FIJI ISLANDS

Capital	Suva	Population	944 720 (157)	% in cities	52%
GDP per capita	$3 800 (159)	Area km²	18 274 km² (156)	GMT +/-	+12
Neighbours (km)	Coast 1129				

RECENT INTERNATIONAL MATCHES PLAYED BY FIJI

2008	Opponents	Score		Venue	Comp	Scorers	Att	Referee
6-09	Vanuatu	W	2-0	Ba	WCq	Salesh Kumar [7], Dunadamu [87]	3 000	Minan PNG
10-09	Vanuatu	L	1-2	Port Vila	WCq	Dunadamu [93+]	1 299	O'Leary NZL
19-11	New Zealand	W	2-0	Lautoka	WCq	Krishna 2 [63 90]	4 500	Fred VAN
2009								

No international matches played in 2009

2010

No international matches played in 2010

OC = Oceania Nations Cup • SP = South Pacific Games • WC = FIFA World Cup
q = qualifier • r1 = first round group • sf = semi-final • f = final • † Not a full international

FIJI 2010

NEW WORLD NATIONAL FOOTBALL LEAGUE

	Pl	W	D	L	F	A	Pts	Ba	Lautoka	Navua	Rewa	Fiji U-20	Suva	Labasa	Nadi	Nadroga	Tavua	Nasinu
Ba	20	17	0	3	72	15	51		2-0	2-1	4-1	7-0	3-1	3-1	6-2	7-1	11-0	3-0
Lautoka †	20	16	2	2	74	15	50	3-1		3-3	1-1	9-0	1-0	7-1	5-1	1-0	7-0	8-2
Navua	20	14	2	4	35	16	44	2-0	0-4		1-0	1-0	4-1	1-0	1-0	2-0	2-0	3-1
Rewa	20	9	4	7	34	24	31	0-2	1-0	0-2		0-1	2-0	4-0	2-1	4-0	4-0	4-1
Fiji U-20	20	9	3	8	29	42	30	0-5	0-4	0-4	3-2		0-2	1-1	0-0	2-2	5-0	4-1
Suva	20	7	2	11	25	30	23	3-1	1-3	0-2	3-0	1-2		0-3	0-1	2-4	1-1	1-1
Labasa	20	6	4	10	21	47	22	0-4	1-3	1-0	1-1	0-3	0-3		2-1	2-2	1-1	0-3
Nadi	20	6	3	11	22	34	21	0-2	0-2	2-0	2-2	0-4	0-1	1-2		3-0	1-2	2-1
Nadroga	20	3	6	11	22	46	15	0-2	0-5	2-2	1-1	1-0	0-1	1-3	1-2		1-3	2-0
Tavua	20	4	3	13	24	56	15	0-2	1-5	0-2	1-3	0-1	0-3	7-0	0-2	1-1		6-2
Nasinu	20	3	3	14	23	56	12	0-5	0-3	0-2	0-2	2-3	2-1	1-2	1-1	3-3	2-1	

19/02/2010 - 26/09/2010 • † Qualified for the O-League

FA CUP TOURNAMENT 2010

First Round		Semi-finals		Final	
Group A	Pts				
Labassa	10				
Lautoka	9	**Ba**	1		
Nadroga	4	Labassa	0		
Suva	3				
Nadi	2				
				Ba	1
Group B	Pts			Navua	0
Navua	12				
Ba	7				
Rewa	7	Lautoka	1	30-05-2010
Tavua	3	**Navua**	2	
Nasinu	0				

BATTLE OF THE GIANTS 2010

First Round		Semi-finals		Final	
Group A	Pts				
Rewa	9				
Navua	8	**Rewa**	4		
Ba	7	Lautoka	0		
Labassa	4				
Tavua	0				
				Rewa	1
Group B	Pts			Navua	0
Nadi	10				
Lautoka	7				
Nadroga	6	Nadi	1	22-08-2010
Suva	4	**Navua**	2	
Nasinu	0				

INTERDISTRICT CHAMPIONSHIP

First Round		Semi-finals		Final	
Group A	Pts				
Navua	9				
Labasa	8	**Rewa**	3		
Nadi	7	Labasa	0		
Nadroga	4				
Tavua	0				
				Rewa	3
Group B	Pts			Lautoka	1
Rewa	12			17-10-2010
Lautoka	9			Scorers - Abraham
Suva	4	Navua	1	Iniga 2 [7 47], Epeli
Ba	4	**Lautoka**	2	Saukuru [18] for Rewa;
Nasinu	0			Jone Vono Junior [25]
				for Lautoka

MEDALS TABLE

		Overall		Lg	ID		BoG		FACT	OFC
		G	S	G	G	S	G	B		
1	Ba	60	22	16	22	15	14	6	8	1
2	Lautoka	22	17	3	16	9	1	5	2	3
3	Nadi	20	22	8	6	15	5	4	1	2	1
4	Suva	17	20	2	11	15	3	3	1	2
5	Rewa	13	11		9	7	4	3	1
6	Nadroga	11	5	3	3	3	3		2	2
7	Labassa	8	14	2	2	3	1	5	3	6
8	Navua	5	3		1		1	2	3	1
9	Tavua	2	3		1			2	1	1
10	Nasinu	1	6		1	3		2		1
11	Taileva		1		1					
12	Rakiraki		1			1				

FIN – FINLAND

FIFA/COCA-COLA WORLD RANKING

1993	1994	1995	1996	1997	1998	1999	2000	2001	2002	2003	2004	2005	2006	2007	2008	2009	2010
45	38	44	79	60	55	56	59	46	43	40	43	46	52	36	55	55	83

	2010												Hi/Lo
	Jan	Feb	Mar	Mar	Apr	May	Jul	Aug	Sep	Oct	Nov	Dec	33
	55	54	52	54	49	52	51	51	64	86	87	83	87

Olli Hutunen got his reign as Finland national team coach off to the best possible start with a record equalling 8-0 thrashing of San Marino in November 2010, but by then the damage had already been done in the qualifiers for Euro 2012. Defeats at the hands of rivals Moldova, Holland and Hungary in the opening three matches led to the departure of Stuart Baxter after two years at the helm but even if Hutunen can rekindle the good form that Finland have shown sporadically over the past decade, the Finns do not look a good bet to make a first appearance at a major finals in Poland and the Ukraine. In club football, HJK Helsinki retained their league crown with a minimum of fuss, finishing four points ahead of surprise package KuPS Kuopio. TPS finished in third place but they did deny HJK a league and cup double. In the Cup Final, goals from Mika Aaritalo and Riku Riski saw the club from Turku win their first trophy for 16 years, thanks largely to a well-run youth set-up. The season's other trophy - the pre-season League Cup - was won by Honka Espoo. At the age of 39, the career of Finland's most famous footballer Jari Litmanen showed no signs of slowing down. He played eight times for his country in 2010 to take his total number of caps to 137 although he couldn't save Lahti, the club he captains and part-owns, from relegation.

FIFA WORLD CUP RECORD
1930-1934 DNE **1938-2010** DNQ

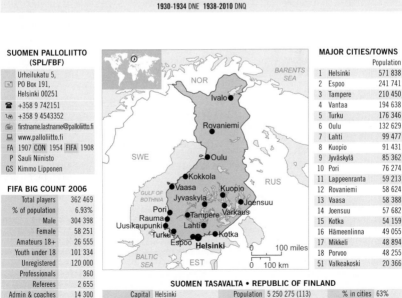

SUOMEN PALLOLIITTO (SPL/FBF)

Urheilukatu 5,
PO Box 191,
Helsinki 00251
☎ +358 9 742151
📠 +358 9 4543352
✉ firstname.lastname@palloliitto.fi
🖥 www.palloliitto.fi
FA 1907 CON 1954 FIFA 1908
P Sauli Niinisto
GS Kimmo Lipponen

FIFA BIG COUNT 2006

Total players	362 469
% of population	6.93%
Male	304 398
Female	58 251
Amateurs 18+	26 555
Youth under 18	101 334
Unregistered	120 000
Professionals	360
Referees	2 655
Admin & coaches	14 300
Number of clubs	990
Number of teams	4 258

MAJOR CITIES/TOWNS

		Population
1	Helsinki	571 838
2	Espoo	241 741
3	Tampere	210 450
4	Vantaa	194 638
5	Turku	176 346
6	Oulu	132 629
7	Lahti	99 477
8	Kuopio	91 431
9	Jyväskylä	85 362
10	Pori	76 274
11	Lappeenranta	59 213
12	Rovaniemi	58 624
13	Vaasa	58 388
14	Joensuu	57 682
15	Kotka	54 159
16	Hämeenlinna	49 055
17	Mikkeli	48 894
18	Porvoo	48 255
51	Valkeakoski	20 366

SUOMEN TASAVALTA • REPUBLIC OF FINLAND

Capital Helsinki	Population 5 250 275 (113)	% in cities 63%
GDP per capita $37 000 (31)	Area km² 338 145 km² (64)	GMT + / - +2
Neighbours (km) Norway 727, Sweden 614, Russia 1313 • Coast 1250		

RECENT INTERNATIONAL MATCHES PLAYED BY FINLAND

2007	Opponents	Score	Venue	Comp	Scorers	Att	Referee
28-03	Azerbaijan	L 0-1	Baku	ECq		14 500	Messina ITA
2-06	Serbia	L 0-2	Helsinki	ECq		33 615	Mejuto Gonzalez ESP
6-06	Belgium	W 2-0	Helsinki	ECq	Johansson [27], Eremenko Jr [71]	34 818	Riley ENG
22-08	Kazakhstan	W 2-1	Tampere	ECq	Eremenko Jr [13], Tainio [61]	13 047	Kassai HUN
8-09	Serbia	D 0-0	Belgrade	ECq		10 530	Braamhaar NED
12-09	Poland	D 0-0	Helsinki	ECq		34 088	Fandel GER
13-10	Belgium	D 0-0	Brussels	ECq		21 393	Kapitanis CYP
17-10	Spain	D 0-0	Helsinki	Fr		8 000	Bre FRA
17-11	Azerbaijan	W 2-1	Helsinki	ECq	Forssell [79], Kuqi [86]	10 325	Hamer LUX
21-11	Portugal	D 0-0	Porto	ECq		49 000	Michel SVK
2008							
6-02	Greece	L 1-2	Nicosia	Fr	Litmanen [66]	500	Kailis CYP
26-03	Bulgaria	L 1-2	Sofia	Fr	Litmanen [22p]	2 500	Tudor ROU
29-05	Turkey	L 0-2	Duisburg	Fr		15 036	Kinhofer GER
2-06	Belarus	D 1-1	Helsinki	Fr	Kallio [90]	6 474	Skomina SVN
20-08	Israel	W 2-0	Tampere	Fr	Johansson 2 [43 88]	4 929	
10-09	Germany	D 3-3	Helsinki	WCq	Johansson [33], Vayrynen [43], Sjolund [53]	37 150	Kassai HUN
11-10	Azerbaijan	W 1-0	Helsinki	WCq	Forssell [61p]	22 124	Collum SCO
15-10	Russia	L 0-3	Moscow	WCq		28 000	Vassaras GRE
19-11	Switzerland	L 0-1	St Gall	Fr		11 500	Kulbakov RUS
2009							
4-02	Japan	L 1-5	Tokyo	Fr	Porokara [50]	34 532	Huang Junjie CHN
11-02	Portugal	L 0-1	Faro-Loule	Fr		19 834	Bertolini SUI
28-03	Wales	W 2-0	Cardiff	WCq	Johansson [43], Kuqi [91+]	22 604	Iturralde ESP
1-04	Norway	L 2-3	Oslo	Fr	Johansson [39], Eremenko Jnr [91+]	16 239	Styles ENG
6-06	Liechtenstein	W 2-1	Helsinki	WCq	Forssell [33], Johansson [71]	20 319	Kovarik CZE
10-06	Russia	L 0-3	Helsinki	WCq		37 028	Plautz AUT
12-08	Sweden	L 0-1	Stockholm	Fr		15 212	Fautrel FRA
5-09	Azerbaijan	W 2-1	Lenkoran	WCq	Tihinen [74], Johansson [85]	12 000	Trifonos CYP
9-09	Liechtenstein	D 1-1	Vaduz	WCq	Litmanen [74p]	3 132	Panic BIH
10-10	Wales	W 2-1	Helsinki	WCq	Porokara [5], Moisander [77]	14 000	Mazic SRB
14-10	Germany	D 1-1	Hamburg	WCq	Johansson [11]	51 500	Atkinson ENG
2010							
18-01	Korea Republic	L 0-2	Malaga	Fr		270	Fernandez ESP
3-03	Malta	W 2-1	Ta'qali	Fr	Eremenko Jnr [66p], Vayrynen [69]		Bergonzi ITA
21-05	Estonia	L 0-2	Tallinn	Fr		5 650	Vad HUN
29-05	Poland	D 0-0	Kielce	Fr		14 200	Avram ROU
11-08	Belgium	W 1-0	Turku	Fr	Porokara [13]	7 451	Hamer LUX
3-09	Moldova	L 0-2	Chisinau	ECq		10 300	Malek POL
7-09	Netherlands	L 1-2	Rotterdam	ECq	Forssell [18]	25 000	Nikolaev POL
12-10	Hungary	L 1-2	Helsinki	ECq	Forssell [86]	18 532	Kelly IRL
17-11	San Marino	W 8-0	Helsinki	ECq	Vayrynen [39], Hamalainen 2 [49 67], Forssell 3 [51 59 78], Litmanen [71p], Porokara [73]	8 192	Matejek POL

Fr = Friendly match • EC = UEFA EURO 2008/2012 • WC = FIFA World Cup • q = qualifier

FINLAND NATIONAL TEAM HISTORICAL RECORDS

Caps
137 - Jari Litmanen 1989- • 105 - Jonatan Johansson 1996- & Sami Hyypia 1992- • 100 - Ari Hjelm 1983-96 • 98 - Joonas Kolkka 1994- • 83 - Erkka Petaja 1983-94 • 76 - Arto Tolsa 1964-81 & Hannu Tihinen 1997-2009 • 75 - Toni Kuivasto 1997- • 72 - Mikael Forssell 1999- • 71 - Mika Nurmela 1992-2007 • 70 - Mika-Matti Paatelainen 1986-2000

Goals
32 - Jari Litmanen 1989-2010 • 24 - Mikael Forssell 1999- • 22 - Jonatan Johansson 1996- • 20 - Ari Hjelm 1983-96 • 18 - Mika-Matti Paatelainen 1986-2000 • 17 - Verner Eklof 1919-27 • 16 - Aulis Koponen 1924-35 & Gunnar Astrom 1923-37 • 13 - Alexei Eremenko 2003- & William Kanerva 1922-38 & Jorma Vaihela 1947-54 & Kai Pahlman 1954-68 • 12 - Kalevi Lehtovirta 1954-59

Past Coaches
Jarl Ohman 1922 • Ferdinand Fabra GER 1936-1937 • Gabor Obitz HUN 1939 • Axel Martensson SWE 1945 • Niilo Tammisalo 1946 • Aatos Lehtonen 1947-1955 • Kurt Weinreich GER 1955-1958 • Aatos Lehtonen 1959-1961 • Olavi Laaksonen 1962-1974 • Martti Kosma 1975 • Aulis Rytkonen 1975-1978 • Esko Malm 1979-1981 • Martti Kuusela 1982-1987 • Jukka Vakkila 1988-1992 • Tommy Lindholm 1993-1994 • Jukka Ikalainen 1994-1996 • Richard Moller Nielsen DEN 1996-1999 • Antti Muurinen 2000-2005 • Jyrki Heliskoski 2005 • Roy Hodgson ENG 2006-2007 • Stuart Baxter SCO 2008-10 • Olli Huttunen 2010-

FINLAND 2010

VEIKKAUSLIIGA (1)

	Pl	W	D	L	F	A	Pts	HJK	KuPS	TPS	Honka	Jaro	Inter	Tampere U	Haka	MyPa-47	VPS	Oulu	Mariehamn	JJK	Lahti
HJK Helsinki †	26	15	7	4	43	19	52		1-2	2-0	0-1	2-1	2-2	3-1	1-1	2-0	3-0	2-0	3-1	1-0	0-0
KuPS Kuopio ‡	26	15	3	8	45	36	48	0-5		2-1	0-2	2-1	2-1	6-2	1-0	2-1	1-2	3-1	0-0	2-0	1-1
TPS Turku ‡	26	13	6	7	46	30	45	0-1	3-0		1-0	0-3	2-2	4-3	1-1	3-0	1-1	5-0	1-4	2-0	3-2
Honka Espoo ‡	26	12	5	9	42	34	41	3-1	2-1	1-0		3-1	1-1	0-2	4-2	3-1	0-0	3-4	3-0	2-3	1-2
Jaro Pietarsaari	26	11	5	10	42	34	38	1-1	0-1	1-3	0-0		0-1	2-2	5-0	3-2	3-2	1-2	2-0	1-3	2-0
Inter Turku	26	10	7	9	34	32	37	0-0	1-3	1-2	2-0	2-0		0-2	1-0	1-1	1-0	0-2	1-1	3-2	1-3
Tampere United	26	10	4	12	37	46	34	2-0	1-3	1-1	2-1	1-4	0-1		2-1	1-1	3-0	3-1	3-4	0-2	0-0
Haka Valkeakoski	26	9	6	11	30	38	33	0-3	2-1	0-0	2-0	4-3	1-3	1-0		0-1	1-1	2-0	2-1	1-2	0-0
MyPa-47 Anjalankoski	26	7	11	8	36	39	32	1-1	1-1	2-2	2-2	0-1	3-2	3-0	2-1		2-2	1-1	2-1	2-4	1-1
VPS Vaasa	26	8	7	11	29	40	31	0-3	2-0	0-3	1-3	1-1	0-3	3-1	2-1	2-1		2-0	1-4	0-1	1-1
AC Oulu	26	8	6	12	31	44	30	1-1	2-5	0-2	2-0	0-1	1-0	3-0	1-1	1-1	1-1		0-0	1-2	1-2
IFK Mariehamn	26	7	7	12	38	43	28	1-2	1-2	2-1	2-2	0-0	3-0	2-3	2-3	1-2	0-3	0-2		3-2	2-2
JJK Jyväskylä	26	8	3	15	34	41	27	1-2	1-3	0-2	0-1	1-2	0-3	0-1	1-2	1-1	0-1	6-1	0-2		2-2
FC Lahti	26	5	11	10	26	37	26	0-1	2-1	1-3	2-4	1-3	1-1	0-1	0-1	0-2	2-1	0-3	1-1	0-0	

16/04/2010 - 23/10/2010 • † Qualified for the UEFA Champions League • ‡ Qualified for the Europa League
Relegation play-off: Viikingit 1-1 0-2 JJK • Top scorers: **16** - Juho Makela, HJK • **12** - Roope Riski, TPS • **11** - Henri Lehtonen, Inter

FINLAND 2010
YKKONEN (2)

	Pl	W	D	L	F	A	Pts
RoPS Rovaniemi	26	15	9	2	61	17	**54**
Viikingit Helsinki	26	15	7	4	49	19	**52**
PoPa Pori	26	15	5	6	48	39	**50**
KPV Kokkola	26	14	5	7	43	31	**47**
OPS-jp Oulu	26	11	7	8	34	29	**40**
FC Espoo	26	10	7	9	32	39	**37**
KooTeePee Kotka	26	10	5	11	28	24	**35**
PK-35 Vantaa	26	10	4	12	36	30	**34**
PS Kemi	26	7	10	9	31	39	**31**
FC Hämeenlinna	26	9	4	13	33	43	**31**
JIPPO Joensuu	26	7	9	10	23	26	**30**
TPV Tampere	26	6	9	11	26	49	**27**
Klubi-04 Helsinki	26	4	5	17	21	50	**17**
MP Mikkeli	26	5	2	19	17	47	**17**

24/04/2010 - 16/10/2010

MEDALS TABLE

		Overall			League			Cup	
		G	S	B	G	S	B	G	S
1	HJK Helsinki	33	18	11	23	13	11	10	5
2	Haka Valkeakoski	21	10	10	9	7	10	12	3
3	TPS Turku	11	17	9	8	12	9	3	5
4	Reipas Lahti	10	9	3	3	6	3	7	3
5	HPS Helsinki	10	7	2	9	6	2	1	1
6	Tampere United	8	4	3	5	1	3	3	3
7	HIFK Helsinki	7	8	4	7	7	4		1
8	KuPS Kuopio	7	9	1	5	9	1	2	
9	FC Lahti	7	8	1	5	4	1	2	4
10	KTP Kotka	6	3	2	2		2	4	3
11	MyPa-47	4	5	3	1	5	3	3	
12	Abo IFK Turku	4	5	1	3	5	1	1	
13	Kronshagen IF Helsinki	4	2	3	4	1	3		1
14	IFK Vaasa	3	2	2	3	2	2		
15	VPS Vaasa	2	6	1	2	5	1		1
16	MP Mikkeli	2	3				3	2	
17	Jazz Pori	2	1	1	2		1	1	1
18	OPS Oulu	2			2				
	Inter Turku	2			1			1	

SUOMEN CUP 2010

Round of 16		Quarter–finals		Semi–finals		Final	
TPS Turku	3						
Jaro Pietarsaari	0	**TPS Turku** *	1				
		Ilves Tampere	2				
Ilves Tampere				**TPS Turku**	2		
				KuPS Kuopio *	1		
Haka Valkeakoski	1						
Sudet Kuovolo	0	Haka Valkeakoski *	0				
MP Mikkeli	0	**KuPS Kuopio**	1				
KuPS Kuopio	2					**TPS Turku** ‡	2
IFK Mariehamn						HJK Helsinki	0
		IFK Mariehamn *	2				
KPV Kokkola	0	Inter Turku	1				
Inter Turku	1			IFK Mariehamn	0		
VPS Vaasa	1			**HJK Helsinki** *	3		
MyPa-47 Anjalankoski	0	VPS Vaasa	0				
Honka Espoo	0	**HJK Helsinki** *	2				
HJK Helsinki	3						

* Home team • ‡ Qualified for the Europa League

CUP FINAL
Sonera (Töölö), Helsinki
25-09-2010, Att: 5137, Ref: Pohjonen
Scorers - Mika Aaritalo 34, Riku Riski 91+

FRA – FRANCE

FIFA/COCA-COLA WORLD RANKING

1993	1994	1995	1996	1997	1998	1999	2000	2001	2002	2003	2004	2005	2006	2007	2008	2009	2010
15	19	8	3	6	2	3	2	1	2	2	2	5	4	7	11	7	18

					2010							Hi/Lo
Jan	Feb	Mar	Mar	Apr	May	Jul	Aug	Sep	Oct	Nov	Dec	1
7	7	7	8	10	9	21	21	27	18	21	18	27

France may have qualified for the 2010 FIFA World Cup in controversial circumstances thanks to Thierry Henry's infamous handball, but that embarrassment was nothing compared to the utter shambles of the French performance in South Africa and the extraordinary off-the-field conflict between coach Raymond Domenech and members of the French squad. An opening goalless draw against a ten-man Uruguay team and defeat at the hands of both Mexico and the hosts meant that the French were one of the first teams on the plane home from South Africa - but not before Nicolas Anelka had been thrown out of the squad following an outburst against the coach during half-time of the Mexico match. That led to a team boycott of training and the limp defeat at the hands of South Africa. Anelka was later given an 18-match ban and all 23 members of the squad were excluded for new coach Laurent Blanc's first match in charge. In club football Marseille won their first championship since the glory days of the early 1990s. Indeed, having gone 16 years without winning a trophy, Marseille, coached by Didier Deschamps, also won the League Cup, beating Laurent Blanc's Bordeaux 3-1 in the final. Paris Saint-Germain beat Monaco 1-0 in the final of the Coupe de France, thanks to an extra-time goal from Guillaume Hoarau, their eighth title overall.

FIFA WORLD CUP RECORD

1930 7 r1 **1934** 9 r1 **1938** 6 QF (hosts) **1950** DNQ **1954** 11 r1 **1958** 3 SF **1962** DNQ **1966** 13 r1 **1970-1974** DNQ **1978** 12 r1
1982 4 SF **1986** 4 SF **1990-1994** DNQ **1998** 1 Winners (hosts) **2002** 28 r1 **2006** 2 Finalists **2010** 29 r1

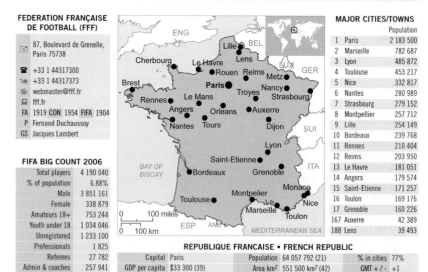

FEDERATION FRANÇAISE DE FOOTBALL (FFF)

87, Boulevard de Grenelle, Paris 75738

☎ +33 1 44317300
📠 +33 1 44317373
✉ webmaster@fff.fr
🖥 fff.fr
FA 1919 CON 1954 FIFA 1904
P Fernand Duchaussoy
GS Jacques Lambert

FIFA BIG COUNT 2006

Total players	4 190 040
% of population	6.88%
Male	3 851 161
Female	338 879
Amateurs 18+	753 244
Youth under 18	1 034 046
Unregistered	1 233 100
Professionals	1 825
Referees	27 782
Admin & coaches	257 941
Number of clubs	18 823
Number of teams	111 760

MAJOR CITIES/TOWNS

		Population
1	Paris	2 183 500
2	Marseille	782 687
3	Lyon	485 872
4	Toulouse	453 217
5	Nice	332 817
6	Nantes	280 989
7	Strasbourg	279 152
8	Montpellier	257 712
9	Lille	254 149
10	Bordeaux	239 768
11	Rennes	210 404
12	Reims	203 950
13	Le Havre	181 051
14	Angers	179 574
15	Saint-Etienne	171 257
16	Toulon	169 176
17	Grenoble	160 226
167	Auxerre	42 389
188	Lens	39 493

REPUBLIQUE FRANCAISE • FRENCH REPUBLIC

Capital	Paris	Population	64 057 792 (21)	% in cities	77%
GDP per capita	$33 300 (39)	Area km²	551 500 km² (42)	GMT +/-	+1
Neighbours (km)	Andorra 56, Belgium 620, Germany 451, Italy 488, Luxembourg 73, Monaco 4, Spain 623, Switzerland 573 • Coast 4668		

RECENT INTERNATIONAL MATCHES PLAYED BY FRANCE

2008	Opponents	Score		Venue	Comp	Scorers	Att	Referee
6-02	Spain	L	0-1	Malaga	Fr		35 000	Asumaa FIN
26-03	England	W	1-0	Paris	Fr	Ribery [32p]	78 500	Meyer GER
27-05	Ecuador	W	2-0	Grenoble	Fr	Gomis 2 [60 86]	20 000	Allaerts BEL
31-05	Paraguay	D	0-0	Toulouse	Fr		33 418	Proenca POR
3-06	Colombia	W	1-0	Paris	Fr	Ribery [25p]	79 727	Dean ENG
9-06	Romania	D	0-0	Zürich	ECr1		30 585	Mejuto Gonzalez ESP
13-06	Netherlands	L	1-4	Berne	ECr1	Henry [71]	30 777	Fandel GER
17-06	Italy	L	0-2	Zürich	ECr1		30 585	Michel SVK
20-08	Sweden	W	3-2	Gothenburg	Fr	Benzema [18], Govou 2 [61 77]	23 263	Braamhaar NED
6-09	Austria	L	1-3	Vienna	WCq	Govou [61]	48 000	Larsen DEN
10-09	Serbia	W	2-1	Paris	WCq	Henry [53], Anelka [63]	53 027	Benquerenca POR
11-10	Romania	D	2-2	Constanta	WCq	Ribery [36], Gourcuff [68]	12 800	De Bleeckere BEL
14-10	Tunisia	W	3-1	Paris	Fr	Henry 2 [40 48], Benzema [58]	74 564	Genov BUL
19-11	Uruguay	D	0-0	Paris	Fr		79 666	Zimmermann SUI
2009								
11-02	Argentina	L	0-2	Marseilles	Fr		60 000	Eriksson SWE
28-03	Lithuania	W	1-0	Kaunas	WCq	Ribery [67]	8 700	Braamhaar NED
1-04	Lithuania	W	1-0	Paris	WCq	Ribery [75]	79 543	Webb ENG
2-06	Nigeria	L	0-1	St-Etienne	Fr		25 000	Bennett ENG
5-06	Turkey	W	1-0	Lyon	Fr	Benzema [39p]	32 000	Grafe GER
12-08	Faroe Islands	W	1-0	Tórshavn	WCq	Gignac [41]	2 974	Koukoulakis GRE
5-09	Romania	D	1-1	Paris	WCq	Henry [48]	78 209	Bebek CRO
9-09	Serbia	D	1-1	Belgrade	WCq	Henry [36]	49 256	Rosetti ITA
10-10	Faroe Islands	W	5-0	Guingamp	WCq	Gignac 2 [34 39], Gallas [53], Anelka [85], Benzema [87]	16 755	Malek POL
14-10	Austria	W	3-1	Paris	WCq	Benzema [18], Henry [26p], Gignac [66]	78 099	Proenca POR
14-11	Republic of Ireland	W	1-0	Dublin	WCq	Anelka [72]	74 103	Brych GER
18-11	Republic of Ireland	D	1-1	Paris	WCq	Gallas [103]	79 145	Hansson SWE
2010								
3-03	Spain	L	0-2	Paris	Fr		79 021	Thomson SCO
26-05	Costa Rica	W	2-1	Lens	Fr	OG [22], Valbuena [83]	40 000	Bezborodov RUS
30-05	Tunisia	D	1-1	Rades/Tunis	Fr	Gallas [62]	55 000	El Raay LBY
4-06	China PR	L	0-1	Saint-Pierre	Fr		10 043	Proenca POR
11-06	Uruguay	D	0-0	Cape Town	WCr1		64 100	Nishimura JPN
17-06	Mexico	L	0-2	Polokwane	WCr1		35 370	Al Ghamdi KSA
22-06	South Africa	L	1-2	Bloemfontein	WCr1	Malouda [70]	39 415	Ruiz COL
11-08	Norway	L	1-2	Oslo	Fr	Ben Arfa [48]	15 165	Velasco ESP
3-09	Belarus	L	0-1	Paris	ECq		76 395	Collum SCO
7-09	Bosnia-Herzegovina	W	2-0	Sarajevo	ECq	Benzema [72], Malouda [78]	28 000	Brych GER
9-10	Romania	W	2-0	Paris	ECq	Remy [83], Gourcuff [93+]	79 299	Proenca POR
12-10	Luxembourg	W	2-0	Metz	ECq	Benzema [22], Gourcuff [76]	24 710	Jug SVN
17-11	England	W	2-1	London	Fr	Benzema [16], Valbuena [55]	85 495	Larsen DEN

Fr = Friendly match • EC = UEFA EURO 2008/2012 • WC = FIFA World Cup

q = qualifier • r1 = first round group • r2 = second round • qf = quarter-final • sf = semi-final • f = final

FRANCE NATIONAL TEAM HISTORICAL RECORDS

Caps

142 - Lilian Thuram 1994-2008 • **123** - Thierry Henry 1997- • **116** - Marcel Desailly 1993-2004 • **108** - Zinedine Zidane 1994-2006 • **107** - Patrick Vieira 1997-2009 • **103** - Didier Deschamps 1989-2000 • **97** - Laurent Blanc 1989-2000 & Bixente Lizarazu 1992-2004 • **92** - Sylvain Wiltord 1999-2006 • **87** - Fabien Barthez 1994-2006 • **84** - William Gallas 2002- • **82** - Manuel Amoros 1982-92 & Youri Djorkaeff 1993-2002 • **79** - Robert Pires 1996-2004 • **76** - Maxime Bossis 1976-86 • **72** - Michel Platini 1976-87

Goals

51 - Thierry Henry 1997- • **41** - Michel Platini 1976-87 • **34** - David Trezeguet 1998-2008 • **31** - Zinedine Zidane 1994-2006 • **30** - Just Fontaine 1953-60 & Jean-Pierre Papin 1986-95 • **28** - Youri Djorkaeff 1993-2002 • **26** - Sylvain Wiltord 1999-2006 • **22** - Jean Vincent 1953-61 • **21** - Jean Nicolas 1933-38 • **20** - Paul Nicolas 1920-31 & Eric Cantona 1987-95 • **19** - Jean Baratte 1944-52 • **18** - Roger Piantoni 1952-61 & Raymond Kopa 1952-62 • **16** - Larent Blanc 1989-2000 • **15** - Eugene Maës 1911-13 & Hervé Revelli 1973-77

Past Coaches

Gaston Barreau 1919-45 • Gabriel Hanot 1945-49 • Paul Baron & Pierre Pibarot 1949-53 • Pierre Pibarot 1953-54 • Jules Bigot & Albert Batteux 1954-56 • Albert Batteux 1956-60 • Albert Batteux & Henri Guérin 1960-64 • Henri Guérin 1964-1966 • José Arribas ESP & Jean Snella 1966 • Just Fontaine 1967 • Louis Dugauguez 1967-1968 • Georges Boulogne 1969-1973 • Stefan Kovács 1973-1975 • Michel Hidalgo 1976-1984 • Henri Michel 1984-1988 • Michel Platini 1988-1992 • Gérard Houllier 1992-1993 • Aimé Jacquet 1994-1998 • Roger Lemerre 1998-2002 • Jacques Santini 2002-2004 • Raymond Domenech 2004-2010 • Laurent Blanc 2010-

FRANCE 2009-10

LIGUE 1 ORANGE

	Pl	W	D	L	F	A	Pts	Marseille	Lyon	Auxerre	Lille	Montpellier	Bordeaux	Lorient	Monaco	Rennes	Valenc'nes	Lens	Nancy	PSG	Toulouse	Nice	Sochaux	St Etienne	Le Mans	Boulogne	Grenoble
Olympique Marseille †	38	23	9	6	69	36	78		2-1	0-2	1-0	4-2	0-0	1-1	1-2	3-1	5-1	1-0	3-1	1-0	1-1	4-1	3-0	1-0	2-1	2-0	2-0
Olympique Lyonnais †	38	20	12	6	64	38	72	5-5		2-1	1-1	1-2	0-1	1-0	3-0	1-1	1-0	1-0	3-1	2-1	2-1	2-0	0-2	1-1	2-0	2-0	2-0
AJ Auxerre ‡	38	20	11	7	42	29	71	0-0	0-3		3-2	2-1	1-0	4-1	2-0	1-0	1-0	0-0	1-3	1-1	1-1	2-0	0-1	1-0	0-2	0-0	
Lille OSC ‡	38	21	7	10	72	40	70	3-2	4-3	1-2		4-1	2-4	1-2	4-0	4-0	1-3	3-1	1-1	1-1	1-1	1-0	4-0	3-0	3-1	1-0	
Montpellier-Hérault ‡	38	20	9	9	50	40	69	2-0	0-1	1-1	2-0		0-1	2-1	0-0	3-1	2-1	1-0	0-2	1-1	1-1	0-2	0-2	1-2	1-1	1-0	1-0
Girondins Bordeaux	38	19	7	12	58	40	64	1-1	2-2	1-2	3-1	1-1		4-1	1-0	1-0	0-1	4-1	1-2	1-0	1-0	4-0	2-0	3-1	3-0	0-0	1-0
FC Lorient	38	16	10	12	54	42	58	1-2	1-3	0-0	2-1	2-2	1-0		2-2	1-1	3-2	1-0	3-1	1-1	1-1	4-1	1-0	4-0	1-0	5-0	2-2
AS Monaco	38	15	10	13	39	45	55	1-2	1-1	0-0	0-4	4-0	0-0	2-0		1-0	2-1	2-0	2-1	2-0	0-0	3-2	2-0	1-2	1-1	1-0	0-0
Stade Rennais	38	14	11	13	52	41	53	1-1	1-2	0-1	1-2	3-0	4-2	1-0	1-0		0-3	1-1	0-0	1-0	4-1	2-2	1-2	1-0	2-1	3-0	4-0
Valenciennes FC	38	14	10	14	50	50	52	3-2	2-2	0-0	1-0	1-1	2-0	0-0	3-1	0-2		0-0	1-3	2-3	1-3	2-1	1-1	1-0	0-1	1-1	2-0
Racing Club Lens	38	12	12	14	40	44	48	1-0	0-2	2-0	1-1	0-1	4-3	1-1	3-0	2-2	1-1		2-1	1-1	0-2	2-0	0-0	1-2	1-3	0-1	1-1
AS Nancy-Lorraine	38	13	9	16	46	53	48	0-3	0-2	0-1	0-4	0-0	0-3	1-0	4-0	1-2	1-1	5-1		0-0	0-0	2-0	2-1	0-1	3-2	1-3	0-4
Paris Saint-Germain ‡	38	12	11	15	50	46	47	0-3	1-1	1-0	3-0	1-3	3-1	0-3	0-1	1-1	2-2	1-1	1-1		1-0	0-1	4-1	3-0	3-1	3-0	4-0
Toulouse FC	38	12	11	15	36	36	47	1-1	0-0	0-3	0-2	0-1	1-2	0-1	0-0	3-2	0-1	1-0	0-0	1-0		0-2	2-0	3-1	2-0	1-0	4-0
OGC Nice	38	11	11	16	41	57	44	1-3	4-1	0-1	1-1	0-3	1-1	1-0	1-3	1-1	3-2	0-0	2-3	1-0	1-0		0-0	1-1	1-0	2-2	2-1
Sochaux-Montbéliard	38	11	8	19	28	52	41	0-1	0-4	1-2	2-1	0-1	2-3	1-0	1-0	2-0	2-5	1-2	1-1	1-4	1-0	1-0		0-2	1-0	0-3	1-0
AS Saint-Etienne	38	10	10	18	27	45	40	0-0	0-1	1-1	1-1	1-0	3-1	0-2	3-0	0-0	0-2	1-4	0-0	0-0	0-1	0-2	0-0		2-0	0-1	1-0
Le Mans UC 72	38	8	8	22	36	59	32	1-2	2-2	0-1	1-2	2-2	2-1	0-3	1-1	1-3	2-1	3-0	2-1	1-0	1-3	0-1	0-0	1-1		1-1	1-0
US Boulogne-sur-mer	38	7	10	21	31	62	31	1-2	0-0	0-2	3-0	2-0	2-0	2-0	1-3	1-0	0-2	2-1	1-2	2-5	1-3	3-3	0-0	0-1	1-3		2-1
Grenoble Foot 38	38	5	8	25	31	61	23	0-2	1-1	5-0	0-2	2-3	1-3	1-2	0-0	4-0	0-1	1-2	1-2	4-0	1-0	1-2	2-1	2-1	1-1	2-0	

8/08/2009 – 15/05/2010 • † Qualified for the UEFA Champions League • ‡ Qualified for the Europa League

Top scorers: **18** – Mamadou Niang SEN, Marseille • **17** – Kevin Gameiro, Lorient • **15** – Lisandro Lopez ARG, Lyon & Mevlut Erding TUR, PSG • **14** – Ireneusz Jelen POL, Auxerre, Loic Remy, Nice & Nene BRA, Monaco • **13** – Gervinho CIV, Lille, Yohan Cabaye, Lille, Pierre-Alan Frau, Lille & Asamoah Gyan GHA, Rennes • **13** – Wendel BRA, Bordeaux, Victor Montano COL, Montpellier & Youssouf Hadji MAR, Nancy

FRANCE 2009-10

LIGUE 2 ORANGE

	Pl	W	D	L	F	A	Pts	Caen	Brest	Arlés	Metz	Angers	Clermont	Le Havre	Laval	Dijon	Nîmes	Tours	Sedan	Ajaccio	Vannes	Nantes	Chât'roux	Istres	Guingamp	Strasbourg	Bastia
SM Caen	38	18	15	5	52	30	69		1-0	1-0	0-2	2-1	2-1	2-0	1-1	1-0	0-0	0-3	1-0	4-2	1-0	1-1	1-2	0-0	0-1	0-0	1-0
Stade Brestois	38	20	7	11	53	34	67	2-0		3-1	2-1	2-0	2-0	2-1	2-1	1-4	1-0	2-0	1-3	0-1	3-4	1-2	2-1	1-0	2-0	1-1	4-0
AC Arlés-Avignon	38	16	12	10	43	39	60	0-0	3-2		2-0	1-1	1-0	1-0	2-0	0-0	2-0	1-2	1-1	1-0	2-1	1-1	1-0	3-0	3-0	1-1	1-1
FC Metz	38	14	14	10	43	39	56	1-3	0-0	1-2		1-0	2-1	2-0	3-2	1-1	1-1	1-2	0-1	0-0	3-1	1-1	2-0	0-1	0-0	2-0	1-0
SC Angers	38	15	10	13	46	43	55	2-2	1-2	3-1	0-1		2-1	0-0	2-1	3-0	1-0	0-1	2-0	0-0	2-0	1-0	1-0	0-0	0-0
Clermont Foot	38	15	9	14	48	41	54	1-3	0-1	1-2	2-0	3-2		1-0	0-0	0-2	0-1	0-0	0-3	3-0	1-0	2-0	2-0	3-1	3-0	0-0
Le Havre AC	38	14	10	14	45	50	52	1-1	1-0	1-2	2-0	3-2	2-1		0-2	1-1	0-2	1-3	1-1	0-0	1-4	0-2	2-2	2-1	2-1	3-0	3-1
Stade Lavallois	38	11	18	9	49	41	51	2-1	1-2	0-1	3-3	2-2	0-0	4-0		2-2	0-0	1-0	1-1	2-2	2-1	0-0	2-2	3-0	3-2	1-1
Dijon FCO	38	12	15	11	52	46	51	1-1	1-3	1-0	1-0	2-2	2-3	1-2	0-0		1-0	2-2	3-1	3-0	0-0	1-2	5-4	1-1	1-0	0-1
Nîmes Olympique	38	13	12	13	37	43	51	0-4	1-0	1-1	1-1	0-1	0-1	1-1	1-1	2-1		1-1	3-0	2-0	1-1	2-1	1-4	2-1	2-0	2-1	2-1
Tours FC	38	11	16	11	47	46	49	1-1	0-1	4-2	1-1	2-0	1-1	2-0	0-3	1-4	0-0		1-3	1-3	1-1	1-1	2-2	4-0	2-0	2-0	0-0
CS Sedan Ardennes	38	11	16	11	46	46	49	0-0	0-0	0-0	1-1	2-2	2-1	1-1	0-0	2-0	2-1	1-0		1-3	0-1	1-1	1-1	0-3	3-1	0-0
AC Ajaccio	38	13	9	16	41	42	48	2-0	0-0	1-0	1-1	0-2	1-1	3-0	1-0	0-2	0-2	2-2	2-0		1-2	1-1	0-1	1-2	2-0	1-1
Vannes Olympique	38	11	13	14	40	49	46	0-3	0-2	0-0	3-0	1-0	1-2	1-1	2-1	2-3	1-0	0-2	1-2	0-2		0-3	1-1	3-2	2-2	2-1	1-3
FC Nantes	38	12	9	17	43	54	45	1-3	1-4	1-0	2-2	1-2	3-2	4-1	0-0	0-1	2-1	2-1	1-3	1-0	0-0		2-2	5-0	0-2	2-1	3-1
LB Châteauroux	38	10	14	14	50	54	44	1-1	1-3	0-1	2-2	0-3	3-1	2-1	1-3	2-0	3-0	1-0	1-2	0-0	2-2		0-2	0-1	2-1	2-2
FC Istres	38	11	11	16	34	52	44	2-1	1-0	1-1	2-2	1-1	1-3	0-1	1-2	1-2	3-1	0-2	1-1	1-0	2-1		0-0	2-1	0-1	0-0
En Avant Guingamp	38	9	16	13	35	40	43	0-0	0-0	4-1	2-1	0-0	1-1	1-2	0-0	1-1	0-0	2-2	2-2	2-1	4-1	2-0	1-1	0-0		2-0	1-1
RC Strasbourg	38	9	15	14	42	49	42	2-2	1-0	1-1	1-1	1-1	2-1	1-1	4-1	3-1	1-1	0-1	2-2	2-0	1-0	1-0	1-2	2-0	2-1		2-1
SC Bastia	38	10	9	19	40	48	39	1-2	1-1	3-0	1-0	3-1	3-1	1-0	0-1	3-4	6-1	3-0	2-0	1-0	1-2	1-1	0-2	0-0	0-1	1-0	

7/08/2009 – 14/05/2010 • Top scorers: **21** – Olivier Giroud, Tours • **20** – Anthony Modeste, Angers • **19** – Sebastian Ribas URU, Dijon

FRANCE 2009-10

NATIONAL (3)

Cross-table opponents (columns): Evian, Reims, Troyes, Créteil, Pacy d'Eure, Paris FC, Beauvais, Fréjus, Cannes, Luzenac, Rouen, Amiens, Bayonne, Plabennec, Rodez, Gueugnon, Moulins, Hyères, Cassis, Louhans

Team	Pl	W	D	L	F	A	Pts	Results
Evian-Thonon Gaillard	38	26	7	5	64	26	**85**	2-1 1-1 3-0 2-1 0-1 1-0 1-0 3-0 2-0 1-1 1-0 5-2 1-0 3-1 1-1 4-1 1-0 3-0
Stade de Reims	38	21	8	9	63	31	**71**	0-1 1-0 1-2 4-1 2-1 3-0 0-1 0-0 4-2 1-1 5-0 1-0 1-2 3-0 2-2 3-2 1-1 5-0 2-0
ES Troyes FC	38	18	15	5	61	31	**69**	4-0 0-0 2-1 2-0 1-0 4-0 1-2 2-2 1-0 1-2 1-0 0-0 5-0 1-1 3-1 2-0 2-0 2-0 2-0
US Créteil-Lusitanos	38	19	6	13	48	37	**63**	0-1 0-1 1-1 4-1 1-0 3-0 1-1 1-0 3-0 0-1 1-0 2-1 0-0 0-2 1-0 3-1 1-1 2-1 2-0
Pacy-sur-Eure	38	17	9	12	60	41	**60**	1-1 0-2 1-1 1-2 1-1 1-1 1-0 3-0 0-1 0-1 6-0 0-0 2-1 2-1 1-0 3-0 0-0 5-2 2-0
Paris FC	38	16	10	12	50	44	**58**	3-1 1-2 2-2 2-1 2-0 0-0 0-0 1-1 2-0 2-1 2-1 2-0 4-4 2-2 4-2 2-0 1-5 2-1 2-3 2-0
AS Beauvais Oise	38	15	11	12	50	48	**56**	1-4 2-0 2-2 1-0 0-1 1-1 1-1 3-2 4-1 1-1 4-1 2-2 2-1 2-0 2-1 0-0 2-1 4-0 0-0
Fréjus Saint-Raphaël	38	14	12	12	44	34	**54**	3-1 2-0 2-2 1-0 1-2 3-0 0-1 0-1 3-0 2-0 2-4 3-0 0-0 1-1 2-0 1-1 1-1 2-1 0-1
AS Cannes	38	13	15	10	37	34	**54**	0-0 0-0 0-0 0-1 0-0 2-1 2-0 1-1 2-1 3-1 2-2 3-0 0-0 2-1 0-1 1-0 1-1 0-2 0-0
US Luzenac	38	15	8	15	51	48	**53**	1-1 0-2 1-1 4-1 2-1 0-0 2-1 0-1 0-1 2-2 1-0 0-1 3-1 2-1 2-0 3-0 4-0 0-2 5-0
FC Rouen	38	12	14	12	47	43	**50**	1-3 0-0 2-0 1-1 1-0 0-3 1-1 2-1 1-1 0-1 3-1 4-0 0-0 1-1 1-1 2-1 2-0 0-0 7-0
Amiens SFC §1	38	14	9	15	55	54	**50**	0-0 0-1 0-0 4-2 1-2 2-1 2-1 2-1 0-1 2-2 0-0 0-1 5-1 2-1 0-0 3-1 3-0 1-0 8-1
Aviron Bayonnais	38	13	11	14	41	47	**50**	0-1 0-3 0-0 1-1 1-1 2-0 1-2 0-0 0-1 2-2 4-2 2-0 2-1 0-1 3-1 4-0 0-0 2-0 3-0
Stade Plabennecois	38	13	11	14	41	57	**50**	0-1 0-4 3-0 2-0 2-1 0-3 3-1 1-0 1-1 0-0 1-0 0-3 0-1 2-1 2-0 2-0 0-0 2-1 2-0
Rodez Aveyron	38	12	9	17	42	45	**45**	0-1 2-0 1-2 0-1 1-1 0-1 2-1 1-0 2-0 1-0 1-0 1-2 2-0 3-1 1-1 1-0 0-0 1-1 2-1
FC Gueugnon	38	11	9	18	41	48	**42**	0-1 0-2 1-2 0-2 1-3 2-0 1-0 0-1 3-3 2-0 1-0 2-0 4-0 0-0 4-3 0-1 2-0 3-0 3-0
AS Moulins	38	9	11	18	37	57	**38**	1-0 1-1 1-1 1-0 0-3 3-1 1-3 1-2 0-1 0-2 2-2 2-2 0-1 1-2 0-0 0 1-0 1-1 0-2
Hyères FC	38	7	14	17	34	55	**35**	0-2 3-1 2-3 0-4 1-3 0-0 1-1 2-0 2-1 0-2 2-1 2-1 1-2 1-1 1-0 1-2 1-2
Cassis-Carnoux	38	8	9	21	39	61	**33**	1-3 1-2 1-2 0-1 2-3 1-1 0-1 1-1 0-3 3-4 0-1 2-1 1-1 1-0 0-3 1-1 2-1 2-0
Louhans-Cuiseaux §5	38	5	6	27	18	85	**16**	0-2 0-2 0-5 0-2 0-6 0-0 1-2 2-2 0-0 1-2 0-2 0-0 1-4 1-3 3-2 0-0 0-3 0-1 2-0

7/08/2009 - 14/05/2010 • § = points deducted • Top scorers: **24** - Cédric Fauré, Reims • **23** - Yassin El-Azzouzi, Pacy-sur-Eure

MEDALS TABLE

		Overall			League			Cup		LC		Europe		
		G	S	B	G	S	B	G	S	G	S	G	S	B
1	Olympique Marseille	21	20	7	9	9	5	10	8	1		1	3	2
2	AS Saint-Etienne	16	7	3	10	3	2	6	3				1	1
3	Paris Saint-Germain	14	11	6	2	6	3	8	3	3	1	1	1	3
4	AS Monaco	13	12	14	7	5	10	5	4	1	1		2	4
5	Girondins Bordeaux	12	19	6	6	9	4	3	6	3	3		1	2
6	Olympique Lyonnais	12	8	7	7	3	5	4	3	1	2			2
7	FC Nantes Atlantique	11	13	4	8	7	2	3	5		1			2
8	Lille OSC	8	11	3	3	7	3	5	4					
9	Stade de Reims	8	6	4	6	3	4	2	1				2	
10	OGC Nice	7	5		4	3		3	1	1				
11	Racing Club Paris	6	4	5	1	2	5	5	2					
12	Racing Club Strasbourg	6	4	3	1	1	3	3	3	2				
13	FC Sochaux-Montbéliard	5	7	5	2	3	4	2	3	1	1			1
14	AJ Auxerre	5	1	6	1		5	4	1					1
15	Red Star 93 Paris	5	1					5	1					
16	FC Sète	4	4	1	2			2	4					
17	FC Metz	3	3	1	1	1		2	1	1	1			
18	Racing Club Lens	2	8	3	1	4	2		3	1	1			1
19	CS Sedan Ardennes	2	3	2		2		2	3					
20	Stade Rennais	2	3					2	3					
21	CO Roubaix-Tourcoing	2	2	1	1		1	1	2					
22	CAS Généraux	2						2						
	AS Nancy-Lorraine	2			1			1		1				
24	SC Bastia	1	4	1			1	1	2	1		1		
25	Toulouse FC	1	1	2	1	2		1						
26	Le Havre AC	1	1	1			1	1	1					
	Montpellier HSC	1	1	1			1	1	1					
28	AS Cannes	1	1			1		1						
	En Avant Guingamp	1	1					1	1					
	FC Lorient	1	1					1		1				
	Cercle Athlétique Paris	1	1					1	1					
	SO Montpellier	1	1					1	1					

FRANCE 2009–10
CFA GROUPE A (4)

	Pl	W	D	L	F	A	Pts
Colmar	36	19	12	5	55	33	105
Alfortville	36	19	10	7	56	37	102
Villemomble	36	15	16	5	45	33	97
Besançon	36	15	11	10	59	48	92
Amnéville	36	15	8	13	58	55	89
Drancy	36	15	7	14	49	51	88
Noisy-le-Sec	36	11	17	8	52	46	86
Épinal	36	13	11	12	45	46	86
Nancy B	36	14	8	14	47	46	86
Lille B	36	11	16	9	55	47	84
Compiègne	36	11	15	10	42	40	84
Raon-l'Étape	36	11	12	13	47	48	81
Mulhouse	36	12	9	15	41	48	81
Sannois Saint-Gratien	36	12	9	15	47	51	81
Lens B	36	12	8	16	40	42	80
Vesoul Haute-Saône	36	9	11	16	29	45	74
Dunkerque	36	10	7	19	45	53	73
Marck	36	8	13	15	43	57	73
Strasbourg B	36	4	12	20	28	59	60

8/08/2009 - 29/05/2010 • Four points for a win, two for a draw and one for a defeat

FRANCE 2009–10
CFA GROUPE B (4)

	Pl	W	D	L	F	A	Pts
Gap	34	17	9	8	58	34	94
Gazélec Ajaccio	34	16	10	8	45	30	92
Jura Sud	34	16	9	9	47	37	91
Lyon B	34	12	15	7	51	38	85
Martigues	34	13	10	11	39	35	83
Marignane	33	13	10	10	34	34	82
Toulon	33	13	11	9	38	31	80
Agde	34	11	13	10	30	39	80
CA Bastia	34	11	11	12	40	38	78
Bourg-Péronnas	34	11	11	12	37	47	78
Sochaux B	34	11	9	14	37	33	76
Montceau Bourgogne	34	12	9	13	42	42	76
Villefranche	34	12	9	13	41	45	76
Andrézieux	34	11	8	15	36	39	75
Lyon-Duchère	34	10	11	13	30	34	75
Le Pontet	34	10	11	13	40	54	75
Montpellier B	34	8	12	14	35	41	70
Grenoble B	34	6	10	18	31	55	61

8/08/2009 - 29/05/2010 • Four points for a win, two for a draw and one for a defeat

FRANCE 2009–10
CFA GROUPE C (4)

	Pl	W	D	L	F	A	Pts
Niort	34	18	11	5	53	23	99
Yzeure	34	16	10	8	37	28	92
Vendée Luçon	34	15	11	8	45	39	90
Paris SG B	34	13	15	6	37	28	88
Albi	34	14	12	8	42	40	88
Montluçon	34	14	10	10	45	36	86
Colomiers	34	13	9	12	33	29	82
Les Herbiers	34	12	12	10	48	44	82
Le Mans Reserves	34	10	14	10	42	34	78
Libourne-Saint-Seurin	34	10	14	10	35	31	78
Red Star	34	11	9	14	38	42	76
Pau	34	9	12	13	30	35	73
Aurillac	34	8	14	12	26	40	72
Genêts d'Anglet	34	9	9	16	29	42	70
Vendée Fontenay	34	6	18	10	31	41	70
Bordeaux B	34	9	10	15	23	32	69
Balma	34	6	12	16	27	41	64
Toulouse Fontaines	34	6	10	18	25	39	62

8/08/2009 - 29/05/2010 • Four points for a win, two for a draw and one for a defeat

FRANCE 2009–10
CFA GROUPE D (4)

	Pl	W	D	L	F	A	Pts
Orléans	34	19	12	3	43	21	103
Vitréenne	34	17	10	7	49	34	95
Le Havre B	34	15	14	5	59	40	93
Cherbourg	34	17	8	9	45	33	93
Quevilly	34	13	9	12	52	46	82
Racing	34	13	11	10	47	36	81
Romorantin	34	12	11	11	59	57	81
Viry-Châtillon	34	13	8	13	50	58	81
Ivry	34	12	10	12	40	37	80
Auxerre B	34	12	9	13	47	42	79
Sénart-Moissy	34	11	12	11	49	47	79
Carquefou	34	12	9	13	37	42	79
Rennes B	34	12	9	13	31	41	76
Caen B	34	9	12	13	46	43	73
Avranches	34	10	9	15	34	44	73
Mantes	34	10	7	17	35	49	71
Quimper	34	6	9	19	24	57	61
Pontivy	34	5	10	19	36	57	59

8/08/2009 - 29/05/2010 • Four points for a win, two for a draw and one for a defeat

COUPE DE LA LIGUE 2009-10

Third Round		Fourth Round		Quarter-finals		Semi-finals		Final	
Olympique Marseille	Bye	Olympique Marseille	3						
OGC Nice	1	AS Saint-Etienne *	2						
AS Saint-Etienne *	4			Olympique Marseille *	2				
Stade Rennais *	2	Stade Rennais	1	Lille OSC	1				
Sochaux-Montbéliard	1	Lille OSC *	3						
Lille OSC	Bye					Olympique Marseille	2		
En Avant Guingamp	Bye	En Avant Guingamp *	1			Toulouse FC *	1		
US Boulogne-sur-mer *	0	Paris Saint-Germain	0						
Paris Saint-Germain	1			En Avant Guingamp *	0				
AS Nancy-Lorraine *	2	AS Nancy-Lorraine	0	Toulouse FC	1				
AS Monaco	0	Toulouse FC *	3						
Toulouse FC	Bye							Olympique Marseille	3
FC Lorient *	1	FC Lorient	2					Girondins Bordeaux	1
Grenoble Foot 38	0	Racing Club Lens *	1						
Montpellier-Hérault *	3			FC Lorient *	1				
Racing Club Lens	4	FC Metz *	0	Olympique Lyonnais	0				
FC Metz *	2	Olympique Lyonnais *	3						
Valenciennes FC	0					FC Lorient *	1		
Olympique Lyonnais	Bye	CS Sedan Ardennes *	1			Girondins Bordeaux	4		
CS Sedan Ardennes *	3	Clermont Foot	0						
AJ Auxerre	1			CS Sedan Ardennes					
Vannes Olympique	1	Le Mans UC 72 *	2	Girondins Bordeaux *					
Clermont Foot *	3	Girondins Bordeaux	3						
Le Mans UC 72 *	3								
Nîmes Olympique	0								
Girondins Bordeaux	Bye								

COUPE DE LA LIGUE FINAL

Stade de France, Paris, 27-03-2010, 20:50
Att: 72,749. Ref: Stephane Lannoy
Scorers – Diawara 61, Valbuena 68
Chalme OG 77 for OM; Sane 85 for Bordeaux
OM - Steve Mandanda – Laurent Bonnart, Souleymane Diawara, Stephane M'Bia, Taye Taiwo - Edouard Cisse – Charles Kabore, Lucho Gonzalez (Fabrice Abriel 74) - Mamadou Niang (c) (Mathieu Valbuena 52), Brandao◊, Hatem Ben Arfa Gabriel Heinze 86). Tr: Didier Deschamps
Bordeaux - Ulrich Rame - Mathieu Chalme, Ludovic Sane◊, Michael Ciani, Benoit Tremoulinas◊ - Alou Diarra◊ (c) - Jaroslav Plasil, Fernando (Jussie 67), Wendel - Yohann Gourcuff (Yoan Gouffran 70), Marouane Chamakh (Fernando Cavenaghi 70). Tr: Laurent Blanc

* Home team • Ligue 1 clubs enter in the third round

COUPE DE FRANCE 2009-10

Round of 64		Round of 32		Round of 16	
Paris Saint-Germain	5				
Aubervilliers *	0	**Paris Saint-Germain** *	3		
Pau *	0	Evian-Thonon Gaillard	1		
Evian-Thonon Gaillard	2			**Paris Saint-Germain**	1
US Raon L'Etape	4			Vesoul Haute-Saône *	0
Saint-Dizier	0	US Raon L'Etape *	0		
Stade Lavallois *	1	**Vesoul Haute-Saône**	1		
Vesoul Haute-Saône	2				
Stade Plabennecois *	2				
OGC Nice	1	**Stade Plabennecois**	2		
Thiers *	1 2p	AS Nancy-Lorraine *	0		
AS Nancy-Lorraine	1 3p			Stade Plabennecois	0
CS Sedan Ardennes	3			**AJ Auxerre** *	4
Saint-Ouen l'Aumône *	0	CS Sedan Ardennes	1 0p		
Amiens SFC *	0	**AJ Auxerre** *	1 3p		
AJ Auxerre	1				
US Boulogne-sur-mer	4				
Seclin *	1	**US Boulogne-sur-mer**	2		
Lille OSC	0 9p	Colmar *	1		
Colmar *	0 10p			**US Boulogne-sur-mer** *	1
Mulhouse	2			En Avant Guingamp	0
Marquette *	1	Mulhouse *	0		
Bonchamp-les-Laval *	0	**En Avant Guingamp**	1		
En Avant Guingamp	2				
Stade Rennais *	2				
SM Caen	0	**Stade Rennais**	4		
US Avranches *	0	Olympique Saumur *	0		
Olympique Saumur	1			Stade Rennais	0
SC Angers	1			**US Quevilly** *	1
Lattes *	0	SC Angers	0		
Saint-Quentin	0	**US Quevilly** *	1		
US Quevilly *	6				
Racing Club Lens	1				
AFC Compiegne *	0	**Racing Club Lens** *	3		
Trélissac *	0	Olympique Marseille	1		
Olympique Marseille	2			**Racing Club Lens** *	2
Toulouse FC	1			Stade Brestois	1
Les Herbiers *	0	Toulouse FC *	0		
Pontivy *	0	**Stade Brestois**	2		
Stade Brestois	1				
Vannes Olympique *	1 8p				
ES Troyes FC	1 7p	**Vannes Olympique** *	4		
Montpellier-Hérault	2	Grenoble Foot 38	3		
Grenoble Foot 38 *	3			Vannes Olympique	0
Villefranche	3			**AS Saint-Etienne** *	2
Grand Motte *	0	Villefranche	2 1p		
FC Lorient	1	**AS Saint-Etienne** *	2 3p		
AS Saint-Etienne *	4				
Sochaux-Montbéliard	1				
Saint-Louis Neuweg *	0	**Sochaux-Montbéliard** *	3		
Valenciennes	0	Le Mans UC 72	0		
Le Mans UC 72 *	1			**Sochaux-Montbéliard**	4
SU Agen	1			AS Beauvais Oise *	1
Chauray *	0	SU Agen	0		
Versailles *	0	**AS Beauvais Oise** *	3		
AS Beauvais Oise	3				
Girondins Bordeaux *	1				
Rodez Aveyron	0	**Girondins Bordeaux** *	5		
AS Cannes	0	AC Ajaccio	1		
AC Ajaccio *	3			Girondins Bordeaux *	0
Olympique Lyonnais	3			**AS Monaco**	2
RC Strasbourg *	1	Olympique Lyonnais	1		
Tours FC	0 3p	**AS Monaco** *	2		
AS Monaco *	0 4p				

* Home team

COUPE DE FRANCE 2009–10

Quarter–finals **Semi–finals** **Final**

| Paris Saint-Germain | 0 6p |
| AJ Auxerre * | 0 5p |

| Paris Saint-Germain † | 1 |
| US Quevilly | 0 |

| US Boulogne-sur-mer | 1 |
| **US Quevilly *** | 3 |

| Paris Saint-Germain ‡ | 1 |
| AS Monaco | 0 |

| **Racing Club Lens *** | 3 |
| AS Saint-Etienne | 1 |

| Racing Club Lens | 0 |
| **AS Monaco ††** | 1 |

| Sochaux-Montbéliard | 3 |
| **AS Monaco *** | 4 |

COUPE DE FRANCE FINAL 2010

Stade de France, Paris, 1-05-2010, Att: 75 000, Ref: Lionel Jaffredo

Paris Saint-Germain 1 Hoarau [105]
AS Monaco 0

PSG - Apoula Edel - Christophe Jallet (Sammy Traore 116), Zoumana Camara, Mamadou Sakho, Sylvain Armand - Claude Makelele● (c) - Stephane Sessegnon, Jeremy Clement, Ludovic Giuly (Peguy Luyindula 77) - Mevlut Erdinc (Ceara 105), Guillaume Hoarau●. Tr: Antoine Kombouare
Monaco - Stephane Ruffier - Francois-Joseph Modesto, Cedric Mongongu●, Sebastien Puygrenier, Djimi Traore - Juan Pablo Pino (Moussa Maazou 86), Eduardo Costa● (Yannick Sagbo 111), Thomas Mangani (Lukman Haruna 55), Nene● - Alejandro Alonso● (c), Park Chu Young. Tr: Guy Lacombe

† Played in Caen • †† Played in Monaco
‡ Qualified for the Europa League

CLUB BY CLUB GUIDE TO THE 2009-10 SEASON IN FRANCE

AUXERRE 2009–10

	No	Opponent	Res	Score	Comp	Scorers	Att
Aug	8	Sochaux	L	0-1	L1		12 562
	15	Lens	L	0-2	L1		34 671
	22	Lyon	L	0-3	L1		13 392
	29	Boulogne	D	0-0	L1		11 090
Sep	13	Nice	W	2-0	L1	Hengbart 31, Niculae 78	8 776
	19	St-Etienne	D	1-1	L1	Lejeune 75	24 309
	23	Sedan	L	1-3	LCr3	Mignot 62	5 811
	26	Grenoble	W	2-0	L1	Pedretti 63, Hengbart 84	8 631
Oct	3	Rennes	W	1-0	L1	Pedretti 17	20 378
	17	Bordeaux	W	1-0	L1	Birsa 72p	16 496
	25	Lille	W	3-2	L1	Jelen 2 36 78, Niculae 82	11 285
	31	Montpellier	W	2-1	L1	Jelen 2 16 29	11 373
Nov	7	Le Mans	W	1-0	L1	OG 51	7 996
	21	Monaco	W	2-0	L1	Coulibaly 45, Ndinga 87	14 951
	28	PSG	L	0-1	L1		34 849
Dec	6	Nancy	L	1-3	L1	Birsa 35	10 483
	12	Lorient	D	0-0	L1		9 091
	15	Val'ciennes	D	0-0	L1		10 946
	20	Toulouse	D	1-1	L1	Contout 90	6 677
	23	Marseille	W	2-0	L1	Oliech 2 40 79	49 966
Jan	11	Amiens	W	1-0	CFr9	Hengbart 47	2 600
	16	Boulogne	D	0-0	L1		10 127
	20	Nice	W	1-0	L1	Jelen 93+	7 001
	26	Sedan	D	1-1	CFr10	Jelen 28, W 3-0p	2 287
	31	St-Etienne	W	1-0	L1	Mignot 78	11 670
Feb	6	Grenoble	L	0-5	L1		12 849
	10	Plabennec	W	4-0	CFr11	Jelen 3 9 57 71, Pedretti 64	3 516
	14	Rennes	W	1-0	L1	Jelen 42	8 689
	28	Lille	W	2-1	L1	Contout 2 19 73	14 717
Mar	6	Val'ciennes	W	1-0	L1	Jelen 38	9 473
	10	Bordeaux	W	2-1	L1	Jelen 2 65 83	20 868
	13	Montpellier	D	1-1	L1	Oliech 45	19 320
	20	Le Mans	W	2-1	L1	Jelen 25, Pedretti 92+	10 159
	23	PSG	D	0-0	CFqf	L 5-6p	BCD
	29	Monaco	D	0-0	L1		6 037
Apr	4	PSG	D	1-1	L1	Niculae 11	16 153
	11	Nancy	W	1-0	L1	Niculae 88	17 041
	17	Lorient	W	4-1	L1	Oliech 35, Jelen 37, Birsa 55, Hengbart 89p	15 439
	25	Toulouse	W	3-0	L1	Pedretti 47, Jelen 2 68 79	21 561
	30	Marseille	D	0-0	L1		20 005
May	5	Lyon	L	1-2	L1	Jelen 15	36 262
	8	Lens	D	0-0	L1		18 080
	15	Sochaux	W	2-1	L1	Hengbart 2 6 90	14 971

KEY TO THE CLUB SECTION

SC = Trophée des Champions (played in Tunis) • L1 = Ligue 1 •
CF = Coupe de France • LC = Coupe de la Ligue • CL = UEFA
Champions League • EL = Europa League • r1 = first round etc •
p3 = third preliminary round •po = preliminary round play-off •
gA = Group A etc •qf = quarter-final • sf = semi-final • f = final
• BCD = Played behind closed doors
Matches that are shaded were played at home; matches with no
shading were played either away or on a neutral ground
The figures for the player appearances and goals consist of three
elements - matches started+appearances as a substitute/goals
scored

AUXERRE APPEARANCES/GOALS 2009-10
Goalkeepers Remy Riou 3 • Olivier Sorin 35
Defenders Jeremy Berthod 13+6/0 • Adama Coulibaly MLI 33/1 •
Stephane Grichting SUI 37/0 • Cedric Hengbart 37/5 •
Kevin Malaga 0+1/0 • Jean-Pascal Mignot 28+4/1
Midfield Valter Birsa SVN 24+11/3 • Aurelien Capoue 16+5/0 • Kamel
Chafni MAR 16+9/0 • Dariusz Dudka POL 17+2/0 • Moussa
Narry GHA 2+1/0 • Delvin Ndinga CGO 23+3/1 • Benoit Pedretti 36/4 •
Alain Traore BFA 0+1/0
Forwards Maxime Bourgeois 0+5/0 • Roy Contout 18+15/3 • Ireneusz
Jelen POL 28+1/14 • Kevin Lejeune 1+7/1 • Daniel Niculae ROU 28+5/4
• Dennis Oliech KEN 23+10/4 • Julien Quercia 0+10/0 •
Yaya Sanogo 0+1/0
Coach Jean Fernandez

GIRONDINS BORDEAUX 2009–10

	No	Opponent	Res	Score	Comp	Scorers	Att
=	25	Guingamp	W	2-0	SC	Cavenaghi 38, Fernando 91+	34 068
Aug	9	Lens	W	4-1	L1	Wendel 12, Gourcuff 2 54 93+, Chamakh 92+	32 725
	15	Sochaux	W	3-2	L1	Chamakh 2 31 80, OG 43	16 689
	23	Nice	W	4-0	L1	Jussie 44, Goucuff 2 53 70, Diarra 76	32 065
	30	Marseille	D	0-0	L1		55 920
Sep	12	Grenoble	W	1-0	L1	Gouffran 18	28 211
	15	Juventus	D	1-1	CLgA	Plasil 75	17 513
	19	Boulogne	W	2-0	L1	Gouffran 34, OG 70	13 178
	27	Rennes	W	1-0	L1	Wendel 24	26 811
	30	Mac. Haifa	W	1-0	CLgA	Ciani 83	28 748
Oct	3	St-Etienne	L	1-3	L1	Jussie 68p	30 049
	4	Auxerre	L	0-1	L1		16 496
	21	Bayern	W	2-1	CLgA	Ciani 27, Planus 40	31 321
	24	Le Mans	W	3-0	L1	OG 3, Chamakh 67, Bellion 83	27 737
	31	Monaco	W	1-0	L1	Planus 62	32 308
Nov	3	Bayern	W	2-0	CLgA	Gourcuff 37, Chamakh 90	66 000
	8	Lille	L	0-2	L1		16 233
	21	Val'ciennes	W	0-1	L1		27 431
	25	Juventus	W	2-0	CLgA	Fernando 54, Chamakh 94+	32 195
	29	Nancy	W	3-0	L1	Fernando 25, Wendel 61, Gouffran 75	18 223
Dec	5	PSG	W	1-0	L1	Plasil 24	32 826
	8	Mac. Haifa	W	1-0	CLgA	Jussie 13	25 800
	13	Lyon	W	1-0	L1	Chamakh 86	36 887
	16	Montpellier	W	1-0	L1	Jussie 57	26 366
Jan	19	Lorient	W	4-1	L1	Bellion 2 12 42, Cavenaghi 52, Goucuff 75	27 599
	23	Toulouse	W	2-1	L1	Chamakh 9, Wendel 75	28 352
	9	Rodez	W	1-0	CFr9	Wendel 77p	6 782
	17	Marseille	D	1-1	L1	OG 45	32 771
	20	Grenoble	W	3-1	L1	Gouffran 53, Chamakh 56, Cavenaghi 83	13 336
	23	Ajaccio	W	5-1	CFr10	Plasil 2, Wendel 38, Cavenaghi 3 42 58 84	8 221
	26	Le Mans	W	3-2	LCr4	Gouffran 14, Gourcuff 36, Plasil 51	8 466
	30	Boulogne	D	0-0	L1		25 288
Feb	2	Sedan	W	1-0	LCqf	Gouffran 50	9 819
	6	Rennes	L	2-4	L1	Gouffran 64, Wendel 68	28 006
	10	Monaco	L	0-2	CFr11		14 062
	14	St-Etienne	W	3-1	L1	Chamakh 13, Wendel 2 27 79	30 084
	17	Lorient	W	4-1	LCsf	Wendel 2 24p 80, Chamakh 29, Gouffran 89	14 168
	23	Olympiacos	W	1-0	CLr2	Ciani 45	29 773
Mar	7	Montpellier	D	1-1	L1	Chamakh 59	27 444
	10	Auxerre	L	1-2	L1	Tremoulinas 7	20 868
	13	Monaco	D	0-0	L1		9 535
	17	Olympiacos	W	2-1	CLr2	Gourcuff 5, Chamakh 88	31 004
	21	Lille	W	3-1	L1	Ciani 40, Jussie 65p, Gourcuff 78	32 952
	27	Marseille	L	1-3	LCf	Sane 85	72 749
	30	Lyon	L	1-3	CLqf	Chamakh 14	37 859
Apr	3	Nancy	L	1-2	L1	Cavenaghi 28	29 985
	7	Lyon	W	1-0	CLqf	Chamakh 45	31 962
	10	PSG	L	1-3	L1	Sane 80	42 127
	14	Le Mans	L	1-2	L1	Henrique 8	11 160
	17	Lyon	D	2-2	L1	Chamakh 26, Plasil 62	32 284
	24	Lorient	L	0-1	L1		15 708
	28	Val'ciennes	L	0-2	L1		11 740
May	2	Toulouse	W	1-0	L1	Ciani 17	28 496
	5	Nice	D	1-1	L1	Wendel 34	8 706
	8	Sochaux	W	2-0	L1	Wendel 65p, Tremoulinas 86	28 146
	15	Lens	L	3-4	L1	Wendel 2 41 80, OG 50	39 201

BORDEAUX LEAGUE APPEARANCES/GOALS 2009-10
Goalkeepers Cedric Carrasso 29 • Abdoulaye Keita 0+1 • Ulrich Rame 9+1
Defenders Matthieu Chalme 33/0 • Michael Ciani 29+1/2 • Henrique
BRA 11+2/1 • Franck Jurietti 2+1/0 • Diego Placente ARG 3/0 • Marc
Planus 26/1 • Ludovic Sane 14+3/1 • Benoit Tremoulinas 35/2
Midfield Alou Diarra 30/1 • Fernando BRA 20+9/1 •
Yoann Gourcuff 26+3/6 • Jaroslav Plasil CZE 27+7/2 • Gregory
Sertic 7+5/0 • Abdou Traore MLI 4+6/0 • Wendel BRA 25+6/11
Forwards David Bellion 6+14/3 • Fernando Cavenaghi ARG 14+16/3 •
Marouane Chamakh MAR 32+6/10 • Yoan Gouffran 22+10/5 •
Jussie BRA 13+17/4 • Henri Saivet 1+2/0
Coach Laurent Blanc

BOULOGNE 2009-10

Mon	Day	Opponent		Score	Comp	Scorers	Att
Aug	8	Rennes	L	0-3	L1		21 462
	16	Grenoble	W	2-1	L1	Thil 2 34 38	10 452
	22	St-Etienne	W	1-0	L1	Cuvillier 37	25 032
	29	Auxerre	D	0-0	L1		11 090
Sep	12	Val'ciennes	D	1-1	L1	Moreira 83	11 769
	19	Bordeaux	L	0-2	L1		13 178
	23	PSG	L	0-1	LCr3		5 809
	26	Montpellier	L	0-1	L1		13 190
Oct	4	Lille	L	2-3	L1	Dembele 33, Blayac 45	10 272
	17	Le Mans	D	1-1	L1	Robert 92+	7 912
	24	Monaco	L	1-3	L1	Blayac 66	13 686
	31	Nancy	L	1-2	L1	Cuvillier 16	12 149
Nov	7	Lorient	L	0-5	L1		9 145
	28	Toulouse	L	0-1	L1		27 430
Dec	2	PSG	L	2-5	L1	Ducatel 36, Ramare 82p	12 346
	6	Lens	W	2-1	L1	Karuru 40, OG 45	13 719
	12	Marseille	L	0-2	L1		47 575
	16	Lyon	L	0-2	L1		37 512
	23	Nice	D	2-2	L1	Perrinelle 58, Blayac 74	7 656
	9	Seclin	W	4-1	CFr9	Lecointe 7, Agouazi 14, Ramare 66p, Cuvillier 87	
Jan	13	Sochaux	D	0-0	L1		11 681
	16	Auxerre	D	0-0	L1		10 127
	20	Val'ciennes	L	0-2	L1		11 085
	27	Colmar	W	2-1	CFr10	Lorca 9, OG 45	3 300
	30	Bordeaux	D	0-0	L1		25 288
	6	Montpellier	L	0-2	L1		11 900
Feb	9	Guingamp	W	1-0	CFr11	Cuvillier 60	3 750
	13	Lille	L	1-3	L1	Edefemi 28	14 817
	20	Le Mans	L	1-3	L1	Yatabare 72	11 269
	27	Monaco	L	0-1	L1		5 926
	6	Lyon	D	0-0	L1		12 358
Mar	13	Nancy	W	3-1	L1	Agouazi 32, Moussilou 71, Cuvillier 77	17 045
	20	Lorient	W	2-0	L1	Marcq 14, OG 52	11 847
	23	Quevilly	L	1-3	CFqf	Agouazi 43	10 490
	28	PSG	L	0-3	L1		BCD
Apr	4	Toulouse	D	1-1	L1	Kapo 36	12 150
	10	Lens	L	0-3	L1		34 218
	17	Marseille	L	1-2	L1	Blayac 82	15 242
	24	Sochaux	W	3-0	L1	Thil 41, Yatabare 81, Blayac 91+	14 112
May	2	Nice	D	3-3	L1	Blayac 81, Kapo 89, Cuvillier 91+	11 694
	5	St-Etienne	L	0-1	L1		12 408
	8	Grenoble	L	0-2	L1		12 863
	15	Rennes	W	1-0	L1	Thil 20p	12 015

GRENOBLE 2009-10

Mon	Day	Opponent		Score	Comp	Scorers	Att
Aug	8	Marseille	L	0-2	L1		19 626
	16	Boulogne	L	1-2	L1	Ljuboja 46	10 452
	23	Lens	L	1-2	L1	Ljuboja 12	15 431
	29	St-Etienne	L	0-1	L1		25 321
Sep	12	Bordeaux	L	0-1	L1		28 211
	19	Rennes	L	0-4	L1		13 154
	22	Lorient	L	0-1	LCr3		7 202
	26	Auxerre	L	0-2	L1		8 631
Oct	3	Montpellier	L	2-3	L1	Ljuboja 47, Dieuze 92+	14 676
	17	Val'ciennes	L	0-2	L1		12 177
	24	Nancy	L	1-2	L1	Ljuboja 53	15 995
	31	Lille	L	0-2	L1		13 104
Nov	7	Monaco	D	0-0	L1		6 347
	21	Lyon	D	1-1	L1	Ljuboja 73	15 563
	28	Lorient	D	2-2	L1	Matsui 63, Juan 71	8 736
	6	Toulouse	W	1-0	L1	Dieuze 81	13 865
Dec	13	Sochaux	L	0-1	L1		10 606
	16	Le Mans	L	0-1	L1		8 020
	19	Nice	D	1-1	L1	Dieuze 75	13 623
	23	PSG	L	0-4	L1		32 548
	16	St-Etienne	L	1-2	L1	OG 42	13 677
	20	Bordeaux	L	1-3	L1	Batlles 45	13 336
Jan	23	Montpellier	W	3-2	CFr9	Matsui 45, Ljuboja 81, Akrour 104	
	26	Vannes	L	3-4	CFr10	Juan 77, Dieuze 82, Paillot 92+	1 723
	30	Rennes	L	0-4	L1		17 515
	6	Auxerre	W	5-0	L1	Ljuboja 8, Akrour 2 10 42, Matsui 2 36 53	12 849
Feb	13	Montpellier	L	0-1	L1		14 122
	20	Val'ciennes	L	0-1	L1		12 660
	27	Nancy	W	2-0	L1	Ravet 2 14 78	14 667
	7	Le Mans	D	1-1	L1	Akrour 2	12 828
	14	Lille	L	0-1	L1		14 000
Mar	20	Monaco	D	0-0	L1		12 949
	27	Lyon	L	0-2	L1		32 323
	3	Lorient	L	1-2	L1	Akrour 3	12 744
	10	Toulouse	L	0-4	L1		13 167
	17	Sochaux	D	2-2	L1	Ljuboja 55, Matsui 63	12 960
	24	Nice	L	1-2	L1	Akrour 23	8 399
Apr	27	PSG	W	4-0	L1	Batlles 26, Dieuze 44, Akrour 65, Ljuboja 68	12 386
May	5	Lens	D	1-1	L1	Courtois 45	32 686
	8	Boulogne	W	2-0	L1	Ljuboja 2 35 82	12 863
	15	Marseille	L	0-2	L1		55 808

BOULOGNE APPEARANCES/GOALS 2009-10

Goalkeepers Florian Bague 1 • Jean-Francois Bedenik 25 • Ibrahim Kone CIV 3 • Matthieu Valverde 9

Defenders Olubayo Adefemi NGA 11+2/1 • Habib Bellaid ALG 9/0 • Guillaume Borne 16+1/0 • Kevin Das Neves 8/0 • Bira Dembele 15+7/1 • Yoann Lachor 29/0 • Antony Lecointe 19+3/0 • Mame N'Diaye SEN 4/0 • Damien Perrinelle 8+3/1 • Nicolas Rabuel 23/0 • Bakary Soumare MLI 18+2/0

Midfield Laurent Agouazi 20+5/1 • Alexandre Cuvillier 28+6/4 • Frederic Da Rocha 18+12/0 • Guillaume Ducatel 19+8/1 • Olivier Kapo 15+1/2 • Ovidy Karuru ZIM 9+5/1 • Dorian Leveque 6/0 • Damien Marcq 33+1/1 • Johann Ramare 6+11/1 • Zargo Toure SEN 13+1/0

Forwards Jeremy Blayac 14+8/6 • Lakdar Boussaha 1+1/0 • Juan Lorca CHI 2+2/0 • Daniel Moreira 4+2/1 • Matt Moussilou 8+7/1 • Fabien Robert 3+13/1 • Gregory Thil 12+3/4 • Mustapha Yatabare MLI 9+8/2

Coach Laurent Guyot

GRENOBLE LEAGUE APPEARANCES/GOALS 2009-10

Goalkeepers Ronan Le Crom 15+1/0 • Brice Maubleu 2 • Jody Viviani 21

Defenders Jean Calve 20+4/0 • Bostjan Cesar SVN 25/0 • Hugo Cianci 2+6/0 • David Jemmali TUN 8/0 • Jimmy Mainfroi 10+4/0 • Francois Marque 5+1/0 • Sandy Paillot 16/0 • Zoran Rendulic SRB 5+4/0 • Martial Robin 14+3/0 • David Sauget 25+2/0 • Milijove Vitakic SRB 14+1/0

Midfield Laurent Batlles 33+1/2 • Mehdi Bourabia 0+2/0 • Laurent Courtois 23+4/1 • Nicolas Dieuze 27+5/4 • Sofiane Feghouli 4+1/0 • Jimmy Juan 11+7/1 • Laurant Macquet 6+1/0 • Daisuke Matsui JPN 25+4/4 • Alaixys Romao TOG 29/0 • Saphir Sliti Taider 1/0 • Jonathan Tinhan 0+6/0

Forwards Nassim Akrour ALG 26+12/6 • Pierre Boya CMR 10+7/0 • Sho Ito JPN 0+1/0 • Mustafa Kucukovic GER 0+4/0 • Danijel Ljuboja SRB 30+4/10 • Yoric Ravet 5+11/2 • Josip Tadic CRO 6+8/0

Coach Mehmed Bazdarevic BIH

LE MANS 2009–10

Month	Date	Opponent	Res	Score	Comp	Scorers	Att
Aug	8	Lyon	D	2-2	L1	Maiga [21], Coutadeur [59p]	10 391
	15	PSG	L	1-3	L1	Helstad [20]	30 558
	22	Nancy	W	2-1	L1	Helstad [44], Le Tallec [53]	8 492
	29	Lorient	L	0-1	L1		11 072
Sep	12	Marseille	L	1-2	L1	Maiga [61]	16 309
	20	Toulouse	L	0-2	L1		13 072
	23	Nimes	W	3-0	LCr3	Lamah [62], Sene [80], Cisse [93+]	7 331
	27	Lens	W	3-0	L1	Thomas 2[14 30], Le Tallec [62]	8 693
Oct	3	Sochaux	L	0-1	L1		10 985
	17	Boulogne	D	1-1	L1	Lamah [63]	7 912
	24	Bordeaux	L	0-3	L1		27 737
Nov	1	Nice	L	0-1	L1		8 993
	7	Auxerre	L	0-1	L1		7 996
	21	Rennes	L	1-2	L1	Lamah [56]	20 292
	29	St-Etienne	D	1-1	L1	Le Tallec [74]	9 799
Dec	5	Montpellier	L	1-2	L1	Le Tallec [62]	13 272
	12	Val'ciennes	W	2-1	L1	Corchia [28], Le Tallec [91+]	7 700
	16	Grenoble	W	1-0	L1	Helstad [8]	8 020
	20	Lille	L	0-3	L1		13 501
	23	Monaco	D	1-1	L1	Le Tallec [37]	8 661
Jan	9	Val'ciennes	W	1-0	CFr9	Le Tallec [24]	
	16	Lorient	L	0-3	L1		8 015
	20	Marseille	L	1-2	L1	Le Tallec [16]	44 907
	26	Bordeaux	L	2-3	LCr4	Le Tallec [5], Joao Paulo [38]	8 466
	30	Toulouse	W	3-1	L1	Ouali [70]	7 144
Feb	3	Sochaux	L	0-3	CFr10		
	6	Lens	L	1-2	L1	Maiga [83]	30 113
	13	Sochaux	D	0-0	L1		7 318
	20	Boulogne	W	3-1	L1	Dossevi [30], Cerdan [32], Maiga [95+]	11 269
	7	Grenoble	W	1-0	L1	Maiga [50]	12 828
Mar	13	Nice	L	0-1	L1		11 014
	20	Auxerre	L	1-2	L1	Helstad [91+]	10 159
	28	Rennes	L	1-3	L1	Dossevi [58]	7 749
Apr	3	St-Etienne	L	0-2	L1		26 540
	10	Montpellier	D	2-2	L1	Lamah 2[1 69]	9 821
	14	Bordeaux	W	2-1	L1	Le Tallec [17], Dossevi [45]	11 160
	17	Val'ciennes	W	1-0	L1	Corchia [93+]	12 362
	24	Lille	L	1-2	L1	Maiga [55]	10 301
	27	Monaco	D	1-1	L1	Dossevi [10]	5 358
May	5	Nancy	L	2-3	L1	Maiga [25], Dossevi [26]	15 015
	8	PSG	W	1-0	L1	OG [9]	8 582
	15	Lyon	L	0-2	L1		37 353

RACING CLUB LENS 2009–10

Month	Date	Opponent	Res	Score	Comp	Scorers	Att
Aug	9	Bordeaux	L	1-4	L1	Jemaa [40]	32 725
	15	Auxerre	W	2-0	L1	Monnet-Paquet [15], Boukari [60]	34 671
	23	Grenoble	W	2-1	L1	Eduardo [7], Boukari [70]	15 431
	29	Rennes	D	2-2	L1	Demont [21p], Jemaa [73]	33 810
Sep	12	Montpellier	L	0-1	L1		16 792
	20	Lille	D	1-1	L1	Boukari [57]	37 511
	23	Montpellier	W	4-3	LCr3	Maoulida [4], Sartre 2[76 103], Boukari [88p]	4 058
	27	Le Mans	L	0-3	L1		8 693
Oct	3	Lyon	L	0-2	L1		39 423
	18	Monaco	L	0-2	L1		7 603
	25	Toulouse	L	0-2	L1		32 576
	31	Lorient	D	1-1	L1	Eduardo [49]	32 741
Nov	7	Sochaux	W	2-1	L1	Sartre [38], Boukari [85]	13 578
	21	Nancy	W	2-1	L1	Jemaa [81], Monnet-Paquet [84]	31 189
	28	Marseille	W	1-0	L1	Eduardo [92+]	41 052
	6	Boulogne	L	1-2	L1	OG [22]	13 719
Dec	12	Nice	W	2-0	L1	Akale [19], Maoulida [36]	30 605
	16	PSG	D	1-1	L1	Maoulida [74]	36 257
	19	Val'ciennes	D	0-0	L1		13 720
	22	St-Etienne	W	1-0	L1	Eduardo [91+]	33 971
Jan	13	Lorient	L	1-2	LCr4	Eduardo [88p]	20 554
	16	Rennes	D	1-1	L1	Monnet-Paquet [64]	21 187
	20	Montpellier	L	0-1	L1		29 784
	23	Compeigne	W	1-0	CFr9	Maoulida [43]	
	30	Lille	L	0-1	L1		16 458
Feb	6	Le Mans	W	2-1	L1	Monnet-Paquet [30], Eduardo [49]	30 113
	10	Marseille	W	3-1	CFr10		27 044
	13	Lyon	L	0-1	L1		33 239
	17	Brest	W	2-1	CFr11	Hermach [31], Ramos [100]	14 062
	20	Monaco	W	3-0	L1	Jemaa [31], Roudet [43], Bedimo [52p]	33 493
	27	Toulouse	L	0-1	L1		14 626
Mar	6	PSG	D	1-1	L1	Roudet [68]	35 157
	13	Lorient	L	0-1	L1		11 650
	20	Sochaux	D	0-0	L1		33 354
	24	St-Etienne	W	3-1	CFqf	Eduardo [36], Yahia [75], Roudet [90]	22 191
	28	Nancy	L	1-5	L1	Jemaa [93+p]	16 231
	4	Marseille	L	0-1	L1		54 839
Apr	10	Boulogne	W	3-0	L1	Maoulida 3[33 50 66]	34 218
	13	Monaco	L	0-1	CFsf		10 382
	17	Nice	D	0-0	L1		8 969
	25	Val'ciennes	D	1-1	L1	Roudet [38]	34 182
	2	St-Etienne	W	4-1	L1	Akale [55], Jemaa [60], Maoulida 2[83 89]	32 684
May	5	Grenoble	D	1-1	L1	Maoulida [68]	32 686
	8	Auxerre	D	0-0	L1		18 080
	15	Bordeaux	W	4-3	L1	Maoulida 2[21 63], Sow [36], Jemaa [61p]	39 201

LE MANS APPEARANCES/GOALS 2009-10

Goalkeepers George Makaridze GEO 2 • Didier Ovono Ebang GAB 32 • Rodolphe Roche 4
Defenders Joao Paulo Andrade POR 18+2/0 • Ludovic Baal 35+3/0 • Saber Ben Frej TUN 0+1/0 • Samuel Bouhours 5/0 • Ibrahima Camara GUI 3/0 • Gregory Cerdan 30/0 • Sebastien Corchia 31+4/2 • Geder BRA 14/0 • Pierre Gibaud 0+1/0 • Cyriaque Louvion 17+2/0
Midfield Almen Abdi SUI 9+4/0 • Mathieu Coutadeur 4/1 • Mathieu Dossevi 19+12/5 • Estigarribia PAR 1+4/0 • Herold Goulon 22+4/0 • Alphousseyni Keita MLI 5+2/0 • Roland Lamah BEL 22+9/4 • Guy Landel GUI 0+1/0 • Guillaume Loriot 18+3/0 • Moussa Narry GHA 12/0 • Marcos Paulo BRA 3/0 • Badara Sene SEN 1+4/0 • Fredrik Stromstad NOR 0+3/0 • Frederic Thomas 30/2 • Mamadou Wague 1+1/0
Forwards Fousseyni Cisse 3+7/0 • Thorstein Helstad NOR 15+16/4 • Anthony Le Tallec 33+3/8 • Modibo Maiga MLI 23+9/7 • Idir Ouali 2+8/1 • Olivier Thomert 4/0
Coach Paulo Duarte POR • Arnaud Cormier (10/12/09)

LENS LEAGUE APPEARANCES/GOALS 2009-10

Goalkeepers Hamdi Kasraoui TUN 6 • Vedran Runje CRO 32
Defenders Christopher Aurier 5/0 • Henri Bedimo CMR 12+3/1 • Eric Chelle MLI 31/0 • Fabien Laurenti 3+2/0 • Marco Ramos POR 27+3/0 • Romain Sartre 12+6/1 • Alassane Toure 0+1/0 • Alaeddine Yahia TUN 34/0
Midfield Kanga Akale CIV 17+11/2 • Abdoulrazak Boukari TOG 20+7/4 • Yohan Demont 37/0 • Adil Hermach MAR 30+4/0 • Nenad Kovacevic SRB 24+2/0 • Dejan Milovanovic SRB 8+8/0 • Steven Joseph-Monrose 0+2/0 • Sebastien Roudet 28+2/3 • Samba Sowz MLI 22+9/1
Forwards Eduardo BRA 18+13/5 • Issam Jemaa TUN 18+11/7 • Toifilou Maoulida 11+13/10 • Kevin Monnet-Paquet 23+9/4
Coach Jean-Guy Wallemme

LILLE OSC 2009-10

	Date	Opponent	Res	Score	Comp	Scorers	Att
=	30	Sevojno	W	2-0	ELp3	Vittek 34, Hazard 39	3 000
Aug	6	Sevojno	W	2-0	ELp3	Cabaye 72, De Melo 85	15 056
	9	Lorient	L	1-2	L1	OG 66	14 710
	16	Marseille	L	0-1	L1		26 965
	23	Genk	W	2-1	ELpo	Dumont 40, Vittek 56	12 278
	23	Toulouse	D	1-1	L1	Vittek 44	14 354
	27	Genk	W	4-2	ELpo	De Melo 2 10 73, Dumont 59, Hazard 70	16 055
	30	PSG	L	0-3	L1		34 439
Sep	12	Sochaux	W	1-0	L1	Frau 70	13 043
	17	Valencia	D	1-1	ELgB	Gervinho 86	14 676
	20	Lens	D	1-1	L1	Rami 93+	37 511
	27	Nice	D	1-1	L1	Frau 89	13 529
Oct	1	Slavia	W	5-1	ELgB	OG 47, Frau 71, Gervinho 2 85 91+, Souquet 88	9 158
	4	Boulogne	W	3-2	L1	Gervinho 42, Frau 2 51 57	10 272
	17	Rennes	D	0-0	L1		14 409
	22	Genoa	W	3-0	ELgB	Obraniak 38, Vittek 63, Hazard 84	16 518
	25	Auxerre	L	2-3	L1	Gervinho 26, Frau 40	11 285
	31	Grenoble	W	2-0	L1	Cabaye 27, Gervinho 90	13 103
Nov	5	Genoa	L	2-3	ELgB	Frau 76, Gervinho 84	18 587
	8	Bordeaux	W	2-0	L1	Cabaye 70, Balmont 86p	16 233
	22	Montpellier	L	0-2	L1		14 376
	28	Val'ciennes	W	4-0	L1	Frau 42, Gervinho 2 52 61, Cabaye 87p	13 367
Dec	2	Valencia	L	1-3	ELgB	Chedjou 91+	26 193
	6	Lyon	W	4-3	L1	Frau 24, Gervinho 2 53 92+, Cabaye 70	14 206
	10	St-Etienne	W	4-0	L1	Frau 33, Cabaye 58p, Gervinho 72, Rami 82	13 592
	13	Monaco	W	4-0	L1	De Melo 2 39 55, Cabaye 71p, Aubameyang 86	6 323
	17	Slavia	W	3-1	ELgB	Cabaye 25, Gervinho 40, Obraniak 80	15 358
	20	Le Mans	W	3-0	L1	Chedjou 12, Gervinho 26, Hazard 27	13 501
	23	Nancy	W	4-0	L1	Hazard 42, Gervinho 2 51 72, Frau 60p	15 649
Jan	13	Rennes	W	3-1	LCr4	Rami 42, De Melo 96, Hazard 113	8 943
	16	PSG	W	3-1	L1	Obraniak 5, Balmont 52, Beria 68	15 340
	20	Sochaux	L	1-2	L1	Vittek 76	10 321
	23	Colmar	D	0-0	CFr9	L 9-10p	
	27	Marseille	L	1-2	LCqf	De Melo 5	19 217
	30	Lens	W	1-0	L1	Hazard 23	16 458
Feb	6	Nice	D	1-1	L1	De Melo 75	7 123
	13	Boulogne	W	3-1	L1	Obraniak 2 6 43, Rami 11	14 817
	18	Fenerbahçe	W	2-1	ELr2	Balmont 3, Frau 52	16 783
	21	Rennes	W	2-1	L1	Frau 10, Aubameyang 89	20 196
	25	Fenerbahçe	D	1-1	ELr2	Rami 85	38 740
	28	Auxerre	L	1-2	L1	Hazard 34	14 717
Mar	6	St-Etienne	D	1-1	L1	Dumont 22	22 463
	11	Liverpool	W	1-0	ELr3	Hazard 84	17 700
	14	Grenoble	W	1-0	L1	OG 46	14 000
	18	Liverpool	L	0-3	ELr3		38 139
	21	Bordeaux	L	1-3	L1	Hazard 24	32 952
	28	Montpellier	W	4-1	L1	Gervinho 17, Cabaye 54p, Frau 59, Toure 79	16 545
Apr	3	Val'ciennes	L	0-1	L1		12 127
	11	Lyon	D	1-1	L1	Frau 62	38 593
	18	Monaco	W	4-0	L1	Chedjou 14, Cabaye 2 45p 75, De Melo 91+	16 894
	24	Le Mans	W	2-1	L1	De Melo 13, Cabaye 77p	10 301
May	2	Nancy	W	3-1	L1	Cabaye 33, Gervinho 35, Frau 49	16 465
	5	Toulouse	W	2-0	L1	Cabaye 34, Obraniak 48	20 893
	8	Marseille	W	3-2	L1	Cabaye 28p, De Melo 81, Debuchy 94+	17 688
	15	Lorient	L	1-2	L1	Costa 33	16 337

LORIENT 2009-10

	Date	Opponent	Res	Score	Comp	Scorers	Att
Aug	9	Lille	W	2-1	L1	Gameiro 33, Vahirua 52	14 710
	15	Montpellier	D	2-2	L1	Gameiro 63, Koscielny 93+	10 167
	22	Monaco	L	0-2	L1		8 016
	29	Le Mans	W	1-0	L1	Vahirua 63	11 072
Sep	12	Lyon	L	0-1	L1		36 600
	19	Nancy	W	3-1	L1	Diarra 42, Gameiro 60, Monterrubio 93+p	9 601
	22	Grenoble	W	1-0	LCr3	Gameiro 71	7 202
	26	PSG	D	1-1	L1	Mvuemba 40	11 192
Oct	4	Toulouse	W	1-0	L1	Monterrubio 90p	25 435
	18	Nice	W	4-1	L1	Mvuemba 39, Vahirua 48, Diarra 77, Gameiro 89	10 562
	24	Sochaux	L	0-1	L1		11 379
	31	Lens	D	1-1	L1	Sosa 42	32 741
Nov	7	Boulogne	W	5-0	L1	Gameiro 2 33 48, Vahirua 2 45 58, Amalfitano 92+	9 145
	22	St-Etienne	W	2-0	L1	Vahirua 4, Sosa 17	24 851
	28	Grenoble	D	2-2	L1	OG 37, Gameiro 92+	8 736
Dec	5	Rennes	L	0-1	L1		24 459
	12	Auxerre	D	0-0	L1		9 091
	16	Marseille	L	1-2	L1	Vahirua 53p	11 625
	19	Bordeaux	L	1-4	L1	Gameiro 88	27 599
	23	Val'ciennes	W	3-2	L1	Amalfitano 2 24 46, Sosa 67	10 991
Jan	13	Lens	W	2-1	LCr4	Marchal 8, Amalfitano 29	20 554
	16	Le Mans	W	3-0	L1	Koscielny 23, Monterrubio 2 44 53	8 015
	20	Lyon	L	1-3	L1	Ducasse 28	15 790
	24	St-Etienne	L	1-4	CFr9	Penalba 84p	
	27	Lyon	W	1-0	LCqf	Gameiro 5	16 758
	30	Nancy	L	0-1	L1		13 878
Feb	6	PSG	W	3-0	L1	Vahirua 24p, Gameiro 26, Amalfitano 36	32 156
	14	Toulouse	D	1-1	L1	Gameiro 56	
	17	Bordeaux	L	1-4	LCsf	Koscielny 12	14 168
	20	Nice	L	0-1	L1		7 105
	27	Sochaux	W	1-0	L1	Diarra 34	13 081
Mar	7	Marseille	D	1-1	L1	Koscielny 65	48 290
	13	Lens	W	1-0	L1	Marchal 79	11 650
	20	Boulogne	L	0-2	L1		11 847
	28	St-Etienne	W	4-0	L1	Amalfitano 35, Gameiro 2 38 73, Dubarbier 48	12 378
Apr	3	Grenoble	W	2-1	L1	Gameiro 32, Fanchone 87	12 744
	10	Rennes	D	1-1	L1	Diarra 13	15 103
	17	Auxerre	L	1-4	L1	Gameiro 83	15 439
	24	Bordeaux	W	1-0	L1	Gameiro 57	15 708
May	2	Val'ciennes	D	0-0	L1		11 164
	9	Monaco	D	2-2	L1	Amalfitano 42, Gameiro 80	15 436
	8	Montpellier	L	1-2	L1	Bourillon 89	18 071
	15	Lille	W	2-1	L1	Gameiro 37, Jouffre 66	16 337

LILLE APPEARANCES/GOALS 2009-10

Goalkeepers Ludovic Butelle 10 • Mickael Landreau 28
Defenders Franck Beria 31+2/1 • Aurelien Chedjou CMR 28+3/2 • Mathieu Debuchy 30+1/1 • Emerson BRA 14+9/0 • Nicolas Plestan 5/0 • Adil Rami 34/3 • Ricardo Costa POR 9+1/1 • Jerry Vandam 1+7/0
Midfield Florent Balmont 35/2 • Yohan Cabaye 30+2/13 • Stephane Dumont 9+14/1 • Rio Mavuba 34+1/0 • Ludovic Obraniak POL 17+12/4 • Arnaud Souquet 1/0
Forwards Pierre Aubameyang GAB 4+10/2 • Pierre-Alain Frau 25+9/13 • Gervinho CIV 28+4/13 • Eden Hazard BEL 31+6/5 • Larsen Toure GUI 1+13/1 • Tulio BRA 9+11/6 • Robert Vittek SVK 4+8/2
Coach Rudi Garcia

LORIENT LEAGUE APPEARANCES/GOALS 2009-10

Goalkeepers Fabien Audard 35 • Lionel Cappone 3
Defenders Maxime Baca 12+3/0 • Gregory Bourillon 8+2/1 • Benjamin Genton 3+5/0 • Laurent Koscielny 35/3 • Arnaud Le Lan 17+3/0 • Sylvain Marchal 31/1 • Jeremy Morel 18+1/0 • Franco Sosa ARG 29/3
Midfield Morgan Amalfitano 37/6 • Maxime Barthelme 0+1/0 • Sigamary Diarra 33+5/4 • Pierre Ducasse 27+3/1 • Yann Jouffre 3+5/1 • Yazid Mansouri ALG 9+11/0 • Olivier Monterrubio 7+12/4 • Arnold Mvuemba 34+3/2 • Gabriel Penalba ARG 2+6/0 • Jonas Sakuwaha ZAM 1+13/0
Forwards Sebastian Dubarbier ARG 6+6/1 • James Fanchone 6+18/1 • Kevin Gameiro 34+1/17 • Marama Vahirua 28+4/8
Coach Christian Gourcuff

OLYMPIQUE LYONNAIS 2009–10

	Date	Opponent	Res	Score	Comp	Scorers	Att
	8	Le Mans	D	2-2	L1	Bodmer 28, Lisandro 90	10 391
	15	Val'ciennes	W	1-0	L1	Gomis 37	31 745
Aug	19	Anderlecht	W	5-1	CLpo	Pjanic 10, Lisandro 15p, Bastos 39, Gomis 2 42 63	37 902
	22	Auxerre	W	3-0	L1	Boumsong 31, Makoun 45, Pjanic 65	15 294
	25	Anderlecht	W	3-1	CLpo	Lisandro 3 26 32 41	16 096
	29	Nancy	W	3-1	L1	Gomis 38, Lisandro 51, Bastos 68	34 193
	12	Lorient	W	1-0	L1	Bastos 72	36 600
	16	Fiorentina	W	1-0	CLgE	Pjanic 76	37 169
Sep	20	PSG	D	1-1	L1	Gomis 85	44 778
	26	Toulouse	W	2-1	L1	Tafer 52, Gomis 71	34 031
	29	Debreceni	W	4-0	CLgE	Kallstrom 3, Pjanic 13, Govou 24, Gomis 51	41 600
	3	Lens	W	2-0	L1	Govou 7, Kallstrom 78	39 423
	17	Sochaux	L	0-2	L1		36 489
Oct	20	Liverpool	W	2-1	CLgE	Gonalons 72, Delgado 91+	41 562
	24	Nice	L	1-4	L1	Ederson 34	10 793
	31	St-Etienne	W	1-0	L1	Gomis 83	34 342
	4	Liverpool	D	1-1	CLgE	Lisandro 90	39 180
	8	Marseille	D	5-5	L1	Pjanic 3, Govou 14, Lisandro 2 80 83p, Bastos 91+	38 018
Nov	21	Grenoble	D	1-1	L1	Delgado 66	15 563
	24	Fiorentina	L	0-1	CLgE		34 301
	29	Rennes	D	1-1	L1	Lisandro 42	35 978
	6	Lille	L	3-4	L1	Lisandro 3 2 22p 35	14 206
	9	Debreceni	W	4-0	CLgE	Gomis 25, Bastos 45, Pjanic 59, Cissokho 76	36 884
Dec	13	Bordeaux	L	0-1	L1		36 887
	16	Boulogne	W	2-0	L1	Pjanic 72, Delgado 91+	37 512
	20	Monaco	D	1-1	L1	Bastos 22	10 620
	23	Montpellier	L	1-2	L1	Gomis 84	37 963
	9	Strasbourg	W	3-1	CFr9	Gomis 11, Bastos 2 14 72	
	13	Metz	W	3-0	LCr4	Toulalan 30, Lisandro 2 87 89	20 010
	16	Nancy	W	2-0	L1	Cris 79, Gonalons 87	16 097
Jan	20	Lorient	W	3-1	L1	Lisandro 63, Kallstrom 2 71 88	15 790
	23	Monaco	L	1-2	CFr10	Boumsong 45	
	27	Lorient	L	0-1	LCqf		16 758
	31	PSG	W	2-1	L1	Gomis 17p, Cris 81	34 157
	7	Toulouse	D	0-0	L1		21 218
	13	Lens	W	1-0	L1	Delgado 78	33 239
Feb	16	RealMadrid	W	1-0	CLr2	Makoun 47	40 327
	21	Sochaux	W	4-0	L1	Bastos 3 5 25 26, Lisandro 80	14 768
	27	Nice	W	2-0	L1	Lisandro 10, OG 92+	33 593
	6	Boulogne	D	0-0	L1		12 358
	10	RealMadrid	D	1-1	CLr2	Pjanic 75	71 569
Mar	13	St-Etienne	D	1-1	L1	Lisandro 79	36 199
	21	Marseille	L	1-2	L1	Gomis 80	52 557
	27	Grenoble	W	2-0	L1	Bastos 48, Delgado 90	32 323
	30	Bordeaux	W	3-1	CLqf	Lisandro 2 10 77p, Bastos 32	37 859
	3	Rennes	W	2-1	L1	Bastos 53, Lisandro 61	28 244
	7	Bordeaux	L	0-1	CLqf		31 962
Apr	11	Lille	D	1-1	L1	Cris 71	38 593
	17	Bordeaux	D	2-2	L1	Ederson 55, Cris 71	32 284
	21	Bayern	L	0-1	CLsf		66 000
	27	Bayern	L	0-3	CLsf		39 414
	2	Montpellier	W	1-0	L1	Bastos 72	25 767
	5	Auxerre	W	2-1	L1	Lisandro 45p, Pjanic 85	36 262
May	8	Val'ciennes	D	2-2	L1	Kallstrom 17, OG 92+	13 206
	12	Monaco	W	3-0	L1	Pjanic 28, Gomis 48, Lisandro 87	38 432
	15	Le Mans	W	2-0	L1	Gomis 45, Pjanic 68	37 353

OLYMPIQUE MARSEILLE 2009–10

	Date	Opponent	Res	Score	Comp	Scorers	Att
	8	Grenoble	W	2-0	L1	Niang 2, Cheyrou 81	19 622
Aug	16	Lille	W	1-0	L1	Brandao 11	26 965
	22	Rennes	D	1-1	L1	Niang 52	28 631
	30	Bordeaux	D	0-0	L1		55 920
	12	Le Mans	W	2-1	L1	Niang 14, Brandao 70	16 309
	15	Milan	L	1-2	CLgC	Heinze 49	55 434
Sep	19	Montpellier	W	4-2	L1	Lucho 31, Niang 34, Cisse 39, Diawara 50	52 351
	26	Val'ciennes	L	2-3	L1	Morientes 13, Niang 22	16 208
	30	RealMadrid	L	0-3	CLgC		67 244
	4	Monaco	L	1-2	L1	Niang 85	48 566
Oct	17	Nancy	W	3-0	L1	Valbuena 5, Brandao 79, Abriel 81	20 057
	21	Zürich	W	1-0	CLgC	Heinze 69	22 300
	31	Toulouse	D	1-1	L1	Brandao 75	53 340
	3	Zürich	W	6-1	CLgC	OG 3, Abriel 11, Niang 51, Hilton 80, Cheyrou 87, Brandao 90	56 282
Nov	8	Lyon	D	5-5	L1	Diawara 11, Cheyrou 44, Kone 47, Brandao 74, OG 92+	38 018
	20	PSG	W	1-0	L1	Heinze 25	55 623
	25	Milan	D	1-1	CLgC	Lucho 16	49 063
	28	Lens	L	0-1	L1		41 052
	5	Nice	W	3-1	L1	Niang 19, Lucho 77, Kone 86	15 047
	8	RealMadrid	L	1-3	CLgC	Lucho 11	55 722
Dec	12	Boulogne	W	2-0	L1	Heinze 48, Taiwo 54p	47 575
	16	Lorient	W	2-1	L1	Ayew 68, Diawara 92+	11 625
	19	St-Etienne	D	0-0	L1		27 614
	23	Auxerre	L	0-2	L1		49 966
	10	Trelissac	W	2-0	CFr9	Ben Arfa 16, Cheyrou 74	
	13	St-Etienne	W	3-2	LCr4	Brandao 2 29 59, Niang 94+	15 774
Jan	17	Bordeaux	D	1-1	L1	Cheyrou 81	32 771
	20	Le Mans	W	2-1	L1	Niang 2 30 56p	44 907
	27	Lille	W	2-1	LCqf	Lucho 10, Valbuena 82	19 217
	30	Montpellier	L	0-2	L1		29 051
	3	Toulouse	W	2-1	LCsf	Brandao 2 86 105	26 548
	7	Val'ciennes	W	5-1	L1	Lucho 33, Brandao 43, Cheyrou 53, Valbuena 77, Niang 91+	46 306
Feb	10	Lens	L	1-3	CFr10	Kabore 63	
	15	Monaco	W	2-1	L1	Niang 37, OG 89	13 063
	18	København	W	3-1	ELr2	Niang 72, Ben Arfa 84, Kabore 90	20 334
	21	Nancy	W	3-1	L1	Niang 3 10 34 67	47 975
	25	København	W	3-1	ELr2	Ben Arfa 43, Kone 2 62 78	27 195
	28	PSG	W	3-0	L1	Ben Arfa 15, Lucho 54, Cheyrou 71	43 813
	1	Lorient	D	1-1	L1	Niang 43	48 290
	11	Benfica	W	1-0	ELr3	Ben Arfa 90	46 635
Mar	14	Toulouse	D	1-1	L1	Brandao 30	27 249
	18	Benfica	L	1-2	ELr3	Niang 70	38 386
	21	Lyon	W	2-1	L1	Kabore 68, Taiwo 81	52 557
	27	Bordeaux	W	3-1	LCf	Diawara 61, Valbuena 68, OG 77	72 059
	4	Lens	W	1-0	L1	Brandao 22	54 839
	7	Sochaux	W	3-0	L1	Heinze 9, Ben Arfa 27p, Kone 91+	48 198
Apr	11	Nice	W	4-1	L1	Kone 42, Mbia 52, Valbuena 70, Diawara 74	51 229
	14	Sochaux	W	1-0	L1	Mbia 88	19 992
	17	Boulogne	W	2-1	L1	Valbuena 44, Taiwo 94+p	15 242
	25	St-Etienne	W	1-0	L1	Valbuena 6	56 056
	30	Auxerre	D	0-0	L1		20 005
May	5	Rennes	W	3-1	L1	Heinze 4, Niang 76, Lucho 78	55 377
	8	Lille	L	2-3	L1	Niang 6, Hilton 45	17 688
	15	Grenoble	W	2-0	L1	Niang 40, Ben Arfa 91+	55 808

LYON APPEARANCES/GOALS 2009-10

Goalkeepers Hugo Lloris 36 • Remy Vercoutre 2

Defenders Jean-Alain Boumsong 19/1 • Aly Cissokho 31/0 • Francois Clerc 5+2/0 • Cris BRA 34/4 • Lamine Gassama 5+1/0 • Fabio Grosso ITA 1/0 • Thimothee Kolodziejczak 1+1/0 • Dejan Lovren CRO 8/0 • Anthony Reveillere 29+1/0

Midfield Mathieu Bodmer 10+4/1 • Cesar Delgado ARG 13+14/4 • Ederson BRA 11+13/2 • Maxime Gonalons 12+3/1 • Clement Grenier 0+3/0 • Kim Kallstrom SWE 28+4/4 • Jean Makoun CMR 25+3/1 • Michel Bastos BRA 22+10/10 • Miralem Pjanic BIH 27+10/6 • Anthony Mounier 1/0 • Jeremy Toulalan 1/0

Forwards Ishak Belfodil 0+3/0 • Bafetimbi Gomis 22+15/10 • Sidney Govou 22+8/2 • Alexandre Lacazette 0+1/0 • Lisandro Lopez ARG 27+6/15 • Yannis Tafer 0+7/1

Coach Claude Puel

MARSEILLE LEAGUE APPEARANCES/GOALS 2009-10

Goalkeepers Elinton Andrade BRA 2+1 • Steve Mandanda 36

Defenders Garry Bocaly 3+1/0 • Laurent Bonnart 30+1/0 • Souleymane Diawara SEN 37/4 • Gabriel Heinze ARG 26+1/4 • Hilton BRA 9+3/1 • Pape M'Bow SEN 0+3/0 • Cyril Rool 1+1/0 • Taye Taiwo NGA 24+3/3

Midfield Fabrice Abriel 18+14/1 • Hatem Ben Arfa 17+12/3 • Benoit Cheyrou 27+5/5 • Edouard Cisse 27+5/1 • Lucho Gonzalez ARG 28+4/5 • Charles Kabore BFA 17+8/1 • Stephane Mbia CMR 26+1/2 • Matthieu Valbuena 19+12/5

Forwards Jordan Ayew 0+4/1 • Brandao BRA 27+3/8 • Bakari Kone CIV 11+16/4 • Morientes ESP 4+8/1 • Mamadou Niang SEN 29+3/18

Coach Didier Deschamps

MONACO 2009–10

Aug	8	Toulouse	W	1-0	L1	Nene [45]	11 260
	15	Nancy	L	0-4	L1		17 099
	22	Lorient	W	2-0	L1	Nimani [22], Nene [33]	8 016
	29	Sochaux	L	0-1	L1		13 141
Sep	13	PSG	W	2-0	L1	Park [85], Nene [88]	10 459
	19	Nice	W	3-1	L1	Nene [8p], Alonso 2 [12 71]	8 430
	23	Nancy	L	0-2	LCr3		15 020
	26	St-Etienne	L	1-2	L1	Puygrenier [56]	8 490
Oct	4	Marseille	W	2-1	L1	Nene [20], Park [42]	48 566
	18	Lens	W	2-0	L1	Nene 2 [9 67p]	7 603
	24	Boulogne	W	3-1	L1	Park [36], Nene 2 [86 92+]	13 686
	31	Bordeaux	L	0-1	L1		32 308
Nov	7	Grenoble	D	0-0	L1		6 347
	21	Auxerre	L	0-2	L1		14 951
Dec	5	Val'ciennes	L	1-3	L1	Nene [50p]	12 464
	13	Lille	L	0-4	L1		6 323
	16	Rennes	W	1-0	L1	Park [20]	5 555
	20	Lyon	D	1-1	L1	Park [35]	10 620
	23	Le Mans	D	1-1	L1	Park [50]	8 661
	9	Tours	D	0-0	CFr9	W 4-3p	
Jan	13	Montpellier	W	4-0	L1	Puygrenier [11], Haruna 2 [55 66], OG [87]	5 763
	16	Sochaux	W	2-0	L1	Nene 2 [84 91+]	5 640
	20	PSG	W	1-0	L1	OG [68]	32 603
	24	Lyon	W	2-1	CFr10	Nene [52p], Park [77]	4 818
	30	Nice	W	3-2	L1	Park 2 [19 60], Nene [62]	10 420
Feb	7	St-Etienne	L	0-3	L1		23 241
	10	Bordeaux	W	2-0	CFr11	Traore [28], Maazou [56]	14 062
	13	Marseille	L	1-2	L1	OG [40]	13 063
	20	Lens	L	0-3	L1		33 493
	27	Boulogne	W	1-0	L1	Maazou [41]	5 926
	6	Rennes	L	0-1	L1		23 177
Mar	13	Bordeaux	D	0-0	L1		9 535
	20	Grenoble	D	0-0	L1		12 949
	24	Sochaux	W	4-3	CFqf	Puygrenier [34], Haruna [38], Pino [93+], Maazou [95]	5 409
	29	Auxerre	D	0-0	L1		6 037
Apr	3	Montpellier	D	0-0	L1		19 675
	10	Val'ciennes	W	2-1	L1	Nene [61], Maazou [78]	6 685
	13	Lens	W	1-0	CFsf	Maazou [110]	10 382
	18	Lille	L	0-4	L1		16 894
	27	Le Mans	D	1-1	L1	Maazou [48]	5 385
May	1	PSG	L	0-1	CFf		75 000
	5	Lorient	D	2-2	L1	Haruna [41], Maazou [72]	15 436
	8	Nancy	W	2-1	L1	OG [7], Maazou [58]	6 878
	12	Lyon	L	0-3	L1		38 432
	15	Toulouse	D	0-0	L1		16 641

MONTPELLIER 2009–10

Aug	8	PSG	D	1-1	L1	Spahic [94+]	29 312
	15	Lorient	D	2-2	L1	Costa [60], Spahic [67]	10 167
	22	Sochaux	W	2-0	L1	Costa [61p], Ait-Fana [93+]	15 295
	29	Nice	W	3-0	L1	Dernis [4], Montano [49], Compan [77]	9 027
Sep	12	Lens	W	1-0	L1	Costa [39p]	16 792
	19	Marseille	L	2-4	L1	Belhanda [75], Camara [88]	52 351
	23	Lens	L	3-4	LCr3	Lacombe 2 [11 45], Ait-Fana [69]	4 058
	26	Boulogne	W	1-0	L1	Dzodic [78]	13 189
Oct	3	Grenoble	W	3-2	L1	Montano 3, Dzodic 2 [13 49]	14 676
	17	St-Etienne	W	2-1	L1	Ait-Fana [55], Camara [61]	22 953
	24	Rennes	L	0-3	L1		23 311
	31	Auxerre	L	0-2	L1		11 373
Nov	7	Val'ciennes	D	1-1	L1	Montano 3	12 633
	22	Lille	W	2-0	L1	Montano 2 [65 87]	14 376
Dec	5	Le Mans	W	2-1	L1	Ait-Fana [12], Compan [72]	13 272
	13	Toulouse	W	1-0	L1	Camara [11]	17 969
	16	Bordeaux	L	0-1	L1		26 366
	19	Nancy	L	0-2	L1		BCD
	23	Lyon	W	2-1	L1	Montano [53], Marveaux [86]	37 963
Jan	13	Monaco	L	0-4	L1		5 763
	16	Nice	W	1-0	L1	Camara [57]	12 958
	20	Lens	W	1-0	L1	Montano [86]	29 784
	23	Grenoble	L	2-3	CFr9	Montano [38p], Ait-Fana [83]	
	30	Marseille	W	2-0	L1	Ait-Fana [49], OG [76]	29 051
Feb	6	Boulogne	W	2-0	L1	Camara [27], Montano [92+]	11 900
	13	Grenoble	W	1-0	L1	Montano [28]	14 129
	20	St-Etienne	L	0-1	L1		24 117
	27	Rennes	W	3-1	L1	Marveaux 2 [25 36], Camara [82]	15 726
Mar	7	Bordeaux	D	1-1	L1	Costa [94+]	27 494
	13	Auxerre	D	1-1	L1	Costa [66]	19 320
	21	Val'ciennes	W	2-1	L1	Montano [5], Marveaux [58]	16 183
	28	Lille	L	1-4	L1	Camara [46]	16 545
Apr	3	Monaco	D	0-0	L1		19 675
	10	Le Mans	D	2-2	L1	Ait-Fana [13], Camara [34p]	9 821
	18	Toulouse	D	1-1	L1	Costa [32]	19 274
	24	Nancy	D	0-0	L1		16 361
May	2	Lyon	L	0-1	L1		25 767
	5	Sochaux	W	1-0	L1	Costa [72]	12 281
	8	Lorient	W	2-1	L1	Montana [29], Camara [43p]	18 071
	15	PSG	W	3-1	L1	Dernis 2 [16 58], Compan [47]	32 124

MONACO APPEARANCES/GOALS 2009-10
Goalkeepers Stephane Ruffier 37 • Yohann Thuram-Ulien 1
Defenders Adriano BRA 15+1/0 • Igor Lolo CIV 8+7/0 • Thomas
Mangani 10+4/0 • Francois Modesto 23+1/0 • Cedric Mongongu
COD 33/0 • Vincent Muratori 12+4/0 • Nicolas N'Koulou CMR 21+3/0 •
Sebastien Puygrenier 36/2 • Djimi Traore MLI 28+1/0
Midfield Alejandro Alonso ARG 27/2 • Mathieu Coutadeur 11+8/0 •
Eduardo Costa BRA 14+1/0 • Jean-Jacques Gosso CIV 7+1/0 • Lukman
Haruna NGA 16+3/3 • Jerko Leko CRO 0+4/0 • Yohan Mollo 7+11/0 •
Nene BRA 34/14 • Diego Perez URU 20+3/0
Forwards Djamel Bakar 4/0 • Serge Gakpe TOG 0+3/0 • Eidur Smari
Gudjohnsen ISL 6+3/0 • Moussa Maazou NIG 10+8/6 •
Frederic Nimani 2+6/1 • Chu Young Park KOR 26+1/8 •
Juan Pino COL 9+5/0 • Yannick Sagbo 1+14/0
Coach Guy Lacombe

MONTPELLIER LEAGUE APPEARANCES/GOALS 2009-10
Goalkeepers Geoffrey Jourdren 38
Defenders Mourad Benhamida 0+3/0 • Garry Bocaly 8+4/0 •
Xavier Collin 9+10/0 • Nenad Dzodic SRB 17/4 •
Abdelhamid El Kaoutari 20+5/0 • Cyril Jeunechamp 28/0 • Emir Spahic
BIH 34/2 • Mapou Yanga-Mbiwa 36/0
Midfield Younes Belhanda 19+14/1 • Tino Costa ARG 31/7 • Bryan
Dabo 0+1/0 • Philippe Delaye 3+1/0 • Geoffrey Dernis 9+6/3 • Gregory
Lacombe 2+6/0 • Joris Marveaux 31/4 • Romain Pitau 36/0 • Jamel
Saihi 7+19/0
Forwards Karim Ait Fana 24+9/5 • Souleymane Camara SEN 30+8/9 •
Lilian Compan 3+10/3 • Bengali-Fode Koita 0+6/0 • Victor Montano
COL 33+3/11
Coach Rene Girard

NANCY 2009–10

Month	Date	Opponent	Res	Score	Comp	Scorers	Att
Aug	8	Val'ciennes	W	3-1	L1	Feret 17, Brison 60, Traore 71p	11 777
Aug	15	Monaco	W	4-0	L1	Dia 31, Andre Luiz 42, Alo'o Efoulou 2 50 80	17 099
Aug	22	Le Mans	L	1-2	L1	Macaluso 94+	8 492
Aug	29	Lyon	L	1-3	L1	Hadji 57	34 193
Sep	12	Toulouse	D	0-0	L1		17 063
Sep	19	Lorient	L	1-3	L1	Alo'o Efoulou 91+	9 601
Sep	23	Monaco	W	2-0	LCr3	Feret 13, Dia 81	15 020
Sep	26	Sochaux	W	2-1	L1	Hadji 2 3 39p	15 329
Oct	3	PSG	D	1-1	L1	Hadji 14	36 779
Oct	17	Marseille	L	0-3	L1		20 057
Oct	24	Grenoble	W	2-1	L1	OG 74, Hadji 89p	15 995
Oct	31	Boulogne	W	2-1	L1	Dia 10, Hadji 82	12 149
Nov	7	St-Etienne	L	0-1	L1		16 076
Nov	21	Lens	L	1-2	L1	Alo'o Efoulou 53	31 189
Nov	29	Bordeaux	L	0-3	L1		18 223
Dec	6	Auxerre	W	3-1	L1	Andre Luiz 25, Ouaddou 51, Hadji 87	10 483
Dec	12	Rennes	L	1-2	L1	Feret 41	16 029
Dec	16	Nice	W	2-0	L1	Feret 50, Malonga 52	15 328
Dec	19	Montpellier	W	2-0	L1	Bakar 32, Berenguer 39	BCD
Dec	23	Lille	L	0-4	L1		15 649
Jan	13	Toulouse	L	0-3	LCr4		5 080
Jan	16	Lyon	L	0-2	L1		16 097
Jan	20	Toulouse	D	0-0	L1		13 937
Jan	24	Thiers	D	1-1	CFr9	Curbelo 66. W 3-2p	
Jan	27	Plabennec	L	0-2	CFr10		4 007
Jan	30	Lorient	W	1-0	L1	Hadji 41	13 878
Feb	6	Sochaux	D	1-1	L1	Dia 32	11 057
Feb	13	PSG	L	0-5	L1		15 650
Feb	21	Marseille	L	1-3	L1	Andre Luiz 13	47 975
Feb	27	Grenoble	L	0-2	L1		14 667
Mar	6	Nice	W	3-2	L1	Bakar 5, Brison 27, Dia 93+	7 504
Mar	13	Boulogne	L	1-3	L1	Malonga 41	17 045
Mar	20	St-Etienne	D	0-0	L1		26 177
Mar	28	Lens	W	5-1	L1	Dia 3 43 45 61, Hadji 59, Berenguer 68	16 231
Apr	3	Bordeaux	W	2-1	L1	Hadji 18, Dia 72	29 985
Apr	11	Auxerre	L	0-1	L1		17 041
Apr	17	Rennes	D	0-0	L1		25 215
Apr	24	Montpellier	D	0-0	L1		16 361
May	2	Lille	L	1-3	L1	Malonga 54	16 465
May	5	Nancy	W	3-2	L1	Feret 2 18 32, Malonga 62	15 015
May	8	Monaco	L	1-2	L1	Sami 75	6 878
May	15	Val'ciennes	D	1-1	L1	Hadji 39	17 103

OGC NICE 2009–10

Month	Date	Opponent	Res	Score	Comp	Scorers	Att
Aug	8	St-Etienne	W	2-0	L1	Traore 39, Remy 88	29 243
Aug	16	Rennes	D	1-1	L1	Ben Saada 44	12 824
Aug	23	Bordeaux	L	0-4	L1		32 065
Aug	29	Montpellier	L	0-3	L1		9 027
Sep	13	Auxerre	L	0-2	L1		8 776
Sep	19	Monaco	L	1-3	L1	Remy 42	8 430
Sep	23	St-Etienne	L	1-4	LCr3	Remy 85	13 636
Sep	27	Lille	D	1-1	L1	Remy 61	13 529
Oct	3	Val'ciennes	W	3-2	L1	Ben Saada 67, Echouafni 73, OG 76	9 443
Oct	18	Lorient	L	1-4	L1	Remy 62	10 562
Oct	24	Lyon	W	4-1	L1	Bagayoko 17, OG 40, Hellebuyck 69, Remy 74	10 793
Nov	1	Le Mans	W	1-0	L1	Gace 40	8 993
Nov	7	PSG	W	1-0	L1	Remy 88	36 300
Nov	22	Toulouse	W	1-0	L1	Remy 51p	9 485
Nov	28	Sochaux	L	0-1	L1		11 333
Dec	5	Marseille	L	1-3	L1	Coulibaly 33	15 047
Dec	12	Lens	L	0-2	L1		30 605
Dec	16	Nancy	L	0-2	L1		15 328
Dec	19	Grenoble	D	1-1	L1	Ben Saada 85	13 623
Dec	23	Boulogne	D	2-2	L1	Pote 2 67 86	7 656
Jan	2	Plabennec	L	1-2	CFr9	Remy 13	
Jan	16	Montpellier	L	0-1	L1		12 958
Jan	20	Auxerre	L	0-1	L1		7 001
Jan	30	Monaco	L	2-3	L1	Ben Saada 54, Digard 80	10 420
Feb	6	Lille	D	1-1	L1	De Melo 75	7 123
Feb	13	Val'ciennes	L	1-2	L1	Remy 75	10 224
Feb	20	Lorient	W	1-0	L1	Remy 57p	7 105
Feb	27	Lyon	L	0-2	L1		33 593
Mar	6	Nancy	L	2-3	L1	Civelli 7, Ben Saada 36	7 504
Mar	13	Le Mans	W	1-0	L1	Remy 76	11 014
Mar	20	PSG	W	1-0	L1	Remy 79	BCD
Mar	28	Toulouse	W	2-0	L1	Mounier 41, Mouloungui 84	16 253
Apr	3	Sochaux	D	0-0	L1		8 079
Apr	11	Marseille	L	1-4	L1	Fae 92+	51 229
Apr	17	Lens	D	0-0	L1		8 969
Apr	24	Grenoble	W	2-1	L1	Mouloungui 37, Fae 76	8 399
May	2	Boulogne	D	3-3	L1	Remy 2 32 57, Hellebuyck 62	11 694
May	5	Bordeaux	D	1-1	L1	Fae 27	8 706
May	8	Rennes	D	2-2	L1	Mounier 12, Fae 77	22 033
May	15	St-Etienne	D	1-1	L1	Remy 2	10 988

NANCY APPEARANCES/GOALS 2009-10
Goalkeepers Gennaro Bracigliano 32 • Damien Gregorini 6
Defenders Andre Luiz BRA 31+1/3 • Michael Chretien MAR 18+2/0 • Reynald Lemaitre 22+3/0 • Jordan Loties 19+3/0 • Damian Macaluso URU 11+1/1 • Florian Marange 12+4/0 • Abdeslam Ouaddou MAR 20+1/1 • Joel Sami COD 19+4/1
Midfield Floyd Ayite TOG 4+2/0 • Pascal Berenguer 29+1/2 • Jonathan Brison 23+3/2 • Bocundii Ca GNB 10+7/0 • Aatif Chahechouhe 0+2/0 • Samba Diakite 2+1/0 • Julien Feret 35+2/5 • Benjamin Gavanon 0+2/0 • Youssouf Hadji MAR 24+2/11 • Cris Malonga 17+8/4 • Alfred N'Diaye 17+6/0 • Bakaye Traore MLI 13+9/1
Forwards Paul Alo'o Efoulou CMR 13+10/4 • Djamel Bakar 13+19/2 • Issdia Dia 28+5/8 • Cheick Diabate MLI 0+2/0
Coach Manager Pablo Correa

NICE LEAGUE APPEARANCES/GOALS 2009-10
Goalkeepers Lionel Letizi 1+1 • Jeremie Moreau 0+1 • David Ospina COL 37
Defenders Onyekachi Apam NGA 23/0 • Julien Berthomier 0+1/0 • Alain Cantareil 5+5/0 • Gerald Cid 10+3/0 • Renato Civelli ARG 17/1 • Drissa Diakite MLI 28+3/0 • Ismael Gace 19+1/1 • Larrys Mabiala COD 19/0 • Gregory Paisley 28+1
Midfield Chaouki Ben Saada TUN 18+10/6 • Kafoumba Coulibaly CIV 24+3/1 • Didier Digard 11+1/1 • Olivier Echouafni 13+7/1 • Emerse Fae CIV 26+3/4 • David Hellebuyck 27+2/2 • Anthony Mounier 23+7/2 • Julien Sable 19+4/0 • Mahamane Traore MLI 7+9/1
Forwards Mamadou Bagayoko MLI 18+5/1 • Habib Bamogo BFA 2+11/0 • Eric Mouloungui GAB 5+12/2 • Mickael Pote BEN 5+7/2 • Abeiku Quansah GHA 0+2/0 • Loic Remy 33+1/14
Coach Didier Olle-Nicolle • Eric Roy (9/03/10)

PARIS SAINT-GERMAIN 2009–10

	Date	Opponent	Res	Score	Comp	Scorers	Att
Aug	8	Montpellier	D	1-1	L1	Giuly 71	29 312
	15	Le Mans	W	3-1	L1	Erding 33, OG 59, Giuly 81	30 558
	22	Val'ciennes	W	3-2	L1	Luyindula 35, Erding 56, Jallet 84	12 927
	30	Lille	W	3-0	L1	Clement 28, Luyindula 78, Jallet 91+	34 439
Sep	13	Monaco	L	0-2	L1		10 459
	20	Lyon	D	1-1	L1	Giuly 29	44 778
	23	Boulogne	W	1-0	LCr3	Maurice 60	5 809
	26	Lorient	D	1-1	L1	Hoarau 45	11 192
Oct	3	Nancy	D	1-1	L1	Sessegnon 18	36 779
	18	Toulouse	L	0-1	L1		23 754
	1	Sochaux	W	4-1	L1	Clement 35, Chantome 56, Erding 75, Luyindula 87	16 405
Nov	7	Nice	L	0-1	L1		36 300
	20	Marseille	L	0-1	L1		55 623
	28	Auxerre	W	1-0	L1	Clement 66	34 849
	2	Boulogne	W	5-2	L1	Chantome 60, Luyindula 63p, Erding 2 67 69, Maurice 86	12 346
	5	Bordeaux	L	0-1	L1		32 826
Dec	13	St-Etienne	W	3-0	L1	Luyindula 11, Sessegnon 13, Erding 39	38 462
	16	Lens	D	1-1	L1	Makelele 70	36 257
	19	Rennes	L	0-1	L1		26 621
	23	Grenoble	W	4-0	L1	Luyindula 9, Armand 18, Erding 65, Jallet 80	32 548
	10	Aubervilliers	W	5-0	CFr9	Luyindula 2 10 38, Erding 23, Chantome 65, Maurice 81p	
	13	Guingamp	L	0-1	LCr4		5 898
Jan	16	Lille	L	1-3	L1	Erding 83	15 340
	20	Monaco	L	0-1	L1		32 603
	24	Evian	W	3-1	CFr10	Erding 2 15 60, Hoarau 94+	15 000
	31	Lyon	L	1-2	L1	Erding 10	34 157
	6	Lorient	L	0-3	L1		32 156
	9	Vesoul	W	1-0	CFr11	Giuly 15	6 000
Feb	13	Nancy	D	0-0	L1		15 650
	20	Toulouse	W	1-0	L1	Hoarau 24p	32 544
	28	Marseille	L	0-3	L1		43 813
	6	Lens	D	1-1	L1	Sessegnon 94+	35 157
	13	Sochaux	W	4-1	L1	Hoarau 17, Erding 3 18 35 70	29 249
Mar	20	Nice	L	0-1	L1		BCD
	23	Auxerre	D	0-0	CFqf	W 6-5p	BCD
	28	Boulogne	W	3-0	L1	OG 27, Hoarau 35p, Kezman 80	BCD
	4	Auxerre	D	1-1	L1	Sankhare 16	16 153
	10	Bordeaux	W	3-1	L1	Armand 35, Erding 74, Hoarau 86	42 127
Apr	14	Quevilly	W	1-0	CFsf	Erding 51	20 523
	18	St-Etienne	D	0-0	L1		26 493
	24	Rennes	D	1-1	L1	Hoarau 64	32 596
	27	Grenoble	L	0-4	L1		12 386
	1	Monaco	W	1-0	CFf	Hoarau 105	75 000
May	5	Val'ciennes	D	2-2	L1	Erding 30, Kezman 90	29 873
	8	Le Mans	L	0-1	L1		8 582
	15	Montpellier	L	1-3	L1	Erding 79	32 124

STADE RENNAIS 2009–10

	Date	Opponent	Res	Score	Comp	Scorers	Att
Aug	8	Boulogne	W	3-0	L1	Bangoura 7, Mangane 45, Leroy 91+	21 462
	16	Nice	D	1-1	L1	Gyan 45p	12 824
	22	Marseille	D	1-1	L1	Leroy 37p	28 631
	29	Lens	D	2-2	L1	Bangoura 4, Gyan 91+	33 810
Sep	13	St-Etienne	W	1-0	L1	Marveaux 62	22 009
	19	Grenoble	W	4-0	L1	Gyan 2 1 61p, Marveaux 7, Mangane 20	13 154
	23	Sochaux	W	2-1	LCr3	Danze 74, Mangane 84	9 317
	27	Bordeaux	L	0-1	L1		26 811
Oct	3	Auxerre	L	0-1	L1		20 378
	17	Lille	D	0-0	L1		14 409
	24	Montpellier	W	3-0	L1	Marveaux 34, Sow 50, Gyan 94+	23 311
	1	Val'ciennes	L	0-3	L1		21 675
Nov	8	Toulouse	L	2-3	L1	Gyan 44, Mangane 84	15 405
	21	Le Mans	W	2-1	L1	Mangane 10, Gyan 81	20 292
	29	Lyon	D	1-1	L1	Gyan 14	35 978
	5	Lorient	W	1-0	L1	Sow 3	24 459
Dec	12	Nancy	W	2-1	L1	OG 49, Marveaux 70	16 029
	16	Monaco	L	0-1	L1		5 555
	19	PSG	W	1-0	L1	Bangoura 40	26 621
	23	Sochaux	L	0-2	L1		10 581
	9	Caen	W	2-0	CFr9	Briand 69, Bangoura 78	
	13	Lille	L	1-3	LCr4	Pagis 59	8 943
Jan	16	Lens	D	1-1	L1	Sow 55	21 187
	19	St-Etienne	D	0-0	L1		21 579
	22	Samur	W	4-0	CFr10	Marveaux 2 40 88, Sow 2 84 92+p	8 000
	30	Grenoble	W	4-0	L1	Danze 3, Marveaux 2 41 47, Bangoura 57	17 515
	6	Bordeaux	W	4-2	L1	Marveaux 3, Briand 17p, Bangoura 48, Gyan 78	28 006
Feb	9	Quevilly	L	0-1	CFr11		12 000
	14	Auxerre	L	0-1	L1		8 689
	21	Lille	L	1-2	L1	Leroy 26	20 196
	27	Montpellier	L	1-3	L1	Briand 70	15 726
	6	Monaco	W	1-0	L1	Bocanegra 28	23 177
Mar	14	Val'ciennes	W	2-0	L1	Marveaux 27, Gyan 39	11 116
	20	Toulouse	W	4-1	L1	Hansson 31, Gyan 2 35 46, Ekoko 91+	18 865
	28	Le Mans	W	3-1	L1	Bangoura 51p, Briand 2 74 86	7 749
	3	Lyon	L	1-2	L1	Gyan 15	28 244
Apr	10	Lorient	D	1-1	L1	Danze 42	15 103
	17	Nancy	D	0-0	L1		25 215
	24	PSG	D	1-1	L1	Leroy 32	32 596
	2	Sochaux	L	1-2	L1	Marveaux 83p	17 265
May	5	Marseille	L	1-3	L1	Briand 38	55 377
	8	Nice	D	2-2	L1	Leroy 60, Marveaux 66	22 033
	15	Boulogne	L	0-1	L1		12 015

PSG APPEARANCES/GOALS 2009-10

Goalkeepers Gregory Coupet 16 • Apoula Edel ARM 22+1/0
Defenders Sylvain Armand 33/2 • Gregory Bourillon 2+4/0 • Zoumana Camara 22+1/0 • Ceara BRA 26+3/0 • Christophe Jallet 24+11/3 • Tripy Makonda 1/0 • Mamadou Sakho 32/0 • Sammy Traore MLI 22+1/0
Midfield Clement Chantome 11+13/2 • Jeremy Clement 33+1/3 • Claude Makelele 31/1 • Granddi Ngoyi 8+8/0 • Younousse Sankhare 7+15/1 • Stephane Sessegnon BEN 27+2/3
Forwards Mevlut Erdinc TUR 30+1/15 • Ludovic Giuly 25+6/3 • Guillaume Hoarau 17+5/6 • Mateja Kezman SRB 3+10/2 • Peguy Luyindula 23+5/6 • Jean-Eudes Maurice 3+20/1
Coach Antoine Kombouare

RENNES LEAGUE APPEARANCES/GOALS 2009-10

Goalkeepers Abdoulaye Diallo 1 • Nicolas Douchez 37
Defenders Lucien Aubey 3/0 • Carlos Bocanegra USA 24+2/1 • Rod Fanni 38/0 • Petter Hansson SWE 34/1 • Kader Mangane SEN 34/4 • Kevin Theophile-Catherine 1+1/0
Midfield Bruno Cheyrou 5+3/0 • Romain Danze 19+13/2 • Tongo Doumbia 0+3/0 • Junichi Inamoto JPN 3+2/0 • Fabien Lemoine 28+3/0 • Jerome Leroy 26+6/5 • Yann M'Vila 33+2/0 • Sylvain Marveaux 33+2/10 • Alexander Tettey NOR 20+4/0
Forwards Ismael Bangoura GUI 21+14/6 • Jimmy Briand 17+6/5 • Asamoah Gyan GHA 27+2/13 • Jires Kembo-Ekoko 4+20/1 • Mickael Pagis 0+3/0 • Moussa Sow 9+15/3 • Olivier Thomert 1+1/0
Coach Frederic Antonetti

SAINT-ETIENNE 2009–10

Month	Date	Opponent	Res	Score	Comp	Scorers	Att
Aug	8	Nice	L	0-2	L1		29 243
	15	Toulouse	L	1-3	L1	Riviere 25	21 202
	22	Boulogne	L	0-1	L1		25 032
	29	Grenoble	W	1-0	L1	Landrin 23	25 321
Sep	13	Rennes	L	0-1	L1		22 009
	19	Auxerre	D	1-1	L1	Bergessio 13	24 309
	23	Nice	W	4-1	LCr3	Bergessio 2 23 80, Sanogo 27, Landrin 37	13 636
	26	Monaco	W	2-1	L1	Sanogo 3, Bergessio 92+	8 490
Oct	3	Bordeaux	W	3-1	L1	Augusto 8, Ilan 29, Payet 94+	30 049
	17	Montpellier	L	1-2	L1	Bergessio 71p	22 953
	24	Val'ciennes	L	0-2	L1		27 621
	31	Lyon	L	0-1	L1		34 342
Nov	7	Nancy	W	1-0	L1	Payet 71	16 076
	22	Lorient	L	0-2	L1		24 851
	29	Le Mans	D	1-1	L1	Ilan 18	9 799
Dec	5	Sochaux	D	0-0	L1		21 518
	10	Lille	L	0-4	L1		13 592
	13	PSG	L	0-3	L1		38 462
	19	Marseille	D	0-0	L1		27 614
	22	Lens	L	0-1	L1		33 971
Jan	3	Marseille	L	2-3	LCr4	Sako 18, Bergessio 31	15 774
	16	Grenoble	W	2-1	L1	Perrin 31, Riviere 40	13 677
	19	Rennes	D	0-0	L1		21 579
	24	Lorient	W	4-1	CFr9	Riviere 10, Payet 2 21 74, Sako 40	
	31	Auxerre	L	0-1	L1		11 670
	3	Villefranche	D	2-2	CFr10	Bergessio 10, Sako 86, W 3-1p	3 000
Feb	7	Monaco	W	3-0	L1	Matuidi 14, Bergessio 74, Riviere 92+	23 241
	10	Vannes	W	2-0	CFr11	Payet 79, Riviere 92+	9 426
	14	Bordeaux	L	1-3	L1	Sako 45	30 084
	20	Montpellier	W	1-0	L1	Riviere 79	24 117
	27	Val'ciennes	L	0-1	L1		12 197
Mar	6	Lille	D	1-1	L1	Riviere 18	22 463
	13	Lyon	D	1-1	L1	Riviere 39	36 199
	20	Nancy	D	0-0	L1		26 177
	24	Lens	L	1-3	CFqf	Mirallas 1	22 191
	28	Lorient	L	0-4	L1		12 378
Apr	3	Le Mans	W	2-0	L1	Varrault 55, Benalouane 76	26 540
	10	Sochaux	W	2-0	L1	Perrin 42, Bergessio 64	14 711
	18	PSG	D	0-0	L1		26 493
	25	Marseille	L	0-1	L1		56 056
May	2	Lens	L	1-4	L1	Diakhate 44	32 684
	5	Boulogne	W	1-0	L1	Riviere 87	12 408
	8	Toulouse	L	0-1	L1		27 103
	15	Nice	D	1-1	L1	Riviere 67	10 988

SOCHAUX 2009–10

Month	Date	Opponent	Res	Score	Comp	Scorers	Att
Aug	8	Auxerre	W	1-0	L1	Sverkos 40	12 562
	15	Bordeaux	L	2-3	L1	Davies 2 62 92+	16 689
	22	Montpellier	L	0-2	L1		15 295
	29	Monaco	W	1-0	L1	Sverkos 20p	13 141
Sep	12	Lille	L	0-1	L1		13 043
	19	Val'ciennes	L	2-5	L1	Brechet 3, Boudebouz 40	11 880
	23	Rennes	L	1-2	LCr3	Boudebouz 68	9 317
	26	Nancy	L	1-2	L1	Martin 82	15 329
Oct	3	Le Mans	W	1-0	L1	Martin 79	10 985
	17	Lyon	W	2-0	L1	Faty 17, Privat 89	36 489
	24	Lorient	W	1-0	L1	Perquis 8	11 379
	1	PSG	L	1-4	L1	Dalmat 86	16 405
Nov	7	Lens	L	1-2	L1	Privat 94+	13 578
	28	Nice	W	1-0	L1	Mikari 29	11 333
Dec	5	St-Etienne	D	0-0	L1		21 518
	10	Toulouse	L	0-2	L1		12 152
	13	Grenoble	W	1-0	L1	Mikari 29	10 606
	23	Rennes	W	2-0	L1	Dalmat 45, Butin 61	10 581
	13	Boulogne	D	0-0	L1		11 681
	16	Monaco	L	0-2	L1		5 640
Jan	20	Lille	W	2-1	L1	Perquis 8, Dalmat 11	10 321
	23	St-Louis N	W	1-0	CFr9	Privat 31	
	31	Val'ciennes	D	1-1	L1	Perquis 54	10 265
	3	Le Mans	W	3-0	CFr10	Boudebouz 36, Ideye 2 56 71	3 009
	6	Nancy	D	1-1	L1	Dalmat 52	11 057
Feb	9	Beauvais	W	4-1	CFr11	Martin 2 14 29, Boudebouz 56p, Mikari 84	3 932
	13	Le Mans	D	0-0	L1		7 318
	21	Lyon	L	0-4	L1		14 768
	27	Lorient	L	0-1	L1		13 081
Mar	6	Toulouse	W	1-0	L1	Boudebouz 84	14 055
	13	PSG	L	1-4	L1	Boudebouz 64p	29 249
	20	Lens	D	0-0	L1		33 354
	24	Monaco	L	3-4	CFqf	Boudebouz 29, Dalmat 48, Ideye 71	5 409
	3	Nice	D	0-0	L1		8 079
	7	Marseille	L	0-3	L1		48 198
Apr	10	St-Etienne	L	0-2	L1		14 711
	14	Marseille	L	0-1	L1		19 992
	17	Grenoble	D	2-2	L1	Ideye 27, Brechet 74	12 960
	24	Boulogne	L	0-3	L1		14 112
May	2	Rennes	W	2-1	L1	OG 27, Gavanon 80	17 265
	5	Montpellier	L	0-1	L1		12 281
	8	Bordeaux	L	0-2	L1		28 146
	15	Auxerre	L	1-2	L1	Ideye 47	14 971

SAINT-ETIENNE APPEARANCES/GOALS 2009-10

Goalkeepers Jeremy Janot 38
Defenders Yoann Andreu 8+4/0 • Mustapha Bayal SEN 8+1/0 • Yohan Benalouane 27+2/1 • Mouhamadou Dabo 23+2/0 • Pape Diakhate SEN 18/1 • Helton Dos Reis 2+2/0 • Sylvain Monsoreau 3+5/0 • Efstathios Tavlaridis GRE 6/0 • Cedric Varrault 23/1
Midfield Gelson Fernandes SUI 29+4/0 • Augusto Fernandez ARG 8+4/1 • Josua Guilavogui 1+1/0 • Yohan Hautcoeur 5+4/0 • Christophe Landrin 15+3/1 • Boubacar Mansaly SEN 1/0 • Blaise Matuidi 35+1/1 • Kevin Mirallas BEL 14+9/0 • Guirane N'Daw SEN 29+5/0 • Dimitri Payet 25+10/2 • Loic Perrin 15+3/2 • Bakary Sako 17+13/1
Forwards Gonzalo Bergessio ARG 26+5/5 • Malick Faye SEN 0+4/0 • David Gigliotti 0+1/0 • Ilan BRA 9+3/2 • Emmanuel Riviere 19+11/8 • Boubacar Sanogo CIV 14+3/1
Coach Alain Perrin • Christophe Galtier (15/12/09)

SOCHAUX LEAGUE APPEARANCES/GOALS 2009-10

Goalkeepers Mathieu Dreyer 7+1 • Teddy Richert 31
Defenders Jeremie Brechet 33/2 • Boukary Drame SEN 22+1/0 • Frederic Duplus 8+2/0 • Jacques Faty 33/1 • Bojan Jokic SVN 5+1/0 • Maxime Josse 3+4/0 • Yassin Mikari TUN 29+1/2 • Damien Perquis 34/3 • Mathieu Peybernes 0+1/0 • Ivan Stevanovic SRB 5+1/0
Midfield Ryad Boudebouz ALG 20+11/3 • Carlao BRA 9+7/0 • Stephane Dalmat 29/4 • Benjamin Gavanon 19+8/1 • Serdar Gurler TUR 0+1/0 • Marvin Martin 34+2/2 • Nicolas Maurice-Belay 34+3/0 • Vincent Nogueira 8+5/0 • Loic Poujol 8+8/0 • Rafael Dias 0+2/0 • Geoffrey Tulasne 0+4/0
Forwards Ideye Brown NGA 17/2 • Edouard Butin 4+18/1 • Charlie Davies USA 6+2/2 • Sloan Privat 1+13/2 • Vaclav Sverkos CZE 19+6/2
Coach Francis Gillot

TOULOUSE 2009–10

Month	Date	Opponent		Score	Comp.	Scorers	Att.
Aug	8	Monaco	L	0-1	L1		11 260
	15	St-Etienne	W	3-1	L1	Machado 10, Gignac 67, Sissoko 81	21 202
	20	Trabzonspor	W	3-1	ELpo	Gignac 2 12 59, Mansare 91+	21 757
	23	Lille	D	1-1	L1	Mbengue 74	14 354
	27	Trabzonspor	L	0-1	ELpo		15 535
	30	Val'ciennes	L	0-1	L1		15 029
Sep	12	Nancy	D	0-0	L1		17 063
	17	Partizan	W	3-2	ELgJ	Sirieix 2 30 38, Devaux 49	13 860
	20	Le Mans	W	2-0	L1	Didot 26, Sissoko 69	13 072
	26	Lyon	L	1-2	L1	Sissoko 8	34 031
Oct	1	ClubBrugge	D	2-2	ELgJ	Gignac 84, Perisic 94+	12 275
	4	Lorient	L	0-1	L1		25 435
	18	PSG	W	1-0	L1	Ebondo 74	23 754
	22	Shakhtar	L	0-4	ELgJ		50 217
	25	Lens	W	2-0	L1	Sissoko 35, Gignac 57	32 576
	31	Marseille	D	1-1	L1	Sissoko 27	53 340
Nov	5	Shakhtar	L	0-2	ELgJ		12 046
	8	Rennes	W	3-2	L1	Sissoko 31, Braaten 59, Gignac 63	15 405
	22	Nice	L	0-1	L1		9 485
	28	Boulogne	W	1-0	L1	Fofana 30	27 430
Dec	3	Partizan	W	1-0	ELgJ	Braaten 54	11 123
	6	Grenoble	L	0-1	L1		13 865
	10	Sochaux	W	2-0	L1	Gignac 2 49 51	12 152
	13	Montpellier	L	0-1	L1		17 969
	16	ClubBrugge	L	0-1	ELgJ		23 668
	20	Auxerre	D	1-1	L1	Luan 21	6 677
	22	Bordeaux	L	1-2	L1	Machado 4	28 352
Jan	9	LesHerbiers	W	1-0	CFr9	Machado 10	
	13	Nancy	W	3-0	LCr4	OG 33, Machado 45, Dupuis 48	5 080
	16	Val'ciennes	W	3-1	L1	Tabanou 2 16 84, Sissoko 87	10 249
	20	Nancy	D	0-0	L1		13 937
	27	Guingamp	W	1-0	LCqf	Ebondo 54	6 494
	30	Le Mans	W	3-1	L1	Machado 52, Gignac 62, Kazim-Richards 85	7 144
Feb	3	Marseille	L	1-2	LCsf	Gignac 60	26 548
	7	Lyon	D	0-0	L1		21 218
	2	Brest	L	0-2	CFr10		5 078
	14	Lorient	D	1-1	L1	Braaten 78	BCD
	20	PSG	L	0-1	L1		32 544
	27	Lens	W	1-0	L1	Dupuis 57	14 626
Mar	6	Sochaux	L	0-1	L1		14 055
	14	Marseille	D	1-1	L1	Machado 40	27 249
	21	Rennes	L	1-4	L1	Braaten 51	18 865
	28	Nice	L	0-2	L1		16 253
Apr	4	Boulogne	D	1-1	L1	Braaten 88	12 150
	10	Grenoble	W	4-0	L1	Machado 9, Tabanou 2 65 75, Gignac 85	13 167
	18	Montpellier	D	1-1	L1	Kazim-Richards 91+	19 274
	25	Auxerre	L	0-3	L1		21 561
May	2	Bordeaux	L	0-1	L1		28 496
	5	Lille	L	0-2	L1		20 893
	8	St-Etienne	W	1-0	L1	Gignac 62	27 103
	15	Monaco	D	0-0	L1		16 641

VALENCIENNES 2009–10

Month	Date	Opponent		Score	Comp.	Scorers	Att.
Aug	8	Nancy	L	1-3	L1	Samassa 6	11 777
	15	Lyon	L	0-1	L1		31 745
	22	PSG	L	2-3	L1	Tiene 59, Mater 91+	12 927
	30	Toulouse	W	1-0	L1	Samassa 87	15 029
Sep	12	Boulogne	D	1-1	L1	Pujol 75	11 769
	19	Sochaux	W	5-2	L1	Sanchez Moreno 24, Pujol 2 49 85, Audel 63, Ben Khalfallah 78	11 880
	23	Metz	L	0-2	LCr3		5 545
	26	Marseille	W	3-2	L1	Bisevac 21, Ducourtioux 28, Rafael 84	16 208
Oct	3	Nice	L	2-3	L1	Samassa 39p, Sanchez Moreno 50	9 443
	17	Grenoble	W	2-0	L1	Samassa 18, Ben Khalfallah 24	12 177
	24	St-Etienne	W	2-0	L1	Audel 17, Ducourtioux 92+	27 621
Nov	1	Rennes	W	3-0	L1	Balde 58, Ben Khalfallah 78, Pujol 85	21 675
	7	Montpellier	D	1-1	L1	Sanchez Moreno 52	12 633
	21	Bordeaux	W	1-0	L1	Samassa 7	27 431
	28	Lille	L	0-4	L1		13 367
Dec	5	Monaco	W	3-1	L1	Ducourtioux 27, Samassa 85, Ben Khalfallah 92+	12 464
	12	Le Mans	L	1-2	L1	Danic 32	7 700
	15	Auxerre	D	0-0	L1		10 946
	19	Lens	D	0-0	L1		13 720
	23	Lorient	L	2-3	L1	Audel 7, Danic 35	10 991
Jan	9	Le Mans	L	0-1	CFr9		
	16	Toulouse	L	1-3	L1	Audel 44	10 249
	20	Boulogne	W	2-0	L1	Bong 49, Ben Khalfallah 92+	11 085
	30	Sochaux	D	1-1	L1	Audel 21	10 265
Feb	7	Marseille	L	1-5	L1	Sanchez Moreno 66	46 306
	13	Nice	W	2-1	L1	Mater 51, Sebo 90	10 224
	20	Grenoble	W	1-0	L1	Sanchez Moreno 32	12 660
	27	St-Etienne	W	1-0	L1	Audel 77	12 197
Mar	6	Auxerre	L	0-1	L1		9 473
	14	Rennes	L	0-2	L1		11 116
	21	Montpellier	L	1-2	L1	Ben Khalfallah 74	16 183
Apr	3	Lille	W	1-0	L1	Samassa 82	12 127
	10	Monaco	L	1-2	L1	Bisevac 37	6 685
	17	Le Mans	L	0-1	L1		12 362
	25	Lens	D	1-1	L1	Pujol 73	34 182
	28	Bordeaux	W	2-0	L1	Pujol 12, Kadir 72	11 740
May	2	Lorient	D	0-0	L1		11 164
	5	PSG	D	2-2	L1	Bong 59, Ben Khalfallah 93+	29 873
	8	Lyon	D	2-2	L1	Audel 72, Cohade 81p	13 206
	15	Nancy	D	1-1	L1	Angoua 65	17 103

TOULOUSE APPEARANCES/GOALS 2009-10
Goalkeepers Olivier Blondel 11+2 • Anthony Loustallot 1 • Yohann Pele 18 • Matthieu Valverde 7+1 • Marc Vidal 1
Defenders Mauro Cetto ARG 16/0 • Daniel Congre 33/0 • Albin Ebondo 27+1/1 • Mohamed Fofana 16+1/1 • Cheikh M'Bengue 30/1 • Dany Nounkeu CMR 17/0 • Jean-Joel Perrier-Doumbe CMR 2+1/0
Midfield Mathieu Berson 14+2/0 • Daniel Omoya Braaten NOR 24+8/4 • Etienne Capoue 30+3/0 • Antoine Devaux 1+2/0 • Etienne Didot 22+4/1 • Colin Kazim-Richards TUR 10+5/2 • Luan BRA 6+8/1 • Fode Mansare GUI 2+6/0 • Paulo Machado POR 27+5/5 • Adrien Regattin 0+5/0 • Francois Sirieix 10+8/0 • Moussa Sissoko 35+2/7 • Franck Tabanou 26+7/4
Forwards Kevin Dupuis 2+4/1 • Andre-Pierre Gignac 30+1/8 • Alexandre N'Gadi Kakou 0+1/0 • Xavier Pentecote 0+6/0 • Ahmed Soukouna 0+3/0
Coach Alain Casanova

VALENCIENNES LEAGUE APPEARANCES/GOALS 2009-10
Goalkeepers Jean-Louis Leca 1 • Guy N'Dy Assembe CMR 17 • Nicolas Penneteau 19 • Gregory Wimbee 1
Defenders Jacques Abardonado 13+2/0 • Brou Angoua CIV 15/1 • Bobo Balde GUI 6+4/1 • Milan Bisevac SRB 31/2 • Gaetan Bong CMR 20+9/2 • David Ducourtioux 26+2/3 • Rudy Mater 28/2 • Rafael Schmitz BRA 8/1 • Siaka Tiene CIV 26+2/1
Midfield Amara Bangoura GUI 0+1/0 • Fahid Ben Khalfallah TUN 24+12/7 • Renaud Cohade 28+4/1 • Gael Danic 20+9/2 • Remi Gomis 31+5/0 • Jose Saez 10+5/0 • Carlos Sanchez COL 28/5 • Nam Tae Hee KOR 0+6/0
Forwards Johan Audel 20+6/7 • Foued Kadir ALG 14+4/1 • Luigi Pieroni BEL 0+2/0 • Gregory Pujol 21+9/6 • Mamadou Samassa MLI 11+6/7 • Filip Sebo SVK 0+11/1
Coach Philippe Montanier

FRO – FAROE ISLANDS

FIFA/COCA-COLA WORLD RANKING

1993	1994	1995	1996	1997	1998	1999	2000	2001	2002	2003	2004	2005	2006	2007	2008	2009	2010
115	133	120	135	117	125	112	117	117	114	126	131	132	181	194	184	117	136

2010												Hi/Lo
Jan	Feb	Mar	Mar	Apr	May	Jul	Aug	Sep	Oct	Nov	Dec	**94**
117	118	118	125	125	125	117	118	138	133	131	136	**198**

In an open and eventful championship HB Tórshavn sacked coach Kristjan Gudmundsson with six games to go and under new coach Julian Hansen secured 16 out of 18 points to clinch the title on the final day of the season. Five of the ten clubs had topped the table at one point during the season but a 2-1 victory over fierce rivals B'36 saw HB secure their 21st title at the expense of runners-up EB/Streymur. For EB/Streymur it was the fourth time in five seasons that they had finished in second place - disappointing certainly, but a testament to their newfound power in Faroese football. Until 2000 they had never even played in the top flight but along with the 2008 league title they have now won three Cup Finals in the past four years, including a 1-0 victory in the 2010 final over IF Fuglafjordur, the winner coming from their Romanian striker Sorin Anghel who was playing his 250th game for the club. At international level, 2010 failed to produce a win for the national team as 2009 had done, and there were four straight defeats at the start of the Euro 2012 qualifying campaign to leave the Faroes rooted to the bottom of the table. The year did end, however, with a morale boosting home draw against Northern Ireland in Toftir which gave them their first points of the campaign.

FIFA WORLD CUP RECORD
1930-1990 DNE **1994-2010** DNQ

**THE FAROE ISLANDS'
FOOTBALL ASSOCIATION
(FSF)**

Gundadalur, PO Box 3028, Tórshavn 110
☎ +298 351979
📠 +298 319079
📧 fsf@football.fo
🖥 www.football.fo
FA 1979 CON 1988 FIFA 1988
P Christian Andreasen
GS Niklas A Lidarenda

FIFA BIG COUNT 2006

Total players	8 094
% of population	17.13%
Male	6 290
Female	1 804
Amateurs 18+	1 654
Youth under 18	4 040
Unregistered	2 000
Professionals	0
Referees	60
Admin & coaches	990
Number of clubs	23
Number of teams	303

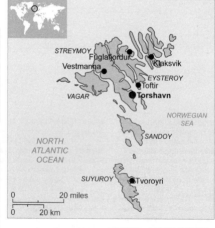

MAJOR CITIES/TOWNS
Population

1	Tórshavn	12 194
2	Klaksvík	4 628
3	Hoyvík	3 200
4	Argir	1 891
5	Fuglafjørður	1 580
6	Vágur	1 406
7	Vestmanna	1 238
8	Tvøroyri	1 213
9	Miðvágur	1 030
10	Sørvágur	988
11	Leirvík	885
12	Saltangará	882
13	Sandavágur	838
14	Strendur	834
15	Kollafjørður	829
16	Toftir	788
17	Skáli	711
18	Hvalba	663
19	Eiði	648

FOROYAR • FAROE ISLANDS

Capital	Tórshavn	Population	48 856 (208)	% in cities	41%
GDP per capita	$31 000 (43)	Area km²	1 393 km² (182)	GMT + / -	0
Neighbours (km)	Coast 1117				

RECENT INTERNATIONAL MATCHES PLAYED BY THE FAROE ISLANDS

2006	Opponents	Score		Venue	Comp	Scorers	Att	Referee
14-05	Poland	L	0-4	Wronki	Fr		4 000	Prus USA
16-08	Georgia	L	0-6	Toftir	ECq		2 114	Ross NIR
2-09	Scotland	L	0-6	Glasgow	ECq		50 059	Egorov RUS
7-10	Lithuania	L	0-1	Tórshavn	ECq		1 982	Buttimer IRL
11-10	France	L	0-5	Sochaux	ECq		19 314	Corpodean ROU
2007								
24-03	Ukraine	L	0-2	Toftir	ECq		717	Skomina SVN
28-03	Georgia	L	1-3	Tbilisi	ECq	Rógvi Jacobsen [57]	12 000	Saliy KAZ
2-06	Italy	L	1-2	Tórshavn	ECq	Rógvi Jacobsen [77]	5 800	Malek POL
6-06	Scotland	L	0-2	Toftir	ECq		4 100	Kasnaferis GRE
12-09	Lithuania	L	1-2	Kaunas	ECq	Rógvi Jacobsen [93+]	5 500	Georgiev BUL
13-10	France	L	0-6	Tórshavn	ECq		1 980	Rossi SMR
17-10	Ukraine	L	0-5	Kyiv	ECq		5 000	Jakov ISR
21-11	Italy	L	1-3	Modena	ECq	Rógvi Jacobsen [83]	16 142	Meyer GER
2008								
16-03	Iceland	L	0-3	Kopavogur	Fr		400	Skjerven NOR
4-06	Estonia	L	3-4	Tallinn	Fr	Holst 2 [63 66], Olsen [70]	2 300	Stalhammar SWE
20-08	Portugal	L	0-5	Aveiro	Fr		22 000	Shandor UKR
6-09	Serbia	L	0-2	Belgrade	WCq		9 615	Nikolaev RUS
10-09	Romania	L	0-1	Tórshavn	WCq		805	Strahonja CRO
11-10	Austria	D	1-1	Tórshavn	WCq	Lokin [47]	1 890	Ceferin SVN
15-10	Lithuania	L	0-1	Kaunas	WCq		5 000	Kapitanis CYP
2009								
22-03	Iceland	W	2-1	Kopavogur	Fr	Benjaminsen [22], Antonuisson OG [42]	553	Riley ENG
10-06	Serbia	L	0-2	Tórshavn	WCq		2 896	Levi ISR
12-08	France	L	0-1	Tórshavn	WCq		2 974	Koukoulakis GRE
5-09	Austria	L	1-3	Graz	WCq	Andreas Olsen [82]	12 300	Borg MLT
9-09	Lithuania	W	2-1	Toftir	WCq	Suni Olsen [13], Arnbiorn Hansen [34]	1 942	Vad HUN
10-10	France	L	0-5	Guingamp	WCq		16 755	Malek POL
14-10	Romania	L	1-3	Piatra-Neamt	WCq	Bo [83]	13 000	Gvardis RUS
2010								
21-03	Iceland	L	0-2	Kopavogur	Fr		312	Larsen DEN
4-06	Luxembourg	D	0-0	Hesperange	Fr		713	Bertolini SUI
11-08	Estonia	L	1-2	Tallinn	ECq	Edmundsson [26]	5 470	Vucemilovic CRO
3-09	Serbia	L	0-3	Tórshavn	ECq		1 847	Toussaint LUX
7-09	Italy	L	0-5	Florence	ECq		19 266	Kulbakov BLR
8-10	Slovenia	L	1-5	Ljubljana	ECq	Mouritsen [93+]	15 750	Todorov BUL
12-10	Northern Ireland	D	1-1	Toftir	ECq	Holst [60]	1 921	Zimmermann SUI
16-11	Scotland	L	0-3	Aberdeen	Fr		10 873	Van Boekel NED

Fr = Friendly match • EC = UEFA EURO 2008/2012 • WC = FIFA World Cup • q = qualifier

FAROE ISLANDS NATIONAL TEAM HISTORICAL RECORDS

Caps
83 - Oli Johannesen 1992-2007 • **69** - Jakup Mikkelsen 1995- • **65** - Jens Martin Knudsen 1988-2006 • **64** - Frodi Benjaminsen 1999- • **62** - Julian Johnsson 1995-2006 & Jakup a Borg 1998- • **57** - John Petersen 1995-2004 • **54** - Allan Morkore 1990-2001 • **52** - Rogvi Jacobsen 1999- • **51** - Ossur Hansen 1992-2002

Goals
10 - Rogvi Jacobsen 1999- • **9** - Todi Jonsson 1991-2005 • **8** - John Petersen 1995-2004 & Uni Arge 1992-2002 • **4** - Julian Johnsson 1995-2006 & Jan Allan Muller 1988-98

Past Coaches
Pall Gudlaugsson ISL 1988-93 • Johan Melle Nielsen & Jogvan Nordbud 1993 • Allan Simonsen DEN 1994-2001 • Henrik Larsen DEN 2002-05 • Jogvan Martin Olsen 2006-08 • Hedin Askham 2009 • Brian Kerr 2009-

FAROE ISLANDS 2010

VODAFONEDEILDIN

	Pl	W	D	L	F	A	Pts	HB	EB	NSI	IF	Vikingur	B'36	B'68	B'71	Sudoroy	AB
HB Tórshavn †	27	16	6	5	49	32	54		5-2	2-1 3-2	2-0	2-0	2-2 2-1	4-3 1-0	1-2	4-4 1-4	2-1 3-0
EB/Streymur ‡	27	14	9	4	65	30	51	0-1 1-1		1-1	3-0	2-2	1-2 4-1 3-0 3-1	8-0	2-0	5-2 2-1	6-0
NSI Runavík ‡	27	14	6	7	60	33	48	2-0	2-1 0-0		1-2 0-0 0-2 0-1	4-3	2-1	2-0 9-1	2-1	3-0	2-1
IF Fuglafjørdur ‡	27	12	7	8	50	41	43	2-1 1-2 1-1 3-3	3-5			0-1	0-5	4-2	1-1 3-0 2-0 3-1		4-4
Víkingur Gøtu/Leirvík	27	12	7	8	44	35	43	0-0 0-1 2-2 0-3	2-3	1-3 1-3			1-3 1-0	0-0	0-0 5-0	4-1	5-3 3-1
B'36 Tórshavn	27	11	7	9	44	36	40	1-0	1-1	1-5 2-1 1-1 1-0	1-2			3-1 3-1	1-1	1-0	1-0
B'68 Toftir	27	8	7	12	42	47	31	2-2	1-1	0-3 3-2 1-0 3-3	5-3 2-0	1-0			5-0 1-1	1-1	1-1 3-0
B'71 Sandur	27	5	8	14	24	65	23	0-1 0-2 2-3 0-4	1-6	0-2	0-0	0-3 0-0	1-0			3-1 2-2	1-0
FC Sudoroy	27	5	7	15	33	54	22	0-3	0-1	1-1 1-1	0-3	1-3 0-2 1-1	2-1 3-1 2-1	2-1			3-3
AB Argir	27	2	8	17	27	65	14	1-1	1-2	0-0	0-2 1-4	1-1	2-2 0-5	1-2	3-3 0-4 1-0 1-0		

31/03/2010 - 23/10/2010 • † Qualified for the UEFA Champions League • ‡ Qualified for the Europa League
Top scorers: 22 - Arnbjorn Hansen, EB & Christian Hogni Jacobsen NSI • 13 - Frodi Benjaminsen, HB

FAROE ISLANDS 2010
1. DEILD (2)

	Pl	W	D	L	F	A	Pts
07 Vestur	27	18	7	2	75	23	61
KI Klaksvík	27	18	4	5	78	26	58
TB Tvøroyri	27	15	6	6	62	34	51
EB/Streymur 2	27	13	6	8	59	42	45
HB Tórshavn 2	27	12	3	12	53	63	39
Víkingur Gøtu/Leirvík 2	27	11	4	12	40	53	37
FC Hoyvík	27	9	6	12	40	49	33
AB Argir 2	27	8	2	17	28	68	26
NSI Runavík 2	27	6	7	14	35	63	25
B'68 Toftir 2	27	1	3	23	19	68	6

31/03/2010 - 23/10/2010 • AB relegated after their first team were relegated to the 1. Deild

MEDALS TABLE

		Overall			League			Cup	
		G	S	B	G	S	B	G	S
1	HB Tórshavn	47	25	4	21	14	4	26	11
2	KI Klaksvík	22	10	8	17	2	8	5	8
3	B'36 Tórshavn	13	14	6	8	4	6	5	10
4	TB Tvøroyri	12	10		7	5		5	5
5	GI Gøtu	12	6	4	6	3	4	6	3
6	EB/Streymur	4	5		1	4		3	1
7	NSI Runavík	3	5	1	1	1	1	2	4
8	B'68 Toftir	3	2	6	3	1	6		1
9	FC Sudoroy (ex VB)	2	3	2	1		2	1	3
10	B'71 Sandur	2	2	1	1	1	1	1	2
11	IF Fuglafjørdur	1	5		1				5
12	SI Sørvagur	1			1				
13	Vikingur Gøta/Leirvik	1		1	1				1
14	Skála		1	1		1	1		
	LIF Leirvik	1							1
16	Royn Valba	1							1
	MB Midvágur		1					1	

FFA CUP 2010

Round of 16		Quarter–finals		Semi–finals		Final	
EB/Streymur *	1						
NSI Runavík	0	EB/Streymur	4				
Skála		FC Sudoroy *	1				
FC Sudoroy *				EB/Streymur	1 2		
FC Hoyvík *	2			B'36 Tórshavn *	2 0		
TB Tvøroyri	0	FC Hoyvík *	1				
HB Tórshavn *	0	B'36 Tórshavn	7			EB/Streymur ‡	1
B'36 Tórshavn	1					IF Fuglafjørdur	0
Vikingur	4						
B'71 Sandur *	2	Vikingur *	1 4p				
KI Klaksvík	1	AB Argir	1 3p				
AB Argir *	3			Vikingur	2 0		
B'68 Toftir *	3			IF Fuglafjørdur *	1 3		
07 Vestur	0	B'68 Toftir	2				
Undri FF *	0	IF Fuglafjørdur *	3	‡ Qualified for the Europa League			
IF Fuglafjørdur	1			* Home team/Home team in the first leg			
First round:							

CUP FINAL

Injector Arena, Klaksvik
6-08-2010, 12:00

Scorer - Sorin Anghel [25]

GAB – GABON

FIFA/COCA-COLA WORLD RANKING

1993	1994	1995	1996	1997	1998	1999	2000	2001	2002	2003	2004	2005	2006	2007	2008	2009	2010
60	64	67	46	63	82	74	89	102	121	111	109	104	95	104	62	48	39

	2010												Hi/Lo
	Jan	Feb	Mar	Mar	Apr	May	Jul	Aug	Sep	Oct	Nov	Dec	30
	48	44	43	43	41	42	34	34	31	39	37	39	125

After heart-breaking elimination by the narrowest of margins in the first round of the 2010 African Nations Cup finals in Angola, oil-rich Gabon turned its attention to co-hosting the 2012 finals. They are guaranteed one of the 16 berths in the final and so have no competitive action over the next two years although the federation has arranged a full programme of matches. Gernot Rohr replaced Alain Giresse as coach of the Azingo Nationale after the finals in Angola and he had six matches in charge in 2010. Gabon played in Algeria, France, Oman and Turkey and have an equally exotic programme for 2011 as they build-up to the 2012 finals. A new stadium, which will host the final, is being built in the capital Libreville with a capacity of 40,000 while the existing national stadium is being renovated as is the stadium in Franceville. In domestic football US Bitam won the championship, finishing four points ahead of Mangasport, and also took the cup with a 2-1 win over Missile FC Libreville in the final. Ulrich Bemangoye proved the hero in the final with both goals for the champions. In continental competition, Stade Mandji went out at the first hurdle in the Champions League while FC 105 Libreville, who had a bye into the second round of the Confederation Cup, were eliminated by Daring Club Motema Pembe from Congo DR.

FIFA WORLD CUP RECORD
1930-1986 DNE **1990-2010** DNQ

FEDERATION GABONAISE DE FOOTBALL (FGF)

Boite postale 181, Libreville

☎ +241 704985

📠 +241 704992

✉ fegafoot@hotmail.fr

🖥 www.les-pantheres.com

FA 1962 CON 1967 FIFA 1963
P Placide Engandzas
GS Barthelemy Moussadji

FIFA BIG COUNT 2006

Total players	69 800
% of population	4.90%
Male	69 800
Female	0
Amateurs 18+	5 500
Youth under 18	2 800
Unregistered	5 500
Professionals	0
Referees	100
Admin & coaches	900
Number of clubs	60
Number of teams	220

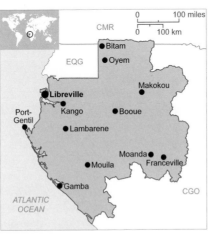

MAJOR CITIES/TOWNS

		Population
1	Libreville	732 885
2	Port-Gentil	138 378
3	Masuku	54 466
4	Oyem	39 132
5	Moanda	38 220
6	Mouila	28 483
7	Lambaréné	26 257
8	Tchibanga	24 547
9	Koulamoutou	20 563
10	Makokou	17 203
11	Bitam	13 053
12	Tsogni	12 621
13	Gamba	12 585
14	Mounana	11 130
15	Ntoum	10 862
16	Nkan	10 808
17	Lastoursville	10 572
18	Okandja	9 070
19	Ndendé	7 860

REPUBLIQUE GABONAISE • GABONESE REPUBLIC

Capital	Libreville	Population	1 514 993 (151)	% in cities	85%
GDP per capita	$14 200 (81)	Area km²	267 667 km² (76)	GMT +/-	+1
Neighbours (km)	Cameroon 298, 1903, Equatorial Guinea 350 • Coast 885				

RECENT INTERNATIONAL MATCHES PLAYED BY GABON

2006	Opponents		Score	Venue	Comp	Scorers	Att	Referee
15-08	Algeria	W	2-0	Aix-en-Provence	Fr	Mouloungui [65], Djissikadie [67]		Mezouar
2-09	Madagascar	W	4-0	Libreville	CNq	Antchouet [40], Cousin [67p], Nzigou 2 [70 71]		Diatta SEN
8-10	Côte d'Ivoire	L	0-5	Abidjan	CNq			Buenkadila COD
15-11	Morocco	L	0-6	Rabat	Fr		5 000	Ousmane Sidebe MLI
2007								
7-03	Congo	D	2-2	N'Djamena	CMr1	Ambourouet [62], Akiremy [89]		
9-03	Equatorial Guinea	D	1-1	N'Djamena	CMr1	Akiremy [15]		
11-03	Chad	W	2-1	N'Djamena	CMsf	Akiremy 2 [44 56]		
16-03	Congo	L	0-1	N'Djamena	CMf			
17-06	Madagascar	W	2-0	Antananarivo	CNq	Akiremy [20], Meye [89]		Mlangeni SWZ
21-08	Benin	D	2-2	Paris	Fr	Nzigou [4], Mouloungui [42p]		
8-09	Côte d'Ivoire	D	0-0	Libreville	CNq			Damon RSA
2008								
25-03	Congo DR	D	0-0	Aubervilliers	Fr			
7-06	Libya	L	0-1	Tripoli	WCq		30 000	Chaibou NIG
14-06	Ghana	W	2-0	Libreville	WCq	Meye [45], Stephane Nguema [59]	13 000	Benouza ALG
22-06	Ghana	L	0-2	Accra	WCq		29 040	Damon RSA
28-06	Lesotho	W	2-0	Libreville	WCq	Fabrice Do Marcolino 2 [45 63]	15 000	Mendy GAM
19-08	Mali	W	1-0	Mantes-La-Ville	Fr	Meye [30]		
7-09	Lesotho	W	3-0	Bloemfontein	WCq	Ecuele [56], Meye [72], Mbanangoye [94+]	1 500	Abd El Fatah EGY
11-10	Libya	W	1-0	Libreville	WCq	Mbanangoye [82]	26 000	Bennett RSA
18-11	Guinea	D	3-3	Compiegne	Fr	Stephane Nguema 2 [13 55], Mouloungui [30]		
2009								
28-03	Morocco	W	2-1	Casablanca	WCq	Pierre Aubameyang [34], Meye [45]	38 000	Diatta SEN
6-06	Togo	W	3-0	Libreville	WCq	Ecuele [11], Meye [67], Brou [81]	20 000	Lwanja MWI
11-08	Benin	D	1-1	Dieppe	Fr	Pierre Aubameyang [1]		
5-09	Cameroon	L	0-2	Libreville	WCq		10 000	Ndinya KEN
9-09	Cameroon	L	1-2	Yaoundé	WCq	Cousin [90]	38 000	Bennaceur TUN
10-10	Morocco	W	3-1	Libreville	WCq	Erbate OG [43], Moulougui [65], Cousin [70]	14 000	Doue CIV
14-11	Togo	L	0-1	Lomé	WCq		10 000	Seechurn MRI
2010								
6-01	Mozambique	W	2-0	Bloemfontein	Fr	Fanuel Massingue [5], Cousin [76]		
13-01	Cameroon	W	1-0	Lubango	CNr1	Cousin [17]	15 000	Bennett RSA
17-01	Tunisia	D	0-0	Lubango	CNr1		16 000	Codjia BEN
21-01	Zambia	L	1-2	Benguela	CNr1	Fabrice Do Marcolino [83]	5 000	Benouza ALG
19-05	Togo	W	3-0	Ajaccio	Fr	Pierre Aubameyang [16], OG [27], Do Marcolino [80]		
11-08	Algeria	W	2-1	Algiers	Fr	Cousin [35], Pierre Aubameyang [55]		Rouaissi MAR
6-09	Burkina Faso	D	1-1	Cannes	Fr	Roger Issakounia [52]		
8-10	Oman	L	0-1	Muscat	Fr			
12-10	Saudi Arabia	L	0-1	Istanbul	Fr			
17-11	Senegal	L	1-2	Saint-Gratien	Fr	Pierre Aubameyang [29]		

Fr = Friendly match • CN = CAF African Cup of Nations • CM = CEMAC Cup • WC = FIFA World Cup
q = qualifier • r1 = first round group • sf = semi-final • 3p = third place play-off • f = final

GABON 2009–10

CHAMPIONNAT NATIONAL DE D1 (LINAF)

	Pl	W	D	L	F	A	Pts	USB	Mangasport	Missiles	Cercle Mbéri	Pélican	Sogéa	USM	Stade Mandji	Variété	Oyem	FC 105	Estuaire	Commerçants	Stade Nynois
US Bitam †	26	18	6	2	47	19	60		3-3	0-1			2-2					2-0	4-1	1-0	3-1
Mangasport Moanda	26	15	11	0	58	14	56	2-0		1-0	5-1	1-0	3-0	5-0	0-0			1-1	2-1		
Missiles Libreville	26	15	8	3	53	25	53	1-1				1-0				0-1	1-1	1-0			
Cercle Mbéri Sportif	26	11	7	8	29	23	40	1-4	2-3				5-0		3-3			1-1		0-1	2-1
AS Pélican	26	11	6	9	32	25	39	0-1	1-3		2-1		0-0			1-0	1-0	0-0	1-1	3-3	
Sogéa FC	26	9	9	8	40	32	36			3-2				0-3			4-0			0-0	
US Mbilanzambi	26	8	8	10	31	36	32	2-2		1-1	1-1	1-0					2-1	1-1		2-3	3-0
AS Stade Mandji	26	8	7	11	23	22	31	0-1					1-2	2-0		4-1	1-1			1-0	1-0
Variété AC Mouila	26	7	8	11	23	30	29	1-2	0-0	0-0	2-1		1-1	1-1			0-0			1-1	
US Oyem	26	6	9	11	22	33	27	0-1	1-3			1-1	0-1					0-0	1-0	0-0	3-0
FC 105 Libreville	26	6	9	11	21	36	27							2-1	1-3	0-0	1-1		1-1	0-2	1-1
En Avant Estuaire	26	6	8	12	30	51	26						2-3	0-0	2-2	3-2	1-0	2-1			0-0
AS Commerçants	26	6	6	14	18	46	24		1-4	0-5	1-3	0-3			0-3				0-5		4-3
Stade Nynois	26	2	6	18	20	55	12		1-1	1-4			1-2	0-3	0-0	1-2					

5/12/2009 - 17/06/2010 • † Qualified for the CAF Champions League • ‡ Qualified for the CAF Confederation Cup

MEDALS TABLE

		Overall			Lge	Cup	Africa			City
		G	S	B	G	G	G	S	B	
1	FC 105	15			10	5				Libreville
2	Mangasport	11			6	5				Moanda
3	AS Sogara	7	1		6	1		1		Port-Gentil
4	US Mbilanzambi (USM)	8			4	4				Libreville
5	Mbilinga	6		1	1	5			1	Port-Gentil
6	US Bitam	5			2	3				Bitam
7	En Avant Estuaire (ex Téléstar)	3				3				Libreville
	Stade Mandji	3			1	2				Port-Gentil
	Vautour Mangoungou	3			2	1				Libreville
10	Aigle Royale	2			2					Libreville
	Olympique Sportif	2			2					Libreville
	Petrosport	2			1	1				Port-Gentil
13	Anges ABC	1			1					Libreville
	Jeunesse AC (JAC)	1			1					Libreville
	AS Police	1			1					Libreville
	AS Solidarité	1			1					Libreville
	Zalang COC	1			1					Libreville
	AO Evizo	1				1				Lambaréné

COUPE DU GABON INTERCLUBS 2010

Round of 16	Quarter-finals	Semi-finals	Final
US Bitam			
	US Bitam — 1		
	Akieni FC — 0		
Akieni FC		US Bitam — 1	
Nzimba FC		Mangasport Moanda — 0	
	Nzimba FC — 0		
	Mangasport Moanda — 2		
Mangasport Moanda			US Bitam — 2
En Avant Estuaire			Missiles Libreville ‡ — 1
	En Avant Estuaire — 1		
	AS Pélican — 0		
AS Pélican		En Avant Estuaire — 0	
Sogea FC		Missiles Libreville — 2	
	Sogea FC — 1		
	Missiles Libreville — 2		
Missiles Libreville			

CUP FINAL

Stade Monédang de Sibang, Libreville, 17-08-2010
Scorers - Ulrich Bemangoye 2 [35][40] for Bitam; Gilbert Momo Epande [43] for Missiles

‡ Qualified for the CAF Confederation Cup

GAM – GAMBIA

FIFA/COCA-COLA WORLD RANKING

1993	1994	1995	1996	1997	1998	1999	2000	2001	2002	2003	2004	2005	2006	2007	2008	2009	2010
125	117	112	128	132	135	151	155	148	143	138	154	164	134	117	88	116	100

2010												Hi/Lo
Jan	Feb	Mar	Mar	Apr	May	Jul	Aug	Sep	Oct	Nov	Dec	65
116	98	95	92	93	93	102	103	91	102	103	100	166

A 2-1 away win over Tunisia in a friendly international at the start of the year went almost unnoticed internationally but came as confirmation of Gambia's improving prospects. Building on the back of youth teams that have competed in recent FIFA tournaments, the small West African nation is now building a competitive national team and is seeking to break new ground by qualifying for the finals of the African Nations Cup. The withdrawal of Mauritania from their group in the 2012 qualifiers left Gambia with only Burkina Faso and Namibia to compete against with the winner progressing to the finals. Home success will be key and a 3-1 win over Namibia in September proved the perfect start but they then lost 3-1 away to Burkina Faso a month later to make the task of qualifying much more difficult. Coach Paul Put from Belgium is now able to put together a team almost exclusively made up of players competing with clubs in Europe and of them Momodou Ceesay enjoys the biggest profile after playing with MSK Zilina of Slovakia in the group stages of the UEFA Champions League. Gambia Ports Authority won the first division by three points from Wallidan for their first success since 2006 while Gamtel won the GFA Cup at the start of 2011 with a 3-0 win over Hawks in the final.

FIFA WORLD CUP RECORD
1930-1978 DNE 1982-1986 DNQ 1990-1994 DNE 1998-2010 DNQ

GAMBIA FOOTBALL ASSOCIATION (GFA)

⌂ Independence Stadium, Bakau, PO Box 523, Banjul

☎ +220 9960437

📠 +220 4494802

✉ info@gambiafa.gm

🖥 www.gambiafa.org

FA 1952 CON 1962 FIFA 1966

P Seedy Kinteh

GS Jammeh Bojang

FIFA BIG COUNT 2006

Total players	68 030
% of population	4.14%
Male	67 400
Female	630
Amateurs 18+	3 080
Youth under 18	1 450
Unregistered	2 500
Professionals	0
Referees	100
Admin & coaches	600
Number of clubs	50
Number of teams	200

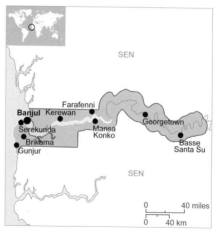

MAJOR CITIES/TOWNS

		Population
1	Serre Kunda	380 416
2	Brikama	93 240
3	Bakau	41 848
4	Banjul	33 422
5	Farafenni	33 305
6	Lamin	32 981
7	Nema Kunku	30 415
8	Brufut	26 724
9	Basse Santa Su	18 414
10	Gunjur	17 520
11	Sukuta	16 832
12	Wellingara	12 744
13	Busumbala	11 189
14	Yundum	10 960
15	Mandinari	10 583
16	Soma	10 211
17	Gambisara	10 102
18	Sabi	8 614
19	Banjulunding	8 505

REPUBLIC OF THE GAMBIA

Capital	Banjul	Population	1 782 893 (148)	% in cities	57%
GDP per capita	$1300 (202)	Area km²	11 295 km² (166)	GMT +/-	0
Neighbours (km)	Senegal 740 • Coast 80				

RECENT INTERNATIONAL MATCHES PLAYED BY GAMBIA

2007	Opponents	Score	Venue	Comp	Scorers	Att	Referee
3-06	Guinea	D 2-2	Conakry	CNq	Edrissa Sonko [53], Pa Modou Jagne [85]		Djaoupe TOG
16-06	Cape Verde Islands	D 0-0	Praia	CNq			Aguidissou BEN
9-09	Algeria	W 2-1	Bakau	CNq	Assan Jatta [71], Mathew Mendy [88]		Imiere NGA
3-12	Cape Verde	D 0-0	Bissau	Fr			
23-12	Sierra Leone	W 2-1	Bakau	Fr	Ebrima Sillah [2], Ebrima Sohna [51]		
2008							
1-06	Liberia	D 1-1	Monrovia	WCq	Mustapha Jarjue [17]	35 000	Keita GUI
8-06	Senegal	D 0-0	Banjul	WCq		24 500	Ncobo RSA
14-06	Algeria	W 1-0	Banjul	WCq	Mustapha Jarjue [19p]	18 000	Coulibaly MLI
20-06	Algeria	L 0-1	Blida	WCq		25 000	Ndume GAB
6-09	Liberia	W 3-0	Banjul	WCq	Njogu Demba 2 [10 76], Ousman Jallow [26]	10 000	Ambaya LBY
11-10	Senegal	D 1-1	Dakar	WCq	Aziz Corr Nyang [85]	50 000	Bennaceur TUN
2009							
No international matches played in 2009							
2010							
3-01	Angola	D 1-1	Vila Real	Fr	Ebrima Sawaneh [4]		
9-01	Tunisia	W 2-1	Rades/Tunis	Fr	Cherno Samba [57], Sainey Nyassi [85]		
30-05	Mexico	L 1-5	Bayreuth	Fr	Ebrima Sohna [65]		
4-09	Namibia	W 3-1	Banjul	CNq	Sainey Nyassi [10], Momoudou Ceesay [12], Ousman Jallow [34]		Ragab Omar LBY
9-10	Burkina Faso	L 1-3	Ouagadougou	CNq	Momoudou Ceesay [75]		Osman EGY

Fr = Friendly match • CN = CAF African Cup of Nations • WC = FIFA World Cup • q = qualifier

GFA CUP 2010

Quarter-finals		Semi-finals		Final	
Gamtel	0 5p				
Real Banjul	0 4p	Gamtel	1 4p		
Bakau United	1 4p	Brikama United	1 3p		
Brikama United	1 5p			Gamtel	3
Africell	1 p			Hawks	0
Seaview	1 p	Africell			
Tallinding Utd	1	**Hawks**			
Hawks	2				

Cup Final: Serrekunda East Mini-Stadium, 23-01-2011
Scorers - Modou Njie Sarr 2 [54 60], Nabi Darboe [87] for Gamtel

MEDALS TABLE

		Overall	Lge	Cup	City
		G	G	G	
1	Wallidan	31	15	16	Banjul
2	Real Banjul	9	8	1	Banjul
3	Ports Authority	8	6	2	Banjul
4	Hawks	4	2	2	Banjul
	Starlight	4	2	2	Banjul
6	Armed Forces	2	2		Banjul
	Augustians	2	2		Banjul
8	Bakau United	1		1	Bakau
	Dingoreh	1		1	
	Mass Sosseh	1		1	
	Steve Biko	1		1	Bakau
	Young Africans	1		1	Banjul

GAMBIA 2010

GFA LEAGUE FIRST DIVISION

	Pl	W	D	L	F	A	Pts	Ports	Wallidan	Samger	Armed Forces	Steve Biko	GAMTEL	Bakau Utd	Interior	Brikama Utd	Real Banjul	Hawks	Sea View
Ports Authority †	22	11	7	4	18	9	40		0-1	2-1	0-0	0-0	1-0	2-0	1-1	2-0	2-1	0-0	2-1
Wallidan	22	11	4	7	23	16	37	0-1		0-1	1-2	2-1	2-1	4-1	0-2	1-0	1-0	0-0	1-1
Samger	22	7	10	5	21	17	31	0-0	1-0		1-1	0-2	3-3	2-0	1-1	1-0	0-0	0-0	1-2
Armed Forces	22	6	12	4	19	17	30	0-0	0-2	2-0		1-0	1-1	1-1	0-0	2-2	0-1	0-0	0-0
Steve Biko	22	7	8	7	13	13	29	1-0	0-1	0-0	3-2		0-1	0-0	0-0	1-1	2-0	0-1	0-1
GAMTEL	22	6	8	8	20	19	26	1-0	0-1	0-0	0-1	0-1		2-0	1-2	1-0	1-1	0-1	0-0
Bakau United	22	6	8	8	16	23	26	0-1	1-0	1-1	1-0	0-0	1-1		1-1	1-0	0-1	1-1	2-1
Interior	22	4	13	5	16	16	25	0-1	2-1	1-1	1-2	0-0	1-1	1-1		0-1	0-1	0-0	0-1
Brikama United	22	5	10	7	19	21	25	1-2	1-1	1-0	1-1	0-0	0-2	2-1	0-0		1-1	1-1	2-1
Real Banjul	22	6	7	9	15	21	25	0-0	1-1	0-2	0-1	3-0	1-0	1-0	0-0	1-4		0-1	1-3
Hawks	22	4	12	6	11	14	24	0-1	0-1	0-2	2-2	0-1	0-0	1-2	1-2	1-1	1-0		0-0
Sea View	22	5	9	8	17	22	24	1-0	0-2	1-3	0-0	0-1	2-4	0-1	1-1	1-1	0-0	1-1	0-0

9/01/2010 - 9/06/2010 • † Qualified for the CAF Champions League

GEO – GEORGIA

FIFA/COCA-COLA WORLD RANKING

1993	1994	1995	1996	1997	1998	1999	2000	2001	2002	2003	2004	2005	2006	2007	2008	2009	2010
-	92	79	95	69	52	66	66	58	90	93	104	104	94	77	108	124	73

2010												Hi/Lo
Jan	Feb	Mar	Mar	Apr	May	Jul	Aug	Sep	Oct	Nov	Dec	42
124	122	124	118	119	120	111	110	89	75	78	73	156

Temuri Ketsbaia's iconic status in Georgian football was further enhanced during his first 12 months at the helm of the national team. In 2009 Georgia failed to win a single match under former boss Hector Cuper but following Ketsbaia's appointment at the start of 2010, they didn't lose a game all year. The about turn in fortunes could not have been more stark although three draws in their opening four qualifiers for Euro 2012 may not prove enough to earn Georgia a place at the final tournament of a major championship for the first time. In club football, Olimpi Rustavi won the league for the second time in four years thanks in part to an influx of Brazilian players on loan from Atlético Paranaense, notably Anderson Aquino. He became the first foreigner to top the goalscoring charts after scoring 26 goals in 31 appearances as Olimpi cruised to the title. In the Cup there was a first meeting in the final between the two major clubs from the capital Tbilisi with WIT Georgia coming out on top after a 1-0 win over rivals Dinamo thanks to a first half goal from Pavle Datunaishvili. It was the first time WIT Georgia had won the Cup and it left Dinamo, the traditional powerhouse of Georgian football, without a trophy in a season for the sixth time since the year 2000, having won six consecutive doubles in the 1990's.

FIFA WORLD CUP RECORD
1930-1994 DNE   1998-2010 DNQ

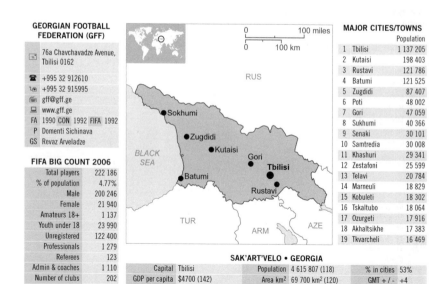

GEORGIAN FOOTBALL FEDERATION (GFF)	
76a Chavchavadze Avenue, Tbilisi 0162	
☎	+995 32 912610
📠	+995 32 915995
✉	gff@gff.ge
🖥	www.gff.ge
FA	1990 CON 1992 FIFA 1992
P	Domenti Sichinava
GS	Revaz Arveladze

FIFA BIG COUNT 2006	
Total players	222 186
% of population	4.77%
Male	200 246
Female	21 940
Amateurs 18+	1 137
Youth under 18	23 990
Unregistered	122 400
Professionals	1 279
Referees	123
Admin & coaches	1 110
Number of clubs	202
Number of teams	522

MAJOR CITIES/TOWNS	
	Population
1 Tbilisi	1 137 205
2 Kutaisi	198 403
3 Rustavi	121 786
4 Batumi	121 525
5 Zugdidi	87 407
6 Poti	48 002
7 Gori	47 059
8 Sukhumi	40 366
9 Senaki	30 101
10 Samtredia	30 008
11 Khashuri	29 341
12 Zestafoni	25 599
13 Telavi	20 784
14 Marneuli	18 829
15 Kobuleti	18 302
16 Tskaltubo	18 064
17 Ozurgeti	17 916
18 Akhaltsikhe	17 383
19 Tkvarcheli	16 469

SAK'ART'VELO • GEORGIA

Capital	Tbilisi	Population	4 615 807 (118)	% in cities	53%
GDP per capita	$4700 (142)	Area km²	69 700 km² (120)	GMT +/-	+4
Neighbours (km)	Armenia 164, Azerbaijan 322, Russia 723, Turkey 252 • Coast 310				

RECENT INTERNATIONAL MATCHES PLAYED BY GEORGIA

2007	Opponents	Score		Venue	Comp	Scorers	Att	Referee
7-02	Turkey	W	1-0	Tbilisi	Fr	Siradze 76	53 000	Lajuks LVA
24-03	Scotland	L	1-2	Glasgow	ECq	Arveladze 41	52 063	Vollquartz DEN
28-03	Faroe Islands	W	3-1	Tbilisi	ECq	Siradze 26, Iashvili 2 46+ 92+	12 000	Saliy KAZ
2-06	Lithuania	L	0-1	Kaunas	ECq		6 400	Circhetta SUI
6-06	France	L	0-1	Auxerre	ECq		19 345	Batista POR
22-08	Luxembourg	D	0-0	Luxembourg	Fr		1 123	Weatherall NIR
8-09	Ukraine	D	1-1	Tbilisi	ECq	Siradze 89	24 000	Hamer LUX
12-09	Azerbaijan	D	1-1	Baku	Fr	Tatanashvili 48	10 000	Kovalenko UZB
13-10	Italy	L	0-2	Genoa	ECq		23 057	Davila ESP
17-10	Scotland	W	2-0	Tbilisi	ECq	Mchedlidze 16, Siradze 64	29 377	Kircher GER
16-11	Qatar	W	2-1	Doha	Fr	Kankava 46, Salukvadze 64		Al Ghabbaz BAH
21-11	Lithuania	L	0-2	Tbilisi	ECq		21 300	Stavrev MKD
2008								
6-02	Latvia	L	1-3	Tbilisi	Fr	Kaladze 46	6 000	Shmolik BKR
26-03	Northern Ireland	L	1-4	Belfast	Fr	Healy OG 55	15 000	Wilmes LUX
27-05	Estonia	D	1-1	Tallinn	Fr	Kenia 82	2 500	Vejlgaard DEN
31-05	Portugal	L	0-2	Viseu	Fr		8 500	Meir ISR
20-08	Wales	W	2-1	Swansea	Fr	Kenia 67, Gotsiridze 90	6 435	Jug SVN
6-09	Republic of Ireland	L	1-2	Mainz	WCq	Kenia 92+	4 500	Szabo HUN
10-09	Italy	L	0-2	Udine	WCq		27 164	Einwaller AUT
11-10	Cyprus	D	1-1	Tbilisi	WCq	Kobiashvili 73	40 000	Matejek CZE
15-10	Bulgaria	D	0-0	Tbilisi	WCq		32 250	Kuipers NED
19-11	Romania	L	1-2	Bucharest	Fr	Martsvaladze 11	2 000	Vassaras GRE
2009								
11-02	Republic of Ireland	L	1-2	Dublin	WCq	Iashvili 1	45 000	Hyytia FIN
28-03	Cyprus	L	1-2	Larnaca	WCq	Kobiashvili 71p	1 500	Fautrel FRA
1-04	Montenegro	D	0-0	Tbilisi	WCq		16 000	Malcolm NIR
6-06	Moldova	L	1-2	Tbilisi	Fr	Khizanishvili 85	8 000	Salyi KAZ
10-06	Albania	D	1-1	Tirana	Fr	Dvalishvili 2	2 000	Stavrev MKD
12-08	Malta	L	0-2	Ta'Qali	Fr			Kailis CYP
5-09	Italy	L	0-2	Tbilisi	WCq		32 000	Borski POL
9-09	Iceland	L	1-3	Reykjavik	Fr	Dvalishvili 33	4 726	Trefoloni ITA
10-10	Montenegro	L	1-2	Podgorica	WCq	Dvalishvili 45	5 420	Dereli TUR
14-10	Bulgaria	L	2-6	Sofia	WCq	Dvalishvili 34, Kobiashvili 51p	700	Jakobsson ISL
2010								
3-03	Estonia	W	2-1	Tbilisi	Fr	Kobiashvili 45p, Siradze 90	40 000	Banari MDA
25-05	Cameroon	D	0-0	Linz	Fr		3 500	Brugger AUT
11-08	Moldova	D	0-0	Chisinau	Fr		3 000	Shvetsov UKR
3-09	Greece	D	1-1	Piraeus	ECq	Iashvili 3	14 794	Clos ESP
7-09	Israel	D	0-0	Tbilisi	ECq		45 000	Kever SUI
8-10	Malta	W	1-0	Tbilisi	ECq	Siradze 91+	38 000	Black NIR
12-10	Latvia	D	1-1	Riga	ECq	Siradze 74	4 330	Neves POR
17-11	Slovenia	W	2-1	Koper	Fr	Guruli 67, Ananidze 68	4 000	Whitby WAL

Fr = Friendly match • EC = UEFA EURO 2008/2012 • WC = FIFA World Cup • q = qualifier

GEORGIA NATIONAL TEAM HISTORICAL RECORDS

Caps
93 - Levan Kobiashvili 1996- • 75 - Kakha Kaladze 1996- • 71 - Zurab Khizanishvili 1999- • 69 - Giorgi Nemsadze 1992-2004 • 62 - Gocha Jamarauli 1994-2004 • 60 - Shota Arveladze 1992-2007 & Aleksander Iashvili 1996- • 59 - Levan Tskitishvili 1995-2009 • 55 - Giorgi Demetradze 1996-2007 • 54 - Giorgi Kinkladze 1992-2005 • 52 - Temuri Ketsbaia 1994-2003

Goals
26 - Shota Arveladze 1992-2007 • 17 - Temuri Ketsbaia 1994-2003 • 14 - Aleksander Iashvili 1996- • 12 - Giorgi Demetradze 1996-2007 • 11 - Levan Kobiashvili 1996- • 9 - Mikheil Kavelashvili 1994-2002 • 8 - Giorgi Kinkladze 1992-2005 • 7 - David Siradze 2004-

Past Coaches
Giga Norakidze 1992 • Aleksandr Chivadze 1993-96 • Vladimir Gutsaev 1996 • David Kipiani 1997 • Vladimir Gutsaev 1998-99 • Johan Boskamp 1999 • David Kipiani & Revaz Dzodzuashvili 2000-01 • Aleksandr Chivadze 2001-03 • Ivo Susak 2003 • Merab Jordania 2003 • Gocha Tqhebuchava 2004 • Alain Giresse 2004-05 • Gayoz Darsadze 2005 • Klaus Toppmoller 2006-08 • Hector Cuper 2008-09 • Temuri Ketsbaia 2010-

GEORGIA 2009–10

UMAGLESI LIGA

	Pl	W	D	L	F	A	Pts
Olimpi Rustavi §3 †	36	25	7	4	69	26	**79**
Dinamo Tbilisi ‡	36	22	8	6	62	19	**74**
FC Zestafoni ‡	36	19	10	7	58	33	**67**
WIT Georgia Tbilisi ‡	36	17	13	6	48	31	**64**
Spartaki Tskhinvali	36	11	10	15	44	58	**43**
Sioni Bolnisi	36	8	14	14	27	43	**38**
FC Samtredia	36	10	7	19	43	68	**37**
Baia Zugdidi	36	7	11	18	29	48	**32**
Lokomotivi Tbilisi	36	5	11	20	19	50	**26**
FC Gagra	36	5	9	22	30	59	**24**

Results grid (Olimpi, Dinamo, Zestafoni, WIT Georgia, Spartaki, Sioni, Samtredia, Baia, Lokomotivi, Gagra):

	Olimpi	Dinamo	Zestafoni	WIT Georgia	Spartaki	Sioni	Samtredia	Baia	Lokomotivi	Gagra
Olimpi Rustavi		1-0 1-1	1-0 3-1	0-0 1-0	1-1 4-0	3-0 0-0	5-0 3-1	2-0 1-0	3-1 2-0	5-0 3-0
Dinamo Tbilisi	4-0 0-0		2-0 2-0	1-2 5-0	2-0 0-2	4-0 2-0	4-1 1-0	3-0 1-0	1-0 2-0	4-1
FC Zestafoni	2-2* 4-1	0-1		2-1 0-1	4-1 0-0	3-0 1-0	4-2 5-1	2-1 4-0	0-0 1-1	1-0 4-1
WIT Georgia Tbilisi	1-2 2-0	0-0 0-2	1-1 1-1		2-0 3-1	2-1 0-0	2-1 1-1	2-1 2-2	1-1 3-0	5-1 2-0
Spartaki Tskhinvali	1-2 4-1	1-1 2-1	3-3 1-4	1-2 0-0		1-1 1-3	2-0 1-1	1-0 2-0	2-0 1-1	3-1 0-0
Sioni Bolnisi	0-6 1-2	0-0 0-1	0-0 0-1	0-1 2-2	1-4 0-1		3-0 2-2	1-0 0-0	2-0 1-0	1-1 2-0
FC Samtredia	0-4 0-1	3-1 0-1	0-2 2-3	2-2 1-0	2-1 2-1	1-1 1-2-1		1-0 0-1	2-0 1-2	4-3 1-0
Baia Zugdidi	1-2 1-1	0-6 1-1	0-1 0-1	1-1 1-4	4-1 0-2	1-0 0-2	2-2 2-0		2-1 0-0	2-2 2-1
Lokomotivi Tbilisi	1-2 0-2	0-3 0-3	0-1 1-1	1-3 0-1	0-0 2-1	0-0 0-1	0-3 3-2	0-0 1-3		1-0 1-1
FC Gagra	0-1 0-2	0-0 0-1	0-1 0-0	4-0 0-1	1-2 4-1	1-1 1-2	1-1 2-1	1-0 1-1	2-0 0-1	

1/08/2009 - 20/05/2010 • † Qualified for the UEFA Champions League • ‡ Qualified for the Europa League • § Points deducted
* Awarded as a defeat to both sides
Top scorers: 26 - Anderson Aquino BRA, Olimpi • 16 - Nikoloz Gelashvili, Zestafoni • 13 - Jaba Dvali, Zestafoni

GEORGIA 2009–10 PIRVELI LIGA (2)

	Pl	W	D	L	F	A	Pts
Torpedo Kutaisi	28	22	4	2	70	12	**70**
Kolkheti Poti	28	19	4	5	63	21	**61**
Merani Martvili	28	17	2	9	44	31	**53**
Guria Lanchkhuti	28	16	5	7	53	32	**53**
Dinamo Batumi	28	15	8	5	44	17	**53**
Chikhura Sachkhere	28	14	7	7	41	28	**49**
SZSU Tbilisi	28	9	7	12	45	40	**34**
Norchi Dinamo Tbilisi	28	9	5	14	38	57	**32**
Mertskhali Ozurgeti	28	9	4	15	29	45	**31**
Kolkheti Khobi	28	9	3	16	36	52	**30**
FC Chiatura	28	9	3	16	36	58	**30**
Meshakhte Tqibuli	28	6	7	15	36	68	**25**
FC 35 Tibilisi	28	6	6	16	30	49	**24**
Hereti Lagodekhi	28	6	5	17	27	60	**23**
Meskheti Akhaltsikhe §3	28	7	4	17	26	48	**22**

21/08/2009 - 23/05/2010 • § Points deducted

MEDALS TABLE

		Overall			League			Cup		Europe		
		G	S	B	G	S	B	G	S	G	S	B
1	Dinamo Tbilisi	22	5	5	13	3	5	9	2			
2	Torpedo Kutaisi	5	6	2	3	3	2	2	3			
3	Lokomotivi Tbilisi	3	3	1		2	1	3	1			
	WIT Georgia Tbilisi	3	3	1	2	3	1	1				
5	Olimpi Rustavi	2	1	2	2			2				1
6	Ameri Tbilisi	2	1	1			1	2	1			
7	Dinamo Batumi	1	5	1	1	1		1	4			
8	FC Zestafoni	1	3	2			2		1	3		
9	Sioni Bolnisi	1	2		1	1		1				
	Guria Lanchkhuti	1	2			2		1				
11	Tskhumi Sukhumi	3			1			2				
12	Kolkheti-1913 Poti	2	3		2	3						
13	Gorda Rustavi	1	2			2		1				
14	Margveti Zestafoni	1			1							
	Samgurali	1						1				
	FC Samtredia	1			1							
	Shevardeni 1906	1			1							
18	Alazani Gurdzhaani		1					1				

GEORGIAN CLUBS IN THE SOVIET UNION

		G	S	B	G	S	B	G	S	G	S	B
6	Dinamo Tbilisi	4	11	13	2	5	13	2	6	1		1

SAKARTVELOS TASI 2009–10

Round of 16

WIT Georgia Tbilisi	3
Lokomotivi Tbilisi *	1
Torpedo Kutaisi *	0
FC Zestafoni	2
Kolkheti Poti *	2
FC Gagra	1
FC Samtredia	0
Merani Martvili *	2
Spartaki Tskhinvali	6
Mertskhali Ozurgeti *	0
Sioni Bolnisi	0
Baia Zugdidi *	3
Chikhura Sachkhere *	1
Olimpi Rustavi	0
FC 35 Tibilisi *	0
Dinamo Tbilisi	1

Quarter-finals

WIT Georgia Tbilisi	0	4
FC Zestafoni *	3	0
Kolkheti Poti	0	1
Merani Martvili *	0	1
Spartaki Tskhinvali	1	2
Baia Zugdidi *	1	1
Chikhura Sachkhere *	1	0
Dinamo Tbilisi	1	0

Semi-finals

WIT Georgia Tbilisi	0	2
Merani Martvili *	1	0
Spartaki Tskhinvali *	0	0
Dinamo Tbilisi	0	3

Final

WIT Georgia Tbilisi ‡	1
Dinamo Tbilisi	0

CUP FINAL
Boris Paichadze, Tbilisi
26-05-2010, 17:45, Ref: Silgava
Scorer - Datunaishvili [41] for WIT

* Home team in the first leg • ‡ Qualified for the Europa League

GER – GERMANY

FIFA/COCA-COLA WORLD RANKING

1993	1994	1995	1996	1997	1998	1999	2000	2001	2002	2003	2004	2005	2006	2007	2008	2009	2010
1	5	2	2	2	3	5	11	12	4	12	19	16	6	5	2	6	3

2010												Hi/Lo
Jan	Feb	Mar	Mar	Apr	May	Jul	Aug	Sep	Oct	Nov	Dec	1
6	6	5	6	6	6	4	4	3	4	4	3	22

Germany's remarkable record at the FIFA World Cup continued as a young and adventurous team thrashed both England and Argentina to reach the semi-finals. There they lost to eventual winners Spain but it was the 12th time in 19 World Cups that the Germans had made it as far as the semis and there is real belief that the team can claim a fourth world title in Brazil in 2014. Poor performances in the 1994 and 1998 World Cups, where they progressed only to the quarter-finals, had prompted a strategic re-think by the DFB and the Bundesliga and the results of that - with an overhauled youth system as a central measure - are now paying dividends. The benefits are also being felt at club level where the Bundesliga continues to be the best-supported league in the world with an average attendance of 41,802 for matches. For Bayern Munich, under coach Louis van Gaal, it was back to business as usual with a domestic double to celebrate - their fifth in just eight seasons - although they fell just short of becoming the first German club to win the treasured 'treble' after losing 2-0 to Inter in the European Cup final in Madrid. Inspired by Arjen Robben, Bayern won the Bundesliga ahead of perennial runners-up Schalke but it was also due in no small measure to the dramatic collapse of Bayer Leverkusen who were unbeaten in their first 24 matches.

FIFA WORLD CUP RECORD

1930 DNE **1934** 3 SF **1938** 10 r1 **1950** DNE **1954** 1 Winners **1958** 4 SF **1962** 7 QF **1966** 2 Finalists **1970** 3 SF **1974** 1 Winners (hosts)
1978 6 r2 **1982** 2 Finalists **1986** 2 Finalists **1990** 1 Winners **1994** 5 QF **1998** 7 QF **2002** 2 Finalists **2006** 3 SF (hosts) **2010** 3 SF

DEUTSCHER FUSSBALL-BUND (DFB)

Otto-Fleck-Schneise 6,
Postfach 71 02 65,
Frankfurt 60528
☎ +49 69 67880
📠 +49 69 6788266
✉ info@dfb.de
🖥 www.dfb.de
FA 1900 CON 1954 FIFA 1904
P Theo Zwanziger
GS Wolfgang Niersbach

FIFA BIG COUNT 2006

Total players	16 308 946
% of population	19.79%
Male	14 438 313
Female	1 870 633
Amateurs 18+	4 221 170
Youth under 18	2 081 912
Unregistered	10 000 000
Professionals	864
Referees	81 372
Admin & coaches	77 800
Number of clubs	25 922
Number of teams	170 480

MAJOR CITIES/TOWNS

		Population
1	Berlin	3 418 983
2	Hamburg	1 773 537
3	Munich/München	1 360 717
4	Cologne/Köln	1 001 499
5	Frankfurt	653 746
6	Stuttgart	596 337
7	Dortmund	586 344
8	Düsseldorf	582 784
9	Essen	578 549
10	Bremen	549 597
11	Dresden	523 592
12	Hanover	517 553
13	Leipzig	513 810
14	Nuremberg	503 786
15	Duisburg	494 215
26	Gelsenkirchen	262 063
27	Mönch'gladbach	257 896
62	Wolfsburg	121 088
83	Kaiserslautern	97 168

BUNDESREPUBLIK DEUTSCHLAND • FEDERAL REPUBLIC OF GERMANY

Capital	Berlin	Population	82 329 758 (16)	% in cities	74%
GDP per capita	$35 500 (33)	Area km²	357 022 km² (62)	GMT + / -	+1
Neighbours (km)	Austria 784, Belgium 167, Czech Republic 646, Denmark 68, France 451, Luxembourg 138, Netherlands 577, Poland 456, Switzerland 334 • Coast 2389				

RECENT INTERNATIONAL MATCHES PLAYED BY GERMANY

2008	Opponents	Score		Venue	Comp	Scorers	Att	Referee
8-06	Poland	W	2-0	Klagenfurt	ECr1	Podolski 2 [20] [72]	30 461	Ovrebø NOR
12-06	Croatia	L	1-2	Klagenfurt	ECr1	Podolski [79]	30 461	De Bleeckere BEL
16-06	Austria	W	1-0	Vienna	ECr1	Ballack [49]	51 428	Mejuto Gonzalez ESP
19-06	Portugal	W	3-2	Basel	ECqf	Schweinsteiger [22], Klose [26], Ballack [61]	39 374	Fröjdfeldt SWE
25-06	Turkey	W	3-2	Basel	ECsf	Schweinsteiger [26], Klose [79], Lahm [90]	39 378	Busacca SUI
29-06	Spain	L	0-1	Vienna	ECf		51 425	Rosetti ITA
20-08	Belgium	W	2-0	Nuremberg	Fr	Schweinsteiger [59p], Marin [77]	34 117	Vejlgaard DEN
6-09	Liechtenstein	W	6-0	Vaduz	WCq	Podolski 2 [21] [48], Rolfes [64], Schweinsteiger [65], Hitzlsperger [75], Westermann [86]	6 021	Gomes POR
10-09	Finland	D	3-3	Helsinki	WCq	Klose 3 [38] [45] [83]	37 150	Kassai HUN
11-10	Russia	W	2-1	Dortmund	WCq	Podolski [9], Ballack [28]	65 607	Frojdfeldt SWE
15-10	Wales	W	1-0	Mönchengladbach	WCq	Trochowski [72]	44 500	Duhamel FRA
19-11	England	L	1-2	Berlin	Fr	Helmes [63]	74 244	Busacca SUI
2009								
11-02	Norway	L	0-1	Düsseldorf	Fr		42 000	Messner AUT
28-03	Liechtenstein	W	4-0	Leipzig	WCq	Ballack [4], Jansen [8], Schweinsteiger [47], Podolski [50]	43 368	Ishchenko UKR
1-04	Wales	W	2-0	Cardiff	WCq	Ballack [11], Williams OG [48]	26 064	Hauge NOR
29-05	China PR	D	1-1	Shanghai	Fr	Podolski [8]	25 000	Lee KOR
2-06	UAE	W	7-2	Dubai	Fr	Westermann [29], Gomez 4 [35] [45] [47] [90], Trochowski [39], Juma OG [52]	7 000	Darwish JOR
12-08	Azerbaijan	W	2-0	Baku	WCq	Schweinsteiger [12], Klose [54]	22 500	Kelly IRL
5-09	South Africa	W	2-0	Leverkusen	Fr	Gomez [35], Ozil [77]	29 569	Circhetta SUI
9-09	Azerbaijan	W	4-0	Hanover	WCq	Ballack [14p], Klose 2 [55] [65], Podolski [71]	35 369	Kakos GRE
10-10	Russia	W	1-0	Moscow	WCq	Klose [35]	72 100	Busacca SUI
14-10	Finland	D	1-1	Hamburg	WCq	Podolski [90]	51 500	Atkinson ENG
18-11	Côte d'Ivoire	D	2-2	Gelsenkirchen	Fr	Podolski 2 [11p] [90]	33 015	Kuipers NED
2010								
3-03	Argentina	L	0-1	Munich	Fr		65 152	Atkinson ENG
13-05	Malta	W	3-0	Aachen	Fr	Cacau 2 [16] [58], OG [61]	27 000	Hamer LUX
29-05	Hungary	W	3-0	Budapest	Fr	Podolski [5p], Gomez [69], Cacau [73]	14 000	Larsen DEN
3-06	Bosnia-Herzegovina	W	3-1	Frankfurt	Fr	Lahm [50], Schweinsteiger 2 [73p] [77p]	48 000	Rizzoli ITA
13-06	Australia	W	4-0	Durban	WCr1	Podolski [8], Klose [26], Muller [68], Cacau [70]	62 660	Rodriguez EX
18-06	Serbia	L	0-1	Port Elizabeth	WCr1		38 294	Undiano ESP
23-06	Ghana	W	1-0	Johannesburg	WCr1	Ozil [60]	83 391	Simon BRA
27-06	England	W	4-1	Bloemfontein	WCr2	Klose [20], Podolski [32], Muller 2 [67] [70]	40 510	Larrionda URU
3-07	Argentina	W	4-0	Cape Town	WCqf	Muller [3], Klose 2 [68] [89], Friedrich [74]	64 100	Irmatov UZB
7-07	Spain	L	0-1	Durban	WCsf		60 960	Kassai HUN
10-07	Uruguay	W	3-2	Port Elizabeth	WC3p	Muller [19], Jansen [56], Khedira [82]	36 254	Archundia MEX
11-08	Denmark	D	2-2	Copenhagen	Fr	Gomez [19], Helmes [73]	19 071	Kelly IRL
3-09	Belgium	W	1-0	Brussels	ECq	Klose [51]	41 126	Hauge NOR
7-09	Azerbaijan	W	6-1	Cologne	ECq	Westermann [28], Podolski [44], Klose 2 [45] [92+], OG [53], Badstuber [86]	43 751	Strombergsson SWE
8-10	Turkey	W	3-0	Berlin	ECq	Klose 2 [42] [87], Ozil [79]	74 244	Webb ENG
12-10	Kazakhstan	W	3-0	Astana	ECq	Klose [48], Gomez [76], Podolski [85]	18 000	Tudor ROU
17-11	Sweden	D	0-0	Gothenburg	Fr		21 959	Velasco ESP

Fr = Friendly match • EC = UEFA EURO 2008/2012 • WC = FIFA World Cup • q = qualifier • r1 = first round group • r2 = second round etc

GERMANY NATIONAL TEAM HISTORICAL RECORDS

Caps
150 - Lothar Matthaus 1980-2000 • 108 - Jurgen Klinsmann 1987-98 • 105 - Miroslav Klose 2001- & Jurgen Kohler 1986-98 • 103 - Franz Beckenbauer 1965-77 • 101 - Thomas Haßler 1988-2000 • 98 - Michael Ballack 1999- • 96 - Berti Vogts 1967-78 • 95 - Sepp Maier 1966-79 & Karl-Heinz Rummenigge 1976-86 • 90 - Rudi Voller 1982-94 • 86 - Andreas Brehme 1984-94 & Oliver Kahn 1995-2006

Goals
68 - Gerd Muller 1966-74 • 58 - Miroslav Klose 2001- • 47 - Jurgen Klinsmann 1987-98 & Rudi Voller 1982-94 • 45 - Karl-Heinz Rummenigge 1976-86 • 43 - Uwe Seeler 1954-70 • 42 - Michael Ballack 1999- & Lukas Podolski 2001- • 37 - Oliver Bierhoff 1996-2002 • 33 - Fritz Walter 1940-58 • 32 - Klaus Fischer 1977-82 • 30 - Ernst Lehner 1933-42 • 29 - Andreas Moller 1988-99 • 27 - Edmund Conen 1934-42 • 24 - Richard Hofmann 1927-33 • 23 - Lothar Matthaus 1980-2000 • 21 - Max Morlock 1950-58 & Helmut Rahn 1951-60

Past Coaches
Committee 1908-28 • Otto Nerz 1928-36 • Sepp Herberger 1936-64 • Helmut Schon 1964-78 • Jupp Derwall 1978-84 • Franz Beckenbauer 1984-90 • Berti Vogts 1990-98 • Erich Ribbeck 1998-2000 • Rudi Voller 2000-04 • Jurgen Klinsmann 2004-06 • Joachim Low 2006-

GERMANY 2009-10

1. BUNDESLIGA

Team	Pl	W	D	L	F	A	Pts	Bayern München	Schalke 04	Werder Bremen	Leverkusen	Bor. Dortmund	VfB Stuttgart	Hamburger SV	VfL Wolfsburg	1.FSV Mainz	Eint. Frankfurt	TSG Hoffenheim	Gladbach	1.FC Köln	SC Freiburg	Hannover 96	1.FC Nürnberg	VfL Bochum	Hertha BSC
Bayern München †	34	20	10	4	72	31	70		1-1	1-1	1-1	3-1	1-2	1-0	3-0	3-0	2-1	2-0	2-1	0-0	2-1	7-0	2-1	3-1	5-2
Schalke 04 †	34	19	8	7	53	31	65	1-2		0-2	2-2	2-1	2-1	3-3	1-2	1-0	2-0	2-0	3-1	2-0	0-1	2-0	1-0	3-0	2-0
Werder Bremen †	34	17	10	7	71	40	61	2-3	0-2		2-2	1-1	2-2	1-1	2-2	3-0	2-3	2-0	3-0	1-0	4-0	0-0	4-2	3-2	2-1
Bayer Leverkusen ‡	34	15	14	5	65	38	59	1-1	0-2	0-0		1-1	4-0	4-2	2-1	4-2	4-0	1-0	3-2	0-0	3-1	3-0	4-0	2-1	1-1
Borussia Dortmund ‡	34	16	9	9	54	42	57	1-5	0-1	2-1	3-0		1-1	1-0	1-1	0-2	2-3	1-1	3-0	1-0	1-0	4-1	4-0	2-0	2-0
VfB Stuttgart ‡	34	15	10	9	51	41	55	0-0	1-2	0-4	2-1	4-1		1-3	3-1	2-2	2-1	3-1	2-1	0-2	2-4	0-0	0-0	1-1	1-1
Hamburger SV	34	13	13	8	56	41	52	1-0	2-2	2-1	0-0	4-1	3-1		1-1	0-1	0-0	0-0	2-3	3-1	2-0	0-0	4-0	0-1	1-0
VfL Wolfsburg	34	14	8	12	64	58	50	1-3	2-1	2-4	2-3	1-3	2-0	2-4		3-3	3-1	4-0	2-1	2-3	2-2	4-2	2-3	4-1	1-5
1.FSV Mainz	34	12	11	11	36	42	47	2-1	0-0	1-2	2-2	1-0	1-1	1-1	0-2		3-3	2-1	1-0	1-0	3-0	1-0	1-0	0-2	1-1
Eintracht Frankfurt	34	12	10	12	47	54	46	2-1	1-4	1-0	3-2	1-1	0-3	1-1	2-2	2-0		1-2	1-2	0-2	1-1	1-1	1-1	2-1	2-2
TSG Hoffenheim	34	11	9	14	44	42	42	1-1	0-0	0-1	0-3	1-2	1-1	5-1	1-2	0-1	1-1		2-2	0-2	1-1	2-1	3-0	3-0	5-1
Bor. Mönchengladbach	34	10	9	15	43	60	39	1-1	1-0	4-3	1-1	0-1	0-0	1-0	0-4	2-0	2-0	2-4		0-0	1-1	5-3	2-1	1-2	2-1
1.FC Köln	34	9	11	14	33	42	38	1-1	1-2	0-0	0-1	2-3	1-5	3-3	1-3	1-0	0-0	0-4	1-1		2-2	0-1	3-0	2-0	0-3
SC Freiburg	34	9	8	17	35	59	35	1-2	0-0	0-6	0-5	3-1	0-1	1-1	1-0	1-0	0-2	0-1	3-0	0-0		1-2	2-1	1-1	0-3
Hannover 96	34	9	6	19	43	67	33	0-3	4-2	1-5	0-0	1-1	0-2	0-1	1-1	2-1	0-1	6-1	1-4	5-2			1-3	2-3	0-3
1.FC Nürnberg	34	8	7	19	32	58	31	1-1	1-2	2-2	3-2	2-3	1-2	0-4	0-2	2-0	1-1	0-0	1-0	1-0	0-1	0-2		0-1	3-0
VfL Bochum	34	6	10	18	33	64	28	1-5	2-2	1-4	1-1	1-4	0-2	1-2	1-1	2-3	1-2	2-1	3-3	0-0	1-2	0-3	0-0		1-0
Hertha BSC Berlin	34	5	9	20	34	56	24	1-3	0-1	2-3	2-2	0-0	0-1	1-0	0-0	0-1	0-4	1-0	1-2	0-0					

7/08/2009 - 8/05/2010 • † Qualified for the UEFA Champions League • ‡ Qualified for the Europa League

Relegation play-off: **1.FC Nürnberg** 1-0 2-0 FC Augsburg

Top scorers: **22** - Edin Dzeko BIH, Wolfsburg • **21** - Stefan Kießling, Bayer Leverkusen • **19** - Lucas Barrios PAR, Dortmund • **18** - Kevin Kuranyi, Schalke • **16** - Claudio Pizarro PER, Werder Bremen & Arjen Robben NED, Bayern München • **13** - Cacau, Stuttgart & Thomas Muller, Bayern München • **12** - Albert Bunjaku SUI, Nürnberg, Eren Derdiyok SUI, Leverkusen & Vedad Ibisevic BIH, Hoffenheim

GERMANY 2009-10

2. BUNDESLIGA (2)

Team	Pl	W	D	L	F	A	Pts	Kaiserslautern	St Pauli	Augsburg	Düsseldorf	Paderborn	MSV Duisburg	Bielefeld	TSV 1860	Cottbus	Karlsruher SC	Greuther Fürth	Union Berlin	Aachen	RW Oberhausen	FSV Frankfurt	Hansa Rostock	TuS Koblenz	Rot-Weiss Ahlen
1.FC Kaiserslautern	34	19	10	5	56	28	67		3-0	1-1	0-2	3-0	4-1	1-0	4-0	4-1	2-0	2-1	1-1	1-1	3-1	1-1	0-1	3-0	0-0
FC St Pauli	34	20	4	10	72	37	64	1-2		3-0	2-1	1-2	2-0	3-1	1-1	2-1	2-2	3-0	1-0	5-3	0-0	2-0	6-1	2-1	
FC Augsburg	34	17	11	6	60	40	62	4-1	3-2		2-0	3-0	2-0	3-1	1-0	3-1	1-1	1-1	1-1	0-1	2-2	2-0	5-2	1-1	3-1
Fortuna Düsseldorf	34	17	8	9	48	31	59	0-0	1-0	1-1		3-0	2-0	3-2	2-0	2-1	1-0	0-0	1-0	0-0	2-0	2-1	1-2	0-0	4-0
SC Paderborn 07	34	14	9	11	49	49	51	0-0	2-1	2-2	1-1		1-3	2-3	5-1	2-0	1-0	3-0	2-1	1-2	0-2	2-1	1-2	2-2	1-1
MSV Duisburg	34	14	8	12	51	46	50	1-1	0-2	2-2	3-0	2-3		0-3	0-1	2-2	0-1	1-1	3-1	0-2	2-2	5-0	3-1	4-1	2-2
Arminia Bielefeld	34	13	10	11	48	41	49	1-2	1-0	1-2	1-1	3-0	1-2		0-1	2-0	0-1	2-1	1-1	1-0	2-1	2-1	3-1	4-2	2-0
TSV 1860 München	34	14	6	14	43	48	48	0-1	2-1	1-0	2-2	0-0	3-1	3-1		1-2	3-3	1-1	2-2	0-1	1-1	3-0	2-0	2-0	0-1
Energie Cottbus	34	13	8	13	55	49	47	1-2	0-1	3-1	4-2	1-2	0-1	4-1	1-0		2-4	1-3	4-2	3-1	3-0	3-0	0-0	1-1	4-1
Karlsruher SC	34	13	7	14	43	45	46	1-3	0-4	1-0	1-1	1-2	0-1	0-2	0-0	0-2		1-1	3-2	1-1	1-1	2-2	2-0	5-2	3-1
SpVgg Greuther Fürth	34	12	8	14	51	50	44	3-0	1-4	4-5	2-1	1-1	0-1	2-4	1-2	1-0	1-4		0-0	0-2	4-0	4-0	1-0	1-2	3-1
1.FC Union Berlin	34	11	11	12	42	45	44	0-2	2-1	0-0	1-0	5-4	0-1	3-0	1-1	1-1	1-1	1-2		0-0	1-0	1-0	3-2	2-1	
Alemannia Aachen	34	10	11	13	37	41	41	0-3	0-5	4-0	0-1	3-2	1-0	0-0	4-1	1-0	0-1	0-3	1-0		2-1	3-0	1-1	0-2	
Rot-Weiß Oberhausen	34	12	5	17	38	52	41	2-1	1-3	0-3	0-1	3-2	1-0	0-0	4-1	1-0	0-3	1-0	1-2	1-4		1-3	2-1	2-0	0-1
FSV Frankfurt	34	9	11	14	29	50	38	1-1	2-3	1-1	2-0	0-0	1-2	0-0	3-2	0-0	2-1	0-5	2-1	1-1	1-0		0-1	1-1	0-0
Hansa Rostock	34	10	6	18	33	45	36	0-1	0-2	0-1	2-1	1-2	3-1	1-1	2-1	0-0	2-1	4-0	0-0	0-2	0-1	2-1		2-1	0-1
TuS Koblenz	34	7	10	17	35	60	31	2-2	1-5	0-1	1-0	2-1	0-3	3-2	2-2	0-2	2-2	2-0	1-1	1-0	0-1	3-2	2-1		1-1
Rot-Weiss Ahlen	34	5	7	22	19	55	22	0-1	0-2	1-3	1-4	0-0	0-1	0-1	0-0	4-1	3-2	1-0	0-0	0-2	1-2	1-0	0-0	0-2	

7/08/2009 - 9/05/2010 • Relegation play-off: **Ingolstadt** 1-0 2-0 Hansa Rostock • Top scorers: **23** - Michael Thurk, Augsburg • **20** - Marius Ebbers, St Pauli • **15** - Erik Jendrisek SVK, Kaiserslautern, Christopher Nothe, Fürth & Mahir Saglik TUR, Paderborn • **14** - Benjamin Auer, Aachen

GERMANY 2009–10

3. BUNDESLIGA (3)

Team	Pl	W	D	L	F	A	Pts	Osnabrück	Aue	Ingolstadt	Braunschweig	Jena	Heidenheim	Offenbach	Bayern	Erfurt	Stuttgart	Unterhaching	Dresden	Werder	Sandhausen	Wehen	Regensburg	Burghausen	Dortmund	Kiel	Wuppertal
VfL Osnabrück	38	20	9	9	55	37	69	—	3-1	5-2	1-0	2-0	3-2	1-0	4-1	3-1	0-1	1-0	1-1	1-0	3-1	0-0	1-0	2-1	4-1	3-1	1-1
Erzgebirge Aue	38	20	8	10	57	41	68	3-0	—	1-0	2-1	0-0	0-1	4-2	2-0	2-0	1-0	2-0	2-0	2-1	3-1	2-2	3-1	2-2	3-0	3-2	3-1
FC Ingolstadt 04	38	18	10	10	72	46	64	0-0	5-1	—	3-3	2-2	4-3	1-0	2-0	5-0	1-1	2-2	0-0	4-1	1-1	5-1	2-2	6-0	0-1	1-0	0-2
Eint. Braunschweig	38	17	11	10	55	37	62	1-0	3-0	2-1	—	2-1	1-1	0-0	3-1	1-1	4-3	1-0	0-1	1-2	6-0	3-1	1-0	1-0	1-2	3-0	
Carl Zeiss Jena	38	16	12	10	54	44	60	1-1	1-0	2-0	2-1	—	1-2	0-0	6-0	0-3	1-2	1-1	0-4	2-2	0-1	2-1	3-1	0-0	2-1	3-0	1-0
1.FC Heidenheim	38	17	8	13	66	56	59	1-0	0-0	0-1	0-1	3-1	—	0-2	4-2	2-2	2-1	4-3	0-1	1-2	1-0	0-2	3-2	6-1	2-1	3-0	2-2
Offenbacher Kickers	38	15	12	11	55	35	57	2-0	0-0	0-1	3-0	4-0	2-1	—	4-1	0-0	2-0	1-3	1-0	4-0	3-3	3-0	0-0	3-0	1-2	2-3	0-1
Bayern München-2	38	15	9	14	55	65	54	1-1	2-3	1-0	1-1	0-0	4-2	2-1	—	1-0	2-0	1-1	0-0	2-1	2-2	0-0	0-5	2-0	3-0	2-1	3-1
Rot-Weiß Erfurt	38	14	11	13	41	41	53	2-0	0-0	2-1	2-1	0-3	1-2	0-2	2-0	—	0-1	1-1	4-1	1-1	1-0	1-2	0-0	1-1	1-0	0-0	1-0
VfB Stuttgart-2	38	16	4	18	53	50	52	0-1	1-2	2-4	1-2	0-1	1-2	2-0	2-4	3-1	—	3-1	2-2	0-1	3-0	3-0	2-3	1-0	2-1	1-0	1-3
SpVgg Unterhaching	38	13	11	14	52	52	50	1-0	2-2	1-2	0-2	0-3	1-0	2-1	0-1	1-1	1-0	—	0-0	1-3	3-4	3-2	1-1	1-3	1-1	3-1	1-0
1.FC Dynamo Dresden	38	14	8	16	39	46	50	0-0	3-0	2-0	1-1	0-3	4-3	2-4	2-0	1-0	0-1	0-2	—	1-0	0-3	3-1	0-2	1-0	3-2	3-0	3-2
Werder Bremen-2	38	13	8	17	49	54	47	0-1	2-1	0-0	0-3	1-2	1-1	0-1	0-3	0-0	0-3	3-1	2-0	—	3-0	5-0	4-1	3-4	1-0	6-1	0-1
SV Sandhausen	38	11	14	13	54	63	47	3-2	0-0	1-2	1-1	2-2	3-0	1-1	4-2	1-2	2-1	3-1	0-0	2-2	—	2-1	2-1	0-0	3-2	1-1	1-3
SV Wehen	38	13	8	17	52	64	47	4-0	2-0	1-5	0-0	1-1	1-2	3-3	1-2	2-0	1-4	2-1	0-1	2-0	2-1	—	0-2	3-1	2-2	2-1	2-3
SSV Jahn Regensburg	38	11	13	14	43	48	46	2-2	2-1	0-2	1-0	1-1	2-2	1-1	1-1	0-2	0-0	1-3	2-1	0-1	1-0	1-0	—	0-0	2-0	2-1	0-1
Wacker Burghausen	38	13	7	18	45	64	46	0-1	0-2	4-2	0-2	2-3	1-3	1-0	2-1	1-3	3-0	3-0	2-0	1-5	2-2	0-1	2-0	—	4-3	0-3	1-0
Borussia Dortmund-2	38	11	6	21	43	58	39	1-2	1-3	0-1	0-0	0-3	1-1	0-0	0-2	1-0	1-2	1-2	1-0	1-2	2-1	1-1	2-0	3-0	—	1-0	2-0
KSV Holstein Kiel	38	9	11	18	43	61	38	1-1	2-1	2-2	1-1	1-1	1-0	0-0	2-2	1-2	2-0	2-1	2-1	2-0	4-0	0-0	1-1	0-0	1-4	—	1-1
Wuppertaler SV	38	10	8	20	40	61	38	0-4	0-2	0-1	1-1	1-1	1-5	3-0	3-0	1-0	1-0	1-0	2-2	2-1	2-0	0-5	3-1	2-2	0-2	5-3	—

25/07/2009 - 8/05/2010 • Top scorers: **22** - Regis Dorn, Sandhausen • **21** - Mortiz Hartmann, Ingolstadt • **17** - Orlando Smeekes ANT, Jena

GERMANY 2009–10

REGIONALLIGA NORD (4)

Team	Pl	W	D	L	F	A	Pts	Babelsberg	Wolfsburg	Chemnitzer	Hallescher	Hamburg	Magdeburg	Plauen	Hannover	Lübeck	Meuselwitz	Hertha	Hansa	Türkiyemspor	Wilhelmshaven	Tennis Borussia	Oberneuland	St Pauli	Goslarer
SV Babelsberg 03	34	23	8	3	54	18	77	—	0-0	2-0	1-0	0-0	3-2	1-0	1-0	2-0	3-0	0-0	2-0	3-2	2-0	0-1	0-0	4-1	1-1
VfL Wolfsburg-2	34	21	7	6	60	20	70	0-0	—	0-1	1-1	0-0	1-0	1-0	2-0	5-0	0-0	2-0	1-0	1-3	2-0	0-0	1-0	3-0	4-0
Chemnitzer FC	34	18	7	9	58	34	61	2-1	1-1	—	1-1	1-0	1-1	1-3	2-0	3-2	3-1	2-2	1-0	3-0	5-1	3-0	4-1	4-0	1-0
Hallescher FC	34	14	14	6	47	25	56	0-1	2-2	0-0	—	0-1	1-1	0-0	1-1	4-0	2-0	3-2	4-0	6-0	1-2	2-0	2-1	1-0	3-0
Hamburger SV-2	34	15	10	9	45	34	55	1-6	2-0	1-2	0-1	—	1-1	1-1	1-0	0-3	1-1	1-2	3-0	1-2	1-1	2-1	2-0	4-0	2-1
1.FC Magdeburg	34	14	9	11	57	38	51	0-1	3-1	1-0	0-1	0-0	—	1-4	2-1	5-2	7-0	5-0	1-0	2-1					
VFC Plauen	34	14	8	12	49	39	50	1-1	0-4	0-1	4-0	2-0	1-4	—	2-1	0-1	0-1	2-1	0-2	1-0	0-1	0-2	1-0	6-0	1-1
Hannover 96-2	34	13	10	11	62	41	49	1-2	3-0	2-0	1-1	0-2	4-1	1-1	—	3-0	1-1	3-3	0-2	2-2	5-2	2-0	5-0	0-0	4-1
VfB Lübeck	34	14	7	13	47	48	49	0-1	1-5	2-0	1-1	0-0	1-1	2-1	1-3	—	0-1	1-1	6-2	1-0	3-0	3-0	1-0	0-0	1-1
ZFC Meuselwitz	34	10	13	11	40	50	43	0-3	1-2	3-1	1-2	2-1	1-0	0-0	1-3	1-3	—	2-1	1-1	1-3	0-4	2-1	1-2	0-0	1-1
Hertha BSC Berlin-2	34	11	9	14	57	55	42	1-4	1-3	2-1	1-1	0-1	3-0	1-3	0-2	1-0	7-3	—	2-3	5-1	1-3	1-1	4-1	3-0	2-1
Hansa Rostock-2	34	11	7	16	36	60	40	0-2	0-1	0-5	0-2	1-2	1-0	0-3	1-1	2-1	0-3	0-0	—	3-1	2-1	0-1	3-2	0-0	1-1
Türkiyemspor	34	10	9	15	51	64	39	0-1	0-3	2-1	0-0	0-1	2-4	2-1	1-2	3-1	5-1	0-0	5-2	—	0-0	0-2	5-0	3-3	3-2
SV Wilhelmshaven	34	10	9	15	45	59	39	1-2	0-1	2-2	0-2	2-2	1-2	1-3	0-5	1-2	0-0	1-1	2-0	1-1	—	1-0	2-3	2-1	3-1
Tennis Borussia Berlin	34	8	10	16	33	55	34	1-1	0-2	0-0	1-1	1-4	3-4	2-2	0-2	3-0	1-2	0-2	1-3	3-1	1-1	—	2-3	2-1	1-0
FC Oberneuland	34	9	6	19	37	71	33	1-2	0-5	0-3	1-0	1-2	1-0	2-2	1-3	0-2	2-0	1-1	2-2	3-1	1-2	0-0	—	0-2	2-1
FC St Pauli-2	34	7	9	18	34	67	30	1-2	1-0	3-1	1-1	0-3	0-3	3-2	2-1	1-3	0-2	3-1	1-2	2-2	0-3	1-1	4-4	—	2-1
Goslarer SC 08	34	4	8	22	33	67	20	2-0	0-4	0-2	0-0	1-2	1-1	1-2	2-1	1-3	0-2	0-4	1-1	4-2	2-2	0-0	1-2	3-2	—

7/08/2009 - 29/05/2010 • Top scorers: **29** - Daniel Frahn, Babelsberg • **19** - Mike Konnecke, Wolfsburg-2

GERMANY 2009-10

REGIONALLIGA WEST (4)

Team	Pl	W	D	L	F	A	Pts	Saarbrücken	Lotte	Bochum	Köln	RW Essen	Pr'ßen Münster	Elversberg	Kaiserslautern	Verl	Bonn	Fortuna	Schalke	Leverkusen	Mannheim	Mainz	Gladbach	Wormatia	Trier
1.FC Saarbrücken	34	20	9	5	53	33	**69**		1-0	1-0	1-1	1-1	2-0	1-0	0-3	3-1	3-1	2-1	2-0	1-1	2-1	1-1	0-0	2-0	1-3
Sportfreunde Lotte	34	17	10	7	48	31	**61**	3-0		0-0	2-1	3-0	1-1	0-0	2-0	2-3	1-2	1-0	0-1	2-2	2-0	2-1	2-1	2-1	1-0
VfL Bochum-2	34	16	9	9	50	32	**57**	2-0	0-2		1-4	5-4	4-1	0-1	1-1	3-0	1-1	2-1	2-1	3-1	0-1	0-0	4-1	2-1	1-2
1.FC Köln-2	34	15	10	9	50	37	**55**	1-3	1-1	0-3		0-1	1-1	4-3	1-0	2-0	0-0	2-2	0-1	0-0	1-1	3-1	1-0	2-1	3-0
Rot-Weiss Essen	34	14	10	10	44	32	**52**	1-2	3-0	2-2	0-2		1-1	2-0	2-0	2-0	1-1	0-1	1-0	1-1	3-1	0-0	0-1	0-3	1-0
Preußen Münster	34	14	9	11	47	37	**51**	0-0	2-0	0-2	1-2	4-0		0-1	2-1	1-2	3-1	1-1	4-1	2-1	2-2	1-2	0-1	2-1	4-0
SV Elversberg	34	14	8	12	41	34	**50**	6-0	1-1	0-2	4-1	0-0	0-1		0-4	1-0	1-1	0-3	2-0	1-0	1-2	2-1	4-0	1-0	0-1
1.FC Kaiserslautern-2	34	14	7	13	43	37	**49**	0-2	1-2	0-0	2-5	1-0	1-0	2-1		2-2	0-2	2-2	0-2	0-0	1-0	1-1	0-2	0-0	3-1
SC Verl	34	12	11	11	41	41	**47**	2-3	0-0	1-0	1-0	0-3	0-0	1-1	0-3		4-1	1-2	3-2	3-0	1-0	2-1	2-1	3-1	1-1
Bonner SC	34	10	13	11	47	45	**43**	0-1	2-3	0-1	0-1	1-1	2-2	0-2	1-0	1-1		1-2	1-1	3-3	4-1	1-1	3-1	5-1	1-0
Fortuna Düsseldorf-2	34	11	8	15	35	50	**41**	0-1	1-0	0-1	1-0	1-2	1-2	2-1	1-3	0-4	0-2		0-4	1-0	0-0	0-3	2-1	1-1	2-1
FC Schalke 04-2	34	11	7	16	42	43	**40**	0-2	1-1	0-1	0-1	1-0	0-2	0-1	2-3	0-0	0-2	3-0		2-1	0-1	1-2	1-1	7-2	3-1
Bayer Leverkusen-2	34	9	13	12	38	45	**40**	1-1	4-0	1-4	1-0	0-0	1-0	2-1	1-0	0-0	2-2	1-1	1-0		2-2	1-1	1-0	1-2	3-2
SV Waldhof Mannheim	34	10	10	14	36	43	**40**	0-2	1-1	1-1	1-0	0-2	0-2	1-1	0-2	1-1	3-2	4-0	0-0	3-1		3-1	0-0	0-3	1-0
1.FSV Mainz 05-2	34	10	10	14	37	46	**40**	0-4	1-7	0-0	1-2	0-3	2-0	1-2	0-1	0-0	0-1	2-0	1-2	2-0	1-0		1-2	4-1	2-0
B. Mönchengladbach-2	34	11	7	16	37	53	**40**	1-1	0-1	1-0	4-0	0-2	1-2	0-1	2-0	1-2	0-1	1-0	1-1	0-3	2-2	3-2		2-1	2-2
VfR Wormatia Worms	34	7	9	18	35	58	**30**	1-4	0-0	2-1	1-1	1-1	0-1	1-1	1-3	0-0	0-0	2-1	1-2	1-0	0-3	0-0	2-3		2-0
Eintracht Trier	34	7	8	19	33	61	**29**	2-2	0-1	0-1	2-2	0-4	2-2	0-0	0-3	3-2	3-2	0-3	2-2	1-2	2-1	0-0	0-2	2-1	

7/08/2009 - 29/05/2010 • Top scorers: **16** - Ercan Aydogmus, Bonner SC & Christian Knappmann, SC Verl

GERMANY 2009-10

REGIONALLIGA SUD (4)

Team	Pl	W	D	L	F	A	Pts	Aalen	Nürnberg	Freiburg	Hessen Kassel	Karlsruher SC	Ulm	TSV 1860	Eintracht	Kickers	Weiden	Fürth	Sonnenhof	Pfullendorf	Reutlingen	Darmstadt	Wehen	Bamberg	Alzenau
VfR Aalen	34	22	8	4	51	19	**74**		0-1	1-1	2-0	2-1	2-2	2-0	0-0	2-0	2-1	3-1	1-0	3-1	2-0	3-0	2-0	1-1	3-0
1.FC Nürnberg-2	34	18	9	7	55	30	**63**	3-1		0-2	1-1	3-0	4-0	0-0	3-1	3-1	1-2	2-0	0-0	1-0	1-0	1-0	3-0	1-1	1-1
SC Freiburg-2	34	17	10	7	63	34	**61**	3-1	1-4		1-1	1-1	3-1	1-0	2-1	0-0	5-1	0-2	2-0	2-0	3-0	1-1	3-3	1-2	3-0
KSV Hessen Kassel	34	15	14	5	63	41	**59**	0-1	4-1	1-1		3-0	1-1	1-1	1-0	0-0	3-1	5-1	3-0	5-2	2-1	2-2	1-0	1-1	1-0
Karlsruher SC-2	34	15	7	12	50	51	**52**	1-2	0-4	2-2	4-3		2-0	0-0	2-0	3-2	2-0	3-2	3-3	3-0	1-0	3-0	3-2	4-1	2-0
SSV Ulm 1846	34	13	12	9	52	45	**51**	0-3	1-1	3-2	0-0	1-3		2-1	2-0	0-1	2-1	3-0	1-2	2-0	1-3	1-0	3-0	3-2	4-0
TSV 1860 München-2	34	13	10	11	51	39	**49**	0-1	2-0	1-1	3-3	3-2	1-1		2-2	2-2	2-1	1-0	1-0	1-1	6-1	4-0	3-2	4-0	1-0
Eintracht Frankfurt-2	34	12	12	10	57	41	**48**	0-0	5-1	1-1	2-2	1-2	2-2	2-0		3-1	5-0	1-2	1-1	1-0	1-1	2-2	1-1	3-0	1-0
Stuttgarter Kickers	34	11	15	8	47	41	**48**	0-0	0-4	2-1	3-3	2-0	0-0	1-1	2-2		2-0	1-0	2-0	2-2	1-1	2-0	1-2	5-4	2-2
SpVgg Weiden	34	15	3	16	57	67	**48**	0-1	1-0	2-1	1-4	4-3	2-0	0-4	1-4	2-2		1-0	2-1	2-1	0-4	0-0	2-0	0-0	1-0
SpVgg Greuther Fürth-2	34	14	5	15	44	58	**47**	1-1	1-4	0-4	1-2	2-1	1-2	3-2	1-0	2-1	2-1		0-4	0-0	2-0	0-0	3-0	3-2	3-2
Sonnenhof Großaspach	34	13	7	14	53	44	**46**	0-1	2-2	3-2	1-2	1-1	0-2	2-0	3-1	2-1	5-3	1-1		2-0	2-0	2-2	2-1	3-1	5-0
SC Pfullendorf	34	10	11	13	39	41	**41**	0-1	2-0	0-1	2-1	1-1	1-1	0-1	3-1	1-0	4-3	0-1	3-1		5-1	1-1	1-2	2-0	1-3
SSV Reutlingen	34	11	7	16	43	56	**40**	1-2	0-0	1-4	1-1	0-1	3-1	0-0	1-3	1-0	2-0	1-3	1-1	6-1		1-2	3-2	2-1	3-0
SV Darmstadt 98	34	8	10	16	39	49	**34**	0-2	1-0	0-1	2-3	3-0	3-1	0-2	1-2	1-2	0-3	3-0	2-1	2-1	0-1		1-3	2-2	3-1
SV Wehen-2	34	7	8	19	32	56	**29**	0-2	1-2	1-1	1-2	1-2	0-0	2-1	1-5	1-1	1-2	0-0	0-1	0-0	0-3	1-0		4-1	1-0
Eintracht Bamberg	34	6	10	18	40	76	**28**	0-1	0-2	0-3	3-1	3-1	1-3	1-0	0-3	1-1	0-3	1-6	0-4	1-1	3-1	2-2	1-4		0-2
Bayern Alzenau	34	5	4	25	23	69	**18**	0-3	1-3	0-1	2-1	0-0	0-3	1-3	1-3	1-3	0-3	2-4	1-1	0-1	1-3	1-0	1-0	1-2	

7/08/2009 - 29/05/2010 • Top scorers: **19** - Abedin Krasniqi, Sonnenhof & Mijo Tunjic, Stuttgarter Kickers

GERMANY 2009–10 OBERLIGA (5)

BAYERN	Pl	Pts
FC Memmingen	36	74
FC Ismaning	36	63
SpVgg Unterhaching 2	36	62
TSV Aindling	36	59
TSV 1896 Rain	36	59
SV Seligenporten	36	58
FC Ingolstadt 04 2	36	58
FSV Erlangen-Bruck	36	56
SpVgg Bayreuth	36	54
SpVgg Bayern Hof	36	52
TSV Buchbach	36	49
TSV 1860 Rosenheim	36	49
SV Schalding-Heining	36	47
TSV Großbardorf	36	44
SpVgg Ansbach	36	42
VfL Frohnlach	36	40
SV Memmelsdorf	36	29
TSG Thannhausen	36	28
1. FC Bad Kötzting	36	24

BREMEN	Pl	Pts
Werder Bremen 3	30	73
Bremer SV	30	71
OSC Bremerhaven	30	64
Brinkumer SV	30	50
FC Bremerhaven	30	43
Türkspor Bremen	30	42
TSV Wulsdorf	30	41
Blumenthaler SV	30	41
Habenhauser FV	30	39
TuS Schwachhausen	30	39
SG Aumund-Vegesack	30	36
VfL Bremen	30	34
FC Oberneuland 2	30	32
TSV Melchiorshausen	30	27
Osterholz-Tenever	30	26
SV Grohn	30	18

NRW	Pl	Pts
SC Wiedenbrück	36	75
Arminia Bielefeld 2	36	71
TSV Germania Windeck	36	67
Schwarz-Weiß Essen	36	59
Rot-Weiss Essen 2	36	53
Almemannia Aachen 2	36	52
Westfalia Herne	36	51
VfB Speldorf	36	51
SV Bergisch Gladbach	36	47
1. FC Kleve	36	45
MSV Duisburg 2	36	44
SSVg. Velbert	36	44
Sportfreunde Siegen	36	44
SV Schermbeck	36	44
Fortuna Köln	36	40
VfB Hüls	36	40
Hammer SpVg	36	37
SG Wattenscheid	36	35
TSG Sprockhövel	36	32

HESSEN	Pl	Pts
FSV Frankfurt 2	36	80
SC Waldgirmes	36	67
KSV Baunatal	36	66
Eintracht Stadtallendorf	36	58
Rot-Weiss Frankfurt	36	57
1.FC Eschborn	36	56
Hünfelder SV	36	56
Viktoria Aschaffenburg	36	55
Kickers Offenbach 2	36	55
RSV Würges	36	53
Viktoria Urberach	36	52
VfB Marburg	36	49
FSV Fernwald	36	46
1.FC Schwalmstadt	36	41
OSC Vellmar	36	40
KSV Klein-Karben	36	39
Germania Ober-Roden	36	36
TSG Wörsdorf	36	27
SVA Bad Hersfeld	36	16

N'SACHSEN EAST	Pl	Pts
Eintracht Braunschweig 2	32	68
TuS Heeslingen	32	66
TSV Ottersberg	32	59
SV Drochtersen/Assel	32	58
Osterholz-Scharmbeck	32	55
Eintracht Northeim	32	55
Hansa Lüneburg	32	52
Borussia Hildesheim	32	51
Göttingen	32	44
Güldenstern Stade	32	42
Lupo-Martini	32	41
Ahlerstedt/Ottendorf	32	40
FT Braunschweig	32	39
Rot-Weiß Cuxhaven	32	27
Gifhorn	32	25
Ölper	32	23
Blau Weiß Bornreihe	32	18

N'SACHSEN WEST	Pl	Pts
Havelse	30	68
VfB Oldenburg	30	65
Schwarz-Weiß Rehden	30	65
BV Cloppenburg	30	56
Kickers Emden	30	48
Eintracht Nordhorn	30	46
SV Meppen	30	43
Ramlingen/Ehlershausen	30	43
SC Langenhagen	30	38
VfL Osnabrück 2	30	37
Bad Rothenfelde	30	36
Preußen Hameln	30	36
Oythe	30	29
Bavenstedt	30	27
VfL Oldenburg	30	22
Bückeburg	30	19

NORDOST - NORD	Pl	Pts
Energie Cottbus 2	30	66
BFC Dynamo	30	58
Brandenburger SC Süd	30	53
FSV 63 Luckenwalde	30	53
Malchower SV	30	53
TSG Neustrelitz	30	52
FSV Optik Rathenow	30	45
Torgelower SV Greif	30	44
SV Germania	30	42
Berlin Ankaraspor Kulübü	30	42
Ludwigsfelder FC	30	36
Lichterfelder FC Berlin	30	32
Reinickendorfer Füchse	30	32
Lichtenrader BC	30	24
Greifswalder SV	30	23
Falkensee-Finkenkrug	30	17

NORDOST - SUD	Pl	Pts
RB Leipzig	30	80
FSV Budissa Bautzen	30	58
FC Carl Zeiss Jena 2	30	53
VfB Auerbach	30	53
SG Dynamo Dresden 2	30	50
FC Sachsen Leipzig	30	48
Rot-Weiß Erfurt 2	30	43
FC Erzgebirge Aue 2	30	40
FSV Zwickau	30	39
VfB Germania Halberstadt	30	39
VfL Halle 1896	30	36
1. FC Lokomotive Leipzig	30	33
SC Borea Dresden	30	28
1. FC Gera	30	25
VfB Pößneck	30	18
SV Schott Jena	30	15

HAMBURG	Pl	Pts
Victoria Hamburg	34	68
TSV Buchholz	34	68
Altona 93	34	66
Curslack-Neuengamme	34	62
Meiendorfer SV	34	59
Oststeinbeker SV	34	54
Uhlenhorster Paloma	34	49
ASV Bergedorf 85	34	46
SC Condor Hamburg	34	45
Eintracht Norderstedt	34	44
Niendorfer TSV	34	42
Wedeler TSV	34	40
HSV Barmbek-Uhlenhorst	34	40
Concordia Hamburg	34	40
SV Lurup	34	39
SV Halstenbek-Rellingen	34	32
VfL Lohbrügge	34	26
TSV Uetersen	34	25

SC'WIG-HOLSTEIN	Pl	Pts
Holstein Kiel 2	34	82
VfR Neumünster	34	75
SV Eichede	34	66
FT Eider Büdelsdorf	34	62
SV Henstedt-Ulzburg	34	59
VfB Lübeck 2	34	56
Eckernförder SV	34	51
Flensburg 08	34	49
Weiche Flensburg	34	44
Heider SV	34	42
Heikendorfer SV	34	42
TSV Kropp	34	42
Schleswig 06	34	40
PSV Union Neumünster	34	39
Klausdorf	34	39
Comet Kiel	34	30
Altenholz	34	30
Itzehoer SV	34	9

B-WURTTEMBERG	Pl	Pts
TSG 1899 Hoffenheim 2	34	77
FC Astoria Walldorf	34	68
Bahlinger SC	34	66
FV Illertissen	34	58
TSG Weinheim	34	58
VfL Kirchheim unter Teck	34	57
1. FC Normannia Gmünd	34	54
SGV Freiberg	34	48
FC Nöttingen	34	47
TSG Balingen	34	45
Kehler FV	34	45
Stuttgarter Kickers 2	34	42
FC 08 Villingen	34	40
ASV Durlach	34	39
SV Spielberg	34	34
FC Denzlingen	34	29
TSV Crailsheim	34	27
SV Bonlanden	34	22

SUDWEST	Pl	Pts
FC 08 Homburg	34	64
FK Pirmasens	34	64
SVN 1929 Zweibrücken	34	59
SC Idar-Oberstein	34	56
SV Auersmacher	34	55
TuS Mechtersheim	34	49
Sportfreunde Eisbachtal	34	49
Alemannia Waldalgesheim	34	48
SC Hauenstein	34	47
Sv Elversberg 2	34	46
SF Köllerbach	34	46
Borussia Neunkirchen	34	45
SG 06 Betzdorf	34	45
SV Roßbach	34	42
Rot-Weiß Hasborn	34	38
SpVgg Wirges	34	32
TuS Mayen	34	30
Hassia Bingen	34	30

MEDALS TABLE

#	Club	Overall G	S	B	League G	S	B	Cup G	S	Europe G	S	B	City
1	Bayern München	43	14	15	22	8	4	15	2	6	4	11	Munich
2	1.FC Nürnberg	13	5	1	9	3		4	2			1	Nuremburg
3	Schalke 04	12	16	4	7	9	2	4	7	1		2	Gelsenkirchen
4	Hamburger SV	11	15	6	6	8	2	3	4	2	3	4	Hamburg
5	Werder Bremen	11	12	8	4	7	5	6	4	1	1	3	Bremen
6	Borussia Dortmund	10	8	8	6	4	5	2	2	2	2	3	Dortmund
7	Borussia Mönchengladbach	10	7	8	5	2	5	3	2	2	3	3	Mönchengladbach
8	VfB Stuttgart	8	8	6	5	4	4	3	2		2	2	Stuttgart
9	1.FC Köln	7	15	9	3	8	2	4	6		1	7	Cologne
10	1.FC Kaiserslautern	6	9	4	4	4	2	2	5			2	Kaiserslautern
11	Eintracht Frankfurt	6	4	7	1	1	5	4	2	1	1	2	Frankfurt
12	Lokomotive Leipzig (VfB)	4	2		3	2		1					Leipzig
13	Dresdner SC	4	1		2	1		2					Dresden
14	Fortuna Düsseldorf	3	7	2	1	1	2	2	5		1		Düsseldorf
15	Karlsruher SC	3	3	1	1	1		2	2			1	Karlsruhe
16	TSV München 1860	3	3		1	2		2			1		Munich
17	SpVgg Fürth	3	1		3	1							Fürth
18	Hannover 96	3			2			1					Hanover
19	Hertha BSC Berlin	2	7	5	2	5	4		2			1	Berlin
20	Bayer 04 Leverkusen	2	7	4		4	3	1	2	1	1	1	Leverkusen
21	Viktoria 89 Berlin	2	2		2	2							Berlin
22	Rot-Weiss Essen	2	1		1			1	1				Essen
23	SK Rapid Wien	2			1			1					Vienna - AUT
24	Holstein Kiel	1	2		1	2							Kiel
	Karlsruher FV	1	2		1	2							Karlsruhe
	Kickers Offenbach	1	2			2		1					Offenbach
27	Blau-Weiß Berlin	1	1		1	1							Berlin
	First Vienna	1	1			1		1					Vienna - AUT
	VfL Wolfsburg	1	1		1							1	Wolfsburg
30	KFC Uerdingen 05	1		2			1	1				1	Krefeld
31	Eintracht Braunschweig	1	1		1	1							Braunschweig
32	Freiburger FC	1			1								Freiburg
	Schwarz-Weiss Essen	1						1					Essen
	VfR Mannheim	1			1								Mannheim
35	MSV Duisburg		5	1		2			3			1	Duisburg
36	TSV Alemania Aachen		4			1			3				Aachen
37	1.FC Saarbrücken		2			2							Saarbrücken
	FSV Frankfurt		2			1			1				Frankfurt
	Stuttgarter Kickers		2			1			1				Stuttgart
	VfL Bochum		2						2				Bochum
	1.FC Union Berlin		2			1			1				Berlin
42	Admira Wien		1			1							Vienna - AUT
	Borussia Neunkirchen		1						1				Neunkirchen
	DFC Prag		1			1							Prague - CZE
	Energie Cottbus		1						1				Cottbus
	Fortuna Köln		1						1				Cologne
	Hertha BSC Berlin am		1						1				Berlin
	1.FC Phorzheim		1			1							Pforzheim
	LSV Groß Hamburg		1			1							Hamburg
	Preußen Münster		1			1							Münster
	Waldhof Mannheim		1						1				Mannheim
52	SC Freiburg			1			1						Freiburg

Leading East German Clubs (1948-91)

#	Club	Overall G	S	B	League G	S	B	Cup G	S	Europe G	S	B	City
1	Dynamo Dresden	15	12	8	8	8	6	7	4			1	Dresden
2	Dynamo Berlin	13	10	4	10	4	3	3	6			1	Berlin
3	1.FC Magdeburg	11	2	6	3	2	6	7		1			Magdeburg
4	Viktoria 91 Frankfurt	8	7	1	6	4	1	2	3				Frankfurt/Oder
5	Carl Zeiss Jena	7	13	6	3	9	5	4	3		1	1	Jena
6	Sachsenring Zwickau	5	1	4	2		3	3	1			1	Zwickau
7	Lokomotive Leipzig	4	8	9		3	8	4	4		1	1	Leipzig

DFB POKAL 2009–10

First Round		Second Round		Third Round	
Bayern München	3				
SpVgg Neckarelz *	1	**Bayern München ***	5		
VfB Speldorf *	0	Rot-Weiß Oberhausen	0		
Rot-Weiß Oberhausen	3			**Bayern München**	4
Alemannia Aachen	4			Eintracht Frankfurt *	0
Torgelower SV Greif *	1	Alemannia Aachen	4		
Kickers Offenbach *	0	**Eintracht Frankfurt ***	6		
Eintracht Frankfurt	3				
VfB Stuttgart	4				
SG Sonnenhof Großaspach	1	**VfB Stuttgart**	3		
1.FSV Mainz	1	VfB Lübeck *	1		
VfB Lübeck *	2			VfB Stuttgart	0
Rot-Weiss Ahlen *	1 5p			**SpVgg Greuther Fürth ***	1
Wacker Burghausen *	1 4p	Rot-Weiss Ahlen *	2		
Wormatia Worms *	0	**SpVgg Greuther Fürth**	3		
SpVgg Greuther Fürth	1				
VfL Osnabrück *	2				
Hansa Rostock	1	**VfL Osnabrück ***	3 4p		
Fortuna Düsseldorf *	3 1p	Hamburger SV	3 2p		
Hamburger SV	3 4p			**VfL Osnabrück ***	3
Karlsruher SC	2			Borussia Dortmund	2
Tennis Borussia Berlin *	0	Karlsruher SC *	0		
SpVgg Weiden *	1	**Borussia Dortmund**	3		
Borussia Dortmund	3				
TSV 1860 München	1				
SC Paderborn 07 *	0	**TSV 1860 München ***	2 4p		
Preußen Munster *	1	Hertha BSC Berlin	2 1p		
Hertha BSC Berlin	3			TSV 1860 München *	0
VfL Bochum	1			**Schalke 04**	3
Sportfreunde Lotte *	0	VfL Bochum *	0		
Germania Windeck *	0	**Schalke 04**	3		
Schalke 04	4				
FC Augsburg	2				
FC Ingolstadt 04 *	1	**FC Augsburg ***	1		
SV Elversberg *	0	SC Freiburg	0		
SC Freiburg	2			**FC Augsburg ***	5
Borussia Mönchengladbach	2			MSV Duisburg	0
FSV Frankfurt *	1	Borussia Mönchengladbach *	0		
Rot-Weiß Erfurt *	1	**MSV Duisburg**	1		
MSV Duisburg	2				
Eintracht Trier *	3				
Hannover 96	1	**Eintracht Trier ***	4		
SpVgg Unterhaching	0	Arminia Bielefeld	2		
Arminia Bielefeld	3			Eintracht Trier *	0
VfL Wolfsburg	4			**1.FC Köln**	3
SV Wehen *	1	VfL Wolfsburg	2		
Kickers Emden *	0	**1.FC Köln ***	3		
1.FC Köln	3				
TSG Hoffenheim	2				
FC Oberneuland *	0	**TSG Hoffenheim**	1		
Dynamo Dresden *	0	1.FC Nürnberg *	0		
1.FC Nürnberg	3			**TSG Hoffenheim ***	4
Energie Cottbus	3			TuS Koblenz	0
1.FC Magdeburg *	1	Energie Cottbus	2		
Concordia Hamburg *	0	**TuS Koblenz ***	4		
TuS Koblenz	4				
1.FC Kaiserslautern	1				
Eintracht Braunschweig *	0	**1.FC Kaiserslautern ***	2		
SV Babelsberg 03 *	0	Bayer Leverkusen	1		
Bayer Leverkusen	1			1.FC Kaiserslautern	0
FC St Pauli	2			**Werder Bremen ***	3
FC 08 Villingen *	0	FC St Pauli	1		
1.FC Union Berlin *	0	**Werder Bremen ***	2		
Werder Bremen	5				

DFB POKAL 2009-10

Quarter–finals	Semi–finals	Final

Bayern München *	6
SpVgg Greuther Fürth	2

Bayern München	1
Schalke 04 *	0

VfL Osnabrück *	0
Schalke 04	1

Bayern München	4
Werder Bremen	0

FC Augsburg *	2
1.FC Köln	0

FC Augsburg	0
Werder Bremen *	2

TSG Hoffenheim	1
Werder Bremen *	2

DFB POKAL FINAL 2010

Olympiastadion, Berlin, 15-05-2010, 20:00, Att: 75 420, Ref: Thorsten Kinhofer

Bayern München	4	Robben [35p], Olic [51], Ribery [63], Schweinsteiger [83]
Werder Bremen	0	

Bayern - Hans-Jorg Butt - Philipp Lahm, Daniel Van Buyten, Martin Demichelis, Holger Badstuber - Mark Van Bommel●, Bastian Schweinsteiger - Arjen Robben (Hamit Altintop 86), Thomas Muller (Anatoliy Tymoshchuk 77), Franck Ribery - Ivica Olic● (Miroslav Klose 80). Tr: Louis Van Gaal

Bremen - Tim Weise - Clemens Fritz●, Per Mertesacker, Naldo, Sebastian Boenisch - Torsten Frings●●◆77, Philippe Bargfrede (Hugo Almeida 46) - Aaron Hunt (Marko Marin 54), Tim Borowski● (Daniel Jensen 70) - Mesut Ozil - Claudio Pizarro. Tr: Thomas Schaaf

* Home team

CLUB BY CLUB GUIDE TO THE 2009-10 SEASON IN GERMANY

BAYER LEVERKUSEN 2009–10

Aug	31	Babelsberg	W	1-0	DPr1	Derdiyok [67]	6 153
	8	Mainz	D	2-2	BL	Derdiyok [42], Kiessling [43]	20 000
	15	Hoffenheim	W	1-0	BL	Kiessling [67]	28 000
	22	Freiburg	W	5-0	BL	Kiessling [35], Barnetta 2 [47 76], Derdiyok 2 [70 84]	22 000
Sep	29	Bochum	W	2-1	BL	Friedrich [41], Kiessling [68]	27 122
	12	Wolfsburg	W	3-2	BL	Rolfes 2 [38 51], Kiessling [58]	30 000
	20	W Bremen	D	0-0	BL		30 210
	23	Kaiser'tern	L	1-2	DPr2	Gekas [86]	33 712
	26	Köln	W	1-0	BL	Rolfes [82]	49 300
Oct	3	Nürnberg	W	4-0	BL	Kroos [2], Rolfes [28], Derdiyok [34], Kiessling [68]	26 785
	17	Hamburg	D	0-0	BL		57 000
	23	B Dortmund	D	1-1	BL	Friedrich [65]	30 210
	31	Schalke	D	2-2	BL	Kroos [29], Kiessling [44]	61 673
Nov	6	E Frankfurt	W	4-0	BL	Kiessling [2], Reinartz [6], Kroos [13], Bender [86]	30 000
	22	Bayern M	D	1-1	BL	Kiessling [14]	69 000
	29	Stuttgart	W	4-0	BL	Kiessling 3 [22 59 87], Derdiyok [38]	30 210
Dec	5	Hannover	D	0-0	BL		34 341
	11	Hertha	D	2-2	BL	Kroos [76], Kaplan [90]	40 474
	19	Gladbach	W	3-2	BL	Kroos 2 [19 69], Derdiyok [60]	30 210
Jan	16	Mainz	W	4-2	BL	Kadlec [15], Barnetta [19], Kroos [30], Derdiyok [88]	28 000
	24	Hoffenheim	W	3-0	BL	Hyypia [11], Kroos [51], Barnetta [72]	29 500
	31	Freiburg	W	3-1	BL	Kiessling [36], Derdiyok [37], Hyypia [40]	26 000
Feb	6	Bochum	D	1-1	BL	Derdiyok [45]	22 176
	13	Wolfsburg	W	2-1	BL	Reinartz [48], Derdiyok [68]	30 000
	21	W Bremen	D	2-2	BL	Derdiyok [29], Kroos [57]	37 500
	27	Köln	D	0-0	BL		30 210
Mar	7	Nürnberg	L	2-3	BL	Kiessling [66], Helmses [73]	40 329
	14	Hamburg	W	4-2	BL	Kiessling 2 [22 62], Derdiyok [55], Castro [84]	30 210
	20	B Dortmund	L	0-3	BL		80 100
	27	Schalke	L	0-2	BL		30 210
Apr	3	E Frankfurt	L	2-3	BL	Kiessling 2 [33 46]	50 900
	10	Bayern M	D	1-1	BL	Vidal [59]	30 210
	17	Stuttgart	L	1-2	BL	Kiessling [13]	41 500
	24	Hannover	W	3-0	BL	Kiessling 2 [25 88], Kaplan [64]	30 210
May	1	Hertha	D	1-1	BL	Friedrich [59]	30 210
	8	Gladbach	D	1-1	BL	Helmes [34]	54 057

BAYER LEVERKUSEN LEAGUE APPEARANCES/GOALS 2009-10

Goalkeepers Rene Adler 31 • Fabian Giefer 3
Defenders Gonzalo Castro 27+2/1 • Manuel Friedrich 31/3 • Sami Hyypia FIN 32/1 • Michal Kadlec CZE 17+6/1 • Stefan Reinartz 23+4/2 Hans Sarpei GHA 2+10/0 • Daniel Schwaab 24+3/0 • Lukas Sinkiewicz 1+6/0 • Assimiou Toure TOG 0+1/0
Midfield Tranquillo Barnetta SUI 31+1/4 • Lars Bender 6+14/1 • Burak Kaplan TUR 2+2/2 • Toni Kroos 26+7/9 • Renato Augusto 11+6/0 Simon Rolfes 8+3/4 • Arturo Vidal CHI 31/1 • Tomasz Zdebel POL 0+8/0
Forwards Eren Derdiyok SUI 32+1/12 • Theofanis Gekas 1+5/0 Patrick Helmes 2+10/2 • Stefan Kießling 33/21
Coach Jupp Heynckes

KEY TO THE CLUB SECTION

BL = Bundesliga • DP = DFB Pokal (German Cup) • CL = UEFA Champions League • EL = Europa League • r1 = first round etc • p3 = third preliminary round •po = preliminary round play-off • gA = Group A etc •qf = quarter-final • sf = semi-final • f = final

Matches that are shaded were played at home; matches with no shading were played either away or on a neutral ground

The figures for the player appearances and goals consist of three elements - matches started+appearances as a substitute/goals scored

BAYERN MUNCHEN 2009–10

Aug	2	Neckarelz	W	3-1	DPr1	Gomez 2 [51 57p], Altintop [82]	30 017
	8	Hoffenheim	D	1-1	BL	Olic [25]	30 150
	15	W Bremen	D	1-1	BL	Gomez [39]	69 000
	22	Mainz	L	1-2	BL	OG [47]	20 300
	29	Wolfsburg	W	3-0	BL	Gpmez [27], Robben 2 [68 80]	69 000
Sep	12	B Dortmund	W	5-1	BL	Gomez [36], Schweinsteiger [49], Ribery [65], Muller 2 [78 88]	80 552
	15	Mac. Haifa	W	3-0	CLgA	Van Buyten [54], Muller 2 [85 88]	38 789
	19	Nürnberg	W	2-1	BL	Olic [55], Van Buyten [82]	69 000
	22	Oberhausen	W	5-0	DPr2	OG [32], Gomez [41], Van Buyten 2 [67 86], Muller [70]	40 000
Oct	26	Hamburg	L	0-1	BL		57 000
	30	Juventus	D	0-0	CLgA		66 000
	3	Köln	D	0-0	BL		69 000
	17	Freiburg	W	2-1	BL	Muller [42], OG [68]	24 500
	21	Bordeaux	L	1-2	CLgA	OG [6]	31 321
	24	E Frankfurt	W	2-1	BL	Robben [70], van Buyten [88]	69 000
	28	E Frankfurt	W	4-0	DPr3	Klose 2 [14 19], Muller [29], Toni [52]	51 500
	31	Stuttgart	D	0-0	BL		42 000
Nov	3	Bordeaux	L	0-2	CLgA		66 000
	7	Schalke	D	1-1	BL	Van Buyten [31]	69 000
	22	Leverkusen	D	1-1	BL	Gomez [8]	69 000
	25	Mac. Haifa	W	1-0	CLgA	Olic [62]	58 000
	29	Hannover	W	3-0	BL	Muller [19], Olic [47], Gomez [90]	49 000
Dec	4	Gladbach	W	2-1	BL	Gomez [19], Badstuber [75]	69 000
	8	Juventus	W	4-1	CLgA	Butt [30p], Olic [52], Gomez [83], Tymoshchuk [92+]	27 801
	12	Bochum	W	5-1	BL	Gomez [23], OG [33], Olic 2 [43 50], Pranjic [56]	30 748
	19	Hertha	W	5-2	BL	Van Buyten [16], Gomez [32], Robben [34], Muller [60], Olic [77]	69 000
Jan	15	Hoffenheim	W	2-0	BL	Demichelis [35], Klose [86]	69 000
	23	W Bremen	W	3-2	BL	Muller [25], Olic [35], Robben [78]	39 100
	30	Mainz	W	3-0	BL	v. Buyten [58], Gomez 75, Robben [86]	69 000
Feb	6	Wolfsburg	W	3-1	BL	Robben [3], v. Buyten [26], Ribery [57]	30 000
	10	Gr'ter Fürth	W	6-2	DPqf	Muller 2 [5 82], Robben [58p], Ribery [61], Lahm [65], OG [89]	53 500
	13	B Dortmund	W	3-1	BL	V. Bommel [21], Robben [50], Gomez [65]	69 000
	17	Fiorentina	W	2-1	CLr2	Robben [45p], Klose [89]	66 000
	20	Nürnberg	D	1-1	BL	Muller [38]	48 548
	28	Hamburg	W	1-0	BL	Ribery [78]	69 000
Mar	6	Köln	D	1-1	BL	Schweinsteiger [58]	50 000
	9	Fiorentina	L	2-3	CLr2	Van Bommel [60], Robben [65]	42 762
	13	Freiburg	W	2-1	BL	Robben 2 [76 83]	69 000
	20	E Frankfurt	L	1-2	BL	Klose [7]	51 500
	24	Schalke	W	1-0	DPsf	Robben [112]	61 673
	27	Stuttgart	L	1-2	BL	Olic [32]	69 000
	30	Man Utd	W	2-1	CLqf	Ribery [77], Olic [92+]	66 000
Apr	3	Schalke	W	2-1	BL	Ribery [25], Muller [26]	61 673
	7	Man Utd	L	2-3	CLqf	Olic [43], Robben [74]	74 482
	10	Leverkusen	D	1-1	BL	Robben [51]	30 210
	17	Hannover	W	7-0	BL	Olic 2 [21 49], Robben 3 [30 50 90], Muller 2 [44 62]	69 000
	21	Lyon	W	1-0	CLsf	Robben [69]	66 000
	24	Gladbach	D	1-1	BL	Klose [73]	54 074
	27	Lyon	W	3-0	CLsf	Olic 3 [26 67 78]	39 414
May	1	Bochum	W	3-1	BL	Muller 3 [18 20 69]	69 000
	8	Hertha	W	3-1	BL	Olic [20], Robben 2 [74 87]	75 420
	15	W Bremen	W	4-0	DPf	Robben [35p], Olic [51], Ribery [63], Schweinsteiger [83]	75 420
	22	Inter	L	0-2	CLf		75 569

BAYERN LEAGUE APPEARANCES/GOALS 2009-10

Goalkeepers Hans-Jorg Butt 31 • Michael Rensing 3
Defenders Holger Badstuber 33/1 • Edson Braafheid NED 5+4/0 Breno BRA 1+2/0 • Diego Contento 8+1/0 • Martin Demichelis ARG 17+4/1 • Philipp Lahm 34/0 • Daniel Van Buyten BEL 31/6
Midfield David Alba AUT 2+1/0 • Alexander Baumjohann 1+2/0 • Hamit Altintop TUR 7+8/0 • Andreas Ottl 1+3/0 • Danijel Pranjic CRO 14+6/1 Franck Ribery FRA 10+9/4 • Arjen Robben NED 18+6/16 • Bastian Schweinsteiger 33/2 • Jose Sosa ARG 2+1/0 • Anatoliy Tymoshchuk UKR 11+10/0 • Mark van Bommel NED 25/1
Forwards Mario Gomez 21+8/10 • Miroslav Klose 11+14/3 • Thomas Muller 29+5/13 • Ivica Olic CRO 23+6/11 • Luca Toni ITA 3+1/0
Coach Louis van Gaal NED

VFL BOCHUM 2009–10

	Date	Opponent		Score	Comp	Scorers	Attendance
Aug	2	Sp. Lotte	W	1-0	DPr1	Klimowicz [50]	4 408
	9	Gladbach	D	3-3	BL	Azaouagh 2 [51][52], Sestak [63]	29 766
	16	Schalke	L	0-3	BL		61 673
	23	Hertha	W	1-0	BL	Yahia [47]	18 853
	29	Leverkusen	L	1-2	BL	Klimowicz [32]	27 122
Sep	12	Hoffenheim	L	0-3	BL		29 500
	19	Mainz	L	2-3	BL	Azaouagh [7], Klimowicz [45]	16 225
	22	Schalke	L	0-3	DPr2		29 592
	25	Nürnberg	W	1-0	BL	Klimowicz [7]	35 376
Oct	3	Wolfsburg	D	1-1	BL	Hashemian [53]	21 710
	8	B Dortmund	L	0-2	BL		72 500
	25	W Bremen	L	1-4	BL	Sestak [1]	25 703
Nov	1	E Frankfurt	L	1-2	BL	OG [25]	37 500
	7	Freiburg	L	1-2	BL	Klimowicz [65]	20 403
	22	Hamburg	W	1-0	BL	Grote [77]	53 838
	27	Köln	D	0-0	BL		29 102
Dec	5	Stuttgart	D	1-1	BL	Fuchs [89]	40 000
	12	Bayern M	L	1-5	BL	Fuchs [76]	30 748
	19	Hannover	W	3-2	BL	Freier [51], Epalle [54], Fuchs [86]	33 875
Jan	16	Gladbach	W	2-1	BL	Sestak [12], Dedic [36]	36 245
	23	Schalke	D	2-2	BL	Hashemian [82], Sestak [90]	29 008
	30	Hertha	D	0-0	BL		38 127
Feb	6	Leverkusen	D	1-1	BL	Dedic [68]	22 176
	13	Hoffenheim	W	2-1	BL	Sestak [24], Dedic [76]	17 104
	20	Mainz	D	0-0	BL		19 000
	27	Nürnberg	D	0-0	BL		24 780
Mar	6	Wolfsburg	L	1-4	BL	Freier [28]	27 152
	13	B Dortmund	L	1-4	BL	Holtby [53]	30 748
	20	W Bremen	L	2-3	BL	Sestak [14], Dedic [63]	36 197
	26	E Frankfurt	L	1-2	BL	Holtby [10]	24 221
Apr	3	Freiburg	D	1-1	BL	Dabrowski [24]	21 500
	11	Hamburg	L	1-2	BL	Dedic [32]	25 780
	16	Köln	L	0-2	BL		46 000
	23	Stuttgart	L	0-2	BL		25 431
May	1	Bayern M	L	1-3	BL	Fuchs [85]	69 000
	8	Hannover	L	0-3	BL		30 748

BORUSSIA DORTMUND 2009–10

	Date	Opponent		Score	Comp	Scorers	Attendance
Aug	1	Weiden	W	3-1	DPr1	Barrios [24], Sahin [46], Zidan [90]	10 000
	8	Köln	W	1-0	BL	OG [75]	78 200
	15	Hamburg	L	1-4	BL	Valdez [4]	57 000
	22	Stuttgart	D	1-1	BL	Valdez [27]	72 100
	29	E Frankfurt	D	1-1	BL	Zidan [62]	51 050
Sep	12	Bayern M	L	1-5	BL	Hummels [10]	80 552
	19	Hannover	D	1-1	BL	Sahin [45]	43 754
	22	Karlsruhe	W	3-0	DPr2	Zidan 2, Barrios 2 [22][51]	24 864
	26	Schalke	L	0-1	BL		80 552
Oct	3	Gladbach	W	1-0	BL	Barrios [38]	53 253
	18	Bochum	W	2-0	BL	Barrios [20], Subotic [51]	72 500
	23	Leverkusen	D	1-1	BL	Barrios [8]	30 210
	27	Osnabruck	L	2-3	DPr3	Barrios [90]	16 130
	30	Hertha	W	2-0	BL	Sahin [60], Barrios [90]	77 000
Nov	8	W Bremen	D	1-1	BL	Barrios [54]	34 906
	21	Mainz	D	0-0	BL		74 600
	28	Hoffenheim	W	2-1	BL	Blaszkowski [3], Sahin [79]	30 150
Dec	5	Nürnberg	W	4-0	BL	Grosskreutz [8], Barrios [13], Zidan [36], Hummels [61]	72 100
	13	Wolfsburg	W	3-1	BL	Barrios 2 [8][10], Owomoyela [36]	30 000
	19	Freiburg	W	1-0	BL	Barrios [19]	80 100
	17	Köln	W	3-2	BL	Hummels 2 [28][45], Grosskreutz [90]	50 000
Jan	23	Hamburg	W	1-0	BL	Valdez [36]	80 552
	31	Stuttgart	L	1-4	BL	Barrios [55]	42 000
Feb	7	E Frankfurt	L	2-3	BL	Hummels [17], Barrios [57]	70 400
	13	Bayern M	L	1-3	BL	Zidan [5]	69 000
	20	Hannover	W	4-1	BL	Subotic [43], OG [60], Valdez [77], Grosskreutz [88]	73 700
	26	Schalke	L	1-2	BL	Sahin [47]	61 673
Mar	6	Gladbach	W	3-0	BL	Grosskreutz [13], Zidan 2 [54][70]	79 800
	13	Bochum	W	4-1	BL	Kehl [18], Zidan [27], Barrios 2 [74][77]	30 748
	20	Leverkusen	W	3-0	BL	Barrios 2 [50][60], Rangelov [87]	80 100
	27	Hertha	D	0-0	BL		60 441
Apr	3	W Bremen	W	2-1	BL	Grosskreutz [9], Subotic [22]	80 552
	10	Mainz	L	0-1	BL		20 300
	18	Hoffenheim	D	1-1	BL	Valdez [57]	80 100
	24	Nürnberg	W	3-2	BL	Barrios 3 [26][62][78]	48 458
May	1	Wolfsburg	D	1-1	BL	Stiepermann [81]	80 300
	8	Freiburg	L	1-3	BL	Barrios [47]	24 000

VFL BOCHUM LEAGUE APPEARANCES/GOALS 2009-10

Goalkeepers Daniel Fernandes POR 1 • Philipp Heerwagen 30 • Andreas Luthe 3

Defenders Philipp Bonig 10/0 • Matias Concha SWE 18+3/0 • Patrick Fabian 1/0 • Christian Fuchs AUT 29+2/4 • Marcel Maltritz 29/0 • Mergim Mavraj 24+3/0 • Marc Pfertzel FRA 18/0 • Antar Yahia ALG 17+1/1

Midfield Mirkan Aydin 0+1/0 • Mimoun Azaouagh 12+5/3 • Christoph Dabrowski 26+3/1 • Joel Epalle CMR 24+3/1 • Paul Freier 15+13/2 • Dennis Grote 5+5/1 • Lewis Holtby 11+3/2 • Daniel Imhof CAN 6/0 • Andreas Johansson SWE 7+9/0 • Milos Maric SRB 13/0 • Shinji Ono JPN 7+2/0 •

Forwards Zlatko Dedic SVN 15+12/5 • Vahid Hashemian IRN 5+20/2 • Diego Klimowicz ARG 9+6/3 • Roman Prokoph 11+4/0 • Stanislav Sestak SVK 28+1/6

Coach Marcel Koller SUI • Frank Heinemann (20/09/09) • Heiko Herrlich (27/10/09) • Dariusz Wosz (29/04/10)

BORUSSIA DORTMUND LEAGUE APPEARANCES/GOALS 2009-10

Goalkeepers Roman Weidenfeller 30 • Marc Ziegler 4+1

Defenders Dede BRA 11+5/0 • Felipe Santana BRA 13+12/0 • Mats Hummels 27+3/5 • Uwe Hunemeier 0+1/0 • Julian Koch 0+2/0 • Patrick Owomoyela 33/1 • Marcel Schmelzer 24+4/0 • Neven Subotic SRB 34/3

Midfield Sven Bender 17+2/0 • Jakub Blaszczykowski POL 30+2/1 • Markus Feulner 1+8/0 • Mario Gotze 0+5/0 • Tamas Hajnal HUN 10+11/0 • Sebastian Kehl 5+1/1 • Nuri Sahin TUR 33/4 • Tinga 7/0 •

Forwards Lucas Barrios PAR 30+3/19 • Kevin Grosskreutz 21+11/5 • Damien Le Tallec FRA 1+3/0 • Dimitar Rangelov BUL 1+9/1 • Marco Stiepermann 0+3/1 • Nelson Valdez PAR 18+10/5 • Mohamed Zidan EGY 24+3/6

Coach Jurgen Klopp

BORUSSIA MONCHENGLADBACH 2009–10

Mon	Day	Opponent	Res	Score	Comp	Scorers	Att
Aug	1	FSV Fr'furt	W	2-1	DPr1	Arango 27, Colautti 59	9 742
	9	Bochum	D	3-3	BL	Arango 19, Colautti 26, Brouwers 40	29 766
	16	Hertha	W	2-1	BL	Brouwers 23, Matmour 52	41 814
	23	W Bremen	L	0-3	BL		34 800
	28	Mainz	W	2-0	BL	Bobadilla 29, Reus 84	42 217
Sep	12	Nürnberg	L	0-1	BL		46 780
	19	Hoffenheim	L	2-4	BL	Arango 10, Colautti 17	46 511
	22	MSV D'burg	L	0-1	DPr2		45 397
	27	Freiburg	L	0-1	BL		24 500
Oct	3	B Dortmund	L	0-1	BL		52 253
	18	Wolfsburg	L	1-2	BL	Bradley 90	30 000
	24	Köln	D	0-0	BL		54 057
	31	Hamburg	W	3-2	BL	Reus 39, Dante 76, Friend 82	57 000
Nov	7	Stuttgart	D	0-0	BL		47 053
	21	E Frankfurt	W	2-1	BL	Russ OG 54, Brouwers 65	50 000
	28	Schalke	W	1-0	BL	Reus 5	54 047
Dec	4	Bayern M	L	1-2	BL	Brouwers 28	69 000
	12	Hannover	W	5-3	BL	OG 3 14 58 90, Friend 22, Bradley 68	43 528
	19	Leverkusen	L	2-3	BL	Brouwers 37, Dante 54	30 210
Jan	16	Bochum	L	1-2	BL	Backer 80	36 245
	23	Hertha	D	0-0	BL		46 090
	30	W Bremen	W	4-3	BL	Reus 4, Colautti 13, Bobadilla 2 18 35	47 458
Feb	7	Mainz	L	0-1	BL		20 300
	12	Nürnberg	W	2-1	BL	Colautti 27, Friend 74	34 297
	19	Hoffenheim	D	2-2	BL	Daems 31, Colautti 51	30 150
	27	Freiburg	D	1-1	BL	Brouwers 72	40 419
Mar	6	B Dortmund	L	0-3	BL		79 800
	13	Wolfsburg	L	0-4	BL		39 128
	19	Köln	D	1-1	BL	Reus 56	50 000
	28	Hamburg	W	1-0	BL	Brouwers 43	52 269
Apr	3	Stuttgart	L	1-2	BL	Reus 33	42 000
	9	E Frankfurt	W	2-0	BL	Reus 6, Dante 55	48 553
	17	Schalke	L	1-3	BL	Bobadilla 16	61 673
	24	Bayern M	D	1-1	BL	Reus 60	54 057
May	1	Hannover	L	1-6	BL	Bruggink 74	49 000
	8	Leverkusen	D	1-1	BL	Brouwers 55	54 057

EINTRACHT FRANKFURT 2009–10

Mon	Day	Opponent	Res	Score	Comp	Scorers	Att
Aug	2	Offenbach	W	3-0	DPr1	Schwegler 71, Caio 75, Meier 86	24 000
	8	W Bremen	W	3-2	BL	Amanatidis 2 6 42, Fenin 71	30 000
	15	Nürnberg	D	1-1	BL	Caio 17	49 000
	22	Köln	D	0-0	BL		49 200
	29	B Dortmund	D	1-1	BL	Amanatidis 68	51 050
Sep	12	Freiburg	W	2-0	BL	Franz 68, Meier 90	23 600
	20	Hamburg	D	1-1	BL	Russ 32	51 500
	23	Aachen	W	6-4	DPr2	Caio 1, Liberopoulos 2 5 50, OG 45, Meier 53, Teber 89	25 450
	26	Stuttgart	L	0-3	BL		49 750
Oct	2	Schalke	L	0-2	BL		61 673
	17	Hannover	W	2-1	BL	Liberopoulos 23, Meier 74	40 700
	24	Bayern M	L	1-2	BL	Meier 60	69 000
	28	Bayern M	L	0-4	DPr3		
Nov	1	Bochum	W	2-1	BL	Caio 14, Franz 53	37 500
	6	Leverkusen	L	0-4	BL		30 000
	21	Gladbach	L	1-2	BL	Schwegler 86	50 000
	28	Hertha	W	3-1	BL	Ochs 11, Franz 70, Meier 75	48 253
Dec	5	Mainz	W	2-0	BL	Franz 29, Meier 90	51 500
	12	Hoffenheim	D	1-1	BL	Schwegler 61	30 150
	19	Wolfsburg	D	2-2	BL	Franz 26, Meier 80	41 700
	16	W Bremen	W	1-0	BL	Russ 57	45 600
Jan	23	Nürnberg	D	1-1	BL	Kohler 40	37 464
	30	Köln	L	1-2	BL	Chris 76	45 100
Feb	7	B Dortmund	W	3-2	BL	Kohler 8, Jung 65, Meier 74	70 400
	14	Freiburg	W	2-1	BL	Kohler 40, Altintop 90	34 900
	20	Hamburg	D	0-0	BL		56 196
	27	Stuttgart	L	1-2	BL	Kohler 39	41 000
Mar	6	Schalke	L	1-4	BL	Meier 52	51 500
	13	Hannover	L	1-2	BL	Altintop 45	38 874
	20	Bayern M	W	2-1	BL	Tsoumou 87	51 500
	26	Bochum	W	2-1	BL	Russ 29, Caio 64	24 221
Apr	3	Leverkusen	W	3-2	BL	Teber 29, Caio 62, Franz 89	50 900
	9	Gladbach	L	0-2	BL		48 553
	18	Hertha	D	2-2	BL	Korkmaz 37, Russ 63	49 800
	24	Mainz	D	3-3	BL	Meier 2 13 19, Korkmaz 63	20 300
May	1	Hoffenheim	L	1-2	BL	Schwegler 20	50 500
	8	Wolfsburg	L	1-3	BL	Fenin 86	30 000

BORUSSIA MONCHENGLADBACH LEAGUE APPEARANCES/GOALS 2009-10

Goalkeepers Logan Bailly BEL 29 • Christofer Heimeroth 5
Defenders Roel Brouwers NED 34/8 • Filip Daems BEL 18/1 • Dante BRA 32/3 • Jean-Sebastien Jaures FRA 14+2/0 • Thomas Kleine 2+12/0 • Tobias Levels 32/0 • Paul Staltieri CAN 2+1/0
Midfield Michael Bradley USA 28+1/2 • Patrick Herrmann 3+1/1 • Tony Jantschke 2+4/0 • Juan Arango VEN 33+1/2 • Thorben Marx 28/0 • Marcel Meeuwis NED 14+4/0 • Roman Neustadter 0+2/0 • Marco Reus 27+6/8
Forwards Fabian Backer 0+2/1 • Raul Bobadilla ARG 25+5/4 • Roberto Colautti ISR 15+8/5 • Rob Friend CAN 11+15/3 • Moses Lamidi 1+2/0 • Karim Matmour ALG 18+7/1 • Oliver Neuville 1+11/0
Coach Michael Frontzeck

EINTRACHT FRANKFURT LEAGUE APPEARANCES/GOALS 2009-10

Goalkeepers Ralf Fahrmann 3 • Oka Nikolov MKD 31 • Jan Zimmermann 0+1
Defenders Chris BRA 29/1 • Maik Franz 25+2/6 • Sebastian Jung 12+2/1 • Patrick Ochs 28/1 • Nikola Petkovic SRB 0+2/0 • Marco Russ 30/4 • Christoph Spycher SUI 27/0 • Aleksandar Vasoski MKD 7/0
Midfield Zlatan Bajramovic BIH 7+4/0 • Caio BRA 15+11/4 • Ricardo Clark USA 3/0 • Marcel Heller 2+7/0 • Benjamin Kohler 21+10/4 • Alexander Meier 34/10 • Christoph Preuss 0+3/0 • Pirmin Schwegler SUI 25/3 • Marcus Steinhofer 3+2/0 • Selim Teber 24+5/1 • Cenk Tosun 0+1/0
Forwards Ioannis Amanatidis GRE 7+1/3 • Martin Fenin CZE 2+15/2 • Halil Altintop TUR 15/3 • Umit Korkmaz AUT 10+8/2 • Nikos Liberopoulos GRE 14+7/1 • Juvhel Tsoumou 0+4/1
Coach Michael Skibbe

SC FREIBURG 2009–10

Mon	Day	Opponent	Res	Score	Comp	Scorers	Att
Aug	1	Elversberg	W	2-0	DPr1	Butscher [30], Reisinger [83]	3 500
	9	Hamburg	D	1-1	BL	Bechmann [65]	24 000
	15	Stuttgart	L	2-4	BL	Idrissou 2 [70 85]	41 500
	22	Leverkusen	L	0-5	BL		22 000
	29	Schalke	W	1-0	BL	Cha [40]	60 198
Sep	12	E Frankfurt	L	0-2	BL		23 600
	20	Hertha	W	4-0	BL	Banovic 2 [6 68], Makiadi [12], Idrissou [42]	38 176
	23	Augsburg	L	0-1	DPr2		12 024
	27	Gladbach	W	3-0	BL	Idrissou [54], Abdessadki [72], Schuster [80]	24 500
Oct	3	Hannover	L	2-5	BL	Banovic [35], Schuster [82]	28 412
	17	Bayern M	L	1-2	BL	Reisinger [90]	24 500
	24	Mainz	L	0-3	BL		20 150
Nov	1	Hoffenheim	L	0-1	BL		24 000
	7	Bochum	W	2-1	BL	Butscher [24], Reisinger [90]	20 403
	21	W Bremen	L	0-6	BL		24 000
	28	Nürnberg	W	1-0	BL	Reisinger [12]	40 824
Dec	5	Wolfsburg	D	2-2	BL	Idrissou [19], Banovic [51]	27 822
	12	Köln	D	0-0	BL		24 000
	19	Dortmund	L	0-1	BL		81 000
Jan	16	Hamburg	L	0-2	BL		51 448
	22	Stuttgart	L	0-1	BL		23 900
	31	Leverkusen	L	1-3	BL	Bastians [66]	26 000
Feb	6	Schalke	D	0-0	BL		24 000
	14	E Frankfurt	L	1-2	BL	Cisse [25]	34 900
	21	Hertha	L	0-3	BL		21 600
	27	Gladbach	D	1-1	BL	Cisse [56]	40 419
Mar	6	Hannover	L	1-2	BL	Abdessadki [70]	19 100
	13	Bayern M	L	1-2	BL	Makiadi [31]	69 000
	20	Mainz	W	1-0	BL	Flum [10]	20 000
	28	Hoffenheim	D	1-1	BL	Idrissou [64]	30 150
Apr	3	Bochum	D	1-1	BL	Cisse [18]	21 500
	10	W Bremen	L	0-4	BL		37 000
	17	Nürnberg	W	2-1	BL	OG [4], Cisse [61]	22 800
	25	Wolfsburg	W	1-0	BL	Makiadi [38]	22 700
May	1	Köln	D	2-2	BL	Idrissou 2 [31 57]	49 200
	8	Dortmund	W	3-1	BL	Idrissou [60], Cisse 2 [70 90]	24 000

HAMBURGER SV 2009–10

Mon	Day	Opponent	Res	Score	Comp	Scorers	Att
Aug	30	Randers	W	4-0	ELp3	Guerrero [11], Boateng [24], Petric [53], Trochowski [80p]	5 755
	3	FDüsseldorf	D	3-3	DPr1	Petric [4], Trochowski 2 [54 94p], W 4-1p	35 600
	6	Randers	L	0-1	ELp3		41 793
	9	Freiburg	D	1-1	BL	Pitroipa [3]	24 000
	15	B Dortmund	W	4-1	BL	Demel [3], Ze Roberto [10], Guerrero [12], Berg [71]	57 000
	20	Guingamp	W	5-1	ELpo	Guerrero [11], Petric 3 [11 26 86], Berg [51]	13 000
	23	Wolfsburg	W	4-2	BL	Guerrero [3], Elia [7], Petric [75], Castelen [90]	30 000
Sep	27	Guingamp	W	3-1	ELpo	Tesche 2 [42 51], Berg [47]	25 798
	30	Köln	W	3-1	BL	Guerrero [19 66], Trochowski [86]	54 112
	12	Stuttgart	W	3-1	BL	Petric [30], Elia [58], Ze Roberto [90]	57 000
	17	Rapid	L	0-3	ELgC		49 500
	20	E Frankfurt	D	1-1	BL	Ze Roberto [8]	51 500
	23	Osnabrück	D	3-3	DPr2	Petric [77], Trochowski [90p], Demel [100], L 2-4p	16 130
Oct	26	Bayern M	W	1-0	BL	Petric [72]	57 000
	1	Hapoel TA	W	4-2	ELgC	Berg 2 [5 12], Elia [41], Ze Roberto [77]	29 976
	4	Hertha	W	3-1	BL	OG [24], Jarolim [38], Ze Roberto [40]	49 208
	17	Leverkusen	D	0-0	BL		57 000
	22	Celtic	W	1-0	ELgC	Berg [63]	40 650
Nov	25	Schalke	D	3-3	BL	Berg 2 [26 80], Trochowski [45]	61 673
	31	Gladbach	L	2-3	BL	Trochowski [13], Ze Roberto [47]	57 000
	5	Celtic	D	0-0	ELgC		45 037
	8	Hannover	D	2-2	BL	Jansen [15], Elia [44]	49 000
	22	Bochum	L	0-1	BL		53 838
	28	Mainz	D	1-1	BL	Torun [3]	20 300
Dec	2	Rapid	W	2-0	ELgC	Jansen [47], Berg [53]	45 737
	5	Hoffenheim	D	0-0	BL		52 725
	12	Nürnberg	W	4-0	BL	Elia 2 [47 74], Jansen [60], Torun [65]	44 865
	17	Hapoel	L	0-1	ELgC		13 552
	20	W Bremen	W	2-1	BL	Mathijsen [9], Jansen [36]	57 000
Jan	16	Freiburg	W	2-0	BL	Jansen [7], Petric [55]	51 448
	23	B Dortmund	L	0-1	BL		80 552
	29	Wolfsburg	D	1-1	BL	Trochowski [90]	51 845
	6	Köln	D	3-3	BL	Jansen 2, Petric 2 [36 50]	50 000
	13	Stuttgart	W	3-1	BL	Berg [23], van Nistelroij 2 [75 77]	41 500
Feb	18	PSV	W	1-0	ELr2	Jansen [26p]	35 672
	20	E Frankfurt	D	0-0	BL		56 196
	25	PSV	L	2-3	ELr2	Petric [46], Trochowski [79p]	32 000
	28	Bayern M	L	0-1	BL		69 000
	6	Hertha	W	1-0	BL	Jansen [40]	53 905
Mar	11	Anderlecht	W	3-1	ELr3	Mathijsen [23], Van Nistelroij [40], Jarolim [76]	34 921
	14	Leverkusen	L	2-4	BL	Ze Roberto [33], Rozehnal [83]	30 210
	18	Anderlecht	L	3-4	ELr3	Boateng [42], Jansen [54], Petric [75]	19 669
	21	Schalke	D	2-2	BL	Van Nistelroij [40], Pitroipa [77]	57 000
	28	Gladback	D	0-1	BL		52 269
Apr	1	Standard	W	2-1	ELqf	Petric [42p], Van Nistelroij [45]	48 437
	4	Hannover	D	0-0	BL		57 000
	8	Standard	W	3-1	ELqf	Petric 2 [20 35], Guerrero [94+]	27 129
	11	Bochum	W	2-1	BL	Tesche [17], OG [88]	25 780
	17	Mainz	L	0-1	BL		55 292
	22	Fulham	D	0-0	ELsf		49 171
	25	Hoffenheim	L	1-5	BL	Tesche [65]	30 150
	29	Fulham	L	1-2	ELsf	Petric [22]	23 705
May	1	Nürnberg	W	4-0	BL	Pitroipa [9], Petric 2 [19 25], Trochowski [73]	53 727
	8	W Bremen	D	1-1	BL	Van Nistelroij [82]	41 150

SC FREIBURG LEAGUE APPEARANCES/GOALS 2009-10
Goalkeepers Oliver Baumann 1 • Simon Pouplin FRA 30 • Manuel Salz 3
Defenders Oliver Barth 12+4/0 • Felix Bastians 33+1/1 Heiko Butscher 29/1 • Cha Du Ri KOR 19+4/1 • Pavel Krmas CZE 15+2/0 Jackson Mendy FRA 6/0 • Mensur Mujdza BIH 9+5/0 • Omer Toprak 10+4/0
Midfield Yacine Abdessadki MAR 20+3/2 • Ivica Banovic CRO 22+3/4 Daniel Caligiuri 9+7/0 • Johannes Flum 22+3/1 • Andreas Glockner 0+2/0 • Hamed Namouchi TUN 10+8/0 • Julian Schuster 18+10/2 David Targamadze GEO 0+2/0 • Eke Uzoma NGA 1+3/0 • Daniel Williams 5+1/0
Forwards Tommy Bechmann DEN 10+11/1 • Squipon Bektasi 0+1/0 Papiss Cisse SEN 13+3/6 • Mohamadou Idrissou CMR 30/9 Jonathan Jager FRA 20+5/0 • Cedric Makiadi COD 27+6/3 • Stefan Reisinger 9+16/3
Coach Robin Dutt

HAMBURG LEAGUE APPEARANCES/GOALS 2009-10
Goalkeepers Wolfgang Hesl 0+1 • Frank Rost 34
Defenders Dennis Aogo 31/0 • Jerome Boateng 26+1/0 • Guy Demel CIV 22+4/1 • Marcell Jansen 15+3/6 • Joris Mathijsen NED 33/1 Bastian Reinhardt 0+1/0 • David Rozehnal CZE 19+4/1
Midfield Tolgay Arslan 2+3/0 • Soren Bertram 0+2/0 • Romeo Castelen NED 0+2/1 • Eljero Elia NED 20+4/5 • David Jarolim CZE 33/1 Jonathan Pitroipa BFA 7+13/3 • Tomas Rincon VEN 14+3/0 • Mickael Tavares SEN 0+3/0 • Robert Tesche 6+10/2 • Piotr Trochowski 25+8/4 Ze Roberto BRA 23/6
Forwards Maximilian Beister 0+2/0 • Marcus Berg SWE 16+14/4 • Jose Guerrero PER 4+2/4 • Mladen Petric 25+1/8 • Tunay Torun TUR 12+7/2 Ruud van Nistelroij NED 7+4/5
Coach Bruno Labbadia • Ricardo Moniz NED (26/04/10)

HANNOVER 96 2009–10

Month	Date	Opponent		Score	Comp	Scorers	Att
Aug	31	Trier	L	1-3	DPr1	Rosenthal 40	6 000
	8	Hertha	L	0-1	BL		42 169
	15	Mainz	D	1-1	BL	Stajner 56	28 952
	22	Nürnberg	W	2-0	BL	Stajner 2 15 86	38 600
	29	Hoffenheim	L	0-1	BL		34 257
Sep	13	W Bremen	D	0-0	BL		34 000
	19	B Dortmund	D	1-1	BL	Ya Konan 48	43 754
	26	Wolfsburg	L	2-4	BL	Balitsch 28, OG 50	30 000
Oct	3	Freiburg	W	5-2	BL	Chahed 7, Bruggink 10, Haggui 45, Ya Konan 85, Pinto 90	28 412
	17	E Frankfurt	L	1-2	BL	Stajner 68	40 700
	24	Stuttgart	W	1-0	BL	Ya Konan 31	34 423
	31	Köln	W	1-0	BL	Rosenthal 37	45 000
Nov	8	Hamburg	D	2-2	BL	Ya Konan 26, Stajner 88	49 000
	21	Schalke	L	0-2	BL		61 505
	29	Bayern M	L	0-3	BL		49 000
Dec	5	Leverkusen	D	0-0	BL		34 341
	12	Gladbach	L	3-5	BL	Ya Konan 2 36 69, Schultz 87	43 528
	19	Bochum	L	2-3	BL	Schlaudraff 2 6 33	33 875
Jan	16	Hertha	L	0-3	BL		28 712
	23	Mainz	L	0-1	BL		20 300
	30	Nürnberg	L	1-3	BL	Stajner 65	26 722
Feb	6	Hoffenheim	L	1-2	BL	Kone 57	28 100
	13	W Bremen	L	1-5	BL	Schultz 59	44 379
	20	B Dortmund	L	1-4	BL	Kone 81	73 700
	28	Wolfsburg	L	0-1	BL		34 312
Mar	6	Freiburg	W	2-1	BL	Elson 63, OG 73	19 100
	13	E Frankfurt	W	2-1	BL	Andreasen 14, Pinto 57	38 847
	20	Stuttgart	L	0-2	BL		41 000
	27	Köln	L	1-4	BL	Cherundulo 82	43 218
	4	Hamburg	D	0-0	BL		57 000
Apr	10	Schalke	W	4-2	BL	OG 17, Ya Konan 2 29 90, Balitsch 80	49 000
	17	Bayern M	L	0-7	BL		69 000
	24	Leverkusen	L	0-3	BL		30 210
May	1	Gladbach	W	6-1	BL	Haggui 16, Pinto 23, Ya Konan 27, Hanke 39, Chahed 53, Bruggink 74	49 000
	8	Bochum	W	3-0	BL	Bruggink 9, Hanke 23, Pinto 45	30 748

HERTHA BSC BERLIN 2009–10

Month	Date	Opponent		Score	Comp	Scorers	Att
	1	Pr Münster	W	3-1	DPr1	Raffael 2 23 120, Domovchiyski 118	18 200
	8	Hannover	W	1-0	BL	Kacar 82	42 169
	16	Gladbach	L	1-2	BL	Kacar 53	41 814
Aug	20	Brøndby	L	1-2	ELpo	Domovchiyski 53	12 050
	23	Bochum	L	0-1	BL		18 853
	27	Brøndby	W	3-1	ELpo	Kacar 2 75 86, Dardai 80	10 000
	30	W Bremen	L	2-3	BL	Piszczek 77, Ebert 90	49 176
	12	Mainz	L	1-2	BL	Nicu 49	20 300
	17	Ventspils	D	1-1	ELgD	Piszczek 34	13 454
Sep	20	Freiburg	L	0-4	BL		38 176
	23	TSV 1860	D	2-2	DPr2	Ramos 76, Domovchiyski 80, L 1-4p	17 000
	27	Hoffenheim	L	1-5	BL	Raffael 45	29 600
	1	Sporting CP	L	0-1	ELgD		16 197
	4	Hamburg	L	1-3	BL	Friedrich 9	49 208
Oct	17	Nürnberg	L	1-3	BL		38 094
	22	Heerenveen	L	0-1	ELgD		13 134
	25	Wolfsburg	D	0-0	BL		36 799
	30	B Dortmund	L	0-2	BL		77 000
Nov	5	Heerenveen	W	3-2	ELgD	Domovchiyski 2 21 52, Wichniarek 91+	20 000
	8	Köln	L	0-1	BL		48 623
	21	Stuttgart	D	1-1	BL	Ramos 49	39 000
	28	E Frankfurt	L	1-3	BL	Ramos 81	48 253
	3	Ventspils	W	1-0	ELgD	Raffael 12	7 200
	6	Schalke	L	0-2	BL		61 000
Dec	11	Leverkusen	D	2-2	BL	Ramos 2 8 90	40 474
	16	Sporting CP	W	1-0	ELgD	Kacar 70	14 174
	19	Bayern M	L	2-5	BL	Ramos 71, Raffael 90	69 000
Jan	14	Hannover	W	3-0	BL	Piszczek 30, Raffael 33, Gekas 80	28 712
	23	Gladbach	D	0-0	BL		46 090
	30	Bochum	D	0-0	BL		38 127
	5	W Bremen	L	1-2	BL	Gekas 68	35 600
	13	Mainz	D	1-1	BL	Ramos 51	36 715
Feb	18	Benfica	D	1-1	ELr2	OG 33	13 684
	21	Freiburg	W	3-0	BL	Ramos 28, Cicero 2 35 57	21 600
	23	Benfica	L	0-4	ELr2		30 402
	27	Hoffenheim	L	0-2	BL		37 391
	6	Hamburg	L	0-1	BL		53 905
	13	Nürnberg	L	1-2	BL	Gekas 36	57 761
Mar	21	Wolfsburg	W	5-1	BL	Gekas 3 6 27 63, Ramos 2 8 84	29 353
	27	B Dortmund	D	0-0	BL		60 441
	3	Köln	W	3-0	BL	Raffael 2 26 45, Cicero 75	46 300
Apr	10	Stuttgart	L	0-1	BL		26 851
	18	E Frankfurt	D	2-2	BL	Kacar 17, Raffael 43	49 800
	24	Schalke	L	0-1	BL		61 902
May	1	Leverkusen	D	1-1	BL	Raffael 12	30 210
	8	Bayern M	L	1-3	BL	Ramos 59	75 420

HANNOVER 96 APPEARANCES/GOALS 2009-10
Goalkeepers Robert Enke 6 • Florian Fromlowitz 28
Defenders Leon Balogun 1+1/0 • Sofian Chahed TUN 9+7/2 • Steve Cherundolo USA 23+3/1 • Constant Djakpa CIV 20+4/0 • Jan Durica SVK 8+1/0 • Mario Eggimann SUI 12+7/0 • Karim Haggui TUN 30/2 • Konstantin Rausch 20+6/0 • Manuel Schmiedebach 11+3/0 • Christian Schulz 33/2
Midfield Leon Andreasen DEN 7/1 • Hanno Balitsch 25+2/2 Arnold Bruggink NED 21+5/3 • Elson BRA 7/1 • Henrik Ernst 0+2/0 Jacek Krzynowek POL 3+8/0 • Altin Lala ALB 3+1/0 • Sergio Pinto POR 20+6/4 • Valdet Rama 4+11/0 • Jan Rosenthal 13+3/1 • Salvatore Zizzo USA 0+1/0
Forwards Florian Buchler 0+1/0 • Mikael Forssell FIN 2/0 • Rubic Ghasemi-Nobakht IRN 0+1/0 • Mike Hanke 5+13/2 • Didier Konan Ya CIV 24+1/9 • Arouna Kone 8/2 • Jaroslaw Lindner POL 0+1/0 • Jan Schlaudraff 5+5/2 • Jiri Stajner CZE 26+4/6
Coach Dieter Hecking • Andreas Bergmann (20/08/09) • Mirko Slomka (19/01/10)

HERTHA BSC LEAGUE APPEARANCES/GOALS 2009-10
Goalkeepers Sascha Burchert 2+1 • Jaroslav Drobny CZE 30 Timo Ochs 2
Defenders Rasmus Bengtsson 3+3/0 • Arne Friedrich 31/1 • Roman Hubnik CZE 7/0 • Christoph Janker 8+7/0 • Kaka BRA 2/0 • Nemanja Pejcinovic SRB 16/0 • Marc Stein 9+1/0 • Steve Von Bergen SUI 24+1/0
Midfield Sascha Bigalke 1/0 • Cesar BRA 0+3/0 • Cicero BRA 28+2/3 Pal Dardai HUN 10+7 • Patrick Ebert 12+4/1 • Lennart Hartmann 1+1/0 • Gojko Kacar SRB 18+4/3 • Levan Kobiashvili GEO 16/0 Florian Kringe 10+2 • Fabian Lustenberger SUI 23/0 • Maximilian Nicu ROU 12+3/1 • Lukasz Piszczek POL 28+3/2
Forwards Valeri Domovchiyski BUL 4+12/0 • Theofanis Gekas GRE 15+2/6 • Raffael BRA 30+1/7 • Adrian Ramos COL 23+6/10 • Artur Wichniarek POL 9+10/0
Coach Lucien Favre SUI • Karsten Heine (29/09/09) • Friedhelm Funkel (31/10/09)

TSG HOFFENHEIM 2009–10

Aug	2	Ob'neuland	W	2-0	DPr1	Obasi [48], Maicosuel [54]	2 743
	8	Bayern M	D	1-1	BL	Obasi [41]	30 150
	15	Leverkusen	L	0-1	BL		28 000
	21	Schalke	D	0-0	BL		30 150
	29	Hannover	W	1-0	BL	Carlos Eduardo [40]	34 257
Sep	12	Bochum	W	3-0	BL	Ba [16], Obasi [58], Compper [79]	29 500
	19	Gladbach	W	4-2	BL	Salihovic [21], Maicosuel [86], Obasi [89], Ba [90]	46 511
	22	Nürnberg	W	1-0	DPr2	Nilsson [35]	26 041
	27	Hertha	W	5-1	BL	Ibisevic 3 [1 4 21], Obasi [58], Carlos Eduardo [63]	29 600
Oct	3	Mainz	L	1-2	BL	Ibertsberger [87]	20 300
	17	W Bremen	L	0-2	BL		33 916
	24	Nürnberg	W	3-0	BL	Eichner [34], Ibisevic [38], Zuculini [64]	30 150
	28	Koblenz	W	4-0	DPr3	Salihovic [50], Ibisevic [67], Maicosuel [71], Compper [90]	18 050
Nov	1	Freiburg	W	1-0	BL	Maicosuel [39]	24 000
	7	Wolfsburg	L	1-2	BL	Ibisevic [23]	29 400
	21	Köln	W	4-0	BL	Carlos Eduardo [5], Obasi [11], Ba [46], Ibisevic [90]	45 000
	28	B Dortmund	L	1-2	BL	Ba [49]	30 150
Dec	5	Hamburg	D	0-0	BL		52 725
	12	E Frankfurt	D	1-1	BL	Salihovic [9]	30 150
	19	Stuttgart	L	1-3	BL	Maiscousuel [44]	41 000
	15	Bayern M	L	0-2	BL		69 000
Jan	24	Leverkusen	L	0-3	BL		29 500
	30	Schalke	L	0-2	BL		60 402
Feb	6	Hannover	W	2-1	BL	Carlos Eduardo [35], Salihovic [40]	28 100
	9	W Bremen	L	1-2	DPqf	Tagoe [73]	25 753
	13	Bochum	L	1-2	BL	Ibisevic [65]	17 104
	19	Gladbach	D	2-2	BL	Ibisevic [69], Carlos Eduardo [89]	30 150
	27	Hertha	W	2-0	BL	Ba [35], Ibisevic [90]	37 391
Mar	7	Mainz	L	0-1	BL		30 150
	14	W Bremen	L	0-1	BL		30 150
	20	Nürnberg	D	0-0	BL		40 421
	28	Freiburg	D	1-1	BL	Simunic [80]	30 150
Apr	4	Wolfsburg	L	0-4	BL		28 107
	10	Köln	L	0-2	BL		26 950
	18	B Dortmund	D	1-1	BL	Ibisevic [89]	80 100
	25	Hamburg	W	5-1	BL	Ibisevic 2 [2 11], Obasi 2 [31 72], Salihovic [77]	30 150
May	1	E Frankfurt	W	2-1	BL	Tagoe 2 [81 88]	50 500
	8	Stuttgart	D	1-1	BL	Vukcevic [44]	30 150

1.FC KOLN 2009–10

Aug	1	Emden	W	3-0	DPr1	Mohamad [37], Sanou [59], Podolski [88]	7 200
	8	B Dortmund	L	0-1	BL	e	78 200
	15	Wolfsburg	L	1-3	BL	Ehret [49]	48 000
	22	E Frankfurt	D	0-0	BL		49 200
	30	Hamburg	L	1-3	BL	Chihi [76]	54 112
Sep	13	Schalke	L	1-2	BL	Podolski [6]	50 000
	19	Stuttgart	W	2-0	BL	Freis [25], Sanou [89]	41 000
	23	Wolfsburg	W	3-2	DPr2	Ishiaku 2 [22 33], Freis [65]	31 500
	26	Leverkusen	L	0-1	BL		49 300
Oct	3	Bayern M	D	0-0	BL		69 000
	17	Mainz	W	1-0	BL	Novakovic [42]	49 000
	24	Gladbach	D	0-0	BL		54 057
	27	Trier	W	3-0	DPr3	Novakovic [25], Mohamad [29], Maniche [52]	10 800
	31	Hannover	L	0-1	BL		45 000
Nov	8	Hertha	W	1-0	BL	Novakovic [79]	48 623
	21	Hoffenheim	L	0-4	BL		45 000
	27	Bochum	D	0-0	BL		29 112
Dec	6	W Bremen	D	0-0	BL		50 000
	12	Freiburg	D	0-0	BL		24 000
	20	Nürnberg	W	3-0	BL	Geromel [37], Novakovic 2 [70 77]	44 500
Jan	17	B Dortmund	L	2-3	BL	McKenna [82], Mohamad [88]	50 000
	24	Wolfsburg	W	3-2	BL	Pezzoni [7], Freis [57], Chihi [74]	27 471
	30	E Frankfurt	W	2-1	BL	Maniche [59], OG [84]	45 100
Feb	6	Hamburg	D	3-3	BL	Mohamad [31], Novakovic [75], Chihi [88]	50 000
	10	Augsburg	L	0-2	DPqf		30 400
	14	Schalke	L	0-2	BL		61 673
	20	Stuttgart	L	1-5	BL	Schorch [44]	45 500
	27	Leverkusen	D	0-0	BL		30 210
Mar	6	Bayern M	D	1-1	BL	Podolski [31]	50 000
	13	Mainz	L	0-1	BL		20 300
	19	Gladbach	D	1-1	BL	Maniche [79]	50 000
	27	Hannover	W	4-1	BL	Tosic 2 [12 71], Petit [21], Novakovic [28]	43 218
Apr	3	Hertha	L	0-3	BL		46 300
	10	Hoffenheim	W	2-0	BL	Matuszyk 2 [46 82]	26 950
	16	Bochum	W	2-0	BL	Tosic 2 [15 78]	46 000
	24	W Bremen	L	0-1	BL		37 900
May	1	Freiburg	D	2-2	BL	Tosic [9], Freis [84]	49 200
	8	Nürnberg	L	0-1	BL		48 548

TSG HOFFENHEIN LEAGUE APPEARANCES/GOALS 2009-10

Goalkeepers Daniel Haas 6 • Timo Hildebrand 28
Defenders Andreas Beck 24+1/0 • Marvin Compper 32/1 • Christian Eichner 22+3/1 • Manuel Gulde 2+4/0 • Andreas Ibertsberger AUT 23/1 • Per Nilsson SWE 5+3/0 • Jukka Raitala FIN 1+1/0 • Josip Simunic CRO 31/1 • Isaac Vorsah GHA 11+5/0
Midfield Carlos Eduardo BRA 32+1/5 • Pascal Gross 0+1/0 • Luiz Gustavo BRA 26+1/0 • Sejad Salihovic 31+1/4 • Boris Vukevic 6+22/1 • Tobias Weis 11+4/0 • Franco Zuculini ARG 2+5/1
Forwards Demba Ba 12+5/5 • Kai Herdling 0+1/0 • Vedad Ibisevic BIH 30+4/12 • Adam Jabiri 0+1/0 • Andreas Ludwig 0+1/0 • Maicosuel BRA 17+10/3 • Chinedu Obasi NGA 21+2/7 • Prince Tagoe GHA 1+11/2 Marco Terrazzino 0+8/0 • Wellington BRA 0+1/0
Coach Ralf Rangnick

1.FC KOLN LEAGUE APPEARANCES/GOALS 2009-10

Goalkeepers Thomas Kessler 2 • Faryd Mondragon COL 32
Defenders Miso Brecko SVN 31+1/0 • Carsten Cullmann 1+2/0 • Geromel BRA 29/1 • Marvin Matip 0+4/0 • Kevin McKenna CAN 11+14/1 • Youssef Mohamad LIB 31/2 • Christopher Schorch 13+4/1 • Pierre Wome CMR 11+1/0 • Reinhold Yabo 0+1/0
Midfield Daniel Brosinski 0+8/0 • Adil Chihi MAR 12+3/3 • Fabrice Ehret FRA 21+8/1 • Maniche POR 26/2 • Adam Matuszczyk POL 9/2 • Petit POR 32/1 • Kevin Pezzoni 18+3/1 • Wilfried Sanou BFA 1+5/1 • Zoran Tosic 9+4/5 • Taner Yalcin TUR 6+1/0
Forwards Sebastian Freis 20+11/3 • Manasseh Ishiaku NGA 6+9/0 • Milivoje Novakovic SVN 26+4/6 • Lukas Podolski 27/2 • Sebastian Zielinsky 0+2/0
Coach Zvonimir Soldo CRO

1.FSV MAINZ 2009–10

=	31 Lübeck	L	1-2	DPr1	Bungert [19]	7 898
	8 Leverkusen	D	2-2	BL	Hoogland [5], Gunkel [82]	20 000
Aug	15 Hannover	D	1-1	BL	Bance [53]	28 952
	22 Bayern M	W	2-1	BL	Ivanschitz [25], Bance [37]	20 300
	28 Gladbach	L	0-2	BL		42 217
	12 Hertha	W	2-1	BL	Ivanschitz [80], Bance [85]	20 300
Sep	19 Bochum	W	3-2	BL	Ivanschitz [45], Schurrle 2 [52 71]	16 225
	26 W Bremen	L	0-3	BL		32 875
	3 Hoffenheim	W	2-1	BL	Ivanschitz [6], Bance [11]	20 300
	17 Köln	L	0-1	BL		49 000
Oct	24 Freiburg	W	3-0	BL	Ivanschitz [24], Hoogland 2 [50 85]	20 150
	31 Wolfsburg	D	3-3	BL	Amri [35], Ivanschitz [41], Hoogland [85]	28 309
	7 Nürnberg	W	1-0	BL	Soto [38]	20 000
Nov	21 B Dortmund	D	0-0	BL		74 600
	28 Hamburg	D	1-1	BL	Hoogland [84]	20 300
	5 E Frankfurt	L	0-2	BL		51 500
Dec	13 Stuttgart	D	1-1	BL	Polanski [90]	20 300
	18 Schalke	L	0-1	BL		60 852
	16 Leverkusen	L	2-4	BL	Hoogland [8], Bungert [67]	28 000
Jan	23 Hannover	W	1-0	BL	Schurrle [4]	20 300
	30 Bayern M	L	0-3	BL		69 000
	7 Gladbach	W	1-0	BL	Svensson [43]	20 300
Feb	13 Hertha	D	1-1	BL	Bance [37]	36 715
	20 Bochum	D	0-0	BL		19 000
	27 W Bremen	L	1-2	BL	Bance [45]	20 300
	7 Hoffenheim	W	1-0	BL	Bance [69]	30 150
Mar	13 Köln	W	1-0	BL	Schurrle [57]	20 300
	20 Freiburg	L	0-1	BL		20 000
	27 Wolfsburg	L	0-2	BL		19 700
	3 Nürnberg	L	0-2	BL		41 222
Apr	10 B Dortmund	W	1-0	BL	Szalai [30]	20 300
	17 Hamburg	W	1-0	BL	Bance [20]	55 292
	24 E Frankfurt	D	3-3	BL	Bance 2 [45 86], Simak [56]	20 300
May	1 Stuttgart	D	2-2	BL	Fathi [52], Schurrle [64]	41 600
	8 Schalke	D	0-0	BL		20 300

1.FC NURNBERG 2009–10

	1 Dy Dresden	W	3-0	DPr1	Kluge [12], Mintal [25], Gundogan [53]	15 460
	8 Schalke	L	1-2	BL	Mintal [88]	46 780
Aug	15 E Frankfurt	D	1-1	BL	Bunjaku [56]	49 000
	22 Hannover	L	0-2	BL		38 600
	29 Stuttgart	D	0-0	BL		42 000
	12 Gladbach	W	1-0	BL	Kluge [6]	46 780
Sep	19 Bayern M	L	1-2	BL	Choupo-Moting [73]	69 000
	22 Hoffenheim	L	0-1	DPr2		26 041
	25 Bochum	L	0-1	BL		35 376
	3 Leverkusen	L	0-4	BL		26 785
Oct	17 Hertha	W	3-0	BL	Gygax [18], Bunjaku 2 [26 60]	38 094
	24 Hoffenheim	L	0-3	BL		30 150
	31 W Bremen	D	2-2	BL	Eigler [3], Bunjaku [33]	42 258
	7 Mainz	L	0-1	BL		20 000
Nov	21 Wolfsburg	W	3-2	BL	Bunjaku 2 [56 64], Kluge [90]	28 736
	28 Freiburg	L	0-1	BL		40 824
	5 B Dortmund	L	0-4	BL		72 100
Dec	12 Hamburg	L	0-4	BL		44 865
	20 Köln	L	0-3	BL		44 500
	17 Schalke	L	0-1	BL		61 515
Jan	23 E Frankfurt	D	1-1	BL	Eigler [27]	37 464
	30 Hannover	W	3-1	BL	Bunjaku 3 [31 64 69]	26 722
	6 Stuttgart	L	1-2	BL	Bunjaku [60]	40 384
Feb	12 Gladbach	L	1-2	BL	Bunjaku [47]	34 297
	20 Bayern M	D	1-1	BL	Gundogan [54]	48 548
	27 Bochum	D	0-0	BL		24 780
	7 Leverkusen	W	3-2	BL	Choupo-Moting 2 [42 45], Tavares [55]	40 329
Mar	13 Hertha	W	2-1	BL	Bunjaku [61], Charistaes [90]	57 761
	20 Hoffenheim	D	0-0	BL		40 421
	27 W Bremen	L	2-4	BL	Frantz [47], Choupo-Moting [63]	36 123
	3 Mainz	W	2-0	BL	Frantz [14], Choupo-Moting [40]	41 222
Apr	11 Wolfsburg	L	0-2	BL		40 593
	17 Freiburg	L	1-2	BL	Maroh [79]	22 800
	24 B Dortmund	L	2-3	BL	Frantz [30], Eigler [84]	48 548
	1 Hamburg	L	0-4	BL		53 727
May	8 Köln	W	1-0	BL	Ottl [88]	48 548
	13 Augsburg	W	1-0	BLpo	Eigler [84]	40 509
	16 Augsburg	W	2-0	BLpo	Gundogan [34], Choupo-Moting [63p]	30 660

1.FSV MAINZ LEAGUE APPEARANCES/GOALS 2009-10

Goalkeepers Heinz Muller **30** • Christian Wetklo **4+1**
Defenders Niko Bungert **21+6/1** • Malik Fathi **14/1** • Tim Hoogland **19+2/6** • Nikolce Noveski MKD **33/0** • Bo Svensson DEN **20+6/1** • Peter van der Heyden BEL **4+4/0** • Radoslav Zabavnik SVK **11+1/0**
Midfield Eugen Gopko **0+1/0** • Daniel Gunkel **0+4/1** • Florian Heller **26+4/0** • Jahmir Hyka **2+6/0** • Andreas Ivanschitz AUT **24+3/6** • Miroslav Karhan SVK **30/0** • Zsolt Low HUN **14+1/0** • Milorad Pekovic MNE **4+7/0** • Eugen Polanski **14+7/1** • Jan Simak CZE **5+3/1** • Elkin Soto COL **28+2/1** • Filip Trojan CZE **3+2/0**
Forwards Chadli Amri ALG **6+13/1** • Aristide Bance BFA **28+2/10** • Felix Borja ECU **0+1/0** • Dragan Bogavac MNE **0+1/0** • Adrian Grimaldi ITA **0+6/0** • Andre Schurrle **25+8/5** • Adam Szalai HUN **8+7/1**
Coach Jorn Andersen NOR • Thomas Tuchel (3/08/09)

1.FC NURNBERG LEAGUE APPEARANCES/GOALS 2009-10

Goalkeepers Raphael Schafer **30** • Alexander Stephan **4+1**
Defenders Pascal Bieler **3/0** • Breno BRA **7/0** • Dennis Diekmeier **30/0** • Dominic Maroh SVN **24+3/1** • Havard Nordtveit NOR **14+5/0** • Javier Pinola **33/0** • Matthew Spiranovic **1/0** • Andreas Wolf **29/0**
Midfield Thomas Broich **2+5/0** • Mike Frantz **20+4/3** • Ilkay Gundogan **19+3/1** • Daniel Gygax SUI **8+2/1** • Juri Judt **8+10/0** • Peer Kluge **17/2** • Marek Mintal SVK **15+7/1** • Jawhar Mnari TUN **3/0** • Andreas Ottl **17/1** • Marcel Riise **10+10/0** • Mickael Tavares SEN **9+2/1**
Forwards Isaac Boakye GHA **4+5/0** • Albert Bunjaku **25+3/12** • Angelos Charisteas GRE **7+11/1** • Eric Choupo-Moting CMR **13+12/5** • Christian Eigler **18+6/3** • Dario Vidosic AUS **4+5/0**
Coach Michael Oenning • Dieter Hecking (22/12/09)

FC SCHALKE 04 2009–10

	Date	Opponent	Res	Score	Comp	Scorers	Att
Aug	1	Windeck	W	4-0	DPr1	Zambrano 10, Kuranyi 43, Kenia 68, Howedes 86	16 000
	8	Nürnberg	W	2-1	BL	Kuranyi 2 36 50	46 780
	16	Bochum	W	3-0	BL	Moritz 39, Westermann 45, Farfan 76	61 673
	21	Hoffenheim	D	0-0	BL		30 150
	29	Freiburg	L	0-1	BL		42 000
Sep	13	Köln	W	2-1	BL	Farfan 2, Kobiaschwili 46	50 000
	18	Wolfsburg	L	1-2	BL	Höwedes 79	60 365
	22	Bochum	W	3-0	DPr2	Westermann 10, Altintop 56, OG 76	29 592
	26	B Dortmund	W	1-0	BL	Farfan 31	80 552
Oct	2	E Frankfurt	W	2-0	BL	Asamoah 66, Farfan 90	61 673
	17	Stuttgart	W	2-1	BL	Rakitic 23, Kuranyi 75	42 000
	25	Hamburg	D	3-3	BL	Kuranyi 2 50 90, Schmitz 62	61 673
	28	TSV 1860	W	3-0	DPr3	Rafinha 41, Howedes 2 48 81	28 500
	31	Leverkusen	D	2-2	BL	Kuranyi 83, Sanchez 88	61 673
Nov	7	Bayern M	D	1-1	BL	Matip 42	69 000
	21	Hannover	W	2-0	BL	Farfan 69, Moravek 90	61 505
	28	Gladbach	L	0-1	BL		54 074
Dec	6	Hertha	W	2-0	BL	Kuranyi 59, Rafinha 90	61 000
	12	W Bremen	W	2-0	BL	Kuranyi 47, Moravek 72	37 000
	18	Mainz	W	1-0	BL	Farfan 12	60 852
Jan	17	Nürnberg	W	1-0	BL	Kuranyi 48	61 515
	23	Bochum	D	2-2	BL	Sanchez 5, Kuranyi 42	29 008
	30	Hoffenheim	W	2-0	BL	Kuranyi 19, Schmitz 49	60 402
Feb	6	Freiburg	D	0-0	BL		24 000
	10	Osnabrück	W	1-0	DPqf	Kuranyi 59	16 130
	14	Köln	W	2-0	BL	Matip 45, Farfan 81	61 673
	21	Wolfsburg	L	1-2	BL	Kuranyi 30	30 000
	26	B Dortmund	W	2-1	BL	Howedes 66, Rakitic 83	61 673
Mar	6	E Frankfurt	W	4-1	BL	Matip 12, Howedes 15, Rakitic 80, Kuranyi 89	51 500
	12	Stuttgart	W	2-1	BL	Edu 46, Kuranyi 55	61 673
	21	Hamburg	D	2-2	BL	Kuranyi 62, Rakitic 68	57 000
	24	Bayern M	L	0-1	DPsf		61 673
	27	Leverkusen	W	2-0	BL	Kuranyi 2 11 28	30 210
Apr	3	Bayern M	L	1-2	BL	Kuranyi 31	61 673
	10	Hannover	L	2-4	BL	Edu 46, Rakitic 52	49 000
	17	Gladbach	W	3-1	BL	Rakitic 2 8 47, Farfan 45	61 673
	24	Hertha	W	1-0	BL	Westermann 87	61 902
May	1	W Bremen	L	0-2	BL		61 673
	8	Mainz	D	0-0	BL		20 300

VFB STUTTGART 2009–10

	Date	Opponent	Res	Score	Comp	Scorers	Att
Aug	1	Großaspach	W	4-1	DPr1	Hitzlsperger 55, Cacau 62, Simak 2 66 88	14 000
	7	Wolfsburg	L	0-2	BL		30 000
	15	Freiburg	W	4-2	BL	Pogrebnjak 53, Elson 2 65 76, Schieber 89	41 500
	18	Timisoara	W	2-0	CLpo	Gebhart 28p, Hleb 30	23 446
	22	B Dortmund	D	1-1	BL	Niedermeier 47	72 100
	26	Timisoara	D	0-0	CLpo		27 500
	29	Nürnberg	D	0-0	BL		42 000
Sep	12	Hamburg	L	1-3	BL	Pogrebnjak 62	57 000
	16	Rangers	D	1-1	CLgG	Pogrebnjak 18	38 000
	19	Köln	L	0-2	BL		41 000
	23	Lübeck	W	3-1	DPr2	Schieber 77, Khedira 109, Cacau 117	16 500
	26	E Frankfurt	W	3-0	BL	Schieber 2 17 31, Hitzlsperger 54	49 750
	29	Unirea	D	1-1	CLgG	Tasci 5	13 557
Oct	4	W Bremen	L	0-2	BL		42 000
	17	Schalke	L	1-2	BL	Cacau 73	42 000
	20	Sevilla	L	1-3	CLgG	Elson 74	37 000
	24	Hannover	L	0-1	BL		34 423
	27	Fürth	L	0-1	DPr3		11 800
	31	Bayern M	D	0-0	BL		42 000
Nov	4	Sevilla	D	1-1	CLgG	Kuzmanovic 79	32 669
	7	Gladbach	D	0-0	BL		47 053
	21	Hertha	D	1-1	BL	Kuzmanovic 82	39 000
	24	Rangers	W	2-0	CLgG	Rudy 16, Kuzmanovic 59	41 468
	29	Leverkusen	L	0-4	BL		30 210
Dec	5	Bochum	D	1-1	BL	Tasci 63	40 000
	9	Unirea	W	3-1	CLgG	Marica 5, Trasch 8, Pogrebnjak 11	37 000
	13	Mainz	D	1-1	BL	Pogrebnjak 11	20 300
	19	Hoffenheim	W	3-1	BL	Marica 32, Cacau 68, Khedira 82	41 000
Jan	16	Wolfsburg	W	3-1	BL	Hibert 28, Pogrebnjak 58, Gebhart 87	37 000
	22	Freiburg	W	1-0	BL	Marica 41	23 900
	31	B Dortmund	W	4-1	BL	Pogrebnjak 14, Kuzmanovic 77, Marica 86, Trasch 89	42 000
Feb	6	Nürnberg	W	2-1	BL	Gebhart 22, Hibert 87	40 384
	13	Hamburg	L	1-3	BL	Trasch 55	41 500
	20	Köln	W	5-1	BL	Cacau 4 13 31 39 74, Pogrebnjak 69	45 500
	23	Barcelona	D	1-1	CLr2	Cacau 25	39 430
	27	E Frankfurt	W	2-1	BL	Cacau 2 41 45	41 000
Mar	6	W Bremen	D	2-2	BL	Pogrebnjak 15, Khedira 42	36 664
	12	Schalke	L	1-2	BL	Tasci 50	61 673
	17	Barcelona	L	0-4	CLr2		88 543
	20	Hannover	W	2-0	BL	Marica 2 36 54	41 000
	27	Bayern M	W	2-1	BL	Trasch 41, Marica 50	69 000
Apr	3	Gladbach	W	2-1	BL	Marica 66, Kuzmanovic 84	42 000
	10	Hertha	W	1-0	BL	Cacau 74	26 851
	17	Leverkusen	W	2-1	BL	Cacau 2 29 85	41 500
	23	Bochum	W	2-0	BL	Cacau 14, Marica 18	25 431
May	1	Mainz	D	2-2	BL	Marica 2 73 75	41 600
	8	Hoffenheim	D	1-1	BL	Cacau 19	30 150

SCHALKE 04 LEAGUE APPEARANCES/GOALS 2009-10

Goalkeepers Manuel Neuer 34
Defenders Bordon BRA 30/0 • Lubos Hanzel SVK 0+1/0 • Benedikt Howedes 32+1/3 • Rafinha BRA 30+1/1 • Tori Reginiussen NOR 0+1/0 • Heiko Westermann 27+2/2 • Carlos Zambrano PER 14+2/0
Midfield Alexander Baumjohann 1+10/0 • Hao Junmin CHN 5+3/0 • Lewis Holtby 4+5/0 • Levan Kenia GEO 4+6/0 • Peer Kluge 13/0 • Levan Kobiashvili GEO 3+1/1 • Joel Matip CMR 17+3/3 • Mineiro BRA 5+2/0 • Jan Moravek CZE 0+7/2 • Christoph Moritz 18+10/1 • Vasilios Pliatsikas GRE 4+4/0 • Ivan Rakitic CRO 25+4/7 • Lukas Schmitz 27+2/2
Forwards Gerald Asamoah 2+6/1 • Edu BRA 7+6/2 • Jefferson Farfan PER 32+1/8 • Mario Gavranovic SUI 0+2/0 • Halil Altintop TUR 2+4/0 • Besart Ibraimi MKD 0+2/0 • Kevin Kuranyi 31+2/18 • Vicente Sanchez URU 7+7/2
Coach Felix Magath

VFB STUTTGART LEAGUE APPEARANCES/GOALS 2009-10

Goalkeepers Jens Lehmann 31 • Sven Ulreich 3+1
Defenders Arthur Boka CIV 12+2/0 • Khalid Boulahrouz NED 5+1/0 • Stefano Celozzi 18+3/0 • Matthieu Delpierre FRA 27/0 • Ludovic Magnin SUI 5+1/0 • Cristian Molinaro ITA 17/0 • Georg Niedermeier 12/1 • Ricardo Osorio MEX 6+1/0 • Serdar Tasci 27/2 • Christian Trasch 28+1/3
Midfield Yildiray Basturk TUR 0+1/0 • Elson BRA 2+9/2 • Timo Gebhart 23+5/2 • Roberto Hilbert 12+11/2 • Thomas Hitzlsperger 11+1/1 • Aleksandr Hleb BLR 24+3/0 • Sami Khedira 24+1/2 • Zdravko Kuzmanovic SRB 14+12/3 • Martin Lanig 0+1/0 • Sebastian Rudy 5+8/0 • Jan Simak CZE 1+1/0 • Clemens Walch AUT 1+1/0
Forwards Cacau 19+6/13 • Ciprian Marica ROU 18+7/10 • Pavel Pogrebnjak RUS 23+5/6 • Julian Schieber 6+13/3
Coach Markus Babbel • Christian Gross SUI (6/12/09)

WERDER BREMEN 2009-10

					Scorers	Att
Aug	2	Union Berlin	W	5-0 DPr1	Sanogo 2 [12 27], Naldo [20], Moreno 2 [85 88]	18 955
	8	E Frankfurt	L	2-3 BL	Ozil [13], Sanogo [44]	33 000
	15	Bayern M	D	1-1 BL	Ozil [39]	69 000
	20	Aktobe	W	6-3 ELpo	Boenisch [17], Ozil 2 [28 67p], Naldo 2 [36 65], Hugo Almeida [60]	21 446
	23	Gladbach	W	3-0 BL	Pizarro 2 [21 38], Naldo [88]	34 800
	27	Aktobe	W	2-0 ELpo	Pizarro 2 [11 45]	11 000
	30	Hertha	W	3-2 BL	Ozil [57], Borowski [74], Naldo [83]	49 176
Sep	13	Hannover	D	0-0 BL		34 000
	17	Nacional	W	3-2 ELgL	Frings [39p], Pizarro 2 [55 85]	3 082
	20	Leverkusen	D	0-0 BL		30 210
	23	St Pauli	W	2-1 DPr2	Hunt [29], Naldo [82]	31 824
	26	Mainz	W	3-0 BL	Hunt [38], Pizarro 2 [71 82]	32 875
Oct	1	Ath Bilbao	W	3-1 ELgL	Hunt [18], Naldo [41], Frings [94+p]	24 305
	4	Stuttgart	W	2-0 BL	Pizarro [3], Hunt [51]	42 000
	17	Hoffenheim	W	2-0 BL	Pizarro [17], Mertesacker [22]	33 916
	22	FK Austria	D	2-2 ELgL	Pizarro 2 [19 63]	11 000
	25	Bochum	W	4-1 BL	Hunt [9], Marin [32], Borowski [76], Ozil [90]	25 703
	28	Kaiser'tern	W	3-0 DPr3	Pasanen [28], Borowski [39], Oehrl [76]	24 094
	31	Nürnberg	D	2-2 BL	Hunt 2 [71 90]	42 258
Nov	5	FK Austria	W	2-0 ELgL	Borowski [81], Hugo Almeida [84]	25 121
	8	B Dortmund	D	1-1 BL	Ozil [36]	34 906
	21	Freiburg	W	6-0 BL	Almeida 2 [33 57], Marin [55], Ozil [67], Naldo [73], Rosenberg [82]	24 000
	28	Wolfsburg	D	2-2 BL	Almeida [62], Mertesacker [90]	34 523
Dec	3	Nacional	W	4-1 ELgL	Rosenberg 2 [31 34], Moreno [84], Marin [92+]	23 784
	6	Köln	D	0-0 BL		50 000
	12	Schalke	L	0-2 BL		37 000
	16	Ath Bilbao	W	3-0 ELgL	Pizarro [13], Naldo [20], Rosenberg [36]	27 500
	20	Hamburg	L	1-2 BL	Naldo [90]	57 000
Jan	16	E Frankfurt	L	0-1 BL		45 600
	23	Bayern M	L	2-3 BL	Hunt [10], Almeida [75]	39 100
	30	Gladbach	L	3-4 BL	Ozil [26], Pizarro [40], Frings [85]	47 458
Feb	5	Hertha	W	2-1 BL	Marin [66], Pizarro [81]	35 600
	9	Hoffenheim	W	2-1 DPqf	Naldo [27], Hugo Almeida [76]	25 753
	13	Hannover	W	5-1 BL	Niemeyer [11], Naldo [18], Andreasen [26], Hunt [44], Pizarro [68]	44 379
	18	Twente	L	0-1 ELr2		22 000
	21	Leverkusen	D	2-2 BL	Pizarro [34], Mertesacker [90]	37 500
	24	Twente	W	4-1 ELr2	Pizarro 3 [15 20 58], Naldo [27]	20 963
	27	Mainz	W	2-1 BL	Borowski [32], Prödl [49]	20 300
Mar	6	Stuttgart	D	2-2 BL	Almeida [75], Frings [82]	36 664
	11	Valencia	L	1-1 ELr3	Frings [24p]	37 223
	14	Hoffenheim	W	1-0 BL	Pizarro [80]	30 150
	18	Valencia	D	4-4 ELr3	Hugo Almeida [26], Frings [57p], Marin [62], Pizarro [84]	24 200
	20	Bochum	W	3-2 BL	Pizarro [58], Marin [65], Frings [81]	36 197
	23	Augsburg	W	2-0 DPsf	Marin [30], Pizarro [84]	31 645
	27	Nürnberg	W	4-2 BL	Mertesacker 2 [1 20], Borowski [36], Fritz [90]	36 123
Apr	3	B Dortmund	L	1-2 BL	Hunt [65]	80 552
	10	Freiburg	W	4-0 BL	Pizarro 2 [35 56], Hunt [53], Ozil [67]	37 000
	17	Wolfsburg	W	4-2 BL	Frings 2 [38 62], Pizarro [49], Almeida [75]	30 000
	24	Köln	W	1-0 BL	Frings [90]	37 900
May	1	Schalke	W	2-0 BL	Ozil [55], Almeida [64]	61 673
	8	Hamburg	D	1-1 BL	Pizarro [58]	41 150
	15	Bayern M	L	0-4 DPf		75 420

WERDER LEAGUE APPEARANCES/GOALS 2009-10

Goalkeepers Sebastian Mielitz 2 • Christian Vander 1+1 • Tim Wiese 31

Defenders Aymen Abdennour TUN 5+1/0 • Sebastian Boenisch 16+1/0 • Clemens Fritz 30+1 • Per Mertesacker 33/5 • Naldo BRA 31/5 • Petri Pasanen FIN 16+3/0 • Sebastian Prodl AUT 5+4/1 • Dusko Tosic SRB 0+1/0

Midfield Philipp Bargfrede 20+3/0 • Tim Borowski 20+8/4 • Torsten Frings 29+1/6 • Said Husejinovic BIH 0+3/0 • Daniel Jensen 5+8/0 • Marko Marin 30+2/4 • Peter Niemeyer 4+7/1 • Mesut Ozil 29+2/9

Forwards Onur Ayik TUR 0+1/0 • Hugo Almeida POR 13+13/7 • Aaron Hunt 26+6/9 • Marcelo Moreno BOL 0+5/0 • Claudio Pizarro PER 23+3/16 • Markus Rosenberg SWE 3+14/1 • Boubacar Sanogo CIV 2/1

Coach Thomas Schaaf

VFL WOLFSBURG 2009-10

					Scorers	Att
Aug	31	Wehen	W	4-1 DPr1	Grafite [26], Misimovic 2 [41 57], Dzeko [51]	7 433
	7	Stuttgart	W	2-0 BL	Misimovic [71], Grafite [82]	30 000
	15	Köln	W	3-1 BL	Dzeko [73], OG [74], Martins [87]	48 000
	23	Hamburg	L	2-4 BL	Misimovic [52], Martins [55]	30 000
	29	Bayern M	L	0-3 BL		69 000
Sep	12	Leverkusen	L	2-3 BL	Misimovic [76], Grafite [80]	30 000
	15	CSKA	W	3-1 CLgB	Grafite 3 [36 41p 87]	25 017
	18	Schalke	W	2-1 BL	Dzeko 2 [55 81]	60 365
	23	Köln	L	2-3 DPr2	Dzeko [54], Riether [66]	31 500
	26	Hannover	W	4-2 BL	Misimovic [8], Gentner [45], Hasebe [48], Dzeko [62]	30 000
Oct	30	Man Utd	L	1-2 CLgB	Dzeko [56]	74 037
	3	Bochum	D	1-1 BL	Martins [75]	21 170
	18	Gladbach	W	2-1 BL	Madlung [45], Gentner [90]	30 000
	21	Besiktas	D	0-0 CLgB		25 778
	25	Hertha	D	0-0 BL		36 799
	31	Mainz	D	3-3 BL	Martins 2 [7 20], Misimovic [64]	28 309
Nov	3	Besiktas	W	3-0 CLgB	Misimovic [14], Gentner [80], Dzeko [87]	18 116
	7	Hoffenheim	W	2-1 BL	Misimovic [52], Grafite [57]	29 400
	21	Nürnberg	L	2-3 BL	Dejagah [59], Grafite [79]	28 736
	25	CSKA	L	1-2 CLgB	Dzeko [19]	13 478
	28	W Bremen	D	2-2 BL	Dzeko 2 [42 85]	34 523
Dec	5	Freiburg	D	2-2 BL	OG [27], Johnson [81]	27 822
	8	Man Utd	L	1-3 CLgB	Dzeko [56]	26 490
	13	B Dortmund	L	1-3 BL	Grafite [55]	30 000
	19	E Frankfurt	D	2-2 BL	Dzeko [38], Josue [69]	41 700
	16	Stuttgart	L	1-3 BL	Dzeko [65]	37 000
Jan	24	Köln	L	2-3 BL	Gentner [22], Ricardo Costa [59]	27 471
	29	Hamburg	D	1-1 BL	Dzeko [34]	51 845
	6	Bayern M	L	1-3 BL	Grafite [90]	30 000
	13	Leverkusen	L	1-2 BL	Dzeko [79]	30 000
	18	Villarreal	D	2-2 ELr2	Grafite 2 [65 84p]	11 384
Feb	21	Schalke	W	2-1 BL	Grafite 2 [71 77]	30 000
	25	Villarreal	W	4-1 ELr2	Dzeko [10], OG [15], Gentner [42], Grafite [64]	16 613
	28	Hannover	W	1-0 BL	Misimovic [78]	34 312
Mar	6	Bochum	W	4-1 BL	Dzeko 2 [60 79], Martins [75], Santana [90]	27 152
	11	Rubin	D	1-1 ELr3	Misimovic [67]	8 432
	13	Gladbach	W	4-0 BL	Misimovic [40], Dzeko 2 [49 80], Gentner [59]	39 128
	18	Rubin	W	2-1 ELr3	Martins [58], Gentner [119]	15 412
	21	Hertha	L	1-5 BL	Grafite [36]	29 353
	24	Mainz	W	2-0 BL	Dzeko 2 [83 90]	19 700
	1	Fulham	L	1-2 ELqf	Madlung [89]	22 307
Apr	4	Hoffenheim	W	4-0 BL	Dzeko 2 [25 75], Barzagli [51], Misimovic [74]	28 107
	8	Fulham	L	0-1 ELqf		24 843
	11	Nürnberg	W	2-0 BL	Dzeko [66], Grafite [78]	40 593
	17	W Bremen	L	2-4 BL	Dzeko [18], Grafite [40]	30 000
	25	Freiburg	L	0-1 BL		22 700
	1	B Dortmund	D	1-1 BL	Dzeko [69]	80 300
May	8	E Frankfurt	W	3-1 BL	Misimovic [21], Riether [30], Dzeko [34]	30 000

WOLFSBURG LEAGUE APPEARANCES/GOALS 2009-10

Goalkeepers Diego Benaglio SUI 22 • Marwin Hitz SUI 5 • Andre Lenz 7+1

Defenders Andrea Barzagli ITA 24/1 • Fabian Johnson 4+6/1 • Alexander Madlung 26+2/1 • Peter Pekarik 10+6/0 • Ricardo Costa POR 10+1/1 • Sascha Riether 33/1 • Marcel Schafer 32/0 • Jan Simunek CZE 4+1/0 • Cristian Zaccardo ITA 0+1/0

Midfield Daniel Baier 0+1/0 • Ashkan Dejagah 4+20/1 • Christian Gentner 34/4 • Makoto Hasebe 19+5/1 • Josue BRA 31/1 • Thomas Kahlenberg DEN 3+9/0 • Zvjezdan Misimovic BIH 31/10 • Jonathan Santana PAR 2+5/1 • Sebastian Schindzielorz 1+1/0 • Karim Ziani ALG 5+5/0

Forwards Edin Dzeko BIH 33+1/22 • Alexander Esswein 0+4/0 • Grafite 27+3/11 • Obafemi Martins NGA 7+9/6

Coach Armin Veh • Lorenz-Gunther Kostner (25/01/10)

GHA – GHANA

FIFA/COCA-COLA WORLD RANKING

1993	1994	1995	1996	1997	1998	1999	2000	2001	2002	2003	2004	2005	2006	2007	2008	2009	2010
37	26	29	25	57	48	48	57	59	61	78	77	50	28	43	25	34	16

					2010							Hi/Lo
	Jan	Feb	Mar	Mar	Apr	May	Jul	Aug	Sep	Oct	Nov	Dec	**14**
	34	27	28	31	32	32	23	23	20	17	17	16	**89**

The Ghana national team received a heroes' welcome on their return to Accra after the FIFA World Cup in South Africa having narrowly missed out on becoming the first African country to reach the semi-finals. With a goal-bound Dominic Adiyiah header fisted away on the line by Uruguay's Luis Suarez in the final seconds of extra-time, it fell to Asamoah Gyan to take the resulting penalty. But he missed and Ghana then lost the resulting penalty shoot-out to the Uruguayans. The absence of Michael Essien from the squad meant that many wrote off Ghana's chances at the start of the tournament, but with key members of the U-20 World Cup winning squad making the move up to the full squad, Ghana surpassed all expectations by reaching the quarter-finals and equalling the best ever performance by an African team at the World Cup. In domestic football there were surprise first time winners of the Ghana Premier League with newly promoted Aduana Stars winning the title ahead of AshantiGold on a better head-to-head record. Remarkably they scored just 19 goals in the 30-game season - the lowest of all the 16 teams and nine less than bottom club Hasaacas. That meant a new world record for the club from the western border town of Dormaa Ahenkro, beating Trabzonspor's total of 25 goals to win a championship set 30 years previously.

FIFA WORLD CUP RECORD
1930-1958 DNE **1962** DNQ **1966** DNE **1970-1978** DNQ **1982** DNE **1986-2002** DNQ **2006** 13 r2 **2010** 7 QF

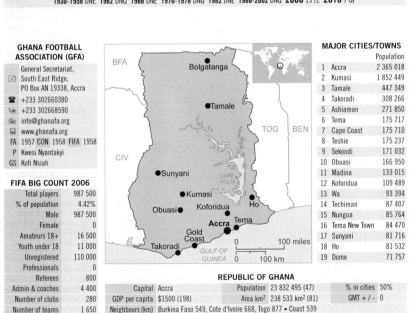

GHANA FOOTBALL ASSOCIATION (GFA)

General Secretariat,
South East Ridge,
PO Box AN 19338, Accra
☎ +233 302660380
📠 +233 302668590
📧 info@ghanafa.org
🖥 www.ghanafa.org
FA 1957 CON 1958 FIFA 1958
P Kwesi Nyantakyi
GS Kofi Nsiah

FIFA BIG COUNT 2006

Total players	987 500
% of population	4.42%
Male	987 500
Female	0
Amateurs 18+	16 500
Youth under 18	11 000
Unregistered	110 000
Professionals	0
Referees	800
Admin & coaches	4 400
Number of clubs	280
Number of teams	1 650

MAJOR CITIES/TOWNS

		Population
1	Accra	2 365 018
2	Kumasi	1 852 449
3	Tamale	447 349
4	Takoradi	308 266
5	Ashiaman	271 850
6	Tema	175 717
7	Cape Coast	175 710
8	Teshie	175 237
9	Sekondi	171 032
10	Obuasi	166 950
11	Madina	133 015
12	Koforidua	109 489
13	Wa	93 394
14	Techiman	87 407
15	Nungua	85 764
16	Tema New Town	84 470
17	Sunyani	81 716
18	Ho	81 532
19	Dome	71 757

REPUBLIC OF GHANA

Capital	Accra	Population	23 832 495 (47)	% in cities	50%
GDP per capita	$1500 (198)	Area km²	238 533 km² (81)	GMT +/-	0
Neighbours (km)	Burkina Faso 549, Cote d'Ivoire 668, Togo 877 • Coast 539				

RECENT INTERNATIONAL MATCHES PLAYED BY GHANA

2008 Opponents	Score		Venue	Comp	Scorers	Att	Referee
1-06 Libya	W	3-0	Kumasi	WCq	Tagoe [17], Agogo [54], Kingston [64]	27 908	Maillet SEY
8-06 Lesotho	W	3-2	Bloemfontein	WCq	Kingston [15], Agogo 2 [41 63]	8 000	Gasingwa RWA
14-06 Gabon	L	0-2	Libreville	WCq		13 000	Benouza ALG
22-06 Gabon	W	2-0	Accra	WCq	Tagoe [31], Muntari [75]	29 040	Damon RSA
20-08 Tanzania	D	1-1	Dar es Salaam	Fr	Kingson [83]		
5-09 Libya	L	0-1	Tripoli	WCq		45 000	Coulibaly MLI
11-10 Lesotho	W	3-0	Sekondi	WCq	Appiah [19], Agogo [24], Amoah [62]	20 000	Rahman SUD
15-10 South Africa	L	1-2	Bloemfontein	Fr	Antwi		Marange ZIM
19-11 Tunisia	D	0-0	Accra	Fr			
2009							
11-02 Egypt	D	2-2	Cairo	Fr	Appiah [52p], Tagoe [77]		
29-03 Benin	W	1-0	Kumasi	WCq	Tagoe [1]	39 000	Bennett RSA
31-05 Uganda	W	2-1	Tamale	Fr	Arko [35], Chibsah [65]		
7-06 Mali	W	2-0	Bamako	WCq	Asamoah [66], Amoah [78]	40 000	Evehe CMR
20-06 Sudan	W	2-0	Omdurman	WCq	Amoah 2 [6 52]	30 000	Ambaya LBY
12-08 Zambia	W	4-1	London	Fr	Muntari [11], Himoonde OG [30], Agogo [41p], Dramani [43]		Marriner ENG
6-09 Sudan	W	2-0	Accra	WCq	Muntari [14], Essien [52]	38 000	Abd El Fatah EGY
9-09 Japan	L	3-4	Utrecht	Fr	Gyan.A 2 [31p 47], Amoah [66]	2 506	Blom NED
30-09 Argentina	L	0-2	Cordoba	Fr			Osses CHI
11-10 Benin	L	0-1	Cotonou	WCq		20 000	Lwanja MWI
15-11 Mali	D	2-2	Kumasi	WCq	Amoah [65], Annan [83]	39 000	Diatta SEN
18-11 Angola	D	0-0	Luanda	Fr			
2010							
5-01 Malawi	D	0-0	Manzini	Fr		2 000	Fakudze SWZ
15-01 Côte d'Ivoire	L	1-3	Cabinda	CNr1	Gyan.A [93+]	23 000	Damon RSA
19-01 Burkina Faso	W	1-0	Luanda	CNr1	Ayew [30]	8 000	Maillet SEY
24-01 Angola	W	1-0	Luanda	CNqf	Gyan.A [15]	50 000	Benouza ALG
28-01 Nigeria	W	1-0	Luanda	CNsf	Gyan.A [21]	7 500	Bennett RSA
31-01 Egypt	L	0-1	Luanda	CNf		50 000	Coulibaly MLI
3-03 Bosnia-Herzegovina	L	1-2	Sarajevo	Fr	Muntari [22]	10 000	Batinic CRO
1-06 Netherlands	L	1-4	Rotterdam	Fr	Gyan.A [78]	45 000	Moen NOR
5-06 Latvia	W	1-0	Milton Keynes	Fr	Owusu-Abeyie [88]	8 108	Clattenburg ENG
13-06 Serbia	W	1-0	Pretoria	WCr1	Gyan.A [85p]	38 833	Baldassi ARG
19-06 Australia	D	1-1	Rustenburg	WCr1	Gyan.A [25p]	34 812	Rosetti ITA
23-06 Germany	L	0-1	Johannesburg	WCr1		83 391	Simon BRA
26-06 USA	W	2-1	Rustenburg	WCr2	Prince Boateng [5], Gyan.A [93]	34 976	Kassai HUN
2-07 Uruguay	D	1-1	Johannesburg	WCqf	Muntari [45]	84 017	Benquerenca POR
11-08 South Africa	L	0-1	Johannesburg	Fr		45 000	
5-09 Swaziland	W	3-0	Lobamba	CNq	Ayew.A [13], Tagoe [69], Sarpei [80]		Seechurn MRI
10-10 Sudan	D	0-0	Kumasi	CNq		39 000	Damon RSA
17-11 Saudi Arabia	D	0-0	Dubai	Fr			

Fr = Friendly match • CN = CAF African Cup of Nations • WC = FIFA World Cup
q = qualifier • r1 = first round group • r2 = second round •qf = quarter-final • sf = semi-final • 3p = third place play-off

GHANA NATIONAL TEAM HISTORICAL RECORDS

Caps
83 -Richard Kingson 1996-

Goals
33 - Abedi Pele 1982-98

Past Coaches
George Ainsley ENG 1958-59 • Andreas Sjoberg SWE 1959-62 • Jozsef Ember HUN 1963 • Charles Gyamfi 1963-65 • Carlos Alberto Pareira BRA 1967 • Karl-Heinz Marotzke GER 1968-70 • Nicolae Dumitru ROU 1974-74 • Karl Weigang GER 1974-75 • Sampaio BRA 1977-78 • Fred Osam-Duodu 1978-81 • Charles Gyamfi 1982-83 • Emmanuel Afranie 1984 • Herbert Addo 1984 • Rudi Gutendorf GER 1986-87 • Fred Osam-Duodu 1988-89 • Burkhard Ziese GER 1990-92 • Otto Pfister GER 1992-93 • Fred Osam-Duodu 1993 • Jorgen Larsen DEN 1993-94 • Edward Aggrey-Fynn 1994 • Petre Gavrilla ROU 1995 • Ismael Kurtz BRA 1996 • Sam Arday 1996-97 • Rinus Israel NED 1997-98 • Giuseppe Dossena ITA 1999-2000 • Fred Osam-Duodu 2000 • Cecil Jones 2001 • Fred Osam-Duodu 2001-02 • Milan Zivadinovic SRB 2002 • Emmanuel Afranie 2002, Burkhard Ziese GER 2003 • Ralf Zumdick GER 2003 • Mariano Barreto 2004 • Sam Arday 2004 • Ratomir Dujkovic SRB 2004-06 • Claude Le Roy FRA 2006-08 • Sellas Tetteh 2008 • Milovan Rajevac SRB 2008-10 • Kwasi Appiah 2010 • Goran Stevanovic SRB 2011-

GHANA 2009-10

GLO PREMIER LEAGUE

	Pl	W	D	L	F	A	Pts	Aduana Stars	AshantiGold	Hearts of Oak	Heart of Lions	Asante Kotoko	All Stars	Arsenal	Chelsea	Kessben	King Faisal	RTU	New Edubiase	Liberty Pros	Olympics	Eleven Wise	Hasaacas
Aduana Stars †	30	15	8	7	19	10	53		1-0	1-0	1-0	1-0	1-0	1-0	0-0	1-0	1-0	2-0	1-0	0-0	1-0	1-0	1-0
AshantiGold ‡	30	15	8	7	36	22	53	0-0		0-0	2-1	1-1	3-1	2-0	1-0	2-1	2-1	1-0	2-1	3-0	1-1	2-0	1-0
Hearts of Oak	30	13	8	9	39	30	47	1-0	0-0		5-6	1-0	1-2	3-0	2-1	1-0	0-2	2-0	1-0	2-3	1-0	2-2	5-0
Heart of Lions	30	13	7	10	38	34	46	1-1	1-0	2-0		1-0	2-1	1-0	2-1	1-0	2-1	0-0	2-1	1-0	2-1	0-0	4-2
Asante Kotoko	30	11	11	8	35	27	44	1-0	0-1	0-1	1-1		0-0	2-2	2-0	2-0	1-1	2-1	2-0	1-0	5-1	2-1	1-1
All Stars	30	12	8	10	33	33	44	0-0	0-2	2-0	0-0	0-0		2-0	2-1	2-0	1-0	1-1	2-1	1-0	2-1	1-1	3-1
Arsenal Berekum	30	12	7	11	27	33	43	1-1	2-1	1-0	0-0	2-0	1-0		1-1	2-1	2-1	1-1	1-1	1-0	2-1	2-1	1-1
Bechem Chelsea	30	11	9	10	26	20	42	0-0	1-0	1-1	1-0	0-1	2-0	2-0		0-0	1-0	0-0	2-0	1-1	0-0	1-0	2-1
Kessben §3	30	14	3	13	39	44	42	1-0	2-1	3-2	1-0	1-1	4-1	2-0	**0-3**		2-1	2-0	1-5	1-1	2-0	2-1	2-0
King Faisal Babes	30	12	6	12	35	27	42	0-0	1-1	1-1	3-1	1-0	1-2	2-0	1-0	1-2		1-0	1-0	1-2	1-1	2-0	2-1
Real Tamale United	30	11	7	12	31	36	40	1-0	1-0	0-0	2-1	0-1	2-1	2-1	1-1	3-1	0-4		2-1	3-0	3-2	2-1	0-0
New Edubiase	30	11	6	13	32	33	39	1-0	1-2	0-0	2-1	3-3	0-0	2-0	0-2	2-1	1-0	1-0		1-0	1-1	2-1	2-0
Liberty Professionals	30	10	8	12	32	29	38	0-1	1-1	0-1	1-1	3-1	2-0	1-2	1-0	4-0	1-1	2-0	1-0		1-1	2-0	4-1
Great Olympics	30	9	7	14	31	40	34	1-0	2-1	0-2	1-0	1-1	4-3	0-1	1-0	2-0	0-1	2-1	2-0	1-0		1-1	1-3
Eleven Wise	30	8	7	15	38	47	31	1-2	1-1	2-3	3-2	1-3	1-1	0-1	2-1	2-3	2-1	4-3	2-2	1-0	2-1		4-1
Hasaacas Sekondi	30	5	6	19	28	54	21	1-0	1-2	1-1	3-2	1-1	1-2	1-0	0-1	3-4	0-2	1-2	0-1	1-1	2-1	0-1	

18/10/2009 - 12/05/2010 • † Qualified for the CAF Champions League • ‡ Qualified for the Confederation Cup • Match in bold awarded
§ = points deducted

MEDALS TABLE

		Overall			League			Cup		Africa			City
		G	S	B	G	S	B	G	S	G	S	B	
1	Asante Kotoko	31	23	6	21	14	3	8	2	2	7	3	Kumasi
2	Hearts of Oak	30	17	8	19	11	6	9	4	2	2	2	Accra
3	Great Olympics	5	4	6	2	3	5	3	1			1	Accra
4	Real Republicans	5		1	1			4					Accra
5	Ashanti Gold	4	6	3	3	4	3	1	1		1		Obuasi
6	Cornerstones	2	6			4		2	2				Kumasi
7	Eleven Wise	2	5	3	1	3	3	1	2				Sekondi
8	Sekondi Hasaacas	2	4	2	1	3	1	1	1			1	Sekondi
9	Cape Coast Dwarfs	2	3	5	1	1	5	1	2				Cape Coast
10	Okwahu United	1	3	2		1	2	1	2				Nkawkaw
11	Ghapoha Tema	1	1					1	1				Tema
12	Aduana Stars	1			1								Dormaa Ahenkro
	Voradep Ho	1						1					Ho
14	Real Tamale United		5	3		2	3	3					Tamale
15	Brong-Ahofu United		2	3		1	3	1					Sunyani
16	Bofoakwa Tano		2	2		1	2	1					Sunyani
17	Great Ashantis		2					2					Kumasi
18	King Faisal Babes		1	3			3	1					Kumasi
19	Akotex Akosombo		1	1			1	1					Akosombo
	Heart of Lions		1	1		1	1						Kpandu

GNB – GUINEA-BISSAU

FIFA/COCA-COLA WORLD RANKING

1993	1994	1995	1996	1997	1998	1999	2000	2001	2002	2003	2004	2005	2006	2007	2008	2009	2010
131	122	118	133	148	165	173	177	174	183	186	190	186	191	171	186	194	147

2010												Hi/Lo
Jan	Feb	Mar	Mar	Apr	May	Jul	Aug	Sep	Oct	Nov	Dec	115
194	195	195	192	189	191	188	188	140	146	148	147	195

Guinea Bissau broke new ground in 2010 with a credible side that won a famous victory at the start of their 2012 African Nations Cup qualifying campaign in September. The 1-0 victory over Kenya in Bissau was only the third win for the former Portuguese colony in a competitive international. Since joining FIFA in 1986, the small west African country has played just 19 competitive internationals, winning three, drawing three and losing the rest. The decision to appoint former Portugal international Norton do Matos as national team coach in April, as well as looking to the large Guinea Bissau community in Portugal for the basis of their national team, saw the country jump over 40 places in the FIFA/Coca-Cola World Ranking. Matos has found it difficult to persuade some players to commit their international careers to Guinea-Bissau but continued to try and persuade the likes of Ivanildo (Portimonense), Eder (Academica) and Yazalde (Rio Ave) to play for the country. Sporting Bissau won a 14th championship title, extending their record by edging out defending champions OS Balantas. Balantas also lost the Cup Final to Sport Bissau e Benfica whose 2-1 victory saw them win the trophy for a record-equalling sixth time. In the 2010 CAF Champions League Balantas lost in the first round to Diffa El Jadida of Morocco.

FIFA WORLD CUP RECORD
1930-1994 DNE **1998-2010** DNQ

FEDERAÇAO DE FUTEBOL DA GUINE-BISSAU (FFGB)

Alto Bandim (Nova Sede),
Case Postale 375,
Bissau 1035
☎ +245 3201918
📠 +245 3206915
📧 ffgb_bissau@hotmail.com
💻
FA 1974 CON 1986 FIFA 1986
P Jose Lobato
GS Simao Da Rocha

FIFA BIG COUNT 2006

Total players	71 900
% of population	4.99%
Male	71 900
Female	0
Amateurs 18+	1 100
Youth under 18	1 200
Unregistered	7 500
Professionals	0
Referees	100
Admin & coaches	300
Number of clubs	40
Number of teams	110

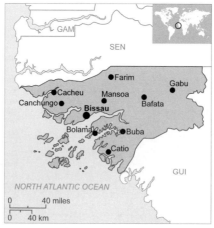

MAJOR CITIES/TOWNS

		Population
1	Bissau	423 478
2	Bafatá	22 791
3	Gabú	14 561
4	Bissorã	12 027
5	Bolama	9 998
6	Cacheu	9 882
7	Catió	9 342
8	Bubaque	9 229
9	Mansôa	7 414
10	Buba	6 867
11	Canchungo	6 456
12	Farim	6 439
13	Quebo	6 243
14	Quinhámel	2 885
15	Fulacunda	1 321

REPUBLICA DA GUINE-BISSAU • REPUBLIC OF GUINEA-BISSAU

Capital Bissau	Population 1 533 964 (150)	% in cities 30%
GDP per capita $600 (224)	Area km² 36 125 km² (137)	GMT + / - 0
Neighbours (km) Guinea 386, Senegal 338 • Coast 350		

RECENT INTERNATIONAL MATCHES PLAYED BY GUINEA-BISSAU

2002 Opponents	Score		Venue	Comp	Scorers	Att	Referee
No international matches played after June 2002							
2003							
10-10 Mali	L	1-2	Bissau	WCq	Dionisio Fernandes [50]	22 000	Sowe GAM
14-11 Mali	L	0-2	Bamako	WCq		13 251	Seydou MTN
2004							
No International matches played in 2004							
2005							
18-11 Guinea	D	2-2	Conakry	ACr1	Manuel Fernandes 2 [35p 49]		
20-11 Sierra Leone	D	1-1	Conakry	ACr1	Agostino Soares [62]		
25-11 Senegal †	D	1-1	Conakry	ACsf			
27-11 Mali †	L	0-1	Conakry	AC3p			
2006							
No international matches played in 2006							
2007							
17-10 Sierra Leone	L	0-1	Freetown	WCq		25 000	Mana NGA
17-11 Sierra Leone	D	0-0	Bissau	WCq		12 000	Lamptey GHA
2-12 Sierra Leone	W	2-0	Bissau	ACr1	Emiliano [8], Suleimane [49]		
7-12 Cape Verde	D	1-1	Bissau	ACsf	Adilson [7]. L 2-3p		
2008							
No international matches played in 2008							
2009							
No international matches played in 2009							
2010							
4-09 Kenya	W	1-0	Bissau	CNq	Dionisio [76]		Bennaceur TUN
9-10 Angola	L	0-1	Luanda	CNq			Coulibaly MLI
16-11 Cape Verde Islands	L	1-2	Lisbon	Fr	Cicero [27]		

AC = Amilcar Cabral Cup • CN = CAF African Cup of Nations • WC = FIFA World Cup
q = qualifier • r1 = first round group • sf = semi-final • 3p = third place play-off • † Not a full international

TACA DA GUINE-BISSAU FINAL
18-07-2010
Sport Bissau e Benfica   0-2   Os Balantas de Mansoa

GRE – GREECE

FIFA/COCA-COLA WORLD RANKING

1993	1994	1995	1996	1997	1998	1999	2000	2001	2002	2003	2004	2005	2006	2007	2008	2009	2010
34	28	34	35	42	53	34	42	57	48	30	18	16	16	11	20	13	11

	2010											Hi/Lo
	Jan	Feb	Mar	Mar	Apr	May	Jul	Aug	Sep	Oct	Nov	Dec	8
	13	12	10	11	12	13	12	12	12	12	11	11	66

The Greeks may have scored a first goal and won a first game at the FIFA World Cup finals, but there can be no disguising the disappointment at their meek exit after the first round in South Africa. With coach Otto Rehhagel's defensive inclinations, perhaps the approach of the team was unsurprising but had Greece committed more to attack, qualification for the second round would have been a real possibility. An opening game defeat at the hands of South Korea set the tone and although the win over Nigeria showed just what the team could achieve, they reverted to type in the 2-0 defeat at the hands of Argentina and were out. Rehhagel's nine year reign came to an end after the tournament and there can be no doubt that he has transformed the fortunes of the national team thanks to the triumph at Euro 2004 but the hope is that new coach Fernando Santos can take the team even further. Santos enjoys a high profile in Greece and in the 2009-10 season took his club PAOK to UEFA Champions League qualification via the end of season play-offs. The title, however, was won by Panathinaikos, ending a run of five championships for fierce rivals Olympiacos. The hiring of coach Nikolaos Nioplias in December 2009, along with the firepower of top scorer Djibril Cisse, transformed their season and they also beat Aris in the Cup Final.

FIFA WORLD CUP RECORD

1930 DNE 1934-1938 DNQ 1950 DNE 1954-1990 DNQ 1994 24 r1 1998-2006 DNQ 2010 25 r1

HELLENIC FOOTBALL FEDERATION (HFF)

Goudi Park,
PO Box 14161,
Athens 11510
☎ +30 210 9306000
📠 +30 210 9359666
📧 epo@epo.gr
💻 www.epo.gr
FA 1926 CON 1954 FIFA 1927
P Sofoklis Pilavios
GS Ioannis Economides

FIFA BIG COUNT 2006

Total players	760 621
% of population	7.12%
Male	705 164
Female	55 457
Amateurs 18+	268 570
Youth under 18	86 779
Unregistered	145 400
Professionals	1 818
Referees	3 230
Admin & coaches	10 100
Number of clubs	5 571
Number of teams	5 899

MAJOR CITIES/TOWNS

		Population
1	Athens	752 573
2	Thessaloníki	348 858
3	Piraeus	178 390
4	Pátra	166 815
5	Peristéri	144 911
6	Irákleio	137 291
7	Lárisa	134 138
8	Kallithéa	111 595
9	Glifáda	102 656
10	Níkaia	101 592
11	Kalamariá	96 986
12	Akharnaí	94 771
13	Ilion	86 984
14	Keratsínion	82 775
15	Vólos	82 046
16	Néa Smírni	81 126
17	Ilioúpoli	80 878
18	Khalándrion	80 854
19	Amaroúsion	79 088

ELLINIKI DHIMOKRATIA • HELLENIC REPUBLIC

Capital	Athens	Population	10 737 428 (74)	% in cities	61%
GDP per capita	$32 100 (40)	Area km²	131 957 km² (96)	GMT + / -	+2
Neighbours (km)	Albania 282, Bulgaria 494, Turkey 206, Macedonia FYR 246 • Coast 13 676				

RECENT INTERNATIONAL MATCHES PLAYED BY GREECE

2008	Opponents	Score		Venue	Comp	Scorers	Att	Referee
6-02	Finland	W	2-1	Nicosia	Fr	Charisteas [67], Katsouranis [72]	500	Kailis CYP
26-03	Portugal	W	3-2	Dusseldorf	Fr	Karagounis 2 [33 59]	25 000	Kirchen GER
19-05	Cyprus	W	2-0	Patras	Fr	Ninis [5], Katsouranis [58p]	16 216	MacDonald SCO
24-05	Hungary	L	2-3	Budapest	Fr	Amanatidis [45], Katsouranis [93+]	7 000	Blom NED
1-06	Armenia	D	0-0	Offenbach/Main	Fr		8 032	Rafati GER
10-06	Sweden	L	0-2	Salzburg	ECr1		31 063	Busacca SUI
14-06	Russia	L	0-1	Salzburg	ECr1		31 063	Rosetti ENG
18-06	Spain	L	1-2	Salzburg	ECr1	Charisteas [42]	30 883	Webb ENG
20-08	Slovakia	W	2-0	Bratislava	Fr	Gekas 2 [61 82]	4 500	Fabian HUN
6-09	Luxembourg	W	3-0	Luxembourg	WCq	Torosidis [36], Gekas [45], Charisteas [76p]	4 596	Hermansen DEN
10-09	Latvia	W	2-0	Riga	WCq	Gekas 2 [10 49]	8 600	Chapron FRA
11-10	Moldova	W	3-0	Piraeus	WCq	Charisteas 2 [32 51], Katsouranis [40]	13 684	Berntsen NOR
15-10	Switzerland	L	1-2	Piraeus	WCq	Charisteas [68]	28 810	Medina ESP
19-11	Italy	D	1-1	Piraeus	Fr	Gekas [50]	7 000	Webb ENG
2009								
11-02	Denmark	D	1-1	Piraeus	Fr	Gekas [62]		Undiano ESP
28-03	Israel	D	1-1	Ramat Gan	WCq	Gekas [41]	38 000	Rosetti ITA
1-04	Israel	W	2-1	Irákleio	WCq	Salpingidis [32], Samaras [66p]	22 794	Benquerença POR
12-08	Poland	L	0-2	Bydgoszcz	Fr		19 000	Sagara JPN
5-09	Switzerland	L	0-2	Basel	WCq		38 500	De Bleeckere BEL
9-09	Moldova	D	1-1	Chisinau	WCq	Gekas [33]	9 870	Stalhammar SWE
10-10	Latvia	W	5-2	Athens	WCq	Gekas 4 [4 47p 57 91+], Samaras [73]	18 981	Ovrebo NOR
14-10	Luxembourg	W	2-1	Athens	WCq	Torosidis [30], Gekas [33]	13 932	Ceferin SVN
14-11	Ukraine	D	0-0	Athens	WCpo		39 045	Duhamel FRA
18-11	Ukraine	W	1-0	Donetsk	WCpo	Salpingidis [31]	31 643	Benquerença POR
2010								
3-03	Senegal	L	0-2	Volos	Fr		10 000	Skomina SVN
25-05	Korea DPR	D	2-2	Altach	Fr	Katsouranis [2], Charisteas [48]	3 000	Schorgenhofer AUT
2-06	Paraguay	L	0-2	Winterthur	Fr		5 200	Circhetta SUI
12-06	Korea Republic	L	0-2	Port Elizabeth	WCr1		31 513	Hester NZL
17-06	Nigeria	W	2-1	Bloemfontein	WCr1	Salpingidis [44], Torosidis [71]	31 593	Ruiz COL
22-06	Argentina	L	0-2	Polokwane	WCr1		38 891	Irmatov UZB
11-08	Serbia	W	1-0	Belgrade	Fr	Salpingidis [45]	10 000	Teixeira ESP
3-09	Georgia	D	1-1	Piraeus	ECq	Spiropoulos [72]	14 794	Clos ESP
7-09	Croatia	D	0-0	Zagreb	ECq		24 399	Larsen DEN
8-10	Latvia	W	1-0	Piraeus	ECq	Torosidis [58]	13 520	Damato ITA
12-10	Israel	W	2-1	Piraeus	ECq	Salpingidis [22], Karagounis [63p]	16 935	Hansson SWE
17-11	Austria	W	2-1	Vienna	Fr	Samaras [49], Fotakis [81]	16 200	Kever SUI

Fr = Friendly match • EC = UEFA EURO 2008/2012 • WC = FIFA World Cup • q = qualifier • r1 = First round group

GREECE NATIONAL TEAM HISTORICAL RECORDS

Caps

120 - Theodoros Zagorakis 1994-2007 • **102** - Giorgos Karagounis 1999- • **100** - Angelos Basinas 1999-2009 • **96** - Stratos Apostolakis 1986-98 • **90** - Antonis Nikopolidis 1999-2008 • **85** - Angelos Charisteas 2001- • **78** - Dimitris Saravakos 1982-94 • **77** - Stelios Giannakopoulos 1997-2008; Tasos Mitropoulos 1978-94 & Kostas Katsouranis 2003- • **76** - Panagiotis Tsalouchidis 1987-95 • **75** - Nikos Anastopoulos 1977-88 • **72** - Giourkas Seitaridis 2002- • **71** - Giannis Kalitzakis 1987-99 & Stelios Manolas 1982-95

Goals

29 - Nikos Anastopoulos 1977-88 • **24** - Angelos Charisteas 2001- • **22** - Dimitris Saravakos 1982-94 • **21** - Mimis Papaioannou 1963-78 • **20** - Theofanis Gekas 2005- • **18** - Nikos Machlas 1993-2002 • **17** - Demis Nikolaidis 1995-2004 • **16** - Panagiotis Tsalouchidis 1987-95

Past Coaches

Ioannis Kalafatis 1920 • Apostolos Nikolaidis 1929 • Jan Kopsiva CZE 1929-30 • Svejik CZE 1930 • Jan Kopsiva CZE 1930 • Committee 1930-31 • Lefteris Panourgias 1932 • Kostas Negrepontis 1933-34 • Apostolos Nikolaidis 1934-35 • Kostas Konstantaras 1935 • Kischler AUT 1936 • Kostas Konstantaras 1936-37 • Kostas Negrepontis 1938 • Bucket ENG 1938 • Kostas Negrepontis 1948-50 • Antonis Migiakis 1951 • Ioannis Chelmis 1951 • Nikos Katrantzos 1951 • Kostas Negrepontis & Antonis Migiakis 1952 • Antonis Migiakis 1952-53 • Kostas Negrepontis 1953 • Ioannis Chelmis 1954 • Antonis Migiakis 1954-55 • Ioannis Chelmis 1955 • Kostas Andritsos 1956 • Rino Martini ITA 1957-58 • Antonis Migiakis 1958 • Paul Barone FRA 1959-60 • Tryfonas Tzanetis 1960-61 • Antonis Migiakis 1961 • Tryfonas Tzanetis 1962-64 • Lakis Petropoulos & Ioannis Magiras 1964-65 • Panos Markovits 1966-67 • Lakis Petropoulos 1967 • Kostas Karapatis 1968 • Dan Georgiadis 1968-69 • Lakis Petropoulos 1969-71 • Bily Bingham NIR 1971-73 • Alketas Panagoulias 1973-76 • Lakis Petropoulos 1976-77 • Alketas Panagoulias 1977-81 • Christos Archontidis 1982-84 • Miltos Papapostolou 1984-88 • Alekos Sofianidis 1988-89 • Antonis Georgiadis 1989-91 • Stefanos Petritsis 1992 • Antonis Georgiadis 1992 • Alketas Panagoulias 1992-94 • Kostas Polychroniou 1994-98 • Anghel Iordanescu ROU 1998-99 • Vassilis Daniil 1999-2001 • Nikos Christidis 2001 • Otto Rehhagel GER 2001-10 • Fernando Santos POR 2010-

GREECE 2009–10

SUPERLEAGUE

Team	Pl	W	D	L	F	A	Pts	Pan	Oly	PAOK	AEK	Aris	Kav	Atr	Lar	Pao	Irk	Erg	Ast	Xan	Lev	PAS	Pth
Panathinaikos †	30	22	4	4	54	17	70		0-1	2-1	1-1	2-1	0-2	3-1	4-0	2-1	2-0	4-1	1-1	1-0	3-0	4-0	2-0
Olympiacos ¥‡	30	19	7	4	47	18	64	2-0		0-1	1-2	2-1	0-0	2-0	2-1	1-0	1-1	2-1	3-0	0-0	5-1	2-2	3-0
PAOK Thessaloníki ¥†	30	19	5	6	41	16	62	2-1	1-2		0-1	4-1	1-0	1-0	1-0	1-0	1-0	4-1	1-0	1-0	3-0	2-0	3-0
AEK Athens ¥‡	30	15	8	7	43	31	53	0-1	1-2	1-0		1-0	3-0	3-3	3-1	1-1	1-0	1-0	2-0	3-1	3-2	3-1	3-2
Aris Thessaloníki ¥‡	30	12	10	8	35	28	46	0-0	1-0	2-0	1-1		0-0	1-0	2-0	1-1	4-2	2-1	0-1	1-0	1-0	1-0	0-2
Kavala	30	10	9	11	31	32	39	2-2	0-0	0-0	2-1	1-1		2-1	3-3	1-1	1-0	1-3	0-1	2-1	2-2	1-0	3-0
Atromitos	30	10	8	12	34	36	38	0-3	0-1	0-0	0-1	0-3	2-0		2-1	1-0	2-1	0-0	0-0	1-0	3-0	2-1	3-1
Larisa	30	10	7	13	31	42	37	0-3	0-2	2-1	1-0	2-2	1-0	2-2		2-2	2-1	1-0	1-0	2-0	1-2	0-0	0-2
Panionios	30	9	10	11	34	35	37	0-2	0-1	0-0	3-1	1-1	1-2	2-1	0-3		0-0	1-1	1-3	3-0	2-2	3-1	3-1
Iraklis Thessaloníki	30	10	7	13	39	41	37	0-1	1-0	1-1	1-1	2-1	1-0	2-2	2-1	0-2		0-2	1-0	2-4	1-1	2-0	3-1
Ergotelis	30	9	9	12	37	41	36	0-3	1-1	0-2	2-2	0-0	1-0	1-1	0-0	0-0	1-3		4-3	1-0	1-0	3-1	4-0
Asteras Tripolis	30	10	6	14	29	36	36	0-1	1-3	1-1	2-1	1-0	2-1	1-0	2-0	2-0	0-4	2-4		0-0	2-1	3-0	3-1
Xánthi	30	10	5	15	27	36	35	1-2	0-1	0-3	1-0	2-1	2-1	2-1	0-1	1-2	4-3	1-0	2-0		1-0	1-1	1-0
Levadiakos	30	9	7	14	31	44	34	0-2	0-3	0-2	0-0	0-2	0-1	1-1	3-0	1-0	1-0	2-2	1-0	2-1		4-1	2-0
PAS Giannina	30	7	7	16	27	46	28	0-1	2-2	0-1	1-1	0-1	2-1	1-0	2-0	2-3	2-3	1-0	1-0	0-0	1-1		2-0
Panthrakikos	30	3	3	24	21	62	12	0-1	0-2	1-2	1-2	1-1	1-3	0-3	1-3	0-1	1-2	3-2	0-0	1-1	0-2	1-2	

22/08/2009 - 18/04/2010 • † Qualified for the UEFA Champions League • ‡ Qualified for the Europa League • ¥ Champions League play-off
Top scorers: 23 - Djibril Cisse, Panathinaikos • 11 - Giorgos Barkoglou, Levadiakos; Victoras Iacob, Iraklis & Javier Campora, Aris • 10 - Benjamin Onwuachi, Kaval & Danijel Cesarec, Asteras • 9 - Kostas Mitroglou, Olympiacos

GREECE 2009–10 BETA ETHNIKI (2)

Team	Pl	W	D	L	F	A	Pts
Olympiacos Volos	34	21	5	8	73	36	68
Kérkira	34	18	9	7	45	25	63
OFI Crete †	34	18	8	8	44	35	62
Ethnikos Piraeus †	34	14	11	9	43	30	53
Panserraikos †	34	14	10	10	36	35	52
Pierikos Katerini †	34	14	8	12	41	31	50
Panetolikos	34	13	11	10	43	36	50
Diagoras Rhodos	34	14	6	14	43	42	48
Illioupoli	34	12	10	12	33	35	46
Agrotikos Asteras	34	10	15	9	36	31	45
Ethnikos Asteras	34	12	9	13	39	37	45
Anagennisi Karditsas	34	10	14	10	29	28	44
Thrasivoulos †	34	9	14	11	42	42	41
Doxa Dramas †	34	10	10	14	37	49	40
Ionikos †	34	10	9	15	32	45	39
Rodos †	34	9	7	18	31	46	34
Kalamata	34	6	10	18	21	49	28
Egaleo	34	5	6	23	19	55	21

11/09/2009 - 16/05/2010 • † Play-offs

CHAMPIONS LEAGUE PLAY-OFFS

Team	Pl	W	D	L	F	A	Pts	PAOK	AEK	Aris	Oly
PAOK Thessaloníki §3	6	4	1	1	7	3	16		1-0	2-0	1-0
AEK Athens §1	6	2	2	2	8	7	9	0-0		4-2	2-1
Aris Thessaloníki	6	2	2	2	8	9	8	3-2	1-1		2-0
Olympiacos §4	6	1	1	4	3	7	8	0-1	2-1	0-0	

28/04/2010 - 19/05/2010 • § = bonus points • PAOK qualified for the Champions League, AEK, Aris and Olympiacos for the UEFA Cup

BETA ETHNIKI PROMOTION PLAY-OFFS

Team	Pl	W	D	L	F	A	Pts	Pan	OFI	Eth	Pie
Panserraikos §1	6	4	1	1	9	3	14		1-1	1-0	2-0
OFI Crete §3	6	2	3	1	9	8	12	0-1		2-1	2-1
Ethnikos Piraeus §1	6	2	2	2	11	11	9	1-0	4-4		2-1
Pierikos Katerini	6	0	2	4	6	13	2	1-4	0-0	3-3	

23/05/2010 - 9/06/2010 • § = bonus points • Panserraikos promoted

BETA ETHNIKI RELEGATION PLAY-OFFS

Team	Pl	W	D	L	F	A	Pts	Doxa	Thr	Ion	Rod
Doxa Dramas §2	6	2	3	1	8	5	11		2-0	2-0	1-1
Thrasivoulos §2	6	2	2	2	8	9	10	1-1		3-1	3-2
Ionikos §1	6	2	2	2	7	8	9	2-1	2-0		1-1
Rodos	6	0	5	1	7	8	5	1-1	1-1	1-1	

23/05/2010 - 9/06/2010 • § = bonus points • Rodos relegated

MEDALS TABLE

	Team	Overall			League			Cup		Europe			City
		G	S	B	G	S	B	G	S	G	S	B	
1	Olympiacos	61	28	10	37	17	10	24	11				Piraeus
2	Panathinaikos	37	30	19	20	19	17	17	10		1	2	Athens
3	AEK	23	26	15	11	19	14	12	7			1	Athens
4	PAOK	6	17	9	2	5	9	4	12				Thessaloníki
5	Aris	4	11	8	3	3	8	1	8				Thessaloníki
6	Larissa	3	3		1	1		2	2				Larissa
7	Panionios	2	6	3		2	3	2	4				Athens
8	Iraklis	1	7	2		3	2	1	4				Thessaloníki
9	OFI Crete	1	2	2		1	2	1	1				Irákleio
10	Ethnikos	1	2			2		1					Piraeus
11	Kastoria	1						1					Kastoria

KYPELLO ELLADOS 2009-10

Third Round

Panathinaikos	3	
Eordiakos *	0	
Ergotelis	2	2p
Pierikos Katerini *	2	4p
Trikala *	1	
Iraklis Thessaloniki	0	
Panthrakikos	0	
Kallithea *	1	
PAOK Thessaloniki	1	
OFI Crete *	0	
Olympiacos	1	
Panserraikos *	3	
Atromitos	0	5p
Visaltikos *	0	4p
Kalamata *	0	
PAS Giannina	3	
Kavala	3	
Agrotikos Asteras *	0	
Ionikos *	1	
Levadiakos	2	
Thrasivoulos *	1	
AEK Athens	0	
Panetolikos *	0	7p
Panionios	0	8p
Xanthi	2	
Ethnikos Piraeus *	1	
Larissa	1	
Olympiacos Volos *	2	
Asteras Tripolis	3	
Egaleo *	0	
Asropyrgos *	3	
Aris Thessaloniki	4	

Fourth Round

Panathinaikos *	2	
Pierikos Katerini	1	
Trikala *	1	3p
Kallithea *	1	4p
PAOK Thessaloniki	2	
Panserraikos *	0	
Atromitos *	0	
PAS Giannina	1	
Kavala	0	4p
Levadiakos *	0	2p
Thrasivoulos *	0	
Panionios	1	
Xanthi *	2	
Olympiacos Volos	0	
Asteras Tripolis	0	
Aris Thessaloniki *	2	

Quarter-finals

Panathinaikos *	2	
Kallithea	0	
PAOK Thessaloniki	0	
PAS Giannina *	4	
Kavala *	1	2
Panionios	0	0
Xanthi *	1	0
Aris Thessaloniki	1	3

Semi-finals

Panathinaikos *	3	0
PAS Giannina	1	0
Kavala	1	1
Aris Thessaloniki *	3	1

Final

Panathinaikos	1
Aris Thessaloniki ‡	0

Superleague clubs enter in the third round • * Home team/home team in the first leg • ‡ Qualified for the Europa League

CUP FINAL

Olympic, Athens
24-04-2010, 20.30. Att: 48 926. Ref: Kakos
Scorer - Leto [63] for Panathinaikos
Panathinaikos - Alexandros Tzorvas - Loukas Vintra, Nikos Spiropoulos●, Cedric Kante - Kostas Katsouranis, Gilberto Silva (c), Simao Mate Junior●, Sotiris Ninis (Stergos Marinos 66), Sebastian Leto● (Lazaros Christodoulopoulos 78) - Dimitris Salpingidis (Giorgos Karagounis 62), Djibril Cisse. Tr: Nikos Nioplias
Aris - Michalis Sifakis - Darcy Dolce Neto, Kristi Vangjeli, Cristian Nasuti, Ronaldo Guiaro - Thanasis Prittas●, Mehdi Nafti (Dario Fernandez 74), Toni Calvo● (Freddy Adu 83), Camel Meriem (Javito 66) - Javier Campora, Sergio Koke (c). Tr: Hector Cuper

GRN – GRENADA

FIFA/COCA-COLA WORLD RANKING

1993	1994	1995	1996	1997	1998	1999	2000	2001	2002	2003	2004	2005	2006	2007	2008	2009	2010
143	142	141	127	111	117	121	143	133	131	154	144	151	163	176	118	138	94

2010												Hi/Lo
Jan	Feb	Mar	Mar	Apr	May	Jul	Aug	Sep	Oct	Nov	Dec	88
138	133	133	128	124	124	133	132	128	125	91	94	176

2010 was another outstanding year for the Grenada national team as they firmly established themselves amongst the elite of Caribbean football by finishing fourth in the 2010 Digicel Caribbean Cup. In 2008 the Spice Boys surprised everyone by making it right through to the final before losing to Jamaica in Kingston. In 2010 they fell in the semi-finals, once again at the hands of the Jamaicans, but not before having seen off traditional powerhouse Trinidad and Tobago in the group stage and having made sure of their qualification for the 2011 Gold Cup in America by reaching the last four. Grenada got their campaign off to a comfortable start, qualifying from a four-team group which they hosted in St George's with strikers Kithson Bain and Delroy Facey in sparkling form. At the final tournament in Martinique it was Bain who provided the main threat, the former Tranmere Rovers striker scoring all of his team's goals, including the only goal of the game against Trinidad. In the semi-final against Jamaica he scored his third of the tournament as Grenada gave a good account of themselves before succumbing 2-1 in extra-time. In club football Eagles Super Strikers beat GBSS 1-0 in the final of the Waggy T Super Knock-out competition whilst Paradise beat Hurricane to the post in a tight championship race.

FIFA WORLD CUP RECORD
1930-1978 DNE 1982 DNQ 1986-1994 DNE 1998-2010 DNQ

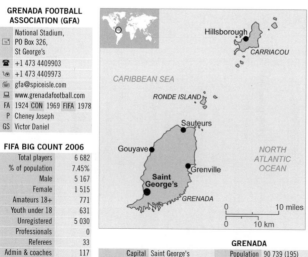

GRENADA FOOTBALL ASSOCIATION (GFA)

National Stadium,
PO Box 326,
St George's
☎ +1 473 4409903
📠 +1 473 4409973
✉ gfa@spiceisle.com
🖥 www.grenadafootball.com

FA	1924	CON	1969	FIFA	1978

P   Cheney Joseph
GS Victor Daniel

FIFA BIG COUNT 2006

Total players	6 682
% of population	7.45%
Male	5 167
Female	1 515
Amateurs 18+	771
Youth under 18	631
Unregistered	5 030
Professionals	0
Referees	33
Admin & coaches	117
Number of clubs	10
Number of teams	52

MAJOR CITIES/TOWNS

		Population
1	Saint George's	5 203
2	Gouyave	3 004
3	Grenville	2 379
4	Victoria	2 276
5	Saint Davids	1 315
6	Sauteurs	1 275
7	Hillsborough	789

GRENADA

Capital	Saint George's	Population	90 739 (195)	% in cities	31%
GDP per capita	$13 200 (85)	Area km²	344 km² (206)	GMT +/-	-4
Neighbours (km)	Coast 121				

RECENT INTERNATIONAL MATCHES PLAYED BY GRENADA

2007	Opponents	Score		Venue	Comp	Scorers	Att	Referee
	No international matches played in 2007							

2008	Opponents	Score		Venue	Comp	Scorers	Att	Referee
20-01	Guyana	W	2-1	Georgetown	Fr	Cassim Langiagne [42], Dennis Rennie [70]	1 500	Persaud GUY
10-02	St Vincent/Grenadines	W	2-1	Kingstown	Fr	Shane Rennie [13], Cassim Langiagne [61]	1 000	Cambridge VIN
15-03	Barbados	D	1-1	St George's	Fr	Shane Rennie [43]	2 500	Phillip GRN
26-03	US Virgin Islands	W	10-0	St George's	WCq	Jason Roberts 2 [3 8], Ricky Charles 4 [9 43 65 87], Shane Rennie [22], Cassim Langiagne [57], Byron Bubb [82], Ferguson OG [89]	3 000	James GUY
27-04	Trinidad and Tobago	L	0-2	Macoya	Fr		400	Brizan TRI
10-06	Jamaica	W	2-1	St George's	Fr	Shalrie Joseph [68], Jason Roberts [76]	5 000	Phillip GRN
14-06	Costa Rica	D	2-2	St George's	WCq	Patrick Modeste [18], Jason Roberts [23]	6 000	Brizan TRI
21-06	Costa Rica	L	0-3	San Jose	WCq		16 000	Marrufo USA
29-07	Aruba	W	3-1	Willemstad	CCq	Jake Rennie [53], Anthony Modeste [76], Shane Rennie [79]	450	Jordan TRI
31-07	Netherlands Antilles	L	0-2	Willemstad	CCq		800	Hospedales TRI
11-10	Martinique †	D	2-2	Abymes	CCq	Shane Rennie 2 [12 43]	1 700	Charles DMA
13-10	Guadeloupe †	L	1-2	Abymes	CCq	Ricky Charles [15]	1 000	Willett ATG
15-10	Cayman Islands	W	4-2	Abymes	CCq	Kithson Bain [43], Shane Rennie [45], Ricky Charles [67], Junior Williams [79]	3 358	Willett ATG
3-12	Trinidad and Tobago	W	2-1	Kingston	CCr1	Kithson Bain [36], Ricky Charles [90]	5 000	James GUY
5-12	Jamaica	L	0-4	Montego Bay	CCr1		4 000	Moreno PAN
7-12	Barbados	W	4-2	Trelawny	CCr1	Kithson Bain 3 [11 26 77], Marcus Julien [20]	9 000	Aguilar SLV
11-12	Cuba	D	2-2	Kingston	CCsf	Ricky Charles [12p], Kithson Bain [80]. W 6-5p	10 000	Moreno PAN
14-12	Jamaica	L	0-2	Kingston	CCf		22 000	Brizan TRI

2009	Opponents	Score		Venue	Comp	Scorers	Att	Referee
8-02	Barbados	L	0-5	Bridgetown	Fr		3 000	Forde BRB
28-06	Antigua and Barbuda	D	2-2	St George's	Fr	Ricky Charles [14], Rimmel Daniel [77]	800	Phillip GRN
4-07	USA	L	0-4	Seattle	GCr1		15 387	Lopez GUA
8-07	Haiti	L	0-2	Washington DC	GCr1		26 079	Moreno PAN
11-07	Honduras	L	0-4	Foxboro	GCr1		24 137	Rodriguez MEX

2010	Opponents	Score		Venue	Comp	Scorers	Att	Referee
17-09	St Vincent/Grenadines	W	1-0	Kingstown	Fr	Shane Rennie [24]	350	Gurley VIN
19-09	St Vincent/Grenadines	D	0-0	Kingstown	Fr		350	Cambridge VIN
22-10	Puerto Rico	W	3-1	St George's	CCq	Kithson Bain 2 [45 68], Ricky Charles [80]	600	Wijngaarde SUR
24-10	St Kitts and Nevis	W	2-0	St George's	CCq	Delroy Facey 2 [17 32]	500	Morrison JAM
26-10	Guadeloupe	L	0-3	St George's	CCq		500	Wijngaarde SUR
26-11	Martinique	D	1-1	Fort de France	CCr1	Kithson Bain [29]	5 000	Bogle JAM
28-11	Trinidad and Tobago	W	1-0	Fort de France	CCr1	Kithson Bain [69]	500	Cruz CRC
30-11	Cuba	D	0-0	Fort de France	CCr1		2 000	Bogle JAM
3-12	Jamaica	L	1-2	Fort de France	CCsf	Kithson Bain [13]	4 000	Taylor BRB
5-12	Cuba	L	0-1	Fort de France	CC3p		4 000	Lopez GUA

Fr = Friendly match • CC = Digicel Caribbean Cup • WC = FIFA World Cup • q = qualifier • r1 = first round group • sf = semi-final • f = final

GRENADA 2010

PREMIER DIVISION	Pl	W	D	L	F	A	Pts	Paradise	Hurricane	Fontenoy	Hard Rock	Eagles	GBSS	Chantimelle	Ball Dogs	South Stars	QPR
ASOMS Paradise	18	13	2	3	41	14	41		2-0	1-2	3-1	3-2	1-2	4-1	3-0	3-2	1-1
Carib Hurricane	17	11	5	1	31	11	38	0-0		3-0	2-1	3-0	2-0	2-0	2-1	3-0	4-1
Fontenoy United	17	9	2	6	28	26	29	2-1	1-2		1-2	0-3		3-2	1-0	3-0	0-0
Hard Rock	18	7	5	6	28	22	26	0-3	1-1	3-4		4-0	3-0	2-0	3-1	1-1	1-1
Eagles Super Strikers	18	6	2	10	23	29	20	0-2	0-1	3-0	1-1		3-1	3-0	3-0	0-3	3-1
Grenada Boys SS	15	5	2	8	19	25	17	0-3	1-1	2-1	0-1	3-0		0-0	2-3	2-3	3-1
Chantimelle	17	4	5	8	22	29	17	0-1	2-2	2-2	0-3	2-0	1-3		2-2	5-1	3-0
Ball Dogs	18	3	7	8	21	32	16	0-4	1-1	2-3	1-1	3-1	2-0	1-1		2-2	1-2
South Stars	15	4	3	8	17	32	15	1-3	0-2	0-4	2-0	1-0			1-1		
Queens Park Rangers	15	3	5	7	12	22	14	0-3		0-1	1-0	1-1		0-1	0-0	3-0	

27/06/2010 - 19/12/2010

GUA – GUATEMALA

FIFA/COCA-COLA WORLD RANKING

1993	1994	1995	1996	1997	1998	1999	2000	2001	2002	2003	2004	2005	2006	2007	2008	2009	2010
120	149	145	105	83	73	73	56	67	78	77	71	56	105	106	109	121	118

	2010												Hi/Lo
	Jan	Feb	Mar	Mar	Apr	May	Jul	Aug	Sep	Oct	Nov	Dec	50
	121	131	129	115	115	114	118	119	115	122	126	118	163

In an attempt to halt a dramatic slump in fortunes, the Guatemala national team turned to experienced coach Ever Almeida but the Paraguayan was unable to make an impression in the 2011 Copa Centroamericana in which Guatemala lost to both Costa Rica and Honduras to exit after the first round. At least there was the consolation of a victory in the fifth place play-off against Nicaragua and qualification for the 2011 CONCACAF Gold Cup, thus avoiding the humiliation of two years previously when defeat to Nicaragua saw them miss out on the tournament for the first time. There was also little to celebrate abroad in club football with Xelajú knocked out in the preliminary round of the 2010-11 CONCACAF Champions League and Municipal failing to qualify from a group containing Mexico's Santos Laguna and Columbus Crew from the States. At home it was back to business as usual with Municipal and Comunicaciones sharing the honours. In the first championship of the year - the 2009-10 Clausura - Municipal comfortably beat Xelajú 7-1 on aggregate in the final in May but they missed out in the opening championship of the 2010-11 season after losing to Comunicaciones on penalties in the final in December after a late Rolando Fonseca goal had levelled the aggregate scores in the second leg.

FIFA WORLD CUP RECORD
1930-1954 DNE 1958-1962 DNQ 1966 DNE 1970-2010 DNQ

FEDERACION NACIONAL DE FUTBOL DE GUATEMALA (FNFG)

2a. Calle 15-57, Zona 15,
Boulevard Vista Hermosa,
Guatemala City 01015

☎ +502 24227777
📠 +502 24227780
✉ info@fedefutguate.com
🖥 www.fedefutguate.com
FA 1919 CON 1961 FIFA 1946
P Bryan Gimenez
GS Byron Duran

FIFA BIG COUNT 2006

Total players	2 006 649
% of population	16.32%
Male	1 847 811
Female	158 838
Amateurs 18+	60 008
Unregistered	1 805 000
Professionals	600
Referees	373
Admin & coaches	5 030
Number of clubs	138
Number of teams	225

MAJOR CITIES/TOWNS
Population

1	Guatemala City	1 089 987
2	Mixco	642 893
3	Villa Nueva	639 709
4	San Juan	312 298
5	Petapa	266 447
6	Villa Canales	265 799
7	Chichicastenango	188 686
8	Quetzaltenango	154 684
9	Chinautla	136 873
10	Escuintla	135 982
11	Totonicapán	133 184
12	Santa Catarina	131 746
13	Huehuetenango	129 252
14	Chimaltenango	123 142
15	San Francisco	115 603
16	San Pedro	95 638
17	Amatitlán	92 851
18	San José Pinula	89 677
19	Jalapa	61 681

REPUBLICA DE GUATEMALA • REPUBLIC OF GUATEMALA

Capital	Guatemala City	Population	13 276 517 (68)	% in cities	49%
GDP per capita	$5300 (136)	Area km²	108 889 km² (106)	GMT + / -	-6
Neighbours (km)	Belize 266, El Salvador 203, Honduras 256, Mexico 962 • Coast 400				

RECENT INTERNATIONAL MATCHES PLAYED BY GUATEMALA

2008	Opponents	Score		Venue	Comp	Scorers	Att	Referee
23-04	Haiti	W	1-0	Guatemala City	Fr	Rodriguez.M [59]	5 000	Lopez GUA
30-05	El Salvador	D	0-0	Washington DC	Fr		38 759	Vaughn USA
1-06	Panama	L	0-1	Fort Lauderdale	Fr		6 800	Geiger USA
4-06	Chile	L	0-2	Rancagua	Fr		7 000	Arias PAR
14-06	St Lucia	W	6-0	Guatemala City	WCq	Rodrigiez.M [5], Ruiz 4 [36 40 58 93+], Trigueros [91+]	24 600	Archundia MEX
21-06	St Lucia	W	3-1	Los Angeles	WCq	Romero 2 [24 43], Trigueros [86]	12 000	Wijngaarde SUR
20-07	El Salvador	D	0-0	Los Angeles	Fr		5 000	Marrufo USA
6-08	Bolivia	W	3-0	Washington DC	Fr	Pezzarossi [51], Ramirez [56], Rodriguez.M [64]	18 000	Toledo USA
20-08	USA	L	0-1	Guatemala City	WCq		26 000	Wijngaarde SUR
6-09	Trinidad and Tobago	D	1-1	Port of Spain	WCq	Gallardo [92+]	9 500	Moreno PAN
10-09	Cuba	W	4-1	Guatemala City	WCq	Ruiz 2 [38 55], Rodriguez.M [85], Contreras [91+]	19 750	Rodriguez MEX
11-10	Trinidad and Tobago	D	0-0	Guatemala City	WCq		29 000	Petrescu CAN
15-10	Cuba	L	1-2	Havana	WCq	Papa [80]	6 000	Campbell JAM
19-11	USA	L	0-2	Commerce City	WCq		9 303	Archundia MEX
2009								
17-01	Haiti	W	1-0	Fort Pierce	Fr	Villatoro [64]	5 000	Jurisvic USA
25-01	Costa Rica	L	1-3	Tegucigalpa	UCr1	Lopez [51]	3 000	Rodriguez MEX
27-01	Panama	L	0-1	Tegucigalpa	UCr1		1 000	Aguilar SLV
29-01	Nicaragua	L	0-2	Tegucigalpa	UC5p		150	Moncada HON
11-02	Venezuela	L	1-2	Maturin	Fr	Pezzarossi [50]	10 000	Perluzzo VEN
28-06	Mexico	D	0-0	San Diego	Fr		27 094	Navarro CAN
30-06	Canada	L	0-3	Oxnard	Fr		200	Singh USA
2010								
3-03	El Salvador	W	2-1	Los Angeles	Fr	Papa [44], Brown [83]	10 000	Salazar USA
31-05	South Africa	L	0-5	Polokwane	Fr		38 000	Ibrahim NIG
4-09	Nicaragua	W	5-0	Fort Lauderdale	Fr	Montepeque 2 [30 58], Figueroa [36], Thompson [42], Flores [54]	5 000	Vaughn USA
7-09	Japan	L	1-2	Osaka	Fr	Rodriguez.M [22]	44 541	Archundia MEX
7-09	El Salvador	W	2-0	Washington DC	Fr	Thompson [45], Montepeque [81]	12 246	Marrufo USA
9-10	Belize	W	4-2	San Jose	Fr	Brown [20], Castellanos [50], Pezzarossi [69], Figueroa [74]	5 500	Bermudez SLV
12-10	Honduras	L	0-2	Los Angeles	Fr		10 000	Hernandez USA
17-11	Guyana	W	3-0	Kennesaw	Fr	Montepeque [23], Ramirez 2 [30 64]	4 124	Okulaja USA
2011								
16-01	Costa Rica	L	0-2	Panama City	UCr1		1 500	Moreno PAN
18-01	Honduras	L	1-3	Panama City	UCr1	Ramirez [24]	10 000	Aguilar SLV
21-01	Nicaragua	W	2-1	Panama City	UCr1	Ruiz [45], Leon [66]	5 000	Garcia MEX

Fr = Friendly match • UC = UNCAF Cup/Copa Centroamericana • GC = CONCACAF Gold Cup • WC = FIFA World Cup

q = qualifier • r1 = first round group • qf = quarter-final • sf = semi-final • 3p = third place play-off • 5p = 5th place play-off

GUATEMALA NATIONAL TEAM HISTORICAL RECORDS

Caps — **97** - Guillermo Ramirez 1997- • **87** - Juan Carlos Plata 1996- & Gustavo Cabrera 2001- • **84** - & Fredy Thompson 2001- • **83** - Carlos Ruiz 1998-2008 • **82** -Julio Giron 1992-2006 • **80** - Edgar Estrada 1995-2003 • **77** - Gonzalo Romero 2000- • **69** - Fredy Garcia 2000-08 & Erick Miranda 1991-2001 • **66** - Juan Manuel Funes 1985-2000 • **62** - Mario Rodriguez 2003- • **60** - Martin Machon 1992-2006

Goals — **41** - Carlos Ruiz 1998-2008 • **35** - Juan Carlos Plata 1996- • **20** - Fredy Garcia 1998-2008- • **15** - Juan Manuel Funes 1985-2000

Past Coaches — Jimmy Elliott ENG 1935 • Manuel Felipe Carrera 1946 • Jose Alberto Cevasco ARG 1948 • Enrique Natalio Pascal Palomini ARG 1950 • Juan Aguirre 1953 • Alfredo Cuevas ARG 1955-57 • Jose Alberto Cevasco ARG 1960-61 • Afro Geronazzo ARG 1961 • Cesar Viccino ARG 1965 • Ruben Amorin URU 1967 • Cesar Viccino ARG 1968-69 • Lorenzo Ausina Tur ESP 1969 • Carmelo Faraone ARG 1971 • Afro Geronazzo ARG 1971-72 • Ruben Amorin URU 1972 • Nestor Valdez CHI 1972 • Ruben Amorin URU 1976 • Carlos Cavagnaro ARG 1976 • Carlos Wellman 1976 • Jose Ernesto Romero 1979 • Ruben Amorin URU 1980 • Carlos Cavagnaro ARG 1983 • Dragoslav Sekularac YUG 1984-85 • Julio Cesar Cortes URU 1987 • Jorge Roldan 1988 • Ruben Amorin URU 1989-90 • Haroldo Cordon 1991 • Miguel Angel Brindisi ARG 1992 • Jorge Roldan 1995 • Juan Ramon Veron ARG 1996 • Horacio Cordero ARG 1996 • Miguel Angel Brindisi ARG 1997-98 • Carlos Bilardo & Eduardo Lujan ARG 1998 • Benjamin Monterroso 1999 • Carlos Miloc URU 2000 • Julio Cesar Cortes URU 2000-03 • Victor Manuel Aguado MEX 2003 • Ramon Maradiaga HON 2004-05 • Hernan Dario Gomez COL 2006-08 • Ramon Maradiaga HON 2008 • Benjamin Monterroso 2008-09 • Ever Almeida PAR 2010-

GUATEMALA 2009-10

LIGA NACIONAL TORNEO CLAUSURA

	Pl	W	D	L	F	A	Pts	Com'ciones	Xelajú	Suc'péquez	Municipal	USAC	Peñarol	Juventud	Jalapa	Marquense	Heredia	Xinabajul	Zacapa
Comunicaciones †	22	12	4	6	37	22	40		1-0	1-2	1-0	1-0	2-0	4-0	2-1	5-1	3-0	3-2	2-0
Xelajú †	22	11	6	5	32	26	39	2-2		0-1	2-1	3-2	1-0	2-0	4-1	0-0	1-0	3-0	2-1
Suchitepéquez †	22	10	6	6	25	22	36	2-1	1-0		2-0	3-0	0-0	1-0	1-3	2-0	1-1	3-2	2-2
Municipal †	22	9	5	8	25	19	32	2-1	0-1	0-2		0-0	1-0	3-0	1-1	1-1	4-0	2-0	1-0
USAC †	22	8	8	6	28	23	32	3-2	0-0	2-0	0-2		1-1	0-0	4-0	1-0	2-0	3-1	4-1
Peñarol La Mesilla †	22	8	7	7	30	25	31	2-2	3-4	1-0	3-1	2-1		3-0	3-3	2-2	1-0	0-0	3-0
Juventud Retalteca	22	9	4	9	20	21	31	2-0	4-1	0-0	0-0	4-1	1-0		2-0	1-0	0-0	2-0	1-0
Deportivo Jalapa	22	6	8	8	24	29	26	1-1	0-0	1-1	0-0	0-0	1-0	1-0		1-1	3-0	4-1	0-1
Deportivo Marquense	22	6	8	8	24	29	26	1-0	4-0	3-1	1-1	1-1	1-2	0-0	1-0		3-2	1-1	2-1
Deportivo Heredia	22	7	3	12	26	34	24	0-1	2-3	4-1	2-1	1-2	1-3	1-0	3-0	2-0		3-1	2-4
Xinabajul	22	5	8	9	25	36	23	1-1	1-0	0-0	2-1	0-0	2-2	2-0	2-1	2-1	1-1		3-1
Deportivo Zacapa	22	6	3	13	24	34	21	0-1	2-2	0-1	0-1	1-1	0-1	2-1	1-2	3-1	1-0	3-1	

15/01/2010 - 25/04/2010 • † Qualified for the play-offs • Top two receive a bye to the semi-finals • Deportivo Jalapa and Deportivo Zacapa were relegated with the worst record over the 2009-10 season (Jalapa were deducted six points which meant Peñarol avoided relegation)

CLAUSURA 2009-10 PLAY-OFFS

Semi-finals

Municipal *	2	1
Comunicaciones	1	1
Suchitepéquez *	2	0 1p
Xelajú	0	2 3p

Finals

Municipal * †	3	4
Xelajú	1	0
(finals 13-05-2010 & 15-05-2010)		

Play-offs first round: Peñarol 1-1 1-2 **Suchitepéquez**
USAC 3-2 0-2 **Municipal**
† Qualified for the CONCACAF Champions League • * Home team in first leg • Top scorer: **15** - Rolando Fonseca CRC, Comunicaciones

APERTURA 2010-11 PLAY-OFFS

Semi-finals

Comunicaciones *	3	3
Deportivo Marquense	0	2
Suchitepéquez *	2	0
Municipal	3	2

Finals

Comunicaciones * †	1	2 4p
Municipal	1	2 3p
(finals 16-12-2010 & 19-12-2010)		

Play-offs first round: **Suchitepéquez** 1-0 3-3 Heredia
Mictlan 1-0 0-3 **Comunicaciones**
† Qualified for the CONCACAF Champions League • * Home team in first leg • Top scorers: **13** - Guillermo Ruiz, Municipal; Henry Hernandez COL, Heredia & Andy Heron CRC, USAC

MEDALS TABLE

		Overall			League			Cup		Cent Am		
		G	S	B	G	S	B	G	S	G	S	B
1	Deportivo Municipal	36	19	7	28	16	6	7		1	1	1
2	Comunicaciones	29	21	10	23	20	7	5		1	2	3
3	Aurora	10	9	6	8	8	5	2	1			1
4	Xelajú	6	6	2	5	4	1	1	2			1
5	Deportivo Jalapa	5	1		2			3	1			
6	Suchitepéquez	3	6	2	1	5	1	2	1			1
7	Tip Nac	3	1		3	1						
8	Cobán Imperial	1	6	2	1	3	2		3			
9	Juventud Retalteca	1	3	2		2	2	1	1			
10	IRCA	1		2		2	1					
11	Hospicio	1		1	1		1					
	Amatitlan	1		1	1		1					
13	Deportivo Marquense		3			3						
14	Universidad		1	4		1	4					
15	Antigua		1	1		1	1					

GUATEMALA 2010-11

LIGA NACIONAL TORNEO APERTURA

	Pl	W	D	L	F	A	Pts	Municipal	Marquense	Heredia	Com'ciones	Mictlán	Suc'péquez	Juventud	Xelajú	Xinabajul	USAC	Malacateco	Peñarol
Municipal †	22	11	5	6	40	22	38		0-0	3-1	0-0	1-0	3-1	0-0	2-1	4-0	4-0	4-0	3-0
Deportivo Marquense †	22	9	6	7	32	27	33	1-0		5-1	0-0	1-0	0-0	2-0	2-1	1-0	2-3	2-1	2-2
Deportivo Heredia †	22	9	5	8	28	30	32	1-2	3-1		0-1	1-0	2-1	1-1	3-2	1-0	1-0	0-0	1-0
Comunicaciones †	22	6	13	3	26	23	31	1-4	2-2	4-1		1-1	1-1	1-1	3-2	2-1	1-1	1-0	1-0
Mictlán †	22	9	4	9	15	18	31	1-3	1-0	2-0	1-0		1-0	1-2	0-1	1-0	1-0	1-0	1-0
Suchitepéquez †	22	8	6	8	32	23	30	3-2	4-3	1-1	0-0	4-0		0-2	2-1	4-2	7-0	0-0	2-0
Juventud Retalteca	22	7	9	6	28	25	30	1-1	3-0	3-1	1-1	0-0	1-0		2-1	1-2	2-3	1-0	1-1
Xelajú	22	9	3	10	27	29	30	1-0	2-1	2-1	1-1	1-1	0-1	2-1		3-2	2-1	3-2	2-1
Xinabajul	22	8	3	11	22	29	27	2-0	0-3	0-2	1-0	1-0	1-0	1-0	1-1		2-1	3-0	1-1
USAC	22	7	6	9	28	36	27	4-1	1-1	0-0	1-1	0-0	1-1	2-1	2-0	1-0		1-1	3-1
Malacateco	22	7	6	9	20	28	27	3-2	1-2	0-3	1-0	1-0	3-1	1-0	2-1	2-1	0-0		0-0
Peñarol La Mesilla	22	5	8	9	22	29	23	1-1	2-1	2-2	2-3	1-2	1-0	2-2	1-0	0-0	3-1	1-0	

24/07/2010 - 28/11/2010 • † Qualified for the play-offs • Top two receive a bye to the semi-finals

GUI – GUINEA

FIFA/COCA-COLA WORLD RANKING

1993	1994	1995	1996	1997	1998	1999	2000	2001	2002	2003	2004	2005	2006	2007	2008	2009	2010
63	66	63	73	65	79	91	80	108	120	101	86	79	23	33	39	73	46

2010												Hi/Lo
Jan	Feb	Mar	Mar	Apr	May	Jul	Aug	Sep	Oct	Nov	Dec	22
73	90	89	85	87	87	101	102	81	47	47	46	123

Frenchman Michel Dussuyer returned to coach the Syli Nationale in May and got the country off to a winning start in their bid to qualify for the 2012 African Nations Cup finals. A 1-0 win over Nigeria in Conakry, with an early goal from former French youth international Kevin Constant, gives Guinea a strong chance of finishing top of their group and qualifying for the tournament in Equatorial Guinea and Gabon. Before beating Nigeria they had sent out a strong signal of their potential with a 4-1 thumping of Ethiopia in their opening group game, away in Addis Ababa. A successful return of captain Pascal Feinduono, absent from the side in recent games, is an added boost to their chances. Former captain Aboubacar 'Titi' Camara was named sports minister in Guinea's post-election government which bodes well for future financial support of the national team and club sides which rely on the government to take part in continental competitions. Fello Star Labe won a fourth successive league title, securing success in the penultimate round, but one of the more successful clubs in recent times AS Kaloum were relegated. In a sign of the shifting nature of club football in the country FC Séquence, a previously unheralded club from the Conakry suburb of Dixinn, won the cup after beating Satellite on post-match penalties in the final.

FIFA WORLD CUP RECORD
1930-1970 DNE 1974-2010 DNQ

FEDERATION GUINEENNE DE FOOTBALL (FGF)

PO Box 3645,
Conakry

☎ +224 20 455878
📠 +224 20 455879
✉ guineefoot59@yahoo.fr
🖥 feguifoot.net
FA 1960 CON 1962 FIFA 1962
P Aboubacar Bruno Bangoura
GS Fode Capi Camara

FIFA BIG COUNT 2006

Total players	410 100
% of population	4.23%
Male	406 600
Female	3 500
Amateurs 18+	10 100
Youth under 18	8 000
Unregistered	90 000
Professionals	0
Referees	433
Admin & coaches	2 400
Number of clubs	150
Number of teams	700

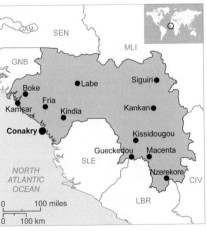

MAJOR CITIES/TOWNS

		Population
1	Conakry	1 931 184
2	Guékédou	250 288
3	Nzérékoré	237 753
4	Kankan	207 390
5	Kindia	189 907
6	Boké	126 668
7	Kissidougou	125 303
8	Fria	119 722
9	Faranah	93 608
10	Macenta	92 569
11	Kamsar	90 341
12	Coyah	86 352
13	Mamou	78 615
14	Lola	67 815
15	Labé	59 110
16	Kérouane	38 224
17	Yomou	31 787
18	Siguiri	28 150

REPUBLIQUE DE GUINEE • REPUBLIC OF GUINEA

Capital	Conakry	Population	10 057 975 (81)	% in cities	34%
GDP per capita	$1100 (208)	Area km²	245 857 km² (78)	GMT +/-	0
Neighbours (km)	Cote d'Ivoire 610, Guinea-Bissau 386, Liberia 563, Mali 858, Senegal 330, Sierra Leone 652, Coast 320				

RECENT INTERNATIONAL MATCHES PLAYED BY GUINEA

2007	Opponents	Score		Venue	Comp	Scorers	Att	Referee
6-02	Côte d'Ivoire	L	0-1	Rouen	Fr			
24-03	Gambia	W	2-0	Bakau	CNq	Diawara [57], Feindouno [69]		Kotey GHA
3-06	Gambia	D	2-2	Conakry	CNq	Jabi [9], Mansare [55]		Djaoupe TOG
16-06	Algeria	W	2-0	Algiers	CNq	Mansare [44], Feindouno [85]		Guezzaz MAR
22-08	Tunisia	D	1-1	Rades	Fr	Diawara [45]		
9-09	Cape Verde Islands	W	4-0	Conakry	CNq	Feindouno [19p], Mohamed Cisse [32], Ibrahima Camara [37], Ismael Bangoura [44]		Trabelsi TUN
14-10	Senegal	L	1-3	Rouen	Fr	Mansare [44]		
20-11	Angola	L	0-3	Melun	Fr			
2008								
11-01	Sudan	W	6-0	Estepona	Fr	Youla 4, Ismael Bangoura, Correa		
20-01	Ghana	L	1-2	Accra	CNr1	Kalabane [65]		Maillet SEY
24-01	Morocco	W	3-2	Accra	CNr1	Feindouno 2 [11 63p], Ismael Bangoura [60]		Damon RSA
28-01	Namibia	D	1-1	Sekondi	CNr1	Youla [62]		Ssegonga UGA
3-02	Côte d'Ivoire	L	0-5	Sekondi	CNqf			Haimoudi ALG
25-03	Togo	W	2-0	Paris	Fr	Doumbouya 2 [80 90]		
1-06	Zimbabwe	D	0-0	Conakry	WCq		12 000	Haimoudi ALG
7-06	Kenya	L	0-2	Nairobi	WCq		35 000	Eyene CMR
14-06	Namibia	W	2-1	Windhoek	WCq	Ismael Bangoura [22], Feindouno [45]	5 000	Imiere NGA
22-06	Namibia	W	4-0	Conakry	WCq	Feindouno [23], Ismael Bangoura 3 [27 55 60]	15 000	Monteiro Lopez CPV
20-08	Côte d'Ivoire	L	1-2	Chantilly	Fr	Ismael Bangoura [13]		
7-09	Zimbabwe	D	0-0	Harare	WCq		23 000	Evehe CMR
9-09	South Africa	W	1-0	Atteridgeville	Fr	Aboubacar Camara [18]		
12-10	Kenya	W	3-2	Conakry	WCq	Ismael Bangoura [31], Bah [51], Zayatte [80]	16 400	Maillet SEY
18-11	Gabon	D	3-3	Compiegne	Fr	Keita [7], Kalabane [36], Ismael Bangoura [75p]		
2009								
11-02	Cameroon	L	1-3	Bondoufle	Fr	Feindouno [84]		
28-03	Burkina Faso	L	2-4	Ouagadougou	WCq	Feindouno [65p], Zayatte [86]	30 000	Benouza ALG
7-06	Côte d'Ivoire	L	1-2	Conakry	WCq	Sambegou Bangoura [65]	14 999	Abd El Fatah EGY
14-06	Angola	D	0-0	Amadora	Fr			
21-06	Malawi	W	2-1	Conakry	WCq	Feindouno 2 [25 43]	14 000	Rahman SUD
12-08	Egypt	D	3-3	Cairo	Fr	Youla 2 [30 40], Diawarra [48]		
5-09	Malawi	L	1-2	Blantyre	WCq	Kalabane [37]	15 000	Codjia BEN
11-10	Burkina Faso	L	1-2	Accra	WCq	Bah [82]	5 000	Ambaya LBY
14-11	Côte d'Ivoire	L	0-3	Abidjan	WCq		28 000	Marange ZIM
2010								
11-08	Mali	W	2-0	Marignane	Fr	Zayatte [52], Constant [34]		
5-09	Ethiopia	W	4-1	Addis Abeba	CNq	Yattara [37], Kalabane [45], Cisse [61], Zayatte [75]		Mnkantjo ZIM
10-10	Nigeria	W	1-0	Conakry	CNq	Constant [5]		El Ahrach MAR
17-11	Burkina Faso	L	1-2	Mantes-La-Ville	Fr	Cisse [10]		

Fr = Friendly match • CN = CAF African Cup of Nations • AC = Amilcar Cabral Cup • WC = FIFA World Cup
q = qualifier • r1 = first round group • sf = semi-final • f = final • † = not a full international

COUPE NATIONALE 2010

Quarter-finals		Semi-finals			Final		
FC Séquence	2						
Sankaran	0	FC Séquence	0	4p			
AS Kaloum Conakry		Fello Star Labe	0	3p			
Fello Star Labe					FC Séquence	0	3p
Hafia Conakry	2				Satellite Conakry	0	1p
Ashanti	0	Hafia Conakry	0				
ASFAG	0	Satellite Conakry	1		Stade du 28 Septembre, Conakry		
Satellite Conakry	1				2-10-2010		

GUM – GUAM

FIFA/COCA-COLA WORLD RANKING

1993	1994	1995	1996	1997	1998	1999	2000	2001	2002	2003	2004	2005	2006	2007	2008	2009	2010
-	-	-	188	191	198	200	199	199	200	201	2005	204	198	201	201	184	188

2010												Hi/Lo
Jan	Feb	Mar	Mar	Apr	May	Jul	Aug	Sep	Oct	Nov	Dec	182
184	184	182	196	193	195	193	193	190	190	189	188	205

With the senior national team out of action for the whole of 2010, it was left to the under-19 and under-16 teams to fly the flag for the country in international competition. Both took part in the Asian championships for their age groups with the under-16s travelling to China for a six-team qualifying group in Xianghe. Teams from Guam are used to being on the wrong end of huge scores - in the 2008 under-19 Asian Championship for instance Guam conceded 72 goals in just four matches - but in China the under-16s re-wrote the rule book by finishing with a goal difference of just minus two despite losing four of their matches. They were competitive throughout scoring nine goals including a 6-0 win over Macau. Most impressive perhaps was their achievement of restricting the Chinese to a 2-0 victory. The under-19s were less successful when they travelled to China for their qualifying group and were on the end of three heavy defeats although they did manage to draw with the Philippines. Club football saw Quality Distributors win the championship for the fourth consecutive season after scoring a staggering 116 goals in the process of winning all their 20 matches. They did lose once during the season, however, in an entertaining Cup Final against Guam Shipyard who won the trophy following a 4-3 victory.

FIFA WORLD CUP RECORD
1930-1998 DNE **2002** DNQ **2006-2010** DNE

GUAM FOOTBALL ASSOCIATION (GFA)

PO Box 5093, Hagatna 96932

☎ +1 671 6374321
📠 +1 671 6374323
✉ info@guamfootball.com
🖥 www.guamfootball.com
FA 1975 CON 1996 FIFA 1996
P Richard Lai
GS Valentino San Gil

FIFA BIG COUNT 2006

Total players	5 460
% of population	3.19%
Male	4 172
Female	1 288
Amateurs 18+	457
Youth under 18	1 943
Unregistered	675
Professionals	0
Referees	21
Admin & coaches	135
Number of clubs	13
Number of teams	195

MAJOR CITIES/TOWNS
Population

1	Tamuning	11 809
2	Yigo	10 533
3	Mangilao	10 071
4	Astumbo	6 536
5	Ordot	4 968
6	Barrigada	4 957
7	Agat	4 780
8	Anderson Air Force Base	4 556
9	Mongmong	4 229
10	Agana Heights	3 953
11	Dededo	3 487
12	Talofofo	3 180
13	Chalan Pago	2 977
14	Marbo Annex	2 344
15	Yona	2 330
16	Apra Harbor	2 265
17	Sinajana	2 123
18	Finegayan Station	1 957

GUAHAN • TERRITORY OF GUAM

Capital	Hagatna	Population	178 430 (187)	% in cities	93%
GDP per capita	$15 000 (74)	Area km²	544 km² (195)	GMT +/-	+10
Neighbours (km)	Coast 125				

RECENT INTERNATIONAL MATCHES PLAYED BY GUAM

2007	Opponents		Score	Venue	Comp	Scorers	Att	Referee
25-03	Northern Marianas †	W	3-2	Saipan	EACq	Jamison [9], Pangelinan 2 [65 78]		
1-04	Northern Marianas †	W	9-0	Hagatna	EACq	Pangelinan 5 [6 21 42 54 61], Mendoza [56], Merfalen [57], Jamison [85], Calvo [90]	1 324	
17-06	Chinese Taipei	L	0-10	Macau	EACq		10	Wan Daxue CHN
21-06	Hong Kong	L	1-15	Macau	EACq	Mendiola [33]	300	Matsuo JPN
23-06	Mongolia	L	2-5	Macau	EACq	Pangelinan [2], Mendiola [8]	100	Wan Daxue CHN
2008								
2-04	Sri Lanka	L	1-5	Taipei	CCq	Mendiola [62]	300	Kovalenko UZB
4-04	Chinese Taipei	L	1-4	Taipei	CCq	Pangelinan [17]	850	Win Cho MYA
6-04	Pakistan	L	2-9	Taipei	CCq	Pangelinan [74], Iltaf OG [80]	200	Auda Lazim IRQ
2009								
11-03	Mongolia	W	1-0	Manenggon Hills	EACq	Mendiola [9]		Kim Jong Hyeuk KOR
13-03	Northern Marianas †	W	2-1	Manenggon Hills	EACq	Borja [10], Mariano [68]		Cheng Oi Cho HKG
15-03	Macao	D	2-2	Manenggon Hills	EACq	Borja [36], Cunliffe [90]		Kim Jong Hyeuk KOR
23-08	Korea DPR	L	2-9	Kaohsiung	EACq	Borja [1], Cunliffe [20]	2 000	Matsuo JPN
25-08	Chinese Taipei	L	2-4	Kaohsiung	EACq	Borja 2 [5 26]	7 500	Matsuo JPN
27-08	Hong Kong	L	0-12	Kaohsiung	EACq		1 500	Tojo JPN
2010								

No international matches played in 2010

EAC = East Asian Championship • AC = AFC Asian Cup • CC = AFC Challenge Cup
q = qualifier • r1 = first round group • † Not an official international

GUAM 2009-10

BUDWEISER SOCCER LEAGUE DIVISION ONE

	Pl	W	D	L	F	A	Pts	Distributors	Strykers	Shipyard	No Ka Oi	Crushers	Masters
Quality Distributors	20	20	0	0	116	26	60		3-2 4-2	7-0 3-0	7-2 5-1	6-1 7-2	9-3 5-0
Paintco Strykers	20	15	1	4	102	30	46	2-5 2-5		6-0 0-0	7-1 5-1	14-4 3-0	8-0 5-1
Guam Shipyard	20	6	4	10	29	42	22	1-2 2-4	0-5 0-3		0-3 8-0	2-1 1-2	3-0 0-0
No Ka Oi Guam	20	6	2	12	49	88	20	3-7 2-7	1-7 1-7	1-6 1-1		2-4 5-4	3-0 3-2
Bank of Guam Crushers	20	6	1	13	49	78	19	1-4 0-3	1-5 3-4	1-3 3-0	5-5 2-11		9-0 0-1
Carpet Masters	20	2	2	16	13	94	8	0-11 0-12	0-10 0-5	0-0 0-2	1-2 3-1	1-3 1-3	

13/09/2009 - 7/03/2010
Top scorers: 28 - Choi Min Sung, Strykers & Matthew Welton, Distributors • 21 - Scott Spindel, Distributors

CARS PLUS GFA CUP 2010

First round		Quarter–finals		Semi–finals		Final	
Guam Shipyard	4						
Big Blue	1	Guam Shipyard	4				
Carpet Masters	0	Islanders	0				
Islanders	3			Guam Shipyard	1		
Espada	7			Paintco Strykers	0		
Rovers	1	Espada	0				
Sheraton	3	Paintco Strykers	3				
Paintco Strykers	7					Guam Shipyard	4
No Ka Oi Guam	8					Quality Distributors	3
Crushers	1	No Ka Oi Guam	4				
DeYo	0	Bank of Guam Crushers	3				
Bank of Guam Crushers	2			No Ka Oi Guam	1		
Paintco Strykers II	6			Quality Distributors	6	28-03-2010	
Han Ma Um	0	Paintco Strykers II	4				
Toyota 4Runners	1	Quality Distributors	11				
Quality Distributors	15						

GUY – GUYANA

FIFA/COCA-COLA WORLD RANKING

1993	1994	1995	1996	1997	1998	1999	2000	2001	2002	2003	2004	2005	2006	2007	2008	2009	2010
136	154	162	153	168	161	171	183	178	169	182	182	167	100	128	131	127	109

	2010												Hi/Lo
	Jan	Feb	Mar	Mar	Apr	May	Jul	Aug	Sep	Oct	Nov	Dec	86
	127	126	120	122	122	122	119	122	120	98	86	109	185

Having missed out on the finals of the 2008 Digicel Caribbean Cup, Guyana made no mistake in the 2010 tournament qualifying for the finals in Martinique with relative ease. Neighbours Suriname hosted a first round qualifying group but it was Guyana who topped it with three wins out of three including a morale boosting 2-0 win over the Surinamese. Wayne Dover's men then travelled to Trinidad for the next qualifying round and although they lost to the hosts they managed to finish above Haiti to qualify for the finals. In Martinique, however, it was a different story as the Guyanese struggled. In their opening match against the much fancied Guadeloupe, Guyana were outplayed but stole a draw with a late equaliser from substitute Dwain Jacobs in what was their only chance of the second half. It turned out to be their only goal of the tournament as they then went down to Antigua and Jamaica. At home, 2010 was Alpha United's year as they successfully defended their league title, finishing the season undefeated. Indeed, by the end of the first two seasons of the GFF sponsored league, Alpha had yet to lose a match. They also won the end of year Kashif and Shanghai Cup, beating Pele in a thrilling final at a packed National Stadium as well as winning the GFF Super 8 tournament with a 2-1 victory over Victoria Kings in August.

FIFA WORLD CUP RECORD
1930-1974 DNE 1978-1998 DNQ 2002 DNE 2006-2010 DNQ

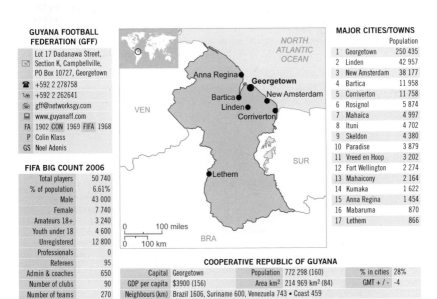

GUYANA FOOTBALL FEDERATION (GFF)

Lot 17 Dadanawa Street,
Section K, Campbellville,
PO Box 10727, Georgetown
☎ +592 2 278758
📠 +592 2 262641
✉ gff@networksgy.com
🖥 www.guyanaff.com
FA 1902 CON 1969 FIFA 1968
P Colin Klass
GS Noel Adonis

FIFA BIG COUNT 2006

Total players	50 740
% of population	6.61%
Male	43 000
Female	7 740
Amateurs 18+	3 240
Youth under 18	4 600
Unregistered	12 800
Professionals	0
Referees	95
Admin & coaches	650
Number of clubs	90
Number of teams	270

MAJOR CITIES/TOWNS

		Population
1	Georgetown	250 435
2	Linden	42 957
3	New Amsterdam	38 177
4	Bartica	11 958
5	Corriverton	11 758
6	Rosignol	5 874
7	Mahaica	4 997
8	Ituni	4 702
9	Skeldon	4 380
10	Paradise	3 879
11	Vreed en Hoop	3 202
12	Fort Wellington	2 274
13	Mahaicony	2 164
14	Kumaka	1 622
15	Anna Regina	1 454
16	Mabaruma	870
17	Lethem	866

COOPERATIVE REPUBLIC OF GUYANA

Capital	Georgetown	Population	772 298 (160)	% in cities	28%
GDP per capita	$3900 (156)	Area km²	214 969 km² (84)	GMT +/-	-4
Neighbours (km)	Brazil 1606, Suriname 600, Venezuela 743 • Coast 459				

RECENT INTERNATIONAL MATCHES PLAYED BY GUYANA

2007	Opponents	Score		Venue	Comp	Scorers	Att	Referee
14-01	St Vincent/Grenadines	L	0-2	Marabella	CCr1		3 000	Angela ARU
16-01	Guadeloupe	W	4-3	Marabella	CCr1	Codrington 3 [23p 60 81], Lowe [66]	1 700	Campbell JAM
18-01	Cuba	D	0-0	Marabella	CCr1		2 000	Moreno PAN
2008								
13-01	St Vincent/Grenadines	W	1-0	Blairmont	Fr	Richardson [11]	1 300	James GUY
20-01	Grenada	L	1-2	Georgetown	Fr	Beveney [45]	1 500	Persaud GUY
27-01	St Vincent/Grenadines	D	2-2	Kingstown	Fr	Mannings [56], Abrams [68]	2 000	Caswell VIN
16-06	Surinam	L	0-1	Paramaribo	WCq		3 000	Guerrero NCA
22-06	Surinam	L	1-2	Georgetown	WCq	Codrington [85]	12 000	Campbell JAM
8-07	Trinidad and Tobago	L	0-2	Macoya	Fr		500	Jordan TRI
8-08	Dominica	W	3-0	Georgetown	CCq	Codrington 2 [20 43], Edmonds [36]	3 000	Forde BRB
10-08	Surinam	D	1-1	Georgetown	CCq	Peters [90]	10 000	Forde BRB
3-09	Trinidad and Tobago	L	0-3	Port of Spain	Fr		1 000	Brizan TRI
21-09	Antigua and Barbuda	L	0-3	St John's	Fr		3 500	Willett ATG
5-11	St Kitts and Nevis	D	1-1	Macoya	CCq	Richardson [35]	750	Cambridge VIN
7-11	Antigua and Barbuda	L	1-2	Macoya	CCq	Jerome [45]	500	Minyetty DOM
9-11	Trinidad and Tobago	D	1-1	Macoya	CCq	Richardson [58p]	1 000	Minyetty DOM
2009								
3-06	Antigua and Barbuda	L	1-2	Paramaribo	Fr	Parks [34]	1 700	Wijngaarde SUR
28-10	Surinam	W	1-0	Paramaribo	Fr	Millington [66]	2 000	Jauregui ANT
30-10	Netherlands Antilles	W	1-0	Paramaribo	Fr	Millington [29]	500	Pinas SUR
1-11	French Guiana †	W	1-0	Paramaribo	Fr	Archer [57]	1 000	Wijngaarde SUR
2010								
26-09	Trinidad and Tobago	D	1-1	Providence	Fr	Dwight Peters [43]	9 000	Lancaster GUY
13-10	St Lucia	W	1-0	Paramaribo	CCq	Christopher Bourne [10]	550	Davis TRI
15-10	Netherlands Antilles	W	3-2	Paramaribo	CCq	Dwight Peters [15], Anthony Abrams [45], Walter Moore [58]	750	Matthew SKN
17-10	Suriname	W	2-0	Paramaribo	CCq	Walter Moore [18p], Devon Millington [90]	2 800	Davis TRI
2-11	Haiti	D	0-0	Marabella	CCq		880	Taylor BRB
4-11	Trinidad and Tobago	L	1-2	Port of Spain	CCq	Shawn Beveney [78]	1 100	Legister JAM
6-11	St Vincent/Grenadines	W	2-0	Port of Spain	CCq	Devon Millington [57], Sean Cameron [81]	850	Taylor BRB
17-11	Guatemala	L	0-3	Kennesaw	Fr		4 124	Okulaja USA
27-11	Guadeloupe	D	1-1	Riviere-Pilote	CCr1	Dwain Jacobs [86]	2 500	Davis TRI
29-11	Antigua and Barbuda	L	0-1	Riviere-Pilote	CCr1		3 000	Wijngaarde SUR
1-12	Jamaica	L	0-4	Riviere-Pilote	CCr1		3 000	Cruz CRC

Fr = Friendly match • CC = Digicel Caribbean Cup • WC = FIFA World Cup • q = qualifier • † Not a full international

GFF SUPER 8 CUP 2010

Quarter-finals		Semi-finals		Final	
Alpha United	2				
Topp XX	0	**Alpha United**	5		
Buxton United		Camptown	3		
Camptown				**Alpha United**	2
Guyana Defence Force				Victoria Kings	1
Milerock		Guyana Defence Force	1		
Rosignol United	1	**Victoria Kings**	2	15-08-2010	
Victoria Kings	2	Third Place: GDF 5-1 Camptown			

GUYANA 2010

GFF SUPER LEAGUE

	Pl	W	D	L	F	A	Pts	Alpha Utd	Milerock	GDF	Rosignol Utd	Camptown	Seawall	Buxton Utd	Victoria Kings	Topp XX	Liquid Gold
Alpha United	16	12	4	0	39	9	40		2-1	4-1	2-2	n/p	1-0	3-0	2-0	3-0	**2-0**
Milerock	18	10	2	6	24	21	32	0-3		0-3	4-1	1-0	2-1	0-2	3-0	2-1	3-1
Guyana Defence Force	18	9	4	5	32	17	31	1-2	2-0		1-1	1-0	2-0	0-0	0-0	6-0	1-0
Rosignol United	18	8	5	5	35	33	29	0-0	3-2	3-1		4-4	2-4	5-4	3-2	2-0	3-0
Camptown	17	8	4	5	36	27	28	1-1	0-1	3-2	4-1		3-2	1-0	1-4	1-1	4-0
Seawall	18	6	3	9	14	21	21	0-0	0-1	1-0	1-0	1-3		0-2	0-2	1-0	0-2
Buxton United	18	4	7	7	23	33	19	1-8	1-1	0-3	2-2	2-1	0-0		3-4	0-0	**2-0**
Victoria Kings	18	5	3	10	27	32	18	2-3	1-1	0-2	1-2	2-4	0-1	1-1		1-2	5-1
Topp XX	18	4	4	10	16	33	16	0-3	0-1	2-2	0-1	1-3	1-1	3-2	2-0		3-1
Liquid Gold	17	3	2	12	15	35	11	n/p	0-1	1-4	1-0	3-3	0-1	1-1	1-1	3-0	

28/02/2010 - 17/11/2010 • Matches in bold awarded

KASHIF & SHANGHAI CUP 2009-10

First round		Quarter-finals		Semi-finals		Final	
Western Tigers	4						
Victoria Kings	0	**Western Tigers**	2				
Netrockers	1 2p	Topp XX	1				
Topp XX	1 3p			**Western Tigers**	0 3p		
Guyana Defence Force	3			Pele	0 1p		
Seawall	1	Guyana Defence Force	1				
Santos	1	**Pele**	2				
Pele	4					**Western Tigers**	2
Camptown	5					Alpha United	0
Buxton United	0	**Camptown**	3				
Rosignol United	1	Riddim Squad	0			CUP FINAL	
Riddim Squad	2			Camptown	0 2p	National Stadium, Providence	
Fruta Conquerors	3			**Alpha United**	0 4p	1-01-2010	
Eagles United	1	Fruta Conquerors	0			Scorers - Devon Millington 84,	
Grove Hi Tech	1	**Alpha United**	4			Dwayne Alli 88	
Alpha United	7			Third place: Camptown 4-2 Pele			

Preliminary Round: Milerock 0-1 **Grove Hi Tech**; **Seawall** 2-1 Rusal; **Riddim Squad** 2-1 Ann's Grove; New Amsterdam Utd 1-3 **Victoria Kings**

KASHIF & SHANGHAI CUP 2010-11

Second round		Quarter-finals		Semi-finals		Final	
Alpha United	6						
Seawall	0	**Alpha United**	5				
Milerock	0	Netrockers	1				
Netrockers	1			**Alpha United**	1 3p		
Guyana Defence Force	2			Topp XX	1 1p		
Rosignol United	0	Guyana Defence Force	1				
Caribbean United	0	**Topp XX**	2				
Topp XX	2					**Alpha United**	3
Camptown	2					Pele	2
Liquid Gold	1	**Camptown**	2				
Buxton United	2	Western Tigers	0			CUP FINAL	
Western Tigers	3			Camptown	0	National Stadium, Providence	
Santos	2			**Pele**	3	1-01-2011, Att: 15 000	
New Amsterdam Utd	1	Santos	2			Scorers - Dwight Peters 15, Howard	
Fruta Conquerors	0	**Pele**	3			Lowe 26, Kurlson Benjamin 90 for	
Pele	3			Third place: Camptown 2-1 Topp XX		Alpha; Devon Millington 14, Gregory	
						Richardson 35 for Pele	

First Round: Riddim Squad 0-0 3-4p **Liquid Gold**; **Netrockers** 2-0 Buxton Stars; **Fruta Conquerors** 3-3 4-3p Victoria Kings; **Topp XX** 2-1 Ann's Grove

HAI – HAITI

FIFA/COCA-COLA WORLD RANKING

1993	1994	1995	1996	1997	1998	1999	2000	2001	2002	2003	2004	2005	2006	2007	2008	2009	2010
145	132	153	114	125	109	99	84	82	72	96	95	98	102	69	102	90	90

2010												Hi/Lo
Jan	Feb	Mar	Mar	Apr	May	Jul	Aug	Sep	Oct	Nov	Dec	66
90	95	90	91	87	91	130	131	123	128	101	90	155

Given the chaos that wracked the country in the aftermath of the devastating earthquake of January 2010, it was remarkable that the football federation in Haiti not only managed to organise a domestic league calendar but also a limited programme for the various national teams. Indeed, for their sheer perseverance in the face of personal tragedy and the death of their coach Jean-Yves Labaze in the disaster, the Haiti women's under-17 team were awarded the FIFA Fair Play prize at the world player gala in January 2011. The men's national team were invited to Argentina for their first game after the earthquake, losing 4-0 against an experimental Argentine team preparing for the World Cup finals, the proceeds of which went to the disaster fund. Haiti also entered the 2010 Digicel Caribbean Cup but finished third in their qualifying group behind Trinidad and Guyana. Needing to avoid defeat by more than 1-0 in their last game against Trinidad, the 2007 Caribbean champions lost 4-0 and missed out on a trip to the finals in Martinique. At home, a cup tournament was organised during May which was won by Victory whilst just seven months after the earthquake, the opening tournament of the 2010 Championnat National kicked-off and was won by Tempête from the town of Saint-Marc, just to the north of the capital Port-au-Prince.

FIFA WORLD CUP RECORD

1930 DNE 1934 DNQ 1938-1950 DNE 1954 DNQ 1958-1966 DNE 1970 DNQ 1974 15 r1 1978-1986 DNQ 1990 DNE 1994-2010 DNQ

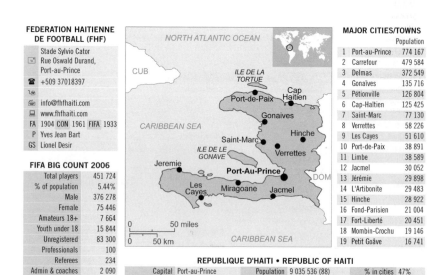

FEDERATION HAITIENNE DE FOOTBALL (FHF)

Stade Sylvio Cator
Rue Oswald Durand,
Port-au-Prince
☎ +509 37018397
🖷
📧 info@fhfhaiti.com
🖥 www.fhfhaiti.com
FA 1904 CON 1961 FIFA 1933
P Yves Jean Bart
GS Lionel Desir

FIFA BIG COUNT 2006

Total players	451 724
% of population	5.44%
Male	376 278
Female	75 446
Amateurs 18+	7 664
Youth under 18	15 844
Unregistered	83 300
Professionals	100
Referees	234
Admin & coaches	2 090
Number of clubs	310
Number of teams	1 200

MAJOR CITIES/TOWNS

		Population
1	Port-au-Prince	774 167
2	Carrefour	479 584
3	Delmas	372 549
4	Gonaïves	135 716
5	Pétionville	126 804
6	Cap-Haïtien	125 425
7	Saint-Marc	77 130
8	Verrettes	58 226
9	Les Cayes	51 610
10	Port-de-Paix	38 891
11	Limbe	38 589
12	Jacmel	30 052
13	Jérémie	29 898
14	L'Artibonite	29 483
15	Hinche	28 922
16	Fond-Parisien	21 004
17	Fort-Liberté	20 451
18	Mombin-Crochu	19 146
19	Petit Goâve	16 741

REPUBLIQUE D'HAITI • REPUBLIC OF HAITI

Capital	Port-au-Prince	Population	9 035 536 (88)	% in cities	47%
GDP per capita	$1300 (203)	Area km²	27 750 km² (147)	GMT +/-	-5
Neighbours (km)	Dominican Republic 360 • Coast 1771				

RECENT INTERNATIONAL MATCHES PLAYED BY HAITI

2008	Opponents	Score		Venue	Comp	Scorers	Att	Referee
26-01	El Salvador	D	0-0	Port au Prince	Fr		3 000	Grant HAI
29-01	El Salvador	D	0-0	Saint Marc	Fr		1 000	Edouard HAI
3-02	Venezuela	L	0-1	Maturin	Fr		20 000	Soto VEN
6-02	Venezuela	D	1-1	Puerto La Cruz	Fr	Brunel [12]	30 000	Perluzzo VEN
27-02	Dominican Republic	W	2-1	San Cristobal	Fr		1 300	Minyetty DOM
28-02	Dominican Republic	W	2-0	San Cristobal	Fr		825	Minyetty DOM
26-03	Ecuador	L	1-3	Latacunga	Fr	Davison [4]	9 000	
23-04	Guatemala	L	0-1	Guatemala City	Fr		5 000	Lopez GUA
7-06	Honduras	L	1-3	La Ceiba	Fr	Germain [77]	10 000	Zelaya HON
15-06	Netherlands Antilles	D	0-0	Port au Prince	WCq		6 000	Aguilar SLV
22-06	Netherlands Antilles	W	1-0	Willemstad	WCq	Martha OG [78]	9 000	Brizan TRI
30-07	Trinidad and Tobago	L	0-2	Macoya	Fr		2 000	Thomas JAM
10-08	Trinidad and Tobago	W	1-0	Port-au-Prince	Fr	Brunnel [48]	6 500	Grant HAI
20-08	Surinam	D	2-2	Port-au-Prince	WCq	Bertin [90], Fucien [94+]	7 800	Navarro CAN
6-09	El Salvador	L	0-5	San Salvador	WCq		21 342	Marrufo USA
10-09	Costa Rica	L	1-3	Port-au-Prince	WCq	Vubert [40]	14 700	Batres GUA
11-10	El Salvador	D	0-0	Port-au-Prince	WCq		10 000	Brizan TRI
15-10	Costa Rica	L	0-2	San Jose	WCq		5 500	Salazar USA
19-11	Surinam	D	1-1	Paramaribo	WCq	Saint-Preux [28]	800	Rodriguez MEX
4-12	Antigua and Barbuda	D	1-1	Montego Bay	CCr1	Norde [53]	2 500	Forde BRB
6-12	Guadeloupe	L	2-3	Trelawny	CCr1	Boucicant [45p], Raymond [68]	1 000	Taylor BRB
8-12	Cuba	W	1-0	Montego Bay	CCr1	Boucicant [37]	1 500	Brizan TRI
2009								
17-01	Guatemala	L	0-1	Fort Pierce	Fr		5 000	Jurisvic USA
11-02	Colombia	L	0-2	Pereira	Fr		20 000	Ruiz COL
31-03	Panama	L	0-4	La Chorrera	Fr		4 500	Amaya PAN
23-05	Jamaica	D	2-2	Fort Lauderdale	Fr	Jerome [39], Saint-Preux [66]	12 000	Marrufo USA
19-06	Panama	D	1-1	Port-au-Prince	Fr	Merceus [74]	2 000	Grant HAI
27-06	Syria	L	1-2	Montreal	Fr	Saint-Preux [29]	4 649	Petrescu CAN
4-07	Honduras	L	0-1	Seattle	GCr1		15 387	Rodriguez MEX
8-07	Grenada	W	2-0	Washington DC	GCr1	Noel [13], Marcelin [79]	26 079	Moreno PAN
11-07	USA	D	2-2	Foxboro	GCr1	Sirin [46], Cherry [48]	24 137	Quesada CRC
19-07	Mexico	L	0-4	Dallas	GCqf		85 000	Campbell JAM
2010								
5-05	Argentina	L	0-4	Cutral Co	Fr		16 500	Osses CHI
2-11	Guyana	D	0-0	Marabella	CCq		880	Taylor BRB
4-11	St Vincent/Grenadines	W	3-1	Port of Spain	CCq	Norde [45], Saint-Preux [62], Charles [83]	1 100	Campbell JAM
6-11	Trinidad and Tobago	L	0-4	Port of Spain	CCq		850	Campbell JAM
18-11	Qatar	W	1-0	Doha	Fr	Monuma Constant [53]	5 000	Al Awaji KSA

Fr = Friendly match • CC = Digicel Caribbean Cup • GC = CONCACAF Gold Cup • WC = FIFA World Cup
q = qualifier • r1 = first round group stage • sf = semi-final • f = final • † Not a full international

HAITI NATIONAL TEAM HISTORICAL RECORDS

Past Coaches: Ernst Nono Baptiste 1999 • Emmanuel Sanon 1999-2000 • Jorge Castelli ARG 2001-02 • Andres Cruciani ARG 2002-03 • Fernando Clavijo USA 2003-05 • Luis Armelio Garcia CUB 2006-07 • Wagneau Eloi 2008 • Jairo Rios Rendon COL 2009-10 • Edson Tavares BRA 2010-

HAITI 2010

CHAMPIONNAT OUVERTURE

	Pl	W	D	L	F	A	Pts	Tempête	America	Aigle Noir	Baltimore	Victory	AS Capoise	AS Carrefour	Racing CH	AS Mirebalais	Saint-Louis	Racing G	Eclair	Cavaly	Violette	Don Bosco	Dynamite
Tempête St Marc	15	10	5	0	23	7	35			3-2				2-1	1-0			1-0	3-0			1-0	1-1
America Cayes	15	8	3	4	13	11	27	1-1			0-3	1-0		3-0			1-0	1-0	1-0		1-0	0-1	
Aigle Noir	15	7	5	3	15	12	26		2-1			1-0	1-1	0-1		0-3	1-0						0-0
Baltimore St Marc	15	7	4	4	18	12	25	0-2					1-0	1-1	1-1		1-1				1-0		1-0
Victory FC	15	6	6	3	15	11	24	0-3					1-1	2-0	1-0	0-0	0-0	3-1					2-1
AS Capoise	15	5	8	2	8	5	23	0-0	0-0						2-1	1-0	1-1				0-0	0-0	2-0
AS Carrefour	15	5	8	2	16	10	23			4-1	0-0		2-1					1-0	1-1		1-1	2-0	
Racing Club Haïtien	15	6	4	5	11	10	20					1-1		0-0			1-0	1-0	4-1		0-0	1-0	0-1
AS Mirebalais	15	4	8	3	11	9	20	1-3	0-0				2-1	0-0	0-0						1-0	1-1	1-1
AS Saint-Louis	15	3	7	5	11	12	16	0-0		0-1					1-1	1-0				4-2	1-1	2-1	
Racing Gônaïves	15	4	3	8	8	15	15		0-1					0-0		0-1	1-0					0-0	1-0
Eclair Gônaïves	15	3	5	7	8	14	14			0-1	3-2	0-0	0-0		0-1	0-0	1-1	0-1			0-2		
Cavaly Léogâne	15	3	5	7	8	13	14	0-0	0-1	0-2	0-3	0-1		0-0					0-1		1-0		
Violette AC	15	2	5	8	10	16	11	1-2					0-2	0-1			1-1						2-1
Don Bosco	15	2	5	8	9	20	11					1-2	0-1	1-1				0-2	0-2	0-3	1-1		2-2
Dynamite St Marc	15	2	5	8	9	16	11		0-1				0-1	0-1			0-0	2-0	1-0	0-2			

31//07/2010 - 8/10/2010

COUPE D'HAITI 2010

Round of 16		Quarter-finals		Semi-finals		Final	
Victory FC	1 0 5p						
Dynamite AC St Marc	0 1 4p	**Victory FC**	1 4				
Violette AC	0 0	ASPDIF Aquin	0 1				
ASPDIF Aquin ‡	0 0			**Victory FC**	1 2		
Valencia Léogâne				Inter Grand-Goâve	0 0		
		Valencia Léogâne	0 0				
Racing Club Haïtien	0 0	**Inter Grand-Goâve**	0 1			**Victory FC**	1
Inter Grand-Goâve	0 3					AS Saint-Louis	0
Baltimore St Marc							
		Baltimore St Marc	0 1 7p				
Racine Gros-Morne		FICA Cap-Haïtien	1 0 6p				
FICA Cap-Haïtien				Baltimore St Marc	0 0		
Triomphe Liancourt	0 3			**AS Saint-Louis**	0 1		
AS Mirebalais	1 0	Triomphe Liancourt					
		AS Saint-Louis					
AS Saint-Louis		‡ ASPDIF won 12-11 on penalties					

CUP FINAL

6-06-2010

HKG – HONG KONG

FIFA/COCA-COLA WORLD RANKING

1993	1994	1995	1996	1997	1998	1999	2000	2001	2002	2003	2004	2005	2006	2007	2008	2009	2010
112	98	111	124	129	136	122	123	137	150	142	133	117	117	125	151	143	146

					2010							Hi/Lo
Jan	Feb	Mar	Mar	Apr	May	Jul	Aug	Sep	Oct	Nov	Dec	90
143	137	142	140	139	140	135	133	136	137	145	146	156

The feel-good factor that hit Hong Kong football following the gold medal-winning performance in the final of the East Asian Games on home soil in 2009 continued into 2010 as the former British colony performed above expectations at the Asian Games in Guangzhou. Hong Kong qualified for the second round of the under-23 tournament having emerged unbeaten from the group stages before losing 3-0 to Oman in the Round of 16. A surprise win over Uzbekistan as well as a victory over Bangladesh and a draw with the United Arab Emirates saw Hong Kong finish in second place in the group, trailing the UAE on goal difference. The upswing in fortunes has prompted the local association to implement an overhaul of the entire set-up of the game at home with David Davies, the former executive director of the Football Association in England overseeing the changes. Club side South China, traditionally the strongest and best-supported club in Hong Kong, sought to bolster their attempts to earn a berth in the 2012 edition of the AFC Champions League by signing up former English Premier League stars Nicky Butt and Mateja Kezman for their 2011 AFC Cup campaign. South China had won both the league and the Senior Shield in 2010 but failed in their attempt to win a clean sweep of trophies when new club TSW Pegasus won the FA Cup.

FIFA WORLD CUP RECORD
1930-1970 DNE **1974-2010** DNQ

THE HONG KONG FOOTBALL ASSOCIATION LTD (HKFA)	
📧	55 Fat Kwong Street, Homantin, Kowloon
☎	+852 27129122
📠	+852 27604303
✉	hkfa@hkfa.com
🖥	www.hkfa.com
FA	1914 CON 1954 FIFA 1954
P	Timothy Tsun Ting Fok
GS	Vincent Yuen

FIFA BIG COUNT 2006	
Total players	149 956
% of population	2.16%
Male	139 960
Female	9 996
Amateurs 18+	2 203
Youth under 18	1 762
Unregistered	50 780
Professionals	211
Referees	149
Admin & coaches	910
Number of clubs	82
Number of teams	582

MAJOR CITIES/TOWNS		
		Population
1	Sha Tin, NT	628 000
2	Eastern, HKI	616 000
3	Kwun Tong, Kw	562 000
4	Tuen Mun, NT	488 000
5	Kwai Tsing, NT	477 000
6	Yuen Long, NT	449 000
7	Wong Tai Sin, Kw	444 000
8	Kowloon City	381 000
9	Sham Shui Po, Kw	353 000
10	Sai Kung, NT	327 000
11	Tai Po, NT	310 000
12	North, NT	298 000
13	Southern, HKI	290 000
14	Yau Tsim Mong, Kw	282 000
15	Tsuen Wan, NT	275 000
16	Central & Western	261 000
	Kw = Kowloon	
	NT = New Territories	
	HKI = Hong Kong Island	

XIANGGANG TEBIE XINGZHENGQU • HONG KONG SPECIAL ADMINISTRATIVE REGION

Capital	Victoria	Population 7 055 071 (100)	% in cities 100%
GDP per capita	$43 800 (15)	Area km² 1 104 km² (183)	GMT +/- +8
Neighbours (km)	China 30 • Coast 733		

RECENT INTERNATIONAL MATCHES PLAYED BY HONG KONG

2007	Opponents	Score	Venue	Comp	Scorers	Att	Referee
1-06	Indonesia	L 0-3	Jakarta	Fr			
10-06	Macau	W 2-1	Hong Kong	Fr	Chan Siu Ki 2 [24 66]		
19-06	Chinese Taipei	D 1-1	Macau	EACq	Lo Chi Kwan [56]	200	Kim Eui Soo KOR
21-06	Guam	W 15-1	Macau	EACq	Chan Siu Ki 5 [5 21 36 42 51], Lo Kwan Yee 2 [8 41], Poon Yiu Cheuk [22], Cheng Siu Wai [31], Lo Chi Kwan [38], Cordeiro [56], OG [69], Law Chun Pong [73], Ambassa Guy [76], Luk Koon Pong [86]	300	Matsuo JPN
24-06	Korea DPR	L 0-1	Macau	EACq		300	Ogiya JPN
21-10	Timor-Leste	W 3-2	Gianyar	WCq	Cheng Siu Wai 2 [25 50], Esteves OG [35]	1 500	Shaharul MAS
28-10	Timor-Leste	W 8-1	Hong Kong	WCq	Lo Kwan Yee [3], Chan Siu Ki 3 [6 79 87], Cheung Sai Ho [50], Cheng Siu Wai 2 [68 71], Lam Ka Wai [84]	1 542	Torky IRN
10-11	Turkmenistan	D 0-0	Hong Kong	WCq		2 823	Mujghef JOR
18-11	Turkmenistan	L 0-3	Ashgabat	WCq		30 000	Al Hilali OMA
2008							
19-11	Macau	W 9-1	Macau	Fr	Lee Wai Lim 3 [5 66 80], Cheng Siu Wai [10], Chan Siu Ki 4 [19 50 55 63], Yiu Chung Au Yeung [30]		
2009							
14-01	India	W 2-1	Hong Kong	Fr	Yiu Chung Au Yeung [70], Ng Wai Chiu [90]	1 200	
21-01	Bahrain	L 1-3	Hong Kong	ACq	Cheng Siu Wai [90]	6 013	Vo Minh Tri VIE
28-01	Yemen	L 0-1	Sana'a	ACq		10 000	Al Hilali OMA
23-08	Chinese Taipei	W 4-0	Kaohsiung	EAq	Lee Wai Lim [38], Chan Wai Ho [45], Chan Siu Ki [60], Ambassa Guy [63]	12 000	Tojo JPN
25-08	Korea DPR	D 0-0	Kaohsiung	EAq		100	Kim Jong Hyeok KOR
27-08	Guam	W 12-0	Kaohsiung	EAq	Man Pei Tak [5], Wong Chin Hung [15], Chan Siu Ki 4 [18 35 75 77], Chao Pengfei 3 [37 71 92+], Leung Chun Pong [41], Poon Yiu Cheuk [89], Chan Wai Ho [90]	1 500	Tojo JPN
8-10	Japan	L 0-6	Shizuoka	ACq		16 028	Torky IRN
18-11	Japan	L 0-4	Hong Kong	ACq		13 254	Green AUS
2010							
6-01	Bahrain	L 0-4	Manama	ACq		1 550	Balideh QAT
7-02	Korea Republic	L 0-5	Tokyo	EAC		2 728	Sato JPN
11-02	Japan	L 0-3	Tokyo	EAC		16 368	Zhao Liang CHN
14-02	China PR	L 0-2	Tokyo	EAC		16 439	Kim Jong Hyeok KOR
3-03	Yemen	D 0-0	Hong Kong	ACq		1 212	Minh Tri Vo VIE
4-10	India	W 1-0	Pune	Fr	Li Haiqiang [76]	8 000	Patwal IND
9-10	Philippines	W 4-2	Kaohsiung	Fr	Chan Man Fai [5], Xu Deshuai [31], Lo Kwan Yee [84], Ju Yingzhi [91+]	650	Kao Jung Fang TPE
10-10	Macau	W 4-0	Kaohsiung	Fr	Tam Lok Hin [38], Xu Deshuai [52], Lam Hok Hei 2 [72 74]	1 200	Yu Ming Hsun TPE
12-10	Chinese Taipei	D 1-1	Kaohsiung	Fr	Lo Kwan Yee [75p]	3 000	Kao Tsai Hu TPE
17-11	Paraguay	L 0-7	Hong Kong	Fr		6 250	Mohd Salleh MAS

Fr = Friendly match • EAC = East Asian Championship • AC = AFC Asian Cup • WC = FIFA World Cup • q = qualifier

HONG KONG NATIONAL TEAM HISTORICAL RECORDS

Past Coaches
Tom Sneddon ENG 1954-56 • Lai Shiu Wing 1958-67 • Chu Wing Keung 1967 • Tang Sum 1968 • Lau Tim 1968 • Hui King Shing 1969-70 • Chan Fai Hung 1970-72 • Ho Ying Fun 1973-75 • Franz van Balkom NED 1976-77 • Chan Yong Chong MAS 1978-79 • Peter McParland ENG 1980 • George Knobel NED 1980 • Lo Tak Kuen 1981 • Kwok Ka Ming 1982-90 • Wong Man Wai 1992 • Chan Hung Ping 1993 • Khoo Luan Khen MAS 1994-95 • Tsang Wai Chung 1996 • Kwok Ka Ming 1997 • Sebastian Araujo BRA 1998 • Chan Hung Ping 1999-2000 • Arie van der Zouwen NED 2000-01 • Casemiro Mior BRA 2002 • Lai Sun Cheung 2003-07 • Lee Kin Wo 2007 • Dejan Antonic SRB & Goran Paulic CRO 2008-09 • Kim Pan Gon KOR 2009 • Liu Chun Fai 2010 • Tsang Wai Chung 2010

HONG KONG 2009-10

COOLPOINT VENTILATION FIRST DIVISION

	Pl	W	D	L	F	A	Pts	South China	Pegasus	Kitchee	Citizen	Sun Hei	Tai Po	Fourway	Tai Chung	Shatin	Happy Valley
South China †	18	13	3	2	51	21	**42**		3-2	2-1	1-0	3-2	1-0	1-0	4-0	6-0	6-1
TSW Pegasus	18	10	5	3	33	21	**35**	2-2		0-0	1-1	1-0	2-1	3-0	2-1	1-0	4-2
Kitchee	18	8	7	3	34	18	**31**	2-1	0-0		2-2	3-2	1-2	3-3	2-0	3-1	6-0
Citizen	18	6	8	4	29	16	**26**	1-1	4-1	0-1		1-1	0-1	1-1	1-0	3-1	7-0
Sun Hei	18	7	3	8	38	27	**24**	3-1	2-3	1-0	0-3		2-3	4-1	3-0	4-0	6-0
Tai Po	18	6	5	7	25	27	**23**	1-3	1-2	2-2	2-2	2-4		1-0	0-1	0-0	4-0
Fourway Rangers	18	4	7	7	19	28	**19**	2-5	1-4	1-1	0-0	2-1	1-1		1-1	1-0	2-0
Tai Chung	18	4	6	8	14	27	**18**	1-1	1-0	1-1	1-3	1-0	1-1	0-2		1-1	1-1
Shatin	18	2	7	9	18	35	**13**	2-2	1-1	0-2	2-0	1-1	4-1	1-1	1-3		1-3
Happy Valley	18	2	5	11	17	58	**11**	2-6	1-4	0-4	0-0	2-2	1-2	1-0	1-1	2-2	

6/09/2009 - 16/05/2010 • † Qualified for the AFC Cup • Tuen Mun disqualified after five matches. Results annulled
Top scorers: **14** - Cahe BRA, Sun Hei • **13** - Itaparica BRA, Pegasus • **11** - Chan Siu Ki, South China • **9** - Sandro BRA, Citizen

HONG KONG 2009-10 SECOND DIVISION

	Pl	W	D	L	F	A	Pts
Hong Kong FC	16	12	1	3	53	19	**37**
Tuen Mun	16	10	3	3	55	17	**33**
Double Flower	16	9	4	3	41	19	**31**
Ongood	16	10	1	5	49	31	**31**
Wing Yee	16	7	1	8	53	38	**25**
Kwai Tsing	16	6	4	6	36	23	**22**
Mutual	16	5	2	9	38	50	**17**
Fukien	16	3	4	9	43	42	**13**
Derico	16	0	0	16	7	136	**0**

12/09/2009 - 18/04/2010

SENIOR SHIELD 2009-10

Quarter-finals		Semi-finals		Final	
South China	3				
Tai Chung	0	**South China**	2		
Tai Po	1	Sun Hei	0		
Sun Hei	2				
TSW Pegasus	3			**South China**	4
Citizen	2	TSW Pegasus	2	Kitchee	2
Fourway Rangers	1	**Kitchee**	3	
Kitchee	3			

Siu Sai Wan Sports Ground
30-01-2010, Att: 2760
Ref: Pau Sai Yin
Scorers - Schutz 68, Leo 2 69 90, Chan Siu Ki 79 for SC; Liang Zicheng 24, Nsue 53 for Kitchee

1st round: Tuen Mun 0-2 **Tai Chung**; **Tai Po** 3-0 Happy Valley; Shatin 0-2 **Citizen**

FA CUP 2009-10

Quarter-finals		Semi-finals		Final	
TSW Pegasus	6				
Happy Valley	1	**TSW Pegasus**	3		
Shatin	1	Tai Po	1		
Tai Po	2				
Fourway Rangers	1 4p			**TSW Pegasus †**	2
Sun Hei	1 3p	Fourway Rangers	1	Citizen	1
South China	0 3p	**Citizen**	2		
Citizen	0 4p				

Hong Kong Stadium
30-05-2010, Att: 3115
Ref: Liu Kwok Man
Scorers - Lee Hong Lim 64, Itaparica 71 for Pegasus; Paulinho 76 for Citizen

1st round: **Shatin** 2-2 3-2p Kitchee; **Citizen** 3-0 Tai Chung
† Qualified for the AFC Cup

MEDALS TABLE

		Overall		Lge		FAC		Shield		VC		LC		Asia	
		G	S	G	B	G	B	G	B	G	B	G	B	G	S
1	South China	71	37	31	15	9	4	21	10	8	7	2			1
2	Seiko	29	8	9	3	6	1	8	2	6	2				
3	Eastern	16	9	4	2	3	1	7	2	2	4				
4	Happy Valley	15	38	6	16	2	5	5	9	1	3	1	5		
5	Kitchee	11	13	3	6		1	5	5			2	1		
6	Sun Hei	11	8	3	2	3	1	1	4			4	1		
7	Rangers	9	8	1		2	3	4	2	2	2	1			
	Sing Tao	9	8	1	4		1	6	2	2	1				
9	Double Flower	6	11	2	2	3	2	4		1	3				
10	Bulova	5	4	2		2	1	1	1	2	1				

HON – HONDURAS

FIFA/COCA-COLA WORLD RANKING

1993	1994	1995	1996	1997	1998	1999	2000	2001	2002	2003	2004	2005	2006	2007	2008	2009	2010
40	53	49	45	73	91	69	46	27	40	49	59	41	56	53	40	37	59

2010												Hi/Lo
Jan	Feb	Mar	Mar	Apr	May	Jul	Aug	Sep	Oct	Nov	Dec	20
37	34	35	36	40	38	46	46	52	54	57	59	95

For Honduras, the major achievement was in qualifying for the FIFA World Cup in South Africa rather than for what they did once there. Although never outclassed, even in a group containing ultimate winners Spain, they limped home after the group stage having failed to score a goal and with only one point in the bag. That came from a 0-0 draw against a Swiss side in their final match having previously lost 1-0 to Chile and 2-0 to Spain. After the tournament the Hondurans found their scoring feet again and at the 2011 Copa Centroamericana in Panama proved that they are currently the best team in the region. Despite being without star players such as Inter's David Suazo and Tottenham's Wilson Palacios, they qualified easily from their group and then beat hosts Panama in the semi-finals, although they needed penalties to do so. In the final Honduras beat seven times champions Costa Rica 2-1 to win the title for only the third time - the first since 1995. At home there were championship wins for Olimpia and Real España in 2010 while Olimpia made a good impression in the 2010-11 CONCACAF Champions League, winning a strong group ahead of Mexico's Toluca, Puerto Rico Islanders and Deportivo FAS from El Salvador to qualify for the knockout rounds.

FIFA WORLD CUP RECORD
1930-1958 DNE 1962-1974 DNQ 1978 DNE **1982** 18 r1 1986-2006 DNQ **2010** 30 r1

FEDERACIÓN NACIONAL AUTÓNOMA DE FÚTBOL DE HONDURAS (FENAFUTH)

Colonia Florencia Norte,
Edificio Plaza América,
Ave. Roble, 1 y 2 Nivel,
Tegucigalpa
☎ +504 2311436
📠 +504 2398826
✉ contacto@fenafuth.com
💻 www.fenafuth.net
FA 1951 CON 1961 FIFA 1951
P Rafael Callejas
GS Alfredo Hawit Banegas

FIFA BIG COUNT 2006

Total players	420 600
% of population	5.74%
Male	360 800
Female	59 800
Amateurs 18+	27 700
Professionals	100
Referees	1 100
Admin & coaches	5 700
Number of clubs	220
Number of teams	1 100

MAJOR CITIES/TOWNS

		Population
1	Tegucigalpa	1 055 298
2	San Pedro Sula	614 912
3	Choloma	206 016
4	La Ceiba	166 835
5	El Progreso	126 396
6	Choluteca	91 193
7	Comayagua	72 802
8	Puerto Cortés	58 914
9	La Lima	57 070
10	Danli	55 169
11	Siguatepeque	53 612
12	Juticalpa	42 523
13	Catacamas	42 370
14	Tocoa	41 028
15	Villanueva	40 235
16	Tela	34 476
17	Olanchito	33 583
18	Santa Rosa	33 479
19	San Lorenzo	27 059

REPUBLICA DE HONDURAS • REPUBLIC OF HONDURAS

Capital Tegucigalpa	Population 7 792 854 (93)	% in cities 48%
GDP per capita $4400 (152)	Area km² 112 090 km² (102)	GMT +/- -6
Neighbours (km) Guatemala 256, El Salvador 342, Nicaragua 922 • Coast 820		

RECENT INTERNATIONAL MATCHES PLAYED BY HONDURAS

2009 Opponents	Score		Venue	Comp	Scorers	Att	Referee
30-01 Panama	L	0-1	Tegucigalpa	UCsf		20 000	Batres GUA
1-02 El Salvador	W	1-0	Tegucigalpa	UC3p	Roger Espinoza [30]	900	Quesada CRC
11-02 Costa Rica	L	0-2	San Jose	WCq		18 000	Aguilar SLV
28-03 Trinidad and Tobago	D	1-1	Port of Spain	WCq	Carlos Pavon [50]	23 500	Quesada CRC
1-04 Mexico	W	3-1	San Pedro Sula	WCq	Carlos Costly 2 [17 79], Carlos Pavon [43]	28 000	Ward CAN
6-06 USA	L	1-2	Chicago	WCq	Carlos Costly [4]	55 647	Morales MEX
10-06 El Salvador	W	1-0	San Pedro Sula	WCq	Carlos Pavon [15]	28 000	Toledo USA
28-06 Panama	W	2-0	Cary	Fr	Allan Lalin [21], Erick Norales [54]	3 766	Vaughn USA
4-07 Haiti	W	1-0	Seattle	GCr1	Carlos Costly [76]	15 387	Rodriguez MEX
8-07 USA	L	0-2	Washington DC	GCr1		26 079	Campbell JAM
11-07 Grenada	W	4-0	Foxboro	GCr1	Walter Martinez [2], Roger Espinoza [25], Melvin Valladares [56], Carlo Costly [66]	24 137	Rodriguez MEX
18-07 Canada	W	1-0	Philadelphia	GCqf	Walter Martinez [35p]	31 087	Aguilar SLV
23-07 USA	L	0-2	Chicago	GCsf		55 173	Campbell JAM
12-08 Costa Rica	W	4-0	San Pedro Sula	WCq	Carlos Costly 2 [30 92+], Carlos Pavon [51], Melvin Valladares [89]	30 000	Rodriguez MEX
5-09 Trinidad and Tobago	W	4-1	San Pedro Sula	WCq	Carlos Pavon 2 [20 28], Amado Guevara [62], David Suazo [83]	38 000	Geiger USA
9-09 Mexico	L	0-1	Mexico City	WCq		97 897	Campbell JAM
10-10 USA	L	2-3	San Pedro Sula	WCq	Julio De Leon 2 [47 78]	37 000	Moreno PAN
14-10 El Salvador	W	1-0	San Salvador	WCq	Carlos Pavon [64]	28 000	Salazar USA
14-11 Latvia	W	2-1	Tegucigalpa	Fr	Carlos Costly [40], George Welcome [87]	10 000	Quesada CRC
18-11 Peru	L	1-2	Miami Gardens	Fr	David Suazo [47]	11 917	Jurisevic USA
2010							
23-01 USA	W	3-1	Carson	Fr	Carlos Pavon [19p], Jerry Palacios [37], Roger Espinoza [53]	18 626	Archundia MEX
3-03 Turkey	L	0-2	Istanbul	Fr		22 000	Olsiak SVK
21-04 Venezuela	L	0-1	San Pedro Sula	Fr		40 000	Moreno PAN
27-05 Belarus	D	2-2	Villach	Fr	Julio De Leon [25], George Welcome [71]	400	Eisner AUT
2-06 Azerbaijan	D	0-0	Zell Am See	Fr		1 000	Drachta AUT
5-06 Romania	L	0-3	St Velt an der Glan	Fr		1 500	Grobelnik AUT
16-06 Chile	L	0-1	Nelspruit	WCr1		32 664	Maillet SEY
21-06 Spain	L	0-2	Johannesburg	WCr1		54 386	Nishimura JPN
25-06 Switzerland	D	0-0	Bloemfontein	WCr1		28 042	Baldassi ARG
4-09 El Salvador	D	2-2	Los Angeles	Fr	Oscar Garcia [58], Roger Rojas [86]. W 4-3p	15 000	Stoica USA
7-09 Canada	L	1-2	Montreal	Fr	Erick Norales [34]	7 525	Geiger USA
9-10 New Zealand	D	1-1	Auckland	Fr	Walter Martinez [64]	18 153	O'Leary NZL
12-10 Guatemala	W	2-0	Los Angeles	Fr	Roger Rojas [21], George Welcome [80]	10 000	Hernandez USA
17-11 Panama	L	0-2	Panama City	Fr		3 646	Cruz CRC
18-12 Panama	W	2-1	San Pedro Sula	Fr	Johny Leveron 2 [7 44]	3 000	Rodas GUA
2011							
14-01 Costa Rica	D	1-1	Panama City	UCr1	Ramon Nunez [90]	6 000	Garcia MEX
18-01 Guatemala	W	3-1	Panama City	UCr1	Ramon Nunez [13], Jorge Claros 2 [42 88]	10 000	Aguilar SLV
21-01 El Salvador	W	2-0	Panama City	UCsf	Johnny Leveron [78], Marvin Chavez [90]	5 000	Quesada CRC
23-01 Costa Rica	W	2-1	Panama City	UCf	Walter Martinez [8], Emil Martinez [52]	2 000	Lopez GUA

Fr = Friendly match • UC = UNCAF Cup/Copa Centroamericana • GC = CONCACAF Gold Cup • WC = FIFA World Cup
q = qualifier • r1 = first round group • qf = quarter-final • 5p = fifth place play-off • sf = semi-final • f = final

HONDURAS NATIONAL TEAM HISTORICAL RECORDS

Caps 137 - Amado Guevara 1994- • 101 - Carlos Pavon 1993- • 88 - Milton Nunez 1994-2008 • 85 - Danilo Turcios 1999- & Ivan Guerrero 1999- • 80 - Noel Valladares 2000- • 77 - Julio Cesar de Leon 1999- • 75 - Maynor Figueroa 2003- • 71 - Wilson Palacios 2003- & Samuel Caballero 1998-

Goals 57 - Carlos Pavon 1993- • 35 - Wilmer Velasquez 1996-2007 • 34 - Milton Nunez 1994-2008 • 29 - Amado Guevara 1994- • 18 - Saul Martinez 2001-08 • 16 - David Suazo 1999- • 15 - Julio Cesar de Leon 1999- • 14 - Carlo Costly 2007- • 13 - Jairo Martinez 1998-

Past Coaches Flavio Ortega 1991-92 • Estanislao Malinowski URU 1993-94 • Carlos Carranza 1995-96 • Miguel Company PER 1997-98 • Ramon Maradiaga 1999-02 • Bora Milutinovic SRB 2003-04 • Jose de la Paz Herrera 2005 • Flavio Ortega 2006 • Reinaldo Rueda COL 2006-10 • Juan de Dios Castillo MEX 2010-

HONDURAS 2009–10

TORNEO APERTURA

	Pl	W	D	L	F	A	Pts	Marathón	Motagua	Olimpia	España	Victoria	Platense	Vida	Savio	Hispano	Juventud
Marathón †	18	11	5	2	32	16	38		2-0	2-2	1-0	3-0	0-2	3-1	1-1	2-1	4-1
Motagua †	18	10	5	3	31	14	35	2-2		0-1	1-0	3-0	2-0	1-2	3-1	1-0	2-0
Olimpia †	18	8	6	4	29	16	30	0-2	0-0		2-0	6-1	1-1	7-1	2-0	1-0	2-1
Real España †	18	9	3	6	26	20	30	3-2	1-2	2-0		2-0	1-2	1-0	2-1	3-2	1-0
Victoria	18	7	5	6	22	27	26	0-0	0-4	2-1	1-1		4-0	2-2	4-1	2-0	1-0
Platense	18	6	6	6	23	25	24	0-1	2-2	1-1	2-3	1-1		3-2	1-1	1-0	1-0
Vida	18	4	6	8	22	33	18	1-1	1-1	1-2	1-1	0-1	0-3		2-2	3-1	1-0
Deportivo Savio	18	4	5	9	13	23	17	0-1	0-2	1-0	1-0	0-1	1-1	0-1		1-0	1-1
Hispano	18	4	3	11	17	28	15	0-2	2-2	0-0	0-3	1-0	2-1	2-2	1-0		3-0
Real Juventud	18	3	4	11	19	32	13	2-3	0-3	1-1	2-2	2-2	3-1	2-1	4-1	4-2	

18/07/2009 - 4/11/2009 • † Qualified for the play-offs • Play-off semi-finals: Real España 1-2 2-1 **Marathón**; **Olimpia** 0-1 2-0 Motagua
Play-off final: Olimpia 1-0 0-2 **Marathón** • **Marathón** are Apertura champions
1st leg. Tiburcio Andino, Tegucigalpa, 22-11-2009, Att: 12 477, Ref: Moncada. Scorer - Jaime Rosales 70 for Olimpia
2nd leg. Olimpico, San Pedro Sula, 25-11-2009, Ref: Pineda. Scorers - Guillermo Ramirez 5, Jerry Palacios 64 for Marathón
Top scorers (including play-offs): **13** - Jerry Palacios, Marathón • **11** - Georgie Welcome, Motagua • **9** - Mauricio Copete COL, Victoria

HONDURAS 2009–10

TORNEO CLAUSURA

	Pl	W	D	L	F	A	Pts	Motagua	Olimpia	Vida	Platense	Hispano	España	Marathón	Juventud	Savio	Victoria
Motagua †	18	11	3	4	28	15	36		1-0	3-2	3-0	1-0	1-0	1-0	3-1	1-1	3-0
Olimpia †	18	8	8	2	26	11	32	0-0		2-1	1-1	4-0	2-0	2-0	0-0	0-0	6-0
Vida †	18	8	4	6	25	20	28	0-1	1-1		1-1	2-1	1-2	2-2	4-1	1-0	2-0
Platense †	18	7	7	4	23	19	28	2-1	0-0	1-1		1-1	3-2	0-1	3-1	3-0	2-0
Hispano	18	8	3	7	22	22	27	3-1	2-0	0-1	1-1		2-1	1-1	1-0	1-0	2-0
Real España	18	7	4	7	28	29	25	2-1	2-2	1-2	3-1	1-0		1-1	2-2	3-4	0-1
Marathón	18	4	7	7	23	24	19	3-4	1-1	0-1	0-1	2-3	1-2		2-1	3-0	2-2
Real Juventud §3	18	6	4	8	25	28	19	0-3	1-2	2-0	2-0	3-1	2-0	1-1		3-2	1-1
Deportivo Savio	18	4	5	9	13	23	17	0-0	0-1	1-0	0-0	2-1	1-2	0-2	0-2		2-0
Victoria	18	2	5	11	15	37	11	1-0	1-0	1-2	1-3	1-3	1-2	2-1	3-2	0-0	

30/01/2010 - 17/04/2010 • † Qualified for the play-offs • Play-off semi-finals: Vida 2-2 1-1 **Olimpia**; Platense 2-2 0-0 **Motagua**
Play-off final: **Olimpia** 3-1 0-1 Motagua • **Olimpia** are Clausura champions
1st leg. Tiburcio Andino, Tegucigalpa, 2-05-2010, Att: 13 819, Ref: Castro. Scorers - Reynaldo Tilguath 23, Roger Rojas 2 40 58 for Olimpia, Marcelo Cabrita 23 for Motagua • 2nd leg. Tiburcio Andino, Tegucigalpa, 8-05-2010, Att: 16 299, Ref: Pineda. Scorer - Georgie Welcome 38 for Motagua
§ = points deducted • Top scorers (including play-offs): **12** - Jerry Bengtson, Vida • **10** - Carlos Pavon, España • **8** - Roger Rojas, Olimpia

HONDURAS 2010–11

TORNEO APERTURA

	Pl	W	D	L	F	A	Pts	Victoria	Marathón	España	Olimpia	Platense	Vida	Motagua	Savio	Necaxa	Hispano
Victoria †	18	10	2	6	26	24	32		0-1	2-1	1-1	2-0	1-2	2-1	3-1	1-0	2-1
Marathón †	18	8	7	3	26	18	31	5-1		0-0	1-0	1-0	0-0	1-0	1-1	0-0	0-2
Real España †	18	7	8	3	28	22	29	1-2	3-2		2-1	2-2	1-0	1-1	3-3	1-2	1-0
Olimpia †	18	7	7	4	29	19	28	1-2	2-2	2-2		2-0	1-0	1-1	5-2	1-1	2-0
Platense	18	8	2	8	20	22	26	2-1	2-2	1-2	1-0		0-2	2-1	2-0	1-0	2-0
Vida	18	7	4	7	26	23	25	1-1	2-3	1-3	1-1	0-1		2-2	4-2	2-1	4-2
Motagua	18	5	6	7	21	25	21	3-0	3-2	1-1	1-2	1-0	0-2		1-0	1-0	2-2
Deportivo Savio	18	5	6	7	22	30	21	1-0	0-2	0-0	1-1	3-1	2-1	2-2		2-1	1-0
Necaxa	18	5	4	9	18	19	19	0-2	0-1	1-1	0-1	2-1	1-2	3-0	3-1		3-0
Hispano	18	3	4	11	17	31	13	2-3	0-3	1-1	1-4	1-2	1-0	1-2	1-0	0-0	

18/07/2009 - 4/11/2009 • † Qualified for the play-offs • Play-off semi-finals: **Real España** 2-2 2-0 Marathón; **Olimpia** 2-0 1-0 Victoria
Play-off final: Olimpia 1-1 1-2 **Real España** • **Real España** are Apertura champions
1st leg. Tiburcio Andino, Tegucigalpa, 5-12-2010, Ref: Matute. Scorers - Jose Dias 7 for Olimpia; Luis Lobo 4 for España • 2nd leg. Francisco Morazan, San Pedro Sula, 11-12-2010, Att: 18 000, Ref: Pineda. Scorers - Christian Martinez 87, Douglas Mattoso 111 for España; Ramiro Bruschi 71 for Olimpia
Top scorers (including play-offs): **12** - Jerry Bengtson, Vida • **11** - Saul Martinez, Victoria • **9** - Rony Flores, Marathón • **8** - Elroy Smith BLZ, Savio

HUN – HUNGARY

FIFA/COCA-COLA WORLD RANKING

1993	1994	1995	1996	1997	1998	1999	2000	2001	2002	2003	2004	2005	2006	2007	2008	2009	2010
50	61	62	75	77	46	45	47	66	56	72	64	74	62	50	47	54	42

2010												Hi/Lo
Jan	Feb	Mar	Mar	Apr	May	Jul	Aug	Sep	Oct	Nov	Dec	36
54	52	48	52	56	57	62	62	51	44	43	42	87

Such has been the dominance of Debreceni VSE in recent years that they have now won a trophy in each season since claiming their first championship in 2005. 2010, however, was the first year in which they claimed the league and cup double, a magnificent achievement for Andras Herczeg's team, coming as it did on the back of the club's first appearance in the group stage of the UEFA Champions League. The title race was a close run affair that went down to the final minutes of the season. Videoton were nine minutes away from forcing a title play-off but conceded a goal by Lazar Stanisic against Györi ETO which handed the title to Debrecen. In the Cup Final, Debreceni had the goals of Frenchman Adamo Coulibaly and Cameroonian Mbengono Yannick to thank for their 3-2 victory over Zalaegerszegi, the former scoring twice to cap a fine season in which he finished as the club's top scorer. The Hungarian national team made a promising enough start to the qualifiers for Euro 2012 under new coach Sandor Egervari, winning three of their first four games, but that only masked the fact that the Hungarians find themselves in a footballing no-mans land - too good for the smaller nations but lacking the strength in depth to seriously challenge the likes of Sweden and the Netherlands - the two nations that block their path to the finals.

FIFA WORLD CUP RECORD

1930 DNE **1934** 6 QF **1938** 2 Finalists 1950 DNE **1954** 2 Finalists **1958** 10 r1 **1962** 5 QF **1966** 6 QF
1970-1974 DNQ **1978** 15 r1 **1982** 14 r1 **1986** 18 r1 1990-2010 DNQ

HUNGARIAN FOOTBALL FEDERATION (MLSZ)

Kanai ut. 314/24,
Budapest 1112

☎ +36 1 5779500
📠 +36 1 5779503
✉ mlsz@mlsz.hu
🌐 www.mlsz.hu
FA 1901 CON 1954 FIFA 1906
P Sandor Csanyi
GS Marton Vagi

FIFA BIG COUNT 2006

Total players	527 326
% of population	5.28%
Male	477 368
Female	49 958
Amateurs 18+	61 208
Youth under 18	63 744
Unregistered	203 100
Professionals	468
Referees	3 615
Admin & coaches	7 150
Number of clubs	2 748
Number of teams	4 631

MAJOR CITIES/TOWNS

		Population
1	Budapest	1 656 358
2	Debrecen	205 042
3	Miskolc	174 574
4	Szeged	161 725
5	Pécs	155 402
6	Györ	130 391
7	Nyíregyháza	115 113
8	Kecskemét	105 498
9	Székesfehérvár	104 486
10	Szombathely	79 976
11	Szolnok	74 604
12	Tatabánya	71 840
13	Kaposvár	66 332
14	Békéscsaba	64 372
15	Érd	63 547
16	Zalaegerszeg	60 622
17	Veszprém	60 225
18	Sopron	56 219
19	Eger	56 036

MAGYAR KOZTARSASAG • REPUBLIC OF HUNGARY

Capital	Budapest	Population	9 905 596 (82)	% in cities	68%
GDP per capita	$19 800 (63)	Area km²	93 028 km² (109)	GMT +/-	+1
Neighbours (km)	Austria 366, Croatia 329, Romania 443, Serbia 166, Slovakia 676, Slovenia 102, Ukraine 103				

RECENT INTERNATIONAL MATCHES PLAYED BY HUNGARY

2008	Opponents	Score		Venue	Comp	Scorers	Att	Referee
6-02	Slovakia	D	1-1	Limassol	Fr	Gera [54]	100	Trattu CYP
26-03	Slovenia	L	0-1	Zalaegerszeg	Fr		7 000	Messner AUT
24-05	Greece	W	3-2	Budapest	Fr	Dzsudzsak [46], Juhasz [59], Vadocz [63]	7 000	Blom NED
31-05	Croatia	D	1-1	Budapest	Fr	Kovac.N OG [45]	10 000	Ledentu FRA
20-08	Montenegro	D	3-3	Budapest	Fr	Priskin [29], Hajnal 2 [55 87p]	4 913	Havrilla SVK
6-09	Denmark	D	0-0	Budapest	WCq		18 984	Hamer LUX
10-09	Sweden	L	1-2	Stockholm	WCq	Rudolf [93+]	28 177	Meyer GER
11-10	Albania	W	2-0	Budapest	WCq	Torghelle [49], Juhasz [82]	18 000	Circhetta SUI
15-10	Malta	W	1-0	Ta'Qali	WCq	Torghelle [23]	4 797	Valgeirsson ISL
19-11	Northern Ireland	W	2-0	Belfast	Fr	Torghelle [57], Gera [71]	6 251	Schoergenhofer AUT
2009								
11-02	Israel	L	0-1	Tel Aviv	Fr		9 500	Borski POL
28-03	Albania	W	1-0	Tirana	WCq	Torghelle [38]	12 000	Kuipers NED
1-04	Malta	W	3-0	Budapest	WCq	Hajnal [7], Gera [81], Juhasz [93+]	34 400	Sukhina RUS
12-08	Romania	L	0-1	Budapest	Fr		9 000	Vnuk SVK
5-09	Sweden	L	1-2	Budapest	WCq	Huszti [79p]	40 169	Rizzoli ITA
9-09	Portugal	L	0-1	Budapest	WCq		42 000	Lannoy FRA
10-10	Portugal	L	0-3	Lisbon	WCq		50 115	Hamer LUX
14-10	Denmark	W	1-0	Copenhagen	WCq	Buzsaky [35]	36 956	Meyer GER
14-11	Belgium	L	0-3	Ghent	Fr		8 000	Piccirillo FRA
2010								
3-03	Russia	D	1-1	Gyor	Fr	Vanczak [39]	10 000	Vucemilovic CRO
29-05	Germany	L	0-3	Budapest	Fr		14 000	Larsen DEN
5-06	Netherlands	L	1-6	Amsterdam	Fr	Dzsudzsak [6]	45 000	Meyer GER
11-08	England	L	1-2	London	Fr	OG [62]	72 024	Lannoy FRA
3-09	Sweden	L	0-2	Stockholm	ECq		32 304	Atkinson ENG
7-09	Moldova	W	2-1	Budapest	ECq	Rudolf [50], Koman [66]	9 209	Kovarik CZE
8-10	San Marino	W	8-0	Budapest	ECq	Rudolf 2 [11 25], Szalai 3 [18 27 48], Koman [60], Dzsudzsak [89], Gera [93+p]	10 596	Kaasik EST
12-10	Finland	W	2-1	Helsinki	ECq	Szalai [50], Dzsudzsak [94+]	18 532	Kelly IRL
17-11	Lithuania	W	2-0	Szekesfehervar	Fr	Priskin [61], Dzsudzsak [80]	4 500	Nijhuis NED

Fr = Friendly match • EC = UEFA EURO 2008/2012 • WC = FIFA World Cup • q = qualifier

HUNGARY NATIONAL TEAM HISTORICAL RECORDS

Caps

101 - Jozsek Bozsik 1947-62 • 92 - Laszlo Fazekas 1968-83 • 86 - Gyula Grosics 1947-62 • 85 - Ferenc Puskas 1945-56 • 82 - Imre Garaba 1980-91 • 81 - Sandor Matrai 1956-67 • 78 - Gabor Kiraly 1998- • 77 - Ferenc Sipos 1957-66 • 76 - Ferenc Bene 1962-79 & Mate Fenyvesi 1954-66 • 75 - Florian Albert 1959-74 & Karoly Sandor 1949-64 • 72 - Lajos Tichy 1955-64 • 70 - Jozsef Kiprich 1984-95 & Tibor Nyilasi 1975-85 • 69 - Nandor Hidegkuti 1945-58 • 68 - Imre Schlosser 1906-27; Sandor Kocsis 1948-56 & Zoltan Gera 2002-

Goals

84 - Ferenc Puskas 1945-56 • 75 - Sandor Kocsis 1948-56 • 59 - Imre Schlosser 1906-27 • 51 - Lajos Tichy 1955-64 • 42 - Gyorgy Sarosi 1931-43 • 39 - Nandor Hidegkuti 1945-58 • 36 - Ferenc Bene 1962-79 • 32 - Gyula Zsengeller 1935-47 & Tibor Nyilasi 1975-85 • 31 - Florian Albert 1959-74 • 29 - Ferenc Deak 1946-49 • 28 - Jozsef Kiprich 1984-95 • 27 - Karoly Sandor 1949-64 • 26 - Jozsef Takacs 1923-33 • 25 - Geza Toldi 1929-40 • 24 - Istvan Avar 1929-35 & Laszlo Fazekas 1968-83 • 21 - Mihaly Pataki 1912-20

Past Coaches

Ferenc Gillemot 1902-04 • Ferenc Stobbe 1904-06 • Alfred Hajos 1906 • Ferenc Stobbe 1907-08 • Frigyes Minder 1908-11 • Ede Herczog 1911-14 • Frigyes Minder 1914-17 • Akos Fehery 1918-19 • Frigyes Minder 1919 • Jozsef Harsady 1920 • Lajos Tibor 1920 • Gyula Kiss 1921-24 • Odon Holits 1924 • Lajos Mariassy 1924-26 • Gyula Kiss 1926-28 • Janos Foldessy 1928-29 • Mihaly Pataki 1930 • Frigyes Minder 1930 • Lajos Mariassy 1930-32 • Odon Nadas 1932-34 • Karoly Dietz 1934-39 • Denes Ginzery 1939-41 • Jozsef Fabian 1941 • Denes Ginzery 1941 • Jozsef Fabian 1942 • Kalman Vaghy 1942-43 • Tibor Gallowich 1945-48 • Gusztav Sebes 1949-56 • Marton Bukovi, Lajos Baroti & Karoly Lakat 1956-57 • Karoly Sos 1957 • Lajos Baroti 1957-66 • Rudolf Illovszky 1966-67 • Karoly Sos 1968-69 • Jozsef Hoffer 1970-71 • Rudolf Illovszky 1971-74 • Jozsef Bozsik 1974 • Ede Moor 1974-75 • Janos Szocs 1975 • Lajos Baroti 1975-78 • Ferenc Kovacs 1978-79 • Karoly Lakat 1979-80 • Kalman Meszoly 1980-83 • Gyorgy Mezey 1983-86 • Imre Komora 1986 • Jozsef Verebes 1987 • Jozsef Garami 1987 • Laszlo Balint 1988 • Gyorgy Mezey 1988 • Bertalan Bicskei 1989 • Kalman Meszoly 1990-91 • Robert Glazer 1991 • Imre Jenei ROU 1992-93 • Ferenc Puskas 1993 • Jozsef Verebes 1993-94 • Kalman Meszoly 1994-95 • Janos Csank 1996-97 • Bertalan Bicskei 1998-01 • Imre Gellei 2001-03 • Lothar Matthaus GER 2004-05 • Peter Bozsik 2006 • Peter Varhidi 2006-08 • Erwin Koeman NED 2008-2010 • Sandor Egervari 2010-

HUNGARY 2009-10

SOPRONI LIGA NB I

	Pl	W	D	L	F	A	Pts	Debrecen	Videoton	Györi ETO	Ujpest	Zalaegerszeg	MTK	Ferencváros	Szombathelyi	Honvéd	Kecskeméti	Pápa	Kaposvár	Vasas	Paksi	Nyiregyháza	Diósgyör
Debreceni VSC †	30	20	2	8	63	37	62		3-2	0-0	1-2	5-3	2-0	2-1	2-1	2-1	1-0	2-0	5-1	3-0	3-1	3-1	3-1
Videoton ‡	30	18	7	5	59	31	61	3-0		0-0	1-1	1-2	0-1	0-0	4-2	2-0	2-0	2-0	2-0	3-0	3-0	1-0	3-2
Györi ETO ‡	30	15	12	3	38	18	57	1-0	1-0		0-0	1-1	2-0	2-1	1-1	2-0	1-0	1-1	1-1	1-1	3-1	2-1	3-1
Ujpest FC	30	17	4	9	48	39	55	2-1	0-1	0-3		2-1	3-2	2-1	3-1	0-1	3-1	0-3	2-1	1-0	3-2	3-1	4-1
Zalaegerszegi TE ‡	30	15	8	7	59	45	53	4-1	2-2	1-1	1-4		1-0	3-3	3-0	0-1	3-2	3-0	0-3	4-1	2-1	4-3	3-0
MTK Hungária	30	12	7	11	52	41	43	2-3	2-2	0-0	4-5	1-0		1-1	0-0	2-1	0-1	0-0	4-0	2-3	1-1	4-0	4-0
Ferencvárosi TC	30	10	11	9	34	35	41	1-0	2-2	1-0	0-1	4-1	2-1		2-1	0-0	3-2	2-0	0-0	1-1	1-1	0-0	0-3
Szombathelyi Haladás	30	10	9	11	46	49	39	0-2	4-3	1-2	1-0	1-1	2-0	0-0		2-2	3-3	4-2	2-1	0-1	4-0	2-0	2-1
Budapest Honvéd	30	9	11	10	38	35	38	1-2	0-0	0-0	1-1	0-1	4-1	2-0	0-0		0-1	1-3	3-1	3-3	1-1	1-1	4-2
Kecskeméti TE	30	10	7	13	50	56	37	1-0	3-6	2-0	2-1	2-2	2-5	3-1	2-3	2-2		2-2	3-1	5-1	1-1	2-2	1-1
Lombard Pápa TFC	30	10	5	15	39	52	35	1-5	0-1	1-0	1-0	1-2	0-1	0-1	1-3	0-3	2-0		3-1	4-1	1-0	5-1	2-1
Kaposvári Rákóczi	30	8	8	14	38	50	32	4-4	1-3	1-3	2-0	1-1	1-2	0-0	3-0	1-0	2-1	3-1		1-0	1-1	1-1	2-2
Vasas SC	30	8	7	15	39	61	31	2-4	2-4	0-2	1-2	2-3	2-0	3-2	0-0	2-2	0-1	2-1	1-0		3-1	2-3	1-0
Paksi SE	30	7	10	13	31	44	31	0-1	1-2	1-1	1-0	1-2	0-2	1-2	2-0	2-1	2-1	2-2	2-0	2-2		1-0	1-0
Nyíregyháza	30	6	9	15	41	60	27	0-3	2-3	1-3	2-2	0-4	1-1	3-1	3-3	0-1	2-3	3-1	2-1	5-1	1-1		1-1
Diósgyöri VTK	30	4	5	21	31	56	17	1-0	0-1	0-1	1-2	1-1	2-5	0-1	1-3	1-2	4-1	3-0	1-3	0-1	0-0	0-1	

24/07/2009 - 23/05/2010 • † Qualified for the UEFA Champions League • ‡ Qualified for the UEFA Cup
Top scorers: 18 - Nemanja Nikolic SRB, Kaposvar/Videoton • 15 - Andre Alves BRA, Videoton • 14 - Peter Kabat, Ujpest; Artjoms Rudnevs LVA, Zalaegerszegi & Adamo Coulibaly FRA, Debrecen • 13 - Janos Lazok, Vasas • 12 - Tibor Montvai, Kecskemeti & Tarmo Kink EST, Gyor

HUNGARY 2009-10 NB II NYUGATI (WEST)

	Pl	W	D	L	F	A	Pts
Bodajk FC Siófok	28	20	3	5	49	20	63
Gyirmót SE	28	19	5	4	56	25	62
Pécsi MFC	28	16	7	5	56	25	55
FC Ajka	28	14	5	9	47	45	47
FC Tatabánya	28	14	3	11	49	41	45
Kozármisleny SE	28	11	8	9	42	35	41
Györi ETO II	28	9	12	7	43	31	39
Szigetszentmiklosi §1	28	10	9	9	43	45	38
Videoton FC II	28	10	6	12	41	43	36
Budaörsi SC	28	9	6	13	38	47	33
Kaposvölgye VSC	28	8	7	13	36	44	31
Budapest-Honvéd II	28	6	9	13	29	54	27
Barcsi FC	28	6	5	17	25	45	23
Hévíz FC	28	5	5	18	23	55	20
Zalaegerszegi TE II	28	4	8	16	29	51	20

7/08/2009 - 12/06/2010 • § = points deducted

HUNGARY 2009-10 NB II KELETI (EAST)

	Pl	W	D	L	F	A	Pts
Szolnoki MAV	28	18	6	4	54	28	60
Debreceni VSC II	28	17	4	7	53	26	55
Dunakanyar-Vac FC	28	15	7	6	47	36	52
Rákospalotai EAC	28	15	5	8	76	36	50
Mezokövesdi SE	28	11	9	8	37	35	42
Vecsési FC	28	11	8	9	45	32	41
Makói FC	28	11	5	12	46	46	38
BKV Elöre	28	9	11	8	38	39	38
Bocsi KSC	28	9	11	8	33	36	38
Hajdúböszörményi TE	28	10	7	11	33	36	37
MTK-Hungária II	28	10	5	13	53	48	35
Kazincbarcika SC	28	9	5	14	35	50	32
Békéscsabai Elore FC	28	7	7	14	31	44	28
Ceglédi VSE	28	6	9	13	40	53	27
Baktalórántgáza VSE §6	28	1	3	24	21	97	0

8/08/2009 - 13/06/2010 • § = points deducted

MEDALS TABLE

		Overall			League			Cup			Europe			City
		G	S	B	G	S	B	G	S	B	G	S	B	
1	Ferencvárosi TC	49	45	22	28	34	20	20	9		1	2	2	Budapest
2	MTK Hungária	35	23	16	23	20	15	12	2		1	1		Budapest
3	Ujpest FC	28	28	20	20	21	18	8	6		1	2		Budapest
4	Budapest Honvéd	20	22	5	13	12	5	7	10					Budapest
5	Vasas SC	10	5	14	6	2	13	4	3		1			Budapest
6	Debreceni VSC	9	3	3	5	1	3	4	2					Debrecen
7	Györi ETO	7	5	6	3	2	5	4	3		1			Györ
8	Csepel SC	4		2	4		2							Budapest
9	Diósgyöri VTK	2	3	1			1	2	3					Miskolc
10	Budapest TC	2	2	3	2	1	3		1					Budapest
11	Videoton	1	5	3		2	3	1	2			1		Székesfehérvár
12	Dunakanyar-Vac	1	5		1	2			3					Vác
13	Pécsi MFC	1	3	1		1	1	1	2					Pécs
14	Zalaegerszeg TE	1	1	1	1		1		1					Zalaegerszeg

MAGYAR KUPA 2009-10

Fourth Round

Team	Score
Debreceni VSC	8
Nírfmadai ISE *	2
Debreceni VSC II	2
Mezőkövesdi SE *	4
Diósgyőri VTK	4
Nyírbátor FC *	0
Turai VSK *	0
MTK-Hungária	6
Győri ETO	5
FC Ajka *	1
Gyirmót SE	1 4p
Kaposvári Rákóczi	1 5p
Szolnoki MAV	4
Rákospalotai EAC *	1
Dunakanyar-Vac FC *	0
Budapest Honvéd	2
Ujpesti FC	4
MTK Hungária II *	0
Ceglédi VSE *	1
Kecskeméti TE	3
Lombard Pápa TFC	2
FC Tatabánya *	1
Pálhalmai SE *	1
Videoton	4
Szigetszentmiklosi	1
Tököl KSK *	0
Paksi SE	0
Kaposvölgye VSC *	1
Szombathelyi Haladás	1
Bajai LSE *	0
Pécsi MFC *	0
Zalaegerszegi TE	1

Round of 16

Team	Score
Debreceni VSC	4 4
Mezőkövesdi SE *	1 3
Diósgyőri VTK	0 0
MTK-Hungária *	3 3
Győri ETO *	1 2
Kaposvári Rákóczi	1 0
Szolnoki MAV *	4 0
Budapest Honvéd	1 3
Ujpesti FC	5 6
Kecskeméti TE *	2 2
Lombard Pápa TFC	0 0
Videoton *	3 0
Szigetszentmiklosi	2 3
Kaposvölgye VSC *	2 2
Szombathelyi Haladás *	0 1
Zalaegerszegi TE	2 1

Quarter-finals

Team	Score
Debreceni VSC *	2 0 5p
MTK-Hungária	0 2 4p
Győri ETO	1 0
Budapest-Honvéd *	1 1
Ujpesti FC	1 1
Videoton *	0 0
Szigetszentmiklosi *	0 1
Zalaegerszegi TE	3 3

Semi-finals

Team	Score
Debreceni VSC	1 2
Budapest-Honvéd *	1 1
Ujpest FC *	0 0
Zalaegerszegi TE	1 0

Final

Team	Score
Debreceni VSC	3
Zalaegerszegi TE ‡	2

CUP FINAL

Puskas Ferenc, Budapest
26-05-2010, 19:00, Att: 5000, Ref: Vad
Scorers - Coulibaly 2 [24] [68], Yannick [30] for DVSC; Pavicevic [41], Rudnevs [70] for ZTE
DVSC - Istvan Verpecz - Csaba Bernath (c), Adam Komlosi●, Mirsad Mijadinoski, Zsolt Laczko● - Peter Szakaly, Adam Bodi (Jozsef Varga 90), Zoltan Szelesi, Peter Czvitkovics (Zoltan Kiss 82) - Mbengono Yannick (Laszlo Rezes● 44), Adamo Coulibaly. Tr: Andras Herczeg
ZTE - Geza Vlaszak - Gergely Kocsardi (c) (Prince Rajcomar 77), Matej Miljatovic, Milan Bogunovic, Peter Mate● - Marian Sluka (Zsolt Balazs 61), Andras Horvath, Dorde Kamber, Gyula Illes - Artjoms Rudnevs, Darko Pavicevic. Tr: Janos Csank

* Home team in the first leg ● ‡ Qualified for the Europa League

IDN – INDONESIA

FIFA/COCA-COLA WORLD RANKING

1993	1994	1995	1996	1997	1998	1999	2000	2001	2002	2003	2004	2005	2006	2007	2008	2009	2010
106	134	130	119	91	87	90	97	87	110	91	91	109	153	133	139	120	127

					2010							Hi/Lo
Jan	Feb	Mar	Mar	Apr	May	Jul	Aug	Sep	Oct	Nov	Dec	76
120	136	137	138	137	137	138	135	131	141	135	127	153

Under former Vietnam and Laos coach Alfred Riedl, Indonesia reached the final of the AFF Suzuki Cup for the fourth time but once again failed to win what is Southeast Asia's premier football tournament. 88,000 expectant fans crammed into the Gelora Bung Karno Stadium in Jakarta for the second leg of the final against Malaysia to see if the Indonesians could overturn a 3-0 defeat from the first leg but a 2-1 victory wasn't enough. Riedl's team had looked certainties to win the title after the group stage in which they had beaten the Malaysians 5-1 but they quickly went off the boil and only just managed to scrape past the Philippines in the semi-finals. Earlier in the year Indonesia had finished bottom of an AFC Asian Cup qualifying group that featured Australia, Oman and Kuwait, missing out on the finals for the first time since 1992. Domestically the game has been hit with controversy off the pitch, with a new league set up to rival the Indonesian Super League, which was won in 2010 by Arema FC. The Indonesia Premier League, which kicked-off in January 2011, is not sanctioned by the Indonesia Football Association but has attracted 19 clubs to its first season - fifteen of them new clubs with four joining from the Super League. Indonesian players who join the league have been told they will not be eligible for national team selection.

FIFA WORLD CUP RECORD

1930-1934 DNE **1938** 15 r1 1950-1954 DNE 1958 DNQ 1962-1970 DNE 1974-2010 DNQ

FOOTBALL ASSOCIATION OF INDONESIA (PSSI)

Gelora Bung Karno,
Pintu X-XI, Senayan,
PO Box 2305, Jakarta 10023

☎ +62 21 5704762
📠 +62 21 5734386
✉ pssi@pssi-football.com
🖥 www.pssi-football.com
FA 1930 CON 1954 FIFA 1952
P Nurdin Halid
GS Nugraha Besoes

FIFA BIG COUNT 2006

Total players	7 094 260
% of population	2.89%
Male	7 094 260
Female	0
Amateurs 18+	2 560
Youth under 18	62 600
Unregistered	6 982 300
Professionals	800
Referees	669
Admin & coaches	400
Number of clubs	73
Number of teams	73

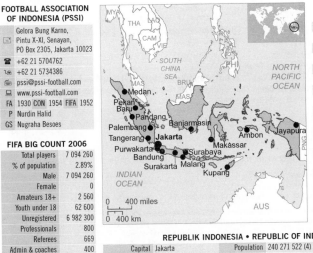

MAJOR CITIES/TOWNS

		Population
1	Jakarta	8 579 263
2	Surabaya	2 336 843
3	Medan	1 772 833
4	Bekasi	1 724 003
5	Bandung	1 601 767
6	Tangerang	1 495 586
7	Depok	1 442 313
8	Makasar	1 440 539
9	Semarang	1 283 279
10	Palembang	1 271 855
11	Padang	960 184
12	BandarLampung	916 561
13	Bogor	834 098
14	Pekan Baru	763 275
15	Malang	755 371
16	Yogyakarta	703 753
17	Banjarmasin	606 831
18	Surakarta	563 208
19	Manado	508 585

REPUBLIK INDONESIA • REPUBLIC OF INDONESIA

Capital	Jakarta	Population	240 271 522 (4)	% in cities	52%
GDP per capita	$3900 (155)	Area km²	1 904 569 km² (16)	GMT +/-	+7
Neighbours (km)	Timor-Leste 228, Malaysia 1782, Papua New Guinea 820 • Coast 54716				

RECENT INTERNATIONAL MATCHES PLAYED BY INDONESIA

2008	Opponents	Score		Venue	Comp	Scorers	Att	Referee
25-04	Yemen	W	1-0	Bandung	Fr	Bambang Pamungkas [30]		
6-06	Malaysia	D	1-1	Surabaya	Fr	Bambang Pamungkas [25p]		
11-06	Vietnam	W	1-0	Surabaya	Fr	Bambang Pamungkas [12p]		
21-08	Cambodia	W	7-0	Jakarta	Fr	Charis Yulianto [8], Budi Sunarsono 4 [11 28 30 36], Muhammad Ilham [51], Bambang Pamungkas [88]	1 200	
25-08	Myanmar	W	4-0	Jakarta	Fr	Arif Suyono 2 [6 19], Budi Sunarsono [48], Bambang Pamungkas [77]		
13-11	Bangladesh	W	2-0	Yangon	Fr	Firman Utina [10], Talaohu Musyafri [45]		
15-11	Myanmar	L	1-2	Yangon	Fr	Ismed Sofyan [38]		
21-11	Myanmar	L	1-2	Yangon	Fr	Moe Win OG [14]	20 000	
5-12	Myanmar	W	3-0	Jakarta	AFFrl	Budi Sunarsono [24], Firman Utina [28], Bambang Pamungkas [64]	40 000	Ramachandran MAS
7-12	Cambodia	W	4-0	Jakarta	AFFrl	Budi Sunarsono 3 [15 54 70], Bambang Pamungkas [76]	30 000	Nafeez MAS
9-12	Singapore	L	0-2	Jakarta	AFFrl		50 000	Ramachandran MAS
16-12	Thailand	L	0-1	Jakarta	AFFsf		70 000	Vo Minh Tri VIE
20-12	Thailand	L	1-2	Bangkok	AFFsf	OG [9]	40 000	Hadimin BRU
2009								
19-01	Oman	D	0-0	Muscat	ACq		13 000	Shamsuzzaman BAN
28-01	Australia	D	0-0	Jakarta	ACq		50 000	Abdul Bashir SIN
4-11	Singapore	L	1-3	Singapore	Fr	Eka Ramdani [12]		
14-11	Kuwait	L	1-2	Kuwait City	ACq	Bambang Pamungkas [33]	16 000	Kovalenko UZB
18-11	Kuwait	D	1-1	Jakarta	ACq	Budi Sunarsono [45]	36 000	Tojo JPN
2010								
6-01	Oman	L	1-2	Jakarta	ACq	Boaz Salossa [45]	45 000	Mohd Salleh MAS
3-03	Australia	L	0-1	Brisbane	ACq		20 422	Ogiya JPN
8-10	Uruguay	L	1-7	Jakarta	Fr	Boaz Salossa [18]	25 000	Daud SIN
12-10	Maldives	W	3-0	Bandung	Fr	Oktavianus Maniani [30], Yongki Aribowo [74], Tony Sucipto [90]	13 000	Palaniyandi SIN
21-11	Timor-Leste	W	6-0	Palembang	Fr	Muhammad Ridwan [12], Oktavianus Maniani [26], Cristian Gonzales 2 [37 46], Bambang Pamungkas [70], Yongki Aribowo [83]		
24-11	Chinese Taipei	W	2-0	Palembang	Fr	Cristian Gonzales [10], Firman Utina [18p]		Singh SIN
1-12	Malaysia	W	5-1	Jakarta	AFFrl	OG [22], Cristian Gonzales [33], Muhammad Ridwan [52], Arif Suyono [76], Irfan Bachdim [94+]	62 000	Vo Min Tri VIE
4-12	Laos	W	6-0	Jakarta	AFFrl	Firman Utina 2 [26p 51], Muhammad Ridwan [33], Irfan Bachdim [63], Arif Suyono [77], Oktavianus Maniani [82]	70 000	Daud SIN
7-12	Thailand	W	2-1	Jakarta	AFFrl	Bambang Pamungkas 2 [82 91+]	65 000	Sato JPN
16-12	Philippines	W	1-0	Jakarta	AFFsf	Cristian Gonzales [32]	70 000	Moradi IRN
19-12	Philippines	W	1-0	Jakarta	AFFsf	Cristian Gonzales [43]	88 000	Ebrahim BHR
26-12	Malaysia	L	0-3	Kuala Lumpur	AFFf		70 000	Toma JPN
29-12	Malaysia	W	2-1	Jakarta	AFFf	Mohammad Nasuha [72], Muhammad Ridwan [88]	88 000	Green AUS

Fr = Friendly match • AFF = ASEAN Football Federation Championship • AC = AFC Asian Cup • WC = FIFA World Cup
q = qualifier • r1 = first round group • sf = semi-final • f = final

INDONESIA NATIONAL TEAM HISTORICAL RECORDS

Caps	**86** - Bambang Pamungkas 1999-
Goals	**31** - Bambang Pamungkas 1999- • **31** - Kurniawan Dwi Yulianto 1995-2005 • **16** - Budi Sudarsono 2001- & Rochy Putiray 1991-2004
Past Coaches	Johannes van Mastenbroek NED 1938 • Choo Seng Quee SIN 1951-53 • Antun Pogacnik YUG 1954-64 • EA Mangindaan 1966-70 • Endang Witarsa 1970 • Djamiaat Dalhar 1971-72 • Suwardi Arland 1972-74 • Aang Witarsa 1974-75 • Wiel Coerver NED 1975-76 • Suwardi Arland 1976-78 • Frans Van Balkom NED 1978-79 • Marek Janota 1979-80 • Bernd Fischer GER 1980-81 • Harry Tjong 1981-82 • Sinyo Aliandoe 1982-83 • M. Basri, Iswadi Idris and Abdul Kadir 1983-84 • Bertje Matulapelwa 1985-87 • Anatoli Polosin URS 1987-91 • Ivan Toplak YUG 1991-93 • Romano Matte ITA 1993-95 • Danurwindo 1995-96 • Henk Wullems NED 1996-97 • Rusdy Bahalwan 1998 • Bernard Schumm 1999 • Nandar Iskandar 1999-00 • Benny Dollo 2000-01 • Ivan Kolev BUL 2002-04 • Peter Withe ENG 2004-07 • Ivan Kolev BUL 2007 • Benny Dollo 2008-10 • Alfred Riedl AUT 2010-

INDONESIA 2009-10

DJARUM INDONESIA SUPER LEAGUE (ISL)

	Pl	W	D	L	F	A	Pts	Arema	Persipura	Persiba	Persib	Persija	Persiwa	PSPS	Sriwijaya	Persijap	Persema	Bontang	Persisam	PSM	Persela	Pelita Jaya	Persik	Persebaya	Persitara
Arema Malang †	34	23	4	7	57	22	**73**		2-1	1-2	0-0	1-0	1-0	0-0	3-0	3-1	3-1	3-0	2-1	3-0	2-1	6-1	3-0	1-0	2-0
Persipura Jayapura ‡	34	18	13	3	62	32	67	4-1		1-1	1-0	0-0	1-1	2-1	1-2	1-0	5-0	5-1	2-2	2-1	2-0	3-1	1-0	2-1	2-2
Persiba Balikpapan	34	15	9	10	44	31	54	1-0	0-0		2-0	2-0	1-0	3-0	4-0	1-0	1-1	0-0	1-0	2-1	3-0	5-0	2-0	1-2	
Persib Bandung	34	16	5	13	50	36	53	1-0	0-0	1-2		0-0	3-0	3-1	1-0	4-0	2-1	2-0	2-0	2-0	2-1	6-1	4-2	2-0	
Persija Jakarta	34	14	10	10	41	36	52	1-5	0-2	3-0	2-2		0-3	2-0	1-0	0-0	1-0	3-0	1-0	2-0	1-0	1-1	0-0	4-3	3-0
Persiwa Wamena	34	15	5	14	57	56	50	0-2	2-2	4-0	2-0	3-0		1-1	3-0	3-1	2-1	4-0	1-0	3-0	5-0	1-0	2-0	1-0	3-0
PSPS Pekanbaru	34	14	7	13	43	37	49	1-1	0-1	2-1	3-0	1-0	5-0		2-0	0-0	2-2	3-0	2-0	3-0	0-0	2-1	1-0	4-1	1-0
Sriwijaya Palembang ‡	34	14	6	14	48	49	48	1-0	1-2	3-3	1-1	1-1	4-1	1-0		4-0	3-0	1-2	3-0	2-0	2-1	3-1	1-1	2-1	3-2
Persijap Jepara	34	13	7	14	40	45	46	0-1	1-2	3-1	2-1	2-1	4-1	1-0	1-1		3-1	1-0	1-1	0-1	3-1	1-0	1-1	1-0	3-0
Persema Malang	34	13	6	15	43	52	45	1-3	2-1	2-1	3-0	1-3	1-0	3-2	1-0	3-1		1-0	0-1	1-1	1-2	2-2	3-1	3-1	3-0
Bontang	34	12	8	14	53	52	44	1-2	2-2	0-0	0-2	2-6	1-0	3-1	4-1	1-2			2-1	3-0	4-1	4-2	3-0	5-1	2-1
Persisam Putra	34	12	8	14	38	41	44	0-1	2-2	2-1	2-1	0-0	2-2	2-0	1-0	5-0	1-0	3-1		1-0	2-0	0-2	1-1	3-1	1-3
PSM Makassar	34	12	7	15	31	46	43	0-2	1-1	1-0	2-1	2-1	2-0	1-2	1-1	1-0	1-1	1-0	3-0		0-0	0-0	5-3	2-0	2-1
Persela Lamongan	34	12	6	16	45	55	42	1-0	1-3	0-1	1-0	3-4	7-2	3-1	3-1	2-2	2-0	1-0	1-0	0-0		2-1	3-1	0-0	1-0
Pelita Jaya Karawang	34	10	9	15	42	53	39	0-2	2-2	2-1	2-1	0-2	3-1	0-0	3-2	1-0	0-0	0-0	1-0	3-1	6-3		1-1	2-2	1-0
Persik Kediri	34	10	9	15	41	55	39	0-1	2-2	1-0	1-3	2-1	3-0	0-1	2-3	2-1	2-2	0-0	4-0	3-2	2-1			0-3	1-1
Persebaya Surabaya	34	10	6	18	42	58	36	2-0	0-1	0-0	2-1	0-0	5-4	0-1	0-2	1-1	1-0	2-2	5-2	2-0	2-0	2-1	0-1		3-2
Persitara Jakarta Utara	34	7	7	20	36	57	28	0-0	0-3	1-1	2-1	0-1	1-1	5-2	5-1	0-2	1-2	1-1	1-0	1-2	2-2	1-0	1-0	1-2	

11/10/2009 - 30/05/2010 • † Qualified for the AFC Champions League • ‡ Qualified for the AFC Cup
Relegation play-off: **Pelita Jaya** 0-0 4-2p Persiram Raja Ampat
Top scorers: **19** - Aldo Barreto PAR, Bontang • **18** - Christian Gonzalez URU, Persib & Alberto Goncalves BRA, Persipura • **17** - Boaz Solossa, Persipura & Lewis Weeks LBR, Persiwa • **16** - Dzumafo Herman CMR, PSPS

DIVISIE UTAMA (2) PLAY-OFFS (DELAPAN BESAR)

First round

Group A (in Bone)

	Pl	W	D	L	F	A	Pts	SP	PB	PSMP
Persiram Raja Ampat†	3	2	1	0	6	3	7	1-1	2-1	3-1
Semem Padang †	3	1	2	0	4	3	5		1-1	2-1
Persiba Bantul	3	1	1	1	6	4	4			4-1
PS Mojokerto Putra	3	0	0	2	3	9	0			

Group B (in Sidoarjo)

	Pl	W	D	L	F	A	Pts	PB	PD	PB
Delta Putra Sidoarjo †	3	2	1	0	5	3	7	2-1	2-1	1-1
Persibo Bojonegoro †	3	2	0	1	3	2	6		1-0	1-0
Persidafon Dafonsoro	3	1	0	2	5	6	3			4-3
Persipasi Bekasi	3	0	1	2	4	6	1			

18/05/2010 -29/05/2010 • † Qualified for the next round • Persibo, Deltras and Semen promoted to ISL

Semi-finals

Persibo Bojonegoro	1
Persiram Raja Ampat	0

Semem Padang	0 2p
Delta Putra Sidoarjo	0 4p

Final

Persibo Bojonegoro	0 3p
Delta Putra Sidoarjo	0 1p

3rd place play-off

Semem Padang	1
Persiram Raja Ampat	0

MEDALS TABLE

		Overall			Lge		Cup		Asia			City
		G	S	B	G	S	G	S	G	S	B	
1	Persija Jakarta	11	6		11	5	1					Jakarta
2	Persis Solo	8	1		8	1						Solo
3	Persebaya Surabaya	7	11		7	11						Surabaya
4	Tiga Berlian	7	1	1	4	1	3				1	Palembang
5	Persib Bandung	6	8		6	8						Bandung
	PSM Makasar	6	8		6	8						Makassar
7	PSMS Medan	6	7		6	7						Medan
8	Arema Malang	4	2		2		2	2				Malang
9	Sriwijaya Palembang	4			1		3					Palembang
10	Pelita Jaya	3	5		3	2	3					Karawang
	Persipura Jayapura	3	5		3	2	3					Jayapura
12	Mitra Kukar	3	2		3	1	1					Tenggarong
13	Arseto	2	1		1	1	1					Solo
	PSIS Semarang	2	1		2	1						Semarang
15	Persik Kediri	2			2							Kediri

PIALA INDONESIA 2009–10

First Stage

	Pts
Sriwijaya Palembang	7
Persikabo Bogor	6
PSPS Pekanbaru	2
Semen Padang	1
Persija Jakarta	7
Persela Lamongan	7
Persikab Bandung	1
Persiba Bantul	1
Persib Bandung	9
Pelita Jaya	6
Persita Tangerang	1
Persipasi Bekasi	1
Persik Kediri	9
Persibo Bojonegoro	6
PSBI Blitar	3
Persitara Jakarta Utara	0
Arema Malang	9
PSMP Mojokerto	6
Persijap Jepara	3
Deltras Sidoarjo	0
Persebaya Surabaya	7
Persidafon Dafonsoro	6
Persema Malang	3
Persipro Probolinggo	1
Persisam Samarinda	9
Bontang FC	4
Persiba Balikpapan	4
Persemalra Tual	0
Persipura Jayapura	9
PSM Makassar	6
Persiwa Wamena	3
Persiram Raja Ampat	0

Round of 16

	Pts
Persija Jakarta	7
Sriwijaya Palembang	5
Persisam Samarinda	4
PSMP Mojokerto	0
Persebaya Surabaya	7
Persib Bandung	5
Persibo Bojonegoro	4
Bontang FC	0
Arema Malang	9
Pelita Jaya	4
Persidafon Dafonsoro	3
Persela Lamongan	1
Persipura Jayapura	9
Persik Kediri	6
PSM Makassar	1
Persikabo Bogor	1

Quarter-finals

Sriwijaya Palembang *	2	0
Persebaya Surabaya	0	1
Pelita Jaya *	1	0
Persipura Jayapura	6	1
Persik Kediri	3	2
Persija Jakarta *	4	0
Persib Bandung	0	2
Arema Malang *	3	0

Semi-finals

Sriwijaya Palembang	2	3p
Persipura Jayapura	2	1p
Persik Kediri	0	
Arema Malang	4	

Final

Sriwijaya Palembang ‡	2
Arema Malang	1

PIALA INDONESIA FINAL

Manahan Stadium, Solo
1-08-2010. Att: 30 000. Ref: Napitupulu
Scorers – Gumbs 47, Solomin 80 for Sriwijaya; Ridhuan 72 for Arema
Sriwijaya – Ferry Rotinsulu (Hendro Kartiko 22) – Ambrizal, Charis Yulianto● (c), Precious Emuejeraye, Isnan Ali● (Mohammad Nasuha 46) – Tony Sucipto, Zah Rahan Krangar, Ponaryo Astaman – Keith Gumbs, Pavel Solomin (Alamsyah Nasution 90), Anoure Richad. Tr: Rahmad Darmawan
Arema – Kurnia Hermansyah – Zulkifli Syukur, Waluyo, Irfan Raditya (Rachmat Affandi 82), Benny Wahyudi – Ahmad Bustomi, Juan Revi● (Ronny Firmansyah 90) – Muhammad Ridhuan●, Roman Chmelo●, Muhammad Fakhrudin (Dendi Santoso 67) – Noh Alam Shah◆19. Tr: Robert Alberts

* Home team in the first leg ● Semi-finals played at Delta Stadium, Sidoarjo
‡ Qualified for the AFC Cup
Third place play-off: Persik Kediri 1-0 Persipura Jayapura

IND – INDIA

FIFA/COCA-COLA WORLD RANKING

1993	1994	1995	1996	1997	1998	1999	2000	2001	2002	2003	2004	2005	2006	2007	2008	2009	2010
100	109	121	120	112	110	106	122	121	127	127	132	127	157	143	143	134	142

2010												Hi/Lo
Jan	Feb	Mar	Mar	Apr	May	Jul	Aug	Sep	Oct	Nov	Dec	**94**
134	130	132	132	132	133	132	138	160	144	142	142	**165**

India returned to the finals of the AFC Asian Cup for the first time since 1984 when they played in the 2011 edition in Qatar but as expected Bob Houghton's team lost all three games in a tough group that featured Australia, Bahrain and Korea Republic. They were able to console themselves with the fact they scored three times during the tournament, with USA-based striker Sunil Chhetri finding the back of the net against the Bahrainis and Koreans but the tournament brought home to the All India Football Federation the stark contrast between the standard of the game in their own nation and elsewhere in Asia. Englishman Houghton, who has been at the helm of the national side since 2006, has regularly highlighted the fact that lack of infrastructure and facilities is holding the game back in India, an opinion shared by both the AFC president, Mohamed bin Hammam, on his visits to India and by various FIFA officials. However, the job of dragging football out from under the shadow of cricket will be a big one. The creation of the I-League in 1997 was an important first step and it is gradually expanding beyond its heartland of Goa and Kolkata but was won for the fourth time in six seasons by Goa's Dempo. The two major cup competitions - the Federation Cup and the Durand Cup were won by East Bengal and Chirag United, both from Kolkata.

FIFA WORLD CUP RECORD
1930-1982 DNE 1986 DNQ 1990 DNE 1994-2010 DNQ

ALL INDIA FOOTBALL FEDERATION (AIFF)

Football House, Sector 19,
Phase 1 Dwarka,
New Delhi 110075

☎ +91 11 28041430
🖷 +91 11 28041434
✉ gsaiff@gmail.com
🖥 www.the-aiff.com
FA 1937 CON 1954 FIFA 1948
P Praful Patel
GS Kushal Das

FIFA BIG COUNT 2006

Total players	20 587 900
% of population	1.88%
Male	19 020 900
Female	1 567 000
Amateurs 18+	71 000
Youth under 18	313 500
Unregistered	2 212 000
Professionals	400
Referees	17 640
Admin & coaches	21 000
Number of clubs	6 500
Number of teams	12 000

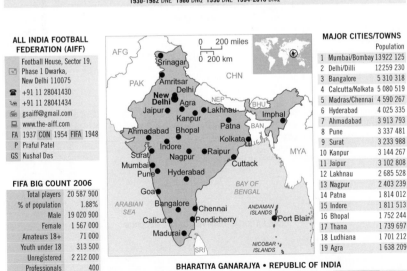

MAJOR CITIES/TOWNS

		Population
1	Mumbai/Bombay	13922 125
2	Delhi/Dilli	12259 230
3	Bangalore	5 310 318
4	Calcutta/Kolkata	5 080 519
5	Madras/Chennai	4 590 267
6	Hyderabad	4 025 335
7	Ahmadabad	3 913 793
8	Pune	3 337 481
9	Surat	3 233 988
10	Kanpur	3 144 267
11	Jaipur	3 102 808
12	Lakhnau	2 685 528
13	Nagpur	2 403 239
14	Patna	1 814 012
15	Indore	1 811 513
16	Bhopal	1 752 244
17	Thana	1 739 697
18	Ludhiana	1 701 212
19	Agra	1 638 209

BHARATIYA GANARAJYA • REPUBLIC OF INDIA

Capital	New Delhi	Population	1 166 079 217 (2)	% in cities	29%
GDP per capita	$2900 (167)	Area km²	3 287 263 km² (7)	GMT +/-	+5.5
Neighbours (km)	Bangladesh 4053, Bhutan 605, China 3380, Myanmar 1463, Nepal 1690, Pakistan 2912 • Coast 7000				

RECENT INTERNATIONAL MATCHES PLAYED BY INDIA

2007	Opponents	Score	Venue	Comp	Scorers	Att	Referee
17-08	Cambodia	W 6-0	New Delhi	Fr	Pradeep 16, Bhutia 45, Dias 2 73 90, Chetri 2 73 90		
20-08	Bangladesh	W 1-0	New Delhi	Fr	Bhutia 5		
23-08	Syria	L 2-3	New Delhi	Fr	Chetri 13, Ajayan 81		
26-08	Kyrgyzstan	W 3-0	New Delhi	Fr	Bhutia 39, Chetri 60, Yadav OG 93+		
29-08	Syria	W 1-0	New Delhi	Fr	Pradeep 44		
8-10	Lebanon	L 1-4	Sidon	WCq	Chetri 30	500	Al Fadhli KUW
30-10	Lebanon	D 2-2	Goa	WCq	Chetri 29, Dias 92+	10 000	Mujghef JOR
2008							
24-05	Chinese Taipei	W 3-0	Goa	Fr	Pradeep 58, Chetri 2 75 89		Arjunan IND
27-05	Chinese Taipei	D 2-2	Chennai	Fr	Pradeep 2		Suresh IND
3-06	Nepal	W 4-0	Male	SAFr1	Pradeep 26, Bhutia 34, Chetri 67, Sushil Singh 67		
5-06	Pakistan	W 2-1	Male	SAFr1	Pradeep 25, Dias 45		
7-06	Maldives	W 1-0	Male	SAFr1	Gouramangi Singh 14		
11-06	Bhutan	W 2-1	Male	SAFsf	Chetri 31, Gouramangi Singh 120		
14-06	Maldives	L 0-1	Colombo	SAFf			
22-07	Malaysia	D 1-1	Hyderabad	Fr	Bhutia 65		Suresh IND
30-07	Afghanistan	W 1-0	Hyderabad	CCr1	Lawrence 92+	300	Iemoto JPN
1-08	Tajikistan	D 1-1	Hyderabad	CCr1	Tuchiev OG 61	350	Shamsuzzaman BAN
3-08	Turkmenistan	W 2-1	Hyderabad	CCr1	Bhutia 2 54 80	1 000	Jasim UAE
7-08	Myanmar	W 1-0	Hyderabad	CCsf	Chetri 82	1 500	Shamsuzzaman BAN
13-08	Tajikistan	W 4-1	Delhi	CCf	Chetri 3 9 23 75, Bhutia 18	10 000	Kovalenko UZB
2009							
14-01	Hong Kong	L 1-2	Hong Kong	Fr	Bhutia 80	1 200	
19-08	Lebanon	L 0-1	New Delhi	Fr			Hannan BAN
23-08	Kyrgyzstan	W 2-1	New Delhi	Fr	Bhutia 43, Chetri 58p		
26-08	Sri Lanka	W 3-1	New Delhi	Fr	Bhutia 25, Gouramangi Singh 69, Dias 85		Adil MDV
29-08	Syria	L 0-1	New Delhi	Fr			Adil MDV
31-08	Syria	D 1-1	New Delhi	Fr	Renedy Singh 114. W 5-4p	20 000	Adil MDV
2010							
4-09	Thailand	L 0-1	Bangkok	Fr			
8-09	Thailand	L 1-2	New Delhi	Fr	Pradeep 60		
15-09	Namibia	W 2-0	New Delhi	Fr	Wadoo 28, Pereira 54		Patwal IND
4-10	Hong Kong	L 0-1	Pune	Fr		8 000	Patwal IND
8-10	Vietnam	W 3-1	Pune	Fr	Chetri 3 25 49 72		Dinesh IND
13-10	Yemen	L 3-6	Pune	Fr	Pereira 21, Yadav 49, Surkurmar Singh 92+		Patwal IND
11-11	Iraq	L 0-2	Sharjah	Fr			
14-11	Kuwait	L 1-9	Abu Dhabi	Fr	Rafi 69		
18-11	UAE	L 0-5	Dubai	Fr			
2011							
10-01	Australia	L 0-4	Doha	ACr1		11 749	Badwawi UAE
14-01	Bahrain	L 2-5	Doha	ACr1	Gouramangi Singh 9, Chetri 52	11 032	Mohd Salleh MAS
18-01	Korea Republic	L 1-4	Doha	ACr1	Chetri 12p	11 366	Al Ghamdi KSA

Fr = Friendly match • SAF = South Asian Football Federation Cup • CC - AFC Confederation Cup • AC = AFC Asian Cup • WC = FIFA World Cup
q = qualifier • r1 = first round group • qf = quarter-final • sf = semi-final • f = final

INDIA NATIONAL TEAM HISTORICAL RECORDS

Caps **108** - Bhaichung Bhutia 1995-

Goals **43** - Bhaichung Bhutia 1995-

Past Coaches Syed Abdul Rahim 1950-62 • Harry Wright ENG 1963-64 • Pradip Kumar Banerjee 1981-82 • Bob Bootland ENG 1983 • Milovan Ciric YUG 1984 • Barry Ford AUS 1984 • Pradip Kumar Banerjee 1985 • Syed Nayeemuddin 1986 • Amal Dutta 1987 • Jozsef Gelei HUN 1990-91 • Syed Nayeemuddin 1992 • Jiri Pesek CZE 1993-94 • Rustam Akramov UZB 1995-96 • Syed Nayeemuddin 1997-98 • Sukhvinder Singh 1999-02 • Stephen Constantine ENG 2002-05 • Syed Nayeemuddin 2005-06 • Bob Houghton ENG 2006-

INDIA 2009-10

ONGC I-LEAGUE

	Pl	W	D	L	F	A	Pts	Dempo	Churchill Bros	Pune	Mahindra Utd	Mohun Bagan	Salgoacar	JCT Mills	Chirag Utd	East Bengal	Viva Kerala	Mumbai	Air India	Sporting	Shillong
Dempo Sports Club †	26	16	6	4	54	31	54		4-2	1-1	2-2	3-1	1-1	2-1	3-1	0-0	3-1	3-2	2-0	3-1	4-1
Churchill Brothers	26	11	10	5	50	35	43	3-2		1-1	1-4	4-0	3-1	6-0	2-0	2-2	2-0	1-1	5-1	0-0	1-0
Pune	26	10	12	4	38	23	42	1-1	4-1		0-0	1-3	1-1	2-0	2-1	0-0	3-1	1-1	0-1	4-0	1-1
Mahindra United	26	10	11	5	45	29	41	3-1	1-1	1-1		1-2	1-2	2-1	2-2	3-2	1-1	0-0	2-1	2-1	5-0
Mohun Bagan	26	10	6	10	48	43	36	1-4	2-2	0-0	3-1		1-1	1-2	2-3	2-1	2-0	1-2	4-0	1-2	1-4
Salgoacar	26	8	9	9	34	38	33	3-2	1-2	1-3	1-4	2-1		0-0	1-2	4-1	1-0	1-0	1-1	1-3	3-1
JCT Mills	26	8	8	10	26	29	32	1-2	1-1	1-2	0-0	0-0	1-1		1-0	1-1	5-1	1-0	0-2	2-0	5-1
Chirag United	26	8	8	10	33	39	32	1-1	2-4	1-1	0-1	1-5	2-0	1-1		1-0	1-1	2-1	3-3	0-1	2-0
East Bengal	26	7	10	9	27	31	31	0-1	3-2	1-1	3-5	1-1	0-0	2-1	1-0		1-1	1-0	0-2	1-1	3-0
Viva Kerala	26	7	9	10	25	36	30	1-0	1-1	0-3	1-1	1-1	1-1	1-0	0-1	0-1		0-1	2-1	4-2	2-1
Mumbai FC	26	6	11	9	24	26	29	1-3	0-0	1-2	0-0	2-0	2-1	2-0	0-2	0-0	0-1		0-0	0-0	3-1
Air India	26	7	7	12	28	46	28	1-3	2-3	1-0	0-4	0-5	2-1	0-1	3-1	0-1	1-1	2-2		1-1	1-1
Sporting Clube Goa	26	6	9	11	30	40	27	1-2	2-1	2-2	3-2	2-2	2-3	1-0	1-1	0-1	1-2	2-2	1-2		0-1
Shillong Lajong	26	6	8	12	23	39	26	0-1	0-0	1-0	2-1	1-2	0-0	0-1	1-1	1-0	1-1	1-1	3-0	0-0	

1/10/2009 - 28/05/2010 • † Qualified for the AFC Champions League
Top scorer: **22** - Odafe Okolie, Churchill Brothers

INDIA 2009-10

NATIONAL LEAGUE 2ND DIVISION

	Pl	W	D	L	F	A	Pts
ONGC Mumbai	7	6	1	0	14	4	19
HAL Bangalore	7	5	1	1	14	7	16
Vasco Sports Club	7	4	1	2	14	5	13
Mohammedan Sporting	7	2	4	1	9	9	10
Malabar United	7	3	1	3	8	9	10
Sesa Academy	7	0	3	4	5	12	3
Oil India	7	0	3	4	6	17	3
NISA Manipur	7	0	2	5	3	10	2

30/04/2010 - 25/05/2010

32ND FEDERATION CUP 2010

First round group stage

Group A (Cuttack)	Pl	W	D	L	F	A	Pts	HAL	Pu	AI
East Bengal	3	3	0	0	6	2	9	2-1	1-0	3-1
HAL SC	3	1	1	1	2	2	4		1-0	0-0
Pune	3	1	0	2	2	2	3			2-0
Air India	3	0	1	2	1	5	1			

Group B (Vasco)	Pl	W	D	L	F	A	Pts	CH	Sesa	VK
Churchill Brothers	3	1	2	0	5	1	5	0-0	1-1	4-0
Chirag United	3	1	2	0	3	2	5		1-0	2-2
Sesa Academy	3	0	2	1	1	2	2			0-0
Viva Kerala	3	0	2	1	2	6	2			

Group C (Ludhiana)	Pl	W	D	L	F	A	Pts	ONGC	AIFF	JCT
Dempo SC	3	2	1	0	7	2	7	5-2	2-0	0-0
ONGC FC	3	2	0	1	6	7	6		2-1	2-1
AIFF XI	3	1	0	2	1	3	3			1-0
JCT Mills	3	0	1	2	1	3	1			

Group D (Cuttack)	Pl	W	D	L	F	A	Pts	Sa	SL	Mu
Mohun Bagan	3	2	1	0	7	1	7	6-1	1-0	0-0
Salgoacar SC	3	1	1	1	5	8	4		2-2	2-0
Shillong Lajong	3	0	2	1	2	3	2			0-0
Mumbai FC	3	0	2	1	0	2	2			

Semi-finals

East Bengal	1
Churchill Brothers	0

Dempo SC	1 3p
Mohun Bagan	1 5p

‡ Qualified for the AFC Cup
Semi-finals played in Cuttack
14/09/2010 - 2/10/2010

Final

East Bengal ‡	1
Mohun Bagan	0

CUP FINAL

Barabati Stadium, Cuttack
2-10-2010

Scorer - R Vashum [53] for East Bengal

123RD DURAND CUP 2010

First round group stage

Group A	Pl	W	D	L	F	A	Pts	AR	MEG
Churchill Brothers	2	2	0	0	7	3	**6**	3-1	4-2
Army Red	2	1	0	1	4	3	**3**		3-0
MEG Bangalore	2	0	0	2	2	7	**0**		

Group B	Pl	W	D	L	F	A	Pts	Pu	IAF
Chirag United	2	1	1	0	5	0	**4**	0-0	5-0
Pune FC	2	1	1	0	2	0	**4**		2-0
Indian Air Force	2	0	0	2	0	7	**0**		

Group C	Pl	W	D	L	F	A	Pts	GH	SP
JCT Mills	2	2	0	0	5	1	**6**	2-1	3-0
Garhwal Heroes	2	1	0	1	3	3	**3**		2-1
Sporting Club Goa	2	0	0	2	1	5	**0**		

Group D	Pl	W	D	L	F	A	Pts	Sa	AI
East Bengal	2	2	0	0	6	2	**6**	2-1	4-1
Salgoacar SC	2	1	0	1	4	3	**3**		3-1
Air India	2	0	0	2	2	7	**0**		

Semi–finals

Chirag United	1
East Bengal	0

Churchill Brothers	0
JCT Mills	1

Played in New Delhi
27/10/2010 - 7/11/2010

Final

Chirag United	1
JCT Mills	0

CUP FINAL

Ambedkar, New Delhi
7-11-2010. Ref: Purkayastha

Scorer - Mohammed Rafique [75] for Chirag United

MEDALS TABLE

		Overall			League			F Cup		D Cup		St		Asia			City	DOF
		G	S	B	G	S	B	G	S	G	S		G	S	B			
1	Mohun Bagan	32	27	2	3	2	1	13	5	16	20	26			1	Kolkata	1889
2	East Bengal FC	25	20	2	3	3	2	7	7	15	10	31				Kolkata	1920
3	JCT Mills	8	8	1	1	1	1	2		5	7	9				Phagwara	1971
4	Border Security Force	8	3					1	1	7	2	3				Jalandhar	
5	Mahindra United	6	6	2	1		2	2	3	3	3	12				Mumbai	1962
6	Salgoacar SC	6	4	2	1	1	2	3	3	2		18				Vasco, Goa	1955
7	Dempo Sports Club	6	4		4	1		1	3	1		10				Panjim, Goa	1968
8	Churchill Brothers SC	3	7	2	1	5	2			2	2	6				Salcete, Goa	1988
9	Mohammedan Sporting	3	6					2	3	1	3	11				Kolkata	1892
10	Kerala Police	2						2				5				Thiruv'puram	
11	Indian Telephone Ind.	1						1				18				Bangalore	
	Chirag United	1								1						Kolkata	1927
13	Sporting Clube de Goa		4	1	1	1		2		1		1				Goa	1999
14	Mafatlal Hills		2					2									
15	Tata Football Academy		1							1						Jamshedpur	1983
16	Shillong Lajong		1					1								Shillong	1983
17	Vasco Sports Club			2				2				6				Vasco, Goa	1951
18	Pune FC			1			1									Balewadi	2007
19	Air India											4				New Delhi	1952
	HAL SC											6				Bangalore	
	State Bank of Travancore											2				Trivandrum	1986
	ONGC FC															Mumbai	
	Viva Kerala														1	Kannur	2004

FC = Federation Cup • D Cup = Durand Cup • St = State championship (not included in overall total)

IRL – REPUBLIC OF IRELAND

FIFA/COCA-COLA WORLD RANKING

1993	1994	1995	1996	1997	1998	1999	2000	2001	2002	2003	2004	2005	2006	2007	2008	2009	2010
10	9	28	36	47	56	35	31	17	14	14	12	24	49	35	38	35	36

	2010											Hi/Lo
Jan	Feb	Mar	Mar	Apr	May	Jul	Aug	Sep	Oct	Nov	Dec	6
35	37	39	44	43	41	36	36	33	32	32	36	57

Although Paul Cook's Sligo Rovers proved to be the revelation of the season in Irish club football, winning a cup double, they could never quite keep pace with Shamrock Rovers and Bohemians in what turned out to be a epic title race that was decided on goal difference. A 1-0 win over Shamrock with four games to go looked to have given Bohemians a decisive advantage, but the pair finished level on points with Shamrock Rovers taking the title with a goal difference that was just two better than their rivals - the closest finish in the history of the league. It was Rovers first title since 1994 and denied Bohemians what would have been their first league hat trick. Against the backdrop of an economy in turmoil, Irish football celebrated the inauguration of the new Aviva Stadium in Dublin with a friendly match against Argentina in August and the hope is that the stadium will raise the profile of the game in the country. That was certainly the case in November as 36,101 turned up for the Cup Final - the biggest crowd since 1968 - to see if Shamrock Rovers could win the cup for the first time since 1987 and complete the double. Instead the goalkeeping heroics of Sligo's Ciaran Kelly denied them and handed Sligo their own double. After a goalless 120 minutes, Kelly saved all four of Rovers' penalties as his side won the shoot-out 2-0.

FIFA WORLD CUP RECORD
1930 DNE **1934-1986** DNQ **1990** 8 QF **1994** 15 r2 **1998** DNQ **2002** 12 r2 **2006-2010** DNQ

THE FOOTBALL ASSOCIATION OF IRELAND (FAI)

National Sports Campus, Abbotstown, Dublin 15
☎ +353 1 8999500
📠 +353 1 8999501
✉ info@fai.ie
🖥 www.fai.ie
FA 1921 CON 1954 FIFA 1923
P Paddy McCaul
GS John Delaney

FIFA BIG COUNT 2006

Total players	421 644
% of population	10.38%
Male	390 444
Female	31 200
Amateurs 18+	77 870
Youth under 18	174 498
Unregistered	98 800
Professionals	476
Referees	1 020
Admin & coaches	6 310
Number of clubs	5 629
Number of teams	15 025

MAJOR CITIES/TOWNS

		Population
1	Dublin	1 064 376
2	Cork	193 328
-	Londonderry	83 652
3	Galway	76 433
4	Waterford	49 094
5	Swords	38 711
6	Limerick	38 439
7	Dundalk	35 867
8	Bray	32 436
9	Drogheda	32 221
10	Navan	29 437
11	Ennis	26 205
12	Kilkenny	23 369
13	Tralee	22 945
14	Naas	21 418
15	Newbridge	20 614
16	Mullingar	20 202
17	Carlow	19 999
18	Sligo	18 926

EIRE • IRELAND

Capital	Dublin	Population	4 203 200 (125)	% in cities	61%
GDP per capita	$45 500 (11)	Area km²	70 273 km² (119)	GMT +/-	0
Neighbours (km)	United Kingdom (Northern Ireland) 360 • Coast 1448				

RECENT INTERNATIONAL MATCHES PLAYED BY THE REPUBLIC OF IRELAND

2007	Opponents	Score	Venue	Comp	Scorers	Att	Referee
7-02	San Marino	W 2-1	Serravalle	ECq	Kilbane [49], Ireland [94+]	3 294	Rasmussen DEN
24-03	Wales	W 1-0	Dublin	ECq	Ireland [39]	73 000	Hauge NOR
28-03	Slovakia	W 1-0	Dublin	ECq	Doyle [13]	71 257	Baskakov RUS
23-05	Ecuador	D 1-1	New Jersey	Fr	Doyle [44]	20 823	
26-05	Bolivia	D 1-1	Foxboro	Fr	Long [13]	13 156	
22-08	Denmark	W 4-0	Aarhus	Fr	Keane 2 [29 40], Long 2 [54 66]	30 000	Einwaller AUT
8-09	Slovakia	D 2-2	Bratislava	ECq	Ireland [7], Doyle [57]	12 360	Farina ITA
12-09	Czech Republic	L 0-1	Prague	ECq		16 648	Vassaras GRE
13-10	Germany	D 0-0	Dublin	ECq		67 495	Hansson SWE
17-10	Cyprus	D 1-1	Dublin	ECq	Finnan [92+]	54 861	Vuorela FIN
17-11	Wales	D 2-2	Cardiff	ECq	Keane [31], Doyle [60]	24 619	Oriekhov UKR
2008							
6-02	Brazil	L 0-1	Dublin	Fr		30 000	Rogalla SUI
24-05	Serbia	D 1-1	Dublin	Fr	Keogh [90]	42 500	Evans WAL
29-05	Colombia	W 1-0	London	Fr	Keane [3]	18 612	Clattenburg ENG
20-08	Norway	D 1-1	Oslo	Fr	Keane [44]	16 037	Whitby WAL
6-09	Georgia	W 2-1	Mainz	WCq	Doyle [13], Whelan [70]	4 500	Szabo HUN
10-09	Montenegro	D 0-0	Podgorica	WCq		12 000	Kaldma EST
15-10	Cyprus	W 1-0	Dublin	WCq	Keane [5]	55 833	Tudor ROU
19-11	Poland	L 2-3	Dublin	Fr	Hunt [88p], Andrews [91+]	50 566	Jakobsson ISL
2009							
11-02	Georgia	W 2-1	Dublin	WCq	Keane 2 [73p 78]	45 000	Hyytia FIN
28-03	Bulgaria	D 1-1	Dublin	WCq	Dunne [1]	60 002	Bebek CRO
1-04	Italy	D 1-1	Bari	WCq	Keane [88]	48 000	Stark GER
29-05	Nigeria	D 1-1	London	Fr	Keane [38]	11 263	Collum SCO
6-06	Bulgaria	D 1-1	Sofia	WCq	Dunne [24]	38 000	Larsen DEN
12-08	Australia	L 0-3	Limerick	Fr		19 000	Burrull ESP
5-09	Cyprus	W 2-1	Nicosia	WCq	Doyle [5], Keane [83]	5 191	Einwaller AUT
8-09	South Africa	W 1-0	Limerick	Fr	Lawrence [37]	11 300	Thomson SCO
10-10	Italy	D 2-2	Dublin	WCq	Whelan [8], St Ledger [87]	70 640	Hauge NOR
14-10	Montenegro	D 0-0	Dublin	WCq		50 212	Hrinak SVK
14-11	France	L 0-1	Dublin	WCpo		74 103	Brych GER
18-11	France	D 1-1	Paris	WCpo	Keane [33]	79 145	Hansson SWE
2010							
2-03	Brazil	L 0-2	London	Fr		40 082	Dean ENG
25-05	Paraguay	W 2-1	Dublin	Fr	Doyle [7], Lawrence [39]	16 722	Laperriere SUI
28-05	Algeria	W 3-0	Dublin	Fr	Green [31], Keane 2 [51 86]	16 888	Braamhaar NED
11-08	Argentina	L 0-1	Dublin	Fr		45 200	Rasmussen DEN
3-09	Armenia	W 1-0	Yerevan	ECq	Fahey [76]	8 600	Szabo HUN
7-09	Andorra	W 3-1	Dublin	ECq	Kilbane [15], Doyle [41], Keane [54]	40 283	Trattou CYP
8-10	Russia	L 2-3	Dublin	ECq	Keane [72p], Long [78]	50 411	Blom NED
12-10	Slovakia	D 1-1	Zilina	ECq	St Ledger [16]	10 892	Undiano ESP
17-11	Norway	L 1-2	Dublin	Fr	Long [5p]	25 000	Jakobsson ISL

Fr = Friendly match • EC = UEFA EURO 2008/2012 • WC = FIFA World Cup • q = qualifier • po = play-off

REPUBLIC OF IRELAND NATIONAL TEAM HISTORICAL RECORDS

Caps
109 - Shay Given 1996- • 108 - Kevin Kilbane 1997- • 104 - Robbie Keane 1998- • 102 - Steve Staunton 1988-2002 • 91 - Niall Quinn 1986-2002 • 88 - Tony Cascarino 1986-2000 • 83 - Paul McGrath 1985-97 • 82 - Damien Duff 1998- • 80 - Pat Bonner 1981-96 • 73 - Ray Houghton 1986-98 • 72 - Kenny Cunningham 1996-2005 & Liam Brady 1975-90 • 71 - Kevin Moran 1980-94 & Frank Stapleton 1977-90 • 70 - Andy Townsend 1989-97 • 69 - John Aldridge 1986-97 • 68 - David O'Leary 1977-93 & John O'Shea 2001- • 67 - Roy Keane 1991-2005

Goals
45 - Robbie Keane 1998- • 21 - Niall Quinn 1986-2002 • 20 - Frank Stapleton 1977-90 • 19 - Don Givens 1969-82; Tony Cascarino 1986-2000 & John Aldridge 1986-97 • 14 - Noel Cantwell 1954-67 • 13 - Jimmy Dunne 1930-39 & Gerry Daly 1973-87

Past Coaches
Doug Livingstone SCO 1951-53 • Alex Stevenson 1953-55 • Johnny Carey 1955-67 • Noel Cantwell 1967 • Charlie Hurley 1967-69 • Mick Meagan 1969-71 • Liam Tuohy 1971-73 • Sean Thomas 1973 • Johnny Giles 1973-80 • Alan Kelly Snr 1980 • Eoin Hand 1980-85 • Jack Charlton ENG 1986-95 • Mick McCarthy 1996-2002 • Don Givens 2002 • Brian Kerr 2003-05 • Steve Staunton 2006-07 • Don Givens 2007-08 • Giovanni Trapattoni ITA 2008-

REPUBLIC OF IRELAND 2010

EIRCOM LEAGUE OF IRELAND PREMIER DIVISION

Team	Pl	W	D	L	F	A	Pts	Shamrock R	Bohemians	Sligo Rov	Sp. Fingal	St Pat's	Dundalk	UCD	Galway Utd	Bray Wand	Drogheda Utd
Shamrock Rovers †	36	19	10	7	57	34	67		1-0 3-0	1-1 1-0	1-1 1-2	0-2 2-1	0-2 4-0	0-0 4-1	2-0 3-0	1-0 4-1	1-1 2-0
Bohemians ‡	36	19	10	7	50	29	67	0-0 1-0		0-0 2-0	1-0 1-1	1-1 1-1	3-0 3-1	0-0 3-1	2-3 0-2	2-0 0-0	1-0 2-0
Sligo Rovers ‡	36	17	12	7	61	36	63	1-1 1-2	1-2 1-1		0-1 4-3	0-0 1-0	2-2 1-0	2-1 4-0	1-0 3-0	5-1 2-1	6-0 2-1
Sporting Fingal ‡	36	16	14	6	62	38	62	1-1 3-3	0-2 0-0	1-1 1-1		2-3 2-2	2-1 1-0	1-2 4-1	2-0 3-1	1-0 2-2	4-1 1-2
St Patrick's Athletic	36	16	9	11	55	33	57	1-2 1-3	3-1 0-1	1-0 0-0	0-0 1-1		1-0 1-2	3-0 2-1	2-0 4-2	3-0 2-0	0-1 0-2
Dundalk	36	14	6	16	46	50	48	2-1 5-1	1-0 1-2	1-0 2-4	1-2 0-2	0-0 0-3		3-0 1-1	0-0 3-0	2-3 0-2	2-2 2-1
University College	36	11	8	17	47	54	41	1-2 3-2	1-2 0-2	0-2 1-2	0-0 1-2	1-0 3-2	3-1 0-2		0-0 0-1	1-0 4-0	2-0 1-1
Galway United	36	9	11	16	38	59	38	0-1 0-1	2-2 3-2	0-0 2-2	2-2 0-1	0-2 1-0	1-1 0-1	1-1 2-2		2-1 2-2	3-1 2-1
Bray Wanderers	36	6	9	21	35	72	27	0-0 2-2	0-2 0-3	2-3 1-3	1-3 0-3	0-4 3-2	0-1 2-0	0-6 2-2	0-2 4-0		2-2 1-1
Drogheda United	36	4	9	23	30	74	21	0-2 0-2	2-4 0-1	2-2 2-3	1-1 0-4	2-1 0-3	1-3 1-3	0-3 1-0	0-1 3-3	0-0 0-2	

5/03/2010 - 29/10/2010 • † Qualified for the UEFA Champions League • ‡ Qualified for the Europa League
Relegation play-off semi-finals: **Galway Utd** 1-0 Bray Wand; Waterford Utd 1-3 **Monaghan Utd** • Final: Monaghan Utd 0-0 1-1 6-7p **Bray Wand**
Galway and Bray remain in the Premier Division, Waterford and Monaghan remain in the first division
Top scorers: **20** - Gary Twigg SCO, Shamrock Rovers • **17** - Padraig Amond, Sligo Rovers • **15** - Ciaran Kilduff, UCD • **14** - Jake Kelly, Bray

REPUBLIC OF IRELAND 2010 FIRST DIVISION

Team	Pl	W	D	L	F	A	Pts
Derry City	33	20	9	4	65	24	69
Waterford United	33	20	6	7	59	27	66
Monaghan United	33	18	8	7	59	29	62
Shelbourne	33	18	7	8	57	31	61
Limerick	33	17	6	10	55	35	57
Cork City FORAS	33	15	7	11	39	31	52
Wexford Youths	33	12	6	15	42	54	42
Finn Harps	33	10	10	13	37	43	40
Longford Town	33	9	8	16	39	53	35
Athlone Town	33	6	13	14	35	50	31
Mervue United	33	5	4	24	34	84	19
Salthill Devon	33	3	6	24	26	86	15

5/03/2010 - 30/10/2010
Relegation play-off: Cobh Ramblers 0-1 1-2 **Salthill Devon**

MEDALS TABLE

#	Team	Overall G	S	B	League G	S	B	Cup G	B	LC G	B
1	Shamrock Rovers	41	28	12	16	14	12	24	9	1	5
2	Bohemian FC	21	24	14	11	14	14	7	7	3	3
3	Shelbourne	21	24	11	13	11	11	7	10	1	3
4	Dundalk	21	19	6	9	10	6	8	5	4	4
5	Derry City	15	10	2	2	4	2	4	4	9	2
6	Cork Athletic	12	8	2	7	2	2	5	6		
7	St. Patrick's Athletic	11	13	2	7	4	2	2	7	2	2
8	Waterford United	10	12	8	6	4	8	2	7	2	1
9	Drumcondra	10	9	4	5	5	4	5	4		
10	Sligo Rovers	7	11	6	2	2	6	3	6	2	3
11	Cork City	7	9	5	2	5	5	2	3	3	1
12	Limerick	7	6	3	2	2	3	2	3	3	1
13	Athlone Town	6	3	3	2	1	3	1		3	2
14	St. James' Gate	4	3		2	1		2	2		
15	Drogheda United	3	3	4	1	1	4	1	2	1	
16	Cork Hibernians	3	3	3	1	1	3	2	2		
17	Galway United	3	3	1		1	1	1	1	2	1
18	Longford Town	3	3					2	2	1	1

LEAGUE OF IRELAND CUP 2010

Round of 16		Quarter-finals		Semi-finals		Final	
Sligo Rovers *	6						
Letterkenny Rovers	0	Sligo Rovers *	4				
Bray Wanderers	0	St Patrick's Athletic	1				
St Patrick's Athletic *	2			Sligo Rovers *	2		
Derry City *	2			Shamrock Rovers	1		
Finn Harps	0	Derry City *	1				
University College *	0	Shamrock Rovers	2				
Shamrock Rovers	1					Sligo Rovers *	1
Dundalk *	2					Monaghan United	0
Sporting Fingal	0	Dundalk	2				
Tralee Dynamos	0	Waterford United *	1				
Waterford United *	9			Dundalk	0		
Limerick	3			Monaghan United *	1		
Cork City FORAS *	0	Limerick *	0				
Bohemians	1 3p	Monaghan United	3				
Monaghan United *	1 4p						

CUP FINAL
The Showgrounds, Sligo
25-09-2010, Att: 3000, Ref: Hanney
Scorer - Matthew Blinkhorn [14]

* Home team

FA OF IRELAND CUP 2010

Third Round

Sligo Rovers *	1		
Athlone Town	0		
Crumlin United	0		
Finn Harps *	3		
Cork City FORAS *	1	1	
Bluebell United	1	0	
FC Carlow *	1	1	
Monaghan United	1	2	
Bray Wanderers	1	3	
Derry City *	1	2	
Drogheda United *	1		
University College	2		
Shelbourne	2		
Dublin Bus *	0		
Glenville *	1		
Bohemians	7		
St Patrick's Athletic *	1		
Dundalk *	0		
Avondale United	1		
Belgrove *	2		
Limerick *	3		
Tolka Rovers	1		
Mervue United	1	0	
Sporting Fingal *	1	4	
Galway United *	5		
Malahide United	0		
Tullamore Town *	1		
Salthill Devon	3		
Longford Town *	1		
Waterford United	0		
Wexford Youths	1		
Shamrock Rovers *	5		

Round of 16

Sligo Rovers	1		
Finn Harps *	0		
Cork City FORAS *	0		
Monaghan United	1		
Bray Wanderers	3		
University College *	2		
Shelbourne	0		
Bohemians *	1		
St Patrick's Athletic *	2		
Belgrove	0		
Limerick *	0	2	3p
Sporting Fingal *	0	2	4p
Galway United *	1	3	
Salthill Devon	1	1	
Longford Town *	1		
Shamrock Rovers	2		

Quarter-finals

Team	Score
Sligo Rovers *	3
Monaghan United	0
Bray Wanderers	0
Bohemians *	3
St Patrick's Athletic *	3
Sporting Fingal	1
Galway United	0
Shamrock Rovers *	6

Semi-finals

Sligo Rovers	1	
Bohemians *	0	
St Patrick's Athletic *	2	0
Shamrock Rovers *	2	1

Final

Sligo Rovers ‡	0	2p
Shamrock Rovers	0	0p

CUP FINAL

Aviva Stadium, Dublin
14-11-2010, 15:30, Att: 36 101. Ref: Connolly
Sligo - Ciaran Kelly - Alan Keane•, Gavin Peers•, Jim Lauchlan, Iarfhlaith Davoran - Romuald Boco, Joseph Ndo•, Danny Ventre• (Connor O'Grady 118), Gary McCabe - John Russell - Eoin Doyle. Tr: Paul Cook
Shamrock - Alan Mannus - Stephen Rice, Craig Sives, Pat Flynn, Enda Stevens - Billy Dennehy, Stephen Bradley•◆111, Chris Turner•, James Chambers (Dessie Baker 69) (Aiden Price 113), Thomas Stewart• (Paddy Kavanagh 102) - Gary Twigg. Tr: Michael O'Neill
Penalties: Doyle ✓; Twigg ✗; Keane ✗; Flynn ✗; O'Grady ✗; Turner ✗; McCabe ✗; Kavanagh ✓

* Home team • ‡ Qualified for the Europa League

IRN – IRAN

FIFA/COCA-COLA WORLD RANKING

1993	1994	1995	1996	1997	1998	1999	2000	2001	2002	2003	2004	2005	2006	2007	2008	2009	2010
59	75	108	83	46	27	49	37	29	33	28	20	19	38	41	43	64	66

2010												Hi/Lo
Jan	Feb	Mar	Mar	Apr	May	Jul	Aug	Sep	Oct	Nov	Dec	15
64	63	67	63	60	61	64	65	57	61	66	66	122

Iran's quest to win a record fourth AFC Asian Cup ended with a quarter-final defeat at the hands of South Korea at the 2011 finals in Qatar, the third time in five tournaments that the Koreans have ended Team Melli's continental hopes. The Iranians had emerged from the group stage as the only team with a 100% record having beaten Iraq, North Korea and the UAE but a tense quarter-final against the South Koreans was decided in extra-time by a goal from Yoon Bit Garam. Coach Afshin Ghotbi stepped down from his post following the team's elimination to take on the role of head coach at Japan's Shimizu S-Pulse, leaving the future direction of the national team in question. There was better news for Iranian football on the continental club scene as Zob Ahan turned out to be the surprise package of the AFC Champions League in 2010 with the Eshfahan-based club reaching the final. Having defeated two-time winners Al Ittihad and defending champions Pohang Steelers, they met South Korea's Seongnam Ilhwa Chunma in the final in Tokyo. Lack of experience took its toll as they failed to become the first Iranian champions since 1993, losing 2-1 to the Koreans. In domestic football cross-town rivals Sepahan emerged as league champions in 2010 while the country's most popular club Pirouzi, who are also known as Persepolis, won the cup.

FIFA WORLD CUP RECORD

1930-1970 DNE 1974 DNQ **1978** 14 r1 1982-1986 DNE 1990-1994 DNQ **1998** 20 r1 2002 DNQ **2006** 26 r1 2010 DNQ

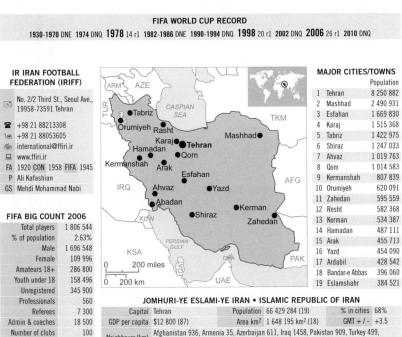

IR IRAN FOOTBALL FEDERATION (IRIFF)

No. 2/2 Third St., Seoul Ave., 19958-73591 Tehran

☎ +98 21 88213308
📠 +98 21 88053605
📧 international@ffiri.ir
🖥 www.ffiri.ir
FA 1920 CON 1958 FIFA 1945
P Ali Kafashian
GS Mehdi Mohammad Nabi

FIFA BIG COUNT 2006

Total players	1 806 544
% of population	2.63%
Male	1 696 548
Female	109 996
Amateurs 18+	286 800
Youth under 18	158 496
Unregistered	345 900
Professionals	560
Referees	7 300
Admin & coaches	18 500
Number of clubs	100
Number of teams	270

MAJOR CITIES/TOWNS

		Population
1	Tehran	8 250 882
2	Mashhad	2 490 931
3	Esfahan	1 669 830
4	Karaj	1 515 368
5	Tabriz	1 422 975
6	Shiraz	1 247 033
7	Ahvaz	1 019 763
8	Qom	1 014 583
9	Kermanshah	807 839
10	Orumiyeh	620 091
11	Zahedan	595 559
12	Resht	582 368
13	Kerman	534 387
14	Hamadan	487 111
15	Arak	455 713
16	Yazd	454 090
17	Ardabil	428 542
18	Bandar-e Abbas	396 060
19	Eslamshahr	384 521

JOMHURI-YE ESLAMI-YE IRAN • ISLAMIC REPUBLIC OF IRAN

Capital	Tehran	Population	66 429 284 (19)	% in cities	68%
GDP per capita	$12 800 (87)	Area km²	1 648 195 km² (18)	GMT +/-	+3.5
Neighbours (km)	Afghanistan 936, Armenia 35, Azerbaijan 611, Iraq 1458, Pakistan 909, Turkey 499, Turkmenistan 992 • Coast 2440				

RECENT INTERNATIONAL MATCHES PLAYED BY IRAN

2009	Opponents	Score		Venue	Comp	Scorers	Att	Referee
9-01	China PR	W	3-1	Tehran	Fr	Borhani [19], Bagheri [26], Mazyar Zare [71p]	10 000	Mozaffari IRN
14-01	Singapore	W	6-0	Tehran	ACq	Gholamnejhad [43], Bagheri [52], Rezaei [55], Mazyar Zare [79], Nouri 2 [82 83]	3 000	Mansour LIB
28-01	Thailand	D	0-0	Bangkok	ACq		10 000	Kovalenko UZB
11-02	Korea Republic	D	1-1	Tehran	WCq	Nekounam [58]	75 000	Williams AUS
14-03	Kenya	W	1-0	Tehran	Fr	Kazemi [54p]	6 500	Jahanbazi IRN
28-03	Saudi Arabia	L	1-2	Tehran	WCq	Shojaei [57]	100000	Nishimura JPN
1-04	Senegal	D	1-1	Tehran	Fr	Madanchi [28]	5 000	Moradi IRN
1-06	China PR	L	0-1	Qinhuangdao	Fr			
6-06	Korea DPR	D	0-0	Pyongyang	WCq		30 000	Sun Baojie CHN
10-06	UAE	W	1-0	Tehran	WCq	Karimi [53]	38 000	Irmatov UZB
17-06	Korea Republic	D	1-1	Seoul	WCq	Shojaei [52]	40 000	Nishimura JPN
5-07	Botswana	D	1-1	Gaborone	Fr	Shirvand [3]		
12-08	Bosnia-Herzegovina	W	3-2	Sarajevo	Fr	Shojaei [79], Borhani [86], Teymourian [90]		
31-08	Bahrain	L	2-4	Manama	Fr	Zandi 2 [37 83p]		
5-09	Uzbekistan	D	0-0	Tashkent	Fr		9 500	Irmatov UZB
10-11	Iceland	W	1-0	Tehran	Fr	Ansarifard [54]		Waleed QAT
14-11	Jordan	W	1-0	Tehran	ACq	Nekounam [72]	15 000	Nishimura JPN
18-11	Macedonia FYR	D	1-1	Tehran	Fr	Teymourian [36]	3 000	Moradi IRN
22-11	Jordan	L	0-1	Amman	ACq		11 000	Al Badwawi UAE
2010								
2-01	Korea DPR	W	1-0	Doha	Fr	Madanchi [43]	1 000	Maillet SEY
6-01	Singapore	W	3-1	Singapore	ACq	Aghili [11p], Madanchi [12], Rezaei [62]	7 356	Sun Baojie CHN
3-03	Thailand	W	1-0	Tehran	ACq	Nekounam [90]	17 000	Balideh QAT
11-08	Armenia	W	3-1	Yerevan	Fr	Aghily 2 [68 90p], Nosrati [71]	3 000	Kvartskhelia GEO
3-09	China PR	W	2-0	Zhengzhou	Fr	Teymourian [38], Gholami [63]	20 000	Kim Jong Hyeok KOR
7-09	Korea Republic	W	1-0	Seoul	Fr	Shojaei [35]	38 642	Mohd Salleh MAS
24-09	Bahrain	W	3-0	Amman	WAr1	Aghili 2 [36 38], Oladi [47]	5 000	Al Ghafari JOR
28-09	Oman	D	2-2	Amman	WAr1	Meydavoudi [15], Teymourian [52]	2 000	Ko Hyung Jin KOR
1-10	Iraq	W	2-1	Amman	WAsf	Hosseini [57], Gholami [82]	10 000	Matsuo JPN
3-10	Kuwait	L	1-2	Amman	WAf	Meydavoudi [95+]	4 000	Al Ghafari JOR
7-10	Brazil	L	0-3	Abu Dhabi	Fr		15 000	Al Marzouqi UAE
28-12	Qatar	D	0-0	Doha	Fr		2 000	Szabo HUN
2011								
2-01	Angola	W	1-0	Al Rayyan	Fr	Nekounam [90]	BCD	
11-01	Iraq	W	2-1	Al Rayyan	ACr1	Rezaei [42], Mobali [84]	10 478	Irmatov UZB
15-01	Korea DPR	W	1-0	Doha	ACr1	Ansarifard [63]	6 488	Shukralla BHR
19-01	UAE	W	3-0	Doha	ACr1	Afshin [67], Nori [83], OG [93+]	5 012	Kim Dong Jin KOR
22-01	Korea Republic	L	0-1	Doha	ACqf		7 111	Irmatov UZB

Fr = Friendly match • WA = West Asian Federation Championship • AC = AFC Asian Cup • WC = FIFA World Cup • q = qualifier

IRAN NATIONAL TEAM HISTORICAL RECORDS

Caps
149 - Ali Daei 1993-2006 • **117** - Javad Nekounam 2000- • **112** - Ali Karimi 1998- • **111** - Mehdi Mahdavikia 1996-2009 • **89** - Hossein Kaebi 2002- • **87** - Karim Bagheri 1993-2010 • **82** - Hamid Reza Estili 1990-2000 • **80** - Javad Zarincheh 1987-2000 • **79** - Ahmad Reza Abedzadeh 1987-98 • **78** - Mohammad Nosrati 2002-

Goals
109 - Ali Daei 1993-2006 • **50** - Karim Bagheri 1993-2010 • **36** - Ali Karimi 1998- • **26** - Javad Nekounam 2000- • **19** - Gholam Hossein Mazloomi 1969-77 & Farshad Pious 1984-1994 • **18** - Ali Ashgar Modir Roosta 1990-98 • **15** - Vahid Hashemian 1998-2009

Past Coaches
Hossein Sadaghiani 1950 • Mostafa Salimi 1951-52 • Edmund Masayufskei AUT 1956-57 • Hossein Sadaghiani 1958 • Ferenc Meszaros HUN 1959 • Hossein Fekri 1962-66 • Gyorgy Szucs HUN 1966 • Hossein Fekri 1967 • Mahmoud Bayati 1968 • Zdravko Rajkov YUG 1969 • Mahmoud Bayati 1970 • Igor Netto URS 1970 • Parviz Dehdari 1971 • Mohammad Ranjbar 1972 • Mahmoud Bayati 1973 • Danny McLennan SCO 1974 • Frank O'Farrell IRL 1974-75 • Heshmat Mohajerani 1976-78 • Hassan Habibi 1980-82 • Naser Ebrahimi 1982 • Jalal Cheraghpour 1982 • Ahmad Tousi 1983-84 • Mahmoud Yavari 1984 • Nasser Ebrahimi 1984-85 • Parviz Dehdari 1986-89 • Reza Vatankhah 1989 • Mehdi Monajati 1989 • Ali Parvin 1989-93 • Hassan Habibi 1994-95 • Stanko Poklepovic CRO 1994 • Mayeli Kohan 1996-97 • Valdeir Viera BRA 1997 • Tomislav Ivic CRO 1998 • Jalal Talebi 1998 • Mansour Pourheidari 1998-2000 • Jalal Talebi 2000 • Ademar Braga 2000-01 • Miroslav Blazevic CRO 2001 • Branko Ivankovic CRO 2002 • Homayoun Shahrokhi 2003 • Branko Ivankovic CRO 2003-6 • Amir Ghalenoei 2006-07 • Parviz Mazloomi 2007 • Mansour Ebrahimzadeh 2008 • Ali Daei 2008-09 • Erich Rutemoller GER 2009 • Mayeli Kohan 2009 • Gholam Peyrovani 2009 • Afshin Ghotbi 2009-

IRAN 2009–10

IRAN PRO LEAGUE

Team	Pl	W	D	L	F	A	Pts	Sepahan	Zob Ahan	Esteghlal	Pirouzi	Steel Azin	Saba	Teraktor-Sazi	Saipa	Mes	Foolad	Paykan	Malavan	Shahin	Rah Ahan	Pass	Moghavemat	AbooMoslem	Esteghlal A
Sepahan †	34	19	10	5	67	30	67		0-1	2-0	2-1	0-1	3-1	3-1	5-1	3-0	1-1	2-1	2-0	2-0	2-0	3-1	5-1	2-0	4-1
Zob Ahan †	34	16	13	5	48	29	61	0-0		1-0	1-1	3-1	2-1	1-0	3-0	0-0	1-0	2-2	3-0	1-0	1-2	0-1	2-0	3-1	5-2
Esteghlal Tehran †	34	16	11	7	49	32	59	1-0	1-0		1-1	2-0	1-1	2-2	2-1	2-0	1-0	2-3	2-2	2-1	1-0	1-0	3-2	3-1	2-3
Pirouzi †	34	13	14	7	46	40	53	1-1	1-1	2-1		0-0	1-0	2-1	0-2	2-0	1-0	1-2	1-1	2-2	1-0	1-0	4-2	2-1	1-1
Steel Azin Tehran	34	13	13	8	55	49	52	2-1	2-2	0-2	2-1		4-3	2-2	4-3	1-1	2-3	0-1	2-2	2-1	1-1	2-2	1-1	0-0	0-1
Saba Qom	34	13	9	12	52	45	48	2-2	1-1	2-1	1-1	4-2		2-1	2-2	1-3	1-1	0-0	0-1	4-0	0-1	2-1	1-2	2-1	2-0
Teraktor-Sazi Tabriz	34	11	14	9	43	42	47	1-1	0-0	1-1	1-1	2-1	3-1		1-2	1-0	1-0	1-0	2-1	1-1	2-1	2-2	0-0	1-0	2-1
Saipa	34	12	10	12	48	53	46	2-2	2-1	1-1	0-2	2-2	2-0	1-0		2-1	1-2	0-2	3-1	1-0	2-3	0-1	1-0	1-1	2-4
Mes Kerman	34	11	9	14	55	56	42	2-3	5-2	1-2	3-3	2-6	0-0	3-2	3-2		2-0	3-3	4-2	1-0	2-2	3-2	0-0	5-2	2-0
Foolad Ahvaz	34	9	15	10	31	34	42	0-0	1-1	1-1	0-0	0-1	2-1	1-1	1-1	0-4		1-1	0-0	0-0	4-0	3-2	1-1	1-0	1-1
Paykan Qazvin	34	9	14	11	40	44	41	1-4	1-1	1-1	1-3	0-1	1-1	1-0	1-1	0-0	1-1		4-0	0-2	1-1	2-2	0-2	2-0	3-1
Malavan	34	10	11	13	41	47	41	0-0	0-1	0-0	1-1	1-3	1-3	1-1	0-2	1-1	1-0	0-1		0-0	2-1	1-0	0-3	1-0	1-0
Shahin Bushehr	34	9	12	13	37	37	39	1-2	1-1	0-1	4-1	1-2	0-1	2-4	2-0	4-1	0-1	0-0	1-1		3-1	1-1	0-0	1-1	0-0
Rah Ahan	34	9	11	14	36	44	38	0-1	0-0	3-2	2-2	1-1	1-3	0-0	0-1	3-2	2-1	3-0	1-2	1-2		0-0	0-0	1-0	1-1
Hamedan-Paas	34	9	11	14	36	44	38	1-1	1-1	0-0	1-2	0-2	2-1	1-1	3-1	1-0	3-1	2-2	1-1	0-1	0-1		3-1	1-0	2-1
Moghavemat Sepasi	34	8	13	13	34	45	37	3-1	0-2	0-0	1-2	1-2	1-4	2-2	0-0	1-1	0-1	1-0	4-0	0-1	2-1	1-0		1-1	3-2
AbooMoslem	34	7	11	16	36	51	32	2-2	1-2	0-5	3-1	2-2	1-3	3-0	1-1	0-1	1-2	1-1	1-1	1-1	0-0	3-0	0-0		2-0
Esteghlal Ahvaz	34	7	9	18	38	60	30	0-5	1-2	0-2	1-0	1-1	0-1	2-3	4-4	1-0	0-1	3-1	2-0	2-2	1-3	0-1	0-0	1-1	

6/08/2009 – 19/05/2010 • † Qualified for the AFC Champions League •
Top scorers: **19** - Emad Mohammed IRQ, Sepahan • **18** - Ibrahima Toure SEN, Sepahan • **14** - Eder Luciano BRA, Mes & Ali Karimi, Steel Azin •
13 - Karim Ansarifard, Saipa & Davoud Haghi, Saba • **12** - Amin Manouchehri, Saipa • **11** - Arash Borhani, Esteghlal & Mohammad Khalatbari, Zob

IRAN 2009–10 — AZADEGAN LEAGUE GROUP A (2)

Team	Pl	W	D	L	F	A	Pts
Shahrdari Tabriz	26	18	8	0	43	11	62
Sanat-Naft Abadan †	26	13	6	7	38	26	45
Tarbyat Badani Yazd	26	12	8	6	29	18	44
Sepahan Novin	26	12	5	9	42	31	41
Mes Rafsanjan	26	9	11	6	30	24	38
Etka Gorgan	26	9	10	7	21	21	37
Shahrdari Bandar Abbas	26	9	9	8	34	25	36
Payam Mashhad	26	9	7	10	33	36	34
Sanati Kaveh	26	9	7	10	27	30	34
IranJavan	26	8	8	10	31	34	32
Damash Tehran	26	7	8	11	23	33	29
Payam Shiraz	26	7	7	12	23	30	28
Shamoushak Noshahr	26	6	8	12	29	37	26
Shahin Ahvaz	26	1	5	20	11	58	8

22/09/2009 - 27/06/2010 • † Qualified for the play-off

Promotion play-off:

Sanat-Naft 5-1 2-1 Damash Gilan

IRAN 2009–10 — AZADEGAN LEAGUE GROUP B (2)

Team	Pl	W	D	L	F	A	Pts
Naft Tehran	26	13	10	3	33	16	49
Damash Gilan †	26	14	6	6	38	26	48
Bargh	26	14	6	6	33	23	48
Aluminium Hormozgan	26	10	10	6	32	33	40
Mes Sarcheshme	26	9	10	7	32	25	37
Shirin-Faraz	26	9	10	7	30	26	37
Nassaji	26	8	10	8	27	26	34
Gostaresh Foolad	26	9	7	10	34	34	34
Mehrkam Pars Tehran	26	9	5	12	22	28	32
Gol Gohar Sirjan	26	8	6	12	30	32	30
Shensa Arak	26	7	8	11	24	29	29
Petroshimi Tabriz	26	7	8	11	23	31	29
Foolad Novin	26	8	5	13	26	36	29
Kousar Lorestan	26	3	8	15	22	41	17

22/09/2009 - 27/06/2010 • † Qualified for the play-off

MEDALS TABLE

	Team	Overall			League			Cup		Asia			City
		G	S	B	G	S	B	G	S	G	S	B	
1	Esteghlal	14	12	7	7	7	4	5	3	2	2	3	Tehran
2	Pirouzi/Persepolis	14	9	7	9	7	4	4	1	1	1	3	Tehran
3	Pas	6	5	2	5	5	2	1					Tehran
4	Sepahan	5	2	2	2	1	2	3			1		Esfahan
5	Saipa	4	2		3	2		1					Karaj
6	Malavan	3	3	2			2	3	3				Bandar Anzali
7	Zob Ahan	2	5	1		3	1	2	1		1		Esfahan
8	Bahman	1	4			2		1	2				Karaj
9	Moghavemat Sepasi	1	2	1			1	1	2				Shiraz
10	Saba Battery	1	1	1			1	1	1				Qom
11	Bargh	1	1					1	1				Shiraz
12	Foolad	1	2		1	2							Ahvaz
13	Shahin	1						1					Ahvaz

JAAM HAZFI 2009-10

Second Stage - First Round

Team	Score
Pirouzi	2
IranJavan *	1
Foolad Ahvaz	0 4p
Aluminium Hormozgan *	0 5p
Bargh *	2
Esteghlal Ahvaz	0
Paykan Qazvin *	1 2p
Petroshimi Tabriz	1 4p
Mes Kerman *	1
Nassaji	0
Sepidrood Rasht	1
Malavan *	2
Sepahan *	3
Sanati Kaveh	0
Foolad Novin Ahvaz *	0
Saba Qom	1
Zob Ahan *	2
Sanat-Naft Abadan	0
Mes Sarcheshme	1
Shahin Bushehr *	3
Esteghlal Tehran *	13
Zoratkaran Parsabad	0
Sepahan Novin	0
Steel Azin Tehran *	2
Mes Rafsanjan *	2
Hamedan-Paas	0
Etka Gorgan	
AbooMoslem *	w/o
Damash Gilan *	1
Moghavemat Sepasi	0
Teraktor-Sazi Tabriz	2
Gostaresh Foolad *	3

Round of 16

Team	Score
Pirouzi *	3
Aluminium Hormozgan	1
Bargh	0 0p
Petroshimi Tabriz *	0 3p
Mes Kerman *	4
Malavan	0
Sepahan	0
Saba Qom *	1
Zob Ahan	3
Shahin Bushehr *	1
Esteghlal Tehran *	4
Steel Azin Tehran *	5
Mes Rafsanjan	2 8p
AbooMoslem *	2 7p
Damash Gilan	0
Gostaresh Foolad *	1

Quarter-finals

Team	Score
Pirouzi	2
Petroshimi Tabriz *	1
Mes Kerman	0
Saba Qom *	1
Zob Ahan *	0 4p
Steel Azin Tehran	0 3p
Mes Rafsanjan *	2
Gostaresh Foolad	4

Semi-finals

Team	Score
Pirouzi *	0 4p
Saba Qom	0 3p
Zob Ahan	0
Gostaresh Foolad *	2

Final

Team	1st	2nd
Pirouzi	1	3
Gostaresh Foolad	0	1

CUP FINAL 1st LEG

Yadegar-e Emam, Tabriz
12-05-2010, Att: 50000, Ref: Afsharian
Scorer - Rezaei [12] for Pirouzi
Gostaresh - Hamed Riahi - Ali Ansarian, Meisam Hosseini, Ahad Shabani - Ruhollah Abdollahi, Morteza Ghorbanpour (Hamedreza Divsalar 65), Amir Nezamipour (Mohsen Dalir 85), Naser Azarkeyvan (Makan Dembele 65), Abbas Aghaei - Silas De Souza, Rasoul Khatibi (c). Tr: Farhad Kazemi
Pirouzi - Alireza Haghighi - Sheys Rezaei (c), Ebrahim Shakouri (Jalal Akbari 30), Alireza Mohammad, Sepehr Heidari - Mehdi Shiri, Hamidreza Aliasgari (Mojtaba Zarei 67), Hossein Badamaki, Hawar Mohammed (Mohammad Mansouri 78), Tiago Alves Fraga - Mohsen Khalili. Tr: Ali Daei

CUP FINAL 2nd LEG

Azadi, Tehran
24-05-2010, Att: 100000, Ref: Afsharian
Scorers - Tiago [31p], Aliasgari [34], Khalili [77] for Pirouzi; Khatibi [73p] for Foolad
Pirouzi - Alireza Haghighi - Alireza Mohammad, Sheys Rezaei (c), Sepehr Heidari, Jalal Akbari (Karim Bagheri 72), Hamidreza Aliasgari, Mehdi Shiri, Mohammad Mansouri (Hawar Mohammed 75) - Hadi Norouzi (Mohsen Khalili 67). Tr: Ali Daei
Gostaresh - Hamed Riahi (Mohammad Torkaman 11 ◆55) - Ali Ansarian, Meisam Hosseini, Thomas Manga - Ruhollah Abdollahi, Morteza Ghorbanpour, Omid Nezamipour, Mohsen Dalir (Naser Azarkeyvan 46), Abbas Aghaei - Silas Feitosa Jose De Souza (Meisam Armian 55), Rasoul Khatibi (c). Tr: Farhad Kazemi

Preliminary Round: Saipa 1-3 **Zob Ahan**; **Sanat Naft Abadan** 4-2 Rah Ahan ● = Home team

IRQ – IRAQ

FIFA/COCA-COLA WORLD RANKING

1993	1994	1995	1996	1997	1998	1999	2000	2001	2002	2003	2004	2005	2006	2007	2008	2009	2010
65	88	110	98	68	94	78	79	72	53	43	44	54	83	68	72	88	101

					2010							Hi/Lo
	Jan	Feb	Mar	Mar	Apr	May	Jul	Aug	Sep	Oct	Nov	Dec	39
	88	86	87	81	82	80	104	106	107	94	99	101	139

Iraq's defence of the Asian Cup title they won in 2007 came to an end at the 2011 tournament in Qatar with a quarter-final defeat at the hands of Australia, thanks to a Harry Kewell goal deep into extra-time. It was deeply frustrating for Wolfgang Sidka's team - who had beaten both North Korea and the UAE to qualify for the knockout stage of the tournament - to lose at the quarter-final stage for the fourth time in five tournaments following on from 1996, 2000 and 2004. Iraq had gone to the Asian Cup off the back of an encouraging performance at the Gulf Cup in Yemen, where they were eliminated by eventual champions Kuwait in a penalty shoot-out in the semi-finals. The result matched the showing at the West Asian Championship, the country's first tournament under the control of Sidka, who was appointed in the summer of 2010. At the Jordan-based event, Iraq won their group games against Palestine and Yemen to qualify for the semi-finals before losing 2-1 to Iran. Iraq played a solitary match on home soil in 2010 - a 1-0 defeat at the hands of Syria in Sulaymaniyah - but there was a full league programme with Duhok winning a first championship after beating Al Talaba in the final. Both teams, along with third placed Arbil, qualified for the 2011 AFC Cup with Iraqi clubs returning having been banned from taking part in the 2010 competition.

FIFA WORLD CUP RECORD
1930-1970 DNE **1974** DNQ **1978** DNE **1982** DNQ **1986** 23 r1 **1990-2010** DNQ

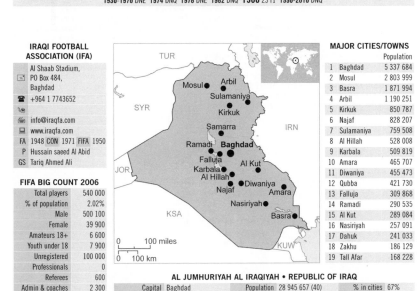

IRAQI FOOTBALL ASSOCIATION (IFA)

Al Shaab Stadium,
PO Box 484,
Baghdad
☎ +964 1 7743652

✉ info@iraqfa.com
🖥 www.iraqfa.com
FA 1948 CON 1971 FIFA 1950
P Hussain saeed Al Abid
GS Tariq Ahmed Ali

FIFA BIG COUNT 2006

Total players	540 000
% of population	2.02%
Male	500 100
Female	39 900
Amateurs 18+	6 600
Youth under 18	7 900
Unregistered	100 000
Professionals	0
Referees	600
Admin & coaches	2 300
Number of clubs	110
Number of teams	170

MAJOR CITIES/TOWNS

		Population
1	Baghdad	5 337 684
2	Mosul	2 803 999
3	Basra	1 871 994
4	Arbil	1 190 251
5	Kirkuk	850 787
6	Najaf	828 207
7	Sulamaniya	759 508
8	Al Hillah	528 008
9	Karbala	509 819
10	Amara	465 707
11	Diwaniya	455 473
12	Qubba	421 730
13	Falluja	309 868
14	Ramadi	290 535
15	Al Kut	289 084
16	Nasiriyah	257 091
17	Dahuk	241 033
18	Zakhu	186 129
19	Tall Afar	168 228

AL JUMHURIYAH AL IRAQIYAH • REPUBLIC OF IRAQ

Capital	Baghdad	Population	28 945 657 (40)	% in cities	67%
GDP per capita	$3200 (162)	Area km²	438 317 km² (58)	GMT +/-	+3
Neighbours (km)	Iran 1458, Jordan 181, Kuwait 240, Saudi Arabia 814, Syria 605, Turkey 352 • Coast 58				

RECENT INTERNATIONAL MATCHES PLAYED BY IRAQ

2009	Opponents	Score		Venue	Comp	Scorers	Att	Referee
15-11	Azerbaijan	W	1-0	Al Ain	Fr	Basem Abbas [88]		
18-11	UAE	W	1-0	Al Ain	Fr	Mahdi Karim [20]		Osman EGY
2010								
16-09	Jordan	L	1-4	Amman	Fr	Nashat Akram [59]		
21-09	Oman	W	3-2	Amman	Fr	Samal Saeed [56], Nashat Akram [68], Ahmad Manajid [19]		
25-09	Yemen	W	2-1	Amman	WAr1	Samal Saeed [49], Hawar Mohammed [72]	3 000	
29-09	Palestine	W	3-0	Amman	WAr1	Mustafa Karim 2 [15 76], Nashat Akram [86p]	4 000	
1-10	Iran	L	1-2	Amman	WAsf	Mustafa Karim [71]		
12-10	Qatar	W	2-1	Doha	Fr	Emad Mohammed 2 [11 57]		
11-11	India	W	2-0	Sharjah	Fr	Mustafa Karim [17p], Mahdi Karim [66]		
17-11	Kuwait	D	1-1	Abu Dhabi	Fr	Younis Mahmoud [45]		
23-11	UAE	D	0-0	Aden	GCr1			Al Qahtani KSA
26-11	Bahrain	W	3-2	Aden	GCr1	Alaa Abdul-Zahra 2 [23 57], Hawar Mohammed [90p]		Allabany YEM
29-11	Oman	D	0-0	Abyan	GCr1			Younis EGY
2-12	Kuwait	D	2-2	Aden	GCsf	Hawar Mohammed [6], Alaa Abdul-Zahra [14]. L 4-5p		Shaaban EGY
18-12	Syria	L	0-1	Sulaymaniyah	Fr			
22-12	Syria	W	1-0	Damascus	Fr	Salam Shakir [88]		
28-12	Saudi Arabia	W	1-0	Dammam	Fr	Younis Mahmoud [24]		
2011								
2-01	China PR	L	2-3	Doha	Fr	Younis Mahmoud 2 [44 50]		
11-01	Iran	L	1-2	Al Rayyan	ACr1	Younis Mahmoud [13]	10 478	Irmatov UZB
15-01	UAE	W	1-0	Al Rayyan	ACr1	Walid Abbas OG [93+]	7 233	Nishimura JPN
19-01	Korea DPR	W	1-0	Al Rayyan	ACr1	Karrar Jassim [22]	4 111	Mohd Salleh MAS
22-01	Australia	L	0-1	Doha	ACqf		7 889	Abdou QAT

Fr = Friendly • WA = West Asian Federation Championship • AC = AFC Asian Cup • GC = Gulf Cup • WC = FIFA World Cup
q = qualifier • r1 = first round group • qf = quarter-final • sf = semi-final • f = final

IRAQ NATIONAL TEAM HISTORICAL RECORDS

Past Coaches

Dhia Habib 1951 • Ismail Mohammed 1957 • Shawqi Aboud 1959 • Hadi Abbas 1959 • Shawqi Aboud 1963-64 • Adil Basher 1964 • Shawqi Aboud 1965 • Adil Basher 1966 • Jalil Shihab 1967 • Abdelilah Mohammed Hassan 1968 • Adil Basher 1968 • Ljubomir Kokeza YUG 1969 • Yuri Illichev URS 1969-71 • Adil Basher 1971-72 • Abdelilah Mohammed Hassan 1972 • Gyula Teleki HUN 1973 • Thamir Muhsin 1973 • Wathiq Naji 1974 • Jalil Shihab 1974 • Thamir Muhsin 1974 • Wathiq Naji 1975 • Danny McLennan SCO 1975-76 • Lenko Grcic YUG 1976-78 • Jamal Salih 1978 • Emmanuel Baba 1978-80 • Wathiq Naji 1980 • Anwar Jassam 1980 • Vojo Gardasevic YUG 1981 • Douglas Aziz 1981 • Emmanuel Baba 1981-84 • Anwar Jassam1985 • Akram Ahmad Salman 1985 • Wathiq Naji 1985 • Jorge Vieira BRA 1985 • Edu BRA 1986 • Ze Mario BRA 1986 • Evaristo de Macedo BRA - 1986 • Akram Ahmad Salman 1986 • Emmanuel Baba 1987-88 • Jamal Salih 1988 • Emmanuel Baba1988-89 • Anwar Jassam1989-90 • Yuri Morozov URS 1990 • Adnan Dirjal 1992-93 • Emmanuel Baba 1993 • Anwar Jassam 1995-96 • Emmanuel Baba 1996 • Yahya Alwan 1996-97 • Ayoub Odisho 1997 • Emmanuel Baba 1997 • Akram Ahmad Salman 1998 • Najih Humoud 1999 • Adnan Hamad 2000 • Milan Zivadinovic SRB 2000-01 • Adnan Hamad 2001 • Rudolf Belin CRO 2001 • Adnan Hamad 2002 • Bernd Stange GER 2002-04 • Adnan Hamad 2004 • Akram Ahmad Salman 2005-07 • Jorvan Vieira BRA 2007 • Egil Olsen NOR 2007-08 • Adnan Hamad 2008 • Jorvan Vieira BRA 2008-09 • Radhi Shenaishil 2009 • Bora Milutinovic SRB 2009 • Nadhim Shaker 2009-10 • Wolfgang Sidka GER 2010

MEDALS TABLE

		Overall			League			Cup			Asia			
		G	S	B	G	S	B	G	S	B	G	S	B	City
1	Al Zawra'a	25	8	2	11	6	2	14	1			1		Baghdad
2	Al Quwa Al Jawia	11	12	9	6	9	9	5	3					Baghdad
3	Al Talaba	7	14	5	5	7	5	2	6			1		Baghdad
4	Al Karkh	5	3	1	3	2	1	2				1		Baghdad
5	Al Jaish	3	6		1	2		2	4					Baghdad
6	Arbil FC	3		1	3		1							Arbil
7	Al Shurta	2	9	8	2	3	8		5			1		Baghdad
8	Al Mina'a	1	1	1	1	1	1							Basra
9	Al Sina'a	1	2				2	1						Baghdad
10	Duhok	1	1	1	1		1							Duhok
11	Salah al Deen	1			1									Tikrit
12	Al Najaf		3	2		3	2							Najaf
13	Al Shabab		3	1			1		3					Baghdad

IRAQ 2009-10

PREMIER LEAGUE GROUP A (NORTH)

	Pl	W	D	L	F	A	Pts	Arbil	Quwa.Jawiya	Duhok	Zawra'a	Nadi	Kahrabaa	Masafi B	Zakho	Ramadi	Mosul	Hindiya	Diyala	Samara'a	Kirkuk	Shirqat	Salah	Masafi J	Pires
Arbil †	33	25	5	3	67	14	80		0-1	1-0	3-0	2-1	3-1	2-0	4-0	1-0	1-0	3-0	5-0	1-0	2-0	2-1	3-0	6-0	1-0
Al Quwa Al Jawiya †	33	22	7	4	60	19	73	0-1		1-0	1-0	2-1	2-2	4-3	3-0	1-1	3-0	2-1	5-0	3-0	3-0	3-1	1-0	4-1	0-0
Duhok †	33	19	7	7	55	23	64	2-2	2-1		3-0	0-1	2-1	3-0	2-0	2-1	2-0	5-0	4-1	1-0	3-2	2-0	3-0	3-0	n/p
Al Zawra'a †	33	19	6	8	39	23	63	2-1	0-3	1-0		2-1	0-0	0-0	1-1	0-0	1-0	0-3	5-0	4-0	0-0	2-1	3-1	2-0	
Nadi Baghdad †	33	15	11	7	42	25	56	2-2	1-1	4-2	1-0		0-0	2-0	1-1	1-1	1-0	1-1	1-0	3-0	1-0	3-0	1-0	n/p	
Kahrabaa †	33	13	14	6	38	25	53	0-0	1-4	1-1	0-1	1-1		2-0	0-0	1-0	0-0	3-1	2-2	0-0	1-1	1-0	0-0	5-0	2-1
Masafi Baghdad	33	12	12	9	40	38	48	0-0	0-1	0-0	1-0	0-1	0-0		3-2	1-3	3-0	3-1	1-0	2-1	2-1	4-3	2-3	0-1	n/p
Zakho	33	12	9	12	33	31	45	0-1	1-0	1-0	1-1	0-1	0-1	0-1		0-2	0-1	3-0	0-0	3-0	2-0	2-0	2-0	2-0	n/p
Ramadi	33	9	13	11	31	33	40	1-4	1-1	0-2	0-0	1-0	0-2	2-1	1-1		4-1	1-1	0-1	1-1	0-1	1-2	3-0	1-0	n/p
Mosul	33	9	11	13	24	32	38	1-0	0-1	0-0	0-1	2-1	1-0	1-1	1-2	0-0		0-1	0-3	0-0	1-0	2-0	3-0	3-0	1-1
Hindiya	33	7	13	13	33	49	34	3-0	0-2	1-1	1-1	0-0	0-2	1-2	1-1	2-2	0-0		3-0	0-1	1-3	3-2	2-2	2-2	n/p
Diyala	33	8	8	17	27	49	32	0-3	0-1	0-1	1-0	1-4	1-2	0-1	3-0	1-1	1-1	0-0		0-0	0-1	1-0	0-1	1-1	1-1
Samara'a	33	6	13	14	24	37	31	0-1	0-1	1-0	0-1	1-0	0-0	1-2	0-1	1-1	0-0	0-0	1-1		2-1	1-0	0-0	1-0	3-0
Kirkuk	33	7	8	18	37	56	29	1-1	0-1	2-3	1-3	1-0	0-2	2-3	2-1	2-1	0-2	0-2	0-1	3-1		1-2	2-2	2-2	1-1
Shirqat	33	5	13	15	20	45	28	1-1	0-1	0-0	0-1	1-0	1-1	0-0	0-0	0-0	0-0	0-0	1-0	1-1	2-2		3-1	3-0	n/p
Salah Al Deen	33	4	13	16	27	51	25	0-2	0-2	0-0	0-2	1-2	1-1	2-1	2-1	2-3	1-0	0-1	1-0	0-0	0-0	1-0		0-0	n/p
Masafi Janob	33	2	8	23	20	76	14	0-3	1-0	0-4	0-1	0-2	0-1	0-0	1-2	1-4	1-2	3-5	1-3	0-3	1-3	0-0	2-2		0-2
Pires Duhok	17	7	5	5	22	13	26	n/p	n/p	0-1	n/p	1-0	n/p	1-0	n/p	1-1	n/p	7-0	n/p	2-1	n/p	2-0	2-1	n/p	

PREMIER LEAGUE GROUP A (NORTH)

	Pl	W	D	L	F	A	Pts	Talaba	Najaf	Sina'a	Karbala	Shurta	Nafit Janob	Mina'a	Naft B	Nafit M	Diwaniya	Karkh	Nasirya	Hassanin	Kufa	Hudod	Sanawa	Itesalat	Maysan
Al Talaba †	34	19	11	4	46	19	68		0-0	2-1	1-0	2-2	1-0	1-1	0-3	4-0	1-0	1-0	1-4	2-1	2-1	1-0	5-1	3-0	4-0
Al Najaf †	34	18	12	4	49	20	66	1-1		1-1	0-3	0-0	0-2	1-0	1-1	0-3	4-0	1-0	1-0	2-1	1-0	2-0	4-0	3-1	1-0
Al Sina'a †	34	19	9	6	52	32	66	1-1	1-3		0-0	0-2	1-0	3-0	2-1	3-1	2-1	2-1	2-1	4-1	1-0	1-0	1-0	3-0	2-1
Karbala †	34	17	13	4	40	18	64	0-0	2-1	1-0		2-5	0-0	0-0	1-0	2-2	0-1	1-1	1-1	1-0	2-0	1-0	4-1	1-0	4-0
Al Shurta †	34	17	11	6	49	33	62	0-1	1-0	2-2	0-1		2-2	1-1	0-0	2-1	0-0	1-1	1-0	2-2	1-0	0-0	1-1	2-0	2-0
Nafit Al Janob †	34	17	10	7	40	22	61	0-0	0-3	1-0	1-4	2-0		1-0	1-2	2-0	2-1	3-0	0-0	2-0	0-0	2-1	3-0	3-0	3-1
Al Mina'a	34	16	11	7	36	23	59	1-0	1-1	4-1	0-0	2-0	0-0		1-0	1-0	1-0	2-1	0-0	2-0	0-3	3-1	2-1	1-0	1-0
Al Naft Baghdad	34	14	6	14	39	34	48	0-2	0-0	1-2	1-3	1-3	0-1	0-1		2-1	3-1	0-0	2-1	3-0	2-0	3-0	1-0	0-1	2-0
Nafit Maysan	34	12	11	11	44	37	47	0-0	1-2	0-0	0-0	2-0	0-0	1-0	2-1		2-0	0-0	1-5	2-2	1-3	0-0	0-0	3-1	5-0
Diwaniya	34	12	7	15	37	44	43	1-2	1-0	2-0	0-0	3-5	1-1	2-1	0-1	0-1		3-1	1-0	2-1	3-2	1-1	1-0	1-3	2-1
Karkh	34	9	14	11	31	35	41	1-1	2-2	0-2	0-0	2-2	2-0	0-0	0-0	2-1	0-1		1-1	4-1	1-0	2-1	1-0	2-1	1-2
Al Nasiriya	34	7	17	10	34	39	38	0-0	1-0	1-1	1-1	0-1	1-1	2-1	3-1	2-4	1-1	2-2		1-3	2-1	0-0	2-1	1-1	1-0
Hassanin	34	9	11	14	32	46	38	0-1	0-0	1-1	1-0	0-1	1-1	0-0	2-3	1-1	1-0	0-0	2-3		2-2	1-1	1-2	1-0	1-0
Kufa	34	8	10	16	32	41	34	1-0	0-2	2-2	0-1	1-1	2-1	1-1	2-1	1-1	3-0	0-0	2-2	1-2		0-0	0-1	1-0	0-0
Hudod	34	6	14	14	19	39	32	0-0	0-0	0-3	0-1	0-0	0-0	0-0	0-0	1-1	1-2	0-1	1-0	2-2	1-3		2-1	1-0	0-0
Samawa	34	6	5	23	30	59	23	0-1	0-3	1-2	0-2	0-3	1-2	0-2	3-1	1-2	0-3	2-1	0-2	0-1	2-2	2-3		2-0	3-0
Itesalat	34	4	8	22	27	51	20	0-1	0-1	1-2	1-3	1-2	0-2	0-3	1-1	0-1	0-0	0-1	1-1	0-1	3-0	0-0	2-2		5-3
Maysan Umara	34	2	8	24	17	58	14	0-1	0-1	0-1	0-1	0-2	1-1	1-3	1-1	0-2	3-0	1-1	1-1	1-0	1-1	1-0	1-1	0-0	

30/12/2009 - 6/07/2010 • † Qualified for the championship play-offs

Play-offs

Group 1

	Pl	W	D	L	F	A	Pts	AZ	AT	AS	NB
Al Zawra'a	6	3	1	2	4		10		1-0	3-1	0-1
Al Talaba	6	3	1	2	6	5	10	2-1		1-2	0-0
Al Sina'a	6	2	1	3	7	9	7	0-1	1-2		2-2
Nadi Baghdad	6	1	3	2	3	4	6	0-0	0-1	0-1	

Group 2

	Pl	W	D	L	F	A	Pts	Ar	AS	Ka	AN
Arbil	6	4	0	2	9	5	12		0-1	3-1	2-1
Al Shurta	6	2	3	1	5	5	9	0-2		1-1	1-0
Kahrabaa	6	2	2	2	6	7	8	1-0	0-0		2-1
Al Najaf	6	1	1	4	7	10	4	1-2	2-2	2-1	

Group 3

	Pl	W	D	L	F	A	Pts	Du	QJ	Ka	NJ
Duhok	6	5	1	0	10	4	16		2-0	3-2	1-0
Al Quwa Al Jawiya	6	2	3	1	7	3	9	0-0		3-0	3-0
Karbala	6	2	1	3	8	11	7	2-3	1-1		2-1
Nafit Al Janob	6	0	1	5	1	8	1	0-1	0-0	0-1	

Semi-finals

Duhok *	5	0
Al Zawra'a	1	1

Arbil * †	0	0
Al Talaba	1	0

† Qualified for the AFC Cup

Final

Duhok †	1
Al Talaba †	0

FINAL

Al Shaab, Baghdad
4-09-2010, Ref: Falah Abid
Scorer - Khalid Musheer 82

15/07/2010 - 4/09/2010 • * Home team in the 1st leg • Third place play-off: Al Zawra'a 2-1 Arbil

ISL – ICELAND

FIFA/COCA-COLA WORLD RANKING

1993	1994	1995	1996	1997	1998	1999	2000	2001	2002	2003	2004	2005	2006	2007	2008	2009	2010
47	39	50	60	72	64	43	50	52	58	58	93	94	93	90	83	92	112

	2010												Hi/Lo
	Jan	Feb	Mar	Mar	Apr	May	Jul	Aug	Sep	Oct	Nov	Dec	37
	92	94	91	90	91	90	79	79	100	110	110	112	117

Sitting in the southern half of what is greater Reykjavík, Kopavogur is classed as the second largest settlement in Iceland after the capital, although to the untrained eye it is impossible to tell where one begins and the other ends. Of greater clarity was the fact that in 98 seasons of league football, the municipality had never witnessed a title-winning team - until 2010 that is. Breidablik may not be one of the most recognisable names in Icelandic football, but as the top team from Kopavogur they wrote themselves into the history books by winning the championship ahead of neighbours FH Hafnarfjördur. It was a close run thing, however, with three teams in with a chance on the final day of the season. Breidablik held a point advantage but nerves got the better of them as they were held to a goalless draw at Stjarnan. Fortunately for Breidablik, IBV lost to Keflavik and so the draw was enough to keep them ahead of FH, 3-0 winners over Fram. FH were gunning for their sixth title in seven years and what would have been their first double, having beaten KR Reykjavík 4-0 the month before in the Cup Final. The Iceland national team had a poor start to the qualifiers for Euro 2012, losing their first three games in a very difficult group containing 2010 World Cup finalists Denmark and Portugal along with Norway and Cyprus.

FIFA WORLD CUP RECORD
1930-1954 DNE 1958 DNQ 1962-1970 DNE 1974-2010 DNQ

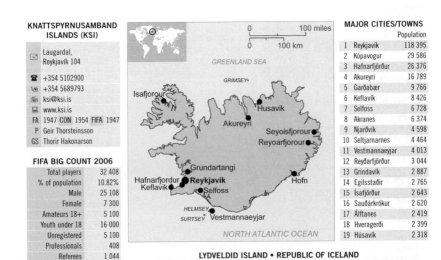

KNATTSPYRNUSAMBAND ISLANDS (KSI)

Laugardal,
Reykjavík 104

☎ +354 5102900
📠 +354 5689793
✉ ksi@ksi.is
🖥 www.ksi.is
FA 1947 CON 1954 FIFA 1947
P Geir Thorsteinsson
GS Thorir Hakonarson

FIFA BIG COUNT 2006

Total players	32 408
% of population	10.82%
Male	25 108
Female	7 300
Amateurs 18+	5 100
Youth under 18	16 000
Unregistered	5 100
Professionals	408
Referees	1 044
Admin & coaches	750
Number of clubs	97
Number of teams	870

MAJOR CITIES/TOWNS
Population

1	Reykjavík	118 395
2	Kópavogur	29 586
3	Hafnarfjörður	26 376
4	Akureyri	16 789
5	Garðabær	9 766
6	Keflavík	8 426
7	Selfoss	6 728
8	Akranes	6 374
9	Njarðvík	4 598
10	Seltjarnarnes	4 464
11	Vestmannaeyjar	4 013
12	Reyðarfjörður	3 044
13	Grindavík	2 887
14	Egilsstaðir	2 765
15	Ísafjörður	2 643
16	Sauðárkrókur	2 620
17	Álftanes	2 419
18	Hveragerði	2 399
19	Húsavík	2 318

LYDVELDID ISLAND • REPUBLIC OF ICELAND

Capital	Reykjavík	Population	306 694 (178)	% in cities	92%
GDP per capita	$42 300 (17)	Area km²	103 000 km² (107)	GMT + / -	0
Neighbours (km)	Coast 4970				

RECENT INTERNATIONAL MATCHES PLAYED BY ICELAND

2007	Opponents		Score	Venue	Comp	Scorers	Att	Referee
22-08	Canada	D	1-1	Reykjavik	Fr	Thorvaldsson [65]	4 359	Asumaa FIN
8-09	Spain	D	1-1	Reykjavik	ECq	Hallfredsson [40]	9 483	Stark GER
12-09	Northern Ireland	W	2-1	Reykjavik	ECq	Armann Bjornsson [6], OG [91+]	7 727	Baskakov RUS
13-10	Latvia	L	2-4	Reykjavik	ECq	Gudjohnsen 2 [4 52]	5 865	Dean ENG
17-10	Liechtenstein	L	0-3	Vaduz	ECq		2 589	Zografos GRE
21-11	Denmark	L	0-3	Copenhagen	ECq		15 393	Benquerenca POR
2008								
2-02	Belarus	L	0-2	Ta'Qali	Fr			
4-02	Malta	L	0-1	Ta'Qali	Fr			
6-02	Armenia	W	2-0	Ta'Qali	Fr	Gudmundsson [45], Thorvaldsson [72]		Attard MLT
16-03	Faroe Islands	W	3-0	Kopavogur	Fr	Saevarsson.J [45], OG [72], Gudmundsson [80]	400	Skjerven NOR
26-03	Slovakia	W	2-1	Zilina	Fr	Thorvaldsson [71], Gudjohnsen [82]	4 120	Lehner AUT
28-05	Wales	L	0-1	Reykjavik	Fr		5 322	McCourt NIR
20-08	Azerbaijan	D	1-1	Reykjavik	Fr	Steinsson [58]	5 133	Evans WAL
6-09	Norway	D	2-2	Oslo	WCq	Helguson [39], Gudjohnsen [69]	17 254	Yefet ISR
10-09	Scotland	L	1-2	Reykjavik	WCq	Gudjohnsen [77p]	9 767	Gumieny BEL
11-10	Netherlands	L	0-2	Rotterdam	WCq		37 500	Trefoloni ITA
15-10	Macedonia FYR	W	1-0	Reykjavik	WCq	Veigar Gunnarsson [15]	5 527	Dereli TUR
19-11	Malta	W	1-0	Corradino	Fr	Helgusson [66]		
2009								
11-02	Liechtenstein	W	2-0	La Manga	Fr	Smarason [28], Gudjohnsen [47]	150	Reinert FRO
22-03	Faroe Islands	L	1-2	Kopavogur	Fr	Saevarsson [91+]	553	Riley ENG
1-04	Scotland	L	1-2	Glasgow	WCq	Indridi Sigurdsson [54]	42 259	Einwaller AUT
6-06	Netherlands	L	1-2	Reykjavik	WCq	Kristian Sigurdsson [88]	9 635	Dean ENG
10-06	Macedonia FYR	L	0-2	Skopje	WCq		7 000	Ennjimmi FRA
12-08	Slovakia	D	1-1	Reykjavik	Fr	Kristian Sigurdsson [60]	5 099	Christoffersen DEN
5-09	Norway	D	1-1	Reykjavik	WCq	Gudjohnsen [29]	7 321	Tudor ROU
9-09	Georgia	W	3-1	Reykjavik	Fr	Johannsson [14], Skulason [18], Veigar Gunnarsson [55p]	4 726	Trefoloni ITA
13-10	South Africa	W	1-0	Reykjavik	Fr	Veigar Gunnarsson [50]	3 253	Moen NOR
10-11	Iran	L	0-1	Tehran	Fr			Waleed QAT
14-11	Luxembourg	D	1-1	Luxembourg	Fr	Johannsson [63]	913	Van Boekel NED
2010								
3-03	Cyprus	D	0-0	Larnaca	Fr			Yordanov.N BUL
21-03	Faroe Islands	W	2-0	Kopavogur	Fr	Vilhjalmsson [10], Sigthorsson [37]	312	Larsen DEN
24-03	Mexico	D	0-0	Charlotte	Fr		63 227	Geiger USA
29-05	Andorra	W	4-0	Reykjavik	Fr	Helguson 2 [32p 51], Veigar Gunnarsson [87p], Sigthorsson [88]	2 567	Reinert FRO
11-08	Liechtenstein	D	1-1	Reykjavik	Fr	Gislason [20]	3 000	Buttimer IRL
3-09	Norway	L	1-2	Reykjavik	ECq		6 137	Banti ITA
7-09	Denmark	L	0-1	Copenhagen	ECq		18 908	McDonald SCO
12-10	Portugal	L	1-3	Reykjavik	ECq		9 767	Einwaller AUT
17-11	Israel	L	2-3	Tel Aviv	Fr	Finnbogason [79], Sigthorsson [85]	4 500	Spathas GRE

Fr = Friendly match • EC = UEFA EURO 2008/2012 • WC = FIFA World Cup • q = qualifier

ICELAND NATIONAL TEAM HISTORICAL RECORDS

Caps
104 - Runar Kristinsson 1987-2004 • 85 - Hermann Hreidarsson 1996- • 80 - Gudni Bergsson 1984-2003 • 74 - Brynjar Bjorn Gunnarsson 1997-& Birkir Kristinsson 1988-2004 • 73 - Arnor Gudjohnsen 1979-97 • 72 - Olafur Thordarson 1984-96 • 71 - Arnar Gretarsson 1991-2004 • 70 - Arni Gautur Arason 1998-& Atli Edvaldsson 1976-91 • 69 - Saevar Jonsson 1980-92 • 67 - Marteinn Geirsson 1971-82

Goals
24 - Eidur Gudjohnsen 1996- • 17 - Rikhardur Jonsson 1947-65 • 14 - Rikhardur Dadason 1991-2004 & Arnor Gudjohnsen 1979-97 • 13 - Thordur Gudjonsson 1993-2004 • 12 - Tryggvi Gudmundsson 1997-2008 • 11 - Petur Petursson 1978-90 & Matthias Hallgrimsson 1968-77

Past Coaches
Frederick Steele & Murdo McDougall 1946 • Roland Bergstrom SWE 1947 • Fritz Buchloh GER 1949 • Oli B. Jonsson 1951 • Franz Kohler 1953 • Karl Gudmundsson 1954-56 • Alexander Wier 1957 • Oli B. Jonsson 1958 • Karl Gudmundsson 1959 • Oli B. Jonsson 1960 • Karl Gudmundsson 1961 • Rikhardur Jonsson 1962 • Karl Gudmundsson 1963-66 • Reynir Karlsson 1967 • Walter Pfeiffer 1968 • Rikhardur Jonsson 1969-71 • Duncan McDowell 1972 • Eggert Johannesson 1972 • Henning Enoksen DEN 1973 • Tony Knapp ENG 1974-77 • Juri Ilitchev URS 1978-79 • Gudni Kjartansson 1980-81 • Johannes Atlason 1982-83 • Tony Knapp ENG 1984-85 • Siegfried Held GER 1986-89 • Gudni Kjartansson 1989 • Bo Johansson SWE 1990-91 • Asgeir Eliasson 1991-95 • Logi Olafsson 1996-97 • Gudjon Thordarson 1997-99 • Atli Edvaldsson 2000-03 • Asgeir Sigurvinsson & Logi Olafsson 2003-05 • Eyjolfur Sverrisson 2006-07 • Olafur Johannesson 2007-

ICELAND 2010

URVALSDEILD (1)

	Pl	W	D	L	F	A	Pts	Breidablik	FH	IBV	KR	Fram	Keflavik	Valur	Stjarnan	Fylkir	Grindavik	Haukar	Selfoss
Breidablik †	22	13	5	4	47	23	44		2-0	1-1	2-1	2-2	0-1	5-0	4-0	1-0	2-3	0-2	3-0
FH Hafnarfjördur ‡	22	13	5	4	48	31	44	1-1		2-3	3-2	4-1	5-3	1-1	1-3	4-2	2-1	3-1	2-1
IBV Vestmannæyjar ‡	22	13	3	6	36	27	42	1-1	1-3		2-4	1-0	2-1	3-1	2-1	2-0	0-1	3-2	3-0
KR Reykjavík ‡	22	11	5	6	45	31	38	1-3	0-1	1-0		2-1	0-0	1-2	3-1	3-0	1-0	2-2	1-2
Fram Reykjavík	22	9	5	8	35	35	32	3-1	0-3	2-0	2-3		2-1	2-2	2-1	1-2	2-0	0-0	3-1
Keflavík	22	8	6	8	30	32	30	0-2	1-1	4-1	0-1	1-1		3-1	2-2	2-1	1-1	1-1	2-1
Valur Reykjavík	22	7	7	8	34	41	28	0-2	2-2	1-1	1-4	1-3	0-2		5-1	5-2	0-0	2-2	2-1
Stjarnan Gardabær	22	6	7	9	39	42	25	0-0	1-4	0-2	2-2	2-3	4-0	1-1		2-1	4-0	2-2	3-2
Fylkir Reykjavík	22	7	3	12	36	42	24	2-4	2-2	1-2	1-4	2-2	1-2	0-1	3-1		2-0	3-0	5-2
Grindavík	22	5	6	11	28	39	21	2-4	3-1	1-2	3-3	3-0	0-1	1-2	1-1	1-2		1-1	1-1
Haukar Hafnarfjördur	22	4	8	10	29	45	20	2-4	0-1	0-3	3-3	2-1	2-0	2-1	0-5	1-1	2-3		2-3
Selfoss	22	5	2	15	32	51	17	1-3	0-2	0-2	0-3	1-2	3-2	2-3	2-3	2-2	1-3	5-2	3-0

10/05/2010 - 25/09/2010 • † Qualified for the UEFA Champions League • ‡ Qualified for the Europa League
Top scorers: 14 - Atli Vidar Bjornsson, FH; Alfred Finnbogason, Breidablik & Gilles Mbang Ondo GAB, Grindavik • 13 - Halldor Bjornsson, Stjarnan

ICELAND 2010
1.DEILD (2)

	Pl	W	D	L	F	A	Pts
Vikingur Reykjavík	22	15	3	4	46	23	48
Thór Akureyri	22	12	7	3	53	23	43
Leiknir Reykjavík	22	13	4	5	32	19	43
Fjölnir Reykjavík	22	12	4	6	42	28	40
IA Akranes	22	9	8	5	44	28	35
IR Reykjavík	22	8	6	8	31	38	30
Thróttur Reykjavík	22	8	5	9	32	37	29
HK Kópavogur	22	7	4	11	30	38	25
KA Akureyri	22	6	6	10	29	43	24
Grótta Seltjarnarnes	22	4	6	12	29	47	18
Fjardabyggd	22	4	5	13	26	47	17
Njardvík	22	3	4	15	14	37	13

9/05/2010 - 18/09/2010

MEDALS TABLE

		Overall			League			Cup		
		G	S	B	G	S	B	G	S	City
1	KR Reykjavík	35	32	12	24	27	12	11	5	Reykjavík
2	Valur	29	20	18	20	17	18	9	3	Reykjavík
3	IA Akranes	27	21	13	18	12	13	9	9	Akranes
4	Fram	25	27	16	18	17	16	7	10	Reykjavík
5	Keflavík IF	8	8	7	4	3	7	4	5	Keflavík
6	IBV Vestmannæyjar	7	12	8	3	6	8	4	6	Vestmannæyjar
7	FH Hafnarfjördur	7	9	1	5	6	1	2	3	Hafnarfjördur
8	Vikingur	6	8	8	5	7	8	1	1	Reykjavík
9	Fylkir	2	2	1		2	1	2		Reykjavík
10	Breidablik UBK	2	1	1	1	1	1	1	1	Kópavogur
11	KA Akureyri	1	3		1				3	Akureyri
12	IBA Akureyri	1		4			4	1		Akureyri
13	Fjölnir		2						2	Reykjavík
14	Leiftur	1	3				3			Olafsfjördur
15	Grindavík	1	2				2	1		Grindavík
16	Vidir Gardur	1							1	Gardi
17	Thór Akureyri		2						2	Akureyri

BIKARKEPPNI 2010

Round of 16		Quarter–finals		Semi–finals		Final	
FH Hafnarfjördur	3						
Keflavík *	2	FH Hafnarfjördur *	3				
Grindavík *	1 4p	KA Akureyri	0				
KA Akureyri	1 5p			FH Hafnarfjördur	3		
Stjarnan Gardabær	2			Vikingur Olafsvík	1		
BI/Bolungarvík *	0	Stjarnan Gardabær	3 4p				
Fjardabyggd	2	Vikingur Olafsvík *	3 5p				
Vikingur Olafsvík *	3					FH Hafnarfjördur ‡	4
Fram Reykjavík	2					KR Reykjavík	0
Fylkir Reykjavík *	0	Fram Reykjavík *	3				
Vikingur Reykjavík *	1	Valur Reykjavík	1				
Valur Reykjavík	3			Fram Reykjavík			
Thróttur Reykjavík	1			KR Reykjavík			
IA Akranes *	0	Thróttur Reykjavík	2				
Fjölnir Reykjavík *	1	KR Reykjavík *	3	Semis played at Laugardalsvøllur			
KR Reykjavík	2			* Home team • ‡ Qualified for the Europa League			

CUP FINAL

Laugardalsvøllur, Reykjavik
14-08-2010, Att: 5438, Ref:Eiriksson
Scorers -
Matthias Vilhjalmsson 2 [35p] [41p], Atli
Vidar Bjornsson [75], Atli Gudnason [86]

ISR – ISRAEL

FIFA/COCA-COLA WORLD RANKING

1993	1994	1995	1996	1997	1998	1999	2000	2001	2002	2003	2004	2005	2006	2007	2008	2009	2010
57	42	42	52	61	43	26	41	49	46	51	48	44	44	26	18	26	50

	2010											Hi/Lo
	Jan	Feb	Mar	Mar	Apr	May	Jul	Aug	Sep	Oct	Nov	Dec	15
	26	27	26	28	24	26	37	38	36	56	55	50	71

Under normal circumstances Maccabi Haifa would have been celebrating a 12th championship at the end of the 2009-10 season but were denied by one of the more bizarre schemes dreamt up by officials to try and make the game more appealing to fans. In this case it was decided that after a full season of 30 games between the 16 Premier League teams, the top six would play a further five matches between themselves but take only half of the points total forward. That meant Maccabi Haifa's six-point lead was cut to three at the start of the play-offs and they eventually lost the title on goal difference to Hapoel Tel Aviv despite having the best record over the 35 games played. For Hapoel, their first title since 2000 came in dramatic circumstances thanks to an injury-time winner through Eran Zhavi against Beitar in the final match as they extended their unbeaten run of 31 matches to the end of the season. Four days earlier Hapoel had beaten Bnei Yehuda 3-1 in the Cup Final and they then qualified for the group stage of the 2010-11 UEFA Champions League to cap a great year for the club. In preparation for the qualifiers for Euro 2012, the football association turned to experienced Frenchman Luis Fernandez as national team coach - only the second foreigner in 20 years to take the reigns - but Israel made an indifferent start in a very winnable group.

FIFA WORLD CUP RECORD
1930 DNE 1934-1966 DNQ **1970** 12 r1 1974-2010 DNQ

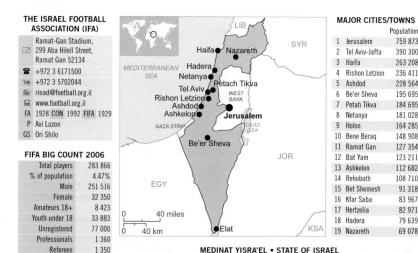

THE ISRAEL FOOTBALL ASSOCIATION (IFA)

Ramat-Gan Stadium,
299 Aba Hilell Street,
Ramat Gan 52134
☎ +972 3 6171500
📠 +972 3 5702044
✉ rinad@football.org.il
🖥 www.football.org.il
FA 1928 CON 1992 FIFA 1929
P Avi Luzon
GS Ori Shilo

FIFA BIG COUNT 2006

Total players	283 866
% of population	4.47%
Male	251 516
Female	32 350
Amateurs 18+	8 423
Youth under 18	33 883
Unregistered	77 000
Professionals	1 360
Referees	1 350
Admin & coaches	10 800
Number of clubs	280
Number of teams	1 400

MAJOR CITIES/TOWNS

		Population
1	Jerusalem	759 873
2	Tel Aviv-Jaffa	390 300
3	Haifa	263 208
4	Rishon Letzion	236 411
5	Ashdod	228 564
6	Be'er Sheva	195 695
7	Petah Tikva	184 695
8	Netanya	181 028
9	Holon	164 285
10	Bene Beraq	148 908
11	Ramat Gan	127 354
12	Bat Yam	123 211
13	Ashkelon	112 682
14	Rehoboth	108 710
15	Bet Shemesh	91 318
16	Kfar Saba	83 967
17	Hertzelia	82 971
18	Hadera	79 639
19	Nazareth	69 078

MEDINAT YISRA'EL • STATE OF ISRAEL

Capital	Jerusalem	Population	7 233 701 (97)	% in cities	92%
GDP per capita	$28 600 (48)	Area km²	22 072 km² (152)	GMT +/-	+2
Neighbours (km)	Egypt 266, Gaza Strip 51, Jordan 238, Lebanon 79, Syria 76, West Bank 307 • Coast 273				

RECENT INTERNATIONAL MATCHES PLAYED BY ISRAEL

2006	Opponents	Score		Venue	Comp	Scorers	Att	Referee
15-08	Slovenia	D	1-1	Celje	Fr	Benayoun [81]	3 000	Kralovec CZE
2-09	Estonia	W	1-0	Tallinn	ECq	Colautti [8]	7 800	Verbist BEL
6-09	Andorra	W	4-1	Nijmegan	ECq	Benayoun [9], Ben Shushan [11], Gershon [43p], Tamuz [69]	400	Zrnic BIH
7-10	Russia	D	1-1	Moscow	ECq	Ben Shushan [84]	22 000	Meyer GER
15-11	Croatia	L	3-4	Tel Aviv	ECq	Colautti 2 [8 89], Benayoun [68]	35 000	Iturralde Gonzalez ESP
2007								
7-02	Ukraine	D	1-1	Tel Aviv	Fr	Badeer [38]	12 000	S. Rodriguez ESP
24-03	England	D	0-0	Tel Aviv	ECq		38 000	Ovrebø NOR
28-03	Estonia	W	4-0	Tel Aviv	ECq	Idan Tal [19], Colautti [29], Sahar 2 [77 80]	21 000	Cüneyt Cakir TUR
2-06	FYR Macedonia	W	2-1	Skopje	ECq	Itzhaki [11], Colautti [44]	12 000	Kircher GER
6-06	Andorra	W	2-0	Andorra-La-Vella	ECq	Tamuz [37], Colautti [53]	680	Stokes IRL
22-08	Belarus	L	1-2	Minsk	Fr	Gershon [29p]	10 000	Malzhinskas LTU
8-09	England	L	0-3	London	ECq		85 372	Vink NED
13-10	Croatia	L	0-1	Zagreb	ECq		30 084	Stark GER
17-10	Belarus	W	2-1	Tel Aviv	Fr	Bruchian [37], Alberman [72]	4 362	Georgiev BUL
17-11	Russia	W	2-1	Tel Aviv	ECq	Barda [10], Golan [92+]	29 787	Farina ITA
21-11	FYR Macedonia	W	1-0	Tel Aviv	ECq	Barda [35]	2 736	Mikulski POL
2008								
6-02	Romania	W	1-0	Tel Aviv	Fr	Golan [25]	8 000	Duarte Gomez POR
26-03	Chile	W	1-0	Tel Aviv	Fr	Benayoun [30]	24 463	Velasco ESP
20-08	Finland	L	0-2	Tampere	Fr		4 929	
6-09	Switzerland	D	2-2	Ramat Gan	WCq	Benayoun [73], Sahar [92+]	29 600	Hansson SWE
10-09	Moldova	W	2-1	Chisinau	WCq	Golan [39], Saban [45]	10 500	Muniz ESP
11-10	Luxembourg	W	3-1	Luxembourg	WCq	Benayoun [2p], Golan [54], Toama [81]	3 562	Egorov RUS
15-10	Latvia	D	1-1	Riga	WCq	Benayoun [50]	7 100	Hrinak SVK
19-11	Côte d'Ivoire	D	2-2	Tel Aviv	Fr	Barda [18], Golan [24]	27 167	
2009								
11-02	Hungary	W	1-0	Tel Aviv	Fr	Benayoun [77]	9 500	Borski POL
28-03	Greece	D	1-1	Ramat Gan	WCq	Golan [55]	38 000	Rosetti ITA
1-04	Greece	L	1-2	Iraklio	WCq	Barda [58]	22 794	Benquerença POR
12-08	Northern Ireland	D	1-1	Belfast	Fr	Barda [27]	10 250	Valgeirsson ISL
5-09	Latvia	L	0-1	Ramat Gan	WCq		20 000	Kircher GER
9-09	Luxembourg	W	7-0	Ramat Gan	WCq	Barda 3 [9 21 43], Baruchyan [15], Golan [58], Sahar 2 [62 84]	7 038	Svendsen DEN
10-10	Moldova	W	3-1	Ramat Gan	WCq	Barda 2 [22 70], Ben Dayan [65]	8 700	Blom NED
14-10	Switzerland	D	0-0	Basel	WCq		38 500	Tudor ROU
2010								
26-05	Uruguay	L	1-4	Montevideo	Fr	Rafaelov [30]	60 000	Osses CHI
30-05	Chile	L	0-3	Concepcion	Fr		25 000	Arias PAR
2-09	Malta	W	3-1	Tel Aviv	ECq	Benayoun 3 [7 64p 75]	17 365	Ennjimi FRA
7-09	Georgia	D	0-0	Tbilisi	ECq		45 000	Kever SUI
9-10	Croatia	L	1-2	Tel Aviv	ECq	Shechter [81]	33 421	Stark Ger
12-10	Greece	L	1-2	Piraeus	ECq	OG [59]	16 935	Hansson SWE
17-11	Iceland	W	3-2	Tel Aviv	Fr	Damari 2 [5 14], Rafaelov [27]	4 500	Spathas GRE

Fr = Friendly match • EC = UEFA EURO 2008/2012 • WC = FIFA World Cup • q = qualifier

ISRAEL NATIONAL TEAM HISTORICAL RECORDS

Caps
94 - Arik Benado 1995-2007 • **88** - Alon Harazi 1992-2006 • **85** - Amir Schelach 1992-2001 • **83** - Mordechai Spiegler (57) 1963-77 & Nir Klinger (76) 1987-97 • **80** - Yossi Benayoun 1998- & Avi Nimni 1992-2006 • **78** - Tal Banin 1990-2002; Itzhak Shum (53) 1969-81 & Eyal Berkovic 1992-2004 • **74** - Walid Badir 1997-2007 • **72** - Alon Hazan 1990-2000 • **70** - Itzik Visoker (43) 1963-76

Goals
33 - Mordechai Spiegler 1963-77 • **24** - Yehoshua Feigenbaum 1966-77 • **23** - Ronen Harazi 1992-99 & Yossi Benayoun 1998- • **22** - Nahum Stelmach 1956-68 • **21** - Gidi Damti 1971-81 • **18** - Giora Spiegel 1965-80 & Yehoshua Glazer 1949-61

Past Coaches
Egon Pollack AUT 1948 • Lajos Hess 1949 • Vladislav Scali HUN 1950 • Jerry Beit haLevi 1953-54 • Jack Gibbons ENG 1956 • Jerry Beit haLevi 1957 • Moshe Varon 1958 • Gyula Mandi HUN 1959-63 • George Ainsley ENG 1963-64 • Yosef Mirmovich YUG 1964 • Gyula Mandi HUN 1964 • Yosef Mirmovich 1964-65 • Milovan Ciric 1965-68 • Emmanuel Scheffer 1968-70 • Edmond Schmilovich 1970-73 • David Schweitzer 1973-77 • Emmanuel Scheffer 1978-79 • Jack Mansell ENG 1980-81 • Yosef Mirmovich 1983-86 • Miljenko Mihic YUG 1986-88 • Itzhak Schneor • Ya'akov Grundman 1988-92 • Shlomo Scharf 1992-2000 • Richard Moller Nielsen DEN 2000-02 • Avram Grant 2002-06 • Dror Kashtan 2006-10 • Eli Ohana 2010 • Luis Fernandez FRA 2010-

Appearances and goals in brackets are totals in games recognised as full internationals by FIFA)

ISRAEL 2009-10

LIGAT HA'AL

	Pl	W	D	L	F	A	Pts	Hapoel TA	Maccabi H	Maccabi TA	Bnei Yehuda	Beitar	Ashdod	Bnei Sakhnin	Maccabi PT	Hapoel BS	Maccabi N	Hapoel H	Hapoel A	Hapoel PT	Hapoel RG	Hapoel R	Maccabi AN
Hapoel Tel Aviv †	35	25	9	1	87	26	49		1-2	1-0	4-0	4-3	2-2	1-0	1-1	4-1	3-3	2-0	5-3	7-1	3-1	5-0	4-0
Maccabi Haifa ‡	35	28	3	4	72	16	49	0-0		1-0	2-0	2-1	1-0	1-0	2-0	4-1	2-0	0-0	2-1	3-0	3-1	3-0	4-1
Maccabi Tel Aviv ‡	35	17	9	9	52	35	34	2-4	1-0		0-0	4-3	2-0	3-1	1-1	1-1	2-2	1-0	1-1	1-0	3-1	2-0	0-1
Bnei Yehuda Tel Aviv ‡	35	14	11	10	43	34	31	0-1	0-2	0-1		0-0	2-3	2-1	2-0	2-2	2-1	2-0	2-1	1-1	1-2	2-1	2-0
Beitar Jerusalem	35	14	7	14	50	44	26	0-0	0-3	0-1	1-0		2-0	1-0	1-2	1-1	3-1	1-1	3-0	1-0	1-0	3-1	5-0
FC Ashdod	35	11	10	14	36	45	22	0-4	0-1	3-1	0-3	2-0		0-0	1-1	5-2	3-0	1-0	1-0	2-1	0-0	0-0	2-1
Hapoel Bnei Sakhnin	33	13	8	12	31	31	27	1-2	2-1	0-0	2-0	0-0	1-0		3-4	1-1	0-3	0-3	1-0	2-0	3-1	1-1	1-1
Maccabi Petah Tikva	33	10	11	12	44	47	24	0-0	0-1	2-1	0-1	1-3	1-1	1-2		3-0	0-3	2-2	2-3	0-0	1-1	2-3	1-0
Hapoel Be'er Sheva	33	11	10	12	49	55	23	1-3	1-3	1-3	0-0	3-2	1-0	1-0	0-1		2-0	2-3	3-2	2-0	1-0	2-1	2-2
Maccabi Netanya	33	10	9	14	44	47	21	0-3	1-0	1-0	1-1	3-0	0-1	1-2	2-2	2-2		1-2	1-0	1-0	2-3	1-1	5-0
Hapoel Haifa	35	10	9	16	44	50	23	1-2	0-1	3-1	0-3	3-2	0-1	0-1	2-0	0-0	0-0		2-4	1-2	1-1	3-1	2-2
Hapoel Acre	35	7	14	14	38	52	23	1-1	0-3	2-3	1-1	0-3	1-1	0-0	2-2	1-3	1-1	2-2		0-0	1-0	1-1	0-1
Hapoel Petah Tikva	35	8	14	13	28	48	23	1-1	0-4	0-2	1-1	0-0	1-1	0-0	1-1	1-0	2-1	2-2	1-1		0-0	2-3	3-0
Hapoel Ramat Gan	35	9	11	15	34	49	22	0-3	0-5	1-4	0-2	0-0	1-1	1-0	0-3	2-2	1-0	3-2	1-1	0-0		1-0	2-3
Hapoel Ranana	35	6	10	19	33	58	18	1-4	1-3	0-3	0-3	1-3	1-1	0-1	3-1	2-2	1-1	2-1	0-1	2-1	0-1		1-1
Maccabi Akhi Nazareth	35	7	7	21	33	81	16	0-4	0-5	3-3	2-2	0-1	1-0	0-2	1-2	1-4	1-3	1-3	1-0	1-2	0-1	2-1	

22/08/2009 - 15/05/2010 • † Qualified for the UEFA Champions League • ‡ Qualified for the Europa League • Points halved after 30 matches
Relegation play-off: **Hapoel Ramat Gan** 1-0 Hapoel Kfar-Saba
Top scorers: **28** - Shlomi Arbeitman, Maccabi Haifa • **22** - Itay Shechter, Hapoel Tel Aviv • **16** - Vladimir Dvalishvili GEO, Maccabi Haifa & Barak Yitzhaki, Beitar • **13** - Dimitar Makriev BUL, Ashdod • **12** - Pedro Galvan ARG, Bnei Yehuda & Toto Tamuz, Beitar

ISRAEL 2009-10 LIGA LEUMIT (2)

	Pl	W	D	L	F	A	Pts
Ironi Kiriat Shmona	35	21	9	5	51	22	41
Hapoel Ashkelon	35	15	11	9	47	42	34
Hapoel Kfar Saba	35	16	9	10	56	47	32
Sektzia Nes Tziona	35	13	15	7	45	29	31
Ironi Ramat Hasharon	35	13	11	11	50	37	27
Ironi Bat Yam	35	14	7	14	43	41	27
Hapoel Upper Nazareth	33	12	14	7	38	24	29
Ironi Rishon Letzion	33	13	7	13	39	31	26
Ahva Arraba §1	33	12	9	12	37	37	23
Maccabi Hertzelia	33	10	12	11	31	28	22
Hakoah Ramat Gan	35	11	14	10	44	42	28
Beitar/Shimshon TA	35	10	13	12	31	47	27
Hapoel Bnei Lod	35	10	15	10	37	34	26
Maccabi Be'er Sheva	35	12	6	17	42	53	24
Hapoel Jerusalem	35	6	11	18	40	66	18
Hapoel Marmorek	35	2	9	24	21	72	8

21/08/2009 - 15/05/2010 • § = points deducted
Relegation play-off: Maccabi Be'er Sheva 2-0 HaShikma

Top group play-offs: Maccabi TA 3-0 Beitar • Hapoel TA 1-0 Bnei Yehuda • Maccabi Haifa 3-1 Ashdod • Bnei Yehuda 0-0 Maccabi Tel-Aviv • Ashdod 1-2 Beitar • Maccabi Haifa 0-1 Hapoel TA • Hapoel TA 4-0 Ashdod • Beitar 0-2 Bnei Yehuda • Maccabi TA 0-2 Maccabi Haifa • Ashdod 2-3 Bnei Yehuda • Hapoel TA 0-0 Maccabi TA • Maccabi Haifa 2-1 Beitar • Beitar 1-2 Hapoel TA • Bnei Yehuda 1-1 Maccabi Haifa • Maccabi TA 2-0 Ashdod
Middle Group play-offs: Bnei Sakhnin 2-0 Mac Petah Tikva • Be'er Sheva 4-0 Netanya • Bnei Sakhnin 1-0 Be'er Sheva • Mac Petah Tikva 3-1 Netanya • Netanya 2-0 Bnei Sakhnin • Be'er Sheva 1-4 Mac Petah Tikva
Relegation group play-offs: Hapoel Haifa 2-2 Akhi Nazareth • H Petah Tikva 1-2 Acre • Ramat Gan 0-0 Ranana • Ranana 4-0 Acre • Akhi Nazareth 3-0 H Petah Tikva • Ramat Gan 0-1 Hapoel Haifa • Acre 3-1 Akhi Nazareth • Hapoel Haifa 1-0 Ranana • H Petah Tikva 2-1 Ramat Gan • Hapoel Haifa 1-2 H Petah Tikva • Ranana 2-0 Akhi Nazareth • Ramat Gan 0-0 Acre • Acre 1-0 Hapoel Haifa • H Petah Tikva 0-0 Ranana • Akhi Nazareth 0-7 Ramat Gan

MEDALS TABLE

		Overall			League			Cup		Asia/Eur			
		G	S	B	G	S	B	G	S	G	S	B	City
1	Maccabi Tel Aviv	42	20	8	18	9	8	22	11	2			Tel Aviv
2	Hapoel Tel Aviv	26	20	6	12	11	6	13	8	1	1		Tel Aviv
3	Maccabi Haifa	16	14	5	11	6	5	5	8				Haifa
4	Beitar Jerusalem	13	9	5	6	6	5	7	3				Jerusalem
5	Hapoel Petach Tikva	8	15	4	6	9	4	2	6				Petach Tikva
6	Maccabi Netanya	6	6	4	5	4	4	1	2				Netanya
7	Hapoel Haifa	4	7	8	1	2	8	3	5				Haifa
8	Hakoah Ramat Gan	4	1	1	2		1	2	1				Ramat Gan
9	Hapoel Kfar Saba	4			1			3					Kfar Saba
10	Bnei Yehuda Tel Aviv	3	7	2	1	3	2	2	4				Tel Aviv
11	Hapoel Beer Sheva	3	2	5	2		5	1	2				Beer Sheva
12	Maccabi Petach Tikva	2	5	1		3	1	2	2				Petach Tikva

G'VIAA H'AMEDINA (STATE CUP) 2009–10

Eighth Round

Team	Score
Hapoel Tel Aviv	3
Hapoel Haifa *	0
Ironi Kiriat Shmona *	0
Maccabi Kabilio Jaffa	1
Maccabi Tel Aviv *	3
Maccabi Netanya	1
Maccabi Be'er Sheva *	1
Beitar Jerusalem	4
Maccabi Petah Tikva	5
Maccabi Akhi Nazareth *	1
Hapoel Marmorek *	0
Hapoel Bnei Lod	2
Hapoel Be'er Sheva *	1
Maccabi Ironi Netivot	0
Beitar Kfar Saba *	0
Ironi Ramat Hasharon	1
FC Ashdod	1
Hakoah Ramat Gan *	0
Ironi Sayid Umm Al Fahm*	0
Hapoel Bnei Sakhnin	2
Hapoel Petah Tikva *	1 8p
Hapoel Ranana	1 7p
Hapoel Arad *	1 4p
Hapoel Upper Nazareth	1 5p
Hapoel Ramat Gan	1
Karmiel Safed *	0
Hapoel Kfar Saba *	0
Maccabi Haifa	5
Hapoel Ashkelon *	2
Sektzia Nes Tziona	1
Hapoel Acre	0
Bnei Yehuda Tel Aviv *	2

Round of 16

Team	Score
Hapoel Tel Aviv	5
Maccabi Kabilio Jaffa *	0
Maccabi Tel Aviv	1 8p
Beitar Jerusalem *	1 9p
Maccabi Petah Tikva	3
Hapoel Bnei Lod *	1
Hapoel Be'er Sheva *	1
Ironi Ramat Hasharon	3
FC Ashdod *	2
Hapoel Bnei Sakhnin	1
Hapoel Petah Tikva *	0 0p
Hapoel Upper Nazareth	0 3p
Hapoel Ramat Gan *	2
Maccabi Haifa	1
Hapoel Ashkelon	0
Bnei Yehuda Tel Aviv *	1

Quarter-finals

Team	Score
Hapoel Tel Aviv *	2
Beitar Jerusalem	0
Maccabi Petah Tikva	1
Ironi Ramat Hasharon *	2
FC Ashdod *	3
Hapoel Upper Nazareth	0
Hapoel Ramat Gan *	0
Bnei Yehuda Tel Aviv	1

Semi-finals

Team	Score
Hapoel Tel Aviv	3
Ironi Ramat Hasharon	1
FC Ashdod	1 3p
Bnei Yehuda Tel Aviv	1 4p

Final

Team	Score
Hapoel Tel Aviv	3
Bnei Yehuda Tel Aviv	1

CUP FINAL

National Stadium, Ramat Gan
11-05-2010, Att: 34,442, Ref: Tabrizi
Scorers - Vermouth 2 25 75, Enyeama 42p for
Hapoel; Douglas 38 for Bnei Yehuda
Hapoel - Vincent Enyeama - Omri Kenda●,
Walid Badir, Douglas, Dedi Ben Dayan - Avihai
Yadin●, Eran Zhavi, Gil Vermouth, Daniel De
Ridder (Shay Abutbol● 74) - Etey Shechter
(Zurab Menteshashvili 88), Ma'aran Al Lala
(Bojan Vrucina 70). Tr: Eli Guttman
Bnei Yehuda - Dele Aiyenugba◆❖42 - Oz Raii
(Mahran Radi 86), Din Mori (Ran Kadosh 42),
Aviv Hadad, Ivan Garrido - Kfir Edri, Liroy Zairi,
Itzhak Azoz, Asi Baldut● - Michael Zandberg
(Moshe Biton 65), Eliran Atar. Tr: Guy Luzon

Premier League clubs enter in the eighth round ● * Home team

ITA – ITALY

FIFA/COCA-COLA WORLD RANKING

1993	1994	1995	1996	1997	1998	1999	2000	2001	2002	2003	2004	2005	2006	2007	2008	2009	2010
2	4	3	10	9	7	14	4	6	13	10	10	12	2	3	4	4	14

	2010											Hi/Lo
	Jan	Feb	Mar	Mar	Apr	May	Jul	Aug	Sep	Oct	Nov	Dec	1
	4	4	4	5	5	5	11	11	13	16	14	14	16

Italy's dismal failure at the 2010 FIFA World Cup in South Africa drew strong comparisons with the previous low-point in the history of the team - the humiliating first round exit in the 1966 World Cup. The defending champions could only draw with both Paraguay and New Zealand and after losing to Slovakia in the final group game they finished bottom of their group. An over reliance by Marcelo Lippi on the players that won the trophy in Germany was seen as the reason for the failure and he quickly resigned after the tournament and was replaced by Cesare Prandelli. In 2006 the national team had provided welcome relief from a club scene in chaos but in 2010 it was the other way around with Internazionale winning the UEFA Champions League for the first time since 1965. Coached by the charismatic Jose Mourinho, Inter claimed the first treble in the history of Italian football, a magnificent achievement for a club that for two decades had lived in the shadow of both Juventus and neighbours Milan. In the Champions League final they beat Bayern Munich 2-0 to complete the treble having earlier beaten Roma 1-0 in the final of the Coppa Italia and having claimed a fifth consecutive Serie A title. Despite the loss of Mourinho to Real Madrid, Inter finished 2010 by claiming the FIFA Club World Cup in Abu Dhabi.

FIFA WORLD CUP RECORD

1930 DNE **1934** 1 Winners (hosts) **1938** 1 Winners **1950** 7 r1 **1954** 10 r1 1958 DNQ **1962** 9 r1 **1966** 9 r1 **1970** 2 Finalists **1974** 10 r1 **1978** 4 r2 **1982** 1 Winners **1986** 11 r2 **1990** 3 SF (hosts) **1994** 2 Finalists **1998** 5 QF **2002** 12 r2 **2006** 1 Winners **2010** 26 r1

FEDERAZIONE ITALIANA GIUOCO CALCIO (FIGC)

Via Gregorio Allegri 14, Roma 00198

☎ +39 06 84912542
📠 +39 06 84912526
✉ international@figc.it
🖳 www.figc.it
FA 1898 CON 1954 FIFA 1905
P Giancarlo Abete
GS Antonio Di Sebastiano

FIFA BIG COUNT 2006

Total players	4 980 296
% of population	8.57%
Male	4 688 929
Female	291 367
Amateurs 18+	877 602
Youth under 18	557 453
Unregistered	3 207 700
Professionals	3 541
Referees	24 981
Admin & coaches	53 500
Number of clubs	16 128
Number of teams	80 864

MAJOR CITIES/TOWNS

		Population
1	Rome	2 491 807
2	Milan	1 324 927
3	Naples	959 303
4	Turin	862 469
5	Palermo	647 870
6	Genoa	585 060
7	Florence	378 158
8	Bologna	371 940
9	Bari	304 594
10	Catania	289 838
11	Venice	265 493
12	Verona	263 899
13	Messina	236 530
14	Padova	215 258
15	Trieste	198 389
16	Brescia	195 448
17	Taranto	190 548
18	Parma	186 566
49	Udine	97 669

REPUBBLICA ITALIANA • ITALIAN REPUBLIC

Capital	Rome	Population	58 126 212 (23)	% in cities	68%
GDP per capita	$31 400 (41)	Area km²	301 340 km² (71)	GMT +/-	+1
Neighbours (km)	Austria 430, France 488, San Marino 39, Slovenia 199, Switzerland 740 • Coast 7600				

RECENT INTERNATIONAL MATCHES PLAYED BY ITALY

2008	Opponents		Score	Venue	Comp	Scorers	Att	Referee
9-06	Netherlands	L	0-3	Berne	ECr1		30 777	Fröjdfeldt SWE
13-06	Romania	D	1-1	Zürich	ECr1	Panucci 56	30 585	Ovrebø NOR
17-06	France	W	2-0	Zürich	ECr1	Pirlo 25p, De Rossi 62	30 585	Michel SVK
22-06	Spain	D	0-0	Vienna	ECqf	L 2-4p	51 178	Fandel GER
20-08	Austria	D	2-2	Nice	Fr	Gilardino 45, Ozcan OG 66	14 000	Coue FRA
6-09	Cyprus	W	2-1	Larnaca	WCq	Di Natale 2 8 92+	6 000	Vink NED
10-09	Georgia	W	2-0	Udine	WCq	DeRossi 2 17 89	27 164	Einwaller AUT
11-10	Bulgaria	D	0-0	Sofia	WCq		35 000	Lannoy FRA
15-10	Montenegro	W	2-1	Lecce	WCq	Aquilani 2 8 29	20 162	Proenca POR
19-11	Greece	D	1-1	Piraeus	Fr	Toni 54	7 000	Webb ENG
2009								
10-02	Brazil	L	0-2	London	Fr		60 077	Webb ENG
28-03	Montenegro	W	2-0	Podgorica	WCq	Pirlo 11p, Pazzini 75	10 500	Atkinson ENG
1-04	Republic of Ireland	D	1-1	Bari	WCq	Iaquinta 10	48 000	Stark GER
6-06	Northern Ireland	W	3-0	Pisa	Fr	Rossi 20, Foggia 53, Pellissier 72	16 583	Blom NED
10-06	New Zealand	W	4-3	Atteridgeville	Fr	Gilardino 2 33 48, Iaquinta 2 68 73	2 000	Bennett RSA
15-06	USA	W	3-1	Pretoria	CCr1	Rossi 2 58 94+, De Rossi 72	34 341	Pozo CHI
18-06	Egypt	L	0-1	Johannesburg	CCr1		52 150	Hansson SWE
21-06	Brazil	L	0-3	Pretoria	CCr1		41 195	Archundia MEX
12-08	Switzerland	D	0-0	Basel	Fr		31 500	Kircher GER
5-09	Georgia	W	2-0	Tbilisi	WCq	Kaladze OG 2 56 66	32 000	Borski POL
9-09	Bulgaria	W	2-0	Turin	WCq	Grosso 11, Iaquinta 40	26 122	Meyer GER
10-10	Republic of Ireland	D	2-2	Dublin	WCq	Camoranesi 26, Gilardino 90	70 640	Hauge NOR
14-10	Cyprus	W	3-2	Parma	WCq	Gilardino 3 78 81 92+	15 009	Yefet ISR
14-11	Netherlands	D	0-0	Pescara	Fr		17 134	Circhetta SUI
18-11	Sweden	W	1-0	Cesena	Fr	Chiellini 29	18 260	Skomina SVN
2010								
3-03	Cameroon	D	0-0	Monte Carlo	Fr		10 752	Ennjimi FRA
3-06	Mexico	L	1-2	Brussels	Fr	Bonucci 89	30 000	Verbist BEL
5-06	Switzerland	D	1-1	Geneva	Fr	Quagliarella 14	30 000	Piccirillo FRA
14-06	Paraguay	D	1-1	Cape Town	WCr1	De Rossi 63	62 869	Archundia MEX
20-06	New Zealand	D	1-1	Nelspruit	WCr1	Iaquinta 29p	38 229	Batres GUA
24-06	Slovakia	L	2-3	Johannesburg	WCr1	Di Natale 81, Quagliarella 92+	53 412	Webb ENG
10-08	Cote d'Ivoire	L	0-1	London	Fr		11 176	Atkinson ENG
3-09	Estonia	W	2-1	Tallinn	ECq	Cassano 60, Bonucci 63	8 600	Velasco ESP
7-09	Faroe Islands	W	5-0	Florence	ECq	Gilardino 11, De Rossi 22, Cassano 27, Quagliarella 81, Pirlo 90	19 266	Kulbakov BLR
8-10	Northern Ireland	D	0-0	Belfast	ECq		15 200	Chapron FRA
12-10	Serbia	W	3-0	Genoa	ECq	Match abanadoned after six minutes at 0-0	28 000	Thomson SCO
17-11	Romania	D	1-1	Klagenfurt	Fr	OG 82	14 000	Einwaller AUT

Fr = Friendly match • EC = UEFA EURO 2008/2012 • WC = FIFA World Cup • q = qualifier • r1 = first round group • qf = quarter-finals

ITALY NATIONAL TEAM HISTORICAL RECORDS

Caps

136 - Fabio Cannavaro 1997- • **126** - Paolo Maldini 1988-2002 • **112** - Dino Zoff 1968-83 • **102** - Gianluigi Buffon 1997- • **97** - Gianluca Zambrotta 1999- • **94** - Giacinto Facchetti 1963-77 • **91** - Alessandro Del Piero 1995-2008 • **81** - Franco Baresi 1982-94, Giuseppe Bergomi 1982-98 & Marco Tardelli 1976-85 • **79** - Demetrio Albertini 1991-2002 • **78** - Alessandro Nesta 1996-2006 & Gaetano Scirea 1975-86 • **73** - Giancarlo Antognoni 1974-83, Antonio Cabrini 1978-87 & Gennaro Gattuso 2000- • **71** - Claudio Gentile 1975-84

Goals

35 - Luigi Riva 1965-74 • **33** - Giuseppe Meazza 1930-39 • **30** - Silvio Piola 1935-52 • **27** - Roberto Baggio 1988-2004 & Alessandro Del Piero 1995-2008 • **25** - Adolfo Baloncieri 1920-30, Filippo Inzaghi 1997-2007 & Alessandro Altobelli • **23** - Christian Vieri 1997-2005 & Francesco Graziani 1975-83 • **22** - Alessandro Mazzola 1963-74 • **20** - Paolo Rossi 1977-86 • **19** - Roberto Bettega 1975-83

Past Coaches

Committee 1910-12 • Vittorio Pozzo 1912 • Committee 1912-24 • Vittorio Pozzo 1924 • Committee 1924-25 • Augusto Rangone 1925-28 • Carlo Carcano 1928-29 • Vittorio Pozzo 1929-48 • Committe - Novo, Bardelli, Copernico & Biancone 1949-59 • Committee - Beretta, Busini & Combi 1951 • Committee - Beretta & G. Meazza 1952-53 • Committee - Czeizler, Schiavio & Piola 1953-54 • Committee - Marmo, Pasquale, Tentorio, Schiavio & Foni 1954-56 • Committee - Foni, Pasquale, Schiavio, Tentorio, Marmo, Biancone 1957-58 • Committee - Ferrari, Mocchetti & Biancone 1958-59 • Giuseppe Viani 1960 • Giovanni Ferrari 1960-61 • Giovanni Ferrari & Paolo Mazza 1962 • Edmondo Fabbri 1962-66 • Helenio Herrera & Ferruccio Valcareggi 1966-67 • Ferruccio Valcareggi 1967-74 • Fulvio Bernardini 1974-75 • Fulvio Bernardini & Enzo Bearzot 1975-77 • Enzo Bearzot 1977-86 • Azeglio Vicini 1986-91 • Arrigo Sacchi 1991-96 • Cesare Maldini 1997-98 • Dino Zoff 1998-2000 • Giovanni Trapattoni 2000-04 • Marcello Lippi 2004-06 • Roberto Donadoni 2006-08 • Marcello Lippi 2008-10 • Cesare Prandelli 2010-

ITALY 2009-10

SERIE A

	Pl	W	D	L	F	A	Pts	Inter	Roma	Milan	Sampdoria	Palermo	Napoli	Juventus	Parma	Genoa	Bari	Fiorentina	Lazio	Catania	Chievo	Udinese	Cagliari	Bologna	Atalanta	Siena	Livorno
Internazionale †	38	24	10	4	75	34	82		1-1	2-0	0-0	5-3	3-1	2-0	2-0	0-0	1-1	1-0	1-0	2-1	4-3	2-1	3-0	3-0	3-1	4-3	3-0
Roma †	38	24	8	6	68	41	80	2-1		0-0	1-2	4-1	2-1	1-3	2-0	3-0	3-1	3-1	1-0	1-0	1-0	4-2	2-1	2-1	2-1	2-1	0-1
Milan †	38	20	10	8	60	39	70	0-4	2-1		3-0	0-2	1-1	3-0	2-0	5-2	0-0	1-1	2-2	1-0	3-2	4-3	1-0	3-1	4-0		1-1
Sampdoria †	38	19	10	9	49	41	67	1-0	0-0	2-1		1-1	1-0	1-1	1-0	0-0	2-0	2-1	1-1	2-1	3-1	1-1	4-1	2-0	4-1	2-0	
Palermo ‡	38	18	11	9	59	47	65	1-1	3-3	3-1	1-1		2-1	2-0	2-1	0-0	1-1	3-0	3-1	1-1	3-1	1-0	2-1	3-1	1-0	1-0	1-0
Napoli ‡	38	15	14	9	50	43	59	0-0	2-2	2-2	1-0	0-0		3-1	2-3	0-0	3-2	1-3	0-0	1-0	2-0	0-0	0-0	2-1	2-0	2-1	3-1
Juventus ‡	38	16	7	15	55	56	55	2-1	1-2	0-3	5-1	0-2	2-3		2-3	3-2	3-0	1-1	1-1	2-1	1-0	1-0	1-0	1-1	2-1	3-3	2-0
Parma	38	14	10	14	46	51	52	1-1	1-2	1-0	1-0	1-0	1-1	1-2		2-3	2-0	1-1	0-2	2-1	2-0	0-0	0-2	2-1	1-0	1-0	4-1
Genoa	38	14	9	15	57	61	51	0-5	3-2	1-0	3-0	2-2	4-1	2-2	2-2		1-1	2-1	1-2	2-1	0-1	0-3	5-3	3-4	2-0	4-2	1-1
Bari	38	13	11	14	49	49	50	2-2	0-1	0-2	2-1	4-2	1-2	3-1	1-1	3-0		2-0	2-0	0-0	1-0	2-0	0-0	1-0	0-4	2-1	1-0
Fiorentina	38	13	8	17	48	47	47	2-2	0-1	1-2	2-0	1-0	0-1	1-2	2-3	3-0	2-1		0-0	3-1	0-2	4-1	1-0	1-2	2-0	1-1	2-1
Lazio	38	11	13	14	39	43	46	0-2	1-2	1-2	1-1	1-1	1-1	0-2	1-1	1-2	0-1	1-1		0-1	1-1	3-1	0-0	1-0	2-0	4-1	1-1
Catania	38	10	15	13	44	45	45	3-1	1-1	0-1	2-1	2-2	0-0	0-1	3-0	1-0	4-0	1-0	1-1		1-2	1-1	2-1	1-0	0-0	2-2	0-1
Chievo Verona	38	12	8	18	37	42	44	0-1	0-2	1-2	1-2	1-0	1-2	1-0	0-0	3-1	1-2	2-1	1-2	1-1		1-1	2-1	1-1	1-1	0-1	2-0
Udinese	38	11	11	16	54	59	44	2-3	2-1	1-0	2-3	3-2	3-1	3-0	2-2	2-0	3-3	0-1	1-1	4-2	0-0		2-1	1-1	3-4	1-2	0
Cagliari	38	11	11	16	56	58	44	1-2	2-2	2-3	2-0	2-2	3-3	2-0	3-2	3-3	2-1	2-2	2-2	1-2	2-2	1-1		3-0	1-3	3-0	
Bologna	38	10	12	16	42	55	42	1-3	0-2	0-0	1-1	3-1	2-1	1-2	2-1	1-3	2-1	1-1	2-3	1-1	0-2	2-1	0-1		2-2	2-1	2-0
Atalanta	38	9	8	21	37	53	35	1-1	1-2	1-1	0-1	1-2	0-2	2-5	3-1	0-1	1-0	2-1	3-0	0-0	0-1	0-0	3-1	1-1		2-0	3-1
Siena	38	7	10	21	40	67	31	0-1	1-2	1-2	1-2	1-0	0-0	1-1	1-0	0-3	2-1	5-1	3-2	0-0	2-1	1-1	1-0	0-2			0-0
Livorno	38	7	8	23	27	61	29	0-2	3-3	0-0	3-1	1-2	0-2	1-1	2-1	1-2	1-1	1-2	3-1	0-2	0-2	0-0	1-1	0-1	1-2		

22/08/2009 - 16/05/2010 • † Qualified for the UEFA Champions League • ‡ Qualified for the Europa League

Top scorers: **29** - Antonio Di Natale, Udinese • **22** - Diego Milito ARG, Inter • **19** - Fabrizio Miccoli, Palermo & Giampaolo Pazzini, Sampdoria • **15** - Alberto Gilardino, Fiorentina • **14** - Barreto BRA, Bari; Marco Borriello, Milan; Francesco Totti, Roma & Mirko Vucinic MNE, Roma • **13** - Alessandro Matri, Cagliari & Edinson Cavani URU, Palermo

ITALY 2009-10

SERIE B (2)

	Pl	W	D	L	F	A	Pts	Lecce	Cesena	Brescia	Sassuolo	Torino	Cittadella	Grosseto	Crotone	Ascoli	Empoli	AlbinoLeffe	Modena	Reggina	Vicenza	Piacenza	Frosinone	Ancona	Triestina	Padova	Mantova	Gallipoli	Salernitana
Lecce	42	20	15	7	66	47	75		1-2	2-2	0-0	2-1	1-5	3-2	0-0	0-0	1-0	2-1	0-0	3-2	1-0	1-0	1-3	3-0	1-1	2-1	2-1	1-0	1-0
Cesena	42	20	14	8	55	29	74	3-1		2-0	0-1	1-1	1-0	2-2	0-2	1-0	2-0	3-0	1-1	3-0	4-0	2-1	2-0	3-1	0-3	1-0	2-0	3-1	3-0
Brescia ‡	42	21	9	12	60	44	72	1-0	0-1		3-1	1-0	1-3	0-2	2-1	2-2	4-1	1-0	0-0	0-1	3-1	3-0	4-0	0-2	4-2	3-2	1-0	0-1	3-0
Sassuolo ‡	42	18	15	9	60	42	69	1-1	1-1	0-2		2-3	1-0	2-3	2-0	0-1	3-2	0-0	0-0	1-1	2-2	1-1	0-2	2-2	1-0	2-2	3-2	1-0	1-2
Torino ‡	42	19	11	12	53	36	68	2-2	1-1	1-1	0-1		1-0	4-1	1-2	1-0	3-0	2-1	0-1	2-0	1-0	1-1	3-1	1-1	1-0	0-1	1-1	2-0	2-3
Cittadella ‡	42	18	12	12	62	43	66	3-0	1-1	1-1	0-0	2-0		1-1	3-0	2-0	2-1	2-1	1-1	1-0	1-1	1-0	1-0	2-0	1-1	6-0	1-2	1-0	2-2
Grosseto	42	14	19	9	66	63	61	0-3	1-1	2-1	2-2	0-3	3-0		0-4	2-1	1-0	2-2	3-1	2-2	4-0	3-3	2-1	2-0	3-1	2-0	3-2	1-2	2-2
Crotone §2	42	17	11	14	53	50	60	1-1	0-0	0-0	1-2	1-0	1-1	0-0		1-2	2-1	0-3	4-2	1-1	1-2	1-0	3-0	2-1	2-0	2-1	2-2	4-2	2-0
Ascoli	42	15	12	15	57	57	57	1-2	1-1	2-0	1-5	1-2	1-1	1-1	3-1		2-1	1-1	2-0	1-3	1-1	1-1	1-2	1-3	1-0	1-0	2-1	1-1	4-2
Empoli	42	15	11	16	66	56	56	2-2	2-0	1-2	1-1	0-0	4-3	2-2	3-1	4-2		1-3	3-0	2-1	0-2	0-2	3-0	3-1	1-4	4-0	4-0	2-2	5-2
AlbinoLeffe	42	14	13	15	59	56	55	1-3	1-2	1-1	0-0	0-2	1-1	1-1	1-1	1-1	2-0		0-3	2-0	2-2	0-1	4-1	1-3	0-3	1-2	1-0	3-2	0-2
Modena	42	14	12	16	39	47	54	0-0	1-0	1-2	1-1	0-2	2-1	1-0	2-1	1-2	2-0	1-1		1-0	1-0	0-3	2-1	2-0	0-0	1-1	3-2	1-0	
Reggina	42	15	9	18	51	56	54	2-4	1-3	4-0	0-2	1-2	1-1	1-1	1-0	1-2	1-3	1-0	1-0		0-2	2-1	1-0	0-3	3-1	1-1	3-1	2-1	3-1
Vicenza	42	12	17	13	40	41	53	0-0	0-0	1-0	1-1	1-0	0-2	0-0	0-0	2-2	2-2	1-1	2-1	1-3	1-0		0-0	2-0	2-2	0-0	0-0	1-1	2-2
Piacenza	42	13	14	15	40	45	53	3-2	0-1	1-3	1-3	0-0	1-0	1-0	1-1	0-2	1-0	0-3	0-0	1-1	0-2		0-2	1-0	0-0	2-1	0-0	2-0	1-0
Frosinone	42	15	8	19	50	67	53	0-4	0-2	1-0	0-3	2-2	2-1	1-0	1-1	1-5	3-1	2-2	0-0	2-0	0-0	1-2	3		1-1	1-1	2-2	1-0	2-0	1-0
Ancona §2	42	15	9	18	55	56	52	1-1	0-0	2-0	2-2	2-1	2-3	1-1	0-1	1-0	2-1	2-0	2-1	2-0	1-2	2-0	2-1	3-1		2-1	2-2	1-1	3-1	2-0
Triestina ‡	42	13	12	17	41	51	51	1-4	0-0	0-1	0-1	2-0	2-0	1-0	0-0	2-0	1-0	2-3	1-1	2-1	0-0	1-0	3-0	3-2			2-1	2-1	1-0	2-0
Padova ‡	42	12	15	15	44	48	51	1-1	1-0	2-1	1-1	0-1	2-2	1-0	2-0	2-3	2-0	3-2	0-2	0-1	1-1	2-1	1-1	2-0	0-0	2-0		3-0	0-3	3-1
Mantova	42	10	18	14	46	58	48	2-2	0-1	2-2	2-1	1-0	1-3	2-0	2-1	0-0	1-1	1-2	1-1	2-1	2-1	1-3	1-2	0-0	2-1			1-0	1-1
Gallipoli	42	10	10	22	43	74	40	0-3	0-2	1-2	1-1	0-1	1-2	2-2	2-3	1-4	0-0	1-5	1-0	2-1	0-5	1-4	2-1	1-0	2-1	1-0	2-0		3-2
Salernitana §6	42	5	8	29	40	80	17	1-2	0-0	1-3	1-4	0-3	1-2	3-4	4-1	0-0	1-0	1-1	1-2	0-2	0-1	1-0	1-2	3-0	1-2	0-0	1-3	1-3	

21/08/2009 - 30/05/2010 • § = points deducted • ‡ = promotion/relegation play-off • Top scorer: **26** - Eder BRA, Empoli

Play-off semis: Cittadella 0-1 1-0 **Brescia** • **Torino** 1-1 2-1 Sassuolo

Play-off final: • Torino 0-0 1-2 **Brescia** • Brescia promoted

Relegation play-off: • **Padova** 0-0 3-0 Triestina • Triestina relegated but were spared when Ancona were later excluded

ITALY 2009–10

LEGA PRO PRIMA DIVISIONE GROUP A (3)

	Pl	W	D	L	F	A	Pts	Novara	Varese	Cremonese	Arezzo	Benevento	Lumezzane	Figline	Alessandria	Sorrento	Monza	Perugia	Como	Foligno	Viareggio	Pergocrema	Pro Patria	Paganese	Lecco
Novara	34	18	13	3	52	24	67		1-1	3-3	0-0	2-0	3-2	1-0	1-0	2-1	1-1	2-1	1-1	2-0	1-1	2-0	1-1	0-1	3-0
Varese ‡	34	17	11	6	53	34	62	1-1		5-1	1-0	1-1	4-2	1-0	1-0	2-1	2-2	2-0	1-0	2-0	4-2	2-1	3-1	5-2	1-0
Cremonese ‡	34	16	13	5	62	47	61	0-2	4-1		5-1	1-0	1-1	5-1	1-1	0-0	1-1	1-0	1-0	4-3	2-0	1-1	4-1	1-0	3-2
Arezzo ‡ - R¹	34	17	10	7	54	35	61	2-1	1-0	2-2		1-0	2-2	3-2	3-0	2-0	1-0	1-1	2-3	3-1	1-1	3-1	1-1	2-0	1-0
Benevento ‡	34	16	8	10	51	37	56	1-0	1-0	1-3	0-1		2-1	1-0	3-1	3-0	3-0	3-1	1-1	2-0	2-0	1-1	1-1	3-0	2-1
Lumezzane	34	14	10	10	47	38	52	1-4	2-0	0-0	1-0	0-0		1-1	1-2	1-0	3-0	1-0	0-0	3-2	1-0	2-0	1-1	2-0	1-0
Figline §1 - R¹	34	12	10	12	45	44	45	0-2	1-1	3-3	1-0	2-2	1-0		2-2	1-0	2-0	2-1	2-0	4-2	1-2	1-0	2-1	2-0	2-2
Alessandria	34	12	7	15	35	46	43	1-3	0-3	2-1	1-0	1-0	1-0	0-2		2-1	1-2	1-0	0-0	1-1	0-0	3-1	2-1	1-0	2-1
Sorrento	34	10	11	13	44	45	41	0-2	1-1	2-1	3-2	3-2	2-2	2-1	2-2		1-2	1-1	0-0	2-1	2-2	0-0	3-0	1-1	4-0
Monza	34	9	14	11	37	45	41	1-1	3-1	3-0	1-6	1-1	2-1	2-2	0-1	3-4		0-0	0-1	2-1	1-1	1-1	2-0	0-2	2-1
Perugia §1 - R¹	34	12	6	16	31	38	41	0-2	1-1	4-0	0-0	1-2	0-2	1-0	2-1	0-1	2-1		3-1	2-1	1-0	1-0	2-1	2-1	2-1
Como	34	9	13	12	27	34	40	0-2	1-1	0-1	0-0	0-2	2-1	0-2	1-0	1-1	0-1	1-1		2-2	1-1	1-1	0-0	3-2	2-1
Foligno	34	10	9	15	53	56	39	1-1	1-1	1-2	1-4	2-0	0-1	3-1	2-0	1-0	1-1	1-2	3-0		4-2	2-0	1-1	3-1	2-3
Viareggio ‡	34	8	14	12	29	39	38	0-0	0-1	1-1	1-0	2-2	2-2	1-0	0-2	0-2	0-0	1-0	0-0	0-2		1-0	2-1	1-0	4-2
Pergocrema ‡	34	9	9	16	35	43	36	1-1	2-0	0-1	3-4	1-2	1-2	1-0	1-2	1-1	2-1	1-1	1-0	2-2	2-0		1-1	1-0	4-0
Pro Patria ‡	34	7	14	13	37	49	35	0-1	1-1	2-2	1-1	3-4	2-1	2-2	1-0	2-2	0-0	2-0	2-0	1-0	4-2	1-0		2-1	0-2
Paganese ‡	34	8	9	17	33	48	33	1-2	0-0	1-1	0-1	1-2	1-2	1-0	2-0	0-1	0-0	3-1	2-1	1-1	2-0	1-3	2-2		1-0
Lecco	34	8	7	19	34	53	31	1-1	0-2	2-1	0-1	1-2	1-2	2-2	3-1	1-0	0-0	1-0	0-1	1-1	0-2	0-1	2-1	1-0	

23/08/2009 - 9/05/2010 • ‡ Entered play-offs • § Points deducted • R¹ Relegated due to bankruptcy or financial issues
Promotion play-off semi-finals: Benevento 2-2 1-2 **Varese** • Arezzo 0-2 2-1 **Cremonese** • Final: Cremonese 1-0 0-2 **Varese** • Varese promoted
Relegation play-offs: Paganese 1-1 1-1 **Viareggio** • Pro Patria 2-2 1-1 **Pergocrema** • Paganese and Pro Patria relegated. Paganese later reprieved

ITALY 2009–10

LEGA PRO PRIMA DIVISIONE GROUP A (3)

	Pl	W	D	L	F	A	Pts	Portosummaga	Pescara	Verona	Rimini	Reggiana	Ternana	SPAL	Taranto	V. Lanciano	Cavese	Cosenza	R. Marcianise	Ravenna	Andria BAT	Foggia	Pescina	Potenza	Giulianova
Portosummaga	34	16	11	7	39	26	59		2-2	0-0	2-1	2-1	1-2	1-0	1-0	1-1	0-0	1-0	0-0	0-1	0-0	1-1	0-0	1-0	2-0
Pescara ‡	34	15	13	6	39	25	58	0-1		0-0	2-0	3-0	2-1	1-0	1-1	0-0	1-2	3-1	2-0	2-1	1-0	0-0	1-0	2-1	1-0
Verona	34	13	16	5	38	20	55	0-1	0-0		0-1	1-2	2-0	1-1	1-0	2-2	1-1	2-1	2-0	2-1	3-1	0-0	5-1	2-2	1-0
Rimini ‡ - R¹	34	15	6	13	39	36	51	2-3	0-0	3-2		1-1	1-1	1-2	0-0	0-1	0-2	0-1	0-2	1-0	2-1	0-1	3-1	2-0	2-1
Reggiana ‡	34	13	10	11	45	38	49	0-1	2-1	0-3	3-1		1-0	0-0	0-1		5-2	3-1	2-2	1-1	3-4	2-0	2-0	1-0	
Ternana	34	14	7	13	34	34	49	1-0	2-0	0-2	3-0	0-1		0-1	2-1	1-1	1-1	0-0	3-0	1-0	2-1	4-1	0-2	3-0	2-0
SPAL	34	10	15	9	37	29	45	2-1	0-1	1-1	1-2	1-1	0-1		0-0	0-1	2-0	1-1	2-3	0-0	2-0	0-0	0-0	1-1	2-0
Taranto	34	10	15	9	24	24	45	1-2	0-1	0-0	1-0	0-0	1-0	0-2		1-1	0-2	1-1	1-0	1-0	0-0	2-0	2-2		0-0
Virtus Lanciano	34	9	17	8	31	36	44	0-2	2-2	0-3	1-0	1-5	0-2	1-3	1-1		0-0	0-1	2-1	1-0	1-0	0-0	2-2	0-0	1-1
Cavese	34	9	16	9	25	25	43	1-2	1-1	0-0	1-0	2-0	1-0	2-2	1-0	0-2		1-1	1-0	1-0	1-1	0-0	2-1	0-1	2-2
Cosenza	34	10	13	11	43	45	43	3-2	2-1	0-0	0-3	1-1	1-0	3-1	0-1	0-0	0-0		1-1	2-2	1-1	4-0	1-1	0-2	3-4
Real Marcianise - R¹	34	11	11	12	44	40	43	1-1	1-2	2-3	1-0	1-1	1-3	4-0	1-0	3-3	2-2	0-0		0-1	3-0	0-0	0-2	3-0	1-2
Ravenna	34	9	13	12	38	36	40	1-1	1-1	0-1	1-2	3-1	0-1	1-1	1-1	0-2	2-3	1-1	0-1		3-1	0-0	3-1	2-1	2-0
Andria BAT ‡	34	9	13	12	31	35	40	1-0	1-0	0-1	0-1	1-0	1-0	0-2	1-0	3-1	0-1	0-0	0-0			0-1	3-0	3-1	1-1
Foggia ‡ §1	34	9	14	11	27	37	40	2-1	1-0	0-1	3-0	2-1	1-2	0-3	0-0	0-0	0-0	1-3	1-3	1-2	0-2		2-0	1-1	1-1
Pescina ‡ - R¹	34	8	10	16	32	49	34	0-1	0-2	1-1	2-0	2-1	3-0	0-3	0-2	1-0	0-0	1-3	3-3	2-1	1-1	2-0		3-2	1-2
Potenza - R¹	34	8	10	16	30	48	34	0-3	0-0	0-2	2-1	0-0	1-1	2-2	0-0	0-2	1-0	0-2	0-2	1-1	3-1	1-0	2-1		2-1
Giulianova ‡	34	6	14	14	28	42	32	2-1	1-1	0-0	0-2	1-0	1-1	1-1	0-0	2-2	0-2	1-2	0-0	2-2	1-1	1-2	0-1	1-0	

23/08/2009 - 9/05/2010 • ‡ Entered play-offs • § Points deducted • R¹ Relegated due to bankruptcy or financial issues
Promotion play-off semi-finals: Reggiana 0-0 0-2 **Pescara** • Rimini 0-1 0-0 **Verona** • Final: Verona 2-2 0-1 **Pescara** • Pescara promoted
Relegation play-offs: Giulianova 1-1 0-1 **Andria BAT** • Pescina 1-2 2-1 **Foggia** • Giulianova and Pescina relegated

MEDALS TABLE

		Overall			League			Cup		Europe		
		G	S	B	G	S	B	G	S	G	S	B
1	Juventus	42	32	19	27	20	13	9	4	6	8	6
2	Milan	31	24	22	17	13	18	5	6	9	5	4
3	Internazionale	30	22	22	18	13	14	6	6	6	3	8
4	Torino	13	17	7	8	9	6	5	7		1	1
5	Roma	13	20	7	3	11	5	9	7	1	2	2
6	Genoa 1893	10	5	2	9	4	1	1	1			1
7	Fiorentina	9	11	7	2	5	5	6	3	1	3	2
8	Bologna	9	4	5	7	4	3	2				2
9	Lazio	8	8	5	2	6	4	5	1	1	1	1
10	Pro Vercelli	7	1		7	1						
11	Napoli	6	8	7	2	4	6	3	4	1		1
12	Sampdoria	6	6	4	1	1	3	4	3	1	2	1
13	Parma	6	4	3		1	2	3	2	3	1	1
14	Hellas-Verona	1	3		1				3			
15	Atalanta	1	2	1				1	2			1
	Venezia	1	2	1	1	1		1	1			
	Vicenza	1	2	1		2		1				1
18	Cagliari	1	1	1	1	1						1
19	Casale	1			1							
	Novese	1			1							
	Vado	1						1				
22	US Milanese		2	1	2	1						
	Udinese		2	1	1	1		1				
24	Alba		2		2							
	Livorno		2		2							
	Palermo		2					2				
27	Alessandria		1	1		1		1				
	Padova		1	1		1		1				
29	Ancona		1					1				
	Catanzaro		1					1				
	Fortitudo		1		1							
	Novara		1					1				
	Perugia		1		1							
	Pisa		1		1							
	Savoia		1		1							
	SPAL Ferrara		1					1				
37	Modena			1		1						

COPPA ITALIA 2009-10

Third Round		Fourth Round		Round of 16	
				Internazionale *	1
				Livorno	0
Livorno *	2				
Torino	0	Livorno	2		
Lecce	2	Sampdoria *	1		
Sampdoria *	6				
Cittadella *	2				
Ascoli	1	Cittadella	0		
Salernitana	0	Napoli *	1		
Napoli *	3			Napoli	0
				Juventus *	3
				Lazio *	2
Palermo *	4			Palermo	0
SPAL	2	Palermo *	4		
Brescia *	0	Reggina	1		
Reggina	1				
Frosinone *	0 7p				
Bologna	0 6p	Frosinone	0		
Mantova	0	Chievo Verona *	2		
Chievo Verona *	3			Chievo Verona	2
				Fiorentina *	3
				Udinese *	2
Lumezzane	3			Lumezzane	0
Ancona *	2	Lumezzane	1		
Cesena *	0	Atalanta *	0		
Atalanta	1				
Siena *	2				
Grosseto	0	Siena *	0		
Parma *	1	Novara	2		
Novara	2			Novara	1
				Milan *	2
Empoli	1 5p				
Bari *	1 4p	Empoli	0		
Cremonese	0	Catania *	2		
Catania *	1			Catania	2
				Genoa *	1
Sassuolo *	2				
Verona	0	Sassuolo	0		
Cagliari	0	Triestina *	1		
Triestina *	1			Triestina	1
				Roma *	3

Clubs playing in Europe enter in the round of 16

COPPA ITALIA 2009–10

Quarter–finals　　　　**Semi–finals**　　　　**Final**

Internazionale *	2
Juventus	1

Internazionale *	1	1
Fiorentina	0	0

Lazio	2
Fiorentina *	3

Internazionale	1
Roma	0

Udinese	1
Milan *	0

Udinese	0	1
Roma *	2	0

COPPA ITALIA FINAL 2010

Stadio Olimpico, Rome, 5-05-2010, 20:45, Att: 55 000, Ref: Nicola Rizzoli

Catania	0
Roma *	1

Internazionale	1	Milito [39]
Roma	0	

Inter - Julio Cesar - Maicon, Ivan Cordoba (Walter Samuel• 39), Marco Materazzi•, Cristian Chivu• - Javier Zanetti (c), Thiago Motta, Esteban Cambiasso - Wesley Sneijder (Balotelli• 5) (Muntari 92) - Samuel Eto'o, Diego Milito. Tr: Jose Mourinho
Roma - Julio Sergio - Nicolas Burdisso• (Marco Motta 51), Juan, Philippe Mexes•, John Arne Riise - Rodrigo Taddei, Simone Perrotta•, David Pizarro (Francesco Totti 51•♦87), Daniele De Rossi (c) - Mirko Vucinic, Luca Toni (Jeremy Menez 69). Tr: Claudio Ranieri

* Home team/Home team in the first leg

CLUB BY CLUB GUIDE TO THE 2009-10 SEASON IN ITALY

ATALANTA 2009–10

	Day	Opponent	Res	Score	Comp	Scorers	Att
Aug	15	Cesena	W	1-0	ICr3	Acquafresca 84	3 799
	23	Lazio	L	0-1	SA		25 000
	30	Genoa	L	0-1	SA		13 324
	13	Sampdoria	L	0-1	SA		13 461
Sep	20	Bari	L	1-4	SA	Bellini 84	16 717
	23	Catania	D	0-0	SA		11 152
	27	Chievo	D	1-1	SA	Tiribocchi 72	7 657
	4	Milan	D	1-1	SA	Tiribocchi 21	15 024
Oct	18	Udinese	W	3-1	SA	Tiribocchi 4, Valdes 69, De Ascentis 73	17 292
	25	Parma	W	3-1	SA	Valdes 43, Tiribocchi 52, Peluso 84	11 575
	28	Livorno	L	0-1	SA		9 065
	1	Cagliari	L	0-3	SA		10 000
Nov	1	Juventus	L	2-5	SA	Valdes 51, Ceravolo 71	20 764
	22	Siena	W	2-0	SA	Tiribocchi 52, Acquafresca 67p	9 528
	26	Lumezzane	L	0-1	ICr4		2 500
	29	Roma	L	1-2	SA	Ceravolo 12	10 752
Dec	6	Fiorentina	L	0-2	SA		24 671
	13	Inter	D	1-1	SA	Tiribocchi 81	14 608
	6	Napoli	L	0-2	SA		11 061
	10	Palermo	L	0-1	SA		18 817
Jan	17	Lazio	W	3-0	SA	Doni 2 59, Padoin 35	10 260
	20	Bologna	D	2-2	SA	Manfredini 37, Chevanton 60	13 727
	24	Genoa	L	0-2	SA		25 875
	31	Sampdoria	L	0-2	SA		22 408
	7	Bari	W	1-0	SA	Tiribocchi 82	12 706
Feb	14	Catania	D	0-0	SA		19 071
	21	Chievo	L	0-1	SA		12 897
	28	Milan	L	1-3	SA	Valdes 56	38 688
	7	Udinese	D	0-0	SA		13 023
	14	Parma	L	0-1	SA		15 560
Mar	21	Livorno	W	3-0	SA	Padoin 13, Chevanton 49, Adriano 54	31 412
	24	Cagliari	W	3-1	SA	Tiribocchi 53, Valdes 2 64p 72	12 597
	28	Juventus	L	1-2	SA	Amoruso 45	20 310
	3	Siena	W	2-0	SA	Valdes 16, Adriano 70	11 908
Apr	11	Roma	L	1-2	SA	Tiribocchi 53	49 803
	18	Fiorentina	W	2-1	SA	Adriano 6, Tiribocchi 69	13 614
	24	Inter	L	1-3	SA	Tiribocchi 5	63 779
May	2	Bologna	D	1-1	SA	Guarente 23	14 105
	9	Napoli	L	0-2	SA		43 111
	16	Palermo	L	1-2	SA	Ceravolo 48	12 147

BARI 2009–10

	Day	Opponent	Res	Score	Comp	Scorers	Att
Aug	15	Empoli	D	1-1	ICr3	Greco 82p, L 3-4p	5 136
	23	Inter	D	1-1	SA	Kutuzov 74	53 369
	29	Bologna	D	0-0	SA		21 336
	13	Palermo	D	1-1	SA	Allegretti 2	20 004
Sep	20	Atalanta	W	4-1	SA	Rivas 7, Barreto 9, Alvarez 39, Donati 61	16 717
	23	Cagliari	L	0-1	SA		20 231
	27	Milan	D	0-0	SA		37 354
Oct	3	Catania	D	0-0	SA		16 778
	18	Chievo	W	2-1	SA	Almiron 4, Ranocchia 65	9 268
	25	Lazio	W	2-0	SA	Barreto 11, Meggiorini 69	20 675
	28	Parma	L	0-2	SA		15 952
	1	Sampdoria	D	0-0	SA		26 180
Nov	8	Livorno	W	1-0	SA	Allegretti 6	15 759
	22	Roma	L	1-3	SA	OG 74	41 248
	29	Siena	W	2-1	SA	Masiello 78, Greco 90	15 445
	6	Napoli	L	2-3	SA	Barreto 49, Ranocchia 62	46 547
Dec	12	Juventus	W	3-1	SA	Meggiorini 7, Barreto 44p, Almiron 81	51 849
	6	Udinese	W	2-0	SA	Meggiorini 6, Barreto 68	17 828
	10	Fiorentina	L	1-2	SA	Barreto 25	25 972
	16	Inter	D	2-2	SA	Barreto 2 60p 63p	51 855
Jan	20	Genoa	D	1-1	SA	Barreto 5	24 863
	24	Bologna	L	1-2	SA	Barreto 40	18 239
	30	Palermo	W	4-2	SA	Bonucci 5, Alvarez 7, Barreto 62p, Koman 84	18 922
	7	Atalanta	L	0-1	SA		12 706
Feb	14	Cagliari	L	1-3	SA	Masiello 52	15 000
	21	Milan	L	0-2	SA		51 943
	27	Catania	L	0-4	SA		18 782
	7	Chievo	W	1-0	SA	Castillo 20	16 071
Mar	14	Lazio	W	2-0	SA	Almiron 51, Alvarez 64	46 942
	21	Parma	D	1-1	SA	Masiello 85	17 305
	24	Sampdoria	W	2-1	SA	Meggiorini 58, Barreto 86	28 368
	28	Livorno	D	1-1	SA	Allegretti 24	9 225
	3	Roma	L	0-1	SA		43 773
Apr	11	Siena	L	2-3	SA	Rivas 13, Castillo 22	9 943
	18	Napoli	L	1-2	SA	Almiron 76	19 507
	25	Juventus	L	0-3	SA		24 147
May	2	Genoa	W	3-0	SA	Meggiorini 57, Castillo 85, Barreto 89	14 783
	9	Udinese	D	3-3	SA	Barreto 18, Koman 39, Almiron 92+	17 968
	16	Fiorentina	W	2-0	SA	Stellini 36, Rivas 95+	23 318

ATALANTA LEAGUE APPEARANCES/GOALS 2009-10

Goalkeepers Andrea Consigli 31 • Ferdinando Coppola 7+1
Defenders Gianpaolo Bellini 29/1 • Paolo Bianco 20+1/0 • Daniele Capelli 10/0 • Gyorgy Garics AUT 28+2/0 • Thomas Manfredini 26/1 Maximiliano Pellegrino ARG 6/0 • Federico Peluso 17+7/1 • Leonardo Talamonti ARG 15+2/0
Midfield Edgar Barreto PAR 3+1/0 • Giacomo Bonaventura 0+1/0 Fabio Caserta 5+9/0 • Diego De Ascentis 14+3/1 • Cristiano Doni 23+7/2 • Ferreira Pinto 21+2/3 • Tiberio Guarente 32/1 • Miguel Layun MEX 0+2/0 • Nicola Madonna 2+4/0 • Simone Padoin 36/2 • Ivan Radovanovic 3+9/0 • Sergio Volpi 1+4/0 • Paolo Zanetti 2/0
Forwards Robert Acquafresca 10+2/1 • Nicola Amoruso 12+3/1 • Fabio Ceravolo 9+18/3 • Ernesto Chevanton 3+9/2 • Manolo Gabbiadini 0+2/0 • Christian Tiboni 0+1/0 • Simone Tiribocchi 28+9/11 • Jaime Valdes CHI 25+8/7
Coach Angelo Gregucci • Antonio Conte (21/09/09) • Walter Bonacina (7/01/10) • Bortolo Mutti (11/01/10)

BARI LEAGUE APPEARANCES/GOALS 2009-10

Goalkeepers Jean-Francois Gillet BEL 37 • Daniele Padelli 1
Defenders Nicola Belmonte 17+1/0 • Leonardo Bonucci 38/1 Souleymane Diamontene MLI 3/0 • Andrea Masiello 37/2 • Alessandro Parisi 13+2/0 • Marco Pisano 0+1/0 • Andrea Ranocchia 17/2 Cristian Stellini 3+6/1
Midfield Riccardo Allegretti 14+2/3 • Sergio Almiron ARG 20+7/5 Edgar Alvarez HON 37/3 • Filippo Antonelli 1+3/0 • Daniele De Vezze 5+4/0 • Massimo Donati 26+6/1 • Alessandro Gazzi 25+7/0 • Pedro Kamata FRA 1+13/0 • Vladimir Koman HUN 11+5/2 • Salvatore Masiello 25+2/1 • Emanuel Rivas ARG 10+10/3 • Alessio Sestu 0+3/0
Forwards Barreto BRA 30+1/14 • Jose Castillo ARG 11+5/3 • Andras Gosztonyi HUN 0+2/0 • Giuseppe Greco 0+6/1 • Vitaliy Kutuzov BLR 10+2/1 • Antonio Langella 2+8/0 • Riccardo Meggiorini 23+8/5 Ferdinando Sforzini 1+7/0
Coach Giampiero Ventura

KEY TO THE CLUB SECTION

SC = Supercoppa (played in Beijing) • SA = Serie A • IC = Coppa Italia • CL = UEFA Champions League • EL = Europa League • r1 = first round etc • p3 = third preliminary round • po = preliminary round play-off • gA = Group A etc • qf = quarter-final • sf = semi-final • f = final • BCD = Played behind closed doors
Matches that are shaded were played at home; matches with no shading were played either away or on a neutral ground
The figures for the player appearances and goals consist of three elements - matches started+appearances as a substitute/goals scored

BOLOGNA 2009-10

Aug	15	Frosinone	D	0-0	ICr3	L 6-7p	2 000
	22	Fiorentina	D	1-1	SA	Osvaldo 24	17 204
	29	Bari	D	0-0	SA		21 336
Sep	13	Chievo	L	0-2	SA		14 896
	20	Milan	L	0-1	SA		35 713
	23	Livorno	W	2-0	SA	Portanova 35, Di Vaio 53	14 452
	27	Juventus	D	1-1	SA	Adailton 93+	24 456
Oct	4	Genoa	L	1-3	SA	Di Vaio 85p	21 622
	18	Napoli	L	1-2	SA	Adailton 15	43 407
	24	Sampdoria	L	1-4	SA	Osvaldo 63	23 376
	28	Siena	W	2-1	SA	Adailton 16, Osvaldo 60	14 034
Nov	1	Roma	L	0-2	SA	Adailton 32	28 022
	8	Palermo	W	3-1	SA	Zalayeta 2 42 49, Di Vaio 90	14 096
	21	Inter	L	1-3	SA	Zalayeta 23	33 067
	29	Lazio	D	0-0	SA		30 489
Dec	6	Udinese	W	2-1	SA	Adailton 27, Di Vaio 65p	14 618
	13	Parma	L	1-2	SA	Mudingayi 44	17 535
	6	Catania	L	0-1	SA		13 057
	10	Cagliari	L	0-1	SA		14 341
Jan	17	Fiorentina	W	2-1	SA	Gimenez 27, Di Vaio 44	25 000
	20	Atalanta	D	2-2	SA	Di Vaio 2 19 34	13 727
	24	Bari	W	2-1	SA	Gimenez 2 54 73	18 239
	31	Chievo	D	1-1	SA	Di Vaio 11	8 913
Feb	7	Milan	D	0-0	SA		27 089
	14	Livorno	W	1-0	SA	Di Vaio 22	10 157
	21	Juventus	L	1-2	SA	Busce 50	25 759
	28	Genoa	W	4-3	SA	Busce 11, Adailton 3 28 56 79p	25 395
Mar	7	Napoli	W	2-1	SA	Zalayeta 7, Adailton 12	21 052
	14	Sampdoria	D	1-1	SA	Raggi 92+	18 573
	21	Siena	L	0-1	SA		11 621
	24	Roma	L	0-2	SA		32 775
	27	Palermo	L	1-3	SA	Adailton 38	27 920
Apr	3	Inter	L	0-3	SA		57 169
	11	Lazio	L	2-3	SA	Guana 12, Portanova 16	20 954
	18	Udinese	D	1-1	SA	OG 3	14 000
	25	Parma	W	2-1	SA	Di Vaio 2 39 50	23 970
May	2	Atalanta	D	1-1	SA	OG 82	14 105
	9	Catania	D	1-1	SA	Di Vaio 15	22 279
	16	Cagliari	D	1-1	SA	Adailton 4	14 700

CAGLIARI 2009-10

Aug	16	Tiestina	L	0-1	ICr3		4 060
	23	Livorno	D	0-0	SA		10 724
	30	Siena	L	1-3	SA	Jeda 76p	10 450
Sep	13	Fiorentina	L	0-1	SA		23 176
	20	Inter	L	1-2	SA	Jeda 16p	18 000
	23	Bari	W	1-0	SA	Nene 77	20 231
	27	Parma	W	2-0	SA	Jeda 8, Dessena 58	15 078
Oct	4	Chievo	L	1-2	SA	Matri 38	10 000
	18	Catania	L	1-2	SA	Dessena 45	11 247
	25	Genoa	W	3-2	SA	Biondini 55, Nene 78p, Lazzari 87	10 000
	28	Lazio	W	1-0	SA	Matri 51	30 000
Nov	1	Atalanta	W	3-0	SA	Nene 2 33 36, Matri 45p	10 000
	8	Sampdoria	W	2-0	SA	Conti 85, Matri 90	15 000
	22	Milan	L	3-4	SA	Matri 9, Lazzari 30, Nene 69	39 821
	29	Juventus	W	2-0	SA	Nene 30, Matri 90	20 000
Dec	6	Palermo	L	1-2	SA	Matri 24	18 963
	12	Napoli	D	3-3	SA	Larrivey 75, Matri 80, Jeda 90	10 000
	6	Roma	D	2-2	SA	Diego Lopez 91+, Conti 93+	20 000
	10	Bologna	W	1-0	SA	Matri 66	14 341
Jan	16	Livorno	W	3-0	SA	Larrivey 2 3 50, Jeda 64	12 000
	24	Siena	D	1-1	SA	Matri 80p	10 057
	31	Fiorentina	D	2-2	SA	Lazzari 35, Astori 48	13 400
Feb	7	Inter	L	0-3	SA		57 079
	14	Bari	W	3-1	SA	Conti 13, Nene 30, OG 53	15 000
	21	Parma	W	2-0	SA	Lazzari 2, Matri 39	15 000
	24	Udinese	L	1-2	SA	Jeda 2	14 922
	28	Chievo	L	1-2	SA	Astori 51	8 678
Mar	7	Catania	D	2-2	SA	Lazzari 4, Cossu 74	12 000
	14	Genoa	L	3-5	SA	Dessena 16, Conti 40, Matri 55p	25 417
	21	Lazio	L	0-2	SA		12 000
	24	Atalanta	L	1-3	SA	Conti 90	12 597
	28	Sampdoria	D	1-1	SA	Nene 80	22 633
Apr	3	Milan	L	2-3	SA	Ragatzu 17, Matri 32	23 200
	11	Juventus	L	0-1	SA		22 634
	18	Palermo	D	2-2	SA	Cossu 28, Jeda 87	10 000
	25	Napoli	D	0-0	SA		41 450
May	2	Udinese	D	2-2	SA	Lazzari 15, Jeda 58	7 500
	9	Roma	L	1-2	SA	Lazzari 73	50 291
	16	Bologna	D	1-1	SA	Ragatzu 65	14 700

BOLOGNA LEAGUE APPEARANCES/GOALS 2009-10

Goalkeepers Roberto Colombo 4 • Emiliano Viviano 34

Defenders Alessandro Bassoli 0+1/0 • Miguel Britos URU 21+2/0 • Salvatore Lanna 33/0 • Francesco Modesto 11+2/0 • Vangelis Moras GRE 17+3/0 • Daniele Portanova 36/2 • Rafael BRA 2/0 • Andrea Raggi 30+1/1 • Cristian Zenoni 12+4/0

Midfield Stephen Appiah GHA 1+1/0 • Davide Bombardini 4+5/0 • Antonio Busce 16+1/2 • Federico Casarini 10+9/0 • Roberto Guana 33+1/1 • Nicola Mingazzini 18+6/0 • Gaby Mudingayi BEL 21+7/1 • Massimo Mutarelli 3+4/0 • Andrea Pisanu 1+1/0 • Giacomo Tedesco 5+3/0 • Francesco Valiani 15+4/0 • Luca Vigiani 6+5/0

Forwards Adailton BRA 24+7/11 • Marco Di Vaio 28+2/12 • Henry Gimenez URU 4+14/3 • Massimo Marazzina 0+4/0 • Savio Nsereko GER 0+2/0 • Pablo Osvaldo 4+9/3 • Davide Succi 2+8/0 • Marcelo Zalayeta URU 23+6/4

Coach Giuseppe Papadopulo • Franco Colomba (20/10/09)

CAGLIARI LEAGUE APPEARANCES/GOALS 2009-10

Goalkeepers Michael Agazzi 3 • Cristiano Lupatelli 1+1 • Federico Marchetti 33 • Mauro Vigorito 1+1

Defenders Alessandro Agostini 38/0 • Lorenzo Ariaudo 8+1/0 • Davide Astori 34/2 • Michele Canini 30/0 • Diego Lopez URU 18/1 • Lino Marzoratti 12+1/0 • Francesco Pisano 7+2/0

Midfield Simone Barone 5+11/0 • Davide Biondini 32+4/1 • Daniele Conti 32/5 • Andrea Cossu 31+2/2 • Daniele Dessena 19+10/3 • Andrea Lazzari 24+9/6 • Radja Nainggolan BEL 2+5/0 • Andrea Parola 7+7/0 • Mikhail Sivakov BLR 0+1/0 • Enrico Verachi 0+1/0

Forwards Mattia Gallon 0+1/0 • Jeda BRA 21+11/8 • Joaquin Larrivey ARG 12+15/3 • Alessandro Matri 30+8/13 • Nene BRA 14+19/8 • Daniele Ragatzu 4+4/2

Coach Massimiliano Allegri • Giorgio Melis (13/04/10)

CATANIA 2009–10

	Date	Opp	Res	Score	Comp	Scorers	Att
Aug	15	Cremonese	W	1-0	ICr3	Mascara 44	8 000
	23	Sampdoria	L	1-2	SA	Morimoto 38	14 325
	30	Parma	L	1-2	SA	Biagianti 15	11 870
Sep	13	Udinese	L	2-4	SA	Morimoto 11, Mascara 34p	15 078
	20	Lazio	D	1-1	SA	Martinez 12	12 150
	23	Atalanta	D	0-0	SA		11 152
	27	Roma	D	1-1	SA	Morimoto 22	12 660
Oct	3	Bari	D	0-0	SA		16 778
	18	Cagliari	W	2-1	SA	Ricchiuti 37, Martinez 88	11 247
	24	Inter	L	1-2	SA	Mascara 84p	57 745
	28	Chievo	L	1-2	SA	Mascara 42p	12 347
Nov	1	Fiorentina	L	1-3	SA	Mascara 48	23 975
	7	Napoli	D	0-0	SA		14 106
	22	Palermo	D	1-1	SA	Martinez 57	25 082
	29	Milan	L	0-2	SA		16 699
Dec	2	Empoli	W	2-0	ICr4	Moretti 8, Morimoto 74p	2 000
	6	Siena	L	2-3	SA	Martinez 2 14 55	9 157
	13	Livorno	L	0-1	SA		12 098
	20	Juventus	W	2-1	SA	Martinez 23p, Izco 87	21 327
Jan	6	Bologna	W	1-0	SA	Spolli 81	13 057
	10	Genoa	L	0-2	SA		24 766
	13	Genoa	W	2-1	ICr5	Plasmati 2 4 7	7 625
	17	Sampdoria	D	1-1	SA	Llama 13	21 095
	23	Parma	W	3-0	SA	Mascara 15, Martinez 71, Morimoto 77	12 733
	26	Roma	L	0-1	ICqf		14 479
	31	Udinese	D	1-1	SA	Biagianti 80	13 321
Feb	7	Lazio	W	1-0	SA	Lopez 63	32 496
	14	Atalanta	D	0-0	SA		19 071
	21	Roma	L	0-1	SA		30 449
	27	Bari	W	4-0	SA	Ricchiuti 4, Llama 40, Morimoto 81, Martinez 90	18 782
Mar	7	Cagliari	D	2-2	SA	Mascara 31p, Lopez 35	12 000
	12	Inter	W	3-1	SA	Lopez 74, Mascara 81p, Martinez 90	20 941
	21	Chievo	D	1-1	SA	Lopez 74p	8 578
	24	Fiorentina	W	1-0	SA	Mascara 2	14 531
	28	Napoli	L	0-1	SA		31 642
Apr	3	Palermo	W	2-0	SA	Lopez 2 14 32	24 500
	11	Milan	D	2-2	SA	Lopez 13, Ricchiuti 43	47 124
	18	Siena	D	2-2	SA	Lopez 11, Biagianti 50	18 106
	25	Livorno	L	1-3	SA	Lopez 87	8 177
May	2	Juventus	D	1-1	SA	Silvestre 24	18 582
	9	Bologna	D	1-1	SA	Lopez 51	22 279
	16	Genoa	W	1-0	SA	Lopez 65	18 448

CHIEVO VERONA 2009–10

	Date	Opp	Res	Score	Comp	Scorers	Att
Aug	15	Mantova	W	3-0	ICr3	Bogdani 48, Pellissier 82, Bentivoglio 90	3 223
	23	Juventus	L	0-1	SA		23 523
	30	Lazio	L	1-2	SA	Pellissier 16	8 581
Sep	13	Bologna	W	2-0	SA	Pinzi 18, Pellissier 29	14 896
	20	Genoa	W	3-1	SA	Marcolini 5p, Bogdani 7, Pellissier 77	9 557
	23	Siena	D	0-0	SA		9 213
	27	Atalanta	D	1-1	SA	Pellissier 77	7 657
Oct	4	Cagliari	W	2-1	SA	Marcolini 2 41 71	10 000
	18	Bari	L	1-2	SA	Bogdani 82	9 268
	25	Milan	L	1-2	SA	Pinzi 7	15 737
	28	Catania	W	2-1	SA	Mantovani 31, Marcolini 70	12 347
Nov	1	Udinese	D	1-1	SA	Yepes 71	8 793
	8	Parma	L	0-2	SA		14 793
	22	Sampdoria	L	1-2	SA	Mantovani 81	21 958
	25	Frosinone	W	2-0	ICr4	Hanine 38, Bentivoglio 90	654
	29	Palermo	W	1-0	SA	Abbruscato 53	8 373
Dec	6	Livorno	W	2-0	SA	Rigoni 12, Bentivoglio 67	8 893
	13	Fiorentina	W	2-1	SA	Pinzi 12, Sardo 24	10 508
	20	Napoli	L	0-2	SA		31 973
	6	Inter	L	0-1	SA		26 000
	9	Roma	L	0-1	SA		29 467
Jan	14	Fiorentina	L	2-3	ICr5	Granoche 7, Bentivoglio 38	7 000
	17	Juventus	W	1-0	SA	Sardo 33	21 132
	24	Lazio	D	1-1	SA	Pellissier 77	30 308
	31	Bologna	D	1-1	SA	Pellissier 49	8 913
Feb	7	Genoa	L	0-1	SA		19 991
	14	Siena	L	0-1	SA		7 741
	21	Atalanta	W	1-0	SA	Pellissier 44	12 897
	28	Cagliari	W	2-1	SA	De Paula 33, Granoche 78	8 678
Mar	7	Bari	L	0-1	SA		16 071
	14	Milan	L	0-1	SA		37 866
	21	Catania	D	1-1	SA	Pellissier 64	8 578
	24	Udinese	D	0-0	SA		14 950
	28	Parma	D	0-0	SA		8 841
	3	Sampdoria	L	1-2	SA	Mantovani 76	10 087
Apr	11	Palermo	L	1-3	SA	De Paula 18	25 917
	17	Livorno	W	2-0	SA	Pellissier 28, Abbruscato 88	9 309
	25	Fiorentina	W	2-0	SA	Pellissier 54, Sardo 75	26 198
May	2	Napoli	L	1-2	SA	Granoche 75	11 049
	9	Inter	L	3-4	SA	OG 12, Granoche 60, Pellissier 74	75 379
	16	Roma	L	0-2	SA		28 136

CATANIA LEAGUE APPEARANCES/GOALS 2009-10

Goalkeepers Mariano Andujar ARG 35 • Andrea Campagnolo 3
Defenders Pablo Alvarez ARG 23+2/0 • Blazej Augustyn POL 6+4/0 • Giuseppe Bellusci 7+5/0 • Ciro Capuano 29+1/0 • Giovanni Marchese 2+2/0 • Alessandro Potenza 14+5/0 • Gennaro Sardo 1/0 • Matias Silvestre ARG 35/1 • Nicolas Spolli ARG 22+4/1 • Christian Terlizzi 15+2/0
Midfield Pablo Barrientos ARG 0+2/0 • Marco Biagianti 35+1/3 • Ezequiel Carboni ARG 26+2/0 • Gennaro Delvecchio 7+10/0 • Mariano Izco ARG 24+8/1 • Pablo Ledesma ARG 6+10/0 • Cristian Llama ARG 18+5/2 • Federico Moretti 0+2/0 • Simone Pesce 1+3/0 • Orazio Russo 0+1/0 • Fabio Sciacca 1+3/0
Forwards Jorge Martinez URU 19+6/9 • Giuseppe Mascara 33+1/8 • Maxi Lopez ARG 17/11 • Takayuki Morimoto JPN 16+11/5 • Gianvito Plasmati 1+12/0 • Adrian Ricchiuti 22+5/3
Coach Gianluca Atzori • Sinisa Mihajlovic SRB (8/12/09)

CHIEVO LEAGUE APPEARANCES/GOALS 2009-10

Goalkeepers Stefano Sorrentino 37 • Lorenzo Squizzi 1
Defenders Nicolas Frey FRA 20+4/0 • Bojan Jokic SVN 5+4/0 • Marco Malago 0+2/0 • Davide Mandelli 19+2/0 • Andrea Mantovani 36/3 • Santiago Morero ARG 23+1/0 • Fabio Moro 0+1/0 • Gennaro Sardo 19+3/3 • Francesco Scardina 2+1/0 • Mario Yepes COL 31/1
Midfield Luca Ariatti 8+23/0 • Simone Bentivoglio 13+22/1 • Yonese Hanine 0+1/0 • Manuel Iori 14+1/0 • Luciano BRA 31+2 • Michele Marcolini 28+2/4 • Giampiero Pinzi 31+1/3 • Luca Rigoni 24/1 • Alessandro Sbaffo 0+2/0
Forwards Elvis Abbruscato 9+6/2 • Erjon Bogdani ALB 12+9/2 • Pablo Granoche URU 10+20/3 • Marcos De Paula 10+6/2 • Sergio Pellissier 35/11
Coach Domenico Di Carlo

FIORENTINA 2009–10

		Opp			Score		Scorers	Att
Aug	18	Sporting CP	D	2-2	CLpo	Vargas [6], Gilardino [79]	27 602
	22	Bologna	D	1-1	SA	Mutu [64]	17 204
	26	Sporting CP	D	1-1	CLpo	Jovetic [54]	30 821
	30	Palermo	W	1-0	SA	Jovetic [29]	24 576
	13	Cagliari	W	1-0	SA	Gilardino [55]	23 176
Sep	16	Lyon	L	0-1	CLgE		37 169
	20	Roma	L	1-3	SA	Gilardino [84]	35 000
	23	Sampdoria	W	2-0	SA	Jovetic [25], Gilardino [66]	26 307
	26	Livorno	W	1-0	SA	Jovetic [76p]	11 915
	29	Liverpool	W	2-0	CLgE	Jovetic 2 [28 37]	33 426
	4	Lazio	D	0-0	SA		26 436
	17	Juventus	D	1-1	SA	Vargas [5]	25 779
Oct	20	Debrecen	W	4-3	CLgE	Mutu 2 [6 20], Gilardino [10], Santana [37]	41 500
	25	Napoli	L	0-1	SA		26 864
	28	Genoa	L	1-2	SA	Marchionni [63]	25 778
	1	Catania	W	3-1	SA	Marchionni 2 [4 69], Gilardino [86]	23 975
Nov	4	Debrecen	W	5-2	CLgE	Mutu [14], Dainelli [52], Montolivio [59], Marchionni [61], Gilardino [74]	19 676
	8	Udinese	W	1-0	SA	Vargas [84]	15 000
	21	Parma	L	2-3	SA	Gilardino 2 [26 62]	25 068
	24	Lyon	W	1-0	CLgE	Vargas [28p]	34 301
	29	Inter	L	0-1	SA		59 471
Dec	6	Atalanta	W	2-0	SA	Vargas [26], Gilardino [88]	24 671
	9	Liverpool	W	2-1	CLgE	Jorgensen [63], Gilardino [92+]	40 863
	13	Chievo	L	0-1	SA	Montolivio [5]	10 508
	6	Siena	W	5-1	SA	Kroldrup [5], Santana [28], Gilardino 2 [35 66], Mutu [79]	9 731
Jan	10	Bari	W	2-1	SA	Mutu [38], Castillo [74]	25 972
	14	Chievo	W	3-2	ICr4	Mutu 2 [35 75], Babacar [75]	7 000
	17	Bologna	L	1-2	SA	Mutu [51]	25 000
	20	Lazio	W	3-2	ICqf	Mutu 2 [9 44], Kroldrup [59]	10 565
	24	Palermo	L	0-3	SA		21 585
	31	Cagliari	D	2-2	SA	Marchionni [8], Jovetic [63]	13 400
	3	Inter	L	0-1	ICsf		15 307
Feb	7	Roma	L	0-1	SA		27 442
	13	Sampdoria	L	0-2	SA		23 485
	17	Bayern	L	1-2	CLr2	Kroldrup [50]	66 000
	21	Livorno	W	2-1	SA	Vargas [62], Gilardino [78]	24 997
	24	Milan	L	1-2	SA	Gilardino [14]	38 389
	27	Lazio	D	1-1	SA	Keirrison [90]	30 708
Mar	6	Juventus	L	1-2	SA	Marchionni [32]	34 805
	9	Bayern	W	3-2	CLr2	Vargas [28], Jovetic 2 [54 64]	42 762
	13	Napoli	W	3-1	SA	Gilardino 2 [60 87], Jovetic [90]	31 986
	20	Genoa	W	3-0	SA	Santana [5], Gilardino [73p], Babacar [86]	25 543
	24	Catania	L	0-1	SA		14 531
	28	Udinese	W	4-1	SA	Vargas [36], Gilardino [55], Santana [68], Jovetic [84]	25 418
Apr	3	Parma	D	1-1	SA	De Silvestri [22]	18 702
	10	Inter	D	2-2	SA	Keirrison [11], Kroldrup [82]	36 981
	13	Inter	L	0-1	ICsf		36 003
	18	Atalanta	L	1-2	SA	Montolivio [75]	13 614
	25	Chievo	L	0-2	SA		26 198
May	1	Milan	L	0-1	SA		47 579
	9	Siena	D	1-1	SA	Marchionni [15]	29 378
	16	Bari	L	0-2	SA		23 318

GENOA 2009–10

		Opp			Score		Scorers	Att
Aug	20	Odense	W	3-1	ELpo	Moretti [9], Figueroa 2 [48 56]	21 889
	23	Roma	W	3-2	SA	Criscito [49], Zapater [69], Biava [83]	25 414
	27	Odense	D	1-1	ELpo	Criscito [53]	10 000
	30	Atalanta	W	1-0	SA	Moretti [45]	13 324
Sep	13	Napoli	W	4-1	SA	Floccari [45p], Mesto [55], Crespo [75], Kharja [88p]	32 245
	17	Slavia	W	2-0	ELgB	Zapater [4], Sculli [39]	17 356
	20	Chievo	L	1-3	SA	Floccari [65p]	9 557
	24	Juventus	D	2-2	SA	Mesto [31], Crespo [75]	31 882
	27	Udinese	L	0-2	SA		15 762
	1	Valencia	L	2-3	ELgB	Floccari [43], Kharja [64p]	21 333
	4	Bologna	W	3-1	SA	Kharja [10p], Sculli [35], Zapater [90]	21 622
Oct	17	Inter	L	0-5	SA		32 942
	22	Lille	L	0-3	ELgB		16 518
	25	Cagliari	L	2-3	SA	Mesto [21], Floccari [60]	10 000
	28	Fiorentina	W	2-1	SA	Palladino [43], Mesto [73]	25 778
Nov	1	Palermo	D	0-0	SA		25 624
	5	Lille	W	3-2	ELgB	Palacio [14], Crespo [58], Sculli [93+]	18 587
	8	Siena	W	4-2	SA	Crespo 2 [2 18], Palladino [35], Floccari [90]	26 000
	22	Livorno	L	1-2	SA	Criscito [63]	11 153
	28	Sampdoria	W	3-0	SA	Milanetto [10p], Rossi [53], Palladino [75p]	33 265
Dec	2	Slavia	D	0-0	ELgB		11 799
	6	Parma	D	2-2	SA	Palacio [13], Palladino [66]	25 869
	13	Lazio	L	0-1	SA		29 489
	17	Valencia	L	1-2	ELgB	Crespo [51]	23 480
	6	Milan	L	2-5	SA	Sculli [25], Suazo [79]	33 043
Jan	10	Catania	W	2-0	SA	Mesto [36], Sculli [71]	24 766
	13	Catania	L	1-2	ICr4	Rossi [57]	7 625
	17	Roma	L	0-3	SA		31 746
	20	Bari	D	1-1	SA	Milanetto [52]	24 863
	24	Atalanta	W	2-0	SA	Palacio [18], Crespo [42]	25 875
	30	Napoli	D	0-0	SA		64 612
Feb	7	Chievo	W	1-0	SA	Rossi [56]	19 991
	14	Juventus	L	2-3	SA	Rossi 2 [16 63]	22 252
	20	Udinese	W	3-0	SA	Acquafresca 2 [30 53p], Palacio [64]	24 831
	28	Bologna	L	3-4	SA	Suazo 2 [8 38], Sculli [18]	25 395
	7	Inter	D	0-0	SA		51 795
Mar	14	Cagliari	W	5-3	SA	Zapater [35p], Palacio [39], Sculli [42], Rossi [45], Milanetto [59]	25 417
	20	Fiorentina	L	0-3	SA		25 543
	24	Palermo	D	2-2	SA	Bocchetti [75], Kharja [90p]	25 772
	28	Siena	D	0-0	SA		13 029
Apr	3	Livorno	D	1-1	SA	Boakye [51]	25 260
	11	Sampdoria	L	0-1	SA		34 494
	18	Parma	W	3-2	SA	Palacio 2 [33 52], Fatic [73]	16 660
	25	Lazio	L	1-2	SA	Palacio [8]	26 082
	2	Bari	L	0-3	SA		14 783
May	9	Milan	W	1-0	SA	Sculli [57]	BCD
	16	Catania	L	0-1	SA		18 448

FIORENTINA LEAGUE APPEARANCES/GOALS 2009-10
Goalkeepers Vlada Avramov SRB 2 • Sebastian Frey FRA 36
Defenders Gianluca Comotto 22+4/0 • Dario Dainelli 11/0 • Lorenzo De Silvestri 17+9/1 • Felipe BRA 16+2/0 • Alessandro Gamberini 16+2/0 • Per Kroldrup 24+1/2 • Cesare Natali 14+3/0 • Manuel Pasqual 18+3/0 Midfield Daniel Agyei GHA 0+1/0 • Mario Bolatti ARG 9+3/0 • Federico Carraro 0+1/0 • Marco Donadel 20+8/0 • Massimo Gobbi 19+6/0 Martin Jorgensen DEN 2+11/0 • Adem Ljajic SRB 3+6/0 • Marco Marchionni 23+5/6 • Riccardo Montolivio 33+3/2 • Mario Santana ARG 21+5/3 • Juan Vargas PER 27+2/5 • Cristiano Zanetti 16+7/0 Forwards Babacar SEN 0+4/1 • Jose Castillo ARG 0+6/1 • Alberto Gilardino 32+4/15 • Stevan Jovetic MNE 26+3/6 • Keirrison BRA 2+8/2 Adrian Mutu ROU 9+2/4
Coach Cesare Prandelli

GENOA LEAGUE APPEARANCES/GOALS 2009-10
Goalkeepers Marco Amelia 30 • Alessio Scarpi 8
Defenders Giuseppe Biava 17+2/1 • Salvatore Bocchetti 25+3/1 • Domenico Criscito 28+1/2 • Dario Dainelle 9+1/0 • Andrea Esposito 2+3/0 • Ivan Fatic MNE 3+7/1 • Emiliano Moretti 28+1/1 • Sokratis Papastathopoulos GRE 25+5/0 • Nenad Tomovic SRB 8+6/0 Midfield Isaac Cofie GHA 0+1/0 • Stephan El Shaarawi 0+2/0 • Bosko Jankovic SRB 0+3/0 • Ivan Juric CRO 15+4/0 • Houssine Kharja MAR 3+4/3 • Dejan Lazarevic SVN 0+2/0 • Giandomenico Mesto 32+4/5 • Omar Milanetto 31+1/3 • Francesco Modesto 8+2/0 • Raffaele Palladino 18+7/4 • Marco Rossi 26+2/5 • Alberto Zapater ESP 19+9/3 Forwards Robert Acquafresca 8+2/2 • Danijel Aleksic SRB 0+1/0 • Richmond Boakye GHA 0+3/1 • Hernan Crespo ARG 6+10/5 • Luciano Figueroa ARG 1+1/0 • Sergio Floccari 7+4/4 • Rodrigo Palacio ARG 23+8/7 • Giuseppe Sculli 27+10/6 • David Suazo HON 11+5/3
Coach Gian Piero Gasperini

INTERNAZIONALE 2009–10

	Date	Opponent	W/D/L	Score	Comp	Scorers	Att
Aug	8	Lazio	L	1-2	SC	Eto'o [77]. Played in Beijing	68 961
	23	Bari	D	1-1	SA	Eto'o [56p]	53 369
	29	Milan	W	4-0	SA	Motta [29], Milito [36p], Maicon [45], Stankovic [67]	78 467
Sep	13	Parma	W	2-0	SA	Eto'o [71], Milito [88]	51 237
	16	Barcelona	D	0-0	CLgF		77 321
	20	Cagliari	W	2-1	SA	Milito 2 [51][55]	18 000
	23	Napoli	W	3-1	SA	Eto'o 2, Milito [5], Lucio [32]	41 695
	26	Sampdoria	L	0-1	SA		30 629
	29	Rubin	D	1-1	CLgF	Stankovic [27]	23 670
Oct	3	Udinese	W	2-1	SA	Stankovic [22], Sneijder [90]	50 000
	17	Genoa	W	5-0	SA	Cambiasso [6], Balotelli [31], Stankovic [45], Vieira [66], Maicon [70]	32 942
	20	Dy'mo Kyiv	D	2-2	CLgF	Stankovic [35], Samuel [47]	34 721
	24	Catania	W	2-1	SA	Muntari [13], Sneijder [31]	57 745
	29	Palermo	W	5-3	SA	Eto'o 2 [7p][43], Balotelli 2 [34][42], Milito [83]	53 261
Nov	1	Livorno	W	2-0	SA	Milito [49], Maicon [80]	15 736
	4	Dy'mo Kyiv	W	2-1	CLgF	Milito [86], Sneijder [89]	15 900
	8	Roma	D	1-1	SA	Eto'o [48]	56 807
	21	Bologna	W	3-1	SA	Milito [22], Balotelli [41], Cambiasso [72]	33 067
	24	Barcelona	L	0-2	CLgF		93 524
	29	Fiorentina	W	1-0	SA	Milito [85p]	59 471
Dec	5	Juventus	L	1-2	SA	Eto'o [26]	25 530
	9	Rubin	W	2-0	CLgF	Eto'o [31], Balotelli [64]	49 539
	13	Atalanta	D	1-1	SA	Milito [15]	14 608
	16	Livorno	W	1-0	ICr5	Sneijder [61]	8 316
	20	Lazio	W	1-0	SA	Eto'o [14]	52 859
	6	Chievo	W	1-0	SA	Balotelli [12]	26 000
Jan	9	Siena	W	4-3	SA	Milito [24], Sneijder 2 [36][88], Samuel [90]	52 979
	16	Bari	D	2-2	SA	Pandev [69], Milito [74p]	51 855
	24	Milan	W	2-0	SA	Milito [10], Pandev [65]	80 018
	28	Juventus	W	2-1	ICqf	Lucio [71], Balotelli [89]	40 000
	3	Fiorentina	W	1-0	ICsf	Milito [34]	15 307
	7	Cagliari	W	3-0	SA	Pandev [6], Samuel [20], Milito [47]	57 079
	10	Parma	D	1-1	SA	Balotelli [59]	20 128
Feb	14	Napoli	D	0-0	SA		56 211
	20	Sampdoria	D	0-0	SA		53 806
	24	Chelsea	W	2-1	CLr2	Milito [3], Cambiasso [55]	78 971
	28	Udinese	W	3-2	SA	Balotelli [5], Maicon [20], Milito [45]	23 604
	7	Genoa	D	0-0	SA		51 795
	2	Catania	L	1-3	SA	Milito [54]	20 941
	16	Chelsea	W	1-0	CLr2	Eto'o [78]	38 112
Mar	20	Palermo	D	1-1	SA	Milito [11p]	35 753
	24	Livorno	W	3-0	SA	Eto'o 2 [36][41], Maicon [61]	53 086
	27	Roma	L	1-2	SA	Milito [66]	61 898
	31	CSKA	W	1-0	CLqf	Milito [65]	69 398
	3	Bologna	W	3-0	SA	Motta 2 [29][85], Balotelli [52]	57 169
	6	CSKA	W	1-0	CLqf	Sneijder [6]	54 400
	10	Fiorentina	D	2-2	SA	Milito [74], Eto'o [81]	36 981
	13	Fiorentina	W	1-0	ICsf	Eto'o [57]	36 003
Apr	16	Juventus	W	2-0	SA	Maicon [75], Eto'o [90]	46 164
	20	Barcelona	W	3-1	CLsf	Sneijder [30], Maicon [48], Milito [61]	79 000
	24	Atalanta	W	3-1	SA	Milito [24], Muntari [35], Chivu [78]	63 779
	28	Barcelona	L	0-1	CLsf		96 214
	2	Lazio	W	2-0	SA	Samuel [45], Motta [70]	50 945
	5	Roma	W	1-0	ICf	Milito [40]	55 000
May	9	Chievo	W	4-3	SA	OG [13], Cambiasso [34], Milito [39], Balotelli [52]	75 379
	16	Siena	W	1-0	SA	Milito [57]	15 373
	22	Bayern	W	2-0	CLf	Milito 2 [35][70]	75 569

INTER LEAGUE APPEARANCES/GOALS 2009-10

Goalkeepers Julio Cesar BRA 38

Defenders Cristian Chivu ROU 16+4/1 • Ivan Cordoba COL 15+6/0 Lucio BRA 30+1/1 • Maicon BRA 33/6 • Marco Materazzi 7+5/0 • Walter Samuel ARG 25+3/3 • Davide Santon 8+4/0 • Javier Zanetti ARG 37/0

Midfield Esteban Cambiasso ARG 26+4/3 • Rene Krhin SVN 1+4/0 Mancini BRA 1+5/0 • McDonald Mariga KEN 3+5/0 • Sulley Muntari GHA 16+11/2 • Ricardo Quaresma POR 3+8/0 • Wesley Sneijder NED 24+2/4 Dejan Stankovic SRB 24+5/3 • Alen Stevanovic 4+1/0 • Thiago Motta BRA 18+8/4 • Patrick Vieira FRA 7+5/1

Forwards Marko Arnautovic AUT 0+3/0 • Mario Balotelli 13+13/9 Samuel Eto'o CMR 27+5/12 • Diego Milito ARG 33+2/22 • Goran Pandev MKD 13+6/3 • David Suazo HON 0+1/0

Coach Jose Mourinho POR

JUVENTUS 2009–10

	Date	Opponent	W/D/L	Score	Comp	Scorers	Att
Aug	23	Chievo	W	1-0	SA	Iaquinta [11]	23 523
	30	Roma	W	3-1	SA	Diego 2 [25][68], Felipe Melo [90]	57 500
Sep	12	Lazio	W	2-0	SA	Caceres [72], Trezeguet [90]	55 000
	15	Bordeaux	D	1-1	CLgA	Iaquinta [63]	17 513
	19	Livorno	W	2-0	SA	Iaquinta [8], Marchisio [30]	22 788
	24	Genoa	D	2-2	SA	Iaquinta [6], Trezeguet [86]	31 882
	27	Bologna	D	1-1	SA	Trezeguet [24]	24 456
	30	Bayern	D	0-0	CLgA		66 000
Oct	4	Palermo	L	0-2	SA		31 606
	17	Fiorentina	D	1-1	SA	Amauri [19]	25 779
	21	Mac. Haifa	W	1-0	CLgA	Chiellini [47]	21 303
	25	Siena	W	1-0	SA	Amauri [72]	15 367
	28	Sampdoria	W	5-1	SA	Amauri 2 [26][62], Chiellini [42], Camoranesi [50], Trezeguet [88]	25 273
	31	Napoli	L	2-3	SA	Trezeguet [35], Giovinco [54]	22 899
Nov	3	Mac. Haifa	W	1-0	CLgA	Camoranesi [45]	39 120
	7	Atalanta	W	5-2	SA	Camoranesi 2 [36][37], Felipe Melo [55], Diego [85], Trezeguet [87]	20 764
	22	Udinese	W	1-0	SA	Grosso [51]	23 609
	25	Bordeaux	L	0-2	CLgA		32 195
	29	Cagliari	L	0-2	SA		20 000
Dec	5	Inter	W	2-1	SA	Chiellini [20], Marchisio [58]	25 530
	8	Bayern	L	1-4	CLgA	Trezeguet [19]	27 801
	12	Bari	L	1-3	SA	Trezeguet [23]	51 849
	20	Catania	L	1-2	SA	Salihamidzic [66]	21 327
	6	Parma	W	2-1	SA	Salihamidzic [3], OG [39]	20 530
	10	Milan	L	0-3	SA		24 165
Jan	13	Napoli	W	3-0	ICr4	Diego [24], Del Piero 2 [77][82p]	10 112
	17	Chievo	L	0-1	SA		21 132
	23	Roma	L	1-2	SA	Del Piero [51]	23 750
	28	Inter	L	1-2	ICqf	Diego [10]	40 000
	31	Lazio	D	1-1	SA	Del Piero [70p]	20 899
Feb	6	Livorno	D	1-1	SA	Legrottaglie [42]	14 867
	14	Genoa	W	3-2	SA	Amauri [42], Del Piero 2 [61][78p]	22 252
	18	Ajax	W	2-1	ELr2	Amauri 2 [32][58]	51 676
	21	Bologna	W	2-1	SA	Diego [4], Candreva [66]	25 759
	25	Ajax	D	0-0	ELr2		16 441
	28	Palermo	L	0-2	SA		20 749
Mar	6	Fiorentina	W	2-1	SA	Diego [2], Grosso [68]	34 805
	11	Fulham	W	3-1	ELr3	Legrottaglie [9], Zebina [25], Salihamidzic [45]	11 406
	14	Siena	D	3-3	SA	Del Piero 2 [2][7], Candreva [10]	22 804
	18	Fulham	L	1-4	ELr3	Trezeguet [2]	23 458
	21	Sampdoria	L	0-1	SA		27 398
	25	Napoli	L	1-3	SA	Chiellini [7]	52 249
	28	Atalanta	W	2-1	SA	Del Piero [30], Felipe Melo [82]	20 310
Apr	3	Udinese	L	0-3	SA		22 390
	11	Cagliari	W	1-0	SA	Chiellini [35]	22 634
	16	Inter	L	0-2	SA		46 164
	25	Bari	W	3-0	SA	Iaquinta 2 [53][87], Del Piero [69p]	24 147
	2	Catania	D	1-1	SA	Marchisio [52]	18 582
May	9	Parma	L	2-3	SA	Del Piero [16], Iaquinta [90]	23 666
	15	Milan	L	0-3	SA		66 108

JUVENTUS LEAGUE APPEARANCES/GOALS 2009-10

Goalkeepers Gianluigi Buffon 27 • Antonio Chimenti 2 • Alexander Manninger AUT 9+2

Defenders Jose Caceres URU 11+4/1 • Fabio Cannavaro 27/0 • Giorgio Chiellini 32/0 • Paolo De Ceglie 14+11/0 • Fabio Grosso 22+4/2 • Zdenek Grygera 15+4/0 • Nicola Legrottaglie 18+1/1 • Cristian Molinaro 4+1/0 • Jonathan Zebina 13+3/0

Midfield Mauro Camoranesi 14+10/3 • Antonio Candreva 8+8/2 • Diego BRA 31+2/5 • Felipe Melo BRA 28+1/3 • Manuel Giandonato 0+1/0 • Sebastian Giovinco 5+10/1 • Claudio Marchisio 27+1/3 • Luca Marrone 0+2/0 • Christian Poulsen DEN 9+6/0 • Hasan Salihamidzic BIH 6+8/2 • Mohamed Sissoko MLI 14+3/0 • Tiago Por 4+3/0

Forwards Amauri BRA 24+6/5 • Alessandro Del Piero 18+5/9 • Vincenzo Iaquinta 12+3/6 • Ciro Immobile 0+2/0 • Michele Paolucci 1+3/0 • David Trezeguet FRA 13+6/7

Coach Ciro Ferrara • Alberto Zaccheroni (29/01/10)

LAZIO 2009-10

						Scorers	Att.
Aug	8	Inter	W	2-1	SC	Matuzalem 63, Rocchi 66	68 961
	20	Elfsborg	W	3-0	ELpo	Kolarov 23, Zarate 35, Mauri 69	18 000
	23	Atalanta	W	1-0	SA	Rocchi 22	25 000
	27	Elfsborg	L	0-1	ELpo		11 693
	30	Chievo	W	2-1	SA	Cruz 2 41p 53	8 581
Sep	12	Juventus	L	0-2	SA		55 000
	17	Salzburg	L	1-2	ELgG	Foggia 59	12 600
	20	Catania	D	1-1	SA	Cruz 57	12 150
	23	Parma	L	1-2	SA	Zarate 42p	30 000
	27	Palermo	D	1-1	SA	Zarate 85	31 109
Oct	1	Levski	W	4-0	ELgG	Matuzalem 22, Zarate 45, Meghni 67, Rocchi 74	10 000
	4	Fiorentina	D	0-0	SA		26 436
	18	Sampdoria	D	1-1	SA	Matuzalem 42	33 103
	22	Villarreal	W	2-1	ELgG	Zarate 20, Rocchi 92+	14 388
	25	Bari	L	0-2	SA		20 675
	28	Cagliari	L	0-1	SA		30 000
Nov	1	Siena	D	1-1	SA	Mauri 9	10 060
	5	Villarreal	L	1-4	ELgG	Zarate 72	14 114
	8	Milan	L	1-2	SA	OG 64	38 207
	22	Napoli	D	0-0	SA		48 524
	29	Bologna	D	0-0	SA		30 489
Dec	2	Salzburg	L	1-2	ELgG	Foggia 57	26 270
	6	Roma	L	0-1	SA		54 273
	13	Genoa	W	1-0	SA	Kolarov 39	29 489
	17	Levski	L	0-1	ELgG		8 051
	20	Inter	L	0-1	SA		52 859
Jan	6	Livorno	W	4-1	SA	Floccari 2 48 54, Rocchi 72, Kolarov 90p	30 865
	10	Udinese	D	1-1	SA	Floccari 16	15 044
	14	Palermo	W	2-0	ICr4	Kolarov 59, Floccari 73	10 000
	17	Atalanta	L	0-3	SA		10 260
	20	Fiorentina	L	2-3	ICqf	Zarate 50, Rocchi 68	10 565
	24	Chievo	D	1-1	SA	Stendardo 18	30 308
	31	Juventus	D	1-1	SA	Mauri 78	20 899
Feb	7	Catania	L	0-1	SA		32 496
	14	Parma	W	2-0	SA	Stendardo 68, Zarate 89	15 313
	21	Palermo	L	1-3	SA	Rocchi 78	23 104
	27	Fiorentina	D	1-1	SA	Siviglia 7	30 708
Mar	7	Sampdoria	L	1-2	SA	Floccari 7	23 919
	14	Bari	L	0-2	SA		46 942
	21	Cagliari	W	2-0	SA	Rocchi 4, Floccari 37	12 000
	24	Siena	W	2-0	SA	Lichtsteiner 6, Cruz 72	41 234
	28	Milan	D	1-1	SA	Borriello 18p	40 393
Apr	3	Napoli	D	1-1	SA	Floccari 4	31 820
	11	Bologna	W	3-2	SA	Mauri 44, Dias 63, Rocchi 68	20 954
	18	Roma	L	1-2	SA	Rocchi 14	61 615
	25	Genoa	W	2-1	SA	Dias 25, Floccari 32	26 082
May	2	Inter	L	0-2	SA		50 945
	9	Livorno	W	2-1	SA	Rocchi 13, Brocchi 43	3 534
	15	Udinese	W	3-1	SA	Hitzlsperger 16, Floccari 45, Brocchi 52	34 455

LIVORNO 2009-10

						Scorers	Att.
Aug	14	Torino	W	2-0	ICr3	Raimondi 73, Dionisi 81	3 821
	23	Cagliari	D	0-0	SA		10 724
	30	Napoli	L	1-3	SA	Lucarelli 47	32 063
Sep	12	Milan	D	0-0	SA		15 982
	19	Juventus	L	0-2	SA		22 788
	23	Bologna	L	0-2	SA		14 452
	26	Fiorentina	L	0-1	SA		11 915
Oct	4	Siena	D	0-0	SA		9 581
	18	Palermo	L	1-2	SA	Danilevicius 54	9 206
	25	Roma	W	1-0	SA	Tavano 40	28 328
	28	Atalanta	W	1-0	SA	Miglionico 67	9 065
	1	Inter	L	0-2	SA		15 736
Nov	8	Bari	L	0-1	SA		15 759
	22	Genoa	W	2-1	SA	Lucarelli 21, Pulzetti 90	11 153
	28	Udinese	L	0-2	SA		14 703
Dec	1	Sampdoria	W	2-1	ICr4	OG 76, Danilevicius 87	4 212
	6	Chievo	L	0-2	SA		8 893
	13	Catania	L	1-0	SA	Danilevicius 88	12 098
	16	Inter	L	0-1	ICr5		8 316
	20	Sampdoria	W	3-1	SA	Rivas 39, Danilevicius 2 47 90	9 371
Jan	6	Lazio	L	1-4	SA	Bergvold 7	30 865
	10	Parma	W	2-1	SA	Tavano 23, Lucarelli 62	8 793
	16	Cagliari	L	0-3	SA		12 000
	24	Napoli	L	0-2	SA		9 883
	31	Milan	D	1-1	SA	Lucarelli 53	34 998
Feb	6	Juventus	D	1-1	SA	Filippini 26	14 867
	14	Bologna	L	0-1	SA		10 157
	21	Fiorentina	L	1-2	SA	Rivas 36	24 997
	28	Siena	L	1-2	SA	Lucarelli 11p	9 487
Mar	7	Palermo	L	0-1	SA		25 018
	14	Roma	D	3-3	SA	Lucarelli 3 9 26 71p	12 358
	21	Atalanta	L	0-3	SA		31 412
	24	Inter	L	0-3	SA		53 086
	28	Bari	D	1-1	SA	Tavano 85	9 225
Apr	3	Genoa	D	1-1	SA	Tavano 88	25 260
	11	Udinese	L	0-2	SA		8 494
	17	Chievo	L	0-2	SA		9 309
	25	Catania	W	3-1	SA	Lucarelli 50p, Bellucci 60, Bergvold 66	8 177
May	2	Sampdoria	L	0-2	SA		25 076
	9	Lazio	L	1-2	SA	Lucarelli 34	3 534
	16	Parma	L	1-4	SA	Danilevicius 72	16 852

LAZIO LEAGUE APPEARANCES/GOALS 2009-10

Goalkeepers Tommaso Berni 2 • Nestor Muslera URU 36
Defenders Andre Dias BRA 12/2 •Giuseppe Biava 10+3/0 • Cribari BRA 7+3/0 • Modibo Diakite FRA 11+8/0 • Aleksandar Kolarov SRB 33/3 Stephan Lichtsteiner SUI 28+5/2 • Alessio Luciani 0+1/0 • Stefan Radu ROU 28/0 • Lionel Scaloni ARG 1+4/0 • Sebastian0 Siviglia 18+2/1 Guglielmo Stendardo 19/2
Midfield Roberto Baronio 22+2/0 • Cristian Brocchi 25+2/2 • Ousmane Dabo FRA 6+6/0 • Eliseu POR 0+2/0 • Fabio Firmani 8+4/0 • Pasquale Foggia 9+7/0 • Thomas Hitzlsperger GER 2+4/1 • Cristian Ledesma ARG 13/0 • Matuzalem BRA 14+4/1 • Stefano Mauri 29+6/3 • Mourad Meghni ALG 3+4/0 • Riccardo Perpetuini 1+1/0
Forwards Julio Cruz ARG 8+17/4 • Simone Del Nero 6+1/0 • Sergio Folccari 17/8 • Simone Inzaghi 0+3/0 • Stephen Makinwa NGA 0+2/0 Tommaso Rocchi 23+9/6 • Mauro Zarate ARG 27+5/3
Coach Davide Ballardini • Edoardo Reja (10/02/10)

LIVORNO LEAGUE APPEARANCES/GOALS 2009-10

Goalkeepers Francesco Bardi 1 • Francesco Benussi 4+1 • Alfonso De Lucia 22+1 • Rubinho BRA 11
Defenders Alessandro Bernardini 4+1/0 • Andrea Esposito 3/0 • Fabio Galante 5+4/0 • Alessandro Grandoni 1/0 • Dario Knezevic CRO 25+2/0 Marcus Diniz BRA 15+6/0 • Leonardo Miglionico URU 12+1/1 Samuele Modica 1+1/0 • Welle Ossou SEN 0+1/0 • Romano Perticone 26+1/0 • Nelson Rivas COL 16/2
Midfield Martin Bergvold DEN 16+7/2 • Antonio Candreva 16+3/0 Antonio Filippini 20+4/1 • Matteo Lignani 1+1/0 • Davide Marchini 4+12/0 • Davide Moro 22+6/0 • Mozart BRA 21+4/0 • Jurgen Prutsch AUT 5+1/0 • Nico Pulzetti 25+4/1 • Cristian Raimondi 32/0 Luigi Vitali 14+8/0
Forwards Claudio Bellucci 12+2/1 • Gaston Cellerino ARG 0+6/0 Alessandro Diamanti 1/0 • Davide Di Gennaro 6+5/0 • Federico Dionisi 0+3/0 • Cristiano Lucarelli 28/10 • Luca Simeoni 0+2/0 • Francesco Tavano 18+6/4
Coach Vittorio Russo • Serse Cosmi (21/10/09) • Gennaro Ruotolo (5/04/10)

MILAN 2009–10

	Date	Opponent		Score	Comp	Scorers	Att
Aug	22	Siena	W	2-1	SA	Pato 2 29 48	15 028
	29	Inter	L	0-4	SA		78 467
Sep	12	Livorno	D	0-0	SA		15 982
	15	Marseille	W	2-1	CLgC	Inzaghi 2 28 74	55 434
	20	Bologna	W	1-0	SA	Seedorf 75	35 713
	23	Udinese	L	0-1	SA		21 000
	27	Bari	D	0-0	SA		37 354
	30	Zürich	L	0-1	CLgC		32 439
Oct	4	Atalanta	D	1-1	SA	Ronaldinho 83	15 024
	18	Roma	W	2-1	SA	Ronaldinho 57p, Pato 67	42 700
	21	Real Madrid	W	3-2	CLgC	Pirlo 62, Pato 2 66 88	71 569
	25	Chievo	W	2-1	SA	Nesta 2 81 90	15 737
	28	Napoli	D	2-2	SA	Inzaghi 2, Pato 5	55 709
	31	Parma	W	2-0	SA	Borriello 2 12 90	33 303
Nov	3	Real Madrid	D	1-1	CLgC	Ronaldinho 35p	75 092
	8	Lazio	W	2-1	SA	Thiago Silva 21, Pato 35	38 207
	22	Cagliari	W	4-3	SA	Seedorf 5, Borriello 38, Pato 40, Ronaldinho 62p	39 821
	25	Marseille	D	1-1	CLgC	Borriello 10	49 063
	29	Catania	D	2-0	SA	Huntelaar 2 89 90	16 699
Dec	5	Sampdoria	W	3-0	SA	Borriello 2, Seedorf 21, Pato 24	42 824
	8	Zürich	D	1-1	CLgC	Ronaldinho 64p	24 100
	13	Palermo	L	0-2	SA		39 253
Jan	6	Genoa	W	5-2	SA	Ronaldinho 32p, Thiago Silva 38, Borriello 2 48 60, Huntelaar 74p	33 043
	10	Juventus	W	3-0	SA	Nesta 29, Ronaldinho 2 71 87	24 165
	13	Novara	W	2-1	ICr4	Inzaghi 12, Flamini 81	15 061
	17	Siena	W	4-0	SA	Ronaldinho 3 12p 72 89, Borriello 28	35 958
	24	Inter	L	0-2	SA		80 018
	27	Udinese	L	0-1	ICqf		5 513
	31	Livorno	D	1-1	SA	Ambrosini 44	34 998
Feb	7	Bologna	D	0-0	SA		27 089
	12	Udinese	W	3-2	SA	Huntelaar 2 7 57, Pato 39	33 837
	16	Man Utd	L	2-3	CLr2	Ronaldinho 3, Seedorf 85	78 587
	21	Bari	W	2-0	SA	Borriello 43, Pato 69	51 943
	24	Fiorentina	W	2-1	SA	Huntelaar 81, Pato 90	38 389
	28	Atalanta	W	3-1	SA	Pato 2 30 41, Borriello 62	38 688
Mar	6	Roma	D	0-0	SA		61 036
	10	Man Utd	L	0-4	CLr2		74 595
	14	Chievo	W	1-0	SA	Seedorf 90	37 866
	21	Napoli	D	1-1	SA	Inzaghi 26	51 044
	24	Parma	L	0-1	SA		20 493
	28	Lazio	D	1-1	SA	Borriello 18p	40 393
Apr	3	Cagliari	W	3-2	SA	Borriello 7, Huntelaar 19, OG 38	23 200
	11	Catania	D	2-2	SA	Borriello 2 48 80	47 124
	18	Sampdoria	L	1-2	SA	Borriello 20	28 763
	24	Palermo	L	1-3	SA	Seedorf 55	25 695
May	1	Fiorentina	W	1-0	SA	Ronaldinho 78p	47 579
	9	Genoa	L	0-1	SA		BCD
	15	Juventus	W	3-0	SA	Antonini 14, Ronaldinho 2 28 67	66 108

NAPOLI 2009–10

	Date	Opponent		Score	Comp	Scorers	Att
Aug	16	Salernitana	W	3-0	ICr3	Maggio 29, Lavezzi 43, Hoffer 84	30 000
	23	Palermo	L	1-2	SA	Hamsik 73	31 236
	30	Livorno	W	3-1	SA	Quagliarella 2 10 83, Hamsik 36	32 063
Sep	13	Genoa	L	1-4	SA	Hamsik 41	32 245
	19	Udinese	D	0-0	SA		36 100
	23	Inter	L	1-3	SA	Lavezzi 37	41 695
	27	Siena	W	2-1	SA	Hamsik 2 49 64	40 209
Oct	4	Roma	L	1-2	SA	Lavezzi 25	27 119
	18	Bologna	W	2-1	SA	Quagliarella 72, Maggio 90	43 407
	25	Fiorentina	W	1-0	SA	Maggio 88	26 864
	28	Milan	D	2-2	SA	Cigarini 91+, Denis 93+	55 709
	31	Juventus	W	3-2	SA	Hamsik 2 59 81, Datolo 64	22 899
Nov	7	Catania	D	0-0	SA		14 106
	22	Lazio	D	0-0	SA		48 524
	26	Cittadella	W	1-0	ICr4	Bogliacino 27	30 000
	29	Parma	D	1-1	SA	Denis 32	19 737
Dec	6	Bari	W	3-2	SA	Quagliarella 2 54 88, Maggio 71	46 547
	12	Cagliari	D	3-3	SA	Lavezzi 21, Pazienza 65, Bogliacino 96+	10 000
	20	Chievo	W	2-0	SA	Hamsik 7p, Quagliarella 87	31 973
	6	Atalanta	W	2-0	SA	Quagliarella 7, Pazienza 58	11 061
	10	Sampdoria	W	1-0	SA	Denis 71	57 692
Jan	13	Juventus	L	0-3	ICr5		10 112
	17	Palermo	D	0-0	SA		66 451
	24	Livorno	W	2-0	SA	Maggio 45, Cigarini 90	9 883
	30	Genoa	D	0-0	SA		64 612
Feb	7	Udinese	L	1-3	SA	Maggio 21	20 084
	14	Inter	D	0-0	SA		56 211
	21	Siena	D	0-0	SA		10 865
	28	Roma	D	2-2	SA	Denis 75, Hamsik 90p	50 832
Mar	7	Bologna	L	1-2	SA	Rinaudo 14	21 052
	13	Fiorentina	L	1-3	SA	Lavezzi 48	31 986
	21	Milan	D	1-1	SA	Campagnaro 13	51 044
	25	Juventus	W	3-1	SA	Hamsik 51, Quagliarella 72, Lavezzi 88	52 249
	28	Catania	W	1-0	SA	Cannavaro 51	31 642
Apr	3	Lazio	D	1-1	SA	Hamsik 38	31 820
	10	Parma	L	2-3	SA	Quagliarella 3, Hamsik 78	36 527
	18	Bari	W	2-1	SA	Lavezzi 2 28 57	19 507
	25	Cagliari	D	0-0	SA		41 450
May	2	Chievo	W	2-1	SA	Denis 45, Lavezzi 86	11 049
	9	Atalanta	W	2-0	SA	Quagliarella 2 43 83	43 111
	16	Sampdoria	L	0-1	SA		30 883

MILAN LEAGUE APPEARANCES/GOALS 2009-10

Goalkeepers Christian Abbiati 8+1/0 • Dida BRA 23/0 • Marco Storari 7/0

Defenders Luca Antonini 20+2/1 • Daniele Bonera 6+1/0 • Andrea De Vito 0+1/0 • Giuseppe Favalli 15+1/0 • Marek Jankulovski CZE 5+7/0 • Kakhaber Kaladze GEO 5+1/0 • Alessandro Nesta 22+1/3 • Massimo Oddo 9+5/0 • Thiago Silva BRA 33/2 • Gianluca Zambrotta 19+5/0

Midfield Ignazio Abate 22+8/0 • Massimo Ambrosini 26+4/1 • David Beckham ENG 7+4/0 • Mathieu Flamini FRA 14+11/0 • Gennaro Gattuso 20+2/0 • Mancini BRA 3+4/0 • Andrea Pirlo 33+1/0 • Clarence Seedorf NED 25+4/5 • Rodney Strasser SLE 0+1/0

Forwards Marco Borriello 27+2/14 • Klass Jan Huntelaar NED 11+14/7 • Filippo Inzaghi 4+20/2 • Alexandre Pato BRA 20+3/12 • Ronaldinho BRA 34+2/12 • Gianmarco Zigoni 0+1/0

Coach Leonardo BRA

NAPOLI LEAGUE APPEARANCES/GOALS 2009-10

Goalkeepers Morgan De Sanctis 38

Defenders Salvatore Aronica 24+2/0 • Hugo Campagnaro ARG 28/1 • Paolo Cannavaro 32+1/1 • Matteo Contini 12+1/0 • Andrea Dossena 3+7/0 • Gianluca Grava 22+2/0 • Leandro Rinaudo 13+7/1 • Erminio Rullo 0+1/0 • Fabiano Santacroce 4/0 • Juan Zuniga COL 15+7/0

Midfield Mariano Bogliacino URU 2+16/1 • Luca Cigarini 11+17/2 • Jesus Datolo ARG 6+7/1 • Walter Gargano URU 35+1/0 • Marek Hamsik SVK 37/12 • Lorenzo Insigne 0+1/0 • Christian Maggio 33+1/5 • Rafael Maiello 0+1/0 • Michele Pazienza 27+6/2

Forwards German Denis ARG 16+13/5 • Erwin Hofer AUT 0+8/0 • Inacio Pia BRA 1+1/0 • Ezequiel Lavezzi ARG 27+3/8 • Fabio Quagliarella 32+2/11

Coach Roberto Donadoni • Walter Mazzarri (6/10/09)

PALERMO 2009-10

	Date	Opponent	Res	Score	Comp	Scorers	Att
Aug	15	SPAL	W	4-1	ICr3	Miccoli 2 32p 37, Simplicio 52, Cavani 71	9 208
	23	Napoli	W	2-1	SA	Cavani 44, Miccoli 75p	31 236
	30	Fiorentina	L	0-1	SA		24 576
Sep	13	Bari	D	1-1	SA	Budan 91+	20 004
	20	Parma	L	0-1	SA		15 032
	23	Roma	D	3-3	SA	Budan 40, Miccoli 45, Nocerino 56	21 111
	27	Lazio	D	1-1	SA	Cavani 75	31 109
Oct	4	Juventus	W	2-0	SA	Cavani 37, Simplicio 42	31 606
	18	Livorno	W	2-1	SA	Miccoli 56, Balzaretti 81	9 206
	25	Udinese	W	1-0	SA	Bovo 87	20 834
	29	Inter	L	3-5	SA	Miccoli 2 49 67, Hernandez 61	53 261
Nov	1	Genoa	D	0-0	SA		25 624
	8	Bologna	L	1-3	SA	Kjaer 45	14 096
	22	Catania	D	1-1	SA	Migliaccio 4	25 082
	26	Reggina	W	4-1	ICr4	Miccoli 27p, Cavani 56, Budan 2 69 73	9 358
	29	Chievo	L	0-1	SA		8 373
Dec	6	Cagliari	W	2-1	SA	Budan 54, Kjaer 64	18 963
		Milan	W	2-0	SA	Miccoli 49, Bresciano 62	39 253
	20	Siena	W	1-0	SA	Cavani 40	19 221
Jan	6	Sampdoria	D	1-1	SA	Cavani 40	21 540
	10	Atalanta	W	1-0	SA	Cavani 70p	18 817
	14	Lazio	L	0-2	ICr5		10 000
	17	Napoli	D	0-0	SA		66 451
	24	Fiorentina	W	3-0	SA	Hernandez 2 28 38, Budan 58	21 585
	30	Bari	L	2-4	SA	Cavani 28, Pastore 54	18 922
Feb	6	Parma	L	2-1	SA	Cavani 62, Simplicio 87	22 252
	13	Roma	L	1-4	SA	Miccoli 80p	37 005
	21	Lazio	W	3-1	SA	Hernandez 1, Miccoli 28p, Nocerino 75	23 104
	28	Juventus	W	2-0	SA	Miccoli 60, Budan 81	20 749
Mar	7	Livorno	W	1-0	SA	Miccoli 81	25 018
	14	Udinese	L	2-3	SA	Simplicio 50, Cavani 80	17 313
	20	Inter	D	1-1	SA	Cavani 24	35 753
	24	Genoa	D	2-2	SA	Hernandez 34, Pastore 78	25 772
	27	Bologna	W	3-1	SA	Miccoli 3 10 43p 79	27 920
Apr	3	Catania	L	0-2	SA		24 500
	11	Chievo	W	3-1	SA	Pastore 28, Miccoli 2 39p 53	25 917
	18	Cagliari	D	2-2	SA	Miccoli 88, Hernandez 95+	10 000
	24	Milan	W	3-1	SA	Bovo 95, Hernandez 18, Miccoli 69	25 695
May	2	Siena	W	2-1	SA	Cavani 24, Miccoli 58	11 156
	9	Sampdoria	D	1-1	SA	Miccoli 68p	35 872
	16	Atalanta	W	2-1	SA	Cavani 2 12 95+p	12 147

PARMA 2009-10

	Date	Opponent	Res	Score	Comp	Scorers	Att
Aug	14	Novara	L	1-2	ICr3	Lucarelli 57	2 751
	23	Udinese	D	2-2	SA	Paloschi 42, Lucarelli 49	15 383
	30	Catania	W	2-1	SA	Galloppa 13, Paloschi 47	11 870
Sep	13	Inter	L	0-2	SA		51 237
	20	Palermo	W	1-0	SA	Zaccardo 17	15 032
	23	Lazio	W	2-1	SA	Bojinov 21, Amoruso 45p	30 000
	27	Cagliari	L	0-2	SA		15 078
Oct	4	Sampdoria	D	1-1	SA	Galloppa 30	25 786
	18	Siena	W	1-0	SA	Bojinov 7	15 126
	25	Atalanta	L	1-3	SA	Paloschi 77	11 575
	28	Bari	W	2-0	SA	Bojinov 58, Paloschi 66	15 952
	31	Milan	L	0-2	SA		33 303
Nov	8	Chievo	W	2-0	SA	Zaccardo 41, Lanzafame 72	14 793
	21	Fiorentina	W	3-2	SA	Amoruso 30, Bojinov 52, Lanzafame 68	25 068
	29	Napoli	D	1-1	SA	Amoruso 86p	19 737
Dec	6	Genoa	D	2-2	SA	Biabiany 2 36 58	25 869
	13	Bologna	W	2-1	SA	Panucci 58, Amoruso 86	17 535
	20	Roma	L	0-2	SA		36 899
Jan	6	Juventus	L	1-2	SA	Amoruso 25	20 530
	10	Livorno	L	1-2	SA	Zaccardo 68	8 793
	17	Udinese	D	0-0	SA		14 839
	23	Catania	L	0-3	SA		12 733
Feb	6	Palermo	L	1-2	SA	Biabiany 72	22 252
	10	Inter	D	1-1	SA	Bojinov 54	20 128
	14	Lazio	L	0-2	SA		15 313
	21	Cagliari	L	0-2	SA		15 000
	28	Sampdoria	W	1-0	SA	Zaccardo 54	18 789
Mar	7	Siena	D	1-1	SA	Biabiany 35	10 151
	14	Atalanta	W	1-0	SA	Bojinov 72	15 560
	21	Bari	D	1-1	SA	OG 36	17 305
	24	Milan	W	1-0	SA	Bojinov 90	20 493
	28	Chievo	D	0-0	SA		8 841
Apr	3	Fiorentina	D	1-1	SA	Bojinov 67	18 702
	10	Napoli	W	3-2	SA	Antonelli 63, Lucarelli 68, Jimenez 87	36 527
	18	Genoa	L	2-3	SA	Zaccardo 60, OG 62	16 660
	25	Bologna	L	1-2	SA	Biabiany 23	23 970
May	1	Roma	L	1-2	SA	Lanzafame 81	35 014
	9	Juventus	W	3-2	SA	Lanzafame 2 20 40, Biabiany 84	23 666
	16	Livorno	W	4-1	SA	Lanzafame 2 45 46, Morrone 49, Crespo 90	16 852

PALERMO LEAGUE APPEARANCES/GOALS 2009-10

Goalkeepers Rubinho BRA 6 • Salvatore Sirigu 32

Defenders Federico Balzaretti 34/1 • Cesare Bovo 29/2 • Marco Calderoni 1/0 • Mattia Cassani 37/0 • Ondrej Celustka CZE 0+1/0 • Dorin Goian ROU 12+2/0 • Simon Kjaer DEN 35/2 • Cristian Melinte ROU 1+1/0

Midfield Nicolas Bertolo ARG 5+16/0 • Manuele Blasi 4+10/0 • Mark Bresciano AUS 18/1 • Fabio Simplicio BRA 21+6/3 • Fabio Liverani 20+1/0 • Giulio Migliaccio 28+2/1 • Antonio Nocerino 32+3/2 • Javier Pastore ARG 27+7/3 • Giovanni Tedesco 0+4/0

Forwards Igor Budan CRO 5+25/5 • Edinson Cavani URU 31+3/13 • Abel Hernandez URU 8+13/7 • Levan Mchedlidze GEO 0+2/0 • Fabrizio Miccoli 32+3/19 • Davide Succi 0+6/0

Coach Walter Zenga • Delio Rossi (23/11/09)

PARMA LEAGUE APPEARANCES/GOALS 2009-10

Goalkeepers Antonio Mirante 37 • Nicola Pavarini 1+1

Defenders Luca Antonelli 13+11/1 • Paolo Castellini 20+8/0 • Hernan Dellafiore 22+1/0 • Abel Gigli 0+1/0 • Alessandro Lucarelli 33/2 • Massimo Paci 23+4/0 • Christian Panucci 19/1 • Cristian Zaccardo 34/5

Midfield Jonathan Biabiany FRA 25+4/6 • Alessandro Budel 0+1/0 • Blerim Dzemaili SUI 17+2/0 • Daniele Galloppa 33+1/2 • Luis Jimenez CHI 10+2/1 • Davide Lanzafame 14+13/7 • Francesco Lunardini 7+11/0 • Alessio Manzoni 0+1/0 • McDonald Maringa KEN 8+1/0 • Stefano Morrone 30+1/1 • Ricardo Pasi 0+1/0 • Francesco Valiani 14/0

Forwards Nicola Amoruso 10+7/5 • Valeri Bojinov BUL 15+15/8 • Hernan Crespo ARG 10+3/1 • Alberto Paloschi 9+8/4

Coach Francesco Guidolin

ROMA 2009–10

=	30	Gent	W	3-1	ELp3	Mexes [56], Toni [73p], Vucinic [85]	38 000
Aug	6	Gent	W	7-1	ELp3	Totti 3 [35 56 64p], De Rossi 2 [58 74], Menez [80], Okaka Chuka [86]	11 800
Aug	20	Kosice	D	3-3	ELpo	Totti 2 [38p 67], Menez [52]	8 450
Aug	23	Genoa	L	2-3	SA	Taddei [54], Totti [64]	25 414
Sep	27	Kosice	W	7-1	ELpo	Totti 3 [1 6 86], Guberti [8], Cerci [17], Menez [18], Riise [70]	16 145
Sep	30	Juventus	L	1-3	SA	De Rossi [35]	57 500
Sep	13	Siena	W	2-1	SA	Mexes [73], Riise [90]	10 045
Sep	17	Basel	L	0-2	ElgE		16 459
Sep	20	Fiorentina	W	3-1	SA	Totti 2 [27p 33], De Rossi [41]	35 000
Sep	23	Palermo	D	3-3	SA	Brighi [20], Burdisso [45], Totti [88p]	21 111
Sep	27	Catania	D	1-1	SA	De Rossi [90]	12 660
Oct	1	CSKA Sofia	W	2-0	ElgE	Okaka Chuka [19], Perrotta [23]	16 027
Oct	4	Napoli	W	2-1	SA	Totti 2 [37 63]	27 119
Oct	18	Milan	L	1-2	SA	Menez [3]	42 700
Oct	22	Fulham	D	1-1	ElgE	Andreolli [93+]	23 561
Oct	25	Livorno	L	0-1	SA		28 328
Oct	28	Udinese	L	1-2	SA	De Rossi [42]	16 563
Nov	1	Bologna	W	2-1	SA	Vucinic [35], Perrotta [52]	28 022
Nov	5	Fulham	W	2-1	ElgE	Riise [69], Okaka Chuka [76]	14 457
Nov	8	Inter	D	1-1	SA	Vucinic [13]	56 807
Nov	22	Bari	W	3-1	SA	Totti 3 [6p 14 28]	41 248
Nov	29	Atalanta	W	2-1	SA	Vucinic [43], Perrotta [64]	10 752
Dec	3	Basel	W	2-1	ElgE	Totti [32p], Vucinic [59]	17 332
Dec	6	Lazio	W	1-0	SA	Cassetti [79]	54 273
Dec	13	Sampdoria	D	0-0	SA		24 073
Dec	16	CSKA Sofia	W	3-0	ElgE	Cerci 2 [45 52], Scardina [89]	9 010
Dec	20	Parma	W	2-0	SA	Burdisso [48], Brighi [90]	36 899
Dec	6	Cagliari	D	2-2	SA	Pizarro [52], Perrotta [65]	20 000
Dec	9	Chievo	W	1-0	SA	De Rossi [1]	29 467
Jan	12	Tiestina	W	3-1	ICr4	Brighi [45], Vucinic [60], Baptista [80]	7 241
Jan	17	Genoa	W	3-0	SA	Perrotta [17], Toni 2 [44 60]	31 746
Jan	23	Juventus	W	2-1	SA	Totti [68p], Riise [90p]	23 750
Jan	26	Catania	W	1-0	ICqf	De Rossi [74]	14 479
Jan	31	Siena	W	2-1	SA	Riise [29], Okaka [88]	30 537
Feb	4	Fiorentina	W	1-0	SA	Vucinic [82]	27 442
Feb	13	Palermo	W	4-1	SA	Brighi 2 [33 62], Baptista [53], Riise [83]	37 005
Feb	18	Pan'nakos	L	2-3	ELr2	Vucinic [29], Pizarro [81p]	54 274
Feb	21	Catania	W	1-0	SA	Vucinic [18]	30 449
Feb	25	Pan'naikos	L	2-3	ELr2	Riise [11], De Rossi [67]	47 825
Feb	28	Napoli	D	2-2	SA	Baptista [59p], Vucinic [65]	50 832
Mar	6	Milan	D	0-0	SA		61 036
Mar	14	Livorno	D	3-3	SA	Perrotta [10], Toni [19], Pizarro [27]	12 358
Mar	20	Udinese	W	4-2	SA	Toni [15], Vucinic 3 [23 66p 82]	34 138
Mar	24	Bologna	W	2-0	SA	Riise [48], Baptista [82]	32 775
Mar	27	Inter	W	2-1	SA	De Rossi [17], Toni [72]	61 898
Apr	3	Bari	W	1-0	SA	Vucinic [19]	43 773
Apr	11	Atalanta	W	2-1	SA	Vucinic [12], Cassetti [27]	49 803
Apr	18	Lazio	W	2-1	SA	Vucinic 2 [53p 63]	61 615
Apr	21	Udinese	L	0-1	ICsf		20 000
Apr	25	Sampdoria	L	1-2	SA	Totti [15]	56 379
May	1	Parma	W	2-1	SA	Totti [5], Taddei [75]	35 014
May	5	Inter	L	0-1	ICf		55 000
May	9	Cagliari	W	2-1	SA	Totti 2 [79 83]	50 291
May	16	Chievo	W	2-0	SA	Vucinic [40], De Rossi [45]	28 136

SAMPDORIA 2009–10

Aug	16	Lecce	W	6-2	ICr3	Pazzini 2 [8 33], Cassano 2 [32 59], Palombo [76p], Padalino [90]	10 240
Aug	23	Catania	W	2-1	SA	Pazzini [9], Gastaldello [90]	14 325
Aug	30	Udinese	W	3-1	SA	Pazzini [11], Mannini [45], Cassano [83]	22 995
Sep	13	Atalanta	W	1-0	SA	Mannini [63]	13 461
Sep	20	Siena	W	4-1	SA	Palombo [23], Mannini [31], Paladino 2 [48 85]	22 859
Sep	23	Fiorentina	L	0-2	SA		26 307
Oct	26	Inter	W	1-0	SA	Pazzini [72]	30 629
Oct	4	Parma	D	1-1	SA	Pazzini [23]	25 786
Oct	18	Lazio	D	1-1	SA	Pazzini [40]	33 103
Oct	24	Bologna	W	4-1	SA	Pazzini [8], Mannini 2 [17 33], Ziegler [26]	23 376
Oct	28	Juventus	L	1-5	SA	Pazzini [63]	25 273
Nov	1	Bari	D	0-0	SA		26 180
Nov	8	Cagliari	L	0-2	SA		15 000
Nov	22	Chievo	W	2-1	SA	Rossi [19], Pazzini [65]	21 958
Nov	28	Genoa	L	0-3	SA		33 265
Dec	1	Livorno	L	1-2	ICr4	Mannini [46]	4 212
Dec	5	Milan	L	0-3	SA		42 824
Dec	13	Roma	D	0-0	SA		24 073
Dec	20	Livorno	L	1-3	SA	Cassano [9]	9 371
Dec	6	Palermo	D	1-1	SA	Cassano [41]	21 540
Dec	10	Napoli	L	0-1	SA		57 692
Jan	17	Catania	D	1-1	SA	Pazzini [44p]	21 095
Jan	24	Udinese	W	3-2	SA	Pazzini [26p], Pozzi [57], Semioli [66]	16 169
Jan	31	Atalanta	W	2-0	SA	Palombo [36], Pazzini [45]	22 408
Feb	7	Siena	W	2-1	SA	Gastaldello [3], Pozzi [77]	10 853
Feb	13	Fiorentina	W	2-0	SA	Semioli [16], Pazzini [40]	23 485
Feb	20	Inter	D	0-0	SA		53 806
Feb	28	Parma	L	0-1	SA		18 789
Mar	7	Lazio	W	2-1	SA	Guberti [29], Pazzini [36]	23 919
Mar	14	Bologna	D	1-1	SA	Gastaldello [86]	18 573
Mar	21	Juventus	W	1-0	SA	Cassano [77]	27 398
Mar	24	Bari	L	1-2	SA	Cassano [19]	28 368
Mar	28	Cagliari	D	1-1	SA	Guberti [47]	22 633
Apr	3	Chievo	W	2-1	SA	Cassano [1], Pazzini [55]	10 087
Apr	11	Genoa	W	1-0	SA	Cassano [23]	34 494
Apr	18	Milan	W	2-1	SA	Cassano [54p], Pazzini [90]	28 763
Apr	25	Roma	W	2-1	SA	Pazzini 2 [52 85]	56 379
May	2	Livorno	W	2-0	SA	Cassano [5], Ziegler [84]	25 076
May	9	Palermo	D	1-1	SA	Pazzini [54p]	35 872
May	16	Napoli	W	1-0	SA	Pazzini [52]	30 883

ROMA LEAGUE APPEARANCES/GOALS 2009-10
Goalkeepers Artur BRA 1 • Doni BRA 7 • Julio Sergio BRA 30 Bogdan Lobont ROU 0+2
Defenders Marco Andreolli 4+4/0 • Nicolas Burdisso ARG 32+1/2 Marco Cassetti 26+3/2 • Cicinho BRA 0+2/0 • Juan BRA 28+1/0 Philippe Mexes FRA 16+3/1 • Marco Motta 13+3/0 • John Arne Riise NOR 34+2/5 • Max Tonetto 0+4/0
Midfield Matteo Brighi 15+9/4 • Alessio Cerci 2+7/0 • Danielle De Rossi 33/7 • Ricardo Faty FRA 2+6/0 • Stefano Guberti 3+3/0 • Jeremy Menez FRA 18+5/1 • Simone Perrotta 31+1/5 • Stefano Pettinari 0+1/0 Adrian Pit ROU 0+2/0 • David Pizarro CHI 31/2 • Rodrigo Taddei 25+8/2
Forwards Julio Baptista BRA 4+19/3 • Stefano Okaka Chuka 0+7/1 Luca Toni 10+5/5 • Francesco Totti 21+2/14 • Mirko Vucinic MNE 32+2/14
Coach Luciano Spalletti • Claudio Ranieri (2/09/10)

SAMPDORIA LEAGUE APPEARANCES/GOALS 2009-10
Goalkeepers Luca Castellazzi 19 • Vincenzo Fiorillo 0+1 Marco Storari 19
Defenders Pietro Accardi 5+9/0 • Fabrizio Cacciatore 5+5/0 • Daniele Gastaldello 33/3 • Stefano Lucchini 25+1/0 • Marco Rossi 17+3/1 Marius Stankevicius LTU 14/0 • Reto Ziegler SUI 31+6/2
Midfield Daniele Franceschini 1+5/0 • Stefano Guberti 12+4/2 Daniele Mannini 25+11/5 • Marco Padalino SUI 6+14/2 • Angelo Palombo 36/2 • Andrea Poli 26+5/0 • Paolo Sammarco 0+1/0 • Franco Semioli 25+1/2 • Fernando Tissone ARG 15+14/0 • Luciano Zauri 25+7/0
Forwards Claudio Bellucci 3+5/0 • Antonio Cassano 30+2/9 Giampaolo Pazzini 37/19 • Nicola Pozzi 7+11/2 • Stefan Scepovic SRB 1+1/0 • Emanuele Testardi 1+4/0
Coach Luigi Del Neri

SIENA 2009–10

Month	Date	Opponent	Res	Score	Comp	Scorers	Att
Aug	22	Milan	L	1-2	SA	Ghezzal 34	15 028
	30	Cagliari	W	3-1	SA	Calaio 2 52 71, Reginaldo 89	10 450
Sep	13	Roma	L	1-2	SA	Maccarone 26	10 045
	20	Sampdoria	L	1-4	SA	Fini 68	22 859
	23	Chievo	D	0-0	SA		9 213
	27	Napoli	L	1-2	SA	Maccarone 56	40 209
	4	Livorno	D	0-0	SA		9 581
Oct	18	Parma	L	0-1	SA		15 126
	25	Juventus	L	0-1	SA		15 367
	28	Bologna	L	1-2	SA	Calaio 88	14 034
	1	Lazio	D	1-1	SA	Maccarone 32	10 060
	8	Genoa	L	2-4	SA	Paolucci 80, Maccarone 82	26 000
Nov	12	Grosseto	W	2-0	ICr3	Calaio 14, Larrondo 81	3 000
	22	Atalanta	L	0-2	SA		9 528
	26	Novara	L	0-2	ICr4		848
	29	Bari	L	1-2	SA	Vergassola 3	15 445
Dec	6	Catania	W	3-2	SA	Calaio 50, Terzi 56, Paolucci 61	9 157
	13	Udinese	W	2-1	SA	Maccarone 66, Ghezzal 90	9 248
	20	Palermo	L	0-1	SA		19 221
	6	Fiorentina	L	1-5	SA	Maccarone 84p	9 731
	9	Inter	L	3-4	SA	Maccarone 2 18 65, Ekdal 37	52 979
Jan	17	Milan	L	0-4	SA		35 958
	24	Cagliari	D	1-1	SA	Calaio 78	10 057
	31	Roma	L	1-2	SA	Vergassola 41	30 537
	7	Sampdoria	L	1-2	SA	Maccarone 82	10 853
Feb	14	Chievo	W	1-0	SA	Reginaldo 75	7 741
	21	Napoli	D	0-0	SA		10 865
	28	Livorno	W	2-1	SA	Calaio 79, Maccarone 90	9 487
	7	Parma	D	1-1	SA	Vergassola 69	10 151
Mar	14	Juventus	D	3-3	SA	Maccarone 16, Ghezzal 2 46 74p	22 804
	21	Bologna	W	1-0	SA	Larrondo 10	11 621
	24	Lazio	L	0-2	SA		41 234
	28	Genoa	D	0-0	SA		13 029
	3	Atalanta	L	0-2	SA		11 908
Apr	11	Bari	W	3-2	SA	Ghezzal 2 18 62, Rosi 66	9 943
	18	Catania	D	2-2	SA	Maccarone 49, Vergassola 69	18 106
	25	Udinese	L	1-4	SA	Calaio 41	16 033
	2	Palermo	L	1-2	SA	Calaio 80	11 156
May	9	Fiorentina	D	1-1	SA	Vergassola 3	29 378
	16	Inter	L	0-1	SA		15 373

UDINESE 2009–10

Month	Date	Opponent	Res	Score	Comp	Scorers	Att
Aug	23	Parma	D	2-2	SA	Di Natale 2 45 89	15 383
	30	Sampdoria	L	1-3	SA	Di Natale 56	22 995
Sep	13	Catania	W	4-2	SA	Flores 29, Di Natale 3 55 69p 79	15 078
	19	Napoli	D	0-0	SA		36 100
	23	Milan	W	1-0	SA	Di Natale 22	21 000
	27	Genoa	W	2-0	SA	Di Natale 81, Pepe 88	15 762
	3	Inter	L	1-2	SA	Di Natale 27	50 000
Oct	18	Atalanta	L	1-3	SA	Lodi 8	17 292
	25	Palermo	L	0-1	SA		20 834
	28	Roma	W	2-1	SA	Flores 2 21 84	16 563
	1	Chievo	D	1-1	SA	Flores 28	8 793
Nov	8	Fiorentina	L	0-1	SA		15 000
	22	Juventus	L	0-1	SA		23 609
	28	Livorno	W	2-0	SA	Di Natale 29, Flores 38	14 703
Dec	6	Bologna	L	1-2	SA	Di Natale 45	14 618
	13	Siena	L	1-2	SA	D'Agostino 90	9 248
	6	Bari	L	0-2	SA		17 828
	10	Lazio	D	1-1	SA	Di Natale 27	15 044
	14	Lumezzane	W	2-0	ICr5	Lodi 44p, Corradi 61	1 794
Jan	17	Parma	D	0-0	SA		14 839
	24	Sampdoria	L	2-3	SA	Di Natale 7p, Isla 44	16 169
	27	Milan	W	1-0	ICqf	Inler 56	5 513
	31	Catania	D	1-1	SA	Flores 32	13 321
	4	Roma	L	0-2	ICsf		19 746
Feb	7	Napoli	W	3-1	SA	Di Natale 3 7 91+ 93+	20 084
	12	Milan	L	2-3	SA	Flores 45, Di Natale 87	33 837
	20	Genoa	L	0-3	SA		24 831
	24	Cagliari	W	2-1	SA	Sanchez 68, Di Natale 70	14 922
	28	Inter	L	2-3	SA	Pepe 2, Di Natale 52p	23 604
Mar	7	Atalanta	D	0-0	SA		13 023
	14	Palermo	W	3-2	SA	Flores 2 44 65, Asamoah 70	17 313
	20	Roma	L	2-4	SA	Di Natale 2 38p 61	34 138
	24	Chievo	D	0-0	SA		14 950
	28	Fiorentina	L	1-4	SA	Pepe 41	25 418
	3	Juventus	W	3-0	SA	Sanchez 9, Pepe 65, Di Natale 77	22 390
Apr	11	Livorno	W	2-0	SA	Sanchez 8, Di Natale 35	8 494
	18	Bologna	D	1-1	SA	Di Natale 90	14 000
	21	Roma	W	1-0	ICsf	Sanchez 81	20 000
	25	Siena	W	4-1	SA	Pepe 2 19 43, Sanchez 61, Di Natale 81	16 033
May	2	Cagliari	D	2-2	SA	Di Natale 26, Sanchez 28	7 500
	9	Bari	D	3-3	SA	Di Natale 2 21 63, Pepe 26	17 968
	15	Lazio	L	1-3	SA	Di Natale 30	34 455

SIENA LEAGUE APPEARANCES/GOALS 2009-10

Goalkeepers Gianluca Curci 36 • Gianluca Pegolo 2+2
Defenders Brandao POR 20+1/0 • Cribari 18/0 • Cristiano Del Grosso 34+2/0 • Daniele Ficagna 10+1 • Marco Malago 4+2/0 • Michael Odibe NGA 4+1/0 • Francesco Pratali 12/0 • Luca Rossettini 2/0 • Andrea Rossi 5+3/0 • Claudio Terzi 17+2/1
Midfield Paul Codrea ROU 22+2/0 • Albin Ekdal SWE 20+6/1 • Michele Fini 11+6/1 • Agostino Garofalo 0+3/0 • Gael Genevier FRA 4/0 • Mato Jajalo CRO 14+11/0 • Lukas Jarolim CZE 6+12/0 • Francesco Parravicini 1/0 • Aleandro Rosi 28+2/1 • Alexandros Tziolis GRE 13/0 • Simone Vergassola 34/5
Forwards Emanuele Calaio 13+20/8 • Abdelkader Ghezzal ALG 26+4/6 • Marcelo Larrondo ARG 5+10/1 • Massimo Maccarone 37/12 • Michele Paolucci 2+8/2 • Reginaldo BRA 18+11/2
Coach Marco Giampaolo • Marco Baroni (29/10/09) • Alberto Malesani (23/11/09)

UDINESE LEAGUE APPEARANCES/GOALS 2009-10

Goalkeepers Samir Handanovic SVN 37 • Rafael Romo VEN 1
Defenders Andrea Coda 24+2/0 • Juan Cuadrado COL 4+7/0 • Maurizio Domizzi 13/0 • Felipe BRA 3/0 • Damiano Ferronetti 8+4/0 • Aleksandar Lukovic SRB 31+2/0 • Giovanni Pasquale 19+3/0 • Cristian Zapata COL 30+1/0
Midfield Emmanuel Agyemang-Badu GHA 0+5/0 • Kwadwo Asamoah GHA 24+1/1 • Dusan Basta SRB 14+2/0 • Gaetano D'Agostino 18+2/1 • Gokhan Inler SUI 32+1/0 • Mauricio Isla 27+3/1 • Jaime ESP 1+3/0 • Francesco Lodi 4+15/1 • Christian Obodo NGA 0+1/0 • Paolo Sammarco 17+9/0 • Siqueira BRA 0+3/0 • Niki Zimling DEN 1/0
Forwards Bernardo Corradi 2+17/0 • Antonio Di Natale 33+2/29 • Antonio Floro Flores 25+7/9 • Alexandre Geijo SUI 0+4/0 • Simone Pepe 25+7/7 • Alexis Sanchez CHI 25+7/5
Coach Pasquale Marino • Gianni De Biasi (22/12/09) • Pasquale Marino (21/02/10)

JAM – JAMAICA

FIFA/COCA-COLA WORLD RANKING

1993	1994	1995	1996	1997	1998	1999	2000	2001	2002	2003	2004	2005	2006	2007	2008	2009	2010
80	96	56	32	39	33	41	48	53	51	46	49	42	57	97	65	81	58

	2010											Hi/Lo
Jan	Feb	Mar	Mar	Apr	May	Jul	Aug	Sep	Oct	Nov	Dec	27
81	78	77	78	79	81	83	82	76	79	82	58	116

Jamaica confirmed their re-emergence as the pre-eminent football nation in the Caribbean when they retained the Digicel Caribbean Cup in Martinique at the end of 2010. It was the Reggae Boyz third triumph in five years and their fifth overall. As the holders they qualified automatically for the finals where they won all three group games in the Stade en Camee in Riviere-Pilote with a team based around a number of professionals playing in Major League Soccer. New York Red Bulls' Dane Richards put the Jamaicans ahead in the semi-final against Grenada although it took and extra-time winner from Jamaica based Troy Smith to see the Jamaicans through to a final against Guadeloupe. With their opponents playing in front of a partisan crowd in what practically amounted to a home fixture, Jamaica went ahead through Omar Cummings, fresh from his MLS triumph with Colorado Rapids, but they conceded soon after and it finished 1-1. In the penalty shoot-out Jamaica scored all five of theirs before Jean Luc Lambourde shot wide to hand the cup to the Reggae Boyz. There was no such joy in Caribbean Club Championship with Jamaican clubs concentrating instead on domestic football where Harbour View won the 2010 championship ahead of defending champions Tivoli Gardens whilst Boy's Town beat Humble Lions 3-2 to win the Cup.

FIFA WORLD CUP RECORD

1930-1962 DNE **1966-1970** DNQ **1974** DNE **1978** DNQ **1982** DNE **1986-1994** DNQ **1998** 22 r1 **2002-2010** DNQ

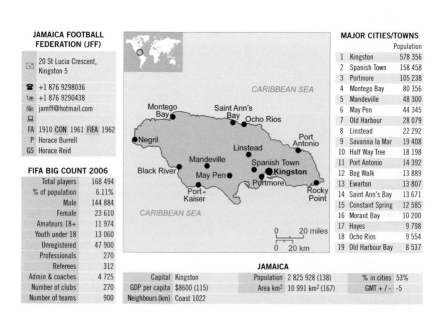

JAMAICA FOOTBALL FEDERATION (JFF)

20 St Lucia Crescent, Kingston 5

☎ +1 876 9298036
📠 +1 876 9290438
✉ jamff@hotmail.com

FA 1910 CON 1961 FIFA 1962
P Horace Burrell
GS Horace Reid

FIFA BIG COUNT 2006

Total players	168 494
% of population	6.11%
Male	144 884
Female	23 610
Amateurs 18+	11 974
Youth under 18	13 060
Unregistered	47 900
Professionals	270
Referees	312
Admin & coaches	4 725
Number of clubs	270
Number of teams	900

MAJOR CITIES/TOWNS

		Population
1	Kingston	578 356
2	Spanish Town	158 458
3	Portmore	105 238
4	Montego Bay	80 356
5	Mandeville	48 300
6	May Pen	44 345
7	Old Harbour	28 079
8	Linstead	22 292
9	Savanna la Mar	19 408
10	Half Way Tree	18 198
11	Port Antonio	14 392
12	Bog Walk	13 889
13	Ewarton	13 807
14	Saint Ann's Bay	13 671
15	Constant Spring	12 585
16	Morant Bay	10 200
17	Hayes	9 798
18	Ocho Rios	9 554
19	Old Harbour Bay	8 537

JAMAICA

Capital	Kingston	Population	2 825 928 (138)	% in cities 53%
GDP per capita	$8600 (115)	Area km²	10 991 km² (167)	GMT + / - -5
Neighbours (km)	Coast 1022		

RECENT INTERNATIONAL MATCHES PLAYED BY JAMAICA

2008	Opponents	Score	Venue	Comp	Scorers	Att	Referee
6-02	Costa Rica	D 1-1	Kingston	Fr	Marshall [88]	30 000	Brizan TRI
26-03	Trinidad and Tobago	D 2-2	Kingston	Fr	King [32], Marshall [38]	19 000	Whittaker CAY
3-06	St Vincent/Grenadines	W 5-1	Kingston	Fr	Phillips [17], King 2 [27p 40], Burton [73], Gardner [87]	20 000	Whittaker CAY
7-06	Trinidad and Tobago	D 1-1	Macoya	Fr	Shelton [90p]	2 500	Small BRB
10-06	Grenada	L 1-2	St George's	Fr	Fuller [20]	5 000	Green GRN
15-06	Bahamas	W 7-0	Kingston	WCq	Gardner [17], Phillips [23], King [34], Shelton 2 [51 66], Goodison [75], Daley [89]	20 000	Navarro CAN
18-06	Bahamas	W 6-0	Greenfield	WCq	Burton 2 [29 55], Shelton 3 [35 37p 42], Marshall [39]	10 500	Archundia MEX
26-07	El Salvador	D 0-0	Frisco	Fr		15 000	Salazar USA
20-08	Canada	D 1-1	Toronto	WCq	Williams [52]	22 000	Batres GUA
6-09	Mexico	L 0-3	Mexico City	WCq		96 000	Toledo USA
10-09	Honduras	L 0-2	San Pedro Sula	WCq		38 000	Moreno PAN
11-10	Mexico	W 1-0	Kingston	WCq	Fuller [34]	27 000	Quesada CRC
15-10	Honduras	W 1-0	Kingston	WCq	Shelton [16]	25 000	Brizan TRI
9-11	Cayman Islands	W 2-0	Grand Cayman	Fr	Cummings [42], Dean [58]	500	Whittaker CAY
19-11	Canada	W 3-0	Kingston	WCq	Shelton [28], King [58p], Cummings [85]	28 000	Aguilar SLV
3-12	Barbados	W 2-1	Kingston	CCr1	Austin [76], Shelton [82]	20 000	Aguilar SLV
5-12	Grenada	W 4-0	Montego Bay	CCr1	Vernan [6], Shelton [18], Williams [53], Phillips [78]	4 000	Moreno PAN
7-12	Trinidad and Tobago	D 1-1	Treawny	CCr1	Vernan [46]	20 000	Moreno PAN
11-12	Guadeloupe †	W 2-0	Kingston	CCsf	Thompson [11], Shelton [57]	23 000	Aguilar SLV
14-12	Grenada	W 2-0	Kingston	CCf	Shelton 2 [16p 70p]	22 000	Brizan TRI
2009							
11-02	Nigeria	D 0-0	London	Fr		8 000	Dean ENG
23-05	Haiti	D 2-2	Fort Lauderdale	Fr	Addley [29], Stewart [88]	12 000	Marrufo USA
30-05	El Salvador	D 0-0	Washington DC	Fr		30 313	Prus USA
7-06	Panama	W 3-2	Kingston	Fr	Johnson [44], Hodges [50], Daley [90]	12 000	Whittaker CAY
28-06	Cayman Islands	W 4-1	Grand Cayman	Fr	Bayliss [22], Wolfe [43], Daley [68], Morrison [82]	900	Holder CAY
3-07	Canada	L 0-1	Carson	GCr1		27 000	Vaughn USA
7-07	Costa Rica	L 0-1	Columbus	GCr1		7 059	Marrufo USA
10-07	El Salvador	W 1-0	Miami	GCr1	Cummings [69]	17 269	Hospedales TRI
12-08	Ecuador	D 0-0	New Jersey	Fr		21 360	Prus USA
16-08	St Kitts and Nevis	W 1-0	Basseterre	Fr	Hodges [55]	5 000	Willett SKN
17-11	South Africa	D 0-0	Bloemfontein	Fr		15 000	Andria'harisoa MAD
2010							
31-01	Canada	W 1-0	Kingston	Fr	Shelton [67]	18 000	Hospedales TRI
10-02	Argentina	L 1-2	Mar Del Plata	Fr	Johnson [46]	20 000	Rivera PER
28-04	South Africa	L 0-2	Offenbach	Fr		562	Sippel GER
11-08	Trinidad and Tobago	W 3-1	Macoya	Fr	Richards [7], Austin [30p], Bryan [52]	4 500	Taylor BRB
5-09	Costa Rica	W 1-0	Kingston	Fr	Johnson [66]	15 000	Brizan TRI
7-09	Peru	L 1-2	Fort Lauderdale	Fr	Cummings [18]	5 217	Vaughn USA
10-10	Trinidad and Tobago	W 1-0	Kingston	Fr	Richards [19p]	7 000	Archundia MEX
17-11	Costa Rica	D 0-0	Fort Lauderdale	Fr		4 000	Renso USA
27-11	Antigua and Barbuda	W 3-1	Riviere-Pilote	CCr1	Shelton 2 [14 37], Richards [40]	3 000	Wijngaarde SUR
29-11	Guadeloupe †	W 2-0	Riviere-Pilote	CCr1	Francis [53], Johnson [93+]	3 000	Lopez GUA
1-12	Guyana	W 4-0	Riviere-Pilote	CCr1	Richards [42], Morgan 2 [49 75], Vernan [90]	3 000	Cruc CRC
3-12	Grenada	W 2-1	Fort de France	CCsf	Richards [7], Smith [96]	4 000	Taylor BRB
5-12	Guadeloupe †	D 1-1	Riviere-Pilote	CCf	Cummings [32], W 5-4p	4 000	Wijngaarde SUR

Fr = Friendly match • CC = Digicel Caribbean Cup • GC = CONCACAF Gold Cup • WC = FIFA World Cup
q = qualifier • r1 = first round group • qf = quarter-final • † Not a full international

JAMAICA NATIONAL TEAM HISTORICAL RECORDS

Past Coaches Geoffrey Maxwell 1989-90 • Carl Brown 1990-94 • Rene Simoes BRA 1994-2000 • Sebastiao Lazaroni BRA 2000 • Clovis De Oliveira BRA 2000-01 • Carl Brown 2001-04 • Sebastiao Lazaroni BRA 2004 • Wendell Downswell 2004-06 • Carl Brown 2006 • Bora Milutinovic 2006-07 • Theodore Whitmore 2007-08 • Rene Simoes BRA 2008 • Theodore Whitmore 2008 • John Barnes ENG 2008-09 • Theodore Whitmore 2009-

JAMAICA 2009-10

DIGICEL PREMIER LEAGUE

	Pl	W	D	L	F	A	Pts	Harbour V	Tivoli G'ns	Waterhouse	St George's	Boys' Town	Village Utd	Portmore U	Arnett G'ns	Sporting	Humble L	Rivoli Utd	August Town
Harbour View	38	23	8	7	53	27	**77**		2-3 2-0	0-2 0-0	1-1 3-1	1-0 2-1	0-1 3-0	1-0 2-0	1-0 2-1	1-1 1-0	1-1 1-1	1-0	1-1
Tivoli Gardens	38	18	12	8	58	32	66	0-1 1-2		1-1 1-0	1-0 3-0	0-2 4-1	4-0 1-0	2-2	1-1	1-1	3-2 2-0	3-3 2-0	4-0 1-0
Waterhouse	38	17	9	12	43	35	60	0-3 1-3	0-2 0-0		0-0 6-1	1-0 2-0	2-0 1-0	1-0	2-0 1-0	2-1	2-1 0-1	1-0	4-1 1-0
St George's	38	12	14	12	32	38	50	0-2 1-2	0-0 2-1	2-0 2-2		0-1 2-0	1-0 1-1	3-1	1-1	2-0 1-0	0-0 0-1	1-0 0-1	2-1
Boys' Town	38	12	13	13	33	36	49	2-2 0-1	1-1 4-3	1-0 1-3	1-1 0-0		1-0 1-0	1-0 1-2	2-0	0-0	2-1	1-0	2-1 1-0
Village United	38	11	15	12	35	40	48	0-2 2-1	0-3 2-0	2-1 3-0	1-1 3-0	0-0 1-3		1-1 2-2	1-1	0-1	1-1 0-0	1-1 0-0	
Portmore United	38	11	14	13	24	28	47	0-1	0-0 1-0	1-1 1-0	0-1 1-1	1-0	0-0 0-1		2-1 0-1	0-1 3-1	0-1 0-0	1-1 1-0	1-0 0-0
Arnett Gardens	38	10	15	13	36	38	45	0-2	1-2 0-1	0-1	0-1 0-0	1-0 1-1	0-0	2-1 0-0		0-2 1-1	1-1 1-0	1-1 0-0	4-1 1-0
Sporting Central Acad.	38	9	16	13	33	34	43	0-0	0-0 0-4	1-3 0-0	0-0	1-2 0-0	0-0 0-1	0-1 0-1	2-1 1-1		3-0 1-1	2-1 2-1	2-0 3-0
Humble Lions	38	9	16	13	32	36	43	1-0	0-2	1-2	0-0	1-0 0-0	1-2 1-2	2-2 0-0	0-1 0-0	0-0 0-0		1-1 4-1	0-1 4-1
Rivoli United	38	9	15	14	36	45	42	0-1 3-2	1-1	2-1 0-0	2-0	0-0 1-0	4-2	2-0 0-0	1-3 0-1	2-2 0-4	1-2 1-1		1-1 3-2
August Town	38	9	9	20	28	54	36	0-1 2-1	0-0	1-0	0-2 2-1	1-1	2-2	0-1 1-0	4-2 4-0	1-0 1-0	2-1 0-0	0-0 0-1	

6/09/2009 - 16/05/2010 • Top scorer: **18** - Devon Hodges, Rivoli United

---

JFF FLOW CHAMPIONS CUP 2009-10

Round of 16
Boys' Town	1
Sporting Central Ac *	0
Reno *	0 3p
Village United	0 5p
Granville	3
York United *	2
Greenwich Town	0
Arnett Gardens *	5
St George's *	1
Portmore United	0
Rivoli United *	1
Harbour View	2
Waterhouse *	1
August Town	0
Tivoli Gardens	0
Humble Lions *	2

Quarter-finals
Boys' Town	1
Village United *	0
Granville *	1
Arnett Gardens	2
St George's	2
Harbour View *	1
Waterhouse	1
Humble Lions *	2

Semi-finals
Boys' Town	4
Arnett Gardens	3
St George's	0
Humble Lions	1

Final
Boys' Town	3
Humble Lions	2

CUP FINAL
Antony Spaulding Complex, Kingston
18-04-2010
Scorers - George Vernal 2 [25 56], Renae Lloyd [105p] for Boys' Town; Kimroy Davis [24], Zico Herrera [43] for Lions

* Home team

MEDALS TABLE

		Overall			League		Cup		City/Town
		G	S	B	G	S	G	S	
1	Portmore United	8	6		4	3	4	3	Portmore
2	Harbour View	7	7		3	5	4	2	Kingston
3	Tivoli Gardens	6	6		4	4	2	2	Kingston
4	Boys' Town	5	4		3	3	2	1	Kingston
5	Reno	5	3		3	3	2		Savannah del Mar
6	Santos	5	1		5	1			Kingston
7	Waterhouse	4	3		2	2	2	1	Kingston
8	Arnett Gardens	3	5		3	4		1	Kingston
9	Seba United	3	4		2	4	1		Montego Bay
10	Wadadah	2	2		2			2	Montego Bay
11	Violet Kickers	2	1		2			1	Montego Bay
12	Olympic Gardens	2					2		Kingston
13	Cavalier	1	3		1	3			Kingston
14	Jamaica Defence Force	1			1				Kingston
15	Naggo's Head	1			1			2	Portmore
16	Black Lions		1		1				
	Constant Spring		1		1				Constant Spring
	Humble Lions		1					1	Clarendon
	Rivoli United		1					1	Spanish Town
	Thunderbolts		1		1				
	Village United		1					1	Falmouth

JOR – JORDAN

FIFA/COCA-COLA WORLD RANKING

1993	1994	1995	1996	1997	1998	1999	2000	2001	2002	2003	2004	2005	2006	2007	2008	2009	2010
87	113	143	146	124	126	115	105	99	77	47	40	86	95	120	124	111	104

	2010											Hi/Lo
	Jan	Feb	Mar	Mar	Apr	May	Jul	Aug	Sep	Oct	Nov	Dec	37
	111	106	106	102	103	104	98	98	99	95	95	104	152

At the 2011 AFC Asian Cup in Qatar, Jordan surprised everyone with a strong run to the quarter-finals - just as they had done at their only previous appearance in the finals seven years before in China. Coached by Iraq's Adnan Hamed - the Asian Coach of the Year in 2004 - the Jordanians almost pulled off one of the biggest shocks of the tournament in their opening game against Japan. With just seconds to go and leading the Japanese 1-0, Maya Yoshida scored from a header to deny Jordan a famous win. The Jordanians bounced back from that disappointment to register a surprise 1-0 win over Saudi Arabia before defeating Syria in their final game to advance to the last eight. Their run ended there after losing 2-1 to Uzbekistan in what was, remarkably, their first ever defeat at the Asian Cup finals, discounting their penalty shoot-out defeat at the hands of Japan in 2004. The Asian Cup performance came off the back of a disappointing showing on home soil in the West Asian Championships, when the Jordanians were unable to move beyond the group stages following draws with both Syria and Kuwait. There was also disappointment in the AFC Cup, a tournament which Jordanian clubs have won three times in the past. In the 2010 competition Al Whidat failed to get past the group stage whilst Shabab Al Ordon were knocked out in the Round of 16.

FIFA WORLD CUP RECORD
1930-1982 DNE   1986-2010 DNQ

JORDAN FOOTBALL ASSOCIATIOM (JFA)

Al-Hussein Youth City,
PO Box 962024,
Amman 11196

☎ +962 6 5657662
📠 +962 6 5657660
✉ info@jfa.com.jo
🖥 www.jfa.com.jo
FA 1949 CON 1970 FIFA 1958
P HRH Prince Ali Al-Hussein
GS Khalil Al-Salem

FIFA BIG COUNT 2006

Total players	121 191
% of population	2.05%
Male	112 856
Female	8 335
Amateurs 18+	3 637
Youth under 18	1 163
Unregistered	40 250
Professionals	21
Referees	161
Admin & coaches	6 070
Number of clubs	93
Number of teams	146

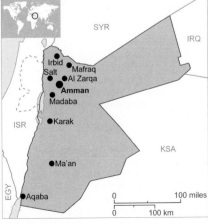

MAJOR CITIES/TOWNS

		Population
1	Amman	1 155 710
2	Al Zarqa	460 007
3	Russeifa	309 152
4	Irbit	302 061
5	Quaismeh	198 777
6	Khelda	179 928
7	Wadi Essier	159 554
8	Khraibet Essooq	133 849
9	Aqaba	99 265
10	Ramtha	92 461
11	Salt	91 385
12	Madaba	86 372
13	Jbaiha	85 732
14	Swaileh	72 705
15	Al Muqabalayn	70 421
16	Mshairfet Ras	60 013
17	Mafraq	58 447
18	Sahab	55 562
19	Um Qsair	54 341

AL MAMLAKAH AL URDUNIYAH AL HASHIMIYA • HASHEMITE KINGDOM OF JORDAN

Capital Amman		Population 6 342 948 (104)	% in cities 78%
GDP per capita $5200 (139)		Area km² 89 342 km² (111)	GMT +/- +2
Neighbours (km) Iraq 181, Israel 238, Saudi Arabia 744, Syria 375, West Bank 97			

RECENT INTERNATIONAL MATCHES PLAYED BY JORDAN

2008	Opponents	Score		Venue	Comp	Scorers	Att	Referee
24-01	Iraq	D	1-1	Dubai	Fr	Shelbaieh [60]		
28-01	Lebanon	W	4-1	Amman	Fr	Awad Ragheb [27], Shelbaieh [78], Amer Deeb [80], Rafat Ali [87]		
31-01	Singapore	W	2-1	Al Zarqa	Fr	Albzour [32], Awad Ragheb [94+]		
6-02	Korea DPR	L	0-1	Amman	WCq		16 000	Shamsuzzaman BAN
16-03	Qatar	L	1-2	Doha	Fr	Alsaify [45]		
22-03	Uzbekistan	L	1-4	Tashkent	Fr	Ala Matalka [11]		
26-03	Turkmenistan	W	2-0	Ashgabat	WCq	Albzzor [34], Bawab [84]	20 000	Tongkhan THA
25-05	China PR	L	0-2	Kunshan City	Fr			
31-05	Korea Republic	D	2-2	Seoul	WCq	Hasan Mahmoud 2 [73 81]	50 000	Shield AUS
7-06	Korea Republic	L	0-1	Amman	WCq		8 000	Moradi IRN
14-06	Korea DPR	L	0-2	Pyongyang	WCq		28 000	Najm LIB
22-06	Turkmenistan	W	2-0	Amman	WCq	Hasan Mahmoud 2 [66 67]	150	Williams AUS
7-08	Syria	D	0-0	Tehran	WAr1			
11-08	Oman	W	3-1	Tehran	WAr1	Hasan Mahmoud [6], Al Nawateer 2 [71 84]		
13-08	Qatar	W	3-0	Tehran	WAsf	Qasem [45], Amer Deeb [71], Alsaify [90]		
15-08	Iran	L	1-2	Tehran	WAf	Amer Deeb [82]	10 000	Zarouni UAE
5-09	Korea Republic	L	0-1	Seoul	Fr		16 537	Ong MAS
26-10	Palestine	D	1-1	Ram	Fr	Al Nawateer [48]		
14-11	Oman	L	0-2	Muscat	Fr			
21-12	China PR	L	0-1	Amman	Fr			
2009								
14-01	Thailand	D	0-0	Amman	ACq		5 000	Racho SYR
28-01	Singapore	L	1-2	Singapore	ACq	Aqel [41p]	6 188	Green AUS
13-05	Zimbabwe	W	2-0	Amman	Fr	Abdullah Deeb [50], Elamaireh [70]		
27-05	Congo	D	1-1	Amman	Fr	Bani Yassen [47]		
3-06	Bahrain	L	0-4	Manama	Fr			
5-09	Malaysia	D	0-0	Amman	Fr			
9-09	New Zealand	L	1-3	Amman	Fr	Aqel [2]		
10-10	Kuwait	L	1-2	Cairo	Fr	Amer Deeb [64]		
14-10	UAE	L	1-3	Dubai	Fr	Abdullah Deeb [60p]		
14-11	Iran	L	0-1	Tehran	ACq		15 000	Nishimura JPN
22-11	Iran	W	1-0	Amman	ACq	Amer Deeb [78]	11 000	Albadwawi USA
30-12	China PR	D	2-2	Jinan	Fr	Shelbaieh 2 [71 78]		
2010								
6-01	Thailand	D	0-0	Bangkok	ACq		15 000	Williams AUS
25-02	Azerbaijan	L	0-2	Amman	Fr			Shaaban EGY
3-03	Singapore	W	2-1	Amman	ACq	Odai Alsaify [9], Bashar Yaseen [60]	17 000	Abdou QAT
16-09	Iraq	W	4-1	Amman	Fr	Ahmad Al Zugheir [6], Abdullah Deeb [19], Hassouneh Qasem [69], Amer Deeb [73]		
19-09	Bahrain	W	2-0	Zarqa	Fr	Moayad Abukeshek [22], Abdullah Deeb [52]		
24-09	Syria	D	1-1	Amman	WAr1	Amer Deeb [13]	18 000	
28-09	Kuwait	D	2-2	Amman	WAr1	Hasan Abdel Fattah 2 [38 51]	18 000	
16-11	Cyprus	D	0-0	Amman	Fr		3 500	Ebrahim BHR
28-12	Bahrain	L	1-2	Dubai	Fr	Baha Suleiman [60]		
2011								
2-01	Uzbekistan	D	2-2	Sharjah	Fr	Amer Deeb [33], Odai Al Saify [75]		Hashmi UAE
9-01	Japan	D	1-1	Doha	ACr1	Hasan Abdel Fattah [45]	6 255	Abdul Bashir SIN
13-01	Saudi Arabia	W	1-0	Al Rayyan	ACr1	Baha Suleiman [42]	17 349	Albadwawi UAE
17-01	Syria	W	2-1	Doha	ACr1	Ali Dyab OG [30], Odai Alsaify [59]	9 849	Abdou QAT
21-01	Uzbekistan	L	1-2	Doha	ACqf	Bashar Yaseen [58]	16 073	Abdul Bashir SIN

Fr = Friendly match • WA = West Asian Federation Championship • AC = AFC Asian Cup • WC = FIFA World Cup
q = qualifier • r1 = first round group

JORDAN 2009-10

FIRST DIVISION

	Pl	W	D	L	F	A	Pts	Al Faysali	Al Wihdat	Shabab	Al Hussein	Kfarsoum	Al Buq'aa	Al Jazeera	Al Ramtha	Al Yarmouk	Al Arabi	Al Karmel	Al Ittihad
Al Faysali ‡	22	17	2	3	43	16	53		0-1	0-0	1-0	2-1	2-0	0-0	2-1	2-0	5-0	3-1	3-0
Al Wihdat ‡	22	16	4	2	39	11	52	2-1		2-0	2-0	1-1	1-0	1-0	2-1	3-0	3-1	4-0	0-0
Shabab Al Ordon	22	12	8	2	35	20	44	2-1	2-1		0-0	3-1	0-0	3-3	5-5	1-0	1-0	4-0	2-0
Al Hussein	22	7	8	7	29	24	29	1-2	2-1	0-1		0-0	0-2	1-1	2-0	1-1	4-0	1-0	5-1
Kfarsoum	22	8	5	9	25	35	29	1-3	0-3	1-1	0-1		0-0	2-0	2-1	1-0	0-4	2-1	3-2
Al Buq'aa	22	6	8	8	22	24	26	2-4	1-1	1-2	3-1	2-2		0-3	0-1	2-2	1-0	4-0	0-0
Al Jazeera	22	7	5	10	27	30	26	1-2	1-3	0-1	1-3	1-2	2-1		3-2	1-0	1-1	4-0	1-0
Al Ramtha	22	6	7	9	31	36	25	0-1	1-1	2-5	2-1	3-0	2-0	0-3		0-0	4-2	1-1	1-1
Al Yarmouk	22	5	7	10	21	29	22	1-4	0-1	0-0	1-1	3-2	1-1	2-0	1-2		1-3	2-0	0-1
Al Arabi	22	6	3	13	31	42	21	2-3	0-3	2-0	1-1	0-1	0-1	1-2	2-2	2-0		2-4	3-2
Al Karmel	22	5	3	14	21	41	18	0-1	0-1	1-2	2-2	1-3	0-0	4-0	2-0	0-3	3-1		1-0
Al Ittihad Al Ramtha	22	3	8	11	15	31	17	0-1	0-2	0-0	2-2	3-0	0-1	0-0	0-0	2-2	0-4	1-0	

24/09/2009 - 17/04/2010 • ‡ Qualified for the AFC Cup

JORDAN 2009-10 SECOND DIVISION (2)

	Pl	W	D	L	F	A	Pts
Mansheyat B. Hasan	11	8	2	1	28	6	26
Al Ahli	11	6	4	1	20	8	22
Shabab Al Hussein	11	6	2	3	17	6	20
Al Sareeh	11	4	4	3	16	14	16
Al Badiah Al Wosta	11	4	3	4	15	14	15
Al Jaleel	11	2	7	2	17	16	13
That Ras	11	3	4	4	12	13	13
Al Salt	11	3	4	4	13	19	13
Ain Karem	11	3	4	4	11	18	13
Al Qouqazy	11	2	5	4	8	14	11
Sahab	11	2	3	6	10	13	9
Al Mugeer	11	1	2	8	8	34	5

29/05/2009 - 7/08/2009

MEDALS TABLE

	Overall G	Overall S	Overall B	Lge G	Cup G	Cup S	SC G	SC S	Asia G	Asia S	Asia B	City
1 Al Faysali	55	11		31	16	5	6	5	2	1		Amman
2 Al Wihdat	27	10	2	11	8	4	8	6			2	Amman
3 Al Ramtha	9	10	1	2	2	9	5	1			1	Irbid
4 Al Ahli	8	1		8	1							Amman
5 Al Jazeera	6	2		3	1	1	2	1				Amman
6 Shabab Al Ordon	5	2		1	2	2	1			1		Zarqa
7 Al Hussein	3	12			5		3	7				Irbid
8 Amman	3	1		1			2	1				Amman
9 Al Arabi	1	2			1	1		1				Irbid
10 Jordan	1			1								Amman
Kfarsoum	1						1					
Al Yarmouk	1											Irbid
13 Al Buq'aa		3				1		2				Amman
Shabab Al Hussein		3				1		2				Amman
15 Al Jalil		1						1				
Al Qadisiya		1						1				

JFA SHIELD 2009-10 FINAL

King Abdullah Stadium, Amman, 1-08-2010

Al Wihdat 2-0 Al Jazeera

JFA CUP 2009-10

First Round			Quarter-finals			Semi-finals			Final		
Al Wihdat *	5	7									
Shehan	0	0	Al Wihdat *	0	4						
Al Karmel	1	2	Al Hussein	0	3						
Al Hussein *	1	3				Al Wihdat *	1	5			
Al Faysali	12	8				Al Ramtha	0	0			
Al Turra *	0	1	Al Faysali	1	3						
Al Yarmouk *	5	1	Al Ramtha *	2	3				Al Wihdat ‡		1
Al Ramtha	5	1							Al Arabi		0
Al Jazeera *	4	4									
Kfarsoum	0	0	Al Jazeera *	0	2						
Mansheyat B. Hasan *	0	0	Shabab Al Ordon	1	1				**CUP FINAL**		
Shabab Al Ordon	1	3				Al Jazeera	2	0			
Al Buq'aa *	3	2				Al Arabi *	1	2	28-05-2010		
Al Ahli	0	1	Al Buq'aa *	1	3						
Al Ittihad *	1	1	Al Arabi	4	3						
Al Arabi	4	0									

* Home team in the first leg • ‡ Qualified for the AFC Cup

JPN – JAPAN

FIFA/COCA-COLA WORLD RANKING

1993	1994	1995	1996	1997	1998	1999	2000	2001	2002	2003	2004	2005	2006	2007	2008	2009	2010
43	36	31	21	14	20	57	38	34	22	29	17	15	47	34	35	43	29

2010												Hi/Lo
Jan	Feb	Mar	Mar	Apr	May	Jul	Aug	Sep	Oct	Nov	Dec	**9**
43	40	46	45	45	45	32	32	30	30	30	29	**66**

After only eight games in charge, Italian Alberto Zaccheroni steered Japan to victory at the 2011 AFC Asian Cup finals in Qatar, the fourth time the Japanese have been crowned kings of Asia. Tadanari Lee's 108th minute goal in Doha's impressive Khalifa Stadium secured the title for Japan with a 1-0 victory over Australia. The appointment of the former Milan coach came in the aftermath of Japan's performance at the World Cup finals in South Africa, where under Takeshi Okada the team pulled off a series of surprises to reach the second round. The Japanese had gone to South Africa with low expectations but victories over Cameroon and Denmark took them into a last-16 meeting with Paraguay. There the two nations played out a dull scoreless draw that the Paraguayans won on penalties, denying the Japanese a place in the quarter-finals for the first time. 2010 saw an increasing number of Japanese players moving to play in Europe which, while it serves as a boost to the national team, will undoubtedly have an impact on the stature of the J.League, which was won in 2010 for the first time by Nagoya Grampus. Defending champions Kashima Antlers had to be content with the Emperor's Cup but both will look to improve on a poor Champions League campaign in 2010 in which Japanese interest ended in the Round of 16.

FIFA WORLD CUP RECORD

1930-1950 DNE **1954** DNQ **1958** DNE **1962** DNQ **1966** DNE **1970-1994** DNQ **1998** 31 r1 **2002** 9 r2 (hosts) **2006** 28 r1 **2010** 9 r2

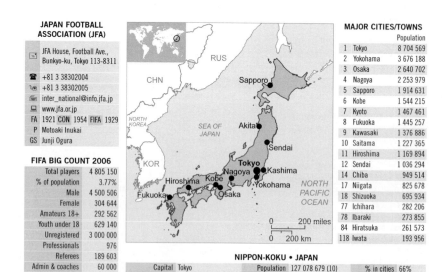

JAPAN FOOTBALL ASSOCIATION (JFA)

JFA House, Football Ave., Bunkyo-ku, Tokyo 113-8311

☎ +81 3 38302004
📠 +81 3 38302005
✉ inter_national@info.jfa.jp
🖥 www.jfa.or.jp

FA 1921 CON 1954 FIFA 1929
P Motoaki Inukai
GS Junji Ogura

FIFA BIG COUNT 2006

Total players	4 805 150
% of population	3.77%
Male	4 500 506
Female	304 644
Amateurs 18+	292 562
Youth under 18	629 140
Unregistered	3 000 000
Professionals	976
Referees	189 603
Admin & coaches	60 000
Number of clubs	1 000
Number of teams	29 132

MAJOR CITIES/TOWNS

		Population
1	Tokyo	8 704 569
2	Yokohama	3 676 188
3	Osaka	2 640 702
4	Nagoya	2 253 979
5	Sapporo	1 914 631
6	Kobe	1 544 215
7	Kyoto	1 467 461
8	Fukuoka	1 445 257
9	Kawasaki	1 376 886
10	Saitama	1 227 365
11	Hiroshima	1 169 894
12	Sendai	1 036 294
14	Chiba	949 514
17	Niigata	825 678
18	Shizuoka	695 934
77	Ichihara	282 206
78	Ibaraki	273 855
84	Hiratsuka	261 573
118	Iwata	193 956

NIPPON-KOKU • JAPAN

Capital Tokyo	Population 127 078 679 (10)	% in cities 66%
GDP per capita $34 100 (37)	Area km² 377 915 km² (61)	GMT +/- +9
Neighbours (km) Coast 29 751		

RECENT INTERNATIONAL MATCHES PLAYED BY JAPAN

2009	Opponents		Score	Venue	Comp	Scorers	Att	Referee
20-01	Yemen	W	2-1	Kumamoto	ACq	Okazaki [7], Tanaka.T [66]	32 000	Tan Hai CHN
28-01	Bahrain	L	0-1	Manama	ACq		11 200	Irmatov UZB
4-02	Finland	W	5-1	Tokyo	Fr	Okazaki 2 [15 32], Kagawa [44], Nakazawa [57]	34 532	Huang Junjie CHN
11-02	Australia	D	0-0	Yokohama	WCq		66 000	Basma SYR
28-03	Bahrain	W	1-0	Saitama	WCq	Nakamura.S [47]	57 276	Kim Dong Jin KOR
27-05	Chile	W	4-0	Osaka	Fr	Okazaki 2 [20 24], Abe [52], Honda [90]	43 531	Hermansen DEN
31-05	Belgium	W	4-0	Tokyo	Fr	Nagamoto [21], Nakamura.K [23], Okazaki [60], Yano [77]	42 520	Styles ENG
6-06	Uzbekistan	W	1-0	Tashkent	WCq	Okazaki [9]	34 000	Basma SYR
10-06	Qatar	D	1-1	Yokohama	WCq	Albinali OG [3]	60 356	Mohd Salleh MAS
17-06	Australia	L	1-2	Melbourne	WCq	Tanaka.MT [39]	69 238	Al Ghamdi KSA
5-09	Netherlands	L	0-3	Enschede	Fr		23 750	Skomina SVN
9-09	Ghana	W	4-3	Utrecht	Fr	Nakamura.K [53], Tamada [78], Okazaki [79], Inamoto [83]	2 506	Blom NED
8-10	Hong Kong	W	6-0	Shizuoka	ACq	Okazaki 3 [18 75 78], Nagamoto [29], Nakazawa [51], Tanaka.MT [67]	16 028	Torky IRN
10-10	Scotland	W	2-0	Yokohama	Fr	Berra OG [83], Honda [90]	61 285	Kim KOR
14-10	Togo	W	5-0	Miyagi	Fr	Okazaki 3 [5 8 65], Morimoto [11], Honda [85]	32 852	Mikulski POL
14-11	South Africa	D	0-0	Port Elizabeth	Fr			Baltazar ANG
18-11	Hong Kong	W	4-0	Hong Kong	ACq	Hasebe [33], Sato [75], Nakamura.S [84], Okazakai [91+]	13 254	Green AUS
2010								
6-01	Yemen	W	3-2	Sana'a	ACq	Hirayama 3 [42 55 79]	10 000	Albadwawi UAE
2-02	Venezuela	D	0-0	Oita	Fr		27 009	Fan Qi CHN
6-02	China PR	D	0-0	Tokyo	EAF		25 964	Delovski AUS
11-02	Hong Kong	W	3-0	Tokyo	EAF	Tamada 2 [41 82], Tanaka.MT [65]	16 368	Zhao Liang CHN
14-02	Korea Republic	L	1-3	Tokyo	EAF	Endo [23p]	42 951	Delovski AUS
3-03	Bahrain	W	2-0	Toyota	ACq	Okazaki [36], Honda [92+]	38 042	Abdul Bashir SIN
7-04	Serbia	L	0-3	Osaka	Fr		46 270	Choi Myung Yong KOR
24-05	Korea Republic	L	0-2	Saitama	Fr		57 873	Attwell ENG
30-05	England	L	1-2	Graz	Fr	Tanaka.MT [7]	15 326	Eisner AUT
4-06	Côte d'Ivoire	L	0-2	Sion	Fr		4 919	Studer SUI
14-06	Cameroon	W	1-0	Bloemfontein	WCr1	Honda [39]	30 620	Benquerenca POR
19-06	Netherlands	L	0-1	Durban	WCr1		62 010	Baldassi ARG
24-06	Denmark	W	3-1	Rustenburg	WCr1	Honda [17], Endo [30], Okazaki [87]	27 967	Damon RSA
29-06	Paraguay	D	0-0	Pretoria	WCr2	L 3-5p	36 742	De Bleeckere BEL
4-09	Paraguay	W	1-0	Yokohama	Fr	Kagawa [70]	65 157	Rodriguez.M MEX
7-09	Guatemala	W	2-1	Osaka	Fr	Morimoto 2 [12 20]	44 541	Archundia MEX
8-10	Argentina	W	1-0	Saitama	Fr	Okazaki [19]	57 735	Gil POL
12-10	Korea Republic	D	0-0	Seoul	Fr		62 503	Irmatov UZB
2011								
9-01	Jordan	D	1-1	Doha	ACr1	Yoshida [92+]	6 255	Abdul Bashir SIN
13-01	Syria	W	2-1	Doha	ACr1	Hasebe [35], Honda [82p]	10 453	Torky IRN
17-01	Saudi Arabia	W	5-0	Al Rayyan	ACr1	Okazaki 3 [8 13 80], Maeda 2 [19 51]	2 022	Irmatov UZB
21-01	Qatar	W	3-2	Doha	ACqf	Kagawa 2 [29 71], Inoha [90]	19 479	Mohd Salleh MAS
25-01	Korea Republic	D	2-2	Doha	ACsf	Maeda [36], Hosogai [97], W 3-0p	16 171	Al Ghamdi KSA
29-01	Australia	W	1-0	Doha	ACf	Lee [109]	37 174	Irmatov UZB

Fr = Friendly match • EAF - East Asian Federation Cup • AC = AFC Asian Cup • WC = FIFA World Cup • q = qualifier

JAPAN NATIONAL TEAM HISTORICAL RECORDS

Caps

122 - Masami Ihara 1988-99 • 116 - Yoshikatsu Kawaguchi 1997- • 110 - Yuji Nakazawa 1999- • 100 - Yasuhito Endo 2002- • 98 - Shunsuke Nakamura 2000-10 • 89 - Kazuyoshi Miura 1990-2000 • 82 - Alessandro dos Santos 2002-06 & Junichi Inamoto 2000- • 78 - Satoshi Tsunami 1980-95 • 77 - Seigo Narazaki 1998-2010 • 72 - Keiji Tamada 2004-

Goals

55 - Kunishige Kamamoto 1964-77 & Kazuyoshi Miura 1990-2000 • 28 - Takuya Takagi 1992-97 • 24 - Shunsuke Nakamura 2000-10 & Hirome Hara 1978-88 • 23 - Naohiro Takahara 2000-08 • 21 - Masashi Nakayama 1990-2003 • 18 - Shiji Okazaki 2008-10

Past Coaches

Hirokazu Ninomiya 1951 • Shigemaru Takenokoshi 1951-56 • Hidetoki Takahashi 1957 • Taizo Kawamoto 1958 • Shigemaru Takenokoshi 1958-59 • Dettmar Cramer (Technical Director) 1960-64 • Hidetoki Takahashi 1960-62 • Ken Naganuma 1962-70 • Shunichiro Okano 1970-72 • Ken Naganuma 1972-76 • Hiroshi Ninomiya 1976-78 • Yukio Shimomura 1979-80 • Masashi Watanabe 1980 • Saburo Kawabuchi 1980-1981 • Takaji Mori 1981-1986 • Yoshinobu Ishii 1986-1987 • Kenzo Yokoyama 1988-1992 • Hans Ooft 1992-1993 • Falcão 1993-94 • Shu Kamo 1995-1997 • Takeshi Okada 1997-1998 • Philippe Troussier 1998-2002 • Zico 2002-2006 • Ivica Osim 2006-2007 • Takeshi Okada 2007-2010 • Alberto Zaccheroni 2010-

JAPAN 2010

J.LEAGUE DIVISION 1

	Pl	W	D	L	F	A	Pts	Nagoya	Gamba	Cerezo	Kashima	Kawasaki	Shimizu	Sanfrecce	Yokohama	Albirex	Urawa	Jubilo	Omiya	Montedio	Vegalta	Vissel	FC Tokyo	Kyoto	Shonan
Nagoya Grampus †	34	23	3	8	54	37	72		3-1	1-0	1-4	2-3	3-3	2-1	1-1	1-1	3-1	2-0	2-1	2-1	2-1	2-0	0-1	1-0	2-1
Gamba Osaka †	34	18	8	8	65	44	62	1-2		3-2	1-1	4-4	1-1	2-0	0-2	0-0	3-2	2-0	5-1	1-0	2-2	2-4	2-0	1-1	2-1
Cerezo Osaka †	34	17	10	7	58	32	61	0-1	1-1		2-1	0-0	1-0	1-1	2-0	2-1	2-3	6-2	2-0	3-0	0-0	2-1	4-1	3-1	2-1
Kashima Antlers †	34	16	12	6	51	31	60	1-0	2-1	0-1		2-1	1-1	0-0	2-0	2-2	2-0	1-2	3-0	3-1	1-0	3-1	1-1	2-1	1-0
Kawasaki Frontale	34	15	9	10	61	47	54	4-0	1-2	1-2	1-2		0-0	2-0	1-3	2-1	1-1	1-1	1-0	0-0	3-2	3-0	2-1	1-0	4-2
Shimizu S-Pulse	34	15	9	10	60	49	54	1-5	0-3	3-2	2-1	2-0		2-1	1-2	0-2	2-1	0-0	2-1	3-0	5-1	1-0	1-2	1-1	5-0
Sanfrecce Hiroshima	34	14	9	11	45	38	51	1-0	0-2	0-5	1-1	0-3	1-1		3-0	4-0	2-1	1-1	1-2	2-1	1-0	1-1	2-1	3-0	3-0
Yokohama F-Marinos	34	15	6	13	43	39	51	0-2	1-0	0-0	1-3	4-0	1-2	2-1		3-0	1-4	1-0	0-2	0-1	0-1	1-1	1-0	1-2	2-2
Albirex Niigata	34	12	13	9	48	45	49	4-1	1-2	1-1	2-1	2-1	4-1	2-2	2-1		0-2	1-1	0-3	1-1	1-1	1-2	1-1	2-1	3-1
Urawa Reds	34	14	6	14	48	41	48	2-1	0-2	2-0	1-1	3-0	1-1	0-1	2-3	2-0		0-1	0-1	0-1	1-1	0-4	1-0	2-0	2-1
Jubilo Iwata	34	11	11	12	38	49	44	1-2	4-3	0-3	2-3	3-1	2-1	2-1	0-0	1-1	2-1		1-1	0-0	3-2	2-1	2-3	3-2	
Omiya Ardija	34	11	9	14	39	45	42	0-1	1-3	3-0	0-1	2-2	3-0	0-0	1-1	2-2	1-2	0-0		2-1	0-3	2-2	0-2	2-1	3-0
Montedio Yamagata	34	11	9	14	29	42	42	0-1	2-1	3-3	1-1	0-0	0-3	1-0	0-1	1-0	1-1	1-0	1-0		3-1	0-0	0-3	1-0	1-1
Vegalta Sendai	34	10	9	15	40	46	39	1-2	1-3	1-1	2-1	1-1	1-3	1-1	0-1	2-3	1-1	3-0	3-1	2-0		0-1	3-2	1-0	2-1
Vissel Kobe	34	9	11	14	37	45	38	1-2	1-3	0-0	0-0	4-1	1-0	1-2	1-1	1-2	1-0	3-0	3-1	0-2	2-0		0-0	2-0	0-0
FC Tokyo	34	8	12	14	36	41	36	0-1	1-1	0-0	1-1	1-2	2-2	0-2	1-0	1-1	0-1	1-1	0-1	1-1	1-1	0-0		1-1	3-0
Kyoto Sanga	34	4	7	23	30	60	19	0-2	1-2	0-1	1-1	3-4	2-4	0-3	1-2	0-2	0-4	0-1	0-2	1-2	2-1	3-0	2-0		0-1
Shonan Bellmare	34	3	7	24	31	82	16	0-1	1-3	0-4	1-1	1-6	3-6	1-3	1-4	2-0	1-4	0-0	1-3	1-1	1-0	2-2	1-3	2-2	

6/03/2010 - 4/12/2010 • † Qualified for the AFC Champions League

Top scorers: **17** - Joshua Kennedy AUS, Nagoya & Ryoichi Maeda, Jubilo • **16** - Edmilson BRA, Urawa & Marcio Richards BRA, Albirex • **14** - Adriano BRA, Cerezo; Shoki Hirai, Gamba & Juninho BRA, Kawasaki • **13** - Jungo Fujimoto, Shimizu; Shinjo Okazaki, Shimizu & Keiji Tamada, Nagoya

JAPAN 2010

J.LEAGUE DIVISION 2

	Pl	W	D	L	F	A	Pts	Kashiwa	Ventforet	Avispa	JEF United	Verdy	Yokohama	Rosso	Tokushima	Sagan	Tochigi	Ehime	Thespa	Consadole	Gifu	Oita	Mito	Fagiano	Kataller	Giravanz
Kashiwa Reysol	36	23	11	2	71	24	80		2-2	1-0	2-2	0-1	2-0	0-0	6-0	2-0	1-1	3-2	5-1	3-0	2-1	1-0	1-1	1-0	1-1	2-1
Ventforet Kofu	36	19	13	4	71	40	70	1-1		2-2	2-0	0-1	0-0	3-3	1-0	0-2	4-3	1-1	2-4	4-1	0-0	3-3	1-1	1-0	5-0	6-0
Avispa Fukuoka	36	21	6	9	63	34	69	0-2	3-1		2-1	3-2	2-1	6-1	1-0	0-1	2-3	2-0	2-1	0-0	0-2	2-1	5-0	0-0	5-0	2-0
JEF United Chiba	36	18	7	11	58	37	61	2-3	1-2	1-1		2-1	4-1	0-2	1-0	2-1	2-0	1-2	3-0	2-0	0-3	2-0	5-0	4-0	2-1	2-1
Tokyo Verdy	36	17	7	12	47	34	58	0-2	1-2	1-1	1-2		1-1	1-2	1-0	3-0	2-0	1-3	1-0	0-1	3-1	1-0	4-0			
Yokohama FC	36	16	6	14	54	47	54	2-2	3-4	1-3	1-0	3-2		1-2	4-0	2-0	0-0	1-0	2-0	0-1	3-1	1-0	0-1	3-1	1-0	4-0
Rosso Kumamoto	36	14	12	10	39	43	54	1-3	0-1	2-1	1-1	3-2	0-2		2-1	2-0	0-2	1-0	0-1	0-0	1-0	0-0	0-0	2-1	1-1	3-0
Tokushima Vortis	36	15	6	15	51	47	51	1-1	0-1	2-3	3-1	2-3	1-0	2-1		2-1	4-0	0-0	1-0	0-0	4-0	0-0	3-3	2-3	1-0	4-4
Sagan Tosu	36	13	12	11	42	41	51	1-1	1-2	0-3	3-1	2-3	1-1	0-1	4-4		3-1	2-1	0-0	1-1	3-0	0-0	1-0	0-0	2-2	3-2
Tochigi SC	36	14	8	14	46	42	50	0-0	0-2	1-2	2-2	0-1	2-1	1-2	1-2	2-0		1-0	0-0	0-1	1-2	2-0	0-1	1-2	1-0	2-0
Ehime FC	36	12	12	12	34	34	48	1-1	1-1	0-2	2-1	3-1	0-1	0-1	0-0	1-2	0-1		1-2	1-1	3-0	0-0	1-0	0-0	2-1	1-1
Thespa Kusatsu	36	14	6	16	36	48	48	0-4	1-4	2-1	2-0	1-0	0-3	1-2	1-4	0-2	2-1	0-1		0-1	1-2	1-1	3-0	0-1	2-1	1-1
Consadole Sapporo	36	11	13	12	37	38	46	1-1	1-1	0-3	1-0	0-0	1-2	4-0	1-0	0-0	4-0	0-1	0-1		0-0	2-1	2-2	0-2	3-1	2-0
FC Gifu	36	13	6	17	32	45	45	0-2	0-0	1-0	3-0	1-0	1-3	0-1	0-1	0-1	4-2	1-1	2-1	3-0		2-0	1-0	1-0	2-1	1-0
Oita Trinita	36	10	11	15	39	49	41	1-0	0-1	0-0	0-2	1-1	2-2	1-1	1-0	3-4	1-4	0-2	1-0	1-2	3-1		1-1	1-0	1-0	0-0
Mito Hollyhock	36	8	14	14	29	45	38	1-4	2-2	1-0	1-0	0-4	3-1	0-1	0-2	0-0	2-1	1-1	1-1	1-1	1-2	2-1		1-1	3-1	0-0
Fagiano Okayama	36	8	8	20	27	51	32	0-2	0-4	1-2	2-1	0-1	0-1	0-0	1-2	1-1	2-1	1-2	1-1	1-0	1-2	2-1	2-1		1-2	0-0
Kataller Toyama	36	8	4	24	39	71	28	1-2	0-3	1-2	0-1	2-3	2-1	0-2	3-3	2-3	1-2	2-1	1-2	3-2	3-2	1-3	0-0	4-0		1-0
Giravanz Kitakyushu	36	1	12	23	20	65	15	0-2	0-0	0-1	0-3	1-0	1-4	2-2	1-3	0-1	1-1	0-3	0-1	0-1	0-1	1-1	1-1	2-1	1-2	

6/03/2010 - 4/12/2010

Top scorers: **20** - Mike Havenaar, Ventforet • **16** - Ricardo Lobo BRA, Tochigi & Tomohiro Tsuda, Tokushima • **15** - Genki Nagasato, Avispa • **14** - Paulinho BRA, Ventforet • **13** - Leandro Domingues BRA, Kashiwa & Yohei Toyoda, Sagan • **12** - Masashi Oguro, Yokohama

JAPAN 2010

9TH JAPAN FOOTBALL LEAGUE (JFL) (3)

Team	Pl	W	D	L	F	A	Pts	Gainare	Sagawa Sh.	Machida	Honda	V-Varen	Sagawa Pr.	Matsumoto	Blaublitz	Zweigen	Ryukyu	MIO Biwako	Yokogawa	Honda Lock	Sony	Tochigi	JEF United	Arte	Ryutsu KU
Gainare Tottori	34	24	5	5	64	31	77		3-1	3-2	1-0	2-1	4-2	3-0	2-0	3-1	3-0	1-0	2-1	0-0	3-1	2-1	2-1	1-0	2-1
Sagawa Shiga	34	17	11	6	69	35	62	4-1		1-1	2-0	1-0	2-0	1-2	4-1	2-2	3-0	3-0	2-2	2-0	1-2	5-1	2-2	1-0	7-0
Machida Zelvia	34	19	4	11	71	44	61	0-1	1-1		1-2	3-0	0-0	6-1	1-0	2-0	1-2	2-0	1-2	1-1	3-1	3-1	2-1	2-3	5-1
Honda FC	34	18	5	11	52	43	59	1-3	2-0	2-1		1-0	2-1	0-3	3-1	2-0	0-1	1-2	2-0	2-0	0-0	4-0	2-1	3-1	0-0
V-Varen Nagasaki	34	15	8	11	50	38	53	1-2	2-1	0-1	1-2		1-1	1-0	1-1	0-1	4-2	1-1	0-1	2-0	1-0	5-2	0-1	1-0	3-1
Sagawa Printing	34	15	8	11	54	46	53	0-0	0-3	1-4	3-4	3-3		0-2	2-1	1-2	2-1	8-2	2-0	1-0	0-1	3-0	1-0	2-1	2-2
Matsumoto Yamaga	34	15	7	12	48	41	52	1-0	0-0	1-2	1-0	1-1	0-1		1-2	1-0	0-2	6-0	1-0	0-2	0-2	2-3	5-1	0-0	2-1
Blaublitz Akita	34	14	9	11	54	41	51	3-2	2-3	1-2	5-0	0-0	1-1	1-3		2-2	2-1	3-0	1-1	1-1	1-0	1-1	3-0	2-0	4-2
Zweigen Kanazawa	34	13	9	12	46	41	48	1-0	2-2	0-1	2-1	2-2	0-1	1-1	0-3		3-0	0-1	1-1	0-1	1-0	1-2	0-1	2-0	4-0
FC Ryukyu	34	14	6	14	51	51	48	1-1	1-1	3-1	2-2	2-1	3-3	0-2	1-0	3-1		4-1	0-1	1-2	2-1	2-2	2-2	1-2	0-2
MIO Biwako Kusatsu	34	13	7	14	51	56	46	5-0	1-2	4-3	0-1	2-3	2-0	2-2	1-0	1-0	2-1		0-2	2-2	2-0	0-1	5-0	3-0	0-1
Yokogawa Musashino	34	12	9	13	34	38	45	0-1	2-1	2-3	1-1	0-0	1-4	0-1	1-3	2-0	1-0	3-0		3-0	1-0	0-2	2-3	0-1	3-2
Honda Lock	34	10	12	12	36	39	42	0-0	0-0	2-1	2-2	1-2	1-0	0-1	2-2	1-1	0-1	3-4	3-0		2-1	1-2	3-0	0-1	3-2
Sony Sendai	34	11	9	14	34	42	42	1-1	1-1	2-1	0-3	2-3	2-3	3-2	1-0	1-0	1-1	2-1	0-0	0-0		0-0	0-1	1-3	3-2
Tochigi Uva	34	7	10	17	41	75	31	0-6	2-3	1-4	4-4	0-2	1-2	2-2	1-5	1-3	2-5	1-1	1-0	0-1	4-0		1-0	2-1	2-2
JEF United Club	34	7	9	18	31	55	30	0-3	0-0	2-3	1-0	1-2	0-0	1-0	1-2	1-3	2-1	0-0	0-1	3-0	1-0	1-1		1-3	1-2
Arte Takasaki	34	7	8	19	28	51	29	0-3	0-2	2-4	1-2	0-2	0-1	2-0	1-1	1-2	1-4	1-0	1-1	0-0	1-1	0-1	1-1		1-0
Ryutsu Keizai Univ.	34	5	4	25	33	80	19	1-3	2-5	0-3	1-2	0-4	0-3	1-2	0-1	2-4	0-3	2-2	0-1	0-2	1-3	2-0	1-2	1-0	

15/03/2010 - 28/11/2010 • Relegation play-off: Sanyo Electric Sumoto 0-3 1-1 **Arte Takasaki**
Top scorers: 27 - Sho Gokyu, Sagawa Shiga • 24 - Masatoshi Matsuda, Blaublitz • 18 - Yosinori Katsumata, Machida

MEDALS TABLE

	Team	Overall G	Overall S	Overall B	J.League G	J.League S	J.League B	JSL G	JSL S	JSL B	EC G	EC S	JLC G	JLC S	Asia G	Asia S	Asia B	City	Former name	Formed
1	Tokyo Verdy	16	8	1	2	1		5	3		5	3	3	1	1		1	Tokyo	Yomiuri	1969
2	Yokohama F.Marinos	14	8	2	3	2	1	2	4		6	1	1		2	1	1	Yokohama	Nissan	1972
3	Kashima Antlers	14	7	3	7	2	2				4	2	3	3			1	Ibaraki	Sumitomo	1947
4	Urawa Reds	13	14	1	1	3		4	6	5	6	3	1	2	1		1	Saitama	Mitsubishi	1950
5	Jubilo Iwata	9	10	3	3	3		1		3	2	2	2	3	1	2		Iwata	Yamaha	1970
6	JEF United	9	4	6			2	2	1	4	4	2	2	1	1			Ichihara	Furukawa	1946
7	Sanfrecce Hiroshima	8	13	2		1		5	1	1	3	10			1		1	Hiroshima	Toyo Kogyo/Mazda	1938
8	Cerezo Osaka	7	12	2			1	4	4	1	3	8						Osaka	Yanmar	1957
9	Shonan Bellmare	7	5	3				3	1	3	3	4			1			Hiratsuka	Fujita	1968
10	Gamba Osaka	6	3	5	1	1	5				3	1	1	1	1			Osaka	Matsushita	1980
11	Kashiwa Reysol	4	4	7			2	1	1	5	2	3	1					Kashiwa	Hitachi	1940
12	Shimizu S-Pulse	3	8	3		1	2				1	4	1	3	1		1	Shimizu		1991
13	Nagoya Grampus	3	3	3	1	1	2				2	1			1		1	Nagoya	Toyota	1939
14	Yokohama Flugels	3	2	3			1				1	1	2	1	1		1	Yokohama	All Nippon Airways	1964
15	FC Tokyo	2											2					Tokyo	Tokyo Gas	1935
	Kyoto Sanga	2									1							Kyoto	Kyoto Shiko	1922
17	Yawata/Nippon Steel	1	5	2				2	2		1	3						Kitakyushi		1950
18	Nippon Kokan	1	4							3	1	1						Kawasaki		1912
19	Oita Trinita	1											1					Oita		1994
20	Kawasaki Frontale		6				3										3	Kawasaki	Fujitsu	1955
21	Honda			2							2							Hamamatsu		1971

The creation of the J.League saw all of the company teams change their names as listed above • In 1998 Yokohama Marinos merged with Yokohama Flugels (previously All Nippon Airways) to form Yokohama F.Marinos. Disgruntled Flugel's fans then formed Yokohama FC in protest

EMPEROR'S CUP 2010

Second Round

Team	Score
Kashima Antlers *	6
Arte Takasaki	0
Ehime FC	1
Rosso Kumamoto *	2
Sony Sendai	1
Vegalta Sendai *	0
Toyama Shinjo Club *	0
Cerezo Osaka	7
Albirex Niigata *	3
Zweigen Kanazawa	0
Tokyo Verdy	0
Machida Zelvia *	1
Consadole Sapporo *	4
Grulla Morioka	1
Chukyo University	0
Nagoya Grampus *	3
Avispa Fukuoka	3
Fagiano Okayama *	2
Dezzola Shimahe	0
Sanfrecce Hiroshima *	4
Oita Trinita *	3
Honda Lock	2
Kamatamere Sanuki	1
Omiya Ardija *	4
JEF United Chiba *	3
FC Ryukyu	0
Sagawa Printing *	2
Kyoto Sanga	3
Giravanz Kitakyushu	3
Thespa Kusatsu *	1
Komazawa University	0
FC Tokyo *	2
Gamba Osaka *	6
Osaka University of H&SS	2
FC Gifu *	2
Tochigi SC	3
Vissel Kobe	2
MIO Biwako Kusatsu *	0
Juntendo University	0
Kashiwa Reysol *	6
Jubilo Iwata *	2
Ehime FC Shimanami	1
Matsumoto Yamaga	0
Ventforet Kofu *	1
Tokushima Vortis *	2
Gainare Tottori	1
Tokyo International University	0
Urawa Reds *	7
Montedio Yamagata *	3
Blaublitz Akita	0
Renofa Yamaguchi	0
Shonan Bellmare *	4
Yokohama FC	2
Kataller Toyama *	1
NIFS Kanoya	0
Kawasaki Frontale *	4
Yokohama F-Marinos *	3
V-Varen Nagasaki	1
Kumamoto Gakuen University	0
Sagan Tosu *	10
Mito Hollyhock *	4
Sagawa Shiga	2
Honda FC	0
Shimizu S-Pulse *	2

Third Round

Team	Score
Kashima Antlers *	2
Rosso Kumamoto	1
Sony Sendai *	0
Cerezo Osaka	3
Albirex Niigata *	2
Machida Zelvia	1
Consadole Sapporo	1
Nagoya Grampus *	2
Avispa Fukuoka	2 6p
Sanfrecce Hiroshima *	2 5p
Oita Trinita	0
Omiya Ardija *	3
JEF United Chiba	4
Kyoto Sanga *	0
Giravanz Kitakyushu *	0
FC Tokyo	2
Gamba Osaka *	3
Tochigi SC	2
Vissel Kobe *	1
Kashiwa Reysol	2
Jubilo Iwata *	2
Ventforet Kofu	1
Tokushima Vortis	0
Urawa Reds *	2
Montedio Yamagata *	1
Shonan Bellmare	3
Yokohama FC	1
Kawasaki Frontale *	2
Yokohama F-Marinos *	2
Sagan Tosu	1
Mito Hollyhock	1
Shimizu S-Pulse *	4

Fourth Round

Team	Score
Kashima Antlers *	2
Cerezo Osaka	1
Albirex Niigata	1 4p
Nagoya Grampus *	1 5p
Avispa Fukuoka	2 4p
Omiya Ardija *	2 3p
JEF United Chiba	0
FC Tokyo *	2
Gamba Osaka *	4
Kashiwa Reysol	1
Jubilo Iwata	0
Urawa Reds *	1
Montedio Yamagata	3 5p
Kawasaki Frontale *	3 4p
Yokohama F-Marinos *	0
Shimizu S-Pulse	3

J.League clubs join in the second round • * Home team

EMPEROR'S CUP 2010

Quarter–finals	Semi–finals	Final

Kashima Antlers * 2
Nagoya Grampus 1

Kashima Antlers ‡ 2
FC Tokyo 1

Avispa Fukuoka * 2
FC Tokyo 3

Kashima Antlers † 2
Shimizu S-Pulse 1

Gamba Osaka * 2
Urawa Reds 1

Gamba Osaka 0
Shimizu S-Pulse †† 3

Montedio Yamagata 1 4p
Shimizu S-Pulse * 1 5p

‡ Played at National Stadium, Tokyo
†† Played at Ecopa Stadium, Shizuoka
† Qualified for the AFC Champions League

90TH EMPEROR'S CUP FINAL 2010

National Stadium, Tokyo, 1-01-2011, 14:00, Att: 41 348, Ref: Masaaki Toma

Kashima Antlers 2 Fellype Gabriel [26], Takuya Nozawa [77]
Shimizu S-Pulse 1 Frode Johsen [59]

Kashima - Hitoshi Sogahata - Toru Araiba (Takefumi Toma 88), Masahiko Inoha, Koji Nakata, Tomohiko Miyazaki - Takeshi Oaki, Mitsuo Ogasawara (c), Takuya Nozawa, Fellype Gabriel (Masashi Motoyama 63) - Yuya Osako (Yasushi Endo 92+), Shinzo Koroki. Tr: Oswaldo Oliveira
Shimizu - Kaito Yamamoto - Daisuke Ichikawa, Keisuke Iwashita (c), Eddy Bosnar, Kosuke Ota - Masaki Yamamoto (Teruyoshi Ito 67), Takuya Honda (Genki Omae 87), Shinji Ono (Kazuki Hara 82) - Shinji Okazaki, Frode Johnson, Jungo Fujimoto. Tr: Kenta Hasegawa

J.LEAGUE YAMAZAKI NABISCO CUP 2010

First Round Groups

	Pl	W	D	L	F	A	Pts	To	VS	KS	AN	OA	NG	CO
FC Tokyo	6	4	1	1	7	4	13				1-0	1-0	2-2	0-0
Vegalta Sendai	6	3	3	0	7	1	12			1-1				0-0
Kyoto Sanga	6	3	2	1	9	5	11	1-0						
Albirex Niigata	6	3	1	2	5	5	10		0-0	0-4		1-0		
Omiya Ardija	6	2	1	3	6	9	7			1-0			2-1	
Nagoya Grampus	6	0	3	3	4	9	3		0-2	1-3		0-1		1-1
Cerezo Osaka	6	0	1	5	4	9	1		1-2	0-1	0-1			

	Pl	W	D	L	F	A	Pts	JI	SSP	MY	YM	UR	VK	SB
Jubilo Iwata	6	4	1	1	12	5	13			5-0	2-1			2-0
Shimizu S-Pulse	6	3	2	1	6	3	11			2-0				0-0
Montedio Yamagata	6	3	1	2	6	6	10		0-0		1-0		3-0	
Yokohama F.Marinos	6	2	3	1	6	3	9	1-0	0-2			0-0	3-0	
Urawa Reds	6	2	2	2	6	6	8	1-1	0-1		3-1		1-1	
Vissel Kobe	6	2	1	3	8	10	7					1-3		
Shonan Bellmare	6	0	0	6	4	15	0		1-2				2-3	

Quarter-finals

Jubilo Iwata *	2	0
Vegalta Sendai	1	0

Kashima Antlers *	2	1
Kawasaki Frontale	1	3

Shimizu S-Pulse	1	0
FC Tokyo *	1	0

Gamba Osaka	1	1
Sanfrecce Hiroshima *	0	2

Semi-finals

Jubilo Iwata *	0	3
Kawasaki Frontale	1	1

Shimizu S-Pulse	1	1
Sanfrecce Hiroshima *	2	1

Final

Jubilo Iwata	5
Sanfrecce Hiroshima *	3

CUP FINAL

National Stadium, Tokyo, 3-11-2010
Att: 39,767. Ref: Takayama. Scorers - Keisuke Funatani 36, Ryoichi Maeda 2 89 109, Minoru Suganuma 102, Ryohei Yamazaki 104 for Jubilo; Tadanari Lee 43, Satoru Yamagishi 48, Tomoaki Makino 105 for Sanfrecce
Jubilo - Yoshikatsu Kawaguchi - Kosuke Yamamoto, Masahiro Koga, Lee Gang Jin (Kentaro Oi 49), Shuto Yamamoto - Daisuke Masu, Kota Ueda•, Norihiro Nishi, Keisuke Funatani (Minoru Suganuma 60) - Gilsinho• (Ryohei Yamazaki 77), Ryoichi Maeda. Tr: Masaaki Yanagishita. **Sanfrecce** - Shusaku Nishikawa - Ryota Moriwaki, Koji Nakajima, Tomoaki Makino - Mihael Mikic (Tsubasa Yokotake 78), Kazuyuki Morisaki• Koji Morisaki (Toshihiro Aoyama 56), Satoru Yamagishi, Yojiro Takahagi (Issei Takayanagi (Masato Yamazaki 46) - Tadanari Lee. Tr: Mihailo Petrovic.

Sanfrecce, Gamba, Kashima and Kawasaki qualified directly for the knock-out stage due to AFC Champions League commitments

* Home team in the first leg

KAZ – KAZAKHSTAN

FIFA/COCA-COLA WORLD RANKING

1993	1994	1995	1996	1997	1998	1999	2000	2001	2002	2003	2004	2005	2006	2007	2008	2009	2010
-	153	163	156	107	102	123	120	98	117	136	147	137	135	112	137	125	138

	2010											Hi/Lo
Jan	Feb	Mar	Mar	Apr	May	Jul	Aug	Sep	Oct	Nov	Dec	**98**
125	123	127	129	129	129	126	125	126	137	137	138	**166**

After coming so close in the past, Tobol Kostanay finally landed the Kazakh league title, finishing a point ahead of rivals FK Aktobe, the team that had beaten them on penalties in the 2008 championship play-off. At one point it looked as if Tobol had blown their chances, letting a 10 point lead slip and when Aktobe trounced them 5-2 at home with three games to go, their fans feared the worst, but the defeat spurred Tobol on and they won their final three matches. After a decade at the club, captain Nurbol Zhumaskaliyev finally got his hands on a championship medal although he missed out on finishing as top scorer to team mate Ulugbek Bakaev. Lokomotiv Astana won their first silverware when they beat Shakhter Karagandy 1-0 in the Cup Final - just two years after being formed. Playing in the spectacular new 30,000 capacity Turkish designed Astana Arena, Lokomotiv have been able to lure players from other clubs in Kazakhstan and from further afield as they look to establish themselves as a force in Kazakhstan. The stadium is also home to the national team and they won for the first time there in a friendly against Oman in August 2010 but with defeats in their first four qualifiers for Euro 2012, coach Bernd Storck made way for compatriot Holger Fach as the Kazakhs aim to build a team worthy of their new home.

FIFA WORLD CUP RECORD
1930-1994 DNE 1998-2010 DNQ

FOOTBALL FEDERATION OF KAZAKHSTAN (FSK)

Satpayev Street 29/3,
Almaty 050 012

☎ +7 71 72 924492
📠 +7 3272 921885
📧 kfo@mail.online.kz
🖥 www.kff.kz
FA 1914 CON 2002 FIFA 1994
P Adilbek Dzhaksybekov
GS Sayan Khamitzhanov

FIFA BIG COUNT 2006

Total players	510 420
% of population	3.35%
Male	437 820
Female	72 600
Amateurs 18+	5 250
Youth under 18	20 500
Unregistered	79 600
Professionals	1 450
Referees	210
Admin & coaches	2 950
Number of clubs	43
Number of teams	300

MAJOR CITIES/TOWNS

		Population
1	Almaty	1 351 521
2	Shymkent	461 798
3	Karagandy	427 906
4	Taraz	406 262
5	Astana	398 753
6	Pavlodar	358 262
7	Oskemen	347 925
8	Semey	314 013
9	Aktobe	289 179
10	Uralsk	260 504
11	Kostanay	252 115
12	Petropavl	206 991
13	Akmechet	186 007
14	Aktau	182 799
15	Temirtau	179 035
16	Ekibastuz	160 492
17	Atyrau	160 008
18	Kokshetau	133 561
19	Rudni	126 839

QAZAQSTAN RESPUBLIKASY • REPUBLIC OF KAZAKHSTAN

Capital	Astana	Population	15 399 437 (62)	% in cities	58%
GDP per capita	$11 500 (96)	Area km²	2 724 900 km² (9)	GMT +/-	+4 +5
Neighbours (km)	China 1533, Kyrgyzstan 1224, Russia 6846, Turkmenistan 379, Uzbekistan 2203				

RECENT INTERNATIONAL MATCHES PLAYED BY KAZAKHSTAN

2007	Opponents	Score		Venue	Comp	Scorers	Att	Referee
7-02	China PR	L	1-2	Suzhou	Fr	Suyumagambetov [14]		
7-03	Kyrgyzstan	W	2-0	Shymkent	Fr	Byakov [3], Chichulin [68]		Irmatov UZB
9-03	Azerbaijan	W	1-0	Shymkent	Fr	Finonchenko [87]	4 500	Mashentsev KGZ
11-03	Uzbekistan	D	1-1	Shymkent	Fr	Suyumagambetov [13]		Mashentsev KGZ
24-03	Serbia	W	2-1	Almaty	ECq	Ashirbekov [47], Zhumaskaliyev [61]	19 600	Hrinák SVK
2-06	Armenia	L	1-2	Almaty	ECq	Baltiev [88p]	17 100	Kralovec CZE
6-06	Azerbaijan	D	1-1	Almaty	ECq	Baltiev [53]	11 800	Toussaint LUX
22-08	Finland	L	1-2	Tampere	ECq	Byakov [23]	13 047	Kassai HUN
8-09	Tajikistan	D	1-1	Almaty	Fr	Nurdauletov [54]		
12-09	Belgium	D	2-2	Almaty	ECq	Byakov [39], Smakov [77p]	18 100	Tudor ROU
13-10	Poland	L	1-3	Warsaw	ECq	Byakov [20]	11 040	Berntsen NOR
17-10	Portugal	L	1-2	Almaty	ECq	Byakov [93+]	25 057	Wegeref NED
21-11	Armenia	W	1-0	Yerevan	ECq	Ostapenko [64]	3 100	Fautrel FRA
24-11	Serbia	L	0-1	Belgrade	ECq		500	Vasaras GRE
2008								
3-02	Azerbaijan	D	0-0	Antalya	Fr			Kamil TUR
6-02	Moldova	L	0-1	Antalya	Fr		300	Lehner AUT
26-03	Armenia	L	0-1	Pernis	Fr			Vink NED
23-05	Russia	L	0-6	Moscow	Fr		10 000	
27-05	Montenegro	L	0-3	Podgorica	Fr		9 000	Tusin LUX
20-08	Andorra	W	3-0	Almaty	WCq	Ostapenko 2 [14 30], Uzdenov [44]	7 700	Banari MDA
6-09	Croatia	L	0-3	Zagreb	WCq		17 424	Johannesson SWE
10-09	Ukraine	L	1-3	Almaty	WCq	Ostapenko [68]	17 000	Brych GER
11-10	England	L	1-5	London	WCq	Kukeyev [68]		
2009								
11-02	Estonia	W	2-0	Antalya	Fr	Baltiyev 2 [33 82]	200	Gocek TUR
1-04	Belarus	L	1-5	Almaty	WCq	Abdulin [10]	19 000	Jech CZE
6-06	England	L	0-4	Almaty	WCq		24 000	Jakobsson ISL
10-06	Ukraine	L	1-2	Kyiv	WCq	Nusserbayev [18]	11 500	Paixao POR
9-09	Andorra	W	3-1	Andorra La Vella	WCq	Khizhnichenko 2 [14 35], Baltiyev [29]	510	Toussaint LUX
10-10	Belarus	L	0-4	Brest	WCq		9 530	Ennjimmi FRA
14-10	Croatia	L	1-2	Astana	WCq	Khizhnichenko [26]	10 250	Circhetta SUI
2010								
3-03	Moldova	L	0-1	Antalya	Fr		500	Bezborodov RUS
11-08	Oman	W	3-1	Astana	Fr	Karpovich [20], Zhumaskaliev [43], OG [62]		Irmatov UZB
3-09	Turkey	L	0-3	Astana	ECq		15 800	Vad HUN
7-09	Austria	L	0-2	Salzburg	ECq		22 500	Strahonja CRO
8-10	Belgium	L	0-2	Astana	ECq		8 500	Borski POL
12-10	Germany	L	0-3	Astana	ECq		18 000	Tudor ROU

Fr = Friendly match • EC = UEFA EURO 2008/2012 • WC = FIFA World Cup • q = qualifier • BCD = behind closed doors

KAZAKHSTAN NATIONAL TEAM HISTORICAL RECORDS

Caps
70 - Ruslan Baltiyev 1997-2009 • 54 - Samat Smakov 2000-09 • 48 - Nurbol Zhumaskaliyev 2001- • 47 - Andrey Karpovich 2000- • 35 - Alexandr Kuchma 2000- & David Loriya 2000-09 • 34 - Alexandr Familtsev 1997-2006 • 33 - Farkhadbek Irismetov 2004- • 32 - Dmitry Byakov 2000-08 • 29 - Maxim Zhalmagambetov 2004-08 • 27 - Igor Avdeyev 1996-2005 & Oleg Litvinenko 1997-2006

Goals
13 - Ruslan Baltiyev 1997-2009 • 12 - Viktor Zubarev 1997-2002 • 8 - Dmitry Byakov 2000-08 • 6 - Igor Avdeyev 1996-2005 & Oleg Litvinenko 1997-2006

Past Coaches
Bakhtiar Baiseitov 1992 • Baurzhan Baimukhammedov 1994 • Serik Berdalin 1995-97 • Sergei Gorokhovadatskiy 1998 • Voit Talgaev 2000 • Vladimir Fomichev 2000 • Vakhid Masudov 2001-02 • Leonid Pakhomov RUS 2003-04 • Sergey Timofeev 2004-05 • Arno Pijpers NED 2006-08 • Bernd Storck GER 2008-10 • Holger Fach GER 2010-

KAZAKHSTAN 2010

SUPERLIGA ALMA TV

	Pl	W	D	L	F	A	Pts	Tobol	Aktobe	Irtysh	Astana	Atyrau	Shakhter	Zhetysu	Ordabasy	Taraz	Kairat	Akzhayuk	Okzhetpes
Tobol Kostanay †	32	19	7	6	53	25	64		2-1 2-5	4-1 4-0	0-1 2-0	2-2 3-0	0-0 1-1	0-1	2-0	1-0	3-1	3-1	4-0
FK Aktobe ‡	32	19	6	7	56	30	63	1-3 2-0		0-0 1-0	1-2 1-1	3-0	2-0 0-1	2-1	1-1	2-1	1-0	4-1	4-1
Irtysh Pavlodar ‡	32	16	8	8	39	30	56	0-0 2-1	2-1 1-1		3-1 3-0	1-0	1-3	1-1	0-0	2-1	0-0	1-0	1-0
Lokomotiv Astana ‡	32	14	8	10	41	28	50	2-0 0-0	0-1 2-2	3-0 0-0		1-0 2-0	4-0 1-0	1-0	1-0	3-0	0-0	2-0	4-0
FK Atyrau	32	13	5	14	36	44	44	1-3 0-2	2-1 2-5	0-3 1-2	2-2 1-0		1-0 1-1	1-2	1-0	1-0	2-0	2-0	1-0
Shakhter Karagandy	32	11	8	13	32	30	41	1-1 0-1	2-0 0-1	0-1 1-1	3-1 0-1	1-1 0-1		1-2	0-1	2-0	1-0	3-2	2-0
Zhetysu Taldykorgan	32	13	10	9	36	26	49	0-0	0-1	0-0	1-0	1-2	0-0		2-1	0-2 3-1	0-2 1-4	0-2 2-2	1-0 0-0
Ordabasy Shymkent	32	12	9	11	37	34	45	1-2	0-2	1-0	3-1	2-1	1-0	2-1 1-1		1-0 1-0	1-1 1-2	1-2 1-4	1-4 1-1
FK Taraz	32	9	10	13	36	40	37	0-1	2-2	1-1	1-0	1-2	1-5	2-2 1-1	0-1 1-1		2-1 1-0	3-2 0-1	2-1 2-3
Kairat Almaty	32	6	11	15	17	38	29	0-1	0-2	0-0	2-2	1-0	0-1	0-3 0-1	1-1 0-5	0-0 0-3		0-0 2-1	1-1 0-1
Akzhayuk Uralsk	32	7	5	20	33	58	26	0-2	1-1	1-4	2-2	1-1	0-3	0-2 0-3	2-1 4-0	2-3 1-2	2-2 2-0		2-0 2-0
Okzhetpes Kokshetau	32	6	7	19	24	57	25	1-3	0-1	2-4	2-1	0-6	0-1	0-0 1-0	3-2 3-1	2-2 0-0	1-1 1-0	1-0	

22/03/2010 - 6/11/2010 • † Qualified for the UEFA Champions League • ‡ Qualified for the Europa League

Top scorers: 16 - Ulugbek Bakaev UZB, Tobol • 15 - Nurbol Zhumaskaliyev, Tobol & Georgi Daskalov BUL, Irtysh • 14 - Moses Sakyi GHA, Akzhayuk

KAZAKHSTAN 2010 — PERVAIA (2)

	Pl	W	D	L	F	A	Pts
Vostock Oskemen	34	27	6	1	91	15	87
Kaisar Kyzylorda	34	25	6	3	74	23	81
Sunkar Kaskelen	34	22	7	5	73	28	73
Spartak Semey	34	19	7	8	68	40	64
Ilie-Saulet	34	18	9	7	73	38	63
Cesna Almaty	34	18	5	11	56	34	59
Kazakmis Satpayev	34	17	6	11	80	45	57
Ekibastuzetc	34	14	9	11	44	37	51
Bulak Talgar	34	14	9	11	48	39	51
Yesil-Bogatyr Petropavl	34	14	4	16	44	57	46
Aktobe-Zhas	34	13	4	17	40	66	43
Lashin Taraz	34	12	8	14	46	54	44
Gefest Karagandy	34	12	2	20	52	83	38
Bolat-AMT Temirtau	34	10	8	16	44	58	38
FK Astana 64 §3	34	9	4	21	41	75	28
Kaspiy Aktau	34	5	5	24	40	79	20
CSKA Almaty	34	5	3	26	32	76	18
Asbest Jitikara	34	0	2	32	11	110	2

1/05/2010 - 24/10/2010 • § = points deducted

MEDALS TABLE

		Overall			League			Cup		City
		G	S	B	G	S	B	G	S	
1	Kairat Almaty	7	2	3	2		3	5	2	Almaty
2	Irtysh Pavlodar	6	5	5	5	3	5	1	2	Pavlodar
3	FK Astana	6	2	1	3		1	3	2	Astana
4	FK Aktobe	5	3		4	2		1	1	Aktobe
5	FK Semey	4		1	3		1	1		Semey
6	Tobol Kostanay	2	5	3	1	4	3	1	1	Kostanay
7	FK Taraz	2	4		1	2		1	2	Taraz
8	Vostock Oskemen	1	2					1	2	Oskemen
9	FK Atyrau	1	2			2		1		Atyrau
10	Kaisar Kyzylorda	1	1					1	1	Kyzylorda
	FK Almaty	1	1					1	1	Almaty
	Lokomotiv Astana	1	1			1		1		Astana
13	Dostyk Almaty	1			1					Almaty
14	Yesil-Bogatyr Petropavl		3	1		2	1		1	Petropavl
	Ordabasy Shymkent		3	1		1	1		2	Shymkent
16	Shakhter Karagandy		2	3			3		2	Karagandy
17	Ekibastuzetc		2			2				Ekibastuz
18	Gornyak Khromtau			1			1			Khromtau

KUBOK KAZAKHSTANA 2010

First round

Lokomotiv Astana	3
Cesna Almaty *	0
Irtysh Pavlodar	0
FK Taraz *	1
FK Atyrau *	9
Okzhetpes Kokshetau	2
Kairat Almaty	0
Zhetysu Taldykorgan *	
Ordabasy Shymkent *	5
Akzhayuk Uralsk	0
Vostock Oskemen *	1
Tobol Kostanay	2
FK Aktobe	2
Lashin Taraz *	0
Gefest Karagandy *	0
Shakhter Karagandy	4

Quarter–finals

Lokomotiv Astana *	1
FK Taraz	0
FK Atyrau	0
Zhetysu Taldykorgan *	3
Ordabasy Shymkent	4
Tobol Kostanay *	1
FK Aktobe	1
Shakhter Karagandy *	2

Semi–finals

Lokomotiv Astana	1 1
Zhetysu Taldykorgan *	0 0
Ordabasy Shymkent	1 1
Shakhter Karagandy *	0 2

Final

Lokomotiv Astana ‡	1
Shakhter Karagandy	0

CUP FINAL

Astana Arena, Astana
14-11-2010, Att: 20 000

Scorer - Mikhail Rozhkov 35

* Home team/Home team in first leg • ‡ Qualified for the Europa League

KEN – KENYA

FIFA/COCA-COLA WORLD RANKING

1993	1994	1995	1996	1997	1998	1999	2000	2001	2002	2003	2004	2005	2006	2007	2008	2009	2010
74	83	107	112	89	93	103	108	104	81	72	74	89	127	110	68	98	120

2010												Hi/Lo
Jan	Feb	Mar	Mar	Apr	May	Jul	Aug	Sep	Oct	Nov	Dec	68
98	112	113	114	114	113	115	116	114	115	116	120	137

The Kenya national team continued its poor run of form with a series of uninspiring results during the course of 2010, notably a 1-0 defeat at the hands of minnows Guinea-Bissau in the qualifiers for the 2012 African Nations Cup. With six coaches in the past three years a lack of stability hasn't helped with Twahir Muhiddin, Jacob Mulee and Zedekiah Otieno all taking the helm during the year. The Kenyans did give themselves some hope in the Nations Cup with a 0-0 draw at home to a Uganda team currently ruling the roost in East Africa but at the East and Central African Senior Challenge Cup in Tanzania at the end of the year, the Kenyans had a disastrous time, losing all three of their first round group matches - the first time that had happened since 1970. The one bright spot of the season was McDonald Mariga's transfer to Internazionale and in March 2010 he became the first Kenyan to play in the UEFA Champions League. Although missing out on the final he did play a minor role as Inter swept to an historic treble. He also came on as a substitute in Inter's victory over TP Mazembe in the Club World Cup final at the end of the year. At home Ulinzi Stars won the Kenyan championship for the first time since their move from Thika to Nakuru, denying traditional giants Gor Mahia in second place what would have been a first title since 1995.

FIFA WORLD CUP RECORD
1930-1970 DNE   1974-2010 DNQ

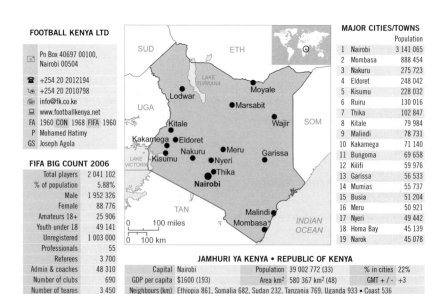

FOOTBALL KENYA LTD

Po Box 40697 00100, Nairobi 00504

☎ +254 20 2012194
📠 +254 20 2010798
📧 info@fk.co.ke
🖥 www.footballkenya.net
FA 1960 CON 1968 FIFA 1960
P Mohamed Hatimy
GS Joseph Agola

FIFA BIG COUNT 2006

Total players	2 041 102
% of population	5.88%
Male	1 952 326
Female	88 776
Amateurs 18+	25 906
Youth under 18	49 141
Unregistered	1 003 000
Professionals	55
Referees	3 700
Admin & coaches	48 310
Number of clubs	690
Number of teams	3 450

MAJOR CITIES/TOWNS

		Population
1	Nairobi	3 141 065
2	Mombasa	888 454
3	Nakuru	275 723
4	Eldoret	248 042
5	Kisumu	228 032
6	Ruiru	130 016
7	Thika	102 847
8	Kitale	79 984
9	Malindi	78 731
10	Kakamega	71 140
11	Bungoma	69 658
12	Kilifi	59 976
13	Garissa	56 533
14	Mumias	55 737
15	Busia	51 204
16	Meru	50 921
17	Nyeri	49 442
18	Homa Bay	45 139
19	Narok	45 078

JAMHURI YA KENYA • REPUBLIC OF KENYA

Capital	Nairobi	Population	39 002 772 (33)	% in cities	22%
GDP per capita	$1600 (193)	Area km²	580 367 km² (48)	GMT +/-	+3
Neighbours (km)	Ethiopia 861, Somalia 682, Sudan 232, Tanzania 769, Uganda 933 • Coast 536				

RECENT INTERNATIONAL MATCHES PLAYED BY KENYA

2008	Opponents	Score		Venue	Comp	Scorers	Att	Referee
31-12	Sudan	D	0-0	Jinja	CCr1			
2009								
2-01	Zambia	D	0-0	Jinja	CCr1			
6-01	Djibouti	W	5-1	Jinja	CCr1	Ouma 3 [4 29 93+], Shikokoti [57], George Owino [92+]		
8-01	Burundi	W	1-0	Kampala	CCr1	Monday [60p]		
11-01	Tanzania	W	2-1	Kampala	CCsf	Ouma [19], Baraza [21]		
13-01	Uganda	L	0-1	Kampala	CCf			
23-01	Egypt	L	0-1	Cairo	Fr			
14-03	Iran	L	0-1	Tehran	Fr			
28-03	Tunisia	L	1-2	Nairobi	WCq	Oliech [70]	27 000	Evehe CMR
7-06	Nigeria	L	0-3	Abuja	WCq		60 000	El Achiri MAR
20-06	Mozambique	W	2-1	Nairobi	WCq	Julius Owino [8], Mariaga [72p]	15 000	Keita GUI
12-08	Malaysia	D	0-0	Kuala Lumpur	Fr			
26-08	Bahrain	L	1-2	Manama	Fr	Pascal Ochieng [43]		
6-09	Mozambique	L	0-1	Maputo	WCq		35 000	Coulibaly MLI
11-10	Tunisia	L	0-1	Rades/Tunis	WCq		50 000	Diatta SEN
3-11	Kuwait	L	0-5	Cairo	Fr			
14-11	Nigeria	L	2-3	Nairobi	WCq	Oliech [15], Wetende [77]	20 000	Maillet SEY
28-11	Zambia	L	0-2	Nairobi	CCr1			
2-12	Djibouti	W	2-0	Nairobi	CCr1	Odhiambo [23], Wetende [44]		
5-12	Ethiopia	W	2-0	Nairobi	CCr1	Barasa [1], Wetende [46]		
7-12	Uganda	L	0-1	Nairobi	CCqf			
2010								
9-01	Cameroon	L	1-3	Nairobi	Fr	Situma [8]		
15-01	Yemen	L	1-3	Sana'a	Fr	Julius Owino [11p]		
11-08	Tanzania	D	1-1	Dar es Salaam	Fr	McDonald Mariga [13]		
18-08	Ethiopia	W	3-0	Addis Abeba	Fr	Allan Wanga 2 [13 55], Levy Muaka [70]		
4-09	Guinea-Bissau	L	0-1	Bissau	CNq			Bennaceur TUN
9-10	Uganda	D	0-0	Nairobi	CNq			Diatta SEN
23-11	Tanzania	L	0-1	Dar es Salaam	Fr			
29-11	Malawi	L	2-3	Dar es Salaam	CCr1	John Baraza [34], Fred Ajwang [45]		
2-12	Ethiopia	L	1-2	Dar es Salaam	CCr1	Fred Ajwang [85]		
5-12	Uganda	L	0-2	Dar es Salaam	CCr1			

Fr = Friendly match • CN = CAF African Cup of Nations • CC = CECAFA Cup • WC = FIFA World Cup
q = qualifier • r1 = first round group • sf = semi-final • 3p = third place play-off • f = final

KENYA 2010

UNIFIED LEAGUE	Pl	W	D	L	F	A	Pts	Ulinizi Stars	Gor Mahia	Tusker	Sofapaka	SonySugar	Mathare Utd	Karuturi	Western Stima	Chemelil S	Thika United	City Stars	AFC Leopards	Posta Rangers	KCB	Red Berets	Mahakama
Ulinizi Stars †	30	16	11	3	37	16	59		1-0	1-0	1-1	2-1	0-2	2-0	0-1	2-1	1-0	1-1	2-0	3-0	3-0	1-0	1-1
Gor Mahia	30	15	11	4	33	15	56	2-0		1-1	1-1	2-0	0-0	1-0	0-0	4-1	2-1	1-0	1-0	1-0	0-1	0-0	2-0
Tusker	30	14	11	5	35	19	53	0-0	0-2		0-1	1-2	0-0	1-0	2-0	0-0	1-0	0-0	0-0	1-1	1-0	3-1	1-0
Sofapaka	30	11	14	5	39	23	47	0-0	1-1	1-1		2-0	0-0	1-0	4-2	0-0	3-0	3-0	0-1	1-1	2-0	0-0	1-1
SonySugar	30	11	8	11	26	26	41	2-2	1-1	1-2	1-1		2-0	2-1	2-0	1-0	1-0	0-0	2-0	0-0	2-0	1-0	0-0
Mathare United	30	7	18	5	31	28	39	0-1	1-1	0-0	1-3	1-0		0-0	2-0	1-1	2-2	2-0	3-3	2-1	3-1	1-2	1-1
Karuturi Sports	30	9	11	10	22	24	38	0-0	0-0	2-1	0-2	0-0	0-0		0-1	1-0	1-1	2-0	3-0	1-1	0-3	0-0	2-1
Western Stima	30	9	11	10	28	31	38	1-2	0-1	0-3	3-0	3-0	1-1	1-1		0-1	2-2	0-0	1-1	1-0	2-2	0-0	3-2
Chemelil Sugar	30	7	13	10	22	26	34	0-1	3-0	0-1	0-0	0-1	1-1	0-0	0-0		**2-0**	3-1	0-0	0-0	0-0	2-1	0-0
Thika United	30	8	10	12	23	30	34	1-1	0-1	1-3	0-0	2-1	1-1	0-1	2-0	2-0		1-0	0-0	0-0	1-0	1-0	1-0
Nairobi City Stars	30	7	13	10	25	34	34	1-1	0-0	2-2	2-0	1-0	2-2	1-1	1-0	2-1	2-2		0-1	1-1	1-1	2-1	0-2
AFC Leopards	30	8	10	12	29	41	34	0-1	1-0	2-4	2-4	0-1	1-1	0-1	1-1	0-2	1-0	1-1		2-1	0-2	2-1	2-1
Posta Rangers	30	7	12	11	28	37	33	0-0	0-2	1-4	3-2	2-1	0-1	2-0	0-1	1-1	2-1	1-3	1-1		2-3	1-1	1-0
KCB	30	9	6	15	29	40	33	0-4	0-2	0-1	2-1	1-0	1-1	1-2	0-2	1-2	0-0	3-0	3-4	2-2		1-0	1-0
Red Berets	30	7	10	13	27	32	31	1-1	1-1	0-0	0-4	1-0	1-1	1-0	1-2	4-0	**2-0**	0-1	2-2	1-2	1-0		3-1
Mahakama	30	5	11	14	21	33	26	0-2	1-3	0-0	0-0	1-1	2-0	1-3	0-0	1-1	0-1	0-0	2-1	0-1	1-0	2-1	

20/02/2010 - 14/11/2010 • † Qualified for the CAF Champions League • Matches in bold awarded

KGZ – KYRGYZSTAN

FIFA/COCA-COLA WORLD RANKING

1993	1994	1995	1996	1997	1998	1999	2000	2001	2002	2003	2004	2005	2006	2007	2008	2009	2010
-	166	172	168	140	151	159	174	164	171	157	150	157	139	139	158	159	174

2010												Hi/Lo
Jan	Feb	Mar	Mar	Apr	May	Jul	Aug	Sep	Oct	Nov	Dec	**119**
159	158	161	151	161	168	165	163	159	173	176	174	**176**

Kyrgyzstan qualified for the finals of the AFC Challenge Cup for the second time but failed to match their performance from 2006 when they reached in the semi-finals. At the 2010 finals in Sri Lanka they were knocked out at the end of the group stage after picking up a solitary win which came in their opening game against India. It was disappointing for a country so used to success at club level in the AFC President's Cup, which in 2010 Dordoi-Dynamo maintained their record of having reached every final since the tournament was inaugurated in 2005. They won a first round group held in Bangladesh and then travelled to Myanmar for the final stages where they beat HTTU Ashgabat 2-0 in the semi-finals. In the final they met home side Yadanabon who were appearing in their first final and it was the team from Myanmar who claimed the trophy with a 1-0 victory after extra-time. That left Dordoi-Dynamo in the runners-up spot for the third year running, unable to add to the two titles won in 2006 and 2007. They also won't be at the 2011 tournament after failing to win the Kyrgyz title. In a season disrupted by political unrest, Neftchi Kochkorata won the title for the first time, ending a run of six successive championships for Dordoi-Dynamo, and they will represent Kyrgyzstan at the 2011 competition.

FIFA WORLD CUP RECORD
1930-1994 DNE 1998-2010 DNQ

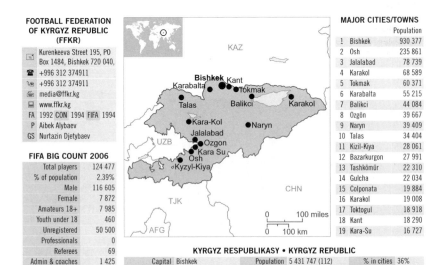

FOOTBALL FEDERATION OF KYRGYZ REPUBLIC (FFKR)

Kurenkeeva Street 195, PO Box 1484, Bishkek 720 040,
☎ +996 312 374911
📠 +996 312 374911
✉ media@ffkr.kg
🖥 www.ffkr.kg
FA 1992 CON 1994 FIFA 1994
P Aibek Alybaev
GS Nurtazin Djetybaev

FIFA BIG COUNT 2006

Total players	124 477
% of population	2.39%
Male	116 605
Female	7 872
Amateurs 18+	7 985
Youth under 18	460
Unregistered	50 500
Professionals	0
Referees	69
Admin & coaches	1 425
Number of clubs	100
Number of teams	500

MAJOR CITIES/TOWNS

		Population
1	Bishkek	930 377
2	Osh	235 861
3	Jalalabad	78 739
4	Karakol	68 589
5	Tokmak	60 371
6	Karabalta	55 215
7	Balikci	44 084
8	Ozgön	39 667
9	Naryn	39 409
10	Talas	34 404
11	Kizil-Kiya	28 061
12	Bazarkurgon	27 991
13	Tashkömür	22 310
14	Gulcha	22 034
15	Colponata	19 884
16	Karakol	19 008
17	Toktogul	18 918
18	Kant	18 290
19	Kara-Su	16 727

KYRGYZ RESPUBLIKASY • KYRGYZ REPUBLIC

Capital	Bishkek	Population	5 431 747 (112)	% in cities	36%
GDP per capita	$2200 (184)	Area km²	199 951 km² (86)	GMT + / -	+6
Neighbours (km)	China 858, Kazakhstan 1224, Tajikistan 870, Uzbekistan 1099				

RECENT INTERNATIONAL MATCHES PLAYED BY KYRGYZSTAN

2005	Opponents	Score		Venue	Comp	Scorers	Att	Referee
No international matches played in 2005								
2006								
2-04	Pakistan	L	0-1	Dhaka	CCr1		2 500	Shamsuzzaman BAN
6-04	Tajikistan	W	1-0	Dhaka	CCr1	Krasnov [22]	2 000	AK Nema IRQ
7-04	Macao	W	2-0	Dhaka	CCr1	Ablakimov [35], Ishenbaev.A [58]	1 000	Tan Hai CHN
9-04	Palestine	W	1-0	Dhaka	CCqf	Djamshidov [91]	150	U Win Cho MYA
13-04	Tajikistan	L	0-2	Dhaka	CCsf		2 000	Tan Hai CHN
5-07	Kazakhstan	L	0-1	Almaty	Fr			
2007								
7-03	Kazakhstan	L	0-2	Shymkent	Fr			Irmatov UZB
9-03	Uzbekistan	L	0-6	Shymkent	Fr			Kister KAZ
11-03	Azerbaijan	L	0-1	Shymkent	Fr			Aliyev AZE
19-08	Cambodia	W	4-3	New Delhi	Fr	Samsaliev [12], Mamatov [17], Djamshidov [48], Harchenko [65]		Suresh IND
21-08	Syria	L	1-4	New Delhi	Fr	OG [13]		Suresh IND
24-08	Bangladesh	W	3-0	New Delhi	Fr	Lutfullaev 2 [28 54], Djamshidov [57]		Suresh IND
26-08	India	L	0-3	New Delhi	Fr			Surendra NEP
18-10	Jordan	W	2-0	Bishkek	WCq	Esenkul Uulu [45], Bokoev [76]	18 000	Sarkar IND
28-10	Jordan	L	0-2	Amman	WCq	L 5-6p	12 000	Ebrahim BHR
2008								
27-04	Oman	L	0-2	Muscat	Fr			
7-05	Afghanistan	L	0-1	Bishkek	CCq		7 000	Shaharul MAS
9-05	Bangladesh	W	2-1	Bishkek	CCq	Kornilov [83], Sydykov [87]	5 000	Al Enezi KUW
2009								
28-03	Nepal	D	1-1	Kathmandu	CCq	Murzaev [86p]	15 000	Jahanbazi IRN
30-03	Palestine	D	1-1	Kathmandu	CCq	Murzaev [20p]	2 000	Yu Ming Hsun
25-07	China PR	L	0-3	Tianjin	Fr			
20-08	Syria	L	0-2	New Dehli	Fr			Singh IND
23-08	India	L	1-2	New Dehli	Fr	Murzaev [90]		
25-08	Lebanon	D	1-1	New Dehli	Fr	Zemlianuhin [48]		Hannan BAN
28-08	Sri Lanka	W	4-1	New Dehli	Fr	Zemlianuhin [34], Amirov [45], Murzaev [65], Usanov [70]		Singh IND
2010								
17-02	India	W	2-1	Colombo	CCr1	Amirov [15], Zemlianuhin [32]	800	Shukralla BHR
19-02	Korea DPR	L	0-4	Colombo	CCr1		300	El Haddad LIB
21-02	Turkmenistan	L	0-1	Colombo	CCr1		100	El Haddad LIB

Fr = Friendly match • CC = AFC Challenge Cup • WC = FIFA World Cup
q = qualifier • r1 = first round group • qf = quarter-final • sf = semi-final

KYRGYZSTAN 2010

PREMIER LEAGUE

	Pl	W	D	L	F	A	Pts	Neftchi	Dordoi-Dynamo	Abdish-Ata	Alga	Sher-Ak	Khimik
Neftchi Kochkorata †	20	12	7	1	36	14	**43**		2-2 1-0	1-1 2-0	2-0 2-1	1-0 4-0	3-0 3-2
Dordoi-Dynamo	20	13	3	4	49	18	42	1-1 1-2		1-0 2-1	0-2 3-1	9-0 1-0	2-0 1-0
Abdish-Ata Kant	20	11	6	3	63	21	**39**	0-0 3-0	4-3 2-2		1-1 3-0	4-1 4-2	9-0 0-0
Alga Bishkek	20	6	4	10	26	33	**22**	0-1 1-1	0-1 1-4	2-2 0-5		3-3 1-0	3-0 4-2
Sher-Ak Dan Bishkek	20	4	3	13	19	58	15	1-1 0-5	0-6 0-3	3-6 1-6	1-3 1-0		0-0 2-1
Khimik Karabalta	20	1	3	16	8	57	**6**	0-3 1-1	0-5 1-2	0-3 0-9	1-0 0-3	0-2 0-2	

27/03/2010 - 15/09/2010 • † Qualified for the AFC President's Cup • Zhastyk Kara-Su, Lokomotiv Jalalabad and Alay Osh withdrew due to the political unrest during 2010

KYRGYZSTAN CUP 2009

Quarter-finals			Semi-finals			Final	
Abdish-Ata Kant	10	5					
Plaza Bishkek	0	0	**Abdish-Ata Kant**	6	1		
			Zhashtyk Kara-Su	2	2		
Zhashtyk Kara-Su						**Abdish-Ata Kant**	2
Kambar Ata Jalalabad	1	0				Alay Osh	0
Jivoe Pivo Kant	0	0	Kambar Ata Jalalabad	0	1		
			Alay Osh	2	3	4-10-2009	
Alay Osh							

KYRGYZSTAN CUP 2010

Quarter-finals			Semi-finals			Final	
Dordoi-Dynamo	0	0					
Sher-Ak Dan Bishkek	2	3	**Dordoi-Dynamo**	1	1		
Alga Bishkek	0	2	Abdish-Ata Kant	0	0		
Abdish-Ata Kant	2	1				**Dordoi-Dynamo**	3
Neftchi Kochkorata-2						Neftchi Kochkorata	0
			Neftchi Kochkorata-2	1	1	Spartak, Bishkek, 31-08-2010	
			Neftchi Kochkorata	10	9	Scorers - Yuri Volos [27], Ildar	
Neftchi Kochkorata						Amirov [31], Mirlan Murzaev [90]	

MEDALS TABLE

		Overall			League			Cup			Asia			City
		G	S	B	G	S	B	G	S	G	S	B		
1	Alga Bishkek	14	7		5	6		9	1				Bishkek
2	Dordoi-Dynamo	13	5	3	6	1	3	5		2	4		Naryn
3	Dinamo Bishkek	3	2		3	1			1				Bishkek
4	Abdish-Ata Kant	2	4	1		4	1	2					Kant
5	Kant-Oil	2			2								Kant
6	Zhashtyk Kara-Su	1	9	5	1	2	5		7				Kara-Su
7	AiK Bishkek	1	2	2		2	2	1					Bishkek
8	Semetey Kyzyl-Kiya	1	2	1		1	1	1	1				Kyzyl-Kiya
9	Neftchi Kochkorata	1	1		1				1				Kochkorata
	Metallurg Kadamjay	1	1		1				1				Kadamjay
11	Ak-Maral Tokmak	1		1		1		1					Tokmak
12	Alay Osh		6	5		5		6					Osh
13	Lokomotiv Jalalabad		1						1				Jalalabad
	SKA Sokuluk		1			1							Sokuluk
	Spartak Tokmak		1			1							Tokmak
16	Polyot Bishkek			2		2							Bishkek

KOR – KOREA REPUBLIC

FIFA/COCA-COLA WORLD RANKING

1993	1994	1995	1996	1997	1998	1999	2000	2001	2002	2003	2004	2005	2006	2007	2008	2009	2010
41	35	46	44	27	17	51	40	42	20	22	22	29	51	42	42	52	40

	2010												Hi/Lo
	Jan	Feb	Mar	Mar	Apr	May	Jul	Aug	Sep	Oct	Nov	Dec	**17**
	52	49	53	49	47	47	44	44	44	40	39	40	**62**

South Korea's status as the leading nation in Asian football is long-held but the country's Asian Cup-winning drought continues after yet another failure to win the continental title at the 2011 AFC Asian Cup in Qatar. Korea last won the tournament 50 years ago and Cho Kwang Rae's team travelled to Qatar determined to end one of the most astonishing records within the Asian game. A young squad bolstered by the likes of Manchester United midfielder Park Ji Sung and former Tottenham and Eintracht defender Lee Young Pyo fell at the semi-final stage, losing in a thrilling clash with Japan that was arguably the game of the tournament. At the 2010 FIFA World Cup finals in South Africa, former coach Huh Jung Moo had taken South Korea to the second round for the first time on foreign soil. Victory over Greece set the Koreans on their way to earning a place in the last 16 but their run was ended when they were beaten 2-1 by Uruguay. Korean clubs continue to dominate the Asian Champions League with Seongnam Ilhwa Chunma defeating Iran's Zob Ahan in the 2010 final in Tokyo - South Korea's ninth title overall. FC Seoul claimed the domestic title, beating of runners-up Jeju United 4-3 on aggregate in the final, as well as the League Cup while Suwon won the FA Cup, beating Busan 1-0 in the final..

FIFA WORLD CUP RECORD
1930-1950 DNE **1954** 15 r1 **1958** DNE **1962** DNQ **1966** DNE **1970-1982** DNQ
1986 20 r1 **1990** 22 r1 **1994** 20 r1 **1998** 30 r1 **2002** 4 SF (co-hosts) **2006** 17 r1 **2010** 15 r2

KOREA FOOTBALL ASSOCIATION (KFA)

1-131 Sinmunno, 2-ga,
Jongno-Gu, Seoul 110-062

☎ +82 2 7377538
📠 +82 2 7352755
✉ kfainfo@kfa.or.kr
🖥 www.kfa.or.kr
FA 1928 CON 1954 FIFA 1948
P Cho Chung Yun
GS Kim Jin Kook

FIFA BIG COUNT 2006

Total players	1 094 227
% of population	2.24%
Male	1 021 677
Female	72 550
Amateurs 18+	12 372
Youth under 18	18 205
Unregistered	423 100
Professionals	550
Referees	948
Admin & coaches	3 700
Number of clubs	96
Number of teams	864

MAJOR CITIES/TOWNS

		Population
1	Seoul	9 660 532
2	Busan	3 351 991
3	Incheon	2 533 513
4	Daegu	2 413 599
5	Goyang	1 518 319
6	Daejeon	1 437 093
7	Suwon	1 374 548
8	Gwangju	1 360 225
9	Seongnam	1 023 219
10	Ulsan	957 963
12	Bucheon	810 980
13	Jeonju	720 987
15	Anyang	623 289
16	Jeongju	619 781
18	Changwon	518 370
19	Kimhae	417 161
35	Gimpo	220 543
48	Gwangyang	138 012
63	Seogwipo	92 056

TAEHAN-MIN'GUK • REPUBLIC OF KOREA

Capital Seoul	Population 48 508 972 (25)	% in cities 81%
GDP per capita $27 700 (50)	Area km² 99 720 km² (108)	GMT +/- +9
Neighbours (km) Korea DPR 238 • Coast 2413		

RECENT INTERNATIONAL MATCHES PLAYED BY KOREA REPUBLIC

2009	Opponents	Score		Venue	Comp	Scorers	Att	Referee
12-08	Paraguay	W	1-0	Seoul	Fr	Park Chu Young [83]	22 631	Toma JPN
5-09	Australia	W	3-1	Seoul	Fr	Park Chu Young [4], Lee Jung Soo [20], Seol Ki Hyeon [86]	40 215	Mohd Salleh MAS
14-10	Senegal	W	2-0	Seoul	Fr	Ki Sung Yueng [42], Oh Beom Seok [80]	31 574	Tan Hai CHN
14-11	Denmark	D	0-0	Esbjerg	Fr		15 789	Hansson SWE
18-11	Serbia	L	0-1	London	Fr		5 117	Attwell ENG
2010								
9-01	Zambia	L	2-4	Johannesburg	Fr	Kim Jung Woo [35], Koo Ja Cheol [83]	2 000	Gornes RSA
18-01	Finland	W	2-0	Malaga	Fr	Oh Beom Seok [39], Lee Jung Soo [61]	270	Fernandez ESP
22-01	Latvia	W	1-0	Malaga	Fr	Kim Jae Sung [55]	150	Velasco ESP
7-02	Hong Kong	W	5-0	Tokyo	EAC	Kim Jung Woo [10], Koo Ja Cheol [24], Lee Dong Gook [32], Lee Seung Yeoul [37], No Byung Jun [93+]	2 728	Sato JPN
10-02	China PR	L	0-3	Tokyo	EAC		3 629	Ng Kai Lam HKG
14-02	Japan	W	3-1	Tokyo	EAC	Lee Dong Gook [33p], Lee Seung Yeoul [39], Kim Jae Sung [70]	42 951	Delovski AUS
3-03	Côte d'Ivoire	W	2-0	London	Fr	Lee Dong Gook [4], Kwak Tae Hwi [90]	6 000	Mariner ENG
16-05	Ecuador	W	2-0	Seoul	Fr	Lee Seung Ryul [71], Lee Chung Yong [83]	62 209	Wongkamdee THA
24-05	Japan	W	2-0	Saitama	Fr	Park Ji Sung [6], Park Chu Young [90]	57 873	Attwell ENG
30-05	Belarus	L	0-1	Kufstein	Fr		1 000	Brugger AUT
3-06	Spain	L	0-1	Innsbruck	Fr		17 400	Schorgenhofer AUT
12-06	Greece	W	2-0	Port Elizabeth	WCr1	Lee Jung Soo [7], Park Ji Sung [52]	31 513	Hester NZL
17-06	Argentina	L	1-4	Johannesburg	WCr1	Lee Chung Yong [45]	82 174	De Bleeckere BEL
22-06	Nigeria	D	2-2	Durban	WCr1	Lee Jung Soo [38], Park Chu Young [49]	61 874	Benquerenca POR
26-06	Uruguay	L	1-2	Port Elizabeth	WCr2	Lee Chung Yong [68]	30 597	Stark GER
11-08	Nigeria	W	2-1	Suwon	Fr	Yoon Bit Garam [17], Choi Hyo Jin [44]	40 331	Nishimura JPN
7-09	Iran	L	0-1	Seoul	Fr		38 642	Mohd Salleh MAS
12-10	Japan	D	0-0	Seoul	Fr		62 503	Irmatov UZB
30-12	Syria	W	1-0	Abu Dhabi	Fr	Ji Dong Won [83]	500	Al Marzouqi UAE
2011								
10-01	Bahrain	W	2-1	Doha	ACr1	Koo Ja Cheol 2 [40 52]	6 669	Al Hilali OMA
14-01	Australia	D	1-1	Doha	ACr1	Koo Ja Cheol [24]	15 526	Abdou QAT
18-01	India	W	4-1	Doha	Acr1	Ji Dong Won 2 [6 23], Koo Ja Cheol [9], Son Heung Min [81]	11 366	Al Ghamdi KSA
22-01	Iran	W	1-0	Doha	ACqf	Yoon Bit Garam [105]	7 111	Irmatov UZB
25-01	Japan	D	2-2	Doha	ACsf	Li Sung Yueng [23p], Hwang Jae Won [120]. L 0-3p	16 171	Al Ghamdi
28-01	Uzbekistan	W	3-2	Doha	AC3p	Koo Ja Cheol [18], Ji Dong Won 2 [28 39]	8 199	Abdul Bashir SIN

Fr = Friendly match • AC = AFC Asian Cup • EAC = East Asian Championship • WC = FIFA World Cup
q = qualifier • r1 = first round group • qf = quarter-final • sf = semi-final • 3p = third place play-off

KOREA REPUBLIC NATIONAL TEAM HISTORICAL RECORDS

Caps
136 - Hong Myung Bo 1990-2002 • **133** - Lee Woon Jae 1994- • **123** - Yoo Sang Chul 1994-2005 • **121** - Cha Bum Kun 1972-86 • **120** - Lee Young Pyo 1999- • **104** - Kim Tae Young 1992-2004 • **103** - Hwang Seon Hong 1993-2002 • **97** - Kim Nam Il 1998- • **96** - Park Ji Sung 2000- • **95** - Choi Soon Hoo 1980-91 & Ha Seok Joo 1991-2001 • **92** - Choi Young Jeung 1975-86 & Park Sung Hwa 1974-84 • **89** - Choi Jong Duk 1975-86 & Seo Jung Won 1990-2001 • **88** - Park Kyung Hoon 1981-90 • **84** - Huh Jung Moo 1974-86 • **83** - Seol Ki Hyeon 2000-09 • **81** - Lee Dong Gook 1998- • **80** - Cho Gwang Rae 1975-86 • **79** - Lee Chun Soo 2000- • **77** - Kim Joo Sung 1985-96 • **76** - Ko Jung Woon 1989-95

Goals
55 - Cha Bum Kun 1972-86 • **50** - Hwang Seon Hong 1993-2002 • **30** - Choi Soon Hoo 1980-91 • **29** - Huh Jung Moo 1974-86 & Kim Do Hoon 1994-2003 • **27** - Choi Yong Soo 1995-2003 & Lee Tae Hoo 1980-91 • **25** - Lee Dong Gook 1998- • **24** - Lee Young Soo 1974-82 & Park Sung Hwa 1974-84 • **23** - Ha Seok Joo 1991-2001 • **22** - Chung Hae Won 1980-90

Past Coaches
Park Jung-Hwi 1948 • Lee Young-Min 1948 • Park Jung-Hwi 1948-50 • Kim Hwa-Jip 1952-54 • Lee Yoo-Hyung 1954 • Kim Yong-Sik 1954 • Park Jung-Hwi 1955 • Lee Yoo-Hyung 1956 • Kim Keun-Chan 1958 • Jeong Kook-Jin 1959 • Kim Yong-Sik 1960 • Wi Hye-Deok 1960 • Lee Yoo-Hyung 1961 • Lee Jong-Gap 1961 • Min Byung-Dae 1962 • Jeong Kook-Jin 1964 • Hong Keon-Pyo 1965 • Min Byung-Dae 1966 • Jang Kyung-Hwan 1967 • Park Il-Gap 1968 • Kim Yong-Sik 1969 • Kang Jun-Young 1969 • Han Hong-Ki 1970-71 • Hong Deok-Young 1971 • Park Byung-Seok 1971-72 • Ham Heung-Cheol 1972 • Min Byung-Dae 1972-73 • Choi Young-Keun 1974 • Ham Heung-Cheol 1974-76 • Mun Jeong-Sik 1976 • Choi Jung-Min 1977 • Kim Jung-Nam 1977 • Ham Heung-Cheol 1978-79 • Jang Kyung-Hwan 1979-80 • Kim Jung-Nam 1980-82 • Choi Eun-Taek 1982 • Kim Jung-Nam 1982-83 • Cho Yoon-Ohk 1983 • Park Jong-Hwan 1983-84 • Mun Jeong-Sik 1984-85 • Kim Jung-Nam 1985-86 • Park Jong-Hwan 1986-88 • Kim Jung-Nam 1988 • Lee Hoi-Taek 1988-90 • Lee Cha-Man 1990 • Park Jong-Hwan 1990-91 • Ko Jae-Wook 1991 • Kim Ho 1992-94 • Anatoliy Byshovets RUS 1994-95 • Park Jong-Hwan 1995 • Huh Jung-Moo 1995 • Jeong Byeong-Tak 1995 • Ko Jae-Wook 1995 • Park Jong-Hwan 1996-97 • Cha Bum-Kun 1997-98 • Kim Pyung-Seok 1998 • Huh Jung-Moo 1998-2000 • Guus Hiddink NED 2001-02 • Kim Ho-Gon 2002 • Humberto Coelho POR 2003-04 • Park Seong-Hwa 2004 • Jo Bonfrere NED 2004-05 • Dick Advocaat NED 2005-06 • Pim Verbeek NED 2006-07 • Huh Jung-Moo 2007-10 • Cho Kwang-Rae 2010-

KOREA REPUBLIC 2010

K-LEAGUE OVERALL

	Pl	W	D	L	F	A	Pts	Seoul	Jeju	Jeonbuk	Ulsan	Seongnam	Gyeongnam	Suwon	Busan	Pohang	Chunnam	Incheon	Gangwon	Daejeon	Gwangju	Daegu
FC Seoul †	28	20	2	6	58	26	62		2-0	0-1	3-0	4-0	3-2	3-1	3-1	1-0	1-0	2-0	2-1	2-1	3-0	4-0
Jeju United ‡	28	17	8	3	54	25	59	1-1		2-2	2-1	1-1	3-2	2-1	1-0	1-1	2-1	0-0	5-0	2-0	4-0	1-0
Jeonbuk Hyundai Motors ‡‡	28	15	6	7	54	36	51	1-0	1-1		1-2	1-1	1-1	3-1	2-1	1-2	3-1	3-2	1-3	3-2	0-0	4-0
Ulsan Hyundai ‡‡	28	15	5	8	47	30	50	1-2	1-0	0-1		0-1	1-0	2-3	0-2	1-1	3-0	3-0	1-0	2-0	2-2	5-0
Seongnam Ilhwa Chunma ‡‡	28	13	9	6	46	26	48	1-2	0-1	1-0	2-0		1-2	0-0	1-1	3-0	4-0	6-0	3-0	0-0	2-2	1-3
Gyeongnam FC ‡‡	28	13	9	6	41	32	48	1-0	1-1	3-2	0-1	2-2		2-1	0-1	3-1	1-1	3-2	1-1	1-0	1-0	1-0
Suwon Samsung Bluewings	28	12	5	11	39	44	41	4-2	0-3	1-5	0-2	1-2	0-2		4-3	2-0	1-0	2-1	1-2	0-0	2-0	2-1
Busan I'Park	28	8	9	11	36	37	33	3-0	0-1	1-0	0-2	0-0	1-2	0-1		4-2	5-3	2-1	1-1	1-1	2-0	0-2
Pohang Steelers	28	8	9	11	39	48	33	1-4	2-5	3-3	1-1	2-0	3-0	1-1	2-2		1-1	3-2	4-0	0-1	1-0	2-1
Chunnam Dragons	28	8	8	12	40	49	32	1-1	4-2	3-2	3-3	0-3	1-1	2-0	2-2	2-2		0-0	2-1	3-0	2-3	2-1
Incheon United	28	8	7	13	42	51	31	1-0	2-3	3-2	1-2	1-4	2-2	2-3	1-1	4-0	1-0		1-3	3-3	2-0	1-1
Gangwon FC	28	8	6	14	36	50	30	0-3	1-4	2-3	2-2	1-2	1-2	1-2	0-0	2-0	5-2	1-2		2-2	1-0	1-0
Daejeon Citizen	28	5	7	16	27	50	22	2-5	1-3	0-4	1-5	0-1	0-3	1-1	2-0	0-1	1-0	0-2	1-2		3-0	1-2
Gwangju Sangmu	28	3	10	15	17	43	19	0-2	0-0	0-1	1-2	2-2	1-1	1-3	2-1	0-2	0-3	1-4	1-1	1-0		0-3
Daegu FC	28	4	7	17	28	57	19	2-3	0-3	0-1	1-2	2-2	1-1	1-3	2-1	0-2	0-3	1-4	2-2	1-3	1-2	

27/02/2010 - 7/11/2010 • † Qualified for the play-off final • ‡ Qualified for the play-off semi-final • ‡‡ Qualified for the play-off first round
Top scorers: 22 - Yoo Byung Soo, Incheon • 17 - Jose Ortigoza PAR, Ulsan • 16 - Eninho BRA, Jeonbuk • 13 - Kim Young Goo, Gangwon; Lucio BRA, Gyeongnam; Kim Eun Jung, Jeju & Dejan Damjanovic MNE, Seoul • 12 - Lee Dong Gook, Jeonbuk; Jung Jo Gook, Seoul & Dzenan Radoncic, MNE S'nam
First round: Jeonbuk 2-0 Gyeongnam; Ulsan 1-3 Seongnam • Second round: Jeonbuk 1-0 Seongnam • Semi-final: Jeju 1-0 Jeonbuk

K-LEAGUE FINAL 2010 1ST LEG

Jeju World Cup Stadium, Seogwipo, 1-12-2010, 18 528, Lee Sang Yong

Jeju United	2	Bae Ki Jong 26, Santos 51
FC Seoul	2	Damjanovic 13, Kim Chi Woo 92+

Jeju - Kim Ho Jun - Lee Sang Ho, Hong Jeong Ho, Kang Min Hyuk, Ma Chul Jun - Park Hyun Beom, Koo Ja Cheol - Bae Ki Jong• (Kim Young Sin 70), Santos (Lee Hyun Ho 78), Danilo Neco (Oh Seung Bum 85) - Kim Eun Jung. Tr: Park Kyung Hoon
Seoul - Kim Yong Dae - Choi Hyo Jin•, Kim Jin Kyu, Kim Dong Woo (Jung Jo Gook 55), Hyun Young Min - Choi Tae Uk, Adilson (Park Yong Ho 71), Ha Dae Sung, Lee Seung Yeoul• (Kim Chi Woo 55) - Server Djeparov, Dejan Damjanovic. Tr: Nelo Vingada

K-LEAGUE FINAL 2010 2ND LEG

World Cup Stadium, Seoul, 5-12-2010, 56 759, Choi Kwang Bo

FC Seoul	2	Jung Jo Gook 27p, Adilson 72
Jeju United	1	Santos 25

Seoul - Kim Yong Dae - Choi Hyo Jin, Kim Jin Kyu, Adilson, Hyun Young Min - Choi Tae Uk (Park Yong Ho 81), Ha Dae Sung, Server Djeparov, Kim Chi Woo• (Lee Seung Yeoul 70) - Jung Jo Gook• (Choi Hyun Tae• 56), Dejan Damjanovic. Tr: Nelo Vingada
Jeju - Kim Ho Jun - Lee Sang Ho, Hong Jeong Ho (Kang Min Hyuk 86), Kang Joon Woo•, Ma Chul Jun• - Park Hyun Beom•, Oh Seung Bum (Koo Ja Cheol• 74) - Bae Ki Jong (Danilo Neco 58), Santos, Kim Young Sin - Kim Eun Jung. Tr: Park Kyung Hoon

FC Seoul win the 2010 K-League and qualify for the AFC Champions League along with Jeju United, Jeonbuk Hyundai Motors and KFA Cup winners Suwon Samsung Bluewings

KOREA REPUBLIC 2010 KOREA NATIONAL LEAGUE (2) OVERALL STANDINGS

	Pl	W	D	L	F	A	Pts
Gangneung City †	28	15	6	7	47	33	51
Goyang KB ‡	28	14	7	7	39	27	49
Suwon City ‡	28	13	10	5	32	22	49
Busan Kyotong	28	13	8	7	45	31	47
Cheonan City	28	14	5	9	44	30	47
Yongin City	28	12	9	7	41	29	45
Ulsan Mipo Dolphins	28	12	8	8	40	24	44
Chungju Hummel	28	13	2	13	48	53	41
Changwon City	28	11	7	10	37	29	40
Daejeon HNP †	28	11	6	11	45	43	39
Incheon Korail	28	9	10	9	40	38	37
Gimhae City	28	10	6	12	25	31	36
Ansan Hallelujah	28	9	1	18	35	48	28
Mokpo City	28	4	8	16	21	38	20
Yesan FC	28	3	1	24	35	97	10

26/03/2010 - 19/11/2010 • † Qualified for play-offs as stage winner • ‡ Qualified for play-offs on overall record
Play-off semi-finals: Gangneung 1-3 Suwon; Daejeon 2-1 Goyang
Play-off final: Daejeon HNP 0-2 1-0 Suwon City

MEDALS TABLE

		Overall			League			Cup			LC			Asia		
		G	S	B	G	S	B	G	S	B	G	S	B	G	S	B
1	Suwon S. Bluewings	15	5	3	4	2	3	3	2		6			2	1	
2	Seongnam I. Chunma	13	11	1	7	3		1	3		3	3		2	2	1
3	Pohang Steelers	11	9	4	4	4	3	2	3		2	2	1	3		
4	Busan I'Park	9	8	7	4	3	2	1	1		3	4	4	1	1	
5	FC Seoul	7	10	1	4	5		1			2	4	1	1		
6	Ulsan Hyundai	6	9	7	2	5	4		1		4	3	1			2
7	Jeonbuk Hyundai	5	1	2	1			3	1		1	1		1	1	1
8	Jeju United	4	7	4	1	4	4		1		3	2				
9	Chunnam Dragons	3	6	1		1	1	3	1		3			1		
10	Daejeon Citizen	1	1						1			1				
11	Gimpo Halleluyah	1			1											
12	Gyeongnam FC		1	1							1			1		
13	Incheon United		1				1									
	Ulsan Mipo Dolphins		1									1				

HANA BANK KOREAN FA CUP 2010

First Round

Team	Score
Suwon Samsung Bluewings*	2
Dongguk University	0
Daegu FC	0
Suwon City*	1
Gangneung City	2
Cheonan City*	1
Jeonju University	0
Jeonbuk Hyundai Motors*	5
Seongnam Ilhwa Chunma*	1
Yongin City	0
Kyunghee University	1
Daejeon Citizen*	3
Ulsan Hyundai*	5
Goyang Kookmin Bank	2
Busan Kyotong*	1
Jeju United	3
Chunnam Dragons*	6
Gimhae City	2
Changwon City*	2
Gyeongnam FC	3
Pohang Steelers*	5
Chungju Hummel	1
Ulsan Mipo Dolphins	0
Gwangju Sangmu*	3
Incheon United	2
Ansan Hallelujah*	1
Gangwon FC	0
Daejeon HNP*	1
FC Seoul*	1 4p
Mokpo City	1 3p
Incheon Korail	1
Busan I'Park*	2

Second Round

Team	Score
Suwon Samsung Bluewings*	4
Suwon City	1
Gangneung City	1
Jeonbuk Hyundai Motors*	2
Seongnam Ilhwa Chunma	3
Daejeon Citizen*	0
Ulsan Hyundai	0
Jeju United*	1
Chunnam Dragons	7
Gyeongnam FC*	4
Pohang Steelers*	1
Gwangju Sangmu*	2
Incheon United*	2
Daejeon HNP	0
FC Seoul	1
Busan I'Park*	2

Quarter-finals

Team	Score
Suwon Samsung Bluewings*	2
Jeonbuk Hyundai Motors	0
Seongnam Ilhwa Chunma*	0
Jeju United	2
Chunnam Dragons*	2
Gwangju Sangmu	1
Incheon United	1
Busan I'Park*	2

Semi-finals

Team	Score
Suwon Samsung Bluewings*	0 4p
Jeju United	0 2p
Chunnam Dragons	2
Busan I'Park*	3

Final

Team	Score
Suwon Samsung Bluewings	1
Busan I'Park*	0

CUP FINAL

Asiad Stadium, Busan
24-10-2010, 16:00
Scorer - Yeom Ki Hun 26

* Home team • † Qualified for the AFC Champions League

POSCO K-LEAGUE CUP 2010

First Round Groups

Group A	Pl	W	D	L	F	A	Pts	JHM	Gy	SSB	CD	Ga
Jeonbuk Hyundai Motors	4	3	1	0	10	4	10		3-1	3-2	1-1	3-0
Gyeongnam FC	4	3	0	1	8	4	9			4-1	1-0	2-0
Suwon Samsung Bluewings	4	2	0	2	7	9	6				2-1	2-1
Chunnam Dragons	4	1	1	2	6	5	4					4-1
Gangwon FC	4	0	0	4	2	11	0					

Group B	Pl	W	D	L	F	A	Pts	Se	JU	UH	SIC	GS
FC Seoul	4	2	2	0	8	2	8		1-1	3-0	1-1	3-0
Jeju United	4	2	1	1	7	7	7			1-4	3-1	2-1
Ulsan Hyundai	4	1	2	1	7	7	5				3-3	0-0
Seongnam Ilhwa Chunma	4	0	3	1	5	7	3					0-0
Gwangju Sangmu	4	0	2	2	1	5	2					

Group C	Pl	W	D	L	F	A	Pts	BIP	Da	PS	IU	DC
Busan I'Park	4	3	0	1	9	5	9		2-3	3-2	1-0	3-2
Daegu FC	4	2	0	2	9	6	6			1-2	3-2	1-1
Pohang Steelers	4	1	2	1	5	5	5				1-1	
Incheon United	4	1	1	2	6	7	4					1-4
Daejeon Citizen	4	1	1	2	7	10	4					

Quarter-finals

FC Seoul *	2	5p
Daegu FC	2	3p

Busan I'Park *	3	5p
Suwon Samsung Bluewings	3	6p

Gyeongnam FC *	1	4p
Jeju United	1	3p

Ulsan Hyundai	0	
Jeonbuk Hyundai Motors *	2	

Semi-finals

FC Seoul *	4
Suwon Samsung Bluewings	2

Gyeongnam FC	1
Jeonbuk Hyundai Motors *	2

Final

FC Seoul	3
Jeonbuk Hyundai Motors *	0

CUP FINAL

World Cup Stadium, Jeonju
25-08-2010, 19:00, Att: 15 891
Scorers - Dejan Damjanovic [47], Jung Jo Gook [55], Lee Seng Ryul [91+]

Top scorer: **6** - Dejan Damjanovic, Seoul • Home team

KSA – SAUDI ARABIA

FIFA/COCA-COLA WORLD RANKING

1993	1994	1995	1996	1997	1998	1999	2000	2001	2002	2003	2004	2005	2006	2007	2008	2009	2010
38	27	54	37	33	30	39	36	31	38	26	28	33	64	61	48	63	81

2010												Hi/Lo
Jan	Feb	Mar	Mar	Apr	May	Jul	Aug	Sep	Oct	Nov	Dec	21
63	59	57	62	66	66	68	70	73	71	68	81	81

For a team that had played in the final of six of the seven AFC Asian Cups held between 1984 and 2007, Saudi Arabia's inglorious performance at the 2011 finals in Qatar was seen as a national disgrace and coming on the back of their failure to qualify for the World Cup in South Africa, the country's status as the leading nation in Middle-East football has all but evaporated. The opening loss against Syria was seen as a shock and Portuguese coach Jose Peseiro paid with his job with Nasser Al Johar stepping in as his replacement. But defeat at the hands of Jordan and then a 5-0 thrashing by Japan saw Saudi Arabia's participation end in ignominy, resulting in King Abdullah firing Prince Sultan bin Fahd, the president of the football federation. There has been little joy, either, on the continental club scene with teams from Saudi unable to match the achievements of South Korean clubs who have won five Asian Champions League titles in the past decade compared to two from Saudi Arabia. In the 2010 tournament Al Shabab lost in the semi-final to Seongnam Ilhwa Chunma while Al Hilal lost at the same stage to Zob Ahan of Iran. Al Hilal's failure to reach the final was disappointing as they had just completed a league and cup double at home and were looking to round off a great year with a treble - a feat no Asian club has ever achieved.

FIFA WORLD CUP RECORD
1930-1974 DNE 1978-1990 DNQ **1994** 12 r2 **1998** 28 r1 **2002** 32 r1 **2006** 28 r1 **2010** DNQ

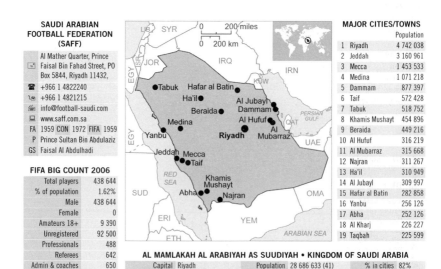

SAUDI ARABIAN
FOOTBALL FEDERATION
(SAFF)

Al Mather Quarter, Prince
Faisal Bin Fahad Street, PO
Box 5844, Riyadh 11432,
☎ +966 1 4822240
+966 1 4821215
info@football-saudi.com
www.saff.com.sa
FA 1959 CON 1972 FIFA 1959
P Prince Sultan Bin Abdulaziz
GS Faisal Al Abdulhadi

FIFA BIG COUNT 2006

Total players	438 644
% of population	1.62%
Male	438 644
Female	0
Amateurs 18+	9 390
Unregistered	92 500
Professionals	488
Referees	642
Admin & coaches	650
Number of clubs	153
Number of teams	780

MAJOR CITIES/TOWNS
Population

1	Riyadh	4 742 038
2	Jeddah	3 160 961
3	Mecca	1 453 533
4	Medina	1 071 218
5	Dammam	877 397
6	Taif	572 428
7	Tabuk	518 752
8	Khamis Mushayt	454 896
9	Beraida	449 216
10	Al Hufuf	316 219
11	Al Mubarraz	315 668
12	Najran	311 267
13	Ha'il	310 949
14	Al Jubayl	309 997
15	Hafar al Batin	282 858
16	Yanbu	256 126
17	Abha	252 126
18	Al Kharj	226 227
19	Taqbah	225 599

AL MAMLAKAH AL ARABIYAH AS SUUDIYAH • KINGDOM OF SAUDI ARABIA

Capital Riyadh	Population 28 686 633 (41)	% in cities 82%
GDP per capita $20 500 (60)	Area km² 2 149 690 km² (14)	GMT +/- +3
Neighbours (km) Iraq 814, Jordan 744, Kuwait 222, Oman 676, Qatar 60, UAE 457, Yemen 1458 • Coast 2640		

RECENT INTERNATIONAL MATCHES PLAYED BY SAUDI ARABIA

2009	Opponents	Score		Venue	Comp	Scorers	Att	Referee
5-02	Thailand	W	2-1	Sendai	Fr	Ryan Belal [61], Sultan Al Numari [64]		
11-02	Korea DPR	L	0-1	Pyongyang	WCq		48 000	Irmatov UZB
22-03	Iran	D	0-0	Riyadh	Fr			
28-03	Iran	W	2-1	Tehran	WCq	Naif Hazazi [79], Osama Al Harbi [87]	100 000	Nishimura JPN
1-04	UAE	W	3-2	Riyadh	WCq	Abdoh Autef [4p], Juma OG [70], Naif Hazazi [85]	70 000	Mohd Salleh MAS
26-05	Qatar	L	1-2	Doha	Fr	Taiseer Al Jassam [44]		
4-06	China PR	W	4-1	Tianjin	Fr	Yasser Al Khatani [6], Mohammed Noor 2 [42 88], Naif Hazazi [72]		
10-06	Korea Republic	D	0-0	Seoul	WCq		32 510	Williams AUS
17-06	Korrea DPR	D	0-0	Riyadh	WCq		65 000	Basma SYR
12-08	Oman	L	1-2	Salalah	Fr	Nassir Al Shamrani [94+p]		
30-08	Malaysia	W	2-1	Riyadh	Fr	Malek Al Hawsawi [36], Abdullatif Al Ghannam [52]		
5-09	Bahrain	D	0-0	Manama	WCq		16 000	Nishimura JPN
9-09	Bahrain	D	2-2	Riyadh	WCq	Nassir Al Shamrani [13], Hamad Al Montashari [91+]	50 000	Irmatov UZB
14-10	Tunisia	W	1-0	Rades/Tunis	Fr	Nassir Al Shamrani [2]		
14-11	Belarus	D	1-1	Dammam	Fr	Nassir Al Shamrani [32]		
2010								
21-05	Congo DR	W	2-0	Schwaz	Fr	Ahmed Al Fraidi [33], Sultan Al Numari [74]		
25-05	Nigeria	D	0-0	Wattens	Fr		1 000	Einwaller AUT
29-05	Spain	L	2-3	Innsbruck	Fr	Osama Hawsawi [17], Mohammad Al Sahlawi [74]	7 200	Einwaller AUT
11-08	Togo	W	1-0	Riyadh	Fr	Saud Kariri [43]		
9-10	Uzbekistan	W	4-0	Jeddah	Fr	Mohannad Aseri 2 [30p 45], Taisser Al Jassam [57], Saleh Bashir [86]		
12-10	Bulgaria	L	0-2	Istanbul	Fr		100	Gocek TUR
12-10	Gabon	W	1-0	Istanbul	Fr	Alaa Al Rishani [4]		
16-11	Uganda	D	0-0	Dubai	Fr			
17-11	Ghana	D	0-0	Dubai	Fr			
22-11	Yemen	W	4-0	Aden	GCr1	Osama Al Harbi [4], Mohammad Al Shalhoub [58], Mohanad Aseri [71p], Mishal Al Saeed [90]		Al Marzouqi UAE
25-11	Kuwait	D	0-0	Abyan	GCr1			Ogiya JPN
28-11	Qatar	D	1-1	Aden	GCr1	OG [89]		Al Marzouqi UAE
2-12	UAE	W	1-0	Aden	GCsf	Ahmad Abbas [55]		Ogiya JPN
5-12	Kuwait	L	0-1	Aden	GCf			Al Harrasi OMA
28-12	Iraq	L	0-1	Dammam	Fr			
31-12	Bahrain	W	1-0	Manama	Fr	Osama Hawsawi [66]		
2011								
4-01	Angola	D	0-0	Dammam	Fr			
9-01	Syria	L	1-2	Al Rayyan	ACr1	Taisser Al Jassam [60]	15 768	Kim Dong Jin KOR
13-01	Jordan	L	0-1	Al Rayyan	ACr1		17 349	Albadwawi UAE
17-01	Japan	L	0-5	Al Rayyan	ACr1		2 022	Irmatov UZB

Fr = Friendly match • AC = AFC Asian Cup • GC = Gulf Cup • WC = FIFA World Cup • q = qualifier • r1 = first round group • sf = semi-final • f = final

SAUDI ARABIA NATIONAL TEAM HISTORICAL RECORDS

Caps
177 -Mohammed Al Deayea 1990-2006 • **161** - Sami Al Jaber 1992-2006 • **139** - Majed Abdullah 1978-94 • **138** - Mohammed Al Khilaiwi 1990-2001 • **122** - Abdullah Zubromawi 1993-2002 • **106** - Hussein Sulimani 1996-2009

Goals
118 - Majed Abdullah 1978-94

Past Coaches
Abdul Rahman Fawzi EGY 1957-62 • Ali Chaouach TUN 1962-70 • George Seknas ENG 1970-72 • Taha Ismail EGY 1972-74 • Abdo Saleh Washash EGY 1974 • Ferenc Puskas HUN 1975 • Bill McGarry ENG 1976-77 • Danny Allison ENG 1978 • David Wallit ENG 1979 • Rubens Minelli BRA 1980 • Mario Zagallo BRA 1981-84 • Khalil Ibrahim Al Zayani 1984-86 • Kosia Tastilo URU 1986 • Osvaldo BRA 1987 • Carlos Galletti BRA 1988 • Omar Borras URU 1988 • Carlos Alberto Parreira BRA 1988-90 • Metin Turel TUR 1990 • Caldinho Garcia BRA 1992 • Veloso BRA 1992 • Candinho BRA 1993 • Leo Beenhakker NED 1993-94 • Mohammed Al Kharashy 1994 • Ivo Wortmann BRA 1994 • Jorge Solari ARG 1994 • Mohammed Al Kharashy 1995 • Ze Mario BRA 1995-96 • Nelo Vingada POR 1996-97 • Otto Pfister GER 1998 • Carlos Alberto Parreira BRA 1998 • Mohammed Al Kharashy 1998 • Otto Pfister GER 1999 • Milan Macala CZE 1999-2000 • Nasser Al Johar 2000 • Slobodan Santrac SRB 2001 • Nasser Al Johar 2001-02 • Gerard van der Lem NED 2002-04 • Nasser Al Johar 2004 • Gabriel Calderon ARG 2004-05 • Marcos Paqueta BRA 2006-07 • Helio dos Anjos BRA 2007-08 • Nasser Al Johar 2008-09 • Jose Peseiro POR 2009-11 • Nasser Al Johar 2011

SAUDI ARABIA 2009-10

SAUDI PREMIER LEAGUE

	Pl	W	D	L	F	A	Pts	Hilal	Ittihad	Nasr	Shabab	Wahda	Ahli	Hazm	Fat'h	Ittifaq	Qadisiya	Ra'ed	Najran
Al Hilal †	22	18	2	2	56	18	56		5-0	2-2	2-2	3-1	3-1	4-0	5-1	1-0	2-1	2-1	5-0
Al Ittihad †	22	14	3	5	46	30	45	2-1		1-2	1-2	2-0	2-1	5-2	1-1	1-1	7-1	3-2	3-1
Al Nasr †	22	12	7	3	38	23	43	2-1	0-1		0-2	1-0	1-1	1-0	3-1	1-0	3-0	4-2	3-2
Al Shabab †	22	11	7	4	36	24	40	1-2	1-0	3-2		2-2	2-1	0-2	2-2	4-1	0-1	2-1	1-0
Al Wahda	22	7	7	8	34	27	28	1-2	1-3	0-2	1-1		1-1	0-0	6-0	2-2	2-1	4-1	2-0
Al Ahli	22	7	7	8	28	29	28	1-2	0-1	3-3	1-1	2-0		2-1	1-1	2-0	3-2	1-0	0-1
Al Hazm	22	6	6	10	29	38	24	0-2	1-2	2-2	1-2	1-2	1-1		2-1	0-2	1-1	2-1	3-1
Al Fat'h	22	6	6	10	26	38	24	0-4	1-2	0-2	2-1	0-0	3-1	1-1		0-3	5-0	2-0	0-1
Al Ittifaq	22	5	7	10	24	30	22	0-2	2-1	1-1	0-0	1-3	0-0	2-3	0-2		0-2	3-0	3-1
Al Qadisiya	22	5	5	12	20	40	20	1-2	3-3	0-2	0-3	1-0	1-2	3-1	0-1	1-1		0-0	1-0
Al Ra'ed	22	3	7	12	19	35	16	0-2	0-2	0-0	1-1	1-1	1-2	1-1	2-1	0-0	2-0		2-2
Najran	22	4	4	14	22	46	16	1-2	2-3	1-1	1-3	0-5	2-1	2-4	1-1	3-2	0-0	0-1	

18/08/2009 - 18/03/2010 • † Qualified for the AFC Champions League
Top scorers: 12 - Mohammad Al Shalhoub, Hilal • 11 - Thiago Neves BRA, Hilal & Mohammad Al Sahlawi, Nasr • 10 - Walid Al Jizani, Hazm

SAUDI ARABIA 2009-10 FIRST DIVISION (2)

	Pl	W	D	L	F	A	Pts
Al Faysali	26	17	7	2	44	12	58
Al Taawun	26	17	5	4	35	18	56
Al Ansar	26	14	8	4	41	26	50
Abha	26	12	5	9	39	36	41
Al Ta'ee	26	12	4	10	30	25	40
Al Khaleej	26	10	4	12	34	34	34
Hajr	26	9	6	11	34	41	33
Al Adala	26	8	7	11	32	33	31
Al Sho'ala	26	7	8	11	36	40	29
Dhemk	26	9	2	15	29	43	29
Al Watani	26	5	12	9	35	44	27
Hitteen	26	8	3	15	38	49	27
Ohod	26	6	7	13	32	41	25
Al Riyadh	26	7	4	15	24	41	25

31/08/2009 - 23/04/2010

THE CUSTODIAN OF THE TWO HOLY MOSQUES CHALLENGE CUP 2010

First round

Al Ittihad *	4	0
Al Hazm	1	0
Al Wahda	0	0
Al Shabab *	1	0
Al Nasr	3	1
Al Ahli *	0	3
Al Fat'h	1	0
Al Hilal *	3	5

Semi-finals

Al Ittihad *	2	2
Al Shabab	0	1
Al Nasr *	3	1
Al Hilal	5	1

Final

Al Ittihad	0	5p
Al Hilal	0	4p

King Fahd International 7-05-2010
* Home team in 1st leg • 3rd Place: Shabab 3-1 Nasr

MEDALS TABLE

		Overall			Lge		Cup		Asia			City
		G	S	B	G	S	G	S	G	S	B	
1	Al Hilal	30	19	3	12	10	14	7	4	2	3	Riyadh
2	Al Ittihad	21	15	2	8	6	10	8	3	1	2	Jeddah
3	Al Ahli	15	13		2	5	13	7	1			Jeddah
4	Al Nasr	14	13		6	5	7	6	1	2		Riyadh
5	Al Shabab	9	12	1	5	5	3	6	1	1	1	Riyadh
6	Al Ittifaq	4	8		2	2	2	6				Dammam
7	Al Wahda	2	5				2	5				Mecca
8	Al Qadisiya	2	1				1	1			1	Khobar
9	Al Riyadh	1	5				1		1	4		Riyadh

CROWN PRINCE CUP 2009-10

First Round

Al Hilal *	2
Al Faysali	1
Al Ra'ed *	0
Al Nasr	2
Al Ansar *	4
Al Hazm	2
Al Ittihad	1
Najran *	2
Al Shabab	2
Al Qadisiya *	1
Al Wahda *	1 4p
Al Ta'ee	1 5p
Al Fat'h *	3
Al Ittifaq	1
Hajr *	2
Al Ahli	3

Quarter-finals

Al Hilal	2
Al Nasr *	1
Al Ansar *	1
Najran	3
Al Shabab *	3
Al Ta'ee	1
Al Fat'h *	0
Al Ahli	2

Semi-finals

Al Hilal	2
Najran	1
Al Shabab	2 3p
Al Ahli	2 5p

Final

Al Hilal	2
Al Ahli	1

Semi-finals played at Prince Faisal Bin Fahd, Riyadh • * Home team

CUP FINAL

King Fahd International, Riyadh 19-02-2010
Scorers - Christian Wilhelmsson 65, Thiago Neves 77 for Hilal; Victor Simoes 43 for Ahli

KUW – KUWAIT

FIFA/COCA-COLA WORLD RANKING

1993	1994	1995	1996	1997	1998	1999	2000	2001	2002	2003	2004	2005	2006	2007	2008	2009	2010
64	54	84	62	44	24	82	74	74	83	48	54	72	78	119	127	104	102

	2010											Hi/Lo
Jan	Feb	Mar	Mar	Apr	May	Jul	Aug	Sep	Oct	Nov	Dec	24
104	92	88	94	96	97	85	85	96	103	105	102	128

Kuwait arrived at the 2011 AFC Asian Cup finals in Qatar as an outside bet for the title on the back of a great year in 2010, having won both the West Asian Championship in Jordan and the Gulf Cup in Yemen. Coach Goran Tufegdzic took a young side to Jordan for the West Asian tournament and, against the odds, they beat a much-more experienced Iran side in the final. At the Gulf Cup in November, first round group victories over Qatar and hosts Yemen and then a penalty shoot-out win over Iraq in the semi-final saw Kuwait qualify for their first final since the current knock out system was adopted in 2004. There they met regional giants Saudi Arabia where an extra-time goal by Waleed Ali Jumah earned Kuwait their first Gulf Cup title since 1998. The Asian Cup, however, was a disaster. It started poorly when Musaed Nada was sent off in the first half against China, who ran out 2-0 winners. A second loss against Uzbekistan meant the Kuwaitis had only a slim chance to progress to the quarter-finals but they were soundly defeated in their final match by hosts Qatar. In club football Al Qadisiya came within a whisker of winning the AFC Cup in 2010 but lost on post-match penalties in the final to Syria's Al Ittihad, having earlier in the year won a league and cup double at home.

FIFA WORLD CUP RECORD
1930-1970 DNE 1974-1978 DNQ **1982** 21 r1 1986-2010 DNQ

KUWAIT FOOTBALL ASSOCIATION (KFA)

Block 5, Street 101,
Building 141 A Jabriya,
PO Box Hawalli 4020,
Kuwait 32071

☎ +965 25 355494
📠 +965 25 355464
📧 info@kfa.org.kw
🖥 www.kfa.org.kw
FA 1952 CON 1962 FIFA 1962
P Shk. Talal Fahad Al Sabah
GS Saho Al Shammari

FIFA BIG COUNT 2006

Total players	45 800
% of population	1.89%
Male	45 800
Female	0
Youth under 18	1 100
Unregistered	6 600
Professionals	0
Referees	100
Admin & coaches	300
Number of clubs	40
Number of teams	110

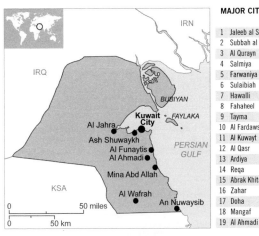

MAJOR CITIES/TOWNS

		Population
1	Jaleeb al Shuyukh	187 884
2	Subbah al Salem	152 780
3	Al Qurayn	141 372
4	Salmiya	138 158
5	Farwaniya	97 640
6	Sulaibiha	88 766
7	Hawalli	87 254
8	Fahaheel	79 779
9	Tayma	76 251
10	Al Fardaws	74 205
11	Al Kuwayt	74 180
12	Al Qasr	64 724
13	Ardiya	62 148
14	Reqa	60 827
15	Abrak Khitan	53 698
16	Zahar	48 364
17	Doha	46 697
18	Mangaf	45 590
19	Al Ahmadi	44 696

DAWLAT AL KUWAYT • STATE OF KUWAIT

Capital	Kuwait City	Population	2 691 158 (139)	% in cities	98%
GDP per capita	$57 500 (6)	Area km²	17 818 km² (157)	GMT +/–	+3
Neighbours (km)	Iraq 240, Saudi Arabia 222 • Coast 499				

RECENT INTERNATIONAL MATCHES PLAYED BY KUWAIT

2009	Opponents	Score		Venue	Comp	Scorers	Att	Referee
5-10	Libya	D	1-1	Cairo	Fr	Mohamad Jarragh [56p]		
10-10	Jordan	W	2-1	Cairo	Fr	Mohamad Jarragh [55], Yousef Nasser [70]		
26-10	Syria	W	1-0	Al Jahra	Fr	Saleh Al Hendi [90]		
3-11	Kenya	W	5-0	Cairo	Fr	Mesaed Al Enezi [22], Ahmed Ajab Al Azemi 2 [77 89], Bader Al Mutwa 2 [84 85p]		
8-11	China PR	D	2-2	Kuwait City	Fr	Abdullah Al Buraiky [42], Mesaed Al Enezi [89]		
14-11	Indonesia	W	2-1	Kuwait City	ACq	Bader Al Mutwa 2 [60 88p]	16 000	Kovalenko UZB
18-11	Indonesia	D	1-1	Jakarta	ACq	Ahmad Ajab Al Azemi [72]	36 000	Tojo JPN
16-12	UAE	D	0-0	Kuwait City	Fr			
2010								
6-01	Australia	D	2-2	Kuwait City	ACq	Hamed Al Enezi [40], Yousef Nasser [44]	20 000	Irmatov UZB
19-02	Syria	D	1-1	Al Ain	Fr	Ahmad Ajab Al Azemi [88]		
25-02	Bahrain	W	4-1	Al Ain	Fr	Ahmad Ajab Al Azemi 2 [33 42], Yousef Nasser [51], Abdullah Buraiki [60]		
3-03	Oman	D	0-0	Muscat	ACq		27 000	Moradi IRN
11-08	Azerbaijan	D	1-1	Baku	Fr	Bader Al Mutwa [82]	9 000	Karasev RUS
3-09	Syria	W	3-0	Kuwait City	Fr	Khaled Matar [7], Bader Al Mutwa [84], Yousef Naser [90]		
7-09	UAE	L	0-3	Abu Dhabi	Fr			
26-09	Syria	W	2-1	Amman	WAr1	Mohammed Rashed [53], Hussain Al Moussawi [71]	1 500	
28-09	Jordan	D	2-2	Amman	WAr1	Yousef Nasser [60], Sauod Al Magmed [78]	18 000	
1-10	Yemen	D	1-1	Amman	WAsf	Ahmed Al Rashidi [73]. W 4-3p		
3-10	Iran	W	2-1	Amman	WAf	Abdulaziz Al Mashaan [10], Yousef Nasser [45]		
8-10	Bahrain	L	1-3	Kuwait City	Fr	Ahmad Ajab Al Azemi [66]		
12-10	Vietnam	W	3-1	Kuwait City	Fr	Khaled Ajab [68], Yousef Al Sulaiman 2 [79 90]		
14-11	India	W	9-1	Abu Dhabi	Fr	Yousef Nasser [20], Bader Al Mutwa 4 [25 55 66 90], Jarah Al Ataiqi [29p], Fahad Al Enezi [51], Khaled Khalaf [56], Hamad Al Enezi [75]		
17-11	Iraq	D	1-1	Abu Dhabi	Fr	Mesaed Al Enezi [67]		
22-11	Qatar	W	1-0	Aden	GCr1	Yousef Nasser [28]		Al Harrasi OMA
25-11	Saudi Arabia	D	0-0	Abyan	GCr1			Ogiya JPN
28-11	Yemen	W	3-0	Abyan	GCr1	Jarah Al Ataiqi [19p], Bader Al Mutwa 2 [34 69]		Abbas BHR
2-12	Iraq	D	2-2	Aden	GCsf	Bader Al Mutwa [1], Fahad Al Enezi [58]. W 5-4p		Shaaban EGY
5-12	Saudi Arabia	W	1-0	Aden	GCf	Waleed Ali Jumah [94]		Al Harrasi OMA
24-12	Korea DPR	W	2-1	6th October City	Fr	Ahmed Al Rashidi [29], Musaed Neda [90]		
27-12	Korea DPR	D	2-2	6th October City	Fr	Ahmad Ajab Al Azemi [23], Talal Al Amer [57]		
31-12	Zambia	W	4-0	Suez	Fr	Yousef Nasser [19], Fahad Al Enezi 2 [21 33], Bader Al Mutwa [25]		
2011								
8-01	China PR	L	0-2	Doha	ACr1		7 423	Williams AUS
12-01	Uzbekistan	L	1-2	Doha	ACr1	Bader Al Mutwa [50p]	3 481	Shukralla BHR
16-01	Qatar	L	0-3	Doha	ACr1		28 339	Abdul Bashir SIN

Fr = Friendly match • AC = AFC Asian Cup • GC = Gulf Cup • WA = West Asian Championship • WC = FIFA World Cup • q = qualifier
r1 = first round group • sf = semi-final • f = final

KUWAIT NATIONAL TEAM HISTORICAL RECORDS

Caps

134 - Bashar Abdullah 1996-2008 • 109 - Wael Sulaiman Al Habashi 1986-96 & Nohair Al Shammari • 108 - Jamal Mubarak 1994-2004

Goals

75 - Bashar Abdullah 1996-2008

Past Coaches

Ali Othman EGY 1955 • Ahmed Abu Taha EGY 1957 • Edmund Majewski AUT 1958 • Ljubisa Brocic SRB 1962 • Mohammed Abdu Saleh Al Wahsh EGY 1964 • Dimitri Tadic URS 1966-69 • Taha Al Touki EGP 1970 • Ljubisa Brocic YUG 1971-73 • Hassen Nasser 1973 • Ljubisa Brocic YUG 1973-75 • Mario Zagallo BRA 1976-78 • Saleh Zakereya 1978 • Carlos Alberto Parreira BRA 1978-83 • Antonio Lopes BRA 1983-85 • Malcolm Allison ENG 1985-86 • Saleh Zakaria 1986 • Gyorgy Mezey HUN 1986-87 • Antonio Vieira BRA 1987-88 • George Armstrong ENG 1988 • Miguel Pereira BRA 1989 • Otacilio BRA 1989-90 • Luiz Felipe Scolari BRA 1990 • Mohammed Karam 1990 • Valmir Louruz BRA 1990-92 • Paulo Luiz Campos BRA 1992-93 • Gildo Rodriguez BRA 1993 • Jawad Maqseed 1993 • Valeriy Lobanovskyi UKR 1993-96 • Milan Macala CZE 1996-99 • Dusan Uhrin CZE 1999-2001 • Berti Vogts GER 2001-02 • Radojko Avramovic SRB 2002-03 • Paulo Cesar Carpegiani BRA 2003-04 • Mohammed Ibrahem 2004 • Slobodan Pavkovic SRB 2005 • Mohammed Ibrahem 2005 • Mihai Stoichita ROU 2005-06 • Saleh Zakaria 2006-07 • Rodion Gacanin CRO 2007-08 • Mohammed Ibrahim 2008-09 • Goran Tufegdzic SRB 2009-

KUWAIT 2009-10

PREMIER LEAGUE

	Pl	W	D	L	F	A	Pts	Qadisiya	Kuwait	Nasr	Kazma	Arabi	Salmiya	Tadamon	Sol'beekhat
Al Qadisiya ‡	21	15	3	3	49	14	48		1-2 1-0	3-0	1-2	1-1	2-0 4-0	5-0	4-1 5-0
Al Kuwait ‡	21	14	4	3	42	16	46	0-2		1-4 0-0	2-2 3-0	0-0	3-1 6-1	2-0	2-0 4-0
Al Nasr ‡	21	12	5	4	29	21	41	3-2 1-1	1-2		2-1 1-0	1-1	2-1	1-0	1-0
Kazma	21	11	4	6	40	26	37	1-2 0-2	0-2	1-0		0-0	2-2 4-1	2-0 3-1	2-1 4-1
Al Arabi	21	7	9	5	31	17	30	0-4 1-2	1-1 0-2	0-0 3-0	2-2 0-2		1-2 4-0	3-0 4-0	4-0 3-0
Salmiya	21	5	5	11	24	44	20	1-1	1-2	0-0 2-3	0-3	0-0		1-0 0-4	4-0
Al Tadamon	21	2	2	17	13	45	8	0-2 0-2	0-3 1-4	0-1 0-1	1-6	0-0	1-1		2-3 0-1
Solaybeekhat	21	2	0	19	15	60	6	1-2	0-1	2-4 1-3	2-3	0-3	0-2 2-4	0-3	

1/12/2009 - 6/05/2010 • ‡ Qualified for the AFC Cup • Relegation play-off: Al Tadamon 1-1 6-7p **Jahra**

KUWAIT 2009-10 FIRST DIVISION (2)

	Pl	W	D	L	F	A	Pts
Al Sahel	20	10	8	2	21	12	38
Jahra	20	10	5	5	27	14	35
Khitan	20	7	7	6	26	21	28
Al Yarmouk	20	7	6	7	32	23	27
Al Shabab	20	3	9	8	19	27	18
Fehayheel	20	3	5	12	14	42	14

30/11/2009 - 7/05/2010

MEDALS TABLE

	Overall			League			Cup			LC		Asia		
	G	S	B	G	S	B	G	S	B	G	S	G	S	B
1 Al Arabi	36	16	3	16	3	3	15	11		5	2			
2 Al Qadisiya	32	16	5	13	7	4	13	7		6	1	1	1	
3 Al Kuwait	24	16	3	10	4	3	9	8		4	4	1		
4 Kazma	11	13	5	4	4	5	6	8		1	1			
5 Salmiya	7	11	5	4	5	5	2	6		1				
6 Al Yarmouk	2	2		1			2	1						
7 Al Jahra	1	2		1				2						

CROWN PRINCE CUP 2009-10

First Round

Al Kuwait	3
Salmiya	0
Solaybeekhat	1
Al Yarmouk	3
Kazma	Bye
Al Sahel	1
Jahra	3
Al Qadisiya	Bye
Khitan	2
Fehayheel	3
Al Tadamon	3
Al Shabab	2
Al Nasr	0
Al Arabi	1

Quarter-finals

Al Kuwait	3
Al Yarmouk	0
Kazma	0
Jahra	1
Al Qadisiya	3
Fehayheel	1
Al Tadamon	0
Al Arabi	1

Semi-finals

Al Kuwait	2
Jahra	1
Al Qadisiya	0
Al Arabi	1

3rd place: Jahra 0-0 5-3p Qadisiya

Final

Al Kuwait	2 3p
Al Arabi	2 2p

CUP FINAL

3-05-2010

EMIR CUP 2009-10

First Round

Al Qadisiya	Bye
Jahra	1
Al Yarmouk	5
Salmiya	2
Khitan	0
Al Tadamon	0
Al Arabi	6
Kazma	1 4p
Al Sahel	1 2p
Solaybeekhat	1
Fehayheel	2
Al Nasr	2
Al Shabab	1
Al Kuwait	Bye

Quarter-finals

Al Qadisiya	2
Al Yarmouk	0
Salmiya	1
Al Arabi	2
Kazma	5
Fehayheel	2
Al Nasr	0
Al Kuwait	1

Semi-finals

Al Qadisiya	4
Al Arabi	1
Kazma	1 3p
Al Kuwait	1 4p

3rd place: Kazma 2-0 Al Arabi

Final

Al Qadisiya	0 4p
Al Kuwait	0 1p

CUP FINAL

17-05-2010

LAO – LAOS

FIFA/COCA-COLA WORLD RANKING

1993	1994	1995	1996	1997	1998	1999	2000	2001	2002	2003	2004	2005	2006	2007	2008	2009	2010
146	160	152	147	143	144	156	165	162	170	167	162	170	151	176	169	178	169

2010												Hi/Lo
Jan	Feb	Mar	Mar	Apr	May	Jul	Aug	Sep	Oct	Nov	Dec	134
178	179	178	177	174	173	173	173	177	175	171	169	190

With a side built around the under-23 squad that had reached the semi-finals of the 2009 South East Asian Games, Laos qualified for the finals of the 2010 AFF Suzuki Cup after winning a qualifying group they had staged in Vientiane, ahead of the Philippines, Cambodia and Timor-Leste. Under Englishman David Booth - who took over as coach following Alfred Riedl's move to Indonesia midway through the year - they showed a vast improvement on previous performances at the finals of Southeast Asia's premier tournament. Against three-time champions Thailand, Laos pulled off one of the surprises of the tournament with a 2-2 draw and were only denied a famous win by an injury-time strike by Thailand's Sarayoot Chaikamdee. Defeats at the hands of Indonesia and eventual champions Malaysia in their remaining games saw Laos exit the competition after which Booth stepped down and was replaced by local coach Bounlap Khenkitisack. Club football in Laos still remains hugely under-developed and teams from the country - like 2010 champions Bank of Laos - have yet to enter the AFC President's Cup which is designed to cater for the lower ranked nations in Asia. However, the success of Yadanarbon from their ASEAN neighbours Myanmar, who won the 2010 tournament, may well act as an incentive for participation in the future.

FIFA WORLD CUP RECORD
1930-1998 DNE 2002-2006 DNQ 2010 DNE

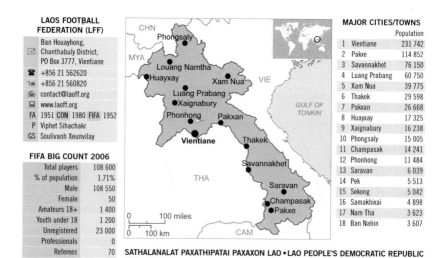

LAOS FOOTBALL FEDERATION (LFF)	
	Ban Houayhong, Chanthabuly District, PO Box 3777, Vientiane
☎	+856 21 562620
⍗	+856 21 560820
✉	contact@laoff.org
🖳	www.laoff.org
FA	1951 CON 1980 FIFA 1952
P	Viphet Sihachakr
GS	Soulivanh Xeunvilay

FIFA BIG COUNT 2006

Total players	108 600
% of population	1.71%
Male	108 550
Female	50
Amateurs 18+	1 400
Youth under 18	1 200
Unregistered	23 000
Professionals	0
Referees	70
Admin & coaches	350
Number of clubs	50
Number of teams	150

MAJOR CITIES/TOWNS

		Population
1	Vientiane	231 742
2	Pakxe	114 852
3	Savannakhet	76 150
4	Luang Prabang	60 750
5	Xam Nua	39 775
6	Thakek	29 598
7	Pakxan	26 668
8	Huayxay	17 325
9	Xaignabury	16 238
10	Phongsaly	15 005
11	Champasak	14 241
12	Phonhong	11 484
13	Saravan	6 039
14	Pek	5 513
15	Sekong	5 042
16	Samakhixai	4 898
17	Nam Tha	3 623
18	Ban Nahin	3 607

SATHALANALAT PAXATHIPATAI PAXAXON LAO • LAO PEOPLE'S DEMOCRATIC REPUBLIC

Capital	Vientiane	Population	6 834 942 (102)	% in cities	31%
GDP per capita	$2100 (186)	Area km²	236 800 km² (83)	GMT +/-	+7
Neighbours (km)	Cambodia 541, China 423, Myanmar 235, Thailand 1754, Vietnam 2130				

RECENT INTERNATIONAL MATCHES PLAYED BY LAOS

2006	Opponents	Score		Venue	Comp	Scorers	Att	Referee
12-11	Philippines	W	2-1	Bacolod	AFFq	Sisomephone [47], Phaphouvanin [49]		
14-11	Cambodia	D	2-2	Bacolod	AFFq	Soukhavong [30], Sisomephone [35]		
16-11	Timor Leste	W	3-2	Bacolod	AFFq	Saysongkham [34], Phothilath [61], Saynakhonevieng [91+]		
18-11	Brunei Darussalam	W	4-1	Bacolod	AFFq	Saysongkham [6], Phaphouvanin [17], Leupvisay [43], Phothilath [55]		
2007								
13-01	Indonesia	L	1-3	Singapore	AFFr1	Xaysongkham [13]		
15-01	Singapore	L	0-11	Singapore	AFFr1		5 224	U Hla Tint MYA
17-01	Vietnam	L	0-9	Singapore	AFFr1		1 005	
22-08	Lesotho	L	1-3	Petaling Jaya	Fr	Visay Phaphouvanin		
25-08	Myanmar	L	0-1	Kuala Lumpur	Fr			
2008								
17-10	Cambodia	L	2-3	Phnom Penh	AFFq	Luanglath [30], Leupvisay [30]		
21-10	Philippines	W	2-1	Phnom Penh	AFFq	Luanglath [56], Phaphouvanin [59]		
23-10	Brunei Darussalam	W	3-2	Phnom Penh	AFFq	Phaphouvanin [8], Singto [89], Saynakhonevieng [93+]		
25-10	Timor-Leste	W	2-1	Phnom Penh	AFFq	Singto [7], Phaphouvanin [50]		
6-12	Malaysia	L	0-3	Phuket	AFFr1		5 000	Nitrorejo IDN
8-12	Thailand	L	0-6	Phuket	AFFr1		10 000	Hadimin BRU
10-12	Vietnam	L	0-4	Phuket	AFFr1			Cho Win MYA
2009								
No international matches played in 2009								
2010								
22-10	Cambodia	D	0-0	Vientiane	AFFq			Abdul Wahab MAS
24-10	Philippines	D	2-2	Vientiane	AFFq	Soukaphone [29], Kanyala [41]		Pechsri THA
26-10	Timor-Leste	W	6-1	Vientiane	AFFq	Kovanh [11], Soukaphone [17], Lamnao [47p], Konekham [59], Kanyala [61], Ketsada [78]		Phung Dinh Dung VIE
1-12	Thailand	D	2-2	Jakarta	AFFr1	Inthammavong [54], Sysomvang [82]		Sato JPN
4-12	Indonesia	L	0-6	Jakarta	AFFr1		70 000	Daud SIN
7-12	Malaysia	L	1-5	Palembang	AFFr1	Lamnao [8]		Vo Minh Tri VIE

AFF = ASEAN Football Federation Championship • AC = AFC Asian Cup 2004 • WC = FIFA World Cup • q = qualifier • r1 = first round group

LBR – LIBERIA

FIFA/COCA-COLA WORLD RANKING

1993	1994	1995	1996	1997	1998	1999	2000	2001	2002	2003	2004	2005	2006	2007	2008	2009	2010
123	127	87	94	94	108	105	95	73	88	110	123	135	115	145	139	161	160

2010												Hi/Lo
Jan	Feb	Mar	Mar	Apr	May	Jul	Aug	Sep	Oct	Nov	Dec	**66**
161	160	160	156	152	150	156	156	139	164	164	160	**164**

A rare investment in the services of a foreign coach held out high hopes for Liberia in their quest to win a place at the 2012 African Nations Cup finals in Equatorial Guinea and Gabon. The Lone Stars have only been to the final tournament twice previously - in 1996 when former World Footballer of the Year George Weah was at the helm of the team and at the peak of his powers and in 2002. The arrival of Bertalan Bicskei, a former technical director of the football federation in his native Hungary, did not however deliver the immediate results hoped for. Playing for the first time in almost two years, Liberia were held at home in their opening group qualifier against Zimbabwe and then lost one month later to Mali in Bamako. Bicskei has already said Liberia have little chance if making it to the finals but with a four-year contract he is hopeful they might have a better tilt in the future. A new 18-team championship got underway in November 2010 in an effort to normalise a fractured club structure in the country but it will be cut down considerably by mass relegation over the next two years. A contract with a cellular company was signed in the first professional sponsorship of its kind for the country, which is still picking up the pieces after their long-standing civil strife.

FIFA WORLD CUP RECORD
1930-1978 DNE 1982-2010 DNQ

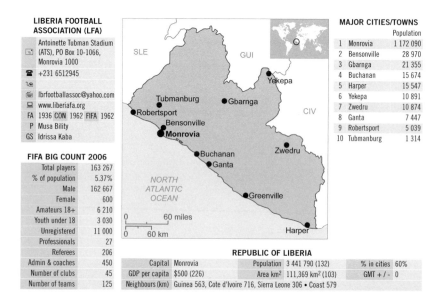

LIBERIA FOOTBALL ASSOCIATION (LFA)

Antoinette Tubman Stadium (ATS), PO Box 10-1066, Monrovia 1000
☎ +231 6512945
✉ lbrfootballassoc@yahoo.com
🖥 www.liberiafa.org
FA 1936 CON 1962 FIFA 1962
P Musa Bility
GS Idrissa Kaba

FIFA BIG COUNT 2006

Total players	163 267
% of population	5.37%
Male	162 667
Female	600
Amateurs 18+	6 210
Youth under 18	3 030
Unregistered	11 000
Professionals	27
Referees	206
Admin & coaches	450
Number of clubs	45
Number of teams	125

MAJOR CITIES/TOWNS

		Population
1	Monrovia	1 172 090
2	Bensonville	28 970
3	Gbarnga	21 355
4	Buchanan	15 674
5	Harper	15 547
6	Yekepa	10 891
7	Zwedru	10 874
8	Ganta	7 447
9	Robertsport	5 039
10	Tubmanburg	1 314

REPUBLIC OF LIBERIA

Capital	Monrovia	Population	3 441 790 (132)	% in cities	60%
GDP per capita	$500 (226)	Area km²	111,369 km² (103)	GMT + / -	0
Neighbours (km)	Guinea 563, Cote d'Ivoire 716, Sierra Leone 306 • Coast 579				

RECENT INTERNATIONAL MATCHES PLAYED BY LIBERIA

2006	Opponents	Score		Venue	Comp	Scorers	Att	Referee
3-09	Equatorial Guinea	L	1-2	Malabo	CNq	Krangar [35]		Agbenyega GHA
8-10	Rwanda	W	3-2	Monrovia	CNq	Doe [27], Makor [68], Williams [76]		Olatunde NGA
2007								
24-03	Cameroon	L	1-3	Yaoundé	CNq	Doe [39]		Djaoupe TOG
3-06	Cameroon	L	1-2	Monrovia	CNq	Mennoh [65]		Coulibaly MLI
17-06	Equatorial Guinea	D	0-0	Monrovia	CNq			Diouf SEN
8-09	Rwanda	L	0-4	Kigali	CNq			Mwanza ZAM
2008								
26-03	Sudan	W	2-0	Omdurman	Fr	Lomell [46], Mennoh [57]		
24-04	Oman	L	0-1	Muscat	Fr			
30-04	Sierra Leone	W	3-1	Paynesville	Fr	Krangar [21], Laffor [58], Zortiah [86]		
27-05	Libya	L	2-4	Tripoli	Fr	Lomell [56], Zortiah [88]		
1-06	Gambia	D	1-1	Monrovia	WCq	Makor [82]	35 000	Keita GUI
6-06	Algeria	L	0-3	Blida	WCq		40 000	Lemghambodj MTN
15-06	Senegal	D	2-2	Monrovia	WCq	Williams [74], Makor [85]	18 000	Djaoupe TOG
21-06	Senegal	L	1-3	Dakar	WCq	Williams [89]	40 000	Chaibou NIG
6-09	Gambia	L	0-3	Banjul	WCq		10 000	Ambaya LBY
11-10	Algeria	D	0-0	Monrovia	WCq		2 000	Ahmed Auda EGY
2009								
No international matches played in 2009								
2010								
5-09	Zimbabwe	D	1-1	Paynesville	CNq	Sekou Oliseh [68]		Codjia BEN
9-10	Mali	L	1-2	Bamako	CNq	Theo Weeks [42]		Djaoupe TOG

CN = CAF African Cup of Nations • WC = FIFA World Cup • q = qualifier

LBY – LIBYA

FIFA/COCA-COLA WORLD RANKING

1993	1994	1995	1996	1997	1998	1999	2000	2001	2002	2003	2004	2005	2006	2007	2008	2009	2010
152	167	175	184	147	147	131	116	116	104	83	61	80	99	95	82	115	72

2010												Hi/Lo
Jan	Feb	Mar	Mar	Apr	May	Jul	Aug	Sep	Oct	Nov	Dec	61
115	115	116	101	102	102	96	94	107	81	81	72	187

Tripoli club Al Ittihad came within a whisker of providing Libya with that elusive place in the final of an African club competition for the first time but were bundled out on the away goals rule in the semi-finals of the 2010 CAF Confederation Cup. They lost 2-1 at home in the first leg of the match against FUS Rabat but recovered to win the return leg 1-0 in Morocco but it wasn't enough to see them through. Ittihad had started the year playing in the 2010 CAF Champions League but were eliminated in the third round by Al Ahly of Egypt, a defeat that meant they took up a place in the Confederation Cup instead. At home Ittihad won a sixth successive Libyan championship, finishing six points ahead of second placed Al Ahli Benghazi, to emphasis their domestic dominance and they also continued to provide the bulk of the players for the national team as Libya got off to a good start in the 2012 African Nations Cup qualifiers. New coach Marcos Paqueta, who had previously won world championships at under-20 and under-17 level with his native Brazil, took over as the team in June but was not afforded any warm-up opportunity before heading to Maputo for a goalless draw with Mozambique. It was followed in October with a 1-0 win over Zambia in Tripoli that could turn out to be the most important result of the group.

FIFA WORLD CUP RECORD

1930-1966 DNE   **1970** DNQ   **1974** DNE   **1978-1990** DNQ   **1994-1998** DNE   **2002-2010** DNQ

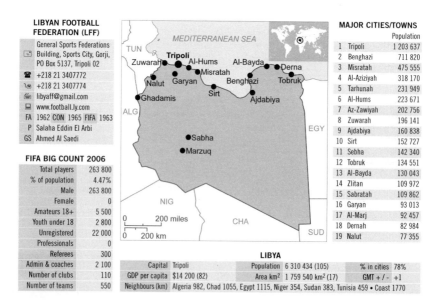

LIBYAN FOOTBALL FEDERATION (LFF)

General Sports Federations Building, Sports City, Gorji, PO Box 5137, Tripoli 02

☎ +218 21 3407772
📠 +218 21 3407774
✉ libyaff@gmail.com
🖥 www.football.ly.com
FA 1962 CON 1965 FIFA 1963
P Salaha Eddin El Arbi
GS Ahmed Al Saedi

FIFA BIG COUNT 2006

Total players	263 800
% of population	4.47%
Male	263 800
Female	0
Amateurs 18+	5 500
Youth under 18	2 800
Unregistered	22 000
Professionals	0
Referees	300
Admin & coaches	2 100
Number of clubs	110
Number of teams	550

MAJOR CITIES/TOWNS

		Population
1	Tripoli	1 203 637
2	Benghazi	711 820
3	Misratah	475 555
4	Al-Aziziyah	318 170
5	Tarhunah	231 949
6	Al-Hums	223 671
7	Az-Zawiyah	202 756
8	Zuwarah	196 141
9	Ajdabiya	160 838
10	Sirt	152 727
11	Sebha	142 340
12	Tobruk	134 551
13	Al-Bayda	130 043
14	Zlitan	109 972
15	Sabratah	109 862
16	Garyan	93 013
17	Al-Marj	92 457
18	Dernah	82 984
19	Nalut	77 355

LIBYA

Capital	Tripoli	Population	6 310 434 (105)	% in cities	78%
GDP per capita	$14 200 (82)	Area km²	1 759 540 km² (17)	GMT +/-	+1
Neighbours (km)	Algeria 982, Chad 1055, Egypt 1115, Niger 354, Sudan 383, Tunisia 459 • Coast 1770				

RECENT INTERNATIONAL MATCHES PLAYED BY LIBYA

2006	Opponents	Score		Venue	Comp	Scorers	Att	Referee
5-08	Sryia	L	1-2	Damascus	Fr	Osman [61]		
16-08	Uganda	W	3-2	Tripoli	Fr	Tarek Tayeb [59], Osman [72], Khaled Hussain [90]		
26-08	Yemen	W	1-0	Sana'a	Fr	Kara [16]		
29-08	Yemen	D	1-1	Sana'a	Fr			
3-09	Ethiopia	L	0-1	Addis Abeba	CNq			AbdelFattah EGY
1-10	Sudan	W	1-0	Tripoli	Fr	El Masli [24]		
8-10	Congo DR	D	1-1	Tripoli	CNq	Khaled Hussain [75]		Pare BFA
15-11	Tunisia	L	0-2	Rades/Tunis	Fr			
2007								
7-02	Algeria	L	1-2	Algiers	Fr	Younus Al Shibani [48]		
20-03	Mauritania	D	0-0	Tripoli	Fr			
25-03	Namibia	W	2-1	Tripoli	CNq	Salem Rewani [12], Tarek Tayeb [66]		Abdelrahman SUD
27-05	Botswana	D	0-0	Gaborone	Fr			
2-06	Namibia	L	0-1	Windhoek	CNq			Ncobo RSA
17-06	Ethiopia	W	3-1	Tripoli	CNq	Ahmed Zuwai 2 [10 47], Salem Rewani [22]		Saadallah TUN
22-08	Sudan	L	0-1	Khartoum	Fr			
8-09	Congo DR	D	1-1	Kinshasa	CNq	Khaled Hussein [51]		Djaoupe TOG
16-10	Bahrain	L	0-2	Al Muharraq	Fr			
18-11	Saudi Arabia	W	2-1	Ismailia	Fr	Osama Al Fazzani [24], Omar Dawood [94+]		
21-11	Egypt	D	0-0	Port Said	Fr			
2008								
26-03	Uganda	D	1-1	Kampala	Fr	Younus Al Shibani [89]		
22-05	Zambia	D	2-2	Tripoli	Fr	Osama Salah 2 [13 61]		
27-05	Liberia	W	4-1	Tripoli	Fr	Ali Rahuma [4], Omar Dawood [11], Mohamed El Mughrby [77], Ali Rahuma [82]		
1-06	Ghana	L	0-3	Kumasi	WCq		27 908	Maillet SEY
7-06	Gabon	W	1-0	Tripoli	WCq	Brou OG [5]	30 000	Chaibou NIG
15-06	Lesotho	W	1-0	Bloemfontein	WCq	Ahmed Osman [85]	3 500	Marange ZIM
20-06	Lesotho	W	4-0	Tripoli	WCq	Osama Salah [3], Omar Dawood [50], Younus Al Shibani [68], Hesham Shaban [80]	30 000	Trabelsi TUN
20-08	Senegal	D	0-0	Tripoli	Fr			
24-08	Chad	W	3-0	Tripoli	Fr	Omar Dawood [19], Mohamed Esnani [77], Nader Kara [80]		
28-08	Niger	W	6-2	Tripoli	Fr	Mohamed El Mughrby 2 [34 76], Ahmed Masli [44], Mohamed Zubya [87]		
5-09	Ghana	W	1-0	Tripoli	WCq	Ahmed Osman [86]	45 000	Coulibaly MLI
11-10	Gabon	L	0-1	Libreville	WCq		26 000	Bennett RSA
2009								
11-02	Uruguay	L	2-3	Tripoli	Fr	Mohamed Esnani [31], Osama Salah [57]		
5-10	Kuwait	D	1-1	Cairo	Fr	Ahmed Kerwaa [88]		
2010								
6-01	Benin	L	0-1	Cotonou	Fr			
3-03	Mali	W	2-1	Tripoli	Fr	Mohamed El Mughrby [35p], Khalid Al Deelawi [81]		
5-09	Mozambique	D	0-0	Maputo	CNq			Bangoura GUI
10-10	Zambia	W	1-0	Tripoli	CNq	Ahmed Osman [36]		Gassama GAM
17-11	Niger	D	1-1	Tripoli	Fr	Mohamed Al-Ghandour [69]. W 4-1p		

Fr = Friendly match • CN = CAF African Cup of Nations • WC = FIFA World Cup • q = qualifier • r1 = first round

LIBYA 2009–10

FIRST DIVISION

	Pl	W	D	L	F	A	Pts	Ittihad	Ahly B	Khaleej	Medina	Akhdar	Nasr	Hilal	Tirsana	Swihli	Shat	Olympique	Najma	Tahaddi	Ahly T
Al Ittihad †	25	15	6	4	45	27	51		3-1	2-1	3-3	3-0	3-0	1-1	1-5	3-1	0-1	3-2	2-0	3-0	2-1
Al Ahly Benghazi §1	25	14	4	7	39	27	45	0-2		0-2	2-1	2-1	2-1	5-0	1-1	1-0	2-3	2-1	2-0		0-0
Khaleej Sirt	25	13	5	7	47	31	44	2-3	1-1		2-2	1-0	2-1	4-0	2-0	2-2	4-1	3-2	1-0	2-3	2-2
Al Medina	25	8	13	4	31	27	37	0-0	0-1	1-1		2-0	2-2	0-0	2-1	**2-0**	1-0	2-1	0-1	1-1	1-1
Al Akhdar	25	9	8	8	29	30	35	2-2	2-1	2-3	2-2		1-0	2-0	2-2	1-1	1-0	1-0	1-0	3-1	2-1
Al Nasr	25	10	4	11	38	30	34	3-1	3-1	4-1	3-1	2-0		2-1	0-1	1-2	1-0	1-1	0-0	3-3	0-1
Al Hilal Benghazi	25	9	6	10	29	33	33	1-1	0-1	1-0	2-2	1-2	0-2		1-2	2-2	3-2	2-2	2-2	0-1	**2-0**
Al Tirsana	25	8	6	11	33	36	30	0-1	2-1	0-1	3-0	0-0	2-1	1-2		2-1	0-0	1-2	0-1	2-0	
Al Swihli	25	8	6	11	27	37	30	2-1	0-1	1-3	0-1	2-1	1-0	1-0	2-1		0-1	0-0	2-1	0-2	
Al Shat	25	8	5	12	25	36	29	1-2	0-2	0-4	1-1	2-1	1-3	1-3	1-1	3-3		1-0	2-1	4-0	
Olympique	25	7	8	10	33	36	29	0-2	1-3	2-1	1-1	0-0	2-1	1-2	3-1	2-1	1-1		1-1	0-1	0-0
Al Najma	25	8	4	13	23	31	28	0-1	2-5	1-0	0-1	1-1	1-0	0-1	2-2	3-0	0-1	4-3		1-2	
Al Tahaddi	25	4	5	16	21	49	17	0-0	1-2	0-2	1-3	1-1	0-4	1-2	2-2	1-2	0-1	1-3	0-1		
Al Ahly Tripoli	13	6	4	3	20	10	22							0-1	3-2	2-0	3-0		3-0	3-0	

8/10/2008 - 1/06/2010 • † Qualified for the CAF Champions League • Matches in bold awarded • § = points deducted
Relegation play-off: Al Wahda 0-1 1-2 **Olympique** • Al Ahly Tripoli expelled from the league on 17/05/2010 and their results from the second half of the season expunged • Top scorer: **15** - Rasheed Al Deasy MAR, Al Shat

LIBYA 2009–10
SECOND DIVISION (2)
CHAMPIONSHIP PLAY-OFF

	Pl	W	D	L	F	A	Pts
Darnes	8	6	1	1	13	7	19
Al Wahda	8	5	2	1	16	5	17
Al Harati	7	1	3	3	6	11	6
Al Jadida	7	1	2	4	7	12	5
Al Jazira	8	1	2	5	10	17	5

21/03/2010 - 25/05/2010

MEDALS TABLE

		Overall			Lge		Cup		Africa			City
		G	S	B	G	S	G	S	G	S	B	
1	Al Ittihad	22	4	3	16	6	4				3	Tripoli
2	Al Ahly	15	1		10	5					1	Tripoli
3	Al Ahly	6			4	2						Benghazi
4	Al Medina	4	3		3		1	3				Tripoli
5	Al Nasr	4	1		1		3				1	Benghazi
6	Al Tahaddi	3	1		3		1					Benghazi
7	Al Mahalah	2			2							Tripoli
	Al Shat	2			1	1						Tripoli
9	Al Hilal	1	3				1	3				Benghazi
10	Olympique	1	1		1		1					Az-Zawiyah
11	Al Dahra	1			1							Tripoli
	Khaleej Sirt	1					1					Sirt
13	Al Akhdar		3								3	Al Bayda
14	Al Swihli		1								1	Misurata

AL FATIH CUP 2009–10

Round of 16		Quarter-finals		Semi-finals		Final	
Al Nasr *	1						
Khaleej Sirt	0	Al Nasr	0 5p				
Rafik Sorman	0 2p	Al Wifak *	0 4p				
Al Wifak *	0 2p			Al Nasr	3		
Al Ittihad *	1			Al Jadida *	1		
Al Mahalah	0	Al Ittihad	1 3p				
Al Charara	0	Al Jadida *	1 5p				
Al Jadida *	1					Al Nasr ‡	2
Al Hiyad *	2 5p					Al Medina	1
Al Soukour	2 3p	Al Hiyad	0 3p				
Alamn Alaam *	0	Al Tahaddi *	0 2p				
Al Tahaddi	1			Al Hiyad *	1		
Al Ahly Tripoli *	1			Al Medina	4		
Al Shat	0	Al Ahly Tripoli *					
Al Akhdar	1	Al Medina	w-0				
Al Medina *	3						

* Home team • ‡ Qualified for the CAF Confederation Cup

CUP FINAL
11 June Stadium, Tripoli
10-06-2010. Ref: Mehraz
Scorers - Abubakr Al Abaidy 62, Ihaab Bouseffi 89 for Nasr; Ismail Bangoura 66 for Medina

LCA – ST LUCIA

1993	1994	1995	1996	1997	1998	1999	2000	2001	2002	2003	2004	2005	2006	2007	2008	2009	2010
139	157	114	134	142	139	152	135	130	112	130	114	128	160	180	176	186	181

2010												Hi/Lo
Jan	Feb	Mar	Mar	Apr	May	Jul	Aug	Sep	Oct	Nov	Dec	**108**
186	187	186	192	189	191	188	188	186	187	182	181	**192**

St Lucia halted a run of eight consecutive defeats with a 2-2 draw against the Netherlands Antilles in the 2010 Digicel Caribbean Cup, but there can be no disguising the continued disappointing form of the national team. In three warm-up games for the tournament the St Lucians lost heavily against St Vincent, Trinidad and Antigua before travelling to Paramaribo for their qualifying group. Against both Guyana and Suriname, Alain Providence's team were content to sit behind the ball in a damage limitation exercise. With just four players with international experience, Providence is building a team for the future and there were signs of promise in the final game against the Dutch Antilles where a late penalty denied them a win after striker Zacchaeus Polius had twice given them the lead. Off the field developments may well help Providence in the future with the go-ahead given to the construction of new offices and a technical centre in Bexon as part of the FIFA Goal project. In club football there was success for Northern United All Stars in the Gold Division of the National League. They beat Big Players of Marchand 2-1 in the final in December whilst Micoud won the 2010 Blackheart/Kashif and Shanghai Cup for regional selections, beating Canaries 1-0 in the final.

FIFA WORLD CUP RECORD
1930-1990 DNE 1994-2010 DNQ

ST LUCIA FOOTBALL ASSOCIATION (SLFA)

La Clery,
PO Box 255,
Castries
☎ +1 758 4530687
📠 +1 758 4590510
🖥 www.saintluciafa.com
FA 1979 CON 1988 FIFA 1988
P Patrick Mathurin
GS TBD

FIFA BIG COUNT 2006

Total players	11 023
% of population	6.54%
Male	9 560
Female	1 463
Amateurs 18+	2 413
Youth under 18	650
Unregistered	1 960
Professionals	0
Referees	66
Admin & coaches	324
Number of clubs	40
Number of teams	125

CARIBBEAN SEA

Gros Islet
Corinthe   Monchy
Castries
Ciceron
Grande Riviere
Dennery
Soufriere
Micoud
Laborie
Vieux Fort

NORTH ATLANTIC OCEAN

0   5 miles
0   5 km

MAJOR CITIES/TOWNS

		Population
1	Castries	9 712
2	Bexon	7 739
3	Babonneau	5 586
4	Ciceron	3 889
5	Dennery	3 671
6	Laborie	3 396
7	Vieux Fort	3 029
8	Monchy	2 985
9	Morne du Don	2 912
10	Marchand	2 800
11	Grande Riviere	2 599
12	Augier	2 465
13	La Clery	2 413
14	Micoud	2 309
15	Corinthe	2 146
16	Marisule	2 029
17	Desruisseaux	1 958
18	Bois d'Orange	1 948
19	Au Leon	1 790

SAINT LUCIA

Capital	Castries	Population	160 267 (187)	% in cities	28%
GDP per capita	$11 100 (99)	Area km²	616 km² (193)	GMT + / -	-4
Neighbours (km)	Coast 158				

RECENT INTERNATIONAL MATCHES PLAYED BY ST LUCIA

2006	Opponents	Score		Venue	Comp	Scorers	Att	Referee
28-07	Guyana	L	2-3	Linden	Fr	Titus Elva [62], Levi Gilbert [70]	1 800	Lancaster GUY
30-07	Guyana	L	0-2	Georgetown	Fr		3 500	James GUY
27-09	Jamaica	L	0-4	Kingston	CCq		4 000	Tamayo CUB
29-09	Haiti	L	1-7	Kingston	CCq	Germal Valcin [90p]	3 000	Callendar BRB
1-10	St Vincent/Grenadines	L	0-8	Kingston	CCq		3 000	Tamayo CUB
2007								
No international matches played in 2007								
2008								
6-02	Turks and Caicos Isl	L	1-2	Providenciales	WCq	Nyhime Gilbert [92+]	2 200	Whittaker CAY
26-03	Turks and Caicos Isl	W	2-0	Vieux Fort	WCq	Kenwin McPhee [28], Titus Elva [85]	1 200	Forde BRB
18-05	Antigua and Barbuda	L	1-6	St John's	Fr	Barnet Bledman [91+]	4 000	Willett ATG
14-06	Guatemala	L	0-6	Guatemala City	WCq		24 600	Archundia MEX
21-06	Guatemala	L	1-3	Los Angeles	WCq	Kenwin McPhee [45]	12 000	Wijngaarde SUR
2009								
No international matches played in 2009								
2010								
10-09	St Vincent/Grenadines	L	1-5	Vieux Fort	Fr	Jamil Joseph [10]	400	St Catherine LCA
21-09	Trinidad and Tobago	L	0-3	St John's	Fr		205	St Catherine LCA
23-09	Antigua and Barbuda	L	0-5	St John's	Fr		500	Willett ATG
13-10	Guyana	L	0-1	Paramaribo	CCq		550	Davis TRI
15-10	Suriname	L	1-2	Paramaribo	CCq	Zacchaeus Polius [77]	750	Baptiste DMA
17-10	Netherlands Antilles	D	2-2	Paramaribo	CCq	Zacchaeus Polius 2 [7 35]	2 800	Willet ATG

Fr = Friendly match • CC = Digicel Caribbean Cup • WC = FIFA World Cup • q = qualifier

ST LUCIA 2010
GOLD DIVISION

Semi-finals		Finals	
Northern United All Stars	2		
VSADC Castries	1		
		Northern United All Stars	2
		Big Players	1
Pakis Micoud	1	5-12-2010	
Big Players	2		

3rd place play-off: VSADC 2-2 5-3p Pakis Micoud

BLACKHEART/KASHIF & SHANGHAI FOOTBALL TOURNAMENT 2010

First Round		Quarter-finals		Semi-finals		Final	
Micoud	2						
Laborie	0	**Micoud**	7				
Anse La Reye	0	Vieux Fort South	0				
Vieux Fort South	3			**Micoud**			
Marchand	2p			Dennery			
Mon Repos	1p	Marchand	1				
South Castries	1	**Dennery**	2				
Dennery	2					**Micoud**	1
Central Castries	2					Canaries	0
Mabouya Valley	1	**Central Castries**	3				
Babonneau	1	Vieux Fort North	0			CUP FINAL	
Vieux Fort North	3			Central Castries	1		
Gros Islet	3			**Canaries**	2	Beausejour Cricket Ground, Gros Islet	
Desruisseuax	2	Gros Islet	2			27-06-2010	
Choiseul	0	**Canaries**	4	3rd place: Dennery 2-0 C. Castries		Scorer - Guy George	
Canaries	9	Played at Beausejour Cricket Ground from 12/06/2010 to 27/06/2010					

LES – LESOTHO

FIFA/COCA-COLA WORLD RANKING

1993	1994	1995	1996	1997	1998	1999	2000	2001	2002	2003	2004	2005	2006	2007	2008	2009	2010
138	135	149	162	149	140	154	136	126	132	120	144	145	160	154	161	150	170

2010												Hi/Lo
Jan	Feb	Mar	Mar	Apr	May	Jul	Aug	Sep	Oct	Nov	Dec	**120**
150	149	148	148	149	152	154	155	157	165	174	170	**174**

Lesotho disbanded their national side after a disappointing 2010 FIFA World Cup qualifying campaign deciding instead to put meagre resources into building a new side from youth level up. It is a decision that paid almost immediate dividends as the small mountain kingdom knocked out giant neighbours South Africa on the way qualifying for the 2011 African Youth Championships in Libya. It is the second time that Lesotho have reached the eight-team final tournament with the prize of a trip to the FIFA U-20 World Cup in Colombia later in the year for the four semi-finalists. National coach Leslie Notsi has been in charge of the under-20 side who have worked together regularly almost like a normal club outfit. Lesotho did not enter the 2012 African Nations Cup but have aspirations of their new generation of talent making a serious tilt at the 2014 event. Matlama, one of the continent's oldest clubs, set a new record for the number of championships won since the league in Lesotho was established in 1970. Founded in 1932, Matlama finished the 2009-10 season four points ahead of runners-up Lioli to claim their ninth title, one more than Lesotho Defence Force, although they almost did not participate after running out of money. A new committee took over the popular club and rescued their status in the top flight.

FIFA WORLD CUP RECORD

1930-1970 DNE **1974** DNQ **1978** DNE **1982** DNQ **1986-1998** DNE **2002-2010** DNQ

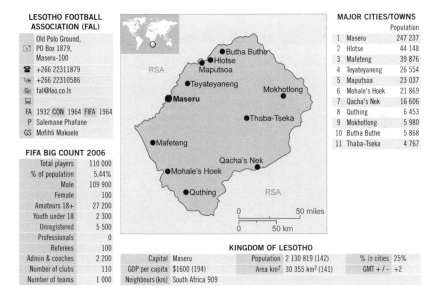

LESOTHO FOOTBALL ASSOCIATION (FAL)

Old Polo Ground,
PO Box 1879,
Maseru-100
☎ +266 22311879
📠 +266 22310586
✉ fal@leo.co.ls
🖥

FA 1932 CON 1964 FIFA 1964
P Salemane Phafane
GS Mofihli Makoele

FIFA BIG COUNT 2006

Total players	110 000
% of population	5.44%
Male	109 900
Female	100
Amateurs 18+	27 200
Youth under 18	2 300
Unregistered	5 500
Professionals	0
Referees	100
Admin & coaches	2 200
Number of clubs	110
Number of teams	1 000

MAJOR CITIES/TOWNS

		Population
1	Maseru	247 237
2	Hlotse	44 148
3	Mafeteng	39 876
4	Teyateyaneng	26 554
5	Maputsoa	23 037
6	Mohale's Hoek	21 869
7	Qacha's Nek	16 606
8	Quthing	6 453
9	Mokhotlong	5 980
10	Butha Buthe	5 868
11	Thaba-Tseka	4 767

KINGDOM OF LESOTHO

Capital	Maseru	Population	2 130 819 (142)	% in cities	25%
GDP per capita	$1600 (194)	Area km²	30 355 km² (141)	GMT +/-	+2
Neighbours (km)	South Africa 909				

RECENT INTERNATIONAL MATCHES PLAYED BY LESOTHO

2008	Opponents	Score		Venue	Comp	Scorers	Att	Referee
8-06	Ghana	L	2-3	Bloemfontein	WCq	Sello Musa [89], Lehlohonolo Seema [90]	8 000	Gasingwa RWA
15-06	Libya	L	0-1	Bloemfontein	WCq		3 500	Marange ZIM
20-06	Libya	L	0-4	Tripoli	WCq		30 000	Trabelsi TUN
28-06	Gabon	L	0-2	Libreville	WCq		15 000	Mendy GAM
20-07	Malawi	L	0-1	Secunda	CCr1			Seechurn MRI
22-07	Namibia	D	1-1	Secunda	CCr1	Thabane Rankara [80]		Seechurn MRI
24-07	Comoros	W	1-0	Secunda	CCr1	Moli Lesesa [50]		Labrosse SEY
30-08	Botswana	L	0-1	Gaborone	Fr			
7-09	Gabon	L	0-3	Bloemfontein	WCq		1 500	Abd El Fatah
11-10	Ghana	L	0-3	Sekondi	WCq		20 000	Rahman SUD
2009								
1-04	Botswana	D	0-0	Maseru	Fr			
19-06	Swaziland	D	1-1	Manzini	Fr	Thapelo Tale [72]		
21-06	Swaziland	D	1-1	Lobamba	Fr	Thapelo Mokhele [41]		
12-08	Zimbabwe	D	1-1	Bulawayo	Fr	Thabo Motsweli [31p]		
11-09	Malaysia	L	0-5	Kuala Lumpur	Fr			
19-10	Zimbabwe	D	2-2	Harare	CCr1	Thabiso Maile 2 [50p 90p]		Ramocha BOT
21-10	Mauritius	W	1-0	Harare	CCr1	Mophane Boakang [88]		Ngosi MWI
2010								

No international matches played in 2010

Fr = Friendly match • CN = CAF African Cup of Nations • CC = COSAFA Castle Cup • WC = FIFA World Cup • q = qualifier • r1 = first round group

VODACOM SPECTACULAR CUP 2009

Quarter-finals		Semi-finals		Final	
Matlama	3 4				
Qalo	0 1	**Matlama**	2		
Lioli	1 1	Likhopo	1		
Likhopo	2 1			**Matlama**	1
LDF Maseru	1 3			LCS Maseru	0
Manamela	0 0	LDF Maseru	0		
Bantu United	0 1	**LCS Maseru**	2	29-11-2009	
LCS Maseru	0 2	3rd place: LCS 3-0 Lioli			

LESOTHO 2009-10

BUDDIE PREMIER LEAGUE

	Pl	W	D	L	F	A	Pts	Matlama	Lioli	LMPS	LDF	LCS	Bantu Utd	Likhopo	Linare	Joy	Mphatlalatsane	Swallows	Lerotholi	Majantja	Nyene Rovers	Roma Rovers	Botha Bothe
Matlama †	30	18	9	3	48	21	63		3-0	1-0	0-1	3-1	2-1	2-0	1-0	3-3	0-0	**3-0**	1-0	2-1	1-0	3-2	5-1
Lioli	30	17	8	5	38	15	59	2-0		1-3	2-0	0-0	0-0	2-0	2-0	0-0	0-0	3-1	0-0	3-0	1-1	2-1	3-0
LMPS Maseru	30	17	5	8	46	32	56	0-2	1-0		2-1	1-0	2-3	1-0	1-1	0-5	1-1	0-0	1-1	1-0	4-2	2-1	8-2
LDF Maseru	30	16	7	7	41	27	55	0-1	0-2	1-0		2-1	0-0	0-0	3-2	0-0	2-1	3-1	1-4	2-0	5-1	2-0	5-1
LCS Maseru	30	15	7	8	49	31	52	1-0	0-1	4-1	0-1		2-0	0-1	3-1	1-1	1-0	5-0	2-0	2-2	3-0	2-1	5-2
Bantu United	30	14	9	7	37	26	51	1-2	1-1	0-2	0-1	4-0		0-0	1-0	3-1	0-0	3-2	0-0	0-0	2-1	3-2	3-1
Likhopo	30	12	7	11	32	32	43	2-2	1-0	1-2	3-0	0-2	1-1		2-2	3-0	1-1	2-1	1-0	4-3	0-1	3-0	0-1
Linare	30	11	8	11	42	31	41	2-2	0-1	1-0	0-1	1-1	2-1	1-2		1-0	0-1	6-1	0-1	1-0	1-0	3-0	
Joy	30	9	11	10	29	25	38	0-0	0-1	0-1	1-1	0-1	1-0	2-0	0-2		1-1	2-0	0-0	1-0	0-1	0-0	1-0
Mphatlalatsane	30	7	15	8	28	25	36	1-1	1-1	2-0	0-1	1-0	1-2	0-0	1-1	0-3		0-1	0-0	1-0	3-2	0-0	5-0
Mazenod Swallows	30	10	5	15	32	46	35	0-1	1-0	1-2	1-1	2-2	0-1	0-1	2-2	0-2	1-0		2-1	**0-3**	2-0	2-1	3-1
Lerotholi Polytechnic	30	8	10	12	29	33	34	1-2	1-2	1-3	2-1	1-1	0-1	3-0	1-1	2-1	1-1	0-1		1-0	0-1	3-0	2-1
Majantja	30	9	6	15	39	47	33	2-2	0-4	0-2	1-3	1-3	1-3	3-1	2-3	2-0	1-1	1-0			1-0	1-1	4-0
Nyene Rovers	30	7	8	15	24	39	29	0-0	0-1	0-2	0-0	1-2	0-0	2-1	0-0	0-2	1-0	1-1	2-2	3-2		**3-0**	
Roma Rovers	30	5	7	18	24	50	19	**0-3**	0-1	0-0	1-1	1-1	1-3	0-1	0-4	1-1	0-2	3-2	1-0	2-3	2-1		2-0
Botha Bothe Roses	30	2	4	24	17	78	10	0-0	0-2	0-3	0-2	2-3	0-1	0-1	0-4	1-1	3-3	0-2	0-1	0-2	1-0	0-4	

19/09/2009 - 23/05/2010 • † Qualified for the CAF Champions League

LIB – LEBANON

FIFA/COCA-COLA WORLD RANKING

1993	1994	1995	1996	1997	1998	1999	2000	2001	2002	2003	2004	2005	2006	2007	2008	2009	2010
108	129	134	97	90	85	111	110	93	119	115	105	125	126	134	150	148	154

				2010								Hi/Lo
Jan	Feb	Mar	Mar	Apr	May	Jul	Aug	Sep	Oct	Nov	Dec	85
148	145	149	149	157	160	151	148	151	157	157	154	161

Lebanon's national team played a reduced programme in 2010 after the West Asian Football Federation moved their 2010 championship away from Beirut to Amman after it deemed that Lebanon was not in a position to host the tournament. As a result the football association didn't enter a team which left the two irrelevant AFC Asian Cup qualifiers at the start of the year as the only games played - with just 50 fans turning up for the home match against Vietnam in Saida. That left the focus on club football with Al Ahed continuing their rise to prominence in the Lebanese game. Since winning their first trophy in 2004 with a Cup Final victory over traditional giants Al Nijmeh, Al Ahed, a club with ties to the local Shia community and to Hezbollah, have since won the cup twice and in 2010 claimed their second league crown becoming only the second club to go through the season unbeaten in the process. Their campaign in the 2010 AFC Cup was rather less impressive, however, after picking up just one point in the group stage. Al Nijmeh, AFC Cup finalists in 2005, also didn't make it past the group stage but they only failed to make the last 16 thanks to a worse head-to-head record with eventual winners Al Ittihad from Syria after the two had finished level on points and despite the fact that Al Nijmeh had the better goal-difference.

FIFA WORLD CUP RECORD
1930-1990 DNE 1994-2010 DNQ

LEBANESE FOOTBALL ASSOCIATION (FLFA)

Verdun Street -
Bristol Radwan Center,
PO Box 4732, Beirut
☎ +961 1 745745
📠 +961 1 349529
✉ libanfa@cyberia.net.lb
🖥

FA 1933 CON 1964 FIFA 1935
P Hachem Haydar
GS Rahif Al Ameh

FIFA BIG COUNT 2006

Total players	318 485
% of population	8.22%
Male	318 385
Female	100
Amateurs 18+	12 240
Youth under 18	6 130
Unregistered	300 000
Professionals	50
Referees	184
Admin & coaches	3 311
Number of clubs	178
Number of teams	877

MAJOR CITIES/TOWNS
		Population
1	Beirut	2 006 452
2	Tripoli	190 793
3	Juniyah	99 581
4	Baalbek	81 842
5	Sidon (Saida)	58 364
6	Zahlah	53 627
7	Kafr Ass	50 478
8	Alayh	45 074
9	Jubayl	44 807
10	Sur (Tyre)	41 824
11	Nabatiyat	35 333
12	Riyak	29 648
13	Talabaya	28 046
14	Ad Damur	27 216
15	Al Hirmil	23 834
16	Ber Al Yaas	23 338
17	Arsal	17 081
18	Bint Jubayl	16 686
19	Amzit	15 629

AL JUMHURIYAH AL LUBNANIYAH • LEBANESE REPUBLIC

Capital Beirut	Population 4 017 095 (126)	% in cities 87%
GDP per capita $11 100 (98)	Area km² 10 400 km² (169)	GMT + / - +2
Neighbours (km) Israel 79, Syria 375 • Coast 225		

RECENT INTERNATIONAL MATCHES PLAYED BY LEBANON

2006 Opponents		Score	Venue	Comp	Scorers	Att	Referee
21-12 Mauritania	D	0-0	Beirut	ARq			Al Khabbaz BHR
24-12 Somalia	W	4-0	Beirut	ARq	Mohammad Ghaddar 2 [4] [28], Nasseredine [72], Paul Rustom [83]		Hazem Hussain IRQ
27-12 Sudan	D	0-0	Beirut	ARq			
2007							
16-06 Syria	L	0-1	Amman	WAr1			
20-06 Jordan	L	0-3	Amman	WAr1			
23-09 UAE	D	1-1	Dubai	Fr	Mahmoud El Ali [17]		
8-10 India	W	4-1	Sidon	WCq	Roda Antar [33], Mohammad Ghaddar 2 [62] [76], Mahmoud El Ali [63]	500	Al Fadhli KUW
30-10 India	D	2-2	Goa	WCq	Mohammad Ghaddar 2 [76p] [88]	10 000	Mujghef JOR
2008							
2-01 Kuwait	L	2-3	Kuwait City	Fr	Mohammad Ghaddar [14p], Mahmoud El Ali [41]		
20-01 China PR	D	0-0	Zhongshan	Fr			
28-01 Jordan	L	1-4	Amman	Fr	Tarek El Ali [77]		
6-02 Uzbekistan	L	0-1	Beirut	WCq		800	Al Hilali OMA
26-03 Singapore	L	0-2	Singapore	WCq		10 118	Takayama JPN
9-04 Maldives	W	4-0	Beirut	ACq	Mahmoud El Ali [5], Ali Yaacoub [11], Abbas Ali Atwi [13p], Mohammad Ghaddar [40]		
23-04 Maldives	W	2-1	Male	ACq	Mohamed Korhani [9], Nasrat Al Jamal [74]		
27-05 Qatar	L	1-2	Doha	Fr	Mohammad Ghaddar [20]		
2-06 Saudi Arabia	L	1-4	Riyadh	WCq	Mahmoud El Ali [42]	8 000	Al Fadhli KUW
7-06 Saudi Arabia	L	1-2	Riyadh	WCq	Mohammad Ghaddar [93+]	2 000	Tongkhan THA
14-06 Uzbekistan	L	0-3	Tashkent	WCq		7 000	Breeze AUS
22-06 Singapore	L	1-2	Beirut	WCq	Khaizan OG [62]	500	Moradi IRN
2009							
14-01 Vietnam	L	1-3	Hanoi	ACq	Akram Moghrabi [73]	13 000	Toma JPN
21-01 Thailand	L	1-2	Phuket	Fr	Mahmoud El Ali [50]	15 000	Veerapool THA
23-01 Korea DPR	W	1-0	Phuket	Fr	Abbas Atwi [2p]		
28-01 Syria	L	0-2	Saida	ACq		300	Balideh QAT
1-04 Namibia	D	1-1	Saida	Fr	Zakaria Shararah [72]		
19-08 India	W	1-0	New Dehli	Fr	Ali Al Saadi [4]		Abdul Hannan BAN
22-08 Sri Lanka	L	3-4	New Dehli	Fr	Akram Moghrabi 9, Ali Al Saadi 45, Korhani [97+p]		Rowan IND
25-08 Kyrgyzstan	D	1-1	New Dehli	Fr	Abbas Atwi [56]		Abdul Hannan BAN
27-08 Syria	L	0-1	New Dehli	Fr			Rowan IND
14-11 China PR	L	0-2	Beirut	ACq		2 000	Albadwawi UAE
22-11 China PR	L	0-1	Zheijang	ACq		21 520	Breeze AUS
2010							
6-01 Vietnam	D	1-1	Saida	ACq	Mahmoud El Ali [19]	50	Kovalenko UZB
3-03 Syria	L	0-4	Damascus	ACq		16 000	Kim Dong Jin KOR

Fr = Friendly match • WA = West Asian Cup • AR = Arab Cup • AC = AFC Asian Cup • WC = FIFA World Cup • q = qualifier
r1 = first round group

LEBANON NATIONAL TEAM HISTORICAL RECORDS

Past Coaches: Joseph Nalbandian 1958-69 • Joseph Abou Murad 1971-73 • Adnan Meckdache 1974-76 • Joseph Abou Murad 1976-78 • Adnan Meckdache 1987-92 • Adnan Al Shargi 1993 • Terry Yorath WAL 1995-97 • Dietmar Werner GER 1998 • Mahmoud Saad EGY 1998-2000 • Josip Skoblar CRO 2000 • Theo Bucker GER 2000-01 • Richard Tardi 2002 • Mohammad Qwid SYR 2004-05 • Adnan Al Shargi 2005 • Emile Rustom 2005-06 • Adnan Meckdache 2006-08 • Emile Rustom 2009-

LEBANON 2009–10

PREMIER LEAGUE

	Pl	W	D	L	F	A	Pts	Ahed	Nijmeh	Safa	Ansar	Racing	Mabarra	Shabab S	Tadamon	Islah	Shabab G	Ahly	Hikma
Al Ahed ‡	22	17	5	0	49	11	**56**		2-0	1-0	1-0	3-1	2-1	7-1	2-0	4-0	1-1	2-0	2-1
Al Nijmeh	22	14	3	5	48	21	**45**	2-2		0-3	0-1	1-0	4-0	2-0	5-1	1-0	2-0	4-0	5-1
Safa	22	13	6	3	42	20	**45**	0-3	3-3		1-1	2-0	5-1	2-0	3-2	1-1	1-0	5-0	4-4
Al Ansar	22	12	8	2	33	14	**44**	1-1	2-1	1-0		1-0	1-0	2-0	1-0	5-1	3-3	1-0	2-3
Racing Club Beirut	22	7	8	7	21	21	**29**	0-0	0-1	1-1	2-2		2-2	0-0	0-1	2-1	3-1	1-0	1-1
Al Mabarra	22	8	5	9	33	37	**29**	0-1	3-1	1-2	1-1	1-2		0-0	2-1	3-2	2-1	0-1	3-1
Shabab Al Sahel	22	6	7	9	20	35	**25**	0-4	1-2	1-2	0-0	2-1	2-2		1-0	4-2	0-2	1-1	3-2
Al Tadamon Tyre	22	7	3	12	21	28	**24**	1-1	1-2	0-0	0-2	0-1	2-2	2-0		1-2	3-0	1-0	1-0
Al Islah	22	5	5	12	23	37	**20**	0-2	1-1	0-1	0-0	0-0	3-2	0-1	1-2		2-3	0-2	3-0
Shabab Al Ghazieh	22	4	6	12	20	37	**18**	0-3	0-3	0-1	0-3	1-2	1-2	1-1	2-1	1-1		1-1	1-0
Al Ahly Saida	22	4	5	13	12	34	**17**	1-3	0-3	0-1	0-3	0-2	1-2	1-1	1-0	0-1	1-1		1-1
Al Hikma	22	2	5	15	18	45	**11**	1-2	0-5	0-4	0-0	0-0	1-3	0-1	0-1	1-2	1-0	0-1	

10/10/2009 - 8/05/2010 • ‡ Qualified for AFC Cup

ELITE CUP 2009

Semi-finals

Safa	1
Al Mabarra	0

Finals

Safa	2
Al Ahed	1

20-09-2009

Al Ansar	0
Al Ahed	5

ELITE CUP 2010

Semi-finals

Al Ahed	1 5p
Al Nijmeh	1 4p

Finals

Al Ahed	0 4p
Al Ansar	0 3p

26-09-2010

Racing Club Beirut	0
Al Ansar	2

MEDALS TABLE

		Overall			Lge			Cup			Asia			City
		G	S	B	G	S	B	G	S	B	G	S	B	
1	Al Ansar	25	3		13			12	3					Beirut
2	Al Nijmeh	12	6	2	7			5	5		1	2		Beirut
3	Homenetmen	10	3		7			3	3					Beirut
4	Al Nahda	9	1		5			4	1					
5	Al Ahed	5	2		2			3	2					Beirut
6	Homenmen	4	4		4				4					Beirut
7	Racing Club	3	2		3				2					Beirut
8	Al Shabiba Mazra	3	1		1			2	1					Beirut
	Sika	3	1		3				1					Beirut
10	American University	3			3									Beirut
11	Safa SC	2	7					2	6		1			Beirut
12	Tripoli SC	2	1		1			1	1					Tripoli
	Helmi Sport	2	1					2	1					
14	Shabab Al Sahel	1	2					1	2					Beirut
15	Al Tadamon Sur	1	1					1	1					Tyre
	Al Mabarra	1	1					1	1					
17	Al Bourj	1												

FA CUP 2009–10

Round of 16

Al Ansar *	2
Trables SC	0
Racing Club Beirut	0 2p
Al Tadamon Tyre *	0 4p
Al Nijmeh	2
Shabab Al Ghazieh *	1
Ijtimai	1
Al Ahed *	8
Al Ikha'a Al Ahli	2
Al Hikma *	1
Al Modha Trables	1
Shabab Al Sahel *	4
Al Islah	1 5p
Al Ahly Sidon *	1 3p
Safa *	2 6p
Al Mabarra	2 7p

Quarter-finals

Al Ansar *	2
Al Tadamon Tyre	0
Al Nijmeh *	1
Al Ahed	3
Al Ikha'a Al Ahli *	1
Shabab Al Sahel	0
Al Islah *	0
Al Mabarra	3

Semi-finals

Al Ansar *	3
Al Ahed	1
Al Ikha'a Al Ahli *	0
Al Mabarra	2

Final

Al Ansar ‡	2
Al Mabarra	1

* Home team • ‡ Qualified for AFC Cup

CUP FINAL

Municipal, Tripoli
16-05-2010

Scorers - Nasrat Al Jamal 2 [89 118] for Ansar; Hassan Hamdan [75] for Mabarra

LIE – LIECHTENSTEIN

FIFA/COCA-COLA WORLD RANKING

1993	1994	1995	1996	1997	1998	1999	2000	2001	2002	2003	2004	2005	2006	2007	2008	2009	2010
160	156	157	154	158	159	125	147	150	147	148	142	122	158	122	149	154	148

	2010												Hi/Lo
	Jan	Feb	Mar	Mar	Apr	May	Jul	Aug	Sep	Oct	Nov	Dec	**118**
	154	153	151	151	148	149	140	141	149	159	158	148	**165**

It's easy to forget just how small a country Liechtenstein is given that the national team continues to hold its own in international competition, but a stark reminder came when the federation pulled its side out of the European Under-17 Championship despite being the host country for the final tournament. The LFV did not consider the team competitive enough and with many of the senior team coming to the end of their careers, the challenge of finding suitable replacements is a real one. Liechtenstein may be the richest country in the world but the harsh reality is that with a population that would only fill the Camp Nou to a third of its capacity, developing players of a high enough standard not to look out of depth against the likes of Spain is imperative. At club level there was almost a huge shock when USV Eschen/Mauren came within a whisker of ending the 12-year winning streak of FC Vaduz in the Liechtensteiner Cup. They held their more illustrious rivals to a 1-1 draw but then lost the resulting shoot-out after national team keeper Peter Jehle saved two of their four penalties. That was a welcome relief for Vaduz who had experienced a mediocre season in the Swiss second division under new Dutch coach Eric Orie, although they did have the satisfaction of knocking out Scottish side Falkirk in the early rounds of the 2009-10 Europa Cup.

FIFA WORLD CUP RECORD
1930-1994 DNE **1998-2010** DNQ

LIECHTENSTEINER FUSSBALLVERBAND (LFV)

	Landstrasse 149,
✉	Postfach 165,
	Vaduz 9490
☎	+423 2374747
📠	+423 2374748
✉	info@lfv.li
🖥	www.lfv.li
FA	1934 CON 1992 FIFA 1976
P	Reinhard Walser
GS	Roland Ospelt

FIFA BIG COUNT 2006

Total players	3 315
% of population	9.75%
Male	2 990
Female	325
Amateurs 18+	795
Youth under 18	1 400
Unregistered	310
Professionals	10
Referees	34
Admin & coaches	240
Number of clubs	7
Number of teams	95

MAJOR CITIES/TOWNS

		Population
1	Schaan	5 747
2	Vaduz	5 070
3	Triesen	4 674
4	Balzers	4 450
5	Eschen	4 141
6	Mauren	3 718
7	Triesenberg	2 566
8	Ruggell	1 920
9	Gamprin	1 463
10	Schellenberg	1 032
11	Planken	387

FUERSTENTUM LIECHTENSTEIN • PRINCIPALITY OF LIECHTENSTEIN

Capital	Vaduz	Population	34 761 (210)	% in cities	14%
GDP per capita	$118 000 (1)	Area km²	160 km² (218)	GMT + / -	+1
Neighbours (km)	Austria 34, Switzerland 41				

RECENT INTERNATIONAL MATCHES PLAYED BY LIECHTENSTEIN

2008	Opponents	Score		Venue	Comp	Scorers	Att	Referee
26-03	Malta	L	1-7	Ta'Qali	Fr	Burgmeier 51	1 600	Collum SCO
30-05	Switzerland	L	0-3	St Gallen	Fr		18 000	Thual FRA
20-08	Albania	L	0-2	Tirana	Fr		1 500	Vlk SVK
6-09	Germany	L	0-6	Vaduz	WCq		6 021	Gomes POR
10-09	Azerbaijan	D	0-0	Baku	WCq		25 000	Georgiev BUL
11-10	Wales	L	0-2	Cardiff	WCq		13 356	Vejlgaard DEN
19-11	Slovakia	L	0-4	Zilina	Fr		2 010	Oriekhov UKR
2009								
11-02	Iceland	L	0-2	La Manga	Fr		150	Reinert FRO
28-03	Germany	L	0-4	Leipzig	WCq		43 368	Ishchenko UKR
1-04	Russia	L	0-1	Vaduz	WCq		5 679	McKeon IRL
6-06	Finland	L	1-2	Helsinki	WCq	Frick.M 13	20 319	Kovarik CZE
12-08	Portugal	L	0-3	Vaduz	Fr		5 525	Bertolini SUI
5-09	Russia	L	0-3	St Petersburg	WCq		21 000	Constantin ROU
9-09	Finland	D	1-1	Vaduz	WCq	Polverino 75	3 132	Panic BIH
10-10	Azerbaijan	L	0-2	Vaduz	WCq		1 635	Radovanovic NME
14-10	Wales	L	0-2	Vaduz	WCq		1 858	Kaldma EST
14-11	Croatia	L	0-5	Vinkovci	Fr		10 000	Fabian HUN
2010								
11-08	Iceland	D	1-1	Reykjavik	Fr	Michael Stocklasa 70	3 000	Buttimer IRL
3-09	Spain	L	0-4	Vaduz	ECq		6 100	Yildirim TUR
7-09	Scotland	L	1-2	Glasgow	ECq	Frick.M 47	37 050	Shvestov UKR
12-10	Czech Republic	L	0-2	Vaduz	ECq		2 555	Sukhina RUS
17-11	Estonia	D	1-1	Tallinn	Fr	Frick.M 35	1 909	Gvardis RUS

Fr = Friendly match • EC = UEFA EURO 2008/2012 • WC = FIFA World Cup • q = qualifier

LIECHTENSTEINER NATIONAL TEAM HISTORICAL RECORDS

Caps
97 - Mario Frick 1993- • **89** - Martin Stocklasa 1996- • **83** - Peter Jehle 1998- • **78** - Daniel Hasler 1993-2007 • **74** - Thomas Beck 1998- • **73** - Martin Telser 1996-2007 • **72** - Ronny Buchel 1998- • **64** - Michael Stocklasa 1998- • **62** - Franz Burgmeier 2001-

Goals
16 - Mario Frick 1993- • 7 - Franz Burgmeier 2001- • **5** - Martin Stocklasa 1996- & Thomas Beck 1998- • **2** - Michael Stocklasa 1998- ; Fabio D'Elia 2001- & Benjamin Fischer 2005-

Past Coaches
Dietrich Weise GER 1994-96 • Alfred Riedl AUT 1997-98 • Ralf Loose 1998-2003 • Walter Hormann 2003-04 • Martin Andermatt SUI 2004-06 • Hans-Peter Zaug 2006-

LIECHTENSTEINER CUP 2009-10

Second Preliminary round		Quarter–finals		Semi–finals		Final		
FC Vaduz	Bye							
		FC Vaduz	8					
FC Triesen-2	0	FC Balzers-2	0					
FC Balzers-2	3			**FC Vaduz**	4			
FC Ruggell	9			FC Balzers	0			
FC Vaduz-2	1	FC Ruggell	2					
		FC Balzers	4					
FC Balzers	Bye					**FC Vaduz** ‡	1	4p
USV Eschen/Mauren-2	6					USV Eschen/Mauren	1	2p
FC Balzers-3	0	**USV Eschen/Mauren-2**	1					
		FC Schaan	0				CUP FINAL	
FC Schaan	Bye			USV Eschen/Mauren-2	2		Rheinparkstadion, Vaduz	
FC Triesenberg	3			**USV Eschen/Mauren**	6		13-05-2010, Att: 1935,	
FC Schaan-2	0	FC Triesenberg	0				Ref: Sperander	
		USV Eschen/Mauren	3				Scorers - Pascal Cerrone 71 for	
USV Eschen/Mauren	Bye						Vaduz; Francesco Clemente 56 for	

* Home team in the first leg • ‡ Qualified for the Europa League
Eschen/Mauren

LTU – LITHUANIA

FIFA/COCA-COLA WORLD RANKING

1993	1994	1995	1996	1997	1998	1999	2000	2001	2002	2003	2004	2005	2006	2007	2008	2009	2010
85	59	43	48	45	54	50	85	97	100	101	100	100	69	59	51	62	55

2010												Hi/Lo
Jan	Feb	Mar	Mar	Apr	May	Jul	Aug	Sep	Oct	Nov	Dec	
62	62	60	58	48	49	52	52	42	48	46	55	**37**
												118

Ekranas Panevezys may have completed the league and cup double for the first time in the 2010 season but the major talking point of the year was the incredible feat achieved by their long time rivals FBK Kaunas of winning maximum points on the way to the second division title. It is one thing to go through a season unbeaten but it is quite remarkable to win all of your games. There have been examples of teams winning every game but rarely have those seasons been more than 20 games. What makes the achievement of Kaunas so extraordinary was that it was done over a 27-game season. They did, however, lose two games in the cup - both legs of the semi-final against Ekranas - who then went on to beat Vetra 2-1 in the final. It was the fourth Cup Final that Vetra had lost and capped a miserable season that saw them expelled from the league two months later as a result of a financial crisis. Having won the cup in May, Ekranas completed the double at the end of the year, securing a hat trick of championships in the process, all three of which were won under their young coach Valdas Urbonas. The national team also saw the appointment of an inexperienced coach with Raimondas Zutautas replacing Portugal's Jose Couceiro after the World Cup qualifiers, though Lithuania face a tough group featuring world champions Spain.

FIFA WORLD CUP RECORD
1930 DNE   1934-1938 DNQ   1950-1990 DNE   1994-2010 DNQ

LITHUANIAN FOOTBALL FEDERATION (LFF)

Seimyniskiu 15,
Vilnius 09312

☎ +370 52638741
📠 +370 52638740
✉ info@lff.lt
🖥 www.lff.lt
FA 1922 CON 1992 FIFA 1992
P Liutauras Varanavicius
GS Julius Kvedaras

FIFA BIG COUNT 2006

Total players	135 874
% of population	3.79%
Male	119 020
Female	16 854
Amateurs 18+	3 510
Youth under 18	9 764
Unregistered	38 100
Professionals	340
Referees	195
Admin & coaches	1 370
Number of clubs	64
Number of teams	367

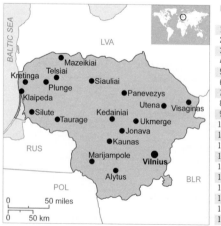

MAJOR CITIES/TOWNS

		Population
1	Vilnius	543 859
2	Kaunas	352 440
3	Klaipeda	183 436
4	Siauliai	127 105
5	Panevézys	113 230
6	Alytus	68 263
7	Marijampolé	46 998
8	Mazeikiai	40 525
9	Jonava	34 203
10	Utena	32 592
11	Kédainiai	31 000
12	Telsiai	29 868
13	Visaginas	28 061
14	Tauragé	27 754
15	Ukmerge	27 426
16	Plungé	23 145
17	Kretinga	21 548
18	Siluté	20 903
19	Radviliskis	19 454

LIETUVOS RESPUBLIKA • REPUBLIC OF LITHUANIA

Capital	Vilnius	Population	3 555 179 (130)	% in cities	67%
GDP per capita	$17 800 (69)	Area km²	65 300 km² (122)	GMT +/-	+2
Neighbours (km)	Belarus 680, Latvia 576, Poland 91, Russia 227 • Coast 90				

RECENT INTERNATIONAL MATCHES PLAYED BY LITHUANIA

2007	Opponents	Score		Venue	Comp	Scorers	Att	Referee
6-02	Mali	L	1-3	La Courneuve	Fr	Jankauskas [28]		Piccirillo FRA
24-03	France	L	0-1	Kaunas	ECq		8 740	Webb ENG
28-03	Ukraine	L	0-1	Odessa	ECq		33 600	Meyer GER
2-06	Georgia	W	1-0	Kaunas	ECq	Mikoliunas [78]	6 400	Circhetta SUI
6-06	Italy	L	0-2	Kaunas	ECq		7 800	Vink NED
22-08	Turkmenistan	W	2-1	Kaunas	Fr	Danilevicius 2 [42 47]		
8-09	Scotland	L	1-3	Glasgow	ECq	Danilevicius [61p]	52 063	Skomina SVN
12-09	Faroe Islands	W	2-1	Kaunas	ECq	Jankauskas [8], Danilevicius [53]	5 500	Georgiev BUL
17-10	France	L	0-2	Nantes	ECq		36 650	Kassai HUN
17-11	Ukraine	W	2-0	Kaunas	ECq	Savenas [41], Danilevicius [67]	3 000	Malcolm NIR
21-11	Georgia	W	2-0	Tbilisi	ECq	Ksanavicius 2 [52 96+]	21 300	Stavrev MKD
2008								
26-03	Azerbaijan	W	1-0	Vilnius	Fr	Klimavicius [38]	1 500	Satchi MDA
27-05	Czech Republic	L	0-2	Prague	Fr		14 220	Hrinak SVK
31-05	Estonia	W	1-0	Jurmala	BC	Mizigurskis [89]	1 300	Lajuks LVA
1-06	Latvia	L	1-2	Riga	BC	Beniusis [81]	3 300	Kaldma EST
4-06	Russia	L	1-4	Burghausen	Fr	Savenas [24]	2 850	Sippel GER
20-08	Moldova	W	3-0	Vilnius	Fr	Poskus 2 [23 54], Danilevicius [61]	2 000	Kaasik EST
6-09	Romania	W	3-0	Cluj	WCq	Stankevicius [31], Mikoliunas [69], Kalonas [86]	14 000	Kelly IRL
10-09	Austria	W	2-0	Marijampole	WCq	Danilevicius 2 [52 58]	4 500	Tagliavento ITA
11-10	Serbia	L	0-3	Belgrade	WCq		22 000	Mejuto ESP
15-10	Faroe Islands	W	1-0	Kaunas	WCq	Danilevicius [20]	5 000	Kapitanis CYP
19-11	Moldova	D	1-1	Tallinn	Fr	Savenas [72p]	100	Tohver EST
22-11	Estonia	D	1-1	Kuressaare	Fr	Kavaliauskas [35]	1 000	Nieminen FIN
2009								
7-02	Poland	D	1-1	Faro-Loule	Fr	Klimavicius [26]	150	Gomes POR
11-02	Andorra	W	3-1	Albufeira	Fr	Velicka [44], Boar [53], Kavaliauskas [83]		Xistra POR
28-03	France	L	0-1	Kaunas	WCq		8 700	Braamhaar NED
1-04	France	L	0-1	Paris	WCq		79 543	Webb ENG
6-06	Romania	L	0-1	Marijampole	WCq		5 850	Eriksson SWE
12-08	Luxembourg	W	1-0	Luxembourg	Fr	Danilevicius [40]	1 000	Black NIR
9-09	Faroe Islands	L	1-2	Toftir	WCq	Danilevicius [22p]	1 942	Vad HUN
10-10	Austria	L	1-2	Innsbruck	WCq	Stankevicius [66]	14 200	Gumienny BEL
14-10	Serbia	W	2-1	Marijampole	WCq	Kalonas [20p], Stankevicius [68p]	2 000	Guenov BUL
2010								
25-05	Ukraine	L	0-4	Kharkov	Fr		42 000	Sukhina RUS
18-06	Latvia	D	0-0	Kaunas	BC		1 000	Kaasik EST
20-06	Estonia	W	2-0	Kaunas	BC	Savenas [31p], Rimkevicius [90]	600	Sipailo LVA
11-08	Belarus	L	0-2	Kaunas	Fr		3 500	Satchi MDA
3-09	Scotland	D	0-0	Kaunas	ECq		5 248	Cakir TUR
7-09	Czech Republic	W	1-0	Olomouc	ECq	Sernas [27]	12 038	Yefet ISR
8-10	Spain	L	1-3	Salamanca	ECq	Sernas [54]	16 800	Rocchi ITA
17-11	Hungary	L	0-2	Szekesfehervar	Fr		4 500	Nijhuis NED

Fr = Friendly match • EC = UEFA EURO 2008/2012 • BC = Baltic Cup • WC = FIFA World Cup • q = qualifier

LITHUANIA NATIONAL TEAM HISTORICAL RECORDS

Caps
79 - Andrius Skerla 1996- • 71 - Deividas Semberas 1996- • 65 - Aurelijus Skarbalius 1991-2005 & Tomas Danilevicius 1998- • 61 - Gintaras Stauce 1992-2004 • 56 - Edgaras Jankauskas 1995-2008 & Andrius Tereskinas 1991-2000 • 55 - Marius Stankevicius 2001- & Tomas Zvirgzdauskas 1998-2008 • 52 - Zydrunas Karcemarskas 2003- • 51 - Igoris Morinas 1997-2007

Goals
19 - Tomas Danilevicius 1998- • 12 - Antanas Lingis 1928-38 • 10 - Edgaras Jankauskas 1995-2008 • 9 - Virginijus Baltusnikas 1990-98 • 8 - Jaroslavas Citavicius 1926-33; Valdas Ivanauskas 1992-2000; Darius Maciulevicius 1991-2005 & Robertas Poskus 1999-

Past Coaches
Benjaminas Zelkevicius 1990-91 • Algimantas Liubinskas 1992-94 • Benjaminas Zelkevicius 1995-97 • Kestutis Latoza 1998-99 • Robertas Tautkus 1999 • Stasys Stankus 1999-2000 • Julius Kvedaras 2000 • Benjaminas Zelkevicius 2000-03 • Algimantas Liubinskas 2003-08 • Jose Couceiro POR 2008-09 • Raimondas Zutautas 2010-

LITHUANIA 2010

A LYGA

	Pl	W	D	L	F	A	Pts	Ekranas	Suduva	Zalgiris	Tauras	Siauliai	Banga	Kruoja	Klaipeda	Mazeikiai	Atletas	Vetra
Ekranas Panevezys †	27	20	3	4	64	19	**63**		1-1	3-0	4-1	3-1 2-1	0-0 2-3	4-1 3-2	2-1 5-0	5-0	1-0	3-2
Suduva Marijampole ‡	27	16	8	3	56	16	**56**	1-1 2-0		0-0	3-1	1-1 0-1	0-0 1-0	2-1 1-2	4-0 7-0	3-0	3-1	
Zalgiris Vilnius ‡	27	16	8	3	47	16	**56**	0-1 1-0	1-1 0-0		1-0	1-0 1-0	2-0	3-1	3-0 6-0	2-0	4-1 3-0	2-1
Tauras Tauarge ‡	27	14	5	8	41	27	**47**	2-1 0-2	0-1 2-1	1-1		0-0	2-0 0-2	4-0 2-2	2-0	5-0	0-0 2-0	0-0
KFK Siauliai	27	11	8	8	37	28	**41**	1-2	0-0	1-3 2-0	0-1 0-1		1-0	2-2	2-1	2-1 1-0	1-1	1-1 0-0
Banga Gargzdai	27	10	9	8	34	30	**39**	0-3	0-2	1-1 1-1	2-1	2-1		0-1	0-3	1-1 2-1	6-1 3-0	1-0 1-1
Kruoja Pakruojis	27	8	11	8	41	45	**35**	0-2	0-2	1-1	2-2	3-3	3-3		2-2 2-3	1-1 1-1	1-0 2-0	1-1 1-1
FC Klaipeda	27	3	6	18	19	74	**15**	1-4	1-6	0-3	0-4	2-3	0-2	0-7 0-3		1-1 1-2	1-1 2-2	1-0 1-3
FK Mazeikiai	27	2	6	19	17	59	**12**	0-2 0-3	1-2	1-3	0-1	1-3	0-3	0-1 2-2	0-2 1-1		1-0 2-2	1-1 1-4
Atletas Kaunas §6	27	0	6	21	14	56	**0**	0-3	0-5 0-5	1-4	0-2	0-1	0-1	1-2 0-0	1-2 0-1	0-1 2-3		1-2 0-3
Vetra Vilnius	16	8	6	2	30	13	**21**	3-1		3-1		2-1		3-0	1-1	3-0	0-0	

21/03/2010 - 14/10/2010 • † Qualified for the UEFA Champions League • ‡ Qualified for the Europa League • § = points deducted
Vetra expelled from the league and all their results annulled
Top scorers: **16** - Povilas Luksys, Suduva • **15** - Vits Rimkus LVA, Ekranas • **12** - Dominykas Galkevicius, Ekranas • **11** - Arturas Jersovas, Zalgiris

LITHUANIA 2010
LFF 1 LYGA (2)

	Pl	W	D	L	F	A	Pts
FBK Kaunas	27	27	0	0	108	16	**81**
Alytis Alytus	27	16	3	8	47	35	**51**
Vidzgiris Alytus	27	14	4	9	69	46	**46**
Nevezis Kedainiai	27	14	3	10	47	47	**45**
Lietava Jonava	27	11	4	12	54	60	**37**
Lifosa Kedainiai	27	10	4	13	48	66	**34**
Atlantas Klaipeda	27	9	6	12	35	33	**33**
FK Silute	27	5	8	14	27	61	**23**
Minija Kretinga	27	6	4	17	29	51	**22**
Lithuania U-19	27	3	4	20	24	73	**13**

9/04/2010 - 30/10/2010

MEDALS TABLE

		Overall			League			Cup	
		G	S	B	G	S	B	G	S
1	FBK Kaunas	12	4	1	8	2	1	4	2
2	Zalgiris Vilnius	8	13	3	3	8	3	5	5
3	Ekranas Panevezys	8	6	4	5	3	4	3	3
4	Kareda Siauliai	4	2		2	2		2	
5	Inkaras Kaunas	3	2	1	2		1	1	2
6	Atlantas Klaipeda	2	3	3		2	3	2	1
7	Suduva Marijampole	2	3	2		2	2	2	1
8	Sirijus Klaipeda	2	1	1	1	1	1	1	1
9	Neris Vilnius	1	1			1		1	
10	ROMAR Mazeikiai	1		1	1			1	
11	Vetra Vilnius		5	3		1	3		4
12	Panerys Vilnius	1	1			1	1		
13	Tauras Siauliai	1							1
	Tauras Taurage	1							1

LFF TAURE 2009–10

Round of 16		Quarter–finals		Semi–finals		Final	
Ekranas Panevezys	Bye						
		Ekranas Panevezys	1 6p				
Kruoja Pakruojis *	1	FK Silute *	1 5p				
FK Silute	2			Ekranas Panevezys	2 2		
KFK Siauliai	Bye			FBK Kaunas *	1 0		
		KFK Siauliai	0				
Banga Gargzdai *	0	FBK Kaunas *	3				
FBK Kaunas	4					Ekranas Panevezys	2
Suduva Marijampole	Bye					Vetra Vilnius	1
		Suduva Marijampole	8				
Zalgiris Vilnius	1	Sakuona Plikiai *	2				
Sakuona Plikiai *	2			Suduva Marijampole	1 2		
Tauras Taurage *	2			Vetra Vilnius *	1 2		
Atletas Kaunas	1	Tauras Taurage *	1 3p				
		Vetra Vilnius	1 4p				
Vetra Vilnius	Bye						

CUP FINAL
S.Darius & S.Girenas, Kaunas
15-05-2010, Ref: Gaigalas

Scorers - Galkevicius [69], Varnas [89] for Ekranas; Raznauskas [45] for Vetra

* Home team/Home team in the first leg

LUX – LUXEMBOURG

FIFA/COCA-COLA WORLD RANKING

1993	1994	1995	1996	1997	1998	1999	2000	2001	2002	2003	2004	2005	2006	2007	2008	2009	2010
111	128	100	123	138	143	124	139	142	148	153	155	150	186	149	121	128	134

2010												Hi/Lo
Jan	Feb	Mar	Mar	Apr	May	Jul	Aug	Sep	Oct	Nov	Dec	**93**
128	124	126	124	127	127	116	117	130	135	133	134	**195**

For only the second time in a decade F91 Dudelange finished the season without a trophy after failing to defend either their league or cup titles. The departure of Michel Leflochmoan, who had led Dudelange to a run of five successive championships, clearly took its toll as the team got off to a slow start under new coach Marc Grosjean and it was Jeunesse d'Esch who claimed the club's 28th title on the final day of the season, despite a valiant run-in by Dudelange which included a 4-0 victory over Jeunesse. In the cup Dudelange were knocked out in the quarter-finals by Jeunesse's cross-town rivals Fola but it was FC Differdange 03 who beat perennial runners-up Grevenmacher in the final. Like Dudelange, Differdange are the result of a recent merger between a number of smaller clubs in an attempt to establish a team capable of winning honours and the cup triumph was the first honour won since the merger in 2003 and the first trophy for the town since Red Boys won the cup in 1985. There was a change in coach for the national team when Guy Hellers resigned in August 2010, just before the qualifiers for Euro 2012 got underway. He was replaced by the U-21 coach Luc Holtz who will have a tough job matching Heller's capacity to inspire his team to the occasional shock result such as the recent away wins over Belarus and Switzerland.

FIFA WORLD CUP RECORD
1930 DNE **1934-2010** DNQ

FEDERATION LUXEMBOURGEOISE DE FOOTBALL (FLF)

PO Box 5,
Monderange 3901
☎ +352 4886651
🖷 +352 48866582
flf@football.lu
www.football.lu
FA 1908 CON 1954 FIFA 1910
P Paul Philipp
GS Joel Wolff

FIFA BIG COUNT 2006

Total players	47 580
% of population	10.03%
Male	44 626
Female	2 954
Amateurs 18+	15 806
Youth under 18	11 874
Unregistered	4 100
Professionals	300
Referees	264
Admin & coaches	1 050
Number of clubs	111
Number of teams	746

MAJOR CITIES/TOWNS

		Population
1	Luxemburg	75 375
2	Esch-sur-Alzette	28 950
3	Dudelange	18 473
4	Schifflange	8 364
5	Bettembourg	7 627
6	Pétange	7 371
7	Ettelbruck	6 466
8	Diekirch	6 343
9	Strassen	6 026
10	Bertrange	5 634
11	Fousbann	5 509
12	Belvaux	5 449
13	Differdange	5 431
14	Soleuvre	5 116
15	Mamer	5 066
16	Wiltz	5 021
17	Echternach	4 901
18	Rodange	4 803
19	Obercorn	4 786

GRAND DUCHE DE LUXEMBOURG

Capital	Luxembourg	Population	491 775 (169)	% in cities	82%
GDP per capita	$81 200 (3)	Area km²	2 586 km² (178)	GMT + / -	+1
Neighbours (km)	Belgium 148, France 73, Germany 138				

RECENT INTERNATIONAL MATCHES PLAYED BY LUXEMBOURG

2007 Opponents	Score	Venue	Comp	Scorers	Att	Referee
7-02 Gambia	W 2-1	Hesperange	Fr	Joachim [65], Sagramola [83]	520	Circhetta SUI
24-03 Belarus	L 1-2	Luxembourg	ECq	Sagramola [68]	2 021	Whitby WAL
28-03 Romania	L 0-3	Piatra-Neamt	ECq		9 120	Lajuks LVA
2-06 Albania	L 0-2	Tirana	ECq		3 000	Silgava GEO
6-06 Albania	L 0-3	Luxembourg	ECq		4 325	Malzinskas LTU
22-08 Georgia	D 0-0	Luxembourg	Fr		1 123	Weatherall NIR
8-09 Slovenia	L 0-3	Luxembourg	ECq		2 012	Berezka UKR
12-09 Bulgaria	L 0-3	Sofia	ECq		4 674	Demirlek TUR
13-10 Belarus	W 1-0	Gomel	ECq	Fons Leweck [95+]	14 000	Svendsen DEN
17-10 Romania	L 0-2	Luxembourg	ECq		3 584	Brych GER
17-11 Netherlands	L 0-1	Rotterdam	ECq		45 000	Hansson SWE
2008						
30-01 Saudi Arabia	L 1-2	Riyadh	Fr	Peters [87p]	2 000	
26-03 Wales	L 0-2	Luxembourg	Fr		1 879	Kuipers NED
27-05 Cape Verde Islands	D 1-1	Luxembourg	Fr	Fons Leweck [77]	2 051	Radovanovic MNE
20-08 Macedonia FYR	L 1-4	Luxembourg	Fr	Kitenge [73]	885	Brugger AUT
6-09 Greece	L 0-3	Luxembourg	WCq		4 596	Hermansen DEN
10-09 Switzerland	W 2-1	Zurich	WCq	Strasser [27], Leweck [87]	20 500	Filipovic SRB
11-10 Israel	L 1-3	Luxembourg	WCq	Peters [14]	3 562	Egorov RUS
15-10 Moldova	D 0-0	Luxembourg	WCq		2 157	Borski POL
19-11 Belgium	D 1-1	Luxembourg	Fr	Mutsch [47]		Riley ENG
2009						
28-03 Latvia	L 0-4	Luxembourg	WCq		2 516	Whitby WAL
1-04 Latvia	L 0-2	Riga	WCq		6 700	Aydinus TUR
12-08 Lithuania	L 0-1	Luxembourg	Fr		1 000	Black NIR
5-09 Moldova	D 0-0	Chisinau	WCq		7 820	Mazeika LTU
9-09 Israel	L 0-7	Ramat Gan	WCq		7 038	Svendsen DEN
10-10 Switzerland	L 0-3	Luxembourg	WCq		8 031	Iturralde ESP
14-10 Greece	L 1-2	Athens	WCq	Papadopoulos OG [90]	13 932	Ceferin SVN
14-11 Iceland	D 1-1	Luxembourg	Fr	Kintziger [75]	913	Van Boekel NED
2010						
3-03 Azerbaijan	L 1-2	Luxembourg	Fr	Strasser [33]	874	Kari FIN
4-06 Faroe Islands	D 0-0	Hesperange	Fr		713	Bertolini SUI
11-08 Wales	L 1-5	Llanelli	Fr	Kitenge [44]	4 904	Gestranius FIN
3-09 Bosnia-Herzegovina	L 0-3	Luxembourg	ECq		7 327	Banari MDA
7-09 Albania	L 0-1	Tirana	ECq		10 000	Trutz SVK
8-10 Belarus	D 0-0	Luxembourg	ECq		1 857	Stavrev MKD
12-10 France	L 0-2	Metz	ECq		24 710	Jug SVN
17-11 Algeria	D 0-0	Luxembourg	Fr		7 033	Sippel GER

Fr = Friendly match • EC = UEFA EURO 2008/2012 • WC = FIFA World Cup • q = qualifier

LUXEMBOURG NATIONAL TEAM HISTORICAL RECORDS

Caps 98 - Jeff Strasser 1993- • 87 - Carlo Weis 1978-98 • 79 - Rene Peters 2000- • 77 - Francois Konter 1955-69 • 73 - Roby Langers 1980-98 • 69 - Manuel Cardoni 1993-2004 & Eric Hoffmann 2002-10 • 67 - Ernest Brenner 1955-65 • 64 - Marcel Bossi 1980-93 & Jeff Saibene 1986-2001 • 63 - Gilbert Dresch 1975-87 • 58 - Jean-Paul Girres 1980-92 • 57 - Fernand Brosius 1956-66 • 56 - Nicolas Kettel 1946-59

Goals 16 - Leon Mart 1936-45 • 15 - Gustave Kemp 1937-45 • 14 - Camille Libar 1938-47 • 13 - Nicolas Kettel 1946-59 • 12 - Francois Muller 1949-54 • 11 - Leon Letsch 1947-62 • (Totals include all matches and not just full internationals)

Past Coaches Ernst Melchior 1969-72 • Louis Pilot 1978-84 • Paul Philipp 1985-2001 • Allan Simonsen 2001-04 • Guy Hellers 2004-10 • Luc Holz 2010-

LUXEMBOURG 2009-10

BGL LIGUE — DIVISION NATIONALE

	Pl	W	D	L	F	A	Pts	Jeunesse	Dudelange	Grevenmacher	Differdange	RM Hamm	Fola	Racing Union	Etzella	Pétange	Swift	Progrès	Käerjeng	Rumelange	Mondercange
Jeunesse d'Esch †	26	17	6	3	45	20	57		1-1	2-0	2-1	1-0	1-0	5-1	1-2	0-0	3-1	2-1	2-0	4-0	2-0
F91 Dudelange ‡	26	16	6	4	62	23	54	4-0		5-0	3-1	3-0	3-3	3-0	1-1	2-0	4-1	2-1	1-1	0-0	1-0
CS Grevenmacher ‡	26	13	4	9	46	40	43	2-5	1-0		2-0	3-2	2-0	1-1	3-1	0-3	2-1	2-1	5-2	4-1	0-1
FC Differdange 03 ‡	26	12	6	8	41	30	42	0-1	4-2	2-2		3-0	1-0	0-5	7-0	2-0	4-1	1-1	1-1	4-0	1-0
RM Hamm Benfica	26	11	8	7	50	29	41	0-1	4-2	2-2	3-0		3-0	1-1	3-1	7-2	0-0	3-3	3-0	0-3	2-0
Fola Esch/Alzette	26	11	8	7	49	38	41	0-1	1-3	3-2	1-1	1-1		1-2	5-4	2-1	4-1	4-1	0-0	4-2	1-1
Racing Union	26	12	5	9	39	47	41	0-2	2-2	2-1	0-1	1-0	2-2		3-4	3-1	1-0	1-2	1-0	3-0	1-0
Etzella Ettelbruck	26	8	8	10	42	43	32	1-1	1-2	1-3	1-0	1-1	0-1	1-1		2-4	1-0	2-2	1-1	1-2	1-0
CS Pétange	26	9	5	12	36	42	32	0-3	0-1	2-0	0-0	1-3	4-1	1-1	6-1		1-3	1-1	3-1	1-3	5-2
Swift Hesperange	26	8	5	13	33	41	29	0-0	0-2	1-3	3-0	0-0	0-1	0-2	2-2	1-3		1-4	1-4	4-1	2-1
Progrès Niedercorn	26	6	10	10	39	44	28	0-2	4-2	0-0	0-0	2-2	1-1	2-2	1-3	0-1	1-4		0-2	3-1	4-2
UN Käerjeng	26	7	7	12	28	36	28	0-0	1-0	1-1	1-4	0-1	1-0	1-3	0-1	0-0	0-2	2-0		1-2	1-1
US Rumelange	26	7	1	18	27	63	22	0-1	0-5	0-2	1-2	0-6	2-4	0-3	1-3	1-0	1-2	0-3	2-3		2-0
FC Mondercange	26	2	7	17	18	58	13	1-1	0-9	1-5	1-1	1-5	2-2	1-2	2-1	0-1	0-2	1-1	0-4	0-2	

1/08/2009 - 21/05/2010 • † Qualified for the UEFA Champions League • ‡ Qualified for the Europa League
Relegation play-off: **UN Käerjeng** 3-1 CS Obercorn • Top scorer: **22** - Daniel Huss, Grevenmacher

---

LUXEMBOURG 2009-10 — EHRENPROMOTION (2)

	Pl	W	D	L	F	A	Pts
FC Wiltz 71	26	17	4	5	66	39	55
Jeunesse Canach	26	14	9	3	53	29	51
CS Obercorn	26	14	6	6	53	27	48
Sporting Steinfort	26	14	4	8	53	32	46
FC 72 Erpeldange	26	12	7	7	53	40	43
Victoria Rosport	26	11	6	9	48	40	39
Koeppchen W'dange	26	10	6	10	43	42	36
Young Boys Diekirch	26	10	5	11	52	50	35
Avenir Beggen	26	8	10	8	36	37	34
Union 05 Kayl Tetange	26	10	4	12	48	50	34
Minerva Lintgen	26	9	5	12	42	46	32
US Hostert	26	9	3	14	41	57	30
Jeunesse Schieren	26	4	4	18	32	60	16
AS Colmarberg	26	3	1	22	15	86	10

22/08/2009 - 2/05/2010
Relegation play-offs: **Eischen** 2-1 Hostert
Sandweiler 0-1 **Minerva**

MEDALS TABLE

		Overall			League			Cup	
		G	S	B	G	S	B	G	S
1	Jeunesse d'Esch/Alzette	40	23	15	28	12	15	12	11
2	Red Boys Differdange	21	19	14	6	10	14	15	9
3	AC Spora Luxembourg	19	18	10	11	10	10	8	8
4	Union Luxembourg	16	18	12	6	8	12	10	10
5	Stade Dudeldange	14	13	6	10	6	6	4	7
6	Avenir Beggen	13	9	3	6	5	3	7	4
7	F'91 Dudelange	12	7		8	4		4	3
8	Fola Esch/Alzette	8	8	4	5	7	4	3	1
9	Progres Niedercorn	7	8	8	3	5	8	4	3
10	CS Grevenmacher	5	12	4	1	7	4	4	5
11	US Hollerich	5	3	2	5	3	2		
12	Aris Bonnevoie	4	6	2	3	1	2	1	5
13	US Rumelange	2	5	1		3	1	2	2
14	Sporting Club Luxembourg	2	3	2	2	3	2		
15	The National Schifflange	2	3		1	2		1	1
16	Alliance Dudelange	2	2		1			2	1
17	Racing Club Luxembourg	2		3	1		3	1	

COUPE DE LUXEMBOURG 2009-10

Round of 16

FC Differdange 03	3
CS Obercorn *	0
Progrès Niedercorn	0 3p
FC Mondercange *	0 4p
Swift Hesperange	2
Young Boys Diekirch *	1
CS Pétange	1
Etzella Ettelbruck *	2
Fola Esch/Alzette *	4
UN Käerjeng	2
RM Hamm Benfica *	1
F91 Dudelange	2
Jeunesse Canach *	0 4p
US Rumelange	0 3p
Etoile Clemency *	1
CS Grevenmacher	4

Quarter-finals

FC Differdange 03 *	3
FC Mondercange	0
Swift Hesperange	1
Etzella Ettelbruck *	2
Fola Esch/Alzette	2 8p
F91 Dudelange *	2 7p
Jeunesse Canach	2
CS Grevenmacher *	4

Semi-finals

FC Differdange 03 *	3
Etzella Ettelbruck	1
Fola Esch/Alzette	1
CS Grevenmacher *	5

Final

FC Differdange 03 ‡	1
CS Grevenmacher	0

CUP FINAL
Josy Barthel, Luxembourg
30-05-2010, Ref: Parage
Scorer - Soraire [89]

* Home team • ‡ Qualified for the Europa League

LVA – LATVIA

FIFA/COCA-COLA WORLD RANKING

1993	1994	1995	1996	1997	1998	1999	2000	2001	2002	2003	2004	2005	2006	2007	2008	2009	2010
86	69	60	82	75	77	62	92	106	79	51	65	69	90	86	67	45	78

2010												Hi/Lo
Jan	Feb	Mar	Mar	Apr	May	Jul	Aug	Sep	Oct	Nov	Dec	45
45	49	47	46	46	46	50	49	68	72	73	78	111

Six years after having set the world record at 14 consecutive league championships, Skonto Riga finally got their hands on the trophy again when they won the 2010 Virsliga ahead of FK Ventspils and Liepajas Metalurgs - the only other clubs to have won the title. Buoyed by the return of Aleksandrs Starkovs, the architect of most of those 14 championship wins, Skonto lost just twice all season with their Brazilian striker Nathan Junior topping the scoring charts alongside Metalurgs' Deniss Rakels. Daugava Daugavpils made sure that it was a four-horse title race instead of the usual three as they look to establish themselves as a force in Latvian football, but the surprise of the season was the Cup Final triumph of FK Jelgava. Twice a winner in the early 1990s when known as RAF Jelgava, they beat FK Jurmala in the final on post-match penalties with their keeper Marks Bogdanovs saving three spot kicks. Starkovs may have had a good year with his club but as coach of the national team he had less joy, winning just one game, a 2-0 victory in Malta in the qualifiers for Euro 2012. Latvia were drawn in a tough group with favourites Croatia and Greece but with Georgia a transformed side under Temuri Ketsbaia and Israel always providing tough opposition, the Latvians are unlikely to repeat their exploits of 2004.

FIFA WORLD CUP RECORD
1930-1934 DNE 1938 DNQ 1950-1990 DNE 1994-2010 DNQ

LATVIAN FOOTBALL FEDERATION (LFF)

Olympic Sports Center,
Grostonas Street 6b,
Riga 1013
☎ +371 67292988
📠 +371 67315604
✉ futbols@lff.lv
🖥 www.lff.lv
FA 1921 CON 1992 FIFA 1992
P Guntis Indriksons
GS Janis Mezeckis

FIFA BIG COUNT 2006

Total players	85 285
% of population	3.75%
Male	73 885
Female	11 400
Amateurs 18+	1 450
Youth under 18	6 550
Unregistered	17 900
Professionals	265
Referees	225
Admin & coaches	430
Number of clubs	68
Number of teams	420

MAJOR CITIES/TOWNS

		Population
1	Riga	711 789
2	Daugavpils	105 520
3	Liepaja	84 492
4	Jelgava	66 120
5	Jurmala	55 061
6	Ventspils	43 098
7	Rezekne	35 680
8	Valmiera	27 339
9	Jekabspils	26 713
10	Ogre	26 167
11	Tukums	19 904
12	Salaspils	18 084
13	Cesis	17 844
14	Kuldiga	12 892
15	Olaine	12 719
16	Saldus	12 353
17	Dobele	11 104
18	Talsi	11 059
19	Sigulda	10 760

LATVIJAS REPUBLIKA • REPUBLIC OF LATVIA

Capital Riga	Population 2 231 503 (141)	% in cities 68%
GDP per capita $17 300 (72)	Area km² 64 589 km² (123)	GMT +/- +2
Neighbours (km) Belarus 171, Estonia 343, Lithuania 576, Russia 292 • Coast 498		

RECENT INTERNATIONAL MATCHES PLAYED BY LATVIA

2007	Opponents	Score		Venue	Comp	Scorers	Att	Referee
6-02	Bulgaria	L	0-2	Larnaca	Fr		500	Andronikou CYP
7-02	Hungary	L	0-2	Limassol	Fr		400	Kailisz CYP
28-03	Liechtenstein	L	0-1	Vaduz	ECq		1 680	Gumienny BEL
2-06	Spain	L	0-2	Riga	ECq		10 000	Thomson SCO
6-06	Denmark	L	0-2	Riga	ECq		7 500	Trefoloni ITA
22-08	Moldova	L	1-2	Riga	Fr	Astafjevs 31		
8-09	Northern Ireland	W	1-0	Riga	ECq	Baird OG 69	7 500	Proença POR
12-09	Spain	L	0-2	Oviedo	ECq		22 560	Yefet ISR
13-10	Iceland	W	4-2	Reykjavík	ECq	Klava 27, Laizans 31, Verpakovskis 2 37 46	5 865	Dean ENG
17-10	Denmark	L	1-3	Copenhagen	ECq	Gorkss 80	19 004	Cakir TUR
17-11	Liechtenstein	W	4-1	Riga	ECq	Karlsons 14, Verpakovskis 30, Laizans 63, Visnakovs 87	4 800	Moen NOR
21-11	Sweden	L	1-2	Stockholm	ECq	Laizans 26	26 218	Stark GER
2008								
6-02	Georgia	W	3-1	Tbilisi	Fr	Karlsons 7, Stepanovs 16, Astafjevs 34		Shmolik BLR
26-03	Andorra	W	3-0	Andorra la Vella	Fr	Ivanovs 10, Pereplotkins 24, Rimkus 41		Rubinos Perez ESP
30-05	Estonia	W	1-0	Riga	BC	Laizans 48p	4 500	Zuta LTU
1-06	Lithuania	W	2-1	Riga	BC	Pereplotkins 57, Alunderis OG 77	3 300	Kaldma EST
20-08	Romania	L	0-1	Urziceni	Fr		10 000	Ovrebo NOR
6-09	Moldova	W	2-1	Tiraspol	WCq	Karlsons.G 8, Astafjevs 22	4 300	Courtney NIR
10-09	Greece	L	0-2	Riga	WCq		8 600	Chapron FRA
11-10	Switzerland	L	1-2	St Gall	WCq	Ivanovs 71	18 026	Batista POR
15-10	Israel	D	1-1	Riga	WCq	Kolesnicenko 89	7 100	Hrinak SVK
12-11	Estonia	D	1-1	Tallinn	Fr	Grebis 75	2 000	Sandmoen NOR
2009								
11-02	Armenia	D	0-0	Limassol	Fr		150	
28-03	Luxembourg	W	4-0	Luxembourg	WCq	Karlsons 24, Cauna 48, Visnakovs 72, Pereplotkins 86	2 516	Whitby WAL
1-04	Luxembourg	W	2-0	Riga	WCq	Zigajevs 43, Verpakovskis 75	6 700	Aydinus TUR
12-08	Bulgaria	L	0-1	Sofia	Fr		2 000	Pamporidis GRE
5-09	Israel	W	1-0	Ramat Gan	WCq	Gorkss 59	20 000	Kircher GER
9-09	Switzerland	D	2-2	Riga	WCq	Cauna 62, Astafjevs 75	8 600	Kralovec CZE
10-10	Greece	L	2-5	Athens	WCq	Verpakovskis 2 12 40	18 981	Ovrebo NOR
14-10	Moldova	W	3-2	Riga	WCq	Rubins 2 32 44, Grebis 76	3 800	Hyytia FIN
14-11	Honduras	L	1-2	Tegucigalpa	Fr	Kolesnicenko 45p		Quesada CRC
2010								
22-01	Korea Republic	L	0-1	Malaga	Fr		150	Velasco ESP
5-06	Ghana	L	0-1	Milton Keynes	Fr		8 108	Clattenburg ENG
18-06	Lithuania	D	0-0	Kaunas	BC		1 000	Kaasik EST
19-06	Estonia	D	0-0	Kaunas	BC		300	Mazeika LTU
11-08	Czech Republic	L	1-4	Liberec	Fr	Cauna 90	7 456	Dankovsky UKR
3-09	Croatia	L	0-3	Riga	ECq		7 600	Kuipers NED
7-09	Malta	W	2-0	Ta'Qali	ECq	Gorkss 43, Verpakovskis 85	6 255	Asumaa FIN
8-10	Greece	L	0-1	Piraeus	ECq		13 520	Damato ITA
12-10	Georgia	D	1-1	Riga	ECq	Cauna 91+	4 330	Neves POR
17-11	China PR	L	0-1	Kunming	Fr		7 500	Ko Hyung Jin KOR

Fr = Friendly match • EC = UEFA EURO 2008/2012 • BC = Baltic Cup • WC = FIFA World Cup
q = qualifier • po = play-off • r1 = first round group

LATVIA NATIONAL TEAM HISTORICAL RECORDS

Caps	**167** - Vitalijs Astafjevs 1992-2010 • **113** - Andrejs Rubins 1998- • **106** - Juris Laizans 1998- & Imants Bleidelis 1995-07 • **105** - Mihails Zemlinskis 1992-2005 • **99** - Igors Stepanovs 1995- • **86** - Aleksandrs Kolinko 1997- • **83** - Maris Verpakovskis 1999- • **81** - Andrejs Stolcers 1994-2005 • **75** - Marian Pahars 1996-2007 • **73** - Vitas Rimkus 1995-2008 • **70** - Oleg Blagonadezdins 1992-2004
Goals	**28** - Maris Verpakovskis 1999- • **24** - Eriks Petersons 1929-39 • **16** - Vitalijs Astafjevs 1992-2010 • **15** - Marian Pahars 1996-2007 & Juris Laizans 1998- • **14** - Alberts Seibelis 1925-39 • **13** - Ilja Vestermans 1935-38 • **12** - Mihails Zemlinskis 1992-2005
Past Coaches	Janis Gilis 1992-97 • Revaz Dzodzuashvili GEO 1998-99 • Gary Johnson ENG 1999-2001 • Aleksandrs Starkovs 2001-04 • Jurijs Andrejevs 2004-07 • Aleksandrs Starkovs 2007-

LATVIA 2010

VIRSLIGA

	Pl	W	D	L	F	A	Pts	Skonto	Ventspils	Metalurgs	Daugava	Jurmala	Jelgava	Blazma	Olimps/RFS	Tranzits	Jauniba
Skonto Riga †	27	22	3	2	86	16	69		1-0 2-2	0-0	1-0 0-1	4-2	4-1 2-1	6-0	6-1 4-0	5-0	7-0 6-0
FK Ventspils ‡	27	20	3	4	68	18	63	2-1		2-4 0-1	1-1	1-0 3-1	2-1	1-0 2-0	7-0	2-0 5-0	5-0 4-1
Liepajas Metalurgs ‡	27	19	4	4	70	20	61	1-2 1-2	0-0		0-1 0-0	1-2	3-1 3-0	4-0	4-0 2-1	2-0	4-0 8-0
Daugava Daugavpils	27	16	8	3	35	16	56	1-1	1-0 0-1	1-1		1-0 2-0	1-1	2-0 3-1	2-0	2-0 1-0	1-0 3-1
FK Jurmala	27	8	4	15	30	45	28	0-4 0-2	1-4	1-2 1-4	0-1		2-1 1-1	0-0	2-2 0-3	2-1	0-1 0-1
FK Jelgava	27	6	7	14	36	45	25	0-5	1-2 2-4	1-2	3-3 0-1	1-2		4-0 2-0	4-0	2-1 0-0	4-1
Blazma Rezekne	27	7	3	17	27	57	24	1-3 1-4	0-5	1-4 2-3	3-1	0-4 2-1	0-0		2-0 1-1	2-0	1-2
Olimps/RFS Riga	27	5	6	16	31	63	21	1-3	0-3 0-3	0-3	1-1 0-2	0-2	2-1 2-1	2-1		0-1 0-2	2-2
Tranzits Ventspils	27	5	4	18	17	56	19	0-2 0-6	0-2	0-4 0-6	0-1	1-1 2-3	1-1	3-1 0-3	2-2		2-0
Jauniba Riga	27	4	4	19	16	80	16	0-3	0-5	2-3	1-1	0-2	1-1 0-1	0-1 0-4	0-9 2-2	1-0 0-1	

10/04/2010 - 7/11/2010 • † Qualified for the UEFA Champions League • ‡ Qualified for the Europa League
Top scorer: **18** - Deniss Rakels, Metalurgs & Nathan Junior BRA, Skonto • **15** - Jurijs Zigajevs, Ventspils • **12** - Kristaps Grebis, Metalurgs

LATVIA 2010 PIRMALIGA (2)

	Pl	W	D	L	F	A	Pts
FB Gulbene	22	21	1	0	84	14	64
FC Jurmala	22	14	4	4	47	19	46
Daugava Riga	22	13	5	4	51	27	44
Liepajas Metalurgs-2	22	13	4	5	55	31	43
FS Metta	22	10	6	6	42	25	36
FK Valmiera	22	9	4	9	33	40	31
Daugava Riga-2	22	7	3	12	28	35	24
FK Auda	22	6	6	10	21	33	24
FK Spartaks	22	6	4	12	32	41	22
FK Tukums	22	4	7	11	33	46	19
FK Jelgava-2	22	4	3	15	21	42	15
FK Kuldiga	22	1	1	20	14	109	4

1/05/2010 - 6/11/2010

MEDALS TABLE

	Overall			League			Cup		City
	G	S	B	G	S	B	G	S	
1 Skonto Riga	22	7	3	15	1	3	7	6	Riga
2 FK Ventspils	7	6	5	3	5	5	4	1	Ventspils
3 Liepajas Metalurgs	3	11	4	2	7	4	1	4	Liepaja
4 FK Jelgava	3	2	2		2	2	3		Jelgava
5 Dinaburg Daugavpils	1	3	2		1	2	1	2	Daugavpils
6 Olimpija Riga	1	1			1		1		Riga
7 FK Riga	1		1			1	1		Riga
8 Daugava Daugavpils	1							1	Daugavpils
9 Daugava Riga		5			3			2	Riga

LATVIJAS KAUSS 2009–10

Round of 16		Quarter–finals		Semi–finals		Final	
FK Jelgava	2						
Tranzits Ventspils	1	FK Jelgava	1 7p				
Daugava Daugavpils	1	Liepajas Metalurgs	1 6p				
Liepajas Metalurgs	4			FK Jelgava	1 5p		
FK Ventspils	4			Skonto Riga	1 3p		
FC Jurmala	0	FK Ventspils	0 6p				
FK Kauguri	0	Skonto Riga	0 7p				
Skonto Riga	W-0					FK Jelgava ‡	2 6p
Olimps/RFS Riga	2					FK Jurmala	2 5p
Coldgel/Varaviksne	0	Olimps/RFS Riga	4				
FS Metta	1	Daugava Riga	0				
Daugava Riga	3			Olimps/RFS Riga			
Blazma Rezekne	5			FK Jurmala			
SK Upesciems	0	Blazma Rezekne	0				
FK Valke	0	FK Jurmala	4				
FK Jurmala	13			‡ Qualified for the Europa League			

CUP FINAL
Skonto, Riga
19-05-2010. Ref: Sipailo
Scorers - Igors Lapkovskis [55],
Valerijs Redjko [85p] for Jelgava;
Dimitrijs Paplavskis [14], Valerijs
Cistjakovs [76] for Jurmala

MAC – MACAU

MAC – MACAU

FIFA/COCA-COLA WORLD RANKING

1993	1994	1995	1996	1997	1998	1999	2000	2001	2002	2003	2004	2005	2006	2007	2008	2009	2010
166	175	180	172	157	174	176	180	180	188	184	188	192	185	190	196	187	193

	2010											Hi/Lo
Jan	Feb	Mar	Mar	Apr	May	Jul	Aug	Sep	Oct	Nov	Dec	**156**
187	188	188	181	196	197	196	196	197	195	194	193	**197**

Macau's disappointing record at international level continued throughout 2010 with the national team failing to pick up a win in the three matches played throughout the year. That means Macau have still only won four matches since the enclave was handed back to China by Portugal in 1999, with those victories coming over fellow minnows Brunei, Guam and twice against Mongolia. All three games in 2010 were played over the space of four days in October at the Long Teng Cup in Chinese Taipei. A 7-1 defeat against the hosts was noteworthy only for Leong Ka Hong scoring Macau's only goal of the year while the other two matches also ended in defeat - 4-0 against Hong Kong and 5-0 against the Philippines - as the team slipped perilously close to the bottom of the FIFA/Coca-Cola World Ranking. At the end of 2010 only Afghanistan, Bhutan and the suspended Brunei stood below them amongst the Asian nations. In local football Windsor Arch Kai I emerged from the nine-game championship unbeaten, finishing three points ahead of runners-up FC Porto. They also completed the league and cup double when they beat Lam Pak - who had finished third in the league - in the final of the Macau Football Association Cup, winning the trophy on post-match penalties.

FIFA WORLD CUP RECORD

1930-1978 DNE 1982-1986 DNQ 1990 DNE 1994-2010 DNQ

MACAU FOOTBALL ASSOCIATION (AFM)

	Avenida Wai Leong Taipa, University of Science and Technology, Football Field, Block I, Taipa, Macau
☎	+853 28830287
📠	+853 28830409
✉	macaufa@macau.ctm.net
🖥	www.macaufa.com
FA	1939 **CON** 1976 **FIFA** 1976
P	Vitor Lup Kwan Cheung
GS	Kam Vai Choi

FIFA BIG COUNT 2006

Total players	14 123
% of population	3.12%
Male	13 423
Female	700
Amateurs 18+	4 130
Unregistered	1 750
Professionals	1
Referees	51
Admin & coaches	703
Number of clubs	96
Number of teams	120

MAJOR CITIES/TOWNS

		Population
1	Macau	559 846

AOMEN TEBIE XINGZHENGQU • MACAU SPECIAL ADMINISTRATIVE REGION

Capital	Macau	Population	559 846 (167)	% in cities	100%
GDP per capita	$30 000 (45)	Area km²	28 km² (235)	GMT + / -	+8
Neighbours (km)	China 0.3 • Coast 41				

RECENT INTERNATIONAL MATCHES PLAYED BY MACAU

2007	Opponents	Score		Venue	Comp	Scorers	Att	Referee
10-06	Hong Kong	L	1-2	Hong Kong	Fr	Chan Kin Seng 29		
17-06	Mongolia	D	0-0	Macau	EAq		300	Matsuo JPN
21-06	Korea DPR	L	1-7	Macau	EAq	Chan Kin Seng 46	300	Wan Daxue CHN
24-06	Chinese Taipei	L	2-7	Macau	EAq	De Sousa 48, Leong Chong In 78	200	Kim Eui Soo KOR
8-10	Thailand	L	1-6	Bangkok	WCq	Chan Kin Seng 23	11 254	Chynybekov KGZ
15-10	Thailand	L	1-7	Macau	WCq	Chan Kin Seng 92+	500	Recho SYR
2008								
25-05	Nepal	L	2-3	Phnom Penh	CCq	Che Chi Man 29p, Chan Kin Seng 59	2 000	Vo Minh Tri VIE
28-05	Cambodia	L	1-3	Phnom Penh	CCq	Che Chi Man 65	3 000	Kurbanov TKM
19-11	Hong Kong	L	1-9	Macau	Fr			
2009								
11-03	Nth Mariana Islands	W	6-1	Manenggon Hills	EAq	Chan Kin Seng 2 13 24, Ho Man Hou 2 33 90, Leong Chong In 40, Loi Wai Hong 62		Sato JPN
13-03	Mongolia	L	1-2	Manenggon Hills	EAq	Ho Man Hou 79		Fan Qi CHN
15-03	Guam	D	2-2	Manenggon Hills	EAq	Chan Kin Seng 2 10 51	1 400	Kim Jong Hyeuk KOR
7-04	Mongolia	W	2-0	Macau	CCpr	Chan Kin Seng 22, Leong Chong In 24	500	Perera SRI
14-04	Mongolia	L	1-3	Ulaan-Baatar	CCpr	Chan Kin Seng 39	3 000	Yu Ming Hsun TPE
16-04	Myanmar	L	0-4	Dhaka	CCq		3 600	Mashentsev KGZ
28-04	Cambodia	L	1-2	Dhaka	CCq	Che Chi Man 75	6 000	Saleem MDV
30-04	Bangladesh	L	0-3	Dhaka	CCq		8 700	Mashentsev KGZ
2010								
9-10	Chinese Taipei	L	1-7	Kaohsiung	Fr	Leong Ka Hang 82	1 000	
10-10	Hong Kong	L	0-4	Kaohsiung	Fr		1 200	Yu Ming Hsun TPE
12-10	Philippines	L	0-5	Kaohsiung	Fr		700	Yu Ming Hsun TPE

Fr = Friendly match • EA = East Asian Championship • AC = AFC Asian Cup • CC = AFC Challenge Cup • WC = FIFA World Cup
q = qualifier • r1 = first round group

MACAU 2010

CAMPEONATO 1° DIVISAO

	Pl	W	D	L	F	A	Pts	Ka I	FC Porto	Lam Pak	Monte Carlo	Policia	U-23	Artilheiros	Hoi Fan	Kuan Tai	Va Luen
Windsor Arch Ka I	9	7	2	0	26	9	23					1-0		2-0		1-1	
FC Porto	9	6	2	1	23	13	20	0-5					4-3	2-0			
Lam Pak	9	6	1	2	21	12	19	1-2	2-3			1-1	1-0				
Monte Carlo	9	4	4	1	18	15	16	3-3	1-1						4-1		2-0
Policia	9	4	1	4	17	7	13			0-2					1-1		
Macau U-23	9	3	1	5	21	17	10	3-5		0-1	6-1	0-1			0-1	1-1	
Artilheiros Pau Peng	9	3	1	5	12	17	10			1-2	2-2	0-2					2-1
Hoi Fan	9	2	2	5	23	30	8	1-4	2-7	3-4			2-3	6-4		3-3	
Kuan Tai	9	0	5	4	12	26	5		0-0	2-4	1-2	0-9		0-2			4-4
Va Luen	9	0	1	8	6	33	1	0-3	0-4	0-5		0-4	1-5		0-4		

9/04/2010 - 4/07/2010

TACA DE ASSOCIACAO DE FUTEBOL DE MACAU 2010

Quarter-finals		Semi-finals		Final	
Windsor Arch	2				
Chao Pak Kei	0	**Windsor Arch**	1 p		
Macau U-18	0	Monte Carlo	1 p		
Monte Carlo	1			**Windsor Arch**	4 p
FC Porto	1			Lam Pak	4 p
Benfica	0	FC Porto	0		
Hong Ngai	1	**Lam Pak**	1		
Lam Pak	2				

MAD – MADAGASCAR

FIFA/COCA-COLA WORLD RANKING

1993	1994	1995	1996	1997	1998	1999	2000	2001	2002	2003	2004	2005	2006	2007	2008	2009	2010
89	111	132	140	163	150	134	114	122	101	118	147	149	184	149	135	158	155

2010												Hi/Lo
Jan	Feb	Mar	Mar	Apr	May	Jul	Aug	Sep	Oct	Nov	Dec	**74**
158	156	157	154	149	148	144	148	154	160	158	155	**188**

Defeat for Madagascar in both their opening qualifiers for the 2012 African Nations Cup effectively ended any chance they had of progress to a first-ever finals appearance and cost French coach Jean-Paul Rabier his job. Two defeats in six matches in the 2010 FIFA World Cup qualifiers played during the course of 2008 had suggested the Barea could be a more forceful opponent but the Malagasy lost, not unexpectedly, to Nigeria away in their opening game and then flopped at home to Ethiopia in October. Rabier's appointment as coach in April displayed a new intent by Madagascar to compete more vociferously in the international arena but by the end of the year those hopes had come to nothing. Madagascar's fractured championship was won by CNaPS Sport, a first success for the club from Itasy. They finished ahead of Academie Ny Antsika, Japan Actuel's and AS Adema of Antananarivo in the four-team play-off with the title decided in the last game at the Mahamasina Stadium in Antananarivo with a 2-1 win over Japan Actuel's. It proved a triumph for former international Etienne 'Titi' Rasoanaivo who has been the driving force behind CNaPS Sport. Adema won the Malagasy Cup beating Japan Actuel's 1-0 in extra time in the final, the winner from Tsiala Kennedy Ganja securing a fourth successive triumph for the club.

FIFA WORLD CUP RECORD
1930-1978 DNE 1982-1986 DNQ 1990 DNE 1994-2010 DNQ

FEDERATION MALAGASY DE FOOTBALL (FMF)

26 rue de Russie, Isoraka,
PO Box 4409, Tananarive
101
☎ +261 20 2268374
📠 +261 20 2268373
📧 fmf@blueline.mg

FA 1961 CON 1963 FIFA 1964
P Ahmad
GS Anselme Rabibisoa

FIFA BIG COUNT 2006

Total players	826 420
% of population	4.44%
Male	787 470
Female	38 950
Amateurs 18+	16 650
Youth under 18	13 700
Unregistered	27 000
Professionals	0
Referees	680
Admin & coaches	4 108
Number of clubs	220
Number of teams	880

MAJOR CITIES/TOWNS

		Population
1	Antananarivo	1 612 632
2	Toamasina	219 669
3	Antsirabé	192 499
4	Fianarantsoa	179 302
5	Mahajanga	162 807
6	Toliary	120 790
7	Antsiranana	86 421
8	Antanifotsy	75 485
9	Ambovombe	70 740
10	Amparafaravola	55 578
11	Taolanaro	47 791
12	Ambatondrazaka	46 532
13	Mananara	44 455
14	Soavinandriana	43 237
15	Mahanoro	43 021
16	Soanierana Ivongo	42 364
17	Faratsiho	40 148
18	Vavatenina	39 824
19	Morondava	38 963

REPUBLIQUE DE MADAGASCAR • REPUBLIC OF MADAGASCAR

Capital	Antananarivo	Population	20 653 556 (55)	% in cities	29%
GDP per capita	$1000 (212)	Area km²	587 041 km² (46)	GMT +/-	+3
Neighbours (km)	Coast 4828				

RECENT INTERNATIONAL MATCHES PLAYED BY MADAGASCAR

2006	Opponents	Score		Venue	Comp	Scorers	Att	Referee
2-09	Gabon	L	0-4	Libreville	CNq			Diatta SEN
2007								
25-03	Côte d'Ivoire	L	0-3	Antananarivo	CNq			Maillet SEY
28-04	Zimbabwe	L	0-1	Maputo	CCr1			Faduco MOZ
29-04	Seychelles	W	5-0	Maputo	CCr1	Voavy 3 [11 14 69], Ramiadamanana [62], Andriatsima [84]		Mpopo LES
3-06	Côte d'Ivoire	L	0-5	Bouaké	CNq			Louzaya CGO
17-06	Gabon	L	0-2	Antananarivo	CNq			Mlangeni SWZ
29-07	Congo DR	D	0-0	Antananarivo	Fr			
14-08	Comoros	W	3-0	Antananarivo	Fr	Voavy 2 [70 89], Ramiadamanana 90		
14-10	Comoros	W	6-2	Antananarivo	WCq	Andriatsima 4 [30 40 49p 57], Rakotomandimby [65], Tsaralaza [79]	7 754	Kaoma ZAM
17-11	Comoros	W	4-0	Moroni	WCq	Nomenjanahary 2 [37 51], Rakotomandimby [61], Robson [73]	1 610	Damon RSA
2008								
9-03	Mauritius	W	2-1	Curepipe	Fr	Rabemananjara 2 [77 81]		
31-05	Botswana	D	0-0	Gaborone	WCq		11 087	Kaoma ZAM
8-06	Côte d'Ivoire	D	0-0	Antananarivo	WCq			Labrosse SEY
15-06	Mozambique	D	1-1	Antananarivo	WCq	Mamihasindrahona [91p]	15 501	Ebrahim RSA
22-06	Mozambique	L	0-3	Maputo	WCq		20 000	Maillet SEY
19-07	Swaziland	D	1-1	Witbank	CCr1	Robson [65]		Nhlapo RSA
21-07	Seychelles	D	1-1	Witbank	CCr1	Rabenandrasana [23]		Kaoma ZAM
23-07	Mauritius	W	2-1	Witbank	CCr1	Rabenandrasana [52], Rabemananjara [63]		Marange ZIM
30-07	Mozambique	L	1-2	Thulamahashe	CCsf	Rabemananjara		Marange ZIM
3-08	Zambia	L	0-2	Thulamahashe	CC3p			
7-09	Botswana	W	1-0	Antananarivo	WCq	Rabemananjara [24]	20 000	Seechurn MRI
11-10	Côte d'Ivoire	L	0-3	Abidjan	WCq		24 000	Benouza ALG
2009								
19-09	South Africa	L	0-1	Kimberley	Fr			
2010								
29-08	Comoros	W	1-0	Mahajanga	Fr			
5-09	Nigeria	L	0-2	Calabar	CNq			Jedidi TUN
10-10	Ethiopia	L	0-1	Antananarivo	CNq			Ngosi MWI

Fr = Friendly match • CN = CAF African Cup of Nations • CC = COSAFA Cup • WC = FIFA World Cup
q = qualifier • r1 = first round group • sf = semi-final • 3p = third place play-off

MADAGASCAR 2010
THB CHAMPIONS LEAGUE
FIRST STAGE

Group A - Ambanja	Pl	W	D	L	F	A	Pts
Racing Nosy Be ‡	3	2	0	1	4	3	6
Joel Sava ‡	3	1	1	1	3	4	4
ASCUM Boeny	3	1	1	1	3	2	4
Herita Antsohihy	3	0	2	1	4	5	2

Group B - Tsiroanomandidy	Pl	W	D	L	F	A	Pts
CNaPS Sport Itasy ‡	3	2	0	1	8	3	6
Maintirano Melaky ‡	3	1	1	1	4	5	4
Tana FC	3	1	1	1	5	5	4
BAS Bongolava	3	0	2	1	3	7	2

Group C - Antsirabe	Pl	W	D	L	F	A	Pts
Académie Ny Antsika ‡	3	3	0	0	13	0	9
Japan Actuel's ‡	3	2	0	1	6	1	6
Maeva Betsiboka	3	1	0	2	2	10	3
Grand Olympique	3	0	0	3	1	11	0

Group D - Manakara	Pl	W	D	L	F	A	Pts
Jirama Fianarantsoa ‡	3	2	0	0	5	0	6
Real Vatovavy ‡	3	1	0	1	3	3	3
Mania Ambositra	3	0	0	2	0	3	0
Vangaindrano			Withdrew				

Group E - Ihosy	Pl	W	D	L	F	A	Pts
3FB Ambatondrazaka ‡	2	1	1	0	2	0	4
Ilakaka Ihorombe ‡	2	1	1	0	1	0	4
Fils Elephant	2	0	0	2	0	3	0
Espoir Ambovombe			Withdrew				

Group F - Ambatondrazaka	Pl	W	D	L	F	A	Pts
Fortior Toamasina ‡	5	3	2	0	5	3	11
Adema Antananarivo ‡	5	2	2	1	13	1	8
Voromaherin Alaotra	5	1	2	2	5	4	5
Esperance Vavatenina	3	0	0	3	0	15	0

Fortior, Adema and Voromaherin all finished on five points so they played each other again in a play-off

15/09/2010 - 21/09/2010 • ‡ Qualified for the second stage

MADAGASCAR 2010
THB CHAMPIONS LEAGUE
SECOND STAGE

Group A - Mahajanga	Pl	W	D	L	F	A	Pts
CNaPS Sport Itasy ‡	2	1	1	0	5	2	4
Racing Nosy Be	2	0	2	0	4	4	2
Real Vatovavy	2	0	1	1	2	5	1

Group B - Toamasina	Pl	W	D	L	F	A	Pts
Japan Actuel's ‡	2	1	0	1	2	1	3
Fortior Toamasina	2	1	0	1	1	1	3
3FB Ambatondrazaka	2	1	0	1	1	2	3

Group C - Antsiranana	Pl	W	D	L	F	A	Pts
Adema Antananarivo ‡	2	1	1	0	3	2	4
Joel Sava	2	0	2	0	2	2	2
Jirama Fianarantsoa	2	0	1	1	2	3	1

Group D - Toliara	Pl	W	D	L	F	A	Pts
Académie Ny Antsika ‡	2	2	0	0	7	2	6
Ilakaka Ihorombe	2	1	0	1	7	3	3
Maintirano Melaky	2	0	0	2	2	11	0

20/10/2010 - 30/10/2010 • ‡ Qualified for the final stage

MADAGASCAR 2010
THB CHAMPIONS LEAGUE
FINAL STAGE (POULE DES AS)

Final Stage - Antananarivo	Pl	W	D	L	F	A	Pts	ANA	JA	AA
CNaPS Sport Itasy †	3	2	1	0	4	7	7	2-1	2-0	0-0
Académie Ny Antsika	3	1	1	1	5	4	4		2-2	2-1
Japan Actuel's	3	1	1	1	4	4	4			2-0
Adema Antananarivo	3	0	1	2	1	1	1			

31/10/2010 - 7/11/2010 • † Qualified for the CAF Champions League

TELMA COUPE DE MADAGASCAR 2010

Round of 16		Quarter–finals		Semi–finals		Final	
Adema Antananarivo	3						
Comato Andrefana	0	Adema Antananarivo	1				
SOS Village Atsinanana	0	ASCUM Boeny	0				
ASCUM Boeny	4			Adema Antananarivo	1		
Ilakaka Ihorombe	3			Académie Ny Antsika	0		
St-Francois	2	Ilakaka Ihorombe	1				
Ajesaia Antananarivo	0	Académie Ny Antsika	3				
Académie Ny Antsika	3					Adema Antananarivo ‡	1
Tana FC	5					Japan Actuel's	0
Ajesaia Ambat'drazaka	1	Tana FC	3				
Andry Bongolava	0	Fortior Toamasina	0				
Fortior Toamasina	1			Tana FC	1 1p		
3FB Ambatondrazaka	1			Japan Actuel's	1 4p		
Kintan'i Boeny	0	3FB Ambatondrazaka	0				
Iarivo Analamanga	0	Japan Actuel's	1				
Japan Actuel's	1						

‡ Qualified for the CAF Confederation Cup

CUP FINAL

Stade Rabemananjara, Mahajanga
19-11-2010, Ref: Nampiandrazana

Scorer - Tsiala Kennedy Ganja [94]

MAR – MOROCCO

FIFA/COCA-COLA WORLD RANKING

1993	1994	1995	1996	1997	1998	1999	2000	2001	2002	2003	2004	2005	2006	2007	2008	2009	2010
30	33	38	27	15	13	24	28	36	35	38	33	36	39	39	41	67	

	2010												Hi/Lo
	Jan	Feb	Mar	Mar	Apr	May	Jul	Aug	Sep	Oct	Nov	Dec	**10**
	67	65	70	68	70	70	82	83	95	77	80	79	**67**

FUS Rabat, a club playing lower league football just two years earlier, became the first Moroccan side in five years to win a continental club title with a thrilling victory in the 2010 CAF Confederation Cup. The club from the capital surprised everyone with their progress to the final but were given little chance of lifting the trophy after they had been held at home to a goalless draw by highly fancied CS Sfaxien of Tunisia in the first leg of the final. Down 2-1 with 15 minutes left in the second leg, Mohamed Zouidi came on to inspire a remarkable comeback. He was involved in the equaliser from Rachid Rokki and then grabbed a spectacular winner two minutes from the end, tearing off on the breakaway and chipping the on-rushing goalkeeper to win the match. Two weeks later FUS won the Coupe du Trone with a 2-1 triumph over Mahgreb Fes in the final. The league was won by Wydad Casablanca but they surprisingly went through four coaches in the calendar year. Belgian Eric Gerets was appointed new national team coach but only able to take up his job in November after his stint at Al Hilal in Saudi Arabia ended. His assistant Dominique Cuperly stood in for him for the two matches at the start of the 2010 African Nations Cup qualifiers - including an embarrassing draw at home to the Central African Republic.

FIFA WORLD CUP RECORD

1930-1958 DNE **1962** DNQ **1966** DNE **1970** 14 r1 **1974-1982** DNQ **1986** 11 r2 **1990** DNQ **1994** 23 r1 **1998** 18 r1 **2002-2010** DNQ

FEDERATION ROYALE MAROCAINE DE FOOTBALL (FRMF)

✉ 51 Bis Avenue Ibn Sina, Agdal, Case Postale 51, Rabat 10 000

☎ +212 37 672706
📠 +212 37 671070
📧 contact@frmf.ma
🖥 www.frmf.ma

FA 1955 CON 1966 FIFA 1960
P Ali Fassi Fihri
GS Khalid Laraichi

FIFA BIG COUNT 2006

Total players	1 628 016
% of population	4.90%
Male	1 553 748
Female	74 268
Amateurs 18+	40 010
Unregistered	165 000
Professionals	601
Referees	2 007
Admin & coaches	6 644
Number of clubs	563
Number of teams	2 815

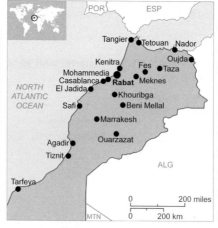

MAJOR CITIES/TOWNS

		Population
1	Casablanca	3 269 962
2	Rabat	1 787 307
3	Fes	1 024 587
4	Marrakesh	903 589
5	Tangier	746 516
6	Meknes	586 197
7	Agadir	556 324
8	Oujda	423 444
9	Kenitra	395 808
10	Tetouan	347 052
11	Safi	301 693
12	Mohammedia	201 880
13	Beni Mellal	179 565
14	Khouribga	172 775
15	El Jadida	160 791
16	Taza	150 761
17	Nador	142 349
18	Settat	129 747
19	Larache	116 051

AL MAMLAKAH AL MAGHRIBIYAH • KINGDOM OF MOROCCO

Capital	Rabat	Population 34 859 364 (35)	% in cities 56%
GDP per capita	$4500 (148)	Area km² 446 550 km² (57)	GMT +/- 0
Neighbours (km)	Algeria 1559, Western Sahara 443, Spain 16 • Coast 1835		

RECENT INTERNATIONAL MATCHES PLAYED BY MOROCCO

2007	Opponents	Score		Venue	Comp	Scorers	Att	Referee
7-02	Tunisia	D	1-1	Casablanca	Fr	Chammakh [29]		
25-03	Zimbabwe	D	1-1	Harare	CNq	Youssef Hadji [7]		Damon RSA
2-06	Zimbabwe	W	2-0	Casablanca	CNq	Chamakh [4], Youssef Hadji [26]		Daami TUN
16-06	Malawi	W	1-0	Blantyre	CNq	El Moubarki [10]		Maillet SEY
8-09	Ghana	L	0-2	Rouen	Fr			
17-10	Namibia	W	2-0	Tangiers	Fr	Alloudi [71], El Karkouri [90]		
16-11	France	D	2-2	Paris	Fr	Sektioui [8], Mokhtari [84]	78 000	Bossen NED
21-11	Senegal	W	3-0	Creteil	Fr	Aboucherouane [23], Mokhtari [64], Azmi [73]		Benoit FRA
2008								
12-01	Zambia	W	2-0	Fes	Fr	Sektioui [51p], Alloudi [60]		
16-01	Angola	W	2-1	Rabat	Fr	Chamakh [44], Aboucherouane [51]		
21-01	Namibia	W	5-1	Accra	CNr1	Alloudi 3 [2 5 28], Sektioui [39p], Zerka [74]		Evehe CMR
24-01	Guinea	L	2-3	Accra	CNr1	Aboucherouane [60], Ouaddou [89]		Damon RSA
28-01	Ghana	L	0-2	Accra	CNr1			Sowe GAM
26-03	Belgium	W	4-1	Brussels	Fr	Alloudi [14], Sektioui [34], El Zhar [85], Benjelloun [89]	24 000	Nijhuis NED
31-05	Ethiopia	W	3-0	Casablanca	WCq	Benjelloun [4], Aboucherouane [13], Kharja [85]	5 000	Diatta SEN
7-06	Mauritania	W	4-1	Nouakchott	WCq	Sektioui [9], Benjelloun [37], Safri [58], Kharja [79]	9 500	Lamptey GHA
14-06	Rwanda	L	1-3	Kigali	WCq	Safri [78]	12 000	Evehe CMR
21-06	Rwanda	W	2-0	Casablanca	WCq	Safri [12p], El Zhar [49]	2 500	Benouza ALG
20-08	Benin	W	3-1	Rabat	Fr	Kharja [21], Safri [57], Zerka [78]		
6-09	Oman	D	0-0	Muscat	Fr			
11-10	Mauritania	W	4-1	Rabat	WCq	Safri [35], Youssef Hadji 2 [55 60], Zemmama [65]	1 472	Aboubacar CIV
19-11	Zambia	W	3-0	Rabat	Fr	Kharja [3], Sektioui [24], Baha [62]		
2009								
11-02	Czech Republic	D	0-0	Casablanca	Fr		38 000	Alakim TUN
28-03	Gabon	L	1-2	Casablanca	WCq	El Hamdaoui [83]	38 000	Diatta SEN
31-03	Angola	W	2-0	Lisbon	Fr	Taarabt [9], Chamakh [51]		
7-06	Cameroon	D	0-0	Yaounde	WCq		35 000	Seechurn MRI
20-06	Togo	D	0-0	Rabat	WCq		22 000	Kaoma ZAM
12-08	Congo	D	1-1	Rabat	Fr	El Ahmadi [44]		
6-09	Togo	D	1-1	Lome	WCq	Taarabt [92+]	24 651	Ssegonga UGA
10-10	Gabon	L	1-3	Libreville	WCq	Taarabt [88]	14 000	Doue CIV
14-11	Cameroon	L	0-2	Fes	WCq		17 000	Bennett RSA
2010								
11-08	Equatorial Guinea	W	2-1	Rabat	Fr	Youssef Hadji 2 [65 79]		
4-09	Central African Rep	D	0-0	Rabat	CNq			Coulibaly MLI
9-10	Tanzania	W	1-0	Dar es Salaam	CNq	El Hamdaoui [42]		Seechurn MRI
17-11	Northern Ireland	D	1-1	Belfast	Fr	Chamakh [55]	15 000	Hagen NOR

Fr = Friendly match • CN = CAF African Cup of Nations • WC = FIFA World Cup
q = qualifier • r1 = first round group • qf = quarter-final • sf = semi-final • f = final

MOROCCO NATIONAL TEAM HISTORICAL RECORDS

Caps	**115** - Noureddine Naybet 1990-2006
Goals	**42** - Ahmed Faras 1965-79
Past Coaches	Larbi Ben Barek, Abdelkader Lohkmiri & Mohamed Kadmiri 1957-61) • Mohamed Massoun & Kader Firoud 1961-64 • Mohamed Massoun & Abderrahmane Belmahjoub 1964-67 • Cluzeau FRA & Abdellah Settati 1968-70 • Blagoja Vidinic YUG 1970-71 • Abderrahmane Belmahjoub 1971 • Jose Barinaga ESP 1972 • Abdallah El Emmani 1972-76 • Gheorghe Mardarescu ROU 1976-77 • Abdallah Ben Barek 1977 • Cluzeau FRA 1979 • Just Fontaine FRA 1979-81 • Yabram Hamidouch 1981 • Jose Faria BRA 1983-88 • Jaime Valente BRA 1988-89 • Antonio Angelillo ARG 1989-90 • Werner Olk GER 1990-92 • Abdelkhalek Louzani 1992 • Abdellah Ajri Blinda 1993-94 • Mohammed Lamari 1994 • Gilson Nunez BRA 1995 • Henri Michel FRA 1995-2000 • Henryk Kasperczak POL 2000 • Mustapha Madih 2001 • Humberto Coelho POR 2002 • Badou Zaki 2002-05 • Philippe Troussier FRA 2005 • Mohamed Fakhir 2005-07 • Henri Michel FRA 2007-08 • Roger Lemerre FRA 2008-09 • Hassan Moumen 2009-10 • Eric Gerets BEL 2010-

MOROCCO 2009–10

CHAMPIONNAT DU GNF1

	Pl	W	D	L	F	A	Pts	WAC	RCA	DHJ	KACM	OCK	HUS	FAR	MAS	KAC	MAT	WAF	FUS	JSM	OCS	IZK	ASS
Wydad Casablanca †	30	15	9	6	36	22	54		0-1	1-2	2-0	1-0	1-0	1-0	1-0	2-2	2-1	3-1	1-0	3-1	1-0	2-1	0-1
Raja Casablanca †	30	14	10	6	39	26	52	1-1		1-1	1-2	2-2	2-1	1-0	2-0	2-0	1-1	1-0	3-2	3-2	3-2	1-1	1-1
Diffa El Jadida ‡	30	12	14	4	30	17	50	0-0	1-2		1-1	0-0	0-0	2-0	1-0	0-1	0-0	4-2	2-0	1-1	2-0	1-0	0-0
Kawkab Marrakech	30	10	14	6	27	19	44	0-2	1-2	1-1		1-0	3-1	1-0	0-0	3-1	1-0	2-0	0-0	0-0	2-0	0-0	3-0
Olympique Khouribga	30	11	10	9	30	26	43	0-0	2-1	0-1	2-1		0-1	2-1	2-1	0-2	1-0	3-0	0-1	2-1	4-2	0-0	
HUS Agadir	30	10	11	9	33	31	41	1-1	0-0	2-1	2-1	2-1		1-1	1-1	2-0	0-1	3-1	0-1	3-1	0-0	2-0	1-1
FAR Rabat	30	10	10	10	21	20	40	1-0	1-0	0-1	0-0	0-1	1-0		1-3	1-1	0-0	3-1	1-0	0-0	4-1	2-1	1-0
Maghreb Fès ‡	30	9	12	9	29	26	39	2-2	1-0	2-3	1-1	0-0	4-1	0-0		1-0	1-0	1-2	1-0	0-1	0-0	2-0	1-0
Kénitra AC	30	10	8	12	28	30	38	0-1	0-3	0-0	1-1	1-0	1-0	0-0	2-2		0-1	2-1	2-1	2-0	0-1	1-0	5-0
MA Tétouan	30	7	15	8	18	18	36	1-0	0-0	0-0	0-0	1-1	1-1	0-0	0-0	2-0		2-0	2-0	1-0	0-1	0-0	1-3
Wydad Fès	30	9	9	12	33	41	36	0-0	1-1	0-0	0-0	2-2	1-3	1-0	1-1	1-1	0-0		3-1	0-0	3-2	1-0	3-0
FUS Rabat ‡	30	9	9	12	24	30	36	2-3	1-0	0-1	0-0	1-1	2-2	0-1	1-0	2-1	1-1	0-2		3-1	1-0	1-0	1-0
JS Massira	30	8	10	12	26	33	34	1-3	1-0	0-2	1-0	2-1	3-1	2-0	1-1	1-0	1-1	1-2	0-0		2-0	0-1	1-1
Olympique Safi	30	8	9	13	29	37	33	1-1	0-2	2-1	0-1	1-2	1-1	0-0	1-0	0-1	0-1	2-3	1-1	1-1		1-0	2-0
IZ Khemisset	30	7	12	11	15	22	33	1-0	0-1	1-1	1-1	0-0	0-0	0-0	2-1	1-1	1-0	0-2	0-0	1-0	1-1		1-0
AS Salé	30	4	12	14	15	35	24	1-1	1-1	0-0	0-0	0-1	0-1	0-2	0-1	1-0	1-1	2-1	1-1	0-0	1-3	0-1	

28/08/2009 - 16/05/2010 • † Qualified for the CAF Champions League • ‡ Qualified for the CAF Confederation Cup

MOROCCO 2009–10
CHAMPIONNAT DU GNF2

	Pl	W	D	L	F	A	Pts
Chabab Kasba Tadla	36	18	11	7	34	23	65
CR Hoceima	36	17	10	9	31	26	61
US Mohammedia	36	15	13	8	38	25	58
COD Meknès	36	14	16	6	38	26	58
TUS Temara	36	14	14	8	39	35	56
Chabab Houara	36	13	14	9	39	28	53
Stade Marocain	36	13	13	10	36	33	52
Racing Casablanca	36	14	10	12	36	36	52
Raja Al Hoceima	36	12	12	12	37	36	48
CAY Berrechid	36	11	10	15	39	35	43
Mouloudia Oujda	36	11	10	15	30	34	43
TAS Casablanca	36	9	15	12	28	26	42
Rachad Bernoussi	36	11	9	16	26	37	42
IR Tanger	36	10	12	14	28	33	42
IR Fkih Ben Salah	36	10	11	15	29	36	41
Chabab Mohammedia §1	36	10	12	14	29	36	41
RS Settat	36	7	17	12	29	40	38
US Sidi Kacem	36	8	12	16	33	37	36
CA Khenifra §4	36	11	7	18	31	46	36

28/08/2009 - 6/06/2010 • § = points deducted

MEDALS TABLE

			Overall			League			Cup		Africa		
			G	S	B	G	S	B	G	S	G	S	B
1	Wydad Casablanca	WAC	23	14	9	12	7	7	9	6	2	1	2
2	FAR Rabat	FAR	25	11	7	12	5	5	11	4	2	2	2
3	Raja Casablanca	RCA	19	12	10	9	7	9	6	4	4	1	1
4	Kawkab Marrakech	KACM	9	8	3	2	6	3	6	2	1		
5	Maghreb Fès	MAS	6	10	2	4	2	2	2	8			
6	FUS Rabat	FUS	6	4	1		2	1	5	2	1		
7	KAC Kénitra	KAC	5	5	1	4	2	1	1	3			
8	Mouloudia Oujda	MCO	5	2	3	1	1	3	4	1			
9	Olympic Casablanca	OC	3	1		1	1		2				
10	Olympique Khouribga	OCK	2	6	3	1	2	3	1	4			
11	Rennaisance Settat	RSS	2	5	3	1	2	3	1	3			
12	Chabab Mohammedia	SCCM	2	2	1	1			1	1	2		
13	Hassania Agadir	HUSA	2	2		2				2			
14	COD Meknès	CODM	2	1	1	1			1	1	1		
15	Racing Casablanca	RAC	1	2					2		1		

COUPE DU TRONE 2010

Round of 16		Quarter-finals		Semi-finals		Final	
FUS Rabat *	2						
Olympique Khouribga	1	FUS Rabat	0 5p				
Raja Casablanca *	1 3p	Chabab Mohammedia*	0 3p				
Chabab Mohammedia	1 4p			FUS Rabat	1		
Olympique Safi	2 5p			Diffa El Jadida	0		
CAY Berrechid *	2 4p	Olympique Safi *	0				
AS Salé	0 4p	Diffa El Jadida	1				
Diffa El Jadida *	0 5p					FUS Rabat ‡	2
Kénitra AC *	0 4p					Maghreb Fès ‡	1
COD Meknès	0 2p	Kénitra AC *	0 5p				
Mouloudia Oujda *	0	MA Tétouan	0 4p				
MA Tétouan	1			Kénitra AC	1 2p		
Stade Marocain	2			Maghreb Fès	1 3p		
HUS Agadir *	0	Stade Marocain	0				
FAR Rabat	1 6p	Maghreb Fès *	1				
Maghreb Fès *	1 7p			Semis played in Casablanca			

* Home team • ‡ Qualified for the CAF Confederation Cup

CUP FINAL

Moulay Abdallah, Rabat
25-11-2010. Ref: Yara
Scorers - Issoufou Dante [35], Hicham El Fatihi [50] for FUS; Idriss Belamri [58] for MAS

MAS – MALAYSIA

FIFA/COCA-COLA WORLD RANKING

1993	1994	1995	1996	1997	1998	1999	2000	2001	2002	2003	2004	2005	2006	2007	2008	2009	2010
79	89	106	96	87	113	117	107	111	128	116	120	123	152	159	156	160	144

2010												Hi/Lo
Jan	Feb	Mar	Mar	Apr	May	Jul	Aug	Sep	Oct	Nov	Dec	75
160	159	146	147	147	146	142	139	144	149	150	144	170

Malaysian football enjoyed one its finest moments at the end of 2010 when the national team were crowned Southeast Asian champions for the first time after winning the AFF Suzuki Cup final 4-2 on aggregate against Indonesia. The Malaysians had not appeared in the final of the biennial event since the inaugural competition in 1996 but led by former Selangor coach K Rajagobal, a young squad overcame the odds to pick up the title to add to the country's gold medal-winning performance at the Southeast Asian Games a year earlier. Victory over the Indonesians saw the Tigers avenge a 5-1 defeat in the opening game of the tournament at the Gelora Bung Karno Stadium in Jakarta, and the turn around in fortunes after that had much to do with striker Safee Sali who finished the tournament as topscorer with five goals. He scored twice against defending champions Vietnam in the semi-final and scored two more in a crucial 3-0 first leg victory in the final before 70,000 ecstatic fans in Kula Lumpur's National Stadium. Safee Sali was also part of the Selangor team which won the Malaysian Super League to become national champions for a record sixth time. The season's other trophies were won by Kelantan who won the prestigious Malaysia Cup for the first time and by Negeri Sembilan who beat Kedah on penalties in the FA Cup Final.

FIFA WORLD CUP RECORD
1930-1970 DNE 1974-2010 DNQ

FOOTBALL ASSOCIATION OF MALAYSIA (FAM)

3rd Floor Wisma FAM, Jalan
SS5A/9, Kelana Jaya,
Petaling Jaya 47301

☎ +60 3 78733100

🖷 +60 3 78757984

✉ gensec@fam.org.my

🖳 www.fam.org.my

FA 1933 CON 1954 FIFA 1956
P HRH Sultan Ahmad Shah
GS Azzuddin Bin Ahmad

FIFA BIG COUNT 2006

Total players	585 730
% of population	2.40%
Male	549 300
Female	36 430
Amateurs 18+	1 430
Youth under 18	7 300
Unregistered	259 800
Professionals	600
Referees	1 810
Admin & coaches	10 000
Number of clubs	11-
Number of teams	550

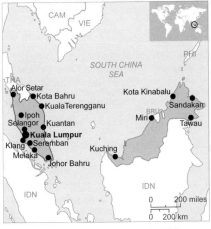

MAJOR CITIES/TOWNS
		Population
1	Kuala Lumpur	1 468 984
2	Subang Jaya	1 321 672
3	Klang	1 055 207
4	Johor Bahru	895 509
5	Ampang Jaya	756 309
6	Ipoh	702 464
7	Kuching	658 562
8	Shah Alam	617 149
9	Kota Kinabalu	579 304
10	Petaling Jaya	543 415
11	Batu Sembilan	515 961
12	Sandakan	479 121
13	Kajang-Sungai	428 131
14	Seremban	419 536
15	Kuantan	407 778
17	Kuala Terengganu	286 433
18	Kota Bahru	277 301
20	Selangor	265 297
25	Alor Setar	213 624

MALAYSIA

Capital	Kuala Lumpur	Population	25 715 819 (46)	% in cities	70%
GDP per capita	$15 200 (75)	Area km²	329 847 km² (66)	GMT +/-	+8
Neighbours (km)	Brunei 381, Indonesia 1782, Thailand 506 • Coast 4675				

RECENT INTERNATIONAL MATCHES PLAYED BY MALAYSIA

2007	Opponents	Score		Venue	Comp	Scorers	Att	Referee
10-07	China PR	L	1-5	Kuala Lumpur	ACr1	Indra Putra [72]	20 000	Basma SYR
14-07	Uzbekistan	L	0-5	Kuala Lumpur	ACr1		7 137	Abdou QAT
18-07	Iran	L	0-2	Kuala Lumpur	ACr1		4 520	Basma SYR
21-10	Bahrain	L	1-4	Manama	WCq	Bunyamin Umar [45]	4 000	Yang Zhiqiang CHN
28-10	Bahrain	D	0-0	Kuala Lumpur	WCq		2 000	Lee Gi Young KOR
2008								
6-06	Indonesia	D	1-1	Surabaya	Fr	Adan [34]		
22-07	India	D	1-1	Hyderabad	Fr	Indra Putra [75]		
10-10	Pakistan	W	4-1	Kuala Lumpur	Fr	Safee Sali [42], Zaquan Abd Radzak [60], Hairuddin Omar [70], Muhymeen [81]		
15-10	Nepal	W	4-0	Petaling Jaya	Fr	Indra Putra [20], Safee Sali 2 [25 48], Muhymeen [52]	1 000	Junji Huang CHN
20-10	Afghanistan	W	6-0	Petaling Jaya	Fr	Ashaari Shamsuddin 2 [21 64], Nizaruddin Yusof [41], Zaquan Abd Radzak [44], Safee Sali [85], Hairuddin [87]	3 000	
23-10	Myanmar	W	4-0	Kuala Lumpur	Fr	Indra Putra 2 [26 76p], Safee Sali [61], Amirul Hadi [83]	20 000	Mahapab THA
18-11	Myanmar	L	1-4	Yangon	Fr	Amirul Hadi [75]	30 000	
29-11	Singapore	D	2-2	Petaling Jaya	Fr	Amirul Hadi [22], Hardi Jaafar [74]		
6-12	Laos	W	3-0	Phuket	AFFr1	Safee Sali 2 [68 87], Indra Putra [73]	5 000	Nitrorejo IDN
8-12	Vietnam	L	2-3	Phuket	AFFr1	Indra Putra 2 [20 85]		Palaniyandi SIN
10-12	Thailand	L	0-3	Phuket	AFFr1		15 000	Abdul Bashir SIN
2009								
21-01	UAE	L	0-5	Kuala Lumpur	ACq		10 000	Williams AUS
12-08	Kenya	D	0-0	Kuala Lumpur	Fr			
15-08	China PR	D	0-0	Kuala Lumpur	Fr			
30-08	Saudi Arabia	L	1-2	Riyadh	Fr	Shakir [85]		
5-09	Jordan	D	0-0	Amman	Fr			
11-09	Lesotho	W	5-0	Kuala Lumpur	Fr	Zaquan Abd Razak [41], Norshahrul Talaha [44], Manaf 2 [78 90], Amirul Hadi [88]		
14-11	Uzbekistan	L	1-3	Tashkent	ACq	Zaquan Abd Razak [68]	5 000	Moradi IRN
18-11	Uzbekistan	L	1-3	Kuala Lumpur	ACq	Baddrol Bin Bakhtiar [70]	2 000	Tan Hai CHN
2010								
6-01	UAE	L	0-1	Dubai	ACq		3 500	Basma SYR
27-02	Yemen	W	1-0	Kuala Lumpur	Fr	Baddrol Bin Bakhtiar [55]		
3-09	Oman	L	0-3	Doha	Fr			
1-12	Indonesia	L	1-5	Jakarta	AFFr1	Norshahrul Talaha [18]	62 000	Vo Min Tri VIE
4-12	Thailand	D	0-0	Jakarta	AFFr1			Win Cho MYA
7-12	Laos	W	5-1	Palembang	AFFr1	Amri Yahyah 2 [4 40], Mohd Zainal [73], Norshahrul Talaha [77], Mahalli Jasuli [90]		Vo Min Tri VIE
15-12	Vietnam	W	2-0	Kuala Lumpur	AFFsf	Safee Sali 2 [60 79]	45 000	Sun Baojie CHN
18-12	Vietnam	D	0-0	Hanoi	AFFsf		40 000	Kim Sang Woo KOR
26-12	Indonesia	W	3-0	Kuala Lumpur	AFFf	Safee Sali 2 [61 73], Ashaari Shamsuddin [68]	70 000	Toma JPN
29-12	Indonesia	L	1-2	Jakarta	AFFf		80 000	Green AUS

Fr = Friendly match • AFF = ASEAN Football Federation Championship • AC = AFC Asian Cup • WC = FIFA World Cup
q = qualifier • r1 = first round group • sf = semi-final • 3p = third place play-off • † not a full international

MALAYSIA NATIONAL TEAM HISTORICAL RECORDS

Past Coaches

Neoh Boon Hean • Edwin Dutton • Choo Seng Quee SIN • Otto Westphal GER • C. De Silva • Peter Velappan • Abdul Ghani Minhat 1969 • Harold Hassall ENG • Dave McLaren AUS 1970-71 • Jalil Che Din 1972 • M. Kuppan 1973-77 • Jalil Che Din 1974 • Chow Kwai Lam 1978 • Karl-Heinz Weigang GER 1979-82 • M. Chandran 1982-83 • Frank Lord ENG 1983-85 • Mohamad Bakar 1985-86 • Jozef Venglos CZE 1986-87 • Abdul Rahman Ibrahim 1987 • Richard Bate ENG 1988 • M. Chandran 1988 • Trevor Hartley ENG 1989 • Ahmad Shafie 1990 • Rahim Abdullah 1991 • Ken Worden AUS 1992-93 • Claude Le Roy FRA 1994-95 • Hatem Souisi TUN 1995 • Wan Jamak Wan Hassan 1996-97 • Hatem Souisi 1998 • Abdul Rahman Ibrahim 1998-2000 • Allan Harris 2001-04 • K. Rajagopal1 2004 • Bertalan Bicskei HUN 2004-05 • Norizan Bakar 2005-07 • B. Sathianathan 2007-09 • K. Rajagopal 2009-

MALAYSIA 2010

MALAYSIAN SUPER LEAGUE (MSL)

	Pl	W	D	L	F	A	Pts	Selangor	Kelantan	Terengganu	Johor FC	Kedah	Negeri	PBDKT	Pahang	KLFA	KL Plus	Perak	Perlis	Johor FA	Penang
Selangor FA	26	20	3	3	62	23	63	–	1-1	2-0	4-1	4-0	4-2	3-0	4-0	4-1	2-1	4-1	2-0	6-0	3-0
Kelantan FA	26	17	8	1	50	14	59	0-0	–	3-0	4-1	0-1	1-0	0-0	2-1	3-0	4-1	2-0	2-1	3-0	3-1
Terengganu FA	26	16	5	5	54	24	53	4-0	0-0	–	**0-3**	1-1	1-1	1-0	2-0	2-0	1-0	2-0	4-0	2-0	4-0
Johor FC	26	12	4	10	41	33	40	1-3	1-3	2-0	–	1-2	1-1	2-2	2-1	0-1	1-0	1-0	2-1	3-0	5-0
Kedah FA	26	10	8	8	34	23	38	2-0	0-0	4-0	0-1	–	0-1	3-1	3-0	0-0	2-3	1-1	0-1	1-0	0-0
Negeri Sembilan FA	26	11	5	10	40	31	38	1-2	1-3	2-1	2-1	2-1	–	0-1	5-0	1-2	2-1	0-0	3-2	3-1	4-0
PBDKT T-Team FC	26	10	8	8	33	26	38	1-2	0-1	1-1	1-0	2-2	2-1	–	1-1	1-0	0-0	1-1	1-0	5-0	1-0
Pahang FA	26	10	3	13	31	50	33	2-3	3-3	0-5	3-0	2-1	2-1	2-1	–	1-0	2-1	2-1	3-2	0-1	2-0
Kuala Lumpur FA	26	8	8	10	20	29	32	2-4	0-2	1-1	0-0	0-2	0-0	1-1	1-1	–	0-2	2-1	1-1	2-1	2-0
KL Plus FC	26	8	6	12	25	30	30	1-0	0-0	1-3	0-3	1-0	2-1	3-0	2-0	0-1	–	0-1	1-1	2-0	4-0
Perak FA	26	8	6	12	25	30	30	1-0	0-3	0-1	1-1	1-1	1-1	1-0	1-2	0-0	0-1	–	1-2	4-0	3-1
Perlis FA	26	8	5	13	32	35	29	1-1	0-0	2-4	0-1	1-1	2-0	0-1	4-0	0-2	0-1	3-0	–	4-2	2-0
Johor FA	26	5	1	20	18	66	16	1-2	1-4	3-6	0-5	0-3	0-2	0-3	2-0	0-1	1-0	0-2	3-2	–	1-0
Penang FA	26	2	4	20	10	67	10	0-1	1-3	1-5	0-5	0-3	0-3	1-6	2-1	1-0	0-4	1-1	0-0	1-1	–

9/01/2010 - 3/08/2010 • Match in bold awarded

Top scorers: **18** - Ashaari Shamsuddin, Terengganu • **12** - Safee Sali, Selangor & Amirul Zainal, Selangor • **11** - Norshahrul Talaha, Kelantan

MALAYSIA 2010 PREMIER LEAGUE (2)

	Pl	W	D	L	F	A	Pts
Felda United FC	22	15	5	2	48	12	50
Sabah FA	22	15	3	4	42	14	48
PKNS FC	22	14	3	5	56	18	45
ATM FA	22	11	9	2	49	18	42
Harimau Muda	22	11	4	7	49	39	37
Sarawak FA	22	11	4	7	42	34	37
PDRM FA	22	8	4	10	37	41	28
Pos Malaysia FC	22	7	3	12	41	43	24
USM FC	22	6	5	11	28	40	23
Muar Mun'pal Council	22	5	3	14	19	68	18
Melaka FA	22	4	3	15	31	68	15
Shahzan Muda	22	1	2	19	15	62	5

11/01/2010 - 23/07/2010 • Harimau Muda is the national U-20 development team and is ineligible for promotion

MEDALS TABLE

		Overall			League			MCup		FAC		Asia		
		G	S	B	G	S	B	G	S	G	S	G	S	B
1	Selangor FA	43	20		6	2		32	15	5	2			1
2	FA of Singapore	26	19		2			24	19					
3	Perak FA	11	15	3	2	1	3	7	11	2	3			
4	Kedah FA	10	10	1	3	3	1	4	6	3	1			
5	Penang FA	8	13		3	2		4	9	1	2			
6	Pahang FA	8	7		5	2		2	4	1	1			
7	Kuala Lumpur FA	8	2		2			3	1	3	1			
8	Negeri Sembilan FA	5	4	3	1	1	3	2	3	2				
9	Johor FA	4	1		1			2	1	1				
10	Perlis FA	3	5	2	1	1	2	2	1					3
11	Terengganu FA	2	7	1		2	1	1	3	1	2			
12	Sabah FA	2	6	2			1	2		3	1			3
13	Sarawak FA	2	3	1	1			1		1	1			2
14	Kelantan FA	1	5	1		1	1	1	3	1				
15	Brunei D'salam	1	1					1	1					
16	Melaka FA	1			1									
	Selangor MPPJ	1						1						
18	ATM FA (Army)		2								2			

MALAYSIA CUP 2010

First Round Groups (Pts)

	Pts
Negeri Sembilan FA	14
Kelantan FA	11
PKNS FC	6
KL Plus FC	2
Terengganu FA	10
Pahang FA	10
Sabah FA	9
Kuala Lumpur FA	4
Johor FC	12
Kedah FA	9
Perak FA	7
ATM FA	3
Selangor FA	18
Perlis FA	9
PBDKT T-Team FC	7
Felda United FC	1

Quarter-finals

- **Kelantan FA**
- Selangor FA *
- Terengganu FA *
- **Kedah FA**
- **Johor FC** *
- Pahang FA
- Perlis FA
- **Negeri Sembilan FA** *

Semi-finals

Kelantan FA	0	1
Kedah FA *	0	0
Johor FC	1	0
Negeri Sembilan FA *	0	2

Final

Kelantan FA	2
Negeri Sembilan FA	1

CUP FINAL
National, Bukit Jalil, Kuala Lumpur
30-10-2010
Scorers - Hairuddin Omar 57, Badri Radzi 65 for Kelantan; Shahruaian Abu Saman 13p for Negeri

* Home team in the first leg

MALAYSIA FA CUP 2010

First Round

Team	Leg 1	Leg 2
Negeri Sembilan FA	2	5
Johor FC *	2	3
Melodi Jaya SC	1	1
PDRM FA *	5	1
Kuala Lumpur FA *	3	0
Johor FA	1	0
Harimau Muda	2	1
KL Plus FC *	1	3
Pos Malaysia FC	1	1
Muar Municipal Council *	0	5
Pahang FA *	1	1
Felda United FC	1	3
PKNS FC	2	1
SDM Kepala Batas FC *	0	0
Selangor FA	Bye	
Terengganu FA	4	3
USM FC *	1	0
Penang FA *	2	0
Sarawak FA	1	1
Perak FA	0	2
Perlis *	0	1
Shahzan Muda FC	0	0
PBDKT T-Team FC *	1	3
ATM FA *	3	3
Melaka FA	0	1
Juara Ban Hoe Leong FC	0	0
UiTM FC *	3	3
Kelantan FA	Bye	
Sabah FA *	0	0
Kedah FA	2	1

Round of 16

Team	Leg 1	Leg 2
Negeri Sembilan FA	3	5
PDRM FA *	2	0
Kuala Lumpur FA	0	1
KL Plus FC *	3	1
Pos Malaysia FC	1	2
Felda United FC *	1	1
PKNS FC	0	1
Selangor FA *	2	0
Terengganu FA	2	2
Sarawak FA *	0	1
Perak FA	1	0
PBDKT T-Team FC *	1	2
ATM FA *	3	3
UiTM FC	0	0
Kelantan FA	0	1
Kedah FA *	0	1

Quarter-finals

Team	Leg 1	Leg 2
Negeri Sembilan FA	0	3
KL Plus FC *	1	1
Pos Malaysia FC	1	0
Selangor FA *	5	3
Terengganu FA	1	4
PBDKT T-Team FC *	3	1
ATM FA *	1	0
Kedah FA	1	5

Semi-finals

Team	Leg 1	Leg 2
Negeri Sembilan FA	2	0
Selangor FA *	1	1
Terengganu FA *	0	1
Kedah FA	2	2

Final

Team	Score	
Negeri Sembilan FA	1	5p
Kedah FA	1	4p

PENALTIES

NS	Ked
✗ Zaquan Adha	
	Shahrulnizam ✓
✓ Norizam Salaman	
	Badrol Bakhtiar ✓
✓ Aidil Zafuan	
	Fadzliata Taib ✗
✓ S. Kunalan	
	Azmi Muslim ✓
✓ Shukor Adan	
	M.Aminuddin ✓
✗ Asyraf Japri	
	Helmi Eliza ✗
✓ Rezal Zambery	
	Sabre Abu ✗

CUP FINAL

National Stadium, Bukit Jalil, Kuala Lumpur
10-04-2010, 20:45. Att: 70 000. Ref: Krishnan
Scorers - Shafik Rahman 38 for Negeri;
Badrol Bakhtiar 26 for Kedah
Negeri - Sani Anuar - Aidil Zafuan, Shukor
Adan, Rahman Zabul, C.H.Aik, S. Kunalan,
Shafik Rahman (Asyraf Japri), K. Thanaraj
(Firdaus Azizul), Idris Karim (Norizam
Salaman), Rezal Zambery (c), Zaquan Adha.
Tr: Wan Jamak Wan Hassan
Kedah - Helmi Eliza - Khairul Helmi, Fadzliata
Taib, Azmi Muslim, V. Thirumurugan,
Shahrulnizam Mustapa (c). Sabre Abu, Badrol
Bakhtiar, Fadly Baharom (Khyril Muhymeen),
Syafiq Jamal (Wan Zaim), Faizal Abu
(M.Aminuddin). Tr: Ahmad Yusof

* Home team/home team in the first leg

MDA – MOLDOVA

FIFA/COCA-COLA WORLD RANKING

1993	1994	1995	1996	1997	1998	1999	2000	2001	2002	2003	2004	2005	2006	2007	2008	2009	2010
-	118	109	117	131	116	93	94	103	111	106	114	107	86	52	97	94	84

					2010								Hi/Lo
	Jan	Feb	Mar	Mar	Apr	May	Jul	Aug	Sep	Oct	Nov	Dec	37
	94	96	100	87	84	89	89	89	80	78	84	84	149

It is said that ten years is a long time in football but it must seem like an eternity for most fans in Moldova because for the tenth consecutive season Sheriff Tiraspol claimed the league title. Only once in those ten years has the title race been a close one - the first in 2001 - and again they strolled over the winning line with plenty to spare despite a change of coach mid-way through the season. Having joined in 2004, Leonid Kuchuk took Sheriff to six of those ten titles, but he left to try his luck in Russian football and was replaced by his assistant Andrei Sosnitskiy. Sheriff were not as impressive in the cup but they still managed to retain the trophy for the third year running despite scraping through in the quarter and semi-finals. In the final they beat Dacia 2-0 with both goals coming from their Brazilian striker Jymmy. In European competition, Sheriff fell at the final hurdle before the Champions League group stage for the second year running, losing in the play-off round of the 2010-11 competition to FC Basel. New national team coach Gavril Balint saw his team get their Euro 2010 qualifying campaign off to a good start with a 2-0 victory over Finland - Moldova's first competitive win in just under three years - with the Romanian targeting a runners-up spot in a group likely to be dominated by The Netherlands and Sweden.

FIFA WORLD CUP RECORD
1930-1994 DNE 1998-2010 DNQ

FOOTBALL ASSOCIATION OF MOLDOVA (FMF)

Federatia Moldoveneasca de Fotbal, Str. Tricolorului nr. 39, Chisinau MD-2012

☎ +373 22 210413
📠 +373 22 210432
✉ fmf@fmf.md
🖥 www.fmf.md
FA 1990 CON 1992 FIFA 1994
P Pavel Cebanu
GS Nicolai Cebotari

FIFA BIG COUNT 2006

Total players	168 570
% of population	3.77%
Male	147 430
Female	21 140
Amateurs 18+	6 629
Youth under 18	2 603
Unregistered	66 150
Professionals	543
Referees	151
Admin & coaches	560
Number of clubs	86
Number of teams	2 036

MAJOR CITIES/TOWNS

		Population
1	Chisinau	586 151
2	Tiraspol	143 977
3	Balti	100 176
4	Tighina	98 001
5	Ribnita	50 345
6	Ungheni	31 344
7	Cahul	30 487
8	Soroca	23 484
9	Edinet	21 944
10	Orhei	21 878
11	Comrat	20 750
12	Causeni	20 433
13	Dubasari	20 199
14	Ocnita	18 556
15	Ciadir Lunga	17 523
16	Straseni	17 459
17	Floresti	15 324
18	Ialoveni	14 311
36	Otaci	8 400

REPUBLICA MOLDOVA • REPUBLIC OF MOLDOVA

Capital Chisinau	Population 4 320 748 (122)	% in cities 42%
GDP per capita $2500 (172)	Area km² 33 851 km² (139)	GMT + / - +2
Neighbours (km) Romania 450, Ukraine 940		

RECENT INTERNATIONAL MATCHES PLAYED BY MOLDOVA

2007	Opponents	Score		Venue	Comp	Scorers	Att	Referee
7-02	Romania	L	0-2	Bucharest	Fr		8 000	Deaconu ROU
24-03	Malta	D	1-1	Chisinau	ECq	Epureanu [85]	8 033	Aliyev AZE
28-03	Hungary	L	0-2	Budapest	ECq		6 150	Ingvarsson SWE
6-06	Greece	L	1-2	Irákleio	ECq	Frunza [80]	22 000	Wegereef NED
22-08	Latvia	W	2-1	Riga	Fr	Frunza [23], Bordian [53]	4 500	Shandor UKR
8-09	Norway	L	0-1	Chisinau	ECq		10 173	Malek POL
12-09	Bosnia-Herzegovina	W	1-0	Sarajevo	ECq	Bugaev [22]	2 000	Hyytiä FIN
13-10	Turkey	D	1-1	Chisinau	ECq	Frunza [11]	9 815	Atkinson ENG
17-10	Malta	W	3-2	Ta'Qali	ECq	Bugaev [24p], Frunza 2 [31 35]	7 069	Ischenko UKR
17-11	Hungary	W	3-0	Chisinau	ECq	Bugaev 13, Josan 23, Alexeev [86]	6 483	Královec CZE
2008								
6-02	Kazakhstan	W	1-0	Antalya	Fr	Bugaev [13]	300	Lehner AUT
24-05	Croatia	L	0-1	Rijeka	Fr		7 000	Ceferin SVN
28-05	Armenia	D	2-2	Tiraspol	Fr	Arakelyan OG [42], Alexeev [74]	3 653	Ischenko UKR
20-08	Lithuania	L	0-3	Vilnius	Fr		2 000	Kaasik EST
6-09	Latvia	L	1-2	Tiraspol	WCq	Alexeev [76]	4 300	Courtney NIR
10-09	Israel	L	1-2	Chisinau	WCq	Picusciac [1]	10 500	Muniz ESP
11-10	Greece	L	0-3	Piraeus	WCq		13 684	Berntsen NOR
15-10	Luxembourg	D	0-0	Luxembourg	WCq		2 157	Borski POL
18-11	Estonia	L	0-1	Tallinn	Fr		1 500	Larsen DEN
19-11	Lithuania	D	1-1	Tallinn	Fr	Bugalov [65]	100	Tohver EST
2009								
11-02	Macedonia FYR	D	1-1	Antalya	Fr	Andronic [60]	600	Salyi KAZ
28-03	Switzerland	L	0-2	Chisinau	WCq		10 500	McDonald SCO
1-04	Switzerland	L	0-2	Geneva	WCq		20 100	Rocchi ITA
6-06	Georgia	W	2-1	Tbilisi	Fr	Sofroni [7], Golovatenco [57]	8 000	Salyi KAZ
10-06	Belarus	D	2-2	Borisov	Fr	Calincov [77], Andronic [82]	2 000	Mazeika LTU
12-08	Armenia	W	4-1	Yerevan	Fr	Golovatenco 2 [34 64], Andronic [82], Epureanu [90p]	1 000	Silagava GEO
5-09	Luxembourg	D	0-0	Chisinau	WCq		7 820	Mazeika LTU
9-09	Greece	D	1-1	Chisinau	WCq	Andronic [90]	9 870	Stalhammar SWE
10-10	Israel	L	1-3	Ramat Gan	WCq	Calincov [92+]	8 700	Blom NED
14-10	Latvia	L	2-3	Riga	WCq	Ovseannicov [25], Sofroni [90]	3 800	Hyytia FIN
2010								
3-03	Kazakhstan	W	1-0	Antalya	Fr	Epureanu [65]	500	Bezborodov RUS
26-05	Azerbaijan	D	1-1	Seekirchen	Fr	Cojocari [81]	200	Lechner AUT
29-05	UAE	L	2-3	Anif	Fr	Tigirlas [14], Bulgaru [80]	200	Schorgenhofer AUT
11-08	Georgia	D	0-0	Chisinau	Fr		3 000	Shvestov UKR
3-09	Finland	W	2-0	Chisinau	ECq	Suvorov [69], Doros [74]	10 300	Malek POL
7-09	Hungary	L	1-2	Budapest	ECq	Suvorov [79]	9 209	Kovarik CZE
8-10	Netherlands	L	0-1	Chisinau	ECq		10 500	Meyer GER
12-10	San Marino	W	2-0	Serravalle	ECq	Josan [20], Doros [86p]	714	Courtney NIR

Fr = Friendly match • EC = UEFA EURO 2008/2012 • WC = FIFA World Cup • q = qualifier

MOLDOVA NATIONAL TEAM HISTORICAL RECORDS

Caps
74 - Radu Rebeja 1991-2008 • 69 - Serghei Clescenco 1991-2006 • 55 - Valeriu Catinsus 1999-2009 • 53 - Ion Testemitanu 1991-2007 • 52 - Serghei Rogaciov 1996-2007 • 46 - Serghei Epureanu 1996-2006 & Serghei Stroenco 1992-2007

Goals
11 - Serghei Clescenco 1991-2006 • 9 - Serghei Rogaciov 1996-2007 • 8 - Iurie Miterev 1992-2006 • 7 - Serghei Dadu • 6 - Viorel Frunza 2002-08 • 5 - Igor Bugaiov 2007- • Ion Testemitanu 1991-2007

Past Coaches
Ion Caras 1991-92 • Eugen Piunovschi 1992 • Ion Caras 1992-97 • Ivan Daniliant 1998-99 • Alexandru Matiura 1999-2001, Alexandra Spiridon 2001 • Viktor Pasulko UKR 2002-06 • Anatol Teslev 2006-07 • Igor Dobrovolski RUS 2007-09 • Gavril Balint Rou 2010-

MOLDOVA 2009-10

DIVIZIA NATIONALA

	Pl	W	D	L	F	A	Pts	Sheriff	Iskra-Stal	Olimpia	Zimbru	Dacia	CSCA Rapid	Academia	Viitorul	Tiraspol	Dinamo	Sfintul	Nistru
Sheriff Tiraspol †	33	27	3	3	75	8	84		5-0 3-0	2-0 1-0	3-0	0-0	1-0 3-1	1-0	3-0 3-1	2-0	5-0 3-0	2-0	5-0 4-0
Iskra-Stal Rîbnita ‡	33	19	8	6	50	25	65	0-1		1-1	1-1 0-0 3-1	0-0	5-0	2-0 1-0	1-0	1-0 3-0	2-0	1-0 5-0 2-1	3-0
Olimpia Balti ‡	33	17	9	7	45	23	60	1-0	0-1 2-1		0-0 1-0	0-1	0-2	2-2 1-0	1-0	1-0 1-0	3-1	4-2 2-0 3-0	3-0
Zimbru Chisinau	33	17	8	8	47	29	59	1-0 0-1	3-1	1-4		2-1 1-0 0-1 1-1	4-1	1-1 1-0	1-1	3-1 2-0	2-1	4-1 2-1	
Dacia Chisinau ‡	33	16	10	7	54	30	58	1-2 0-0	1-2	1-1 2-4	1-0		4-0 2-2	1-0	2-0 2-1	1-0	3-2 0-0	1-0	1-1 3-0
CSCA Rapid Ghidighici	33	12	9	12	40	39	45	0-6	0-2 0-0 0-0 0-0	0-1	0-2		4-1 0-1	1-0	1-2 4-1	2-1	1-1 2-0	1-0	6-0
Academia Chisinau	33	11	9	13	36	37	42	0-0 0-1	1-1	2-1	2-2 0-2 1-1 3-1	0-1		0-2 3-0	1-1	1-1 1-0	3-0		1-0
Viitorul Orhei	33	10	6	17	32	45	36	0-3	0-3 1-3 0-1 2-0	0-3		1-5	2-2 1-0	2-0		1-0 0-0	3-2	1-0 3-3	0-0
FC Tiraspol	33	8	10	15	20	34	34	1-0 0-2	0-0		0-1	1-0 0-2 0-3 0-2	0-0	1-1 0-0	0-0		4-1 2-0	2-0	1-0
Dinamo Bender	33	9	5	19	36	66	32	0-5	2-1 1-1 1-1 0-0	3-1		2-3	2-1 0-4	1-4	1-0 1-0	2-1		0-2 5-3	1-2
Sfintul Gheorghe	33	6	6	21	29	67	24	2-5 0-2	0-1	0-0 0-1 1-5 0-0 2-2	0-3	1-3 1-0	0-7	2-0 0-0	2-1				3-0
Nistru Otaci	33	2	5	26	13	74	11	0-1	1-2	0-6	0-0	0-6	0-0	1-2 0-2 0-2 0-1 1-0 1-0 1-1 3-2 0-1 3-3					

5/07/2009 - 23/05/2010 • † Qualified for the UEFA Champions League • ‡ Qualified for the Europa League • No relegation
Top scorers: 13 - Alexandru Maximov, Viitorul & Jymmy BRA, Sheriff • 12 - Oleksandr Zgura UKR, Dacia • 11 - Alexandr Erokhin RUS, Sheriff

MOLDOVA 2009-10
DIVIZIA A (2)

	Pl	W	D	L	F	A	Pts
FC Costuleni	30	24	2	4	90	27	74
Lilcora Suruceni	30	22	6	2	77	32	72
Gagauziya Comrat	30	18	4	8	62	32	58
FC Cahul 2005	30	16	5	9	44	33	53
Intersport	30	15	7	8	43	26	52
Sheriff-2 Tiraspol	30	15	6	9	38	26	51
Zimbru-2 Chisinau	30	14	5	11	44	34	47
Podis Inesti	30	12	10	8	37	28	46
Lokomotiva Balti	30	13	2	15	47	58	41
Dinamo-2 Bender	30	10	8	12	42	40	38
MIPAN Chisinau	30	9	9	12	38	41	36
CSCA Buiucani	30	7	9	14	46	50	30
Olimp Ungheni	30	6	6	18	34	66	24
Sfintul Gheorghe-2	30	5	5	20	33	60	20
Olimpia-2 Tiligul	30	5	4	21	36	82	19
Academia-2 Chisinau	30	5	0	25	26	102	15

7/08/2009 - 26/05/2010 • Lilorca were refused promotion

MEDALS TABLE

		Overall			League			Cup		
		G	S	B	G	S	B	G	S	City
1	Sheriff Tiraspol	17	2		10	1		7	1	Tiraspol
2	Zimbru Chisinau	13	7	2	8	5	2	5	2	Chisinau
3	Tiligul-Tiras	3	8	3		6	3	3	2	Tiraspol
4	FC Tiraspol	3	3	4	1	1	4	2	2	Tiraspol
5	Nistru Otaci	1	11	3		3	3	1	8	Otaci
6	Bugeac Comrat	1		1		1		1		Comrat
7	Dacia Chisnau		5	1		2	1		3	Chisinau
8	Iskra-Stal Ribnita		1	1		1	1			Ribnita
9	Dinamo Chisinau		1						1	Chisinau
10	Olimpia Balti			2			2			Balti
11	Codru Calarasi			1			1			Calarasi
	Moldova Boroseni			1			1			Boroseni

CUPA MOLDOVEI 2009-10

Round of 16		Quarter-finals			Semi-finals			Final		
Sheriff Tiraspol *	5									
CSCA Rapid Ghidighici	0	**Sheriff Tiraspol** *	0	1						
Nistru Otaci *	0	Academia Chisinau	0	0						
Academia Chisinau	2				**Sheriff Tiraspol** *	0	1			
Dinamo Bender	1				Iscra-Stali Rîbnita	0	1			
Cricova *	0	Dinamo Bender *	0	0						
Olimp Ungheni *	0	**Iscra-Stali Rîbnita**	2	3						
Iscra-Stali Rîbnita	1							**Sheriff Tiraspol**	2	
Olimpia Balti *	2							Dacia Chisinau ‡	0	
Lilcora Suruceni	1	**Olimpia Balti** *	3	0						
Universitatea Agrara	0	Zimbru Chisinau	1	0			**CUP FINAL**		
Zimbru Chisinau *	8				Olimpia Balti	2	0			
FC Tiraspol *	3				**Dacia Chisinau** *	4	1	Zimbru, Chisinau		
FC Cahul 2005	2	FC Tiraspol *	0	1				30-05-2010, Ref: Banari		
Viitorul Orhei *	0	**Dacia Chisinau**	0	3				Scorer - Jymmy 2 27 52 for Sheriff		
Dacia Chisinau	2	* Home team/home team in the first leg • ‡ Qualified for the Europa League								

MDV – MALDIVES

FIFA/COCA-COLA WORLD RANKING

1993	1994	1995	1996	1997	1998	1999	2000	2001	2002	2003	2004	2005	2006	2007	2008	2009	2010
148	162	169	176	160	166	143	154	147	152	141	139	133	158	151	154	137	162

2010												Hi/Lo
Jan	Feb	Mar	Mar	Apr	May	Jul	Aug	Sep	Oct	Nov	Dec	126
137	140	140	139	143	142	145	143	143	148	146	162	183

With the national team playing just a single match at the end of the year and with both the under-16 and under-19 teams being withdrawn from the Asian Championships for their age groups, football in the Maldives during 2010 was centred almost exclusively on club football. Victory and VB Sports dominated the domestic scene with the two clubs claiming both of the country's slots for the 2011 AFC Cup after once again after sharing the trophies between them at home. VB Sports took top spot in the Dhiraagu Dhivehi League, comfortably clinching the title ahead of Victory, who were 11 points adrift of the leaders on the final day of the season. The pair - along with Maziya and New Radiant - qualified for the President's Cup where Victory managed to extract some revenge defeating VB Sports 5-2 in the final. Victory then went on to win the FA Cup, seeing off Valencia in a penalty shootout in the semi-finals before defeating New Radiant 2-1 the final. Neither club, however, had much luck in the 2010 AFC Cup. Victory finished bottom of their group, picking up just one win but VB Sports only narrowly missed out on a place in the knock-out phase earning a pair of wins over Indonesia's Persiwa Wamena as well as a victory over Hong Kong's South China, but still finished two points short of second-placed Muangthong United.

FIFA WORLD CUP RECORD
1930-1994 DNE   1998-2010 DNQ

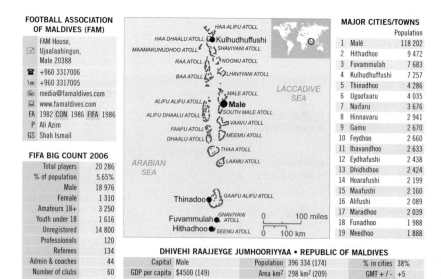

FOOTBALL ASSOCIATION OF MALDIVES (FAM)

FAM House,
Ujaalaahingun,
Male 20388
☎ +960 3317006
🖷 +960 3317005
✉ media@famaldives.com
🖳 www.famaldives.com
FA 1982 CON 1986 FIFA 1986
P Ali Azim
GS Shah Ismail

FIFA BIG COUNT 2006

Total players	20 286
% of population	5.65%
Male	18 976
Female	1 310
Amateurs 18+	3 250
Youth under 18	1 616
Unregistered	14 800
Professionals	120
Referees	134
Admin & coaches	44
Number of clubs	60
Number of teams	367

MAJOR CITIES/TOWNS

		Population
1	Malé	118 202
2	Hithadhoo	9 472
3	Fuvammulah	7 683
4	Kulhudhuffushi	7 257
5	Thinadhoo	4 286
6	Ugoofaaru	4 035
7	Naifaru	3 676
8	Hinnavaru	2 941
9	Gamu	2 670
10	Feydhoo	2 660
11	Ihavandhoo	2 633
12	Eydhafushi	2 438
13	Dhidhdhoo	2 424
14	Hoarafushi	2 199
15	Maafushi	2 160
16	Alifushi	2 089
17	Maradhoo	2 039
18	Funadhoo	1 988
19	Meedhoo	1 888

DHIVEHI RAAJJEYGE JUMHOORIYYAA • REPUBLIC OF MALDIVES

Capital	Male	Population	396 334 (174)	% in cities	38%
GDP per capita	$4500 (149)	Area km²	298 km² (209)	GMT + / -	+5
Neighbours (km)	Coast 644				

RECENT INTERNATIONAL MATCHES PLAYED BY THE MALDIVES

2006	Opponents	Score		Venue	Comp	Scorers	Att	Referee
No international matches played in 2006								
2007								
2-10	Oman	L	0-1	Muscat	Fr			
8-10	Yemen	L	0-3	Sana'a	WCq		3 000	Mansour LIB
28-10	Yemen	L	0-2	Male	WCq		8 900	Sarkar IND
2008								
9-04	Lebanon	L	0-4	Beirut	ACq			
23-04	Lebanon	L	1-2	Male	ACq	Shamveel Qasim 22		
3-06	Pakistan	W	3-0	Male	SAFr1	Mohamed Shifan 45, Ahmed Thariq 48, Akram OG 90		
5-06	Nepal	W	4-1	Male	SAFr1	Ismail Mohamed 2 10 47, Ibrahim Fazeel 2 51 62		
7-06	India	L	0-1	Male	SAFr1			
11-06	Sri Lanka	W	1-0	Colombo	SAFsf	Ibrahim Fazeel 70		
14-06	India	W	1-0	Colombo	SAFf	Mukhtar Naseer 87		
2009								
28-03	Sri Lanka	D	1-1	Colombo	Fr	Ibrahim Fazeel 19		
14-04	Turkmenistan	L	1-3	Male	CCq	Ibrahim Fazeel 61p	9 000	Al Ghafary JOR
16-04	Philippines	W	3-2	Male	CCq	Ibrahim Fazeel 26p, Ali Ashfaq 45, Mukhthar Naseer 82	9 000	Faghani IRN
18-04	Bhutan	W	5-0	Male	CCq	Ali Ashfaq 2 4 36, Ibrahim Fazeel 45p 47, Mohamed Umair 80	9 000	Lazeem IRQ
5-12	Nepal	D	1-1	Dhaka	SAFr1	Ahmed Thariq 61		
7-12	Afghanistan	W	3-1	Dhaka	SAFr1	Ahmed Thariq 52, Ali Ashfaq 2 69 89		
9-12	India †	W	2-0	Dhaka	SAFr1	Ahmed Thariq 15, Ibrahim Fazeel 82		
11-12	Sri Lanka	W	5-1	Dhaka	SAFsf	Ahmed Thariq 21, Ibrahim Fazeel 2 63 85p, Ali Ashfaq 76, Ali Ashad 87		
13-12	India †	D	0-0	Dhaka	SAFf	L 1-3p		
2010								
12-10	Indonesia	L	0-3	Bandung	Fr			

Fr = Friendly match • SAF = South Asian Football Federation Cup • CC = AFC Challenge Cup • AC = AFC Asian Cup • WC = FIFA World Cup
q = qualifier • r1 = first round group • sf = semi-final • f = final • † Not a full international

MALDIVES 2010

DHIRAAGU DHIVEHI LEAGUE

	Pl	W	D	L	F	A	Pts	VB Sports	Victory	Maziya	Radiant	Valencia	Vyansa	Thoddoo	AYL
VB Sports ‡	21	16	5	0	66	17	53		0-0 2-2	1-1 4-1	2-1 3-0	5-0 4-1	1-0 6-1	8-0 6-2	5-2 2-0
Victory	21	12	6	3	35	16	42	1-1		0-0 1-3	2-1 2-1	1-1 0-0	1-3 4-1	3-0 3-0	2-0 2-0
Maziya	21	10	8	3	35	17	38	1-1	0-1		0-0 0-0	3-2 1-0	1-1	2-1 3-1	3-1 4-1
New Radiant	21	11	3	7	44	31	36	2-3	2-1	0-1		4-1 3-1	2-4 1-0	1-0 3-1	6-1 5-3
Valencia	21	8	6	7	34	32	28	1-3	1-2	0-0 1-0	4-4		1-1 0-0	7-1 1-0	2-0 2-1
Vyansa	21	4	5	12	19	37	17	1-3	0-1	0-3	1-2	0-3		0-2 1-4	0-0 1-1
Thoddoo	21	4	0	17	16	60	12	0-1	4-0	0-7	0-2	0-2	0-2		1-0 2-4
All Youth Linkage	21	1	3	17	16	55	6	0-5	0-2	1-1	1-4	0-3	0-2	0-1	

26/03/2010 - 25/09/2010 • Top four qualify for the President's Cup • ‡ Qualified for the AFC Cup

PRESIDENT'S CUP 2010

Preliminary round		Semi–final		Final	
		VB Sports	5		
Maziya	2	New Radiant	0		
New Radiant	4			**VB Sports**	5
		Final Qualifier		Victory	2
		VB Sports	1		
		Victory	2		

Final: Galolhu, Malé, 28-10-2010. Scorers - Ali Ashfaq 4 [32 43 63p 81], Ashad Ali [38] for VB; Samuel Tye Smith 2 [51 68] for Victory

FA CUP 2010

Quarter–finals		Semi–finals		Final	
Victory	3				
Vyansa	1	**Victory**	2 4p		
Maziya	1 1p	Valencia	2 1p		
Valencia	1 3p			**Victory** ‡	2
VB Sports	1			New Radiant	1
Thoddoo	0	VB Sports	0		
Al Youth Linkage	1	**New Radiant**	2	‡ Qualified for AFC Cup	
New Radiant	7	Third place: VB Sports 3-1 Valencia			

Final: Galolhu, Malé, 18-10-2010. Scorers - Hussain Niyaz [27], Mohamed Jameel [81] for Victory; Ahmed Thoriq [36] for New Radiant

MEDALS TABLE

		Overall			Lge	PC	FAC		CW	Asia			City/Town
		G	S	B	G	G	G	S	G	G	S	B	
1	Victory SC	29	3		2	20	4	3	3				Malé
2	New Radiant SC	22	7	1	1	7	10	7	4		1		Malé
3	Club Valencia	20	8		5	5	4	8	6				Malé
4	VB Sports	10	3		2	3	5	3					Malé
5	Hurriyya	1	2		1		2						Malé

VB Sports previously known as Club Lagoons and Island FC • LGE = Dhivehi League • PC = President's Cup (also known historically as the National Championship) • FAC = FA Cup • CW = Cup Winners Cup

MEX – MEXICO

FIFA/COCA-COLA WORLD RANKING

1993	1994	1995	1996	1997	1998	1999	2000	2001	2002	2003	2004	2005	2006	2007	2008	2009	2010
16	15	12	11	5	10	10	12	9	8	7	7	5	20	15	26	17	27

2010												Hi/Lo
Jan	Feb	Mar	Mar	Apr	May	Jul	Aug	Sep	Oct	Nov	Dec	**4**
17	17	15	17	17	17	24	25	28	28	28	27	**33**

For the fifth tournament in a row Mexico's World Cup campaign ended in the first knockout round. As in Germany four years previously, the Mexicans were beaten by Argentina but there was a good deal of controversy surrounding the defeat with Carlos Tevez's opening goal clearly offside. The challenge for Mexican football now has to be to shift up a gear and compete with the major nations of world football on a consistently equal footing. With exciting talent like Manchester United's Javier Hernandez starting to make an impact there is certainly the potential to do so and the French, for example, were comfortably beaten during the group stage in South Africa - Hernandez scoring a goal just as his grandfather Tomas Balcazar had done against them at the 1954 World Cup. Hernandez's old club Chivas Guadalajara became only the second Mexican team to reach the final of South America's Copa Libertadores, but there was huge disappointment for the full house at their brand new Estadio Omnilife in the first leg when they lost 2-1 before losing the second leg 3-2 in Porto Alegre. Pachuca emerged as winners from an all-Mexican last four in the CONCACAF Champions League, consigning Cruz Azul to another runners-up spot, whilst at home Toluca and Monterrey won domestic league honours, both at the expense of Santos Laguna.

FIFA WORLD CUP RECORD

1930 13 r1 **1934** DNQ **1938** DNE **1950** 12 r1 **1954** 13 r1 **1958** 16 r1 **1962** 11 r1 **1966** 12 r1 **1970** 6 QF (hosts) **1974** DNQ
1978 16 r1 **1982** DNQ **1986** 6 QF (hosts) **1990** DNE **1994** 13 r2 **1998** 13 r2 **2002** 11 r2 **2006** 15 r2 **2010** 14 r2

FEDERACION MEXICANA DE FUTBOL ASOCIACION, A.C. (FMF)

Colima No. 373, Colonia
Roma, Mexico D.F. 06700

☎ +52 55 52410166
📠 +52 55 52410191
📧 ddemaria@femexfut.org.mx
🖥 www.femexfut.org.mx
FA 1927 CON 1961 FIFA 1929
P Justino Compean
GS Decio De Maria

FIFA BIG COUNT 2006

Total players	8 479 595
% of population	7.89%
Male	7 151 688
Female	1 327 907
Amateurs 18+	186 954
Youth under 18	129 006
Unregistered	7 000 000
Professionals	4 593
Referees	522
Admin & coaches	32 600
Number of clubs	302
Number of teams	16 957

MAJOR CITIES/TOWNS

		Population
1	Mexico City	8 587 132
2	Ecatepec	1 956 531
3	Guadalajara	1 605 520
4	Tijuana	1 595 681
5	Juárez	1 585 034
6	Puebla	1 483 341
7	Nezahualcóyotl	1 216 077
8	León	1 197 771
9	Monterrey	1 113 114
10	Zapopan	1 060 417
11	Naucalpan	846 554
12	Guadalupe	767 167
13	Mérida	760 249
14	Chihuahua	750 039
15	San Luis Potosí	718 137
17	Aguascalientes	712 682
19	Cancún	700 394
30	Toluca	571 143
33	Torreon	540 078

ESTADOS UNIDOS MEXICANOS • UNITED MEXICAN STATES

Capital	Mexico City	Population	111 211 789 (11)	% in cities	77%
GDP per capita	$14 300 (79)	Area km²	1 964 375 km² (15)	GMT + / -	-6
Neighbours (km)	Belize 250, Guatemala 962, US 3141 • Coast 9330				

RECENT INTERNATIONAL MATCHES PLAYED BY MEXICO

2009	Opponents	Score		Venue	Comp	Scorers	Att	Referee
5-07	Nicaragua	W	2-0	Oakland	GCr1	Noriega [45p], Barrera [86]	32 700	Ward CAN
9-07	Panama	D	1-1	Houston	GCr1	Sabah [10]	47 713	Aguilar SLV
12-07	Guadeloupe †	W	2-0	Phoenix	GCr1	Torrado [42], Sabah [85]	23 876	Brizan TRI
19-07	Haiti	W	4-0	Dallas	GCqf	Sabah 2 [23 63], Dos Santos [42], Barrera [83]	85 000	Campbell JAM
23-07	Costa Rica	D	1-1	Chicago	GCsf	Franco [88]. W 5-3p	55 173	Moreno PAN
26-07	USA	W	5-0	New Jersey	GCf	Torrado [56], Dos Santos [62], Vela [67], Jose Castro [79], Franco [90]	79 156	Campbell JAM
12-08	USA	W	2-1	Mexico City	WCq	Israel Castro [19], Sabah [82]	104 499	Moreno PAN
5-09	Costa Rica	W	3-0	San Jose	WCq	Dos Santos [45], Franco [62], Guardado [71]	20 000	Brizan TRI
9-09	Honduras	W	1-0	Mexico City	WCq	Blanco [76p]	97 897	Campbell JAM
30-09	Colombia	L	1-2	Dallas	Fr	Aguilar [88]	50 000	Salazar USA
10-10	El Salvador	W	4-1	Mexico City	WCq	OG [25], Blanco [71], Palencia [85], Vela [90]	104 000	Batres GUA
14-10	Trinidad and Tobago	D	2-2	Port of Spain	WCq	Esqueda [57], Salcido [65]	2 000	Quesada CRC
2010								
24-02	Bolivia	W	5-0	San Francisco	Fr	Barrera [3], Hernandez 2 [13 20], Luna [18], Aguilar [51]	20 000	Vaughn USA
3-03	New Zealand	W	2-0	Pasadena	Fr	Hernandez [54], Vela [57]	90 526	Marrufo USA
17-03	Korea DPR	W	2-1	Torreon	Fr	Blanco [51], Hernandez [69]	30 000	Moreno PAN
24-03	Iceland	D	0-0	Charlotte	Fr		70 000	Geiger USA
7-05	Ecuador	D	0-0	New Jersey	Fr		77 507	Depiero CAN
10-05	Senegal	W	1-0	Chicago	Fr	Medina [60]	60 610	Salazar USA
13-05	Angola	W	1-0	Houston	Fr	Guardado [52]	70 099	Toledo USA
16-05	Chile	W	1-0	Mexico City	Fr	Medina [13]	100 000	Geiger USA
24-05	England	L	1-3	London	Fr	Franco [45]	88 638	Toma JPN
26-05	Netherlands	L	1-2	Freiburg	Fr	Hernandez [73]	22 000	Graefe GER
30-05	Gambia	W	5-1	Bayreuth	Fr	Hernandez 2 [18 50], Bautista 2 [59 74], Medina [80]	15 000	Brych GER
3-06	Italy	W	2-1	Brussels	Fr	Vela [17], Medina [84]	30 000	Verbist BEL
11-06	South Africa	D	1-1	Johannesburg	WCr1	Rafael Marquez [79]	84 490	Irmatov UZB
17-06	France	W	2-0	Polokwane	WCr1	Hernandez [64], Blanco [79p]	35 370	Al Ghamdi KSA
22-06	Uruguay	L	0-1	Rustenburg	WCr1		33 425	Kassai HUN
27-06	Argentina	L	1-3	Johannesburg	WCr2	Hernandez [71]	84 377	Rosetti ITA
11-08	Spain	D	1-1	Mexico City	Fr	Hernandez [10]	100 000	Moreno PAN
4-09	Ecuador	L	1-2	Guadalajara	Fr	OG [40]	43 800	Quesada CRC
7-09	Colombia	W	1-0	Monterrey	Fr	Hernandez [89]	43 000	Pineda HON
12-10	Venezuela	D	2-2	Juarez	Fr	Hernandez [33], Dos Santos [60]	20 000	Aguilar SLV

Fr = Friendly match • GC = CONCACAF Gold Cup • CA = Copa America • CC = FIFA Confederations Cup • WC = FIFA World Cup
q = qualifier • r1 = first round group • r2 = second round • qf = quarter-final • sf = semi-final • f = final

MEXICO NATIONAL TEAM HISTORICAL RECORDS

Caps
177 - Claudio Suarez 1992-2006 • 145 - Pavel Pardo 1996-2009 • 129 - Jorge Campos 1991-2003 • 121 - Ramon Ramirez 1991-2000 & Gerardo Torrado 1999- • 119 - Cuauhtemoc Blanco 1995- • 108 - Alberto Garcia-Aspe 1988-2002 • 98 - Oswaldo Sanchez 1996- & Rafael Marquez 1997- • 90 - Carlos Hermosillo 1984-97 • 89 - Jared Borgetti 1997-2008 • 85 - Luis Hernandez 1995-2002 • 84 - Zague 1988-2002; Salvador Carmona 1996-2005 & Duilio Davino 1996-2006 • 82 - Gustavo Pena 1961-74 • 81 - Miguel Espana 1984-94 & Carlos Salcido • 80 - Ricardo Osorio 2003- • 79 - Juan Palencia 1996-2009 • 78 - Luis Garcia 1991-99 • 70 - Jesus Arellano 1996-2006

Goals
46 - Jared Borgetti 1997-2008 • 39 - Cuauhtemoc Blanco 1995- • 35 - Carlos Hermosillo 1984-97 & Luis Hernandez 1995-2002 • 31 - Enrique Borja 1966-75 • 30 - Zague 1988-2001 • 29 - Luis Flores 1983-93; Luis Garcia 1991-98 & Hugo Sanchez 1977-98 • 28 - Benjamin Galindo 1983-97 • 21 - Francisco Fonseca 2004-08 & Alberto Garcia-Aspe 1988-2002 • 19 - Javier Fragoso 1965-70 • 16 - Isidoro Diaz 1960-70 & Ricardo Pelaez 1989-99 • 15 - Horacio Casarin 1937-56; Ramon Ramirez 1991-2000 & Omar Bravo 2003-

Past Coaches
Adolfo Frias Beltran 1923 • Alfonso Rojo de la Vega 1928 • Juan Luque de Serrallonga ESP 1930 • Rafael Garza Gutierrez 1934 • Alfred Crowle ENG 1935 • Rafael Garza Gutierrez 1937-38 • Jorge Orth HUN 1947 • Rafael Garza Gutierrez 1949 • Octavio Vial 1950 • Antonio Lopez Herranz ESP 1950 • Antonio Lopez Herranz ESP 1952 • Horacio Casarin 1953 • Antonio Lopez Herranz ESP 1953-54 • Antonio Lopez Herranz ESP 1956-58 • Ignacio Trelles 1958 • Fernando Marcos 1959 • Ignacio Trelles 1960-69 • Arpad Fekete HUN 1963 • Diego Mercado 1969 • Javier de la Torre 1970-73 • Ignacio Juaregui 1974 • Ignacio Trelles 1975-76 • Jose Antonio Roca 1977-78 • Jose Moncebaez 1979 • Gustavo Pena 1979 • Raul Cardenas 1979-81 • Bora Milutinovic YUG 1983-86 • Mario Velarde 1987-89 • Alberto Guerra 1989 • Manuel Lapuente 1990-91 • Cesar Luis Menotti ARG 1991-92 • Miguel Mejia Baron 1993-95 • Bora Milutinovic YUG 1995-97 • Manuel Lapuente 1997-2000 • Mario Carrillo 1999 • Gustavo Vargas 1999 • Enrique Meza 2000-01 • Javier Aguirre 2001-02 • Ricardo La Volpe ARG 2002-06 • Hugo Sanchez 2006-08 • Jesus Ramirez 2008 • Sven-Goran Eriksson SWE 2008-09 • Javier Aguirre 2009-10 • Enrique Meza 2010 • Efrain Flores 2010 • Jose Manuel de la Torre 2010-

MEXICO 2009-10 PRIMERA DIVISION NACIONAL (CLAUSURA)

Grupo 1	Pl	W	D	L	F	A	Pts
Guadalajara †	17	10	2	5	28	21	32
Toluca †	17	8	6	3	27	15	30
Atlas	17	7	3	7	26	23	24
Querétaro	17	6	3	8	13	25	21
Indios	17	4	3	10	10	29	15
San Luis	17	3	5	9	18	29	14

Grupo 2	Pl	W	D	L	F	A	Pts
Monterrey †	17	10	6	1	30	15	36
América †	17	7	4	6	29	20	25
Morelia †	17	7	4	6	22	13	25
Pachuca †	17	7	4	6	27	26	25
Jaguares	17	4	7	6	22	24	19
Puebla	17	5	4	8	28	31	19

Grupo 3	Pl	W	D	L	F	A	Pts
Pumas UNAM †	17	7	7	3	20	10	28
Santos Laguna †	17	8	4	5	27	25	28
Cruz Azul	17	7	4	6	20	20	25
Estudiantes Tecos	17	5	4	8	26	32	19
Tigres UANL	17	5	4	8	19	26	19
Atlante	17	4	4	9	21	29	16

16/01/2010 - 25/04/2010 • † Qualified for the play-offs
Top scorers (inc play-offs): **10** - Javier Hernandez, Guadalajara; Johan Fano PER, Atlante & Herculez Gomez USA, Puebla • **9** - Jackson Martinez COL, Jaguares

MEXICO 2010-11 PRIMERA DIVISION NACIONAL (APERTURA)

Grupo 1	Pl	W	D	L	F	A	Pts
Monterrey †	17	9	5	3	29	20	32
Santos Laguna †	17	9	3	5	28	19	30
Tigres UANL	17	6	6	5	24	16	24
Guadalajara	17	4	10	3	16	15	22
Necaxa	17	4	4	9	14	21	16
Estudiantes Tecos	17	4	3	10	18	36	15

Grupo 2	Pl	W	D	L	F	A	Pts
América †	17	7	6	4	22	16	27
San Luis †	17	8	2	7	21	19	26
Pachuca †	17	7	4	6	27	28	25
Toluca	17	5	7	5	18	20	22
Atlante	17	4	4	9	17	27	16
Atlas	17	3	4	10	18	27	13

Grupo 3	Pl	W	D	L	F	A	Pts
Cruz Azul †	17	12	3	2	33	13	39
Jaguares †	17	6	7	4	21	14	25
Pumas UNAM †	17	7	4	6	23	24	25
Morelia	17	5	6	6	17	16	21
Puebla	17	5	4	8	21	26	19
Querétaro	17	5	4	8	18	28	19

23/07/2010 - 14/11/2010 • † Qualified for the play-offs
Top scorers (inc play-offs): **16** - Christian Benitez ECU, Santos • **15** - Humberto Suazo CHI, Monterrey • **9** - Johan Fano PER, Atlante & Itamar BRA, UNAL

CLAUSURA 2009-10 PLAY-OFFS

Quarter–finals		Semi–finals		Final	
Toluca					
América *		Toluca	2 1		
Monterrey	0 1	Pachuca *	2 0		
Pachuca *	1 2			Toluca	2 0 4p
Morelia *	4 1			Santos Laguna *	2 0 5p
Guadalajara	2 0	Morelia *	3 1		
UNAM Pumas		Santos Laguna	3 7		
Santos Laguna *					

* Home team in 1st leg • † Qualified on overall record

CLAUSURA 2009-10 FINAL
Estadio Corona, Torreón, 20-05-2010, 20:00, Att: 30 0000, Ref: Rodriguez.M

Santos Laguna	2	Quintero [14], Vuoso [84]
Toluca	2	Novaretti [22], Zinha [67]

Santos - Oswaldo Sanchez - Jorge Estrada, Felipe Baloy, Jonathan Lacerda, Jose Olvera (Daniel Luduena 36) - Walter Jimenez (Francisco Torres 73), Carlos Morales - Fernando Arce, Jose Maria Cardenas (Vicente Vuoso 46) - Oribe Peralta•, Carlos Darwin Quintero. Tr: Ruben Omar Romano
Toluca - Alfredo Talavera - Jose Cruzalta•, Diego Novaretti, Edgar Duenas•, Manuel de la Torre♦92+ - Martin Romagnoli, Antonio Rios - Carlos Esquivel, Antonio Naelson 'Zinha' (Manuel Perez 78), Nestor Calderon (Vladimir Marin 68) - Hector Raul Mancilla• (Raul Nava 84). Tr: Jose Manuel de la Torre

Estadio Nemesio Diez, Toluca, 23-05-2010, 12:00, Att: 27 000, Ref: Archundia

Toluca	0 4p	(see page 576 for penalty details)
Santos Laguna	0 3p	

Toluca - Alfredo Talavera - Jose Cruzalta (Francisco Gamboa Gomez 81), Diego Novaretti, Edgar Duenas•, Osvaldo Gonzalez - Martin Romagnoli, Antonio Rios - Carlos Esquivel (Isaac Brizuela 99), Antonio Naelson 'Zinha'•, Nestor Calderon (Vladimir Marin 74) - Hector Raul Mancilla•. Tr: Jose Manuel de la Torre
Santos - Oswaldo Sanchez - Jorge Estrada (Rafael Figueroa 83), Felipe Baloy•, Jonathan Laserda, Carlos Morales• - Juan Pablo Rodriguez•, Francisco Torres (Vicente Vuoso 45) - Fernando Arce, Jose Cardenas (Daniel Ludena 70) - Carlos Darwin Quintero, Oribe Peralta•. Tr: Ruben Omar Romano

APERTURA 2010-11 PLAY-OFFS

Quarter–finals		Semi–finals		Final	
Monterrey	1 3				
Pachuca *	1 3	Monterrey	0 2		
Cruz Azul	2 0	UNAM Pumas *	0 0		
UNAM Pumas *	1 2			Monterrey	2 3
América	0 4			Santos Laguna *	3 0
San Luis *	0 1	América *	1 3		
Jaguares *	1 0	Santos Laguna	2 3		
Santos Laguna	1 1				

* Home team in 1st leg • † Qualified on overall record

APERTURA 2010-11 FINAL
Estadio Corona, Torreón, 2-12-2010, 20:00, Ref: Chacon

Santos Laguna	3	Estrada [23], Quintero [41], OG [85]
Monterrey	2	Suazo [37], Cardozo [54]

Santos - Oswaldo Sanchez - Jorge Estrada (Jose Cardenas 77), Rafael Figueroa, Jonathan Lacerda, Jose Olvera - Francisco Torres, Carlos Morales - Fernando Arce, Daniel Luduena (Jaime Toledo 86) - Christian Benitez, Carlos Darwin Quintero (Rodrigo Ruiz 83). Tr: Ruben Omar Romano
Monterrey - Jonathan Orozco - Ricardo Osorio (Sergio Perez• 45), Jose Basanta, Duilio Davino, Hiriam Mier•, Walter Ayovi - Osvaldo Martinez, Jesus Zavala•, Neri Cardozo (Sergio Santana 81) - Aldo de nigris (William Paredes 73), Humberto Suazo. Tr: Victor Manuel Vucetich

Tecnologico, Monterrey, 5-12-2010, 18:00, Ref: Archundia

Monterrey	3	Suazo 2 [28 85], Basanta [72]
Santos Laguna	0	

Monterrey - Jonathan Orozco - Sergio Perez, Jose Basanta•, Duilio Davino, Hiriam Mier, William Paredes (Severo Meza 46) - Neri Cardozo (Hector Morales 81), Jesus Zavala, Walter Ayovi - Aldo de Nigris• (Sergio Santana 87), Humberto Suazo. Tr: Victor Manuel Vucetich
Santos - Oswaldo Sanchez - Jorge Estrada, Rafael Figueroa (Daniel Luduena 78), Felipe Baloy, Jonathan Lacerda, Jose Olvera - Fernando Arce, Carlos Morales• (Juan Rodriguez 78), Francisco Torres• (Jose Cardenas 52) - Carlos Darwin Quintero, Christian Benitez. Tr: Ruben Omar Romano

MEXICO 2009-10

PRIMERA DIVISION NACIONAL RESULTS AND RELEGATION TABLE

	Pl	Pts	Av	Toluca	Santos	Guadalajara	Cruz Azul	Pachuca	Monterrey	Morelia	UNAM	San Luis	América	Atlante	Puebla	Tecos	Jaguares	Atlas	Querétaro	Tigres	C. Juarez
Toluca	102	189	1.8529		3-0	4-3	2-3	3-0	1-1	1-0	3-0	1-1	3-1	2-0	2-1	5-0	1-1	2-0	2-0	1-1	3-0
Santos Laguna	102	168	1.6471	1-0		1-0	3-2	4-0	1-1	3-2	1-1	2-1	1-1	4-2	2-1	3-3	0-3	1-2	2-0	2-2	1-0
Guadalajara	102	161	1.5842	3-1	6-2		0-1	2-2	1-0	0-3	0-0	2-0	1-0	2-0	3-2	3-2	1-0	0-2	2-0	1-3	2-2
Cruz Azul	102	153	1.5	1-2	0-2	1-1		2-2	2-0	1-0	0-0	4-2	2-3	3-1	4-0	3-1	0-2	3-1	1-0	4-0	2-3
Pachuca	102	152	1.4902	1-1	0-3	0-1	1-3		1-3	1-0	0-3	2-0	2-1	5-1	1-2	3-0	4-0	0-2	3-1	1-1	1-0
Monterrey	102	149	1.4608	1-0	2-1	2-1	2-0	3-0		1-1	1-0	1-1	1-2	3-0	2-1	2-2	1-2	3-0	3-0	2-1	4-0
Morelia	102	144	1.4118	0-0	1-1	3-1	0-3	2-0	1-1		0-0	2-1	2-0	0-1	1-1	2-0	1-2	3-0	5-0	2-1	5-0
Pumas UNAM	102	143	1.402	0-0	1-0	1-1	0-3	1-2	2-1	2-0		0-0	3-2	1-0	4-1	1-1	2-0	2-0	3-0	1-2	1-1
San Luis	102	140	1.3725	2-3	4-2	4-0	1-2	3-0	0-3	0-2	1-0		1-1	2-1	0-0	1-1	0-3	3-1	3-0	0-3	1-1
América	102	136	1.3333	7-2	1-0	1-0	2-0	2-2	1-0	1-2	0-0	5-1		1-0	0-0	5-0	1-1	2-1	6-0	2-2	1-0
Atlante	102	133	1.3039	2-1	1-0	0-1	3-1	1-0	0-2	0-1	2-1	1-0	2-3		2-2	1-1	0-0	2-0	2-0	0-0	1-2
Puebla	102	124	1.2157	0-2	3-3	2-2	4-1	3-5	1-1	2-1	1-1	1-0	2-1	1-0		1-1	3-3	1-0	1-2	0-1	1-2
Tecos	102	123	1.2059	2-1	2-4	1-2	2-1	2-3	3-4	0-2	3-0	1-1	1-2	3-2	2-3		3-0	1-2	2-0	0-0	4-1
Jaguares	102	121	1.1863	0-2	1-1	4-0	0-1	2-2	1-1	1-2	0-2	1-1	1-3	1-1	0-1	0-1		2-3	0-1	2-2	1-0
Atlas	102	120	1.1765	1-1	2-1	1-4	0-1	1-1	3-0	0-2	1-0	0-0	1-0	3-3	0-2	0-1	1-1		0-1	2-1	7-1
Querétaro	34	39	1.1471	0-1	1-0	0-2	2-1	1-0	1-3	1-1	3-2	4-0	0-0	1-2	1-1	1-0	2-2	2-1		1-0	3-1
Tigres UANL	102	116	1.1373	0-1	1-2	1-3	2-0	1-2	1-2	0-3	2-2	1-0	1-1	4-0	1-1	2-2	0-1	0-1	2-1		0-0
Ciudad Juarez	68	63	0.9265	0-1	0-0	1-0	0-0	1-2	0-0	0-1	2-0	1-1	0-1	0-2	0-2	1-2	0-1	1-1	1-0	0-1	

The relegation averages are worked out over three years. This table lists the results of the 2009-10 season - the Apertura played in the second half of 2009 and the Clausura in the first half of 2010. For details of the Apertura see Oliver's Almanack of World Football 2010. The Apertura results are in the shaded boxes

MEDALS TABLE

		Overall			League			Cup			CON'CAF			Sth Am			City
		G	S	B	G	S	B	G	S	B	G	S	B	G	S	B	
1	Club América	25	14	9	14	10	5	6	3		5			1	3		Mexico City
2	Real Club España	20	5	4	15	5	4	5									
3	Necaxa	16	8	9	7	7	7	7			2	1	1		1		Aguascalientes
4	Cruz Azul	15	14		8	9		2	2		5	2			1		Mexico City
5	CD Guadalajara	14	17	9	11	9	4	2	5		1	2	1		1	4	Guadalajara
6	CD Toluca	14	8	5	10	5	2	2	1		2	2	2		1		Toluca
7	CF Pachuca	14	7	6	7	7	5	2			4		1	1			Pachuca
8	Asturias	11	4	3	3	4	3	8									
9	CF Atlante	10	13	5	5	8	3	3	4		2	1					Mexico City
10	León	10	10	6	5	5	4	5	4			1	2				León
11	UNAM Pumas	10	8	1	6	6		1			3	1	1		1		Mexico City
12	Reforma	8	3	2	6	3	2	2									
13	Puebla FC	7	4	3	2	2	3	4	2		1						Puebla
14	CF Monterrey	5	5	5	4	3	2	1	2				3				Monterrey
15	CF Atlas	5	4	4	1	3	4	4	1								Guadalajara
16	Santos Laguna	4	4	2	4	4						1			1		Torreón
17	Tigres UANL	4	4	1	2	3		2	1			1					Monterrey
18	CD Zacatepec	4	3	1	2	1	1	2	2								Zacatepec
19	UAG Tecos	3	6		1	4		1	2		1						Zapopan
20	CD Veracruz	3	3	3	2	3		1	3								Veracruz
21	Club Mexico	3	1	1	1	1	1	2									
22	Marte FC	3		1	3		1										Xochitepec
23	Tampico Madero	2	4		1	2		1	2								Tampico Madero
24	British Club	2	3	5	1	3	5	1									
25	Moctezuma	2		3				3	2								
26	Oro Jalisco	1	6		1	5			1								
27	Monarcas Morelia	1	5		1	2			1		2						Morelia
28	Rovers	1	1	1	1	1	1										
29	Mexico Cricket Club	1			1												
	Orizaba	1			1												

CLAUSURA 2009-10 FINAL PENALTIES TOLUCA WON 4-3

Tol		San
✗[1] Zinha		
		Rodriguez ✓
✓ Marin		
		Ludena ✓
✗[1] Mancilla		
		Lacerda ✓
✓ Novaretti		
		Vuoso ✗[2]
✓ Romagnoli		
		Morales ✗[1]
✓ Duenas		
		Arce ✗[1]

✗[1] = saved; ✗[2] = wide

MGL – MONGOLIA

FIFA/COCA-COLA WORLD RANKING

1993	1994	1995	1996	1997	1998	1999	2000	2001	2002	2003	2004	2005	2006	2007	2008	2009	2010
-	-	-	-	-	196	198	196	187	193	179	185	179	181	178	192	171	182

2010												Hi/Lo
Jan	Feb	Mar	Mar	Apr	May	Jul	Aug	Sep	Oct	Nov	Dec	**170**
171	170	170	172	180	179	182	180	180	183	183	182	**200**

Mongolia's sporadic involvement in the international scene remained just that as the national side did not play at all during 2010 while both the under-16 and under-19 teams were withdrawn from the Asian championships for their age groups. 2011 promises some action with entry to the 2012 AFC Challenge Cup with the Mongolians drawn against the Philippines in a pre-qualifying play-off. With much of the country snow-bound for at least six months of each year and where summer temperatures can climb to over 40 degrees, the climate in Mongolia makes playing football a challenge. As a result the Mongolian league has to squeeze itself into a three-month window between July and September. Organised by the Mongolia Football Federation since 1996, the League's most successful club have been Erchim from the capital Ulaan-Baatar but in 2010 it was won by Khangarid who claimed top spot in the first stage of the championship on goal-difference from Mazaalai. Bizarrely, the top six in the seven-team league progressed to the championship playoffs with only last-placed Khasiin Khulguud missing out. After a second group phase and then semi-finals, the top two teams from the first stage made it through to the final with Khangarid beating Mazaalai 2-1 to claim the title for the third time.

FIFA WORLD CUP RECORD
1930-1998 DNE 2002-2010 DNQ

MONGOLIA FOOTBALL FEDERATION (MFF)

PO Box 259,
Ulaan-Baatar 210646

☎ +976 11 345968
📠 +976 11 345966
✉ mongolianff@the-mff.mn

FA	1959	CON	1998	FIFA	1998
P	Ganbold Buyannemekh				
GS	Terbaatar Dambiijav				

FIFA BIG COUNT 2006

Total players	51 200
% of population	1.81%
Male	51 200
Female	0
Amateurs 18+	800
Youth under 18	3 020
Unregistered	11 000
Professionals	200
Referees	30
Admin & coaches	73
Number of clubs	10
Number of teams	70

MAJOR CITIES/TOWNS

		Population
1	Ulaan Baatar	922 127
2	Erdenet	90 353
3	Darchan	78 254
4	Choybalsan	46 525
5	Saynshand	31 784
6	Olgiy	31 747
7	Moron	29 536
8	Ulaan Gom	29 529
9	Hovd	29 486
10	Uliastay	27 657
11	Suche Baatar	25 906
12	Bayanhongor	24 148
13	Arvaiheer	21 929
14	Dzuunharaa	19 949
15	Tsetserleg	19 675
16	Altay	19 344
17	Dzuunmod	19 024
18	Bulgan	18 239
19	Nalajh	17 311

MOGOL ULS • MONGOLIA

Capital	Ulaan-Baatar	Population	3 041 142 (136)	% in cities	57%
GDP per capita	$3200 (163)	Area km²	1 564 116 km² (19)	GMT +/-	+8
Neighbours (km)	China 4677, Russia 3543				

RECENT INTERNATIONAL MATCHES PLAYED BY MONGOLIA

2004	Opponents		Score	Venue	Comp	Scorers	Att	Referee
	No international matches played in 2004							
2005								
5-03	Hong Kong	L	0-6	Taipei	EAq			
7-03	Korea DPR	L	0-6	Taipei	EAq			
9-03	Guam	W	4-1	Taipei	EAq	Tugsbayer 2 [31] [34], Bayarzorig [46], Buman-Uchral [81]		
13-03	Chinese Taipei	D	0-0	Taipei	EAq			
2006								
	No international matches played in 2006							
2007								
17-06	Macau	D	0-0	Macau	EAq		300	Matsuo JPN
19-06	Korea DPR	L	0-7	Macau	EAq		300	Ogiya JPN
23-06	Guam	W	5-2	Macau	EAq	OG [24], Davaa 2 [37] [42], Bayasgalan [46], Batchuluun [75]	100	Wan Daxue CHN
21-10	Korea DPR	L	1-4	Ulaan-Baatar	WCq	Selenge [93+]	4 870	Takayama JPN
28-10	Korea DPR	L	1-5	Pyongyang	WCq	Donorov [41]	5 000	Gosh BAN
2008								
	No international matches played in 2008							
2009								
11-03	Guam	L	0-1	Manenggon Hills	EAq			Kim Jong Hyeuk KOR
13-03	Macau	W	2-1	Manenggon Hills	EAq	Norjmoo [67], Donorov [69]		Fan Qi CHN
15-03	Northern Marianas†	W	4-1	Manenggon Hills	EAq	Donorov [16], Sukhbaatar [42], Norjmoo [71], Battsagaan [90]	700	Sato JPN
7-04	Macau	L	0-2	Macau	CCq		500	Perera SRI
14-04	Macau	W	3-1	Ulaan-Baatar	CCq	Altankhuyag [55], De Sousa OG [77], Donorov [89]	3 000	Yu Ming Hsun TPE
2010								
	No international matches played in 2010							

EA = EAFF East Asian Championship • AC = AFC Asian Cup • CC = AFC Challenge Cup • WC = FIFA World Cup • q = qualifier

MONGOLIA 2010

MONGOLIA PREMIER LEAGUE FIRST STAGE

	Pl	W	D	L	F	A	Pts	Mazaalai	Erchim	Khoromkhon	Ulaanbaatar	Selenge Press	Khasiin
Khangarid †	6	4	1	1	13	5	13	0-1	1-1	2-0	5-2	3-0	2-1
Mazaalai †	6	4	1	1	12	8	13		3-1	3-1	0-1	5-4	0-0
Erchim †	6	3	2	1	9	6	11			1-1	1-0	3-0	2-1
Khoromkhon †	6	2	1	3	6	10	7				0-2	1-0	3-2
Ulaanbaatar DS †	6	2	0	4	9	12	6					2-3	2-3
Selenge Press †	6	2	0	4	12	18	6						5-4
Khasiin Khulguud	6	1	1	4	11	14	4						

30/07/2010 - 26/08/2010 • † Qualified for the play-offs

PLAY-OFFS

Quarter-final group stage

Group A	Pl	W	D	L	F	A	Pts	Kh	Er
Ulaanbaatar DS	2	1	0	1	3	1	3	3-0	0-1
Khangarid	2	1	0	1	2	3	3		2-0
Erchim	2	1	0	1	1	2	3		

Group B	Pl	W	D	L	F	A	Pts	Ma	Kh
Selenge Press	2	2	0	0	7	3	6	2-1	5-2
Mazaalai	2	1	0	1	4	3	3		3-1
Khoromkhon	2	0	0	2	3	8	0		

Semi-finals

Khangarid	3
Selenge Press	2

Ulaanbaatar DS	1 4p
Mazaalai	1 5p

29/08/2010- 11/09/2010

Final

Khangarid	2
Mazaalai	1

3rd Place

Ulaanbaatar DS	2 5p
Selenge Press	2 4p

MKD – FYR MACEDONIA

FIFA/COCA-COLA WORLD RANKING

1993	1994	1995	1996	1997	1998	1999	2000	2001	2002	2003	2004	2005	2006	2007	2008	2009	2010
-	90	94	86	92	59	68	76	89	85	92	92	87	54	58	56	65	76

2010												Hi/Lo
Jan	Feb	Mar	Mar	Apr	May	Jul	Aug	Sep	Oct	Nov	Dec	46
65	64	64	65	60	61	66	66	71	70	76	76	147

Although a rare occurrence, there have been a number of examples of defending champions suffering relegation in the following season, but Macedonia went one further in 2010 with the top two from 2009 losing their top flight status - an almost unprecedented occurrence in world football. There were mitigating circumstances in the case of both Makedonija Skopje - the 2009 champions - and Sloga Jugomagnat in that both relegations were self inflicted, the result of a dispute that severely disrupted the season in the aftermath of elections at the federation. After refusing to turn up for two fixtures Makedonija and Sloga were expelled and there was further disruption when Pobeda were expelled from the league after 28 games and all their results annulled after the implementation of a worldwide eight-year ban for match fixing in European competition. That left the field free for Renova, a previously unheralded village team from the outskirts of Tetovo in the northwest, to secure an unlikely title triumph. It proved to be a good year for Tetovo with the more established Teteks also winning their first trophy after beating Rabotniki from the capital Skopje 3-2 in the Cup Final. One event that united the country, however, was Inter's UEFA Champions League win with Macedonia's Goran Pandev playing a full role in helping Inter to the treble.

FIFA WORLD CUP RECORD
1930-1994 DNE **1998-2010** DNQ

FOOTBALL FEDERATION OF MACEDONIA (FFM)

8-ma Udarna brigada 31-a,
PO Box 84,
Skopje 1000
☎ +389 23 129291
🖷 +389 23 165448
✉ ffm@ffm.com.mk
🖳 www.ffm.com.mk
FA 1908 CON 1994 FIFA 1994
P Haralampie Hadji-Risteski
GS Igor Klimper

FIFA BIG COUNT 2006

Total players	93 896
% of population	4.58%
Male	82 546
Female	11 350
Amateurs 18+	14 530
Youth under 18	7 760
Unregistered	19 000
Professionals	356
Referees	740
Admin & coaches	1 125
Number of clubs	456
Number of teams	615

MAJOR CITIES/TOWNS

		Population
1	Skopje	480 678
2	Kumanovo	114 283
3	Bitola	85 622
4	Tetovo	75 045
5	Prilep	73 648
6	Veles	57 623
7	Ohrid	55 021
8	Gostivar	52 406
9	Stip	48 425
10	Strumica	45 591
11	Kavadarci	38 944
12	Struga	37 656
13	Kocani	34 668
14	Kicevo	32 161
15	Lipkovo	29 259
16	Saraj	26 726
17	Zelino	26 586
18	Radovis	25 387
47	Kratavo	9 906

REPUBLIKA MAKEDONIJA • REPUBLIC OF MACEDONIA

Capital	Skopje	Population	2 066 718 (144)	% in cities	67%
GDP per capita	$9100 (111)	Area km²	25 713 km² (149)	GMT +/-	+1
Neighbours (km)	Albania 151, Bulgaria 148, Greece 246, Kosovo 159, Serbia 62				

RECENT INTERNATIONAL MATCHES PLAYED BY FYR MACEDONIA

2007 Opponents		Score	Venue	Comp	Scorers	Att	Referee
7-02 Albania	W	1-0	Tirana	Fr	Ristic [33]	8 000	Bertini ITA
24-03 Croatia	L	1-2	Zagreb	ECq	Sedloski [38]	29 969	Plautz AUT
2-06 Israel	L	1-2	Skopje	ECq	Stojkov [13]	12 000	Kircher GER
22-08 Nigeria	D	0-0	Skopje	Fr			
8-09 Russia	L	0-3	Moscow	ECq		23 000	Ovrebø NOR
12-09 Estonia	D	1-1	Skopje	ECq	Maznov [30]	5 000	Trattou CYP
17-10 Andorra	W	3-0	Skopje	ECq	Naumoski [30], Sedloski [44], Pandev [59]	17 500	Malzinskas LTU
17-11 Croatia	W	2-0	Skopje	ECq	Maznov [71], Naumoski [83]	14 500	De Bleeckere BEL
21-11 Israel	L	0-1	Tel Aviv	ECq		2 736	Mikulski POL
2008							
6-02 Serbia	D	1-1	Skopje	Fr	Novevski [58]	12 000	
26-03 Bosnia-Herzegovina	D	2-2	Zenica	Fr	Maznov 2 [40 45]		Svilokos CRO
26-05 Poland	D	1-1	Reutlingen	Fr	Maznov [45]	2 200	Brych GER
20-08 Luxembourg	W	4-1	Luxembourg	Fr	Pandev 2 [6 45], Grozdanoski [33], Naumoski [49]	885	Brugger AUT
6-09 Scotland	W	1-0	Skopje	WCq	Naumoski [5]	9 000	Kralovec CZE
10-09 Netherlands	L	1-2	Skopje	WCq	Pandev [77]	11 000	Gilewski POL
15-10 Iceland	L	0-1	Reykjavík	WCq		5 527	Dereli TUR
19-11 Montenegro	L	1-2	Podgorica	Fr	Popov [85]		Panic BIH
2009							
11-02 Moldova	D	1-1	Antalya	Fr	Pandev [54]	600	Saliy KAZ
1-04 Netherlands	L	0-4	Amsterdam	WCq		47 750	Rasmussen DEN
6-06 Norway	D	0-0	Skopje	WCq		7 000	Tagliavento ITA
10-06 Iceland	W	2-0	Skopje	WCq	Stojkov [9], Ivanovski [85]	7 000	Ennjimmi FRA
12-08 Spain	L	2-3	Skopje	Fr	Pandev 2 [8 33]	25 000	Vink NED
5-09 Scotland	L	0-2	Glasgow	WCq		50 214	Stark GER
9-09 Norway	L	1-2	Oslo	WCq	Grncarov [79]	14 766	Paixao POR
11-10 Qatar	W	2-1	Skopje	Fr	Pandev 2 [25 40]	5 000	Georgiev BUL
14-11 Canada	W	3-0	Strumica	Fr	Sedloski [48], Pandev 2 [61p 90p]	6 000	Genov BUL
18-11 Iran	D	1-1	Tehran	Fr	Pandev [49]	3 000	Moradi IRN
2010							
3-03 Montenegro	W	2-1	Skopje	Fr	Naumoski [27], Pandev [31]	7 000	Janku ALB
29-05 Azerbaijan	W	3-1	Villach	Fr	Trickovski [8], Despotovski [66], Djurovski [88]	100	Drabek AUT
2-06 Romania	W	1-0	Bischofshofen	Fr	Sikov [28]	1 000	Krassnitzer AUT
11-08 Malta	D	1-1	Ta'Qali	Fr	Trickovski [36]		Rossi SMR
3-09 Slovakia	L	0-1	Bratislava	ECq		5 980	Circhetta SUI
7-09 Armenia	D	2-2	Skopje	ECq	Gjurovski [42], Naumoski [96+p]	9 000	Berntsen NOR
8-10 Andorra	W	2-0	Andorra La Vella	ECq	Naumoski [42], Sikov [60]	550	Mazeika LTU
12-10 Russia	L	0-1	Skopje	ECq		10 500	Johannesson SWE
17-11 Albania	D	0-0	Korce	Fr		12 000	Gocek TUR
22-12 China PR	L	0-1	Guangzhou	Fr		8 000	

Fr = Friendly match • EC = UEFA EURO 2008/2012 • WC = FIFA World Cup • q = qualifier

FYR MACEDONIA NATIONAL TEAM HISTORICAL RECORDS

Caps
100 - Goce Sedloski 1996- • **73** - Artim Sakiri 1996-2006 • **71** - Velice Sumulikoski 2002- • **69** - Igor Mitreski 2001- • **59** - Petar Milosevski 1998-2008 • **56** - Goran Pandev 2001- • **48** - Georgi Hristov 1995-2003 • **46** - Vlatko Grozdanoski 2001- • **44** - Toni Micevski 1993-2002 • **43** - Goran Maznov 2001- • **42** - Nikolce Noveski 2004- & Igor Nikolovski • **41** - Goran Stavrevski

Goals
23 - Goran Pandev 2001- • **16** - Georgi Hristov 1995-2003 • **15** - Artim Sakiri 1996-2009 • **10** - Goran Maznov 2001- • **9** - Ilco Naumoski 2003- • **8** - Goce Sedloski 1996- & Sasa Ciric 1996-2003 • **5** - Aco Stojkov 2002- ; Mitko Stojkovski 1994-2002 & Zoran Boskovski 1993-98

Past Coaches
Andon Doncevski 1993-95 • Gjoko Hadzievski 1996-99 • Dragan Kanatlarovski 1999-2001 • Gjore Jovanovski 2001-02 • Nikola Ilievski 2002-03 • Dragan Kanatlarovski 2003-05 • Slobodan Santrac SRB 2005 • Boban Babunski 2005-06 • Srecko Katanec SVN 2006-09 • Mirsad Jonuz 2009-

FYR MACEDONIA 2009-10

PRVA LIGA

	Pl	W	D	L	F	A	Pts	Renova	Rabotnicki	Metalurg	Pelister	Sileks	Vardar	Teteks	Turnovo	Milano	Makedonija	Sloga	Pobeda
Renova Cepciste †	26	17	4	5	45	21	55		2-0 0-1	3-1	1-0 3-1	3-1	3-2	1-0	3-2 2-0	4-0 1-0	1-0	3-1	2-1 2-1
Rabotnicki Skopje ‡	26	15	5	6	38	20	50	2-1		1-1 1-2	3-0	1-1	1-2 1-0	1-3 1-1	3-1 2-1	1-0	5-1	1-1	6-2
Metalurg Skopje ‡	26	12	11	3	35	16	47	3-1 1-0	1-1		1-2 1-0	2-2	3-0	4-0	3-0	1-1 4-0	3-0	0-0	2-1 3-0
Pelister Bitola	26	11	6	9	28	27	39	1-1	1-0 1-0	3-0		1-1	1-0 0-1	0-1 3-1	0-0	1-2	3-1	0-0	1-0 1-0
Sileks Kratovo	26	8	8	10	29	33	32	0-5 0-0	2-0	0-1 0-1	1-0		1-1	1-0	3-0	1-1 4-0	1-1	2-1	0-1 3-0
Vardar Skopje §3	26	9	6	11	31	28	30	1-1 2-0	1-2	0-0 0-0	1-0	3-1 2-0		3-1	1-3 0-1	2-0	3-0		0-0
Teteks	26	8	6	12	31	30	30	0-1 0-1	0-1	0-0 0-0	1-2	1-1 2-1	0-1 0-1		1-0	6-0	2-2	3-0	3-1
Turnovo §3	26	8	5	13	27	35	26	2-2	0-2 0-1	1-1	4-3 0-1	2-0	0-1 0-2	0-1		3-1 2-1	0-1	2-0	3-1
Milano Kumanovo	26	1	3	22	14	81	6	0-2	0-2 0-2	0-0	3-0 2-2	1-4	0-4 0-5	1-2	5-2 2-4		0-2		0-3 3-2
Makedonija GP Skopje	10	5	4	1	23	5	0	0-1		0-0	2-0	5-0	1-0			8-0		4-1	0-3
Sloga Jugomagnat	10	3	2	5	9	16	0			0-3	0-1		1-3	0-3	0-1	1-0	1-0		1-1
Pobeda Prilep	*Excluded after round 28*							0-4	4-2	0-1	0-0	2-2	2-1	2-0	2-0 0-1	0-0 1-0	4-1	0-0	2-0

1/08/2009 - 15/05/2010 • † Qualified for the UEFA Champions League • ‡ Qualified for the Europa League • § = points deducted • Results in bold were annulled • Podeba were excluded from the league after round 28 • Makedonija and Sloga excluded but their first 10 matches were retained
Relegation play-off: **Bregalnica Stip** 2-1 Milano
Top scorers: 14 - Bobi Bozinovski, Rabotnicki • 12 - Dusan Savic, Rabotnicki & Besart Ibraimi, Renova

FYR MACEDONIA 2009-10 — VTORA LIGA (2)

	Pl	W	D	L	F	A	Pts
Shkendija Tetovo §6	26	20	3	3	57	15	57
Skopje	26	17	6	3	49	22	57
Napredok Kicevo	26	17	3	6	55	32	54
Bregalnica Stip	26	15	7	4	49	20	52
Drita Bogovinje	26	12	5	9	36	34	41
Miravci	26	11	3	12	31	31	36
11 Oktomvri Prilep	26	10	4	12	30	34	34
Belasica Strumica	26	10	3	13	27	40	33
Novaci 2005	26	8	7	11	26	37	31
Lokomotiva Skopje	26	8	5	13	29	30	29
Vlaznimi TL Struga	26	7	7	12	26	42	28
Cementarnica Skopje	26	7	5	14	21	40	26
Vlazrimi Kicevo	26	3	5	18	16	49	14
Ohrid 2004 §3	26	5	1	20	26	52	13

15/08/2009 - 19/05/2010 • § = points deducted

MEDALS TABLE

		Overall			League			Cup		City
		G	S	B	G	S	B	G	S	
1	Vardar Skopje	10	3	3	5	2	3	5	1	Skopje
2	Sloga Jugomagnat	6	7	2	3	2	2	3	5	Skopje
3	Sileks Kratovo	5	6		3	5		2	1	Kratovo
4	Rabotnicki Skopje	5	3	1	3	2	1	2	1	Skopje
5	Pobeda Prilep	3	4	4	2	2	4	1	2	Prilep
6	Makedonija Skopje	2	2	2	1	1	2	1	1	Skopje
7	Pelister Bitola	1	2	1			1	1	2	Bitola
8	Cementarnica Skopje	1	1	1			1	1	1	Skopje
9	Renova Cepciste	1		1	1		1			Tetovo
10	Baskimi Kumanovo	1						1		Kumanovo
	Teteks	1						1		Tetovo
12	Milano Kumanovo		3			2			1	Kumanovo
13	Belasica Strumica		2			2				Strumica
14	Madzari Skopje		1						1	Skopje
	Napredok Kicevo		1						1	Kicevo
	Shkendija Tetovo		1						1	Tetovo
17	Balkan Skopje			1			1			Skopje
	Balkan Stokokomerc			1			1			Skopje
	Metalurg Skopje			1			1			Skopje

MAKEDONSKI CUP 2009-10

Round of 16

Teteks	3	1
Belasica Strumica	1	0
Sileks	1	1
Makedonija GP Skopje	1	2
Metalurg Skopje	1	0 4p
Pobeda Prilep	0	1 3p
11 Oktomvri Prilep	1	1
Skopje	3	0
Pelister Bitola	2	3
Ohrid 2004	0	0
Vlaznimi TL Struga	0	1
Drita Bogovinje	1	1
Renova Cepciste	3	3
Lokomotiva Skopje	0	0
Fortuna	0	0
Rabotnicki Skopje	6	3

Quarter-finals

Teteks	0	3
Makedonija GP Skopje	2	0
Metalurg Skopje	0	2
Skopje	0	2
Pelister Bitola	2	1
Drita Bogovinje	2	0
Renova Cepciste	0	0
Rabotnicki Skopje	4	1

Semi-finals

Teteks	0	2
Skopje	0	1
Pelister Bitola	1	0 4p
Rabotnicki Skopje	0	1 5p

Final

Teteks ‡	3
Rabotnicki Skopje	2

3-0 results in bold were awarded
* Home team in the first leg • ‡ Qualified for the Europa League

CUP FINAL
Gradski, Skopje
26-05-2010, Ref: Kiprijanovski
Scorers - Srgan Zaharievski 47p, Genc Iseni 49, Aleksandar Stojanovski 63 for Teteks; Nikola Gligorov 69, Filip Petkovski 83 for Rabotnicki

MLI – MALI

FIFA/COCA-COLA WORLD RANKING

1993	1994	1995	1996	1997	1998	1999	2000	2001	2002	2003	2004	2005	2006	2007	2008	2009	2010
70	52	52	67	80	70	72	98	112	73	54	51	63	36	46	45	47	67

	2010												Hi/Lo
	Jan	Feb	Mar	Mar	Apr	May	Jul	Aug	Sep	Oct	Nov	Dec	35
	47	53	54	57	54	54	55	55	65	64	64	67	117

Mali made a miraculous recovery in a dramatic opening game at the Nations Cup finals against Angola in what was one of the most extraordinary games played during 2010, but the tournament ended in an early exit and the unceremonious departure of coach Stephen Keshi. Frenchman Alain Giresse replaced him in April but made a horrendous start to the 2012 Nations Cup qualifiers with defeat in the Cape Verde islands. Mali needed an own goal to win their next match in October against Liberia but face a tough battle in their bid to qualify for a fifth finals appearance in the last six tournaments. Stade Malien's historic triumph in the 2009 CAF Confederation Cup saw them take part in the African Super Cup in February but they were beaten 2-0 by TP Mazembe Englebert in Lubumbashi and there were to be no repeat heroics in 2010 for either Stade Malien or Djoliba. In a close title race at home, Stade Malien pipped Djoliba to the championship by two points - their eighth title in the past 11 seasons. In the cup Djoliba were looking for a fourth consecutive triumph but were beaten in the semi-finals by CSF who then lost 1-0 in the final to Real Bamako. For Real, one of the historic names of football in Mali and one of only three teams to have won the league, it was their first trophy in nearly two decades.

FIFA WORLD CUP RECORD
1930-1998 DNE 2002-2010 DNQ

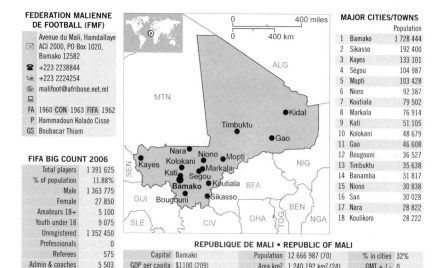

FEDERATION MALIENNE DE FOOTBALL (FMF)

Avenue du Mali, Hamdallaye
ACI 2000, PO Box 1020, Bamako 12582
☎ +223 2238844
📠 +223 2224254
📧 malifoot@afribone.net.ml
🖥
FA 1960 CON 1963 FIFA 1962
P Hammadoun Kolado Cisse
GS Boubacar Thiam

FIFA BIG COUNT 2006

Total players	1 391 625
% of population	11.88%
Male	1 363 775
Female	27 850
Amateurs 18+	5 100
Youth under 18	9 075
Unregistered	1 352 450
Professionals	0
Referees	575
Admin & coaches	5 503
Number of clubs	140
Number of teams	700

MAJOR CITIES/TOWNS

Population

1	Bamako	1 728 444
2	Sikasso	192 400
3	Kayes	133 101
4	Ségou	104 987
5	Mopti	103 428
6	Nioro	92 387
7	Koutiala	79 502
8	Markala	76 914
9	Kati	51 105
10	Kolokani	48 679
11	Gao	46 608
12	Bougouni	36 527
13	Timbuktu	35 638
14	Banamba	31 817
15	Niono	30 838
16	San	30 028
17	Nara	28 822
18	Koulikoro	28 222

REPUBLIQUE DE MALI • REPUBLIC OF MALI

Capital	Bamako	Population	12 666 987 (70)	% in cities	32%
GDP per capita	$1100 (209)	Area km²	1 240 192 km² (24)	GMT +/-	0
Neighbours (km)	Algeria 1376, Burkina Faso 1000, Guinea 858, Cote d'Ivoire 532, Mauritania 2237, Niger 821, Senegal 419				

RECENT INTERNATIONAL MATCHES PLAYED BY MALI

2008	Opponents		Score	Venue	Comp	Scorers	Att	Referee
10-01	Egypt	L	0-1	Abu Dhabi	Fr			
21-01	Benin	W	1-0	Sekondi	CNr1	Kanoute [49p]		Damon RSA
25-01	Nigeria	D	0-0	Sekondi	CNr1			El Arjoun MAR
29-01	Côte d'Ivoire	L	0-3	Accra	CNr1			Maillet SEY
1-06	Congo	W	4-2	Bamoko	WCq	Seydou Keita 2 [1 61], Adama Coulibaly [32], Soumaila Coulibaly [42]	40 000	Bennaceur TUN
7-06	Chad	W	2-1	N'Djamena	WCq	Kanoute 2 [4 22]	15 000	Aguidissou BEN
14-06	Sudan	L	2-3	Khartoum	WCq	Kanoute 2 [63 94+]	15 000	Abdelfattah EGY
22-06	Sudan	W	3-0	Bamoko	WCq	Kanoute [23], Seydou Keita 2 [58 66]	25 000	Doue CIV
19-08	Gabon	L	0-1	Mantes-La-Ville	Fr			
7-09	Congo	L	0-1	Brazzaville	WCq		16 000	Haimoudi ALG
11-10	Chad	W	2-1	Bamako	WCq	Sidi Yaya Keita 2 [44 82]	40 000	Keita GUI
18-11	Algeria	D	1-1	Rouen	Fr	Cheick Diabate [13]		
2009								
11-02	Angola	W	4-0	Bois-Guillaume	Fr	Ismail Coulibaly [14], Yatabare [18], Kanoute [35], Seydou Keita [66]		
28-03	Sudan	D	1-1	Omdurman	WCq	Kanoute [19]	35 000	Maillet SEY
25-04	Equatorial Guinea	W	3-0	Bamako	Fr	Sekou Camara [18], Idrissa Traore [38], Diamoutene [86]		
7-06	Ghana	L	0-2	Bamako	WCq		40 000	Evehe CMR
21-06	Benin	W	3-1	Bamako	WCq	Maiga [29], Mamadou Diallo [76], Kanoute [84]	40 000	Abd El Fatah EGY
12-08	Burkina Faso	W	3-0	Le Petit Quevilly	Fr	Mamadou Diallo 2 [20 35], Maiga [25]		
6-09	Benin	D	1-1	Cotonou	WCq	Samassa [72]	33 000	Damon RSA
11-10	Sudan	W	1-0	Bamako	WCq	Kanoute [89]	15 000	Benouza ALG
15-11	Ghana	D	2-2	Kumasi	WCq	Fane [23], Ndiaye [68]	39 000	Diatta SEN
27-12	Korea DPR	L	0-1	Doha	Fr			
30-12	Iran	W	2-1	Doha	Fr	Ndiaye [29], Bakaye Traore [30]		
2010								
2-01	Qatar	D	0-0	Doha	Fr			
4-01	Egypt	L	0-1	Dubai	Fr			
10-01	Angola	D	4-4	Luanda	CNr1	Seydou Keita 2 [79 93+], Kanoute [88], Yattabare [94+]	45 000	Abd El Fatah EGY
14-01	Algeria	L	0-1	Luanda	CNr1		4 000	Ssegonga UGA
18-01	Malawi	W	3-1	Cabinda	CNr1	Kanoute [1], Seydou Keita [3], Bagayoko [85]	21 000	Seechurn MRI
3-03	Libya	L	1-2	Tripoli	Fr	Bakary Coulibaly [15]		
11-08	Guinea	L	0-2	Marignane	Fr			
4-09	Cape Verde Islands	L	0-1	Praia	CNq			Benouza ALG
9-10	Liberia	W	2-1	Bamako	CNq	Abdou Traore [2], OG [51]		Djaoupe TOG
17-11	Congo DR	W	3-1	Evreux	Fr	Maiga [48], Abdou Traore [54], Ndiaye [75p]		

Fr = Friendly match • CN = CAF African Cup of Nations • WC = FIFA World Cup • q = qualifier

MALI 2010

PREMIERE DIVISION

	Pl	W	D	L	F	A	Pts	Stade Malien	Djoliba	CSK	COB	Jeanne d'Arc	Réal	Police	ASKO	O. Créateurs	Duguwolofila	USFAS	Bakaridjan	Sigui	Stade Sik'so
Stade Malien †	26	20	1	5	48	17	61		0-1	0-2	2-1	1-0	2-0	3-0	2-0	4-0	**	2-1	2-0	4-1	7-1
Djoliba †	26	17	8	1	34	9	59	0-0		1-0	1-0	1-0	1-0	1-1	2-1	1-0	2-0	1-1	3-0	0-0	3-0
Centre Salif Keita ‡	26	14	4	8	31	21	46	2-0	0-1		1-0	0-0	3-0	1-1	2-0	2-1	1-0	0-1	0-3	2-1	2-1
Cercle Olympique	26	12	3	11	33	29	39	2-3	0-0	1-1		1-0	3-3	0-1	0-4	1-0	2-0	1-0	3-2	3-1	3-0
Jeanne d'Arc	26	11	4	11	32	29	37	1-0	0-1	1-2	1-2		2-0	**	2-0	3-2	1-0	5-2	1-5	3-1	2-1
Réal Bamako ‡	26	8	11	7	28	23	35	0-1	0-0	2-0	1-0	1-1		0-0	0-1	3-0	1-1	1-1	**	2-0	1-0
Police Bamako	26	8	8	10	23	34	32	0-2	1-1	0-3	1-2	1-2	0-4		D	3-1	3-2	1-2	2-1	0-0	3-1
AS Korofina Bamako	26	8	7	11	24	26	31	**0-2**	2-0	0-1	2-1	0-0	0-0	3-1		1-2	1-2	2-0	1-1	0-1	1-1
Onze Créateurs	26	8	4	14	31	40	28	1-3	1-2	1-1	0-3	2-1	2-2	2-1	0-1		**2-0**	0-1	0-2	5-1	2-0
Duguwolofila Koulikoro	26	7	8	12	20	30	28	0-1	0-3	2-1	1-0	1-1	0-0	0-1	1-1	0-2		1-0	1-1	2-0	3-1
USFAS Bamako	26	6	9	11	21	31	27	0-1	0-2	2-1	0-2	1-2	2-2	0-0	1-2	0-0	1-1		0-0	2-2	1-0
Bakaridjan Ségou	26	6	7	13	25	31	25	0-2	0-0	0-1	1-2	0-3	**0-2**	2-0	0-1	0-1	0-0	1-1		4-2	0-1
Sigui Kayes	26	5	6	15	19	45	21	1-2	0-0	0-2	**	1-0	0-2	1-1	1-0	1-1	**2-0**	1-0	0-2		0-3
Stade Sikasso	26	5	5	16	21	45	20	1-2	2-4	**	1-0	1-0	1-1	0-1	1-1	2-4	1-0	0-1	0-0	1-1	

13/12/2009 - 11/08/2010 • † Qualified for the CAF Champions League • ‡ Qualified for the CAF Confederation Cup • Matches in bold awarded
** Awarded as 2-0 defeats for both clubs

MEDALS TABLE

		Overall			Lge		Cup		Africa			City
		G	S	B	G	S	G	S	G	S	B	
1	Djoliba AC	40	10	3	21		19	10			3	Bamako
2	Stade Malien	34	9		16		17	8	1	1		Bamako
3	Real Bamako	16	8		6		10	7		1		Bamako
4	Cercle Olympique	2	2				2	2				Bamako
5	AS Bamako	1	1				1	1				Bamako
6	AS Sigui Kayes	1					1					Kayes
7	Avenir Ségou		4					4				Ségou
8	AS Nianan Koulikoro		3					3				Koulikoro
9	Kayésienne		2					2				Kayes
	USFAS Bamako		2					2				Bamako

COUPE DU MALI 2010

Round of 16

Round of 16		Quarter-finals		Semi-finals		Final	
Réal Bamako	2						
Stade Sikasso	0	Réal Bamako	2				
Attar Club Kidal	1	Sigui Kayes	0				
Sigui Kayes	4			Réal Bamako	2		
AS Korofina Bamako	2			Stade Malien	0		
Cercle Olympique	0	AS Korofina Bamako	0				
Balanzan Segou	0	Stade Malien	1				
Stade Malien	4					Réal Bamako ‡	1
Djoliba	3					Centre Salif Keita	0
Tata National Sikasso	0	Djoliba	3				
Bakaridjan Ségou	1	Nianan Koulikoro	0				
Nianan Koulikoro	2			Djoliba	0		
AS Bamako	2			Centre Salif Keita	2		
Duguwolofila Koulikoro	1	AS Bamako	4 5p				
USFAS Bamako	1	Centre Salif Keita	4 6p				
Centre Salif Keita	4						

CUP FINAL

Stade Modibo Keita, Bamako
31-07-2010, Ref: Sidibe

Scorer - Ibrahim Kader Coulibaly 25

‡ Qualified for the CAF Confederation Cup

MLT – MALTA

FIFA/COCA-COLA WORLD RANKING

1993	1994	1995	1996	1997	1998	1999	2000	2001	2002	2003	2004	2005	2006	2007	2008	2009	2010
83	78	90	122	133	130	116	119	131	122	129	134	118	119	136	147	146	164

2010												Hi/Lo
Jan	Feb	Mar	Mar	Apr	May	Jul	Aug	Sep	Oct	Nov	Dec	66
146	144	150	158	154	157	152	151	150	168	169	164	169

Four years after last winning the championship, Birkirkara claimed the title for the third time in the club's history, although they had the peculiar system on which the Premier League is organised to thank for their triumph. Under normal circumstances Valletta would have been crowned champions. The two teams had identical records but Valletta had a much better goal difference, but, as is the case in Israel, the points totals are halved after the first 18 games of the season in preparation for a further round in a 'championship' group. With 40 points after 18 games, Valletta took 20 points forward as did Birkirkara despite only having 39 points. The system of rounding up gave Birkirakara an 'extra' point which made all the difference at the end of the season. For Birkirkara coach Paul Zammit it must have seemed like poetic justice having been sacked by Valletta at the end of the previous season, but there was consolation for Valletta when they won the FA Trophy for the first time in nine years, beating Qormi 2-1 in the final. Qormi were the surprise team of the season after not only making it to the final for the first time in their 49-year history but also finishing third in the league, thanks in no small part to the goals of their striker Camilo. The Brazilian scored 24 goals in just 21 starts to finish the season as the league's top scorer.

FIFA WORLD CUP RECORD
1930-1970 DNE 1974-2010 DNQ

MALTA FOOTBALL ASSOCIATION (MFA)

	Millenium Stand, Floor 2, National Stadium, Ta'Qali, ATD 400
☎	+356 23 386000
📠	+356 23 386900
✉	info@mfa.com.mt
🖥	www.mfa.com.mt
FA	1900 CON 1960 FIFA 1959
P	Norman Darmanin Demajo
GS	Joseph Gauci

FIFA BIG COUNT 2006

Total players	24 853
% of population	6.21%
Male	22 451
Female	2 402
Amateurs 18+	7 000
Youth under 18	2 773
Unregistered	3 100
Professionals	430
Referees	99
Admin & coaches	2 105
Number of clubs	51
Number of teams	325

MAJOR CITIES/TOWNS

		Population
1	Birkirkara	20 737
2	Mosta	19 152
3	St Paul's Bay	16 507
4	Qormi	15 743
5	Zabbar	14 519
6	San Gwann	12 741
7	Naxxar	12 704
8	Sliema	12 595
9	Marsascala	11 335
10	Zebbug	11 335
11	Fgura	11 196
12	Zejtun	11 129
13	Rabat	10 684
14	Attard	10 523
15	Zurrieq	10 002
16	Birzebugia	9 057
17	Hamrun	8 665
18	Paola	8 330
38	Marsaxlokk	3 302

REPUBBLIKA TA' MALTA • REPUBLIC OF MALTA

Capital	Valletta	Population	405 165 (173)	% in cities	94%
GDP per capita	$24 600 (52)	Area km²	316 km² (207)	GMT +/-	+1
Neighbours (km)	Coast 196				

RECENT INTERNATIONAL MATCHES PLAYED BY MALTA

2007 Opponents		Score	Venue	Comp	Scorers	Att	Referee
7-02 Austria	D	1-1	Ta'Qali	Fr	Agius [8]	3 000	Bartolini SUI
24-03 Moldova	D	1-1	Chisinau	ECq	Mallia [73]	8 033	Aliyev AZE
28-03 Greece	L	0-1	Ta'Qali	ECq		8 700	Garcia POR
2-06 Norway	L	0-4	Oslo	ECq		16 364	Granat POL
6-06 Bosnia-Herzegovina	L	0-1	Sarajevo	ECq		10 500	Richards WAL
22-08 Albania	L	0-3	Tirana	Fr			
8-09 Turkey	D	2-2	Ta'Qali	ECq	Said [41], Schembri [76]	10 500	Messner AUT
12-09 Armenia	L	0-1	Ta'Qali	Fr		2 000	Richmond SCO
13-10 Hungary	L	0-2	Budapest	ECq		7 633	Nalbandyan ARM
17-10 Moldova	L	2-3	Ta'Qali	ECq	Scerri [71], Mifsud [84p]	7 069	Ishchenko UKR
17-11 Greece	L	0-5	Athens	ECq		31 332	Kaldma EST
21-11 Norway	L	1-4	Ta'Qali	ECq	Mifsud [53]	7 000	Baskakov RUS
2008							
2-02 Armenia	L	0-1	Ta'Qali	Fr			
4-02 Iceland	W	1-0	Ta'Qali	Fr	Frendo [18]		
6-02 Belarus	L	0-1	Ta'Qali	Fr			Tshagharyan ARM
26-03 Liechtenstein	W	7-1	Ta'Qali	Fr	Mifsud 5 [2p 17 21p 59 69], Pace [35], Said [86]		Collum SCO
30-05 Austria	L	1-5	Graz	Fr	Mifsud [41]	14 200	Krajnc SVN
20-08 Estonia	L	1-2	Tallinn	Fr	Azzopardi [9]	2 700	Gilewski POL
6-09 Portugal	L	0-4	Ta'Qali	WCq		11 000	Blom NED
10-09 Albania	L	0-3	Tirana	WCq		7 400	Schoergenhofer AUT
11-10 Denmark	L	0-3	Copenhagen	WCq		33 124	Paniashvili GEO
15-10 Hungary	L	0-1	Ta'Qali	WCq		4 797	Valgeirsson ISL
19-11 Iceland	L	0-1	Corradino	Fr			Demarco ITA
2009							
11-02 Albania	D	0-0	Ta'Qali	WCq		2 041	Deaconu ROU
28-03 Denmark	L	0-3	Ta'Qali	WCq		6 235	Mikulski POL
1-04 Hungary	L	0-3	Budapest	WCq		34 400	Sukhina RUS
5-06 Czech Republic	L	0-1	Jablonec	Fr		6 019	Fautrel FRA
10-06 Sweden	L	0-4	Gothenburg	WCq		25 271	Murray SCO
12-08 Georgia	W	2-0	Ta'Qali	Fr	Mifsud 2 [64 73]		Kailis CYP
4-09 Cape Verde Islands	L	0-2	Ta'Qali	Fr			Banti ITA
9-09 Sweden	L	0-1	Ta'Qali	WCq		4 705	McCourt NIR
10-10 Angola	L	1-2	Vila Real	Fr	Cohen [13]		Almeida POR
14-10 Portugal	L	0-4	Guimaraes	WCq		29 350	Kelly IRL
18-11 Bulgaria	L	1-4	Paola	Fr	Mifsud [46]		Nijhuis NED
2010							
3-03 Finland	L	1-2	Ta'Qali	Fr	Mifsud [17]		Bergonzi ITA
13-05 Germany	L	0-3	Aachen	Fr		27 000	Hamer LUX
11-08 FYR Macedonia	D	1-1	Ta'Qali	Fr	Mifsud [47]		Rossi ITA
2-09 Israel	L	1-3	Tel Aviv	ECq	Pace [38]	17 365	Ennjimi FRA
7-09 Latvia	L	0-2	Ta'Qali	ECq		6 255	Asumaa FIN
8-10 Georgia	L	0-1	Tbilisi	ECq		38 000	Black NIR
17-11 Croatia	L	0-3	Zagreb	ECq		9 000	Gomes POR

Fr = Friendly match • EC = UEFA EURO 2008/2012 • WC = FIFA World Cup • q = qualifier

MALTA NATIONAL TEAM HISTORICAL RECORDS

Caps
121 - David Carabott 1987-2005 & Gilbert Agius 1993- • 111 - Carmel Busuttil 1982-2001 • 102 - Joe Brincat 1988-2004 • 95 - John Buttigieg 1984-2000 • 91 - Brian Said 1996- • 90 - Silvio Vella 1988-2000 • 79 - Michael Mifsud 2000- • 74 - Michael Degiorgio 1981-92 • 70 - Hubert Suda 1988-2003 • 69 - Jeffrey Chetcuti 1994-2005

Goals
25 - Michael Mifsud 2000- • 23 - Carmel Busuttil 1982-2001 • 12 - David Carabott 1987-2005 • 8 - Gilbert Agius 1993- & Hubert Suda 1988-2003 • 6 - Kristian Laferla 1986-98; Raymond Xuereb 1971-85 & Joe Brincat 1988-2004 • 5 - George Mallia 1999- & Brian Said 1996-

Past Coaches
Joe A. Griffiths 1957-61 • Carm Borg 1961-64 • Janos Bedl HUN 1966 • Tony Formosa 1966 • Joseph Attard 1969 • Saviour Cuschieri 1970 • Victor Scerri 1973 • Terrenzio Polverini ITA 1974-76 • John Calleja 1976-78 • Victor Scerri 1978-83 • Guentcho Dobrev BUL 1984-87 • Horst Heese GER 1988-91 • Pippo Psaila 1991-93 • Pietro Ghedin ITA 1993-95 • Robert Gatt 1996 • Milorad Kosanovic YUG 1996-97 • Josif Ilic YUG 1997-2001 • Sigfried Held GER 2001-03 • Horst Heese GER 2003-06 • Dusan Fitzel CZE 2006-09 • John Buttigieg 2009-

MALTA 2009-10

PREMIER LEAGUE

Team	Pl	W	D	L	F	A	Pts	Birkirkara	Valletta	Qormi	Sliema W	Tarxien	Hibernians	Floriana	Hamrun Sp	Dingli	Msida SJ
Birkirkara (20) †	28	20	4	4	64	32	**45**	—	1-3 1-0	2-0 3-1	0-1 2-1	5-1 1-0	2-2 2-1	0-1	2-1	2-0	4-1
Valletta (20) ‡	28	20	4	4	71	25	**44**	1-1 4-2	—	1-0 3-0	1-3 2-0	2-2 3-0	0-1 2-1	6-0	4-0	4-1	0-0
Qormi (18)	28	15	2	11	53	36	**30**	2-5 0-2	0-2 1-2	—	1-0 3-0	0-2 2-0	3-1 3-0	6-2	2-0	4-0	3-0
Sliema Wanderers (15) ‡	28	14	2	12	41	37	**30**	0-3 0-3	0-1 2-1	1-2 0-4	—	4-2 2-0	2-2 3-0	3-0	5-0	3-1	2-0
Tarxien Rainbows (13)	28	10	6	12	41	50	**23**	0-2 3-3	2-2 2-6	1-2 3-2	3-1 0-2	—	1-2 2-0	2-1	0-1	2-1	3-1
Hibernians (14)	28	8	6	14	40	51	**17**	2-2 4-5	2-4 1-3	2-2 1-0	0-1 1-2	0-1 0-1	—	2-3	4-2	2-1	3-0
Floriana (12)	24	10	6	8	35	41	**25**	1-2	0-4	1-1	1-1	1-1	1-1	—	1-1 1-0	1-2 4-2	4-2 2-1
Hamrun Spartans (11)	24	10	4	10	41	39	**24**	0-2	2-3	1-2	3-0	2-2	2-2	0-1 2-1	—	3-0 2-1	1-0 2-2
Dingli Swallows (2)	24	2	0	22	23	71	**5**	1-3	0-6	1-4	0-2	1-4	1-2	0-2 0-3	1-3 0-6	—	1-2 5-2
Msida St Joseph (6) §10	24	4	4	16	24	51	**1**	1-2	0-1	0-3	1-0	1-1	0-1	1-2 1-1	0-2 3-5	2-1 3-2	—

21/08/2009 - 5/05/2010 • † Qualified for the UEFA Champions League • ‡ Qualified for the Europa League • Points taken forward for the final round in brackets • § = points deducted • Top scorers: 24 - Camilo BRA, Qormi • 20 - Terence Scerri, Valletta • 17 - Ryan Darmanin, Floriana

MALTA 2009-10 FIRST DIVISION (2)

Team	Pl	W	D	L	F	A	Pts
Marsaxlokk	18	12	5	1	42	14	**41**
Vittoriosa Stars	18	11	3	4	28	13	**36**
Balzan Youth	18	9	4	5	26	18	**31**
St George's	18	9	2	7	28	32	**29**
Mosta	18	7	6	5	31	28	**27**
Mqabba	18	5	6	7	30	30	**21**
Melita	18	5	4	9	21	31	**19**
Pietà Hotspurs	18	4	5	9	15	25	**17**
St Patrick	18	5	2	11	14	34	**17**
San Gwann	18	2	5	11	21	31	**11**

20/11/2009 - 3/05/2010

MEDALS TABLE

#	Team	Overall			League			Cup		City
		G	S	B	G	S	B	G	S	
1	Sliema Wanderers	46	50	19	26	31	19	20	19	Sliema
2	Floriana	43	23	13	25	11	13	18	12	Floriana
3	Valletta	31	28	20	19	16	20	12	12	Valletta
4	Hibernians	18	19	9	10	9	9	8	10	Paola
5	Hamrun Spartans	13	13	13	7	10	13	6	3	Hamrun
6	Birkirkara	7	9	5	3	6	5	4	3	Birkirkara
7	Rabat Ajax	3	2	1	2	1	1	1	1	Rabat
8	St. Georges	1	6	5	1	4	5		2	Cospicua
9	Zurrieq	1	2	2			2	1	2	Zurrieq
10	Marsaxlokk	1	2	1	1	1	1		1	Marsaxlokk
	Melita St. Julians	1	2	1		1	1	1	1	Melita
12	Gzira United	1						1	1	Gzira
13	KOMR Militia	1			1					

FA TROPHY 2009-10

Round of 16		Quarter-finals		Semi-finals		Final	
Valletta	Bye						
		Valletta	3				
		Birkirkara	1				
Birkirkara	Bye			**Valletta**	0 6p		
Sliema Wanderers	Bye			Hamrun Spartans	0 5p		
		Sliema Wanderers	2				
Marsaxlokk	0	**Hamrun Spartans**	5				
Hamrun Spartans	1					**Valletta** ‡	2
Tarxien Rainbows	4					Qormi	1
Floriana	1	**Tarxien Rainbows**	2				
Dingli Swallows	1	Balzan Youths	0				
Balzan Youths	2			Tarxien Rainbows	0		
Hibernians	Bye			**Qormi**	2		
		Hibernians	1 3p				
St Patrick	1	**Qormi**	1 4p				
Qormi	5						

‡ Qualified for the Europa League

CUP FINAL
National, Ta'Qali
23-05-2010. Ref: Pisani
Scorers - Michael Mifsud 8, Terence Scerri 21 for Valletta; Camilo 78p for Qormi

MNE – MONTENEGRO

FIFA/COCA-COLA WORLD RANKING

1993	1994	1995	1996	1997	1998	1999	2000	2001	2002	2003	2004	2005	2006	2007	2008	2009	2010
-	-	-	-	-	-	-	-	-	-	-	-	-	-	172	112	74	25

	2010												Hi/Lo
	Jan	Feb	Mar	Mar	Apr	May	Jul	Aug	Sep	Oct	Nov	Dec	25
	74	72	71	69	65	64	72	73	40	26	26	25	199

With just four short years of history behind it, the national team of Montenegro is already starting to make an impact and coach Zlatko Kranjcar could not have hoped for a better start to the qualifiers for Euro 2012. With Wales and Switzerland beaten at home and with a victory over Bulgaria in Sofia, many expected Montenegro to lose their 100% record against England at Wembley. They did - but they still held the English to a draw to finish the year in pole position in the group and with the very real possibility of qualifying for the finals. That would be a staggering achievement should it happen given that the population of Montenegro is less than 700,000. That would make them comfortably the smallest nation to have qualified for the finals although with Montenegrins spread throughout the former Yugoslavia, the numbers of players available is not quite so restricted. At home a pecking order of clubs is emerging with Rudar, from the town of Pljevlja in the north, winning the double in 2010. With three trophies overall in the first four years of the league and cup they now head the honours list, followed by Mogren and then Buducnost from the capital Podgorica. Buducnost are starting to earn a reputation for finishing as runners-up and in 2010 they came a close second behind Rudar in the league as well as losing to them in the Cup Final.

FIFA WORLD CUP RECORD
1930-2006 DNE 2010 DNQ

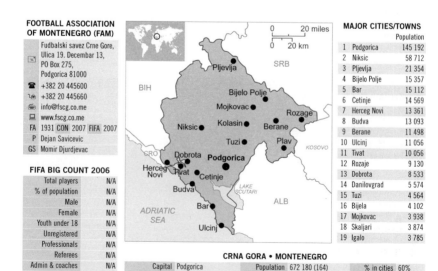

FOOTBALL ASSOCIATION OF MONTENEGRO (FAM)

Fudbalski savez Crne Gore, Ulica 19. Decembar 13, PO Box 275, Podgorica 81000
☎ +382 20 445600
📠 +382 20 445660
📧 info@fscg.co.me
🖥 www.fscg.co.me
FA 1931 CON 2007 FIFA 2007
P Dejan Savicevic
GS Momir Djurdjevac

FIFA BIG COUNT 2006

Total players	N/A
% of population	N/A
Male	N/A
Female	N/A
Youth under 18	N/A
Unregistered	N/A
Professionals	N/A
Referees	N/A
Admin & coaches	N/A
Number of clubs	N/A
Number of teams	N/A

MAJOR CITIES/TOWNS

		Population
1	Podgorica	145 192
2	Niksic	58 712
3	Pljevlja	21 354
4	Bijelo Polje	15 357
5	Bar	15 112
6	Cetinje	14 569
7	Herceg Novi	13 361
8	Budva	13 093
9	Berane	11 498
10	Ulcinj	11 056
11	Tivat	10 056
12	Rozaje	9 130
13	Dobrota	8 533
14	Danilovgrad	5 574
15	Tuzi	4 564
16	Bijela	4 102
17	Mojkovac	3 938
18	Skaljari	3 874
19	Igalo	3 785

CRNA GORA • MONTENEGRO

Capital Podgorica	Population 672 180 (164)	% in cities 60%
GDP per capita $10 100 (104)	Area km² 13 812 km² (161)	GMT +/- +1
Neighbours (km) Albania 172, Bosnia-Herzegovina 225, Croatia 25, Kosovo 79, Serbia 124 • Coast 293		

RECENT INTERNATIONAL MATCHES PLAYED BY MONTENEGRO

2007	Opponents	Score		Venue	Comp	Scorers	Att	Referee
24-03	Hungary	W	2-1	Podgorica	Fr	Vucinic [64p], Burzanovic [82p]	11 000	Kranjc SVN
1-06	Japan	L	0-2	Shizuoka	Fr		28 635	Svendsen DEN
3-06	Colombia	L	0-1	Matsumoto	Fr		10 070	Ogiya JPN
22-08	Slovenia	D	1-1	Podgorica	Fr	Vucinic [28p]		
12-09	Sweden	L	1-2	Podgorica	Fr	Vucinic [15]	9 000	Brugger AUT
17-10	Estonia	W	1-0	Tallinn	Fr	Vucinic [41]	2 000	Fröjdfeldt SWE
2008								
26-03	Norway	W	3-1	Podgorica	Fr	Burzanovic [7], Boskovic [37], Dalovic [59]	9 000	Stavrev MKD
27-05	Kazakhstan	W	3-0	Podgorica	Fr	Dalovic 2 [15 45], Drincic [21]	9 000	Tusin LUX
31-05	Romania	L	0-4	Bucharest	Fr		8 000	Tudor ROU
20-08	Hungary	D	3-3	Budapest	Fr	Jovetic 2 [45p 68], Vukevic [51]	4 913	Havrilla SVK
6-09	Bulgaria	D	2-2	Podgorica	WCq	Vucinic [61], Jovetic [82p]	9 000	Oriekhov UKR
10-09	Republic of Ireland	D	0-0	Podgorica	WCq		12 000	Kaldma EST
15-10	Italy	L	1-2	Lecce	WCq	Vucinic [19]	20 162	Proenca POR
19-11	Macedonia FYR	W	2-1	Podgorica	Fr	Dzudovic [24], Jovetic [33p]		Panic BIH
2009								
28-03	Italy	L	0-2	Podgorica	WCq		10 500	Atkinson ENG
1-04	Georgia	D	0-0	Tbilisi	WCq		16 000	Malcolm NIR
6-06	Cyprus	D	2-2	Larnaca	WCq	Damjanovic 2 [65 77]	3 000	Velasco ESP
12-08	Wales	W	2-1	Podgorica	Fr	Jovetic [31p], Dalovic [45]	5 000	Mazic SRB
5-09	Bulgaria	L	1-4	Sofia	WCq	Jovetic [9]	7 543	Asumaa FIN
9-09	Cyprus	D	1-1	Podgorica	WCq	Vucinic [56p]	4 000	Zimmermann SUI
10-10	Georgia	W	2-1	Podgorica	WCq	Batak [14], Delibasic [78]	5 420	Dereli TUR
14-10	Republic of Ireland	D	0-0	Dublin	WCq		50 212	Hrinal SVK
18-11	Belarus	W	1-0	Podgorica	Fr	Vucinic [80]	5 000	Stavrev MKD
2010								
3-03	FYR Macedonia	L	1-2	Skopje	Fr	Basa [62]	7 000	Janku ALB
25-05	Albania	L	0-1	Podgorica	Fr		7 000	Strahonja CRO
29-05	Norway	L	1-2	Oslo	Fr	Vucinic [82]	13 132	Eriksson SWE
11-08	Northern Ireland	W	2-0	Podgorica	Fr	Dalovic 2 [43 59]	5 000	Jovanetic SRB
3-09	Wales	W	1-0	Podgorica	ECq	Vucinic [30]	7 442	Kakos GRE
7-09	Bulgaria	W	1-0	Sofia	ECq	Zverotic [36]	9 470	Bezborodov RUS
8-10	Switzerland	W	1-0	Podgorica	ECq	Vucinic [68]	10 750	Iturralde ESP
12-10	England	D	0-0	London	ECq		73 451	Grafe GER
17-11	Azerbaijan	W	2-0	Podgorica	Fr	Pejovic [62], Beciraj [74]	3 000	Stavrev MKD

Fr = Friendly match • EC = UEFA EURO 2012 • WC = FIFA World Cup • q = qualifier

MONTENEGRO NATIONAL TEAM HISTORICAL RECORDS

Caps
25 - Simon Vukcevic 2007- • **24** - Mirko Vucinic 2007- & Savo Pavicevic 2007- • **22** - Vladimir Bozovic 2007-; Branko Boskovic 2007- & Milorad Petkovic 2007- • **21** - Radoslav Batak 2007- • **20** - Luka Pejovic 2007-

Goals
11 - Mirko Vucinic 2007- • **6** - Radomir Dalovic 2007- & Stevan Jovetic 2007-

Past Coaches
Zoran Filipovic 2007-10 • Zlatko Kranjcar 2010-

MONTENEGRO 2009-10

PRVA CRNOGORSKA LIGA

	Pl	W	D	L	F	A	Pts	Rudar	Buducnost	Mogren	Zeta	Grbalj	Lovcen	Sutjeska	OFK	Decic	Mornar	Berane	Kom
Rudar Pljevlja †	33	22	5	6	56	26	71		1-0 2-1	2-0 3-1	2-4	1-0 3-0	0-1	3-1 2-0 3-1	2-2	1-1	1-0	1-0	1-0 3-0
Buducnost Podgorica ‡	33	21	6	6	67	35	69	0-0		1-2	4-2 3-1	4-1	3-1 4-0	2-1	3-2	2-1 1-1-0-2	4-0-2-1	2-0 3-0 3-1	
Mogren Budva ‡	33	16	9	8	49	34	57	0-0	0-0 2-2		0-0	0-2 1-3 1-0	4-0	1-1	0-2 1-04-0 0-04-0	2-03-1 2-1			
Zeta Golubovci ‡	33	17	6	10	43	33	57	0-1 3-2	2-4 0-3 1-0			1-0 2-2	2-1	3-0-0-0-2-0 1-1	2-1	1-0	1-0	2-0 2-0	
Grbalj Radanovici	33	15	8	10	66	42	53	4-2	0-4 1-1 2-4 3-5	0-2			4-0	0-0	2-0	0-0 1-0 2-0 3-1 5-0	5-0 1-0 0-11-0		
Lovcen Cetinje	33	15	7	11	32	37	52	0-3 0-3	1-2	0-0	2-1 1-0-0-0-2-1			0-0 3-2 1-0 1-0	1-1	1-0	2-1	1-0 2-1	
Sutjeska Niksic	33	11	7	15	33	36	40	1-2	3-1 2-0 4-0 2-0	2-1	2-2 0-2 1-1		1-0		2-0	1-2 3-0 1-0 0-0 1-0			
OFK Petrovac	33	10	6	17	38	49	36	0-4	1-1 1-2 1-2 1-2	0-1	0-2 1-2	0-2	1-0 2-1			1-3	4-2 3-1	1-2	2-0
Decic Tuzi	33	8	11	14	27	35	35	0-1 2-2	0-1	1-1	0-2 2-1	1-3	2-1 0-1-0-1	0-0 1-0-0-2 2-3			0-0	2-1	2-1
Mornar Bar §1	33	9	8	16	29	49	34	0-1 2-1	2-3	1-2	0-0-0-0 3-3	1-1 1-0	1-0	1-3 0-0 2-0		0-2 2-1		0-3	
FK Berane	33	8	6	19	28	49	30	0-1 2-0	1-3	0-0	1-2 0-1	2-2	1-2 1-0 2-1	1-1 0-1 1-0 1-1	1-2				3-0
Kom Podgorica	33	5	3	25	16	59	18	0-2	0-1	0-2	1-0	1-0	0-0 1-0 0-1 1-2 0-2 0-1	1-00-2 1-1 2-3 0-0					

7/08/2009 - 29/05/2010 • † Qualified for the UEFA Champions League • ‡ Qualified for the Europa League • § = points deducted • Match in bold awarded • Relegation play-offs: **OFK Bar** 1-1 1-1 5-4p FK Berane • Bratstvo Cijevna 0-1 1-2 **Mornar Bar**
Top scorers: 21 - Ivan Boskovic, Grbalj • 17 - Ivan Vukovic, Buducnost • 15 - Predrag Randelovic SRB, Rudar • 11 - Zarko Korac, Zeta

MONTENEGRO 2009-10 II LIGA (2)

	Pl	W	D	L	F	A	Pts
Mladost Podgorica	33	21	8	4	75	32	71
OFK Bar ‡	33	18	11	4	40	10	65
Bratstvo Cijevna ‡	33	15	11	7	35	24	56
Bokelj Kotor	33	13	12	8	52	25	51
Zabjelo Podgorica	33	12	9	12	33	34	45
Jedinstvo Bijelo Polje	33	11	10	12	42	43	43
Jezero Plav	33	11	7	15	41	50	40
Celik Niksic	33	11	6	16	36	51	39
Ibar Rozaje	33	10	7	16	27	44	37
Otrant Ulcinj	33	8	12	13	28	35	36
Crvena stijena	33	9	9	15	30	44	36
Gusinje	33	5	6	22	19	66	21

15/08/2009 - 29/05/2010 • ‡ Promotion play-off

MEDALS TABLE

		Overall			League			Cup		City
		G	S	B	G	S	B	G	S	
1	Rudar Pljevlja	3			1				2	Pljevlja
2	Mogren Budva	2	2		1	2			1	Budva
3	Buducnost Podgorica	1	5		1	3			2	Podgorica
4	Zeta Golubovci	1	1		1	1				Golubovci
5	OFK Petrovac	1							1	Petrovac
6	Sutjeska Niksic		1	1			1		1	Niksic
7	Lovcen Cetinje	1							1	Cetinje
8	Grbalj Radanovici			1			1		1	Radanovici

KUPA CRNE GORE 2009-10

Round of 16			Quarter-finals			Semi-finals			Final	
Rudar Pljevlja	2	1								
Jedinstvo Bijelo Polje*	0	1	**Rudar Pljevlja**	0	6					
Celik Niksic *	1	0	Mornar Bar *	0	1					
Mornar Bar	3	2				**Rudar Pljevlja ***	2	0		
OFK Bar	2	0				OFK Petrovac	1	0		
Zeta Golubovci *	0	1	OFK Bar	1	1					
Drezga Piperi *	0	0	**OFK Petrovac ***	1	3					
OFK Petrovac	3	4							**Rudar Pljevlja**	2
Grbalj Radanovici	4	4							Buducnost Podgorica‡	1
Bokelj Kotor *	0	1	**Grbalj Radanovici**	2	4					
Jezero Plav *	1	3	Mladost Podgorica *	1	3					
Mladost Podgorica	4	6				Grbalj Radanovici *	0	2		
Sutjeska Niksic	1	2				**Buducnost Podgorica**	1	3		
Decic Tuzi *	0	0	Sutjeska Niksic	1	0					
Lovcen Cetinje	0	0	**Buducnost Podgorica ***	1	1					
Buducnost Podgorica *	2	2								

* Home team in the first leg • ‡ Qualified for the Europa League

CUP FINAL
Pod Goricom, Podgorica
19-05-2010, Att: 5000,
Ref: Kaluderovic
Scorers - Predrag Randelovic 4p,
Blazo Igumanovic 36 for Rudar; Ilija
Stolica 84 for Buducnost

MOZ – MOZAMBIQUE

FIFA/COCA-COLA WORLD RANKING

1993	1994	1995	1996	1997	1998	1999	2000	2001	2002	2003	2004	2005	2006	2007	2008	2009	2010
104	94	76	85	67	80	101	112	128	125	127	126	130	128	75	95	72	96

2010												Hi/Lo
Jan	Feb	Mar	Mar	Apr	May	Jul	Aug	Sep	Oct	Nov	Dec	66
72	82	84	89	89	85	80	80	86	90	98	96	134

The construction of a new national stadium to host the 2011 All-Africa Games, but to be primarily used by football thereafter, dominated the year for the southern African country. The Estadio Zimpeto, with a 42,000 capacity, will be smaller than the concrete Machava but the distinguished old stadium where both Eusebio and Pele once played is now more than 70 years old. The Zimpeto will be the new home for the national team which returned from the 2010 African Nations Cup finals in Angola to a row over the future of coach Mart Nooij. A new contract for the Dutchman was proposed by the government but the Mozambican Football Federation sought instead to look for a new man. It was a battle that FMF president Feizal Sidat lost, although the impasse lasted several months which meant former international Chiquinho Conde was caretaker for the prestige friendly against Portugal in Johannesburg before the start of the World Cup finals in neighbouring South Africa. Nooij returned for the start of the 2012 Nations Cup qualifiers, where the Mambas dropped valuable points in their opening game against Libya. In the MocamBola, Liga Muculmana won a first-ever title, finishing seven points clear of Maxaquene who beat Vilankulo in the Cup Final to win the trophy for the ninth time, just two short of the record held by Costa do Sol.

FIFA WORLD CUP RECORD
1930-1978 DNE **1982** DNQ **1986-1990** DNE **1994-2010** DNQ

FEDERACAO MOCAMBICANA DE FUTEBOL (FMF)

Av. Samora Machel,
Número 11, PO Box 1467,
Maputo 1467
☎ +258 21 300366
📠 +258 21 300367
📧 fmfbol@tvcabo.co.mz
🖥 www.fmf.co.mz
FA 1976 CON 1978 FIFA 1980
P Feizal Sidat
GS Filipe Lucas Johane

FIFA BIG COUNT 2006

Total players	885 700
% of population	4.50%
Male	885 600
Female	100
Amateurs 18+	19 500
Unregistered	55 000
Professionals	400
Referees	1 000
Admin & coaches	5 100
Number of clubs	170
Number of teams	850

MAJOR CITIES/TOWNS

		Population
1	Maputo	1 120 245
2	Matola	729 469
3	Nampula	515 320
4	Beira	441 957
5	Chimoio	253 259
6	Nacala	217 479
7	Quelimane	200 788
8	Tete	164 201
9	Lichinga	155 277
10	Pemba	153 900
11	Garue	127 074
12	Gurué	119 598
13	Xai-Xai	118 667
14	Maxixe	107 292
15	Cuamba	98 719
16	Angoche	84 356
17	Dondo	78 639
18	Montepuez	77 515

REPUBLICA DE MOCAMBIQUE • REPUBLIC OF MOZAMBIQUE

Capital	Maputo	Population	21 669 278 (52)	% in cities	37%
GDP per capita	$900 (215)	Area km²	799 380 km² (35)	GMT +/-	+2
Neighbours (km)	Malawi 1569, South Africa 491, Swaziland 105, Tanzania 756, Zambia 419, Zimbabwe 1231 • Coast 2470				

RECENT INTERNATIONAL MATCHES PLAYED BY MOZAMBIQUE

2006 Opponents	Score	Venue	Comp	Scorers	Att	Referee
2-09 Senegal	L 0-2	Dakar	CNq			Sule NGA
8-10 Tanzania	D 0-0	Maputo	CNq			Kaoma ZAM
2007						
24-03 Burkina Faso	D 1-1	Ouagadougou	CNq	Mano 2		Imiere NGA
28-04 Seychelles	W 2-0	Maputo	CCr1	Bino 2 51 77		Mpopo LES
29-04 Zimbabwe	D 0-0	Maputo	CCr1	W 5-4p		Seechun MRI
3-06 Burkina Faso	W 3-1	Maputo	CNq	Dario 6p, Tico-Tico 2 34 46		Raolimanana MAD
17-06 Senegal	D 0-0	Maputo	CNq			Seechurn MRI
20-08 Zimbabwe	D 0-0	Beira	Fr	W 3-1p		
8-09 Tanzania	W 1-0	Dar es Salaam	CNq	Tico-Tico 2		Guezzaz MAR
29-09 Zambia	L 0-3	Atteridgeville	CCsf			Bennett RSA
2008						
13-01 South Africa	L 0-2	Durban	Fr			
21-05 Lesotho	L 2-3	Maputo	Fr	Fanuel 9, Tico-Tico 43		
1-06 Côte d'Ivoire	L 0-1	Abidjan	WCq		20 000	Auda EGY
8-06 Botswana	L 1-2	Maputo	WCq	Miro 60	30 000	Faudze SWZ
15-06 Madagascar	D 1-1	Antananarivo	WCq	Dario 33	15 501	Ebrahim RSA
22-06 Madagascar	W 3-0	Maputo	WCq	Tico-Tico 23, Carlitos 52, Domingues 64	20 000	Maillett SEY
27-07 Botswana	W 2-0	Secunda	CCqf	Momed Hagi 18, Txuma 89		Katjimune NAM
30-07 Madagascar	W 2-1	Thulamahashe	CCsf	Tico-Tico 19, Momed Hagi 66		Marange ZIM
20-08 Swaziland	W 3-0	Maputo	Fr	Dario 2 4 12, Domingues 35		
7-09 Côte d'Ivoire	D 1-1	Maputo	WCq	Miro 56	35 000	El Achiri MAR
11-10 Botswana	W 1-0	Gaborone	WCq	Genito 6	2 000	Seck SEN
19-11 Tanzania	L 0-1	Dar es Salaam	Fr			
2009						
11-02 Malawi	W 2-0	Maputo	Fr	Dario 31, Domingues 90		
29-03 Nigeria	D 0-0	Maputo	WCq		35 000	Eyob ERI
6-06 Tunisia	L 0-2	Rades/Tunis	WCq		30 000	Djaoupe TOG
20-06 Kenya	L 1-2	Nairobi	WCq	Domingues 49	15 000	Keita GUI
12-08 Swaziland	W 1-0	Maputo	Fr	Miro 39		
6-09 Kenya	W 1-0	Maputo	WCq	Tico-Tico 66	35 000	Coulibaly MLI
11-10 Nigeria	L 0-1	Abuja	WCq		13 000	Abdel Rahman SUD
25-10 Malawi	W 1-0	Harare	CCqf	Josemar 35		Ramocha BOT
29-10 Zambia	L 0-2	Bulawayo	CCsf			Ramocha BOT
14-11 Tunisia	W 1-0	Maputo	WCq	Dario 83	30 000	Doue CIV
19-12 Malawi	L 0-1	Tete	Fr			
28-12 Zambia	L 0-1	Johannesburg	Fr			
2010						
6-01 Gabon	L 0-2	Bloemfontein	Fr			
12-01 Benin	D 2-2	Benguela	CNr1	Miro 29, Fumo 54	15 000	Abdel Rahman SUD
16-01 Egypt	L 0-2	Benguela	CNr1		16 000	Djaoupe TOG
20-01 Nigeria	L 0-3	Lubango	CNr1		10 000	Coulibaly MLI
3-03 Botswana	L 0-1	Maputo	Fr			
8-06 Portugal	L 0-3	Johannesburg	Fr		34 000	Dyer RSA
11-08 Swaziland	W 2-1	Maputo	Fr	Domingues 9p, Miro 51		
5-09 Libya	D 0-0	Maputo	CNq			Bangoura GUI
9-10 Comoros	W 1-0	Moroni	CNq	Josemar 90		Ibada TAN

Fr = Friendly match • CN = CAF African Cup of Nations • CC = COSAFA Cup • WC = FIFA World Cup • q = qualifier

MOZAMBIQUE 2010

CAMPEONATO NACIONAL DA 1ª DIVISAO

	PI	W	D	L	F	A	Pts	Muçulmana	Maxaquene	Ferro Maputo	HCB Songo	Matchedje	Vilankulo	Desportivo	Costa do Sol	Sporting	Ferro Beira	Atlético	Textáfrica	Lichinga	Ferro Pemba
Liga Muçulmana †	26	18	4	4	44	13	58		1-0	1-0	1-0	3-0	2-0	2-1	1-1	4-0	1-1	1-0	2-1	5-0	3-0
Maxaquene ‡	26	15	6	5	27	14	51	1-0		1-0	0-0	1-0	2-0	2-1	1-0	2-1	1-0	0-0	2-0	1-0	1-0
Ferroviário Maputo	26	14	7	5	41	20	49	0-0	1-0		2-2	1-2	4-0	1-1	0-0	5-2	3-0	1-0	1-0	4-0	2-0
HCB de Songo	26	12	10	4	30	21	46	0-2	2-1	2-0		1-0	0-0	2-0	2-1	3-0	1-1	2-1	3-1	2-0	3-2
Matchedje Maputo	26	9	7	10	19	24	34	2-1	0-0	0-1	1-1		0-0	1-0	1-0	0-1	1-0	1-0	0-1	2-1	3-2
Vilankulo	26	8	9	9	19	24	33	1-2	2-1	1-2	0-0	1-1		3-0	1-0	0-2	1-1	0-2	2-0	1-0	1-0
Desportivo Maputo	26	7	10	9	17	23	31	0-2	2-2	0-2	2-0	1-1	0-0		0-0	2-1	1-0	0-1	1-1	1-0	2-0
Costa do Sol	26	8	7	11	30	26	31	1-4	1-2	3-1	4-0	2-0	0-0	0-1		2-1	3-4	5-0	1-0	3-0	1-1
Sporting Beira	26	8	6	12	28	35	30	0-1	0-1	2-2	1-1	2-1	3-2	0-0	2-0		1-1	4-1	0-0	2-1	0-1
Ferroviário Beira	26	7	8	11	21	26	29	2-1	1-0	0-1	0-1	2-0	0-0	0-1	2-0	0-0		0-1	2-0	1-0	1-0
Atlético Muçulmano	26	6	10	10	18	27	28	0-0	0-2	1-1	0-0	2-1	0-1	2-0	1-1	2-1	1-1		1-1	1-1	0-1
Textáfrica Chimoio	26	6	8	12	16	26	26	0-1	1-0	1-3	0-0	0-0	1-0	0-0	0-0	0-1	3-1	0-0		3-1	0-2
Lichinga	26	5	9	12	13	31	24	1-0	1-1	1-1	0-0	0-1	1-1	0-0	1-0	1-0	1-0	1-1	1-0		0-0
Ferroviário Pemba	26	6	5	15	17	30	23	1-3	0-1	0-2	1-2	0-0	0-1	0-0	0-1	2-1	2-0	1-0	1-2	0-0	

20/03/2010 - 7/11/2010 • † Qualified for the CAF Champions League

MEDALS TABLE

		Overall	Lge		Cup		City/Town
		G	G		G	S	
1	Costa do Sol	20	9		11	3	Maputo
2	Ferroviário Maputo	13	9		4	4	Maputo
3	Maxaquene	13	4		9	3	Maputo
4	Desportivo Maputo	8	6		2	1	Maputo
5	Matchedje	3	2		1	1	Maputo
6	Ferroviário Nampula	2	1		1	1	Nampula
7	Têxtil Púnguè	1	1			3	Beira
	Textáfrica Chimoio	1	1			3	Chimoio
9	Palmeiras Beira	1			1	3	Beira
10	Ferroviário Beira	1			1	2	Beira
11	Clube de Gaza	1			1	1	Xai-Xai
12	Liga Muçulmana	1	1				Maputo
13	Atlético Muçulmano	1				1	Matola

TACA NACIONAL 2010

Round of 16		Quarter–finals		Semi–finals		Final	
Maxaquene	3						
Ferroviário Gaza	0	Maxaquene	1				
Pipeline da Maforga	0	Chingale Tete	0				
Chingale Tete	2			Maxaquene	5		
Costa do Sol	1			Textáfrica Chimoio	0		
Liga Muçulmana	0	Costa do Sol	0				
MuçulmanaQuelimane	0 2p	Textáfrica Chimoio	2				
Textáfrica Chimoio	0 4p					Maxaquene ‡	2
Lichinga	1 4p					Vilankulo	0
Ferroviário Pemba	1 3p	Lichinga	2				
Têxtil Púnguè	0	Sporting Beira	1			CUP FINAL	
Sporting Beira	1			Lichinga	1	Machada, Maputo	
Ferroviário Maputo	2			Vilankulo	2	14-11-2010. Ref: Rachide	
Incomati	0	Ferroviário Maputo	0			Scorers - Eusebio 60, Alvarito 70 for	
Aguuias Especiais	0	Vilankulo	1			Maxaquene	
Vilankulo	2			‡ Qualified for the CAF Confederation Cup			

Cup Final line-ups: **Maxaquene** - Soarito - Vasil - Campira, Gabito, Eusebio - Liberty, Macamito, Alvarito e Kito (Mustafa) - Eboh (Reginaldo), Tony (Nelsinho) • **Vilankulo** - Fumo (Jaimito) - Mambucho, Joe, Charles, Bila - Titos (Felio), Jossias, Goncalves, Belo - Edgar, Ivo (Sergito).

MRI – MAURITIUS

FIFA/COCA-COLA WORLD RANKING

1993	1994	1995	1996	1997	1998	1999	2000	2001	2002	2003	2004	2005	2006	2007	2008	2009	2010
133	146	154	150	151	148	118	118	124	126	123	140	143	138	158	170	181	191

2010												Hi/Lo
Jan	Feb	Mar	Mar	Apr	May	Jul	Aug	Sep	Oct	Nov	Dec	112
181	178	177	176	173	172	177	183	193	193	192	191	193

Three years and 16 games on from their last victory, the Mauritius national team saw their position in the FIFA/Coca-Cola World Ranking slump to an all-time low of 193 in October 2010 - just ten places off the bottom. They were also handed a nightmare draw for the 2012 African Nations Cup qualifiers, with Cameroon, Congo DR and Senegal all potential group winners. That left the islanders with a damage limitation exercise as coach Akbar Patel attempts to build a new team in the wake of the retirement of several long-standing stalwarts. In the new-look squad is Jonathan Bru, who plays in Europe with second division Oliveirense in Portugal, a rare phenomenon for footballers from the Indian Ocean Island. His penalty was the only goal scored by Mauritius in 2010 as they shipped 10 goals in the first two of their Nations Cup qualifiers. Pamplemousse SC won both the Premier League and the Republic Cup, which marks the start of the new season. It proved a dream debut season in charge for Henri Speville, the former national team captain still competing as player-coach at the age of 38. The Mauritius Football Association Cup was won by AS Vacoas-Phoenix, their first success in the competition. Coached by former Madagascar coach Maurice Andriamandrato, they beat PAS Mates in the final with a goal from Jean-Francois Nadal.

FIFA WORLD CUP RECORD

1930-1970 DNE **1974** DNQ **1978-1982** DNE **1986** DNQ **1990-1994** DNE **1998-2010** DNQ

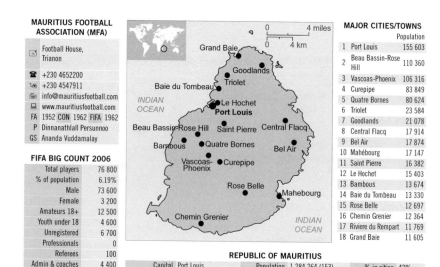

MAURITIUS FOOTBALL ASSOCIATION (MFA)

Football House, Trianon

☎ +230 4652200
📠 +230 4547911
✉ info@mauritiusfootball.com
🖥 www.mauritiusfootball.com
FA 1952 CON 1962 FIFA 1962
P Dinnanathlall Persunnoo
GS Ananda Vuddamalay

FIFA BIG COUNT 2006

Total players	76 800
% of population	6.19%
Male	73 600
Female	3 200
Amateurs 18+	12 500
Youth under 18	4 600
Unregistered	6 700
Professionals	0
Referees	100
Admin & coaches	4 400
Number of clubs	70
Number of teams	700

MAJOR CITIES/TOWNS

		Population
1	Port Louis	155 603
2	Beau Bassin-Rose Hill	110 360
3	Vascoas-Phoenix	106 316
4	Curepipe	83 849
5	Quatre Bornes	80 624
6	Triolet	23 584
7	Goodlands	21 078
8	Central Flacq	17 914
9	Bel Air	17 874
10	Mahébourg	17 147
11	Saint Pierre	16 382
12	Le Hochet	15 403
13	Bambous	13 674
14	Baie du Tombeau	13 330
15	Rose Belle	12 697
16	Chemin Grenier	12 364
17	Riviere du Rempart	11 769
18	Grand Baie	11 605

REPUBLIC OF MAURITIUS

Capital	Port Louis	Population	1 284 264 (153)	% in cities	42%
GDP per capita	$12 100 (91)	Area km²	2040 km² (180)	GMT +/-	+4
Neighbours (km)	Coast 177				

RECENT INTERNATIONAL MATCHES PLAYED BY MAURITIUS

2006	Opponents	Score		Venue	Comp	Scorers	Att	Referee
3-09	Tunisia	D	0-0	Curepipe	CNq			Ncobo RSA
7-10	Seychelles	L	1-2	Roche Caiman	CNq	Godon [53]		Raolimanana MAD
2007								
21-03	Côte d'Ivoire	L	0-3	Bellevue	Fr			
25-03	Sudan	L	1-2	Curepipe	CNq	Naboth [61]		Mwanza ZAM
26-05	Swaziland	D	0-0	Mbabane	CCr1	W 6-5p		Labrosse SEY
27-05	South Africa	L	0-2	Mbabane	CCr1			Mufeti NAM
2-06	Sudan	L	0-3	Omdurman	CNq			Lwanja MWI
16-06	Tunisia	L	0-2	Rades/Tunis	CNq			Benouza ALG
14-08	Seychelles	W	3-0	Antananarivo	Fr	Jeannot 2 [24 64], Appou [40]		
9-09	Seychelles	D	1-1	Curepipe	CNq	Perle [62]		Mwandike TAN
2008								
9-03	Madagascar	L	1-2	Curepipe	Fr	Marquette [68]		
31-05	Tanzania	D	1-1	Dar es Salaam	WCq	Marquette [39]	35 000	Marange ZIM
8-06	Cameroon	L	0-3	Curepipe	WCq		2 400	Martins ANG
15-06	Cape Verde Islands	L	0-1	Curepipe	WCq		1 400	Kaoma ZAM
22-06	Cape Verde Islands	L	1-3	Praia	WCq	Sophie [67]	2 850	Coulibaly MLI
19-07	Seychelles	L	0-7	Witbank	CCr1			Kaoma ZAM
21-07	Swaziland	D	1-1	Witbank	CCr1	Marmitte [35]		Nhlapo RSA
23-07	Madagascar	L	1-2	Witbank	CCr1	Marquette [34]		Marange ZIM
6-09	Tanzania	L	1-4	Curepipe	WCq	Marquette [13]	103	Ndinya KEN
11-10	Cameroon	L	0-5	Yaounde	WCq		12 000	Lemghambodj MTN
2009								
2-10	Egypt	L	0-4	Cairo	Fr			
17-10	Zimbabwe	L	0-3	Harare	CCr1			Ebrahim RSA
21-10	Lesotho	L	0-1	Harare	CCr1			Ngosi MWI
2010								
4-09	Cameroon	L	1-3	Bellevue	CNq	Bru [45p]		Damon RSA
9-10	Senegal	L	0-7	Dakar	CNq			Bennett RSA

Fr = Friendly match • CN = CAF African Cup of Nations • CC = COSAFA Cup • IO = Indian Ocean Games • WC = FIFA World Cup
q = qualifier • r1 = first round group

MAURITIUS 2010

BARCLAYS PREMIER LEAGUE

	Pl	W	D	L	F	A	Pts	Pamplemousses	ASPL 2000	Petite Rivière	ASVP	CSSC	Savanne	CTNFB	PAS Mates	Entente	Faucon Flacq	Rivière Rempart	Etoile	USBBRH
Pamplemousses SC	24	16	4	4	48	17	**52**		1-3	1-1	1-0	1-1	0-2	1-1	3-0	5-0	1-0	2-0	3-1	6-0
AS Port-Louis 2000	24	13	7	4	41	20	**46**	1-2		1-0	1-1	1-1	0-1	2-0	0-1	1-1	3-0	3-1	3-1	1-0
Petite Rivière Noire	24	11	7	6	53	29	**40**	0-1	2-2		3-3	1-0	1-2	4-2	1-0	5-1	3-0	5-2	3-2	2-2
AS Vacoas-Phoenix	24	11	7	6	48	25	**40**	0-2	0-1	1-1		1-1	2-1	5-1	2-2	4-0	2-1	2-2	3-0	1-0
Curepipe Starlight	24	11	6	7	32	28	**39**	2-0	1-2	1-0	1-0		0-1	1-2	3-4	2-1	1-0	1-1	0-3	1-1
Savanne SC	24	11	5	8	31	33	**38**	1-4	1-0	1-0	1-4	1-5		0-1	1-2	0-1	1-0	1-0	3-2	3-0
CTNFB	24	10	5	9	43	37	**35**	1-1	0-1	1-2	1-0	1-2	1-1		5-0	3-0	3-1	1-3	5-1	1-2
Pointe-aux-Sables	24	8	8	8	39	44	**32**	0-3	2-2	1-7	0-3	1-1	0-0	2-2		3-1	2-3	1-1	6-0	4-0
Entente Boulet Rouge	24	6	9	9	28	45	**27**	0-2	1-1	2-1	1-1	0-1	0-0	3-2	4-2		0-2	1-1	7-6	0-0
Faucon Flacq SC	24	6	6	12	23	34	**24**	1-0	2-2	0-1	1-0	0-1	2-3	2-2	1-1	0-1		1-1	2-2	3-1
Etoile de l'Ouest	24	5	7	12	30	40	**22**	1-2	1-3	2-2	0-1	1-2	4-2	1-2	0-1	1-1	0-1	1-4		1-0
Beau-Basin/Rose Hill	24	3	6	15	19	62	**15**	1-3	0-6	0-7	0-8	4-1	3-3	1-2	0-3	0-0	0-0	**0-2**	2-1	

21/03/2010 - 28/11/2010 • Match in bold awarded

REPUBLIC CUP 2010

Quarter–finals		Semi–finals		Final	
Pamplemousses SC	5				
Curepipe Starlight	1	**Pamplemousses SC**	2		
Pointe-aux-Sables	2	AS Rivière Rempart	1		
AS Rivière Rempart	3			**Pamplemousses SC**	0 6p
AS Vacoas-Phoenix	1			Petite Rivière Noire	0 5p
Savanne SC	0	AS Vacoas-Phoenix	0		
AS Port-Louis 2000	0	**Petite Rivière Noire**	1		
Petite Rivière Noire	1				

CUP FINAL

Anjalay, Belle Vue
18-07-2010, Ref: Ramchurn

First round: **Petite Rivière Noire** 2-1 Entente Boulet Rouge •
USBBRH 0-1 **Rivière Rempart** • Faucon Flacq 1-5 **AS Vacoas-Phoenix**
• Etoile de l'Ouest 0-4 **Pamplemousses SC**

SKYLINE MFA CUP 2010

Round of 16		Quarter–finals		Semi–finals		Final	
AS Vacoas-Phoenix							
Cercle de Joachim		**AS Vacoas-Phoenix**					
Etoile de l'Ouest		Curepipe Starlight					
Curepipe Starlight				**AS Vacoas-Phoenix**			
Le Cure Sylvester				Savanne SC			
Entente Boulet Rouge		Le Cure Sylvester					
Bolton City		**Savanne SC**					
Savanne SC						**AS Vacoas-Phoenix**	1
Petite Rivière Noire	2					Pointe-aux-Sables	0
Rodrigues SC	1	**Petite Rivière Noire**					
Mangalkhan		Pamplemousses SC					
Pamplemousses SC				Petite Rivière Noire			
AS Rivière Rempart	2			**Pointe-aux-Sables**			
Faucon Flacq SC	0	AS Rivière Rempart					
Black Horns		**Pointe-aux-Sables**					
Pointe-aux-Sables							

CUP FINAL

Germain Comarmond, Bambous
18-12-2010, Ref: Chuttoree

Scorer - Jean-Francois Nadal [10]

MSR – MONTSERRAT

FIFA/COCA-COLA WORLD RANKING

1993	1994	1995	1996	1997	1998	1999	2000	2001	2002	2003	2004	2005	2006	2007	2008	2009	2010
-	-	-	-	-	-	201	202	203	203	204	202	202	198	201	201	203	203

	2010											Hi/Lo
Jan	Feb	Mar	Mar	Apr	May	Jul	Aug	Sep	Oct	Nov	Dec	**196**
203	203	203	202	202	202	202	202	203	203	203	203	**205**

46-year-old Kenny Dyer has emerged as the driving force behind the Montserrat national team in recent years, not only as coach - a position he has held since 2008 - but also as the chief recruitment driver for the team. His tireless quest for players with some connection to the island is beginning to pay dividends with a number of English non-league players pledging their future to the team. A single World Cup qualifier in 2008 had been the only international action for five years prior to 2010 but with the FIFA Financial Assistance Programme giving countries like Montserrat the financial backing to enter international competitions, Montserrat took part in the 2010 Digicel Caribbean Cup and were drawn in a preliminary round group containing St Vincent, Barbados and St Kitts. Predictably, Montserrat had a struggle on their hands as they lost to all three in Kingstown, the capital of St Vincent, with the large home crowd celebrating a comfortable 7-0 win in the opening match. With Dyer playing in all three matches, Montserrat managed to improve as the group progressed, restricting Barbados to five and St Kitts to four but they failed to find the back of the net in all three games. For Montserrat, however, this was all about taking part and not the result although as the team gains experience, the hope is that they can provide stiffer competition.

FIFA WORLD CUP RECORD
1930-1998 DNE **2002-2010** DNQ

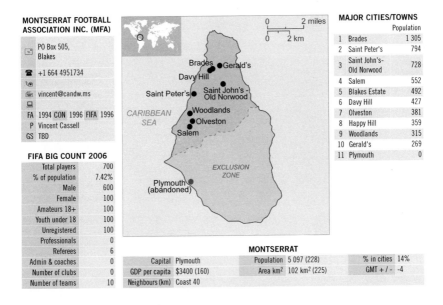

MONTSERRAT FOOTBALL ASSOCIATION INC. (MFA)

PO Box 505,
Blakes

☎ +1 664 4951734

✉ vincent@candw.ms

FA	1994	CON	1996	FIFA	1996
P	Vincent Cassell				
GS	TBD				

FIFA BIG COUNT 2006

Total players	700
% of population	7.42%
Male	600
Female	100
Amateurs 18+	100
Youth under 18	100
Unregistered	100
Professionals	0
Referees	6
Admin & coaches	0
Number of clubs	0
Number of teams	10

MAJOR CITIES/TOWNS

		Population
1	Brades	1 305
2	Saint Peter's	794
3	Saint John's-Old Norwood	728
4	Salem	552
5	Blakes Estate	492
6	Davy Hill	427
7	Olveston	381
8	Happy Hill	359
9	Woodlands	315
10	Gerald's	269
11	Plymouth	0

MONTSERRAT

Capital	Plymouth	Population	5 097 (228)	% in cities	14%
GDP per capita	$3400 (160)	Area km²	102 km² (225)	GMT +/-	-4
Neighbours (km)	Coast 40				

RECENT INTERNATIONAL MATCHES PLAYED BY MONTSERRAT

2002	Opponents	Score		Venue	Comp	Scorers	Att	Referee
No international matches played in 2002 after June								
2003								
No international matches played in 2003								
2004								
29-02	Bermuda	L	0-13	Hamilton	WCq		3 000	Kennedy USA
21-03	Bermuda	L	0-7	Plymouth	WCq		250	Charles DMA
31-10	St Kitts and Nevis	L	1-6	Basseterre	CCq	Adams [81]		Bedeau GRN
2-11	Antigua and Barbuda	L	4-5	Basseterre	CCq	Tesfaye Bramble [36], Fox [41], Mendes [50], Farrel [61]		Phillip GRN
4-11	St Lucia	L	0-3	Basseterre	CCq	Not played. St Lucia awarded the match 3-0		
2005								
No international matches played in 2005								
2006								
No international matches played in 2006								
2007								
No international matches played in 2007								
2008								
26-03	Surinam	L	1-7	Macoya	WCq	Vladimir Farrell [48]	100	Aguilar SLV
2009								
No international matches played in 2009								
2010								
6-10	St Vincent/Grenadines	L	0-7	Kingstown	CCq		5 000	Pinas PUR
8-10	Barbados	L	0-5	Kingstown	CCq		350	Pinas PUR
10-10	St Kitts And Nevis	L	0-4	Kingstown	CCq		1 100	Elskamp SUR

Fr = Friendly match • CC = Digicel Caribbean Cup • WC = FIFA World Cup • q = qualifier

MTN – MAURITANIA

FIFA/COCA-COLA WORLD RANKING

1993	1994	1995	1996	1997	1998	1999	2000	2001	2002	2003	2004	2005	2006	2007	2008	2009	2010
144	137	85	113	135	142	160	161	177	180	165	175	178	133	130	158	169	180

						2010							Hi/Lo
	Jan	Feb	Mar	Mar	Apr	May	Jul	Aug	Sep	Oct	Nov	Dec	85
	169	161	162	168	165	164	168	168	169	180	181	180	182

Mauritania unexpectedly pulled out of the 2012 African Nations Cup qualifiers just two weeks before their campaign was due to kick-off, earning themselves a ban from entering the next edition of the continental championship. The team had been preparing for their first match against Burkina Faso in September and had even invited Palestine to Nouakchott for a preparatory international in August, playing to a goalless draw, but officials felt the side was not properly prepared after a long hiatus in domestic league. Officials also claimed there were problems in bringing back the country's small group of foreign-based professionals with the Mauritania football federation president Mohamed Salem Ould Boukhreiss also hinting at the financial burden. There had been a six-month hiatus in the league with an effort in the new 2010-11 campaign to introduce semi professionalism to the eight clubs from Nouakchott, three from Nouadhibou and one from Zuwarat. CF Cansado from Nouadhibou, previously known as AS SNIM, had won the league in May while runners-up FC Tevragh-Zeina won the Mauritania Cup in October with a 3-0 win over Ecole Feu Mini, an academy run by a former Mauritania international in the capital. Tevragh-Zeina then beat Cansado in the first Super Cup to mark the start of the new season, winning 3-1 in late November.

FIFA WORLD CUP RECORD
1930-1974 DNE 1978 DNQ 1982-1994 DNE 1998-2010 DNQ

FEDERATION DE FOOT-BALL DE LA REPUBLIQUE ISLAMIQUE DE MAURITANIE (FFM)

- BP 566, Nouakchott
- +222 35 241860
- +222 35 241861
- dmassa59@yahoo.fr
- www.ffrim.com
- FA 1961 CON 1968 FIFA 1964
- P Mohamed Salem Boukhreiss
- GS Massa Diarra

FIFA BIG COUNT 2006

Total players	137 920
% of population	4.34%
Male	137 920
Female	0
Amateurs 18+	3 520
Youth under 18	1 600
Unregistered	14 300
Professionals	0
Referees	177
Admin & coaches	700
Number of clubs	68
Number of teams	250

MAJOR CITIES/TOWNS

		Population
1	Nouakchott	798 725
2	Nouadhibou	83 277
3	Kifah	80 612
4	Rusu	72 400
5	Kayhaydi	54 593
6	Zuwarat	50 949
7	an-Na'mah	41 583
8	Bu Tilimit	37 812
9	Silibabi	33 084
10	Atar	31 958
11	Buqah	27 859
12	Tinbadgah	27 562
13	Guérou	27 031
14	Magta' Lahjar	26 026
15	Alak	25 140
16	Ayun	24 991
17	Tintane	19 118
18	Tijiqjah	18 375
19	Adel Bagrou	16 004

AL JUMHURIYAH AL ISLAMIYAH AL MAURITANIYAH • ISLAMIC REPUBLIC OF MAURITANIA

Capital Nouakchott	Population 3 129 486 (135)	% in cities 41%
GDP per capita $2100 (187)	Area km² 1 030 700 km² (29)	GMT + / - 0
Neighbours (km) Algeria 463, Mali 2237, Senegal 813, Western Sahara 1561 • Coast 754		

RECENT INTERNATIONAL MATCHES PLAYED BY MAURITANIA

2006	Opponents	Score		Venue	Comp	Scorers	Att	Referee
3-09	Botswana	W	4-0	Nouakchott	CNq	Seydou Mbodji [3], Moussa Karamoko 2 [8 23], Yohan Langlet [83]		Djaoupe TOG
8-10	Burundi	L	1-3	Bujumbura	CNq	Mohamed Benyachou [51]		Abdelrahman SUD
21-12	Lebanon	D	0-0	Beirut	ARr1			Al Jannaz BHR
24-12	Sudan	L	0-2	Beirut	ARr1			Ebel KUW
27-12	Somalia	W	8-2	Beirut	ARr1			
2007								
20-03	Libya	D	0-0	Tripoli	Fr			
25-03	Egypt	L	0-3	Cairo	CNq			Benouza ALG
3-06	Egypt	D	1-1	Nouakchott	CNq	Yohan Langlet [70]		Sowe GAM
16-06	Botswana	L	1-2	Gaborone	CNq	Yohan Langlet [74]		Gasingwa RWA
13-10	Burundi	W	2-1	Nouakchott	CNq	Dominique Da Silva [32], Ahmed Teguedi [47]		Aboubacar CIV
2008								
31-05	Rwanda	L	0-3	Kigali	WCq		12 000	Doue CIV
7-06	Morocco	L	1-4	Nouakchott	WCq	Ahmed Teguedi [82p]	9 500	Lamptey GHA
13-06	Ethiopia	L	0-1	Nouakchott	WCq		5 000	Ambaya EGY
22-06	Ethiopia	L	1-6	Addis Abeba	WCq	Voulani Ely [44]	13 000	Lwanja MWI
6-09	Rwanda	L	0-1	Nouackchott	WCq		1 000	Bennaceur TUN
11-10	Morocco	L	1-4	Rabat	WCq	Ahmed Teguedi [67]	1 472	Aboubacar CIV
2009								
No international matches played in 2009								
2010								
11-08	Palestine	D	0-0	Nouakchott	Fr			

Fr = Friendly match • CN = CAF African Cup of Nations • AR = Arab Cup • WC = FIFA World Cup • q = qualifier • r1 = first round group

MAURITANIA 2010

CHAMPIONNAT NATIONAL	Pl	W	D	L	F	A	Pts	Cansado	Tevragh	Concorde	Ksar	Nouadhibou	Kédia	NASR	Mauritel	El Ahmedi	Teyarett	Dar El Barka	Dar Naim
CF Cansado †	22	13	7	2	30	13	46		1-1	2-0	1-0	1-1	1-2	1-1	3-0	0-0	4-1	2-1	0-0
Tevragh Zeina ‡	22	14	3	5	48	14	45	0-1		1-0	1-1	1-0	7-0	3-0	1-0	1-2	5-0	2-1	5-0
ASAC Concorde	22	12	4	6	39	22	40	0-1	2-1		2-0	2-2	2-2	1-0	1-3	2-0	4-0	4-2	2-0
ACS Ksar	22	9	8	5	23	14	35	2-2	1-2	0-0		1-0	1-2	1-0	3-0	0-0	1-1	1-0	4-0
FC Nouadhibou	22	9	6	7	21	17	33	1-0	2-0	1-0	1-0		1-0	0-3	2-0	1-1	2-0	1-2	0-0
Kédia Zouératt	22	9	6	7	27	30	33	0-2	0-0	2-1	1-1	2-1		3-2	1-2	0-1	0-0	1-0	4-1
NASR Sebkha	22	9	5	8	32	27	32	1-2	1-0	1-2	0-2	1-0	3-2		1-1	2-2	3-2	2-0	3-0
Mauritel	22	9	4	9	26	27	31	0-1	1-2	2-2	0-0	0-2	2-1	3-2		0-0	1-2	2-0	0-2
El Ahmedi Sebkha	22	5	8	9	14	22	23	1-1	0-1	0-1	0-1	0-1	0-1	0-3	0-3		1-2	1-0	0-0
ACAS Teyarett	22	5	7	10	19	32	22	0-1	1-3	0-1	0-0	1-1	0-0	0-0	0-1	1-2		3-1	3-1
ASC Dar El Barka	22	4	2	16	18	46	14	1-2	0-7	1-7	1-2	2-1	1-2	1-2	0-3	0-0	0-0		1-0
Dar Naim	22	1	6	15	10	43	9	0-1	0-4	1-3	0-1	0-0	1-1	1-1	1-2	1-3	0-2	1-3	

22/01/2010 - 21/05/2010 • † Qualified for the CAF Champions League • ‡ Qualified for the Confederation Cup
SNIM Nouadhibou were renamed CF Cansado

COUPE DU PRESIDENT DE LA REPUBLIQUE 2010

Quarter–finals		Semi–finals		Final	
Tevragh Zeina	1				
Trarza Rosso	0	**Tevragh Zeina**	1 3p		
FC Nouadhibou	0	ASAC Concorde	1 2p		
ASAC Concorde	1			**Tevragh Zeina** ‡	3
Kédia Zouératt	0 p			Feu Mini Nouakchott	0
Renaissance	0 p	Kédia Zouératt	1		
Assaba Kiffa	1	**Feu Mini Nouakchott**	3	Olympique, Nouakchott
Feu Mini Nouakchott	3	‡ Qualified for the Confederation Cup		15-10-2010	

MWI – MALAWI

FIFA/COCA-COLA WORLD RANKING

1993	1994	1995	1996	1997	1998	1999	2000	2001	2002	2003	2004	2005	2006	2007	2008	2009	2010
67	82	89	88	97	89	114	113	120	95	105	109	106	104	138	104	99	86

2010												Hi/Lo
Jan	Feb	Mar	Mar	Apr	May	Jul	Aug	Sep	Oct	Nov	Dec	53
99	82	82	81	82	86	74	74	78	84	77	86	138

The year began for Malawi with only their second-ever appearance in the African Nations Cup finals where they caused an upset with a win over World Cup-bound Algeria but in the end the Flames were eliminated at the first hurdle in Angola. It marked the start of a furious year of international activity for Kinnah Phiri's side, who went unbeaten through their first four games of the 2012 Nations Cup qualifiers and then competed at the year-ending CECAFA Cup in Tanzania, playing 14 internationals in total. In the 2012 Nations Cup qualifiers, there were satisfactory draws away in Togo and Tunisia but points dropped at home to surprise group leaders Botswana mean that Malawi will have a tough fight on their hands to finish in second place to secure a spot in the finals in Gabon and Equatorial Guinea. In the CECAFA Cup, where they were guest competitors, Malawi were unbeaten in the first round group but then lost in the quarter-finals to Cote d'Ivoire, who sent their 'A' team to the tournament. In club football Silver Strikers won the Super League by a point from Escom United in early 2010 but lost in the President's Cup Final to CIVO United in September with Gerald Mkungula scoring a late winner in Lilongwe. However, neither they nor Silver Strikers elected to play in the 2011 African club competitions.

FIFA WORLD CUP RECORD
1930-1974 DNE 1978-1990 DNQ 1994 DNE 1998-2010 DNQ

FOOTBALL ASSOCIATION OF MALAWI (FAM)

Cimwembe Technical Centre, Cimwembe, Limbe
PO Box 51657, Blantyre
☎ +265 1 842204
📠 +265 1 842204
✉ fam@africa-online.net
🖥 www.fam.mw
FA 1966 CON 1968 FIFA 1967
P Walter Nyamilandu Manda
GS Charles Nyirenda

FIFA BIG COUNT 2006

Total players	515 800
% of population	3.96%
Male	515 600
Female	200
Amateurs 18+	11 400
Youth under 18	8 700
Unregistered	29 700
Professionals	0
Referees	600
Admin & coaches	1 800
Number of clubs	70
Number of teams	120

MAJOR CITIES/TOWNS

		Population
1	Lilongwe	922 894
2	Blantyre	760 064
3	Mzuzu	187 151
4	Zomba	105 264
5	Kasungu	64 433
6	Mangochi	54 509
7	Karonga	44 112
8	Salima	42 651
9	Nkhotakota	34 741
10	Liwonde	31 218
11	Rumphi	29 803
12	Nsanje	28 246
13	Mzimba	27 778
14	Mchinji	27 135
15	Balaka	25 169
16	Mulanje	21 890
17	Luchenza	16 350
18	Dedza	15 681
19	Nkhata Bay	15 294

DZIKO LA MALAWI • REPUBLIC OF MALAWI

Capital	Lilongwe	Population	14 268 711 (66)	% in cities	19%
GDP per capita	$800 (220)	Area km²	118 484 km² (99)	GMT +/-	+2
Neighbours (km)	Mozambique 1569, Tanzania 475, Zambia 837				

RECENT INTERNATIONAL MATCHES PLAYED BY MALAWI

2007	Opponents	Score		Venue	Comp	Scorers	Att	Referee
26-05	South Africa	D	0-0	Mbabane	CCr1	L 4-5p		Dlamini SWZ
27-05	Swaziland	L	0-1	Mbabane	CCr1			Labrosse SEY
10-06	Senegal	L	2-3	Blantyre	Fr	Mwafulirwa [75], Mkhandawire [78]		
16-06	Morocco	L	0-1	Blantyre	CNq			Maillet SEY
6-07	Namibia	L	1-2	Blantyre	Fr	Kafoteka [48]		
9-09	Zimbabwe	L	1-3	Bulawayo	CNq	Kanyenda [43]		Hicuburundi BDI
18-11	Swaziland	W	3-0	Manzini	Fr	Mwafulirwa [31], Kanyenda [45], Mkandawire [60]		
2008								
26-03	Namibia	W	3-1	Windhoek	Fr	Nyondo [29], Chirambo [38], Mwakasungula [61]		
25-05	Tanzania	D	1-1	Dar es Salaam	Fr	Kanyenda [56]		
31-05	Djibouti	W	8-1	Blantyre	WCq	Kafoteka [3], Kanyenda 3 [19 46 48], Kamwendo [66], Chavula [73], Ngambi [78], Mkandawire [83]	35 000	Katjimune NAM
8-06	Congo DR	L	0-1	Kinshasa	WCq		35 000	Abdelkadir SUD
14-06	Egypt	W	1-0	Blantyre	WCq	Msowoya [93+]	40 000	Keita GUI
22-06	Egypt	L	0-2	Cairo	WCq			Diatta SEN
20-07	Lesotho	W	1-0	Secunda	CCr1	Msowoya [75]		Rajindraparsad MRI
22-07	Comoros	W	1-0	Secunda	CCr1	Kondowe [62]		Marange ZIM
24-07	Namibia	L	0-1	Secunda	CCr1			Marange ZIM
5-09	Djibouti	W	3-0	Djibouti	WCq	Msowoya [30], Chavula [63], Nyondo [67]	700	Carvalho ANG
30-09	South Africa	L	0-3	Johannesburg	Fr			
11-10	Congo DR	W	2-1	Blantyre	WCq	Ngambi [56], Msowoya [83]	50 000	Codjia BEN
2009								
11-02	Mozambique	L	0-2	Maputo	Fr			
21-03	Uganda	L	1-2	Kampala	Fr	Nyondo [37]		
29-03	Côte d'Ivoire	L	0-5	Abidjan	WCq		34 000	Haimoudi ALG
30-05	Rwanda	W	2-0	Blantyre	Fr	Msowoya 2 [63 82]		
6-06	Burkina Faso	L	0-1	Blantyre	WCq		25 000	Bennaceur TUN
21-06	Guinea	L	1-2	Conakry	WCq	Msowoya [88]	14 000	Abdul Rahman SUD
6-07	Swaziland	W	3-1	Blantyre	Fr	Maziya OG [19], Wadabwa 2 [43 86]		
5-09	Guinea	W	2-1	Blantyre	WCq	Msowoya 2 [46 59]	15 000	Codjia BEN
10-10	Côte d'Ivoire	D	1-1	Blantyre	WCq	Ngwira [64]	25 000	El Achiri MAR
25-10	Mozambique	L	0-1	Harare	CCqf			Ramocha BOT
14-11	Burkina Faso	L	0-1	Ouagadougou	WCq		20 000	Abd El Fatah EGY
19-12	Mozambique	W	1-0	Tete	Fr	Nyirenda [88]		
29-12	Egypt	D	1-1	Cairo	Fr	Msowoya [87]		
2010								
5-01	Ghana	D	0-0	Manzini	Fr			
11-01	Algeria	W	3-0	Luanda	CNr1	Mwafulirwa [17], Kafoteka [35], Banda [48]	1 000	Diatta SEN
14-01	Angola	L	0-2	Luanda	CNr1		48 500	Doue CIV
18-01	Mali	L	1-3	Luanda	CNr1	Mwafulirwa [58]	21 000	Seechurn MRI
3-03	Zimbabwe	L	1-2	Harare	Fr	Makandawire [13]		
12-05	Yemen	L	0-1	Sana'a	Fr			
9-07	Togo	D	1-1	Lome	CNq	Mwakasungula [18]		Bennett RSA
11-08	Botswana	D	1-1	Blantyre	CNq	Banda [75]		Carvalho ANG
4-09	Tunisia	D	2-2	Rades/Tunis	CNq	Msowoya [45], Kanyenda [82p]		Lamptey GHA
9-10	Chad	W	6-2	Blantyre	CNq	Zakazaka [13], Kanyenda 2 [21 52], Msowoya 2 [68 79], Ngambi [85]		Kirwa KEN
17-11	Rwanda	W	2-1	Blantyre	Fr	Banda [56], Nyirenda [76]		
29-11	Kenya	W	3-2	Dar es Salaam	CFr1	Nyirenda [1], Banda 2 [26 81]		
2-12	Uganda	D	1-1	Dar es Salaam	CFr1	Nyirenda [2]		
4-12	Ethiopia	D	1-1	Dar es Salaam	CFr1	Kabichi [27]		

Fr = Friendly match • CN = CAF African Cup of Nations • CC = COSAFA Cup • CF = CECAFA Cup • WC = FIFA World Cup
q = qualifier • r1 = first round group • qf = quarter-final • sf = semi-final • f = final

MALAWI 2009-10

SUPER LEAGUE

	Pl	W	D	L	F	A	Pts	Silver Strikers	Escom Utd	MTL Wanderers	CIVO Utd	Tigers	Bullets	Red Lions	Moyale Barracks	Eagle Strikers	Blue Eagles	Blackpool	Zomba Utd	EPAC Utd	Dwangwa Utd	Nkhata Bay Utd
Silver Strikers	28	18	5	5	56	18	59		0-0	2-2	0-1	2-3	0-1	1-0	3-0	2-1	3-2	3-2	3-0	1-0	5-0	2-0
Escom United	28	15	13	0	44	12	58	0-0		1-1	1-1	2-1	1-0	1-1	0-0	0-0	1-0	2-2	1-1	1-0	4-0	8-0
MTL Wanderers	28	14	11	3	39	22	53	1-4	1-1		2-1	0-1	1-0	1-2	0-0	1-1	2-1	2-2	0-0	6-1	1-0	1-0
CIVO United	28	14	6	8	43	22	48	1-2	0-1	1-1		0-1	1-0	1-0	1-1	1-0	0-0	1-0	2-1	1-0	1-0	7-0
Tigers FC	28	14	6	8	42	29	48	1-0	1-1	0-0	2-1		1-3	1-0	1-3	3-2	2-2	2-0	4-2	1-0	1-1	9-0
Bullets	28	13	7	8	38	27	46	0-3	0-2	0-1	2-2	1-1		1-0	2-0	1-1	2-0	1-2	3-2	2-1	4-1	7-1
Red Lions	28	12	7	9	37	25	43	0-0	1-2	1-3	1-0	1-0	3-0		3-3	1-2	2-1	1-1	0-0	1-1	2-1	0-0
Moyale Barracks	28	10	10	8	36	37	40	0-0	0-1	1-2	0-5	1-0	2-2	1-0		2-1	0-0	2-3	1-2	3-2	2-0	1-0
Eagle Strikers	28	9	9	10	33	30	36	1-0	0-0	0-1	2-2	2-0	0-0	0-1	2-2		1-0	1-1	5-2	3-0	1-0	3-0
Blue Eagles	28	8	11	9	25	23	35	0-1	1-1	0-0	0-2	0-0	0-2	0-0	**0-2**	0-0		2-0	0-0	2-0	2-1	1-1
Blackpool	28	9	7	12	36	36	34	0-2	0-2	0-1	0-1	1-0	1-2	0-0	2-3	2-3	1-1		1-2	1-0	3-0	4-1
Zomba United	28	9	3	16	31	43	30	1-2	0-2	0-1	2-0	3-1	0-1	0-1	2-2	2-1	0-1	0-1		0-1	3-1	2-1
EPAC United	28	6	4	18	23	38	22	0-3	0-1	0-1	0-2	1-0	1-3	2-1	0-2	3-0	1-1	0-1	2-3		1-1	5-1
Dwangwa United	28	6	4	18	25	55	22	0-1	1-2	2-2	1-5	0-1	0-1	0-4	1-0	2-0	0-1	2-1	0-1	2-0		4-1
Nkhata Bay United	28	1	1	26	13	104	4	1-11	0-5	0-3	1-3	0-2	0-1	0-5	2-4	0-2	0-5	1-4	1-2	1-0	1-3	

27/06/2009 - 27/02/2010 • Match in bold awarded

PRESIDENT'S CUP 2008-09

Quarter-finals		Semi-finals		Final	
MTL Wanderers	1				
Moyale Barracks	0	**MTL Wanderers**	0 4p		
Tigers	1	Bullets	0 3p		
Bullets	2			**MTL Wanderers**	1 2p
Silver Strikers	1			Escom United	1 1p
Eagle Strikers	0	Silver Strikers	0	Kamuzu, Blantyre	
Pakeeza	1	**Escom United**	1	25-04-2009	
Escom United	2	3rd Place: Strikers 1-0 Bullets			

MEDALS TABLE

		Overall G	Lge G	Cup G	City/Town
1	Bullets	45	11	34	Blantyre
2	Wanderers	23	4	19	Blantyre
3	Silver Strikers	16	3	13	Lilongwe
4	MDC United	9	1	8	Blantyre
5	Tigers	7	1	6	Blantyre
6	CIVO United	5	1	4	Lilongwe
7	Moyale Barracks	3		3	Mzuzu
	Red Lions	3		3	Zomba
	Sucoma	3		3	Chikwawa
	MITCO	3		3	Lilongwe
	Michuru Castles	3		3	Blantyre
12	Escom United	2	1	1	Blantyre

PRESIDENT'S CUP 2010

First Round		Quarter-finals		Semi-finals		Final	
CIVO United	5						
Mangochi Medicals	0	**CIVO United**	0 5p				
Airborne Rangers	1	Tigers	0 4p				
Tigers	2			**CIVO United**	1		
Bullets	1			Escom United	0		
Juke Box	0	**Bullets**	1				
Blantyre United	0 3p	**Escom United**	4				
Escom United	0 4p					**CIVO United** ‡	1
Red Lions	3 4p					Silver Strikers	0
Super Eagles	3 2p	**Red Lions**	1 4p				
White Eagles	1	Moyale Barracks	1 2p			CUP FINAL	
Moyale Barracks	2			Red Lions	0	CIVO Stadium, Lilongwe	
Blue Eagles	1			**Silver Strikers**	3	11-09-2010	
Eagle Strikers	0	**Blue Eagles**	0				
Support Batallion	1	**Silver Strikers**	3			Scorer - Gerald Mkungula 84 for CIVO	
Silver Strikers	2						

3rd place: ESCOM 1-1 6-5p Lions

MYA – MYANMAR

FIFA/COCA-COLA WORLD RANKING

1993	1994	1995	1996	1997	1998	1999	2000	2001	2002	2003	2004	2005	2006	2007	2008	2009	2010
110	124	115	104	114	115	126	124	151	162	140	144	147	154	157	156	140	149

					2010							Hi/Lo
Jan	Feb	Mar	Mar	Apr	May	Jul	Aug	Sep	Oct	Nov	Dec	97
140	141	139	141	142	147	143	140	141	145	144	149	165

The story of the year in Myanmar was the unexpected success of club side Yadanarbon in winning the AFC President's Cup - the first continental honour for the country since the glory days of the late 1960s. In a tournament reserved for the lowest ranked nations in Asia, Yadanarbon broke the stranglehold of the Tajik and Kyrgyz clubs who between them had won all the five previous competitions. Most impressive of all was their 1-0 victory in the final over two-time champions Dordoi-Dynamo, with Ivorian striker Lassina Kone scoring the only goal in a packed Thuwunna stadium in Yangon. The national team also performed well at the 2010 AFC Challenge Cup in Sri Lanka when Tin Myint Aung's team reached the semi-finals of the second-tier continental competition. There they came up against World Cup-bound North Korea and were comprehensively beaten 5-0 before losing the third place play-off to Tajikistan. Myanmar's struggles continued at the regional AFF Suzuki Cup at the end of the year with the team unable to progress - once again - beyond the group stages of Southeast Asia's leading football tournament. Myanmar picked up just one point in a draw with the Philippines after losing 1-0 to Singapore and 7-1 to Vietnam. Following the tournament Myint Aung was replaced as head coach by the veteran Serb Milan Zivadinovic.

FIFA WORLD CUP RECORD
1930-2006 DNE 2010 DNQ

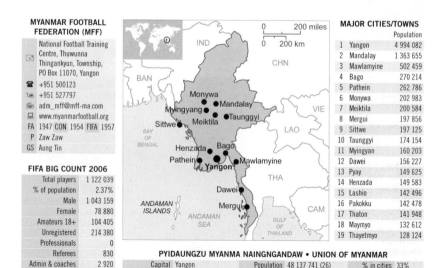

MYANMAR FOOTBALL FEDERATION (MFF)

National Football Training Centre, Thuwunna Thingankyun, Township, PO Box 11070, Yangon
☎ +951 500123
📠 +951 527797
📧 adm_mff@mff-ma.com
🖥 www.myanmarfootball.org
FA 1947 CON 1954 FIFA 1957
P Zaw Zaw
GS Aung Tin

FIFA BIG COUNT 2006

Total players	1 122 039
% of population	2.37%
Male	1 043 159
Female	78 880
Amateurs 18+	104 405
Unregistered	214 380
Professionals	0
Referees	830
Admin & coaches	2 920
Number of clubs	598
Number of teams	4 200

MAJOR CITIES/TOWNS

		Population
1	Yangon	4 994 082
2	Mandalay	1 363 655
3	Mawlamyine	502 459
4	Bago	270 214
5	Pathein	262 786
6	Monywa	202 983
7	Meiktila	200 584
8	Mergui	197 856
9	Sittwe	197 125
10	Taunggyi	174 154
11	Myingyan	160 203
12	Dawei	156 227
13	Pyay	149 625
14	Henzada	149 583
15	Lashio	142 496
16	Pakokku	142 478
17	Thaton	141 948
18	Maymyo	132 612
19	Thayetmyo	128 124

PYIDAUNGZU MYANMA NAINGNGANDAW • UNION OF MYANMAR

Capital	Yangon	Population	48 137 741 (26)	% in cities	33%
GDP per capita	$1200 (206)	Area km²	676 578 km² (40)	GMT +/-	+6.5
Neighbours (km)	Bangladesh 193, China 2185, India 1463, Laos 235, Thailand 1800 • Coast 1930				

RECENT INTERNATIONAL MATCHES PLAYED BY MYANMAR

2008	Opponents		Score	Venue	Comp	Scorers	Att	Referee
5-12	Indonesia	L	0-3	Jakarta	AFFrl		40 000	Ramachandran MAS
7-12	Singapore	L	1-3	Jakarta	AFFrl	Min Tun Myo [28]	21 000	Phung VIE
9-12	Cambodia	W	3-2	Bandung	AFFrl	Mo Win [29], Win Thein Yaza [35], Min Tun Myo [85]		Martinez PHI
2009								
26-04	Macau	W	4-0	Dhaka	CCq	Maung Lwin Khin [3], Win Thein Yaza [15], Phyo Oo Pyaye [48], Min Tun Myo [59]	3 600	Mashentsev KGZ
28-04	Bangladesh	W	2-1	Dhaka	CCq	Soe Pae 2 [68 77]	14 000	Matsuo JPN
30-04	Cambodia	W	1-0	Dhaka	CCq	Win Thein Yaza [94+]	2 500	Mozaffari IRN
2010								
16-02	Sri Lanka	W	4-0	Colombo	CCrl	Thi Ha Kyaw [39], Paing Yan [71], Soe Pai [81], Min Tun Myo [87]	3 000	Faghani IRN
18-02	Bangladesh	W	2-1	Colombo	CCrl	Tun Win Tun [16], Soe Pai [32]	500	Al Yarimi YEM
20-02	Tajikistan	L	0-3	Colombo	CCrl		100	Shukralla BHR
24-02	Korea DPR	L	0-5	Colombo	CCsf		400	Al Yarimi YEM
27-02	Tajikistan	L	0-1	Colombo	CC3p		300	El Haddad LIB
2-12	Vietnam	L	1-7	Hanoi	AFFrl	Kyaw Moe Aung [16]	40 000	Patwal IND
5-12	Singapore	L	1-2	Hanoi	AFFrl	Maung Lwin Khin [13]		Tao Ranchang CHN
8-12	Philippines	D	0-0	Nam Dinh	AFFrl			Patwal IND

Fr = Friendly match • AFF = AFF Championship • CC = AFC Challenge Cup • q = qualifier • rl = 1st round group • † Not a full international

MYANMAR 2009-10

MYANMAR NATIONAL LEAGUE

	Pl	W	D	L	F	A	Pts	Yadanarbon	Delta Utd	Kanbawza	Yangon Utd	Zeyar	Okktha Utd	Magway	Sth Myanmar
Yadanarbon †	14	9	2	3	24	13	29		1-2	1-0	0-2	1-0	3-1	2-1	2-2
Delta United	14	8	2	4	22	15	26	0-1		1-1	2-1	3-2	1-1	1-0	2-1
Kanbawza	14	7	3	4	25	18	24	1-3	3-1		1-1	1-0	1-1	2-0	3-2
Yangon United	14	7	2	5	24	16	23	1-2	1-0	4-2		1-2	2-0	2-1	4-1
Zeyar Shwe Myay	14	5	2	7	19	19	17	2-1	1-3	0-1	1-3		3-1	0-2	4-1
Okktha United	14	3	6	5	11	20	15	0-2	1-0	0-4	1-1	0-0		2-2	2-1
Magway	14	3	5	6	11	18	14	0-0	1-5	0-2	1-0	1-1	0-0		2-1
Southern Myanmar Utd	14	2	2	10	16	33	8	1-5	0-1	4-3	2-1	0-3	0-1	0-0	

5/09/2009 - 17/01/2010 • † Qualified for the AFC President's Cup

MYANMAR 2010

MYANMAR NATIONAL LEAGUE

	Pl	W	D	L	F	A	Pts	Yadanarbon	Zeyar	Yangon Utd	Kanbawza	Magway	Sth Myanmar	Okktha Utd	Delta Utd	Manaw Myay	Nay Pyi Taw	Zwekapin Utd
Yadanarbon †	20	13	5	2	44	16	44		0-3	0-0	0-0	2-2	1-0	3-1	3-2	5-0	2-0	4-0
Zeyar Shwe Myay	20	13	5	2	41	18	44	1-2		1-0	1-0	1-0	3-2	2-2	1-0	4-1	0-0	4-1
Yangon United	20	11	6	3	44	12	39	4-1	0-1		0-0	1-0	3-1	0-0	3-3	3-0	2-0	7-0
Kanbawza	20	11	5	4	28	11	38	0-0	1-0	0-0		1-3	2-3	1-1	1-0	2-0	2-0	3-0
Magway	20	10	2	8	37	36	32	0-3	1-3	0-7	0-3		1-2	2-1	0-0	5-3	3-1	4-2
Okktha United	20	9	3	8	34	34	30	1-4	2-2	1-1	0-2	3-2		0-1	2-0	1-2	4-2	1-0
Southern Myanmar Utd	20	6	7	7	32	29	25	0-1	2-2	0-2	3-2	2-3	2-2		0-2	0-1	1-1	6-1
Delta United	20	7	3	10	28	34	24	0-3	3-3	2-1	0-3	1-2	2-1	0-2		2-4	2-1	0-1
Manaw Myay	20	6	1	13	24	50	19	0-2	0-3	1-4	0-2	0-5	0-1	2-2	2-4		1-2	2-0
Nay Pyi Taw	20	3	3	14	25	36	12	1-1	1-2	1-2	0-2	0-2	1-3	1-2	1-2	1-2		5-1
Zwekapin Utd	20	1	0	19	13	74	3	1-7	0-4	0-4	0-1	0-2	3-4	1-4	0-3	2-3	0-6	

13/03/2010 - 10/11/2010 • † Qualified for the AFC President's Cup

NAM – NAMIBIA

FIFA/COCA-COLA WORLD RANKING

1993	1994	1995	1996	1997	1998	1999	2000	2001	2002	2003	2004	2005	2006	2007	2008	2009	2010
156	123	116	103	86	69	80	87	101	123	144	158	161	116	114	115	113	138

	2010											Hi/Lo
Jan	Feb	Mar	Mar	Apr	May	Jul	Aug	Sep	Oct	Nov	Dec	68
113	109	111	112	112	111	119	115	116	140	141	138	167

Despite reviving the fortunes of the Namibian national team since taking over in 2008 the 37-year-old Belgian coach Tom Santfiet was shown the door after a 3-1 loss to Gambia in the qualifiers for the 2012 African Nations Cup. Under Santfiet Namibia's Brave Warriors were beginning to show signs of the accomplished and settled atmosphere which saw them qualify for the 2008 Nations Cup finals in Ghana with the Belgian losing just three of his 13 matches in charge. The withdrawal of Mauritania leaves new coach Brian Isaacs with a reduced schedule in the qualifying group from which Burkina Faso are expected to qualify. The high cost of participating in continental club competition meant that African Stars were absent from the 2010 African Champions League and they also declined to enter the 2011 tournament after successfully defending their league crown in 2010. Coached by Bobby Samara, Stars finished two points ahead of Orlando Pirates to win the title for only the second time in their history but then followed that up with a 1-0 victory over fellow Windhoek club Civics in the Cup Final, who they beat with an extra time goal from Rudi Louw. Remarkably, it was the first time that a club had achieved a league and cup double in Namibian football since independence in 1990.

FIFA WORLD CUP RECORD
1930-1994 DNE **1998-2010** DNQ

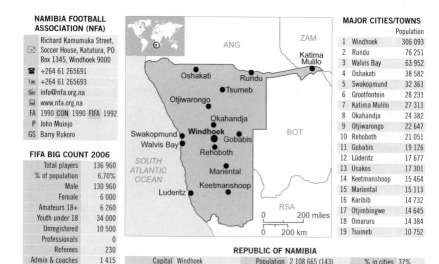

NAMIBIA FOOTBALL ASSOCIATION (NFA)

Richard Kamumuka Street, Soccer House, Katutura, PO Box 1345, Windhoek 9000

☎ +264 61 265691
📠 +264 61 265693
✉ info@nfa.org.na
🖥 www.nfa.org.na
FA 1990 CON 1990 FIFA 1992
P John Muinjo
GS Barry Rukoro

FIFA BIG COUNT 2006

Total players	136 960
% of population	6.70%
Male	130 960
Female	6 000
Amateurs 18+	6 260
Youth under 18	34 000
Unregistered	10 500
Professionals	0
Referees	230
Admin & coaches	1 415
Number of clubs	100
Number of teams	250

MAJOR CITIES/TOWNS

		Population
1	Windhoek	306 093
2	Rundu	76 251
3	Walvis Bay	63 952
4	Oshakati	38 582
5	Swakopmund	32 361
6	Grootfontein	28 231
7	Katima Mulilo	27 311
8	Okahandja	24 382
9	Otjiwarongo	22 647
10	Rehoboth	21 051
11	Gobabis	19 126
12	Lüderitz	17 677
13	Usakos	17 301
14	Keetmanshoop	15 464
15	Mariental	15 113
16	Karibib	14 732
17	Otjimbingwe	14 645
18	Omaruru	14 384
19	Tsumeb	10 752

REPUBLIC OF NAMIBIA

Capital	Windhoek	Population	2 108 665 (143)	% in cities	37%
GDP per capita	$6400 (129)	Area km²	824 292 km² (34)	GMT +/-	+1

Neighbours (km) Angola 1376, Botswana 1360, South Africa 967, Zambia 233 • Coast 1572

RECENT INTERNATIONAL MATCHES PLAYED BY NAMIBIA

2006	Opponents	Score		Venue	Comp	Scorers	Att	Referee
22-07	Seychelles	D	1-1	Katutura	CCr1	Khaiseb 18. L 2-4p		Simisse MRI
23-07	Malawi	W	3-2	Katutura	CCr1	Iasaacks 44, Bester 47, Botes 66p		Simisse MRI
16-08	South Africa	L	0-1	Katutura	Fr			
3-09	Congo DR	L	2-3	Kinshasa	CNq	Plaatjies 2 34 60		Evehe CMR
7-10	Ethiopia	W	1-0	Katutura	CNq	Jacobs 20p		Moeketsi LES
15-11	Zimbabwe	L	2-3	Harare	Fr	Helu 36, Khaiseb 55p		
2007								
6-02	Botswana	L	0-1	Gaborone	Fr			
25-03	Libya	L	1-2	Tripoli	CNq	Benjamin 85		
26-05	Zambia	L	1-2	Windhoek	Fr	Shatimuene 89		
2-06	Libya	W	1-0	Windhoek	CNq	Benjamin 4		Ncobo RSA
16-06	Congo DR	D	1-1	Windhoek	CNq	Pienaar 38		Mwanza ZAM
6-07	Malawi	W	2-1	Blantyre	Fr	Katjatenja 23, Bester 65		
28-07	Botswana	L	0-1	Gaborone	CCr1			Lwanja MWI
29-07	Lesotho	W	3-2	Gaborone	CCr1	Katupose 53, Brendell 2 67 77		Disang BOT
8-09	Ethiopia	W	3-2	Addis Abeba	CNq	Bester 2 64 81, Katupose 89		Auda EGY
17-10	Morocco	L	0-2	Tanger	Fr			
2-11	Saudi Arabia	L	0-1	Riyadh	Fr			
17-11	Tunisia	L	0-2	Rades	Fr			
2008								
5-01	Egypt	L	0-3	Aswan	Fr			
12-01	Senegal	L	1-3	Dakar	Fr	Brendell 62		
21-01	Morocco	L	1-5	Accra	CNr1	Brendell 23		Evehe CMR
24-01	Ghana	L	0-1	Accra	CNr1			Bennaceur TUN
28-01	Guinea	D	1-1	Sekondi	CNr1	Brendell 80		Ssegonga UGA
26-03	Malawi	L	1-3	Windhoek	Fr	Tuyeni 53		
31-05	Kenya	W	2-1	Windhoek	WCq	Risser 14, Khaiseb 89	6 000	Ssegonga UGA
8-06	Zimbabwe	L	0-2	Harare	WCq		27 979	Lwanja MWI
14-06	Guinea	L	1-2	Windhoek	WCq	Bester 42	5 000	Imiere NGA
22-06	Guinea	L	0-4	Conakry	WCq		15 000	Monteiro Lopes CPV
20-07	Comoros	W	3-0	Secunda	CCr1	Kaimbi 25, Jacobs 2 43 74		Labrosse SEY
22-07	Lesotho	D	1-1	Secunda	CCr1	Ngatjizeko 23		Seechurn MRI
24-07	Malawi	W	1-0	Secunda	CCr1	Kaimbi 50		Marange ZIM
6-09	Kenya	L	0-1	Nairobi	WCq		40 000	Hicuburundi BDI
11-10	Zimbabwe	W	4-2	Windhoek	WCq	Risser 2 18 53, Bester 30, Shipanga 43	4 000	Coulibaly MLI
2009								
21-03	Botswana	D	0-0	Keetmanshoop	Fr			
1-04	Lebanon	D	1-1	Saida	Fr	Bester 70		
4-04	Angola	D	0-0	Dundo	Fr			
6-06	Congo DR	W	4-0	Windhoek	Fr	Jacobs 34, Bester 49, Isaacks 2 73 84		
5-09	Swaziland	D	1-1	Windhoek	Fr	Bester 28		
25-10	Zambia	L	0-1	Harare	CCqf			Ebrahim RSA
2010								
3-03	South Africa	D	1-1	Durban	Fr	Bester 42	35 000	Nguluwe MWI
21-03	Botswana	D	0-0	Windhoek	Fr			
4-09	Gambia	L	1-3	Banjul	CNq	Risser 90		Ragab LBY
15-09	India	L	0-2	New Delhi	Fr			

Fr = Friendly match • CN = CAF African Cup of Nations • CC = COSAFA Cup • WC = FIFA World Cup • q = qualifier • r1 = first round group

NAMIBIA 2009–10

TAFEL LAGER PREMIER LEAGUE

	Pl	W	D	L	F	A	Pts	African Stars	Pirates	Black Africa	Tigers	Eleven Arrows	Blue Waters	SK Windhoek	Civics	Oshakati City	Ramblers	Hotspurs	United Stars
African Stars	22	12	8	2	31	13	44		1-0	1-1	2-0	2-1	1-0	4-0	0-1	3-1	1-1	1-1	2-0
Orlando Pirates	22	12	6	4	37	24	42	0-2		0-0	1-2	1-1	3-2	3-1	1-0	0-0	3-1	2-1	6-1
Black Africa	22	10	7	5	43	24	37	1-1	5-1		0-1	1-1	2-2	1-2	3-1	3-0	5-0	0-0	2-2
United Africa Tigers	22	10	7	5	21	14	37	0-0	1-1	2-3		0-0	1-0	1-0	1-1	2-1	2-0	1-0	2-0
Eleven Arrows	22	9	7	6	19	15	34	1-0	0-1	1-0	1-0		0-0	1-1	3-0	0-0	0-3	1-0	2-0
Blue Waters	22	9	6	7	27	23	33	1-1	0-2	2-0	2-1	1-0		2-0	1-0	1-1	2-0	1-0	1-1
SK Windhoek	22	8	5	9	31	35	29	0-1	1-1	2-4	0-0	2-0	2-0		2-1	1-0	0-3	1-0	9-3
Civics	22	8	4	10	42	31	28	1-1	1-2	2-0	0-2	0-0	3-1	3-0		1-2	4-0	4-4	7-1
Oshakati City	22	6	6	10	23	39	24	0-1	1-4	2-5	2-1	1-0	0-4	0-0	3-2		1-1	2-1	3-1
Ramblers	22	4	8	10	23	37	20	1-1	1-1	0-4	0-0	1-2	1-2	1-2	0-2	1-1		1-1	2-2
Hotspurs	22	4	4	14	24	35	16	2-4	0-1	1-2	0-1	1-2	3-1	2-1	2-1	4-2	0-2		1-2
United Stars	22	3	6	13	28	59	15	0-1	2-3	0-1	0-0	0-2	1-1	4-4	2-7	3-0	1-3	2-0	

11/09/2009 - 22/05/2010

MEDALS TABLE

		Overall G	S	B	Lge G	S	Cup G	S	City/Town
1	Black Africa	7	2		4		3	2	Winhoek
2	Chief Santos	6			2		4		Tsumeb
3	Civics	5	1		3		2	1	Windhoek
4	African Stars	4	2		2		2	2	Windhoek
5	Orlando Pirates	4	2		1		3	2	Windhoek
6	Blue Waters	4	1		3		1	1	Walvis Bay
7	United Africa Tigers	2	5				2	5	Windhoek
8	Ramblers	2			1		1		Windhoek
9	Liverpool	2			1		1		Okahandja
10	Eleven Arrows	1	1		1			1	Walvis Bay
11	Life Fighters		2					2	Otjiwarongo
12	Young Ones		2				2		Windhoek
13	SK Windhoek			1				1	Windhoek

LEO NFA CUP 2010

Round of 16

African Stars	3
Young Rangers	0
African Lions	0
SK Windhoek	3
Eleven Arrows	2
Spoilers	0
United Stars	1
Black Africa	5
Mighty Gunners	3
Chief Santos	1
Try Again	0
Eleven Warriors	3
Ramblers	2
Unam Ogongo	1
Orlando Pirates	2 5p
Civics	2 6p

Quarter–finals

African Stars	1
SK Windhoek	0
Eleven Arrows	1 8p
Black Africa	1 9p
Mighty Gunners	6
Eleven Warriors	2
Ramblers	3 1p
Civics	0 3p

Semi–finals

African Stars	2
Black Africa	0
Mighty Gunners	2
Civics	3

Semi-finals played in Gobabis
‡ Qualified for the CAF Confederation Cup

Final

African Stars	1
Civics	0

CUP FINAL

Independence, Windhoek
29-05-2010

Scorer - Rudi Louw [106] for African Stars

NCA – NICARAGUA

FIFA/COCA-COLA WORLD RANKING

1993	1994	1995	1996	1997	1998	1999	2000	2001	2002	2003	2004	2005	2006	2007	2008	2009	2010
155	168	174	179	182	188	193	191	188	186	173	158	152	168	161	181	133	158

2010												Hi/Lo
Jan	Feb	Mar	Mar	Apr	May	Jul	Aug	Sep	Oct	Nov	Dec	**132**
133	162	159	160	155	155	161	161	158	161	161	158	**193**

When the national team travelled to Panama for the 2011 Copa Centroamericana - the renamed UNCAF Cup - there was to be no repeat of the heroics in the 2009 tournament which had seen Nicaragua qualify for the CONCACAF Gold Cup for the first time. In Panama, Nicaragua reverted to type, losing to both El Salvador and Panama in their first-round group and only managing a draw against rank outsiders Belize - the one team in the region over which Nicaragua can claim to be stronger. They did, however, finish above Belize in the group which meant a fifth-place play-off against Guatemala for a place in the 2011 Gold Cup. It was Guatemala that Nicaragua beat in 2009 but this time they lost 2-1 despite taking a first half lead through Felix Rodriguez. At home Nicaragua remains one of the few countries in the Americas that has resisted the temptation to adopt fully the two seasons per year league system with the winners of the Apertura and Clausura playing off for the title. The 2010 final in May was a repeat of the Clausura final the previous week and was settled on away goals with Real Estelí managing a 1-1 draw in Managua against Walter Ferreti following a 0-0 draw at home. There was consolation for Walter Ferreti when they qualified for the 2011 final - beating Diriangen in the Apertura final in December.

FIFA WORLD CUP RECORD
1930-1990 DNE   1994-2010 DNQ

FEDERACION NICARAGUENSE DE FUTBOL (FENIFUT)

Estadio Nacional de Futbol ubicado frente a la Universad Nacional de Managua, Managua

☎ +505 22774087
📠 +505 22774089
📧 fenifut@yahoo.com
🖥 www.fenifut.org.ni
FA 1931 CON 1968 FIFA 1950
P Julio Rocha Lopez
GS Florencio Leiva

FIFA BIG COUNT 2006

Total players	467 031
% of population	8.38%
Male	408 081
Female	58 950
Unregistered	190 354
Professionals	0
Referees	1 372
Admin & coaches	4 398
Number of clubs	1 270
Number of teams	4 221

MAJOR CITIES/TOWNS

		Population
1	Managua	925 313
2	León	144 179
3	Estelí	97 488
4	Chinandega	93 996
5	Tipitapa	93 080
6	Masaya	93 053
7	Matagalpa	89 132
8	Granada	81 674
9	Ciudad Sandino	75 610
10	Puerto Cabezas	48 491
11	Jinotega	45 580
12	Juigalpa	44 686
13	El Viejo	41 110
14	Bluefields	40 297
15	Ocotal	38 148
16	Diriamba	36 827
17	Chichigalpa	36 186
18	Jinotepe	33 604
19	Mateare	32 114

REPUBLICA DE NICARAGUA • REPUBLIC OF NICARAGUA

Capital Managua	Population 5 891 199 (108)	% in cities 57%
GDP per capita $2900 (165)	Area km² 130 370 km² (97)	GMT +/- -6
Neighbours (km) Costa Rica 309, Honduras 922 • Coast 910		

RECENT INTERNATIONAL MATCHES PLAYED BY NICARAGUA

2006	Opponents	Score		Venue	Comp	Scorers	Att	Referee
No international matches played in 2006								
2007								
8-02	Guatemala	L	0-1	San Salvador	UCr1		10 000	Pineda HON
10-02	El Salvador	L	1-2	San Salvador	UCr1	Wilson [53]	20 000	Arredondo MEX
12-02	Belize	W	4-2	San Salvador	UCr1	Palacios 3 [12 20 68], Bustos [28]	5 000	Quesada CRC
15-02	Honduras	L	1-9	San Salvador	UC5p	Wilson [31]	3 000	Aguilar SLV
2008								
6-02	Netherlands Antilles	L	0-1	Diriamba	WCq		7 000	Lopez GUA
26-03	Netherlands Antilles	L	0-2	Willemstad	WCq		9 000	Wijngaarde SUR
2009								
22-01	El Salvador	D	1-1	Tegucigalpa	UCr1	Medina [85]	20 000	Batres GUA
24-01	Honduras	L	1-4	Tegucigalpa	UCr1	Reyes [30]	20 000	Batres GUA
26-01	Belize	D	1-1	Tegucigalpa	UCr1	Barrera [66]	8 000	Moncada HON
29-01	Guatemala	W	2-0	Tegucigalpa	UC5p	Wilson 2 [39 85]	150	Moncada HON
5-07	Mexico	L	0-2	Oakland	GCr1		32 700	Ward CAN
9-07	Guadeloupe	L	0-2	Houston	GCr1		47 713	Moncada HON
12-07	Panama	L	0-4	Phoenix	GCr1		23 876	Pineda HON
2010								
4-09	Guatemala	L	0-5	Fort Lauderdale	Fr		5 000	Vaughn USA
2011								
14-01	El Salvador	L	0-2	Panama City	UCr1		2 000	Quesada CRC
16-01	Panama	L	0-2	Panama City	UCr1		7 747	Lopez GUA
18-01	Belize	D	1-1	Panama City	UCr1	Espinoza [10p]	10 000	Brea CUB
21-01	Guatemala	L	1-2	Panama City	UC5p	Rodriguez [24]	5 000	Garcia MEX

Fr = Friendly match • UC = UNCAF Cup/Copa Centroamericana • GC = CONCACAF Gold Cup • WC = FIFA World Cup • q = qualifier
r1 = first round group • 5p = fifth place play-off

NICARAGUA 2009-10

XXVI CAMPEONATO NACIONAL PRIMERA DIVISION TORNEO CLAUSURA

	Pl	W	D	L	F	A	Pts	Real Esteli	Walter Ferreti	Chinandega	Diriangén	Ocotal	Xilotepelt	Chinandega	Real Madriz
Real Estelí †	14	9	3	2	25	7	30		1-1	0-1	1-0	1-0	4-0	4-0	3-0
Dep. Walter Ferreti †	14	7	5	2	22	10	26	2-2		4-0	1-1	1-1	2-0	1-0	3-0
VCP Chinandega †	14	7	2	5	22	29	23	3-2	3-1		3-2	1-1	1-3	1-2	2-1
Diriangén †	14	7	1	6	25	15	22	0-1	0-3	6-0		2-1	2-0	3-0	2-1
Deportivo Ocotal	14	4	7	3	18	14	19	0-3	0-0	0-0	2-2		2-0	3-0	1-0
Xilotepelt	14	6	1	7	23	26	19	0-1	1-1	6-3	1-4	0-3		3-0	3-1
Chinandega FC	14	3	3	8	11	25	12	0-0	1-2	1-2	1-0	2-2	1-2		2-2
Real Madriz	14	1	2	11	9	29	5	0-2	1-0	0-2	0-2	2-2	1-4	0-1	

10/01/2010 - 2/05/2010 • † Qualified for the Clausura play-offs • Chinandega FC relegated on season record • América Managua bought the licence of VCP Chinandega for the 2010-11 season • Relegation play-off: América Managua 1-1 1-3 **Real Madriz**

CLAUSURA SEMI-FINALS

	Pl	W	D	L	F	A	Pts	RE	WF	Di	Ch
Real Estelí †	6	4	1	1	9	5	13		1-0	0-0	3-2
Dep. Walter Ferreti †	6	4	0	2	12	6	12	3-2		2-0	5-1
Diriangén	6	3	1	2	7	6	10	0-1	1-0		3-1
VCP Chinandega	6	0	0	6	7	18	0	0-2	1-2	2-3	

7/04/2010 - 14/03/2010 • † Qualified for the Clausura final

CLAUSURA FINAL

Olimpico, Managua, 5-05-2010
Dep. Walter Ferreti 1-1 Real Estelí
Scorers: Carlos Mendieta OG 72 for Ferreti; Samuel Wilson 32 for Esteli

Somoto, 9-05-2010
Real Estelí 0-0 Dep. Walter Ferreti

Real Estelí win the Clausura on away goals and qualify to meet Walter Ferreti, winners of the 2009-10 Aperura (see **Oliver's Almanack 2010**) in the 2009-10 Grand Final

2009-10 GRAND FINAL

Independencia, Estelí, 12-05-2010
Real Estelí 0-0 Dep. Walter Ferreti

Olimpico, Managua, 16-05-2010
Dep. Walter Ferreti 1-1 **Real Estelí**
Scorers: Ronald Perez 18 for Ferreti; Rudel Calero 35 for Esteli
Real Estelí are Nicaraguan champions for 2009-10 on away goals

MEDALS TABLE

		Overall G	Lge G	City/Town
1	Diriangén	25	25	Diriamba
2	Real Estelí	9	9	Estelí
3	Santa Cecilia	5	5	Diriamba
4	UCA Managua	4	4	Managua
5	Aduana	3	3	Managua
6	América Managua	3	3	Managua

NICARAGUA 2010-11

XXVII CAMPEONATO NACIONAL PRIMERA DIVISION TORNEO APERTURA

	Pl	W	D	L	F	A	Pts	Walter Ferreti	Diriangén	Managua	Real Madriz	Real Esteli	Xilotepelt	Ocotal	América
Dep. Walter Ferreti †	14	8	3	3	26	18	27		2-1	4-1	2-2	1-0	1-3	1-0	3-0
Diriangén †	14	8	2	4	29	17	26	1-2		0-3	1-0	1-0	6-2	2-1	4-0
Managua FC †	14	8	2	4	22	15	26	4-1	0-3		4-0	0-2	3-0	2-0	1-0
Real Madriz †	14	6	4	4	16	19	22	1-1	2-1	1-1		2-1	1-0	2-1	2-1
Real Estelí	14	6	3	5	13	11	21	2-1	2-1	1-2	1-0		0-0	2-1	0-0
Xilotepelt	14	3	4	7	17	22	13	1-1	1-2	0-1	4-0	0-1		3-3	2-1
Deportivo Ocotal	14	3	4	7	17	23	13	1-3	1-1	1-1	1-1	2-1	2-1		2-1
América Managua	14	1	4	9	9	24	7	1-3	3-3	0-1	0-2	0-0	0-0	2-1	

25/07/2010 - 16/10/2010 • † Qualified for the Apertura play-offs
Top scorers (overall): 15 - Herbert Cabrera, Diriangén • 9 - Raul Leguias PAN, Managua FC

APERTURA SEMI-FINALS

	Pl	W	D	L	F	A	Pts	Di	WF	Ma	RM
Diriangén †	6	5	1	0	9	1	16		1-0	0-0	2-0
Dep. Walter Ferreti †	6	3	1	2	12	4	10	0-1		1-1	4-0
Managua FC	6	2	2	2	5	3	8	1-2	0-1		5-0
Real Madriz	6	0	0	6	0	18	0	0-3	0-3	0-1	

24/10/2010 - 29/11/2010 • † Qualified for the Clausura final

APERTURA FINAL

Olimpico, Managua, 6-12-2010, Ref: Jarquin
Dep. Walter Ferreti 1-0 Diriangén
Scorer: Juan Barrera 77

Cacique, Diriangén, 12-12-2010, Ref: Guerrero
Diriangén 2-1 **Dep. Walter Ferreti**
Scorers: Marocos Roman 41, Remi Vanegas 88 for Diriangén; Denis Espinoza 65p for Ferreti. Walter Ferreti win the Apertura on away goals and qualify for the 2010-11 Grand Final (see **Oliver's Almanack 2012**)

NCL – NEW CALEDONIA

FIFA/COCA-COLA WORLD RANKING

1993	1994	1995	1996	1997	1998	1999	2000	2001	2002	2003	2004	2005	2006	2007	2008	2009	2010
-	-	-	-	-	-	-	-	-	-	-	186	187	176	118	130	147	156

2010												Hi/Lo
Jan	Feb	Mar	Mar	Apr	May	Jul	Aug	Sep	Oct	Nov	Dec	**95**
147	146	145	146	146	145	162	154	145	154	156	156	**188**

One of the peculiarities of the French Cup is that clubs from around the francophone world are given entries and in 2010 New Caledonia Cup winners Magenta caused something of a sensation when they beat Dunkerque in Noumea to reach the eighth round - the furthest any team from New Caledonia had progressed in 42 years. The victory meant a trip to Paris to play Paris FC but that's where the dream ended with a 4-0 defeat. Magenta had qualified for the Coupe de France by winning the Coupe de Caledonie, a tournament they won in the most dramatic of fashions. Trailing Gaïtcha by a goal three minutes into added-time they scored twice to seal an unlikely victory, the second coming from an own goal after captain Pierre Wajoka had hit a long hopeful ball forward as the clock ran down. Magenta also won the Grand Terre Super Ligue to qualify for the OFC Champions League but lost to Mont Dorre in the less prestigious national championship - the Championnat des Iles. The only international action of the year came in the second Coupe de l'Outre-Mer, held in Paris, France. Games against Guadeloupe, Martinique and Tahiti failed to produce a win and New Caledonia finished bottom of the group but with the South Pacific Games coming to Noumea in August 2011, it should prove to be a worthwhile experience.

FIFA WORLD CUP RECORD
1930-2002 DNE 2006-2010 DNQ

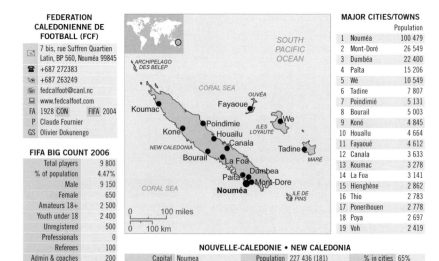

FEDERATION CALEDONIENNE DE FOOTBALL (FCF)

7 bis, rue Suffren Quartier Latin, BP 560, Nouméa 99845
☎ +687 272383
📠 +687 263249
✉ fedcalfoot@canl.nc
🖥 www.fedcalfoot.com

FA	1928 CON	FIFA 2004
P	Claude Fournier	
GS	Olivier Dokunengo	

FIFA BIG COUNT 2006

Total players	9 800
% of population	4.47%
Male	9 150
Female	650
Amateurs 18+	2 500
Youth under 18	2 400
Unregistered	500
Professionals	0
Referees	100
Admin & coaches	200
Number of clubs	100
Number of teams	250

MAJOR CITIES/TOWNS

		Population
1	Nouméa	100 479
2	Mont-Doré	26 549
3	Dumbéa	22 400
4	Païta	15 206
5	Wé	10 549
6	Tadine	7 807
7	Poindimié	5 131
8	Bourail	5 003
9	Koné	4 845
10	Houaïlu	4 664
11	Fayaoué	4 612
12	Canala	3 633
13	Koumac	3 278
14	La Foa	3 141
15	Hienghène	2 862
16	Thio	2 783
17	Ponerihouen	2 778
18	Poya	2 697
19	Voh	2 419

NOUVELLE-CALEDONIE • NEW CALEDONIA

Capital	Noumea	Population	227 436 (181)	% in cities	65%
GDP per capita	$15 000 (76)	Area km²	18 575 km² (155)	GMT + / -	+11
Neighbours (km)	Coast 2254				

RECENT INTERNATIONAL MATCHES PLAYED BY NEW CALEDONIA

2006 Opponents	Score		Venue	Comp	Scorers	Att	Referee
No international matches played in 2006							
2007							
17-07 Vanuatu	W	5-3	Noumea	Fr	Mapou [40], Toto 2 [47 62], Hmae.J [56], Wajoka [69p]		
19-07 Vanuatu	L	0-2	Noumea	Fr			
25-08 Tahiti	W	1-0	Apia	WCq	Wajoka [9p]	400	Hester NZL
27-08 Tuvalu †	W	1-0	Apia	WCq	Kabeu [52]	250	Sogo SOL
29-08 Cook Islands	W	3-0	Apia	WCq	Kabeu 3 [35 51 85]	200	Fox NZL
3-09 Fiji	D	1-1	Apia	WCq	Wajoka [44]	1 000	Fred VAN
5-09 Solomon Islands	W	3-2	Apia	WCq	Kabeu [37], Toto [54], Mercier [94+]	600	Minan PNG
7-09 Fiji	W	1-0	Apia	WCq	Hmae.J [61]	400	Hester NZL
17-11 Fiji	D	3-3	Ba	WCq	Djamali [67], Kaudre [83], Hmae.M [88]	1 500	O'Leary NZL
21-11 Fiji	W	4-0	Noumea	WCq	Wajoka [28p], Hmae.M 2 [30 55], Mapou [59]		Breeze AUS
2008							
14-06 Vanuatu	D	1-1	Port Vila	WCq	Djamali [73]	4 000	Varman FIJ
21-06 Vanuatu	W	3-0	Noumea	WCq	Wajoka [36], Hmae.M [60], Diaike [87]	2 700	Hester NZL
6-09 New Zealand	L	1-3	Noumea	WCq	Hmae.M [55]	2 589	Varman FIJ
10-09 New Zealand	L	0-3	Auckland	WCq		8 000	Hauata TAH
24-09 Tahiti	W	1-0	Paris	Fr	Hmae.M [91+]		
27-09 Guadeloupe †	L	0-4	Paris	Fr			Alain GYF
30-09 Martinique †	D	1-1	Paris	Fr	Lolohea		Alain GYF
3-10 Mayotte	W	3-2	Paris	Fr	Wajoka 2 [53 87p], Kai [58]		Touraine GLP
2009							
No international matches played in 2009							
2010							
23-09 Guadeloupe †	D	1-1	Paris	Fr	Hmae.M		Prevot FRA
26-09 Martinique †	L	0-4	Paris	Fr			Tetauira FRA
29-09 Tahiti	D	1-1	Paris	Fr	Watrone [6], L 3-5p		Fouquet FRA

Fr = Friendly match • OC = OFC Oceania Nations Cup • SP = South Pacific Games • WC = FIFA World Cup
q = qualifier • r1 = first round group • sf = semi-final • f = final • † Not a full international

NEW CALEDONIA 2010

GRAND TERRE SUPER LIGUE

	Pl	W	D	L	F	A	Pts	Magenta	Mont-Dore	Lössi	Gaïtcha	Hienghène	Mouli	Kunié	Baco
AS Magenta	14	11	1	2	41	17	48		4-2	5-1	0-1	3-1	2-1	4-0	3-2
AS Mont-Dore	14	10	0	4	56	27	44	1-3		5-4	5-1	9-2	6-3	0-1	8-2
AS Lössi	14	8	1	5	29	24	39	1-2	0-1		0-2	3-2	3-1	3-1	1-0
Gaïtcha FCN	14	6	4	4	27	28	36	0-3	0-4	2-2		2-2	0-1	2-2	4-0
Hienghène Sports	14	4	4	6	35	38	30	2-2	2-3	1-2	1-2		4-3	1-1	4-3
Mouli Sport	14	4	1	9	28	40	27	2-3	3-2	1-2	2-4	0-4		2-1	3-2
AS Kunié	14	3	2	9	17	42	25	3-2	1-6	0-3	1-2	2-6	3-2		1-5
JS Baco	14	2	3	9	32	49	23	0-5	1-4	1-4	5-5	3-3	4-4	4-0	

11/02/2010 - 21/08/2010 • Top four qualify for the Championnat des Iles

NEW CALEDONIA 2010

CHAMPIONNAT DES ILES

	Pl	W	D	L	F	A	Pts	Mont-Dore	Magenta	Gaïtcha	Lössi	Kirikitr
AS Mont-Dore †	7	7	0	0	23	11	28		2-1	4-2	4-1	5-4
AS Magenta	8	6	0	2	20	12	26	0-2		3-1	4-1	3-2
Gaïtcha FCN	7	3	0	4	17	17	16		1-3		2-3	3-2
AS Lössi	7	2	0	5	12	20	13	1-3	2-3	1-3		3-1
AS Kirikitr	7	0	0	7	13	25	7	2-3	1-3	1-5		

4/09/2010 - 28/11/2010 • † Qualified for the O-League

COUPE DE CALEDONIE 2010

Round of 16 / Quarter-finals / Semi-finals / Final

Round of 16:
- AS Magenta / AS Lössi
- Mouli / Traput
- AS Kuné
- Ravel'sport / Tiga
- USC 2 / Saint-Louis 0
- JS Baco
- Hienghène Sports 4 / AS Kirikitr 1
- AS Mont-Dore 0 / Gaïtcha FCN 3

Quarter-finals:
- AS Magenta 2 / Traput 1
- AS Kuné 2 / Tiga 3
- USC 1 / JS Baco 0
- Hienghène Sports 2 / Gaïtcha FCN 3

Semi-finals:
- AS Magenta / Tiga
- USC / Gaïtcha FCN

Final:
- AS Magenta 2 / Gaïtcha FCN 1

CUP FINAL
Stade Numa-Daly, Nouméa
14-08-2010, Ref: Yann Faye

Scorers - Judicael Ixoee [93+], Emile Bearune OG [94+] for Magenta; Georges Bearune [61] for Gaïtcha

Cup Final line-ups: **Magenta** - Hne - Ixoee, B. Longue, J. Dokunengo, S. Longue - Wea (Sinedo 66), R. Kayara (Xewe-Lamo 52), Bako, Poatinda (Saiko 70), Wajoka (c) - Watrone. Tr: Alain Moizan • **Gaïtcha** - Nyikeine - Lolohea, E. Bearune, Ouka (c), Qaeze - J. Siapo, F. Ausu (Hnanganyan 81), Wangane, G. Bearune, Passil - J-L Toto (J. Xolawawa 55). Tr: Adrien Ausu

NED – NETHERLANDS

FIFA/COCA-COLA WORLD RANKING

1993	1994	1995	1996	1997	1998	1999	2000	2001	2002	2003	2004	2005	2006	2007	2008	2009	2010
7	6	6	9	22	11	19	8	8	6	4	6	3	7	9	3	3	2

	2010											Hi/Lo
Jan	Feb	Mar	Mar	Apr	May	Jul	Aug	Sep	Oct	Nov	Dec	2
3	3	3	3	4	4	2	2	2	2	2	2	25

A quick look at their record through the course of 2009 and 2010 shows that it was no fluke that the Netherlands made it to the final of the FIFA World Cup in South Africa. In the 25 games leading up to the final the Dutch won 20 and drew five - but then, with the eyes of the world on them, Bert Marwijk's team undid all the good work with a thoroughly un-Dutch display in losing 1-0 to Spain in Johannesburg. The Dutch were lucky to go in at half-time will 11 players still on the field as they tried to intimidate the Spanish into submission, a tactic that left Johan Cruijff furious at the damage done to the reputation of Dutch football. The fact that the team had played some outstanding football on the way to the final, with Wesley Sneijder one of the stars of the tournament, made the sense of a lost opportunity even stronger. By the end of the year the final was the only game the Netherlands had lost with Klaas-Jan Huntelaar hitting a rich scoring vein as qualification for Euro 2012 was all but assured. At home the Eredivisie witnessed a truly historic season with former England coach Steve McClaren leading Twente Enschede to a first league title. Only four other teams had been crowned champions since 1964 and it was the first time since the 1950s that Ajax, PSV or Feyenoord had not won the title over the course of two seasons.

FIFA WORLD CUP RECORD

1930 DNE **1934** 9 r1 **1938** 14 r1 1950-1954 DNE 1958-1970 DNQ **1974** 2 Finalist **1978** 2 Finalist
1982-1986 DNQ **1990** 15 r2 **1994** 7 QF **1998** 4 SF 2002 DNQ **2006** 11 r2 **2010** 2 Finalist

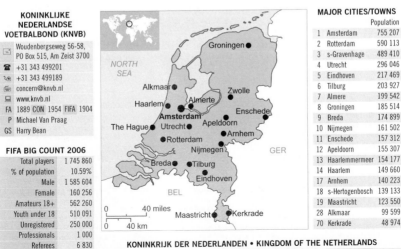

KONINKLIJKE NEDERLANDSE VOETBALBOND (KNVB)

Woudenbergseweg 56-58,
PO Box 515, Am Zeist 3700

☎ +31 343 499201
🖷 +31 343 499189
✉ concern@knvb.nl
🖥 www.knvb.nl
FA 1889 CON 1954 FIFA 1904
P Michael Van Praag
GS Harry Bean

FIFA BIG COUNT 2006

Total players	1 745 860
% of population	10.59%
Male	1 585 604
Female	160 256
Amateurs 18+	562 260
Youth under 18	510 091
Unregistered	250 000
Professionals	1 000
Referees	6 830
Admin & coaches	4 408
Number of clubs	3 656
Number of teams	55 060

MAJOR CITIES/TOWNS

		Population
1	Amsterdam	755 207
2	Rotterdam	590 113
3	s-Gravenhage	489 410
4	Utrecht	296 046
5	Eindhoven	217 469
6	Tilburg	203 927
7	Almere	199 542
8	Groningen	185 514
9	Breda	174 899
10	Nijmegen	161 502
11	Enschede	157 312
12	Apeldoorn	155 307
13	Haarlemmermeer	154 177
14	Haarlem	149 660
17	Arnhem	140 223
18	s-Hertogenbosch	139 133
19	Maastricht	123 550
28	Alkmaar	99 599
70	Kerkrade	48 974

KONINKRIJK DER NEDERLANDEN • KINGDOM OF THE NETHERLANDS

Capital The Hague	Population 16 715 999 (59)	% in cities 82%
GDP per capita $40 500 (20)	Area km² 41 543 km² (134)	GMT + / - +1
Neighbours (km) Belgium 450, Germany 577 • Coast 451		

RECENT INTERNATIONAL MATCHES PLAYED BY THE NETHERLANDS

2008	Opponents	Score		Venue	Comp	Scorers	Att	Referee
20-08	Russia	D	1-1	Moscow	Fr	Van Persie [25]	25 000	Frojdfeldt SWE
6-09	Australia	L	1-2	Eindhoven	Fr	Huntelaar [5]	22 500	Atkinson ENG
10-09	Macedonia FYR	W	2-1	Skopje	WCq	Heitinga [46], Van der Vaart [60]	11 000	Gilewski POL
11-10	Iceland	W	2-0	Rotterdam	WCq	Mathijsen [15], Huntelaar [64]	37 500	Trefoloni ITA
15-10	Norway	W	1-0	Oslo	WCq	Van Bommel [63]	23 840	Plautz AUT
19-11	Sweden	W	3-1	Amsterdam	Fr	Van Persie 2 [32 48], Kuyt [93+]	26 750	Szabo HUN
2009								
11-02	Tunisia	D	1-1	Rades/Tunis	Fr	Huntelaar [61]	17 000	Abdel Fattah EGY
28-03	Scotland	W	3-0	Amsterdam	WCq	Huntelaar [30], Van Persie [45], Kuyt [77p]	50 000	Duhamel FRA
1-04	Macedonia FYR	W	4-0	Amsterdam	WCq	Kuyt 2 [16 41], Huntelaar [25], Van der Vaart [88]	47 750	Rasmussen DEN
6-06	Iceland	W	2-1	Reykjavik	WCq	De Jong [10], Van Bommel [17]	9 635	Dean ENG
10-06	Norway	W	2-0	Rotterdam	WCq	Ooijer [33], Robben [51]	45 600	Baskakov RUS
12-08	England	D	2-2	Amsterdam	Fr	Kuyt [10], Van der Vaart [37]	48 000	Rizzoli ITA
5-09	Japan	W	3-0	Enschede	Fr	Van Persie [69], Sneijder [73], Huntelaar [87]	23 750	Skomina SVN
9-09	Scotland	W	1-0	Glasgow	WCq	Elia [82]	51 230	Larsen DEN
10-10	Australia	D	0-0	Sydney	Fr		40 537	Minoru JPN
14-11	Italy	D	0-0	Pescara	Fr		17 134	Chirchetta ITA
18-11	Paraguay	D	0-0	Heerenveen	Fr		25 000	Hrinak SVK
2010								
3-03	USA	W	2-1	Amsterdam	Fr	Kuyt [40p], Huntelaar [73]	46 630	Cakir TUR
26-05	Mexico	W	2-1	Freiburg	Fr	Van Persie 2 [17 41]	22 000	Grafe GER
1-06	Ghana	W	4-1	Rotterdam	Fr	Kuyt [30], Van der Vaart [72], Sneijder [81], Van Persie [87p]	45 000	Moen NOR
5-06	Hungary	W	6-1	Amsterdam	Fr	Van Persie [21], Sneijder [55], Robben 2 [64 78], Van Bommel [71], Elia [74]	45 000	Meyer GER
14-06	Denmark	W	2-0	Johannesburg	WCr1	Agger OG [46], Kuyt [85]	83 465	Lannoy FRA
19-06	Japan	W	1-0	Durban	WCr1	Sneijder [53]	62 010	Baldassi ARG
24-06	Cameroon	W	2-1	Cape Town	WCr1	Van Persie [36], Huntelaar [83]	63 093	Pozo CHI
28-06	Slovakia	W	2-1	Durban	WCr2	Robben [18], Sneijder [84]	61 962	Undiano ESP
2-07	Brazil	W	2-1	Port Elizabeth	WCqf	Sneijder 2 [53 68]	40 186	Nishimura JPN
6-07	Uruguay	W	3-2	Cape Town	WCsf	Van Bronckhorst [18], Sneijder [70], Robben [73]	62 479	Irmatov UZB
11-07	Spain	L	0-1	Johannesburg	WCf		84 490	Webb ENG
11-08	Ukraine	D	1-1	Donetsk	Fr	Lens [73]	18 051	Skomina SVN
3-09	San Marino	W	5-0	Serravalle	ECq	Kuyt [16p], Huntelaar 3 [38 48 66], Van Nistelrooy [90]	4 127	Evans WAL
7-09	Finland	W	2-1	Rotterdam	ECq	Huntelaar 2 [7 16p]	25 000	Nikolaev RUS
8-10	Moldova	W	1-0	Chisinau	ECq	Huntelaar [37]	10 500	Meyer GER
12-10	Sweden	W	4-1	Amsterdam	ECq	Huntelaar 2 [4 55], Afellay 2 [37 59]	46 000	Lannoy FRA
17-11	Turkey	W	1-0	Amsterdam	Fr	Huntelaar [52]	35 500	Kassai HUN

Fr = Friendly match • EC = UEFA EURO 2008/2012 • WC = FIFA World Cup • q = qualifier • r1 = first round group • qf = quarter-final

NETHERLANDS NATIONAL TEAM HISTORICAL RECORDS

Caps

130 - Edwin van der Sar 1995-2008 • **112** - Frank de Boer 1990-2004 • **106** - Giovanni van Bronckhorst 1996-2010 • **101** - Phillip Cocu 1996-2006 • **88** - Rafael van der Vaart 2001- • **87** - Clarence Seedorf 1994-2008 • **86** - Marc Overmars 1993-2004 • **84** - Aron Winter 1987-2000 • **83** - Ruud Krol 1969-83 • **79** - Patrick Kluivert 1994-2004 & Dennis Bergkamp • **78** - Ronald Koeman 1983-94 • **74** - Edgar Davids 1994-2005 • **73** - Hans van Breukelen 1980-92; Dirk Kuyt 2004- ; Frank Rijkaard 1981-94 & Wesley Sneijder 2003-

Goals

40 - Patrick Kluivert 1994-2004 • **37** - Dennis Bergkamp 1990-2000 • **35** - Faas Wilkes 1946-61 • **34** - Ruud van Nistelrooy 1998- • **33** - Abe Lenstra 1940-59 & Johan Cruijff 1966-77 • **28** - Beb Bakhuys 1928-37 • **26** - Kick Smit 1935-46 • **25** - Klaas-Jan Huntelaar 2006- • **24** - Marco van Basten 1983-92 • **19** - Leen Vente 1933-40; Robin van Persie 2005- & Wesley Sneijder 2003-

Past Coaches

Cees van Hasselt 1905-08 • Edgar Chadwick ENG 1908-13 • Jimmy Hogan ENG 1910 • Tom Bradshaw ENG 1913 • Billy Hunter SCO 1914 • Jack Reynolds ENG 1919 • Fred Warburton ENG 1919-23 • Jim Waites ENG 1921 • Bob Glendenning ENG 1923 • Billy Townley ENG 1924 • J.E. Bollington ENG 1924 • Bob Glendenning ENG 1925-40 • Karel Kaufman 1946 • Jesse Carver ENG 1947-48 • Tom Sneddon SCO 1948 • Karel Kaufman 1949 • Jaap van der Leck 1949-54 • Karel Kaufman 1954-55 • Friedrich Donenfeld AUT 1955 • Max Merkel AUT 1955-56 • Heinrich Muller AUT 1956 • Friedrich Donenfeld AUT 1956-57 • George Hardwick ENG 1957 • Elek Schwartz ROU 1957-64 • Denis Neville ENG 1964-66 • Georg Kessler GER 1966-70 • Frantisek Fadrhonc CZE 1970-74 • Rinus Michels 1974 • George Knobel 1974-76 • Jan Zwartkruis 1976-77 • Ernst Happel AUT 1977-78 • Jan Zwartkruis 1978-81 • Kees Rijvers 1981-84 • Rinus Michels 1984-85 • Leo Beenhakker 1985-86 • Rinus Michels 1986-88 • Thijs Libregts 1988-90 • Leo Beenhakker 1990 • Rinus Michels 1990-92 • Dick Advocaat 1992-95 • Guus Hiddink 1995-98 • Frank Rijkaard 1998-2000 • Louis van Gaal 2000-02 • Dick Advocaat 2002-04 • Marco van Basten 2004-08 • Bert van Marwijk 2008-

NETHERLANDS 2009-10

EREDIVISIE

	Pl	W	D	L	F	A	Pts	FC Twente	Ajax	PSV	Feyenoord	AZ Alkmaar	Heracles	Utrecht	Groningen	Roda	NAC Breda	Heerenveen	VVV Venlo	NEC	Vitesse	ADO	Sparta	Willem II	Waalwijk
FC Twente Enschede †	34	27	5	2	63	23	86		1-0	1-1	2-0	3-2	2-0	3-2	4-0	2-0	3-1	2-0	2-1	2-1	1-0	3-1	3-0	1-0	2-1
Ajax †	34	27	4	3	106	20	85	3-0		4-1	5-1	1-0	4-0	4-0	3-0	4-0	6-0	5-1	7-0	3-0	4-0	3-0	0-0	4-0	4-1
PSV Eindhoven ‡	34	23	9	2	72	29	78	1-1	4-3		0-0	1-0	4-0	2-1	3-1	3-0	1-0	3-3	3-0	1-0	2-0	1-1	3-1	5-1	
Feyenoord ‡	34	17	12	5	54	31	63	1-1	1-1	1-3		1-2	1-1	0-0	3-1	4-0	0-0	6-2	1-0	2-0	2-1	2-2	3-0	1-0	3-0
AZ Alkmaar ‡	34	19	5	10	64	34	62	1-0	2-4	1-1	1-1		3-2	2-0	0-1	2-0	1-0	4-1	2-0	0-1	1-2	3-0	2-0	2-1	6-2
Heracles Almelo	34	17	5	12	54	49	56	1-3	0-3	0-1	0-1	3-2		3-1	4-3	3-2	3-0	3-1	1-0	2-0	1-2	4-2	2-1	3-2	4-1
FC Utrecht ‡	34	14	11	9	39	33	53	0-0	2-0	0-0	1-0	0-0		1-1	2-1	3-1	2-3	2-2	1-0	2-2	1-0	2-0	3-1	4-0	2-1
FC Groningen	34	14	7	13	48	47	49	0-0	0-2	0-2	2-3	0-1	4-1	0-0		1-0	1-2	2-0	1-0	2-2	1-0	2-0	3-1	4-0	2-1
Roda JC Kerkrade	34	14	5	15	56	60	47	1-2	2-2	0-1	2-4	2-4	2-1	2-0	1-1		2-0	4-2	4-2	1-0	3-4	1-1	2-1	3-2	5-1
NAC Breda	34	12	10	12	42	49	46	0-2	1-1	2-1	0-2	1-1	0-0	0-2	0-3	1-0		2-0	2-0	3-3	4-0	3-0	2-2	4-0	1-0
SC Heerenveen	34	11	4	19	44	64	37	0-2	0-2	2-2	0-2	1-2	2-0	0-1	2-0	0-0	0-0		1-1	4-1	1-0	3-0	4-1	4-2	3-1
VVV Venlo	34	8	11	15	43	57	35	0-2	0-4	2-4	1-1	3-3	1-0	0-1	2-1	1-1	1-1	3-1		2-0	2-0	2-2	5-0	2-1	3-0
NEC Nijmegen	34	8	9	17	35	59	33	3-4	1-4	0-4	0-0	0-0	0-2	1-1	0-2	0-2	4-2	4-1	1-1		2-1	1-1	1-0	2-1	0-1
Vitesse Arnhem	34	8	8	18	38	62	32	1-2	1-5	0-0	0-0	0-3	0-2	2-2	3-0	2-5	1-1	0-1	2-0	2-2		1-3	2-0	2-1	3-1
ADO Den Haag	34	7	9	18	38	59	30	0-1	0-1	1-5	0-2	2-1	1-4	0-1	1-1	1-2	1-2	2-1	0-0	2-3	1-1		2-3	3-4	4-0
Sparta Rotterdam	34	6	8	20	30	66	26	0-2	0-3	2-3	2-1	0-1	1-0	3-2	4-1	2-2	2-0	2-0	1-0	0-0	1-1	0-0		2-1	1-0
Willem II Tilburg	34	7	2	25	36	70	23	1-3	0-2	0-1	2-3	0-3	0-1	0-3	2-1	1-3	1-2	4-1	2-1	1-1	3-1	1-3	1-3		2-1
RKC Waalwijk	34	5	0	29	30	80	15	0-1	1-5	0-2	0-1	0-6	0-1	0-1	3-1	4-1	0-1	1-2	1-2	0-1	4-1	0-2	4-1	0-1	

31/07/2009 - 2/05/2010 • † Qualified for the UEFA Champions League • ‡ Qualified for the Europa League
Top scorers: **35** - Luis Suarez URU, Ajax • **24** - Bryan Ruiz CRC, FC Twente • **21** - Mads Junker DEN, Roda • **20** - Mounir El Hamdaoui MAR, Alkmaar • **16** - Marko Pantelic SRB, Ajax • **14** - Bas Dost, Heracles; Everton BRA, Heracles & Balazs Dzsudzsak HUN, PSV
Europa League play-off semi-finals: **Utrecht** 3-1 2-0 Groningen; **Roda JC** 1-1 2-1 Heracles • Final: Roda JC 0-2 1-4 **Utrecht**

NACOMPETITIE

			Willem II Tilburg	2	1			
FC Eindhoven	1	3	FC Eindhoven	1	1	**Willem II Tilburg**	0	3
AGOVV Apeldoorn	0	2	Cambuur-Leeuwarden	0	1	Go Ahead Eagles	1	0
			Go Ahead Eagles	2	0			
			Sparta Rotterdam	1	2			
Helmond Sport	1 2	5p	Helmond Sport	2	0	Sparta Rotterdam	0	1
FC Den Bosch	2 1	4p	FC Zwolle	0	3	**Excelsior Rotterdam**	0	1
			Excelsior Rotterdam	1	4	* Home team in 1st leg		

NETHERLANDS 2009-10
EERSTE DIVISIE

	Pl	W	D	L	F	A	Pts
De Graafschap	36	25	6	5	85	34	81
Cambuur-Leeuwarden ††	36	21	8	7	78	48	71
Excelsior Rotterdam †	36	20	5	11	77	49	65
FC Zwolle ††	36	19	8	9	59	37	65
Go Ahead Eagles †	36	18	9	9	53	33	63
AGOVV Apeldoorn ††§2	36	16	9	11	63	52	55
FC Den Bosch ††	36	14	12	10	66	54	54
Helmond Sport ††	36	16	6	14	63	53	54
BV Veendam §1	36	14	11	11	57	48	52
MVV Maastricht §1	36	14	7	15	59	67	48
RBC Roosendaal	36	12	10	14	47	53	46
FC Eindhoven †	36	13	7	16	63	81	46
FC Dordrecht	36	13	4	19	54	59	43
FC Omniworld Almere	36	11	7	18	40	65	40
FC Emmen	36	10	8	18	51	79	38
FC Volendam	36	8	11	17	61	81	35
Fortuna Sittard	36	7	9	20	31	57	30
Telstar	36	7	8	21	45	65	29
FC Oss	36	6	11	19	42	79	29
Haarlem	23	3	4	16	26	61	13

7/08/2009 - 23/05/2010 • † Qualified for Nacompetitie as stage winners • †† Qualified for Nacompetitie on overall record • § = points deducted

MEDALS TABLE

		Overall			League			Cup		Europe		
		G	S	B	G	S	B	G	S	G	S	B
1	Ajax	53	29	14	29	21	11	18	4	6	3	3
2	PSV Eindhoven	31	20	17	21	13	13	8	7	2		4
3	Feyenoord	28	23	16	14	19	12	11	4	3		4
4	HVV Den Haag	9	3		8			1	3			
5	Sparta Rotterdam	9	2	5	6			5		3	2	
6	HBS Den Haag	5	5		3					2	5	
7	AZ Alkmaar	5	4	6	2	2	5	3	1	1		1
8	Willem II Tilburg	5	2	5	3	1	5	2	1			
9	Quick Den Haag	5			1			4				
10	ADO Den Haag	4	6	4	2		4	2	6			
	Go Ahead Eagles	4	6	4	4	5	4	1				
12	RCH Heemstede	4			2			2				
13	Twente Enschede	3	7	9	1	2	7	2	4	1	2	
14	Roda JC Kerkrade	3	6		1	2		2	4			
15	Haarlem	3	3	1	1		1	2	3			
16	FC Utrecht	3	2	1	1			3	2			
17	RAP Amsterdam	3	1		2			1	1			
18	HFC Haarlem	3						3				
19	NAC Breda	2	7	3	1	4	3	1	3			
20	Fortuna Sittard	2	3	1	1	1		2	2			

KNVB BEKER 2009-10

Second Round

Ajax	2
AGOVV Apeldoorn *	1
Fortuna Sittard	2
FC Dordrecht *	3
VV Gemert	1
Achilles '29 *	0
AFC *	0
VV WHC	1
FC Groningen	4
FC Utrecht *	2
FC Oss	2
Vitesse Arnhem *	5
Excelsior Rotterdam	6 7p
Haaglandia/Winston *	6 6p
FC Eindhoven *	2
NEC Nijmegan	3
NAC Breda	3
Willem II Tilburg *	2
BV Veendam	0
De Treffers *	2
FC Zwolle	2 4p
Sparta Nijkerk *	2 2p
Cambuur-Leeuwarden	0
Jong de Graafschap *	1
Heracles Almelo *	1
RKC Waalwijk	0
Telstar *	1
Haarlem	3
FC Emmen	6
AFC '34 *	1
Rijnsburgse Boys *	1
Go Ahead Eagles	4
FC Twente Enschede	8
SC Joure *	0
RKVV Westlandia	0
VV Capelle *	4
ASWH *	2
GVVV	1
FC Omniworld Almere *	1
Helmond Sport	3
VV Baronie *	1 6p
BVV Barendrecht	1 5p
VV Bennekom	2
Excelsior Maassluis *	4
VVV Venlo *	3
ADO Den Haag	0
FC Volendam *	1
Sparta Rotterdam	2
PSV Eindhoven *	2
De Graafschap	1
IJsselmeervogels *	1
Roda JC Kerkrade	2
RBC Roosendaal	5
LRC Leerdam *	1
SDC Putten *	0
SC Heerenveen	7
AZ Alkmaar *	2
Jong Ajax	0
MVV Maastricht *	2
SV Spakenburg	3
FC Den Bosch	4
FC Lisse *	0
Harkemase Boys	0
Feyenoord	5

Third Round

Ajax	2
FC Dordrecht *	1
VV Gemert *	2 5p
VV WHC	2 6p
FC Groningen	5
Vitesse Arnhem *	1
Excelsior Rotterdam	1
NEC Nijmegan *	2
NAC Breda	6
De Treffers *	1
FC Zwolle	0
Jong de Graafschap *	1
Heracles Almelo *	3
Haarlem	0
FC Emmen	2
Go Ahead Eagles *	4
FC Twente Enschede *	3
VV Capelle	0
ASWH	0
Helmond Sport *	5
VV Baronie *	1
Excelsior Maassluis	0
VVV Venlo	1 4p
Sparta Rotterdam *	1 5p
PSV Eindhoven	2
Roda JC Kerkrade *	0
RBC Roosendaal	2
SC Heerenveen *	4
AZ Alkmaar *	5
SV Spakenburg	2
FC Den Bosch	0
Feyenoord *	2

Fourth Round

Ajax	14
VV WHC *	1
FC Groningen *	0
NEC Nijmegan	2
NAC Breda	2
Jong de Graafschap *	0
Heracles Almelo *	0
Go Ahead Eagles	2
FC Twente Enschede *	3
Helmond Sport	0
VV Baronie *	0
Sparta Rotterdam	5
PSV Eindhoven	3
SC Heerenveen *	1
AZ Alkmaar	0
Feyenoord *	1

KNVB BEKER 2009-10

Quarter–finals	Semi–finals	Final

KNVB BEKER FINAL 2010 1ST LEG

De Kuip, Amsterdam ArenA, Amsterdam, 25-04-2010, 18:00, Att: 37 283, Ref: Eric Braamhaar

Ajax	2	De Jong 2 [67]
Feyenoord	0	

Ajax - Maarten Stekelenburg - Gregory van der Wiel, Jan Vertonghen, Toby Alderweireld, Vurnon Anita - Demy de Zeeuw●, Siem de Jong, Eyong Enoh - Luis Suarez●, Marko Pantelic (Dennis Rommedahl 70), Urby Emanuelson (Christian Eriksen 80). Tr: Martin Jol
Feyenoord - Erwin Mulder - Stefan de Vrij, Ron Vlaar (Bart Schenkeveld 72), Bahia●, Giovanni van Bronckhorst - Georginio Wijnaldum, Denny Landzaat, Leroy Fer, Luigi Bruins●, Karim El Ahmadi (Kelvin Leerdam 85) - John Dahl Tomasson (Sekou Cisse 73). Tr: Mario Been

Ajax *	3
NEC Nijmegan	2

Ajax	6
Go Ahead Eagles *	0

NAC Breda *	1
Go Ahead Eagles	2

Ajax	2	4
Feyenoord	0	1

FC Twente Enschede	4
Sparta Rotterdam *	0

FC Twente Enschede	1
Feyenoord *	2

KNVB BEKER FINAL 2010 2ND LEG

De Kuip, Rotterdam, 6-05-2010, 18:30, Att: 35 000, Ref: Roelof Luinge

PSV Eindhoven *	0
Feyenoord	3

Feyenoord	1	Tomasson [72]
Ajax	4	Suarez 2 [4 82], De Jong 2 [64 77]

Feyenoord - Erwin Mulder - Stefan de Vrij (Bart Schenkeveld 46), Bahia, Ron Vlaar, Tim de Cler (Kevin Hofland 75) - Karim El Ahmadi●, Denny Landzaat (Jonathan de Guzman 46), Leroy Fer, Georginio Wijnaldum - Jon Dahl Tomasson, Roy Makaay. Tr: Mario Been
Ajax - Maarten Stekelenburg - Gregory van der Wiel, Jan Vertonghen, Toby Alderweireld●, Vurnon Anita - Eyong Enoh, Siem de Jong (Nicolas Lodeiro 84), Demy de Zeeuw, Luis Suarez●, Marko Pantelic (Dennis Rommedahl 78), Urby Emanuelson (Christian Eriksen 62). Tr: Martin Jol

NEP – NEPAL

FIFA/COCA-COLA WORLD RANKING

1993	1994	1995	1996	1997	1998	1999	2000	2001	2002	2003	2004	2005	2006	2007	2008	2009	2010
124	138	147	151	155	176	157	166	156	165	165	177	175	170	186	174	152	172

					2010							Hi/Lo
Jan	Feb	Mar	Mar	Apr	May	Jul	Aug	Sep	Oct	Nov	Dec	**124**
152	152	151	160	161	161	156	159	156	163	163	172	**188**

Football fans in Nepal were able to enjoy league football for the first time since 2006 as stability returned to the Himalayan kingdom following the fall of the monarchy in 2008. The league kicked off in February 2010 with Nepal Police Club emerging as the new champions four months later, finishing seven points clear of nearest rivals Three Star Club. Both have represented the country with distinction at past tournaments of AFC President's Cup with Police Club reaching the final in 2007, but at the 2010 tournament Nepal was represented by New Road Team who were appearing for the first time. They found the going tough at a qualifying group held in Bangladesh and were knocked out although they did win a seven-goal thriller against Chinese Taipei's Hasus NTCPE with two goals in the final 13 minutes from Jeevan Sinkemana and Nabin Neupane. The national team's inactivity throughout 2010 came as a result of the failure to qualify for the finals of the AFC Challenge Cup but with a busier programme ahead of them in 2011 the All Nepal Football Association sought out a new coach and appointed former England international Graham Roberts at the start of the year after the ex-Tottenham Hotspur and Rangers midfielder had had a brief stint working in Pakistan.

FIFA WORLD CUP RECORD

1930-1982 DNE 1986-1990 DNQ 1994 DNE 1998-2002 DNQ 2006 DNE 2010 DNQ

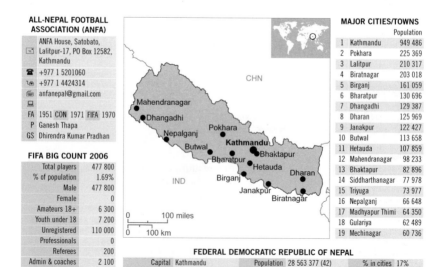

ALL-NEPAL FOOTBALL ASSOCIATION (ANFA)

✉ ANFA House, Satobato, Lalitpur-17, PO Box 12582, Kathmandu
☎ +977 1 5201060
📠 +977 1 4424314
📧 anfanepal@gmail.com
🖥
FA 1951 CON 1971 FIFA 1970
P Ganesh Thapa
GS Dhirendra Kumar Pradhan

FIFA BIG COUNT 2006

Total players	477 800
% of population	1.69%
Male	477 800
Female	0
Amateurs 18+	6 300
Youth under 18	7 200
Unregistered	110 000
Professionals	0
Referees	200
Admin & coaches	2 100
Number of clubs	110
Number of teams	440

MAJOR CITIES/TOWNS

		Population
1	Kathmandu	949 486
2	Pokhara	225 369
3	Lalitpur	210 317
4	Biratnagar	203 018
5	Birganj	161 059
6	Bharatpur	130 696
7	Dhangadhi	129 387
8	Dharan	125 969
9	Janakpur	122 427
10	Butwal	113 658
11	Hetauda	107 859
12	Mahendranagar	98 233
13	Bhaktapur	82 896
14	Siddharthanagar	77 978
15	Triyuga	73 977
16	Nepalganj	66 648
17	Madhyapur Thimi	64 350
18	Gulariya	62 489
19	Mechinagar	60 736

FEDERAL DEMOCRATIC REPUBLIC OF NEPAL

Capital	Kathmandu	Population	28 563 377 (42)	% in cities	17%
GDP per capita	$1100 (210)	Area km²	147 181 km² (93)	GMT +/-	+5.75
Neighbours (km)	China 1236, India 1690				

RECENT INTERNATIONAL MATCHES PLAYED BY NEPAL

2006	Opponents		Score	Venue	Comp	Scorers	Att	Referee
2-04	Bhutan	W	2-0	Chittagong	CCr1	Pradeep Maharjan 2 [52 68]	3 500	Gosh BAN
4-04	Brunei Darussalam	L	1-2	Chittagong	CCr1	Tashi Tsering [60]	2 500	Al Ghatrifi OMA
6-04	Sri Lanka	D	1-1	Chittagong	CCr1	Pradeep Maharjan [75p]	2 500	Lee Gi Young KOR
9-04	India	W	3-0	Chittagong	CCqf	Pradeep Maharjan 2 [16 26], Basanta Thapa [28]	3 000	Gosh BAN
12-04	Sri Lanka	D	1-1	Chittagong	CCsf	Basanta Thapa [82]. L 3-5p	2 500	Lee Gi Young KOR
2007								
8-10	Oman	L	0-2	Muscat	WCq		15 000	Al Marzouqi UAE
28-10	Oman	L	0-2	Kathmandu	WCq		10 000	Tongkhan THA
2008								
25-03	Pakistan	W	2-1	Pokhara	Fr	Bharat Khawas [77], Anil Gurung [86]		
27-03	Pakistan	L	0-2	Pokhara	Fr			
20-05	Thailand	L	0-7	Bangkok	Fr			
25-05	Macau	W	3-2	Phnom Penh	CCq	Sandip Rai [43], Ju Manu Rai 2 [57 65]	2 000	Vo Minh Tri VIE
26-05	Cambodia	W	1-0	Phnom Penh	CCq		3 000	Torky IRN
3-06	India	L	0-4	Male	SAFr1			
5-06	Maldives	L	1-4	Male	SAFr1	Vishad Gauchan Thakali [11]		
7-06	Pakistan	W	4-1	Male	SAFr1	Raju Tamang [3], Nirajan Rayajhi [5], Ju Manu Rai 2 [67 87]		
31-07	Myanmar	L	0-3	Hyderabad	CCr1		150	Jassim UAE
2-08	Korea DPR	L	0-1	Hyderabad	CCr1		100	Iemoto JPN
4-08	Sri Lanka	W	3-0	Hyderabad	CCr1	Santosh Shahukhala [14], Ju Manu Rai [55], Anjan [68]	200	Saleem MDV
15-10	Malaysia	L	0-4	Petaling Jaya	Fr			
17-10	Afghanistan	D	2-2	Petaling Jaya	Fr	Anil Gurung [63], Bijay Gurung [78]		
2009								
26-03	Palestine	D	0-0	Kathmandu	CCq		12 000	El Haddad LIB
28-03	Kyrgyzstam	D	1-1	Kathmandu	CCq	Biraj Maharjan [2]	15 000	Jahanbazi IRN
29-11	Bhutan	W	2-1	Calcutta	Fr	Anil Gurung [70], Bijay Gurung [80]		
5-12	Maldives	D	1-1	Dhaka	SAFr1	Ju Manu Rai [68]		
7-12	India †	L	0-1	Dhaka	SAFr1			
9-12	Afghanistan	W	3-0	Dhaka	SAFr1	Anil Gurung 2 [55 73], Bijay Gurung [56]		
2010								

No international matches played in 2010

Fr = Friendly match • SAF = South Asian Football Federation Cup • CC = AFC Challenge Cup • AC = AFC Asian Cup
q = qualifier • r1 = first round group • qf = quarter-final • sf = semi-final

NEPAL 2010

ANFA A DIVISION	Pl	W	D	L	F	A	Pts	Police	Three Star	New Road	Army	Manang	Machhindra	Jawalakhel	Friends Club	Ranipokhari	Armed Police	Boys Union	Sankata
Nepal Police Club †	22	14	8	0	35	8	50		0-0	1-0	1-1	1-0	0-0	2-2	3-0	1-1	2-0	3-0	1-0
Three Star Club	22	12	7	3	41	15	43	0-0		0-1	1-1	0-1	1-1	6-0	3-2	1-0	1-1	4-0	4-1
New Road Team	22	12	4	6	39	29	40	1-2	1-2		1-0	2-0	0-0	4-3	3-2	3-1	5-3	2-0	2-1
Tribhuvan Army Club	22	11	6	5	38	21	39	0-0	1-1	2-0		1-0	1-0	4-1	0-1	3-2	1-2	4-0	1-0
Manang Marsyangdi	22	8	6	8	30	32	30	0-2	0-3	5-3	0-2		0-4	1-1	1-0	1-2	4-1	2-2	1-0
Machhindra FC	22	7	6	9	20	27	27	1-2	1-0	0-3	1-1	1-1		0-1	3-1	1-0	0-8	0-1	3-1
Jawalakhel Youth Club	22	7	6	9	27	43	27	1-1	1-2	1-0	1-5	3-3	2-1		0-1	0-0	3-0	1-0	1-2
Friends Club	22	7	4	11	27	41	25	0-4	0-4	2-2	3-1	3-3	0-1	0-1		3-2	3-1	2-1	0-4
Ranipokhari Corner	22	6	5	11	24	31	23	0-2	1-3	2-2	0-2	0-1	1-2	3-1	0-0		0-2	2-1	1-1
Armed Police Force	22	6	4	12	28	36	22	1-3	0-2	0-1	2-1	1-3	0-0	1-1	0-0	1-3		2-0	0-1
Boys Union Club	22	6	4	12	28	39	22	0-2	1-1	2-3	3-3	0-0	1-0	7-1	3-2	0-2	0-1		3-1
Sankata Kathmandu	22	5	2	15	20	35	17	0-2	1-2	0-0	1-3	0-3	2-0	0-1	1-2	0-1	0-2	3-2	

20/02/2010 - 19/06/2010 • † Qualified for the AFC President's Cup • First tournament played since the 2006-07 season

NGA – NIGERIA

FIFA/COCA-COLA WORLD RANKING

1993	1994	1995	1996	1997	1998	1999	2000	2001	2002	2003	2004	2005	2006	2007	2008	2009	2010
18	12	27	63	71	65	76	52	40	29	35	21	24	9	20	19	22	32

	2010												Hi/Lo
	Jan	Feb	Mar	Mar	Apr	May	Jul	Aug	Sep	Oct	Nov	Dec	5
	22	15	21	22	20	21	30	30	34	34	33	32	82

Nigeria gave a perfect lesson in how not to prepare for a World Cup finals when after finishing third at the African Nations Cup in Angola, coach Shaibu Amidu was fired, a decision that smacked of vindictiveness rather than desperation. It meant Nigeria had to scramble to find a coach for the finals with former Sweden manager Lars Lagerback having less than two months to prepare the Super Eagles for the tournament in South Africa. It came as no surprise when Nigeria went home without making much of an impact, having lost their opening two matches and then drawing with South Korea. Lagerback was offered a chance to stay on after the World Cup but declined and after several months limbo, Samson Siasia was promoted up from his job in charge of the under-23 side. Nigeria won their opening qualifying match for the 2012 Nations Cup finals, albeit without much fanfare at home, but they lost their second group game away to Guinea - both with caretaker Austin Eguavoen in charge. In club football Enyimba won the Premier League for the sixth time in the past ten seasons but missed out on a double when they lost the Cup Final to Kaduna United on post-match penalties. In the 2010 CAF Champions League, Bayelsa United suffered a humiliating first round exit against Gazelle from Chad whilst Heartland finished bottom of their group.

FIFA WORLD CUP RECORD
1930-1958 DNE   **1962** DNQ   **1966** DNE   **1970-1990** DNQ   **1994** 9 r2   **1998** 12 r2   **2002** 27 r1   **2006** DNQ   **2010** 27 r1

NIGERIA FOOTBALL ASSOCIATION (NFA)

	Plot 2033, Olusegun Obasanjo Way, Zone 7, Wuse Abuja, PO Box 5101 Garki, Abuja
☎	+234 9 5237326
📠	+234 9 5237327
✉	nigeria_fa@yahoo.com
💻	www.nigeriaff.com
FA	1945 CON 1959 FIFA 1959
P	Sani Abdullahi
GS	Bolaji Ojo-Oba

FIFA BIG COUNT 2006

Total players	6 653 710
% of population	5.05%
Male	6 344 600
Female	309 110
Amateurs 18+	26 170
Unregistered	565 000
Professionals	2 440
Referees	522
Admin & coaches	32 600
Number of clubs	522
Number of teams	522

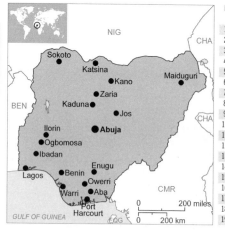

MAJOR CITIES/TOWNS

		Population
1	Lagos	9 733 876
2	Ibadan	5 003 747
3	Kano	2 359 248
4	Benin	2 324 188
5	Port Harcourt	1 999 375
6	Kaduna	1 994 242
7	Aba	1 529 729
8	Abuja	1 243 152
9	Maiduguri	1 096 414
10	Ilorin	1 050 031
11	Warri	893 929
12	Onitsha	871 554
13	Akure	804 104
14	Abeokuta	771 585
15	Enugu	698 136
16	Zaria	667 446
17	Oshogbo	647 652
18	Jos	619 122
19	Ife	599 924

FEDERAL REPUBLIC OF NIGERIA

Capital Abuja	Population 149 229 090 (8)	% in cities 48%
GDP per capita $2300 (182)	Area km² 923 768 km² (32)	GMT +/- +1
Neighbours (km) Benin 773, Cameroon 1690, Chad 87, Niger 1497 • Coast 853		

RECENT INTERNATIONAL MATCHES PLAYED BY NIGERIA

2008	Opponents	Score		Venue	Comp	Scorers	Att	Referee
9-01	Sudan	W	2-0	Estepona	Fr	Ike Uche, Ishiaku		
21-01	Côte d'Ivoire	L	0-1	Sekondi	CNr1			Benouza ALG
25-01	Mali	D	0-0	Sekondi	CNr1			El Arjoune MAR
29-01	Benin	W	2-0	Sekondi	CNr1	Mikel [52], Yakubu [86]		Bennaceur TUN
3-02	Ghana	L	1-2	Accra	CNqf	Yakubu [35p]		Benouza ALG
27-05	Austria	D	1-1	Graz	Fr	Kalu Uche [19]	15 000	Gumienny BEL
1-06	South Africa	W	2-0	Abuja	WCq	Ike Uche [10], Nwaneri [44]	50 000	Coulibaly MLI
7-06	Sierra Leone	W	1-0	Freetown	WCq	Yobo [89]	25 000	Korti LBR
15-06	Equatorial Guinea	W	1-0	Malabo	WCq	Yobo [5]	15 200	Mendy GAM
21-06	Equatorial Guinea	W	2-0	Abuja	WCq	Yakubu [45], Ike Uche [84]	20 000	Ambaya LBY
6-09	South Africa	W	1-0	Port Elizabeth	WCq	Ike Uche [69]	25 000	Lwanja MWI
11-10	Sierra Leone	W	4-1	Abuja	WCq	Obodo [20], Obinna [34], Odemwingie [45], Odiah [50]	20 000	Kaoma ZAM
19-11	Colombia	L	0-1	Cali	Fr		10 000	Duarte COL
2009								
11-02	Jamaica	D	0-0	London	Fr			Dean ENG
29-03	Mozambique	D	0-0	Maputo	WCq		35 000	Eyob ERI
29-05	Republic of Ireland	D	1-1	London	Fr	Eneramo [30]	11 263	Collum SCO
2-06	France	W	1-0	St Etienne	Fr	Akpala [32]	25 000	Bennett ENG
7-06	Kenya	W	3-0	Abuja	WCq	Ike Uche [2], Obinna 2 [72p 77]	60 000	El Achiri MAR
20-06	Tunisia	D	0-0	Rades/Tunis	WCq		45 000	Coulibaly MLI
6-09	Tunisia	D	2-2	Abuja	WCq	Odemwingie [23], Eneramo [80]	52 000	Bennett RSA
11-10	Mozambique	W	1-0	Abuja	WCq	Obinna [93+]	13 000	Abdel Rahman SUD
14-11	Kenya	W	3-2	Nairobi	WCq	Martins 2 [60 81], Yakubu [64]	20 000	Maillet SEY
2010								
12-01	Egypt	L	1-3	Benguela	CNr1	Obassi [12]	18 000	Seechurn MRI
16-01	Benin	W	1-0	Benguela	CNr1	Yakubu [42p]	8 000	Carvalho ANG
20-01	Mozambique	W	3-0	Lubango	CNr1	Odemwingie 2 [45 47], Martins [86]	10 000	Coulibaly MLI
25-01	Zambia	D	0-0	Lubango	CNqf	W 5-4p	10 000	Abd El Fatah EGY
28-01	Ghana	L	0-1	Luanda	CNsf		7 500	Bennett RSA
30-01	Algeria	W	1-0	Benguela	CN3p	Obinna [56]	12 000	Diatta SEN
3-03	Congo DR	W	5-2	Abuja	Fr	Utaka [11], Idehen 2 [28 65], Ezimorah [31], Obinna [52]	5 000	
25-05	Saudi Arabia	D	0-0	Wattens	Fr		1 000	Einwaller AUT
30-05	Colombia	D	1-1	Milton Keynes	Fr	Haruna [70]	BCD	Atkinson ENG
6-06	Korea DPR	W	3-1	Johannesburg	Fr	Yakubu [15], Obinna [62p], Martins [88]	20 000	
12-06	Argentina	L	0-1	Johannesburg	WCr1		55 686	Stark GER
17-06	Greece	L	1-2	Bloemfontein	WCr1	Kalu Uche [16]	31 593	Ruiz COL
22-06	Korea Republic	D	2-2	Durban	WCr1	Kalu Uche [12], Yakubu [69p]	61 874	Benquerenca POR
11-08	Korea Republic	L	1-2	Suwon	Fr	Odemwingie [26]	40 331	Nishimura JPN
5-09	Madagascar	W	2-0	Calabar	CNq	Martins [19], Eneramo [45]		Jedidi TUN
10-10	Guinea	L	0-1	Conakry	CNq			El Ahrach MAR

Fr = Friendly match • CN = CAF African Cup of Nations • WC = FIFA World Cup • q = qualifier • r1 = first round group

NIGERIA NATIONAL TEAM HISTORICAL RECORDS

Caps

86 - Nwankwo Kanu 1995-2010 • **80** - Muda Lawal 1976-84 • **63** - • **61** - • **56** - • **54** - • **53** - • **51** - • **49** -

Goals

37 - Rashidi Yekini 1986-98 • **23** - Segun Odegbami 1976-89 • **21** - Yakubu Aiyegbeni 2000- • **18** - Obafemi Martins 2004- • **17** - Sunday Oyarekhua 1971-75 • **14** - Daniel Amokachi 1990-99; Jay-Jay Okocha 1993-2006 & Julius Agahowa 1999- • **13** - Nwankwo Kanu 1995-2010; Samson Siasia 1989-98 & Thompson Usiyen 1976-78 • **12** - Asuquo Ekpe 1960-65 & Muda Lawal 1976-84

Past Coaches

John Finch ENG 1949 • Daniel Anyiam 1954-56 • Les Courtier ENG 1956-60 • Moshe Beth-Halevi ISR 1960-61 • George Vardar HUN 1961-63 • George Penna BRA 1963-64 • Daniel Anyiam 1964-65 • Joseph Ember HUN 1965-68 • Peter 'Eto' Amaechina 1969-70 • Heinz Marotze GER 1970-71 • George Penna BRA 1972-73 • Heinz Marotze GER 1974 • Jelisavcic 'Tiki' Tihomir YUG 1974-78 • Otto Gloria BRA 1979-82 • Gottlieb Goller GER 1981 • Adegboyega Onigbinde 1983-84 • Chris Udemezue 1984-86 • Patrick Ekeji 1985 • Paul Hamilton 1987-89 • Manfred Hoener GER 1988-89 • Clemens Westerhof NED 1989-94 • Shaibu Amodu 1994-95 • Jo Bonfere NED 1995-96 • Shaibu Amodu 1996-97 • Philippe Troussier FRA 1997-98 • Monday Sinclar 1997-98 • Bora Milutinovic SRB 1998 • Thijs Libregts NED 1999 • Jo Bonfrere NED 1999-2001 • Shaibu Amodu 2001-02 • Adegboyega Onigbinde 2002 • Christian Chukwu 2002-05 • Augustine Eguavoen 2005-07 • Berti Vogts GER 2007-08 • James Peters 2008 • Shaibu Amodu 2008-10 • Lars Lagerback SWE 2010 • Augustine Eguavoen 2010 • Samson Siasia 2010-

NIGERIA 2009–10

NIGERIAN FOOTBALL LEAGUE

	Pl	W	D	L	F	A	Pts	Eny	KanP	SunS	KwaU	EnuR	WarW	NigT	Hrt	GomU	KadU	ShoS	Dol	LobS	OceB	ZamU	Shk	WikT	BayU	Gat	RanB
Enyimba	38	20	10	8	43	25	70		2-1	2-1	2-0	1-0	1-0	3-1	0-0	1-0	1-1	1-0	1-0	0-0	2-1	1-0	2-1	2-0	2-0	2-0	4-0
Kano Pillars	38	19	9	10	48	29	66	2-0		1-0	3-0	1-0	4-0	2-0	4-0	2-1	1-0	1-0	1-1	2-0	5-1	3-0	2-1	1-0	1-1	1-0	2-1
Sunshine Stars	38	19	7	12	39	30	64	3-1	2-1		1-0	2-1	2-0	1-0	0-0	2-0	2-1	1-0	1-0	0-0	1-0	2-0	3-1	4-0	1-0	2-1	1-0
Kwara United	38	18	6	14	43	34	60	0-0	0-2	0-0		0-0	2-0	2-0	2-1	0-0	1-0	2-0	0-0	1-0	3-0	1-0	1-0	2-1	2-0		6-0
Enugu Rangers	38	15	13	10	34	22	58	0-0	1-0	0-0	2-0		1-1	1-0	2-1	2-0	1-0	2-0	0-0	1-0	1-1	3-1	1-0	1-0	4-0	2-0	
Warri Wolves	38	17	7	14	50	43	58	0-1	3-0	2-0	3-1	1-1		2-1	3-2	1-0	4-0	2-0	2-1	1-0	2-0	5-0	1-0	1-0	2-0	2-1	1-0
Niger Tornadoes	38	16	7	15	42	38	55	3-2	1-1	1-0	2-0	2-0	2-1		1-0	1-0	3-0	0-0	2-0	1-0	1-3	1-0	0-0	2-0	0-0		
Heartland	38	16	6	16	37	33	54	1-0	2-0	3-0	3-1	1-0	2-0	1-1		1-0	2-0	2-1	1-0	1-0	2-0	2-1	0-1	0-0	2-1	2-0	
Gombe United	38	16	4	18	34	33	52	1-1	2-0	2-1	1-0	0-0	1-0	1-2	2-1		1-0	2-0	2-0	2-0	3-0	2-0	1-0	1-0	1-0	2-0	
Kaduna United	38	15	7	16	40	45	52	1-0	0-0	1-1	1-2	1-1	1-0	1-0	3-2	2-1		3-0	3-0	2-0	2-0	0-0	0-1	1-0	2-0	2-0	2-1
Shooting Stars	38	14	10	14	27	33	52	0-0	0-0	2-0	1-0	0-0	2-1	2-1	1-0	1-0	3-1		1-1	0-0	0-0	2-0	1-0	2-0	1-0	0-0	
Dolphin	38	13	12	13	39	39	51	1-1	3-1	1-1	1-0	1-1	1-1	1-0	1-0	2-1	2-0		1-0	1-1	2-1	1-1	2-1	3-1	3-0	2-0	
Lobi Stars	38	14	9	15	34	37	51	0-1	1-1	2-0	2-1	2-1	3-1	2-0	1-1	2-1	1-1	2-0	2-1		2-0	1-1	1-0	0-0	2-1	2-0	
Ocean Boys	38	14	8	16	32	36	50	1-1	1-0	1-0	1-0	1-1	1-0	1-1	1-1	1-0	2-0	1-2	3-0	2-0		2-0	1-0	1-1	1-0	3-0	
Zamfara United	38	13	10	15	30	46	49	1-0	0-0	1-0	1-0	0-2	0-1	1-0	1-0	1-0	1-1	1-1	3-2	2-1	1-1		0-0	0-0	1-0	1-0	2-0
Sharks	38	14	6	18	45	41	48	2-3	2-0	0-1	1-0	0-1	0-0	2-0	1-0	5-0	2-0	0-0	3-1	1-0	4-2		2-0	2-1	2-1	4-0	
Wikki Tourists	38	13	8	17	40	38	47	1-0	0-1	1-1	3-4	2-1	3-1	2-0	**3-0**	2-0	2-1	0-0	0-0	0-1	0-1	0-3	1-1		3-0	2-0	4-0
Bayelsa United	38	13	8	17	40	46	47	1-1	2-1	1-0	1-2	1-0	2-2	1-1	1-0	2-0	3-1	3-1	1-1	4-1	2-1	1-0	2-1	1-1		2-1	3-1
Gateway	38	11	7	20	33	46	40	1-0	1-1	1-2	1-0	0-2	2-1	0-0	2-1	1-0	1-2	1-1	1-0	2-0	1-0	4-1	2-1	2-0			4-0
Ranchers Bees	38	10	6	22	23	59	36	0-1	0-1	0-0	2-0	1-3	1-2	1-0	0-0	1-0	0-2	2-0	1-2	1-0	0-1	2-1	2-1	2-1	2-1	0-0	

20/09/2009 - 7/07/2010 • † Qualified for the CAF Champions League • ‡ Qualified for the CAF Confederation Cup • Match in bold awarded

FEDERATION CUP 2010

Quarter-finals		Semi-finals		Final	
Kaduna United	1 5p				
Ocean Boys	1 3p	Kaduna United	0 5p		
Dolphin	2 5p				
Enugu Rangers	2 6p	Enugu Rangers	0 4p		
				Kaduna United	3 3p
Sunshine Stars	1			Enyimba	3 2p
Niger Tornadoes	0	Sunshine Stars	0		
Heartland	0			Sani Abacha, Kano	
Enyimba	2	Enyimba	1	15-08-2010	

Round of 16 played in four groups of four

3rd Place: Enugu Rangers 2-1 Sunshine Stars

Cup Final scorers - Bola Bello 2 [28p] [40], Siman Yusuf [35] for Kaduna; Magnus Iwuoha [37p], Valentine Nwabili [45], Atanda Sakibu [52] for Enyimba

MEDALS TABLE

		Overall G	S	B	Lge G	S	Cup G	S	Africa G	S	B	City
1	Shooting Stars	15	4	1	5		8	2	2	2	1	Ibadan
2	Enugu Rangers	11	8	4	5		5	7	1	1	4	Enugu
3	Enyimba	10	1	1	6		2	1	2		1	Aba
4	Lagos Railways	7	1				7	1				Lagos
5	Heartland	6	4	3	5		1	2		2	3	Owerri
6	Bendel Insurance	6	3	2	2		3	2	1	1	2	Benin City
7	BCC Lions	6	2		1		4	1	1	1		Gboko
8	Dolphin	6	1		2		4			1		Port Harcourt
9	Stationery Stores	5	3	1	1		4	2		1	1	Lagos
10	Julius Berger	4	3		2		2	1		2		Lagos
11	Port Harcourt FC	3	3				3	3				Port Harcourt
12	Leventis United	3	1		1		2			1		Ibadan
13	Lagos ECN	3					3					Lagos
14	Abiola Babes	2	2	1			2	2			1	Mashood
	Kano Pillars	2	2	1	1		1	2			1	Kano

NIG – NIGER

FIFA/COCA-COLA WORLD RANKING

1993	1994	1995	1996	1997	1998	1999	2000	2001	2002	2003	2004	2005	2006	2007	2008	2009	2010
81	70	93	129	150	154	164	182	191	184	164	173	177	147	155	143	163	94

2010												Hi/Lo
Jan	Feb	Mar	Mar	Apr	May	Jul	Aug	Sep	Oct	Nov	Dec	68
163	162	164	165	161	162	147	145	154	100	102	94	196

Association Sportive des Forces Armees Nigeriennes completed a dream year by becoming the first side from the arid Sahara nation to get to the group phase of a continental club competition. But the euphoria over their giant-killing progress to the last eight of the CAF Confederation Cup was then usurped by a famous win for the national side in the 2012 African Nations Cup qualifiers. A swiftly taken goal from burly striker Moussa Maazou handed Niger a 1-0 win over Egypt in Niamey in October - without doubt the biggest win to date for the under-performing country. Earlier in the year, Niger had beaten Nigeria in the African Nations Championship qualifiers with almost the same side, save for their small foreign-based contingent. Maazou has become a veritable ambassador for his country and in 2010 moved from CSKA Moskva on loan to Monaco for the second half of the French season and then later joined Bordeaux, where he had less success. AS-FAN, his old club, caused a sensation with their progress through the early rounds of the CAF Confederation Cup with wins over Tunisian powerhouse Etoile du Sahel, then Daring Club Motema Pembe of the Congo DR and finally Al Mererikh of Sudan to qualify for the group phase where they garnered only two points. They did also take the domestic league and cup double.

FIFA WORLD CUP RECORD
1930-1974 DNE 1978-1982 DNQ 1986-1990 DNE 1994 DNQ 1998-2002 DNE 2006-2010 DNQ

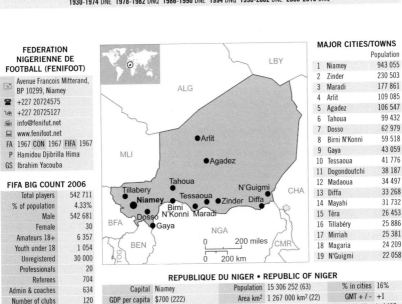

FEDERATION NIGERIENNE DE FOOTBALL (FENIFOOT)

Avenue Francois Mitterand, BP 10299, Niamey
☎ +227 20724575
📠 +227 20725127
✉ info@fenifut.net
🖥 www.fenifut.net
FA 1967 CON 1967 FIFA 1967
P Hamidou Djibrilla Hima
GS Ibrahim Yacouba

FIFA BIG COUNT 2006

Total players	542 711
% of population	4.33%
Male	542 681
Female	30
Amateurs 18+	6 357
Youth under 18	1 054
Unregistered	30 000
Professionals	20
Referees	704
Admin & coaches	634
Number of clubs	120
Number of teams	1 010

MAJOR CITIES/TOWNS

		Population
1	Niamey	943 055
2	Zinder	230 503
3	Maradi	177 861
4	Arlit	109 085
5	Agadez	106 547
6	Tahoua	99 432
7	Dosso	62 979
8	Birni N'Konni	59 518
9	Gaya	43 059
10	Tessaoua	41 776
11	Dogondoutchi	38 187
12	Madaoua	34 497
13	Diffa	33 268
14	Mayahi	31 732
15	Téra	26 453
16	Tillabéry	25 886
17	Mirriah	25 381
18	Magaria	24 209
19	N'Guigmi	22 058

REPUBLIQUE DU NIGER • REPUBLIC OF NIGER

Capital	Niamey	Population	15 306 252 (63)	% in cities	16%
GDP per capita	$700 (222)	Area km²	1 267 000 km² (22)	GMT +/-	+1
Neighbours (km)	Algeria 956, Benin 266, Burkina Faso 628, Chad 1175, Libya 354, Mali 821, Nigeria 1497				

RECENT INTERNATIONAL MATCHES PLAYED BY NIGER

2007	Opponents	Score		Venue	Comp	Scorers	Att	Referee
25-03	Lesotho	L	1-3	Maseru	CNq	Daouda Kamilou [41]		Lwanja MWI
3-06	Lesotho	W	2-0	Niamey	CNq	Hamidou Djibo [3], Souleymane Dela Sacko [13]		Kotey GHA
17-06	Nigeria	L	1-3	Niamey	CNq	Daouda Kamilou [68]		Pare BFA
8-09	Uganda	L	1-3	Kampala	CNq	Idrissa Hasseydou [44]		Marange ZIM
21-11	Equatorial Guinea	D	1-1	Malabo	Fr	Ouwo Moussa Maazou [74]		
2008								
31-05	Uganda	L	0-1	Kampala	WCq		25 000	Evehe CMR
8-06	Angola	L	1-2	Niamey	WCq	Ismael Alassane [3]	23 000	Jedidi TUN
14-06	Benin	L	0-2	Niamey	WCq		5 000	Haimoudi ALG
22-06	Benin	L	0-2	Cotonou	WCq		25 000	Niyongabo BDI
28-08	Libya	L	2-6	Tripoli	Fr			
7-09	Uganda	W	3-1	Niamey	WCq	Ilssoufou Alhassane 2 [68 86], Daouda Kamilou [88]	5 000	Lamptey GHA
12-10	Angola	L	1-3	Luanda	WCq	Mallam [19]	3 200	Gasingwa RWA
2009								
No international matches played in 2009								
2010								
19-06	Chad	D	1-1	Niamey	Fr	Koffi Dan Kowa [90]		
11-08	Benin	D	0-0	Porto Novo	Fr			
4-09	South Africa	L	0-2	Nelspruit	CNq			Abdul Rahman SUD
10-10	Egypt	W	1-0	Niamey	CNq	Moussa Maazou [34]		Doue CIV
17-11	Libya	D	1-1	Tripoli	Fr	Moussa Maazou [77]. L 1-4p		

Fr = Friendly match • CN = CAF African Cup of Nations • WC = FIFA World Cup • q = qualifier

NIGER 2010											
SUPER LIGUE PLAY-OFFS								Sahel	Akokana	D Kassawa	
	Pl	W	D	L	F	A	Pts				
AS-FAN Niamey	3	2	1	0	7	2	**7**	1-1	1-0	5-1	
Sahel SC Niamey	3	2	1	0	6	2	**7**		2-1	3-0	
Akokana Arlit	3	0	1	2	2	4	1			1-1	
Dan Kassawa Maradi	3	0	1	2	2	9	1				

17/08/2010 - 21/08/2010 • † Qualified for the CAF Champions League

COUPE NATIONALE 2010 FINAL

Stade Seyni Kountche, Niamey, 3-08-2010

AS-FAN Niamey   2-1   AS Garde Nationale

Scorers - Scorers - Mohamed Abdoulaye [57], Hinsa Issoufou [62]
for ASFAN; Issiakou Koudize [83p] for ASGNN

NIR – NORTHERN IRELAND

FIFA/COCA-COLA WORLD RANKING

1993	1994	1995	1996	1997	1998	1999	2000	2001	2002	2003	2004	2005	2006	2007	2008	2009	2010
39	45	45	64	93	86	84	93	88	103	122	107	103	48	32	52	40	43

2010												Hi/Lo
	Jan	Feb	Mar	Mar	Apr	May	Jul	Aug	Sep	Oct	Nov	Dec	27
	40	40	39	50	57	56	59	59	45	41	42	43	124

Linfield completed a fourth league and Irish Cup double in five years and as they continued their dominance of club football in Northern Ireland and they now stand just one short of becoming only the second club in world football to win 50 league titles. On April 24, 2010, Noel Bailie created his own landmark for the club when he made his 1000th appearance in all competitions in a career stretching back to March 1989. In the following two weeks the 39-year old Linfield captain was also celebrating a ninth championship success following a 1-0 win over Cliftonville in the penultimate round and a sixth cup winners medal after Linfield beat Portadown 2-1 in the final at Windsor Park. 2009 champions Glentoran claimed the season's other major trophy when they beat Coleraine in the League Cup final - their 50th trophy in Northern Ireland's three main club competitions. A quick look at the national team's record of just one win and five goals in the 15 games played to the end of 2010 would suggest that Nigel Worthington's team are going through a rough patch but Northern Ireland actually made a positive start to the qualifiers for Euro 2012. They began with an excellent win in Slovenia and then held Italy to a 0-0 draw in Belfast but then ended the year with a disappointing draw away to the Faroe Islands.

FIFA WORLD CUP RECORD

1930-1938 DNE **1950-1954** DNQ **1958** 8 QF **1962-1978** DNQ **1982** 9 r2 **1986** 21 r1 **1990-2010** DNQ

IRISH FOOTBALL ASSOCIATION (IFA)

20 Windsor Avenue,
Belfast, BT9 6EG,
United Kingdom

☎ +44 28 90669458
📠 +44 28 90667620
✉ enquiries@irishfa.com
🖥 www.irishfa.com

FA	1880	CON	1954	FIFA	1911

P   Jim Shaw
GS Patrick Nelson

FIFA BIG COUNT 2006

Total players	92 320
% of population	4.84%
Male	83 220
Female	9 100
Amateurs 18+	22 600
Youth under 18	16 000
Unregistered	10 500
Professionals	220
Referees	553
Admin & coaches	11 557
Number of clubs	820
Number of teams	1 570

MAJOR CITIES/TOWNS

		Population
1	Belfast	260 735
2	Londonderry	89 915
3	Lisburn	83 172
4	Newtownabbey	65 869
5	Bangor	62 364
6	Craigavon	61 920
7	Castlereagh	57 093
8	Newtownards	29 583
9	Carrickfergus	29 535
10	Ballymena	29 438
11	Newry	28 146
12	Coleraine	24 321
13	Omagh	22 507
14	Antrim	22 064
15	Larne	18 777
16	Banbridge	18 012
17	Enniskillen	15 592
18	Armagh	15 126
19	Strabane	15 060

NORTHERN IRELAND (PART OF THE UNITED KINGDOM)

Capital	Belfast	Population	1 716 942 (149)	% in cities	90%
GDP per capita	$36 700 (32)	Area km²	14 120 km² (160)	GMT +/-	0
Neighbours (km)	Republic of Ireland 360 • Coast 539				

RECENT INTERNATIONAL MATCHES PLAYED BY NORTHERN IRELAND

2006	Opponents		Score	Venue	Comp	Scorers	Att	Referee
16-08	Finland	W	2-1	Helsinki	Fr	Healy [32], Lafferty [64]	12 500	Svendsen DEN
2-09	Iceland	L	0-3	Belfast	ECq		13 522	Skjerven NOR
6-09	Spain	W	3-2	Belfast	ECq	Healy 3 [20 64 80]	13 885	De Bleeckere BEL
7-10	Denmark	D	0-0	Copenhagen	ECq		41 482	Plautz AUT
11-10	Latvia	W	1-0	Belfast	ECq	Healy [35]	13 500	Fleischer GER
2007								
6-02	Wales	D	0-0	Belfast	Fr		13 500	Richmond SCO
24-03	Liechtenstein	W	4-1	Vaduz	ECq	Healy 3 [52 75 83], McCann [92+]	4 340	Oriekhov UKR
28-03	Sweden	W	2-1	Belfast	ECq	Healy 2 [31 58]	13 500	Braamhaar NED
22-08	Liechtenstein	W	3-1	Belfast	ECq	Healy 2 [5 35], Lafferty [56]	13 544	Matejek CZE
8-09	Latvia	L	0-1	Riga	ECq		7 500	Proença POR
12-09	Iceland	L	1-2	Reykjavík	ECq	Healy [72p]	7 727	Baskakov RUS
17-10	Sweden	D	1-1	Stockholm	ECq	Lafferty [72]	33 112	Layec FRA
17-11	Denmark	W	2-1	Belfast	ECq	Feeney [62], Healy [80]	12 997	Vink NED
21-11	Spain	L	0-1	Las Palmas	ECq		30 339	Fandel GER
2008								
6-02	Bulgaria	L	0-1	Belfast	Fr		11 000	McDonald SCO
26-03	Georgia	W	4-1	Belfast	Fr	Lafferty 2 [25 36], Healy [33], Thompson [87]	15 000	Wilmes LUX
20-08	Scotland	D	0-0	Glasgow	Fr		28 072	Vollquartz DEN
6-09	Slovakia	L	1-2	Bratislava	WCq	Durica OG [81]	5 445	Ivanov.N RUS
10-09	Czech Republic	D	0-0	Belfast	WCq		12 882	Bebek CRO
11-10	Slovenia	L	0-2	Maribor	WCq		12 385	Iturralde ESP
15-10	San Marino	W	4-0	Belfast	WCq	Healy [31], McCann [43], Lafferty [56], Davis [75]	12 957	Kari FIN
19-11	Hungary	L	0-2	Belfast	Fr		6 251	Schoergenhofer AUT
2009								
11-02	San Marino	W	3-0	Serravalle	WCq	McAuley [7], McCann [33], Brunt [63]	1 942	Stankovic SRB
28-03	Poland	W	3-2	Belfast	WCq	Feeney [10], Evans [47], Zewlakow.M OG [62]	13 357	Hansson SWE
1-04	Slovenia	W	1-0	Belfast	WCq	Feeney [73]	13 243	Yefet ISR
6-06	Italy	L	0-3	Pisa	Fr		16 583	Blom NED
12-08	Israel	D	1-1	Belfast	Fr	McCann [19]	10 250	Valgeirsson ISL
5-09	Poland	D	1-1	Chorzow	WCq	Lafferty [38]	38 914	Mejuto ESP
9-09	Slovakia	L	0-2	Belfast	WCq		13 019	Kuipers NED
14-10	Czech Republic	D	0-0	Prague	WCq		8 002	Duhamel FRA
14-11	Serbia	L	0-1	Belfast	Fr		13 500	Toussaint LUX
2010								
3-03	Albania	L	0-1	Tirana	Fr		7 500	Pilav BIH
26-05	Turkey	L	0-2	New Britain	Fr		4 000	Vaughn USA
30-05	Chile	L	0-1	Chillan	Fr		12 000	Prudente URU
11-08	Montenegro	L	0-2	Podgorica	Fr		5 000	Jovanetic SRB
3-09	Slovenia	W	1-0	Maribor	ECq	Evans [70]	12 000	Balaj ROU
8-10	Italy	D	0-0	Belfast	ECq		15 200	Chapron FRA
12-10	Faroe Islands	D	1-1	Toftir	ECq	Lafferty [76]	1 921	Zimmermann SUI
17-11	Morocco	D	1-1	Belfast	Fr	Patterson [86p]	15 000	Hagen NOR

Fr.= Friendly match • EC = UEFA EURO 2008/2012 • WC = FIFA World Cup • q = qualifier

NORTHERN IRELAND NATIONAL TEAM HISTORICAL RECORDS

Caps
119 - Pat Jennings 1964-86 • **91** - Mal Donaghy 1980-94 • **88** - Sammy McIlroy 1972-87 • **87** - Maik Taylor 1999- • **86** - Keith Gillespie 1996-2008 • **84** - David Healy 2000- • **75** - Aaron Hughes 1998- • **73** - Jimmy Nicholl 1976-86 • **71** - Michael Hughes 1992-2004 • **67** - David McCreery 1976-90 • **66** - Nigel Worthington • **64** - Martin O'Neill 1972-85 • **63** - Gerry Armstrong 1977-86

Goals
35 - David Healy 2000- • **13** - Billy Gillespie 1913-32 & Colin Clarke 1986-93 • **12** - Joe Bambrick 1928-40; Gerry Armstrong 1977-86; Jimmy Quinn 1985-96 & Iain Dowie 1990-2000 • **11** - Olphie Stanfield 1887-97 • **10** - Billy Bingham 1951-64; Jimmy McIlroy 1952-66; Peter McParland 1954-62 & Johnny Crossan 1960-68

Past Coaches
Peter Doherty 1951-62 • Bertie Peacock 1962-67 • Billy Bingham 1967-71 • Terry Neill 1971-75 • Dave Clements 1975-76 • Danny Blanchflower 1976-79 • Billy Bingham 1980-94 • Bryan Hamilton 1994-98 • Lawrie McMenemy ENG 1998-99 • Sammy McIlroy 2000-03 • Lawrie Sanchez 2004-07 • Nigel Worthington 2007-

NORTHERN IRELAND 2009-10

IFA JJB SPORTS PREMIERSHIP

	Pl	W	D	L	F	A	Pts	Linfield	Cliftonville	Glentoran	Crusaders	Swifts	Portadown	Coleraine	Glenavon	Newry City	Ballymena	Distillery	Institute
Linfield †	38	22	8	8	78	37	74		1-2	1-0 2-1	3-1 0-1	0-4	1-1 1-5-0	2-4	4-1 1-2 3-0	5-0 1-0	1-0	2-0	2-2
Cliftonville ‡	38	21	6	11	69	42	69	4-0 1-1		1-2 1-2 1-0	1-0 4-1	2-1 2-1 0-1	0-1	3-2	3-2	0-2	3-0	1-4-0	1-3-0
Glentoran ‡	38	19	8	11	58	46	65	2-2-2-2 1-0-3	0-1 0-0 1-0-1-0		1-0	2-0	0-6	2-0	0-1	1-2-3-0	1-0-2-0	1-1-2-1	
Crusaders	38	17	9	12	57	52	60	0-4 0-0-2-3 1-2 1-1-2-1				2-3 2-3-3-1 3-2-1-0	2-5-3-0 3-0-1-1	4-1	2-2	2-0	1-2		
Dungannon Swifts	38	16	9	13	56	58	57	2-2 0-1-1 1-0-2-1 1-2-0-1-2 1-1					2-8 4-1-0-1-1	4-0	0-0	2-1-2-1	2-1	2-1	
Portadown ‡	38	15	10	13	70	55	55	1-0-1-0-2-2-0-1 2-2-1-1-2-2-2-1 4-1-2						4-0-3-1	2-0	0-0	2-0 6-1	1-3-0	0-3-1
Coleraine	38	16	9	13	76	62	57	1-2	3-2-0-2-2-1-3 3-3 0-1-4-3 4-1		2-1		3-3		3-0 1-0-3-0	2-3-3-2 3-1-2-1	1-1	1-1	0-2-2-1 1-2-1-1 1-3-0 1-1-2
Glenavon	38	12	7	19	47	67	43	1-2	3-2-0-2-2-1-3	3-3 0-1-4-3	4-1	2-1	3-3			3-0 1-0-3-0	2-3-3-2 3-1-2-1	1-1	1-1-0-2-2-1-1-2-1-1-3-0-1-1-2
Newry City	38	10	12	16	38	63	42	0-6	1-2-1-1-2-0-3	0-1	0-1-4-0-0-1-5-2	1-0-0-0-3-3-2		3-2	1-0-0		1-2-2-3-1	0-0	
Ballymena United	38	11	7	20	46	56	40	2-0	0-1-2-1	2-3	1-2-2-0	0-1	2-1-0-1-3-2 2-4-0-3-1-0-1-2		0-0		0-1-1-2-1	1-3-0	
Lisburn Distillery	38	11	6	21	45	76	39	1-2-0-5	0-5	0-4	0-1-2-0-0-2-5	0-3	3-2-1-1-2-3-0-0-2-4	3-0-0-2-2-2					2-1-2-1
Institute	38	6	13	19	36	62	31	1-2-0-3	1-1	0-3	1-0-1-3-0-1-2-0	1-1	2-2-1-1-0-1-1-2-0-0 1-0-1-2-2-2-1	2-3					

8/08/2009 - 1/05/2010 • † Qualified for the UEFA Champions League • ‡ Qualified for the Europa League
Relegation play-off: **Donegal Celtic** 0-0 1-0 Institute
Top scorers: **30** - Rory Patterson, Coleraine • **17** - Darren Boyce, Coleraine & George McMullen, Cliftonville • **16** - Liam Boyce, Cliftonville

NORTHERN IRELAND 2009-10
IFA CHAMPIONSHIP (2)

	Pl	W	D	L	F	A	Pts
Loughgall	26	19	3	4	60	24	60
Donegal Celtic	26	19	2	5	59	21	59
Limavady United	26	18	3	5	56	29	57
Ards	26	13	6	7	49	27	45
Carrick Rangers	26	12	5	9	37	39	41
Ballinamallard United	26	10	8	8	36	29	38
Ballymoney United	26	10	8	8	39	33	38
Larne	26	11	4	11	34	37	37
Banbridge Town	26	8	3	15	33	48	27
Glebe Rangers	26	7	6	13	30	56	27
Bangor	26	7	5	14	36	48	26
Ballyclare Comrades	26	7	5	14	34	46	26
Coagh United	26	6	4	16	38	62	22
Armagh City	26	2	4	20	20	62	10

8/08/2009 - 5/05/2010 • Loughgall ineligible for promotion

MEDALS TABLE

		Overall			League			Cup		LC	
		G	S	B	G	S	B	G	B	G	B
1	Linfield	98	43	14	49	20	14	40	20	9	3
2	Glentoran	50	48	24	23	24	24	20	19	7	5
3	Belfast Celtic	22	8	8	14	4	8	8	4		
4	Lisburn Distillery	18	15	9	6	8	9	12	7		
5	Cliftonville	12	18	6	3	6	6	8	10	1	2
6	Glenavon	9	21	6	3	10	6	5	10	1	1
7	Portadown	9	17	7	4	9	7	3	7	2	1
8	Coleraine	7	19	9	1	9	9	5	6	1	4
9	Crusaders	8	6	4	4	2	4	3	1	1	3

CIS INSURANCE LEAGUE CUP 2009-10

Round of 16

Glentoran *	2	3
Glenavon	2	2
Newry City *	2	0
Linfield	2	0
Ballinamallard Utd *	0	1
Limavady United	0	0
Crusaders	1	3
Portadown *	2	4
Dungannon Swifts *	3	5
Larne	1	3
Ballymena United	1	1
Institute *	2	2
Cliftonville	1	2
Donegal Celtic *	0	1
Lisburn Distillery *	1 0 4p	
Coleraine	0 1 5p	

Quarter-finals

Glentoran *	0	2
Linfield	1	1
Ballinamallard Utd *	0	3
Portadown	5	1
Dungannon Swifts *	6	1
Institute	2	0
Cliftonville *	2	1
Coleraine	3	1

Semi-finals

Glentoran ‡‡	1
Portadown	0
Dungannon Swifts	0
Coleraine †	2

Final

Glentoran ‡	2 4p
Coleraine	2 1p

‡ Qualified for the Europa League
* Home team in 1st leg • † Played at The Oval • ‡‡ Played at Windsor Park

CUP FINAL
Windsor Park, Belfast
27-03-2010, Att: 4500, Ref: Courtney
Scorers - Cairan Martyn [6], Colin Nixon [45] for Glentoran; Darren Boyce [7], Rory Patterson [31] for Coleraine

IRISH CUP 2009–10

Fifth Round		Round of 16		Quarter–finals		Semi–finals		Final	
Linfield	4								
Donegal Celtic *	0	Linfield *	4						
Malachians	0	Dungannon Swifts	0	Linfield	3				
Dungannon Swifts *	6			Glentoran *	1				
Ballyclare Comrades *	5	Ballyclare Comrades	1						
Islandmagee	1	Glentoran *	2			Linfield †	4		
Omagh United	0					Coleraine	2		
Glentoran *	5								
Newry City *	2	Newry City *	1 1					Linfield	2
Larne	1	Loughgall *	1 0	Newry City	2			Portadown ‡	1
Ards Rangers	1			Coleraine *	3				
Loughgall *	3								
Nortel *	2 2 5p	Nortel	0						
Bryansburn Rangers	2 2 3p	Coleraine *	6						
Dundela *	0								
Coleraine	2								
Ballymena United *	0 1	Ballymena United *	5						
Ards	0 0	Ballinamallard United	2						
Glebe Rangers *	0			Ballymena United	3 2				
Ballinamallard United	3			Glenavon *	3 0				
Institute *	1 1	Institute	1						
Ballymoney United	1 0	Glenavon *	2			Ballymena United	1 3p		
HW Welders	1					Portadown ††	1 4p		
Glenavon *	5								
Crusaders *	5	Crusaders *	4						
Bangor	1	Coagh United	0	Crusaders *	1 0				
Tobermore United	1			Portadown	1 1				
Coagh United	1								
Cliftonville	2	Cliftonville	1						
Lisburn Distillery *	0	Portadown *	2						
Carrick Rangers *	1 0								
Portadown	1 1								

* Home team in the first leg • † Played at The Oval • †† Played at Windsor Park • ‡ Qualified for the Europa League

CUP FINAL

Windsor Park, Belfast
8-05-2010, Att: 8000, Ref: Courtney
Scorers - Peter Thompson 1, Philip Lowry 11 for Linfield; Kevin Braniff 13 for Portadown
Linfield - Alan Blayney - Michael Gault, William Murphy, Damien Curran, Philip Lowry (Jamie Mulgrew 71), Peter Thompson, Noel Bailie, Aaron Burns, Robert Garrett, Mark McAllister (Paul Munster 45), John Gallagher. Tr: David Jeffrey
Portadown - David Miskelly - Ross Redman, Richard Clarke (Alan Teggart 82), Darren Kelly, Wesley Boyle, Kevin Braniff, Tim Mouncey, Jordan Baker (Richard Lecky 66), Andy Hunter (Ryan McCluskey 57), Johnny Topley, Sean Mackie. Tr: Ronny McFall

NOR – NORWAY

FIFA/COCA-COLA WORLD RANKING

1993	1994	1995	1996	1997	1998	1999	2000	2001	2002	2003	2004	2005	2006	2007	2008	2009	2010
4	8	10	14	13	14	7	14	26	26	42	35	38	50	29	59	32	12

						2010						Hi/Lo
Jan	Feb	Mar	Mar	Apr	May	Jul	Aug	Sep	Oct	Nov	Dec	2
32	32	33	24	22	22	22	22	14	13	12	12	59

In his first two years back in charge of the Norwegian national team Egil Olsen has overseen a dramatic rise in fortunes that his designated successor Stale Solbakken will find hard to live up to. Solbakken, currently the coach of FC København, will take over from Olsen after the Euro 2012 qualifiers although if the Norwegians carry on in the manner they have started the campaign, that may well have to be delayed until after the finals should they qualify for what would only be the second time. At club level, Solbakken continued to carve out a name for himself after leading København to the knock-out stage of the 2010-11 UEFA Champions League whilst another of the Norwegian coaching legends, Nils Arne Eggen, created his own bit of history when he led Rosenborg to the Tippeligaen title without losing a game - the first time a team has gone through the season unbeaten. Rosenborg have now won the title 16 times - all of them in the last 20 years. Remarkably, captain Roar Strand has been part of all 16 title-winning teams (and five cup winning teams) but after 440 league games the 40-year old finally decided to hang up his boots, content with what is a truly astonishing world record. Rosenborg did lose in the cup, to second division Follo FK in the semi-final, who then went on to lose to Strømgodset in the final.

FIFA WORLD CUP RECORD
1930-1934 DNE **1938** 12 r1 1950 DNE 1954-1990 DNQ **1994** 17 r1 **1998** 15 r2 2002-2010 DNQ

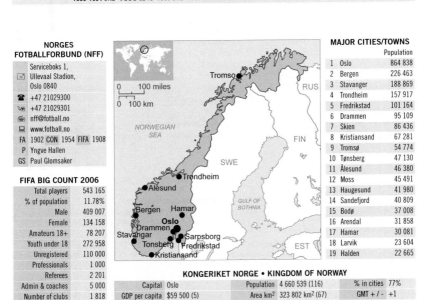

NORGES FOTBALLFORBUND (NFF)

Serviceboks 1,
Ullevaal Stadion,
Oslo 0840
☎ +47 21029300
📠 +47 21029301
✉ nff@fotball.no
🖥 www.fotball.no
FA 1902 CON 1954 FIFA 1908
P Yngve Hallen
GS Paul Glomsaker

FIFA BIG COUNT 2006

Total players	543 165
% of population	11.78%
Male	409 007
Female	134 158
Amateurs 18+	78 207
Youth under 18	272 958
Unregistered	110 000
Professionals	1 000
Referees	2 201
Admin & coaches	5 000
Number of clubs	1 818
Number of teams	19 841

MAJOR CITIES/TOWNS

		Population
1	Oslo	864 838
2	Bergen	226 463
3	Stavanger	188 869
4	Trondheim	157 917
5	Fredrikstad	101 164
6	Drammen	95 109
7	Skien	86 436
8	Kristiansand	67 281
9	Tromsø	54 774
10	Tønsberg	47 130
11	Ålesund	46 380
12	Moss	45 491
13	Haugesund	41 980
14	Sandefjord	40 809
15	Bodø	37 008
16	Arendal	31 858
17	Hamar	30 081
18	Larvik	23 604
19	Halden	22 665

KONGERIKET NORGE • KINGDOM OF NORWAY

Capital Oslo	Population 4 660 539 (116)	% in cities 77%
GDP per capita $59 500 (5)	Area km² 323 802 km² (67)	GMT + / - +1
Neighbours (km) Finland 727, Sweden 1619, Russia 196 • Coast 25 148		

RECENT INTERNATIONAL MATCHES PLAYED BY NORWAY

2007 Opponents	Score	Venue	Comp	Scorers	Att	Referee
7-02 Croatia	L 1-2	Rijeka	Fr	Moen [86]	8 000	Kalt FRA
24-03 Bosnia-Herzegovina	L 1-2	Oslo	ECq	Carew [50p]	16 987	Riley ENG
28-03 Turkey	D 2-2	Frankfurt	ECq	Brenne [31], Andresen [40]	BCD	Farina ITA
2-06 Malta	W 4-0	Oslo	ECq	Hæsted [31], Helstad [73], Iversen [79], Riise [91+]	16 364	Granat POL
6-06 Hungary	W 4-0	Oslo	ECq	Iversen [22], Braaten [57], Carew 2 [60 78]	19 198	Iturralde Gonzalez ESP
22-08 Argentina	W 2-1	Oslo	Fr	Carew 2 [11p 58]	23 932	Ceferin SVN
8-09 Moldova	W 1-0	Chisinau	ECq	Iversen [48]	10 173	Malek POL
12-09 Greece	D 2-2	Oslo	ECq	Carew [15], Riise [39]	24 080	Busacca SUI
17-10 Bosnia-Herzegovina	W 2-0	Sarajevo	ECq	Hagen [5], Riise.B [74]	1 500	Lannoy FRA
17-11 Turkey	L 1-2	Oslo	ECq	Hagen [12]	23 783	Merk GER
21-11 Malta	W 4-1	Ta'Qali	ECq	Iversen 3 [25 27p 45], Pedersen [75]	7 000	Baskakov RUS
2008						
6-02 Wales	L 0-3	Wrexham	Fr		7 553	McKeon IRL
26-03 Montenegro	L 1-3	Podgorica	Fr	Carew [72]	9 000	Stavrev MKD
28-05 Uruguay	D 2-2	Oslo	Fr	Elyounoussi [55], Riise [84]	12 246	Buttimer IRL
20-08 Republic of Ireland	D 1-1	Oslo	Fr	Reginiussen [61]	16 037	Whitby WAL
6-09 Iceland	D 2-2	Oslo	WCq	Iversen 2 [36p 50]	17 254	Yefet ISR
11-10 Scotland	D 0-0	Glasgow	WCq		50 205	Busacca SUI
15-10 Netherlands	L 0-1	Oslo	WCq		23 840	Plautz AUT
19-11 Ukraine	L 0-1	Dnepropetrovsk	Fr		10 000	Lajuks LVA
2009						
11-02 Germany	W 1-0	Dusseldorf	Fr	Grindheim [63]	42 000	Messner AUT
28-03 South Africa	L 1-2	Rustenburg	Fr	Pedersen [27]	30 000	Fleischer GHA
1-04 Finland	W 3-2	Oslo	Fr	Riise.JA [56], Hoiland [90], Pedersen [92+]	16 239	Styles ENG
6-06 Macedonia FYR	D 0-0	Skopje	WCq		7 000	Tagliavento ITA
10-06 Netherlands	L 0-2	Rotterdam	WCq		45 600	Baskakov RUS
12-08 Scotland	W 4-0	Oslo	WCq	Riise.JA [35], Pedersen 2 [45 90], Huseklepp [60]	24 493	Hamer LUX
5-09 Iceland	D 1-1	Reykjavik	WCq	Riise.JA [11]	7 321	Tudor ROU
9-09 Macedonia FYR	W 2-1	Oslo	WCq	Helstad [2], Riise.JA [25]	14 766	Paixao POR
10-10 South Africa	W 1-0	Oslo	Fr	Waehler [48]	13 504	Collum SCO
14-11 Switzerland	W 1-0	Geneva	Fr	Carew [48p]	16 000	Whitby WAL
2010						
3-03 Slovakia	W 1-0	Zilina	Fr	Moldskred [67]	9 756	Nijhuis NED
29-05 Montenegro	W 2-1	Oslo	Fr	Grindheim [44], Pedersen [89]	13 132	Eriksson SWE
2-06 Ukraine	L 0-1	Oslo	Fr		10 178	Blom NED
11-08 France	W 2-1	Oslo	Fr	Huseklepp 2 [51 71]	15 165	Velasco ESP
3-09 Iceland	W 2-1	Reykjavík	ECq	Hangeland [58], Abdellaoue [75]	6 137	Banti ITA
7-09 Portugal	W 1-0	Oslo	ECq	Huseklepp [21]	24 535	Duhamel FRA
8-10 Cyprus	W 2-1	Larnaca	ECq	Riise.JA [2], Carew [42]	7 648	Gumienny BEL
12-10 Croatia	L 1-2	Zagreb	Fr	Abdellaoue [21]	3 000	Skomina SVN
17-11 Republic of Ireland	W 2-1	Dublin	Fr	Pedersen [34], Huseklepp [86]	25 000	Jakobsson ISL

Fr = Friendly match • EC = UEFA EURO 2008/2012 • WC = FIFA World Cup • q = qualifier • po = qualifying play-off

NORWAY NATIONAL TEAM HISTORICAL RECORDS

Caps
104 - Thorbjorn Svenssen 1947-62 • 100 - Henning Berg 1992-2004 • 97 - Erik Thorstvedt 1982-96 • 92 - John Arne Riise 2000- • 86 - Oyvind Leonhardsen 1990-2003 & John Carew 1998- • 83 - Kjetil Rekdal 1987-2000 • 78 - Erik Mykland 1990-2000 & Steffen Iversen 1998- • 77 - Svein Grondalen 1973-84 • 76 - Tore Andre Flo 1995-2004 • 75 - Stig Inge Bjornebye 1989-2000

Goals
33 - Jorgen Juve 1928-37 • 26 - Einar Gundersen 1917-28 • 25 - Harald Hennum 1949-60 • 23 - Ole Gunnar Solskjær 1995-2007; Tore Andre Flo 1995-2004 & John Carew 1998- • 22 - Gunnar Thoresen 1946-59 • 21 - Steffen Iversen 1998- • 20 - Jan Age Fjortoft 1986-96 • 19 - Odd Iversen 1967-79; Olav Nilsen 1962-71 & Oyvind Leonhardsen 1990-2003

Past Coaches
Willibald Hahn AUT 1953-55 • Ron Lewin ENG 1956-57 • Edmund Majowsky 1958 • Ragnar Larsen 1958 • Kristian Henriksen 1959 • Wilhelm Kment AUT 1960-62 • Ragnar Larsen 1962-66 • Wilhelm Kment AUT 1967-69 • Oivind Johannessen 1970-71 • George Curtis ENG 1972-74 • Kjell Schou-Andreassen & Nils Arne Eggen 1975-77 • Tor Roste Fossen 1978-87 • Tord Grip SWE 1987-88 • Ingvar Stadheim 1988-90 • Egil Olsen 1990-98 • Nils Johan Semb 1998-2003 • Age Hareide 2003-08 • Egil Olsen 2009-

NORWAY 2010

TIPPELIGAEN

	Pl	W	D	L	F	A	Pts	Rosenborg	Vålerenga	Tromsø	Aalesund	Odd	Haugesund	Strømgodset	Start	Viking	Lillestrøm	Molde	Stabæk	Brann	Hønefoss	Kongsvinger	Sandefjord
Rosenborg BK †	30	19	11	0	58	24	68		3-1	1-0	2-2	1-1	4-3	3-0	3-3	1-1	0-0	3-1	2-0	3-0	3-0	4-0	1-0
Vålerenga IF ‡	30	19	4	7	69	36	61	0-0		3-0	3-0	6-1	5-2	4-1	8-1	2-0	2-1	2-1	3-2	1-0	0-0	5-2	3-0
Tromsø IL ‡	30	14	8	8	36	30	50	0-0	2-1		0-1	3-1	2-0	2-1	1-0	1-0	0-0	0-1	3-0	0-3	2-0	1-0	2-1
Aalesunds SK	30	14	5	11	46	37	47	1-1	1-0	2-0		2-3	2-1	3-1	2-0	3-1	3-0	0-0	2-2	3-1	1-3	2-0	2-2
Odd Grenland	30	12	10	8	48	41	46	1-3	1-2	1-1	2-1		4-1	2-0	2-1	2-1	2-1	1-1	2-3	0-0	1-0	0-0	5-0
SK Haugesund	30	12	9	9	51	39	45	0-0	2-0	0-0	2-1	3-0		2-2	4-2	4-0	3-3	1-2	2-1	1-1	5-1	3-0	2-0
IF Strømgodset ‡	30	13	4	13	51	59	43	1-1	1-0	2-1	3-1	0-4	2-1		3-1	2-1	5-4	1-3	1-3	1-1	4-1	2-0	4-2
IK Start	30	11	9	10	57	60	42	2-3	5-3	1-1	1-0	1-1	3-3	4-2		1-1	2-3	1-1	3-2	3-1	2-0	3-0	2-0
Viking FK	30	10	11	9	48	41	41	1-2	3-4	1-1	1-3	3-1	1-0	3-1	2-2		0-0	4-1	2-0	4-0	4-0	3-1	0-0
Lillestrøm SK	30	9	13	8	51	44	40	1-2	1-4	2-0	1-0	2-2	1-1	3-1	3-2	1-1		1-1	0-0	3-2	6-0	2-2	4-0
Molde FK	30	10	10	10	42	45	40	1-2	0-1	2-3	2-1	0-0	2-1	3-2	1-2	2-2	3-3		1-0	3-2	1-0	2-0	0-0
Stabæk Fotball	30	11	6	13	46	47	39	1-2	1-1	0-1	2-1	0-3	0-0	1-2	3-0	2-3	2-1	4-3		2-1	0-1	4-2	2-1
SK Brann	30	8	10	12	48	50	34	2-3	1-1	0-1	2-1	1-1	0-0	4-0	3-4	3-3	1-1	1-1	2-2		3-2	3-1	3-2
Hønefoss BK	30	7	6	17	28	62	27	0-2	3-1	2-2	0-2	2-1	0-2	1-1	0-0	0-1	3-2	1-1	0-4	2-0		1-2	1-0
Kongsvinger IL	30	4	8	18	27	58	20	0-0	1-2	1-1	1-2	1-2	0-1	0-2	3-3	1-1	0-0	0-1	3-1	1-1	1-4		1-0
Sandefjord Fotball	30	2	6	22	25	58	12	1-3	0-1	3-5	0-1	1-1	0-1	0-3	1-2	0-0	0-1	3-1	1-1	1-4	6-1	0-1	

13/03/2010 - 7/11/2010 • † Qualified for the UEFA Champions League • ‡ Qualified for the Europa League • Play-off: **Fredrikstad** 2-0 Løv-Ham; **Hønefoss** 2-1 Ranheim • Final: Hønefoss 1-4 0-4 **Fredrikstad** • Top scorers: **16** - Baye Djiby Fall SEN, Molde • **15** - Mohammed Abdellaoue, Vålerenga

MEDALS TABLE

		Overall			League			Cup		City
		G	S	B	G	S	B	G	S	
1	Rosenborg BK	31	10	1	22	5	1	9	5	Trondheim
2	Fredrikstad FK	20	16	1	9	9	1	11	7	Fredrikstad
3	Viking SK	13	7	8	8	2	8	5	5	Stavanger
4	Odd Grenland	12	10			2		12	8	Skien
5	Lillestrøm SK	10	16	3	5	8	3	5	8	Lillestrøm
6	FC Lyn	10	10	4	2	4	4	8	6	Oslo
7	SK Brann	9	12	3	3	5	3	6	7	Bergen
8	FK Skeid	9	8	1	1	5	1	8	3	Oslo
9	Vålerenga IF	9	5	3	5	3	3	4	2	Oslo
10	FK Sarpsborg	6	6	2				6	6	Sarpsborg
11	IF Stromsgodset	6	2	3	1		3	5	2	Drammen
12	FK Orn-Horten	4	4					4	4	Horten
13	Mjøndalen IF	3	7			2		3	5	Mjøndalen

NORWAY 2010

ADECCOLIGAEN (2)

	Pl	W	D	L	F	A	Pts	Sogndal	Sarpsborg	Fredrikstad	Løv-Ham	Ranheim	Bodø-Glimt	Strømmen	Alta	Bryne	Mjøndalen	Nybergsund	Follo	Sandnes	Tromsdalen	Moss	Lyn
Sogndal IL	28	17	5	6	51	28	56		1-2	2-0	2-0	2-1	1-0	5-1	2-1	2-2	3-0	1-1	4-3	0-1	5-0	2-0	
Sarpsborg 08	28	16	6	6	54	36	54	4-0		3-0	3-2	3-1	1-1	0-3	4-0	0-0	1-0	1-0	0-0	2-1	1-0	4-1	
Fredrikstad FK	28	14	8	6	53	37	50	2-0	1-1		1-0	2-3	0-0	1-0	3-0	3-3	2-2	1-3	3-1	2-1	1-1	1-1	**3-1**
Løv-Ham Bergen	28	13	4	11	46	38	43	2-0	2-1	0-1		1-1	0-1	1-2	4-2	1-2	0-2	3-1	1-3	2-2	0-0	3-0	**4-1**
Ranheim IL	28	12	7	9	38	38	43	2-2	0-3	2-2	1-3		2-1	0-0	2-0	1-0	2-1	0-2	1-0	3-1	2-2	1-0	
FK Bodø-Glimt	28	12	6	10	41	28	42	0-1	4-0	1-2	3-0	3-1		2-0	2-0	0-5	0-2	5-0	4-0	1-2	2-0	0-0	**4-1**
Strømmen IF	28	12	4	12	43	42	40	1-2	2-1	3-2	2-3	1-0	2-1		6-1	6-3	1-2	1-3	0-2	2-0	2-2	2-2	**1-1**
Alta IF	28	10	6	12	41	51	36	0-1	4-4	1-0	1-1	2-2	0-1	3-1		2-1	7-3	1-1	3-1	1-0	1-2	3-1	**2-0**
Bryne FK	28	10	5	13	57	52	35	2-5	3-1	2-2	2-5	0-1	1-2	1-2	4-1		5-1	5-1	5-1	1-3	0-1	5-0	**3-1**
Mjøndalen IF	28	10	5	13	41	49	35	0-1	3-1	2-5	0-2	1-0	1-0	0-0	0-1	3-1		3-1	0-0	2-2	4-0	1-3	
Nybergsund IL-Trysil	28	9	8	11	38	47	35	0-2	2-3	0-0	1-4	3-1	2-2	0-2	0-1	2-2	2-1		4-1	0-1	1-0	4-2	
Follo FK	28	8	8	12	35	43	32	1-1	2-2	1-2	0-1	0-1	1-1	2-0	0-0	0-2	1-1	3-2		1-3	4-0	0-4	
Sandnes Ulf	28	8	7	13	33	40	31	0-0	2-3	0-1	1-2	1-1	1-1	0-1	2-2	1-2	0-2	1-1	3-2		2-1	1-2	
Tromsdalen UIL	28	8	4	16	33	50	28	1-0	1-3	2-5	2-0	1-2	1-2	1-0	0-2	5-0	5-3	1-2	0-2	0-1		4-2	**1-1**
FK Moss	28	7	5	16	32	56	26	1-4	0-2	2-5	1-3	1-3	2-1	2-0	2-0	0-3	1-1	0-1	1-2	1-0	0-0		**2-3**
FC Lyn Oslo	Relegated to 6th level									**3-1**	**1-2**	**2-3**									**1-1**	**2-4**	

5/04/2010 - 7/11/2010 • Matches in bold annulled. Lyn withdrew after 11 games • Top scorers: **17** - Marius Heele, Bryne • **16** - Sindre Marøy, Løv-Ham

NM SAS BRAATHENS CUPEN 2010

Third Round

Team	Score
IF Strømgodset	4
FC Lyn Oslo	2
Bryne FK	1
SK Haugesund *	6
Tromsø IL	2
Tromsdalen UIL *	0
FK Bodø-Glimt *	1
Ranheim IL	2
Viking FK	4
Fyllingen Fotball *	1
Nybergsund IL-Trysil	1
Kongsvinger IL *	2
Hønefoss BK	2 5p
Sarpsborg 08 *	2 3p
Mjøndalen IF	2
Odd Grenland *	6
Rosenborg BK *	3
Alta IF	1
FK Moss	2
Sandefjord Fotball *	4
Fredrikstad FK	5
Strømmen IF *	2
Sandnes Ulf	0
IK Start *	2
Sogndal IL	3
Molde FK *	1
Aalesunds SK	1
Løv-Ham Bergen *	2
FK Tønsberg	3 4p
Stabæk Fotball *	3 3p
Lillestrøm SK	2
Follo FK *	4

Round of 16

Team	Score
IF Strømgodset *	3
SK Haugesund	0
Tromsø IL *	0
Ranheim IL	2
Viking FK *	2
Kongsvinger IL	0
Hønefoss BK *	1
Odd Grenland	5
Rosenborg BK	4
Sandefjord Fotball *	1
Fredrikstad FK *	0
IK Start	1
Sogndal IL *	3
Løv-Ham Bergen	1
FK Tønsberg *	0
Follo FK	2

Quarter-finals

Team	Score
IF Strømgodset	2
Ranheim IL *	1
Viking FK	1
Odd Grenland *	2
Rosenborg BK *	4
IK Start	3
Sogndal IL	1
Follo FK *	3

Semi-finals

Team	Score
IF Strømgodset *	2
Odd Grenland	0
Rosenborg BK	2
Follo FK *	3

Final

Team	Score
IF Strømgodset ‡	2
Follo FK	0

CUP FINAL

Ullevaal, Oslo
14-11-2010. Att: 24 500. Ref: Hagen
Scorers - Ola Kamara 30, Glenn Andersen 42
Strømgodset - Adam Larsen - Lars Vilsvik, Alexander Aas, Glenn Andersen, Joel Riddez - Øyvind Storflor (Gardar Johansson 86), Andre Hanssen (Alfred Sankoh 71), Jason Morrison, Fredrik Nordkvelle - Jo Inge Berget (Petar Rnkovic 78), Ola Kamara. Tr: Ronny Deila
Follo - Glenn Arne Hansen - Jens Skogmo, Edvard Skagestad, Christian Petersen, Benjamin Dahl Hagen - Alban Shipshani (Patrik Karoliussen 70), Øystein Grini•, Anders Jahnsen (Mads Clausen 90), Alexander Tveter - Eirik Markegard, Bonaventure Maruti• (Christian Bwamy 89). Tr: Hans Eriksen

* Home team • ‡ Qualified for the Europa League

NZL – NEW ZEALAND

FIFA/COCA-COLA WORLD RANKING

1993	1994	1995	1996	1997	1998	1999	2000	2001	2002	2003	2004	2005	2006	2007	2008	2009	2010
77	99	102	132	120	103	100	91	84	49	88	95	120	131	95	86	82	63

2010												Hi/Lo
Jan	Feb	Mar	Mar	Apr	May	Jul	Aug	Sep	Oct	Nov	Dec	47
82	79	80	79	78	78	54	54	49	51	59	63	156

New Zealand remaining unbeaten at the World Cup... you could be forgiven for thinking it was a reference to the rugby union All Blacks, but even they haven't done that since winning the first rugby World Cup in 1987. For football's All Whites it may have been backs-to-the-wall but they emerged from South Africa 2010 with three draws including one against defending champions Italy. The tone for New Zealand's tournament was set with a dramatic injury-time equaliser by Winston Reid against Slovakia and when Shane Smeltz scored after seven minutes in the next match against Italy, Ricki Herbert's team were in uncharted territory. The Italians equalised not long after but New Zealand held on for a famous draw which meant that a win against Paraguay would see them through to the knockout rounds. Content to contain the Paraguayans for much of the match the Kiwis never looked like scoring the crucial goal. The match finished 0-0 and they were out. Australia's decision to leave the OFC may have made World Cup qualification more of a reality but in club football the 2010 champions Waitakere United were on the receiving end of a nasty shock when they lost the final of the OFC Champions League to Papua New Guinea's Hekari United - the first time a club outside of Australia and New Zealand had won the trophy.

FIFA WORLD CUP RECORD
1930-1966 DNE 1970-1978 DNQ **1982** 23 r1 1986-2006 DNQ **2010** 22 r1

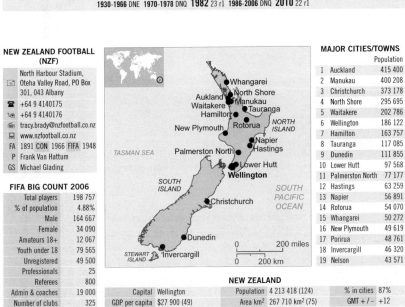

NEW ZEALAND FOOTBALL (NZF)

North Harbour Stadium, Oteha Valley Road, PO Box 301, 043 Albany
☎ +64 9 4140175
📠 +64 9 4140176
✉ tracy.brady@nzfootball.co.nz
🖥 www.nzfootball.co.nz
FA 1891 CON 1966 FIFA 1948
P Frank Van Hattum
GS Michael Glading

FIFA BIG COUNT 2006

Total players	198 757
% of population	4.88%
Male	164 667
Female	34 090
Amateurs 18+	12 067
Youth under 18	79 565
Unregistered	49 500
Professionals	25
Referees	800
Admin & coaches	19 000
Number of clubs	325
Number of teams	7 524

MAJOR CITIES/TOWNS

		Population
1	Auckland	415 400
2	Manukau	400 208
3	Christchurch	373 178
4	North Shore	295 695
5	Waitakere	202 786
6	Wellington	186 122
7	Hamilton	163 757
8	Tauranga	117 085
9	Dunedin	111 855
10	Lower Hutt	97 568
11	Palmerston North	77 177
12	Hastings	63 259
13	Napier	56 891
14	Rotorua	54 070
15	Whangarei	50 272
16	New Plymouth	49 619
17	Porirua	48 761
18	Invercargill	46 320
19	Nelson	43 571

NEW ZEALAND

Capital	Wellington
GDP per capita	$27 900 (49)
Neighbours (km)	Coast 15 134

Population	4 213 418 (124)
Area km²	267 710 km² (75)

% in cities	87%
GMT +/-	+12

RECENT INTERNATIONAL MATCHES PLAYED BY NEW ZEALAND

2005	Opponents	Score		Venue	Comp	Scorers	Att	Referee
9-06	Australia	L	0-1	London	Fr		9 023	Dean ENG
2006								
19-02	Malaysia	W	1-0	Christchurch	Fr	Old [87]	10 100	O'Leary NZL
23-02	Malaysia	W	2-1	Albany	Fr	Banks [18], Barron [88]	8 702	Fox NZL
25-04	Chile	L	1-4	Rancagua	Fr	Smeltz [14]	8 000	Osorio CHI
27-04	Chile	L	0-1	La Calera	Fr			Acosta CHI
24-05	Hungary	L	0-2	Budapest	Fr		5 000	Hrinak SVK
27-05	Georgia	W	3-1	Altenkirchen	Fr	Coveny 2 [35 53], Killen [37]	1 000	
31-05	Estonia	D	1-1	Tallinn	Fr	Hay [27]	3 000	Rasmussen DEN
4-06	Brazil	L	0-4	Geneva	Fr		32 000	Laperriere SUI
2007								
7-02	Tahiti	D	0-0	Auckland	Fr			Hester NZL
24-03	Costa Rica	L	0-4	San Jose	Fr		15 000	Rodriguez CRC
28-03	Venezuela	L	0-5	Maracaibo	Fr		12 000	
26-05	Wales	D	2-2	Wrexham	Fr	Smeltz 2 [2 24]	7 819	Skjerven DEN
17-10	Fiji	W	2-0	Lautoka	WCq	Vicelich [37], Smeltz [86]	6 000	Marrufo USA
17-11	Vanuatu	W	2-1	Port Vila	WCq	Smeltz [52], Mulligan [93+]	8 000	Minan PNG
21-11	Vanuatu	W	4-1	Wellington	WCq	Mulligan 2 [14 81], Smeltz 2 [29p 34]	2 500	Jacques TAH
2008								
6-09	New Caledonia	W	3-1	Noumea	WCq	Sigmund [16], Smeltz 2 [66 76]	2 589	Varman FIJ
10-09	New Caledonia	W	3-0	Auckland	WCq	Smeltz 2 [49 76], Christie [69]	8 000	Hauata TAH
19-11	Fiji	L	0-2	Lautoka	WCq		4 500	Fred VAN
2009								
28-03	Thailand	L	1-3	Bangkok	Fr	Elliott [14]		
3-06	Tanzania	L	1-2	Dar es Salaam	Fr	Smeltz [10p]		
6-06	Botswana	D	0-0	Gaborone	Fr			
10-06	Italy	L	3-4	Atteridgeville	Fr	Smeltz [13], Killen 2 [42 57p]	2 000	Bennett RSA
14-06	Spain	L	0-5	Rustenburg	CCr1		21 649	Codjia BEN
17-06	South Africa	L	0-2	Rustenburg	CCr1		36 598	Archundia MEX
20-06	Iraq	D	0-0	Johannesburg	CCr1		23 295	Webb ENG
9-09	Jordan	W	3-1	Amman	Fr	Smeltz 2 [17p 65], Fallon [45]		
10-10	Bahrain	D	0-0	Manama	WCq		37 000	Kassai HUN
14-11	Bahrain	W	1-0	Wellington	WCq	Fallon [45]	36 500	Larrionda URU
2010								
3-03	Mexico	L	0-2	Pasadena	Fr		90 526	Marrufo USA
24-05	Australia	L	1-2	Melbourne	Fr	Killen [16]	55 659	Salazar USA
29-05	Serbia	W	1-0	Klagenfurt	Fr	Smeltz [22]	14 000	Drachta AUT
4-06	Slovenia	L	1-3	Maribor	Fr	Fallon [20]	10 965	Kakkos GRE
15-06	Slovakia	D	1-1	Rustenburg	WCr1	Reid [93+]	23 871	Damon RSA
20-06	Italy	D	1-1	Nelspruit	WCr1	Smeltz [7]	38 229	Batres GUA
24-06	Paraguay	D	0-0	Polokwane	WCr1		34 850	Nishimura JPN
9-10	Honduras	D	1-1	Auckland	Fr	Wood [45]	18 153	O'Leary NZL
12-10	Paraguay	L	0-2	Wellington	Fr		16 477	Cross NZL

Fr = Friendly match • OC = OFC Oceania Nations Cup • CC = FIFA Confederations Cup • WC = FIFA World Cup
q = qualifier • r1 = first round group • sf = semi-final • f = final

NEW ZEALAND NATIONAL TEAM HISTORICAL RECORDS

Caps
71 - Ivan Vicelich 1995- • **68** - Simon Elliott 1995- • **64** - Vaughn Coveny 1992-2007 • **61** - Ricki Herbert 1980-89 • **60** - Chris Jackson 1995-2003 • **59** - Brian Turner 1967-82 • **53** - • **51** - • **49** -

Goals
28 - Vaughn Coveny 1992-2007 • **22** - Steve Sumner 1976-88 • **21** - Brian Turner 1967-82 • **17** - Shane Smeltz 2003- • **16** - Jock Newall 1951-52 & Keith Nelson 1977-83 • **9** -

Past Coaches
Matthew Robinson AUS 1947-56 • Ken Armstrong ENG 1957-64 • Lou Brocic YUG 1965-66 • Juan Schwanner CHI 1967-68 • Lou Brocic YUG 1969 • Barrie Truman 1970-76 • Wally Hughes 1977-78 • John Adshead ENG 1979-82 • Allan Jones 1983-84 • Kevin Fallon 1985-88 • John Adshead ENG 1989 • Ian Marshall SCO 1990-93 • Bobby Clark SCO 1994-95 • Keith Pritchett SCO 1996-97 • Joe McGrath IRL 1997-98 • Ken Dugdale 1998-2002 • Mick Waitt ENG 2002-04 • Ricki Herbert 2005-

NEW ZEALAND 2009-10

NEW ZEALAND FOOTBALL CHAMPIONSHIP (NZFC)	Pl	W	D	L	F	A	Pts	Auckland	Waitakere	Wellington	Canterbury	Otago Utd	Hawkes Bay	YoungHeart	Waikato
Auckland City †	14	9	4	1	33	13	31		2-1	3-1	1-1	5-0	1-4	2-1	5-0
Waitakere United †	14	9	2	3	31	22	29	1-1		2-1	1-0	4-0	3-2	4-1	4-2
Team Wellington	14	7	0	7	22	24	21	0-1	4-3		2-1	0-2	0-4	0-1	2-1
Canterbury United	14	5	3	6	23	16	18	1-3	4-0	1-4		2-0	6-0	1-1	2-0
Otago United	14	5	3	6	16	22	18	0-0	1-2	3-1	1-3		1-1	1-0	2-2
Hawkes Bay United	14	4	3	7	18	27	15	1-1	0-1	0-2	0-0	0-3		1-0	2-3
YoungHeart Manawatu	14	4	4	6	19	24	16	1-6	2-2	0-2	2-1	2-1	2-2		3-0
Waikato	14	3	1	10	19	33	10	1-2	2-3	2-3	1-0	0-1	1-2	4-2	

1/11/2009 - 14/03/2010 • Top four qualified for the play-offs • † Qualified for OFC Champions League • Top scorer: **9** - Seule Soromon, YoungHeart
Play-off Semi-finals: **Canterbury United** 1-2 3-0 Auckland City; Team Wellington 3-2 1-2 **Waitakere United**
Grand Final: **Waitakere United** 3-1 Canterbury United. **Waitakere United** are the 2010 NZFC champions
Final details: Fred Taylor Park, Waitakere, 24-04-2010, Att: 1535, Ref: Cross. Scorers - Benjamin Totori 2 34 73, Allan Pearce 57 for Waitakere; Tom
Lancaster 6 for Canterbury • **Waitakere** - Danny Robinson - Jason Rowley● (Jack Pelter 91+), Tim Myers, Martin Bullock●, Brent Fisher, Benjamin
Totori, Allan Pearce (Dakota Lucas 91+), Neil Sykes●, Roy Krishna (Ryan De Vries 79), Neil Emblem, Jake Butler (c). Tr: Neil Emblem • **Canterbury** -
Tom Batty - Dan Terris (c), Gareth Rowe, Matt Boyd, Andy Pitman (Andy Barton 80), Aaron Clapham, Russel Kamo (Hue Frame 88), Tom Lancaster,
Nick Wortelboer, Paul Dirou◆37, Glen Collins (Dareen Overton 59). Tr: Keith Braithwaite

MEDALS TABLE

		Overall		Lge		OFC		City/Town
		G	S	G	S	G	S	
1	Auckland City	6		4		2		Auckland
2	Waitakere United	4	4	2	3	2	1	Waitakere
3	Canterbury United		2		2			Christchurch
4	Team Wellington		1		1			Wellington
5	Hawke's Bay United							Napier
	Otago United							Dunedin
	Waikato FC							Hamilton
	YoungHeart Manawatu							Palmerston North

CHATHAM CUP 2010

Round of sixteen		Quarter–finals		Semi–finals		Final	
Miramar Rangers	2						
Napier City Rovers *	1	**Miramar Rangers ***	3				
Upper Hutt City *	0	Wellington United	1				
Wellington United	4			**Miramar Rangers ***	2		
Glenfield Rovers *	3			East Coast Bays	1		
Birkenhead United	1	Glenfield Rovers	1				
Three Kings United *	1	**East Coast Bays ***	2			**Miramar Rangers**	3
East Coast Bays	2					Bay Olympic	1
Caversham AFC *	8						
Roslyn-Wakari	2	**Caversham AFC**	7			
Western AFC *	1 3p	Ferrymead Bays *	3			
Ferrymead Bays	1 4p			**Caversham AFC ***	3 1p	
Forrest Hill Milford *	3			**Bay Olympic**	3 4p	
Albany United	1	Forrest Hill Milford *	0			
Waitakere City	1	**Bay Olympic**	2			
Bay Olympic *	3					

CUP FINAL
North Harbour, Auckland
12-09-2010, Ref: Benischke
Scorers - Tim Schaeffers 12,
Campbell Parkin 20, Michael White 75
for Miramar; Nathan Strom 34 for
Olympic

* Home team

OMA – OMAN

FIFA/COCA-COLA WORLD RANKING

1993	1994	1995	1996	1997	1998	1999	2000	2001	2002	2003	2004	2005	2006	2007	2008	2009	2010
97	71	98	91	81	58	92	106	91	96	62	56	91	72	84	96	79	99

	2010												Hi/Lo
	Jan	Feb	Mar	Mar	Apr	May	Jul	Aug	Sep	Oct	Nov	Dec	50
	79	93	93	96	97	91	81	81	92	96	97	99	117

2010 proved to be a bitterly disappointing year for Claude Le Roy's Omani national team. It started off with the failure to qualify for the Asian Cup finals in Qatar. In their final qualifying match Oman had to beat Kuwait to make it to their third consecutive finals but they could only muster a 0-0 draw in Muscat that saw the Kuwaitis qualify instead. In September Oman didn't get past the group stage at the West Asian Championship in Jordan but it was the lacklustre performance at the Gulf Cup in Yemen that was most disappointing for fans in the country. Having won the title on home soil at the start of 2009, the Omanis travelled to neighbouring Yemen in December as defending champions but they scored just a single goal in drawing all three of their first round matches, against Bahrain, UAE and Iraq, and were out. The run of poor form saw Le Roy and the Oman FA part company in January 2011, with no replacement announced to fill the Frenchman's position. In club football there were surprise first time champions when Al Suwaiq won the title finishing two points ahead of the more established Dhofar. Suwaiq, who first came to prominence when they won the Sultan Qaboos Cup in 2008, originate from a small coastal town to the north-west of Muscat but they played their home matches in and around the capital.

FIFA WORLD CUP RECORD
1930-1986 DNE 1990-2010 DNQ

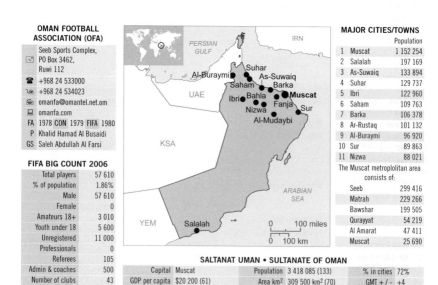

OMAN FOOTBALL ASSOCIATION (OFA)
Seeb Sports Complex,
PO Box 3462,
Ruwi 112
☎ +968 24 533000
📠 +968 24 534023
✉ omanfa@omantel.net.om
🖥 omanfa.com
FA 1978 CON 1979 FIFA 1980
P Khalid Hamad Al Busaidi
GS Saleh Abdullah Al Farsi

FIFA BIG COUNT 2006
Total players	57 610
% of population	1.86%
Male	57 610
Female	0
Amateurs 18+	3 010
Youth under 18	5 600
Unregistered	11 000
Professionals	0
Referees	105
Admin & coaches	500
Number of clubs	43
Number of teams	129

MAJOR CITIES/TOWNS
		Population
1	Muscat	1 152 254
2	Salalah	197 169
3	As-Suwaiq	133 894
4	Suhar	129 737
5	Ibri	122 960
6	Saham	109 763
7	Barka	106 378
8	Ar-Rustaq	101 132
9	Al-Buraymi	96 920
10	Sur	89 863
11	Nizwa	88 021

The Muscat metroplolitan area consists of:
Seeb	299 416
Matrah	229 266
Bawshar	199 505
Qurayyat	54 219
Al Amarat	47 411
Muscat	25 690

SALTANAT UMAN • SULTANATE OF OMAN
Capital	Muscat	Population	3 418 085 (133)	% in cities	72%
GDP per capita	$20 200 (61)	Area km²	309 500 km² (70)	GMT +/-	+4
Neighbours (km)	Saudi Arabia 676, UAE 410, Yemen 288 • Coast 2092				

RECENT INTERNATIONAL MATCHES PLAYED BY OMAN

2008	Opponents	Score		Venue	Comp	Scorers	Att	Referee
9-08	Syria	L	1-2	Tehran	WArl	Hashim Saleh [47]		
11-08	Jordan	L	1-3	Tehran	WArl	Mohamed Katkut [26]		
20-08	Uzbekistan	W	2-0	Muscat	Fr	Fouzi Bashir [25], Amad Ali [36]		
6-09	Morocco	D	0-0	Muscat	Fr			
10-09	Zimbabwe	W	3-2	Muscat	Fr	Hashim Saleh [27], Al Ajmi [29], Hassan Rabia [49]		
14-11	Jordan	W	2-0	Muscat	Fr	Hassan Rabia 2 [33 64]		
19-11	Paraguay	L	0-1	Muscat	Fr			
17-12	China PR	W	3-1	Muscat	Fr	Hashim Saleh 2 [47 84], Fouzi Bashir [74]		
19-12	Ecuador	W	2-0	Muscat	Fr	Hassan Rabia [3], Amad Ali [75]		
22-12	Senegal	W	1-0	Muscat	Fr			
2009								
4-01	Kuwait	D	0-0	Muscat	GCr1			
7-01	Iraq	W	4-0	Muscat	GCr1	Hassan Rabia 3 [23 65 79], Amad Ali [50]		
10-01	Bahrain	W	2-0	Muscat	GCr1	Badr Al Maimani [14], Fouzi Bashir [71]		
14-01	Qatar	W	1-0	Muscat	GCsf	Hassan Rabia [18]		
17-01	Saudi Arabia	D	0-0	Muscat	GCf	W 6-5p		
19-01	Indonesia	D	0-0	Muscat	ACq		13 000	Shamsuzzaman BAN
28-01	Kuwait	W	1-0	Kuwait City	ACq	Hassan Rabia [63]	22 000	Al Saeedi UAE
28-03	Senegal	W	2-0	Muscat	Fr	Mohammed Sheiba [10], Saad Obaid [88]		
30-05	Egypt	L	0-1	Muscat	Fr			
9-06	Bosnia-Herzegovina	L	1-2	Cannes	Fr	Ahmed Hadid [31]		
12-08	Saudi Arabia	W	2-1	Salalah	Fr	Hassan Rabia 2 [47 63]		
9-09	Qatar	D	1-1	Doha	Fr	Hassan Rabia [63]		
14-10	Australia	L	0-1	Melbourne	ACq		20 595	Toma JPN
14-11	Australia	L	1-2	Muscat	ACq	Khalifa Ayil [16]	12 000	Sun Baojie CHN
17-11	Brazil	L	0-2	Muscat	Fr			
31-12	Singapore	W	4-1	Singapore	Fr	Fouzi Bashir [15], Yacoob Abdul Karim [20], Hussein Al Hadhri [34], Osama Hadid [69]		
2010								
6-01	Indonesia	W	2-1	Jakarta	ACq	Fouzi Bashir [32], Ismail Sulaiman [52]	45 000	Mohd Salleh MAS
20-01	Sweden	L	0-1	Muscat	Fr		1 000	Shukralla BHR
3-03	Kuwait	D	0-0	Muscat	ACq		27 000	Moradi IRN
18-05	Yemen	W	1-0	Sana'a	Fr	Ahmed Manaa [24]		
11-08	Kazakhstan	L	1-3	Astana	Fr	Hussein Ali [64]		Irmatov UZB
3-09	Malaysia	W	3-0	Doha	Fr	Hassan Rabia [3], Amad Ali 2 [38 44]		
7-09	Qatar	D	1-1	Doha	Fr	Amad Ali [56]		
21-09	Iraq	L	2-3	Amman	Fr	Hassan Rabia [42], Osama Hadid [88]		
26-09	Bahrain	L	0-2	Amman	WArl		500	
28-09	Iran	D	2-2	Amman	WArl	Osma Hadid [40], Yacoob Abdul Karim [45]	3 000	
8-10	Gabon	W	1-0	Muscat	Fr	Hassan Rabia [9]		
12-10	Chile	L	0-1	Muscat	Fr		9 000	Blooshi KUW
17-11	Belarus	L	0-4	Muscat	Fr		1 000	Al Amri KSA
23-11	Bahrain	D	1-1	Aden	GCr1	Amad Ali [37]		Al Enezi KUW
26-11	UAE	D	0-0	Aden	GCr1			Shaaban EGY
29-11	Iraq	D	0-0	Abyan	GCr1			Younis EGY

Fr = Friendly match • GC = Gulf Cup • WA = West Asian Championship • AC = AFC Asian Cup • WC = FIFA World Cup
q = qualifier • r1 = first round group • sf = semi-final • f = final

OMAN NATIONAL TEAM HISTORICAL RECORDS

Past Coaches: Mamadoh Al Khafaji EGY 1974-76 • George Smith ENG 1979 • Hamed El Dhiab TUN 1980-82 • Mansaf El Meliti TUN 1982 • Paulo Heiki BRA 1984 • Antonio Clemente BRA 1986 • Jorge Vitorio BRA 1986-88 • Karl-Heinz Heddergott GER 1988-89 • Bernd Patzke GER 1990-92 • Heshmat Mohajerani IRN 1992-94 • Rashid Jaber Al Yafi'i 1995-96 • Mahmoud El Gohary EGY 1996 • Jozef Venglos SVK 1996-97 • Ian Porterfield SCO 1997 • Valdeir Vieira BRA 1998-99 • Carlos Alberto Torres BRA 2000-01 • Milan Macala CZE 2001 • Bernd Stange GER 2001 • Rashid Jaber Al Yafi'i 2002 • Milan Macala CZE 2003-05 • Srecko Juricic CRO 2005-06 • Hamad Al Azani 2006 • Milan Macala CZE 2006-07 • Gabriel Calderon ARG 2007-08 • Julio Cesar Ribas URU 2008 • Hamad Al Azani 2008 • Claude Le Roy FRA 2008-

OMAN 2009-10

OFA OMAN MOBILE LEAGUE

	Pl	W	D	L	F	A	Pts	Suwaiq	Dhofar	Nahda	Muscat	Tali'aa	Saham	Nasr	Shabab	Oman Club	Urooba	Khaboora	Seeb
Al Suwaiq ‡	22	13	5	4	30	18	44		2-0	2-0	1-1	0-1	1-0	2-1	0-4	3-1	0-1	1-0	2-0
Dhofar Salalah	22	12	5	5	33	26	41	3-4		2-2	1-0	1-2	2-1	1-0	1-0	2-1	2-1	0-0	1-2
Al Nahda	22	12	4	6	29	21	40	2-1	1-2		0-2	2-0	1-0	1-0	2-1	0-0	3-2	1-0	2-1
Muscat	22	7	9	6	26	22	30	1-1	2-2	0-0		0-0	1-2	1-1	2-1	3-1	0-2	1-1	2-0
Al Tali'aa	22	7	6	9	21	28	27	0-2	1-2	0-3	0-0		0-1	4-2	3-2	1-1	0-0	0-2	1-0
Saham	22	7	6	9	19	26	27	0-0	0-1	1-2	0-3	2-2		2-2	2-1	1-2	2-1	0-2	1-0
Al Nasr Salalah	22	6	8	8	25	27	26	1-1	1-2	0-3	1-0	2-0	0-0		1-0	0-2	0-0	2-0	3-0
Al Shabab	22	7	4	11	30	25	25	0-2	1-1	2-0	0-1	2-1	0-1	2-3		1-1	2-0	5-0	0-0
Oman Club	22	6	7	9	27	29	25	0-1	1-1	1-2	3-0	0-2	4-0	1-1	1-3		1-0	2-1	2-2
Al Urooba Sur ‡	22	6	7	9	18	22	25	2-3	0-2	1-0	2-1	1-1	0-0	0-0	1-1	2-1		0-1	0-1
Khaboora	22	5	9	8	20	27	24	0-0	1-3	2-2	1-1	3-1	0-1	3-2	0-2	1-1	1-1		1-1
Seeb	22	6	6	10	19	26	24	0-1	3-1	1-0	1-4	0-1	1-1	2-2	2-0	**2-0**	0-1	0-0	

12/09/2009 - 7/05/2010 • ‡ Qualified for the AFC Cup • Match in bold awarded • Relegation play-off: **Urooba** 0-0 2-1 Fanja

OMAN 2009-10
FIRST DIVISION (2)

Group A

	Pl	W	D	L	F	A	Pts
Al Ahli Sidab	7	5	1	1	9	3	16
Fanja	7	3	4	0	7	3	13
Al Masnaah	7	3	3	1	15	12	12
Bahla	7	3	2	2	11	10	11
Mirbat	7	2	3	2	11	11	9
Bashayer	7	2	2	3	9	10	8
Sohar	7	1	2	4	5	9	5
Jalan	7	0	1	6	5	14	1

Group B

	Pl	W	D	L	F	A	Pts
Al Hilal	7	5	2	0	12	3	17
Al Ittihad	7	5	1	1	21	14	16
Al Mudhaibi	7	4	2	1	17	8	14
Al Wahda	7	2	5	0	12	9	11
Sur	7	3	1	3	14	14	10
Samail	7	2	1	4	11	13	7
Majees	7	0	1	6	4	14	1
Al Salam	7	0	1	6	5	21	1

3/03/2010 - 15/04/2010
Play-off semis: Ittihad 2-2 1-1 **Ahli**; Fanja 2-2 0-1 **Hilal** •
3rd Place **Fanja** 3-1 Ittihad • Final: **Ahli** 1-0 Hilal

MEDALS TABLE

		Overall G	Overall S	Overall B	Lge G	Cup G	Asia G	Asia S	Asia B	City
1	Dhofar	16			9	7				Salalah
2	Fanja	15			7	8				Fanja
3	Al Nasr	9			5	4				Salalah
4	Al Ahli	6			1	5				Sidab
5	Al Urooba	6			3	3				Sur
6	Sur	5			2	3				Sur
7	Muscat	4			3	1				Muscat
8	Oman Club	3	1		1	2	1			Muscat
9	Seeb	3				3				Seeb
10	Al Nahda	2	1		2				1	Al Buraimi
11	Al Suwaiq	2			1	1				Al Suwaiq
12	Al Tali'aa	1				1				Sur
	Saham	1				1				Saham

SULTAN QABOOS CUP 2010

Round of 16		Quarter-finals		Semi-finals		Final	
Al Urooba Sur	2						
Al Msnaa *	0	**Al Urooba Sur**	1 3				
Bahla *	0	Muscat *	2 1				
Muscat	2			**Al Urooba Sur**	2 0		
Al Tali'aa	4			Dhofar Salalah *	1 1		
Mirbat *	3	Al Tali'aa *	0 1				
Al Bashaeer	0	**Dhofar Salalah**	1 1				
Dhofar Salalah *	2						
Al Ahli Sidab *	2					**Al Urooba Sur ‡**	1 5p
Yanqil	0	**Al Ahli Sidab**	1 0 4p			Fanja	1 3p
Seeb	0 3p	Al Shabab *	0 1 3p				
Al Shabab *	0 4p			Al Ahli Sidab *	1 0		
Khaboora	2			**Fanja**	1 0		
Samail *	1	Khaboora	1 0				
Al Nahda	0 1p	**Fanja ***	1 1				
Fanja *	0 4p						

* Home team/Home team in the first leg • ‡ Qualified for the AFC Cup

CUP FINAL

Wattayah Stadium, Muscat
12-12-2010, Att: 15 000

Scorers - Hamad Hamdan OG [46] for Urooba; Adel Al Hiedbiy [39] for Fanja

PAK – PAKISTAN

FIFA/COCA-COLA WORLD RANKING

1993	1994	1995	1996	1997	1998	1999	2000	2001	2002	2003	2004	2005	2006	2007	2008	2009	2010
142	158	160	173	153	168	179	190	181	178	168	177	158	164	163	165	156	171

					2010							Hi/Lo
Jan	Feb	Mar	Mar	Apr	May	Jul	Aug	Sep	Oct	Nov	Dec	141
156	156	156	153	166	165	163	164	162	169	167	171	192

After missing out on a place at the finals of the 2010 AFC Challenge Cup in Sri Lanka, Pakistan had a low-key programme for much of the year with the country sending an under-23 team to China for the Asian Games in Guangzhou. There was little joy for the Pakistanis, however, with the team exiting the competition in the group stages after failing to score in any of their three games. Austrian George Kottan, who had taken over as national team coach in February 2009, left a year later and was replaced by former England international Graham Roberts. The ex-Tottenham Hotspur and Rangers midfielder was named coach in late 2010 but the Englishman was only in charge for a matter of months before moving to Kathmandu to take on the role of national team coach of Nepal. Khan Research Laboratory's emergence as a force in Pakistani club football continued in the wake of their first championship success in 2009 and although they lost their league title to WAPDA, KRL claimed the Pakistan Challenge Cup by comfortably beating Pakistan Navy 4-0 in the final. They also took part in the 2010 AFC President's Cup travelling to Myanmar for a first round group in Yangon. Although KRL beat Cambodia's Naga Corp they lost to both Sri Lanka's Renown and group winners Vakhsh from Tajikistan to make a quick exit.

FIFA WORLD CUP RECORD
1930-1986 DNE 1990-2010 DNQ

PAKISTAN FOOTBALL FEDERATION (PFF)

PFF Football House,
Nashar Park,
Ferozepur Road,
Lahore

☎ +92 42 9230821
📠 +92 42 9230823
✉ mail@pff.com.pk
🖥 www.pff.com.pk
FA 1948 CON 1954 FIFA 1948
P Makhdoom Saleh Hayat
GS Ahmed Yar Khan Lodhi

FIFA BIG COUNT 2006

Total players	2 975 400
% of population	1.79%
Male	2 975 400
Female	0
Amateurs 18+	40 700
Unregistered	880 000
Professionals	0
Referees	2 500
Admin & coaches	7 400
Number of clubs	720
Number of teams	2 830

MAJOR CITIES/TOWNS

		Population
1	Karachi	12 827 927
2	Lahore	6 936 563
3	Faisalabad	2 793 721
4	Rawalpindi	1 933 933
5	Multan	1 566 932
6	Hyderabad	1 536 398
7	Gujranwala	1 526 168
8	Peshawar	1 390 874
9	Quetta	859 973
10	Islamabad	673 766
11	Sargodha	586 922
12	Bahawalpur	530 438
13	Sialkot	502 721
14	Sukkur	476 776
15	Larkana	435 817
16	Shekhupura	411 834
17	Jhang	365 198
18	Mardan	340 898
19	Rahim Yar Khan	340 810

JAMHURYAT ISLAMI PAKISTAN • ISLAMIC REPUBLIC OF PAKISTAN

Capital Islamabad	Population 176 242 949 (6)	% in cities 36%
GDP per capita $2500 (173)	Area km² 796 095 km² (36)	GMT +/- +5
Neighbours (km) Afghanistan 2430, China 523, India 2912, Iran 909 • Coast 1046		

RECENT INTERNATIONAL MATCHES PLAYED BY PAKISTAN

2006	Opponents	Score		Venue	Comp	Scorers	Att	Referee
18-02	Palestine	L	0-3	Manama	Fr			
22-02	Jordan	L	0-3	Amman	ACq			Basma SYR
1-03	United Arab Emirates	L	1-4	Karachi	ACq	Muhammad Essa [60]	10 000	Tongkhan THA
2-04	Kyrgyzstan	W	1-0	Dhaka	CCr1	Muhammad Essa [59]	2 500	Shamsuzzaman BAN
4-04	Tajikistan	L	0-2	Dhaka	CCr1		5 000	Tan Hai CHN
6-04	Macau	D	2-2	Dhaka	CCr1	Adeel [12], Muhammad Essa [43]	1 000	Shamsuzzaman BAN
16-08	Oman	L	1-4	Quetta	ACq	Muhammad Essa [79p]	4 000	Torky IRN
6-09	Oman	L	0-5	Muscat	ACq		10 000	Nema IRQ
11-10	Jordan	L	0-3	Lahore	ACq		4 000	Orzuev TJK
15-11	UAE	L	2-3	Abu Dhabi	ACq	Naveed Akram [22], Tanveer Ahmed [67]	6 000	Sarkar IND
2007								
22-10	Iraq	L	0-7	Lahore	WCq		2 500	Chynybekov KGZ
28-10	Iraq	D	0-0	Damascus	WCq		8 000	Al Fadhli KUW
2008								
25-03	Nepal	L	1-2	Pokhara	Fr	Muhammad Essa [21]		
27-03	Nepal	W	2-0	Pokhara	Fr	Muhammad Qasim [46], Muhammad Rasool [90]		
2-04	Chinese Taipei	W	2-1	Taipei	CCq	Muhammad Essa [13], Michael Masih [34]	800	Iemoto JPN
4-04	Sri Lanka	L	1-7	Taipei	CCq	Adnan Farooq Ahmed [17]	300	Kovalenko UZB
6-04	Guam	W	9-2	Taipei	CCq	Jamshed Anwar 2 [9 18], Farooq Shah [28], Muhammad Qasim 3 [44 72 82], Ahmed Tanveer [62], Zahid Hameed [65p], Abdul Rehman [85]	200	Auda Lazim IRQ
3-06	Maldives	L	0-3	Male	SAFr1			
5-06	India	L	1-2	Male	SAFr1	Adnan Farooq Ahmed [88]		
7-06	Nepal	L	1-4	Male	SAFr1	Samar Ishaq [54]		
10-10	Malaysia	L	1-4	Kuala Lumpur	Fr	Arif Mehmood [86]		
2009								
4-04	Chinese Taipei	D	1-1	Colombo	CCq	Adnan Ahmed [53]	400	Tseytlin UZB
6-04	Brunei Darussalam	W	6-0	Colombo	CCq	Safiullah Khan 4 [19 61 68 78], Pathan Khan [31], Adnan Ahmed [84]	200	Orzuev TJK
8-04	Sri Lanka	D	2-2	Colombo	CCq	Safiullah Khan [82], Atif Bashir [84]	3 000	Tseytlin UZB
4-12	Sri Lanka	L	0-1	Dhaka	SAFr1			
6-12	Bangladesh	D	0-0	Dhaka	SAFr1			
8-12	Bhutan	W	7-0	Dhaka	SAFr1	Muhammad Essa 2 [21 54], Reis Ashraf [23], Arif Mehmood 3 [28 35 66], Shabir Khan [45]		
2010								

No international matches played in 2010

Fr = Friendly match • SAF = South Asian Federation Cup • AC = AFC Asian Cup • CC = AFC Challenge Cup • WC = FIFA World Cup
q = qualifier • r1 = first round group • sf = semi-final • 3p = third place play-off

PAKISTAN 2010

NATIONAL FOOTBALL LEAGUE PREMIER LEAGUE

	Pl	W	D	L	F	A	Pts	WAPDA	KRL	PIA	KESC	Army	KPT	PAF	Afghan	Navy	PEL	Boloch	NBP	HBL	PMC	SSGC	Young Blood
WAPDA †	30	21	4	5	60	21	67		1-0	1-0	2-1	1-1	5-2	1-0	1-0	0-1	4-1	1-0	0-2	3-0	4-1	4-0	6-1
Khan Research Labs	30	17	7	6	37	16	58	1-3		1-3	3-0	0-2	1-0	0-0	0-1	1-1	1-1	0-0	0-0	1-0	2-0	1-0	2-0
Pakistan Int. Airlines	30	16	9	5	49	23	57	1-0	0-0		1-1	2-1	0-0	2-2	2-0	2-3	1-0	0-1	3-3	1-2	2-0	3-1	5-0
Karachi Electric SC	30	16	7	7	58	28	55	2-1	0-1	0-1		1-1	2-0	0-2	4-2	1-1	3-0	1-0	1-1	2-0	5-0	6-1	0-0
Pakistan Army	30	15	9	6	41	22	54	1-2	1-1	0-1	0-0		4-0	0-1	2-0	0-1	2-1	2-2	3-1	1-0	1-0	1-0	1-0
Karachi Port Trust	30	15	6	9	54	41	51	1-0	0-1	2-1	1-3	2-2		0-1	2-2	0-1	2-0	4-3	2-2	3-0	4-2	2-1	6-1
Pakistan Air Force	30	12	9	9	31	30	45	0-2	0-2	1-2	0-1	1-3	1-2		1-0	0-0	0-2	3-0	2-0	2-0	0-0	3-2	1-0
Afghan FC	30	12	6	12	43	34	42	0-0	0-1	0-3	3-2	0-0	0-3	3-0		3-0	1-2	2-1	4-1	1-0	0-1	3-0	6-1
Pakistan Navy	30	11	9	10	33	35	42	0-0	0-2	1-1	1-2	0-1	1-4	0-0	2-1		1-2	3-1	2-1	1-0	6-0	1-1	
Pak Electron Limited	30	11	5	14	36	47	38	2-2	0-4	1-2	1-3	1-2	2-1	2-2	1-1	1-0		2-0	0-1	2-1	1-0	1-3	2-1
Boloch Nushki	30	8	10	12	31	34	34	1-2	1-2	0-0	0-0	0-1	0-0	3-0	0-0	3-0	0-3		0-0	1-0	1-2	3-0	2-0
Nat. Bank of Pakistan	30	7	13	10	35	45	34	1-3	0-2	1-2	1-4	0-0	2-4	0-0	1-4	1-1	3-1	2-2		0-0	2-1	1-0	4-1
Habib Bank Ltd	30	6	7	17	26	40	25	0-2	0-2	0-0	0-3	0-2	1-2	2-2	1-1	3-0	2-0	0-1	0-0		4-1	1-1	3-0
PMC Club Faisalabad	30	5	6	19	22	54	21	0-3	1-2	1-1	1-2	1-1	1-1	0-1	0-1	0-3	2-1	1-1	1-1	1-0		2-1	1-2
SSGC	30	5	5	20	36	72	20	1-2	0-3	0-5	1-6	1-4	1-2	0-2	2-1	3-0	0-0	1-2	1-1	3-3	5-1		6-2
Young Blood	30	4	6	20	23	73	18	0-4	1-0	0-2	1-3	2-1	0-2	2-0	3-0	0-0	2-3	2-2	1-2	0-2	1-0	1-1	

16/09/2010 - 30/12/2010 • † Qualified for the AFC Presidents Cup • Top scorers: 21 - Arif Mehmood, WAPDA • 16 - Asim Faiz, SSGC • 13 - Abdul Rehman, KESC & Muhammad Younus, KPT • 12 - Muhammad Essa, KESC

PAKISTAN 2010

GEO SUPER FOOTBALL LEAGUE

	Pl	W	D	L	F	A	Pts	Karachi	Quetta	Lahore	Islamabad	Peshawar
Karachi Energy	8	4	3	1	11	6	15		1-0	0-0	2-2	3-1
Quetta Zorawar	8	3	3	2	8	5	12	2-1		3-0	0-0	1-0
Lahore Lajpaals	8	3	3	2	8	6	12	0-1	2-2		0-0	1-0
Islamabad United	8	1	4	3	5	9	7	0-2	1-0	0-2		0-1
Tribe Peshawar	8	1	3	4	5	11	6	1-1	0-0	0-3	2-2	

11/06/2010 - 31/07/2010 • All matches played at People's Football Stadium, Karachi • Top scorer: 6 - Muhammad Rasool, Karachi
Semi-finals: Lahore 1-2 Quetta ; Karachi 1-1 4-2p Islamabad
Final: Karachi Energy 1-0 Quetta Power. Scorer - Muhammad Rasool 83 •
Karachi Energy are the 2010 Geo Super League champions

MEDALS TABLE

		All		Lge		Cup	
		G	S	G	S	G	S
1	Pakistan Int. Airlines	10	6	9	5	1	1
2	WAPDA	8	8	8	5		3
3	Punjab	8	1	8	1		
4	Allied Bank Limited	7	3	3	2	4	1
5	Pakistan Army	6	8	4	7	2	1
6	Karachi	6	5	6	5		
7	Crescent Textile Mills	4		2		2	
8	Khan Research Labs	3	5	1	2	2	3
9	Balochistan	3	1	3	1		
10	Pakistan Railways	2	9	2	9		
11	Habib Bank Limited	2	3	1	3	1	

PAKISTAN NATIONAL FOOTBALL CHALLENGE CUP 2010

Round of 16		Quarter-finals		Semi-finals		Final	
	Pts						
Pakistan Air Force	6	Khan Research Labs	2				
WAPDA	3	Pakistan Int. Airlines	0				
Pakistan Railways	0			Khan Research Labs	1 5p		
				WAPDA	1 3p		
Pakistan Army	9	Nat. Bank of Pakistan	0				
Pakistan Int. Airlines	6	WAPDA	3			Khan Research Labs	4
Sui Southern Gas Co	3					Pakistan Navy	0
Pakistan Police	0						
Khan Research Labs	9	Pakistan Army	0 4p				
Karachi Electric SC	6	Karachi Electric SC	0 1p				
Habib Bank	3			Pakistan Army	0		
Ashraf Sugar Mills	0			Pakistan Navy	1		
Nat. Bank of Pakistan	9						
Pakistan Navy	6	Pakistan Air Force	1 6p				
Pak Electron Limited	3	Pakistan Navy	1 7p				
DFA Multan	0						

Third place: Army 3-3 WAPDA. Army won on penalties.

CUP FINAL

Qila Kuhna Qasim Bagh, Multan
29-04-2010
Scorers - Samar Ishaq 2,
Kalim Ullah 22, Zubair Ahmed 63,
Abid Ghafoor 76 for KRL

PAN – PANAMA

FIFA/COCA-COLA WORLD RANKING

1993	1994	1995	1996	1997	1998	1999	2000	2001	2002	2003	2004	2005	2006	2007	2008	2009	2010
132	140	126	101	119	131	138	121	109	129	125	100	78	81	67	88	70	64

2010												Hi/Lo
	Jan	Feb	Mar	Mar	Apr	May	Jul	Aug	Sep	Oct	Nov	Dec	50
	70	77	78	76	76	74	94	97	70	59	64	64	150

Panama hoped to consolidate their emergence as a genuine football power in Central America by retaining the Copa Centroamericana when they staged the tournament at the beginning of 2011 but not for the first time they were denied by penalties, losing out to Costa Rica after the semi-final between them had finished all-square. There was the consolation of victory in the third place play-off against El Salvador and qualification for the CONCACAF Gold Cup later on in the year, yet there was bitter disappointment at not reaching the final, a measure of the huge progress that has been made in the past few years. At club level, however, Panama still has much catching up to do but with a national league only being created in 1988 and the fully professional Liga Professional de Futbol only two years old, that is perhaps to be expected. Arabe Unido did reach the quarter-finals of the 2009-10 CONCACAF Champions League - the best performance of any Panamanian club to do date - but Cruz Azul won the tie 4-0 on aggregate and in the 2010-11 tournament they finished bottom of their group. At home, Gary Stempel's San Francisco reached the final of both championships but were beaten by Arabe Unido in the Clausura final in May 2010 and then lost to Tauro in the Apertura final in December.

FIFA WORLD CUP RECORD
1930-1974 DNE **1978-2010** DNQ

FEDERACION PANAMENA DE FUTBOL (FEPAFUT)

Urbanizacion Chanis
Calle f53, Edif. Christine PB,
Apartado postal 0827-00391
Zona 8, Panama
☎ +507 2333896
🖷 +507 2330582
✉ info@fepafut.com
🖥 www.fepafut.com
FA 1937 CON 1961 FIFA 1938
P Pedro Chaluja Arauz
GS Ariel Alvarado

FIFA BIG COUNT 2006

Total players	203 400
% of population	6.37%
Male	176 000
Female	27 400
Amateurs 18+	28 800
Unregistered	30 800
Professionals	300
Referees	300
Admin & coaches	1 700
Number of clubs	570
Number of teams	950

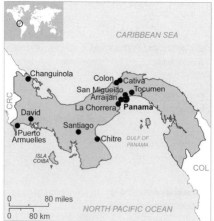

MAJOR CITIES/TOWNS

		Population
1	Panama	425 557
2	San Miguelito	366 201
3	Arraiján	102 355
4	Tocumen	100 800
5	Las Cumbres	93 590
6	David	93 351
7	Colón	87 838
8	La Chorrera	70 297
9	Pacora	63 218
10	Santiago	52 432
11	Chitré	50 122
12	Vista Alegre	47 570
13	Chilibre	38 179
14	Cativá	35 471
15	Nuevo Arraiján	26 861
16	Changuinola	25 496
17	Alcalde Díaz	22 390
18	La Cabima	22 081
19	Puerto Armuelles	20 648

REPUBLICA DE PANAMA • REPUBLIC OF PANAMA

Capital	Panama City	Population	3 360 474 (134)	% in cities	73%
GDP per capita	$11 800 (94)	Area km²	75 420 km² (117)	GMT +/-	-5
Neighbours (km)	Colombia 225, Costa Rica 330 • Coast 2490				

RECENT INTERNATIONAL MATCHES PLAYED BY PANAMA

2007	Opponents	Score		Venue	Comp	Scorers	Att	Referee
22-08	Guatemala	W	2-1	Panama City	Fr	Blanco [31], Herrera [52p]	8 700	Rodriguez CRC
12-09	Venezuela	D	1-1	Puerto La Cruz	Fr	Escobar [67]	30 000	Buitriago COL
14-10	Honduras	L	0-1	Tegucigalpa	Fr		23 139	Zelaya HON
21-11	Costa Rica	D	1-1	Panama City	Fr	Marin OG [41]	3 500	Rodas GUA
2008								
1-06	Guatemala	W	1-0	Fort Lauderdale	Fr	Garces [67]	6 800	Geiger USA
4-06	Canada	D	2-2	Sunrise	Fr	Tejada [44p], Garces [48]	BCD	
7-06	Chile	D	0-0	Valparaiso	Fr		15 000	Fagundes BRA
15-06	El Salvador	W	1-0	Panama City	WCq	Tejada [21]	22 150	Wijngaarde SUR
22-06	El Salvador	L	1-3	San Salvador	WCq	Garces [14]	27 420	Rodriguez MEX
20-08	Bolivia	L	0-1	Santa Cruz	Fr			Antequera BOL
2009								
23-01	Costa Rica	L	0-3	Tegucigalpa	UCr1		2 000	Campbell JAM
27-01	Guatemala	W	1-0	Tegucigalpa	UCr1	Zapata [31]	1 000	Aguilar SLV
30-01	Honduras	W	1-0	Tegucigalpa	UCsf	Phillips [40]	20 000	Batres GUA
1-02	Costa Rica	D	0-0	Tegucigalpa	UCf	W 5-3p	900	Batres GUA
18-03	Trinidad and Tobago	L	0-1	Marabella	Fr		2 000	Jordan TRI
31-03	Haiti	W	4-0	La Chorrera	Fr	Tejada [4], Blas Perez 3 [57 68 81]	4 500	Amaya PAN
20-05	Argentina	L	1-3	Santa Fe	Fr	Barahona [29]	20 000	Antequera BOL
7-06	Jamaica	L	2-3	Kingston	Fr	Blas Perez [12], Tejada [81]	12 000	Whittaker CAY
19-06	Haiti	D	1-1	Port-au-Prince	Fr	Machada [84]	2 000	Grant HAI
28-06	Honduras	L	0-2	Cary	Fr		3 766	Vaughn USA
5-07	Guadeloupe	L	1-2	Oakland	GCr1	Barahona [68]	32 700	Brizan TRI
9-07	Mexico	D	1-1	Houston	GCr1	Blas Perez [29]	47 713	Aguilar SLV
12-07	Nicaragua	W	4-0	Phoenix	GCr1	Blas Perez [35], Gomez [56], Tejada 2 [77 88]	23 876	Pineda HON
18-07	USA	L	1-2	Philadelphia	GCqf	Blas Perez [45]	32 000	Archundia MEX
2010								
20-01	Chile	L	1-2	Coquimbo	Fr	Roberto Brown [87]	15 000	Vasquez URU
3-03	Venezuela	W	2-1	Barquisimeto	Fr	Roman Torres [9], Blas Perez [51]	37 000	Buitrago COL
11-08	Venezuela	W	3-1	Panama City	Fr	Luis Tejada [75], Blas Perez [88], Edwin Aguilar [90]	2 000	Quesada CRC
3-09	Costa Rica	D	2-2	Panama City	Fr	Luis Tejada 2 [27 38]	23 005	Delgadillo MEX
7-09	Trinidad and Tobago	W	3-0	Panama City	Fr	Edwin Aguilar [13], Luis Tejada [75], Gavilan Gomez [87]	6 645	Cruz CRC
8-10	El Salvador	W	1-0	Panama City	Fr	Blas Perez [61]	16 175	Ruiz COL
12-10	Peru	W	1-0	Panama City	Fr	Gabriel Torres [76]	8 528	Cerdas CRC
26-10	Cuba	L	0-3	Panama City	Fr		2 116	Moreno PAN
17-11	Honduras	W	2-0	Panama City	Fr	Luis Tejada [25], Aramis Haywood [52]	3 646	Cruz CRC
18-12	Honduras	L	1-2	San Pedro Sula	Fr	Edwin Aguilar [40]	3 000	Rodas GUA
2011								
14-01	Belize	W	2-0	Panama City	UCr1	Edwin Aguilar [21], Roberto Brown [28]	10 000	Pineda HON
16-01	Nicaragua	W	2-0	Panama City	UCr1	Armando Cooper [16], Luis Renteria [80]	7 747	Lopez GUA
18-01	El Salvador	W	2-0	Panama City	UCr1	Edwin Aguilar [24], Armando Cooper [78]	10 000	Garcia MEX
21-01	Costa Rica	D	1-1	Panama City	UCsf	Blas Perez [76]. L 2-4p	10 000	Aguilar SLV
23-01	El Salvador	D	0-0	Panama City	UC3p	W 5-4p	2 000	Pineda HON

Fr = Friendly match • UC = UNCAF Cup/Copa Centroamericana • GC = CONCACAF Gold Cup • WC = FIFA World Cup
q = qualifier • r1 = first round group • qf = quarter-final • sf = semi-final • 3p = third place play-off • f = final

PANAMA NATIONAL TEAM HISTORICAL RECORDS

Past Coaches: Romeo Parravicini URU 1938 • Rogelio Diaz 1952 • Renato Panay CHI 1976 • Omar Muraco ARG 1978 • Edgardo Bone Baldi URU 1979 • Luis Borghini URU 1980 • Ruben Cardenas 1980 • Orlando Munoz 1984 • Carlos Cavagnaro ARG 1984 • Juan Colecchio ARG 1986-88 • Gustavo de Simone URU 1992 • Orlando Munoz 1996 • Cesar Maturana COL 1996 • Oscar Aristizabel COL 1999 • Miguel Mansilla URU 2000 • Leopoldo Lee 2000 • Ezequiel Fernandez 2000 • Mihai Stoichita ROU 2001 • Carlos Alberto Daluz BRA 2002-03 • Jose Eugenio Hernandez COL 2004-05 • Julio Dely Valdes & Jorge Dely Valdes 2006 • Victor Rene Mendieta 2006 • Alexandre Guimaraes CRC 2006-08 • Gary Stempel ENG 2008-09 • Julio Dely Valdes 2010-

PANAMA 2009-10

LIGA PROFESIONAL DE FUTBOL CLAUSURA

	Pl	W	D	L	F	A	Pts	Chiriquí	Arabe Unido	Chorrillo	San Francisco	Alianza	Plaza Amador	Tauro	Sporting	Chepo	Veragüense
Atlético Chiriquí †	18	10	3	5	28	21	33		2-1	2-1	2-1	1-0	1-0	1-1	2-0	4-1	1-0
Arabe Unido †	18	8	7	3	24	18	31	2-1		1-0	1-1	2-0	1-0	1-0	1-1	0-0	1-2
Chorrillo †	18	8	4	6	19	16	28	2-1	0-2		0-2	0-2	2-1	2-1	0-0	0-0	1-1
San Francisco †	18	7	5	6	32	15	26	1-2	2-0	0-1		1-1	0-0	1-2	0-1	1-1	7-1
Alianza	18	7	5	6	22	18	26	0-2	1-1	1-0	1-0		1-1	4-1	2-0	1-2	3-1
Plaza Amador	18	5	7	6	23	21	22	1-1	1-1	1-1	0-4	1-1		1-2	1-2	2-1	2-0
Tauro	18	6	4	8	20	24	22	1-0	2-3	0-3	2-2	0-0	0-3		0-0	2-0	1-2
Sporting San Miguelito	18	5	6	7	19	20	21	2-1	2-3	1-2	0-1	2-3	1-1	0-1		1-1	4-0
Chepo	18	4	6	8	17	28	18	5-2	0-0	0-1	0-5	1-0	2-3	1-0	1-1		0-3
Atlético Veragüense	18	5	3	10	19	42	18	2-2	3-3	0-3	0-3	2-1	0-4	0-4	0-1	2-1	

15/01/2010 - 14/05/2010 • † Qualified for the play-offs • Play-off semi-finals: Chorrillo 1-0 0-2 **Arabe Unido**; **San Francisco** 1-0 2-2 At. Chiriqui
Final: Arabe Unido 1-0 San Francisco. **Arabe Unido** are the Apertura Champions
Estadio Rommel Fernandez, Panama City, 14-05-2010, Att: 20 125, Ref: Vidal. Scorer - Jose Justavino 46 for Arabe Unido
Arabe Unido - Carlos Bejarano - Eric Davis, Andres Santamaria, Harold Cummings, David Daniels - Alejandro Velez• - Armando Cooper (c), Angel Luis Rodriguez, Jose Justavino• (Camilo Aguirre 75) - Rene Victor Mendieta (Orlando Rodriguez 65), Publio Rodriguez◆49. Tr: Richard Parra
San Francisco - William Negrete - Osvaldo Gonzalez (Boris Alfaro 65), Rolando Algandona, Carlos Rivera, Wess Torres• - Juan Ramon Solis•, Manuel Torres• (c) - Ricardo Phillips, Victor Herrera - Johan De Avila•, Alberto Zapata (Luis Olivardia 80). Tr: Gary Stempel
Top scorers: **10** - Johan de Avila COL, San Francisco • **9** - Luis Renteria, Tauro • **7** - Auriel Gallardo, At. Chiriqui

MEDALS TABLE

		Overall			Lge		City/Town
		G	S	B	G	S	
1	Tauro FC	8	8		8	8	Panama City
2	San Francisco FC	6	6		6	6	La Chorrera
3	Deportivo Arabe Unido	6	3		6	3	Colon
4	CD Plaza Amador	5	2		5	2	Panama City
5	AFC Euro Kickers	1	2		1	2	Panama City
6	Panama Viejo FC	1			1		Panama City
7	Chorrillo FC		1			1	Panama City
8	Sporting Colon		1			1	Colon
9	Projusa		1			1	
		27	24		27	24	

PANAMA 2010-11

LIGA PROFESIONAL DE FUTBOL APERTURA

	Pl	W	D	L	F	A	Pts	Tauro	Arabe Unido	San Francisco	Chorrillo	Sporting	Plaza Amador	Alianza	Chiriquí	Chepo	Veragüense
Tauro †	18	11	4	3	27	14	37		3-1	1-2	1-1	0-0	2-0	1-0	2-2	2-0	1-0
Arabe Unido †	18	10	4	4	22	17	34	1-1		1-0	1-0	0-1	2-1	2-1	1-1	1-0	2-1
San Francisco †	18	9	6	3	26	18	33	2-0	2-1		2-2	0-0	2-2	1-1	0-1	3-0	1-0
Chorrillo †	18	7	6	5	23	20	27	0-3	0-1	1-1		1-1	1-2	1-0	4-1	1-0	2-0
Sporting San Miguelito	18	7	5	6	23	19	26	2-3	0-2	0-1	0-1		2-1	1-2	5-1	1-0	1-0
Plaza Amador	18	7	3	8	24	28	24	1-2	2-3	2-3	5-4	1-0		1-0	2-1	2-1	0-1
Alianza	18	6	5	7	21	18	23	1-2	2-0	1-2	0-0	2-3	1-1		2-1	1-0	1-1
Atlético Chiriquí	18	4	7	7	22	29	19	0-1	1-1	2-2	1-1	2-2	3-0	0-0		2-1	2-4
Chepo	18	4	2	12	12	21	14	1-0	1-2	2-0	1-1	0-0	0-2	0-1			2-1
Atlético Veragüense	18	3	2	13	13	29	11	1-0	0-1	0-2	1-2	1-3	0-1	1-4	1-0	0-3	

30/07/2010 - 17/12/2010 • † Qualified for the play-offs • Play-off semi-finals: Chorrillo 0-0 0-0 2-4p **Tauro**; San Francisco 0-0 0-0 2-3p **Arabe Un**
Final: **Tauro** 1-0 San Francisco • **Tauro** are the Clausura Champions
Estadio Rommel Fernandez, Panama City, 17-12-2010, Ref: Rodriguez. Scorer - Marcos Sanchez 45 for Tauro
Tauro - Varcan Sterling - Luis Moreno, Leonel Parrish, Eduardo Dasent, Juan Perez - Jhoan Melo (Carlos Martinez 72), Jean McLean, Marcos Sanchez, Alexander Moreno (Cristian Vega 62) - Temistocles Perez, Luis Renteria (Sergio Thompson 79). Tr: Juan Cubilla
San Francisco - Eric Hughes - Osvaldo Gonzalez (Ricardo Phillips 61), Rolando Algandona, Amir Withe, Wess Torres - Roderick Miller, Manuel Torres - Amilcar James, Roberto Brown - Johan De Avila, Gabriel Torres (Edgardo Panezo 67). Tr: Gary Stempel
Top scorer: **8** - Gabriel de los Rios, At. Chiriqui

PAR – PARAGUAY

FIFA/COCA-COLA WORLD RANKING

1993	1994	1995	1996	1997	1998	1999	2000	2001	2002	2003	2004	2005	2006	2007	2008	2009	2010
61	87	64	38	29	25	17	10	13	18	22	30	30	35	21	17	29	24

	2010											Hi/Lo
Jan	Feb	Mar	Mar	Apr	May	Jul	Aug	Sep	Oct	Nov	Dec	8
29	29	29	23	30	31	16	15	17	24	23	24	103

Paraguay may have only scored three goals at the 2010 FIFA World Cup in South Africa but that shouldn't detract from their best-ever performance at the finals. Under the astute guidance of their Argentine coach Gerardo Martino, the Paraguayans matched both Brazil and Argentina by reaching the quarter-finals before they were narrowly beaten 1-0 by Spain. Had a perfectly good first half goal from Nelson Valdez not been disallowed or had Oscar Cardozo scored from the penalty spot on the hour, matters may have been very different for the Paraguayans. They successfully disrupted the usual flow of the Spanish game and when the Spanish goal did come, it hit the post three times before finally crossing the line. Next stop for Paraguay - the 2011 Copa América in neighbouring Argentina and the hope of a first appearance in the final since last winning it in 1979. At home, Guaraní were the surprise champions in the 2009-10 Clausura which finished just prior to the World Cup. It was their first title for just over a quarter of a century and followed hot on the heels of Nacional's first title since 1949 - the two clubs ending a series of 10 championships won by either Libertad or Cerro Porteño. For the 2010-11 Apertura, however, it was back to business as usual with Libertad winning their seventh title since 2002, pipping Cerro Porteño to the post.

FIFA WORLD CUP RECORD

1930 9 r1 **1934-1938** DNE **1950** 11 r1 **1954** DNQ **1958** 12 r1 **1962-1982** DNQ **1986** 13 r2
1990-1994 DNQ **1998** 14 r2 **2002** 16 r2 **2006** 18 r1 **2010** 8 QF

ASOCIACION PARAGUAYA DE FUTBOL (APF)

Estadio de los Defensores del Chaco, Calle Mayor Martinez 1393, Asuncion
☎ +595 21 480120
📠 +595 21 480124
📧 secretaria@apf.org.py
🖥 www.apf.org.py
FA 1906 CON 1921 FIFA 1925
P Juan Angel Napout
GS Arturo Filartiga

FIFA BIG COUNT 2006

Total players	1 037 435
% of population	15.94%
Male	886 966
Female	150 469
Amateurs 18+	53 667
Youth under 18	29 984
Unregistered	950 000
Professionals	590
Referees	802
Admin & coaches	3 200
Number of clubs	1 696
Number of teams	3 500

MAJOR CITIES/TOWNS

		Population
1	Asunción	539 795
2	Ciudad del Este	338 885
3	Luque	293 267
4	Capiatá	291 591
5	San Lorenzo	283 280
6	Limpio	150 879
7	Ñemby	146 409
8	Lambaré	143 479
9	Fernando de la Mora	136 121
10	Itauguá	106 406
11	San Antonio	103 593
12	Mariano Roque Alonso	88 618
13	Villa Elisa	88 459
14	Encarnación	87 581
15	Pedro Juan Caballero	76 816
16	Hernandaríaz	73 115
17	Presidente Franco	68 493
18	Caaguazú	65 263
19	Coronel Oviedo	59 757

REPUBLICA DEL PARAGUAY • REPUBLIC OF PARAGUAY

Capital	Asunción	Population	6 995 655 (101)	% in cities	60%
GDP per capita	$4200 (153)	Area km²	406 752 km² (59)	GMT +/-	-4
Neighbours (km)	Argentina 1880, Bolivia 750, Brazil 1365				

RECENT INTERNATIONAL MATCHES PLAYED BY PARAGUAY

2008	Opponents	Score		Venue	Comp	Scorers	Att	Referee
15-06	Brazil	W	2-0	Asuncion	WCq	Santa Cruz [26], Cabanas [49]	38 000	Larrionda URU
18-06	Bolivia	L	2-4	La Paz	WCq	Santa Cruz [56], Valdez [82]	8 561	Gaciba BRA
20-08	Saudi Arabia	D	1-1	Nyon	Fr	Riveros [9]		Devoug SUI
6-09	Argentina	D	1-1	Buenos Aires	WCq	Heinze OG [13]	46 250	Simon BRA
9-09	Venezuela	W	2-0	Asuncion	WCq	Riveros [28], Valdez [45]	31 867	Baldassi ARG
11-10	Colombia	W	1-0	Bogota	WCq	Cabanas [9]	26 000	Lunati ARG
15-10	Peru	W	1-0	Asuncion	WCq	Cardozo [81]	31 545	Fagundes BRA
19-11	Oman	W	1-0	Muscat	Fr	Vera [37]		
2009								
11-02	Peru	W	1-0	Lima	Fr	Riveros [19]		Buckley PER
28-03	Uruguay	L	0-2	Montevideo	WCq		45 000	Simon BRA
1-04	Ecuador	D	1-1	Quito	WCq	Benitez [92+]	36 853	Roldan COL
6-06	Chile	L	0-2	Asuncion	WCq		34 000	Pezzotta ARG
10-06	Brazil	L	1-2	Recife	WCq	Cabanas [25]	56 682	Ruiz COL
12-08	Korea Republic	L	0-1	Seoul	Fr		22 631	Toma JPN
5-09	Bolivia	W	1-0	Asuncion	WCq	Cabanas [45p]	25 094	Carrillo PER
9-09	Argentina	W	1-0	Asuncion	WCq	Valdez [27]	38 000	Fagundes BRA
10-10	Venezuela	W	2-1	Puerto Ordaz	WCq	Cabanas [56], Cardozo [80]	41 680	Chandia CHI
14-10	Colombia	L	0-2	Asuncion	WCq		17 503	De Oliveira BRA
13-11	Qatar	L	0-2	Rouen	Fr			Lesage FRA
18-11	Netherlands	D	0-0	Heerenveen	Fr		25 000	Hrinak SVK
2010								
31-03	South Africa	D	1-1	Asuncion	Fr	Estigarribia [38]	7 738	Fagundes BRA
15-05	Korea DPR	W	1-0	Nyon	Fr	Santa Cruz [85p]	1 000	Bertolini SUI
25-05	Republic of Ireland	L	1-2	Dublin	Fr	Barrios [57]	16 722	Laperriere SUI
30-05	Côte d'Ivoire	D	2-2	Thonon-les-Bains	Fr	Barrios [75], Torres [90]	2 000	Bien FRA
2-06	Greece	W	2-0	Winterthur	Fr	Vera [9], Barrios [25]	5 200	Circhetta SUI
14-06	Italy	D	1-1	Cape Town	WCr1	Antolin Alcaraz [39]	62 869	Archundia MEX
20-06	Slovakia	W	2-0	Bloemfontein	WCr1	Enrique Vera [27], Cristian Riveros [86]	26 643	Maillet SEY
24-06	New Zealand	D	0-0	Polokwane	WCr1		34 850	Nishimura JPN
29-06	Japan	D	0-0	Pretoria	WCr2	W 5-3p	36 742	De Bleeckere BEL
3-07	Spain	L	0-1	Johannesburg	WCqf		55 359	Batres GUA
11-08	Costa Rica	W	2-0	Asuncion	Fr	Vera [8], Riveros [73]	22 000	Beligoy ARG
4-09	Japan	L	0-1	Yokohama	Fr		65 157	Rodriguez MEX
7-09	China PR	D	1-1	Nanjing	Fr	Barrios [8]	30 000	Wang Di CHN
9-10	Australia	L	0-1	Sydney	Fr		25 210	Nishimura JPN
12-10	New Zealand	W	2-0	Wellington	Fr	Valdez [22p], Martinez [28]	16 477	Cross NZL
17-11	Hong Kong	W	7-0	Hong Kong	Fr	Roque Santa Cruz 2 [4 32], Edgar Barreto [30], Jose Ortigoza 2 [46 54], Marcos Riveros [75], Cristian Riveros [90]	6 250	Mohd Salleh MAS

Fr = Friendly match • CA = Copa América • WC = FIFA World Cup • q = qualifier • r1 = 1st round • qf = quarter-final

PARAGUAY NATIONAL TEAM HISTORICAL RECORDS

Caps
110 - Carlos Gamarra 1993-2006 • 100 - Denis Caniza 1996- • 97 - Roberto Acuna 1993-2006 • 85 - Celso Ayala 1993-2003 • 83 - Justo Villar 1999- • 82 - Jose Cardozo 1991-2006 & Paulo Da Silva 2000- • 79 - Roque Santa Cruz 1999- • 78 - Roberto Fernandez 1976-89 • 77 - Juan Torales 1979-89 • 74 - Jose Luis Chilavert 1989-2003; Carlos Paredes 1998-2008 & Estanislao Struway 1991-2002 • 70 - Carlos Bonet 2002- & Julio Cesar Enciso 1995-2004 • 64 - Julio Cesar Caceres 2002- • 61 - Francisco Arce 1994-2004

Goals
25 - Jose Cardozo 1991-2006 • 23 - Roque Santa Cruz 1999- • 13 - Saturnino Arrua 1969-80 & Julio Cesar Romero 1979-86 • 12 - Carlos Gamarra 1993-2006 & Gerardo Rivas 1921-26 • 11 - Miguel Benitez 1996-99; Roberto Cabanas 1981-93 & Cristian Riveros 2005-

Past Coaches
Jose Laguna ARG 1921-22 • Manuel Fleitas Solich 1922-29 • Jose Laguna ARG 1929-45 • Manuel Fleitas Solich 1945-46 • Aurelio Gonzalez 1946-47 • Manuel Fleitas Solich 1947-51 • Julio Ramirez 1951-55 • Aurelio Gonzalez 1955-59 • Benjamin Laterza 1959-62 • Manuel Fleitas Solich 1962-65 • Aurelio Gonzalez 1965-74 • Benjamin Benitez 1974-76 • Ramon Rodriguez 1976-80 • Carlos Monin 1980-83 • Ranulfo Miranda 1983-85 • Cayetano Re 1986-88 • Eduardo Manera ARG 1988-89 • Ruben Valdez ESP 1990 • Carlos Kiese 1991-92 • Sergio Markarian URU 1992-93 • Alicio Solalinde 1993-94 • Laszlo Kubala ESP 1995 • Paulo Cesar Carpegiani BRA 1996-98 • Ever Almeida 1998-99 • Sergio Markarian URU 1999-2001 • Cesare Maldini ITA 2001-02 • Anibal Ruiz URU 2002-06 • Raul Amarilla 2006-07 • Gerardo Martino ARG 2007-

PARAGUAY 2010

DIVISION PROFESIONAL APERTURA

	Pl	W	D	L	F	A	Pts	Guaraní	Cerro	Olimpia	Libertad	Rubio Nu	Nacional	Luqueño	Sol	Trinidense	3 Febrero	Colombia	Tacuary
Guaraní †	22	15	4	3	43	20	49		1-2	2-1	1-0	3-2	2-2	2-0	3-1	2-0	1-1	1-0	5-2
Cerro Porteño	22	14	3	5	37	23	45	1-3		0-0	0-2	1-1	3-0	1-0	1-0	4-1	2-1	4-1	1-0
Olimpia	22	11	6	5	32	18	39	0-0	3-2		0-2	1-1	1-0	2-1	1-2	3-1	1-0	2-1	3-2
Libertad	22	11	5	6	33	15	38	2-1	3-0	0-0		2-1	0-0	0-1	3-4	0-1	3-0	3-0	0-0
Rubio Nu	22	10	8	4	36	25	38	1-1	0-3	1-0	2-1		4-1	0-0	5-0	1-1	0-2	2-1	3-1
Nacional	22	10	5	7	31	22	35	1-0	0-3	0-0	1-0	0-0		3-0	1-2	2-0	2-1	1-2	4-0
Sportivo Luqueño	22	5	10	7	26	30	25	1-2	3-1	1-1	1-2	2-2	1-1		1-0	3-3	0-0	2-3	3-3
Sol de América	22	7	4	11	27	39	25	0-1	1-2	2-1	1-4	0-1	2-5	1-1		1-1	3-1	1-2	1-0
Sportivo Trinidense	22	4	7	11	19	34	19	0-3	1-2	0-3	1-1	1-1	0-1	2-2	2-0		0-1	1-0	0-1
3 de Febrero	22	5	4	13	17	32	19	1-2	0-1	0-1	0-0	2-3	0-3	0-0	0-2	1-3		2-0	1-0
Sport Colombia	22	4	5	13	21	40	17	1-3	1-1	0-4	0-1	2-4	1-0	0-1	2-2	0-0	2-3		0-0
Tacuary	22	3	5	14	20	44	14	1-4	1-2	0-4	0-4	0-1	0-3	1-2	1-1	2-0	3-0	2-2	

30/01/2010 - 30/05/2010 • † Qualified for the Copa Libertadores
Top scorers: **16** - Rodrigo Teixeira BRA, Guarani & Pablo Zeballos, Cerro Porteño • **8** - Guillermo Beltran, Nacional & Nelson Cuevas, Olimpia

PARAGUAY 2010
DIVISION INTERMEDIA (2)

	Pl	W	D	L	F	A	Pts
General Caballero	26	14	8	4	38	22	50
Independiente	26	12	10	4	33	26	46
Sportivo San Lorenzo	26	11	9	6	31	24	42
Fernando de la Mora	26	9	10	7	34	25	37
Atlético Colegiales	26	10	7	9	29	31	37
Deportivo Caaguazú	26	9	8	9	32	36	35
Cerro Porteño PF	26	8	8	10	31	31	32
General Díaz	26	7	10	9	36	36	31
12 de Octubre	26	9	4	13	34	39	31
Deportivo Santaní	26	7	9	10	25	28	30
Sportivo Iteño	26	6	11	9	21	25	29
Deportivo Capiatá	26	6	11	9	27	36	29
2 de Mayo	26	6	10	10	27	35	28
Cerro Corá	26	6	9	11	27	31	27

20/03/2010 - 19/09/2010

MEDALS TABLE

		Overall			Lge		Sth Am			
		G	S	B	G	S	G	S	B	City
1	Olimpia	42	23	8	38	19	4	4	8	Asunción
2	Cerro Porteño	28	27	6	28	27			6	Asunción
3	Libertad	15	20	2	15	20			2	Asunción
4	Guaraní	10	12	1	10	12			1	Asunción
5	Nacional	7	9		7	9				Asunción
6	Sol de América	2	12		2	12				Vila Elisa
7	Sportivo Luqueño	2	4		2	4				Luque
8	Presidente Hayes	1			1					Tacumbu
9	Atlántida		3			3				Asunción
	River Plate		3			3				Asunción
11	12 de Octubre	1			1					Itaugua
12	Atlético Colegiales		1						1	Asunción

PARAGUAY 2010

DIVISION PROFESIONAL CLAUSURA

	Pl	W	D	L	F	A	Pts	Libertad	Cerro	Nacional	Guaraní	Olimpia	Rubio Nu	Colombia	Tacuary	Sol	3 Febrero	Trinidense	Luqueño
Libertad †	22	16	1	5	46	15	49		2-0	1-0	2-0	2-2	2-1	4-0	3-0	5-0	7-0	3-1
Cerro Porteño † ‡	22	13	7	2	36	18	46	2-0		1-1	2-1	1-1	2-0	0-0	1-3	2-0	3-0	3-1	1-1
Nacional ‡	22	12	6	4	29	18	42	1-0	0-0		0-1	0-2	0-0	4-3	1-0	2-0	1-0	4-1	2-0
Guaraní	22	10	6	6	29	22	36	2-0	1-2	0-0		0-0	1-2	3-0	1-0	1-0	2-1	0-1	1-0
Olimpia ‡	22	7	11	4	31	23	32	0-2	2-2	1-2	2-2		1-4	3-0	2-1	0-0	2-0	1-1	1-1
Rubio Nu	22	7	7	8	25	32	28	1-3	1-2	1-1	2-2	2-2		1-0	1-2	2-1	1-1	1-0	2-2
Sport Colombia	22	5	9	8	23	30	24	1-0	1-1	1-2	1-1	0-0	2-0		1-3	2-0	1-1	1-1	0-0
Tacuary	22	6	5	11	20	29	23	0-1	0-1	1-2	1-1	1-4	0-0	2-1		1-1	2-0	0-1	0-3
Sol de América	22	5	5	12	20	28	20	0-1	1-2	1-0	1-2	1-0	4-0	1-2	0-1		0-1	2-2	2-1
3 de Febrero	22	4	7	11	19	34	19	2-1	0-1	1-2	4-0	0-3	3-0	0-3	0-0	1-1		0-2	0-0
Sportivo Trinidense	22	3	9	10	25	46	18	1-2	1-5	3-3	1-4	1-2	1-2	2-2	1-1	1-3	1-1		2-2
Sportivo Luqueño	22	2	11	9	21	29	17	1-2	1-3	0-1	0-3	0-0	0-1	1-1	2-0	1-1	3-3	0-0	

16/07/2010 - 5/12/2010 • † Qualified for the Copa Libertadores • ‡ Qualified for the Copa Sudamericana
Sport Colombia & Trinidense relegated on three season average • Top scorers: **12** - Juan Carlos Ferreyra ARG, Olimpia & Roberto Nanni ARG, Cerro

PER – PERU

FIFA/COCA-COLA WORLD RANKING

1993	1994	1995	1996	1997	1998	1999	2000	2001	2002	2003	2004	2005	2006	2007	2008	2009	2010
73	72	69	54	38	72	42	45	43	82	74	66	66	70	63	75	68	68

	2010											Hi/Lo
Jan	Feb	Mar	Mar	Apr	May	Jul	Aug	Sep	Oct	Nov	Dec	34
68	68	61	60	53	53	38	39	48	55	52	68	91

With the national team restricted to a few friendlies in the second half of the year as the team prepared for the 2011 Copa América under new coach Sergio Makarian, attention was focused on club football with a major talking point the mass brawl during the championship final between León de Huanuco and Universidad San Martin. Under former international Franco Navarro, Huanuco, a small team from the mountains to the north of Lima, were making their first appearance in the final. After half an hour of the first leg in a packed stadium in Huanuco, a seemingly innocuous challenge led to an almighty fight between both teams which involved riot police trying to restore order. Four players were sent off before calm was restored and the match was resumed. Huanuco took the lead early in the second half but a late goal by San Martin's German Alemanno gave the club from the capital the advantage for the return. San Martin, who were only formed in 2004 and have almost no supporters, were aiming for a third title in four years but despite the majority of the crowd in the Monumental supporting Huanaco, the dentists, as San Martin are known, won 2-1 to claim the title. Earlier in the year they had become the first Peruvian team since 2004 to make it out of the group stages of the Copa Libertadores, but they then lost to Grêmio.

FIFA WORLD CUP RECORD

1930 10 r1 **1934** DNE **1938** DNQ **1950-1954** DNE **1958-1966** DNQ **1970** 7 QF **1974** DNQ **1978** 8 r2 **1982** 20 r1 **1986-2010** DNQ

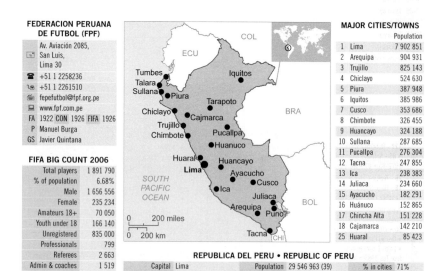

FEDERACION PERUANA DE FUTBOL (FPF)

Av. Aviación 2085,
San Luis,
Lima 30
☎ +51 1 2258236
📠 +51 1 2261510
✉ fepefutbol@fpf.org.pe
🖥 www.fpf.com.pe
FA 1922 CON 1926 FIFA 1926
P Manuel Burga
GS Javier Quintana

FIFA BIG COUNT 2006

Total players	1 891 790
% of population	6.68%
Male	1 656 556
Female	235 234
Amateurs 18+	70 050
Youth under 18	166 140
Unregistered	835 000
Professionals	799
Referees	2 663
Admin & coaches	1 519
Number of clubs	1 800
Number of teams	3 000

MAJOR CITIES/TOWNS

		Population
1	Lima	7 902 851
2	Arequipa	904 931
3	Trujillo	825 143
4	Chiclayo	524 630
5	Piura	387 948
6	Iquitos	385 986
7	Cusco	353 686
8	Chimbote	326 455
9	Huancayo	324 188
10	Sullana	287 685
11	Pucallpa	276 304
12	Tacna	247 855
13	Ica	238 383
14	Juliaca	234 660
15	Ayacucho	182 291
16	Huánuco	152 865
17	Chincha Alta	151 228
18	Cajamarca	142 210
25	Huaral	85 423

REPUBLICA DEL PERU • REPUBLIC OF PERU

Capital	Lima	Population 29 546 963 (39)	% in cities 71%
GDP per capita	$8500 (116)	Area km² 1 285 216 km² (20)	GMT + / - -5
Neighbours (km)	Bolivia 1075, Brazil 2995, Chile 171, Colombia 1800, Ecuador 1420 • Coast 2414		

RECENT INTERNATIONAL MATCHES PLAYED BY PERU

2007	Opponents	Score		Venue	Comp	Scorers	Att	Referee
22-08	Costa Rica	D	1-1	San Jose	Fr	Garcia.P 57		Mena CRC
8-09	Colombia	D	2-2	Lima	Fr	Guerrero 2 49 90	20 000	Carpio ECU
12-09	Bolivia	W	2-0	Lima	Fr	Vargas 15, Guerrero 36	15 000	Rivera PER
13-10	Paraguay	D	0-0	Lima	WCq		50 000	Simon BRA
17-10	Chile	L	0-2	Santiago	WCq		58 000	Ruiz COL
18-11	Brazil	D	1-1	Lima	WCq	Vargas 71	45 847	Torres PAR
21-11	Ecuador	L	1-5	Quito	WCq	Mendoza 86	28 557	Chandia CHI
2008								
6-02	Bolivia	L	1-2	La Paz	Fr	Garcia.P 70		
26-03	Costa Rica	W	3-1	Iquitos	Fr	Rengifo 32, Zambrano 46, Hidalgo 51		Buckley PER
31-05	Spain	L	1-2	Huelva	Fr	Rengifo 74	17 500	Meckarovski MKD
8-06	Mexico	L	0-4	Chicago	Fr			Geiger USA
14-06	Colombia	D	1-1	Lima	WCq	Marino 40	25 000	Torres PAR
17-06	Uruguay	L	0-6	Montevideo	WCq		20 016	Pozo CHI
6-09	Venezuela	W	1-0	Lima	WCq	Alva 39	25 500	Maldonado BOL
10-09	Argentina	D	1-1	Lima	WCq	Fano 93+	40 000	Amarilla PAR
11-10	Bolivia	L	0-3	La Paz	WCq		23 147	Buitrago COL
15-10	Paraguay	L	0-1	Asuncion	WCq		31 545	Fagundes BRA
2009								
6-02	El Salvador	L	0-1	Los Angeles	Fr			
11-02	Paraguay	L	0-1	Lima	Fr			Buckley PER
29-03	Chile	L	1-3	Lima	WCq	Fano 34	48 700	Amarilla PAR
1-04	Brazil	L	0-3	Porto Alegre	WCq		55 000	Pezzotta ARG
7-06	Ecuador	L	1-2	Lima	WCq	Vargas 52	17 050	Torres PAR
10-06	Colombia	L	0-1	Medellin	WCq		32 300	Simon BRA
5-09	Uruguay	W	1-0	Lima	WCq	Rengifo 86	15 000	Chandia CHI
9-09	Venezuela	L	1-3	Puerto La Cruz	WCq	Fuenmayor OG 41	31 703	Vera ECU
10-10	Argentina	L	1-2	Buenos Aires	WCq	Rengifo 89	38 019	Ortube BOL
14-10	Bolivia	W	1-0	Lima	WCq	Fano 54	4 373	Soto VEN
18-11	Honduras	W	2-1	Miami Gardens	Fr	Izaguirre OG 40, Rengifo 63		Jurisevic USA
2010								
4-09	Canada	W	2-0	Toronto	Fr	Jose Carlos Fernandez 68, Jean Tragodara 72	10 619	Jurisevic USA
7-09	Jamaica	W	2-1	Fort Lauderdale	Fr	OG 4, Jose Carlos Fernandez 85	5 217	Vaughn USA
8-10	Costa Rica	W	2-0	Lima	Fr	Luis Ramirez 3, Hernan Rengifo 5	15 000	Ponce ECU
12-10	Panama	L	0-1	Panama City	Fr		8 528	Cerdas CRC
17-11	Colombia	D	1-1	Bogota	Fr	Luis Ramirez 32	6 900	Laverni ARG

Fr = Friendly match • CA = Copa América • WC = FIFA World Cup • q = qualifier

PERU NATIONAL TEAM HISTORICAL RECORDS

Caps
127 - Roberto Palacios 1992-2009 • 104 - Hector Chumpitaz 1965-81 • 100 - Jorge Soto PER 1992-2005 • 97 - Juan Jose Jayo 1994-2008 • 95 - Nolberto Solano 1994-2009 • 89 - Ruben Diaz 1972-85 • 84 - Juan Reynoso • 83 - Percy Olivares 1987-2001 • 82 - Jose Velasquez 1972-85 • 81 - Teofilo Cubillas 1968-82 • 75 - Jose Soto 1992-2003 • 74 - Jose Del Solar 1986-2001 • 64 - Juan Carlos Oblitas 1973-85

Goals
26 - Teofilo Cubillas 1968-82 • 24 - Teodoro Fernandez 1935-47 • 20 - Nolberto Solano 1994-2009 • 19 - Roberto Palacios 1992-2009 • 18 - Hugo Sotil 1970-79 • 17 - Oswaldo Ramirez 1969-82 • 16 - Franco Navarro 1980-89 • 15 - Pedro Leon 1963-73 • 14 - Oscar Gomez Sanchez 1953-59 • 13 - Jorge Alcalde 1935-39 & Claudio Pizarro 1999-2007 • 12 - Jefferson Farfan 2003- & Jose Velasquez 1972-85

Past Coaches
Pedro Olivieri URU 1927 • Julio Borrelli URU 1929 • Francisco Bru ESP 1930-33 • Telmo Carbajo 1934-35 • Alberto Denegri 1936-37 • Jack Greenwell ENG 1938-39 • Domingo Arrillaga ESP 1940-41 • Angel Fernandez ARG 1942-45 • Jose Arana 1946-47 • Arturo Fernandez 1948-50 • Alfonso Huapaya 1951-52 • William Cook ENG 1953 • Angel Fernandez ARG 1953 • Juan Valdivieso 1954-55 • Arturo Fernandez 1956 • Gyorgy Orth HUN 1957-59 • Jorge de Almeyda BRA 1963 • Dan Georgiadis GRE 1964-65 • Marcos Calderon 1965-67 • Didi BRA 1968-70 • Lajos Baroti HUN 1971-72 • Roberto Scarone URU 1972-73 • Marcos Calderon 1975-79 • Jose Chiarella 1979 • Tim BRA 1980-82 • Juan Jose Tan 1983 • Moises Barack 1984-85 • Roberto Challe 1985-87 • Fernando Cuellar 1987 • Marcos Calderon 1987 • Pepe BRA 1988-89 • Miguel Company 1991 • Vladimir Popovic YUG 1992-93 • Miguel Company 1994-95 • Juan Carlos Oblitas 1996-99 • Francisco Maturana COL 1999-2000 • Julio Cesar Uribe 2000-02 • Paulo Autuori BRA 2003-05 • Freddy Ternero 2005-06 • Franco Navarro 2006 • Julio Cesar Uribe 2007 • Jose del Solar 2007-10 • Sergio Markarian URU 2010-

PERU 2010

PRIMERA DIVISION — FIRST STAGE

Column opponents (left→right): San Martin, Alianza, Universitario, Sp. Cristal, Inti Gas, Colegio Nac., José Gálvez, Total Chalaco, Huanuco, César Vallejo, Juan Aurich, Huancayo, Sport Boys, FBC Melgar, Cienciano, Alianza At.

Liguilla A

	Pl	W	D	L	F	A	Pts
Univ. San Martin †	44	28	7	9	87	39	92
Alianza Lima †	44	22	12	10	70	48	78
Universitario ‡	44	21	11	12	55	31	72
Sporting Cristal	44	18	10	16	58	54	64
Inti Gas Deportes	44	17	5	22	63	69	56
Colegio Nacional	44	16	8	20	58	71	52
José Gálvez	44	10	13	21	31	67	43
Total Chalaco	44	10	12	22	41	64	40

Results vs Liguilla B opponents (Huanuco, César Vallejo, Juan Aurich, Huancayo, Sport Boys, FBC Melgar, Cienciano, Alianza At.):
- Univ. San Martin: 3-2 1-0 1-0 2-1 2-1 0-1 3-0 4-0
- Alianza Lima: 4-3 0-2 1-0 4-0 4-1 2-1 2-1 3-0
- Universitario: 1-1 2-0 1-0 3-0 3-0 3-1 2-0 2-1
- Sporting Cristal: 1-0 0-1 1-1 4-1 1-1 3-1 0-1 2-1
- Inti Gas Deportes: 1-2 1-2 3-0 2-1 2-1 0-1 3-1 4-1
- Colegio Nacional: 2-4 0-1 1-1 3-1 5-1 1-0 3-0 2-1
- José Gálvez: 0-3 0-1 1-0 2-1 1-1 1-0 0-0
- Total Chalaco: 1-0 0-1 1-2 3-2 1-1 1-2 3-0 0-0

Liguilla B

	Pl	W	D	L	F	A	Pts
León de Huanuco †	44	24	9	11	77	44	81
Univ.César Vallejo ‡	44	19	11	14	64	48	70
Juan Aurich ‡	44	19	11	14	62	47	68
Sport Huancayo	44	17	8	19	64	60	59
Sport Boys	44	15	8	21	54	78	53
FBC Melgar	44	13	11	20	53	72	50
Cienciano	44	13	10	21	50	69	47
Alianza Atlético	44	10	14	20	45	71	44

Results vs Liguilla A opponents (San Martin, Alianza, Universitario, Sp. Cristal, Inti Gas, Colegio Nac., José Gálvez, Total Chalaco):
- León de Huanuco: 4-2 1-0 1-0 6-0 3-0 2-1 1-1 0-1
- Univ.César Vallejo: 2-0 1-1 0-1 2-3 1-0 2-0 3-0 1-2
- Juan Aurich: 1-1 1-1 2-1 2-2 1-0 1-1 3-0 2-1
- Sport Huancayo: 1-2 2-0 1-0 0-1 3-0 4-0 1-0 2-2
- Sport Boys: 0-1 2-1 1-2 1-2 1-1 2-4 2-1 3-2
- FBC Melgar: 1-4 4-2 0-4 1-1 2-1 1-1 2-0 1-1
- Cienciano: 1-3 2-1 1-1 3-3 2-0 4-0 0-3 5-2
- Alianza Atlético: 0-3 1-1 1-0 0-0 1-1 0-1 0-0 3-0

13/02/2010 - 5/12/2010 • Universidad San Martin and Leon de Huanuco qualified for the final • † Qualified for the Copa Libertadores • ‡ Qualified for the Copa Sudamericana • Stage One played over two rounds between all 16 teams. Teams are then split into two groups of eight with points taken forward to the second stage • Top scorers: 24 - Heber Arriola ARG, San Martin • 22 - Luis Perea COL, Huanuco • 21 - Sergio Almiron ARG, Colegio Nacional & Leonardo Mina Polo COL, Inti Gas • 19 - Miguel Ximenez URU, Sporting Cristal • 17 - Irvin Avila, Huancayo • 16 - Luis Tejada PAN, Juan Aurich & German Alemanno ARG, San Martin • 15 - Ricardo Ciciliano COL, Juan Aurich & Franco Mendoza ARG, Total Chalaco

CHAMPIONSHIP FINAL 2010

Heraclio Tapia, Huanuco, 8-12-2010, 13:30, Att: 18090, Ref: Garay

Huanuco	1	Zegarra 51
San Martin	1	Alemanno 89

Huanuco - Juan Angel Flores - Luis Guadalupe (c), Luis Cardoza, Gianfranco Espinoza, Gustavo Rodas◆34, Jean Ferrari, Carlos Zegarra (Daniel Hidalgo 92+), Victor Pena, Ever Chavez (Giulia Portilla 87), Luis Perea, Ronaille Calheira◆34. Tr: Franco Navarro

San Martin - Ricardo Farro - Orlan Contreras, Adan Balbin● (Atilio Muente 46), Aldo Corzo●, Christian Ramos◆34, Ronal Quinteros (Christian Cueva● 65), John Hinostroza (c), Carlo Fernandez, Pablo Vitti (Pedro Garcia 74), German Alemanno, Heber Arriola◆34. Tr: Anibal Ruiz

CHAMPIONSHIP FINAL 2010

Monumental, Lima, 12-12-2010, 15:30, Att: 35768, Ref: Rivera

San Martin	2	Garcia 14, Rodriguez 75
Huanuco	1	Perea 29

San Martin - Ricardo Farro - Guill Guizasola, Orlan Contreras, Atilio Muente, Adan Balbin, Aldo Corzo, Pedro Garcia (Braian Rodriguez 75), Ronal Quinteros, John Hinostroza (c), Pablo Vitti, German Alemanno. Tr: Anibal Ruiz

Huanuco - Juan Angel Flores● - Luis Guadalupe (c), Luis Cardoza, Guillermo Salas (Fernando Garcia● 44), Giulia Portilla (Daniel Hidalgo 70), Gianfranco Espinoza, Jean Ferrari, Carlos Zegarra●, Victor Pena (Christian Sanchez 25), Ever Chavez, Luis Perea●. Tr: Franco Navarro

San Martin, Huanco and Alianza Lima qualified for the Copa Libertadores

PERU 2010 — SEGUNDA DIVISION (2)

	Pl	W	D	L	F	A	Pts
Cobresol	18	12	5	1	36	7	41
Sport Ancash	18	12	2	4	33	17	38
Hijos de Acosvinchos	18	11	3	4	37	22	36
Deportivo Coopsol	18	9	5	4	32	14	32
Coronel Bolognesi	18	6	6	6	28	23	24
Atlético Mineiro	18	5	5	8	36	37	20
Atlético Torino	18	5	5	8	18	30	20
América Cochahuayco	18	5	3	10	22	22	18
Univ'dad San Marcos	18	5	2	11	20	27	17
Tecnologico	18	2	0	16	9	71	6

28/05/2010 - 17/10/2010

COPA PERU 2010

Semi-finals

Unión Comercio	2	4
Dep. Hospital *	0	1

* Home team in 1st leg

As. Dep. Tarma	0	2
Alianzia P-U *	3	0

Finals

Unión Comercio *	2	2
Alianza P-U	0	4

Union promoted to the Primera Division

MEDALS TABLE

		Overall			League			Sth Am			City
		G	S	B	G	S	B	G	S	B	
1	Universitario	25	14	18	25	13	14		1	4	Lima
2	Alianza	20	18	12	20	18	9			3	Lima
3	Sporting Cristal	15	16	6	15	15	6		1		Lima
4	Sport Boys	6	7	5	6	7	5				Callao
5	Universidad San Martin	3			3						Lima
6	Deportivo Municipal	4	7	6	4	7	6				Lima
7	Atlético Chalaco	2	5	4	2	5	4				Callao
8	Mariscal Sucre	2	2	2	2	2	2				Lima
9	Unión Huaral	2	1		2	1					Huaral
10	Cienciano	1		4			4	1			Cusco
11	FBC Melgar	1	1	2	1	1	2				Arequipa
12	Defensor Lima	1		4	1		3			1	Lima
13	Centro Iqueño	1		3	1		3				Chancay
14	Colegio San Agustín	1	1		1	1					Lima
15	Sport Progreso	1			1						Lima
16	Juan Aurich		1	3		1	3				Chiclayo
17	Defensor Arica		1	2		1	2				Arica

PHI – PHILIPPINES

FIFA/COCA-COLA WORLD RANKING

1993	1994	1995	1996	1997	1998	1999	2000	2001	2002	2003	2004	2005	2006	2007	2008	2009	2010
163	171	166	166	175	175	181	179	175	181	189	188	191	171	179	160	167	150

	2010												Hi/Lo
	Jan	Feb	Mar	Mar	Apr	May	Jul	Aug	Sep	Oct	Nov	Dec	**150**
	167	167	169	167	170	169	167	165	165	152	151	150	**195**

The Philippines national team took part in the very first international match on Asian soil way back in 1913 when they beat China 2-1 in the Far-Eastern Games but for almost all of the 97 years since football has barely registered in the national psyche. The national team's extraordinary 2-0 victory over Vietnam in the 2010 AFF Suzuki Cup in Hanoi may just start to change that. American magazine Sports Illustrated listed the Philippines victory in its top ten soccer stories of 2010 but it is a story that can trace its roots back to the other side of the world in England, where players with Filipino roots have been encouraged to play for the national team. Key figures in this have been the Younghusband brothers, products of the Chelsea youth system, and the Greatwich brothers from Brighton who have persuaded the likes of goalkeeper Neil Etheridge of Fulham to join the ranks. At the AFF Suzuki Cup - Southeast Asia's premier football tournament - the victory over hosts Vietnam saw the Philippines, coached by Englishman Simon McMenemy, qualify for the semi-finals for the first time. Lack of a suitable stadium in Manila meant that home advantage was ceded against Indonesia and both matches in Jakarta ended in 1-0 defeats. However, almost 100 years after their first match, the Philippines national team is finally starting to make waves.

FIFA WORLD CUP RECORD
1930-1994 DNE 1998-2002 DNQ 2006-2010 DNE

PHILIPPINE FOOTBALL FEDERATION (PFF)

No 27 Danny Floro, Corner Capt Henry Javiers Sts., Pasig City, Metro Manila 1600

☎ +63 2 5712871

📠 +63 2 5712872

✉ philippine_football_federation @yahoo.com

🖥 www.the-pff.com

FA 1907 CON 1954 FIFA 1930

P Mariano Araneta

GS Ramon Manuel

FIFA BIG COUNT 2006

Total players	1 548 746
% of population	1.87%
Male	1 548 746
Female	120 019
Amateurs 18+	20 910
Unregistered	340 090
Professionals	0
Referees	167
Admin & coaches	132
Number of clubs	75
Number of teams	229

MAJOR CITIES/TOWNS

		Population
1	Manila	11 165 131
2	Davao	1 627 171
3	Cebu	821 499
4	Zamboanga	762 624
5	Dasmariñas	711 476
6	Dadiangas	657 891
7	Antipolo	628 923
8	Calamba	560 456
9	Cagayan	545 873
10	Bacolod	484 099
11	Bacoor	469 925
12	Iloilo	421 924
13	San Jose	397 951
14	Mandaue	394 174
15	Batangas	388 989
16	Cainta	370 873
17	Iligan	367 763
18	Cabanatuan	357 768
19	Butuan	354 151

REPUBLIKA NG PILIPINAS • REPUBLIC OF THE PHILIPPINES

Capital Manila	Population 97 976 603 (12)	% in cities 65%
GDP per capita $3300 (161)	Area km² 300 000 km² (72)	GMT +/- +8
Neighbours (km) Coast 36 289		

RECENT INTERNATIONAL MATCHES PLAYED BY THE PHILIPPINES

2006 Opponents		Score	Venue	Comp	Scorers	Att	Referee
26-03 Thailand	L	0-5	Chonburi	Fr			
1-04 Chinese Taipei	L	0-1	Chittagong	CCrl		4 000	Lee Gi Young KOR
3-04 India	D	1-1	Chittagong	CCrl	Valeroso [19]	2 000	Mujghef JOR
5-04 Afghanistan	D	1-1	Chittagong	CCrl	Valeroso [59]	3 000	Mujghef JOR
12-11 Laos	L	1-2	Bacolod	AFFq	Greatwich [62]		
14-11 Timor Leste	W	7-0	Bacolod	AFFq	Younghusband 4 [22 25p 36 69], Greatwich [30], Zerrudo [51], Caligdong [82]		
18-11 Cambodia	W	1-0	Bacolod	AFFq	Borromeo [81p]		
20-11 Brunei Darussalam	W	4-1	Bacolod	AFFq	Del Rosario [25], Younghusband 2 [59 90], Caligdong [73]		
2007							
7-01 Singapore	L	1-4	Singapore	Fr	Younghusband [19p]	2 000	
12-01 Malaysia	L	0-4	Bangkok	AFFq		5 000	Daud SIN
14-01 Thailand	L	0-4	Bangkok	AFFq		30 000	
16-01 Myanmar	D	0-0	Bangkok	AFFq		500	Daud SIN
2008							
13-05 Brunei Darusalam	W	1-0	Iloilo City	CCq	Caligdong [28]	3 500	Saleem MDV
15-05 Tajikistan	D	0-0	Iloilo City	CCq		4 500	Al Badwawi UAE
17-05 Bhutan	W	3-0	Iloilo City	CCq	Gould [41], Younghusband [43], Pema OG [58]	7 000	Saleem MDV
17-10 Timor-Leste	W	1-0	Phnom Penh	AFFq	Borromeo [68]	15 000	
19-10 Brunei-Darussalam	D	1-1	Phnom Penh	AFFq	Gould [40]	12 000	
21-10 Laos	L	1-2	Phnom Penh	AFFq	Araneta [32]		
23-10 Cambodia	W	3-2	Phnom Penh	AFFq	Borromeo [19], Greatwich [36], Gould [53]	15 000	
2009							
14-04 Bhutan	W	1-0	Male	CCq	Gould [13]	200	Lazeem IRQ
16-04 Maldives	L	2-3	Male	CCq	Borromeo [11], Gould [92+]	9 000	Faghani IRN
18-04 Turkmenistan	L	0-5	Male	CCq		400	Al Ghafary JOR
2010							
16-01 Chinese Taipei	D	0-0	Kaohsiung	Fr			
9-10 Hong Kong	L	2-4	Kaohsiung	Fr	Younghusband.P 2 [58p 69]	650	Kao Jung Fang TPE
10-10 Chinese Taipei	D	1-1	Kaohsiung	Fr	Araneta [93+]	890	Kao Tsai Hu TPE
12-10 Macau	W	5-0	Kaohsiung	Fr	Caligdong [6], Araneta 3 [13 54 90], Younghusband.J [48]	700	Yu Ming Hsun TPE
22-10 Timor-Leste	W	5-0	Vientiane	AFFq	Araneta 3 [27 41 57], Younghusband.P [30p], Del Rosario [32]		Leow SIN
24-10 Laos	D	2-2	Vientiane	AFFq	Younghusband.P [76p], Younghusband.J [94+]	2 000	Pechsri THA
26-10 Cambodia	D	0-0	Vientiane	AFFq			Abdul Wahab MAS
2-12 Singapore	D	1-1	Hanoi	AFFr1	Greatwich [93+]		Mahapab THA
5-12 Vietnam	W	2-0	Hanoi	AFFr1	Greatwich [38], Younghusband.P [79]	40 000	Napitupulu IDN
8-12 Myanmar	D	0-0	Nam Dinh	AFFr1			Patwal IND
16-12 Indonesia	L	0-1	Jakarta	AFFsf		70 000	Moradi IRN
19-12 Indonesia	L	0-1	Jakarta	AFFsf		88 000	Ebrahim BHR

Fr = Friendly match • AFF = ASEAN Football Federation Championship • CC = AFC Challenge Cup • q = qualifier • r1 = 1st round

PHILIPPINES NATIONAL TEAM HISTORICAL RECORDS

Past Coaches Alan Rogers ENG 1962-63 • Danny McLennan SCO 1963 • Carlos Cavagnaro ARG 1989 • Eckhard Krautzun GER 1991-92 • Noel Casilao 1993-96 • Juan Cutillas ESP 1996-2000 • Rodolfo Alicante 2000 • Masataka Imai JPN 2001 • Sugao Kambe JPN 2002-03 • Aris Caslib 2004-07 • Norman Fegidero 2008 • Juan Cutillas ESP 2008-09 • Aris Caslib 2009 • Des Bulpin ENG 2009-10 • Simon McMenemy ENG 2010 • Michael Weiss GER 2011-

PLE – PALESTINE

FIFA/COCA-COLA WORLD RANKING

1993	1994	1995	1996	1997	1998	1999	2000	2001	2002	2003	2004	2005	2006	2007	2008	2009	2010
-	-	-	-	-	184	170	171	145	151	139	126	137	128	165	179	173	177

2010												Hi/Lo
Jan	Feb	Mar	Mar	Apr	May	Jul	Aug	Sep	Oct	Nov	Dec	**115**
173	172	173	173	174	173	171	171	173	178	178	177	**191**

Palestine made significant strides forward in 2010 especially behind the scenes with PFA president Jibril Al Rajoub and former FIFA official Jerome Champagne charged with overhauling the administration of the game in the territories and with planning the launch of a professional league. At present Palestinian clubs play in competitions that are restricted to either the West Bank or the Gaza Strip and forming a unified structure is made difficult by the travel restrictions imposed by the Israelis. In a major breakthrough Palestinian clubs will take part in AFC competitions for the first time in 2011, with participation in the AFC President's Cup. In 2010 Jabal Mukabar won the West Bank Premier League for the first time while Gaza Sports Club beat Al Sadaqa in the final of the Gaza Strip Sport Union Championship. The major cup competition, the Yasser Arafat Cup was won by Wadi Al Neiss who in 2009 had represented Palestine in the Arab Champions League. Having qualified for the 2010 tournament as the 2009 West Bank champions they were denied the chance of taking part when the tournament was cancelled. It was a quiet year for the Palestinian national team with just four matches played, two of them at the West Asian Championship in Jordan, but they were knocked out at the end of the group stage after losing to Yemen and Iraq.

FIFA WORLD CUP RECORD
1930-1998 DNE 2002-2010 DNQ

PALESTINE FOOTBALL ASSOCIATION (PFA)

PO Box 4373,
Ramallah-Al Bireh

☎ +972 2 2959102
📠 +972 2 2959101
✉ info@pfa.ps
🖥 www.pfa.ps
FA 1928 CON 1998 FIFA 1998
P Jibril Al Rajoub
GS Abdelmajeed Hijjeh

FIFA BIG COUNT 2006

Total players	92 160
% of population	2.43%
Male	87 060
Female	5 100
Amateurs 18+	5 500
Youth under 18	13 200
Unregistered	22 100
Professionals	0
Referees	301
Admin & coaches	494
Number of clubs	40
Number of teams	66

MAJOR CITIES/TOWNS

		Population
1	Gaza	674 309
2	Jabaliya	251 324
3	Khan Yunis	250 817
4	Hebron	229 258
5	Nablus	182 734
6	Rafah	181 619
7	al-Nusayrat	89 954
8	Dayr al-Balah	86 229
9	Bayt Lahya	85 096
10	Tulkarm	62 006
11	Qalqilya	61 903
12	Yatta	59 240
13	al-Birah	54 954
14	al-Burayj	50 681
15	Jenin	48 813
16	Bayt Hanun	46 028
17	Bani Suhalyah	45 651
18	Bethlehem	41 176
19	Ramallah	35 439

PALESTINE

Capital	Ramallah	Population	3 636 195 (130)	% in cities	72%
GDP per capita	$2900 (164)	Area km²	6 200 km² (171)	GMT +/-	+2
Neighbours (km)	For the West Bank and Gaza: Israel 358, Jordan 97, Egypt 11 • Coast 40				

RECENT INTERNATIONAL MATCHES PLAYED BY PALESTINE

2008 Opponents	Score		Venue	Comp	Scorers	Att	Referee
7-08 Iran	L	0-3	Tehran	WAr1		5 000	Delo SYR
9-08 Qatar	L	0-1	Tehran	WAr1			
26-10 Jordan	D	1-1	Ram	Fr	Keshkesh [4]		
2009							
26-03 Nepal	D	0-0	Kathmandu	CCq		12 000	El Haddad LIB
30-03 Kyrgyzstan	D	1-1	Kathmandu	CCq	Said Alsbakhi [29]	2 000	Yu Ming Hsun TPE
10-07 Iraq	L	0-3	Arbil	Fr			
13-07 Iraq	L	0-4	Baghdad	Fr			
18-07 China PR	L	1-3	Tianjin	Fr	Keshkesh [88p]		
10-10 UAE	D	1-1	Dubai	Fr	Al Amour [35]		
2010							
4-06 Sudan	D	1-1	Omdurman	Fr	Jamal [45]		
11-08 Mauritania	D	0-0	Nouakchott	Fr			
27-09 Yemen	L	1-3	Amman	WAr1	Obeid [79]	4 500	
29-09 Iraq	L	0-3	Amman	WAr1		4 000	

Fr = Friendly match • AC = AFC Asian Cup • CC = AFC Challenge Cup • WA = West Asian Championship • WC = FIFA World Cup
q = qualifier • r1 = 1st round

PALESTINE NATIONAL TEAM HISTORICAL RECORDS

Past Coaches
Ricardo Carugati ARG 1998 • Ricardo Carugati ARG & Azmi Nassar 1999 • Azmi Nassar 2000 • Mansour Hamid El Bouri EGY 2000 • Mustafa Abdel Ghali Yacoub EGY 2001 • Andrzej Wisniewski POL 2002 • Nicola Hadwa Shahwan 2002-04 • Alfred Riedl AUT 2004 • Ghassan Balawi 2004 • Tamas Viczko HUN 2004 • Azmi Nassar 2005-07 • Nelson Dekmak 2007 • Naeem Swerky 2008 • Izzat Hamza 2008-09 • Jamal Daraghmeh 2009 • Mousa Bezaz ALG 2009-

PALESTINE 2009-10
GAZA STRIP SPORT UNION CHAMPIONSHIP

Quarter-finals		Semi-finals		Final	
Gaza SC	1				
Al Salah	0	**Gaza SC**	1 3p		
Al Shejaia	0	Khidmat Rafah	1 0p		
Khidmat Rafah	2			**Gaza SC**	3
Shabab Rafah	2			Al Sadaqa	0
S. Khan Younes	1	Shabab Rafah	1 4p		
Jama'ee Rafah	1	**Al Sadaqa**	1 5p	18-07-2010	
Al Sadaqa	2				

YASSER ARAFAT CUP 2010

Semi-finals		Finals	
Wadi Al-Neiss	2		
Shabab Al Khalil	1		
		Wadi Al-Neiss	1
		Shabab Al-Am'ari	0
Jabal Mukabar	1		
Shabab Al Am'ari	2	18-08-2010	

PALESTINE 2009-10

WEST BANK PREMIER LEAGUE	Pl	W	D	L	F	A	Pts	Jabal Mukabar	Hilal Jerusalem	Shabab Al-Am'ari	Wadi Al-Neiss	Thagafi Tulkarm	Shabab Al Khalil	Markaz Tulkarm	Al-Thahriyeh	Al-Bireh	Shabab Ubeidieh	Beit Ummar	Al-Khader
Jabal Mukabar	22	15	4	3	43	19	49		2-1	2-1	2-1	1-0	3-1	0-1	1-0	2-3	2-1	6-1	7-1
Hilal Jerusalem	22	12	6	4	43	19	42	1-1		0-0	3-0	1-0	2-0	2-1	4-1	6-0	1-0	3-2	3-2
Shabab Al-Am'ari	22	13	3	6	42	22	42	0-1	2-2		2-1	3-0	0-1	4-1	4-2	1-0	6-0	3-2	2-0
Wadi Al-Neiss	22	11	6	5	36	23	39	0-1	1-1	1-0		1-0	0-1	0-0	1-1	2-0	5-1	3-1	2-0
Thagafi Tulkarm	22	11	2	9	39	31	35	1-0	0-2	1-2	1-2		1-1	2-1	1-1	3-2	4-1	3-2	3-2
Shabab Al Khalil	22	9	7	6	36	26	34	2-2	1-1	2-1	0-2	2-0		0-0	1-2	3-2	5-1	1-0	3-0
Markaz Tulkarm	22	9	5	8	25	32	32	1-1	0-6	2-1	1-2	0-1	1-1		2-0	0-1	3-1	1-0	2-1
Al-Thahriyeh	22	8	6	8	32	28	30	1-2	1-1	1-2	1-2	3-1	2-0	0-1		1-1	1-1	1-0	2-1
Al-Bireh	22	8	5	9	36	32	29	0-1	1-0	1-3	1-1	1-2	3-2	5-1	0-0		0-0	2-2	8-0
Shabab Al Ubeidieh	22	4	8	10	24	47	20	0-1	1-0	1-1	3-3	3-5	2-2	3-3	1-4	1-0		0-0	1-0
Beit Ummar	22	2	3	17	20	52	9	2-2	0-3	0-2	2-4	0-1	0-6	0-1	0-3	1-3	0-1		1-0
Al-Khader	22	1	3	18	19	64	6	0-3	2-0	1-2	1-1	1-9	1-1	1-2	1-4	0-2	1-1	3-5	

16/08/2004 - 9/04/2010

PNG – PAPUA NEW GUINEA

FIFA/COCA-COLA WORLD RANKING

1993	1994	1995	1996	1997	1998	1999	2000	2001	2002	2003	2004	2005	2006	2007	2008	2009	2010
-	-	-	169	167	172	183	192	196	167	172	161	166	178	183	201	203	203

2010												Hi/Lo
Jan	Feb	Mar	Mar	Apr	May	Jul	Aug	Sep	Oct	Nov	Dec	**160**
203	203	203	202	202	202	202	202	203	203	203	203	**203**

2010 turned out to be an extraordinary year for football in Papua New Guinea, a year that fans in the country hope will see the start of a boom in the game. Having won a third consecutive National Soccer League title in 2009, Hekari United secured their ticket for the 2009-10 OFC Champions League. Grouped once again in the non-New Zealand half of the draw, there was genuine hope of qualifying for the final having come so close in 2009. A defeat at home to Fiji's Lautoka in the second match seemed to have scuppered Hekari's hopes, especially after having drawn the opener against Tafea, but they stormed through the rest of the group winning their last four games to qualify for the final against New Zealand's Waitakere United. No-one gave them a chance against a team containing former English football League professionals, but in the first leg in Port Moresby they stunned the Kiwis with a 3-0 victory. It was a result that ranked amongst the most notable of the year and although they lost the return 2-1, Hekari were crowned Oceania champions and had unbelievably qualified for the FIFA Club World Cup in Abu Dhabi. That adventure didn't last long with defeat at the hands of the UAE's Al Wahda, but for the first time ever Papua New Guinea had enjoyed a brief moment in the spotlight, the first they hope of many.

FIFA WORLD CUP RECORD
1930-1994 DNE 1998 DNQ 2002 DNE 2006 DNQ 2010 DNE

PAPUA NEW GUINEA FOOTBALL ASSOCIATION (PNGFA)

📠 PO Box 957, Lae 411, Morobe Province
☎ +675 4751398
📠 +675 4751399
✉ pngfa@yahoo.com
🖥 www.pngfootball.com.pg
FA 1962 CON 1966 FIFA 1963
P David Chung
GS Dimirit Mileng

FIFA BIG COUNT 2006

Total players	196 900
% of population	3.47%
Male	188 900
Female	8 000
Amateurs 18+	7 700
Youth under 18	59 200
Unregistered	57 100
Professionals	0
Referees	1 200
Admin & coaches	5 200
Number of clubs	440
Number of teams	1 100

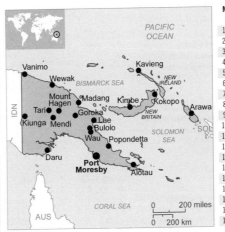

MAJOR CITIES/TOWNS

		Population
1	Port Moresby	307 643
2	Lae	72 967
3	Arawa	39 741
4	Mount Hagen	39 003
5	Popondetta	37 793
6	Mendi	37 163
7	Kokopo	32 957
8	Madang	26 897
9	Kimbe	22 811
10	Bulolo	19 106
11	Goroka	18 192
12	Daru	17 288
13	Kavieng	17 248
14	Wewak	16 698
15	Wau	16 350
16	Kiunga	14 879
17	Alotau	13 928
18	Tari	12 457
19	Vanimo	12 129

PAPUANIUGINI • PAPUA NEW GUINEA

Capital	Port Moresby	Population	6 057 263 (106)	% in cities	12%
GDP per capita	$2300 (181)	Area km²	462 840 km² (54)	GMT +/-	+10
Neighbours (km)	Indonesia 820 • Coast 5152				

RECENT INTERNATIONAL MATCHES PLAYED BY PAPUA NEW GUINEA

2004 Opponents	Score	Venue	Comp	Scorers	Att	Referee
10-05 Vanuatu	D 1-1	Apia	WCq	Wasi 73	500	Breeze AUS
12-05 Fiji	L 2-4	Apia	WCq	Davani 12, Komboi 44	400	Diomis AUS
17-05 American Samoa	W 10-0	Apia	WCq	Davani 4 23 24 40 79, Lepani 3 26 28 64, Wasi 34 Komboi 37, Lohai 71	150	Afu SOL
19-05 Samoa	W 4-1	Apia	WCq	Davani 16, Lepani 2 37 55, Komeng 68	300	Diomis AUS

2005

No international matches played in 2005

2006

No international matches played in 2006

2007

| 13-07 Solomon Islands | L 1-2 | Honiara | Fr | Davani | | |

2008

No international matches played in 2008

2009

No international matches played in 2009

2010

No international matches played in 2010

Fr = Friendly match • OC = OFC Nations Cup • SP = South Pacific Games • WC = FIFA World Cup • q = qualifier • r1 = first round group

PAPUA NEW GUINEA 2009-10

NATIONAL SOCCER LEAGUE

	Pl	W	D	L	F	A	Pts	Hekari	Rapatona	Gigira	Inter	Eastern	Tukoko	Gelle Hills	Madang	Besta
Hekari United †	15	13	1	1	59	14	**40**		1-1	3-1	2-0	5-1	3-1	5-1	N/p	10-0
Rapatona Tigers †	16	6	8	2	30	23	**26**	2-6		2-0	1-1	2-2	6-2	0-0	3-1	1-2
Gigira Laitepo Morobe†	16	7	4	5	29	23	**25**	0-3	2-2		2-2	3-4	1-0	2-0	3-0	3-0
University Inter †	16	6	6	4	25	18	**24**	1-0	0-0	1-0		2-3	2-3	4-1	2-0	1-1
Eastern Stars	16	7	3	6	37	36	**24**	3-4	1-2	1-5	2-0		1-1	1-2	3-2	3-1
Tukoko University	16	6	5	5	30	34	**23**	1-5	1-1	1-1	1-1	1-3		3-0	5-3	3-3
Gelle Hills United	16	4	3	9	14	29	**15**	0-3	1-2	1-2	0-0	2-1	0-1		0-2	2-2
Madang Niupetro Fox	15	2	4	9	22	33	**10**	1-3	1-1	2-2	2-4	2-2	1-2	1-2		1-1
Besta (PNGFA U-20)	16	1	4	11	19	55	**7**	1-6	2-4	1-2	0-4	2-6	3-4	0-2	0-3	

14/11/2009 - 3/04/2010 • † Qualified for the play-off semi-finals

PLAY-OFFS

Semi-finals

Hekari United	7
University Inter	1

Rapatona Tigers	0
Gigira Laitepo Morobe	1

Finals

Hekari United †	5
Gigira Laitepo Morobe	0

† Qualified for OFC Champions League

Final: Lloyd Robson Oval, Port Moresby, 24-04-2010
Scorers - Kema Jack 2 30 32, Alick Maemae 40p, David Muta 65, Benjamin Mela 85

MEDALS TABLE

		Overall G	S	Lge G	S	OFC G	S	Town
1	Hekari United	5		4		1		Port Moresby
2	Gelle Hills United		2	2				Port Moresby
3	Rapatona Tigers		1	1				Port Moresby
4	Gigira Rapatona Morobe		1	1				Lae
5	Eastern Stars							Milne Bay
	Madang Niupetro Fox							Madang
	Tukoko University							Lae
	University Inter							Port Moresby

POL – POLAND

FIFA/COCA-COLA WORLD RANKING

1993	1994	1995	1996	1997	1998	1999	2000	2001	2002	2003	2004	2005	2006	2007	2008	2009	2010
28	29	33	53	48	31	32	43	33	34	25	25	22	24	22	34	58	73

2010												Hi/Lo
Jan	Feb	Mar	Mar	Apr	May	Jul	Aug	Sep	Oct	Nov	Dec	16
58	57	59	59	58	58	56	56	66	69	71	73	73

Wisla Krakow were denied a hat trick of league titles by a resurgent Lech Poznan team in what proved to be an exciting end to the season. In the penultimate match, long-time league leaders Wisla were ahead against local rivals Cracovia heading into injury-time but conceded an own goal through Mariusz Jop to level the scores. At the same moment Lech midfielder Sergei Krivets scored a dramatic winner against Ruch Chorzow to put them a point ahead going into the final round. They then made certain of their first title since 1993 with a 2-0 victory against Zaglebie Lubin. There were first time winners in the Cup with Jagiellonia Bialystok beating second division Pogon Szczecin 1-0 in the final thanks to a goal from their Lithuanian defender Andrius Skerla. Jagiellonia also managed to avoid relegation from the Ekstraklasa, despite starting the season with a ten-point penalty. With Euro 2012 looming, Polish preparations for the tournament were on schedule off the pitch - if not on it. Franciszek Smuda's first year as coach of the national team saw victories over a number of lesser ranked nations but a 6-0 defeat at the hands of soon to be world champions Spain mid-way through a run of eight games without a win, left Polish fans fearing the worst when the cream of Europe's teams descend on the country in June 2012.

FIFA WORLD CUP RECORD

1930 DNE **1934** DNQ **1938** 11 r1 **1950-1954** DNE **1958-1970** DNQ **1974** 3 r2 **1978** 5 r2
1982 3 SF **1986** 14 r2 **1990-1998** DNQ **2002** 25 r1 **2006** 21 r1 **2010** DNQ

POLISH FOOTBALL ASSOCIATION (PZPN)

Bitwy Warszawskiej 1920 r.7, Warsaw 02-366

☎ +48 22 5512253
📠 +48 22 5512240
✉ pzpn@pzpn.pl
🖥 www.pzpn.pl
FA 1919 CON 1954 FIFA 1923
P Grzegorz Lato
GS Zdzislaw Krecina

FIFA BIG COUNT 2006

Total players	2 000 264
% of population	5.19%
Male	1 817 819
Female	182 445
Amateurs 18+	465 854
Youth under 18	185 808
Unregistered	424 300
Professionals	1 202
Referees	11 658
Admin & coaches	60 100
Number of clubs	5 690
Number of teams	13 245

MAJOR CITIES/TOWNS

		Population
1	Warsaw	1 707 566
2	Kraków	755 192
3	Lódz	743 898
4	Wroclaw	631 154
5	Poznan	557 972
6	Gdánsk	453 404
7	Szczecin	405 539
8	Bydgoszcz	357 833
9	Lublin	350 387
10	Katowice	308 170
11	Bialystok	296 227
12	Gdynia	249 946
13	Czestochowa	241 063
14	Radom	223 424
15	Sosnowiec	219 551
16	Torun	204 891
17	Kielce	204 550
18	Zabrze	187 349
36	Chorzow	111 794

RZECZPOSPOLITA POLSKA • REPUBLIC OF POLAND

Capital	Warsaw	Population	38 482 919 (34)	% in cities	61%
GDP per capita	$17 800 (69)	Area km²	312 685 km² (69)	GMT +/-	+1
Neighbours (km)	Belarus 605, Czech Republic 615, Germany 456, Lithuania 91, Russia 432, Slovakia 420, Ukraine 428 • Coast 440				

RECENT INTERNATIONAL MATCHES PLAYED BY POLAND

2008 Opponents		Score	Venue	Comp	Scorers	Att	Referee
8-06 Germany	L	0-2	Klagenfurt	ECr1		30 461	Ovrebø NOR
12-06 Austria	D	1-1	Vienna	ECr1	Guerreiro 30	51 428	Webb ENG
16-06 Croatia	L	0-1	Klagenfurt	ECr1		30 461	Vassaras GRE
20-08 Ukraine	L	0-1	Lviv	Fr		22 000	Nalbandian ARM
6-09 Slovenia	D	1-1	Wroclaw	WCq	Zewlakow 17p	7 300	Jakobsson ISL
10-09 San Marino	W	2-0	Serravalle	WCq	Smolarek 36, Lewandowski.R 66	2 374	Zografos GRE
11-10 Czech Republic	W	2-1	Chorzow	WCq	Brozek 27, Blaszczykowski 53	38 293	Stark GER
15-10 Slovakia	L	1-2	Bratislava	WCq	Smolarek 70	17 650	Layec FRA
19-11 Republic of Ireland	W	3-2	Dublin	Fr	Lewandowski.M 3, Guerreiro 47, Lewandowski.R 89	50 566	Jakobsson IRL
14-12 Serbia	W	1-0	Antalya	Fr	Boguski 56	100	Dereli TUR
2009							
7-02 Lithuania	D	1-1	Faro-Loule	Fr	Brozek 11	150	Pereira POR
11-02 Wales	W	1-0	Vila Real	Fr	Guerreiro 80	487	Duarte POR
28-03 Northern Ireland	L	2-3	Belfast	WCq	Jelen 27, Saganowski 91+	13 357	Hansson SWE
1-04 San Marino	W	10-0	Kielce	WCq	Boguski 2 1 27, Smolarek 4 18 60 72 81, Lewandowski.R 43, Jelen 51, Lewandowski.M 63, Saganowski 88	15 200	Kulbakou BLR
6-06 South Africa	L	0-1	Johannesburg	Fr		8 000	Bwanya ZIM
9-06 Iraq	D	1-1	Cape Town	Fr	Guerreiro 71	2 000	Damon RSA
12-08 Greece	W	2-0	Bydgoszcz	Fr	Obraniak 2 47 79	19 000	Sagara JPN
5-09 Northern Ireland	D	1-1	Chorzow	WCq	Lewandowski.M 80	38 914	Mejuto ESP
9-09 Slovenia	L	0-3	Maribor	WCq		10 226	Collum SCO
10-10 Czech Republic	L	0-2	Prague	WCq		14 010	Larsen DEN
14-10 Slovakia	L	0-1	Chorzow	WCq		5 000	Eriksson SWE
14-11 Romania	L	0-1	Warsaw	Fr		8 000	Mashiah ISR
18-11 Canada	W	1-0	Bydgoszcz	Fr	Rybus 19	10 400	Christoffersen DEN
2010							
20-01 Thailand	W	3-1	Nak'n Ratchasima	Fr	Glik 43, Malecki 52, Robak 87	20 000	Mbaga TAN
23-01 Singapore	W	6-1	Nak'n Ratchasima	Fr	Lewandowski.R 2 26p 37, Iwanski 45p, Brozek.Pi 69, OG 80, Nowak.T 88p		Amwayi KEN
3-03 Bulgaria	W	2-0	Warsaw	Fr	Blaszczykowski 42, Lewandowski.R 62	6 800	Kever SUI
29-05 Finland	D	0-0	Kielce	Fr		14 200	Avram ROU
2-06 Serbia	D	0-0	Kufstein	Fr		2 000	Drabek AUT
8-06 Spain	L	0-6	Murcia	Fr		30 000	Koukoulakis GRE
11-08 Cameroon	L	0-3	Szczecin	Fr		17 000	Asumaa FIN
4-09 Ukraine	D	1-1	Lodz	Fr	Jelen 41	6 500	Irmatov UZB
7-09 Australia	L	1-2	Krakow	Fr	Lewandowski.R 18	17 000	Bebek CRO
9-10 USA	D	2-2	Chicago	Fr	Matuszczyk 29, Blaszczykowski 72	31 696	Depiero CAN
12-10 Ecuador	D	2-2	Montreal	Fr	Smolarek 60, Obraniak 70	1 000	Navarro CAN
17-11 Cote d'Ivoire	W	3-1	Poznan	Fr	Lewandowski.R 2 19 80, Obraniak 65	42 000	Toma JPN
10-12 Bosnia-Herzegovina	D	2-2	Antalya	Fr	Brozek.Pa 2 7 52	100	Ogretmenoglu TUR

Fr = Friendly match • EC = UEFA EURO 2008 • WC = FIFA World Cup • q = qualifier • r1 = first round group

POLAND NATIONAL TEAM HISTORICAL RECORDS

Caps
101 - Michal Zewlakow 1998- • **100** - Grzegorz Lato 1971-84 • **97** - Kazimierz Deyna 1968-78 • **96** - Jacek Bak 1993-2008 & Jacek Krzynowek 1999-2009 • **91** - Wladislaw Zmuda 1973-86 • **82** - Antoni Szymanowski 1970-80 • **80** - Zbigniew Boniek 1976-88 • **75** - Wlodzimierz Lubanski 1963-80 • **74** - Tomasz Waldoch 1991-2002 • **72** - Maciej Zurawski 1998-2008 • **70** - Piotr Swierczewski 1992-2003

Goals
48 - Wlodzimierz Lubanski 1963-80 • **45** - Grzegorz Lato 1971-84 • **41** - Kazimierz Deyna 1968-78 • **39** - Ernst Pol 1955-65 • **32** - Andrzej Szarmach 1973-82 • **27** - Gerard Cieslik 1947-58 • **24** - Zbigniew Boniek 1976-88 • **21** - Ernest Willimowski 1934-39 • **20** - Dariusz Dziekanowski 1981-90 & Euzebiusz Smolarek 2002- • **19** - Roman Kosecki 1988-95 • **18** - Lucjan Brychczy 1954-69

Past Coaches
Jozef Szkolnikowski 1921-22 • Jozef Lustgarten 1922 • Kazimierz Glabisz 1923 • Adam Obrubanski 1924 • Tadeusz Kuchar 1925 • Tadeusz Synowiec 1925-27 • Tadeusz Kuchar 1928 • Stefan Loth 1928-31 • Jozef Kaluza 1932-39 • Henryk Reyman 1947 • Andrzej Przeworski 1947 • Zygmunt Alfus 1948 • Andrzej Przeworski 1948 • Mieczyslaw Szymkowiak 1949-50 • Ryszard Koncewicz 1953-56 • Alfred Nowakowski 1956 • Czeslaw Krug 1956 • Henryk Reyman 1957-58 • Czeslaw Krug 1959-62 • Wieslaw Motoczynski 1963-65 • Ryszard Koncewicz 1966 • Antoni Brzezanczyk 1966 • Alfred Nowakowski 1966 • Michal Matyas 1966-67 • Ryszard Koncewicz 1968-70 • Kazimierz Gorski 1971-76 • Jacek Gmoch 1976-78 • Ryszard Kulesza 1978-80 • Antoni Piechniczek 1981-86 • Wojciech Lazarek 1986-89 • Andrzej Strejlau 1989-93 • Leslaw Cmikiewicz 1993 • Henryk Apostel 1994-95 • Wladyslaw Stachurski 1996 • Antoni Piechniczek 1996-97 • Krzysztof Pawlak 1997 • Janusz Wojcik 1997-99 • Jerzy Engel 2000-02 • Zbigniew Boniek 2002 • Pawel Janas 2003-06 • Leo Beenhakker 2006-09 • Stefan Majewski 2009 • Franciszek Smuda 2009-

POLAND 2009-10

LIGA POLSKA ORANGE EKSTRAKLASA

	Pl	W	D	L	F	A	Pts	Lech	Wisla	Ruch	Legia	GKS	Korona	Polonia B	Lechia	Slask	Zaglebie	Jagiellonia	Cracovia	Polonia W	Arka	Odra	Piast
Lech Poznan †	30	19	8	3	51	20	65		1-0	3-1	1-0	2-2	2-0	3-0	2-1	1-0	2-0	2-0	3-1	2-4	2-0	1-0	1-1
Wisla Krakow ‡	30	19	5	6	48	20	62	0-0		2-0	0-1	3-0	0-1	1-1	3-0	1-0	1-0	2-1	0-1	2-1	0-1	1-1	2-1
Ruch Chorzów ‡	30	16	5	9	40	30	53	1-2	1-3		1-0	1-0	0-0	2-1	1-0	0-0	0-2	5-2	2-0	2-0	1-0	3-2	2-0
Legia Warszawa	30	15	7	8	36	22	52	2-0	0-3	2-0		2-2	5-2	1-0	2-0	1-1	4-0	2-1	0-0	1-1	1-0	0-1	3-0
GKS Belchatow	30	13	9	8	37	27	48	1-1	1-0	2-1	0-1		1-0	2-2	2-1	2-0	1-3	1-1	3-0	3-0	1-0	3-0	0-1
Korona Kielce	30	9	10	11	35	41	37	0-5	2-3	3-0	0-1	1-1		1-0	1-0	1-1	3-3	1-0	1-1	4-0	1-2	1-1	3-2
Polonia Bytom	30	9	10	11	29	31	37	1-1	1-3	0-1	1-0	1-0	1-0		1-1	0-0	2-1	1-1	1-2	1-0	3-1	1-1	4-0
Lechia Gdansk	30	9	10	11	30	32	37	0-0	0-1	1-1	2-3	0-2	1-1	0-0		1-1	1-0	2-0	1-0	1-1	2-1	0-2	0-1
Slask Wroclaw	30	8	12	10	32	33	36	0-3	1-3	0-0	0-0	0-0	1-1	2-1	1-2		2-0	1-2	2-0	1-0	2-1	4-0	2-1
Zaglebie Lubin	30	8	11	11	30	38	35	0-1	1-4	0-1	0-0	1-1	2-2	2-0	2-2	1-1		0-0	0-0	2-0	0-2	2-1	1-1
Jagiellonia Bialystok§10	30	11	11	8	29	27	34	2-3	0-0	1-0	2-0	2-1	2-0	0-0	0-0	2-0	0-0		0-0	1-0	2-1	2-1	2-0
Cracovia	30	9	7	14	25	39	34	1-0	1-1	1-4	1-2	0-1	3-0	1-2	2-6	1-0	1-1	0-1		1-2	1-1	1-0	3-2
Polonia Warszawa	30	9	6	15	25	38	33	0-3	0-1	1-1	1-0	0-0	1-1	1-0	0-1	3-2	0-1	2-0	0-1		2-1	2-1	0-2
Arka Gdynia	30	7	7	16	28	39	28	1-1	0-1	0-3	0-1	2-1	1-2	2-2	1-2	1-1	0-2	0-0	2-0	0-0		2-0	2-1
Odra Wodzislaw Slaski	30	7	6	17	27	45	27	0-0	1-3	1-3	1-0	0-1	0-2	0-1	0-0	2-4	1-2	2-2	1-0	2-1	2-1		2-0
Piast Gliwice	30	7	6	17	30	50	27	1-3	1-4	1-2	1-1	1-2	1-0	1-0	0-2	2-2	4-1	0-0	0-1	0-2	2-2	2-1	

31/07/2009 - 15/05/2010 • † Qualified for the UEFA Champions League • ‡ Qualified for the Europa League • § = points deducted
Top scorers: **18** - Robert Lewandowski, Lech Poznan • **14** - Iliyan Mitsanski BUL, Zaglebie Lubin • **11** - Tomasz Frankowski, Jagiellonia

MEDALS TABLE

		Overall			League			Cup			Europe		
		G	S	B	G	S	B	G	S	B	G	S	B
1	Legia Warszawa	21	17	14	8	11	12	13	6			2	
2	Górnik Zabrze	20	12	7	14	4	7	6	7		1		
3	Wisla Kraków	17	18	9	13	12	9	4	6				
4	Ruch Chorzów	16	10	8	13	5	8	3	5				
5	Lech Poznan	11	1	4	6		4	5	1				
6	Widzew Lódz	5	7	4	4	7	3	1				1	
7	Cracovia	5	2		5	2							
8	Zaglebie Sosnowiec	4	5	2			4	2	4	1			
9	Pogon Lwow	4	3		4	3							
	Polonia Warszawa	4	3		2	3		2					
11	GKS Katowice	3	9	4		4	4	3	5				
12	LKS Lódz	3	2	2	2	1	2	1	1				
13	Slask Wroclaw	3	2	1	1	2	1	2					

POLAND 2009-10

I LIGA POLSKA

	Pl	W	D	L	F	A	Pts	Widzew	Górnik	Sandecja	LKS	Pogon	MKS	Flota	Ostrowiec	Gorzów	Warta	Górnik L	Podbesk'zie	GKS	Dolcan	Wisla	Znicz	Stal	Motor
Widzew Lodz	34	23	8	3	62	17	77		3-0	1-0	2-1	2-1	3-2	0-0	1-1	2-0	1-0	0-0	2-2	2-1	3-0	3-0	7-0	3-0	1-1
Górnik Zabrze	34	18	7	9	47	30	61	0-1		1-0	1-1	1-3	3-2	1-1	3-1	1-0	2-3	1-0	0-3	0-2	0-0	1-0	3-1	2-0	2-0
Sandecja Nowy Sacz	34	17	8	9	55	42	59	1-6	2-1		4-1	3-1	4-0	1-0	3-0	2-1	1-1	2-2	1-1	1-0	2-2	2-2	3-1	3-0	2-0
LKS Lodz	34	16	7	11	51	45	55	1-4	1-4	1-3		2-2	0-0	1-1	1-0	2-1	1-0	4-2	2-2	1-2	3-0	1-0	3-0	2-1	5-2
Pogon Szczecin	34	13	12	9	46	35	51	1-2	0-2	4-0	0-2		0-1	0-0	2-1	1-0	1-1	2-2	2-2	3-0	2-0	3-3	1-0	2-0	2-0
MKS Kluczbork	34	12	10	12	43	37	46	2-0	0-1	1-1	0-0	2-0		0-2	2-1	1-2	1-2	0-0	1-3	3-0	1-1	0-0	1-0	3-0	0-2
Flota Swinoujscie	34	12	10	12	33	36	46	1-0	0-0	3-0	1-0	1-1	1-4		2-1	2-0	1-0	0-3	1-0	1-0	3-1	1-2	1-0	2-0	
Ostrowiec	34	13	7	14	37	46	46	0-2	2-1	3-1	1-0	0-1	0-2	2-0		0-1	2-1	2-0	1-0	1-1	1-0	1-1	1-0	2-0	1-0
Gorzów Wielkopolski	34	11	12	11	34	33	45	0-0	1-0	0-0	1-2	1-0	1-1	1-1	1-1		2-0	1-0	1-2	2-0	3-0	1-1	2-2	0-0	2-2
Warta Poznan	34	12	8	14	49	45	44	0-2	2-1	1-0	1-2	1-2	1-3	2-0	6-0	2-3		1-1	4-1	3-3	1-1	2-0	2-3	0-1	
Górnik Leczna	34	11	11	12	38	45	44	0-2	1-1	0-1	1-0	0-3	2-1	1-0	3-1	2-1	2-2		2-0	1-0	1-1	0-3	2-1	2-2	3-0
Podbeskidzie	34	10	14	10	45	38	44	0-1	0-1	1-2	2-1	0-0	1-1	1-2	0-1	0-0	3-0	2-2		1-3	4-0	0-0	1-1	2-2	0-0
GKS Katowice	34	11	10	13	41	41	43	0-3	0-0	0-1	4-1	2-2	0-1	2-1	4-1	1-1	2-0	0-0	0-1		0-0	0-0	2-0	1-1	2-0
Dolcan Zabki	34	10	12	12	37	43	42	1-0	0-1	1-1	0-0	1-1	1-1	3-0	0-0	3-1	1-2	4-0	0-3	3-2		3-1	2-1	1-1	0-1
Wisla Plock	34	9	13	12	43	51	40	0-1	1-2	2-4	1-2	0-1	0-4	2-1	1-3	1-0	1-3	3-3	3-1		3-1		1-0	1-1	0-1
Znicz Pruszkow	34	11	6	17	32	48	39	1-0	0-0	1-0	0-1	0-0	2-0	1-2	3-2	1-0	1-0	2-0	0-1	0-2	0-1	1-1		2-1	2-0
Stal Stalowa Wola	34	5	10	19	32	58	25	0-1	1-3	2-0	2-3	0-0	2-2	2-0	1-1	0-1	1-0	1-3	2-4	1-2	1-4	0-1	3-2		3-3
Motor Lubin	34	4	11	19	27	62	23	0-0	0-3	1-4	0-3	3-2	1-0	1-1	2-2	0-1	1-4	0-2	1-1	0-2	0-0	3-4	1-1	0-2	

1/08/2009 - 9/06/2010 • Top scorers: **18** - Marcin Robak, Widew Lodz • **16** - Piotr Reiss, Warta Poznan & Adrian Swiatek, LKS Lodz/Gornik Zabrze

PUCHAR POLSKI 2009-10

Third Round		Fourth Round	Quarter-finals		Semi-finals		Final	
Jagiellonia Bialystok	1	**Jagiellonia Bialystok**						
GKS Tychy *	0							
Okocimski Brzesko *	1	Arka Gdynia *						
Arka Gdynia	2							
Dolcan Zabki *	1 5p	Dolcan Zabki *	**Jagiellonia Bialystok**	1 3				
Slask Wroclaw	1 4p		Korona Kielce *	3 0				
GKS Belchatow	1	**Korona Kielce**			**Jagiellonia Bialystok**	2 1		
Korona Kielce *	3				Lechia Gdansk *	1 1		
Wisla Krakow	3	**Wisla Krakow**						
Hetman Zamosc *	0							
Polonia Bytom	1	Bytovia Bytow *	Wisla Krakow	0 1				
Bytovia Bytow *	2		Lechia Gdansk *	0 3				
Odra Wodzislaw Slaski	2	Odra Wodzislaw Slaski						
Olimpia Grudziadz *	1							
Nielba Wagrowiec *	1	Lechia Gdansk *						
Lechia Gdansk	3							
Ruch Chorzów	1	**Ruch Chorzów**						
Widzew Lodz *	0							
LKS Lodz	2	Start Otwock *	**Ruch Chorzów ***	1 1				
Start Otwock *	3		Legia Warszawa	0 2				
Cracovia	1 4p	Cracovia			**Ruch Chorzów ***	1 0		
Piast Kobylin *	1 2p				**Pogon Szczecin**	1 0		
Gorzów Wielkopolski *	0	**Legia Warszawa ***						
Legia Warszawa	2							
Zaglebie Sosnowiec *	2	**Zaglebie Sosnowiec ***						
Górnik Zabrze	0							
Lech Poznan	0 1p	Stal Stalowa Wola	Zaglebie Sosnowiec *	0 1				
Stal Stalowa Wola *	0 4p		**Pogon Szczecin**	3 1				
Piast Gliwice	2	Piast Gliwice						
Polonia Slubice *	1							
Polonia Warszawa	0	**Pogon Szczecin ***					**Jagiellonia Bialystok ‡**	1
Pogon Szczecin *	2						Pogon Szczecin	0

CUP FINAL

Zdzislaw Krzyszkowiak, Bydgoszcz
22-05-2010, 15:30, Att: 13 300, Ref: Malek
Scorer - Skerla [49] for Jagiellonia

Jagiellonia - Gikiewicz - Lewczuk (Burkhardt 66), Skerla, Sidgy (Jezierski 73), Norambuena, Bruno, Grzyb, Hermes, Lato, Grosicki, Frankowski (Jarecki 81). Tr: Michal Probierz

Pogon - Janukiewicz - Nowak (Lebedynski 60), Hrymowicz, Jarun, Wozniak, Rogalski, Mandrysz (Wolkiewicz 82), Mysiak, Pietruszka, Bojarski (Dziuba 68), Moskalewicz. Tr: Piotr Mandrysz

* Home team/home team in the 1st leg • ‡ Qualified for the Europa League

POR – PORTUGAL

FIFA/COCA-COLA WORLD RANKING

1993	1994	1995	1996	1997	1998	1999	2000	2001	2002	2003	2004	2005	2006	2007	2008	2009	2010
20	20	16	13	30	36	15	6	4	11	17	9	10	8	8	11	5	8

	2010											Hi/Lo
	Jan	Feb	Mar	Mar	Apr	May	Jul	Aug	Sep	Oct	Nov	Dec	3
	5	5	6	4	3	3	8	8	8	8	8	8	43

For a tournament that had promised so much, the 2010 FIFA World Cup in South Africa proved to be a massive disappointment for a Portuguese side that only briefly showed the flashes of brilliance that it was capable of. Astonishingly, although touted as potential winners at the start, the 2006 semi-finalists failed to score in three of their four matches while captain Cristiano Ronaldo, billed as the best player on the planet alongside Argentina's Lionel Messi, ploughed a lonesome furrow up front, often looking isolated and discontent. A 7-0 victory over North Korea was the only highlight of a tournament which saw the team limp to 0-0 draws with the Côte d'Ivoire and Brazil, before meekly bowing out against neighbours Spain in the first knockout round in a 1-0 defeat. At home, Jorge Jesus lead Benfica to only their second title in 14 years whilst his previous club Sporting Braga were the surprise of the season after finishing as runners-up. That meant that for only the third time since 1997, FC Porto failed to finish in the top two and so missed out on a place in the 2010-11 UEFA Champions League. However, both they and Sporting sailed through their Europa League groups and going into 2011 were joined by both Benfica and Braga in the knockout stage after the latter two failed to progress beyond the group stage of the Champions League.

FIFA WORLD CUP RECORD

1930 DNE 1934-1962 DNQ **1966** 3 SF 1970-1982 DNQ **1986** 17 r1 1990-1998 DNQ **2002** 21 r1 **2006** 4 SF **2010** 11 r2

FEDERACAO PORTUGUESA DE FUTEBOL (FPF)

Rua Alexandre Herculano, no.58, Apartado 24013, Lisbon 1250-012

☎ +351 21 3252700
📠 +351 21 3252780
✉ secretario_geral@fpf.pt
🖥 www.fpf.pt

FA 1914 CON 1954 FIFA 1923
P Gilberto Madail
GS Angelo Brou

FIFA BIG COUNT 2006

Total players	547 734
% of population	5.16%
Male	488 787
Female	58 947
Amateurs 18+	40 351
Unregistered	210 000
Professionals	1 663
Referees	4 471
Admin & coaches	34 000
Number of clubs	2 284
Number of teams	8 786

MAJOR CITIES/TOWNS

		Population
1	Lisbon	482 678
2	Porto	237 448
3	Amadora	181 377
4	Braga	130 300
5	Setúbal	121 668
6	Queluz	120 811
7	Coimbra	110 764
8	Cacém	109 120
9	Funchal	93 938
10	Mem Martins	89 121
11	Rio de Mouro	65 237
12	Corroios	59 395
13	Aveiro	57 459
14	Odivelas	55 544
15	Amora	55 047
16	Rio Tinto	53 068
17	Leiria	50 087
18	Guimarães	43 062
19	Faro	42 301

REPUBLICA PORTUGUESA • PORTUGUESE REPUBLIC

Capital	Lisbon	Population	10 707 924 (75)	% in cities	59%
GDP per capita	$22 200 (54)	Area km²	92 090 km² (110)	GMT +/-	0
Neighbours (km)	Spain 1214 • Coast 1793				

RECENT INTERNATIONAL MATCHES PLAYED BY PORTUGAL

2008 Opponents	Score	Venue	Comp	Scorers	Att	Referee
6-02 Italy	L 1-3	Zurich	Fr	Quaresma 77	30 500	Kever SUI
26-03 Greece	L 1-2	Dusseldorf	Fr	Nuno Gomes 75	25 000	Kirchen GER
31-05 Georgia	W 2-0	Viseu	Fr	Joao Moutinho 19, Simão 44p	8 500	Meir ISR
7-06 Turkey	W 2-0	Geneva	ECr1	Pepe 61, Raul Meireles 93+	29 016	Fandel GER
11-06 Czech Republic	W 3-1	Geneva	ECr1	Deco 8, Ronaldo 63, Quaresma 91+	29 016	Vassaras GRE
15-06 Switzerland	L 0-2	Basel	ECr1		39 730	Plautz AUT
19-06 Germany	L 2-3	Basel	ECqf	Nuno Gomes 40, Postiga 87	39 374	Fröjdfeldt SWE
20-08 Faroe Islands	W 5-0	Aveiro	Fr	Carlos Martins 23, Simao 48, Duda 86, Bruno Alves 89, Nani 91+	22 000	Shandor UKR
6-09 Malta	W 4-0	Ta'Qali	WCq	Said OG 26, Hugo Almeida 61, Simao 72, Nani 78	11 000	Blom NED
10-09 Denmark	L 2-3	Lisbon	WCq	Nani 42, Deco 86p	33 000	Webb ENG
11-10 Sweden	D 0-0	Stockholm	WCq		33 241	Rosetti ITA
15-10 Albania	D 0-0	Braga	WCq		29 500	Kircher GER
19-11 Brazil	L 2-6	Gama	Fr	Danny 4, Simao 62	19 157	Larrionda URU
2009						
11-02 Finland	W 1-0	Faro-Loule	Fr	Ronaldo 78p	19 834	Bertolini SUI
28-03 Sweden	D 0-0	Porto	WCq		40 200	De Bleckere BEL
31-03 South Africa	W 2-0	Lausanne	Fr	Bruno Alves 4, Thwala OG 56	14 659	Busacca ITA
6-06 Albania	W 2-1	Tirana	WCq	Hugo Almeida 28, Bruno Alves 92+	13 320	Meyer GER
10-06 Estonia	D 0-0	Tallinn	Fr		6 350	Svendson DEN
12-08 Liechtenstein	W 3-0	Vaduz	Fr		5 525	Bertolini SUI
5-09 Denmark	D 1-1	Copenhagen	WCq	Liedson 86	37 998	Busacca SUI
9-09 Hungary	W 1-0	Budapest	WCq	Pepe 10	42 000	Lannoy FRA
10-10 Hungary	W 3-0	Lisbon	WCq	Simao 2 18 79, Liedson 74	50 115	Hamer LUX
14-10 Malta	W 4-0	Guimaraes	WCq	Nani 14, Simao 45, Miguel Veloso 52, Edinho 90	29 350	Kelly IRL
14-11 Bosnia-Herzegovina	W 1-0	Lisbon	WCq	Bruno Alves 31	60 588	Atkinson ENG
18-11 Bosnia-Herzegovina	W 1-0	Zenica	WCq	Raul Meireles 56	15 000	Rosetti ITA
2010						
24-05 Cape Verde Islands	D 0-0	Covilha	Fr		6 000	Clos ESP
1-06 Cameroon	W 3-1	Covilha	Fr	Raul Meireles 2 32 47, Nani 82	6 125	Weiner GER
8-06 Mozambique	W 3-0	Johannesburg	Fr	Danny 52	34 000	Dyer RSA
15-06 Côte d'Ivoire	D 0-0	Port Elizabeth	WCr1		37 034	Larrionda URU
21-06 Korea DPR	W 7-0	Cape Town	WCr1	Raul Meireles 29, Simao 53, Hugo Almeida 56, Tiago 2 60 89, Liedson 81, Cristiano Ronaldo 87	63 644	Pozo CHI
25-06 Brazil	D 0-0	Durban	WCr1		62 712	Archundia MEX
29-06 Spain	L 0-1	Cape Town	WCr2		62 955	Baldassi ARG
3-09 Cyprus	D 4-4	Guimaraes	ECq	Hugo Almeida 8, Raul Meireles 29, Danny 50, Manuel Fernandes 60	9 100	Clattenburg ENG
7-09 Norway	L 0-1	Oslo	ECq		24 535	Duhamel FRA
8-10 Denmark	W 3-1	Porto	ECq	Nani 2 29 30, Cristiano Ronaldo 85	27 117	Braamhaar NED
12-10 Iceland	W 3-1	Reykjavik	ECq	Cristiano Ronaldo 3, Raul Meireles 27, Postiga 72	9 767	Einwaller AUT
17-11 Spain	W 4-0	Lisbon	Fr	Carlos Martins 45, Postiga 2 49 68, Hugo Almeida 90	38 000	Gautier FRA

Fr = Friendly match • EC = UEFA EURO 2008/2012 • WC = FIFA World Cup • q = qualifier • r1 = first round group • qf = quarter-final

PORTUGAL NATIONAL TEAM HISTORICAL RECORDS

Caps
127 - Luis Figo 1991-2006 • 110 - Fernando Couto 1990-2004 • 94 - Rui Costa 1993-2004 • 88 - Pauleta 1997-2006 • 85 - Simao 1998- • 81 - Joao Pinto 1991-2002 • 80 - Vitor Baia 1990-2002 • 79 - Cristiano Ronaldo 2003- & Ricardo 2001-08 • 77 - Nuno Gomes 1996- • 73 - Deco 2003- • 72 - Ricardo Carvalho 2003- • 70 - Joao Pinto 1983-96 • 66 - Nene 1971-84 • 64 - Eusebio 1961-73 & Humberto 1968-83

Goals
47 - Pauleta 1997-2006 • 41 - Eusebio 1961-73 • 32 - Luis Figo 1991-2006 • 29 - Nuno Gomes 1996- • 26 - Rui Costa 1993-2004 • 25 - Cristiano Ronaldo 2003- • 23 - Joao Pinto 1991-2002 • 22 - Nene 1971-84 & Simao 1998- • 15 - Rui Jordao 1972-89 & Peyroteo 1938-49

Past Coaches
Committee 1921-23 • Ribeiro dos Reis 1925-26 • Candido de Oliveira 1926-29, 1935-45, 1952 • Maia Loureiro 1929 • Laurindo Grijo 1930 • Tavares da Silva 1931, 1945-47, 1951, 1955-57 • Salvador do Carmo 1932-33, 1950, 1953-54 • Virgilio Paula 1947-48 • Armando Sampaio 1949 • Jose Maria Antunes 1957-60, 1962-64 • Armando Ferreira 1961 • Fernando Peyroteo 1961 • Armando Ferreira 1962-64 • Manuel da Luz Afonso 1964-66 • Jose Gomes da Silva 1967 • Jose Maria Antunes 1968-69 • Jose Gomes da Silva 1970-71 • Jose Augusto 1972-73 • Jose Maria Pedroto 1974-76 • Juca 1977-78 • Mario Wilson 1978-80 • Juca 1980-82 • Otto Gloria 1982-83 • Fernando Cabrita 1983-84 • Jose Augusto Torres 1984-86 • Rui Seabra 1986-87 • Juca 1987-89 • Artur Jorge 1990-91 • Carlos Queiroz 1991-93 • Nelo Vingada 1994 • Antonio Oliveira 1994-96 • Artur Jorge 1996-97 • Humberto Coelho 1997-2000 • Antonio Oliveira 2000-02 • Agostinho Oliveira 2002 • Luiz Felipe Scolari 2003-08 • Carlos Queiroz 2008-10 • Paulo Bento 2010-

PORTUGAL 2009–10

LIGA SAGRES

	Pl	W	D	L	F	A	Pts	Benfica	Braga	Porto	Sporting CP	Marítimo	Vitória SC	Nacional	Naval	União	Paços	Académica	Rio Ave	Olhanense	Vitória FC	Belenenses	Leixões
SL Benfica †	30	24	4	2	78	20	76		1-0	1-0	2-0	1-1	3-1	6-1	1-0	3-0	3-1	4-0	2-1	5-0	8-1	1-0	5-0
Sporting Braga †	30	22	5	3	48	20	71	2-0		1-0	1-0	2-1	3-2	2-0	0-0	2-0	1-0	1-0	1-0	3-1	2-0	3-1	3-1
FC Porto ‡	30	21	5	4	70	26	68	3-1	5-1		1-0	4-1	3-0	3-0	3-0	3-2	1-1	3-2	2-1	2-2	2-0	1-1	4-1
Sporting CP ‡	30	13	9	8	42	26	48	0-0	1-2	3-0		1-1	3-1	3-2	0-1	0-1	1-0	1-2	5-0	3-2	2-1	0-0	1-0
CS Marítimo ‡	30	11	8	11	42	43	41	0-5	1-2	1-0	3-2		0-1	1-1	1-2	1-0	3-1	0-0	0-1	5-2	2-0	3-3	1-0
Vitória SC Guimarães	30	11	8	11	31	34	41	0-1	1-0	1-4	1-1	1-2		2-0	3-0	2-2	1-2	1-0	1-0	1-1	2-2	2-0	2-0
CD Nacional	30	10	9	11	36	46	39	0-1	1-1	0-4	1-1	2-1	2-0		1-1	2-0	1-1	4-3	1-1	1-1	2-1	1-0	1-0
Naval 1º de Maio	30	10	6	14	20	35	36	2-4	0-4	1-3	0-1	2-1	0-0	0-0		1-0	1-0	0-1	3-2	0-0	0-1	1-0	1-0
União de Leiria	30	9	8	13	35	41	35	1-2	1-2	1-4	1-1	0-0	0-1	1-2	2-0		2-1	1-1	1-1	2-0	3-3	1-0	2-1
Paços de Ferreira	30	8	11	11	32	37	35	1-3	0-1	1-1	0-0	1-0	0-0	2-1	1-3	0-1		2-1	1-1	2-2	5-3	0-0	1-1
Académica Coimbra	30	8	9	13	37	42	33	2-3	0-2	1-2	0-2	2-4	2-0	3-3	2-0	0-0	1-1		0-1	1-1	3-0	1-1	2-0
Rio Ave FC	30	6	13	11	22	33	31	0-1	1-1	0-1	2-2	0-0	0-0	2-0	0-0	0-2	1-2	0-0		1-5	1-0	0-0	2-0
SC Olhanense	30	5	14	11	31	46	29	2-2	0-1	0-3	0-0	1-2	0-2	1-0	1-0	0-0	1-1	2-1	0-1		2-2	1-3	1-0
Vitória FC Setúbal	30	5	10	15	29	57	25	1-1	0-0	2-5	0-2	3-2	0-0	2-1	0-1	0-4	0-1	1-1	2-2	0-0		1-2	1-0
Os Belenenses	30	4	11	15	23	44	23	0-4	1-3	0-3	0-4	2-2	0-1	0-1	2-0	5-2	0-3	1-2	0-0	0-0	0-0		1-3
Leixões	30	5	6	19	25	51	21	0-1	0-1	1-1	1-0	0-1	1-2	1-2	3-1	2-4	1-0	3-2	2-0	1-3	0-0	2-2	

14/08/2009 - 9/05/2010 • † Qualified for the UEFA Champions League • ‡ Qualified for the UEFA Cup
Top scorers: **26** - Oscar Cardozo PAR, Benfica • **25** - Radamel Falcao COL, Porto • **13** - Liedson, Sporting CP

MEDALS TABLE

		Overall			League			Cup			Europe		
		G	S	B	G	S	B	G	S	B	G	S	B
1	SL Benfica	61	40	18	32	24	15	27	10		2	6	3
2	FC Porto	46	39	12	24	24	11	19	14		3	1	1
3	Sporting Clube Portugal	38	36	27	18	19	25	19	16		1	1	2
4	OS Belenenses	7	11	14	1	3	14	6	8				
5	Boavista FC	6	4	2	1	3	1	5	1				1
6	Vitória FC Setúbal	3	9	3		1	3	3	8				
7	Académica de Coimbra	1	5			1		1	4				
8	Sporting Clube Braga	1	4			1		1	3				
9	Atlético Clube Portugal	1	3	2			2	1	3				
10	CS Marítimo	1	2					1	2				
11	SC Olhanense	1	1					1	1				
	Leixoes SC	1	1					1	1				
	SC Beira Mar	1	1					1	1				
14	CF Estrella Amadora	1						1					
15	Vitória SC Guimaraes		4	4			4		4				

PORTUGAL 2009–10

LIGA DE HONRA (2)

	Pl	W	D	L	F	A	Pts	Beira-Mar	Portimonense	Feirense	Santa Clara	Oliveirense	Trofense	Penafiel	Fátima	Aves	Gil Vicente	Estoril	Freamunde	Varzim	Sp. Covilha	Chaves	Carregado
SC Beira-Mar	30	16	6	8	44	30	54		2-0	1-1	1-0	1-2	1-2	0-1	3-2	2-1	3-1	1-3	3-0	0-1	2-1	1-0	
Portimonense SC	30	16	6	8	43	34	54	2-1		1-0	0-0	3-1	1-3	1-3	3-3	1-1	0-3	2-1	1-0	3-2	2-0	2-1	1-0
CD Feirense	30	14	10	6	37	24	52	0-2	2-1		2-1	2-1	3-0	1-1	1-1	1-0	0-1	1-1	1-1	4-0	3-2	1-0	1-0
GD Santa Clara	30	13	12	5	45	29	51	1-1	3-0	1-1		1-2	3-1	0-1	1-0	0-0	0-0	1-1	3-2	0-0	2-1	1-0	1-0
UD Oliveirense	30	14	7	9	38	27	49	2-1	0-1	0-0	1-0		3-1	2-0	1-0	3-1	1-1	0-0	2-1	3-0	3-0	1-3	3-0
CD Trofense	30	13	6	11	44	45	45	0-1	0-3	0-2	5-2	1-0		0-0	1-0	2-2	2-4	1-1	4-0	2-1	2-2	2-1	3-0
SC Penafiel	30	10	11	9	35	34	41	0-2	1-0	1-1	2-2	0-2	0-1		2-1	1-1	0-0	1-0	2-3	0-0	1-0	2-0	1-1
CD Fátima	30	8	14	8	31	31	38	1-2	0-1	1-0	2-5	1-1	2-1	2-2		1-0	0-0	1-1	0-0	3-0	0-0	1-2	
Desportivo Aves	30	9	11	10	33	33	38	1-3	1-1	1-1	0-0	2-1	1-0	3-2	0-1		2-2	0-1	1-2	2-0	0-0	2-2	2-1
Gil Vicente FC	30	9	11	10	36	32	38	1-1	0-2	1-1	0-0	1-0	4-0	3-1	1-1	0-2		0-2	1-1	1-2	3-0	0-3	0-1
GD Estoril-Praia	30	7	14	9	26	29	35	2-0	1-3	1-2	0-0	0-1	1-1	0-0	0-1	1-0	0-2		0-0	1-1	1-0	2-2	1-1
SC Freamunde	30	9	8	13	43	50	35	1-2	0-3	1-2	1-0	2-3	1-3	1-1	0-0	3-2	0-2	2-2		1-0	3-2	0-0	3-0
Varzim SC	30	6	13	11	25	38	31	1-1	0-0	2-1	1-2	0-0	0-1	2-2	1-0	0-0	0-2	2-2	2-2		1-0	1-0	1-1
Sporting Covilha	30	7	9	14	35	49	30	2-2	3-1	1-1	2-2	1-1	2-1	2-1	2-2	1-2	1-2	3-1	2-3	0-0		2-0	1-0
GD Chaves	30	6	10	14	28	37	28	1-1	1-1	0-1	0-3	0-0	1-1	2-0	0-0	0-1	1-1	1-1	1-1	0-1	3-1		2-0
AD Carregado	30	6	6	18	26	47	24	0-2	1-3	0-1	1-2	4-1	2-3	0-3	1-1	0-0	1-0	1-2	3-2	3-2	1-1	1-2	

13/08/2009 - 8/05/2010 • Top scorers: **15** - Reguila, Trofense • **14** - Joao Silva, Desportivo Aves • **13** - Leandro Tatu BRA, Santa Clara

TAÇA DE PORTUGAL 2009–10

Round of 64			Round of 32			Round of 16		
FC Porto *	4							
Sertanense	0		FC Porto	2				
Tondela *	1		UD Oliveirense *	0				
UD Oliveirense	2					FC Porto	2	10p
Valenciano *	1	4p				Os Belenenses *	2	9p
SC Olhanense	1	2p	Valenciano *	0				
Oriental	1		Os Belenenses	1				
Os Belenenses *	3							
Mafra	1							
Vieira *	0		Mafra *	1	3p			
Alcains	0		União da Madeira	1	2p			
União da Madeira *	2					Mafra	3	
Pescadores	1	3p				Sporting CP *	4	
Cinfães *	1	1p	Pescadores *	1				
SC Penafiel	0		Sporting CP	4				
Sporting CP *	3							
Sporting Braga	1							
Sporting Covilhã *	0		Sporting Braga *	3				
Atlético CP *	0		Vitória FC Setúbal	0				
Vitória FC Setúbal	2					Sporting Braga	3	
União de Leiria	2					SC Freamunde *	1	
Merelinense FC *	1		União de Leiria	2				
AD Carregado	0		SC Freamunde *	3				
SC Freamunde *	3							
Vitória SC Guimarães *	3							
CD Feirense	1		Vitória SC Guimarães	1				
Monsanto *	0		Benfica *	0				
Benfica	6					Vitória SC Guimarães	2	2p
GD Santa Clara *	2					Rio Ave FC *	2	4p
CS Marítimo	1		GD Santa Clara	0				
Esmoriz	1		Rio Ave FC *	1				
Rio Ave FC *	2							
Naval 1° de Maio *	1							
Padroense FC	0		Naval 1° de Maio *	3				
SL Nelas	1		Gil Vicente FC	2				
Gil Vicente FC *	6					Naval 1° de Maio	1	
Leixões *	2					Aliados do Lordelo *	0	
Casa Pia	1		Leixões	0				
AD Machico	0		Aliados do Lordelo *	1				
Aliados do Lordelo *	2							
AD Camacha *	3							
Paredes	1		AD Camacha *	1				
Cruzado Canicense *	1		Vigor da Mocidade	0				
Vigor da Mocidade	4					AD Camacha *	0	
Oeiras *	6					CD Pinhalnovense	1	
CD Operário	1		Oeiras *	1				
Sintrense *	0	3p	CD Pinhalnovense	2				
CD Pinhalnovense	0	4p						
Paços de Ferreira *	3							
Mineiro Aljustrelense	1		Paços de Ferreira	0	10p			
Oliveira do Bairro	0		Tirsense *	0	9p			
Tirsense *	1					Paços de Ferreira	2	
CD Fátima *	3					CD Nacional *	1	
AC Vila Meã	0		CD Fátima	0	3p			
Varzim SC *	1		CD Nacional *	0	4p			
CD Nacional	2							
SC Beira-Mar *	4							
Torre de Moncorvo	0		SC Beira-Mar	2				
Portimonense SC	1		Académica Coimbra *	1				
Académica Coimbra *	2					SC Beira-Mar	0	
União da Serra *	3					GD Chaves *	1	
Coimbrões	2		União da Serra	0				
Leça FC *	0		GD Chaves *	2				
GD Chaves	3							

TAÇA DE PORTUGAL 2009–10

Quarter–finals	Semi–finals	Final

FC Porto * — 5
Sporting CP — 2

FC Porto	3 4
Rio Ave FC *	1 0

Sporting Braga * — 0 5p
Rio Ave FC — 0 6p

FC Porto ‡	2
GD Chaves	1

Naval 1° de Maio — 3
CD Pinhalnovense * — 1

Naval 1° de Maio	0 1
GD Chaves *	1 2

TAÇA DE PORTUGAL FINAL 2010

Estadio Nacional, Lisbon, 16-05-2010, 17:00, Att: 25 000, Ref: Pedro Proenca

Paços de Ferreira * — 1
GD Chaves — 2

FC Porto	2	Guarin [13], Falcao [23]
CD Chaves	1	Clemente [85]

Porto - Helton - Miguel Lopes (Christian Rodriguez 62), Rolando, Bruno Alves◆90, Alvaro Pereira - Fernando, Fernando Belluschi, Raul Meireles (Tomas Costa 46), Freddy Guarin (Diego Valeri 72) - Hulk, Falcao. Tr: Jesualdo Ferreira
Chaves - Rui Rego - Danilo, Lameirao, Ricardo Rocha◆90, Eduardo - Siaka Bamba, Edu, Bruno Magalhaes, Castanheira (Flavio Igor 61) - Samson (Diego 61), Mbaye Diop (Clemente 78). Tr: Tulipa

* Home team/home team in the 1st leg
‡ Qualified for the Europa League

PRK – KOREA DPR

FIFA/COCA-COLA WORLD RANKING

1993	1994	1995	1996	1997	1998	1999	2000	2001	2002	2003	2004	2005	2006	2007	2008	2009	2010
62	84	117	144	166	158	172	142	136	124	117	95	82	113	115	113	86	108

	2010												Hi/Lo
	Jan	Feb	Mar	Mar	Apr	May	Jul	Aug	Sep	Oct	Nov	Dec	57
	86	85	102	105	106	105	103	100	106	111	107	108	181

Korea DPR's preparations for taking part in the FIFA World Cup finals after an absence of 44 years took the team on a long and elaborate journey to South Africa. Along the way they failed to qualify for the East Asian Championship after failing to beat Hong Kong in a preliminary tournament in Chinese Taipei; they travelled to Sri Lanka to take part in the 2010 AFC Challenge Cup - a tournament for the lower ranked nations on the continent which they won, beating Turkmenistan on penalties in the final; and they played friendlies in South America, Central America, the Middle-East, Europe and Africa before finally arriving in Johannesburg for their opening match of the World Cup finals against Brazil. Perhaps it was the fear of being heavily beaten but the people of North Korea weren't able to watch the match live which was a pity for them because their team played very well, only just losing to the Brazilians. Emboldened, the authorities relented and the next match against Portugal was the first-ever live televised game in the country's history. They lost 7-0 and it wasn't long before Hong Yong Jo and his team were on a plane back home to a less than rapturous reception. At the start of 2011 the Koreans stepped back into the limelight again when they took part in the Asian Cup in Qatar but they failed to progress beyond the first round.

FIFA WORLD CUP RECORD

1930-1962 DNE **1966** 8 QF **1970** DNE **1974** DNQ **1978** DNE **1982-1994** DNQ **1998-2002** DNE **2006** DNQ **2010** 32 r1

DPR KOREA FOOTBALL ASSOCIATION (PRK)

Kumsongdong, Kwangbok Street, Mangyongdae Dist., PO Box 56, Pyongyang

☎ +850 2 3814334
🖷 +850 2 3814434
📧 gs-prkfa@hotmail.com
🖳

FA	1945 CON 1974 FIFA 1958
P	Ri Ryong Nam
GS	Kim Jong Man

FIFA BIG COUNT 2006

Total players	502 912
% of population	2.18%
Male	436 956
Female	65 956
Amateurs 18+	7 200
Youth under 18	7 712
Unregistered	170 000
Professionals	0
Referees	360
Admin & coaches	1 498
Number of clubs	170
Number of teams	850

MAJOR CITIES/TOWNS

		Population
1	Pyongyang	3 198 937
2	Hamhung	580 914
3	Nampo	467 044
4	Hungnam	359 613
5	Kaesong	351 503
6	Wonsan	340 174
7	Chongjin	329 382
8	Sinuiju	285 903
9	Haeju	227 231
10	Kanggye	207 807
11	Kimchaek	197 552
12	Sariwon	161 058
13	Songnim	158 441
14	Pyongsong	123 489
15	Hyesan	98 212
16	Sinpo	79 415
17	Hongwon	73 696
18	Chongpyong	72 384
19	Tanchon	71 457

DEMOCRATIC PEOPLE'S REPUBLIC OF KOREA

Capital Pyongyang	Population 22 665 345 (50)	% in cities 63%
GDP per capita $1800 (189)	Area km² 120 538 km² (98)	GMT + / - +9
Neighbours (km) China 1416, Korea Republic 238, Russia 19 • Coast 2495		

RECENT INTERNATIONAL MATCHES PLAYED BY KOREA DPR

2008	Opponents	Score		Venue	Comp	Scorers	Att	Referee
2-08	Nepal	W	1-0	Hyderabad	CCr1	Pak Song Chol [39]	100	Iemoto JPN
4-08	Myanmar	W	1-0	Hyderabad	CCr1	Ro Hak Su [15]	100	Shamsuzzaman BAN
7-08	Tajikistan	L	0-1	Hyderabad	CCsf		600	Iemoto JPN
13-08	Myanmar	W	4-0	New Delhi	CC3p	Pak Song Chol 3 [10 12 44p], Ro Hak Su [53]	1 000	Jasim UAE
24-08	Qatar	L	1-2	Doha	Fr	Ri Kum Chol [67p]		
29-08	Uzbekistan	D	0-0	Tashkent	Fr			Saidov UZB
6-09	UAE	W	2-1	Abu Dhabi	WCq	Choe Kum Chol [72], An Chol Hyok [80]	10 000	Irmatov UZB
10-09	Korea Republic	D	1-1	Shanghai	WCq	Hong Yong Jo [64p]	3 000	Basma SYR
15-10	Iran	L	1-2	Tehran	WCq	Jong Tae Se [72]	60 000	Al Hilali OMA
28-10	Thailand	L	0-1	Hanoi	Fr			
30-10	Vietnam	D	0-0	Hanoi	Fr			
2009								
23-01	Lebanon	L	0-1	Phuket	Fr			
11-02	Saudi Arabia	W	1-0	Pyongyang	WCq	Mun In Guk [29]	48 000	Irmatov UZB
28-03	UAE	W	2-0	Pyongyang	WCq	Pak Nam Chol [51], Mun In Guk [93+]	50 000	Breeze AUS
1-04	Korea Republic	L	0-1	Seoul	WCq		48 000	Al Hilali OMA
6-06	Iran	D	0-0	Pyongyang	WCq		30 000	Sun Baojie CHN
17-06	Saudi Arabia	D	0-0	Riyadh	WCq		65 000	Basma SYR
23-08	Guam	W	9-2	Kaohsiung	EAq	Kim Yong Jun [8], Pak Nam Chol [12], Mun In Guk [45] An Chol Hyok 4 [20 74 78 89], Choe Kum Chol 2 [28 41]	2 000	Matsuo JPN
25-08	Hong Kong	D	0-0	Kaohsiung	EAq		100	Kim Jong Hyeok KOR
27-08	Chinese Taipei	W	2-1	Kaohsiung	EAq	Jong Tae Se [23p], Ji Yun Nam [61]	10 000	Matsuo JPN
13-10	Congo	D	0-0	Le Mans	Fr			
21-11	Zambia	L	1-4	Lusaka	Fr	Mun In Guk [86p]	10 129	Mpanisi ZAM
27-12	Mali	W	1-0	Doha	Fr	Hong Yong Jo [55]	127	Abdou QAT
30-12	Qatar	W	1-0	Doha	Fr	Choe Chol Man [59]	1 223	Shukralla BHR
2010								
2-01	Iran	L	0-1	Doha	Fr		224	Maillet SEY
17-02	Turkmenistan	D	1-1	Colombo	CCr1	Ryang Yong Gi [51]	400	Mahapab THA
19-02	Kyrgyzstan	W	4-0	Colombo	CCr1	Pak Song Chol [29], Pak Kwang Ryong [47], Choe Myong Ho [65], Ri Chol Myong [68]	300	El Haddad LIB
21-02	India †	W	3-0	Colombo	CCr1	Ryang Yong Gi 2 [36 72], Choe Chol Man [57]	300	Tan Hai CHN
24-02	Myanmar	W	5-0	Colombo	CCsf	Choe Myong Ho [6], Choe Chol Man 2 [12 73], Pak Song Chol [13], Kim Seong Yong [85]	400	Al Yarimi YEM
27-02	Turkmenistan	D	1-1	Colombo	CCf	Ryang Yong Gi [75]. W 5-4p	3 000	Faghani IRN
6-03	Venezuela	L	1-2	Puerto La Cruz	Fr		10 000	Buitrago COL
17-03	Mexico	L	1-2	Torreon	Fr	Choe Kum Chol [56]	30 000	Moreno PAN
22-04	South Africa	D	0-0	Taunusstein-Wehen	Fr		628	Brych GER
15-05	Paraguay	L	0-1	Nyon	Fr		1 000	Bertolini SUI
25-05	Greece	D	2-2	Altach	Fr	Jong Tae Se 2 [24 51]	3 000	Schorgenhofer AUT
6-06	Nigeria	L	1-3	Johannesburg	Fr	Cha Jong Hyok [64]	20 000	
15-06	Brazil	L	1-2	Johannesburg	WCr1	Ji Yun Nam [89]	54 331	Kassai HUN
21-06	Portugal	L	0-7	Cape Town	WCr1		63 644	Pozo CHI
25-06	Côte d'Ivoire	L	0-3	Nelspruit	WCr1		34 763	Undiano ESP
24-09	Vietnam	D	0-0	Hanoi	Fr			
2-11	Singapore	W	2-1	Hanoi	Fr	Ri Kwang Chon [80], Hong Yong Jo [90]		
6-11	Vietnam	W	2-0	Hanoi	Fr	Myong Cha Hyon [55], Ri Jin Hyok [67]		
10-11	Yemen	D	1-1	Aden	Fr	Ri Chol Myong [2]		
24-12	Kuwait	L	1-2	6th October City	Fr	Ri Chol Myong [33]		
27-12	Kuwait	D	2-2	6th October City	Fr			
31-12	Qatar	W	1-0	Doha	Fr	Ryang Yong Gi [70p]		
2011								
4-01	Bahrain	W	1-0	Riffa	Fr	An Chol Hyok [59]		
11-01	UAE	D	0-0	Doha	ACr1		3 639	Mohd Salleh MAS
15-01	Iran	L	0-1	Doha	ACr1		6 488	Shukralla BHR
19-01	Iraq	L	0-1	Al Rayyan	ACr1		4 111	Mohd Salleh MAS

Fr = Friendly match • CC = AFC Challenge Cup • EA = East Asian Championship • WC = FIFA World Cup • q = qualifier

PUR – PUERTO RICO

FIFA/COCA-COLA WORLD RANKING

1993	1994	1995	1996	1997	1998	1999	2000	2001	2002	2003	2004	2005	2006	2007	2008	2009	2010
105	112	128	149	169	182	186	195	195	198	200	194	195	195	196	142	165	133

	2010											Hi/Lo
Jan	Feb	Mar	Mar	Apr	May	Jul	Aug	Sep	Oct	Nov	Dec	97
165	166	167	169	168	166	170	170	170	129	130	133	202

Following the recent surge of interest surrounding football in Puerto Rico, there were definite signs of progress on the pitch at both national team and club level. With club side Puerto Rico Islanders spearheading the transformation of the game, they secured a first-ever international title for football in the country when they won the 2010 CFU Caribbean Club Championship in Trinidad in May, finishing above Trinidad's Joe Public and San Juan Jabloteh. That also gave them a berth in the 2010-11 CONCACAF Champions League where they faced three former winners - Mexico's Toluca, Olimpia from Honduras and El Salvador's Deportivo FAS. Both Toluca and FAS were beaten at home in Bayamon but a last day defeat to Olimpia in Tegucigalpa meant the Islanders just missed out on qualifying for the knockout rounds. Although economic difficulties saw a much reduced domestic championship in 2010, Puerto Rico Islanders finished the year on a high by winning the USSF Pro League - the second tier of club football in the USA - after beating Carolina RailHawks in the final. Coach Colin Clarke also lead the national team in the 2010 Digicel Caribbean Championship, winning all three matches in a first round group staged in Bayamon but then disappointingly losing all three in a second round group in Grenada.

FIFA WORLD CUP RECORD
1930-1970 DNE   1974 DNQ   1978-1982 DNE   1986-2002 DNQ   2006 DNE   2010 DNQ

**FEDERACION
PUERTORRIQUENA DE
FUTBOL (FPF)**

Calle Los Angeles Final
Plaza de Santurce
Apartado postal 367567
San Juan PR 00902

☎ +1 787 7652895
📠 +1 787 7672288
✉ info@fedefutbolpr.com
🖥 www.fedefutbolpr.com
FA 1940 CON 1962 FIFA 1960
P Eric Labrador
GS Frankie Gautier

FIFA BIG COUNT 2006

Total players	222 670
% of population	5.67%
Male	187 470
Female	35 200
Unregistered	43 900
Professionals	45
Referees	601
Admin & coaches	9 016
Number of clubs	75
Number of teams	350

MAJOR CITIES/TOWNS

		Population
1	San Juan	407 386
2	Bayamón	197 009
3	Carolina	167 303
4	Ponce	145 676
5	Caguas	82 148
6	Guaynabo	80 952
7	Mayagüez	72 042
8	Trujillo Alto	54 862
9	Arecibo	47 550
10	Fajardo	33 717
11	Vega Baja	28 930
12	Levittown	28 563
13	Cataño	25 486
14	Guayama	20 749
15	Yauco	20 280
16	Humacao	19 561
17	Candelaria	17 348
18	Cayey	17 263
19	Manatí	15 448

COMMONWEALTH OF PUERTO RICO

Capital San Juan	Population 3 971 020 (128)	% in cities 98%
GDP per capita $17 800 (70)	Area km² 13 790 km² (162)	GMT + / - -4
Neighbours (km) Coast 501		

RECENT INTERNATIONAL MATCHES PLAYED BY PUERTO RICO

2006 Opponents	Score	Venue	Comp	Scorers	Att	Referee
No international matches played in 2006						
2007						
No international matches played in 2007						
2008						
16-01 Bermuda	W 2-0	Hamilton	Fr	Taylor Graham [47], Andres Cabrero [67]	500	Mauchette BER
18-01 Bermuda	W 1-0	Hamilton	Fr	Noah Delgado [13]	325	Raynor BER
26-01 Trinidad and Tobago	D 2-2	Bayamon	Fr	Kupono Low [15], Chris Mesaloudis [33]	4 500	Santos PUR
26-03 Dominican Republic	W 1-0	Bayamon	WCq	Petter Villegas [96p]	8 000	Morales MEX
4-06 Honduras	L 0-4	San Pedro Sula	WCq		20 000	Campbell JAM
14-06 Honduras	D 2-2	Bayamon	WCq	Christopher Megaloudis [31], Petter Villegas [41]	5 000	Lopez GUA
2009						
No international matches played in 2009						
2010						
2-10 Anguilla	W 3-1	Bayamon	CCq	Hansen [28], Megaloudis 2 [32 81]	2 050	Thomas JAM
4-10 Saint Martin †	W 2-0	Bayamon	CCq	Krause [26], Arrieta [80]	1 800	Legister JAM
6-10 Cayman Islands	W 2-0	Bayamon	CCq	Megaloudis [26], Figueroa [89]	3 800	Campbell JAM
22-10 Grenada	L 1-3	St George's	CCq	Nieves [81]	600	Wijngaarde SUR
24-10 Guadeloupe †	L 2-3	St George's	CCq	Megaloudis [65], Villegas [74]	200	Baptiste DMA
26-10 St Kitts and Nevis	L 0-1	St George's	CCq		500	Morrison JAM

Fr = Friendly match • CC = Digicel Caribbean Cup • WC = FIFA World Cup • q = qualifier • † Not an official internatiuonal

PUERTO RICO 2010
SUPERCOPA DIRECTV

First Round Group Stage

Group A	Pl	W	D	L	F	A	Pts	RP	Ma	Fl	Fa
River Plate	6	6	0	0	29	2	**18**		1-0	4-1	7-0
Mayagüez	6	2	1	3	10	5	**7**	0-1		4-0	5-0
Fluminense	6	2	1	3	12	19	**7**	1-9	3-1		6-0
Fajardo	6	0	2	4	1	26	**2**	0-7	0-0	1-1	

Group B	Pl	W	D	L	F	A	Pts	PRI	Se	PRU	Hu
PR Islanders	6	5	1	0	27	2	**16**		1-1	4-0	6-0
Sevilla	6	4	1	1	10	5	**13**	1-2		3-0	1-0
Puerto Rico Utd	6	1	0	5	5	15	**3**	0-3	0-1		1-4
Huracán	6	1	0	5	6	26	**3**	0-11	2-3	0-4	

30/10/2010 - 12/12/2010

Semi-finals

River Plate	1 1
Sevilla	0 1

Mayagüez	1 0
PR Islanders	2 2

Final

River Plate	1 2
PR Islanders	0 0

QAT – QATAR

FIFA/COCA-COLA WORLD RANKING

1993	1994	1995	1996	1997	1998	1999	2000	2001	2002	2003	2004	2005	2006	2007	2008	2009	2010
54	60	83	69	70	60	107	102	80	62	65	66	95	58	87	84	86	114

	2010												Hi/Lo
	Jan	Feb	Mar	Mar	Apr	May	Jul	Aug	Sep	Oct	Nov	Dec	51
	86	89	92	97	95	96	98	98	104	109	113	114	114

Qatar had plenty of high profile people like Zinedine Zidane backing their bid to host the FIFA World Cup finals in 2022 but it was to general surprise when FIFA president Sepp Blatter pulled their name out of the envelope. It was certainly a bold bid, full of innovation in order to tackle the searing heat of the summer months when the tournament will be played although immediately rumours were started about rescheduling the tournament. Ironically, just a month after the decision Qatar played host to the AFC Asian Cup where they highlighted their ability to organise top class events with a well-organised tournament. On the pitch, however, it was a different story. Bruno Metsu's team lost to Uzbekistan in the opening match of the tournament and there can be no doubt that the small player pool available from a population of less than a million could seriously restrict the progress of the team as it builds towards the finals in 2022. Wins over China PR and Kuwait saw the Qataris sneak into the quarter-finals where their progress was halted in dramatic fashion by eventual winners Japan. Despite twice leading and with Japan down to 10 men, a late Masahiko Inoha's goal not only ended Qatar's involvement in the tournament but also Metsu's tenure as coach. For the next 12 years, expect to hear much more about this tiny but super rich Gulf state.

FIFA WORLD CUP RECORD
1930-1974 DNE   1978-2010 DNQ

QATAR FOOTBALL ASSOCIATION (QFA)

7th Floor, QNOC Building, West Bay, PO Box 5333, Doha

☎ +974 44944411
📠 +974 44944424
✉ info@qfa.com.qa
🖥 www.qfa.com.qa
FA 1960 CON 1972 FIFA 1970
P Shk Hamad Al Thani
GS Saoud Al Mohannadi

FIFA BIG COUNT 2006

Total players	18 156
% of population	2.05%
Male	18 020
Female	136
Amateurs 18+	2 236
Youth under 18	4 320
Unregistered	2 600
Professionals	0
Referees	98
Admin & coaches	432
Number of clubs	16
Number of teams	160

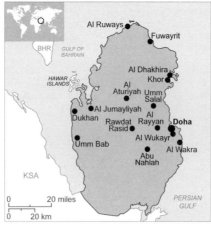

MAJOR CITIES/TOWNS

		Population
1	Doha	410 494
2	Al Rayyan	367 026
3	Umm Salal	39 905
4	Al Wakra	31 922
5	Khor	27 260
6	Al Dhakhira	21 268
7	Al Shahniya	15 240
8	Musayid	12 080
9	Dukhan	9 408
10	Al Hisah	6 456
11	Al Wukayr	5 952
12	Rawdat Rasid	4 532
13	Al Ruways	4 119
14	Abu Nahlah	3 335
15	Umm Bab	3 085
16	Al Guwariyah	2 784
17	Al Jumayliyah	2 283
18	Al Kiranah	1 727
19	Fuwayrit	1 663

DAWLAT QATAR • STATE OF QATAR

Capital	Doha	Population	833 285 (158)	% in cities	96%
GDP per capita	$111 000 (2)	Area km²	11 586 km² (165)	GMT + / -	+3
Neighbours (km)	Saudi Arabia 60 • Coast 563				

RECENT INTERNATIONAL MATCHES PLAYED BY QATAR

2008	Opponents	Score		Venue	Comp	Scorers	Att	Referee
6-09	Uzbekistan	W	3-0	Doha	WCq	Majdi Siddiq [37], Magid Hassan [72], Talal Alblboushi [89]	8 000	Mohd Salleh MAS
10-09	Bahrain	D	1-1	Doha	WCq	Soria [6]	7 000	Kim Dong Jin KOR
15-10	Australia	L	0-4	Brisbane	WCq		34 320	Al Ghamdi KSA
9-11	Iran	L	0-1	Doha	Fr			
14-11	Korea Republic	D	1-1	Doha	Fr	Montesin [73]		
19-11	Japan	L	0-3	Doha	WCq		13 000	Sun Baojie CHN
2009								
5-01	Saudi Arabia	D	0-0	Muscat	GCr1			
8-01	UAE	D	0-0	Muscat	GCr1			
11-01	Yemen	W	2-1	Muscat	GCr1	Musa Jama [13], Majdi Siddiq [98+]		
14-01	Oman	L	0-1	Muscat	GCsf			
17-03	Kuwait	W	1-0	Doha	Fr	Nasser Nabil Salem [56]		
21-03	Syria	W	2-1	Aleppo	Fr	Quintana 2 [56 74]		
28-03	Uzbekistan	L	0-4	Tashkent	WCq		18 000	Moradi IRN
1-04	Bahrain	L	0-1	Manama	WCq		20 000	Sun Baojie CHN
26-05	Saudi Arabia	W	2-1	Doha	Fr	Ali Yahya [63p], Ibrahim Abdulmajed [87]		
6-06	Australia	D	0-0	Doha	WCq		7 000	Bashir SIN
10-06	Japan	D	1-1	Yokohama	WCq	Ali Yahya [53p]	60 256	Mohd Salleh MAS
9-09	Oman	D	1-1	Doha	Fr	Ali Yahya [44]		
8-10	Croatia	L	2-3	Rijeka	Fr	Kovac.R OG [43], Soria [69]		
11-10	Macedonia FYR	L	1-2	Skopje	Fr	Musa Jama [24]		
14-10	Congo DR	D	2-2	Sannois St Gratien	Fr	Ali Yahya [60], Magid Hassan [75]		
13-11	Paraguay	W	2-0	Rouen	Fr	Montesin 2 [57 81]		
17-11	Belgium	L	0-2	Sedan	Fr			
28-12	Iran	W	3-2	Doha	Fr	Ali Yahya [7], Magid Hassan 2 [10 94+]		
30-12	Korea DPR	L	0-1	Doha	Fr			
2010								
2-01	Mali	D	0-0	Doha	Fr			
3-03	Slovenia	L	1-4	Maribor	Fr	Fabio Cesar [41]	4 900	Van Boekel NED
10-08	Bosnia-Herzegovina	D	1-1	Sarajevo	Fr	Wesam Rizik [58p]	18 000	Vuckov CRO
3-09	Bahrain	D	1-1	Doha	Fr	Majdi Siddiq [41]		
7-09	Oman	D	1-1	Doha	Fr	Fabio Cesar [68]		
12-10	Iraq	L	1-2	Doha	Fr	Magid Hassan [33]		
18-11	Haiti	L	0-1	Doha	Fr			
22-11	Kuwait	L	0-1	Aden	GCr1			Al Rashid OMA
25-11	Yemen	W	2-1	Abyan	GCr1	Jaralla Al Marri 2 [35 55]		Abid Iddan IRQ
28-11	Saudi Arabia	D	1-1	Aden	GCr1	Ibrahim Al Ghanim [84]		Al Marzouqi UAE
16-12	Egypt	W	2-1	Doha	Fr	Soria [21], OG [43]		
22-12	Estonia	W	2-0	Doha	Fr	Soria 2 [37 78]		
28-12	Iran	D	0-0	Doha	Fr			
31-12	Korea DPR	L	0-1	Doha	Fr			
2011								
7-01	Uzbekistan	L	0-2	Doha	ACr1		37 143	Nishimura JPN
12-01	China PR	W	2-0	Doha	ACr1	Yusef Ahmed 2 [27 45]	30 778	Kim Dong Jin KOR
16-01	Kuwait	W	3-0	Doha	ACr1	Bilal Mohammed [12], Mohamed El Sayed [16], Fabio Cesar [86]	28 339	Abdul Bashir SIN
21-01	Japan	L	2-3	Doha	ACqf	Soria [13], Fabio Cesar [63]	19 479	Mohd Salleh MAS

Fr = Friendly match • AC = AFC Asian Cup • GC = Gulf Cup • WC = FIFA World Cup

QATAR NATIONAL TEAM HISTORICAL RECORDS

Past Coaches

Mohammed Hassan Kheiri 1969-72 • Helmi Hussein Mahmoud 1974 • Frank Wignall ENG 1975-76 • Hassan Othman 1979 • Evaristo de Macedo BRA 1980-86 • Procopio Cardoso BRA 1987-88 • Anatoly Prokopenko URS 1988 • Cabralzinho BRA 1989 • Dino Sani BRA 1989-90 • Evaristo de Macedo BRA 1992 • Ivo Wortmann BRA 1992 • Sebastiao Lapola BRA 1992-93 • Abdul Mallalah 1993 • Dave Mackay SCO 1994-95 • Jorgen Larsen DEN 1995-96 • Jo Bonfrere NED 1996-97 • Dzemal Hadziabdic YUG 1997 • Ze Mario BRA 1998 • Luiz Gonzaga Milioli 1998 • Dzemal Hadziabdic YUG 2000-01 • Paulo Luiz Campos BRA 2001 • Pierre Lechantre FRA 2002-03 • Philippe Troussier FRA 2003-04 • Dzemaludin Musovic BIH 2004-07 • Jorge Fossati URU 2007-08 • Bruno Metsu FRA 2008-11

QATAR 2009-10

QATAR STARS LEAGUE

	Pl	W	D	L	F	A	Pts	Gharafa	Sadd	Arabi	Qatar SC	Rayyan	Khritiyat	Umm Salal	Wakra	Khor	Ahli	Siliya	Shamal
Al Gharafa †	22	16	5	1	55	16	53	–	4-1	2-1	0-0	4-1	2-0	1-0	2-3	4-1	4-0	1-0	8-1
Al Sadd	22	15	5	2	55	22	50	1-1	–	3-3	3-0	4-3	1-1	5-0	0-0	2-1	3-0	2-1	5-1
Al Arabi	22	12	4	6	52	30	40	1-1	0-2	–	2-3	0-5	1-2	2-1	3-2	2-1	1-2	2-2	6-2
Qatar SC	22	11	5	6	32	23	38	3-3	1-1	1-3	–	5-2	3-1	0-0	1-0	2-0	2-0	3-0	0-3
Al Rayyan	22	11	4	7	41	30	37	0-3	1-4	3-1	1-3	–	0-1	0-0	5-2	2-1	2-0	0-0	3-0
Al Khritiyat	22	8	5	9	23	36	29	0-4	0-2	0-6	0-2	0-1	–		4-2	0-1	2-1	1-0	1-2
Umm Salal	22	7	7	8	27	30	28	1-3	1-0	1-3	0-1	1-1	3-3	–	2-2	1-0	3-2	1-0	4-1
Al Wakra	22	8	3	11	44	44	27	1-4	1-3	0-1	0-1	0-4	1-1	3-2	–	4-1	5-2	1-2	7-0
Khor	22	5	5	12	21	30	20	0-1	0-2	0-0			2-0		1-0	–	1-1	1-1	1-1
Al Ahli	22	6	2	14	31	53	20	0-0	2-6	0-4	1-0	1-2	2-3	1-4	4-5	3-2	–	1-2	6-2
Al Siliya	22	4	7	11	16	28	19	0-1	1-3	0-2	1-0	0-2	0-0	0-0	0-3	1-2	0-1	–	1-1
Shamal	22	2	2	18	17	72	8	1-2	0-2	0-7	0-3	0-3	0-1	1-1	1-2	1-5		0-3	–

12/09/2009 - 4/04/2010 • † Qualified for AFC Champions League • Top scorers: 21 - Younis Mahmoud IRQ, Al Gharafa & Cabore BRA, Al Arabi • 20 - Leandro Montera Da Silva BRA, Al Sadd • 17 - Adil Ramzi MAR, Al Wakra • 15 - Klemerson BRA, Al Gharafa & Sebastian Soria QAT, Qatar SC Relegation play-off: **Al Siliya** 2-0 Mseimeer. **Lekhwia** promoted from the second division
Crown Prince Cup: Semi-finals: **Al Gharafa** 2-1 Qatar SC; Al Sadd 0-1 **Al Arabi** • Final: Al Arabi 0-5 **Al Gharafa.** The Crown Prince Cup is a tournament played at the end of the season between the top four of the league but it is not part of the league season

MEDALS TABLE

		Overall G	S	B	Lg G	Cup G	S	CP	QC	QS	Asia G	S	B	City
1	Al Sadd	42	6	1	12	12	6	5	12			1	1	Doha
2	Al Arabi	21	4	1	7	8	3	1	5			1	1	Doha
3	Al Gharrafa	19	3		7	6	3	2	3	1				Doha
4	Al Rayyan	16	9	1	7	4	9	3	2				1	Al Rayyan
5	Qatar SC	13	3		3	3	3	3	4					Doha
6	Al Wakra	7	6		2		6	1	4					Al Wakra
7	Al Oruba	5			5									
8	Al Ahli	4	5			4	5							Doha
9	Umm Salal	3	1	1		1	1		2				1	Umm Salal
10	Al Maref	3			3									
11	Khor	2	2					2	1	1				Khor
12	Al Shamal	1							1					
13	Al Shabab	1							1					

Name changes: Al Ittihad → Al Gharrafa • Al Taawun → Khor • Al Oruba merged with Qatar SC to form Al Esteqlal but renamed to Qatar SC in 1981 Cup = Emir's Cup • CP = Crown Prince Cup • QC = Sheikh Qassim Cup • QS = Qatar Stars Cup

SHEIKH JASSIM CUP 2010

Group A	Pts
Lekhwia	12
Khor	9
Al Gharafa	6
Al Rayyan	3
Markheya	0

Group B	Pts
Al Wakra	12
Qatar SC	9
Al Jaish	6
Maitheer	3
Al Shamal	0

Group C	Pts
Al Sadd	7
Umm Salal	7
Al Ahli	3
Mseimeer	0

Group D	Pts
Al Arabi	7
Al Khritiyat	7
Al Siliya	3
Shahaniya	0

Semi-finals:
Al Arabi 2 4p — Al Wakra 2 3p
Al Sadd 1 — Lekhwia 2

Final:
Al Arabi 1 — Lekhwia 0

Final: Doha Stadium, 5-09-2010
Scorer - Everaldo [85] for Al Arabi

QATAR STARS CUP 2010

Group A	Pts
Al Siliya	12
Al Arabi	10
Al Sadd	7
Qatar SC	7
Umm Salal	4
Al Shamal	3

Group B	Pts
Al Ahli	12
Al Gharafa	10
Al Rayyan	8
Al Wakra	4
Khor	4
Al Khritiyat	3

Semi-finals:
Al Gharafa 3 — Al Siliya 2
Al Arabi 1 — Al Ahli 2

Final:
Al Gharafa 5 — Al Ahli 0

Final: Grand Hamad, Doha, 5-01-2010
Scorers - Clemerson 3 [9 39 78], Younis Mahmoud 2 [45 71] for Al Gharafa

EMIR'S CUP 2009–10

Round of 16		Quarter–finals		Semi–finals		Final	
Al Rayyan	1						
Al Siliya	0	Al Rayyan	2				
		Al Gharafa	1				
Al Gharafa	Bye			Al Rayyan	2		
Al Ahli	3			Al Sadd	1		
Al Wakra	2	Al Ahli	0				
		Al Sadd	2				
Al Sadd	Bye					Al Rayyan †	1
Qatar SC	Bye					Umm Salal	0
		Qatar SC	2				
Khor	1	Al Khritiyat	1				
Al Khritiyat	3			Qatar SC	0		
Al Arabi	Bye			Umm Salal	1		
		Al Arabi	1 3p				
Shamal	2	Umm Salal	1 4p				
Umm Salal	3						

CUP FINAL
Khalifa International, Doha
15-05-2010, Att: 50 000
Scorer - Afonso Alves 82

† Qualified for AFC Champions League

CLUB BY CLUB GUIDE TO THE 2009-10 SEASON IN QATAR

AL AHLI 2009–10

Aug	23	Al Rayyan	L	1-5 SJg3	Mesha Abdulla 25p
	26	Umm Salal	L	1-5 SJg3	Mesha Abdulla 25
	29	Mseimeer	W	2-0 SJg3	Thia Oleviea 2 10 34
Sep	13	Al Shamal	W	1-0 QSL	Fernando Dienns 65
	18	Al Sadd	L	0-3 QSL	
	3	Al Wakra	L	4-5 QSL	Ahmed Dad 19, Adel Ahmed 33, Julio Cesar 36, OG 56
Oct	9	Al Rayyan	W	3-0 SCgB	Adel Ahmed 2 20 68, Mesha Abdulla 90
	16	Al Wakra	W	1-0 SCgB	Mesha Abdulla
	23	Al Rayyan	L	1-2 QSL	Julio Cesar 91+
	30	Al Khritiyat	L	2-3 QSL	Rahman Rezaei 39, Thia Oleviea 41
	6	Al Arabi	W	2-1 QSL	Wegnar Renato 11, Fernando Almeda 27
Nov	13	Khor	L	0-1 SCgB	
	17	Al Khritiyat	W	4-2 SCgB	Julio Cesar 2 18 49, Mesha Abdulla 53p, Shahin Ali 91+
	22	Khor	D	1-1 QSL	Julio Cesar 18
	1	Qatar SC	W	1-0 QSL	Mesha Abdulla 54
Dec	6	Umm Salal	L	2-3 QSL	Wegnar Renato 50, Mesha Abdulla 56
	11	Al Siliya	W	1-0 QSL	Emad Nasser 51
	21	Al Gharafa	L	0-4 QSL	
	29	Al Gharafa	W	3-0 SCgB	Julio Cesar 2 2p 10, Abdulrahman 27
	1	Al Arabi	W	2-1 SCsf	Julio Cesar 74, Mesha Abdulla 92
	5	Al Gharafa	L	0-5 SCf	
Jan	9	Al Shamal	W	6-2 QSL	Julio Cesar 3 20 34 62, Theo Oleviea 58, Abdulla Mostafa 67, Khalifa Ayil 82p
	15	Al Sadd	L	2-6 QSL	Thia Oleviea 2 42 85
	23	Umm Salal	L	1-4 QSL	Julio Cesar 26
	28	Al Wakra	L	2-5 QSL	Thia Oleviea 86, Julio Cesar 89
Feb	3	Al Rayyan	L	0-2 QSL	
	8	Al Khritiyat	L	1-2 QSL	Wegnar Renato 53
	14	Al Arabi	L	0-4 QSL	
	20	Khor	W	3-2 QSL	Wegnar Renato 2 44 91+, Julio Cesar 65
Mar	14	Qatar SC	L	0-2 QSL	
	20	Al Siliya	L	1-2 QSL	Abdulla Mostafa 55
	4	Al Gharafa	D	0-0 QSL	
Apr	15	Mseimeer	W	2-1 ECr2	Thia Oleviea 24, Wegnar Renato 88
	26	Al Wakra	W	3-2 ECr3	Thia Oleviea 3, Julio Cesar 44, Khalifa Ayil 90
My	2	Al Sadd	L	0-2 ECqf	

AL ARABI 2009–10

Aug	22	Shahaniya	W	3-0 SJg2	Salman Issa 5, Leonardo 46, Salem Al Mal 79
	28	Al Sadd	L	2-4 SJg2	Carlos Diaz 2 69 87
Sep	13	Al Siliya	D	2-2 QSL	Leonardo 40, Ali Fartous 78
	19	Qatar SC	W	3-1 QSL	Salman Issa 5, Moaz Yousif 42, Leonardo 58
	26	Al Gharafa	D	1-1 QSL	Leonardo 8
Oct	3	Al Khritiyat	W	6-0 QSL	Salman Issa 3, Everaldo 9, Carlos Diaz 39, OG 42, Everaldo 2 79 93+
	8	Umm Salal	W	3-0 SCgA	Ali Fartous 2 66 91+, Al Mal 76
	15	Al Siliya	W	3-2 SCgA	Ali Fartous 2 48 86, Al Mal 75
	31	Khor	W	2-1 QSL	Salman Issa 22, Ali Fartous 88p
Nov	6	Al Ahli	L	1-2 QSL	Everaldo 52
	13	Al Sadd	D	3-3 SCgA	Everaldo 52, Al Mal 64, Mousa Haroun 90
	16	Qatar SC	W	3-1 SCgA	Everaldo 3 48 54 95+
	24	Al Sadd	D	3-3 QSL	Everaldo 36, Abdulaziz Al Sulaiti 48, Al Mal 52
Dec	1	Al Shamal	W	7-0 QSL	Abdulaziz Hatim 38, Everaldo 3 40 52 88, Carlos Diaz 64, Al Mal 72, Omer Al Ansari 90
	11	Al Rayyan	L	0-5 QSL	
	16	Umm Salal	W	2-1 QSL	Everaldo 2 18 85
	22	Al Wakra	W	1-0 QSL	Everaldo 75p
	29	Al Shamal	L	1-2 SCgA	Hadi Al Marri 4
	1	Al Ahli	L	1-2 SCsf	Ali Fartous 72
Jan	10	Al Siliya	W	2-0 QSL	Abdulaziz Hatim 2 56 69
	15	Qatar SC	W	3-0 QSL	
	22	Al Gharafa	L	1-2 QSL	Everaldo 85
	28	Al Khritiyat	L	1-2 QSL	Everaldo 40p
	4	Umm Salal	W	3-1 QSL	Daniel Carvalho 32, Everaldo 50, Al Mal 58
Feb	9	Khor	D	0-0 QSL	
	14	Al Ahli	W	4-0 QSL	Carlos Diaz 26, Carvalho 2 54 91+, Everaldo 66
	19	Al Sadd	L	0-2 QSL	
Mar	13	Al Shamal	W	6-2 QSL	Everaldo 4 31 69 76 86, Mojtaba Said Ja 72, Ali Fartous 87
	20	Al Rayyan	L	1-3 QSL	Abdulaziz Al Sulati 27
	3	Al Wakra	W	3-2 QSL	Everaldo 2 41 91+, Al Mal
Apr	18	Al Sadd	W	1-0 CPsf	Everaldo 64
	24	Al Gharafa	L	0-5 CPf	
	30	Umm Salal	D	1-1 ECqf	Joji Boualem 110, L 3-4p

QSL = Qatar Stars League • SJ = Sheikh Jassim Cup • SC = Qatar Stars Cup • CP = Crown Prince Cup • EC = Emir's Cup • CL = AFC Champions League • gA = group A etc • r1 = first round etc • qf = quarter-final • sf = semi-final • f = final
Clubs use a variety of stadia. Matches in the 2009 Sheik Jassim Cup were played either at the Suheim Bin Hamad Stadium or the Grand Hamad Stadium in Doha with the final staged at the Doha Stadium • Matches in the 2009-10 Qatar Stars Cup were played either at the Suheim Bin Hamad Stadium or the Grand Hamad Stadium in Doha with the final staged at the later • All matches in the 2010 Crown Prince Cup were played at the Jassim Bin Hamad Stadium • Matches in the 2010 Emir's Cup were played either at the Suheim Bin Hamad Stadium or the Grand Hamad Stadium in Doha with the final staged at the Khalifa International Stadium • League matches were played at a variety of venues. The matches with no shading were technically 'away' matches.

AL GHARAFA 2009–10

Month	Date	Opponent	Res	Score	Comp	Scorers
Aug	22	Al Wakra	W	3-2	SJg1	Younis Mahmoud 28, Clemerson Araujo 44, Juninho Pernambuco 74
	25	Al Markheya	W	8-0	SJg1	Younis M. 3 5 13 62, Clemerson 2 7 19, Juninho P. 2 30p 77, Mergani Al Zain 58
	28	Al Siliya	W	2-0	SJg1	Clemerson 2 10 45
	1	Umm Salal	L	2-3	SJsf	Ibrahim Al Ganim 29, Mergani Al Zain 62
Sep	12	Khor	W	4-1	QSL	Anas Mobarak 37, Clemerson 2 45 88, Younis M. 48
	17	Al Shamal	W	2-1	QSL	Younis M. 2 32 51
	26	Al Arabi	D	1-1	QSL	Younis M. 21
	5	Al Siliya	W	1-0	QSL	Juninho P. 96+
Oct	9	Al Khritiyat	W	3-2	SCgB	Anas Mobarak 36, Saoud Al Shammari 43, Juninho P. 54
	16	Al Rayyan	D	3-3	SCgB	Mohammed Al Hajj 38, Saoud AS 60, Klemerson 77
	24	Qatar SC	D	3-3	QSL	Younis M. 33, Juninho P. 45, Bilal Mohammed 55
Nov	1	Al Rayyan	W	4-1	QSL	Younis M. 28p, Clemerson 3 47 80 83
	7	Al Khritiyat	W	2-0	QSL	Ibrahim Al Ganim 10, Clemerson 78
	12	Al Wakra	W	2-1	SCgB	Clemerson 3, Othman El Assas 72
	17	Khor	W	5-1	SCgB	Othman EA 17, Clemerson 3 26 61 75, Georges Koussy 60
	23	Umm Salal	W	3-1	QSL	Klemerson 15, Anas Mobarak 2 74 92+
	30	Al Wakra	L	2-3	QSL	Saoud AS 2, Younis M. 90
Dec	12	Al Sadd	D	1-1	QSL	Klemerson 56
	21	Al Ahli	W	4-0	QSL	Younis M. 2 34p 47, Juninho P. 41, Mergani Al Zain 49
	29	Al Ahli	L	0-3	SCgB	
Jan	1	Al Siliya	W	3-2	SCsf	OG 11, Younis M. 62, Clemerson 84p
	5	Al Ahli	W	5-0	SCf	Clemerson 3 9 39 78, Younis M. 2 45 71
	10	Khor	W	1-0	QSL	Nasser Kamil 79
	16	Al Shamal	W	8-1	QSL	Saoud AS 37, Younis M 3 49 73 82, Juninho P. 62, Clemerson 3 70 80 90
	22	Al Arabi	W	2-1	QSL	Younis M. 2 28p 64
	30	Al Siliya	W	1-0	QSL	Fuhaid Al Shammeri 81
Feb	4	Qatar SC	D	0-0	QSL	
	9	Al Rayyan	W	3-0	QSL	Younis M. 2 8 48, Mergani AZ 20
	13	Al Khritiyat	W	4-0	QSL	Younis M. 2 19 35p, Clemerson 32, Othman EA 59
	18	Umm Salal	W	1-0	QSL	Clemerson 54
	23	Al Jazira	W	2-1	CLgA	Othman EA 17, Younis M. 53
	9	Al Ahli KSA	W	3-2	CLgA	Mergani AZ 2, Saoud AS 79, Clemerson 81
	13	Al Wakra	W	4-1	QSL	Younis M. 30, Clemerson 35, Juninho P 2 50 86
Mar	19	Al Sadd	W	4-1	QSL	Clemerson 14, Saoud AS 59, Younis M 2 60 64
	23	Esteghlal	L	0-3	CLgA	
	31	Esteghlal	D	1-1	CLgA	Younis M. 45
	4	Al Ahli	D	0-0	QSL	
Apr	14	Al Jazira	W	4-2	CLgA	Clemerson 3 11 41 46, Othman EA 65
	19	Qatar SC	W	2-1	CPsf	Mergani AZ 15, Clemerson 30
	24	Al Arabi	W	5-0	CPf	Clemerson 2 3 49, Younis M. 2 15 44,
	28	Al Ahli KSA	W	1-0	CLgA	Nasser Kamil 92+
May	3	Al Rayyan	L	1-2	ECqf	Mergani AZ 7
	11	Pakhtakor	W	1-0	CLr2	Clemerson 86p

KHOR 2009–10

Month	Date	Opponent	Res	Score	Comp	Scorers
Aug	23	Maitheer	W	4-1	SJg4	Moumouni Dagano 2 32 44, Ibrahim Awwal 2 45 62
	26	Khor	W	4-0	SJg4	Dagano 3 31 35 73, Sayed Adnan 75
Sep	29	Qatar SC	D	1-1	SJg4	Dagano 62
	1	Al Sadd	D	2-2	SJsf	W 3-1p. Kasula 60, Nasser Jalal 97+
	4	Umm Salal	L	0-2	SJf	
	12	Al Gharafa	L	1-4	QSL	Rafik Saifi 84
	18	Al Siliya	D	1-1	QSL	Sayed Adnan 75
	24	Al Shamal	L	0-1	QSL	
Oct	4	Qatar SC	L	0-2	QSL	
	9	Khor	L	0-1	SCgB	
	16	Al Khritiyat	D	1-1	SCgB	
	22	Al Khritiyat	W	1-0	QSL	Rafik Saifi 79
	31	Al Arabi	L	1-2	QSL	Dagano 40
Nov	6	Umm Salal	L	0-1	QSL	
	13	Al Ahli	W	1-0	QSL	Safar Yazal Somara 78
	17	Al Gharafa	L	1-5	SCgB	Ibrahim Awwal 67
	22	Al Ahli	D	1-1	QSL	Dagano 33
	29	Al Rayyan	D	0-0	QSL	
Dec	12	Al Wakra	W	1-0	QSL	Salam Shakir 90
	22	Al Sadd	L	1-2	QSL	Mohamed Kasoula 82
	29	Al Rayyan	L	2-3	SCgB	Ibrahim Awwal 33, Nasser Jalal Moussa 71
	10	Al Gharafa	L	0-1	QSL	
Jan	14	Al Siliya	W	2-1	QSL	Sayad Adnan 28, Ibrahim Awwal 58
	22	Al Shamal	W	5-1	QSL	Sayad Adnan 2 9 51, Mustafa Jalal 12, Ibrahim Awwal 2 64 93+
	29	Qatar SC	D	1-1	QSL	Abdoulaye Cisse 7
Feb	4	Al Khritiyat	W	2-0	QSL	Sayad Adnan 2 59p 73
	9	Al Arabi	D	0-0	QSL	
	14	Umm Salal	L	0-1	QSL	
Mar	20	Al Ahli	L	2-3	QSL	Dagano 39, Sayed Adnan 90
	12	Al Rayyan	L	1-2	QSL	Dagano 5
	19	Al Wakra	L	1-4	QSL	Dagano 51
	4	Al Sadd	L	0-2	QSL	
Apr	16	Maitheer	W	5-2	ECr2	Dagano 6, Cisse 2 45 58, Adnan 61, Abdulla Bari 72
	26	Al Khritiyat	L	1-3	ECr3	Hashim Edris 87

AL KHRITIYAT 2009–10

Month	Date	Opponent	Res	Score	Comp	Scorers
Aug	22	Al Sadd	L	0-5	SJg2	
	25	Al Arabi	D	0-0	SJg2	
	28	Shahaniya	W	1-0	SJg2	
Sep	12	Al Wakra	D	1-1	QSL	Yahia Kiepi 14
	19	Al Rayyan	L	0-1	QSL	
	25	Al Sadd	D	1-1	QSL	Alaa Abdul Zahra 66
	3	Al Arabi	L	0-6	QSL	
Oct	9	Al Gharafa	L	2-3	SCgB	Jar Al Marri 2 26 29
	16	Khor	D	1-1	SCgB	Hassan Shami 15
	22	Khor	L	0-1	QSL	
	30	Al Ahli	W	3-2	QSL	Alaa Abdul Zahra 2 21 62, Yahia Kiepi 65
	7	Al Gharafa	L	0-2	QSL	
Nov	13	Al Rayyan	D	2-2	SCgB	Yahia Kiepi 83, Suliman Kita 97+p
	17	Al Ahli	L	2-4	SCgB	Yahia Kiepi 2 13 66
	23	Al Siliya	D	1-1	QSL	Yahia Kiepi 33
	29	Umm Salal	W	1-0	QSL	Yahia Kiepi 60
Dec	11	Al Shamal	W	1-0	QSL	Alaa Abdul Zahra 42
	20	Qatar SC	L	1-3	QSL	Bilal Abdulrahman 49
	26	Al Wakra	D	0-0	SCgB	
Jan	9	Al Wakra	W	4-2	QSL	Alaa Abdul Zahra 22, Jar Al Mari 3 31 34 56
	14	Al Rayyan	W	1-0	QSL	Yahia Kiepi 78
	21	Al Sadd	L	0-2	QSL	
	28	Al Arabi	W	2-1	QSL	Jar Al Marri 69, Alaa Abdul Zahra 77
	4	Khor	L	0-2	QSL	
Feb	8	Al Ahli	W	2-1	QSL	Alaa Abdul Zahra 2 39 56
	13	Al Gharafa	L	0-4	QSL	
	20	Al Siliya	D	0-0	QSL	
Mar	12	Umm Salal	D	3-3	QSL	Alaa Abdul Zahra 2 15 38, Yahia Kiepi 40
	18	Al Shamal	W	2-1	QSL	Jar Al Marri 2 20 28
	3	Qatar SC	L	0-2	QSL	
Apr	26	Khor	W	3-1	ECr3	Alaa Abdul Zahra 9, Jar Allah Al Mari 36, Yahia Kiepi 46
My	1	Qatar SC	L	1-2	ECqf	Alaa Abdul Zahra 91+

QATAR SC 2009–10

Month	Date	Opponent		Score	Comp	Scorers
Aug	23	Al Shamal	W	1-0	SJg4	Sebastian Soria 76
	26	Maitheer	W	4-1	SJg4	Marcio Olivira 2 28 88, Abdulla Saad Al Kawari 2 50 65
	29	Khor	D	1-1	SJg4	Soria 87p
Sep	12	Al Rayyan	W	5-2	QSL	Marcio Olivira 2 41 78p, Al Kawari 57, Soria 2 59 87
	19	Al Arabi	L	1-3	QSL	Soria 34
	25	Al Wakra	W	1-0	QSL	Yousef Ali 60
Oct	4	Khor	W	2-0	QSL	Marcio Olivira 51, Soria 77
	8	Al Siliya	L	0-1	SCgA	
	15	Al Sadd	W	2-1	SCgA	Marcio Olivira 16, Qusai Muneer 72
	24	Al Gharafa	D	3-3	QSL	Soria 10, Qusai Muneer 14, Yousef Ali 74
	31	Al Sadd	L	0-3	QSL	
Nov	5	Al Siliya	L	0-1	QSL	
	11	Al Shamal	W	3-0	SCgA	Marcio Olivira 2 6 35, Youssef Safri 15
	16	Al Arabi	L	1-3	SCgA	Ali Hasan Kamal 26
	22	Al Shamal	L	0-3	QSL	
Dec	1	Al Ahli	L	0-1	QSL	
	12	Umm Salal	W	1-0	QSL	Soria 66p
	20	Al Khritiyat	W	3-1	QSL	Marcio Olivira 17, Soria 53, Talal El Karkouri 73
	26	Umm Salal	D	0-0	SCgA	
Jan	9	Al Rayyan	W	3-1	QSL	El Karkouri 38, Soria 2 42 59
	15	Al Arabi	L	0-3	QSL	
	23	Al Wakra	W	1-0	QSL	Soria 29
	29	Khor	D	1-1	QSL	Mohammed Omar 85
Feb	4	Al Gharafa	D	0-0	QSL	
	9	Al Sadd	D	1-1	QSL	Fadhel Omar 90
	13	Al Siliya	W	3-0	QSL	El Kharkouri 57, Jasim Al Buaenain 69, Soria 78
	18	Al Shamal	W	3-0	QSL	Soria 23, Qusai Muneer 25, El Kharkouri 92+
Mar	14	Al Ahli	W	2-0	QSL	Al Kawari 65, Soria 94+p
	18	Umm Salal	D	0-0	QSL	
Apr	3	Al Khritiyat	W	2-0	QSL	Soria 2 12 80
	19	Al Gharafa	L	1-2	CPsf	Soria 4
May	1	Al Khritiyat	W	2-1	ECqf	Soria 1, Qusai Muneer 72
	8	Umm Salal	L	0-1	ECsf	

AL RAYYAN 2009–10

Month	Date	Opponent		Score	Comp	Scorers
Aug	23	Al Ahli	W	5-1	SJg3	Sayyed Ali Basheer 16, Amara Diane 2 30 42, Aadel Lami 32, Saud Khamis Sultan 80
	26	Mseimeer	W	9-0	SJg3	Diane 2 5 70, Basheer 2 23 39, Marcilo Tavarease 2 42 68, Hamed Ismaeel 67, Saud Salem 74, Saud Khamis Sultan 85
Sep	29	Umm Salal	L	1-2	SJg3	Mohammad Yasser 30
	12	Qatar SC	L	2-5	QSL	Pascal Feindouno 6, Basheer 18
	19	Al Khritiyat	W	1-0	QSL	Diane 64
	24	Al Siliya	D	0-0	QSL	
Oct	5	Umm Salal	D	1-1	QSL	Feindouno 28
	9	Al Ahli	L	0-3	SCgB	
	16	Al Gharafa	D	3-3	SCgB	Daniel Allsopp 2 10 24, Morad Abdulla 91+
	23	Al Ahli	W	2-1	QSL	Allsopp 15, Daniel Gouma 33
Nov	1	Al Gharafa	L	1-4	QSL	Basheer 35
	7	Al Sadd	L	1-4	QSL	Feindouno 23
	13	Al Khritiyat	D	2-2	SCgB	Basheer 49, Abdulla Taleb Afifa 81
	17	Al Wakra	W	1-0	SCgB	Diane 85
	24	Al Wakra	W	5-2	QSL	Diane 2 22 77, Allsopp 2 31 54, Feindouno 74
	29	Khor	D	0-0	QSL	
Dec	11	Al Arabi	W	5-0	QSL	Ismaeel 2 24 46, Mostafa Abdi 38, Allsopp 45, Diane 54
	20	Al Shamal	W	3-0	QSL	Feindouno 4, Diane 12, Afifa 35
	29	Khor	W	3-2	SCgB	Afifa 13, Salem Al Ali 23 55p
Jan	9	Qatar SC	L	1-3	QSL	Diane 73p
	14	Al Khritiyat	L	0-1	QSL	
	21	Al Siliya	W	2-0	QSL	Abdulgafour Abdulla 35, Diane 88
	29	Umm Salal	D	0-0	QSL	
Feb	3	Al Ahli	W	2-0	QSL	OG 9, Marcilo 80
	9	Al Gharafa	L	0-3	QSL	
	14	Al Sadd	L	3-4	QSL	Afonso Alves 11, Ismaeel 79, OG 86
	19	Al Wakra	W	4-0	QSL	Afonso Alves 2 16 50, Imad Al Hosni 2 39 41
Mar	12	Khor	W	2-1	QSL	OG 23, Afonso Alves 33
	20	Al Arabi	W	3-1	QSL	Afonso Alves 2 17 47, Imad Al Hosni 43
Apr	3	Al Shamal	W	3-0	QSL	Salem Al Ali 37, Ali Al Hosni, Afonso Alves 83p
	25	Al Siliya	W	1-0	ECr3	Afonso Alves 12
May	3	Al Gharafa	W	2-1	ECqf	Basheer 63, Fabio Cesar 90
	7	Al Sadd	W	2-1	ECsf	Imad Ali Al Hosni 42, Younus Ali 54
	15	Umm Salal	W	1-0	ECf	Afonso Alves 82

AL SADD 2009–10

Month	Date	Opponent		Score	Comp	Scorers
Aug	22	Al Khritiyat	W	5-0	SJg2	Agyemang Opoku 13, Felipe Goerge 39p, Ali Hassan Afif 50, Majed Mohammed 80, Nasser Nabil Salem 90
	25	Shahaniya	W	4-0	SJg2	Talal Al Bloushi 19, Majed M. 20, Afif 89, Agyemang 92+
	28	Al Arabi	W	4-2	SJg2	Goerge 2 47 70, Majed M. 79, Hassan Al Haidos 83
Sep	1	Khor	D	2-2	SJsf	Al Haidos 31, Yusef Ahmad Ali 107, L 1-3p
	13	Umm Salal	W	5-0	QSL	Al Haidos 2 38 52, Leandro Da Silva 2 59 70, OG 82
	18	Al Ahli	W	3-0	QSL	Afif 5, Al Haidos 44, Leandro 67
	25	Al Khritiyat	D	1-1	QSL	Leandro 95+
Oct	4	Al Shamal	W	2-0	QSL	OG 85, Nasser Nabil Salem 94+
	8	Al Shamal	W	5-0	SCgA	Leandro 3 31 80 92+, Afonso Alves 26, Humood Al Yazeedi 48
	15	Qatar SC	L	1-2	SCgA	Leandro 21p
	24	Al Wakra	W	3-1	QSL	Tahir Zakaria 56, Afonso Alves 71, Al Yazeedi 92+
	31	Qatar SC	W	3-0	QSL	Leandro 2 24p 84, Afif 82
Nov	7	Al Rayyan	W	4-1	QSL	Leandro 26, Afif 2 52 68, Afonso Alves 60
	11	Al Arabi	D	3-3	SCgA	Leandro 3 32 69 70
	16	Umm Salal	W	2-1	SCgA	Leandro 2 62 85
	24	Al Arabi	D	3-3	QSL	Leandro 75, Ibrahim Majid 80, Al Haidos 93+
	30	Al Saliya	W	3-1	QSL	Leandro 18p, Goerge 46, Al Haidos 55
Dec	12	Al Gharafa	D	1-1	QSL	Leandro 28
	22	Khor	W	2-1	QSL	Leandro 7, Ibrahim Majid 75
	29	Al Siliya	L	1-2	SCgA	Goerge 48
Jan	10	Umm Salal	L	0-1	QSL	
	15	Al Ahli	W	6-2	QSL	Al Bloushi 17, Al Haidos 28, Afif 50, Leandro 2 53 72, OG 89
	21	Al Khritiyat	W	2-0	QSL	Goerge 17, Leandro 76
	30	Al Shamal	W	5-1	QSL	Leandro 14, Ibrahim Khalfan 2 35 59, Majed M. 2 40 47
Feb	3	Al Wakra	D	0-0	QSL	
	9	Qatar SC	D	1-1	QSL	Leandro 87
	14	Al Rayyan	W	4-3	QSL	Leandro 33, Majed M. 2 66 92+, Mesaad Al Hamad 83
	19	Al Arabi	W	2-0	QSL	Leandro 2 60 69
	24	Al Hilal	L	0-3	CLgA	
Mar	10	Al Ahli UAE	W	5-0	CLgA	Afif 36, Leandro 3 44 45 76, Yusef Ali 64
	14	Al Saliya	W	2-0	QSL	Goerge 2 1 91+
	19	Al Gharafa	L	1-4	QSL	Leandro 45
	24	Mes Kerman	W	4-1	CLgA	Leandro 2 46 49, Felipe 53, Al Bloushi 60
	30	Mes Kerman	L	1-3	CLgA	Ibrahim Majid 7
Apr	4	Khor	W	2-0	QSL	Ibrahim Majid 58, Abdulaziz Al Ansari 92+
	13	Al Hilal	D	0-0	CLgA	
	18	Al Arabi	L	0-1	CPsf	
	27	Al Ahli UAE	D	2-2	CLgA	Ibrahim Majid 16, Al Bloushi 20
May	2	Al Ahli	W	2-0	ECqf	Ibrahim Majid 21, Goerge 48
	7	Al Rayyan	L	1-2	ECsf	Al Haidos 71

AL SHAMAL 2009–10

Mon	Day	Opponent	Res	Score	Comp	Scorers
Aug	23	Qatar SC	L	0-1	SJg4	
	26	Khor	L	0-4	SJg4	
	29	Maitheer	D	1-1	SJg4	
	13	Al Ahli	L	0-1	QSL	
Sep	17	Al Ghafara	L	1-2	QSL	Samir Mujbel 27
	24	Khor	W	1-0	QSL	Hamad Al Sada 75
	4	Al Sadd	L	0-2	QSL	
Oct	8	Al Sadd	L	0-5	SCgA	
	15	Umm Salal	L	1-2	SCgA	De Lima 36
	22	Al Siliya	L	0-3	QSL	
	1	Umm Salal	L	1-4	QSL	De Lima 75
	5	Al Wakra	L	0-7	QSL	
Nov	11	Qatar SC	L	0-3	SCgA	
	16	Al Siliya	L	0-2	SCgA	
	22	Qatar SC	W	3-0	QSL	De Lima 2 27 76, Mohammed Salem 50
	1	Al Arabi	L	0-7	QSL	
Dec	11	Al Khritiyat	L	0-1	QSL	
	20	Al Rayyan	L	0-3	QSL	
	29	Al Arabi	W	2-1	SCgA	Mohammed Salem 87, Adel Darweesh 91+
	9	Al Ahli	L	2-6	QSL	Abdullah Al Mansoori 29 80
Jan	16	Al Ghafara	L	1-8	QSL	Samir Mujbel 52
	22	Khor	L	1-5	QSL	Bong Tkwi Bitron 77p
	30	Al Sadd	L	1-5	QSL	Mahmoud Abdurrahman 86
	3	Al Siliya	D	1-1	QSL	Abdullah Al Mansoori 74
Feb	8	Umm Salal	D	1-1	QSL	Gader Mousa 67
	13	Al Wakra	L	1-2	QSL	Abdurrahman 6
	18	Qatar SC	L	0-3	QSL	
Mar	3	Al Arabi	L	2-6	QSL	Abdurrahman 49, Yemen Ben Zekri 64
	18	Al Khritiyat	L	1-2	QSL	Abdurrahman 45
	3	Al Rayyan	L	0-3	QSL	
Apr	15	Lekhwia	W	1-0	ECr3	Yemen Ben Zekri 90
	25	Umm Salal	L	2-3	ECqf	Bakhit Al Marri 31, Abdurrahman 38

AL SILIYA 2009–10

Mon	Day	Opponent	Res	Score	Comp	Scorers
Aug	22	Markheya	W	3-0	SJg1	Emanue Efa 2 50 60, Waleed Al Deen 52
	25	Al Wakra	W	2-0	SJg1	Efa 33p, Al Deen 66
	28	Al Gharafa	L	0-2	SJg1	
	13	Al Arabi	D	2-2	QSL	Roger Flores 84, Mujeeb Hamed 92+
Sep	18	Khor	D	1-1	QSL	Efa 90
	24	Al Rayyan	D	0-0	QSL	
	5	Al Ghafara	L	0-1	QSL	
	8	Qatar SC	W	1-0	SCgA	Roger Flores 76p
Oct	15	Al Arabi	L	2-3	SCgA	Hamad Al Marri 67 82
	22	Al Shamal	W	3-0	QSL	Roger Flores 35, Barro Babo Seddiqi 79, Hamad Al Marri 83
	30	Al Wakra	L	0-3	QSL	
	5	Qatar SC	W	1-0	QSL	Ismaiel Ali 77
Nov	12	Umm Salal	W	3-1	SCgA	Waleed Al Deen 8, Efa Amanue 30, Abdul Karim Dawood 36
	16	Al Shamal	W	2-0	SCgA	Ali Rahma Al Marri 5, Roger Flores 34p
	23	Al Khritiyat	D	1-1	QSL	Barro Babo Seddiqi 1
	30	Al Sadd	L	1-3	QSL	Efa 77p
	11	Al Ahli	L	0-1	QSL	
Dec	21	Umm Salal	L	0-1	QSL	
	29	Al Sadd	W	2-1	SCgA	Barro Babo Seddiqi 38, Roger Flores 45p
	1	Al Gharafa	L	2-3	SCsf	Roger Flores 2 8 78p
	10	Al Arabi	L	0-2	QSL	
Jan	14	Khor	L	1-2	QSL	Barro Babo Seddiqi 52
	21	Al Rayyan	L	0-2	QSL	
	30	Al Ghafara	L	0-1	QSL	
	3	Al Shamal	D	1-1	QSL	Mostafa Dabo 95+
Feb	8	Al Wakra	W	2-1	QSL	Mustafa Kareem 2 46 57
	13	Qatar SC	L	0-3	QSL	
	20	Al Khritiyat	D	0-0	QSL	
	14	Al Sadd	L	1-2	QSL	Alexander Souza 34
Mar	20	Al Ahli	W	2-1	QSL	Faozi Ayish 19, Alexander Souza 56
	4	Umm Salal	D	0-0	QSL	
Apr	15	Al Jaish	W	2-1	ECr2	Alexander Souza 9, AR Al Marri 64
	25	Al Rayyan	L	0-1	ECr3	

UMM SALAL 2009–10

Mon	Day	Opponent	Res	Score	Comp	Scorers
Aug	23	Mseimeer	W	5-1	SJg3	Magno Alves 3 13 15 43, Fabio Cesar 53, Davi Jose Silva 59
	26	Al Ahli	W	5-1	SJg3	Fabio 2 5 45, Davi 40, Alves 2 70 85
	29	Al Rayyan	W	2-1	SJg3	Davi 72, Jeddo 84
	1	Al Gharafa	W	3-2	SJsf	Fabio 2 52p 85p, Davi 102
	4	Khor	W	2-0	SJf	Alves 2 24 67p
Sep	13	Al Sadd	L	0-5	QSL	
	17	Al Wakra	L	2-3	QSL	Alves 29, Davi 54
	23	FC Seoul	W	3-2	CLqf	Alves 2 55 85, Fabio Cesar 84
	30	FC Seoul	D	1-1	CLqf	Aziz Ben Askar 14
	5	Al Rayyan	D	1-1	QSL	Askar 37
Oct	8	Al Arabi	L	0-3	SCgA	
	15	Al Shamal	W	2-1	SCgA	Abdulaziz Kareem 78 83
	21	Pohang	L	0-2	CLsf	
		Pohang	L	1-2	CLsf	Ibrahima Nadiya 93+
	1	Al Shamal	W	4-1	QSL	Davi 3 10 20 90, Alves 45
	6	Khor	W	1-0	QSL	Fabio Cesar 71
Nov	12	Al Siliya	L	1-2	SCgA	Ahmad Rahmatallah 49
	16	Al Sadd	L	1-2	SCgA	Alves 51
	23	Al Ghafara	L	1-3	QSL	Nadiya 12
	29	Al Khritiyat	L	0-1	QSL	
	6	Al Ahli	W	3-2	QSL	Nadiya 30, Davi 65, Kaream 87
	12	Qatar SC	L	0-1	QSL	
Dec	16	Al Arabi	L	1-2	QSL	Dhahi Al Noubi 28
	21	Al Siliya	W	1-0	QSL	Alves 7
	26	Qatar SC	D	0-0	SCgA	
	10	Al Sadd	W	1-0	QSL	Jeddo 15
Jan	16	Al Wakra	D	2-2	QSL	Nadiya 41p, Davi 72
	23	Al Ahli	W	4-1	QSL	Alves 4 24p 39 45 70
	29	Al Rayyan	D	0-0	QSL	
	4	Al Arabi	L	1-3	QSL	Alves 11
Feb	8	Al Shamal	D	1-1	QSL	Alves 62
	14	Khor	W	1-0	QSL	Davi
	18	Al Gharafa	L	0-1	QSL	
Mar	12	Al Khritiyat	D	3-3	QSL	Alves 2 5 45, Aadel Lami 85
	18	Qatar SC	D	0-0	QSL	
	4	Al Siliya	D	0-0	QSL	
Apr	25	Al Shamal	W	3-2	ECr3	Abdulmottalib 12, Tushoka 60, Alves 77
	30	Al Arabi	D	1-1	ECqf	Tamer Jamal Othman 101, W 4-3p
May	8	Qatar SC	W	1-0	ECsf	Alves 105
	15	Al Rayyan	L	0-1	ECf	

AL WAKRA 2009–10

Mon	Day	Opponent	Res	Score	Comp	Scorers
Aug	22	Al Gharafa	L	2-3	SJg1	Hasan Al Qadi 27, Omar Musa 46
	25	Al Siliya	L	0-2	SJg1	
	28	Markheya	W	6-0	SJg1	Kaled Moftah 3 2 60 84, Youness Hawassi 31
	12	Al Khritiyat	D	1-1	QSL	Ali Edan 90
Sep	17	Umm Salal	W	3-2	QSL	Hawassi 2 70 90, Ali Qassim 73
	25	Qatar SC	L	0-1	QSL	
	3	Al Ahli	W	5-4	QSL	Tom Caluwe 50, Qassim 63, Adil Ramzi 68, Hawassi 79, Moftah 82
Oct	9	Khor	W	1-0	SCgB	Adil Ramzi 7
	16	Al Ahli	L	0-1	SCgB	
	24	Al Sadd	L	1-3	QSL	Ramzi 49
	30	Al Siliya	W	3-0	QSL	Ramzi 49, Hawassi 68, Qassim 89
	5	Al Shamal	W	7-0	QSL	Ramzi 4 9 22 76 91+, Hawassi 2 26 63, OG 79
	12	Al Gharafa	L	1-2	SCgB	Tom Caluwe 65
Nov	17	Al Rayyan	L	0-1	SCgB	
	24	Al Rayyan	L	2-5	QSL	Ramzi 2 39 59
	30	Al Gharafa	W	3-2	QSL	Caluwe 24, Al Qadi 51, Moftah 57
	2	Khor	L	0-1	QSL	
Dec	22	Al Arabi	L	0-1	QSL	
	26	Al Khritiyat	D	0-0	SCgB	
	9	Al Khritiyat	L	2-4	QSL	Hawassi 4, Moftah 60
	16	Umm Salal	D	2-2	QSL	Naif Al Khater 14, Moftah 54
Jan	23	Qatar SC	L	0-1	QSL	
	28	Al Ahli	W	5-2	QSL	Qassim 11, Moftah 19, Ramzi 2 25 47, Caluwe 34
	3	Al Sadd	D	0-0	QSL	
Feb	8	Al Siliya	L	1-2	QSL	Hawassi 1
	13	Al Shamal	W	2-1	QSL	Ramzi 2 21 71
	19	Al Rayyan	L	0-4	QSL	
Mar	13	Al Gharafa	L	1-4	QSL	Ramzi 74
	19	Khor	W	4-1	QSL	Ramzi 2 5 30p, Moftah 8, Qassim 10
	3	Al Arabi	L	2-3	QSL	Al Qadi, Ramzi
Apr	26	Al Ahli	L	2-3	ECr3	Tom Caluwe 2 11 66

ROU – ROMANIA

FIFA/COCA-COLA WORLD RANKING

1993	1994	1995	1996	1997	1998	1999	2000	2001	2002	2003	2004	2005	2006	2007	2008	2009	2010
13	11	11	16	7	12	8	13	15	24	27	29	27	19	13	21	36	56

2010												Hi/Lo
Jan	Feb	Mar	Mar	Apr	May	Jul	Aug	Sep	Oct	Nov	Dec	3
36	38	36	32	28	28	42	42	46	50	52	56	56

For the first time since 1972 and for only the second time since organised league football began in the 1930's, there were no clubs from Bucharest in the top three league positions as the capital remained trophyless for the third consecutive season. Instead it was CFR Cluj who secured their second league and cup double in three years. Coached by Italian Andrea Mandorlini, the Railwaymen's fortunes have been transformed over the past five years with owner Arpad Paszkany's largesse responsible for the creation of a multi-national squad that has lifted the club game in Romania. At the start of 2008 Cluj didn't have a trophy to their name but after a Cup Final penalty shoot-out victory over Vaslui not only secured the double but also a hat-trick of cup wins, they now have five. At a European level, Romanian clubs have a significantly higher profile than they have had for many years thanks to an automatic place in the group stages of the UEFA Champions League but repeating the heroics of the European Cup winning Steaua team of the 1980s looks an unlikely dream as none of Steaua, Cluj or Unirea have in recent seasons managed to make it through to the knockout stage. The national team continues to struggle in the wake of a disastrous FIFA World Cup qualifying campaign with a tepid start to qualifying for Euro 2012.

FIFA WORLD CUP RECORD

1930 8 r1 **1934** 12 r1 **1938** 9 r1 1950 DNE 1954-1958 DNQ 1962 DNE 1966 DNQ **1970** 11 r1
1974-1986 DNQ **1990** 12 r2 **1994** 6 QF **1998** 11 r2 2002-2010 DNQ

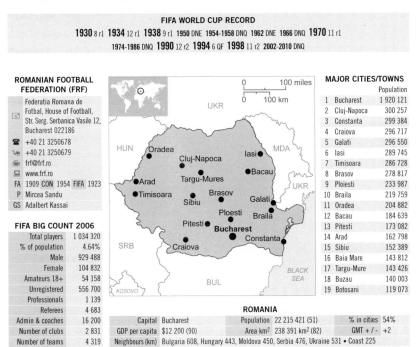

ROMANIAN FOOTBALL FEDERATION (FRF)

Federatia Romana de Fotbal, House of Football, Str. Serg. Serbanica Vasile 12, Bucharest 022186

☎ +40 21 3250678
🖷 +40 21 3250679
✉ frf@frf.ro
🖥 www.frf.ro
FA 1909 CON 1954 FIFA 1923
P Mircea Sandu
GS Adalbert Kassai

FIFA BIG COUNT 2006

Total players	1 034 320
% of population	4.64%
Male	929 488
Female	104 832
Amateurs 18+	54 158
Unregistered	556 700
Professionals	1 139
Referees	4 683
Admin & coaches	16 200
Number of clubs	2 831
Number of teams	4 319

MAJOR CITIES/TOWNS

		Population
1	Bucharest	1 920 121
2	Cluj-Napoca	300 257
3	Constanta	299 384
4	Craiova	296 717
5	Galati	296 550
6	Iasi	289 745
7	Timisoara	286 728
8	Brasov	278 817
9	Ploiesti	233 987
10	Braila	219 759
11	Oradea	204 882
12	Bacau	184 639
13	Pitesti	173 082
14	Arad	162 798
15	Sibiu	152 389
16	Baia Mare	143 812
17	Targu-Mure	143 426
18	Buzau	140 003
19	Botosani	119 073

ROMANIA

Capital	Bucharest	Population	22 215 421 (51)	% in cities	54%
GDP per capita	$12 200 (90)	Area km²	238 391 km² (82)	GMT +/-	+2
Neighbours (km)	Bulgaria 608, Hungary 443, Moldova 450, Serbia 476, Ukraine 531 • Coast 225				

RECENT INTERNATIONAL MATCHES PLAYED BY ROMANIA

2007	Opponents	Score		Venue	Comp	Scorers	Att	Referee
22-08	Turkey	W	2-0	Bucharest	Fr	Dica 61, Mutu 70	12 000	Merk GER
8-09	Belarus	W	3-1	Minsk	ECq	Mutu 2 16 77p, Dica 42	19 320	Fröjdfeldt SWE
12-09	Germany	L	1-3	Cologne	Fr	Goian 3	44 500	Rizzoli ITA
13-10	Netherlands	W	1-0	Constanta	ECq	Goian 71	12 595	Vassaras GRE
17-10	Luxembourg	W	2-0	Luxembourg	ECq	Petre.F 42, Marica 61	3 584	Brych GER
17-11	Bulgaria	L	0-1	Sofia	ECq		6 000	Plautz AUT
21-11	Albania	W	6-1	Bucharest	ECq	Dica 2 22 71p, Tamas 53, Niculae.D 2 62 65, Marica 69p	23 427	Trivkovic CRO
2008								
6-02	Israel	L	0-1	Tel Aviv	Fr		8 000	Duarte Gomez POR
26-03	Russia	W	3-0	Bucharest	Fr	Marica 45, Niculae.D 60, Niculae.M 75	10 000	Kenan ISR
31-05	Montenegro	W	4-0	Bucharest	Fr	Mutu 15, Ghionea 49, Dica 2 55 69	8 000	Tudor ROU
9-06	France	D	0-0	Zurich	ECr1		30 585	Mejuto Gonzalez ESP
13-06	Italy	D	1-1	Zurich	ECr1	Mutu 55	30 585	Ovrebø NOR
17-06	Netherlands	L	0-2	Berne	ECr1		30 777	Busacca SUI
20-08	Latvia	W	1-0	Urziceni	Fr	Dica 51	10 000	Ovrebo NOR
6-09	Lithuania	L	0-3	Cluj	WCq		14 000	Kelly IRL
10-09	Faroe Islands	W	1-0	Tórshavn	WCq	Cocis 59	805	Strahonja CRO
11-10	France	D	2-2	Constanta	WCq	Petre 5, Goian 16	12 800	De Bleeckere BEL
19-11	Georgia	W	2-1	Bucharest	Fr	Marica 62, Goian 70	2 000	Vassaras GRE
2009								
11-02	Croatia	L	1-2	Bucharest	Fr	Marica 22		Balaj ROU
28-03	Serbia	L	2-3	Constanta	WCq	Marica 50, Stoica 74	12 000	Trefoloni ITA
1-04	Austria	L	1-2	Klagenfurt	WCq	Tanase 24	23 000	Thomson SCO
6-06	Lithuania	W	1-0	Marijampole	WCq	Marica 39	5 850	Eriksson SWE
12-08	Hungary	W	1-0	Budapest	Fr	Ghioane 42	9 000	Vnuk SVK
5-09	France	D	1-1	Paris	WCq	Escude OG 55	78 209	Bebek CRO
9-09	Austria	D	1-1	Bucharest	WCq	Bucur 54	7 505	Atkinson ENG
10-10	Serbia	L	0-5	Belgrade	WCq		39 839	Kapitanis CYP
14-10	Faroe Islands	W	3-1	Piatra-Neamt	WCq	Apostal 16, Bucur 65, Mazilu 87	13 000	Gvardis RUS
14-11	Poland	W	1-0	Warsaw	Fr	Niculae 59	8 000	Mashiah ISR
2010								
29-05	Ukraine	L	2-3	Lviv	Fr	Tamas 54, Niculae 63	22 000	Kralovec CZE
2-06	Macedonia FYR	L	0-1	Bischofshofen	Fr		1 000	Krassnitzer AUT
5-06	Honduras	W	3-0	St Velt An Der Glan	Fr	Niculae 20, Florescu 45, Radoi 76p	700	Grobelnik AUT
11-08	Turkey	L	0-2	Istanbul	Fr		15 000	Mazic SRB
3-09	Albania	D	1-1	Piatra-Neamt	ECq	Stancu 80	13 400	Schorgenhofer AUT
7-09	Belarus	D	0-0	Minsk	ECq		26 354	Kralovec CZE
9-10	France	L	0-2	Paris	ECq		79 299	Proenca POR
17-11	Italy	D	1-1	Klagenfurt	Fr	Marica 34	14 000	Einwaller AUT

Fr = Friendly match • EC = UEFA EURO 2008/2012 • WC = FIFA World Cup • q = qualifier • r1 = first round group

ROMANIA NATIONAL TEAM HISTORICAL RECORDS

Caps
134 - Dorinel Munteanu 1991-2007 • 125 - Gheorghe Hagi 1983-2000 • 115 - Gheorghe Popescu 1988-2003 • 108 - Ladislau Boloni 1975-88 • 95 - Dan Petrescu 1989-2000 • 91 - Bogdan Stelea 1988-2005 • 90 - Michael Klein 1981-91 • 84 - Marius Lacatus 1984-98 • 83 - Mircea Rednic 1981-91 • 78 - Bogdan Lobont 1998- • 77 - Silviu Lung 1979-93 • 75 - Rodion Camataru 1978-90 & Cristian Chivu 1999-

Goals
35 - Gheorghe Hagi 1983-2000 • 31 - Iuliu Bodola 1931-39 • 29 - Adrian Mutu 2000- • 26 - Anghel Iordanescu 1971-81 • 25 - Viorel Moldovan 1993-2005 & Ladislau Boloni 1975-88 • 22 - Rodion Camataru 1978-90 • 21 - Dudu Georgescu 1973-80 & Florin Raducioiu 1988-96 • 20 - Stefan Dobay 1930-39 & Ilie Dumitrescu 1989-98 • 19 - Ioan Ganea 1998-2006

Past Coaches
Valentin Stanescu 1973-75 • Cornel Dragusin 1975 • Stefan Kovacs 1976-79 • Florin Halagian 1979 • Constantin Cernaianu 1979 • Stefan Kovacs 1980 • Valentin Stanescu 1980-1981 • Mircea Lucescu 1981-86 • Emerich Jenei 1986-90 • Gheorghe Constantin 1990 • Mircea Radulescu 1990-92 • Cornel Dinu 1992-93 • Anghel Iordanescu 1993-98 • Victor Piturca 1998-99 • Emerich Jenei 2000 • Ladislau Boloni 2000-01 • Gheorghe Hagi 2001-02 • Anghel Iordanescu 2002-04 • Victor Piturca 2005-09 • Razvan Lucescu 2009-

ROMANIA 2009-10

LIGA I BURGER

	Pl	W	D	L	F	A	Pts	CFR Cluj	Unirea	Vaslui	Steaua	Timisoara	Dinamo	Rapid	Otelul	Brasov	Gaz Metan	Gloria	International	Un Craiova	Astra	Pandurii	Iasi	Ceahlaul	Unirea
CFR 1907 Cluj †	34	20	9	5	46	23	69		2-0	0-0	1-1	0-0	2-2	1-0	2-1	2-0	1-0	2-1	2-0	1-0	2-1	1-0	1-0	1-1	2-0 3-2
Unirea Urziceni †	34	18	12	4	53	26	66	0-1		1-2	2-2	0-0	4-4	1-0	0-0	1-0	1-1	2-0	1-0	3-2	4-1	3-0	2-0	4-0	1-0
SC Vaslui ‡	34	18	8	8	44	28	62	2-0	1-1		2-1	0-1	2-0	1-0	1-1	2-2	2-1	0-1	1-0	0-1	3-1	2-1	2-1	1-0	3-0
Steaua Bucuresti ‡	34	18	8	8	49	36	62	2-2	0-1	2-1		3-3	0-1	1-1	1-0	1-0	2-0	1-1	3-2	2-0	2-0	1-0	2-1	1-3	2-0
FC Timisoara ‡	34	15	14	5	55	27	59	1-1	0-0	0-1	0-1		2-0	1-0	2-1	1-2	0-2	1-0	0-0	1-1	0-0	1-0	2-1	6-0	6-0
Dinamo Bucuresti ‡	34	13	14	7	48	37	53	1-0	2-1	1-1	2-0	1-2		1-1	0-1	0-0	1-0	1-1	2-1	3-3	1-1	1-1	1-1	2-0
Rapid Bucuresti	34	14	10	10	53	38	52	1-4	1-1	3-2	5-1	0-3	2-2		3-0	2-1	4-1	2-1	4-0	0-1	0-1	1-0	4-1	1-1	2-0
Otelul Galati	34	14	8	12	38	38	50	1-0	1-4	1-0	0-1	3-3	2-3	0-0		1-1	0-1	3-0	1-0	1-0	3-2	1-1	4-0	0-0	1-0
FC Brasov	34	12	10	12	40	30	46	0-1	0-0	1-1	0-0	1-0	0-1	1-1	3-0		3-2	6-0	1-2	2-0	0-0	2-0	2-0	1-0	2-1
Gaz Metan Medias	34	9	15	10	33	37	42	0-0	0-0	0-0	2-4	2-6	1-0	0-0	0-1	1-1		1-1	0-0	2-1	0-0	1-0	1-0	2-0	5-0
Gloria Bistrita	34	10	11	13	35	46	41	0-2	0-0	1-3	1-2	0-0	3-2	1-1	2-1	2-1	1-1		0-1	2-1	3-1	1-0	5-0	1-0	1-1
International C. Arges	34	10	6	18	32	49	36	0-1	1-2	1-2	0-2	0-3	1-3	1-2	0-1	0-3	2-4	2-1		0-1	2-1	0-0	0-2	2-0	2-1
Universitatea Craiova	34	11	3	20	44	52	36	2-3	1-4	1-2	1-2	1-2	0-0	3-4	3-0	3-0	1-2	5-1	1-3		1-0	2-0	2-1	3-2	3-1
Astra Ploesti	34	8	12	14	33	45	36	1-0	0-2	0-0	2-1	1-3	1-1	3-1	1-0	0-2	0-0	1-1	3-1		0-1	1-1	1-1	4-2
Pandurii Târgu Jiu	34	7	13	14	19	30	34	1-0	0-0	1-0	0-0	0-0	0-0	1-1	2-3	1-0	0-0	1-1	3-1	0-0	0-2		1-1	0-0	2-0
Politehnica Iasi	34	7	10	17	28	50	31	0-2	1-2	1-3	0-2	1-1	1-3	2-1	1-1	0-0	1-1	0-0	0-0	1-0	2-0	1-0		2-0	1-0
Ceahlaul Piatra Neamt	34	6	10	18	28	57	28	2-4	2-3	0-1	0-2	1-1	0-4	0-1	2-1	0-0	2-1	2-2	2-1	0-0	1-2	1-0			1-1
Unirea Alba Iulia	34	7	5	22	33	62	26	1-1	1-2	2-0	2-1	3-3	1-2	0-1	3-1	0-1	0-0	1-2	2-1	3-2					

31/07/2009 - 22/05/2010 • † Qualified for the UEFA Champions League • ‡ Qualified for the Europa League • Top scorers: **16** - Andrei Cristea, Dinamo • **15** - Pantelis Kapetanos GRE, Steaua • **12** - Dorin Goga, Timisoara; Wesley BRA, Vaslui; Marius Bilasco, Unirea

ROMANIA 2009-10 — LIGA II SERIE 1 (2)

	Pl	W	D	L	F	A	Pts
Victoria Branesti	34	21	8	5	62	28	71
Sportul Studentesc	34	20	8	6	65	26	68
Petrolul Ploiesti	34	18	13	3	58	20	67
FC Snagov	34	18	6	10	62	41	60
Delta Tulcea	34	17	8	9	41	23	59
Sageata Stejaru	34	17	7	10	46	29	58
Concordia Chiajna	34	16	6	12	51	36	54
Farul Constanta	34	16	5	13	52	48	53
Dunarea Giurgiu	34	14	7	13	43	41	49
FC Botosani	34	13	10	11	45	36	49
Dunarea Galati	34	13	6	15	37	39	45
FCM Bacau	34	12	7	15	47	57	43
Steaua Bucuresti-2	34	10	11	13	36	36	41
Gloria Buzau §8	34	12	7	15	39	44	35
Dinamo Bucuresti-2	34	8	5	21	36	67	29
Tricolorul Breaza	34	8	4	22	31	66	28
Râmnicu Sarat	34	4	7	23	14	68	19
Cetatea Suceava	34	2	9	23	16	76	15

15/08/2009 - 12/06/2010 • § = points deducted

ROMANIA 2009-10 — LIGA II SERIE 2 (2)

	Pl	W	D	L	F	A	Pts
Târgu Mures	32	20	9	3	52	20	69
Universitatea Cluj	32	21	6	5	62	23	69
Dacia Mioveni	32	19	9	4	46	20	66
UTA Arad	32	16	10	6	50	26	58
Arges Pitesti	32	16	5	11	47	32	53
CS Otopeni §3	32	15	8	9	59	40	50
Gaz Metan Craiova	32	12	9	11	39	36	45
Baia Mare	32	11	11	10	34	35	44
Bihor Oradea	32	10	12	10	49	40	42
Ariesul Turda	32	13	3	16	40	43	42
Silvania Simleu	32	10	7	15	31	46	37
Minerul Lupeni	32	8	12	12	33	41	36
Râmnicu Vâlcea	32	9	9	14	51	51	36
Muresul Deva	32	9	4	19	28	50	31
Fortuna Covaci	32	7	5	20	37	59	26
Jiul Petrosani	31	7	5	19	21	59	26
Drobeta Turnu Severin	31	5	2	24	12	70	17
CFR Timisoara							Expelled

15/08/2009 - 12/06/2010 • § = points deducted

MEDALS TABLE

		Overall			League			Cup		Europe		
		G	S	B	G	S	B	G	S	G	S	B
1	Steaua Bucuresti	45	21	9	23	13	7	21	7	1	1	2
2	Dinamo Bucuresti	31	31	11	19	20	9	12	11			2
3	Rapid Bucuresti	16	19	8	3	14	8	13	5			
4	Universitatea Craiova	10	10	8	4	5	7	6	5			1
5	UT Arad	8	3	1	6	1	1	2	2			
6	Venus Bucuresti	8	1	1	8	1		1				
7	Petrolul Ploiesti	6	4	2	4	3	2	2	1			
	Ripensia Timisoara	6	4	2	4	2	2	2	2			
9	Chinezul Timisoara	6	1		6			1				
10	CFR 1907 Cluj	5		1	2		1	3				
11	FC Timisoara	2	7	5		1	5	2	6			
12	FC Arges Pitesti	2	3	4	2	2	4	1				
13	FC Bihor Oradea	2	3	1	1	2	1	1	1			
14	FCM Resita	2	1		1	1		1				

CUPA ROMANIEI 2009-10

First Round

Team	Score
CFR 1907 Cluj	2
Dunarea Galati *	0
Ceahlaul Piatra Neamt *	1 2p
Gaz Metan Craiova	1 3p
Politehnica Iasi *	3
Pandurii Targu Jiu	1
Gloria Bistrita-2	3
Universitatea Craiova *	4
Astra Ploesti	2
Farul Constanta	1
Sanatatea Cluj	0
FC Timisoara *	7
Otelul Galati *	1 4p
Unirea Alba Iulia	1 3p
CS Zlatna *	0
Dinamo Bucuresti	5
FC Brasov *	4
CS Otopeni	0
Sportul Studentesc	0
Unirea Urziceni *	3
Steaua Bucuresti	2
FCM Bacau *	0
Dunarea Giurgiu	0
Gloria Bistrita *	3
International C. Arges	1 5p
Minerul Valea Copcii *	1 3p
Bihor Oradea *	0
Rapid Bucuresti	2
Gaz Metan Medias *	1 5p
Ramnicu Valcea	1 4p
Chimia Brazi *	0
FC Vaslui	5

Second Round

Team	Score
CFR 1907 Cluj	
Gaz Metan Craiova *	
Politehnica Iasi *	0
Universitatea Craiova	3
Astra Ploesti *	2 6p
FC Timisoara	2 5p
Otelul Galati	0
Dinamo Bucuresti *	1
FC Brasov	1
Unirea Urziceni *	0
Steaua Bucuresti	0 4p
Gloria Bistrita *	0 5p
International C. Arges *	2
Rapid Bucuresti	1
Gaz Metan Medias *	0
FC Vaslui	1

Quarter-finals

Team	Score
CFR 1907 Cluj	1
Universitatea Craiova *	0
Astra Ploesti *	1
Dinamo Bucuresti	2
FC Brasov *	3
Gloria Bistrita	0
International C. Arges	0
FC Vaslui *	1

Semi-finals

Team	Score
CFR 1907 Cluj	1 1
Dinamo Bucuresti *	1 2
FC Brasov *	1 0
FC Vaslui	0 4

Final

Team	Score
CFR 1907 Cluj	0 5p
FC Vaslui ‡	0 4p

CUP FINAL

Emil Alexandrescu, Iasi
26-05-2010, 21:00, Att: 11 000, Ref: Deaconu
Cluj - Nuno Claro - Cristian Panin, Cadu (c), Felice Piccolo, Edimar - Roberto De Zerbi (Cristian Bud 92), Gabriel Muresan - Sixto Peraita ● (Davide Bottone 83), Emmanuel Culio, Ciprian Deac - Yssouf Kone (Nicolae Dica 116). Tr. Andrea Mandorlini
Vaslui - Cristian Haisan - Zhivko Milanov, Gladstone Pereira, Paul Papp ● Hugo Luz - Milos Pavlovic ● - Adrian Gheorghiu Raul Costin, Wesley (c), Lucian Sanmartean - Lucian Burdujan ●. Tr: Marius Lacatus

* Home team/home team in the 1st leg ● ‡ Qualified for the Europa League

RSA – SOUTH AFRICA

FIFA/COCA-COLA WORLD RANKING

1993	1994	1995	1996	1997	1998	1999	2000	2001	2002	2003	2004	2005	2006	2007	2008	2009	2010
95	56	40	19	31	26	30	20	35	30	36	38	49	67	77	76	85	51

2010												Hi/Lo
	Jan	Feb	Mar	Mar	Apr	May	Jul	Aug	Sep	Oct	Nov	Dec	16
	85	81	81	88	90	83	66	66	58	52	50	51	124

South Africa enjoyed the global spotlight with their hosting of the 2010 FIFA World Cup given a resounding seal of approval after a month-long festival of fun where some of the football and the weather proved indifferent but the sights and sounds did not - even against the backdrop of the monotonous tone of the dreaded vuvuzela. Despite extensive pre-tournament training in Brazil and Germany under veteran coach Carlos Alberto Parreira, Bafana Bafana were not expected to make an impact at their own tournament with the ambition being to avoid the ignominy of becoming the first host nation to be eliminated at the first hurdle of a World Cup. But a devastating defeat by Uruguay in Pretoria after a dramatic 1-1 draw in the opening match against Mexico effectively ended home interest. A 2-1 win over France in their last group game provided some consolation for South Africa, who notched up their first win over a top-ranked nation. Parreira departed after the World Cup to be replaced by Pitso Mosimane, his long-time assistant who has already had a spell in charge of Bafana Bafana. SuperSport United won a third successive title to become only the second side to achieve the distinction while BidVest Wits won the cup in a match watched by over 70,000 at Soccer City as it was officially re-opened before the start of the World Cup.

FIFA WORLD CUP RECORD

1930-1990 DNE 1994 DNQ **1998** 24 r1 **2002** 17 r1 **2006** DNQ **2010** 20 r1

SOUTH AFRICAN FOOTBALL ASSOCIATION (SAFA)

125 Samuel Evans Road, Aeroton, Johannesburg
☎ +27 11 4943522
📠 +27 11 4943013
📧 raymond.hack@safa.net
🖥 www.safa.net
FA 1991 CON 1992 FIFA 1992
P Kirsten Nematandani
GS Pinky Lehoko

FIFA BIG COUNT 2006

Total players	4 540 410
% of population	10.28%
Male	4 423 300
Female	117 110
Amateurs 18+	165 560
Youth under 18	1 300 400
Unregistered	2 025 000
Professionals	1 000
Referees	4 020
Admin & coaches	16 537
Number of clubs	450
Number of teams	3 200

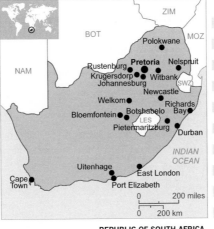

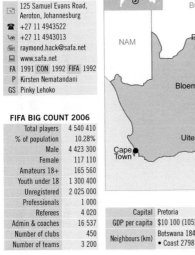

MAJOR CITIES/TOWNS

		Population
1	Cape Town	3 569 359
2	Durban	3 409 081
3	Johannesburg	2 023 456
4	Soweto	1 755 247
5	Pretoria	1 679 164
6	Port Elizabeth	1 146 350
7	Pietermaritzburg	891 607
8	Benoni	654 509
9	Welkom	584 719
10	Bloemfontein	583 253
11	Tembisa	573 022
12	Vereeniging	473 975
13	Boksburg	473 121
14	Sihlangu	463 706
15	East London	453 207
16	Krugersdorp	422 884
43	Polokwane	136 107
53	Nelspruit	116 705
59	Rustenburg	108 483

REPUBLIC OF SOUTH AFRICA

Capital	Pretoria	Population	49 052 489 (24)	% in cities	61%
GDP per capita	$10 100 (105)	Area km²	1 219 090 km² (25)	GMT +/-	+2
Neighbours (km)	Botswana 1840, Lesotho 909, Mozambique 491, Namibia 967, Swaziland 430, Zimbabwe 225 • Coast 2798				

RECENT INTERNATIONAL MATCHES PLAYED BY SOUTH AFRICA

2009	Opponents	Score		Venue	Comp	Scorers	Att	Referee
14-06	Iraq	D	0-0	Johannesburg	CFr1		48 837	Larrionda URU
17-06	New Zealand	W	2-0	Rustenburg	CFr1	Parker 2 [21 52]	36 598	Archundia MEX
20-06	Spain	L	0-2	Bloemfontein	CFr1		38 212	Pozo CHI
25-06	Brazil	L	0-1	Johannesburg	CFsf		48 049	Busacca SUI
28-06	Spain	L	2-3	Rustenburg	CF3p	Mphela 2 [73 93+]	31 788	Breeze AUS
12-08	Serbia	L	1-3	Atteridgeville	Fr	Mphela [90]	10 000	Maullet SEY
5-09	Germany	L	0-2	Leverkusen	Fr		29 569	Circhetta SUI
8-09	Republic of Ireland	L	0-1	Limerick	Fr		11 300	Thomson SCO
19-09	Madagascar	W	1-0	Kimberley	Fr	Mphela [64]		
10-10	Norway	L	0-1	Oslo	Fr		13 504	Collum SCO
13-10	Iceland	L	0-1	Reykjavik	Fr		3 253	Moen NOR
14-11	Japan	D	0-0	Port Elizabeth	Fr		44 000	Baltazar ANG
17-11	Jamaica	D	0-0	Bloemfontein	Fr		15 000	Andriamiharisoa MAD
2010								
27-01	Zimbabwe	W	3-0	Durban	Fr	Tshabalala [49], Mbuyane [76], Thwala [90]	35 000	Nhleko SWZ
3-03	Namibia	D	1-1	Durban	Fr	Mphela [70]	35 000	Nguluwe MWI
31-03	Paraguay	D	1-1	Asuncion	Fr	Tshabalala [71]	7 738	Fagundes BRA
22-04	Korea DPR	D	0-0	Taunusstein-Wehen	Fr		628	Brych GER
28-04	Jamaica	W	2-0	Offenbach/Main	Fr	Moriri [51], Nomvete [85]	562	Sippel GER
16-05	Thailand	W	4-0	Nelspruit	Fr	Tshabalala [22], Mphela 2 [30 33], Parker [89]	30 000	Kipngetich KEN
24-05	Bulgaria	D	1-1	Johannesburg	Fr	Sangweni [20]	25 000	Kakou RSA
27-05	Colombia	W	2-1	Johannesburg	Fr	Modise [18p], Mphela [58p]	76 000	Kipngetich KEN
31-05	Guatemala	W	5-0	Polokwane	Fr	Mphela 2 [12p 56p], Letsholonyane [25], Moriri [48], Parker [82]	45 000	Chaibou RSA
5-06	Denmark	W	1-0	Atteridgeville	Fr	Mphela [75]	25 000	Mbata RSA
11-06	Mexico	D	1-1	Johannesburg	WCr1	Tshabalala [55]	84 490	Irmatov UZB
16-06	Uruguay	L	0-3	Pretoria	WCr1		42 658	Busacca SUI
22-06	France	W	2-1	Bloemfontein	WCr1	Khumalo [20], Mphela [37]	39 415	Ruiz COL
11-08	Ghana	W	1-0	Johannesburg	Fr	Mphela [42]	47 000	
4-09	Niger	W	2-0	Nelspruit	CNq	Mphela [12], Parker [45]	40 000	Abdel Rahman SUD
10-10	Sierra Leone	D	0-0	Freetown	CNq		60 000	Lemghaifry MTN
17-11	USA	L	0-1	Cape Town	Fr		52 000	Kirwa KEN

Fr = Friendly match • CN = CAF African Cup of Nations • CC = COSAFA Cup • CF = FIFA Confederations Cup • WC = FIFA World Cup
q = qualifier • r1 = first round group • sf = semi-final • 3p = 3rd place play-off

SOUTH AFRICA NATIONAL TEAM HISTORICAL RECORDS

Caps
105 - Aaron Mokoena 1999- • **79** - Benni McCarthy 1997- & Siyabonga Nomvete 1999- • **74** - Shaun Bartlett 1995-2005 • **73** - John Moshoeu 1992-2004 & Delron Buckley 1999-2008 • **70** - Lucas Radebe 1992-2003 • **67** - Andre Arendse 1995-2004 & Sibusiso Zuma 1998-2008 • **62** - Mark Fish 1993-2004 • **58** - Phil Masinga 1992-2001 & MacBeth Sibaya 2001- • **52** - Neil Tovey 1992-97

Goals
32 - Benni McCarthy 1997- • **29** - Shaun Bartlett 1995-2005 • **18** - Phil Masinga 1992-2001 & Katlego Mphela 2005- • **16** - Siyabonga Nomvete 1999- • **13** - Sibusiso Zuma 1998-2008 • **10** - Teko Modise 2007- , Delron Buckley 1999-2008 & Bernard Parker 2007-

Past Coaches
Stanley Tshabalala 1992 • Ephraim Mashaba 1992 • Augusto Palacios PER 1992-94 • Clive Barker 1994-97 • Jomo Sono 1998 • Philippe Troussier FRA 1998 • Trott Moloto 1998-2000 • Carlos Queiroz POR 2000-02 • Jomo Sono 2002 • Ephraim Mashaba 2002-03 • April Phumo 2004 • Stuart Baxter SCO 2004-05 • Ted Dumitru ROU 2005-06 • Pitso Mosimane 2006 • Carlos Alberto Parreira BRA 2007-08 • Joel Santana BRA 2008-09 • Carlos Alberto Parreira BRA 2009-10 • Pitso Mosimane 2010-

MEDALS TABLE

		Overall			League			Cup		T8		LCup		Africa			City
		G	S	B	G	S	B	G	S					G	S	B	
1	Kaizer Chiefs	49	19	4	10	6	4	12	5	14	5	12	3	1			Johannesburg
2	Orlando Pirates	22	21	8	7	5	6	6	7	8	4		5	1	2		Johannesburg
3	Mamelodi Sundowns	16	16	3	8	3	3	3	4	3	5	2	3		1		Pretoria
4	Moroka Swallows	7	8	1		1	1	5	1	2	4		2				Johannesburg
5	SuperSport United	6	7	1	3	2	1	2	1	1	2		2				Pretoria
6	BidVest Wits	6	5	2		2		2	1	2	3	2	1				Johannesburg
7	Jomo Cosmos	5	8	1	1	1		1	4	1	1	2	2			1	Johannesburg
8	Bush Bucks	4	2	1	1	1	1					3	1				Umtata
9	Santos	4	1	1	1		1	2		1			1				Cape Town
10	Ajax Cape Town	3	7			2		1	1		2	2	2				Cape Town
11	AmaZulu	2	7	2	1		2		6		1	1					Durban

SOUTH AFRICA 2009-10

PREMIER SOCCER LEAGUE — THE ABSA PREMIERSHIP

	Pl	W	D	L	F	A	Pts	SuperSport	Sundowns	Chiefs	Santos	Pirates	Celtic	Ajax	Swallows	AmaZulu	Wits	Maritzburg	Arrows	Free State	Platinum S	Black Aces	Cosmos
SuperSport United †	30	16	9	5	51	25	57		0-1	1-0	2-2	3-0	0-0	0-1	4-2	4-2	1-2	3-2	1-1	2-0	1-1	3-0	3-0
Mamelodi Sundowns	30	16	8	6	43	24	56	1-1		2-2	0-0	2-0	0-0	1-2	3-3	2-0	1-0	1-0	4-0	1-1	1-0	2-0	3-1
Kaizer Chiefs	30	14	9	7	39	25	51	0-2	1-2		0-0	0-0	1-1	2-1	1-2	1-0	0-1	0-1	2-0	2-1	3-1	2-0	2-2
Santos	30	12	11	7	34	20	47	1-2	1-0	0-1		0-0	0-1	1-0	2-0	1-0	0-0	4-0	1-1	2-2	2-0	1-0	1-1
Orlando Pirates	30	10	14	6	26	18	44	0-0	0-0	0-0	0-1		3-1	3-0	2-2	2-0	1-1	1-1	1-0	0-0	1-0	1-0	4-0
Bloemfontein Celtic	30	9	15	6	38	35	42	1-1	0-2	1-0	1-1	1-1		4-2	1-1	1-1	3-0	0-2	2-2	2-2	2-0	2-5	3-3
Ajax Cape Town	30	11	9	10	27	29	42	1-1	0-1	0-3	0-2	0-1	1-0		2-0	0-0	1-1	1-1	0-0	0-0	2-0	1-1	1-0
Moroka Swallows	30	11	9	10	30	36	42	0-3	0-1	0-1	0-0	0-0	0-0	2-1		0-4	0-2	2-0	0-0	2-1	1-0	1-1	1-0
AmaZulu	30	11	6	13	30	35	39	3-0	0-3	2-3	0-2	2-1	2-1	0-1	2-1		2-2	0-1	0-1	1-0	2-1	0-0	0-0
BidVest Wits	30	7	14	9	32	38	35	1-2	4-2	0-3	0-3	0-0	1-1	0-2	0-0	1-2		1-1	2-1	1-1	2-0	0-1	3-1
Maritzburg United	30	8	11	11	28	39	35	1-1	1-5	1-3	0-1	2-1	2-4	2-1	1-1	2-0	1-1		1-0	1-1	1-3	1-0	1-1
Golden Arrows	30	6	14	10	25	33	32	1-0	1-0	0-0	1-1	0-0	1-1	1-1	1-3	1-2	3-3	1-1		0-1	1-1	2-1	2-0
Free State Stars	30	5	16	9	29	30	31	0-1	2-2	0-1	3-3	0-0	0-1	1-1	0-1	1-0	1-0	0-0	3-1		0-1	2-0	2-2
Platinum Stars	30	5	16	9	29	34	31	0-1	2-0	0-1	1-0	0-1	1-2	0-1	0-1	3-1	1-0	2-1	0-3	0-1		2-0	2-2
Mpuma'ga Black Aces	30	5	11	14	20	38	26	0-5	0-1	3-3	1-2	1-1	0-0	1-2	2-1	2-0	1-1	1-0	0-0	1-1			0-0
Jomo Cosmos	30	4	12	14	21	40	24	1-3	2-0	1-2	1-0	1-0	0-1	0-1	1-2	1-1	0-0	0-0	0-1	0-0	0-0	2-1	

7/08/2009 - 6/03/2010 • † Qualified for the CAF Champions League • Top scorers: **17** - Katlego Mphela, Sundowns • **13** - Prince Olomu NGA, Celtic

---

SOUTH AFRICA 2009-10 — NATIONAL FIRST DIVISION (2)

Inland	Pl	W	D	L	F	A	Pts
Black Leopards †	21	11	5	5	31	20	38
African Warriors	21	9	9	3	31	19	36
Witbank Spurs	21	10	5	6	20	19	35
Batau	21	7	6	8	30	30	27
Dynamos	21	6	9	6	29	29	27
Pretoria University	21	6	7	8	21	26	25
United FC	21	5	5	11	18	28	20
Winners Park	21	4	6	11	23	32	18

Coastal	Pl	W	D	L	F	A	Pts
Vasco da Gama †	21	13	2	6	42	22	41
Nathi Lions	21	12	4	5	29	22	40
Bay United	21	10	4	7	32	28	34
Carara Kicks	21	7	7	7	29	25	28
Thanda Royal Zulu	21	7	5	9	21	29	26
FC Cape Town	21	7	4	10	23	29	25
Hanover Park	21	6	7	8	21	29	23
Ikapa Sporting	21	5	3	13	26	39	18

21/08/2009 - 13/02/2010 • † Championship play-off

National First Division Championship: Black Leopards 1-1 1-2 **Vasco da Gama**
Vasco da Gama are First Division champions. Black Leopards enter the play-offs

Play-off semis: **Mpumalanga Black Aces** 2-2 2-0 Nathi Lions
Black Leopards 4-0 2-3 African Warriors
Play-off final: Black Leopards 2-1 1-2 3-5p **Mpumalanga Black Aces**
Black Aces remain in the Premier Soccer League

MTN 8 CUP 2009

First Round		Semi-finals		Final	
Golden Arrows	1				
Free State Stars	0	**Golden Arrows**	2 2		
SuperSport Utd	2 3p	AmaZulu	1 0		
AmaZulu	2 4p			**Golden Arrows**	6
Kaizer Chiefs	3			Ajax Cape Town	0
Bidvest Wits	1	Kaiser Chiefs	0 3		
Orlando Pirates	1	**Ajax Cape Town**	1 3	24-10-2009	
Ajax Cape Town	2				

TELKOM KNOCK-OUT LEAGUE CUP 2010

First Round		Quarter-finals		Semi-finals		Final	
Kaizer Chiefs	0 4p						
Santos	0 2p	**Kaizer Chiefs**	1				
Free State Stars	3	Mamelodi Sundowns	0				
Mamelodi Sundowns	4			**Kaizer Chiefs**	0 3p		
Jomo Cosmos	2			Orlando Pirates	0 0p		
BidVest Wits	0	Jomo Cosmos	1				
Bloemfontein Celtic	1	**Orlando Pirates**	2				
Orlando Pirates	2					**Kaizer Chiefs**	2
AmaZulu	1					Ajax Cape Town	1
Maritzburg United	0	**AmaZulu**	2 4p				
Mpuma'ga Black Aces	1	SuperSport United	2 1p				
SuperSport United	5			AmaZulu	0		
Golden Arrows	2			**Ajax Cape Town**	2		
Platinum Stars	1	Golden Arrows	1				
Moroka Swallows	0	**Ajax Cape Town**	2				
Ajax Cape Town	1						

CUP FINAL
Absa Park, Durban
10-04-2010
Scorers - Mandla Masango [19],
Knowlwedge Musona [46] for Chiefs;
Diyo Sibisi [85] for Ajax

NEDBANK FA CUP 2009-10

First Round

Team	Score
BidVest Wits	3
Nathi Lions *	2
Peace Lovers	1
Thanda Royal Zulu *	2
Kaiser Chiefs	2
SuperSport United *	1
Ikapa Sporting	1
FC Cape Town	2
Mpumalanga Black Aces	2 5p
FC Royals *	2 3p
Price Parkhurst *	1
Winners Park	3
Ajax Cape Town *	5
Wings United	0
Tower United *	1
Free State Stars	6
Mamelodi Sundowns	3
Island *	1
Methlareng Tigers *	1
Black Leopards	2
Als Puk Tawana	3
Platinum Stars *	2
Bloemfontein Celtic	1
Orlando Pirates *	2
Pretoria University *	5
Vasco da Gama	1
Santos *	1 4p
Jomo Cosmos	1 5p
Moroka Swallows *	2 5p
Golden Arrows	1
Maritzburg United *	0
AmaZulu	1

Second Round

Team	Score
BidVest Wits *	4
Thanda Royal Zulu	1
Kaiser Chiefs	0
FC Cape Town *	2
Mpumalanga Black Aces	1
Winners Park *	0
Ajax Cape Town *	1 2p
Free State Stars	1 4p
Mamelodi Sundowns *	1
Black Leopards	0
Als Puk Tawana	0
Orlando Pirates *	4
Pretoria University	1 4p
Jomo Cosmos *	1 2p
Moroka Swallows *	2 5p
AmaZulu	2 6p

Quarter-finals

Team	Score
BidVest Wits *	0 4p
FC Cape Town	0 3p
Mpumalanga Black Aces	0
Free State Stars *	2
Mamelodi Sundowns *	3
Orlando Pirates	1
Pretoria University	1
AmaZulu *	2

Semi-finals

Team	Score
BidVest Wits †	3
Free State Stars	1
Mamelodi Sundowns	1 3p
AmaZulu ††	1 4p

Final

Team	Score
BidVest Wits ‡	3
AmaZulu	0

CUP FINAL
Soccer City, Johannesburg
22-05-2010, Att: 71 956, Ref: Damon
Scorers - Rodrigues 76, Vilakazi 2 91+ 92+
Wits - Francis Chansa - Tefu Mashamaite, Patrick Phungwayo, Timothy Batabaire, Nyiko Tshabangu, Sibusiso Vilakazi, Sipho Mngomezulu, Sifiso Myeni, Marawaan Bantam (Fabrice Rodrigues 50), Mark Haskins (Calvin Kadi 75), Michael Morton. Tr: Roger de Sa
AmaZulu - Nick Gindre - Pere Ariweriyai, Simangaliso Biyela, Siphiwe Mkhonza, Abdullahi Ishaka, Thami Sangweni, Nhlanhla Zwane (Bradley Ritson 84), Tsweu Mokoro, Litha Ngxabi (Sthembiso Dlamini 74), Ayanda Dlamini, Dumisani Ngwenya (Sboniso Gumede 81). Tr: Neil Tovey

‡ Qualified for the CAF Confederation Cup

* Home team • † played in Olen Park, Potchefstroom • †† played in King's Park, Durban

RUS – RUSSIA

FIFA/COCA-COLA WORLD RANKING

1993	1994	1995	1996	1997	1998	1999	2000	2001	2002	2003	2004	2005	2006	2007	2008	2009	2010
14	13	5	7	12	40	18	21	21	23	24	32	34	22	23	9	12	13

	2010											Hi/Lo
Jan	Feb	Mar	Mar	Apr	May	Jul	Aug	Sep	Oct	Nov	Dec	3
12	13	12	12	11	11	17	16	25	10	13	13	40

By winning the right to host the 2018 FIFA World Cup Russia took a major step on the road to establishing itself as a major footballing power. Both the national team, with its patchy record of qualification for major tournaments, and club football will for the first time take centre stage in a sporting landscape that has always placed so much emphasis on individual athletic prowess. Central to the development of the game will be the 13 new stadia to be built to replace the crumbling and inhospitable Soviet era structures, stadia that should transform the Russian Premier League. The League is already very cosmopolitan and standards are improving - Zenit St Petersburg used players from ten different countries on the way to their 2010 title success and were coached by the Italian Luciano Spalletti - but crowds are still small compared with the major leagues in Western Europe. FIFA chose Russia for the potential that exists in the country and the football authorities there now have the big task of delivering on the promises made. If all goes to plan there is the very real prospect that European football will have a new centre of power at both club and national team level, although Russia's defeat at home to Slovakia in the Euro 2012 qualifiers showed just how much there is to do. These are exciting times for Russian football.

FIFA WORLD CUP RECORD

1930-1954 DNE **1958** 7 QF **1962** 6 QF **1966** 4 SF **1970** 5 QF 1974-1978 DNQ **1982** 7 r2 **1986** 10 r2 **1990** 17 r1 (as the Soviet Union) **1994** 18 r1 **1998** DNQ **2002** 22 r1 2006-2010 DNQ (as Russia)

FOOTBALL UNION OF RUSSIA (RFU)

House of Football,
Ulitsa Narodnaya 7,
Moscow 115 172
☎ +7 495 9261300
📠 +7 501 9261305
📧 info@rfs.ru
🖥 www.rfs.ru
FA 1912 CON 1992 FIFA 1992
P Sergey Fursenko
GS TBD

FIFA BIG COUNT 2006

Total players	5 802 536
% of population	4.06%
Male	5 105 014
Female	697 522
Amateurs 18+	582 383
Youth under 18	196 170
Unregistered	1 443 800
Professionals	3 724
Referees	36 530
Admin & coaches	223 300
Number of clubs	13 840
Number of teams	55 350

MAJOR CITIES/TOWNS

		Population
1	Moscow	10 494 522
2	Saint Petersburg	4 523 802
3	Novosibirsk	1 380 638
4	Yekaterinburg	1 305 070
5	Nizhniy Novgorod	1 263 758
6	Omsk	1 128 973
7	Samara	1 122 068
8	Kazan	1 118 623
9	Chelyabinsk	1 090 454
10	Rostov-na-Donu	1 048 157
11	Ufa	1 021 381
12	Perm	986 851
13	Volgograd	979 720
14	Krasnoyarsk	929 136
15	Voronezh	844 448
16	Saratov	835 418
17	Tolyatti	709 482
18	Krasnodar	702 427
56	Vladikavkaz	313 354

ROSSIYSKAYA FEDERATSIYA • RUSSIAN FEDERATION

Capital	Moscow	Population 140 041 247 (9)	% in cities 73%
GDP per capita	$16 100 (71)	Area km² 17 098 242 km² (1)	GMT + / - +2 to +12

Neighbours (km): Azerbaijan 284, Belarus 959, China 3645, Estonia 290, Finland 1313, Georgia 723, Kazakhstan 6846, Korea DPR 17, Latvia 292, Lithuania 227, Mongolia 3441, Norway 196, Poland 432, Ukraine 1576 • Coast 37 653

RECENT INTERNATIONAL MATCHES PLAYED BY RUSSIA

2007	Opponents	Score		Venue	Comp	Scorers	Att	Referee
7-02	Netherland	L	1-4	Amsterdam	Fr	Bystrov [76]	24 589	Clattenburg ENG
24-03	Estonia	W	2-0	Tallinn	ECq	Kerzhakov.A 2 [66 78]	8 212	Ceferin SVN
2-06	Andorra	W	4-0	St Petersburg	ECq	Kerzhakov.A 3 [8 16 49], Sychev [71]	21 520	Skjerven NOR
6-06	Croatia	D	0-0	Zagreb	ECq		36 194	Michel SVK
22-08	Poland	D	2-2	Moscow	Fr	Sychev [21], Pavlyuchenko [34]	15 000	Hrinak SVK
8-09	Macedonia	W	3-0	Moscow	ECq	Berezutski.V [6], Arshavin [83], Kerzhakov [86]	23 000	Ovrebø NOR
12-09	England	L	0-3	London	ECq		86 106	Hansson SWE
17-10	England	W	2-1	Moscow	ECq	Pavlyuchenko 2 [69p 73]	75 000	Cantalejo ESP
17-11	Israel	L	1-2	Tel Aviv	ECq	Bilyaletdinov [61]	29 787	Farina ITA
21-11	Andorra	W	1-0	Andorra la Vella	ECq	Sychev [38]	780	Hauge NOR
2008								
26-03	Romania	L	0-3	Bucharest	Fr		10 000	Kenan ISR
23-05	Kazakhstan	W	6-0	Moscow	Fr	Pogrebnyak [27p], Bystrov [44], Zyryanov [57], Torbinsky [85], Bilyaletdinov [85p], Sychev [89]	10 000	
28-05	Serbia	W	2-1	Berghausen	Fr	Pogrebnyak [12], Pavlyuchenko [48]	4 030	Stark GER
4-06	Lithuania	W	4-1	Berghausen	Fr	Zyryanov [33], Arshavin [52], Pavlyuchenko [64], Bystrov [80]	2 850	Sippel GER
10-06	Spain	L	1-4	Innsbruck	ECr1	Pavlyuchenko [86]	30 772	Plautz AUT
14-06	Greece	W	1-0	Salzburg	ECr1	Zyryanov [33]	31 063	Rosetti ITA
18-06	Sweden	W	2-0	Innsbruck	ECr1	Pavlyuchenko [24], Arshavin [50]	30 772	De Bleeckere BEL
21-06	Netherlands	W	3-1	Basel	ECqf	Pavlyuchenko [56], Torbinski [112], Arshavin [116]	38 374	Michel SVK
26-06	Spain	L	0-3	Vienna	ECsf		51 428	De Bleeckere BEL
20-08	Netherlands	D	1-1	Moscow	Fr	Zyryanov [78p]	25 000	Frojdfeldt SWE
10-09	Wales	W	2-1	Moscow	WCq	Pavlyuchenko [22p], Pogrebnyak [81]	28 000	Skomina SVN
11-10	Germany	L	1-2	Dortmund	WCq	Arshavin [51]	65 607	Frojdfeldt SWE
15-10	Finland	W	3-0	Moscow	WCq	Pasanen OG [23], Lampi OG [65], Arshavin [88]	28 000	Vassaras GRE
2009								
28-03	Azerbaijan	W	2-0	Moscow	WCq	Pavlyuchenko [32], Zyrianov [71]	62 000	Gumienny BEL
1-04	Liechtenstein	W	1-0	Vaduz	WCq	Zyrianov [38]	5 679	McKeon IRL
10-06	Finland	W	3-0	Helsinki	WCq	Kerzhakov 2 [27 53]	37 028	Plautz AUT
12-08	Argentina	L	2-3	Moscow	Fr	Semshov [17], Pavlyuchenko [78]	28 800	De Bleeckere BEL
5-09	Liechtenstein	W	3-0	St Petersburg	WCq	Berezutsky.V [17], Pavlyuchenko 2 [40p 45p]	21 000	Constantin ROU
9-09	Wales	W	3-1	Cardiff	WCq	Semshov [36], Ignashevich [71], Pavlyuchenko [91+]	14 505	De Sousa POR
10-10	Germany	L	0-1	Moscow	WCq		72 100	Busacca SUI
14-10	Azerbaijan	D	1-1	Baku	WCq	Arshavin [13]	17 000	Webb ENG
14-11	Slovenia	W	2-1	Moscow	WCpo	Bilyaletdinov 2 [40 52]	71 600	Larsen DEN
18-11	Slovenia	L	0-1	Maribor	WCpo		12 510	Hauge NOR
2010								
3-03	Hungary	D	1-1	Gyor	Fr	Bilyaletdinov [59]	10 000	Vucemilovic CRO
11-08	Bulgaria	W	1-0	St Petersburg	Fr	Shirokov [6]	8 200	Rizzoli ITA
3-09	Andorra	W	2-0	Andorra La Vella	ECq	Pogrebnyak 2 [14 64p]	1 100	Borg MLT
7-09	Slovakia	L	0-1	Moscow	ECq		27 052	De Bleeckere BEL
8-10	Republic of Ireland	W	3-2	Dublin	ECq	Kerzakhov [11], Dzagoev [29], Shirokov [50]	50 411	Blom NED
12-10	Macedonia FYR	W	1-0	Skopje	ECq	Kerzhakov [8]	10 500	Johannesson SWE
17-11	Belgium	L	0-2	Voronezh	Fr		31 743	Kaasik EST

Fr = Friendly match • EC = UEFA EURO 2008/2012 • WC = FIFA World Cup • q = qualifier
r1 = first round group • qf = quarter-final • sf = semi-final

RUSSIA NATIONAL TEAM HISTORICAL RECORDS

Caps
109 - Viktor Onopko 1992-2004 • **72** - Valeri Karpin 1992-2003 • **71** - Vladimir Beschastnykh 1992-2003 • **65** - Sergei Semak 1997- • **62** - Sergei Ignashevich 2002- • **57** - Andrei Arshavin 2002- • **55** - Dmitri Alenichev 1996-2005, Yuri Nikiforov 1993-2002 & Alexey Smertin 1998-2006 • **54** - Aleksandr Anyukov 2004- • **53** - Dmitriy Khokhlov 1996-2005 • **52** - Aleksandr Kerzhakov 2002-

Goals
26 - Vladimir Beschastnykh 1992-2003 • **17** - Valeri Karpin 1992-2003 & Aleksandr Kerzhakov 2002- • **16** - Andrei Arshavin 2002- • **15** - Roman Pavlyuchenko 2003- & Dmitri Sychev 2002- • **12** - Igor Kolyvanov 1992-98 • **10** - Sergei Kiryakov 1992-98 & Aleksandr Mostovoi 1992-2004 • **9** - Igor Simutenkov 1994-98 & Dmitriy Bulykin

Past Coaches
Pavel Sadyrin 1992-94 • Oleg Romantsev 1994-96 • Boris Ignatyev 1996-98 • Anatoli Byshovets 1998 • Oleg Romantsev 1999-2002 • Valeri Gazzaev 2002-03 • Georgi Yartsev 2003-05 • Yuri Semin 2005 • Aleksandr Borodyuk 2006 • Guus Hiddink 2006-10 • Dick Advocaat 2010-

RUSSIA 2010

PREMIER LEAGUE

	Pl	W	D	L	F	A	Pts	Zenit	CSKA	Rubin	Spartak M	Lokomotiv	Spartak N	Dinamo	Tom	Rostov	Saturn	Anzhi	Terek	Krylya	Amkar	Alania	SIBIR
Zenit St Petersburg †	30	20	8	2	61	21	**68**		1-3	2-0	1-1	1-0	3-1	1-1	2-0	5-0	6-1	2-1	0-0	0-0	2-0	3-0	2-0
CSKA Moskva †	30	18	8	4	51	22	**62**	0-2		0-0	3-1	1-1	1-2	0-0	3-1	2-0	1-1	4-0	4-1	4-3	1-0	2-1	1-0
Rubin Kazan †	30	15	13	2	37	16	**58**	2-2	0-1		1-1	2-0	1-1	2-0	2-1	2-1	2-0	0-0	0-0	3-0	3-0	1-0	1-0
Spartak Moskva ‡	30	13	10	7	43	33	**49**	1-0	1-2	0-1		2-1	0-0	0-0	4-2	2-1	2-1	3-0	2-1	0-0	2-2	3-0	5-3
Lokomotiv Moskva ‡	30	13	9	8	34	29	**48**	0-3	1-0	0-0	2-3		1-0	3-2	2-1	0-1	0-1	2-1	2-1	3-0	2-0	3-0	1-1
Spartak Nalchik	30	12	8	10	40	37	**44**	2-3	1-1	1-1	0-2	1-1		1-0	2-1	5-2	2-0	1-3	2-1	1-0	2-1	2-1	4-2
Dinamo Moskva	30	9	13	8	38	31	**40**	1-2	0-0	2-2	1-1	3-0	0-3		0-0	3-2	1-0	4-0	3-1	1-1	1-1	2-0	4-1
Tom Tomsk	30	7	13	10	35	43	**37**	0-0	0-3	0-1	2-2	1-1	1-0	1-0		2-1	2-2	1-4	2-1	1-1	1-0	1-1	3-2
FK Rostov	30	10	4	16	27	44	**34**	1-3	1-0	0-2	1-0	1-2	1-1	1-1	0-2		1-0	1-0	1-0	1-2	2-1	0-1	0-1
Saturn Ramenskoe	30	8	10	12	27	38	**34**	0-1	1-1	0-0	0-0	0-1	3-1	3-2	1-2	0-2		1-0	1-0	1-1	2-2	1-1	1-1
Anzhi Makhachkala	30	9	6	15	29	39	**33**	3-3	1-2	0-1	0-1	0-0	1-1	0-0	1-1	1-0	1-2		1-2	1-0	0-0	2-0	1-0
Terek Groznyi	30	8	9	13	28	34	**33**	0-0	0-3	1-1	2-0	0-0	1-1	1-1	1-0	1-1	2-0	1-3		2-0	1-3	2-0	1-1
Krylya Sovetov Samara	30	7	10	13	28	40	**31**	0-1	0-1	0-2	0-0	0-0	2-0	1-0	2-3	1-2	2-1	3-0	1-3		1-1	1-0	1-1
Amkar Perm	30	8	6	16	24	35	**30**	0-2	0-0	0-1	0-2	1-2	3-1	0-1	2-1	1-0	0-1	1-0	2-0	2-1		1-0	3-1
Alania Vladikavkaz	30	7	9	14	25	41	**30**	1-3	1-3	1-1	5-2	0-0	1-0	0-2	1-1	0-0	1-1	0-0	2-1	2-3	0-0		2-1
SIBIR Novosibirsk	30	4	8	18	34	58	**20**	2-5	1-4	2-2	0-0	2-2	0-2	2-2	0-1	2-0	1-0	2-4	0-2	4-1	1-0	1-2	

12/03/2010 - 28/11/2010 • † Qualified for the UEFA Champions League • ‡ Qualified for the Europa League

Top scorers: **19** - Welliton BRA, Spartak Moskva • **14** - Oleksandr Aliyev UKR, Lokomotiv & Sergei Kornilenko BLR, Tom/Rubin • **13** - Aleksandr Kerzhakov, Zenit • **10** - Vladimir Dyadyun, Spartak Nalchik; Danny POR, Zenit & Artem Dzyuba, Tom Tomsk

RUSSIA 2010

FIRST DIVISION (2)

	Pl	W	D	L	F	A	Pts	Kuban	Volga	Nizhniy N'rod	KamAZ	Krasnodar	Mordovia	Ural	Zhemchuzhina	Volgar	Shinnik	SKA	Luch	Khimki	Dinamo Bry	Baltika	Dinamo St P	Salyut	Rotor	Irtysh	Avangard
Kuban Krasnodar	38	24	8	6	51	20	**80**		1-0	0-0	0-1	3-0	0-2	3-0	0-1	6-1	1-1	1-0	3-0	1-0	1-0	0-0	2-0	0-0	3-0	2-1	2-0
Volga Nizhniy Novgorod	38	19	14	5	62	25	**71**	0-0		3-0	2-2	4-1	3-0	3-0	3-1	1-0	2-0	2-2	2-0	1-1	4-1	3-0	1-0	0-0	3-0	2-3	2-0
FC Nizhniy Novgorod	38	21	7	10	60	41	**70**	3-1	2-2		3-1	4-3	0-1	1-0	0-0	0-0	1-0	2-0	3-1	2-0	3-1	2-0	3-1	0-0	3-0	3-2	3-2
KamAZ Chelny	38	19	9	10	55	43	**66**	1-2	1-1	3-2		1-0	2-1	1-1	2-0	3-1	1-2	1-1	1-0	1-1	1-1	2-1	2-0	2-1	2-0	1-2	2-0
FK Krasnodar	38	17	10	11	60	44	**61**	0-1	3-3	4-2	2-2		4-1	1-0	1-1	2-0	2-1	3-0	3-0	1-5	1-3	1-0	2-0	3-0	2-0	0-0	0-0
Mordovia Saransk	38	16	10	12	53	40	**58**	3-0	2-0	3-1	1-2	1-2		1-1	1-1	1-1	1-0	0-0	2-0	2-0	1-3	2-1	0-1	3-1	2-1	0-1	1-0
Ural Yekaterinburg	38	14	16	8	38	28	**58**	0-0	0-1	3-0	1-1	3-1	1-0		1-1	2-0	0-0	1-0	0-0	2-3	3-3	1-0	2-0	0-4	0-1	0-0	1-0
Zhemchuzhina Sochi	38	16	9	13	45	44	**57**	0-1	0-2	2-2	3-2	2-0	2-1	2-2		1-0	2-1	1-0	0-0	2-1	2-1	1-2	3-1	2-2	2-2	2-1	3-2
Volgar Astrakhan	38	16	9	13	45	48	**57**	2-1	1-0	2-1	0-1	2-1	0-3	0-0	0-3		0-1	1-0	2-1	2-2	3-2	2-3	2-2	0-0	0-2	0-3	1-0
Shinnik Yaroslavl	38	13	13	11	43	31	**55**	0-1	0-0	1-1	0-2	0-0	3-1	1-0	1-2	0-1		3-0	3-2	0-0	1-0	1-0	0-0	1-1	1-1	1-0	2-0
SKA Khabarovsk	38	15	8	15	37	39	**53**	0-0	1-2	0-1	0-2	1-0	3-1	0-0	2-3	1-0	2-3		0-0	1-0	0-0	1-0	0-0	1-2	1-0	0-1	4-3
Luch Vladivostock	38	13	13	12	42	42	**52**	0-1	1-1	3-1	0-1	1-1	2-0	1-0	2-1	0-1	3-1	0-0		0-0	0-3	2-1	1-0	2-0	1-1	1-1	4-3
FK Khimki	38	11	17	10	39	38	**50**	0-1	1-0	1-1	0-2	0-0	3-1	1-1	1-1	1-0	0-1	1-0	0-1		2-2	1-0	4-1	1-0	1-3	1-1	3-0
Dinamo Bryansk	38	11	11	16	53	54	**44**	0-1	1-0	1-1	0-2	0-0	3-1	1-1	1-1	1-0	0-1	1-1	2-2	1-0		4-1	1-0	1-3	1-1	3-0	2-0
Baltika Kaliningrad	38	11	10	17	38	47	**43**	0-1	0-0	1-0	2-4	1-1	2-2	1-0	1-1	0-1	1-0	3-1	1-2	0-0	1-0		2-0	0-0	3-2	2-1	2-1
Dynamo St Petersburg	38	9	10	19	32	53	**37**	0-0	1-1	0-1	1-1	0-0	1-3	1-1	0-1	1-1	2-5	2-1	1-2	0-2	0-0	0-2		2-0	4-1	2-0	1-0
Salyut Belgorod	38	7	13	18	30	47	**34**	1-2	0-0	0-1	2-0	1-2	1-1	1-1	1-0	1-2	0-0	2-4	0-1	1-2	4-2	1-1	1-2		2-1	1-0	0-0
Rotor Volgograd	38	9	7	22	27	64	**34**	0-3	1-4	0-2	1-0	0-6	1-2	1-0	0-1	1-0	0-0	2-2	0-1	1-0	1-0	1-0	1-2	0-1		0-0	1-0
Irtysh Omsk	38	6	10	22	26	52	**28**	2-3	1-1	0-0	0-0	0-0	0-1	0-0	1-0	1-4	1-1	0-1	0-3	0-1	4-2	0-0	2-1	1-1	2-0		2-1
Avangard Kursk	38	7	6	25	31	67	**27**	1-2	1-0	1-5	2-1	1-2	1-1	0-1	1-0	1-0	1-6	1-5	1-2	0-1	1-2	1-1	0-0	2-0	1-3	2-1	

27/03/2010 - 6/11/2010 • Top scorers: **21** - Otari Martsvaladze GEO, Volga NN • **18** - Spartak Gogniyev, KamAZ/Krasnodar

MEDALS TABLE

		Overall			League			Cup			Europe		
		G	S	B	G	S	B	G	S	B	G	S	B
1	Spartak Moskva	12	6	4	9	4	2	3	2				2
2	CSKA Moskva	9	8	2	3	5	2	5	3		1		
3	Lokomotiv Moskva	7	5	6	2	4	4	5	1				2
4	Zenit St Petersburg	5	2	2	2	1	2	2	1		1		
5	Rubin Kazan	2	1	2	2	1	2						
6	Dinamo Moskva	1	3	4		1	4	1	2				
7	Spartak Vladikavkaz	1	2		1	2							
8	Topedo Moskva	1		1				1		1			
9	Terek Groznyi	1						1					

Russian Clubs in the Soviet League and Cup

		Overall			League			Cup			Europe		
		G	S	B	G	S	B	G	S	B	G	S	B
2	Spartak Moskva	22	17	10	12	12	9	10	5				1
3	Dinamo Moskva	17	17	7	11	11	5	6	6			1	2
4	CSKA Moskva	12	7	6	7	4	6	5	3				
5	Torpedo Moskva	9	12	6	3	3	6	6	9				
10	Zenit Leningrad	2	3	1	1		1	1		3			
11	Lokomotiv Moskva	2	2		1			2	1				
12	SKA Rostov	1	3		1			1	2				

KUBOK ROSSII 2009–10

Fourth Round

Team	
Zenit St Petersburg	Bye
Shinnik Yaroslavl	0
Torpedo Vladimir *	1
Spartak Nalchik	Bye
Saturn-2 Moskva Oblast *	2
FK Nizhniy Novgorod	3
Baltika Kaliningrad	3
Torpedo Moskva *	0
FK Khimki	Bye
Rubin Kazan	Bye
Rossii Moskva	0
Volga Tver *	1
FK Moskva	Bye
FK Volgograd *	0
Salyut Belgorod	1
FK Krasnodar *	1
Chernomorets Novorossiyisk	0
Spartak Moskva	Bye
Avangard Podolsk *	1
Metallurg Lipetsk	0
FK Rostov	Bye
Avangard Kursk *	2
Vityaz Podolsk	0
Amkar Perm	Bye
Alania Vladikavkaz *	3
Anzhi Makhachkala	0
Tom Tomsk	Bye
Dinamo Moskva	Bye
Zhemchuzhina Sochi *	1
Volgar Astrakhan	2
FK Chelyabinsk *	2
KamAZ Chelny	1
Krylya Sovetov Samara	Bye
Terek Groznyi	Bye
Volga Nizhniy Novgorod	1
Mordovia Saransk *	2
Luch Vladivostock	4
Amur Blagoveshchensk *	1
Saturn Ramenskoe	Bye
Lokomotiv Moskva	Bye
FK Chita	0
SKA Khabarovsk *	1
Ural Yekaterinburg	2
NoSta Novotroitsk *	1
CSKA Moskva	Bye
Kuban Krasnodar	Bye
Dinamo Barnaul *	0
SIBIR Novosibirsk	2

Fifth Round

Zenit St Petersburg	2
Torpedo Vladimir *	0
Spartak Nalchik	0
FK Nizhniy Novgorod *	2
Baltika Kaliningrad *	2
FK Khimki	1
Rubin Kazan	3
Volga Tver *	4
FK Moskva	2
Salyut Belgorod *	0
FK Krasnodar *	1
Spartak Moskva	2
Avangard Podolsk *	4
FK Rostov	2
Avangard Kursk *	1
Amkar Perm	2
Alania Vladikavkaz *	1
Tom Tomsk	0
Dinamo Moskva	0
Volgar Astrakhan *	2
FK Chelyabinsk *	2
Krylya Sovetov Samara	1
Terek Groznyi	1
Mordovia Saransk *	2
Luch Vladivostock *	3
Saturn Ramenskoe	0
Lokomotiv Moskva	1
SKA Khabarovsk *	2
Ural Yekaterinburg *	1
CSKA Moskva	0
Kuban Krasnodar	0
SIBIR Novosibirsk *	1

Sixth Round

Zenit St Petersburg *	2
FK Nizhniy Novgorod	1
Baltika Kaliningrad	2 2p
Volga Tver *	2 4p
FK Moskva	2
Spartak Moskva *	1
Avangard Podolsk	1
Amkar Perm *	2
Alania Vladikavkaz *	2
Volgar Astrakhan	1
FK Chelyabinsk *	0
Mordovia Saransk	2
Luch Vladivostock *	2
SKA Khabarovsk	1
Ural Yekaterinburg *	1
SIBIR Novosibirsk	2

The 16 Premier League teams enter in the fifth round and are drawn away to the 16 qualifiers

KUBOK ROSSII 2009-10

Quarter-finals	Semi-finals	Final

Zenit St Petersburg *   2
Volga Tver   0

Zenit St Petersburg   0   4p
Amkar Perm *   0   2p

FK Moskva
Amkar Perm   W-O

Zenit St Petersburg   1
SIBIR Novosibirsk ‡   0

Alania Vladikavkaz   3
Mordovia Saransk *   0

Alania Vladikavkaz   0
SIBIR Novosibirsk *   3

Luch Vladivostock   0
SIBIR Novosibirsk *   3

KUBOK ROSSI FINAL 2010

Olimp-2, Rostov-na-Donu, 16-05-2010, 14:00, Att: 15 400, Ref: Aleksandr Kolobayev

Zenit St Petersburg   1   Shirokov 60p
SIBIR Novosibirsk   0

Zenit - Vyacheslav Malafeyev - Aleksandr Anyukov• (c), Ivica Krizanac•, Nicolas Lombaerts, Tomas Hubocan - Igor Denisov, Constantin Zyryanov (Viktor Fayzulin 80) - Wladimir Bystrov (Alessandro Rosina 90), Roman Shirokov, Danny - Aleksandr Kerzhakov (Maksim Kanunnikov 83). Tr: Luciano Spalletti
SIBIR - Wojciech Kowalewski• - Nikola Valentic•, Denis Bukhryakov, Yegor Filipenko•, Arunas Klimavicius (Ivan Nagibin 75), Dmitriy Molosh - Aleksei Aravin•, Aleksandr Makarenko, Tomas Cizek (Aleksei Vasilyev 61) - Aleksei Medvedev (c) - Aleksandr Degtyaryov (Aleksandr Antipenko• 70). Tr: Igor Kriushenko

* Home team • ‡ Qualified for the Europa League

CLUB BY CLUB GUIDE TO THE 2010 SEASON IN RUSSIA

ALANIA VLADIKAVKAZ 2010

Mon	Date	Opponent	R	Score	Comp	Scorers	Att
Mar	14	Saturn	D	1-1	PL	Kirillov 23	28 000
	19	Sp Nalchik	L	1-2	PL	Bazayev 67p	10 000
	26	Amkar	D	0-0	PL		22 000
Apr	3	Anzhi	L	0-2	PL		12 500
	11	CSKA	L	1-3	PL	Kuznetsov 57	24 000
	17	Sibir	W	2-1	PL	Kirillov 72, Marenich 87	17 500
	25	Rostov	W	1-0	PL	Stoyanov 13	12 000
May	2	Rubin	D	1-1	PL	Stoyanov 32	17 000
	5	Krylya	L	0-1	PL		9 200
	10	Spartak M	W	5-2	PL	Marenich 5, Gabulov 2 9 69, Hubulov 88, Ohanyan 91+	20 000
	14	Dinamo	L	0-2	PL		7 053
	9	Zenit	L	1-3	PL	Ivanov 79	20 000
	13	KamAZ	D	0-0	KRr5	W 4-2p	5 700
Jul	18	Lokomotiv	L	0-3	PL		11 423
	24	Tom Tomsk	W	2-1	PL	Marenich 59, Gnanou 70	11 500
	31	Terek	L	0-2	PL		6 300
	8	Sp Nalchik	W	1-0	PL	Nizamutdinov 42	12 500
Aug	15	Amkar	L	0-1	PL		16 500
	22	Anzhi	D	0-0	PL		10 000
	29	CSKA	L	1-2	PL	Florescu 90p	8 000
	11	Sibir	W	2-1	PL	Gnanou 90, Babatunde 90	6 500
Sep	18	Rostov	D	0-0	PL		10 000
	22	Gornjak	D	0-0	KRr6	W 5-4p	4 000
	25	Rubin	L	0-1	PL		14 630
	2	Krylya	L	2-3	PL	Marenich 75, Bikmaev 78	8 000
Oct	15	Spartak M	L	0-1	PL		10 500
	23	Dinamo	D	0-0	PL		13 000
	31	Zenit	L	0-3	PL		20 500
	7	Lokomotiv	D	0-0	PL		15 000
Nov	13	Tom Tomsk	D	1-1	PL	Gabulov 65	8 000
	20	Terek	W	2-1	PL	Bikmaev 63, Gabulov 77	15 000
	28	Saturn	D	1-1	PL	Ivanov 13	2 000

ANZHI MAKHACHKALA 2010

Mon	Date	Opponent	R	Score	Comp	Scorers	Att
Mar	13	Sp Nalchik	D	0-0	PL		13 000
	20	Amkar	L	0-1	PL		11 800
	26	CSKA	L	1-2	PL	Streltsov 11	15 200
Apr	3	Alania	W	2-0	PL	Streltsov 24p, Holenda 53	12 500
	11	Sibir	W	4-2	PL	Tsorayev 2 21 93+, Holenda 2 34 48	10 000
	19	Rostov	L	1-2	PL	Tsorayev 47	12 000
	25	Rubin	D	0-0	PL		8 120
	30	Krylya	D	0-0	PL		10 000
May	6	Spartak M	L	0-3	PL		19 000
	11	Dinamo	D	1-1	PL	Mamayev 33	13 000
	4	Zenit	L	1-2	PL	Tagirbekov 66	21 380
	10	Lokomotiv	L	1-2	PL	Tagirbekov 91+	3 000
	14	FK Pskov	W	2-1	KRr5	Timonov 22p, OG 82	3 150
Jul	18	Tom Tomsk	W	4-1	PL	Agalarov 19, Josan 45, Gajibekov 71, Tsorayev 77	9 800
	25	Terek	W	1-0	PL	Tsorayev 75	6 000
	30	Saturn	L	0-1	PL		6 000
	7	Amkar	W	1-0	PL	Josan 43p	9 700
Aug	15	CSKA	L	0-4	PL		4 500
	22	Alania	D	0-0	PL		10 000
	30	Sibir	W	1-0	PL	Tsorayev 51p	10 000
	12	Rostov	L	0-1	PL		11 500
Sep	19	Rubin	L	0-1	PL		12 000
	27	Krylya	L	0-3	PL		10 100
	3	Spartak M	L	0-1	PL		11 000
	17	Dinamo	L	0-4	PL		5 269
Oct	24	Zenit	D	3-3	PL	Holenda 3, Josan 79, Bakaev 89	12 000
	31	Lokomotiv	L	0-1	PL		12 000
	6	Tom Tomsk	W	1-0	PL	Strelkov 23	8 700
Nov	13	Terek	W	3-1	PL	Holenda 16, Josan 61, Tsoraev 66	7 000
	20	Saturn	L	1-2	PL	Tsoraev 69p	7 500
	28	Sp Nalchik	W	3-1	PL	Streltsov 45, Kukharchuk 2 63 75	7 000

KEY TO THE CLUB SECTION

SC = Super Cup • PL = Premier League • KR = Russian Cup (Kubok Rossi) • CL = UEFA Champions League • EL = Europa League Matches that are shaded were played at home; matches with no shading were played either away or on a neutral ground

ALANIA LEAGUE APPEARANCES/GOALS 2010

Goalkeepers Mikhail Kerzhakov 14+2 • Dmitriy Khomich 16
Defenders Simeon Bulgaru MDA 12/0 • Ibrahim Gnanou BFA 24+1/2 • Da Costa Goore CIV 26/0 • Nariman Gusalov 1/0 • Ivan Ivanov BUL 23+1/2 • Juri Kirillov 15+8/2 • Abdoul Mamah TOG 11+2/0
Midfield Dzhambulat Bazayev 6/1 • Georgiy Bazayev 4+2/0 • Shota Bibilov 0+1/0 • Vitaliy Chochiev 3+2/0 • George Florescu ROU 20/1 • Georgiy Gabulov 24+2/4 • Sani Kaita NGA 6/0 • Arsen Khubulov 0+8/1 • Aslan Mashukov 15/0 • Eldar Nizamutdinov 19+4/1 • Ivan Stoyanov BUL 21+3/2 • Francisco Zuela 6/0
Forwards Aleksandr Alkhazov 0+2/0 • Collins Babatunde NGA 7+3/1 • Marat Bikmaev UZB 7+6/2 • Atsamaz Buran 0+1/0 • Sergei Dadu MDA 0+4/1 • Georgi Gogichaev 4+4/0 • Sergey Kuznetsov UKR 7+3/1 • Aleksandr Marenich 18+8/4 • Karen Oganyan 1+9/0 • Aleksandr Tikhonovetskiy 3+3/0 • Taras Tsarikaev 3+4/0 • Dioh Williams LBR 1/0
Coach Vladimir Shevchuk

AMKAR LEAGUE APPEARANCES/GOALS 2010

Goalkeepers Sergey Narubin 16 • Igor Usminskiy 14
Defenders Dmitriy Belorukov 24/1 • Miklos Gaal HUN 12+2/0 • Vadim Gagloev 0+3/0 • Vyacheslav Kalashnikov 3+3/0 • Mikhail Makagonov 1/0 • Aleksey Popov KAZ 22+3/0 • Zahari Sirakov BUL 22/1
Midfield Ivan Cherenchikov 19/2 • Denis Dedechko UKR 5/0 • Vitaliy Grishin 19+5/1 • Josip Knezevic CRO 9+4/0 • Alexander Kolomeitsev 19/1 • Mitar Novakovic MNE 29/3 • Georgi Peev BUL 23/4 • Nika Piliev 4+1/0 • Alexei Pomerko 3+3/0 • Andrey Sekretov 0+5/0 • Dmitry Sokolov 6+1/1 • Andrey Topchu 12+8/4 • Luka Zinko SVN 0+3/0
Forwards Nikita Burmistrov 6+2/0 • Vitaliy Fedoriv UZB 12+1/0 • Martin Kushev BUL 15+7/1 • Seiichiro Maki JPN 4+5/0 • Stevica Ristic MKD 10/4 • Damir Sadikov 1+3/0 • Vito ITA 2+4/0 • Sergey Volkov 18+2/2
Coach Rashid Rakhimov TJK

AMKAR PERM 2010

Mon	Date	Opponent	R	Score	Comp	Scorers	Att
Mar	12	CSKA	L	0-1	PL		6 700
	20	Anzhi	W	1-0	PL	Cherenchikov 74	11 800
	26	Dinamo	D	0-0	PL		22 000
Apr	3	Sibir	W	3-1	PL	Volkov 10, Peev 2 23 92+	12 500
	11	Rostov	L	1-2	PL	Sokolov 51	9 500
	17	Rubin	L	0-1	PL		12 000
	21	Zent	D	0-0	KRsf	L 2-4p	15 400
	26	Krylya	D	1-1	PL	Novakovic 66	12 100
	2	Spartak M	L	0-1	PL		13 700
May	5	Dinamo	D	1-1	PL	Grishin 55	3 637
	10	Zenit	L	0-2	PL		11 900
	15	Lokomotiv	L	0-2	PL		11 123
	10	Tom Tomsk	W	2-1	PL	Kushev 71p, Kolomeitsev 93+	8 200
	14	Cherno'rets	W	1-0	KRr5	Knezevic 7p	9 000
Jul	18	Terek	L	0-1	PL		7 200
	25	Saturn	L	0-1	PL		8 200
	30	Sp Nalchik	L	1-2	PL	Sirakov 74	10 000
	7	Anzhi	L	0-1	PL		9 700
Aug	15	Alania	W	1-0	PL	Volkov 65	16 500
	22	Sibir	L	0-1	PL		9 000
	28	Rostov	W	1-0	PL	Peev 24	8 200
	11	Rubin	L	0-3	PL		13 400
Sep	18	Krylya	W	2-1	PL	Ristic 15, OG 47	6 400
	24	Spartak M	D	2-2	PL	Novakovic 23, Cherenchikov 54	12 700
	2	Dinamo	L	0-1	PL		9 200
	16	Zenit	L	0-2	PL		20 500
Oct	24	Lokomotiv	L	1-2	PL	Topchu 24	7 000
	31	Tom Tomsk	L	0-1	PL		14 500
	6	Terek	W	2-0	PL	Novakovic 24, Ristic 46	14 100
Nov	12	Saturn	D	2-2	PL	Ristic 55, Peev 89	5 000
	20	Sp Nalchik	W	3-1	PL	Ristic 16, Topchu 57, Belorikov 74	14 500
	28	CSKA	D	0-0	PL		11 600

ANZHI LEAGUE APPEARANCES/GOALS 2010

Goalkeepers Ilya Abaev 16 • Nukri Revishvili GEO 14
Defenders Ali Gadzhibekov 19/1 • Ibra Kebe SEN 23/0 • Otar Khizaneishvili GEO 6+2/0 • Dato Kvirkvelia GEO 13/0 • Oskars Klava LVA 7+4/0 • Mitar Pekovic SRB 19/0 • Mahir Shukurov AZE 20/0 • Rasim Tagirbekov 28/2
Midfield Kamil Agalarov 27/1 • Zurab Arziani GEO 5+6/0 • Mikhail Bakaev 28+1/1 • Shamil Burziev 0+7/0 • Dmitri Ivanov 10+4/0 • Nicolae Josan MDA 18+4/4 • Gocha Khodzhava GEO 4+5/0 • Eldar Mamaev 1+7/1 • Muhammad Sharif 0+2/0 • Andrey Streltsov 12+6/3 • Todor Timonov BUL 1+10/0 • David Tsoraev 28/8
Forwards Revaz Barabadze GEO 1+1/0 • Jan Holenda CZE 16+3/5 • David Iluridze 1+4/0 • Ilya Kukharchuk 3+9/2 • Magomed Magomedov 0+4/0 • Igor Strelkov 10+3/1
Coach Omari Tetradze • Arsen Akaev (18/04/2010) • Gadzhi Gadzhiev (19/04/2010)

CSKA MOSKVA 2010

Mar	24 Sevilla	D	1-1	CLr2	Gonzalez 66	28 600
	7 Rubin	L	0-1	SC		17 000
	12 Amkar	W	1-0	PL	Honda 93+	6 700
	16 Sevilla	W	2-1	CLr2	Necid 39, Honda 55	29 666
	21 Dinamo	D	0-0	PL		13 000
Apr	26 Anzhi	W	2-1	PL	Honda 49, Necid 62	15 200
	31 Inter	L	0-1	CLqf		69 398
	6 Inter	L	0-1	CLqf		54 400
	11 Alania	W	3-1	PL	Gonzalez 6, Krasic 45, Dzagoyev 45p	24 000
	17 Lokomotiv	D	1-1	PL	Milhomen 7	14 000
	24 Sibir	W	4-1	PL	Ignashevich 11, Milhomen 45, Necid 54, Dzagoyev 73	12 400
	28 Zenit	L	0-2	PL		13 600
May	2 Tom Tomsk	W	3-1	PL	Krasic 20, Milhomen 2 72 92+	6 500
	6 Rostov	L	0-1	PL		14 300
	10 Terek	W	4-1	PL	Odiah 47, Gonzalez 53, Dzagoyev 2 57 62	10 500
	14 Rubin	W	1-0	PL	Gonzalez 38	25 200
Jul	10 Saturn	D	1-1	PL	Dzagoyev 27	5 365
	14 Torpedo M	W	2-0	KRr5	Milhomen 2 9 12	9 000
	19 Krylya	W	1-0	PL	Dzagoyev 9p	16 050
	25 Sp Nalchik	L	1-2	PL	Necid 45	5 100
Aug	1 Spartak M	W	2-1	PL	Ignashevich 83, Vagner Love 93+	65 000
	15 Anzhi	W	4-0	PL	Oliseh 2 12 44, Vagner Love 20, Tosic 36	4 500
	19 Anorthosis	W	4-0	ELpo	Doumbia 2 13 20, Tosic 2 48 74	6 000
	24 Anorthosis	W	2-1	ELpo	Doumbia 85, Gonzalez 89	4 000
	29 Alania	W	2-1	PL	Doumbia 4, Tosic 69	8 000
Sep	12 Lokomotiv	L	0-1	PL		20 608
	16 Lausanne	W	3-0	ELgF	Vagner Love 2 22 80p, Ignashevich 68	9 531
	20 Sibir	W	1-0	PL	Oliseh 73	4 500
	26 Tom Tomsk	W	3-0	PL	Vagner Love 1, Doumbia 40, Necid 90	14 000
Oct	30 Sp Praha	W	3-0	ELgF	Doumbia 2 72 86, Gonzalez 84p	12 900
	3 Rostov	W	2-0	PL	Vagner Love 2 35 43p	4 740
	17 Terek	W	3-0	PL	Doumbia 17, Vagner Love 76, Honda 90	9 300
	21 Palermo	W	3-0	ELgF	Doumbia 2 34 59, Necid 82	17 548
	24 Rubin	D	0-0	PL		11 000
	27 Dinamo	D	0-0	PL		9 153
	31 Saturn	D	1-1	PL	Necid 39	12 000
Nov	4 Palermo	W	3-1	ELgF	Honda 47, Necid 2 50 54	11 980
	7 Krylya	W	4-3	PL	Berezutskiy 3, Necid 2 8 89, Tosic 66	4 500
	10 Zenit	W	3-1	PL	Vagner Love 14, Gonzalez 34, Doumbia 52	20 500
	14 Spartak N	D	1-1	PL	Vagner Love 59p	14 200
	20 Spartak M	W	3-1	PL	Honda 57, Doumbia 66, Vagner Love 90	14 800
	28 Amkar	D	0-0	PL		11 600
Dec	1 Lausanne	W	5-1	ELgF	Necid 2 18 82, Oliseh 22, Tosic 40, Dzagoev 71	4 500
	15 Sp Praha	D	1-1	ELgF	Dzagoev 15	12 707

DINAMO MOSKVA 2010

Mar	14 Spartak M	W	1-0	PL	Semshov 72	43 000
	21 CSKA	D	0-0	PL		13 000
	27 Zenit	L	1-2	PL	Kombarov.D 66p	13 480
Apr	4 Lokomotiv	L	2-3	PL	Voronin 22, Kombarov.D 88p	17 823
	10 Tom Tomsk	D	0-0	PL		5 177
	18 Terek	D	1-1	PL	Kombarov.D 60	10 000
	24 Saturn	W	1-0	PL	Epureanu 72	4 326
May	1 Sp Nalchik	L	0-1	PL		9 000
	5 Amkar	D	1-1	PL	Voronin 14p	3 637
	11 Anzhi	D	1-1	PL	Semshov 30	13 000
	15 Alania	W	2-0	PL	Kombarov.K 2 19 49	7 053
	9 Sibir	D	2-2	PL	Kombarov.D 7, Fernandez 68	11 100
	13 Mordovia	W	2-1	KRr5	Khokhlov 34, Semshov 35	13 000
Jul	17 Rostov	W	3-2	PL	Kolodin 23, Voronin 31, Granat 55	5 517
	24 Rubin	L	0-2	PL		15 100
	31 Krylya	D	1-1	PL	Semshov 66	6 638
Aug	14 Zenit	D	1-1	PL	Kuranyi 26	21 200
	22 Lokomotiv	W	3-0	PL	Kuranyi 2 42 73, Cesnauskis 90	10 224
	29 Tom Tomsk	L	0-1	PL		12 000
Sep	12 Terek	W	3-1	PL	Kuranyi 43, Samedov 66, Semshov 73	6 213
	18 Saturn	L	2-3	PL	Kuranyi 43, Dujmovic 83	9 500
	22 Volga NN	W	4-1	KRr6	Cesnauskis 43, Semshov 60, Dujmovic 74, Samedov 76	3 083
	26 Sp Nalchik	L	0-3	PL		6 391
Oct	2 Amkar	W	1-0	PL	Kuranyi 90	9 200
	17 Anzhi	W	4-0	PL	Kuranyi 37p, Fernandez 40, Cesnauskis 80, Voronin 90p	5 269
	23 Alania	D	0-0	PL		13 000
	27 CSKA	D	0-0	PL		9 153
	30 Sibir	W	4-1	PL	Kuranyi 64, Fernandez 67, Samedov 86, Semshov 90	4 484
Nov	6 Rostov	D	1-1	PL	Samedov 51	10 000
	13 Rubin	D	2-2	PL	Epureanu 23, Kuranyi 36	7 322
	20 Krylya	L	0-1	PL		28 500
	28 Spartak M	D	1-1	PL	Khokhlov 40	12 378

DINAMO LEAGUE APPEARANCES/GOALS 2010

Goalkeepers Vladimir Gabulov 21 • Anton Shunin 9
Defenders Alexandru Epureanu MDA 23/2 • Leandro Fernandez ARG 20/3 • Vladimir Granat 19+3/1 • Denis Kolodin 14+1/1 • Marcin Kowalczyk POL 4+4/0 • Marko Lomic SRB 10+1/0
Midfield Edgaras Cesnauskis LTU 14+8/2 • Tomislav Dujmovic CRO 12+1/1 • Dmitriy Khokhlov 13+7/1 • Dimitriy Kombarov 12+4/4 • Kirill Kombarov 8+3/2 • Aleksey Rebko 9+10/0 • Adrian Ropotan ROU 14+6/0 • Igor Semshov 27+2/5 • Luke Wilkshire AUS 26/0
Forwards Martin Jakubko SVK 0+11/0 • Aleksandr Kokorin 9+15/0 • Kevin Kuranyi GER 16/9 • Irakli Logua 0+1/0 • Aleksandr Samedov AZE 27/3 • Fedor Smolov 0+2/0 • Andriy Voronin UKR 23+3/4
Coach Andrei Kobelev • Miodrag Bozovic MNE (27/04/2010)

CSKA LEAGUE APPEARANCES/GOALS 2010

Goalkeepers Igor Akinfeev 28 • Sergey Chepchugov 2
Defenders Vasiliy Berezutskiy 21/0 • Sergei Ignashevich 28/2 • Kirill Nababkin 12+1/0 • Chidi Odiah NGA 9+2/1 • Deividas Semberas LTU 21+5/0 • Georgiy Shchennikov 24+1/0 • Anton Vlasov 1/0
Midfield Evgeniy Aldonin 6+8/0 • Alan Dzagoev 19+5/6 • Mark Gonzalez CHI 12+9/3 • Keisuke Honda JPN 23+5/4 • Milos Krasic SRB 9+5/2 • Pavel Mamayev 18+9 • Sekou Oliseh NGA 13+3/3 • Elvir Rahimic BIH 3+8/0 • Zoran Tosic SRB 11+4/3
Forwards Seydou Doumba CIV 11/5 • Guilherme BRA 9+3/5 • Tomas Necid CZE 12+12/7 • Vagner Love BRA 14/9
Coach Leonid Slutskiy

KRYLYA SOVETOV SAMARA 2010

Mon	Date	Opponent	Res	Score	Comp	Scorers	Att
Mar	13	Zenit	L	0-1	PL		16 500
	20	Lokomotiv	L	0-3	PL		14 923
	27	Tom Tomsk	L	2-3	PL	OG 5, OG 12	13 000
Apr	4	Terek	L	0-2	PL		10 000
	10	Saturn	W	2-1	PL	Bobyor 10, Dordevic 79	9 800
	18	Sp Nalchik	L	0-1	PL		9 000
	26	Amkar	D	1-1	PL	Ajinjal 9	12 100
	30	Anzhi	D	0-0	PL		10 000
May	5	Alania	W	1-0	PL	Strelkov 50	9 200
	10	Sibir	L	1-4	PL	Tkachov 6	10 000
	14	Rostov	L	1-2	PL	Alhazov 59	10 300
Jul	9	Rubin	L	0-3	PL		12 900
	13	Shinnik	L	1-2	KRr5	Drmic 39	4 200
	19	CSKA	L	0-1	PL		16 050
	25	Spartak M	D	0-0	PL		16 500
	31	Dinamo	D	1-1	PL	OG 86	6 638
Aug	7	Lokomotiv	D	0-0	PL		13 757
	14	Tom Tomsk	D	1-1	PL	Savin 62	10 000
	21	Terek	L	1-3	PL	Leilton 23	12 327
	28	Saturn	D	1-1	PL	Taranov 84	4 000
Sep	12	Sp Nalchik	W	2-0	PL	Dordevic 72, Yakovlev 86	10 300
	18	Amkar	L	1-2	PL	Savin 45	6 400
	27	Anzhi	W	3-0	PL	Samsonov 3, Ivanov 29, Savin 42p	10 100
Oct	2	Alania	W	3-2	PL	Samsonov 32, Tsallagov 40, Yakovlev 74	8 000
	17	Sibir	D	1-1	PL	Yakovlev 48	15 400
	24	Rostov	W	2-1	PL	Dordevic 12, Yakovlev 70	9 800
	29	Rubin	L	0-2	PL		14 450
Nov	7	CSKA	L	3-4	PL	Ivanov 71, Leilton 81p, Tkachev 90	4 500
	14	Spartak M	D	0-0	PL		12 554
	20	Dinamo	W	1-0	PL	Savin 54	28 500
	28	Zenit	D	0-0	PL		21 300

KRYLYA LEAGUE APPEARANCES/GOALS 2010

Goalkeepers Eduardo Lobos CHI 25 • Mykola Tsygan UKR 3 • David Yurchenko 2

Defenders Aleksandr Belozerov 15+1/0 • Goran Drmic BIH 10/0 • Nenad Dordevic SRB 23+1/3 • Aleksey Kontsedalov 2/0 • Leilton BRA 14+3/2 • Roman Polovov 0+1/0 • Ivan Taranov 24+2/1 • Farkhod Vasiev TJK 1+2/0

Midfield Ruslan Adzhindzhal 16/1 • Anton Bober 16+8/1 • Aleksandr Budanov 2/0 • Sergey Budylin 19/0 • Juan Escobar COL 0+3/0 • Daniil Gridnev 10+6/0 • Oleg Ivanov 14+1/2 • Vladimir Khozin 2/0 • Dmitri Kostyayev 1+1/0 • Denis Kovba BLR 4/0 • Sergey Kuznetsov 15/0 • Branimir Petrovic SRB 10+1/0 • Artur Rylov 0+2/0 • Oleg Samsonov 17+3/2 • Anton Sosnin 10+1/0 • Sergey Tkachev 12+4/2 • Ibrahima Tsallagov 20+3/1

Forwards Aleksandr Alhazov 1+7/1 • Dragan Jelic SVN 2+4/0 • Aleksandr Khramov 0+1/0 • Aleksey Popov 0+1/0 • Aleksandr Salugin 1+3/0 • Evgeniy Savin 23+5/4 • Aleksandr Stavpets 3+4/0 • Igor Strelkov 5+3/1 • Pavel Yakovlev 12+4/4

Coach Yuri Gazaev • Aleksandr Tarkhanov (25/07/2010)

FK ROSTOV 2010

Mon	Date	Opponent	Res	Score	Comp	Scorers	Att
Mar	13	Tom Tomsk	L	0-2	PL		9 000
	20	Terek	D	1-1	PL	Ahmetovic 81	9 350
	28	Saturn	W	1-0	PL	Pavlenko 17	9 200
Apr	3	Sp Nalchik	L	2-5	PL	Ahmetovic 64, Adamov 79p	9 500
	11	Amkar	W	2-1	PL	Ahmetovic 13, Andelkovic 83	9 500
	19	Anzhi	W	2-1	PL	Adamov 61, Kalachou 85	12 000
	25	Alania	L	0-1	PL		12 000
	2	Sibir	L	0-2	PL		10 000
May	6	CSKA	W	1-0	PL	Ahmetovic 68	14 300
	10	Rubin	L	0-2	PL		12 500
	14	Krylya	W	2-1	PL	Adamov 2 21 46	10 300
Jul	9	Spartak M	W	1-0	PL	Kulchy 13	14 500
	13	Salyut	W	4-0	KRr5	Adamov 75, Akimov 82, Hagush 87, Lebedenko 89	8 000
	17	Dinamo	L	2-3	PL	Adamov 11, Lebedenko 42	5 517
	24	Zenit	L	1-3	PL	Lebedenko 89p	14 500
	1	Lokomotiv	W	1-0	PL	Valikayev 35	12 517
Aug	7	Terek	W	1-0	PL	Pavlenko 75	12 000
	15	Saturn	W	2-0	PL	Adamov 1, Lebedenko 73	6 500
	20	Sp Nalchik	D	1-1	PL	Adamov 87p	13 500
	28	Amkar	L	0-1	PL		8 200
Sep	12	Anzhi	W	1-0	PL	Kalachev 56	11 500
	18	Alania	D	0-0	PL		10 000
	22	Volgar Ast.	W	2-0	KRr6	Pavlenko 2 49 63	4 500
	26	Sibir	L	0-1	PL		11 000
Oct	3	CSKA	L	0-2	PL		4 740
	16	Rubin	L	1-2	PL	Pavlenko 3	11 480
	24	Krylya	L	1-2	PL	Adamov 37	9 800
	30	Spartak M	L	1-2	PL	Khagush 25	10 900
Nov	6	Dinamo	D	1-1	PL	Yankov 36	10 000
	14	Zenit	L	0-5	PL		20 500
	20	Lokomotiv	L	1-2	PL	Blatnjak 59	8 200
	28	Tom Tomsk	L	1-3	PL	Yankov 55	10 000

LOKOMOTIV MOSKVA 2010

Mon	Date	Opponent	Res	Score	Comp	Scorers	Att
Mar	14	Rubin	L	0-2	PL		8 123
	20	Krylya	W	3-0	PL	Aliyev 2 50p 57, Sychev 54p	14 923
	28	Spartak M	L	1-2	PL	Aliyev 28	48 000
Apr	4	Dinamo	W	3-2	PL	Aliyev 2 45 68, Tarasov 85	17 823
	11	Zenit	L	0-1	PL		20 300
	17	CSKA	D	1-1	PL	Kuzmin 89	14 000
	24	Tom Tomsk	W	2-1	PL	Glushakov 33, Aliyev 43	13 600
May	1	Terek	D	0-0	PL		9 000
	5	Saturn	L	0-1	PL		11 118
	11	Sp Nalchik	D	1-1	PL	Dujmovic 42	8 500
	15	Amkar	W	2-0	PL	Aliyev 17, Maicón Marques 80	11 123
Jul	10	Anzhi	W	2-1	PL	Dujmovic 17, Aliyev 68	3 000
	14	Gornyak	L	0-1	KRr5		3 113
	18	Alania	W	3-0	PL	Aliyev 15, Sychev 2 45 47	11 423
	25	Sibir	D	2-2	PL	Aliyev 2 16 31	12 000
Aug	1	Rostov	L	0-1	PL		12 517
	7	Krylya	D	0-0	PL		13 757
	15	Spartak M	L	2-3	PL	Aliyev 20, Sychev 88	23 123
	19	Lausanne	D	1-1	ELpo	Sychev 65	11 200
	22	Dinamo	L	0-3	PL		10 224
Sep	26	Lausanne	D	1-1	ELpo	Aliev 85, L 3-4p	11 053
	29	Zenit	L	0-3	PL		14 187
	12	CSKA	W	1-0	PL	Maicon 25	20 608
	19	Tom Tomsk	D	1-1	PL	Gatagov 39	12 000
	26	Terek	W	2-1	PL	Aliev 3p, Maicon 28	8 867
Oct	3	Saturn	W	1-0	PL	Loskov 85	6 000
	17	Sp Nalchik	W	1-0	PL	Sychev 70	10 700
	24	Amkar	W	2-1	PL	Aliev 78p, Rodolfo 88	7 000
	31	Anzhi	W	1-0	PL	Sychev 89	12 000
Nov	7	Alania	D	0-0	PL		15 000
	14	Sibir	D	1-1	PL	Sychev 63	12 170
	20	Rostov	W	2-1	PL	Sychev 54, Rodolfo 61	8 200
	28	Rubin	D	0-0	PL		14 046

LOKOMOTIV LEAGUE APPEARANCES/GOALS 2010

Goalkeepers Guilherme BRA 30

Defenders Marko Basa MNE 22/0 • Taras Burlak 1+2/0 • Jan Durica SVK 9+1/0 • Alan Gatagov 5+13/1 • Branko Ilic SVN 1/0 • Ruslan Kambolov 1/0 • Oleg Kuzmin 10/1 • Rodolfo BRA 10+6/2 • Dmitriy Sennikov 1/0 • Roman Shishkin 15/0 • Igor Smolnikov 6+8/0

Midfield Aleksandr Aliev UKR 25/14 • Malchaz Asatiani GEO 19+3/0 • Charles BRA 3+1/0 • Haminu Dramani GHA 1+1/0 • Tomislav Dujmovic CRO 12+1/2 • Denis Glushakov 21+7/1 • Dmitriy Loskov 11+2/1 • Magomed Ozdoev 0+3/0 • Dmitriy Tarasov 21+5/1 • Dmitriy Torbinskiy 13+4/0 • Wagner BRA 7+7/0 • Renat Yanbaev 30/0

Forwards Maicon BRA 15+3/3 • Peter Odemwingie 8+2/0 • Dmitriy Sychev 28/8 • Dramane Traore MLI 6+11/0

Coach Yuriy Semin

ROSTOV LEAGUE APPEARANCES/GOALS 2010

Goalkeepers Anton Amelichenko BLR 23 • Dejan Radic SRB 7
Defenders Dusan Andelkovic SRB 26/1 • Aleksandr Cherkes 15/0 • Sorin Ghionea ROU 18/0 • Gia Grigalava 8+1/0 • Henri Hagba 0+1/0 • Anri Khagush 16+4/1 • Roman Lengyel CZE 1+1/0 • Isaac Okoronkwo NGA 22/0 • Andrey Proshin UKR 1+2/0 • Arthur Valikaev 5+2/1 • Ivan Zivanovic SRB 14+1/0
Midfield Alexandru Gatcan MDA 24/0 • Stanislav Ivanov MDA 6+3/0 • Tsimafei Kalachev BLR 16+1/2 • Aleksandr Kulchiy BLR 25/1 • Aleksandr Pavlenko 18+5/3 • Sergei Tumasyan 0+2/0 • Chavdar Yankov BUL 8+3/2
Forwards Roman Adamov 24/8 • Mersudin Ahmetovic BIH 5+22/4 • Dmitriy Akimov 5+6/0 • Dragan Blatnjak BIH 12+11/1 • Hong Yong Jo PRK 0+1/0 • Igor Lebedenko 29+1/3 • Evgeniy Lutsenko 2+3/0 • Alexandr Sugak 0+2/0
Coach Oleg Protasov UKR

RUBIN KAZAN 2010

	Date	Opponent	Res	Score	Comp	Scorers	Att
	18	Hapoel TA	W	3-0	ELr2	Bukharov 2 [14 23], Semak [69]	10 200
	25	Hapoel TA	D	0-0	ELr2		12 864
	7	CSKA	W	1-0	SC		17 000
	11	Wolfsburg	D	1-1	ELr3	Noboa [29]	16 700
	14	Lokomotiv	W	2-0	PL	Gorbanets [88], Bukharov [90]	8 123
	18	Wolfsburg	L	1-2	ELr3	Kasaev [21]	15 412
	22	Tom Tomsk	W	1-0	PL	Bukharov [76]	14 000
	28	Terek	D	0-0	PL		10 072
	4	Saturn	D	0-0	PL		7 500
Apr	12	Sp Nalchik	D	1-1	PL	Noboa [60]	10 230
	17	Amkar	W	1-0	PL	Natkho [20]	12 000
	25	Anzhi	D	0-0	PL		8 120
May	2	Alania	D	1-1	PL	Kasaev [88]	17 000
	8	Sibir	W	1-0	PL	Noboa [51]	5 200
	10	Rostov	W	2-0	PL	Semak [63], Bukharov [76]	12 500
	14	CSKA	L	0-1	PL		25 200
	9	Krylya	W	3-0	PL	Kasaev [33], Bukharov [79], Ryazantsev [91+p]	12 900
Jul	13	Volgar	L	0-1	KRr5		10 500
	17	Spartak M	W	1-0	PL	Noboa [3]	16 000
	24	Dinamo	W	2-0	PL	Kasaev 2 [55 63]	15 100
	31	Zenit	L	0-2	PL		21 500
	8	Tom Tomsk	W	2-1	PL	Ryazantsev [36], Orekhov [64]	13 975
Aug	15	Terek	D	1-1	PL	Noboa [52p]	7 500
	22	Saturn	W	2-0	PL	Noboa [32p], Medvedev [69]	15 400
	28	Sp Nalchik	D	1-1	PL	Kasaev [15]	11 000
	11	Amkar	W	3-0	PL	Carlos Eduardo 2 [26 53], Martins [86p]	13 400
	13	København	L	0-1	CLgD		29 661
Sep	19	Anzhi	W	1-0	PL	Gokdeniz [90]	12 000
	25	Alania	W	1-0	PL	Bocchetti [37]	14 630
	28	Barcelona	D	1-1	CLgD	Noboa [30p]	23 950
	3	Sibir	D	2-2	PL	Noboa [50p], Bocchetti [81]	8 000
	16	Rostov	W	2-1	PL	Natcho [10], Martins [12]	11 480
Oct	19	Panath'kos	D	0-0	CLgD		36 748
	24	CSKA	D	0-0	PL		11 000
	29	Krylya	W	2-0	PL	Kornilenko 2 [47 58]	14 450
	1	Panath'kos	D	0-0	CLgD		16 400
	8	Spartak M	D	1-1	PL	Kornilenko [90]	20 450
	13	Dinamo	D	2-2	PL	Noboa 2 [49 65]	7 322
Nov	20	Zenit	D	2-2	PL	Navas [61], Medvedev [67]	18 400
	23	København	W	1-0	CLgD	Noboa [45p]	18 720
	28	Lokomotiv	D	0-0	PL		14 046
	7	Barcelona	L	0-2	CLgD		50 436

SATURN RAMENSKOYE 2010

	Date	Opponent	Res	Score	Comp	Scorers	Att
Mar	14	Alania	D	1-1	PL	Ivanov [10]	28 000
	20	Sibir	D	1-1	PL	Ivanov [73]	7 000
	28	Rostov	L	0-1	PL		9 200
Apr	4	Rubin	D	0-0	PL		7 500
	10	Krylya	L	1-2	PL	Nemov [85]	9 800
	18	Spartak M	D	0-0	PL		14 300
	24	Dinamo	L	0-1	PL		4 326
	2	Zenit	L	0-1	PL		8 500
May	5	Lokomotiv	W	1-0	PL	Kirichenko [51]	11 118
	11	Tom Tomsk	L	1-2	PL	Kirichenko [59]	5 000
	14	Terek	L	0-2	PL		7 500
	10	CSKA	D	1-1	PL	Kirichenko [7]	5 365
	13	Sakhalin	D	1-1	KRr5	Jakubko [67], W 4-3p	4 700
Jul	19	Sp Nalchik	W	3-1	PL	Kirichenko 2 [9p 41], Sapeta [33]	6 500
	25	Amkar	W	1-0	PL	Boyarintsev [22]	8 200
	30	Anzhi	W	1-0	PL	Sapeta [67]	6 000
	8	Sibir	W	1-0	PL	Nemov [85]	10 000
Aug	14	Rostov	L	0-2	PL		6 500
	22	Rubin	L	0-2	PL		15 400
	28	Krylya	D	1-1	PL	Taranov [84]	4 000
	11	Spartak M	L	1-2	PL	Kirichenko [22]	13 500
Sep	18	Dinamo	W	3-2	PL	Nemov 2 [38 63], Kirichenko [45]	9 500
	22	Luch Vlad.	W	2-1	KRr6	Topic 2 [14 25]	4 500
	25	Zenit	L	1-6	PL	Kirichenko [45]	21 000
	3	Lokomotiv	L	0-1	PL		6 000
Oct	16	Tom Tomsk	D	2-2	PL	Katyaka [25], Topic [66]	8 000
	23	Terek	W	1-0	PL	Sapeta [79]	4 000
	31	CSKA	D	1-1	PL	Ivanov [46]	12 000
	5	Sp Nalchik	L	0-2	PL		8 000
Nov	12	Amkar	D	2-2	PL	Topic [48], Karyaka [65]	5 000
	20	Anzhi	W	2-1	PL	Makhmudov [51], Topic [62]	7 500
	28	Alania	D	1-1	PL	Zelao [32]	2 000

SATURN LEAGUE APPEARANCES/GOALS 2010

Goalkeepers Vitaliy Chilyushkin 3+1 • Antonin Kinsky CZE 20 • Artem Rebrov 7
Defenders Benoit Angbwa CMR 23+1/0 • Sergei Bryzgalov 1/0 • Dmitry Grachev 15+2/0 • Denis Halilovic SVN 2/0 • Ruslan Nakhushev 21+1/0 • Dmytro Parfyonov UKR 13/0 • Vadim Yevseyev 17+3/1 • Zelao BRA 21+1/1 • Dmitriy Zinovich 0+1/0
Midfield Denis Boyarintsev 9+7/1 • Aleksey Igonin 21/0 • Aleksey Ivanov 29/3 • Andrey Karyaka 25+1/2 • Kamil Kopunek SVK 3+4/0 • Dmitriy Kudryashov 0+1/0 • Dmitriy Loskov 0+2/0 • Emin Makhmudov 16+5/1 • Pyotr Nemov 24+2/4 • Aleksandr Sapeta 17+7/3 • Vladimir Sobolev 0+2/0 • Roman Vorobiev 5+9/0
Forwards Martin Jakubko SVK 6+6/0 • Dmitriy Kirichenko 21+8/8 • Leonid Kovel BLR 0+4/0 • Vladimir Kuzmichev 4+7/0 • Marko Topic BIH 3+6/3
Coach Andrey Gordeev

RUBIN LEAGUE APPEARANCES/GOALS 2010

Goalkeepers Giedrius Arlauskis LTU 2 • Sergey Ryzhikov 28
Defenders Cristian Ansaldi ARG 19+1/0 • Salvatore Bocchetti ITA 6+1/2 • Cesar Navas ESP 29/1 • Jordi ESP 7+1/0 • Vitaliy Kaleshin 14+1/0 • Oleg Kuzmin 12+1/0 • Aleksandr Orekhov 19/1 • Lasha Salukvadze GEO 9+1/0 • Roman Sharonov 2/0
Midfield Alexandru Antoniuc MDA 0+1/0 • Evgeniy Balyaykin 4+9/0 • Petr Bystrov 7+11/0 • Carlos Eduardo BRA 6/2 • Vagiz Galiulin UZB 7/0 • Andrey Gorbanets 7+10/1 • Gokdeniz Karadeniz TUR 11+6/1 • Alan Kasaev 27+1/5 • Rafal Murawski POL 20+3/0 • Bebars Natcho ISR 10+4/2 • Christian Noboa ECU 26+1/8 • Aleksandr Ryazantsev 9+4/2 • Sergey Semak 8/1 • Macbeth Sibaya RSA 5+2/0
Forwards Aleksandr Bukharov 11+1/4 • Fatih Tekke TUR 2+3/0 • Hasan Kabze TUR 2+3/0 • Sergey Kornilenko BLR 5+3/3 • Obafemi Martins NGA 9+3/2 • Aleksey Medvedev 6+7/2 • Bakhodir Nasimov UZB 1+1/0 • Igor Portnyagin 0+4/0
Coach Kurban Berdiyev TKM

SIBIR NOVOSIBIRSK 2010

Mar	14	Terek	L 0-2	PL		11 500
	20	Saturn	D 1-1	PL	Medvedev 45	7 000
	27	Sp Nalchik	L 0-2	PL		9 000
	3	Amkar	L 1-3	PL	Molash 34	10 500
	7	Luch Vlad.	W 3-0	KRqf	Bliznyuk 2 51 54p, Astafyev 69	7 000
Apr	11	Anzhi	L 2-4	PL	Medvedev 58, Astafyev 60	10 000
	17	Alania	L 1-2	PL	Cizek 46	17 500
	21	Alania	W 3-0	KRsf	Medvedev 3 13 67 91+	12 000
	24	CSKA	L 1-4	PL	Cizek 74	12 400
	2	Rostov	W 2-0	PL	Medvedev 57, Nagibin 87	10 000
	6	Rubin	L 0-1	PL		5 200
May	10	Krylya	W 4-1	PL	Cizek 8, Medvedev 17, Klimavicius 67, Astafyev 80	10 000
	16	Zenit	L 0-1	KRf		15 400
	9	Dinamo	D 2-2	PL	Shevchenko 58, Nagibin 80	11 100
	13	Avangard K	W 5-2	KRr5	Shevchenko 2 50 115, Molash 83p, Medvedev 107, Cizek 120	5 500
Jul	17	Zenit	L 0-2	PL		18 500
	21	Spartak M	L 3-5	PL	Antipenko 70 Cizek 73, Astafyev 73	11 000
	25	Lokomotiv	D 2-2	PL	Medvedev 49, Molash 67	12 000
	29	Apollon	W 1-0	ELp3	Medvedev 74	10 000
	2	Tom Tomsk	L 2-3	PL	Medvedev 22, Shevchenko 24	13 500
	5	Apollon	L 1-2	ELp3	Shevchenko 63	6 000
	8	Saturn	L 0-1	PL		10 000
Aug	14	Sp Nalchik	L 2-4	PL	Shevchenko 14, Molash 68	10 000
	19	PSV	W 1-0	ELpo	Degtyarev 92+	11 500
	22	Amkar	W 1-0	PL	Shevchenko 80	9 000
	26	PSV	L 0-5	ELpo		20 900
	30	Anzhi	L 0-1	PL		10 000
Sep	11	Alania	L 1-2	PL	Zinoviev 12	6 500
	20	CSKA	L 0-1	PL		4 500
	26	Rostov	W 1-0	PL	Grzelak 37	11 000
	3	Rubin	D 2-2	PL	Reinette 29, Belyaev 82	8 000
Oct	17	Krylya	D 1-1	PL	Oyewole 42	15 400
	23	Spartak	D 0-0	PL		12 000
	30	Dinamo	L 1-4	PL	Grzelak 61	4 484
	7	Zenit	L 2-5	PL	Nagibin 2, Grzelak 6	12 100
Nov	14	Lokomotiv	D 1-1	PL	Molosh 86	12 170
	20	Tom Tomsk	L 0-1	PL		5 000
	28	Terek	D 1-1	PL	Cizek 70	7 000

SPARTAK MOSKVA 2010

Mar	14	Dinamo	L 0-1	PL		43 000
	21	Zenit	D 1-1	PL	Welliton 12	19 450
	28	Lokomotiv	W 2-1	PL	Suchy 11, Ari da Silva 18	48 000
	4	Tom Tomsk	D 2-2	PL	Welliton 29, Ibson 47	14 500
Apr	10	Terek	W 2-1	PL	OG 58, Welliton 88	17 100
	18	Saturn	D 0-0	PL		14 300
	25	Sp Nalchik	D 0-0	PL		18 500
	2	Amkar	W 2-0	PL	Ari da Silva 39, Welliton 50	13 700
May	6	Anzhi	W 3-0	PL	Welliton 2 42 67, Alex 86	19 000
	10	Alania	L 2-5	PL	Welliton 7, OG 30	20 000
	9	Rostov	L 0-1	PL		14 500
	13	Metallurg L	W 1-0	KRr5	Alex 54p	14 000
Jul	17	Rubin	L 0-1	PL		16 000
	21	Sibir	W 5-3	PL	Ari da Silva 2 5 52, Ananidze 2 23 67, Jiranek 76	11 000
	25	Krylya	D 0-0	PL		16 500
	1	CSKA	L 1-2	PL	OG 72	65 000
Aug	15	Lokomotiv	W 3-2	PL	Welliton 2 18 31, OG 66	23 123
	21	Tom Tomsk	W 4-2	PL	Welliton 3 52 55 58, Alex 87	14 000
	28	Terek	L 0-2	PL		9 500
Sep	11	Saturn	W 2-1	PL	Welliton 2 8 74	13 500
	15	O. Marseille	W 1-0	CLgF	OG 81	45 729
	20	Sp Nalchik	W 2-0	PL	Ari 2 20 78	12 000
	24	Amkar	D 2-2	PL	Welliton 37, McGeady 77	12 700
	28	MSK Zilina	W 3-0	CLgF	Ari 2 34 61, Ibson 89	37 000
Oct	3	Anzhi	W 1-0	PL	Sheshukov 21	11 000
	15	Alania	W 3-0	PL	Ari 24, Alex 39, OG 52	10 500
	19	Chelsea	L 0-2	CLgF		70 012
	23	Sibir	D 0-0	PL		12 000
Nov	27	Zenit	W 1-0	PL	Kombarov 88p	27 100
	30	Rostov	W 2-1	PL	Welliton 39, McGeady 90p	10 900
	3	Chelsea	L 1-4	CLgF	Bazhenov 86	40 477
	8	Rubin	D 1-1	PL	Welliton 41	20 450
	14	Krylya	D 0-0	PL		12 554
	20	CSKA	L 1-3	PL	Ibson 17	14 800
	23	O. Marseille	L 0-3	CLgF		43 217
	28	Dinamo	D 1-1	PL	Welliton 28	12 378
	8	MSK Zilina	W 2-1	CLgF	Alex 54, Ibson 61	7 208

SIBIR LEAGUE APPEARANCES/GOALS 2010

Goalkeepers Wojciech Kowalewski POL 14 • Aleksey Solosin 10+2 • Petr Vasek CZE 6

Defenders Denis Bukhryakov 11/0 • Egor Filipenko BLR 15+3/0 • Martin Horak CZE 1/0 • Steeve Joseph-Reinette FRA 13/1 • Arunas Klimavicius LTU 7+4/1 • Dmitriy Molosh BLR 22/4 • Adessoye Oyewole 6+1/1 • Nikola Valentic SRB 10+2/0 • Tomas Vychodil CZE 23/0

Midfield Aleksey Aravin 19+4/0 • Roger Canas COL 9+4/0 • Tomas Cizek CZE 19+5/4 • Vagiz Galiulin UZB 9+2/0 • Aleksandr Makarenko 9+2/0 • Ivan Nagibin 15+9/3 • Mantas Savenas LTU 0+1/0 • Aleksandr Shulenin 10+2/0 • Aleksandr Shumov 0+1/0 • Velice Sumulikoski MKD 13/0 • Aleksey Vasiliev 2+7/0 • Leonid Zuev 1/0

Forwards Aleksandr Antipenko 10+8/1 • Maksim Astafyev 18+5/3 • Roman Belyaev 0+7/1 • Gennadiy Bliznyuk 5/0 • Aleksandr Degtyarev 8+10/0 • Bartlomiej Grzelak POL 8/3 • Aleksey Medvedev 15/6 • Igor Shevchenko 14+5/4 • Evgeniy Zinoviev 8+3/1

Coach Igor Kriushenko BLR

SPARTAK MOSKVA LEAGUE APPEARANCES/GOALS 2010

Goalkeepers Alexander Belenov 1 • Andrey Dikan UKR 12 • Soslan Dzhanaev 12 • Sergey Pesyakov 5

Defenders Andrey Ivanov 11+1/0 • Martin Jiranek CZE 10/1 • Anton Khodyrev 2+1/0 • Fedor Kudryasov 8+1/0 • Nicolas Pareja ARG 10+1/0 • Renat Sabitov 11+7/0 • Aleksandr Sheshukov 22+1/1 • Martin Stranzl AUT 14+1/0 • Marek Suchy CZE 25/1

Midfield Alex BRA 21+1/3 • Zhano Ananidze GEO 12+11/2 • Nikola Drincic MNE 2+2/0 • Pavel Golishev 0+1/0 • Ibson BRA 27+1/2 • Igor Kireev 0+1/0 • Dmitriy Kombarov 11+1/1 • Kirill Kombarov 2/0 • Cristian Maidana ARG 4+6/0 • Evgeniy Makeev 19+3/0 • Filip Ozobic CRO 0+1/0 • Sergey Parshivlyuk 21/0 • Aleksandr Zotov 2+2/0

Forwards Ari BRA 18+6/7 • Nikita Bazhenov 4+8/0 • Artem Dzyuba 0+2/0 • Alexandr Kozlov 0+12/0 • Aiden McGeady IRL 11/2 • Ivan Saenko 8+2/0 • Welliton BRA 24+1/19 • Pavel Yakolev 1+5/0

Coach Valeriy Karpin

SPARTAK NALCHIK 2010

	Date	Opp	Res		Comp	Scorers	Att
Mar	13	Anzhi	D	0-0	PL		13 000
	19	Alania	W	2-1	PL	Shchanitsin 23, Gogua 45	10 000
	27	Sibir	W	2-0	PL	Dyadyun 2 17 53	9 000
Apr	3	Rostov	W	5-2	PL	Siradze 4, Leandro 13p, Amisulashvili 52p, Dyadyun 2 67 81	9 500
	12	Rubin	D	1-1	PL	Rusic 87	10 230
	18	Krylya	W	1-0	PL	Kisenkov 27	9 000
	25	Spartak M	D	0-0	PL		18 500
May	1	Dinamo	W	1-0	PL	Malyarov 66	9 000
	6	Zenit	L	1-3	PL	Malyarov 90	21 405
	11	Lokomotiv	D	1-1	PL	Leandro 21	8 500
	15	Tom Tomsk	L	0-1	PL		14 000
	9	Terek	W	2-1	PL	Kontsedalov 16, Leandro 40p	9 500
Jul	13	Volga NN	L	0-5	KRr5		7 100
	19	Saturn	L	1-3	PL	Bikmoyev 69	6 500
	25	CSKA	W	2-1	PL	Siradze 8, Gogua 44	5 100
	30	Amkar	W	2-1	PL	Kontsedalov 9, Leandro 11	10 000
Aug	8	Alania	L	0-1	PL		12 500
	14	Sibir	W	4-2	PL	Dyadyun 23, Leandro 2 40p 83p, Leandro 93+	10 000
	20	Rostov	D	1-1	PL	Kontsedalov 5	13 500
	28	Rubin	D	1-1	PL	Jovanovic 29	11 000
Sep	12	Krylya	L	0-2	PL		10 300
	20	Spartak M	L	0-2	PL		12 000
	26	Dinamo	W	3-0	PL	Dyadun 3 31 50 89	6 391
Oct	3	Zenit	L	2-3	PL	Golic 45, Vasin 89	10 000
	17	Lokomotiv	L	0-1	PL		10 700
	23	Tom Tomsk	W	2-1	PL	Dyadun 60, Siradze 90	7 000
	31	Terek	D	1-1	PL	Dyadun 87	5 800
Nov	5	Saturn	W	2-0	PL	Kontsedalov 45p, Goshokov 65	8 000
	14	CSKA	D	1-1	PL	Goshokov 88	14 200
	20	Amkar	L	1-3	PL	Golic 30	14 500
	28	Anzhi	L	1-3	PL	Mitrishev 73	7 000

TEREK GROZNY 2010

	Date	Opp	Res		Comp	Scorers	Att
Mar	13	Sibir	W	2-0	PL	Kobenko 40, Asildarov 55	11 500
	20	Rostov	D	1-1	PL	Asildarov 4	9 350
	27	Rubin	D	0-0	PL		10 072
Apr	4	Krylya	W	2-0	PL	Bracamonte 2 19 34	10 000
	11	Spartak M	L	1-2	PL	Asildarov 15	17 100
	18	Dinamo	D	1-1	PL	Lahiyalov 96+p	10 000
	25	Zenit	D	0-0	PL		21 000
May	2	Lokomotiv	D	0-0	PL		9 000
	6	Tom Tomsk	L	1-2	PL	Asildarov 47	10 500
	10	CSKA	L	1-4	PL	Georgiev 26	10 500
	15	Saturn	W	2-0	PL	Mauricio Junior 19, Bracamonte 53	7 500
	8	Sp Nalchik	L	1-2	PL	Gvazava 50	9 500
	13	Luch Vlad.	L	0-4	KRr5		4 900
Jul	18	Amkar	W	1-0	PL	Asildarov 42	7 200
	25	Anzhi	L	0-1	PL		6 000
	31	Alania	W	2-0	PL	Mauricio Junior 57, Utsiyev 83	6 300
Aug	6	Rostov	L	0-1	PL		12 000
	15	Rubin	D	1-1	PL	Bracamonte 30	7 500
	21	Krylya	W	3-1	PL	Mauricio Junior 3, Lahiyalov 43, Asildarov 73	12 327
	28	Spartak M	W	2-0	PL	Asildarov 49, Utsiev 82	9 500
Sep	12	Dinamo	L	1-3	PL	Lakhiyalov 34	6 213
	20	Zenit	D	0-0	PL		10 150
	26	Lokomotiv	L	1-2	PL	Mauricio 20	8 867
Oct	2	Tom Tomsk	W	1-0	PL	Asildarov 22p	7 500
	17	CSKA	L	0-3	PL		9 300
	23	Saturn	L	0-1	PL		4 000
	31	Sp Nalchik	D	1-1	PL	Mauricio 13	5 800
Nov	6	Amkar	L	0-2	PL		14 100
	13	Anzhi	L	1-3	PL	Sadaev 13	7 000
	20	Alania	L	1-2	PL	OG 45	15 000
	28	Sibir	D	1-1	PL	Asildarov 6	7 000

SPARTAK NALCHIK LEAGUE APPEARANCES/GOALS 2010

Goalkeepers Otto Fredrikson FIN 22 • Aleksandrs Kolinko LVA 8
Defenders Roman Amirkhanov 1/0 • Aleksandr Amisulashvili GEO 11/1 • Miodrag Dzudovic MNE 28/0 • Valentin Filatov 12/0 • Milan Jovanovic MNE 12/1 • Vladislav Khatazenkov 2+2/0 • Vladimir Kisenko 16/1 • Aleksandr Khokhlov 1/0 • Zaurbek Pliev 3+1/0 • Viktor Vasin 18+2/1 • Andrey Vasyanovich 12+1/0
Midfield Aslan Dyshekov 3+2/0 • Kazbek Geteriev KAZ 23+1/0 • Gogita Gogua GEO 21+5/3 • Jovan Golic SRB 9+6/2 • Roman Kontsedalov 24/4 • Leandro BRA 24+2/6 • Nikita Malyarov 8+9/2 • Artur Rylov 1+6/0 • Aleksandr Shchanitsin 10+6/1 • David Siradze GEO 19+6/3
Forwards Marat Bikmoyev UZB 3+9/1 • Vladimir Dyadyun 28/10 • Patrick Echkini CGO 1+4/0 • Arsen Goshokov 6+11/2 • Nazir Kazharov 1/0 • Magomed Mitrishev 0+1/1 • Ricardo Jesus BRA 2+4/0 • Dejan Rusic SVN 1+6/1
Coach Yuriy Krasnozhan

TEREK LEAGUE APPEARANCES/GOALS 2010

Goalkeepers Andrey Dikan UKR 18 • Soslan Dzhanaev 3 • Yaroslav Godzyur UKR 9
Defenders Antonio Ferreira BRA 25+1/0 • Timur Dzhabrailov 0+1/0 • Ismail Ediev 8+1/0 • Ze'ev Haymovich ISR 8/0 • Sergey Omelyanchuk BLR 24+2/0 • Dmitriy Yatchenko 30/0 • Herve Zengue CMR 2+3/0
Midfield Guy Essame CMR 16+5/0 • Blagoy Georgiev BUL 17+2/1 • Levan Gvazava GEO 8+11/1 • Adlan Katsaev 8+10/0 • Andrey Kobenko 14+7/1 • Shamil Lakhiyalov 23+1/3 • Mauricio BRA 25+3/5 • Rizvan Utsiev 24+1/2
Forwards Juan Arce BOL 16+4/0 • Shamil Asildarov 28+1/9 • Hector Bracamonte ARG 21+7/4 • Rodrigo Tiui BRA 0+8/0 • Zaur Sadaev 3+13/1
Coach Anatoliy Baydachniy

TOM TOMSK 2010

Mar	13	Rostov	W 2-0	PL	Karnilenka 2 [63 87]	9 000
	22	Rubin	L 0-1	PL		14 000
	27	Kryla	W 3-2	PL	Michkov [24p], Covalciuc [32], Jokic [39]	13 000
Apr	4	Spartak M	D 2-2	PL	Karnilenka [8p], Klimov [39]	14 500
	10	Dinamo	D 0-0	PL		5 177
	17	Zenit	D 0-0	PL		14 500
	24	Lokomotiv	L 1-2	PL	Karnilenka [83]	13 600
May	2	CSKA	L 1-3	PL	Kharitonov [15]	6 500
	6	Terek	W 2-1	PL	Karnilenka [22p], Dzyuba [85]	10 500
	11	Saturn	W 2-1	PL	Gultyayev [48], Karnilenka [85]	5 000
	15	Sp Nalchik	W 1-0	PL	Karnilenka [66p]	14 000
	10	Amkar	L 1-2	PL	Karnilenka [67p]	8 200
Jul	14	Krasnodar	L 1-2	KRr5	Dzyuba [42]	3 500
	18	Anzhi	L 1-4	PL	Dzyuba [74]	9 800
	24	Alania	L 1-2	PL	Karnilenka [14p]	11 500
	2	Sibir	W 3-2	PL	Dzyuba 2 [3 21], Smirnov [94+]	13 500
Aug	8	Rubin	L 1-2	PL	Dzyuba [37]	13 975
	14	Krylya	D 1-1	PL	Jioyev [54]	10 000
	21	Spartak M	L 2-4	PL	Karnilenka 2 [68 95+]	14 000
	29	Dinamo	W 1-0	PL	Dzyuba [49p]	12 000
Sep	11	Zenit	L 0-2	PL		20 500
	19	Lokomotiv	D 1-1	PL	OG [44]	12 000
	26	CSKA	L 0-3	PL		14 000
Oct	2	Terek	L 0-1	PL		7 500
	16	Saturn	D 2-2	PL	Dzyuba 2 [18 55]	8 000
	23	Sp Nalchik	L 1-2	PL	Starikov [55]	7 000
	31	Amkar	W 1-0	PL	Kharitonov [53]	14 500
Nov	6	Anzhi	L 0-1	PL		8 700
	13	Alania	D 1-1	PL	Dzyuba [5p]	8 000
	20	Sibir	W 1-0	PL	Dzyuba [52p]	5 000
	28	Rostov	W 3-1	PL	Kharitonov 2 [58 79], Kovalchuk [90]	10 000

ZENIT ST PETERSBURG 2010

Mar	13	Krylya	W 1-0	PL	Danny [65]	16 500
	21	Spartak M	D 1-1	PL	Lombaerts [88]	19 450
	27	Dinamo	W 2-1	PL	Danny [12], Bystrov [33]	13 480
	7	Volga Tver	W 2-0	KRqf	Huszti [25p], Bystrov [59]	20 500
	11	Lokomotiv	W 1-0	PL	Bystrov [53]	20 300
Apr	17	Tom Tomsk	D 0-0	PL		14 500
	21	Amkar	D 0-0	KRsf	W 4-2p	15 400
	25	Terek	D 0-0	PL		21 000
	28	CSKA	W 2-0	PL	Krizanac [5], Kerzhakov [65]	13 600
	2	Saturn	W 1-0	PL	Lombaerts [88]	8 500
May	6	Sp Nalchik	W 3-1	PL	Bystrov [65], Shirokov [71p], Danny [74]	21 405
	10	Amkar	W 2-0	PL	Kanunnikov [85], Danny [89]	11 900
	16	Sibir	W 1-0	KRf	Shirokov [60p]	15 400
	4	Anzhi	W 2-1	PL	Bystrov [15], Zyryanov [87]	21 380
	9	Alania	W 3-1	PL	Shirokov [26p], Bystrov [34], Lazovic [39]	20 000
	13	Dinamo SP	W 3-1	KRr3	Kanunnikov [16], Rosina 2 [55 59]	10 500
Jul	13	Sibir	W 2-0	PL	Lombaerts [30], Shirokov [54]	10 500
	24	Rostov	W 3-1	PL	Kerzhakov [45], Danny [50], Fayzulin [70]	14 500
	27	Unirea	D 0-0	CLp3		12 000
	31	Rubin	W 2-0	PL	Kerzhakov 2 [45 65]	21 500
	4	Unirea	W 1-0	CLp3	Danny [33]	21 100
	14	Dinamo	D 1-1	PL	Lazovic [34]	21 200
Aug	17	Auxerre	W 1-0	CLpo	Kerzhakov [3]	21 405
	25	Auxerre	L 0-2	CLpo		15 277
	29	Lokomotiv	W 3-0	PL	Danny [17], Bukharov [67], Shirokov [77]	14 187
	11	Tom Tomsk	W 2-0	PL	OG [3], Bukharov [45]	20 500
	16	Anderlecht	W 3-1	ELgG	Kerzhakov 3 [8 33 44]	13 336
	20	Terek	D 0-0	PL		10 150
Sep	25	Saturn	W 6-1	PL	Kerzhakov 3 [25 46 54], Danny [32p], Lazovic [34], Rosina [83]	21 000
	30	AEK Athens	W 4-2	ELgG	Hubocan [1], Bruno Alves [13], Lazovic 2 [43p 57]	19 000
	3	Spartak N	W 3-2	PL	Kerzhakov 2 [2 22], Shirokov [49]	10 000
	16	Amkar	W 2-0	PL	Kerzhakov [49], Shirokov [64p]	20 500
Oct	21	Hajduk	W 2-0	ELgG	Bukharov [25], Danny [68]	19 500
	24	Anzhi	D 3-3	PL	Danny 2 [8 63], Zyryanov [40]	12 000
	27	Spartak M	L 0-1	PL		27 100
	31	Alania	W 3-0	PL	Lazovic [15], Kerzhakov 2 [41 52]	20 500
	4	Hajduk	W 3-2	ELgG	Ionov [31], Huszti [47p], Rosina [50]	28 000
	7	Sibir	W 5-2	PL	Bystrov [13], OG [15], Danny [61], Semak [63], Anyukov [67]	12 100
Nov	10	CSKA	L 1-3	PL	Rosina [90]	20 500
	14	Rostov	W 5-0	PL	Lazovic [39], Semak [75], Kerzhakov [82], Bukharov 2 [90 90]	20 500
	20	Rubin	D 2-2	PL	Fayzulin [19], Huszti [54]	18 400
	28	Krylya	D 0-0	PL		21 300
Dec	1	Anderlecht	W 3-1	ELgG	Ionov [12], Bukharov [65], Huszti [88]	15 000
	16	AEK Athens	W 3-0	ELgG	Bukharov [43], Rosina [67], Denisov [67]	13 605

TOM TOMSK LEAGUE APPEARANCES/GOALS 2010
Goalkeepers Sergei Pareiko EST 26 • Aleksey Polyakov UZB 4
Defenders Georgiy Dzhioev 16+4/1 • Ilya Gultyaev 24+2/0 • Andrey Ivanov 11+2/0 • Djordje Jokic SRB 25/1 • Vladislav Khatazenkov 4+4/0 • Fedor Kudryashov 9+1/0 • Nikola Petkovic SRB 7/0 • Dmitriy A. Smirnov 1/0 • Viktor Stroev 1+7/0
Midfield Serghei Covalciuc MDA 20+4/0 • Aleksandr Kharitonov 22+2/5 • Kim Nam Il KOR 24/0 • Valeriy Klimov 24+3/1 • Kyrylo Kovalchuk UKR 4+10/2 • Daisuke Matsui JPN 3+4/0 • Dmitriy Michkov 29+1/1 • Norbert Nemeth HUN 0+1/0 • Sergey Skoblyakov 13+7/0 • Dmitriy N. Smirnov 15+5/1 • Viktor Svezhov 0+1/0
Forwards Artem Dzyuba 22+2/10 • Denis Kiselev 0+2/0 • Sergey Kornilenko BLR 12+3/11 • Goran Maznov MKD 8+9/0 • Aleksandr Prudnikov 0+6/0 • Evgeniy Starikov 6+3/1
Coach Valeriy Nepomnyashchiy

ZENIT LEAGUE APPEARANCES/GOALS 2010
Goalkeepers Dimitry Borodin 1 • Vyacheslav Malafeev 21 • Yuriy Zhevnov BLR 8
Defenders Aleksandr Anyukov 26+1/1 • Bruno Alves POR 14/0 • Fernando Meira POR 7+4/0 • Tomas Hubocan SVK 23/0 • Ivica Krizanac CRO 13+1/1 • Nicolas Lombaerts BEL 26/3 • Aleksandar Lukovic SRB 10+1/0 • Michael Lumb DEN 1+1/0
Midfield Vladimir Bystrov 22+3/6 • Viktor Fayzulin 3+11/2 • Szabolcs Huszti HUN 3+10/1 • Aleksey Ionov 2+9/0 • Alessandro Rosina ITA 5+10/2 • Sergey Semak 10+2/2 • Roman Shirokov 17+4/6 • Konstantin Zyryanov 23+5/2
Forwards Aleksandr Bukharov 4+5/4 • Danny POR 27/10 • Igor Denisov 24/0 • Maksim Kannunikov 0+12/1 • Aleksandr Kerzhakov 26+2/13 • Danko Lazovic SRB 14+6/5
Coach Luciano Spalletti ITA

RWA – RWANDA

FIFA/COCA-COLA WORLD RANKING

1993	1994	1995	1996	1997	1998	1999	2000	2001	2002	2003	2004	2005	2006	2007	2008	2009	2010
-	-	168	159	172	107	146	128	144	130	109	99	89	121	99	78	102	132

					2010							Hi/Lo
Jan	Feb	Mar	Mar	Apr	May	Jul	Aug	Sep	Oct	Nov	Dec	**78**
102	107	105	107	107	107	113	111	112	118	127	132	**178**

Rwanda's biggest achievement of the year was to qualify for the 2011 African Nations Championship in Sudan, a tournament created by the CAF for national sides comprising only home-based players. Rwanda needed just a victory over Tanzania to reach the finals but it gave new coach Sellas Tetteh a false sense of confidence in his home grown talent and for the September start to the 2012 African Nations Cup qualifiers, he picked a squad with no foreign-based professionals. The tactic backfired badly with a 3-0 defeat in Abidjan that proved a devastating blow to their hopes of reaching the finals in Equatorial Guinea and Gabon. It was followed by a 3-0 home defeat by Benin that has rendered their chances virtually nil. More disappointment followed in the end-of-year East and Central African Senior Challenge Cup in Tanzania where the side did not win and were bundled out in the first round without a goal in any of their three games. There was much better news in club football when APR FC - league and cup double winners at home - won the CECAFA Club Cup in May on home turf. They had a six-game winning run through the tournament and secured the trophy with a 2-0 win over St George of Ethiopia in the final, with extra time goals from Malawian imports Chiukepo Msowoya and Victor Nyirenda.

FIFA WORLD CUP RECORD
1930-1994 DNE 1998-2010 DNQ

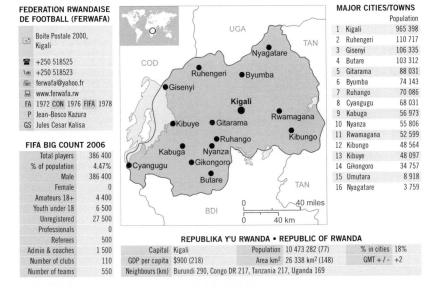

FEDERATION RWANDAISE DE FOOTBALL (FERWAFA)

Boite Postale 2000, Kigali

☎ +250 518525
📠 +250 518523
📧 ferwafa@yahoo.fr
🖥 www.ferwafa.rw
FA 1972 CON 1976 FIFA 1978
P Jean-Bosco Kazura
GS Jules Cesar Kalisa

FIFA BIG COUNT 2006

Total players	386 400
% of population	4.47%
Male	386 400
Female	0
Amateurs 18+	4 400
Youth under 18	6 500
Unregistered	27 500
Professionals	0
Referees	500
Admin & coaches	1 500
Number of clubs	110
Number of teams	550

MAJOR CITIES/TOWNS
Population

1	Kigali	965 398
2	Ruhengeri	110 717
3	Gisenyi	106 335
4	Butare	103 312
5	Gitarama	88 031
6	Byumba	74 143
7	Ruhango	70 086
8	Cyangugu	68 031
9	Kabuga	56 973
10	Nyanza	55 806
11	Rwamagana	52 599
12	Kibungo	48 564
13	Kibuye	48 097
14	Gikongoro	34 757
15	Umutara	8 918
16	Nyagatare	3 759

REPUBLIKA Y'U RWANDA • REPUBLIC OF RWANDA

Capital	Kigali	Population	10 473 282 (77)	% in cities	18%
GDP per capita	$900 (218)	Area km²	26 338 km² (148)	GMT +/-	+2
Neighbours (km)	Burundi 290, Congo DR 217, Tanzania 217, Uganda 169				

RECENT INTERNATIONAL MATCHES PLAYED BY RWANDA

2007	Opponents	Score		Venue	Comp	Scorers	Att	Referee
8-09	Liberia	W	4-0	Kigali	CNq	Bokota [21], Abedi Said [29], Witakenge [85], Karekezi [89]		Mwanza ZAM
9-12	Eritrea	W	2-1	Dar es Salaam	CCr1	Niyonzima [6], Bokota [40]		
11-12	Uganda	L	0-2	Dar es Salaam	CCr1			
13-12	Djibouti	W	9-0	Dar es Salaam	CCr1	Karekezi 2 [17 84], Abdi OG [25], Bokota 3 [36 42 77], Tuyisenge [47], Uzamukunda [54], Ngoma [62]		
18-12	Zanzibar †	D	0-0	Dar es Salaam	CCqf			
20-12	Uganda	W	1-0	Dar es Salaam	CCsf	Tuyisenge [118]		
22-12	Sudan	D	2-2	Dar es Salaam:	CCf	Niyonzima [48], Mulenda [59]. L 2-4p		
2008								
6-02	Burundi	D	0-0	Bujumbura	Fr			
31-05	Mauritania	W	3-0	Kigali	WCq	Karekezi [15], Abedi Said [67p], Bokota [72]	12 000	Doue CIV
8-06	Ethiopia	W	2-1	Addis Abeba	WCq	Abedi Said [59], Karekezi [82]	18 000	Ndinya KEN
14-06	Morocco	W	3-1	Kigali	WCq	Abedi Said [15], Bokota [68], Karekezi [93+]	12 000	Evehe CMR
21-06	Morocco	L	0-2	Casablanca	WCq		2 500	Benouza ALG
6-09	Mauritania	W	1-0	Nouakchott	WCq	Bobo [79]	1 000	Bennaceur TUN
19-11	Togo	L	0-1	Lomé	Fr			
2009								
1-01	Uganda	L	0-4	Kampala	CCr1			
5-01	Somalia	W	3-0	Kampala	CCr1	Gasana 2 [20 40], Labama [86]		
7-01	Tanzania	L	0-2	Kampala	CCr1			
9-01	Zanzibar †	W	3-0	Kampala	CCr1	Lomami [12], Mabula [17], Gasana [39]		
28-03	Algeria	D	0-0	Kigali	WCq		22 000	Codjia BEN
30-05	Malawi	L	0-2	Blantyre	Fr			
6-06	Zambia	L	0-1	Chililabombwe	WCq		28 000	Seck SEN
5-07	Egypt	L	0-3	Cairo	WCq		18 000	Imiere NGA
12-08	Tanzania	L	1-2	Kigali	Fr	Mwiseneza [68]		
5-09	Egypt	L	0-1	Kigali	WCq		20 000	Lamptey GHA
11-10	Algeria	L	1-3	Blida	WCq	Mutesa [19]	22 000	Keita GUI
14-11	Zambia	D	0-0	Kigali	WCq		18 000	Ambaya LBY
29-11	Somalia	W	1-0	Nairobi	CCr1	Mwalimu OG [4]		
3-12	Eritrea	W	2-1	Nairobi	CCr1	Ndayishimiye [20], Wolday OG [45]		
5-12	Zimbabwe †	W	1-0	Nairobi	CCr1	Ndayishimiye [20]		
8-12	Zimbabwe †	W	4-1	Nairobi	CCqf	Ndayishimiye [30], Ndamuhanga 2 [67 76], Niyonzima [90]		
10-12	Tanzania	W	2-1	Nairobi	CCsf	Ndayishimiye [68], Mafisango [77]		
13-12	Uganda	L	0-2	Nairobi	CCf			
2010								
7-01	Côte d'Ivoire	L	0-2	Dar es Salaam	Fr			
4-09	Côte d'Ivoire	L	0-3	Abidjan	CNq			Maillet SEY
9-10	Benin	L	0-3	Kigali	CNq			Haimoudi ALG
17-11	Malawi	L	1-2	Blantyre	Fr	Birori [8]		
1-12	Sudan	D	0-0	Dar es Salaam	CCr1			
3-12	Zanzibar	D	0-0	Dar es Salaam	CCr1			
8-12	Tanzania	L	0-1	Dar es Salaam	CCqf			

Fr = Friendly match • CN = CAF African Cup of Nations • CC = CECAFA Cup • WC = FIFA World Cup
q = qualifier • r1 = first round group • sf = semi-final • f = final • † Not a full international

RWANDA NATIONAL TEAM HISTORICAL RECORDS

Past Coaches: Ratomir Dujkovic SRB 2001-04 • Roger Palmgren SWE 2004-05 • Michael Nees GER 2006-07 • Josip Kuze CRO 2007-08 • Branco Tucak 2008-09 • Eric Nhsimiyimana 2009-10 • Sellas Tetteh GHA 2010-

RWANDA 2009-10

PRIMUS NATIONAL SOCCER LEAGUE PREMIER DIVISION

	Pl	W	D	L	F	A	Pts	APR	ATRACO	Etincelles	Rayon	Kiyovu	Police	Electrogaz	Mukura	Amagaju	AS Kigali	Marines	Musanze
APR FC †	22	17	3	2	48	19	54		1-1	4-1	2-2	2-0	3-2	0-0	4-1	1-0	4-1	2-0	3-1
ATRACO	22	13	4	5	35	23	43	0-3		0-1	0-3	1-1	1-2	3-1	2-0	0-0	1-0	1-0	3-0
Etincelles Gisenyi ‡	22	12	6	4	27	21	42	1-2	0-2		1-0	1-0	1-1	3-2	1-0	1-0	1-1	1-1	2-1
Rayon Sport	22	11	5	6	33	21	38	2-0	1-2	1-2		1-1	0-3	2-1	**3-0**	2-0	2-2	3-0	2-0
Kiyovu Sport	22	10	6	6	25	19	36	0-3	0-3	0-0	3-2		2-1	0-1	1-0	0-0	0-0	5-0	2-0
Police FC Kibungo	22	8	6	8	34	28	30	2-3	2-3	1-1	2-2	0-1		0-1	2-1	1-0	3-1	2-1	4-2
Electrogaz	22	8	6	8	30	31	30	0-2	1-4	1-1	0-1	3-2	1-1		1-2	3-2	1-1	5-1	2-1
Mukura Victory	22	7	2	13	20	30	23	1-0	**3-0**	1-0	0-1	0-1	1-0	2-3		1-3	0-1	1-2	2-1
Amagaju Nyamagabe	22	4	7	11	21	27	19	1-2	1-2	2-3	1-0	0-2	1-1	2-2	1-1		3-0	2-1	0-0
AS Kigali	22	4	7	11	21	35	19	2-3	2-4	0-2	0-0	1-3	1-0	0-1	2-0	1-0		1-1	0-1
Marines FC Gisenyi	22	5	3	14	22	43	18	1-3	1-2	1-2	1-2	0-0	1-4	1-0	0-2	2-1	3-2		**3-0**
Musanze	22	2	7	13	13	32	13	0-1	0-0	0-1	0-1	0-1	0-0	0-0	1-1	1-1	2-2	2-1	

17/10/2009 - 27/06/2010 • † Qualified for the CAF Champions League • ‡ Qualified for the Confederation Cup • Matches in bold awarded
ATRACO and Electrogaz withdrew at the end of the season so Marines and Musanze escaped relegation

RWANDA 2009-10 SECOND DIVISION GROUP A (2)

	Pl	W	D	L	F	A	Pts
Nyanza Huye †	14	12	2	0	25	6	38
Kibuye FC †	14	12	0	2	32	10	36
Pepinière	14	6	3	5	26	21	21
SORWATHE Kinikira	14	4	5	5	22	22	17
Intare Butare	14	5	1	8	10	20	16
ASPOR Kigali	14	4	2	8	19	24	14
Etoile de l'Est Kibungo	14	3	1	10	14	30	10
Zèbres FC Byumba	14	1	4	9	9	24	7

29/11/2009 - 3/04/2010 • † Qualified for the play-offs

RWANDA 2009-10 SECOND DIVISION GROUP B (2)

	Pl	W	D	L	F	A	Pts
Muhanga Gitarama †	14	8	4	2	25	10	28
La Jeunesse †	14	8	3	3	23	16	27
UNR Kigali	14	8	2	4	22	20	26
Interforce	14	7	4	3	25	17	25
Union Nyamirambo	14	6	4	4	22	16	22
Espoir FC Cyangugu	14	4	3	7	19	24	15
Stella Maris Gisenye	14	4	2	8	15	25	14
ISAE Busogo	14	2	1	11	20	31	7

29/11/2009 - 3/04/2010 • † Qualified for the play-offs

SECOND DIVISION PLAY-OFFS

Semi-finals

Muhanga	1	1
Kibuye *	0	0
Nyanza	0	1
La Jeunesse *	0	1

Final

Muhanga	1	4p
La Jeunesse	1	3p

Both finalists promoted • * Home team in the 1st leg

COUPE AMAHORO 2010

Round of 16

APR FC *	4
ISAE	0
Police FC Kibungo *	2 1p
AS Kigali	2 4p
Mukura Victory *	3
UNR Kigali	1
AS Muhanga	0
Electrogaz *	5
ATRACO *	6
Pepinière	0
Amagaju Nyamagabe *	2 0p
Etincelles	2 3p
Kiyovu Sports *	2
Musanze	1
Marines FC Gisenyi	0
Rayon Sports *	4

Quarter-finals

APR FC *	2
AS Kigali	0
Mukura Victory *	1 p
Electrogaz	1 p
ATRACO *	2
Etincelles	1
Kiyovu Sports	0
Rayon Sports *	2

Semi-finals

APR FC	3
Electrogaz *	2
ATRACO	
Rayon Sports	w-o

Final

APR FC	1
Rayon Sports	0

CUP FINAL

Amahoro, Kigali
4-07-2010

Scorer - Patrick Mafisango 90 for APR

* Home team in the 1st leg • Third place: Electrogaz w-o ATRACO

SAM – SAMOA

FIFA/COCA-COLA WORLD RANKING

1993	1994	1995	1996	1997	1998	1999	2000	2001	2002	2003	2004	2005	2006	2007	2008	2009	2010
-	-	-	177	183	164	180	173	172	163	176	179	182	187	146	176	182	185

2010												Hi/Lo
Jan	Feb	Mar	Mar	Apr	May	Jul	Aug	Sep	Oct	Nov	Dec	**146**
182	182	181	180	179	177	176	176	181	185	185	185	**191**

Football in Samoa took significant steps forward in 2010 most notably with the successful staging of the National league. Although two clubs - Central United and USP - fell by the wayside during the campaign, the tournament concluded in May with village team Moaula United being crowned champions for the first time. In the 20-match campaign they won 18 of their games and lost just once to finish five points ahead of Cruz Azul. Two weeks later in the newly launched Samoa Cup, Moaula faced Kiwi in the final. Kiwi had been the only team to beat Moaula during the league campaign and they did it again in the final, beating the champions 3-1 to deny them the double. Moaula were not given a slot in the OFC Champions League, however, with clubs from Samoa unable to fulfill the criteria needed for entry and they have yet to make an appearance since the competition was relaunched in 2007. The Samoan national team went a third consecutive year in 2010 without playing an international with their last match abroad back in 2004, but 2011 will see the team travel to Noumea in New Caledonia for the 2011 Pacific Games in late August, early September. Having failed to get past the group stage in 2007 when they hosted the tournament - then known as the South Pacific Games - Samoa will have their work cut out to make an impression.

FIFA WORLD CUP RECORD
1930-1994 DNE 1998-2010 DNQ

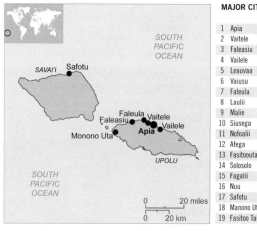

FOOTBALL FEDERATION SAMOA (FFS)

PO Box 1682, Apia

☎ +685 29993
📠 +685 27895
✉ stoe@samoa.ws
🖥 www.footballsamoa.ws
FA 1968 CON 1984 FIFA 1986
P Toetu Petana
GS Frederick Young

FIFA BIG COUNT 2006

Total players	5 700
% of population	3.22%
Male	5 400
Female	300
Amateurs 18+	1 100
Youth under 18	1 100
Unregistered	1 100
Professionals	0
Referees	100
Admin & coaches	300
Number of clubs	60
Number of teams	220

MAJOR CITIES/TOWNS

		Population
1	Apia	36 679
2	Vaitele	7 061
3	Faleasiu	3 780
4	Vailele	3 188
5	Leauvaa	3 145
6	Vaiusu	2 303
7	Faleula	2 197
8	Laulii	2 070
9	Malie	2 004
10	Siusega	1 951
11	Nofoalii	1 823
12	Afega	1 789
13	Fasitoouta	1 765
14	Solosolo	1 686
15	Fagalii	1 650
16	Nuu	1 504
17	Safotu	1 473
18	Manono Uta	1 420
19	Fasitoo Tai	1 371

MALO SA'OLOTO TUTO'ATASI O SAMOA • INDEPENDENT STATE OF SAMOA

Capital	Apia	Population	219 998 (184)	% in cities	23%
GDP per capita	$4700 (143)	Area km²	2831 km² (177)	GMT +/-	-11
Neighbours (km)	Coast 403				

RECENT INTERNATIONAL MATCHES PLAYED BY SAMOA

2004	Opponents	Score	Venue	Comp	Scorers	Att	Referee
5-05	Cook Islands	D 0-0	Auckland	Fr			
10-05	American Samoa	W 4-0	Apia	WCq	Bryce [12], Fasavalu 2 [30 53], Michael [66]	500	Afu SOL
15-05	Vanuatu	L 0-3	Apia	WCq		650	Breeze AUS
17-05	Fiji	L 0-4	Apia	WCq		450	Diomis AUS
19-05	Papua New Guinea	L 1-4	Apia	WCq	Michael [69]	300	Diomis AUS
2005							
No international matches played in 2005							
2006							
No international matches played in 2006							
2007							
25-08	Vanuatu	L 0-4	Apia	WCq		300	Jacques TAH
27-08	America Samoa	W 7-0	Apia	WCq	Tumua 2 [24 51], Faaiuaso [29], Cahill 2 [43p 67], Fonotti [61], Michael [76]	2 800	Minan PNG
29-08	Tonga	W 2-1	Apia	WCq	Faaiuaso [45], Taylor [83]	1 850	Sosongan PNG
3-09	Solomon Islands	L 0-3	Apia	WCq		200	Hester NZL
2008							
No international matches played in 2008							
2009							
No international matches played in 2009							
2010							
No international matches played in 2010							

Fr = Friendly match • WC = FIFA World Cup • q = qualifier

SAMOA 2009-10

SFSF–NC NATIONAL LEAGUE

	Pl	W	D	L	F	A	Pts	Moaula Utd	Cruz Azul	Kiwi	Goldstar	Apia Youth	Adidas	Vaivase-Tai	Togafuafua	Moataa	Strickland	Central Utd	USP
Moaula United	20	18	1	1	90	26	55		6-4	2-3	3-3	3-1	8-4	6-1	12-0	3-0	9-2	5-1	3-0
Cruz Azul	20	16	2	2	68	27	50	1-2		1-0	3-2	4-2	10-1	2-2	5-4	4-1	3-1		
Kiwi	20	15	2	3	70	20	47		0-1		0-0	8-1	4-0	3-2	7-1	2-0	9-1	3-0	3-0
Goldstar Sogi	20	11	5	4	44	29	38	1-5	1-5	0-0		4-4	1-0	1-1	4-1		3-0		3-0
Apia Youth	20	9	3	8	51	45	30	2-6	0-2	2-5			4-4	0-0	3-0	1-0	3-2	9-1	3-0
Adidas	20	7	3	10	44	57	24				2-4	3-1	2-5		2-3	1-3	4-1	3-0	4-3	3-0
Vaivase-Tai	20	6	5	9	34	45	23	0-3	1-7		2-4	1-3	0-3		3-0	2-1	3-0	2-1	8-5
Togafuafua Saints	20	5	1	14	37	80	16	3-6	1-4	4-13	2-5		3-4	3-3		3-0	3-0	3-4	1-0
Moataa	20	4	3	13	24	42	15	0-5		1-2	0-2	1-3	3-3	0-0	4-1		2-1	2-1	5-5
Strickland Brothers	20	5	0	15	28	65	15	0-3	1-7	2-4	0-3	2-5	4-1	1-0	2-1	0-3		6-0	3-0
Central United	11	2	0	9	20	44	6		1-3		0-6								8-1
USP	11	0	1	10	12	42	1												

5/09/2009 - 8/05/2010 • † Qualified for OFC Champions League

SAMOA CUP 2009-10

Group A	Pts
Kiwi	13
Moaula Utd	10
Moataa	6
Goldstar	4
Adidas	4
Strickland	3

Semi-finals

Kiwi	2
Apia Youth	1

Final

Kiwi	3
Moaula Utd	1

Group B	Pts
Cruz Azul	10
Apia Youth	10
Vaivase-Tai	7
Togafuafua	7
USP	3
Central Utd	3

Cruz Azul	1
Moaula Utd	2

22-05-2010

SCO – SCOTLAND

FIFA/COCA-COLA WORLD RANKING

1993	1994	1995	1996	1997	1998	1999	2000	2001	2002	2003	2004	2005	2006	2007	2008	2009	2010
24	32	26	29	37	38	20	25	50	59	54	86	60	25	14	33	46	52

	2010												Hi/Lo
	Jan	Feb	Mar	Mar	Apr	May	Jul	Aug	Sep	Oct	Nov	Dec	13
	46	46	45	41	44	43	41	41	47	57	54	52	88

When Motherwell won the Scottish championship in 1932 they ended an extraordinary run of 27 consecutive titles for either Rangers or Celtic. By winning the 2010 championship, Rangers ensured that the two Glasgow giants extended their current spell of domination to a quarter of a century, just two seasons short of that long-standing record and there is little to suggest that the record won't be broken. But despite the domination of Rangers and Celtic at home, the standing of Scottish football overall has rarely been lower. Scottish clubs are set to lose their automatic place in the group stage of the UEFA Champions League for the 2011-12 season thanks to a string of poor performances in recent years and it was only Rangers' guaranteed group berth that saw Scottish representation in Europe extend beyond the end of August as the 2010-11 tournament got underway. Amongst the casualties were Celtic, who endured a disappointing 2010, having finished the season trophyless for the first time since 2003. Rangers, under coach Walter Smith, won the League and League Cup double but it was Dundee United who won the Scottish FA Cup after a convincing 3-0 win over First Division Ross County in the final. It was only the second time Dundee United had won the Cup and marked their first trophy since their last triumph in 1994.

FIFA WORLD CUP RECORD
1930-1938 DNE 1950 withdrew **1954** 15 r1 **1958** 14 r1 1962-1970 DNQ
1974 9 r1 **1978** 11 r1 **1982** 15 r1 **1986** 19 r1 **1990** 19 r1 1994 DNQ **1998** 27 r1 2002-2010 DNQ

THE SCOTTISH FOOTBALL ASSOCIATION (SFA)

Hampden Park,
Glasgow G42 9AY,
United Kingdom
☎ +44 141 6166000
📠 +44 141 6166001
✉ info@scottishfa.co.uk
🖥 www.scottishfa.co.uk
FA 1873 CON 1954 FIFA 1910
P George Peat
GS Stewart Regan

FIFA BIG COUNT 2006

Total players	420 589
% of population	8.31%
Male	374 075
Female	46 514
Amateurs 18+	39 234
Youth under 18	67 123
Unregistered	302 500
Professionals	4 132
Referees	2 097
Admin & coaches	8 500
Number of clubs	6 600
Number of teams	8 200

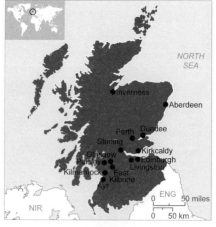

MAJOR CITIES/TOWNS

		Population
1	Glasgow	578 725
2	Edinburgh	449 058
3	Aberdeen	166 927
4	Dundee	141 616
5	East Kilbride	74 604
6	Paisley	71 730
7	Livingston	58 968
8	Cumbernauld	54 003
9	Dunfermline	51 456
10	Hamilton	47 979
11	Kirkcaldy	47 649
12	Ayr	45 899
13	Kilmarnock	45 163
14	Perth	44 201
15	Greenock	42 695
16	Coatbridge	41 454
17	Inverness	41 111
18	Glenrothes	38 862
19	Airdrie	35 309

SCOTLAND (PART OF THE UNITED KINGDOM)

Capital Edinburgh	Population 5 057 400 (114)	% in cities 89%
GDP per capita $39 680 (20)	Area km² 77 000 km² (117)	GMT +/- 0
Neighbours (km) England 164 • Coast 9911		

RECENT INTERNATIONAL MATCHES PLAYED BY SCOTLAND

2006	Opponents	Score		Venue	Comp	Scorers	Att	Referee
2-09	Faroe Islands	W	6-0	Glasgow	ECq	Fletcher [7], McFadden [10], Boyd 2 [24p 38], Miller.K [30p], O'Connor [85]	50 059	Egorov RUS
6-09	Lithiania	W	2-1	Kaunas	ECq	Dailly [46], Miller.K [62]	8 000	Hrinák SVK
7-10	France	W	1-0	Glasgow	ECq	Caldwell.G [67]	50 456	Busacca SUI
11-10	Ukraine	L	0-2	Kyiv	ECq		50 000	Hansson SWE
2007								
24-03	Georgia	W	2-1	Glasgow	ECq	Boyd [11], Beattie [89]	52 063	Vollquartz DEN
28-03	Italy	L	0-2	Bari	ECq		37 600	De Bleeckere BEL
30-05	Austria	W	1-0	Vienna	Fr	O'Connor [59]	13 200	Szabo HUN
6-06	Faroe Islands	W	2-0	Toftir	ECq	Maloney [31], O'Connor [35]	4 100	Kasnaferis GRE
22-08	South Africa	W	1-0	Aberdeen	Fr	Boyd [71]	13 723	Atkinson ENG
8-09	Lithuania	W	3-1	Glasgow	ECq	Boyd [31], McManus [77], McFadden [85]	52 063	Skomina SVN
12-09	France	W	1-0	Paris	ECq	McFadden [64]	43 342	Plautz AUT
13-10	Ukraine	W	3-1	Glasgow	ECq	Miller.K [4], McCulloch [10], McFadden [68]	52 063	Vink NED
17-10	Georgia	L	0-2	Tbilisi	ECq		29 377	Kircher GER
17-11	Italy	L	1-2	Glasgow	ECq	Ferguson [65]	51 301	Mejuto Gonzalez ESP
2008								
26-03	Croatia	D	1-1	Glasgow	Fr	Miller.K [31]	28 821	Hauge NOR
30-05	Czech Republic	L	1-3	Prague	Fr	Clarkson [85]	11 314	Braamhaar NED
20-08	Northern Ireland	D	0-0	Glasgow	Fr		28 072	Vollquartz DEN
6-09	Macedonia FYR	L	0-1	Skopje	WCq		9 000	Kralovec CZE
10-09	Iceland	W	2-1	Reykjavík	WCq	Broadfoot [19], McFadden [59]	9 767	Gumienny BEL
11-10	Norway	D	0-0	Glasgow	WCq		50 205	Busacca SUI
19-11	Argentina	L	0-1	Glasgow	Fr		32 492	Brych GER
2009								
28-03	Netherlands	L	0-3	Amsterdam	WCq		50 000	Duhamel FRA
1-04	Iceland	W	2-1	Glasgow	WCq	McCormack [39], Fletcher.S [65]	42 259	Einwaller AUT
12-08	Norway	L	0-4	Oslo	WCq		24 493	Hamer LUX
5-09	Macedonia FYR	W	2-0	Glasgow	WCq	Brown [56], McFadden [80]	50 214	Stark GER
9-09	Netherlands	L	0-1	Glasgow	WCq		51 230	Larsen DEN
10-10	Japan	L	0-2	Yokohama	Fr		61 285	Kim KOR
14-11	Wales	L	0-3	Cardiff	Fr		13 844	Zimmermann SUI
2010								
3-03	Czech Republic	W	1-0	Glasgow	Fr	Brown [62]	26 530	Fautrel FRA
11-08	Sweden	L	0-3	Stockholm	Fr		25 249	Rocchi ITA
3-09	Lithuania	D	0-0	Kaunas	ECq		5 248	Cakir TUR
7-09	Liechtenstein	W	2-1	Glasgow	ECq	Miller.K [63], McManus [97+]	37 050	Shvetsov UKR
8-10	Czech Republic	L	0-1	Prague	ECq		14 922	Bebek CRO
12-10	Spain	L	2-3	Glasgow	ECq	Naismith.S [58], OG [66]	51 322	Busacca SUI
16-11	Faroe Islands	W	3-0	Aberdeen	Fr	Wilson [24], Commons [31], Mackie [45]	10 873	Van Boekel NED

Fr = Friendly match • EC = UEFA EURO 2008/2012 • WC = FIFA World Cup • q = qualifier

SCOTLAND NATIONAL TEAM HISTORICAL RECORDS

Caps

102 - Kenny Dalglish 1971-86 • **91** - Jim Leighton 1982-98 • **77** - Alex McLeish 1980-93 • **76** - Paul McStay 1983-97 • **72** - Tom Boyd 1990-2001 • **69** - David Weir 1997- • **67** - Christian Dailly 1997-2008 • **65** - Willie Miller 1975-89 • **62** - Danny McGrain 1973-82 • **61** - Richard Gough 1983-93 & Ally McCoist 1985-98 • **58** - John Collins 1988-2000 • **57** - Roy Aitken 1980-92 & Gary McAllister 1990-99 • **55** - Denis Law 1959-74 & Maurice Malpas 1984-93 • **54** - Billy Bremner 1965-76 & Graeme Souness 1976-86

Goals

30 - Kenny Dalglish 1971-86 & Denis Law 1959-74 • **24** - Hughie Gallacher 1924-35 • **22** - Lawrie Reilly 1948-57 • **19** - Ally McCoist 1985-98 • **15** - Robert Hamilton 1899-1911 & James McFadden 2002 • **14** - Mo Johnston 1984-91 • **13** - Robert Smyth McColl 1896-1908

Past Coaches

Committee 1872-54 • Andy Beattie 1954 • Committee 1954-58 • Dawson Walker 1958 • Matt Busby 1958 • Andy Beattie 1959-60 • Ian McColl 1960-65 • Jock Stein 1965-66 • John Prentice 1966 • Malcolm MacDonald 1966-67 • Bobby Brown 1967-71 • Tommy Docherty 1971-72 • Willie Ormond 1973-77 • Ally MacLeod 1977-78 • Jock Stein 1978-85 • Alex Ferguson 1985-86 • Andy Roxburgh 1986-93 • Craig Brown 1993-2002 • Berti Vogts GER 2002-04 • Tommy Burns 2004 • Walter Smith 2004-07 • Alex McLeish 2007 • George Burley 2008-09 • Craig Levein 2009-

SCOTLAND 2009–10

CLYDESDALE BANK PREMIER LEAGUE

	Pl	W	D	L	F	A	Pts	Results
Rangers †	38	26	9	3	82	28	87	2-1 1-0 7-1 **2-1** 1-1 3-0 6-1 3-3 1-1 2-0 4-1 1-0 3-0 0-0 3-1 2-1 3-1 3-0 4-1 3-0
Celtic †	38	25	6	7	75	39	81	1-1 2-1 1-1 1-0 1-2 3-2 0-0 2-1 2-1 2-0 2-0 5-2 3-0 3-0 3-1 3-0 3-1 1-1
Dundee United ‡	38	17	12	9	55	47	63	0-1 0-0 2-1 0-2 1-0 0-2 0-1 3-0 2-0 1-0 1-1 0-2 3-3 0-1 3-2 0-0 2-1 3-0
Hibernian ‡	38	15	9	14	58	55	54	1-4 0-1 0-1 0-1 1-1 2-4 2-0 **6-6** 1-1 1-2 5-1 3-0 1-1 2-0 2-2 2-1 2-1 1-0 1-0 2-0
Motherwell ‡	38	13	14	11	52	54	53	0-0 1-1 2-3 **0-4** 2-2 2-3 1-3 1-0 1-0 3-1 1-0 1-3 1-1 2-0 3-1 1-0 1-0 0-1
Heart of Midlothian	38	13	9	16	35	46	48	1-2 1-4 2-1 1-2 0-0 0-0 0-0 2-1 1-0 2-1 2-0 1-2 0-3 1-0 1-0 1-0 0-0 3-2
Hamilton Academical	38	13	10	15	39	46	49	0-1 1-2 0-1 0-1 2-0 4-1 2-2 0-0 2-1 0-2 1-0 0-3 1-1 1-0 0-0 3-0 0-0 2-2
St Johnstone	38	12	11	15	57	61	47	1-2 4-1 1-4 2-3 0-1 5-1 2-2 1-2 2-2 1-0 1-1 2-3 1-0 1-1 1-0 2-2 0-1 **2-1** 3-1 1-1
Aberdeen	38	10	11	17	36	52	41	1-0 1-3 4-1 0-2 2-2 0-2 0-0 0-3 1-1 0-1 1-2 1-3 2-1 1-3 1-0 2-1 1-0 1-2 0-1 1-0
St Mirren	38	7	13	18	36	49	34	0-2 0-2 4-0 0-0 1-2 1-1 3-3 0-0 2-1 1-1 1-0 2-0 0-1 1-1 0-0-1 1-0 1-0 1-1 **1-1**
Kilmarnock	38	8	9	21	29	51	33	0-0 0-2 1-0 0-2 4-4 1-1 0-3 1-2 3-0 1-2 2-1 3-2 1-1 2-0 1-2 1-1 1-2 0-0
Falkirk	38	6	13	19	31	57	31	1-3 3-3 0-2 1-4 1-3 1-3 0-0 0-1 2-0 0-1 1-2 0-0 0-0 3-1 1-3 2-1 0-0 0-1

15/08/2009 – 9/05/2010 • † Qualified for the UEFA Champions League • ‡ Qualified for the Europa League • Matches in bold are away matches

Top scorers: **23** - Kris Boyd, Rangers • **21** - Anthony Stokes IRL, Hibs • **18** - Kenny Miller, Rangers • **13** - Jon Daly IRL, Dundee U & Derek Riordan, Hibs

SCOTLAND 2009–10

IRN–BRU FIRST DIVISION (2)

	Pl	W	D	L	F	A	Pts	Results
Inverness Caley Thistle	36	21	10	5	72	32	73	1-1 1-0 1-1 2-0 1-3 3-1 1-3 3-0 2-3 2-1 1-0 4-3 4-1 1-0 2-0 4-0 0-0 3-3
Dundee	36	16	13	7	48	34	61	2-2 2-2 1-0 3-2 0-0 1-1 2-0 0-1 2-0 1-0 2-1 1-0 1-0 3-1 2-1 0-3 3-1 3-0
Dunfermline Athletic	36	17	7	12	54	44	58	0-1 0-0 1-1 2-1 1-4 3-1 3-3 1-2 3-1 1-2 0-2 2-1 3-1 4-1 2-0 2-0 3-1 0-1
Queen of the South	36	15	11	10	53	40	56	1-1 1-3 2-0 1-1 1-2 2-0 2-0 1-0 1-0 1-0 1-3 0-2 3-1 2-3 1-2 3-0 2-2 2-0 3-0
Ross County	36	15	11	10	46	44	56	2-1 0-0 0-1 1-1 0-0 2-2 3-2 1-1 2-2 1-2 0-1 1-0 3-1 2-1 1-2 1-5 3-2 1-1 1-0
Partick Thistle	36	14	6	16	43	40	48	2-1 0-1 0-2 0-1 2-0 1-4 2-2 1-0 0-0 1-2 1-2 0-0 5-0 1-0 2-0 2-0 0-0 2-0 0-1
Raith Rovers	36	11	9	16	36	47	42	0-1 0-4 2-2 1-0 1-2 1-2 1-0 0-0 2-1 4-1 1-1 1-0 3-0 1-2 1-1 0-1 0-0 1-1
Greenock Morton	36	11	4	21	40	65	37	0-3 0-2 0-1 2-2 0-2 1-2 1-2 3-3 0-1 1-1 0-2 1-0 5-0 1-1 1-0 2-1 1-0 2-1
Airdrie United †	36	8	9	19	41	56	33	1-1 0-1 1-1 1-1 1-0 1-1 0-1 1-1 0-1 0-1 1-1 2-5 2-0 1-2 3-0 2-4 3-0 3-1 1-1
Ayr United	36	7	10	19	29	60	31	1-5 0-7 2-2 1-1 1-0 1-2 0-1 3-0 1-1 0-1 1-1 1-0 1-0 0-2 2-2 0-0 1-1 1-4

8/08/2009 – 1/05/2010 • † Play-off (see second division)

SCOTLAND 2009–10

IRN–BRU SECOND DIVISION (3)

	Pl	W	D	L	F	A	Pts	Results
Stirling Albion	36	18	11	7	68	48	65	0-1 0-3 2-2 1-0 1-0 6-2 2-1 2-0 2-2 1-2 3-0 3-3 0-0 1-1 2-2 2-2 1-1 1-0
Alloa Athletic †	36	19	8	9	49	35	65	1-0 2-1 2-1 3-1 2-1 2-3 1-0 2-1 1-3 1-2 0-0 2-0 1-4 2-1 0-1 1-0 2-0 2-2
Cowdenbeath †	36	16	11	9	60	41	59	1-2 3-3 1-1 1-1 0-0 4-0 5-0 1-3 2-1 0-0 2-1 6-2 2-1 1-1 0-1 2-2 1-1 0-3 1-0
Brechin City †	36	15	9	12	47	42	54	1-0 1-1 2-1 1-1 3-1 3-3 3-0 1-2 3-1 0-1 3-2 1-0 1-0 2-2 0-0 0-0 2-2 2-3 1-1
Peterhead	36	15	6	15	45	49	51	3-2 1-1 0-0 2-0 0-2 1-0 1-0 0-3 1-2 2-1 1-1 3-1 2-2 0-1 1-2 3-0 2-0 0-0
Dumbarton	36	14	6	16	49	58	48	2-3 2-4 1-3 3-1 0-3 2-1 0-0 0-1 1-0 1-2 0-3 0-1 0-0 2-1 1-0 0-2 3-3 3-3
East Fife	36	10	11	15	46	53	41	1-2 0-3 0-2 0-1 1-1 2-2 2-2 0-1 2-3 0-0 1-2 3 2-1 1-1 1-1 3-1 1-0 1-1
Stenhousemuir	36	9	13	14	38	42	40	1-2 1-3 1-0 0-2 0-2 0-0 1-1 1-2 2-0 1-1 0-3 1-0 1-1 1-1 3-0 1-1 0-0 3
Arbroath †	36	10	10	16	41	55	40	3-4 2-4 2-2 0-0 0-1 1-1 1-4 1-0 0-1 1-4 3-1 3-1 0-1 2-2 0-3 1-1 0-3 2-0
Clyde	36	8	7	21	37	57	31	0-1 1-2 0-1 0-2 0-1 1-2 1-0 0-3 1-3 3-1 0-2 4-2 1-3 2-1 2-1 0-2 1-0 0-2

8/08/2009 – 1/05/2010 • † Play-off • **Brechin** 2-1 1-0 Airdrie; **Cowdenbeath** 1-1 2-0 Alloa • Final: **Cowdenbeath** 0-0 3-0 Brechin

SCOTLAND 2009-10

IRN–BRU THIRD DIVISION (4)

	Pl	W	D	L	F	A	Pts	Livingston	Forfar Ath	East Stirling	Queen's Park	Albion Rov	Berwick Rang	Stranraer	Annan Ath	Elgin City	Montrose
Livingston	36	24	6	6	63	25	**78**		1-2 2-3	2-0 1-0	2-1 2-0	2-0 2-0	1-1 0-0	3-0 2-1	2-0 3-2	3-2 1-0	2-0 1-0
Forfar Athletic †	36	18	9	9	59	44	**63**	0-1 2-2		5-1 4-1	0-1 1-1	2-2 1-1	2-0 3-0	1-0 2-0	2-1 1-5	3-3 1-0	2-2 2-0
East Stirling †	36	19	4	13	50	46	**61**	3-1 0-2	2-1 4-0		1-0 0-3	2-0 3-1	1-0 3-2	1-1 2-0	1-3 3-1	1-1 1-2	0-1 0-2 3
Queen's Park †	36	15	6	15	42	42	**51**	1-2 0-1	2-2 1-3	1-0 2-0		0-1 1-0	2-0 2-3	1-2 2-5	0-0 3-2	0-3 0-1	3-2 3-0
Albion Rovers	36	13	11	12	35	35	**50**	1-0 0-2	1-1 0-1	3-0 2-1	0-1 1-0		2-1 4-1	3-1 0-0	0-0 1-0	1-1 1-2	0-0 1-0
Berwick Rangers	36	14	8	14	46	50	**50**	1-0 1-1	0-1 0-4	0-1 2-2	1-0 1-1	2-0 1-2		1-0 1-0	2-1 0-2	2-0 2-1	2-0 0-2
Stranraer	36	13	8	15	48	54	**47**	0-3 1-1	1-0 2-0	1-2 2-2	1-1 0-0	1-1 2-4	3-1		2-0 3-2	0-2 2-1	2-0 0-2
Annan Athletic	36	11	10	15	41	42	**43**	0-0 2-0	1-0 1-1	0-1 1-0	3-1 0-2	0-0 1-2	1-1 0-1	1-0 3-2		0-2 3-3	2-0 0-0
Elgin City	36	9	7	20	46	59	**34**	1-6 0-1	0-2 0-2	1-2 0-1	0-1 0-1	0-2 3-1	3-3 1-5	1-2 2-3	1-1 1-0		0-1 5-2
Montrose	36	5	9	22	30	63	**24**	0-3 0-5	1-2 4-0	0-3 0-1	1-2 1-2	0-0 0-0	1-3 1-1	1-1 4-5	0-0 1-2	1-1 0-4	

8/08/2009 - 1/05/2010 • † Play-off • Semis: Queen's Park 0-4 2-2 **Arbroath**; East Stirling 0-1 2-2 **Forfar** • Final: Arbroath 0-0 0-2 **Forfar**

MEDALS TABLE

		Overall			League			Cup		LC		Europe			Town/City
		G	S	B	G	S	B	G	S	G	S	G	S	B	
1	Rangers	113	56	19	53	29	17	33	17	26	7	1	3	2	Glasgow
2	Celtic	91	63	21	42	30	17	34	18	14	13	1	2	4	Glasgow
3	Aberdeen	17	28	9	4	13	8	7	8	5	7	1		1	Aberdeen
4	Heart of Midlothian	15	22	16	4	14	16	7	6	4	2				Edinburgh
5	Queen's Park	10	2					10	2						Glasgow
6	Hibernian	9	21	15	4	6	13	2	9	3	6			2	Edinburgh
7	Dundee United	5	12	9	1		8	2	7	2	4	1	1		Dundee
8	Dundee	5	11	3	1	4	1	1	4	3	3			2	Dundee
9	Kilmarnock	4	14	4	1	4	3	3	5		5			1	Kilmarnock
10	Motherwell	4	11	7	1	5	7	2	4	1	2				Motherwell
11	East Fife	4	2	2		2		1	2	3					Methil
12	St. Mirren	3	5	2		2		3	3		2				Paisley
	Third Lanark	3	5	2	1		2	2	4		1				Glasgow
14	Dumbarton	3	5		2			1	5						Dumbarton
15	Vale of Leven	3	4					3	4						Alexandria
16	Clyde	3	3	3		3		3	3						Cumbernauld
17	Dunfermline Athletic	2	6	3		2		2	3		3			1	Dunfermline
18	Falkirk	2	5	1	2	1		2	2		1				Falkirk
19	Partick Thistle	2	4	3		3		1	1	1	3				Glasgow
20	Renton	2	3					2	3						Renton
21	Airdrie United	1	7	1		4	1	1	3						Airdrie
22	Morton	1	3	2		1	2	1	1		1				Greenock
23	Raith Rovers	1	2	1			1		1	1	1				Kirkcaldy
24	St. Bernard's	1		1			1	1	1						Edinburgh
	Livingston	1		1			1			1					Livingston
26	St. Johnstone		2	2		2				2					Perth
27	Hamilton Academical		2						2						Hamilton
28	Albion Rovers		1						1						Coatbridge
	Ayr United		1							1					Ayr
	Cambuslang		1						1						Cambuslang
	Clydesdale		1						1						Glasgow
	Gretna		1						1						Gretna
	Queen of the South		1						1						Dumfries
	Ross County		1						1						Dingwall
	Thornliebank		1						1						Glasgow

708 PART TWO – THE NATIONS OF THE WORLD

SCOTTISH CUP 2009–10

Third Round

Forfar Athletic	1	
Spartans *	0	
Cowdenbeath *	0	0
Alloa Athletic	0	1
Clyde *	1	1
Livingston	1	7
Brechin City	4	4
Wick Academy *	4	2
Deveronvale *	0	
Ayr United	1	
Airdrie United *	4	
Queen of the South	0	
Peterhead	0	1
Raith Rovers *	0	4
Dumbarton	0	0
Greenock Morton *	0	1
Stenhousemuir *	5	
Cove Rangers	0	
Arbroath	0	
Irvine Meadow XI *	1	
Edinburgh City *	3	
Keith	1	
East Fife	1	
Montrose	2	
Stirling Albion *	2	
Auchinleck Talbot	1	
Elgin City	0	
Albion Rovers *	1	
Inverurie Loco Works	2	
Threave Rovers *	1	
Berwick Rangers	1	
Ross County *	5	

Fourth Round

Dundee United	2	
Partick Thistle *	0	
Forfar Athletic *	0	
St Johnstone	3	
St Mirren *	3	
Alloa Athletic	1	
Hamilton Academical *	3	0
Rangers	3	2
Dundee	1	
Livingston *	0	
Brechin City	0	
Ayr United *	1	
Aberdeen *	2	
Heart of Midlothian	0	
Airdrie United	1	1
Raith Rovers *	1	3
Celtic	1	
Greenock Morton *	0	
Stenhousemuir	1	1
Dunfermline Athletic * †	7	2
Inverness Caledonian Thistle *	2	
Motherwell	0	
Falkirk	0	
Kilmarnock *	1	
Hibernian *	3	
Irvine Meadow XI	0	
Edinburgh City *	1	
Montrose	3	
Stirling Albion	0	3
Albion Rovers *	0	1
Inverurie Loco Works	0	
Ross County *	4	

Fifth Round

Dundee United	1	
St Johnstone *	0	
St Mirren *	0	0
Rangers	0	1
Dundee *	2	
Ayr United	1	
Aberdeen	1	0
Raith Rovers *	1	1
Celtic	4	
Dunfermline Athletic *	2	
Inverness Caledonian Thistle	0	
Kilmarnock *	3	
Hibernian *	5	
Montrose	1	
Stirling Albion	0	
Ross County *	9	

† Original match declared void. Replay at Stenhousemuir • * Home team

SCOTTISH CUP 2009-10

Quarter–finals			Semi–finals		Final	
Dundee United	3	1				
Rangers *	3	0				
			Dundee United	2		
			Raith Rovers	0		
Dundee *		1				
Raith Rovers		2				
					Dundee United ‡	3
					Ross County	0
Celtic		3				
Kilmarnock *		0				
			Celtic	0		
			Ross County	2		
Hibernian *	2	1				
Ross County	2	2				

Top 16 teams from the previou season enter in the fourth round. Clubs positioned 17-32 enter in the third round
Both semi-finals played at Hampden Park
‡ Qualified for the Europa League

SCOTTISH FA CUP FINAL 2010

Hampden Park, Glasgow, 15-05-2010, 15:00, Att: 47 122, Ref: Dougie McDonald

Dundee United	3	Goodwillie [61], Conway 2 [75] [86]
Ross County	0	

Dundee Utd - Dusan Pernis - Sean Dillon, Andy Webster, Garry Kenneth, Michael Kovacevic (Keith Watson 83) - Craig Conway, Danny Swanson (Scott Robertson 74), Prince Buaben, Morgaro Gomis• - Jon Daly, David Goodwillie• (David Robertson 78). Tr: Peter Houston
Ross Co - Michael McGovern - Gary Miller•, Scott Boyd, Jimmy Scott• (Garry Wood 79), Scott Morrison - Alex Keddie, Michael Gardyne (Paul di Giacomo 77), Steven Craig (Paul Lawson 52), Richard Brittain, Ian Vigurs - Andrew Barrowman. Tr: Derek Adams

CO-OPERATIVE INSURANCE SCOTTISH LEAGUE CUP 2009-10

Second Round

Team	Score
Rangers	Bye
Partick Thistle *	1
Queen of the South	2
Aberdeen	Bye
Forfar Athletic *	2
Dundee	4
Dundee United	2
Alloa Athletic *	0
Hamilton Academical	1
Ross County *	2
Hibernian *	3
Brechin City	0
Arbroath *	0
St Johnstone	6
Heart of Midlothian	Bye
Raith Rovers	1
Dunfermline Athletic *	3
Falkirk	Bye
Celtic	Bye
Motherwell	Bye
Albion Rovers	0
Inverness Caley Thistle	4
Kilmarnock *	3
Greenock Morton	1
Ayr United *	0
St Mirren	2

Third Round

Team	Score
Rangers	2
Queen of the South *	1
Aberdeen	2
Dundee *	3
Dundee United	2
Ross County *	0
Hibernian *	1
St Johnstone	3
Heart of Midlothian *	2
Dunfermline Athletic	1
Falkirk	0
Celtic	4
Motherwell *	3
Inverness Caley Thistle	2
Kilmarnock *	1
St Mirren	2

Quarter-finals

Team	Score
Rangers	3
Dundee *	1
Dundee United	1
St Johnstone *	2
Heart of Midlothian	1
Celtic *	0
Motherwell	0
St Mirren *	3

Semi-finals

Team	Score
Rangers †	2
St Johnstone	0
Heart of Midlothian	0
St Mirren ‡	2

Final

Team	Score
Rangers	1
St Mirren	0

LEAGUE CUP FINAL

Hampden Park, Glasgow
21-03-2010, 15:00
Att: 44 538, Ref: Craig Thomson
Scorer - Millar 84 for Rangers
Rangers - Neil Alexander - Steven Whittaker●, David Weir (c), Danny Wilson◆71, Sasa Papac - Steven Davis (Maurice Edu 45), Lee McCulloch●, Kevin Thomson◆53, Nacho Novo (Steven Smith 89) - Kris Boyd (Steven Naismith 79), Kenny Miller●. Tr: Walter Smith
St Mirren - Paul Gallacher - Jack Ross, Lee Mair●, John Potter (c), David Barron - Graham Carey, Hugh Murray● Andy Dorman 60, Steven Thomson, Garry Brady● (Stephen O'Donnell 85) - Billy Mehmet (Craig Dargo 70), Michael Higdon. Tr: Gus MacPherson

* Home team ● † Played at Hampden Park, Glasgow ● ‡ Played at Fir Park, Motherwell
Premier League clubs enter in the second round while those in European competition enter in the third round

SEN – SENEGAL

FIFA/COCA-COLA WORLD RANKING

1993	1994	1995	1996	1997	1998	1999	2000	2001	2002	2003	2004	2005	2006	2007	2008	2009	2010
56	50	47	58	85	95	79	88	65	27	33	31	30	41	38	50	89	70

					2010							Hi/Lo
Jan	Feb	Mar	Mar	Apr	May	Jul	Aug	Sep	Oct	Nov	Dec	**26**
89	91	94	72	77	75	91	91	79	73	75	70	**95**

The emergence of a new generation of players with the potential to match, or even better, the exploits of the 2002 side which reached the FIFA World Cup quarter-finals has given Senegalese football a new energy. After failure to qualify for the 2010 African Nations Cup finals in Angola, the Lions of Teranga unveiled a new and potentially deadly strike force at the start of the 2012 qualifiers. A 4-2 win away over the Democratic Republic of Congo was a resounding warning shot, followed up by a 7-1 pasting of Mauritius. Senegal must still meet Cameroon in the group but are heavily fancied to progress to the finals in Equatorial Guinea and Gabon. French-born Moussa Sow transferred his allegiance to the Senegal team before the start of the preliminaries and with Mamadou Niang and Papiss Cisse they have arguably the most exciting attack in African football. Amara Traore, who had been the senior member of the 2002 side, is now national coach and quickly sounded an independent note when he rejected widespread calls for a return to the side of El Hadji Diouf and he led Senegal to wins in five of their seven internationals in 2010. In domestic football Diaraf Dakar won the title for the first time in six years while the cup was won by second division Toure Kounda Mbour, who won promotion to the top flight at the same time.

FIFA WORLD CUP RECORD
1930-1966 DNE 1970-1986 DNQ 1990 DNE 1994-1998 DNQ **2002** 7 QF 2006-2010 DNQ

FEDERATION SENEGALAISE DE FOOTBALL (FSF)

VDN-Ouest-Foire en face du CICES, Case Postale 13021, Dakar
☎ +221 33 8692828
📠 +221 33 8200592
📧 fsf@senegalfoot.sn
🖥 www.senegalfoot.sn
FA 1960 CON 1963 FIFA 1962
P Augustin Senghor
GS Victor Cisse

FIFA BIG COUNT 2006

Total players	661 685
% of population	5.52%
Male	661 226
Female	459
Amateurs 18+	15 145
Unregistered	70 000
Professionals	100
Referees	2 960
Admin & coaches	2 064
Number of clubs	191
Number of teams	12 200

MAJOR CITIES/TOWNS

		Population
1	Dakar	2 535 431
2	Thiès	270 065
3	Mbour	207 286
4	Kaolack	180 409
5	Saint-Louis	175 988
6	Ziguinchor	165 027
7	Diourbel	105 713
8	Louga	85 344
9	Tambacounda	82 412
10	Kolda	65 714
11	Mbacké	57 731
12	Tivaouane	56 345
13	Richard Toll	50 102
14	Joal-Fadiouth	42 024
15	Kaffrine	30 846
16	Dahra	29 590
17	Bignona	26 603
18	Fatick	25 318
19	Vélingara	24 687

REPUBLIQUE DU SENEGAL • REPUBLIC OF SENEGAL

Capital	Dakar	Population	13 711 597 (67)	% in cities	42%
GDP per capita	$1600 (141)	Area km²	196 722 km² (87)	GMT +/-	0
Neighbours (km)	Gambia 740, Guinea 330, Guinea-Bissau 338, Mali 419, Mauritania 813 • Coast 531				

RECENT INTERNATIONAL MATCHES PLAYED BY SENEGAL

2008	Opponents	Score		Venue	Comp	Scorers	Att	Referee
12-01	Namibia	W	3-1	Dakar	Fr	Diomansy Kamara 2 [9 73], Henri Camara [83]		
16-01	Benin	W	2-1	Ouagadougou	Fr	Mendy [13], Gueye [82]		
23-01	Tunisia	D	2-2	Tamale	CNr1	Sall [44], Diomansy Kamara [66]		Nichimura JPN
27-01	Angola	L	1-3	Tamale	CNr1	Abdoulaye Faye [20]		Haimoudi ALG
31-01	South Africa	D	1-1	Kumasi	CNr1	Henri Camara [37]		Kotey GHA
31-05	Algeria	W	1-0	Dakar	WCq	Ibrahima Faye [80]	50 000	Kotey GHA
8-06	Gambia	D	0-0	Banjul	WCq		24 500	Ncobo RSA
15-06	Liberia	D	2-2	Monrovia	WCq	Diouf [47], Gueye [55]	18 000	Djaoupe TOG
21-06	Liberia	W	3-1	Dakar	WCq	Sonko [8], Diouf [32], Henri Camara [63]	40 000	Chaibou NIG
20-08	Libya	D	0-0	Tripoli	Fr			
5-09	Algeria	L	2-3	Blida	WCq	Dia [53], Sougou [91+]	35 000	Maillet SEY
11-10	Gambia	D	1-1	Dakar	WCq	Mangane [65]	50 000	Bennaceur TUN
22-12	Oman	L	0-1	Muscat	Fr			
2009								
28-03	Oman	L	0-2	Muscat	Fr			
1-04	Iran	D	1-1	Tehran	Fr	Papiss Cisse [77]		
12-08	Congo DR	W	2-1	Blois	Fr	Papiss Cisse 2 [66 69]		
5-09	Angola	D	1-1	Portimao	Fr	Mamadou Niang [54]		
14-10	Korea Republic	L	0-2	Seoul	Fr		31 574	Tan Hai CHN
2010								
3-03	Greece	W	2-0	Volos	Fr	Mamadou Niang [71], Guirane N'Daw [80]	10 000	Skomina SVN
10-05	Mexico	L	0-1	Chicago	Fr		60 610	Salazar USA
27-05	Denmark	L	0-2	Aalborg	Fr		14 112	Nijhuis NED
11-08	Cape Verde Islands	W	1-0	Dakar	Fr	Mame Biram Diouf [46]		
5-09	Congo DR	W	4-2	Kinshasa	CNq	Moussa Sow [6], Mamadou Niang 3 [12 22 57p]		Haimoudi ALG
9-10	Mauritius	W	7-0	Dakar	CNq	Papiss Cisse 3 [8 38 76], Mamadou Niang 2 [22 62], Moussa Sow [47], OG [90]		Bennett RSA
17-11	Gabon	W	2-1	Sannois St Gratien	Fr	Papiss Cisse [37], Issiar Dia [57]		

Fr = Friendly match • CN = CAF African Cup of Nations • WC = FIFA World Cup • q = qualifier • r1 = first round group • qf = quarter-final

SENEGAL NATIONAL TEAM HISTORICAL RECORDS

Past Coaches — Peter Schnittger GER 1999-2000 • Bruno Metsu FRA 2000-02 • Guy Stephan FRA 2002-05 • Abdoulaye Sarr 2005-06 • Henryk Kasperczak POL 2006-08 • Lamine N'Diaye 2008 • Amara Traore 2009-

COUPE NATIONALE 2009

Round of 16		Quarter–finals		Semi–finals		Final	
ASC Diaraf							
DUC Dakar		**ASC Diaraf**	3				
ASC Niary Tally Dakar	0	ETICS Mboro	0				
ETICS Mboro	1			**ASC Diaraf**	0 4p		
Saint-Louis FC	2			Guédiawaye FC Dakar	0 2p		
Stade Mbour	0	Saint-Louis FC	0				
Deggo Ouakam	0	**Guédiawaye FC Dakar**	2				
Guédiawaye FC Dakar	1					**ASC Diaraf ‡**	1
Jeanne d'Arc	1 3p					ASC Cambérène	0
Espoirs Bignona	1 2p	**Jeanne d'Arc**	1				
Thiès FC		US Ouakem	0				
US Ouakem				Jeanne d'Arc	0	**CUP FINAL**	
ASC Médiour Rufisque	3			**ASC Cambérène**	1	Demba Diop, Dakar 27-12-2010, Ref: Diatta	
CSS Richard Toll	1	ASC Médiour Rufisque	0				
ASC Yakaar		**ASC Cambérène**	1			Scorer - Pape Macou Sarr [13] for Diaraf	
ASC Cambérène				‡ Qualified for the CAF Confederation Cup			

SENEGAL 2010

CHAMPIONNAT PROFESSIONNEL LIGUE NATIONAL 1 POULE A

	Pl	W	D	L	F	A	Pts	Niary Tally	HLM	Douanes	DUC	Jeanne d'Arc	Richard Toll	La Linguère	Pt Autonome	Stade Mbour
ASC Niary Tally Dakar †	16	9	5	2	19	9	32		2-0	0-1	1-1	0-0	0-0	0-0	3-1	2-0
ASC HLM Dakar	16	7	5	4	16	14	26	0-2		1-1	1-1	1-1	0-2	1-0	2-1	2-0
AS Douanes	16	5	8	3	13	12	23	0-2	1-3		1-1	2-0	0-0	1-0	1-2	1-0
DUC Dakar	16	5	8	3	15	10	23	0-1	0-0	0-0		0-1	2-0	0-2	2-1	5-1
Jeanne d'Arc	16	5	8	3	11	11	23	0-1	1-1	0-1	1-1		2-1	0-0	0-0	
CSS Richard Toll	16	4	6	6	14	15	18	3-0	0-1	1-1	0-1	0-0		0-2	2-1	2-0
ASC La Linguère	16	5	5	6	10	10	20	0-1	0-1	0-1	0-0	1-2	2-2			2-1
UCST Port Autonome	16	3	4	9	13	18	13	1-2	0-1	1-1	0-1	1-0	3-1	0-1		0-0
Stade Mbour	16	1	7	8	10	22	10	2-2	2-1	1-1	0-0	2-3	0-0	0-0	1-1	

20/02/2010 - 20/07/2010 • † Qualified for the Championship final

SENEGAL 2010

CHAMPIONNAT PROFESSIONNEL LIGUE NATIONAL 1 POULE B

	Pl	W	D	L	F	A	Pts	Diaraf	Casa Sport	Ouakem	Gorée	Yakaar	Pikine	Guédiawaye	RS Yoff	Saloum
ASC Diaraf	16	8	7	1	22	3	31		**2-0**	0-0	1-0	6-0	0-0	3-0	1-1	3-0
Casa Sport	16	7	5	4	28	13	26	0-3		3-0	2-0	6-1	1-1	1-1	2-3	2-0
US Ouakem	16	6	6	4	12	12	24	1-0	0-2		0-0	2-0	**0-2**	0-0	1-1	0-0
US Gorée	16	5	7	4	11	12	22	1-1	1-0	1-0		1-0	0-0	0-0	3-2	0-0
ASC Yakaar	16	6	2	8	12	31	20	0-0	0-7	0-2	**2-0**		2-1	0-1	0-3	4-0
AS Pikine	16	4	7	5	13	11	19	0-1	0-0	1-1	1-2	3-0		0-0	2-1	2-0
Guédiawaye FC Dakar	16	4	6	6	11	15	18	0-0	0-0	2-3	2-1	0-1	1-0		1-2	2-0
Renaissance Yoff	16	3	7	6	14	16	16	0-0	0-1	0-1	0-0	0-0	0-0	1-2		0-0
AS Saloum Kaolack	16	3	5	8	8	18	14	0-1	1-1	0-1	1-1	0-1	2-0	2-0	2-0	

20/02/2010 - 28/07/2010 • † Qualified for the Championship final • Matches in bold awarded

FINAL 1ST LEG
Demba Diop, Dakar, 31-07-2010
ASC Niary Tally 1-0 ASC Diaraf
Scorer - Abdoulaye Badiane 72 for Niary Tally

FINAL 2ND LEG
Demba Diop, Dakar, 31-07-2010
ASC Diaraf 3-1 ASC Niary Tally
Scorers - Dieylani Fall 2 19 84, Mor Soumare 55 for Diaraf; Ass Mandaw Sy 87 for Niary Tally

MEDALS TABLE

		Overall			Lge	Cup		Africa			City
		G	S	B	G	G	S	G	S	B	
1	ASC Diaraf	25	6	1	11	14	6			1	Dakar
2	Jeanne d'Arc	16	5	3	10	6	4		1	3	Dakar
3	AS Douanes	11	2		5	6	2				Dakar
4	US Gorée	7	6	2	3	4	6			2	Dakar
5	ASC La Linguère	5	3		1	4	3				St-Louis
	SUNEOR	5	3		4	1	3				Diourbel

COUPE NATIONALE 2010

Round of 16		Quarter-finals		Semi-finals		Final	
Touré Kounda Mbour	4						
Walydan Thiès	1	Touré Kounda Mbour	0 5p				
CNEPS Thiès	0 3p	Diambars Diourbel	0 4p				
Diambars Diourbel	0 4p			Touré Kounda Mbour	1		
Avenir Kolda	3			CSS Richard Toll	0		
Zig Inter	2	Avenir Kolda	0 0p				
Bargueth	2 1p	CSS Richard Toll	0 3p				
CSS Richard Toll	2 4p					Touré Kounda Mbour ‡	0 5p
ASC Yeggo Dakar	1					US Gorée	0 4p
ASC Diaraf	0	ASC Yeggo Dakar	1				
US Guinguenéo	0	AS Pikine	0				
AS Pikine	1			ASC Yeggo Dakar	0		
Casa Sport	3			US Gorée	1		
ASC La Linguère	1	Casa Sport	1				
Ndar Guédj	2	US Gorée	2				
US Gorée	3						

CUP FINAL
Demba Diop, Dakar
16-10-2010, Ref: Fall

‡ Qualified for the CAF Confederation Cup

SEY – SEYCHELLES

FIFA/COCA-COLA WORLD RANKING

1993	1994	1995	1996	1997	1998	1999	2000	2001	2002	2003	2004	2005	2006	2007	2008	2009	2010
157	175	176	175	181	181	192	188	192	185	163	173	176	130	163	166	178	196

2010												Hi/Lo
Jan	Feb	Mar	Mar	Apr	May	Jul	Aug	Sep	Oct	Nov	Dec	**129**
178	175	174	175	174	178	177	185	184	196	195	195	**196**

A run of poor form at international level over the past four years, which has seen the country plummet from 129th to 195th in the FIFA/Coca-Cola World Ranking - the worst position of any of the 52 African nations - led to the decision to suspend participation in international tournaments for the national side. The island nation failed to enter the 2012 African Nations Cup qualifiers, having lost all six group games in the 2010 FIFA World Cup preliminaries, but Ralph Jean Louis was appointed coach to prepare a team for the next Indian Ocean Island Games. Traditionally, the football tournament of this multi-sport event is the title that the Seychelles national team most aspires to win and in 2011 Seychelles will host the games giving an added incentive to the preparations. In club football St Michel United won the league title, finishing 10 points ahead of second placed La Passe. They also won the League Cup but were denied a clean sweep of all the silverware when they were bundled out in the quarter-finals of the FA Cup, which St Louis Suns won with a 1-0 extra time win in the final over La Passe with Fabien Cadeau scoring the winner. La Passe competed in the 2010 African Champions League and won their home leg against Curepipe Starlight of Mauritius, but lost the return leg to be bundled out 3-2 on aggregate.

FIFA WORLD CUP RECORD
1930-1998 DNE   2002-2010 DNQ

SEYCHELLES FOOTBALL FEDERATION (SFF)

Maison Football,
Roche Caiman,
PO Box 843, Mahe
☎ +248 601160
📠 +248 601163
✉ sff@seychelles.net
🖥 www.sff.sc
FA 1979 CON 1986 FIFA 1986
P Suketu Patel
GS Jemmy Adela

FIFA BIG COUNT 2006

Total players	5 860
% of population	7.19%
Male	5 675
Female	185
Amateurs 18+	1 225
Youth under 18	835
Unregistered	800
Professionals	0
Referees	70
Admin & coaches	320
Number of clubs	20
Number of teams	60

MAJOR CITIES/TOWNS

		Population
1	Victoria	25 500
2	Anse Royal	3 700
3	Cascade	2 400
4	Takamaka	2 200
5	Anse Boileau	2 000

REPUBLIC OF SEYCHELLES

Capital	Victoria	Population	87 476 (197)	% in cities	54%
GDP per capita	$21 000 (59)	Area km²	455 km² (198)	GMT +/-	+4
Neighbours (km)	Coast 491				

RECENT INTERNATIONAL MATCHES PLAYED BY THE SEYCHELLES

2006	Opponents	Score		Venue	Comp	Scorers	Att	Referee
22-07	Namibia	D	1-1	Katutura	CCr1	Wilnes Brutus [18]. W 4-2p		Simisse MRI
23-07	Zambia	L	0-2	Katutura	CCr1			Ngobo RSA
3-09	Sudan	L	0-3	Khartoum	CNq			Kidane ERI
7-10	Mauritius	W	2-1	Roche Caiman	CNq	Wilnes Brutus 2 [23 81]		Raolimanana MAD
2007								
24-03	Tunisia	L	0-3	Victoria	CNq			Ssegonga UGA
28-04	Mozambique	L	0-2	Maputo	CCr1			Mpopo LES
29-04	Madagascar	L	0-5	Maputo	CCr1			Mpopo LES
2-06	Tunisia	L	0-4	Rades/Tunis	CNq			Diatta SEN
16-06	Sudan	L	0-2	Roche Caiman	CNq			Dlamini SWZ
14-08	Mauritius	L	0-3	Antananarivo	Fr			
9-09	Mauritius	D	1-1	Curepipe	CNq	Godfrey Denis [43p]		Mwandike TAN
2008								
1-06	Burundi	L	0-1	Bujumbura	WCq		4 000	Imiere NGA
7-06	Tunisia	L	0-2	Victoria	WCq		2 033	Faduco MOZ
14-06	Burkina Faso	L	2-3	Victoria	WCq	Philip Zialor [47], Don Annacoura [53]	1 000	Seechurn MRI
21-06	Burkina Faso	L	1-4	Ouagadougou	WCq	Bernard St Ange [44]	12 500	Lamptey GHA
19-07	Mauritius	W	7-0	Witbank	CCr1	Colin Laporte [14], Philip Zialor 4 [35 51 59 88], Don Annacoura [66], Trevor Poiret [87]		Kaoma ZAM
21-07	Madagascar	D	1-1	Witbank	CCr1	Godfrey Denis [48]		Kaoma ZAM
23-07	Swaziland	L	0-1	Witbank	CCr1			Katjimune NAM
6-09	Burundi	L	1-2	Victoria	WCq	Philip Zialor [63]	3 000	Djaoupe TOG
11-10	Tunisia	L	0-5	Tunis/Rades	WCq		10 000	Diatta SEN
2009								
18-10	Swaziland	L	1-2	Bulawayo	CCr1	Nelson Laurence [8]		Carvalho ANG
20-10	Comoros	L	1-2	Bulawayo	CCr1	Don Anacoura [54]		Rachide MOZ
22-10	Botswana	L	0-2	Bulawayo	CCr1			Seechurn MRI
2010								
No international matches played in 2010								

Fr = Friendly match • CN = CAN African Cup of Nations • IO = Indian Ocean Games • CC = COSAFA Castle Cup • WC = FIFA World Cup
q = qualifier • r1 = first round group

SEYCHELLES 2010

BARCLAYS LEAGUE DIVISION ONE

	Pl	W	D	L	F	A	Pts	St Michel Utd	La Passe	Anse Reunion	St Louis Suns	Light Stars	St Francis	Dynamo	St Roch Utd
St Michel United †	21	17	3	1	52	11	54		0-0 2-1	7-0 3-0	0-0	3-0 7-2	2-2 4-0	4-1	4-1
La Passe	21	14	2	5	46	14	44	2-0		1-0	1-0 3-0	3-0 1-0	3-0	1-0 1-1	6-1 7-0
Anse Reunion	21	10	4	7	42	37	34	0-1	2-1 1-2		1-1	2-1 5-2	1-1	2-1 2-4	3-1
St Louis Suns United	21	9	6	6	34	24	33	1-2 0-2	1-0	1-3 2-2		3-0 0-0	1-0	3-2	4-1
Light Stars	21	6	5	10	20	37	23	0-1	0-4	1-1	1-1		0-0	3-1 1-0	3-1 1-0
St Francis	21	5	6	10	16	39	21	0-1	1-0 0-4	0-6 3-2	1-4 1-0	2-1 0-1		1-2	2-1 0-0
Northern Dynamo	21	5	4	12	27	35	19	0-2 0-2	3-2	1-2	1-1 1-2	0-1	2-2 0-0		2-0
St Roch United	21	2	2	17	23	63	8	0-3 1-2	2-3	0-2 3-5	0-5 2-4	2-2	4-0	0-3 3-2	

26/02/2010 - 23/10/2010 • † Qualified for the CAF Champions League
Relegation play-off: **Northern Dynamo** 5-3 The Lions

SEYCHELLES 2010 DIVISION TWO

	Pl	W	D	L	F	A	Pts
Côte d'Or	18	13	3	2	52	23	42
The Lions	18	12	4	2	48	14	40
St John Bosco	18	10	2	6	48	36	32
Mont Buxton	18	7	3	8	23	27	24
Fire Brigade	18	7	1	10	37	32	22
Cadets U–20	18	6	3	9	35	44	21
SPDF	18	5	5	8	24	38	20
Super Magic Brothers	18	5	4	9	24	36	19
Foresters	18	5	3	10	33	41	18
Mont Fleuri	18	4	4	10	25	48	16

26/02/2010 - 23/10/2010

AIRTEL LEAGUE CUP 2010

Semi-finals		Final	
St Michel United	3		
Anse Reunion	0		
		St Michel United	0 4p
		Light Stars	0 3p
La Passe	1		
Light Stars	3	17-07-2010	

MEDALS TABLE

		Overall			League			Cup		LC		City
		G	S	B	G	S	B	G	S	G	S	
1	St Michel United	20	6		9	5		7		4	1	Anse aux Pins
2	Red Star	8	6	4	2	2	4	4	3	2	1	Anse aux Pins
3	La Passe	5	4	4	4	2	4		1	1	1	La Passe
4	St Louis Suns Utd †	4	10	4	1	3	4	3	4		3	Victoria
5	Anse Reunion	3	5	3	1	1	3	1	3	1	1	Anse Reunion
6	Seychelles MB	1	1		1			1				Victoria
7	Light Stars			2					1		1	Grand Anse

LAND MARINE FA CUP 2010

Round of 16		Quarter–finals		Semi–finals		Final	
St Louis Suns	6						
Mont Buxton	0	**St Louis Suns**	3				
West Coast Brothers	0	Cadets U–20	0				
Cadets U–20	5			**St Louis Suns**	4		
St Michel United	2			St Roch United	1		
Northern Dynamo	1	St Michel United	1 2p				
Anse Reunion	0	**St Roch United**	1 4p				
St Roch United	1					**St Louis Suns**	1
Light Stars						La Passe	0
Quincy		**Light Stars**	3				
Mont Fleuri	0	St Francis	1				
St Francis	7			Light Stars	1		
Seychelles MB	2			**La Passe**	2		
St John Bosco	1	Seychelles MB	1				
Foresters	0	**La Passe**	6				
La Passe	9						

CUP FINAL
Stade Linite, Victoria
7-11-2010
Scorer - Fabien Cadeau 98 for St Louis Suns

SIN – SINGAPORE

FIFA/COCA-COLA WORLD RANKING

1993	1994	1995	1996	1997	1998	1999	2000	2001	2002	2003	2004	2005	2006	2007	2008	2009	2010
75	95	104	92	103	81	104	101	115	118	106	112	92	111	126	132	110	140

2010												Hi/Lo
Jan	Feb	Mar	Mar	Apr	May	Jul	Aug	Sep	Oct	Nov	Dec	73
110	120	120	127	127	127	121	120	119	127	138	140	140

Singapore's status among the elite of the game in Southeast Asia suffered a blow as Raddy Avramovic's side failed to progress beyond the group stages of the AFF Suzuki Cup at the end of the year. Having appeared in four of the seven finals played before the tournament - winning three of them - the outcome was a sobering one. Many within the squad were involved in the back-to-back victories in 2004 and 2006 but time has taken it toll and draws with Myanmar and the Philippines left the Singaporeans needing to win against hosts and defending champions Vietnam but they lost 1-0 and were knocked out at the group stage for the first time since 2002. It left the long-serving Avramovic complaining about the lack of preparation time with his squad due to an increasing number of them having left the local S-League to play elsewhere in Southeast Asia. Having earlier failed to qualify for the 2011 AFC Asian Cup in Qatar the football association took the drastic decision to disband the team in January 2011. Avramovic certainly has a point with regard to the S-League which has become something of a nursery for foreign teams. In 2010 it was won by Etoile FC, a team made up of French nationals. Etoile were the eighth 'foreign' team to have joined the league but the first to win it as the squeeze on Singaporean players intensifies.

FIFA WORLD CUP RECORD
1930-1974 DNE 1978-2010 DNQ

FOOTBALL ASSOCIATION OF SINGAPORE (FAS)

100 Tyrwhitt Road,
Jalan Besar Stadium, 01-02,
Singapore 207542
☎ +65 63483477
📠 +65 63921194
✉ winstonlee@fas.org.sg
🖥 www.fas.org.sg
FA 1892 CON 1954 FIFA 1952
P Zainudin Nordin
GS Winston Lee

FIFA BIG COUNT 2006

Total players	197 003
% of population	4.39%
Male	188 626
Female	8 377
Amateurs 18+	1 250
Youth under 18	7 300
Unregistered	181 000
Professionals	233
Referees	171
Admin & coaches	1 345
Number of clubs	41
Number of teams	104

MAJOR CITIES/TOWNS

		Population
1	Singapore	4 657 542

The Sinagore metropolitan area contains various centres including

Ang Mo Kio	174 700
Bedok	289 000
Bukit Batok	141 600
Bukit Merah	149 900
Choa Chu Kang	165 800
Geylang	117 900
Hougang	211 500
Jurong West	243 000
Pasir Ris	127 200
Queenstown	97 200
Sengkang	139 500
Tampines	257 400
Woodlands	228 800
Yishun	179 300

REPUBLIC OF SINGAPORE

Capital	Singapore	Population	4 657 542 (117)	% in cities	100%
GDP per capita	$51 600 (8)	Area km²	697 km² (192)	GMT +/-	+8
Neighbours (km)	Coast 193				

RECENT INTERNATIONAL MATCHES PLAYED BY SINGAPORE

2008	Opponents	Score		Venue	Comp	Scorers	Att	Referee
6-02	Saudi Arabia	L	0-2	Riyadh	WCq		10 000	Basma SYR
22-03	Australia	D	0-0	Singapore	Fr		6 282	Prayoon THA
26-03	Lebanon	W	2-0	Singapore	WCq	Duric [8], Fazrul Shahul [23]	10 118	Takayama JPN
28-05	Bahrain	L	0-1	Singapore	Fr			
2-06	Uzbekistan	L	3-7	Singapore	WCq	Duric [16], Fahrudin [31p], Wilkinson [73]	28 750	Albadwawi UAE
7-06	Uzbekistan	L	0-1	Tashkent	WCq		12 867	Kim Dong Jin KOR
14-06	Saudi Arabia	L	0-2	Singapore	WCq		23 000	Williams AUS
22-06	Lebanon	W	2-1	Beirut	WCq	Dayoub OG [72], Wilkinson [73]	500	Moradi IRN
14-10	Vietnam	D	0-0	Hanoi	Fr			
29-11	Malaysia	D	2-2	Petaling Jaya	Fr	Duric 2 [10 45]		
5-12	Cambodia	W	5-0	Jakarta	AFFr1	Casmir 2 [44 73], Fahrudin [61p], Indra [71], Shah [89]	18 000	Mahapab THA
7-12	Myanmar	W	3-1	Jakarta	AFFr1	Shah [1], Casmir 2 [16 74]	21 000	Phung VIE
9-12	Indonesia	W	2-0	Jakarta	AFFr1	Khaizan [3], Jiayi [50]	50 000	Ramachandran MAS
17-12	Vietnam	D	0-0	Hanoi	AFFsf		40 000	Ramachandran MAS
21-12	Vietnam	L	0-1	Singapore	AFFsf		55 000	Mohd Salleh MAS
2009								
14-01	Iran	L	0-6	Tehran	ACq		3 000	Mansour LIB
28-01	Jordan	W	2-1	Singapore	ACq	Casmir [21], Shah [63]	6 188	Green AUS
12-08	China PR	D	1-1	Singapore	Fr	Shah [7]. L 3-4p		
22-10	Turkmenistan	W	4-2	Ho Chi Minh City	Fr	Duric 2 [9 38], Masturi [60] Khairul Amri [77]		
24-10	Vietnam	D	2-2	Ho Chi Minh City	Fr	Duric [26], Fazrul Shahul [51]		
4-11	Indonesia	W	3-1	Singapore	Fr	Fahrudin [85]		
14-11	Thailand	L	1-3	Singapore	ACq	Fahrudin [84p]	22 183	Takayama JPN
18-11	Thailand	W	1-0	Bangkok	ACq	Duric [37]	30 000	Balideh QAT
31-12	Oman	L	1-4	Singapore	Fr	Daud [76]		
2010								
6-01	Iran	L	1-3	Singapore	ACq	Shah [31]	7 356	Sun Baojie CHN
17-01	Thailand	L	0-1	Nakhon Ratch'ma	Fr		20 000	Mbaga TAN
20-01	Denmark	L	1-5	Nakhon Ratch'ma	Fr	Fazrul Nawaz [84]		
23-01	Poland	L	1-6	Nakhon Ratch'ma	Fr	Shi Jiayi [39]		Amwayi KEN
3-03	Jordan	L	1-2	Amman	ACq	Shah [48]	17 000	Abdou QAT
11-08	Thailand	L	0-1	Nonthaburi	Fr			Aonrak THA
2-11	Korea DPR	L	1-2	Hanoi	Fr	Duric [41]		
4-11	Vietnam	D	1-1	Hanoi	Fr	Shi Jiayi [24]		
2-12	Philippines	D	1-1	Hanoi	AFFr1	Duric [65]		Mahapab THA
5-12	Myanmar	W	2-1	Hanoi	AFFr1	Duric [62], Casnir [94+]		Tao Ranchang CHN
8-12	Vietnam	L	0-1	Hanoi	AFFr1		40 000	Mahapab THA

Fr = Friendly match • AC = AFC Asian Cup • AFF = ASEAN Football Federation Championship • WC = FIFA World Cup
q = qualifier • r1 = first round group • sf = semi-final • f = final

SINGAPORE NATIONAL TEAM HISTORICAL RECORDS

Caps 121 - Aide Iskandar 1995-2007 • 115 - Shunmugham Subramani 1996-2007 • 100 - Nasri Nasir 1990-2004

Goals 52 - Fandi Ahmad 1978-97

Past Coaches Hussein Aljunied 1984-86 • Seak Poh Leong 1986-88 • Jita Singh 1988-89 • Robin Chan 1990-92 • Milous Kvacek CZE 1992 • PN Sivaji 1992-94 • Ken Worden ENG 1994 • Douglas Moore ENG 1994-96 • Barry Whitbread ENG 1996-98 • Vincent Subramaniam 1998-2000 • Jan Poulsen DEN 2000-02 • Radojko Avramovic SRB 2003-

SINGAPORE 2010

S.LEAGUE

	Pl	W	D	L	F	A	Pts	Etoile	Tampines	Home Utd	SAFFC	Geylang	Gombak	Albirex	Balestier	Lions	Beijing G	Senkang	Woodlands
Etoile FC	33	21	7	5	54	23	70		4-0	1-0	3-0 0-3	2-2 1-0	0-0	0-1	1-0 3-0	2-0 3-0	0-0	2-2 1-0	4-0 2-0
Tampines Rovers ‡	33	21	6	6	68	30	69	1-1 1-2		0-0 0-3	1-1 2-0	0-1 2-1	3-3	3-0	3-2 4-1	3-0 1-1	4-0	3-0	5-0
Home United	33	18	11	4	55	31	65	3-3 1-0	1-0		1-1 0-0	3-0 1-0	2-0	1-0	2-2 0-0	2-2 2-1	3-2	2-1	2-0 2-2
S'pore Armed Forces	33	16	5	12	56	41	53	2-3	0-1	2-5		1-1 0-2	0-1	3-0 1-2	2-1 0-2	5-2	3-0 4-2	2-1	3-1 1-0
Geylang United	33	12	11	10	32	30	47	0-1	0-0	0-3	0-3		0-0 0-0	1-1 1-1	0-0	0-0	1-3 3-0	3-2 4-1	1-0 0-1
Gombak United	33	12	10	11	33	25	46	1-0 0-1	0-1 0-2	1-0 1-1	1-0 0-2	1-0		3-1	0-1	2-0 1-1	0-1	3-0	5-0
Albirex Niigata	33	9	10	14	31	42	37	0-0 2-4	1-3 0-1	1-2 2-2	1-3	1-2	0-0 1-2		0-1	1-2 1-1	1-0	1-1	1-0
Balestier Khalsa	33	10	7	16	26	40	37	0-3	0-2	0-1	1-1	0-2 0-1	1-2 0-0	1-0 1-1		0-3	1-0 3-0	1-0	0-1 1-1
Young Lions §5	33	9	12	12	37	45	34	1-2	2-1	2-1	4-3 1-0	0-1 2-2	1-0	1-1	3-0 0-2		0-0 1-1	0-1 0-1	2-2 1-0
Beijing Guoan §5	33	10	6	17	30	49	31	0-1 3-1	1-2 2-5	4-1 0-3	1-2	0-1	1-0 1-1	0-1 2-1	3-1	1-0		1-1 1-0	2-1
Senkang Punggol	33	7	6	20	24	48	27	0-1	0-3 1-3	0-1	1-3 0-1	0-2	2-1 0-0	1-0 1-0	1-1 2-1	0-2	2-2	1-0	0-1
Woodlands Wellington	33	4	7	22	18	60	19	0-2	0-4 2-4	2-2 1-2	0-4	0-0	2-1 0-3	1-2 0-0	1-2	1-1	0-0 0-1	0-1 0-1	

1/02/2010 - 12/11/2010 • ‡ Qualified for the AFC Cup • ‡ Qualified for the AFC Cup • § = points deducted
Top scorers: 21 - Frederic Mendy FRA, Etoile • 20 - Aleksandar Duric, Tampines • 17 - Shahril Ishak, Home Utd • 15 - Qiu Li, Tampines

SINGAPORE LEAGUE CUP 2010

Quarter-finals		Semi-finals		Final	
Etoile FC	3				
Geylang United	2	Etoile FC	1		
SAFFC	1	Senkang P'ggol	0		
Senkang P'ggol	3			Etoile FC	3
Gombak United	1			Woodlands W	1
Home United	0	Gombak United	2 3p		
Tampines Rov	0	Woodlands W	2 4p		
Woodlands W	1				

Preliminary round: Etoile 2-0 Balestier ; Geylang Utd 0-0 4-2p Young Lions;
Sengkang Punggol 3-1 Beijing Guoan; Woodlands Wellington 0-0 4-3p Abirex
Final: Jalan Besar, 7-03-2010, Att: 2814, Ref: Pandian. Scorers - Matthias
Verschave 2 [50] [84], Leeroy Anton [90] for Etoile; Abdelhadi Laakkad [45] for Woodlands

MEDALS TABLE

		All	Lge	Cup	LC
		G	G	G	G
1	Singapore Armed Forces	19	11	8	
2	Geylang United	18	11	7	
3	Tanjong Pagar United	9	2	7	
4	Tampines Rovers	8	5	3	
	Home United	8	3	5	
6	Farrer Park United	4	1	3	
7	Toa Payoh United	2		2	
	Etoile FC	2	1		1
9	Perth Kangaroos	1	1		
	Bangkok Glass	1		1	
	Balestier United	1		1	
	Jurong Town	1		1	
	Woodlands Wellington	1			1
	Gombak United	1			1
	DPMM Brunei	1			1

RHB SINGAPORE CUP 2010

First round		Quarter–finals		Semi–finals		Final	
Bangkok Glass	5						
S'pore Armed Forces	3	Bangkok Glass	3 3				
Gombak United	1	South Melbourne *	1 3				
South Melbourne	2			Bangkok Glass *	1 2		
Kitchee SC	2			Etoile FC	1 0		
Beijing Guoan	1	Kitchee SC	0 4				
Phnon Penh Crown	1	Etoile FC *	2 4				
Etoile FC	2					Bangkok Glass	1
Young Lions	2					Tampines Rovers	0
Home United	0	Young Lions *	1 0				
Senkang Punggol	0	Albirex Niigata	0 0				
Albirex Niigata	1			Young Lions	0 0		
Balestier Khalsa	2			Tampines Rovers *	2 1		
Geylang United	1	Balestier Khalsa	0 1				
Woodlands Wellington	1	Tampines Rovers *	3 3	3rd place: Etoile 3-0 Young Lions			
Tampines Rovers	2			* Home Team in the first leg			

CUP FINAL

Jalan Besar, Singapore
14-11-2010, Att: 3943
Ref: Ng Kai Lam

Scorer - Benoit Croissant OG [57]

SKN – ST KITTS AND NEVIS

FIFA/COCA-COLA WORLD RANKING

1993	1994	1995	1996	1997	1998	1999	2000	2001	2002	2003	2004	2005	2006	2007	2008	2009	2010
166	175	150	121	127	132	137	146	129	109	134	118	129	143	160	152	156	121

	2010											Hi/Lo
Jan	Feb	Mar	Mar	Apr	May	Jul	Aug	Sep	Oct	Nov	Dec	**108**
156	155	151	149	151	151	147	145	151	129	122	121	**176**

Almost a decade on since their last appearance in the finals of the Digicel Caribbean Cup, St Kitts and Nevis are beginning to make their presence felt again in Caribbean football although they fell short of reaching the 2010 finals in Martinique. With star striker Atiba Harris helping his club side FC Dallas reach the MLS Cup Final for the first time, coach Lester Harris went into the first qualifying round in St Vincent relying on another foreign-based striker, Keith Gumbs, to bolster the ranks of local-based players and they topped the group ahead of the hosts, Barbados and Montserrat. Gumbs, who has carved a successful career for himself in Indonesia - he won the cup with his club Sriwijaya in 2010 - missed the second round group in Grenada, however, and his experience was missed as St Kitts lost to Guadeloupe and Grenada before salvaging some pride with a victory over Puerto Rico in the final match. At home it was a great season for the most successful club on the island, Newtown United. They topped both the first and second rounds of the championship before comfortably beating St Peters Strikers 7-1 on aggregate in the final in May. Earlier in the month, striker Ian Lake - a consistent scorer for the national team - had helped inspire Newtown to a 2-0 victory over St Pauls in the Cup Final.

FIFA WORLD CUP RECORD
1930-1994 DNE 1998-2010 DNQ

ST KITTS AND NEVIS FOOTBALL ASSOCIATION (SKNFA)

Warner Park, PO Box 465, Basseterre
☎ +1 869 4668502
📠 +1 869 4659033
✉ info@sknfa.com
🖥 www.sknfa.com
FA 1932 CON 1992 FIFA 1992
P Anthony Johnson
GS Stanley Jacobs

FIFA BIG COUNT 2006

Total players	3 500
% of population	8.94%
Male	3 100
Female	400
Amateurs 18+	900
Youth under 18	600
Unregistered	600
Professionals	0
Referees	0
Admin & coaches	100
Number of clubs	30
Number of teams	40

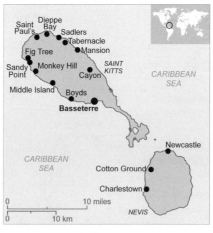

MAJOR CITIES/TOWNS

		Population
1	Basseterre	13 243
2	Charlestown	2 093
3	Saint Paul's	1 319
4	Sadlers	1 037
5	Middle Island	905
6	Tabernacle	830
7	Cayon	806
8	Mansion	798
9	Sandy Point	758
10	Boyds	749
11	Monkey Hill	728
12	Dieppe Bay	622
13	Gingerland	572
14	Newcastle	570
15	Fig Tree	490
16	Cotton Ground	422

FEDERATION OF SAINT KITTS AND NEVIS

Capital	Basseterre	Population	40 131 (209)	% in cities	32%
GDP per capita	$19 100 (65)	Area km²	261 km² (211)	GMT +/-	-4
Neighbours (km)	Coast 135				

SKN – ST KITTS AND NEVIS

RECENT INTERNATIONAL MATCHES PLAYED BY ST KITTS AND NEVIS

2006	Opponents	Score		Venue	Comp	Scorers	Att	Referee
20-09	Barbabdos	D	1-1	St John's	CCq	Atiba Harris [60]	300	Campbell JAM
22-09	Anguilla	W	6-1	St John's	CCq	George Isaac 2 [14 68], Ian Lake 3 [30 46 79], Jevon Francis [81]	500	Phillips GRN
24-09	Antigua and Barbuda	L	0-1	St John's	CCq		2 800	Wijngaarde SUR
2007								
18-11	Antigua and Barbuda	W	3-0	Basseterre	Fr	Jevon Francis [36], Christian OG [43], Aiden Nurse [44]	3 000	Matthew SKN
1-12	Antigua and Barbuda	L	0-2	St John's	Fr		3 800	Willett ATG
14-12	Bermuda	W	2-1	Hamilton	Fr	Jevon Francis [25], Ian Lake [38]	800	Mauchette BER
16-12	Bermuda	L	2-4	Hamilton	Fr	Imran Ponteen [44], Stedro Charles	1 500	Raynor BER
2008								
6-02	Belize	L	1-3	Guatemala City	WCq	Gerard Williams [13]	500	Stennet JAM
26-03	Belize	D	1-1	Basseterre	WCq	Orlando Mitchum [84]	2 000	Brizan TRI
8-06	Antigua and Barbuda	L	0-2	St John's	Fr		4 000	Willett ATG
24-09	British Virgin Islands	W	4-0	Basseterre	CCq	Jevon Francis [15], Zevon Archibald [21], Venton James OG [52], Ian Lake [77]	500	Charles DMA
28-09	Barbados	L	1-3	Basseterre	CCq	George Isaac [13]	500	Charles DMA
5-11	Guyana	D	1-1	Macoya	CCq	Ian Lake [29]	750	Cambridge VIN
7-11	Trinidad and Tobago	L	1-3	Macoya	CCq	Jevon Francis [86]		Wijngaarde SUR
9-11	Antigua and Barbuda	L	3-4	Macoya	CCq	Jevon Francis 3 [57 70 80]	1 000	Wijngaarde SUR
2009								
12-07	Trinidad and Tobago	L	2-3	Basseterre	Fr	Ian Lake [48], Gerard Williams [62]	3 100	Matthew SKN
16-08	Jamaica	L	0-1	Basseterre	Fr		5 000	Willett ATG
5-09	St Vincent/Grenadines	W	3-0	Kingstown	Fr	Stephen Clarke [50], Tishan Hanley [55], Alexis Saddler [81]	3 500	Cambridge VIN
20-09	St Vincent/Grenadines	D	1-1	Basseterre	Fr	Shashi Isaac [10]	1 600	Matthew SKN
2010								
28-08	Antigua and Barbuda	D	1-1	Basseterre	Fr	Ian Lake [30]	500	Matthew SKN
6-10	Barbados	D	1-1	Kingstown	CCq	George Isaac [62]	250	Elskamp SUR
8-10	St Vincent/Grenadines	D	1-1	Kingstown	CCq	Jevon Francis [40]	1 600	Jauregui ANT
10-10	Montserrat	W	4-0	Kingstown	CCq	Alexis Saddler 2 [18 31], Keith Gumbs [21], Ian Lake [90]	1 100	Elskamp SUR
22-10	Guadeloupe	L	1-2	St George's	CCq	Jevon Francis [83p]	300	Taylor BRB
24-10	Grenada	L	0-2	St George's	CCq		500	Morrison JAM
26-10	Puerto Rico	W	1-0	St George's	CCq	Jevon Francis [90]	500	Morrison JAM

Fr = Friendly match • CC = Digicel Caribbean Cup • WC = FIFA World Cup • q = qualifier

ST KITTS AND NEVIS NATIONAL TEAM HISTORICAL RECORDS

Past Coaches: Ces Podd 1999-2002 • Elvis Browne 2002-04 • Lenny Lake 2004-07 • Lester Morris 2008-

ST KITTS 2009–10

SKNFA DIGICEL SUPER LEAGUE FIRST STAGE

	Pl	W	D	L	F	A	Pts	Newtown	St Pauls	St Peters	Conaree	Superstars	Hotspurs	Mantab	Challengers	CFBC	WAHS
Newtown United †	18	13	4	1	63	6	43		2-3	0-0	2-0	1-1	4-0	3-0	8-0	1-0	9-0
St Pauls United †	18	11	6	1	43	14	39	1-1		3-1	0-1	0-0	2-2	3-1	4-1	2-1	6-1
St Peters Strikers †	18	8	7	3	42	16	31	0-3	0-3		1-0	1-1	0-0	3-1	5-0	5-1	6-0
Conaree United †	18	9	4	5	36	18	31	0-0	0-2	1-1		2-2	2-3	1-1	8-1	3-0	1-0
Village Superstars	18	7	9	2	38	18	30	0-2	2-2	1-1	2-1		1-2	1-1	4-0	2-0	4-0
Garden Hotspurs	18	6	6	6	21	26	24	0-5	0-0	1-1	1-2	0-0		1-2	1-2	2-1	2-0
Mantab United	18	5	6	7	24	28	21	1-2	1-1	0-2	1-2	2-2	1-1		2-1	3-0	3-0
Challengers United	18	4	0	14	24	57	12	0-3	0-4	1-2	0-3	1-5	3-2	0-1		6-2	7-0
Clarence Fitzroy BC	18	3	2	13	17	49	11	0-2	0-6	0-0	1-4	2-6	0-2	3-1	1-0		1-1
Washington Archibald	18	1	2	15	9	85	5	0-15	0-1	0-13	0-5	0-4	0-1	2-2	2-1	3-4	

1/11/2009 - 18/04/2010 • † Qualified for play-offs

SKNFA DIGICEL SUPER LEAGUE SUPER FOUR PLAY-OFFS

	Pl	W	D	L	F	A	Pts
Newtown United †	3	2	1	0	8	2	7
St Peters Strikers †	3	2	0	1	3	4	6
St Pauls United	3	1	1	1	4	3	4
Conaree United	3	0	0	3	1	7	0

15/05/2010 - 23/05/2010 • † Qualified for the final

SKNFA DIGICEL SUPER LEAGUE FINAL

Champions	Score	Runners-up
Newtown United	3-0 4-1	St Peters Strikers

1st leg. 26-05-2010. Scorers - Kiethroy Richards [35], Kennedy Isles [48], Alexis Saddler [54] for Newtown; 2nd leg. 29-05-2010. Scorers - Orlando Mitchum [26], Ian Lake [31], Jason Isaac [77], Zevon Archibald [80] for Newtown; Kirkland Harris [1] for St Peters

MEDALS TABLE

		Overall	Lge	Cup	Town
		G	G	G	
1	Newtown United	17	15	2	Basseterre
2	Village Superstars	7	5	2	Basseterre
3	Garden Hotspurs	4	4		Basseterre
4	St Pauls United	2	2		Basseterre
	Cayon Rockets	2	1	1	Cayon

SKNFA CUP 2010

Eighth-finals	Quarter-finals	Semi-finals	Final
Newtown United			
Trafalgar Southstars	**Newtown United**		
Lodge Patriots	Mantab United		
Mantab United w-0		**Newtown United** 2	
Washington Archibald w-0		Conaree United 1	
St Kitts & Nevis U–18	Washington Archibald 0		
St Kitts & Nevis U–16 0	**Conaree United** 2		
Conaree United 6			**Newtown United** 2
Molineaux 1			St Pauls United 0
St Peters Strikers 0	**Molineaux**		
Rivers of Living Waters	Parson Ground School		
Parson Ground School		Molineaux 1	
Village Superstars 2		**St Pauls United** 2	
St Thomas Strikers 0	Village Superstars 0		
Garden Hotspurs 2 3p	**St Pauls United** 1		
St Pauls United 2 4p			

CUP FINAL

8-05-2010

Scorers - Ian Lake [51], Maliva Harris [89] for Newtowmn

SLE – SIERRA LEONE

FIFA/COCA-COLA WORLD RANKING

1993	1994	1995	1996	1997	1998	1999	2000	2001	2002	2003	2004	2005	2006	2007	2008	2009	2010
76	76	58	84	84	111	120	129	138	133	146	160	163	148	156	116	138	125

2010												Hi/Lo
Jan	Feb	Mar	Mar	Apr	May	Jul	Aug	Sep	Oct	Nov	Dec	51
138	132	135	135	133	130	139	137	132	122	125	125	172

The era of Sierra Leone's most famous player Mohamed Kallon has come to an end with injuries forcing the former Internazionale forward to call time on his playing days at the age of 31. For a country like Sierra Leone, beset by decades of civil strife, with no sporting infrastructure to speak of and with little pedigree on the African football circuit, it is a big loss but remarkably as Kallon exits the stage so enters Rodney Strasser, a 20-year-old who featured for Milan for the first time in 2010. Along with Mohamed Bangura, who plays for AIK Stockholm in Sweden, the pair hold the hopes of a nation in their hands as the national team looks to become more competitive in the international arena. Sierra Leone's only two matches in 2010 both ended in draws but both were against top ranked teams in what is a very difficult qualifying group for the 2012 African Nations Cup. In September they held African champions Egypt to a 1-1 draw in Cairo and followed that in October with a 0-0 draw against South Africa in Freetown. In the last five years, the Leone Stars have won just three internationals but they could turn out to be key players in a group that also contains Niger. In the Sierra Leone league defending champions East End Lions retained their league title and are now just one behind record holders Mighty Blackpool with 15.

FIFA WORLD CUP RECORD

1930-1970 DNE 1974-1986 DNQ 1990-1994 DNE 1998-2010 DNQ

SIERRA LEONE FOOTBALL ASSOCIATION (SLFA)

21 Battery Street, Kingtom, PO Box 672, Freetown
☎ +232 22 240071
📠 +232 22 241339
✉ starssierra@yahoo.com
🖥 slfa.1hwy.com
FA 1967 CON 1967 FIFA 1967
P Nahim Khadi
GS Abdul Rahman Swaray

FIFA BIG COUNT 2006

Total players	259 630
% of population	4.32%
Male	247 240
Female	12 390
Amateurs 18+	840
Youth under 18	5 640
Unregistered	15 150
Professionals	0
Referees	263
Admin & coaches	2 200
Number of clubs	24
Number of teams	196

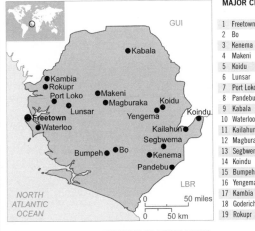

MAJOR CITIES/TOWNS

		Population
1	Freetown	827 985
2	Bo	206 769
3	Kenema	164 125
4	Makeni	99 549
5	Koidu	91 042
6	Lunsar	23 609
7	Port Loko	22 397
8	Pandebu	19 378
9	Kabala	18 616
10	Waterloo	17 469
11	Kailahun	17 210
12	Magbaraka	15 770
13	Segbwema	15 714
14	Koindu	15 659
15	Bumpeh	14 825
16	Yengema	13 225
17	Kambia	12 282
18	Goderich	12 178
19	Rokupr	12 166

REPUBLIC OF SIERRA LEONE

Capital	Freetown	Population	6 440 053 (103)	% in cities	38%
GDP per capita	$900 (217)	Area km²	71 740 km² (118)	GMT +/-	0
Neighbours (km)	Guinea 652, Liberia 306 • Coast 402				

RECENT INTERNATIONAL MATCHES PLAYED BY SIERRA LEONE

2006	Opponents	Score		Venue	Comp	Scorers	Att	Referee
3-09	Mali	D	0-0	Freetown	CNq			Mbera GAB
8-10	Benin	L	0-2	Cotonou	CNq			Sowe GAM
2007								
24-03	Togo	L	1-3	Lomé	CNq	Gibrilla Woobay [77]		Pare BFA
3-06	Togo	L	0-1	Freetown	CNq			Imiere NGA
17-06	Mali	L	0-6	Bamako	CNq			Lemghambodj MTN
12-10	Benin	L	0-2	Freetown	CNq			Ambaya LBY
17-10	Guinea-Bissau	W	1-0	Freetown	WCq	Kewullay Conteh [17]	25 000	Mana NGA
17-11	Guinea-Bissau	D	0-0	Bissau	WCq		12 000	Lamptey GHA
2-12	Guinea-Bissau	L	0-2	Bissau	ACr1			
23-12	Gambia	L	1-2	Bakau	Fr	Alex Sesay [87]		
2008								
30-04	Liberia	L	1-3	Paynesville	Fr	Kemokai Kallon [65]		
1-06	Equatorial Guinea	L	0-2	Malabo	WCq		13 000	Codjia BEN
7-06	Nigeria	L	0-1	Freetown	WCq		25 000	Korti LBR
14-06	South Africa	W	1-0	Freetown	WCq	Mohammed Kallon [21p]	15 000	Pare BFA
21-06	South Africa	D	0-0	Atteridgeville	WCq		12 000	Evehe CMR
6-09	Equatorial Guinea	W	2-1	Freetown	WCq	Kewullay Conteh [30], Sheriff Suma [73]	22 000	Doue CIV
11-10	Nigeria	L	1-4	Abuja	WCq	Yobo OG [31]	20 000	Kaoma ZAM
2009								
No international matches played in 2009								
2010								
5-09	Egypt	D	1-1	Cairo	CNq	Mustapha Bangura [56]		Diatta SEN
10-10	South Africa	D	0-0	Freetown	CNq			Lemghaifry MTN

Fr = Friendly match • CN = CAF African Cup of Nations • AC = Amilcar Cabral Cup • WC = FIFA World Cup • q = qualifier

MEDALS TABLE

		Overall	Lge	Cup
		G	G	G
1	Mighty Blackpool	15	11	4
2	East End Lions	14	11	3
3	Kallon FC	5	4	1
4	Real Republicans	4	3	1
	Ports Authority	4	2	2
6	Old Edwardians	3	1	2
7	Bai Bureh Warriors	2		2
	Kamboi Eagles	2		2
9	Freetown United	1	1	
	Diamond Stars	1		1
	Wusum Stars	1		1

SLV – EL SALVADOR

FIFA/COCA-COLA WORLD RANKING

1993	1994	1995	1996	1997	1998	1999	2000	2001	2002	2003	2004	2005	2006	2007	2008	2009	2010
66	80	82	65	64	92	96	83	86	94	95	106	124	156	134	111	78	117

					2010							Hi/Lo
Jan	Feb	Mar	Mar	Apr	May	Jul	Aug	Sep	Oct	Nov	Dec	50
78	71	72	74	71	72	90	86	110	114	117	117	169

After the resignation of their Mexican coach Carlos de los Cobos at the end of 2009 following a three year spell in charge, the national team turned to his assistant Jose Luis Rugamas on an interim basis but he could do little to improve fortunes with the team losing four and drawing one of their five matches in 2010. His contract was extended for the duration of the 2011 Copa Centroamericana in Panama City and El Salvador got off to a good start with victories over both Belize and Nicaragua to qualify for a semi-final against Honduras. In the past the tie would have been an even match but once again the Hondurans proved themselves a cut above their neighbours with a 2-0 victory. A place in the 2011 CONCACAF Gold Cup in the USA was a reward for the semi-final spot with the objective of progressing beyond the group stage for the first time since 2003. At home, Isidro-Metapan continued to emerge as one of the best-run clubs in the country, winning both championships played in 2010. Since winning their first title in 2007, the club have now won five - all of them under coach Edwin Portillo. In May 2010 they beat traditional powerhouse Aguila 3-1 in the 2009-10 Clausura final and then at the end of the year beat Alianza in the 2010-11 Apertura final, although it took a penalty shoot-out to secure the title.

FIFA WORLD CUP RECORD

1930-1966 DNE **1970** 16 r1 1974-1978 DNQ **1982** 24 r1 1986-2010 DNQ

FEDERACION SALVADORENA DE FUTBOL (FESFUT)

Avenida José Matias Delgado, Frente al Centro Español, Colonia Escalón, Zona 10, San Salvador CA 1029

☎ +503 22096200
📠 +503 22637528
✉ cmendez@fesfut.org.sv
🖥 www.fesfut.org.sv
FA 1935 CON 1961 FIFA 1938
P Carlos Mendez
GS Gladis Guerra

FIFA BIG COUNT 2006

Total players	459 692
% of population	6.74%
Male	401 040
Female	58 652
Unregistered	225 900
Professionals	200
Referees	315
Admin & coaches	5 538
Number of clubs	68
Number of teams	2 828

MAJOR CITIES/TOWNS

		Population
1	San Salvador	550 828
2	Soyapango	402 198
3	Santa Ana	189 014
4	San Miguel	174 467
5	Mejicanos	165 652
6	Apopa	136 818
7	N'va San Salvador	131 971
8	Delgado	87 335
9	San Marcos	66 623
10	Sonsonate	63 729
11	Usulután	55 041
12	Cuscatancingo	54 124
13	Cojutepeque	51 348
14	San Martín	48 015
15	Antiguo Cuscatlán	44 829
16	Zacatecoluca	42 234
17	San Vicente	39 742
18	Quezaltepeque	38 348
27	La Libertad	22 890

REPUBLICA DE EL SALVADOR • REPUBLIC OF EL SALVADOR

Capital San Salvador	Population 7 185 218 (99)	% in cities 61%
GDP per capita $6200 (131)	Area km² 21 041 km² (153)	GMT + / - -6
Neighbours (km) Guatemala 203, Honduras 342 • Coast 307		

RECENT INTERNATIONAL MATCHES PLAYED BY EL SALVADOR

2009 Opponents		Score	Venue	Comp	Scorers	Att	Referee
22-01	Nicaragua	D 1-1	Tegucigalpa	UCr1	OG [18]	20 000	Batres GUA
24-01	Belize	W 4-1	Tegucigalpa	UCr1	Pacheco 2 [11p 30p], Sanchez [75], Ayala [88]	20 000	Quesada CRC
26-01	Honduras	L 0-2	Tegucigalpa	UCr1		20 000	Quesada CRC
30-01	Costa Rica	L 0-1	Tegucigalpa	UCsf		2 500	Moreno PAN
1-02	Honduras	L 0-1	Tegucigalpa	UC3p		900	Quesada CRC
6-02	Peru	W 1-0	Los Angeles	Fr	Romero [24]	5 000	Jurisevic USA
11-02	Trinidad and Tobago	D 2-2	San Salvador	WCq	Romero 2 [82 93+]	25 000	Rodriguez MEX
28-03	USA	D 2-2	San Salvador	WCq	Quintanilla [19], Castillo [72]	30 350	Archundia MEX
1-04	Costa Rica	L 0-1	San Jose	WCq		19 200	Marrufo USA
27-05	Ecuador	W 3-1	Los Angeles	Fr	Romero 2 [11 51], Corrales [45]	11 000	Salazar USA
30-05	Jamaica	D 0-0	Washington DC	Fr		30 313	Prus USA
6-06	Mexico	W 2-1	San Salvador	WCq	Julio Martinez [12], Quintanilla [85p]	33 000	Quesada CRC
10-06	Honduras	L 0-1	San Pedro Sula	WCq		28 000	Toledo USA
3-07	Costa Rica	W 2-1	Carson	GCr1	Romero 2 [19 87]	27 000	Archundia MEX
7-07	Canada	L 0-1	Columbus	GCr1		7 059	Garcia MEX
10-07	Jamaica	L 0-1	Miami	GCr1		17 269	Hospedales TRI
7-08	Colombia	L 1-2	Houston	Fr	Moscoso [63]	20 418	Marrufo USA
12-08	Trinidad and Tobago	L 0-1	Port of Spain	WCq		16 000	Vaughn USA
5-09	USA	L 1-2	Sandy	WCq	Castillo [31]	19 066	Pineda HON
9-09	Costa Rica	W 1-0	San Salvador	WCq	Corrales [91+]	18 000	Archundia MEX
10-10	Mexico	L 1-4	Mexico City	WCq	Julio Martinez [89]	104 000	Batres GUA
14-10	Honduras	L 0-1	San Salvador	WCq		28 000	Salazar USA
2010							
24-02	USA	L 1-2	Tampa	Fr	Corrales [59]	21 737	Petrescu CAN
3-03	Guatemala	L 1-2	Los Angeles	Fr	Quintanilla [89]	10 000	Salazar USA
4-09	Honduras	D 2-2	Los Angeles	Fr	Zelaya 2 [42 90], L 3-4p	15 000	Stoica USA
8-10	Panama	L 0-1	Panama City	Fr		16 175	Ruiz COL
12-10	Costa Rica	L 1-2	Quesada	Fr	Burgos [53]	4 000	Rodriguez PAN
2011							
14-01	Nicaragua	W 2-1	Panama City	UCr1	Alas [71], Burgos [76]	2 000	Quesada CRC
16-01	Belize	W 5-2	Panama City	UCr1	Romero [15], Burgos 2 [25 46], Alas [54], Umanzor [59]	1 500	Cerdas CRC
18-01	Panama	L 0-2	Panama City	UCr1		10 000	Garcia MEX
21-01	Honduras	L 0-2	Panama City	UCsf		5 000	Quesada CRC
23-01	Panama	D 0-0	Panama City	UC3p	L 4-5p	2 000	Pineda HON

Fr = Friendly match • UC = UNCAF Cup/Copa Centroamericana • GC = CONCACAF Gold Cup • WC = FIFA World Cup • q = qualifier

EL SALVADOR NATIONAL TEAM HISTORICAL RECORDS

Caps
89 - Luis Guevara Mora 1979-96 • 77 - Marvin Gonzalez 2002- • 74 - Guillermo Rivera 1988-2002 • 72 - Alfredo Pacheco 2002- •
71 - Rudis Corrales 1999- • 68 - Mauricio Cienfuegos 1987-2003 • 66 - Ronald Cerritos 1995-2008 • 65 - Jorge Rodriguez 1994-2005 •
64 - Juan Francisco Barraza 1953-69 • 63 - Ramon Sanchez 2001-

Goals
39 - Raul Diaz Arce 1991-2000 • 22 - Jose Maria Rivas 1979-89 • 21 - Jorge Gonzalez 1976-98 • 17 - Luis Ramirez Zapata 1971-89 •
16 - Norberto Huezo 1973-87; Miguel Cruz 1935-43 & Rudis Corrales 1999- • 14 - Eliseo Quinanilla 2007- • 13 - Juan Francisco Barraza
1953-69 & Ever Hernandez 1976-85 • 12 - Rafael Corado 1943-55 & Gustavo Marroquin 1927-30

Past Coaches
Mark Scott Thompson USA 1930-35 • Pablo Ferre Elias ESP 1935-38 • Maximo Garay ARG 1940-41 • Slade 1941-43 • Amaricano Gonzalez
1943-48 • Rodolfo Orlandini ARG 1949-51 • Marcelo Estrada 1953 • Carbilio Tomasino 1954-59 • Milo Guardado 1959-60 • Conrado
Miranda 1961 • Luis Comitante URU 1962-63 • Hernan Vivanco CHI 1965-67 • Rigoberto Guzman 1968 • Gregorio Bundio ARG 1968-70 •
Hernan Vivanco CHI 1970 • Conrado Miranda 1971 • Hector D'Angelo ARG 1972 • Jorge Tupinamba BRA 1973 • Pipo Rodriguez 1973-74 •
Conrado Miranda 1975 • Marcelo Estrada 1975-76 • Raul Magana 1976 • Aurelio Pinto Beltrao BRA 1976 • Roberto Porta URU 1977 • Julio
Contreras Cardona 1977 • Ricardo Tomasino 1978 • Raul Magana 1979 • Pipo Rodriguez 1979-82 • Armando Contreras 1983 • Raul
Magana 1984 • Juan Quarterone ARG 1984-85 • Paulo Roberto Cabrera 1986 • Raul Magana 1987 • Milovan Doric YUG 1988 • Miroslav
Vukasinovic YUG 1988-89 • Conrado Miranda 1989 • Kiril Dojcinovski YUG 1989 • Oscar Emigdio Benitez 1991 • Jorge Aude URU 1991-92
• Anibal Ruiz URU 1992 • Jorge Vieira BRA 1993-94 • Jose Omar Pastoriza ARG 1995-96 • Armando Contreras 1996-97 • Milovan Doric
YUG 1997-98 • Kiril Dojcinovski YUG 1998 • Marinho Peres BRA 1998 • Oscar Emigdio Benitez 1999-2000 • Carlos Recinos 2000-02 •
Juan Ramon Paredes 2002-04 • Armando Contreras 2004 • Carlos Cavagnaro ARG 2005 • Miguel Aguilar 2005-06 • Carlos de los Cobos
MEX 2006-09 • Jose Luis Rugamas 2010-

EL SALVADOR 2009-10

PRIMERA DIVISION PROFESIONAL CAMPEONATO CLAUSURA	Pl	W	D	L	F	A	Pts	LA Firpo	Aguila	V. Hermosa	I-Metapán	At. Balboa	Alianza	FAS	Municipal	At. Marte	Alacranes
Luis Angel Firpo †	18	10	5	3	28	17	35		1-1	0-0	2-2	1-2	2-0	2-1	1-0	4-1	1-0
CD Aguila †	18	7	10	1	24	9	31	2-2		3-0	0-0	0-0	2-0	2-2	0-0	1-1	3-0
Vista Hermosa †	18	7	8	3	25	17	29	1-0	0-0		1-0	0-0	1-1	3-1	5-2	1-0	2-1
CD Isidro-Metapán †	18	6	10	2	24	20	28	1-1	1-1	0-0		1-1	3-1	4-0	0-0	3-2	3-1
Atlético Balboa	18	6	9	3	18	17	27	0-1	0-1	1-0	0-0		3-1	3-0	3-3	2-1	2-1
Alianza	18	6	6	6	22	18	24	2-1	0-2	1-1	7-1	0-0		3-0	3-1	2-0	1-0
Deportivo FAS	18	5	5	8	19	25	20	1-2	1-0	2-0	0-1	0-0	0-0		2-0	3-1	4-1
Municipal Limeño	18	3	9	6	20	27	18	1-2	1-2	3-3	1-1	1-1	0-0	1-0		1-1	3-2
Atlético Marte	18	3	7	8	22	27	16	0-2	0-0	2-2	1-1	6-0	1-0	2-2	0-1		2-1
Nejapa	18	0	5	13	12	37	5	2-3	0-4	0-5	1-2	0-0	0-0	0-0	1-1	1-1	

9/01/2010 - 25/04/2010 • † Qualified for the play-offs • Nejapa relegated due to the worst record over the 2009-20 season. Atlético Marte had the second worst record and entered a play-off. Relegation play-off: Municipal Limeño 1-1 0-1 Once Municipal. Municipal relegated
Top scorers: **11** - Jose Oliveira de Souza BRA, Alianza • **10** - Leonardo da Silva BRA, Vista Hermosa

CLAUSURA PLAY-OFFS

Semi-finals			Finals	
CD Isidro-Metapán *	2	2		
Luis Angel Firpo	2	1	CD Isidro-Metapán	3
Vista Hermosa *	0	0	CD Aguila	1
CD Aguila	1	0	* At home in the first leg	

CHAMPIONSHIP FINAL CLAUSURA 2010

Estadio Cuscatlan, San Salvador, 23-05-2010, Ref: Joel Aguilar

Isidro-Metapán 3 Blanco 2 [22] [45], Suarez [96+]
Aguila 1 Corrales [63]

I-Metapán - Misael Alfaro• - Ernesto Aquino, Alexander Escobar• (Mario Aguilar 94+), Ricardo Alvarado, Omar Mejia - Oscar Jimenez, Andres Flores, Josue Flores• (Gabriel Garcete 91+), Emerson Umana - Lester Blanco (Milton Molina 76), Paolo Suarez•. Tr: Edwin Portillo
Aguila - Miguel Montes - Hermes Martinez, Isaac Zelaya•, Luis Hernandez (Shawn Martin 52), William Cabrera - Gilberto Murgas, Eliseo Salamanca, Darwin Bonilla (Francisco Alvarez 32), William Torres - Rudis Corrales, Nelson Reyes (Arturo Albarran 81). Tr: Ruben Alonso

EL SALVADOR 2010-11

PRIMERA DIVISION PROFESIONAL TORNEO APERTURA	Pl	W	D	L	F	A	Pts	I-Metapán	Alianza	LA Firpo	Aguila	At. Balboa	V. Hermosa	At. Marte	FAS	UES	Once
CD Isidro-Metapán †	18	10	4	4	34	27	34		3-0	2-2	3-0	4-2	2-1	4-3	2-0	2-1	1-2
Alianza †	18	9	6	3	26	13	33	0-0		5-0	4-0	0-0	2-0	2-1	4-0	2-2	1-0
Luis Angel Firpo †	18	8	7	3	24	17	31	1-1	0-0		1-2	2-0	3-1	2-2	1-0	1-0	2-0
CD Aguila †	18	9	4	5	22	19	31	4-1	0-2	1-1		2-0	2-1	2-1	3-1	1-0	1-0
Atlético Balboa	18	7	8	3	21	16	29	3-0	2-0	2-0	1-0		2-2	1-1	1-1	1-0	3-2
Vista Hermosa	18	3	9	6	20	25	18	1-1	1-1	0-0	1-1	0-0		2-1	2-2	1-0	2-1
Atlético Marte	18	4	5	9	22	28	17	1-2	0-1	0-2	0-2	0-0	3-2		1-1	3-1	0-1
Deportivo FAS	18	4	5	9	19	28	17	1-2	3-0	0-2	2-1	0-1	1-0	0-1		2-2	1-1
Univ'dad El Salvador	18	3	7	8	23	27	16	3-1	1-2	1-1	0-0	1-1	3-3	2-2	2-1		4-2
Once Municipal	18	3	5	10	16	27	14	2-3	0-0	0-3	0-0	1-1	0-0	1-2	2-3	1-0	

31/07/2010 - 28/11/2010 • † Qualified for the play-offs
Top scorers: **9** - Alexander Campos, Balboa & Rodolfo Zelaya, Alianza • **8** - Alcides Bandera URU, Marte

APERTURA PLAY-OFFS

Semi-finals			Finals	
CD Isidro-Metapán	2	0		
CD Aguila *	1	0	CD Isidro-Metapán	0 4p
Luis Angel Firpo *	2	0	Alianza	0 3p
Alianza	1	1	* At home in the first leg	

CHAMPIONSHIP FINAL APERTURA 2010

Estadio Cuscatlan, San Salvador, 19-12-2010, Ref: Joel Aguilar

Isidro-Metapán 0 4p
Alianza 0 3p

I-Metapán - Fidel Mondragon - Ricardo Alvarado, Milton Molina, Ernesto Aquino (Carlos Carrillo 85), Omar Mejia - Andres Flores• (Emerson Umana 112), Oscar Jimenez, Paolo Suarez, Jorge Moran• - Lester Blanco, Anel Canales (Elias Montes 115). Tr: Edwin Portillo
Alianza - Rafel Fuentes - Mauricio Quintanilla, Marcelo Messias, Edwin Martinez, Carlos Arevalo• - Hector Salazar, Julio Martinez, Herbert Sosa• (Juan Lazo 83), Cristian Castillo• - Carlos Ayala (Willer Souza 67), Rodolfo Zelaya•. Tr: Milos Miljanic

SMR – SAN MARINO

FIFA/COCA-COLA WORLD RANKING

1993	1994	1995	1996	1997	1998	1999	2000	2001	2002	2003	2004	2005	2006	2007	2008	2009	2010
121	131	951	165	173	179	150	168	158	160	162	164	155	194	197	201	203	203

2010												Hi/Lo
Jan	Feb	Mar	Mar	Apr	May	Jul	Aug	Sep	Oct	Nov	Dec	**118**
203	203	203	202	202	202	202	202	203	203	203	203	**203**

October 12th, 2010 was an historic day in world football with San Marino breaking the world record for the number of consecutive defeats. Their 2-0 loss at the hands of Moldova that night was their 37th in a row, surpassing the old record which they had established after a spell of 36 defeats between 1993 and 2001. Their current run began in September 2004 with a 3-0 loss against Serbia and while it is tempting to say that things can only get better, it is difficult to see where the next goal is coming from, let alone a draw or a victory. Andy Selva remains the great hope of the team and in 2010 he helped his club side, former Italian champions Hellas Verona, to push for promotion from the third tier of Italian football, but despite leading the table in spring, Verona finished third and missed out on a place in Serie B. In San Marino the season was dominated by Tre Fiore who won the double for the first time in their history and with it joined Domagnano as the most successful club in the country with 12 trophies. They beat Tre Penne 2-1 in the final of both the championship and the Coppa Titano with 39-year old veteran forward Sossio Aruta scoring the winner in extra-time in both matches. Tre Penne had finished as comfortably the best team in the regular season but a first championship success was not to be.

FIFA WORLD CUP RECORD
1930-1990 DNE 1994-2010 DNQ

FEDERAZIONE SAMMARINESE GIUOCO CALCIO (FSGC)

Strada di Montecchio 17, San Marino 47890

☎ +378 054 9990515
📠 +378 054 9992348
✉ fsgc@omniway.sm
🖥 www.fsgc.sm
FA 1931 CON 1988 FIFA 1988
P Giorgio Crescentini
GS Luciano Casadei

FIFA BIG COUNT 2006

Total players	2 836
% of population	9.70%
Male	2 421
Female	415
Amateurs 18+	763
Youth under 18	823
Unregistered	650
Professionals	0
Referees	35
Admin & coaches	225
Number of clubs	16
Number of teams	56

MAJOR CITIES/TOWNS

		Population
1	Serravalle	9 894
2	Borgo Maggiore	6 058
3	San Marino	4 433
4	Domagnano	2 872
5	Fiorentino	2 250
6	Acquaviva	1 914
7	Murata	1 580
8	Faetano	1 175
9	Chiesanuova	1 042
10	Montegiardino	837

REPUBBLICA DI SAN MARINO • REPUBLIC OF SAN MARINO

Capital	San Marino	Population	30 324 (212)	% in cities	94%
GDP per capita	$41 900 (19)	Area km^2	61 km^2 (228)	GMT +/-	+1
Neighbours (km)	Italy 39				

RECENT INTERNATIONAL MATCHES PLAYED BY SAN MARINO

2004	Opponents		Score	Venue	Comp	Scorers	Att	Referee
28-04	Liechtenstein	W	1-0	Serravalle	Fr	Andy Selva [5]	700	Sammut MLT
4-09	Serbia & Montenegro	L	0-3	Serravalle	WCq		1 137	Kholmatov KAZ
8-09	Lithuania	L	0-4	Kaunas	WCq		4 000	Jareci ALB
13-10	Serbia & Montenegro	L	0-5	Belgrade	WCq		4 000	Isaksen FRO
17-11	Lithuania	L	0-1	Serravalle	WCq		1 457	Nalbandyan ARM
2005								
9-02	Spain	L	0-5	Almeria	WCq		12 580	Clark SCO
30-03	Belgium	L	1-2	Serravalle	WCq	Andy Selva [41]	871	Kasnaferis GRE
4-06	Bosnia-Herzegovina	L	1-3	Serravalle	WCq	Andy Selva [39]	750	Demirlek TUR
7-09	Belgium	L	0-8	Antwerp	WCq		8 207	Stokes IRL
8-10	Bosnia-Herzegovina	L	0-3	Zenica	WCq		8 500	Hamer LUX
12-10	Spain	L	0-6	Serravalle	WCq		3 426	Meyer GER
2006								
16-08	Albania	L	0-3	Serravalle	Fr			
6-09	Germany	L	0-13	Serravalle	ECq		5 090	Dereli TUR
7-10	Czech Republic	L	0-7	Liberec	ECq		9 514	Aliyev AZE
15-11	Republic of Ireland	L	0-5	Dublin	ECq		34 018	Isaksen FRO
2007								
7-02	Republic of Ireland	L	1-2	Serravalle	ECq	Manuel Marani [86]	3 294	Rasmussen DEN
28-03	Wales	L	0-3	Cardiff	ECq		18 752	Tchagharyan ARM
2-06	Germany	L	0-6	Nuremberg	ECq		43 967	Asumaa FIN
22-08	Cyprus	L	0-1	Serravalle	ECq		552	Janku ALB
8-09	Czech Republic	L	0-3	Serravalle	ECq		3 412	Filipovic SRB
12-09	Cyprus	L	0-3	Nicosia	ECq		1 000	Kulbakov BLR
13-10	Slovakia	L	0-7	Dubnica n. Vahom	ECq		2 576	Wilmes LUX
17-10	Wales	L	1-2	Serravalle	ECq	Andy Selva [73]	1 182	Zammit MLT
21-11	Slovakia	L	0-5	Serravalle	ECq		538	Sipailo LVA
2008								
10-09	Poland	L	0-2	Serravalle	WCq		2 374	Zografos GRE
11-10	Slovakia	L	1-3	Serravalle	WCq	Andy Selva [45]	1 037	Kever SUI
15-10	Northern Ireland	L	0-4	Belfast	WCq		12 957	Kari FIN
19-11	Czech Republic	L	0-3	Serravalle	WCq		1 318	Kaasik EST
2009								
11-02	Northern Ireland	L	0-3	Serravalle	WCq		1 942	Stankovic SRB
1-04	Poland	L	0-10	Kielce	WCq		15 200	Kulbakou BLR
6-06	Slovakia	L	0-7	Bratislava	WCq		6 652	Efong Nzolo BEL
12-08	Slovenia	L	0-5	Maribor	WCq		4 400	Meckarovski MKD
9-09	Czech Republic	L	0-7	Uherske Hradiste	WCq		8 121	Amirkhanyan ARM
14-10	Slovenia	L	0-3	Serravalle	WCq		1 745	Szabo HUN
2010								
3-09	Netherlands	L	0-5	Serravalle	ECq		4 127	Evans WAL
7-09	Sweden	L	0-6	Malmo	ECq		21 083	McKeon IRL
8-10	Hungary	L	0-8	Budapest	ECq		10 596	Kaasik EST
12-10	Moldova	L	0-2	Serravalle	ECq		714	Courtney NIR
17-11	Finland	L	0-8	Helsinki	ECq		8 192	Matejek CZE

Fr = Friendly match • EC = UEFA EURO 2008/2012 • WC = FIFA World Cup • q = qualifier

SAN MARINO NATIONAL TEAM HISTORICAL RECORDS

Caps	**58** - Damiano Vannucci 1996- • **50** - Simone Bacchiocchi 1997- & Andy Selva 1998- • **48** - Mirco Gennari 1992-2003 • **44** - Ivan Matteoni 1990-2003 • **43** - Paolo Montagna 1995- • **41** - Federico Gasperoni 1996-2005 • **40** - Luca Gobbi 1990-2002 • **39** - Nicola Albani 2001-
Goals	**8** - Andy Selva 1998-
Past Coaches	Giorgio Leoni 1990-95 • Massimo Bonini 1996-98 • Giampaolo Mazza 1998-

SAN MARINO 2009-10

CAMPIONATO SAMMARINESE DI CALCIO

Group A	Pl	W	D	L	F	A	Pts	Cosmos	Domagnano	Juvenes/D	Murata	La Fiorita	Virtus	Cailungo	S. Giovanni	Tre Penne	Faetano	Tre Fiori	Pennarossa	Libertas	Fiorentino	Folgore
Cosmos †	21	11	5	5	32	24	38		1-0	0-2	1-0	0-0	1-1	1-0	4-3		2-2	2-1		2-1		
Domagnano †	21	10	7	4	32	21	37	1-1		1-1	1-0	4-1	2-2	2-1	6-1				0-0	1-0		1-1
Juvenes/Dogana †	21	10	6	5	34	20	36	1-0	0-1		2-2	1-1	0-2	4-0	4-1			0-0	2-2	1-2		
Murata	21	9	6	6	35	21	33	0-1	2-1	2-2		1-1	2-1	4-0	5-0			1-1		0-0	0-2	6-1
La Fiorita	21	8	8	5	33	30	32	2-1	1-1	0-1	1-3		1-0	3-0	1-1	2-3	1-2		3-2		3-2	
Virtus	21	7	5	9	27	29	26	1-1	1-2	0-1	1-1	1-1		2-1	1-0	3-4	0-3				2-1	3-2
Cailungo	21	2	3	16	12	43	9	0-2	1-2	1-3	1-3	1-2	0-1		1-1	0-4	0-2					2-2
San Giovanni	21	1	5	15	18	50	8	1-3	1-2	0-3	0-1	3-3	3-1	0-1		0-4		0-2	0-3		0-1	

Group B	Pl	W	D	L	F	A	Pts	Cosmos	Domagnano	Juvenes/D	Murata	La Fiorita	Virtus	Cailungo	S. Giovanni	Tre Penne	Faetano	Tre Fiori	Pennarossa	Libertas	Fiorentino	Folgore
Tre Penne †	20	15	3	2	55	22	48	5-2	2-1	3-1	3-0						0-3	2-1	1-1	2-2	6-0	2-1
Faetano †	20	12	4	4	41	20	40		3-0	0-1	0-2				1-0	3-2		1-0	1-1	2-2	4-2	2-0
Tre Fiori †	20	11	5	4	26	14	38		0-0			0-0	1-0	2-0		1-4	3-2		2-1	1-0	2-0	3-0
Pennarossa	20	9	7	4	30	25	34	3-2			1-0		2-1	2-0		0-4	0-5	0-0		1-1	2-0	2-1
Libertas	20	3	10	7	22	29	19					1-2	0-3	0-0	2-2	1-1	4-3	1-3	1-1		1-1	1-1
Fiorentino	20	4	1	15	17	45	13	0-2	1-3	1-0				1-2		0-2	0-2	0-2	0-4	1-2		4-3
Folgore/Falciano	20	2	5	13	21	42	11	0-3		1-4		2-4			3-0	1-1	0-1	0-0	0-1	1-2	1-0	

19/09/2009 - 18/04/2010 • † Qualified for the play-offs

PLAY-OFFS WINNERS BRACKET

Tre Penne	Bye			
		Tre Penne	3	
		Cosmos	0	
Cosmos	Bye			
			Tre Penne	1
Tre Fiori	2		Faetano	0
Domagnano	0	Tre Fiori	0 0p	
Domagnano	0	Faetano	0 3p	
Faetano	2	Losing teams drop down to the losers bracket		

† Qualified for the UEFA Champions League • ‡ Qualified for the Europa League

FINAL

Olimpico, Serravalle
31-05-2010
Scorers - Aruta 2 [18] [103] for Tre Fiori; Palazzi [81] for Tre Penne

Tre Fiori †	2
Tre Penne ‡	1

PLAY-OFFS LOSERS BRACKET

Teams losing in the losers bracket are eliminated having lost twice overall

			Tre Fiori	2
			Faetano	1
		Tre Fiori	1	
		Cosmos	0	
	Tre Fiori	3		
	Domagnano	0		
Juvenes/Dogana	2			
Domagnano	4			

Tre Fiori qualify to meet Tre Penne in the final • Faetano qualified for the Europa League

COPPA TITANO 2009-10

Quarter-finals		Semi-finals		Final	
Tre Fiori	2				
Domagnano	0	Tre Fiori	3		
Folgore/FalcianO	0	Murata	0		
Murata	3			Tre Fiori	2
Virtus	2			Tre Penne	1
Juvenes/Dogana	1	Virtus	0	Olimpico, 31-05-2010	
Libertas	1	Tre Penne	1	Scorers - Giunta [61], Aruta [95] for Fiori; Valli [14] for Penne	
Tre Penne	3				

MEDALS TABLE

		Overall G	Lge G	Cup G
1	Domagnano	12	4	8
	Tre Fiori	12	6	6
3	Libertas	11	1	10
4	Faetano	6	3	3
	Murata	6	3	3
6	Cosmos	5	1	4
	Juvenes	5		5
	Tre Penne	5		5
9	La Fiorita	3	2	1
	Folgore Falciano	3	3	
	Pennarossa	3	1	2
12	Dogana	2		2
13	Juvenes/Dogana	1		1
	Fiorentino	1	1	

SOL – SOLOMON ISLANDS

FIFA/COCA-COLA WORLD RANKING

1993	1994	1995	1996	1997	1998	1999	2000	2001	2002	2003	2004	2005	2006	2007	2008	2009	2010
149	163	170	171	130	128	144	130	134	142	156	130	140	160	123	163	172	177

	2010											Hi/Lo
	Jan	Feb	Mar	Mar	Apr	May	Jul	Aug	Sep	Oct	Nov	Dec	**120**
	172	171	171	170	169	170	169	169	175	177	178	177	**178**

There had been high hopes in the Solomon Islands that one of their clubs would be the first from outside of Australia or New Zealand to win the OFC Champions League, but in 2010 those hopes were dashed when Papua New Guinea's Hekari United sensationally beat New Zealand's Waitakere United in the final. Marist were hoping to follow in the footsteps of Kossa and Koloale and make it a hat trick of appearances in the final but they had a disastrous campaign and finished bottom of their group with just a single point. At home the 2010 National Club Championship was won by Koloale from Honiara. Played over the course of two weeks in May at the Lawson Tama Stadium in the capital, Koloale were comfortably the best team in the tournament with Marist struggling to regain the form that saw them win the title in 2009. Koloale beat them 3-1 in the quarter-finals and then beat 2007 champions Kossa 3-0 in the semi-finals. In the final they faced surprise package Solomon Warriors who had had the benefit of an easier draw but the underdogs put up a spirited fight before going down to goals from star striker Benjamin Totori and midfielder Henry Faarodo. It was Koloale's third title since the introduction of the National Club Championship in 2003, making them the most successful club to date.

FIFA WORLD CUP RECORD
1930-1990 DNE 1994-2010 DNQ

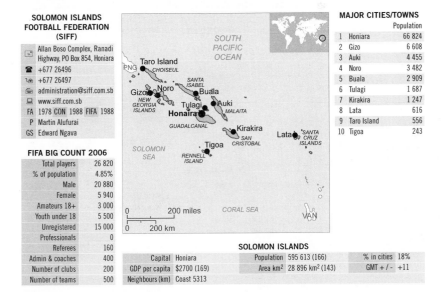

SOLOMON ISLANDS FOOTBALL FEDERATION (SIFF)

Allan Boso Complex, Ranadi Highway, PO Box 854, Honiara
☎ +677 26496
📠 +677 26497
✉ administration@siff.com.sb
🖥 www.siff.com.sb
FA 1978 CON 1988 FIFA 1988
P Martin Alufurai
GS Edward Ngava

FIFA BIG COUNT 2006

Total players	26 820
% of population	4.85%
Male	20 880
Female	5 940
Amateurs 18+	3 000
Youth under 18	5 500
Unregistered	15 000
Professionals	0
Referees	160
Admin & coaches	400
Number of clubs	200
Number of teams	500

MAJOR CITIES/TOWNS

		Population
1	Honiara	66 824
2	Gizo	6 608
3	Auki	4 455
4	Noro	3 482
5	Buala	2 909
6	Tulagi	1 687
7	Kirakira	1 247
8	Lata	616
9	Taro Island	556
10	Tigoa	243

SOLOMON ISLANDS

Capital	Honiara	Population	595 613 (166)	% in cities	18%
GDP per capita	$2700 (169)	Area km²	28 896 km² (143)	GMT +/-	+11
Neighbours (km)	Coast 5313				

RECENT INTERNATIONAL MATCHES PLAYED BY THE SOLOMON ISLANDS

2006	Opponents	Score	Venue	Comp	Scorers	Att	Referee
No international matches played in 2006							
2007							
13-07	Papua New Guinea	W 2-1	Honiara	Fr	Iniga, Maemae		
25-08	American Samoa	W 12-1	Apia	WCq	Totori 2 [12 15], Menapi 4 [20p 41 75 82], Faarodo [43], Waita 2 [58 85], Bebeu [69], Molea [77], Taka [92+]	300	Sosongan PNG
27-08	Tonga	W 4-0	Apia	WCq	Menapi 2 [5 12], Faarodo [51], Maemae [66]	350	Aimaasu SAM
1-09	Vanuatu	W 2-0	Apia	WCq	Bebeu [60], Faarodo [64]	1 000	Jacques TAH
3-09	Samoa	W 3-0	Apia	WCq	Totori 2 [1 37], Maemae [69]	200	Hester NZL
5-09	New Caledonia	L 2-3	Apia	WCq	Faarodo [40], Menapi [47]	600	Minan PNG
7-09	Vanuatu	L 0-2	Apia	WCq		200	Jacques TAH
2008							
7-07	Vanuatu	L 1-2	Honiara	Fr			
2009							
No international matchesplayed in 2009							
2010							
No international matchesplayed in 2010							

Fr = Friendly match • OC = OFC Oceania Nations Cup • SP = South Pacific Games • WC = FIFA World Cup
q = qualifier • r1 = first round group • f = final • † Not a full international

SOLOMON ISLANDS NATIONAL TEAM HISTORICAL RECORDS

Past Coaches: Edward Ngara 1995-96 • Wilson Maelaua 1996 • Alexander Napa 1998 • George Cowie SCO 2000-03 • Alan Gillett ENG 2004-05 • Airton Andrioli BRA • Jacob Moli 2010-

SOLOMON ISLANDS 2010
NATIONAL TELEKOM CLUB CHAMPIONSHIP

First Round Group Stage

Group A	Pl	W	D	L	F	A	Pts	So	Ma	Si	Na
Kossa	4	4	0	0	14	3	**12**	5-1	2-1	3-0	4-1
Soloso	4	2	1	1	9	10	7		2-1	2-2	4-2
Marist	4	1	1	2	6	7	**4**			3-2	1-1
Sipa	4	0	2	2	6	10	2				2-2
Naha	4	0	2	2	6	11	2				

Group B	Pl	W	D	L	F	A	Pts	RD	NU	HL	Ka
Koloale	4	3	1	0	18	0	**10**	0-0	4-0	6-0	8-0
Rendova Devon	4	2	2	0	0	0	**8**	‡	0-0	W	
Northern Utd	4	2	0	2	6	5	**6**			2-0	4-1
Harbour Lights	4	1	1	2	3	9	4				3-1
Ka'arua	4	0	0	4	2	15	0	‡ awarded to RD			

Group C	Pl	W	D	L	F	A	Pts	Wa	GU	SC
Makuru	3	3	0	0	7	1	**9**	2-0	4-1	1-0
Warriors	3	1	1	1	3	4	**4**		2-2	1-0
Gizo United	3	0	2	1	4	7	2			1-1
South Central	3	0	1	2	1	3	1			

Quarter-finals

Koloale	3
Marist	1

Northern Utd	1
Kossa	2

Soloso	1
Warriors	3

Rendova Devon	2
Makuru	1

Semi-finals

Koloale	3
Kossa	0

Rendova Devon	1
Warriors	5

Final

Koloale	2
Warriors	1

3rd place play-off

Kossa	4
Rendova Devon	2

17/05/2010 - 29/05/2010 • † Qualified for the O-League
Final: Lawson Tama, Honiara, 29-05-2010. Scorers - Benjamin Totori, Henry Faarodo for Koloale; Coleman Wasi for Solomon Warriors

SOM – SOMALIA

FIFA/COCA-COLA WORLD RANKING

1993	1994	1995	1996	1997	1998	1999	2000	2001	2002	2003	2004	2005	2006	2007	2008	2009	2010
-	159	165	178	187	190	197	194	197	190	191	193	184	193	195	200	170	182

2010												Hi/Lo
Jan	Feb	Mar	Mar	Apr	May	Jul	Aug	Sep	Oct	Nov	Dec	158
170	179	178	177	174	173	173	173	176	178	180	182	200

Somalia's notoriety in recent years as a failed state providing a safe-haven for pirates hijacking ships in the Indian Ocean has meant little contact with the outside world, with the exception it would seem of football. The Somali Football Federation kept up its commitment to participate in the annual East and Central African Senior Challenge Cup sending a national side to the 2010 edition at the end of the year in Tanzania where they lost all three group games without scoring and conceding 11 goals in the process. There was, however, a sensational victory for Somalia over Kenya at under-17 level in the first round of the African U-17 Championship qualifiers. Somalia beat their Kenyan counterparts 3-1 in neutral Djibouti in the first leg and then drew 0-0 in Nairobi in the return. They then faced Egypt and with the benefit of a spell spent training in Qatar, won widespread plaudits for their plucky spirit despite an aggregate 7-2 defeat in the two matches in Cairo. The country was not able to send a side to the regional CECAFA Club Cup in Kigali but it did host a national tournament in Garoowe at the end of the year, won by Banadir with a 1-0 win over Bari. Reports from the Somali capital Mogadishu during the World Cup claimed the death of two supporters killed by Islamic extremists for the crime of watching a World Cup match.

FIFA WORLD CUP RECORD
1930-1978 DNE 1982 DNQ 1986-1994 DNE 1998-2010 DNQ

SOMALI FOOTBALL FEDERATION (SFF)

DHL Mogadishu, Mogadishu BN 03040

☎ +252 1 216199
📠 +252 1 600601
✉ sofofed@hotmail.com
🖥 www.somsoccer.com
FA 1951 CON 1968 FIFA 1960
P Mohamud Nur
GS Abdiqani Said Arab

FIFA BIG COUNT 2006

Total players	546 268
% of population	6.16%
Male	522 433
Female	23 835
Amateurs 18+	12 460
Youth under 18	13 450
Unregistered	137 400
Professionals	3
Referees	1 300
Admin & coaches	6 030
Number of clubs	48
Number of teams	205

MAJOR CITIES/TOWNS

		Population
1	Mogadishu	1 663 223
2	Hargeysa	443 539
3	Burco	153 988
4	Beledweyne	109 935
5	Boosaaso	109 825
6	Baydhabo	90 138
7	Gaalkacyo	86 680
8	Berbera	72 343
9	Boorama	70 004
10	Kismaayo	68 042
11	Laascaanood	41 259
12	Jawhar	38 421
13	Garoowe	34 251
14	Baardheere	33 518
15	Qardho	28 116
16	Ceerigaabo	25 696
17	Dhusa Harreb	22 746
18	Marka	22 012
19	Wanlaweyn	19 949

JAMHUURIYADA DEMUQRAADIGA SOOMAALIYEED • SOMALIA

Capital Mogadishu	Population 9 832 017 (83)	% in cities 37%	
GDP per capita $600 (225)	Area km² 637 657 km² (43)	GMT + / - +3	
Neighbours (km) Djibouti 58, Ethiopia 1600, Kenya 682 • Coast 3025			

RECENT INTERNATIONAL MATCHES PLAYED BY SOMALIA

2003	Opponents	Score		Venue	Comp	Scorers	Att	Referee
16-11	Ghana	L	0-5	Accra	WCq		19 447	Bebou TOG
19-11	Ghana	L	0-2	Kumasi	WCq		12 000	Chaibou NIG
2004								
12-12	Uganda	L	0-2	Addis Abeba	CCr1			
14-12	Kenya	L	0-1	Addis Abeba	CCr1			
18-12	Sudan	L	0-4	Addis Abeba	CCr1			
2005								
27-11	Djibouti	W	2-1	Kigali	CCr1	Abdul Hakim 28, Mahmoud Sharki 87		
29-11	Sudan	L	1-4	Kigali	CCr1	Abdullahi Sheikh Mohamed 37		
1-12	Uganda	L	0-7	Kigali	CCr1			
5-12	Ethiopia	L	1-4	Kigali	CCr1			
2006								
27-11	Rwanda	L	0-3	Addis Abeba	CCr1			
30-11	Sudan	L	0-3	Addis Abeba	CCr1			
3-12	Uganda	L	0-2	Addis Abeba	CCr1			
21-12	Sudan	L	1-6	Beirut	ARr1	Mohammed Abdulaziz 93+		
24-12	Lebanon	L	0-4	Beirut	ARr1			
27-12	Mauritania	L	2-8	Beirut	ARr1	Abdulaziz Ali 2 26 67		
2007								
16-11	Djibouti	L	0-1	Djibouti	WCq		10 000	Abdul Rahman SUD
10-12	Burundi	L	0-1	Dar es Salaam	CCr1			
12-12	Tanzania	L	0-1	Dar es Salaam	CCr1			
14-12	Kenya	L	0-2	Dar es Salaam	CCr1			
2008								
23-12	Djibouti	W	3-2	Djibouti	Fr	Isse Midnimo, Ali Baashi, Ismail Yusuf		
2009								
1-01	Zanzibar †	L	0-2	Kampala	CCr1			
3-01	Tanzania	W	1-0	Kampala	CCr1	Abshir Cisse 14		
5-01	Rwanda	L	0-3	Kampala	CCr1			
7-01	Uganda	L	0-4	Kampala	CCr1			
29-11	Rwanda	L	0-1	Nairobi	CCr1			
3-12	Zimbabwe †	L	0-2	Nairobi	CCr1			
5-12	Eritrea	L	1-3	Nairobi	CCr1	Mohamed Hassan 70		
2010								
28-11	Burundi	L	0-2	Dar es Salaam	CCr1			
30-11	Tanzania	L	0-3	Dar es Salaam	CCr1			
3-12	Zambia	L	0-6	Dar es Salaam	CCr1			

Fr = Friendly match • CC = CECAFA Cup • AR = Arab Cup • WC = FIFA World Cup
q = qualifier • r1 = first round group • † Not a full international

SOMALIA 2010
NATIONAL TOURNAMENT

Quarter-finals		Semi-finals		Final	
Banadir	2				
Hiiraan	1	**Banadir**	1 5p		
Mudug	1	Nugal	1 3p		
Nugal	2			**Banadir**	1
Lower Jubba	0 4p			Bari	0
Mid Shabelle	0 2p	Lower Jubba	1		
Bay	2	**Bari**	3		
Bari	3	3rd place: Nugal 3-1 Lower Jubba			

Played in Garoowe from 15-12-2010 to 31-12-2010 • The first round was
playedin four groups with the top two qualifying for the quarter-finals

SRB – SERBIA

FIFA/COCA-COLA WORLD RANKING

1993	1994	1995	1996	1997	1998	1999	2000	2001	2002	2003	2004	2005	2006	2007	2008	2009	2010
-	-	-	-	-	-	-	-	-	19	41	46	47	33	27	30	19	23

2010												Hi/Lo
Jan	Feb	Mar	Mar	Apr	May	Jul	Aug	Sep	Oct	Nov	Dec	**13**
19	19	13	15	16	15	13	13	15	22	25	23	**47**

A year that began with so much promise ended in turmoil for Serbia. At the 2010 FIFA World Cup in South Africa the national team failed to get past the group stage for the second tournament running, while fans all but destroyed the team's chances of making it to the finals of Euro 2012 after hooligans caused the qualifier against Italy in Genoa to be abandoned after just six minutes. The match was awarded to the Italians and with Serbia already having lost at home to Estonia, their hopes of reaching the finals looked slim. At the World Cup the Serbs had got off to a terrible start with a self inflicted 1-0 defeat at the hands of Ghana although they seemed to have salvaged their campaign with a spirited win over Germany. In the final group match, a 2-1 defeat at the hands of Australia, the Serbs claimed a late penalty for handball which could have seen them through but it wasn't given and they were out. At home, Partizan completed a hat trick of League titles after going through the season unbeaten for the second time in six years. In the 2010-11 UEFA Champions League they made it back to the group stage for the first time since 2003 but proved to be the whipping boys in a group containing Shakhtar, Arsenal and Braga. In the Serbian Cup there was some consolation for league runners-up Red Star after beating Vojvodina 3-0 in the final.

FIFA WORLD CUP RECORD

1930 4 SF **1934-1938** DNQ **1950** 5 r1 **1954** 7 QF **1958** 5 QF **1962** 4 SF **1966-1970** DNQ **1974** 7 r2 **1978** DNQ **1982** 16 r1
1986 DNQ **1990** 5 QF **1994** DNE **1998** 9 r2 **2002** DNQ (as Yugoslavia) **2006** 32 r1 (as Serbia & Montenegro) **2010** 23 r1 (as Serbia)

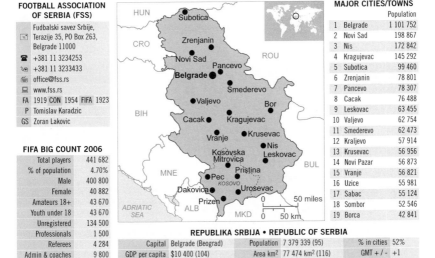

FOOTBALL ASSOCIATION OF SERBIA (FSS)

Fudbalski savez Srbije,
Terazije 35, PO Box 263,
Belgrade 11000
☎ +381 11 3234253
🖷 +381 11 3233433
✉ office@fss.rs
🖳 www.fss.rs
FA 1919 CON 1954 FIFA 1923
P Tomislav Karadzic
GS Zoran Lakovic

FIFA BIG COUNT 2006

Total players	441 682
% of population	4.70%
Male	400 800
Female	40 882
Amateurs 18+	43 670
Youth under 18	43 670
Unregistered	134 500
Professionals	1 500
Referees	4 284
Admin & coaches	9 800
Number of clubs	2 076
Number of teams	4 450

MAJOR CITIES/TOWNS

		Population
1	Belgrade	1 101 752
2	Novi Sad	198 867
3	Nis	172 842
4	Kragujevac	145 292
5	Subotica	99 460
6	Zrenjanin	78 801
7	Pancevo	78 307
8	Cacak	76 488
9	Leskovac	63 455
10	Valjevo	62 754
11	Smederevo	62 473
12	Kraljevo	57 914
13	Krusevac	56 956
14	Novi Pazar	56 873
15	Vranje	56 821
16	Uzice	55 981
17	Sabac	55 124
18	Sombor	52 546
19	Borca	42 841

REPUBLIKA SRBIJA • REPUBLIC OF SERBIA

Capital	Belgrade (Beograd)	Population	7 379 339 (95)	% in cities	52%
GDP per capita	$10 400 (104)	Area km²	77 474 m² (116)	GMT +/-	+1
Neighbours (km)	Bosnia-Herzegovina 302, Bulgaria 318, Croatia 241, Hungary 151, Kosovo 352, Macedonia 62, Montenegro 124, Romania 476				

INTERNATIONAL MATCHES PLAYED BY SERBIA

2008 Opponents	Score		Venue	Comp	Scorers	Att	Referee
6-02 FYR Macedonia	D	1-1	Skopje	Fr	Lazovic [43]	12 000	Georgiev BUL
26-03 Ukraine	L	0-2	Odessa	Fr		8 000	Lajuks LVA
24-05 Republic of Ireland	D	1-1	Dublin	Fr	Pantelic [75]	42 500	Evans WAL
28-05 Russia	L	1-2	Burghausen	Fr	Pantelic [40]	4 030	Stark GER
31-05 Germany	L	1-2	Gelsenkirchen	Fr	Jankovic [18]	53 951	Fautrel FRA
6-09 Faroe Islands	W	2-0	Belgrade	WCq	Jacobsen OG [30], Zigic [88]	9 615	Nikolaev RUS
10-09 France	L	1-2	Paris	WCq	Ivanovic [75]	53 027	Benquerenca POR
11-10 Lithuania	W	3-0	Belgrade	WCq	Ivanovic [6], Krasic [34], Zigic [82]	22 000	Mejuto ESP
15-10 Austria	W	3-1	Vienna	WCq	Krasic [14], Jovanovic [18], Obradovic [24]	47 998	Riley ENG
19-11 Bulgaria	W	6-1	Belgrade	Fr	Jovanovic 2 [9 27], Milosevic 2 [28 34], Milijas [57], Lazovic [67]	6 000	Sippel GER
14-12 Poland	L	0-1	Antalya	Fr		100	Dereli TUR
2009							
10-02 Cyprus	W	2-0	Nicosia	Fr	Jovanovic [25], Lazovic [42]		Kakkos GRE
11-02 Ukraine	L	0-1	Nicosia	Fr		500	Kakkos GRE
28-03 Romania	W	3-2	Constanta	WCq	Jovanovic [18], Stoica OG [44], Ivanovic [59]	12 000	Trefoloni ITA
1-04 Sweden	W	2-0	Belgrade	Fr	Zigic [1], Jankovic [82]	17 830	Perez ESP
6-06 Austria	W	1-0	Belgrade	WCq	Milijas [7p]	41 000	Vink NED
10-06 Faroe Islands	W	2-0	Tórshavn	WCq	Jovanovic [44], Subotic [69]	2 896	Levi ISR
12-08 South Africa	W	3-1	Atteridgeville	Fr	Tosic 2 [58 78], Lazovic [69]	10 000	Maillet SEY
9-09 France	D	1-1	Belgrade	WCq	Milijas [12p]	49 256	Rosetti ITA
10-10 Romania	W	5-0	Belgrade	WCq	Zigic [36], Pantelic [50], Kuzmanovic [77], Jovanovic 2 [87 93+]	39 839	Kapitanis CYP
14-10 Lithuania	L	1-2	Marijampole	WCq	Tosic [60]	2 000	Guenov BUL
14-11 Northern Ireland	W	1-0	Belfast	Fr	Lazovic [57]	13 500	Toussaint LUX
18-11 Korea Republic	W	1-0	London	Fr	Zigic [7]	5 117	Attwell ENG
2010							
7-04 Japan	W	3-0	Osaka	Fr	Mrda 2 [15 23], Tomic [60]	46 270	Choi Myung Yong KOR
29-05 New Zealand	L	0-1	Klagenfurt	Fr		14 000	Drachta AUT
2-06 Poland	D	0-0	Kufstein	Fr		2 000	Drabek AUT
5-06 Cameroon	W	4-3	Belgrade	Fr	Krasic [16], Stankovic [25], Milijas [44p], Pantelic [45]	30 000	Trattou CYP
13-06 Ghana	L	0-1	Pretoria	WCr1		38 833	Baldassi ARG
18-06 Germany	W	1-0	Port Elizabeth	WCr1	Jovanovic [38]	38 294	Undiano ESP
23-06 Australia	L	1-2	Nelspruit	WCr1	Pantelic [84]	37 836	Larrionda URU
11-08 Greece	L	0-1	Belgrade	Fr		10 000	Teixeira ESP
3-09 Faroe Islands	W	3-0	Torshavn	ECq	Lazovic [14], Stankovic [18], Zigic [91+]	1 847	Toussaint LUX
7-09 Slovenia	D	1-1	Belgrade	ECq	Zigic [86]	24 028	Benquerenca POR
8-10 Estonia	L	1-3	Belgrade	ECq	Zigic [60]	12 000	Layushkin RUS
12-10 Italy	L	0-3	Genoa	ECq	Match awarded to Italy. Abandoned after 6'	28 000	Thomson SCO
17-11 Bulgaria	W	1-0	Sofia	Fr	Zigic [80]	1 500	Avram ROU

Fr = Friendly match • EC = UEFA EURO 2008/2012 • WC = FIFA World Cup • q = qualifier

SERBIA NATIONAL TEAM HISTORICAL RECORDS

Caps — 102 - Savo Milosevic 1994-2008 • 95 - Dejan Stankovic 1998- • 84 - Dragan Stojkovic 1983-2001 • 73 - Predrag Mijatovic 1989-2003 • 64 - Slavisa Jokanovic 1991-2002 • 63 - Sinisa Mihajlovic 1991-2003 • 59 - Mladen Krstajic 1999-2008 & Zoran Mirkovic 1995-2003 • 58 - Darko Kovacevic 1994-2004 • 56 - Dejan Savicevic 1986-1999 (based on internationals played since 1994 only)

Goals — 37 - Savo Milosevic 1994-2008 • 28 - Predrag Mijatovic 1989-2003 • 20 - Nikola Zigic 2004- • 19 - Dejan Savicevic 1986-2003 • 17 - Mateja Kezman 2000-2006 • 15 - Dragan Stojkovic 1983-2001 & Dejan Stankovic 1998- • 11 - Danko Lazovic 2002- • 10 - Milan Jovanovic 2007- & Darko Kovacevic 1994-2004 (based on internationals played since 1994 only)

Past Coaches — Slobodan Santrac 1994-98 • Milan Zivadinovic 1998-99 • Vujadin Boskov 1999-2000 • Ilija Petkovic 2000-01 • Milovan Doric 2001 • Vujadin Boskov, Ivan Curkovic & Dejan Savicevic 2001 • Dejan Savicevic 2001-03 • Ilija Petkovic 2003-06 • Javier Clemente ESP 2006-07 • Miroslav Dukic 2007-08 • Radomir Antic 2008-10 • Vladimir Petrovic 2010-

SERBIA 2009–10

JELEN SUPERLIGA

	Pl	W	D	L	F	A	Pts	Partizan	Red Star	OFK	Spartak	Vojvodina	Jagodina	Javor	Rad	Metalac	Smederevo	Borac	BSK Borca	Cukaricki	Hajduk	Napredak	Mladi
Partizan Beograd †	30	24	6	0	63	14	78		1-0	3-0	2-0	1-0	3-0	0-0	2-1	3-1	2-1	5-0	2-1	3-0	1-0	3-1	6-0
Crvena Zvezda ‡	30	23	2	5	53	17	71	1-2		2-1	5-2	3-0	1-0	0-1	1-0	3-0	2-1	1-0	1-3	4-0	1-0	2-1	4-1
OFK Beograd ‡	30	15	5	10	38	33	50	0-3	0-2		0-1	2-2	1-0	0-0	3-2	3-2	1-0	3-2	0-2	4-1	2-1	1-1	3-0
Spartak Subotica ‡	30	14	7	9	34	27	49	1-1	0-1	0-1		0-1	1-1	0-0	1-0	0-0	2-0	1-0	2-1	1-0	1-1	2-0	2-0
Vojvodina Novi Sad	30	13	6	11	51	30	45	1-2	0-1	0-0	0-1		4-1	0-1	2-3	1-0	1-1	3-0	2-0	4-0	3-2	7-0	3-0
Jagodina	30	12	7	11	38	34	43	0-0	0-3	3-2	3-1	2-2		2-0	1-0	3-1	2-0	0-1	2-0	2-0	2-0	1-1	2-0
Javor Ivanjica	30	8	14	8	22	23	38	1-1	0-2	0-1	1-0	1-1	0-0		2-2	2-0	1-0	1-1	1-0	2-2	1-1	1-0	0-0
Rad Beograd	30	10	7	13	38	39	37	2-3	1-2	0-2	1-3	1-0	1-0	3-2		3-0	3-2	0-0	2-0	2-0	1-1	2-1	3-2
Metalac G. Milanovac	30	10	5	15	24	39	35	0-2	2-1	2-1	0-0	3-1	2-3	1-0	1-1		0-2	1-0	1-3	0-1	2-1	1-0	1-0
FC Smederevo	30	8	10	12	23	30	34	0-2	0-3	0-1	2-0	1-0	2-0	1-1	2-1	0-1		0-0	1-1	1-0	0-0	1-1	1-0
Borac Cacak	30	9	7	14	21	34	34	0-3	0-0	2-0	1-2	0-0	2-1	1-0	0-0	1-0	3-1		2-0	2-1	1-1	0-1	1-0
BSK Borca	30	9	6	15	27	37	33	1-2	0-1	1-0	0-2	0-4	1-4	1-0	0-0	0-0	0-0	2-0		2-0	3-0	1-1	2-3
Cukaricki Stankom	30	9	5	16	25	46	32	1-1	0-3	0-0	0-3	1-3	2-1	0-1	2-1	0-1	0-0	1-0	1-0		1-0	2-1	1-1
Hajduk Kula	30	7	9	14	28	40	30	0-2	0-1	0-2	2-1	0-3	1-1	1-1	2-1	1-1	1-2	2-0	0-0	2-1		3-1	2-0
Napredak Krusevac	30	7	8	15	30	44	29	0-1	1-1	1-2	2-3	2-0	2-1	1-1	2-1	2-0	2-2	2-0	1-2	0-2	2-0		0-0
Mladi R'nik Pozarevac	30	5	10	15	19	47	25	1-1	0-1	1-1	0-0	1-0	1-3	0-0	1-0	0-0	1-0	0-0	2-1	2-0	1-4	1-3	

15/08/2009 - 16/05/2010 • † Qualified for the UEFA Champions League • ‡ Qualified for the Europa League

Top scorers: 22 - Dragan Mrda, Vojvodina • 17 - Andrija Kaluderovic, Rad • 14 - Cleo BRA, Partizan & Lamine Diarra SEN, Partizan • 12 - Dejan Lekic, Red Star & Milan Bojovic, Jagodina • 10 - Aleksandar Jevtic, Red Star; Vojo Ubiparip, Spartak & Dusan Tadic, Vojvodina

SERBIA 2009–10
PRVA LIGA TELEKOM SRBIJA (2)

	Pl	W	D	L	F	A	Pts
Indjija	34	17	9	8	47	26	60
Sevojno	34	17	7	10	40	24	58
Kolubara Lazarevac	34	14	14	5	37	28	56
Bezanija Novi Beograd	34	14	11	9	34	28	53
Novi Sad	34	14	9	11	34	29	51
Teleoptik Zemun	34	13	8	12	35	31	47
Proleter Novi Sad	34	13	7	14	41	35	46
Srem Sremska Mitrovica	34	12	10	12	34	37	46
Novi Pazar	34	13	7	14	33	38	46
Banat Zrenjanin	34	11	12	11	31	28	45
Radnicki Sombor	34	12	9	13	30	32	45
FK Zemun §2	34	11	12	11	39	36	43
Dinamo Vranje	34	12	7	15	32	38	43
Mladost Lucani	34	9	15	10	33	31	42
Radnicki Nis	34	9	14	11	33	35	41
Slog Kraljevo	34	9	12	13	28	32	39
CSK Pivara Celarevo	34	6	14	14	32	48	32
Mladost Apatin	34	7	7	20	24	61	28

15/08/2009 - 6/06/2010 • § = points deducted

MEDALS TABLE

		Overall			League			Cup		City/Town
		G	S	B	G	S	B	G	S	
1	Crvena Zvezda	18	14	2	7	10	2	11	4	Belgrade
2	Partizan	17	10	1	11	7	1	6	3	Belgrade
3	Obilic	1	3	2	1	1	2		2	Belgrade
4	FK Smederevo	1	1	1			1	1	1	Smederevo
5	Zeleznik	1	1					1		Belg:ade
6	Vojvodina		4	8		1	8		3	Novi Sad
7	OFK Beograd		1	2					2	Belgrade
8	Spartak Subotica	1						1		Subotica
	Napredak Krusevac	1						1		Krusevac
	Buducnost Dvor	1						1		Banatski Dvor
	FK Zemun	1						1		Belgrade
	Sevojno	1						1		Sevojno
13	Vozdovac Beograd			1			1			Belgrade
	Zeta Golubovci			1			1			Podgorica

From 1992, the season after Croatian clubs left the Yugoslav league

SERBIAN CLUBS IN YUGOSLAVIA UNTIL 1991

		Overall			League			Cup		Europe		
		G	S	B	G	S	B	G	S	G	S	B
1	Crvena Zvedza (Red Star)	31	17	11	18	8	7	12	8	1	1	4
2	Partizan Beograd	16	14	8	11	9	8	5	4		1	
3	OFK Beograd	9	6	5	5	6	4	4				1
4	Vojvodina Novi Sad	2	4	1	2	3	1		1			
5	Yugoslavia Beograd	2	3	3	2	3	3					
6	Nasa Krila Zemun	2						2				
7	FK Radnicki	1	2						2	1		
8	FK Bor	1						1				
9	Spartak Subotica	1						1				
	Trepca Mitrovica	1						1				
11	Radnicki Nis			3			2					1
12	Belgrade Select XI	1								1		
	Vozdovac Beograd			1			1					

LAV KUP SRBJE 2009-10

First Round		Round of 16		Quarter-finals		Semi-finals		Final	
Crvena Zvezda *	6								
Mladost Apatin	1	Crvena Zvezda	1						
Mladi Radnik Pozarevac	1	Novi Pazar *	0						
Novi Pazar *	2			Crvena Zvezda *	3				
Banat Zrenjanin	3			Spartak Subotica	2				
Radnicki Svilajnac *	1	Banat Zrenjanin *	0						
Bezanija Novi Beograd	0	Spartak Subotica	2			Crvena Zvezda *	1		
Spartak Subotica *	3					OFK Beograd	0		
Borac Cacak	1 4p								
Srem Sremska Mitrovica *	1 1p	Borac Cacak	1						
Cukaricki Stankom *	1 3p	Metalac G. Milanovac *	0						
Metalac G. Milanovac	1 5p			Borac Cacak *	0				
Partizan K. Mitrovica *	0 5p			OFK Beograd	2				
Napredak Krusevac	0 4p	Partizan K. Mitrovica	1						
Novi Sad	1 4p	OFK Beograd *	3						
OFK Beograd *	1 5p							Crvena Zvezda *	1
								OFK Beograd	0
Partizan Beograd *	3								
Indjija	0	Partizan Beograd	2						
Javor Ivanjica	1	Proleter Novi Sad *	1						
Proleter Novi Sad *	3			Partizan Beograd	2				
Sevojno	1 5p			Jagodina *	1				
BSK Borca *	1 4p	Sevojno	0						
Vozdovac Beograd *	0	Jagodina *	1			Partizan Beograd *	1		
Jagodina	1					Vojvodina Novi Sad	3		
FC Smederevo *	4								
Kolubara Lazarevac	0	FC Smederevo *	3						
CSK Pivara Celarevo	1 3p	Hajduk Kula	0						
Hajduk Kula *	1 5p			FC Smederevo	0				
Mladost Lucani	3			Vojvodina Novi Sad *	1				
Rad Beograd *	2	Mladost Lucani *	1						
Dinamo Vranje	0	Vojvodina Novi Sad	3						
Vojvodina Novi Sad *	4								

Crvena Zvezda ‡	3
Vojvodina Novi Sad	0

CUP FINAL

Partizan, Belgrade
5-05-2010, Att: 20 000, Ref: Stankovic
Scorers - Jevtic [14] Cadu [62] Trifunovic [71]
Red Star - Sasa Stamenkovic, Pavle Ninkov,
Slavoljub Dordevic, Milan Vilotic, Milos Reljic,
Darko Lazetic (Slavko Perovic 69), Vladimir
Bogdanovic, Savio, Cadu (Milos Trifunovic 66),
Dejan Lekic, Aleksandar Jevtic (Marko
Blazic 80). Tr: Ratko Dostanic
Vojvodina - Zeljko Brkic, Miroslav Vulicevic,
Marcelo Pletsch, Dejan Karan, Janko
Tumbasevic, Nnaemeka Ajuru, Slobodan
Medojevic (Ognjen Mudrinski 75), Slobodan
Novakovic (Slaven Stjepanovic 67), Mario
Djurovski (Vuk Mitosevic 58), Dusan Tadic,
Dragan Mrda. Tr: Milan Duricic

* Home team • ‡ Qualified for the Europa League

SRI – SRI LANKA

FIFA/COCA-COLA WORLD RANKING

1993	1994	1995	1996	1997	1998	1999	2000	2001	2002	2003	2004	2005	2006	2007	2008	2009	2010
126	139	135	126	136	134	153	149	143	139	135	140	144	145	167	163	151	163

2010												Hi/Lo
Jan	Feb	Mar	Mar	Apr	May	Jul	Aug	Sep	Oct	Nov	Dec	**122**
151	151	154	157	156	159	155	153	148	153	153	163	**170**

Having lost in the final of the first AFC Challenge Cup in 2006, Sri Lanka were hoping to go one better when they hosted the 2010 tournament but there was bitter disappointment after a poor performance saw them eliminated at the end of the first round group stage. They did salvage some pride with a 3-0 victory over Bangladesh in their final game but by then they had lost to both Myanmar and Tajikistan in what were the only three games they played during the course of the year. At club level Renown Sports Club fared little better in the 2010 AFC President's Cup, finishing bottom of their first round group to complete a miserable year for Sri Lanka in continental competitions. The performance of the 2009 champions was perhaps not surprising given that they finished 10th in the 12-team Sri Lankan championship in 2010, well-adrift of new champions Don Bosco. In a close finish Don Bosco, from the capital Colombo, collected their first-ever trophy thanks to a 2-1 win over Air Force on the final day of a season that had crept over into the new year. The previous June Don Bosco had lost to Navy in the semi-finals of the Holcim FA Cup and in a year of firsts Navy then went on to beat Nandamithra in the final at the Police Grounds in Colombo to win the trophy in their first appearance in the final.

FIFA WORLD CUP RECORD
1930-1990 DNE 1994-2010 DNQ

FOOTBALL FEDERATION OF SRI LANKA (FFSL)

100/9 Independence Avenue, Colombo 07

☎ +94 11 2686120
📠 +94 11 2682471
✉ ffsl@srilankafootball.com
🖥 www.srilankafootball.com
FA 1939 CON 1958 FIFA 1950
P Sarath Weerasekera
GS Anton Thangeswaran

FIFA BIG COUNT 2006

Total players	429 150
% of population	2.12%
Male	397 000
Female	32 150
Amateurs 18+	23 200
Youth under 18	26 800
Unregistered	68 000
Professionals	0
Referees	390
Admin & coaches	1 830
Number of clubs	580
Number of teams	1 100

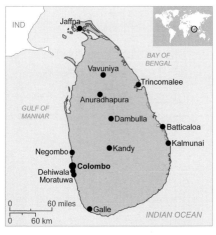

MAJOR CITIES/TOWNS

		Population
1	Colombo	682 046
2	Dehiwala	232 220
3	Moratuwa	202 021
4	Negombo	142 451
5	Trincomalee	131 954
6	Kotte	125 914
7	Kandy	119 186
8	Kalmunai	103 879
9	Vavuniya	101 143
10	Jaffna	98 193
11	Galle	97 209
12	Batticaloa	95 489
13	Katunayaka	90 231
14	Battaramulla	84 200
15	Dambulla	75 290
16	Daluguma	74 129
17	Maharagama	74 117
18	Kotikawatta	71 879
19	Anuradhapura	66 951

SHRI LAMKA • SRI LANKA

Capital	Colombo	Population	21 324 791 (53)	% in cities	15%
GDP per capita	$4400 (150)	Area km²	65 610 km² (121)	GMT +/-	+5.5
Neighbours (km)	Coast 1340				

RECENT INTERNATIONAL MATCHES PLAYED BY SRI LANKA

2006	Opponents	Score		Venue	Comp	Scorers	Att	Referee
2-04	Brunei Darusalaam	W	1-0	Chittagong	CCr1	Kasun Weerarathna [74]	2 000	Saidov UZB
4-04	Bhutan	W	1-0	Chittagong	CCr1	Karu [45]		Saidov UZB
6-04	Nepal	D	1-1	Chittagong	CCr1	Izzadeen [19]	2 500	Lee Gi Young KOR
8-04	Chinese Taipei	W	3-0	Chittagong	CCqf	Izzadeen [44], Sanjaya [70], Ratnayaka [90]	2 500	Al Ghatrifi OMA
12-04	Nepal	D	1-1	Chittagong	CCsf	Kasun Weerarathna [65]. W 5-3p	2 500	Lee Gi Young KOR
16-04	Tajikistan	L	0-4	Dhaka	CCf		2 000	Mombini IRN
2007								
21-10	Qatar	L	0-1	Colombo	WCq		6 500	Bashir SIN
28-10	Qatar	L	0-5	Doha	WCq		3 000	Al Ghamdi KSA
2008								
2-04	Guam	W	5-1	Taipei	CCq	Channa Edrib'nage [54], Chathura Weerasinghe 2 [55 64], Safras Mohamed [82], Kasun Weerarathna [91+]	300	Kavalenko UZB
4-04	Pakistan	W	7-1	Taipei	CCq	Chathura Weerasinghe 4 [2 7 9 42], Channa Edribandanage 2 [13p 82], Fernando 2 [72 77]	300	Kavalenko UZB
6-04	Chinese Taipei	D	2-2	Taipei	CCq	Chen Po Liang OG [59], Kasun Weerarathna [86]	900	Iemoto JPN
4-06	Afghanistan	D	2-2	Colombo	SAFr1	Chathura Weerasinghe [8], Channa Edribandanage [80p]		
6-06	Bhutan	W	2-0	Colombo	SAFr1	Chathura Weerasinghe 2 [25 39]		
8-06	Bangladesh	W	1-0	Colombo	SAFr1	Rawme Mohideen [73]		
11-06	Maldives	L	0-1	Colombo	SAFsf			
31-07	Korea DPR	L	0-3	Hyderabad	CCr1		100	Vo Minh Tri VIE
2-08	Myanmar	L	1-3	Hyderabad	CCr1	Kasun Weerarathna [51]	100	Kovalenko UZB
4-08	Nepal	L	0-3	Hyderabad	CCr1		200	Saleem MDV
2009								
28-03	Maldives	D	1-1	Colombo	Fr	Channa Edribandanage [37]		
4-04	Brunei Darussalam	W	5-1	Colombo	CCq	Kasun Weerarathna 4 [23 53 67 73], Moh'd Asmeer [32]	700	Zhao Liang CHN
6-04	Chinese Taipei	W	2-1	Colombo	CCq	Kasun Weerarathna [35], Rohana Ruwan Dinesh [39]	1 400	Al Zahrani KSA
8-04	Pakistan	D	2-2	Colombo	CCq	Rohana Ruwan Dinesh [2], Sanjeev Shanmugarajah [88]	3 000	Tseytlin UZB
22-08	Lebanon	W	4-3	New Delhi	Fr	Moh'd Izzadeen 3 [6 80 88], Chathura Weerasinghe [83]		Rowan IND
24-08	Syria	L	0-4	New Delhi	Fr			Singh IND
26-08	India	L	1-3	New Delhi	Fr	Rohana Ruwan Dinesh [62]		Ali Adil MDV
28-08	Kyrgyzstan	L	1-4	New Delhi	Fr	Chathura Weerasinghe [53]		Singh IND
4-12	Pakistan	W	1-0	Dhaka	SAFr1	Chathura Gunarathna [23]		
6-12	Bhutan	W	6-0	Dhaka	SAFr1	Channa Ediri 2 [7 25], Kasun Weerarathna 3 [39 66 78], Chathura Gunarathna [90]		
8-12	Bangladesh	L	1-2	Dhaka	SAFr1	Channa Ediri [42]		
11-12	Maldives	L	1-5	Dhaka	SAFsf	Channa Ediri [62]		
2010								
16-02	Myanmar	L	0-4	Colombo	CCr1		3 000	Faghani IRN
18-02	Tajikistan	L	1-3	Colombo	CCr1	Philip Dalpethado [78]	1 000	Tan Hai CHN
20-02	Bangladesh	W	3-0	Colombo	CCr1	Mohamed Kaiz [7], Chathura Gunarathna [43], Sanjeev Shanmugarajah [79]	600	Mahapab THA

Fr = Friendly match • SAF = South Asian Federation Cup • CC = AFC Challenge Cup • WC = FIFA World Cup • q = qualifier

SRI LANKA 2010

DIALOG CHAMPIONS LEAGUE

	Pl	W	D	L	F	A	Pts	Don Bosco	Army	Police	Ratnam	New Young	Blue Star	Air Force	Saunders	Java Lane	Renown	Kalutara Park	Jupiters
Don Bosco †	22	13	5	4	37	17	44		0-0	1-1	1-1	2-0	2-0	2-1	1-0	2-0	4-1	1-0	4-0
Army	22	11	9	2	44	16	42	0-2		1-1	1-1	3-0	2-0	0-0	1-1	1-1	1-1	5-0	5-0
Police	21	11	7	3	41	21	40	2-1	0-2		4-1	6-1	0-0	0-2	3-0	2-0	1-0	5-2	4-1
Ratnam	21	11	5	5	41	32	38	2-1	0-0	1-3		3-2	1-0	0-1	1-2	5-3	2-2	n/p	5-1
New Young	21	10	4	7	38	34	34	3-1	2-4	3-3	2-2		1-0	2-0	2-0	1-0	2-0	0-2	7-0
Blue Star	21	8	7	6	21	16	31	2-1	1-0	0-0	2-3	n/p		1-0	1-0	0-0	2-2	2-0	5-0
Air Force	21	8	6	7	24	21	30	0-1	1-3	2-1	2-0	1-2	0-1		2-0	n/p	1-0	1-0	2-2
Saunders	20	6	6	9	17	23	22	0-1	2-2	1-2	0-1	1-1	0-2	0-0		0-0	2-1	4-1	1-0
Java Lane	21	4	8	9	26	34	20	1-5	0-1	1-1	2-3	2-0	1-1	2-2	1-2		2-1	5-2	4-1
Renown	20	4	5	11	33	41	17	2-2	1-3	n/p	1-2	3-4	3-1	2-2	n/p	3-2		5-2	4-1
Kalutara Park	21	3	7	11	20	40	16	1-1	1-4	1-1	0-2	1-1	0-0	0-2	0-0	1-1	3-1		3-1
Jupiters	22	2	3	17	17	64	9	0-1	1-5	0-1	2-5	0-2	0-0	2-2	0-1	1-3	2-0	2-1	

31/09/2010 - 8/01/2011 • † Qualified for the AFC President's Cup

MEDALS TABLE

		Overall	Lge	Cup		City
		G	G	G	S	
1	Saunders	18	12	6	4	Colombo
2	Ratnam	10	4	6	1	Kotahena
3	Renown	9	4	5	3	Colombo
4	Negombo Youth	3	2	1	2	Negombo
5	Old Bens	2	1	1	2	Colombo
6	Police	1		1	2	Colombo
7	Army	1	1	1		Colombo
8	Blue Stars	1	1			Kalutara
	Don Bosco	1	1			Colombo
	Navy	1		1		Colombo
	Pettah United	1	1			Colombo
	York	1		1		Kandy

HOLCIM FA CUP 2010

Round of 16	Quarter-finals	Semi-finals	Final
Navy			
	Navy 1 3p		
Old Bens 0	Ratnam 1 1p		
Ratnam 4		Navy 2 4p	
Renown		Don Bosco 2 3p	
	Renown 0 2p		
Maligawatte 0	Don Bosco 0 4p		
Don Bosco 1			Navy 2
Police 4			Nandamithra 1
Colombo SC 0	Police 0 3p		
Saunders 0	Java Lane 0 1p		**CUP FINAL**
Java Lane 1		Police 0	
Army		Nandimithra 2	Police Grounds, Colombo
	Army 1		18-06-2010
	Nandimithra 2		
Nandimithra			

STP – SAO TOME E PRINCIPE

FIFA/COCA-COLA WORLD RANKING

1993	1994	1995	1996	1997	1998	1999	2000	2001	2002	2003	2004	2005	2006	2007	2008	2009	2010
-	-	-	-	-	194	187	181	186	191	192	195	197	198	-	-	-	-

2010												Hi/Lo
Jan	Feb	Mar	Mar	Apr	May	Jul	Aug	Sep	Oct	Nov	Dec	179
Not Ranked												200

There was no international football for Africa's second smallest nation for a seventh successive year as the former Portuguese colony remained an isolated outpost. The national side has not played since 2003 and as a result is the only one of the 208 nations affiliated to FIFA that is absent from the FIFA Coca-Cola World Ranking. At club level there were also no entries in the two annual continental club competitions; none in the continental junior championships at under-20 and under-17 level or in the regional CEMAC Cup. The costs of leaving the island, with its limited flight connections, holds back participation although the recent discovery of substantial oil reserves could give the country the same boost enjoyed by nearby Equatorial Guinea. Contacts were kept with Portugal and Brazil, where three of the country's more promising footballers were sent for training and trials whilst plans were also announced to renovate stadiums. The domestic championship was decided between the champions from the two rival islands and provided only a second triumph for a team from Principe as Desportivo Roca Sundy beat Vitoria Riboque in Santo Antonio. The game was not completed as Riboque walked off in protest at a penalty awarded against them in the second half. Military team 6 de Setembro won the National Cup.

FIFA WORLD CUP RECORD
1930-1998 DNE 2002-2006 DNQ 2010 DNE

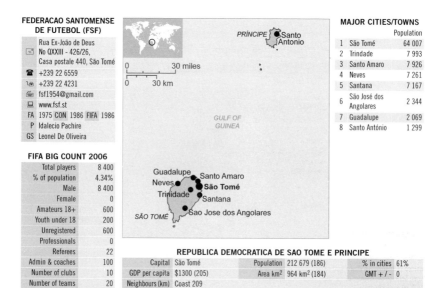

FEDERACAO SANTOMENSE DE FUTEBOL (FSF)

Rua Ex-João de Deus
No QXXIII - 426/26,
Casa postale 440, São Tomé
☎ +239 22 6559
📠 +239 22 4231
✉ fsf1954@gmail.com
🖳 www.fsf.st
FA 1975 CON 1986 FIFA 1986
P Idalecio Pachire
GS Leonel De Oliveira

FIFA BIG COUNT 2006

Total players	8 400
% of population	4.34%
Male	8 400
Female	0
Amateurs 18+	600
Youth under 18	200
Unregistered	600
Professionals	0
Referees	22
Admin & coaches	100
Number of clubs	10
Number of teams	20

MAJOR CITIES/TOWNS

		Population
1	São Tomé	64 007
2	Trindade	7 993
3	Santo Amaro	7 926
4	Neves	7 261
5	Santana	7 167
6	São José dos Angolares	2 344
7	Guadalupe	2 069
8	Santo António	1 299

REPUBLICA DEMOCRATICA DE SAO TOME E PRINCIPE

Capital	São Tomé	Population	212 679 (186)	% in cities	61%
GDP per capita	$1300 (205)	Area km²	964 km² (184)	GMT + / -	0
Neighbours (km)	Coast 209				

RECENT INTERNATIONAL MATCHES PLAYED BY SAO TOME E PRINCIPE

2000	Opponents	Score		Venue	Comp	Scorers	Att	Referee
8-04	Sierra Leone	W	2-0	São Tomé	WCq			
22-04	Sierra Leone	L	0-4	Freetown	WCq			
2-07	Gabon	D	1-1	São Tomé	CNq			
15-07	Gabon	L	1-4	Libreville	CNq			
2001								
No international matches played in 2001								
2002								
No international matches played in 2002								
2003								
11-10	Libya	L	0-1	São Tomé	WCq		4 000	Yameogo JPN
12-11	Equatorial Guinea	L	1-3	Malabo	Fr			
16-11	Libya	L	0-8	Benghazi	WCq		20 000	Guirat TUN
2004								
No international matches played in 2004								
2005								
No international matches played in 2005								
2006								
No international matches played in 2006								
2007								
No international matches played in 2007								
2008								
No international matches played in 2008								
2009								
No international matches played in 2009								
2010								
No international matches played in 2010								

Fr = Friendly match • CN = CAF African Cup of Nations • WC = FIFA World Cup • q = qualifier

SAO TOME E PRINCIPE 2009
SAO TOME CHAMPIONSHIP

	Pl	W	D	L	F	A	Pts
Vitória FC Riboque	26						55
DM 6 de Setembro	26						53
Desportivo Oque d'El Rei	26						46
Sporting Club Praia Cruz	26						44
Santana FC	26						39
Barrios Unidos Caixão Grande	26						38
UDRA São João dos Angolares	26						36
UDESCAI Agua Ize	26						32
Agrosport Monte Café	26						29
Desportivo Guadalupe	26						28
Inter Bom Bom	26						28
Aliança Nacional Pantufo	26						24
Cruz Vermelha Almeirim	26						24
Andorinha Ponta Mina	26						13

Started 14-02-2009

CAMPEONATO NACIONAL 2010
Santo Antonio de Príncipe, 6-03-2010

Des. Roca Sundy   3-1   Vitória FC Riboque

Awarded to Sundy after Vitoria walked off after 56'
Played between the winners of the 2009 championships in
São Tomé and in Príncipe

TACA NACIONAL FINAL 2010
Estadio Nacional, São Tomé, 6-03-2010

6 de Setembro   2-1   Sporting do Príncipe

SUD – SUDAN

FIFA/COCA-COLA WORLD RANKING

1993	1994	1995	1996	1997	1998	1999	2000	2001	2002	2003	2004	2005	2006	2007	2008	2009	2010
119	116	86	74	108	114	132	132	118	106	103	114	92	120	92	93	108	92

	2010												Hi/Lo
	Jan	Feb	Mar	Mar	Apr	May	Jul	Aug	Sep	Oct	Nov	Dec	74
	108	109	109	121	121	118	121	120	101	93	96	92	137

Sudan's national side broke a sequence of 10 matches without a victory when they beat Congo 2-0 at home in September at the start of their 2012 African Nations Cup qualifiers. But it was a goalless draw the following month away against Ghana, who just 12 months earlier had hammered Sudan both home and away in the World Cup qualifiers, that gave the squad a major boost. The year had started with Stephen Constantine as coach but ended with Mohamed 'Mazda' Abdallah back in charge of the national side as the brief experiment with foreign coaches was brought to a close. The turmoil in the national team again contrasted with the increasing competitiveness of Sudan's top two clubs in African competition. Both Al Hilal and Al Merreikh made it to the third round of the Champions League but were then both eliminated and dropped down to the CAF Confederation Cup. Al Merreikh suffered a surprise setback to supposedly inferior opposition from Niger but Al Hilal qualified for group phase, going on to win their group but were then beaten in the semi-final on post-match penalties by Tunisia's CS Sfaxien. Consolation for Al Hilal came in the form of yet another championship title, but league runners-up Al Merreikh denied them the double with a 2-0 win in the cup as the pair met in the final for the seventh year running.

FIFA WORLD CUP RECORD
1930-1954 DNE **1958** DNQ **1962-1966** DNE **1970-1974** DNQ **1978** DNE **1982-1990** DNQ **1994** DNE **1998-2010** DNQ

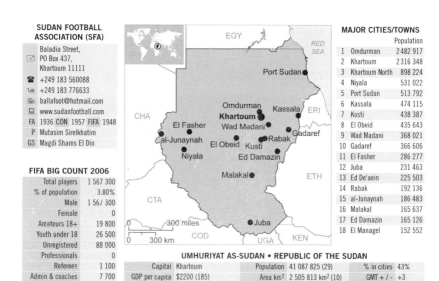

SUDAN FOOTBALL ASSOCIATION (SFA)

Baladia Street,
PO Box 437,
Khartoum 11111
☎ +249 183 560088
📠 +249 183 776633
📧 ballafoot@hotmail.com
🖥 www.sudanfootball.com
FA 1936 CON 1957 FIFA 1948
P Mutasim Sirelkhatim
GS Magdi Shams El Din

FIFA BIG COUNT 2006

Total players	1 567 300
% of population	3.80%
Male	1 56/ 300
Female	0
Amateurs 18+	19 800
Youth under 18	26 500
Unregistered	88 000
Professionals	0
Referees	1 100
Admin & coaches	7 700
Number of clubs	440
Number of teams	2 750

MAJOR CITIES/TOWNS

		Population
1	Omdurman	2 482 917
2	Khartoum	2 316 348
3	Khartoum North	898 224
4	Niyala	531 022
5	Port Sudan	513 792
6	Kassala	474 115
7	Kusti	438 387
8	El Obeid	435 643
9	Wad Madani	368 021
10	Gadaref	366 606
11	El Fasher	286 277
12	Juba	231 463
13	Ed De'aein	225 503
14	Rabak	192 136
15	al-Junaynah	186 483
16	Malakal	165 637
17	Ed Damazin	165 126
18	El Managel	152 552

UMHURIYAT AS-SUDAN • REPUBLIC OF THE SUDAN

Capital	Khartoum	Population	41 087 825 (29)	% in cities	43%
GDP per capita	$2200 (185)	Area km²	2 505 813 km² (10)	GMT +/-	+3
Neighbours (km)	Central African Republic 1165, Chad 1360, Congo DR 628, Egypt 1273, Eritrea 605, Ethiopia 1606, Kenya 232, Libya 383, Uganda 435 • Coast 853				

RECENT INTERNATIONAL MATCHES PLAYED BY SUDAN

2007	Opponents	Score		Venue	Comp	Scorers	Att	Referee
13-12	Zanzibar †	D	2-2	Arusha	CCr1	Abdil Ahmed 2 56 81		
15-12	Ethiopia	D	0-0	Arusha	CCr1			
17-12	Tanzania	W	2-1	Dar es Salaam	CCqf	Abdelhamid Amari 2 9 35		
19-12	Burundi	W	2-1	Dar es Salaam	CCsf	Saifeldin Ali Idris 2, Abdelhamid Amari 45		
22-12	Rwanda	D	2-2	Dar es Salaam	CCf	Abdelhamid Amari 23, Modather Eltaab 46. W 4-2p		
2008								
9-01	Nigeria	L	0-2	Estepona	Fr			
11-01	Guinea	L	0-6	Estepona	Fr			
22-01	Zambia	L	0-3	Kumasi	CNr1			Diatta SEN
26-01	Egypt	L	0-3	Kumasi	CNr1			Codja BEN
30-01	Cameroon	L	0-3	Tamale	CNr1			Djaoupe TOG
26-03	Liberia	L	0-2	Omdurman	Fr			
22-05	Yemen	D	1-1	Sana'a	Fr	Haitham Tambal 15		
8-06	Congo	L	0-1	Brazzaville	WCq		25 000	Mana NGA
14-06	Mali	W	3-2	Khartoum	WCq	Alaeldin Yousif 46, Mohamed Tahir 70, Haytham Kamal 90	15 000	Abd El Fatah EGY
22-06	Mali	L	0-3	Bamako	WCq		25 000	Doue CIV
20-08	Egypt	W	4-0	Omdurman	Fr	OG 35, Mudathir El Tahir 2 81 90, Ahmed Adil 88		
6-09	Chad	L	1-2	Cairo	WCq	Haytham Kamal 75	4 000	Trabelsi TUN
10-09	Chad	W	3-1	Cairo	WCq	Ahmed Adil 4, Faisal Agab 48p, Saifeldin Ali 76	10 000	Diatta SEN
11-10	Congo	W	2-0	Omdurman	WCq	Mohamed Tahir 30, Faisal Agab 74	27 000	Ambaya LBY
31-12	Kenya	D	0-0	Jinja	CCr1			
2009								
4-01	Djibouti	D	1-1	Jinja	CCr1	El Tayeb El Mahi 16		
6-01	Burundi	L	0-1	Jinja	CCr1			
8-01	Zambia	W	2-0	Kampala	CCr1	Abdelhameed Amarri 33, El Tayeb El Mahi 61		
7-03	Uganda	L	0-2	Khartoum	Fr			
28-03	Mali	D	1-1	Omdurman	WCq	Mudathir El Tahir 23	35 000	Maillet SEY
28-05	Tunisia	L	0-4	Rades/Tunis	Fr			Omar LBY
7-06	Benin	L	0-1	Cotonou	WCq		26 000	Marange ZIM
20-06	Ghana	L	0-2	Omdurman	WCq		30 000	Ambaya LBY
6-09	Ghana	L	0-2	Accra	WCq		38 000	Abd El Fatah EGY
11-10	Mali	L	0-1	Bamako	WCq		15 000	Benouza ALG
14-11	Benin	L	1-2	Omdurman	WCq	Hassan Abakar 45	600	Jedidi TUN
2010								
4-06	Palestine	D	1-1	Omdurman	Fr	Tarek Mukhtar 12		
20-06	Tunisia	L	2-6	Omdurman	Fr	Mudathir El Tahir 59p, Mohannad Tahir 83		
4-09	Congo	W	2-0	Khartoum	CNq	Mudathir El Tahir 2 11 90p		Kaoma ZAM
10-10	Ghana	D	0-0	Kumasi	CNq			Damon RSA
28-11	Zanzibar †	L	0-2	Dar es Salaam	CCr1			
1-12	Rwanda	D	0-0	Dar es Salaam	CCr1			

Fr = Friendly match • CN = CAF African Cup of Nations • CC = CECAFA Cup • WC = FIFA World Cup • † Not a full international
q = qualifier • r1 = first round group • sf = semi-final • f = final

SUDAN 2010

PREMIER LEAGUE

	Pl	W	D	L	F	A	Pts	Hilal O	Merreikh	Khartoum	Nil	Mawrada	Jazeerat	Hay Al Arab	Hilal PS	Hilal K	A.al	Ahli K	Ittihad	Ahli WM	Merghani
Al Hilal Omdurman †	26	23	1	2	70	13	**70**		3-2	2-1	2-0	6-0	3-2	4-0	2-0	5-0	3-0	4-1	7-0	2-0	6-0
Al Merreikh †	26	22	1	3	65	19	**67**	0-2		1-0	6-1	2-1	3-0	2-1	2-0	3-0	3-0	4-2	1-0	2-0	4-0
Khartoum-3 ‡	26	10	10	6	33	31	**40**	1-5	0-3		1-1	1-2	3-2	2-1	1-1	2-0	0-0	4-2	1-0	2-2	2-0
Al Nil Hasahisa ‡	26	11	6	9	36	32	**39**	1-2	1-3	1-0		0-0	2-0	2-0	1-0	3-1	1-1	5-1	2-0	1-1	3-0
Al Mawrada Omdurman	26	7	11	8	26	35	**32**	0-1	1-4	3-4	2-1		1-0	2-1	0-0	2-1	1-1	0-0	1-1	0-0	1-2
Jazeerat Al-Feel	26	8	7	11	28	30	**31**	0-1	1-2	0-0	2-2	0-0		4-1	1-0	0-1	2-0	1-0	0-1	1-1	1-0
Hay Al Arab	26	7	10	9	28	34	**31**	2-0	1-3	0-0	0-1	1-1	2-2		1-0	2-1	2-1	3-0	0-0	0-0	4-2
Al Hilal Port Sudan	26	7	9	10	23	24	**30**	0-1	1-2	1-1	3-1	2-0	0-0	0-0		0-0	5-2	0-0	2-0	1-1	2-3
Al Hilal Kadugli	26	8	6	12	19	32	**30**	2-0	2-4	0-1	1-0	0-0	1-0	1-1	1-2		1-0	1-0	0-0	1-1	1-0
Al Amal Atbara	26	7	7	12	28	34	**28**	0-0	2-0	1-1	1-2	2-2	3-2	1-1	0-1	0-1		0-1	2-1	1-2	2-0
Al Ahli Khartoum	26	6	9	11	28	46	**27**	0-2	0-5	2-2	2-0	1-2	2-2	2-2	1-1	1-1	0-1		2-1	2-2	2-2
Al Ittihad Wad Medani	26	7	5	14	14	34	**26**	0-3	0-0	0-1	2-1	1-0	0-1	0-1	2-0	1-0	2-1	0-1		1-0	1-0
Al Ahli Wad Medani	26	4	11	11	20	30	**23**	1-2	0-2	0-1	1-3	1-1	0-1	2-0	1-0	2-1	0-1	0-1	0-0		1-1
Al Merghani Kassala	26	6	5	15	23	47	**23**	0-2	0-2	1-1	0-0	2-3	1-3	1-1	2-0	1-0	1-0	1-2	1-2	2-1	

18/02/2009 - 25/11/2009 • † Qualified for the CAF Champions League • ‡ Qualified for the CAF Confederations Cup

MEDALS TABLE

		Overall	Lge	Cup	Africa			City
		G	G	G	G	S	B	
1	Al Merreikh	38	17	20	1	1	2	Omdurman
2	Al Hilal	33	26	7		2	4	Omdurman
3	Al Mourada	6	1	5			1	Omdurman
4	Burri	1	1					Khartoum
	Al Hilal	1	1					Port Sudan
	Al Ahly	1		1				Wad Medani
	Al Ittihad	1		1				Wad Medani
	Hay Al Arab	1		1				Port Sudan
	Al Nil	1		1				Khartoum

FA CUP 2010

Quarter-finals		Semi-finals		Final	
Al Merreikh	5				
Al Ittihad Wad Medani	0	**Al Merreikh**	4		
Al Hilal Port Sudan	0	Al Amal Atbara	0		
Al Amal Atbara	2			**Al Merreikh**	2
Khartoum-3	2 5p			Al Hilal Omdurman	0
Al Nil Hasahisa	2 4p	Khartoum-3	1		
Al Ahli Khartoum	0	**Al Hilal Omdurman**	4		
Al Hilal Omdurman	5				

SUI – SWITZERLAND

FIFA/COCA-COLA WORLD RANKING

1993	1994	1995	1996	1997	1998	1999	2000	2001	2002	2003	2004	2005	2006	2007	2008	2009	2010
12	7	18	47	62	83	47	58	63	44	44	51	35	17	44	24	18	22

	2010												Hi/Lo
	Jan	Feb	Mar	Mar	Apr	May	Jul	Aug	Sep	Oct	Nov	Dec	**3**
	18	18	15	20	26	24	18	17	21	23	21	22	**83**

Switzerland couldn't have made a more dramatic entrance at the 2010 FIFA World Cup in South Africa. In their opening match they beat the overwhelming favourites and eventual winners Spain but they then froze in the spotlight and were on the plane back home at the end of the group stage. Coach Ottmar Hitzfeld looked to have pulled off a masterstroke in the game against the Spanish, an early second half goal from Gelson Fernandez giving the Swiss a lead that they fought doggedly to hold on to. Why they flopped in the next two games against Chile and Honduras is open to debate. The harsh sending off of Valon Behrami against Chile didn't help and perhaps they were too well drilled defensively to be an effective attacking unit. They did after all beat the World Cup record for minutes without conceding a goal in the match against Chile. At home there was yet another exciting climax to the league with Young Boys looking odds-on for only a second championship in 50 years but four defeats in the run in saw their lead whittled away and in the last game they faced Basel with both teams level on points. Basel had just thrashed Lausanne in the Cup Final and they secured the double in Thorsten Fink's first season in charge with a 2-0 victory thanks to their young star Valentin Stocker and Aussie striker Scott Chipperfield.

FIFA WORLD CUP RECORD

1930 DNE **1934** 7 QF **1938** 7 QF **1950** 6 r1 **1954** 8 QF (hosts) **1958** DNQ **1962** 16 r1 **1966** 16
1970-1990 DNQ **1994** 16 r2 **1998-2002** DNQ **2006** 10 r2 **2010** 19 r1

**SCHWEIZERISCHER
FUSSBALL-VERBAND
(SFV/ASF)**

✉	Worbstrasse 48,
Postfach Bern 3000
☎	+41 31 9508111
📠	+41 31 9508181
✉	sfv.asf@football.ch
🖥	www.football.ch
FA	1895 CON 1954 FIFA 1904
P	Peter Gillieron
GS	Alex Miescher

FIFA BIG COUNT 2006

Total players	571 700
% of population	7.60%
Male	507 900
Female	63 800
Amateurs 18+	103 700
Youth under 18	127 700
Unregistered	240 000
Professionals	550
Referees	4 783
Admin & coaches	25 300
Number of clubs	1 412
Number of teams	13 005

MAJOR CITIES/TOWNS

		Population
1	Zürich	353 485
2	Geneva	179 019
3	Basel	160 663
4	Berne	121 042
5	Lausanne	118 606
6	Winterthur	96 851
7	Saint Gall	69 713
8	Luzern	57 913
9	Lugano	55 907
10	Biel	49 089
11	Thun	41 754
12	Köniz	37 644
13	La Chaux-de-Fonds	36 853
14	Schaffhausen	33 519
15	Fribourg	33 293
16	Neuchâtel	32 390
17	Chur	32 251
18	Uster	31 296
62	Grenchen	16 060

SCHWEIZ • SUISSE • SVIZZERA • SWITZERLAND

Capital	Bern	Population	7 604 467 (94)	% in cities	73%
GDP per capita	$42 000 (18)	Area km²	41 277 km² (135)	GMT + / -	+1
Neighbours (km)	Austria 164, France 573, Italy 740, Liechtenstein 41, Germany 334		

RECENT INTERNATIONAL MATCHES PLAYED BY SWITZERLAND

2007	Opponents	Score		Venue	Comp	Scorers	Att	Referee
22-08	Netherlands	W	2-1	Geneva	Fr	Barnetta 2 [9p 51]	24 000	Duhamel FRA
7-09	Chile	W	2-1	Vienna	Fr	Barnetta [13], Streller [55]	2 500	Stuchlik AUT
11-09	Japan	L	3-4	Klagenfurt	Fr	Magnin [11], N'Kufo [13p], Djourou [81]	19 500	Messner AUT
13-10	Austria	W	3-1	Zurich	Fr	Streller 2 [2 55], Hakan Yakin [36]	22 500	Hamer LUX
17-10	USA	L	0-1	Basel	Fr		16 500	De Bleeckere BEL
20-11	Nigeria	L	0-1	Zurich	Fr		12 700	Bebek CRO
2008								
6-02	England	L	1-2	London	Fr	Derdiyok [58]	86 857	Brych GER
26-03	Germany	L	0-4	Basel	Fr		38 500	Bramhaar NED
24-05	Slovakia	W	2-0	Lugano	Fr	Behrami [56], Frei [63]	10 150	Kelly IRL
30-05	Liechtenstein	W	3-0	St Gall	Fr	Frei 2 [24 31], Vonlanthen [68]	18 000	Thual FRA
7-06	Czech Republic	L	0-1	Basel	ECr1		39 730	Rosetti ITA
11-06	Turkey	L	1-2	Basel	ECr1	Hakan Yakin [32]	39 730	Michel SVK
15-06	Portugal	W	2-0	Basel	ECr1	Hakan Yakin 2 [71 83p]	39 730	Plautz AUT
20-08	Cyprus	W	4-1	Geneva	Fr	Stocker [8], Hakan Yakin [27], Nef [73], Vonlanthen [81]	14 500	Ceferin SVN
6-09	Israel	D	2-2	Ramat Gan	WCq	Hakan Yakin [45], N'Kufo [56]	29 600	Hansson SWE
10-09	Luxembourg	L	1-2	Zurich	WCq	N'Kufo [43]	20 500	Filipovic SRB
11-10	Latvia	W	2-1	St Gall	WCq	Frei [63], N'Kufo [73]	18 026	Batista POR
15-10	Greece	W	2-1	Piraeus	WCq	Frei [41p], N'Kufo [77]	28 810	Medina ESP
19-11	Finland	W	1-0	St Gall	Fr	Ziegler [84]	11 500	Kulbakov RUS
2009								
11-02	Bulgaria	D	1-1	Geneva	Fr	Huggel [45]	9 500	Duarte POR
28-03	Moldova	W	2-0	Chisinau	WCq	Frei [32], Fernandes [92+]	10 500	McDonald SCO
1-04	Moldova	W	2-0	Geneva	WCq	N'Kufo [20], Frei [52]	20 100	Rocchi ITA
12-08	Italy	D	0-0	Basel	Fr		31 500	Kircher GER
5-09	Greece	W	2-0	Basel	WCq	Grichting [84], Padalino [87]	38 500	De Bleeckere BEL
9-09	Latvia	D	2-2	Riga	WCq	Frei [43], Derdiyok [80]	8 600	Kralovec CZE
10-10	Luxembourg	W	3-0	Luxembourg	WCq	Senderos 2 [6 8], Huggel [22]	8 031	Iturralde ESP
14-10	Israel	D	0-0	Basel	WCq		38 500	Tudor ROU
14-11	Norway	L	0-1	Geneva	Fr		16 000	Whitby WAL
2010								
3-03	Uruguay	L	1-3	St Gall	Fr	Gokhan Inler [29p]	12 500	Rizzoli ITA
1-06	Costa Rica	L	0-1	Sion	Fr		11 300	Buttimer IRL
5-06	Italy	D	1-1	Geneva	Fr	Gokhan Inler [10]	30 000	Piccirillo FRA
16-06	Spain	W	1-0	Durban	WCr1	Fernandes [52]	62 453	Webb ENG
21-06	Chile	L	0-1	Port Elizabeth	WCr1		34 872	Al Ghamdi KSA
25-06	Honduras	D	0-0	Bloemfontein	WCr1		28 042	Baldassi ARG
11-08	Austria	W	1-0	Klagenfurt	Fr	Costanzo [73]	18 000	Rubinos ESP
3-09	Australia	D	0-0	St Gall	Fr		14 660	Einwaller AUT
7-09	England	L	1-3	Basel	ECq	Shaqiri [71]	37 500	Rizzoli ITA
8-10	Montenegro	L	0-1	Podgorica	ECq		10 750	Iturralde ESP
12-10	Wales	W	4-1	Basel	ECq	Stocker 2 [8 89], Streller [21], Gokhan Inler [82p]	26 000	Hamer LUX
17-11	Ukraine	D	2-2	Geneva	Fr	Frei 2 [40 62]	11 100	Gumienny BEL

Fr = Friendly match • EC = UEFA EURO 2008 • WC = FIFA World Cup • q = qualifier • po = play-off

SWITZERLAND NATIONAL TEAM HISTORICAL RECORDS

Caps
117 - Heinz Hermann 1978-91 • 112 - Alain Geiger 1980-96 • 103 - Stephane Chapuisat 1989-2004 • 94 - Johann Vogel 1995-2007 • 86 - Hakan Yakin 2000- • 82 - Alexander Frei 2001- • 81 - Patrick Muller 1998-2008 • 80 - Severino Minelli 1930-43 • 79 - Andre Egli 1979-94 & Ciriaco Sforza 1991-2001 • 75 - Raphael Wicky 1996-2007 • 72 - Stephane Henchoz 1993-2005 • 71 - Alfred Bickel 1936-54

Goals
42 - Alexander Frei 2001- • 34 - Max Abegglen 1922-37 & Kubilay Turkyilmaz 1988-2001 • 29 - Andre Abegglen 1927-43 & Jacques Fatton 1946-55 • 26 - Adrian Knupp 1989-96 • 23 - Josef Hugi 1951-61 • 22 - Charles Antenen 1948-62 • 21 - Lauro Amado 1935-48 & Stephane Chapuisat 1989-2004 • 20 - Hakan Yakin 2000- • 19 - Robert Ballaman • 15 - Alfred Bickel 1936-54 & Heinz Hermann 1978-91

Past Coaches
Karl Rappan AUT 1960-63 • Alfredo Foni ITA 1964-67 • Erwin Ballabio 1967-69 • Louis Maurer 1970-71 • Rene Hussy 1973-76 • Miroslav Blazevic YUG 1976-77 • Roger Vonlanthen 1977-79 • Leo Walker 1979-80 • Paul Wolfisberg 1981-85 • Daniel Jeandupeux 1986-89 • Uli Stielike GER 1989-91 • Roy Hodgson ENG 1992-95 • Artur Jorge POR 1996 • Rolf Fringer AUT 1996-97 • Gilbert Gress FRA 1998-99 • Enzo Trossero ENG 2000-01 • Jakob Kuhn 2001-08 • Ottmar Hitzfeld GER 2008-

SWITZERLAND 2009-10

AXPO SUPER LEAGUE

	Pl	W	D	L	F	A	Pts	Results (Basel · Young Boys · Grasshopper · Luzern · Sion · St Gallen · Zürich · Neuchâtel · Bellinzona · Aarau)
FC Basel †	36	25	5	6	90	46	80	1-2 4-0 3-1 1-2 1-1 5-0 5-0 4-3 4-0 3-2 1-1 4-1 4-1 3-0 3-2 4-0 2-1 2-1
BSC Young Boys †	36	25	2	9	78	47	77	2-0 0-2 2-0 4-0 1-1 2-1 3-1 1-0 1-1 2-1 3-0 2-1 1-0 4-1 4-2 2-1 4-0 3-1
Grasshopper-Club ‡	36	21	2	13	65	43	65	3-1 4-0 2-1 2-1 0-0 0-1 3-1 2-0 1-3 2-1 1-0 4-0 1-1 3-2 1-7 0-2 4-0 2-0
FC Luzern ‡	36	17	7	12	66	55	58	4-5 0-1 1-2 5-1 2-1 4-2 1-2 1-1 3-1 2-3 1-0 4-1 2-1 2-1 2-0 2-1 6-0 4-0
FC Sion	36	14	9	13	63	57	51	1-2 2-2 3-1 4-1 2-3 1-0 3-1 5-2 2-1 5-1 3-3 1-1 1-0 1-1 3-1 2-1 1-1 4-0
FC St Gallen	36	13	7	16	53	56	46	2-0 2-4 2-3 1-2 1-0 0-1 1-3 1-1 1-0 1-3 1-1 1-0 1-2 0-4 1-2 0-2 0-0 1-1
FC Zürich	36	12	9	15	55	58	45	2-2 1-2 2-3 0-2 4-3 3-2 4-0 1-0 1-1 2-0 1-0 1-1 1-2 0-3 3-0 3-3 4-1 2-0 3-3 2-1
Neuchâtel Xamax	36	11	8	17	55	57	41	2-2 1-1 3-0 1-0 0-1 0-1 1-1 1-2 1-3 4-1 4-2 0-3 3-0 3-3 4-1 2-0 3-3 2-1
AC Bellinzona ††	36	7	4	25	42	92	25	2-3 0-2 1-7 1-3 0-0 1-2 1-2 0-0 3-1 2-1 0-5 0-2 3-2 1-4 1-1 3-2 4-1 1-2
FC Aarau	36	6	5	25	32	88	23	0-2 0-3 0-3 1-5 1-0 1-4 2-4 1-2 0-0 0-3 0-2 2-0 1-1 1-3 0-4 1-0 1-2 6-3

11/07/2009 - 16/05/2010 • † Qualified for the UEFA Champions League • ‡ Qualified for the Europa League • †† Relegation play-off
Top scorers: **30** - Seydou Doumbia CIV, Young Boys • **21** - Marco Streller, Basel; Cristian Ianu ROU, Luzern & Emile Mpenza BEL, Sion •
15 - Alexander Frei, Basel • **14** - Moreno Costanzo, St Gallen & Gonzalo Zarate ARG, Grasshopper-Club • **13** - Scott Chipperfield AUS, Basel
Relegation play-off: **Bellinzona** 2-1 0-0 Lugano

SWITZERLAND 2009-10

CHALLENGE LEAGUE (2)

	Pl	W	D	L	F	A	Pts	Results (Thun · Lugano · Winterthur · Servette · Kriens · Wil · Biel-Bienne · Vaduz · Yverdon-Sp · Lausanne · Schaffh'sen · Wohlen · Locarno · Nyon · Le Mont · Gossau)
FC Thun	30	18	6	6	70	36	60	1-0 4-0 1-1 4-2 1-3 2-2 1-1 5-3 2-0 1-0 1-1 3-2 9-0 1-2 4-0
FC Lugano †	30	17	8	5	65	29	59	1-2 2-0 2-1 2-1 0-0 1-1 1-1 1-0 4-1 4-2 2-1 2-2 2-1 3-0 7-0
FC Winterthur	30	16	8	6	69	46	56	2-1 1-2 0-0 1-0 4-1 1-1 4-3 2-2 5-2 3-0 4-3 2-2 5-1 3-0 3-1
Servette FC	30	14	10	6	49	37	52	2-1 2-0 2-1 1-2 1-0 1-0 1-1 3-3 0-0 4-0 2-2 2-3 3-1 4-2 2-1
SC Kriens	30	12	10	8	50	41	46	0-2 1-1 0-1 1-0 0-1 3-0 2-0 1-1 3-3 3-0 3-2 6-2 5-3 3-3 1-1
FC Wil 1900	30	12	9	9	44	37	45	0-1 3-3 0-0 1-1 3-3 1-1 1-1 1-2 4-2 1-1 1-0 1-1 3-3 1-0 4-0
FC Biel-Bienne	30	10	12	8	54	39	42	1-1 2-1 3-3 2-2 4-1 1-2 1-0 2-1 2-2 0-0 1-0 4-2 3-0 4-0 8-0
FC Vaduz	30	11	8	11	44	43	41	0-1 1-1 3-2 1-2 1-1 3-2 2-0 3-2 0-1 1-3 4-1 2-1 1-0 **0-3** 2-0
Yverdon-Sport	30	10	9	11	50	38	39	3-3 1-1 1-3 1-2 0-1 0-1 2-0 3-0 1-1 1-2 0-5 1-0 1-2 0-0 1-2 4-0
Lausanne-Sport	30	9	12	9	40	43	39	3-1 0-5 3-0 1-3 0-0 2-1 2-0 2-2 0-0 1-0 1-2 2-0 0-0 1-2 4-0
FC Schaffhausen	30	11	6	13	42	51	39	1-2 0-5 0-0 2-2 1-2 3-2 3-2 1-1 0-0 1-0 0-2 3-1 1-3 3-0 3-1
FC Wohlen	30	8	7	15	44	55	31	0-1 0-4 4-4 1-1 2-1 1-2 1-5 0-2 2-4 1-0 2-4 3-1 1-1 0-0 2-0
FC Locarno	30	7	10	13	46	65	31	0-2 3-2 1-4 3-0 0-0 1-2 1-1 4-1 2-6 0-2 2-2 1-0 1-2 1-0 2-2
Stade Nyonnais	30	8	7	15	36	64	31	1-3 1-3 2-7 2-0 0-0 0-0 1-1 1-0 0-4 1-0 2-3 1-3 1-1 2-1 1-0
FC Le Mont	30	8	3	19	30	56	27	2-4 0-2 1-2 1-2 0-1 0-1 1-0 0-3 1-0 1-1 3-2 1-5 0-1 1-2 3-2
FC Gossau	30	2	7	21	27	80	13	2-6 0-1 1-2 1-2 2-3 1-1 2-2 1-4 1-0 1-1 1-1 1-3 3-3 0-3 1-2

24/07/2009 - 15/05/2010 • † Promotion play-off • Match in bold awarded

MEDALS TABLE

		Overall			League			Cup		Europe			City
		G	S	B	G	S	B	G	S	G	S	B	
1	Grasshopper-Club	45	32	14	27	19	13	18	13			1	Zürich
2	Servette FC	24	28	12	17	16	12	7	12				Geneva
3	FC Basel	23	12	5	13	6	5	10	6				Basel
4	FC Zürich	19	9	9	12	8	7	7	1			2	Zürich
5	BSC Young Boys	17	23	10	11	16	9	6	7			1	Berne
6	Lausanne-Sport	16	16	9	7	8	8	9	8			1	Lausanne
7	FC Sion	13	2	6	2	2	6	11					Sion
8	FC La Chaux-de-Fonds	9	4	7	3	3	7	6	1				La Chaux-de-Fonds
9	AC Lugano	6	9	10	3	5	10	3	4				Lugano
10	FC Aarau	4	3	3	3	1	3	1	2				Aarau
11	Neuchâtel Xamax FC	3	8	9	3	3	9				5		Neuchâtel
12	FC Luzern	3	4	1	1	1	1	2	3				Luzern
13	FC Winterthur	3	4	1	3	2	1			2			Wintherthur
14	FC St Gallen	3	3	3	2		3	1	3				St Gallen

SCHWEIZER CUP / COUPE DE SUISSE 2009-10

First Round

FC Basel	3	FC Le Mont*	1
FC Locarno	0	FC Zürich	7
FC Rapperswil-Jona*	4	FC Wohlen	1
FC Aarau	2	FC Biel-Bienne*	3
FC Thun*	2	FC Sion	1
FC Tuggen*	1	FC Winterthur	3
FC Solothurn	3	FC Härkingen*	1
AC Bellinzona	4	SC Kriens	5
FC St Gallen*	2	FC Wil	1
Etoile-Carouge*	0	Servette FC	3
FC Töss	3	FC Muotathal*	0
FC Linth	1	FC Luzern	4
BSC Young Boys	3	Yverdon-Sport*	1
FC Serrières	2	Neuchâtel Xamax*	0
FC Lugano*	1	Grasshopper-Club	0
Stade Nyonnais*	1	Lausanne-Sport	2

Round of 16

FC Basel*	4
FC Zürich	2
FC Rapperswil-Jona*	3
FC Biel-Bienne	5
FC Thun	4
FC Winterthur*	2
FC Solothurn*	2
SC Kriens	4
FC St Gallen	2
Servette FC*	1
FC Töss*	1
FC Luzern	2
BSC Young Boys	1
Neuchâtel Xamax*	0
FC Lugano*	1
Lausanne-Sport	2

Quarter-finals

FC Basel*	3
FC Biel-Bienne	1
FC Thun	1
SC Kriens*	2
FC St Gallen	4
FC Luzern*	1
BSC Young Boys*	1
Lausanne-Sport	4

Semi-finals

FC Basel	1
SC Kriens*	0
FC St Gallen*	1
Lausanne-Sport	2

Final

FC Basel	6
Lausanne-Sport ‡	0

* Home team • ‡ Qualified for the Europa League

CUP FINAL

St Jakob-Park, Basel
9-05-2010, Att: 30 100, Ref: Sascha Kever
Scorers - Stocker 2 28 75, Shaqiri 30 Zoua 46, Chipperfield 52, Huggel 89 for Basel
Basel - Franco Costanzo - Samuel Inkoom (Reto Zanni 54), David Abraham, Beg Ferati, Behrang Safari, Benjamin Huggel, Jacques Zoua, Antonio da Silva, Xherdan Shaqiri (Federico Almeraes 79), Scott Chipperfield (Alexander Frei 67), Valentin Stocker. Tr: Thorsten Fink
Lausanne - Anthony Favre - Nelson (Fabian Geiser 53), Baptiste Buntschu, Sebastien Meoli, Jerome Sonnerat, Bertrand Ndzomo, Nicolas Marazzi, Abdul Carrupt, Rodrigo, Luis Pimenta (Dylan Stadelmann 70), Odirlei Gaspar (Nicolas Helin 83). Tr: Arpad Soos

SUR – SURINAME

FIFA/COCA-COLA WORLD RANKING

1993	1994	1995	1996	1997	1998	1999	2000	2001	2002	2003	2004	2005	2006	2007	2008	2009	2010
117	104	124	131	145	160	162	164	141	141	158	149	152	122	153	129	144	115

	2010											Hi/Lo
	Jan	Feb	Mar	Mar	Apr	May	Jul	Aug	Sep	Oct	Nov	Dec	**84**
	144	142	143	141	140	137	123	126	137	113	121	115	**168**

A decade ago there were only two clubs that really mattered in Surinamese football - Transvaal and Robinhood and in terms of honours won they are still by far and away the most successful teams in the country. Both have represented Suriname in the final of the CONCACAF Champions' Cup with Transvaal twice winning the trophy, way back in 1973 and 1981. Of the 41 league titles won by the two clubs, only one, however, has come since the turn of the century. Indeed, the past six years have seen a total transformation of the club scene in Suriname with two clubs - the Paramaribo based Walking Bout Co (WBC) and Inter Moengotapoe from the town of Moengo - at the forefront of the revolution with the latter winning their third title in four years in the 2010 championship. There were also first time cup winners in 2010 with second division Excelsior picking up their first silverware as well as winning promotion to the top division. The national team had a disappointing year after failing yet again to reach the finals of the Digicel Caribbean Cup. Not since 1996 have they made it to the finals and for the third tournament running they made it through the first round of qualifying only to fall at the second stage - this time finishing third in their group behind Antigua and Cuba.

FIFA WORLD CUP RECORD
1930-1958 DNE 1962-1986 DNQ 1990 DNE 1994-2010 DNQ

SURINAAMSE VOETBAL BOND (SVB)

Letitia Vriesdelaan 7,
✉ PO Box 1223,
Paramaribo
☎ +597 473112
📠 +597 479718
✉ svb@sr.net
🖥 www.svb.sr
FA 1920 CON 1964 FIFA 1929
P Louis Giskus
GS Antonius Stienstra

FIFA BIG COUNT 2006

Total players	35 250
% of population	8.03%
Male	31 950
Female	3 300
Amateurs 18+	6 655
Youth under 18	1 395
Unregistered	14 000
Professionals	0
Referees	100
Admin & coaches	275
Number of clubs	30
Number of teams	292

MAJOR CITIES/TOWNS

		Population
1	Paramaribo	236 398
2	Lelydorp	19 281
3	Nieuw Nickerie	13 470
4	Moengo	7 179
5	Meerzorg	6 781
6	Nieuw Amsterdam	5 118
7	Marienburg	4 592
8	Wageningen	4 248
9	Albina	4 045
10	Groningen	3 435
11	Brownsweg	3 018
12	Brokopondo	2 594
13	Onverwacht	2 259
14	Totness	1 706

REPUBLIEK SURINAME • REPUBLIC OF SURINAME

Capital	Paramaribo	Population	481 267 (170)	% in cities	75%
GDP per capita	$8900 (113)	Area km²	163 820 km² (91)	GMT +/-	-3
Neighbours (km)	Brazil 593, French Guiana 510, Guyana 600 • Coast 386				

RECENT INTERNATIONAL MATCHES PLAYED BY SURINAME

2009	Opponents		Score	Venue	Comp	Scorers	Att	Referee
28-10	Guyana	L	0-1	Paramaribo	Fr		2 000	Jaurequi ANT
30-10	French Guiana †	W	4-0	Paramaribo	Fr	Emanelson, Pinas 3	2 000	
1-11	Netherlands Antilles	D	1-1	Paramaribo	Fr	Valies 9	2 500	
2010								
13-10	Netherlands Antilles	W	2-1	Paramaribo	CCq	Vlijter 31, Aloema 90p	800	Willet ATG
15-10	St Lucia	W	2-1	Paramaribo	CCq	Rijssel 14, Vlijter 38p	750	Baptiste DMA
17-10	Guyana	L	0-2	Paramaribo	CCq		2 800	Davis TRI
31-10	Netherlands Antilles	D	2-2	Willemstad	Fr	OG 20, Emanelson 36. W 6-5p		
10-11	Antigua and Barbuda	L	1-2	St John's	CCq	Emanelson 34	2 000	Morrison JAM
12-11	Cuba	D	3-3	St John's	CCq	Christopher 8, Rijssel 50, Garden 80	400	Campbell JAM
14-11	Dominica	W	5-0	St John's	CCq	Kwasie 45, Vlijter 45p, Limon 56, Emanelson 75, Rijssel 88p	500	Lancaster GUY

Fr = Friendly match • CC = Digicel Caribbean Cup • WC = FIFA World Cup • q = qualifier • † Not a full international

SURINAME 2009-10

HOOFDKLASSE

	Pl	W	D	L	F	A	Pts	Inter	WBC	Leo Victor	Robinhood	Voorwarts	Transvaal	Boskamp	Brothers	Hanuman	Nacional
Inter Moengotapoe	17	13	1	3	46	22	40		2-3	5-1	3-1	3-1	2-1	3-0	4-2	5-2	2-1
Walking Bout Co	17	10	3	4	37	21	33	1-2		5-1	2-0	3-0	2-1	6-1	3-2	2-2	**3-5**
Leo Victor	17	8	6	3	31	25	30	4-2	0-0		3-0	2-1	1-1	1-1	3-1	3-1	3-2
Robinhood	17	7	4	6	29	26	25	1-1	2-3	3-2		1-3	2-1	1-2	3-2	1-0	5-1
Voorwarts	17	6	6	5	27	23	24	2-0	0-2	0-0	1-1		3-2	6-1	2-1	1-1	**4-2**
Transvaal	17	6	4	7	23	27	22	1-2	1-0	0-3	0-2	2-1		1-1	2-1	3-3	2-2
Boskamp	17	5	5	7	19	31	20	1-3	1-3	0-0	1-1	0-0	0-1		0-1	3-0	**3-2**
The Brothers	17	3	3	11	24	36	12	0-3	2-1	2-3	1-1	2-2	2-3	2-3		3-1	**3-1**
Jai Hanuman	17	1	7	9	19	37	10	0-4	4-1	1-1	0-4	1-1	0-1	2-3	0-0		1-1
FCS Nacional	9	1	3	5	10	17	6	**2-4**	0-0	**3-3**	n/p	1-3	**1-3**	0-1	**2-0**	**1-1**	

7/10/2009 - 15/05/2010 • Nacional withdrew a week before the end of the season. Their matches in the second half of the season were annulled (indicated in bold) • Relegation play-off: **Excelsior** 3-0 0-2 Jai Hanuman

SURINAME 2009-10 EERSTE KLASSE

	Pl	W	D	L	F	A	Pts
Kamal Dewaker	24	15	5	4	56	24	50
Excelsior	24	15	4	5	66	32	49
SNL	24	13	7	4	45	20	46
Tammenga	24	14	2	8	75	46	41
Randjiet Boys	24	11	4	9	50	34	37
Notch Moengo	24	11	3	10	33	27	36
Takdier Boys	24	10	6	8	42	40	36
Inter Rica	24	10	3	11	34	41	33
De Ster	24	8	5	11	39	49	26
Peto Ondro	24	5	9	10	30	50	24
Royal '95	24	4	7	13	27	46	19
Young Rhythm	24	5	2	17	22	68	17
Super Red Eagles	24	3	7	14	31	73	16

8/10/2009 - 30/05/2010 • § = points deducted

MEDALS TABLE

		Overall	Lge	Cup	CON'CAF		
		G	G	G	G	S	B
1	Robinhood	27	22	5		5	3
2	Transvaal	24	19	3	2	3	
3	Voorwaarts	6	6				
	Leo Victor	6	5	1			
5	Walking Bout Co	4	3	1			
	Cicerone	4	4				
7	Inter Moengotapoe	3	3				
8	FCS Nacional	2	1	1			

SVB BEKER VAN SURINAME 2009-10

Quarter–finals			Semi–finals			Final		
Excelsior		4						
Walking Bout Co		3	**Excelsior**		2			
Leo Victor	1	4p	Voorwarts		0			
Voorwarts	1	5p				**Excelsior**		2
Boskamp	1	4p				Takdier Boys		0
Peto Ondro	1	3p	Boskamp	2	4p			
Real Saramacca	0	2p	**Takdier Boys**	2	5p	6-06-2010		
Takdier Boys	0	4p						

SVK – SLOVAKIA

FIFA/COCA-COLA WORLD RANKING

1993	1994	1995	1996	1997	1998	1999	2000	2001	2002	2003	2004	2005	2006	2007	2008	2009	2010
150	43	35	30	34	32	21	24	47	55	50	53	45	37	53	44	33	20

					2010							Hi/Lo
Jan	Feb	Mar	Mar	Apr	May	Jul	Aug	Sep	Oct	Nov	Dec	16
33	36	31	33	38	34	27	27	16	20	18	20	150

Slovakia's victory over World Champions Italy at the FIFA World Cup in South Africa is a match that will live long in the memories of football fans in the country as the national team finally emerged from the shadows of the Czech Republic. Together the two nations shared a rich history in the World Cup and it should be remembered that the European championship winning team of 1976 had more than its far share of Slovaks in the side, but South Africa 2010 was the first time Slovakia had made an impression on its own. The tournament didn't start well. New Zealand scored a last minute equaliser in the first match and that was followed by a 2-0 defeat at the hands of Paraguay. Against Italy, however, the Slovaks came of age in a pulsating match in which they built a solid lead and then survived a spirited fight back. In the Round of 16 Slovakia could never quite match the guile and skill of the Netherlands and lost 2-1, but the tournament gave them a valuable platform for the future. At club level, there was success for champions MSK Zilina who qualified for the 2010-11 UEFA Champions League group stage although they were then hopelessly outgunned by Chelsea, Marseille and Spartak Moscow and failed to pick up a point. Zilina had won the title in a close battle with Slovan Bratislava who had the consolation of winning the Cup.

FIFA WORLD CUP RECORD
1930-1994 DNE 1998-2006 DNQ **2010** 16 r2

SLOVAK FOOTBALL ASSOCIATION (SFZ)

Trnavska 100,
Il Bratislava 821 01

☎ +421 2 48206000
📠 +421 2 48206099
✉ office@futbalsfz.sk
🖥 www.futbalsfz.sk
FA 1993 CON 1994 FIFA 1907
P Jan Kovacik
GS Jozef Kliment

FIFA BIG COUNT 2006

Total players	622 668
% of population	11.45%
Male	596 135
Female	26 533
Amateurs 18+	252 435
Youth under 18	169 561
Unregistered	68 700
Professionals	489
Referees	2 437
Admin & coaches	16 300
Number of clubs	2 417
Number of teams	7 353

MAJOR CITIES/TOWNS

		Population
1	Bratislava	423 415
2	Kosice	234 125
3	Presov	91 169
4	Zilina	85 488
5	Nitra	83 983
6	Banska Bystrica	80 291
7	Trnava	68 024
8	Martin	58 867
9	Trencin	56 221
10	Poprad	54 756
11	Prievidza	50 548
12	Zvolen	42 879
13	Povazska Bystrica	42 019
14	Nove Zamky	40 818
15	Michalovce	39 944
16	Spisska Nova Ves	39 242
22	Ruzomberok	29 717
44	Puchov	18 520
50	Senec	15 919

SLOVENSKA REPUBLIKA • SLOVAK REPUBLIC

Capital Bratislava	Population 5 463 046 (111)	% in cities 56%
GDP per capita $22 000 (55)	Area km² 49 035 km² (130)	GMT + / - +1

Neighbours (km) Austria 91, Czech Republic 197, Hungary 676, Poland 420, Ukraine 90

RECENT INTERNATIONAL MATCHES PLAYED BY SLOVAKIA

2008	Opponents	Score		Venue	Comp	Scorers	Att	Referee
6-02	Hungary	D	1-1	Limassol	Fr	Sestak [64]	100	Trattu CYP
26-03	Iceland	L	1-2	Zilina	Fr	Mintál [86]	4 120	Lehner AUT
20-05	Turkey	L	0-1	Bielefeld	Fr		13 100	Weiner GER
24-05	Switzerland	L	0-2	Lugano	Fr		10 150	Kelly IRL
20-08	Greece	L	0-2	Bratislava	Fr		4 500	Fabian HUN
6-09	Northern Ireland	W	2-1	Bratislava	WCq	Skrtel [47], Hamsik [70]	5 445	Ivanov.N RUS
10-09	Slovenia	L	1-2	Maribor	WCq	Jakubko [83]	9 900	Moen NOR
11-10	San Marino	W	3-1	Serravalle	WCq	Sestak [33], Kozak [39], Karhan [51]	1 037	Kever SUI
15-10	Poland	W	2-1	Bratislava	WCq	Sestak 2 [84 86]	17 650	Layec FRA
19-11	Liechtenstein	W	4-0	Zilina	Fr	Hamsik 2 [43 72], Vittek [75], Jez [90]	2 010	Oriekhov UKR
2009								
10-02	Ukraine	L	2-3	Limassol	Fr	Vittek 42, Hamsik 69		Kallis CYP
11-02	Cyprus	L	2-3	Nicosia	Fr	Jez [88], Jendrisek [90]	300	
28-03	England	L	0-4	London	Fr		85 512	Hamer LUX
1-04	Czech Republic	W	2-1	Prague	WCq	Sestak [22], Jendrisek [82]	14 956	Undiano ESP
6-06	San Marino	W	7-0	Bratislava	WCq	Cech 2 [3 32], Pekarik [12], Stoch [35], Kozak [42], Jakubko [63], Hanzel [68]	6 652	Efong Nzolo BEL
12-08	Iceland	D	1-1	Reykjavik	Fr	Vittek [35]	5 099	Christoffersen DEN
5-09	Czech Republic	D	2-2	Bratislava	WCq	Sestak [59], Hamsik [73p]	23 800	Ovrebo NOR
9-09	Northern Ireland	W	2-0	Belfast	WCq	Sestak [15], Holosko [67]	13 019	Kuipers NED
10-10	Slovenia	L	0-2	Bratislava	WCq		23 800	Stark GER
14-10	Poland	W	1-0	Chorzow	WCq	Gancarczyk OG [3]	5 000	Eriksson SWE
14-11	USA	W	1-0	Bratislava	Fr	Hamsik [26p]	7 200	Messner AUT
17-11	Chile	L	1-2	Zilina	Fr	Sestak [17]	11 072	Vad HUN
2010								
3-03	Norway	L	0-1	Zilina	Fr		9 756	Nijhuis NED
29-05	Cameroon	D	1-1	Klagenfurt	Fr	Kopunek [6]	10 000	Lechner AUT
5-06	Costa Rica	W	3-0	Bratislava	Fr	OG [16], Vittek [47], Sestak [88p]	12 000	Messner AUT
15-06	New Zealand	D	1-1	Rustenburg	WCr1	Vittek [50]	23 871	Damon RSA
20-06	Paraguay	L	0-2	Bloemfontein	WCr1		26 643	Maillet SEY
24-06	Italy	W	3-2	Johannesburg	WCr1	Vittek 2 [25 73], Kopunek [89]	53 412	Webb ENG
28-06	Netherlands	L	1-2	Durban	WCr2	Vittek [94+]	61 962	Undiano ESP
11-08	Croatia	D	1-1	Bratislava	Fr	Stoch [50]	6 366	Matejek CZE
3-09	FYR Macedonia	W	1-0	Bratislava	ECq	Holosko [91+]	5 980	Circhetta SUI
7-09	Russia	W	1-0	Moscow	ECq	Stoch [27]	27 052	De Bleeckere BEL
8-10	Armenia	L	1-3	Yerevan	ECq	Weiss [37]	8 500	Orsato ITA
12-10	Republic of Ireland	D	1-1	Zilinia	ECq	Durica [36]	10 892	Undiano ESP
17-11	Bosnia-Hercegovina	L	2-3	Bratislava	Fr	Sebo [3], Grajciar [63]	7 822	Mikulski POL

Fr = Friendly match • EC = UEFA EURO 2008/2012 • WC = FIFA World Cup • q = qualifier • po = play-off

SLOVAKIA NATIONAL TEAM HISTORICAL RECORDS

Caps
101 - Miroslav Karhan 1995- • 75 - Robert Vittek 2001- • 59 - Szilard Nemeth 1996-2006 • 55 - Stanislav Varga 1997-2006 • 52 - Robert Tomaschek 1994-2001 & Radoslav Zabavnik 2003- • 47 - Martin Skrtel 2004- • 45 - Peter Dzurik 1997-2003; Filip Holosko 2005- ; Miroslav Konig 1997-2004 & Marek Mintal 2002-09 • 44 - Jan Durica 2004- & Dusan Tittel 1994-98

Goals
23 - Robert Vittek 2001- • 22 - Szilard Nemeth 1996-2006 • 14 - Marek Mintal 2002-09 • 13 - Miroslav Karhan 1995- • 12 - Peter Dubovsky 1994-2000 • 11 - Stanislav Sestak 2004- • 9 - Tibor Jancula 1995-2001 & Lubomir Reiter 2001-05 • 8 - Marek Hamsik 2007-

Past Coaches
Jozef Venglos 1993-95 • Jozef Jankech 1995-98 • Dusan Radolsky 1998 • Josef Adamec 1999-2001 • Ladislav Jurkemik 2002-03 • Dusan Galis 2004-06 • Jan Kocian 2006-08 • Vladimir Weiss 2008-

SLOVAKIA 2009-10

SUPER LIGA

	Pl	W	D	L	F	A	Pts
MSK Zilina †	33	23	4	6	59	17	73
Slovan Bratislava ‡	33	21	7	5	54	24	70
Dukla Banska Bystrica‡	33	15	11	7	45	30	56
FC Nitra ‡	33	14	6	13	42	40	48
MFK Ruzomberok	33	13	8	12	33	35	47
FK Senica	33	12	7	14	34	44	43
Spartak Trnava	33	12	5	16	52	46	41
Tatran Presov	33	11	5	17	32	38	38
MFK Dubnica	33	8	12	13	27	42	36
DAC Dunajská Streda	33	7	12	14	28	47	33
MFK Kosice	33	8	9	16	32	57	33
MFK Petrzalka	33	7	8	18	33	51	29

Results grid (row team vs column team):

	Zilina	Slovan	Dukla	Nitra	Ruzomberok	Senica	Spartak	Tatran	Dubnica	DAC	Kosice	Petrzalka
MSK Zilina	—	2-0	3-1	1-1 0-1	1-0 3-0	2-1 2-1	5-1 1-0	1-0	4-0	1-0 4-0	4-1	2-0
Slovan Bratislava	2-1 2-0	—	3-0 2-0	2-1	0-2	3-0 2-0	1-1	3-1	1-1 2-2	2-0	3-0 0-0	1-1 1-1
Dukla Banska Bystrica	1-0 1-1	2-1	—	0-3 3-1	1-1	1-0	1-0	2-1	3-0 1-1	2-0 0-0	2-2 3-0	4-0
FC Nitra	0-1	0-1 2-5	0-0	—	2-0 3-1	2-1	1-0 2-2	1-0	4-2	0-1 2-0	1-0 4-0	1-3
MFK Ruzomberok	0-3	1-3 2-0	1-1 1-0	1-0	—	0-1 2-1	2-1 2-1	2-0	1-1 1-0	0-0	2-0	2-0 1-0
FK Senica	0-1	0-2	2-2	2-1 0-0	1-2 2-1	—	0-0	3-2 1-2	2-1 1-1	0-1 2-2	2-2	2-0
Spartak Trnava	1-1	0-2 0-3	0-2	0-1 1-2	3-1	3-0 1-2	—	2-0	1-0 0-1	7-0	5-4 4-0	2-0 3-0
Tatran Presov	1-0	3-0	0-1 0-1	3-1	1-0 0-0	0-0	1-2 3-0	—	0-0 2-0	0-0	1-1	2-0
MFK Dubnica	0-1 1-1	0-1	1-2	3-0 1-0	1-2	0-1	2-1	1-0	—	1-3	1-1 1-0	1-0 0-2
DAC Dunajská Streda	0-2	0-0 0-1	0-2 1-1	2-2	1-1 0-0	1-2	2-1 2-1	3-0 2-1	1-1	—	1-1	3-2
MFK Kosice	0-2 0-4	1-2	0-5	0-1 2-0	3-1 2-0	0-1 2-0	1-4	0-1 3-1	1-1	2-0 2-1	—	1-0
MFK Petrzalka	1-0 0-4	0-2	1-1	0-0 3-2	2-2	1-2 1-2	2-1 2-1	0-1 2-3	7-0	1-0 1-0	1-3 0-0 0-0	—

10/07/2009 - 15/05/2010 • † Qualified for the UEFA Champions League • ‡ Qualified for the Europa League
Top scorers: 18 - Robert Rak, Nitra • 13 - Ivan Lietava, Zilina • 12 - Jan Novak, Kosice

SLOVAKIA 2009-10
II LIGA (2)

	Pl	W	D	L	F	A	Pts
ViOn Zlaté Moravce	27	18	5	4	54	21	59
AS Trenčín	27	13	11	3	53	21	50
FK Púchov	27	15	5	7	38	31	50
LAFC Lucenec	27	10	8	9	36	28	38
Dolny Kubin	27	10	7	10	39	31	37
Zemplin Michalovce	27	8	6	13	23	33	30
MFK Ruzomberok B	27	8	5	14	23	45	29
Rimavska Sobota	27	7	7	13	21	36	28
Tatran Lip'sky Mikulas	27	7	5	15	27	42	26
Slovan Duslo Sala	27	4	11	12	15	41	23
Mesto Prievidza	Withdrew after 17 games						
Sport Podbrezova	Withdrew after 5 games						

11/07/2009 - 29/05/2010

MEDALS TABLE

		Overall			League			Cup		City
		G	S	B	G	S	B	G	S	
1	Slovan Bratislava	9	3	3	5	2	3	4	1	Bratislava
2	MSK Zilina	5	3		5	3				Zilina
3	Inter Bratislava	5	2	3	2	2	3	3		Bratislava
4	MFK Petrzalka	4	5		2	3		2	2	Senec
5	MFK Kosice	3	5	1	2	3	1	1	2	Kosice
6	MFK Ruzomberok	2	1	2	1		2	1	1	Ruzomberok
7	Spartak Trnava	1	6	4		2	4	1	4	Trnava
8	Dukla Banská Bystrica	1	2	2		1	2	1	1	Banská Bystrica
9	Matador Púchov	1	2			1		1	1	Púchov
10	FC Senec	1	1					1	1	Senec
11	1.HFC Humenné	1							1	Humenné
	ViOn Zlaté Moravce	1							1	Zlaté Moravce
13	Tatran Presov		2						2	Presov
14	DAC Dunajská Streda	1	1				1		1	Dunajská Streda
15	Trans Licartovce	1							1	
16	FC Nitra			1			1			Nitra

MEDALS TABLE FOR SLOVAK CLUBS IN CZECHOSLOVAKIAN FOOTBALL

		Overall			League			Cup		Europe		
		G	S	B	G	S	B	G	S	G	S	B
3	Slovan Bratislava	14	16	3	8	10	3	5	6	1		
5	Spartak Trnava	9	2	2	5	1	1	4	1		1	
7	Lokomotíva Kosice	2	1	2			2	2	1			
8	TJ Internacional	1	6	5	1	3	5		3			
9	1.FC Kosice	1	4	2		1	2	1	3			
14	DAC Dunajská Streda	1		1			1	1				
17	Tatran Presov		4	1		2	1		2			
18	Jednota Trencin		2	1		1	1	1				
20	FC Nitra	1	1		1	1						
22	SK Zilina	1							1			
	Dukla Banská Bystrica	1							1			

SLOVENSKY POHAR 2009-10

Third Round

Slovan Bratislava	7
MFK Vrbove *	0
Tatran Liptovsky Mikulas	1
Rimavska Sobota *	3
MFK Ruzomberok	3
MFK Banska Bystrica *	1
FK Senica	0 6p
Spartak Myjava *	0 7p
MFK Kosice	3
MFK Snina *	0
Sport Podbrezova	0
MSK Zilina *	3
FC Nitra *	5
Mesto Prievidza	0
FK Cadca *	0
Dukla Banska Bystrica	1
DAC Dunajská Streda	1 4p
SFM Senec *	1 2p
LAFC Lucenec	0
Tatran Presov	5
Spisska Nova Ves *	1
MFK Dubnica	0
HFC Humenné *	1
Bodva Moldava	2
MFK Petrzalka	6
Nove Mesto nad Vahom *	1
Moravany nad Vahom *	0
AS Trencin	3
ViOn Zlaté Moravce	4
SKF Sered *	1
FK Raca	0
Spartak Trnava *	5

Fourth Round

Slovan Bratislava *	2
Rimavska Sobota	1
MFK Ruzomberok	1
Spartak Myjava *	2
MFK Kosice	2
MSK Zilina *	1
FC Nitra	0
Dukla Banska Bystrica *	1
DAC Dunajská Streda *	1
Tatran Presov	0
Spisska Nova Ves	0
Bodva Moldava *	1
MFK Petrzalka *	4
AS Trencin	0
ViOn Zlaté Moravce	0
Spartak Trnava *	5

Quarter-finals

Slovan Bratislava	3	0
Spartak Myjava *	0	0
MFK Kosice *	0	0
Dukla Banska Bystrica	2	1
DAC Dunajská Streda *	3	3
Bodva Moldava	0	1
MFK Petrzalka *	3	0
Spartak Trnava	2	3

Semi-finals

Slovan Bratislava	1	1
Dukla Banska Bystrica *	0	0
DAC Dunajská Streda *	0	0
Spartak Trnava	1	2

Final

Slovan Bratislava ‡	6
Spartak Trnava	0

FINAL
Mestsky Stadion, Michalovce
11-05-2010, Ref: Vlk
Scorers - Salata 11, Bozic 17, Sylvestr 33, Brezanik 64, Guede 67, Dobrotka 87 for Slovan
Slovan - Matus Putnocky - Martin Dobrotka, Kornel Salata, Radek Dosoudil, Marian Had, Branislav Obzera, Karim Guede, Mario Bozic (Erik Grendel 53), Michal Brezanic (Milan vana 73), Pavol Masaryk, Jakub Sylvestr (Marek Kuzma 81). Tr: Dusan Tittel
Spartak - Jan Slovenciak - Milos Juhasz, Patrik Banovic (Lukas Hlavatovic 68), Vladimir Kozuch, Peter Schmidt, Roman Prochazka, Kamil Kopunek, Neto (Igor Sukennik 21), Martin Mikovic, Peter Styvar (Pitio 46), Martin Guldan. Tr: Milan Malatinsky

* Home team/home team in the 1st leg • ‡ Qualified for the Europa League

SVN – SLOVENIA

FIFA/COCA-COLA WORLD RANKING

1993	1994	1995	1996	1997	1998	1999	2000	2001	2002	2003	2004	2005	2006	2007	2008	2009	2010
134	81	71	77	95	88	40	35	25	36	31	42	68	77	83	57	31	17

2010												Hi/Lo
Jan	Feb	Mar	Mar	Apr	May	Jul	Aug	Sep	Oct	Nov	Dec	15
31	33	27	29	23	25	19	19	19	15	15	17	134

At the FIFA World Cup in South Africa, Slovenia twice came close to qualifying for the knockout stage but were denied in the most cruel of fashions after setting the pace in a group from which they were not expected to qualify. Having beaten Algeria in their opening game they led the USA 2-0 at half-time in their next. With just eight minutes to go they were still ahead and on their way to winning the group but the Slovenes then conceded an equaliser by Michael Bradley. It was to prove costly after Slovenia then lost a very close final group match against England. Despite the defeat, Slovenia still looked to have qualified but then news filtered through of an injury-time winner for the USA against Algeria that denied Matjaz Kek's team a place in the second round. Amongst the sea of disappointed faces there was also the realisation of a missed opportunity. Had they held on against the Americans and won the group Slovenia would have fancied their chances of making the semi-finals given the lack of an established power in that quarter of the draw. In club football there was an unlikely first league title for FC Koper who were inspired by veteran midfielder Miran Pavlin. They finished well ahead of Maribor who won a thrilling Cup Final 3-2 against Domzale, David Bunderla scoring the winner in the final seconds of extra-time.

FIFA WORLD CUP RECORD
1930-1994 DNE 1998 DNQ 2002 30 r1 2006 DNQ 2010 18 r1

FOOTBALL ASSOCIATION OF SLOVENIA (NZS)

Nogometna Zveza Slovenije,
Cerinova 4, PO Box 3986,
Ljubljana 1001
☎ +386 1 5300400
📠 +386 1 5300410
📧 fas@nzs.si
🖥 www.nzs.si
FA 1920 CON 1992 FIFA 1992
P Aleksander Ceferin
GS Ales Zavrl

FIFA BIG COUNT 2006

Total players	116 925
% of population	5.82%
Male	107 255
Female	9 670
Amateurs 18+	9 410
Youth under 18	20 831
Unregistered	55 200
Professionals	284
Referees	818
Admin & coaches	5 000
Number of clubs	328
Number of teams	1 060

MAJOR CITIES/TOWNS

		Population
1	Ljubljana	194 727
2	Maribor	88 349
3	Celje	36 723
4	Kranj	34 782
5	Velenje	26 857
6	Koper	24 725
7	Novo mesto	22 941
8	Ptuj	19 014
9	Trbovlje	15 637
10	Kamnik	13 698
11	Jesenice	13 433
12	Domzale	12 465
13	Nova Gorica	12 407
14	Skofja Loka	12 254
15	Murska Sobota	12 135
16	Izola	11 403
17	Kocevje	9 111
18	Postojna	8 867
27	Adajdovscina	6 972

REPUBLIKA SLOVENIJA • REPUBLIC OF SLOVENIA

Capital Ljubljana	Population 2 005 692 (145)	% in cities 48%
GDP per capita $29 600 (47)	Area km² 20 273 km² (154)	GMT +/- +1
Neighbours (km) Austria 330, Croatia 455, Hungary 102, Italy 199 • Coast 46		

RECENT INTERNATIONAL MATCHES PLAYED BY SLOVENIA

2007 Opponents	Score		Venue	Comp	Scorers	Att	Referee
7-02 Estonia	W	1-0	Domzale	Fr	Lavric [34p]	3 000	Ledentu FRA
24-03 Albania	D	0-0	Shkoder	ECq		7 000	Attard MLT
28-03 Netherlands	L	0-1	Celje	ECq		10 000	Mejuto ESP
2-06 Romania	L	1-2	Celje	ECq	Vrsic [94+]	6 500	Dougal SCO
6-06 Romania	L	0-2	Timisoara	ECq		17 850	Yefet ISR
22-08 Montenegro	D	1-1	Podgorica	Fr	Vrsic [42]	8 000	Circhetta SUI
8-09 Luxembourg	W	3-0	Luxembourg	ECq	Lavric 2 [7 47], Novakovic [37]	2 012	Berezka UKR
12-09 Belarus	W	1-0	Celje	ECq	Lavric [3p]	3 500	Banari MDA
13-10 Albania	D	0-0	Celje	ECq		3 700	Gomes POR
17-10 Netherlands	L	0-2	Eindhoven	ECq		32 500	Rizzoli ITA
21-11 Bulgaria	L	0-2	Celje	ECq		3 700	Webb ENG
2008							
6-02 Denmark	L	1-2	Nova Gorica	Fr	Novakovic [37]	1 700	Kinhofer GER
26-03 Hungary	W	1-0	Zalaegerszeg	Fr	Sisic [59]	7 000	Messner AUT
26-05 Sweden	L	0-1	Gothenburg	Fr		21 118	Collum SCO
20-08 Croatia	L	2-3	Maribor	Fr	Suler [3], Sisic [55p]	11 500	Circhetta SUI
6-09 Poland	D	1-1	Wroclaw	WCq	Dedic [35]	7 300	Jakobsson ISL
10-09 Slovakia	W	2-1	Maribor	WCq	Novakovic 2 [22 81]	9 900	Moen NOR
11-10 Northern Ireland	W	2-0	Maribor	WCq	Novakovic [83], Ljubijankic [84]	12 385	Iturralde ESP
15-10 Czech Republic	L	0-1	Teplice	WCq		15 220	Atkinson ENG
19-11 Bosnia-Herzegovina	L	3-4	Maribor	Fr	Koren [27], Novakovic 2 [64p 75]	10 000	Kari FIN
2009							
11-02 Belgium	L	0-2	Genk	Fr		13 135	Kever SUI
28-03 Czech Republic	D	0-0	Maribor	WCq		12 500	Proenca POR
1-04 Northern Ireland	L	0-1	Belfast	WCq		13 243	Yefet ISR
12-08 San Marino	W	5-0	Maribor	WCq	Koren 2 [19 74], Radosavljevic [39], Kirm [54], Ljubijankic [93+]	4 400	Meckarovski MKD
5-09 England	L	1-2	London	Fr	Ljubijankic [85]	67 232	Eriksson SWE
9-09 Poland	W	3-0	Maribor	WCq	Dedic [13], Novakovic [44], Birsa [62]	10 226	Collum SCO
10-10 Slovakia	W	2-0	Bratislava	WCq	Birsa [56], Pecnik [93+]	23 800	Stark GER
14-10 San Marino	W	3-0	Serravalle	WCq	Novakovic [24], Stevanovic [68], Suler [81]	1 745	Szabo HUN
14-11 Russia	L	1-2	Moscow	WCpo	Pecnik [88]	71 600	Larsen DEN
18-11 Russia	W	1-0	Maribor	WCpo	Dedic [44]	12 510	Hauge NOR
2010							
3-03 Qatar	W	4-1	Maribor	Fr	Novakovic [14], Cesar [30], Kirm [34], Jokic [67]	4 900	Van Boekel NED
4-06 New Zealand	W	3-1	Maribor	Fr	Novakovic 2 [7 30], Kirm [44]	10 965	Kakkos GRE
13-06 Algeria	W	1-0	Polokwane	WCr1	Koren [79]	30 325	Batres GUA
18-06 USA	D	2-2	Johannesburg	WCr1	Birsa [13], Ljubijankic [42]	45 573	Coulibaly MLI
23-06 England	L	0-1	Port Elizabeth	WCr1		36 893	Stark GER
11-08 Australia	W	2-0	Ljubljana	Fr	Dedic [78], Ljubijankic [90]	16 135	Tagliavento ITA
3-09 Northern Ireland	L	0-1	Maribor	ECq		12 000	Balaj ROU
7-09 Serbia	D	1-1	Belgrade	ECq	Novakovic [63]	24 028	Benquerenca POR
8-10 Faeroe Islands	W	5-1	Ljubljana	ECq	Matavz 3 [25 36 65], Novakovic [72p], Dedic [84]	15 750	Todorov BUL
12-10 Estonia	W	1-0	Tallinn	ECq	OG [67]	5 722	Skjerven NOR
17-11 Georgia	L	1-2	Koper	Fr	Cesat [51]	4 000	Whitby WAL

Fr = Friendly match • EC = UEFA EURO 2008/2012 • WC = FIFA World Cup • q = qualifier • po = play-off

SLOVENIA NATIONAL TEAM HISTORICAL RECORDS

Caps
80 -Zlatko Zahovic 1992-2004 • **74** - Milenko Acimovic 1998-2007 & Ales Ceh 1992-2002 • **71** - Dzoni Novak 1992-2002 • **66** - Marinko Galic 1994-2002 & Aleksander Knavs 1998-2006 • **65** - Mladen Rudonja 1994-2002 • **64** - Amir Karic 1996-2004 • **63** - Miran Pavlin 1994-2004 • **57** - Marko Simeunovic 1992-2004 • **55** - Robert Koren 2003- • **51** - Bostjan Cesar 2003-

Goals
35 - Zlatko Zahovic 1992-2004 • **18** - Milvoje Novakovic 2006- • **16** - Saso Udovic 1993-2000 • **14** - Ermin Siljak 1994-2005 • **13** - Milenko Acimovic 1998-2007 • **10** - Primoz Gliha 1993-98 • **8** - Milan Osterc 1997-2002

Past Coaches
Bojan Prasnikar 1991-93 • Zdenko Verdenik 1994-97 • Bojan Prasnikar 1998 • Srecko Katanec 1998-2002 • Bojan Prasnikar 2002-04 • Branko Oblak 2004-06 • Matjaz Kek 2007-

SLOVENIA 2009-10

SIMOBIL LIGA

	Pl	W	D	L	F	A	Pts	Koper	Maribor	Gorica	Olimpija	Celje	Nafta	Rudar	Domzale	Interblock	Drava
FC Koper †	36	21	10	5	59	35	**73**		1-3 0-0	1-1 3-2	2-1 1-0	1-0 4-0	3-1 2-0	2-2 2-1	0-1 1-3	2-1 0-0	0-0 1-1
NK Maribor ‡	36	18	8	10	58	44	**62**	1-2 2-2		0-1 3-1	1-0 2-1	3-3 1-1	3-1 1-2	0-2 0-1	1-2 1-1	1-0 1-0	2-2 3-2
ND Gorica ‡	36	16	7	13	74	60	**55**	1-2 1-2	2-3 3-3		1-2 1-1	1-1 3-0	3-1 3-1	1-3 2-1	1-1 2-3	4-3 6-1	1-2 2-1
Olimpija Ljubljana ‡ §2	36	16	7	13	51	33	**53**	0-1 3-1	0-1 1-1	1-1 5-0		4-2 1-3	2-0 0-0	0-1 0-1	3-1 1-1	1-3 2-0	3-0 2-0
NK Celje	36	14	9	13	53	56	**51**	0-1 1-3	2-1 0-2	2-0 1-4	1-1 1-0		2-2 3-2	0-4 0-0	2-3 1-0	3-1 5-1	1-0 3-0
Nafta Lendava	36	14	7	15	51	53	**49**	3-1 1-2	2-4 3-1	2-1 0-1	1-0 0-1	2-2 2-1		5-2 2-0	2-2 2-0	0-1 3-1	3-1 1-0
Rudar Velenje	36	15	4	17	46	52	**49**	2-2 0-2	1-0 0-2	0-3 2-3	0-3 1-3	2-0 3-1	2-0 0-1		4-1 0-2	2-1 1-2	0-3 4-2
Domzale	36	12	9	15	51	59	**45**	1-1 0-1	1-3 2-3	1-4 2-3	1-2 1-2	1-5 2-2	2-1 3-1	2-0 1-1		1-0 2-1	2-2 2-0
Interblock Ljubljana	36	9	6	21	35	64	**33**	0-1 0-5	2-1 0-1	3-1 0-5	0-1 2-1	1-2 0-0	1-1 1-3	1-0 1-0	0-0 2-1		2-1 0-2
Drava Ptuj	36	7	9	20	34	56	**30**	1-3 1-1	0-2 0-1	1-1 2-4	0-3 0-0	0-1 0-1	1-2 0-0	1-0 0-1	2-1 2-1	1-1 3-1	

17/07/2009 - 16/05/2010 • † Qualified for the UEFA Champions League • ‡ Qualified for the Europa League • § = points deducted
Play-off: Interblock 0-1 0-3 **Triglav**
Top scorers: **23** - Milan Osterc, Gorica • **15** - Dragan Jelic, Maribor • **12** - Mitja Brulc, Koper & Dalibor Volas, Nafta

SLOVENIA 2009-10
2.SNL (2)

	Pl	W	D	L	F	A	Pts
Primorje Ajdovscina	27	15	10	2	51	16	**55**
Triglav Gorenjska	27	14	5	8	33	25	**47**
Aluminij Kidricevo	27	14	4	9	67	34	**46**
Dravinja Kostroj	27	11	6	10	44	32	**39**
Bela Krajina	27	11	6	10	28	36	**39**
Mura Murska Sobota	27	9	7	11	36	51	**34**
Garmin Sencur	27	7	11	9	31	35	**32**
Krsko	27	6	10	11	27	45	**28**
Livar Ivacna Gorica	27	7	6	14	27	43	**27**
Mladi Sentjur	27	5	7	15	29	56	**22**

8/08/2009 - 16/05/2010

MEDALS TABLE

		Overall			League			Cup		City
		G	S	B	G	S	B	G	S	
1	NK Maribor	14	6	3	8	4	3	6	2	Maribor
2	Olimpija Ljubljana	8	6	1	4	3	1	4	3	Ljubljana
3	ND Gorica	6	5	5	4	4	5	2	1	Nova Gorica
4	FC Koper	3	2	2	1	1	2	2	1	Koper
5	NK Domzale	2	3		2	2			1	Domzale
6	Interblock Ljubljana	2							2	Ljubljana
7	NK Celje	1	5	1		1	1	1	4	Celje
8	Mura Murska Sobota	1	3	2		2	2	1	1	Murska Sobota
9	Rudar Velenje	1		3			3	1		Velenje
10	Primorje Ajdovscina		5	1		2	1		3	Ajdovscina
11	Korotan Prevalje		1						1	Prevalje
	Aluminij Kidricevo		1						1	Kidricevo
	NK Dravograd		1						1	Dravograd
14	Izola Belvedur			1		1				Izola

POKAL HERVIS 2009-10

First Round

Team	Score
NK Maribor	Bye
Kalcer V'term Radomlje *	1
Olimpija Ljubljana	5
Primorje Ajdovscina	0 4p
Ankaran HMT *	0 3p
Aluminij	1
Triglav Gorenjska *	2
Rudar Velenje	Bye
Idrija *	0
FC Koper	4
Mura Murska Sobota	5
Gostilna Lobnik Silvnica *	0
Zrece *	0
NK Celje	8
Nafta Lendava	4
Jadran Dekani *	0
Bela Krajina	0
Stojnci *	1
Odranci *	2
Dravinja Kostroj	1
Interblock Ljubljana	Bye
ND Gorica	Bye
Tolmin	1 5p
Crensovci *	1 6p
Drava Ptuj	3
Zeleznicar *	0
Koroska Dravograd *	0
Domzale	5

Round of 16

Team	Score
NK Maribor	1
Olimpija Ljubljana *	0
Primorje Ajdovscina	0
Triglav Gorenjska *	4
Rudar Velenje	4
FC Koper *	2
Mura Murska Sobota *	3
NK Celje	5
Nafta Lendava	6
Stojnci *	2
Odranci *	0
Interblock Ljubljana	2
ND Gorica	5
Crensovci *	0
Drava Ptuj *	2
Domzale	3

Quarter-finals

Team	Score
NK Maribor *	5 2
Triglav Gorenjska	1 2
Rudar Velenje *	0 0
NK Celje	1 1
Nafta Lendava	1 3
Interblock Ljubljana *	1 0
ND Gorica	1 0
Domzale *	1 1

Semi-finals

Team	Score
NK Maribor *	4 3
NK Celje	1 3
Nafta Lendava *	1 0
Domzale	1 3

Final

Team	Score
NK Maribor ‡	3
Domzale	2

FINAL

Ljudski Vrt, Maribor
8-05-2010, Att: 6000, ref: Skomina
Scorers - Marcos Tavares 2 42 55, Bunderla 120 for Maribor; Brezovacki 31, Pekic 45 for Domzale.
Maribor - Marko Ranilovic - Ales Mejac (Janez Aljancic 83), Elvedin Dzinic, Sinisa Andjelkovic, Suad Filekovic, Armin Bacinovic, Dejan Mezga, Dejan Skolnik (Flavio 78), Marcos Tavares, Dragan Jelic (Vito Plut 115), David Bunderla. Tr: Darko Milanic
Domzale - Nejc Vidmar - Blaz Brezovacki, Rok Hanzic, Jovan Vidovic, Matic Seferovic (Zeljko Filipovic 62), Tadej Apatic, Dalibor Teinovic (Mato Simunovic 102), Marko Drevensek, Darko Topic (Jani Sturm 76), Mitja Zatkovic, Damir Pekic. Tr: Darko Birjukov

Preliminary round: Kalcer 2-1 Kranj; Zeleznicar 8-4 Kleparstvo • * Home team/home team in the 1st leg • ‡ Qualified for the Europa League

SWE – SWEDEN

FIFA/COCA-COLA WORLD RANKING

1993	1994	1995	1996	1997	1998	1999	2000	2001	2002	2003	2004	2005	2006	2007	2008	2009	2010
9	3	13	17	18	18	16	23	16	25	19	13	14	14	24	32	42	33

2010												Hi/Lo
Jan	Feb	Mar	Mar	Apr	May	Jul	Aug	Sep	Oct	Nov	Dec	2
42	43	42	40	37	37	35	35	32	36	35	33	43

The major trend in club football for the past decade has undoubtedly been the rise of the super-club with power in many countries concentrated in the hands of just one or two clubs - just think Barca and Real in Spain or Bayern in Germany. Bizarrely, however, the exact opposite has been true in Sweden. For the past decade it has been almost impossible to predict which team would emerge as champions with nine different clubs winning the title in the past 12 seasons. In 2010 coach Roland Nilsson turned Malmö from from mid-table no-hopers in 2009 to champions in one easy leap. It has certainly been good news for fans around the country and once again the league race went right to the final day with Helsingborg conceding a title that for much of the season seemed theirs for the taking. Both they and Malmö went into their final games level on points, but with Malmö having the comfort of a better goal difference they cruised to an easy win over Mjallby whilst Helsingborg were held by Kalmar. The following week there was the consolation for Helsingborg of victory in the 2010 Swedish Cup Final over Hammarby but concerns remain that such an even playing field is restricting progress in Europe with teams unable to build a winning momentum. In the 2010-11 European tournaments there were no Swedish representatives beyond the end of August.

FIFA WORLD CUP RECORD

1930 DNE **1934** 8 QF **1938** 4 SF **1950** 3 r2 **1954** DNQ **1958** 2 Finalists (hosts) **1962-1966** DNQ
1970 9 r1 **1974** 5 r2 **1978** 13 r1 **1982-1986** DNQ **1990** 21 r1 **1994** 3 SF **1998** DNQ **2002** 13 r2 **2006** 14 r2 **2010** DNQ

SVENSKA FOTBOLLFORBUNDET (SVFF)

PO Box 1216,
Solna 17 123
☎ +46 8 7350900
📠 +46 8 7350901
✉ svff@svenskfotboll.se
🖳 www.svenskfotboll.se
FA 1904 CON 1954 FIFA 1904
P Lars-Ake Lagrell
GS Mikael Santoft

FIFA BIG COUNT 2006

Total players	1 006 939
% of population	11.17%
Male	791 612
Female	215 327
Amateurs 18+	231 399
Youth under 18	319 599
Unregistered	375 000
Professionals	2 001
Referees	14 750
Admin & coaches	10 200
Number of clubs	3 236
Number of teams	31 000

MAJOR CITIES/TOWNS

		Population
1	Stockholm	1 272 874
2	Göteborg	519 409
3	Malmö	263 797
4	Uppsala	131 919
5	Västerås	108 107
6	Örebro	99 927
7	Linköping	99 229
8	Helsingborg	93 673
9	Jönköping	85 989
10	Norrköping	83 962
11	Umeå	78 448
12	Gävle	69 274
13	Borås	64 364
14	Eskilstuna	61 606
15	Södertälje	60 728
16	Karlstad	59 862
17	Växjö	58 049
18	Halmstad	56 956
19	Kalmar	35 900

KONUNGARIKET SVERIGE • KINGDOM OF SWEDEN

Capital	Stockholm	Population	9 059 651 (87)	% in cities	85%
GDP per capita	$38 200 (25)	Area km²	450 295 km² (55)	GMT +/-	+1
Neighbours (km)	Finland 614, Norway 1619 • Coast 3218				

RECENT INTERNATIONAL MATCHES PLAYED BY SWEDEN

2008	Opponents	Score		Venue	Comp	Scorers	Att	Referee
13-01	Costa Rica	W	1-0	San Jose	Fr	Holmen [49]	7 000	Batres GUA
19-01	USA	L	0-2	Carson	Fr		14 878	Navarro CAN
6-02	Turkey	D	0-0	Istanbul	Fr		20 000	Tagliavento ITA
26-03	Brazil	L	0-1	London	Fr		60 021	Riley ENG
26-05	Slovenia	W	1-0	Gothenburg	Fr	Linderoth [41]	21 118	Collum SCO
1-06	Ukraine	L	0-1	Stockholm	Fr		25 203	Einwaller AUT
10-06	Greece	W	2-0	Salzburg	ECr1	Ibrahimovic [67], Hansson [72]	31 063	Busacca SUI
14-06	Spain	L	1-2	Innsbruck	ECr1	Ibrahimovic [34]	30 772	Vink NED
18-06	Russia	L	0-2	Innsbruck	ECr1		30 772	De Bleeckere BEL
20-08	France	L	2-3	Gothenburg	Fr	Henrik Larsson [5], Kallstrom [85p]	23 263	Braamhaar NED
6-09	Albania	D	0-0	Tirana	WCq		13 522	Undiano ESP
10-09	Hungary	W	2-1	Stockholm	WCq	Kallstrom [55], Holmen [64]	28 177	Meyer GER
11-10	Portugal	D	0-0	Stockholm	WCq		33 241	Rosetti ITA
19-11	Netherlands	L	1-3	Amsterdam	Fr	Kallstrom [50]	26 750	Szabo HUN
2009								
24-01	USA	L	2-3	Carson	Fr	Nannskog [73], Dahlberg [89]	9 918	Petrescu CAN
28-01	Mexico	W	1-0	Oakland	Fr	Farnerud [52]	46 550	Ward USA
11-02	Austria	W	2-0	Graz	Fr	Elm [58], Kallstrom [63]	11 800	Kassai HUN
28-03	Portugal	D	0-0	Porto	WCq		40 200	De Bleeckere BEL
1-04	Serbia	L	0-2	Belgrade	Fr		17 830	Perez ESP
6-06	Denmark	L	0-1	Stockholm	WCq		33 619	Riley ENG
10-06	Malta	W	4-0	Gothenburg	WCq	Kallstrom [21], Majstorovic [52], Ibrahimovic [56], Berg [58]	25 271	Murray SCO
12-08	Finland	W	1-0	Stockholm	Fr	Elmander [42]	15 212	Fautrel FRA
5-09	Hungary	W	2-1	Budapest	WCq	Mellberg [9], Ibrahimovic [93+]	40 169	Rizzoli ITA
9-09	Malta	W	1-0	Ta'Qali	WCq	Azzopardi OG [82]	4 705	McCourt NIR
10-10	Denmark	L	0-1	Copenhagen	WCq		37 800	Mejuto ESP
14-10	Albania	W	4-1	Stockholm	WCq	Mellberg 2 [6 42], Berg [40], Svensson [86]	25 342	Ivanov.N RUS
18-11	Italy	L	0-1	Cesena	Fr		18 260	Skomina SVN
2010								
20-01	Oman	W	1-0	Muscat	Fr	Svensson [35]	1 000	Shukralla BHR
23-01	Syria	D	1-1	Damascus	Fr	Ranegie [87]	10 000	Najm LIB
3-03	Wales	W	1-0	Swansea	Fr	Elmander [44]	8 258	Black NIR
29-05	Bosnia-Herzegovina	W	4-2	Stockholm	Fr	Toivonen [44], Olsson 2 [68 82], Berg [90]	22 589	Grafe GER
2-06	Belarus	W	1-0	Minsk	Fr	Wilhelmsson [48]	12 000	Nikolaev RUS
11-08	Scotland	W	3-0	Stockholm	Fr	Ibrahimovic [4], Bajrami [39], Toivonen [56]	25 249	Rocchi ITA
3-09	Hungary	W	2-0	Stockholm	ECq	Wernbloom 2 [51 73]	32 304	Atkinson ENG
7-09	San Marino	W	6-0	Malmo	ECq	Ibrahimovic 2 [7 77], OG 2 [11 26], Granqvist [51], Berg [92+]	21 083	McKeon IRL
12-10	Netherlands	L	1-4	Amsterdam	ECq	Granqvist [69]	46 000	Lannoy FRA
17-11	Germany	D	0-0	Gothenburg	Fr		21 959	Velasco ESP

Fr = Friendly match • EC = UEFA EURO 2008/2012 • WC = FIFA World Cup • q = qualifier • r1 = first round group • r2 = second round

SWEDEN NATIONAL TEAM HISTORICAL RECORDS

Caps
143 - Thomas Ravelli 1981-97 • 116 - Roland Nilsson 1986-2000 • 115 - Bjorn Nordqvist 1963-78 • 110 - Anders Svensson 1999- • 109 - Niclas Alexandersson 1993-2008 • 106 - Henrik Larsson 1993-2009 • 104 - Olof Mellberg 2000- • 96 - Patrik Andersson 1991-2002 • 94 - Orvar Bergmark 1951-65 • 86 - Teddy Lucic 1995-2006 • 83 - Kennet Andersson 1990-2000 • 80 - Andreas Isaksson 2002- • 78 - Kim Kallstrom 2001- • 77 - Ronnie Hellstrom 1968-80 • 76 - Tobias Linderoth 1999-2008 • 75 - Joachim Bjorklund 1991-2000; Fredrik Ljungberg 1998-2008 & Jonas Thern 1987-97 • 74 - Marcus Allback 1999-2008; Daniel Andersson 1997-2009 & Hakan Mild 1991-2001

Goals
49 - Sven Rydell 1923-32 • 43 - Gunnar Nordahl 1942-48 • 37 - Henrik Larsson 1993-2009 • 32 - Gunnar Gren 1940-58 • 31 - Kennet Andersson 1990-2000 • 29 - Marcus Allback 1999-2008 & Martin Dahlin 1991-2000 • 27 - Agne Simonsson 1957-67 • 26 - Tomas Brolin 1990-95 • 25 - Zlatan Ibrahimovic 2001- • 23 - Per Kaufeldt 1922-29 • 22 - Karl Gustafsson 1908-18 • 21 - Albin Dahl 1920-30 • 20 - Sven Jonasson 1934-40; Erik Persson 1932-39 & Nils-Ake Sandell • 19 - Herbert Karlsson 1919-21 • 18 - Arne Nyberg 1935-46

Past Coaches
Ludvig Kornerup 1908 • Wilhelm Friberg 1909-11 • John Ohlson 1912 • Ruben Gelbord 1912-13 • Hugo Leevin 1914-15 • Frey Svenson 1916 • Anton Johanson 1917-20 • John Pettersson 1921-24 • Jozsef Nagy HUN 1924-27 • John Pettersson 1927-34 • Jozsef Nagy HUN 1934 • John Pettersson 1934-36 • Carl Linde 1937 • Jozsef Nagy HUN 1938 • Gustaf Carlsson 1938-42 • Selection Committee 1942 • Rudolf Kock 1943-46 • George Raynor ENG 1946-54 • Rudolf Kock 1954-56 • George Raynor ENG 1956-58 • Eric Person 1958-61 • George Raynor ENG 1961 • Lennart Nyman 1962-65 • Orvar Bergmark 1966-70 • Georg Ericson 1971-79 • Lars Arnesson 1980-85 • Olle Nordin 1986-90 • Nils Andersson 1990 • Tommy Svensson 1991-97 • Tommy Soderberg 1998-99 • Tommy Soderberg & Lars Lagerback 2000-04 • Lars Lagerback 2004-09 • Erik Hamren 2009-

SWEDEN 2010

ALLSVENSKAN

	Pl	W	D	L	F	A	Pts	Malmö	Helsingborg	Orebro	Elfsborg	Trelleborg	Mjällby	Göteborg	Hacken	Kalmar	Djurgården	AIK	Halmstad	GAIS	Gefle	Atvidaberg	Bro'pojkarna
Malmö FF †	30	21	4	5	59	24	67		2-0	3-0	1-0	2-0	2-0	2-1	3-1	0-1	2-1	1-0	1-1	1-0	2-0	3-1	2-1
Helsingborgs IF ‡	30	20	5	5	49	26	65	2-1		2-1	2-1	1-0	2-1	2-0	3-1	0-0	3-3	1-0	2-1	0-1	3-1	3-0	1-0
Orebro SK ‡	30	16	4	10	40	30	52	0-3	3-0		3-0	2-0	0-2	2-1	2-0	1-0	1-0	1-0	3-0	0-2	3-1	2-0	1-1
IF Elfsborg ‡	30	12	11	7	55	40	47	2-2	1-3	3-3		4-1	2-0	1-1	0-0	4-1	3-1	4-0	6-0	1-0	1-0	4-1	1-0
Trelleborgs IF	30	13	5	12	39	42	44	0-3	0-0	1-0	1-1		2-1	2-1	3-2	1-1	3-1	4-1	1-0	2-0	2-1	0-3	0-1
Mjällby AIF	30	11	10	9	36	29	43	4-2	0-1	1-0	2-0	1-1		0-0	2-2	0-0	3-0	0-0	2-0	3-0	1-3	2-1	0-0
IFK Göteborg	30	10	10	10	42	29	40	0-2	0-0	0-0	5-1	1-2	0-0		0-1	3-1	1-1	4-0	3-0	2-1	2-2	3-0	1-1
BK Hacken Göteborg	30	11	7	12	40	42	40	0-4	2-1	2-1	1-1	4-2	0-1	1-5		1-1	2-1	0-1	2-0	0-2	0-2	0-0	5-0
Kalmar FF	30	10	10	10	36	38	40	2-3	1-0	4-1	2-2	2-1	1-1	0-3	1-3		0-1	0-3	1-0	3-1	1-1	1-2	3-0
Djurgårdens IF	30	11	7	12	35	42	40	1-0	0-1	2-1	4-4	3-0	1-0	2-0	0-3	0-2		2-1	0-2	1-1	2-1	1-0	2-1
AIK Stockholm	30	10	5	15	29	36	35	2-0	2-3	0-1	2-0	1-0	0-0	1-2	1-1	0-1	1-2		0-1	1-0	2-0	4-1	2-1
Halmstads BK	30	10	5	15	31	42	35	0-2	2-4	1-1	1-3	0-0	1-2	1-0	1-2	2-1	2-0	1-2		3-0	1-0	4-0	2-0
GAIS Göteborg	30	8	8	14	24	35	32	0-0	0-0	0-1	0-2	1-3	3-2	0-0	2-1	2-2	0-1	3-1	1-1		2-1	0-0	1-1
Gefle IF	30	7	8	15	33	46	29	1-3	1-3	1-3	1-0	1-3	3-3	0-0	0-2	0-0	2-2	1-0	1-2	1-0		4-2	2-0
Atvidabergs FF	30	7	8	15	32	51	29	3-3	0-3	0-2	1-1	3-1	1-2	2-1	0-0	0-0	2-1	1-1	1-0	1-0	0-1		4-1
IF Brommapojkarna	30	6	7	17	20	48	25	0-4	1-3	0-1	2-2	0-3	1-0	1-2	2-1	2-3	0-1	0-0	1-0	1-0	2-1	0-2	

13/03/2010 - 7/11/2010 • † Qualified for the UEFA Champions League • ‡ Qualified for the Europa League
Relegation play-off: Sundsvall 0-1 0-2 **Gefle**
Top scorers: 20 - Alexander Gerndt, Gefle/Helsingborg • 19 - Denni Avdic, Elfsborg • 12 - Mathias Ranegie, Hacken • 11 - Agon Mehmeti, Malmö

MEDALS TABLE

		Overall			League			Cup		Europe			City
		G	S	B	G	S	B	G	S	G	S	B	
1	Malmö FF	30	19	6	16	15	6	14	3			1	Malmö
2	IFK Göteborg	25	16	14	18	10	13	5	6	2		1	Gothenburg
3	AIK Stockholm	19	19	9	11	12	9	8	7				Solna, Stockholm
4	IFK Norrköping	18	14	4	12	10	4	6	4				Norrköping
5	Djurgårdens IF	15	14	8	11	11	8	4	3				Stockholm
6	Örgryte IS Göteborg	15	6	5	14	5	5	1	1				Gothenburg
7	Helsingborgs IF	10	12	8	6	10	8	4	2				Helsingborg
8	IF Elfsborg Borås	7	9	4	5	6	4	2	3				Borås
9	GAIS Göteborg	7	5	3	6	4	3	1	1				Gothenburg
10	Östers IF Växjö	5	7	4	4	3	4	1	4				Växjö

SWEDEN 2010

SUPERETTAN (2)

	Pl	W	D	L	F	A	Pts	Syrianska	Norrköping	Sundsvall	Assyriska	Landskrona	Ljungskile	Falkenberg	Hammarby	Orgryte	Degerfors	Brage	Angelholm	Jönköping	Oster	Trollhättan	Väsby Utd
Syrianska FC	30	16	8	6	46	27	56		2-0	2-0	3-2	1-1	2-0	4-0	0-2	2-3	2-1	1-0	0-0	2-1	3-0	3-0	1-0
IFK Norrköping	30	17	5	8	51	33	56	3-2		1-1	0-0	0-3	2-1	0-2	1-0	1-1	3-2	0-0	0-1	3-0	3-0	3-0	4-0
GIF Sundsvall	30	13	12	5	56	39	51	5-2	1-1		3-1	1-2	3-2	3-3	2-2	2-1	2-2	2-1	0-1	1-1	5-0	1-1	3-2
Assyriska FF	30	13	7	10	48	42	46	2-0	2-1	1-0		4-1	2-1	1-1	0-3	1-3	5-2	1-0	3-1	0-0	1-0	5-2	1-2
Landskrona BoIS	30	13	6	11	40	39	45	1-2	3-1	0-0	2-3		2-1	2-1	0-1	0-0	1-0	2-0	1-0	0-3	4-0	3-0	2-0
Ljungskile SK	30	11	11	8	47	35	44	1-1	2-1	0-0	2-0	0-0		1-0	2-2	1-1	2-0	5-1	2-2	2-0	1-2	4-2	1-0
Falkenbergs FF	30	11	11	8	46	34	44	1-2	2-3	0-1	4-1	4-0	1-1		0-0	1-1	1-2	0-2	3-1	1-1	2-0	5-0	3-1
Hammarby IF	30	12	7	11	45	40	43	0-0	2-3	2-1	3-2	4-1	1-1	0-0		1-2	2-1	0-1	2-1	1-1	0-1	3-0	2-0
Orgryte IS Göteborg	30	9	15	6	43	35	42	1-1	0-1	0-0	1-1	1-1	0-0	1-2	3-0		2-1	0-1	3-3	0-1	2-0	3-3	1-1
Degerfors IF	30	12	6	12	43	45	42	0-0	1-3	0-2	2-1	3-2	5-3	2-2	4-2	0-1		1-0	1-0	2-2	1-0	2-0	2-1
IK Brage	30	11	8	11	36	38	41	2-1	2-3	2-3	2-2	2-1	0-3	1-1	2-0	2-2	1-1		1-0	4-1	3-1	0-0	2-1
Angelholms FF	30	9	10	11	39	39	37	0-0	1-2	3-3	2-1	0-1	0-0	1-1	3-2	1-1	1-0	2-0		2-0	2-3	4-2	2-2
Jönköpings Sodra	30	9	9	12	40	47	36	0-1	2-1	2-2	0-1	4-1	0-3	1-2	2-1	0-2	1-2	0-0	1-3		4-3	3-0	2-1
Osters IF Växjö	30	8	5	17	30	54	29	1-1	0-1	0-2	1-1	2-0	2-2	0-1	3-4	1-3	1-1	0-1	1-1	1-1		0-3	2-0
FC Trollhättan	30	5	8	17	32	66	23	0-2	0-4	2-3	0-0	0-2	0-1	1-1	0-2	4-2	1-0	3-3	2-1	2-2	1-2		1-0
Väsby United	30	4	6	20	31	60	18	0-3	0-2	2-4	0-3	1-1	3-2	0-1	3-1	2-2	1-2	1-0	1-1	3-4	1-3	2-2	

10/04/2010 - 23/10/2010
Relegation play-offs: Qviding 0-2 1-2 **Oster**; Sirius 0-1 0-3 **Jönköping**

SVENSKA CUPEN 2010

Third Round		Fourth Round		Quarter-finals		Semi-finals		Final	
Helsingborgs IF	3								
Hammarby TFF *	1	Helsingborgs IF *	2						
Ostersunds FK *	0	BK Hacken Göteborg	1						
BK Hacken Göteborg	5			Helsingborgs IF	1 4p				
Angelholms FF *	1			AIK Stockholm *	1 3p				
Halmstads BK	0	Angelholms FF *	1						
Osters IF Växjö *	1	AIK Stockholm	2						
AIK Stockholm	3					Helsingborgs IF *	2		
Orebro SK	2					Mjällby AIF	0		
IFK Norrköping *	0	Orebro SK	2						
Atvidabergs FF	1	Jönköpings Sodra *	0						
Jönköpings Sodra *	2			Orebro SK *	0				
Malmö FF	1			Mjällby AIF	3				
Syrianska FC *	0	Malmö FF	1						
IF Limhamm/Bunkeflo *	0	Mjällby AIF *	4					Helsingborgs IF ‡	1
Mjällby AIF	1							Hammarby IF	0
Kalmar FF *	3								
FC Trollhättan	0	Kalmar FF	4						
Vasby United *	0	IFK Göteborg *	3						
IFK Göteborg	2			Kalmar FF *	3				
Ljungskile SK *	2			Gefle IF	1				
Djurgårdens IF	0	Ljungskile SK *	0						
Orgryte IS Göteborg *	0	Gefle IF	1						
Gefle IF	1					Kalmar FF	2 3p		
IF Brommapojkarna	3					Hammarby IF *	2 4p		
Falkenbergs FF *	0	IF Brommapojkarna	0 4p						
GIF Sundsvall *	1	GAIS Göteborg *	0 3p						
GAIS Göteborg	2			IF Brommapojkarna	2 4p				
IF Elfsborg	2			Hammarby IF *	2 5p				
Degerfors IF *	0	IF Elfsborg	1						
Trelleborgs IF *	1	Hammarby IF *	3						
Hammarby IF *	3								

FINAL

Söderstadion, Stockholm
13-11-2010, Att: 12 357, Ref: Stalhammar
Scorer - Jonsson 80 for Helsingborg
Hammarby - Par Hansson - Christoffer Andersson (Ardian Gashi 46), Marcus Nilsson, Joel Ekstrand, Erik Edman - Rasmus Jonsson (Hannu Patronen 90), May Mahlangu, Marcus Lantz (c), Rachid Bouaouzan (Erik Wahlstedt 46) - Erik Sundin, Alexander Gerndt. Tr: Conny Karlsson
Helsingborg - Johannes Hopf• - David Johansson, Marcus Tornstrand (Patrik Gerhbrand 46), Jose Monteiro (c), Fadi Malke - Petter Olsen (Christer Gustafsson• 76), Christian Traore- Andreas Dahl, Maic Sema - Sebastian Castro-Tello•, Max Forsberg (Simon Helg 81). Tr: Roger Franzen

* Home team • ‡ Qualified for the Europe League

SWZ – SWAZILAND

FIFA/COCA-COLA WORLD RANKING

1993	1994	1995	1996	1997	1998	1999	2000	2001	2002	2003	2004	2005	2006	2007	2008	2009	2010
99	125	148	160	165	149	127	137	132	116	114	126	134	148	148	138	135	160

	2010											Hi/Lo
Jan	Feb	Mar	Mar	Apr	May	Jul	Aug	Sep	Oct	Nov	Dec	**92**
135	138	134	132	131	131	134	136	142	154	165	160	**174**

Young Buffaloes were the toast of tiny Swaziland in 2010, emerging as Premier League winners for the first time. They beat long-standing challengers Mbabane Swallows to the championship by a single point. The army side spent liberally in purchasing players, including a record E120,000 - the equivalent of around 12,000 Euros - for the transfer of striker Ndoda Mtsetfwa from Manzini Wanderers, and coach Zenzele Dlamini was able to muster a formidable outfit that stayed top of the standings from the first round to last. Relegation from the top flight was annulled before the start of the new campaign, increasing to 15 the number of Premier League clubs. Both Hub Sundowns and Eleven Men in Flight were able to stay up while Manzini Sundowns and Hellenic were promoted. At the end of the 2010-11 season, however, it is planned that four teams will be relegated. Swaziland's most successful club Mbabane Highlanders retained the cup with a 1-0 victory over Umbelebele in the final, winning the trophy for the seventh time. Ephraim Mashaba quit as the coach of the Swaziland national team in mid-year to head back to South Africa and was replaced by Musa Zwane, whose first four games in charge all ended in defeat. They included losses to Ghana and Congo in the first two games of their 2012 African Nations Cup qualifiers.

FIFA WORLD CUP RECORD
1930-1990 DNE 1994-2010 DNQ

NATIONAL FOOTBALL ASSOCIATION OF SWAZILAND (NFAS)

Sigwaca House, Plot 582,
Sheffield Road, PO Box 641,
Mbabane H100

☎ +268 4046852
📠 +268 4046206
✉ info@nfas.org.sz
🖥 www.nfas.org.sz
FA 1968 CON 1976 FIFA 1978
P Adam Mthethwa
GS Frederick Mngomezulu

FIFA BIG COUNT 2006

Total players	54 900
% of population	4.83%
Male	54 900
Female	0
Amateurs 18+	3 300
Unregistered	3 900
Professionals	0
Referees	100
Admin & coaches	800
Number of clubs	60
Number of teams	220

MAJOR CITIES/TOWNS

		Population
1	Manzini	93 374
2	Mbabane	61 391
3	Malkerns	7 902
4	Nhlangano	6 991
5	Mhlume	6 876
6	Big Bend	6 835
7	Siteki	5 910
8	Simunye	5 520
9	Hluti	5 387
10	Pigg's Peak	4 548
11	Ngomane	3 824
12	Lobamba	3 736
13	Mpaka	3 571
14	Vuvulane	3 522
15	Kwaluseni	2 784
16	Bulembu	2 321
17	Hlatikulu	2 271
18	Bhunya	2 187
19	Mhlambanyatsi	2 167

UMBUSO WESWATINI • KINGDOM OF SWAZILAND

Capital	Mbabane	Population	1 123 913 (156)	% in cities	25%
GDP per capita	$4400 (151)	Area km²	17 364 km² (158)	GMT +/-	+1
Neighbours (km)	Mozambique 105, South Africa 430				

RECENT INTERNATIONAL MATCHES PLAYED BY SWAZILAND

2006	Opponents	Score		Venue	Comp	Scorers	Att	Referee
26-08	Lesotho	W	3-1	Mbabane	Fr	Mduduzi Mdluli 2 28 49, Salebona Jele 64		
3-09	Angola	L	0-2	Mbabane	CNq			Maillet SEY
7-10	Eritrea	D	0-0	Asmara	CNq			Gasingwa RWA
15-11	Botswana	L	0-1	Gaborone	Fr			
2007								
13-02	Lesotho	W	1-0	Maseru	Fr	Bheki Msimango 5		
18-03	Lesotho	L	0-1	Lobamba	Fr			
25-03	Kenya	L	0-2	Nairobi	CNq			Seechurn MRI
26-05	Mauritius	D	0-0	Mbabane	CCr1	L 5-6p		Labrosse SEY
27-05	Malawi	W	1-0	Mbabane	CCr1	Mphile Tsabedze 85		Labrosse SEY
3-06	Kenya	D	0-0	Mbabane	CNq			Katjimune NAM
17-06	Angola	L	0-3	Luanda	CNq			Marange ZIM
9-09	Eritrea	D	0-0	Manzini	CNq			Ssegonga UGA
18-11	Malawi	L	0-3	Manzini	Fr			
2008								
9-02	Botswana	L	1-4	Mbabane	Fr	Tony Tsabedze 77		
10-02	Lesotho	D	2-2	Mbabane	Fr	Barry Steenkamp 48, Baiano Kunene 58. L 1-4p		
23-05	Lesotho	D	1-1	Mbabane	Fr	Felix Badenhorst 20		
8-06	Togo	W	2-1	Mbabane	WCq	Siza Dlamini 55, Collen Salelwako 73	5 819	Niyongabo BDI
15-06	Zambia	D	0-0	Mbabane	WCq		7 462	Kotey GHA
21-06	Zambia	L	0-1	Chililabombwe	WCq		14 458	Marange ZIM
19-07	Madagascar	D	1-1	Witbank	CCr1	Phinda Dlamini 39		Nhlapo RSA
21-07	Mauritius	D	1-1	Witbank	CCr1	Gcina Mazibuko 51		Nhlapo RSA
23-07	Seychelles	W	1-0	Witbank	CCr1	Mfanzile Dlamini 89		Katjimune NAM
20-08	Mozambique	L	0-3	Maputo	Fr			
11-10	Togo	L	0-6	Accra	WCq		8 000	Evehe CMR
2009								
19-06	Lesotho	D	1-1	Manzini	Fr	Mxolisi Mthethwa 74		
21-06	Lesotho	D	1-1	Lobamba	Fr	Mfanafuthi Bhembe 83		
6-07	Malawi	L	1-3	Blantyre	Fr	Thokozani Mkhulisi 77p		
12-08	Mozambique	L	0-1	Maputo	Fr			
5-09	Namibia	D	1-1	Windhoek	Fr	Mxolisi Mthethwa 38		
18-10	Seychelles	W	2-1	Bulawayo	CCr1	Mathokoza Twala 72, Mfanzile Dlamini 74		Carvalho ANG
20-10	Botswana	L	0-1	Bulawayo	CCr1			Seechurn MRI
22-10	Comoros	W	3-0	Bulawayo	CCr1	Mathokoza Twala 37, Mxolisi Mthethwa 46, Mfanzile Dlamini 67		Carvalho ANG
2010								
11-08	Mozambique	L	1-2	Maputo	Fr	Siza Dlamini 29		
5-09	Ghana	L	0-3	Lobamba	CNq			Seechurn MRI
10-10	Congo	L	1-3	Brazzaville	CNq	Darren Christie 37		Ssegonga UGA
27-10	Botswana	L	0-2	Lobatse	Fr			

Fr = Friendly match • CN = CAF African Cup of Nations • CC = COSAFA Castle Cup • WC = FIFA World Cup
q = qualifier • r1 = first round group • qf = quarter-final • sf = semi-final

SWAZILAND 2009-10

MTN PREMIER LEAGUE

	Pl	W	D	L	F	A	Pts	Buffaloes	Swallows	Chiefs	Mambas	Leopards	Wanderers	Umbelebele	Highlanders	Rovers	Pirates	Sundowns	XI Men IF
Young Buffaloes †	22	14	5	3	29	15	47		0-1	2-0	2-1	1-0	2-1	2-3	0-0	1-0	0-0	2-0	3-1
Mbabane Swallows	22	14	4	4	33	17	46	3-0		0-1	1-1	1-2	1-0	2-1	0-0	2-0	2-1	3-2	3-1
Malanti Chiefs	22	12	5	5	26	14	41	1-1	1-1		2-0	0-0	3-0	1-0	0-1	0-2	0-0	0-1	2-0
Green Mamba	22	12	4	6	33	23	40	0-2	2-1	1-1		6-2	2-1	3-2	2-0	2-1	0-0	1-0	2-0
Royal Leopards	22	11	4	7	35	27	37	1-2	1-0	1-2	2-1		1-3	0-2	2-0	1-2	3-0	2-1	1-1
Manzini Wanderers	22	9	3	10	25	26	30	0-1	1-1	2-0	2-1	2-4		1-0	1-2	1-0	1-0	1-0	1-1
Umbelebele	22	9	2	11	27	30	29	1-1	1-2	0-2	1-3	1-3	1-3		1-2	2-1	2-0	0-0	3-0
Mbabane Highlanders	22	7	7	8	18	19	28	1-2	0-1	0-2	3-0	0-1	1-1	0-1		0-0	1-0	0-0	2-2
Mhlambanyatsi Rovers	22	6	5	11	22	28	23	0-1	1-3	0-1	0-0	0-0	2-0	3-1	1-2		2-2	3-2	1-2
Moneni Pirates	22	5	6	11	15	26	21	0-0	0-1	1-2	0-2	1-5	2-0	0-1	0-0	1-2		1-0	2-1
Hub Sundowns	22	4	3	15	16	34	15	0-2	0-1	0-3	0-2	1-1	1-4	0-1	1-3	3-0	1-3		2-1
Eleven Men in Flight	22	3	4	15	16	36	13	1-2	1-3	1-2	0-1	0-2	0-0	1-2	1-0	1-1	0-1	0-1	

22/08/2009 - 8/05/2010 • † Qualified for the CAF Champions League

SWAZILAND 2009-10 NATIONAL FIRST DIVISION (2)

	Pl	W	D	L	F	A	Pts
Manzini Sundowns	17	13	2	2	41	20	41
Hellenic FC	18	12	4	2	36	15	40
Bush Bucks	16	8	5	3	26	21	29
Midas Mbabane City	16	8	4	4	23	15	28
Masibini Red Lions	16	7	2	7	17	24	23
Tambankulu Callies	16	7	1	8	25	23	22
Manzini Sea Birds	15	6	2	7	20	18	20
Manchester United	16	4	8	4	14	12	20
RSSC United	16	3	5	8	15	29	14
Russian Bombers	16	3	4	9	17	31	13
Illovo FC	15	2	5	8	13	21	11
Mfishane Never Die	17	0	6	11	13	31	6

23/08/2009 - 18/04/2010

MEDALS TABLE

		Overall G	Lge G	Cup G	City/Town
1	Mbabane Highlanders	19	12	7	Mbabane
2	Manzini Wanderers	7	6	1	Manzini
3	Mbabane Swallows	5	3	2	Mbabane
	Eleven Men in Flight	5	2	3	Siteki
	Manzini Sundowns	5	2	3	Manzini
6	Royal Leopards	4	3	1	Simunye
7	Mhlambanyatsi Rovers	2	1	1	Mhlambanyatsi
	Bulembu Young Aces	2		2	Bulembu
	Moneni Pirates	2		2	Manzini
10	Peacemakers	1	1		Mhlume
	Young Buffaloes	1	1		Matsapha
	Green Mamba	1		1	Matsapha
	Hub Sundowns	1		1	
	Malanti Chiefs	1		1	Pigg's Peak
	Mhlume United	1		1	Mhlume

SWAZI BANK CUP 2010

Round of 16

Mbabane Highlanders	1
Royal Leopards	0
Moneni Pirates	0
Amagagasi	1
Malanti Chiefs	4
Manchester United	2
Illovo FC	2
Green Mamba	3
Hellenic FC	5p
Eleven Men in Flight	4p
Bush Bucks	2p
Manzini Sundowns	4p
Manzini Wanderers	1 3p
Young Buffaloes	1 0p
Hub Sundowns	5p
Umbelebele	6p

Quarter-finals

Mbabane Highlanders	3
Amagagasi	0
Malanti Chiefs	0
Green Mamba	1
Hellenic FC	5p
Manzini Sundowns	4p
Manzini Wanderers	1
Umbelebele	2

Semi-finals

Mbabane Highlanders	1
Green Mamba	0
Hellenic FC	1
Umbelebele	3

Final

Mbabane Highlanders‡	1
Umbelebele	0

CUP FINAL

Somhlolo National, Mbabane
11-04-2010

Scorer - Muma Losper 23

‡ Qualified for the CAF Confederation Cup

SYR – SYRIA

FIFA/COCA-COLA WORLD RANKING

1993	1994	1995	1996	1997	1998	1999	2000	2001	2002	2003	2004	2005	2006	2007	2008	2009	2010
82	105	136	115	98	84	109	100	90	91	85	85	98	112	107	105	91	107

	2010												Hi/Lo
	Jan	Feb	Mar	Mar	Apr	May	Jul	Aug	Sep	Oct	Nov	Dec	**78**
	91	100	101	97	98	98	92	92	94	105	109	107	**145**

Syria returned to the finals of the AFC Asian Cup for the first time since 1996 but, as with their previous appearances at the continental championship, they missed out on a place in the knockout phase of the competition. The Syrians, though, did pull off one of the biggest shocks of the tournament, defeating three-time champions Saudi Arabia 2-1 in their opening game before pushing Japan close in their next match, which they lost as a result of a late Keisuke Honda penalty. Defeat at the hands of neighbours Jordan ended their run at the tournament, but the results were still better than expected after the national association removed Ratomir Dujkovic from his role as head coach just three weeks before the tournament. The Serb was replaced at short notice by Romanian Tita Valeriu, fresh off the back of his success in leading Al Ittihad to the AFC Cup in November. Based in the city of Aleppo, close to the Turkish border, Al Ittihad had only just scraped through from the group stage ahead of Lebanon's Al Nijmeh but then beat three Kuwaiti teams on the way to winning their first continental title. In the final in Kuwait City they beat home team Al Qadisiya on post-match penalties after the it had finished 1-1. Domestic honours went to army club Al Jaish in the league and to Al Karama who beat Al Nwair on penalties in the Cup Final.

FIFA WORLD CUP RECORD
1930-1954 DNE 1958 DNQ 1962-1970 DN E 1974 DNQ 1978 DNE 1982-2010 DNQ

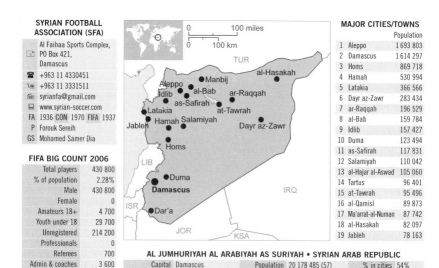

SYRIAN FOOTBALL ASSOCIATION (SFA)

Al Faihaa Sports Complex,
PO Box 421,
Damascus
☎ +963 11 4330451
🖷 +963 11 3331511
🖷 syrianfa@gmail.com
🖳 www.syrian-soccer.com
FA 1936 CON 1970 FIFA 1937
P Forouk Sereih
GS Mohamed Samer Dia

FIFA BIG COUNT 2006

Total players	430 800
% of population	2.28%
Male	430 800
Female	0
Amateurs 18+	4 700
Youth under 18	29 700
Unregistered	214 200
Professionals	0
Referees	700
Admin & coaches	3 600
Number of clubs	170
Number of teams	760

MAJOR CITIES/TOWNS

		Population
1	Aleppo	1 693 803
2	Damascus	1 614 297
3	Homs	869 718
4	Hamah	530 994
5	Latakia	366 566
6	Dayr az-Zawr	283 434
7	ar-Raqqah	196 529
8	al-Bab	159 784
9	Idlib	157 427
10	Duma	123 494
11	as-Safirah	117 831
12	Salamiyah	110 042
13	al-Hajar al-Aswad	105 060
14	Tartus	96 401
15	at-Tawrah	95 496
16	al-Qamisl	89 873
17	Ma'arrat-al-Numan	87 742
18	al-Hasakah	82 097
19	Jableh	78 163

AL JUMHURIYAH AL ARABIYAH AS SURIYAH • SYRIAN ARAB REPUBLIC

Capital Damascus	Population 20 178 485 (57)	% in cities 54%
GDP per capita $4600 (146)	Area km² 185 180 km² (88)	GMT +/- +2
Neighbours (km) Iraq 605, Israel 76, Jordan 375, Lebanon 375, Turkey 822 • Coast 193		

RECENT INTERNATIONAL MATCHES PLAYED BY SYRIA

2008	Opponents	Score		Venue	Comp	Scorers	Att	Referee
7-08	Jordan	D	0-0	Tehran	WAr1			
9-08	Oman	W	2-1	Tehran	WAr1	Mohanand Ibrahim [11], Mohammad Abadi [71]		
13-08	Iran	L	0-2	Tehran	WAsf		4 000	Balideh QAT
20-08	Venezuela	L	1-4	Puerto La Cruz	Fr	Younes Hamida [83]	2 500	Gomez VEN
13-11	Japan	L	1-3	Kobe	Fr	Mohamed Al Zeno [78p]	25 004	Choi Myung Yong KOR
27-12	Saudi Arabia	D	1-1	Dammam	Fr	Raja Rafe [50]		
29-12	Bahrain	D	2-2	Manama	Fr	OG 41, Mohamed Al Zeno [68]		
2009								
14-01	China PR	W	3-2	Aleppo	ACq	Maher Al Said 2 [8p 24], Firas Al Khatib [39p]	7 000	Torky IRN
18-01	Turkmenistan	W	5-1	Kuwait City	Fr	Ali Diab [42], Raja Rafe [53], Tarab Bakri [67], Firas Al Khatib 2 [70 83]		
23-01	Kuwait	W	3-2	Kuwait City	Fr	Raja Rafe [29p], Feras Ismael [52], Firas Al Khatib [65]		
28-01	Lebanon	W	2-0	Saida	ACq	Jehad Alhoussain 37, Firas Al Khatib [77]	300	Balideh QAT
1-02	Korea Republic	D	1-1	Dubai	Fr	Yehya Al Rashed [90]		Aljunaibi UAE
21-03	Qatar	L	1-2	Aleppo	Fr	Majed Al Haj [79]		
27-06	Haiti	W	2-1	Montreal	Fr	Mohamed Al Zeno [8], Firas Al Khatib [26]		
20-08	Kyrgyzstan	W	2-0	New Delhi	Fr	Mohamed Al Zeno [9], Abdul Al Agha [72]		Patwal IND
24-08	Sri Lanka	W	4-0	New Delhi	Fr	Mohamed Al Zeno [26], Abdulrazak Al Hussein [33], Abdul Al Agha 2 [37 55]		Patwal IND
27-08	Lebanon	W	1-0	New Delhi	Fr	Mohamed Al Zeno [23]		Arumughan IND
29-08	India	W	1-0	New Delhi	Fr	Ali Diab [18]		Ali Adil MDV
31-08	India	D	1-1	New Delhi	Fr	Ali Diab [123+] L 4-5p	20 000	Ali Adil MDV
26-10	Kuwait	L	0-1	Al Jahra	Fr			
8-11	Thailand	D	1-1	Bangkok	Fr	Raja Rafe [35p]		
14-11	Vietnam	W	1-0	Hanoi	ACq	Raja Rafe [94+]	30 000	Williams AUS
18-11	Vietnam	D	0-0	Aleppo	ACq		19 000	Al Hilali OMA
2010								
6-01	China PR	D	0-0	Zheijang	ACq		29 570	Toma JPN
23-01	Sweden	D	1-1	Damascus	Fr	Raja Rafe [5]	10 000	Najm LIB
19-02	Kuwait	D	1-1	Al Ain	Fr	Abdelrazaq Al Hussain [81]		
3-03	Lebanon	W	4-0	Damascus	ACq	Mohamed Al Zeno [4], Abdul Al Agha [10], Jehad Alhoussain [47], Abdelrazak Al Hussain [60]	16 000	Kim Dong Jin KOR
3-09	Kuwait	L	0-3	Kuwait City	Fr			
7-09	Yemen	L	1-2	Sana'a	Fr	Adib Barakat [29]		
24-09	Jordan	D	1-1	Amman	WAr1	Mohamed Al Zeno [82]	18 000	
26-09	Kuwait	L	1-2	Amman	WAr1	Ahmad Al Omaier [83]	1 500	
8-10	China PR	L	1-2	Kunming	Fr	Adel Abdullah [60]		
14-11	Bahrain	W	2-0	Riffa	Fr	Mohamed Al Zeno [48], Oday Jaffal [78]		
18-12	Iraq	W	1-0	Sulaymaniyah	Fr	Taha Dyab [86]		
22-12	Iraq	L	0-1	Damascus	Fr			
30-12	Korea Republic	L	0-1	Abu Dhabi	Fr		500	Al Marzouqi UAE
2011								
2-01	UAE	L	0-2	Al Ain	Fr		2 400	Abdul BAKI OMA
9-01	Saudi Arabia	W	2-1	Al Rayyan	ACr1	Abdelrazaq Al Hussain 2 [38 63]	15 768	Kim Dong Jin KOR
13-01	Japan	L	1-2	Doha	ACr1	Firas Al Khatib [76p]	10 453	Torky IRN
17-01	Jordan	L	1-2	Doha	ACr1	Mohamed Al Zeno [15]	9 849	Abdou QAT

Fr = Friendly match • WA = West Asian Championship • WG = West Asian Games • AC = AFC Asian Cup • WC = FIFA World Cup
q = qualifier • r1 = first round group • sf = semi-final • 3p = third place play-off • f = final

SYRIA NATIONAL TEAM HISTORICAL RECORDS

Past Coaches: Jalal Talebi IRN 2001-02 • Janusz Wojcik 2003 • Ahmed Rifaat EGY 2003-04 • Miloslav Radenovic SRB 2005-06 • Fajr Ibrahim 2006-08 • Mohamed Qwayed 2008 • Fajr Ibrahim 2008-10 • Ayman Hakeem 2010 • Ratomir Dujkovic SRB 2010 • Tita Valeriu ROU 2010-

SYRIA 2009-10

PREMIER DIVISION

	Pl	W	D	L	F	A	Pts	Jaish	Karama	Teshrin	Ittihad	Wathba	Shorta	Majd	Umayya	Taliya	Wahda	Nwair	Jazira	Jabala	Efrin
Al Jaish ‡	26	18	4	4	56	22	**58**		1-1	1-2	1-0	4-0	1-2	1-2	4-1	5-0	3-0	2-0	3-2	2-1	2-1
Al Karama ‡	26	16	8	2	40	16	**56**	0-1		0-0	0-0	1-0	0-0	1-0	1-0	2-0	3-2	1-0	2-0	3-3	2-0
Teshrin	26	14	6	6	36	23	**48**	1-1	1-2		3-0	1-2	0-1	1-2	2-0	1-0	1-0	2-0	1-0	2-1	1-0
Al Ittihad	26	13	6	7	40	29	**45**	1-3	0-0	0-1		4-2	1-0	4-0	3-2	2-1	1-1	1-1	2-0	2-0	1-0
Al Wathba	26	12	7	7	35	27	**43**	0-2	2-0	2-1	1-0		2-1	1-1	0-1	3-1	4-0	3-2	5-1	1-0	1-1
Al Shorta	26	11	7	8	34	26	**40**	1-1	0-3	0-1	4-2	0-1		3-0	3-3	1-1	2-1	3-0	3-1	0-0	1-0
Al Majd	26	11	7	8	36	29	**40**	2-3	0-1	1-2	1-1	0-0	2-1		1-2	2-1	1-1	0-0	5-1	3-0	
Umayya	26	9	9	8	32	36	**36**	0-3	1-1	1-1	2-1	1-1	0-2	1-0		1-0	1-2	1-0	2-2	2-1	2-1
Al Taliya	26	10	5	11	36	34	**35**	2-0	1-1	1-1	1-1	0-1	2-3	1-2	3-2		4-1	1-0	2-0	1-0	5-1
Al Wahda	26	6	9	11	32	43	**27**	1-2	1-2	1-1	3-5	1-1	1-0	0-3	1-1	1-0		4-1	2-2	5-2	2-1
Al Nwair	26	4	10	12	20	34	**22**	0-0	0-2	2-2	0-1	1-0	2-2	1-4	0-0	1-1	1-1		2-1	2-0	3-0
Al Jazira	26	3	10	13	24	44	**19**	1-3	1-2	3-2	1-2	3-2	0-0	0-0	2-2	0-1	0-0	0-0		2-2	1-0
Jabala	26	4	6	16	19	42	**18**	1-4	0-3	0-1	0-1	0-0	1-0	1-1	0-2	1-2	0-0	2-0	2-0		1-0
Efrin	26	1	6	19	16	51	**9**	0-3	2-6	2-4	1-4	0-0	0-1	0-1	1-1	1-4	0-0	0-0	1-1	2-0	

9/10/2009 - 7/05/2010 • ‡ Qualified for the AFC Cup

Top scorers: **15** - Firas Kashosh, Taliya • **12** - Abdul Rahman Akari, Teshrin; Amar Zakour, Umayya & Samer Awad, Majd • **11** - Majed Al Haj, Jaish

MEDALS TABLE

		Overall	Lge	Cup	Asia			City/Town
		G	G	G	G	S	B	
1	Al Jaish	18	11	6	1			Damascus
2	Al Karama	16	8	8		2		Homs
3	Al Ittihad	15	6	8	1			Aleppo
4	Al Foutoua	6	2	4				Dayr az-Zawr
5	Jabala	5	4	1				Jableh
	Al Shorta	5	1	4				Damascus
7	Al Wahda	3	1	2			1	Damascus
	Al Horriya	3	2	1				Aleppo
9	Barada	2	2					Damascus
	Teshrin	2	2					Latakia
	Rmeilan	2		2				
12	Al Ahly	1		1				Cairo
	Hottin	1		1				Latakia
	Al Maghazel	1		1				
	Al Majd	1		1				Damascus
	Al Yarmouk	1		1				Aleppo

FASF CUP 2009-10

Round of 16			Quarter-finals			Semi-finals			Final		
Al Karama	3	5									
Efrin *	0	0	**Al Karama ***	3	1						
Al Foutoua *	2	0	Al Wathba	0	3						
Al Wathba	2	4									
Al Sadd *	1	1				Al Karama	4	3			
Banyas	0	0	Al Sadd *	2	0	Jabala *	3	0			
Mleha *	1	0	**Jabala**	1	3						
Jabala	1	3									
Teshrin	2	2							**Al Karama ‡**	1	4p
Mouhafaza *	0	2	**Teshrin ***	0	3				Al Nwair	1	3p
Al Nidhal	0	1	Al Jaish	0	3						
Al Jaish *	4	6									
Al Jazira	2	w				Teshrin *	3	0			
Hottin *	2	o	Al Jazira	1	1	**Al Nwair**	1	2			
Umayya	2	1	**Al Nwair ***	1	2						
Al Nwair *	0	3									

CUP FINAL

Abbasiyyin, Damascus
15-06-2010

* Home team in the first leg • ‡ Qualified for the AFC Cup

TAH – TAHITI

FIFA/COCA-COLA WORLD RANKING

1993	1994	1995	1996	1997	1998	1999	2000	2001	2002	2003	2004	2005	2006	2007	2008	2009	2010
141	148	156	158	161	123	139	131	127	115	133	124	141	173	162	188	194	184

	2010											Hi/Lo
Jan	Feb	Mar	Mar	Apr	May	Jul	Aug	Sep	Oct	Nov	Dec	**111**
194	195	195	192	189	191	188	188	194	184	184	184	**195**

It remains to be seen what effect the Coupe de l'Outre-Mer will have on the standard of the Tahiti national team but with the rest of the Pacific islands largely restricted to a series of internationals once every four years, the tournament for French oversees territories is giving the team valuable experience. 2010 saw the second staging of the competition and once again Tahiti emerged without a win. In 2008 they had lost to Guadeloupe, Martinique and New Caledonia and in the 2010 tournament, staged again in Paris, Tahiti opened with a 4-1 defeat at the hands of Martinique. Against Guadeloupe and New Caledonia, however, they managed to draw both games and even technically won both of them via penalty shoot-outs but it was not enough to see them progress. In club football, 2009 champions Manu Ura had a miserable time in the OFC Champions League, finishing bottom of a group dominated by New Zealand clubs Auckland City and Waitakere United, both of whom stand in the way of 2010 champions Tefana in the 2010-11 tournament. Tefana qualified after an outstanding domestic season that saw them win the double. Based in Faa'a on the outskirts of the capital it was their second league triumph whilst their 2-0 victory over Dragons in the Polynesian Cup Final was their third in four years.

FIFA WORLD CUP RECORD
1930-1990 DNE 1994-2010 DNQ

FEDERATION TAHITIENNE DE FOOTBALL (FTF)

	Rue Coppenrath,
	Stade de Fautaua,
	BP 50358, Pirae 98716
☎	+689 540954
	+689 419629
@	contact@ftf.pf
💻	www.ftf.pf
FA	1989 CON 1990 FIFA 1990
P	TBD
GS	Vaiata Friedman

FIFA BIG COUNT 2006

Total players	16 396
% of population	6.66%
Male	15 391
Female	1 005
Amateurs 18+	4 429
Youth under 18	5 367
Unregistered	4 500
Professionals	0
Referees	64
Admin & coaches	64
Number of clubs	164
Number of teams	650

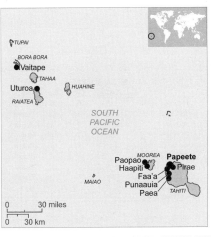

MAJOR CITIES/TOWNS

		Population
1	Faa'a (T)	30 448
2	Punaauia (T)	26 286
3	Papeete (T)	25 980
4	Mahina (T)	14 845
5	Pirae (T)	14 489
6	Paea (T)	12 139
7	Papara (T)	11 121
8	Arue (T)	9 543
9	Afaahiti (T)	5 720
10	Vaitape (BB)	5 182
11	Mataiea (T)	4 580
12	Paopao (M)	4 448
13	Papeari (T)	4 385
14	Haapiti (M)	4 264
15	Uturoa (R)	3 863
	(T) = Tahiti	
	(BB) = Bora Bora	
	(M) = Moorea	
	(R) = Raiatea	

POLYNESIE FRANCAISE • FRENCH POLYNESIA

Capital	Papete	Population	287 032 (179)	% in cities 52%
GDP per capita	$18 000 (68)	Area km²	4167 km² (174)	GMT + / - -10
Neighbours (km)	Coast 2525			

RECENT INTERNATIONAL MATCHES PLAYED BY TAHITI

2004	Opponents	Score		Venue	Comp	Scorers	Att	Referee
10-05	Cook Islands	W	2-0	Honiara	WCq	Temataua [2], Moretta [80]	12 000	Singh FIJ
12-05	New Caledonia	D	0-0	Honiara	WCq		14 000	Rakaroi FIJ
17-05	Tonga	W	2-0	Honiara	WCq	Wajoka [1], Temataua [78]	400	Sosongan PNG
19-05	Solomon Islands	D	1-1	Honiara	WCq	Simon [30]	18 000	Rakaroi FIJ
29-05	Fiji	D	0-0	Adelaide	WCq		3 000	Farina ITA
31-05	Australia	L	0-9	Adelaide	WCq		1 200	Attison VAN
2-06	Solomon Islands	L	0-4	Adelaide	WCq		50	Rakaroi FIJ
4-06	New Zealand	L	0-10	Adelaide	WCq		200	Shield AUS
6-06	Vanuatu	W	2-1	Adelaide	WCq	Temataua [40], Wajoka [89]	300	Rakaroi FIJ
2005								
No international matches played in 2005								
2006								
No international matches played in 2006								
2007								
25-08	New Caledonia	L	0-1	Apia	WCq		400	Hester NZL
29-08	Tuvalu †	D	1-1	Apia	WCq	Williams [45]	100	Lengeta SOL
1-09	Fiji	L	0-4	Apia	WCq		200	Fox NZL
3-09	Cook Islands	W	1-0	Apia	WCq	Tinorua [64]	100	Aimaasu SAM
2008								
24-09	New Caledonia	L	0-1	Paris	Fr			
27-09	Martinique †	L	0-1	Paris	Fr			
30-09	Guadeloupe †	L	0-1	Paris	Fr			
2009								
No international matches played in 2009								
2010								
23-09	Martinique †	L	1-4	Paris	Fr	Li Fung Kee [27]		Panot FRA
26-09	Guadeloupe †	D	1-1	Paris	Fr	Tehau [57]		Fouquet FRA
29-09	New Caledonia	D	1-1	Paris	Fr	William [30], W 5-3p		Fouquet FRA

Fr = Friendly match • OC = OFC Oceania Cup • SP = South Pacific Games • WC = FIFA World Cup
q = qualifier • r1 = first roundgroup • sf = semi-final • 3p = third place play-off • † Not a full international

	MEDALS TABLE	Overall	Lge	Cup	Town
		G	G	G	
1	AS Central Sport	38	20	18	Papeete
2	AS Venus	15	9	6	Mahina
3	AS Pirae	15	7	8	Pirae
4	AS Fei Pi	15	7	8	Papeete
5	AS Excelsior	11	7	4	Papeete
6	AS Jeunes Tahitiens	8	3	5	Papeete
7	AS Manu Ura	7	5	2	Papeete
8	AS Tefana	5	2	3	Faa'a
9	AS Dragon	3			Papeete
10	AS PTT	3	1	2	Papeete
11	AS Tamarii Punaruu	3	1	2	Papeete
12	AS Arue	2	1	1	Arue
13	CAICT	1		1	
14	Marine	1		1	
15	AS Temanava	1		1	Moorea
16	AS Vaiete	1		1	Papeete

TAHITI 2009-10

DIVISION FEDERALE STAGE ONE

	Pl	W	D	L	F	A	Pts	Manu Ura	Tefana	Dragon	Pirae	Vaiete	Tamarii	Vénus	Jeunes	TAC
AS Manu Ura †	16	9	5	2	27	11	50		1-1	1-2	1-1	4-1	2-0	1-0	3-0	3-0
AS Tefana †	16	9	2	5	36	20	49	0-1		1-3	3-0	0-1	1-4	1-0	6-0	4-0
AS Dragon †	16	9	2	5	41	24	47	1-1	2-3		7-1	3-0	4-0	1-2	5-2	2-0
AS Pirae †	16	8	3	5	37	34	43	1-1	2-0	3-2		2-0	0-6	3-2	6-0	2-3
AS Vaiete †	16	7	2	7	21	23	39	1-2	2-4	3-1	2-3		2-0	2-0	0-0	3-1
AS Tamarii Faa'a †	16	6	3	7	34	32	39	1-0	2-4	4-4	3-2	1-1		4-1	1-3	5-2
AS Vénus	16	6	1	9	22	24	37	0-2	1-2	2-1	1-3	1-2	2-0		3-0	2-0
AS Jeunes Tahitiens	16	3	2	11	17	48	29	1-3	0-5	0-1	1-6	0-1	3-2	0-3		2-2
AS Taravao AC	16	2	6	8	18	37	28	1-1	1-1	1-2	2-2	1-0	1-1	2-2	1-5	

4/09/2009 - 17/02/2010 • † Qualified for play-offs • Top six split off for a Championship play-off along with the champions of Mooréa, Temanava, while the bottom four join the top four of the second division in a relegation/promotion play-off group • Four points for a win, two points for a draw and one point for a defeat

CHAMPIONSHIP PLAY-OFF

	Pl	W	D	L	F	A	Pts	Tefana	Vaiete	Tamarii	Pirae	Manu	Tam'va	Dragon
AS Tefana †	12	9	1	2	24	3	42		1-1	2-0	4-0	0-1	3-0	5-0
AS Vaiete	12	5	4	3	18	17	33	0-1		3-2	2-2	0-3	2-1	1-1
AS Tamarii Faa'a	12	5	4	3	16	16	33	1-0	2-2		1-6	1-1	2-0	1-1
AS Pirae	12	5	2	5	25	24	31	0-2	1-3	0-1		4-1	1-0	4-3
AS Manu Ura	12	3	3	6	15	18	28	0-2	1-2	1-1	2-2		2-0	0-1
AS Tamanava	12	4	0	8	10	21	26	0-3	0-1	0-2	3-2	3-2		1-0
AS Dragon	12	3	2	7	13	22	25	0-1	2-1	0-2	2-3	2-1	1-2	

26/02/2010 - 4/06/2010 • † Qualified for the OFC Champions League • Bonus points in brackets

RELEGATION/PROMOTION PLAY-OFF

	Pl	W	D	L	F	A	Pts	Venus	Ex'sior	Vairao	Central	TAC	Roniu	Aorai	JT
AS Vénus	14	12	0	2	25	11	56		3-1	2-1	2-0	2-1	0-1	3-0	1-0
AS Excelsior	14	7	4	3	27	18	42	1-2		2-2	2-0	2-1	1-1	0-0	3-0
AS Vairao	14	6	3	5	32	19	41	1-2	1-1		1-0	3-3	1-1	6-2	5-0
AS Central Sport	14	5	4	5	24	18	37	4-1	0-3	1-2		1-0	0-0	1-3	6-0
AS Taravao AC	14	6	2	6	27	25	37	1-2	3-1	3-2	1-5		3-2	6-2	2-2
AS Roniu	14	4	5	5	20	20	33	0-2	1-2	2-1	1-1	1-0		2-2	5-2
AS Aorai	14	3	4	7	21	34	29	0-1	4-4	0-1	2-2	0-3	2-1		3-4
AS Jeunes Tahitiens	14	1	2	11	10	41	23	0-2	0-3	0-6	0-1	0-1	2-2	0-1	

27/02/2010 - 6/06/2010 • Top four play the 2010-11 season in the Division Federal

COUPE DE POLYNESIE 2009-10

Round of 16		Quarter-finals		Semi-finals		Final	
AS Tefana	1						
AS Excelsior *	0	**AS Tefana**	5 6				
AS Tamarii Faa'a *	0	AS Roniu	2 2				
AS Roniu	3			**AS Tefana**	1 1 9p		
AS Jeunes Tahitiens *	4			AS Pirae	1 1 8p		
AS Vairao	2	AS Jeunes Tahitiens	1 0				
AS Samine *	1	**AS Pirae**	5 6			**AS Tefana**	2
AS Pirae	7					AS Dragon	0
AS Vénus	4						
AS Vaiete *	3	**AS Vénus**	2 3			CUP FINAL	
Olympique Mahina	0	AS Mira	4 0				
AS Mira *	2			AS Vénus	2 1		
AS Taravao AC	3 5p			**AS Dragon**	1 4		
AS Manu Ura *	3 4p	AS Taravao AC	0 1			12-06-2010	
AS Punaruu *	1	**AS Dragon**	3 7				
AS Dragon	4			* Home team/home team in the 1st leg			

TAN – TANZANIA

FIFA/COCA-COLA WORLD RANKING

1993	1994	1995	1996	1997	1998	1999	2000	2001	2002	2003	2004	2005	2006	2007	2008	2009	2010
98	74	70	89	96	118	128	140	149	153	159	172	165	110	89	99	106	116

						2010							Hi/Lo
	Jan	Feb	Mar	Mar	Apr	May	Jul	Aug	Sep	Oct	Nov	Dec	65
	106	108	108	109	108	108	112	111	111	120	124	116	175

Tanzania won the East and Central African Senior Challenge Cup for the first time since 1994 when they hosted the tournament in December, overcoming a losing start to beat Cote d'Ivoire's 'B' team in the final. Remarkably it was only the third time that they had won the tournament in the 32 editions played since the current format was adopted in 1973. It came at the end of a busy year for the Taifa Stars who also played host to Brazil, the five-time world champions winning 5-1 in Dar-es-Salaam during a day-long visit in June as they prepared for the FIFA World Cup finals in South Africa. Danish coach Jan Poulsen took over from the Brazilian Marcio Maximo in mid-year, seeking to continue the improvements of recent years. Tanzania were drawn in a tough 2012 African Nations Cup qualifying group which gave them limited scope for qualifying for the finals but a draw away in Algeria in their opening game was a measure of the country's potential. Simba SC pipped perennial rivals Young Africans by three points to the Premier League title to win the Tanzania Bara (Mainland) championship for only the third time since 2004. Both Simba and Yanga now have 17 championship titles apiece and have dominated the league since 1999 when Prisons were the last side apart from the Dar es Salaam duo to win the league.

FIFA WORLD CUP RECORD

1930-1970 DNE **1974** DNQ **1978** DNE **1982-1986** DNQ **1990** DNE **1994-2010** DNQ

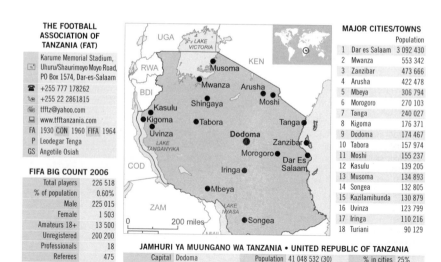

THE FOOTBALL ASSOCIATION OF TANZANIA (FAT)

Karume Memorial Stadium, Uhuru/Shaurimoyo Moyo Road, PO Box 1574, Dar-es-Salaam
☎ +255 777 178262
📠 +255 22 2861815
✉ tfftz@yahoo.com
🖥 www.tfftanzania.com
FA 1930 CON 1960 FIFA 1964
P Leodegar Tenga
GS Angetile Osiah

FIFA BIG COUNT 2006

Total players	226 518
% of population	0.60%
Male	225 015
Female	1 503
Amateurs 18+	13 500
Unregistered	200 200
Professionals	18
Referees	475
Admin & coaches	8 300
Number of clubs	200
Number of teams	5 000

MAJOR CITIES/TOWNS

		Population
1	Dar es Salaam	3 092 430
2	Mwanza	553 342
3	Zanzibar	473 666
4	Arusha	422 478
5	Mbeya	306 794
6	Morogoro	270 103
7	Tanga	240 027
8	Kigoma	176 371
9	Dodoma	174 467
10	Tabora	157 974
11	Moshi	155 237
12	Kasulu	139 205
13	Musoma	134 893
14	Songea	132 805
15	Kazilamihunda	130 879
16	Uvinza	123 799
17	Iringa	110 216
18	Turiani	90 129

JAMHURI YA MUUNGANO WA TANZANIA • UNITED REPUBLIC OF TANZANIA

Capital	Dodoma	Population	41 048 532 (30)	% in cities	25%
GDP per capita	$1400 (201)	Area km²	947 300 km² (31)	GMT +/-	+3
Neighbours (km)	Burundi 451, Congo DR 459, Kenya 769, Malawi 475, Mozambique 756, Rwanda 217, Uganda 396, Zambia 338 • Coast 1424				

RECENT INTERNATIONAL MATCHES PLAYED BY TANZANIA

2009	Opponents	Score		Venue	Comp	Scorers	Att	Referee
3-01	Somalia	L	0-1	Kampala	CCr1			
5-01	Zanzibar †	W	2-1	Kampala	CCr1	Danny Mrwanda [13], Athuman Iddy [78]		
7-01	Rwanda	W	2-0	Kampala	CCr1	Mrisho Ngasa [8], Athuman Iddy [37]		
9-01	Uganda	L	1-2	Kampala	CCr1	Salum Swedi [47p]		
11-01	Kenya	L	1-2	Kampala	CCsf	Danny Mrwanda [80]		
13-01	Burundi	W	3-2	Kampala	CC3p	Mrisho Ngasa [3], Jerson Tegete [70], Danny Mrwanda [75]		
11-02	Zimbabwe	D	0-0	Dar es Salaam	Fr			
9-05	Congo DR	L	0-2	Dar es Salaam	Fr			
3-06	New Zealand	W	2-1	Dar es Salaam	Fr	Jerson Tegete [55], Mwinyi Kazimoto [89]		
12-08	Rwanda	W	2-1	Kigali	Fr	Rashid Gumbo [59], Jerson Tegete [70]		
5-11	Egypt	L	1-5	Aswan	Fr	Kigi Makasi [45]		
8-11	Yemen	D	1-1	Sana'a	Fr	John Boko [69]		
11-11	Yemen	L	1-2	Sana'a	Fr	Abdelhalim Mahmoud [34]		
29-11	Uganda	L	0-2	Mumias	CCr1			
1-12	Zanzibar †	W	1-0	Mumias	CCr1	Mrisho Ngasa [18]		
4-12	Burundi	W	1-0	Mumias	CCr1	Mrisho Ngasa [49]		
8-12	Eritrea	W	4-0	Nairobi	CCqf	John Boko 61, Mrisho Ngasa 3 [64 77 84]		
10-12	Rwanda	L	1-2	Nairobi	CCsf	Mussa Mgosi [78]		
13-12	Zanzibar †	L	0-1	Nairobi	CC3p			
2010								
4-01	Côte d'Ivoire	L	0-1	Dar es Salaam	Fr		60 000	Mbaga TAN
3-03	Uganda	L	2-3	Mwanza	Fr	Nadir Haroub [55], Mrisho Ngasa [68]		
7-06	Brazil	L	1-5	Dar es Salaam	Fr	Jabir Aziz [86]	35 000	Ssegonga UGA
11-08	Kenya	D	1-1	Dar es Salaam	Fr	Mrisho Ngasa [59]		
3-09	Algeria	D	1-1	Blida	CNq	Idrissa Rajab [32]		Djaoupe TOG
9-10	Morocco	L	0-1	Dar es Salaam	CNq			Seechurn MRI
23-11	Kenya	W	1-0	Dar es Salaam	Fr	Gaudence Mwaikimba [1]		
27-11	Zambia	L	0-1	Dar es Salaam	CCr1			Batte UGA
30-11	Somalia	W	3-0	Dar es Salaam	CCr1	Henry Shindika [41p], John Boko [76], Nurdin Bakari [89]		
4-12	Burundi	W	2-0	Dar es Salaam	CCr1	Nurdin Bakari 2 [12 77]		
8-12	Rwanda	W	1-0	Dar es Salaam	CCqf	Shadrack Nsajigwa [62p]		
10-12	Uganda	D	0-0	Dar es Salaam	CCsf	W 5-4p		
12-12	Côte d'Ivoire 'B' †	W	1-0	Dar es Salaam	CCf	Shadrack Nsajigwa [41p]		

Fr = Friendly match • CN = CAF African Cup of Nations • CC = CECAFA Cup • WC = FIFA World Cup
q = qualifier • r1 = first round group • sf = semi-final • f = final • † Not a full international

TANZANIA 2009–10																		
PREMIER LEAGUE (LIGI KUU TANZANIA BARA)	Pl	W	D	L	F	A	Pts	Simba	Yanga	Azzam United	Mtibwa Sugar	African Lyon	Ruvu Stars	Kagera Sugar	Maji Maji	Toto Africa	Manyema	Prisons	Moro United
Simba SC †	22	20	2	0	50	12	62		1-0	1-0	3-1	1-0	3-1	2-0	2-0	3-1	2-0	3-1	2-1
Young Africans ‡	22	15	4	3	46	18	49	3-4		2-1	3-1	1-1	2-2	2-1	3-0	6-0	3-0	4-2	1-0
Azzam United	22	8	9	5	30	23	33	0-2	1-1		0-0	2-2	1-1	1-1	3-0	1-0	4-0	2-0	2-1
Mtibwa Sugar	22	9	6	7	24	23	33	0-4	1-2	0-1		0-1	1-0	0-0	0-0	2-1	2-1	3-1	2-1
African Lyon	22	6	7	9	22	24	25	1-1	0-2	0-2	0-2		1-1	1-2	2-0	6-1	2-1	0-0	0-1
JKT Ruvu Stars	22	6	7	9	26	29	25	1-4	0-1	1-1	0-1	4-2		0-1	1-1	2-1	1-1	2-0	1-2
Kagera Sugar	22	5	9	8	13	20	24	1-1	0-2	3-2	0-0	0-0	1-0		0-0	0-2	0-0	1-0	1-1
Maji Maji	22	6	6	10	14	27	24	0-2	1-0	1-1	1-0	2-1	0-1	1-0		1-2	0-0	0-1	0-3
Toto Africa	22	6	5	11	25	36	23	0-2	0-1	2-2	1-1	0-1	2-1	3-1	0-0		3-1	3-0	2-2
Manyema Rangers	22	6	5	11	19	36	23	0-2	1-3	0-0	2-5	0-1	2-2	1-0	2-1	1-0		2-1	2-0
Prisons SC	22	5	6	11	19	28	21	0-1	1-1	3-0	1-1	1-0	1-2	1-0	1-2	1-1	3-0		0-0
Moro United	22	4	6	12	19	31	18	1-4	0-3	2-3	0-1	0-0	0-2	0-0	2-3	1-0	1-2	0-0	

23/08/2009 - 21/04/2010 • † Qualified for the CAF Champions League • ‡ Qualified for the CAF Confederation Cup
Top scorer: 18 - Musa Hassan Mgosi, Simba

TCA – TURKS AND CAICOS ISLANDS

FIFA/COCA-COLA WORLD RANKING

1993	1994	1995	1996	1997	1998	1999	2000	2001	2002	2003	2004	2005	2006	2007	2008	2009	2010
-	-	-	-	-	-	196	200	200	202	203	203	203	169	181	168	177	187

	2010												Hi/Lo
	Jan	Feb	Mar	Mar	Apr	May	Jul	Aug	Sep	Oct	Nov	Dec	158
	177	174	186	186	185	184	182	180	186	187	188	187	204

Like many of the smallest national associations affiliated to FIFA, the majority of the work undertaken by the Turks and Caicos Islands Football Association revolves around simply providing an infrastructure for ordinary people to play the game - at youth level and for both men and women. Not always does the senior men's national team come top of their priorities and that was the case in 2010 with the TCIFA declining to take up its place in the Digicel Caribbean Cup - the second tournament in a row that they have been absent. The hope is that the momentum from the stunning victory over St Lucia in the 2010 World Cup qualifiers is not lost, a situation not helped by the transfer of team captain and former LA Galaxy and Dallas striker Gavin Glinton to Nam Dinh in Vietnam in March 2010. Over the past decade the economic boom in the Turks and Caicos Islands, fuelled by the tourism and financial industries, has seen the population double, many of them immigrants from neighbouring countries like Haiti. With them they have brought an interest in football that was in short supply in the country before and nowhere has this been more beneficial than in the four-team league and cup competitions. In 2010 AFC Academy won their first league title, whilst Provopool, who had merged with OHS Express at the start of the season, won the cup.

FIFA WORLD CUP RECORD
1930-1998 DNE 2002-2010 DNQ

TURKS AND CAICOS ISLANDS FOOTBALL ASSOCIATION (TCIFA)

Tropicana Plaza, Leeward Highway, PO Box 626, Providenciales

☎ +1 649 9415532
📠 +1 649 9415554
📧 tcifa@tciway.tc
🖥 www.football.tc
FA 1996 CON 1998 FIFA 1998
P Christopher Bryan
GS Sonia Bien-Aime

FIFA BIG COUNT 2006

Total players	2 155
% of population	10.19%
Male	1 540
Female	615
Amateurs 18+	165
Unregistered	1 000
Professionals	0
Referees	12
Admin & coaches	35
Number of clubs	9
Number of teams	9

MAJOR TOWNS

Grand Turk
Cockburn Town (3 691)
Salt Cay
Balfour Town
Providenciales
Providenciales
North Caicos
Bottle Creek
Kew
Whitby
Sandy Point
Middle Caicos
Conch Bar
Lorimers
Bambarra
Turks Islands
Balfour Town

TURKS AND CAICOS ISLANDS

Capital	Cockburn Town	Population	22 942 (216)	% in cities	92%
GDP per capita	$11 500 (97)	Area km²	948 km² (185)	GMT +/-	-5
Neighbours (km)	Coast 389				

RECENT INTERNATIONAL MATCHES PLAYED BY TURKS AND CAICOS

2004	Opponents	Score		Venue	Comp	Scorers	Att	Referee
18-02	Haiti	L	0-5	Miami †	WCq		3 000	Stott USA
21-02	Haiti	L	0-2	Hialeah †	WCq		3 000	Valenzuela USA
2005								
No international matches played in 2005								
2006								
2-09	Cuba	L	0-6	Havana	CCq		2 000	Campbell JAM
4-09	Cayman Islands	W	2-0	Havana	CCq	Gavin Glinton [14], Maxime Fleuriot [72]	100	Stennett JAM
6-09	Bahamas	L	2-3	Havana	CCq	Gavin Glinton 2 [51 72]	120	Campbell JAM
2007								
No international matches played in 2007								
2008								
6-02	St Lucia	W	2-1	Providenciales	WCq	David Lowery [31], Gavin Glinton [74]	2 200	Whittaker CAY
26-03	St Lucia	L	0-2	Vieux Fort	WCq		1 200	Forde BRB
2009								
No international matches played in 2009								
2010								
No international matches played in 2010								

CC = Digicel Caribbean Cup • WC = FIFA World Cup • q = qualifier • † Both matches played in the USA

TURKS AND CAICOS ISLANDS 2009–10										
COXCO MEN'S LEAGUE	Pl	W	D	L	F	A	Pts	AFC Academy	Provopool	AFC National	SWA Sharks
AFC Academy	12	5	4	3	31	25	**19**		1-5 2-1	0-1 3-3	4-5 6-3
Provopool FC	12	5	3	4	36	20	18	2-3 2-2		0-3 1-1	7-0 4-1
AFC National	12	4	5	3	22	17	17	1-1 0-0	1-3 0-0		2-4 2-0
SWA Sharks	12	4	0	8	26	53	12	1-3 1-6	1-8 5-3	5-2 0-6	

10/10/2009 - 27/02/2010 • Top scorer: **17** - Horace James, SWA Sharks

PRESIDENT'S CUP 2010

Semi-finals			Finals	
Provopool	3	0		
AFC Academy	0	0		
			Provopool	4
			SWA Sharks	0
AFC National	2	1		
SWA Sharks	5	3	6-03-2010	

TGA – TONGA

FIFA/COCA-COLA WORLD RANKING

1993	1994	1995	1996	1997	1998	1999	2000	2001	2002	2003	2004	2005	2006	2007	2008	2009	2010
-	-	-	164	174	163	178	185	173	175	180	183	185	188	170	188	188	188

	2010												Hi/Lo
Jan	Feb	Mar	Mar	Apr	May	Jul	Aug	Sep	Oct	Nov	Dec		163
188	189	189	187	186	186	186	186	190	190	189	188		193

The Tonga Football Association has set itself the target of making football the number one sport in the country by the year 2020 - an ambitious task given the huge popularity of rugby, although the women's game does already enjoy a good profile. Central to those plans is the OFC's Just Play scheme in which teams of instructors have gone into primary schools to train teachers the basics of football coaching and to distribute equipment. Although Just Play is a scheme covering a number of countries in the Pacific, it was launched in Tonga in October 2009. Backed by the Australian government to the tune of AU$4 million it has involved the instructors themselves travelling to the OFC headquarters in New Zealand to attend courses as they prepared to introduce the scheme into 82 primary schools in the country as football seeks to win the hearts and minds of the 6-12 year olds in order to promote a healthy lifestyle. If successful football may well indeed be the most popular game in the country by 2020. In 2010, women's football enjoyed the higher profile with the men not in action until the 2011 Pacific Games which are likely to act as qualifiers for the 2014 FIFA World Cup in Brazil. The women's team took part in the qualifiers for their World Cup in Germany but despite beating Fiji lost to both the Solomon Islands and Papua New Guinea.

FIFA WORLD CUP RECORD
1930-1994 DNE 1998-2010 DNQ

TONGA FOOTBALL ASSOCIATION (FTF)

Loto Tonga Soko Center, Off Valungafulu Road - 'Atele, PO Box 852, Nuku'alofa

☎ +676 30233
✆ +676 30240
📠 tfa@kalianet.to
💻 www.tongafootball.com
FA 1965 CON 1994 FIFA 1994
P Hon Veehala
GS TBD

FIFA BIG COUNT 2006

Total players	5 000
% of population	4.36%
Male	4 600
Female	400
Amateurs 18+	2 100
Youth under 18	1 100
Professionals	0
Referees	100
Admin & coaches	100
Number of clubs	100
Number of teams	220

MAJOR CITIES/TOWNS

		Population
1	Nuku'alofa	24 184
2	Mu'a	5 140
3	Neiafu	3 969
4	Haveloloto	3 518
5	Vaini	3 064
6	Tofoa-Koloua	2 610
7	Pangai	1 591
8	Ohonua	1 252
9	Hihifo	671

PULE'ANGA TONGA • KINGDOM OF TONGA

Capital	Nuku'alofa	Population	120 898 (188)	% in cities	25%
GDP per capita	$4600 (145)	Area km²	747 km² (189)	GMT + / -	+13
Neighbours (km)	Coast 419				

RECENT INTERNATIONAL MATCHES PLAYED BY TONGA

2002	Opponents	Score		Venue	Comp	Scorers	Att	Referee
No international matches played in 2002 after June								
2003								
1-07	Papua New Guinea	D	2-2	Suva	SPr1	Unaloto-Ki-Atenoa Feao 2 [62 75]	3 000	Singh FIJ
3-07	New Caledonia	L	0-4	Suva	SPr1		700	Shah FIJ
5-07	Micronesia †	W	7-0	Nausori	SPr1	Ipeni Fonua [5], Maamaloa Tevi [15], Mark Uhatahi 2 [22 36], Unaloto-Ki-Atenoa Feao 2 [34 55], Kilifi Uele [72]	1 000	Moli SOL
7-07	Tahiti	L	0-4	Lautoka	SPr1		3 000	Shah FIJ
2004								
10-05	Solomon Islands	L	0-6	Honiara	WCq		12 385	Attison VAN
15-05	Cook Islands	W	2-1	Honiara	WCq	Mark Uhatahi [46], Viliami Vaitaki [61]	15 000	Sosongan PNG
17-05	Tahiti	L	0-2	Honiara	WCq		400	Sosongan PNG
19-05	New Caledonia	L	0-8	Honiara	WCq		14 000	Fred VAN
2005								
No international matches played in 2005								
2006								
No international matches played in 2006								
2007								
27-08	Solomon Islands	L	0-4	Apia	WCq		350	Aimaasu SAM
29-08	Samoa	L	1-2	Apia	WCq	Unaloto-Ki-Atenoa Feao [54]	1 850	Sosongan PNG
1-09	American Samoa	W	4-0	Apia	WCq	Lafaele Moala [38], Pio Palu 2 [56 63], Kaisani Uhatahi [86]	200	Minan PNG
3-09	Vanuatu	L	1-4	Apia	WCq	Malakai Savieti [50]	50	Minan PNG
2008								
No international matches played in 2008								
2009								
11-06	Cook Islands	D	1-1	Atele	Fr	Mark Uhatahi [35]		
13-06	Cook Islands	L	1-2	Atele	Fr	Mark Uhatahi [48]		
2010								
No international matches played in 2010								

Fr = Friendly match • SP = South Pacific Games • WC = FIFA World Cup • q = qualifier • r1 = first round group • † Not a full international

THA – THAILAND

FIFA/COCA-COLA WORLD RANKING

1993	1994	1995	1996	1997	1998	1999	2000	2001	2002	2003	2004	2005	2006	2007	2008	2009	2010
69	85	77	57	54	45	60	61	61	66	60	79	111	137	121	126	105	121

	2010											Hi/Lo
	Jan	Feb	Mar	Mar	Apr	May	Jul	Aug	Sep	Oct	Nov	Dec	43
	105	98	99	104	105	106	105	104	102	108	114	121	137

2010 was a year the Thai national team will want to quickly put behind them after their failure to qualify for the AFC Asian Cup and their abject performance at the regional AFF Suzuki Cup at the end of the year. It left coach Bryan Robson facing mounting pressure for him to stand down after he was roundly blamed for the poor performances. A 1-0 defeat at the hands of Iran in March saw the Thais miss out on the Asian Cup finals for the first time since 1988 but having assured the Thai football-watching public his team would perform at a higher level at the AFF Suzuki Cup, Robson saw his team put in their worst-ever performance in a tournament that they have won three times. A draw with minnows Laos was a poor start that would have been worse had Sarayoot Chaikamdee not scored an injury-time equalizer while a scoreless draw with Malaysia left the Thais needing to win their final game against Indonesia to progress which they failed to do, losing 2-1. The one bright point of the season was the continued emergence of Muangthong United as a serious force in club football. Not only did they retain their league title but they also put in a great performance in the 2010 AFC Cup where they reached the semi-finals before losing to the eventual winners Al Ittihad from Syria. Muangthong missed out on the double after losing the Cup Final to Chonburi.

FIFA WORLD CUP RECORD
1930-1970 DNE 1974-2010 DNQ

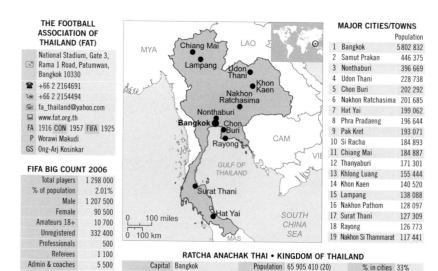

THE FOOTBALL ASSOCIATION OF THAILAND (FAT)

National Stadium, Gate 3, Rama 1 Road, Patumwan, Bangkok 10330

☎ +66 2 2164691
📠 +66 2 2154494
📧 fa_thailand@yahoo.com
🖥 www.fat.org.th
FA 1916 CON 1957 FIFA 1925
P Worawi Makudi
GS Ong-Arj Kosinkar

FIFA BIG COUNT 2006

Total players	1 298 000
% of population	2.01%
Male	1 207 500
Female	90 500
Amateurs 18+	10 700
Unregistered	332 400
Professionals	500
Referees	1 100
Admin & coaches	5 500
Number of clubs	150
Number of teams	1 790

MAJOR CITIES/TOWNS

		Population
1	Bangkok	5 802 832
2	Samut Prakan	446 375
3	Nonthaburi	396 669
4	Udon Thani	228 738
5	Chon Buri	202 292
6	Nakhon Ratchasima	201 685
7	Hat Yai	199 062
8	Phra Pradaeng	196 644
9	Pak Kret	193 071
10	Si Racha	184 893
11	Chiang Mai	184 887
12	Thanyaburi	171 301
13	Khlong Luang	155 444
14	Khon Kaen	140 520
15	Lampang	138 088
16	Nakhon Pathom	128 097
17	Surat Thani	127 309
18	Rayong	126 773
19	Nakhon Si Thammarat	117 441

RATCHA ANACHAK THAI • KINGDOM OF THAILAND

Capital	Bangkok	Population	65 905 410 (20)	% in cities	33%
GDP per capita	$8400 (118)	Area km²	513 120 km² (50)	GMT +/-	+7
Neighbours (km)	Myanmar 1800, Cambodia 803, Laos 1754, Malaysia 506 • Coast 3219				

RECENT INTERNATIONAL MATCHES PLAYED BY THAILAND

2008	Opponents	Score	Venue	Comp	Scorers	Att	Referee
6-12	Vietnam	W 2-0	Phuket	AFFr1	Suksomkit [34], Nutnum [45]	20 000	Abdul Bashir SIN
8-12	Laos	W 6-0	Phuket	AFFr1	Rangsiyo [19], Phetphun [30], Sunthornpit 2 [20 52], Sangsanoi 2 [79 89]	10 000	Hadimin BRU
10-12	Malaysia	W 3-0	Phuket	AFFr1	Suksomkit [23], Dangda 2 [46 76]	15 000	Abdul Bashir SIN
16-12	Indonesia	W 1-0	Jakarta	AFFr1	Dangda [6]	70 000	Vo Minh Tri VIE
20-12	Indonesia	W 2-1	Bangkok	AFFsf	Winothai [73], Rangsiyo [89]	40 000	Hadimin BRU
24-12	Vietnam	L 1-2	Bangkok	AFFf	Rangsiyo [75]	50 000	Ramachandran MAS
28-12	Vietnam	D 1-1	Hanoi	AFFf	Dangda [21]	40 000	Abdul Bashir SIN
2009							
14-01	Jordan	D 0-0	Amman	ACq		5 000	Racho SYR
21-01	Lebanon	W 2-1	Phuket	Fr	Dangda [12], Nutnum [22]		
28-01	Iran	D 0-0	Bangkok	ACq		10 000	Kovalenko UZB
5-02	Saudi Arabia	L 1-2	Sendai	Fr	Dangda [89]		
28-03	New Zealand	W 3-1	Bangkok	Fr	Dangda 2 [12 74], Sripan [21]		
8-11	Syria	D 1-1	Bangkok	Fr	Winothai [59]		
14-11	Singapore	W 3-1	Singapore	ACq	Suksomkit 2 [12p 81], Therdsak [76]	22 183	Takayama JPN
18-11	Singapore	L 0-1	Bangkok	ACq		30 000	Balideh QAT
29-12	Zimbabwe	W 3-0	Bangkok	Fr	Sutinun 2 [27 81], Kirati [84]		
2010							
6-01	Jordan	D 0-0	Bangkok	ACq		15 000	Williams AUS
17-01	Singapore	W 1-0	N'hon Ratchasima	Fr	Suksomkit [59]		Mbaga TAN
20-01	Poland	L 1-3	N'hon Ratchasima	Fr	Chaiman [90p]	20 000	Mbaga TAN
23-01	Denmark	L 0-3	N'hon Ratchasima	Fr			
3-03	Iran	L 0-1	Tehran	ACq		17 000	Balideh QAT
16-05	South Africa	L 0-4	Nelspruit	Fr		30 000	Kipngetich KEN
11-08	Singapore	W 1-0	Nonthaburi	Fr	Chaikamdee [28]		Aonrak THA
4-09	India	W 1-0	Bangkok	Fr	Chaikamdee [72]		Mahapab THA
8-09	India	W 2-1	New Delhi	Fr	Winothai [48], Keawsombut [64]		
1-12	Laos	D 2-2	Jakarta	AFFr1	Chaikamdee 2 [67 91+]		Sato JPN
4-12	Malaysia	D 0-0	Jakarta	AFFr1			Win Cho MYA
7-12	Indonesia	L 1-2	Jakarta	AFFr1	Sukha Suree [68]	65 000	Sato JPN

Fr = Friendly match • AFF = ASEAN Football Federation Championship • AC = AFC Asian Cup • WC = FIFA World Cup • q = qualifier • r1 = 1st round

THAILAND NATIONAL TEAM HISTORICAL RECORDS

Past Coaches Burkhard Ziese GER 1985-86 • Carlos Roberto de Carvalho BRA 1989-91 • Peter Stubbe GER 1992-94 • Worawit Sumpachanyasathit 1994 • Chatchai Paholpat 1994-95 • Arj-han Srongngamsub 1996 • Thawatchai Sartjakul 1996 • Dettmar Cramer GER 1997 • Withaya Laohakul 1997-98 • Peter Withe ENG 1998-2002 • Carlos Roberto de Carvalho BRA 2003-04 • Chatchai Paholpat 2004-04 • Siegfried Held GER 2004-05 • Charnwit Polcheewin 2005-08 • Peter Reid ENG 2008-09 • Bryan Robson ENG 2009-

MEDALS TABLE

		Overall			League			Asia			City
		G	S	B	G	S	B	G	S	B	
1	BEC Tero Sasana	2	3	5	2	2	5	1			Bangkok
2	Air Force United	2	2		2	2					Rangsit
3	Krung Thai Bank	2	1		2	1					Bangkok
4	Thai Farmers Bank	2		2			1	2		1	Bangkok
5	Muangthong United	2		1	2					1	Nonthaburi
6	Chonburi	1	2	1	1	2	1				Chonburi
7	Buriram PEA	1	2		1	2					Buriram
8	Chula United	1	1		1	1					Bangkok
9	Bangkok Bank	1		2	1		2				Bangkok
10	Bangkok University	1			1						Bangkok
11	TTM Phichit	1			1						Phichit
12	Osotspa		2	2		2	2				Saraburi
13	Thai Port		1	1		1	1				Bangkok
14	Stock Exchange		1			1					Bangkok
15	Bangkok Glass			1			1				Pathumthani

THAILAND 2010

PROFESSIONAL LEAGUE

	Pl	W	D	L	F	A	Pts	Muangthong U	Buriram PEA	Chonburi	Thai Port	Bangkok Glass	Pattaya United	Osotspa	Samut	BEC Tero	Rajnavy Rayong	Police United	TOT–CAT	TTM Phichit	Sisaket	Bangkok United	Army United
Muangthong United †	30	20	7	3	64	19	67		0-0	4-1	1-0	2-0	1-0	4-1	5-0	2-0	1-0	1-0	4-0	2-2	6-0	5-1	3-3
Buriram PEA	30	17	12	1	51	19	63	1-0		3-1	0-0	3-1	3-1	2-0	3-1	1-1	4-2	4-2	0-0	2-0	1-0	0-0	3-1
Chonburi	30	17	9	4	57	28	60	0-0	2-2		2-1	2-1	2-2	0-0	0-0	2-0	1-1	3-3	2-0	5-1	3-1	2-1	3-0
Thai Port	30	13	9	8	41	29	48	1-4	0-0	1-2		2-1	2-0	1-1	1-0	1-0	3-0	3-2	1-1	1-1	2-0	3-2	5-0
Bangkok Glass	30	12	9	9	48	38	45	1-0	0-3	0-0	0-0		3-1	0-0	3-1	2-2	5-0	1-0	1-1	2-2	3-1	4-0	3-1
Pattaya United	30	12	9	9	43	38	45	2-2	3-3	1-2	0-1	1-1		0-0	2-0	3-1	3-1	2-0	1-0	4-1	2-1	1-2	1-0
Osotspa Saraburi	30	10	12	8	32	30	42	0-3	0-1	1-1	1-0	4-1	0-0		0-0	0-0	1-1	2-1	1-0	1-1	6-3	1-2	0-1
Samut Songkhram	30	11	9	10	27	32	42	0-0	0-0	0-0	0-3	1-0	1-0	2-0		0-1	1-0	1-1	2-0	0-0	1-0	0-2	4-2
BEC Tero Sasana	30	9	8	13	39	42	35	0-1	1-4	1-4	4-2	0-1	2-3	3-1	2-1		0-0	2-0	1-0	2-2	2-3	3-0	2-1
Rajnavy Rayong	30	8	9	13	35	52	33	1-2	0-0	0-4	2-4	3-3	1-1	1-2	0-0	3-1		1-0	3-2	1-2	4-3	1-1	2-1
Police United	30	9	6	15	40	45	33	1-0	1-1	0-4	0-1	3-2	2-2	1-2	1-2	1-2	2-3		1-0	4-1	0-1	1-1	0-0
TOT–CAT	30	9	6	15	23	42	33	1-2	0-2	0-2	2-1	2-0	1-3	0-0	2-1	0-5	1-0	0-2		1-3	3-2	1-0	0-0
TTM Phichit	30	7	11	12	32	46	32	0-2	0-0	0-2	0-0	0-0	3-0	2-1	1-3	0-0	0-2	0-1	0-1		0-0	2-1	3-1
Sisaket ‡	30	6	8	16	36	54	26	1-2	0-3	0-1	1-1	1-2	1-1	0-0	1-1	1-0	4-1	2-4	1-1	4-0		1-1	0-1
Bangkok United ‡	30	5	9	16	25	52	24	0-3	2-0	3-1	1-1	1-4	0-1	1-4	0-0	1-1	0-0	0-4	1-2	0-3	0-1		0-1
Army United ‡	30	5	7	18	27	54	22	2-2	0-2	1-0	0-2	1-3	0-2	1-2	0-2	1-3	1-1	0-1	1-2	0-1	3-2	2-2	

20/03/2010 - 24/10/2010 • † Qualified for the AFC Champions League • ‡ Relegation/promotion play-offs
Top scorers: 17 - Kengne Ludovick CMR, Pattaya • 15 - Dagno Siaka CIV, Muangthong • 14 - Anon Sangsanoi, BEC Tero • 13 - Sarayoot Chaikamdee, Thai Port • 11 - Chakrit Buathong, BEC Tero/Police & Suchao Nuchnum, Buriram PEA

THAILAND 2010
DIVISION 1 (2)

	Pl	W	D	L	F	A	Pts
Sriracha	30	19	5	6	62	33	62
Khon Kaen	30	15	9	6	51	35	54
Chiangrai United	30	15	8	7	44	32	53
Nakhon Pathom ‡	30	12	15	3	55	36	51
Songkhla ‡	30	14	9	7	47	34	51
Air Force United ‡	30	13	9	8	48	33	48
Suvarnabhumi Customs	30	12	9	9	42	37	45
Thai-Honda	30	11	7	12	32	32	40
Rajpracha-Nonthaburi	30	11	6	13	33	40	39
Chula United	30	10	8	12	59	48	38
PTT	30	9	11	10	47	51	38
Chanthaburi	30	9	10	11	38	40	37
Prachinburi	30	10	5	15	29	36	35
RBAC Mittraphap	30	7	6	17	35	65	27
Suphanburi	30	5	8	17	31	53	23
Narathiwat	30	4	3	23	16	64	15

17/03/2010 - 23/10/2010 • ‡ Relegation/promotion play-offs

RELEGATION/PROMOTION PLAY-OFFS GROUP A

	Pl	W	D	L	F	A	Pts	Si	NP	AFU
Sisaket	4	2	2	0	4	1	8		2-0	2-1
Nakhon Pathom	4	2	1	1	5	3	7	0-0		3-0
Air Force United	4	0	1	3	2	7	1	0-0	1-2	

27/11/2010 - 31/12/2010 • All teams remain at their previous level

RELEGATION/PROMOTION PLAY-OFFS GROUP B

	Pl	W	D	L	F	A	Pts	AU	BU	So
Army United	4	2	2	0	5	2	8		0-0	2-0
Bangkok United	4	1	2	1	3	3	5	0-2		1-1
Songkhla	4	0	2	2	2	6	2	1-1	0-2	

27/11/2010 - 25/12/2010 • Army United and Songkhla remain at their previous level; Bangkok United relegated

THAI FA CUP 2010

Quarter-finals		Semi-finals		Final	
Chonburi	2				
Pattaya United	0	Chonburi	2		
Nakhon Pathom	1	Army United	0		
Army United	4			Chonburi	2
Rajnavy Rayong	2			Muangthong United	1
Sisaket	1	Rajnavy Rayong	0		
Rajpracha-Nonthaburi	0	Muangthong United	1		
Muangthong United	4				

Cup Final. Suphachalasai, Bangkok, 28-11-2010, Ref: Sura Sriart. Scorers - Therdsak 44, Pipob 120 for Chonburi; Datsajorn 59 for Muangthong.
Chonburi - Sinthaweechai Hathairattanakool - Jetsadakorn Hemdaeng, Cholratit Jantakam, Suttinan Phuk-hom, Natthaphong Samana - Ekaphan Inthasen (Suphasek Kaikaew 115), Adul Lahso, Therdsak Chaiman (Jules Baga 72), Phuritad Jarikanon - Arthit Sunthornpit• (Phanuwat Jinta 67), Pipob On Mo• (c). Tr: Jadet Meelarp; **Muangthong** - Thanongsak Panpipat - Jakkraphan Kaewprom, Panupong Wongsa• (Jetsada Jitsawad 53), Nattaporn Phanrit (c), Piyachart Tamaphan - Naruphol Ar Romsawa (Amorn Thammanarm 45), Datsakorn Thonglao, Dagno Siaka, Pichitphong Choeichiu - Teerasil Dangda, Ronnachai Rangsiyo (Mohamed Kone 25). Tr: Rene Desaeyere

TJK – TAJIKISTAN

FIFA/COCA-COLA WORLD RANKING

1993	1994	1995	1996	1997	1998	1999	2000	2001	2002	2003	2004	2005	2006	2007	2008	2009	2010
-	155	164	163	118	120	119	134	154	168	137	136	141	124	137	146	165	145

2010												Hi/Lo
Jan	Feb	Mar	Mar	Apr	May	Jul	Aug	Sep	Oct	Nov	Dec	**114**
165	148	128	130	135	135	137	148	145	150	149	145	**180**

Tajikistan's hopes of winning more continental silverware came to nothing in 2010 when the national team could only finish in third place in the 2010 AFC Challenge Cup in Sri Lanka while in the AFC President's Cup Vakhsh Qurghonteppa were eliminated in the semi-finals. These two competitions have given football in Tajikistan a strong focus. In 2006 the national team won the inaugural AFC Challenge Cup in Bangladesh and then were runners-up two years later in India. In Sri Lanka they surprisingly lost their opening match to Bangladesh but qualified for the semi-finals for a third time with wins over Myanmar and hosts Sri Lanka. In the semi-finals they faced Turkmenistan, a country against whom they have a great record at club level in the AFC President's Cup but in Colombo they were beaten 2-0 and had to settle for a victory in the third place play-off against Myanmar. Tajik club Regar TadAz are the most successful club in the history of the AFC President's Cup but they were not present to defend their title at the 2010 tournament and they have new challengers at home in Esteghlal. In 2010 Esteghlal became the first club from the capital to win the championship for a decade and they went through the season unbeaten. They also added the cup to their trophy cabinet after a 5-0 victory over Hujand in the final.

FIFA WORLD CUP RECORD
1930-1994 DNE **1998-2010** DNQ

TAJIKISTAN FOOTBALL FEDERATION (TFF)

14/3 Ainy Street,
Dushanbe 734 025

☎ +992 372 212447
📠 +992 372 510157
📧 tajikfootball@yahoo.com
💻
FA 1936 CON 1994 FIFA 1994
P Suhrob Qosimov
GS Sherali Davlatov

FIFA BIG COUNT 2006

Total players	132 893
% of population	1.82%
Male	123 563
Female	9 330
Amateurs 18+	980
Youth under 18	2 135
Unregistered	32 150
Professionals	428
Referees	56
Admin & coaches	267
Number of clubs	40
Number of teams	260

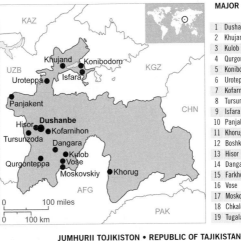

MAJOR CITIES/TOWNS

		Population
1	Dushanbe	703 969
2	Khujand	147 483
3	Kulob	85 467
4	Qurgonteppa	64 709
5	Konibodom	57 792
6	Uroteppa	56 874
7	Kofarnihon	45 693
8	Tursunzoda	40 435
9	Isfara	40 073
10	Panjakent	38 575
11	Khorug	32 470
12	Boshkengash	27 495
13	Hisor	27 200
14	Dangara	26 435
15	Farkhor	25 145
16	Vose	25 145
17	Moskovskiy	22 631
18	Chkalovsk	21 634
19	Tugalan	21 373

JUMHURII TOJIKISTON • REPUBLIC OF TAJIKISTAN

Capital Dushanbe	Population 7 349 145 (96)	% in cities 26%
GDP per capita $1800 (190)	Area km² 143 100 km² (95)	GMT +/- +5
Neighbours (km) Afghanistan 1206, China 414, Kyrgyzstan 870, Uzbekistan 1161		

RECENT INTERNATIONAL MATCHES PLAYED BY TAJIKISTAN

2006 Opponents	Score		Venue	Comp	Scorers	Att	Referee
10-04 Bangladesh	W	6-1	Dhaka	CCqf	Rabimov [2], Makhmudov [20], Muhidinov [31], Hakimov [51], Rabiev [65], Nematov [81]	15 000	AK Nema IRQ
13-04 Kyrgyzstan	W	2-0	Dhaka	CCsf	Rabiev 2 [51 92+]	2 000	Tan Hai CHN
16-04 Sri Lanka	W	4-0	Dhaka	CCf	Muhidinov 3 [1 61 71], Makhmudov [45]	2 000	Mombini IRN
2-07 Kazakhstan	L	1-4	Almaty	Fr	Saidov [75]		
2007							
22-08 Azerbaijan	L	2-3	Dushanbe	Fr	Barotov [18], Saidov [31]		
8-09 Kazakhstan	D	1-1	Almaty	Fr	Saidov [42]		
8-10 Bangladesh	D	1-1	Dhaka	WCq	Hakimov [58p]	700	Al Hilali OMA
28-10 Bangladesh	W	5-0	Dushanbe	WCq	Hakimov 3 [46 47 76p], Muhidinov [49], Vasiev [70]	10 000	Chynybekov KGZ
9-11 Singapore	L	0-2	Singapore	WCq		6 606	Kwon Jong Chul KOR
18-11 Singapore	D	1-1	Dushanbe	WCq	Ismailov [2]	21 500	Shield AUS
16-12 Oman	L	2-4	Muscat	Fr	Makhmudov [26], Shohzukhurov [47]		
2008							
13-05 Bhutan	W	3-1	Barotac	CCq	Hakimov [27p], Rabiev [60]	5 000	Ng Chiu Kok HKG
15-05 Philippines	D	0-0	Iloilo City	CCq		4 500	Albadwawi UAE
17-05 Brunei Darussalam	W	4-0	Iloilo City	CCq	Rabiev 2 [47 87], Muhidinov [61], Hakimov [69]	450	Albadwawi UAE
30-07 Turkmenistan	D	0-0	Hyderabad	CCr1		150	Kovalenko UZB
1-08 India	D	1-1	Hyderabad	CCr1	Rabiev [11]	350	Shamsuzzaman BAN
3-08 Afghanistan	W	4-0	Hyderabad	CCr1	Rabiev 3 [14 44 56], Tukhtasunov [39]	150	Vo Minh Tri VIE
7-08 Korea DPR	W	1-0	Hyderabad	CCsf	Muhidinov [39]	600	Iemoto JPN
13-08 India	L	1-4	New Delhi	CCf	Fatkhuloev [44]	10 000	Kovalenko UZB
20-08 Qatar	L	0-5	Doha	Fr			
2009							
30-12 Yemen	L	1-2	Sana'a	Fr	Rabimov [35]		
2010							
2-01 Yemen	W	1-0	Sana'a	Fr	Tukhtasunov [70]		
16-02 Bangladesh	L	0-1	Colombo	CCr1	Rabiev [70]	1 000	Matsuo JPN
18-02 Sri Lanka	W	3-1	Colombo	CCr1	Rabimov [13], Fatkhuloev 2 [32 92+]	1 000	Tan Hai CHN
20-02 Myanmar	W	3-0	Colombo	CCr1	Rabimov [33], Hakimov [52], Rabiev [88]	100	Shukralla BHR
24-02 Turkmenistan	L	0-2	Colombo	CCsf		300	Faghani IRN
27-02 Myanmar	W	1-0	Colombo	CC3p	Hakimov [11]	300	El Haddad LIB
26-06 China PR	L	0-4	Kunming	Fr			
17-11 Afghanistan	W	1-0	Dushanbe	Fr	Choriev [33]		

Fr = Friendly match • AC = AFC Asian Cup • CC = AFC Challenge Cup • WC = FIFA World Cup
q = qualifier • r1 = first round group • qf = quarter-final • sf = semi-final • f = final

TAJIKISTAN NATIONAL TEAM HISTORICAL RECORDS

Goals 16 - Yusuf Rabiev 2003- & Numonjon Hakimov 2003- • 10 - Tokhirjon Muminov 1993-2000 • 7 - Djomikhon Mukhidinov 2003- • 6 - Alier Ashurmamadov 1992-2005 & Chukhrat Djabarov 1997-2000

Past Coaches Sharif Nazarov 1992-94 • Vladimir Gulyamkhaydarov 1994-95 • Abdulla Muradov 1996 • Sharif Nazarov 2003 • Zoir Babaev 2004 • Sharif Nazarov 2004-06 • Makhmadjon Khabibulloev 2007 • Pulod Kodirov 2008-

TAJIKISTAN 2010

PREMIER LEAGUE

	Pl	W	D	L	F	A	Pts	Esteghlal	Regar TadAZ	Vakhsh	Xayr	Energetik	SKA Pamir	Hujand	Parvoz	Ravshan
Esteghlal Dushanbe †	32	26	6	0	76	17	84		2-1 2-0	1-1 1-0	2-0 3-1	2-1 1-0	0-0 2-0	5-0 2-0	3-0 3-0	5-0 5-0
Regar TadAZ	32	22	5	5	81	24	71	1-1 1-1		2-0 5-0	0-2 2-1	4-1 1-2	0-0 2-1	2-0 2-1	4-1 6-0	5-0 3-0
Vakhsh Qurghonteppa	32	16	8	8	42	27	56	2-3 1-2	0-0 1-0		1-0 3-1	1-0 1-0	3-0 0-0	2-1 0-0	2-1 4-1	1-0 3-0
Xayr Vahdat	32	16	6	10	59	42	54	0-2 1-2	0-4 1-2	0-0 2-1		3-0 1-0	3-2 3-3	3-1 4-1	2-1 4-0	5-0 6-1
Energetik Dushanbe	32	12	4	16	41	44	40	0-4 0-1	0-4 0-3	1-0 0-0	2-3 3-0		1-1 1-2	1-1 3-0	3-0 4-0	4-1 2-0
SKA Pamir Dushanbe	32	9	10	13	35	51	37	0-2 1-5	0-5 1-3	1-0 0-2	1-1 1-1	2-1 1-3		3-2 2-0	0-0 1-0	4-0 2-0
FK Hujand	32	8	8	16	42	58	32	0-1 2-2	1-4 1-2	2-2 1-2	1-1 0-2	1-1 3-1	2-0 3-0		3-1 2-2	1-0 3-0
Parvoz B'jon Gafurov	32	6	6	20	35	71	24	1-2 0-2	1-4 2-2	1-1 1-3	1-2 1-1	2-1 1-2	1-1 2-1	1-1 2-1		3-0 3-0
Ravshan Kulob	32	1	3	28	18	95	6	2-2 1-5	1-5 0-2	0-1 0-4	0-3 1-2	0-1 0-2	2-3 1-1	1-1 3-4	4-1 0-3	

3/04/2010 - 24/11/2010 • † Qualified for the AFC President's Cup • Matches in bold awarded
Top scorer: **30** - Yusuf Rabiev, Esteghlal

MEDALS TABLE

		Overall			League			Cup			Asia			City
		G	S	B	G	S	B	G	S	B	G	S	B	
1	Regar TadAZ	14	8	1	7	5		4	3		3		1	Tursunzoda
2	Vakhsh Qurgonteppa	5	4	5	3	1	4	2	2			1	1	Qurgonteppa
3	Varzob Dushanbe	5	1		3			2	1					Dushanbe
4	FK Hujand	3	6	4		3	4	3	3					Khujand
5	SKA Pamir Dushanbe	3	3	1	2	2	1	1	1					Dushanbe
6	Sitora Dushanbe	3	1	1	2	1	1	1						Dushanbe
7	Esteghlal Dushanbe	3			1			2						Dushanbe
8	Parvoz	2	2	3		2	3	2						Bobojon Gafurov
9	Ravshan Kulob	1	2	1		1		1	2					Kulob
10	Pakhtakor	1						1						Dzhabarrasulovsk
11	Dinamo Dushanbe	1			1									Dushanbe

TAJIKISTAN CUP 2010

Quarter-finals			Semi-finals			Final		
Esteghlal Dushanbe *	3	1						
Energetik Dushanbe	3	0	Esteghlal Dushanbe *	3	1			
Xayr Vahdat	0	1	Regar TadAZ	0	4			
Regar TadAZ *	2	1				Esteghlal Dushanbe	5	
Sitora-2010	1	4				FK Hujand	0	
Shodmon *	1	1	Sitora-2010	3	1			
Hylbyk Bose	0	0	FK Hujand *	4	2	5-10-2010		
FK Hujand *	3	6	* Home team in the first leg					

TKM – TURKMENISTAN

FIFA/COCA-COLA WORLD RANKING

1993	1994	1995	1996	1997	1998	1999	2000	2001	2002	2003	2004	2005	2006	2007	2008	2009	2010
-	108	133	141	134	122	129	125	114	134	99	98	116	155	127	148	141	135

	2010												Hi/Lo
	Jan	Feb	Mar	Mar	Apr	May	Jul	Aug	Sep	Oct	Nov	Dec	86
	141	134	130	134	137	139	136	133	129	142	134	135	174

There was huge disappointment in Turkmenistan when the national team came within touching distance of a first continental trophy only to lose the final of the 2010 AFC Challenge Cup to North Korea on post-match penalties. In their first appearance at the finals in 2008 Turkmenistan had been knocked out in the first round but in Sri Lanka they made steady progress to the final, beating India, Kyrgyzstan and Tajikistan. They had also drawn 1-1 with the World Cup-bound Koreans in the group stage and that was the score in the final too where a missed penalty by Arslanmyrat Amanov in the first round of sudden-death in the shoot-out cost Turkmenistan the title. Hopes of a first-ever continental title at club level also came to nothing at the 2010 AFC President's Cup in Myanmar. Clubs from Turkmenistan had not made it past the semi-finals in the previous five tournaments and HTTU were unable to break that sequence when they lost at that stage to Dordoi-Dynamo of Kyrgyzstan. Balkan Balkanabat will represent the country in the 2011 tournament after their outstanding year in 2010. They won both the league and the cup, beating Altyn Asyr into second place in both. It was the club's second double having previously won it in 2004 when they were known as Nebitchi Balkanabat.

FIFA WORLD CUP RECORD
1930-1994 DNE 1998-2010 DNQ

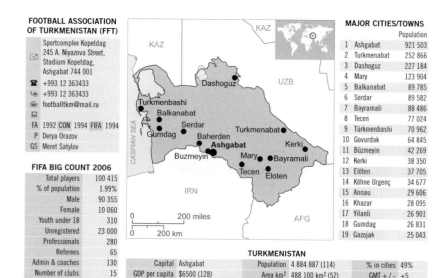

FOOTBALL ASSOCIATION OF TURKMENISTAN (FFT)

Sportcomplex Kopetdag
245 A. Niyazova Street,
Stadium Kopetdag,
Ashgabat 744 001

☎ +993 12 363433
🖷 +993 12 363433
✉ footballtkm@mail.ru

FA 1992 CON 1994 FIFA 1994
P Derya Orazov
GS Meret Satylov

FIFA BIG COUNT 2006

Total players	100 415
% of population	1.99%
Male	90 355
Female	10 060
Youth under 18	310
Unregistered	23 000
Professionals	280
Referees	65
Admin & coaches	130
Number of clubs	15
Number of teams	98

MAJOR CITIES/TOWNS

		Population
1	Ashgabat	921 503
2	Turkmenabat	252 866
3	Dashoguz	227 184
4	Mary	123 904
5	Balkanabat	89 785
6	Serdar	89 582
7	Bayramali	88 486
8	Tecen	77 024
9	Türkmenbashi	70 962
10	Govurdak	64 845
11	Büzmeyin	42 269
12	Kerki	38 350
13	Elöten	37 705
14	Köhne Urgenç	34 677
15	Annau	29 606
16	Khazar	28 095
17	Yilanli	26 901
18	Gumdag	26 831
19	Gazojak	25 043

TURKMENISTAN

Capital	Ashgabat	Population	4 884 887 (114)	% in cities	49%
GDP per capita	$6500 (128)	Area km²	488 100 km² (52)	GMT +/-	+5
Neighbours (km)	Afghanistan 744, Iran 992, Kazakhstan 379, Uzbekistan 1621 • Caspian Sea 1768				

RECENT INTERNATIONAL MATCHES PLAYED BY TURKMENISTAN

2007 Opponents	Score	Venue	Comp	Scorers	Att	Referee
11-10 Cambodia	W 1-0	Phnom Penh	WCq	Karadanov 85	3 000	Gosh BAN
28-10 Cambodia	W 4-1	Ashgabat	WCq	Nasyrov 41, Gevorkyan 2 50 66, Karadanov 74	5 000	Saidov UZB
10-11 Hong Kong	D 0-0	Hong Kong	WCq		2 823	Mujghef JOR
18-11 Hong Kong	W 3-0	Ashgabat	WCq	Nasyrov 42, Bayramov 53, Mirzoev 80	30 000	Al Hilali OMA
2008						
6-02 Korea Republic	L 0-4	Seoul	WCq		25 738	Najm LIB
26-03 Jordan	L 0-2	Ashgabat	WCq		20 000	Tongkhan THA
18-05 Oman	L 1-2	Nizwa	Fr	Saparov 53		
2-06 Korea DPR	D 0-0	Ashgabat	WCq		20 000	Al Ghamdi KSA
7-06 Korea DPR	L 0-1	Pyongyang	WCq		25 000	Al Saeedi UAE
14-06 Korea Republic	L 1-3	Ashgabat	WCq	Ovekov 77p	11 000	Takayama JPN
22-06 Jordan	L 0-2	Amman	WCq		150	Williams AUS
30-07 Tajikistan	D 0-0	Hyderabad	CCr1		150	Kovalenko UZB
1-08 Afghanistan	W 5-0	Hyderabad	CCr1	Ovekov 4 1 41 77 80, Krendelev 23	100	Saleem MDV
3-08 India	L 1-2	Hyderabad	CCr1	Orazmamedov 84	1 000	Jasim UAE
3-10 Mynamar	W 2-1	Ho Chi Minh	Fr			
5-10 Vietnam	W 3-2	Ho Chi Minh	Fr			
2009						
18-01 Syria	L 1-5	Kuwait City	Fr	Bablin 12		
20-01 Kuwait	L 0-2	Kuwait City	Fr			
14-04 Maldives	W 3-1	Male	CCq	Nasyrov 42, Shamuradov 49, Mirzoev 68p	9 000	Al Ghafary JOR
16-04 Bhutan	W 7-0	Male	CCq	Atayev 3 13 67 79, Chonkayev 16, Urazov 47, Mingazov 62, Mirzoev 93+	300	Perera SRI
18-04 Philippines	W 5-0	Male	CCq	OG 26, Shamuradov 2 54 63, Nasyrov 58, Urazov 65	400	Al Ghafary JOR
20-10 Vietnam	L 0-1	Ho Chi Minh	Fr			
22-10 Singapore	L 2-4	Ho Chi Minh	Fr	Shamuradov 14p, Ovekov 84		
2010						
17-02 Korea DPR	D 1-1	Colombo	CCr1	Karadanov 36	400	Mahapab THA
19-02 India	W 1-0	Colombo	CCr1	Karadanov 24p	450	Matsuo JPN
21-02 Kyrgyzstan	W 1-0	Colombo	CCr1	Nurmuradov 70	100	El Haddad LIB
24-02 Tajikistan	W 2-0	Colombo	CCsf	Amanov 33, Urazov 42	300	Faghani IRN
27-02 Korea DPR	D 1-1	Colombo	CCf	Shamuradov 33. L 4-5p	3 000	Faghani IRN

Fr = Friendly match • AC = AFC Asian Cup • CC = AFC Challenge Cup • WC = FIFA World Cup • q = qualifier • r1 = first round group

TURKMENISTAN 2010

YOKARY LIGA

	Pl	W	D	L	F	A	Pts	Balkan	Altyn	Lebap	Merv	HTTU	Ashgabat	Sagadam	Ahal	Dasoguz	Talyp
Balkan Balkanabat †	18	12	4	2	35	8	40		2-0	2-1	1-0	0-0	1-2	3-0	3-0	4-1	3-0
Altyn Asyr	18	10	5	3	34	20	35	2-1		3-2	1-0	2-2	5-2	2-0	3-0	0-0	0-0
Lebap Türkmenabat	18	10	4	4	29	12	34	0-1	1-0		1-1	2-0	2-2	2-0	3-0	4-0	3-0
Merv Mary	18	9	6	3	33	15	33	1-1	6-0	2-1		1-1	3-1	5-2	3-0	1-1	3-2
HTTU Ashgabat	18	7	7	4	26	16	28	0-0	1-1	0-1	2-2		2-0	3-2	0-0	1-0	2-0
FK Ashgabat	18	7	5	6	29	19	26	0-1	1-1	0-0	1-0	3-0		0-0	4-0	5-1	6-0
Sagadam Turkmenbasy	18	6	5	7	15	22	23	0-0	1-4	0-0	0-0	1-0	1-0		1-0	1-0	1-1
Ahal	18	5	1	12	13	33	16	1-3	0-4	1-2	0-1	0-3	1-2	2-0		2-0	0-0
FK Dasoguz	18	2	3	13	7	37	9	0-7	1-4	0-1	0-1	0-3	1-0	0-1	1-2		0-0
Talyp Sporty Ashgabat	18	0	4	14	4	40	4	0-2	0-2	0-3	0-3	1-6	0-0	0-1	0-1	0-1	

2/04/2010 - 11/12/2010 • † Qualified for the AFC President's Cup • Nebitchi Balkanabat renamed Balkan

Top scorer: 11 - Berdi Samyradov, HTTU • 10 - Didargylyc Urazov, Balkan; Amir Gurbani, Altyn & Gahrymanberdi Conkayev, Altyn

MEDALS TABLE

	Club	Overall			League			Cup			Asia			City
		G	S	B	G	S	B	G	S	B	G	S	B	
1	Kopetdag Ashgabat	12	6		6	3		6	3					Ashgabat
2	Balkan Balkanabat	5	8	6	2	5	6	3	3					Balkanabat
3	Nisa Ashgabat	5	8	1	4	5	1	1	3					Ashgabat
4	HTTU Ashgabat	4	3	1	3	2		1	1				1	Ashgabat
5	Merv Mary	2	3	3			3	2	3					Mary
6	Sagadam Turkmenbasy	2	1	1	1			1	1					Turkmenbasy
7	FK Ashgabat	2		3	2	1							2	Ashgabat
8	Altyn Asyr	1	2			1		1	1					Asyr
9	FK Dasoguz	1	1					1	1					Dasoguz
10	Garagam Türkmenabad	1			1	1								Türkmenabad

TURKMENISTAN CUP 2010

First round

Balkan Balkanabat *	6	2
Balkan-2	0	0
Gayrat	3	2
Dasoguz *	5	8
Lebap Türkmenabat *	4	3
Bezirgen	1	0
Gökje	0	1
Merv Mary *	2	7
Talyp Sporty Ashgabat *	0	2
FK Ashgabat	0	1
Bagyr	0	2
Ahal *	3	2
Sagadam Turkmenbasy	w-o	
Melik		
HTTU Ashgabat	0	1
Altyn Asyr *	0	1

Quarter-finals

Balkan Balkanabat *	2	1
Dasoguz	0	0
Lebap Türkmenabat	0	1
Merv Mary *	1	2
Talyp Sporty Ashgabat	2	2
Ahal *	2	1
Sagadam Turkmenbasy	2	1
Altyn Asyr *	5	5

Semi-finals

Balkan Balkanabat	1
Merv Mary	0
Talyp Sporty Ashgabat	0
Altyn Asyr	2

Final

Balkan Balkanabat	3
Altyn Asyr	2

CUP FINAL

Dasoguz Stadium, Dasoguz
17-12-2010, Att: 9500
Scorers - Didargylyc Urazov 3, Arif Mirzoev 16, Gurbangeldi Batyrov 75 for Balkan; Amir Gurbani 2 67 87 for Altyn

* Home team in the first leg

TLS – TIMOR–LESTE

FIFA/COCA-COLA WORLD RANKING

1993	1994	1995	1996	1997	1998	1999	2000	2001	2002	2003	2004	2005	2006	2007	2008	2009	2010
-	-	-	-	-	-	-	-	-	-	-	-	-	198	201	197	200	201

					2010							Hi/Lo
Jan	Feb	Mar	Mar	Apr	May	Jul	Aug	Sep	Oct	Nov	Dec	**197**
200	**200**	**200**	**200**	**200**	**200**	**200**	**200**	**201**	**201**	**201**	**201**	**202**

It has been eight years since Timor-Leste's independence from Indonesia after what was at times a brutal and bloody conflict but in a sign of how times have changed the two countries met on the football field for the first time in an international friendly in Palembang in November. The hastily arranged fixture was played with little fanfare as part of Indonesia's preparations for the AFF Suzuki Cup the following month and although the Indonesians comfortably won 6-0 it still represented a landmark event. The previous month Timor-Leste had travelled to Laos to take part in a qualifying round for the Suzuki Cup but they lost all three games - against the Philippines, Cambodia and Laos to miss out on the finals. The Timorese have struggled at full national level since being admitted into the AFC in 2005 but there was a major breakthrough at youth level in 2010 when the U-16 side qualified for the AFC U-16 Championship in Uzbekistan. They qualified for the finals by finishing second in their qualifying group behind China PR. They emerged unbeaten with wins over Hong Kong, Singapore, Guam and Macau while also drawing with the Chinese to finish second on goal-difference. In Uzbekistan they found the step up in quality at the finals difficult to handle and lost all three games in the group stage against Japan, Australia and Vietnam.

FIFA WORLD CUP RECORD
1930-2006 DNE 2010 DNQ

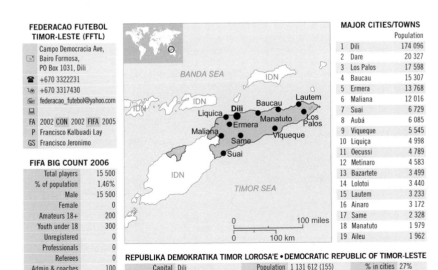

FEDERACAO FUTEBOL TIMOR-LESTE (FFTL)

Campo Democracia Ave,
✉ Bairo Formosa,
PO Box 1031, Dili
☎ +670 3322231
📠 +670 3317430
📧 federacao_futebol@yahoo.com
▢
FA 2002 CON 2002 FIFA 2005
P Francisco Kalbuadi Lay
GS Francisco Jeronimo

FIFA BIG COUNT 2006

Total players	15 500
% of population	1.46%
Male	15 500
Female	0
Amateurs 18+	200
Youth under 18	300
Unregistered	0
Professionals	0
Referees	0
Admin & coaches	100
Number of clubs	10
Number of teams	20

MAJOR CITIES/TOWNS

		Population
1	Dili	174 096
2	Dare	20 327
3	Los Palos	17 598
4	Baucau	15 307
5	Ermera	13 768
6	Maliana	12 016
7	Suai	6 729
8	Aubá	6 085
9	Viqueque	5 545
10	Liquiça	4 998
11	Oecussi	4 789
12	Metinaro	4 583
13	Bazartete	3 499
14	Lolotoi	3 440
15	Lautem	3 233
16	Ainaro	3 172
17	Same	2 328
18	Manatuto	1 979
19	Aileu	1 962

REPUBLIKA DEMOKRATIKA TIMOR LOROSA'E • DEMOCRATIC REPUBLIC OF TIMOR-LESTE

Capital Dili	Population 1 131 612 (155)	% in cities 27%
GDP per capita $2300 (180)	Area km² 14 874 km² (159)	GMT + / - +9
Neighbours (km) Indonesia 228 • Coast 706		

RECENT INTERNATIONAL MATCHES PLAYED BY TIMOR–LESTE

2002	Opponents	Score		Venue	Comp	Scorers	Att	Referee
No international matches played before 2003								
2003								
21-03	Sri Lanka	L	2-3	Colombo	ACq			
23-03	Chinese Taipei	L	0-3	Colombo	ACq			
2004								
8-12	Malaysia	L	0-5	Kuala Lumpur	AFFr1			
12-12	Thailand	L	0-8	Kuala Lumpur	AFFr1			
14-12	Philippines	L	1-2	Kuala Lumpur	AFFr1	Anai [14]		
16-12	Myanmar	L	1-3	Kuala Lumpur	AFFr1	Simon Diamantino [15p]		
2005								
No international matches played in 2005								
2006								
12-11	Brunei	L	2-3	Bacolod	AFFq	Adelio Maria Costa [33], Anatacio Belo [77]		
14-11	Philippines	L	0-7	Bacolod	AFFq			
16-11	Laos	L	2-3	Bacolod	AFFq	Antonio Ximenes [82], Adelio Maria Costa [89]		
20-11	Cambodia	L	1-4	Bacolod	AFFq	Adelio Maria Costa [63]		
2007								
21-10	Hong Kong	L	2-3	Gianyar	WCq	Emilio Da Silva 2 [41 69]	1 500	Shaharul MAS
28-10	Hong Kong	L	1-8	Hong Kong	WCq	Emilio Da Silva	1 542	Torky IRN
2008								
17-10	Philippines	L	0-1	Phnom Penh	AFFq		15 000	
19-10	Cambodia	D	2-2	Phnom Penh	AFFq	Anggisu Barbosa [45], Jose Perreira [67p]	12 000	
21-10	Brunei Darussalam	L	1-4	Phnom Penh	AFFq	Rosito Soares [80]		
25-10	Laos	L	1-2	Phnom Penh	AFFq	Alfredo Esteves [44]		
2009								
No international matches played in 2009								
2010								
22-10	Philippines	L	0-5	Vientiane	AFFq			Leow SIN
24-10	Cambodia	L	2-4	Vientiane	AFFq	Chiquito Do Carmo [5], Anggisu Barbosa [85]		Phung Dinh Dung VIE
26-10	Laos	L	1-6	Vientiane	AFFq	Chiquito Do Carmo [9]		
21-11	Indonesia	L	0-6	Palembang	Fr			

AC = AFC Asian Cup • AFF = ASEAN Football Federation Championship
q = qualifier • r1 = first round group • Matches played before September 2005 are not full internationals

TOG – TOGO

FIFA/COCA-COLA WORLD RANKING

1993	1994	1995	1996	1997	1998	1999	2000	2001	2002	2003	2004	2005	2006	2007	2008	2009	2010
113	86	92	87	78	68	87	81	71	86	94	89	56	60	72	86	71	103

							2010						Hi/Lo
	Jan	Feb	Mar	Mar	Apr	May	Jul	Aug	Sep	Oct	Nov	Dec	46
	71	70	69	73	73	76	75	75	87	87	107	103	123

Togo battled off the field with the absurdity of a suspension from the next two African Nations Cup finals imposed on them after their squad left the finals in Angola following the deadly attack on their team which took the lives of two officials and effectively ended goalkeeper Kodjovi Obilale's career. The Confederation of African Football was roundly condemned for the heavy-handed reaction and almost complete lack of sympathy with the plight of the players and officials. CAF insisted that as Togo had not fulfilled their obligations and that president Issa Hayatou's plea to stay having been refused, a mandatory ban on the team was unavoidable. The subsequent adverse publicity proved a major blow to CAF and was only ended when FIFA president Sepp Blatter stepped in to broker an agreement between them and the Togo federation, who had taken their appeal against the decision to the Swiss-based Court for Arbitration in Sport. As a result, the ban was lifted and Togo belatedly allowed to enter the 2012 Nations Cup qualifiers, where they made a modest start. Star player Emmanuel Adebayor announced his retirement from the international arena and coach Huber Velud quit in May to go to Creteil in the French league. His place was taken by Thierry Frogger but he was sacked just before Christmas.

FIFA WORLD CUP RECORD
1930-1970 DNE **1974-1982** DNQ **1986-1990** DNE **1994-2002** DNQ **2006** 30 r1 **2010** DNQ

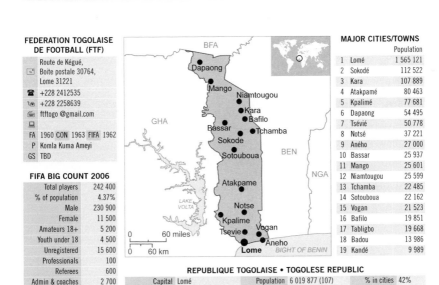

FEDERATION TOGOLAISE DE FOOTBALL (FTF)

Route de Kégué,
Boite postale 30764,
Lome 31221

☎ +228 2412535
🖷 +228 2258639
✉ ftftogo @gmail.com
🖳

FA	1960	CON 1963	FIFA 1962
P	Komla Kuma Ameyi		
GS	TBD		

FIFA BIG COUNT 2006

Total players	242 400
% of population	4.37%
Male	230 900
Female	11 500
Amateurs 18+	5 200
Youth under 18	4 500
Unregistered	15 600
Professionals	100
Referees	600
Admin & coaches	2 700
Number of clubs	100
Number of teams	620

MAJOR CITIES/TOWNS

		Population
1	Lomé	1 565 121
2	Sokodé	112 522
3	Kara	107 889
4	Atakpamé	80 463
5	Kpalimé	77 681
6	Dapaong	54 495
7	Tsévié	50 778
8	Notsé	37 221
9	Aného	27 000
10	Bassar	25 937
11	Mango	25 601
12	Niamtougou	25 599
13	Tchamba	22 485
14	Sotouboua	22 162
15	Vogan	21 523
16	Bafilo	19 851
17	Tabligbo	19 668
18	Badou	13 986
19	Kandé	9 989

REPUBLIQUE TOGOLAISE • TOGOLESE REPUBLIC

Capital Lomé	Population 6 019 877 (107)	% in cities 42%
GDP per capita $900 (216)	Area km² 56 785 km² (125)	GMT +/- 0
Neighbours (km) Benin 644, Burkina Faso 126, Ghana 877 • Coast 56		

RECENT INTERNATIONAL MATCHES PLAYED BY TOGO

2006	Opponents	Score		Venue	Comp	Scorers	Att	Referee
13-06	Korea Republic	L	1-2	Frankfurt	WCr1	Kader Coubadja [31]	48 000	Poll ENG
19-06	Switzerland	L	0-2	Dortmund	WCr1		65 000	Amarilla PAR
23-06	France	L	0-2	Cologne	WCr1		45 000	Larrionda URU
15-08	Ghana	L	0-2	London	Fr			Dean ENG
29-08	Niger	D	1-1	Lomé	Fr	Komlan Amewou [55]		
3-09	Benin	W	2-1	Lomé	CNq	Thomas Dossevi [13], Komlan Amewou [78]		Louzaya CGO
8-10	Mali	L	0-1	Bamako	CNq			Benouza ALG
15-11	Luxembourg	D	0-0	Luxembourg	Fr		1 417	Richards WAL
2007								
7-02	Cameroon	D	2-2	Lomé	Fr	Adekanmi Olufade [25], Emmanuel Adebayor [40]		
25-03	Sierra Leone	W	3-1	Lomé	CNq	Emmanuel Adebayor 2 [38 85], Adekanmi Olufade [62]		Pare BFA
3-06	Sierra Leone	W	1-0	Freetown	CNq	Junior Senaya [48]		Imiere NGA
17-06	Benin	L	1-4	Cotonou	CNq	Adekanmi Olufade [75]		Evehe CMR
22-08	Zambia	W	3-1	Lomé	Fr	Jonathan Ayite 2 [29 41], Adekanmi Olufade [84]		
12-10	Mali	L	0-2	Lomé	CNq			Abdelfattah EGY
18-11	Ghana	L	0-2	Accra	Fr			
21-11	UAE	W	5-0	Accra	Fr	Nouhoun Moutawakilou [19], Sapol Mani [73], OG [77], Thomas Dossevi [83], Emmanuel Adebayor [84]		
2008								
25-03	Guinea	L	0-2	Paris	Fr			
31-05	Zambia	W	1-0	Accra	WCq	Adekanmi Olufade [16]	15 000	Pare BFA
8-06	Swaziland	L	1-2	Mbabane	WCq	Adekanmi Olufade [88]	5 819	Niyongabo BDI
20-08	Congo DR	L	1-2	Dreux	Fr	Emmanuel Adebayor [47p]		
10-09	Zambia	L	0-1	Chililabombwe	WCq		10 500	Damon RSA
11-10	Swaziland	W	6-0	Accra	WCq	Moustapha Salifou [16], Emmanuel Adebayor 4 [29 47 72 85], Adekanmi Olufade [44]	8 000	Evehe CMR
19-11	Rwanda	W	1-0	Lome	Fr	Floyd Ayite [33]		
2009								
11-02	Burkina Faso	D	1-1	Le Petit-Quevilly	Fr	Senah Mangoh [77]		
28-03	Cameroon	W	1-0	Accra	WCq	Emmanuel Adebayor [11]	26 450	Abd El Fatah EGY
6-06	Gabon	L	0-3	Libreville	WCq		20 000	Lwanja MWI
20-06	Morocco	D	0-0	Rabat	WCq		22 000	Kaoma ZAM
12-08	Angola	L	0-2	Lisbon	Fr		7 000	Proenca POR
6-09	Morocco	D	1-1	Lomé	WCq	Moustapha Salifou [3]	24 651	Ssegonga UGA
10-10	Cameroon	L	0-3	Yaoundé	WCq		36 401	Kaoma ZAM
14-10	Japan	L	0-5	Miyagi	Fr		32 852	Mikulski POL
6-11	Bahrain	L	1-5	Manama	Fr	Dove Wome [69]		
14-11	Gabon	W	1-0	Lomé	WCq	Floyd Ayite [71]	10 000	Seechurn MRI
2010								
19-05	Gabon	L	0-3	Ajaccio	Fr			
1-07	Chad	D	2-2	N'Djamena	CNq	Sapol Mani [25], Backer Aloenouvo [68]		Benouza ALG
9-07	Malawi	D	1-1	Lomé	CNq	Backer Aloenouvo [75]		Bennett RSA
11-08	Saudi Arabia	L	0-1	Riyadh	Fr			
4-09	Botswana	L	1-2	Gaborone	CNq	Serge Gakpe [44]		Kagabo RWA
10-10	Tunisia	L	1-2	Lomé	CNq	Sapol Mani [40]		Abdul Rahman SUD
17-11	Chad	D	0-0	Lomé	CNq			Coulibaly MLI

Fr = Friendly match • CN = CAF African Cup of Nations • WC = FIFA World Cup • q = qualifier • r1 = first round group

TPE – CHINESE TAIPEI

FIFA/COCA-COLA WORLD RANKING

1993	1994	1995	1996	1997	1998	1999	2000	2001	2002	2003	2004	2005	2006	2007	2008	2009	2010
161	170	178	174	154	169	174	162	170	166	150	155	156	166	169	167	162	153

2010												Hi/Lo
Jan	Feb	Mar	Mar	Apr	May	Jul	Aug	Sep	Oct	Nov	Dec	**144**
162	162	162	163	166	167	166	165	170	156	155	153	**180**

2010 was a quiet year for the Chinese Taipei national team with just five games played - three of them over the space of four days in the Long Teng Cup, a friendly tournament staged in Kaohsiung City involving Macau, the Philippines and a youthful Hong Kong side preparing for the Asian Games in Guangzhou. In January 2011 national team captain Chen Po Liang made the move to Hong Kong when he become one of only a handful of players from the island to play professionally abroad, the 22-year-old signing for Hong Kong side TSW Pegasus. In November Chinese Taipei made a rare sortie outside of the country for a friendly when they travelled to Palembang in Indonesia, a match they lost 2-0. Club football in Chinese Taipei saw an exciting climax to the season in the local Intercity Football League. The nine-team tournament saw four clubs enter the final round of fixtures with title aspirations but it was Kaohsiung Taipower who prevailed to become champions for the 16th time. Taipei PEC asics had gone into the games a point ahead of Taipower, NSTC and three-time champions Tatung. The game between Taipei PEC asics and Tatung finished 1-1 which meant that Taipower's 3-1 win over NSTC (National Sports Training Center) saw them clinch the title by a point and book a place in the 2011 AFC President's Cup.

FIFA WORLD CUP RECORD
1930-1954 DNE **1954** DNQ **1958-1974** DNE **1978-2010** DNQ

**CHINESE TAIPEI
FOOTBALL ASSOCIATION
(CTFA)**

Room 210, 2F, 55 Chang Chi
Street, Tatung District,
Taipei 10363
☎ +886 2 25961184
📠 +886 2 25951594
✉ ctfa7155@ms59.hinet.net
🖥 www.ctfa.com.tw
FA 1924 CON 1954 FIFA 1954
P Lu Kun Shan
GS Lin Der Chia

FIFA BIG COUNT 2006

Total players	458 460
% of population	1.99%
Male	424 400
Female	34 060
Amateurs 18+	5 960
Unregistered	75 900
Professionals	0
Referees	102
Admin & coaches	374
Number of clubs	60
Number of teams	600

MAJOR CITIES/TOWNS

		Population
1	Taipei	2 655 423
2	Kaohsiung	1 525 999
3	Taizhong	1 078 348
4	Tainan	772 279
5	Banqiao	547 444
6	Zhonghe	414 984
7	Taoyuan	405 289
8	Xinzhu	401 991
9	Xinzhuang	400 647
10	Jilong	389 737
11	Sanchong	380 859
12	Zhongli	367 943
13	Fengshan	343 332
14	Xindian	293 572
15	Jiayi	274 657
16	Zhanghua	239 716
17	Tucheng	237 795
18	Yonghe	236 448
19	Pingdong	217 819

CHINESE TAIPEI

Capital	Taipei	Population	22 974 347 (49)	% in cities	69%
GDP per capita	$31 100 (42)	Area km²	35 980 km² (138)	GMT +/-	+8
Neighbours (km)	Coast 1566				

RECENT INTERNATIONAL MATCHES PLAYED BY CHINESE TAIPEI

2007	Opponents	Score	Venue	Comp	Scorers	Att	Referee
17-06	Guam	W 10-0	Macau	EAq	Lo Chih En 4 [7 28 72 88], Tsai Hui Kai [20], Feng Pao Hsing 2 [25 38], Chen Po Liang 2 [52 68], Huang Cheng Tsung [74]	10	Wan Daxue CHN
19-06	Hong Kong	D 1-1	Macau	EAq	Huang Wei Yi [51]	200	Kim Eui Soo KOR
24-06	Macau	W 7-2	Macau	EAq	Huang Wei Yi [3], Feng Pao Hsing [42], Kuo Chun Yi [52], Chen Po Liang [56], Lo Chih En 2 [57 90], Lo Chih An [71]	200	Kim Eui Soo KOR
13-10	Uzbekistan	L 0-9	Tashkent	WCq		7 000	Albadwawi UAE
28-10	Uzbekistan	L 0-2	Taipei	WCq		800	Shamsuzzaman UZB
2008							
2-04	Pakistan	L 1-2	Taipei	CCq	Lo Chi An [5]	800	Iemoto JPN
4-04	Guam	W 4-1	Taipei	CCq	Chang Han [20], Huang Wei Yi [28], Chen Po Liang [33], Chiang Shih Lu [44]	850	Win Cho MYA
6-04	Sri Lanka	D 2-2	Taipei	CCq	Chang Han [28], Tsai Hsien Tang [74]	900	Iemoto JPN
24-05	India	L 0-3	Goa	Fr			
27-05	India	D 2-2	Chennai	Fr	Chen Po Liang [4], Hsieh Meng Hsuan [48]		
2009							
4-04	Pakistan	D 1-1	Colombo	CCq	Chang Han [21]	400	Tseytlin UZB
6-04	Sri Lanka	L 1-2	Colombo	CCq	Huang Wei Yi [80]	1 400	Al Zahrani KSA
8-04	Brunei Darussalam	W 5-0	Colombo	CCq	Chen Po Liang 3 [11 13 58], Huang Wei Yi [30], Kuo Chun Yi [80]	1 000	Al Zahrani KSA
23-08	Hong Kong	L 0-4	Kaohsiung	EAq		12 000	Tojo JPN
25-08	Guam	W 4-2	Kaohsiung	EAq	Chen Po Liang 2 [45 68], Chang Han [61], Lo Chih En [75]	7 500	Matsuo JPN
27-08	Korea DPR	L 1-2	Kaohsiung	EAq	Chang Han [49]	10 000	Matsuo JPN
2010							
16-01	Philippines	D 0-0	Kaohsiung	Fr			
9-10	Macau	W 7-1	Kaohsiung	Fr	Lin Cheng Yi [16], Lo Chih En [43], Lo Chih An [45], Chen Po Hao 2 [46 77], Chang Han [55], Chen Po Liang [67]	1 000	San Hua Nien TPE
10-10	Philippines	D 1-1	Kaohsiung	Fr	Lo Chih An [48]	890	Kao Tsai Hu TPE
12-10	Hong Kong	D 1-1	Kaohsiung	Fr	Lo Chih An [40]	3 000	Kao Tsai Hu TPE
24-11	Indonesia	L 0-2	Palembang	Fr			Singh SIN

Fr = Friendly match • EA = East Asian Championship • AC = AFC Asian Cup • CC = AFC Challenge Cup • WC = FIFA World Cup • q = qualifier

CHINESE TAIPEI NATIONAL TEAM HISTORICAL RECORDS

Past Coaches: Lee Wai Tong 1954-58 • Law Pak 1977-81 • Chiang Chia 1981-85 • Lo Chih Tsung 1985-88 • Huang Jen Cheng 1988-93 • Chiang Mu Tsai 1994-2000 • Huang Jen Cheng 2000-01 • Lee Po Houng 2001-05 • Dido BRA 2005 • Toshiaki Imai JPN 2005-07 • Chen Sing An 2008-09 • Lo Chih Tsung 2009-

CHINESE TAIPEI 2010

INTERCITY FOOTBALL LEAGUE DIVISION A

	Pl	W	D	L	F	A	Pts	Taipower	Taipei PEC	Tatung	NSTC	Hasus TSU	Taipei County	Ming Chuan	Yilan County	I-Shou Univ
Kaohsiung Taipower ‡	13	8	3	2	41	15	27		2-2	1-1	3-1	2-0	7-1	5-1	7-1	0-0
Taipei PEC asics	13	7	5	1	35	15	26	3-1		0-0	0-0	1-1	7-2		2-0	
Taipei City Tatung	13	7	4	2	30	11	25	1-2	1-1		0-1	3-1	4-1	6-1	3-1	9-2
NSTC	13	7	3	3	24	15	24	0-6	4-1	1-1		3-1	5-1	2-1		
Hasus TSU	13	6	1	6	38	18	19	4-2	0-1	0-3	0-2		3-1	8-0		5-0
Taipei County	13	3	1	9	13	38	10	0-3	0-3	1-2	1-0	0-2				
Ming Chuan University	8	1	2	5	12	30	5		2-5					2-2		3-0
Yilan County	8	1	2	5	7	27	5			0-0	0-10	0-1	2-2			
I-Shou University	8	0	1	7	4	35	1			0-5		0-8	0-2		2-3	

10/04/2010 - 30/10/2010 • ‡ Qualified for the AFC President's Cup • Kaohsiung renamed Hasus TSU; Tianan County renamed Taipei PEC

TRI – TRINIDAD AND TOBAGO

FIFA/COCA-COLA WORLD RANKING

1993	1994	1995	1996	1997	1998	1999	2000	2001	2002	2003	2004	2005	2006	2007	2008	2009	2010
88	91	57	41	56	51	44	29	32	47	70	63	50	91	81	77	82	89

	2010											Hi/Lo
Jan	Feb	Mar	Mar	Apr	May	Jul	Aug	Sep	Oct	Nov	Dec	**25**
82	84	85	93	91	95	76	76	97	106	78	89	**106**

Since appearing in the finals of the 2006 FIFA World Cup in Germany, the national team of Trinidad and Tobago has had to undergo a huge process of rebuilding as a number of its most established stars have reached the end of their careers. It has been a bumpy road with the team struggling to find any consistency and 2010 was a case in point. In nine warm-up games for the 2010 Digicel Caribbean Cup coach Russell Latapy saw his team win just three times - all against much weaker opposition. Then in the qualifying round of the tournament there were three impressive wins that saw Trinidad qualify for the finals in Martinique and had fans of the Socawarriors dreaming of a ninth regional title. Unable to call on England-based Kenwyne Jones and Carlos Edwards, Trinidad's largely home-based squad had a disastrous time in Martinique, losing to both Cuba and Grenada, and were knocked out after the group phase for the second tournament running. Bearing in mind that in the 13 tournaments to 2007 Trinidad had never finished lower than third, the current predicament is clear. Trinidad also lost its grip on the CFU Caribbean Club Cup with Joe Public finishing as runners-up to Puerto Rico Islanders. At home Defence Force won their first title since 1999 whilst San Juan Jabloteh won the FA Trophy and Joe Public the League Cup.

FIFA WORLD CUP RECORD
1930-1962 DNE 1966-2002 DNQ **2006** 27 r1 2010 DNQ

TRINIDAD AND TOBAGO FOOTBALL FEDERATION (TTFF)

43 Dundonald Street, PO Box 400, Port of Spain
☎ +1 868 6237312
📠 +1 868 6238109
📧 richardgroden@aol.com
🖥 www.ttffonline.com
FA 1908 CON 1964 FIFA 1963
P Oliver Camps
GS Richard Groden

FIFA BIG COUNT 2006

Total players	84 600
% of population	7.94%
Male	71 150
Female	13 450
Amateurs 18+	4 250
Youth under 18	11 600
Unregistered	16 000
Professionals	250
Referees	250
Admin & coaches	650
Number of clubs	95
Number of teams	380

MAJOR CITIES/TOWNS

		Population
1	Chaguanas	76 136
2	San Juan	58 815
3	San Fernando	57 032
4	Port of Spain	50 044
5	Arima	37 332
6	Marabella	26 624
7	Tunapuna	18 826
8	Point Fortin	18 748
9	Sangre Grande	17 156
10	Tacarigua	15 973
11	Arouca	12 779
12	Princes Town	10 969
13	Siparia	8 355
14	Couva	5 316
15	Peñal	5 058
16	Saint Joseph	4 979
17	Scarborough	4 734
18	Mucurapo	4 542
19	Tabaquite	3 402

REPUBLIC OF TRINIDAD AND TOBAGO

Capital Port of Spain	Population 1 229 953 (154)	% in cities 13%
GDP per capita $23 600 (53)	Area km² 5 128 km² (173)	GMT +/- -4
Neighbours (km) Coast 362		

RECENT INTERNATIONAL MATCHES PLAYED BY TRINIDAD AND TOBAGO

2008	Opponents	Score		Venue	Comp	Scorers	Att	Referee
5-11	Antigua and Barbuda	W	3-2	Macoya	CCq	Cornell Glen [69], Arnold Dwarika [73], Andre Toussaint [88]	750	Pinas SUR
7-11	St Kitts and Nevis	W	3-1	Macoya	CCq	Keon Daniel [37], Khaleem Hyland [65], Devon Jorsling [66]		Wijngaarde SUR
9-11	Guyana	D	1-1	Macoya	CCq	Devon Jorsling [85]	1 000	Minyetty DOM
19-11	Cuba	W	3-0	Port of Spain	WCq	Kenwyne Jones [67], Dwight Yorke [69], Keon Daniel [89]	18 000	Wijngaarde SUR
3-12	Grenada	L	1-2	Kingston	CCr1	Dwayne Leo [70]	5 000	James GUY
5-12	Barbados	W	2-1	Montego Bay	CCr1	Errol McFarlene 2 [42p 73p]	4 000	Jauregui ANT
7-12	Jamaica	D	1-1	Trelawny	CCr1	Errol McFarlene [80]	9 000	Moreno PAN
2009								
11-02	El Salvador	D	2-2	San Salvador	WCq	Carlos Edwards [7], Dwight Yorke [26p]	25 000	Rodriguez MEX
18-03	Panama	W	1-0	Marabella	Fr	Cornell Glen [74p]	2 000	Jordan TRI
28-03	Honduras	D	1-1	Port of Spain	WCq	Khaleem Hyland [88]	23 500	Quesada CRC
1-04	USA	L	0-3	Nashville	WCq		27 958	Moreno PAN
6-06	Costa Rica	L	2-3	Bacolet	WCq	Carlos Edwards [30], Collin Samuel [63]	8 000	Campbell JAM
10-06	Mexico	L	1-2	Mexico City	WCq	Hayden Tinto [45]	92 000	Pineda HON
12-07	St Kitts and Nevis	W	3-2	Basseterre	Fr	Radanfah Abubakr [21], Ataullah Guerra [27], Kerry Baptiste [72]	3 100	Matthew SKN
12-08	El Salvador	W	1-0	Port of Spain	WCq	Cornell Glen [7]	16 000	Vaughn USA
5-09	Honduras	L	1-4	San Pedro Sula	WCq	Kerry Baptiste [86]	38 000	Geiger USA
9-09	USA	L	0-1	Port of Spain	WCq		4 700	Aguilar SLV
10-10	Costa Rica	L	0-4	San Jose	WCq		10 000	Marrufo USA
14-10	Mexico	D	2-2	Port of Spain	WCq	Kerry Baptiste 2 [23p 61]	2 000	Quesada CRC
2010								
5-05	Chile	L	0-2	Iquique	Fr		10 000	Antequera BRA
21-07	Antigua and Barbuda	W	4-1	Macoya	Fr	Kevon Carter 2 [10 30], Kerry Baptiste [18], Devon Jorsling [67]	1 700	Brizan TRI
11-08	Jamaica	L	1-3	Macoya	Fr	Devon Jorsling [28]	4 500	Taylor BRB
7-09	Panama	L	0-3	Panama City	Fr		6 645	Cruz CRC
10-09	Belize	D	0-0	Belmopan	Fr		5 000	Mejia SLV
19-09	Antigua and Barbuda	W	1-0	St John's	Fr	Devon Jorsling [70]	500	Willett ATG
21-09	St Lucia	W	3-0	St John's	Fr	Devon Jorsling [22], Jamal Gay [53], Hughton Hector [86]	205	St Catherine LCA
26-09	Guyana	D	1-1	Providence	Fr	Devon Jorsling [35]	9 000	Lancaster GUY
10-10	Jamaica	L	0-1	Kingston	Fr		7 000	Archundia MEX
2-11	St Vincent/Grenadines	W	6-2	Marabella	CCq	Devon Jorsling 3 [2 35 59], Kerry Baptiste 2 [57 67], Hughton Hector [90]	1 100	Peterkin JAM
4-11	Guyana	W	2-1	Marabella	CCq	Lester Peltier [34], Devorn Jorsling [42]	1 100	Legister JAM
6-11	Haiti	W	4-0	Marabella	CCq	Hughton Hector 2 [4 33], Devon Jorsling [8], Kerry Baptiste [29]	850	Campbell JAM
26-11	Cuba	L	0-2	Fort de France	CCr1		5 000	Lancaster GUY
28-11	Grenada	L	0-1	Fort de France	CCr1		500	Cruz CRC
30-11	Martinique	W	1-0	Fort de France	CCr1	Hughton Hector [47]	2 000	Taylor BRB

Fr = Friendly match • CC = Digicel Caribbean Cup • GC = CONCACAF Gold Cup • WC = FIFA World Cup • q = qualifier • r1 = first round group

TRINIDAD AND TOBAGO NATIONAL TEAM HISTORICAL RECORDS

Caps
113 - Angus Eve 1994-2005 • **109** - Stern John 1995-2009 • **101** - Marvin Andrews 1996-2009 • **89** - Dennis Lawrence 2000- •
79 - Clayton Ince 1997-2009 • **78** - Carlos Edwards 1999- & Russell Latapy 1988-2009 • **74** - Arnold Dwarika 1993-2008 • **72** - Dwight
Yorke 1989-2009 & Keyeno Thomas 1998-2009 • **70** - Avery John 1996-2009 • **69** - Ansil Elcock 1994-2004 • **67** - Anthony Rougier 1995-
2005 • **62** - Cornell Glen 2002- • **61** - Stokely Mason 1996-2004 • **59** - Cyd Gray 2001-08 • **57** - Nigel Pierre 1999-2008

Goals
69 - Stern John 1995- • **34** - Angus Eve 1994-2005 • **29** - Russell Latapy 1988-2009 • **28** - Arnold Dwarika 1993-2008 • **23** - Cornell Glen
2002- • **22** - Nigel Pierre 1999-2008 • **21** - Leonson Lewis 1988-96 • **19** - Dwight Yorke 1989-2009 • **16** - Steve David 1972-76

Past Coaches
Bertille St. Clair 1997-2000 • Ian Porterfield SCO 2000-01 • Rene Simoes BRA 2001-02 • Hannibal Najjar 2002-03 • Zoran Vranes SRB
2003 • Stuart Charles Fevrier LCA 2003-04 • Bertille St. Clair 2004-05 • Leo Beenhakker NED 2005-06 • Wim Rijsbergen NED 2006-07 •
Francisco Maturana COL 2008-09 • Russell Latapy 2009-11 • Johan Neeskens NED 2011-

TRINIDAD AND TOBAGO 2010

DIGICEL PRO LEAGUE

	Pl	W	D	L	F	A	Pts	Defence	Caledonia	Joe Public	W Connection	Ma Pau	San Juan	NE Stars	St Ann's	Police	South End	Tobago
Defence Force	18	13	2	3	38	13	41		2-0	1-2	2-1	2-1	2-0	4-3	3-0	3-0	1-0	
Caledonia AIA	18	11	3	4	30	18	36	0-3		1-1	2-1	2-1	3-2	0-0	4-2	5-0	1-2	3-0
Joe Public	18	10	5	3	30	22	35	1-3	0-2		1-1	2-1	3-1	3-2	2-1	2-1	2-1	
W Connection	18	9	4	5	35	13	31	0-0	0-1	3-0		2-0	0-0	0-1	4-1	4-0	2-1	
Ma Pau	18	8	5	5	24	16	29	1-0	2-0	1-1	2-2		0-1	0-0	1-0	3-1	2-0	3-1
San Juan Jabloteh	18	7	6	5	25	14	27	0-0	0-0	1-1	0-1	0-1		2-0	2-0	4-0	4-1	
North East Stars	18	7	6	5	29	24	27	2-1	1-2	1-1	2-1	1-3	1-1		2-0	6-3	2-1	
St Ann's Rangers	18	2	4	12	14	36	10	2-4	0-4	0-3	0-2	0-0	0-0	0-0		1-1	2-1	
Police	18	2	3	13	20	54	9	0-3	0-1	1-3	0-5	2-2	1-4	2-2	2-5		3-1	
South End	18	2	0	16	10	45	6	0-4	1-2	0-2	0-6	0-3	1-4	0-3	1-0	0-3		2-0
Tobago United	Withdrew after 10 rounds							0-3		1-4	0-2		0-4	2-2	3-0	3-1		

23/04/2010 - 1/02/2011
Top scorers: **12** - Devorn Jorsling, Defence • **8** - Errol McFarlane, NE Stars • **6** - Anthony Wolfe, Ma Pau

TRINIDAD AND TOBAGO 2010 SPORTWORLD NATIONAL SUPER LEAGUE (2)

	Pl	W	D	L	F	A	Pts
T&TEC Sports Club	18	14	4	0	54	12	46
Angostura Phoenix	19	10	6	3	32	20	36
WASA	19	11	2	6	33	20	35
Joe Public B	19	8	4	7	30	24	28
Defence Force B	19	7	6	6	34	28	27
Stokely Vale	19	8	2	9	34	43	26
Club Sando	20	7	3	10	28	34	24
St Francois Nationals	19	6	4	9	26	32	22
Harvard Sports Club	20	5	5	10	23	37	20
Queen's Park CC	20	4	5	11	28	40	17
Valtrin United	20	5	1	14	22	54	16

18/07/2010 - 19/12/2010

MEDALS TABLE

		All	Pro	Nat	Cup	LC	CL	CC
		G	G	G	G		G	S
1	Defence Force	32	4	17	6	2	2	1
2	Maple Club	20		13	7			
3	W Connection	15	3		3	6		3
	Casuals	15		11	4			
5	Shamrock	13		9	4			
6	Malvern United	9		2	7			
	San Juan Jabloteh	9	4		2	2		1
	Joe Public	9	3		3	1		2
9	Everton	7		3	4			
	Colts	7		4	3			
11	Police	6		3	3			
	Sporting Club	6		5	1			
	United British	6			6			
	United Petrotin	6		5				1
15	Notre Dame	4		3	1			

FA TROPHY 2010

First round		Quarter–finals		Semi–finals		Final	
San Juan Jabloteh	2						
Joe Public	0	**San Juan Jabloteh**	5				
Queen's Park CC	2	La Brea All Stars	0				
La Brea All Stars	3			**San Juan Jabloteh**	2 7p		
Joe Public B	2			Caledonia AIA	2 6p		
Mason Hall USSS	0	Joe Public B	2 4p				
Defence Force B	1	**Caledonia AIA**	2 5p			**San Juan Jabloteh**	1
Caledonia AIA	2					North East Stars	0
Defence Force	7						
Damarie Hill United	1	**Defence Force**	3				
Valencia United	1	St Ann's Rangers	1			CUP FINAL	
St Ann's Rangers	5			Defence Force	0		
Ma Pau	3			**North East Stars**	2		
Santa Rosa	0	Ma Pau	0			4-02-2011	
Bacolet Goal City	1	**North East Stars**	1				
North East Stars	3						

TUN – TUNISIA

FIFA/COCA-COLA WORLD RANKING

1993	1994	1995	1996	1997	1998	1999	2000	2001	2002	2003	2004	2005	2006	2007	2008	2009	2010
32	30	22	23	23	21	31	26	28	41	45	35	28	32	47	46	53	45

	2010											Hi/Lo
	Jan	Feb	Mar	Mar	Apr	May	Jul	Aug	Sep	Oct	Nov	Dec	**19**
	53	55	55	56	55	55	65	64	56	45	44	45	**65**

In their long quest for a second African Champions League title Esperance made it to the final for the third time since winning the tournament in 1994. The Tunis club seemed to have done the hard work by eliminating five-time champions Al Ahly of Egypt in the semi-finals on the away goals rule but then suffered a humiliating 5-0 defeat in first leg of the final to holders TP Mazembe. It was a controversial defeat that led to scenes of vitriol aimed at CAF president Issa Hayatou and other officials during the second leg in Tunisia which ended in a draw. The violence during and after the game earned the club a heavy fine and a home ground ban for the 2011 tournament which they had qualified for by winning the Tunisian championship in 2010. CS Sfaxien then compounded Tunisian misery by losing the final of the CAF Confederation Cup to Morocco's FUS Rabat. Having drawn the first leg 0-0 in Rabat, Sfaxien looked odds-on to win the trophy for a third time in the last four years but lost the return 3-2 at home in Sfax. The national team endured a poor year in 2010 with their French coach Bertrand Marchand given the sack in November after losing to Botswana in the 2012 African Nations Cup qualifiers. Having already lost to the Botswanans earlier in the year it left the Tunisians in a perilous position in their bid to qualify for the finals.

FIFA WORLD CUP RECORD

1930-1958 DNE **1962** DNQ **1966** DNE **1970-1974** DNQ **1978** 9 r1 **1982-1994** DNQ **1998** 27 r1 **2002** 29 r1 **2006** 24 r1 **2010** DNQ

FEDERATION TUNISIENNE DE FOOTBALL (FTF)

Stade annexe d'El Menzah, Cité Olympique, Tunis 1003
☎ +216 71 793760
📠 +216 71 783843
✉ directeur@ftf.org.tn
🖥 www.ftf.org.tn
FA 1956 CON 1960 FIFA 1960
P Ali Jeddi
GS Ridha Kraiem

FIFA BIG COUNT 2006

Total players	525 264
% of population	5.16%
Male	500 636
Female	24 628
Amateurs 18+	29 404
Youth under 18	20 950
Unregistered	42 435
Professionals	1 075
Referees	998
Admin & coaches	6 626
Number of clubs	250
Number of teams	1 512

MAJOR CITIES/TOWNS

		Population
1	Tunis	741 427
2	Sfax	284 027
3	Ariana	277 114
4	At Tadaman	198 854
5	Sousse	195 100
6	Kairouan	124 505
7	Gabès	123 600
8	Bizerte	118 714
9	El Mourouj	91 693
10	Gafsa	89 492
11	Kasserine	81 443
12	Monastir	80 847
13	Ben Arous	78 601
14	La Marsa	78 585
15	Zarzis	73 142
16	Hammamet	66 065
17	Masakin	65 603
18	Tatouine	65 436
19	Béja	56 517

AL JUMHURIYAH AT TUNISIYAH • TUNISIAN REPUBLIC

Capital	Tunis	Population	10 486 339 (76)	% in cities	67%
GDP per capita	$7900 (122)	Area km²	163 610 km² (92)	GMT +/-	+1
Neighbours (km)	Algeria 965, Libya 459 • Coast 1148				

RECENT INTERNATIONAL MATCHES PLAYED BY TUNISIA

2007	Opponents	Score		Venue	Comp	Scorers	Att	Referee
22-08	Guinea	D	1-1	Radès/Tunis	Fr	Mnari [23]		
9-09	Sudan	L	2-3	Omdurman	CNq	Mugahid OG [55], Santos [81p]		Codjia BEN
17-10	UAE	W	1-0	Abu Dhabi	Fr	Belaid [29]		
17-11	Namibia	W	2-0	Radès/Tunis	Fr	Yahia [57], Jomaa [76]		
21-11	Austria	D	0-0	Vienna	Fr		13 800	Olsiak SVK
2008								
6-01	Zambia	L	1-2	Radès/Tunis	Fr	Chikhaoui [47]		
8-01	Zambia	W	1-0	Radès/Tunis	Fr	Chikhaoui [72]		
23-01	Senegal	D	2-2	Tamale	CNr1	Jomaa [9], Traoui [82]		Nichimura JPN
27-01	South Africa	W	3-1	Tamale	CNr1	Santos 2 [8 34], Ben Saada [32]		Djaoupe TOG
31-01	Angola	D	0-0	Tamale	CNr1			Codjia BEN
4-02	Cameroon	L	2-3	Tamale	CNqf	Ben Saada [35], Chikhaoui [81]		Coulibaly MLI
26-03	Côte d'Ivoire	W	2-0	Bondoufle	Fr	Belaid [58], Felhi [83]		
1-06	Burkina Faso	L	1-2	Radès/Tunis	WCq	Belaid [38]	15 000	Ambaya LBY
7-06	Seychelles	W	2-0	Victoria	WCq	Jomaa [9], Ben Saada [43]	2 033	Faduco MOZ
15-06	Burundi	W	1-0	Bujumbura	WCq	Jaidi [70]	7 000	Damon RSA
21-06	Burundi	W	2-1	Radès/Tunis	WCq	Ben Saada [21p], Jomaa [44]	6 000	Younis EGY
20-08	Angola	D	1-1	Monastir	Fr	Chermite [45]		
6-09	Burkina Faso	D	0-0	Ouagadougou	WCq		10 000	Katjimune NAM
11-10	Seychelles	W	5-0	Radès/Tunis	WCq	Essifi 2 [5 68], Mikari [18], Frej [20], Khalfallah [43]		
14-10	France	L	1-3	Paris	Fr	Jomaa [30]	74 564	Genov BUL
19-11	Ghana	D	0-0	Accra	Fr			
2009								
11-02	Netherlands	D	1-1	Radès/Tunis	Fr	Saihi [66]	17 000	Abd El Fatah EGY
28-03	Kenya	W	2-1	Nairobi	WCq	Jemal [6], Jomaa [79]	27 000	Evehe CMR
28-05	Sudan	W	4-0	Radès/Tunis	Fr	Darragi [11], Allagui [17], Jaidi [20], Falhi [55]		Ragab LBY
6-06	Mozambique	W	2-0	Radès/Tunis	WCq	Ben Yahia [21p], Darragi [89]	30 000	Djaoupe TOG
20-06	Nigeria	D	0-0	Radès/Tunis	WCq		45 000	Coulibaly MLI
12-08	Côte d'Ivoire	D	0-0	Sousse	Fr			
6-09	Nigeria	D	2-2	Abuja	WCq	Nabil [24], Darragi [89]	52 000	Bennett RSA
11-10	Kenya	W	1-0	Radès/Tunis	WCq	Jomaa [1]	50 000	Diatta SEN
14-10	Saudi Arabia	L	0-1	Radès/Tunis	Fr			
14-11	Mozambique	L	0-1	Maputo	WCq		30 000	Doue CIV
2010								
9-01	Gambia	L	1-2	Radès/Tunis	Fr	Chermite [94+]		
13-01	Zambia	D	1-1	Lubango	CNr1	Dhaouadi [40]	17 000	Coulibaly MLI
17-01	Gabon	D	0-0	Lubango	CNr1		16 000	Codjia BEN
21-01	Cameroon	D	2-2	Lubango	CNr1	Chermiti [1], Chedjou OG [63]	19 000	Doue CIV
30-05	France	D	1-1	Radès/Tunis	Fr	Jomaa [6]	55 000	El Raay LBY
20-06	Sudan	W	6-2	Omdurman	Fr	Ben Yahia [10], Allagui [37], Haggui [46p], Jomaa 2 [55 57], Akaichi [70]		
1-07	Botswana	L	0-1	Tunis	CNq			Diatta SEN
11-08	Chad	W	3-1	N'Djamena	CNq	Korbi [9], Ben Khalfallah 2 [43 81]		Doue CIV
4-09	Malawi	D	2-2	Rades	CNq	Jomaa 2 [11 26]		Lamptey GHA
10-10	Togo	W	2-1	Lomé	CNq	Jomaa [34], Chermiti [90]		Abdul Rahman SUD
17-11	Botswana	L	0-1	Gaborone	CNq			Kaoma ZAM

Fr = Friendly match • CN = CAF African Cup of Nations • WC = FIFA World Cup • q = qualifier • r1 = first round group • qf = quarter-final

TUNISIA NATIONAL TEAM HISTORICAL RECORDS

Past Coaches

Rachid Turki 1956-57 • Hachemi Cherif 1957-60 • Milan Kristic YUG 1960-61 • Frane Matosic YUG 1961-63 • Andre Gerard FRA 1963-65 • Mokhtar Ben Nacef 1965-68 • Rado Radocijic YUG 1968-69 • Beogovic Sereta YUG 1969 • Rado Radocijic YUG 1970 • Hameur Hizem 1970-74 • Andre Nagy HUN 1974-75 • Abdelmajid Chetali 1975-78 • Hameur Hizem 1978-79 • Ahmed Dhib 1979-80 • Hameur Hizem 1980-81 • Ryszard Kulesza POL 1981-83 • Youssef Zouaoui 1984-86 • Jean Vincent FRA 1986-87 • Taoufik Ben Othman 1987-88 • Antoni Piechniczek POL 1988 • Mokhtar Tlili 1988-89 • Antoni Piechniczek POL 1989 • Mrad Moujab 1989-93 • Youssef Zouaoui 1993-94 • Faouzi Benzarti 1994 • Henryk Kasperczak POL 1994-98 • Francesco Scoglio ITA 1998-01 • Eckhard Krautzun GER 2001 • Henri Michel FRA 2001-02 • Ammar Souayah 2002 • Youssef Zouaoui 2002 • Roger Lemerre FRA 2002-08 • Humberto Coelho POR 2008-09 • Faouzi Benzarti 2009-10 • Sami Trabelsi 2010 • Bertrand Marchand FRA 2010 • Faouzi Benzarti 2010-2011 • Ammar Souayah 2011-

TUNISIA 2009-10

LIGUE NATIONALE A

	Pl	W	D	L	F	A	Pts	Espérance	Club Africain	Etoile	Bizertin	Stade	Sfaxien	Olympique	Kairouan	Hammam Lif	Zarzis	Gafsa	H-Sousse	Kasserine	Monastir
Espérance Tunis †	26	16	6	4	56	24	54		1-1	0-0	2-4	1-0	4-0	1-0	4-0	3-3	7-0	3-0	1-2	4-0	2-0
Club Africain †	26	14	8	4	28	15	50	0-0		3-0	2-0	1-1	1-0	2-2	1-0	1-0	1-0	1-0	1-0	2-0	2-1
Etoile du Sahel ‡	26	13	7	6	41	27	46	0-1	2-2		3-1	0-0	2-1	3-0	2-0	0-0	1-1	3-0	3-2	2-3	2-1
CA Bizertin	26	11	7	8	36	33	40	2-2	1-0	2-1		0-1	1-1	1-0	3-2	1-3	2-0	1-1	1-0	0-0	2-2
Stade Tunisien	26	10	9	7	22	16	39	4-2	0-0	0-1	1-2		0-0	1-0	0-0	0-1	0-0	2-0	1-2	3-0	1-0
CS Sfaxien	26	10	7	9	32	26	37	1-3	1-2	2-0	4-2	2-1		2-1	1-0	1-1	0-1	3-0	2-0	6-1	1-1
Olympique Béjà ‡	26	8	8	10	28	32	32	0-1	0-1	1-1	1-1	0-0	0-0		3-1	2-1	1-0	0-0	1-1	3-1	2-0
JS Kairouan	26	9	4	13	22	34	31	1-3	1-0	2-1	0-3	0-1	0-1	1-2		1-0	1-0	2-2	0-0	1-0	2-1
CS Hammam Lif	26	8	6	12	30	32	30	1-3	1-2	1-2	1-0	0-1	2-0	1-2	0-1		0-0	3-2	2-3	2-0	0-0
Espérance Zarzis	26	6	11	9	17	26	29	0-1	0-0	1-3	0-0	1-2	0-0	2-2	1-1	2-0		1-0	1-1	2-0	1-1
EGS Gafsa	26	7	7	12	29	39	28	1-3	0-0	1-1	3-2	2-0	0-2	4-1	1-0	2-4	1-1		2-0	3-0	0-1
ES Hammam-Sousse	26	7	6	13	28	36	27	2-2	2-0	1-5	0-1	1-1	1-0	4-1	3-4	0-1	1-0	1-1		1-2	0-0
AS Kasserine	26	8	3	15	22	46	27	1-0	2-1	1-2	2-1	0-1	1-0	0-2	0-1	2-1	0-1	**0-2**	2-1		2-2
US Monastir	26	5	11	10	25	30	26	1-2	0-1	0-1	1-2	0-0	1-1	2-1	1-0	1-1	1-1	4-1	1-0	2-2	

26/07/2009 - 15/05/2010 • † Qualified for the CAF Champions League • ‡ Qualified for the CAF Confederation Cup • Match in bold awarded
Top scorers: **12** - Mickeal Eneramo NGA, Espérance • **11** - Ahmed Akaichi, Etoile & Sabeur Khlifa, Hammam-Lif

TUNISIA 2009-10
LIGUE NATIONAL B (2)

	Pl	W	D	L	F	A	Pts
AS Marsa	26	19	2	5	44	17	59
AS Gabés	26	15	7	4	42	23	52
Stade Gabésien	26	13	6	7	29	19	45
ES Béni Khalled	26	13	4	9	30	23	43
CS Masakin	26	12	3	11	32	32	39
LPTA Tozeur	26	11	4	11	29	30	37
Jendouba Sport	26	10	7	9	27	30	37
AS Djerba	26	10	5	11	34	30	35
US Ben Guerdane	26	8	10	8	25	27	34
Olympique Kef	26	8	6	12	29	34	30
EA Mateur	26	8	5	13	19	31	29
CS Korba	26	8	5	13	19	26	29
El Makarem Mahdia	26	8	4	14	21	29	28
SA Menzel Bourguiba	26	1	8	17	20	49	11

9/08/2009 - 7/05/2010

MEDALS TABLE

			Overall			League			Cup		Africa			City
			G	S	B	G	S	B	G	S	G	S	B	
1	Espérance Sportive de Tunis	EST	37	20	12	22	10	9	12	6	3	4	3	Tunis
2	Club Africain	CA	22	34	14	10	20	12	11	12	1	2	2	Tunis
3	Etoile Sportive du Sahel	ESS	21	28	15	8	15	15	7	8	6	5		Sousse
4	Club Sportif Sfaxien	CSS	14	8	6	7	1	5	4	5	3	2	1	Sfax
5	Stade Tunisien	ST	10	8	6	4	3	6	6	5				Tunis
6	Avenir Sportif de la Marsa	ASM	5	8	2		1	2	5	7				Marsa, Tunis
7	Club Athlétique Bizertin	CAB	4	3	2	1	2	1	2	1	1		1	Bizerte
8	Club Sportif de Hammam Lif	CSHL	3	1	2	1			2	1			1	Hammam Lif
9	Olympique de Béjà	OB	2	2					2	2				Béjà
10	Jeunesse Sportive Kairouan	JSK	1	2		1	1			1				Kairouan
	Sfax Railways Sport	SRS	1	2		1				2				Sfax
12	Club Olympique Transports	COT	1	1	2		1	2	1					Tunis
13	Espérance Sportive de Zarzis	ESZ	1							1				Zarzis
14	Stade Soussien	SS		2			1			1				Sousse
15	EM Mehdia	EMM	1							1				Mehdia
	Union Sportive Monastir	USMo	1							1				Monastir
17	US Tunisien	UST			2					2				Tunis

COUPE DE TUNISIE 2009-10

Round of 32

Team	Score
Olympique Béjà *	3
Stade Gabésien	0
SA Menzel Bourguiba *	2
ES Hammam-Sousse	1
CS Korba	3
US Ksour Sef *	0
US Siliana	0
US Ben Guerdane *	2
US Monastir	2 3p
JS Kairouan *	2 4p
CS Hammam Lif	0
ES Béni Khalled *	1
AS Djerba	3
El Makarem Mahdia *	0
Espérance Zarzis *	1
Stade Tunisien	2
Club Africain *	2 4p
El Ahly Mateur	2 2p
JS Soukra *	0
Stade Sfaxien	1
AS Kasserine *	2
Ahly Sfaxien	0
Etoile du Sahel	0 4p
AS Marsa *	0 5p
CA Bizertin *	0 4p
CS Masakin	0 3p
Stade Soussien	1
Jendouba Sport *	4
Espérance Tunis	2
EGS Gafsa *	0
AS Gabés	0
CS Sfaxien *	1

Round of 16

Team	Score
Olympique Béjà *	2
ES Hammam-Sousse	1
CS Korba	0
US Ben Guerdane *	1
US Monastir	4
ES Béni Khalled *	3
AS Djerba *	0
Stade Tunisien	1
Club Africain *	5
Stade Sfaxien	0
AS Kasserine	0 2p
AS Marsa *	0 3p
CA Bizertin	1
Jendouba Sport *	0
Espérance Tunis *	1
CS Sfaxien	2

Quarter-finals

Team	Score
Olympique Béjà *	1
US Ben Guerdane	0
US Monastir *	1
Stade Tunisien	2
Club Africain	3
AS Marsa *	1
CA Bizertin	0 2p
CS Sfaxien *	0 4p

Semi-finals

Team	Score
Olympique Béjà †	1
Stade Tunisien	0
Club Africain	2
CS Sfaxien †	4

Final

Team	Score
Olympique Béjà ‡	1
CS Sfaxien	0

CUP FINAL

Stade 7 noviembre, Rades
22-05-2010. Ref: Slim Jedidi
Scorer - Mehdi Hard 24p for Olympique

Olympique - Sami Nefzi - Rodrigue Mandongua, Ali Hammami●, Anis Matar Bacha, Nizar Nefzi (Kais Makhlouf 56), Ibrahima Camara, Saber Mehammedi, Nizar Guerbouj (Constand Mombley 72), Sameh Derhali (Khalil Jelassi 89), Mehdi Harb, Aymen Soltani. Tr: Rachid Belhout

Sfaxien - Jassem Khaloufi - Hamdi Rouid, Fateh Gharbi, Chaker Bergaoui, Mamane Issoufou●, Ali Maaloul (Heykel Guemamdia), Chadi Hammami, Ibrahima Toure (Uche Agba 77), Hamza Younes, Kamel Zaiem, Mahmoud Ben Salah. Tr: Luca Peruzovic

* Home team ● † Played at Rades ‡ Qualified for the CAF Confederation Cup

TUR – TURKEY

FIFA/COCA-COLA WORLD RANKING

1993	1994	1995	1996	1997	1998	1999	2000	2001	2002	2003	2004	2005	2006	2007	2008	2009	2010
52	48	30	31	43	57	29	30	23	9	8	14	11	26	16	10	41	31

						2010							Hi/Lo
Jan	Feb	Mar	Mar	Apr	May	Jul	Aug	Sep	Oct	Nov	Dec		5
41	42	41	35	33	29	28	28	21	29	29	31		67

2010 was an historic year for Turkish club football, a year in which the Istanbul monopoly on trophies was well and truly smashed. With Bursaspor winning the league and Trabzonsor lifting the cup, it meant that Istanbul ended the season trophyless for the first time since 1984 and for only the fifth time in total. Bursaspor's league triumph was particularly remarkable as they became only the fifth team to have been crowned champions in the 52-year history of the competition. Under former Besiktas coach Ertugrul Saglam, Bursapor clinched the title on the last day in dramatic fashion, overtaking Fenerbahçe who were held to a draw at home by Trabzonspor. Fenerbahçe, who had won their previous eight games, started the day a point ahead and even took the lead but a 2-1 victory for Bursaspor at home to Besiktas sparked wild celebrations across the Sea of Marmara in Bursa - only the third city in the country to boast a championship-winning side. It also marked the first time since 1976 that a club had won a maiden league title and the first time that four different clubs had won the title in as many years. Nine days earlier Trabzonspor had also ended Fenerbahçe's dreams of a first cup triumph in 27 years after a 3-1 victory in the final consigned the Istanbul club to a seventh runners-up spot since last winning it in 1983.

FIFA WORLD CUP RECORD

1930 DNE 1934 DNQ 1938 DNE **1950** Withdrew **1954** 9 r1 1958-1998 DNQ **2002** 3 SF 2006-2010 DNQ

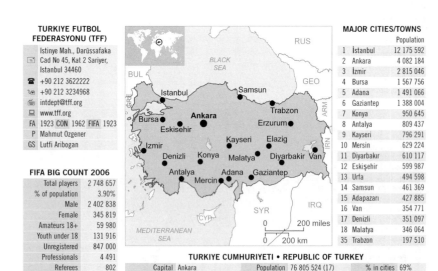

TURKIYE FUTBOL FEDERASYONU (TFF)

Istinye Mah., Darüssafaka
Cad No 45, Kat 2 Sariyer, Istanbul 34460
☎ +90 212 3622222
📠 +90 212 3234968
✉ intdept@tff.org
🖳 www.tff.org
FA 1923 CON 1962 FIFA 1923
P Mahmut Ozgener
GS Lutfi Aribogan

FIFA BIG COUNT 2006

Total players	2 748 657
% of population	3.90%
Male	2 402 838
Female	345 819
Amateurs 18+	59 980
Youth under 18	131 916
Unregistered	847 000
Professionals	4 491
Referees	802
Admin & coaches	20 725
Number of clubs	4 298
Number of teams	9 823

MAJOR CITIES/TOWNS

		Population
1	İstanbul	12 175 592
2	Ankara	4 082 184
3	İzmir	2 815 046
4	Bursa	1 567 756
5	Adana	1 491 066
6	Gaziantep	1 388 004
7	Konya	950 645
8	Antalya	809 437
9	Kayseri	796 291
10	Mersin	629 224
11	Diyarbakır	610 117
12	Eskişehir	599 987
13	Urfa	494 598
14	Samsun	461 369
15	Adapazarı	427 885
16	Van	354 771
17	Denizli	351 097
18	Malatya	346 064
35	Trabzon	197 510

TURKIYE CUMHURIYETI • REPUBLIC OF TURKEY

Capital	Ankara	Population	76 805 524 (17)	% in cities	69%
GDP per capita	$11 200 (100)	Area km²	783 562 km² (37)	GMT + / -	+2
Neighbours (km)	Armenia 268, Azerbaijan 9, Bulgaria 240, Georgia 252, Greece 206, Iran 499, Iraq 352, Syria 822 • Coast 7200				

RECENT INTERNATIONAL MATCHES PLAYED BY TURKEY

2008	Opponents	Score		Venue	Comp	Scorers	Att	Referee
6-02	Sweden	D	0-0	Istanbul	Fr		20 000	Tagliavento ITA
26-03	Belarus	D	2-2	Minsk	Fr	Tuncay Sanli 38, Tumer Metin 71	12 000	Malzinskas LTU
20-05	Slovakia	W	1-0	Bielefeld	Fr	Hakan Balta 63	13 100	Weiner GER
25-05	Uruguay	L	2-3	Bochum	Fr	Arda Turan 13, Nihat Kahveci 51		Meyer GER
29-05	Finland	W	2-0	Duisburg	Fr	Tuncay Sanli 15, Semih Senturk 88	15 036	Kinhofer GER
7-06	Portugal	L	0-2	Geneva	ECr1		29 016	Fandel GER
11-06	Switzerland	W	2-1	Basel	ECr1	Semih Senturk 57, Arda Turan 92+	39 730	Michel SVK
15-06	Czech Republic	W	3-2	Geneva	ECr1	Arda Turan 75, Nihat Kahveci 2 87 89	29 016	Fröjdfeldt SWE
20-06	Croatia	D	1-1	Vienna	ECqf	Semih Senturk 122+. W 3-1p	51 428	Rosetti ITA
25-06	Germany	L	2-3	Basel	ECsf	Ugur Boral 22, Semih Senturk 86	39 378	Busacca SUI
20-08	Chile	W	1-0	Izmit	Fr	Halil Altintop 75		Kakos GRE
6-09	Armenia	W	2-0	Yerevan	WCq	Tuncay Sanli 61, Semih Senturk 77	30 000	Ovrebo NOR
10-09	Belgium	D	1-1	Istanbul	WCq	Emre Belozoglu 74p	34 097	Lannoy FRA
11-10	Bosnia-Herzegovina	W	2-1	Istanbul	WCq	Arda Turan 51, Mevlut Erdinc 66	23 628	Kassai HUN
15-10	Estonia	D	0-0	Tallinn	WCq		6 500	Malek POL
19-11	Austria	W	4-2	Vienna	Fr	Mehmet Aurelio 38, Tuncay Sanli 3 41 47 62	23 100	Grafe GER
2009								
11-02	Côte d'Ivoire	D	1-1	Izmir	Fr	Gokhan Unal 11		Corpodean ROU
28-03	Spain	L	0-1	Madrid	WCq		73 820	Busacca SUI
1-04	Spain	L	1-2	Istanbul	WCq	Semih Senturk 26	19 617	Riley ENG
2-06	Azerbaijan	W	2-0	Kayseri	Fr	Halil Altintop 70, Ibrahim Uzulmez 75		Vlk SVK
5-06	France	L	0-1	Lyon	Fr		32 000	Grafe GER
12-08	Ukraine	W	3-0	Kyiv	Fr	Tuncay Sanli 58, Servet Cetin 63, Hamit Altintop 65		Ceferin SVN
5-09	Estonia	W	4-2	Kayseri	WCq	Tuncay Sanli 2 27 72, Sercan Yildirim 37, Arda Turan 62	28 569	Skjerven NOR
9-09	Bosnia-Herzegovina	D	1-1	Zenica	WCq	Emre Belozoglu 4	14 000	Benquerença POR
10-10	Belgium	L	0-2	Brussels	WCq		30 131	Trefoloni ITA
14-10	Armenia	W	2-0	Bursa	WCq	Halil Altintop 16, Servet Cetin 28	16 200	Hansson SWE
2010								
3-03	Honduras	W	2-0	Istanbul	Fr	Emre Gungor 41, Hamit Altintop 55	17 000	Olsiak SVK
22-05	Czech Republic	W	2-1	Harrison	Fr	Arda Turan 31, Nihat Kahveci 48	16 371	Geiger USA
26-05	Northern Ireland	W	2-0	New Britain	Fr	Sercan Yildirim 48, Semih Senturk 72	4 000	Vaughn USA
29-05	USA	L	1-2	Philadelphia	Fr	Arda Turan 27	55 407	Petrescu CAN
11-08	Romania	W	2-0	Istanbul	Fr	Emre Belozoglu 4	15 000	Mazic SRB
3-09	Kazakhstan	W	3-0	Astana	ECq	Arda Turan 24, Hamit Altintop 26, Nihat Kahveci 76	15 800	Vad HUN
7-09	Belgium	W	3-2	Istanbul	ECq	Hamit Altintop 48, Semih Senturk 66, Arda Turan 78	43 538	Skomina SVN
8-10	Germany	L	0-3	Berlin	ECq		74 244	Webb ENG
12-10	Azerbaijan	L	0-1	Baku	ECq		29 500	Deaconu ROU
17-11	Netherlands	L	0-1	Amsterdam	Fr		35 500	Kassai HUN

Fr = Friendly match • EC = UEFA EURO 2008/2012 • WC = FIFA World Cup • q = qualifier
r1 = first round group • qf = quarter-final • sf = semi-final

TURKEY NATIONAL TEAM HISTORICAL RECORDS

Caps
119 - Rustu Recber 1994-2009 • 112 - Hakan Sukur 1992-2008 • 102 - Bulent Korkmaz 1990-2005 • 94 - Tugay Kerimoglu 1990-2007 • 90 - Alpay Ozlan 1995-2005 • 79 - Tuncay Sanli 2002- • 76 - Ogun Temizkanoglu 1990-2002 • 74 - Emre Belozoglu • 71 - Abdullah Ercan 1992-2003 • 70 - Oguz Cetin 1988-98 • 69 - Nihat Kahveci 2000- • 64 - Hamit Akyel 1997-2004 • 62 - Hamit Altintop 2004- • 60 - Arif Erdem 1994-2003 • 56 - Recep Cetin 1988-97 • 54 - Okan Buruk 1992-2005 • 53 - Cetin Servet 2003- • 51 - Fatih Terim 1975-84

Goals
51 - Hakan Sukur 1992-2008 • 22 - Tuncay Sanli 2002- • 21 - Lefter Kucukandonyadis 1948-61 • 19 - Nihat Kahveci 2000- ; Oktay Metin 1956-65 & Turan Cemil 1969-79 • 15 - Zeki-Riza Sporel 1923-32 • 11 - Arif Erdem 1994-2003 & Ertugrul Saglam 1993-97

Past Coaches
Ali Sami Yen 1923 • Billy Hunter SCO 1924-26 • Bela Toth HUN 1927-32 • Fred Pagnam ENG 1932 • James Elliot ENG 1936-37 • Ignac Molnar HUN 1948 • Ulvi Yenal 1948 • Pat Molloy ENG 1948-49 • Cihat Arman 1949 • Pat Molloy ENG 1950 • Jimmy McCormick ENG 1950-51 • Rebii Erkal 1951 • Sadri Usuoglu 1952 • Sandro Puppo ITA 1952-54 • Gunduz Kilic 1954 • Zarko Mihajlovic YUG 1955 • Giovanni Varglien ITA 1955-56 • Cihat Arman 1956 • Laszlo Szekely HUN 1957 • Leandro Remondini ITA 1958-59 • Ignac Molnar HUN 1960 • Sandro Puppo ITA 1960-62 • Seref Gorkey 1962 • Ljubisa Spajic YUG 1962 • Sandro Puppo ITA 1963-64 • Cihat Arman 1964 • Sandro Puppo ITA 1965 • Dogan Andac 1965 • Sandro Puppo ITA 1965-66 • Adnan Suvari 1966-69 • Abdullah Gegic 1969 • Cihat Arman 1970-71 • Nicolae Petrescu ROU 1971 • Dogan Andac 1972-76 • Dogan Andac 1976 • Metin Turel 1977-78 • Sabri Kiraz 1978-80 • Ozkan Sumer 1980-81 • Fethi Demircan 1981 • Coskun Ozari 1982-84 • Candan Tarhan 1984 • Yilmaz Gokdel 1984-85 • Kalman Meszoly HUN 1985 • Coskun Ozari 1985-86 • Mustafa Denizli 1987 • Tinaz Tirpan 1988-89 • Fatih Terim 1990 • Sepp Piontek GER 1990-93 • Fatih Terim 1993-96 • Mustafa Denizli 1996-2000 • Senol Gunes 2000-04 • Unal Karaman 2004 • Ersun Yanal 2004-05 • Fatih Terim 2005-09 • Oguz Cetin 2010 • Guus Hiddink NED 2010-

TURKEY 2009–10

TURKCELL SUPER LIG

Team	Pl	W	D	L	F	A	Pts	Bursaspor	Fenerbahçe	Galatasaray	Besiktas	Trabzonspor	Istanbul BB	Eskisehirspor	Kayserispor	Antalyaspor	Gençlerbirligi	Kasimpasa	Ankaragücü	Gaziantepspor	Manisaspor	Sivasspor	Diyarbakirspor	Denizlispor	Ankaraspor
Bursaspor †	34	23	6	5	65	26	75		0-1	1-0	2-1	1-1	6-0	3-1	2-0	2-1	1-2	2-1	1-0	2-0	2-0	3-0	4-0	2-1	3-0
Fenerbahçe †	34	23	5	6	61	28	74	2-3		3-1	1-0	1-1	1-0	2-0	2-0	1-0	3-0	1-3	3-2	1-0	2-1	3-0	1-1	3-1	3-0
Galatasaray ‡	34	19	7	8	61	35	64	0-0	0-1		3-0	4-3	1-1	1-1	4-1	1-2	1-0	4-1	3-0	1-0	1-1	2-0	4-1	4-1	3-0
Besiktas ‡	34	18	10	6	47	25	64	2-3	3-0	1-1		0-0	2-0	3-2	0-1	2-0	4-1	2-1	1-0	0-0	2-0	2-2	0-0	1-0	3-0
Trabzonspor ‡	34	16	9	9	53	32	57	1-1	0-1	1-0	0-2		0-0	2-1	2-1	3-1	3-1	2-0	3-0	0-0	3-0	3-1	1-2	2-1	3-0
Istanbul BB	34	16	8	10	47	44	56	2-1	2-1	0-1	1-1	1-6		0-0	1-2	1-0	1-3	4-2	1-1	1-1	1-1	1-0	1-0	3-1	3-0
Eskisehirspor	34	15	10	9	44	34	55	3-2	2-1	2-1	0-1	1-0	2-1		0-1	2-1	0-0	2-0	0-0	3-2	1-0	1-1	0-0	2-0	3-0
Kayserispor	34	14	9	11	45	37	51	3-0	1-1	0-0	1-2	1-0	1-1	1-2		1-2	1-1	0-0	3-0	1-1	1-2	2-2	2-0	2-0	3-0
Antalyaspor	34	14	7	13	49	38	49	1-1	1-2	2-3	0-1	1-1	1-3	1-2	4-0		2-0	2-0	1-0	1-0	0-0	3-0	4-1	2-1	0-1
Gençlerbirligi	34	12	11	11	38	35	47	0-0	0-0	2-1	0-0	2-2	3-1	2-2	0-0	0-4		0-2	0-1	1-1	2-0	1-0	2-0	2-0	3-0
Kasimpasa	34	10	11	13	50	53	41	0-2	0-1	1-3	2-2	3-1	1-3	1-3	1-1	2-2	2-2		0-4	2-0	3-0	3-1	2-2	1-0	3-0
MKE Ankaragücü	34	9	14	11	39	40	41	0-1	0-3	3-0	0-0	1-0	2-2	3-1	3-0	2-2	1-2	2-2		0-0	1-1	2-3	0-0	1-0	3-0
Gaziantepspor	34	9	13	12	38	39	40	0-1	2-1	2-3	0-0	1-1	2-3	1-0	1-1	1-1	1-1	1-0	1-3		0-0	2-2	2-1	2-1	1-1
Manisaspor	34	8	13	13	27	34	37	0-2	2-2	1-2	1-1	1-0	0-0	0-0	1-2	0-0	0-0	0-0	0-1	0-0		3-1	2-1	0-0	3-0
Sivasspor	34	8	10	16	42	59	34	1-3	1-5	1-1	0-1	1-2	0-1	2-1	2-4	2-0	0-2	1-1	3-3	3-0	1-0		0-2	2-0	3-0
Diyarbakirspor	34	6	9	19	28	54	27	0-3	1-3	1-2	1-3	1-2	1-3	0-2	0-3	1-0	1-0	2-2	2-2	1-3	0-0	1-1		0-2	3-0
Denizlispor	34	6	8	20	30	49	26	2-3	0-2	1-0	0-1	0-1	0-1	0-1	1-0	1-0	1-1	2-0	3-3	0-0	1-1	1-1	1-0		3-0
Ankaraspor	34	0	0	34	0	102	0	0-3	0-3	0-3	0-2	0-3	0-3	0-3	0-3	0-3	0-3	0-3	1-1	0-3	0-3	0-3	0-3	0-3	

7/08/2009 - 16/05/2010 • † Qualified for the UEFA Champions League • ‡ Qualified for the Europa League • Ankaraspor relegated after four games. All their matches were awarded as 3-0 wins for their opponents
Top scorers: 21 - Ariza Makukula POR, Kayserispor • 13 - Julio Cesar BRA, Gaziantepspor • 12 - Bobo BRA, Besiktas & Necati Ates, Antalyaspor

PROMOTIONPLAY-OFFS

Team	Pl	W	D	L	F	A	Pts	Ko	Al	Ka	Ad
Konyaspor	3	2	1	0	6	3	7			1-0	3-1
Altay Izmir	3	1	2	0	4	3	5	2-2			2-1
Karsiyaka	3	0	2	1	2	3	2		0-0		
Adanaspor	3	0	1	2	4	7	1			2-2	

16/08/2004 - 15/05/2005

MEDALS TABLE

#	Team	Overall G	Overall S	Overall B	League G	League S	League B	Cup G	Cup S	Cup B	Europe G	Europe S	Europe B
1	Galatasaray	32	14	17	17	9	16	14	5		1		1
2	Fenerbahçe	21	26	6	17	17	6	4	9				
3	Besiktas	19	20	8	11	14	8	8	6				
4	Trabzonspor	14	12	6	6	7	6	8	5				
5	Altay Izmir	2	5	2				2	5				
6	Gençlerbirligi	2	3	2				2	2	3			
7	Bursaspor	2	3		1			1	3				
	MKE Ankaragücü	2	3					2	3				

TURKEY 2009–10

BANK ASYA 1.LIG (2)

Team	Pl	W	D	L	F	A	Pts	Karabükspor	Bucaspor	Adanaspor	Altay Izmir	Karsiyaka	Konyaspor	Giresunspor	Orduspor	Boluspor	Samsunspor	Erciyesspor	Gaziantep BB	Mersin IY	Kartalspor	Rizespor	Hacettepe	Dardanelspor	Kocaelispor
Karabükspor	34	23	8	3	74	28	77		3-0	1-0	3-0	3-0	4-1	1-0	1-1	2-1	2-1	4-2	2-2	0-0	3-0	3-0	4-2	1-0	1-0
Bucaspor	34	19	7	8	69	40	64	1-2		4-1	2-1	3-2	3-1	1-0	3-2	2-2	3-0	4-0	0-0	1-3	1-1	6-1	2-1	2-1	4-0
Adanaspor †	34	18	10	6	42	30	64	3-1	0-3		2-2	1-0	0-0	2-0	1-0	2-1	2-0	1-1	1-0	3-2	1-0	3-4	1-0	2-1	1-0
Altay Izmir †	34	17	8	9	48	36	59	1-1	1-1	0-1		0-2	4-1	1-4	1-1	3-0	1-0	1-0	0-0	1-0	0-1	0-0	2-0	3-2	1-0
Karsiyaka †	34	17	5	12	48	35	56	0-0	2-0	1-1	1-4		2-2	0-1	0-0	2-1	1-2	3-0	0-1	3-0	0-1	3-0	0-1	2-1	2-0
Konyaspor †	34	15	10	9	42	37	55	1-0	3-2	0-0	2-0	0-1		2-1	1-1	1-1	0-1	1-2	0-1	1-0	2-0	2-1	1-1	0-2	3-0
Giresunspor	34	15	6	13	51	42	51	0-0	0-2	0-1	3-4	0-1	3-2		1-1	1-1	3-2	2-1	0-1	2-1	1-2	3-0	0-1	3-0	3-1
Orduspor	34	11	11	12	33	32	44	3-1	0-0	1-2	0-2	1-0	1-1	0-1		0-1	1-3	0-1	2-1	0-2	0-0	1-0	0-0	1-0	1-0
Boluspor	34	12	7	15	48	53	43	1-1	4-1	3-1	2-0	0-4	0-1	2-1	2-4		0-2	1-2	0-0	2-1	5-2	2-1	1-2	2-1	2-2
Samsunspor	34	12	6	16	49	47	42	3-3	0-3	0-0	1-2	0-0	1-0	0-3	1-3	3-0		1-1	0-1	1-3	2-0	2-0	4-1	1-2	4-0
Kayseri Erciyesspor	34	10	11	13	42	53	41	1-2	0-3	0-0	1-2	2-2	0-0	1-1	3-2	2-0	1-5		3-0	1-0	1-1	3-1	3-1	2-4	2-2
Gaziantep BB	34	11	8	15	31	38	41	0-4	1-2	0-2	0-0	2-0	0-1	0-2	0-0	0-4	0-1	3-0		2-0	1-0	3-0	0-1	1-2	1-1
Mersin Idman Yurdu	34	11	8	15	36	44	41	1-6	1-0	1-2	1-1	0-2	3-1	4-1	0-1	2-1	1-2	0-0	0-0		2-0	0-0	1-0	1-2	3-0
Kartalspor	34	11	8	15	32	43	41	0-1	3-0	2-4	1-0	2-0	0-0	1-1	1-0	2-1	2-3	0-2	1-0	0-0		2-0	2-1	1-0	2-1
Caykur Rizespor	34	10	10	14	37	53	40	0-3	0-0	0-0	1-1	0-2	2-1	2-1	0-2	2-1	2-2	2-0	1-2	4-0	2-1		1-1	3-3	1-1
Hacettepe	34	10	8	16	38	50	38	2-4	2-2	0-0	1-3	4-1	0-1	1-1	0-3	0-1	1-0	4-2	2-5	1-1	3-1	0-0		2-1	1-0
Dardanelspor	34	10	5	19	37	53	35	0-2	0-3	0-0	0-3	1-5	1-2	3-2	1-0	0-0	2-2	0-1	1-1	0-1	1-0	0-1	1-0		2-1
Kocaelispor	34	2	8	24	23	66	14	1-5	2-4	0-0	2-3	1-2	0-2	1-2	0-2	1-2	0-4	1-1	3-1	1-0	0-0	1-3	1-1	0-2	

22/08/2009 - 9/05/2010 • † Qualified for the promotion play-offs

TURKIYE KUPASI 2009-10

Second Round

Antalyaspor	2	7p
Mersin Idman Yurdu*	2	6p
Ankaraspor	2	
Tokatspor*	3	
Altay Izmir*	4	
Samsunspor	0	
Yalovaspor*	1	
Eskisehirspor	3	
Galatasaray*	2	
Bucaspor	1	
Karsiyaka Izmir*	2	
MKE Ankaragücü	3	
Orduspor*	1	
Belediye Vanspor	0	
Kastamonuspor	1	
Denizli BSK *	2	
Bursaspor	1	
Güngören BS *	0	
Gaziantepspor	1	
Denizlispor *	4	
Giresunspor*	2	
Caykur Rizespor	1	
Diyarbakir *	0	
Tarsus Idman Yurdu	1	
Istanbul BB *	1	4p
Genclerbirligi	1	2p
Kayserispor *	0	2p
Manisaspor	0	4p
Kasimpasa *	4	
Kayseri Erciyesspor	1	
Adanaspor	2	
Konya Sekerspor *	3	

Third round groups

Group 1

	Pl	W	D	L	F	A	Pts	Fe	An	To	Al	Es
Fenerbahçe	4	3	0	1	10	6	9		3-2	3-0		1-0
Antalyaspor	4	2	0	2	6	4	8	4-3		1-1		1-2
Tokatspor*	4	1	1	2	6	7	4					
Altay Izmir	4	1	1	2	2	9	4			0-0		0-5
Eskisehirspor	4	1	0	3	6	4	3	0-1	1-2			

Group 2

	Pl	W	D	L	F	A	Pts	Ga	Tr	MKE	Or	De
Galatasaray	4	3	1	0	10	2	10			2-1	6-0	
Trabzonspor	4	3	0	1	11	3	9			2-1	5-1	
MKE Ankaragücü	4	2	1	1	4	3	7				0-2	
Orduspor	4	1	0	3	4	8	3	0-3		1-2		
Denizili BSK	4	0	0	4	2	15	0					

Group 3

	Pl	W	D	L	F	A	Pts	Bu	De	Si	Gi	TIy
Bursaspor	4	3	1	0	9	3	10			4-0		2-1
Denizlispor	4	2	2	0	4	2	8	1-1		0-0		1-0
Sivasspor	4	2	1	1	5	7	7				4-3	1-0
Giresunspor	4	1	0	3	6	8	3		1-2	0-1		1-2
Tarsus Idman Yurdu	4	0	0	4	3	7	0					

Group 4

	Pl	W	D	L	F	A	Pts	Is	Ma	Ka	Be	KS
Istanbul BB	4	3	1	0	4	0	10			1-0	1-0	
Manisaspor	4	2	2	0	5	2	8			0-0		2-1
Kasimpasa	4	1	1	2	6	8	4					
Besiktas	4	1	0	3	6	8	3		1-3			1-3
Konya Sekerspor	4	1	0	3	4	7	3	0-0		0-1	2-1	

Quarter-finals

Trabzonspor	1	1
Istanbul BB *	1	0
Galatasaray	1	3
Antalyaspor *	2	2
Manisaspor *	4	1
Denizlispor	1	0
Bursaspor	0	3
Fenerbahçe *	3	1

Semi-finals

Trabzonspor *	2	0
Antalyaspor	0	1
Manisaspor	0	1
Fenerbahçe *	2	1

Final

Trabzonspor ‡	3
Fenerbahçe	1

CUP FINAL

Sanliurfa GAP, Sanliurfa
5-05-2010. Ref: Cuneyt Cakir
Scorers – Umut 66, Engin 80, Colman 94+ for Trabzon; Alex 55 for Fenerbahçe

Trabzon – Onur Kivrak• – Serkan Balci•, Egemen Korkmaz•, Rigobert Song (c), Hrvoje Cale – Burak Yilmaz•, Gustavo Colman, Selcuk Inan (Sezer Badur 83), Engin Baytar (Ceyhun Gulselam 86) – Alanzinho (Remzi Giray Kacar 91), Umut Bulut. Tr: Senol Gunes

Fenerbahçe – Volkan Demirel – Gokhan Gonul (Gokhan Unal 87), Diego Lugano, Fabio Bilica•, Gokcek Vederson – Emre Belozoglu• (Deivid de Souza 68), Selcuk Sahin – Mehmet Topuz, Alex (c), Ozer Hurmaci – Daniel Guiza. Tr: Christoph Daum

Galatasaray, Fenerbahçe, Besiktas and Sivasspor entered at the group stage • * Home team in the first leg • ‡ Qualified for the Europa League

2a+4

UAE – UNITED ARAB EMIRATES

FIFA/COCA-COLA WORLD RANKING

1993	1994	1995	1996	1997	1998	1999	2000	2001	2002	2003	2004	2005	2006	2007	2008	2009	2010
51	46	75	60	50	42	54	64	60	89	75	82	85	87	100	110	112	105

2010												Hi/Lo
Jan	Feb	Mar	Mar	Apr	May	Jul	Aug	Sep	Oct	Nov	Dec	42
112	113	115	102	100	101	88	90	90	99	104	105	124

At face value, the United Arab Emirates' showing at the 2011 AFC Asian Cup finals in Qatar in January would suggest that the country has made little or no progress in recent years. The Srecko Katanec-coached national side finished bottom of their group in the tournament, failing to score a goal and picking up just a point in a draw with North Korea before losing to both Iran and Iraq. However, the nature of the performances and the youthful make-up of much of their squad will have the decision-makers in Abu Dhabi and Dubai quietly confident that the game in the Emirates is moving in the right direction. Youngsters such as midfielder Amer Abdulrahman and Ahmed Khalil impressed at the tournament just months after the country's under-23 side reached the final of the football tournament at the Asian Games, where they lost narrowly to Japan in the gold medal match. With the game in the Middle East generally falling far behind the eastern half of the continent, it could be that the UAE presents the most likely spearhead for a western challenge in the future. In club football the UAE Pro League, won in 2010 by Al Wahda, continues to improve but the performance of the local clubs in the AFC Champions League continues to be a concern, with none of the nation's four participants reaching the knockout phase of the 2010 edition.

FIFA WORLD CUP RECORD
1930-1982 DNE   1986 DNQ   **1990** 24 r1   1994-2010 DNQ

UNITED ARAB EMIRATES FOOTBALL ASSOCIATION (UAEFA)

Wadi Al Amrdi Building, 271-574 Near Murshif Park, PO Box 916, Abu Dhabi
☎ +971 2 4445600
📠 +971 2 4448558
✉ info@uaefa.ae
🖥 www.uaefootball.ae
FA 1971 CON 1974 FIFA 1972
P Mohamed Al Rumaithi
GS Yousuf Mohd Abdullah

FIFA BIG COUNT 2006

Total players	82 776
% of population	3.18%
Male	82 776
Female	0
Youth under 18	6 689
Unregistered	11 000
Professionals	67
Referees	150
Admin & coaches	836
Number of clubs	31
Number of teams	156

MAJOR CITIES/TOWNS

		Population
1	Dubai	1 770 533
2	Abu Dhabi	896 751
3	Sharjah	845 617
4	Al Ain	651 904
5	Ajman	372 923
6	Ras Al Khaima	171 903
7	Al Fujairah	107 940
8	Umm al Quwain	69 936
9	Khor Fakkan	49 635

AL IMARAT AL ARABIYAH AL MUTTAHIDAH • UNITED ARAB EMIRATES

Capital Abu Dhabi	Population 4 798 491 (115)	% in cities 78%
GDP per capita $44 600 (12)	Area km² 83 600 km² (114)	GMT + / - +4
Neighbours (km) Oman 410, Saudi Arabia 457 • Coast 1318		

RECENT INTERNATIONAL MATCHES PLAYED BY THE UNITED ARAB EMIRATES

2009	Opponents	Score		Venue	Comp	Scorers	Att	Referee
5-01	Yemen	W	3-1	Muscat	GCr1	Mohamed Omar 6p, Ismael Al Hammadi 53, Mohamed Al Shehhi 67		
8-01	Qatar	D	0-0	Muscat	GCr1			
11-01	Saudi Arabia	L	0-3	Muscat	GCr1			
21-01	Malaysia	W	5-0	Kuala Lumpur	ACq	Mohamed Omar 2 29 45p, Ismael Matar 2 62 76, Ahmed Khalil 85	10 000	Williams AUS
28-01	Uzbekistan	L	0-1	Sharjah	ACq		15 000	Nishimura JPN
28-03	Korea DPR	L	0-2	Pyongyang	WCq		50 000	Breeze AUS
1-04	Saudi Arabia	L	2-3	Riyadh	WCq	Mohamed Al Shehhi 38, Ismael Matar 45	70 000	Mohd Salleh MAS
2-06	Germany	L	2-7	Dubai	Fr	Ismael Al Hammadi 53, Nawaf Mubarak 73	7 000	Darwish JOR
6-06	Korea Republic	L	0-2	Dubai	WCq		4 000	Balideh QAT
10-06	Iran	L	0-1	Tehran	WCq		38 000	Irmatov UZB
10-10	Palestine	D	1-1	Dubai	Fr	Saeed Al Kas 47		
14-10	Jordan	W	3-1	Dubai	Fr	Mohamed Al Shehhi 35, Ahmad Khamis 56, Mohammed Suroor 80p		
15-11	Czech Republic	D	0-0	Al Ain	Fr	W 3-2p	5 000	Dalkam JOR
18-11	Iraq	L	0-1	Al Ain	Fr			Osman EGY
16-12	Kuwait	D	0-0	Kuwait City	Fr			
2010								
6-01	Malaysia	W	1-0	Dubai	ACq	Ahmed Khalil 93+	3 500	Basma SYR
3-03	Uzbekistan	W	1-0	Tashkent	ACq	Sultan Al Menhali 93+	20 000	Shamsuzzaman BAN
29-05	Moldova	W	3-2	Anif	Fr	Fares Juma 26, Mohamed Al Shehhi 31, Ahmed Khalil 89	200	Schorgenhofer AUT
5-06	Algeria	L	0-1	Fürth	Fr		12 500	Grafe GER
7-09	Kuwait	W	3-0	Abu Dhabi	Fr	Ahmed Khalil 22, Ismael Matar 42, Saeed Al Kuthairi 91+		
9-10	Chile	L	0-2	Abu Dhabi	Fr		500	Al Ghamdi KSA
12-10	Angola	L	0-2	Abu Dhabi	Fr			
18-11	India	W	5-0	Dubai	Fr	Saeed Al Kas 15, Amir Mubarak 35, Ali Al Wehaibi 2 61 73, Ahmed Jumaa 72		
23-11	Iraq	D	0-0	Aden	GCr1			Al Qatani KSA
26-11	Oman	D	0-0	Aden	GCr1			Shaaban EGY
29-11	Bahrain	W	3-1	Aden	GCr1	Subait Khater 4, Fares Juma 8, Ahmed Juma 64		Al Marry BHR
2-12	Saudi Arabia	L	0-1	Aden	GCsf			Ogiya JPN
2011								
2-01	Syria	W	2-0	Al Ain	Fr	Saeed Al Kathiri 63, Theyab Awana 89	2 400	Abdul Baki OMA
5-01	Australia	D	0-0	Al Ain	Fr			Shaban KUW
11-01	Korea DPR	D	0-0	Doha	ACr1		3 639	Mohd Salleh MAS
15-01	Iraq	L	0-1	Al Rayyan	ACr1		7 233	Nishimura JPN
19-01	Iran	L	0-3	Doha	ACr1		5 012	Kim Dong Jin KOR

Fr = Friendly match • AC = AFC Asian Cup • GC = Gulf Cup • WC = FIFA World Cup • q = qualifier • r1 = first round group • sf = semi-final

UAE NATIONAL TEAM HISTORICAL RECORDS

Caps
162 - Adnan Al Talyani 1984-97 • 115 - Abdulraheem Jumaa 1998- • 112 - Zuhair Bilal 1988-2002 • 110 - Abdulsalam Jumaa 1997- • 106 - Mushin Faraj 1988-99

Goals
53 - Adnan Al Talyani 1984-97 • 26 - Ismael Matar 2003-

Past Coaches
Mohammed Sheita EGY 1972-73 • Jumaa Gharib 1973 • Mohammed Sheita EGY 1973-74 • Mimi El Sherbini EGY 1975 • Jumaa Gharib 1975-76 • Dimitri Tadic YUG 1976 • Don Revie ENG 1977-80 • Heshmat Mohajerani IRN 1980-84 • Carlos Alberto Parreira BRA 1984-88 • Mario Zagallo BRA 1988-90 • Bernhard Blaut POL 1990 • Valery Lobanovsky UKR 1990-92 • Antoni Piechniczek POL 1992-95 • Tomislav Ivic CRO 1995-96 • Lori Sandri BRA 1997 • Milan Macala CZE 1997 • Lori Sandri BRA 1998 • Carlos Queiroz POR 1998-99 • Srecko Juricic CRO 1999 • Dr Abdullah Masfar 2000 • Henri Michel FRA 2000-01 • Abdullah Saqr 2001 • Tini Ruijs NED 2001 • Jo Bonfrere NED 2001-02 • Roy Hodgson ENG 2002-04 • Aad De Mos NED 2004-05 • Dick Advocaat NED Aug 2005 • Bruno Metsu FRA 2006-08 • Dominique Bathenay FRA 2008-09 • Srecko Katanec SVN 2009-

UNITED ARAB EMIRATES 2009-10

PRO LEAGUE

	Pl	W	D	L	F	A	Pts	Wahda	Jazeera	Ain	Bani-Yas	Wasl	Sharjah	Shabab	Ahli	Dhafra	Nasr	Emirates	Ajman
Al Wahda †	22	19	1	2	42	15	58		2-1	1-0	1-0	2-0	1-0	4-1	2-1	2-0	3-0	3-1	3-2
Al Jazeera †	22	15	6	1	48	26	51	1-0		2-2	5-3	2-1	1-1	2-1	1-0	2-2	2-0	3-2	2-1
Al Ain	22	14	3	5	57	29	45	0-1	0-1		3-1	1-3	2-1	4-0	5-1	1-1	2-0	5-3	3-2
Bani-Yas	22	10	6	6	44	37	36	1-2	1-1	1-6		2-1	3-3	4-0	1-0	4-1	2-3	4-0	1-1
Al Wasl	22	8	5	9	41	40	29	1-0	2-2	1-3	3-3		0-2	2-0	0-0	2-0	0-0	5-0	2-1
Sharjah	22	7	7	8	37	36	28	0-3	2-4	1-1	0-1	4-2		1-2	1-0	1-5	2-1	1-1	4-1
Al Shabab	22	8	4	10	35	44	28	1-1	1-2	2-5	1-1	4-3	1-1		3-1	1-2	3-2	3-2	3-0
Al Ahli Dubai	22	7	5	10	42	43	26	1-3	2-4	1-5	2-2	1-1	1-1	1-0		4-4	4-2	2-1	8-0
Dhafra	22	7	5	10	47	55	26	1-2	0-2	2-1	0-1	2-3	1-1	2-3	5-4		4-6	4-3	4-2
Al Nasr	22	7	2	13	37	49	23	0-1	1-5	0-2	1-2	3-1	1-4	3-2	1-2	3-3		4-1	2-0
Emirates Club	22	4	2	16	37	57	14	1-2	1-2	0-1	1-2	4-5	3-2	1-1	1-3	2-3	4-1		2-0
Ajman	22	2	2	18	29	68	8	2-5	1-1	4-5	2-4	5-4	1-4	0-2	0-3	4-1	0-3	1-3	

25/09/2009 - 15/05/2010 • † Qualified for the AFC Champions League
Top scorers: **24** - Jose Sand ARG, Al Ain • **18** - Fernando Baiano BRA, Wahda & Carlos Tenorio ECU, Al Nasr • **15** - Marcelinho BRA, Sharjah

UNITED ARAB EMIRATES 2009-10 SECOND DIVISION GROUP A

	Pl	W	D	L	F	A	Pts
Al Ittihad	14	9	0	5	30	24	27
Dubai	14	7	4	3	32	20	25
Al Sha'ab	14	7	3	4	21	18	24
Al Ahli Fujeira	14	5	5	4	25	21	20
Al Urooba	14	5	4	5	23	23	19
Al Khaleej	14	5	4	5	23	25	19
Hatta	14	4	3	7	20	24	15
Dibba Al Hisn	14	2	1	11	17	36	7

6/02/2010 - 6/05/2010

UNITED ARAB EMIRATES 2009-10 SECOND DIVISION GROUP B

	Pl	W	D	L	F	A	Pts
Dibba	12	8	3	1	28	9	27
Thaid	12	6	5	1	26	12	23
Al Arabi	12	6	4	2	26	19	22
Ras Al Khaima	12	5	3	4	20	14	18
Masafi	12	2	5	5	12	19	11
Ramms	12	1	3	8	9	26	6
Al Jazira Al Hamra	12	1	3	8	13	35	6

6/02/2010 - 6/05/2010

MEDALS TABLE

		Overall			Lge	Cup	Asia			City
		G	S	B	G	G	G	S	B	
1	Al Ain	15	1	1	9	5	1	1	1	Al Ain
2	Sharjah	13			5	8				Sharjah
3	Al Ahli	12			5	7				Dubai
4	Al Wasl	9	1		7	2			1	Dubai
5	Al Shabab	7	1		3	4			1	Dubai
6	Al Nasr	6			3	3				Dubai
7	Al Wahda	5	1		4	1			1	Abu Dhabi
8	Al Sha'ab	1	1			1			1	Sharjah
	Ajman	1				1				Ajman
	Bani Yas	1				1				Abu Dhabi
	Emirates Club	1				1				Ras Al Khaima

PRESIDENT'S CUP 2009-10

Round of 16

Emirates Club	2
Al Wasl	1
Al Ain	0 3p
Ajman	0 4p
Al Nasr	5
Ittihad	2
Bani-Yas	0
Al Wahda	4
Al Jazeera	3
Al Sha'ab	0
Al Urooba	1
Dhafra	2
Al Ahli Dubai	4
Sharjah	2
Al Khaleej	1
Al Shabab	3

Quarter-finals

Emirates Club	1
Ajman	0
Al Nasr	3
Al Wahda	5
Al Jazeera	3
Dhafra	0
Al Ahli Dubai	0
Al Shabab	2

Semi-finals

Emirates Club	1
Al Wahda	0
Al Jazeera	0 0p
Al Shabab	0 3p

Final

| Emirates Club † | 3 |
| Al Shabab | 1 |

† Qualified for the AFC Champions League

CUP FINAL

Sheikh Zayed, Abu Dhabi
19-04-2010
Scorers - Nabil Daoudi 2 [48] [77], Karim Kerkar [93+] for Emirates; Renato [11] for Shabab

UGA – UGANDA

FIFA/COCA-COLA WORLD RANKING

1993	1994	1995	1996	1997	1998	1999	2000	2001	2002	2003	2004	2005	2006	2007	2008	2009	2010
94	93	74	81	109	105	108	103	119	102	103	109	101	103	76	71	75	80

					2010								Hi/Lo
Jan	Feb	Mar	Mar	Apr	May	Jul	Aug	Sep	Oct	Nov	Dec		63
75	74	74	74	74	73	70	69	63	63	69	80		121

2010 proved to be yet another outstanding year for the Cranes of Uganda as they rose to their highest-ever position of 63rd in the FIFA/Coca-Cola World Ranking. The Cranes went through 12 matches without defeat in 2010 and by the end of the year had lost just one international in their last 25 games. Scottish coach Bobby Williamson continues to make a huge impact in the East African country, his biggest win to date coming in September at the start of the 2012 African Nations Cup qualifiers with an emphatic 3-0 win over Angola. A match played in a torrential downpour in Kampala proved one of Uganda's best performances in years and has set the platform for a serious bid to qualify for the finals for the first time since 1978. Uganda were not able to successfully defend their East and Central African Senior Challenge Cup title but made a gallant effort at the tournament in Tanzania. They lost to the home nation on post-match penalties in their semi-final but won bronze with a 4-3 triumph over Ethiopia. Bunamwaya FC of Wakiso won a first-ever Super League title just five years after promotion to the top flight. They were third in the 2009 but after recruiting several internationals to bolster their squad secured the 2010 championship. Victor FC from Jinja were the cup winners after beating Simba on penalties in the final.

FIFA WORLD CUP RECORD

1930-1974 DNE **1978** DNQ **1982** DNE **1986-1990** DNQ **1994** DNE **1998-2010** DNQ

FEDERATION OF UGANDA FOOTBALL ASSOCIATIONS (FUFA)

FUFA House, Plot No. 879,
Kyadondo Block 8,
Mengo Wakaliga Road,
PO Box 22518, Kampala
☎ +256 41 4272702
📠 +256 41 4272702
✉ fufaf@yahoo.com
🖥 www.fufa.co.ug
FA 1924 CON 1959 FIFA 1959
P Lawrence Mulindwa
GS Edgar Watson Suubi

FIFA BIG COUNT 2006

Total players	1 191 514
% of population	4.23%
Male	1 186 014
Female	5 500
Amateurs 18+	28 000
Professionals	14
Referees	600
Admin & coaches	5 000
Number of clubs	400
Number of teams	2 000

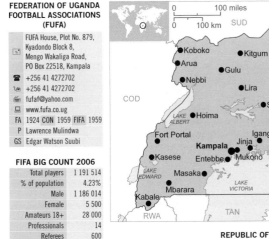

MAJOR CITIES/TOWNS

		Population
1	Kampala	1 560 080
2	Gulu	208 268
3	Lira	174 630
4	Mukono	111 058
5	Jinja	101 604
6	Mbarara	93 969
7	Kasese	91 906
8	Mbale	84 215
9	Kitgum	83 233
10	Njeru	75 380
11	Arua	71 226
12	Masaka	70 273
13	Entebbe	70 052
14	Koboko	59 430
15	Kabale	58 269
16	Iganga	56 074
17	Tororo	55 366
18	Hoima	52 670
19	Mityana	50 612

REPUBLIC OF UGANDA

Capital	Kampala	Population	32 369 558 (38)	% in cities	13%
GDP per capita	$1300 (204)	Area km²	241 038 km² (80)	GMT + / –	+3
Neighbours (km)	Congo DR 765, Kenya 933, Rwanda 169, Sudan 435, Tanzania 396				

RECENT INTERNATIONAL MATCHES PLAYED BY UGANDA

2007 Opponents	Score		Venue	Comp	Scorers	Att	Referee
9-12 Djibouti	W	7-0	Dar es Salaam	CCr1	Hamis Kitagenda 3 [19 31 27], Dan Wagaluka [41], Ronald Muganga [45], Tony Odur [60], Vincent Kayizi [80]		
11-12 Rwanda	W	2-0	Dar es Salaam	CCr1	Simeon Masaba [69], Assani Bajope [86]		
14-12 Eritrea	L	2-3	Dar es Salaam	CCr1	Ronald Muganga [54], Dan Wagaluka [74p]		
20-12 Rwanda	L	0-1	Dar es Salaam	CCsf			
22-12 Burundi	W	2-0	Dar es Salaam	CC3p	Hamis Kitagenda 2 [60 89]		
2008							
26-03 Libya	D	1-1	Kampala	Fr	Ceasar Okhuti [47]		
31-05 Niger	W	1-0	Kamapala	WCq	Ibrahim Sekajja [53]	25 000	Evehe CMR
8-06 Benin	L	1-4	Cotonou	WCq	Eugene Sepuya [9]	10 200	Karembe MLI
14-06 Angola	W	3-1	Kampala	WCq	Eugene Sepuya [6], Andrew Mwesigwa [18], Dan Wagaluka [73]	20 000	Maillet SEY
23-06 Angola	D	0-0	Luanda	WCq		16 000	Mana NGA
7-09 Niger	L	1-3	Niamey	WCq	David Obua [33]	5 000	Lamptey GHA
12-10 Benin	W	2-1	Kampala	WCq	Geofrey Massa 2 [50 53]	2 913	Abd El Fatah EGY
2009							
1-01 Rwanda	W	4-0	Kampala	CCr1	Tony Mawejje [59], Simeon Masaba [67p], Brian Omwony [85], Stephen Bengo [87]		
3-01 Zanzibar †	D	0-0	Kampala	CCr1			
7-01 Somalia	W	4-0	Kampala	CCr1	Tony Mawejje 2 [31 65], Owen Kasule [38], Geofrey Massa [75]		
9-01 Tanzania	W	2-1	Kampala	CCr1	Brian Omwony [11], Stephen Bengo [27]		
11-01 Burundi	W	5-0	Kampala	CCsf	Brian Omwony 2 [30 84], Andrew Mwesigwa [45], Stephen Bengo [46], Geofrey Massa [64]		
13-01 Kenya	W	1-0	Kampala	CCf	Brian Omwony [18]		
7-03 Sudan	W	2-0	Khartoum	Fr	Brian Omwony 2 [9 37]		
21-03 Malawi	W	2-1	Kampala	Fr	Brian Omwony 44, Patrick Ochan [57]		
31-05 Ghana	L	1-2	Tamale	Fr	Geofrey Serunkuma [88]		
29-11 Tanzania	W	2-0	Mumias	CCr1	Owen Kasule [3], Mike Sserumagga [88]		
2-12 Burundi	W	2-0	Mumias	CCr1	Geofrey Massa [12], Dan Wagaluka [67]		
5-12 Zanzibar †	D	0-0	Nairobi	CCr1			
7-12 Kenya	W	1-0	Nairobi	CCqf	Robert Sentongo [64]		
9-12 Zanzibar †	W	2-1	Nairobi	CCsf	Stephen Bengo [2], Hamoud OG [10]		
13-12 Rwanda	W	2-0	Nairobi	CCf	Dan Wagaluka [40], Emmanuel Okwi [73]		
2010							
3-03 Tanzania	W	3-2	Mwanza	Fr	Sula Matovu [12], Saddam Juma [79], Owen Kasule [84]		
11-08 Zambia	D	1-1	Kampala	Fr	Mike Sserumagga [39]		
4-09 Angola	W	3-0	Kampala	CNq	David Obua [35], Andrew Mwesigwa [57], Geofrey Serunkuma [88]		Osman EGY
9-10 Kenya	D	0-0	Nairobi	CNq			Diatta SEN
7-11 Yemen	D	2-2	Aden	Fr	Mike Sserumagga [32], Patrick Edema [90]		
10-11 Bahrain	D	0-0	Riffa	Fr			
16-11 Saudi Arabia	D	0-0	Dubai	Fr			
29-11 Ethiopia	W	2-1	Dar es Salaam	CCr1	Simeon Masaba [35p], Henry Kisseka [46]		
2-12 Malawi	D	1-1	Dar es Salaam	CCr1	Okwi Emmanuel [80]		
5-12 Kenya	W	2-0	Dar es Salaam	CCr1	Okwi Emmanuel [81], Andrew Mwesigwa [92+p]		
8-12 Zanzibar †	D	2-2	Dar es Salaam	CCqf	Mike Sserumaga [13], Okwi Emmanuel [47p]. W 5-3p		
10-12 Tanzania	D	0-0	Dar es Salaam	CCsf	L 4-5p		
12-12 Ethiopia	W	4-3	Dar es Salaam	CC3p	Henry Kisseka [5], Okwi Emmanuel [48], Tony Mawejje [53], Sula Matovu [72]		

Fr = Friendly match • CN = CAF African Cup of Nations • CC = CECAFA Cup • WC = FIFA World Cup
q = qualifier • r1 = first round group • qf = quarter-final • sf = semifinal • 3p = third place play-off • f = final • † Not a full international

UGANDA 2009-10

SUPER LEAGUE

	Pl	W	D	L	F	A	Pts	Bun	Exp	URA	KCC	Sim	Pol	Vil	Nal	Mas	Fir	Kin	CRO	Vic	Bor	Maj	Iga	Hoi	Aru
Bunamwaya Wakiso	34	21	11	2	61	22	**74**		3-3	2-3	0-0	3-0	0-0	2-0	2-1	1-1	5-0	3-1	0-0	2-1	1-1	2-2	3-0	4-1	3-1
Express RE Kampala	34	21	9	4	44	15	**72**	0-1		0-0	0-1	2-0	2-1	0-0	0-0	2-0	1-0	1-0	5-0	0-0	3-0	1-0	1-0	1-0	4-0
URA Kampala	34	20	10	4	53	23	**70**	3-0	2-1		1-0	0-0	1-1	0-0	2-1	3-1	1-2	2-2	2-0	3-0	3-2	1-1	1-0	3-0	
Kampala City Council	34	14	15	5	41	14	**57**	0-1	2-2	1-0		1-2	0-0	0-0	0-1	5-0	0-0	0-1	5-0	3-0	0-0	3-1	4-0	2-1	4-0
Simba	34	14	8	12	34	34	**50**	1-2	1-2	1-0	0-0		1-0	0-0	1-0	2-0	1-4	0-1	3-0	0-0	0-0	0-0	2-0	2-1	3-1
Uganda Police Kampala	34	13	9	12	34	32	**48**	0-1	1-0	1-1	1-2	2-1		2-0	1-2	3-1	2-0	1-1	2-1	0-2	1-1	0-1	2-0	1-0	1-0
SC Villa Kampala	34	12	15	7	32	27	**45**	2-2	0-1	2-3	0-0	1-0	2-0		2-0	3-0	1-1	2-1	0-3	1-3	5-1	2-0	1-0	3-0	1-0
Nalubaale Buikwe	34	12	8	14	34	34	**44**	0-1	1-2	2-1	0-1	2-3	1-0	2-2		0-0	0-0	2-1	0-1	0-1	0-3	2-1	0-0	1-0	5-1
Masaka Local Council	34	12	8	14	30	42	**44**	1-2	0-1	0-3	0-2	2-1	2-0	1-1	0-1		0-0	2-0	2-1	0-0	1-0	0-1	1-0	2-0	3-0
Fire Masters	34	11	10	13	30	37	**43**	0-4	0-1	0-1	1-1	1-0	2-0	0-0	1-0	2-0		0-0	1-0	1-0	2-2	2-3	2-0	2-1	0-0
Kinyara Sugar	34	10	12	12	32	33	**42**	0-0	0-1	0-3	1-1	3-1	1-2	0-0	0-0	1-1	1-0		0-0	1-0	1-0	1-1	3-3	1-0	7-0
CRO Mbale	34	10	11	13	32	35	**41**	0-0	0-0	0-0	0-0	1-1	0-1	1-1	2-0	3-1	2-0	2-0		1-0	0-2	2-0	0-1	2-0	7-0
Victors Jinja	34	9	14	11	25	30	**41**	0-4	0-0	0-1	0-0	1-1	1-2	0-0	0-0	1-1	3-0	1-0	0-0		1-0	2-1	1-2	3-0	2-1
Boroboro Tigers Lira	34	9	13	12	29	40	**37**	0-0	0-1	0-0	1-1	0-1	1-0	0-2	1-1	0-0	2-1	0-1	3-1	0-0		2-1	1-0	3-1	3-1
Maji FC Kampala	34	8	10	16	33	45	**34**	0-2	0-2	1-1	0-0	0-1	1-1	1-2	1-2	2-1	1-2	2-1	2-2	0-1	0-0		1-1	4-3	3-1
Iganga Town Council	34	7	10	17	25	40	**31**	0-1	0-0	0-0	0-0	2-0	1-1	1-1	1-2	1-2	2-1	0-1	0-0	3-0	1-2	0-0		2-1	3-2
Hoima	34	7	3	24	24	53	**24**	0-2	0-1	1-2	0-1	1-2	0-2	2-1	1-4	0-1	0-2	2-0	2-1	0-0	2-0	1-0	1-0		0-0
Arua Central	34	5	6	23	20	72	**15**	0-1	2-3	0-2	0-1	1-2	1-2	0-0	0-2	1-2	1-1	2-1	2-0	2-2	3-0	1-0	1-0	1-1	

1710/2009 - 15/07/2010

SUPER EIGHT 2009

Quarter-finals		Semi-finals		Final	
Villa	1 5p				
Police	1 3p	Villa	0 5p		
Bunamwaya	1	Victors	0 4p		
Victors	2			Villa	3
Express	w-o			URA	2
Kampala CC		Express	0		
Maji	0 3p	**URA**	3	Nakivubo, Kampala	
URA	0 4p			19-09-2009	

MEDALS TABLE

		Overall			Lge		Cup		Africa		
		G	S	B	G	S	G	S	G	S	B
1	Villa	24	5		16		8	3		2	
2	Kampala CC	16	5	1	8		8	5			1
3	Express	15	4	1	5		10	4			1
4	URA	4	1		3		1	1			
5	Simba	3	4		2		1	3		1	
6	Coffee	2	2				2	2			
7	Mbale Heroes	2	1				2	1			
8	Prisons	2			2						
	Victors	2					2				
10	Nile Breweries	1	4		1			4			
11	UCB	1	3		1			3			
12	Police	1	1		1			1			
	Umeme	1	1				1	1			
14	Bunamwaya	1			1						

KAKUNGULU CUP 2010

Round of 16		Quarter-finals		Semi-finals		Final	
Victors Jinja	0 4p						
Iganga Town Council	0 2p	**Victors Jinja**	1				
Ex Internationals FA	0	Kinyara Sugar	0	**Victors Jinja**	1 1		
Kinyara Sugar	1			Masaka Local Council	0 1		
Gulu United	0 5p						
Nalubaale Buikwe	0 4p	Gulu United	0				
Jogoo Young		**Masaka Local Council**	3			**Victors Jinja** ‡	1 5p
Masaka Local Council						Simba	1 4p
Uganda Police	4						
CRO Mbale	1	**Uganda Police**	3				
Buganda Royal Inst.		Express RE Kampala	0	Uganda Police	1 ?	**CUP FINAL**	
Express RE Kampala				Simba	0 ?		
Bunamwaya Wakiso	2 3p					17-07-2010	
URA Kampala	2 2p	Bunamwaya Wakiso	0				
Corporate XI	0	**Simba**	1				
Simba	2						

‡ Qualified for the CAF Confederation Cup

UKR – UKRAINE

FIFA/COCA-COLA WORLD RANKING

1993	1994	1995	1996	1997	1998	1999	2000	2001	2002	2003	2004	2005	2006	2007	2008	2009	2010
90	77	71	59	49	47	27	34	45	45	60	57	40	13	30	15	22	34

	2010											Hi/Lo
	Jan	Feb	Mar	Mar	Apr	May	Jul	Aug	Sep	Oct	Nov	Dec	11
	22	24	24	26	25	23	25	24	26	35	36	34	132

Preparing to host a major international sports tournament in the middle of a global financial crisis has been a major headache for the Ukraine with UEFA voicing concerns over the readiness of the Euro 2012 final venue in Kyiv, along with the state of the road and airport infrastructures and the lack of hotels for visiting fans. In May 2010 UEFA President Michel Platini issued a warning that Germany and Hungary could step in as replacements but since then the government has pulled out all the stops to avoid a 'national embarrassment'. UEFA's worries may have largely been dealt with but there are concerns over how well prepared the national team will be, a situation not helped by the resignation of coach Myron Markevych in August 2010 after just seven months in the job. He was replaced by Yuriy Kalitvintsev who had led the under-19 team to the European title in 2009 but only in a caretaker capacity. In club football, Shakhtar Donetsk boss Mircea Lucescu suffered a heart attack three days before the start of the season but was soon back to steer his club to a fourth league title under his guidance - their fifth in all - with a team boasting a Brazilian sextuplet of Fernandinho, Douglas Costa, Ilsinho, Jadson, Luiz Adriano and Willian. In the Cup Final Tavria Simferopol beat Metalurh Donetsk to claim their first honour since winning the league in 1992.

FIFA WORLD CUP RECORD
1930-1994 DNE 1998-2002 DNQ **2006** 8 QF 2010 DNQ

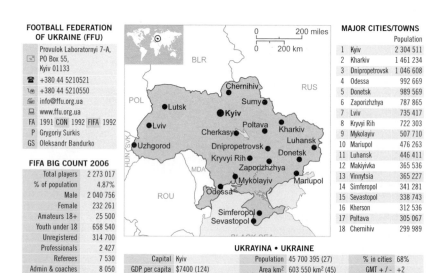

FOOTBALL FEDERATION OF UKRAINE (FFU)

	Provulok Laboratornyi 7-A, PO Box 55, Kyiv 01133
☎	+380 44 5210521
📠	+380 44 5210550
✉	info@ffu.org.ua
🖥	www.ffu.org.ua
FA	1991 CON 1992 FIFA 1992
P	Grygoriy Surkis
GS	Oleksandr Bandurko

FIFA BIG COUNT 2006

Total players	2 273 017
% of population	4.87%
Male	2 040 756
Female	232 261
Amateurs 18+	25 500
Youth under 18	658 540
Unregistered	314 700
Professionals	2 427
Referees	7 530
Admin & coaches	8 050
Number of clubs	68
Number of teams	6 500

MAJOR CITIES/TOWNS

		Population
1	Kyiv	2 304 511
2	Kharkiv	1 461 234
3	Dnipropetrovsk	1 046 608
4	Odessa	992 669
5	Donetsk	989 569
6	Zaporizhzhya	787 865
7	Lviv	735 417
8	Kryvyi Rih	722 303
9	Mykolayiv	507 710
10	Mariupol	476 263
11	Luhansk	446 411
12	Makiyivka	365 536
13	Vinnytsia	365 227
14	Simferopol	341 281
15	Sevastopol	338 743
16	Kherson	312 536
17	Poltava	305 067
18	Chernihiv	299 989

UKRAYINA • UKRAINE

Capital	Kyiv	Population	45 700 395 (27)	% in cities	68%
GDP per capita	$7400 (124)	Area km²	603 550 km² (45)	GMT + / -	+2
Neighbours (km)	Belarus 891, Hungary 103, Moldova 940, Poland 428, Romania 538, Russia 1576, Slovakia 90 • Coast 2782				

RECENT INTERNATIONAL MATCHES PLAYED BY UKRAINE

2007	Opponents	Score	Venue	Comp	Scorers	Att	Referee
22-08	Uzbekistan	W 2-1	Kyiv	Fr	Hladkiy [30], Rotan [65]	4 000	Banari MDA
8-09	Georgia	D 1-1	Tbilisi	ECq	Shelayev [7]	24 000	Hamer LUX
12-09	Italy	L 1-2	Kyiv	ECq	Shevchenko [71]	41 500	Webb ENG
13-10	Scotland	L 1-3	Glasgow	ECq	Shevchenko [24]	52 063	Vink NED
17-10	Faroe Islands	W 5-0	Kyiv	ECq	Kalynychenko 2 [40 49], Gusev 2 [43 45], Vorobey [64]	5 000	Jakov ISR
17-11	Lithuania	L 0-2	Kaunas	ECq		3 000	Malcolm NIR
21-11	France	D 2-2	Kyiv	ECq	Voronin [14], Shevchenko [46]	7 800	Ovrebø NOR
2008							
6-02	Cyprus	D 1-1	Nicosia	Fr	Milevskyi [71]	500	Kasnaferis CYP
26-03	Serbia	W 2-0	Odessa	Fr	Shevchenko [54], Nazarenko [57]	8 000	Lajuks LVA
24-05	Netherlands	L 0-3	Rotterdam	Fr		40 000	Circhetta SUI
1-06	Sweden	W 1-0	Stockholm	Fr	Nazarenko [82]	25 203	Einwaller AUT
20-08	Poland	W 1-0	Lviv	Fr	Kravchenko [45]	22 000	Nalbandian ARM
6-09	Belarus	W 1-0	Lviv	WCq	Shevchenko [94+p]	24 000	Rizzoli ITA
10-09	Kazakhstan	W 3-1	Almaty	WCq	Nazarenko 2 [45 80], Shevchenko [54]	17 000	Brych GER
11-10	Croatia	D 0-0	Kharkov	WCq		38 500	Braamhaar NED
19-11	Norway	W 1-0	Dnepropetrovsk	Fr	Seleznov [26p]	10 000	Lajuks LVA
2009							
10-02	Slovakia	W 3-2	Limassol	Fr	Valyayev [10], Seleznov [47], Milevskiy [83p]		Kailis CYP
11-02	Serbia	W 1-0	Nicosia	Fr	Nazarenko [16]	500	Kokas GRE
1-04	England	L 1-2	London	WCq	Shevchenko [74]	87 548	Larsen DEN
6-06	Croatia	D 2-2	Zagreb	WCq	Shevchenko [13], Gay [54]	32 073	Hauge NOR
10-06	Kazakhstan	W 2-1	Kyiv	WCq	Nazarenko 2 [32 47]	11 500	Paixao POR
12-08	Turkey	L 0-3	Kyiv	Fr			Ceferin SVN
5-09	Andorra	W 5-0	Kyiv	WCq	Yarmolenko [18], Milevskiy 2 [45 92+p], Shevchenko [72p], Seleznov [94+p]	14 870	Sipailo LVA
9-09	Belarus	D 0-0	Minsk	WCq		21 727	Kassai HUN
10-10	England	W 1-0	Dnepropetrovsk	WCq	Nazarenko [30]	31 000	Skomina SVN
14-10	Andorra	W 6-0	Andorra La Vella	WCq	Shevchenko [22], Gusev [61], Lima.l OG [69], Rakits Kyy [80], Seleznov [81], Yarmolenko [83]	820	Thomson SCO
14-11	Greece	D 0-0	Athens	WCpo		39 045	Duhamel FRA
18-11	Greece	L 0-1	Donetsk	WCpo		31 643	Benquerença POR
2010							
25-05	Lithuania	W 4-0	Kharkov	Fr	Aliev 2 [10 17], Shevchenko 2 [68p 78]	42 000	Sukhina RUS
29-05	Romania	W 3-2	Lviv	Fr	Aliev [15], Konoplyanka [75], OG [78]	22 000	Kralovec CZE
2-06	Norway	W 1-0	Oslo	Fr	Zozulya [78]	10 178	Blom NED
11-08	Netherlands	D 1-1	Donetsk	Fr	Aliev [75]	18 051	Skomina SVN
4-09	Poland	D 1-1	Lodz	Fr	Seleznev [90]	6 500	Irmatov UZB
7-09	Chile	W 2-1	Kyiv	Fr	Rakitskiy [36], Aliev [52]	10 000	Sevastsyanik BLR
8-10	Canada	D 2-2	Kyiv	Fr	Milevskiy [59], Tymoshchuk [80]	10 000	Mikulski
11-10	Brazil	L 0-2	Derby	Fr		13 088	Atkinson ENG
17-11	Switzerland	D 2-2	Geneva	Fr	Aliev [48], Konoplyanka [75]	11 100	Gumienny BEL

Fr = Friendly match • EC = UEFA EURO 2008 • WC = FIFA World Cup • q = qualifier

UKRAINE NATIONAL TEAM HISTORICAL RECORDS

Caps
101 - Anatoliy Tymoschuk 2000- • **100** - Andriy Shevchenko 1995- • **86** - Olexandr Shovkovskiy 1994-2009 • **75** - Serhiy Rebrov 1992-2006 • **71** - Andriy Gusin 1993-2006 • **68** - Andriy Vorobei 2000-08 • **67** - Andriy Nesmachnyi 2000- • **64** - Andriy Voronin 2002- • **63** - Vladyslav Vashchuk 1996-2007 • **61** - Oleh Gusev 2003- • **58** - Olexandr Holovko 1995-2004 • **54** - Serhiy Popov 1993-2003

Goals
45 - Andriy Shevchenko 1995- • **15** - Serhiy Rebrov 1992-2006 • **11** - Serhiy Nazarenko 2003- • **9** - Andriy Vorobei 2000-08 & Andriy Gusin 1993-2006 • **8** - Tymerlan Guseynov 1993-97 • **7** - Maksym Kalynychenko 2002- & Oleh Gusev 2003-

Past Coaches
Viktor Prokopenko 1992 • Nikolay Pavlov 1992 • Oleh Bazilevich 1993-94 • Nikolay Pavlov 1994 • Jozsef Szabo 1994 • Anatoliy Konkov 1995 • Jozsef Szabo 1996-99 • Valery Lobanovsky 2000-01 • Leonid Buryak 2002-03 • Oleh Blokhin 2003-07 • Olexiy Mykhailychenko 2008-09 • Myron Markevych 2010 • Yuriy Kalitvintsev 2010-

UKRAINE 2009–10

VYSCHA LIHA

Team	Pl	W	D	L	F	A	Pts	Shakhtar	Dynamo	Metalist	Dnipro	Karpaty	Tavriya	Arsenal	Metalurh D	Metalurh Z	Vorskla	Obolon	Illychivets	Zorja	Kryvbas	Chernomorets	Zakarpattya
Shakhtar Donetsk †	30	24	5	1	62	18	77		1-0	2-1	0-0	5-1	3-0	3-1	4-1	2-0	1-0	4-0	2-1	3-1	3-0	3-0	1-0
Dynamo Kyiv †	30	22	5	3	61	16	71	3-0		3-0	2-1	1-1	6-0	3-1	3-1	3-0	1-0	2-1	3-1	2-0	1-0	5-0	2-0
Metalist Kharkiv ‡	30	19	5	6	49	23	62	1-1	1-2		3-2	1-0	1-1	1-0	2-0	4-0	1-0	0-1	3-1	2-0	1-0	5-1	2-1
Dnipro Dnipropetrovsk ‡	30	15	9	6	48	25	54	2-2	0-2	2-0		3-0	3-1	1-1	2-0	2-0	2-2	2-0	4-1	2-2	3-1	3-1	1-0
Karpaty Lviv ‡	30	13	11	6	44	35	50	0-2	1-0	2-1	1-0		1-0	3-3	2-2	3-3	1-0	5-0	2-2	4-0	0-2	1-1	1-0
Tavriya Simferopol ‡	30	12	9	9	38	38	45	2-3	2-3	0-0	2-1	1-1		2-2	1-0	2-0	1-0	0-0	3-3	0-1	3-1	2-1	3-2
Arsenal Kyiv	30	11	9	10	44	41	42	2-4	0-1	1-2	1-1	0-0	1-6		2-0	2-0	2-0	4-1	3-1	1-1	2-1	2-0	0-0
Metalurh Donetsk	30	11	7	12	41	33	40	0-1	1-1	0-1	0-0	1-0	0-0	3-0		3-0	1-3	5-0	4-1	0-0	0-1	2-0	4-1
Metalurh Zaporizhya	30	10	5	15	31	48	35	0-2	0-0	0-2	1-3	0-1	0-1	2-1	3-2		1-1	2-1	2-0	3-1	2-1	1-0	3-0
Vorskla Poltava	30	6	13	11	29	32	31	1-1	1-1	0-0	1-1	1-2	0-1	1-5	1-2	1-1		3-2	3-0	2-0	0-0	0-0	2-0
Obolon Kyiv	30	9	4	17	26	50	31	0-1	0-4	0-2	1-0	1-3	1-0	0-0	2-1	4-1	1-1		1-1	3-0	1-2	1-0	0-1
Illychivets Mariupil	30	7	8	15	31	56	29	0-2	1-1	0-2	0-3	2-2	2-2	1-2	0-4	2-1	0-0	1-0		1-0	0-3	2-0	1-0
Zorja Luhansk	30	7	7	16	23	47	28	0-2	0-2	1-4	0-1	0-2	0-0	0-0	1-1	3-1	2-1	2-0	3-2		1-0	0-1	2-0
Kryvbas Kryvyi Rih	30	7	4	19	31	47	25	0-2	1-3	2-2	0-0	1-2	0-1	0-1	0-1	1-3	1-1	3-2	0-2	4-0		2-3	3-1
Chernomorets Odessa	30	5	9	16	21	44	24	0-1	0-1	0-2	0-1	1-1	2-0	1-3	1-1	0-0	0-0	0-1	1-1	1-1	3-1		0-0
Zakarpattya Uzhgorod	30	5	4	21	18	44	19	1-1	1-0	0-2	0-2	1-1	0-1	2-1	0-1	0-1	1-3	0-1	0-1	0-1	2-1	3-0	1-1

17/07/2009 - 9/05/2010 • † Qualified for the UEFA Champions League • ‡ Qualified for the Europa League
Top scorers: 17 - Artem Milevsky, Dynamo Kyiv • 16 - Jackson Coelho BRA, Metalist • 13 - Yevhen Seleznyov, Shakhtar/Dnipro

MEDALS TABLE

	Overall			League			Cup			Europe		
	G	S	B	G	S	B	G	S	B	G	S	B
1 Dynamo Kyiv	22	8	2	13	6		9	2				2
2 Shakhtar Donetsk	12	14		5	10		6	4	1			
3 Chernomorets Odessa	2	2	3		2	3	2					
4 Tavriya Simferopol	2	1			1		1	1				
5 Vorskla Poltava	1		1			1	1					
6 Dnipro Dnipropetrovsk	4	4		1	4					3		
7 Karpaty Lviv	2	1			1		2					
8 CSCA Kyiv	2						2					
9 Metallist Kharkiv	1	4			4		1					
10 Metalurh Donetsk	1	3			3		1					

Ukrainian Clubs in the Soviet era

	Overall			League			Cup			Europe		
	G	S	B	G	S	B	G	S	B	G	S	B
1 Dynamo	24	13	5	13	11	3	9	2		2		2
7 Shakhtar	4	6	2		2	2	4	4				
9 Dnipro	3	2	2	2	2	2	1					
13 Zorya	1	2		1				2				
15 Metallist	1	1					1	1				
16 Karpaty	1						1					
21 Chernomorets		1						1				

UKRAINE 2009–10

PERSHA LIHA (2)

Team	Pl	W	D	L	F	A	Pts	Sevastopol	Volyn	Stal	Lviv	Oleksandrija	Krymteplytsja	Naftovyk	Desna	Arsenal	Helios	Dnister	Zirka	Dynamo-2	Feniks	Enerhetyk	Prykarpattija	FC Kharkiv	Nyva
FC Sevastopol	34	24	4	6	68	27	76		1-1	3-4	1-0	1-0	3-2	2-0	1-0	2-0	4-2	2-0	4-0	5-0	3-1	4-0	3-0	1-0	3-1
Volyn Lutsk	34	22	8	4	71	30	74	2-1		1-1	0-0	1-3	0-0	1-0	2-1	3-2	4-0	3-0	4-0	1-1	4-0	4-1	5-1	2-0	2-1
Stal Alchevsk	34	19	8	7	55	35	65	2-1	0-1		0-2	2-1	0-0	0-1	3-0	1-1	3-0	1-0	3-3	1-0	3-1	0-0	2-0	2-1	1-0
FK Lviv	34	19	6	9	49	22	63	0-1	0-1	3-2		1-2	3-1	2-0	0-0	0-1	3-2	2-1	1-0	3-1	1-0	3-1	4-0	2-1	3-0
FK Oleksandrija	34	19	6	9	58	34	63	2-1	0-1	1-2	0-0		0-3	0-0	1-1	5-1	3-2	1-1	2-1	1-1	4-1	4-0	5-0	3-0	
Krymteplytsja	34	17	8	9	53	28	59	1-2	3-2	3-2	0-1	3-0		2-1	0-1	1-2	0-1	0-0	1-1	1-0	3-0	2-1	4-0	4-1	4-0
Naftovyk-Ukrnafta	34	17	6	11	45	37	57	0-1	2-3	1-2	2-0	0-1	1-0		0-0	2-2	2-1	1-0	3-1	1-0	1-1	2-1	1-0	1-1	2-1
Desna Chernihiv	34	12	12	10	38	30	48	0-2	0-1	0-1	0-0	2-1	1-1	1-2		2-1	1-1	1-2	0-0	0-0	0-1	4-0	3-4	4-1	4-0
Arsenal Bila Tserkva	34	12	10	12	48	44	46	2-7	2-0	1-0	1-3	3-0	1-1	4-0	2-2		0-1	0-0	0-0	2-1	1-0	0-0	3-4	4-1	4-0
Helios Kharkiv	34	12	10	12	42	47	46	0-1	2-2	1-1	3-3	2-2	0-4	1-0	0-0	1-0		2-2	1-2	0-3	3-1	1-0	2-0	0-1	2-0
Dnister Ovidiopol	34	12	8	14	44	47	44	4-1	1-5	0-2	0-1	0-1	0-2	0-1	2-1	1-1	1-2		0-0	3-1	2-2	1-1	5-2	2-0	4-1
Zirka Kirovohrad	34	11	13	10	38	40	43	0-0	2-2	1-0	0-1	0-0	2-1	2-1	1-1	1-1	1-2		0-1	2-0	1-2	0-3	2-1	3-2	
Dynamo Kyiv-2	34	12	5	17	35	46	41	1-0	0-2	1-2	2-1	0-3	1-1	2-0	0-1	1-2	0-2	2-0		0-1	1-2	3-1	2-1	3-2	
Feniks-Illichovets	34	10	7	17	39	52	37	1-1	1-1	3-4	1-0	0-1	1-0	1-2	1-2	2-2	2-0	0-1	1-2	1-1		3-0	2-1	4-2	2-0
Enerhetyk Burshtyn	34	8	11	15	32	49	35	1-2	0-3	2-2	1-0	2-1	0-1	0-1	1-1	1-0	0-0	2-1	0-1	3-4	1-1		1-1	1-1	1-1
Prykarpattija I-Frank'sk	34	5	7	22	26	68	22	0-1	0-2	2-2	0-0	0-2	0-1	3-3	0-1	2-0	2-1	1-2	0-1	1-0	2-0	0-1		1-1	1-1
FC Kharkiv	34	3	5	26	23	76	14	0-3	1-3	0-1	1-0	1-1	1-2	1-4	0-4	0-4	0-5	1-3	0-0	1-2	3-0	1-2			1-0
Nyva Ternopil	34	3	4	27	18	72	7	0-2	1-2	0-3	0-4	0-2	0-1	0-4	0-1	0-1	1-2	2-0	1-1	0-1	1-2	2-2	1-0	1-0	

17/07/2009 - 5/06/2010 • Desna Chernihiv withdrew after of the season • § = points deducted • Top scorer: 19 - Serhiy Kucherenko, Krymteplitsia

KUBOK UKRAINY 2009-10

First Round		Second Round		Quarter-finals		Semi-finals		Final	
Tavriya Simferopol	4	**Tavriya Simferopol ***	4	**Tavriya Simferopol ***	4	**Tavriya Simferopol**	2	**Tavriya Simferopol ‡**	3
Stal Dniprodzerzhinsk *	0	Illychivets Mariupil	2	Obolon Kyiv	0	Volyn Lutsk *	1	Metalurh Donetsk	2
Shakhtar Sverdlovsk *	1								
Illychivets Mariupil	3								
Stal Alchevsk *	1	Stal Alchevsk *	0						
Chernomorets Odessa	0	**Obolon Kyiv**	3						
CSCA Kyiv *	3 2p								
Obolon Kyiv	3 4p								
Metalurh Zaporizhya	3	**Metalurh Zaporizhya**	2	Metalurh Zaporizhya	1				
Vorskla Poltava *	2	Krymteplytsja *	1	**Volyn Lutsk ***	2				
MFC Mykolajiv *	0								
Krymteplytsja	1								
Kryvbas Kryvyi Rih *	5	Kryvbas Kryvyi Rih *	1						
Zorja Luhansk	0	**Volyn Lutsk ***	2						
FK Oleksandrija *	2								
Volyn Lutsk	3								
Shakhtar Donetsk	6	**Shakhtar Donetsk**	3	**Shakhtar Donetsk ***	2	Shakhtar Donetsk	1		
Dnister Ovidiopol *	1	Jednist Plysky *	1	Dynamo Kyiv	0	**Metalurh Donetsk ***	2		
Nyva Ternopil	1								
Jednist Plysky *	2								
Metalist Kharkiv	1	Metalist Kharkiv *	0						
Enerhetyk Burshtyn *	0	**Dynamo Kyiv**	1						
Arsenal Kyiv *	1								
Dynamo Kyiv	2								
Dnipro Dnipropetrovsk	3	**Dnipro Dnipropetrovsk**	2	Dnipro Dnipropetrovsk *	1				
Zakarpattya Uzhgorod *	2	Feniks-Illichovets *	1	**Metalurh Donetsk**	2				
FC Poltava *	0								
Feniks-Illichovets	2								
Karpaty Lviv	5	Karpaty Lviv	1						
FC Kharkiv *	1	**Metalurh Donetsk ***	2						
Naftovyk-Ukrnafta *	1 2p								
Metalurh Donetsk	1 4p								

CUP FINAL

OSK Metalist, Kharkiv
16-05-2010, Att: 21 000, Ref: Dereyynskiy
Scorers - Feshtchuk 2, Kovpak 40p, Idahor 97 for
Tavriya; Mkhitaryan 50, Sergio 75 for Metalurh
Tavriya - Maksym Startsev - Slobodan
Markovic●●♦121+, Sasha Juricic●●♦94,
Anton Monakhov●, Ilya Haliuza● (Ivan Matyazh
84) - Andriy Kornev●, Yevhen Lutsenko●, Zeljko
Ljubenovic (Vasil Gigiadze 70), Denys Holaydo,
Maksym Feschuk (Lucky Idahor● 62) -
Oleksandr Kovpak (c). Tr: Serhiy Puchkov
Metalurh - Vladimir Disljenkovic - Vyacheslav
Checher (c), Oleksandr Volovyk, Oleksiy Hodin,
Mario Sergio●, Boaventura● (Ciprian Tanasa
106) - Velizar Dimitrov, Vasyl Pryima (Chavdar
Yankov● 67, Kingsley (Ze Soares 75) - Musa
Mguni●, Henrikh Mkhitaryan. Tr: Nikolay Kostov

* Home team ● ‡ Qualified for the Europa League

URU – URUGUAY

FIFA/COCA-COLA WORLD RANKING

1993	1994	1995	1996	1997	1998	1999	2000	2001	2002	2003	2004	2005	2006	2007	2008	2009	2010
17	37	32	43	40	76	46	32	22	28	21	16	18	29	28	23	20	7

2010												Hi/Lo
Jan	Feb	Mar	Mar	Apr	May	Jul	Aug	Sep	Oct	Nov	Dec	6
20	21	19	18	18	16	6	6	7	7	7	7	76

Often written off as a relic from a long forgotten past age of football, Uruguay revived former glories with a sensational run to the semi-finals of the 2010 FIFA World Cup in South Africa, illuminating the tournament with some wonderful football and a never-say-die attitude. With a population of just three and a half million, the country continues to produce footballers of high quality and few teams in South Africa could boast a better forward line than Luis Suarez and joint top scorer Diego Forlan who was also voted as the best player at the tournament. Uruguay broke South African hearts in the group stage with a 3-0 win over the hosts and by finishing top of their group they found themselves in the most open quarter of the draw. A 2-1 win over South Korea in the round of 16 was followed by an epic quarter-final clash with Ghana that was not without controversy. In the very last seconds of extra-time Luis Suarez stopped a certain Stephen Appiah winner with his hand and after Asamoah Gyan missed the resulting penalty Uruguay then won the penalty shoot-out. The dream of a third World Cup final was ended in the semi-finals after another thrilling game, against the Netherlands, but Uruguay did more than any other team to liven up the tournament and in the process put themselves firmly back on the map of world football.

FIFA WORLD CUP RECORD

1930 1 Winners (hosts) **1934-1938** DNE **1950** 1 Winners **1954** 4 SF **1958** DNQ **1962** 13 r1 **1966** 7 QF **1970** 4 SF **1974** 13 r1 **1978-1982** DNQ **1986** 16 r2 **1990** 16 r2 **1994-1998** DNQ **2002** 26 r1 **2006** DNQ **2010** 4 SF

ASOCIACION URUGUAYA DE FUTBOL (AUF)

Guayabo 1531, Montevideo 11200

☎ +59 82 4004814
📠 +59 82 4090550
✉ auf@auf.org.uy
🖥 www.auf.org.uy
FA 1900 CON 1916 FIFA 1923
P Sebastian Bauza
GS Anibal De Oliveira

FIFA BIG COUNT 2006

Total players	241 300
% of population	7.03%
Male	214 000
Female	27 300
Amateurs 18+	30 000
Youth under 18	8 000
Unregistered	94 500
Professionals	1 100
Referees	400
Admin & coaches	2 200
Number of clubs	1 210
Number of teams	2 200

MAJOR CITIES/TOWNS

		Population
1	Montevideo	1 328 600
2	Salto	106 286
3	Ciudad de la Costa	101 047
4	Paysandú	77 767
5	Las Piedras	77 484
6	Rivera	69 744
7	Maldonado	63 061
8	Tacuarembó	54 263
9	Melo	53 852
10	Mercedes	44 307
11	Artigas	44 275
12	Minas	39 200
13	San José	39 100
14	Durazno	35 432
15	Florida	33 522
16	San Carlos	28 608
17	Treinta y Tres	27 017
18	Pando	26 869
19	Rocha	26 820

REPUBLICA ORIENTAL DEL URUGUAY • ORIENTAL REPUBLIC OF URUGUAY

Capital	Montevideo	Population	3 494 382 (131)	% in cities	92%
GDP per capita	$12 400 (89)	Area km²	176 215 km² (90)	GMT +/-	-3
Neighbours (km)	Argentina 580, Brazil 1068 • Coast 660				

RECENT INTERNATIONAL MATCHES PLAYED BY URUGUAY

2008	Opponents	Score		Venue	Comp	Scorers	Att	Referee
6-02	Colombia	D	2-2	Montevideo	Fr	Cavani [77], Suarez [85]		
25-05	Turkey	W	3-2	Bochum	Fr	Suarez 2 [31p 78], Rodriguez [85p]		Meyer GER
28-05	Norway	D	2-2	Oslo	Fr	Suarez [44], Eguren [69]	12 246	Buttimer IRL
14-06	Venezuela	D	1-1	Montevideo	WCq	Lugano [12]	41 831	Intriago ECU
17-06	Peru	W	6-0	Montevideo	WCq	Forlan 3 [8 37p 56], Bueno 2 [61 69], Abreu [90]	20 016	Pozo CHI
20-08	Japan	W	3-1	Sapporo	Fr	Eguren [55], Ignacio Gonzalez [83], Abreu [93+]	31 133	Borski POL
6-09	Colombia	W	1-0	Bogota	WCq	Eguren [15]	35 024	Gaciba BRA
10-09	Ecuador	D	0-0	Montevideo	WCq		45 000	Ruiz COL
11-10	Argentina	L	1-2	Buenos Aires	WCq	Lugano [39]	42 421	Torres PAR
14-10	Bolivia	D	2-2	La Paz	WCq	Bueno [64], Abreu [88]	21 075	Baldassi ARG
19-11	France	D	0-0	Paris	Fr		79 666	Zimmermann SUI
2009								
11-02	Libya	W	3-2	Tripoli	Fr	Eguren [14], Martinez [71], Barragan [75]		
28-03	Paraguay	W	2-0	Montevideo	WCq	Forlan [28], Lugano [57]	45 000	Simon BRA
1-04	Chile	D	0-0	Santiago	WCq		55 000	Baldassi ARG
6-06	Brazil	L	0-4	Montevideo	WCq		52 000	Laverni ARG
10-06	Venezuela	D	2-2	Puerto Ordaz	WCq	Suarez [60], Forlan [72]	37 000	Fagundes BRA
12-08	Algeria	L	0-1	Algiers	Fr		20 000	Harzi TUN
5-09	Peru	L	0-1	Lima	WCq		15 000	Chandia CHI
9-09	Colombia	W	3-1	Montevideo	WCq	Suarez [7], Scotti [77], Eguren [87]	30 000	Torres PAR
10-10	Ecuador	W	2-1	Quito	WCq	Suarez [69], Forlan [93+p]	42 700	Fagundes BRA
14-10	Argentina	L	0-1	Montevideo	WCq		50 000	Amarilla PAR
14-11	Costa Rica	W	1-0	San Jose	WCpo	Lugano [21]	19 500	Undiano ESP
18-11	Costa Rica	D	1-1	Montevideo	WCpo	Abreu [70]	55 000	Busacca SUI
2010								
3-03	Switzerland	W	3-1	St Gall	Fr	Forlan [35], Suarez [50], Cavani [87]	12 500	Rizzoli ITA
26-05	Israel	W	4-1	Montevideo	Fr	Forlan [15], Pereira [37], Abreu 2 [75 81]	60 000	Osses CHI
11-06	France	D	0-0	Cape Town	WCr1		64 100	Nishimura JPN
16-06	South Africa	W	3-0	Pretoria	WCr1	Forlan 2 [24 80p], Alvaro Pereira [95+]	42 658	Busacca SUI
22-06	Mexico	W	1-0	Rustenburg	WCr1	Suarez [43]	33 425	Kassai HUN
26-06	Korea Republic	W	2-1	Port Elizabeth	WCr2	Suarez 2 [8 80]	30 597	Stark GER
2-07	Ghana	D	1-1	Johannesburg	WCqf	Forlan [55]. W 4-2p	84 017	Benquerenca POR
6-07	Netherlands	L	2-3	Cape Town	WCsf	Forlan [41], Maximiliano Pereira [92+]	62 479	Irmatov UZB
10-07	Germany	L	2-3	Port Elizabeth	WC3p	Cavani [28], Forlan [51]	36 254	Archundia MEX
11-08	Angola	W	2-0	Lisbon	Fr	Cavani [84], Hernandez [90]	1 500	Miguel POR
8-10	Indonesia	W	7-1	Jakarta	Fr	Cavani 3 [35 80 83], Suarez 3 [43 54 69p], Eguren [58]	25 000	Daud SIN
12-10	China PR	W	4-0	Wuhan	Fr	OG [70], Cavani [78], Rodriguez [81], Fernandez [84]	50 000	Lee Dong Jun KOR
17-11	Chile	L	0-2	Santiago	Fr		45 000	Torres PAR

Fr = Friendly match • CA = Copa America • WC = FIFA World Cup
q = qualifier • po = play-off • r1 = first round group • qf = quarter-final • sf = semi-final • 3p = third place play-off

---

URUGUAY NATIONAL TEAM HISTORICAL RECORDS

Caps
79 - Rodolfo Rodriguez 1976-86 • **74** - Fabian Carini 1999-2009 • **72** - Enzo Francescoli 1982-97 • **70** - Diego Forlan 2002- • **69** - Alvaro Recoba 1995-2007 • **68** - Angel Romano 1911-27 & Pablo Gabriel Garcia 1997-2008 • **65** - Carlos Aguilera 1982-97 • **61** - Sebastian Abreu 1996-, Jorge Barrios 1980-92 & Paolo Montero 1991-2005 • **60** - Diego Perez 2001-

Goals
31 - Hector Scarone 1917-30 • **29** - Diego Forlan 2002- • **28** - Angel Romano 1911-27 • **27** - Oscar Miguez 1950-58 • **26** - Sebastian Abreu 1996- • **24** - Pedro Petrone 1924-30 • **23** - Carlos Aguilera 1983-97 • **22** - Fernando Morena 1971-83 • **20** - Jose Piendibene 1909-23 • **19** - Severino Varela 1935-42 • **18** - Hector Castro 1926-35 & Carlos Scarone 1909-21

Past Coaches
Jorge Pacheco 1916 • Alfredo Foglino 1916 • Julián Bértola 1917-18 • Severino Castillo 1919-20 • Ernesto Fígoli 1920-22 • Pedro Olivieri 1922-23 • Leonardo De Lucca 1923-1924 • Ernesto Meliante 1924-26 • Andrés Mazali 1926 • Ernesto Fígoli 1926 • Luis Grecco 1927-28 • Alberto Suppici 1928-32 • Raúl Blanco 1932-33 • Alberto Suppici 1933-41 • Pedro Cea 1941-42 • José Nasazzi 1942-45 • Aníbal Tejada 1945-46 • Guzmán Vila Gomensoro 1946 • Juan López 1946-55 • Juan Carlos Corazzo 1955 • Hugo Bagnulo 1955-57 • Juan López 1957-59 • Héctor Castro 1959 • Juan Corazzo 1959-61 • Enrique Fernández 1961-62 • Juan Corazzo 1962-64 • Rafael Milans 1964-65 • Ondino Viera 1965-67 • Enrique Fernández 1967-69 • Juan Hohberg 1969-70 • Hugo Bagnulo 1969-70 • Roberto Porta 1974-74 • Juan Alberto Schiaffino 1974-75 • José María Rodríguez 1975-77 • Juan Hohberg 1977 • Raúl Bentancor 1977-79 • Roque Máspoli 1979-82 • Omar Borrás 1982-87 • Roberto Fleitas 1987-88 • Oscar Tabárez 1988-90 • Luis Cubilla 1990-93 • Ildo Maneiro 1993-94 • Héctor Núñez 1994-96 • Juan Ahuntcháin 1996-97 • Roque Máspoli 1997-98 • Víctor Púa 1998-2000 • Daniel Passarella 2000-01 • Víctor Púa 2001-03 • Juan Ramón Carrasco 2003-04 • Jorge Fossati 2004-06 • Juan Ferrín 2006 • Óscar Tabárez 2006-

URUGUAY 2009–10

PRIMERA DIVISION PROFESSIONAL TABLA ANUAL

	Pl	W	D	L	F	A	Pts	Rel	Peñarol	Nacional	Liverpool	River Plate	Defensor	Rampla Jun	Wanderers	Cerro	Danubio	Racing	Fénix	C Español	Tacuarembó	Cerrito	Cerro Largo	Atenas
Peñarol † ‡	30	21	6	3	68	34	69	120		0-0	3-1	2-2	1-1	3-0	4-2	1-1	2-3	3-0	1-0	2-0	1-0	3-1	5-0	3-2
Nacional §3 †	30	21	3	6	63	26	63	118	3-0		2-1	1-4	0-1	3-0	2-1	2-0	2-1	3-2	1-1	5-1	1-0	3-1	3-1	6-0
Liverpool †	30	14	9	7	53	35	51	103	2-2	0-2		1-1	3-0	3-1	1-1	2-0	1-0	2-0	0-0	0-2	7-1	4-3	3-0	2-0
River Plate ‡	30	12	10	8	55	42	46	96	2-3	1-0	1-4		1-2	1-1	2-1	0-1	3-0	4-1	0-1	3-3	3-1	3-0	1-4	1-0
Defensor †	30	13	7	10	49	44	46	110	2-3	0-3	2-2	1-1		2-0	2-0	1-0	0-1	1-1	2-0	3-4	2-3	1-0	0-0	5-1
Rampla Juniors	30	13	7	10	36	37	46	63	1-2	1-0	2-0	1-1	1-3		2-1	2-2	2-0	0-0	2-1	0-0	1-0	1-0	0-3	4-1
Wanderers	30	11	8	11	49	39	41	76	0-2	4-0	0-0	2-2	2-2	0-1		3-1	1-3	1-2	2-0	1-1	2-1	1-2	7-1	0-0
Cerro	30	11	7	12	46	49	40	92	1-2	3-1	5-1	2-3	1-4	1-1	1-2		1-0	1-0	3-2	1-2	1-1	0-2	1-1	3-2
Danubio	30	12	3	15	47	50	39	86	1-2	0-2	2-2	2-2	3-0	1-2	2-3	4-2		2-3	1-2	2-0	4-5	1-0	2-0	0-1
Racing CM	30	11	6	13	43	51	39	89	2-1	0-3	2-0	0-2	3-3	2-1	0-4	3-3	1-2		0-2	1-0	4-1	1-1	1-2	3-1
Fénix	30	9	8	13	31	37	35	68	1-2	0-1	1-1	0-3	3-0	1-0	2-1	2-0	4-1	0-2		2-2	0-2	0-0	1-1	1-4
Central Español	30	8	10	12	37	48	34	66	2-3	0-2	0-0	2-2	0-4	0-3	1-1	1-2	2-0	1-1	1-0		4-1	2-2	1-2	1-0
Tacuarembó	30	10	4	16	39	52	34	63	1-3	1-1	0-1	2-1	0-1	0-1	0-1	3-3	1-2	2-0	1-1	3-1		1-0	3-0	2-0
Cerrito	30	8	8	14	37	48	32	62	2-2	2-5	1-4	1-1	2-0	1-1	1-2	1-4	2-2	3-0	1-0	1-2	1-3		1-1	2-0
Cerro Largo	30	7	7	16	28	52	28	56	1-2	0-1	1-0	2-1	1-3	1-1	0-0	0-1	2-3	1-3	1-0	0-1	1-2	0-1		0-2
Atenas	30	6	3	21	25	62	21	42	0-5	0-5	1-2	0-2	3-1	1-2	0-2	0-1	0-2	0-5	1-1	0-0	2-0	0-1	2-0	

22/08/2009 - 2/05/2010 • † Qualified for the Copa Libertadores • ‡ Qualified for the Copa Sudamericana • § = points deducted
Apertura matches are in the shaded boxes • Relegation calculated over two seasons (promoted clubs have season total doubled)
Championship play-offs: Peñarol qualified for the final as the overall leading points scorer. The winners of the Apertura (Nacional) and Clausura (Peñarol) played off for the right to meet Peñarol in the final • **Nacional** 2-0 Peñarol. Nacional qualified to meet Peñarol in the final. (see below)
Top scorers: **22** - Antonio Pacheco, Peñarol • **16** - Diego Ifran, Danubio & Fabricio Nunez, Cerro Largo

URUGUAY 2009–10 TORNEO APERTURA

	Pl	W	D	L	F	A	Pts
Nacional † §3	15	13	0	2	36	11	36
Liverpool	15	8	5	2	31	14	29
Defensor	15	8	5	2	28	16	29
Wanderers	15	7	5	3	24	13	26
Peñarol	15	7	5	3	28	19	26
Danubio	15	7	2	6	26	25	23
Rampla Juniors	15	7	3	5	18	19	24
River Plate	15	6	5	4	24	23	23
Racing CM	15	5	5	5	25	22	20
Cerrito	15	4	6	5	20	21	18
Cerro Largo	15	4	4	7	15	18	16
Tacuarembó	15	5	1	9	17	24	16
Central Español	15	2	6	7	13	28	12
Cerro	15	2	5	8	18	31	11
Atenas	15	3	2	10	9	32	11
Fénix	15	1	3	11	10	26	6

22/08/2009 - 13/12/2009 • † Qualified for play-off

URUGUAY 2009–10 TORNEO CLAUSURA

	Pl	W	D	L	F	A	Pts
Peñarol †	15	14	1	0	40	15	43
Cerro	15	9	2	4	28	18	29
Fénix	15	8	5	2	21	11	29
Nacional	15	8	3	4	27	15	27
River Plate	15	6	5	4	31	19	23
Central Español	15	6	4	5	24	20	22
Liverpool	15	6	4	5	22	21	22
Rampla Juniors	15	6	4	5	18	18	22
Racing CM	15	6	1	8	18	29	19
Tacuarembó	15	5	3	7	22	28	18
Defensor	15	5	2	8	21	28	17
Danubio	15	5	1	9	21	25	16
Wanderers	15	4	3	8	25	26	15
Cerrito	15	4	2	9	17	27	14
Cerro Largo	15	3	3	9	13	34	12
Atenas	15	3	1	11	16	30	10

23/01/2010 - 2/05/2010 • † Qualified for play-off

CHAMPIONSHIP FINAL 2010

1st leg. Centenario, Montevideo, 15-05-2010, 16:00
Att: 35 000, Ref: Hector Martinez

Nacional 0
Peñarol 1 Pacheco [24]

Nacional - Rodrigo Munoz - Alvaro Gonzalez (Matias Cabrera 73♦77), Alejandro Lembo●, Sebastian Coates●, Christian Nunez - Oscar Javier Morales (c), Raul Ferro (Maximiliano Calzada 46♦63) - Gustavo Varela●, Angel Morales (Diego Vera 75) - Santiago Garcia●, Mario Regueiro●. Tr: Eduardo Acevedo
Peñarol - Sebastian Sosa - Matias Aguirregaray, Alejandro Gonzalez●, Guillermo Rodriguez, Dario Rodriguez● - Jonathan Urretaviscaya♦72, Egidio Arevalo, Sergio Orteman, Gaston Ramirez (Diego Alonso 75) - Antonio Pacheco (c) (Silvio Frontan 67), Alejandro Martinuccio (Ruben Olivera 83♦94+). Tr: Diego Aguirre

CHAMPIONSHIP FINAL 2010

2nd leg. Centenario, Montevideo, 18-05-2010, 16:00
Att: 40 000, Ref: Dario Ubriaco

Peñarol 1 Aguirregaray [68]
Nacional 1 Lembo [35]

Peñarol - Sebastian Sosa - Emiliano Albin●, Alejandro Gonzalez, Guillermo Rodriguez●, Dario Rodriguez - Matias Aguirregaray● (Marcel Roman 94+), Egidio Arevalo, Sergio Orteman, Gaston Ramirez●●♦79 - Antonio Pacheco (c) (Marcelo Sosa 74), Alejandro Martinuccio (Diego Alonso 89). Tr: Diego Aguirre
Nacional - Rodrigo Munoz - Gustavo Varela●, Alejandro Lembo●, Sebastian Coates, Christian Nunez - Raul Ferro (Sebastian Balsas 80), Oscar Javier Morales - Alvaro Gonzalez (Mauricio Pereyra● 72), Angel Morales (Sergio Blanco 77♦88), Mario Regueiro● - Santiago Garcia. Tr: Eduardo Acevedo

URUGUAY 2009-10
SEGUNDA DIVISION (2)
TORNEO APERTURA

	Pl	W	D	L	F	A	Pts
Miramar Misiones †	11	9	2	0	25	7	29
Juventud Las Piedras	11	6	3	2	18	12	21
El Tanque Sisley	11	6	2	3	16	10	20
Bella Vista	11	4	3	4	18	18	15
Progreso	11	4	2	5	15	11	14
Maldonado	11	3	5	3	17	15	14
Rocha	11	3	5	3	7	8	14
Boston River	11	3	4	4	9	14	13
Sud América	11	4	1	6	9	14	13
Durazno	11	3	3	5	16	19	12
Rentistas	11	2	4	5	13	20	10
Plaza Colonia	11	0	4	7	7	22	4

12/09/2009 - 5/12/2009 • † Qualified for play-off

URUGUAY 2009-10
SEGUNDA DIVISION (2)
TORNEO CLAUSURA

	Pl	W	D	L	F	A	Pts
Bella Vista †	11	8	1	2	22	11	25
El Tanque Sisley	11	7	3	1	16	10	24
Rentistas	11	5	2	4	20	13	17
Rocha	11	5	2	4	19	12	17
Progreso	11	4	4	3	18	13	16
Juventud Las Piedras	11	4	3	4	20	14	15
Sud América	11	4	3	4	21	21	15
Miramar Misiones	11	3	4	4	19	20	13
Maldonado	11	3	4	4	9	14	13
Boston River	11	3	2	6	15	17	11
Plaza Colonia	11	3	1	7	13	28	10
Durazno	11	2	1	8	10	29	7

20/02/2010 - 4/05/2010 • † Qualified for play-off

URUGUAY 2009-10
SEGUNDA DIVISION (2)
TABLA ANUAL

	Pl	W	D	L	F	A	Pts
El Tanque Sisley	22	13	5	4	32	20	44
Miramar Misiones	22	12	6	4	44	27	42
Bella Vista	22	12	4	6	40	29	40
Juventud Las Piedras †	22	10	6	6	38	26	36
Rocha †	22	8	7	7	26	20	31
Progreso †	22	8	6	8	33	24	30
Sud América	22	8	4	10	30	35	28
Rentistas	22	7	6	9	33	33	27
Maldonado	22	6	9	7	26	29	27
Boston River	22	6	6	10	24	31	24
Durazno	22	5	4	13	26	48	19
Plaza Colonia	22	3	5	14	20	50	14

12/09/2009 - 5/12/2009 • † Qualified for play-off • Tanque
Sisley promoted with the best overall record

FIRST PROMOTION PLAY-OFF

Played between Apertura and Clausura winners

Bella Vista   0-0 2-1   Miramar Misiones

Bella Vista promoted • Miramar to the Second Promotion Play-off

SECOND PROMOTION PLAY-OFF

Semi-finals			Finals
Miramar Misiones	1	1	
Progreso	0	1	

Miramar Misiones	1	2
Juventud Las Piedras	1	0

Rocha	2	2
Juventud Las Piedras	2	6

Miramar Promoted

MEDALS TABLE

		Overall			League			Sth Am		
		G	S	B	G	S	B	G	S	B
1	Peñarol	53	46	18	48	40	5	5	6	13
2	Nacional	45	45	22	42	41	12	3	4	10
3	Montevideo Wanderers	4	6	14	4	6	14			
4	Defensor Sporting	4	6	8	4	6	8			
5	River Plate	4	1	1	4	1	1			
6	Danubio	3	4	5	3	4	4			1
7	Rampla Juniors	1	5	14	1	5	14			
8	Bella Vista	1	1	2	1	1	2			
9	Central Español	1		4	1		4			
10	Progreso	1			1					
11	Cerro		1	6		1	6			
12	Universal		1	4		1	4			
13	CA River Plate		1	2		1	2			
14	Albion		1	1		1	1			
15	Rocha		1			1				
16	CA Fénix			3			3			
	Liverpool			3			3			
18	Deutscher			2			2			
	Lito			2			2			
20	Dublin			1			1			
	Huracán			1			1			
	Miramar Misiones			1			1			
	Racing Club de Montevideo			1			1			
	Uruguay Montevideo			1			1			

USA – UNITED STATES OF AMERICA

FIFA/COCA-COLA WORLD RANKING

1993	1994	1995	1996	1997	1998	1999	2000	2001	2002	2003	2004	2005	2006	2007	2008	2009	2010
22	23	19	18	26	23	22	16	24	10	11	11	8	31	19	22	14	18

	2010												Hi/Lo
	Jan	Feb	Mar	Mar	Apr	May	Jul	Aug	Sep	Oct	Nov	Dec	4
	14	14	18	16	14	14	13	18	18	25	24	18	35

At the 2010 FIFA World Cup finals in South Africa, the USA showed remarkable grit and determination in winning their first round group after finding themselves behind against both England and Slovenia in their opening two matches. They fought back to force draws in both games but looked on the way out of the tournament before an injury-time winner from Landon Donovan against Algeria saw them leapfrog England to qualify in first place. That left the Americans in the most open quarter of the draw with a potential semi-final place for the taking. Against Ghana in the round of 16, however, they again found themselves behind and the energy spent constantly chasing games finally took its toll as they went down 2-1 after extra-time. The tournament proved that the USA has matured as a football nation and that the 2002 World Cup quarter-final appearance wasn't just a flash in the pan. One weakness of the game in America is the lack of progress in international club competition and in the 2009-10 CONCACAF Champions League Mexican teams once again ruled the roost. At home Colorado Rapids won the MLS Cup for the first time after beating FC Dallas 2-1 in the final - the seventh different winners in the past eight years - whilst expansion team Seattle Sounders retained the US Open Cup.

FIFA WORLD CUP RECORD

1930 3 SF **1934** 16 r1 **1938** DNE **1950** 10 r1 **1954** DNE **1958-1986** DNQ
1990 23 r1 **1994** 14 r2 (hosts) **1998** 32 r1 **2002** 8 QF **2006** 25 r1 **2010** 12 r2

US SOCCER FEDERATION (USSF)

US Soccer House,
1801 S. Prairie Avenue,
Chicago IL 60616
☎ +1 312 8081300
🖷 +1 312 8081301
✉ communications@ussoccer.org
🖳 www.ussoccer.com
FA 1913 CON 1961 FIFA 1914
P Sunil Gulati
GS Dan Flynn

FIFA BIG COUNT 2006

Total players	24 472 778
% of population	8.20%
Male	17 416 859
Female	7 055 919
Amateurs 18+	260 928
Youth under 18	3 907 065
Unregistered	13 466 000
Professionals	1 513
Referees	140 000
Admin & coaches	656 300
Number of clubs	5 000
Number of teams	400 000

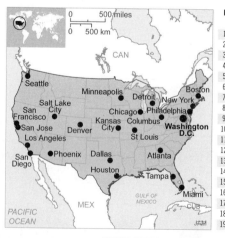

MAJOR CITIES/TOWNS

		Population
1	New York	8 459 053
2	Los Angeles	3 878 732
3	Chicago	2 878 957
4	Houston	2 307 889
5	Phoenix	1 635 801
6	Philadelphia	1 445 991
7	San Antonio	1 402 014
8	San Diego	1 309 752
9	Dallas	1 304 933
10	San Jose	977 894
11	Detroit	901 163
12	Jacksonville	822 422
13	San Francisco	817 244
14	Indianapolis	803 933
15	Austin	792 779
16	Columbus	768 665
17	Fort Worth	751 151
18	Charlotte	723 518
19	Memphis	662 997

UNITED STATES OF AMERICA

Capital	Washington DC	Population	307 212 123 (3)	% in cities	82%
GDP per capita	$47 500 (10)	Area km²	9 826 675 km² (3)	GMT +/-	-5 to -11
Neighbours (km)	Canada 8893, Mexico 3141 • Coast 19 924				

RECENT INTERNATIONAL MATCHES PLAYED BY THE USA

2009	Opponents	Score		Venue	Comp	Scorers	Att	Referee
24-01	Sweden	W	3-2	Carson	Fr	Klejstan 3 [17 40p 74]	9 918	Petrescu CAN
11-02	Mexico	W	2-0	Columbus	WCq	Bradley 2 [43 92+]	23 776	Batres GUA
28-03	El Salvador	D	2-2	San Salvador	WCq	Altidore [77], Hejduk [88]	30 350	Archundia MEX
1-04	Trinidad and Tobago	W	3-0	Nashville	WCq	Altidore 3 [13 71 89]	27 958	Moreno PAN
3-06	Costa Rica	L	1-3	San Jose	WCq	Donovan [90]	19 200	Brizan TRI
6-06	Honduras	W	2-1	Chicago	WCq	Donovan [41p], Bocanegra [67]	55 647	Morales MEX
15-06	Italy	L	1-3	Pretoria	CCr1	Donovan [41p]	34 341	Pozo CHI
18-06	Brazil	L	0-3	Pretoria	CCr1		39 617	Busacca SUI
21-06	Egypt	W	3-0	Rustenburg	CCr1	Davies [21], Bradley [63], Dempsey [71]	23 140	Hester NZL
24-06	Spain	W	2-0	Bloemfontein	CCsf	Altidore [27], Dempsey [74]	35 369	Larrionda URU
28-06	Brazil	L	2-3	Johannesburg	CCf	Dempsey [10], Donovan [27]	52 291	Hansson SWE
4-07	Grenada	W	4-0	Seattle	GCr1	Adu [7], Holden [31], Rogers [60], Davies [69]	15 387	Lopez GUA
8-07	Honduras	W	2-0	Washington DC	GCr1	Quaranta [74], Ching [79]	26 079	Campbell JAM
11-07	Haiti	D	2-2	Foxboro	GCr1	Arnaud [5], Holden [90]	24 137	Quesada CRC
18-07	Panama	W	2-1	Philadelphia	GCqf	Beckerman [49], Cooper [106p]	32 000	Archundia MEX
23-07	Honduras	W	2-0	Chicago	GCsf	Goodson [45], Cooper [90]	55 173	Campbell JAM
26-07	Mexico	L	0-5	New Jersey	GCf		79 156	Campbell JAM
12-08	Mexico	L	1-2	Mexico City	WCq	Davies [9]	104 499	Moreno PAN
5-09	El Salvador	W	2-1	Sandy	WCq	Dempsey [41], Altidore [45]	19 066	Pineda HON
9-09	Trinidad and Tobago	W	1-0	Port of Spain	WCq	Clark [61]	4 700	Aguilar SLV
10-10	Honduras	W	3-2	San Pedro Sula	WCq	Casey 2 [50 66], Donovan [71]	37 000	Moreno PAN
14-10	Costa Rica	D	2-2	Washington DC	WCq	Bradley [71], Bornstein [94+]	26 243	Archundia MEX
14-11	Slovakia	L	0-1	Bratislava	Fr		7 200	Messner AUT
18-11	Denmark	L	1-3	Aarhus	Fr	Cunningham [26]	15 172	Thomson SCO
2010								
23-01	Honduras	L	1-3	Carson	Fr	Goodson [70]	18 626	Archundia MEX
24-02	El Salvador	W	2-1	Tampa	Fr	Ching [75], Kljestan [90]	21 737	Petrescu CAN
3-03	Netherlands	L	1-2	Amsterdam	Fr	Bocanegra [88]	46 630	Cakir TUR
25-05	Czech Republic	L	2-4	East Hartford	Fr	Edu [17], Gomez [66]	36 218	Morales MEX
29-05	Turkey	W	2-1	Philadelphia	Fr	Altidore [58], Dempsey [75]	55 407	Petrescu CAN
5-06	Australia	W	3-1	Roodepoort	Fr	Buddle 2 [4 31], Gomez [90]	6 000	Ebrahim RSA
12-06	England	D	1-1	Rustenburg	WCr1	Dempsey [40]	38 646	Simon BRA
18-06	Slovenia	D	2-2	Johannesburg	WCr1	Donovan [48], Bradley [82]	45 573	Coulibaly MLI
23-06	Algeria	W	1-0	Pretoria	WCr1	Donovan [91+]	35 827	De Bleeckere BEL
26-06	Ghana	L	1-2	Rustenburg	WCr2	Donovan [62p]	34 976	Kassai HUN
10-08	Brazil	L	0-2	New Jersey	Fr		77 223	Brizan TRI
9-10	Poland	D	2-2	Chicago	Fr	Altidore [13], Onyewu [52]	31 696	Depiero CAN
12-10	Colombia	D	0-0	Chester	Fr		8 823	Garcia MEX
17-11	South Africa	W	1-0	Cape Town	Fr	Agudelo [85]	52 000	Kirwa KEN

Fr = Friendly match • GC = CONCACAF Gold Cup • CC = FIFA Confederations Cup • WC = FIFA World Cup
q = qualifier • r1 = first round group • qf = quarter-final • sf = semi-final • f = final

USA NATIONAL TEAM HISTORICAL RECORDS

Caps
164 - Cobi Jones 1992-2004 • **134** - Jeff Agoos 1988-2003 • **128** - Landon Donovan 2000- & Marcelo Balboa 1988-2000 • **112** - Claudio Reyna 1994-2006 • **110** - Paul Caligiuri 1984-97 • **106** - Eric Wynalda 1990-2000 • **102** - 1990-2007 • **101** - Earnie Stewart 1990-2004 • **100** - Tony Meola 1988-2006 & Joe-Max Moore 1992-2002 • **96** - Alexi Lalas 1990-98 • **95** - Brian McBride 1993-2006 • **93** - DaMarcus Beasley 2001- • **90** - John Harkes 1987-2000 • **86** - Bruce Murray 1985-93 • **85** - Frankie Hejduk 1997-2009

Goals
45 - Landon Donovan 2000- • **34** - Eric Wynalda 1990-2000 • **30** - Brian McBride 1993-2006 • **24** - Joe-Max Moore 1992-2002 • **21** - Bruce Murray 1985-93 • **19** - Clint Dempsey 2004-10 • **17** - DaMarcus Beasley 2001- & Earnie Stewart 1990-2004 • **15** - Cobi Jones 1992-2004

Past Coaches
Thomas Cahill 1916-24 • George Burford 1924-25 • Nat Agar 1925-26 • George Burford 1928 • Robert Millar 1929-33 • David Gould 1933-34 • Bill Lloyd 1934-37 • Andrew Brown 1947-48 • Walter Giesler 1948-49 • Bill Jeffrey 1949-52 • John Wood 1952-53 • Erno Schwarz 1953-55 • George Meyer 1957 • Jim Reed 1959-61 • John Herberger 1964 • George Meyer 1965 • Phil Woosnam 1968 • Gordon Jago 1969 • Bob Kehoe 1971-72 • Max Wosniak 1973 • Eugene Chyzowych 1973 • Gordon Bradley 1973 • Dettmar Cramer 1974 • Al Miller 1975 • Manny Schellscheidt 1975 • Walter Chyzowych 1976-80 • Bob Gansler 1982 • Alkis Panagoulias 1983-85 • Lothar Osiander 1986-88 • Bob Gansler 1989-91 • John Kowalski 1991 • Bora Milutinovic 1991-95 • Steve Sampson 1995-98 • Bruce Arena 1998-2006 • Bob Bradley 2006-

USA 2010

MAJOR LEAGUE SOCCER REGULAR SEASON

Eastern Conference	Pl	W	D	L	F	A	Pts	New York	Columbus	Kansas	Chicago	Toronto	NE Revs	Philadelphia	DC United	LA Galaxy	Salt Lake	Dallas	Seattle	Colorado	San Jose	Houston	Chivas
New York Red Bulls †	30	15	6	9	38	29	51		1-3	1-0	1-0	1-0	2-0	2-1	0-0	0-1	0-0	2-1	0-1	3-1	2-0	2-1	1-0
Columbus Crew †	30	14	8	8	40	34	50	2-0		0-1	2-1	2-0	3-2	3-1	2-0	0-2	1-0	0-0	0-4	3-1	0-0	3-0	1-0
Kansas City Wizards	30	11	6	13	36	35	39	0-3	0-1		2-2	1-0	4-1	2-0	4-0	0-0	1-1	1-3	1-2	1-0	4-1	4-3	0-1
Chicago Fire	30	9	9	12	37	38	36	0-0	2-0	0-2		0-0	2-1	2-1	0-0	1-1	0-1	1-1	0-1	2-2	1-2	2-0	1-1
Toronto FC	30	9	8	13	33	41	35	1-4	2-2	0-0	4-1		1-0	2-1	0-1	0-0	0-0	1-1	2-0	1-0	2-3	1-1	2-1
New England Revs	30	9	5	16	32	50	32	3-2	2-2	1-0	0-1	4-1		1-2	1-0	2-0	1-2	1-1	3-1	1-2	0-0	1-0	0-4
Philadelphia Union	30	8	7	15	35	49	31	2-1	1-2	1-1	1-0	2-1	1-1		3-2	0-1	1-1	1-1	3-1	1-1	1-2	1-1	3-0
DC United	30	6	4	20	21	47	22	0-2	0-1	2-1	0-2	2-3	0-2	2-0		1-2	0-0	1-3	0-1	0-1	0-2	1-3	3-2
Western Conference	Pl	W	D	L	F	A	Pts																
Los Angeles Galaxy †	30	18	5	7	44	26	59	0-2	3-1	0-2	2-3	0-0	1-0	3-1	2-1		2-1	2-1	3-1	1-3	2-2	4-1	2-0
Real Salt Lake †	30	15	11	4	45	20	56	0-0	2-0	4-1	1-0	2-1	5-0	3-0	3-0	1-0		2-0	3-1	1-1	0-0	3-1	1-1
FC Dallas †	30	12	14	4	42	28	50	2-2	2-1	1-0	3-0	1-0	2-2	3-1	1-0	0-1	2-0		2-2	2-2	2-0	1-1	1-1
Seattle Sounders †	30	14	6	10	39	35	48	0-1	1-1	3-2	2-1	3-2	3-0	2-0	2-3	0-4	0-0	1-1		1-1	0-1	2-0	2-1
Colorado Rapids †	30	12	10	8	44	32	46	1-1	1-0	1-1	2-2	3-1	3-0	4-1	0-1	0-1	2-2	1-1	1-0		1-0	3-0	3-0
San Jose E'quakes †	30	13	7	10	34	33	46	4-0	2-2	1-0	0-3	1-3	2-0	1-0	1-1	1-0	0-3	0-0	0-1	1-0		0-1	3-0
Houston Dynamo	30	9	6	15	40	49	33	2-2	0-0	0-2	4-3	1-2	1-2	2-3	2-0	3-0	2-1	0-1	2-1	2-2	1-2		3-0
Chivas USA	30	8	4	18	31	45	28	2-0	3-1	1-2	1-4	3-0	2-0	1-1	1-0	1-2	1-2	1-2	0-0	0-1	3-2	0-2	

25/03/2010 - 24/10/2010 • † Qualified for the play-offs • Top scorers: 18 - Chris Wondolowski, San Jose • 17 - Edson Buddle, LA Galaxy 15 - Dwayne De Rosario CAN, Toronto • 14 - Omar Cummings JAM, Colorado & Sebastian Le Toux FRA, Philadelphia • 13 - Juan Pablo Angel COL, New York & Conor Casey, Colorado • 12 - Alvaro Saborio CRC, Salt Lake • 11 - Jeff Cunningham, Dallas

MLS PLAY-OFFS 2010

Quarter-finals		Semi-finals		Final	
Colorado	1 1 5p				
Columbus	0 2 4p	**Colorado**	1		
NY Red Bulls	1 1	San Jose	0		
San Jose	0 3			**Colorado**	2
LA Galaxy	1 2			Dallas	1
Seattle	0 1	LA Galaxy	0		
Salt Lake	1 1	**Dallas**	3		
Dallas	2 1				

MLS CUP 2010

BMO Field, Toronto, 21-11-2010, 20:30,
Att: 21 700, Ref: Baldomero Toledo

Colorado Rapids 2 Casey [57], John OG [107]
FC Dallas 1 Ferreira [35]

Colorado - Matt Pickens - Kosuke Kimura, Marvell Wynne, Drew Moor, Anthony Wallace• (Wells Thompson 90) - Brian Mullan, Pablo Mastroeni (c), Jeff Larentowicz, Jamie Smith• (Julien Baudet 90) - Omar Cummings (Macoumba Kandji 98), Conor Casey•. Tr: Gary Smith
Dallas - Kevin Hartman - Jackson Goncalves (Zach Lloyd 34), George John, Ugo Ihemelu, Jair Benitez• - Dax McCarty, Daniel Hernandez (c) - Marvin Chavez (Eric Avila 105), David Ferreira, Brek Shea (Jeff Cunningham 64) - Atiba Harris. Tr: Schellas Hyndman

USA 2010
USSF DIVISION 2 PRO LEAGUE (2)

	Pl	W	D	L	F	A	Pts
Rochester Rhinos ‡	30	16	8	6	38	24	54
Carolina RailHawks ‡	30	13	9	8	44	32	47
Austin Aztex ‡	30	15	7	8	53	40	53
Portland Timbers ‡	30	13	7	10	34	23	49
Vancouver Whitecaps ‡	30	10	5	15	32	22	45
Montreal Impact ‡	30	12	11	7	36	30	43
Minnesota Stars ‡	30	11	12	7	32	36	40
Puerto Rico Islanders ‡	30	9	11	10	37	35	37
Miami FC Blues	30	7	11	12	37	49	33
FC Tampa Bay	30	7	12	11	41	46	32
AC St Louis	30	7	15	8	32	48	29
C. Palace Baltimore	30	6	18	6	24	55	24

10/04/2010 - 30/10/2010 • ‡ Qualified for the play-offs
Quarter-finals: **Puerto Rico Islanders** 2-0 1-2 Rochester Rhinos; **Vancouver Whitecaps** 2-0 0-1 Portland Timbers; **Montreal Impact** 2-0 2-3 Austin Aztex; Minnesota Stars 0-0 0-4 **Carolina RailHawks**
Semi-finals: **Puerto Rico Islanders** 0-0 2-0 Vancouver Whitecaps; Montreal Impact 1-0 0-2 **Carolina RailHawks** •
Final: **Puerto Rico Islanders** 2-0 1-1 Carolina RailHawks
Puerto Rico Islanders are the 2010 champions

MEDALS TABLE

		Overall			Lge		Cup		CON'CAF		
		G	S	B	G	S	G	S	G	S	B
1	DC United	7	3	6	4	1	2	2	1		6
2	Los Angeles Galaxy	5	7		2	4	2	2	1	1	
3	Chicago Fire	5	3	2	1	2	4	1			2
4	Columbus Crew	2	2		1		1	2			
5	Kansas City Wizards	2	1	1	1	1	1				1
6	Houston Dynamo	2		2	2						2
7	San Jose Earthquakes	2			2						
	Seattle Sounders	2						2			
9	New England Revolution	1	5		4	1	1				
10	FC Dallas	1	3		1		1	2			
11	Colorado Rapids	1	2		1	1	1				
12	Rochester Rhinos	1	1				1	1			
13	Real Salt Lake	1			1						
14	New York Red Bulls		2			1		1			
15	Charleston Battery		1					1			
	Miami Fusion		1					1			

LAMAR HUNT US OPEN CUP 2010

Second Round		Third Round		Quarter-finals		Semi-finals		Final	
Seattle Sounders	Bye	**Seattle Sounders**	1 4p						
Kitsap Pumas*	1	Portland Timbers*	1 3p						
Portland Timbers	4			**Seattle Sounders***	2				
AC St Louis	1	AC St Louis	0	LA Galaxy	0				
Minnesota Stars*	0	**LA Galaxy***	2						
LA Galaxy	Bye					**Seattle Sounders** *‡	3		
Houston Dynamo	Bye	**Houston Dynamo***	1			Chivas USA	1		
FC Tampa Bay	1	Miami FC	0	Houston Dynamo*	1				
Miami FC*	2			**Chivas USA**	3				
Austin Aztex*	3	Austin Aztex*	0					**Seattle Sounders**	2
Arizona Sahuaros	1	**Chivas USA***	1					Columbus Crew	1
Chivas USA	Bye								
DC United	Bye	**DC United***	2						
Real Maryland Monarchs	1	Richmond Kickers	0	**DC United***	2				
Richmond Kickers*	3			Harrisburg City Islanders	0				
New York Red Bulls	Bye	New York Red Bulls	0						
Long Island Rough Riders	0	**Harrisburg City Islanders***	1			DC United*	1		
Harrisburg City Islanders*	1					**Columbus Crew** †	2		
Charleston Battery*	2	**Charleston Battery**	0 3p						
Carolina RailHawks	1	Chicago Fire*	0 0p	Charleston Battery	0				
Chicago Fire	Bye			**Columbus Crew***	3				
Rochester Rhinos*	3	Rochester Rhinos	1						
Pittsburgh Riverhounds	0	**Columbus Crew***	2						
Columbus Crew	Bye								

CUP FINAL

Qwest Field, Seattle, 5-10-2010, 19:50
Att: 31 311, Ref: Kennedy
Scorers - Nyassi 2 38 66 for Seattle; Burns [24]

Seattle - Casey Keller (c) - James Riley*, Patrick Ianni, Jeff Parke, Tyson Wahl - Sanna Nyassi* (Alvaro Fernandez 79), Nathan Sturgis, Osvaldo Alonso*, Steve Zakuani (Roger Levesque 90) - Blaise N'Kufo, Fredy Montero (Nate Jaqua 93+). Tr: Sigi Schmid

Crew - Andy Gruenebaum - Frankie Hejduk (c), Chad Marshall, Andy Iro, Shaun Francis* - Emmanuel Ekpo, Brian Carroll*, Kevin Burns (Andres Mendoza 78), Eddie Gaven (Robbie Rogers 81) - Guillermo Barros Schelotto*, Steven Lenhart (Emilio Renteria 78). Tr: Robert Warzycha

* Home team • † Played at RFK, Washington • ‡ Played at Starfire Sports Complex, Tukwila

CLUB BY CLUB GUIDE TO THE 2010 SEASON IN THE USA

CHICAGO FIRE 2010

	Date	Opp	Res	Score	Comp	Scorers	Att
Apr	27	New York	L	0-1	MLS		24 572
	3	Colorado	D	2-2	MLS	John 26, McBride 50p	11 641
	10	San Jose	L	1-2	MLS	Pappa 52	20 276
	17	DC United	W	2-0	MLS	Pappa 80, McBride 89	18 407
	24	Houston	W	2-0	MLS	Husidic 45, Lowry 67	11 312
May	1	Chivas USA	D	1-1	MLS	Husidic 52	13 224
	8	Toronto	L	1-4	MLS	Pause 51	20 060
	15	Kansas City	D	2-2	MLS	Martinez 15, McBride 48	8 155
	27	Dallas	D	1-1	MLS	McBride 40	12 522
Jun	5	Philadelphia	W	2-1	MLS	Husidic 14, Pappa 74	14 658
	9	Colorado	D	2-2	MLS	Pappa 2 24 45	13 607
	27	NE Revs	W	1-0	MLS	Pappa 29	12 306
	29	Charleston	D	0-0	OCr3	L 0-3p	2 526
Jul	3	Columbus	L	1-2	MLS	OG 44	14 017
	8	Salt Lake	L	0-1	MLS		17 847
Aug	1	LA Galaxy	W	3-2	MLS	Pappa 3, John 5, Banner 19	20 348
	4	New York	D	0-0	MLS		21 868
	18	NE Revs	W	2-1	MLS	Husidic 32, Carr 85	14 056
	21	Houston	L	3-4	MLS	Carr 55, OG 69, Conde 81	18 890
	28	Seattle	L	1-2	MLS	Thorrington 27p	36 386
	4	LA Galaxy	D	1-1	MLS	John 87	21 068
	8	Toronto	D	0-0	MLS		12 891
Sep	11	Philadelphia	L	0-1	MLS		18 563
	18	Salt Lake	L	0-1	MLS		14 440
	25	Seattle	L	0-1	MLS		17 477
	29	San Jose	W	3-0	MLS	Kinney 39, Ljungberg 72, Nyarko 90	9 829
	2	Dallas	L	0-3	MLS		10 615
Oct	3	Columbus	W	2-0	MLS	Lowry 31, McBride 53	15 124
	12	Kasas City	D	0-0	MLS		12 230
	16	DC United	D	0-0	MLS		19 056
	23	Chivas USA	W	4-1	MLS	McBride 40, Ljungberg 47, Carr 68, Husidic 90	14 825

CHIVAS USA 2010

	Date	Opp	Res	Score	Comp	Scorers	Att
Apr	26	Colorado	L	0-1	MLS		18 653
	1	LA Galaxy	L	0-2	MLS		19 805
	10	New York	W	2-0	MLS	OG 47, Padilla 90	12 597
	17	Houston	L	0-3	MLS		14 843
	24	San Jose	W	3-2	MLS	Kljestan 25, Braun 54, Chijindu 88	14 389
May	1	Chicago	D	1-1	MLS	Maicon 78	13 224
	5	NE Revs	W	4-0	MLS	Padilla 2 27 49, Braun 34, Gavin 81	5 990
	8	Houston	L	0-2	MLS		12 577
	15	Columbus	L	0-1	MLS		15 027
	22	Salt Lake	L	1-2	MLS	Braun 81	14 287
	27	DC United	L	2-3	MLS	Braun 16, Galindo 80	13 043
	5	New York	L	0-1	MLS		18 815
Jun	26	Dallas	L	1-2	MLS	Romero 59	14 173
	29	Austin	W	1-0	OCr3	Padilla 13	
	3	Philadelphia	D	1-1	MLS	Gavin 42	14 479
	6	Houston	W	3-1	OCqf	Braun 2 5 90, Lahoud 65	1 097
Jul	10	Kansas City	W	2-0	MLS	Braun 2 55 87	10 288
	24	Salt Lake	D	1-1	MLS	Padilla 70	19 469
	31	Columbus	W	3-1	MLS	Braun 37, Gavin 45, Borja 54	13 419
	7	Toronto	L	1-2	MLS	Maldonado 66p	20 648
Aug	14	Seattle	D	0-0	MLS		13 839
	21	Dallas	L	0-1	MLS		10 309
	29	DC United	W	1-0	MLS	Braun 13	12 517
	1	Seattle	L	1-3	OCsf	Padilla 66	4 547
	4	Colorado	L	0-3	MLS		10 321
Sep	10	NE Revs	W	2-0	MLS	Braun 6, Nagamura 37	10 783
	19	Kansas City	L	0-2	MLS		15 382
	25	Philadelphia	L	0-3	MLS		16 481
	2	LA Galaxy	L	1-2	MLS	Gordon 63	24 283
	9	Toronto	W	3-0	MLS	Flores 51, Padilla 88, Espinoza 90	12 426
Oct	15	Seattle	L	0-2	MLS	Padilla 90	36 356
	20	San Jose	L	0-3	MLS		9 633
	23	Chicago	L	1-4	MLS	Maldonado 58	14 825

CHICAGO MLS APPEARANCES/GOALS 2010

Goalkeepers Andrew Dykstra 17 • Sean Johnson 13
Defenders CJ Brown 26/0 • Wilman Conde COL 22+3/1 • Steven Kinney 10+3/1 • Krzysztof Krol POL 17+2/0 • Dasan Robinson 17/0 • Gonzalo Segares CRC 6/0 • Tim Ward 6/0 • Kwame Watson-Siriboe 10+3/0
Midfield Mike Banner 9+9/1 • Corben Bone 1+4/0 • Nery Castillo MEX 6+2/0 • Baggio Husidic BIH 18+4/5 • Freddie Ljungberg SWE 13+2/2 • Justin Mapp 6+4/0 • Marco Pappa GUA 23+2/7 • Logan Pause 26/1 • Bratislav Ristic SRB 8/0 • John Thorrington 5/1 • Deris Umanzor SLV 5+5/0
Forwards Calen Carr 4+10/3 • Stefan Dimitrov BUL 1+4/0 • Collins John NED 10+7/3 • Peter Lowry 12+3/2 • Julio Martínez SLV 2+1/1 • Brian McBride 18+8/6 • Patrick Nyarko GHA 22+5/1
Coach Carlos De los Cobos MEX

CHIVAS MLS APPEARANCES/GOALS 2010

Goalkeepers Kevin Guppy 1 • Dan Kennedy 6+1 • Zach Thornton 23
Defenders Jonathan Bornstein 17+4/0 • Yamith Cuesta COL 3+3/0 • Dario Delgado CRC 21+1/0 • Ante Jazic CAN 21/0 • Michael Umana CRC 28/0 • Alex Zotinca ROU 1/0
Midfield Carlos Borja MEX 4+4/1 • Bryan de la Fuente 0+1/0 • Rodolfo Espinoza MEX 14+1/1 • Jorge Flores 6+2/1 • Blair Gavin 16/3 • Sacha Kljestan 10/1 • Michael Lahoud 20+3/0 • Jose Macotelo CRC 0+3/0 • Marcelo Saragosa BRA 9+5/0 • Paulo Nagamura BRA 15/1 • Osael Romero SLV 5+4/1 • Mariano Trujillo MEX 28/0 • Ben Zemanski 17+5/0 • Salvatore Zizzo 1+9/0
Forwards Justin Braun 24+4/9 • Maykel Galindo CUB 4+2/1 • Ian Gordon 8+1/1 • Maicon BRA 3+5/1 • Giancarlo Maldonado VEN 7+3/2 • Jesús Padilla MEX 14+12/6
Coach Martin Vasquez MEX

KEY TO THE CLUB SECTION

MLS = Major League Soccer • PO = MLS Play-offs • OC = Lamar Hunt US Open Cup • CL = CONCACAF Champions League • pr = preliminary round • gA = Group A etc • qf = quarter-final • sf = semi-final • f = final
Matches that are shaded were played at home; matches with no shading were played either away or on a neutral ground
The figures for the player appearances and goals consist of three elements - matches started+appearances as a substitute/goals scored and include matches played in the play-offs

COLORADO RAPIDS 2010

	26 Chivas USA	W	1-0	MLS	Cummings [55]	18 653
	3 Chicago	D	2-2	MLS	Cummings [13], Casey [40p]	11 641
	10 Kansas City	L	0-1	MLS		10 228
Apr	14 Kansas City	W	2-1	OCq	Thompson 2 [24 80]	1 226
	18 Toronto	W	3-1	MLS	Casey 2 [23p 85p], Larentowicz [71]	9 928
	24 NE Revs	W	2-1	MLS	Ballouchy [13], Mastroeni [74]	8 142
	1 San Jose	L	0-1	MLS		8 674
	5 LA Galaxy	L	0-1	MLS		9 882
May	15 DC United	W	1-0	MLS	Ballouchy [66]	13 570
	26 New York	L	0-3	OCq		2 637
	29 Seattle	W	1-0	MLS	Casey [64]	18 166
Jun	5 Columbus	W	1-0	MLS	Moor [85]	14 318
	9 Chicago	D	2-2	MLS	Cummings [21], Casey [90]	13 607
	26 Houston	D	2-2	MLS	Casey [45], OG [72]	13 744
	4 New York	D	1-1	MLS	Cummings [15]	18 363
	10 Toronto	L	0-1	MLS		21 836
Jul	17 Kansas City	W	1-0	MLS	Casey [75]	12 825
	25 Seattle	L	1-2	MLS	Cummings [9]	36 333
	31 Dallas	D	1-1	MLS	Ballouchy [26p]	10 596
	7 San Jose	W	1-0	MLS	OG [26]	12 701
Aug	14 Philadelphia	D	1-1	MLS	Larentowicz [59]	17 749
	21 Columbus	L	1-3	MLS	Mastroeni [45]	16 063
	28 Houston	W	3-0	MLS	Smith [2], Cummings [16], Casey [23]	11 511
	4 Chivas USA	W	3-0	MLS	Casey [52], Cummings 2 [68 81]	10 321
	11 New York	L	1-3	MLS	Cummings [52]	19 014
Sep	18 NE Revs	W	3-0	MLS	Cummings [6], Casey [35], Thompson [83]	16 314
	25 Salt Lake	D	1-1	MLS	Casey [37]	18 317
	29 Philadelphia	W	4-1	MLS	Cummings 2 [7 14], Thompson [67], Amarikwa [85]	10 165
	2 DC United	L	0-1	MLS		15 478
	9 Dallas	D	2-2	MLS	Larentowicz 2 [14 52]	10 119
Oct	16 LA Galaxy	W	3-1	MLS	OG [18], Casey [31] Cummings [67]	27 000
	23 Salt Lake	D	2-2	MLS	Cummings [16], Casey [51]	17 729
	28 Columbus	W	1-0	POqf	Mastroeni [23]	11 872
	6 Columbus	L	1-2	POqf	Casey [85], W 5-4p	10 322
Nov	13 San Jose	W	1-0	POsf	Kimura [43]	17 779
	21 Dallas	W	2-1	POf	Casey [56], OG [107]	21 700

COLUMBUS CREW 2010

Mar	10 Toluca	D	2-2	CLqf	Lenhart 2 [65 83]	4 402
	18 Toluca	L	2-3	CLqf	Schelotto 2 [45p 70]	6 946
	27 Toronto	W	2-0	MLS	Iro [29], Schelotto [87]	13 536
	10 Dallas	D	2-2	MLS	Moffat [52], Schelotto [80]	10 556
Apr	24 Salt Lake	W	1-0	MLS	Schelotto [37p]	14 322
	1 Seattle	D	1-1	MLS	Lenhart [45]	36 219
	8 NE Revs	W	3-2	MLS	Gaven [31], OG [35], Rogers [90]	10 197
May	15 Chivas USA	W	1-0	MLS	Schelotto [90p]	15 027
	20 New York	W	3-1	MLS	Gaven [35], Iro [38], Renteria [83]	11 940
	23 Kansas City	W	1-0	MLS	Renteria [64]	10 385
	29 LA Galaxy	L	0-2	MLS		18 139
	2 San Jose	D	2-2	MLS	Gaven [5], Wondolowski [79]	8 033
Jun	5 Colorado	L	0-1	MLS		14 318
	26 DC United	W	2-0	MLS	Schelotto [57], Brunner [87]	15 335
	29 Rochester	W	2-1	OCr3	Iro [30], Lenhart [94+]	1 760
	3 Chicago	W	2-1	MLS	Moffat [43], Garey [45]	14 017
	6 Charleston	W	3-0	OCqf	Renteria [38p], Lenhart [70], Gaven [87]	1 847
	10 Houston	D	0-0	MLS		13 486
Jul	14 Kansas City	L	0-1	MLS		11 304
	17 New York	W	2-0	MLS	Renteria [20], Carroll [48]	14 378
	24 Houston	W	3-0	MLS	Renteria [34], Iro [84], Griffit [90]	13 585
	31 Chivas USA	L	1-3	MLS	Lenhart [88]	13 419
	5 Philadelphia	W	2-1	MLS	Lenhart 2 [43 50]	18 001
	14 Salt Lake	L	0-2	MLS		16 906
Aug	18 Municipal	W	1-0	CLgB	Ekpo [14]	5 745
	21 Colorado	W	3-1	MLS	Schelotto [6p], Garey [53], Lenhart [80]	16 063
	24 S. Laguna	L	0-1	CLgB		4 700
	28 Dallas	D	0-0	MLS		16 708
	1 DC United	W	2-1	OCsf	Iro [89], Schelotto [98p]	3 411
	4 DC United	W	1-0	MLS	Schelotto [23]	12 075
	11 LA Galaxy	L	1-3	MLS	Mendoza [85]	19 482
Sep	14 Joe Public	W	3-0	CLgB	Griffit [47], Garey [51], Lenhart [79]	5 445
	18 Seattle	L	0-4	MLS		17 144
	21 S. Laguna	W	1-0	CLgB	Mendoza [87]	6 298
	25 NE Revs	D	2-2	MLS	OG [62], Schelotto [80p]	13 533
	29 Municipal	L	1-2	CLgB	Iro [44]	3 545
	2 San Jose	D	0-0	MLS		10 867
	5 Seattle	L	1-2	OCf	Burns [24]	31 311
	8 Chicago	L	0-2	MLS		15 124
Oct	16 Toronto	D	2-2	MLS	Marshall [15], Hesmer [90]	18 084
	21 Joe Public	W	4-1	CLgB	Mendoza [20], Renteria 2 [50p 81], Oughton [92+]	500
	24 Philadelphia	W	3-1	MLS	Schelotto [15p], Renteria [42], Mendoza [80]	19 006
	28 Colorado	L	0-1	POqf		11 872
Nov	6 Colorado	W	2-1	POqf	Gaven 21, Rogers 69. L 4-5p	10 322

COLORADO MLS APPEARANCES/GOALS 2010

Goalkeepers Ian Joyce • Matt Pickens 33
Defenders Julien Baudet FRA 14+8/0 • Danny Earls IRL 15+3/0 • Jeff Larentowicz 33+1/4 • Pablo Mastroeni 33/3 • Drew Moor 34/1 • Scott Palguta 5+11/0 • Marvell Wynne 31/0
Midfield Medhi Ballouchy MAR 19+2/3 • Colin Clark 9+7/0 • Kosuke Kimura JPN 25+2/1 • Ross LaBauex 1+4/0 • Brian Mullan 9+2/0 • Jamie Smith SCO 18+6/1 • Wells Thompson 15+15/2 • Anthony Wallace 11/0
Forwards Andre Akpan 0+1/0 • Quincy Amarikwa 2+12/1 • Conor Casey 30+1/15 • Omar Cummings JAM 32+1/14 • Macoumba Kandji 4+6/0 • Claudio Lopez ARG 11+1/0
Coach Gary Smith

COLUMBUS MLS APPEARANCES/GOALS 2010

Goalkeepers Andy Gruenebaum 2 • Will Hesmer 30/1
Defenders Eric Brunner 14+1/1 • Shaun Francis JAM 12+2/0 • Andy Iro ENG 25+1/3 • Chad Marshall 26/2 • Duncan Oughton NZL 0+3/0 • Gino Padula ARG 13+2/0 • Jed Zayner 3+5/0
Midfield Kevin Burns 4+7/0 • Brian Carroll 29+1/1 • Dilly Duka 2+1/0 • Emmanuel Ekpo NGA 15+11/0 • Eddie Gaven 30/4 • Leandre Griffit FRA 0+3/1 • Frankie Hejduk 22/0 • Adam Moffat SCO 23+1/2 • Danny O'Rourke 14+3/0 • Robbie Rogers 19+3/2 • Guillermo Barros Schelotto ARG 31/9
Forwards Jason Garey 9+15/2 • Sergio Herrera COL 0+1/0 • Steven Lenhart 28+11/5 • Andres Mendoza PER 2+8/2 • Emilio Renteria VEN 9+10/5
Coach Robert Warzycha POL

DC UNITED 2010

	Date	Opponent		Score	Comp	Scorers	Att
Apr	27	Kansas City	L	0-4	MLS		10 385
	3	NE Revs	L	0-2	MLS		20 664
	10	Philadelphia	L	2-3	MLS	Quaranta 63, Moreno 71	34 870
	17	Chicago	L	0-2	MLS		18 407
	28	Dallas	W	4-2	OCq	Cristman 2 4 59, Castillo 39, Najar 51	2 804
May	1	New York	L	0-2	MLS		12 089
	5	Kansas City	W	2-1	MLS	Allsopp 2 12 35	10 038
	8	Dallas	L	0-1	MLS		10 323
	15	Colorado	L	0-1	MLS		13 570
	22	Houston	L	0-2	MLS		24 471
	29	Chivas	W	3-2	MLS	Najar 26, Cristman 76, Talley 90p	13 043
Jun	2	Salt Lake	W	2-1	OCq	Emilio 74p, Najar 107	3 074
	5	Salt Lake	D	0-0	MLS		15 328
	10	Seattle	W	3-2	MLS	Pontius 3 39 44 80	36 146
	26	Columbus	L	0-2	MLS		15 335
	30	Richmond	W	2-0	OCr3	Moreno 47, Quaranta 56	2 985
Jul	3	San Jose	D	1-1	MLS	Najar 54	10 304
	10	New York	D	0-0	MLS		16 239
	15	Seattle	L	0-1	MLS		13 716
	18	LA Galaxy	L	1-2	MLS	Najar 54	17 688
	21	Harrisburg	W	2-0	OCqf	Boskovic 1, Khumalo 47	2 089
	31	Salt Lake	L	0-3	MLS		17 719
Aug	7	NE Revs	L	0-2	MLS		12 218
	14	Dallas	L	1-3	MLS	OG 80	12 474
	22	Philadelphia	W	2-0	MLS	Allsopp 2 23 62	12 165
	29	Chivas	L	0-1	MLS		12 517
Sep	1	Columbus	L	1-2	OCsf	Hernandez 13p	3 411
	4	Columbus	L	0-1	MLS		12 075
	11	Toronto	W	1-0	MLS	James 80	20 395
	18	LA Galaxy	L	1-2	MLS	Najar 60	20 094
	25	Houston	L	1-3	MLS	Najar 29	13 828
Oct	2	Colorado	W	1-0	MLS	Allsopp 45	15 478
	9	San Jose	L	0-2	MLS		14 822
	16	Chicago	D	0-0	MLS		19 056
	23	Toronto	L	2-3	MLS	Quaranta 2, Moreno 39	18 071

FC DALLAS 2010

	Date	Opponent		Score	Comp	Scorers	Att
Apr	27	Houston	D	1-1	MLS	Harris 38	8 016
	10	Columbus	D	2-2	MLS	Cunningham 29p, Avila 90	10 556
	17	New York	L	1-2	MLS	McCarty 10	13 667
	22	Seattle	D	2-2	MLS	Cunningham 2 27p 90p	8 512
	28	DC United	L	2-4	OCq	Guarda 52, McCarty 57p	2 804
May	1	NE Revs	D	1-1	MLS	Harris 66	10 057
	5	Houston	W	1-0	MLS	Ihemelu 79	13 231
	8	DC United	W	1-0	MLS	Cunningham 68	10 323
	15	Philadelphia	D	1-1	MLS	Shea 13	25 038
	20	LA Galaxy	L	0-1	MLS		10 947
Jun	27	Chicago	D	1-1	MLS	Ferreira 6	12 522
	5	San Jose	W	2-0	MLS	Shea 2 58 60	14 331
	26	Chivas	W	2-1	MLS	OG 45, Ferreira 61p	14 173
	3	Kansas City	W	1-0	MLS	Ferreira 58p	15 993
Jul	11	Seattle	D	1-1	MLS	Ferreira 87	36 091
	17	Salt Lake	W	2-0	MLS	Shea 69, Harris 76	11 170
	24	Toronto	D	1-1	MLS	Rodriguez 77	19 743
	31	Colorado	D	1-1	MLS	OG 23	10 596
Aug	8	Philadelphia	W	3-1	MLS	Ferreira 23p, Cunningham 2 75 81	8 732
	14	DC United	W	3-1	MLS	Ferreira 36, Alexander 49, Cunningham 90	12 474
	21	Chivas	W	1-0	MLS	Shea 71	10 309
	28	Columbus	D	0-0	MLS		16 708
Sep	4	Toronto	W	1-0	MLS	Cunningham 47	10 033
	11	San Jose	D	0-0	MLS		10 342
	16	New York	D	2-2	MLS	Rodriguez 23, Alexander 68	15 105
	22	NE Revs	D	2-2	MLS	Ferreira 80p, Cunningham 90	7 468
	25	Kansas City	W	3-1	MLS	Chavez 4, Rodriguez 12, Cunningham 82	10 385
Oct	2	Chicago	W	3-0	MLS	Rodriguez 19, Chavez 46, Cunningham 67p	10 615
	9	Colorado	D	2-2	MLS	Rodriguez 27, Ferreira 37	10 119
	16	Salt Lake	L	0-2	MLS		20 236
	24	LA Galaxy	L	1-2	MLS	Harris 23	24 933
	30	Salt Lake	W	2-1	POqf	Cunningham 44, Avila 88	11 003
Nov	6	Salt Lake	D	1-1	POqf	McCarty 18	19 324
	14	LA Galaxy	W	3-0	POsf	Ferreira 26, John 54, Chavez 72	27 000
	21	Colorado	L	1-2	POf	Ferreira 35	21 700

DC UNITED MLS APPEARANCES/GOALS 2010

Goalkeepers Bill Hamid 8 • Troy Perkins 22
Defenders Marc Burch 4/0 • Jordan Graye 20/0 • Julius James TRI 16+6/1 • Juan Pena BOL 9+1/0 • Barry Rice 1+1/0 • JP Rodrigues GUY 0+1/0 • Carey Talley 13+2/1 • Jed Zayner 9/0
Midfield Brandon Barklage 2+1/0 • Branko Boskovic MNE 8+5/0 • Junior Carreiro BRA 0+3/0 • Dejan Jakovic CAN 18+1/0 • Stephen King 16+4/0 • Devon McTavish 16+3/0 • Kurt Morsink CRC 18+2/0 • Andy Najar HON 22+4/5 • Clyde Simms 18+2/0 • Carlos Varela ESP 1+5/0 • Rodney Wallace 11/0
Forwards Danny Allsopp AUS 18+5/5 • Cristian Castillo 8+2/0 • Adam Cristman 8+9/1 • Emilio BRA 1+3/0 • Pablo Hernandez ARG 13+1/0 • Thabiso Khumalo RSA 3+5/0 • Jaime Moreno BOL 8+13/2 • Chris Pontius 13+4/3 • Santino Quaranta 26+1/2
Coach Curt Onalfo

DALLAS MLS APPEARANCES/GOALS 2010

Goalkeepers Kevin Hartman 24 • Dario Sala ARG 10+1
Defenders Jair Benitez COL 32/0 • Kyle Davies 2+1/0 • Edson Edward CAN 0+1/0 • Jackson Goncalves BRA 13+3/0 • Daniel Hernandez 28/0 • Ugo Ihemelu 22+1/1 • George John 28/1 • Heath Pearce 27+1/0
Midfield Eric Alexander 12+7/2 • Eric Avila 1+19/2 • Marvin Chavez HON 14+6/3 • David Ferreira COL 34/10 • Bruno Guarda BRA 2+7/0 • Bryan Levya 0+1/0 • Zach Loyd 20+8/0 • Dax McCarty 22+3/2 • Brek Shea 24+5/5 • Anthony Wallace 0+2/0
Forwards Jeff Cunningham 14+16/12 • Atiba Harris SKN 31+1/4 • Ruben Luna MEX 0+5/0 • Milton Rodriguez COL 14/5 • Jason Yeisley 0+5/0
Coach Schellas Hyndman

HOUSTON DYNAMO 2010

	Date	Opponent		Score	Comp	Scorers	Att
	27	Dallas	D	1-1	MLS	Chabala 36	8 016
	1	Salt Lake	W	2-1	MLS	Davis 2 53p 55p	18 197
Apr	10	LA Galaxy	L	0-2	MLS		16 459
	17	Chivas	W	3-0	MLS	Cameron 11, Palmer 19, Oduro 66	14 843
	24	Chicago	L	0-2	MLS		11 312
	1	Kansas City	W	3-0	MLS	Landin 24, Mullan 53, Appiah 88	16 042
	5	Dallas	L	0-1	MLS		13 231
May	8	Chivas	W	2-0	MLS	Davis 4, Serioux 8	12 577
	13	Salt Lake	L	1-3	MLS	Mullan 72	12 945
	22	DC United	W	2-0	MLS	Cruz 9, Oduro 55	24 471
	29	Philadelphia	L	2-3	MLS	Ching 52, Robinson 59	13 555
	2	New York	L	1-2	MLS	Ching 64	11 462
Jun	5	LA Galaxy	L	1-4	MLS	Weaver 7	20 826
	26	Colorado	D	2-2	MLS	Cruz 17, Ngwenya 79	13 744
	29	Miami	W	1-0	OCr3	Palmer 80	832
	1	Toronto	D	1-1	MLS	Ching 72	21 374
	6	Chivas	L	1-3	OCqf	Oduro 86	1 097
Jul	10	Columbus	D	0-0	MLS		13 486
	24	Columbus	L	0-3	MLS		13 585
	31	New York	D	2-2	MLS	Davis 23p, Mullan 90	24 740
	8	Seattle	L	0-2	MLS		36 111
Aug	14	NE Revs	L	0-1	MLS		11 546
	21	Chicago	W	4-3	MLS	Ching 3 31 59 85, Palmer 49	18 890
	28	Colorado	L	0-3	MLS		11 511
	5	San Jose	L	1-2	MLS	Davis 45	15 073
Sep	18	Toronto	L	1-2	MLS	Ching 18	16 435
	22	Kansas City	L	3-4	MLS	Weaver 14, Oduro 34, Serioux 37	9 679
	25	DC United	W	3-1	MLS	OG 66, Cameron 70, Oduro 90	13 828
	2	Philadelphia	D	1-1	MLS	Hainault 11	16 115
Oct	10	NE Revs	L	1-2	MLS	Oduro 59	16 479
	16	San Jose	W	1-0	MLS	Hainault 23	10 597
	23	Seattle	W	2-1	MLS	Cameron 27, Weaver 46	23 990

KANSAS CITY 2010

	Date	Opponent		Score	Comp	Scorers	Att
	27	DC United	W	4-0	MLS	Kamara 9, Arnaud 35, Smith 53, Jewsbury 69p	10 385
	10	Colorado	W	1-0	MLS	Kamara 49	10 228
	13	Colorado	L	1-2	OCq	Bunbury 4	1 226
Apr	17	Seattle	L	0-1	MLS		35 924
	24	LA Galaxy	D	0-0	MLS		10 045
	1	Houston	L	0-3	MLS		16 042
	5	DC United	L	1-2	MLS	Kamara 90	10 038
May	15	Chicago	D	2-2	MLS	Kamara 2 51 89	8 155
	23	Columbus	L	0-1	MLS		10 385
	29	Salt Lake	L	1-4	MLS	Wolff 42	15 588
	5	Toronto	D	0-0	MLS		21 583
Jun	10	Philadelphia	W	2-0	MLS	Kamara 9, Zusi 35	10 176
	26	New York	L	0-3	MLS		10 385
	3	Dallas	L	0-1	MLS		15 993
	10	Chivas	L	0-2	MLS		10 288
Jul	14	Columbus	W	1-0	MLS	Bunbury 14	11 304
	17	Colorado	D	1-1	MLS	Arnaud 20	12 825
	31	Toronto	W	1-0	MLS	Bunbury 62	10 385
	7	Salt Lake	D	1-1	MLS	Kamara 21	10 385
	14	San Jose	L	0-1	MLS		8 619
Aug	21	NE Revs	W	4-1	MLS	Diop 2 16 27, Kamara 65, Jewsbury 69	10 385
	28	LA Galaxy	W	2-0	MLS	Kamara 13, Conrad 70	20 112
	4	Philadelphia	D	1-1	MLS	Arnaud 70	17 182
	19	Chivas	W	2-0	MLS	Kamara 70, Bunbury 83	15 382
Sep	22	Houston	W	4-3	MLS	Kamara 35, Bunbury 60, OG 72, Wolff 90	9 679
	25	Dallas	L	1-3	MLS	Smith 57	10 385
	2	New York	L	0-1	MLS		24 799
	9	Seattle	L	1-2	MLS	Arnaud 83p	11 522
Oct	12	Chicago	W	2-0	MLS	Arnaud 45, Bunbury 80	12 230
	16	NE Revs	L	0-1	MLS		18 298
	23	San Jose	W	4-1	MLS	Diop 3 36 61 76, OG 90	11 518

HOUSTON MLS APPEARANCES/GOALS 2010
Goalkeepers Tyler Deric 2 • Tally Hall 5 • Pat Onstad CAN 23
Defenders Bobby Boswell 26/0 • Mike Chabala 22+3/1 • Ryan Cochrane 5+7/0 • Andrew Hainault CAN 26+2/2 • Eddie Robinson 19+4/1 • Adrian Serioux CAN 7+6/2 • Craig Waibel 3+1/0
Midfield Samuel Appiah GHA 0+2/1 • Corey Ashe 19+8/0 • Geoff Cameron 15+1/3 • Francisco Navas Cobo 0+1/0 • Danny Cruz 14+11/2 • Brad Davis 25+2/5 • Brian Mullan 17+5/3 Richard Mulrooney 19+4/0 • Anthony Obodai GHA 4/0 • Lovell Palmer JAM 24+2/2
Forwards Brian Ching 16+4/7 • Luis Landin MEX 5+4/1 Joseph Ngwenya ZIM 6+6/1 • Dominic Oduro GHA 19+8/5 Cameron Weaver 9+5/3
Coach Dominic Kinnear

KANSAS MLS APPEARANCES/GOALS 2010
Goalkeepers Eric Kronberg 1 • Jimmy Nielsen DEN 29
Defenders Olukorede Aiyegbusi 1+4/0 • Matt Besler 10+2/0 • Jimmy Conrad 26/1 • Pablo Escobar COL 7/0 • Michael Harrington 29/0 • Aaron Hohlbein 1+1/0 • Jonathan Leathers 3+5/0 • Chance Myers 6+9/0 • Shavar Thomas JAM 16/0
Midfield Davy Arnaud 27/6 • Stephane Auvray FRA 21/0 • Birahim Diop SEN 7+7/5 • Roger Espinoza HON 25/0 • Santiago Hirsig ARG 1+0/0 • Jack Jewsbury 17+12/2 • Craig Rocastle GRN 18+5/0 • Ryan Smith ENG 25+1/2 • Graham Zusi 4+15/1
Forwards Teal Bunbury 13+13/5 • Kei Kamara SLE 27+2/10 • Josh Wolff 16+9/2
Coach Peter Vermes

LA GALAXY 2010

	Date	Opponent	Res	Score	Comp	Scorers	Att
Apr	27	NE Revs	W	1-0	MLS	Buddle [5]	21 376
	1	Chivas	W	2-0	MLS	Buddle 2 [7 86]	19 805
	10	Houston	W	2-0	MLS	Buddle 2 [26 44]	16 459
	17	Salt Lake	W	2-1	MLS	Buddle 2 [12 76]	20 344
	24	Kansas City	D	0-0	MLS		10 045
	1	Philadelphia	W	3-1	MLS	DeLaGarza [1], Buddle 2 [27 45]	15 453
	5	Colorado	W	1-0	MLS	Gordon [22]	9 882
May	8	Seattle	W	4-0	MLS	Kirovski [22], Gonzalez [53], Dunivant [57], Donovan [68]	36 273
	15	Toronto	D	0-0	MLS		20 007
	20	Dallas	W	1-0	MLS	Magee [18]	10 947
	29	Columbus	W	2-0	MLS	Stephens [10], Bowen [88]	18 139
Jun	5	Houston	W	4-1	MLS	Kirovski 2 [1 21], Bowen [49], Cazumba [57]	20 826
	9	Salt Lake	L	0-1	MLS		19 513
	26	Toronto	D	0-0	MLS		18 809
	29	St Louis	W	2-0	OCr3	Klein [69], Juninho [80]	2 179
Jul	4	Seattle	W	3-1	MLS	Buddle [19], Juninho [48], OG [77]	27 000
	7	Seattle	L	0-2	OCqf		4 512
	10	NE Revs	L	0-2	MLS		20 155
	18	DC United	W	2-1	MLS	Buddle [38], Donovan [57p]	17 688
	22	San Jose	D	2-2	MLS	Buddle [59], Donovan [90]	17 712
	27	PR Islanders	L	1-4	CLpr	OG [83]	6 783
Aug	1	Chicago	L	2-3	MLS	Donovan 2 [37p 80p]	20 348
	4	PR Islanders	W	2-1	CLpr	OG [37], Franklin [84]	12 993
	14	New York	W	1-0	MLS	Buddle [10]	25 000
	21	San Jose	L	0-1	MLS		10 799
	28	Kansas City	L	0-2	MLS		20 112
	4	Chicago	D	1-1	MLS	Gonzalez [90]	21 068
Sep	11	Columbus	W	3-1	MLS	Buddle [14], Kovalenko [36], Kirovski [55]	19 482
	18	DC United	W	2-1	MLS	Donovan 2 [82 86]	20 094
	24	New York	L	0-2	MLS		27 000
Oct	3	Chivas	W	2-1	MLS	Buddle [24], Beckham [38]	24 283
	7	Philadelphia	W	1-0	MLS	Buddle [27]	18 799
	16	Colorado	L	1-3	MLS	Buddle [9]	27 000
	24	Dallas	W	2-1	MLS	Beckham [33], Juninho [46]	24 933
	31	Seattle	W	1-0	POqf	Buddle [38]	35 521
Nov	7	Seattle	W	2-1	POqf	Buddle [19], Gonzalez [27]	27 000
	14	Dallas	L	0-3	POsf		27 000

NEW ENGLAND REVOLUTION 2010

	Date	Opponent	Res	Score	Comp	Scorers	Att
Apr	27	LA Galaxy	L	0-1	MLS		21 376
	3	DC United	W	2-0	MLS	Mansally 2 [79 81]	20 664
	10	Toronto	W	4-1	MLS	Schilawski 3 [48 52 58], Nyassi [67]	12 798
	17	San Jose	L	0-2	MLS		9 082
	24	Colorado	L	1-2	MLS	Perovic [18]	8 142
	1	Dallas	D	1-1	MLS	Schilawski [42]	10 057
	5	Chivas	L	0-4	MLS		5 990
May	8	Columbus	L	2-3	MLS	Boggs 2 [29 40]	10 197
	12	New York	L	0-3	OCq		1 935
	15	San Jose	D	0-0	MLS		13 611
	22	Toronto	L	0-1	MLS		20 672
	29	New York	W	3-2	MLS	Perovic [8], OG [24], Schilawski [80]	11 316
Jun	5	Seattle	L	0-3	MLS		36 344
	27	Chicago	L	0-1	MLS		12 306
Jul	2	Salt Lake	L	0-5	MLS		19 101
	10	LA Galaxy	W	2-0	MLS	Perovic [67], Nyassi [74]	20 155
	31	Philadelphia	D	1-1	MLS	Perovic [71]	18 137
Aug	7	DC United	W	1-0	MLS	Phelan [42]	12 218
	14	Houston	W	1-0	MLS	Stolica [62]	11 546
	18	Chicago	L	1-2	MLS	Perovic [16]	14 056
	21	Kansas	L	1-4	MLS	Mansally [37]	10 385
	28	Philadelphia	L	1-2	MLS	Stolica [31]	13 578
	4	Seattle	W	3-1	MLS	Tierney [71], Perovic [73], Dube [82]	13 124
Sep	10	Chivas	L	0-2	MLS		10 783
	18	Colorado	L	0-3	MLS		16 314
	22	Dallas	D	2-2	MLS	Joseph [5], Stolica [66]	7 468
	25	Columbus	D	2-2	MLS	Phelan 2, Joseph [56]	13 533
	2	Salt Lake	L	1-2	MLS	Mansally [82]	18 130
Oct	10	Houston	W	2-1	MLS	Joseph [42], Dube [73]	16 479
	16	Kansas City	W	1-0	MLS	Joseph [31]	18 298
	21	New York	L	0-2	MLS		15 866

LA GALAXY MLS APPEARANCES/GOALS 2010

Goalkeepers Donovan Ricketts JAM 32 • Josh Saunders 1
Defenders Alex Cazumba BRA 8+11/1 • Gregg Berhalter 16+1/0 • AJ DeLaGarza 17+3/1 • Todd Dunivant 27+1/1 • Sean Franklin 27+1/0 • Omar Gonzalez 31/3 • Leonardo BRA 10/0 • Yohance Marshall TRI 2/0
Midfield David Beckham ENG 8+2/2 • Chris Birchall TRI 23+5/0 • Landon Donovan 27/7 • Juninho BRA 28/2 • Chris Klein 3+8/0 • Dema Kovalenko 11+1/1 • Eddie Lewis 4+12/0 • Clint Mathis 0+9/0 • Michael Stephens 21+4/1
Forwards Tristan Bowen 10+8/2 • Edson Buddle 28/19 • Alan Gordon 4+8/1 • Bryan Jordan 2+6/0 • Jovan Kirovski 11+12/4 • Mike Magee 12+7/1
Coach Bruce Arena

NEW ENGLAND MLS APPEARANCES/GOALS 2010

Goalkeepers Preston Burpo 11 • Matt Reis 14 • Bobby Shuttleworth 5+1
Defenders Kevin Alston 22/0 • Darrius Barnes 20+1/0 • Cory Gibbs 25/0 • Seth Sinovic 18+2/0 • Chris Tierney 26+1/1
Midfield Nico Colaluca 0+1/0 • Jason Griffiths ENG 4+6/0 • Shalrie Joseph GRN 22/4 • Roberto Linck BRA 0+2/0 • Joseph Niouky SEN 11+2/0 • Sainey Nyassi GAM 27+1/2 • Emmanuel Osei GHA 18+3/0 • Marko Perovic SRB 24+1/6 • Pat Phelan 25+3/2
Forwards Zak Boggs 4+5/2 • Kheli Dube ZIM 12+8/2 • Edgaras Jankauskas LTU 0+4/0 • Kenny Mansally GAM 8+13/4 • Zack Schilawski 15+10/5 • Khano Smith BER 6+10/0 • Ilija Stolica SRB 13+1/3
Coach Steve Nicol SCO

NEW YORK RED BULL 2010

		Date	Opponent	Res	Score	Comp	Scorers	Att
		27	Chicago	W	1-0	MLS	Lindpere [40]	24 572
		3	Seattle	W	1-0	MLS	Kandji [21]	36 066
		10	Chivas	L	0-2	MLS		12 597
Apr		17	Dallas	W	2-1	MLS	Angel 2 [57 90p]	13 667
		24	Philadelphia	W	2-1	MLS	Ibrahim [51], Angel [67p]	15 619
		27	Philadelphia	W	2-1	OCq	Chinn 2 [16 41]	3 015
		1	DC United	W	2-0	MLS	Ibrahim [51], Angel [60]	12 089
		8	San Jose	L	0-4	MLS		9 711
		12	NE Revs	W	3-0	OCq	Wolyniec 2 [36 64], Ubiparipovic [62]	1 935
May		15	Seattle	L	0-1	MLS		17 900
		20	Columbus	L	1-3	MLS	Tchani [81]	11 940
		26	Colorado	W	3-0	OCq	Wolyniec 2 [11 43], Chinn [56]	2 637
		29	NE Revs	L	2-3	MLS	Stammler [20], Angel [49]	11 316
		2	Houston	W	2-1	MLS	Ubiparipovic [14], Angel [90]	11 462
Jun		5	Chivas	W	1-0	MLS	Stammler [27]	18 815
		26	Kansas City	W	3-0	MLS	Ibrahim [55], Angel 2 [83 90]	10 385
		29	Harrisburg	W	1-0	MLS		1 868
		4	Colorado	D	1-1	MLS	Angel [34]	18 363
		10	DC United	D	0-0	MLS		16 239
Jul		17	Columbus	L	0-2	MLS		14 378
		31	Houston	D	2-2	MLS	Angel 2 [10 58]	24 740
		8	Chicago	D	0-0	MLS		21 868
		11	Toronto	W	1-0	MLS	Lindpere [23]	19 035
Aug		14	LA Galaxy	L	0-1	MLS		25 000
		21	Toronto	W	4-1	MLS	Marquez [35], OG [40], Angel [61p], Robinson [78]	22 108
		28	San Jose	W	2-0	MLS	Richards [46], Henry [63]	21 859
		4	Salt Lake	L	0-1	MLS		19 115
		11	Colorado	W	3-1	MLS	Henry [17], Ream [33], Richards [58]	19 014
Sep		16	Dallas	D	2-2	MLS	Ballouchy [23], OG [82]	15 105
		24	LA Galaxy	W	2-0	MLS	Richards [36], Angel [60p]	27 000
		2	Kansas City	W	1-0	MLS	Richards [6]	24 799
		9	Salt Lake	D	0-0	MLS		20 829
Oct		16	Philadelphia	L	1-2	MLS	Borman [47]	18 578
		21	NE Revs	W	2-0	MLS	Richards [17], Lindpere [90]	15 866
		30	San Jose	W	1-0	POqf	Lindpere [55]	10 525
Nv		4	San Jose	L	1-3	POqf	Angel [78]	22 839

PHILADELPHIA UNION 2010

		Date	Opponent	Res	Score	Comp	Scorers	Att
		25	Seattle	L	0-2	MLS		36 241
		10	DC United	W	3-2	MLS	Le Toux 3 [5 40 80]	34 870
		15	Toronto	L	1-2	MLS	Harvey [45]	21 978
Apr		24	New York	L	1-2	MLS	Le Toux [59]	15 619
		27	New York	L	1-2	OCq	Le Toux [68]	3 015
		1	LA Galaxy	L	1-3	MLS	McInerney [84]	15 453
		8	Salt Lake	L	0-3	MLS		14 224
May		15	Dallas	D	1-1	MLS	Mwanga [90]	25 038
		29	Houston	W	3-2	MLS	Salinas [39], Le Toux [69], Mwanga [90]	13 555
		5	Chicago	L	1-2	MLS	Mwanga [90]	14 658
Jun		10	Kansas City	L	0-2	MLS		10 176
		27	Seattle	W	3-1	MLS	Le Toux [55p], Fred [78], Mwanga [84]	18 755
		3	Chivas	D	1-1	MLS	Mwanga [22]	14 479
		10	San Jose	L	1-2	MLS	Fred [14]	17 158
Jul		17	Toronto	W	2-1	MLS	Orozco [61], Le Toux [90p]	17 251
		31	NE Revs	D	1-1	MLS	Le Toux [25]	18 137
		5	Columbus	L	1-2	MLS	Le Toux [45p]	18 001
		8	Dallas	L	1-3	MLS	Moreno [9]	8 732
		11	Salt Lake	L	1-1	MLS	Mwanga [8]	16 128
Aug		14	Colorado	D	1-1	MLS	Mwanga [73]	17 749
		22	DC United	L	0-2	MLS		12 165
		28	NE Revs	W	2-1	MLS	McInerney [82], Mapp [90]	13 578
		4	Kansas City	D	1-1	MLS	Le Toux [33]	17 182
		11	Chicago	W	1-0	MLS	Le Toux [36]	18 563
Sep		15	San Jose	L	0-1	MLS		8 106
		25	Chivas	W	3-0	MLS	Moreno [26], Fred [45], Le Toux [69]	16 481
		29	Colorado	L	1-4	MLS	McInerney [89]	10 165
		2	Houston	D	1-1	MLS	Le Toux [40]	16 115
Oct		7	LA Galaxy	L	0-1	MLS		18 799
		16	New York	W	2-1	MLS	Fred [8], Orozco [28]	18 578
		24	Columbus	L	1-3	MLS	Le Toux [87]	19 006

NEW YORK MLS APPEARANCES/GOALS 2010

Goalkeepers Bouna Coundoul SEN 29 • Greg Sutton CAN 3
Defenders Chris Albright 20/0 • Rafael Marquez MEX 12/1 • Carlos Mendes 22+1/0 • Roy Miller CRC 23+4/0 • Mike Petke 11+5/0 • Tim Ream 32/1 • Luke Sassano 2+1/0 • Carey Talley 1/0
Midfield Medhi Ballouchy MAR 8/1 • Danleigh Borman RSA 13+5/1 • Jeremy Hall 9+6/0 • Joel Lindpere EST 31/4 • Brian Nielsen DEN 1+1/0 • Dane Richards JAM 25+2/5 • Carl Robinson WAL 3+8/1 • Seth Stammler 17+4/2 • Tony Tchani CMR 17+10/1 • Sinisa Ubiparipovic BIH 11+7/1
Forwards Juan Agudelo 2+2/0 • Juan Pablo Angel COL 31+1/14 • Conor Chinn 0+5/0 • Thierry Henry FRA 11+1/2 • Salou Ibrahim BEL 8+12/3 • Macoumba Kandji SEN 8+5/1 • John Wolyniec 2+2/0
Coach Hans Backe SWE

PHILADELPHIA MLS APPEARANCES/GOALS 2010

Goalkeepers Brad Knighton 8 • Chris Seitz 22+1
Defenders Christian Arrieta 15+1/0 • Danny Califf 28/0 • Diego Gonzalez COL 7/0 • Jordan Harvey 29+1/1 • Dave Myrie CRC 1/0 • Michael Orozco 29/2 • Shavar Thomas JAM 0+1/0 • Sheanon Williams 8/0
Midfield Eduardo Coudet FRA 9/0 • Fred BRA 24+1/4 • Andrew Jacobson 13+12/0 • Justin Mapp 10+5/1 • Stefani Miglioranzi BRA 25+1/0 • Kyle Nakazawa 8+6/0 • Amobi Okugo 4+7/0 • Shea Salinas 7+10/1 • Toni Stahl FIN 1/0 • Roger Torres COL 10+11/0 • Nick Zimmermann 1+7/0
Forwards Sebastien Le Toux FRA 28/14 • Jack McInerney 1+16/3 • Alejandro Moreno VEN 25+1/2 • Danny Mwanga COD 17+7/7
Coach Piotr Nowak POL

REAL SALT LAKE 2010

Month	Date	Opponent	Result	Score	Comp	Scorers	Attendance
Apr	27	San Jose	W	3-0	MLS	Morales 2 14 54, Espindola 27	10 589
	1	Houston	L	1-2	MLS	Morales 17	18 197
	10	Seattle	D	2-2	MLS	Johnson 52, Saborio 90	19 970
	14	San Jose	D	3-3	OCq	Findley 7, Gonzalez 60, Borchers 117. W 5-3p	2 718
	17	LA Galaxy	L	1-2	MLS	Beckerman 41	20 344
	24	Columbus	L	0-1	MLS		14 322
May	1	Toronto	W	2-1	MLS	Olave 14, Williams 43	12 659
	8	Philadelphia	W	3-0	MLS	Beckerman 27, Olave 52, Saborio 70	14 224
	13	Houston	W	3-1	MLS	Findley 3, Saborio 2 25 60	12 945
	22	Chivas	W	2-1	MLS	Wingert 45, Espindola 90	14 287
	29	Kansas City	W	4-1	MLS	Espindola 31, Saborio 34, Russell 83, Grabavoy 90	15 588
Jun	2	DC United	L	1-2	OCq	Johnson 81p	3 074
	5	DC United	D	0-0	MLS		15 328
	9	LA Galaxy	W	1-0	MLS	Morales 80	19 513
	25	San Jose	D	0-0	MLS		16 216
Jul	2	NE Revs	W	5-0	MLS	Espindola 27, Olave 45, Saborio 2 52 57, Findley 85	19 101
	8	Chicago	W	1-0	MLS	Findley 40p	17 847
	17	Dallas	L	0-2	MLS		11 170
	2	Chivas	D	1-1	MLS	Grabavoy 66	19 469
	31	DC United	W	3-0	MLS	Saborio 14, Findley 79, Gonzalez 90	17 719
Aug	7	Kansas City	D	1-1	MLS	Findley 33	10 385
	11	Philadelphia	D	1-1	MLS	Espindola 17	16 128
	14	Columbus	W	2-0	MLS	Morales 2 12 60	16 906
	18	Arabe Un.	W	2-1	CLgA	Saborio 2 45 94+	10 626
	25	Cruz Azul	L	4-5	CLgA	Saborio 2 23p 43, Espindola 64, Johnson 92+	3 400
	28	Toronto	D	0-0	MLS		21 047
Sep	4	New York	W	1-0	MLS	Espindola 4	19 115
	9	Seattle	D	0-0	MLS		36 078
	15	Toronto	W	4-1	CLgA	Beckerman 21, Olave 40, Saborio 69p, Araujo 80	11 579
	18	Chicago	W	1-0	MLS	Saborio 45p	14 440
	22	Arabe Un	W	3-2	CLgA	Johnson 2 10 43, Saborio 36	500
	25	Colorado	D	1-1	MLS	Borchers 90	18 317
	28	Toronto	D	1-1	CLgA	Morales 67	10 581
Oct	2	NE Revs	W	2-1	MLS	Borchers 68, Saborio 84	18 130
	9	New York	D	0-0	MLS		20 829
	16	Dallas	W	2-0	MLS	Grabavoy 59, Morales 89	20 236
	19	Cruz Azul	W	3-1	CLgA	Araujo 2 43 67, Warner 69	20 463
	23	Colorado	D	2-2	MLS	Saborio 2 89p 90	17 729
	30	Dallas	L	1-2	POqf	Espindola 5	11 003
Nv	6	Dallas	D	1-1	POqf	Findley 79	19 324

SAN JOSE EARTHQUAKES 2010

Month	Date	Opponent	Result	Score	Comp	Scorers	Attendance
Apr	27	Salt Lake	L	0-3	MLS		10 589
	10	Chicago	W	2-1	MLS	Alvarez 50, Opara 82	20 276
	14	Salt Lake	D	3-3	OCq	Leitch 68, Alvarez 88, Burling 108, L 3-5p	2 718
	17	NE Revs	W	2-0	MLS	Wondolowski 58, Opara 72	9 082
	24	Chivas	L	2-3	MLS	Wondolowski 41p, Beitashour 90	14 389
May	1	Colorado	W	1-0	MLS	Wondolowski 34	8 674
	8	New York	W	4-0	MLS	Johnson 44, Gjertson 54, Wondolowski 77, Burling 85	9 711
	15	NE Revs	D	0-0	MLS		13 611
	22	Seattle	W	1-0	MLS	Wondolowski 11	35 953
	27	Toronto	L	1-3	MLS	Corrales 76	10 214
Jun	2	Columbus	D	2-2	MLS	Alvarez 6, Wondolowski 79	8 033
	5	Dallas	L	0-2	MLS		14 331
	25	Salt Lake	D	0-0	MLS		16 216
Jul	3	DC United	D	1-1	MLS	Opara 15	10 304
	10	Philadelphia	W	2-1	MLS	Glen 45, Alvarez 90	17 158
	22	LA Galaxy	D	2-2	MLS	Convey 2, McDonald 71	17 712
	31	Seattle	L	0-1	MLS		10 351
Aug	7	Colorado	L	0-1	MLS		12 701
	14	Kansas City	W	1-0	MLS	Wondolowski 35	8 619
	21	LA Galaxy	W	1-0	MLS	Wondolowski 3	10 799
	28	New York	L	0-2	MLS		21 859
Sep	5	Houston	W	2-1	MLS	Stephenson 5, Geovanni 64	15 073
	11	Dallas	D	0-0	MLS		10 342
	15	Philadelphia	W	1-0	MLS	Wondolowski 69	8 106
	25	Toronto	W	3-2	MLS	Wondolowski 3 4p 53 67	20 064
	29	Chicago	L	0-3	MLS		9 829
Oct	2	Columbus	D	0-0	MLS		10 867
	9	DC United	W	2-0	MLS	Wondolowski 2 45 55	14 822
	16	Houston	L	0-1	MLS		10 597
	20	Chivas	W	3-0	MLS	Wondolowski 3 54p 59 72	9 633
	23	Kansas City	L	1-4	MLS	Wondolowski 70	11 518
	30	New York	L	0-1	POqf		10 525
Nv	4	New York	W	3-1	POqf	Convey 2 7 77, Wondolowski 82	22 839
	13	Colorado	L	0-1	POsf		17 779

SALT LAKE MLS APPEARANCES/GOALS 2010

Goalkeepers Kyle Reynish 3 • Nick Rimando 29
Defenders Tony Beltran 18+1/0 • Rauwshan McKenzie 2+2/0 • Jamison Olave COL 29/3 • Robbie Russell 23+1/1 • Chris Schuler 1/0 • Chris Wingert 23+2/1
Midfield Jean Alexandre HAI 5+11/0 • Kyle Beckerman 23+1/2 • Nat Borchers 32/2 • Nelson Gonzalez ARG 3+9/1 • Ned Grabavoy 20+5/3 • Javi Morales ARG 26+1/7 • Paulo Araujo BRA 0+4/0 • Collen Warner 4+10/0 • Andy Williams JAM 22+10/1
Forwards Fabian Espindola ARG 21+3/7 • Robbie Findley 15+11/6 • Will Johnson CAN 25+5/1 • Pablo Campos BRA 3+13/0 • Alvaro Saborio CRC 25+4/12
Coach Jason Kreis

SAN JOSE MLS APPEARANCES/GOALS 2010

Goalkeepers Jon Busch 21 • Joe Cannon 12
Defenders Bobby Burling 16+2/1 • Ramiro Corrales 20+2/1 • Jason Hernandez 30/0 • Chris Leitch 16/0 • Justin Morrow 0+3/0 • Ike Opara 10+1/3 • Tim Ward 15+1/0
Midfield Andre Luiz BRA 9/0 • Steve Beitashour 7+1/1 • Bobby Convey 31/3 • Sam Cronin 19+1/0 • Geovanni BRA 11+4/1 • Omar Jasseh 0+4/0 • Brandon McDonald 31+1/1 • Brad Ring 4+7/0 • Javier Robles ARG 1+1/0 • Ramon Sanchez SLV 1+2/0 • Khari Stephenson JAM 11+2/1
Forwards Arturo Alvarez 11+11/3 • Quincy Amarikwa 0+1/0 • Eduardo BRA 2+9/0 • Joey Gjertsen 16+2/1 • Cornell Glen TRI 10+11/1 • Ryan Johnson JAM 22+8/1 • Scott Sealy TRI 8+10/0 • Chris Wondolowski 29+2/19
Coach Frank Yallop CAN

SEATTLE SOUNDERS 2010

Month	Day	Opponent	Res	Comp	Scorers	Att
Apr	25	Philadelphia	W 2-0	MLS	Evans 12, Montero 43	36 241
	3	New York	L 0-1	MLS		36 066
	10	Salt Lake	D 2-2	MLS	Zakuani 11, Noonan 72	19 970
	17	Kansas City	W 1-0	MLS	Fucito 90	35 924
	22	Dallas	D 2-2	MLS	Zakuani 38, Montero 55	8 512
	25	Toronto	L 0-2	MLS		18 394
May	1	Columbus	D 1-1	MLS	Zakuani 6	36 219
	8	LA Galaxy	L 0-4	MLS		36 273
	15	New York	W 1-0	MLS	Montero 85	17 900
	22	San Jose	L 0-1	MLS		35 953
	29	Colorado	L 0-1	MLS		18 166
Jun	5	NE Revs	W 3-0	MLS	Gonzalez 5, Zakuani 24, Montero 42	36 344
	10	DC United	L 2-3	MLS	Riley 90, Montero 90	36 146
	27	Philadelphia	L 1-3	MLS	Noonan 45	18 755
	30	Portland	D 1-1	OCr3	Jaqua 13, W 4-3p	15 422
	4	LA Galaxy	L 1-3	MLS	Zakuani 66	27 000
	7	LA Galaxy	W 2-0	OCqf	Jaqua 2 50 62	4 512
	11	Dallas	D 1-1	MLS	Montero 14	36 091
Jul	15	DC United	W 1-0	MLS	Levesque 89	13 716
	25	Colorado	W 2-1	MLS	Zakuani 2 8 16	36 333
	28	IsidroM'pan	W 1-0	CLpr	Montero 60	17 228
	31	San Jose	W 1-0	MLS	Montero 27	10 351
	3	IsidroM'pan	D 1-1	CLpr	Fernandez 74	1 083
	8	Houston	W 2-0	MLS	Montero 63, Fernandez 87	36 111
Aug	4	Chivas	D 0-0	MLS		13 839
	19	Marathón	L 1-2	CLgC	Levesque 17	1 990
	25	Monterrey	L 0-2	CLgC		22 513
	28	Chicago	W 2-1	MLS	Montero 2 36 90	36 386
	1	Chivas	W 3-1	OCsf	Jaqua 2 10 90, Montero 59	4 547
	4	NE Revs	L 1-3	MLS	Zakuani 59	13 124
	9	Salt Lake	D 0-0	MLS		36 078
Sep	14	Saprissa	L 0-2	CLgC		3 000
	18	Columbus	W 4-0	MLS	Nkyfo 3 4 39 75, Sturgis 41p	17 144
	22	Monterrey	L 2-3	CLgC	OG 28, Fucito 44	19 697
	25	Chicago	W 1-0	MLS	Nkufo 88	17 477
	29	Marathón	W 2-0	CLgC	Fucito 2 21 68	11 768
	2	Toronto	W 3-2	MLS	Zakuani 20, Nkufo 26, Nyassi 59	36 079
	5	Columbus	W 2-1	OCf	Nyassi 2 38 66	31 311
	9	Kansas City	W 2-1	MLS	Nyassi 66, Fernandez 79	11 522
Oct	15	Chivas	W 2-1	MLS	Zakuani 9, Alonso 26	36 356
	3	Saprissa	L 1-2	CLgC	Jaqua 17	11 434
	23	Houston	L 1-2	MLS	Riley 12	23 990
	31	LA Galaxy	L 0-1	POqf		35 521
Nv	7	LA Galaxy	L 1-2	POqf	Zakuani 86	27 000

TORONTO FC 2010

Month	Day	Opponent	Res	Comp	Scorers	Att
Apr	27	Columbus	L 0-2	MLS		13 536
	10	NE Revs	L 1-4	MLS	De Rosario 29	12 798
	15	Philadelphia	W 2-1	MLS	De Rosario 2 35 81p	21 978
	18	Colorado	L 1-3	MLS	De Rosario 58p	9 928
	25	Seattle	W 2-0	MLS	De Rosario 58, White 76	18 394
	28	Montreal	W 2-0	CC	Harden 12, Barrett 61	21 346
	1	Salt Lake	L 1-2	MLS	De Rosario 88p	12 659
	8	Chicago	W 4-1	MLS	LaBrocca 25, White 47, Barrett 2 66 69	20 060
May	12	Montreal	W 1-0	CC	De Rosario 73	10 737
	15	LA Galaxy	D 0-0	MLS		20 007
	19	Vancouver	D 0-0	CC		4 928
	22	NE Revs	W 1-0	MLS	Barrett 52	20 672
	29	San Jose	W 3-1	MLS	Barrett 31, De Rosario 2 66 90	10 214
	2	Vancouver	D 0-0	CC		15 176
Jun	5	Kansas City	D 0-0	MLS		21 583
	26	LA Galaxy	D 0-0	MLS		18 809
	1	Houston	D 1-1	MLS	Gargan 84	21 374
	10	Colorado	W 1-0	MLS	Ibrahim 61	21 836
	17	Philadelphia	L 1-2	MLS	Barrett 81	17 251
Jul	24	Dallas	D 1-1	MLS	Maicon 61	19 743
	27	Motagua	W 1-0	CLpr	Barrett 20	18 891
	31	Kansas City	L 0-1	MLS		10 385
	3	Motagua	D 2-2	CLpr	De Rosario 59, Barrett 79	8 000
	7	Chivas	W 2-1	MLS	Attakora-Gyan 21, Barrett 32	20 648
	11	New York	L 0-1	MLS		19 035
Aug	17	Cruz Azul	W 2-1	CLgA	Saric 3, Mista 44	16 862
	21	New York	L 1-4	MLS	De Rosario 49	22 108
	24	Arabe Un	L 0-1	CLgA		501
	28	Salt Lake	D 0-0	MLS		21 047
	4	Dallas	L 0-1	MLS		10 033
	8	Chicago	D 0-0	MLS		12 891
	11	DC United	L 0-1	MLS		20 395
Sep	15	Salt Lake	L 1-4	CLgA	Maicon 8	11 579
	18	Houston	W 2-1	MLS	De Rosario 2 60 90	16 435
	21	Cruz Azul	D 0-0	CLgA		5 280
	25	San Jose	L 2-3	MLS	De Rosario 66, Maicon 80	20 064
	28	Salt Lake	D 1-1	CLgA	Peterson 20	10 581
	2	Seattle	L 2-3	MLS	De Rosario 17, Barrett 88	36 079
	9	Chivas	L 0-3	MLS		12 426
Oct	16	Columbus	D 2-2	MLS	Maicon 29, Peterson 38	18 084
	19	Arabe Un	W 1-0	CLgA	Attakora-Gyan 30	10 385
	23	DC United	W 3-2	MLS	Maicon 23, De Rosario 2 48 65	18 071

SEATTLE MLS APPEARANCES/GOALS 2010

Goalkeepers Terry Boss PUR 0+1 • Kasey Keller 32
Defenders Leonardo Gonzalez CRC 29/1 • Taylor Graham 0+1/0 • John Hurtado COL 9/0 • Patrick Ianni 26+1/0 • Tyrone Marshall JAM 15+7/0 • Jeff Parke 21/0 • James Riley 29/2 • Santiago Santiago 1/0 • Nathan Sturgis 18+4/1 • Tyson Wahl 2+2/0
Midfield Osvaldo Alonso CUB 22+2/1 • Alvaro Fernandez URU 4+10/2 • Michel Fucito 0+5/1 • Freddie Ljungberg SWE 14+1/0 • Sanna Nyassi GAM 16+10/2 • Zach Scott 3/0 • Mike Seamon 3+5/0 • Santiago Sommariva 1/0 • Peter Vagenas 7/0 • Steve Zakuani COD 29+2/11
Forwards David Estrada MEX 1+2/0 • Brad Evans 11+1/1 • Nate Jaqua 3+14/0 • Roger Levesque 5+11/1 • Miguel Montano COL 1+5/0 • Fredy Montero COL 29+2/10 • Blaise Nkufo SUI 13/5 • Pat Noonan 8+4/2
Coach Sigi Schmid

TORONTO MLS APPEARANCES/GOALS 2010

Goalkeepers Jon Conway USA 1 • Stefan Frei SUI 28 • Milos Kocic SRB 1+1
Defenders Nana Attakora-Gyan CAN 24+1/1 • Adrian Cann CAN 26/0 • Gabe Gala CAN 1+9/0 • Nick Garcia USA 20+3/0 • Ty Harden USA 10+2/0 • Doneil Henry CAN 0+1/0 • Raivis Hscanovics LVA 10+1/0 • Maksim Usanov RUS 13+1/0
Midfield Jim Brennan CAN 1/0 • Sam Cronin 4+2/0 • Julian de Guzman CAN 21+4/0 • Dan Gargan USA 25+2/1 • Nick LaBrocca USA 24+4/1 • Nicholas Lindsay CAN 2+2/0 • Joseph Nane CMR 8+3/0 • Jacob Peterson USA 15+9/1 • Amadou Sanyang GAM 12+1/0 • Martin Saric ARG 15+2/0
Forwards Chad Barrett USA 18+4/7 • Dwayne De Rosario CAN 24+3/15 • Fuad Ibrahim USA 3+5/1 • Maicon dos Santos BRA 10+3/4 • Mista ESP 5+4/0 • O'Brian White CAN 9+15/2
Coach Preki Radosavljevic USA

UZB – UZBEKISTAN

FIFA/COCA-COLA WORLD RANKING

1993	1994	1995	1996	1997	1998	1999	2000	2001	2002	2003	2004	2005	2006	2007	2008	2009	2010
-	78	97	109	79	66	55	71	62	98	81	47	59	45	64	72	76	109

	2010												Hi/Lo
	Jan	Feb	Mar	Mar	Apr	May	Jul	Aug	Sep	Oct	Nov	Dec	45
	76	75	75	95	94	94	87	88	97	96	106	109	119

At the start of 2010 the Uzbekistan national team made sure of maintaining their record of having qualified for the finals of every AFC Asian Cup since becoming an independent nation in the early 1990s and at the 2011 finals in Qatar they improved upon their quarter-final finishes of 2004 and 2007 by reaching the last four. Vadim Abramov's team handed hosts Qatar a 2-0 loss in the opening game of the competition before defeating Kuwait and drawing with China PR to advance to the last eight unbeaten. There they beat Jordan 2-1 to reach the semi-finals for the first time before suffering a crushing 6-0 defeat at the hands of Australia. That left a third place play-off against Korea Republic with the winners qualifying automatically for the 2015 finals in Australia. It was a match the Uzbeks lost although by a much more respectable margin of 3-2. Domestically Bunyodkor remain the country's leading club even though their big spending days appear to be behind them following the departure of major names such as Luiz Felipe Scolari and Rivaldo. Under former national team midfielder Mirdjalal Kasimov, Bunyodkor completed a hat trick of league titles and lost just once all season on the way to completing the double. There was disappointment, however, with a defeat at the hands of Saudi's Al Hilal in the last-16 of the 2010 AFC Champions League.

FIFA WORLD CUP RECORD
1930-1994 DNE 1998-2010 DNQ

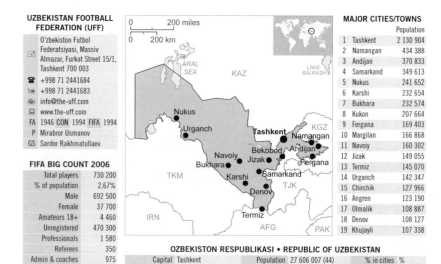

UZBEKISTAN FOOTBALL FEDERATION (UFF)

O'zbekiston Futbol Federatsiyasi, Massiv Almazar, Furkat Street 15/1, Tashkent 700 003

☎ +998 71 2441684
📠 +998 71 2441683
📧 info@the-uff.com
🖥 www.the-uff.com
FA 1946 CON 1994 FIFA 1994
P Mirabror Usmanov
GS Sardor Rakhmatullaev

FIFA BIG COUNT 2006

Total players	730 200
% of population	2.67%
Male	692 500
Female	37 700
Amateurs 18+	4 460
Unregistered	470 300
Professionals	1 580
Referees	350
Admin & coaches	975
Number of clubs	216
Number of teams	24 000

MAJOR CITIES/TOWNS

		Population
1	Tashkent	2 130 904
2	Namangan	434 388
3	Andijan	370 833
4	Samarkand	349 613
5	Nukus	241 652
6	Karshi	232 654
7	Bukhara	232 574
8	Kukon	207 664
9	Fergana	169 403
10	Margilan	166 868
11	Navoiy	160 302
12	Jizak	149 055
13	Termiz	145 070
14	Urganch	142 347
15	Chirchik	127 966
16	Angren	123 190
17	Olmalik	108 887
18	Denov	108 127
19	Khujayli	107 338

OZBEKISTON RESPUBLIKASI • REPUBLIC OF UZBEKISTAN

Capital	Tashkent	Population	27 606 007 (44)	% in cities	%
GDP per capita	$2600 (171)	Area km²	447 400 km² (56)	GMT + / -	+5
Neighbours (km)	Afghanistan 137, Kazakhstan 2203, Kyrgyzstan 1099, Tajikistan 1161, Turkmenistan 1621				

RECENT INTERNATIONAL MATCHES PLAYED BY UZBEKISTAN

2008	Opponents	Score		Venue	Comp	Scorers	Att	Referee
6-02	Lebanon	W	1-0	Beirut	WCq	Ahmedov [44]	800	Al Hilali OMA
22-03	Jordan	W	4-1	Tashkent	Fr	Djeparov [4], Innomov [36], Farhod Tadjiyev [49], Zayntdin Tadjiyev [63]		
26-03	Saudi Arabia	W	3-0	Tashkent	WCq	Kapadze [46], Shatskikh [66], Djeparov [68]	17 000	Mohd Salleh MAS
2-06	Singapore	W	7-3	Singapore	WCq	Kapadze [10], Karpenko [21], Djeparov 2 [34 44], Denisov [42], Ibragimov [62], Shatskikh [88]	28 750	Albadwawi UAE
7-06	Singapore	W	1-0	Tashkent	WCq	Geynrikh [80]	12 867	Kim Dong Jin KOR
14-06	Lebanon	W	3-0	Tashkent	WCq	Ahmedov 2 [51 62], Djeparov [94+]	7 000	Breeze AUS
22-06	Saudi Arabia	L	0-4	Riyadh	WCq		5 000	Nishimura JPN
20-08	Oman	L	0-2	Muscat	Fr		1 000	
29-08	Korea DPR	D	0-0	Tashkent	Fr			Saidov UZB
6-09	Qatar	L	0-3	Doha	WCq		8 000	Mohd Salleh MAS
10-09	Australia	L	0-1	Tashkent	WCq		34 000	Al Fadhli KUW
11-10	Korea Republic	L	0-3	Suwon	Fr		21 194	
15-10	Japan	D	1-1	Saitama	WCq	Shatskikh [27]	55 142	Albadwawi UAE
2009								
28-01	UAE	W	1-0	Sharjah	ACq	Farhod Tadjiyev [30]	15 000	Nishimura JPN
1-02	Azerbaijan	D	1-1	Dubai	Fr	Kurbanov [80]		Ali Hamed UAE
11-02	Bahrain	L	0-1	Tashkent	WCq		30 000	Mohd Salleh MAS
28-03	Qatar	W	4-0	Tashkent	WCq	Farhod Tadjiev 3 [34 45 53], Soliev [62]	18 000	Moradi IRN
1-04	Australia	L	0-2	Sydney	WCq		57 292	Albadwawi UAE
1-06	Bosnia-Herzegovina	D	0-0	Tashkent	Fr		15 000	Kovalenko UZB
6-06	Japan	L	0-1	Tashkent	WCq		34 000	Basma SYR
17-06	Bahrain	L	0-1	Manama	WCq		14 100	Moradi IRN
5-09	Iran	D	0-0	Tashkent	Fr		9 500	Irmatov UZB
14-11	Malaysia	W	3-1	Tashkent	ACq	Djeparov [46], Geynrikh 2 [57 65]	5 000	Moradi IRN
18-11	Malaysia	W	3-1	Kuala Lumpur	ACq	Gafurov [32], Nasimov [58], Kapadze [73]	2 000	Tan Hai CHN
2010								
3-03	UAE	L	0-1	Tashkent	ACq		20 000	Shamsuzzaman BAN
25-05	Armenia	L	1-3	Yerevan	Fr	Geynrikh [70]	20 000	Kvaratskhelia GEO
11-08	Albania	L	0-1	Durres	Fr		8 000	Radovanovic MNE
7-09	Estonia	D	3-3	Tallinn	Fr	Shatskikh [40], Geynrikh [55], Salomov [86]	2 055	Jones WAL
9-10	Saudi Arabia	L	0-4	Jeddah	Fr			
12-10	Bahrain	W	4-2	Manama	Fr	Haydarov [5], Navkarov [12], Ahmedov [44], Shatskikh [45]		
25-12	Bahrain	D	1-1	Dubai	Fr	Geynrikh [15]		
2011								
2-01	Jordan	D	2-2	Sharjah	Fr	Hasanov [70], Navkarov [77]		
7-01	Qatar	W	2-0	Doha	ACr1	Ahmedov [59], Djeparov [77]	37 143	Nishimura JPN
12-01	Kuwait	W	2-1	Doha	ACr1	Shatskikh [41], Djeparov [65]	3 481	Shukralla BHR
16-01	China PR	D	2-2	Doha	ACr1	Ahmedov [30], Geynrikh [46]	3 529	Al Hilali OMA
21-01	Jordan	W	2-1	Doha	ACqf	Bakaev 2 [47 49]	16 073	Abdul Bashir SIN
25-01	Australia	L	0-6	Doha	ACsf		24 826	Albadwawi UAE
28-01	Korea Republic	L	2-3	Doha	AC3p	Geynrikh 2 [45p 53]	8 199	Abdul Bashir SIN

Fr = Friendly match • AC = AFC Asian Cup • WC = FIFA World Cup
q = qualifier • po = play-off • r1 = first round group • qf = quarter-final • po = play-off

UZBEKISTAN NATIONAL TEAM HISTORICAL RECORDS

Caps
72 - Timur Kapadze 2002- • **67** - Mirdjalal Kasimov 1992-2005 • **64** - Server Djeparov 2002- & Andrei Fedorov 1994-2006 • **63** - Nikolai Shirshov 1996-2005 & Asror Alikulov 1999-2008 • **54** -Bahtiyor Ashurmatov 1997-2008 • **53** - Alexander Geynrikh 2002- • **52** - Fevzi Davletov 1994-2005 • **50** - Maksim Shatskikh 1999- & Aleksander Khvostunov 1997-2004

Goals
32 - Maksim Shatskikh 1999- • **31** - Mirdjalal Kasimov 1992-2005 • **20** - Igor Shkvyrin 1992-2000 • **19** - Alexander Geynrikh 2002- • **15** - Jafar Irismetov 1997-2007 • **13** - Nikolai Shirshov 1996-2005 & Server Djeparov 2002-

Past Coaches
Makhmud Rahimov 1999-2002 • Viktor Borisov 2000 • Pavel Sadyrin RUS 2000 • Yuri Sarkisyan 2000-04 • Hans-Jurgen Gede GER 2004 • Ravshan Haydarov 2004-05 • Bob Houghton ENG 2005 • Valeri Nepomniachi RUS 2006 • Rauf Inileyev 2007-08 • Mirdjalal Kasimov 2008-10 • Vadim Abramov 2010-

UZBEKISTAN 2010

O'ZBEKISTON CHEMPIONATI OLIY LIGA

	Pl	W	D	L	F	A	Pts	Bunyodkor	Pakhtakor	Nasaf	Shurton	Mashal	Metallurg	Andijan	Kizilgum	Navbahor	Neftchi	Olmalik	Dinamo	Lokomotiv	Horezm
Bunyodkor Tashkent †	26	20	5	1	45	10	65		2-1	5-0	1-1	3-0	2-1	1-0	1-1	2-0	1-0	1-0	2-1	1-0	4-1
Pakhtakor Tashkent †	26	17	6	3	41	19	57	0-0		2-0	2-0	1-0	2-0	0-0	0-0	3-1	1-0	2-0	1-0	4-2	3-0
Nasaf Karshi	26	13	7	6	30	20	46	0-1	1-1		0-0	3-1	2-0	3-1	1-0	1-0	2-0	4-0	2-1	2-0	2-1
Shurton Guzor	26	12	6	8	35	28	42	0-0	1-2	1-0		1-0	2-2	2-1	0-0	2-0	2-0	5-3	2-0	3-2	4-1
Mashal Muborak	26	10	7	9	22	24	37	0-2	1-2	1-0	1-0		1-1	1-0	0-2	2-0	3-0	1-0	2-1	1-0	0-0
Metallurg Bekobod	26	9	8	9	29	31	35	0-1	1-1	0-0	2-1	1-0		2-1	0-0	0-2	2-2	1-0	0-0	1-0	3-1
FK Andijan	26	9	7	10	28	29	34	0-0	1-1	1-0	2-1	1-1	2-1		2-1	5-1	1-0	3-2	1-0	2-0	0-0
Kizilgum Zarafshon	26	9	7	10	25	28	34	1-0	0-1	1-2	3-1	1-1	0-1	2-1		1-0	2-1	1-0	3-1	0-1	1-0
Navbahor Namangan	26	9	4	13	32	32	31	1-2	0-1	1-1	4-0	0-0	2-0	2-0	1-1		1-1	0-1	2-0	2-0	4-1
Neftchi Fergana	26	8	5	13	36	45	29	0-3	3-3	1-2	0-2	3-0	3-3	1-1	4-2	4-3		3-0	3-2	2-1	1-0
Olmalik FK	26	8	5	13	32	41	29	1-3	2-3	0-0	1-0	0-0	3-2	2-1	5-1	2-1	0-1		3-1	1-1	3-1
Samarkand Dinamo	26	6	9	11	28	33	27	1-2	2-1	0-0	1-1	1-1	0-0	2-0	0-0	1-0	3-1	4-2		2-0	1-1
Lokomotiv Tashkent	26	6	5	15	20	38	23	0-4	0-2	0-0	1-0	1-0	1-0	2-0	1-0	1-3	3-1	0-0	2-2		2-1
Horezm Urganch	26	2	7	17	21	46	13	0-1	0-1	1-2	0-2	1-2	2-3	1-1	3-1	0-1	2-1	1-1	1-1	1-1	

13/03/2010 - 31/10/2010 • † Qualified for the AFC Champions League
Top scorers: 13 - Alisher Khalikov, Neftchi & Nosir Otaquziyev, Olmalik • 11 - Jafar Irismetov, Samarkand & Shukhrat Mirkholdshoyev, Andijan

UZBEKISTAN 2010
BIRINCHI LIGA (2)

	Pl	W	D	L	F	A	Pts
FK Bukhara	30	24	2	4	72	21	74
Sogdiana Jizak	30	21	3	6	60	21	66
Guliston	30	18	3	9	59	31	57
Zarafshon Navai	30	16	5	9	53	38	53
Xiva	30	16	4	10	60	46	52
Lokomotiv BFK T'kent	30	14	6	10	33	23	48
Dinamo-Hamkor Termiz	30	14	4	12	32	27	46
Imkon	30	14	4	12	42	41	46
Lochin Shorchi	30	12	7	11	37	45	43
Mashal-Akademiya	30	11	8	11	42	29	41
Oqtepa	30	13	2	15	48	49	41
Kosonsoy Zakovat	30	9	5	16	30	66	32
Chust Pakhtakor	30	7	5	18	32	68	26
Spartak Tashkent	30	6	7	17	23	38	25
Dormon-Sport	30	7	1	22	22	63	22
Osiyo Tashkent	30	4	2	24	25	64	14

13/03/2010 - 31/10/2010

MEDALS TABLE

		Overall			League			Cup			Asia		
		G	S	B	G	S	B	G	S	B	G	S	B
1	Pakhtakor Tashkent	18	7	2	8	5		10	2				2
2	Neftchi Fergana	7	14	2	5	9	1	2	5				1
3	Bunyodkor Tashkent	5	3	1	3	1		2	2				1
4	Navbahor Namangan	4	1	8	1		8	3	1				
5	Dustlik Tashkent	3			2			1					
6	MHSK Tashkent	1	2	1	1	1	1		1				
7	Mashal Muborak		2	1		1	1		1				
8	Nasaf Karshi	1	6			6		1					
	Nurafshon Bukhara	1						1					
	Samarkand Dinamo	1						1					
	Shurton Guzor	1						1					
	Temirulchi Kukon	1						1					
13	Traktor Tashkent	1						1					
	FK Yangier	1						1					
15	Kizilgum Zarafshon		1			1							
	Sogdiana Jizak		1			1							

UZBEKISTAN CUP 2010

Second Round

Bunyodkor Tashkent	2	1
Nasaf Karshi *	1	1
Kosonsoy Zakovat *	1	0
FK Andijan	5	4
Lokomotiv BFK	w-0	
Mashal Muborak		
Olmalik FK	2	1
Neftchi Fergana	4	0
Lokomotiv Tashkent	4	5
Nasaf-2 Karshi	1	0
Navbahor Namangan	1	3
Samarkand Dinamo *	2	3
Pakhtakor Tashkent	3	4
Metallurg Bekobod *	4	2
Kizilgum Zarafshon *	0	1
Shurton Guzor	2	4

Quarter-finals

Bunyodkor Tashkent *	4	3
FK Andijan	1	1
Lokomotiv BFK	0	2
Neftchi Fergana *	3	4
Samarkand Dinamo	1	2
Lokomotiv Tashkent *	3	1
Pakhtakor Tashkent *	1	1
Shurton Guzor	2	1

Semi-finals

Bunyodkor Tashkent	3	4
Neftchi Fergana *	2	1
Lokomotiv Tashkent *	2	0
Shurton Guzor	0	4

Final

Bunyodkor Tashkent	1
Shurton Guzor	0

CUP FINAL

18-08-2010

Scorer - Stevico Ristic 63 for Bunyodkor

* Home team/Home team in the first leg

VAN – VANUATU

FIFA/COCA-COLA WORLD RANKING

1993	1994	1995	1996	1997	1998	1999	2000	2001	2002	2003	2004	2005	2006	2007	2008	2009	2010
164	172	179	180	186	177	184	167	168	156	160	143	146	167	140	141	155	167

	2010											Hi/Lo
Jan	Feb	Mar	Mar	Apr	May	Jul	Aug	Sep	Oct	Nov	Dec	**131**
155	154	155	155	153	153	163	162	166	170	172	167	**188**

After setting a world record 15 consecutive championships in 2009, Tafea failed to add to that total after finishing second best to rivals Amicale in all three tournaments played during 2010 - the Port Vila Championship, the National Soccer League and the TVL Cup. It was a dramtic reversal of fortunes for a club that had for so long dominated the game in Vanuatu but with football becoming increasingly popular, clubs like Amicale are starting to establish themselves within the community and are reaping the rewards of successful youth development schemes. Selected by FIFA as one of six countries to take part in the pilot scheme for the new Goal Football project, the football association is able to identify promising youngsters and put them on an intensive two year training scheme as part of their education at the national academy, all paid for by the Goal Programme. Amicale are already seeing the benefits of their own youth schemes after having an outstanding year in 2010. The week before the start of the 2009-10 season they beat Tafea 1-0 in the 2009 TVL Cup Final. They then went unbeaten in the 14-game Port Vila League to win the title for the first time, qualifying for the inaugural National Soccer League in which they again consigned Tafea to second place. They then capped a memorable year by beating Tafea 2-1 in the 2010 TVL Cup Final.

FIFA WORLD CUP RECORD

1930-1990 DNE 1994-2010 DNQ

VANUATU FOOTBALL FEDERATION (VFF)

	VFF House, Anabrou,
✉	PO Box 266,
	Port Vila
☎	+678 27239
📠	+678 25236
📧	lambertmatlock@yahoo.com
💻	www.vanuafoot.vu
FA 1934	CON 1988 FIFA 1988
P	Lambert Maltock
GS	Fabien Hoeppe

FIFA BIG COUNT 2006

Total players	27 400
% of population	13.12%
Male	25 600
Female	1 800
Amateurs 18+	4 050
Youth under 18	1 250
Unregistered	21 000
Professionals	0
Referees	110
Admin & coaches	206
Number of clubs	200
Number of teams	400

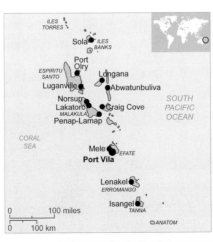

MAJOR CITIES/TOWNS

		Population
1	Port Vila	47 510
2	Luganville	13 800
3	Port Olry	2 897
4	Mele	2 484
5	Norsup	2 374
6	Isangel	1 695
7	Lenakel	1 473
8	Palikulo	1 450
9	Litslits	1 346
10	Lakatoro	1 247
11	Penap-Lamap	1 236
12	Leviamp	1 180
13	Hog Harbour	1 174
14	Abwatunbuliva	1 071
15	Sola	1 065
16	Craig Cove	1 063
17	Longana	648

RIPABLIK BLONG VANUATU • REPUBLIC OF VANUATU

Capital	Port Vila	Population	218 519 (185)	% in cities	25%
GDP per capita	$4600 (144)	Area km²	12 189 km² (163)	GMT +/-	+11
Neighbours (km)	Coast 2528				

RECENT INTERNATIONAL MATCHES PLAYED BY VANUATU

2006 Opponents	Score	Venue	Comp	Scorers	Att	Referee
No international matches played in 2006						
2007						
17-07 New Caledonia	L 3-5	Noumea	Fr	Gete [34], Masauvakalo [83], Soromon [92+]		
19-07 New Caledonia	W 2-0	Noumea	Fr	Naprapol [7], Mermer [19]		
25-08 Samoa	W 4-0	Apia	WCq	Iwai [21], Naprapol [43], Poida [66], Soromon [92+]	300	Jacques TAH
29-08 American Samoa	W 15-0	Apia	WCq	Poida [19], Mermer 4 [24 44 45 68], Sakama 3 [43 79 91+], Chichirua [56], Iwai [62], Tomake [72], Soromon 4 [81 84 86 92+]	200	Hester NZL
1-09 Solomon Islands	L 0-2	Apia	WCq		1 000	Jacques TAH
3-09 Tonga	W 4-1	Apia	WCq	Soromon 3 [24 34 41], Maleb [76]	50	Minan PNG
5-09 Fiji	L 0-3	Apia	WCq		600	Hester NZL
7-09 Solomon Islands	W 2-0	Apia	WCq	Soromon [45], Sakama [51]	200	Jacques TAH
17-11 New Zealand	L 1-2	Port Vila	WCq	Naprapol [26]	8 000	Minan PNG
21-11 New Zealand	L 1-4	Wellington	WCq	Sakama [50]	2 500	Jacques TAH
2008						
14-06 New Caledonia	D 1-1	Port Vila	WCq	Mermer [77]	4 000	Varman FIJ
21-06 New Caledonia	L 0-3	Noumea	WCq		2 700	Hester NZL
7-07 Solomon Islands	W 2-1	Honiara	Fr			
6-09 Fiji	L 0-2	Ba	WCq		3 000	Minan PNG
10-09 Fiji	W 2-1	Port Vila	WCq	Sakama [59], Malas [92+]	1 200	O'Leary NZL
2009						
No international matches played in 2009						
2010						
No international matches played in 2010						

Fr = Friendly match • WC = FIFA World Cup • q = qualifierf • † Not a full international

VANUATU 2009-10 PVFA LIK PREMIA DIVISEN

	Pl	W	D	L	F	A	Pts
Amicale	14	11	3	0	43	8	36
Tafea	14	9	4	1	31	13	31
Spirit 08	14	6	5	3	24	14	23
Teouma Academy	14	6	1	7	16	21	19
Tupuji Imere	13	4	3	6	19	36	15
Yatel	14	3	2	9	19	38	11
Seveners United	14	3	1	10	22	35	10
Westtan Broncos	13	2	3	8	11	20	9

10/09/2009 - 19/02/2010

TVL CUP 2009

Semi-finals		Finals	
Amicale			
		Amicale	1
		Tafea	0
Yatel	0	6-09-2009	
Tafea	4		

TVL CUP 2010

Semi-finals		Finals	
Amicale	2		
Shepherds United	0		
		Amicale	2
		Tafea	1
Spirit 08	1	11-09-2010	
Tafea	2		

VANUATU 2010

NATIONAL SOCCER LEAGUE

	Pl	W	D	L	F	A	Pts	Amicale	Tafea	Spirit 08	Teouma Academy	Tupuji Imere
Amicale †	8	6	1	1	18	8	19		1-0	2-0	3-0	3-1
Tafea	7	4	2	1	14	8	14	3-0		2-1	1-1	2-1
Spirit 08	8	3	2	3	17	12	11	0-3	3-3		3-1	4-0
Teouma Academy	7	0	4	3	7	16	4	2-2	n/p	1-1		1-5
Tupuji Imere	8	1	1	6	11	23	3	2-4	1-3	0-5	1-1	

16/04/2010 - 25/05/2010 • † Qualified for the OFC Champions League

VEN – VENEZUELA

FIFA/COCA-COLA WORLD RANKING

1993	1994	1995	1996	1997	1998	1999	2000	2001	2002	2003	2004	2005	2006	2007	2008	2009	2010
93	110	127	111	115	129	110	111	81	69	57	62	67	73	62	65	50	

2010												Hi/Lo
Jan	Feb	Mar	Mar	Apr	May	Jul	Aug	Sep	Oct	Nov	Dec	**47**
50	47	49	48	49	49	47	47	60	57	56	60	**129**

In the past it was quite common for Venezuela not to play a single international in the years when there were no Copa America or World Cup qualifiers but the new found enthusiasm for football saw a full programme of 13 matches played as coach Cesar Farias sought to prepare the team for the 2011 Copa America in Argentina. Although the 2-0 victory over Peru in 2007 saw their first win at the Copa America since 1967, that was done on home soil and the hope is that the tournament in Argentina will bring them their first win away from home since 1967, although they have been drawn in a tough group containing Brazil, Paraguay and Ecuador. After some encouraging performances by Venezuelan clubs in continental competitions in recent seasons, the 2010 Copa Libertadores was a big disappointment with Tachira knocked out in the preliminary round and both Deportivo Italia and Caracas finishing bottom of their groups. Caracas had the consolation of further reinforcing their dominance at home by comfortably beating Tachira in the 2010 championship final. A 1-0 victory at home was followed by a resounding 4-1 victory in San Cristobal as they won a seventh title in the past ten seasons - and a record 11th overall. In the 2010 Copa Venezuela, Trujillanos beat Zamora on away goals in the final to win the trophy for the second time.

FIFA WORLD CUP RECORD
1930-1962 DNE **1966-1970** DNQ **1974** DNE **1978-2010** DNQ

FEDERACION VENEZOLANA DE FUTBOL (FVF)

Avda. Santos Erminy Ira, Calle las Delicias Torre Mega II, Agregar PH Quitar PH, Caracas 1050

☎ +58 212 7624472

📠 +58 212 7620596

📧 sec_presidencia_fvf@cantv.net

💻

FA 1926 CON 1965 FIFA 1952

P Rafael Esquivel

GS Serafin Boutureira

FIFA BIG COUNT 2006

Total players	1 490 573
% of population	5.79%
Male	1 270 894
Female	219 679
Amateurs 18+	9 897
Unregistered	516 400
Professionals	546
Referees	832
Admin & coaches	8 300
Number of clubs	717
Number of teams	2 449

MAJOR CITIES/TOWNS

		Population
1	Maracaibo	2 637 443
2	Caracas	1 966 466
3	Valencia	1 855 268
4	Barquisimeto	1 157 843
5	Ciudad Guayana	1 019 336
6	Maracay	628 194
7	Barcelona	621 131
8	Maturín	593 285
9	Petare	568 325
10	Ciudad Bolívar	480 077
11	Turmero	455 679
12	Barinas	428 395
13	Puerto la Cruz	372 800
14	San Cristóbal	364 743
15	Cabimas	351 804
16	Cumaná	333 364
17	Santa Teresa	313 960
18	Mérida	311 314
19	Acarigua	222 321

REPUBLICA BOLIVARIANA DE VENEZUELA • BOLIVARIAN REPUBLIC OF VENEZUELA

Capital Caracas	Population 26 814 843 (45)	% in cities 93%
GDP per capita $13 500 (84)	Area km² 912 050 km² (33)	GMT + / - -4
Neighbours (km) Brazil 2200, Colombia 2050, Guyana 743 • Coast 2800		

RECENT INTERNATIONAL MATCHES PLAYED BY VENEZUELA

2008 Opponents	Score		Venue	Comp	Scorers	Att	Referee
3-02 Haiti	W	1-0	Maturin	Fr	Rojas [10]	20 000	Soto VEN
6-02 Haiti	D	1-1	Puerto La Cruz	Fr	Alexander Rondon [31]	30 000	Perluzzo VEN
23-03 El Salvador	W	1-0	Puerto Ordaz	Fr	Jose Rondon [33]	5 000	Gomez VEN
26-03 Bolivia	L	0-1	Puerto La Cruz	Fr		16 000	Buitrago COL
30-04 Colombia	L	2-5	Bucaramanga	Fr	Gabriel Cichero [10], Lucena [43]	25 000	Carillo PER
30-05 Honduras	D	1-1	Fort Lauderdale	Fr	Maldonado [78p]	10 000	Wiemckowski USA
6-06 Brazil	W	2-0	Boston	Fr	Maldonado [6], Vargas [44]	68 000	Marrufo USA
9-06 Netherlands Antilles	W	1-0	Willemstad	Fr	Arismendi [74]		
14-06 Uruguay	D	1-1	Montevideo	WCq	Vargas [55]	41 831	Intriago ECU
19-06 Chile	L	2-3	Puerto La Cruz	WCq	Maldonado [59], Arango [80]	38 000	Silvera URU
20-08 Syria	W	4-1	Puerto La Cruz	Fr	Vielma [14], Maldonado [53], Rojas [56], Moreno [62]	2 500	Gomez VEN
6-09 Peru	L	0-1	Lima	WCq		25 500	Maldonado BOL
9-09 Paraguay	L	0-2	Asuncion	WCq		31 867	Baldassi ARG
12-10 Brazil	L	0-4	San Cristobal	WCq		38 000	Rivera PER
15-10 Ecuador	W	3-1	Puerto La Cruz	WCq	Maldonado [48], Moreno [56], Arango [67]	10 581	Osses CHI
19-11 Angola	D	0-0	Barinas	Fr		15 000	Argote VEN
2009							
11-02 Guatemala	W	2-1	Maturin	Fr	Maldonado [65], Jose Rondon [92+]	10 000	Perluzzo VEN
28-03 Argentina	L	0-4	Buenos Aires	WCq		46 085	Rivera PER
31-03 Colombia	W	2-0	Puerto Ordaz	WCq	Fedor [78], Arango [82]	35 000	Pozo CHI
13-05 Costa Rica	D	1-1	San Cristobal	Fr	Velasquez [24]	10 000	Escalente VEN
6-06 Bolivia	W	1-0	La Paz	WCq	Rivero OG [32]	23 427	Vera ECU
10-06 Uruguay	D	2-2	Puerto Ordaz	WCq	Maldonado [9], Rey [74]	37 000	Fagundes BRA
24-06 Mexico	L	0-4	Atlanta	Fr		40 000	Vaughn USA
27-06 Costa Rica	L	0-1	San Jose	Fr		17 000	Zelaya HON
12-08 Colombia	W	2-1	New Jersey	Fr	Rey [34], Vizcarrondo [72]		Prus USA
5-09 Chile	D	2-2	Santiago	WCq	Maldonado [33], Rey [45]	44 000	Ortube BOL
9-09 Peru	W	3-1	Puerto La Cruz	WCq	Fedor 2 [33 52], Vargas [65]	31 703	Vera ECU
10-10 Paraguay	L	1-2	Puerto Ordaz	WCq	Jose Rondon [85]	41 680	Chandia CHI
14-10 Brazil	D	0-0	Campo Grande	WCq		30 000	Carrillo PER
2010							
2-02 Japan	D	0-0	Oita	Fr		27 009	Fan Qi CHN
3-03 Panama	L	1-2	Barquisimeto	Fr	Gonzalez [90p]	37 000	Buitrago COL
6-03 Korea DPR	W	2-1	Puerto La Cruz	Fr	Granados [8], Sanchez [90]	10 000	Buitrago COL
31-03 Chile	D	0-0	Temuco	Fr		20 000	Silvera URU
21-04 Honduras	W	1-0	San Pedro Sula	Fr	Flores [51]	40 000	Moreno PAN
20-05 Aruba	W	3-0	Oranjestad	Fr	Chourio 2 [10 32], Farias [50]	3 500	Jauregui ANT
29-05 Canada	D	1-1	Merida	Fr	Chourio [44]	20 000	Buitrago COL
11-08 Panama	L	1-3	Panama City	Fr	Vizcarrondo [70]	2 000	Quesada CRC
3-09 Colombia	L	0-2	Puerto La Cruz	Fr		30 000	Moreno PAN
7-09 Ecuador	W	1-0	Barquisimeto	Fr	Fedor [86]	37 262	Torres PAN
7-10 Bolivia	W	3-1	Santa Cruz	Fr	Chourio 2 [10 37], Vizcarrondo [28]	35 000	Chaibou NIG
12-10 Mexico	D	2-2	Juarez	Fr	Arango 2 [6 40]	20 000	Aguilar SLV
17-11 Ecuador	L	1-4	Quito	Fr	Maldonado [49p]	9 000	Chaibou NIG

Fr = Friendly match • CA = Copa América • WC = FIFA World Cup • q = qualifier

VENEZUELA NATIONAL TEAM HISTORICAL RECORDS

Caps
110 - Jose Manuel Rey 1997- • 91 - Jorge Rojas 1999- & Juan Arango 1999- • 81 - Miguel Mea Vitali 1999- • 77 - Gabriel Urdaneta 1996-2005 & Luis Vallenilla 1996-2007 • 65 - Ruberth Moran 1996-2007 • 64 - Leopoldo Jimenez 1999-2005 & Ricardo Paez 2000-07 • 58 - Leonel Vielma 2000-07 • 57 - Rafael Dudamel 1993-2007 • 53 - Hector Gonzalez 2001-07 & Luis Vera • 51 - Giancarlo Maldonado 2003-

Goals
20 - Giancarlo Maldonado 2003- • 18 - Juan Arango 1999- • 14 - Ruberth Moran 1996-2007 • 11 - Jose Manuel Rey 1997- • 9 - Gabriel Urdaneta 1996-2005 & Daniel Arismendi 2006- • 7 - Juan Enrique Garcia 1993-2007 & Ricardo Paez 2000-07 • 6 -Jose Dolgetta 1993-97

Past Coaches
Vittorio Godigna ITA 1938 • Alvaro Cartea 1947-48 • Orlando Fantoni BRA 1956 • Rafael Franco ARG 1965-69 • Gregorio Gomez ARG 1969-72 • Walter Roque 1975 • Dan Georgiadis GRE 1975-77 • Jose Hernandez 1979 • Walter Roque 1979-85 • Rafael Santana 1987 • Luis Mendoza 1989 • Carlos Moreno ARG 1989 • Victor Pignanelli 1991 • Ratomir Dujkovic SRB 1992-95 • Lino Alonso 1995 • Rafael Santana 1996 • Eduardo Borrero COL 1997 • Omar Pastoriza ARG 1999-2001 • Richard Paez 2001-07 • Cesar Farias 2007-

VENEZUELA 2009-10
PRIMERA DIVISION
TORNEO APERTURA 2009

	Pl	W	D	L	F	A	Pts
Deportivo Táchira †	17	11	4	2	25	7	37
Deportivo Italia	17	11	3	3	26	14	36
Caracas FC	17	11	2	4	35	14	35
Deportivo Lara	17	8	6	3	23	13	30
Trujillanos FC	17	8	4	5	31	21	28
Deportivo Anzoátegui	17	8	2	7	22	19	26
Mineros de Guayana	17	7	4	6	22	21	25
Sport Zulia	17	7	3	7	27	29	24
Estudiantes Mérida	17	5	8	4	21	15	23
Atlético El Vigía	17	7	2	8	26	31	23
Zamora FC	17	6	4	7	19	27	22
Monagas SC	17	6	3	8	32	32	21
Yaracuyanos FC	17	6	3	8	20	29	21
Aragua FC	17	4	7	6	11	18	19
Real Esppor	17	4	5	8	12	21	17
Centro Italo Venezolano	17	3	5	9	19	26	14
Carabobo FC	17	2	7	8	16	29	13
Llaneros Guanare	17	1	4	12	18	39	7

9/08/2009-13/12/2009 • † Qualified for the final

VENEZUELA 2009-10
PRIMERA DIVISION
TORNEO CLAUSURA 2010

	Pl	W	D	L	F	A	Pts
Caracas FC †	17	10	5	2	31	16	35
Deportivo Táchira	17	10	5	2	28	15	35
Deportivo Italia	17	10	3	4	36	16	33
Deportivo Lara	17	7	8	2	26	17	29
Sport Zulia	17	9	2	6	26	21	29
Trujillanos FC	17	8	4	5	21	16	28
Zamora FC	17	8	4	5	26	22	28
Atlético El Vigía	17	7	3	7	26	29	24
Deportivo Anzoátegui	17	6	5	6	17	10	23
Aragua FC	17	7	1	9	22	27	22
Real Esppor	17	6	3	8	27	27	21
Monagas SC	17	5	4	8	19	30	19
Carabobo FC	17	4	6	7	16	23	18
Estudiantes Mérida	17	3	8	6	17	23	17
Mineros de Guayana	17	3	8	6	17	24	17
Llaneros Guanare	17	4	3	10	20	28	15
Yaracuyanos FC	17	3	5	9	20	27	14
Centro Italo Venezolano	17	3	3	11	17	29	12

17/01/2010-16/05/2010 • † Qualified for the final

VENEZUELA 2009-10

AGGREGATE TABLE

	Pl	W	D	L	F	A	Pts	Táchira	Caracas	Dep Italia	Lara	Trujillanos	Zulia	Zamora	Anzoátegui	El Vigía	Mineros	Aragua	Estud Mérida	Monagas	Real Esppor	Yaracuyanos	Carabobo	Centro Italo	Llaneros
Deportivo Táchira †	34	21	9	4	53	22	72		1-0	1-0	0-0	0-0	2-0	2-0	2-0	2-1	4-1	2-1	3-0	3-1	0-0	4-3	2-0	1-0	3-1
Caracas FC † ‡	34	21	7	6	66	30	70	1-0		0-1	2-0	3-1	4-0	4-0	1-1	6-0	2-1	4-0	1-0	3-1	3-2	2-0	2-1	2-1	1-1
Deportivo Italia †	34	21	6	7	62	31	69	0-3	3-1		0-1	2-1	2-0	2-1	2-0	2-0	1-1	1-1	0-0	7-1	2-0	4-1	4-0	3-1	2-1
Deportivo Lara ‡	34	15	14	5	49	30	59	2-0	1-1	2-2		2-2	2-1	1-1	2-1	1-0	2-0	1-1	1-1	2-2	1-0	1-1	3-0	2-1	2-1
Trujillanos FC ‡	34	16	8	10	52	37	56	0-0	1-1	1-0	1-3		2-0	0-0	2-1	3-1	1-0	3-1	1-0	3-0	2-1	5-1	7-2	0-1	2-1
Sport Zulia	34	16	5	13	53	50	53	3-2	4-2	1-1	2-1	3-1		1-1	0-1	0-0	0-0	1-0	2-1	0-0	1-0	2-1	0-0	2-1	2-1
Zamora FC	34	14	8	12	45	49	50	1-1	3-1	0-2	1-1	1-2	2-1		0-1	0-1	1-1	2-3	2-0	4-3	3-2	3-2	1-0	4-1	4-3
Deportivo Anzoátegui	34	14	7	13	39	39	49	2-1	2-0	0-1	1-0	0-2	4-3	0-2		2-1	1-1	1-0	0-0	2-1	2-3	2-2	1-0	1-0	4-1
Atlético El Vigía	34	14	5	15	52	60	47	2-2	1-6	1-3	0-2	2-1	3-1	2-0	2-0		1-1	4-2	2-2	2-3	1-2	4-2	4-2	4-2	3-1
Mineros de Guayana	34	10	12	12	39	45	42	1-2	0-1	0-1	1-0	2-1	0-1	1-5	2-1	1-0		1-0	1-1	6-2	0-0	1-0	2-0	1-1	3-2
Aragua FC	34	11	8	15	33	45	41	0-0	0-1	0-2	2-1	0-1	2-4	0-0	0-2	2-1	1-0		1-1	1-0	1-0	2-0	0-1	1-0	1-0
Estudiantes Mérida	34	8	16	10	38	38	40	0-0	1-2	3-2	1-1	3-2	2-2	6-0	0-0	2-0	3-1	0-2		1-2	0-0	1-2	2-1	1-0	2-2
Monagas SC	34	11	7	16	51	52	40	0-1	1-1	5-3	1-0	1-0	2-2	0-2	1-1	2-1	1-1	3-2	2-0	1		5-0	2-1	0-0	2-1	3-0
Real Esppor	34	10	8	16	39	48	38	1-2	0-3	2-0	0-1	0-0	0-1	3-2	0-1	1-1	2-3	2-2	2-1		3-0	0-0	2-0	3-1	
Yaracuyanos FC	34	9	8	17	40	56	35	0-2	0-1	0-1	0-0	1-1	0-3	1-2	3-1	1-0	1-1	1-0	2-0	2-1	1-3		2-0	0-0	3-1
Carabobo FC	34	6	13	15	32	52	31	0-0	0-0	0-1	2-2	1-1	2-1	0-0	0-1	3-1	3-0	1-1	0-0	3-2	3-3	2-2		2-2	2-1
Centro Italo Venezolano	34	6	8	20	36	55	26	1-3	1-3	2-2	1-3	2-1	0-1	2-0	1-2	2-3	2-2	3-1	0-0	1-2	1-1	2-3	2-0		1-2
Llaneros Guanare	34	5	7	22	38	67	22	1-0	1-1	0-3	0-4	1-1	3-4	1-2	0-2	1-2	3-1	0-1	1-1	0-2	2-0	2-1	1-1	1-2	

9/08/2009-16/05/2010 • † Qualified for the Copa Libertadores • ‡ Qualified for the Copa Sudamericana • Apertura matches in shaded boxes
Top scorers: 20 - Norman Cabrera COL, Atlético El Vigia • 17 - Heatklif Castillo, Monagas • 17 - Cesar Alzate COL, Atlético El Vigia

CHAMPIONSHIP FINAL 2010

1st leg. Olimpico, Caracas, 23-05-2010, 16:00
Att: 18 200, Ref: Rafael Lopez

Caracas FC 1 Romero [15]
Deportivo Táchira 0

Caracas - Renny Vega - Alejandro Gonzalez, Jairo Bustamante, Giovanni Romero, Gabriel Cichero - Franklin Lucena, Edgar Jimenez, Jesus Gomez (Dario Figueroa 67), Alejandro Guerra (Cesar Gonzalez 76) - Rafael Castellin (Alejandro Cichero 87), Zamir Valoyes. Tr: Ceferino Bencomo
Táchira - Manuel Sanhouse - Gerzon Chacon, Harold Viafara, Julio Machado, Jose Luis Granados - Javier Villafraz (Nicolas Diez 79), Pedro Fernandez, Maurice Cova, Jorge Rojas - Edgar Perez Greco (Jonathan del Valle 68), Daniel Arismendi (Solari 56). Tr: Carlos Maldonado

CHAMPIONSHIP FINAL 2010

2nd leg. Pueblo Nuevo, San Cristobal, 29-05-2010, 17:00
Att: 45 000. Ref: Jose Hoyos

Deportivo Táchira 1 Villafraz [37]
Caracas FC 4 Cichero [10], Gomes [13], Castellin [60], Guerra [66]

Táchira - Manuel Sanhouse - Gerzon Chacon, Pedro Boada, Julio Machado, Laudemir Valera (Maurice Cova 43) (Marlon Fernandez 57) - Pedro Fernandez, Javier Villafraz, Edgar Perez Greco, Jorge Rojas - Anderson Arias, Jonathan Del Valle (Armando Maita 64). Tr: Carlos Maldonado
Caracas - Renny Vega - Alejandro Gonzalez, Jaime Bustamante, Giovanni Romero, Gabriel Cichero - Franklin Lucena, Edgar Jimenez (Luis Vera 80), Jesus Gomez (Cesar Gonzalez 68), Alejandro Guerra (Dario Figueroa 72) - Zamir Valoyes, Rafael Castellin. Tr: Ceferino Bencomo

COPA VENEZUELA 2009

Round of 16			Quarter–finals			Semi–finals			Final		
Caracas FC	4	3									
Centro Italo *	0	1	Caracas FC	5	1						
Real Esppor *	1	1	Deportivo Italia *	1	0						
Deportivo Italia	2	0				Caracas FC	2	3			
Deportivo Anzoátegui *	0	2				Monagas SC *	1	0			
Atlético Venezuela	1	0	Deportivo Anzoátegui *	2	1						
Mineros de Guayana	0	2	Monagas SC	3	1						
Monagas SC *	1	1							Caracas FC		1 3
Deportivo Táchira	3	3							Trujillanos *		0 0
Estudiantes Mérida *	0	0	Deportivo Táchira	1	2						
Llaneros Guanare *	0	1	Zamora FC *	2	0						
Zamora FC	1	4				Deportivo Táchira	1	1			
Carabobo FC *	1	2				Trujillanos *	2	1			
Deportivo Lara	0	2	Carabobo FC	1	1						
Zulia FC	2	0	Trujillanos *	2	1						
Trujillanos *	2	2									

CUP FINAL

1st leg. Jose Perez, Valera
25-11-2009
2nd leg. Olimpico, Caracas
2-12-2009

* Home team in the 1st leg • ‡ Qualified for the Copa Sudamericana

COPA VENEZUELA 2010

Round of 16			Quarter–finals			Semi–finals			Final		
Trujillanos *	3	0									
Deportivo Táchira	1	0	Trujillanos	1	0						
Aragua FC	0	1	Deportivo Anzoátegui *	1	0						
Deportivo Anzoátegui *	2	0				Trujillanos	1	3			
Mineros de Guayana *	1	1				Deportivo Lara *	2	1			
Deportivo Petare	0	0	Mineros de Guayana *	0	0						
Yaracuyanos FC *	1	0	Deportivo Lara	0	2						
Deportivo Lara	1	1							Trujillanos * ‡		0 1
Carabobo FC	1	2							Zamora FC		0 1
Real Esppor *	1	0	Carabobo FC *	4	2						
Dep. San Antonio	0	2	Real Bolívar	0	3						
Real Bolívar *	1	1				Carabobo FC	0	1			
Caracas FC	6	2				Zamora FC *	1	0			
Monagas SC *	1	1	Caracas FC *	1	0						
Lara FC *	1	1	Zamora FC	2	1						
Zamora FC	1	2									

CUP FINAL

1st leg. Jose Perez, Valera
2-12-2010
2nd leg. Barinas
9-12-2010

* Home team in the 1st leg • ‡ Qualified for the Copa Sudamericana

MEDALS TABLE

		Overall			Lge		Cup		Sth Am			City
		G	S	B	G	B	G	B	G	S	B	
1	Caracas FC	16	4	1	11	2	5	2	1			Caracas
2	Deportivo Galicia	9	6		4	5	5	1				Caracas
3	Deportivo Italia	8	8		5	7	3	1				Caracas
4	Portuguesa FC	8	4	1	5	3	3	1	1			Acarígua
5	Deportivo Tachira	7	9		6	8	1	1				San Cristobal
6	Unión SC	7	3		7	3						
7	Dos Caminos SC	6	8		6	7	1					
8	Deportivo Portugués	6	3		4	2	2	1				
9	CS Maritimo	6	1		4	1	2					Caracas
10	Estudiantes Merida	5	9		2	7	3	2				Merida
11	Centro Atlético	4	7		4	7						
12	Loyola SC	4	5		4	5						
13	Universidad de Los Andes	4	2	1	3	1	1	1	1			Merida
14	Deportivo Venezuela	4			4							
15	Valencia	3	5		1	2	2	3				
16	Unión Deportivo Canarias	3	3		1		2	3				
	Universidad Central	3	3		3	3						
18	Trujillanos	2	4			2	2	2				Valera

VGB – BRITISH VIRGIN ISLANDS

FIFA/COCA-COLA WORLD RANKING

1993	1994	1995	1996	1997	1998	1999	2000	2001	2002	2003	2004	2005	2006	2007	2008	2009	2010
-	-	-	-	180	187	161	172	163	161	175	165	171	190	192	180	191	176

						2010						Hi/Lo
Jan	Feb	Mar	Mar	Apr	May	Jul	Aug	Sep	Oct	Nov	Dec	**160**
191	191	191	195	192	194	191	191	188	175	177	176	**195**

2010 is a year that the British Virgin Islands national team will want to forget as quickly as possible after a torrid outing in the Digicel Caribbean Cup which saw the BVI suffer the heaviest defeat in the entire history of international football in the Americas. And yet their preparations couldn't have got off to a better start at the end of September when they made the short trip across to Saint Martin where they met Anguilla for a friendly match. After just eight minutes the BVI were two goals up, eventually winning the game 2-1 - their first international victory since 2004. Three weeks later they travelled to San Cristobal for their Caribbean Cup matches against hosts Dominican Republic and Dominica. It didn't get off to the best of starts when passports and eligibility concerns meant that the opening game against the Dominican Republic had to be put back 24 hours. What followed was a slaughter with the BVI losing by a record-breaking scoreline of 17-0. The previous record had been Bermuda's 13-0 mauling of Montserrat in 2004 and the BVI came close to matching that again in the next game when Dominica hit double figures in a 10-0 victory which saw the fastest goal ever in the history of the competition after just 26 seconds. The hope is that this was just a blip and not part of a deeper malaise for football in the BVI.

FIFA WORLD CUP RECORD
1930-1998 DNE 2002-2010 DNQ

BRITISH VIRGIN ISLANDS FOOTBALL ASSOCIATION (BVIFA)

Botanic Station Road, Road Town, PO Box 4269, Tortola
☎ +1 284 4945655
📠 +1 284 4948968
🖂 bvifa@surfbvi.com
🖥 www.bvifa.com
FA 1974 CON 1996 FIFA 1996
P Franka Pickering
GS James Shearman

FIFA BIG COUNT 2006

Total players	1 555
% of population	6.73%
Male	1 240
Female	315
Amateurs 18+	190
Youth under 18	245
Unregistered	120
Professionals	0
Referees	5
Admin & coaches	16
Number of clubs	0
Number of teams	14

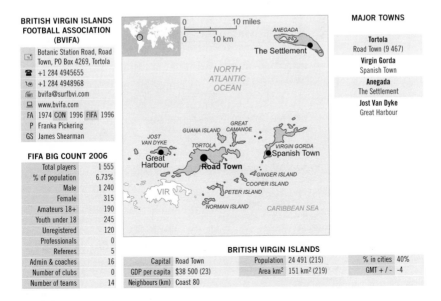

MAJOR TOWNS

Tortola
Road Town (9 467)
Virgin Gorda
Spanish Town
Anegada
The Settlement
Jost Van Dyke
Great Harbour

BRITISH VIRGIN ISLANDS

Capital	Road Town	Population	24 491 (215)	% in cities	40%
GDP per capita	$38 500 (23)	Area km²	151 km² (219)	GMT + / -	-4
Neighbours (km)	Coast 80				

RECENT INTERNATIONAL MATCHES PLAYED BY THE BRITISH VIRGIN ISLANDS

2004	Opponents	Score		Venue	Comp	Scorers	Att	Referee
28-01	Dominica	L	0-1	Tortola	Fr		405	Matthew SKN
30-01	US Virgin Islands	W	5-0	Tortola	Fr	OG [18], Williams [24], Morris 2 [26 56], Ferron [88]	350	Charles DMA
1-02	Dominica	L	1-2	Tortola	Fr	Morris [28]	280	Charles DMA
22-02	St Lucia	L	0-1	Tortola	WCq		800	Stewart JAM
20-03	St Kitts and Nevis	L	0-4	Basseterre	Fr		2 500	Matthew SKN
28-03	St Lucia	L	0-9	Vieux Fort	WCq		665	Corrivault CAN
25-09	US Urgin Islands	W	2-1	Tortola	Fr	Heileger [48], Ettienne [55]	300	Frederick VIR
24-11	St Vincent/Grenadines	D	1-1	Kingstown	CCq	Haynes [53]	300	Prendergast JAM
26-11	Cayman Islands	L	0-1	Kingstown	CCq		1 000	Matthew SKN
28-11	Bermuda	W	2-0	Kingstown	CCq	James 2 [12 24]	400	Matthew SKN
12-12	Trinidad and Tobago	L	0-4	Tortola	CCq		16 000	Arthur LCA
19-12	Tinidad and Tobago	L	0-2	Tunapuna	CCq		2 000	Lancaster GUY
2005								
No international matches played in 2005								
2006								
No international matches played in 2006								
2007								
No international matches played in 2007								
2008								
14-03	US Virgin Islands	D	0-0	Tortola	Fr		300	
15-03	US Virgin Islands	D	1-1	Tortola	Fr		350	
26-03	Bahamas	D	1-1	Nassau	WCq	Lennon [68]	450	Moreno PAN
30-03	Bahamas	D	2-2	Nassau	WCq	Williams 2 [72 90p]	940	Suazo DOM
24-09	St Kitts and Nevis	L	0-4	Basseterre	CCq		500	Charles DMA
26-09	Barbados	L	1-2	Basseterre	CCq	Lennon [23]	150	Baptiste DMA
2009								
5-12	Dominica	L	0-4	Roseau	Fr		600	Baptiste DMA
2010								
25-09	Anguilla	W	2-1	Saint-Martin	Fr	Henroy Mitchell 2 [5 8]	100	
14-10	Dominican Republic	L	0-17	San Cristobal	CCq		200	Lebron PUR
15-10	Dominica	L	0-10	San Cristobal	CCq		200	Santos PUR

Fr = Friendly match • CC = Digicel Caribbean Cup • WC = FIFA World Cup • q = qualifier

BRITISH VIRGIN ISLANDS 2010 FOOTBALL LEAGUE PLAY-OFFS

Semi-finals		Finals
Islanders FC	w-0	
Hairoun Stars		
		Islanders FC — 6
		St Lucian Stars — 1
Sugar Boys		Shirley Ground, Tortola
St Lucian Stars	w-0	7-03-2010

TERRY EVANS KNOCK-OUT CUP 2010

Quarter-finals		Semi-finals		Final	
Islanders FC	4				
Virgin Gorda Utd	2	**Islanders FC**	2		
BVI Under-23	2	HBA Panthers	0		
HBA Panthers	4			**Islanders FC**	3
St Lucian Stars	3			Wolues FC	2
Hairoun Stars	2	St Lucian Stars	1 2p		
Old Madrid	0	**Wolues FC**	1 3p	Shirley Ground, Tortola
Wolues FC	7			25-04-2010

VIE – VIETNAM

VIE – VIETNAM

FIFA/COCA-COLA WORLD RANKING

1993	1994	1995	1996	1997	1998	1999	2000	2001	2002	2003	2004	2005	2006	2007	2008	2009	2010
135	151	122	99	104	98	102	99	105	108	98	103	120	172	142	155	123	137

2010												Hi/Lo
Jan	Feb	Mar	Mar	Apr	May	Jul	Aug	Sep	Oct	Nov	Dec	84
123	116	114	119	118	117	127	127	125	139	139	137	172

Vietnam's two-year reign as champions of Southeast Asia came to an end in December 2010 when Henrique Calisto's side lost in the semi-finals of the AFF Suzuki Cup to Malaysia. The Vietnamese had won the title in 2008 by defeating Thailand in front of a sold-out crowd at Hanoi's My Dinh Stadium but there was to be no repeat performance as Calisto's injury-hit team lacked the sparkle of two years before. After kicking-off the tournament with a 7-1 hammering of Myanmar, Vietnam suffered a shock 2-0 loss in Hanoi at the hands of the Philippines. However, they responded in their final game by beating Singapore 1-0 thanks to a goal from Nguyen Vu Phong to qualify for the semi-final against the Malaysians. A 2-0 defeat in Kuala Lumpur proved to be the difference between the two teams with a scoreless draw in Hanoi ensuring Malaysia qualified for their first final since 1996. After a number a heavy defeats in the AFC Champions League in past years, Vietnamese clubs seem to have found their niche in the AFC Cup with Da Nang winning their first round group and making it to the quarter-finals before losing to Bahrain's Riffa. At home there was a first league title for Hanoi T&T in a close race that saw just seven points separating the top seven clubs. Song Lam Nghe An were the cup winners beating HAGL 1-0 in the final.

FIFA WORLD CUP RECORD

1930-1970 DNE **1974** DNQ **1978-1990** DNE **1994-2010** DNQ

VIETNAM FOOTBALL FEDERATION (VFF)

National Youth Football Training Centre, Le Quang Dao Str, My Dinh, Tu Liem, Hanoi
☎ +84 43 8452480
📠 +84 43 8233119
✉ thanhhavff@yahoo.com
🖥 www.vff.org.vn
FA 1962 CON 1954 FIFA 1964
P Nguyen Trong Hy
GS Tran Quoc Tuan

FIFA BIG COUNT 2006

Total players	1 874 350
% of population	2.22%
Male	1 755 000
Female	119 350
Amateurs 18+	20 850
Unregistered	793 200
Professionals	100
Referees	152
Admin & coaches	10 500
Number of clubs	27
Number of teams	10 000

MAJOR CITIES/TOWNS

		Population
1	Ho Chi Minh City	3 873 661
2	Hanoi	1 491 404
3	Hai Phong	635 820
4	Da Nang	490 700
5	Bien Hoa	446 476
6	Hue	305 721
7	Nhatrang	304 167
8	Can Tho	270 754
9	Rach Gia	267 561
10	Vung Tau	235 642
11	Binh Dinh	224 336
12	Nam Dinh	200 516
13	Phan Thiet	169 992
14	Long Xuyen	164 659
15	Buon Ma Thuot	160 360
16	Cam Ranh	155 748
17	Ha Long	155 006
18	Cam Pha	154 894
19	Thai Nguyen	138 555

CONG HOA XA HOI CHU NGHIA VIET NAM • SOCIALIST REPUBLIC OF VIETNAM

Capital	Hanoi	Population	86 967 524 (13)	% in cities	28%
GDP per capita	$2800 (168)	Area km²	331 210 km² (65)	GMT +/-	+7
Neighbours (km)	Cambodia 1228, China 1281, Laos 2130 • Coast 3444				

RECENT INTERNATIONAL MATCHES PLAYED BY VIETNAM

2007	Opponents	Score		Venue	Comp	Scorers	Att	Referee
8-07	UAE	W	2-0	Hanoi	ACr1	Hyung Quang Thanh [63], Le Cong Vinh [73]	39 450	Najm LIB
12-07	Qatar	D	1-1	Hanoi	ACr1	Phan Thanh Binh [32]	40 000	Moradi IRN
16-07	Japan	L	1-4	Hanoi	ACr1	Suzuki OG [8]	40 000	Breeze AUS
21-07	Iraq	L	0-2	Bangkok	ACqf		9 720	Nishimura JPN
8-10	UAE	L	0-1	Hanoi	WCq		20 000	Nishimura JPN
28-10	UAE	L	0-5	Abu Dhabi	WCq		12 000	Mohd Salleh MAS
2008								
11-06	Indonesia	L	0-1	Surabaya	Fr			
1-10	Mynamar	L	2-3	Ho Chi Minh City	Fr	Le Cong Vinh 2 [63] [91+]		
5-10	Turkmenistan	L	2-3	Ho Chi Minh City	Fr	Nguyen Minh Phuong [20], Le Cong Vinh [89]		
14-10	Singapore	D	0-0	Hanoi	Fr			
30-10	Korea DPR	D	0-0	Hanoi	Fr			
16-11	Thailand	D	2-2	Hanoi	Fr	Viet Thang [52], Nguyen Minh Phuong [87]		
6-12	Thailand	L	0-2	Phuket	AFFr1		20 000	Abdul Bashir SIN
8-12	Malaysia	W	3-2	Phuket	AFFr1	Pham Thanh Lurong [17], Nguyen Vu Phong 2 [73] [88]		Palaniyandi SIN
10-12	Laos	W	4-0	Phuket	AFFr1	Nguyen Viet Thang [49], Pham Thanh Lurong [63], Huynh Quang Thanh [66], Phan Thanh Binh [81]		Cho Win MYA
17-12	Singapore	D	0-0	Hanoi	AFFsf		40 000	Ramachandran MAS
21-12	Singapore	W	1-0	Singapore	AFFsf	Nguyen Quang Hai [74]	55 000	Mohd Salleh MAS
24-12	Thailand	W	2-1	Bangkok	AFFf	Nguyen Vu Phong [40], Le Cong Vinh [42]	50 000	Ramachandran MAS
28-12	Thailand	D	1-1	Hanoi	AFFf	Le Cong Vinh [93+]	40 000	Abdul Bashir SIN
2009								
14-01	Lebanon	W	3-1	Hanoi	ACq	Nguyen Minh Phuong [11], Le Cong Vinh [30], Nguyen Vu Phong [69]	13 000	Toma JPN
21-01	China PR	L	1-6	Zheijang	ACq		15 300	Kim Dong Jin KOR
31-05	Kuwait	W	1-0	Kuwait City	Fr	Nguyen Trong Hoang [36]		
20-10	Turkmenistan	W	1-0	Ho Chi Minh City	Fr	Nguyen Quang Hai [58]		
24-10	Singapore	D	2-2	Ho Chi Minh City	Fr	Nguyen Quang Hai [18], Vu Nhu Thanh [85p]		
14-11	Syria	L	0-1	Hanoi	ACq		30 000	Williams AUS
18-11	Syria	D	0-0	Aleppo	ACq		19 000	Al Hilali OMA
2010								
6-01	Lebanon	D	1-1	Saida	ACq	Pham Thanh Luong [39]	50	Kovalenko UZB
17-01	China PR	L	1-2	Hanoi	ACq	Le Cong Vinh [76p]	3 000	Abdul Bashir SIN
24-09	Korea DPR	D	0-0	Hanoi	Fr			
8-10	India	L	1-3	Pune	Fr	Vu Nhu Thanh [62]		
12-10	Kuwait	L	1-3	Kuwait City	Fr	Nguyen Minh Phuong [57]		
4-11	Singapore	D	1-1	Hanoi	Fr	Phan Van Tai Em [76]		
6-11	Korea DPR	L	0-2	Hanoi	Fr			
2-12	Myanmar	W	7-1	Hanoi	AFFr1	Nguyen Minh Phuong [30], Nguyen Anh Duc 2 [13] [56], Le Tan Tai [51], Nguyen Trong Hoang 2 [13] [56], Nguyen Vu Phong [94+]	40 000	Patwal IND
5-12	Philippines	L	0-2	Hanoi	AFFr1		40 000	Napitupulu IDN
8-12	Singapore	W	1-0	Hanoi	AFFr1	Nguyen Vu Phong [32]	40 000	Mahaprab THA
15-12	Malaysia	L	0-2	Kuala Lumpur	AFFsf		45 000	Sun Baojie CHN
18-12	Malaysia	D	0-0	Hanoi	AFFsf		40 000	Kim Sang Woo KOR

Fr = Friendly match • AFF = ASEAN Football Federation Championship • AC = AFC Asian Cup • WC = FIFA World Cup
q = qualifier • r1 = first round group • sf = semi-final • 3p = third place play-off

VIETNAM NATIONAL TEAM HISTORICAL RECORDS

Caps	**63** - Le Huynh Duc 1995-2004
Goals	**30** - Le Huynh Duc 1995-2004
Past Coaches	Tran Duy Long 1995 • Edson Tavares BRA 1995 • Karl-Heinz Weigang GER 1995-97 • Colin Murphy ENG 1997 • Alfred Riedl AUT 1998-2001 • Henrique Calisto 2002 • Alfred Riedl AUT 2003 • Edson Tavares BRA 2004 • Tran Van Khanh 2004 • Alfred Riedl AUT 2006-07 • Henrique Calisto POR 2008-

VIETNAM 2010

V-LEAGUE

	Pl	W	D	L	F	A	Pts	T&T Hanoi	Hai Phong	Dong Thap	Khanh Hoa	Dong Tam	Da Nang	HAGL	Binh Duong	SLNA	Hoa Phat	Ninh Binh	Than Hoa	Navibank	Nam Dinh
T&T Hanoi †	26	14	4	8	35	25	46	–	1-2	1-0	5-1	4-1	1-0	1-0	2-1	0-0	1-2	2-1	2-1	0-0	2-0
Hai Phong	26	14	3	9	41	34	45	0-1	–	1-0	2-0	2-0	3-1	2-2	2-1	3-2	2-0	1-0	0-0	1-0	2-0
Dong Thap	26	13	5	8	43	34	44	2-1	1-0	–	1-1	0-6	2-0	1-0	2-1	2-2	4-1	5-2	2-1	2-1	2-0
Khanh Hoa	26	13	4	9	42	42	43	1-3	2-1	2-1	–	2-1	4-1	4-2	5-1	0-0	1-3	2-0	0-0	4-3	1-0
Dong Tam Long An	26	13	4	9	43	31	43	2-0	2-1	3-1	0-1	–	4-1	0-2	3-2	1-1	4-1	3-1	0-1	1-1	1-0
Da Nang	26	12	4	10	41	44	40	2-0	3-2	1-1	2-0	2-1	–	3-0	2-2	2-3	1-1	1-1	3-1	1-0	3-2
Hoang Anh Gia Lai	26	11	6	9	34	27	39	4-1	2-0	1-0	0-2	1-0	0-2	–	2-0	0-0	1-2	0-1	3-1	0-1	5-0
Binh Duong	26	11	4	11	48	40	37	0-2	3-1	2-4	4-0	0-1	2-0	1-1	–	2-1	0-0	4-0	5-2	0-0	2-1
Song Lam Nghe An	26	9	10	7	36	26	37	0-0	2-4	2-0	2-4	0-1	5-0	1-2	0-1	–	2-1	0-0	4-1	1-1	2-0
Hoa Phat Hanoi	26	10	6	10	41	44	36	1-2	4-3	2-1	1-1	4-3	3-4	1-1	4-2	0-1	–	0-2	3-2	3-1	1-0
Ninh Binh	26	8	10	8	33	34	34	1-1	2-2	0-3	5-1	0-0	0-1	1-1	2-1	0-0	1-1	–	4-2	3-0	2-0
Than Hoa	26	8	7	11	36	46	31	2-1	4-1	0-0	3-2	0-0	2-4	2-0	2-6	1-2	2-1	1-1	–	1-0	1-1
Navibank Saigon	26	4	8	14	21	39	20	1-0	0-1	1-4	0-2	1-2	3-1	1-1	1-3	0-0	1-1	1-2	0-0	–	1-4
Nam Dinh	26	3	3	20	19	47	12	0-1	1-2	2-2	0-1	3-1	0-2	1-2	0-2	0-3	1-0	1-1	1-3	1-2	–

31/01/2010 - 22/08/2010 • † Qualified for the AFC Cup • Play-off: **Navibank** 2-0 Than Quang Ninh • Top scorers: **19** - Gaston Merlo ARG, Da Nang • **16** - Evaldo Goncalves BRA, HAGL • **14** - Huynh Kesley Alves BRA/VIE, Binh Duong & Tomothy Anjembe NGA, Hoa Phat

The Cong Hanoi were renamed Viettel • Quan Khu 4 were renemed Navibank Saigon

VIETNAM 2010 SECOND DIVISION

	Pl	W	D	L	F	A	Pts
Hanoi ACB	24	13	6	5	50	33	45
Than Quang Ninh	24	12	7	5	38	27	43
Binh Dinh	24	12	4	8	44	32	40
An Giang	24	11	6	7	35	28	39
Quang Nam	24	11	5	8	28	22	38
Can Tho	24	8	9	7	27	28	33
TDC Binh Duong	24	8	5	11	35	37	29
Tay Ninh	24	7	8	9	39	51	29
Viettel	24	7	6	11	36	43	27
Ho Chi Minh City	24	7	6	11	28	42	27
Huda Hue	24	7	6	11	27	38	27
Dong Nai	24	6	8	10	27	31	26
Tien Giang	24	8	2	14	31	33	26

30/01/2010 - 21/08/2010 • The Cong Hanoi renamed Viettel • Cang Saigon renamed Ho Chi Minh City

MEDALS TABLE

	Overall			League			Cup		Asia		
	G	S	B	G	S	B	G	S	G	S	B
1 Cang Saigon	6	3	3	4		3	2	3			
2 The Cong Hanoi	5	5	6	5	2	6		3			
3 Song Lam Nghe An	4	3	2	2	3	2	2				
4 Cong An Thanh Pho	3	5	2	1	3	2	2	2			
5 Dong Tam Long An	3	4	1	2	3	1	1	1			
6 Binh Duong	3	3	2	2	2	1	1	1			1
Hai Quan	3	3	2	1	2	2	2	1			
8 Quang Nam Da Nang	2	2	1	1	2		1				1
9 Hoang Anh Gia Lai	2	1	1	2		1		1			
Binh Dinh	2	1	1			1	2	1			
11 Da Nang	2	1		1	1		1				
Hanoi ACB	2	1		1			1	1			
13 Dong Thap	2		1	2		1					
14 Hai Phong	1	4	2		3	2	1	1			
15 Cong An Hanoi	1	3	2	1	1	2		2			
16 Nam Dinh	1	2	1		2	1	1				
17 Hanoi T&T	1			1							
Hoa Phat Hanoi	1						1				

VIETNAM CUP 2010

Round of 16

Song Lam Nghe An	3
Viettel	0
Hai Phong	0 4p
Hoa Phat Hanoi	0 5p
Ninh Binh	3
Than Hoa	0
Hanoi ACB	0
Nam Dinh	1
Da Nang	2
Can Tho	0
Dong Nai	0
Dong Thap	2
Binh Duong	1
Khanh Hoa	0
Dong Tam Long An	1 4p
Hoang Anh Gia Lai	1 5p

Quarter-finals

Song Lam Nghe An	2
Hoa Phat Hanoi	1
Ninh Binh	0
Nam Dinh	1
Da Nang	4
Dong Thap	0
Binh Duong	1 5p
Hoang Anh Gia Lai	1 6p

Semi-finals

Song Lam Nghe An	3
Nam Dinh	0
Da Nang	1 2p
Hoang Anh Gia Lai	1 4p

Final

Song Lam Nghe An †	1
Hoang Anh Gia Lai	0

CUP FINAL

Hang Day, Hanoi
28-08-2010
Scorer - Abdulrazak Ekopoki [25]

† Qualified for the AFC Cup

VIN – ST VINCENT AND THE GRENADINES

FIFA/COCA-COLA WORLD RANKING

1993	1994	1995	1996	1997	1998	1999	2000	2001	2002	2003	2004	2005	2006	2007	2008	2009	2010
129	144	95	93	122	138	141	127	125	144	169	137	130	85	101	133	152	142

2010												Hi/Lo
Jan	Feb	Mar	Mar	Apr	May	Jul	Aug	Sep	Oct	Nov	Dec	73
152	168	168	166	164	163	160	160	153	126	139	142	170

The St Vincent and Grenadines national team played a full calendar of matches in 2010 with some success, qualifying for the second round of qualifiers in the Digicel Caribbean Cup. Vincey Heat hosted a first round qualifying group in Kingstown and got off to a great start with a 7-0 victory over minnows Montserrat, star player Shandel Samuel scoring a hat trick in front of a Victoria Park packed to it's 5,000 capacity. The large margin of victory was to prove crucial. With St Vincent, St Kitts and Barbados drawing the three matches between them, Vincey Heat qualified on goal difference ahead of Barbados who only managed to score five against an improving Montserrat. The next round saw Vincey Heat cast as the underdogs in a group played in Trinidad and predictably all three matches were lost against the hosts, Haiti and Guyana which meant there was to be no repeat of their finals appearance from three years earlier in 2007. In domestic football the 2009-10 National Championship had kicked-off in September 2009 amid much fanfare and with a friendly international match against St Lucia, with the aim of establishing a unified competition in a country where the distances between the islands makes this difficult. Won by Avenues United in January 2010, the following edition kicked off almost a whole year later in mid-October.

FIFA WORLD CUP RECORD
1930-1990 DNE 1994-2010 DNQ

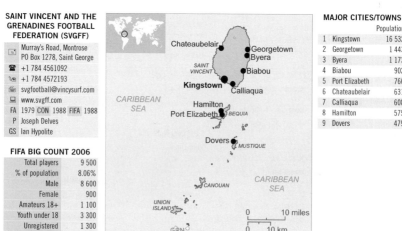

SAINT VINCENT AND THE GRENADINES FOOTBALL FEDERATION (SVGFF)

Murray's Road, Montrose
PO Box 1278, Saint George
☎ +1 784 4561092
🖷 +1 784 4572193
✉ svgfootball@vincysurf.com
🖳 www.svgff.com
FA 1979 CON 1988 FIFA 1988
P Joseph Delves
GS Ian Hypolite

FIFA BIG COUNT 2006

Total players	9 500
% of population	8.06%
Male	8 600
Female	900
Amateurs 18+	1 100
Youth under 18	3 300
Unregistered	1 300
Professionals	0
Referees	5
Admin & coaches	500
Number of clubs	50
Number of teams	300

MAJOR CITIES/TOWNS

		Population
1	Kingstown	16 532
2	Georgetown	1 443
3	Byera	1 173
4	Biabou	902
5	Port Elizabeth	766
6	Chateaubelair	631
7	Calliaqua	608
8	Hamilton	575
9	Dovers	479

SAINT VINCENT AND THE GRENADINES

Capital	Kingstown	Population	104 574 (192)	% in cities	47%
GDP per capita	$10 200 (103)	Area km²	389 km² (202)	GMT +/-	-4
Neighbours (km)	Coast 84				

RECENT INTERNATIONAL MATCHES PLAYED BY ST VINCENT AND THE GRENADINES

2007	Opponents	Score		Venue	Comp	Scorers	Att	Referee
14-01	Guyana	W	2-0	Marabella	CCr1	Shandel Samuel [4], Sean Glynn [85]	3 000	Angela ARU
16-01	Cuba	L	0-3	Marabella	CCr1		1 700	Angela ARU
18-01	Guadeloupe †	L	0-1	Marabella	CCr1		2 000	Brizan TRI
30-05	Haiti	L	0-3	Port of Spain	Fr		500	Jordan TRI
2008								
13-01	Guyana	L	0-1	Blairmont	Fr		1 300	James GUY
27-01	Guyana	D	2-2	Kingstown	Fr	Randolph Williams [6], George Emerald [80]	2 000	Cambridge VIN
10-02	Grenada	L	1-2	Kingstown	Fr	Alwyn Guy [49]	1 000	Cambridge VIN
13-03	Barbados	L	0-2	Kingstown	Fr		1 050	Cambridge VIN
3-06	Jamaica	L	1-5	Kingston	Fr	Marlon James [56]	20 000	Whittaker CAY
7-06	Cuba	L	0-1	Havana	Fr		400	Duran CUB
15-06	Canada	L	0-3	Kingstown	WCq		5 000	Batres GUA
20-06	Canada	L	1-4	Montreal	WCq	Marlon James [75]	11 500	Aguilar SLV
15-09	Martinique †	L	0-3	Fort de France	CCq		250	George LCA
17-09	Anguilla	W	3-1	Fort de France	CCq	Theon Gordon [35], Darren Hammlet [39], Myron Samuel [80]	100	Fanus LCA
2009								
5-09	St Kitts and Nevis	L	0-3	Kingstown	Fr		3 500	Cambridge VIN
20-09	St Kitts and Nevis	D	1-1	Basseterre	Fr	Wendell Cuffy [47]	1 600	Matthew SKN
2010								
10-09	St Lucia	W	5-1	Vieux Fort	Fr	Norrel George [19], Myron Samuel 2 [21 43], Romano Snagg [57], Wendell Cuffy [72]	400	St Catherine LCA
17-09	Grenada	L	0-1	Kingstown	Fr		350	Gurley VIN
19-09	Grenada	D	0-0	Kingstown	Fr		350	Cambridhe VIN
6-10	Montserrat	W	7-0	Kingstown	CCq	Shandel Samuel 3 [25p 26 66], Damon Francis [56], Cornelius Stewart [63], Chad Balcombe [70], Romano Snagg [89]	5 000	Pinas SUR
8-10	St Kitts and Nevis	D	1-1	Kingstown	CCq	Keith James [73]	1 600	Jauregui ANT
10-10	Barbados	D	0-0	Kingstown	CCq		5 420	Jauregui ANT
2-11	Trinidad and Tobago	L	2-6	Marabella	CCq	Shandel Samuel [28], Cornelius Stewart [45]	1 100	Peterkin JAM
4-11	Haiti	L	1-3	Port of Spain	CCq	Shandel Samuel [64]	1 100	Campbell JAM
6-11	Guyana	L	0-2	Port of Spain	CCq		850	Taylor BRB

Fr = Friendly match • CC = Digicel Caribbean Cup • WC = FIFA World Cup • q = qualifier • r1 = first round group • † Not a full international

ST VINCENT AND THE GRENADINES NATIONAL TEAM HISTORICAL RECORDS

Past Coaches
Jorge Ramos BRA 1992 • Lenny Taylor JAM 1995-96 • Bertile St Clair ATG 1996 • Lenny Taylor JAM 2000-01 • Elvis Brown JAM 2002 • Adrian Shaw ENG 2003 • Zoran Vranes SRB 2004-07 • Roger Gurley 2008 • John Hall 2009 • Carrington

ST VINCENT/GRENADINES 2009–10 NLA/SVG CLUB CHAMPIONSHIP

	Pl	W	D	L	F	A	Pts
Avenues United	11	10	1	0	63	14	**31**
System 3	11	8	2	1	33	10	**26**
Nemwil Hope International	11	8	1	2	40	15	**25**
Prospect United	11	7	2	2	38	18	**23**
Digicel Jebelle FC	11	6	1	4	33	14	**19**
Toni Store Jugglers	11	4	4	3	21	19	**16**
Camdonia Chelsea SC	11	3	5	3	18	22	**14**
Zodiac FC Bequia	11	4	1	6	21	48	**13**
JG & Sons Stingers FC	11	3	1	7	17	27	**10**
Predators of Fitz Hughes	11	1	1	9	12	36	**4**
Cane End United	11	2	1	8	13	39	**4**
United Force FC Bequia	11	0	0	11	2	49	**0**

6/09/2009 - 8/01/2010

VIR – US VIRGIN ISLANDS

FIFA/COCA-COLA WORLD RANKING

1993	1994	1995	1996	1997	1998	1999	2000	2001	2002	2003	2004	2005	2006	2007	2008	2009	2010
-	-	-	-	-	-	194	198	198	197	199	196	196	198	201	195	199	200

2010												Hi/Lo
Jan	Feb	Mar	Mar	Apr	May	Jul	Aug	Sep	Oct	Nov	Dec	**190**
199	199	199	199	199	199	199	199	200	200	200	200	**202**

The decision of the US Virgin Islands not to enter the 2010 Digicel Caribbean Cup saw the national team edge ever closer to the bottom of the FIFA/Coca-Cola World Ranking with the two draws against neighbours British Virgin Islands in March 2008 - the only results to keep the USVI off the bottom of the rankings - starting to lose their significance when the rankings are calculated. With no matches having been played after the 10-0 World Cup qualifying defeat against Grenada later that month, the USVI has now missed out on two successive Caribbean Cups, the first time that has happened since the late 1990s but the federation will certainly have been chastened by the experience of the British Virgin Islands who lost their two Caribbean Cup matches in 2010 by 17-0 and 10-0. In club football, Helenites saw their ten-year winning streak in the Saint Croix championship come to an end when they were deposed by Unique FC. On Saint Thomas - the other of the two major islands that comprise the USVI - Positive Vibes regained their league crown from New Vibes. For the first time since 2004, however, the traditional end of season play-offs between the top clubs from both islands didn't take place and for the 2010-11 season there was no league competition at all in Saint Thomas with a seven-a-side tournament held in its place.

FIFA WORLD CUP RECORD
1930-1998 DNE 2002-2010 DNQ

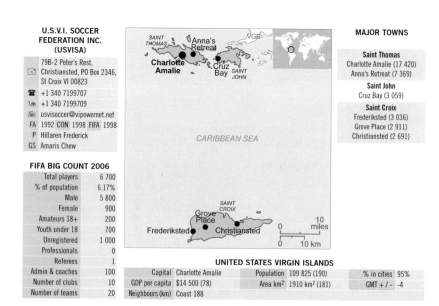

U.S.V.I. SOCCER FEDERATION INC. (USVISA)

79B-2 Peter's Rest,
Christiansted, PO Box 2346,
St Croix VI 00823
☎ +1 340 7199707
📠 +1 340 7199709
📧 usvisoccer@vipowernet.net
FA 1992 CON 1998 FIFA 1998
P Hillaren Frederick
GS Amaris Chew

FIFA BIG COUNT 2006

Total players	6 700
% of population	6.17%
Male	5 800
Female	900
Amateurs 18+	200
Youth under 18	700
Unregistered	1 000
Professionals	0
Referees	1
Admin & coaches	100
Number of clubs	10
Number of teams	20

MAJOR TOWNS

Saint Thomas
Charlotte Amalie (17 420)
Anna's Retreat (7 369)
Saint John
Cruz Bay (3 059)
Saint Croix
Frederiksted (3 036)
Grove Place (2 911)
Christiansted (2 691)

UNITED STATES VIRGIN ISLANDS

Capital	Charlotte Amalie	Population	109 825 (190)	% in cities	95%
GDP per capita	$14 500 (78)	Area km²	1910 km² (181)	GMT + / -	-4
Neighbours (km)	Coast 188				

RECENT INTERNATIONAL MATCHES PLAYED BY THE US VIRGIN ISLANDS

2004	Opponents	Score		Venue	Comp	Scorers	Att	Referee
30-01	British Virgin Islands	L	0-5	Road Town	Fr		350	Charles DMA
31-01	Dominica	L	0-5	Road Town	Fr		550	Matthew SKN
18-02	St Kitts and Nevis	L	0-4	Charlotte Amalie	WCq		225	Brizan TRI
31-03	St Kitts and Nevis	L	0-7	Basseterre	WCq		800	Recinos SLV
25-09	British Virgin Islands	L	1-2	Road Town	Fr	Challenger [65]	300	Frederick VIR
24-11	Haiti	L	0-11	Kingston	CCq		250	Piper TRI
26-11	Jamaica	L	1-11	Kingston	CCq	Lauro [72]	4 200	Piper TRI
28-11	St Martin †	D	0-0	Kingston	CCq		200	Brizan TRI
2005								
No international matches played in 2005								
2006								
27-09	Bermuda	L	0-6	Charlotte Amalie	CCq		150	Small BRB
1-10	Dominican Republic	L	1-6	Charlotte Amalie	CCq	Pierre [7]	250	Davis TRI
2007								
No international matches played in 2007								
2008								
14-03	British Virgin Islands	D	0-0	Road Town	Fr		300	
15-03	British Virgin Islands	D	1-1	Road Town	Fr		350	
26-03	Grenada	L	0-10	St George's	WCq		3 000	James GUY
2009								
No international matches played in 2009								
2010								
No international matches played in 2010								

Fr = Friendly match • CC = Digicel Caribbean Cup • WC = FIFA World Cup • q = qualifier • † Not a full international

WAL – WALES

FIFA/COCA-COLA WORLD RANKING

1993	1994	1995	1996	1997	1998	1999	2000	2001	2002	2003	2004	2005	2006	2007	2008	2009	2010
29	41	61	80	102	97	98	109	100	52	66	68	71	73	57	60	77	112

	2010												Hi/Lo
	Jan	Feb	Mar	Mar	Apr	May	Jul	Aug	Sep	Oct	Nov	Dec	27
	77	76	76	77	75	77	84	84	84	104	111	112	113

After six often turbulent years as the Welsh coach, John Toshack called it a day after defeat to Montenegro in the opening qualifying match for Euro 2012. Two defeats under caretaker Brian Flynn left Wales facing the prospect of yet another unsuccessful campaign in their quest for a first appearance at a championship finals for over 50 years. With attacking defender Gareth Bale receiving rave reviews around Europe for his UEFA Champions League displays with Tottenham, the disappointment of Welsh fans was tangible, especially given the recent optimism surrounding the team. Toshack pinpointed the continual absence of many players from friendly matches as a major problem and that is something new coach Gary Speed will have to try and tackle. At club level, Cardiff City just missed out on the chance of a return to the top level of English football for the first time in almost 50 years, after losing the play-off final at Wembley to Blackpool, while in the FAW League of Wales there was a return to winning ways for The New Saints as they picked up a fifth title. They also retained their League Cup crown beating Rhyl 2-0 in the final - the fourth time in six years the club from the north coast has lost in the final. In the Welsh Cup their neighbours Bangor City completed a hat trick of wins with a 3-2 win over Port Talbot Town.

FIFA WORLD CUP RECORD
1930-1938 DNE 1950-1954 DNQ **1958** 7 QF 1962-2010 DNQ

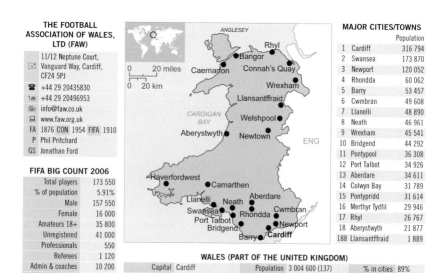

THE FOOTBALL ASSOCIATION OF WALES, LTD (FAW)		
11/12 Neptune Court, Vanguard Way, Cardiff, CF24 5PJ		
☎ +44 29 20435830		
📠 +44 29 20496953		
📧 info@faw.co.uk		
🖥 www.faw.org.uk		
FA 1876	CON 1954	FIFA 1910
P Phil Pritchard		
GS Jonathan Ford		

FIFA BIG COUNT 2006

Total players	173 550
% of population	5.91%
Male	157 550
Female	16 000
Amateurs 18+	35 800
Unregistered	41 000
Professionals	550
Referees	1 120
Admin & coaches	10 200
Number of clubs	1 900
Number of teams	4 500

MAJOR CITIES/TOWNS

		Population
1	Cardiff	316 794
2	Swansea	173 870
3	Newport	120 052
4	Rhondda	60 062
5	Barry	53 457
6	Cwmbran	49 608
7	Llanelli	48 890
8	Neath	46 961
9	Wrexham	45 541
10	Bridgend	44 292
11	Pontypool	36 308
12	Port Talbot	34 926
13	Aberdare	34 611
14	Colwyn Bay	31 789
15	Pontypridd	31 614
16	Merthyr Tydfil	29 946
17	Rhyl	26 767
18	Aberystwyth	21 877
188	Llansantffraid	1 889

WALES (PART OF THE UNITED KINGDOM)

Capital	Cardiff	Population	3 004 600 (137)	% in cities	89%
GDP per capita	$30 546 (45)	Area km²	20 779 km² (154)	GMT + / -	0
Neighbours (km)	England 468 • Coast 627				

RECENT INTERNATIONAL MATCHES PLAYED BY WALES

2007	Opponents	Score	Venue	Comp	Scorers	Att	Referee
6-02	Northern Ireland	D 0-0	Belfast	Fr		13 500	Richmond SCO
24-03	Republic of Ireland	L 0-1	Dublin	ECq		72 539	Hauge NOR
28-03	San Marino	W 3-0	Cardiff	ECq	Giggs [3], Bale [20], Koumas [63p]	18 752	Tchagharyan ARM
26-05	New Zealand	D 2-2	Wrexham	Fr	Bellamy 2 [18 38]	7 819	Skjerven NOR
2-06	Czech Republic	D 0-0	Cardiff	ECq		30 174	Allaerts BEL
22-08	Bulgaria	W 1-0	Burgas	Fr	Eastwood [45]	15 000	Germanakos GRE
8-09	Germany	L 0-2	Cardiff	ECq		27 889	Mejuto Gonzalez ESP
12-09	Slovakia	W 5-2	Trnava	ECq	Eastwood [22], Bellamy 2 [34 41], OG [78], Davies.S [90]	5 846	Duhamel FRA
13-10	Cyprus	L 1-3	Nicosia	ECq	Collins [21]	2 852	Bertolini SUI
17-10	San Marino	W 2-1	Serravalle	ECq	Earnshaw [13], Ledley [36]	1 182	Zammit MLT
17-11	Republic of Ireland	D 2-2	Cardiff	ECq	Koumas 2 [23 89p]	24 619	Oriekhov UKR
21-11	Germany	D 0-0	Frankfurt	ECq		49 262	Balaj ROU
2008							
6-02	Norway	W 3-0	Wrexham	Fr	Fletcher [15], Koumas 2 [62 89]	7 553	McKeon IRE
26-03	Luxembourg	W 2-0	Luxembourg	Fr	Eastwood 2 [37 46]	3 000	Kuipers NED
28-05	Iceland	W 1-0	Reykjavik	Fr	Evans [45]	5 322	McCourt NIR
1-06	Netherlands	L 0-2	Rotterdam	Fr		48 500	Brych GER
20-08	Georgia	L 1-2	Swansea	Fr	Koumas [17]	6 435	Jug SVN
6-09	Azerbaijan	W 1-0	Cardiff	WCq	Vokes [83]	17 106	Stavrev MKD
10-09	Russia	L 1-2	Moscow	WCq	Ledley [67]	28 000	Skomina SVN
11-10	Liechtenstein	W 2-0	Cardiff	WCq	Edwards [42], Frick OG [80]	13 356	Vejlgaard DEN
15-10	Germany	L 0-1	Mönchengladbach	WCq		44 500	Duhamel FRA
19-11	Denmark	W 1-0	Brøndby	Fr	Bellamy [77]	10 271	Weiner GER
2009							
11-02	Poland	L 0-1	Vila Real	Fr		487	Paixao POR
28-03	Finland	L 0-2	Cardiff	WCq		22 604	Iturralde ESP
1-04	Germany	L 0-2	Cardiff	WCq		26 064	Hauge NOR
29-05	Estonia	W 1-0	Llanelli	Fr	Earnshaw [26p]	4 071	Thorisson ISL
6-06	Azerbaijan	W 1-0	Baku	WCq	Edwards [42]	25 000	Strombergsson SWE
12-08	Montenegro	L 1-2	Podgorica	Fr	Vokes [47]	5 000	Mazic SRB
9-09	Russia	L 1-3	Cardiff	WCq	Collins [53]	14 505	De Sousa POR
10-10	Finland	L 1-2	Helsinki	WCq	Bellamy [17]	14 000	Mazic SRB
14-10	Liechtenstein	W 2-0	Vaduz	WCq	Vaughan [16], Ramsey [80]	1 858	Kaldma EST
14-11	Scotland	W 3-0	Cardiff	Fr	Edwards [17], Church [32], Ramsey [35]	13 844	Zimmermann SUI
2010							
3-03	Sweden	L 0-1	Swansea	Fr		8 258	Black NIR
23-05	Croatia	L 0-2	Osijek	Fr		15 000	Vincic SVN
11-08	Luxembourg	W 5-1	Llanelli	Fr	Cotterill [35], Ledley [47p], King [55], Williams [78], Bellamy [82]	4 904	Gestranius FIN
3-09	Montenegro	L 0-1	Podgorica	ECq		7 442	Kakos GRE
8-10	Bulgaria	L 0-1	Cardiff	ECq		14 061	Eriksson SWE
12-10	Switzerland	L 1-4	Basel	ECq	Bale [13]	26 000	Hamer LUX

Fr = Friendly match • EC = UEFA EURO 2008/2012 • WC = FIFA World Cup • q = qualifier

WALES NATIONAL TEAM HISTORICAL RECORDS

Caps
92 - Neville Southall 1982-98 • **85** - Gary Speed 1990-2004 • **75** - Dean Saunders 1986-2001 • **73** - Peter Nicholas 1979-91 & Ian Rush 1980-96 • **72** - Mark Hughes 1984-99 & Joey Jones 1975-86 • **68** - Ivor Allchurch 1950-66 • **66** - Brian Flynn 1974-84 • **65** - Andy Melville 1989-2004 • **64** - Ryan Giggs 1991-2007 • **62** - David Phillips 1984-98 • **59** - Barry Horne 1988-96, Cliff Jones 1954-70, Kevin Ratcliffe 1981-93 & Terry Yorath 1970-81 • **58** - Craig Bellamy 1998-, Simon Davies 2001- & Leighton Phillips 1971-82

Goals
28 - Ian Rush 1980-96 • **23** - Ivor Allchurch 1950-66 & Trevor Ford 1947-57 • **22** - Dean Saunders 1986-2001 • **17** - Craig Bellamy 1998- • **16** - Mark Hughes 1984-99 & Cliff Jones 1954-70 • **15** - John Charles 1950-65 • **14** - Robert Earnshaw 2002- & John Hartson 1997-2005 • **13** - John Toshack 1969-80 • **12** - Ryan Giggs 1991-2007 & Billy Lewis 1885-1898 • **11** - Billy Meredith 1895-1920

Past Coaches
Committee 1876-1954 • Wally Barnes 1954-55 • Jimmy Murphy 1956-64 • Trevor Morris 1964 • Dave Bowen 1964-74 • Mike Smith ENG 1974-79 • Mike England 1979-87 • David Williams 1988 • Terry Yorath 1988-93 • John Toshack 1994 • Mike Smith ENG 1994-95 • Bobby Gould ENG 1995-99 • Mark Hughes 1999-2004 • John Toshack 2004-10 • Brian Flynn 2010 • Gary Speed 2010-

WALES 2009-10

LEAGUE OF WALES

Team	Pl	W	D	L	F	A	Pts	New Saints	Llanelli	Port Talbot	Aberystwyth	Bangor City	Rhyl	Airbus UK	Prestatyn	Neath	Carmarthen	Bala Town	Haverfordwest	Newtown	Connah's Quay	Porthmadog	Welshpool	Caersws	Cefn Druids
The New Saints †	34	25	7	2	69	13	82		1-0	1-0	4-0	2-1	4-0	2-1	5-0	2-2	2-0	0-0	4-0	2-2	3-0	5-0	4-0	4-0	4-0
Llanelli ‡	34	25	5	4	79	26	80	0-2		1-0	4-0	3-2	3-1	2-2	4-1	2-1	1-0	2-0	1-1	3-2	5-0	5-0	2-1	7-1	4-0
Port Talbot Town ‡	34	19	8	7	56	23	65	2-0	0-0		1-2	2-1	2-1	2-1	1-1	2-0	0-1	0-0	1-0	2-1	1-0	5-0	3-0	4-0	7-0
Aberystwyth Town	34	19	7	8	54	41	64	1-3	1-1	2-1		2-1	2-2	0-3	2-3	1-1	1-2	1-0	2-1	2-1	1-2	1-0	1-1	3-2	4-1
Bangor City ‡	34	19	6	9	75	45	63	0-1	2-3	1-1	0-1		3-1	3-0	4-0	3-1	3-2	6-3	3-2	0-0	0-0	2-0	3-2	7-1	3-1
Rhyl	34	18	8	8	74	43	62	1-2	0-0	2-0	1-1	5-1		2-1	1-1	0-1	2-1	5-2	1-2	4-2	4-1	4-0	4-1	3-1	6-0
Airbus UK Broughton	34	12	13	9	49	37	49	0-0	0-1	0-0	2-0	1-5	2-2		2-0	1-1	2-2	0-1	3-1	2-0	4-0	1-2	1-2	3-0	1-1
Prestatyn Town	34	12	12	10	53	53	48	0-1	1-5	0-3	0-2	1-1	0-0	2-2		0-0	0-0	2-1	3-0	1-1	3-2	1-1	2-1	1-0	2-0
Neath Athletic	34	12	11	11	41	38	47	0-1	2-1	0-2	1-3	0-1	2-0	0-0	1-1		1-1	2-1	1-2	1-1	1-1	3-2	4-0	5-3	1-1
Carmarthen Town	34	12	9	13	45	38	45	1-2	1-2	3-1	0-0	2-2	0-0	1-1	1-2	0-1		2-1	2-2	1-2	1-0	1-3	1-1	1-0	4-0
Bala Town	34	12	9	13	39	47	45	0-1	0-1	1-1	1-1	2-1	0-4	1-2	2-4	1-0	1-3		1-1	1-1	2-2	0-0	2-1	2-0	1-0
Haverfordwest County	34	11	11	12	47	43	44	0-0	0-1	1-1	0-1	2-2	2-4	1-1	3-3	1-2	2-1	1-1		1-2	1-0	2-0	1-0	3-1	1-0
Newtown	34	10	11	13	54	57	41	0-2	0-2	2-2	1-2	2-5	2-4	3-3	3-2	1-0	0-0	0-1	2-1		0-0	1-3	4-1	4-1	4-2
Connah's Quay Nomads	34	11	8	15	31	42	41	1-0	1-0	0-3	0-3	0-1	0-2	0-1	1-1	2-0	0-0	0-1	1-1	3-1		3-0	0-0	5-0	3-1
Porthmadog	34	6	6	22	23	66	24	1-1	0-4	0-1	0-1	0-2	0-2	0-1	2-0	1-4	1-4	0-2	0-0	1-1	0-1		2-3	1-1	1-0
Welshpool Town	34	6	5	23	30	70	23	0-1	1-2	0-2	1-3	1-2	1-2	0-0	0-5	0-0	1-3	1-2	1-3	1-5	0-1	2-0		3-1	2-1
Caersws	34	3	4	27	26	94	13	0-3	0-2	1-2	0-4	1-3	2-2	0-4	1-5	0-1	0-3	1-3	0-2	1-1	1-0	1-2	1-2		1-0
NEWI Cefn Druids	34	1	6	27	16	77	9	0-0	2-5	0-1	0-3	0-1	1-1	0-1	0-5	0-1	1-2	0-1	0-1	1-2	1-0	2-0	1-1	1-1	

14/08/2009 - 24/04/2010 • † Qualified for the UEFA Champions League • ‡ Qualified for the Europa League • Rhyl refused a licence for 2010-11
Top scorers: **30** - Rhys Griffiths, Llanelli • **24** - Jamie Reed ENG, Bangor • **23** - Chris Sharp SCO, New Saints • **20** - Matthew Williams, Rhyl • **17** - Luke Bowen, Aberystwyth • **16** - Marc Lloyd-Williams, Airbus UK & Martin Rose ENG, Port Talbot • **15** - Mark Connolly ENG, Rhyl & Lee Hunt ENG, Bangor

WALES 2009-10
WELSH LEAGUE DIVISION 1 (2)

	Pl	W	D	L	F	A	Pts
Goytre United	34	19	12	3	86	47	69
Cambrian & Clydach	34	19	11	4	73	42	68
Afan Lido	34	19	6	9	74	37	63
Caldicot Town	34	16	7	11	78	54	55
Bryntirion Athletic	34	15	9	10	67	60	54
Taffs Well	34	15	5	14	72	60	50
Barry Town	34	12	13	9	46	41	49
Pontardawe Town	34	13	8	13	59	56	47
Bridgend Town	34	12	9	13	57	55	45
Aberaman Athletic	34	12	8	14	56	68	44
West End	34	12	8	14	62	84	44
Cardiff Corinthians	34	12	7	15	63	69	43
Garden Village	34	12	6	16	46	52	42
Ton Pentre	34	11	8	15	56	65	41
Ely Rangers	34	10	6	18	46	67	36
Bettws	34	9	9	16	38	59	36
Dinas Powys	34	9	4	21	50	83	31
Caerleon	34	8	6	20	37	67	30

15/08/2009 - 22/05/2010

WALES 2009-10
CYMRU ALLIANCE (2)

	Pl	W	D	L	F	A	Pts
Llangefni Town	32	25	4	3	95	27	79
Flint Town United	32	23	6	3	84	29	75
Llandudno	32	19	8	5	73	31	65
Buckley Town	32	17	9	6	57	30	60
Penrhyncoch	32	16	7	9	51	46	55
Guilsfield	32	12	9	11	54	54	45
Ruthin Town	32	13	5	14	48	61	44
Holyhead Hotspur	32	13	4	15	53	52	40
Denbigh Town	32	10	9	13	56	56	39
Bethesda Athletic	32	10	9	13	70	59	39
Llangollen Town	32	11	3	18	59	78	36
Berriew	32	10	5	17	49	74	35
Mold Alexandra	32	11	2	19	53	80	35
Lex XI	32	9	7	16	45	70	34
Llanfairpwll	32	9	5	18	38	60	32
Caernarfon Town	32	8	5	19	50	69	26
Gresford Athletic	32	5	5	22	28	87	20

14/08/2009 - 8/05/2010

LOOSEMORES CHALLENGE CUP (LEAGUE CUP) 2009-10

Quarter-finals		Semi-finals		Final	
The New Saints	4				
Llanelli	1	The New Saints	0 2		
Welshpool	1	Port Talbot Town	0 0		
Port Talbot Town	3			The New Saints	2
Connah's Quay	3			Rhyl	0
Balla Town	2	Connah's Quay	2 0		
Porthmadog	1	Rhyl	1 4	Airfield, Broughton	
Rhyl	4			27-04-2010	

MEDALS TABLE

		Overall			League			Cup	
		G	S	B	G	S	B	G	S
1	Wrexham	28	25					23	22
2	Cardiff City	23	12	1				22	10
3	Barry Town	18	3		7	1		6	1
4	Swansea City	12	10					10	8
5	The New Saints	12	6	1	5	4	1	2	2
6	Bangor City	10	14	3	2		3	8	8
7	Rhyl	8	11	2	2	2	2	4	4
8	NEWI Cefn Druids	8	5					8	5
9	Shrewsbury Town	6	3					6	3
10	Chirk	5	1					5	1

Overall totals also include the League Cup and Premier Cup

WELSH CUP 2009–10

Third Round		Fourth Round		Quarter-finals		Semi-finals		Final	
Bangor City	1								
Flint Town United *	0	Bangor City *	3						
Ely Rangers	0	Aberaman Athletic	1	Bangor City *	2				
Aberaman Athletic *	2			Llanelli	0				
Holyhead Hotspur	6	Holyhead Hotspur	0			Bangor City †	2		
Llangeinor *	1	Llanelli *	4			Prestatyn Town	0		
Carmarthen Town	1								
Llanelli *	3							Bangor City ‡	3
Rhyl *	4	Rhyl *	7					Port Talbot Town	2
Bridgend Town	2	Pontardawe Town *	0	Rhyl	4 3p				
Llandudno Town	0			Prestatyn Town *	4 5p				
Pontardawe Town *	2								
Porthmadog *	3	Porthmadog	0						
Rhydymwyn	1	Prestatyn Town *	1						
Cardiff Bay Harlequins	0								
Prestatyn Town *	3								
Bala Town *	2	Bala Town *	2						
Llanrug United	0	Caersws	0	Bala Town *	2				
Coedpoeth United	1			Afan Lido	0				
Caersws *	4								
Connah's Quay Nomads *	3	Connah's Quay Nomads	1			Bala Town	0		
Airbus UK Broughton	2	Afan Lido *	2			Port Talbot Town ††	1		
Caerau Ely *	1								
Afan Lido	2								
The New Saints	2	The New Saints	6						
Cambrian & Clydach *	0	Llandudno Junction *	0	The New Saints *	2 3p				
Llangollen Town *	1			Port Talbot Town	2 4p				
Llandudno Junction	3								
Aberystwyth Town	2	Aberystwyth Town *	0						
Haverfordwest County *	1	Port Talbot Town	2						
Caldicot Town *	0								
Port Talbot Town	3								

* Home team ● † Played in Newtown ● †† Played in Aberystwyth ● ‡ Qualified for the Europa League

CUP FINAL

Parc y Scarlets, Llanelli
1-05-2010, Att: 1303, Ref: Dean John
Scorers - Hunt [6], Reed [16], Morley [91+] for Bangor City; Fahiya [57], McCreesh [85] for Port Talbot

Bangor - Paul Smith - Peter Hoy, Chris Roberts, Dave Morley●, Jamie Brewerton, Craig Garside, Jamie Reed (Les Davies 90), Michael Johnston●, Eddie Jebb (Sion Edwards 69), Mark Smyth● (Marc Limbert 80), Lee Hunt.
Tr: Neville Powell

Port Talbot - Lee Kendall - Leigh De-Vulgt● (Nicky Holland 63), Scott Barrow, Gareth Phillips●, Matthew Rees, Lee Surman, Drew Fahiya (Lee John 66), Lloyd Grist, Martin Rose, Liam McCreesh, Daniel Thomas (Karl Lewis 66).
Tr: Mark Jones

YEM – YEMEN

FIFA/COCA-COLA WORLD RANKING

1993	1994	1995	1996	1997	1998	1999	2000	2001	2002	2003	2004	2005	2006	2007	2008	2009	2010
91	103	123	139	128	146	158	160	135	145	132	124	139	141	144	145	130	126

2010												Hi/Lo
Jan	Feb	Mar	Mar	Apr	May	Jul	Aug	Sep	Oct	Nov	Dec	90
130	105	107	108	109	112	109	109	107	117	122	126	163

Yemen's hosting of the Gulf Cup in November and December 2010 was the first time the nation had played host to a major event since North and South Yemen became one country in 1990. Concerns about security had been voiced in the build up to the tournament but they proved groundless as the tournament passed off peacefully. The artificial pitch at the May 22 Stadium in Aden was the main venue for the event along with the town of Zinjibar in Abyan province further down the coast. It was won by Kuwait who beat Saudi Arabia in the final with Yemen failing to progress beyond the group stage after losing all three of their matches - against Saudi Arabia, Qatar and Kuwait. Coached by Srecko Juricic, who previously had led Bahrain to a fourth place at the 2004 Asian Cup, Yemen had high hopes for the tournament having only just missed out on a place in the West Asian Championship earlier in a year in Jordan where they lost to Kuwait in the semi-finals on post-match penalties. Veteran striker Ali Al-Nono remained as prolific as ever, scoring four times to finish as the tournament's top scorer but he failed to find the back of the net at the Gulf Cup. Domestic honours were won by Al Saqr from Taizz who won the league title five points ahead of cup winners Al Tilal from Aden. In the final they beat Al Shabab Al Baydaa 2-1.

FIFA WORLD CUP RECORD
1930-1982 DNE **1986-1990** DNQ (as North Yemen) **1930-1982** DNE **1986-1990** DNQ (as South Yemen) **1994-2010** DNQ

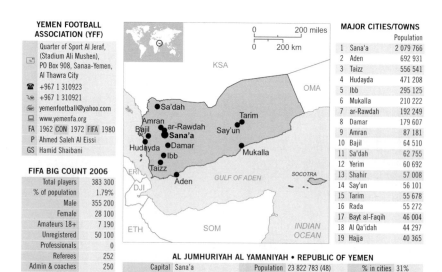

YEMEN FOOTBALL ASSOCIATION (YFF)

Quarter of Sport Al Jeraf, (Stadium Ali Mushen), PO Box 908, Sanaa-Yemen, Al Thawra City
☎ +967 1 310923
📠 +967 1 310921
✉ yemenfootball@yahoo.com
🖥 www.yemenfa.org
FA 1962 CON 1972 FIFA 1980
P Ahmed Saleh Al Eissi
GS Hamid Shaibani

FIFA BIG COUNT 2006

Total players	383 300
% of population	1.79%
Male	355 200
Female	28 100
Amateurs 18+	7 190
Unregistered	50 100
Professionals	0
Referees	252
Admin & coaches	250
Number of clubs	110
Number of teams	220

MAJOR CITIES/TOWNS

		Population
1	Sana'a	2 079 766
2	Aden	692 931
3	Taizz	556 541
4	Hudayda	471 208
5	Ibb	295 125
6	Mukalla	210 222
7	ar-Rawdah	192 249
8	Damar	179 607
9	Amran	87 181
10	Bajil	64 510
11	Sa'dah	62 755
12	Yerim	60 692
13	Shahir	57 008
14	Say'un	56 101
15	Tarim	55 678
16	Rada	55 272
17	Bayt al-Faqih	46 004
18	Al Qa'idah	44 297
19	Hajja	40 365

AL JUMHURIYAH AL YAMANIYAH • REPUBLIC OF YEMEN

Capital	Sana'a	Population	23 822 783 (48)	% in cities	31%
GDP per capita	$2500 (175)	Area km²	527 968 km² (49)	GMT +/-	+3
Neighbours (km)	Oman 288, Saudi Arabia 1458 • Coast 1906				

RECENT INTERNATIONAL MATCHES PLAYED BY YEMEN

2007	Opponents	Score	Venue	Comp	Scorers	Att	Referee
7-01	Eritrea	W 4-1	Sana'a	Fr	Akram Al Worafi [54], Fekri Al Hubaishi [71], Yaser Basuhai [73], Nashwan Al Haggam [79]		
12-01	Bahrain	L 0-4	Dubai	Fr			
17-01	Kuwait	D 1-1	Abu Dhabi	GCr1	Ali Al Omqy [16]		
20-01	UAE	L 1-2	Abu Dhabi	GCr1	Ala Al Sasi [90]		
23-01	Oman	L 1-2	Abu Dhabi	GCr1	Mohammed Salem [9]		
8-10	Maldives	W 3-0	Sana'a	WCq	Mohammed Salem [43], Fekri Al Hubaishi [66], Haitham Thabit [80]	3 000	Mansour LIB
28-10	Maldives	L 0-2	Male	WCq		8 900	Sarkar IND
9-11	Thailand	D 1-1	Sana'a	WCq	Ali Al Nono [43]	12 000	Al Ghamdi KSA
18-11	Thailand	L 0-1	Bangkok	WCq		29 000	Matsumura JPN
2008							
26-01	Bahrain	L 1-2	Manama	Fr	Abdullah Yaslam [67]		
4-04	Tanzania	W 2-1	Sana'a	Fr	Abdullah Yaslam 2 [2 50]		
25-04	Indonesia	L 0-1	Bandung	Fr			
3-05	Oman	D 0-0	Muscat	Fr			
22-05	Sudan	D 1-1	Sana'a	Fr	Muaz Assaj [47]		
2009							
5-01	UAE	L 1-3	Muscat	GCr1	Ali Al Nono [90]		
8-01	Saudi Arabia	L 0-6	Muscat	GCr1			
11-01	Qatar	L 1-2	Muscat	GCr1	Ali Al Nono [30p]		
20-01	Japan	L 1-2	Kumamoto	ACq	Zaher Al Fadhli [47]	32 000	Tan Hai CHN
28-01	Hong Kong	W 1-0	Sana'a	ACq	Akram Al Selwi [51]	10 000	Al Hilali OMA
8-11	Tanzania	D 1-1	Sana'a	Fr	Ali Mubarak [78]		
11-11	Tanzania	W 2-1	Sana'a	Fr	Tamer Hanash [13p], Akram Al Worafi [37]		
18-11	Bahrain	L 0-4	Manama	ACq		1 000	Basma SYR
30-12	Tajikistan	W 2-1	Sana'a	Fr	Khaled Baleid [71], Ali Al Nono [85]		
2010							
2-01	Tajikistan	L 0-1	Sana'a	Fr			
6-01	Japan	L 2-3	Sana'a	ACq	Basem Al Aqel [13], Salem Abbod [39]	10 000	Albadwawi UAE
15-01	Kenya	W 3-1	Sana'a	Fr	Ali Al Nono [45], Ala Al Sasi 2 [48 50]		
20-01	Bahrain	W 3-0	Sana'a	ACq	Ali Al Nono 2 [5 25], Mohammed Al Abidi [86]	7 000	Torky IRN
27-02	Malaysia	L 0-1	Kuala Lumpur	Fr			
3-03	Hong Kong	D 0-0	Hong Kong	ACq		1 212	Minh Tri Vo VIE
12-05	Malawi	W 1-0	Sana'a	Fr			
18-05	Oman	L 0-1	Sana'a	Fr			
7-09	Syria	W 2-1	Sana'a	Fr	Ali Al Nono 2 [18p 55]		
18-09	Zambia	L 0-1	Sana'a	Fr			
25-09	Iraq	L 1-2	Amman	WAr1	Ali Al Nono [10]		
27-09	Palestine	W 3-1	Amman	WAr1	Ali Al Nono 2 [43p 83], Haitham Thabit [63]		
1-10	Kuwait	D 1-1	Amman	WAsf	Ali Al Nono [55]. L 3-4p		
13-10	India	W 6-3	Pune	Fr	Haitham Thabit [9], Khaled Baleid [28], Akram Al Worafi [61], Ala Al Sasi 2 [77 88], Yasser Basuhai [93+]		
7-11	Uganda	D 2-2	Sana'a	Fr	Ali Al Nono 2 [9 11]		
10-11	Korea DPR	D 1-1	Sana'a	Fr	Akram Al Worafi [42]		
22-11	Saudi Arabia	L 0-4	Aden	GCr1			Al Marzouqi UAE
25-11	Qatar	L 1-2	Zinjibar	GCr1	Akram Al Worafi [17]		Abid IRQ
28-11	Kuwait	L 0-3	Zinjibar	GCr1			Abbas BHR

Fr = Friendly match • GC = Gulf Cup • AC = AFC Asian Cup • WC = FIFA World Cup • q = qualifier • r1 = first round group

YEMEN 2010

PREMIER LEAGUE

	Pl	W	D	L	F	A	Pts	Saqr	Tilal	Shabab	Ahly S	Ahly T	Urooba	Wahda S	Ittihad	Sha'ab	Hilal	Shula	Wahda A	Salam	Yarmuk
Al Saqr Taizz ‡	26	16	4	6	43	23	52		2-1	3-1	4-0	0-1	3-1	2-0	3-1	1-0	4-2	2-0	1-0	2-1	0-0
Al Tilal Aden ‡	26	14	5	7	43	26	47	2-2		1-0	2-2	2-0	1-0	1-1	3-0	2-1	1-4	5-0	4-0	2-0	1-0
Al Shabab Al Baydaa	26	14	2	10	31	23	44	2-0	1-0		2-0	3-0	2-1	2-0	2-1	1-0	1-0	1-1	2-0	1-0	2-0
Al Ahly Sana'a	26	12	7	7	29	23	43	2-0	3-2	2-0		0-2	1-1	0-0	3-1	2-0	0-1	2-1	2-0	0-0	2-0
Al Ahly Taizz	26	13	2	11	34	32	41	0-2	0-1	1-0	0-1		2-1	3-0	2-1	2-3	1-0	7-3	2-3	2-0	0-0
Al Urooba	26	12	3	11	36	30	39	1-2	3-0	1-0	2-2	2-0		1-0	2-1	1-2	3-1	1-0	1-0	4-1	1-0
Al Wahda Sana'a	26	9	10	7	28	24	37	0-1	1-1	2-1	1-1	3-0	2-1		0-0	1-1	1-0	1-0	1-0	1-1	4-0
Al Ittihad Ibb	26	9	9	8	22	25	36	1-3	0-0	3-1	1-0	2-0	0-0	1-1		1-0	1-0	0-0	1-0	2-2	2-1
Al Sha'ab Ibb	26	8	7	11	29	30	31	0-0	0-1	3-2	1-0	2-0	0-1	2-2	0-0		0-1	1-1	2-0	3-0	0-1
Al Hilal Hudayda	26	9	4	13	26	31	31	2-0	0-4	2-0	0-1	1-0	1-0	3-0	0-1	2-4		1-0	0-1	1-1	2-2
Shula Aden	26	7	9	10	25	39	30	1-1	2-1	1-0	0-0	2-3	**3-0**	1-3	0-0	2-2	1-0		0-0	1-1	2-1
Al Wahda Aden	26	8	4	14	23	39	28	1-0	1-3	0-2	1-0	0-1	2-1	0-0	0-0	3-1	2-0	0-1		1-1	4-2
Salam Al Garfa	26	5	12	9	27	33	27	1-0	3-1	0-0	1-0	2-4	1-0	1-1	0-1	1-1	0-0	1-2	7-2		1-1
Al Yarmuk Sana'a	26	4	6	16	26	44	18	2-5	0-1	1-2	0-1	0-1	2-5	0-3	0-1	2-0	2-2	5-0	4-2	0-0	

5/11/2009 - 4/06/2010 • ‡ Qualified for the AFC Cup • Match in bold awarded

YEMEN 2010
SECOND DIVISION GROUP A (2)

	Pl	W	D	L	F	A	Pts
Hassan Abyan	18	14	2	2	35	12	44
Al Rasheed Taizz	18	11	7	0	24	6	40
Al Tadamun Shabwa	18	10	4	4	23	14	34
Al Nasir Al Dalaa	18	8	5	5	18	13	29
May 22 Sana'a	18	7	5	6	32	19	26
Al Taawun Badan	18	5	8	5	14	18	23
Al Sharara Lahaj	18	6	3	9	22	26	21
Samoon	18	1	8	9	11	25	11
Al Tadamun Mukalla	18	2	4	12	13	31	10
Al Shabab Al Zaydiya	18	2	2	14	8	36	8

16/12/2009 - 2/05/2010

YEMEN 2010
SECOND DIVISION GROUP B (2)

	Pl	W	D	L	F	A	Pts
Al Sha'ab Sana'a	18	12	2	4	45	12	38
Al Sha'ab Hadramaut	18	12	2	4	30	16	38
Saioon	18	11	5	2	26	13	38
Khanfar	18	10	0	8	26	25	30
Shamshan Aden	18	8	3	7	31	25	27
Doan	18	8	2	8	18	20	26
Al Ahli Hudayda	18	7	5	6	23	19	26
September 26	18	5	3	10	19	28	18
Al Nahda	18	3	2	13	13	35	11
Al Shabab Amran	18	1	2	15	7	45	5

16/12/2009 - 2/05/2010

PRESIDENTS CUP 2010

Round of 16			Quarter–finals			Semi–finals			Final	
Al Tilal Aden *	1	4								
Al Taawun Badan	0	1	**Al Tilal Aden ***	5	2					
September 26 *	1	1	Salam Al Garfa	1	0					
Salam Al Garfa	1	2				**Al Tilal Aden**	0	3		
Al Sha'ab Ibb	0	1				Al Urooba *	2	0		
Al Ittihad Ibb *	0	0	Al Sha'ab Ibb *	0	0					
Al Sha'ab Sana'a *	2	3	**Al Urooba**	4	3					
Al Urooba	4	2							**Al Tilal Aden ‡**	2
Al Hilal Hudayda	2	6							Al Shabab Al Baydaa	1
Al Tadamun Mukalla *	2	2	**Al Hilal Hudayda ***	2	4					
Al Yarmuk Sana'a	1	2	Al Wahda Aden	1	1					
Al Wahda Aden *	4	1				Al Hilal Hudayda	0	1		
Al Ahly Sana'a *	3	2				**Al Shabab Al Baydaa ***	0	1		
Al Wahda Sana'a	1	2	Al Ahly Sana'a	0	1					
Al Saqr Taizz *	1	1	**Al Shabab Al Baydaa ***	3	2					
Al Shabab Al Baydaa	3	0								

CUP FINAL

18-07-2010
Scorers - Almi Antana 10, Murad Gardi 90 for Al Tilal; Mohammed Abdullah Alabidi 71 for Shabab

* Home team in the first leg • ‡ Qualified for the AFC Cup

ZAM – ZAMBIA

FIFA/COCA-COLA WORLD RANKING

1993	1994	1995	1996	1997	1998	1999	2000	2001	2002	2003	2004	2005	2006	2007	2008	2009	2010
27	21	25	20	21	29	36	49	64	67	68	70	58	62	65	72	84	76

						2010							Hi/Lo
Jan	Feb	Mar	Mar	Apr	May	Jul	Aug	Sep	Oct	Nov	Dec		15
84	73	73	71	71	71	73	72	74	76	69	76		96

Zambia continued to be able to lay claim to the title of Africa's most consistent side after participating in the African Nations Cup finals for the 10th time in the past 11 tournaments. In Angola they added some icing to the achievement by making it through to the quarter-finals for the first time since 1996. French coach Herve Renard departed after the tournament for a similar job in neighbouring Angola and was replaced by former Italian international Dario Bonetti. At the East and Central African Senior Challenge Cup at the end of the year, where Zambia were again invited as guest competitors despite being from outside the CECAFA region, there was the disappointment of losing again in the quarter-finals as they had done in 2009, this time at the hands of Ethiopia. Domestic tournaments were severely disrupted at the end of 2010 by a bitter dispute when FIFA-backed football association president Kalusha Bwalya came under attack from a breakaway faction who, supported by some of the Premier League clubs, even voted in a new Executive Committee. The Premier League staggered to a close with Zesco United having done enough to win the title despite the full programme not having been completed. The 2010 Barclays Cup Final between Zanaco and Zesco United was delayed and rescheduled for the new year.

FIFA WORLD CUP RECORD
1930-1966 DNE   1970-2010 DNQ

FOOTBALL ASSOCIATION OF ZAMBIA (FAZ)

Football House, Alick Nkhata Road, Long Acres, PO Box 34751, Lusaka

☎ +260 211 250940
📠 +260 211 250946
📧 faz@zamnet.zm
🖥 www.fazfootball.com
FA 1929 CON 1964 FIFA 1964
P Kalusha Bwalya
GS George Kasengele

FIFA BIG COUNT 2006

Total players	1 024 817
% of population	8.91%
Male	992 786
Female	32 031
Amateurs 18+	19 560
Youth under 18	9 050
Unregistered	975 606
Professionals	101
Referees	524
Admin & coaches	11 035
Number of clubs	470
Number of teams	2 350

MAJOR CITIES/TOWNS

		Population
1	Lusaka	1 460 566
2	Kitwe	526 937
3	Ndola	495 004
4	Kabwe	215 015
5	Chingola	178 092
6	Mufulira	141 056
7	Livingstone	133 936
8	Luanshya	132 117
9	Kasama	111 588
10	Chipata	109 344
11	Kalulushi	100 712
12	Mazabuka	95 723
13	Chililabombwe	71 876
14	Mongu	69 379
15	Choma	59 151
16	Kapiri Mposhi	56 860
17	Kansanshi	51 986
18	Kafue	47 838

REPUBLIC OF ZAMBIA

Capital	Lusaka	Population	11 862 740 (71)	% in cities	35%
GDP per capita	$1500 (200)	Area km²	752 618 km² (39)	GMT +/-	+2
Neighbours (km)	Angola 1110, Congo DR 1930, Malawi 837, Mozambique 419, Namibia 233, Tanzania 338, Zimbabwe 797				

RECENT INTERNATIONAL MATCHES PLAYED BY ZAMBIA

2008	Opponents	Score		Venue	Comp	Scorers	Att	Referee
27-07	Zimbabwe	D	0-0	Secunda	CCqf	W 5-4p		Nhlapo RSA
3-08	Madagascar	W	2-0	Thulamahashe	CC3p	Emmanuel Mayuka 56, Francis Kombe 70		Marange ZIM
10-09	Togo	W	1-0	Chililabombwe	WCq	Felix Katongo 31	10 500	Damon RSA
19-11	Morocco	L	0-3	Rabat	Fr			
31-12	Djibouti	W	3-0	Jinja	CErl	Given Singuluma 2 25 38, Jonas Sakuwaha 44		
2009								
2-01	Kenya	D	0-0	Jinja	CErl			
4-01	Burundi	D	1-1	Jinja	CErl	Rodgers Kola 60		
8-01	Sudan	L	0-2	Kampala	CErl			
27-01	South Africa	L	0-1	Atteridgeville	Fr		10 125	Seechurn MRI
29-03	Egypt	D	1-1	Cairo	WCq	Francis Kasonde 56	70 000	Coulibaly MLI
6-06	Rwanda	W	1-0	Chililabombwe	WCq	Rainford Kalaba 78	28 000	Seck SEN
20-06	Algeria	L	0-2	Chililabombwe	WCq		9 000	Evehe CMR
12-08	Ghana	L	1-4	London	Fr	Stophira Sunzu 32		Marriner ENG
6-09	Algeria	L	0-1	Blida	WCq		30 000	Seechurn MRI
10-10	Egypt	L	0-1	Chililabombwe	WCq		10 000	Djaoupe TOG
25-10	Namibia	W	1-0	Harare	CCqf	Stophira Sunzu 86		Ebrahim RSA
29-10	Mozambique	W	2-0	Bulawayo	CCsf	Ennoch Sakala 8, Felix Sunzu 84		Ramocha BOT
1-11	Zimbabwe	L	1-3	Harare	CCf	Henry Banda 24		Carvalho ANG
14-11	Rwanda	D	0-0	Kigali	WCq		18 000	Ambaya LBY
21-11	Korea DPR	W	4-1	Lusaka	Fr	James Chamanga 3 10 13 70, Felix Sunzu 90		
28-11	Kenya	W	2-0	Nairobi	CErl	James Chamanga 88, Stophira Sunzu 90		
2-12	Ethiopia	W	1-0	Nairobi	CErl	James Chamanga 30		
4-12	Djibouti	W	6-0	Nairobi	CErl	Kennedy Chola 3 4 49 89, Felix Sunzu 33, Kebby Hachipaka 65, Charles Siyanga 74		
7-12	Zanzibar †	D	0-0	Nairobi	CEqf	L 3-4p		
28-12	Mozambique	W	1-0	Johannesburg	Fr	Collins Mbesuma 76		
2010								
9-01	Korea Republic	W	4-2	Johannesburg	Fr	Felix Katongo 6, Rainford Kalaba 14, James Chamanga 63, Noah Chivuta 72p	2 000	Gomes RSA
13-01	Tunisia	D	1-1	Lubango	CNrl	Jacob Mulenga 19	17 000	Coulibaly MLI
17-01	Cameroon	L	2-3	Lubango	CNrl	Jacob Mulenga 8, Chris Katongo 81p	15 000	Al Ghamdi KSA
21-01	Gabon	W	2-1	Benguela	CNrl	Rainford Kalaba 28, James Chamanga 62	5 000	Benouza ALG
25-01	Nigeria	D	0-0	Lubango	CNqf	L 4-5p	10 000	Abd El Fatah EGY
26-05	Chile	L	0-3	Calama	Fr		12 000	Favale ARG
11-08	Uganda	D	1-1	Kampala	Fr	OG 22		
5-09	Comoros	W	4-0	Lusaka	CNq	Rainford Kalaba 5, Fwayo Tembo 21, James Chamanga 30, Emmanuel Mayuka 82		Eyob ERI
18-09	Yemen	W	1-0	Sana'a	Fr	Rainford Kalaba 15		
10-10	Libya	L	0-1	Tripoli	CNq			Gassama GAM
27-11	Tanzania	W	1-0	Dar es Salaam	CErl	Kennedy Mudenda 24		
30-11	Burundi	D	0-0	Dar es Salaam	CErl			
3-12	Somalia	W	6-0	Dar es Salaam	CErl	Felix Sunzu 4 25 27 43 49p, Alan Mukuka 28, Venecious Mapande 81		
7-12	Ethiopia	L	1-2	Dar es Salaam	CEqf	Felix Sunzu 58		
31-12	Kuwait	L	0-4	Suez	Fr			

Fr = Friendly match • CC = COSAFA Cup • CE = CECAFA Cup • CN = CAF African Cup of Nations • WC = FIFA World Cup • BCD = Behind closed doors
q = qualifier • rl = first round group • qf = quarter-final • sf = semi-final • f = final • † Not an official international

ZAMBIA NATIONAL TEAM HISTORICAL RECORDS

Caps 102 - Kalusha Bwalya 1983-2000

Goals 50 - Kalasha Bwalya 1983-2000

Past Coaches Jochen Figge GER 1992-93 • Godfrey Chitalu 1993 • Ian Porterfield SCO 1993-94 • Roald Poulsen DEN 1994-96 • George Mungwa 1996-97 • Obby Kapita 1997 • Burkhard Ziese GER 1997-98 • Ben Bamfuchile 1998-2001 • Jan Brouwer NED 2001 • Roald Poulsen DEN 2002 • Kalusha Bwalya 2003-06 • Patrick Phiri 2006-08 • Herve Renard FRA 2008-10 • Dario Bonetti ITA 2010-

ZAMBIA 2010

KONKOLA COPPER MINES PREMIER LEAGUE

	Pl	W	D	L	F	A	Pts	ZESCO	Nchanga	Buffaloes	Dynamos	Zanaco	Nkana	Nkwazi	Red Arrows	Konkola	Kabwe	Roan United	Choma	Rangers	City of Lusaka	L Dynamos	Nat Assembly
ZESCO United †	29	17	9	3	41	16	60		1-0	1-0	3-1	0-0	2-1	2-0	0-0	1-1	2-0	3-1	4-1	n/p	2-0	2-0
Nchanga Rangers ‡	29	15	8	6	34	20	53	1-2		1-2	0-0	2-1	0-0	3-1	n/p	2-1	1-0	1-0	1-0	1-0	2-0	1-0
Green Buffaloes	28	14	8	6	37	17	50	2-0	2-0		0-0	0-2	n/p	1-1	1-2	2-0	1-0	1-0	1-1	0-0	5-0	1-1	1-0
Power Dynamos	30	13	11	6	36	21	50	1-1	2-2	1-2		1-0	1-1	4-0	2-0	2-0	1-0	0-2	3-0	1-1	2-0	1-1	2-1
Zanaco	27	13	5	9	37	20	44	2-2	0-1	1-0	0-1		8-1	1-0	2-0	2-0		1-0	3-1	3-0	2-0	2-1
Nkana	28	11	9	8	27	24	42	0-0	1-1	2-1	1-2	1-0		2-1	1-1	0-1	2-0	1-0	2-1	2-2	4-2	2-0	2-0
Nkwazi	30	8	13	9	24	37	37	1-3	1-1	1-1	1-0	1-0	0-0		0-0	1-0	1-1	1-0	1-1	0-0	0-2	1-0	1-1
Red Arrows	28	8	11	9	31	30	35	1-1	2-1	1-1	2-0	1-1	3-0	0-0		1-0	2-2	0-1	1-1	4-1	0-1	1-0	3-2
Konkola Blades	28	8	11	9	25	30	35	2-1	2-2	0-3	1-1	2-1	1-0	2-1	n/p		1-1	1-1	1-1	0-0	1-1	4-0	1-0
Kabwe Warriors	28	8	10	10	24	23	34	0-1	2-0	0-0	0-1	0-0	1-0	0-1	3-1	2-0		n/p	0-0	1-1	1-1	3-0	1-3
Roan United	27	9	7	11	17	26	34	0-3	0-2	0-2	1-0	0-2	0-1	2-1	1-1	1-1	1-0		1-0	0-0	0-0	1-0	n/p
Choma Eagles	29	6	14	9	22	24	32	0-0	0-0	1-0	1-1	1-0	2-0	0-0	3-2	n/p	0-2	0-0		0-1	4-0	3-0	0-0
Forest Rangers	28	6	12	10	21	29	30	0-2	0-1	n/p	1-1	0-0	2-1	1-2	1-0	2-0	0-1	0-0	0-0		1-0	1-2	1-1
City of Lusaka	27	6	6	15	15	37	24	1-0	0-0	0-2	1-2		0-1	1-0	0-0	n/p	0-1	1-1	1-0		0-1	0-2
Lusaka Dynamos	30	5	8	17	20	43	23	0-1	0-2	0-1	0-0	1-2	1-0	1-1	1-1	1-1	1-1	1-2	0-1	1-3	2-3		1-1
National Assembly	28	4	10	14	24	38	22	0-0	0-3	1-4	0-3	0-0	0-0	1-1	1-1	1-2	0-1	5-2	0-0	n/p	1-0	1-2	

13/03/2010 - 19/12/2010 • † Qualified for the CAF Champions League • ‡ Qualified for the CAF Confederation Cup

MEDALS TABLE

		Overall			Lg	C	T8	LC	BC	Africa			City
		G	S	B	G	G	G	G		G	S	B	
1	Mufulira Wanderers	27		3	9	9	9					3	Mufulira
2	Nkana	24	1	5	11	6	7				1	5	Kitwe
3	Kabwe Warriors	19			5	5	8	1					Kabwe
4	Power Dynamos	16	1		5	6	2	1	1	1	1		Kitwe
5	Green Buffaloes	12			6	1	5						Lusaka
6	Zanaco	11			5	1	3	2					Lusaka
7	Roan United	8			1	4	3						Luanshya
8	ZESCO United	7			3	1		1	2				Ndola
9	Nchanga Rangers	6		1	2	1	3					1	Chingola
10	City of Lusaka	5			1	2	2						Lusaka
11	Red Arrows	3			1	1	1						Lusaka
	Konkola Blades	3				3							Chililabombwe
13	Mufulira Blackpool	2				2							Mufulira
	Ndola United	2				1	1						Ndola
	Kitwe United	2					2						Kitwe
16	Chambishi	1						1					Kitwe
	Forest Rangers	1					1						Ndola
	Lusaka Celtic	1				1							Lusaka
	Strike Rovers	1				1							Ndola
	Vitafoam United	1				1							Ndola
	Zamsure	1				1							Lusaka
	Lusaka Dynamos	1					1						Lusaka

Lge = Premier League • C = Castle/Independence/Mosi Cup (1961-2007) • T8 = Top 8 Cup (1962-2008) •
LC = Coca Cola League Cup (2001-07) • BC = Barclays Cup (2007-)

ZIM - ZIMBABWE

1993	1994	1995	1996	1997	1998	1999	2000	2001	2002	2003	2004	2005	2006	2007	2008	2009	2010
46	51	59	71	74	74	67	68	68	57	53	60	53	76	87	97	109	119

	2010											Hi/Lo
Jan	Feb	Mar	Mar	Apr	May	Jul	Aug	Sep	Oct	Nov	Dec	**40**
109	117	117	113	113	110	110	113	118	118	118	119	**131**

Political intrigue and economic meltdown has meant difficult times for football in Zimbabwe but the country's footballers have lost none of their grit and fight. This was exemplified by Harare club Dynamos who qualified against expectations for the group phase of the 2010 African Champions League despite any real resources and having to beg and borrow scarce foreign currency at every turn to keep their campaign going. Ultimately player demands for unpaid wages and promised bonuses sidetracked the fairytale run but it still emphasised the potential that exists in the country were it not blighted by civil turmoil. Dynamos also made a late charge for the Premier League title but Motor Action held on for their first-ever championship on a dramatic last day of the season. Belgian coach Tom Saintfiet was appointed head of the national side before the start of the 2012 African Nations Cup qualifiers, only to be deported just days after arrival because he did not have the necessary paperwork. It appeared he was the victim of a factional fight between football officials. He had taken over from Norma Mapeza and was later replaced on a interim basis by another former international Madinda Ndlovu. The highlight of the season was without question the visit of the Brazil national team to Harare for an international prior to the World Cup.

ZIMBABWE FOOTBALL ASSOCIATION (ZIFA)

53 Livingstone Avenue, Causeway, PO Box CY 114, Harare
☎ +263 4 798631
📠 +263 4 798626
✉ zifa@africaonline.co.zw
🖥 www.zimbabwesoccer.com
FA 1965 CON 1965 FIFA 1965
P Cuthbert Dube
GS TBD

FIFA BIG COUNT 2006

Total players	651 400
% of population	5.32%
Male	622 300
Female	29 100
Amateurs 18+	28 600
Youth under 18	5 900
Unregistered	46 800
Professionals	100
Referees	800
Admin & coaches	2 300
Number of clubs	350
Number of teams	1 250

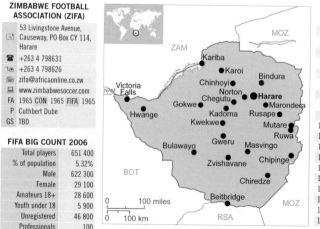

MAJOR CITIES/TOWNS

		Population
1	Harare	1 727 713
2	Bulawayo	748 883
3	Chitungwiza	357 280
4	Mutare	185 238
5	Gweru	141 793
6	Epworth	140 645
7	Kwekwe	99 561
8	Kadoma	77 485
9	Masvingo	72 132
10	Norton	67 177
11	Marondera	63 717
12	Chinhoyi	61 289
13	Chegutu	46 359
14	Bindura	42 488
15	Zvishavane	34 851
16	Ruwa	34 693
17	Redcliff	34 601
18	Hwange	34 177
19	Beitbridge	33 763

REPUBLIC OF ZIMBABWE

Capital	Harare	Population	11 392 629 (73)	% in cities	37%
GDP per capita	$200 (229)	Area km²	390 757 km² (60)	GMT +/-	+2
Neighbours (km)	Botswana 813, Mozambique 1231, South Africa 225, Zambia 797				

RECENT INTERNATIONAL MATCHES PLAYED BY ZIMBABWE

2006	Opponents	Score		Venue	Comp	Scorers	Att	Referee
17-09	Angola	L	1-2	Harare	CCsf	Francis Chandida [64]		Kaoma ZAM
7-10	Malawi	L	0-1	Blantyre	CNq			Seechun MRI
15-11	Namibia	W	3-2	Harare	Fr	Gwekwerere [11], Mushangazhike [17], Matawu [50]		
2007								
25-03	Morocco	D	1-1	Harare	CNq	Esrom Nyandoro [81]		Damon RSA
28-04	Madagascar	W	1-0	Maputo	CCr1	Kingston Nkhata [8]		Faduco MOZ
29-04	Mozambique	D	0-0	Maputo	CCr1	L 4-5p		Seechun MRI
25-05	Lesotho	D	1-1	Masvingo	Fr	Quincy Antipas [57]		
29-05	Burkina Faso	D	1-1	Masvingo	Fr	Shingi Kawondera [45]		
2-06	Morocco	L	0-2	Casablanca	CNq			Daami TUN
20-08	Mozambique	D	0-0	Beira	Fr	L 1-3p		
9-09	Malawi	W	3-1	Bulawayo	CNq	Kingston Nkhata [24], Richard Mteki [54], Method Mwanjili [61]		Hicuburundi BDI
2008								
11-03	South Africa	L	1-2	Johannesburg	Fr	Gilbert Mushangazhike [12]		
26-03	Botswana	W	1-0	Gaborone	Fr	Cuthbert Malajila [48]		
1-06	Guinea	D	0-0	Conakry	WCq		12 000	Haimoudi ALG
8-06	Namibia	W	2-0	Harare	WCq	Gilbert Mushangazhike 2 [26 85]	27 979	Lwanja MWI
14-06	Kenya	L	0-2	Nairobi	WCq		27 500	Diatta SEN
22-06	Kenya	D	0-0	Harare	WCq		23 000	Kotey GHA
27-07	Zambia	D	0-0	Thulamahashe	CCqf	L 4-5p		Nhlapo RSA
20-08	Botswana	W	1-0	Harare	Fr	Edward Sadomba [30]		
7-09	Guinea	D	0-0	Harare	WCq		23 000	Evehe CMR
10-09	Oman	L	2-3	Muscat	Fr	Pride Tafirenyika [15], Justice Majabvi [67]		
11-10	Namibia	L	2-4	Windhoek	WCq	Esrom Nyandoro [58], Cuthbert Malajila [85]	4 000	Coulibaly MLI
2009								
11-02	Tanzania	D	0-0	Dar es Salaam	Fr			
23-03	Bahrain	L	2-5	Manama	Fr	Ashley Rambanapasi [86p], Tito Marfumo [91+]		
13-05	Jordan	L	0-2	Amman	Fr			
12-08	Lesotho	D	1-1	Bulawayo	Fr	Guthrie Zhokinyu [80]		
17-10	Mauritius	W	3-0	Harare	CCr1	Cuthbert Malajila 2 [48 57], Method Mwanjale [87]		Ebrahim RSA
19-10	Lesotho	D	2-2	Harare	CCr1	Cuthbert Malajila [6], Sello OG [62]		Ramocha BOT
26-10	Botswana	W	1-0	Bulawayo	CCqf	Mthulisi Maphosa [88]		Carvalho ANG
28-10	South Africa †	D	1-1	Harare	CCsf	Phillip Marufu [54]. W 3-2p		Seechurn MRI
1-11	Zambia	W	3-1	Harare	CCf	Nyasha Mushekwi 2 [26 35], Cuthbert Malajila [45]		Carvalho ANG
1-12	Eritrea †	D	0-0	Nairobi	CFr1			
3-12	Somalia †	W	2-0	Nairobi	CFr1	Tapiwa Mangezi [30], Guthrie Zhokinyi [46]		
5-12	Rwanda †	L	0-1	Nairobi	CFr1			
8-12	Rwanda †	L	1-4	Nairobi	CFqf	Lionel Mtizwa [8]		
29-12	Thailand	L	0-3	Bangkok	Fr			
2010								
27-01	South Africa	L	0-3	Durban	Fr		35 000	Nhleko SWZ
3-03	Malawi	W	2-1	Harare	Fr	OG [17], Tafadzwa Rusike [25]		
2-06	Brazil	L	0-3	Harare	Fr		30 000	Martins ANG
4-08	Botswana	L	0-2	Selibe-Phikwe	Fr			
5-09	Liberia	D	1-1	Paynesville	CNq	Knowledge Musona [30]		Codjia BEN
10-10	Cape Verde Islands	D	0-0	Harare	CNq			Ndume GAB

Fr = Friendly match • CN = CAF African Cup of Nations • CC = COSAFA Cup • CF = CECAFA Cup • WC = FIFA World Cup
q = qualifier • r1 = first round group • qf = quarter-final • sf = semi-final • f = final • † Not a full international

ZIMBABWE 2010

NATIONAL PREMIER SOCCER LEAGUE

	Pl	W	D	L	F	A	Pts	Motor Action	Dynamos	Highlanders	Gunners	Hwange	CAPS United	Monomatapa	Shabanie	Kiglon Bird	Eagles	Shooting Stars	Black Mambas	Lengthens	Warriors	Bantu Rovers	Victoria
Motor Action †	30	20	6	4	52	18	66		1-2	0-0	1-1	2-0	1-0	4-0	3-0	1-0	2-0	0-0	3-0	3-1	2-0	5-0	3-0
Dynamos †	30	20	6	4	43	13	66	1-2		1-0	1-1	0-1	0-0	1-0	4-0	0-1	1-1	1-0	2-1	1-0	4-0	1-0	1-0
Highlanders ‡	30	17	6	7	32	20	57	2-3	**0-3**		1-0	3-1	1-0	1-0	1-0	1-1	1-0	1-0	2-1	2-1	4-1	0-0	**3-0**
Gunners	30	14	11	5	44	25	53	1-1	1-0	1-2		1-0	1-2	1-1	1-0	2-1	0-1	0-0	0-0	2-2	1-0	4-1	5-1
Hwange	30	14	8	8	43	33	50	0-1	0-2	1-0	1-1		1-0	2-1	2-3	3-1	3-1	2-0	5-2	1-1	**3-0**	2-0	3-1
CAPS United	30	13	9	8	41	28	48	2-4	1-2	3-1	1-1	0-0		2-3	2-0	2-2	0-1	3-0	2-0	1-1	0-0	1-1	3-0
Monomatapa United	30	13	8	9	43	29	47	2-0	0-2	0-0	2-2	1-2	1-1		2-0	0-0	0-1	1-0	1-0	3-0	0-1	3-0	**3-0**
Shabanie Mine	30	12	7	11	34	35	43	1-1	1-1	1-0	1-2	1-1	1-0	2-0		5-1	1-1	1-1	2-1	2-0	2-1	0-0	1-0
Kiglon Bird	30	8	13	9	29	30	37	1-1	0-0	1-0	2-0	2-3	0-1	1-1	0-1		0-0	0-1	5-0	1-1	1-0	1-0	0-2
Eagles Chitungwiza	30	8	13	9	18	24	37	1-0	0-2	0-0	0-1	2-1	1-4	0-0	1-1	1-1		0-0	1-1	1-1	0-0	1-0	2-1
Shooting Stars	30	8	9	13	22	31	33	0-2	0-2	0-1	1-2	0-0	0-1	2-1	3-1	0-2	1-0		0-0	1-0	2-2	1-0	2-1
Black Mambas	30	7	8	15	30	35	29	0-1	0-1	0-0	0-0	0-1	2-2	1-3	1-0	0-0	0-1	2-0		1-0	3-0	2-0	8-0
Lengthens	30	7	8	15	27	47	29	0-1	0-1	0-1	0-5	1-1	2-3	1-5	2-1	2-0	1-0	1-0	2-1		2-0	2-0	0-3
Douglas Warriors	29	4	8	17	15	46	20	1-0	1-1	0-1	0-3	1-1	0-1	1-4	0-2	1-2	0-0	0-4	1-1	0-0		2-1	2-1
Bantu Rovers	30	3	9	18	12	37	18	1-2	0-2	0-1	0-1	0-0	0-1	0-0	1-2	1-1	1-0	0-0	2-0	1-1	1-0		0-0
Victoria	29	4	5	20	25	59	17	1-2	1-3	1-2	1-2	3-0	0-1	1-3	1-3	0-0	1-1	1-1	0-2	3-3	n/p	1-0	

17/04/2010 - 19/12/2010 • † Qualified for the CAF Champions League • ‡ Qualified for the CAF Confederation Cup • Matches in Bold awarded

ABC SUPER EIGHT 2010

First Round

Dynamos	1
Hwange	0
Monomatapa United	0
Highlanders	1
Lengthens	1 1
Gunners	1 0
Shooting Stars	3 1p
CAPS United	3 3p

Semi-finals

Dynamos †	
Highlanders	
Lengthens	0 2p
CAPS United	0 3p

Final

Dynamos	3
CAPS United	2

National Stadium, Harare
11-12-2010. Scorers - Dylan Chivandire 49, Archford Gutu 54, Milton Makopa 60 for Dynamos; Joel Luphahla 13, Vincent Nzombe 83 for CAPS

† Original match abandoned. Awarded to Dynamos

UHURU CUP 2010

Semi-finals

Dynamos	0 4p
Gunners	0 3p
Bantu Rovers	0
Highlanders	2

Finals

Dynamos	2
Highlanders	0

3rd place: Bantu Rovers 3-1 Gunners
Final: National Stadium, Harare, 18-04-2010
Scorers - Guthrie Zhokinyu 35p, Cuthbert Malajila 90 for Dynamos

MEDALS TABLE

		Overall G	Overall S	Overall B	Lg G	C G	IT G	LC G	Africa G	Africa S	Africa B	City
1	Dynamos	35	1	1	18	9	6	2		1	1	Harare
2	CAPS United	22			4	9	4	5				Harare
3	Highlanders	15			7	2	5	1				Bulawayo
4	Zimbabwe Saints	6			2	3	1					Bulawayo
5	Black Rhinos	5			2	1	2					Mutare
	Black Aces (ex Chibuku)	5			2	2		1				Harare
7	Masvingo United	4					2	2				Masvingo
8	Hwange (ex Wankie)	3				3						Hwange
	Arcadia United	3			1	2						Harare
	Bulawayo Rovers	3				2	1					Bulawayo

Lge = League • C = Castle/Unity/CBZ Cup • IT = Independence Trophy/Uhuru Cup • LC = League Cup

PART THREE

THE
CONTINENTAL
CONFEDERATIONS

THE
CONTINENTAL
CONFEDERATIONS

AFC

ASIAN FOOTBALL CONFEDERATION

2010 proved to be a memorable year for Asian football with both Japan and Korea Republic confirming their status amongst the world's leading football nations with mature performances at the 2010 FIFA World Cup in South Africa, a tournament which saw both qualify for the last 16. It was the first time either had progressed beyond the group stage when not hosting the tournament with the Japanese unlucky not to progress further after losing against Paraguay on penalties. Of Asia's two other representatives at the finals, Australia missed out on qualifying from their group on goal difference having suffered a heavy defeat at the hands of Germany in their opening match, whilst for North Korea there was to be no repeat of their heroics in 1966, a 7-0 thrashing at the

THE FIFA BIG COUNT OF 2006 FOR ASIA

	Male	Female		Total
Number of players	80 075 000	5 102 000	Referees and Assistant Referees	263 000
Professionals	11 000		Admin, Coaches, Technical, Medical	410 000
Amateurs 18+	1 531 000		Number of clubs	20 000
Youth under 18	2 322		Number of teams	145 000
Unregistered	81 136 000		Clubs with women's teams	3 000
Total Players	85 849		Players as % of population	2.22%

hands of Portugal bringing them down to earth. Notable for their absence from the finals were any nations from the Middle-East but that was more than made up for when Qatar won the right to host the 2022 FIFA World Cup, a bold decision by FIFA which should give football in the region a much needed boost. Ironically, a month after the decision Qatar played host to the 2011 AFC Asian Cup but it wasn't a good tournament for the Middle-East who were without a representative beyond the quarter-finals. By beating Australia in the final, Japan became the most successful nation in the history of the tournament with four titles - all of them won since 1992. It's a tournament Korea Republic haven't won since 1960 but they continue to dominate at club level with Seongnam winning the 2010 AFC Champions League - the fifth Korean success in the past decade.

Asian Football Confederation (AFC)
AFC House, Jalan 1/155B, Bukit Jalil, 57000 Kuala Lumpur, Malaysia
Tel +60 3 89943388   Fax +60 3 89946168
media@the-afc.com   www.the-afc.com
President: Mohamed Bin Hammam QAT   General Secretary: Alex Soosay MAS
AFC Formed: 1954

AFC EXECUTIVE COMMITTEE
President: Mohamed Bin Hammam QAT   Vice-President: Yousuf Al Serkal UAE   Vice-President: Zhang Jilong CHN
Vice-President: Tengku Abdullah Ahmad Shah MAS   Vice-President: Ganesh Thapa NEP

Hon Treasurer: Farouk Bouzo SYR
FIFA Vice-President: Prince Ali Bin Al Hussein JOR   FIFA ExCo Member: Worawi Makudi THA   FIFA ExCo Member: Vernon Manilal Fernando SRI

MEMBERS OF THE EXECUTIVE COMMITTEE
Shk. Ali Bin Khalifa Al Khalifa BHR   Hafez I. Al Medlej KSA   Sayyid Khalid Hamed Al Busaidi OMA
Praful Patel IND   Makhdoom Syed Faisal Saleh Hayat PAK   Ali Azim MDV
Lee Boo Aun Winston SIN   Tran Quoc Tuan VIE   Zaw Zaw MYA
Ganbold Buyannemekh MGL   Kohzo Tashima JPN   Richard Lai GUM
Mahfuza Akhter Kiron BAN

MAP OF AFC MEMBER NATIONS

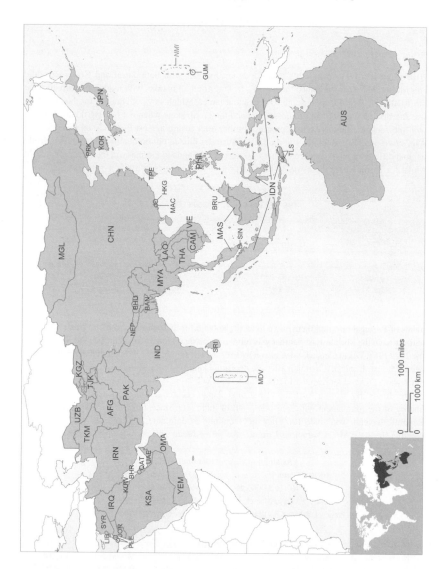

AFC MEMBER ASSOCIATIONS (46)

AFG - **Afghanistan** • AUS - **Australia** • BHR - **Bahrain** • BAN - **Bangladesh** • BHU - **Bhutan** • BRU - **Brunei Darussalam** • CAM - **Cambodia**
CHN - **China PR** • TPE - **Chinese Taipei** • GUM - **Guam** • HKG - **Hong Kong** • IND - **India** • IDN - **Indonesia** • IRN - **Iran** • IRQ - **Iraq**
JPN - **Japan** • JOR - **Jordan** • PRK - **Korea DPR** • KOR - **Korea Republic** • KUW - **Kuwait** • KGZ - **Kyrgyzstan** • LAO - **Laos** • LIB - **Lebanon**
MAC - **Macau** • MAS - **Malaysia** • MDV - **Maldives** • MGL - **Mongolia** • MYA - **Myanmar** • NEP - **Nepal** • OMA - **Oman** • PAK - **Pakistan**
PLE - **Palestine** • PHI - **Philippines** • QAT - **Qatar** • KSA - **Saudi Arabia** • SIN - **Singapore** • SRI - **Sri Lanka** • SYR - **Syria** • TJK - **Tajikistan**
THA - **Thailand** • TLS - **Timor Leste** • TKM - **Turkmenistan** • UAE - **United Arab Emirates** • UZB - **Uzbekistan** • VIE - **Vietnam** • YEM - **Yemen**

AFC PROVISIONAL ASSOCIATE MEMBER ASSOCIATION (1)
MNI - **Northern Mariana Islands** • Not affiliated to FIFA

ASIAN NATIONAL TEAM TOURNAMENTS

AFC ASIAN CUP

Year	Host Country	Winners	Score	Runners-up	Venue
1956	Hong Kong	Korea Republic	2-1	Israel	Government Stadium, Hong Kong
1960	Korea Republic	Korea Republic	3-0	Israel	Hyochang Park, Seoul
1964	Israel	Israel	2-0	India	Bloomfield, Jaffa
1968	Iran	Iran	3-1	Burma	Amjadieh, Tehran
1972	Thailand	Iran	2-1	Korea Republic	Suphachalasai, Bangkok
1976	Iran	Iran	1-0	Kuwait	Azadi, Tehran
1980	Kuwait	Kuwait	3-0	Korea Republic	Kuwait City
1984	Singapore	Saudi Arabia	2-0	China PR	National Stadium, Singapore
1988	Qatar	Saudi Arabia	0-0 4-3p	Korea Republic	Khalifa, Doha
1992	Japan	Japan	1-0	Saudi Arabia	Main Stadium, Hiroshima
1996	UAE	Saudi Arabia	0-0 4-2p	United Arab Emirates	Zayed, Abu Dhabi
2000	Lebanon	Japan	1-0	Saudi Arabia	Camille Chamoun, Beirut
2004	China PR	Japan	3-1	China PR	Workers' Stadium, Beijing
2007	ASEAN co-hosts	Iraq	1-0	Saudi Arabia	Gelora Bung Karno, Jakarta
2011	Qatar	Japan	1-0	Australia	Khalifa International, Doha

From 1956 to 1968 the tournament was played as a league. The result listed is that between the winners and runners-up.

AFC ASIAN CUP MEDALS TABLE

	Country	G	S	B	F	SF
1	Japan	4			4	5
2	Saudi Arabia	3	3		6	6
3	Iran	3		4	2	7
4	Korea Republic	2	3	4	3	6
5	Israel	1	2	1		
6	Kuwait	1	1	1	2	4
7	Iraq	1			1	2
8	China PR		2	2	2	6
9	Utd Arab Emirates		1		1	2
10	Australia		1		1	1
11	India		1			
	Myanmar		1			
13	Thailand			1		1
	Chinese Taipei			1		
	Hong Kong			1		
16	Bahrain					1
	Cambodia					1
	Korea DPR					1
	Uzbekistan					1
		15	15	14	22	44

This table represents the Gold (winners), Silver (runners-up) and Bronze (semi-finalists) placings of countries in the AFC Asian Cup, along with the number of appearances in the final and semi-finals

FOOTBALL TOURNAMENT OF THE ASIAN GAMES

Year	Host Country	Winners	Score	Runners-up	Venue
1951	India	India	1-0	Iran	New Delhi
1954	Philippines	Chinese Taipei	5-2	Korea Republic	Manilla
1958	Japan	Chinese Taipei	3-2	Korea Republic	Tokyo
1962	Indonesia	India	2-1	Korea Republic	Djakarta
1966	Thailand	Burma	1-0	Iran	Bangkok
1970	Thailand	Burma/KoreaRepublic	0-0		Bangkok
1974	Iran	Iran	1-0	Israel	Tehran
1978	Thailand	Korea Rep/Korea DPR	0-0		Bangkok
1982	India	Iraq	1-0	Kuwait	New Dehli
1986	Korea Republic	Korea Republic	2-0	Saudi Arabia	Seoul

FOOTBALL TOURNAMENT OF THE ASIAN GAMES (CONT'D)

Year	Host Country	Winners	Score	Runners-up	Venue
1990	China PR	Iran	0-0 4-1p	Korea DPR	Beijing
1994	Japan	Uzbekistan	4-2	China PR	Hiroshima
1998	Thailand	Iran	2-0	Kuwait	Bangkok
2002	Korea Republic	Iran	2-1	Japan	Busan
2006	Qatar	Qatar	1-0	Iraq	Doha
2010	China PR	Japan	1-0	UAE	Guangzhou

AFC CHALLENGE CUP

Year	Host Country	Winners	Score	Runners-up	Venue
2006	Bangladesh	Tajikistan	4-0	Sri Lanka	Bangabandhu, Dhaka
2008	India	India	4-1	Tajikistan	Ambedkar, Delhi
2010	Sri Lanka	Korea DPR	1-1 5-4p	Turkmenistan	Sugathadasa, Colombo

ASEAN FOOTBALL FEDERATION CHAMPIONSHIP

Year	Host Country	Winners	Score	Runners-up	Venue
1996		Thailand	1-0	Malaysia	
1998	Vietnam	Singapore	1-0	Vietnam	Hanoi Stadium, Hanoi
2000	Thailand	Thailand	4-1	Indonesia	Bangkok
2002	Indonesia/Sin'pore	Thailand	2-2 4-2p	Indonesia	Gelora Senayan, Jakarta
2004	Malaysia/Vietnam	Singapore	3-1 2-1	Indonesia	Jakarta, Singapore
2007	Singapore/Th'land	Singapore	2-1 1-1	Thailand	Singapore, Bangkok
2008	Indonesia/Th'land	Vietnam	2-1 1-1	Thailand	Bangkok, Hanoi
2010	Indonesia/Vietnam	Malaysia	3-0 1-2	Indonesia	Kuala Lumpur, Jakarta

SOUTH ASIAN FOOTBALL FEDERATION CUP

Year	Host Country	Winners	Score	Runners-up	Venue
1993	Pakistan	India	2-0	Sri Lanka	Lahore
1995	Sri Lanka	Sri Lanka	1-0	India	Colombo
1997	Nepal	India	5-1	Maldives	Dasharath Rangashala, Kathmandu
1999	Goa	India	2-0	Bangladesh	Margao
2003	Bangladesh	Bangladesh	1-1 5-3p	Maldives	Bangabandu, Dhaka
2005	Pakistan	India	2-0	Bangladesh	Karachi
2008	Sri Lanka/Maldives	Maldives	1-0	India	Sugathadhasa, Colombo
2009	Bangladesh	India	0-0 3-1p	Maldives	Bangabandhu, Dhaka

EAST ASIAN CHAMPIONSHIP

Year	Host Country	Winners	Score	Runners-up	Venue
2003	Japan	Korea Republic	0-0	Japan	International, Yokohama
2005	Korea Republic	China PR	2-2	Japan	World Cup Stadium, Daejeon
2008	China PR	Korea Republic	1-1	Japan	Sports Centre, Chongqing
2010	Japan	China PR	3-0	Korea Republic	Ajinomoto & National, Tokyo

Tournament played as a league. The result listed is that between the winners and runners-up

WEST ASIAN FOOTBALL FEDERATION CHAMPIONSHIP

Year	Host Country	Winners	Score	Runners-up	Venue
2000	Jordan	Iran	1-0	Syria	Malek Abdullah, Amman
2002	Syria	Iraq	3-2	Jordan	Al Abbassiyyine, Damascus
2004	Iran	Iran	4-1	Syria	Tehran
2007	Jordan	Iran	2-1	Iraq	International, Amman
2008	Iran	Iran	2-1	Jordan	Tehran
2010	Jordan	Kuwait	2-1	Iran	King Abdullah, Amman

FOOTBALL TOURNAMENT OF THE SOUTH EAST ASIAN GAMES

Year	Host Country	Winners	Score	Runners-up	Venue
1959	Thailand	Vietnam	3-1	Thailand	Bangkok
1961	Burma	Malaysia	2-0	Burma	Rangoon
1965	Malaysia	Burma	2-2†	Thailand	Kuala Lumpur
1967	Thailand	Burma	2-1	South Vietnam	Bangkok
1969	Burma	Burma	3-0	Thailand	Rangoon

FOOTBALL TOURNAMENT OF THE SOUTH EAST ASIAN GAMES

Year	Host Country	Winners	Score	Runners-up	Venue
1971	Malaysia	Burma	2-1	Malaysia	Kuala Lumpur
1973	Singapore	Burma	2-1	South Vietnam	Singapore
1975	Thailand	Thailand	2-1	Malaysia	Bangkok
1977	Malaysia	Malaysia	2-0	Thailand	Kuala Lumpur
1979	Indonesia	Malaysia	1-0	Indonesia	Jakarta
1981	Philippines	Thailand	2-1	Malaysia	Manila
1983	Singapore	Thailand	2-1	Singapore	Singapore
1985	Thailand	Thailand	2-0	Singpaore	Bangkok
1987	Indonesia	Indonesia	1-0	Malaysia	Jakarta
1989	Malaysia	Malaysia	3-1	Singapore	Merdeka, Kuala Lumpur
1991	Philippines	Indonesia	0-0 4-3p	Thailand	Manila
1993	Singapore	Thailand	4-3	Myanmar	Singapore
1995	Thailand	Thailand	4-0	Vietnam	Chiang Mai
1997	Indonesia	Thailand	1-1 4-2p	Indonesia	Jakarta
1999	Brunei	Thailand	2-0	Vietnam	Bandar Seri Begawan
2001	Malaysia	Thailand	1-0	Malaysia	Kuala Lumpur
2003	Vietnam	Thailand	2-1	Vietnam	Hanoi
2005	Philippines	Thailand	3-0	Vietnam	Manila
2007	Thailand	Thailand	2-0	Myanmar	Korat
2009	Laos	Malaysia	1-0	Vietnam	Vientiane

† Gold medal shared • Until 2001 the SEA Games featured full national teams but is now a U-23 event

FOOTBALL TOURNAMENT OF THE EAST ASIAN GAMES

Year	Host Country	Winners	Score	Runners-up	Venue
1993	China PR	Korea Republic	1-1†	Korea DPR	Shanghai
1997	Korea Republic	Korea Republic	0-1†	Japan	Pusan
2001	Japan	Japan	2-1	Australia	Nagai, Osaka
2005	Macao	China PR	1-0	Korea DPR	Macau Stadium, Macau
2009	Hong Kong	Hong Kong	1-1 4-2p	Japan	Hong Kong

† Played on a league basis. The result listed is between the top two teams, both of which ocurred in the last round of games • U-23 event

FOOTBALL TOURNAMENT OF THE SOUTH ASIAN GAMES

Year	Host Country	Winners	Score	Runners-up	Venue
1984	Nepal	Nepal	4-2	Bangladesh	Dasharath Rangashala, Kathmandu
1985	Bangladesh	India	1-1 4-1p	Bangladesh	Dhaka
1987	India	India	1-0	Nepal	Salt Lake, Calcutta
1989	Pakistan	Pakistan	1-0	Bangladesh	Islamabad
1991	Sri Lanka	Pakistan	2-0	Maldives	Colombo
1993	Bangladesh	Nepal	2-2 4-3p	India	Dhaka
1995	India	India	1-0	Bangladesh	Madras
1999	Nepal	Bangladesh	1-0	Nepal	Dasharath Rangashala, Kathmandu
2004	Pakistan	Pakistan	1-0	India	Jinnah Stadium, Islamabad
2006	Sri Lanka	Pakistan	1-0	Sri Lanka	Colombo
2010	Bangladesh	Bangladesh	4-0	Afghanistan	Bangabandhu, Dhaka

GULF CUP

Year	Host Country	Winners	Runners-up
1970	Bahrain	Kuwait	Bahrain
1972	Saudi Arabia	Kuwait	Saudi Arabia
1974	Kuwait	Kuwait	Saudi Arabia
1976	Qatar	Kuwait	Iraq
1979	Iraq	Iraq	Kuwait
1982	UAE	Kuwait	Bahrain
1984	Oman	Iraq	Qatar
1986	Bahrain	Kuwait	UAE
1988	Saudi Arabia	Iraq	UAE
1990	Kuwait	Kuwait	Qatar

GULF CUP

Year	Host Country	Winners	Runners-up
1992	Qatar	Qatar	Bahrain
1994	UAE	Saudi Arabia	UAE
1996	Oman	Kuwait	Qatar
1998	Bahrain	Kuwait	Saudi Arabia
2002	Saudi Arabia	Saudi Arabia	Qatar
2004	Kuwait	Saudi Arabia	Bahrain
2005	Qatar	Qatar	Oman
2007	UAE	UAE	Oman
2009	Oman	Oman	Saudi Arabia
2010	Yemen	Kuwait	Saudi Arabia

ASIAN CLUB TOURNAMENTS

AFC CHAMPIONS LEAGUE

Year	Winners	Country	Score	Country	Runners-up
1967	Hapoel Tel Aviv	ISR	2-1	MAS	Selangor
1968	Maccabi Tel Aviv	ISR	1-0	KOR	Yangzee
1970	Taj Club	IRN	2-1	ISR	Hapoel Tel Aviv
1971	Maccabi Tel Aviv	ISR	W-0	IRQ	Police Club
1986	Daewoo Royals	KOR	3-1	KSA	Al Ahly
1987	Furukawa	JPN	4-3	KSA	Al Hilal
1988	Yomiuri	JPN	W-0	KSA	Al Hilal
1989	Al Saad	QAT	2-3 1-0	IRQ	Al Rasheed
1990	Liaoning	CHN	2-1 1-1	JPN	Nissan
1991	Esteghlal SC	IRN	2-1	CHN	Liaoning
1992	Al Hilal	KSA	1-1 4-3p	IRN	Esteghlal SC
1993	Pas	IRN	1-0	KSA	Al Shabab
1994	Thai Farmers Bank	THA	2-1	OMA	Omani Club
1995	Thai Farmers Bank	THA	1-0	QAT	Al Arabi
1996	Ilhwa Chunma	KOR	1-0	KSA	Al Nasr
1997	Pohang Steelers	KOR	2-1	KOR	Ilhwa Chunma
1998	Pohang Steelers	KOR	0-0 6-5p	CHN	Dalian
1999	Jubilo Iwata	JPN	2-1	IRN	Esteghlal SC
2000	Al Hilal	KSA	3-2	JPN	Jubilo Iwata
2001	Suwon Samsung Bluewings	KOR	1-0	JPN	Jubilo Iwata
2002	Suwon Samsung Bluewings	KOR	0-0 4-2p	KOR	Anyang LG Cheetahs
2003	Al Ain	UAE	2-0 0-1	THA	BEC Tero Sasana
2004	Al Ittihad	KSA	1-3 5-0	KOR	Seongnam Ilhwa Chunma
2005	Al Ittihad	KSA	1-1 4-2	UAE	Al Ain
2006	Jeonbuk Hyundai Motors	KOR	2-0 1-2	SYR	Al Karama
2007	Urawa Reds	JPN	1-1 2-0	IRN	Sepahan
2008	Gamba Osaka	JPN	3-0 2-0	AUS	Adelaide United
2009	Pohang Steelers	KOR	2-1	KSA	Al Ittihad
2010	Seongnam Ilhwa Chunma	KOR	3-1	IRN	Zob Ahan

AFC CHAMPIONS LEAGUE MEDALS TABLE

	Country	G	S	B	F	SF
1	Korea Republic	9	4	5	13	21
2	Japan	5	3	4	8	13
3	Saudi Arabia	4	6	3	10	13
4	Iran	3	4	5	7	14
5	Israel	3	1		4	4
6	Thailand	2	1	1	3	4
7	China PR	1	2	3	3	8
8	UAE	1	1	3	2	6
9	Qatar	1	1	2	2	4
10	Iraq		2		2	4
11	Syria	1	1	1	1	2
12	Australia			1	1	1
	Malaysia		1		1	1

AFC CHAMPIONS LEAGUE MEDALS TABLE (CONT'D)

	Country	G	S	B	F	SF
	Oman		1		1	1
15	Uzbekistan			4		5
16	Indonesia		1			3
17	Lebanon		1		1	
	Korea DPR		1		1	1
	Kuwait		1		1	1
20	India					1
	Kazakstan					1
		29	29	35	58	109

This table represents the Gold (winners), Silver (runners-up) and Bronze (semi-finalists) placings of clubs representing the above countries in the AFC Champions League, along with the number of appearances in the final and semi-finals

AFC CHAMPIONS LEAGUE MEDALS TABLE

	Club		G	S	B
1	Pohang Steelers	KOR	3		
2	Esteghlal	IRN	2	2	3
3	Al Hilal	KSA	2	2	2
4	Seongnam Ilhwa Chunma	KOR	2	2	1
5	Al Ittihad	KSA	2	1	
6	Thai Farmers Bank	THA	2		1
7	Maccabi Tel Aviv	ISR	2		
	Suwon Samsung Bluewings	KOR	2		
9	Jubilo Iwata	JPN	1	2	
10	Al Ain	UAE	1	1	1
	Liaoning	CHN	1	1	1
12	Hapoel Tel Aviv	ISR	1	1	
13	Busan I'Park	KOR	1		1
	Jeonbuk Hyundai Motors	KOR	1		1
	Urawa Reds	JPN	1		1
	Tokyo Verdy	JPN	1		1
17	Al Saad	QAT	1		
	Gamba Osaka	JPN	1		
	JEF United	JPN	1		
	Pass	IRN	1		
21	Dalian	CHN		1	1
	Al Shabab	KSA		1	1
23	Adelaide United	AUS		1	
	Al Ahli	KSA		1	
	Al Arabi	QAT		1	
	Al Karama	SYR		1	
	Al Nasr	KSA		1	

AFC CHAMPIONS LEAGUE MEDALS TABLE (CONT'D)

	Club		G	S	B
	Al Rasheed	IRQ		1	
	Anyang LG Cheetahs	KOR		1	
	BEC Tero Sasana	THA		1	
	Omani Club	OMA		1	
	Police	IRQ		1	
	Selangor	MAS		1	
	Sepahan	IRN		1	
	Yangzee	KOR		1	
	Yokohama Marinos	JPN		1	
	Zob Ahan	IRN		1	
38	Pirouzi	IRN			3
39	Pakhtakor Tashkent	UZB			2
40	Al Qadisiya	KUW			1
	Al Rayyan	QAT			1
	Al Wasl	UAE			1
	April 25th	PRK			1
	Bunyodkor Tashkent	UZB			1
	Homenetmen	LIB			1
	Nagoya Grampus	JPN			1
	Neftchi Fergana	UZB			1
	Sanfrecce Hiroshima	JPN			1
	Shenzhen	CHN			1
	Tiga Berlian	IDN			1
	Tungsten Mining	KOR			1
	Ulsan Hyundai Horang-i	KOR			1
	Umm Salal	QAT			1
	Al Wahda	UAE			1
			29	29	35

ASIAN CUP WINNERS' CUP

Year	Winners	Country	Score	Country	Runners-up
1991	Pirouzi	IRN	0-0 1-0	BHR	Al Muharraq
1992	Nissan	JPN	1-1 5-0	KSA	Al Nasr
1993	Nissan	JPN	1-1 1-0	IRN	Pirouzi
1994	Al-Qadisiyah	KSA	4-2 2-0	HKG	South China
1995	Yokohama Flugels	JPN	2-1	UAE	Al Shaab
1996	Bellmare Hiratsuka	JPN	2-1	IRQ	Al Talaba
1997	Al Hilal	KSA	3-1	JPN	Nagoya Grampus Eight
1998	Al Nasr	KSA	1-0	KOR	Suwon Samsung Bluewings
1999	Al Ittihad	KSA	3-2	KOR	Chunnam Dragons
2000	Shimizu S-Pulse	JPN	1-0	IRQ	Al Zawra
2001	Al Shabab	KSA	4-2	CHN	Dalian Shide
2002	Al Hilal	KSA	2-1	KOR	Chonbuk Hyundai Motors

CUP WINNERS CUP MEDALS TABLE

	Country	G	S	B	F	SF
1	Saudi Arabia	6	1	3	7	10
2	Japan	5	1	4	6	10
3	Iran	1	1		2	4
4	Korea Republic		3	1	3	4
5	Iraq		2		2	3
6	China PR		1	1	1	3
7	United Arab Emirates		1	1	1	2
8	Bahrain		1		1	1
	Hong Kong		1		1	1
10	Qatar			2		2
11	Thailand			1		2

CUP WINNERS CUP MEDALS TABLE

	Country	G	S	B	F	SF
12	Indonesia			1		1
	Jordan			1		1
	Vietnam			1		1
15	Uzbekistan					1
	Kuwait					1
	Turkmenistan					1
		12	12	16	24	48

This table represents the Gold (winners), Silver (runners-up) and Bronze (semi-finalists) placings of clubs representing the above countries in the Cup Winners Cup, along with the number of appearances in the final and semi-finals

ASIAN CUP WINNERS CUP MEDALS TABLE

	Club		G	S	B
1	Yokohama Marinos (Nissan)	JPN	2		1
2	Al Hilal	KSA	2		1
3	Pirouzi	IRN	1	1	
	Al Nasr	KSA	1	1	
5	Al Ittihad	KSA	1		2
6	Yokohama Flugels	JPN	1		1
	Shimizu S-Pulse	JPN	1		1
8	Al Qadisiyah	KSA	1		
	Bellmare Hiratsuka	JPN	1		
	Al Shabab	KSA	1		
11	Al Shaab	UAE		1	
	Al Talaba	IRQ		1	
	Al Zawra	IRQ		1	
	Chunnam Dragons	KOR		1	
	Jeonbuk Hyundai Motors	KOR		1	
	Dalian	CHN		1	

ASIAN CUP WINNERS CUP MEDALS TABLE (CONT'D)

	Club		G	S	B
	Muharraq	BHR		1	
	Nagoya Grampus Eight	JPN		1	
	South China	HKG		1	
	Suwon Samsung Bluewings	KOR		1	
21	Al Shabab	UAE			1
	Al Ramtha	JOR			1
	Bangkok Bank	THA			1
	Pupuk Kaltim	IDN			1
	Quang Nam Danang	VIE			1
	Al Arabi	QAT			1
	Al Sadd	QAT			1
	Ulsan Hyundai	KOR			1
	Beijing Guoan	CHN			1
	Kashima Antlers	JPN			1
			12	12	16

AFC CUP

Year	Winners	Country	Score	Country	Runners-up
2004	Al Jaish	SYR	3-2 0-1	SYR	Al Wahda
2005	Al Faysali	JOR	1-0 3-2	LIB	Al Nejmeh
2006	Al Faysali	JOR	3-0 2-4	BHR	Muharraq
2007	Shabab Al Ordun	JOR	1-0 1-1	JOR	Al Faysali
2008	Muharraq	BHR	5-1 5-4	LIB	Safa
2009	Al Kuwait	KUW	2-1	SYR	Al Karama
2010	Al Ittihad Aleppo	SYR	1-1 4-2p	KUW	Al Qadisiya

AFC CUP MEDALS TABLE

	Country	G	S	B	F	SF
1	Jordan	3	1	2	4	6
2	Syria	2	2		4	4
3	Bahrain	1	1	1	2	3
4	Kuwait	1			2	2
5	Lebanon		2	2	2	4
6	Singapore			2		2
	Hong Kong			2		2
8	Maldives			1		1
	India			1		1
	Oman			1		1
	Thailand			1		1
	Vietnam			1		1
		7	7	14	14	28

This table represents the Gold (winners), Silver (runners-up) and
Bronze (semi-finalists) placings of clubs representing the above
countries in the AFC Cup, along with the number of appearances in
the final and semi-finals

AFC CUP MEDALS TABLE

	Club		G	S	B
1	Al Faysali	JOR	2	1	
2	Muharraq	BHR	1	1	
3	Al Ittihad Aleppo	SYR	1		
	Al Jaish	SYR	1		
	Al Kuwait	KUW	1		
	Al Shabab Al Ordun	JOR	1		
7	Al Nijmeh	LIB		1	2
8	Al Karama	SYR		1	
	Al Qadisiya	KUW		1	
	Safa	LIB		1	
	Al Wahda	SYR		1	
12	Al Wihdat	JOR			2
13	Binh Duong	VIE			1
	Dempo SC	IND			1
	Geylang United	SIN			1
	Home United	SIN			1
	Muangthong United	THA			1
	Al Nahda	OMA			1
	New Radiant	MDV			1
	Riffa	BHR			1
	South China	HGK			1
	Sun Hei	HKG			1
			7	7	14

AFC PRESIDENT'S CUP

Year	Winners	Country	Score	Country	Runners-up
2005	Regar TadAZ	TJK	3-0	KGZ	Dordoi-Dynamo
2006	Dordoi-Dynamo	KGZ	2-1	TJK	Vakhsh Qurgonteppa
2007	Dordoi-Dynamo	KGZ	2-1	NEP	Mahendra Police Club
2008	Regar TadAZ	TJK	1-1 4-3p	KGZ	Dordoi-Dynamo
2009	Regar TadAZ	TJK	2-0	KGZ	Dordoi-Dynamo
2010	Yadanabon	MYA	1-0	KGZ	Dordoi-Dynamo

AFC PRESIDENT'S CUP MEDALS TABLE

	Country	G	S	B	F	SF
1	Tajikistan	3	1	2	4	6
2	Kyrgyzstan	2	4		6	6
3	Myanmar	1			1	1
4	Nepal		1	2	1	3
5	Sri Lanka			2		2
	Turkmenistan			3		3
7	Cambodia			1		1
	Chinese Taipei			1		1
	Pakistan			1		1
		6	6	12	12	24

This table represents the Gold (winners), Silver (runners-up) and Bronze (semi-finalists) placings of clubs representing the above countries in the AFC President's Cup, along with the number of appearances in the final and semi-finals

AFC PRESIDENT'S CUP MEDALS TABLE

	Club		G	S	B
1	Regar TadAZ	TJK	3		1
2	Dordoi-Dynamo	KGZ	2	4	
3	Yadanabon	MYA	1		
4	Nepal Police Club	NEP		1	1
	Vakhsh Qurgonteppa	TJK		1	1
6	FK Ashgabat	TKM			2
7	Blue Star Club	SRI			1
	HTTU Ashgabat	TKM			1
	Khmera	CAM			1
	Ratnam SC	SRI			1
	Tatung	TPE			1
	Three Star Club	NEP			1
	WAPDA	PAK			1
			6	6	12

ASIAN YOUTH TOURNAMENTS

AFC U-19 CHAMPIONSHIP

Year	Host Country	Winners	Score	Runners-up	Venue
1959	Malaysia	Korea Republic	2-1	Malaysia	Kuala Lumpur
1960	Malaysia	Korea Republic	4-0	Malaysia	Kuala Lumpur
1961	Thailand	Burma	0-0†	Indonesia	Bangkok
1962	Thailand	Thailand	2-1	Korea Republic	Bangkok
1963	Malaysia	Burma	2-2†	Korea Republic	Penang
1964	Vietnam	Burma	0-0†	Israel	Saigon
1965	Japan	Israel	5-0	Burma	Tokyo
1966	Philippines	Burma	1-1	Israel	Manila
1967	Thailand	Israel	3-0	Indonesia	Bangkok
1968	Korea Republic	Burma	4-0	Malaysia	Seoul
1969	Thailand	Burma	2-2†	Thailand	Bangkok
1970	Philippines	Burma	3-0	India	Manila
1971	Japan	Israel	1-0	Korea Republic	Tokyo
1972	Thailand	Israel	1-0	Korea Republic	Bangkok
1973	Iran	Iran	2-0	Japan	Tehran
1974	Thailand	Iran	2-2†	India	Bangkok
1975	Kuwait	Iran	0-0†	Iraq	Kuwait City
1976	Thailand	Iran	0-0†	Korea DPR	Bangkok
1977	Iran	Iraq	4-3	Iran	Tehran
1978	Bangladesh	Iraq	1-1†	Korea Republic	Dhaka
1980	Thailand	Korea Republic	4-1‡	Qatar	Bangkok
1982	Thailand	Korea Republic	1-1‡	China PR	Bangkok
1984	UAE	China PR	2-2‡	Saudi Arabia	Abu Dhabi
1986	Saudi Arabia	Saudi Arabia	2-0	Bahrain	Riyadh
1988	Qatar	Iraq	1-1 5-4p	Syria	Doha

AFC U-19 CHAMPIONSHIP (CONT'D)

Year	Host Country	Winners	Score	Runners-up	Venue
1990	Indonesia	Korea Republic	0-0 4-3p	Korea DPR	Jakarta
1992	UAE	Saudi Arabia	2-0	Korea Republic	Dubai
1994	Indonesia	Syria	2-1	Japan	Jakarta
1996	Korea Republic	Korea Republic	3-0	China PR	Suwon
1998	Thailand	Korea Republic	2-1	Japan	Chiang Mai
2000	Iran	Iraq	2-1	Japan	Tehran
2002	Qatar	Korea Republic	1-0	Japan	Doha
2004	Malaysia	Korea Republic	2-0	China PR	Kuala Lumpur
2006	India	Korea DPR	1-1 5-3p	Japan	Kolkata
2008	Saudi Arabia	UAE	2-1	Uzbekistan	Damman
2010	China PR	Korea DPR	3-2	Australia	Zibo

† Title shared between both finalists • ‡ Played on a league system so the match indicated was not a final

AFC U-16 CHAMPIONSHIP

Year	Host Country	Winners	Score	Runners-up	Venue
1984	Qatar	Saudi Arabia	4-3	Qatar	Doha
1986	Qatar	Korea Republic	0-0 5-4p	Qatar	Doha
1988	Thailand	Saudi Arabia	2-0	Bahrain	Bangkok
1990	UAE	Qatar	2-0	UAE	Dubai
1992	Saudi Arabia	China PR	2-2 8-7p	Qatar	Riyadh
1994	Qatar	Japan	1-0	Qatar	Doha
1996	Thailand	Oman	1-0	Thailand	Bangkok
1998	Qatar	Thailand	1-1 3-2p	Qatar	Doha
2000	Vietnam SR	Oman	1-0	Iran	Danang
2002	UAE	Korea Republic	1-1 5-3p	Yemen	Abu Dhabi
2004	Japan	China PR	1-0	Korea DPR	Shizuoka
2006	Singapore	Japan	4-2	Korea DPR	Singapore
2008	Uzbekistan	Iran	2-1	Korea Republic	Tashkent
2010	Uzbekistan	Korea DPR	2-0	Uzbekistan	Tashkent

ASIAN WOMENS TOURNAMENTS

WOMEN'S FOOTBALL TOURNAMENT OF THE ASIAN GAMES

Year	Host Country	Winners	Score	Runners-up	Venue
1990	China PR	China PR	5-0	Japan	Beijing
1994	Japan	China PR	2-0	Japan	Hiroshima
1998	Thailand	China PR	1-0	Korea DPR	Bangkok
2002	Korea Republic	Korea DPR	0-0	China PR	Busan
2006	Qatar	Korea DPR	0-0 4-2p	Japan	Doha
2010	China PR	Australia	1-1 5-4p	Korea DPR	Chengdu

In 1990, 1994 and 2002 the tournament was played as a league. The result listed is that between the winners and runners-up

AFC U-19 WOMEN'S CHAMPIONSHIP

Year	Host Country	Winners	Score	Runners-up	Venue
2002	India	Japan	2-1	Chinese Taipei	
2006	Malaysia	China PR	1-0	Korea DPR	
2007	China PR	Korea DPR	1-0	Japan	Sports Centre, Chongqing
2009	China PR	Japan	2-1	Korea Republic	Hankou Sports Stadium, Wuhan

AFC U-16 WOMEN'S CHAMPIONSHIP

Year	Host Country	Winners	Score	Runners-up	Venue
2005	Korea Republic	Japan	1-1 3-1p	China PR	Namhae
2007	Malaysia	Korea DPR	3-0	Japan	MPPJ Stadium, Petaling Jaya
2009	Thailand	Korea Republic	4-0	Korea DPR	Supachalasai, Bangkok

NATIONAL TEAM TOURNAMENTS IN ASIA 2010–11

AFC ASIAN CUP QATAR 2011

Qualifying groups		First Round		Quarter-finals		Semi-finals		Final	
Group A	Pts								
Japan	15								
Bahrain	12								
Yemen	7	**Group A**	Pts						
Hong Kong	1	**Uzbekistan**	7						
		Qatar	6	**Japan**	3				
Group B	Pts	China PR	4	Qatar	2				
Australia	11	Kuwait	0						
Kuwait	9					**Japan**	2 3p		
Oman	8	**Group B**	Pts			Korea Republic	2 0p		
Indonesia	3	**Japan**	7						
		Jordan	7	Iran	0				
Group C	Pts	Syria	3	**Korea Republic**	1				
UAE	9	Saudi Arabia	0						
Uzbekistan	9							**Japan**	1
Malaysia	0	**Group C**	Pts					Australia	0
		Australia	7						
		Korea Republic	7	**Uzbekistan**	2				
Group D	Pts	Bahrain	3	Jordan	1				
Syria	14	India	0						
China PR	13					Uzbekistan	0		
Vietnam	5	**Group D**	Pts			**Australia**	6		
Lebanon	1	**Iran**	9						
		Iraq	6	Iraq	0				
Group E	Pts	Korea DPR	1	**Australia**	1				
Iran	13	UAE	1						
Jordan	8								
Thailand	6								
Singapore	6								

Iraq, Saudi Arabia and Korea Republic received byes to the finals as the top three finishers from the previous tournament in 2007. India also received a bye as the winners of the 2010 AFC Challenge Cup

Top scorers (Finals): 5 - Koo Ja Cheol KOR • 4 - Ismaeel Abdullatif BHR & Ji Dong Won KOR

3rd Place Play-off

Korea Republic	3
Uzbekistan	2

PRELIMINARY ROUND

Sports City, Beirut
9-04-2008, 18:00, 200, Al Ghafary JOR

Lebanon **4**

El Ali [5], Yaacoub [11], Atwi [13], Ghaddar [39]

Larry Mehanna - Khaled Hamieh (Nasrat Al Jamal 77), Ali Al Saadi, Hussein Amine, Bilal Najjarin, Mohamad Korhani, Abbas Atwi, Amer Khan•, Ali Yaacoub•, Mahmoud El Ali (Khodor Salame 65), Mohamad Ghaddar (Paul Rustom 64). Tr: Adnan Mekdache

Maldives **0**

Imran Mohamed• - Mohamed Jameel•, Assadh Abdul Ghani, Akram Abdul Ghani, Sabah Ibrahim (Ibrahim Amil 46), Mohamed Shifan, Ahmed Saeed, Shinaz Hilmy• (Mohamed Arif 82), Ibrahim Fazeel, Ali Ashfaq (Ismail Mohamed 36), Ali Umar•. Tr: Jozef Jankech

National Stadium, Male
23-04-2008, 12:00, 6000, Shahrul MAS

Maldives **1**

Qasim [22]

Imran Mohamed - Assadh Abdul Ghani, Akram Abdul Ghani (Mukhtar Naseer 60), Mohamed Shifan, Shamweel Qasim, Mohamed Jameel, Sabah Ibrahim, Ahmed Saeed (Shinaz Hilmy 69), Ali Ashfaq, Ali Umar (Ahmed Thariq 46), Ibrahim Fazeel. Tr: Jozef Jankech

Lebanon **2**

Korhani [9], Al Jamal [75]

Larry Mehanna - Ali Al Saadi, Hussein Amine, Bilal Najjarin, Mohamad Korhani, Abbas Atwi (Nasrat Al Jamal 57), Amer Khan, Ali Yaacoub (Ali El Atat 67), Mahmoud M. Younes, Mahmoud El Ali, Paul Rustom (Tarek El Ali 82). Tr: Adnan Mekdache

QUALIFYING GROUP A

		Pl	W	D	L	F	A	Pts	JPN	BHR	YEM	HKG
Japan	JPN	6	5	0	1	17	4	**15**		2-0	2-1	6-0
Bahrain	BHR	6	4	0	2	12	6	**12**	1-0		4-0	4-0
Yemen	YEM	6	2	1	3	7	9	**7**	2-3	3-0		1-0
Hong Kong	HKG	6	0	1	5	1	18	**1**	0-4	1-3	0-0	

KKWing Stadium, Kumamoto
20-01-2009, 19:20, 30 654, Tan Hai CHN

Japan 2

Okazaki [7], Tatsuya Tanaka [66]

Eiji **Kawashima** - Shuhei **Terada**, Yuichi **Komano•**, Atsuto **Uchida**, Kazumichi **Takagi**, Kengo **Nakamura**, Shinji **Kagawa** (Mu **Kanazaki** 88), Takeshi **Aoki**, Tatsuya **Tanaka** (Takashi **Inui** 79), Shinzo **Koroki** (Seiichito **Maki** 60), Shinji **Okazaki**. Tr: Takeshi **Okada**

Yemen 1

Al Fadhli [47]

Salem **Saeed** - Mohammed **Salem**, Zaher **Al Fadhli**, Ahmed **Al Wadi**, Omar **Awsan**, Mohammed **Al Ammari**, Akram **Al Worafi** (Haitham **Thabit** 73), Ala **Mohammed**, Ali **Yousef** (Saleh **Al Shekri** 84), Yaser **Ba Suhai**, Ali **Al Nono** (Basem **Al Aqel** 67). Tr: Sami **Saleh**

National Stadium, Manama
28-01-2009, 18:15, 11 200, Irmatov UZB

Bahrain 1

Isa 24

Sayed **Jaffer** - Salman **Isa**, Sayed **Adnan**, Hussain **Baba**, Abdulla **Fatadi**, Mohamed **Salmeen**, Abdullah **Omar** (Mahmood **Abdulrahman** 70), Rashid **Abdulrahman** (Abbas **Ayyad** 90), Faouzi **Aaish**, Mohamed **Hubail**, Ismaeel **Latif** (Jaycee **Okwunwanne** 74). Tr: Milan **Macala**

Japan 0

Eiji **Kawashima** - Shuhei **Terada•**, Atsuto **Uchida**, Yuji **Nakazawa**, Yuto **Nagatomo**, Junichi **Inamoto**, Kengo **Nakamura**, Keisuke **Honda** (Shinji **Kagawa** 63), Tatsuya **Tanaka** (Seiichiro **Maki** 82), Keiji **Tamada**, Shinji **Okazaki** (Shinzo **Koroki•** 76). Tr: Takeshi **Okada**

Hong Kong Stadium, Hong Kong
21-09-2009, 19:30, 6013, Minh Tri Vo VIE

Hong Kong 1

Cheng Siu Wai [90]

Zhang Chunhui - **Lee** Chi Ho, **Cheung** Kin Fung, **Liu** Quankun• (**Gao** Wen 57), Cristiano **Cordeiro**, **Chan** Siu Ki, **Au** Yeung Yiu Chung, **Lee** Wai Lim (**Xu** Deshuai 75), **Chao** Pengfei (**Cheng** Siu Wai 65). Tr: Dejan Antonic

Bahrain 3

Latif [10], Fatadi [37], Isa [87]

Sayed **Jaffer** -Salman **Isa**, Sayed **Adnan**, Hussain **Baba**, Abdulla **Fatadi**, Mohamed **Salmeen**, Abdullah **Omar** (Abbas **Ayyad** 74), Rashid **Abdulrahman** (Abdullah Abdi **Omar** 81), Faouzi **Aaish**, Mohamed **Hubail**, Ismaeel **Latif** (Sayed **Hashem** 89). Tr: Milan **Macala**

Nihondaira, Shizuoka
8-10-2009, 19:20, 16 028, Torky IRN

Japan 6

Okazaki 3 [18 75 78], Nagatomo [29], Nakazawa [51], Marcus Tulio Tanaka [67]

Shusaku **Nishikawa** - Yuichi **Komano** (Yuhei **Tokunaga** 60), Marcus Tulio **Tanaka•**, Yuji **Nakazawa**, Yuto **Nagatomo**, Yasuhito **Endo**, Shunsuke **Nakamura**, Makoto **Hasebe**, Keiji **Tamada** (Daisuke **Matsui** 33), Yoshito **Okubo** (Hisato **Sato** 75), Shinji **Okazaki** . Tr: Takeshi **Okada**

Hong Kong 0

Zhang Chunhui - **Lee** Chi Ho, **Deng** Jinghuang, Cristiano **Cordeiro•**, **Sham** Kwok Fai (**Lee** Wai Lun 53), **Kwan** Yee Lo, **Lam** Ka Wai (**Lee** Wai Lim 69), **Lee** Hong Lim, **Bai** He, **Chan** Siu Ki, **Chao** Pengfei 46). Tr: Kim Pan Gon

---

Ali Mohsen, Sana'a
28-01-2009, 16:15, 10 000, Al Hilali OMA

Yemen 1

Al Selwi [51]

Salem **Saeed** - Mohammed **Salem**, Zaher **Al Fadhli**, Ahmed **Al Wadi**, Omar **Awsan**, Mohammed **Al Ammari•** (Akram **Al Selwi** 46), Akram **Al Worafi**, Ala **Mohammed**, Ali **Yousef** (Haitham **Thabit** 84), Yaser **Ba Suhai**, Ali **Al Nono**. Tr: Sami **Saleh**

Hong Kong 0

Zhang Chunhui - **Lee** Chi Ho (**Lo** Kwan Yee 65), Gerard Ambassa Guy, **Ng** Wai Chiu, **Cheung** Kin Fung, Cristiano **Cordeiro•** (**Cheng** Siu Wai 50), **Gao** Wen•, **Xu** Deshuai, **Chan** Siu Ki, **Au** Yeung Yiu Chung (**Chao** Pengfei 78), **Lee** Wai Lim. Tr: Dejan Antonic

---

Hong Kong Stadium, Hong Kong
18-11-2009, 18:30, 13 254, Green AUS

Hong Kong 0

Zhang Chunhui - **Lee** Chi Ho, Gerard Ambassa Guy•, **Ng** Wai Chiu, **Chan** Wai Ho, **Poon** Yiu Cheuk (**Wong** Chin Hung 36), **Li** Haiqiang (**Au** Yeung Yiu Chung 46), **Lo** Kwan Yee, **Kwok** Kin Pong, **Bai** He, **Chan** Siu Ki. Tr: Kim Pan Gon

Japan 4

Hasebe [33], Sato [75], Nakamura [84], Okazaki [91+]

Eiji **Kawashima** - Yuichi **Komano** (Yuhei **Tokunaga** 84), Marcus Tulio **Tanaka•**, Yuji **Nakazawa**, Yasuhito **Endo** (Yuki **Abe** 86), Daisuke **Matsui**, Shunsuke **Nakamura**, Makoto **Hasebe**, Yoshito **Okubo** (Hisato **Sato** 60), Shinji **Okazaki**. Tr: Takeshi **Okada**

National Stadium, Manama
18-11-2009, 17:45, 1000, Basma SYR

Bahrain 4

Latif [20], Fatadi [28], Salman [64], Al Dali OG [75]

Abbas **Ahmed** - Mohamed **Husain•**, Hussain **Baba** (Ali **Abdulwahab** 81), Ebrahim **Al Mishkhas**, Abdulla **Fatadi** (Ahmed **Taleb** 46), Mohamed **Salmeen**, Abdullah **Omar**, Mahmood **Abdulrahman** (Husein **Salman** 63), Ismaeel **Latif**, Jaycee **Okwunwanne**. Tr: Milan **Macala**

Yemen 0

Saoud **Al Sowadi** - Zaher **Al Fadhli**, Khaled **Baleid**, Aref **Al Dali**, Abdulqader **Al Roatde**, Ahmed **Al Khamri**, Akram **Al Worafi** (Basem **Al Aqel** 59), Munassar **Ba Haj**, Hamada **Al Zubairi**, Ali **Yousef•** (Ala **Mohammed** 69), Ali **Al Nono** (Tamer **Hanash** 83). Tr: Sami **Saleh**

Ali Mohsen, Sana'a
6-01-2010, 16:15, 10 000, Albadwawi UAE

Yemen 2

Al Aqel [13], Abbod [39]

Salem **Saeed** - Basem **Al Aqel** (Hamada **Al Zubairi** 71), Zaher **Al Fadhli**, Khaled **Baleid**, Aref **Al Dali**, Ahmed **Al Khamri**, Akram **Al Worafi** (Mohammed **Al Abidi** 83), Ala **Mohammed**, Salem **Abbod** (Hussein **Al Ghazi** 77), Munassar **Ba Haj**, Ali **Al Nono**. Tr: Sami **Saleh**

Japan 3

Hirayama 3 [42 55 79]

Shuichi **Gonda** - Maya **Yoshida**, Tomoaki **Makino•**, Kosuke **Ota**, Mu **Kanazaki**, Naoki **Yamada** (Sota **Hirayama** 21), Takuji **Yonemoto•**, Kazuya **Yamamura** (Takashi **Inui** 46), Naoya **Kikuchi•**, Yosuke **Kashiwagi**, Kazuma **Watanabe** (Kensuke **Nagai** 85). Tr: Takeshi **Okada**

National Stadium, Manama
6-01-2010, 18:00, 1550, Balideh QAT

Bahrain 4

Latif 3 [34 40 43], Al Dakeel [79]

Sayed **Jaffer** - Mohamed **Husain**, Salman **Isa** (Mahmood **Abdulrahman** 46), Sayed **Adnan**, Hussain **Baba**, Mohamed **Salmeen**, Husein **Salman** (Abdulla **Al Dakeel** 67), Faouzi **Aaish**, Ahmed **Taleb**, Ali **Abdulwahab**, Ismaeel **Latif** (Husain **Ahmed** 82). Tr: Milan **Macala**

Hong Kong 0

Tse Tak Him - **Lee** Wai Lun, **Poon** Yiu Cheuk, **Deng** Jinghuang, **Fung** Kai Hong, **Man** Pei Tak, **So** Loi Keung, **Ip** Chung Long, **Lai** Yiu Cheong (**Sham** Kwok Fai 46), **Leung** Tsz Chun (**Leung** Hinson 46), **Cheng** Lai Hin (**Cheng** Siu Wai 73). Tr: Kim Pan Gon

---

Ali Mohsen, Sana'a
20-01-2010, 16:15, 7000, Torky IRN

Yemen 3

Al Nono 2 [5 25], Al Abdi [86]

Salem **Saeed** - Zaher **Al Fadhli**, Khaled **Baleid** (Ahmed **Al Khamri** 90), Aref **Al Dali•**, Mohammed **Al Ammari**, Akram **Al Worafi**, Ala **Mohammed**, Munassar **Ba Haj**, Hamada **Al Zubairi**, Hesham **Al Asbahi** (Salem **Abbod** 72), Ali **Al Nono** (Mohammed **Al Abidi** 83). Tr: Sami **Saleh**

Bahrain 0

Abbas **Ahmed** - Dawood **Saad**, Ahmed **Matar**, Sayed **Jalal**, Mohamed **Salmeen**, Rashid **Abdulrahman** (Abdulla **Al Dakeel** 46), Ahmed **Taleb**, Ali **Abdulwahab**, Saleh **Mahmeedi** (Abbas **Ayyad** 51), Ismaeel **Latif**, Husain **Ahmed** (Sayed **Hashem** 73). Tr: Milan **Macala**

Toyota Stadium, Toyota
3-03-2010, 19:00, 38 042, Abdul Bashir SIN

Japan 3

Okazaki [36], Honda [92+]

Seigo **Narazaki** - Marcus Tulio **Tanaka**, Atsuto **Uchida•**, Yuji **Nakazawa**, Yuto **Nagatomo**, Yasuhito **Endo•**, Daisuke **Matsui** (Takayuki **Morimoto** 67), Shunsuke **Nakamura** (Keiji **Tamada** 87), Makoto **Hasebe**, Keisuke **Honda**, Shinji **Okazaki**. Tr: Takeshi **Okada**

Bahrain 0

Sayed **Jaffer** - Mohamed **Husain**, Salman **Isa•**, Sayed **Adnan**, Mohamed **Salmeen** (Husein **Salman** 72), Mahmood **Abdulrahman**, Mohamed **Hubail•**, Saleh **Mahmeedi** (Husain **Ahmed** 83), Ismaeel **Latif**, Sayed **Hashem** (Abbas **Ayyad** 89). Tr: Milan **Macala**

Hong Kong Stadium, Hong Kong
3-03-2010, 19:30, 1212, Minh Tri Vo VIE

Hong Kong 0

Yapp Hung Fai - **Lee** Chi Ho, **Chan** Wai Ho, **Wong** Chin Hung (**Leung** Chun Pong 67), **Chak** Ting Fung, **Fung** Kai Hong (**Cheng** Lai Hin 56), **Xu** Deshuai, **Kwok** Kin Pong (**Leung** Hinson 40), **Lau** Nim Yat, **Au** Yeung Yiu Chung, **Chao** Pengfei. Tr: Kim Pan Gon

Yemen 0

Salem **Saeed** - Khaled **Baleid** (Salem **Abbod** 76), Aref **Al Dali**, Ahmed **Al Khamri**, Mohammed **Al Ammari**, Haitham **Thabit**, Akram **Al Worafie**, Ala **Mohammed** (Mohammed **Al Abidi** 64), Munassar **Ba Haj**, Hamada **Al Zubairi** (Basem **Al Aqel** 82), Ali **Al Nono**. Tr: Sami **Saleh**

QUALIFYING GROUP B		Pl	W	D	L	F	A	Pts	AUS	KUW	OMA	IDN
Australia	AUS	6	3	2	1	6	4	11		0-1	1-0	1-0
Kuwait	KUW	6	2	3	1	6	5	9	2-2		0-1	2-1
Oman	OMA	6	2	2	2	4	4	8	1-2	0-0		0-0
Indonesia	IDN	6	0	3	3	3	6	3	0-0	1-1	1-2	

Sultan Qaboos, Muscat
19-01-2009, 19:30, 13 000, Shamsuzzaman

Oman   0

Mohammed **Al Hooti** - Mohamed **Rabia**, Mohamed **Al Balushi** (Hashim **Saleh** 58), Hassan **Mudhafar**, Khalifa **Ayil**, Fouzi **Bashir**, Ahmed **Mubarak**, Hassan **Rabia**, Ahmed **Hadid** (Mansoor **Al Nuaimi** 74), Ismail **Al Ajmi**, Amad Ali **Al Hosni•**. Tr: Claude **Le Roy**

Indonesia   0

Markus **Rihihina•** - Charis **Yulianto**, Isnan **Ali**, Ricardo **Salampessy**, Maman **Abdurahman**, Ponaryo **Astaman**, Budi **Sudarsono** (Talaohu 46), Firman **Utina** (Nova **Arianto** 65), **Harione**, Boaz **Salossa•** (Erol **Iba** 83), Bambang **Pamungkas•**. Tr: Benny **Dollo**

Gelora Bung Karno, Jakarta
28-01-2009, 19:30, 50 000, Abdul Bashir SIN

Indonesia   0

Markus **Rihihina** - Charis **Yulianto**, Isnan **Ali**, Ricardo **Salampessy**, Maman **Abdurahman•**, Ponaryo **Astaman**, Budi **Sudarsono** (Erol **Iba** 83), Firman **Utina**, **Harione**, Boaz **Salossa** (Bambang **Pamungkas** 71), **Talaohu•** (Elie **Aiboy** 64). Tr: Benny **Dollo**

Australia   0

Eugene **Galekovic** - Craig **Moore**, Rodrigo **Vargas**, Dean **Heffernan** (Michael **Zullo** 74), Matt **Thompson**, Matt **McKay**, Paul **Reid**, Scott **Jamieson•**, Tom **Pondeljak** (Billy **Celeski** 68), Archie **Thompson**, Danny **Allsopp** (Matt **Simon•** 57). Tr: Pim **Verbeek**

Al Sadaqua, Kuwait City
28-01-2009, 18:00, 22 000, Al Saeedi UAE

Kuwait   0

Nawaf **Al Khaldi** - Yaqoub **Abdullah**, Hussain Fadhel **Ali**, Mesaed **Al Enezi•**, Mohammad **Sinad**, Saleh **Al Hendi** (Mohammad **Jarragh** 61), Talal **Al Enezi•**, Jarah **Al Ataiqi** (Waleed **Jumah** 77), Ahmad Ajab **Al Azemi**, Khaled **Matar** (Hamad **Al Enezi** 80), Bader **Al Mutwa**. Tr: Mohammed **Ibrahim**

Oman   1

Hassan **Rabea** 63

Mohammed **Al Hooti** - Mohamed **Rabia•**, Mohamed **Al Balushi** (Said **Al Shoon** 46), S'ad **Suhail**, Hassan **Mudhafar**, Fouzi **Bashir•**, Ahmed **Mubarak**, Hassan **Rabia**, Ismail **Al Ajmi**, Amad Ali **Al Hosni**, Mansoor **Al Nuaimi**. Tr: Claude **Le Roy**

Canberra Stadium, Canberra
5-03-2009, 20:00, 20 032, Moradi IRN

Australia   0

Eugene **Galekovic** - Craig **Moore** (Robert **Cornthwaite** 86), Rodrigo **Vargas**, Matt **Thompson**, Daniel **Mullen**, Matt **McKay**, Paul **Reid** (Mitch **Nichols** 62), Tom **Pondeljak**, Michael **Zullo•**, (Fabian **Barbiero** 68), Archie **Thompson**, Matt **Simon•**. Tr: Pim **Verbeek**

Kuwait   1

Mesaed **Al Enezi** 37

Nawaf **Al Khaldi** - Yaqoub **Abdullah**, Hussain Fadhel **Ali**, Mesaed **Al Enezi**, Waleed **Jumah•** (Saleh **Al Hendi** 86), Fahad **Shaheen**, Fahad **Al Ebrahim** (Mohammad **Jarragh** 77), Jarah **Al Ataiqi**, Talal **Al Amer**, Hamad **Al Enezi•** (Khaled **Matar** 65), Bader **Al Mutwa**. Tr: Goran **Tufegdzic**

Etihad, Melbourne
14-10-2009, 19:30, 20 595, Toma JPN

Australia   1

Cahill 73

Mark **Schwarzer** - Lucas **Neill**, Craig **Moore**, Tim **Cahill** (Mile **Jedinak** 89), Jason **Culina**, Brett **Emerton**, Luke **Wilkshire**, Harry **Kewell** (David **Carney** 79), Scott **Chipperfield**, Carl **Valeri** (Dario **Vidosic** 71), Joshua **Kennedy**. Tr: Pim **Verbeek**

Oman   0

Ali **Al Habsi** - Mohamed **Rabia**, Mohamed **Al Balushi•**, Hassan **Mudhafar**, Khalifa **Ayil**, Fouzi **Bashir**, Ahmed **Mubarak** (Badr **Al Maimani** 86), Hassan **Rabia•**, Ahmed **Hadid**, Ismail **Al Ajmi** (Hashim **Saleh** 83), Amad Ali **Al Hosni**. Tr: Claude **Le Roy**

Sultan Qaboos, Muscat
14-11-2009, 18:00, 12 000, Sun Baojie CHN

Oman   1

Khalifa Ayil 16

Ali **Al Habsi** - Mohamed **Rabia**, Mohamed **Al Balushi•**, Hassan **Mudhafar**, Khalifa **Ayil**, Fouzi **Bashir**, Hassan **Rabia** (Hashim **Saleh** 69), Ahmed **Hadid•**, Qasim **Said** (Yacoob **Abdul Karim** 87), Ismail **Al Ajmi**, Amad Ali **Al Hosni•**. Tr: Claude **Le Roy**

Australia   2

Wilkshire 43, Emerton 83

Mark **Schwarzer** - Lucas **Neill**, Craig **Moore•**, Rhys **Williams◆**15, Tim **Cahill** (Brett **Holman** 67), Jason **Culina**, Brett **Emerton**, Luke **Wilkshire•**, Harry **Kewell** (Patrick **Kisnorbo** 89), Scott **Chipperfield**, Mark **Bresciano** (David **Carney•** 67). Tr: Pim **Verbeek**

Al Kuwait Sports Club, Kuwait City
14-11-2009, 18:30, 16 000, Kovalenko UZB

Kuwait   2

Bader Al Mutwa 2 60 88p

Nawaf **Al Khaldi** - Yaqoub **Abdullah**, Mesaed **Al Enezi**, Waleed **Jumah**, Fahad **Shaheen**, Ahmad **Al Eidan**, Fahad **Al Ebrahim** (Mohammad **Jarragh** 46), Talal **Al Amer**, Abdullah **Al Buraiki** (Hamad **Al Enezi** 68), Ahmad Ajab **Al Azemi** (Jarah **Al Ataiqi•** 90), Bader **Al Mutwa**. Tr: Goran **Tufegdzic**

Indonesia   1

Pamungkas 33

Markus **Rihihina** - Charis **Yulianto**, Isnan **Ali** (Muhammad **Ridwan** 26), Maman **Abdurahman**, Ponaryo **Astaman** (**Harione** 66), Ismet **Sofyand**, Syamsul **Bachri**, Muhammad **Ilham**, Eka **Ramdani** (Firman **Utina** 78), **Talaohu**, Bambang **Pamungkas**. Tr: Benny **Dollo**

Gelora Bung Karno, Jakarta
18-11-2009, 18:30, 36 000, Tojo JPN

Indonesia   1

Sudarsono 45

Markus **Rihihina** -Charis **Yulianto**, Nova **Arianto•**, Maman **Abdurahman•**, Ponaryo **Astaman•**, Budi **Sudarsono**, Ismet **Sofyand••**46, Firman **Utina** (Syamsul **Bachri** 80), Muhammad **Ridwan** (Isnan **Ali** 23), Boaz **Salossa**, Bambang **Pamungkas** (Rachmat **Latif** 58). Tr: **Dollo**

Kuwait   1

Ahmad Ajab Al Azemi 72

Nawaf **Al Khaldi** - Yaqoub **Abdullah**, Mesaed **Al Enezi**, Waleed **Jumah•**, Fahad **Shaheen**, Ahmad **Al Eidan**, Fahad **Al Ebrahim** (Saleh **Al Hendi** 54), Talal **Al Amer**, Abdullah **Al Buraiki** (Mohammad **Jarragh** 82), Ahmad Ajab **Al Azemi**, Bader **Al Mutwa** (Hamad **Al Enezi** 46). Tr: Goran **Tufegdzic**

Gelora Bung Karno, Jakarta
6-01-2010, 18:30, 45 000, Mohd Salleh MAS

Indonesia   1

Salossa 45

Markus **Rihihina** - Charis **Yulianto•**, Isnan **Ali** (Mohamad **Roby** 66), Nova **Arianto**, Marthen **Worabai**, Ponaryo **Astaman**, Budi **Sudarsono** (**Talaohu** 36), Firman **Utina**, Syamsul **Bachri•** (**Harione** 70), Boaz **Salossa•**, Bambang **Pamungkas**. Tr: Benny **Dollo**

Oman   2

Fouzi Bashir 32, Ismail Al Ajmi 53

Ali **Al Habsi** - Mohamed **Rabia**, Mohamed **Al Balushi**, S'ad **Suhail**, Hassan **Mudhafar**, Fouzi **Bashir•**, Hassan **Rabia•**, Ahmed **Hadid**, Qasim **Said**, Ismail **Al Ajmi**, Yacoob **Abdul Karim** (Hashim **Saleh** 64). Tr: Claude **Le Roy**

Al Kuwait Sports Club, Kuwait City
6-01-2010, 17:30, 20 000, Irmatov UZB

Kuwait   2

Hamad Al Enezi 40, Yousuf Nasser 44

Nawaf **Al Khaldi** - Yaqoub **Abdullah**, Hussain Fadhel **Ali**, Fahad **Shaheen**, Saleh **Al Hendi**, Talal **Al Enezi**, Jarah **Al Ataiqi** (Abdulaziz **Al Enezi** 24), Talal **Al Amer**, Hamaad **Aman•** (Ahmad **Al Eidan** 78), Yousef **Nasser** (Mohammad **Jarragh** 72), Bader **Al Mutwa**. Tr: Goran **Tufegdzic**

Australia   2

Wilkshire 3, Heffernan 5

Eugene **Galekovic** - Craig **Moore**, Dean **Heffernan**, Luke **Wilkshire**, Nick **Carle** (Matt **Thompson** 89), Mile **Sterjovski** (Nikita **Rukavytsya** 60), Mile **Jedinak**, Simon **Colosimo**, Dario **Vidosic**, Matthew **Kemp**, Archie **Thompson** (Bruce **Djite** 90). Tr: Pim **Verbeek**

Suncorp, Brisbane
3-03-2010, 19:00, 20 422, Ogiya JPN

Australia   1

Milligan 42

Eugene **Galekovic** - Mark **Milligan**, Shannon **Cole** (Matt **Thompson** 72), Jason **Culina**, Luke **Wilkshire**, Mile **Sterjovski** (Matt **McKay** 46), Jacob **Burns** (David **Williams** 89), Simon **Colosimo**, Scott **Jamieson**, Joshua **Kennedy**, Tommy **Oar•**. Tr: Pim **Verbeek**

Indonesia   0

Markus **Rihihina** -Charis **Yulianto**, Nova **Arianto**, Maman **Abdurahman**, Ponaryo **Astaman**, Budi **Sudarsono** (Arif **Suyono** 83), Ismet **Sofyand**, Firman **Utina** (Eka **Ramdani•** 58), Syamsul **Bachri** (**Harione** 59), Muhammad **Ridwan**, Bambang **Pamungkas**. Tr: Benny **Dollo**

Sultan Qaboos, Muscat
3-03-2010, 19:30, 27 000, Moradi IRN

Oman   0

Ali **Al Habsi** - Mohamed **Al Balushi•**, S'ad **Suhail•** (Hashim **Saleh** 87), Hassan **Mudhafar** (Khalifa **Ayil**, Fouzi **Bashir**, Ahmed **Mubarak** (Badr **Al Maimani** 71), Hassan **Rabia** (Qasim **Said** 70), Ahmed **Hadid•**, Ismail **Al Ajmi**, Amad Ali **Al Hosni**. Tr: Claude **Le Roy**

Kuwait   0

Nawaf **Al Khaldi** - Yaqoub **Abdullah**, Hussain Fadhel **Ali**, Mesaed **Al Enezi•**, Waleed **Jumah** (Khaled **Matar** 68), Fahad **Shaheen**, Saleh **Al Hendi•**, Talal **Al Amer**, Abdullah **Al Buraiki** (Talal **Al Enezi** 56), Yousuf **Nasser**, Bader **Al Mutwa** (Jarah **Al Ataiqi** 84). Tr: Goran **Tufegdzic**

QUALIFYING GROUP C

		Pl	W	D	L	F	A	Pts	UAE	UZB	MAS
United Arab Emirates	UAE	6	3	0	1	7	1	9		0-1	1-0
Uzbekistan	UZB	6	3	0	1	7	3	9	0-1		3-1
Malaysia	MAS	6	0	0	4	2	12	0	0-5	1-3	
India	IND	India qualified automatically for the finals by winning the 2008 AFC Challenge Cup									

KLFA Stadium, Kuala Lumpur
21-01-2009, 20:45, 10 000, Williams AUS
Malaysia   0

Mohammad Mohd Mustafa• (Syed Hussein 68), Fauzie Nan, Norhafiz Misbah, Veeran Thirumurugan, Mohamad Aidil Abd Radzak, Mohammad Hardi Jaafar•, Mohd Zainal (Hairuddin Omar 77), Mohamad Zaquan Abd Radzak• (Mohd Ashaari Shamsuddin 85), Mohd Safee Sali, Indra Putra Mahayuddin, Mohd Zambri. Tr: Bhaskaran Sathianathan

United Arab Emirates   5
Omar 2 ²⁹ ⁴⁵ᵖ, Matar 2 ⁶² ⁷⁶, Khalil ⁸⁵

Majed Naser - Haidar Ali, Walid Abbas Al Balooshi, Ismail Hamdan, Mohammed Fayez, Abdulraheem Jumaa, Abdulsalam Jumaa, Mohammed Omar (Ahmed Khalil 46), Ismael Matar, Ismail Al Hammadi (Mahmoud Khamis 46), Mohamed Al Shehhi. Tr: Dominique Bathenay

Al Sharjah Stadium, Sharjah
28-01-2009, 19:00, 15 000, Nishimura JPN
United Arab Emirates   0

Majed Naser - Haidar Ali (Ismail Al Hammadi 82), Walid Abbas Al Balooshi, Ismail Hamdan, Mohammed Fayez, Abdulraheem Jumaa (Abdulla Malallah 63), Abdulsalam Jumaa, Ali Al Wehaibi, Mohammed Omar (Ahmed Khalil 69), Ismael Matar, Mohamed Al Shehhi. Tr: Dominique Bathenay

Uzbekistan   1
Farhod Tadjiyev ³⁰

Ignatiy Nesterov - Anvar Gafurov, Anzur Ismailov•, Sakhob Jurayev, Islom Tuhtahujaev, Server Djeparov, Odil Ahmedov, Timur Kapadze, Jasur Hasanov (Ruslan Melziddinov 90), Ildar Magdeev•, Farhod Tadjiyev (Shakuboz Erkinov 65). Tr: Mirdjalol Kasimov

JAR, Tashkent
14-11-2009, 16:00, 5000, Moradi IRN
Uzbekistan   3
Djeparov ⁴⁶, Geynrikh 2 ⁵⁷ ⁶⁵

Ignatiy Nesterov - Anvar Gafurov, Murod Khalmukhamedov, Kamoliddin Tadjiyev, Aziz Ibragimov (Alexander Geynrikh 46), Azizbek Haydarov, Server Djeparov, Odil Ahmedov (Timur Kapadze 71), Jasur Hasanov (Zohir Pirimov 82), Vitaliy Denisov, Anvarjon Soliev. Tr: Mirdjalol Kasimov

Malaysia   1
MZ Abd Radzak ⁶⁸

Mohd Farizal (Syed Hussein 80) - Mohamad Sabree Abu, Norhafiz Misbah, Mohamad Aidil Abd Radzak, Mohd Nasriq•●85, Amar Rohidan (Norshahrul Idlan Talaha 60), Safiq Rahim, Mohamad Zaquan Abd Radzak•, Mohd Amri Yahyah, Baddrol Bakhtiar, Amad Faqri Saarani (Subramaniam Kunalan73). Tr: Rajagobal Krishnasamy

---

National Stadium, Kuala Lumpur
18-11-2009, 17:30, 2000, Tan Hai CHN
Malaysia   1
Bakhtiar ⁷⁰

Mohd Farizal - Mohamad Sabree Abu, Norhafiz Misbah, Mohamad Aidil Abd Radzak, Mahalli Jasuli (Mohd Azmi Muslim 67), Subramaniam Kunalan, Safiq Rahim, Norshahrul Idlan Talaha (Ahmad Shakir Mohd Ali 55), Mohd Amri Yahyah•, Baddrol Bakhtiar•, Amad Faqri Saarani (Mohd Muslim Ahmad 75). Tr: Rajagobal Krishnasamy

Uzbekistan   3
Gafurov ³², Nasimov ⁵⁸, Kapadze ⁷³

Timur Juraev - Anvar Gafurov, Murod Khalmukhamedov, Kamoliddin Tadjiyev, Aziz Ibragimov (Stanislav Andreev 55), Azizbek Haydarov, Timur Kapadze, Jasur Hasanov (Zohir Pirimov 71), Vitaliy Denisov, Bakhodir Nasimov (Lochinbek Soliyev 78), Anvarjon Soliev. Tr: Mirdjalol Kasimov

Al Shabab, Dubai
6-01-2010, 19:00, 3500, Basma SYR
United Arab Emirates   1
Ahmed Khalil ⁹³⁺

Majed Naser - Haidar Ali (Ahmed Khalil 46), Mohammad Qassim•, Ismail Hamdan•, Mahmoud Khamis, Abdulsalam Jumaa, Ali Al Wehaibi, Amir Mubarak (Sultan Al Menhali• 71), Yousif Jaber (Fares Juma 24), Ismael Matar, Mohamed Al Shehhi. Tr: Srecko Katanec

Malaysia   0

Mohd Farizal - Norhafiz Misbah (Amar Rohidan• 45), Mohamad Aidil Abd Radzak•, Mohd Azmi Muslim, Mohd Muslim Ahmad, Mohd Nasriq•, Subramaniam Kunalan, Safiq Rahim, Mohamad Zaquan Abd Radzak•, Norshahrul Idlan Talaha, Amad Faqri Saarani (Mohd Zainal 63). Tr: Rajagobal Krishnasamy

Pakhtakor, Tashkent
3-03-2010, 18:00, 20 000, Shamsuzzaman
Uzbekistan   0

Ignatiy Nesterov - Anvar Gafurov, Islom Innomov, Anzur Ismailov, Azizbek Haydarov, Server Djeparov•, Odil Ahmedov, Jasur Hasanov, Vitaliy Denisov, Bakhodir Nasimov (Farhod Tadjiyev 62), Alexander Geynrikh• (Timur Kapadze 81). Tr: Mirdjalol Kasimov

United Arab Emirates   1
Sultan Al Menhali ⁹³⁺

Majed Naser - Subait Khater (Ahmed Khalil 85), Fares Juma, Walid Abbas Al Balooshi, Ismail Hamdan, Fahed Masoud (Sultan Al Menhali 61), Ali Al Wehaibi, Amir Mubarak•, Yousif Jaber, Mohamed Al Shehhi•, Saeed Al Kas (Saeed Salem 57). Tr: Srecko Katanec

QUALIFYING GROUP D

		Pl	W	D	L	F	A	Pts	SYR	CHN	VIE	LIB
Syria	SYR	6	4	2	0	10	2	14		3-2	0-0	4-0
China PR	CHN	6	4	1	1	13	5	13	0-0		6-1	1-0
Vietnam	VIE	6	1	2	3	6	11	5	0-1	1-2		3-1
Lebanon	LIB	6	0	1	5	2	13	1	0-2	0-2	1-1	

My Dinh National, Hanoi
14-01-2009, 19:00, 13 000, Iemoto JPN

Vietnam   **3**

Nguyen Minh Phuong [11], Le Cong Vinh [30], Nguyen Vu Phong [69]

Duong Hong Son - **Doan** Viet Cuong, Le Phuoc Tu, **Vu Nhu** Thanh, **Huynh** Quang Thanh (**Nguyen** Minh Duc 81), **Nguyen** Minh Phuong (**Nguyen** Minh Chau 63), Le Tan Tai (**Nguyen** Quang Hai 54), **Nguyen** Vu Phong, **Phan** Van Tai Em, Le Cong Vinh•♦54, **Nguyen** Viet Thang. Tr: **Calisto**

Lebanon   **1**

Akram Moghrabi [73]

Lary **Mehanna** - Ali **Al Saadi**, Ramez **Dayoub**, Ali **El Atat**, Hassan **Matouk** (Zakaria Yehya **Charara** 46), Mohamad **Korhani**• (Nasrat **Al Jamal** 60), Abbas **Atwi**, Ali **Yaacoub**•, Mahmoud M. **Younes**• (Mohamad **Ghaddar** 60), Ali **Hamam**, Akram **Moghrabi**•. Tr: Emile **Rustom**

International, Aleppo
14-01-2009, 14:00, 7000, Torky IRN

Syria   **3**

Maher Al Said 2 [8p] [24], Firas Al Khatib [39p]

Radwan **Al Azhar** - Ali **Diab**, Omar **Hemidi**•, Feras **Ismail**, Bakri **Tarab**, Aatef **Jenyat**, Bassel **Hamamieh**, Yehya **Al Rashed** (Adel **Abdellah** 63), Maher **Al Said** (Jehad **Alhoussain** 71), Firas **Al Khatib** (Ziad **Chabo** 86), Raja **Rafe**. Tr: **Ebrahim Fajer**

China PR   **2**

Qu Bo [51], Liu Jian [94+]

Song Zhen Yu• - Du Wei•, **Wang** Xiao•, Cao Yang, Zhang Yaokun, Huang Bowen (Liu Jian 80), Du Zhenyu•, **Wang** Dong (Qu Bo 46), Zhou Haibin, Gao Lin•, Jiang Ning•. Tr: **Yin Tiesheng**

Yellow Dragon, Hangzhou
21-01-2009, 19:35, 15 300, Kim Dong Jin KOR

China PR   **6**

Gao Lin 3 [2] [20] [84], Du Wei [27], Jiang Ning [37], Hao Junmin [47]

Song Zhen Yu - Du Wei, Cao Yang, Wu Hao, Jiao Zhe, Huang Bowen, Du Zhenyu• (Qu Bo 46), Hao Junmin (Shen Longyuan 64), Zhou Haibin, Gao Lin, Jiang Ning. Tr: **Yin Tiesheng**

Vietnam   **1**

Nguyen Vu Phong [11]

Tran Duc Cuong - **Doan** Viet Cuong, Le Phuoc Tu, **Vu Nhu** Thanh, **Huynh** Quang Thanh (**Chu** Ngoc Anh 46), **Nguyen** Minh Chau (**Nguyen** Quang Hai 46), **Nguyen** Minh Phuong, Le Tan Tai•, **Nguyen** Vu Phong, **Phan** Van Tai Em, **Nguyen** Viet Thang. Tr: Henrique **Calisto**

International, Saida
28-01-2009, 17:00, 300, Balideh QAT

Lebanon   **0**

Lary **Mehanna** - **Al Saadi**, Hussein **Amine** (Zakaria Yehya **Charara** 46), Ramez **Dayoub**, Bilal **Najarin**, Mohamad **Korhani**, Abbas **Atwi**, Ali **Yaacoub**, Mahmoud M. **Younes** (Ali **El Atat** 76), Roda **Antar**, Akram **Moghrabi** (Paul **Rustom** 59). Tr: Emile **Rustom**

Syria   **2**

Jehad Alhoussain [37], Firas Al Khatib [77]

Mosab **Balhous** - Belal **Abduldaim**, Ali **Diab**, Omar **Hemidi**•, Bakri **Tarab**, Jehad **Alhoussain** (Maher **Al Said** 88), Adel **Abdellah**•, Wael **Ayan**•, Yehya **Al Rashed** (Hamzeh **Al Aitoni** 76), Firas **Al Khatib**, Raja **Rafe** (Mohamed **Al Zeno** 73). Tr: **Ebrahim Fajer**

My Dinh National, Hanoi
14-11-2009, 19:00, 30 000, Williams AUS

Vietnam   **0**

Duong Hong Son - **Doan** Viet Cuong, Le Phuoc Tu, **Vu Nhu** Thanh, **Vo** Hoang Quang, **Nguyen** Minh Phuong, Le Tan Tai•, **Nguyen** Vu Phong (**Pham** Thanh Luong 37), **Tran** Duy Quang, Le Cong Vinh•, **Nguyen** Viet Thang• (**Nguyen** Quang Hai 86). Tr: Henrique **Calisto**

Syria   **1**

Raja Rafe [94+]

Mosab **Balhous** - Ali **Diab**, Feras **Ismail**, Ahmad **Deeb**, Bakri **Tarab**, Jehad **Alhoussain**, Abdelrazaq **Al Hussain**, Aatef **Jenyat**, Meaataz **Kailouni** (Raja **Rafe** 77), Firas **Al Khatib**, Abdul **Al Agha** (Mohamed **Al Zeno** 65). Tr: **Ebrahim Fajer**

Municipal, Beirut
14-11-2009, 17:00, 2000, Albadwawi UAE

Lebanon   **0**

Lary **Mehanna** - **Al Saadi** (Hussein **Amine** 65), Bilal **Najarin**, Ali **El Atat**, Hassan **Matouk**, Mohamad **Korhani**•, Ali **Yaacoub** (Akram **Moghrabi** 52), Ali **Hamam**, Roda **Antar**•, Hamze **Abboud**, Mahmoud **El Ali** (Ahmad **Zreik** 60). Tr: Emile **Rustom**

China PR   **2**

Yu Hai [44], Qu Bo [72]

Yang Zhi - Du Wei, Feng Xiaoting, Zhao Peng•, Zhao Xuri•, Hao Junmin (Zheng Zhi 57), Yang Hao, Rong Hao, Yu Hai, Gao Lin (Zheng Long 90), Jiang Ning• (Qu Bo 66). Tr: **Gao Hongbo**

International, Aleppo
18-11-2009, 14:00, 19 000, Al Hilali OMA

Syria   **0**

Mosab **Balhous** - Ali **Diab**, Feras **Ismail**, Ahmad **Deeb**, Bakri **Tarab** (Yasser **Shahen** 86), Jehad **Alhoussain**, Abdelrazaq **Al Hussain**, Aatef **Jenyat**, Meaataz **Kailouni** (Mohamed **Al Zeno** 59), Firas **Al Khatib**, Abdul **Al Agha** (Raja **Rafe** 78). Tr: **Ebrahim Fajer**

Vietnam   **0**

Bui Tan Truong - **Doan** Viet Cuong•, Le Phuoc Tu, **Vu Nhu** Thanh, **Vo** Hoang Quang, **Nguyen** Minh Chau, **Pham** Thanh Luong (**Nguyen** Minh Duc 80), **Nguyen** Trong Hoang, **Phan** Thanh Hung (**Nguyen** Vu Phong 46), Le Cong Vinh••♦69, **Nguyen** Viet Thang (**Nguyen** Quang Hai 46). Tr: Henrique **Calisto**

Yellow Dragon, Hangzhou
22-11-2009, 20:05, 21 520, Breeze AUS

China PR   **1**

Du Wei [19]

Yang Zhi - Du Wei (**Sun** Xiang 83), Feng Xiaoting, Zhao Peng, Zhao Xuri, Huang Bowen, Deng Zhuoxiang, Hao Junmin (Qu Bo 40), Rong Hao•, Yu Hai, Gao Lin (Han Peng 62). Tr: **Gao Hongbo**

Lebanon   **0**

Lary **Mehanna** - Hussein **Amine**, Bilal **Najarin**, Ahmad **El Khodor**, Ali **El Atat** (Mouhamad **Chamass** 60), Hassan **Matouk**, Amer **Khan**, Ali **Hamam**• (Mootaz **Jounaidi** 63), Hamze **Abboud**•, Akram **Moghrabi**•, Mahmoud **El Ali** (Ahmad **Zreik** 87). Tr: Emile **Rustom**

Yellow Dragon, Hangzhou
6-01-2010, 19:30, 29 570, Toma JPN

China PR   **0**

Yang Zhi - Du Wei, Zhao Peng, Zhao Xuri, Zhang Linpeng, Yang Hao, Rong Hao, Yu Hai (Mao Jianqing 89), Shao Jiayi, Jiang Ning (Hao Junmin 60), Peng Han (Qu Bo 73). Tr: **Gao Hongbo**

Syria   **0**

Mosab **Balhous** - Belal **Abduldaim**, Ali **Diab**, Omar **Hemidi**, Feras **Ismail** (Mahmoud **Nezaa** 89), Bakri **Tarab**•, Jehad **Alhoussain**, Adel **Abdellah**, Wael **Ayan**, Firas **Al Khatib** (Abdelrazaq **Al Hussain** 82), Mohamed **Al Zeno**•. Tr: **Ebrahim Fajer**

International, Saida
6-01-2010, 50, Kovalenko UZB

Lebanon   **1**

Mahmoud El Ali [19]

Elias **Freije** - Bilal **Najarin**, Mootaz **Jounaidi**, Ahmad **El Khodor**, Hassan **Matouk**, Mohamad **Korhani**•, Ali **Yaacoub** (Mouhamad **Chamass** 76), Ali **Hamam**, Hamze **Abboud**, Ahmad **Zreik** (Hussein **Dakik** 71), Mahmoud **El Ali** (Amer **Khan** 72). Tr: Emile **Rustom**

Vietnam   **1**

Pham Thanh Luong [39]

Tran Duc Cuong - Le Phuoc Tu, **Vu Nhu** Thanh, **Truong** Dinh Luat•, **Tran** Dinh Dong, **Nguyen** Minh Phuong, Le Tan Tai (**Phan** Thanh Hung 29), **Nguyen** Vu Phong (Mai Tien Thanh 73), **Pham** Thanh Luong, **Tran** Duy Quang (**Nguyen** Trong Hoang• 42), **Nguyen** Viet Thang. Tr: Henrique **Calisto**

My Dinh National, Hanoi
17-01-2010, 19:00, 3000, Abdul Bashir SIN

Vietnam   **1**

Le Cong Vinh [76p]

Bui Tan Truong - **Doan** Viet Cuong, Le Phuoc Tu•, **Vu Nhu** Thanh, **Truong** Dinh Luat• (**Tran** Dinh Dong 72), **Nguyen** Minh Chau•, **Nguyen** Minh Phuong•, **Pham** Thanh Luong•, **Phan** Thanh Hung• (**Nguyen** Trong Hoang 70), Le Cong Vinh, **Nguyen** Viet Thang•♦55. Tr: Henrique **Calisto**

China PR   **2**

Yang Xu [35], Zhang Linpeng [43]

Yang Zhi - Feng Xiaoting, Zhao Peng, Zhao Xuri (Huang Bowen• 69), Zhang Linpeng•, Deng Zhuoxiang, Hao Junmin (Gao Lin 71), Yang Hao, Rong Hao, Yu Hai, Yang Xu• (**Sun** Xiang 85). Tr: **Gao Hongbo**

Abbasiyyin, Damascus
3-03-2010, 15:00, 16 000, Kim Dong Jin KOR

Syria   **4**

Mohamed Al Zeno [4], Abdul Al Agha [10], Jehad Alhoussain [47], Abdelrazaq Al Hussain [60]

Mosab **Balhous** - Belal **Abduldaim**, Ali **Diab**•, Omar **Hemidi**, Feras **Ismail**, Bakri **Tarab** (Mahmoud **Nezaa** 64), Jehad **Alhoussain**, Adel **Abdellah** (Abdelrazaq **Al Hussain** 51), Wael **Ayan**, Mohamed **Al Zeno**, Abdul **Al Agha** (Ahmad **Al Omair** 83). Tr: **Ebrahim Fajer**

Lebanon   **0**

Lary **Mehanna** - Bilal **Najarin**, Walid **Ismail** (Hassan **Daher** 80), Ahmad **El Khodor**, Ali **El Atat**, Hassan **Matouk**, Mohamad **Korhani**, Amer **Khan** (Mouhamad **Chamass** 66), Ali **Hamam** (Nour **Mansour** 16), Hussein **Dakik**, Mahmoud **El Ali**. Tr: Emile **Rustom**

QUALIFYING GROUP E

		Pl	W	D	L	F	A	Pts	IRN	JOR	THA	SIN
Iran	IRN	6	4	1	1	11	2	**13**		1-0	1-0	6-0
Jordan	JOR	6	2	2	2	4	4	**8**	1-0		0-0	2-1
Thailand	THA	6	1	3	2	3	3	**6**	0-0	0-0		0-1
Singapore	SIN	6	2	0	4	6	15	**6**	1-3	2-1	1-3	

Azadi, Tehran
14-01-2009, 15:00, 3000, Mansour LIB

Iran 6

Gholamnejhad [43], Bagheri [52], Rezaei [55], Mazyar Zare [79], Nori 2 [82 83]

Seyed **Rahmati** - Seyed Hosseini, Hadi Aghili, Hassan Ashjari, Mageed **Gholamnejhad** (Mohammad **Nori** 68), Karim **Bagheri** (Sattar Zare 68), Hossein **Kaebi** (Seyed-Mehdi Salehi 80), Gholamreza **Rezaei**, Mohammad Khalatbari•, Mazyar Zare, Arash Borhani. Tr: Ali Daei

Singapore 0

Lewis **Lionel** - Baihakki **Khaizan**, Precious **Emuejeraye**, Daniel **Bennett**, Ismail Yunos, Mohammad Bin Abdul•, John **Wilkinson**• (Agu Casmir 67), Mustafic **Fahrudin**, Shahril **Ishak** (Jumaat Jantan 57), Noh Alam **Shah**, Indra **Sahdan** (Ridhuan Muhamad 46). Tr: Raddy Avramovic

---

International, Amman
14-01-2009, 17:00, 5000, Racho SYR

Jordan 0

Amer **Sabbah** - Mohammed Al Mutasim (Qusai Abu Alieh 46), Bashar Bani Yaseen, Ala Matalka, Hatem **Aqel**, Baha Suleiman•, Amer Khalil **Deeb**, Abdallah **Salim**, Mahmoud Shelbaieh (Odai Alsaify 58), Mohamad **Maharmeh** (Moayad Abukeshek 65), Abdul Hadi Al Maharmeh. Tr: Nelo Vingada

Thailand 0

Kosin **Hathairattanakool**• - Suree **Sukha**, Nattaporn **Phanrit**, Natthaphong **Samana**, Cholratit Jantakam, Suchao **Nutnum**, Sukha **Surat** (Salahudin Arware 68), Pichitpong **Choechiu**•, Datsakorn **Thonglao** (Anon Sangsanoi 87), Teerasil **Dangda** (Ronnachai Rangsiyo 76), Sutee **Suksomkit**•. Tr: Peter Reid

---

National Stadium, Singapore
28-01-2009, 19:30, 6188, Green AUS

Singapore 2

Agu Casmir [21], Noh Alam Shah [63]

Hassan **Sunny** - Baihakki **Khaizan**, Noh **Rahman**, Daniel **Bennett**, Shaiful **Esah**, Ridhuan **Muhamad** (Rosman Sulaiman 81), John **Wilkinson**, Mustafic **Fahrudin**•, Shahril **Ishak** (Shi Jiayi 69), Noh Alam **Shah**• (Precious **Emuejeraye** 89), Agu **Casmir**. Tr: Raddy Avramovic

Jordan 1

Hatem Aqel [41p]

Amer **Sabbah** - Bashar Bani Yaseen, Ala Matalka, Hatem **Aqel**, Anas **Bani** (Mohammad Al Mutasim 46), Baha Suleiman, Amer Khalil **Deeb**, Qusai Abu Alieh, Abdallah **Salim** (Raed Abdelrahman 73), Odai Alsaify, Abdul Hadi Al **Maharmeh** (Mahmoud Shelbaieh• 57). Tr: Nelo Vingada

---

Rajamangala, Bangkok
28-01-2009, 18:30, 10 000, Kovalenko UZB

Thailand 0

Kosin **Hathairattanakool** - Suree **Sukha**, Nattaporn **Phanrit**, Natthaphong **Samana**•, Cholratit Jantakam, Suchao **Nutnum**, Sukha **Surat**, Pichitpong **Choechiu**•, Datsakorn **Thonglao**• (Rangsiyo Ronnachai 82), Teerasil **Dangda** (Teeratep Winothai 76), Sutee **Suksomkit** (Rangsan Vivatchaichok• 63). Tr: Peter Reid

Iran 0

Seyed **Rahmati** - Seyed Hosseini, Hadi Aghili , Hassan Ashjari, Mageed **Gholamnejhad**, Karim **Bagheri** (Mohammad **Nori** 71)•, Hossein **Kaebi**•, Gholamreza **Rezaei** (Seyed-Mehdi Salehi 71), Mohammad Khalatbari, Mazyar Zare (Kianoush Rahmati 57), Arash Borhani. Tr: Ali Daei

---

National Stadium, Singapore
14-11-2009, 19:30, 22 183, Takayama JPN

Singapore 1

Mustafic Fahrudin [84p]

Hassan **Sunny** - Baihakki **Khaizan**, Noh **Rahman**, Daniel **Bennett**, Shaiful **Esah**, Ridhuan **Muhamad**, John **Wilkinson**, Mustafic **Fahrudin**, Shahril **Ishak** (Indra **Sahdan** 72), Noh Alam **Shah**• (Khairul **Amri** 51), Aleksandar **Duric**. Tr: Raddy Avramovic

Thailand 3

Sutee **Suksomkit** 2 [12p 81], Therdsak Chaiman [76]

Kosin **Hathairattanakool**• - Suree **Sukha**, Nattaporn **Phanrit**•, Natthaphong **Samana**•, Panupong **Wongsa**, Suchao **Nutnum**, Sukha **Surat** (Peter Lang 54), Datsakorn **Thonglao** (Nirut Surasiang 80), Teerasil **Dangda**, Sutee **Suksomkit**, Pipat **Thonkanya** (Therdsak **Chaiman**• 61). Tr: Bryan Robson

---

Rajamangala, Bangkok
18-11-2009, 18:30, 30 000, Balideh QAT

Thailand 0

Kittisak **Rawangpa** - Suree **Sukha**, Nattaporn **Phanrit**, Panupong **Wongsa**, Rangsan **Vivatchaichok**, Suchao **Nutnum**, Nirut **Surasiang** (Teeratep Winothai 68), Datsakorn **Thonglao**• (Therdsak **Chaiman** 61), Teerasil **Dangda**, Sutee **Suksomkit**, Pipat **Thonkanya** (Peter Lang 84). Tr: Bryan Robson

Singapore 1

Duric [37]

Hassan **Sunny** - Baihakki **Khaizan**, Precious **Emuejeraye**, Daniel **Bennett**, Shaiful **Esah**, Ridhuan **Muhamad** (Rosman Sulaiman• 86), Mustafic **Fahrudin** (Noh **Rahman** 34), Shahril **Ishak** (John **Wilkinson**• 70), Hariss **Harun**, Aleksandar **Duric**, Khairul **Amri**•. Tr: Raddy Avramovic

---

King Abdullah, Amman
22-11-2009, 18:00, 11 000, Albadwawi UAE

Jordan 1

Amer Khalil Deeb [78]

Amer **Sabbah** - Bashar Bani **Yaseen**, Hatem **Aqel**, Anas **Bani**, Basem **Othman**, Baha **Suleiman**, Amer **Khalil Deeb**, Mohammad **Jarrar** (Ahmad Al Zugheir 73), Odai Alsaify•, Mohammad **Omar** (Moayad Abukeshek 57), Hassouneh **Qasem**• (Abdallah Salim 46). Tr: Adnan Hamad

Iran 0

Seyed **Rahmati** - Hadi **Aghili**, Mohammad Nosrati, Khosro Heydari (Hashem Beikzadeh 77), Hossein **Kaebi**, Andranik Teymourian, Ehsan Hajy-Safi, Pejman **Nouri**, Mohammad Khalatbari, Eman Mobali (Milad Midavoudi 60), Karim Ansarifard (Arash Borhani 85).

National Stadium, Singapore
6-01-2010, 19:30, 7356, Sun Baojie CHN

Singapore 0

Hassan **Sunny** - Baihakki **Khaizan**, Precious **Emuejeraye**, Daniel **Bennett**, Shaiful **Esah**•, Ridhuan **Muhamad**, Mustafic **Fahrudin**• (Noh **Rahman** 75), Hariss **Harun**, Noh Alam **Shah**•, Aleksandar **Duric** (Indra Sahdan **Daud** 60), Fazrul **Nawaz** (Khairul Amri 46). Tr: Raddy Avramovic

Iran 3

Aghili [11p], Madanchi [12], Rezaei [62]

Seyed **Rahmati** - Seyed Hosseini, Hadi **Aghili**, Khosro **Heydari**, Mehrzad **Madanchi**, Andranik Teymourian•, Ehsan Hajy-Safi, Pejman **Nouri**, Mohammad **Khalatbari** (Hossein **Kaebi** 90), Milad **Zanidpour** (Gholamreza **Rezaei** 57), Milad **Midavoudi** (Karim Ansarifard 70). Tr: Afshin Ghotbi

---

Rajamangala, Bangkok
6-01-2010, 19:00, 15 000, Williams AUS

Thailand 0

Kosin **Hathairattanakool** - Suree **Sukha**, Nattaporn **Phanrit**, Natthaphong **Samana**, Panupong **Wongsa**, Rangsan **Vivatchaichok** (Keerati Keawsombat 74), Suchao **Nutnum** (Pipat Thonkanya 88), Pichitpong **Choechiu**•, Narongchai **Vachiraban**, Teeratep Winothai, Sutee **Suksomkit** (Therdsak **Chaiman** 76). Tr: Robson

Jordan 0

Amer **Sabbah** - Bashar Bani Yaseen, Hatem **Aqel**, Anas **Bani**, Basem **Othman**•, Baha **Suleiman**, Amer **Khalil Deeb**, Abdallah **Salim** (Ahmad Al Zugheir• 59), Mohammad **Jarrar**•, Odai Alsaify (Mohammed Al Jamal 86), Mahmoud Shelbaieh• (Moayad Abukeshek 53). Tr: Adnan Hamad

---

Azadi, Tehran
3-03-2010, 19:30, 17 000, Balideh QAT

Iran 1

Javad Nekounam [90]

Seyed **Rahmati** - Seyed Hosseini, Hadi **Aghili**, Khosro **Heydari**, Mehrzad **Madanchi**• (Milad Zanidpour 24), Andranik Teymourian•, Ehsan Hajy-Safi, Mohammad **Khalatbari** (Gholamreza **Rezaei** 73), Javad **Nekounam**, Ali **Karimi**, Masoud Shojaei (Karim Ansarifard• 64). Tr: Afshin Ghotbi

Thailand 0

Kawin **Thammasatchanan** - Suree **Sukha**, Nattaporn **Phanrit**, Natthaphong **Samana**, Panupong **Wongsa**, Suchao **Nutnum** (Datsakorn Thonglao 69), Sukha **Surat** (Cholratit Jantakam 26), Pichitpong **Choechiu**, Teeratep **Winothai**• (Pipat Thonkanya 69), Sutee **Suksomkit**, Keerati **Keawsombat**. Tr: Bryan Robson

---

International, Amman
3-03-2010, 18:00, 17 000, Abdou QAT

Jordan 2

Odai Alsaify [9], Bashar Bani Yaseen [60]

Amer **Sabbah** - Bashar Bani **Yaseen**, Hatem **Aqel**, Anas **Bani**, Basem **Othman**•, Amer **Khalil Deeb** (Mohamad Maharmeh 85), Moayad Abukeshek (Ahmad Al Zugheir 56), Mohammad **Jarrar**, Odai Alsaify (Qusai Abu Alieh 90), Hassouneh **Qasem**. Tr: Adnan Hamad

Singapore 1

Noh Alam Shah [48]

Lewis **Lionel** - Baihakki **Khaizan**, Noh **Rahman** (Rosman Sulaiman• 29), Precious **Emuejeraye**, Daniel **Bennett**, Ridhuan **Muhamad** (Shahril Ishak 86), Shi Jiayi, Hariss **Harun**, Noh Alam **Shah**, Aleksandar **Duric**, Li Qiu. Tr: Raddy Avramovic

AFC ASIAN CUP QATAR 2011
FINAL TOURNAMENT

	GROUP A	PL	W	D	L	F	A	PTS		QAT	CHN	KUW
1	Uzbekistan	3	2	1	0	6	3	7		2-0	2-2	2-1
2	Qatar	3	2	0	1	5	2	6			2-0	3-0
3	China PR	3	1	1	1	4	4	4				2-0
4	Kuwait	3	0	0	3	1	7	0				

Khalifa International, Doha, 7-01-2011, 19:15, 37 143, Nishimura JPN

Qatar 0

1 Qasem Burhan - 2 Hamid Ismail, 6 Bilal Mohammed, 18 Ibrahim Al Ghanim, 13 Ibrahim Majed - 11 Fabio Cesar (12 Yusef Ali Ahmed 80), 4 Lawrence Quaye, 7 Wesam Rizik•, 10 Hussain Yasser (14 Khalfan Ibrahim 61) - 9 Jaralla Al Marri (16 Mohammed Mubarak El Sayed 62), 23 Sebastian Soria. Tr: Bruno Metsu

Uzbekistan 2
Odil Ahmedov 59, Server Djeparov 77

12 Ignatiy Nesterov - 22 Viktor Karpenko, 4 Anzur Ismailov, 9 Odil Ahmedov, 6 Sakhob Jurayev (14 Stanislav Andreev 54) - 16 Maksim Shatskikh, 7 Azizbek Haydarov, 8 Server Djeparov, 18 Timur Kapadze, 19 Jansur Hasanov (17 Sanzhar Tursunov 66) - 15 Alexander Geynrikh (13 Olim Navkarov 89). Tr: Vadim Abramov

Al Gharafa, Doha, 12-01-2011, 16:15, 3481, Shukralla BHR

Uzbekistan 2
Maksim Shatskikh 41, Server Djeparov 65

12 Ignatiy Nesterov - 22 Viktor Karpenko, 4 Anzur Ismailov, 9 Odil Ahmedov, 14 Stanislav Andreev - 18 Timur Kapadze, 7 Azizbek Haydarov - 17 Sanzhar Tursunov (23 Vagiz Galiulin 90), 16 Maksim Shatskikh (19 Jansur Hasanov• 54), 8 Server Djeparov - 15 Alexander Geynrikh• (Olim Navkarov 74). Tr: Vadim Abramov

Kuwait 1
Bader Al Mutwa 50p

22 Nawaf Al Khaldi - 2 Yaqoub Al Taher, 4 Hussein Fadhel•, 6 Amer Matoug Al Fadhel, 3 Fahad Awad Shaheen (5 Ahmad Ajab Alzemi 80) - 7 Fahad Al Enezi, 14 Talal Al Amer, 18 Jarah Al Ateeqi (16 Hamad Nayef Al Enezi 46), 15 Waleed Jumah Ali (Abdulaziz Mashan Al Enezi 71) - 17 Bader Al Mutwa, 20 Yousef Naser. Tr: Goran Tufegdzic

Khalifa International, Doha, 16-01-2011, 19:15, 28 339, Bashir SIN

Qatar 3
Bilal Mohammed 12, Mohamed El Sayed 16, Fabio Cesar 86

1 Qasem Burhan - 3 Mohammed Kasola• (8 Mesaad Ali Al Hamad 88), 6 Bilal Mohammed, 18 Ibrahim Al Ghanim, 13 Ibrahim Majed - 2 Hamid Ismail•, 4 Lawrence Quaye, 7 Wesam Rizik, 16 Mohammed El Sayed (20 Ali Hasan Yahya Afif 80) - 12 Yusef Ali Ahmed• (11 Fabio Cesar 72), 23 Sebastian Soria. Tr: Bruno Metsu

Kuwait 0

22 Nawaf Al Khaldi - 2 Yaqoub Al Taher (5 Ahmad Ajab Alzemi 46), 4 Hussein Fadhel•, 19 Ahmad Al Rashidi, 6 Amer Matoug Al Fadhel• - 7 Fahad Al Enezi, 14 Talal Al Amer•, 8 Saleh Al Sheikh• (21 Abdulaziz Mashan Al Enezi 62), 15 Waleed Jumah Ali - 17 Bader Al Mutwa, 16 Hamad Nayef Al Enezi (10 Khaled Khalaf Al Rashidi 79). Tr: Goran Tufegdzic

Al Gharafa, Doha, 8-01-2011, 16:15, 7423, Williams AUS

Kuwait 0

22 Nawaf Al Khaldi - 2 Yaqoub Al Taher•, 4 Hussein Fadhel, 13 Mesaed Neda Al Enezi♦36, 6 Amer Matoug Al Fadhel - 17 Bader Al Mutwa, 7 Fahad Al Enezi (16 Hamad Nayef Al Rashidi 84), 14 Talal Al Amer, 15 Waleed Jumah Ali (21 Abdulaziz Mashan Al Enezi 71) - 18 Jarah Al Ateeqi•, 20 Yousef Naser (3 Fahad Awad Shaheen 36). Tr: Goran Tufegdzic

China PR 2
Zhang Linpeng 58, Deng Zhuoxiang 67

1 Yang Zhi - 17 Zhang Linpeng, 5 Du Wei, 4 Zhao Peng (13 Liu Jianye 58), 20 Rong Hao - 7 Zhao Xuri (15 Yu Tao 77), 19 Yang Hao - 11 Qu Bo• (8 Hao Junmin 46), 10 Deng Zhuoxiang, 21 Yu Hai - 9 Yang Xu. Tr: Gao Hongbo

Khalifa International, Doha, 12-01-2011, 19:15, 30 778, Kim Dong Jin KOR

Qatar 2
Yusef Ahmed 2 27 45

1 Qasem Burhan - 3 Mohammed Kasola• (8 Mesaad Ali Al Hamad 61), 6 Bilal Mohammed•, 18 Ibrahim Al Ghanim, 13 Ibrahim Majed - 20 Ali Hasan Yahya Afif 90), 4 Lawrence Quaye, 7 Wesam Rizik, 16 Mohammed El Sayed - 12 Yusef Ali Ahmed (9 Jaralla Al Marri 64), 23 Sebastian Soria. Tr: Bruno Metsu

China PR 0

22 Zeng Cheng - 17 Zhang Linpeng•, 5 Du Wei, 4 Zhao Peng, 20 Rong Hao - 15 Yu Tao (6 Zhou Haibin 59), 19 Yang Hao• - 11 Qu Bo•, 10 Deng Zhuoxiang, 21 Yu Hai (8 Hao Junmin 46) - 18 Gao Lin (9 Yang Xu 42). Tr: Gao Hongbo

Al Gharafa, Doha, 16-01-2011, 19:15, 3529, Al Hilali OMA

China PR 2
Yu Hai 6, Hao Junmin 56

1 Yang Zhi - 17 Zhang Linpeng•, 5 Du Wei, 2 Li Xuepeng, 20 Rong Hao - 7 Zhao Xuri (13 Liu Jianye 46), 19 Yang Hao (10 Deng Zhuoxiang 73) - 8 Hao Junmin•, 14 Wang Song, 21 Yu Hai (9 Yang Xu 60) - 18 Gao Lin. Tr: Gao Hongbo

Uzbekistan 2
Odil Ahmedov 30, Alexander Geynrikh 46

12 Ignatiy Nesterov - 22 Viktor Karpenko (Shavkatjon Mulladjanov 74), 4 Anzur Ismailov•, 9 Odil Ahmedov, 14 Stanislav Andreev - 18 Timur Kapadze•, 7 Azizbek Haydarov• - 13 Olim Navkarov (Sanzhar Tursunov 62), 16 Maksim Shatskikh, 8 Server Djeparov (Shavkat Salomov 85) - 15 Alexander Geynrikh. Tr: Vadim Abramov

	GROUP B	PL	W	D	L	F	A	PTS		JOR	SYR	KSA
1	Japan	3	2	1	0	8	2	7		1-1	2-1	5-0
2	Jordan	3	2	1	0	4	2	7			2-1	1-0
3	Syria	3	1	0	2	4	5	3				2-1
4	Saudi Arabia	3	0	0	3	1	8	0				

Qatar Sports Club, Doha, 9-01-2011, 16:15, 6255, Abdul Bashir SIN

Japan 1

Maya Yoshida [92+]

1 Eiji Kawashima – 6 Atsuto Uchida, 22 Maya Yoshida, 4 Yasuyuki Konno, 5 Yuto Nagatomo – 7 Yasuhito Endo, 17 Makoto Hasebe – 8 Daisuke Matsui (9 Shinji Okazaki 58), 18 Keisuke Honda (14 Jungo Fujimoto 70), 10 Shinji Kagawa – 11 Ryoichi Maeda (Tadanari Lee 46). Tr: Alberto Zaccheroni

Jordan 1

Hasan Abdel Fattah [45]

1 Amer Sabah – 3 Suleiman Salman, 8 Bashar Bani Yaseen, 17 Hatem Aqel• (5 Mohammad Al Dumeiri 80), 16 Basem Fatahi – 7 Amer Deeb, 4 Baha'a Abdul Rahman, 15 Shadi Abu Hashhash, 18 Hasan Abdel Fattah•, 9 Odai Al Saify – 14 Abdallah Salim Deeb (21 Ahmad Abdelhalim 72). Tr: Adnan Hamad

Ahmed Bin Ali, Al Rayyan, 13-01-2011, 16:15, 17 349, Albadwawi UAE

Jordan 1

Baha Abdelrahman [42]

1 Amer Sabah – 3 Suleiman Salman, 8 Bashar Bani Yaseen, 2 Mohammad Moneer, 16 Basem Fatahi• – 7 Amer Deeb• (23 Anas Hajjeh 90), 4 Baha'a Abdul Rahman, 15 Shadi Abu Hashhash, 9 Odai Al Saify• – 14 Abdallah Salim Deeb (10 Moayyad Abu Keshek• 69), 18 Hasan Abdel Fattah (21 Ahmad Abdelhalim 83). Tr: Adnan Hamad

Saudi Arabia 0

1 Waleed Abdullah – 2 Abdullah Al Shuhail (16 Abdulaziz Al Dosari 87), 3 Osama Hawsawi, 5 Osama Al Harbi•, 7 Kamil Al Mousa – 15 Abdoh Autef (11 Nasser Al Shamrani 46), 14 Saud Khariri, 17 Taisir Al Jassim, 10 Mohammad Al Shalhoub (18 Nawaf Al Abed 65) – 9 Naif Hazazi, 20 Yasser Al Kahtani. Tr: Nasser Al Johar

Ahmed Bin Ali, Al Rayyan, 17-01-2011, 16:15, 2022, Irmatov UZB

Saudi Arabia 0

1 Waleed Abdullah – 2 Abdullah Al Shuhail, 3 Osama Hawsawi, 5 Osama Al Harbi, 7 Kamil Al Mousa• – 15 Abdoh Autef (8 Manaf Abushgeer 28), 6 Ahmed Ateef, 17 Taisir Al Jassim, 10 Mohammad Al Shalhoub – 20 Yasser Al Kahtani, 9 Naif Hazazi (13 Motaz Al Mosa• 46). Tr: Nasser Al Johar

Japan 5

Shinji Okazaki 3 [8 13 80], Ryoichi Maeda 2 [19 51]

21 Shusaku Nishikawa – 6 Atsuto Uchida (2 Masahiko Inoha 46), 22 Maya Yoshida (3 Daiki Iwamasa 63), 4 Yasuyuki Konno, 5 Yuto Nagatomo – 17 Makoto Hasebe, 7 Yasuhito Endo (15 Takuya Honda 87) – 9 Shinji Okazaki, 16 Yosuke Kashiwagi, 10 Shinji Kagawa – 11 Ryoichi Maeda. Tr: Alberto Zaccheroni

Ahmed Bin Ali, Al Rayyan, 9-01-2011, 19:15, 15 768, Kim Dong Jin KOR

Saudi Arabia 1

Taiseer Al Jassam [60]

1 Waleed Abdullah – 2 Abdullah Al Shuhail, 3 Osama Hawsawi, 14 Saud Khariri, 5 Osama Al Harbi – 6 Ahmed Ateef•, 15 Abdoh Autef (17 Taisir Al Jassim 46), 8 Manaf Abushgeer (18 Nawaf Al Abed 68), 12 Mishal Al Saeed• – 11 Nasser Al Shamrani (9 Naif Hazazi 57), 20 Yasser Al Kahtani. Tr: Jose Peseiro

Syria 1

Abdulrazak Al Hussein 2 [38 63]

1 Mosab Balhous – 2 Belal Abduldaim•, 3 Ali Diab, 17 Abdulkader Dakka, 13 Nadim Sabagh – 7 Abdelrazag Al Hussain•, 5 Feras Esmaeel – 6 Jehad Al Hussain• (9 Qusay Habib 76), 19 Sanharib Malki (11 Adel Abdullah 65), 14 Wael Ayan (23 Samer Awad 83) – 12 Mohamed Al Zeno, Tr: Valeriu Tita

Qatar Sports Club, Doha, 13-01-2011, 19:15, 10 453, Torky IRN

Syria 1

Firas Al Khatib [76p]

1 Mosab Balhous – 2 Belal Abduldaim, 3 Ali Diab•, 17 Abdulkader Dakka•, 13 Nadim Sabagh•♦90 – 7 Abdelrazag Al Hussain, 5 Feras Esmaeel – 6 Jehad Al Hussain (18 Abdul Fattah Al Agha• 77), 23 Samer Awad• (10 Firas Al Khatib 46), 14 Wael Ayan – 12 Mohamed Al Zeno (19 Sanharib Malki 64). Tr: Valeriu Tita

Japan 2

Makoto Hasebe [35], Keisuke Honda [82p]

1 Eiji Kawashima♦72 – 6 Atsuto Uchida•, 22 Maya Yoshida•, 4 Yasuyuki Konno, 5 Yuto Nagatomo – 7 Yasuhito Endo, 17 Makoto Hasebe – 8 Daisuke Matsui• (13 Hajime Hosogai 90), 18 Keisuke Honda, 10 Shinji Kagawa (9 Shinji Okazaki 65) – 11 Ryoichi Maeda (21 Shusaku Nishikawa 75). Tr: Alberto Zaccheroni

Qatar Sports Club, Doha, 17-01-2011, 16:15, 9849, Abdou QAT

Jordan 2

Ali Dyab OG [30], Odai Al Saify [59]

1 Amer Sabah – 3 Suleiman Salman, 8 Bashar Bani Yaseen, 16 Basem Fatahi• – 7 Amer Deeb, 4 Baha'a Abdul Rahman, 15 Shadi Abu Hashhash, 9 Odai Al Saify (23 Anas Hajjeh 90) – 14 Abdallah Salim Deeb• (10 Moayyad Abu Keshek 62), 18 Hasan Abdel Fattah (21 Ahmad Abdelhalim 88). Tr: Adnan Hamad

Syria 1

Mohamad Al Zeno [15]

1 Mosab Balhous• – 2 Belal Abduldaim• (9 Qusay Habib 78), 3 Ali Diab (20 Louay Chanko 63), 17 Abdulkader Dakka, 19 Sanharib Malki – 7 Abdelrazag Al Hussain, 5 Feras Esmaeel – 6 Jehad Al Hussain, 23 Samer Awad (10 Firas Al Khatib 63), 14 Wael Ayan – 12 Mohamed Al Zeno. Tr: Valeriu Tita

	GROUP C	PL	W	D	L	F	A	PTS		KOR	BHR	IND
1	Australia	3	2	1	0	6	1	7		1-1	1-0	4-0
2	Korea Republic	3	2	1	0	7	3	7			2-1	4-1
3	Bahrain	3	1	0	2	6	5	3				5-2
4	India	3	0	0	3	3	13	0				

Al Saad, Doha, 10-01-2011, 16:15, 9783, Albadwawi UAE

India 0

1 Subrata Pal – 17 Surkumar Singh, 19 Gouramangi Singh, 5 Anwar Ali, 12 Deepak Kumar Mondal – 23 Steven Dias (8 Renedy Singh 79), 20 Climax Lawrence, 7 Pappachan Pradeep (16 Mehrjajuddin Wadoo 61), 22 Syed Rahim Nabi – 18 Mohammed Rafi (9 Abhishek Yadav 63), 11 Sunil Chhetri. Tr: Bob Houghton

Australia 4

Tim Cahill 2 [12 65], Harry Kewell [25], Brett Holman [45]

1 Mark Schwarzer – 2 Lucas Neill, 3 David Carney, 6 Sasa Ognenovski, 8 Luke Wilkshire, 4 Tim Cahill, 5 Jason Culina, 7 Brett Emerton (Nathan Burns 77), 10 Harry Kewell (Scott McDonald 79), 14 Brett Holman, 15 Mile Jedinak (Matt McKay 62). Tr: Holger Osieck

Al Gharafa, Doha, 10-01-2011, 19:15, 6669, Al Hilali OMA

Korea Republic 2

Koo Ja Cheol 2 [40 52]

1 Jung Sung Ryong – 22 Cha Du Ri, 5 Kwak Tae Hwi♦83, 14 Lee Jung Soo•, 12 Lee Young Pyo – 16 Ki Sung Yueng, 6 Lee Yong Rae – 17 Lee Chung Yong, 7 Park Ji Sung, 13 Koo Ja Cheol (19 Yeom Ki Hun 78) – 10 Ji Dong Won (11 Son Heung Min 68) 4 Cho Yong Hyung 85). Tr: Cho Kwang Rae

Bahrain 1

Faouzi Aaish [86p]

1 Mahmood Mansour – 15 Abdullah Omar, 3 Abdulla Marzooq, 23 Ebrahim Al Mishkhas, 2 Rashed Khalil Al Hooti – 11 Ismaeel Abdullatif (20 Abdulla Al Dakeel 79), 4 Abdulla Fatadi, 12 Faouzi Aaish•, 17 Hussain Ali Baba (7 Hamad Rakea 12), 13 Mahmood Abdulrahman (6 Abbas Ayyad 69) – 8 Jaycee John Okwunwanne. Tr: Salman Sharida

---

Al Gharafa, Doha, 14-01-2011, 16:15, 15 526, Abdou QAT

Australia   **1**

Mile Jedinak [62]

1 Mark **Schwarzer** - 8 Luke **Wilkshire** (13 Jade **North** 68), 2 Lucas **Neill**, 6 Sasa **Ognenovski**•, 3 David **Carney** - 7 Brett **Emerton**•, 5 Jason **Culina** (16 Carl **Valeri** 46), 15 Mile **Jedinak**, 14 Brett **Holman** (17 Matt **McKay** 89) - 10 Harry **Kewell**, 4 Tim **Cahill**•. Tr: Holger **Osieck**

Korea Republic   **1**

Koo Ja Cheol [24]

1 Jung Sung Ryong - 22 **Cha** Du Ri•, 14 **Lee** Jung Soo, 3 **Hwang** Jae Won, 12 **Lee** Young Pyo - 16 **Ki** Sung Yueng•, 6 **Lee** Yong Rae - 17 **Lee** Chung Yong, 7 **Park** Ji Sung, 13 **Koo** Ja Cheol (19 **Yeom** Ki Hun 67) - 10 **Ji** Dong Won (9 **Yoo** Byung Soo 67) (8 **Yoon** Bit Garam 89). Tr: **Kim** Shin Wook

---

Al Gharafa, Doha, 18-01-2011, 16:15, 11 366, Al Ghamdi KSA

Korea Republic   **4**

Ji Dong Won [6 23], Koo Ja Cheol [9], Son Heung Min [81]

1 Jung Sung Ryong - 22 **Cha** Du Ri (2 **Choi** Hyo Jin 46), 3 **Hwang** Jae Won, 5 **Kwak** Tae Hwi, 12 **Lee** Young Pyo - 16 **Ki** Sung Yueng (11 **Son** Heung Min 46), 6 **Lee** Yong Rae - 17 **Lee** Chung Yong, 7 **Park** Ji Sung (8 **Yoon** Bit Garam 76), 13 **Koo** Ja Cheol - 10 **Ji** Dong Won. Tr: **Cho** Kwang Rae

India   **1**

Sunil Chhetri [12p]

1 Subrata **Pal** - 17 Surkurmar **Singh**, 19 Gouramangi **Singh**, 5 Anwar **Ali**, 8 Renedy **Singh** (12 Deepak Kumar **Mondal** 5) - 23 Steven **Dias**, 20 Climax **Lawrence**, 7 Pappachan **Pradeep** (16 Mehrjajuddin **Wadoo** 56), 22 Syed Rahim **Nabi**• - 11 Sunil **Chhetri**, 9 Abhishek **Yadav** (15 Baichung **Bhutia** 78). Tr: Bob **Houghton**

Al Saad, Doha, 14-01-2011, 19:15, 11 032, Mohd Salleh MAS

Bahrain   **5**

Faouzi Aaish [8p], Ismaeel Abdulatif 4 [16 20 35 77]

1 Mahmood **Mansour**, 15 Abdullah **Omar**, 3 Abdulla **Marzooq**, 23 Ebrahim **Al Mishkhas**, 14 Salman **Isa** - 11 Ismaeel **Abdullatif** (16 Dawood **Saad** 83), 18 Abdulwahab **Ali** Al Safi, 20 Abdulla **Al Dakeel** (13 Mahmood **Abdulrahman** 67), 7 Hamad **Rakea**, 12 Faouzi **Aaish**•◆[62] - 8 Jaycee **John** Okwunwanne (4 Abdulla **Fatadi** 78), Tr: Salman **Sharida**

India   **2**

Gouramangi Singh [10], Sunil Chhetri [53]

1 Subrata **Pal** - 17 Surkurmar **Singh**, 19 Gouramangi **Singh**, 5 Anwar **Ali**, 22 Syed Rahim **Nabi** - 23 Steven **Dias**•, 20 Climax **Lawrence**, 7 Pappachan **Pradeep** (12 Deepak Kumar **Mondal** 74), 8 Renedy **Singh** (16 Mehrjajuddin **Wadoo** 74) - 9 Abhishek **Yadav**, 11 Sunil **Chhetri**•. Tr: Bob **Houghton**

Al Saad, Doha, 18-01-2011, 16:15, 3919, Nishimura JPN

Australia   **1**

Mile Jedinak [37]

1 Mark **Schwarzer** - 13 Jade **North** (22 Neil **Kilkenny** 80), 2 Lucas **Neill**, 6 Sasa **Ognenovski**, 15 Mile **Jedinak** - 7 Brett **Emerton**•, 16 Carl **Valeri**, 17 Matt **McKay**, 14 Brett **Holman**• - 10 Harry **Kewell** (9 Scott **McDonald** 76), 4 Tim **Cahill** (23 Robbie **Kruse** 90). Tr: Holger **Osieck**

Bahrain   **0**

1 Mahmood **Mansour**, 15 Abdullah **Omar**, 3 Abdulla **Marzooq**, 23 Ebrahim **Al Mishkhas**•, 14 Salman **Isa** (9 Abdulwahab **Al Malood** 90) - 11 Ismaeel **Abdullatif**, 7 Hamad **Rakea**, 13 Mahmood **Abdulrahman** (2 Rashed Khalil **Al Hooti** 55), 18 Abdulwahab **Ali** Al Safi•, 4 Abdulla **Fatadi**• - 8 Jaycee **John** Okwunwanne• (20 Abdulla **Al Dakeel** 66), Tr: Salman **Sharida**

	GROUP D	PL	W	D	L	F	A	PTS	IRQ	KOR	UAE
1	Iran	3	3	0	0	6	1	9	2-1	1-0	3-0
2	Iraq	3	2	0	1	3	6	6		1-0	1-0
3	Korea DPR	3	0	1	2	0	2	1			0-0
4	UAE	3	0	1	2	0	4	1			

Qatar Sports Club, Doha, 11-01-2011, 16:15, 3639, Mohd Salleh MAS

Korea DPR   **0**

1 **Ri** Myong Guk - 2 **Cha** Jong Hyok•, 14 **Pak** Nam Chol•, 5 **Ri** Kwang Chon, 12 **Kwang** Ik Jon - 23 **Kim** Kuk Jin, 17 **An** Young Hak, 7 **Ryang** Yong Gi, 4 **Pak** Nam Chol (6 **Choe** Myong Ho 79) - 10 **Hong** Yong Jo (19 **An** Chol Hyok 48), 9 **Jong** Tae Se (21 **Pak** Chol Min 83). Tr: **Jo** Tong Sop

United Arab Emirates   **0**

1 Majed **Nasser** - 2 Khalid **Ibrahim** Sabeel, 8 Hamdan **Al Kamali**•, 14 Waleed **Abbas** Yousuf, 17 Yousef **Jaber** - 5 Amer **Abdulrahman**, 4 Subait **Khater** - 7 Ali **Al Wehaibi** (23 Omar **Abdulrahman** 90), 10 Ismail **Matar** (9 Mohamed **Al Shehhi** 90), 15 Ismail **Al Hammadi** - 11 Ahmed **Khalil** (20 Saeed **Al Kathiri** 77). Tr: Srecko **Katanec**

Qatar Sports Club, Doha, 15-01-2011, 16:15, 6488, Shukralla BHR

Iran   **1**

Karim Ansarifard [63]

1 Seyed **Rahmati**, 20 Mohammad **Nosrati** (7 Gholamreza **Rezaei** 61), 5 Hadi **Aghily**, 4 Jalal **Hosseini**, 11 Ehsan **Hajsafi** - 2 Khosro **Heydari**•, 6 Javad **Nekounam**, 18 Pejman **Nouri**•, 23 Eman **Mobali** (17 Mohammad **Nouri** 46), 9 Mohammad Reza **Khalatbari** - 10 Karim **Ansarifard**• (19 Mohamad **Gholami** 90). Tr: Afshin **Ghotbi**

Korea DPR   **0**

1 **Ri** Myong Guk - 2 **Cha** Jong Hyok, 3 **Ri** Jun Il, 5 **Ri** Kwang Chon, 12 **Jon** Kwang Ik - 11 **Mun** In Guk (7 **Ryang** Yong Gi 61), 17 **An** Young Hak, 4 **Pak** Nam Chol•, 23 **Kim** Kuk Jin - 9 **Jong** Tae Se (21 **Pak** Chol Min 65), 10 **Hong** Yong Jo•. Tr: **Jo** Tong Sop

---

Ahmed Bin Ali, Al Rayyan, 11-01-2011, 19:15, 10 478, Irmatov UZB

Iraq   **1**

Younis Mahmood [13]

12 Mohammed **Gassid** - 14 Salam **Shakir** (21 Ahmad **Ibrahim** Khalaf 46), 16 Samal **Saeed**, 15 Ali **Rehema**, 18 Mahdi **Karim** - 4 Qusay **Munir** (9 Mustafa **Karim** 88), 5 Nashat **Akram**, 17 Alaa **Abdul Zahra**, 11 Hawar **Mohammed** - 7 Emad **Mohammed** (8 Samer **Saeed**• 82), 10 Younis **Mahmoud**. Tr: Wolfgang **Sidka**

Iran   **2**

Gholamreza Rezaei [42], Iman Mobali [84]

1 Seyed **Rahmati** - 20 Mohammad **Nosrati**, 5 Hadi **Aghily**, 4 Jalal **Hosseini**, 11 Ehsan **Hajsafi** - 7 Gholamreza **Rezaei**, 6 Javad **Nekounam**, 14 Andranik **Teymourian**, 23 Eman **Mobali** (18 Pejman **Nouri** 87) - 19 Mohamad **Gholami** (10 Karim **Ansarifard** 83), 8 Masoud **Shojaei** (9 Mohammad Reza **Khalatbari** 69). Tr: Afshin **Ghotbi**

Ahmed Bin Ali, Al Rayyan, 15-01-2011, 19:15, 7233, Nishimura JPN

United Arab Emirates   **0**

1 Majed **Nasser** - 2 Khalid **Ibrahim** Sabeel, 8 Hamdan **Al Kamali**, 14 Waleed **Abbas** Yousuf, 17 Yousef **Jaber** - 5 Amer **Abdulrahman**, 4 Subait **Khater** (16 Amir **Mubarak** 84) - 7 Ali **Al Wehaibi** (21 Mahmoud **Khamis** 74), 10 Ismail **Matar**•, 15 Ismail **Al Hammadi** - 11 Ahmed **Khalil** (Saeed **Al Kas** 68). Tr: Srecko **Katanec**

Iraq   **1**

Walid Abbas OG [93+]

12 Mohammed **Gassid** - 21 Ahmad **Ibrahim** Khalaf•, 16 Samal **Saeed**, 15 Ali **Rehema**, 18 Mahdi **Karim** - 4 Qusay **Munir**, 5 Nashat **Akram**, 17 Alaa **Abdul Zahra** (9 Mustafa **Karim** 74), 11 Hawar **Mohammed** (3 Bassim **Abbas** 64) - 7 Emad **Mohammed** (13 Karrar **Jassim** 61), 10 Younis **Mahmoud**. Tr: Wolfgang **Sidka**

Ahmed Bin Ali, Al Rayyan, 19-01-2011, 19:15, 4111, Mohd Salleh MAS

Iraq	1
	Karrar Jasim [22]

12 Mohammed **Gassid** - 16 Samal **Saeed**, 15 Ali **Rehema**, 21 Ahmad **Ibrahim** Khalaf, 3 Bassim **Abbas** - 18 Mahdi **Karim**, 4 Qusay **Munir**, 5 Nashat **Akram**, 13 Karrar **Jassim** (11 Hawar **Mohammed** 77) - 9 Mustafa **Karim** (17 Alaa **Abdul Zahra** 73), 10 Younis **Mahmoud** (20 Muthana **Khalid** 90). Tr: Wolfgang Sidka

Korea DPR	0

1 **Ri** Myong Guk - 2 **Cha** Jong Hyok, 3 **Ri** Jun Il (14 **Pak** Nam Chol 48), 5 **Ri** Kwang Chon, 12 **Jon** Kwang Ik - 23 **Kim** Kuk Jin (11 **Mun** In Guk 70), 17 **An** Young Hak, 4 **Pak** Nam Chol, 7 **Ryang** Yong Gi - 10 **Hong** Yong Jo●, 9 **Jong** Tae Se. Tr: **Jo** Tong Sop

Qatar Sports Club, Doha, 19-01-2011, 19:15, 5012, Kim Dong Jin KOR

United Arab Emirates	0

1 Majed **Nasser**● - 2 Khalid Ibrahim **Sabeel**●◆79, 8 Hamdan **Al Kamali**, 14 Waleed **Abbas** Yousuf, 17 Yousef **Jaber** - 4 Subait **Khater**, 5 Amer **Abdulrahman** (9 Mohamed **Al Shehhi** 64) - 7 Ali **Al Wehaibi** (23 Omar **Abdulrahman** 53), 10 Ismail **Matar**, 15 Ismail **Al Hammadi** - 11 Ahmed **Khalil** (20 Saeed **Al Kathiri** 75). Tr: Srecko Katanec

Iran	3
	Arash Afshin [67], Mohammad Nori [83], Walid Abbas OG [93+]

22 Shahab **Gordan** - 2 Khosro **Heydari**, 3 Farsheed **Talebi**, 13 Mohsen **Bengar**●, 11 Ehsan **Hajsafi** (16 Mohammad **Nosrati** 59) - 14 Andranik **Teymourian** - 21 Arash **Afshin**●◆75, 17 Mohammad **Nouri**, 15 Ghasem **Hadadifar**, 8 Masoud **Shojaei** (7 Gholamreza **Rezaei**● 46) - 19 Mohamad **Gholami** (16 Reza **Norouzi** 84). Tr: Afshin Ghotbi

QUARTER-FINALS

Al Gharafa, Doha, 21-01-2011, 16:25, 19 479, Mohd Salleh MAS

Japan	3
	Shinji Kagawa 2 [29 71], Masahiko Inoha [90]

1 Eiji **Kawashima** - 2 Masahiko **Inoha**, 22 Maya **Yoshida**●◆63, 4 Yasuyuki **Konno**, 5 Yuto **Nagatomo** - 7 Yasuhito **Endo**, 17 Makoto **Hasebe** - 9 Shinji **Okazaki**, 18 Keisuke **Honda**, 10 Shinji **Kagawa** (20 Mitsuru **Nagata** 90) - 11 Ryoichi **Maeda** (3 Daiki **Iwamasa** 64). Tr: Alberto Zaccheroni

Qatar	2
	Sebastian [13], Fabio Cesar [63]

1 Qasem **Burhan** - 13 Ibrahim **Majed** (19 Khaled **Muftah** 14), 6 Bilal **Mohammed**, 18 Ibrahim **Al Ghanim**●, 8 Yusef **Ali** (9 Jaralla **Al Marri** 90) - 2 Hamid **Ismail**, 4 Lawrence **Quaye**, 7 Wesam **Rizik**, 16 Mohammed Mubarak **El Sayed** (11 **Fabio Cesar** 59) - 12 Mesaad **Al Hamad**, 23 Sebastian **Soria**. Tr: Bruno Metsu

Khalifa International, Doha, 21-01-2011, 19:25, 16 073, Bashir SIN

Uzbekistan	2
	Ulugbek Bakaev 2 [47 49]

12 Ignatiy **Nesterov** (1 Temur **Juraev** 62) - 3 Shavkatjon **Mulladjanov**, 9 Odil **Ahmedov**, 6 Sakhob **Jurayev** - 17 Sanzhar **Tursunov**●, 18 Timur **Kapadze**, 7 Azizbek **Haydarov**, 8 Server **Djeparov**, 19 Jansur **Hasanov** (14 Stanislav **Andreev** 57) - 2 Ulugbek **Bakaev**●, 15 Alexander **Geynrikh** (4 Anzur **Ismailov** 70). Tr: Vadim Abramov

Jordan	1
	Bashar Bani Yaseen [58]

1 Amer **Sabah** - 2 Mohammad **Moneer**, 3 Suleiman **Salman**●, 5 Mohammad **Al Dumeiri**, 8 Bashar **Bani Yaseen**, 15 Shadi **Abu Hashhash** (14 Abdallah **Salim** 64), 4 Baha'a **Abdul Rahman**, Amer **Deeb**, 18 Hasan **Abdel Fattah**, 21 Ahmad **Abdelhalim**, 10 Moayyad **Abu Keshek** (23 Anas **Hajjeh** 76). Tr: Adnan Hamad

Al Saad, Doha, 22-01-2011, 16:25, 7889, Abdou QAT

Australia	1
	Harry Kewell [118]

1 Mark **Schwarzer** - 8 Luke **Wilkshire**, 2 Lucas **Neill**●, 6 Sasa **Ognenovski**, 3 David **Carney**● (22 Neil **Kilkenny** 109) - 14 Brett **Holman** (11 Nathan **Burns** 102), 15 Mile **Jedinak**●, 16 Carl **Valeri**, 17 Matt **McKay** - 10 Harry **Kewell**●, 4 Tim **Cahill** (9 Scott **McDonald** 90). Tr: Holger Osieck

Iraq	0

12 Mohammed **Gassid** - 15 Ali **Rehema**●, 16 Samal **Saeed**, 14 Salam **Shakir** (21 Ahmad **Ibrahim** Khalaf 75), 3 Bassim **Abbas**● - 18 Mahdi **Karim** (9 Mustafa **Karim** 63), 4 Qusay **Munir**, 5 Nashat **Akram**●, 11 Hawar **Mohammed** (17 Alaa **Abdul Zahra** 86) - 7 Emad **Mohammed**, 10 Younis **Mahmoud**●. Tr: Wolfgang Sidka

Qatar Sports Club, Doha, 22-01-2011, 19:25, 7111, Irmatov UZB

Iran	0

1 Seyed **Rahmati** - 20 Mohammad **Nosrati** (2 Khosro **Heydari** 46), 5 Hadi **Aghily**, 4 Jalal **Hosseini**, 11 Ehsan **Hajsafi** - 6 Javad **Nekounam**, 18 Pejman **Nouri** (19 Mohamad **Gholami** 109), 14 Andranik **Teymourian**●, 9 Mohammad Reza **Khalatbari** - 7 Gholamreza **Rezaei**, 10 Karim **Ansarifard** (8 Masoud **Shojaei**● 75). Tr: Afshin Ghotbi

Korea Republic	1
	Yoon Bit Garam [105]

1 Jung Sung Ryong - 22 **Cha** Du Ri, 3 **Hwang** Jae Won, 14 **Lee** Jung Soo●, 12 **Lee** Young Pyo - 16 **Ki** Sung Yueng (15 **Hong** Jeong Ho 111), 6 **Lee** Yong Rae - 17 **Lee** Chung Yong●, 7 **Park** Ji Sung (19 **Yeom** Ki Hun 117), 13 **Koo** Ja Cheol (8 **Yoon** Bit Garam● 81) - 10 **Ji** Dong Won. Tr: **Cho** Kwang Rae

SEMI-FINALS

Al Gharafa, Doha, 25-01-2011, 16:25, 16 171, Al Ghamdi KSA

Japan	2 3p
	Ryoichi Maeda [36], Hajime Hosogai [97]

1 Eiji **Kawashima** - 6 Atsuto **Uchida**●, 3 Daiki **Iwamasa**●, 4 Yasuyuki **Konno**, 5 Yuto **Nagatomo**● - 7 Yasuhito **Endo**, 17 Makoto **Hasebe** (15 Takuya **Honda** 117) - 9 Shinji **Okazaki**, 18 Keisuke **Honda**, 10 Shinji **Kagawa** (13 Hajime **Hosogai** 87) - 11 Ryoichi **Maeda** (2 Masahiko **Inoha** 105). Tr: Alberto Zaccheroni

Korea Republic	2 0p
	Ki Sung Yueng [23p], Hwang Jae Won [120]

1 **Jung** Sung Ryong - 22 **Cha** Du Ri●, 3 **Hwang** Jae Won, 4 **Cho** Yong Hyung● (**Kim** Shin Wook 103), 12 **Lee** Young Pyo - 16 **Ki** Sung Yueng, 6 **Lee** Yong Rae - 17 **Lee** Chung Yong (**Son** Heung Min 82), 7 **Park** Ji Sung●, 13 **Koo** Ja Cheol - 10 **Ji** Dong Won (**Hong** Jeong Ho 66). Tr: **Cho** Kwang Rae

Khalifa International, Doha, 25-01-2011, 19:25, 24 826, Albadwawi UAE

Australia	6
	Harry Kewell [5], Sasa Ognenovski [35], David Carney [65], Brett Emerton [73], Carl Valeri [82], Robbie Kruse [83]

1 Mark **Schwarzer** - 8 Luke **Wilkshire**●, 2 Lucas **Neill**, 6 Sasa **Ognenovski**, 3 David **Carney**● - 14 Brett **Holman** (7 Brett **Emerton** 61), 15 Mile **Jedinak**, 16 Carl **Valeri**●, 17 Matt **McKay** - 10 Harry **Kewell** (23 Robbie **Kruse** 53), 4 Tim **Cahill** (22 Neil **Kilkenny** 71). Tr: Holger Osieck

Uzbekistan	0

1 Temur **Juraev** - 22 Victor **Karpenko** (5 Aziz **Ibragimov** 71), 4 Anzur **Ismailov**, 9 Odil **Ahmedov**, 6 Sakhob **Jurayev** - 18 Timur **Kapadze**, 7 Azizbek **Haydarov**, 19 Jansur **Hasanov** (11 Marat **Bikmaev** 55) - 16 Maksim **Shatskikh** (17 Sanzhar **Tursunov** 59), 2 Ulugbek **Bakaev**●◆67, 8 Server **Djeparov**. Tr: Vadim Abramov ◆57

See page 890 for details of the Japan v Korea Republic penalty shoot-out and the third place play-off between Korea Republic and Uzbekistan

AFC Asian Cup Final	Khalifa International Stadium Doha	Saturday 29-01-2011
Kick-off: 18:00	Very good weather 20°	Attendance: 37 174

JAPAN   1   0   AUSTRALIA

Tadanari Lee [109]

JAPAN

Blue shirts, White shorts, Blue socks
Tr: Alberto Zaccheroni

Eiji Kawashima

| 120 | Asuto Uchida Masahiko Inoha | Maya Yoshida | Yasuyuki Konno | Yuto Nagatomo |

Makoto Hasebe (c)   Yasuhito Endo

Keisuke Honda

| 56 | Jungo Fujimoto Daiki Iwamasa | | Shinji Okazaki |

| 98 | Ryoichi Maeda Tadanari Lee |

| 109 | Tim Cahill Neil Kilkenny | | 103 | Harry Kewell Robbie Kruse |

Matt McKay [112]

| 65 | Brett Holman [39] Brett Emerton |

Carl Valeri [16]   Mile Jedinak

David Carney   Sasa Ognenovski   Lucas Neill (c)   Luke Wilkshire

Mark Schwarzer

Tr: Holger Osieck
Yellow shirts, Green shorts, Yellow socks

AUSTRALIA

MATCH STATS

JPN		AUS
9	Shots	20
3	Shots on Goal	8
14	Fouls Committed	22
6	Corner Kicks	9
1	Caught Offside	3
55%	Possession	45%

MATCH OFFICIALS

REFEREE
Ravshan Irmatov UZB

ASSISTANTS
Abdukhamidullo Rasulov UZB
Rafael Ilyasov UZB

4TH OFFICIAL
Subkhiddin Mohd Salleh MAS

(C) Captain † Man of the Match

In attack we played with speed and accuracy, that's the main feature this team has at the moment and we improved all the way to the final. Australia played really aggressive football and are a fantastic team as well. I wanted to strengthen the midfield so I pushed Nagatomo up and from that point Australia looked kind of loose. I was surprised because they were so compact before. After changing the position of Nagatomo, we looked better.

Alberto Zaccheroni

We have seen a very exciting game between two very good teams. You can imagine we are disappointed, we definitely had our opportunities but unfortunately we couldn't convert. We had six games in an intense tournament and twice we had to go into extra time so if there was no fatigue, then the players must be robots. I congratulate Japan on their victory. They have a new generation coming up and they are definitely on a good path.

Holger Osieck

AFC CHALLENGE CUP SRI LANKA 2010

Qualifying groups

Group A	Pts
Myanmar	9
Bangladesh	6
Cambodia	3
Macau	0

Group B	Pts
Turkmenistan	9
Maldives	6
Philippines	3
Bhutan	0

Group C	Pts
Kyrgyzstan	2
Nepal	2
Palestine	2
Afghanistan	-

Group D	Pts
Sri Lanka	7
Pakistan	5
Chinese Taipei	4
Brunei	0

First round groups

Group A	Pts
Tajikistan	6
Myanmar	6
Sri Lanka	3
Bangladesh	3

Group B	Pts
Korea DPR	7
Turkmenistan	7
Kyrgyzstan	3
India	0

Macau beat Mongolia in a preliminary qualifying round
India, Tajikistan and Korea DPR qualified automatically for the finals
Finals held in Colombo Sri Lanka from 16-02-2010 to 17-02-2010
Top scorers (Finals): 4 - Ryang Yong Gi PRK • 3 - Choe Chol Man PRK

Semi–finals

Korea DPR	5
Myanmar	0

Tajikistan	0
Turkmenistan	2

Final

Korea DPR	1 5p
Turkmenistan	1 4p

Tajikistan	1
Myanmar	0

QUALIFYING GROUP A

		Pl	W	D	L	F	A	Pts		BAN	CAM	MAC
Myanmar	MYA	3	3	0	0	7	1	9		2-1	1-0	4-0
Bangladesh	BAN	3	2	0	1	5	2	6			1-0	3-0
Cambodia	CAM	3	1	0	2	2	3	3				2-1
Macau	MAC	3	0	0	3	1	9	0				

Bangabandhu, Dhaka
26-04-2009, 15:30, 3600, Mashentsev KGZ

Myanmar 4

Maung Lwin Khin [3], Win Thien Yaza [15], Phyo Oo Pyaye [48], Min Tun Myo [59]

Zin Htet **Kyaw** - Win **Moe**, Maung Lwin **Khin** (Win Aung **Han** 70), Min Htut **Win**, Zaw Tun **Myo** - Myo Thant **Aung**, Min Tun **Myo**, Thiha Aung **Soe** (Htet Aung **Zaw** 66) - Bo Aung **Bo**, Win Thien **Yaza**, Phyo Oo **Pyaye** (Kyaw Myo **Aung** 60). Tr: Myint Aung **Tin**

Macau 0

Leong Chon Kit - **Lei** Weng Chi, Geofredo **De Sousa**, **Kwok** Siu Tin, **Lei** Kam Hong, **Choi** Keng Sang - Leong Lap San (**Che** Chi Man 49), **Chan** Man Hei, **Lei** Ka Kei (**Sio** Ka Un 63) - **Chan** Kin Seng, **Chong** Chi Chio (**Loi** Wai Hong 56). Tr: **Leung** Sui Wing

Bangabandhu, Dhaka
26-04-2009, 18:00, 8060, Yazdi IRN

Bangladesh 1

Enamul Hoque [73]

Aminul **Hoque** - Mohamed **Islam**, Mohammed **Miah**, Rajani **Barman**, Mohammed **Faisal**, Atiqur **Rahaman** **Meshu** - Aziz **Arman**•, Mohammed **Al Mamun**• (Mohammad **Chowdhury** 79), Mezbabul **Manik**•, Emon **Mahmud** (Mohammed **Hossain** 57) - Mohammed Enamul **Hoque**. Tr: Saiful Bari **Titu**

Cambodia 0

Samreth **Seiha** - Kim Chan **Bunrith**, Lay **Raksmey**, Tieng **Tiny** - Pok Chan **Than**, San **Narith** (Ly **Ravy** 77), Sun **Sovannarith**• - Khim **Borey** (Keo **Sokngorn** 66), Teab **Vathanak** (Khuon **Laboravy** 30), Kouch **Sokumpheak**, Samel **Nasa**. Tr: Prak **Sovannara**

Bangabandhu, Dhaka
28-04-2009, 15:30, 6000, Saleem MDV

Cambodia 2

Vathanak [12], Sokngorn [66]

Samreth **Seiha** - Kim Chan **Bunrith** (San **Narith** 62), Lay **Raksmey** (Lar **Pichseyla** 33), Tieng **Tiny**, Om **Thavrak** - Sun **Sovannarith** - Khim **Borey**, Keo **Sokngorn**, Teab **Vathanak**, Khuon **Laboravy**, Samel **Nasa** (Kouch **Sokumpheak**• 36). Tr: Prak **Sovannara**

Macau 1

Che Chi Man [75]

Leong Chon Kit (**Tam** Heng Wa 93+) - **Ku** Weng Nin (**Sio** Ka Un• 46), Geofredo **De Sousa**, **Kwok** Siu Tin, **Lei** Kam Hong, **Choi** Keng Sang, **Lau** Pak Meng - **Che** Chi Man, **Chan** Man Hei, **Lei** Ka Kei (**Loi** Wai Hong 34) - **Chan** Kin Seng. Tr: **Leung** Sui Wing

Bangabandhu, Dhaka

28-04-2009, 18:00, 14 000, Matsuo JPN

Bangladesh   **1**
Enamul Hoque [12]

Aminul **Hoque** - Mohamed **Islam**•◆87, Mohammed **Miah**• (Mohammed **Sujan** 62), Rajani **Barman**, Mohammed **Faisal**, Atiqur Rahaman **Meshu** - Aziz **Arman**, Mohammed **Al Mamun** (Mohamed **Hasan** 78), Mezbabul **Manik**•, Emon **Mahmud** (Mohammed **Hossain** 55) - Mohammed **Enamul Hoque**. Tr: Saiful Bari **Titu**

Myanmar   **2**
Soe Pai 2 [68 77]

Zin Htet **Kyaw** - Win **Moe**•, Maung Lwin **Khin** (Win Aung **Han** 95+), Zaw Tun **Myo**, Min Htut **Win** - Htet Aung **Zaw**, Myo Thant **Aung**, Min Tun **Myo** - Bo Aung **Bo** (Soe Pai 63), Win Thien **Yaza**, Phyo Oo **Pyaye**• (Kyaw Myo **Aung** 80). Tr: Myint Aung **Tin**

Bangabandhu, Dhaka

30-04-2009, 15:30, 2500, Yazdi IRN

Myanmar   **1**
Win Thien Yaza [94+]

Zin Htet **Kyaw** - Win **Moe**•, Maung Lwin **Khin**, Min Htut **Win**, Zaw Tun **Myo** - Htet Aung **Zaw**, Myo Thant **Aung** (San Aye 93+), Min Tun **Myo** (Tun Win **Tun** 89), Soe Pai - Win Thien **Yaza**, Phyo Oo **Pyaye** (Kyaw Myo **Aung** 33). Tr: Myint Aung **Tin**

Cambodia   **0**

Samreth **Seiha** - Kim Chan **Bunrith** (Keo **Sokngorn** 61), Lay **Raksmey**, Tieng **Tiny**, Om **Thavrak** - San **Narith** (Ly **Ravy** 73), Sun **Sovannarith**• - Khim **Borey**, Teab **Vathanak**, Kouch **Sokumpheak**, Khuon **Laboravy** (Samel **Nasa** 46). Tr: Prak **Sovannara**

Bangabandhu, Dhaka

30-04-2009, 18:00, 8700, Mashentsev KGZ

Bangladesh   **3**
Al Mumum [38], Mohammed Hossain 2 [68 71]

Aminul **Hoque** - Mohammed **Miah**, Rajani **Barman**, Mohammed **Faisal**, Atiqur Rahaman **Meshu**• (Mohamed **Hasan** 61), Mohammed **Rashed** - Aziz **Arman**, Mohammed **Al Mamun**, Motiur **Munna** (Mohammed **Hossain**• 33), Emon **Mahmud** (Anamul **Hoque** 74) - Mohammed **Enamul Hoque**. Tr: Saiful Bari **Titu**

Macau   **0**

Tam Heng **Wa** - **Ku** Weng Nin•, **Kwok** Siu Tin, Lei Kam Hong (Lei Weng Chi 68), **Choi** Keng Sang, Lau Pak Meng - **Che** Chi Man• (**Leong** Lap San 73), **Chan** Man Hei, **Loi** Wai Hong - **Chan** Kin Seng, **Chong** Chi Chio (**Sio** Ka Un 53). Tr: **Leung** Sui Wing

---

QUALIFYING GROUP B

		Pl	W	D	L	F	A	Pts	MDV	PHI	BHU
Turkmenistan	TKM	3	3	0	0	15	1	**9**	3-1	5-0	7-0
Maldives	MDV	3	2	0	1	9	5	**6**		3-2	5-0
Philippines	PHI	3	1	0	2	3	8	**3**			1-0
Bhutan	BHU	3	0	0	3	0	13	**0**			

Galolhu, Malé

14-04-2009, 16:00, 9000, Al Ghafari JOR

Turkmenistan   **3**
Nasyrov [42], Shamuradov [49], Mirzoev [68p]

Pavel **Harchik** - Guvanch **Rejepov**, Begli **Annageldiyev**•, Omar **Berdiyev** - Mekan **Nasyrov**, Nazar **Choliyev**, Nazar **Bayramov**, Begli **Nurmuradov**• (Ahmed **Allaberdiev**• 55), Bahtiyar **Hojaahmedov** - Berdy **Shamuradov** (Ruslan **Mingazov** 73), Didarklych **Urazov** (Arif **Mirzoev** 46). Tr: Boris **Grigoryants**

Maldives   **1**
Fazeel [61p]

Mohamed **Shinan** - Sabah **Ibrahim**, Mohamed **Jameel**, Assad **Ghani** - Arif **Mohamed** (Ahmed **Thariq** 57), Shamweel **Qasim**, Akram **Ghani**• (Adam **Lareef** 79) - Ali **Ashfaq**•, Mukhthar **Naseer**•, Ali **Ashad**, Ibrahim **Fazeel**. Tr: Bela **Urbanyi**

Galolhu, Malé

14-04-2009, 21:00, 200, Lazim IRQ

Philippines   **1**
Gould [13]

Neil **Etheridge**• - Gerald **Orcullo**, Robert **Gier**, Alexander **Borromeo** - Simon **Greatwich**• (Anton **Del Rosario** 65), Christopher **Greatwich**, Bongbong **Dorlas**, Jason **De Jong** (Emelio **Caligdong** 46), James **Younghusband** - Chad **Gould**, Ian **Araneta** (Francis **Gustilo** 75). Tr: Jose **Caslib**

Bhutan   **0**

Puspa Lal **Sharma** - Sangay **Khandu**, **Pema**, Pema **Rinchen** - Passang **Tshering**, Nima **Sangay**, Kinley **Dorji** - Nawang **Dendup**, **Gyeltshen** (Chimi **Dorji** 57), **Chencho**, Yeshey **Dorji** (Tshewang **Gyeltshen**• 72). Tr: Gyotoku **Koji**

Galolhu, Malé

16-04-2009, 16:00, 9000, Faghani IRN

Maldives   **3**
Fazeel [26p], Ashfaq [45], Naseer [82]

Hassan **Rameez** - Ahmed **Ashfan**•, Mohamed **Umair**, Sabah **Ibrahim**◆80, Mohamed **Jameel**, Assad **Ghani** - Shamweel **Qasim**•, Akram **Ghani** (Ali **Umar**• 64) - Ali **Ashfaq** (Ali **Ashad** 87), Mukhthar **Naseer** (Abdulla **Hanif** 83), Ibrahim **Fazeel**•. Tr: Bela **Urbanyi**

Philippines   **2**
Borromeo [11], Gould [92+]

Neil **Etheridge** - Anton **Del Rosario**, Robert **Gier**, Jason **Cordova**•, Alexander **Borromeo**◆24 - Simon **Greatwich**, Bongbong **Dorlas**•, James **Younghusband** - Emelio **Caligdong**• (Chad **Gould** 74), Ian **Araneta** (Christopher **Greatwich** 36), Jovanie **Simpron** (Jason **De Jong**• 61). Tr: Jose **Caslib**

Galolhu, Malé

16-04-2009, 21:00, 300, Perera SRI

Turkmenistan   **7**
Atayev 3 [13 67 79], Chonkayev [16], Urazov [47], Mingazov [62], Mirzoyev [93+]

Rahmanberdi **Alyhanov** - Guvanch **Rejepov** (Ilyas **Minhairov** 65), Aleksey **Pronchenko**, Bayramdurdy **Meredov**, Omar **Berdiyev** (Nazar **Choliyev** 58) - Serdar **Geldiyev**, Guvanch **Hangeldiyev**, Ruslan **Mingazov** - Gahrymanberdi **Chonkayev** (Arif **Mirzoev** 68), Dovletmyrat **Atayev**, Didarklych **Urazov**. Tr: Boris **Grigoryants**

Bhutan   **0**

Puspa Lal **Sharma**• - Sangay **Khandu** (Kelzang **Dorji** 92+), **Pema**, Pema **Rinchen** - Passang **Tshering**, Nima **Sangay**, Kinley **Dorji**•, Chimi **Dorji** - Nawang **Dendup**, **Chencho**, Yeshey **Dorji**. Tr: Gyotoku **Koji**

Galolhu, Malé

18-04-2009, 16:00, 400, Al Ghafari JOR

Turkmenistan   **5**
Del Rosario OG [26], Shamuradov 2 [54 63], Nasyrov [58], Urazov [65]

Pavel **Harchik** - Guvanch **Rejepov**, Begli **Annageldiyev**, Omar **Berdiyev** - Mekan **Nasyrov**, Nazar **Choliyev**•, Begli **Nurmuradov**, Bahtiyar **Hojaahmedov**, Ahmed **Allaberdiev** (Dovletmyrat **Atayev**• 67), Gahrymanberdi **Chonkayev** (Arif **Mirzoev** 62). Tr: Boris **Grigoryants**

Philippines   **0**

Neil **Etheridge** - Anton **Del Rosario**, Robert **Gier**, Jason **Cordova**• (Eduardo **Gempisaw** 60) - Simon **Greatwich**, Christopher **Greatwich**, Bongbong **Dorlas**•, Francis **Gustilo** (Jovanie **Simpron** 54), James **Younghusband**• - Chad **Gould**• (Jason **De Jong** 68), Emelio **Caligdong**. Tr: Jose **Caslib**

Galolhu, Malé

18-04-2009, 21:00, 9000, Lazim IRQ

Maldives   **5**

Mohamed **Faisal** - Abdulla **Haneef**, Ahmed **Ashfan**, Mohamed **Umair**, Mohamed **Jameel**, Assad **Ghani** (Ahmed **Thariq** 60) - Shamweel **Qasim** - Ali **Ashfaq**, Ali **Umar** (Hassan **Adhuham** 46), Mukhthar **Naseer** (Adam **Lareef** 69), Ibrahim **Fazeel**. Tr: Bela **Urbanyi**

Bhutan   **0**

Puspa Lal **Sharma** (Hari **Gurung** 45) - Sangay **Khandu** (Jigme **Tenzin**• 54), **Pema**••79, Pema **Rinchen** - Passang **Tshering**, Nima **Sangay**, Kinley **Dorji**, Chimi **Dorji** - Nawang **Dendup** (Kinley **Wangchuk** 80), **Chencho**•, Yeshey **Dorji**. Tr: Gyotoku **Koji**

QUALIFYING GROUP C

		Pl	W	D	L	F	A	Pts		NEP	PLE
Kyrgyzstan	KGZ	2	0	2	0	2	2	2		1-1	1-1
Nepal	NEP	2	0	2	0	1	1	2			0-0
Palestine	PLE	2	0	2	0	1	1	2			
Afghanistan	AFG			Withdrew							

Dasarath Rangasala, Kathmandu
26-03-2009, 15:00, 12 000, El Haddad LIB

Nepal 0

Bikash **Malla** - Rakesh Shrestha (Deepak Bhusal 55), Biraj **Maharjan**, Rohit **Chand**, Sagar Thapa - Bijay **Gurung**, Sandip Rai (Santosh Shahukhala 72), Raju **Tamang** - Anil **Gurung**, Ju Manu **Rai**, Chetan Ghimire. Tr: Yogamber Man **Suwal**

Palestine 0

Mohammed **Shbair** - Ammar **Abuseleisel** (Mohammed Ashour 67), Abdallatif **Bahdari**, Nadim **Barghouthi**, Roberto Bishara **Adauy**•, Majed **Abusidu** (Ayman Al **Hendi** 77) - Mali **Kaware**•, Ismail **Alamour**• (Ashraf Al **Fawaghra** 63), Khader **Yusef** - Fahed **Attal**, Ahmed **Keshkesh**. Tr: Izzat **Hamzeh**

Dasarath Rangasala, Kathmandu
28-03-2009, 15:00, 15 000, Jahanbazi IRN

Nepal 1
Biraj Maharjan [2]

Bikash **Malla**• - Biraj **Maharjan**, Rohit **Chand**, Sagar **Thapa**, Deepak Bhusal - Bijay **Gurung**, Raju **Tamang** - Anil **Gurung**, Ju Manu **Rai**, Santosh **Shahukhala**, Chetan **Ghimire**. Tr: Yogamber Man **Suwal**

Kyrgyzstan 1
Murzaev [86p]

Pavel **Matiash** - Talant **Samsaliev**• (Faruh Abitov 80), Ruslan **Sydykov**, Vaicheslav **Amin** (Rustem Usanov 65), Kursanbek **Sheratov**• - Cholponbek **Esenkul-Uulu**, Vadim **Harchenko** (Ruslan Djamshidov 61), Aibek **Bokoev**, Pavel **Sidorenko** - Mirlan **Murzaev**, Anton **Zemlianuhin**. Tr: Anarbek **Ormombekov**

Dasarath Rangasala, Kathmandu
30-03-2009, 15:00, 2000, Yu Ming Hsun TPE

Kyrgyzstan 1
Murzaev [20p]

Maksim **Agapov** - Faruh Abitov• (Rustamjan Zakirov 84), Ruslan **Sydykov**• (Davron Askarov 69), Rustem Usanov - Vadim **Harchenko**, Aibek **Bokoev**•, Pavel **Sidorenko**, Artem **Muladjanov**• - Mirlan **Murzaev**• (Ildar Amirov 75), Anton **Zemlianuhin**. Tr: Anarbek **Ormombekov**

Palestine 1

Mohammed **Shbair** - Abdallatif **Bahdari**, Nadim **Barghouthi** (Suleiman **Obeid** 82), Roberto Bishara **Adauy**, Majed **Abusidu** - Mali **Kaware** (Mohammed **Eid** 61), Ismail **Alamour** (Ahmed **Aliwisat** 80), Khader **Yusef** - Said Al **Sobakhi**, Fahed **Attal**, Ahmed **Keshkesh**. Tr: Izzat **Hamzeh**

QUALIFYING GROUP D

		Pl	W	D	L	F	A	Pts		PAK	TPE	BRU
Sri Lanka	SRI	3	2	1	0	9	4	7		2-1	2-1	5-1
Pakistan	PAK	3	1	2	0	9	3	5			1-1	6-0
Chinese Taipei	TPE	3	1	1	1	7	3	4				5-0
Brunei Darussalam	BRU	3	0	0	3	1	16	0				

Sugathadasa, Colombo
4-04-2009, 16:00, 700, Zhao Liang CHN

Sri Lanka 5
Kasun Jayasuriya 4 [23 53 67 73], A.Mohamed [32]

Herath **Kumara** - Rohana **Dinesh**, **Hettiharachchige**, Sanjaya **Kumara**, Chathura **Gunarathna** - Chatura **Weerasinghe**, Asmeer Lathif **Mohamed** (Sameera Perera 68), Mohamed **Mohideen** (Sanjeev **Shanmugarajah**• 81) - Channa Ediri, Kasun Jayasura, Anton Nimal **Fernando** (Rajitha Jayawilal 63). Tr: Sampath **Kolonnage**

Brunei Darussalam 1
Kamarul Ramlee [82]

Muhammad **Mumtazali** - Mohd Zulkhairi **Salleh** (Naasiruddeen Wahab 38), Micky **Gindi**, Mohd Hendra **Idris** - Mohd Hardyman **Lamit** (Aqmal Hamid 46), Nurul **Nordin**, Awangku **Ramlee**, Ratano **Tuah** - Riwandi **Wahit**, Adie Arsham **Salleh** (Hamizan **Sulaiman** 56). Tr: Muhammad **Mustapa**

Sugathadasa, Colombo
4-04-2009, 18:30, 400, Tseytlin UZB

Pakistan 1
Adnan Ahmed [53]

Amir **Gul** - Samar **Ishaq**, Muhammad **Shahid**, Yasir **Sabir** (Mahmood Khan 46) - Abdul **Aziz**, **Ateequllah** (Jadeed Khan 46), Muhammad **Essa**, Adnan **Ahmed**, Atif **Bashir**• - Safiullah **Khan**, Muhammad **Rasool** (Muhammad **Asif** 73). Tr: Akhtar **Mohiuddin**

Chinese Taipei 1
Chang Han [21]

Lu Kun Chi - **Lee** Meng Chian, **Chiang** Ming Han, **Chen** Yu Lin, **Kuo** Chun Yi - **Chen** Po Liang, **Hung** Kai Chun, **Chan** Che Yuan - **Hsieh** Meng Hsuan (**Chen** Yi Wei 62), **Chang** Han (**Huang** Wei Yi 86), **Lo** Chih An (**Chiang** Shih Lu• 64). Tr: **Chen** Sing An

Sugathadasa, Colombo
6-04-2009, 16:00, 200, Orzuev TJK

Pakistan 6
S Kahn 4 [19 61 68 78], J Khan [81], A Ahmed [84]

Amir **Gul**• - Mahmood **Khan**, Samar **Ishaq**•, Muhammad **Shahid** - Muhammad **Essa** (Nasrullah **Khan** 46), Abdul **Aziz** (**Ateequllah**• 46), Jadeed **Khan**, Adnan **Ahmed**, Atif **Bashir** - Muhammad **Rasool** (Muhammad **Asif**• 46), Safiullah **Khan**. Tr: Akhtar **Mohiuddin**

Brunei Darussalam 0

Muhammad **Mumtazali** - Micky **Gindi**, Mohd Hendra **Idris** (Philip Anak Ahar 88) - Mardi **Bujang** (Naasiruddeen Wahab 64), Mohd Hardyman **Lamit** (Adie Arsham **Salleh** 46), Nurul **Nordin**•◆51, Awangku **Ramlee**, Ratano **Tuah** - Aqmal **Hamid**, Hamizan **Sulaiman**, Riwandi **Wahit**. Tr: Muhammad **Mustapa**

Sugathadasa, Colombo
6-04-2009, 18:30, 1400, Al Zahrani KSA

Sri Lanka 2
Kasun Jayasuriya [35], Rohana Dinesh [39]

Herath **Kumara** - Rohana **Dinesh**, **Hettiharachchige**, Sanjaya **Kumara**, Chathura **Gunarathna** - Chatura **Weerasinghe**, Asmeer Lathif **Mohamed**, Mohamed **Mohideen** (Mohamed **Izzadeen** 88) - Channa **Ediri**, Kasun Jayasura◆61, Anton Nimal **Fernando**. Tr: Sampath **Kolonnage**

Chinese Taipei 1

Lu Kun Chi - **Chang** Yung Hsien•, **Lee** Meng Chian, **Chen** Yi Wei, **Chen** Yu Lin (**Hsieh** Meng Hsuan 80), **Kuo** Chun Yi - **Chen** Po Liang, **Hung** Kai Chun•, **Chan** Che Yuan (**Lo** Chih An 73) - **Chang** Han (**Huang** Wei Yi 64), **Chiang** Shih Lu. Tr: **Chen** Sing An

Sugathadasa, Colombo
8-04-2009, 16:00, 1000, Al Zahrani KSA

Chinese Taipei 5
Chen Po Liang 3 [11 13 58], Huang Wei Yi [30], Kuo Chun Yi [80]

Chung Kuang Tien - **Chang** Yung Hsien, **Lee** Meng Chian, **Chen** Yi Wei•, **Chiang** Ming Han, **Kuo** Chun Yi - **Chen** Po Liang, **Hung** Kai Chun - **Chang** Han (**Chan** Che Yuan• 46), **Huang** Wei Yi (**Lo** Chih An 46), **Chiang** Shih Lu (**Lo** Chih En 78). Tr: **Chen** Sing An

Brunei Darussalam 0

Muhammad **Mumtazali** - Mohd Zulkhairi **Salleh**• (Philip Anak Ahar 80), Micky **Gindi**•, Naasiruddeen **Wahab**, Mohd Hendra **Idris** (Mardi **Bujang** 86) - Awangku **Ramlee**, Ratano **Tuah** - Aqmal **Hamid**, Hamizan **Sulaiman**, Riwandi **Wahit**, Adie Arsham **Salleh**. Tr: Muhammad **Mustapa**

Sugathadasa, Colombo
8-04-2009, 18:30, 3000, Tseytlin UZB

Sri Lanka 2
Rohana Dinesh [2], Shanmugarajah [88]

Herath **Kumara** - Rohana **Dinesh**, **Hettiharachchige**, Sanjaya **Kumara**•, Chathura **Gunarathna** - Chatura **Weerasinghe**, Asmeer Lathif **Mohamed**, Mohamed **Mohideen** (Sanjeev **Shanmugarajah** 77), Mohamed **Izzadeen** (Sameera **Perera** 89) - Channa **Ediri**, Anton Nimal **Fernando**. Tr: Sampath **Kolonnage**

Pakistan 2
S Khan [82], Atif Bashir [84]

Amir **Gul** - Samar **Ishaq**, Muhammad **Shahid**, Yasir **Sabir** (Mahmood Khan• 47) - **Ateequllah**•◆90, Muhammad **Essa**, Abdul **Aziz** (Jadeed **Khan** 46), Adnan **Ahmed**, Atif **Bashir**• - Muhammad **Rasool**, Safiullah **Khan**. Tr: Akhtar **Mohiuddin**

AFC CHALLENGE CUP SRI LANKA 2010
FINAL TOURNAMENT

GROUP A		PL	W	D	L	F	A	PTS		MYA	SRI	BAN
1	Tajikistan	3	2	0	1	7	3	**6**		3-0	3-1	1-2
2	Myanmar	3	2	0	1	6	4	**6**			4-0	2-1
3	Sri Lanka	3	1	0	2	4	7	**3**				3-0
4	Bangladesh	3	1	0	2	3	6	**3**				

Sugathadasa, Colombo
16-02-2010, 16:00, 1000, Matsuo JPN

Bangladesh   **2**

Hoque 67, Meshu 74

Aminul **Hoque** - Mohamed **Islam**, Mohammed **Faisal**, Mintu **Sheikh**, Razaul **Karim•**, Atiqur Rahaman **Meshu** - Mohammed **Al Mamun•**, Shakil **Ahmed** (Mohammad **Chowdhury** 85), Anamul **Hoque** (Mithun **Chowdhury** 91+) - Mohammed **Hasan**, Abdul Baten **Komal•** (Tawhidul **Sabuz** 70). Tr: Saiful Bari **Titu**

Tajikistan   **1**

Rabiev 70

Alisher **Tuychiev** - Naim **Nasirov**, Davronjon **Ergashev•**, Sohib **Savankulov**, Farrukh **Choriev♦**79 - Ibragim **Rabimov•**, Khurshed **Makhmudov**, Dilshod **Vasiev** (Dzhamikhon **Muhinov** 61), Fatkhullo **Fatkhuloev** (Asatullo **Nurulloev** 88) - Davrondzhon **Tukhtasunov•**, Yusuf **Rabiev** (Numordzhon **Hakimov** 70). Tr: Pulod **Kodirov**

Sugathadasa, Colombo
16-02-2010, 19:00, 3000, Faghani IRN

Sri Lanka   **0**

Viraj **Asanka** - Bandara **Warakagoda**, Rohana **Dinesh**, Thuwan **Rahem♦**79, Nirantha Perera - Kolitha **Lankesara**, Madushka **Peiris** (Philip **Dalpethado** 61), Fazlur Abdul **Azeez**, Chathura **Gunarathna** (Mohamed **Izzadeen** 75) - Sanjeev **Shanmugarajah** (Mohammed **Kaiz** 46), Nadeeka **Pushpakumara**. Tr: Mohamed **Amunulla**

Myanmar   **4**

Thi Ha Kyaw 39, Paing Yan 71, Soe Pai 81, Min Tun Myo 87

Si Thu **Thiha** - Min Htut **Win**, Maung Lwin **Khin•** (Hlaing Win **Shwe** 82), Maung Tun **Khin**, Lynn Tun **Zaw** - Htat Aung **Zaw**, Win Tun **Tun**, Min Tun **Myo** - Kyaw Moe **Aung**, **Paing Yan•** (Phyo Oo **Pyaye** 74), Thi Ha **Kyaw•** (Soe **Pai** 64). Tr: Myint Aung **Tin**

Sugathadasa, Colombo
18-02-2010, 16:00, 1000, Tan Hai CHN

Sri Lanka   **1**

Dalpethado 78

Viraj **Asanka** - Bandara **Warakagoda**, Rohana **Dinesh**, Kolitha **Lankesara** (Tuwan **Rizni** 46), Madushka **Peiris•** (Philip **Dalpethado•** 61), Nirantha Perera - Fazlur Abdul **Azeez•** (Malik **Migara** 71), Chathura **Gunarathna•** - Mohamed **Izzadeen**, Sanjeev **Shanmugarajah**, Nadeeka **Pushpakumara**. Tr: Mohamed **Amunulla**

Tajikistan   **3**

Rabimov 13, Fatkhuloev 2 32 92+

Alisher **Tuychiev** - Naim **Nasirov**, Davronjon **Ergashev**, Eradzh **Radzhabov**, Sohib **Savankulov** - Ibragim **Rabimov** (Dilshod **Vasiev** 75), Khurshed **Makhmudov**, Fatkhullo **Fatkhuloev** - Numordzhon **Hakimov**, Dzhamikhon **Muhidinov** (Asatullo **Nurulloev** 68), Yusuf **Rabiev** (Davrondzhon **Tukhtasunov** 68). Tr: Pulod **Kodirov**

Sugathadasa, Colombo
18-02-2010, 19:00, 500, Al Yarimi YEM

Myanmar   **2**

Tun Win Tun 16, Soe Pai 32

Si Thu **Thiha** - Min Htut **Win**, Maung Lwin **Khin**, Maung Tun **Khin•**, Lynn Tun **Zaw•** - Htat Aung **Zaw**, Win Tun **Tun** (San Aye 86), Min Tun **Myo**, Soe **Pai** - Kyaw Moe **Aung•** (Aung **Htay** 78), Paing **Yan•** (Phyo Oo **Pyaye** 49). Tr: Myint Aung **Tin**

Bangladesh   **1**

Hossain 49

Aminul **Hoque** - Mohamed **Islam**, Mohammed **Faisal**, Mintu **Sheikh**, Razaul **Karim•**, Atiqur Rahaman **Meshu** - Mohammed **Al Mamun**, Shakil **Ahmed** (Tawhidul **Sabuz** 55) - Anamul **Hoque** (Imtiaz **Jitu** 79), Mohammed **Hasan**, Abdul Baten **Komal** (Mohammed **Hossain** 35). Tr: Saiful Bari **Titu**

CR & FC Grounds, Colombo
20-02-2010, 15:00, 100, Shukralla BHR

Tajikistan   **3**

Rabimov 33, Hakimov 52, Rabiev 88

Alisher **Tuychiev** - Davronjon **Ergashev**, Eradzh **Radzhabov•**, Sohib **Savankulov**, Farrukh **Choriev** - Ibragim **Rabimov**, Khurshed **Makhmudov**, Fatkhullo **Fatkhuloev** (Asatullo **Nurulloev** 62) - Numordzhon **Hakimov** (Kamil **Saidov** 71), Dzhamikhon **Muhidinov** (Alisher **Ulmasov** 57), Yusuf **Rabiev**. Tr: Pulod **Kodirov**

Myanmar   **0**

Aung Oo **Aung** - Win Aung **Han**, Min Htut **Win•**, Maung Lwin **Khin**, Lynn Tun **Zaw** - Htat Aung **Zaw**, Min Tun **Myo** (Maung Tun **Khin** 67), Soe **Pai** - Phyo Oo **Pyaye** (Thi Ha **Kyaw** 80), Kyaw Moe **Aung•**, Min Oo **Soe** (Tun Win **Tun** 56). Tr: Myint Aung **Tin**

Sugathadasa, Colombo
20-02-2010, 15:00, 600, Mahapab THA

Sri Lanka   **3**

Kaiz 7, Gunarathna 43, Shanmugarajah 79

Viraj **Asanka•** - Bandara **Warakagoda•**, Rohana **Dinesh**, Mohamed **Imtiyas**, Thuwan **Rahem** - Fazlur Abdul **Azeez** (Tuwan **Rizni** 94+), Chathura **Gunarathna** - Mohamed **Izzadeen** (Philip **Dalpethado** 66), Sanjeev **Shanmugarajah**, Mohamed **Kaiz** (Malik **Migara•** 81), Nadeeka **Pushpakumara**. Tr: Mohamed **Amunulla**

Bangladesh   **0**

Aminul **Hoque♦**37 - Mohamed **Islam**, Mohammed **Faisal**, Mintu **Sheikh**, Atiqur Rahaman **Meshu** - Mohammed **Al Mamun**, Shakil **Ahmed•** (Abdul Baten **Komal** 61), Mohammd **Hossain** (Tawdidul **Sabuz** 72) - Anamul **Hoque** (Biplob Bhatta **Charjee** 41), Mohammed **Hasan**, Mohammad **Chowdhury**. Tr: Saiful Bari **Titu**

GROUP B		PL	W	D	L	F	A	PTS		TKM	KGZ	IND
1	Korea DPR	3	2	1	0	8	1	**7**		1-1	4-0	3-0
2	Turkmenistan	3	2	1	0	3	1	**7**			1-0	1-0
3	Kyrgyzstan	3	1	0	2	2	6	**3**				2-1
4	India	3	0	0	3	1	6	**0**				

Sugathadasa, Colombo
17-02-2010, 16:00, 800, Shukralla BHR

Kyrgyzstan   **2**

Amirov 15, Zemlianuhin 32

Vladislav **Volkov** - Azamat **Baimatov**, Faruh **Abitov**, Davron **Askarov•**, Rustem **Usanov** (Sergey **Chikishev** 86) - Sergey **Kaleutin•** (Kaiumzhan **Sharipov** 77), Vadim **Harchenko**, Aibek **Bokoev♦**46, Pavel **Sidorenko** - Anton **Zemlianuhin**, Ildar **Amirov** (Artem **Muladjanov** 59). Tr: Anarbek **Ormombekov**

India   **1**

Franco 58p

Karanjit **Singh** - Rowilson **Rodrigues**, Dharmaraj **Ravanan•**, Robert **Lalthlamuana•** (Debabrata **Roy** 41), Denzil **Franco•** - Balwant **Singh** (Jeje **Lalpekhlua** 79), Joaquim **Abranches**, Khangembam **Singh** (Lalrindika **Ralte** 67), Jewel Raja **Shaikh**, Baljit **Sahni•** - Shushil Kumar **Singh**. Tr: Sukhvinder **Singh**

Sugathadasa, Colombo
17-02-2010, 19:00, 400, Mahapab THA

Korea DPR   **2**

Ryang Yong Gi 51

Ju Kwang Min - **Ryang** Myong Il, Pak Yong Jin, **Pak** Nam Chol, **Ri** Kwang Hyok - Pak Song Chol, **Sin** Yong Nam, Ri Chol **Myong•** (**Yun** Yong Il 78), **Ryang** Yong Gi - **Choe** Chol Man (**Pak** Kwang Ryong 78), **Chae** Tu Yong (**Pak** Chol Min 26). Tr: **Jo** Tong Sop

Turkmenistan   **1**

Karadanov 36

Bayramniyaz **Berdiyev** - Begli **Annageldiyev**, Maksim **Belyh**, Omar **Berdiyev••♦**67, Bayramdurdy **Meredov** - Nazar **Bayramov**, Dovlet **Bayramov•** (Ruslan **Mingazov** 60) - Berdy **Shamuradov**, Didarklych **Urazov•** (David **Sarkisov** 70), Mamedaly **Karadanov**, Arslanmyrat **Amanov** (Guvanch **Rejepov** 83). Tr: Yazguly **Hojageldiyev**

Sugathadasa, Colombo
19-02-2010, 16:00, 300, El Haddad LIB

Korea DPR   **4**

Pak Song Chol 29, Pak Kwang Ryong 47, Choe Myong Ho 65, Ri Chol Myong 68

Ju Kwang Min - Pak Yong Jin, Jon Kwang IK, Kim Song Gi (Pak Nam Chol 29), Ri Kwang Hyok - Pak Song Chol (**Ryang** Yong Gi 68), **Yun** Yong Il, Ri Chol **Myong**, Choe Myong Ho - Pak Song Ryong•, **Chae** Tu Yong (**Kim** Song Yong 68). Tr: **Jo** Tong Sop

Kyrgyzstan   **0**

Vladislav **Volkov** - Azamat **Baimatov•**, Faruh **Abitov** (Vladimir **Kasian** 46), Davron **Askarov**, Kursanbek **Sheratov**, Rustem **Usanov** - Vadim **Harchenko** (Islam **Shamshiev** 70), Pavel **Sidorenko**, Artem **Muladjanov** - Anton **Zemlianuhin•** (Kaiumzhan **Sharipov** 72), Ildar **Amirov•**. Tr: Anarbek **Ormombekov**

Sugathadasa, Colombo
19-02-2010, 19:00, 450, Matsuo JPN

Turkmenistan 1

Karadanov [24p]

Bayramniyaz **Berdiyev** - Begli **Annageldiyev**, Maksim **Belyh**, Azat **Garajayev** (Nazar **Bayramov** 53), Begli **Nurmuradov**, Bayramdurdy **Meredov**, David **Sarkisov** - Dovlet **Bayramov** (Dovran **Allanazarov**• 30), Ruslan **Mingazov**• - Guvanchmuhamed **Ovekov**, Mamedaly **Karadanov**. Tr: Yazguly **Hojageldiyev**

India 0

Karanjit **Singh** - Nirmal **Chettri**, Rowilson **Rodrigues**, Denzil **Franco**, Debabrata **Roy**••♦77 - Khangembam **Singh**, Lalrindika **Ralte** (Jagtar **Singh** 74), Jewel Raja **Shaikh**, Baljit **Sahni** - Shushil Kumar **Singh** (Balwant **Singh** 85), Jeje **Lalpekhlua** (Gurwinder **Singh** 80). Tr: Sukhvinder **Singh**

CR & FC Grounds, Colombo
21-02-2010, 15:00, 300, Tan Hai CHN

Korea DPR 3

Ryang Yong Gi 2 [36 72], Choe Chol Man [57]

Ju Kwang Min - **Ryang** Mong Il (Jon Kwang Ik 63), Pak Yong Jin, **Pak** Nam Chol (**Kim** Song Gi 72), **Ri** Kwang Hyok - Pak Song Chol (**Yun** Yong Il 72), Sin Yong Nam•, **Ri** Chol Myong, **Ryang** Yong Gi - **Choe** Chol Man, Chae Tu Yong. Tr: **Jo** Tong Sop

India 0

Karanjit **Singh** - Chettri Nirmal, Thokchom **Singh**, Denzil **Franco** - Joaquim Abranches (Lalrindika **Ralte** 36), Khangembam **Singh** (Jagtar **Singh** 84), Jewel Raja **Shaikh**, Baljit **Sahni**, Gurwinder **Singh** - Shushil Kumar **Singh**♦82, Jeje **Lalpekhlua** (Balwant **Singh** 74). Tr: Sukhvinder **Singh**

Sugathadasa, Colombo
21-02-2010, 15:00, 100, El Haddad LIB

Turkmenistan 1

Nurmuradov [70]

Bayramniyaz **Berdiyev** - Begli **Annageldiyev**, Maksim **Belyh** (Omar **Berdiyev**• 15), Begli **Nurmuradov**, David **Sarkisov** - Nazar **Choliyev**, Mihail **Muhammedov**•, Ruslan **Mingazov**• (Dovran **Allanazarov** 91+) - Berdy **Shamuradov**, Guvanchmuhamed **Ovekov** (Mamedaly **Karadanov** 63), Arslanmyrat **Amanov**. Tr: Yazguly **Hojageldiyev**

Kyrgyzstan 0

Vladislav **Volkov**• - Azamat **Baimatov**•, Faruh **Abitov** (Sergey **Chikishev** 86), Davron **Askarov**•, Kursanbek **Sheratov**, Rustem **Usanov** - Serget **Kaleutin**, Vadim **Harchenko** (Artem **Muladjanov** 46), Pavel **Sidorenko** - Anton **Zemlianuhin**, Almazbek **Mirzaliev** (Ildar **Amirov** 74). Tr: Anarbek **Ormombekov**

SEMI-FINALS

Sugathadasa, Colombo
24-02-2010, 19:00, 400, Al Yarimi YEM

Korea DPR 5

Choe Myong Ho [6], Choe Chol Man 2 [12 73], Pak Song Chol [13], Kim Seong Yong [85]

Ju Kwang Min - **Ryang** Myong Il, Pak Yong Jin (**Yun** Yong Il 57), **Pak** Nam Chol, **Ri** Kwang Hyok (**Kim** Myong Gyu 56) - Pak Song Chol (**Kim** Song Yong 56), **Ri** Chol Myong•, **Choe** Myong Ho, **Ryang** Yong Gi - **Choe** Chol Man•, **Pak** Kwang Ryong. Tr: **Jo** Tong Sop

Myanmar 0

Si Thu **Thiha** - Min Htut **Win**, Maung Lwin **Khin**•, Maung Tun **Khin**, Hlaing Win **Shwe**, Lynn Tun **Zaw** (Win **Moe** 55) - Htat Aung **Zaw** (Aung **Htay** 62), Tun Win **Tun**•, Soe **Pai** - Paing **Yan** (Ko Ko **Kyaw** 46). Tr: Myint Aung **Tin**

Sugathadasa, Colombo
24-02-2010, 15:30, 300, Faghani IRN

Turkmenistan 2

Amanov [33], Urazov [42]

Bayramniyaz **Berdiyev** - Begli **Annageldiyev**, Omar **Berdiyev** (David **Sarkisov** 52), Begli **Nurmuradov**, Bayramdurdy **Meredov** - Nazar **Choliyev**, Mihail **Muhammedov**• (Guvanch **Rejepov** 70), Dovran **Allanazarov** - Didarklych **Urazov**, Mamedaly **Karadanov** (Berdy **Shamuradov** 76), Arslanmyrat **Amanov**. Tr: Yazguly **Hojageldiyev**

Tajikistan 0

Alisher **Tuychiev** - Davronjon **Ergashev**•, Eradzh **Radzhabov**, Sohib **Savankulov**, Farrukh **Choriev** - Ibragim **Rabimov**, Khurshed **Makhmudov**, Fatkhullo **Fatkhuloev** (Asatullo **Nurulloev** 71) - Numordzhon **Hakimov**, Dzhamikhon **Muhidinov** (Dilshod **Vasiev** 81), Yusuf **Rabiev** (Davrondzhon **Tukhtasunov** 76). Tr: Pulod **Kodirov**

THIRD PLACE PLAY-OFF

Sugathadasa, Colombo
27-02-2010, 15:30, 300, El Haddad LIB

Tajikistan 1

Hakimov [11]

Alisher **Dodov** - Davrondzhon **Ergashev**, Eradzh **Radzhabov**, Sohib **Savankulov**, Farrukh **Choriev** - Ibragim **Rabimov** (Dilshod **Vasiev** 83), Khurshed **Makhmudov**, Fatkhullo **Fatkhuloev** - Davrondzhon **Tukhtasunov**, Numordzhon **Hakimov** (Kamil **Saidov** 90), Dzhamikhon **Muhidinov** (Asatullo **Nurulloev** 70). Tr: Pulod **Kodirov**

Myanmar 0

Si Thu **Thiha** - Min Htut **Win**, Win **Moe**, Maung Lwin **Khin**, Maung Tun **Khin**, Hlaing Win **Shwe**, Aung **Htay** (Min Tun **Myo** 73) - Soe **Pai** - Kyaw Moe **Aung** (Phyo Oo **Pyaye** 85), Paing **Yan**, Ko Ko **Kyaw** (Tun Win **Tun** 45). Tr: Myint Aung **Tin**

FINAL

Sugathadasa, Colombo
17-02-2010, 19:00, 3000, Faghani IRN

Korea DPR 1 5p

Ryang Yong Gi [75]

Ju Kwang Min• - **Ryang** Myong Il••♦32, Pak Yong Jin, **Pak** Nam Chol, Pak Song Chol, Sin Yong Nam• (Yun Yong Il 74), **Ri** Chol Myong, **Ryang** Yong Gi - **Choe** Chol Man (Jon Kwang Ik 42), **Pak** Kwang Ryong (**Chae** Tu Yong 61). Tr: **Jo** Tong Sop

Turkmenistan 1 4p

Shamuradov [33]

Bayramniyaz **Berdiyev**• - Begli **Annageldiyev**, Maksim **Belyh**, Azat **Garajayev**, Begli **Nurmuradov**•, David **Sarkisov**• - Nazar **Choliyev**• (Guvanch **Rejepov** 69), Ruslan **Mingazov**• (Guvanchmuhamed **Ovekov**• 80) - Berdy **Shamuradov**, Didarklych **Urazov** (Mamedaly **Karadanov** 46), Arslanmyrat **Amanov**. Tr: Yazguly **Hojageldiyev**

FINAL PENALTIES

Korea DPR	Turkmenistan
✓ Pak Song Chol	
	Ovekov ✓
✓ Ryang Yong Gi	
	Karadanov ✗[1]
✓ Chae Tu Yong	
	Shamuradov ✓
✓ Pak Yong Jin	
	Rejepov ✓
✗[2] Ri Chol Myong	
	Nurmuradov ✓
✓ Ri Kwang Hyok	
	Amanov ✗[3]

[1] crossbar • [2] wide • [3] saved

FOOTBALL TOURNAMENT OF THE 2010 GUANGZHOU ASIAN GAMES

First round groups

Group A	Pts	CHN	MAS	KGZ
Japan	9	3-0	2-0	3-0
China PR	6		3-0	2-1
Malaysia	3			2-1
Kyrgyzstan	0			

Group B	Pts	TKM	VIE	BHR
Iran	9	4-1	1-0	1-0
Turkmenistan	4		6-2	1-1
Vietnam	3			3-1
Bahrain	1			

Group C	Pts	KOR	PLE	JOR
Korea DPR	9	1-0	3-0	3-0
KoreaRepublic	6		3-0	4-0
Palestine	1			0-0
Jordan	1			

Group D	Pts	KUW	IND	SIN
Qatar	7	2-0	2-1	0-0
Kuwait	6		2-0	2-0
India	3			4-1
Singapore	1			

Group E	Pts	HKG	UZB	BAN
UAE	7	1-1	3-0	3-0
Hong Kong	7		1-0	4-1
Uzbekistan	3			3-0
Bangladesh	0			

Group F	Pts	THA	MDV	PAK
Oman	7	1-1	3-0	2-0
Thailand	5		0-0	6-0
Maldives	2			0-0
Pakistan	1			

Round of 16

Japan	5	India	0
Turkmenistan	0	Thailand	1
Oman	3	Hong Kong	0
Malaysia	1	Iran	3
Korea Rep	3	China PR	0
Qatar	0	Uzbekistan	1
Korea DPR	2	Vietnam	0
Kuwait	0	UAE	2

Quarter-finals

Japan	1	Thailand	0
Oman	0	Iran	1
Korea Rep	3	Uzbekistan	1
Korea DPR	0 8p	UAE	0 9p

Semi-finals

Japan	2	Iran	1
Korea Rep	0	UAE	1

Final

Japan	1	UAE	0

3rd place play-off

Korea Rep	4	Iran	3

A U-23 event with three overage players per team

Top scorer: 5 - Kensuke Nagai, Japan

WEST ASIAN FEDERATION CHAMPIONSHIP JORDAN 2010

First Round Group Stage

	Pl	W	D	L	F	A	Pts	BHR	OMA
Iran	2	1	1	0	5	2	4	3-0	2-2
Bahrain	2	1	0	1	2	3	3		2-0
Oman	2	0	1	1	2	4	1		

	Pl	W	D	L	F	A	Pts	JOR	SYR
Kuwait	2	1	1	0	4	3	4	2-2	2-1
Jordan	2	0	2	0	3	3	2		1-1
Syria	2	0	1	1	2	3	1		

	Pl	W	D	L	F	A	Pts	YEM	PLE
Iraq	2	2	0	0	5	1	6	2-1	3-0
Yemen	2	1	0	1	4	3	3		3-1
Palestine	2	0	0	2	1	6	0		

Semi-finals

Kuwait	1 4p	Yemen	1 3p
Iraq	1	Iran	2

Final

Kuwait	2	Iran	1

Held in Amman, Jordan from 24-09-2010 to 3-10-2010 • Top scorer: 4 - Ali Al Nono, Yemen

GULF CUP OF NATIONS YEMEN 2010

First Round Group Stage

	Pl	W	D	L	F	A	Pts	KSA	QAT	YEM
Kuwait	3	2	1	0	4	0	7	0-0	1-0	3-0
Saudi Arabia	3	1	2	0	5	1	5		1-1	4-0
Qatar	3	1	1	1	3	3	4			2-1
Yemen	3	0	0	3	1	9	0			

	Pl	W	D	L	F	A	Pts	IRQ	OMA	BHR
UAE	3	1	2	0	3	1	5	0-0	0-0	3-1
Iraq	3	1	2	0	3	2	5		0-0	3-2
Oman	3	0	3	0	1	1	3			1-1
Bahrain	3	0	1	2	4	7	1			

Semi-finals

Kuwait	2 5p
Iraq	2 4p

UAE	0
Saudi Arabia	1

Final

Kuwait	1
Saudi Arabia	0

Held in Aden, Yemen from 22-11-2010 to 4-12-2010 • Top scorers: **3** - Badr Al Mutawa, Kuwait & Alaa Abdul Zahra, Iraq

SOUTH ASIAN FEDERATION GAMES BANGLADESH 2010

First Round Group Stage

	Pl	W	D	L	F	A	Pts	IND	SRI	PAK
Afghanistan	3	3	0	0	5	1	9	1-0	2-0	2-1
India	3	1	1	1	5	2	4		0-0	5-1
Sri Lanka	3	1	1	1	1	2	4			1-0
Pakistan	3	0	0	3	2	8	0			

	Pl	W	D	L	F	A	Pts	MDV	NEP	BHU
Bangladesh	3	3	0	0	8	0	9	1-0	3-0	4-0
Maldives	3	2	0	1	2	1	6		1-0	1-0
Nepal	3	1	0	2	2	4	3			2-0
Bhutan	3	0	0	3	0	9	0			

Semi-finals

Bangladesh	1
India	0

Maldives	0
Afghanistan	1

Final

Bangladesh	4
Afghanistan	0

Held in Dhaka and Chittagong, Bangladesh from 29-01-2010 to 8-02-2010 • A U-23 tournament although India played with a U-19 team

AFC ASIAN CUP THIRD PLACE PLAY–OFF
AND SEMI-FINAL PENALTY SHOOT-OUT

Al Saad, Doha, 28-01-2011, 18:00, 8199, Abdul Bashir SIN

Uzbekistan — **2**

Alexander Geynrikh 2 45p 53

12 Ignatiy **Nesterov** - 22 Viktor **Karpenko** (19 Jansur **Hasanov** 87), 3 Shavkatjon **Mulladjanov**•, 9 Odil **Ahmedov**, 14 Stanislav **Andreev** - 17 Sanzhar **Tursunov**, 17 Azizbek **Haydarov**, 18 Timur **Kapadze**, 8 Server **Djeparov** - 15 Alexander **Geynrikh**•, 13 Olim **Navkarov** (10 Shavkat **Salomov**• 77). Tr: Vadim **Abramov**

Korea Republic — **3**

Koo Ja Cheol 18, Ji Dong Won 2 28 39

1 **Jung** Sung Ryong - 22 **Cha** Du Ri, 3 **Hwang** Jae Won•, 14 **Lee** Jung Soo, 12 **Lee** Young Pyo• - 16 **Ki** Sung Yueng•, 15 **Hong** Jeong Ho (5 **Kwak** Tae Hwi 79) - 6 **Lee** Yong Rae, 13 **Koo** Ja Cheol (8 **Yoon** Bit Garam 53), 17 **Lee** Chung Yong (11 **Son** Heung Min 60) - 10 **Ji** Dong Won. Tr: **Cho** Kwang Rae

Continued from page 882

SEMI-FINAL PENALTIES JPV V KOR

JPN		KOR
✓	Honda	
	Koo Ja Cheol	✗[1]
✓	Okazaki	
	Lee Yong Rae	✗[1]
✗[2]	Nagatomo	
	Hong Jeong Ho	✗[2]
✓	Konno	

[1] Saved; [2] Missed

AFF SUZUKI CUP INDONESIA/VIETNAM 2010

Preliminary group

First round groups

Group A	MAS	THA	LAO	Pts
Indonesia	5-1	2-1	6-0	**9**
Malaysia		0-0	5-1	**4**
Thailand			2-1	**2**
Laos				**1**

Semi-finals

Malaysia	2	0
Vietnam	0	0

Final

	PHI	CAM	TLS	Pts
Laos	2-2	0-0	6-1	**5**
Philippines		0-0	5-0	**5**
Cambodia			4-2	**5**
Timor-Leste				**0**

Malaysia	3	1
Indonesia	0	2

Preliminary round held in Vientiane, Laos,
16-10-2010 to 24-10-2010

Group B	PHI	SIN	MYA	Pts
Vietnam	0-2	1-0	7-1	**6**
Philippines		1-1	0-0	**5**
Singapore			2-1	**4**
Myanmar				**1**

Philippines	0	0
Indonesia	1	1

Top scorers: **5** - Mhd Safee Sali, Malaysia • **3** - Christian Gonzalez, Indonesia & Muhammad Ridwan, Indonesia

PRELIMINARY GROUP

		Pl	W	D	L	F	A	Pts		PHI	CAM	TLS
Laos	LAO	3	1	2	0	8	3	**5**		2-2	0-0	6-1
Philippines	PHI	3	1	2	0	7	2	**5**			0-0	5-0
Cambodia	CAM	3	1	2	0	4	2	**5**				4-2
Timor-Leste	TLS	3	0	0	3	3	15	**0**				

National Sports Complex, Vientiane
22-10-2010, 16:00, Leow SIN

Philippines 5

Araneta 3 27 41 57, Younghusband.P 30p, Del Rosario 32

Neil Etheridge - Robert Gier•, Anton Del Rosario•, James Younghusband (Joebel Bermejo 72), Manuel Gelito Ott (Nestorio Margase 80), Philip Younghusband (Yanti Barsales 65), Alexander Borromeo (c), Emelio Calidong, Jason De Jong•, Ian Araneta, Ray Jonsson. Tr: Simon McMenemy

Timor-Leste 0

Diamantino Leong - Lamberto Gama•, Miguel Soares, Helder Ricardo• (c), Eusebio De Almeida, Joao Pereira•, Emilio Da Silva•, Chiquito Do Carmo (Cipriano Branco• 62), Zeferino Martins, Anggisu Barbosa, Vicente Freitas (Marcelino Fernandes 70). Tr: Pedro De Almeida

---

National Sports Complex, Vientiane
22-10-2010, 18:30, Abdul Wahab MAS

Laos 0

Sengphachan Bounthisanh - Kitsada (c), Ketsada Souksavanh, Khamla Pinkeo, Phatthana Syvilay (Konekham 80), Lamnao Singtao (Visay 80), Kanlaya Sysomvang, Keoviengphet Lithideth, Kaysone Soukhavong, Kovanh Namthavixay, Khampeng Sayavutthi (Soukhaphone 52). Tr: David Booth

Cambodia 0

Ouk Mic (c) - Lay Raksmey, Tieng Tiny, Khim Borey, San Narith, Kouch Sokumpheak, Keo Sokngon (Nuth Sinoun 84), Khoun Laboravy (Phourng Soksana 89), Rang Borin, Chhun Sothearath (Tum Saray 77), Sun Sophana•. Tr: Lee Tae Hon

---

National Sports Complex, Vientiane
24-10-2010, 16:00, Phung Dinh Dung VIE

Cambodia 4

Borey 3 26 29 40, Sinoun 75

Ouk Mic (c) - Lay Raksmey, Tieng Tiny, Khim Borey, San Narith, Kouch Sokumpheak, Keo Sokngon (Tum Saray• 54), Khoun Laboravy (Nuth Sinoun 65), Rang Borin (Sok Rithy 24), Chhun Sothearath, Sun Sophana•. Tr: Lee Tae Hon

Timor-Leste 2

Chiquito 5, Anggisu 85

Leonel Da Silva Araujo - Elijeu Soares (Zeferino Martins 61), Juvitu Da Silva, Helder Ricardo (c), Eusebio De Almeida, Joao Pereira, Cipriano Branco, Marcelino Fernandes (Vicente Freitas 46), Chiquito Do Carmo (Emilio Da Silva 68), Anggisu Barbosa, Carlo Ximenes. Tr: Pedro De Almeida

---

National Sports Complex, Vientiane
24-10-2010, 18:30, Pechsri THA

Laos 2

Soukaphone 29, Kanyala 41

Sengphachan Bounthisanh - Saynakhonevieng Phommapanya•, Kitsada• (c), Ketsada Souksavanh, Lamnao Singtao (Khampeng 90), Kanlaya Sysomvang•, Keoviengphet Lithideth, Kaysone Soukhavong, Konekham• (Phatthana 67), Kovanh Namthavixay, Soukaphone (Visay 83). Tr: David Booth

Philippines 2

Younghusband.P 76p, Younghusband.J 94+

Neil Etheridge• - Robert Gier, Anton Del Rosario•, James Younghusband•, Manuel Gelito Ott•, Philip Younghusband, Alexander Borromeo (c), Emelio Calidong (David 32), Jason De Jong•, Ian Araneta, Ray Jonsson. Tr: Simon McMenemy

---

National Sports Complex, Vientiane
26-10-2010, 16:00, Abdul Wahab MAS

Philippines 0

Neil Etheridge• - Robert Gier, Anton Del Rosario•, Roel Gener, James Younghusband, Manuel Gelito Ott•, Philip Younghusband, Alexander Borromeo• (c), Ian Araneta• (Yanti Barsales 87), David Basa• (Emilio Caligdon 51), Ray Jonsson•. Tr: Simon McMenemy

Cambodia 0

Ouk Mic (c) - Lay Raksmey, Tieng Tiny, Sok Rithy, Khim Borey• (Phourng Soksana 83), San Narith, Kouch Sokumpheak, Khoun Laboravy (Nuth Sinoun 75), Keo Sokngon (Tum Saray 64), Sun Sophana•, Pheak Rady. Tr: Lee Tae Hon

---

National Sports Complex, Vientiane
26-10-2010, 18:30, Phung Dinh Dung VIE

Laos 6

Kovanh 11, Soukaphone 17, Lamnao 47p, Konekham 59, Kanyala 61, Ketsada 78

Seng Somvang - Kitsada (c), Ketsada Souksavanh, Khamla Pinkeo, Lamnao Singtao, Kanlaya Sysomvang (Manolom 80), Keoviengphet Lithideth, Kaysone Soukhavong, Konekham Inthammavong, Kovanh Namthavixay (Saynakhonevieng 77), Soukaphone Vongchiengkham• (Visay 66). Tr: David Booth

Timor-Leste 1

Chiquito 9

Diamantino Leong - Elijeu Soares, Juvitu Da Silva, Helder Ricardo (c), Eusebio De Almeida•, Joao Pereira, Cipriano Branco (Zeferino Martins• 69), Marcelino Fernandes (Vicente Freitas 69), Chiquito Do Carmo, Anggisu Barbosa, Carlo Ximenes

FINAL TOURNAMENT GROUP A

		Pl	W	D	L	F	A	Pts		MAS	THA	LAO
Indonesia	IDN	3	3	0	0	13	2	**9**		5-1	2-1	6-0
Malaysia	MAS	3	1	1	1	6	6	**4**			0-0	5-1
Thailand	THA	3	0	2	1	3	4	**2**				2-1
Laos	LAO	3	0	1	2	3	13	**1**				

Gelora Bung Karno, Jakarta
1-12-2010, 17:00, Sato JPN

Thailand	**2**
	Chaikamdee 2 [67] [91+]

Kosin Hathairattanakool - Suttinun Phukhom, Rangsan Vivatchaichok•, Theerarathon Boonmathan•, Suree Sukha, Therdsak Chaiman (Naruphol Ar-Romsawa 70), Sutee Suksomkit, Cholratit Jantakam, Suchao Nutnum (Teerasil Dangda 68), Teeratep Winothai (Datsakorn Thonglao 70), Sarayoot Chaikamdee. Tr: Bryan Robson

Laos	**2**
	Inthammavong [54], Sysomvang [82]

Sengphachan Bounthisanh - Saynakhonevieng Phommapanya, Kitsada, Ketsada Souksavanh, Khamla Pinkeo, Keoviengphet Lithideth, Kaysone Soukhavong, Konekham Inthammavong, Soukaphone Vongchiengkham, Lamnao Singtao (Kanlaya Sysomvang 75), Khampheng Sayavutthi (Visay 88). Tr: David Booth

Gelora Bung Karno, Jakarta
1-12-2010, 19:30, 62 000, Vo Min Tri VIE

Indonesia	**5**
Omar OG [22], Gonzales [33], Ridwan [52],	
Suyono [76], Bachdim [94+]	

Markus Rihihina - Maman Abdurahman, Hamka Hamzah, Zulkifli Syukur, Muhammad Ridwan (Arif Suyono 75), Mohammad Nasuha, Firman Utina•, Oktavianus Maniani, Ahmed Bustomi (Tony Sucipto 70), Irfan Bachdim, Cristian Gonzales (Bambang Pamungkas 86). Tr: Alfred Riedl

Malaysia	**1**
	Talaha [18]

Mohd Ramli - Mohd Roslan (Amar Rohidan 62), Mohd Putra Omar (Mohamad Sabree Abu 77), Mohd Muslim Ahmad, Mohamad Mohd Shas, Norshahrul Idlan Talaha, Mohd Zainal, Safiq Rahim•, Mohd Amri Yahyah (Mohd Ashaari Shamsuddin 62), Subramaniam Kunalan, Mohd Safee Sali. Tr: Rajagobal Krishnasamy

Gelora Bung Karno, Jakarta
4-12-2010, 19:30, 70 000, Daud SIN

Indonesia	**6**
Utina 2 [26p] [51], Ridwan [33], Bachdim [63],	
Suyono [77], Maniani [82]	

Markus Rihihina - Maman Abdurahman, Hamka Hamzah, Zulkifli Syukur (Beny Wahyudi 75), Muhammad Ridwan (Arif Suyono 70), Mohammad Nasuha, Firman Utina, Oktavianus Maniani, Ahmed Bustomi•, Irfan Bachdim, Cristian Gonzales (Bambang Pamungkas 67). Tr: Alfred Riedl

Laos	**0**

Sengphachan Bounthisanh - Saynakhonevieng Phommapanya• (Kovanh Namthavixay 54), Kitsada, Ketsada Souksavanh•, Khamla Pinkeo, Kanlaya Sysomvang (Soukaphone Vongchiengkham 55), Keoviengphet Lithideth, Kaysone Soukhavong, Konekham Inthammavong, Lamnao Singtao, Khampheng Sayavutthi (Visay 64). Tr: David Booth

Gelora Bung Karno, Jakarta
4-12-2010, 17:00, Win Cho MYA

Thailand	**0**

Kosin Hathairattanakool• - Nattaporn Phanrit•, Natthaphong Samana•, Panupong Wongsa, Suree Sukha, Datsakorn Thonglao (Therdsak Chaiman 85), Sutee Suksomkit (Keerati Keawsombat 77), Pichitpong Choechiu, Suchao Nutnum•, Teerasil Dangda, Sarayoot Chaikamdee. Tr: Bryan Robson

Malaysia	**0**

Khairul Che Mat - Mohd Putra Omar, Mahalli Jasuli (Mohamad Sabree Abu 66), Mohd Muslim Ahmad, Mohamad Mohd Shas, Norshahrul Idlan Talaha, Mohd Zainal (Mohd Zambri 39), Amar Rohidan, Safiq Rahim, Subramaniam Kunalan, Mohd Safee Sali• (Mohd Amri Yahyah 73). Tr: Rajagobal Krishnasamy

Gelora Sriwijaya, Palembang
7-12-2010, 19:30, Vo Minh Tri VIE

Malaysia	**5**
Yahyah 2 [4] [40], Zainal [73], Talaha [77] Jasuli [90]	

Khairul Che Mat - Mohamad Sabree Abu, Mahalli Jasuli, Mohd Muslim Ahmad, Mohd Faizal Muhammad, Mohd Zambri (Mohd Zainal 39), Norshahrul Idlan Talaha (Izzak Ramlan 80), Amar Rohidan, Safiq Rahim, Mohd Amri Yahyah (Gurusamy Kandasamy 68), Subramaniam Kunalan. Tr: Rajagobal Krishnasamy

Laos	**1**
	Lamnao Singto 8

Sengphachan Bounthisanh - Kitsada, Ketsada Souksavanh, Khamla Pinkeo, Kovanh Namthavixay, Kanlaya Sysomvang (Saynakhonevieng Phommapanya 55), Keoviengphet Lithideth, Kaysone Soukhavong (Manolom 55), Konekham Inthammavong (Khampheng Sayavutthi 47), Soukaphone Vongchiengkham, Lamnao Singtao. Tr: David Booth

Gelora Bung Karno, Jakarta
7-12-2010, 19:30, 65 000, Sato JPN

Indonesia	**2**
	Pamungkas 2 [82] [91+]

Markus Rihihina - Maman Abdurahman, M. Roby, Zulkifli Syukur, Muhammad Ridwan, Mohammad Nasuha, Eka Ramdani (Ahmed Bustomi 83), Tony Sucipto, Oktavianus Maniani (Arif Suyono 69), Irfan Bachdim (Bambang Pamungkas 58), Cristian Gonzales. Tr: Alfred Riedl

Thailand	**1**
	Sukha Suree [68]

Kosin Hathairattanakool - Nattaporn Phanrit, Natthaphong Samana, Suttinun Phukhom, Rangsan Vivatchaichok, Panupong Wongsa•• ♦ [87], Suree Sukha• (Suchao Nutnum 76), Datsakorn Thonglao (Therdsak Chaiman 67), Teerasil Dangda•, Naruphol Ar-Romsawa, Keerati Keawsombat (Sarayoot Chaikamdee• 73). Tr: Bryan Robson

FINAL TOURNAMENT GROUP B

		Pl	W	D	L	F	A	Pts		PHI	SIN	MYA
Vietnam	VIE	3	2	0	1	8	3	**6**		0-2	1-0	7-1
Philippines	PHI	3	1	2	0	3	1	**5**			1-1	0-0
Singapore	SIN	3	1	1	1	3	3	**4**				2-1
Myanmar	MYA	3	0	1	2	2	9	**1**				

My Dinh, Hanoi
2-12-2010, 17:00, Mahapab THA

Singapore	**1**
	Duric [65]

Hassan Sunny - Daniel Bennett, Noh Rahman•, Baihakki Khaizan, Fazrul Nawaz (Ridhuan Muhamad 47), Jumaat Jantan, Shahril Ishak, Shahdan Sulaiman•, Mustafic Fahrudin (Isa Halim• 88), Aleksandar Duric, Noh Alam Shah• (Khairul Amri 68). Tr: Raddy Avramovic

Philippines	**1**
	Greatwich [93+]

Neil Etheridge - Robert Gier, Alexander Borromeo, Anton Del Rosario, Ray Jonsson, James Younghusband, Jason De Jong, Christopher Greatwich•, Ian Araneta (Joebel Bermejo 78), Emilio Caligdong (Roel Gener 83), Philip Younghusband•. Tr: Simon McMenemy

My Dinh, Hanoi
2-12-2010, 19:30, 40 000, Patwal IND

Vietnam	**7**
Nguyen Minh Phuong [30], Nguyen Anh Duc 2 [13] [56],	
Le Tan Tai [51], Nguyen Trong Hoang 2 [13] [56],	
Nguyen Vu Phong [94+]	

Duong Hong Son - Doan Viet Cuong, Huynh Quang Thanh, Vu Nhu Thanh, Le Phuoc Tu, Le Tan Tai (Nguyen Trong Hoang 72), Nguyen Minh Phuong (Nguyen Minh Chau 90), Phan Van Tai Em, Nguyen Vu Phong, Pham Thanh Luong• (Dinh Thanh Trung 78), Nguyen Anh Duc•. Tr: Henrique Calisto

Myanmar	**1**
	Kyaw Moe Aung [16]

Zin Htet Kyaw - Min Htut Win, Maung Lwin Khin, Maung Tun Khin, Lynn Tun Zaw, Tun Win Tun Tun (Maung Nai 61), Min Tun Myo• (Ko Ko Kyaw 46), Kyaw Moe Aung, Myo Thant Aung (Khing Win Kyaw 61), Paing Yan, Win Thein Yaza. Tr: Myint Aung Tim

My Dinh, Hanoi
5-12-2010, 17:00, Tao Ranchang CHN

Singapore	**2**
	Duric [62], Agu Casmir [94+]

Hassan Sunny - Noh Rahman•, Baihakki Khaizan, Precious Emuejeraye, Jumaat Jantan, Shahril Ishak, Ridhuan Muhamad (Khairul Amri 46), Mustafic Fahrudin, Isa Halim (Shahdan Sulaiman 62), Aleksandar Duric, Noh Alam Shah (Agu Casmir 46). Tr: Raddy Avramovic

Myanmar	**1**
	Maung Lwin Khin [13]

Si Thu Thiha - Win Moe, Maung Lwin Khin, San Aye, Lynn Tun Zaw•, Aung Win Na, Na Lwin Nya (Ko Ko Kyaw 69), Kyaw Moe Aung (Myo Thant Aung 72), Paing Yan, Win Thein Yaza• (Khing Win Kyaw 77), Aih Naing Mai. Tr: Myint Aung Tim

My Dinh, Hanoi	Thien Truong, Nam Dinh	My Dinh, Hanoi

My Dinh, Hanoi
5-12-2010, 19:30, 40 000, Napitupulu IDN
Vietnam   0

Duong Hong Son - **Huynh** Quang Thanh, **Vu Nhu Thanh** (Nguyen Quang Hai 81), **Le** Phuoc Tu●, **Tran** Dinh Dong● (Le Sy Manh 71), **Le** Tan Tai (**Nguyen** Trong Hoang 62), **Nguyen** Minh Phuong, **Phan** Van Tai Em, Nguyen Vu Phong, **Pham** Thanh Luong, **Nguyen** Anh Duc. Tr: Henrique **Calisto**

Philippines   2
Greatwich [38], Phil Younghusband [79]

Neil **Etheridge●** - Robert **Gier**, Alexander **Borromeo**, Anton **Del Rosario**, Ray **Jonsson**, James **Younghusband**, Jason **De Jong●**, Christopher **Greatwich**, Roel **Gener** (Yanti **Barsales** 90), Ian **Araneta**, Philip **Younghusband** (Nestorio **Margase** 86). Tr: Simon **McMenemy**

Thien Truong, Nam Dinh
8-12-2010, 19:30, Patwal IND
Philippines   0

Neil **Etheridge** - Robert **Gier**, Alexander **Borromeo**, Anton **Del Rosario**, James **Younghusband●**, Jason **De Jong**, Christopher **Greatwich**, Roel **Gener** (Emilio **Caligdong** 86), Ian **Araneta**, Philip **Younghusband**, David **Basa**. Tr: Simon **McMenemy**

Myanmar   0

Si Thu **Thiha** - Win **Moe**, Maung Lwin **Khin**, Maung Tun **Khin**, San Aye, Soe **Paing**, Kyaw Moe **Aung** (Zeyar Win **Kyaw** 78), Myo Thant **Aung**, Ko Ko **Kyaw**, Win Thein **Yaza** (Paing **Yan** 60), Aih Naing **Mai** (Tun Win **Tun** 89). Tr: Myint Aung **Tim**

My Dinh, Hanoi
8-12-2010, 19:30, 40 000, Mahaprab THA
Vietnam   1
Nguyen Vu Phong [32]

Bui Tan Truong - **Doan** Viet Cuong● (**Tran** Dinh Dong 78), **Huynh** Quang Thanh (**Truong** Dinh Luat 67), **Vu** Nhu Thanh, **Le** Phuoc Tu, **Nguyen** Minh Phuong, **Phan** Van Tai Em●, **Nguyen** Vu Phong, **Pham** Thanh Luong (**Nguyen** Minh Chau), **Nguyen** Trong Hoang●◆64, Nguyen Anh Duc. Tr: Henrique **Calisto**

Singapore   0

Hassan **Sunny●** - Baihakki **Khaizan●**, Precious **Emuejeraye**, Safuwan **Baharudin** (Khairul **Amri** 47), Jumaat **Jantan**, Rosman **Sulaiman**, Shahril **Ishak**, Mustafic **Fahrudin●**, Aleksandar **Duric**, Agu **Casmir**, Noh Alam **Shah**. Tr: Raddy **Avramovic**

SEMI-FINALS

Bukit Jalil, Kuala Lumpur
15-12-2010, 20:00, 45 000, Sun Baojie CHN
Malaysia   2
Safee Sali 2 [60] [79]
Khairul Che **Mat** - Mohd Putra **Omar**, Mahalli **Jasuli●** (Mohamad Sabree **Abu** 56), Mohd Muslim **Ahmad**, Mohamad Mohd **Shas**, Norshahrul Idlan **Talaha** (Amri **Yahyah** 68), Mohd **Zainal**, Amar **Rohidan**, Safiq **Rahim**, Subramaniam **Kunalan** (Mohd **Zambri** 84), Mohd Safee **Sali●**. Tr: Rajagobal **Krishnasamy**

Vietnam   0

Bui Tan Truong - **Vu** Nhu Thanh, **Nguyen** Huy Hoang , **Le** Phuoc Tu●, **Tran** Dinh Dong●, **Le** Tan Tai (**Nguyen** Viet Thang 70), **Nguyen** Minh Phuong, **Nguyen** Vu Phong , **Pham** Thanh Luong (**Nguyen** Minh Chau 46), **Phan** Thanh Hung (**Nguyen** Minh Chau 46), Nguyen Anh Duc. Tr: Henrique **Calisto**

My Dinh
18-12-2010, 19:00, 40 000, Kim Sang Woo KOR
Vietnam   0

Duong Hong Son - **Doan** Viet Cuong●, **Vu** Nhu Thanh, **Le** Phuoc Tu●, **Tran** Dinh Dong (**Nguyen** Quang Hai 71), **Nguyen** Minh Phuong, **Phan** Van Tai Em (**Le** Tan Tai 13), **Nguyen** Vu Phong, **Pham** Thanh Luong●●◆72, **Nguyen** Trong Hoang, **Nguyen** Viet Thang (**Nguyen** Anh Duc 63). Tr: Henrique **Calisto**

Malaysia   0

Khairul Che **Mat** - Mohd Putra **Omar**, Mohamad Sabree **Abu** (Mahalli **Jasuli** 85), Mohd Muslim **Ahmad**, Mohamad Mohd **Shas**, Norshahrul Idlan **Talaha** (Amri **Yahyah** 71), Mohd **Zainal●** (Ashaari **Shamsuddin** 70), Amar **Rohidan**, Safiq **Rahim**, Subramaniam **Kunalan**, Mohd Safee **Sali**. Tr: Rajagobal **Krishnasamy**

Gelora Bung Karno, Jakarta
16-12-2010, 19:00, 70 000, Moradi IRN
Philippines   0

Neil **Etheridge●** - Robert **Gier**, Alexander **Borromeo**, Anton **Del Rosario**, Ray **Jonsson**, James **Younghusband●**, Jason **De Jong●**, Christopher **Greatwich**, Roel **Gener**, Ian **Araneta** (Emilio **Caligdong** 59), Philip **Younghusband**. Tr: Simon **McMenemy**

Indonesia   1
Gonzales [32]
Markus **Rihihina** - Hamka **Hamzah**, Maman **Abdurahman**, Zulkifli **Syukur**, Muhammad **Ridwan**, Mohammad **Nasuha** (Beny **Wahyudi** 85), Firman **Utina**, Oktavianus **Maniani●**, Ahmed **Bustomi**, Irfan **Bachdim** (Bambang **Pamungkas** 68), Cristian **Gonzales●**. Tr: Alfred **Riedl**

Gelora Bung Karno, Jakarta
19-12-2010, 19:00, 88 000, Ebrahim BHR
Indonesia   1
Gonzales [43]
Markus **Rihihina** - Maman **Abdurahman**, Hamka **Hamzah●**, Zulkifli **Syukur**, Muhammad **Ridwan●**, Mohammad **Nasuha**, Firman **Utina**, Oktavianus **Maniani** (Arif **Suyono** 85), Ahmed **Bustomi●**, Yongky **Aribowo**, Cristian **Gonzales** (Bambang **Pamungkas** 90). Tr: Alfred **Riedl**

Philippines   0

Neil **Etheridge** - Robert **Gier●**, Alexander **Borromeo**, Anton **Del Rosario**, Ray **Jonsson**, James **Younghusband** (Yanti **Barsales** 84), Jason **De Jong**, Christopher **Greatwich●**, Roel **Gener** (Nestorio **Margase** 57), Ian **Araneta●** (Emilio **Caligdong** 76), Philip **Younghusband**. Tr: Simon **McMenemy**

FINAL

Bukit Jalil, Kuala Lumpur
26-12-2010, 20:00, 70 000, Toma JPN
Malaysia   3
Safee Sali 2 [61] [73], Shamsuddin [68]
Khairul Che **Mat** - Mohd Putra **Omar●**, Mahalli **Jasuli●** (Mohamad Sabree **Abu** 90), Mohd Muslim **Ahmad**, Mohamad Mohd **Shas**, Norshahrul Idlan **Talaha**, Mohd **Zainal●** (Mohd Ashaari **Shamsuddin** 53), Amar **Rohidan**, Safiq **Rahim**, Subramaniam **Kunalan**, Mohd Safee **Sali** (Amri **Yahyah** 81). Tr: Rajagobal **Krishnasamy**

Indonesia   0

Markus **Rihihina** - Maman **Abdurahman**, Hamka **Hamzah**, Zulkifli **Syukur**, Muhammad **Ridwan**, Mohammad **Nasuha**, Firman **Utina**, Oktavianus **Maniani●** (Arif **Suyono** 70), Ahmed **Bustomi**, Yongky **Aribowo** (Irfan **Bachdim** 65), Cristian **Gonzales** (Bambang **Pamungkas**). Tr: Alfred **Riedl**

Gelora Bung Karno, Jakarta
29-12-2010, 19:00, 88 000, Green AUS
Indonesia   2
Nasuha [72], Ridwan [88]
Markus **Rihihina** - Maman **Abdurahman**, Hamka **Hamzah**, Zulkifli **Syukur●**, Muhammad **Ridwan**, Mohammad **Nasuha**, Firman **Utina** (Bambang **Pamungkas** 56), Ahmed **Bustomi●**, Arif **Suyono●** (Tony **Sucipto** 72), Irfan **Bachdim** (Eka **Ramdani** 56), Cristian **Gonzales** Tr: Alfred **Riedl**

Malaysia   1
Safee Sali [54]
Khairul Che **Mat** - Mohd Putra **Omar**, Mohamad Sabree **Abu●**, Mohd Muslim **Ahmad**, Mohamad Mohd **Shas**, Norshahrul Idlan **Talaha**, Amar **Rohidan** (Mohd **Roslan** 62), Safiq **Rahim**, M. **Shamsuddin** (Amri **Yahyah** 78), Subramaniam **Kunalan●**, Mohd Safee **Sali** (Izzak **Ramlan** 90). Tr: Rajagobal **Krishnasamy**

AFC U-19 CHAMPIONSHIP 2010 – QUALIFIERS

Qualifying Group A

(In Nepal)	Pl	W	D	L	F	A	Pts	YEM	TJK	PLE	NEP	KGZ
Jordan	5	4	1	0	12	6	13	2-2	2-0	3-1	3-2	2-1
Yemen	5	3	2	0	13	5	11		3-0	2-2	3-0	3-1
Tajikistan	5	3	0	2	9	6	9			3-0	2-1	4-0
Palestine	5	1	1	3	7	11	4				4-1	0-2
Nepal	5	1	0	4	6	13	3					2-1
Kyrgyzstan	5	1	0	4	5	11	3					

Qualifying Group B

(In UAE)	Pl	W	D	L	F	A	Pts	SYR	BHR	QAT	SRI
UAE	4	4	0	0	13	4	12	2-1	4-1	3-2	4-0
Syria	4	2	1	1	8	4	7		3-1	1-1	3-0
Bahrain	4	2	0	2	7	7	6			1-0	4-0
Qatar	4	1	1	2	11	5	4				8-0
Sri Lanka	4	0	0	4	0	19	0				
Bhutan	Withdrew										

Qualifying Group C

(In Iraq)	Pl	W	D	L	F	A	Pts	KSA	OMA	IND	KUW	AFG
Iraq	5	4	1	0	13	0	13	3-0	2-0	5-0	0-0	3-0
Saudi Arabia	5	3	1	1	9	5	10		0-0	3-1	1-0	5-1
Oman	5	2	2	1	9	6	8			4-3	1-1	4-0
India	5	2	0	3	11	13	6				3-0	4-1
Kuwait	5	1	2	2	5	6	5					4-1
Afghanistan	5	0	0	5	3	20	0					

Qualifying Group D

(In Iran)	Pl	W	D	L	F	A	Pts	IRN	PAK
Uzbekistan	2	1	1	0	6	1	4	1-1	5-0
Iran	2	1	1	0	5	1	4		4-0
Pakistan	2	0	0	2	0	9	0		
Turkmenistan	Withdrew								
Lebanon	Withdrew								
Maldives	Withdrew								

Qualifying Group E

(In Thailand)	Pl	W	D	L	F	A	Pts	THA	VIE	BAN	MAC	LAO
Korea Republic	5	4	0	1	18	3	12	2-1	0-1	5-0	5-1	6-0
Thailand	5	4	0	1	9	2	12		1-0	3-0	3-0	1-0
Vietnam	5	4	0	1	9	2	12			1-0	3-0	4-1
Bangladesh	5	1	1	3	6	14	4				3-2	3-3
Macau	5	1	0	4	7	17	3					4-3
Laos	5	0	1	4	7	18	1					

Qualifying Group F

(In Indonesia)	Pl	W	D	L	F	A	Pts	AUS	IDN	HGK	SIN	TPE
Japan	5	5	0	0	19	2	15	3-2	7-0	3-0	2-0	4-0
Australia	5	3	1	1	17	4	10		0-0	3-1	8-0	4-0
Indonesia	5	2	1	2	10	9	7			4-1	0-1	6-0
Hong Kong	5	2	0	3	7	13	6				2-1	3-2
Singapore	5	2	0	3	5	13	6					3-1
Chinese Taipei	5	0	0	5	3	20	0					

Qualifying Group G

(In China PR)	Pl	W	D	L	F	A	Pts	PRK	MAS	MYA	PHI	GUM
China PR	5	5	0	0	29	1	15	3-0	3-1	2-0	13-0	8-0
Korea DPR	5	4	0	1	25	5	12		2-1	4-0	8-0	11-1
Malaysia	5	3	0	2	19	7	9			4-0	4-2	9-0
Myanmar	5	2	0	3	9	12	6				6-0	3-2
Philippines	5	0	1	4	4	33	1					2-2
Guam	5	0	1	4	5	33	1					

AFC U-19 CHAMPIONSHIP CHINA PR 2010

First round groups

Group A

Group A	Pl	W	D	L	F	A	Pts	KSA	SYR	THA
China PR	3	2	1	0	6	2	7	3-1	2-0	1-1
Saudi Arabia	3	2	0	1	3	3	6		1-0	1-0
Syria	3	1	0	2	1	3	3			1-0
Thailand	3	0	1	2	1	3	1			

Group B

Group B	Pl	W	D	L	F	A	Pts	PRK	BHR	IRQ
Uzbekistan	3	3	0	0	4	0	9	1-0	1-0	2-0
Korea DPR	3	2	0	1	5	1	6		2-0	3-0
Bahrain	3	1	0	2	2	4	3			2-1
Iraq	3	0	0	3	1	7	0			

Group C

Group C	Pl	W	D	L	F	A	Pts	UAE	VIE	JOR
Japan	3	3	0	0	9	1	9	2-1	4-0	3-0
UAE	3	1	1	1	5	2	4		4-0	0-0
Vietnam	3	1	0	2	2	9	3			2-1
Jordan	3	0	1	2	1	5	1			

Group D

Group D	Pl	W	D	L	F	A	Pts	KOR	IRN	YEM
Australia	3	2	1	0	7	1	7	0-0	3-0	4-1
Korea Republic	3	2	1	0	3	0	7		2-0	1-0
Iran	3	1	0	2	2	5	3			2-0
Yemen	3	0	0	3	1	7	0			

Quarter-finals

Korea DPR	2
China PR	0

Japan	2
Korea Republic	3

Saudi Arabia	2
Uzbekistan	1

UAE	2
Australia	4

Semi-finals

Korea DPR	2
Korea Republic	0

Saudi Arabia	0
Australia	2

Final

Korea DPR	3
Australia	2

Held in Zibo and Linzi, China PR from 3-10-2010 to 17-10-2010 • Korea DPR, Australia, Saudi Arabia and Korea Republic qualified for the FIFA U-20 World Cup Colombia 2011

AFC U-16 CHAMPIONSHIP 2010 – QUALIFIERS

Qualifying Group A

(In Malaysia)	Pl	W	D	L	F	A	Pts	KUW	KSA	PAK	AFG
Uzbekistan	4	3	1	0	10	0	10	3-0	0-0	3-0	4-0
Kuwait	4	3	0	1	8	3	9		1-0	1-0	6-0
Saudi Arabia	4	2	1	1	3	1	7			2-0	1-0
Pakistan	4	0	1	3	1	7	1				1-1
Afghanistan	4	0	1	3	1	12	1				
Sri Lanka	Withdrew										

Qualifying Group B

(In Nepal)	Pl	W	D	L	F	A	Pts	TJK	BHR	NPL	LIB
Iran	4	3	1	0	9	0	10	0-0	2-0	3-0	4-0
Tajikistan	4	3	1	0	9	0	10		2-0	4-0	3-0
Bahrain	4	2	0	2	7	5	6			5-0	2-1
Nepal	4	1	0	3	3	12	3				3-0
Lebanon	4	0	0	4	1	12	0				
Maldives	Withdrew										

Qualifying Group C

(In Yemen)	Pl	W	D	L	F	A	Pts	IRQ	YEM	QAT	PLE	BHU
Syria	5	5	0	0	23	0	15	1-0	1-0	2-0	9-0	10-0
Iraq	5	4	0	1	15	3	12		1-0	4-0	3-1	7-1
Yemen	5	3	0	2	12	3	9			2-1	3-0	7-0
Qatar	5	2	0	3	6	8	6				1-0	4-0
Palestine	5	1	0	4	3	17	3					2-1
Bhutan	5	0	0	5	2	30	0					

Qualifying Group D

(In the UAE)	Pl	W	D	L	F	A	Pts	JOR	OMA	KGZ	IND	TKM
UAE	5	4	1	0	19	4	13	0-0	2-1	3-0	6-3	8-0
Jordan	5	3	2	0	12	5	11		1-1	2-1	6-1	3-2
Oman	5	3	1	1	8	3	10			2-0	2-0	2-0
Kyrgyzstan	5	1	1	3	4	8	4				0-0	3-1
India	5	1	1	3	6	15	4					2-1
Turkmenistan	5	0	0	5	4	18	0					

Qualifying Group E

(In Philippines)	Pl	W	D	L	F	A	Pts	IDN	TPE	BAN	PHI
Japan	4	4	0	0	26	0	12	3-0	5-0	6-0	12-0
Indonesia	4	2	1	1	10	3	7		1-0	0-0	9-0
Chinese Taipei	4	2	0	2	6	8	6			2-1	4-1
Bangladesh	4	1	1	2	2	8	4				1-0
Philippines	4	0	0	4	1	26	0				
Mongolia	Withdrew										

Qualifying Group F

(In China PR)	Pl	W	D	L	F	A	Pts	TLS	HKG	SIN	GUM	MAC
China PR	5	4	1	0	29	0	13	0-0	6-0	7-0	2-0	14-0
Timor-Leste	5	4	1	0	22	0	13		3-0	3-0	3-0	13-0
Hong Kong	5	2	1	2	16	13	7			1-1	3-2	12-1
Singapore	5	2	1	2	8	12	7				3-1	4-0
Guam	5	1	0	4	9	11	3					6-0
Macau	5	0	0	5	1	49	0					

Qualifying Group G

(In Thailand)	Pl	W	D	L	F	A	Pts	VIE	THA	KOR	MYA	CAM
Korea DPR	5	4	1	0	15	4	13	2-1	1-1	2-1	5-1	5-0
Vietnam	5	2	2	1	12	6	8		1-0	3-3	0-0	7-1
Thailand	5	2	2	1	13	4	8			2-2	2-0	8-0
Korea Republic	5	1	3	1	17	7	6				0-0	11-0
Myanmar	5	1	2	2	4	8	5					3-1
Cambodia	5	0	0	5	2	34	0					

Qualifying Group H

(In Thailand)	Pl	W	D	L	F	A	Pts	AUS	LAO	MAS
Australia	4	3	1	0	17	3	10		7-0	2-2
Laos	4	1	1	2	10	17	4	0-6		6-0
Malaysia	4	0	2	2	7	14	2	1-2	4-4	

AFC U-16 CHAMPIONSHIP UZBEKISTAN 2010

First round groups

Group A

	Pl	W	D	L	F	A	Pts	JOR	IDN	TJK
Uzbekistan	3	2	1	0	11	1	7	0-0	3-0	8-1
Jordan	3	1	2	0	2	1	5		1-0	1-1
Indonesia	3	1	0	2	4	5	3			4-1
Tajikistan	3	0	1	2	3	13	1			

Group B

	Pl	W	D	L	F	A	Pts	SYR	IRN	OMA
Korea DPR	3	2	1	0	5	2	7	1-1	2-0	2-1
Syria	3	1	2	0	3	2	5		1-1	1-0
Iran	3	1	1	1	6	4	4			5-1
Oman	3	0	0	3	2	8	0			

Group C

	Pl	W	D	L	F	A	Pts	JPN	VIE	TLS
Australia	3	2	1	0	8	1	7	0-0	3-1	5-0
Japan	3	2	1	0	7	0	7		6-0	1-0
Vietnam	3	1	0	2	4	10	3			3-1
Timor-Leste	3	0	0	3	1	9	0			

Group D

	Pl	W	D	L	F	A	Pts	UAE	KUW	CHN
Iraq	3	2	0	1	6	2	6	1-2	3-0	2-0
UAE	3	1	2	0	3	2	5		0-0	1-1
Kuwait	3	1	1	1	1	3	4			1-0
China PR	3	0	1	2	1	4	1			

Quarter-finals

Korea DPR	4
Jordan	0
Iraq	1
Japan	3
Australia	3
UAE	2
Syria	1
Uzbekistan	2

Semi-finals

Korea DPR	2
Japan	1
Australia	1
Uzbekistan	2

Final

Korea DPR	2
Uzbekistan	0

Held in Tashkent, Uzbekistan from 24-10-2010 to 7-11-2010 • Korea DPR, Uzbekistan, Japan & Australia qualified for the FIFA U-17 World Cup Mexico 2011

CLUB TOURNAMENTS IN ASIA 2010

AFC CHAMPIONS LEAGUE 2010

First Round

Round of 16

Group A

		Pl	W	D	L	F	A	Pts	QAT	IRN	KSA	UAE
Al Gharafa	QAT	6	4	1	1	11	9	**13**		1-1	3-2	4-2
Esteghlal Tehran	IRN	6	3	2	1	9	5	**11**	3-0		2-1	0-0
Al Ahli	KSA	6	2	0	4	11	9	**6**	0-1	1-2		5-1
Al Jazira	UAE	6	1	1	4	6	14	**4**	1-2	2-1	0-2	

Seongnam I. Chunma *   3
Gamba Osaka   0

Group B

		Pl	W	D	L	F	A	Pts	IRN	UZB	KSA	UAE
Zob Ahan	IRN	6	4	1	1	8	3	**13**		3-0	1-0	1-0
Bunyodkor	UZB	6	3	1	2	10	7	**10**	0-1		3-0	4-1
Al Ittihad	KSA	6	2	2	2	9	7	**8**	2-2	1-1		4-0
Al Wahda	UAE	6	1	0	5	3	13	**3**	1-0	1-2	0-2	

Beijing Guoan   0
Suwon Bluewings *   2

Group C

		Pl	W	D	L	F	A	Pts	KSA	UZB	IRN	UAE
Al Shabab	KSA	6	3	1	2	10	8	**10**		2-1	1-1	3-2
Pakhtakor Tashkent	UZB	6	3	0	3	8	10	**9**	1-3		2-1	3-2
Sepahan	IRN	6	2	2	2	5	5	**8**	1-0	2-0		0-0
Al Ain	UAE	6	2	1	3	8	8	**7**	2-1	0-1	2-0	

Jeonbuk Hy. Motors   3
Adelaide United   2

Group D

		Pl	W	D	L	F	A	Pts	KSA	IRN	QAT	UAE
Al Hilal	KSA	6	3	2	1	11	7	**11**		3-1	0-0	1-1
Mes Kerman	IRN	6	3	0	3	13	13	**9**	3-1		3-1	4-2
Al Sadd	QAT	6	2	2	2	12	9	**8**	0-3	4-1		2-2
Al Ahli	UAE	6	1	2	3	9	16	**5**	2-3	2-1	0-5	

Esteghlal Tehran   2
Al Shabab *   3

Group E

		Pl	W	D	L	F	A	Pts	KOR	CHN	JPN	AUS
Seongnam I. Chunma	KOR	6	5	0	1	11	6	**15**		3-1	2-0	3-2
Beijing Guoan	CHN	6	3	1	2	7	5	**10**	0-1		2-0	1-0
Kawasaki Frontale	JPN	6	2	0	4	8	8	**6**	3-0	1-3		4-0
Melbourne Victory	AUS	6	1	1	4	3	10	**4**	0-2	0-0	1-0	

Al Hilal *   3
Bunyodkor   0

Group F

		Pl	W	D	L	F	A	Pts	JPN	KOR	CHN	IDN
Kashima Antlers	JPN	6	6	0	0	14	3	**18**		2-1	1-0	5-0
Jeonbuk Hy. Motors	KOR	6	4	0	2	17	6	**12**	1-2		1-0	8-0
Changchun Yatai	CHN	6	1	0	5	10	7	**3**	0-1	1-2		9-0
Persipura Jayapura	IDN	6	1	0	5	4	29	**3**	1-3	1-4	2-0	

Pakhtakor Tashkent   0
Al Gharafa *   1

Group G

		Pl	W	D	L	F	A	Pts	KOR	JPN	SIN	CHN
Suwon Bluewings	KOR	6	4	1	1	13	4	**13**		0-0	6-2	2-0
Gamba Osaka	JPN	6	3	3	0	11	5	**12**	2-1		3-0	1-1
Singapore A. Forces	SIN	6	1	1	4	6	16	**4**	0-2	2-4		2-1
Henan Jianye	CHN	6	0	3	3	3	8	**3**	0-2	1-1	0-0	

Pohang Steelers   1
Kashima Antlers *   0

Group H

		Pl	W	D	L	F	A	Pts	AUS	KOR	JPN	CHN
Adelaide United	AUS	6	3	1	2	6	4	**10**		1-0	3-2	0-1
Pohang Steelers	KOR	6	3	1	2	8	7	**10**	0-0		2-1	1-0
Sanfrecce Hiroshima	JPN	6	3	0	3	11	11	**9**	1-0	4-3		0-1
Shandong Luneng	CHN	6	2	0	4	5	8	**6**	0-2	1-2	2-3	

Mes Kerman   0
Zob Ahan *   1

AFC CHAMPIONS LEAGUE 2010

Quarter-finals	Semi-finals	Final

Seongnam Ilhwa Chunma *   4   0
Suwon Samsung Bluewings   1   2

Seongnam Ilhwa Chunma   3   1
Al Shabab *   4   0

Jeonbuk Hyundai Motors *   0   1
Al Shabab   2   0

Seongnam Ilhwa Chunma   3
Zob Ahan   1

Al Hilal *   3   2
Al Gharafa   0   4

Al Hilal   0   0
Zob Ahan *   1   1

Pohang Steelers   1   1
Zob Ahan *   2   1

* Home team/Home team in the first leg

Top scorers: **9** - Jose Mota BRA, Suwon • **7** - Mauricio Molina COL, Seognam • **5** - Mohammad Khalatbari, Zob Ahan; Denilson BRA, Bunyodkor; Farhad Majidi IRN, Esteghlal; Leandro BRA, Al Sadd; Flavio ANG, Al Shabab; Araujo BRA, Al Gharafa; Eninho BRA, Jeonbuk; Mehdi Rajabzadeh IRN, Mes Kerman/Zob Ahan & Yasser Al Khatani KSA, Hilal

AFC CHAMPIONS LEAGUE 2010 QUALIFYING

West Asia Semi-finals

Al Wahda	UAE	1
Al Karama *	SYR	0

West Asia Final

Al Wahda *	5
Churchill Brothers	2

Churchil Brothers	IND	Bye

East Asia Semi-finals

Singapore Armed Forces *	SIN	3
Sriwijaya	IDN	0

East Asia Final

Singapore Armed Forces *	0	4p
Muangthong United	0	3p

Da Nang *	VIE	0
Muangthong United	THA	3

* Home team • Al Wahda and Singapore Armed Forces qualified for the first round proper

West Asia Qualifying

Semi-Final. Khaled Bin Waled, Homs
30-01-2010, 19:00, 30 000, Kovalenko UZB

Al Karama 0

Mosab **Balhous** - Naser **Al Sebai**, Ahmad **Deeb** (Fahad **Al Rashidi** 76), Belal **Abduldaim**, Richard **Etiege**, Hasan **Abdel Fattah**, Fahad **Oudah** (Mohanad **Al Ibrahim** 61), Alaa **Al Shbli**, Aatef **Jenyat**, Yazid **Kaissi**, Mohamad **Al Hamawi**. Tr: Mohamed **Kwid**

Al Wahda 1
Mahmoud Khamis [72]

Adel **Al Hosani** - Yaqoub **Al Hosani** (Abdulraheem **Jumaa** 81), Hassan **Mudhafar**, Basheer **Saeed**, Haidar **Ali**, Mahmoud **Khamis**, Hamdan **Al Kamali**, Magrao, Ismail **Matar**, Mohamed **Al Shehhi** (Talal **Abdulla** 90), **Fernando** Baiano. Tr: Josef **Hickersberger**

Final. Al Nahyan, Abu Dhabi
6-02-2010, 19:00, 3000, Torky IRN

Al Wahda 5
Fernando 2 [45] [65], Khamis [46], Jumaa [63], Matar [85]

Adel **Al Hosani** - Yaqoub **Al Hosani**, Talal **Abdulla**, Hassan **Mudhafar**, Basheer **Saeed**•, Mahmoud Khamis (Ahmed **Ali** 76), Eisa **Ahmed**, Ismail **Matar**, Fahed **Masoud**, Abdulraheem **Jumaa** (Pinga 71), **Fernando** Baiano• (Mohamed **Al Shehhi** 80). Tr: Josef **Hickersberger**

Churchill Brothers 2
Ito [42], Dhanachandra Singh [77]

Arindam **Bhattacharya** - Rowilson **Rodrigues**, Robert **Lalthalma**, Gouramangi **Singh**, Thokchom **Singh**, Ogba **Nnanna**•, Reisangmei **Vashum** (Dan Ito 23), Nacimento **Silveira** (Dhanachandra **Singh** 71), Felix **Chimaokwu** (Jaison **Vales** 47), Odafe **Okolie**, Charan **Rai**. Tr: Carlos **da Silva**

East Asia Qualifying

Semi-final. Jalan Besar, Singapore
30-01-2010, 19:30, 2057, Williams AUS

Singapore Armed Forces 3
Akiyoshi [7], Martinez [63p], Sahdan [88p]

Rezal **Hassan** - Shaiful **Esah**, Niklas **Sandberg**, Ivan **Lovric**, Daniel **Bennett**, Noh **Rahman**•, Ahmad **Latiff** (Mustaqim **Manzur** 77), John **Wilkinson**, Taisuke **Akiyoshi**•, Federico **Martinez**• (Rhysh Roshan **Rai** 82), Indra **Sahdan**. Tr: Richard **Bok**

Sriwijaya 0

Feri **Rotinsulu** - Charis **Yulianto**, Precious **Emuejeraye**, Marthen Christian **Worabai**◆62, Isnan **Ali**, Toni **Sucipto** (Ambrizal 66), Zah **Krangar**, Ponaryo **Astaman**•, Arif **Suyono** (Muhammad **Nashua**• 74), Rachmat **Rivai** (Anoure **Obiora** 55), Keith **Gumbs**. Tr: Rahmad **Darmawan**

Semi-final. Chi Lang, Da Nang
31-01-2010, 16:00, 14 000, Mohd Salleh MAS

Na Nang 0

Tran Duc Cuong - **Tran** Van Hoc••◆49, **Vo** Hoang Quang, Le Phuoc Vinh Chau, **Tran** Hai Lam, **Phan** Thanh Phuc (Truong Quang Tuan 64), **Pham** Nguyen Sa (**Ha** Ngoc Quoc• 24), **Rogerio**••◆89, **Phan** Thanh Hung•, Huynh Quoc Anh (**Nguyen** Van Meo 72), Gaston **Merlo**•. Tr: Jose **Almeida**

Muangthong United 3
Wongsa [32], Kouakou [44], Winothai [78]

Kawin **Thammasatchanan** - Prakasit **Sansook**•, Panupong **Wongsa**, Nattaporn **Phanrit**, Piyachart **Tamaphan**, Moussa **Sylla**, Phichitpong **Choeichiu**, Yaya **Soumahoro**• (Jakkraphan **Kaewprom** 67), Christian **Kouakou** (Nobuyuki **Zaizen** 84), Teerathep **Winothai**, Amorn **Thammanarm** (Wisarut **Pannasri**• 71). Tr: Rene **Desaeyere**

Final. Jalan Besar, Singapore
6-02-2010, 19:30, 2809, Kim Dong Jin KOR

Singapore Armed Forces 0 4p

Shahril **Jantan** - Shaiful **Esah**, Niklas **Sandberg**, Ivan **Lovric** (Rhysh Roshan **Rai** 91), Daniel **Bennett**•, Noh **Rahman**, Ahmad **Latiff**, John **Wilkinson**, Mustaqim **Manzur** (Erwan Gunawan **Suherman** 114), Taisuke **Akiyoshi**, Indra **Sahdan**. Tr: Richard **Bok**

Muangthong United 0 3p

Kawin **Thammasatchanan** - Prakasit **Sansook**•, Panupong **Wongsa**, Nattaporn **Phanrit**, Piyachart **Tamaphan**•, Moussa **Sylla**, Phichitpong **Choeichiu** (Jakkraphan **Kaewprom** 54), Yaya **Soumahoro** (Wisarut **Pannasri** 98), Christian **Kouakou**, Teerathep **Winothai**•, Amorn **Thammanarm** (Nobuyuki **Zaizen** 69). Tr: Rene **Desaeyere**

PENALTIES (SAF WON 4-3)

Sahdan ✓; Tamaphan ✓; Wilkinson ✓;
Wongsa ✗; Sandberg ✓; Winothai ✓; Bennett
✓; Zaizen ✓; Akiyoshi ✗; Sansook ✗

GROUP A		Pl	W	D	L	F	A	Pts	QAT	IRN	KSA	UAE
Al Gharafa	QAT	6	4	1	1	11	9	13		1-1	3-2	4-2
Esteghlal Tehran	IRN	6	3	2	1	9	5	11	3-0		2-1	0-0
Al Ahli Jeddah	KSA	6	2	0	4	11	9	6	0-1	1-2		5-1
Al Jazira	UAE	6	1	1	4	6	14	4	1-2	2-1	0-2	

Bin Zayed, Abu Dhabi
23-02-2010, 19:15, 5810, Nishimura JPN
Al Jazira 1
Rafael Sobis 56
Ali Khasif - Juma **Abdulla**, Marcio Rozario (Saleh Basheer 24), Abdulla Mousa, Salim **Al Abri**, Abdulsalam **Jumaa•**, Yaser Matar (Ali Mabkhout 46), Subait Khater, Ibrahim Diaky, Mohamed Rashid (Abdulla Qasim 66), Rafael Sobis. Tr: Abel **Braga**
Al Gharafa 2
El Assas 17, Younis Mahmoud 53
Qasem Burhan - Ibrahim **Al Ghanim**, Hamed Shami, Ahmed **Al Binali•** (Fahid **Al Shammari** 64), George Kwesi Semakor•, Saud Sabah, Juninho Pernambucano•, Othmane El Assas, Younis **Mahmoud•** (Muayed Hassan 90), Clemerson, Mirghani **Al Zain•** (Saad Al Shammari 81). Tr: Caio Junior

Al Gharafa, Doha
9-03-2010, 18:40, 6091, Basma SYR
Al Gharafa 3
Al Zain 2, Fahid Al Shammari 79, Clemerson 81
Abdulaziz Ali - Ibrahim **Al Ghanim**, Hamed Shami, Ahmed **Al Binali**, George Kwesi Semakor, Saud Sabah (Fahid Al Shammari 73), Juninho Pernambucano♦89, Othmane El Assas, Younis **Mahmoud**, Clemerson, Mirghani Al Zain (Saad Al Shammari 65). Tr: Caio Junior
Al Ahli Jeddah 2
Marcinho 45, Jaizawi 64
Abdullah **Al Muaiouf** - Saif Ghezal•, Muhammed Massad•, Waleed Jahdali, Mansour Al Harbi, Motaz Al Mosa (Ahmed Al Safri 85), Marcinho, Ahmed **Mubarak•**, Abdulraheem Jaizawi• (Hassan Al Raheb 72), Victor Simoes, Malek Mouath (Hamoud Abbas 68). Tr: Gustavo **Alfaro**.

Al Gharafa, Doha
31-03-2010, 18:45, 6023, Green AUS
Al Gharafa 1
Younis Mahmoud 45
Qasem Burhan - Ibrahim **Al Ghanim**, Hamed Shami, George Kwesi Semakor, Bilal Mohammed, Saud Sabah (Ahmed **Al Binali** 73), Juninho Pernambucano, Othmane El Assas•, Fahid Al Shammari (Mirghani Al Zain 59), Younis Mahmoud, Clemerson. Tr: Caio Junior
Esteghlal Tehran 1
Salehi 59
Mohammad Mohammadi - Hanif Omranzadeh, Amir-Hossein Sadeghi•, Khosro Heydari, Mohsen Yousefi, Kianoush Rahmati, Pejman Montazeri, Fabio Januario, Farhad Majidi (Arash Borhani 79), Siavash Akbarpour, Mehdi Seyed Salehi (Rinaldo Cruzado 90). Tr: Samad Marfavi

Al Gharafa, Doha
14-04-2010, 19:00, 5432, Kim DJ KOR
Al Gharafa 4
Clemerson 3 11 41 46, El Assas 65
Qasem Burhan - Ibrahim **Al Ghanim•**, Hamed Shami, George Kwesi Semakor, Bilal Mohammede (Ahmed Al Binali 62), Saud Sabah (Fahid Al Shammari 81), Juninho Pernambucano•, Othmane El Assas, Younis Mahmoud (Muayed Hassan 72), Clemerson, Mirghani Al Zain. Tr: Caio Junior
Al Jazira 2
Rafael Sobis 74, Abdulla Mousa 88
Ali Khasif - Marcio Rozario, Abdulla Mousa•, Salim Al Abri, Ali Salem Ahmed Faraj, Abdulsalam Jumaa•, Yaser Matar (Tariq Ahmed 46), Subait Khater, Ahmed Muhad (Ahmed Jumaa 81), Ali Mabkhout (Mohamed Salem 87), Rafael Sobis. Tr: Abel Braga

---

Prince Abdullah, Jeddah
23-02-2010, 20:20, 16 000, Takayama JPN
Al Ahli Jeddah 1
Al Raheb 85
Abdullah **Al Muaiouf** - Saif Ghezal•, Muhammed Massad, Waleed Jahdali, Mansour Al Harbi (Abdulraheem Jaizawi 21), Motaz Al Mosa, Taisir Al Jassim•, **Marcinho•** (Ahmed Al Raheb 75), Ahmed Mubarak, Victor Simoes, Malek Mouath• (Mohammed Al Safri 66). Tr: Gustavo Alfaro
Esteghlal Tehran 2
Farhad Majdi 2 17 75
Mohammad Mohammadi• - Mehdi Amirabadi (Amir-Hossein Sadeghi 90), Hadi Shakouri, Hanif Omranzadeh, Khosro Heydari, Hossein Kazemi, Kianoush Rahmati, Pejman Montazeri, Fabio Januario (Hashem Beikzadeh 71), Farhad Majidi• (Mehdi Seyed Salehi 85), Siavash Akbarpour. Tr: Samad Marfavi

Azadi, Tehran
23-03-2010, 17:30, 60 000, Kovalenko UZB
Esteghlal Tehran 3
Farhad Majdi 2 12 54, Pejman Montazeri 79
Mohammad Mohammadi - Hanif Omranzadeh, Amir-Hossein Sadeghi, Khosro Heydari, Hossein Kazemi•, Mohsen Yousefi, Pejman Montazeri, Fabio Januario (Milad Noori• 85), Farhad Majidi, Siavash Akbarpour, Mehdi Seyed Salehi (Arash Borhani 77). Tr: Samad Marfavi
Al Gharafa 0
Abdulaziz Ali - Ibrahim **Al Ghanim**, Hamed Shami• (Fahid **Al Shammari** 55), Saad Al Shammari (Ahmed Al Binali 64), George Kwesi Semakor, Bilal Mohammed, Saud Sabah, Othmane El Assas, Younis Mahmoud, Clemerson, Mirghani Al Zain. Tr: Caio Junior

Bin Zayed, Abu Dhabi
31-03-2010, 19:30, 2006, Abdul Bashir SIN
Al Jazira 0
Khalid Eisa - Marcio Rozario, Saleh Basheer, Michael Beauchamp, Salim **Al Abri** (Khalid Sabeel 81), Yaser Matar, Tariq Ahmed, Sultan **Al Menhali♦**35, Abdulla **Qasim•** (Ahmed Jumaa 46), Mohamed Rashid• (Mohamed Salem 73), Ali Mabkhout. Tr: Abel Braga
Al Ahli Jeddah 2
Victor Simoes 2 7 50
Yaser Al Mosailem - Mahmoud Moad, Muhammed Massad•, Waleed Jahdali♦83, Ibrahim Hazzazi•, Mansour Al Harbi (Jufain Al Bishi 66), Motaz Al Mosa, Marcinho (Ahmed Darwesh 86), Ahmed Mubarak (Sahib Al Abdulla 82), Abdulraheem Jaizawi, Victor Simoes. Tr: Gustavo Alfaro

Bin Zayed, Abu Dhabi
28-04-2010, 19:45, 2129, Tojo JPN
Al Jazira 2
Saleh Basheer 51, Tariq Ahmed 53
Ali Khasif - Marcio Rozario, Saleh Basheer, Michael Beauchamp, Salim **Al Abri•**, Yaser Matar, Tariq Ahmed•, Eid **Ibrahim•**, Abdulla Qasim (Ali Mabkhout 61), Ahmed Muhad (Subait Khater 79), Rafael Sobis (Ahmed Jumaa 84). Tr: Abel Braga
Esteghlal Tehran 1
Farhad Majidi 38
Mohammad Mohammadi - Mehdi Amirabadi (Hashem Beikzadeh 74), Hanif Omranzadeh, Amir-Hossein Sadeghi, Khosro Heydari, Hossein Kazemi, Pejman Montazeri, Fabio Januario, Farhad Majidi, Arash Borhani (Mehdi Seyed Salehi 69), Siavash Akbarpour (Mojtaba Jabbari 81). Tr: Samad Marfavi

---

Azadi, Tehran
9-03-2010, 17:30, 32 000, Choi MY KOR
Esteghlal Tehran 0
Mohammad Mohammadi - Mehdi Amirabadi (Mohsen Yousefi 84), Hanif Omranzadeh, Amir-Hossein Sadeghi, Khosro Heydari, Hossein Kazemi•, Kianoush Rahmati (Mehdi Seyed Salehi 74), Pejman Montazeri, Fabio Januario (Arash Borhani 90), Farhad Majidi, Siavash Akbarpour. Tr: Samad Marfavi
Al Jazira 0
Ali Khasif• - Saleh Basheer, Abdulla Mousa•, Khalid Sabeel (Salim Al Abri 88), Ali Salem Ahmed Faraj, Abdulsalam Jumaa, Subait Khater, Abdulla Qasim (Sultan Al Menhali 52), Ibrahim Diaky, Mohamed Rashid (Ali Mabkhout 46), Rafael Sobis•. Tr: Abel Braga

Prince Abdullah, Jeddah
23-03-2010, 20:30, 11 000, Irmatov UZB
Al Ahli Jeddah 5
Simoes 2, Marcinho 2 55 78, Jaizawi 2 57 92+
Yaser Al Mosailem - Mahmoud Moad, Muhammed Massad (Taisir Al Jassim 64), Waleed Jahdali, Ibrahim Hazzazi•, Mansour Al Harbi•, Motaz Al Mosa, Marcinho•, Ahmed Mubarak, Abdulraheem Jaizawi, Victor Simoes (Hassan Al Raheb 66). Tr: Gustavo Alfaro
Al Jazira 1
Koutouan 62
Ali Khasif• - Marcio Rozario, Abdulla Mousa, Khalid Sabeel (Sultan Al Menhali 66), Ali Salem Ahmed Faraj, Abdulsalam Jumaa• (Ahmed Muhad• 46), Helal Saeed, Abdulla Qasim (Mohamed Rashid 46), Ibrahim Diaky, Antonin Koutouan, Ali Mabkhout. Tr: Abel Braga

Azadi, Tehran
14-04-2010, 17:30, 64 840, Sun Baojie CHN
Esteghlal Tehran 2
Salehi 24, Sadeghi 44
Mohammad Mohammadi - Hanif Omranzadeh•, Amir-Hossein Sadeghi, Khosro Heydari, Hossein Kazemi•, Mohsen Yousefi, Pejman Montazeri, Fabio Januario (Rinaldo Cruzado 90), Farhad Majidi (Arash Borhani• 75), Siavash Akbarpour, Mehdi Seyed Salehi (Kianoush Rahmati 84). Tr: Samad Marfavi
Al Ahli Jeddah 1
Victor Simoes 35p
Yaser Al Mosailem - Saif Ghezal (Ahmed Darwesh 46), Jufain Al Bishi, Marcinho, Ahmed Mubarak•, Sahib Al Abdulla•, Ahmed Darwesh, Alaa Al Rishani•, Hamoud Abbas (Abdulraheem Jaizawi 54), Victor Simoes, Malek Mouath (Hassan Al Raheb 67). Tr: Gustavo Alfaro

Prince Abdullah, Jeddah
28-04-2010, 20:40, 500, Williams AUS
Al Ahli Jeddah 0
Yaser Al Mosailem - Saif Ghezal (Ahmed Darwesh 26), Muhammed Massad, Waleed Jahdali, Ibrahim Hazzazi•, Taisir Al Jassim (Waleed Rashid 83), Marcinho, Sahib Al Abdulla, Abdulraheem Jaizawi• (Hassan Al Raheb 74), Alaa Al Rishani•, Victor Simoes•. Tr: Gustavo Alfaro
Al Gharafa 1
Nasser Mubarak 92+
Abdulaziz Ali - Ibrahim **Al Ghanim•**, Marcone Amaral, Saad Al Shammari, Ahmed **Al Binali•**, Saghayer Al Shammari• (Nasser Mubarak 81), Saud Sabah, Abdul Aziz Wadi, Mohammed Shaker (Mirghani Al Zain 46), Fahid Al Shammari, Mohammed Harees (Muayed Hassan 66). Tr: Caio Junior

GROUP B		Pl	W	D	L	F	A	Pts	IRN	UZB	KSA	UAE
Zob Ahan	IRN	6	4	1	1	8	3	**13**		3-0	1-0	1-0
Bunyodkor	UZB	6	3	1	2	10	7	**10**	0-1		3-0	4-1
Al Ittihad Jeddah	KSA	6	2	2	2	9	7	**8**	2-2	1-1		4-0
Al Wahda	UAE	6	1	0	5	3	13	**3**	1-0	1-2	0-2	

JAR, Tashkent
23-02-2010, 16:00, 7500, Williams AUS

Bunyodkor 3
Rivaldo [3], Hasanov [21], Denilson [66]

Ignatiy Nesterov - Anvar Gafurov, Sakhob Jurayev•, Anzur Ismailov•, Aziz Haydarov•, Rivaldo•, Jansur Hasanov (Timur Kapadze 88), Viktor Karpenko, Joao Victor, Server Djeparov (Anvarjon Solyiev 90), Denilson. Tr: Luiz Felipe Scolari

Al Ittihad Jeddah 0

Tisir Al Antaif - Obaid Al Shamrani•, Saleh Al Saqri, Hamad Al Montashari, Osama Al Harbi, Manaf Abushgeer, Ahmed Hadid (Rashid Al Raheeb 63), Saud Khariri, Mohammed Noor•, Abdelmalek Ziaya (Sultan Al Nemari 84), Hicham Aboucherouane (Amine Chermiti 67). Tr: Enzo Trossero

---

Prince Abdullah, Jeddah
9-03-2010, 20:35, 15 343, Abdou QAT

Al Ittihad Jeddah 2
Ziaya [13], Noor [41]

Tisir Al Antaif - Mohammed Saadem, Obaid Al Shamrani (Rashid Al Raheeb 69), Saleh Al Saqri•, Hamad Al Montashari, Manaf Abushgeer, Saud Khariri, Mohammed Noor, Sultan Al Nemari (Amine Chermiti 72), Abdelmalek Ziaya•, Hicham Aboucherouane (Talal Al Meshal 83). Tr: Enzo Trossero

Zob Ahan 2
Farhadi [50], Ghazi [52]

Shahabeddin Gordan - Farsheed Talebi•, Mohammad Salsali, Hassan Ashjari, Seyed Hosseini•, Mohammad Mansori (Mohammad Ahmadi 90), Ghasem Hadadifar (Gabriel Iribarren 81), Sina Ashori, Mohammad Reza Khalatbari, Esmail Farhadi (Igor 63), Mohammad Ghazi. Tr: Mansour Ebrahimsadeh

---

JAR, Tashkent
30-03-2010, 17:00, 9000, Sun Baojie CHN

Bunyodkor 0

Ignatiy Nesterov - Anvar Gafurov•, Sakhob Jurayev, Anzur Ismailov, Aziz Haydarov (Anvarjon Solyiev 65), Rivaldo•67, Jansur Hasanov, Viktor Karpenko, Joao Victor (Timur Kapadze 78), Server Djeparov, Denilson. Tr: Luiz Felipe Scolari

Zob Ahan 1
Khalatbari [29]

Shahabeddin Gordan - Mohamad Ahmadi• (Mostafa Salehi 71), Farsheed Talebi, Hassan Ashjari, Seyed Hosseini•, Mohammad Mansori• (Mohsen Mosalman 88), Sina Ashori•, Mohammad Reza Khalatbari, Esmail Farhadi (Igor 61), Mohammad Ghazi. Tr: Mansour Ebrahimsadeh

---

Prince Abdullah, Jeddah
14-04-2010, 20:50, 17 500, Nishimura JPN

Al Ittihad Jeddah 1
Noor [38]

Mabrouk Zaid - Rashid Al Raheeb, Redha Tukar (Hamad Al Montashari 66), Mishal Al Saeed, Saleh Al Saqri•, Manaf Abushgeer, Ahmed Hadid, Saud Khariri, Mohammed Noor, Sultan Al Nemari (Hicham Aboucherouane 72), Abdelmalek Ziaya•. Tr: Enzo Trossero

Bunyodkor 1
Solyiev [62]

Ignatiy Nesterov - Hayrulla Karimov, Anzur Ismailov•, Ruslan Melzididinov• (Aleksandr Kovalev 84), Aziz Haydarov, Timur Kapadze (Anvarjon Solyiev 61), Jansur Hasanov, Viktor Karpenko, Joao Victor, Server Djeparov, Denilson (Shavkat Salomov 88). Tr: Luiz Felipe Scolari

---

Foolad Shahr, Isfahan
23-02-2010, 17:30, 4568, Tojo JPN

Zob Ahan 1
Igor [60]

Shahabeddin Gordan - Farsheed Talebi, Mohammad Salsali, Hassan Ashjari, Seyed Hosseini, Mohammad Mansori (Mostafa Salehi 90), Ghasem Hadadifar (Mohsen Mosalman 86), Sina Ashori•, Mohammad Reza Khalatbari, Igor, Mohammad Ghazi (Esmail Farhadi 74). Tr: Mansour Ebrahimsadeh

Al Wahda 0

Adel Mohamed - Fahed Masoud (Salem Saleh 70), Hassan Mudhafar, Basheer Saeed, Eisa Ahmed, Hamdan Al Kamali, Magrao, Mahmoud Khamis (Khalid Jalal 46), Mohamed Saeed (Hasan Ameen76), Fernando Baiano•, Saeed Salem. Tr: Josef Hickersberger

---

Foolad Shahr, Isfahan
24-03-2010, 18:00, 5250, Choi MY KOR

Zob Ahan 3
Hosseini [38], Ghazi [54], Khalatbari [80]

Shahabeddin Gordan - Mohamad Ahmadi, Farsheed Talebi, Hassan Ashjari, Seyed Hosseini, Mohammad Mansori (Mohsen Mosalman 90), Ghasem Hadadifar, Sina Ashori, Mohammad Reza Khalatbari, Igor (Esmail Farhadi 75), Mohammad Ghazi (Mostafa Salehi 83). Tr: Mansour Ebrahimsadeh

Bunyodkor 0

Ignatiy Nesterov - Anvar Gafurov•, Anzur Ismailov, Aziz Haydarov, Timur Kapadze, Jansur Hasanov (Shavkat Salomov 67), Viktor Karpenko, Server Djeparov, Aleksandr Kovalev (Ruslan Melzididinov 70), Denilson• (Anvar Rakhimov 81), Anvarjon Solyiev. Tr: Luiz Felipe Scolari

---

Prince Abdullah, Jeddah
30-03-2010, 20:45, 15 500, Mahapab THA

Al Ittihad Jeddah 2
Ziaya [12], Khariri 2 [17 19], Al Nemari [32]

Mabrouk Zaid - Rashid Al Raheeb, Redha Tukar, Mishal Al Saeed•, Saleh Al Saqri, Manaf Abushgeer, Ahmed Hadid (Ali Al Zubaidi 70), Saud Khariri (Hicham Aboucherouane 65), Mohammed Noor, Sultan Al Nemari, Abdelmalek Ziaya (Amine Chermiti 67). Tr: Enzo Trossero

Al Wahda 0

Adel Mohamed - Omar Ali, Talal Abdulla, Hassan Mudhafar•, Haider Alo Ali, Eisa Ahmed, Yaqoub Yousif, Ismail Matar, Hasan Ameen• (Salem Saleh 72), Saeed Salem (Amer Bazuhair 60), Ahmed Ali (Mohamed Ahmed 76). Tr: Josef Hickersberger

---

JAR, Tashkent
28-04-2010, 18:00, 7992, Kim DJ KOR

Bunyodkor 4
Rivaldo [29], Denilson 2 [31 57], Haydarov [79]

Ignatiy Nesterov• - Hayrulla Karimov, Anvar Gafurov•, Sakhob Jurayev (Ruslan Melzididinov 74), Aziz Haydarov, Rivaldo, Jansur Hasanov, Viktor Karpenko•, Joao Victor (Timur Kapadze 62), Server Djeparov (Anvarjon Solyiev 82), Denilson•. Tr: Luiz Felipe Scolari

Al Wahda 1
Talal Abdulla [92+p]

Ali Mohamed - Omar Ali, Talal Abdulla•, Eisa Ahmed (Arwan Mohamed 33), Yaqoub Yousif• (Mohamed Othman 58), Hasan Ameen•, Mahmoud Khamis, Amer Bazuhair, Khalid Jalal, Saeed Salem (Mohamed Ahmed 72), Ahmed Ali. Tr: Josef Hickersberger

---

Al Nahyan, Abu Dhabi
9-03-2010, 19:20, 5000, Balideh QAT

Al Wahda 1
Saeed Salem [89]

Adel Mohamed - Hassan Mudhafar, Basheer Saeed, Haider Alo Ali•, Hamdan Al Kamali•, Yaqoub Yousif (Khalid Jalal 73) (Saeed Salem• 83), Ismail Matar•, Pinga, Abdulraheem Jumaa, Mohamed Saeed (Ahmed Ali 60), Fernando Baiano. Tr: Josef Hickersberger

Bunyodkor 2
Denilson 2 [37 85]

Ignatiy Nesterov• - Anvar Gafurov, Sakhob Jurayev• (Aleksandr Kovalev 84), Anzur Ismailov, Aziz Haydarov, Rivaldo, Jansur Hasanov•, Viktor Karpenko, Joao Victor•, Server Djeparov (Timur Kapadze 86), Denilson (Anvar Rakhimov 90). Tr: Luiz Felipe Scolari

---

Al Nahyan, Abu Dhabi
24-03-2010, 19:30, 8553, Tan Hai CHN

Al Wahda 0

Adel Mohamed - Hassan Mudhafar (Abdulraheem Jumaa 46), Basheer Saeed, Eisa Ahmed (Talal Abdulla 89), Hamdan Al Kamali, Yaqoub Yousif (Saeed Salem 64), Magrao, Ismail Matar, Mahmoud Khamis, Mohamed Saeed, Fernando Baiano•. Tr: Josef Hickersberger

Al Ittihad Jeddah 2
Ziaya [17], Noor [92+]

Mabrouk Zaid - Rashid Al Raheeb, Redha Tukar, Mishal Al Saeed, Saleh Al Saqri (Hamad Al Montashari 81), Manaf Abushgeer (Hicham Aboucherouane• 75), Ahmed Hadid, Saud Khariri•, Mohammed Noor, Sultan Al Nemari•, Abdelmalek Ziaya (Amine Chermiti 78). Tr: Enzo Trossero

---

Al Nahyan, Abu Dhabi
14-04-2010, 19:35, 1575, Shukralla BHR

Al Wahda 1
Hasan Ameen [72]

Adel Mohamed - Omar Ali, Talal Abdulla, Haider Alo Ali, Yaqoub Yousif (Khalid Jalal 73), Hasan Ameen, Abdulraheem Jumaa, Mahmoud Khamis, Mohamed Saeed (Eisa Ahmed 79), Fernando Baiano (Mohamed Ahmed 83), Saeed Salem. Tr: Josef Hickersberger

Zob Ahan 0

Shahabeddin Gordan (Abbas Ghasemi 26) - Mohamad Ahmadi, Farsheed Talebi, Hassan Ashjari, Mostafa Salehi, Mohammad Mansori, Gabriel Iribarren, Ghasem Hadadifar•, Mohammad Reza Khalatbari, Esmail Farhadi (Igor 61), Mohammad Ghazi (Mohsen Mosalman• 77). Tr: Mansour Ebrahimsadeh

---

Foolad Shahr, Isfahan
28-04-2010, 18:30, 5961, Green AUS

Zob Ahan 1
Khalatbari [56]

Shahabeddin Gordan - Mohamad Ahmadi, Farsheed Talebi•, Hassan Ashjari, Seyed Hosseini, Mohammad Mansori, Mohsen Mosalman (Mostafa Salehi 90), Sina Ashori, Mohammad Reza, Mohammad Reza Khalatbari• (Keivan Amraei 90), Esmail Farhadi, Mohammad Ghazi (Igor 85). Tr: Mansour Ebrahimsadeh

Al Ittihad Jeddah 0

Mabrouk Zaid - Rashid Al Raheeb, Mishal Al Saeed, Adnan Falatah (Naif Hazazi 61), Hamad Al Montashari, Manaf Abushgeer•, Ahmed Hadid (Amine Chermiti 78), Saud Khariri, Mohammed Noor•, Sultan Al Nemari (Hicham Aboucherouane 46), Talal Al Meshal. Tr: Enzo Trossero

GROUP C		Pl	W	D	L	F	A	Pts	KSA	UZB	IRN	UAE
Al Shabab	KSA	6	3	1	2	10	8	10		2-1	1-1	3-2
Pakhtakor Tashkent	UZB	6	3	0	3	8	10	9	1-3		2-1	3-2
Sepahan	IRN	6	2	2	2	5	5	8	1-0	2-0		0-0
Al Ain	UAE	6	2	1	3	8	8	7	2-1	0-1	2-0	

Khalifa International, Al Ain
24-02-2010, 19:20, 6405, Sun Baojie CHN
Al Ain   **0**

Waleed Salem• - Helal Saeed, Msalam Fayez, Faris Juma, Ali Al Wehaibi•, Jorge Valdivia, Shehab Ahmed (Ahmed Mathaad 64), Saif Mohammed, Abdullah Malalla (Mohammed Abdulrahman 80), Ho Lee, Jose Sand•. Tr: Toninho Cerezo

Pakhtakor Tashkent   **1**
                      Gevorkyan [60]
Temur Juraev - Bojan Miladinovic, Kamoliddin Tadjiev, Ilhomjon Suyunov, Darko Markovic•, Akmal Kholmatov (Stanislav Andreev• 75), Asqar Jadigerov (Sherzodbek Karimov 80), Artur Gevorkyan, Alexandr Kletskov (Odil Ahmedov, Milorad Janjus (Farhod Tadjiyev 85). Tr: Miodrag Radulovic

---

Foolad Shahr, Isfahan
10-03-2010, 17:00, 8000, Abdul Bashir SIN
Sepahan   **0**

Seyed Rahmati - Hadi Aghily, Jalal Hosseini, Mohsen Bengar, Mehdi Karimian (Hossein Papi 86), Shahin Kheiri, Armando Sa (Moharram Navidkia 46), Ehsan Hajysafi, Ali Molaei (Mehdi Jafarpour 46), Ibrahima Toure, Ahmad Jamshidian. Tr: Amir Ghalenoei

Al Ain   **0**

Waleed Salem - Helal Saeed, Msalam Fayez, Mohnad Salem, Faris Juma (Fawzi Fayez 84), Ali Al Wehaibi, Jorge Valdivia•, Saif Mohammed (Hazza Salem 72) (Ahmed Mathaad 90), Abdullah Malalla, Ho Lee•, Jose Sand. Tr: Toninho Cerezo

---

Foolad Shahr, Isfahan
31-03-2010, 18:00, 9570, Balideh QAT
Sepahan   **2**
            Toure [74], Bengar [75]
Seyed Rahmati - Hadi Aghily•, Jalal Hosseini, Mohsen Bengar•, Moharram Navidkia (Farzad Hatami 46), Mehdi Karimian (Mehdi Jafarpour 67), Shahin Kheiri, Ehsan Hajysafi, Emad Mohammed (Hossein Papi 84), Ibrahima Toure, Ahmad Jamshidian. Tr: Amir Ghalenoei

Pakhtakor Tashkent   **0**

Temur Juraev - Bojan Miladinovic, Kamoliddin Tadjiev, Ilhomjon Suyunov•, Darko Markovic, Asqar Jadigerov (Akmal Kholmatov 78), Artur Gevorkyan, Alexandr Kletskov, Odil Ahmedov, Stanislav Andreev (Murod Khalmukhamedov 69), Milorad Janjus (Alisher Azizov 45). Tr: Miodrag Radulovic

---

Foolad Shahr, Isfahan
13-04-2010, 18:30, 9500, Mohd Salleh MAS
Sepahan   **1**
                 Jamsidian [9]
Seyed Rahmati - Hadi Aghily, Jalal Hosseini, Ahmad Alenemeh, Moharram Navidkia (Hossein Papi 88), Mehdi Karimian, Shahin Kheiri, Ehsan Hajysafi•, Emad Mohammed, Ibrahima Toure• (Farzad Hatami 90), Ahmad Jamshidian• (Mehdi Jafarpour 84). Tr: Amir Ghalenoei

Al Shabab   **0**

Waleed Abdullah• - Naif Al Qadi, Ziad Al Mowalad (Abdullah Al Shuhail 82), Sanad Shrahilee (Ahmad Kabee 66), Mesaed Al Enezi, Camacho, Ahmed Ateef•, Abdulmalek Al Khaibri• (Faisal bin Sultan 73), Tarik El Taib, Ali Ataif, Flavio Amado. Tr: Jaime Pacheco

---

King Fahd International, Riyadh
24-02-2010, 20:20, 7000, Abdou QAT
Al Shabab   **1**
          Faisal bin Sultan [69]
Waleed Abdullah - Abdullah Al Astaa (Naji Majrashi 66), Hassan Muath, Mesaed Al Enezi, Majed Al Marhoum, Camacho, Ahmed Ateef, Abdulmalek Al Khaibri•, Ali Ataif, Flavio Amado (Waleed Al Gizani 81), Faisal bin Sultan (Sanad Shrahilee 89). Tr: Jaime Pacheco

Sepahan   **1**
                 Hosseini [14]
Seyed Rahmati - Hadi Aghily, Jalal Hosseini, Mohsen Bengar, Mehdi Jafarpour• (Hossein Papi 71), Mehdi Karimian, Shahin Kheiri, Ehsan Hajysafi, Emad Mohammed, Ibrahima Toure, Ahmad Jamshidian (Ahmad Alenemeh 84). Tr: Amir Ghalenoei

---

Pakhtakor, Tashkent
23-03-2010, 17:00, 9500, Basma SYR
Pakhtakor Tashkent   **2**
          Gevorkyan [38], Geynrikh [71]
Temur Juraev - Bojan Miladinovic, Murod Khalmukhamedov•, Kamoliddin Tadjiev, Ilhomjon Suyunov, Darko Markovic, Asqar Jadigerov (Aleksandr Geynrikh 70), Artur Gevorkyan, Alexandr Kletskov, Stanislav Andreev (Gulom Urunov 81), Milorad Janjus• (Sherzodbek Karimov 88). Tr: Miodrag Radulovic

Sepahan   **1**
               Jamshidian [45]
Seyed Rahmati - Hadi Aghily (Armando Sa 27), Jalal Hosseini•, Mohsen Bengar•, Moharram Navidkia, Mehdi Jafarpour (Hossein Papi 77), Mehdi Karimian (Farzad Hatami 83), Shahin Kheiri, Ehsan Hajysafi, Ibrahima Toure, Ahmad Jamshidian•. Tr: Amir Ghalenoei

---

King Fahd International, Riyadh
31-03-2010, 20:30, 10 000, Basma SYR
Al Shabab   **3**
     Flavio Amado 2 [12 66], Camacho [83]
Waleed Abdullah - Abdullah Al Astaa•, Hassan Muath, Sanad Shrahilee (Abdoh Autef 60), Mesaed Al Enezi•, Majed Al Marhoum, Camacho, Ahmed Ateef, Tarik El Taib (Bader Al Hagbani 88), Flavio Amado, Abdulaziz bin Saran (Faisal bin Sultan 61). Tr: Jaime Pacheco

Al Ain   **2**
          Sand [31], Al Enezi OG [58]
Waleed Salem - Msalam Fayez, Ismaeel Ahmed, Faris Juma (Fawzi Fayez 84), Abdulaziz Fayez• (Hazza Salem 37) (Ahmed Mathaad 85), Ali Al Wehaibi, Saif Mohammed, Abdullah Malalla, Ho Lee, Emerson, Jose Sand•. Tr: Toninho Cerezo

---

Pakhtakor, Tashkent
10-03-2010, 17:00, 12 000, Tojo JPN
Pakhtakor Tashkent   **1**
                    Azizov [77]
Temur Juraev - Bojan Miladinovic•, Kamoliddin Tadjiev, Ilhomjon Suyunov, Darko Markovic, Akmal Kholmatov (Alisher Azizov 70), Asqar Jadigerov (Stanislav Andreev 56), Artur Gevorkyan, Alexandr Kletskov (Ruzimbay Ahmedov 85), Odil Ahmedov, Milorad Janjus. Tr: Miodrag Radulovic

Al Shabab   **3**
    Flavio Amado 2 [61 74], Ahmad Kabee [97+]
Waleed Abdullah• - Abdullah Al Astaa, Hassan Muath, Sanad Shrahilee (Ahmad Kabee 87), Hadi Yahya, Majed Al Marhoum, Camacho•, Ahmed Ateef, Abdulmalek Al Khaibri, Flavio Amado (Faisal bin Sultan 90), Abdulaziz bin Saran (Majed Al Amri 81). Tr: Jaime Pacheco

---

Khalifa International, Al Ain
23-03-2010, 19:30, 4607, Kim DJ KOR
Al Ain   **2**
           Emerson [14], Sand [23]
Waleed Salem - Helal Saeed•, Ismaeel Ahmed, Faris Juma, Ali Al Wehaibi (Abdulaziz Fayez 89), Jorge Valdivia••71, Saif Mohammed, Abdullah Malalla, Ho Lee (Msalam Fayez 90), Emerson•, Jose Sand (Ahmed Mathaad 82). Tr: Toninho Cerezo

Al Shabab   **1**
                  Saran [45]
Waleed Abdullah - Abdullah Al Astaa, Sanad Shrahilee, Hadi Yahya, Majed Al Marhoum•, Camacho, Ahmed Ateef, Abdulmalek Al Khaibri• (Faisal bin Sultan 81), Flavio Amado, Abdulaziz bin Saran, Abdulaziz Yousef (Tarik El Taib 69). Tr: Jaime Pacheco

---

Pakhtakor, Tashkent
13-04-2010, 18:00, 14 600, Breeze AUS
Pakhtakor Tashkent   **3**
               Ahmedov 3 [9 12 29]
Eldor Tadjibaev - Bojan Miladinovic, Murod Khalmukhamedov (Sherzodbek Karimov• 37), Kamoliddin Tadjiev, Ilhomjon Suyunov•, Darko Markovic•, Asqar Jadigerov, Alexandr Kletskov, Odil Ahmedov (Oybek Kilichev 90), Stanislav Andreev, Aleksandr Geynrikh (Alisher Azizov 88). Tr: Radulovic

Al Ain   **2**
     Jorge Valdivia [2], Suyunov OG [20]
Waleed Salem - Msalam Fayez•, Ismaeel Ahmed•, Faris Juma, Abdulaziz Fayez (Mohammed Abdulrahman 69), Ali Al Wehaibi, Jorge Valdivia•, Saif Mohammed• (Mohnad Salem 46), Abdullah Malalla, Ho Lee (Ahmed Mathaad 46), Emerson•. Tr: Toninho Cerezo

---

Khalifa International, Al Ain
27-04-2010, 19:50, 1543, Takayama JPN
Al Ain   **2**
              Sand 2 [43 71]
Yousif Abdulrahman• - Helal Saeed, Mohnad Salem, Fawzi Fayez, Faris Juma, Omar Abdulrahman• (Ahmed Mathaad 65), Ali Al Wehaibi•, Shehab Ahmed (Abdulaziz Fayez 71), Abdullah Malalla, Ho Lee• (Mohammed Abdulrahman 87), Jose Sand. Tr: Toninho Cerezo

Sepahan   **2**

Seyed Rahmati - Hadi Aghily, Jalal Hosseini, Mohsen Bengar, Ahmad Alenemeh (Mehdi Jafarpour 46), Moharram Navidkia, Mehdi Karimian, Shahin Kheiri• (Hossein Papi 75), Ehsan Hajysafi, Emad Mohammed, Ibrahima Toure. Tr: Amir Ghalenoei

---

King Fahd International, Riyadh
27-04-2010, 20:40, 7251, Choi MY KOR
Al Shabab   **2**
     Camacho [64p], Flavio Amado [86]
Hussain Al Shian - Naif Al Qadi, Hassan Muath• (Ziad Al Mowalad 46), Abdullah Al Shuhail, Mesaed Al Enezi, Camacho, Ahmed Ateef, Abdulmalek Al Khaibri (Abdoh Autef 46), Tarik El Taib, Flavio Amado• (Faisal bin Sultan (Waleed Al Gizani 75). Tr: Jaime Pacheco

Pakhtakor Tashkent   **1**
                   Karimov [31]
Temur Juraev - Bojan Miladinovic, Kamoliddin Tadjiev (Murod Khalmukhamedov 6), Alexandr Kletskov, Asqar Jadigerov (Oybek Kilichev 57), Sherzodbek Karimov, Artur Gevorkyan, Alexandr Kletskov••35, Odil Ahmedov, Stanislav Andreev•, Aleksandr Geynrikh• (Alisher Azizov 69). Tr: Miodrag Radulovic

GROUP D		Pl	W	D	L	F	A	Pts	KSA	IRN	QAT	UAE
Al Hilal	KSA	6	3	2	1	11	7	11		3-1	0-0	1-1
Mes Kerman	IRN	6	3	0	3	13	13	9	3-1		3-1	4-2
Al Sadd	QAT	6	2	2	2	12	9	8	0-3	4-1		2-2
Al Ahli Dubai	UAE	6	1	2	3	9	16	5	2-3	2-1	0-5	

Bin Hamad, Doha
24-02-2010, 17:55, 11 100, Irmatov UZB

Al Sadd 0

Saad Al Sheeb - Mohamed Rabee, Mohammed Kasoula, Mesaad Al Hamad• (Mosaab Mahmoud Al Hassan 82), Abdulrab Al Yazidi, Talal Al Bloushi, Nasser Nabil Salem, Felipe, Leandro, Magid Mohammed (Opoku Agyemang• 46), Khalfan Ibrahim (Ali Afif 71). Tr: Cosmin Olaroiu

Al Hilal 3

Al Khatani 2 [9 66], Thiago [93+]

Mohammed Al Deayea - Osama Hawsawi, Abdullah Al Zori•, Mirel Radoi (Omar Al Ghamdi 90), Lee Young Pyo, Majed Al Marshadi, Khaled Aziz, Thiago Neves, Christian Wilhelmsson•, Mohammad Al Shalhoub (Nawaf Al Abed 46), Yasser Al Khatani (Essa Al Mehyani 89). Tr: Eric Gerets

Shahid Bahonar, Kerman
24-02-2010, 19:00, 10 000, Kovalenko UZB

Mes Kerman 4

Sayfi [20], Rajabzadeh 2 [75 85], Samereh [70]

Saman Safa - Reza Ghanizadeh, Ghasem Dehnavi, Pirouz Ghorbani, Farhad Salari (Paulo Zaltron 58), Hamid Azizzadeh, Amir Hossein Yousefi, Farzad Ashoubi, Mostafa Sayfi (Rouhollah Bigdeli 72), Faraz Fatemi (Ali Samereh 70), Mehdi Rajabzadeh. Tr: Luka Bonacic

Al Ahli Dubai 2

Salem Khamis [45], Madanchi [57]

Mohd Obaid - Bader Yaqoot•, Abdulla Saleh, Obaid Mesmari, Hosny Abd Rabou, Yousef Jaber, Mehrzad Madanchi, Salem Khamis• (Salmin Khamis 77), Ali Hussain (Ahmad Khalil 89), Cesar•, Bare. Tr: Henk ten Cate

Al Rashid, Dubai
10-03-2010, 19:15, 1351, Kim DJ KOR

Al Ahli Dubai 0

Mohd Obaid - Saad Surour, Mohammad Qassim, Obaid Mesmari, Ali Abbas (Mehrzad Madanchi 46), Hosny Abd Rabou, Yousef Jaber, Salem Khamis (Mohamed Fawzi 46), Ali Hussain, Salmin Khamis, Ahmad Khalil (Abdulla Abdulrahman 85). Tr: Henk ten Cate

Al Sadd 5

Ali Afif [36], Leandro 3 [44 45 76], Yusef Ali [64]

Mohammed Saqr• - Taher Zakaria, Mosaab Mahmoud Al Hassan, Mohamed Rabee, Mesaad Al Hamad, Abdulrab Al Yazidi (Khalfan Ibrahim 72), Talal Al Bloushi, Felipe, Leandro (Mohammed Kasoula 79), Hasan Al Haidos, Ali Afif• (Yusef Ali 51). Tr: Cosmin Olaroiu

King Fahd International, Riyadh
10-03-2010, 20:25, 22 000, Tan Hai CHN

Al Hilal 3

Wilhelmsson [3], Hawsawi [15], Al Khatani [81]

Mohammed Al Deayea - Osama Hawsawi, Abdullah Al Zori, Mirel Radoi, Lee Young Pyo, Majed Al Marshadi, Khaled Aziz, Thiago Neves (Essa Al Mehyani 83), Christian Wilhelmsson (Mohammad Al Shalhoub 86), Ahmed Al Fraidi (Nawaf Al Abed 66), Yasser Al Khatani. Tr: Eric Gerets

Mes Kerman 1

Ali Samereh [93+]

Saman Safa - Ghasem Dehnavi•, Pirouz Ghorbani, Hamid Azizzadeh, Mojtaba Ensafi (Mostafa Sayfi 46) (Farhad Salari 80), Amir Hossein Yousefi•, Farzad Ashoubi, Farzad Hossainkhani, Paulo Zaltron, Mehdi Rajabzadeh•, Milad Sheikhfakhroddini (Ali Samereh• 46). Tr: Luka Bonacic

Bin Hamad, Doha
24-03-2010, 18:10, 5672, Takayama JPN

Al Sadd 4

Leandro 2 [46 49], Felipe [53], Al Bloushi [60]

Mohammed Saqr - Taher Zakaria, Mohamed Rabee, Ibrahim Majid (Abdulaziz Rashid 84), Mesaad Al Hamad, Abdulrab Al Yazidi•, Talal Al Bloushi, Felipe (Mohammed Kasoula 62), Leandro, Hasan Al Haidos, Yusef Ali (Khalfan Ibrahim 33). Tr: Cosmin Olaroiu

Mes Kerman 1

Edinho [21]

Saman Safa - Reza Ghanizadeh, Ghasem Dehnavi, Pirouz Ghorbani, Amir Hossein Yousefi (Mojtaba Ensafi 77), Farzad Ashoubi, Farzad Hossainkhani, Paulo Zaltron, Mehdi Rajabzadeh, Edinho (Milad Sheikhfakhroddini 53), Ali Samereh (Farhad Salari• 54). Tr: Luka Bonacic

King Fahd International, Riyadh
24-03-2010, 20:30, 12 000, Shukralla BHR

Al Hilal 1

Al Mehyani [48]

Mohammed Al Deayea - Osama Hawsawi, Abdullah Al Zori•, Mirel Radoi, Lee Young Pyo, Majed Al Marshadi, Thiago Neves (Abdullatif Al Ghannam 72), Mohammad Al Shalhoub (Nawaf Al Abed 46) Ahmed Al Fraidi (Omar Al Ghamdi 80), Essa Al Mehyani, Yasser Al Khatani. Tr: Eric Gerets

Al Ahli Dubai 1

Abd Rabou [91+]

Yosif Abdalla - Saad Surour, Mohammad Qassim, Ali Abbas, Hosny Abd Rabou, Yousef Jaber, Mehrzad Madanchi•, Salem Khamis, Cesar, Ahmad Khalil, Mohamed Fawzi. Tr: Mohammed Ahmad

Shahid Bahonar, Kerman
30-03-2010, 18:00, 9000, Williams AUS

Mes Kerman 3

Edinho [37], Ali Samereh [48], Zaltron [83]

Saman Safa - Ghasem Dehnavi• (Rouhollah Bigdeli 90), Pirouz Ghorbani, Farhad Salari (Amir Hossein Yousefi 46), Mojtaba Ensafi, Farzad Ashoubi, Farzad Hossainkhani•, Mostafa Sayfi (Paulo Zaltron• 69), Edinho, Milad Sheikhfakhroddini, Ali Samereh. Tr: Luka Bonacic

Al Sadd 1

Khalfan Ibrahim [7]

Mohammed Saqr - Taher Zakaria•, Mohamed Rabee, Ibrahim Majid•, Mesaad Al Hamad, Abdulrab Al Yazidi, Talal Al Bloushi (Ali Afif 62), Felipe (Ali Asadalla Thaimn 90), Leandro, Hasan Al Haidos (Magid Mohammed 76), Khalfan Ibrahim. Tr: Cosmin Olaroiu

Al Rashid, Dubai
30-03-2010, 19:25, 4000, Nishimura JPN

Al Ahli Dubai 2

Ahmad Khalil [43], Cesar [65]

Yosif Abdalla - Saad Surour, Mohammad Qassim•, Ali Abbas•, Hosny Abd Rabou•, Yousef Jaber, Mehrzad Madanchi, Salem Khamis (Faisal Khalil 59), Cesar, Ahmad Khalil, Mohamed Fawzi. Tr: Mohammed Ahmad

Al Hilal 3

Al Khatani [10], Wilhelmsson [15], Lee Young Pyo [92+]

Mohammed Al Deayea - Osama Hawsawi, Mirel Radoi, Lee Young Pyo, Mohammed Nami, Hasan Khairat•, Khaled Aziz (Abdullatif Al Ghannam 90), Thiago Neves, Christian Wilhelmsson (Essa Al Mehyani 82), Yasser Al Khatani, Nawaf Al Abed (Abdulaziz Al Dosari 68). Tr: Eric Gerets

Al Rashid, Dubai
13-04-2010, 19:35, 1223, Basma SYR

Al Ahli Dubai 2

Hossainkhani OG [30], Ahmad Khalil [83p]

Yosif Abdalla - Saad Surour•, Mohammad Qassim, Bader Yaqoot, Ali Abbas, Hosny Abd Rabou, Yousef Jaber, Mehrzad Madanchi (Bare 78), Ahmad Khalil (Ali Hussain 90), Faisal Khalil (Salem Khamis 67), Mohamed Fawzi. Tr: Mohammed Ahmad

Mes Kerman 1

Rajabzadeh [75]

Saman Safa - Pirouz Ghorbani, Farhad Salari• (Ali Samereh 61), Mojtaba Ensafi, Amir Hossein Yousefi, Farzad Ashoubi, Farzad Hossainkhani, Mostafa Sayfi (Rouhollah Bigdeli 46), Paulo Zaltron (Milad Sheikhfakhroddini 46), Mehdi Rajabzadeh, Edinho. Tr: Luka Bonacic

King Fahd International, Riyadh
13-04-2010, 20:35, 17 000, Al Hilali OMA

Al Hilal 0

Mohammed Al Deayea - Osama Hawsawi, Abdullah Al Zori (Mohammed Nami 83), Mirel Radoi•, Lee Young Pyo, Majed Al Marshadi, Khaled Aziz•, Thiago Neves, Christian Wilhelmsson, Yasser Al Khatani, Nawaf Al Abed (Mohammad Al Shalhoub 46). Tr: Eric Gerets

Al Sadd 0

Mohammed Saqr - Mosaab Mahmoud Al Hassan, Mohamed Rabee•, Ibrahim Majid, Mohammed Kasoula, Mesaad Al Hamad, Talal Al Bloushi, Felipe, Leandro (Abdulrab Al Yazidi 90), Hasan Al Haidos (Yusef Ali• 31), Magid Mohammed (Khalfan Ibrahim 61). Tr: Cosmin Olaroiu

Shahid Bahonar, Kerman
27-04-2010, 18:00, 11 100, Toma JPN

Mes Kerman 3

Edinho [1], Zaltron [76], Rajabzadeh [92+]

Abbas Mohammadi - Ghasem Dehnavi•, Pirouz Ghorbani, Mojtaba Ensafi, Amir Hossein Yousefi, Farzad Ashoubi (Paulo Zaltron 70), Farzad Hossainkhani, Mehdi Rajabzadeh, Edinho (Rouhollah Bigdeli 82), Milad Sheikhfakhroddini•, Ali Samereh (Reza Ghanizadeh 46). Tr: Luka Bonacic

Al Hilal 1

Al Mehyani [51]

Mohammed Al Deayea - Abdullah Al Dosari, Hasan Khairat•, Abdullatif Al Ghannam, Abdulaziz Al Dosari (Ahmed Al Swaileh 87), Omar Al Ghamdi, Ahmed Al Fraidi•89, Saleh Ali Al Dosari (Khaled Aziz 46), Salman Al Faraj, Essa Al Mehyani, Nawaf Al Abed. Tr: Eric Gerets

Bin Hamad, Doha
27-04-2010, 18:25, 5100, Mahapab THA

Al Sadd 2

Felipe [16], Al Bloushi [20]

Mohammed Saqr - Mosaab Mahmoud Al Hassan•, Mohamed Rabee, Ibrahim Majid, Mohammed Kasoula, Mesaad Al Hamad, Talal Al Bloushi, Felipe, Leandro, Hasan Al Haidos (Khalfan Ibrahim 59), Ali Afif (Magid Mohammed 76). Tr: Cosmin Olaroiu

Al Ahli Dubai 2

Bare [14], Ali Abbas [93+]

Yosif Abdalla - Saad Surour• (Mohamed Fawzi 84), Mohammad Qassim, Bader Yaqoot, Ali Abbas, Hosny Abd Rabou•, Yousef Jaber•, Salem Khamis (Faisal Khalil 62), Cesar (Mehrzad Madanchi 88), Bare•, Ahmad Khalil. Tr: Mohammed Ahmad

GROUP E		Pl	W	D	L	F	A	Pts	KOR	CHN	JPN	AUS
Seongnam Ilhwa Chunma	KOR	6	5	0	1	11	6	15		3-1	2-0	3-2
Beijing Guoan	CHN	6	3	1	2	7	5	10	0-1		2-0	1-0
Kawasaki Frontale	JPN	6	2	0	4	8	8	6	3-0	1-3		4-0
Melbourne Victory	AUS	6	1	1	4	3	10	4	0-2	0-0	1-0	

Tancheon, Seongnam
23-02-2010, 19:00, 4983, Mohd Salleh MAS
Seongnam Ilhwa Chunma   **2**
Molina [35], Radoncic [78]

Jung Sung Ryong - Sasa Ognenovski•, Cho Byong Kuk, Jeon Gwang Jin, Kim Sung Hwan•, Jang Hack Young, Fabricio Souza (Song Ho Young 90), Mauricio Molina, Kim Chul Ho (Ko Jae Seong 67), Dzenan Radoncic, Kim Jin Yong (Do Nam Gung 71). Tr: Shin Tae Yong

Kawasaki Frontale   **0**

Eiji Kawashima - Hiroki Ito, Takanobu Komiyama•, Shuhei Terada•, Kengo Nakamura, Yusuke Mori, Junichi Inamoto, Hiroyuki Taniguchi (Takuro Yajima 87), Masaru Kurotsu (Yusuke Tasaka 80), Jong Tae Se•, Renatinho (Kyohei Noborizato 80). Tr: Tsutomu Takahata

Workers Stadium, Beijing
23-02-2010, 19:30, 31 000, Albadwawi UAE
Beijing Guoan   **1**
Griffiths [52]

Yang Zhi - Wo Hao, Zhou Ting, Xu Yunlong, Maurice Ross, Darko Matic, Xu Liang• (Wang Changqing 90), Zhu Yifan (Huang Bowen• 61), Valdo•, Yan Xiangchuang•, Joel Griffiths (Wang Xiaolong 86). Tr: Hong Yuanshuo

Melbourne Victory   **0**

Mitchell Langerak - Kevin Muscat, Surat Sukha• (Evan Berger 46), Rodrigo Vargas, Adrian Leijer•, Leigh Broxham (Marvin Angulo 82), Grant Brebner, Tom Pondeljak, Carlos Hernandez, Nick Ward, Nik Mrdja. Tr: Ernie Merrick

Etihad Stadium, Melbourne
9-03-2010, 19:30, 7899, Shukralla BHR
Melbourne Victory   **0**

Mitchell Langerak - Surat Sukha (Carlos Hernandez 46), Rodrigo Vargas, Matthew Foschini•, Evan Berger (Mate Dugandzic 82), Adrian Leijer, Leigh Broxham, Nick Ward•, Marvin Angulo, Robbie Kruse, Nik Mrdja (Archie Thompson 58). Tr: Ernie Merrick

Seongnam Ilhwa Chunma   **2**
Ognenovski [40], Yun Young Sun [85]

Jung Sung Ryong - Yun Young Sun, Sasa Ognenovski, Jeon Gwang Jin•, Kim Sung Hwan•, Hong Chul (Jo Jae Cheol 80), Fabricio Souza, Mauricio Molina, Kim Chul Ho (Ko Jae Seong 46), Dzenan Radoncic, Kim Jin Yong• (Song Ho Young 74). Tr: Shin Tae Yong

Todoroki, Kawasaki
9-03-2010, 19:00, 6606, Yazdi IRN
Kawasaki Frontale   **1**
Kikuchi [40]

Eiji Kawashima - Hiroki Ito, Takanobu Komiyama, Yusuke Tasaka (Yuji Kimura 88), Kosuke Kikuchi, Yusuke Mori, Junichi Inamoto•, Hiroyuki Taniguchi, Masaru Kurotsu (Kyohei Noborizato 88), Jong Tae Se, Renatinho (Takuro Yajima 70). Tr: Tsutomu Takahata

Beijing Guoan   **3**
Griffiths [37], Wang Changqing 2 [65] [86]

Yang Zhi - Zhou Ting, Xu Yunlong, Zhang Yonghai, Maurice Ross, Darko Matic, Xu Liang (Wang Changqing 46), Huang Bowen, Valdo (Lang Zheng 81), Yan Xiangchuang• (Lu Jiang 90), Joel Griffiths. Tr: Hong Yuanshuo

Tancheon, Seongnam
23-03-2010, 19:00, 1224, Moradi IRN
Seongnam Ilhwa Chunma   **3**
Song Ho Young [79], Radoncic [87], Jo Jae Cheol [97+]

Jung Sung Ryong - Ko Jae Seong, Sasa Ognenovski, Cho Byong Kuk, Jeon Gwang Jin•, Jang Hack Young, Mauricio Molina, Kim Chul Ho, Park Sang He (Song Ho Young 65), Dzenan Radoncic, Kim Jin Yong (Jo Jae Cheol 89). Tr: Shin Tae Yong

Beijing Guoan   **1**
Ross [18]

Yang Zhi•[93+] - Lang Zheng, Zhou Ting, Xu Yunlong, Maurice Ross, Darko Matic, Xu Liang• (Du Wenhui 53), Wang Changqing (Lu Jiang 78), Huang Bowen, Valdo (Wu Hao 90), Joel Griffiths. Tr: Hong Yuanshuo

Todoroki, Kawasaki
23-03-2010, 19:00, 9728, Al Ghamdi KSA
Kawasaki Frontale   **4**
Jong 3, Kurotsu [11], Renatinho [22], Taniguchi [90]

Eiji Kawashima - Hiroki Ito, Yusuke Igawa•, Takanobu Komiyama, Yusuke Tasaka (Jumpei Kusukami 86), Yusuke Mori, Junichi Inamoto (Tomonobu Yokoyama 78), Hiroyuki Taniguchi•, Masaru Kurotsu (Kyohei Noborizato 90), Jong Tae Se•♦45, Renatinho. Tr: Tsutomu Takahata

Melbourne Victory   **0**

Glen Moss - Surat Sukha, Rodrigo Vargas, Evan Berger• (Matthew Foschini 55), Adrian Leijer•, Leigh Broxham•♦93+, Grant Brebner•, Carlos Hernandez, Nick Ward (Mate Dugandzic 80), Robbie Kruse (Marvin Angulo 56), Nik Mrdja. Tr: Ernie Merrick

Workers Stadium, Beijing
31-03-2010, 19:30, 31 200, Al Ghamdi KSA
Beijing Guoan   **0**

Zhang Sipeng - Lang Zheng, Zhou Ting, Zhang Yonghai♦72, Maurice Ross (Wang Xiaolong 84), Darko Matic•, Wang Changqing (Valdo 68), Huang Bowen, Du Wenhui•, Yan Xiangchuang• (Xu Yunlong 78), Joel Griffiths. Tr: Hong Yuanshuo

Seongnam Ilhwa Chunma   **1**
Molina [73]

Jung Sung Ryong - Ko Jae Seong, Yun Young Sun, Sasa Ognenovski••♦94+, Kim Sung Hwan, Hong Chul, Fabricio Souza (Jo Jae Cheol 64), Mauricio Molina, Kim Chul Ho•, Dzenan Radoncic (Do Nam Gung 87), Kim Jin Yong (Song Ho Young 59). Tr: Shin Tae Yong

Etihad Stadium, Melbourne
31-03-2010, 19:30, 6011, Yazdi IRN
Melbourne Victory   **1**
Muscat [60p]

Mitchell Langerak• - Kevin Muscat, Surat Sukha, Rodrigo Vargas, Matthew Foschini, Adrian Leijer, Grant Brebner, Carlos Hernandez, Nick Ward (Evan Berger 71), Marvin Angulo (Diogo Ferreira 88), Robbie Kruse (Nik Mrdja 73). Tr: Ernie Merrick

Kawasaki Frontale   **0**

Eiji Kawashima - Hiroki Ito, Yusuke Igawa•, Takanobu Komiyama, Yusuke Tasaka (Yuji Kimura 90), Yusuke Mori, Junichi Inamoto, Hiroyuki Taniguchi (Jumpei Kusukami 62), Masaru Kurotsu, Kyohei Noborizato (Vitor Junior 69), Renatinho. Tr: Tsutomu Takahata

Todoroki, Kawasaki
14-04-2010, 19:00, 10 403, Abdou QAT
Kawasaki Frontale   **3**
Taniguchi [4], Tasaka [21], Renatinho [69p]

Eiji Kawashima - Hiroki Ito•, Takanobu Komiyama, Shuhei Terada•, Yusuke Tasaka (Vitor Junior 66), Yusuke Mori, Junichi Inamoto (Tomonobu Yokoyama 82), Hiroyuki Taniguchi, Masaru Kurotsu, Kyohei Noborizato (Kengo Nakamura 66), Renatinho. Tr: Tsutomu Takahata

Seongnam Ilhwa Chunma   **0**

Jung Sung Ryong - Ko Jae Seong•, Yun Young Sun•, Jeon Gwang Jin, Kim Sung Hwan, Hong Chul, Fabricio Souza (Song Ho Young 72), Kim Chul Ho, Dzenan Radoncic, Do Nam Gung (Mauricio Molina 46), Kim Jin Yong (Jo Jae Cheol 46). Tr: Shin Tae Yong

Etihad Stadium, Melbourne
14-04-2010, 19:30, 6394, Abdul Bashir SIN
Melbourne Victory   **0**

Mitchell Langerak - Kevin Muscat•, Surat Sukha• (Diogo Ferreira 61), Rodrigo Vargas•, Matthew Foschini, Evan Berger, Leigh Broxham, Carlos Hernandez (Marvin Angulo 53), Nick Ward (Luke Pilkington 83), Robbie Kruse, Nik Mrdja. Tr: Ernie Merrick

Beijing Guoan   **0**

Yang Zhi - Lang Zheng, Zhou Ting, Xu Yunlong, Maurice Ross, Darko Matic•, Xu Liang• (Wang Changqing 73), Huang Bowen, Valdo (Du Wenhui 59), Yan Xiangchuang (Wang Xiaolong 80), Joel Griffiths. Tr: Hong Yuanshuo

Tancheon, Seongnam
28-04-2010, 19:00, 502, Zarouni UAE
Seongnam Ilhwa Chunma   **3**
Jeon Gwang Jin [28], Do Nam Gung [74], Jo Jae Cheol [84]

Jung Sung Ryong - Ko Jae Seong, Sasa Ognenovski, Cho Byong Kuk, Jeon Gwang Jin•, Kim Sung Hwan (Kim Chul Ho 61), Hong Chul (Song Ho Young 66), Jang Hack Young, Fabricio Souza (Park Sang He 86), Jo Jae Cheol, Do Nam Gung. Tr: Shin Tae Yong

Melbourne Victory   **2**
Dugandzic [46], Pondeljak [78]

Mitchell Langerak - Kevin Muscat, Matthew Foschini (Luke Pilkington 46), Adrian Leijer, Diogo Ferreira, Leigh Broxham, Grant Brebner, Tom Pondeljak, Carlos Hernandez, Nick Ward (Mate Dugandzic 46), Marvin Angulo (Evan Berger 65). Tr: Ernie Merrick

Workers Stadium, Beijing
28-04-2010, 19:30, 42 690, Kovalenko UZB
Beijing Guoan   **2**
Griffiths [26], Valdo [47]

Yang Zhi - Zhou Ting, Xu Yunlong, Zhang Yonghai, Maurice Ross, Xu Liang, Huang Bowen (Yang Hao 52), Wang Ke, Valdo (Du Wenhui 68), Yan Xiangchuang, Joel Griffiths (Wang Changqing 77). Tr: Hong Yuanshuo

Kawasaki Frontale   **0**

Eiji Kawashima - Hiroki Ito, Yusuke Igawa•, Takanobu Komiyama, Yusuke Tasaka (Vitor Junior (Jumpei Kusukami 71), Kengo Nakamura, Yusuke Mori, Hiroyuki Taniguchi (Yuji Kimura 59), Masaru Kurotsu, Renatinho (Kyohei Noborizato 39). Tr: Tsutomu Takahata

GROUP F		Pl	W	D	L	F	A	Pts	JPN	KOR	CHN	IDN
Kashima Antlers	JPN	6	6	0	0	14	3	18		2-1	1-0	5-0
Jeonbuk Hyundai Motors	KOR	6	4	0	2	17	6	12	1-2		1-0	8-0
Changchun Yatai	CHN	6	1	0	5	10	7	3	0-1	1-2		9-0
Persipura Jayapura	IDN	6	1	0	5	4	29	3	1-3	1-4	2-0	

Gelora Bung Karno, Jakarta
23-02-2010, 19:00, 7534, Abdul Bashir SIN
Persipura Jayapura 1
Pae 68
Jendry Christian **Pitoy** - Ricardo **Salampessy**, **Kim** Jong Kyung (Jack **Komboy** 57), Ortizan **Salossa**, Paulin **Bio**•, Eduard **Ivakdalam** (Edison **Ames** 77), Gerald **Pangkali**, Boaz **Salossa** (Stevie **Bonsapia** 44), **Beto**, Ian **Kabes**, Tinus **Pae**. Tr: Jacksen **Tiago**
Jeonbuk Hyundai Motors 4
Kim Seong Yong 17p, Lovrek 3 26 67 82
Kwon Sun Tae - **Son** Seung Jun, **Jung** Hun•, **Lee** Yo Han, **Shin** Kwang Hoon•, **Jin** Kyung Sun, **Kang** Seung Jo• (**Lim** Sang Hyub75), **Seo** Jung Jin• (Krunoslav **Lovrek** 24), **Kim** Seung Yong, **Sim** Woo Yeon (**Lee** Gwang Jae 57), Luis **Henrique**. Tr: **Choi** Kang Hee

---

World Cup Stadium, Jeonju
9-03-2010, 19:00, 3800, Kovalenko UZB
Jeonbuk Hyundai Motors 1
Eninho 42
Kwon Sun Tae - **Choi** Chul Soon, **Kim** Sang Sik•, **Jung** Hun•, **Feng** Xiaoting, **Shin** Kwang Hoon, **Lim** You Hwan, **Eninho** (Krunoslav **Lovrek** 63), Luis **Henrique**, **Choi** Tae Uk (**Kim** Seung Yong 62), **Lee** Dong Gook. Tr: **Choi** Kang Hee
Kashima Antlers 2
Koji Nakata 70, Endoh 90
Hitoshi **Sogahata** - Atsuto **Uchida**, Daiki **Iwamasa**•, Koji **Nakata**•, Toru **Araiba** (**Gilton** 86), Masahiko **Inoha**, Takuya **Nozawa** (Takeshi **Aoki** 90), Fellype **Gabriel** (Yasushi **Endo** 86), Mitsuo **Ogasawara**, Shinzo **Koroki**, **Marquinhos**•. Tr: Oswaldo de **Oliveira**

Gelora Bung Karno, Jakarta
30-03-2010, 19:00, 732, Shukralla BHR
Persipura Jayapura 1
Pae 19
Ricardo **Salampessy** - Jack **Komboy**, Ortizan **Salossa** (Eduard **Ivakdalam** 40), Paulin **Bio**, Gerald **Pangkali** (David **Laly** 69), **Ferdiansyah**, Hendra **Ridwan** (Stevie **Bonsapia** 24), Boaz **Salossa**, **Beto**, Ian **Kabes**, Tinus **Pae**. Tr: Jacksen **Tiago**
Kashima Antlers 3
Endoh 1, Koroki 26, Uchida 34
Hitoshi **Sogahata** - Atsuto **Uchida**, Daiki **Iwamasa**, **Gilton**, Koji **Nakata**, **Jung** Soo Lee, Takuya **Nozawa**•, Yasushi **Endo** (Takeshi **Aoki** 64), Mitsuo **Ogasawara** (Masahiko **Inoha** 80), Yuya **Osako**, Shinzo **Koroki**• (Ryuta **Sasaki** 60). Tr: Oswaldo de **Oliveira**

World Cup Stadium, Jeonju
14-04-2010, 19:00, 1862, Balideh QAT
Jeonbuk Hyundai Motors 8
Eninho 2 12 56, Sim Woo Yeon 3 30 80 85, Lee Dong Gook 40p, Seo Jung Jin 59, Lim Sang Hyub 81
Kim Min Sik - **Kim** Sang Sik, **Feng** Xiaoting (**Jin** Kyung Sun 46), **Shin** Kwang Hoon, **Lim** You Hwan, **Eninho**, **Seo** Jung Jin, **Park** Won Jae, **Sim** Woo Yeon, **Choi** Tae Uk (Luis **Henrique** 46), **Lee** Dong Gook (**Lim** Sang Hyub 64). Tr: **Choi** Kang Hee
Persipura Jayapura 0
Ricardo **Salampessy** (Imanuel **Wanggai** 54), Jack **Komboy**•, Victor **Igbonefo**, Paulin **Bio**•, Stevie **Bonsapia**, Gerald **Pangkali** (Boaz **Salossa** 64), Brian **Sainyakit** (Edison **Ames** 71), **Ferdiansyah**, Hendra **Ridwan**, Ian **Kabes**•, Tinus **Pae**. Tr: Jacksen **Tiago**

Kashima Stadium, Kashima
23-02-2010, 19:00, 5757, Moradi IRN
Kashima Antlers 1
Koji Nakata 42
Hitoshi **Sogahata** - Atsuto **Uchida** (**Gilton** 84), Daiki **Iwamasa**, Koji **Nakata**•, Toru **Araiba** (**Lee** Jung Soo, Takuya **Nozawa**, Fellype **Gabriel** (Yasushi **Endo**74), Takeshi **Aoki**, Shinzo **Koroki**, **Marquinhos** (Yuya **Osako** 88). Tr:Oswaldo de **Oliveira**
Changchun Yatai 0
An Qi - **Wang** Wanpeng, Samuel **Caballero**, **Lee** Se In, **Wang** Dong, **Jiang** Pengxiang, **Du** Zhenyu• (**Zhang** Wenzhao 46), **Zhang** Xiaofei, **Yan** Feng, Johnny **Lambert** (**Liu** Weidong 46), **Gao** Jian. Tr: **Shen** Xiangfu

---

City Stadium, Changchun
24-03-2010, 14:30, 18 000, Al Hilali OMA
Changchun Yatai 1
Du Zhenyu 65
Mi Tianhe - **Wang** Wanpeng, Samuel **Caballero**, **Lee** Se In, **Lu** Jianjun, **Wang** Dong, **Zhang** Xiaofei, **Yan** Feng•, Johnny **Lambert**•, **Cao** Tianbao (**Liu** Weidong 64), **Gao** Jian (**Du** Zhenyu 46). Tr: **Shen** Xiangfu
Jeonbuk Hyundai Motors 2
Choi Tae Uk 75, Lee Dong Gook 86
Kwon Sun Tae - **Kim** Sang Sik, **Son** Seung Jun, **Feng** Xiaoting•, **Shin** Kwang Hoon, **Eninho** (**Choi** Tae Uk 54), **Park** Won Jae•, **Kim** Seung Yong (**Seo** Jung Jin 61), Luis **Henrique**•, Krunoslav **Lovrek** (**Lee** Gwang Jae76), **Lee** Dong Gook. Tr: **Choi** Kang Hee

---

World Cup Stadium, Jeonju
30-03-2010, 19:00, 5860, Torky IRN
Jeonbuk Hyundai Motors 1
Lee Dong Gook 55
Kwon Sun Tae - **Kim** Sang Sik, **Son** Seung Jun, **Feng** Xiaoting, **Shin** Kwang Hoon, **Kang** Seung Jo•, **Seo** Jung Jin (**Eninho** 65), **Park** Won Jae, **Sim** Woo Yeon (Krunoslav **Lovrek** 75), **Choi** Tae Uk (**Lim** Sang Hyub 90), **Lee** Dong Gook. Tr: **Choi** Kang Hee
Changchun Yatai 0
Mi Tianhe - **Wang** Wanpeng, Samuel **Caballero**, **Lee** Se In, **Wang** Dong, **Jiang** Pengxiang, **Du** Zhenyu (**Gao** Jian 58), **Zhang** Xiaofei•, **Yan** Feng (**Zhang** Wenzhao 61), Johnny **Lambert**, **Cao** Tianbao (Ricardo **Steer** 70). Tr: **Shen** Xiangfu

---

Gelora Bung Karno, Jakarta
28-04-2010, 19:00, 500, Shamsuzzaman BAN
Persipura Jayapura 2
Ivakdalam 27, Pae 65
Jendry Christian **Pitoy** - Erol **Iba**•, Ricardo **Salampessy**, Ortizan **Salossa**, Victor **Igbonefo**, David **Laly** (Imanuel **Wanggai** 67), Eduard **Ivakdalam**, Gerald **Pangkali**, Hendra **Ridwan**• (Stevie **Bonsapia** 57), Ian **Kabes**, Tinus **Pae**. Tr: Jacksen **Tiago**
Changchun Yatai 0
Zong Lei - **Ai** Zhibo, **Zhang** Baofeng, **Lu** Jianjun•, **Zhang** Tianhan, **Yan** Feng, **Liu** Xiadong (**Wen** Chenghua 72), Ricardo **Steer** (**Yang** Haibo 70), **Zhang** Wenzhao, **Cao** Tianbao•, **Liu** Weidong. Tr: **Shen** Xiangfu

---

City Stadium, Changchun
9-03-2010, 14:30, 15 000, Mahapab THA
Changchun Yatai 9
Gao Jian 3 23 34 57, Lambert 3 45 52 59, Liu Weidong 2 65 91+, Wang Bo 84
Mi Tianhe - **Wang** Wanpeng, Samuel **Caballero**, **Lee** Se In (**Wang** Bo 46), **Wang** Dong•, **Jiang** Pengxiang, **Zhang** Xiaofei, **Yan** Feng, Johnny **Lambert**, **Cao** Tianbao (**Liu** Weidong 60), **Gao** Jian• (**Zhang** Wenzhao 59). Tr: **Shen** Xiangfu
Persipura Jayapura 0
Jendry Christian **Pitoy** - Ricardo **Salampessy**, Jack **Komboy** (Edison **Ames** 63), Ortizan **Salossa**, Paulin **Bio**, Stevie **Bonsapia** (David **Laly** 81), Eduard **Ivakdalam**, Gerald **Pangkali** (Boaz **Salossa** 41), **Beto**, Ian **Kabes**, Tinus **Pae**. Tr: Jacksen **Tiago**

Kashima Stadium, Kashima
24-03-2010, 19:00, 4708, Zarouni UAE
Kashima Antlers 5
Araiba 39, Marquinhos 2 45 77, Ogasawara 66p, Osako 68
Hitoshi **Sogahata** - Atsuto **Uchida**, Daiki **Iwamasa**, Toru **Araiba** (**Gilton**74), Masahiko **Inoha**, Takuya **Nozawa** (Kenji **Koyano** 80), Takeshi **Aoki**, Mitsuo **Ogasawara**, Yuya **Osako**, Shinzo **Koroki**, **Marquinhos** (Yasushi **Endo** 77). Tr: Oswaldo de **Oliveira**
Persipura Jayapura 0
Erol **Iba** (Tinus **Pae** 46), Ricardo **Salampessy**, Jack **Komboy**, Ortizan **Salossa**, Paulin **Bio**, Stevie **Bonsapia**, Gerald **Pangkali** (Eduard **Ivakdalam** 81), **Ferdiansyah**, Hendra **Ridwan** (**Beto**72), Boaz **Salossa**, Ian **Kabes**. Tr: Jacksen **Tiago**

City Stadium, Changchun
14-04-2010, 14:30, 6000, Albadwawi UAE
Changchun Yatai 0
Mi Tianhe - Samuel **Caballero** (**Lee** Se In 75), **Zhang** Baofeng, **Lu** Jianjun (**Zhang** Wenzhao 78), **Wang** Bo, **Zhang** Xiaofei, **Yan** Feng, **Liu** Xiadong, Ricardo **Steer**, **Cao** Tianbao, **Liu** Weidong (**Wang** Dong 46). Tr: **Shen** Xiangfu
Kashima Antlers 1
Koroki 37
Hitoshi **Sogahata** - Atsuto **Uchida** (Masahiko **Inoha** 88), Daiki **Iwamasa**, Koji **Nakata**, Toru **Araiba**, **Lee** Jung Soo, Takuya **Nozawa**, Yasushi **Endo** (Takeshi **Aoki** 68), Mitsuo **Ogasawara**, Shinzo **Koroki** (Yuya **Osako** 90), **Marquinhos**. Tr: Oswaldo de **Oliveira**

Kashima Stadium, Kashima
28-04-2010, 19:00, 6490, Moradi IRN
Kashima Antlers 2
Lee Jung Soo 20, Nozawa 22
Hitoshi **Sogahata** - Atsuto **Uchida** (Masahiko **Inoha** 73), Daiki **Iwamasa**, Koji **Nakata**, Toru **Araiba**, **Lee** Jung Soo, Takuya **Nozawa**, Fellype **Gabriel** (Takeshi **Aoki** 68), Mitsuo **Ogasawara**, Shinzo **Koroki** (Ryuta **Sasaki** 86), **Marquinhos**. Tr: Oswaldo de **Oliveira**
Jeonbuk Hyundai Motors 1
Jin Kyung Sun 77
Kwon Sun Tae - **Kim** Sang Sik• (**Lee** Dong Gook 54), **Feng** Xiaoting, **Shin** Kwang Hoon, **Lim** You Hwan, **Jin** Kyung Sun•, **Eninho** (**Lim** Sang Hyub 61), **Seo** Jung Jin (**Sim** Woo Yeon• 79), **Park** Won Jae, Luis **Henrique**•, **Choi** Tae Uk. Tr: **Choi** Kang Hee

GROUP G		Pl	W	D	L	F	A	Pts	KOR	JPN	SIN	CHN
Suwon Samsung Bluewings	KOR	6	4	1	1	13	4	**13**		0-0	6-2	2-0
Gamba Osaka	JPN	6	3	3	0	11	5	**12**	2-1		3-0	1-1
Singapore Armed Forces	SIN	6	1	1	4	6	16	**4**	0-2	2-4		2-1
Henan Jianye	CHN	6	0	3	3	8	8	**3**	0-2	1-1	0-0	

World Cup Stadium, Suwon
24-02-2010, 19:30, 17 264, Breeze AUS
Suwon Samsung Bluewings   0

Lee Woon Jae - Juninho, Li Weifeng, Kang Min Soo•, Kwak Hee Ju, Kim Do Heon, Cho Won Hee, Song Chong Gug (Hong Soon Hak 42), Baek Ji Hoon, Jose Mota• (Lee Hyun Jin 74), Reinaldo (Yang Joon A 67). Tr: Cha Bum Kun

Gamba Osaka   0

Yosuke Fujigaya - Sota Nakazawa, Kazumichi Takagi, Michihiro Yasuda (Shunya Suganuma 42), Akira Kaji•, Yasuhito Endo, Takahiro Futagawa, Tomokazu Myojin, Hideo Hashimoto (Takashi Usami 77), Lucas Severino, Shoki Hirai (Cho Jae Jin 77). Tr: Akira Nishino

---

Hanghai, Zhengzhou
24-02-2010, 20:00, 20 893, Torky IRN
Henan Jianye   0

Zeng Cheng - Song Tae Lim, Zhao Peng, Tan Wangsong (Zhi Xiao 53), Milos Bajalica, Lu Feng, Xu Yang, Zhang Lu, Li Zhaonan, Leandro Netto, Amado Dialo (Su Jingyu 86). Tr: Tang Yaodong

Singapore Armed Forces   0

Shahril Jantan - Hafiz Osman, Niklas Sandberg, Ivan Lovric•, Daniel Bennett, Noh Rahman, Ahmad Latiff, Rhysh Roshan Rai (Razaleigh Khalik 90), Taisuke Akiyoshi, Federico Martinez• (Mustaqim Manzur 81), Indra Sahdan. Tr: Richard Bok

---

Expo '70, Osaka
10-03-2010, 19:00, 7598, Albadwawi UAE
Gamba Osaka   1
Lucas [35p]

Atsushi Kimura - Sota Nakazawa•, Kazumichi Takagi, Takumi Shimohira (Michihiro Yasuda 69), Akira Kaji, Yasuhito Endo, Takahiro Futagawa, Hideo Hashimoto (Hayato Sasaki 84), Lucas Severino, Pedro Junior (Ze Carlos 69), Cho Jae Jin. Tr: Akira Nishino

Henan Jianye   1
Zhang Lu [4]

Zeng Cheng - Song Tae Lim, Zhao Peng, Tan Wangsong (Wang Shouting 76), Milos Bajalica, Lu Feng, Xu Yang (Su Jingyu 88), Zhang Lu, Li Zhaonan•, Leandro Netto, Amado Dialo (Xiao Zhi 56). Tr: Tang Yaodong

---

Jalan Besar, Singapore
10-03-2010, 19:30, 2674, Zarouni UAE
Singapore Armed Forces   0

Shahril Jantan - Razaleigh Khalik•, Hafiz Osman, Niklas Sandberg•, Ivan Lovric••♦57, Daniel Bennett, Ahmad Latiff, Rhysh Roshan Rai, Taisuke Akiyoshi, Federico Martinez, Indra Sahdan (Mustaqim Manzur 68). Tr: Richard Bok

Suwon Samsung Bluewings   2
Juninho [45], Mota [72]

Lee Woon Jae - Juninho, Li Weifeng•, Oh Jae Seok (Song Chong Gug 54), Yang Joon A (Lee Hyun Jin 73), Yang Sang Min, Kwak Hee Ju, Cho Won Hee, Lee Kil Hoon (Baek Ji Hoon 60), Jose Mota, Seo Dong Hyeon. Tr: Cha Bum Kun

---

Jalan Besar, Singapore
23-03-2010, 19:30, 3226, Abdou QAT
Singapore Armed Forces   2
Suherman [32], Sandberg [62]

Shahril Jantan (Hyrulnizam Jumaat 89), Razaleigh Khalik, Hafiz Osman, Niklas Sandberg, Daniel Bennett, Ahmad Latiff, Rhysh Roshan Rai, Mustaqim Manzur, Taisuke Akiyoshi, Erwan Gunawan Suherman (Syaiful Iskandar 63), Indra Sahdan. Tr: Richard Bok

Gamba Osaka   4
Hirai 3 [6 46 81], Nakazawa [70]

Yosuke Fujigaya - Sota Nakazawa (Hayato Sasaki 46), Akira Kaji, Takahiro Futagawa (Takuya Takei 80), Tomokazu Myojin, Hideo Hashimoto, Shoki Hirai, Cho Jae Jin (Ze Carlos 68). Tr: Akira Nishino

---

Hanghai, Zhengzhou
10-03-2010, 20:00, 20 666, Shamsuzzaman BAN
Henan Jianye   0

Zeng Cheng - Song Tae Lim•, Zhao Peng•, Tan Wangsong, Milos Bajalica, Lu Feng, Xu Yang, Zhang Lu, Xiao Zhi, Leandro Netto, Su Jingyu (Amado Dialo 59). Tr: Tang Yaodong

Suwon Samsung Bluewings   2
Mota 2 [47 59]

Lee Woon Jae - Juninho (Ha Tae Gyun 82), Li Weifeng, Kang Min Soo, Yang Joon A (Lee Kil Hoon 65), Yang Sang Min, Kwak Hee Ju, Cho Won Hee, Song Chong Gug, Jose Mota (Lee Dong Sik 72), Seo Dong Hyeon. Tr: Cha Bum Kun

---

Expo '70, Osaka
31-03-2010, 19:00, 7526, Kovalenko UZB
Gamba Osaka   3
Yasuda [28], Hirai [55], Ze Carlos [93+]
Atsushi Kimura - Kazumichi Takagi, Satoshi Yamaguchi, Michihiro Yasuda, Akira Kaji, Hayate Sasaki, Takahiro Futagawa, Tomokazu Myojin, Hideo Hashimoto (Takumi Shimohira 80), Shoki Hirai (Ze Carlos• 75), Cho Jae Jin (Shohei Otsuka 75). Tr: Akira Nishino
Singapore Armed Forces   0

Shahril Jantan - Razaleigh Khalik (Zulfadli Abidin 82), Hafiz Osman, Niklas Sandberg, Ivan Lovric, Daniel Bennett, Syaiful Iskandar, Ahmad Latiff, Rhysh Roshan Rai, Erwan Gunawan Suherman, Indra Sahdan (Federico Martinez 80). Tr: Richard Bok

---

World Cup Stadium, Suwon
31-03-2010, 19:30, 11 456, Irmatov UZB
Suwon Samsung Bluewings   2
Mota [11], Kim Dae Eui [91+]

Kim Dae Hwan - Li Weifeng, Kang Min Soo, Oh Jae Seok (Kwak Hee Ju 72), Yang Sang Min, Cho Won Hee, Baek Ji Hoon, Lee Kil Hoon (Kim Dae Eui 46), Jose Mota (Yeo Seung Won 61), Lee Hyun Jin, Seo Dong Hyeon. Tr: Cha Bum Kun

Henan Jianye   0

Zeng Cheng - Song Tae Lim, Zhao Peng, Milos Bajalica, Yao Bing, Wang Shouting (Lu Zhang 54), Feng Lu, Yang Xu (Zhi Xiao 65), Zhaonan Li, Leandro Netto (Tan Wangsong 78), Amado Dialo. Tr: Tang Yaodong

---

Expo '70, Osaka
13-04-2010, 19:00, 12 311, Moradi IRN
Gamba Osaka   2
Futagawa [61], Usami [92+]

Yosuke Fujigaya - Sota Nakazawa, Kazumichi Takagi, Takumi Shimohira, Michihiro Yasuda, Akira Kaji, Takahiro Futagawa, Tomokazu Myojin, Takuya Takei, Takashi Usami, Shohei Otsuka• (Hayato Sasaki 72). Tr: Akira Nishino

Suwon Samsung Bluewings   1
Mota [58]

Lee Woon Jae - Juninho (Baek Ji Hoon 81), Li Weifeng, Yang Sang Min, Kwak Hee Ju, Cho Won Hee, Song Chong Gug, Jose Mota, Ha Tae Gyun, Lee Hyun Jin (Yang Joon A 70), Kim Dae Eui (Seo Dong Hyeon 70). Tr: Cha Bum Kun

---

Jalan Besar, Singapore
13-04-2010, 19:30, 2278, Williams AUS
Singapore Armed Forces   2
Bennett [65], Suherman [77]

Shahril Jantan - Razaleigh Khalik, Hafiz Osman, Niklas Sandberg•, Ivan Lovric, Daniel Bennett, John Wilkinson (Syaiful Iskandar 79), Rhysh Roshan Rai, Taisuke Akiyoshi, Indra Sahdan (Erwan Gunawan Suherman 46). Tr: Richard Bok

Henan Jianye   1
Yu Le [72]

Zeng Cheng - Song Tae Lim, Qiao Wei•, Milos Bajalica, Lu Feng, Zhang Lu, Li Zhaonan, Leandro Netto, Yu Le (Tan Wangsong 84), Amado Dialo (Xiao Zhi 46), Su Jingyu (Yang Xu 57). Tr: Tang Yaodong

---

World Cup Stadium, Suwon
27-04-2010, 19:30, 2963, Basma SYR
Suwon Samsung Bluewings   6
Mota 2 [11 38], Lee Hyun Jin [13], Kwak Hee Ju [28], Yeom Ki Hun 2 [46 92+]

Lee Woon Jae - Li Weifeng (Choi Sung Hwan 46), Lee Dong Sik, Kwak Hee Ju, Heo Jae Won, Cho Won Hee, Song Chong Gug, Jose Mota (Yeom Ki Hun 46), Lee Hyun Jin, Yeo (Ha Tae Gyun 61), Kim Dae Eui. Tr: Cha Bum Kun

Singapore Armed Forces   2
Martinez [5], Lovric [69]

Shahril Jantan - Razaleigh Khalik, Ivan Lovric, Daniel Bennett•, Noh Rahman, Ahmad Latiff (Hafiz Osman 33), John Wilkinson•, Rhysh Roshan Rai•, Taisuke Akiyoshi•, Federico Martinez (Erwan Gunawan Suherman 85), Indra Sahdan. Tr: Richard Bok

---

Hanghai, Zhengzhou
27-04-2010, 20:00, 17 645, Balideh QAT
Henan Jianye   1
Song Tae Lim [92+]

Zeng Cheng - Zhao Peng, Qiao Wei, Milos Bajalica, Yao Bing (Su Jingyu 77), Wang Shouting (Song Tae Lim• 46), He Bin, Xu Yang, Zhang Lu•, Yu Le, Amado Dialo (Leandro Netto 55). Tr: Tang Yaodong

Gamba Osaka   1
Usami [39]

Yosuke Fujigaya - Sota Nakazawa, Kazumichi Takagi, Takumi Shimohira, Michihiro Yasuda, Hayato Sasaki, Takuya Takei, Takashi Usami (Shigeru Yokotani 83), Lucas Severino (Tomokazu Myojin 65), Kenta Hoshihara, Shohei Otsuka (Takahiro Futagawa 65). Tr: Akira Nishino

GROUP H		Pl	W	D	L	F	A	Pts	AUS	KOR	JPN	CHN
Adelaide United	AUS	6	3	1	2	6	4	10		1-0	3-2	0-1
Pohang Steelers	KOR	6	3	1	2	8	7	10	0-0		2-1	1-0
Sanfrecce Hiroshima	JPN	6	3	0	3	11	11	9	1-0	4-3		0-1
Shandong Luneng	CHN	6	2	0	4	5	8	6	0-2	1-2	2-3	

Big Arch, Hiroshima
24-02-2010, 19:00, 11 955, Balideh QAT
Sanfrecce Hiroshima 0

Shusaku Nishikawa - Ilian Stoyanov, Tomoaki Makino, Ryota Moriwaki, Kazuyuki Morisaki, Yojiro Takahagi, Satoru Yamagishi, Kota Hattori• (Kohei Shimizu 84), Koji Nakajima, Tadanari Lee (Issei Takayanagi 81), Hisato Sato. Tr: Mihailo Petrovic

Shandong Luneng 1
Han Peng 77

Li Leilei - Liu Jindong, Carlos Santos, Yuan Weiwei, Jiao Zhe•, Zhou Haibin• (Ma Long• 62), Cui Peng, Wang Yongpo (Deng Zhuoxiang 77), Roda Antar, Han Peng, Lu Zheng (Gao Di 71). Tr: Branko Ivankovic

Hindmarsh, Adelaide
24-02-2010, 19:30, 8 374, Basma SYR
Adelaide United 1
Leckie 45

Eugene Galekovic - Robert Cornthwaite, Iain Fyfe•, Daniel Mullen•, Scott Jamieson, Michael Marrone (Adam Griffiths 63), Lucas Pantelis (Adam Hughes 90), Travis Dodd, Mathew Leckie, Marcos Flores (Fabian Barbiero 76), Sergio van Dijk. Tr: Aurelio Vidmar

Pohang Steelers 0

Shin Hwa Yong - Kim Gwang Seok, Hwang Jae Won•, Kim Hyung Il, Park Hee Chul, Kim Tae Su (Almir 82), Kim Jae Sung (Hwang Jin Sung71), Shin Hyung Min, Alexsandro, Mota, No Byung Jun (Yoo Chang Hyun 64). Tr: Waldemar Lemos

Shandong Stadium, Jinan
10-03-2010, 15:30, 22 176, Faghani IRN
Shandong Luneng 0

Li Leilei - Liu Jindong, Carlos Santos, Yuan Weiwei, Jiao Zhe, Zhou Haibin (Fred Benson 64), Cui Peng•, Wang Yongpo, Roda Antar, Han Peng, Lu Zheng (Li Jinyu 75). Tr: Branko Ivankovic

Adelaide United 2
Van Dijk 28, Leckie 70

Eugene Galekovic - Robert Cornthwaite•, Iain Fyfe, Daniel Mullen, Scott Jamieson, Michael Marrone, Lucas Pantelis• (Adam Griffiths 90), Travis Dodd, Mathew Leckie•, Marcos Flores (Adam Hughes• 82), Sergio van Dijk (Cassio 78). Tr: Aurelio Vidmar

Steelyard, Pohang
10-03-2010, 19:30, 10 293, Torky IRN
Pohang Steelers 2
Hwang Jae Won 54, Almir 92+

Shin Hwa Yong - Kim Gwang Seok, Hwang Jae Won•, Kim Hyung Il, Kim Tae Su, Kim Jae Sung (Choi Hyun Yeon 86), Kim Jung Kyum, Shin Hyung Min, Alexsandro (Almir 73), Mota, No Byung Jun. Tr: Waldemar Lemos

Sanfrecce Hiroshima 1
Stoyanov 89

Shusaku Nishikawa - Ilian Stoyanov, Tomoaki Makino, Ryota Moriwaki, Koji Morisaki (Tadanari Lee• 61), Kazuyuki Morisaki, Yojiro Takahagi, Satoru Yamagishi, Kota Hattori, Koji Nakajima (Tsubasa Yokotake 52), Hisato Sato. Tr: Mihailo Petrovic

Hindmarsh, Adelaide
24-03-2010, 19:30, 12 841, Mohd Salleh MAS
Adelaide United 3
Dodd 11, Cornthwaite 77, Cassio 82

Eugene Galekovic - Robert Cornthwaite, Iain Fyfe, Daniel Mullen, Scott Jamieson, Michael Marrone, Lucas Pantelis (Cassio 71), Travis Dodd• (Nigel Boogaard• 87), Mathew Leckie, Marcos Flores (Fabian Barbiero 71), Sergio van Dijk. Tr: Aurelio Vidmar

Sanfrecce Hiroshima 2
Kazuyuki Morisaki 55, Takayanagi 75

Shusaku Nishikawa - Ilian Stoyanov♦82, Ryota Moriwaki• (Issei Takayanagi 46), Koji Morisaki, Kazuyuki Morisaki, Satoru Yamagishi (Kohei Shimizu 87), Kota Hattori (Tadanari Lee 69), Tsubasa Yokotake•, Koji Nakajima, Hisato Sato, Masato Yamazaki. Tr: Mihailo Petrovic

Steelyard, Pohang
24-03-2010, 19:30, 10 128, Albadwawi UAE
Pohang Steelers 1
No Byung Jin 5

Shin Hwa Yong - Kim Gwang Seok•, Okayama Kazunari, Kim Hyung Il, Kim Tae Su, Kim Jae Sung, (Song Chang Ho 90), Kim Jung Kyum•, Shin Hyung Min, Alexsandro (Yoo Chang Hyun 78), Mota, No Byung Jun (Almir 66). Tr: Waldemar Lemos

Shandong Luneng 0

Li Leilei - Liu Jindong, Carlos Santos, Yuan Weiwei, Zheng Zheng•, Zhou Haibin (Lu Zheng 68), Cui Peng•, Wang Yongpo (Deng Zhuoxiang 79), Roda Antar (Xia Ningning 46), Han Peng, Fred Benson•. Tr: Branko Ivankovic

Big Arch, Hiroshima
30-03-2010, 19:00, 12 094, Albadwawi UAE
Sanfrecce Hiroshima 1
Sato 45

Shusaku Nishikawa - Ryota Moriwaki, Koji Morisaki, Kazuyuki Morisaki, Issei Takayanagi (Shinichiro Kuwada 76), Satoru Yamagishi, Kota Hattori, Tsubasa Yokotake•, Koji Nakajima, Hisato Sato (Tadanari Lee 85), Masato Yamazaki (Takuya Marutani 90). Tr: Mihailo Petrovic

Adelaide United 0

Eugene Galekovic - Robert Cornthwaite, Iain Fyfe•, Daniel Mullen, Scott Jamieson (Paul Reid 78), Michael Marrone, Lucas Pantelis (Fabian Barbiero 78), Travis Dodd, Mathew Leckie (Cassio 59), Marcos Flores, Sergio van Dijk. Tr: Aurelio Vidmar

Shandong Stadium, Jinan
30-03-2010, 19:30, 11 810, Mohd Salleh MAS
Shandong Luneng 1
Li Jinyu 74

Yang Cheng - Liu Jindong, Carlos Santos, Yuan Weiwei, Zheng Zheng• (Wang Liang 78), Zhou Haibin, Wang Yongpo (Li Jinyu 66), Roda Antar, Xia Ningning (Lu Zheng• 55), Han Peng, Fred Benson. Tr: Branko Ivankovic

Pohang Steelers 2
Kim Jae Sung 51, Kim Tae Su 86

Shin Hwa Yong - Kim Gwang Seok, Okayama Kazunari, Kim Hyung Il, Kim Tae Su, Kim Jae Sung, Kim Jung Kyum (Song Chang Ho 88), Shin Hyung Min•, Alexsandro (Almir 90), Mota, No Byung Jun (Ko Ki Gu 84). Tr: Waldemar Lemos

Shandong Stadium, Jinan
13-04-2010, 19:30, 8876, Al Ghamdi KSA
Shandong Luneng 2
Han Peng 45, Benson 85

Yang Cheng - Liu Jindong, Carlos Santos, Sinisa Radanovic••♦89, Yuan Weiwei, Zhou Haibin, Cui Peng (Xia Ningning• 58), Roda Antar, Han Peng (Wang Yongpo 72), Fred Benson, Lu Zheng (Li Jinyu 78). Tr: Branko Ivankovic

Sanfrecce Hiroshima 3
Koji Morisaki 72, Lee 2 79 92+

Shusaku Nishikawa - Tomoaki Makino, Ryota Moriwaki•, Kazuyuki Morisaki, Issei Takayanagi (Tadanari Lee 74), Satoru Yamagishi (Hironori Ishikawa 72), Kota Hattori, Tsubasa Yokotake, Koji Nakajima, Hisato Sato, Masato Yamazaki (Junya Osaki 86). Tr: Mihailo Petrovic

Steelyard, Pohang
13-04-2010, 19:30, 8217, Irmatov UZB
Pohang Steelers 0

Shin Hwa Yong - Kim Gwang Seok, Hwang Jae Won, Kim Hyung Il, Kim Tae Su, Kim Jae Sung, Kim Jung Sung (Aurelio Vidmar 88), Kim Jung Kyum•, Shin Hyung Min, Mota, Almir (Ko Ki Gu 88). Tr: Waldemar Lemos

Adelaide United 0

Eugene Galekovic - Robert Cornthwaite, Nigel Boogaard, Daniel Mullen•, Cassio, Scott Jamieson•, Michael Marrone, Lucas Pantelis•, Travis Dodd (Mathew Leckie 62), Marcos Flores (Adam Hughes• 67), Sergio van Dijk (Fabian Barbiero 87). Tr: Aurelio Vidmar

Big Arch, Hiroshima
27-04-2010, 19:00, 5612, Al Hilali OMA
Sanfrecce Hiroshima 4
Osaki 1, Lee 30, Kuwada 42, Makino 81p

Hirotsugu Nakabayashi• - Tomoaki Makino, Shinichiro Kuwada•, Tsubasa Yokotake, Hironori Ishikawa, Tomotaka Okamoto (Issei Takayanagi 65) Koji Nakajima, Tadanari Lee, Junya Osaki (Satoru Yamagishi 69), Kohei Shimizu (Hisato Sato 69),Takuya Marutani. Tr: Mihailo Petrovic

Pohang Steelers 3
Kim Jae Sung 2 4 47, Shin Hyung Min 62

Shin Hwa Yong - Kim Gwang Seok, Kazunari Okayama, Hwang Jae Won, Park Hee Chul•, Kim Tae Su••♦80, Kim Jae Sung, Shin Hyung Min, Alexsandro (Hwang Jin Sung 89), Mota (Ko Ki Gu 89), Almir (Choi Hyun Yeon 89). Tr: Waldemar Lemos

Hindmarsh, Adelaide
27-04-2010, 19:30, 10 313, Shukralla BHR
Adelaide United 0

Eugene Galekovic - Robert Cornthwaite, Iain Fyfe, Cassio, Michael Marrone•, Adam Griffiths•, Paul Reid, Travis Dodd (Scott Jamieson 78), Mathew Leckie•, Marcos Flores (Fabian Barbiero 81), Sergio van Dijk•. Tr: Aurelio Vidmar

Shandong Luneng 1
Li Wei 52

Yang Cheng - Liu Jindong, Yuan Weiwei, Zheng Zheng, Zhou Haibin, Roda Antar•, Wang Liang, Li Wei• (Xia Ningning 64), Ma Long (Fred Benson 67), Han Peng, Gao Di• (Ma Xingyu 87). Tr: Branko Ivankovic

ROUND OF SIXTEEN

Tancheon, Seongnam
11-05-2010, 19:30, 9368, Al Hilali OMA

Seongnam Ilhwa Chunma   **3**

Molina 2 [75p] [91+], Song Ho Young [84]

Jung Sung Ryong - Sasa **Ognenovski**, Cho Byong Kuk, Jeon Gwang Jin, **Kim** Sung Hwan, **Hong** Chul (**Song** Ho Young 58), **Jang** Hack Young, Fabricio **Souza** (**Kim** Chul Ho 69), Mauricio **Molina**, Jo Jae Cheol, Dzenan **Radoncic** (**Do** Nam Gung 90). Tr: **Shin** Tae Yong

Gamba Osaka   **0**

Yosuke **Fujigaya** - Sota **Nakazawa**, Kazumichi **Takagi** (Shoki **Hirai** 46), Satoshi **Yamaguchi**, Michihiro **Yasuda**, Akira **Kaji**, Yasuhito **Endo**, Takahiro **Futagawa**, Tomokazu **Myojin•**, Takashi **Usami** (Hayato **Sasaki** 80), Lucas Severino. Tr: Akira **Nishino**

World Cup Stadium, Suwon
11-05-2010, 19:30, 5693, Albadwawi UAE

Suwon Samsung Bluewings   **2**

Mota 2 [28] [85]

Jae Lee Woon - **Li** Weifeng, **Kang** Min Soo, **Kwak** Hee Ju, **Cho** Won Hee•, **Lee** Sang Ho (**Kim** Do Heon78), **Song** Chong Gug, **Park** Tae Min (**Yang** Sang Min 46), Jose **Mota**, **Kim** Dae Eui, **Yeom** Ki Hun. Tr: **Cha** Bum Kun

Beijing Guoan   **0**

Yang Yang - **Lang** Zheng, **Zhou** Ting•, **Xu** Yunlong, Maurice **Ross•**, Darko **Matic**, **Wang** Changqing (**Xu** Liang 56), **Huang** Bowen, **Valdo** (**Du** Wenhui 56), **Yan** Xiangchuang (**Wang** Ke 76), Joel **Griffiths**. Tr: **Hong** Yuanshuo

---

Hindmarsh, Adelaide
12-05-2010, 19:30, 12 015, Abdou QAT

Adelaide United   **2**

Cornthwaite [78], Van Dijk [95+]

Eugene **Galekovic** - Robert **Cornthwaite**, Iain **Fyfe**, Daniel **Mullen**, **Cassio••♦**120, Adam **Griffiths**, Lucas **Pantelis** (Francesco **Monterosso** 63), Travis **Dodd•**, Fabian **Barbiero** (Michael **Marrone** 75), Marcos **Flores** (Adam **Hughes** 90), Sergio **van Dijk**. Tr: Aurelio **Vidmar**

Jeonbuk Hyundai Motors   **3**

Eninho 2 [38] [87], Lee Dong Gook [116]

Kwon Sun Tae• - **Sung** Jong Hyun•, **Son** Seung Jun, **Jung** Hun (Krunoslav **Lovrek** 68), **Lim** You Hwan•, **Jin** Kyung Sun•, **Eninho•** (**Lee** Kwang Hyeon 90), **Kang** Seung Jo•, **Park** Won Jae, **Sim** Woo Yeon (**Lee** Dong Gook 68), **Choi** Tae Uk. Tr: **Choi** Kang Hee

---

King Fahd International, Riyadh
11-05-2010, 20:45, 6853, Toma JPN

Al Shabab   **3**

Sultan [22], El Taib [48], Al Gizani [88]

Waleed **Abdullah** - Abdullah **Al Shuhail**, Ziad **Al Mowalad•** (Hassan **Muath** 64), Mesaed **Al Enezi**, Majed **Al Marhoum**, Camacho, Ahmed **Ateef**, Abdulmalek **Al Khaibri** (Abdoh **Autel** 46), Tarik **El Taib**, Flavio **Amado** (Waleed **Al Gizani** 79), Faisal bin **Sultan**. Tr: Jaime **Pacheco**

Esteghlal Tehran   **2**

Akbarpour [24p], Kazemi [31]

Mohammad **Mohammadi** - Hanif **Omranzadeh**, Amir-Hossein **Sadeghi**, Khosro **Heydari**, Hossein **Kazemi•** (Arash **Borhani** 90), Mohsen **Yousefi•**, Kianoush **Rahmati**, Pejman **Montazeri**, **Fabio** Januario (Mojtaba **Jabbari** 69), Farhad **Majidi**, Siavash **Akbarpour**. Tr: Samad **Marfavi**

King Fahd International, Riyadh
12-05-2010, 20:45, 52 129, Williams AUS

Al Hilal   **3**

Al Marshadi [9], Wilhelmsson [57], Thiago Neves [61]

Mohammed **Al Deayea** - Osama **Hawsawi**, Abdullah **Al Zori**, Mirel **Radoi**, Lee Young Pyo, Majed **Al Marshadi** (Omar **Al Ghamdi•** 85), Khaled **Aziz**, **Thiago** Neves (Abdullatif **Al Ghannam** 76), Christian **Wilhelmsson•** (Nawaf **Al Abed** 81), Mohammad **Al Shalhoub**, Yasser **Al Khatani**. Tr: Eric **Gerets**

Bunyodkor   **0**

Murad **Zukhurov** - Anvar **Gafurov**, Sakhob **Jurayev** (Timur **Kapadze** 70), Anzur **Ismailov**, Aziz **Haydarov**, **Rivaldo**, Jansur **Hasanov**, Viktor **Karpenko**, Joao **Victor**, Server **Djeparov**, Anvarjon **Solyiev** (Shavkat **Salomov** 76). Tr: Luiz Felipe **Scolari**

Al Gharafa, Doha
11-05-2010, 19:20, 7283, Basma SYR

Al Gharafa   **1**

Clemerson [86p]

Qasem **Burhan** - Marcone **Amaral**, Hamed **Shami**, George Kwesi **Semakor**, Bilal **Mohammed**, Saud **Sabah** (Fahid **Al Shammari** 60), **Juninho** Pernambucano, Othmane **El Assas**, Younis **Mahmoud**, **Clemerson**, Mirghani **Al Zain** (Saad **Al Shammari** 78). Tr: **Caio** Junior

Pakhtakor Tashkent   **0**

Temur **Juraev** (Eldor **Tadjibaev** 85) - Bojan **Miladinovic**, Murod **Khalmukhamedov•**, Ilhomjon **Suyunov**, Darko **Markovic•**, Akmal **Kholmatov**, Asqar **Jadigerov** (Sanat **Shikhov** 88), Sherzodbek **Karimov•**, Artur **Gevorkyan**, Odil **Ahmedov**, Alisher **Azizov** (Milorad **Janjus** 66). Tr: Miodrag **Radulovic**

Kashima Stadium, Kashima
12-05-2010, 19:00, 9794, Kovalenko UZB

Kashima Antlers   **0**

Hitoshi **Sogahata** - Atsuto **Uchida**, Daiki **Iwamasa**, Koji **Nakata•**, Toru **Araiba**, Lee Jung Soo, Takuya **Nozawa** (Yuya **Osako** 83), Fellype **Gabriel** (Yasushi **Endo•** 61), Mitsuo **Ogasawara**, Shinzo **Koroki**, Marquinhos. Tr: Oswaldo de Oliveira

Pohang Steelers   **1**

Mota [29]

Shin Hwa Yong - **Kim** Gwang Seok, **Hwang** Jae Won, **Kim** Hyung Il, **Kim** Jae Sung, **Kim** Jung Kyum (**Cho** Hong Kyu 53), **Shin** Hyung Min, **Mota•**, Almir, **No** Byung Jun (**Jung** Seok Min• 71), **Cho** Chan Ho (**Hwang** Jin Sung 74). Tr: **Park** Chang Hyun

---

Foolad Shahr, Isfahan
12-05-2010, 19:00, 6700, Choi Myung Yong KOR

Zob Ahan   **1**

Igor [85]

Shahabeddin **Gordan** - Mohamad **Ahmadi**, Hassan **Ashjari**, Seyed **Hosseini**, Mostafa **Salehi**, Mohammad **Mansori**, Ghasem **Hadadifar** (Seyed Ahmad **Mohammadpour** 90), Sina **Ashori**, Mohammad Reza **Khalatbari•**, Esmail **Farhadi** (Mohsen **Mosalman** 90), Mohammad **Ghazi** (**Igor•** 73). Tr: Mansour **Ebrahimzadeh**

Mes Kerman   **0**

Abbas **Mohammadi** - Reza **Ghanizadeh**, Ghasem **Dehnavi••♦**47, Pirouz **Ghorbani**, Marcio **Giovanini•** (Ali **Samereh** 88), Reza **Torabian** (Amir Hossein **Yousefi** 54), Farzad **Ashoubi**, Farzad **Hossainkhani** (Milad **Sheikhfakhroddini** 76), Paulo **Zaltron**, Mehdi **Rajabzadeh**, **Edinho**. Tr: Luka **Bonacic**

QUARTER-FINALS

Tancheon, Seongnam
15-09-2010, 19:30, 7462, Abdou QAT

Seongnam Ilhwa Chunma   4
Radoncic 2 [8 66], Molina [33], Yang Sang Min OG [82]

Jung Sung Ryong - Sasa **Ognenovski**, Cho Byong Kuk, Jeon Gwang Jin, **Kim** Sung Hwan, **Hong** Chul, Mauricio **Molina**, Kim Chul Ho (Jo Jae Cheol 90), Dzenan **Radoncic**, **Song** Ho Young (**Moon** Dae Seung 88), **Do** Nam Gung (**Cho** Dong Geon 79). Tr: **Shin** Tae Yong

Suwon Samsung Bluewings   1
Yeom Ki Hun [17]

Lee Woon Jae - **Li** Weifeng, **Yang** Sang Min, Kwak Hee Ju, **Hwang** Jae Won, Cho Won Hee, **Lee** Sang Ho (**Kim** Do Heon 81), **Baek** Ji Hoon (**Lee** Hyun Jin 69), Jose Mota, **Ha** Tae Gyun (**Shin** Young Rok 54), Yeom Ki Hun. Tr: **Cha** Bum Kun

World Cup Stadium, Suwon
22-09-2010, 19:30, 13 076, Basma SYR

Suwon Samsung Bluewings   2
Yeom Ki Hun [32], Lee Sang Ho [59]

Ha Kang Jin - **Li** Weifeng, **Kang** Min Soo, **Yang** Sang Min•, Kwak Hee Ju•, **Hwang** Jae Won, **Kim** Do Heon, **Baek** Ji Hoon (Lee Sang Ho 18), **Shin** Young Rok (Takahara **Naohiro** 76), Yeom Ki Hun, **Im** Kyung Hyun (Marcio **Diogo** 55). Tr: **Cha** Bum Kun

Seongnam Ilhwa Chunma   0

Jung Sung Ryong - Sasa **Ognenovski**, Cho Byong Kuk, Jeon Gwang Jin, **Kim** Sung Hwan, **Hong** Chul, Mauricio **Molina**, Kim Chul Ho, Dzenan **Radoncic**• (**Cho** Dong Geon 90), **Song** Ho Young, **Do** Nam Gung (Jo Jae Cheol 62). Tr: **Shin** Tae Yong

World Cup Stadium, Jeonju
15-09-2010, 19:00, 6784, Torky IRN

Jeonbuk Hyundai Motors   0

Kim Min Sik - **Choi** Chul Soon, Kim Sang Sik, **Son** Seung Jun (**Kang** Seung Jo 69), Feng Xiaoting, Cho Sung Hwan, Eninho, Kim Ji Woong (Luis **Henrique** 53), **Park** Won Jae, Sim Woo Yeon (Krunoslav **Lovrek** 53), **Lee** Dong Gook•. Tr: **Choi** Kang Hee

Al Shabab   2
Fahad Hamad [68], Olivera [90]

Waleed **Abdullah**• - Marcelo **Tavares**•, Hassan **Muath**, Ziad **Al Mowalad** (Abdullah **Al Astaa** 45), Sanad **Shrahilee**•, Omar **Al Ghamdi**, Ahmed **Ateef**•, Abdulmalek **Al Khaibri**••◆87, Abdoh **Autef** (**Camacho** 58), Fahad **Hamad**, Nasser **Al Shamrani** (Juan **Olivera** 77). Tr: Jorge **Fossati**

King Fahd International, Riyadh
22-09-2010, 20:15, 8340, Kovalenko UZB

Al Shabab   0

Waleed **Abdullah** - Abdullah **Al Astaa**, Marcelo **Tavares**•, Hassan **Muath**, Sanad **Shrahilee**, Omar **Al Ghamdi**, **Camacho**, Ahmed **Ateef** (Song Chong Gug• 61), Abdoh **Autef** (Majed **Al Amri** 82), Fahad **Hamad** (Juan **Olivera** 70), Nasser **Al Shamrani**. Tr: Jorge **Fossati**

Jeonbuk Hyundai Motors   1
Kim Ji Woong [24]

Kim Min Sik - **Choi** Chul Soon, Feng Xiaoting, Jin Kyung Sun, Eninho (Cho Sung Hwan 85), **Kang** Seung Jo• (Luis **Henrique** 52), Kim Ji Woong• (Seo Jung Jin 51), **Park** Won Jae, **Sim** Woo Yeon, Krunoslav **Lovrek**, **Lee** Dong Gook. Tr: **Choi** Kang Hee

King Fahd International, Riyadh
15-09-2010, 20:35, 53 241, Toma JPN

Al Hilal   3
Al Shaloub [13], Al Fraidi [59], Al Gizani [85]

Hassan **Al Otaibi** - Osama **Hawsawi**, Mirel **Radoi** (Abdullatif **Al Ghannam** 12), Lee Young Pyo, Mohammad **Al Nakhli**, Hasan **Khairat**, Thiago Neves, Mohammad **Al Shalhoub**, Ahmed **Al Fraidi** (Waleed **Al Gizani** 72), Essa **Al Mehyani** (Nawaf **Al Abed** 72), Yasser **Al Khatani**•. Tr: Eric **Gerets**

Al Gharafa   0

Abdulaziz **Ali** - Ibrahim **Al Ghanim**, Hamed **Shami**•, George Kwesi Semakor, Bilal **Mohammed**, Saud Sabah (Mirghani **Al Zain** 46), Lawrence **Quaye**• (Bilal **Abdulrahman** 81), **Juninho** Pernambucano (Ahmed **Al Binali** 90), Othmane **El Assas**, Younis **Mahmoud**, Clemerson. Tr: Caio **Junior**

Al Gharafa, Doha
22-09-2010, 18:30, 13 632, Abdul Bashir SIN

Al Gharafa   4
Al Zain [2], Younis Mahmoud 2 [38 102], El Assas [41]

Abdulaziz **Ali** - Ibrahim **Al Ghanim**, Hamed **Shami**• (Ahmed **Al Binali** 71), Meshaal **Abdilla** (Fahid **Al Shammari** 68), George Kwesi **Semakor** (Bilal **Abdulrahman** 91+ • •◆120), Bilal **Mohammed**, Lawrence **Quaye**, Othmane **El Assas**, Younis **Mahmoud**•, **Clemerson**, Mirghani **Al Zain**•. Tr: Caio **Junior**

Al Hilal   2
Al Khatani [117], Al Mehyani [119]

Hassan **Al Otaibi** - Osama **Hawsawi**, **Lee** Young Pyo, Mohammad **Al Nakhli**•, Hasan **Khairat**, Abdullatif **Al Ghannam**• (Sultan **Al Bargan**• 73), Thiago Neves, Christian **Wilhelmsson** (Essa **Al Mehyani** 81), Mohammad **Al Shalhoub**, Ahmed **Al Fraidi** (Nawaf **Al Abed** 46), Yasser **Al Khatani**. Tr: Eric **Gerets**

Foolad Shahr, Isfahan
15-09-2010, 18:30, 9156, Al Hilali OMA

Zob Ahan   2
Igor [18], Rajabzadeh [76p]

Shahabeddin **Gordan** - Mohamad **Ahmadi**, Farsheed **Talebi**• (Mohammad **Salsali** 90), Seyed Ahmad **Mohammadpour**, Seyed **Hosseini**, Ghasem **Hadadifar**, Shahin Kheiri, Esmail **Farhadi** (Sina Ashori 90), **Igor**, Mohammad **Ghazi**• (Jalal **Rafkhaei** 77), Mehdi **Rajabzadeh**. Tr: Mansour **Ebrahimsadeh**

Pohang Steelers   1
Mota [56]

Shin Hwa Yong - **Shin** Kwang Hoon, **Jung** Hong Youn•, **Kim** Hyung Il, **Kim** Won Il, **Kim** Tae Su•, (**Hwang** Jin Sung 52), **Kim** Jae Sung, **Shin** Hyung Min (**Song** Chang Ho• 76), **Mota**, Seol Ki Hyeon, Almir (Yoo Chang Hyun 81). Tr: **Park** Chang Hyun

Steelyard, Pohang
22-09-2010, 19:30, 8617, Williams AUS

Pohang Steelers   1
Kim Jae Sung [10]

Shin Hwa Yong - **Ahn** Tae Eun (Song Chang Ho 75), Jung Hong Youn, **Kim** Hyung Il, **Kim** Won Il•, **Kim** Jae Sung, **Hwang** Jin Sung• (Yoo Chang Hyun 83), Shin Hyung Min, **Mota**, Seol Ki Hyeon, Lee Jin Ho (Almir 67). Tr: **Park** Chang Hyun

Zob Ahan   1
Khalatbari [80]

Shahabeddin **Gordan** - Mohamad **Ahmadi**, Farsheed **Talebi**, Seyed Ahmad **Mohammadpour** (Hossain **Mahini** 79), Seyed **Hosseini**, Ghasem **Hadadifar**, Shahin **Kheiri**•, Mohammad Reza **Khalatbari**, **Igor** (Sina Ashori 88), Mohammad **Ghazi** (Esmail **Farhadi** 64), Mehdi **Rajabzadeh**••◆86. Tr: Mansour **Ebrahimsadeh**

SEMI-FINALS

King Fahd International, Riyadh
5-10-2010, 20:00, 9300, Breeze AUS

Al Shabab 4

Olivera 2 15 83, Al Shamrani 57, Sultan 89

Waleed **Abdullah** - Majed **Al Amri•**, Hassan **Muath**, Abdullah **Al Shuhail**, Sanad **Shrahilee** (Abdoh **Autef•** 70), **Camacho**, Ahmed **Ateef•** (Fahad **Hamad** 86), Abdulmalek **Al Khaibri**, **Song** Chong Gug (Faisal bin **Sultan** 82), Juan **Olivera**, Nasser **Al Shamrani**. Tr: Jorge **Fossati**

Seongnam Ilhwa Chunma 3

Molina 2 4 69, Jo Jae Cheol 26

Jung Sung Ryong - Sasa **Ognenovski**, Cho Byong Kuk•, **Jeon** Gwang Jin, **Kim** Sung Hwan, **Hong** Chul, Mauricio **Molina**, Kim Chul Ho, **Jo** Jae Cheol, **Cho** Dong Geon (**Do** Nam Gung 80), Dzenan **Radoncic** (**Song** Ho Young 65). Tr: **Shin** Tae Yong

---

Tancheon, Seongnam
20-10-2010, 19:30, 10 996, Albadwawi UAE

Seongnam Ilhwa Chunma 1

Cho Dong Geon 31

Jung Sung Ryong - **Ko** Jae Seong, Sasa **Ognenovski**, Cho Byong Kuk, **Jeon** Gwang Jin• (Jo Jae Cheol• 83), **Kim** Sung Hwan, **Hong** Chul, Mauricio **Molina**, Kim Chul Ho, **Cho** Dong Geon (**Song** Ho Young 66) (**Moon** Dae Seung 90), Dzenan **Radoncic•**. Tr: **Shin** Tae Yong

Al Shabab 0

Waleed **Abdullah** - Marcelo Tavares•, Majed **Al Amri**, Naif **Al Qadi**, Hassan Muath, Abdullah **Al Shuhail** (Abdoh **Autef** 80), **Camacho**, Abdulmalek **Al Khaibri•**, **Song** Chong Gug (Faisal bin **Sultan** 87), Juan **Olivera**, Nasser **Al Shamrani**. Tr: Jorge **Fossati**

Foolad Shahr, Isfahan
6-10-2010, 17:00, 9811, Mohd Salleh MAS

Zob Ahan 1

Hadadifar 57

Shahab **Gordan** - Mohamad **Ahmadi•**, Farsheed **Talebi**, Seyed Ahmad **Mohammadpour** (Hossain **Mahini** 52), Seyed **Hosseini**, Ghasem **Hadadifar**, Shahin **Kheiri**, Mohammad Reza **Khalatbari•**, Esmail **Farhadi** (Mohammad **Salsali** 90), **Igor**, Mohammad **Ghazi** (Jalal **Rafkhaei** 79). Tr: Mansour **Ebrahimsadeh**

Al Hilal 0

Hassan **Al Otaibi** - Osama **Hawsawi**, Abdullah **Al Zori**, Lee Young Pyo, Majed **Al Marshadi•**, Christian **Wilhelmsson** (Abdulaziz **Al Dosari** 83), Ahmed **Al Fraidi**, Salman **Al Faraj** (Mohammad **Al Shalhoub** 76), Sultan **Al Bargan**, Yasser **Al Khatani** (Essa **Al Mehyani•** 48), Nawaf **Al Abed**. Tr: Eric **Gerets**

King Fahd International, Riyadh
20-10-2010, 20:00, 68 752, Irmatov UZB

Al Hilal 0

Hassan **Al Otaibi** - Osama **Hawsawi**, Abdullah **Al Zori**, Mirel **Radoi**, Lee Young Pyo•71, Majed **Al Marshadi**, **Thiago** Neves• (Abdulaziz **Al Dosari** 78), Mohammad **Al Shalhoub**, Ahmed **Al Fraidi•** (Christian **Wilhelmsson** 46), Essa **Al Mehyani** (Waleed **Al Gizani** 74), Yasser **Al Khatani**. Tr: Eric **Gerets**

Zob Ahan 1

Igor 55

Shahab **Gordan** - Mohamad **Ahmadi**, Farsheed **Talebi**, Hossain **Mahini**, Seyed **Hosseini**, Ghasem **Hadadifar•**, Shahin **Kheiri**, Mohammad Reza **Khalatbari** (Mohammad **Salsali** 90), **Igor**, Mohammad **Ghazi** (Omid **Abolhassani** 83), Mehdi **Rajabzadeh** (Esmail **Farhadi** 90). Tr: Mansour **Ebrahimsadeh**

AFC Champions League Final	National Stadium Tokyo	Saturday 13-11-2010
Kick-off: 19:00	Clear night 17°	Attendance: 27 308

SEONGNAM IC   3   1   ZOB AHAN

Sasa Ognenovski [29], Cho Byong Kuk [53], Kim Chul Ho [83]

Mohammad Reza Khalatbari [67]

SEOGNGNAM ILHWA CHUNMA

Yellow shirts, Red shorts, Red socks

Tr: Shin Tae Yong

Jung Sung Ryong

Ko Jae Seong   Cho Byong Kuk   Sasa Ognenovski (c) †   Kim Tae Yoon

Kim Chul Ho

Kim Sung Hwan   Jo Jae Cheol [71]

Mauricio Molina

[88] Cho Dong Geon   [80] Song Ho Young
Nam Kung Do   Kim Jin Ryong

[69] Mehdi Rajabzadeh
Esmail Farhadi

Mohammad Ghazi [81]   Hossein Mahini [81]

[87] Igor Castro
Ghasem Hadadifar (c)   Mohammad Salsali   [56] Shahin Kheiri
Sina Ashouri [86]

Mohammad Reza Khalatbari   Seyed Hosseini

Farsheed Talebi   Mohamad Ahmadi [81]

Shahab Gordan

Tr: Mansour Ebrahimzadeh

White shirts with green trimmings, White shorts, White socks

ZOB AHAN

MATCH OFFICIALS
REFEREE
Yuichi Nishimura JPN
ASSISTANTS
Toru Sagara JPN
Toshiyuki Nagi JPN
4TH OFFICIAL
Hiroyoshi Takayama JPN

(C) Captain † Man of the Match

I have won this title as a player in 1995 and now as a coach, but I am happier tonight. I am almost speechless and very happy. This was the first time since I was named coach of this team that I spent a lot of time analysing the other team. Before the match I told them that they had to be careful of them and their defence and I think it worked well. We will play in the Club World Cup and we want to show people that Asian football is at a high level.

Shin Tae Wong

They played very well with very good football but unfortunately we made simple mistakes. When we first joined the AFC Champions League nobody imagined that we would get this far but now we are runners-up and I think people know about us now. We conceded goals in a disappointing way. Tomorrow is the first day of the rest of our lives and we will go back to Iran and look to do well in the Iranian League.

Mansour Ebrahimzadeh

AFC PRESIDENT'S CUP 2010

First round groups

Group A (In Dhaka BAN)

		Pl	W	D	L	F	A	Pts	BAN	NEP	TPE
Dordoi-Dynamo	KGZ	3	2	1	0	8	0	**7**	0-0	3-0	5-0
Abahani Dhaka	BAN	3	1	2	0	2	0	**5**		2-0	0-0
New Road Team	NEP	3	1	0	2	4	8	**3**			4-3
Kaohsiung Yaoti	TPE	3	0	1	2	3	9	**1**			

Group B (In Yangon MYA)

		Pl	W	D	L	F	A	Pts	PAK	CAM	SRI
Vakhsh Qurghonteppa	TJK	3	3	0	0	10	0	**9**	1-0	3-0	6-0
Khan Research Labs	PAK	3	1	0	2	3	4	**3**		2-1	1-2
Naga Corp	CAM	3	1	0	2	5	7	**3**			4-2
Renown	SRI	3	1	0	2	4	11	**3**			

Group C (In Yangon MYA)

		Pl	W	D	L	F	A	Pts	TKM	BHU
Yadanabon	MYA	2	1	1	0	11	0	**4**	0-0	11-0
HTTU Ashgabat	TKM	2	1	1	0	8	0	**4**		8-0
Druk Star	BHU	2	0	0	2	0	19	**0**		

HTTU Ashgabat qualified for the semi-finals as the best runner-up

Semi-finals

Yadanabon	2
Vakhsh Qurghonteppa	0

HTTU Ashgabat	0
Dordoi-Dynamo	2

Top scorer: **5** - Rustom Usmonov, Vakhsh

Final

Yadanabon	1
Dordoi-Dynamo	0

CUP FINAL

Thuwunna, Yangon
26-09-2010, Att: 23 720, Ref: Salleh MAS
Scorer - Kone 98 for Yadanabon

Yadanabon - Yin Ming Aung●- Kyaw Khing Win, Khin Maung Tun, Jean Gnonsian, Chit San Maung (Aung Chan Moe 67) - Lassina Kone●, Tun Tun Win●, Aung Kyaw Moe - Thet Naing (Pai Soe 56), Yan Paing, Ye Zaw Htet Aung●.
Tr: Zaw Lay Aung

Dordoi - Vladislav Volkov - Ruslan Sydykov●, Azamat Baimatov●, Daniel Tagoe●, Faruh Abitov (Talant Samsaliev 59) - Davron Askarov, Ildar Amirov (Yury Volos 46), Vadim Kharchenko, Anatolii Vlasichev - Mirlan Murzaev, David Tetteh (Sergey Kniazev● 83).
Tr: Serget Dvoryankov

AFC CUP 2010

First Round   **Round of 16**

Group A

		Pl	W	D	L	F	A	Pts	SYR	JOR	OMA	YEM
Al Karama	SYR	6	4	2	0	12	4	**14**		1-1	2-0	2-0
Shabab Al Ordun	JOR	6	3	3	0	13	5	**12**	2-2		3-1	6-1
Saham	OMA	6	1	2	3	5	11	**5**	1-4	0-0		1-0
Al Ahly Sana'a	YEM	6	0	1	5	3	13	**1**	0-1	0-1	2-2	

Al Ittihad Aleppo 1 5p
Al Kuwait * 1 4p

Group B

		Pl	W	D	L	F	A	Pts	KUW	IND	YEM
Al Kuwait	KUW	4	2	2	0	13	5	**8**		7-1	2-2
Churchill Brothers	IND	4	2	1	1	6	10	**7**	2-2		1-0
Al Hilal Hudaya	YEM	4	0	1	3	3	7	**1**	0-2	1-2	

Shabab Al Ordun 1 5p
Kazma * 1 6p

Group C

		Pl	W	D	L	F	A	Pts	KUW	UZB	SYR	LIB
Kazma	KUW	6	4	1	1	6	3	**13**		0-0	0-1	1-0
Nasaf Qarshi	UZB	6	3	2	1	12	4	**11**	1-2		2-1	4-0
Al Jaish	SYR	6	2	2	2	10	8	**8**	0-1	1-1		6-3
Al Ahed	LIB	6	0	1	5	5	18	**1**	1-2	0-4	1-1	

Al Karama * 1
Nasaf Karshi 0

Group D

		Pl	W	D	L	F	A	Pts	KUW	SYR	LIB	IND
Al Qadisiya	KUW	6	4	2	0	14	5	**14**		3-0	1-1	4-1
Al Ittihad Aleppo	SYR	6	3	1	2	10	8	**10**	0-0		4-2	2-1
Al Nijmeh	LIB	6	3	1	2	12	8	**10**	1-3	1-0		3-0
East Bengal	IND	6	0	0	6	5	20	**0**	2-3	1-4	0-4	

Al Rayyan * 1 2p
Muangthong United 1 4p

Group E

		Pl	W	D	L	F	A	Pts	QAT	BHR	JOR	OMA
Al Rayyan	QAT	6	5	0	1	16	7	**15**		0-2	3-0	3-2
Riffa	BHR	6	4	1	3	7	5	**13**	1-4		2-1	1-0
Al Wihdat	JOR	6	2	1	3	8	10	**7**	2-4	0-0		2-0
Al Nahda	OMA	6	0	0	6	3	12	**0**	0-2	0-1	1-3	

Riffa 3
South China * 1

Group F

		Pl	W	D	L	F	A	Pts	IDN	VIE	MAS	MDV
Sriwijaya	IDN	6	4	1	1	17	3	**13**		1-0	6-1	5-0
Binh Duong	VIE	6	4	1	1	14	2	**13**	2-1		4-0	3-0
Selangor	MAS	6	1	1	4	7	16	**4**	0-4	0-0		5-0
Victory	MDV	6	1	1	4	2	19	**4**	0-0	0-5	2-1	

Binh Duong 3
Da Nang * 4

Group G

		Pl	W	D	L	F	A	Pts	HKG	THA	MDV	IDN
South China	HKG	6	4	1	1	12	5	**13**		0-0	3-1	6-3
Muangthong	THA	6	3	2	1	12	7	**11**	0-1		3-1	4-1
VB Sports	MDV	6	3	0	3	12	11	**9**	1-0	2-3		4-0
Persiwa Wamena	IDN	6	0	1	5	8	21	**1**	0-2	2-2	2-3	

Thai Port 4
Sriwijaya * 1

Group H

		Pl	W	D	L	F	A	Pts	VIE	THA	SIN	HKG
Da Nang	VIE	6	4	2	0	12	6	**14**		0-0	3-2	3-0
Thai Port	THA	6	3	2	1	8	5	**11**	2-3		2-2	2-0
Geyland United	SIN	6	0	4	2	7	9	**4**	1-1	0-1		1-1
Tai Po	HKG	6	0	2	4	3	10	**2**	1-2	0-1	1-1	

Churchill Brothers 1
Al Qadisiya * 2

Top scorers: **9** - Afonso Alves BRA, Al Rayyan • **8** - Gaston Merlo ARG, Da Nang • **7** - Fabio Cesar Montesin BRA/QAT, Al Rayyan; Huynh Kesley Alves BRA/VIE, Binh Duong & Bader Al Mutwa KUW, Al Qadisiya • **6** - Khaled Al Azemi KUW, Al Kuwait

AFC CUP 2010

Quarter-finals	Semi-finals	Final

Al Ittihad Aleppo *	3	1
Kazma	2	0

Al Ittihad Aleppo	0	2
Muangthong United *	1	0

Al Karama *	1	0
Muangthong United	0	2

Al Ittihad Aleppo	1	4p
Al Qadisiya	1	2p

Riffa *	3	5
Da Nang	0	3

FINAL PENALTIES

Qadisiya		Ittihad
✓	Al Mutwa	
	Hemidi	✓
✓	Al Mejmed	
	Dyab	✓
✗[1]	Al Khatib	
	Dakka	✓
✗[2]	Alebrahim	
	Kalaji	✓

[1] saved • [2] over bar

Riffa *	2	1
Al Qadisiya	0	4

AFC CUP FINAL 2010

Jaber International, Kuwait City, 6-11-2010, 19:00, 58 604, Al Ghamdi KSA

Al Qadisiya	1	2p	Al Enezi [29]
Al Ittihad	1	4p	Dyab [53]

Qadisiya - Nawaf Al Khaldy - Mohammed Sanad (Ali Alnamash 111), Hussain Ali•, Amer Al Fadhel, Mesaed Alenzi - Jehad Al Hussein (Soud Almgamad 120), Fahed Alebrahim, Talal Al Amer••♦75, Abdulaziz Alenezi• - Bader Al Mutwa, Hamad Alenezi• (Firas Al Khatib 78). Tr: Mohammad Ibrahim

Ittihad - Khaled Othman - Majeddin Homsi, Omar Hemidi, Abdalkader Dakka•, Ahmmad Kalasi (Mouhamad Kalaji 84) - Jude Kongnyuy, Mohammed Fares (Salah Chahrour• 91), Taha Dyab, Ahmad Haj Muhmad•, Mohamad Alhasan♦92+ - Tamer Rashed (Ayman Salal• 72). Tr: Tita Valeriu

Thai Port *	0	0
Al Qadisiya	0	3

* Home team/Home team in the first leg

CAF

CONFEDERATION AFRICAINE DE FOOTBALL

The 2010 FIFA World Cup in South Africa was a great success on a number of fronts both on and off the pitch, a success that reflected well on Africa as a whole. However, there can be no doubting the fact that the performances of the African teams, with the exception of Ghana, were deeply disappointing. The South Africans started and finished brightly - notably the morale boosting 2-1 victory over France - but a 3-0 defeat at the hands of Uruguay completely scuppered their chances. Nigeria, Algeria and Cameroon never really looked as if they were at the races whilst Côte d'Ivoire had the misfortune of having both Brazil and Portugal in their group. With all four falling at the first hurdle it was left to Ghana to carry the torch for Africa. They managed to do it with some style and were desperately unlucky not to become the first African team to reach the

THE FIFA BIG COUNT OF 2006 FOR AFRICA

	Male	Female		Total
Number of players	44 940 000	1 361 000	Referees and Assistant Referees	50 000
Professionals	7 000		Admin, Coaches, Technical, Medical	580 000
Amateurs 18+	926 000		Number of clubs	12 000
Youth under 18	2 156 000		Number of teams	71 000
Unregistered	43 199 000		Clubs with women's teams	1 000
Total Players	46 930 000		Players as % of population	5.16%

semi-finals, denied a place there when Uruguay's Luis Suarez stopped a certain goal with his hands to deny Ghana a winner in the last minute of extra-time. Asamoah Gyan's miss from the resulting penalty will haunt him for the rest of his years. There was a major breakthrough for African club football at the end of the year when Congo's TP Mazembe beat Internacional of Brazil in the semi-final of the FIFA Club World Cup to become the first African team to qualify for the final. They then lost the final to Internazionale but just being there crowned a glorious 2010 for the club after having retained their CAF Champions League title thanks to an outstanding 5-0 victory over Tunisia's Esperance in the first leg of the final. Morocco's FUS Rabat also contributed to Tunisian woes after beating Sfaxien 3-2 on aggregate in the CAF Confederation Cup final.

Confédération Africaine de Football (CAF)

PO Box 23, 3 Abdel Khalek Sarwat Street, El Hay El Motamayez, 6th October City, Egypt

Tel +20 2 8371000   Fax +20 2 8370006

info@cafonline.com   www.cafonline.com

President: Issa Hayatou CMR   General Secretary: Hicham El Amrani MAR

CAF Formed: 1957

CAF EXECUTIVE COMMITTEE

President: Issa Hayatou CMR   1st Vice-President: Seyi Memene TOG   2nd Vice-President: Molefi Oliphant RSA

ORDINARY MEMBERS OF THE EXECUTIVE COMMITTEE

Amadou Diakité MLI	Adoum Djibrine CHA	Amos Adamu NGA
Mohamed Raouraoua ALG	Suketu Patel SEY	Hani Abu Rida EGY
Almamy Kabele Camara GUI	Celestin Musabyimana RWA	Thierry Kamach CTA
	Magdi Shams El Din SUD	
Co-opted: Slim Aloulou TUN	FIFA Exco: Jacques Anouma CIV	General Secretary: Hicham El Amrani MAR

MAP OF CAF MEMBER NATIONS

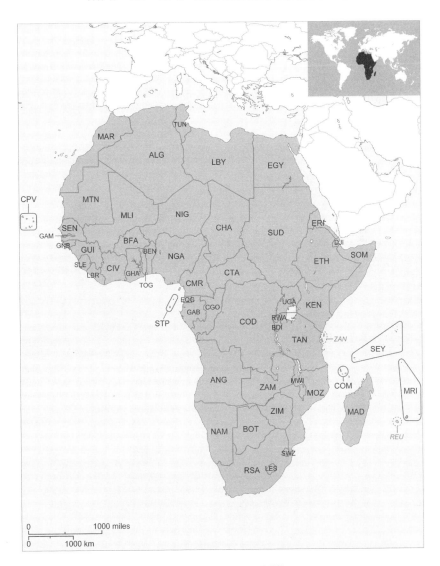

CAF MEMBER ASSOCIATIONS (53)

ALG - **Algeria** • ANG - **Angola** • BEN - **Benin** • BOT - **Botswana** • BFA - **Burkina Faso** • BDI - **Burundi** • CMR - **Cameroon** • CPV - Cape Verde Islands
CTA - **Central African Republic** • CHA - **Chad** • COM - **Comoros** • CGO - **Congo** • COD - **Congo DR** • CIV - **Côte d'Ivoire** • DJI - **Djibouti**
EGY - **Egypt** • EQG - **Equatorial Guinea** • ERI - **Eritrea** • ETH - **Ethiopia** • GAB - **Gabon** • GAM - **Gambia** • GHA - **Ghana** • GUI - **Guinea**
GNB - **Guinea-Bissau** • KEN - **Kenya** • LES - **Lesotho** • LBR - **Liberia** • LBY - **Libya** • MAD - **Madagascar** • MWI - **Malawi** • MLI - **Mali**
MTN - **Mauritania** • MRI - **Mauritius** • MAR - **Morocco** • MOZ - **Mozambique** • NAM - **Namibia** • NIG - **Niger** • NGA - **Nigeria** • RWA - **Rwanda**
STP - **São Tomé e Príncipe** • SEN - **Senegal** • SEY - **Seychelles** • SLE - **Sierra Leone** • SOM - **Somalia** • RSA - **South Africa** • SUD - **Sudan**
SWZ - **Swaziland** • TAN - **Tanzania** • TOG - **Togo** • TUN - **Tunisia** • UGA - **Uganda** • ZAM - **Zambia** • ZIM - **Zimbabwe**

CAF ASSOCIATE MEMBER ASSOCIATIONS (2)

REU - **Reunion** • ZAN - Zanzibar • Neither of these two nations is affiliated to FIFA

AFRICAN NATIONAL TEAM TOURNAMENTS

CAF AFRICA CUP OF NATIONS

Year	Host Country	Winners	Score	Runners-up	Venue
1957	Sudan	Egypt	4-0	Ethiopia	Municipal, Khartoum
1959	Egypt	Egypt	2-1	Sudan	Al Ahly Stadium, Cairo
1962	Ethiopia	Ethiopia	2-0	Egypt	Haile Selassie, Addis Abeba
1963	Ghana	Ghana	3-0	Sudan	Accra Stadium, Accra
1965	Tunisia	Ghana	3-2	Tunisia	Zouiten, Tunis
1968	Ethiopia	Congo Kinshasa	1-0	Ghana	Haile Selassie, Addis Abeba
1970	Sudan	Sudan	1-0	Ghana	Municipal, Khartoum
1972	Cameroon	Congo	3-2	Mali	Omnisports, Yaoundé
1974	Egypt	Zaire	2-2 2-0	Zambia	International, Cairo
1976	Ethiopia	Morocco	1-1	Guinea	Addis Abeba Stadium
1978	Ghana	Ghana	2-0	Uganda	Accra Stadium, Accra
1980	Nigeria	Nigeria	3-0	Algeria	Surulere, Lagos
1982	Libya	Ghana	1-1 7-6p	Libya	11th June Stadium, Tripoli
1984	Côte d'Ivoire	Cameroon	3-1	Nigeria	Houphouët Boigny, Abidjan
1986	Egypt	Egypt	0-0 5-4p	Cameroon	International, Cairo
1988	Morocco	Cameroon	1-0	Nigeria	Mohamed V, Casablanca
1990	Algeria	Algeria	1-0	Nigeria	Stade Olympique, Algiers
1992	Senegal	Côte d'Ivoire	0-0 11-10p	Ghana	Stade de l'Amite, Dakar
1994	Tunisia	Nigeria	2-1	Zambia	El Menzah, Tunis
1996	South Africa	South Africa	2-0	Tunisia	Soccer City, Johannesburg
1998	Burkina Faso	Egypt	2-0	South Africa	Stade du 4 Août, Ouagadougou
2000	Ghana/Nigeria	Cameroon	2-2 4-3p	Nigeria	Surulere, Lagos
2002	Mali	Cameroon	0-0 3-2p	Senegal	Stade du 26 Mars, Bamako
2004	Tunisia	Tunisia	2-1	Morocco	Rades, Tunis
2006	Egypt	Egypt	0-0 4-2p	Côte d'Ivoire	International, Cairo
2008	Ghana	Egypt	1-0	Cameroon	Ohene Djan, Accra
2010	Angola	Egypt	1-0	Ghana	Cidade Universitária, Luanda

CAF AFRICA CUP OF NATIONS MEDALS TABLE

	Country	G	S	B	F	SF
1	Egypt	7	1	3	7	11
2	Ghana	4	4	1	8	8
3	Cameroon	4	2	1	6	8
4	Nigeria	2	4	7	6	12
5	Zaire	2		1	2	4
6	Tunisia	1	2	1	3	5
7	Sudan	1	2	1	3	2
8	Côte d'Ivoire	1	1	4	2	7
9	Algeria	1	1	2	2	6
10	South Africa	1	1	1	2	3
11	Morocco	1	1	1	1	4
12	Ethiopia	1	1	1	1	3
13	Congo	1			1	2
14	Zambia		2	3	2	5
15	Mali		1		1	4
16	Senegal		1		1	3
17	Uganda		1		1	2
18	Libya		1		1	1
19	Guinea		1			
20	Burkina Faso					1
		27	27	27	50	91

This table represents the Gold (winners), Silver (runners-up) and Bronze (semi-finalists) placings of nations in the Africa Cup of Nations, along with the number of appearances in the final and semi-finals.

FOOTBALL TOURNAMENT OF THE AFRICAN GAMES

Year	Host Country	Winners	Score	Runners-up	Venue
1965	Congo	Congo	0-0 †	Mali	Brazzaville
1973	Nigeria	Nigeria	2-0	Guinea	Lagos
1978	Algeria	Algeria	1-0	Nigeria	Algiers
1987	Kenya	Egypt	1-0	Kenya	Nairobi
1991	Egypt	Cameroon	1-0	Tunisia	Cairo
1995	Zimbabwe	Egypt	3-1	Zimbabwe	Harare
1999	South Africa	Cameroon	0-0 4-3p	Zambia	Johannesburg
2003	Nigeria	Cameroon	2-0	Nigeria	Abuja
2007	Algeria	Cameroon	1-0	Guinea	Algiers

† Decided on number of corner-kicks awarded. Congo won 7-2

CECAFA CUP

Year	Host Country	Winners	Score	Runners-up	Venue
1973	Uganda	Uganda	2-1	Tanzania	
1974	Tanzania	Tanzania	1-1 5-3p	Uganda	
1975	Zambia	Kenya	0-0 5-4p	Malawi	
1976	Zanzibar	Uganda	2-0	Zambia	
1977	Somalia	Uganda	0-0 5-3p	Zambia	
1978	Malawi	Malawi	3-2	Zambia	
1979	Kenya	Malawi	3-2	Kenya	
1980	Sudan	Sudan	1-0	Tanzania	
1981	Tanzania	Kenya	1-0	Tanzania	
1982	Uganda	Kenya	1-1 5-3p	Uganda	
1983	Kenya	Kenya	1-0	Zimbabwe	
1984	Uganda	Zambia	0-0 3-0p	Malawi	Kampala
1985	Zimbabwe	Zimbabwe	2-0	Kenya	Rufaro, Harare
1986	Sudan	Not held			
1987	Ethiopia	Ethiopia	1-1 5-4p	Zimbabwe	
1988	Malawi	Malawi	3-1	Zambia	
1989	Kenya	Uganda	3-3 2-1	Malawi	Nyayo, Nairobi
1990	Zanzibar	Uganda	2-0	Sudan	
1991	Uganda	Zambia	2-0	Kenya	Kampala
1992	Tanzania	Uganda	1-0	Tanzania	Mwanza
1993	Uganda	Not held			
1994	Kenya	Tanzania	2-2 4-3p	Uganda	Nairobi
1995	Uganda	Zanzibar	1-0	Uganda	
1996	Sudan	Uganda	1-0	Sudan	
1997		Not held			
1998	Rwanda	Not held			
1999	Rwanda	Rwanda B	3-1	Kenya	Amahoro, Kigali
2000	Uganda	Uganda	2-0	Uganda B	Nakivubo, Kampala
2001	Rwanda	Ethiopia	2-1	Kenya	Amahoro, Kigali
2002	Tanzania	Kenya	3-2	Tanzania	Memorial, Arusha
2003	Sudan	Uganda	2-0	Rwanda	Khartoum
2004	Ethiopia	Ethiopia	3-0	Burundi	Addis Abeba
2005	Rwanda	Ethiopia	1-0	Rwanda	Amahoro, Kigali
2006	Ethiopia	Zambia	0-0 11-10p	Sudan	Addis Abeba
2007	Tanzania	Sudan	2-2 4-2p	Rwanda	Dar es Salaam
2008	Uganda	Uganda	1-0	Kenya	Kampala
2009	Kenya	Uganda	2-0	Rwanda	Nairobi
2010	Tanzania	Tanzania	1-0	Côte d'Ivoire	Dar es Salaam

COSAFA CUP

Year	Host Country	Winners	Score	Runners-up	Venue
1997	Home and away	Zambia	1-1	Namibia	Windhoek
1998	Home and away	Zambia	1-0	Zimbabwe	Harare
1999	Home and away	Angola	1-0 1-1	Namibia	Luanda & Windhoek
2000	Home and away	Zimbabwe	3-0 3-0	Lesotho	Maseru & Bulawayo

COSAFA CUP (CONT'D)

Year	Host Country	Winners	Score	Runners-up	Venue
2001	Home and away	Angola	0-0 1-0	Zimbabwe	Luanda & Harare
2002	Home and away	South Africa	3-1 1-0	Malawi	Blantyre & Durban
2003	Home and away	Zimbabwe	2-1 2-0	Malawi	Blantyre & Harare
2004	Home and away	Angola	0-0 5-4p	Zambia	Lusaka
2005	Home and away	Zimbabwe	1-0	Zambia	Mafikeng
2006	Home and away	Zambia	2-0	Angola	Lusaka
2007	Home and away	South Africa	0-0 4-3p	Zambia	Bloemfontein
2008	Home and away	South Africa	2-1	Mozambique	Thulamahashe
2009	Zimbabwe	Zimbabwe	3-1	Zambia	Harare
2010	Angola	Cancelled			

COUPE CEMAC

Year	Host Country	Winners	Score	Runners-up	Venue
2003	Congo	Cameroon	3-2	Central African Rep.	Brazzaville
2005	Gabon	Cameroon	1-0	Chad	Libreville
2006	Equat. Guinea	Equatorial Guinea	1-1 4-2p	Cameroon	Bata
2007	Chad	Congo	1-0	Gabon	N'Djamena
2008	Cameroon	Cameroon	3-0	Congo	Yaounde
2009	Cent'l African Rep	Central African Rep.	3-0	Equatorial Guinea	Bangui
2010	Congo	Congo	1-1 9-8p	Cameroon	Brazzaville

COPA AMILCAR CABRAL

Year	Host Country	Winners	Score	Runners-up	Venue
1979	Guinea-Bissau	Senegal	1-0	Mali	Bissau
1980	Gambia	Senegal	1-0	Gambia	Banjul
1981	Mali	Guinea	0-0 6-5p	Mali	Bamako
1982	Cape Verde	Guinea	3-0	Senegal	Praia
1983	Mauritania	Senegal	3-0	Guinea-Bissau	Nouakchott
1984	Sierra Leone	Senegal	0-0 5-3p	Sierra Leone	Freetown
1985	Gambia	Senegal	1-0	Gambia	Banjul
1986	Senegal	Senegal	3-1	Sierra Leone	Dakar
1987	Guinea	Guinea	1-0	Mali	Conakry
1988	Guinea-Bissau	Guinea	3-2	Mali	Bissau
1989	Mali	Mali	3-0	Guinea	Bamako
1991	Senegal	Senegal	1-0	Cape Verde Islands	Dakar
1993	Sierra Leone	Sierra Leone	2-0	Senegal	Freetown
1995	Mauritania	Sierra Leone	0-0 4-2p	Mauritania	Nouakchott
1997	Gambia	Mali	1-0	Senegal	Banjul
2000	Cape Verde	Cape Verde Islands	1-0	Senegal	Praia
2001	Mali	Senegal	3-1	Gambia	Bamako
2005	Guinea	Guinea	1-0	Senegal	Conakry
2007	Guinea-Bissau	Mali	2-1	Cape Verde Islands	Bissau

AFRICAN CLUB TOURNAMENTS

CAF CHAMPIONS LEAGUE

Year	Winners	Country	Score	Country	Runners-up
1965	Oryx Douala	CMR	2-1	MLI	Stade Malien
1966	Stade Abidjan	CIV	1-3 4-1	MLI	AS Real Bamako
1967	Tout Puissant Englebert	COD	1-1 2-2	GHA	Asante Kotoko
1968	Tout Puissant Englebert	COD	5-0 1-4	TOG	Etoile Filante
1969	Al Ismaili	EGY	2-2 3-1	COD	Tout Puissant Englebert
1970	Asante Kotoko	GHA	1-1 2-1	COD	Tout Puissant Englebert
1971	Canon Yaoundé	CMR	0-3 2-0 1-0	GHA	Asante Kotoko
1972	Hafia FC Conakry	GUI	4-2 3-2	UGA	Simba FC

CAF CHAMPIONS LEAGUE (CONT'D)

Year	Winners	Country	Score	Country	Runners-up
1973	AS Vita Kinshasa	COD	2-4 3-0	GHA	Asante Kotoko
1974	CARA Brazzaville	CGO	4-2 2-1	EGY	Mehalla Al Kubra
1975	Hafia FC Conakry	GUI	1-0 2-1	NGA	Enugu Rangers
1976	Mouloudia d'Algiers	ALG	3-0 0-3 4-1p	GUI	Hafia FC Conakry
1977	Hafia FC Conakry	GUI	1-0 3-2	GHA	Hearts of Oak
1978	Canon Yaoundé	CMR	0-0 2-0	GUI	Hafia FC Conakry
1979	Union Douala	CMR	0-1 1-0 5-3p	GHA	Hearts of Oak
1980	Canon Yaoundé	CMR	2-2 3-0	COD	AS Bilima
1981	JE Tizi-Ouzou	ALG	4-0 1-0	COD	AS Vita Kinshasa
1982	Al Ahly Cairo	EGY	3-0 1-1	GHA	Asante Kotoko
1983	Asante Kotoko	GHA	0-0 1-0	EGY	Al Ahly Cairo
1984	Zamalek	EGY	2-0 1-0	NGA	Shooting Stars
1985	FAR Rabat	MAR	5-2 1-1	COD	AS Bilima
1986	Zamalek	EGY	2-0 0-2 4-2p	CIV	Africa Sports
1987	Al Ahly Cairo	EGY	0-0 2-0	SUD	Al Hilal
1988	Entente Setif	ALG	0-1 4-0	NGA	Iwuanyanwu Owerri
1989	Raja Casablanca	MAR	1-0 0-1 4-2p	ALG	Mouloudia d'Oran
1990	JS Kabylie	ALG	1-0 0-1 5-3p	ZAM	Nkana Red Devils
1991	Club Africain	TUN	5-1 1-1	UGA	Nakivubo Villa
1992	Wydad Casablanca	MAR	2-0 0-0	SUD	Al Hilal
1993	Zamalek	EGY	0-0 0-0 7-6p	GHA	Asante Kotoko
1994	Espérance Tunis	TUN	0-0 3-1	EGY	Zamalek
1995	Orlando Pirates	RSA	2-2 1-0	CIV	ASEC Mimosas
1996	Zamalek	EGY	1-2 2-1 4-2p	NGA	Shooting Stars
1997	Raja Casablanca	MAR	0-1 1-0 5-4p	GHA	Obuasi Goldfields
1998	ASEC Mimosas	CIV	0-0 4-1	ZIM	Dynamos
1999	Raja Casablanca	MAR	0-0 0-0 4-3p	TUN	Espérance Tunis
2000	Hearts of Oak	GHA	2-1 3-1	TUN	Espérance Tunis
2001	Al Ahly Cairo	EGY	1-1 3-0	RSA	Mamelodi Sundowns
2002	Zamalek	EGY	0-0 1-0	MAR	Raja Casablanca
2003	Enyimba	NGA	2-0 0-1	EGY	Al Ismaili
2004	Enyimba	NGA	1-2 2-1 5-3p	TUN	Etoile du Sahel
2005	Al Ahly Cairo	EGY	0-0 3-0	TUN	Etoile du Sahel
2006	Al Ahly Cairo	EGY	1-1 1-0	TUN	CS Sfaxien
2007	Etoile du Sahel	TUN	0-0 3-1	EGY	Al Ahly Cairo
2008	Al Ahly Cairo	EGY	2-0 2-2	CMR	Cotonsport
2009	TP Mazembe	COD	1-2 1-0	NGA	Heartland
2010	TP Mazembe	COD	5-0 1-1	TUN	Espérance Tunis

CAF CHAMPIONS LEAGUE MEDALS TABLE

	Country	G	S	B	F	SF
1	Egypt	12	5	9	17	26
2	Congo DR	5	5	5	10	15
3	Cameroon	5	1	6	6	12
4	Morocco	5	1	3	6	7
5	Algeria	4	1	5	5	10
6	Ghana	3	8	6	11	15
7	Tunisia	3	6	4	9	11
8	Guinea	3	2	3	5	8
9	Nigeria	2	5	9	7	16
10	Côte d'Ivoire	2	2	6	4	9
11	South Africa	1	1	1	2	3
12	Congo	1			1	1
13	Sudan		2	3	2	5
14	Mali		2	1	2	3
	Uganda		2	1	2	3

CAF CHAMPIONS LEAGUE MEDALS TABLE

	Country	G	S	B	F	SF
16	Zambia		1	6	1	7
17	Togo		1	3	1	4
18	Zimbabwe		1	1	1	1
19	Senegal			5		5
20	Ethiopia			2		2
	Kenya			2		2
22	Angola			1		1
	Libya			1		1
	Tanzania			1		1
		46	46	84	92	168

This table represents the Gold (winners), Silver (runners-up) and Bronze (semi-finalists) placings of clubs representing the above countries in the CAF Champions League, along with the number of appearances in the final and semi-finals

CAF CHAMPIONS LEAGUE MEDALS TABLE

	Club		G	S	B
1	Al Ahly Cairo	EGY	6	2	3
2	Zamalek	EGY	5	1	2
3	TP Mazembe	COD	4	2	2
4	Hafia FC Conakry	GUI	3	2	
5	Raja Casablanca	MAR	3	1	1
6	Canon Yaoundé	CMR	3		2
7	Asante Kotoko	GHA	2	5	3
8	Jeunesse Sportive Kabylie	ALG	2		3
9	Enyimba	NGA	2		1
10	Esperance Tunis	TUN	1	3	3
11	Hearts of Oak	GHA	1	2	1
12	Etoile du Sahel	TUN	1	2	
13	ASEC Mimosas	CIV	1	1	5
14	Ismaily	EGY	1	1	3
15	AS Vita Club Kinshasa	COD	1	1	1
16	FAR Rabat	MAR	1		2
17	Oryx Douala	CMR	1		1
	Union Douala	CMR	1		1
19	CARA Brazzaville	CGO	1		
	Mouloudia Alger	ALG	1		
	Club Africain	TUN	1		
	Entente Setif	ALG	1		
	Orlando Pirates	RSA	1		
	Stade Abidjan	CIV	1		
	Wydad Casablanca	MAR	1		
26	Al Hilal	SUD		2	3
27	Heartland Owerri	NGA		2	2
28	AS Bilima	COD		2	
	Shooting Stars	NGA		2	
30	Nkana Red Devils	ZAM		1	5
31	Enugu Rangers	NGA		1	3
32	Dynamos	ZIM		1	1
	Ghazl Al Mehalla	EGY		1	1
	Mouloudia Oran	ALG		1	1
	CS Sfaxien	TUN		1	1
36	Africa Sports	CIV		1	

CAF CHAMPIONS LEAGUE MEDALS TABLE

	Club		G	S	B
	Cotonsport	CMR		1	
	Etoile Filante	TOG		1	
	Nakivubo Villa	UGA		1	
	AS Real Bamako	MLI		1	
	Obuasi Goldfields	GHA		1	
	Mamelodi Sundowns	RSA		1	
	Simba FC	UGA		1	
	Stade Malien	MLI		1	
45	US Goree	SEN			2
	AS Kaloum Star	GUI			2
	Lomé I	TOG			2
	Jeanne d'Arc	SEN			2
49	Bendel Insurance	NGA			1
	Kenya Breweries	KEN			1
	Cotton Club	ETH			1
	ASC Diaraf	SEN			1
	Djoliba AC	MLI			1
	Express FC	UGA			1
	Great Olympics	GHA			1
	DC Motema Pembe	COD			1
	Al Ittihad	LBY			1
	Kakimbo FC	GUI			1
	Kano Pillars	NGA			1
	AFC Leopards	KEN			1
	Leopard Douala	CMR			1
	FC Lupopo	COD			1
	Mufulira Wanderers	ZAM			1
	Petro Atlético	ANG			1
	Real Republicans	GHA			1
	St. Georges	ETH			1
	Semassi Sokode	TOG			1
	SC Simba	TAN			1
	Stationery Stores	NGA			1
	Tonnerre Yaoundé	CMR			1
	USM Alger	ALG			1
			46	46	84

CAF CUP WINNERS' CUP

Year	Winners	Country	Score	Country	Runners-up
1975	Tonnerre Yaoundé	CMR	1-0 4-1	CIV	Stella Abidjan
1976	Shooting Stars	NGA	4-1 0-1	CMR	Tonnerre Yaoundé
1977	Enugu Rangers	NGA	4-1 1-1	CMR	Canon Yaoundé
1978	Horoya AC Conakry	GUI	3-1 2-1	ALG	MA Hussein-Dey
1979	Canon Yaoundé	CMR	2-0 6-0	KEN	Gor Mahia
1980	TP Mazembe	COD	3-1 1-0	CIV	Africa Sports
1981	Union Douala	CMR	2-1 0-0	NGA	Stationery Stores
1982	Al Mokaoulum	EGY	2-0 2-0	ZAM	Power Dynamos
1983	Al Mokaoulum	EGY	1-0 0-0	TOG	Agaza Lomé
1984	Al Ahly Cairo	EGY	1-0 0-1 4-2p	CMR	Canon Yaoundé
1985	Al Ahly Cairo	EGY	2-0 0-1	NGA	Leventis United
1986	Al Ahly Cairo	EGY	3-0 0-2	GAB	AS Sogara
1987	Gor Mahia	KEN	2-2 1-1	TUN	Espérance Tunis
1988	CA Bizerte	TUN	0-0 1-0	NGA	Ranchers Bees
1989	Al Merreikh	SUD	1-0 0-0	NGA	Bendel United

CAF CUP WINNERS' CUP

Year	Winners	Country	Score	Country	Runners-up
1990	BCC Lions	NGA	3-0 1-1	TUN	Club Africain
1991	Power Dynamos	ZAM	2-3 3-1	NGA	BCC Lions
1992	Africa Sports	CIV	1-1 4-0	BDI	Vital'O
1993	Al Ahly Cairo	EGY	1-1 1-0	CIV	Africa Sports
1994	DC Motema Pembe	COD	2-2 3-0	KEN	Kenya Breweries
1995	JS Kabylie	ALG	1-1 2-1	NGA	Julius Berger
1996	Al Mokaoulum	EGY	0-0 4-0	COD	Sodigraf
1997	Etoile du Sahel	TUN	2-0 0-1	MAR	FAR Rabat
1998	Espérance Tunis	TUN	3-1 1-1	ANG	Primeiro Agosto
1999	Africa Sports	CIV	1-0 1-1	TUN	Club Africain
2000	Zamalek	EGY	4-1 0-2	CMR	Canon Yaoundé
2001	Kaiser Chiefs	RSA	1-1 1-0	ANG	Inter Luanda
2002	Wydad Casablanca	MAR	1-0 1-2	GHA	Asante Kotoko
2003	Etoile du Sahel	TUN	0-2 3-0	NGA	Julius Berger

Discontinued after the 2003 tournament and replaced by the CAF Confederation Cup

CUP WINNERS CUP MEDALS TABLE

	Country	G	S	B	F	SF
1	Egypt	8		6	8	14
2	Tunisia	4	3	2	7	9
3	Nigeria	3	7	4	10	14
4	Cameroon	3	4	3	7	10
5	Côte d'Ivoire	2	3	2	5	7
6	Congo DR	2	1	2	3	5
7	Kenya	1	2	2	3	5
8	Algeria	1	1	4	2	6
9	Morocco	1	1	2	2	4
10	Zambia	1	1	2	2	4
11	Guinea	1		2	1	3
	Sudan	1		2	1	3
	South Africa	1		2	1	3
14	Angola		2		2	2
15	Ghana		1	2	1	3
16	Burundi		1	1	1	2
	Gabon		1	1	1	2
	Togo		1	1	1	2
19	Libya			3		3
20	Burkina Faso			2		2
	Congo			2		2
	Mali			2		2
	Mozambique			2		2
	Reunion			2		2
25	Benin			1		1
	Madagascar			1		1
	Rwanda			1		1
	Senegal			1		1
	Zimbabwe			1		1
		29	29	58	58	116

This table represents the Gold (winners), Silver (runners-up) and Bronze (semi-finalists) placings of clubs representing the above countries in the Cup Winners Cup, along with the number of appearances in the final and semi-finals

CUP WINNERS CUP MEDALS TABLE

	Club		G	S	B
1	Al Ahly Cairo	EGY	4		
2	Mokawloon	EGY	3		1
3	Africa Sports	CIV	2	2	1
4	Etoile du Sahel	TUN	2		
5	Canon Yaoundé	CMR	1	3	1
6	Gor Mahia	KEN	1	1	1
7	BCC Lions	NGA	1	1	
	Power Dynamos	ZAM	1	1	
	Tonnerre Yaoundé	CMR	1	1	
	Esperance Tunis	TUN	1	1	
11	Horoya AC Conakry	GUI	1		2
	Al Merreikh	SUD	1		2
	Wydad Casablanca	MAR	1		2
14	Daring Club Motema Pembe	COD	1		1
	Shooting Stars	NGA	1		1
	Zamalek	EGY	1		1
17	CA Bizerte	TUN	1		
	Enugu Rangers	NGA	1		
	Jeunesse Sportive Kabylie	ALG	1		
	Kaiser Chiefs	RSA	1		
	TP Mazembe	COD	1		
	Union Douala	CMR	1		
23	Club Africain	TUN		2	1
24	Julius Berger	NGA		2	
25	NA Hussein-Dey	ALG		1	1
	Agaza Lomé	TOG		1	1
	Bendel Insurance	NGA		1	1
28	Asante Kotoko	GHA		1	
	FAR Rabat	MAR		1	
	Inter Clube	ANG		1	
	Kenya Breweries	KEN		1	
	Leventis United	NGA		1	
	Primeiro de Agosto	ANG		1	
	Ranchers Bees	NGA		1	
	Sodigraf	COD		1	
	AS Sogara	GAB		1	
	Stationery Stores	NGA		1	

CUP WINNERS CUP MEDALS TABLE (CONT'D)

	Club		G	S	B
	Stella Abidjan	CIV	1		
	Vital'O	BDI	1		
40	Djoliba AC	MLI			2
	Kadiogo	BFA			2
	Mufulira Wanderers	ZAM			2
	St Louisienne	REU			2
44	Abiola Babes	NGA			1
	APR FC	RWA			1
	ASEC Mimosas	CIV			1
	CR Belouizdad	ALG			1
	BFV FC	MAD			1
	Blackpool	ZIM			1
	Diamant Yaoundé	CMR			1
	Dragons de l'Ouème	BEN			1
	Al Ahly Tripoli	LBY			1
	Al Ittihad	EGY			1
	Al Ittihad	LBY			1
	Al Nasr	LBY			1
	CS Hammam-Lif	TUN			1
	Hearts of Oak	GHA			1

CUP WINNERS CUP MEDALS TABLE (CONT'D)

Club		G	S	B
Inter Club	CGO			1
Inter Star	BDI			1
Ismaily	EGY			1
ASC Jeanne d'Arc	SEN			1
Jomos Cosmos	RSA			1
El Kanemi Warriors	NGA			1
Kumbo Strikers	CMR			1
AFC Leopards	KEN			1
Mansoura	EGY			1
Al Masry	EGY			1
Desportivo Maputo	MOZ			1
Maxaquene	MOZ			1
Mbilinga	GAB			1
Orlando Pirates	RSA			1
AS Police	CGO			1
Sekondi Hasaacas	GHA			1
Entente Setif	ALG			1
USM Alger	ALG			1
AS Vita Club Kinshasa	COD			1
		29	29	58

CAF CUP

Year	Winners	Country	Score	Country	Runners-up
1992	Shooting Stars	NGA	0-0 3-0	UGA	Nakivubo Villa
1993	Stella Abidjan	CIV	0-0 2-0	TAN	SC Simba
1994	Bendel Insurance	NGA	0-1 3-0	ANG	Primeiro de Maio
1995	Etoile du Sahel	TUN	0-0 2-0	GUI	Kaloum Star
1996	Kawkab Marrakech	MAR	1-3 2-0	TUN	Etoile du Sahel
1997	Esperance Tunis	TUN	0-1 2-0	ANG	Petro Atlético
1998	CS Sfaxien	TUN	1-0 3-0	SEN	ASC Jeanne d'Arc
1999	Etoile du Sahel	TUN	1-0 1-2	MAR	Wydad Casablanca
2000	JS Kabylie	ALG	1-1 0-0	EGY	Al Ismaili
2001	JS Kabylie	ALG	1-2 1-0	TUN	Etoile du Sahel
2002	JS Kabylie	ALG	4-0 0-1	CMR	Tonnerre Youndé
2003	Raja Casablanca	MAR	2-0 0-0	CMR	Cotonsport Garoua

Discontinued after the 2003 tournament and replaced by the CAF Confederation Cup

CAF CUP MEDALS TABLE

	Country	G	S	B	F	SF
1	Tunisia	4	2	2	6	8
2	Algeria	3			3	3
3	Morocco	2	1		3	3
4	Nigeria	2		3	2	5
5	Côte d'Ivoire	1		3	1	4
6	Cameroon		2	2	2	4
7	Angola		2	1	2	3
8	Egypt		1	2	1	3
9	Tanzania		1	1	1	2
	Uganda		1	1	1	2
11	Guinea		1		1	1
	Senegal		1		1	1
13	Congo DR			2		2

CAF CUP MEDALS TABLE

	Country	G	S	B	F	SF
14	Congo			1		1
	Ethiopia			1		1
	Kenya			1		1
	Mozambique			1		1
	Reunion			1		1
	Sudan			1		1
	Zambia			1		1
		12	12	24	24	48

This table represents the Gold (winners), Silver (runners-up) and Bronze (semi-finalists) placings of clubs representing the above countries in the CAF Cup, along with the number of appearances in the final and semi-finals

CAF CUP MEDALS TABLE

	Club		G	S	B
1	JS Kabylie	ALG	3		
2	Etoile du Sahel	TUN	2	2	
3	Bendel Insurance	NGA	1		
	Espérance Tunis	TUN	1		
	Kawkab AC Marrakech	MAR	1		
	CS Sfaxien	TUN	1		
	Raja Casablanca	MAR	1		
	Shooting Stars	NGA	1		
	Stella Club Abidjan	CIV	1		
10	Cotonsport	CMR		1	1
11	Ismaily	EGY		1	
	Jeanne d'Arc	SEN		1	
	AS Kaloum	GUI		1	
	Nakivubo Villa	UGA		1	
	Petro Atlétco	ANG		1	
	Primeiro de Maio	ANG		1	
	Simba SC	TAN		1	
	Tonnerre Yaoundé	CMR		1	
	Wydad Casablanca	MAR		1	
20	Africa Sports	CIV			1
	Atletico Sport Aviacao	ANG			1
	CA Bizerte	TUN			1

CAF CUP MEDALS TABLE

Club		G	S	B
Canon Yaoundé	CMR			1
Club Africain	TUN			1
DC Motema Pembe	COD			1
Enugu Rangers	NGA			1
Ferroviarrio Maputo	MOZ			1
Insurance	ETH			1
Inter Club	CGO			1
Iwuanyanwu Nationale	NGA			1
Jasper United	NGA			1
Kampala CC	UGA			1
Kenya Breweries	KEN			1
Malindi	TAN			1
Al Masry	EGY			1
El Mourada	SUD			1
Nchanga Rangers	ZAM			1
Saint Denis	REU			1
Satelitte	CIV			1
Stade Abidjan	CIV			1
AS Vita Kinshasa	COD			1
Zamalek	EGY			1
		12	12	24

CAF CONFEDERATION CUP

Year	Winners	Country	Score	Country	Runners-up
2004	Hearts of Oak	GHA	1-1 1-1 8-7p	GHA	Asante Kotoko
2005	FAR Rabat	MAR	0-1 3-0	NGA	Dolphin Port Harcourt
2006	Etoile du Sahel	TUN	1-1 0-0	MAR	FAR Rabat
2007	CS Sfaxien	TUN	4-2 1-0	SUD	Al Merreikh
2008	CS Sfaxien	TUN	0-0 2-2	TUN	Etoile du Sahel
2009	Stade Malien	MLI	0-2 2-0 3-2p	ALG	Entente Sétif
2010	FUS Rabat	MAR	0-0 3-2	TUN	CS Sfaxien

CAF CONFEDERATION CUP MEDALS TABLE

	Country	G	S	B	F	SF
1	Tunisia	3	2		5	1
2	Morocco	2	1		3	1
3	Ghana	1	1		2	
4	Mali	1			1	1
5	Nigeria		1	1	1	1
	Sudan		1	1	1	1
7	Algeria		1		1	1
8	Egypt			1	1	
	Libya			1		1
		7	7	4	14	8

This table represents the Gold (winners) and Silver (runners-up) placings of clubs representing the above countries in the CAF Confederation Cup, along with the number of appearances in the final. There were no semi-finals in the Confederation Cup before 2009

CAF CONFEDERATION CUP MEDALS TABLE

	Club		G	S	B
1	CS Sfaxien	TUN	2	1	
2	FAR Rabat	MAR	1	1	
	Etoile du Sahel	TUN	1	1	
4	FUS Rabat	MAR	1		
	Hearts of Oak	GHA	1		
	Stade Malien	MLI	1		
7	Entente Sétif	ALG		1	
	Asante Kotoko	GHA		1	
	Dolphin	NGA		1	
	Al Merreikh	SUD		1	
11	Bayelsa United	NGA			1
	ENPPI	EGY			1
	Al Hilal	SUD			1
	Al Ittihad	LBY			1
			6	7	4

CECAFA CLUB CHAMPIONSHIP

Year	Winners	Country	Score	Country	Runners-up
1974	Simba SC	TAN	1-0 †	KEN	Abaluhya FC
1975	Young Africans	TAN	2-0	TAN	Simba SC
1976	Luo Union	KEN	2-1	TAN	Young Africans
1977	Luo Union	KEN	2-1	SOM	Horsed
1978	Kamapala City Council	UGA	0-0 3-2p	TAN	Simba SC
1979	Abaluhya FC	KEN	1-0	UGA	Kampala City Council
1980	Gor Mahia	KEN	3-2	KEN	Abaluhya FC
1981	Gor Mahia	KEN	1-0	TAN	Simba SC
1982	AFC Leopards	KEN	1-0	ZIM	Rio Tinto
1983	AFC Leopards	KEN	2-1	MWI	Admarc Tigers
1984	AFC Leopards	KEN	2-1	KEN	Gor Mahia
1985	Gor Mahia	KEN	2-0	KEN	AFC Leopards
1986	Al Merreikh	SUD	2-2 4-2p	TAN	Young Africans
1987	Nakivubo Villa	UGA	1-0	SUD	Al Merreikh
1988	Kenya Breweries	KEN	2-0	SUD	Al Merreikh
1989	Kenya Breweries	KEN	3-0	TAN	Coastal Union
1990	Not held				
1991	Simba SC	TAN	3-0	UGA	Nikivubo Villa
1992	Simba SC	TAN	1-1 5-4p	TAN	Young Africans
1993	Young Africans	TAN	2-1	UGA	Nakivubo Villa
1994	Al Merreikh	SUD	2-1	UGA	Express FC
1995	Simba SC	TAN	1-1 5-3p	UGA	Express FC
1996	Simba SC	TAN	1-0	RWA	APR FC
1997	AFC Leopards	KEN	1-0	KEN	Kenya Breweries
1998	Rayyon Sport	RWA	2-1	ZAN	Mlandege
1999	Young Africans	TAN	1-1 4-1p	UGA	SC Villa
2000	Tusker FC	KEN	3-1	RWA	APR FC
2001	Tusker FC	KEN	0-0 3-0p	KEN	Oserian
2002	Simba SC	TAN	1-0	BDI	Prince Louis
2003	SC Villa	UGA	1-0	TAN	Simba SC
2004	APR FC	RWA	3-1	KEN	Ulinzi Stars
2005	SC Villa	UGA	3-0	RWA	APR FC
2006	Police FC	UGA	2-1	TAN	Moro United
2007	APR FC	RWA	2-1	UGA	URA Kampala
2008	Tusker	KEN	2-1	UGA	URA Kampala
2009	ATRACO	RWA	1-0	SUD	Al Merreikh
2010	APR FC	RWA	2-0	ETH	Saint George

AFRICAN YOUTH TOURNAMENTS

AFRICAN YOUTH CHAMPIONSHIP

Year	Host Country	Winners	Score	Runners-up	Venue
1979		Algeria	2-1 2-3	Guinea	Algiers, Conakry
1981		Egypt	1-1 2-0	Cameroon	Douala, Cairo
1983		Nigeria	2-2 2-1	Côte d'Ivoire	Abidjan, Lagos
1985		Nigeria	1-1 2-1	Tunisia	Tunis, Lagos
1987		Nigeria	2-1 3-0	Togo	Lomé, Lagos
1989		Nigeria	2-1 2-0	Mali	Bamako, Lagos
1991	Egypt	Egypt	2-1	Côte d'Ivoire	Cairo
1993	Mauritius	Ghana	2-0	Cameroon	Bellevue
1995	Nigeria	Cameroon	4-0	Burundi	Lagos
1997	Morocco	Morocco	1-0	South Africa	Meknès
1999	Ghana	Ghana	1-0	Nigeria	Accra

AFRICAN YOUTH CHAMPIONSHIP (CONT'D)

Year	Host Country	Winners	Score	Runners-up	Venue
2001	Ethiopia	Angola	2-0	Ghana	Addis Abeba
2003	Burkina Faso	Egypt	4-3	Côte d'Ivoire	Ouagadougou
2005	Benin	Nigeria	2-0	Egypt	Cotonou
2007	Congo	Congo	1-0	Nigeria	Brazzaville
2009	Rwanda	Ghana	2-0	Cameroon	Kigali

AFRICAN U–17 CHAMPIONSHIP

Year	Host Country	Winners	Score	Runners-up	Venue
1995	Mali	Ghana	3-1	Nigeria	Bamako
1997	Botswana	Egypt	1-0	Mali	Gaborone
1999	Guinea	Ghana	3-1	Burkina Faso	Conakry
2001	Seychelles	Nigeria	3-0	Burkina Faso	Victoria
2003	Swaziland	Cameroon	1-0	Sierra Leone	Mbabane
2005	Gambia	Gambia	1-0	Ghana	Bakau
2007	Togo	Nigeria	1-0	Togo	Lome
2009	Algeria	Gambia	3-1	Algeria	Algiers

AFRICAN WOMEN'S TOURNAMENTS

CAF AFRICAN WOMEN'S CHAMPIONSHIP

Year	Host Country	Winners	Score	Runners-up	Venue
1991		Nigeria	2-0 4-0	Cameroon	
1995		Nigeria	4-1 7-1	South Africa	
1998	Nigeria	Nigeria	2-0	Ghana	Abeokuta
2000	South Africa	Nigeria	2-0	South Africa	Johannesburg
2002	Nigeria	Nigeria	2-0	Ghana	Lagos
2004	South Africa	Nigeria	5-0	Cameroon	Johannesburg
2006	Nigeria	Nigeria	1-0	Ghana	Warri
2008	Equatorial Guinea	Equatorial Guinea	2-1	South Africa	Malabo
2010	South Africa	Nigeria	4-2	Equatorial Guinea	Daveyton

WOMEN'S FOOTBALL TOURNAMENT OF THE AFRICAN GAMES

Year	Host Country	Winners	Score	Runners-up	Venue
2003	Nigeria	Nigeria	1-0	South Africa	Abuja
2007	Algeria	Nigeria	4-0	South Africa	Algiers

AFRICAN WOMEN'S U–20 CHAMPIONSHIP

Year	Host Country	Winners	Score	Runners-up	Venue
2002		Nigeria	6-0 3-2	South Africa	
2004		Nigeria	1-0 0-0	South Africa	

AFRICAN WOMEN'S U–17 CHAMPIONSHIP

Year	Host Country	Winners	Score	Runners-up	Venue
2008	Home & Away	Nigeria	4-2 0-1	Ghana	

REGIONAL TOURNAMENTS IN AFRICA 2010

CECAFA CUP TANZANIA 2010

First round groups

Group A	Pl	W	D	L	F	A	Pts	TAN	BDI	SOM
Zambia	3	2	1	0	7	0	**7**	1-0	0-0	6-0
Tanzania	3	2	0	1	5	1	**6**		2-0	3-0
Burundi	3	1	1	1	2	2	**4**			2-0
Somalia	3	0	0	3	0	11	**0**			

Group B	Pl	W	D	L	F	A	Pts	RWA	ZAN	SUD
Côte d'Ivoire	3	2	0	1	5	2	**6**	1-2	1-0	3-0
Rwanda	3	1	2	0	2	1	**5**		0-0	0-0
Zanzibar	3	1	1	1	2	1	**4**			2-0
Sudan	3	0	1	2	0	5	**1**			

Group C	Pl	W	D	L	F	A	Pts	MWI	ETH	KEN
Uganda	3	2	1	0	5	2	**7**	1-1	2-1	2-0
Malawi	3	1	2	0	5	4	**5**		1-1	3-2
Ethiopia	3	1	1	1	4	4	**4**			2-1
Kenya	3	0	0	3	3	7	**0**			

Quarter-finals

Tanzania	1
Rwanda	0
Zanzibar	2 3p
Uganda	2 5p
Ethiopia	2
Zambia	1
Malawi	0
Côte d'Ivoire	1

Semi-finals

Tanzania	0 5p
Uganda	0 4p
Ethiopia	0
Côte d'Ivoire	1

Final

Tanzania	1
Côte d'Ivoire	0

Third place play-off

Uganda	4
Ethiopia	3

Top scorer: **5** - Felix Sunzu ZAM

Played in Dar es Salaam, Tanzania from 27-11-2010 to 12-12-2010 • None of the matches played by Côte d'Ivoire are full internationals

CECAFA KAGAME INTER-CLUB CUP RWANDA 2010

First round groups

Group A		Pl	W	D	L	F	A	Pts	BDI	DJI	COD
APR FC	RWA	2	2	0	0	8	2	**6**	2-1	6-1	1-0‡
Vital'O	BDI	2	1	0	1	4	3	**3**		3-1	1-2
Ali Sabieh	DJI	2	0	0	2	2	9	**0**			0-8
TP Mazembe	COD		Disqualified								

‡ Abandoned after 38 miniutes

Group B		Pl	W	D	L	F	A	Pts	RWA	ZAN
Saint George	ETH	2	1	1	0	7	2	**4**	2-2	5-0
Rayon Sport	RWA	2	1	1	0	5	2	**4**		3-0
Mafunzo	ZA	2	0	0	2	0	8	**0**		

Group C		Pl	W	D	L	F	A	Pts	RWA	TAN	UGA
Sofapaka	KEN	3	3	0	0	7	0	**9**	3-0	1-0	3-0
ATRACO	RWA	3	1	0	2	5	5	**3**		1-2	4-0
Simba SC	TAN	3	1	0	2	3	4	**3**			1-2
URA	UGA	3	1	0	2	3	8	**3**			

Quarter-finals

APR FC	2
Simba SC	1
Rayon Sport	0 6p
Sofapaka	0 7p
ATRACO	2
Vital'O	0
Ali Sabieh	0
Saint George	5

Semi-finals

APR FC	1
Sofapaka	0
ATRACO	1
Saint George	3

Final

APR FC	2
Saint George	0

Third place play-off

Sofapaka	2
ATRACO	1

Played in Kigali, Rwanda from 15-05-2010 to 29-05-2010
Final: Amahoro, Kigali, 29-05-2010. Scorers - Chiukepo Msowya [92], Victor Nyirenda [98] for APR

CAF AFRICA CUP OF NATIONS GABON/EQUATORIAL GUINEA 2012

Qualifying groups		First Round		Quarter-finals	Semi-finals	Final

Group A — Seed

	Seed
Mali	1
Cape Verde Isl	2
Zimbabwe	3
Liberia	4

Group A — Pts
Equat. Guinea

Group B

	Seed
Nigeria	1
Guinea	2
Ethiopia	3
Madagascar	4

Group C

	Seed
Zambia	1
Mozambique	2
Libya	3
Comoros	4

Group D

	Seed
Algeria	1
Morocco	2
Tanzania	3
C. African Rep	4

Group B — Pts

Group E

	Seed
Cameroon	1
Senegal	2
Congo DR	3
Mauritius	4

Group F

	Seed
Burkina Faso	1
Gambia	2
Namibia	3

Group G

	Seed
Egypt	1
South Africa	2
Niger	3
Sierra Leone	4

Group C — Pts

Group H

	Seed
Cote d'Ivoire	1
Benin	2
Rwanda	3
Burundi	4

Group I

	Seed
Ghana	1
Congo	2
Sudan	3
Swaziland	4

Group J

	Seed
Angola	1
Uganda	2
Kenya	3
Guinea-Bissau	4

Group D — Pts
Gabon

Group K

	Seed
Tunisia	1
Malawi	2
Botswana	3
Chad	4
Togo	

Gabon and Equatorial Guinea qualified automatically as hosts • Togo were initially refused entry but were later rea-admitted • Group winners qualify along with the top two in Group K along with the two best runners-up

3rd Place Play-off

CLUB TOURNAMENTS IN AFRICA IN 2010

MTN CAF CHAMPIONS LEAGUE 2010

First Round

Team	Code	Score
TP Mazembe	COD	Bye
Recreativo Libolo	ANG	2 0
APR FC *	RWA	2 1
ASC La Linguère *	SEN	2 0 4p
Asante Kotoko	GHA	0 2 2p
Al Ahly Benghazi	LBY	0 0
Djoliba *	MLI	1 0
Zanaco	ZAM	0 4
URA Kampala *	UGA	1 0
ASEC Mimosas	CIV	Bye
Union Douala	CMR	Bye
Diables Noirs *	CGO	3 0
ES Sétif	ALG	2 2
Dynamos	ZIM	Bye
Young Africans *	TAN	2 0
St Eloi Lipopo	COD	3 1
Curepipe Starlight	MRI	0 3
La Passe *	SEY	1 1
Orlando Pirates	RSA	0 2
Gaborone United *	BOT	0 2
Petro Atlético	ANG	3 6
Sony de Ela Nguema *	EQG	2 1
Fello Star Labe *	GUI	1 1
Raja Casablanca	MAR	3 1
Club Africain	TUN	1 1
Sahel SC *	NIG	2 0
Armed Forces *	GAM	1 0
JS Kabylie	ALG	2 3
Al Ahly Cairo	EGY	Bye
Mafunzo *	ZAN	1 0
Gunners	ZIM	2 4
Diffa El Jadida	MAR	0 3
Os Balantas *	GNB	0 0
Tempête Mocaf *	CTA	1 0
Al Ittihad Tripoli	LBY	2 6
Al Hilal Omdurman	SUD	Bye
Africa Sports	CIV	Bye
Stade Tamponnaise *	REU	2 3
Ajesaia	MAD	1 1
Sofapaka *	KEN	0 0
Ismaily	EGY	0 2
Heartland	NGA	Bye
Vital'O *	BDI	2 2 3p
Tiko United	CMR	2 2 5p
Ferroviário Maputo	MOZ	5 4
Apaches Mitsamiouli *	COM	3 1
Mbabane Swallows *	SWZ	1 2
Supersport United	RSA	3 2
Al Merreikh Omdurman	SUD	1 3
Saint George *	ETH	1 1
Bayelsa United	NGA	0 2
Gazelle FC *	CHA	1 2
ASFA/Yennenga	BFA	2 4
Stade Mandji *	GAB	0 1
East End Lions *	SLE	2 2
Espérance Tunis	TUN	2 3

Second Round

Team	Score
TP Mazembe	0 2
APR FC *	1 0
ASC La Linguère	0 1 3p
Djoliba *	1 0 4p
Zanaco *	1 1
ASEC Mimosas	0 1
Union Douala *	0 0
ES Sétif	2 5
Dynamos	1 1
St Eloi Lipopo *	0 0
Curepipe Starlight *	0 0
Gaborone United	3 3
Petro Atlético	1 1
Raja Casablanca *	1 0
Club Africain *	1 0
JS Kabylie	1 1
Al Ahly Cairo	0 2
Gunners *	1 0
Diffa El Jadida	1 1 3p
Al Ittihad Tripoli *	1 1 4p
Al Hilal Omdurman	0 4
Africa Sports *	0 1
Stade Tamponnaise	1 1
Ismaily *	3 0
Heartland	2 1
Tiko United *	2 1
Ferroviário Maputo	0 2
Supersport United *	3 0
Al Merreikh Omdurman	1 2
Gazelle FC *	1 0
ASFA/Yennenga	1 1
Espérance Tunis *	4 3

Third Round

Team	Score
TP Mazembe	1 3
Djoliba *	0 0
Zanaco	0 2
ES Sétif *	1 2
Dynamos *	4 0
Gaborone United	1 1
Petro Atlético	0 2
JS Kabylie *	0 1
Al Ahly Cairo	0 3
Al Ittihad Tripoli *	2 0
Al Hilal Omdurman *	0 1
Ismaily	1 3
Heartland	1 3
Supersport United *	1 1
Al Merreikh Omdurman	0 1
Espérance Tunis *	3 1

* Home team in the first leg • Losing teams in the third round enter the Confederation Cup

MTN CAF CHAMPIONS LEAGUE 2010

Champions League Stage   **Semi-finals**   **Final**

Group A	Pl	W	D	L	F	A	Pts	TUN	COD	ALG	ZIM
Espérance Tunis	6	4	1	1	9	4	**13**		3-0	2-2	1-0
TP Mazembe	6	3	2	1	8	7	**11**	2-1		2-2	2-1
ES Sétif	6	1	3	2	7	6	**6**	0-1	0-0		3-0
Dynamos	6	1	0	5	2	9	**3**	0-1	0-2	1-0	

TP Mazembe *	3	0
JS Kabylie	1	0

TP Mazembe *	5	1
Espérance Tunis	0	1

Al Ahly Cairo *	2	0
Espérance Tunis	1	1

Group B	Pl	W	D	L	F	A	Pts	ALG	EGY	EGY	NGA
JS Kabylie	6	4	2	0	6	2	**14**		1-0	1-0	1-0
Al Ahly Cairo	6	2	2	2	8	9	**8**	1-1		2-1	2-1
Ismaily	6	2	0	4	7	8	**6**	0-1	4-2		1-0
Heartland	6	1	2	3	5	7	**5**	1-1	1-1	2-1	

FIRST ROUND

Amahoro, Kigali, 13-02-2010, Kirwa KEN
APR FC 2 Twite Kabange 18, Vivtor Nyirenda 85
Recreativo Libolo 2 Fuxito 2 53 90

Patrice Lumumba, Libolo, 27-02-2010, Dyr RSA
Recreativo Libolo 0
APR FC 1 Selly Rogba 78

Stade de Linguère, Saint-Louis, 13-02-2010, Ould MTN
ASC La Linguère 2 Serigne Diouck 51, Ahmeth Diallo 60
Asante Kotoko 0

Baba Yara, Kumasi, 28-02-2010, Aguidissou BEN
Asante Kotoko 2 Kabiru Imoro 33, Isaac Amoako 51p
ASC La Linguère 0 ASC La Linguère won 4-2p

Hérémakono, Bamoko, 14-02-2010, 14:00, Fall SEN
Djoliba 1 Jean Goua 67
Al Ahly Benghazi 0

March 28th, Benghazi, 28-02-2010, 19:00, Grisha EGY
Al Ahly Benghazi 0
Djoliba 0

Mandela National, Kampala, 12-02-2010, 16:00, Munyemana RWA
URA Kampala 1 Kameesa Manco 90
Zanaco 0

Sunset Stadium, Lusaka, 27-02-2010, Mnkantjo ZIM
Zanaco 4 Alan Mukuka 16, Makundika Sakala 2 37 54, Winston Kalewgo 49
URA Kampala 0

Stade Marchand, Brazzaville, 14-02-2010, 15:00, Cordier CHA
Diables Noirs 3 Fabrice N'Guessi 3, Noelly 2 11 13
ES Sétif 2 Lamouri Djediat 16, Lazhar Aissa 81

8 Mai 1945, Sétif, 27-02-2010, 18:00, Dembele CIV
ES Sétif 2 Mourad Delhoum 2 25 40
Diables Noirs 0

Mkapa National, Dar es Salaam, 13-02-2010, 16:00, Gasinzigwa BDI
Yound Africans 2 Kigi Makasi 51, Mrisho Ngassa 69
St Eloi Lupopo 3 Garrington Gonba 4, Philip Narufu 38, Ntonbo Ivtete 82

Stade de la Kenya, Lubumbashi, 27-02-2010, Alioum CMR
St Eloi Lupopo 1 Kayembe Mukendi 77
Yound Africans 0

Stade Linité, Victoria, 13-02-2010, Fakudze SWZ
La Passe 1 Hassman Abdou 55
Curepipe Starlight 0

Auguste Vollaire, Flacq, 28-02-2010, Rakotonjanahary MAD
Curepipe Starlight 3 Sanhaboa Tomy 45, Olayeni Fashina 62, Dawoochano Sewraj 80
La Passe 1 Hassman Abdou 37

University of Botswana, Gaborone, 13-02-2010, 15:30, Raphael MWI
Gaborone United 0
Orlando Pirates 0

Mandela Bay, Port Elizabeth, 28-02-2010, 15:30, Nunkoo MRI
Orlando Pirates 2 Katlego Mashego 50, Bennett Chenene 54
Gaborone United 2 OG 84, Stephen Maposa 85

Internacional, Malabo, 14-02-2010, 15:30, Mouandjo CMR
Ela Nguema 2 OG 68, Ibrahim Toure 73p
Petro Atlético 3 Santana 2 15 90, Mabina 18

11 de Novembro, Luanda, 28-02-2010, 16:00, Bondo BOT
Petro Atlético 6 Ntui Etah Michel 33, Yamba Asha 51, Joka 3 57 64 80, Ricardo Job 86
Ela Nguema 1 Valentin Eyama 86

28 Septembre, Conakry, 14-02-2010, 16:30, Parkinson SLE
Fello Star Labe 1 Alpha Oumar Diallo 89
Raja Casablanca 3 Omar Najdi 11, Dia Cire 72, OG 76

Mohamed V, Casablanca, 28-02-2010, 17:00, Jedidi TUN
Raja Casablanca 2 Omar Najdi 16
Fello Star Labe 1 Abass Cisse 90

Seyni Kountche, Niamey, 14-02-2010, Wokoma NGA
Sahel 2 Ba Amadou 29, Abubakart Abdul Latif 41
Club Africain 1 Mohamed Traore 88

El Menzah, Tunis, 26-02-2010, 19:00, Bichari ALG
Club Africain 1 Khaled Melliti 41
Sahel 0

Independence, Baku, 13-02-2010, 14:00, El Achiri MAR
Armed Forces 1 OG 85
JS Kabylie 2 Fares Hamiti 48, Mohamed Amine Aoudia 56

1er Novembre, Tizi-Ouzou, 27-02-2010, 15:00, Sidibe MLI
JS Kabylie 3 Nassim Oussalah 24, Rabie Meftah 53p, Mohamed Seguer 83
Armed Forces 0

Uhuru, Dar es Salaam, 14-02-2010, Mohamed Hussein SUD
Mafunzo 1 Makaay Ayoub 90
Gunners 2 David Rediyoni 45, Norman Maroto 49

Dzivaresekwa, Harare, 28-02-2010, Seechurn MRI
Gunners 4 Norman Maroto 41, Ramson Zhuwawo 2 44 70, Ali Sadiki 92+
Mafunzo 0

Estadio de Mansoa, Mansoa, 13-02-2010, 16:00, Kona LBR
Os Balantas 0
Diffa El Jadida 0

El Abdi, El Jadida, 27-02-2010, 20:00, Lamptey GHA
Diffa El Jadida 3 Cheick Oumar Dabo 2 9 40, Said Makasi 33
Os Balantas 0

Bathelemy Boganda, Bangui, 14-02-2010, 15:00, Ndume GAB
Tempête Mocaf 1 Igor Mandjao 21
Al Ittihad Tripoli 2 Daouda Kamilou 71, Mohamed Esnani 81

June 11, Tripoli, 27-02-2010, 19:30, Chaibou NIG
Al Ittihad Tripoli 6 Ali Rahuma 2, Ahmed Zuway 2 14 42, Marwan Mabrouk 20, Pierre Koulibaly 2 31 38
Tempête Mocaf 0

Klebert Picard, Le Tampon, 13-02-2010, 20:00, Ebrahim RSA
Stade Tampon'se 2 Johan Boulard 15, Jean-Michel Fontaine 28
Ajesaia 1 Lalaina Nomenjanahary 81

Mahamasina, Antananarivo, 28-02-2010, Benstrong SEY
Ajesaia 1 Voavy Kassah 14
Stade Tampon'se 3 Johan Boulard 8, Mamadou Diallo 64, Mohamed El Magadarhi 67

Nyayo, Nairobi, 13-02-2010, 16:00, Waziri TAN
Sofapaka 0
Ismaily 0

Ismailia Stadium, Ismailia, 27-02-2010, 19:30, El Raay LBY
Ismaily 2 Mohamed Homos 54, Abdallah Said 67
Sofapaka 0

Rwagasore, Bujumbura, 13-02-2010, Ali Farah DJI
Vital'O 2 Leopold Nkurikiye 2 12p 79
Tiko United 2 Edingue Tombe 36, Njounkou Job 40

Moliko, Tiko, 27-02-2010, 15:30, Leya COD
Tiko United 2 Njounkou Job 6, Francis Evambe 75
Vital'O 2 Tambwe Amissi 56, Matembe Type 59

Mahamasina, Antananarivo, 12-02-2010, 15:00, Eyob ERI
Apaches 3 Adinane Moumine 2 48 53, Ahmed Radjab 48, Italo Fernandes 6, Jeremias Sitoe 45,
Ferroviário Maputo 5 Jorge Manjate 60, Carlos Parruaue 75, Michael Nymukasa 87

Machava, Maputo, 27-02-2010, Dos Santos ANG4
Ferroviário Maputo 4 Adnan Gurbuz 7, Jeremias Sitoe 2 51 81, Carlos Parruaue 62
Apaches 1 Ahmed Radjab 87

Somhlolo National, Lobamba, 14-02-2010, 15:30, Phomane LES
M'bane Swallows 1 Lwazi Maziya 84
Supersport Utd 3 Tebogo Langerman 7, Thabo Mongalo 20, Dario Monteiro 67

Super Stadium, Atteridgeville, 27-02-2010, 20:15, Tiyeho NAM

Supersport Utd	2	Brian Umony [35], Brent Carelse [64]
M'bane Swallows	2	Bougania Cisse [61], Ndzimandze Mfanfikile [61]

Addis Abeba Stadium, 14-02-2010, 16:00, Ngobi UGA

Saint George	1	Mohammed Nasser [75]
Al Merreikh	1	Abdelhamid Ammari [19]

Al Merreikh Stadium, Omdurman, 27-02-2010, 20:00, Onyango KEN

Al Merreikh	3	Abdelhamid Ammari 2 [45 83], Endurance Idahor [53]
Saint George	1	Adane Girma [35]

Stade Nacional, N'Djamena, 14-02-2010, Ngbokaye CTA

Gazelle	1	Henri Djikoloum [24]
Bayelsa United	0	

Samson Siasia, Yenagoa, 28-02-2010, Bangoura GUI

Bayelsa United	2	Gbemi Akinrolabu [43], Mannir Ubale [69p]
Gazelle	2	Greyanda Fiacre [24], Madalngue Cesar [89p]

Divounguy, Port-Gentile, 14-02-2010, Moukoko CGO

Stade Mandji	0	
ASFA/Yennenga	2	Ocansey Mandela 2 [23 68]

4-août, Ouagadougou, 28-02-2010, Atsoo TOG

ASFA/Yennenga	4	Asante Solomon [25], Ocansey Mandela 2 [28 69], Plange Nii Adamah [45]
Stade Mandji	1	Nkoua Junior [65]

National, Freetown, 13-02-2010, 16:30, Gassama GAM

East End Lions	2	Issa Kamara [19], Mohamed Kabia [24]
Espérance Tunis	2	Khaled Ayari [39], Skander Cheikh [45]

7 Novembre, Rades, Tunis, 26-02-2010, 16:00, Ilboudo BFA

Espérance Tunis	3	Guy-Roger Toindouba [4], Wajdi Bouazzi [34], Michael Eneramo [88]
East End Lions	2	Mohamed Kabia [10], Dauda Kanu [86]

SECOND ROUND

Amahoro, Kigali, 20-03-2010, 15:30, Bennett RSA

APR FC	1	Albeir Ngabo [87]
TP Mazembe	0	

Stade de la Kenya, Lubumbashi, 4-04-2010, Kaoma ZAM

TP Mazembe	2	Tresor Mputu [7], Patou Kabangu [72]
APR FC	0	

Heremakono, Bamako, 21-03-2010, 16:30, Bangoura GUI

Djoliba	1	Koffi Pascal Nguessan [25]
ASC La Linguère	0	

Stade de Linguère, Saint-Louis, 5-04-2010, Doue CIV

ASC La Linguère	1	Mbaye Thiam [39]
Djoliba	0	Djoliba won 4-3p

Nkoloma, Lusaka, 20-03-2010, 15:00, Seechurn MRI

Zanaco	1	Makundika Sakala [75]
ASEC Mimosas	0	

Houphouet-Boigny, Abidjan, 4-04-2010, 15:30, Lamptey GHA

ASEC Mimosas	1	Mangoua Kesse [44]
Zanaco	1	Trinity Chalanshi [53]

Reunification, Douala, 21-03-2010, 14:30, Munyemana RWA

Union Douala	0	
ES Sétif	2	Lazhar Aissa [19], Lamouri Djediat [39]

8 Mai 1945, Sétif, 2-04-2010, 19:00, Coulibaly MLI

ES Sétif	5	Lazhar Aissa [15], Lamouri Djediat [40], Mehdi Kacem [63], Smail Diss [72], Seghir Ferradji [84]
Union Douala	0	

Stade de la Kenya, Lubumbashi, 21-03-2010, Abdel Rahman SUD

St Eloi Lupopo	0	
Dynamos	1	Cuthbert Malajila [73]

National, Harare, 4-04-2010, 15:00, Carvalho ANG

Dynamos	1	Thabani Kamusoko [69]
St Eloi Lupopo	0	

Stade George V, Curepipe, 20-03-2010, 16:15, Ibrahim COM

Curepipe Starlight	0	Mandla Mgadla [52]
Gaborone Utd	3	Vincent Puri [6], Ronald Chikoma [45],

University of Botswana, Gaborone, 2-04-2010, 15:30, Phomane LES

Gaborone Utd	3	OG [30], Mandla Mgadla [49], Otlaadisa
Curepipe Starlight	0	Mohambi [86]

Mohamed V, Casablanca, 21-03-2010, 17:00, Benouza ALG

Raja Casablanca	1	Mouhssine Moutouali [48p]
Petro Atlético	0	Avex [43]

11 de Novembro, Luanda, 4-04-2010, 16:00, Ngosi MWI

Petro Atlético	1	Joka [65]
Raja Casablanca	0	

El Menzah, Tunis, 19-03-2010, 17:00, Ennouni MAR

Club Africain	1	Mohamed Traore [85]
JS Kabylie	1	Idriss Ech-Chergui [30]

1er Novembre, Tizi-Ouzou, 2-04-2010, 16:00, El Raay LBY

JS Kabylie	1	Sid Yahia Cherif [36]
Club Africain	0	

Rufaro, Harare, 20-03-2010, 16:00, Maillet SEY

Gunners	1	Norman Maroto [23]
Al Ahly Cairo	0	

International, Cairo, 2-04-2010, 19:30, Jiyed MAR

Al Ahly Cairo	2	Ahmed Shoukry [21], Mohamed Samir [45]
Gunners	0	

June 11, Tripoli, 19-03-2010, 18:30, Djaoupe TOG

Al Ittihad Tripoli	1	Ahmed Zuway [58]
Diffa El Jadida	1	Cheick Ouinar Dabo [74]

El Abdi, El Jadida, 2-04-2010, 19:00, Jedidi TUN

Diffa El Jadida	1	Cheick Oumar Dabo [67]
Al Ittihad Tripoli	1	Daouda Kamilou [73]. Ittihad won 4-3p

Houphouet-Boigny, Abidjan, 20-03-2010, 15:30, Diedhiou SEN

Africa Sports	0	
Al Hilal	0	

Al Hilal Stadium, Omdurman, 4-04-2010, Eyob ERI

Al Hilal	4	Sef Masawi 2 [29 50], Blaise Mbele 2 [72 93+]
Africa Sports	1	Djedjed Landry [92+]

Ismailia Stadium, Ismailia, 20-03-2010, 19:30, El Achiri MAR

Ismaily	3	Ahmed Farag 2 [16 80], Mohamed Abougrisha [70]
Stade Tampon'se	1	Mohamed Modghary [33]

Klebert Picard, Le Tampon, 3-04-2010, 20:00, Kirwa KEN

Stade Tampon'se	1	Mamadou Diallo [31]
Ismaily	0	

Reunification, Douala, 20-03-2010, 15:30, Karembe MLI

Tiko United	2	Ackey Ambino [60], Tamen Nghanthy [85]
Heartland	2	Signs Chibambo 2 [76 90]

Dan Anyiam, Owerri, 4-04-2010, 16:00, Nahi CIV

Heartland	1	Emmanuel Omodiagbe [85]
Tiko United	1	Njondong Joel [30]

Rand Stadium, Johannesburg, 20-03-2010, 20:15, Mohamadou CMR

Supersport Utd	3	Tebogo Langerman 2 [37 61], Anthony Laffor [44]
Ferroviário Maputo	0	

Machava, Maputo, 3-04-2010, 15:00, Mbaga TAN

Ferroviário Maputo	2	Jeremia Sitoe [12], Momed Hagy [26]
Supersport Utd	0	

Nacional, N'Djamena, 21-03-2010, 16:00, Moukoko CGO

Gazelle	1	OG [80]
Al Merreikh	1	Kelechi Osunwa [70]

Al Merreikh Stadium, Omdurman, 3-04-2010, 20:00, Ndayisenga BDI

Al Merreikh	2	Kelechi Osunwa [10], OG [61]
Gazelle	0	

7 Novembre, Rades, Tunis, 20-03-2010, 17:00, Amalou ALG

Espérance Tunis	4	Khaled Ayari [13], Michael Eneramo [20], Wajdi Bouazzi [26], Sameh Derbali [26]
ASFA/Yennenga	1	OG [41]

4-août, Ouagadougou, 3-04-2010, Keita GUI

ASFA/Yennenga	1	Ocansey Mandela [19]
Espérance Tunis	3	Michael Eneramo [2], Khaled Ayari [19], Wajdi Bouazzi [80]

THIRD ROUND

Heremakono, Bamako, 25-04-2010, 17:00, Benouza ALG

| Djoliba | 0 | |
| TP Mazembe | 1 | Tresor Mputu 53p |

Stade de la Kenya, Lubumbashi, 9-05-2010, 16:30, Djaoupe TOG

| TP Mazembe | 3 | Alain Kaluyituka 2 27p 60, Tresor Mputu 28 |
| Djoliba | 0 | |

8 Mai 1945, Sétif, 24-04-2010, 19:00, Diatta SEN

| ES Sétif | 1 | Mourad Delhoum 73 |
| Zanaco | 0 | |

Nkoloma, Lusaka, 8-05-2010, 15:00, Abdel Rahman SUD

| Zanaco | 2 | Makundika Sakala 53, Kennedy Nketani 78 |
| ES Sétif | 2 | Nabil Hemani 61, Lazhar Aissa 77 |

National, Harare, 25-04-2010, 16:00, Ssegonga UGA

| Dynamos | 4 | Dylan Chivandre 42, Benjamin Marere 44, Farai Vimisayi 56, Evans Gwekwerere 83 |
| Gaborone Utd | 1 | Mandla Mgadla 29 |

University of Botswana, Gaborone, 8-05-2010, 15:30, Eyob ERI

| Gaborone Utd | 1 | Ofentse Nato 84 |
| Dynamos | 0 | |

1er Novembre, Tizi-Ouzou, 25-04-2010, 17:00, Mailett SEY

| JS Kabylie | 2 | Fares Hamiti 51, Mohamed Aoudia 90 |
| Petro Atlético | 0 | |

11 de Novembro, Luanda, 9-05-2010, 16:00, Bennett RSA

| Petro Atlético | 2 | Magalhaes 5, Ricardo Job 13 |
| JS Kabylie | 1 | Mohamed Aoudia 54 |

June 11, Tripoli, 23-04-2010, 20:30, Coulibaly MLI

| Al Ittihad Tripoli | 2 | Younes Al Shibani 13, Ahmed Zuway 73 |
| Al Ahly Cairo | 0 | |

International, Cairo, 9-05-2010, 20:00, Doue CIV

| Al Ahly Cairo | 3 | Emad Moteab 60, Mohamed Fadl 74, Shehab Ahmed 94+ |
| Al Ittihad Tripoli | 0 | |

Al Hilal Stadium, Omdurman, 25-04-2010, 20:00, Damon RSA

| Al Hilal | 0 | |
| Ismaily | 1 | Mohamed Homos 45 |

Ismailia Stadium, Ismailia, 9-05-2010, 18:00, Seechurn MRI

| Ismaily | 3 | Mohamed Homos 65, Ahmed Farag 76, Ahmed Khairy 90 |
| Al Hilal | 1 | Edward Sadomba 27 |

Rand Stadium, Johannesburg, 24-04-2010, 20:15, Lamptey GHA

| Supersport Utd | 1 | Thabo September 39 |
| Heartland | 1 | Thankgod Ike 3 |

Dan Anyiam, Owerri, 9-05-2010, 15:00, Haimoudi ALG

| Heartland | 3 | Emeka Nwanna 39, John Owoeri 70, Bello Kofarmata 75 |
| Supersport Utd | 1 | Brian Umony 80 |

7 Novembre, Rades, Tunis, 23-04-2010, 16:00, Rouassi MAR

| Espérance Tunis | 3 | Eneramo 8, Ben Omar 23, Darragi 28p |
| Al Merreikh | 0 | |

Al Merreikh Stadium, Omdurman, 8-05-2010, 20:00, El Raay LBY

| Al Merreikh | 1 | OG 45 |
| Espérance Tunis | 1 | Bouazzi 52 |

GROUP STAGE

GROUP A											
		Pl	W	D	L	F	A	Pts	TUN	COD	ALG	ZIM
Espérance Tunis	TUN	6	4	1	1	9	4	13		3-0	2-2	1-0
TP Mazembe	COD	6	3	2	1	8	7	11	2-1		2-2	2-1
ES Sétif	ALG	6	1	3	2	7	6	6	0-1	0-0		3-0
Dynamos	ZIM	6	1	0	5	2	9	3	0-1	0-2	1-0	

8 Mai, Sétif
16-07-2010, 2-:30, Bennett RSA

| ES Sétif | 0 |

Mohamed **Ferradji** - Slimane **Raho**, Mourad **Delhoum•**, Abdelkader **Laifaoui** - Bouazza **Feham** (Mehdi **Kacem** 64), Farouk **Belkaid**, Khaled **Lemmouchia**, Abdelmoumene **Djabou**, Hocine **Metref** (Moustapha **Djallit** 64) - Mokhtar **Benmoussa** (Abderrahmane **Hachoud** 46), Youcef **Ghazali**. Tr: Noureddine Zekri

| Espérance Tunis | 1 |
| | Wajdi Bouazzi 53 |

Wassim **Naouara** - Harrison **Afful•** (Walid **Hicheri** 90), Aymen **Ben Amor**, Khalil **Chemmam•**, Zied **Derbali**, Syam **Ben Youssef** - Mejdi **Traoui•**, Wajdi **Bouazzi** (Youssef **Msekni** 60), Khaled **Korbi•** - Borhene **Ghannem** (Khaled **Ayari** 76), Oussama **Darragi**. Tr: Faouzi Benzarti

National Stadium, Harare
18-07-2010, 15:00, Lamptey GHA

| Dynamos | 0 |

Washington **Arubi** - Ttafadzwa **Maingire** (Thabani **Kamusoko** 43), George **Magariro**, Guthrie **Zhokinyi**, Phillip **Sithole** - Benjamin **Marere**, Wonder **Sithole•** (Desmond **Maringwa** 63), Ashley **Rambanepasi•**, Kumbulani **Banda** (Brighton **Tuwaya** 77) - Evans **Gwekwerere**, Cuthbert **Malajila**. Tr: Elvis Chiweshe

| TP Mazembe | 2 |
| | Given Singuluma 2 15 32 |

Robert **Kidiaba** - Hichani **Himoonde**, Jean **Kasusula•**, Eric **Nkulukuta•**, Stopila **Sunzu**, Joel **Kimwaki** - Pamphile **Mihayo**, Hugues **Bedi** (Ngandu **Kasongo** 83) - Tresor **Mputu** (Darryl **Nyandoro** 90), Alain **Kaluyituka** (Guy **Lusadisu** 74), Given **Singuluma**. Tr: Diego Garzitto

7 Novembre, Rades, Tunis
31-07-2010, 20:30, Djaoupe TOG

| Espérance Tunis | 1 |
| | Darragi 83p |

Wassim **Naouara** - Harrison **Afful** (Aymen **Ben Amor**, Khalil **Chemmam** (Borhene **Ghannem** 65), Zied **Derbali•**, Syam **Ben Youssef** - Mejdi **Traoui**, Khaled **Korbi** - Oussama **Darragi** (Guy-Roger **Toindouba** 87), Youssef **Msekni**, Khaled **Ayari** (Walid **Hicheri** 90). Tr: Faouzi Benzarti

| Dynamos | 0 |

Washington **Arubi** - Brighton **Tuwaya•**, George **Magariro•**, Guthrie **Zhokinyi**, David **Kutyauripo** - Benjamin **Marere**, Milton **Makopa**, Ashley **Rambanepasi**, Farai **Vimisayi**, Isaac **Pitamuja** (Desmond **Maringwa** 46) - Cuthbert **Malajila**. Tr: Elvis Chiweshe

Stade de la Kenya, Lubumbashi
1-08-2010, 15:30, Carvalho ANG

TP Mazembe   **2**
Hugues Bedi [17], Tresor Mputu [55]

Robert Kidiaba - Hichani Himoonde, Jean Kasusula (Aime Bakula 78), Bawaka Mabele, Stopila Sunzu, Joel Kimwaki• - Pamphile Mihayo (Guy Lusadisu 65), Hugues Bedi - Tresor Mputu, Alain Kaluyituka, Given Singuluma (Deo Kanda 85). Tr: Diego Garzitto

ES Sétif   **2**
Nabil Hemani 2 [49 50]

Fawzi Chaouchi - Slimane Raho•, Mohamed Yekhlef (Abderrahmane Hachoud 13), Mourad Delhoum•, Abdelkader Laifaoui - Bouazza Feham, Lazhar Aissa (Moustapha Djallit 76), Farouk Belkaid, Khaled Lemmouchia•, Abdelmoumene Djabou (Antar Boucherit• 82) - Nabil Hemani♦56. Tr: Noureddine Zekri

---

National Stadium, Harare
15-08-2010, 15:00, Maillet SEY

Dynamos   **1**
Wonder Sithole [30]

Washington Arubi - Brighton Tuwaya, George Magariro, Guthrie Zhokinyi, David Kutyauripo - Benjamin Marere•, Milton Makopa•, Wonder Sithole, Ashley Rambanepasi - Farai Vimisayi•, Divani Chivandire (Edmore Mashiri 67). Tr: Elvis Chiweshe

ES Sétif   **0**
Mohamed Ferradji - Abderrahmane Hachoud (Bouazza Feham 41), Smail Diss, Ryad Benchadi (Mehdi Kacem 66), Slimane Raho• - Lazhar Aissa, Farouk Belkaid, Khaled Lemmouchia, Abdelmoumene Djabou - Antar Boucherit, Youcef Ghazali (Moustapha Djallit 67). Tr: Noureddine Zekri

---

Stade de la Kenya, Lubumbashi
15-08-2010, 15:30, Seechurn MRI

TP Mazembe   **2**
Alain Kaluyituka [44], Ngandu Kasongo [87]

Robert Kidiaba - Hichani Himoonde (Mukinaye Tshani 17), Jean Kasusula, Eric Nkulukuta•, Stopila Sunzu (Ngandu Kasongo 74) - Narcisse Ekanga, Pamphile Mihayo, Hugues Bedi - Alain Kaluyituka, Patou Kabangu (Ghislain Mvete 90), Given Singuluma. Tr: Diego Garzitto

Espérance Tunis   **1**
Michael Eneramo [41]

Wassim Naouara• - Harrison Afful, Aymen Ben Amor, Khalil Chemmam, Zied Derbali, Syam Ben Youssef - Mejdi Traoui•, Khaled Korbi - Michael Eneramo (Khaled Ayari 69), Oussama Darragi, Youssef Msekni (Guy-Roger Toindouba 84). Tr: Faouzi Benzarti

---

8 Mai, Sétif
27-08-2010, 22:00, El Achiri MAR

ES Sétif   **3**
Bouazza Feham 2 [32 74], Youcef Ghazali [77]

Fawzi Chaouchi - Abderrahmane Hachoud, Mourad Delhoum, Abdelkader Laifaoui - Bouazza Feham, Lazhar Aissa (Smail Diss 89), Farouk Belkaid, Khaled Lemmouchia, Abdelmoumene Djabou (Mehdi Kacem 84) - Moustapha Djallit (Francis Ambane 66), Youcef Ghazali•. Tr: Giovanni Solinas

Dynamos   **0**
Washington Arubi• - Brighton Tuwaya♦66, George Magariro•, Guthrie Zhokinyi, Phillip Sithole - Benjamin Marere•, Milton Makopa, Wonder Sithole (Kumbulani Banda 76), Ashley Rambanepasi•, Farai Vimisayi• - Divani Chivandire♦90 . Tr: Elvis Chiweshe

---

7 Novembre, Rades, Tunis
28-08-2010, 22:00, Maillet SEY

Espérance Tunis   **3**
Michael Eneramo 2 [19 46], Walid Hicheri [86]

Wassim Naouara - Harrison Afful, Walid Hicheri•, Aymen Ben Amor, Khalil Chemmam, Syam Ben Youssef• - Khaled Korbi - Michael Eneramo (Saber Khelifa 72), Oussama Darragi (Zied Derbali 86), Youssef Msekni, Guy-Roger Toindouba. Tr: Faouzi Benzarti

TP Mazembe   **0**
Robert Kidiaba - Jean Kasusula, Boule Tshizeu, Eric Nkulukuta, Stopila Sunzu (Ngandu Kasongo 51), Joel Kimwaki - Pamphile Mihayo, Narcisse Ekanga (Deo Kanda 79), Hugues Bedi - Alain Kaluyituka•, Patou Kabangu (Mukinaye Tshani 79), Given Singuluma•. Tr: Diego Garzitto

---

7 Novembre, Rades, Tunis
11-09-2010, 20:30, Diatta SEN

Espérance Tunis   **2**
Oussama Darragi [41], Mejdi Traoui [58]

Wassim Naouara - Harrison Afful, Walid Hicheri, Aymen Ben Amor (Khaled Ayari 89), Khalil Chemmam, Syam Ben Youssef - Mejdi Traoui (Guy-Roger Toindouba 88), Khaled Korbi - Michael Eneramo•, Oussama Darragi•, Youssef Msekni (Saber Khelifa 72). Tr: Faouzi Benzarti

ES Sétif   **2**
Youcef Ghazali 2 [5 85]

Fawzi Chaouchi - Abderrahmane Hachoud, Slimane Raho (Hocine Metref 72), Mourad Delhoum (Francis Ambane 46), Abdelkader Laifaoui• - Bouazza Feham, Lazhar Aissa (Moustapha Djallit 67), Farouk Belkaid•, Khaled Lemmouchia, Abdelmoumene Djabou - Youcef Ghazali. Tr: Giovanni Solinas

---

Stade de la Kenya, Lubumbashi
12-09-2010, 15:30, Ssegonga UGA

TP Mazembe   **2**
Alain Kaluyituka [60], Given Singuluma [63]

Robert Kidiaba - Jean Kasusula, Eric Nkulukuta, Mukinaye Tshani, Joel Kimwaki - Pamphile Mihayo, Narcisse Ekanga• (Ngandu Kasongo• 40), Hugues Bedi - Alain Kaluyituka, Patou Kabangu (Marcellin Tamboulas 80), Given Singuluma (Deo Kanda 66). Tr: Lamine N'Diaye

Dynamos   **1**
Munyaradzi Diya - Guthrie Zhokinyi, Augustine Mbara, Matthew Mahala, David Kutyauripo - Desmond Maringwa, Edmore Mashiri (Phillip Sithole 68), Milton Makopa, Wonder Sithole, Kumbulani Banda (Thabani Kamusoko 58) - Evans Gwekwerere (Nicholas Alifandika 68. Tr: Elvis Chiweshe

---

National Stadium, Harare
18-09-2010, 15:00, Mohamadou CMR

Dynamos   **0**
Washington Arubi - Brighton Tuwaya, Guthrie Zhokinyi, Matthew Mahala, David Kutyauripo (Thabani Kamusoko 66) - Desmond Maringwa, Edmore Mashiri, Milton Makopa•, Wonder Sithole (Nicholas Alifandika 66), Farai Vimisayi - Evans Gwekwerere (Kumbulani Banda 76). Tr: Elvis Chiweshe

Espérance Tunis   **1**
Oussama Darragi [21]

Moez Ben Chrifia - Harrison Afful, Aymen Ben Amor•, Khalil Chemmam, Zied Derbali, Mohamed Ben Mansour - Mejdi Traoui, Saber Khelifa - Oussama Darragi (Walid Hicheri 89), Khaled Ayari (Borhene Ghannem 46), Guy-Roger Toindouba (Oussama Boughanmi 75). Tr: Faouzi Benzarti

---

8 Mai, Sétif
18-09-2010, 14:00, Doue CIV

ES Sétif   **0**
Fawzi Chaouchi - Abderrahmane Hachoud•, Smail Diss, Abdelkader Laifaoui•, Lazhar Aissa - Khaled Lemmouchia, Abdelmoumene Djabou, Antar Boucherit•, Hocine Metref - Mokhtar Benmoussa (Moustapha Djallit 67), Youcef Ghazali. Tr: Giovanni Solinas

TP Mazembe   **0**
Robert Kidiaba - Jean Kasusula, Eric Nkulukuta, Mukinaye Tshani, Joel Kimwaki - Pamphile Mihayo, Hugues Bedi, Christopher Semakweri (Ghislain Mvete 60) - Alain Kaluyituka, Patou Kabangu (Deo Kanda 83), Given Singuluma (Stopila Sunzu 75). Tr: Lamine N'Diaye

GROUP B

		Pl	W	D	L	F	A	Pts	ALG	EGY	EGY	NGA
JS Kabylie	ALG	6	4	2	0	6	2	14		1-0	1-0	1-0
Al Ahly Cairo	EGY	6	2	2	2	8	9	8	1-1		2-1	2-1
Ismaily	EGY	6	2	0	4	7	8	6	0-1	4-2		1-0
Heartland	NGA	6	1	2	3	5	7	5	1-1	1-1	2-1	

Dan Anyiam, Owerri
18-07-2010, 15:00, Diatta SEN
Heartland   **1**
Bello Kofarmata 49

Austin Brown - ThankGod Ike, Orji Okagbue, Joseph Jackson, Joseph Eyimofe, Emmanuel Olowo• - Joshua Obaje, Emeka Nwanna - John Dwoeri, Bello Kofarmata•, Julius Ubido. Tr: Samson Siasia

Al Ahly Cairo   **1**
Mohamed Aboutrika 75p

Sherif Ekrami• - Ahmed Fathi, Wael Gomaa, Sayed Moawad•, Sherif Abdul Fadil, Ahmed El Sayed - Ahmed Hassan (Hossam Ghaly 59), Mohamed Aboutrika (Mostafa Shebeta 86), Hossam Ashour, Ahmed Shokri (Mohamed Barakat 55) - Mohamed Fadl•. Tr: Hossam El Badry

---

Ismailia Stadium, Ismailia
18-07-2010, 20:00, Doue CIV
Ismaily   **0**

Mohamed Sobhi - Ibrahim Yehia•, Ahmed Sedik (Mohab Saied 68), Shadi Mohamed - Abdallah Shahat, Ahmed Ali, Ahmed Khairi (Ahmed Hegazi 82), Ahmed Samir Farag, Mohamed Soliman - Amr Al Sulaya•, Mohamed Abougreisha. Tr: Mark Wotte

JS Kabylie   **1**
Essaid Belkalem 75

Malik Asselah• - Ali Rial•, Drissa Coulibaly, Nassim Oussalah•, Essaid Belkalem, Chemseddine Nessakh - Lamara Douicher (Billal Naili 65), Saad Tedjar (Mohamed Khoutir-Ziti 88), Abdennour El Ouazzani - Mohamed Aoudia, Fares Hamiti (Nabil Yalaoui 83). Tr: Alain Geiger

---

1er Novembre, Tizi-Ouzou
31-07-2010, 21:00,, Ssegonga UGA
JS Kabylie   **1**
Fares Hamiti 55

Malik Asselah - Ali Rial•, Drissa Coulibaly (Mohamed Khoutir-Ziti 35), Nassim Oussalah, Essaid Belkalem - Lamara Douicher, Billal Naili•, Saad Tedjar - Mohamed Aoudia, Fares Hamiti• (Isu Asuka• 56), Sid Yahia Cherif (Chemseddine Nessakh 83). Tr: Alain Geiger

Heartland   **0**

Austin Brown - ThankGod Ike, Orji Okagbue, Chinedu Efugh, Joseph Jackson•, Emmanuel Olowo - Joshua Obaje (Onyekachi Okoye 67), Philip Obhafuoso - John Dwoeri•, Ikechukwu Ibenegbu (Emeka Nwanna 78), Bello Kofarmata (Adama Odey 80), Julius Ubido. Tr: Samson Siasia

---

International Stadium, Cairo
1-08-2010, 20:30, Coulibaly MLI
Al Ahly Cairo   **2**
Mohamed Talaat 58, Wael Gomaa 90

Sherif Ekrami - Ahmed Fathi (Ahmed Shokri 75), Wael Gomaa, Sayed Moawad, Sherif Abdul Fadil (Mohamed Nagi Geddo 46), Ahmed El Sayed - Hossam Ghaly, Ahmed Hassan, Mohamed Aboutrika•, Hossam Ashour (Shehab Ahmed 71) - Mohamed Talaat. Tr: Hossam El Badry

Ismaily   **1**
Mohamed Abougreisha 80

Mohamed Sobhi - Ahmed Sedik, Moatasem Salem, Ahmed Hegazi - Abdallah Shahat, Ahmed Ali (Abdessalam Benjelloun 70), Ahmed Khairi•, Ahmed Samir Farag, Mohamed Soliman (Shadi Mohamed 86) - Amr Al Sulaya, Ndubuisi Ezeh (Mohamed Abougreisha• 63). Tr: Mark Wotte

---

Ismailia Stadium, Ismailia
15-08-2010, 21:30, Abdel Rahman SUD
Ismaily   **1**
Ndubuisi Ezeh 15

Mohamed Sobhi• - Ahmed Sedik, Moatasem Salem, Shadi Mohamed - Abdallah Shahat, Ahmed Ali (Mohamed Abougreisha 60), Ahmed Khairi, Ahmed Samir Farag, Mohamed Soliman - Amr Al Sulaya (Abdullah Saied 88), Ndubuisi Ezeh (Abdessalam Benjelloun 75). Tr: Mark Wotte

Heartland   **0**

Austin Brown - Orji Okagbue, Joseph Jackson•, Kingsley Udoh, Emmanuel Olowo – Emmanuel Omodiagbe, John Dwoeri - Ikechukwu Ibenegbu, Okechukwu Nwadike, Julius Ubido, Chibuzor Ozurumba (Bello Kofarmata 40). Tr: Samson Siasia

---

1er Novembre, Tizi-Ouzou
15-08-2010, 22:00, Djaoupe TOG
JS Kabylie   **1**
Mohamed Khoutir-Ziti 24

Mourad Berrefane - Drissa Coulibaly, Nassim Oussalah, Essaid Belkalem, Mohamed Khoutir-Ziti, Chemseddine Nessakh - Lamara Douicher (Belkacem Remache 80), Billal Naili, Saad Tedjar (Hocine El Orfi 80) - Mohamed Aoudia, Sid Yahia Cherif (Koceila Berchiche 90). Tr: Alain Geiger

Al Ahly Cairo   **0**

Sherif Ekrami - Ahmed Fathi, Wael Gomaa•, Sayed Moawad, Sherif Abdul Fadil, Ahmed El Sayed - Hossam Ghaly••90, Mohamed Aboutrika (Ahmed Hassan 62), Hossam Ashour• (Mohamed Shawki 85), Mohamed Barakat• - Mohamed Nagi Geddo (Mohamed Talaat 46). Tr: Hossam El Badry

---

Dan Anyiam, Owerri
29-08-2010, 15:00, Bennaceur TUN
Heartland   **2**
ThankGod Ike 38, Chinedu Efugh 85

Austin Brown - ThankGod Ike (Damian Udeh 73), Orji Okagbue, Kingsley Udoh (Chinedu Efugh 25), Emmanuel Olowo - Joshua Obaje (Singwonders Chibambo 60) - John Dwoeri, Ikechukwu Ibenegbu, Julius Ubido, Chibuzor Ozurumba, Emmanuel Nwachi. Tr: Samson Siasia

Ismaily   **1**
Mohamed Soliman 29

Mohamed Sobhi - Ahmed Sedik, Moatasem Salem, Shadi Mohamed• - Abdallah Shahat, Ahmed Ali (Mohamed Abougreisha 60), Ahmed Khairi, Ahmed Samir Farag, Mohamed Soliman - Amr Al Sulaya, Ndubuisi Ezeh. Tr: Mark Wotte

---

International Stadium, Cairo
29-08-2010, 21:30, Kaoma ZAM
Al Ahly Cairo   **1**
Geddo 20

Sherif Ekrami - Ahmed Fathi (Ahmed El Sayed 64), Wael Gomaa, Sayed Moawad, Sherif Abdul Fadil - Mohamed Aboutrika (Ahmed Hassan 77), Hossam Ashour, Mohamed Barakat•, Shehab Ahmed - Mohamed Fadl (Osama Hosni 55), Mohamed Nagi Geddo. Tr: Hossam El Badry

JS Kabylie   **1**
Saad Tedjar 29

Malik Asselah - Ali Rial, Drissa Coulibaly, Nassim Oussalah, Essaid Belkalem, Chemseddine Nessakh• - Lamara Douicher (Mohamed Khoutir-Ziti 90), Billal Naili• (Hocine El Orfi 58), Saad Tedjar (Belkacem Remache 66) - Mohamed Aoudia, Sid Yahia Cherif••♦43. Tr: Alain Geiger

---

1er Novembre, Tizi-Ouzou
10-09-2010, 22:00, El Raay LBY
JS Kabylie   **1**
Isu Asuka 86

Malik Asselah• - Ali Rial, Drissa Coulibaly, Nassim Oussalah•, Essaid Belkalem, Chemseddine Nessakh - Lamara Douicher (Abdennour El Ouazzani 69), Nabil Yalaoui (Isu Asuka 69), Saad Tedjar (Belkacem Remache 76) - Hocine El Orfi•, Mohamed Aoudia. Tr: Alain Geiger

Ismaily   **0**

Mohamed Sobhi - Moatasem Salem, Shadi Mohamed - Abdallah Shahat, Abdullah Saied, Ahmed Ali (Mohamed Abougreisha 77), Ahmed Khairi (Mohab Saied 84), Ahmed Samir Farag, Mohamed Soliman - Amr Al Sulaya, Ndubuisi Ezeh. Tr: Mark Wotte

International Stadium, Cairo
12-09-2010, 20:00, Eyob ERI

Al Ahly Cairo	2

Ahmed Fathi [20], Mohamed Fadl [51]

Sherif Ekrami - Ahmed Fathi, Wael Gomaa, Sayed Moawad, Sherif Abdul Fadil - Mohamed Aboutrika (Ahmed Shokri 83), Hossam Ashour, Mohamed Talaat, Shehab Ahmed - Mohamed Fadl (Mohamed Ghaddar 75), Mohamed Nagi Geddo (Mohamed Shawki 67). Tr: Hossam El Badry

Heartland	1

Emmanuel Nwachi [57]

Ikechukwu Ezenwa - Chinedu Efugh, Orji Okagbue, Joseph Jackson, Kingsley Udoh (Emmanuel Olowo 73) - Damian Udeh (Singwonders Chibambo 54) - John Owoeri, Ikechukwu Ibenegbu, Bello Kofarmata (Emeka Nwanna 63), Julius Ubido, Emmanuel Nwachi. Tr: Samson Siasia

---

Dan Anyiam, Owerri
19-09-2010, 16:00, Bennett RSA

Heartland	1

Emeka Nwanna [30p]

Daniel Akpeyi - Chinedu Efugh•, Joseph Jackson, Peter Ambrose, Emmanuel Olowo - Damian Udeh, Joshua Obaje (Onyekachi Okoye• 83), Emeka Nwanna (Chibuzor Ozurumba 78) - John Owoeri•, Bello Kofarmata (Singwonders Chibambo 84), Julius Ubido. Tr: Samson Siasia

JS Kabylie	1

Nabil Yalaoui [50]

Malik Asselah - Ali Rial, Belkacem Remache, Drissa Coulibaly (Mohamed Khoutir-Ziti 80), Essaid Belkalem, Chemseddine Nessakh - Billal Naili, Nabil Yalaoui, Abdennour El Ouazzani - Sid Yahia Cherif• (Fares Hamiti 70), Isu Asuka (Koceila Berchiche 46). Tr: Alain Geiger

---

Ismailia Stadium, Ismailia
19-09-2010, 18:00, Damon RSA

Ismaily	4

Abdallah Shahat [5], Ahmed Ali 2 [36 74], Moatasem Salem [70]

Mohamed Sobhi - Ahmed Sedik, Moatasem Salem•, Shadi Mohamed - Abdallah Shahat, Abdullah Saied (Abdessalam Benjelloun 68), Ahmed Ali (Mohamed Abougreisha 85), Ahmed Khairi, Ahmed Samir Farag, Mohamed Soliman - Ndubuisi Ezeh (Ibrahim Yehia 90). Tr: Mark Wotte

Al Ahly Cairo	2

Mohamed Barakat [35], Mohamed Talaat [87]

Ahmed Abdul Monem - Ahmed Fathi• (Mohamed Samir 78), Sherif Abdul Fadil, Ahmed El Sayed, Ayman Ashraf - Mohamed Shawki, Mohamed Barakat, Shehab Ahmed, Mohamed Talaat - Francis Doe, Mohamed Nagi Geddo (Ahmed Shokri 29). Tr: Hossam El Badry

SEMI-FINALS

Stade de la Kenya, Lubumbashi
3-10-2010, 15:30, Diatta SEN

TP Mazembe	3

Kaluyituka 2 [6 89], Kasongo [85]

Robert Kidiaba• - Joel Kimwaki, Jean Kasusula, Pamphile Mihayo (Bawaka Mabele 46), Eric Nkulukuta - Narcisse Ekanga (Ngandu Kasongo 80), Darryl Nyandoro, Hugues Bedi - Alain Kaluyituka, Patou Kabangu, Given Singulama (Deo Kanda 62). Tr: Lamine N'Diaye

JS Kabylie	1

Nabil Yalaoui [69]

Malik Asselah• - Ali Rial, Belkacem Remache (Saad Tedjar 80), Drissa Coulibaly, Nassim Oussalah, Essaid Belkalem - Chemseddine Nessakh, Billel Naili•, Hocine El Orfi (Lamara Douicher 63) - Mohamed Aoudia, Sid Yahia Cherif (Nabil Yalaoui 62). Tr: Alain Geiger

---

Stade 1er Novembre, Tizi-Ouzou
16-10-2010, 20:15, Damon RSA

JS Kabylie	0

Malik Asselah - Ali Rial, Belkacem Remache, Drissa Coulibaly (Koceila Berchiche• 46), Nassim Oussalah - Chemseddine Nessakh (Sid Yahia Cherif 69), Lamara Douicher, Billel Naili•• ◆61, Saad Tedjar - Mohamed Aoudia, Isu Asuka (Nabil Yalaoui• 46). Tr: Alain Geiger

TP Mazembe	0

Robert Kidiaba - Joel Kimwaki, Jean Kasusula•, Pamphile Mihayo, Eric Nkulukuta• - Narcisse Ekanga, Stopila Sunzu•, Hugues Bedi - Alain Kaluyituka, Patou Kabangu, Given Singulama• (Ngandu Kasongo 76). Tr: Lamine N'Diaye

---

International, Cairo
3-10-2010, 19:30, El Raay LBY

Al Ahly Cairo	2

Mohamed Fadl [38], Ahmed Fathy [68]

Sherif Ekramy - Ahmed Fathi, Wael Gomaa, Sherif Abdel Fadil, Ahmed El Sayed - Mohamed Aboutrika, Hossam Ashour•, Mohamed Barakat, Shehab Ahmed• (Mohamed Shawki 70) - Mohamed Fadl (Mohamed Talaat 59), Francis Doe (Ahmed Shokri 81). Tr: Hossam El Badry

Esperance Tunis	1

Oussama Darragi [72]

Wassim Naouara - Harrisson Afful, Walid Hicheri•, Khalil Chemmam, Aymen Ben Amour• (Youssef Msekni 61) - Mejdi Traoui, Saber Khifa, Khaled Korbi (Khaled Ayari 80), Mohamed Ben Mansour - Michael Eneramo, Oussama Darragi (Zied Derbali 90). Tr: Faouzi Benzarti

---

Stade 7 Novembre, Rades, Tunis
17-10-2010, 19:15, Lamptey GHA

Esperance Tunis	1

Eneramo [1]

Wassim Naouara - Harrisson Afful, Walid Hicheri, Khalil Chemmam (Zied Derbali 84), Mohamed Ben Mansour - Mejdi Traoui•, Saber Khifa (Khaled Ayari 72), Khaled Korbi - Michael Eneramo, Oussama Darragi•, Youssef Msekni (Syam Ben Youssef 90). Tr: Faouzi Benzarti

Al Ahly Cairo	0

Sherif Ekramy - Ahmed Fathi, Wael Gomaa•, Sayed Moawad (Mohamed Fadl 55), Sherif Abdel Fadil•, Ahmed El Sayed - Hossam Ghaly•, Mohamed Aboutrika (Shehab Ahmed 70), Hossam Ashour•, Mohamed Barakat◆28 - Mohamed Fadl, Mohamed Nagy Geddo. Tr: Hossam El Badry

CAF Champions League Final 1st Leg	Stade de la Kenya Lubumbashi	Sunday 31-10-2010
Kick-off: 15:30		Attendance: 50 000

TP MAZEMBE 5 0 ESPERANCE

Ngandu Kasongo 2 18 74, Alain Kaluyituka 45p,
Given Singuluma 2 56 59

TOUTE PUISSANT MAZEMBE

White shirts with black stripes, Black shorts, White socks

Tr: Lamine N'Diaye SEN

Robert Kidiaba

Joel Kimwaki   Jean Kasusula   Pamphile Mihayo (c)   Eric Nkulukuta

Sebastien Mwanza   Stopila Sunzu

77 Ngandu Kasongo
Deo Kanda

Given Singulama   86 Patou Kabangu
Christopher Semakweri

Alain Kaluyituka

35 Oussama Darragi   65 Michael Eneramo 17   87 Youssef Msekni
Zied Derbali 41   Khaled Ayari   Guy-Roger Toindouba

Khaled Korbi   Saber Khlifa   Mejdi Traoui

Mohamed Ben Mansour 24   Khalil Chemmam   Walid Hicheri   Harrisson Afful

Wassim Naouara

Tr: Faouzi Benzarti

Red and yellow striped shirts, Red shorts, Red socks

ESPERANCE

MATCH OFFICIALS
REFEREE
Kokou Djaoupe TOG
ASSISTANTS
Djoukere Biagui TOG
Ayena Mathias TOG
4TH OFFICIAL
Atsoo Kokou TOG

CAF Champions League Final 2nd Leg	Stade 7 Novembre Rades, Tunis	Saturday 13-11-2010
Kick-off: 15:30		Attendance: 50 000

ESPERANCE　　1　1　TP MAZEMBE

Harrisson Afful [24]　　　　　　　　　　　　　　　　　　Deo Kanda [67]

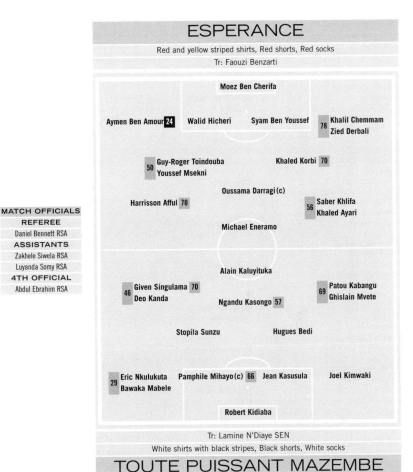

ESPERANCE
Red and yellow striped shirts, Red shorts, Red socks
Tr: Faouzi Benzarti

Moez Ben Cherifa

Aymen Ben Amour [24]　Walid Hicheri　Syam Ben Youssef　[78] Khalil Chemmam / Zied Derbali

[50] Guy-Roger Toindouba / Youssef Msekni　　Khaled Korbi [70]

Oussama Darragi (c)

Harrisson Afful [70]　　　　　　[56] Saber Khlifa / Khaled Ayari

Michael Eneramo

MATCH OFFICIALS
REFEREE
Daniel Bennett RSA
ASSISTANTS
Zakhele Siwela RSA
Luyanda Somy RSA
4TH OFFICIAL
Abdul Ebrahim RSA

Alain Kaluyituka

[46] Given Singulama [70] / Deo Kanda　　　　　[69] Patou Kabangu / Ghislain Mvete

Ngandu Kasongo [57]

Stopila Sunzu　　　　Hugues Bedi

[29] Eric Nkulukuta / Bawaka Mabele　Pamphile Mihayo (c) [66]　Jean Kasusula　Joel Kimwaki

Robert Kidiaba

Tr: Lamine N'Diaye SEN
White shirts with black stripes, Black shorts, White socks

TOUTE PUISSANT MAZEMBE

I took over the reigns of the team in August from Frenchman Diego Garzitto and my target was the Champions League title. I have a talented side backed up by their mental toughness. My players are very dedicated and the result is this success.
Lamine N'Diaye
I very happy to have scored my first goal in two years - in the Champions League final! In Lubumbashi everybody will be very happy at the moment.
Deo Kanda

We have a young team with an average age of 20. We must move on and get over our disappointment. I don't think our players were psychologically ill-prepared. The expulsion of Ben Amor was unfortunate - it was always going to be difficult to score four more goals with only 10 men although we did miss a number of opportunities
Maher Kanzari (Assistant Coach of Esperance)

CAF CONFEDERATION CUP 2010

First Round

FUS Rabat	MAR	1 2
ASC Diaraf *	SEN	2 0
Benfica Bissau *	GNB	0 2
AS Baraka Djoma	GUI	0 3
Séwé San Pedro *	CIV	2 1
US Forces Armées	BFA	1 0
Stade Malien	MLI	Bye
Al Amal Atbarra	SUD	0 2 11p
ATRACO *	RWA	2 0 10p
Uniao Flamengo Santos	BOT	0 1
Costa do Sol *	MOZ	2 3
FAR Rabat	MAR	Bye
Al Tirsana *	LBY	1 1
CR Belouizdad	ALG	1 2
AS-FAN Niamey *	NIG	2 1
Issia Wazi	CIV	0 2
Etoile du Sahel	TUN	Bye
FC 105 Libreville	GAB	Bye
Anges de Fatima	CTA	0 1
DC Motema Pembe *	COD	3 1
Cotonsport	CMR	Bye
Dragón CF Bata *	GNB	2 0
AC Léopard Dolisie	CGO	3 4
Cercle Olympique Bamako	MLI	0 4
Central Parade *	SLE	0 0
Primeiro de Agosto	ANG	Bye
CAPS United *	ZIM	1 0 8p
Mbabane Highlanders	SWZ	0 1 7p
Pamplemousses SC *	MRI	1 0
Moroka Swallows	RSA	2 3
ZESCO United	ZAM	Bye
Atlético Olympic *	BDI	1 0
Warri Wolves	NGA	1 1
AS Vita Club Kinshasa	COD	Bye
Panthère Bangangté	CMR	Bye
Académica Soyo	ANG	Bye
Enyimba	NGA	Bye
Haras Al Hedod	EGY	Bye
AFC Leopards *	KEN	3 0
Banks	ETH	1 3
Lengthens *	ZIM	2 0
Adema Antananarivo	MAD	1 0
Simba SC	TAN	Bye
Petrojet	EGY	2 2
Miembeni *	ZAN	2 0
SC Villa Kampala *	UGA	
Khartoum-3	SUD	w-o
Al Ahly Tripoli	LBY	0 2
Coton Tchad *	CHA	0 0
CS Sfaxien	TUN	Bye

Second Round

FUS Rabat		0 1
AS Baraka Djoma *		0 0
Séwé San Pedro *		2 0 3p
Stade Malien		0 2 4p
Al Amal Atbarra *		4 2
Costa do Sol		2 3
FAR Rabat		0 1
CR Belouizdad *		1 1
AS-FAN Niamey *		1 1
Etoile du Sahel		0 2
FC 105 Libreville		0 0
DC Motema Pembe *		0 1
Cotonsport		1 2
AC Léopard Dolisie *		3 0
Cercle Olympique Bamako*		0 0
Primeiro de Agosto		0 3
CAPS United *		1 1
Moroka Swallows		1 0
ZESCO United		0 2
Warri Wolves *		3 0
AS Vita Club Kinshasa		1 3
Panthère Bangangté *		1 2
Académica Soyo *		2 0
Enyimba		0 3
Haras Al Hedod		1 5
Banks *		1 0
Lengthens *		0 1
Simba SC		3 2
Petrojet *		3 2
Khartoum-3		0 1
Al Ahly Tripoli *		0 0
CS Sfaxien		0 1

Third Round

FUS Rabat *		2 0
Stade Malien		0 0
Al Amal Atbarra *		1 0
CR Belouizdad		0 2
AS-FAN Niamey *		1 0
DC Motema Pembe		0 0
Cotonsport *		1 0
Primeiro de Agosto		2 0
CAPS United		1 2
Warri Wolves *		2 0
AS Vita Club Kinshasa *		3 0 4p
Enyimba		0 3 5p
Haras Al Hedod		1 5
Simba SC *		2 1
Petrojet *		1 0
CS Sfaxien		1 1

CAF CONFEDERATION CUP 2010

Intermediate Round   **Group Stage**   **Final**

FUS Rabat	MAR	1	1
SuperSport United * †	RSA	2	0

FINAL FIRST LEG

Stade Prince Moulay Abdellah, Rabat, 28-11-2010, Ref: Mohamed Benouza ALG
FUS - Issam Badda - Abdelfattah Boukhris, Mohamed Benchrifa, Mourad Zitouni●, Daniel Monshare, Mohamed Amine Bekkali (Souleymane Dembele 57), Hemani, Ayoub El Khalqi, Rachid Rokki (Chemseddine Chtibi 59), Hicham Fatihi●, Hassan Youssoufo. Tr: Houcine Ammouta
CSS - Jassem Khalloufi - Chadi Hammami, Hamdi Rouied, Fatih Gharbi, Amine Abbas, Mahmoud Bensaleh●, Chaker Bargaoui●, Ibrahima Toure, Kamal Zaiem (Kamoune 92+), Hamza Younes, Uche Agba (Dominique Da Silva 63). Tr: Pierre Lechantre FRA

CR Belouizdad	ALG	0	1
Djoliba * †	MLI	0	1

AS-FAN Niamey	NIG	2	2
Al Merreikh * †	SUD	2	1

Group A	Pts	SUD	LBY	MLI	NIG
Al Hilal	13		2-0	2-1	4-2
Al Ittihad	12	1-2		2-0	4-0
Djoliba	7	2-0	0-1		1-0
AS-FAN Niamey	2	0-0	1-3	0-0	

FUS Rabat	2	0
Al Ittihad *	1	1

Primeiro de Agosto	ANG	0	2
Al Ittihad Tripoli * †	LBY	2	1

FUS Rabat	0	3
CS Sfaxien	0	2

Al Hilal Omdurman * †	SUD	5	1
CAPS United	ZIM	0	3

Group B	Pts	MAR	TUN	ZAM	EGY
FUS Rabat	13		2-1	1-0	1-0
CS Sfaxien	10	3-0		2-1	3-1
Zanaco	6	1-1	1-0		1-1
Haras Al Hedod	3	1-2	0-0	1-1	

Al Hilal	0 1 3p
CS Sfaxien *	1 0 5p

Enyimba	NGA	0	2
Zanaco * †	AZM	4	0

FINAL SECOND LEG

Stade Taieb Mhiri, Sfax, 4-12-2010, Att: 25 000, Ref: Jerome Damon RSA. Scorers - Hamdi Rouied [43], Kamal Zaiem [47p] for CSS; Abdelfattah Boukhriss [9], Mohamed Zouidi 2 [75][89] for FUS
CSS - Jassem Khalloufi - Hamdi Rouied●, Fatih Gharbi, Ali Maaloul (Mouaz Alloulo 46), Chaker Bargaoui, Chadi Hammami, Kamal Zaiem●, Assaad Dridi (Youssofo 46), Dominique Da Silva, Mahmoud Bensaleh, Hamza Younes. Tr: Pierre Lechantre FRA
FUS - Issam Badda - Abdelfattah Boukhris●, Mohamed Benchrifa●, Mohamed Amine Bekkali, Ayoub El Khalqi, Daniel Monshare, Oussama Gharib (Mohamed Zouidi 71), Mourad Zitouni, Hicham Fatihi, Rachid Rokki, Hassan Youssoufo (Jamal Triki 72). Tr: Houcine Ammouta

Haras Al Hedod	EGY	0	8
Gaborone United * †	BOT	1	1

Petro Atlético * †	ANG	0	1
CS Sfaxien	TUN	0	3

* Home team in the first leg ● † Champions League third round losers that entered at the Intermediate round

CONCACAF

CONFEDERATION OF NORTH, CENTRAL AMERICAN AND CARIBBEAN ASSOCIATION FOOTBALL

Whilst not exactly setting the 2010 FIFA World Cup alight, both the United States and Mexico put in positive performances in South Africa, with both qualifying for the Round of 16. The Americans showed a never-say-die attitude that saw them top their first-round group when at one point that looked distinctly unlikely. Indeed, it took an injury-time winner against Algeria in their final group game to avoid an early trip home but against Ghana in the next round they were forced once again to chase a game and it proved too much. As in 2006, Mexico lost to Argentina in the first knock-out round - the fifth tournament in a row that they have bowed out in the round of 16, seemingly unable to take the next step needed to compete on level terms with the likes of Argentina, Germany, Italy, Brazil and co. For Honduras just being at the finals was good experience despite failing to score a goal and early in 2011 they reaped the benefits by beating Costa Rica in the final of the

THE FIFA BIG COUNT OF 2006 FOR NORTH AND CENTRAL AMERICA AND THE CARIBBEAN

	Male	Female		Total
Number of players	33 071 000	10 038 000	Referees and Assistant Referees	172 000
Professionals	9 000		Admin, Coaches, Technical, Medical	961 000
Amateurs 18+	884 000		Number of clubs	17 000
Youth under 18	5 163 000		Number of teams	490 000
Unregistered	36 988 000		Clubs with women's teams	7 000
Total Players	44 242 000		Players as % of population	8.53%

Copa Centroamericana - previously known as the UNCAF Cup - winning the trophy for the first time since 1995. The tournament acted as a qualifier for the 2011 CONCACAF Gold Cup in the USA, as did the 2010 Digicel Caribbean Cup. With the Caribbean accounting for 25 of the 35 members of CONCACAF, the Caribbean Cup is a hugely significant event in the region, especially as none of those 25 countries has a realistic chance of success in the Gold Cup. The 2010 tournament was won by a resurgent Jamaica, their third title in the past four tournaments. At club level the 2010 CONCACAF Champions League was won by Mexico's Pachuca. It was also their third title in the past four tournaments as Mexican clubs made a clean sweep of the semi-final places. It meant another crack at the FIFA Club World Cup for Pachuca but they went out at the first hurdle after losing 1-0 to Congo's TP Mazembe.

Confederation of North, Central American and Caribbean Association Football (CONCACAF)
725, Fifth Avenue, Trump Tower, 17th Floor, New York, NY 1022, USA
Tel +1 212 3080 044   Fax +1 212 3081 851
mail@concacaf.net   www.concacaf.com
President: Jack A. Warner TRI   General Secretary: Chuck Blazer USA
CONCACAF Formed: 1961

CONCACAF EXECUTIVE COMMITTEE
President: Jack A. Warner TRI
Vice-President: Lisle Austin BRB   Vice-President: Alfredo Hawit Banegas HON   Vice-President: Guillermo Canedo White MEX
ORDINARY MEMBERS OF THE EXECUTIVE COMMITTEE
Horace Burrell JAM   Ariel Alvarado PAN   Sunil Gulati USA
FIFA Exco: Rafael Salguero GUA   FIFA Exco: Chuck Blazer USA

MAP OF CONCACAF MEMBER NATIONS

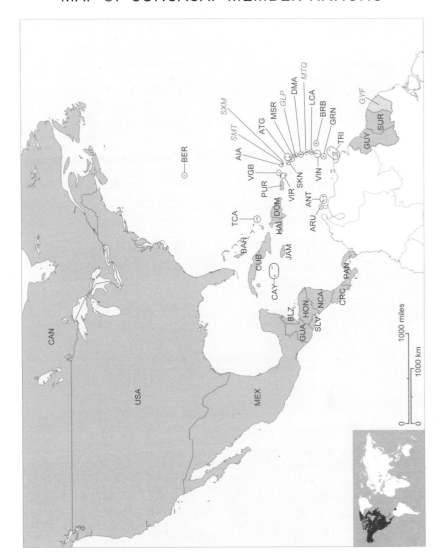

CONCACAF MEMBER ASSOCIATIONS (35)

AIA - Anguilla • ATG - Antigua and Barbuda • ARU - Aruba • BAH - Bahamas • BRB - Barbados • BLZ - Belize • BER - Bermuda
VGB - British Virgin Islands • CAN - Canada • CAY - Cayman Islands • CRC - Costa Rica • CUB - Cuba • DMA - Dominica
DOM - Dominican Republic • SLV - El Salvador • GRN - Grenada • GUA - Guatemala • GUY - Guyana • HAI - Haiti • HON - Honduras
JAM - Jamaica • MEX - Mexico • MSR - Montserrat • ANT - Netherlands Antilles • NCA - Nicaragua • PAN - Panama • PUR - Puerto Rico
SKN - St Kitts and Nevis • LCA - St Lucia • VIN - St Vincent/Grenadines • SUR - Suriname • TRI - Trinidad and Tobago
TCA - Turks and Caicos Islands • VIR - US Virgin Islands • USA - United States of America

CONCACAF ASSOCIATE MEMBER ASSOCIATIONS (5)

GYF - French Guiana • GLP - Guadeloupe • MTQ - Martinique • SMT - Saint Martin • SMX - Sint Maarten
None of these five nations are affiliated to FIFA

CENTRAL AMERICAN, NORTH AMERICAN AND CARIBBEAN NATIONAL TEAM TOURNAMENTS

CONCACAF GOLD CUP

Year	Host Country	Winners	Score	Runners-up	Venue
1991	USA	USA	0-0 4-3p	Honduras	Coliseum, Los Angeles
1993	Mexico/USA	Mexico	4-0	USA	Azteca, Mexico City
1995	USA	Mexico	2-0	Brazil	Coliseum, Los Angeles
1998	USA	Mexico	1-0	USA	Coliseum, Los Angeles
2000	USA	Canada	2-0	Colombia	Coliseum, Los Angeles
2002	USA	USA	2-0	Costa Rica	Rose Bowl, Pasadena
2003	Mexico/USA	Mexico	1-0	Brazil	Azteca, Mexico City
2005	USA	USA	0-0 3-1p	Panama	Giants Stadium, New Jersey
2007	USA	USA	2-1	Mexico	Soldier Field, Chicago
2009	USA	Mexico	5-0	USA	Giants Stadium, New Jersey

CONCACAF GOLD CUP MEDALS TABLE

	Country	G	S	B	F	SF
1	Mexico	5	1	1	6	7
2	USA	4	3	2	7	9
3	Canada	1		2	1	3
4	Costa Rica		1	2	1	5
5	Honduras		1	2	1	3
6	Panama		1		1	1
7	Jamaica			1		2
8	Guadeloupe			1		1
	Trinidad and Tobago			1		1
10	Guatemala					1
		10	7	12	17	33

This table represents the Gold (winners), Silver (runners-up) and Bronze (semi-finalists) placings in the CONCACAF Gold Cup, along with the number of appearances in the final and semi-finals. It does not include nations from outside of CONCACAF

CCCF CHAMPIONSHIP

Year	Host Country	Winners	Score	Runners-up	Venue
1941	Costa Rica	Costa Rica	3-1	El Salvador	San José
1943	El Salvador	El Salvador	2-1	Guatemala	San Salvador
1946	Costa Rica	Costa Rica	1-4	Guatemala	San José
1948	Guatemala	Costa Rica	2-3	Guatemala	Guatemala City
1951	Panama	Panama	2-0	Costa Rica	Panama City
1953	Costa Rica	Costa Rica	4-1	Honduras	San José
1955	Honduras	Costa Rica	2-1	Netherlands Antilles	Tegucigalpa
1957	Curaçao	Haiti	3-1	Curaçao	Willemstad
1960	Cuba	Costa Rica	4-1†	Netherlands Antilles	Havana
1961	Costa Rica	Costa Rica	4-0	El Salvador	San José

All tournaments played on a league basis. The result listed is the match played between the top two • † Play-off after both teams finished level

CONCACAF NATIONS CUP

Year	Host Country	Winners	Score	Runners-up	Venue
1963	El Salvador	Costa Rica	4-1	El Salvador	San Salvador
1965	Guatemala	Mexico	2-1	Guatemala	Guatemala City
1967	Honduras	Guatemala	1-0	Mexico	Tegucigalpa
1969	Costa Rica	Costa Rica	1-1	Guatemala	San José
1971	Trinidad & T	Mexico	0-0	Haiti	Port of Spain

All tournaments played on a league basis. The result listed is the match played between the top two

CONCACAF NATIONS CUP/FIFA WORLD CUP QUALIFIERS

Year	Host Country	Winners	Score	Runners-up	Venue
1973	Haiti	Haiti	2-1	Trinidad	Port-au-Prince
1977	Mexico	Mexico	4-1	Haiti	Mexico City
1981	Honduras	Honduras	0-0	El Salvador	Tegucigalpa
1985	Home & Away	Canada	2-1	Honduras	Saint John's
1989	Home & Away	Costa Rica	1-0	USA	San José

All tournaments played on a league basis. The result listed is the match played between the top two

CARIBBEAN CUP

Year	Host Country	Winners	Score	Runners-up	Venue
1989	Barbados	Trinidad & Tobago	2-1	Grenada	Bridgetown
1990	Trinidad	Not completed			
1991	Jamaica	Jamaica	2-0	Trinidad & Tobago	Kingston
1992	Trinidad	Trinidad & Tobago	3-1	Jamaica	Port of Spain
1993	Jamaica	Martinique	0-0 6-5p	Jamaica	Kingston
1994	Trinidad	Trinidad & Tobago	7-2	Martinique	Port of Spain
1995	Cayman/Jamaica	Trinidad & Tobago	5-0	St Vincent/Grenadines	George Town
1996	Trinidad	Trinidad & Tobago	2-0	Cuba	Port of Spain
1997	Antigua/St Kitts	Trinidad & Tobago	4-0	St Kitts and Nevis	St John's
1998	Jamaica/Trinidad	Jamaica	2-1	Trinidad & Tobago	Port of Spain
1999	Trinidad	Trinidad & Tobago	2-1	Cuba	Port of Spain
2001	Trinidad	Trinidad & Tobago	3-0	Haiti	Port of Spain
2005	Barbados	Jamaica	1-0†	Cuba	Waterford
2007	Trinidad	Haiti	2-1	Trinidad & Tobago	Port of Spain
2008	Jamaica	Jamaica	2-0	Grenada	Kingston
2010	Martinique	Jamaica	1-1 5-4p	Guadeloupe	Fort-de-France

† Final tournament played as a league. The match listed is between the top two.

UNCAF CUP/COPA CENTROAMERICANA

Year	Host Country	Winners	Score	Runners-up	Venue
1991	Costa Rica	Costa Rica	2-0†	Honduras	San José
1993	Honduras	Honduras	2-0†	Costa Rica	Tegucigalpa
1995	El Salvador	Honduras	3-0	Guatemala	San Salvador
1997	Guatemala	Costa Rica	1-1†	Guatemala	Mateo Flores, Guatemala City
1999	Costa Rica	Costa Rica	1-0†	Guatemala	San José
2001	Honduras	Guatemala	2-0†	Costa Rica	Tegucigalpa
2003	Panama	Costa Rica	1-1†	Guatemala	Rommel Fernández, Panama City
2005	Guatemala	Costa Rica	1-1 7-6p	Honduras	Mateo Flores, Guatemala City
2007	El Salvador	Costa Rica	1-1 4-1p	Panama	Cuscatlán, San Salvador
2009	Honduras	Panama	0-0 5-3p	Costa Rica	Tiburcio Andino, Tegucigalpa

† Final tournament played as a league. The match listed is between the top two.

CENTRAL AMERICAN, NORTH AMERICAN AND CARIBBEAN NATIONAL CLUB TOURNAMENTS

CONCACAF CHAMPIONS LEAGUE

Year	Winners	Country	Score	Country	Runners-up
1962	Guadalajara	MEX	1-0 5-0	GUA	Comunicaciones
1963	Racing Club Haïtienne	HAI	W-O	MEX	Guadalajara
1964	Not completed				
1965	Not completed				
1966	Not held				
1967	Alianza	SLV	1-2 3-0 5-3	ANT	Jong Colombia
1968	Toluca	MEX	W-O †		
1969	Cruz Azul	MEX	0-0 1-0	GUA	Comunicaciones
1970	Cruz Azul	MEX	W-O †		
1971	Cruz Azul	MEX	5-1	CRC	LD Alajuelense

CONCACAF CHAMPIONS LEAGUE

Year	Winners	Country	Score	Country	Runners-up
1972	Olimpia	HON	0-0 2-0	SUR	Robinhood
1973	Transvaal	SUR	W-0 †		
1974	Municipal	GUA	2-1 2-1	SUR	Transvaal
1975	Atletico Español	MEX	3-0 2-1	SUR	Transvaal
1976	Aguila	SLV	6-1 2-1	SUR	Robinhood
1977	América	MEX	1-0 0-0	SUR	Robinhood
1978	UAG Tecos	MEX	W-0 †		
1979	Deportivo FAS	SLV	1-0 8-0	ANT	Jong Colombia
1980	UNAM Pumas	MEX	2-0 ‡	HON	Universidad de Honduras
1981	Transvaal	SUR	1-0 1-1	SLV	Atlético Marte
1982	UNAM Pumas	MEX	2-2 3-0	SUR	Robinhood
1983	Atlante	MEX	1-1 5-0	SUR	Robinhood
1984	Violette	HAI	W-0 †		
1985	Defence Force	TRI	2-0 0-1	HON	Olimpia
1986	LD Alajuelense	CRC	4-1 1-1	SUR	Transvaal
1987	América	MEX	2-0 1-1	TRI	Defence Force
1988	Olimpia	HON	2-0 2-0	TRI	Defence Force
1989	UNAM Pumas	MEX	1-1 3-1	CUB	Piñar del Rio
1990	América	MEX	2-2 6-0	CUB	Piñar del Rio
1991	Puebla	MEX	3-1 1-1	TRI	Police FC
1992	América	MEX	1-0	CRC	LD Alajuelense
1993	Deportivo Saprissa	CRC	2-2 ‡	MEX	Leon
1994	Cartagines	CRC	3-2	MEX	Atlante
1995	Deportivo Saprissa	CRC	1-0 ‡	GUA	Municipal
1996	Cruz Azul	MEX	1-1 ‡	MEX	Necaxa
1997	Cruz Azul	MEX	5-3	USA	Los Angeles Galaxy
1998	DC United	USA	1-0	MEX	Toluca
1999	Necaxa	MEX	2-1	CRC	LD Alajuelense
2000	LA Galaxy	USA	3-2	HON	Olimpia
2001	Not completed				
2002	Pachuca	MEX	1-0	MEX	Monarcas Morelia
2003	Toluca	MEX	3-3 2-1	MEX	Monarcas Morelia
2004	LD Alajuelense	CRC	1-1 4-0	CRC	Deportivo Saprissa
2005	Deportivo Saprissa	CRC	2-0 1-2	MEX	UNAM Pumas
2006	América	MEX	0-0 2-1	MEX	Toluca
2007	Pachuca	MEX	2-2 0-0 7-6p	MEX	Guadalajara
2008	Pachuca	MEX	1-1 2-1	CRC	Deportivo Saprissa
2009	Atlante	MEX	2-0 0-0	MEX	Cruz Azul
2010	Pachuca	MEX	1-2 1-0	MEX	Cruz Azul

† 1968 Toluca were declared champions after Aurora GUA and Transvaal SUR were disqualified • 1970 Cruz Azul were declared champions after Deportivo Saprissa CRC and Transvaal SUR withdrew • 1973 Transvaal were declared champions after LD Alajuelense CRC and Deoprtivo Saprissa CRC withdrew • 1978 UAG Tecos were joint winners with Comunicaciones GUA and Defence Force TRI • 1984 Violette were declared champions after Guadalajara and New York Freedoms were disqualified • ‡ 1980 1993 1995 & 1996 finals played as a league with the match listed between the top two

CONCACAF CHAMPIONS LEAGUE MEDALS TABLE

	Country	G	S	B	F	SF
1	Mexico	26	12	14	38	52
2	Costa Rica	6	5	11	11	22
3	El Salvador	3	1	2	4	6
4	Surinam	2	8	3	10	13
5	Guatemala	2	3	7	5	12
6	Honduras	2	3	3	5	8
7	Trinidad and Tobago	2	3	2	5	7
8	USA	2	1	12	3	15
9	Haiti	2			2	2

CONCACAF CHAMPIONS LEAGUE MEDALS TABLE

	Country	G	S	B	F	SF
10	Netherlands Antilles		2	4	2	6
11	Cuba		2		2	2
12	Martinique			3		3
13	Bermuda			1		1
	Puerto Rico			1		1
		47	40	63	87	150

This table represents the Gold (winners), Silver (runners-up) and Bronze (semi-finalists) placings of clubs representing the above countries in the CONCACAF Champions' Cup, along with the number of appearances in the final and semi-finals.

CONCACAF CHAMPIONS LEAGUE MEDALS TABLE

	Club		G	S	B
1	Cruz Azul	MEX	5	2	
2	América	MEX	5		1
3	Pachuca	MEX	4		1
4	Deportivo Saprissa	CRC	3	2	6
5	UNAM Pumas	MEX	3	1	1
6	LD Alajuelense	CRC	2	3	4
7	Transvaal	SUR	2	3	
8	Toluca	MEX	2	2	2
9	Olimpia	HON	2	2	1
10	Defence Force	TRI	2	2	
11	Atlante	MEX	2	1	
12	Comunicaciones	GUA	1	2	3
13	Guadalajara	MEX	1	2	1
14	Municipal	GUA	1	1	1
	Necaxa	MEX	1	1	1
16	Los Angeles Galaxy	USA	1	1	
17	DC United	USA	1		6
18	Alianza	SLV	1		2
19	Aguila	SLV	1		
	Atlético Español	MEX	1		
	CS Cartagines	CRC	1		
	Deportivo FAS	SLV	1		
	Puebla	MEX	1		
	Racing Club Haïtienne	HAI	1		
	UAG Tecos	MEX	1		
	Violette	HAI	1		
27	Robinhood	SUR		5	3
28	Jong Colombia	ANT		2	1

CONCACAF CHAMPIONS LEAGUE MEDALS TABLE

	Club		G	S	B
29	Piñar del Rio	CUB		2	
	Monarcas Morelia	MEX		2	
31	Leon	MEX		1	2
32	Atlético Marte	SLV		1	
	Police FC	TRI		1	
	Universidad de Honduras	HON		1	
35	Monterrey	MEX			3
36	Chicago Fire	USA			2
	Houston Dynamo	USA			2
	SUBT	ANT			2
	Trintoc	TRI			2
40	Aurora	GUA			1
	Herediano	CRC			1
	Kansas City Wizards	USA			1
	L'Aiglon	MTQ			1
	Marathon	HON			1
	Pembrooke	BER			1
	Philidelphia Ukrainians	USA			1
	Puerto Rico Islanders	PUR			1
	Real España	HON			1
	Riviere-Pilote	MTQ			1
	US Robert	MTQ			1
	Santos Laguna	MEX			1
	Sithoc	ANT			1
	Suchitepequez	GUA			1
	Tigres UANL	MEX			1
	Xelaju	GUA			1
			47	40	63

TORNEO INTERCLUBES DE UNCAF

Year	Winners	Country	Score	Country	Runners-up
1999	Olimpia	HON	2-0 †	CRC	LD Alajuelense
2000	Olimpia	HON	0-0 †	CRC	LD Alajuelense
2001	Municipal	GUA	1-1 †	CRC	Deportivo Saprissa
2002	LD Alajuelense	CRC	4-0 †	PAN	Arabe Unido
2003	Deportivo Saprissa	CRC	3-2	GUA	Comunicaciones
2004	Municipal	GUA	1-0 †	CRC	Deportivo Saprissa
2005	LD Alajuelense	CRC	1-0 0-1 4-2p	HON	Olimpia
2006	Puntarenas FC	CRC	3-2 0-1 3-1p	HON	Olimpia
2007	CD Motagua	HON	1-1 1-0	CRC	Deportivo Saprissa

CFU CLUB CHAMPIONS CUP

Year	Winners	Country	Score	Country	Runners-up
1997	United Petrotin	TRI	2-1	JAM	Seba United
1998	Joe Public	TRI	1-0	TRI	Caledonia AIA
2000	Joe Public	TRI	1-0 †	TRI	W Connection
2003	San Juan Jabloteh	TRI	2-1 1-2 4-2p	TRI	W Connection
2004	Harbour View	JAM	1-1 2-1	JAM	Tivoli Gardens
2005	Portmore United	JAM	1-2 4-0	SUR	Robinhood
2006	W Connection	TRI	1-0	TRI	San Juan Jabloteh
2007	Harbour View	JAM	2-1	TRI	Joe Public
2008	Not held				
2009	W Connection	TRI	2-1	PUR	Puerto Rico Islanders
2010	Puerto Rico Islanders	PUR	1-1 †	TRI	Joe Public

† Played on a league system. The match listed was between the top two

CENTRAL AMERICAN, NORTH AMERICAN AND CARIBBEAN YOUTH TOURNAMENTS

CONCACAF U-20 TOURNAMENT

Year	Host Country	Winners	Runners-up
1954	Costa Rica	Costa Rica	Panama
1956	El Salvador	El Salvador	Neth. Antilles
1958	Guatemala	Guatemala	Honduras
1960	Honduras	Costa Rica	Honduras
1962	Panama	Mexico	Guatemala
1964	Guatemala	El Salvador	
1970	Cuba	Mexico	Cuba
1973	Mexico	Mexico	Guatemala
1974	Canada	Mexico	Cuba
1976	Puerto Rico	Mexico	Honduras
1978	Honduras	Mexico	Canada

CONCACAF U-20 TOURNAMENT

Year	Host Country	Winners	Runners-up
1980	USA	Mexico	USA
1982	Guatemala	Honduras	USA
1984	Trinidad	Mexico	Canada
1986	Trinidad	Canada	USA
1988	Guatemala	Costa Rica	Mexico
1990	Guatemala	Mexico	Trinidad
1992	Canada	Mexico	USA
1994	Honduras	Honduras	Costa Rica
1996	Mexico	Canada	Mexico
2009	Trinidad & T	Costa Rica	USA

CONCACAF U-17 TOURNAMENT

Year	Host Country	Winners	Runners-up
1983	Trinidad	USA	Trinidad
1985	Mexico	Mexico	Costa Rica
1987	Honduras	Mexico	USA
1988	Trinidad	Cuba	USA

CONCACAF U-17 TOURNAMENT

Year	Host Country	Winners	Runners-up
1991	Trinidad	Mexico	USA
1992	Cuba	USA	Mexico
1994	El Salvador	Costa Rica	USA
1996	Trinidad	Mexico	USA

CENTRAL AMERICAN, NORTH AMERICAN AND CARIBBEAN WOMEN'S TOURNAMENTS

CONCACAF WOMEN'S GOLD CUP

Year	Host Country	Winners	Score	Runners-up	Venue
1991	Haiti	USA	5-0	Canada	Port au Prince
1993	USA	USA	1-0	Canada	Long Island
1994	Canada	USA	6-0	Canada	Montreal
1998	Canada	Canada	1-0	Mexico	Toronto
2000	USA	USA	1-0	Brazil	Foxboro, Boston
2002	USA/Canada	USA	2-1	Canada	Rose Bowl, Pasadena
2006	USA	USA	2-1	Canada	Home Depot Center, Los Angeles
2010	Mexico	Canada	1-0	Mexico	Quintana Roo, Cancun

CONCACAF WOMEN'S U-20 CHAMPIONSHIP

Year	Host Country	Winners	Score	Runners-up	Venue
2004	Canada	Canada	2-1	USA	Frank Clair, Ottawa
2006	Mexico	USA	3-2	Canada	Luis Fuentes, Veracruz
2008	Mexico	Canada	1-0	USA	Cuauhtémoc, Puebla
2010	Guatemala	USA	1-0	Mexico	Cementos Progreso, Guatemala City

CONCACAF WOMEN'S U-17 CHAMPIONSHIP

Year	Host Country	Winners	Score	Runners-up	Venue
2008	Trinidad & Tobago	USA	4-1	Costa Rica	Marvin Lee, Macoya
2010	Costa Rica	Canada	1-0	Mexico	Alejandro Morera Soto, Alajuela

NATIONAL TEAM TOURNAMENTS 2010

DIGICEL CARIBBEAN CHAMPIONSHIP 2010 QUALIFYING

First Round Groups

Group A	Pl	W	D	L	F	A	Pts	CAY	AIA	SMT
Puerto Rico	3	3	0	0	7	1	**9**	2-0	3-1	2-0
Cayman Islands	3	1	1	1	5	4	**4**		4-1	1-1
Anguilla	3	1	0	2	4	8	**3**			2-1
Saint-Martin	3	0	1	2	2	5	**1**			

Group B	Pl	W	D	L	F	A	Pts	VIN	BRB	MSR
St Kitts and Nevis	3	1	2	0	6	2	**5**	1-1	1-1	4-0
St Vincent/Grenadines	3	1	2	0	8	1	**5**		0-0	7-0
Barbados	3	1	2	0	6	1	**5**			5-0
Montserrat	3	0	0	3	0	16	**0**			

Group C	Pl	W	D	L	F	A	Pts	SUR	ANT	LCA
Guyana	3	3	0	0	6	2	**9**	2-0	3-2	1-0
Suriname	3	2	0	1	4	4	**6**		2-1	2-1
Netherlands Antilles	3	0	1	2	5	7	**1**			2-2
St Lucia	3	0	1	2	3	5	**1**			

Group D	Pl	W	D	L	F	A	Pts	DOM	VGB	
Dominica	2	2	0	0	11	0	**6**	1-0	10-0	
Dominican Republic	2	1	0	1	17	1	**3**		17-0	
British Virgin Islands	2	0	0	2	0	27	**0**			

Second Round Groups

Group E	Pl	W	D	L	F	A	Pts	GRN	SKN	PUR
Guadaloupe	3	3	0	0	8	3	**9**	3-0	2-1	3-2
Grenada	3	2	0	1	5	4	**6**		2-0	3-1
St Kitts and Nevis	3	1	0	2	2	4	**3**			1-0
Puerto Rico	3	0	0	3	3	7	**0**			

Group F	Pl	W	D	L	F	A	Pts	GUY	HAI	VIN
Trinidad and Tobago	3	3	0	0	12	3	**9**	2-1	4-0	6-2
Guyana	3	1	1	1	3	2	**4**		0-0	2-0
Haiti	3	1	1	1	3	5	**4**			3-1
St Vincent/Grenadines	3	0	0	3	3	11	**0**			

Group G	Pl	W	D	L	F	A	Pts	ATG	SUR	DMA
Cuba	3	1	2	0	7	5	**5**	0-0	3-3	4-2
Antigua and Barbuda	3	1	2	0	2	1	**5**		2-1	0-0
Suriname	3	1	1	1	9	5	**4**			5-0
Dominica	3	0	1	2	2	9	**1**			

Martinique qualified for the finals as hosts, Jamaica as holders

Grenada, Guadaloupe, Cuba, Haiti, Antigua & Barbuda and Trinidad & Tobago received byes to the second round
Top scorers (overall including finals): 7 - Kurlson Benjamin DMA • 5 - Darly Batista DOM; Shandel Samuel VIN & Devon Jorsling TRI

GROUP A		Pl	W	D	L	F	A	Pts	CAY	AIA	SMT
Puerto Rico	PUR	3	3	0	0	7	1	**9**	2-0	3-1	2-0
Cayman Islands	CAY	3	1	1	1	5	4	**4**		4-1	1-1
Anguilla	AIA	3	1	0	2	4	8	**3**			2-1
Saint-Martin	SMT	3	0	1	2	2	5	**1**			

Juan Ramon Loubriel, Bayamon
2-10-2010, 19:00, 600, Campbell JAM

Saint Martin ... **1**
Derville Virgile 55

David Saintil - Joel Richardson♦45, Jean Kevin Avril (Henry Emile 75), Jude Sainval, Cedric Adam, Jerome Beausol (c), Mickael Mazzoli, Derville Virgile, Nicolas Chamlet (Omar Morales 72), Jonathan Vigneau (Maxime Chevreul 75), Elvis Fleming•. Tr: Richards Jean Louis

Cayman Islands ... **1**
Paul Brown 18p

Jermaine Brown••♦47 - Paul Brown• (Nicholas Ebanks 86), Oneil Taylor•, Lugi Hernandez, Donald Solomon, Ian Lindo (c) (Ramon Sealy 47), Theron Wood, Mark Ebanks•, Andre McFarlene, Tex Whitelocke (Mario Carter 69), Leighton Elliot. Tr: Carl Brown

---

Juan Ramon Loubriel, Bayamon
2-10-2010, 21:00, 2050, Thomas JAM

Puerto Rico ... **3**
Joshua Hansen 28, Chris Megaloudis 2 32 81

Terence Boss - Richard Martinez, Noah Delgado (c), Alexis Rivera, Andres Cabrero (Tyler Wilson 78), Petter Villegas (Isaac Nieves 86), Christopher Megaloudis, John Krause, Gadiel Figueroa, Cristian Arrieta•, Joshua Hansen (Christopher Feigenbaum 81). Tr: Adrian Whitbread

Anguilla ... **1**
Walwyn Benjamin 54p

Ryan Liddie - Lester Connor, Jarden Abbot, Adonijah Richardson, Leon Jeffers, Walwyn Benjamin (Lester Connor 73), Ian Edwards (c), Gracen Richardson (Javille Brooks 63), Terrence Rogers•, Romare Kelsick, Andre Griffith (Kevin Hawley 67). Tr: Scott Cooper

---

Juan Ramon Loubriel, Bayamon
4-10-2010, 19:00, 500, Davis TRI

Cayman Islands ... **4**
Mark Ebanks 2 45p 49, Theron Wood 57, Paul Brown 59

Ramon Sealy - Paul Brown (Ron Douglas 77), Oneil Taylor, Lugi Hernandez, Donald Solomon, Ian Lindo (c) (Nicholas Ebanks 65), Theron Wood (Tex Whitelocke 73), Mark Ebanks, Mario Rene Carter, Andre McFarlene, Leighton Elliot. Tr: Carl Brown

Anguilla ... **1**
Javelle Brooks 32

Ryan Liddie - Girdon Connor, Romare Kelsick, Walwyn Benjamin, Leon Jeffers (Khaloni Richardson 60), Javille Brooks (Damian Bailey 75), Terrence Rogers, Ian Edwards (c) (Gracen Richardson 60), Adonijah Richardson, Jarden Abbot•, Kevin Hawley. Tr: Scott Cooper

Juan Ramon Loubriel, Bayamon
4-10-2010, 21:00, 1800, Legister JAM

Puerto Rico 2

John Krause [26], Cristian Arrieta [80]

Terence Boss - Noah Delgado (Eloy Matos 64), Alexis Rivera (c), Tyler Wilson, Christopher Megaloudis, John Krause•, Gadiel Figueroa, Joan Morales•, Christopher Feigenbaum (Hector Ramos 83), Cristian Arrieta, Joshua Hansen (Petter Villegas 64). Tr: Colin Clarke

Saint Martin 0

David Saintil - Jean Kevin Avril, Jude Sainval, Cedric Adam, Jerome Beausol (c) (Marceau Magras 83), Mickael Mazzoli, Derville Virgile, Henry Emile (Willy Elien 83), Nicolas Chamlet (Maxime Chevreul 66), Jonathan Vigneau, Elvis Fleming. Tr: Richards Jean Louis

---

Juan Ramon Loubriel, Bayamon
6-10-2010, 19:00, 500, Davis TRI

Anguilla 2

Javille Brooks [19], Terrence Rogers [38]

Ryan Liddie - Girdon Connor, Romare Kelsick, Walwyn Benjamin (Khaloni Richardson 78), Leon Jeffers, Javille Brooks, Terrence Rogers, Damian Bailey, Adonijah Richardson, Jarden Abbot, Kevin Hawley. Tr: Scott Cooper

Saint Martin 1

Derville Virgile [15]

Franck Martin - Joel Richardson, Jude Sainval, Cedric Adam, Mickael Mazzoli•, Derville Virgile (Gregory Seguin 84), Nicolas Chamlet• (Jean Kevin Avril 78), Jonathan Vigneau, Elvis Fleming, Willy Elien (Omar Morales 78), Marceau Magras. Tr: Richards Jean Louis

---

Juan Ramon Loubriel, Bayamon
6-10-2010, 21:00, 3800, Campbell JAM

Puerto Rico 2

Chris Megaloudis [26], Gadiel Figueroa [89]

Terence Boss - Elliot Velez, Tyler Wilson (Isaac Nieves 85), Andres Cabrero, Petter Villegas, Christopher Megaloudis• (c) (Hector Ramos• 76), John Krause•, Gadiel Figueroa, Joan Morales, Christopher Feigenbaum, Cristian Arrieta (Steven Enrichs 67). Tr: Colin Clarke

Cayman Islands 0

Jermaine Brown - Paul Brown (Nicholas Ebanks 43), Oneil Taylor, Lugi Hernandez, Donald Solomon, Ian Lindo (c) (Ron Douglas 74), Mark Ebanks, Mario Rene Carter• 72, Theron Wood (Tex Whitelocke 79), Andre McFarlene, Leighton Elliot. Tr: Carl Brown

---

GROUP B

		Pl	W	D	L	F	A	Pts		VIN	BRB	MSR
St Kitts and Nevis	SKN	3	1	2	0	6	2	5		1-1	1-1	4-0
St Vincent/Grenadines	VIN	3	1	2	0	8	1	5			0-0	7-0
Barbados	BRB	3	1	2	0	6	1	5				5-0
Montserrat	MSR	3	0	0	3	0	16	0				

Victoria Park, Kingstown
6-10-2010, 17:00, 250, Elskamp SUR

Barbados 1

Rashida Williams [14]

Alvin Rouse - Barry Skeete, Brian Neblett (Terry Adamson 79), Omar Archer•, Rommel Burgess, Riviere Williams (Mario Harte 60), Norman Forde (c) (Jason Carter 90), Jonathan Straker•, Sheridan Grosvenor, Rashida Williams, John Paris. Tr: Thomas Jordan

St Kitts and Nevis 1

George Isaac [62]

Akil Byron - Keithroy Richards (Joel Jeffers 34), Earl Jones•, Kareen Mitchum•, Jevon Francis (Orlando Mitchum 68), Ian Lake (Alexis Saddler 86), Tiran Hanley, George Isaac•, Thirzen Leader•, Gerard Williams, Keith Gumbs (c). Tr: Clinton Percival

---

Victoria Park, Kingstown
6-10-2010, 19:00, 5000, Pinas SUR

St Vincent/Grenadines 7

Shandel Samuel 3 [25p 26 66], Damon Francis [56], Cornelius Stewart [63], Chad Balcombe [70], Romano Snagg [89]

Dwaine Sandy - Oscar Nero, Chester Morgan, Darren Hamlet, Myron Samuel, Shandel Samuel• (Chad Balcombe 68), Seinad Bowens (Romano Snagg 46), Damol Francis (Emerald George 60), Jolanshoy McDonald•, Keith James, Cornelius Stewart. Tr: Samuel Carrington

Montserrat 0

Micah Hamilton - Clifford Joseph, Linbert Wright, (Kenneth Dyer 46), Stanford Jarrett•, Pete Phyll•, Julian Wade, Junior Mendes, Steve Stewart (Sinclair Anderson 46), Benjamin Manning (Vlaimer Farrell 61), Ellis Remy••♦68, Leovan Garro. •Tr: Kenneth Dyer

---

Victoria Park, Kingstown
8-10-2010, 18:00, 350, Pinas SUR

Barbados 5

Norman Forde 2 [19 83], Riviere Williams [36], Terry Adamson [53], Kadeem Atkins [90]

Alvin Rouse - Barry Skeete, Omar Archer, Rommel Burgess•, Jason Carter•, Riviere Williams (Terry Adamson 53), Norman Forde, Sheridan Grosvenor (Brian Neblett 27), Rashida Williams, Mario Harte (Kadeem Atkins 63), John Paris. Tr: Thomas Jordan

Montserrat 0

Micah Hamilton - Julian Wade, Stanford Jarrett, Clifford Joseph•, Linbert Wright, Vlaimer Farrell, Rowan Taylor (Syclair Anderson 41), Ellery White, Pete Phyll• (Andrew Julius 46), Kenneth Dyer, Leovan Garro• (Benjamin Manning 77). Tr: Kenneth Dyer

---

Victoria Park, Kingstown
8-10-2010, 20:30, 1600, Jauregui ANT

St Vincent/Grenadines 1

Keith James [73]

Dwaine Sandy - Seinad Bowens•, Damol Francis (Emerald George 68), Darren Hamlet, Keith James, Jolanshoy McDonald•, Chester Morgan•, Oscar Nero, Myron Samuel• (Romano Snagg 70), Shandel Samuel (Joel George 89), Cornelius Stewart. Tr: Samuel Carrington

St Kitts and Nevis 1

Jevon Francis [40]

Akil Byron - Kareen Mitchum, Jevon Francis (Tishan Hanley• 87), Joel Jeffers•, Ian Lake (Alexis Saddler 75), Tiran Hanley (Orlando Mitchum 72), Earl Jones, George Isaac, Thirzen Leader, Gerard Williams, Keith Gumbs. Tr: Clinton Percival

---

Victoria Park, Kingstown
10-10-2010, 18:00, 1100, Elskamp SUR

St Kitts and Nevis 4

Alexis Saddler 2 [18 31], Keith Gumbs [21], Ian Lake [90]

Akil Byron - Alexis Saddler, Kareem Mitchum, Jevon Francis (Ian Lake• 72), Joel Jeffers, Tiran Hanley (Orlando Mitchum 63), Earl Jones, George Isaac (Tishan Hanley 80), Thirzen Leader, Gerard Williams, Keith Gumbs (c). Tr: Clinton Percival

Montserrat 0

Jermain Sweeny - Julian Wade, Benjamin Manning, Andrew Julius (Linbert Wright 69), Junior Mendes (c) (Standford Jarrett 80), Clifford Joseph, Steve Stewart (Sinclair Anderson 60), Vlaimer Farrell, Ellery White, Kenneth Dyer•, Leovan O'Garro. Tr: Kenneth Dyer

---

Victoria Park, Kingstown
10-10-2010, 20:30, 5420, Jauregui ANT

St Vincent/Grenadines 0

Dwaine Sandy - Chad Balcombe (Damol Francis 46), Emerald George••♦69, Joel George, Darren Hamlet (Seinad Bowens 46), Keith James♦89, Chester Morgan• (c), Roy Richards, Reginal Richardson, Romano Snagg (Oscar Nero 85), Cornelius Stewart. Tr: Samuel Carrington

Barbados 0

Alvin Rouse••♦90 - Barry Skeete, Brian Neblett• (Mario Harte 31), Omar Archer•, Rommel Burgess•, Jason Carter (Kadeem Atkins 78), Norman Forde (c)♦89, Jonathan Straker, Sheridan Grosvenor, Rashida Williams, Mario Harte, John Paris••♦90. Tr: Thomas Jordan

GROUP C

		Pl	W	D	L	F	A	Pts		SUR	ANT	LCA
Guyana	GUY	3	3	0	0	6	2	9		2-0	3-2	1-0
Suriname	SUR	3	2	0	1	4	4	6			2-1	2-1
Netherlands Antilles	ANT	3	0	1	2	5	7	1				2-2
St Lucia	LCA	3	0	1	2	3	5	1				

Andre Kamperveen, Paramaribo
13-10-2010, 19:00, 550, Davis TRI

Guyana 1
Christopher Bourne [10]

Ronson **Williams** - Howard **Lowe** (c), Christopher **Bourne**, Walter **Moore**, Jake **Newton**, Dwain **Jacobs**, Anthony **Abrams**, Charles **Pollard**, Sean **Cameron•**, Shawn **Beveney** (Dwayne **Ali** 75), Devon **Millington** (Dwight **Peters** 75). Tr: Wayne **Dover**

St Lucia 0

Iran **Cassius** - Shervon **Jack** (Hanif **Dolor•** 72), Fabian **Joseph** (c), Kurt **Frederick**, Nathan **Justin**, Vernus **Abbott**, Guy **George**, Enderson **George**, Hiram **Hunte** (Troy **Prosper** 46), Zacchaeus **Polius**, Magnam **Valcin•** (Cornelius **Butcher** 89). Tr: Alain **Providence**

Andre Kamperveen, Paramaribo
13-10-2010, 21:00, 800, Willet ATG

Suriname 2
Ives **Vlijter** [31], Rony **Aloema** [90p]

Rony **Aloema** - Derrick **Garden** (c), Marlon **Felter**, Foline **Abauna**, Emelio **Limon** (Giovanni **Alleyne** 52), Ives **Vlijter**, Stefano **Rijssel** (Galgyto **Talea** 90), Stefan **Baneti**, Wensley **Christoph** (Reguillo **Kemper** 82), Kenneth **Moenno**, Naldo **Kwasie**. Tr: Ricardo **Winter**

Netherlands Antilles 1
Lacey **Pauletta** [81]

Marcello **Pisas** (c) - Bryan **Anastatia**, Hujoybert **Delando**, Genaro **Cicilia**, Richenel **Doran** (Giandro **Steba** 78), Vilyson **Lake**, Everon **Espacia**, Rilove **Janga** (Lacey **Pauletta** 58), Kenneth **Kunst**, Mirco **Colina**, Ramiro **Griffith** (Lisandro **Trenidad** 67). Tr: Henry **Caldera**

Andre Kamperveen, Paramaribo
15-10-2010, 19:00, 750, Matthew SKN

Guyana 3
Dwight **Peters** [15], Anthony **Abrams** [45], Walter **Moore** [58]

Ronson **Williams** - Howard **Lowe** (c), Christopher **Bourne** (Devon **Millington** 63), Walter **Moore**, Jake **Newton**, Dwain **Jacobs**, Dwayne **Ali** (Shawn **Beveney** 73), Dwight **Peters**, Anthony **Abrams**, John **Rodrigues**, Sean **Cameron** (Philbert **Moffat** 86). Tr: Wayne **Dover**

Netherlands Antilles 2
Hujoybert **Delando** [74p], Kenneth **Kunst** [84]

Marcello **Pisas** (c) - Bryan **Anastatia**, Hujoybert **Delando**, Genaro **Cicilia**, Richenel **Doran** (Lisandro **Trenidad** 46), Vilyson **Lake**, Everon **Espacia**, Rilove **Janga** (Giandro **Steba** 67), Kenneth **Kunst**, Mirco **Colina** (Shurwendel **Roosje** 67), Lacey **Pauletta**. Tr: Henry **Caldera**

Andre Kamperveen, Paramaribo
15-10-2010, 21:00, 750, Baptiste DMA

Suriname 2
Stefano **Rijssel** [14], Ives **Vlijter** [38p]

Obrendo **Huiswoud** - Derrick **Garden** (c), Marlon **Felter**, Foline **Abauna**, Emelio **Limon** (Germaine **Van Dijck** 62), Ives **Vlijter•**, Stefano **Rijssel**, Stefan **Baneti** (Giovanni **Alleyne** 67), Wensley **Christoph** (Galgyto **Talea•** 80), Kenneth **Moenno**, Naldo **Kwasie**. Tr: Ricardo **Winter**

St Lucia 1
Zacchaeus **Polius** [77]

Iran **Cassius** - Shervon **Jack** (Pernal **Williams** 46), Fabian **Joseph** (c), Kurt **Frederick**, Nathan **Justin•**, Vernus **Abbott•**, Enderson **George**, Hiram **Hunte**, Zacchaeus **Polius**, Magnam **Valcin** (Hanif **Dolor** 82), Cornelius **Butcher•** (Troy **Prosper** 70). Tr: Alain **Providence**

Andre Kamperveen, Paramaribo
17-10-2010, 19:00, 2800, Willet ATG

St Lucia 2
Zacchaeus **Polius** 2 [7 35]

Iran **Cassius** - Fabian **Joseph** (c), Kurt **Frederick**, Pernal **Williams•** (Andreas **Willie** 59), Nathan **Justin**, Vernus **Abbott**, Guy **George** (Rickson **Augustin** 79), Enderson **George**, Hiram **Hunte**, Zacchaeus **Polius**, Troy **Prosper** (Magnam **Valcin** 61). Tr: Alain **Providence**

Netherlands Antilles 2
Lisandro **Trenidad** [30], Bryan **Anastatia** [89p]

Marcello **Pisas** (c) - Bryan **Anastatia**, Hujoybert **Delando**, Genaro **Cicilia**, Vilyson **Lake**, Everon **Espacia**, Kenneth **Kunst**, Giandro **Steba** (Mirco **Colina** 21), Lisandro **Trenidad** (Rilove **Janga** 63), Lacey **Pauletta** (Shurwendel **Roosje** 78), Glenciene **Gregoria**. Tr: Henry **Caldera**

Andre Kamperveen, Paramaribo
17-10-2010, 21:00, 2800, Davis TRI

Suriname 0

Obrendo **Huiswoud** - Derrick **Garden** (c), Marlon **Felter•**, Foline **Abauna**, Emelio **Limon** (Germaine **Van Dijck** 58), Ives **Vlijter**, Stefano **Rijssel** (Reguillo **Kemper** 76), Stefan **Baneti•**, Wensley **Christoph** (Galgyto **Talea** 64), Kenneth **Moenno**, Naldo **Kwasie**. Tr: Ricardo **Winter**

Guyana 2
Walter **Moore** [18p], Devon **Millington** [90]

Ronson **Williams** - Howard **Lowe** (c), Christopher **Bourne**, Walter **Moore•**, Jake **Newton**, Dwain **Jacobs**, Dwayne **Ali** (Shawn **Beveney•** 76), Dwight **Peter** (Philbert **Moffat** 67), Anthony **Abrams** (Devon **Millington** 84), John **Rodrigues•**, Charles **Pollard**. Tr: Wayne **Dover**

GROUP D

		Pl	W	D	L	F	A	Pts		DOM	VGB
Dominica	DMA	2	2	0	0	11	0	6		1-0	10-0
Dominican Republic	DOM	2	1	0	1	17	1	3			17-0
British Virgin Islands	VGB	2	0	0	2	0	27	0			

Panamericano, San Cristobal
14-10-2010, 11:00, 200, Lebron PUR

Dominican Republic 17
Darly **Batista** 5 [4 67 68 72 78], Domingo **Peralta** 3 [21 43 76], Inoel **Navarro** 3 [26 47 81], Manuel **Reinoso** 2 [60 73], Kerwin **Severino** [63], Erick **Obuna** 2 [83 90], Gonzalo **Frechilla** [90]

Miguel **Baez** - Rafael **Ramirez**, Orlando **Belen**, Johan **Cruz** (Erick **Ozuna** 45), Cesar **Garcia**, Kervin **Severino**, Jobdwin **Rosario** (Manuel **Reinoso** 45), Gonzalo **Frechilla**, Inoel **Navarro**, Jonathan **Fana Farias** (Domingo **Peralta** 17), Darly **Batista**. Tr: Domingo **Hernandez**

British Virgin Islands 0

Dowlyn **Daly** - Christopher **Telemache**, Javier **Smith**, Trevor **Peters**, Chevon **Russell•** (Estavan **Jefferson** 82), Joel **Fahie**, Jhon **Samuel**, Jevon **Demmons**, Gregory **James**, Troy **Caesar** (Damien **Farrell** 63), Andraes **Norford**. Tr: Avon **Dale**

Panamericano, San Cristobal
15-10-2010, 16:00, 200, Santos PUR

Dominica 10
Mitchel **Joseph** 3 [1 12 13], Kurlson **Benjamin** 5 [47 71 81 84 85], Chad **Bertrand** [55], Donald **Jervier** [87]

Glenson **Prince** - Colin **Bernard**, Prince **Austrie**, Jerome **Thomas**, Elmond **Derrick**, Raschid **Bertrand**, Chad **Bertrand** (Wayne **George** 71), Glenworth **Elize•** (Lester **Langlais** 46), Kelrick **Walter** (Donald **Javier** 79), Kurlson **Benjamin•**, Mitchel **Joseph**. Tr: Kirt **Hector**

British Virgin Islands 0

Gerard **Vanterpool•** (Dowl **Daly** 74) - Andraes **Norford**, Troy **Caesar**, Gregory **James•**, Jevon **Demmons**, Jhon **Samuel•**, Joel **Fahie•**, Chevon **Russell** (Christopher **Telemache** 47), Rushedo **Robinson**, Javier **Smith**, Trevor **Peters**. Tr: Avon **Dale**

Panamericano, San Cristobal
17-10-2010, 16:00, 600, Lebron PUR

Dominican Republic 0

Miguel **Baez** - Rafael **Ramirez**, Orlando **Belen•**, Johan **Cruz•** (Ramon **Mariano** 75), Cesar **Garcia**, Domingo **Peralta**, Kervin **Severino**, Gonzalo **Frechilla** (Erick **Ozuna** 52), Inoel **Navarro•** (Francisco **Jimenez** 62), Manuel **Reinoso**, Darly **Batista**. Tr: Domingo **Hernandez**

Dominica 1
Elmond **Derrick** [66]

Glenson **Prince** - Colin **Bernard•**, Prince **Austrie**, Elmond **Derrick•**, Carlyn **Cristopher•**, Raschid **Bertrand** (Wayne **George** 43), Chad **Bertrand•**, Kelrick **Walter**, Kurlson **Benjamin**, Lester **Langlais**, Mitchel **Joseph** (Donald **Javier** 31) (Cheston **Dangleben** 66). Tr: Kirt **Hector**

GROUP E

		Pl	W	D	L	F	A	Pts	GRN	SKN	PUR
Guadaloupe	GLP	3	3	0	0	8	3	9	3-0	2-1	3-2
Grenada	GRN	3	2	0	1	5	4	6		2-0	3-1
St Kitts and Nevis	SKN	3	1	0	2	4	4	3			1-0
Puerto Rico	PUR	3	0	0	3	3	7	0			

National Stadium, St George's
22-10-2010, 15:00, 300, Taylor BRB

Guadaloupe 2

Gregory Gendrey [13], Jean-Luc Lambourde [87]

Yohan Bus - Mathias Babel, Eddy Viator, Mathieu Bemba (Dmitri Fautrai 85), Larry Clavier◆25, Stephane Auvray• (c), Gregory Gendrey•, Jean-Luc Lambourde, Lerry Hanany (Kevin Lacroix 55), Vidian Valerius (Cedric Collet 55), Julien Ictoi. Tr: Roger Salnot

St Kitts and Nevis 1

Jevon Francis [83p]

Akil Byron◆85 - Shashi Isaac (GK 85'), Kareem Mitchum, George Isaac• (Austin Lewis 77), Alexis Saddler•, Jevon Francis, Ian Lake, Thrizen Leader (c), Tiran Hanley (Tishan Hanley 70), Errol O'Loughlin, Gerard Williams (Orlando Mitchum 58). Tr: Clinton Percival

---

National Stadium, St George's
22-10-2010, 17:00, 600, Wijngaarde SUR

Grenada 3

Kithson Bain 2 [45 68], Ricky Charles [80]

Desmond Noel - Shannon Phillip, Curt Rennie, Cassim Langaigne, Mark Marshall, Delroy Facey (Marcus Julien 46), Ricky Charles, Kithson Bain (Rimmel Daniel 77), Anthony Modeste, Patrick Modeste, Shane Rennie (Ian Perrotte 40◆45). Tr: Franklyn Simpson

Puerto Rico 1

Isaac Nieves [81]

Alessandro Perez◆46 - Elliot Velez (Christopher Megaloudis 50), Alexis Rivera (GK 61'), Tyler Wilson, Andres Cabrero (Isaac Nieves 59), Petter Villegas, Gadiel Figueroa (Eloy Matos 63), Joan Morales, Christopher Feigenbaum, Cristian Arrieta, Hector Ramos. Tr: Adrian Whitbread

---

National Stadium, St George's
24-10-2010, 15:00, 200, Baptiste DMA

Guadaloupe 3

Gregory Gendrey [1], Lodovic Gotin [11], Stephane Auvray [58]

Yohan Bus• - Kevin Lacroix, Eddy Viator, Stephane Auvray• (c), Lodovic Gotin•, Gregory Gendrey (Mathieu Bemba 60), Cedric Collet (Michel LaFortune 73), Jean-Luc Lambourde, Willy Laurence (Lerry Hanany 87), Dmitri Fautrai, Julien Ictoi•. Tr: Roger Salnot

Puerto Rico 2

Chris Megaloudis [65], Petter Villegas [74]

Jose Vila Torres - Raphel Ortiz (c), Elliot Velez (Eloy Matos 90), Tyler Wilson (Carlos Morales 65), Petter Villegas, John Krause•, Joan Morales, Christopher Feigenbaum• (Christopher Megaloudis 46), Isaac Nieves, Cristian Arrieta, Hector Ramos. Tr: Adrian Whitbread

---

National Stadium, St George's
24-10-2010, 17:00, 500, Morrison JAM

Grenada 2

Delroy Facey 2 [17 32]

Andre Baptiste - Shannon Phillip, Curt Rennie, Cassim Langaigne, Mark Marshall, Delroy Facey (Denron Daniel 66), Ricky Charles, Kithson Bain (Lashley Cyrus 74), Anthony Modeste (c), Patrick Modeste (Kyle Joseph 66), Shane Rennie. Tr: Franklyn Simpson

St Kitts and Nevis 0

Alexis Richards - Shashi Isaac (Tishan Hanley 77), Kareem Mitchum, George Isaac, Alexis Saddler•, Jevon Francis (Stephen Clarke 63), Ian Lake◆85, Thrizen Leader (c), Tiran Hanley (Orlando Mitchum 70), Errol O'Loughlin•, Gerard Williams. Tr: Clinton Percival

---

National Stadium, St George's
26-10-2010, 15:00, 500, Morrison JAM

St Kitts and Nevis 1

Jevon Francis [90]

Akil Byron - Keithroy Richards, Shashi Isaac, Kareem Mitchum, Tishan Hanley (Jevon Francis 46), Orlando Mitchum, Stephen Clarke (George Isaac 46), Austin Lewis (Gerard Williams 74), Thrizen Leader, Tiran Hanley, Errol O'Loughlin. Tr: Clinton Percival

Puerto Rico 0

Salvatore Perez - Raphel Ortiz, Carlos Morales, Andres Cabrero (Elliot Velez 78), Elroy Matos (Hector Ramos 61) Christopher Megaloudis, John Krause, Gadiel Figueroa•, Joan Morales, Isaac Nieves (Christopher Feigenbaum 56), Cristian Arrieta. Tr: Jack Stefahowski

---

National Stadium, St George's
26-10-2010, 17:00, 500, Wijngaarde SUR

Grenada 0

Desmond Noel - Shannon Phillip, Michael Mark, Curt Rennie, Cassim Langaigne, Mark Marshall (Shane Rennie 38), Delroy Facey•, Ricky Charles, Marcus Julien, Henson Cuffie (Ian Perrotte 72), Lashley Cyrus (Kyle Joseph 57). Tr: Franklyn Simpson

Guadaloupe 3

Johnny Tacita 2 [2 78], George Gendrey [68]

Yohan Bus - Kevin LaCroix (Mathias Babel 65), Eddy Viator, Larry Clavier, Gregory Gendrey, Jean-Luc Lambourde, Willy Laurence (Mathieu Bemba 57), Lerry Hanany, Johnny Tacita, Dimitri Fautrai (Cedric Collet 71), Julien Ictoi. Tr: Roger Salnot

---

GROUP F

		Pl	W	D	L	F	A	Pts	GUY	HAI	VIN
Trinidad and Tobago	TRI	3	3	0	0	12	3	9	2-1	4-0	6-2
Guyana	GUY	3	1	1	1	3	2	4		0-0	2-0
Haiti	HAI	3	1	1	1	3	5	4			3-1
St Vincent/Grenadines	VIN	3	0	0	3	3	11	0			

Manny Ramjohn, Marabella
2-11-2010, 18:00, 880, Taylor BRB

Haiti 0

Steward Ceus - Mechack Jerome (Wildedonald Guerrier 44), Parnal Guerrier• (c), Harold Milord, Versailles Kenold, Sony Norbe (Jacqueson Jean 79), Eliphene Cadet (Ricardo Charles 65), Leonel Saint Preux•, Constant Jean Junior Monuma, Pascal Millien, Rubin Jean Garry. Tr: Edson Tavares

Guyana 0

Ronson Williams - Chris Nurse, Howard Lowe (c), Christopher Bourne, Jake Newton, Dwain Jacobs, Dwight Peters••◆67, Anthony Abrams (Shawn Beveney 69), Charles Pollard, Sean Cameron (Dwain Ali 76), Devon Millington (Warren Gilkes 82). Tr: Wayne Dover

---

Manny Ramjohn, Marabella
2-11-2010, 20:30, 1100, Peterkin JAM

Trinidad and Tobago 6

Devon Jorsling 3 [2 35 59], Kerry Baptiste 2 [57 67], Hughton Hector [90]

Jan Micheal Williams - Clyde Leon (c), Kern Cupid, Daniel Cyrus, Trent Noel (Hughton Hector 65), Devon Jorsling, Kendall Jagdeosingh, Jovin Jones, Lester Peltier (Keon Daniel 71), Julius James, Jamal Gay (Kerry Baptiste 53). Tr: Russell Latapy

St Vincent/Grenadines 1

Shandel Samuel [28], Cornelius Stewart [45]

Dwayne Sandy• - Roy Richards, Oscar Nero, Wesley Charles (c), Cornelius Stewart, Dorren Hamlet (Paul Farrell 78), Myron Samuel•, Shandel Samuel (Windell Cuffy 73), Seinard Bownes, Damol Francis (Joel George 62), Reginal Richardson. Tr: Samuel Carrington

---

Manny Ramjohn, Marabella
4-11-2010, 18:00, 1100, Campbell JAM

Haiti 3

Sony Norde [45], Leonel Saint Preux [62], Ricardo Charles [83]

Steward Ceus - Parnal Guerrier• (c), Harold Milord•, Fabien Vorbe (Leonel Saint Preux 61), Sony Norbe, Ricardo Charles, Constant Jean Junior Monuma (Jacqueson Jean 82) Pascal Millien, Rubin Jean Garry•, Wildedonald Guerrier (Joseph Nicodeme Beauge 61), Junior Clairssainvil. Tr: Edson Tavares

St Vincent/Grenadines 1

Shandel Samuel [64]

Kenyan Lynch - Roy Richards, Wesley Charles (c), Cornelius Stewart•, Dorren Hamlet (Chad Balcombe 46), Myron Samuel (Narel George 55), Shandel Samuel, Seinard Bownes, Jolanshoy McDowald (Oscar Nero 46), Reginal Richardson•, Emerald George. Tr: Samuel Carrington

---

Manny Ramjohn, Marabella
4-11-2010, 20:30, 1100, Legister JAM

Trinidad and Tobago   2
Lester Peltier [34], Devon Jorsling [42]

Jan Micheal **Williams** - Clyde **Leon** (c) (Densil **Theobald** 52), Yohance **Marshall•**, Daniel **Cyrus•**, Trent **Noel**, Devon **Jorsling**, Jovin **Jones** (Anthony **Wolfe** 58), Lester **Peltier** (Keon **Daniel** 67), Julius **James**, Jamal **Gay**, Kevin **Molino•**. Tr: Russell **Latapy**

Guyana   1
Shawn Beveney [78]

Ronson **Williams** - Chris **Nurse**, Howard **Lowe** (c), Christopher **Bourne**, Walter **Moore**, Jake **Newton**, Dwain **Jacobs** (Shawn **Beveney** 75), Anthony **Abrams**, John **Rodrigues•**, Sean **Cameron** (Dwain **Ali** 61), Devon **Millington**. Tr: Wayne **Dover**

Manny Ramjohn, Marabella
6-11-2010, 17:00, 850, Taylor BRB

Guyana   2
Devon Millington [57], Sean Cameron [81]

Ronson **Williams** - Chris **Nurse** (Charles **Pollard** 32), Howard **Lowe** (c), Christopher **Bourne**, Walter **Moore**, Jake **Newton**, Dwight **Peters**, Anthony **Abrams•** (Shawn **Beveney** 58), John **Rodrigues**, Sean **Cameron**, Devon **Millington** (Dwain **Ali** 58). Tr: Wayne **Dover**

St Vincent/Grenadines   0

Kenyan **Lynch** - Roy **Richards** (Chad **Balcombe** 90), Oscar **Nero**, Wesley **Charles** (c), Cornelius **Stewart**, Myron **Samuel**, Narel **George** (Seinard **Bowens** 79), Damol **Francis•**, Reginal **Richardson**, Emerald **George** (Joel **George** 46), Paul **Farrell**. Tr: Samuel **Carrington**

Manny Ramjohn, Marabella
6-11-2010, 19:30, 850, Campbell JAM

Trinidad and Tobago   4
Hughton Hector 2 [4 33], Devon Jorsling [8], Kerry Baptiste [29]

Marvin **Phillip** - Yohance **Marshall**, Kerry **Baptiste•**, Kern **Cupid•**, Hughton **Hector**, Devon **Jorsling** (c) (Shahdon **Winchester** 46), Anthony **Wolfe•**, Julius **James**, Densil **Theobald**, Keon **Daniel** (Kendall **Jagdeosingh** 46), Kevin **Molino**. Tr: Russell **Latapy**

Haiti   0

Steward **Ceus** - Mechack **Jerome**, Harold **Milord•** (c), Sony **Norbe**, Ricardo **Charles**, Constant **Jean** Junior **Monuma**, Jacqueson **Jean** (Fabien **Vorbe** 71), Pascal **Millien** (Leonel **Saint Preux** 34), Rubin **Jean** Garry, Wildedonald **Guerrier**, Junior **Clairssainvil**. Tr: Edson **Tavares**

GROUP G

		Pl	W	D	L	F	A	Pts	ATG	SUR	DMA
Cuba	CUB	3	1	2	0	7	5	**5**	0-0	3-3	4-2
Antigua and Barbuda	ATG	3	1	2	0	2	1	**5**		2-1	0-0
Suriname	SUR	3	1	1	1	9	5	**4**			5-0
Dominica	DMA	3	0	1	2	2	9	**1**			

Recreation Ground, St John's
10-11-2010, 500, Lancaster GUY

Cuba   4
Armando Curuneaux [9], Reysander Fernandez [20], Yoel Colome [27], Marcel Hernandez [35]

Vismel **Castellano** - Yenier **Marquez**, Reysander **Fernandez** (Hanier **Dranguet** 88), Joel **Colome•**, Jaime **Colome** (c), Alianni **Urgelles**, Alain **Cervantes** (Leonel **Duarte** 74), Roberto **Linares**, Alain **Cervantes** (Dagoberto **Quesada** 77), Marcel **Hernandez**. Tr: Raul **Gonzalez**

Dominica   2
Kurlson Benjamin 2 [11 87]

Owen **Oscar** - Colin **Bernard•** (c) (Kurtney **McKenzie** 55), Prince **Austrie**, Jerome **Thomas**, Carlyn **Christopher•**, Elmond **Derrick**, Rasheed **Bertrand** (Wayne **George** 30), Chad **Bertrand**, Glenworth **Elizee** (Cheston **Dangleben** 46), Lester **Langlais**, Kurlson **Benjamin**. Tr: Kirt **Hector**

Recreation Ground, St John's
10-11-2010, 16:30, 2000, Morrison JAM

Antigua and Barbuda   2
Randolph Burton [18], Justin Cochrane [64]

Keita **Decastro** - George **Dublin** (c), Karanja **Mack•** (Roy **Gregory** 80), Joshua **Parker**, Mikele **Leightwood**, Akeem **Thomas•** (Quinton **Griffith** 73), Peter **Byers**, Gason **Gregory** (Kerry **Skepple** 87), Dave **Carr**, Justin **Cochrane**, Randolph **Burton**. Tr: Rowan **Benjamin**

Suriname   1
Roche Emanelson [34]

Obrendo **Huiswoud** - Foline **Abauna**, Roche **Emanelson**, Marlon **Felter**, Derrick **Garden•** (Germaine **Van Dijck•** 69), Stefan **Baneti** (Germaine **Van Dijck•** 69), Stefan **Baneti** (Emilio **Limon** (Gregory **Rigters** 81), Ives **Vlijter**, Stefano **Rijssel**. Tr: Ricardo **Winter**

Recreation Ground, St John's
12-11-2010, 14:30, 400, Campbell JAM

Suriname   3
Wensley Christopher [8], Stefano Rijssel [50], Derrick Garden [80]

Obrendo **Huiswoud** - Derrick **Garden** (c), Marlon **Felter**, Foline **Abauna**, Roche **Emanelson**, Emilio **Limon** (Gregory **Rigters** 90), Ives **Vlijter** (Stefan **Baneti** 74), Stefano **Rijssel•**, Wensly **Christopher**, Giovanni **Waal** (Naldo **Kwasie** 38), Germaine **Van Dijck**. Tr: Ricardo **Winter**

Cuba   3
Armando Curuneaux [45], Alain Cervantes [65], Adonis Ramos [87]

Vismel **Castellano** - Hanier Humberto **Dranguet**, Joel **Colome•**, Marcel **Hernandez** (Leonel **Duarte** 60), Jaime **Colome** (c), Alain **Cervantes•** (Adonis **Ramos** 79), Sander **Fernandez**, Alianni **Urgelles**, Armando **Curuneaux** (Roberto **Linares** 60), Reysander **Fernandez**, Yenier **Marquez**. Tr: Raul **Gonzalez**

Recreation Ground, St John's
12-11-2010, 16:30, 400, Purser JAM

Antigua and Barbuda   0

Keita **Decastro** - Ranja **Christian** (Jamie **Thomas** 56), Karanja **Mack**, Dave **Carr•**, Joshua **Parker•**, Gason **Gregory•** (Kerry **Skepple•** 49), Justin **Cochrane**, Mikele **Leightwood**, Randolph **Burton**, Peter **Byers**, George **Dublin** (c). Tr: Rowan **Benjamin**

Dominica   0

Glenson **Prince** - Prince **Austrie**, Elmond **Derrick**, Colin **Bernard** (c), Wayne **George** (Rasheed **Bertrand** 56), Jerome **Thomas**, Lester **Langlais** (Cheston **Dangleben•** 68) (Kerry **Alleyne** 90), Mitchell **Joseph**, Kurlson **Benjamin**, Donan **Jervier**, Chad **Bertrand**. Tr: Kirt **Hector**

Recreation Ground, St John's
14-11-2010, 14:30, 500, Lancaster GUY

Suriname   5
Naldo Kwasie [45], Ives Vlijter [45p], Emilio Limon [56], Roche Emanelson [75], Stefano Rijssel [88p]

Obrendo **Huiswoud** - Derrick **Garden** (c), Marlon **Felter**, Foline **Abauna**, Roche **Emanelson**, Emilio **Limon**, Ives **Vlijter** (Stefan **Baneti** 77), Stefano **Rijssel** (Gregory **Rigters** 90), Wensly **Christopher**, Naldo **Kwasie** (Kenneth **Moennoe** 88), Germaine **Van Dijck•**. Tr: Ricardo **Winter**

Dominica   0

Glenson **Prince** (c) (Owen **Oscar** 58) - Prince **Austrie•**, Elmond **Derrick**, Colin **Bernard**, Jerome **Thomas**, Lester **Langlais**, Mitchell **Joseph•**, Kurlson **Benjamin**, Donan **Jervier** (Kerry **Alleyne** 65), Chad **Bertrand•**, Carlyn **Christopher** (Wayne **George** 72). Tr: Kirt **Hector**

Recreation Ground, St John's
14-11-2010, 16:30, 500, Campbell JAM

Antigua and Barbuda   0

Keita **Decastro** - Karanja **Mack**, Dave **Carr**, Joshua **Parker**, Jamie **Thomas•** (Gason **Gregory** 75), Justin **Cochrane**, Mikele **Leightwood**, Randolph **Burton** (Quinton **Griffith** 90), Peter **Byers** (Kerry **Skepple** 81), George **Dublin** (c), Akeem **Thomas**. Tr: Rowan **Benjamin**

Cuba   0

Odelin **Molina** - Carlos Francisco **Serrano**, Hanier Humberto **Dranguet**, Marcel **Hernandez** (Dagoberto **Quesada** 90), Jaime **Colome** (c), Sander **Fernandez** (Adonis **Ramos** 82), Alianni **Urgelles**, Armando **Curuneaux**, Reysander **Fernandez•**, Leonel **Duarte** (Roberto **Linares** 70), Yenier **Marquez**. Tr: Raul **Gonzalez**

DIGICEL CARIBBEAN CHAMPIONSHIP MARTINIQUE 2010

First Round Group Stage

Group A		Pl	W	D	L	F	A	Pts	GRN	TRI	MTQ
Cuba		3	2	1	0	3	0	7	0-0	2-0	1-0
Grenada		3	1	2	0	2	1	5		1-0	1-1
Trinidad and Tobago		3	1	0	2	1	3	3			1-0
Martinique		3	0	1	2	1	3	1			

Semi-finals

Jamaica	2
Grenada	1
Cuba	1
Guadeloupe	2

Final

Jamaica	1	5p
Guadeloupe	1	4p

Group B		Pl	W	D	L	F	A	Pts	GLP	ATG	GUY
Jamaica		3	3	0	0	9	1	9	2-0	3-1	4-0
Guadeloupe		3	1	1	1	2	3	4		1-0	1-1
Antigua and Barbuda		3	1	0	2	2	4	3			1-0
Guyana		3	0	1	2	1	6	1			

Third place play-off

Cuba	1
Grenada	0

Held in Martinique from 26-11-2010 to 5-12-2010 • Top scorers: 3 - Kithson Bain GRN & Dane Richards JAM
Jamaica, Guadeloupe Cuba & Grenada qualified for the CONCACAF Gold Cup 2011

GROUP A

		Pl	W	D	L	F	A	Pts		GRN	TRI	MTQ
Cuba	CUB	3	2	1	0	3	0	7		0-0	2-0	1-0
Grenada	GRN	3	1	2	0	2	1	5			1-0	1-1
Trinidad and Tobago	TRI	3	1	0	2	1	3	3				1-0
Martinique	MTQ	3	0	1	2	1	3	1				

Stade Pierre-Aliker, Fort de France
26-11-2010, 18:00, 5000, Lancaster GUY

Trinidad and Tobago 0

Jan Michael Williams - Trent Noel (Hughton **Hector** 69), Julius **James**, Yohance **Marshall** (Daniel **Cyrus** 46), Joevin **Jones•** - Kern **Cupid**, Clyde Leon (C), Kerry **Baptiste•** (Jamal **Gay** 46), Lester **Peltier♦**84 Keon **Daniel** - Devorn Jorsling. Tr: Russell **Latapy**

Cuba 2
Joel Colome [23], Roberto Linares [79]

Odelin Molina - Aliannis Urgelles, Yenier Marquez, Sander Fernandez (Adonis Ramos 78), Hanier Dranguet, Joel **Colome•** - Carlos Serrano, Marcel Hernandez, Jaime **Colome•** (C) - Armando Curuneaux, Leonel **Duarte** (Roberto Linares 78). Tr: Raul **Gonzalez**

Stade Pierre-Aliker, Fort de France
26-11-2010, 20:30, 5000, Bogle JAM

Martinique 1
Jose Goron [79p]

Eddy Heurlie - Ludovic **Clement•**, Stephane Suedile, Fabrice Reuperne (Manuel **Mence** 70) - Sebastien Cretinoir, Daniel Herelle, Steve Gustan, Rodrigue Cesar, Kevin Parsemain (Sebastien **Carole** 59), Gaetan Sidney (Jose Goron 77) - Patrick Percin (c). Tr: Jocelyn **Germe**

Grenada 1
Kithson Bain [29]

Andray Baptiste - David **Cyrus**, Shannon Phillip (Cassim Langaigne 66), Arkenson Neckles (Bradley Bubb 57), Marc **Marshall** - Ricky Charles, Anthony Modeste (c), Craig Rocastle, Patrick Modeste - Kithson Bain, Delroy Facey (Shane Rennie 78). Tr: Franklyn **Simpson**

Stade Pierre-Aliker, Fort de France
28-11-2010, 16:00, 500, Cruz CRC

Grenada 1
Kithson Bain [69]

Andray Baptiste - Marc Marshall (Curt Rennie 53), David Cyrus, Craig **Rocastle•** (Cassim Langaigne 75) - Arkenson **Neckles** (Shanon **Phillip** 67) - Patrick **Modeste**, Anthony Modeste (c), Ricky Charles, Delroy **Facey** - Kithson Bain, Bradley **Bubb**. Tr: Franklyn **Simpson**

Trinidad and Tobago 0

Marvin Phillip (c) - Trent Noel, Daniel Cyrus, Julius **James•**, Yohance **Marshall**, Joevin Jones (Densil Theobald 74) - Anthony Wolfe, Hughton Hector (Cornell Glen 65), Kevin Molino - Kendall Jagdeosingh (Keon **Daniel** 50), Devorn Jorsling. Tr: Russell **Latapy**

Stade Pierre-Aliker, Fort de France
28-11-2010, 18:30, 500, Taylor BRB

Martinique 0

Eddy Heurlie - Ludovic Clement, Stephane **Suedile** (Manuel **Mence** 68), Fabrice Reuperne (Jose Goron 57) - Sebastien **Cretinoir**, Daniel Herelle, Steve **Gustan•**, Rodrigue Cesar, Kevin Parsemain, Sebastien Carole (Gaetan Sidney 47) - Patrick **Percin** (c). Tr: Guy Nisas

Cuba 1
Yenier Marquez [28]

Odelin Molina - Aliannis Urgelles, Yenier **Marquez**, Sander Fernandez (Reysandri Fernandez 60), Hanier **Dranguet••♦**54, Joel Colome - Carlos Serrano, Marcel Hernandez♦39, Jaime **Colome•** (c) - Armando Curuneaux (Adonise Ramos 83), Leonel **Duarte•** (Roberto Linares 62). Tr: Raul **Gonzalez**

Stade Pierre-Aliker, Fort de France
30-11-2010, 18:00, 2000, Bogle JAM

Cuba 0

Odelin Molina - Jorge Clavelo, Reysandri Fernandez, Alianni Urgelles, Yenier Marquez (c), Joel Colome - Carlos Serrano, Sander Fernandez (Adonis Ramos 76) - Armando **Curuneaux**, Roberto Linares (Leonel Duarte 76). Tr: Raul **Gonzalez**

Grenada 0

Andray Baptiste - David **Cyrus** (Cassim Langaigne 46), Curt Rennie, Craig Rocastle (Shane Rennie 61) - Anthony Modeste (c), Byron Bubb, Delroy Facey, Ricky Charles (Marcus Julien 46), Patrick Modeste - Kithson Bain, Bradley **Bubb**. Tr: Franklyn **Simpson**

Stade Pierre-Aliker, Fort de France
30-11-2010, 20:30, 2000, Taylor BRB

Martinique 0

Eddy Heurlie - Fabrice **Reuperne•**, Joan Deluge, Sebastien Cretinoir, Daniel **Herelle•**, Steve **Gustan•**, Rodrigue **Cesar•**, Rodrigue Audel - Manuel Mence (Livaye **Aliker** 75), Jose Goron (Kevin Parsemain 61), Patrick Percin (c) (Gaetsan Sidney 46). Tr: Jocelyn **Germe**

Trinidad and Tobago 1
Hector [47]

Marvin Phillip - Julius James, Daniel Cyrus, Kern Cupid (Joevin Jones 76), Densil Theobald - Clyde Leon (c), Hughton **Hector•**, Kevin Molino, Anthony Wolfe, Keon Daniel (Kendall Jagdeosingh 75) - Devorn Jorsling (Cornell **Glen** 70). Tr: Russell **Latapy**

GROUP B

		Pl	W	D	L	F	A	Pts		GLP	ATG	GUY
Jamaica	JAM	3	3	0	0	9	1	9		2-0	3-1	4-0
Guadeloupe	GLP	3	1	1	1	2	3	4			1-0	1-1
Antigua and Barbuda	ATG	3	1	0	2	2	4	3				1-0
Guyana	GUY	3	0	1	2	1	6	1				

Stade En Camee, Riviere-Pilote

27-11-2010, 17:00, 2500, Davis TRI

Guyana   **1**

Dwain Jacobs [86]

Ronson **Williams** - Howard **Lowe** (c), Charles **Pollard**, Jake **Newton**, Chris **Bourne**, Kester **Jacobs** - Philbert **Moffat**, Walter **Moore**, Nigel **Codrington** (Dwain **Jacobs** 59) - Dwight **Peters** (Howard **Newton** 59), Devon **Millington** (Anthony **Abrams** 78). Tr: Wayne **Dover**

Guadeloupe   **1**

Loic Loval [70]

Yohanne **Bus** - Kevin **Lacroix**, Ulick **Lupede**•, Julien **Ictoi** - Jean Luc **Lamboude**, Fabien **Belson** (Cedril **Collet** 46), Stephane **Auvray**• (c) - Mickael **Nicoise** (Gregory **Gendrey** 67), Livio **Nabab** (Ludovic **Gotin** 90), Larry **Clavier**•, Loic **Loval**. Tr: Roger **Salnot**

Stade En Camee, Riviere-Pilote

27-11-2010, 19:30, 3000, Wijngaarde SUR

Jamaica   **3**

Luton Shelton 2 [14 37], Dane Richards [40]

Dwayne **Miller** - Shavar **Thomas**• (c), Jermaine **Taylor**, Adrian **Reid**•, Shaun **Francis** - Rodolph **Austin**• (Keneil **Moodie** 90), Richard **Edwards**•, Lovel **Palmer** - Keammar **Daley** (O'Brian **Woodbine** 74), Dane **Richards** (Eric **Vernan** 81), Luton **Shelton**. Tr: Theodore **Whitmore**

Antigua and Barbuda   **1**

Gason Gregory [49]

Keita **Decastro** - Martin **McCoy**, Dave **Carr** - Joshua **Parker**, Justin **Cochrane**•, Kieran **Murtagh**•, Randolph **Burton**• (Ranja **Christian** 70), George **Dublin** (c), Akeem **Thomas** (Quinton **Griffith** 90), Jamie **Thomas** (Gason **Gregory** 46) - Peter **Byers**. Tr: Rowan **Benjamin**

Stade En Camee, Riviere-Pilote

29-11-2010, 18:00, 3000, Wijngaarde SUR

Antigua and Barbuda   **1**

Gason Gregory [69]

Molvin **James** - Karanja **Mack**, Joshua **Parker** (Desmond **Bleau** 46), Gason **Gregory**, Justin **Cochrane**•, Kieran **Murtagh**•, Kerry **Skepple** (Randolph **Burton** 59), George **Dublin** (c), Martin **McCoy**, Akeem **Thomas** - Peter **Byers** (Ranja **Christian** 89). Tr: Rowan **Benjamin**

Guyana   **0**

Ronson **Williams** - Howard **Lowe** (c),Charles **Pollard**•, Jake **Newton**, Chris **Bourne**, Walter **Moore** (Dwight **Peters** 72), Kester **Jacobs** - Dwain **Jacobs**, Nigel **Codrington** - Anthony **Abrams** (Shawn **Beveney** 65), Devon **Millington** (Warren **Gilkes** 90). Tr: Wayne **Dover**

Stade En Camee, Riviere-Pilote

29-11-2010, 20:30, 3000, Lopez GUA

Guadeloupe   **0**

Yohanne **Bus** - Eddy **Viator**•, Ulick **Lupede**, Julien **Ictoi** - Jean Luc **Lomboude**, Larry **Hanany** (Fabien **Belson** 52), Dominique **Mocka** (Cedric **Collet** 58), Stephane **Auvray** (c) - Ludovic **Gotin** (Livio **Nabab** 67), Larry **Clavier**, Loic **Loval**. Tr: Roger **Salnot**

Jamaica   **2**

Shaun Francis [53], Ryan Johnson [93+]

Dwayne **Miller** - Shavar **Thomas**• (c), Jermaine **Taylor**, Adrian **Reid**, Shaun **Francis** (Troy **Smith**• 74) - Rodolph **Austin**•, Lovel **Palmer**, Dane **Richards** (Richard **Edwards** 81) - Keammar **Daley**, Omar **Cummings** (Ryan **Johnson** 64), Luton **Shelton**. Tr: Theodore **Whitmore**

Stade En Camee, Riviere-Pilote

1-12-2010, 18:00, 3000, Lopez GUA

Guadeloupe   **1**

Jean Luc Lambourde [41]

Yohanne **Bus** - Eddy **Viator**, Ulick **Lupede** (Kevin **Lacroix** 46), Julien **Ictoi** - Jean Luc **Lamboude**, Stephane **Auvray**• (c), Gregory **Gendrey**, Cedril **Collet**• (Larry **Clavier** 69) - Mickael **Nicoise** (Dominique **Mocka** 79), Livio **Nabab**•, Loic **Loval**•. Tr: Roger **Salnot**

Antigua and Barbuda   **0**

Molvin **James** - Martin **McCoy**•, Ranja **Christian**• (Randolph **Burton** 61), Dave **Carr**••♦85 - Joshua **Parker**, Gason **Gregory**, Desmond **Bleau** (Kerry **Skepple** 74), George **Dublin** (c), Karanja **Mack**, Akeem **Thomas**• - Peter **Byers** (Jamie **Thomas** 90). Tr: Rowan **Benjamin**

Stade En Camee, Riviere-Pilote

1-12-2010, 20:30, 3000, Cruz CRC

Guyana   **0**

Ronson **Williams** - Howard **Lowe** (c), Charles **Pollard**, Chris **Bourne**, Jake **Newton**•, Kester **Jacobs**• (Philbert **Moffat** 78) - Dwain **Jacobs**, Winston **Ali**, Shawn **Beveney** (Anthony **Abrams** 81), Nigel **Codrington** - Dwight **Peters** (Walter **Moore** 30), Tr: Wayne **Dover**

Jamaica   **4**

Richards [42], Morgan 2 [49 75], Vernan [90]

Richard **McCallum** - Troy **Smith**, Eric **Vernan**, Jermaine **Taylor** (c), Adrian **Reid** - Keneil **Moodie**, Richard **Edwards** (Sergio **Campbell** 46), Dane **Richards** (Marvin **Morgan** 46) - Ryan **Johnson**•, Keammar **Daley**, Luton **Shelton** (O'Brian **Woodbine**• 53). Tr: Theodore **Whitmore**

SEMI-FINALS & 3RD PLACE PLAY-OFF

S/F. Pierre-Aliker, Fort de France

3-12-2010, 17:30, 2000, Wijngaarde SUR

Cuba   **1**

Reysandri Fernandez [34]

Odelin **Molina** - Reysandri **Fernandez**, Alianni **Urgelles**, Yenier **Marquez**, Sander **Fernandez** (Adonis **Ramos** 81), Joel **Colome** - Jaime **Colome**• (c), Carlos Francisco **Serrano**, Marcel **Hernandez** - Armando **Curuneaux**• (Roberto **Linares** 68), Leonel **Duarte** (Yosneil **Mesa** 83). Tr: Raul **Gonzalez**

Guadeloupe   **2**

Gendrey [55p], Lambourde [78]

Yohanne **Bus** - Eddy **Viator**, Kevin **Lacroix**, Julien **Ictoi**, Dominique **Mocka** (Mickael **Antoine-Currier** 68), Gregory **Gendrey**, Cedric **Collet**• (Mathias **Babel** 90), Jean Luc **Lomboude**• (c), Larry **Hanany** (Fabien **Belson** 59) - Ludovic **Gotin**, Larry **Clavier**•. Tr: Roger **Salnot**

S/F. Pierre-Aliker, Fort de France

3-12-2010, 20:30, 4000, Taylor BRB

Jamaica   **2**

Dane Richards [7], Troy Smith [96]

Dwayne **Miller** - Shavar **Thomas** (c), Jermaine **Taylor**, Adrian **Reid**•, Shaun **Francis** (Troy **Smith** 73) - Rodolph **Austin**•, Richard **Edwards** (Sergio **Campbell** 106♦111), Lovel **Palmer** - Ryan **Johnson** (Omar **Cummings** 28), Dane **Richards**, Luton **Shelton**. Tr: Theodore **Whitmore**

Grenada   **1**

Kithson Bain [13]

Andray **Baptiste** - David **Cyrus**, Shanon **Phillip**, Cassim **Langaigne** (Arkenson **Neckles** 103), Marc **Marshall** - Byron **Bubb** (Curt **Rennie** 101), Anthony **Modeste** (c), Craig **Rocastle**, Patrick **Modeste** (Bradley **Bubb**• 75) - Delroy **Facey**, Kithson **Bain**. Tr: Franklyn **Simpson**

3P/PO. Pierre-Aliker, Fort de France

5-12-2010, 16:00, 4000, Lopez GUA

Cuba   **1**

Roberto Linares [12]

Odelin **Molina** - Carlos Francisco **Serrano**, Yenier **Marquez**, Hanier **Dranguet**, Joel **Colome**, Marcel **Hernandez**, Jaime **Colome**• (c), Roberto **Linares** (Leonel **Duarte** 78), Adonis **Ramos** (Sander **Fernandez** 72), Alianni **Urgelles**•, Reysandri **Fernandez**. Tr: Raul **Gonzalez**

Grenada   **0**

Andray **Baptiste** - Shanon **Phillip**, Curt **Rennie**, Cassim **Langaigne** - Byron **Bubb**, Anthony **Modeste** (c), Craig **Rocastle**, Patrick **Modeste** (Arkenson **Neckles** 46), Shane **Rennie** (Rimmel **Daniel** 63) - Delroy **Facey**• (Lancaster **Keller** 75), Kithson **Bain**. Tr: Franklyn **Simpson**

FINAL

Stade En Camee, Riviere-Pilote

5-12-2010, 19:00, 4000, Enrico Wijngaarde SUR; Goddard BRB & Louisville SUR

Jamaica   **1 5p**

Omar Cummings [32]

Dwayne **Miller** - Shavar **Thomas** (c) (O'Brian **Woodbine** 117), Jermaine **Taylor**, Eric **Vernan**, Troy **Smith**, Adrian **Reid** (Keneil **Moodie** 85) - Richard **Edwards** (Lovel **Palmer** 68), Rodolph **Austin** - Dane **Richards**, Omar **Cummings**, Luton **Shelton**. Tr: Theodore **Whitmore**

Guadeloupe   **1 4p**

Ludovic Gotin [37]

Yohanne **Bus** - Eddy **Viator**, Ulick **Lupede**, Julien **Ictoi** - Jean Luc **Lomboude**, Stephane **Auvray** (c), Cedric **Collet**, Gregory **Gendrey**, Larry **Hanany** (Fabien **Belson** 78) - Ludovic **Gotin** (Mickael **Antoine-Currier** 105), Larry **Clavier**. Tr: Roger **Salnot**

PENALTY SHOOT-OUT GRENADA V CUBA FINAL JAMAICA WON 5-4		
Jamaica		Guadeloupe
Austin	✓ ✓	Clavier
Shelton	✓ ✓	Gendrey
Woodbine	✓ ✓	Collet
Vernan	✓ ✓	A-Currier
Smith	✓ ✗	Lomboude

CLUB TOURNAMENTS 2010

CONCACAF CHAMPIONS LEAGUE 2009-10

Preliminary Round   **Group Phase**

| Pachuca * | MEX | 3 | 7 |
| Deportivo Jalapa | GUA | 0 | 1 |

Group A		Pl	W	D	L	F	A	Pts	MEX	PAN	USA	SLV
Pachuca	MEX	6	5	0	1	15	4	**15**		2-0	2-0	5-0
Arabe Unido	PAN	6	3	1	2	13	9	**10**	4-1		1-1	4-1
Houston Dynamo	USA	6	2	1	3	9	8	**7**	0-1	5-1		1-0
Isidro Metapán	SLV	6	1	0	5	3	19	**3**	0-4	0-1	3-2	

| Olimpia * | HON | 2 | 0 |
| **Arabe Unido** | PAN | 1 | 1 |

| DC United * | USA | 1 | 1 5p |
| Luis Angel Firpo | SLV | 1 | 1 4p |

Group B		Pl	W	D	L	F	A	Pts	MEX	HON	USA	TRI
Toluca	MEX	6	4	1	1	15	4	**13**		7-0	1-1	3-0
Marathón	HON	6	4	0	2	12	14	**12**	2-0		3-1	3-1
DC United	USA	6	3	1	2	12	8	**10**	1-3	3-0		5-1
San Juan Jabloteh	TRI	6	0	0	6	4	17	**0**	0-1	2-4	0-1	

| San Francisco * | PAN | 2 | 0 |
| **San Juan Jabloteh** | TRI | 0 | 3 |

| Cruz Azul | MEX | 6 | 0 |
| CS Herediano | CRC | 2 | 0 |

Group C		Pl	W	D	L	F	A	Pts	MEX	USA	CRC	PUR
Cruz Azul	MEX	6	5	1	0	16	4	**16**		5-0	2-0	2-0
Columbus Crew	USA	6	2	2	2	5	9	**8**	0-2		1-1	2-0
Deportivo Saprissa	CRC	6	1	2	3	6	8	**5**	1-2	0-1		3-1
Puerto Rico Islanders	PUR	6	0	3	3	6	12	**3**	3-3	1-1	1-1	

| Toronto FC * | CAN | 0 | 0 |
| **Puerto Rico Islanders** | PUR | 0 | 1 |

| W Connection * | TRI | 2 | 2 |
| New York Red Bulls | USA | 2 | 1 |

Group D		Pl	W	D	L	F	A	Pts	MEX	GUA	TRI	HON
UNAM Pumas	MEX	6	4	1	1	15	6	**13**		1-0	2-1	4-0
Comunicaciones	GUA	6	3	0	3	6	8	**9**	2-1		0-3	2-0
W Connection	TRI	6	2	1	3	10	9	**7**	2-2	1-2		3-2
Real España	HON	6	2	0	4	6	14	**6**	1-5	2-0	1-0	

| Liberia Mia * | CRC | 3 | 0 |
| **Real España** | HON | 0 | 6 |

Match details for the preliminary round and group phase can be found in *Oliver's Almanack of World Football 2010*

CONCACAF CHAMPIONS LEAGUE 2009–10

Quarter-Finals				Semi-finals			Final		
Pachuca	MEX	1	2						
Communicaciones *	GUA	1	1						
				Pachuca	1	1			
				Toluca *	1	0			
Columbus Crew *	USA	2	2						
Toluca	MEX	2	3						
							Pachuca	2	0
							Cruz Azul *	1	1
UNAM Pumas	MEX	0	6						
Marathón *	HON	2	1						
				UNAM Pumas *	1	0			
				Cruz Azul	0	5			
Arabe Unido *	PAN	0	0						
Cruz Azul	MEX	1	3		* Home team in the first leg					

Top scorers: **9** - Ulises **Mendivil** MEX, Pachuca • **8** - Orlando **Rodriguez** PAN, Arabe Unido • **6** - Javier **Orozco** MEX, Cruz Azul • **5** - Jonathan **Fana Frias** DOM, W Connection; Carlos **Pavon** HON, Real España; Rolando **Fonseca** GUA, Comunicaciones; Paul **Aguilar** MEX, Pachuca; Pablo **Zeballos** PAR, Pachuca, Walter **Martinez** HON, Marathón & Edgar **Benitez** PAR, Pachuca • **4** - Douglas **Caetano** BRA; Real España, Christian **Gomez** ARG, DC United; Francisco **Palencia** MEX, UNAM; Jerry **Palacios** HON, Marathón & Ismael **Iniguez** MEX, UNAM

QUARTER-FINALS

Mateo Flores, Guatemala City

10-03-2010, 22:00, 7438, Moreno PAN

Comunicaciones 1

Fonseca [73]

David Guerra - Carlos **Gallardo**, Edwin **Enriquez•**, Erwin **Morales•** - Rigoberto **Gomez**, Jean **Marquez** (Edgar **Chinchilla** 46), Luis **Bradley** (Jairo **Arreola** 81), Fredy **Thompson** - Transito **Montepeque**, Rolando **Fonseca**, Abner **Trigueros** (Marco Tulio **Ciani** 70). Tr: Julio **Gonzalez**

Pachuca 1

Aguilar [1]

Miguel **Calero** (c) - Leonardo **Lopez•**, Paul **Aguilar**, Javier **Munoz**, Carlos **Rodriguez•** (Dario **Cvitanich** 57) - Gregorio **Torres•**, Juan Carlos **Rojas**, Raul **Martinez**, Damian **Manso** (Edy **Brambila** 75) - Juan Carlos **Cacho** (Damian **Alvarez** 66), Edgar **Benitez**. Tr: Guillermo **Rivarola**

Crew Stadium, Columbus

9-03-2010, 20:00, 4402, Campbell JAM

Columbus Crew 2

Lenhart 2 [65 83]

William **Hesmer** - Daniel **O'Rourke**, Andrew **Iro**, Gino **Padula**, Eric **Brunner** - Robbie **Rogers** (Jason **Garey** 78), Eddie **Gaven**, Brian **Carroll** (c), Adam **Moffat** (Kevin **Burns** 78) - Emmanuel **Ekpo** (Emilio **Renteria** 72), Steven **Lenhart**. Tr: Robert **Warzycha**

Toluca 2

Sinha [19], Rios [44]

Alfredo **Talavera** - Manuel **Cruzalta**, Osvaldo **Gonzalez**, Carlos **Galeana**, Diego **Novaretti** - Antonio **Naelson Zinha** (c) (Manuel **De La Torre** 82), Vladimir **Marin•** (Carlos **Esquivel** 78), Martin **Romagnoli**, Antonio **Rios** - Raul **Nava**, Isaac **Brizuela•**. Tr: Jose Manuel **De La Torre**

Olimpico, San Pedro Sula

10-03-2010, 20:00, 12 297, Quesada CRC

Marathón 2

Martinez [18p], Mejia [53p]

Orlin **Vallecillo** - Luis **Crisanto**, Milton **Palacios**, Astor **Henriquez**, Juan Carlos **Garcia**, Erick **Norales** - Mariano **Acevedo**, Guillermo **Ramirez** (Mario **Rodriguez** 81), Reinier **Mayorquin** (Arnol **Solorzano** 85) - Walter **Martinez•** (c), Carlos **Mejia** (Israel **Solis** 83). Tr: Nicolas **Suazo**

UNAM Pumas 0

Alejandro **Palacios** - Fernando **Espinoza**, Luis **Fuentes**, Humberto **Gonzalez**, David **Cabrera**, Jose Antonio **Garcia•** - Alex Diego **Tejado** (Carlos **Campos** 46), Fernando **Santana•**, Oscar **Rojas** (Javier **Cortes** 79) - Juan Francisco **Palencia** (c), Ismael **Iniguez** (Alfonso **Nieto** 81). Tr: Ricardo **Ferretti**

Armando Dely Valdez, Colón

11-03-2010, 20:00, 2500, Lopez GUA

Arabe Unido 0

Jose **Marin** - Reynaldo **Lewin**, Nahil **Carroll**, David **Daniels** - Angel **Rodriguez** (c) (Roderick **Paul** 63), Alejandro **Velez**, Camilo **Aguirre**, Andres **Santamaria•**, Nicolas **Munoz** (Mauricio **Gonzalez** 46) - Jose **Justavino**, Victor **Mendieta** (Orlando **Rodriguez** 69). Tr: Richard **Parra**

Cruz Azul 1

Riveros [70]

Yosgart **Gutierrez** - Melvin **Brown**, Julio Cesar **Dominguez**, Rogelio **Chavez** (Alejandro **Castro** 79), Adrian **Cortes•**, Horacio **Cervantes** - Cristian **Riveros** (c), Gerardo **Lugo** (Javier **Orozco** 57), Hector **Gutierrez** - Cesar **Villaluz** (Alejandro **Vela** 57), Mario **Ortiz**. Tr: Enrique **Meza**

Estadio Hidalgo, Pachuca

16-03-2010, 22:00, 13 000, Vaughn USA

Pachuca 2

Aguilar [72], Montes [88]

Miguel **Calero** (c) - Leobardo **Lopez**, Paul **Aguilar**, Javier **Munoz•** (Luis **Montes** 70), Carlos **Rodriguez**, Juan Carlos **Rojas** - Raul **Martinez**, Jose Francisco **Torres•**, Damian **Manso** (Edy **Brambila** 75) - Dario **Cvitanich•**, Ulises **Mendivil** (Edgar **Benitez** 60). Tr: Guillermo **Rivarola**

Comunicaciones 1

Fonseca [75p]

David Guerra - Carlos **Castrillo**, Carlos **Gallardo♦**64, Edwin **Enriquez**, Erwin **Morales** - Rigoberto **Gomez** (Jairo **Arreola** 90), Luis **Bradley**, Fredy **Thompson♦**66 - Transito **Montepeque**, Rolando **Fonseca** (c), Abner **Trigueros** (Edgar **Chinchilla** 63). Tr: Julio **Gonzalez**

Nemesio Diez, Toluca

17-03-2010, 20:00, 6946, Ward CAN

Toluca 3

Mancilla [47p], Sinha 2 [57 72]

Alfredo **Talavera** - Edgar **Duenas•**, Osvaldo **Gonzalez•**, Diego **Novaretti** - Antonio **Naelson Zinha•** (c) (Manuel **Perez** 90), Martin **Romagnoli**, Antonio **Rios** - Hector **Mancilla**, Nestor **Calderon**, Raul **Nava** (Manuel **De La Torre** 83), Isaac **Brizuela** (Carlos **Esquivel** 66). Tr: Jose Manuel **De La Torre**

Columbus Crew 2

Schelotto 2 [45p 70]

William **Hesmer** - Frankie **Hejduk** (c) (Jason **Garey** 84), Daniel **O'Rourke**, Andrew **Iro**, Eric **Brunner** - Robbie **Rogers** (Emmanuel **Ekpo** 78), Eddie **Gaven** (Emilio **Renteria** 75), Brian **Carroll•**, Adam **Moffat** - Guillermo **Barros Schelotto•**, Steven **Lenhart•♦**80. Tr: Robert **Warzycha**

Olimpico Universitario, Mexico City

18-03-2010, 22:00, 8500, Brizan TRI

UNAM Pumas 6

Barrera [3], Iñiguez 2 [20 35], Bravo [50], Palencia 2 [63 90]

Alejandro **Palacios** - Efrain **Velarde**, Marco **Palacios**, Humberto **Gonzalez**, Israel **Castro•** (c) - Jehu **Chiapas** (David **Cabrera** 89), Pablo **Barrera** (Oscar **Rojas** 68), Efrain **Juarez**, Juan Francisco **Palencia** - Ismael **Iniguez**, Martin **Bravo** (Luis **Fuentes** 82). Tr: Ricardo **Ferretti**

Marathón 1

Chiapas OG [53]

Orlin **Vallecillo** - Luis **Crisanto**, Astor **Henriquez•** (Arnol **Solorzano** 73), Juan Carlos **Garcia**, Erick **Norales**, Mariano **Acevedo**, Pastor **Martinez**, Guillermo **Ramirez** (Fernando **Castillo** 78), Wilmer **Fuentes**, Walter **Martinez** (c) - Israel **Solis** (Luis **Lopez** 68). Tr: Nicolas **Suazo**

Estadio Azul, Mexico City

17-03-2010, 22:00, 3140, Pineda HON

Cruz Azul 3

Orozco 2 [50 75], Villaluz [64]

Yosgart **Gutierrez** - Julio Cesar **Dominguez**, Adrian **Cortes**, Horacio **Cervantes**, Javier **Orozco**, Alejandro **Castro** - Gerardo **Torrado** (c), Hector **Gutierrez** (Cristian **Riveros** 59), Cesar **Villaluz•**, Alejandro **Vela** (Felix **Gonzalez** 67) - Mario **Ortiz** (Emmanuel **Villa** 46). Tr: Enrique **Meza** (Eugenio **Villazon**)

Arabe Unido 0

Carlos **Bejarano** - Reynaldo **Lewin**, Nahil **Carroll**, Eric **Davis•**, David **Daniels** - Angel **Rodriguez**, Alejandro **Velez** (Roderick **Paul** 72), Armando **Cooper**, Andres **Santamaria**, Mauricio **Gonzalez** (Victor **Mendieta** 55) - Jose **Justavino** (Publio **Rodriguez** 59). Tr: Richard **Parra**

SEMI-FINALS

Estadio Nemesio Diez, Toluca
30-03-2010, 22:00, 13 898, Arellano MEX

Toluca	**1**
	Dueñas [78]

Alfredo **Talavera** - Manuel **De La Torre** (Raul **Nava** 60), Edgar **Duenas**, Miguel **Almazan**••♦78, Diego **Novaretti**••♦81 - Antonio Naelson **Zinha** (c), Martin **Romagnoli**, Antonio **Rios**• (Vladimir **Marin** 75) - Hector **Mancilla**, Nestor **Calderon**, Isaac **Brizuela** (Carlos **Esquivel** 55). Tr: Jose Manuel **De La Torre**

Pachuca	**1**
	Cvitanich [34]

Rodolfo **Cota** - Leobardo **Lopez**, Paul **Aguilar**, Javier **Munoz**, Carlos Gerardo **Rodriguez**, Juan Carlos **Rojas** - Jaime **Correra** (c), Jose Francisco **Torres**• (Hector **Hernandez** 67), Damian **Manso**• (Gregorio **Torres** 72) - Dario **Cvitanich** (Ulises **Mendivil** 52), Edgar **Benitez**. Tr: Guillermo **Rivarola**

Estadio Hidalgo, Pachuca
7-04-2010, 20:00, 25 000, Orozco MEX

Pachuca	**1**
	Brambila [6]

Miguel **Calero** (c) - Leobardo **Lopez**, Javier **Munoz**•, Carlos Gerardo **Rodriguez**, Juan Carlos **Rojas** - Jaime **Correa**, Raul **Martinez**, Edy **Brambila** (Damian **Alvarez** 61), Damian **Manso** (Luis **Montes** 71) - Dario **Cvitanich**• (Juan Carlos **Cacho** 79), Edgar **Benitez**. Tr: Guillermo **Rivarola**

Toluca	**0**

Alfredo **Talavera** - Manuel **De La Torre** (Raul **Nava** 72), Edgar **Duenas**, Manuel **Cruzalta** (Francisco **Gamboa** 10), Osvaldo **Gonzalez**• - Antonio Naelson **Zinha**• (c), Martin **Romagnoli**•, Antonio **Rios**• (Vladimir **Marin** 32) - Hector **Mancilla**, Carlos **Esquivel**, Nestor **Calderon**. Tr: Jose Manuel **De La Torre**

Olimpico Universitario, Mexico City
31-03-2010, 22:00, 32 177, Soto MEX

UNAM Pumas	**1**
	Barrera [24]

Alejandro **Palacios** - Dario **Veron**, Marco Antonio **Palacios**, Luis **Fuentes**, Israel **Castro** (c) - Jehu **Chiapas**, Leandro Augusto **Oldoni**, Pablo **Barrera** (Ismael **Iniguez** 89), Efrain **Juarez** - Juan Francisco **Palencia** (Martin **Bravo** 66), Dante **Lopez**. Tr: Ricardo **Ferretti**

Cruz Azul	**0**

Yosgart **Gutierrez** - Edcarlos **Concencao**, Fausto **Pinto**, Melvin **Brown** (Jaime **Lozano** 53), Horacio **Cervantes** - Javier **Orozco** (Cesar **Villaluz** 76), Alejandro **Castro**, Cristian **Riveros**, Gerardo **Torrado** (c) - Emanuel **Villa**, Alejandro **Vela** (Maxi **Biancucchi** 58). Tr: Enrique **Meza**

Estadio Azul, Mexico City
6-04-2010, 22:00, 28 900, Morales MEX

Cruz Azul	**5**
	Riveros [37], Cervantes [74], Cortes [77],
	Chavez [84], Lugo [90]

Yosgart **Gutierrez**• - Fausto **Pinto**•, Melvin **Brown**, Adrian **Cortes**•, Horacio **Cervantes**, Alejandro **Castro** (Rogelio **Chavez** 44) - Cristian **Riveros** (c), Hector **Gutierrez** - Javier **Orozco** (Alejandro **Vela** 63), Emanuel **Villa**, Maxi **Biancucchi** (Gerardo **Lugo** 81). Tr: Enrique **Meza**

UNAM Pumas	**0**

Sergio **Bernal** (c) - Dario **Veron**••♦75, Fernando **Espinoza**, Luis **Fuentes**, Victor **Rosales**• - Humberto **Gonzalez**•, Jehu **Chiapas**•, Leandro Augusto **Oldoni** - Juan Francisco **Palencia** (Martin **Bravo** 45), Ismael **Iniguez**, Dante **Lopez**. Tr: Ricardo **Ferretti**

CONCACAF Champions League Final	Estadio Azul Mexico City	Wednesday 21-11-2010
Kick-off: 22:00		Attendance: 16 186

CRUZ AZUL   2 1   PACHUCA

Emanuel Villa [20], Carlos Rodriguez OG [24]

Damian Alvarez [69]

CRUZ AZUL

Blue shirts, White shorts, Blue socks

Tr: Enrique Meza

Jose de Jesus Corona

Julio Dominguez [67]   Horacio Cervantes   Melvin Brown

Rogelio Chavez [88]   Jaime Lozano
Alejandro Castro

Hector Gutierrez   Cristian Riveros (c)

Maxi Biancucchi [67]   Emanuel Villa   Javier Orozco [74]
Cesar Villaluz [83]   Mario Ortiz

Ulises Mendivil [32]   Edgar Benitez
Damian Manso

Damian Alvarez   Jose Francisco Torres

Edy Brambila [36]
[60] Juan Carlos Cacho

Raul Martinez [74]   Juan Rojas

Gregorio Torres [84]   Carlos Rodriguez   Leobardo Lopez [61]
Luis Montes

Miguel Calero (c)

Tr: Guillermo Rivarola

Gold shirts with black striped, Black shorts, Black and gold socks

PACHUCA

MATCH STATS

Cruz Azul		Pachuca
11	Shots	8
9	Shots on Goal	7
15	Fouls Committed	9
7	Corner Kicks	7
1	Caught Offside	4
52%	Possession	48%

MATCH OFFICIALS
REFEREE
Benito Archundia MEX
ASSISTANTS
Marvin Torrentera MEX
Hector Delgadillo MEX
4TH OFFICIAL
Mauricio Morales MEX

We scored two goals on their mistakes and finished the first half well. We then stopped moving the ball and doing the things we needed to do. In the end I am not happy because I didn't like my team today. With the 2-1 advantage if we think we've won, we will be very mistaken.

Enrique Meza

The result is not what we wanted but it is not bad. We were able to come back and therefore I am happy. It is 180-minute match and there are 90 minutes left. We committed two key errors but I am happy with the team. The team played a great second half.

Guillermo Rivarola

CONCACAF Champions League Final	Estadio Hidalgo Pachuca	Wednesday 28-04-2010
Kick-off: 20:00		Attendance: 26 500

PACHUCA   1   0   CRUZ AZUL

Pachuca won on away goals

Edgar Benitez 93+

PACHUCA

Tr: Guillermo Rivarola

Blue shirts with white stripes, White shorts, White socks

Miguel Calero (c)

88 Juan Rojas / Pedro Cortez   Marco Perez   Javier Munoz   Carlos Rodriguez

Damian Manso   81 Jose Francisco Torres / Victor Manon   Raul Martinez   Damian Alvarez

55 Dario Cvitanich 36 / Ulises Mendivil   Edgar Benitez 93+

69 Javier Orozco / Alejandro Vela   Emanuel Villa   61 Maxi Biancucchi / Edgar Lugo

Jaime Lozano   Cristian Riveros (c)   Hector Gutierrez

Fausto Pinto   Melvin Brown   Horacio Cervantes   78 Alejandro Castro / Rogelio Chavez

Jose de Jesus Corona

Tr: Enrique Meza

Pale yellow shirts, Navy blue shorts, Navy blue socks

CRUZ AZUL

MATCH STATS

Pachuca		Cruz Azul
19	Shots	8
8	Shots on Goal	3
9	Fouls Committed	7
7	Corner Kicks	3
1	Caught Offside	5
51%	Possession	49%

MATCH OFFICIALS

REFEREE
Marco Antonio Rodriguez MEX

ASSISTANTS
Jose Carmargo MEX
Marcos Quintero MEX

4TH OFFICIAL
Roberto Garcia MEX

We knew that it was going to be tough but we never gave up. We kept fighting until the end. It was the last play. I turned, shot and it went in...
Edgar Benitez

When we saw the ball hit the net, it was madness. There was tons of emotion. We all wanted to hug each other as the goal gave us the championship and the ticket to the Club World Cup. I really can't describe it.
Guillermo Rivarola

Life isn't over. Cruz Azul will keep on fighting. It's true that we have been through some tough times but we are professionals and you have to keep your head held high.
Enrique Meza

CFU CLUB CHAMPIONS CUP 2010

First Round Groups

Group A (In ANT)

Team		Pl	W	D	L	F	A	Pts	HAI	ANT	ANT
River Plate	PUR	3	3	0	0	12	2	**9**	3-1	4-0	5-1
Racing Gonaïves	HAI	3	1	1	1	3	4	**4**		1-0	1-1
Centro Barber	ANT	3	1	0	2	3	6	**3**			3-1
Hubentut Fortuna	ANT	3	0	1	2	3	9	**1**			

16/03/2010 - 20/03/2010

Group B (In PUR)

Team		Pl	W	D	L	F	A	Pts	PUR	VIN
Bayamón	PUR	2	1	1	0	6	2	**4**		2-2
Systems 3	VIN	2	0	1	1	2	6	**1**	0-4	
Defence Force	GUY				Moved to Group D					
Elite SC	CAY				Withdrew					

27/03/2010 - 28/03/2010

Group C (In VIN)

Team		Pl	W	D	L	F	A	Pts	VIN	SUR	BER
Joe Public	TRI	3	3	0	0	18	5	**9**	6-0	4-3	8-2
Avenues United	VIN	3	1	1	1	5	9	**4**		3-1	2-2
Leo Victor	SUR	3	1	0	2	9	9	**3**			5-2
Devonshire Cougars	BER	3	0	1	2	6	15	**1**			

19/03/2010 - 23/03/2010

Group D (In GUY)

Team		Pl	W	D	L	F	A	Pts	SUR	GUY
Alpha United	GUY	2	1	1	0	4	2	**4**	1-1	3-1
Walking Bout Co	SUR	2	1	1	0	3	2	**4**		2-1
Defence Force	GUY	2	0	0	2	2	5	**0**		
Centre Bath Estate	DMA				Withdrew					

26/03/2010 - 30/03/2010

Second round groups

Group E (In PUR)

Team		Pl	W	D	L	F	A	Pts	PUR	HAI
Puerto Rico Islanders	PUR	2	2	0	0	5	0	**6**		2-0
Racing Gonaïves	HAI	2	0	0	2	0	5	**0**	0-3	
Leo Victor					Withdrew					

16/04/2010 - 18/04/2010

Group F (In PUR)

Team		Pl	W	D	L	F	A	Pts	PUR	VIN
Bayamón	PUR	2	2	0	0	8	2	**6**		3-0
Avenues United	VIN	2	0	0	2	2	8	**0**	2-5	
Tempête St Marc					Withdrew					

13/04/2010 - 15/04/2010

Group G (In TRI)

Team		Pl	W	D	L	F	A	Pts	PUR	GUY
San Juan Jabloteh	TRI	2	2	0	0	3	0	**6**	1-0	2-0
River Plate		2	0	1	1	1	2	**1**		1-1
Alpha United		2	0	1	1	1	3	**1**		

14/04/2010 - 18/04/2010

Group G (In TRI)

Team		Pl	W	D	L	F	A	Pts	SUR	VIN
Joe Public		2	2	0	0	8	1	**6**	5-0	3-1
Walking Bout Co		2	1	0	1	2	5	**3**		2-0
Systems 3		2	0	0	2	1	5	**0**		

14/04/2010 - 18/04/2010

Final Round Group

Team	Pl	W	D	L	F	A	Pts	TRI	TRI	PUR
Puerto Rico Islanders	3	2	1	0	5	1	**7**	1-1	1-0	3-0
Joe Public	3	1	1	1	4	4	**4**		1-0	1-3
San Juan Jabloteh	3	1	0	2	3	3	**3**			4-1
Bayamón	3	1	0	2	4	8	**3**			

At Marvin Lee Stadium, Trinidad and Tobago from 5/05/2010 to 9-05-2010
Top three qualify for the 2010-11 CONCACAF Champions League

Puerto Rico Islanders PUR, Tempête St Marc HAI and San Juan Jabloteh TRI all received byes to the second round • Top scorers: **9** - Kerry Baptiste TRI, Joe Public • **5** - Jason Marcano TRI, San Juan Jabloteh & Krdail Watson CRC, Bayamon

CONCACAF CHAMPIONS LEAGUE 2010-11

Preliminary Round

Cruz Azul	MEX	3	6
San Francisco *	PAN	2	0
Toronto FC *	CAN	1	2
Motagua	HON	0	2
Santos Laguna	MEX	1	5
SanJuan Jabloteh*	TRI	0	0
Joe Public	TRI	2	4
Brujas Escazú *	CRC	2	2
Marathón	HON	3	1
Tauro *	PAN	0	2
Seattle Sounders *	USA	1	1
Isidro-Metapán	SLV	0	1
P. Rico Islanders	PUR	4	1
LA Galaxy *	USA	1	2
Deportivo FAS	SLV	1	2
Xelajú	GUA	1	0

Group Phase

Group A		Pl	W	D	L	F	A	Pts	USA	MEX	CAN	PAN
Real Salt Lake	USA	6	4	1	1	17	11	**13**		3-1	4-1	2-1
Cruz Azul	MEX	6	3	1	2	15	9	**10**	5-4		0-0	2-0
Toronto FC	CAN	6	2	2	2	5	7	**8**	1-1	2-1		1-0
Arabe Unido	PAN	6	1	0	5	4	14	**3**	2-3	0-6	1-0	

Group B		Pl	W	D	L	F	A	Pts	MEX	USA	GUA	TRI
Santos Laguna	MEX	6	4	1	1	19	7	**13**		1-0	6-1	5-1
Columbus Crew	USA	6	4	0	2	10	4	**12**	1-0		1-0	3-0
Municipal	GUA	6	2	2	2	9	13	**8**	2-2	2-1		1-1
Joe Public	TRI	6	0	1	5	7	21	**1**	2-5	1-4	2-3	

Group C		Pl	W	D	L	F	A	Pts	MEX	CRC	HON	USA
Monterrey	MEX	6	5	1	0	11	4	**16**		1-0	2-0	3-2
Dep. Saprissa	CRC	6	3	1	2	11	7	**10**	2-2		4-1	2-0
Marathón	HON	6	2	0	4	5	11	**6**	0-1	2-1		2-1
Seattle Sounders	USA	6	1	0	5	6	11	**3**	0-2	1-2	2-0	

Group D		Pl	W	D	L	F	A	Pts	HON	MEX	PUR	SLV
Olimpia	HON	6	4	1	1	12	7	**13**		2-1	3-0	2-0
Toluca	MEX	6	3	1	2	15	5	**10**	4-0		3-0	5-0
P. Rico Islanders	PUR	6	2	2	2	8	10	**8**	1-1	3-2		4-1
Deportivo FAS	SLV	6	0	2	4	2	15	**2**	1-4	0-0	0-0	

Quarter-finals

Cruz Azul *
Santos

Toluca *
Monterrey

Columbus Crew*
Real Salt Lake

Dep. Saprissa *
Olimpia

* Home team in the first leg • Quarter-finals to be played 22-24/02/2011 & 1-3/03/2011 • Semi-finals to be played 15-17/03/2011 & 5-7/04/2011
Final to be played on 19-21/04/2011 & 26-28/04/2011

CONCACAF CHAMPIONS LEAGUE 2010-11
PRELIMINARY ROUND

Augustin Sanchez, La Chorrera
27-07-2010, 22:00, 725, Brizan TRI

San Francisco — **2**
Jimenez [20], Torres [44]

William **Negrete** - Rolando **Algandona**•, Amir **White**• (Boris **Alfaro** 60), Osvaldo **Gonzalez**•, Edgardo **Panezo** (Wess **Torres** 67) - Manuel **Torres**, Ricardo **Phillips**•, Eduardo **Jimenez**•, James **Sanches** - Gabriel **Torres** (Luis **Olivardia** 73), Johan **De Avila**. Tr: Gary **Stempel**

Cruz Azul — **3**
Villa 3 [3 54 71]

Yosgart **Gutierrez** - Julio Cesar **Dominguez**, Horacio **Cervantes**, Alejandro **Castro** - Gonzalo **Pineda**•, Hector **Gutierrez**•, Gienir **Garcia**•, Cesar **Villaluz** - Maxi **Biancucchi** (Christian **Gimenez** 54), Alejandro **Vela** (Alam **Bello** 54), Emmanuel **Villa**. Tr: Enrique **Meza**

Estadio Azul, Mexico City
3-08-2010, 20:00, 5000, Quesada CRC

Cruz Azul — **6**
Orozco 3 [11 45 84], Biancucchi 2 [18 92+], Garcia [71]

Yosgart **Gutierrez** (c) - Joel **Huiqui** (Hiram **Mondragon** 23), Julio **Dominguez**, Javier **Orozco**, Alejandro **Castro**• - Cesar **Villaluz**, Hector **Gutierrez**, Gienir **Garcia** - Maxi **Biancucchi**, Christian **Gimenez** (Luis **Alanis** 66), Alejandro **Vela** (Javier **Aquino** 57). Tr: Enrique **Meza**

San Francisco — **0**

William **Negrete** - Carlos **Rivera**, Rolando **Algandona** (Amir **White** 24), Osvaldo **Gonzalez**, Wess **Torres** (Luis Felipe **Olivardia** 66) - Manuel **Torres**• (c), Ricardo **Phillips**•, James **Sanches**, Eduardo **Jimenez** - Gabriel **Torres**, Johan **De Avila** (Edgardo **Panezo** 46). Tr: Gary **Stempel**

BMO Field, Toronto
27-07-2010, 20:00, 18 891, Vaughn USA

Toronto FC — **1**
Barrett [20]

Stefan **Frei** - Nana **Attakora**, Adrian **Cann**, Joseph **Nane**, Max **Usanov** (Dan **Gargan** 46), Nick **Garcia** - Julian **DeGuzman**, Jacob **Peterson**, Dwayne **DeRosario** - O'Brian **White** (Miguel Angel **Ferrer** 63), Chad **Barrett** (Maicon **Dos Santos**• 46). Tr: Preki **Radosaljevic**

Motagua — **0**

Donaldo **Morales** - Guillermo **Diaz**, Emilio **Izaguirre**, Sergio **Mendoza**, Johnny **Leveron**• - Mauricio **Weber** (Milton **Reyes** 76), Mario Ivan **Guerrero**, Amado **Guevara** (Ronald **Martinez** 46), Jorge **Claros** - Georgie **Welcome**, Charles **Cordoba** (Javier **Portillo** 46). Tr: Ramon **Maradiaga**

Tiburcio Andino, Tegucigalpa
3-08-2010, 20:00, 8000, Rodriguez PAN

Motagua — **2**
Guevara 2 [6 64]

Donaldo **Morales** - Emilio **Izaguirre**, Sergio **Mendoza**, Guillermo **Diaz** (Milton **Reyes** 84), Johnny **Leveron** - Jorge **Claros**, Mario Ivan **Guerrero**, Mauricio **Weber** (Javier **Portillo** 65), Amado **Guevara** (c) - Charles **Cordoba** (Shannon **Welcome** 62), **Marcelo Dos Santos**. Tr: Ramon **Maradiaga**

Toronto FC — **2**
De Rosario [59], Barrett [79]

Stefan **Frei**• - Nana **Attakora**, Dan **Gargan**, Adrian **Cann**, Joseph **Nane**, Nick **Garcia** - Julian **DeGuzman**, Dwayne **DeRosario** (c), Nick **LaBrocca** (Jacob **Peterson**• 72), Doneil **Henry**• (Maicon **Dos Santos** 30) - Chad **Barrett** (Miguel Angel **Ferrer** 81). Tr: Preki **Radosaljevic**

Marvin Lee, Tunapuna
27-07-2010, 20:00, 763, Lancaster GUY

San Juan Jabloteh	0

Cleon John - Robert Primus, Noel Williams, Sheldon Bateau, Leslie Russell (Karlon Murray 4), Jamal Jack - Marvin Oliver (c), Kennedy Hinkson (Atualla Guerra 58), Ronaldo - Jason Marcano, Hector Sam (Willis Plaza 64). Tr: Terry Fenwick

Santos Laguna	1
	Ruiz 83

Miguel Becerra (c) - Juan Pablo Santiago, Rafael Figueroa, Jose Antonio Olvera• (Carlos Morales 68), Uriel Alvarez - Jose Reyes• (Jose Maria Cardenas 64), Francisco Torres, Jaime Toledo - Rodrigo Ruiz•, Rodolfo Salinas (Jorge Estrada 72), Oribe Peralta. Tr: Ruben Omar Romano

---

Marvin Lee, Tunapuna
5-08-2010, 20:00, 500, Ledgister JAM

Joe Public	4
	Baptiste 8, Mitchell 39, Lewis 45, Toussaint 76

Glenroy Samuel - Trent Noel, Carlyle Mitchell, Makan Hislop, Keion Goodridge• - Kerry Baptiste (Marcus Joseph 75), Hayden Tinto (Andre Toussaint 64), Kareem Young, Yu Hoshide, Jevon Morris• - Micah Lewis (Nigel Daniel• 78). Tr: Derek King

Brujas Escazú	2
	Arias 63, Nunez 72

Danny Carvajal - Andres Nunez, Heiner Mora (Yendrik Ruiz 46), Roy Smith, Brandon Poltronieri - Keilor Soto, Yosimar Arias, Fabricio Chavarria - Pablo Brenes, William Sunsing (Jose Luis Cordero 78), Bryan Vega (Christian Lagos• 58). Tr: Jose Luis Torres

---

Qwest Field, Seattle
28-07-2010, 22:00, 17 228, Arellano MEX

Seattle Sounders	1
	Montero 60

Kasey Keller - Leonardo Gonzalez, Tyrone Marshall, James Riley•, Taylor Graham - Peter Vagenas• (Osvaldo Alonso• 15), Sanna Nyassi•, Michael Seamon - Jonathan Jaqua (Fredy Montano 60), Roger Levesque, Miguel Montano (Steve Zakuani 57). Tr: Sigi Schmid

Isidro-Metapán	0

Alvaro Misael Alfaro - Ernesto Aquino, Erick Prado•, Moises Menendez (Mark Blanco 63) - Jose Alvarado, Rodolfo Suarez• (Andres Flores 80), Hector Mejia, Oscar Jimenez, Emerson Umana• - Anel Canales, Josue Odir Flores (Jorge Moran 87). Tr: Edwin Portillo

---

Juan Ramon Loubriel, Bayamon
4-08-2010, 20:00, 12 993, Taylor BRB

Puerto Rico Islanders	1
	Foley 33p

William Gaudette - David Horst, Marco Velez, Scott Jones (Kevon Villaroel 44), Richard Martinez - Noah Delgado (Logan Emory 69), Osei Telesford•, Christopher Nurse - Joshua Hansen, Nicholas Addlery, David Foley (Kendall Jagdeosingh 80). Tr: Colin Clarke

Los Angeles Galaxy	2
	Velez OG 37, Franklin 84

Donovan Ricketts - Todd Dunivant, Alex Cazumba•, Sean Franklin, Omar Gonzalez - Landon Donovan, Dema Kovalenko - Edson Buddle• (Chris Klein 75), Bryan Jordan (Alan Gordon• 58), Tristan Bowen (Michael Magee 67), Leonardo Da Silva•. Tr: Bruce Arena

---

Corona, Torreón
4-08-2010, 22:00, 10 000, Ward CAN

Santos Laguna	5
	Reyes 2 3 80, Salinas 46, Quintero 73,
	Gonzalez 83

Miguel Becerra (c) - Juan Santiago, Rafael Figueroa, Jose Olvera, Uriel Alvarez (Jonathan Lacerda 54) - Jose Reyes•, Francisco Torres, Jaime Toledo• - Rodrigo Ruiz, Rodolfo Salinas (Arnulfo Gonzalez 64), Oribe Peralta (Carlos Quintero 52). Tr: Ruben Omar Romano

San Juan Jabloteh	0

Cleon John - Robert Primus, Sheldon Bateau, Leslie Russell, Jamal Jack - Elijah Manners (Johan Peltier 74), Marvin Oliver• (c), Atualla Guerra, Ronaldo - Jason Marcano• (Jerrel Britto 74), Hector Sam (Willis Plaza 48). Tr: Terry Fenwick

---

Rommel Fernandez, Panama City
28-07-2010, 20:00, 1237, Mejia SLV

Tauro	0

Varcan Sterling - Luis Moreno, Leonel Parris•, Eduardo Dasent•, Jassir Arango - Juan Perez (Cristian Vega 39), Jean McLean•, Marcos Sanchez, Luis Renteria•, Alexander Moreno (Isaias Olmedo 64) - Temistocles Perez (Eusebio Paredes 65). Tr: Juan Carlos Cubilla

Marathón	3
	Cardozo 2 24 59, Palacios 35

Shane Orio - Milton Palacios, Astor Henriquez, Erick Norales, Mariano Acevedo, Carlos Palacios•, Adolfo Machado - Mario Berrios (Fernando Castillo 85), Reinier Mayorquin• (Carlos Mejia 75) - Randy Diamond (Hector Amarilla 76), Claudo Cardozo. Tr: Nicolas Suazo

---

Cuscatlan, San Salvador
3-08-2010, 22:00, 1083, Pineda HON

Isidro-Metapán	1
	Canales 17

Jose Luis Gonzalez - Ernesto Aquino•, Erick Prado, Milton Molina - Jose Ricardo Alvarado (Cesar Larios 79), Rodolfo Suarez (c), Hector Mejia, Oscar Jimenez (Andres Flores 89), Emerson Umana (Mark Blanco• 71) - Anel Canales, Josue Odir Flores. Tr: Edwin Portillo

Seattle Sounders	1
	Fernandez 74

Kasey Keller - Leonardo Gonzalez, Patrick Ianni, Nathan Sturgis, Tyrone Marshall•, James Riley - Osvaldo Alonso, Sanna Nyassi• (Alvaro Fernandez 63), Steve Zakuani (Jonathan Jaqua 63) - Fredy Montero, Roger Levesque• (Michael Seamon 74). Tr: Sigi Schmid

---

Cuscatlan, San Salvador
29-07-2010, 22:00, 4200, Chacon MEX

Deportivo FAS	1
	Reyes 44

Luis Contreras - Mardoqueo Henriquez•, Victor Velasquez (c), Juan Carlos Moscoso•, Miguel Granadino (Ramon Solis 70), Carlos Aparicio - Rodolfo Cordoba (Gilberto Murgas 57), Roberto Pena, Christian Alvarez - Williams Reyes (Ricardo Ulloa 85), Alejandro Bentos•. Tr: Alberto Rujana

Xelajú	1
	Crossa 42

Marvin Barrios - Carlos De Castro♦ 56, Miguel Fernandez, Johny Giron• - Milton Leal - Hector De Mata, Carlos Figueroa (Gregory Ruiz 71), Edgar Cotto, Julio Estacuy (c) - Israel Silva (Kristian Guzman 63), Nelson Crossa (Minor Lopez 86). Tr: Horacio Cordero

---

Eladio Cordero, Heredia
28-07-2010, 22:00, 253, Guerra GUA

Brujas Escazú	2
	Nunez 2, Cordero 66

Luis Sequeira - Andres Nunez, Heiner Mora, Esteban Maitland (c) (Jameson Scott 63), Roy Smith - Jose Luis Cordero (Brandon Poltronieri• 76), Keilor Soto, Yosimar Arias, Fabricio Chavarria - William Sunsing, Steven Calderon• (Christian Lagos 80). Tr: Jose Luis Torres

Joe Public	2
	Baptiste 13, Noel 91+

Glenroy Samuel - Trent Noel, Carlyle Mitchell, Makan Hislop, Keion Goodridge - Kerry Baptiste• (c), Hayden Tinto• (Conrad Smith 80), Kareem Young, Yu Hoshide (Marcus Joseph 69), Jevon Morris• - Andre Toussaint• (Micah Lewis 74). Tr: Derek King

---

Olimpico, San Pedro Sula
4-08-2010, 22:00, 2528, Geiger USA

Marathón	1
	Cardozo 24

Shane Orio - Milton Palacios, Astor Henriquez•, Erick Norales•, Mariano Acevedo, Carlos Palacios (Fernando Castillo 63), Adolfo Machado - Mario Berrios (c), Reinier Mayorquin• (Carlos Mejia 52) - Randy Diamond (Luis Santa Maria 83), Claudo Cardozo. Tr: Nicolas Suazo

Tauro	2
	Renteria 2 26 45

Varcan Sterling - Luis Moreno (c), Leonel Parris, Sergio Thompson•, Jassir Arango - Cristian Vega (Juan De Dios Perez 76), Jhoan Melo• (Eusebio Paredes 68), Marcos Sanchez, Luis Renteria, Alexander Moreno (Isaias Olmedo 55) - Temistocles Perez•. Tr: Juan Carlos Cubilla

---

Home Depot Center, Carson
27-07-2010, 22:00, 6783, Bogle JAM

Los Angeles Galaxy	1
	Martinez OG 83

Joshua Saunders - Gregg Berhalter (Tristan Bowen 63), Sean Franklin, Adolph De La Garza (Michael Stephens 38) - Chris Birchall, Landon Donovan, Eddie Lewis, Vitor Pereira Juninho - Alan Gordon (Alex Cazumba 63), Edson Buddle, Leonardo Da Silva. Tr: Bruce Arena

Puerto Rico Islanders	4
	Foley 26, Addlery 2 45 81, Hansen 56

William Gaudette - David Horst, Marco Velez, Scott Jones, Richard Martinez - Noah Delgado• (Kevon Villaroel 71), Osei Telesford, Christopher Nurse - Joshua Hansen (Logan Emory 86), Nicholas Addlery, David Foley (Kendall Jagdeosingh 78). Tr: Colin Clarke

---

Mateo Flores, Guatemala City
5-08-2010, 22:00, 8000, Cruz CRC

Xelajú	0

Marvin Barrios - Miguel Fernandez•, Johny Giron, Milton Leal• - Hector De Mata• (Osmar Lopez 45), Carlos Figueroa, Edgar Cotto (Marco Ciani 77), Julio Estacuy (c), Kristian Guzman• (Minor Lopez 66) - Israel Silva, Nelson Crossa. Tr: Horacio Cordero

Deportivo FAS	2
	Bentos 2 41 77

Luis Contreras - Mardoqueo Henriquez, Manuel Salazar, Victor Velasquez (c), Juan Carlos Moscoso, Miguel Granadino, Carlos Aparicio (Gilberto Murgas• 66) - Roberto Pena•, Christian Alvarez (Rodolfo Cordoba 82) - Williams Reyes (Eliseo Salamanca 71), Alejandro Bentos•. Tr: Alberto Rujana

GROUP A		Pl	W	D	L	F	A	Pts	USA	MEX	CAN	PAN
Real Salt Lake	USA	6	4	1	1	17	11	13		3-1	4-1	2-1
Cruz Azul	MEX	6	3	1	2	15	9	10	5-4		0-0	2-0
Toronto FC	CAN	6	2	2	2	5	7	8	1-1	2-1		1-0
Arabe Unido	PAN	6	1	0	5	4	14	3	2-3	0-6	1-0	

BMO Field, Toronto
17-08-2010, 20:00, 16 862, Campbell JAM

Toronto FC — **2**

Saric [3], Mista [44]

Jon Conway - Nana Attakora, Raivis Hscanovics, Max Usanov, Adrian Cann - Julian DeGuzman, Dwayne DeRosario•(c), Martin Saric (Jacob Peterson• 65), Nick LaBrocca - Miguel Angel Ferrer (Joseph Nane 67), O'Brian White (Fuad Ibrahim 78). Tr: Preki Radosaljevic

Cruz Azul — **1**

Gimenez [90]

Yosgart Gutierrez (c) - Fausto Pinto•, Julio Dominguez, Horacio Cervantes, Alejandro Castro - Gonzalo Pineda (Gerardo Torrado• 46), Hector Gutierrez (Javier Orozco 63), Cesar Villaluz - Emmanuel Villa, Alejandro Vela (Christian Gimenez• 46), Maxi Bianchucchi. Tr: Enrique Meza

Estadio Azul, Mexico City
25-08-2010, 20:00, 3400, Moncada HON

Cruz Azul — **5**

Orozco 4 [5 76 87 89], Gimenez [93+]

Yosgart Gutierrez (c) - Fausto Pinto, Julio Cesar Dominguez, Horacio Cervantes•, Javier Orozco, Alejandro Castro - Gonzalo Pineda (Rogelio Chavez 75), Gerardo Torrado, Cesar Villaluz (Christian Gimenez 46) - Emmanuel Villa•, Maxi Bianchucchi• (Alejandro Vela 45). Tr: Enrique Meza

Real Salt Lake — **4**

Saborio 2 [23p 43], Espindola [64], Johnson [92+]

Nick Rimando - Christopher Wingert, Nathaniel Borchers, Rauwshan McKenzie - Will Johnson, Kyle Beckerman (c), Robert Russell, Javier Morales (Andrew Williams 73), Nelson Gonzalez (Ned Grabavoy 45) - Alvaro Saborio, Edgar Espindola (Robert Findley• 66). Tr: Jason Kreis

Estadio Azul, Mexico City
21-09-2010, 22:00, 5280, Guerra GUA

Cruz Azul — **0**

Yosgart Gutierrez - Fausto Pinto•♦80, Horacio Cervantes (c), Javier Orozco, Alejandro Castro (Rogelio Chavez 71), Nestor Araujo - Gonzalo Pineda, Hector Gutierrez (Christian Gimenez• 64), Cesar Villaluz (Gerardo Torrado• 53) - Alejandro Vela, Maxi Bianchucchi. Tr: Enrique Meza

Toronto FC — **0**

Jon Conway• - Nick Garcia•, Ty Harden, Raivis Hscanovics, Adrian Cann (c), Joseph Nane (Martin Saric 9) (Dwayne DeRosario 30) - Julian DeGuzman•, Jacob Peterson, Nicholas Lindsay• (Dan Gargan• 57) - Fuad Ibrahim•, O'Brian White. Tr: Nick Dasovic

Estadio Azul, Mexico City
28-09-2010, 20:00, 5015, Quesada CRC

Cruz Azul — **2**

Villa [1], Cortes [47p]

Jose Corona - Julio Dominguez, Joel Huiqui, Rogelio Chavez (Alejandro Castro 83), Adrian Cortes, Javier Orozco (Javier Aquino 62) - Gonzalo Pineda•, Hector Gutierrez•, Cesar Villaluz (c) (Alejandro Vela 78) - Emmanuel Villa, Maxi Bianchucchi. Tr: Enrique Meza

Arabe Unido — **0**

Jose Calderon - Reynaldo Anderson•, Eric Davis, Harold Cummings•, Felix Gondola• - Armando Cooper (c), Andres Santamaria, Paul Roderick (Axel Garude 88), Luis Jaramillo - Mario Angulo (Manuel Mosquera• 53), Williams Aguilar (Oscar Londono 63). Tr: Richard Parra

Rio Rinto Stadium, Sandy
18-08-2010, 22:00, 10 626, Ward CAN

Real Salt Lake — **2**

Saborio 2 [45 94+]

Nick Rimando - Christopher Wingert•, Nathaniel Borchers, Jamison Olave - Will Johnson (Nelson Gonzalez 57), Kyle Beckerman (c), Andrew Williams•, Robert Russell• (Ned Grabavoy 73), Javier Morales - Robert Findley (Edgar Espindola 45), Alvaro Saborio. Tr: Jason Kreis

Arabe Unido — **1**

OG [13]

Jose Calderon - Nahil Carroll•28, Eric Davis, Rolan De La Cruz - Armando Cooper• (c) (Paul Roderick 53), Andres Santamaria•♦90, Luis Jaramillo (Reynaldo Anderson 32) - Jose Justavino•, Victor Mendieta (Publio Rodriguez• 25), Mario Angulo, Fidel Caesar•. Tr: Richard Parra

Rommel Fernandez, Panama City
15-09-2010, 22:00, 2975, Vaughn USA

Arabe Unido — **0**

Jose Calderon - Nahil Carroll, Rolan De La Cruz (Publio Rodriguez 54), Harold Cummings - Armando Cooper• (c), Andres Santamaria, Jose Justavino (Mario Angulo 54) - Manuel Mosquera•, Victor Mendieta, Fidel Caesar, Oscar Londono (Luis Jaramillo 37). Tr: Richard Parra

Cruz Azul — **6**

Orozco 3 [10 22 27], Villa 2 [67 80], Biancucchi [86]

Jose de Jesus Corona - Fausto Pinto, Julio Dominguez, Horacio Cervantes (Maxi Bianchucchi 60), Alejandro Castro - Gerardo Torrado (Cesar Villaluz 46), Hector Gutierrez - Emmanuel Villa•, Christian Gimenez (Adrian Cortes 71), Alejandro Vela. Tr: Enrique Meza

Rommel Fernandez, Panama City
22-09-2010, 20:00, 500, Archundia MEX

Arabe Unido — **2**

Aguilar [2], Angulo [51p]

Jose Marin - Nahil Carroll• (Manuel Mosquera 46), Harold Cummings - Andres Santamaria, Paul Roderick (Rolan De La Cruz• 46), Luis Jaramillo•, Jose Justavino• - Mario Angulo, Fidel Caesar, Williams Aguilar, Oscar Londono (Publio Rodriguez 46). Tr: Richard Parra

Real Salt Lake — **3**

Johnson 2 [10 43], Saborio [36]

Nick Rimando - Anthony Beltran, Jamison Olave, Christopher Schuler - Will Johnson, Kyle Beckerman (c), Ned Grabavoy, Robert Russell, Nelson Gonzalez• (Collen Warner 81) - Alvaro Saborio (Jean Alexandre• 74), Edgar Espindola•♦87 (Robert Findley 60). Tr: Jason Kreis

BMO Field, Toronto
19-10-2010, 20:00, 10 385, Orozco MEX

Toronto FC — **2**

Attakora [30]

Jon Conway - Dan Gargan•, Nick Garcia•, Nana Attakora (Ty Harden 46), Doneil Henry•, Ashtone Morgan• - Julian DeGuzman (Oscar Cordon 66), Dwayne DeRosario (c), Nick LaBrocca, Nicholas Lindsay• (O'Brian White 80) - Fuad Ibrahim. Tr: Nick Dasovic

Arabe Unido — **0**

Jose Calderon - Harold Cummings, Felix Gondola• - Armando Cooper, Paul Roderick, Jose Gomez, Rigoberto Nino (Luis Jaramillo 55) - Mario Angulo, Jose Gonzalez (Andres Santamaria 46), Fidel Caesar•, Oscar Londono• (Sabat Gerardo 76). Tr: Richard Parra

Agustin Sanchez, La Chorrera
24-08-2010, 22:00, 501, Mejia SLV

Arabe Unido — **1**

Cesar [40]

Jose Calderon - Reynaldo Anderson•, Eric Davis (Publio Rodriguez 32), Harold Cummings, Rolan De La Cruz - Armando Cooper (c), Jose Justavino (Jose Gomez 86) - Manuel Mosquera, Mario Angulo, Fidel Caesar, Oscar Londono• (Paul Roderick 61). Tr: Richard Parra

Toronto FC — **0**

Milos Kocic - Ty Harden, Nana Attakora, Raivis Hscanovics•, Max Usanov• - Julian DeGuzman (c), Martin Saric (Joseph Nane 60), Nick Labrocca•50, Andres Santamaria•♦90, O'Brian White (Dwayne DeRosario 46). Tr: Preki Radosaljevic

Rio Rinto Stadium, Sandy
15-09-2010, 22:00, 11 579, Morales MEX

Real Salt Lake — **4**

Beckerman [21], Olave [40], Saborio [69p], Araujo [80]

Nick Rimando - Christopher Wingert, Nathaniel Borchers, Jamison Olave - Will Johnson, Kyle Beckerman• (c), Andrew Williams, Robert Russell (Anthony Beltran 28), Nelson Gonzalez (Ned Grabavoy 67) - Robert Findley, Alvaro Saborio (Paulo De Araujo 73). Tr: Jason Kreis

Toronto FC — **1**

Santos [8]

Stefan Frei - Dan Gargan, Nick Garcia, Ty Harden, Adrian Cann - Julian DeGuzman, Jacob Peterson (Miguel Ferrer 60♦65), Dwayne DeRosario (c), Martin Saric• (Nicholas Lindsay 45) - Maicon Dos Santos, O'Brian White (Chad Barrett 72). Tr: Nick Dasovic

BMO Field, Toronto
28-09-2010, 20:00, 10 581, Taylor BRB

Toronto FC — **1**

Peterson [20]

Jon Conway - Dan Gargan, Nick Garcia, Nana Attakora, Max Usanov•, Adrian Cann - Julian DeGuzman, Jacob Peterson (Miguel Ferrer 65), Dwayne DeRosario (c), Nick LaBrocca (O'Brian White 77) - Maicon Dos Santos (Chad Barrett 31). Tr: Nick Dasovic

Real Salt Lake — **1**

Morales [67]

Nick Rimando - Christopher Wingert, Nathaniel Borchers, Jamison Olave - Will Johnson (Ned Grabavoy 62), Kyle Beckerman• (c), Andrew Williams, Robert Russell, Collen Warner• (Javier Morales 46) - Robert Findley, Alvaro Saborio (Jean Alexandre 83). Tr: Jason Kreis

Rio Rinto Stadium, Sandy
19-10-2010, 22:00, 20 463, Aguilar SLV

Real Salt Lake — **3**

Araujo 2 [43 67], Warner [69]

Kyle Reynish - Nathaniel Borchers (c), Anthony Beltran, Rauwshan McKenzie - Will Johnson, Andrew Williams, Jean Alexandre•, Paulo De Araujo (Javier Morales 77), Luis Gil (Ned Grabavoy 46), Collen Warner• - Pablo Campos (Robert Findley 66). Tr: Jason Kreis

Cruz Azul — **1**

Villaluz [71]

Yosgart Gutierrez - Julio Dominguez (Rogelio Chavez 75), Joel Huiqui•, Adrian Cortes (Fausto Pinto 55), Horacio Cervantes, Javier Orozco, Alejandro Castro - Gerardo Torrado (c), Cesar Villaluz, Christian Gimenez• - Javier Aquino (Alejandro Vela 63). Tr: Enrique Meza♦76

GROUP B		Pl	W	D	L	F	A	Pts	MEX	USA	GUA	TRI
Santos Laguna	MEX	6	4	1	1	19	7	**13**		1-0	6-1	5-1
Columbus Crew	USA	6	4	0	2	10	4	**12**	1-0		1-0	3-0
Municipal	GUA	6	2	2	2	9	13	**8**	2-2	2-1		1-1
Joe Public	TRI	6	0	1	5	7	21	**1**	2-5	1-4	2-3	

Marvin Lee, Tunapuna
18-08-2010, 20:00, 900, Moreno PAN

Joe Public — 2
Hislop [11], Hoshide [44]

Glenroy **Samuel** - Trent **Noel**, Makan **Hislop**, Nigel **Daniel**, Keion **Goodridge** - Kerry **Baptiste** (c) (Andre **Toussaint** 71), Hayden **Tinto** (Gason **Gregory** 56), Marcus **Joseph** (Jason **Springer**• 31), Kareem **Young**, Yu **Hoshide** - Micah **Lewis**. Tr: Derek King

Santos Laguna — 5
Cardenas 4 [9 24 66 76], Enriquez [90]

Miguel **Becerra** (c) - Juan Pablo **Santiago**, Rafael **Figueroa**, Jose **Olvera** - Francisco **Torres**, Jaime **Toledo** - Rodrigo **Ruiz**, Jose Maria **Cardenas**, Rodolfo **Salinas** (Enrique **Lopez** 66), Oribe **Peralta** (Juan Carlos **Enriquez** 80), Alejandro **Martinez** (Jose **Hoyo** 55). Tr: Ruben Omar **Romano**

Crew Stadium, Columbus
18-08-2010, 20:00, 5745, Orozco MEX

Columbus Crew — 1
Ekpo [14]

Andrew **Gruenebaum** - Chad **Marshall**, Frankie **Hejduk** (c), Daniel **O'Rourke**•, Andrew **Iro**, Shawn **Francis** - Eddie **Gaven**, Adam **Moffat** (Emilio **Renteria**• 70), Emmanuel **Ekpo** (Leandre **Griffit** 84) - Jason **Garey**, Guillermo **Barros Schelotto**. Tr: Robert **Warzycha**

Municipal — 0

Jaime **Penedo** - Gustavo **Cabrera**, Yony **Flores**, Pablo **Melgar** (Juan Jose **Castillo** 46), Pablo **Solorzano** (Marvin **Avila** 46), Jaime **Vides** - Guillermo **Ramirez**• (Carlos **Castillo** 75), Mario **Rodriguez**, Sergio **Guevara**, Cristian **Noriega**, Gonzalo **Romero** (c). Tr: Guilherme **Farinha**

Nueva Corona, Torreón
24-08-2010, 20:00, 4700, Rodriguez PAN

Santos Laguna — 1
Estrada [93+]

Miguel **Becerra** (c) - Juan Pablo **Santiago**• (Carlos **Morales**• 45), Rafael **Figueroa**, Jose **Olvera**, Jonathan **Lacerda** - Fernando **Arce**, Francisco **Torres** (Jorge **Estrada** 71), Jaime **Toledo** (Carlos **Quintero** 58) - Rodrigo **Ruiz**, Jose Maria **Cardenas**, Oribe **Peralta**. Tr: Ruben Omar **Romano**

Columbus Crew — 0

Andrew **Gruenebaum**• - Andrew **Iro**•, Eric **Brunner**, Shawn **Francis** - Leandre **Griffit**• (Eddie **Gaven** 67), Duncan **Oughton**, Brian **Carroll** (c), Kevin **Burns**, Dilaver **Duka** (Emmanuel **Ekpo** 74) - Emilio **Renteria**• (Jason **Garey**• 71), Steven **Lenhart**. Tr: Robert **Warzycha**

Mateo Flores, Guatemala City
26-08-2010, 22:00, 2498, Toledo USA

Municipal — 1
Rodriguez [77]

Jaime **Penedo** - Gustavo **Cabrera**, Yony **Flores**, Jaime **Vides** - Guillermo **Ramirez** (Carlos **Castillo** 88), Mario **Rodriguez**, Sergio **Guevara**, Cristian **Noriega**, Gonzalo **Romero** (c) (Pedro **Samayoa** 58) - Marvin **Avila** (Darwin **Oliva** 70), Juan Jose **Castillo**•. Tr: Guilherme **Farinha**

Joe Public — 1
Lewis [93+]

Marvin **Phillip** - Trent **Noel**, Jason **Springer**• (Keion **Goodridge** 75), Carlyle **Mitchell**, Makan **Hislop** - Kerry **Baptiste** (c), Gason **Gregory**, Kareem **Young**, Yu **Hoshide** (Nigel **Daniel** 66), Jevon **Morris**•80 - Andre **Toussaint** (Micah **Lewis** 56). Tr: Derek **King**

Crew Stadium, Columbus
14-09-2010, 20:00, 5445, Lopez GUA

Columbus Crew — 3
Griffit [47], Garey [51], Lenhart [79]

Andrew **Gruenebaum** - Chad **Marshall** (Andrew **Iro** 80), Eric **Brunner**, Shawn **Francis**• - Leandre **Griffit**, Duncan **Oughton** (c), Kevin **Burns**, Adam **Moffat**, Emmanuel **Ekpo** (Dilaver **Duka** 62) - Jason **Garey**, Andres **Mendoza** (Steven **Lenhart** 65). Tr: Robert **Warzycha**

Joe Public — 0

Marvin **Phillip** - Carlyle **Mitchell**• (Kareem **Moses** 85), Makan **Hislop**, Nigel **Daniel**, Keion **Goodridge** - Kerry **Baptiste** (c), Gason **Gregory**, Hayden **Tinto**, Marcus **Joseph**, Yu **Hoshide** (Kenaz **Williams**• 80) - Micah **Lewis** (Marvin **Manswell** 74). Tr: Derek **King**

Mateo Flores, Guatemala City
14-09-2010, 22:00, 10 414, Quesada CRC

Municipal — 2
Rodriguez [28], Castillo [87p]

Jaime **Penedo**• - Gustavo **Cabrera**•, Yony **Flores**, Jaime **Vides** - Guillermo **Ramirez** (Darwin **Oliva** 45), Mario **Rodriguez**•, Sergio **Guevara**, Cristian **Noriega**, Gonzalo **Romero** (c) - Marvin **Avila** (Carlos **Castillo** 61), Juan Jose **Castillo** (David **Aroche** 63). Tr: Guilherme **Farina**

Santos Laguna — 2
Ruiz [8p], Peralta [13]

Miguel **Becerra** (c) - Juan Pablo **Santiago**, Rafael **Figueroa**, Jose **Olvera**, Jonathan **Lacerda**• - Fernando **Arce**•, Francisco **Torres** (Carlos **Morales** 63), Jaime **Toledo** (Jorge **Estrada** 61) - Rodrigo **Ruiz**, Rodolfo **Salinas** (Jose Maria **Cardenas** 45), Oribe **Peralta**•. Tr: Ruben Omar **Romano**

Crew Stadium, Columbus
21-09-2010, 20:00, 6298, Campbell JAM

Columbus Crew — 1
Mendoza [87]

Andrew **Gruenebaum** - Chad **Marshall** (Eric **Brunner** 67), Frankie **Hejduk**• (c), Andrew **Iro**, Shawn **Francis** - Eddie **Gaven**•, Brian **Carroll**, Kevin **Burns**•, Emmanuel **Ekpo** - Andres **Mendoza** (Steven **Lenhart** 88), Emilio **Renteria** (Jason **Garey** 46). Tr: Robert **Warzycha**

Santos Laguna — 0

Miguel **Becerra** - Juan Pablo **Santiago**, Jorge **Estrada** (c), Rafael **Figueroa**, Jose **Olvera** (Jose Maria **Cardenas** 68), Jonathan **Lacerda** - Francisco **Torres** (Fernando **Arce** 71), Jaime **Toledo** - Rodrigo **Ruiz**, Oribe **Peralta**•, Carlos **Quintero** (Daniel **Luduena** 46). Tr: Ruben Omar **Romano**

Marvin Lee, Tunapuna
23-09-2010, 20:00, 500, Aguilar SLV

Joe Public — 2
Toussaint 2 [15 67]

Marvin **Phillip** - Trent **Noel** (Marcus **Joseph** 55), Jason **Springer**, Makan **Hislop**, Kareem **Moses**♦11 - Kerry **Baptiste** (c) (Yu **Hoshide** 62), Gason **Gregory**, Hayden **Tinto** (Micah **Lewis** 59), Kareem **Young**, Jevon **Morris** - Andre **Toussaint**. Tr: Derek **King**

Municipal — 3
Ramirez 2 [17 48], Guevara [92+]

Rony **Alvarez** - Gustavo **Cabrera**•, Yony **Flores**, Jaime **Vides**• - Guillermo **Ramirez** (Pablo **Hutt** 87), Mario **Rodriguez**, Sergio **Guevara**, Cristian **Noriega**•, Gonzalo **Romero** (c) (Pedro **Samayoa** 66) - Marvin **Avila** (Carlos **Castillo** 55), Juan **Castillo**. Tr: Guilherme **Farinha**

Mateo Flores, Guatemala City
29-09-2010, 22:00, 3545, Pineda HON

Municipal — 2
Ramirez 2 [19 39]

Rony **Alvarez** - Yony **Flores**, Pablo **Melgar**, Jaime **Vides** - Guillermo **Ramirez**, Mario **Rodriguez** (Pedro **Samayoa** 90), Sergio **Guevara**, Cristian **Noriega**, Gonzalo **Romero**• (c) (Pablo **Solorzano** 87) - Marvin **Avila**, Juan Jose **Castillo** (Diego **Alfonso** 72). Tr: Guilherme **Farinha**

Columbus Crew — 1
Iro [44]

Andrew **Gruenebaum** - Andrew **Iro**, Gino **Padula**•, Eric **Brunner**, Joshua **Williams** (Steven **Lenhart**• 67) - Leandre **Griffit** (Kevin **Burns** 65), Duncan **Oughton** (c), Adam **Moffat**•, Dilaver **Duka** (Shawn **Francis** 79) - Jason **Garey**, Andres **Mendoza**. Tr: Robert **Warzycha**

Nueva Corona, Torreón
29-09-2010, 22:00, 7000, Geiger USA

Santos Laguna — 5
Reyes [4], Torres [14], Quintero [60], Cardenas [67], Figueroa [79]

Miguel **Becerra** (c) - Juan Pablo **Santiago**, Rafael **Figueroa**, Jose **Olvera** (Carlos **Quintero** 52), Uriel **Alvarez** - Jose **Reyes** (Christian **Benitez** 52), Francisco **Torres**, Jaime **Toledo** - Rodrigo **Ruiz** (Daniel **Ludueña** 67), Jose Maria **Cardenas**, Rodolfo **Salinas**. Tr: Ruben Omar **Romano**

Joe Public — 1
Baptiste [32]

Glenroy **Samuel** - Trent **Noel** (Devon **Jamerson** 76), Jason **Springer**•, Carlyle **Mitchell**♦90, Nigel **Daniel**• (Marvin **Manswell** 71) - Kerry **Baptiste** (c), Gason **Gregory**, Hayden **Tinto**, Marcus **Joseph**, Yu **Hoshide** (Micah **Lewis** 67) - Jevon **Morris**•. Tr: Derek **King**

Nueva Corona, Torreón
19-10-2010, 20:00, 3600, Moreno PAN

Santos Laguna — 6
Peralta 2 [20 51], Ludena 2 [27 87], Ruiz [40], Quintero [81]

Oswaldo **Sanchez** (c) - Felipe **Baloy**, Jorge **Estrada**, Rafael **Figueroa**, Jonathan **Lacerda** - Fernando **Arce** (Jose Maria **Cardenas** 75), Carlos **Morales**, Daniel **Ludueña**, Francisco **Torres** - Rodrigo **Ruiz** (Christian **Benitez** 64), Oribe **Peralta** (Carlos **Quintero** 64). Tr: Ruben Omar **Romano**

Municipal — 1
Castillo [39]

Jaime **Penedo** (Rony **Alvarez** 60) - Gustavo **Cabrera**, Yony **Flores**, Jaime **Vides** (Juan Carlos **Plata** 67) - Guillermo **Ramirez**, Mario **Rodriguez**•, Sergio **Guevara**, Cristian **Noriega**, Gonzalo **Romero** (c) - Marvin **Avila** (Pablo **Hutt** 75), Juan Jose **Castillo**. Tr: Guilherme **Farina**

Marvin Lee, Tunapuna
21-10-2010, 20:00, 500, Lancaster GUY

Joe Public — 1
Noel [27p]

Glenroy **Samuel** - Trent **Noel** (c) (Kerry **Baptiste** 71), Jason **Springer**, Makan **Hislop**, Keion **Goodridge**, Kareem **Moses** - Gason **Gregory** (Marvin **Manswell** 77), Devon **Jamerson**, Hayden **Tinto** (Yu **Hoshide** 55) - Andre **Toussaint**, Micah **Lewis**. Tr: Derek King

Columbus Crew — 4
Mendoza [20], Renteria 2 [50p 81], Oughton [92+]

Andrew **Gruenebaum** - Gino **Padula**, Eric **Bunner**, Joshua **Williams** (Shawn **Francis** 82) - Leandre **Griffit**, Duncan **Oughton** (c), Kevin **Burns** (Brian **Carroll** 69), Adam **Moffat**, Dilaver **Duka** - Jason **Garey**, Andres **Mendoza** (Emilio **Renteria** 46). Tr: Robert **Warzycha**

GROUP C		Pl	W	D	L	F	A	Pts	MEX	CRC	HON	USA
Monterrey	MEX	6	5	1	0	11	4	**16**		1-0	2-0	3-2
Deportivo Saprissa	CRC	6	3	1	2	11	7	**10**	2-2		4-1	2-0
Marathón	HON	6	2	0	4	5	11	**6**	0-1	2-1		2-1
Seattle Sounders	USA	6	1	0	5	6	11	**3**	0-2	1-2	2-0	

Tecnologico, Monterrey
17-08-2010, 22:00, 12 042, Salazar USA

Monterrey 1

De Nigris [25]

Jonathan Orozco - Severo Meza (Ricardo Osorio 66), Sergio Perez, Duilio Davino, Hector Morales - Luis Perez (c), Neri Cardozo (Walter Ayovi 73), Jesus Zavala, Osvaldo Martinez - Jesus De Nigris (Humberto Suazo 65), Abraham Carreno. Tr: Victor Manuel Vucetich

Deportivo Saprissa 0

Fausto Gonzalez - Jervis Drummond, Victor Cordero (c), Yader Balladares, Alexander Robinson (Ricardo Blanco 46), Jose Mena• - Walter Centeno, Douglas Sequeira, Armando Alonso - Josue Martinez (Mauricio Castillo 76), Alejandro Sequeira (Jairo Arrieta 53). Tr: Roy Myers

Olimpico, San Pedro Sula
19-08-2010, 22:00, 1990, Guerra GUA

Marathón 2

Paz [27], Cardozo [45p]

Shane Orio - Milton Palacios (Luis Santa Maria 76), Astor Henriquez, Erick Norales, Carlos Palacios, Adolfo Machado - Mario Berrios• (Orvin Paz - Hector Amarilla (Rony Flores 46), Randy Diamond (Carlos Mejia 68), Claudio Cardozo. Tr: Nicolas Suazo

Seattle Sounders 1

Levesque [17]

Kasey Keller (c) - Leonardo Gonzalez•, Nathan Sturgis, Tyrone Marshall•, James Riley, Jeff Parke - Osvaldo Alonso, Alvaro Fernandez (Michael Seamon 68) - Blaise Nkufo (Jonathan Jaqua 62), Fredy Montero, Roger Levesque (David Estrada 86). Tr: Sigi Schmid

Qwest Field, Seattle
25-08-2010, 22:00, 22 513, Aguilar SLV

Seattle Sounders 0

Kasey Keller - Leonardo Gonzalez, Patrick Ianni, Nathan Sturgis (Michael Seamon 67), James Riley, Jeff Parke - Osvaldo Alonso, Alvaro Fernandez (Roger Levesque 72), Sanna Nyassi - Blaise Nkufo (Jonathan Jaqua• 46), Fredy Montero. Tr: Sigi Schmid

Monterrey 2

Cardozo [41], De Nigris [58]

Jonathan Orozco - Jose Maria Basanta, Sergio Perez, Hector Morales, Hiram Mier, Ricardo Osorio - Neri Cardozo• (Sergio Santana 70), Jesus Zavala•, Osvaldo Martinez (Luis Perez 82) - Jesus De Nigris (Humberto Suazo 75), Abraham Carreno. Tr: Victor Manuel Vucetich

Ricardo Saprissa, San José
26-08-2010, 22:00, 2899, Delgadillo MEX

Deportivo Saprissa 4

Sequeira [34], Arrieta [52], Martinez [77], Alonso [86]

Fausto Gonzalez - Gabriel Badilla•, Jervis Drummond (Allan Aleman 73), Victor Cordero• (c) - Walter Centeno, Douglas Sequeira• (David Guzman 85), Armando Alonso, Ricardo Blanco, Mauricio Castillo - Jairo Arrieta, Alejandro Sequeira (Josue Martinez 69). Tr: Roy Myers

Marathón 1

Berrios [32]

Shane Orio - Milton Palacios, Astor Henriquez, Erick Norales, Carlos Palacios, Adolfo Machado• - Mario Berrios• (c), Orvin Paz (Carlos Mejia• 61), Reinier Mayorquin• - Randy Diamond♦45, Claudio Cardozo (Rony Flores 73). Tr: Nicolas Suazo

Tecnologico, Monterrey
14-09-2010, 20:00, 9628, Bogle JAM

Monterrey 2

De Nigris [23], Paredes [55]

Juan de Dios Ibarra - Jose Maria Basanta (Luis Perez 73), Severo Meza, William Paredes, Pierre Ibarra, Hector Morales•, Hiram Mier - Jesus Zavala• (Humberto Suazo 62) - Jose de Jesus Arellano (c), Jesus De Nigris, Abraham Carreno (Neri Cardozo 82). Tr: Victor Manuel Vucetich

Marathón 0

Shane Orio - Luis Crisanto, Erick Norales (c), Elder Valladares, Carlos Palacios, Adolfo Machado - Fernando Castillo (Mariano Acevedo 68), Orvin Paz (Mario Rodriguez 60), Reinier Mayorquin - Carlos Mejia (Astor Henriquez 74), Claudio Cardozo. Tr: Edwin Pavon

Ricardo Saprissa, San José
14-09-2010, 22:00, 3000, Rodriguez MEX

Deportivo Saprissa 2

Guzman [56], Aleman [81]

Fausto Gonzalez - Gabriel Badilla, Victor Cordero (c), Jose Mena (Josue Martinez 46) - Walter Centeno•, David Guzman (Jose Luis Lopez 73), Fernando Paniagua, Esteban Sirias, Armando Alonso (Allan Aleman 63), Ricardo Blanco - Jairo Arrieta. Tr: Roy Myers

Seattle Sounders 0

Terence Boss• - Leonardo Gonzalez♦38, Nathan Sturgis (Alvaro Fernandez• 64), Tyrone Marshall, Taylor Graham, Zach Scott - Osvaldo Alonso, Sanna Nyassi, Steve Zakuani (Tyson Wahl• 46) - Fredy Montero, Roger Levesque• (Michael Fucito 72). Tr: Sigi Schmid

Tecnologico, Monterrey
22-09-2010, 20:00, 19 697, Mejia HON

Monterrey 3

De Nigris [74], Suazo [75], Perez [78p]

Jonathan Orozco - Severo Meza, William Paredes (Humberto Suazo 63), Sergio Perez (Neri Cardozo• 46), Duilio Davino (Luis Perez 46), Hector Morales, Hiram Mier - Walter Ayovi - Jose de Jesus Arellano•♦90 (c), Jesus De Nigris, Abraham Carreno. Tr: Victor Manuel Vucetich

Seattle Sounders 2

OG [28], Fucito [44]

Terence Boss - Tyson Wahl, Tyrone Marshall (c), Taylor Graham, Zach Scott• - Alvaro Fernandez, David Estrada, Michael Seamon - Jonathan Jaqua (Fredy Montero 72), Michael Fucito, Miguel Montano (Sanna Nyassi 75). Tr: Sigi Schmid

Olimpico, San Pedro Sula
22-09-2010, 22:00, 1820, Moreno PAN

Marathón 2

Berrios [49], OG [64]

Shane Orio - Milton Palacios, Erick Norales, Mariano Acevedo, Nahun Avila (Astor Henriquez 72), Elder Valladares, Carlos Palacios, Adolfo Machado - Mario Berrios (c) - Carlos Mejia (Rony Flores 80), Claudio Cardozo (Randy Diamond 54). Tr: Edwin Pavon

Deportivo Saprissa 1

Arrieta [66]

Fausto Gonzalez - Gabriel Badilla, Victor Cordero• (c) (Jose Mena 82), Alexander Robinson - Walter Centeno•, Fernando Paniagua, Armando Alonso, Ricardo Blanco (Esteban Sirias 60), Mauricio Castillo - Jairo Arrieta, Josue Martinez (David Guzman 85). Tr: Roy Myers

Ricardo Saprissa, San José
28-09-2010, 22:00, 1635, Vaughn USA

Deportivo Saprissa 2

OG [16], Mena [65]

Fausto Gonzalez - Gabriel Badilla, Alexander Robinson, Jose Mena - David Guzman, Fernando Paniagua•, Esteban Sirias (Joel Campbell 62), Ricardo Blanco, Mauricio Castillo (Josue Martinez 55) - Jairo Arrieta, Alejandro Sequeira (c) (Armando Alonso 66). Tr: Roy Myers

Monterrey 2

Rodriguez [5], Carreno [31]

Juan Ibarra - Severo Meza•, William Paredes (Jesus Nigris 71), Pierre Ibarra, Sergio Perez, Hector Morales•, Hiram Mier - Jesus Zavala•, Cesar Martinez (Ricardo Osorio 63), Luis Rodriguez (Eduardo Guevara 77) - Abraham Carreno•. Tr: Victor Manuel Vucetich

Qwest Field, Seattle
29-09-2010, 22:00, 11 768, Ward CAN

Seattle Sounders 2

Fucito 2 [21 68]

Terence Boss - Tyson Wahl, Tyrone Marshall (c), Taylor Graham, Zach Scott - Alvaro Fernandez (Peter Vagenas 61), David Estrada, Michael Seamon - Roger Levesque, Michael Fucito (Sanna Nyassi 70), Miguel Montano (Leonardo Gonzalez 82). Tr: Sigi Schmid

Marathón 0

Shane Orio - Milton Palacios (Rony Flores 72), Astor Henriquez, Erick Norales, Mariano Acevedo, Elder Valladares, Carlos Palacios, Adolfo Machado - Mario Berrios (c) - Carlos Mejia, Hector Amarilla (Randy Diamond 73). Tr: Edwin Pavon

Qwest Field, Seattle
19-10-2010, 22:00, 11 434, Brizan TRI

Seattle Sounders 1

Jaqua [17]

Kasey Keller (c) - Tyson Wahl, Tyrone Marshall, Taylor Graham, Zach Scott - Peter Vagenas (Miguel Montano• 63), Alvaro Fernandez, Michael Seamon - Jonathan Jaqua• (Sanna Nyassi 84), Roger Levesque (David Estrada 76), Michael Fucito. Tr: Sigi Schmid

Deportivo Saprissa 2

Arrieta [26], Martinez [89]

Minor Alvarez - Gabriel Badilla•, Javier Loaiza (Luis Cordero 73), Alexander Robinson•♦89, Jose Mena• - Walter Centeno, David Guzman, Ricardo Blanco•, Mauricio Castillo (Alonso Solis 69) - Jairo Arrieta, Alejandro Sequeira (c) (Josue Martinez 56). Tr: Roy Myers

Olimpico, San Pedro Sula
20-10-2010, 22:00, 500, Lopez GUA

Marathón 0

Orlin Vallecillo - Luis Crisanto, Erick Norales, Mariano Acevedo, Adolfo Machado - Mario Rodriguez (Carlos Palacios• 46), Mario Berrios• (c), Fernando Castillo (Carlos Mejia 46), Orvin Paz (Randy Diamond 72), Reinier Mayorquin - Rony Flores. Tr: Edwin Pavon

Monterrey 1

Santana [69]

Juan Ibarra - Severo Meza, William Paredes, Pierre Ibarra, Sergio Perez• (Jose Maria Basanta 72), Hiram Mier, Eduardo Guevara - Cesar Martinez - Jose Arellano (c) (Jesus Corona 81), Sergio Santana (Brayan Martinez 80), Abraham Carreno. Tr: Victor Manuel Vucetich

GROUP D		Pl	W	D	L	F	A	Pts	HON	MEX	PUR	SLV
Olimpia	HON	6	4	1	1	12	7	**13**		2-1	3-0	2-0
Toluca	MEX	6	3	1	2	15	5	**10**	4-0		3-0	5-0
Puerto Rico Islanders	PUR	6	2	2	2	8	10	**8**	1-1	3-2		4-1
Deportivo FAS	SLV	6	0	2	4	2	15	**2**	1-4	0-0	0-0	

Juan Ramon Loubriel, Bayamon
17-08-2010, 20:00, 2632, Rodriguez MEX

Puerto Rico Islanders   **1**

Addlery [40]

William **Gaudette** - David **Horst**, Marco **Velez•**, Kevon **Villaroel**, Richard **Martinez** - Keon **Daniel**, Noah **Delgado** (Kendall **Jagdeosingh** 83), Joseph **Salem** - Joshua **Hansen** (Sandy **Gbandi** 83), Nicholas **Addlery**, David **Foley•** (Jonathan **Fana Farias** 77). Tr: Colin **Clarke**

Olimpia   **1**

Copete [68]

Noel **Valladares** - Oscar **Garcia**, Juan Carlos **Garcia**, Jose **Arevalo**, Wilfredo **Barahona**, Johnny **Palacios•** - Walter **Castro**, Reynaldo **Tiguath** (Miguel **Castillo** 85), Bany **Lozano** (Alexander **Lopez** 64) - Washington **Bruschi** (Andres **Copete•** 61), Roger **Rojas**. Tr: Carlos **Restrepo**

Cuscatlan, San Salvador
18-08-2010, 22:00, 3500, Quesada CRC

Deportivo FAS   **0**

Luis **Contreras** - Mardoqueo **Henriquez**, Manuel **Salazar•**, Victor **Velasquez** (c), Juan Carlos **Moscoso**, Miguel **Granadino**, Eliseo **Salamanca** (Carlos **Aparicio** 54) - Gilberto **Murgas**, Roberto **Pena**, Christiam **Alvarez** - Williams **Reyes** (Ricardo **Ulloa** 78). Tr: Alberto **Rujana**

Toluca   **0**

Alfredo **Talavera** - Mario **Mendez**, Edgar **Duenas•** (c), Francisco **Gamboa** (Osvaldo **Gonzalez** 78), Carlos **Galeana**, Diego **Novaretti** - Juan **Cuevas** (Nestor **Calderon** 66), Manuel **Perez**, Martin **Romagnoli** - Emmanuel **Cerda** (Carlos **Esquivel** 58), Raul **Nava**. Tr: Jose Manuel **De La Torre**

Juan Ramon Loubriel, Bayamon
25-08-2010, 20:00, 2050, Brizan TRI

Puerto Rico Islanders   **4**

Foley [16], Fana 2 [22 45], Addlery [84]

William **Gaudette** - David **Horst**, Marco **Velez**, Kevon **Villaroel**, Richard **Martinez** - Keon **Daniel** (Joseph **Salem** 71), Osei **Telesford** (Sandy **Gbandi** 79) - Joshua **Hansen**, Nicholas **Addlery** (c), David **Foley**, Jonathan **Fana Farias•** (Kendall **Jagdeosingh•** 85). Tr: Colin **Clarke**

Deportivo FAS   **1**

Reyes [24]

Luis **Contreras** - Mardoqueo **Henriquez** (Carlos **Aparicio•** 45), Manuel **Salazar**, Victor **Velasquez•** (c), Juan Carlos **Moscoso**, Miguel **Granadino** - Gilberto **Murgas** (Pablo **Quandt** 57), Roberto **Pena**, Christiam **Alvarez•** - Williams **Reyes** (Ramon **Solis** 79), Alejandro **Bentos**. Tr: Alberto **Rujana**

Nemesio Diez, Toluca
26-08-2010, 20:00, 7463, Cruz CRC

Toluca   **4**

Cuevas 2 [4 10], Mancilla [63], OG [86]

Alfredo **Talavera** - Mario **Mendez**, Edgar **Duenas** (c) (Hector **Acosta** 45), Osvaldo **Gonzalez**, Carlos **Galeana•**, Diego **Novaretti** - Juan **Cuevas**, Manuel **Perez** (Antonio **Naelson** 57), Martin **Romagnoli** - Hector **Mancilla**, Emmanuel **Cerda** (Isaac **Brizuela** 65). Tr: Jose Manuel **De La Torre**

Olimpia   **0**

Donis **Escober** - Oscar **Garcia•**, Juan Carlos **Garcia**, Jose **Arevalo**, Wilfredo **Barahona**, Johnny **Palacios** - Walter **Castro•**, Reynaldo **Tiguath** (c) (Miguel **Angel Castillo** 57), Bany **Lozano** - Washington **Bruschi** (Andres **Copete** 57), Roger **Rojas** (Alexander **Lopez** 67). Tr: Carlos **Restrepo**

Nemesio Diez, Toluca
15-09-2010, 20:00, 5165, Pineda HON

Toluca   **3**

Gonzalez [18], Cuevas [76p], Cerda [93+]

Alfredo **Talavera** - Mario **Mendez**, Edgar **Duenas**, Osvaldo **Gonzalez**, Carlos **Galeana**, Diego **Novaretti** - Antonio **Naelson Zinha** (c) (Nestor **Calderon** 61), Juan **Cuevas**, Martin **Romagnoli** - Hector **Mancilla•** (Emmanuel **Cerda** 74), Isaac **Brizuela** (Carlos **Esquivel** 56). Tr: Jose Manuel **De La Torre**

Puerto Rico Islanders   **0**

William **Gaudette** - David **Horst**, Marco **Velez•**, Kevon **Villaroel**, Richard **Martinez** - Noah **Delgado** (c) (Keon **Daniel** 79), Osei **Telesford** (Jonathan **Fana Farias** 64), Joseph **Salem** (Sandy **Gbandi** 71) - Joshua **Hansen**, Kendall **Jagdeosingh**, David **Foley•**. Tr: Colin **Clarke**

Tiburcio Andino, Tegucigalpa
16-09-2010, 20:00, 9200, Cruz CRC

Olimpia   **2**

Rojas 2 [14 81]

Noel **Valladares** - Oscar **Garcia**, Jose **Arevalo•**, Fabio **De Souza**, Wilfredo **Barahona**, Johnny **Calderon** (Juan Carlos **Garcia** 60) - Elvis **Turcios** (c), Walter **Castro**, Reynaldo **Tiguath** (Alexander **Lopez** 46) - Washington **Bruschi** (Andres **Copete** 68), Roger **Rojas**. Tr: Carlos **Restrepo**

Deportivo FAS   **0**

Luis **Contreras** - Mardoqueo **Henriquez**, Victor **Velasquez** (c), Juan Carlos **Moscoso•**, Eliseo **Salamanca**, Carlos **Aparicio•** (Pablo **Quandt** 57) - Gilberto **Murgas** (Williams **Reyes** 66), Gustavo **Lopez** (William **Maldonado** 87), Roberto **Pena**, Christiam **Alvarez** (Alejandro **Bentos**. Tr: Alberto **Rujana**

Cuscatlan, San Salvador
22-09-2010, 22:00, 3500, Delgadillo MEX

Deportivo FAS   **0**

Luis **Contreras** - Mardoqueo **Henriquez**, Manuel **Salazar**, Victor **Velasquez** (c), Eliseo **Salamanca** - Gilberto **Murgas** (Pablo **Quandt•** 51), Gustavo **Lopez** (Donny **Valle** 63), Roberto **Pena**, Christiam **Alvarez•** - Williams **Reyes** (Oscar **Ulloa** 81), Alejandro **Bentos**. Tr: Jorge **Abrego**

Puerto Rico Islanders   **0**

William **Gaudette** - David **Horst**, Alexis **Rivera•**, Richard **Martinez**, Logan **Emory** - Keon **Daniel•** (Anthony **Allison** 87), Noah **Delgado**, Osei **Telesford**, Christopher **Nurse** - Joshua **Hansen** (Sandy **Gbandi** 75), Jonathan **Fana Farias** (Kendall **Jagdeosingh** 75). Tr: Colin **Clarke**

Olimpico, San Pedro Sula
23-09-2010, 22:00, 4654, Lopez GUA

Olimpia   **2**

Garcia [14], Rojas [25]

Donis **Escober** - Oscar **Garcia**, Jose **Arevalo**, Fabio **De Souza•**, Wilfredo **Barahona** - Elvis **Turcios•** (c) (Alexander **Lopez** 66), Walter **Castro**, Reynaldo **Tiguath•** (Miguel **Castillo** 80), Bany **Lozano•** - Andres **Copete** (Washington **Bruschi** 61), Roger **Rojas**. Tr: Carlos **Restrepro**

Toluca   **1**

Cuevas [39p]

Alfredo **Talavera•** - Mario **Mendez** (c), Francisco **Gamboa**, Osvaldo **Gonzalez**, Carlos **Galeana** (Erbin **Trejo** 36), Diego **Novaretti** - Juan **Cuevas**, Manuel **Perez•** (Nestor **Calderon** 46), Antonio **Rios•** - Emmanuel **Cerda**, Isaac **Brizuela** (Carlos **Esquivel** 69). Tr: Jose Manuel **De La Torre**

Juan Ramon Loubriel, Bayamon
29-09-2010, 20:00, 4122, Bogle JAM

Puerto Rico Islanders   **2**

Foley [54], Horst 2 [70 91+]

William **Gaudette** - David **Horst**, Marco **Velez** (c), Kevon **Villaroel** (Alexis **Rivera** 81), Richard **Martinez** - Osei **Telesford** (Sandy **Gbandi** 77), Christopher **Nurse** - Joshua **Hansen**, Kendall **Jagdeosingh** (Anthony **Allison** 87), David **Foley•**, Jonathan **Fana Farias**. Tr: Colin **Clarke**

Toluca   **2**

Mancilla 2 [10 23]

Alfredo **Talavera** - Mario **Mendez** (Edgar **Duenas** 72), Manuel **De La Torre**, Osvaldo **Gonzalez**, Diego **Novaretti** - Antonio **Naelson Zinha** (c), Martin **Romagnoli**, Antonio **Rios** - Hector **Mancilla**, Nestor **Calderon•** (Erbin **Trejo** 88), Isaac **Brizuela** (Carlos **Esquivel** 60). Tr: Jose Manuel **De La Torre**

Cuscatlan, San Salvador
30-09-2010, 22:00, 1000, Marrufo USA

Deportivo FAS   **1**

Lopez [72]

Luis **Contreras** - Mardoqueo **Henriquez**, Manuel **Salazar**, Victor **Velasquez** (c), Juan Carlos **Moscoso•**, Eliseo **Salamanca** - Gilberto **Murgas** (William **Maldonado** 67), Gustavo **Lopez**, Roberto **Pena•** - Williams **Reyes** (Carlos **Aparicio** 50), Alejandro **Bentos** (Ricardo **Ulloa** 80). Tr: Jorge **Abrego**

Olimpia   **4**

Bruschi 2 [29 45], Barahona [52], Lozano [89]

Noel **Valladares** - Oscar **Garcia**, Jose **Arevalo**, Fabio **De Souza**, Wilfredo **Barahona** - Elvis **Turcios** (c) (Jose Carlos **Dias** 69), Walter **Castro**, Reynaldo **Tiguath** (Miguel **Castillo** 75), Bany **Lozano** - Washington **Bruschi** (Anthony **Lozano** 69), Roger **Rojas**. Tr: Carlos **Restrepo**

Nemesio Diez, Toluca
20-10-2010, 20:00, 3985, Geiger USA

Toluca   **5**

Mancilla 3 [19 56 90], Cuevas [55p], Calderon [87]

Alfredo **Talavera** - Manuel **De La Torre**, Edgar **Duenas**, Osvaldo **Gonzalez**, Diego **Novaretti•** (Emmanuel **Cerda** 76) - Antonio **Naelson Zinha** (c), Juan **Cuevas•**, Martin **Romagnoli**, Antonio **Rios** (Nestor **Calderon** 60) - Hector **Mancilla**, Carlos **Esquivel** (Isaac **Brizuela** 65). Tr: Jose Manuel **De La Torre**

Deportivo FAS   **0**

Daniel **Arroyo** - Mardoqueo **Henriquez**, Manuel **Salazar**, Victor **Velasquez** (c) (Donny **Valle** 59), Juan Carlos **Moscoso**, Miguel **Granadino**, Carlos **Aparicio** - Gilberto **Murgas**, Christiam **Alvarez** (Gustavo **Lopez** 70) - Alejandro **Bentos**, Pablo **Quandt** (Eliseo **Salamanca** 58). Tr: Jorge **Abrego**

Tiburcio Andino, Tegucigalpa
20-10-2010, 22:00, 5550, Archundia MEX

Olimpia   **3**

Rojas 2 [53 77], De Souza [81]

Noel **Valladares** - Oscar **Garcia**, Jose **Arevalo**, Fabio **De Souza**, Johnny **Palacios** - Elvis **Turcios** (c) (Miguel **Castillo** 81), Walter **Castro**, Reynaldo **Tiguath**, Bany **Lozano** - Washington **Bruschi** (Alexander **Lopez** 68), Roger **Rojas** (Anthony **Lozano** 85). Tr: Carlos **Restrepo**

Puerto Rico Islanders   **0**

William **Gaudette** - David **Horst**, Alexis **Rivera** (Joshua **Hansen** 62), Kevon **Villaroel**, Richard **Martinez**, Logan **Emory** - Keon **Daniel**, Noah **Delgado** (c) (David **Foley** 62), Sandy **Gbandi**, Christopher **Nurse** (Joseph **Salem** 78) - Kendall **Jagdeosingh**. Tr: Colin **Clarke**

CONMEBOL

CONFEDERACION SUDAMERICANA DE FUTBOL

At one point during the 2010 FIFA World Cup it looked as if the South Americans could do no wrong, with the continent's five representatives winning ten and drawing four of the 15 games they played during the first-round group stage. But if ever there was a case of peaking to soon this was it. Chile were the first to fall - at the hands of Brazil in the first knockout round but it was in the quarter-finals where the damage was done with Brazil, Argentina and Paraguay all well beaten by European opposition. It had always been a matter of some pride in South America that Argentina and Brazil were the only nations to have won a World Cup outside of their own confederation but any hopes of that run continuing rested on tiny Uruguay, controversial winners of their quarter-final against Ghana, thanks to a Luis Suarez handball stopping a certain winner for Ghana in the

THE FIFA BIG COUNT OF 2006 FOR SOUTH AMERICA

	Male	Female		Total
Number of players	24 703	3 074	Referees and Assistant Referees	32 000
Professionals	25 000		Admin, Coaches, Technical, Medical	136 000
Amateurs 18+	980 000		Number of clubs	47 000
Youth under 18	2 346 000		Number of teams	162 000
Unregistered	24 018 000		Clubs with women's teams	1 000
Total involved in football	27 946 000		Players as % of population	7.47%

dying seconds of extra-time. Their luck finally ran out in the semi-final against the Netherlands despite yet another plucky performance and South America's treasured record was gone. There was further disappointment at the end of the year when the 2010 Copa Libertadores winners Internacional from Porto Alegre in Brazil lost to Congo's TP Mazembe in the semi-final of the FIFA Club World Cup. Since the introduction of the Intercontinental Cup in 1960 between the European Cup and Copa Libertadores winners, South American clubs had more than held their own against the European champions, even after the launch of the FIFA Club World Cup in 2000. To miss out on the chance to play Internazionale was deeply disappointing for South American fans. The one consolation, perhaps, was Argentina's Lionel Messi comfortably winning the first FIFA Ballon d'Or ahead of Spain's Andres Iniesta and Xavi.

Confederación Sudamericana de Fútbol (CONMEBOL)

Autopista Aeropuerto Internacional y Leonismo Luqueño, Luque, Gran Asuncion, Paraguay
Tel +595 21 645781   Fax +595 21 645791
conmebol@conmebol.com.py   www.conmebol.com
President: Dr Nicolas Leoz PAR   General Secretary: Eduardo Deluca ARG
CONMEBOL Formed: 1916

CONMEBOL EXECUTIVE COMMITTEE

President: Dr Nicolas Leoz PAR

Vice-President: Eugenio Figueredo URU   General Secretary: Eduardo Deluca ARG   Treasurer: Romer Osuna BOL

DIRECTORS OF THE EXECUTIVE COMMITTEE

Rafael Esquivel VEN	Nicolas Delfino PER	Oscar Harrison PAR
Nabi Abi Chedid BRA	Luis Chiriboga ECU	Alvaro Fina COL
	Jose Abdalah CHI	

MAP OF CONMEBOL MEMBER NATIONS

CONMEBOL MEMBER ASSOCIATIONS (10)
ARG - **Argentina** • BOL - **Bolivia** • BRA - **Brazil** • CHI - **Chile** • COL - **Colombia**
ECU - **Ecuador** • PAR - **Paraguay** • PER - **Peru** • URU - **Uruguay** • VEN - **Venezuela**

SOUTH AMERICAN
NATIONAL TEAM TOURNAMENTS

COPA AMERICA

Year	Host Country	Winners	Score	Runners-up	Venue
1910	Argentina ††	Argentina	4-1	Uruguay	‡ Racing Club, Buenos Aires
1916	Argentina †	Uruguay	0-0	Argentina	‡ Racing Club, Buenos Aires
1917	Uruguay	Uruguay	1-0	Argentina	‡ Parque Pereira, Montevideo
1919	Brazil	Brazil	1-0	Uruguay	§ Laranjeiras, Rio de Janeiro
1920	Chile	Uruguay	1-1	Argentina	* Sporting Club, Vina del Mar
1921	Argentina	Argentina	1-0	Brazil	* Sportivo Barracas, Buenos Aires
1922	Brazil	Brazil	3-0	Paraguay	§ Laranjeiras, Rio de Janeiro
1923	Uruguay	Uruguay	2-0	Argentina	‡ Parque Central, Montevideo
1924	Uruguay	Uruguay	0-0	Argentina	‡ Parque Central, Montevideo
1925	Argentina	Argentina	2-2	Brazil	‡ Bombonera, Buenos Aires
1926	Chile	Uruguay	2-0	Argentina	* Sport de Nunoa, Santiago
1927	Peru	Argentina	3-2	Uruguay	* Estadio Nacional, Lima
1929	Argentina	Argentina	4-1	Paraguay	* San Lorenzo, Buenos Aires
1935	Peru †	Uruguay	3-0	Argentina	‡ Estadio Nacional, Lima
1937	Argentina	Argentina	2-0	Brazil	‡ San Lorenzo, Buenos Aires
1939	Peru	Peru	2-1	Uruguay	‡ Estadio Nacional, Lima
1941	Chile †	Argentina	1-0	Uruguay	* Estadio Nacional, Santiago
1942	Uruguay	Uruguay	1-0	Argentina	‡ Centenario, Montevideo
1945	Chile †	Argentina	3-1	Brazil	* Estadio Nacional, Santiago
1946	Argentina †	Argentina	2-0	Brazil	‡ Monumental, Buenos Aires
1947	Ecuador	Argentina	6-0	Paraguay	* Estadio Capwell, Guayaquil
1949	Brazil	Brazil	7-0	Paraguay	§ Sao Januario, Rio de Janeiro
1953	Lima	Paraguay	3-2	Brazil	§ Estadio Nacional, Lima
1955	Chile	Argentina	1-0	Chile	‡ Estadio Nacional, Santiago
1956	Uruguay †	Uruguay	1-0	Argentina	‡ Centenario, Montevideo
1957	Peru	Argentina	3-0	Brazil	‡ Estadio Nacional, Lima
1959	Argentina	Argentina	1-1	Brazil	‡ Monumental, Buenos Aires
1959	Ecuador †	Uruguay	5-0	Argentina	* Modelo, Guayaquil
1963	Bolivia	Bolivia	5-4	Brazil	‡ Felix Capriles, Cochabamba
1967	Uruguay	Uruguay	1-0	Argentina	‡ Centenario, Montevideo
1975		Peru	0-1 2-0 1-0	Colombia	Bogota, Lima, Caracas
1979		Paraguay	3-0 0-1 0-0	Chile	Asuncion, Santiago, Buenos Aires
1983		Uruguay	2-0 1-1	Brazil	Montevideo & Salvador
1987	Argentina	Uruguay	1-0	Chile	Monumental, Buenos Aires
1989	Brazil	Brazil	1-0	Uruguay	‡ Maracana, Rio de Janeiro
1991	Chile	Argentina	3-2	Brazil	* Estadio Nacional, Santiago
1993	Ecuador	Argentina	2-1	Mexico	Monumental, Guayaquil
1995	Uruguay	Uruguay	1-1 5-3p	Brazil	Centenario, Montevideo
1997	Bolivia	Brazil	3-1	Bolivia	Hernando Siles, La Paz
1999	Paraguay	Brazil	3-0	Uruguay	Defensores del Chaco, Asuncion
2001	Colombia	Colombia	1-0	Mexico	El Campin, Bogota
2004	Peru	Brazil	2-2 4-2p	Argentina	Estadio Nacional, Lima
2007	Venezuela	Brazil	3-0	Argentina	Pachencho Romero, Maracaibo
2011	Argentina				Monumental, Buenos Aires

† Extraordinario tournaments are recognised as official tournaments though the teams did not compete for the Copa America • †† Unofficial tournament that is not part of the official records. CONMEBOL refer to it as The South American Championship although it was known at the time as the Copa Centenario • ‡ Tournament played on a league system. The final game was between the top two teams • * Tournament played on a league system. The game listed between the top two teams was not the final match in the tournament • § Tournament played on a league system. The game listed was a play-off after the top two teams finished level on points.

COPA AMERICA MEDALS TABLE

	Country	G	S	B	F	SF
1	Argentina	14	12	4	3	4
2	Uruguay	14	6	7	4	8
3	Brazil	8	11	7	6	8
4	Paraguay	2	5	8	1	2
5	Peru	2		4	1	4
6	Colombia	1	1	3	2	6
7	Bolivia	1	1		1	1
8	Chile		4	5	2	3
9	Mexico		2	3	2	5
10	Honduras			1		1
11	Ecuador					1
	United States					1
		42	42	42	22	42

This table represents the Gold (winners), Silver (runners-up) and Bronze (semi-finalists) placings of nation in the Copa América, along with the number of appearances in the final and semi-finals. It does not include the 1910 tournament and does not distinguish between official and extraordinario tournaments

SOUTH AMERICAN CLUB TOURNAMENTS

COPA LIBERTADORES DE AMERICA

Year	Winners	Country	Score	Country	Runners-up
1960	Peñarol	URU	1-0 1-1	PAR	Olimpia
1961	Peñarol	URU	1-0 1-1	BRA	Palmeiras
1962	Santos	BRA	2-1 2-3 3-0	URU	Peñarol
1963	Santos	BRA	3-2 2-1	ARG	Boca Juniors
1964	Independiente	ARG	0-0 1-0	URU	Nacional Montevideo
1965	Independiente	ARG	1-0 1-3 4-1	URU	Peñarol
1966	Peñarol	URU	2-0 2-3 4-2	ARG	River Plate
1967	Racing Club	ARG	0-0 0-0 2-1	URU	Nacional Montevideo
1968	Estudiantes LP	ARG	2-1 1-3 2-0	BRA	Palmeiras
1969	Estudiantes LP	ARG	1-0 2-0	URU	Nacional Montevideo
1970	Estudiantes LP	ARG	1-0 0-0	URU	Peñarol
1971	Nacional Montevideo	URU	0-1 1-0 2-0	ARG	Estudiantes LP
1972	Independiente	ARG	0-0 2-1	PER	Universitario
1973	Independiente	ARG	1-1 0-0 2-1	CHI	Colo Colo
1974	Independiente	ARG	1-2 2-0 1-0	BRA	São Paulo FC
1975	Independiente	ARG	0-1 3-1 2-0	CHI	Union Española
1976	Cruzeiro	BRA	4-1 1-2 3-2	ARG	River Plate
1977	Boca Juniors	ARG	1-0 0-1 0-0 5-4p	BRA	Cruzeiro
1978	Boca Juniors	ARG	0-0 4-0	COL	Deportivo Cali
1979	Olimpia	PAR	2-0 0-0	ARG	Boca Juniors
1980	Nacional Montevideo	URU	0-0 1-0	BRA	Internacional
1981	Flamengo	BRA	2-1 0-1 2-0	CHI	Cobreloa
1982	Peñarol	URU	0-0 1-0	CHI	Cobreloa
1983	Grêmio	BRA	1-1 2-1	URU	Peñarol
1984	Independiente	ARG	1-0 0-0	BRA	Grêmio
1985	Argentinos Juniors	ARG	1-0 0-1 1-1 5-4p	COL	América Cali
1986	River Plate	ARG	2-1 1-0	COL	América Cali
1987	Peñarol	URU	0-2 2-1 1-0	COL	América Cali
1988	Nacional Montevideo	URU	0-1 3-0	ARG	Newell's Old Boys
1989	Atlético Nacional Medellín	COL	0-2 2-0 5-4p	PAR	Olimpia
1990	Olimpia	PAR	2-0 1-1	ECU	Barcelona
1991	Colo Colo	CHI	0-0 3-0	PAR	Olimpia

COPA LIBERTADORES DE AMERICA (CONT'D)

Year	Winners	Country	Score	Country	Runners-up
1992	São Paulo FC	BRA	1-0 0-1 3-2p	ARG	Newell's Old Boys
1993	São Paulo FC	BRA	5-1 0-2	CHI	Universidad Catolica
1994	Velez Sarsfield	ARG	1-0 0-1 5-3p	BRA	São Paulo FC
1995	Grêmio	BRA	3-1 1-1	COL	Atlético Nacional Medellin
1996	River Plate	ARG	0-1 2-0	COL	América Cali
1997	Cruzeiro	BRA	0-0 1-0	PER	Sporting Cristal
1998	Vasco da Gama	BRA	2-0 2-1	ECU	Barcelona
1999	Palmeiras	BRA	0-1 2-1 4-3p	COL	Deportivo Cali
2000	Boca Juniors	ARG	2-2 0-0 4-2p	BRA	Palmeiras
2001	Boca Juniors	ARG	1-0 0-1 3-1p	MEX	Cruz Azul
2002	Olimpia	PAR	0-1 2-1 4-2p	BRA	São Caetano
2003	Boca Juniors	ARG	2-0 3-1	BRA	Santos
2004	Once Caldas	COL	0-0 1-1 2-0p	ARG	Boca Juniors
2005	São Paulo FC	BRA	1-1 4-0	BRA	Atlético Paranaense
2006	Internacional	BRA	2-1 2-2	BRA	São Paulo FC
2007	Boca Juniors	ARG	3-0 2-0	BRA	Grêmio
2008	LDU Quito	ECU	4-2 1-3 3-1p	BRA	Fluminense
2009	Estudiantes LP	ARG	0-0 2-1	BRA	Cruzeiro
2010	Internacional	BRA	2-1 3-2	MEX	Guadalajara

COPA LIBERTADORES MEDALS TABLE - NATIONS

	Country	G	S	B	F	SF
1	Argentina	22	8	31	30	61
2	Brazil	14	15	22	29	51
3	Uruguay	8	7	18	15	33
4	Paraguay	3	3	13	6	19
5	Colombia	2	7	18	9	27
6	Chile	1	5	14	6	20
7	Ecuador	1	2	9	3	12
8	Peru		2	6	2	8
9	Mexico		2	5	2	7
9	Bolivia			3		3
	Venezuela			3		3
		51	51	142	102	244

This table represents the Gold (winners), Silver (runners-up) and
Bronze (semi-finalists) placings of clubs representing the above
countries in the Copa Libertadores, along with the number of
appearances in the final and semi-finals

COPA LIBERTADORES MEDALS TABLE - CLUBS

	Club		G	S	B
1	Independiente	ARG	7		5
2	Boca Juniors	ARG	6	3	4
3	Peñarol	URU	5	4	10
4	Estudiantes La Plata	ARG	4	1	1
5	Nacional Montevideo	URU	3	3	7
6	Olimpia	PAR	3	3	5
7	São Paulo FC	BRA	3	3	3
8	River Plate	ARG	2	2	11
9	Grêmio	BRA	2	2	3
10	Cruzeiro	BRA	2	2	2
11	Santos FC	BRA	2	1	3
12	Internacional	BRA	2	1	2
13	SE Palmeiras	BRA	1	3	2
14	Colo Colo	CHI	1	1	3
15	At. Nacional Medellín	COL	1	1	2

COPA LIBERTADORES MEDALS TABLE (CONT'D)

	Club		G	S	B
16	Flamengo	BRA	1		2
	LDU Quito	ECU	1		2
	Racing Club Avellaneda	ARG	1		2
19	Argentinos Juniors	ARG	1		1
	Vélez Sarsfield	ARG	1		1
21	Once Caldas	COL	1		
	Vasco da Gama	BRA	1		
23	América Cali	COL		4	6
24	Barcelona	ECU		2	5
25	Deportivo Cali	COL		2	2
26	Cobreloa	CHI		2	1
27	Newell's Old Boys	ARG		2	
28	Universidad Catolica	CHI		1	4
29	Universitario	PER		1	3
30	Chivas Guadalajara	MEX		1	2

COPA LIBERTADORES MEDALS TABLE (CONT'D)

	Club		G	S	B
31	Union Española	CHI		1	1
32	Atlético Paranaense	BRA		1	
	Cruz Azul	MEX		1	
	Fluminense	BRA		1	
	São Caetano	BRA		1	
	Sporting Cristal	PER		1	
37	Cerro Porteño	PAR			5
38	CF América	MEX			3
	Millonarios	COL			3
	San Lorenzo de Almagro	ARG			3
	Universidad de Chile	CHI			3
42	Alianza	PER			2
	Botafogo	BRA			2
	Rosario Central	ARG			2
	Libertad	PAR			2
46	Atlético Junior	COL			1
	Atlético Mineiro	BRA			1
	Atlético San Cristobal	VEN			1
	Blooming	BOL			1

COPA LIBERTADORES MEDALS TABLE (CONT'D)

	Club		G	S	B
	Bolivar	BOL			1
	Corinthians	BRA			1
	Cúcuta Deportiva	COL			1
	Danubio	URU			1
	Defensor Lima	PER			1
	Deportes Tolima	COL			1
	Emelec	ECU			1
	Guarani Asuncion	PAR			1
	Guarani Campinas	BRA			1
	Huracán	ARG			1
	Independiente Medellin	COL			1
	Independiente Santa Fé	COL			1
	Jorge Wilsterman	BOL			1
	El Nacional Quito	ECU			1
	O'Higgins	CHI			1
	Palestino	CHI			1
	Portuguesa	VEN			1
	ULA Merida	VEN			1
			51	51	142

SUPERCOPA JOAO HAVELANGE

Year	Winners	Country	Score	Country	Runners-up
1988	Racing Club	ARG	2-1 1-1	BRA	Cruzeiro
1989	Boca Juniors	ARG	0-0 0-0 5-3p	ARG	Independiente
1990	Olimpia	PAR	3-0 3-3	URU	Nacional Montevideo
1991	Cruzeiro	BRA	0-2 3-0	ARG	River Plate
1992	Cruzeiro	BRA	4-0 0-1	ARG	Racing Club
1993	São Paulo FC	BRA	2-2 2-2 5-3p	BRA	Flamengo
1994	Independiente	ARG	1-1 1-0	ARG	Boca Juniors
1995	Independiente	ARG	2-0 0-1	BRA	Flamengo
1996	Velez Sarsfield	ARG	1-0 2-0	BRA	Cruzeiro
1997	River Plate	ARG	0-0 2-1	BRA	São Paulo FC

SUPERCOPA MEDALS TABLE - NATIONS

	Country	G	S	B	F	SF
1	Argentina	6	4	4	10	14
2	Brazil	3	5	6	8	14
3	Paraguay	1		2	1	3
4	Uruguay		1	4	1	5
5	Chile			2		2
	Colombia			2		2
		10	10	20	20	40

This table represents the Gold (winners), Silver (runners-up) and Bronze (semi-finalists) placings of clubs representing the above countries in the Supercopa, along with the number of appearances in the final and semi-finals

SUPERCOPA MEDALS TABLE - CLUBS (CONT'D)

	Club		G	S	B
1	Cruzeiro	BRA	2	2	2
2	Independiente	ARG	2	1	
3	River Plate	ARG	1	1	2
4	São Paulo FC	BRA	1	1	1
5	Boca Juniors	ARG	1	1	
	Racing Club	ARG	1	1	
7	Olimpia	PAR	1		2
8	Velez Sarsfield	ARG	1		
9	Flamengo	BRA		2	1
10	Nacional Montevideo	URU		1	2
11	Colo Colo	CHI			2
	Peñarol	URU			2
	At. Nacional Medellin	COL			2
14	Argentinos Juniors	ARG			1
	Estudiantes LP	ARG			1
	Santos	BRA			1
	Grêmio	BRA			1
			10	10	20

COPA CONMEBOL

Year	Winners	Country	Score	Country	Runners-up
1992	Atlético Mineiro	BRA	2-0 0-1	PAR	Olimpia
1993	Botafogo	BRA	1-1 2-2 3-1p	URU	Peñarol
1994	São Paulo FC	BRA	6-1 0-3	URU	Peñarol
1995	Rosario Central	ARG	0-4 4-0 4-3p	BRA	Atlético Mineiro
1996	Lanús	ARG	2-0 0-1	COL	Independiente Santa Fé
1997	Atlético Mineiro	BRA	4-1 1-1	ARG	Lanús
1998	Santos	BRA	1-0 0-0	ARG	Rosario Central
1999	Talleres Córdoba	ARG	2-4 3-0	BRA	CSA

COPA CONMEBOL MEDALS TABLE - NATIONS

	Country	G	S	B	F	SF
1	Brazil	5	2	6	7	13
2	Argentina	3	2	4	5	9
3	Uruguay		2		2	2
4	Paraguay		1	1	1	2
	Colombia		1	1	1	2
6	Chile			2		2
7	Ecuador			1		1
	Peru			1		1
		8	8	16	16	32

This table represents the Gold (winners), Silver (runners-up) and Bronze (semi-finalists) placings of clubs representing the above countries in the Copa Conmebol, along with the number of appearances in the final and semi-finals

COPA CONMEBOL MEDALS TABLE - CLUBS

	Club		G	S	B
1	Atlético Mineiro	BRA	2	1	2
2	Lanus	ARG	1	1	
3	Rosario Central	ARG	1	1	1
4	Botafogo	BRA	1		
	Santos	BRA	1		

COPA CONMEBOL MEDALS TABLE - CLUBS (CONT'D)

	Club		G	S	B
	São Paulo FC	BRA	1		
	Talleres Cordoba	ARG	1		
8	Peñarol	URU		2	
9	CSA	BRA		1	
	Independiente Santa Fé	COL		1	
	Olimpia	PAR		1	
12	Corinthians	BRA			1
	Deportes Concepcion	CHI			1
	Gimnasia y Esgrima	ARG			1
	El Nacional Quito	ECU			1
	San Lorenzo	ARG			1
	América Cali	COL			1
	Colón Santa Fé	ARG			1
	Atlético Colegiales	PAR			1
	Sampaio Correa	BRA			1
	São Raimundo	BRA			1
	Vasco da Gama	BRA			1
	Universitario	PER			1
	Universidad de Chile	CHI			1
			8	8	16

COPA MERCOSUR

Year	Winners	Country	Score	Country	Runners-up
1998	Palmeiras	BRA	1-2 3-1 1-0	BRA	Cruzeiro
1999	Flamengo	BRA	4-3	BRA	Palmeiras
2000	Vasco da Gama	BRA	2-0 0-1 4-3	BRA	Palmeiras
2001	San Lorenzo	ARG	0-0 1-1 4-3p	BRA	Flamengo

COPA MERCOSUR MEDALS TABLE - NATIONS

	Country	G	S	B	F	SF
1	Brazil	3	4	3	7	10
2	Argentina	1		3	1	4
3	Paraguay			1		1
	Uruguay			1		1
		4	4	8	8	16

This table represents the Gold (winners), Silver (runners-up) and Bronze (semi-finalists) placings of clubs representing the above countries in the Copa Mercosur, along with the number of appearances in the final and semi-finals

COPA MERCOSUR MEDALS TABLE

	Club		G	S	B
1	Palmeiras	BRA	1	2	-
2	Flamengo	BRA	1	1	-
3	San Lorenzo	ARG	1	-	2
4	Vasco da Gama	BRA	1	-	-
5	Cruzeiro	BRA	-	1	-
6	Atlético Mineiro	BRA	-	-	1
	Corinthians	BRA	-	-	1
	Grêmio	BRA	-	-	1
	Olimpia	PAR	-	-	1
	Peñarol	URU	-	-	1
	River Plate	ARG	-	-	1
			4	4	8

COPA MERCONORTE

Year	Winners	Country	Score	Country	Runners-up
1998	Atlético Nacional Medellin	COL	3-1 1-0	COL	Deportivo Cali
1999	América Cali	COL	1-2 1-0	COL	Independiente Santa Fé
2000	Atlético Nacional Medellin	COL	0-0 2-1	COL	Millonarios
2001	Millonários	COL	1-1 1-1 3-1p	ECU	Emelec

COPA MERCONORTE MEDALS TABLE - NATIONS

	Country	G	S	B	F	SF
1	Colombia	4	3	1	7	8
2	Ecuador		1	2	1	3
3	Mexico			3		3
4	Peru			1		1
	Venezuela			1		1
		4	4	8	8	16

This table represents the Gold (winners), Silver (runners-up) and Bronze (semi-finalists) placings of clubs representing the above countries in the Copa Merconorte, along with the number of appearances in the final and semi-finals

COPA MERCONORTE MEDALS TABLE

	Club		G	S	B
1	Atlético Nacional Medellin	COL	2		
2	Millonarios	COL	1	1	1
3	América Cali	COL	1		
4	Emelec	ECU		1	1
5	Deportivo Cali	COL		1	
	Independiente Santa Fé	COL		1	
7	Alianza Lima	PER			1
	Caracas FC	VEN			1
	Chivas Guadalajara	MEX			1
	El Nacional Quito	ECU			1
	Necaxa	MEX			1
	Santos Laguna	MEX			1
			4	4	8

COPA SUDAMERICANA

Year	Winners	Country	Score	Country	Runners-up
2002	San Lorenzo	ARG	4-0 0-0	COL	Atlético Nacional Medellin
2003	Cienciano	PER	3-3 1-0	ARG	River Plate
2004	Boca Juniors	ARG	0-1 2-0	BOL	Bolivar
2005	Boca Juniors	ARG	1-1 1-1 4-3p	MEX	Pumas UNAM
2006	Pachuca	MEX	1-1 2-1	CHI	Colo Colo
2007	Arsenal	ARG	3-2 1-2	MEX	America
2008	Internacional	BRA	1-0 1-1	ARG	Estudiantes LP
2009	LDU Quito	ECU	5-1 0-3	BRA	Fluminense
2010	Independiente	ARG	0-2 3-1 5-3p	BRA	Goiás EC

COPA SUDAMERICANA MEDALS TABLE - NATIONS

	Country	G	S	B	F	SF
1	Argentina	5	2	4	7	11
2	Mexico	1	2	2	3	5
3	Brazil	1	2	4	3	7
4	Ecuador	1		2	1	3
5	Peru	1			1	1
6	Colombia		1	2	1	3
7	Bolivia		1	1	1	2
	Chile		1	1	1	2
9	Paraguay			1		1
	Uruguay			1		1
		9	9	18	18	36

This table represents the Gold (winners), Silver (runners-up) and Bronze (semi-finalists) placings of clubs representing the above countries in the Copa Sudamericana, along with the number of appearances in the final and semi-finals

COPA SUDAMERICANA MEDALS TABLE - CLUBS

	Club		G	S	B
1	Boca Juniors	ARG	2		
2	LDU Quito	ECU	1		2
3	Internacional	BRA	1		1
4	Arsenal	ARG	1		
	Cienciano	PER	1		
	Independiente	ARG	1		

COPA SUDAMERICANA MEDALS TABLE - CLUBS

	Club		G	S	B
	Pachuca	MEX	1		
	San Lorenzo	ARG	1		
9	River Plate	ARG		1	2
10	Atlético Nacional Medellin	COL		1	1
	Bolivar	BOL		1	1
12	CF América	MEX		1	
	Colo Colo	CHI		1	
	Estudiantes LP	ARG		1	
	Fluminense	BRA		1	
	Goiás EC	BRA		1	
	Pumas UNAM	MEX		1	
18	Argentinos Juniors	ARG			1
	Atlético Paranaense	BRA			1
	Cerro Porteño	PAR			1
	Guadalajara	MEX			1
	Millonarios	COL			1
	Nacional Montevideo	URU			1
	Palmeiras	BRA			1
	São Paulo FC	BRA			1
	Universidad Catolica	CHI			1
	Toluca	MEX			1
	Velez Sarsfield	ARG			1
			8	8	16

SOUTH AMERICAN YOUTH TOURNAMENTS

SUDAMERICANA SUB-20

Year	Host Country	Winners	Runners-up
1954	Venezuela	Uruguay	Brazil
1958	Chile	Uruguay	Argentina
1964	Colombia	Uruguay	Paraguay
1967	Paraguay	Argentina	Paraguay
1971	Paraguay	Paraguay	Uruguay
1974	Chile	Brazil	Uruguay
1975	Peru	Uruguay	Chile
1977	Venezuela	Uruguay	Brazil
1979	Uruguay	Uruguay	Argentina
1981	Ecuador	Uruguay	Brazil
1983	Bolivia	Brazil	Uruguay
1985	Paraguay	Brazil	Paraguay

SUDAMERICANA SUB-20 (CONT'D)

Year	Host Country	Winners	Runners-up
1987	Colombia	Colombia	Brazil
1988	Argentina	Brazil	Colombia
1991	Venezuela	Brazil	Argentina
1992	Colombia	Brazil	Uruguay
1995	Bolivia	Brazil	Argentina
1997	Chile	Argentina	Brazil
1999	Argentina	Argentina	Uruguay
2001	Ecuador	Brazil	Argentina
2003	Uruguay	Argentina	Brazil
2005	Colombia	Colombia	Brazil
2007	Paraguay	Brazil	Argentina
2009	Venezuela	Brazil	Paraguay

SOUTH AMERICA PRE-OLIMPICO

Year	Host Country	Winners	Runners-up
1960	Peru	Argentina	Peru
1964	Peru	Argentina	Brazil
1968	Colombia	Brazil	Colombia
1971	Colombia	Brazil	Colombia
1976	Brazil	Brazil	Uruguay
1980	Colombia	Argentina	Colombia
1984	Ecuador	Brazil	Chile
1987	Bolivia	Brazil	Argentina
1992	Paraguay	Paraguay	Colombia
1996	Argentina	Brazil	Argentina
2000	Brazil	Brazil	Chile
2004	Chile	Argentina	Paraguay
2008	Paraguay	Brazil	Argentina

Open to non-professionals only prior to 1984 • The 1987 tournament was open to any player who had not played in a FIFA World Cup™ match • Since 1992 it has been an U-23 tournament

SUDAMERICANA SUB-17

Year	Host Country	Winners	Runners-up
1985	Argentina	Argentina	Brazil
1986	Peru	Bolivia	Brazil
1988	Ecuador	Brazil	Argentina
1991	Paraguay	Brazil	Uruguay
1993	Colombia	Colombia	Chile
1995	Peru	Brazil	Argentina
1997	Paraguay	Brazil	Argentina
1999	Uruguay	Brazil	Paraguay
2002	Peru	Brazil	Argentina
2003	Bolivia	Argentina	Brazil
2005	Venezuela	Brazil	Uruguay
2007	Ecuador	Brazil	Colombia
2009	Brazil	Argentina	Chile

From 1985-1988 the championship was a U-16 tournament but since 1991 it has operated as an U-17 championship

SOUTH AMERICAN WOMEN'S TOURNAMENTS

SOUTH AMERICAN WOMEN'S CHAMPIONSHIP

Year	Host Country	Winners	Runners-up
1991	Brazil	Brazil	Chile
1995	Brazil	Brazil	Argentina
1998	Argentina	Brazil	Argentina
2003	Peru	Brazil	Argentina
2006	Argentina	Argentina	Brazil
2010	Ecuador	Brazil	Colombia

SOUTH AMERICAN WOMEN'S U-20 CHAMPIONSHIP

Year	Host Country	Winners	Runners-up
2004		Brazil	Paraguay
2006	Chile	Brazil	Argentina
2008	Brazil	Brazil	Argentina
2010	Colombia	Brazil	Colombia

SOUTH AMERICAN WOMEN'S U-17 CHAMPIONSHIP

Year	Host Country	Winners	Runners-up
2008	Chile	Colombia	Brazil
2010	Brazil	Brazil	Chile

CLUB TOURNAMENTS IN SOUTH AMERICA IN 2010

COPA SANTANDER LIBERTADORES 2010

Preliminary Round

Group Stage

Grupo 1		Pts	BRA	URU	COL	PAR
Corinthians	BRA	16		2-1	1-0	2-1
Racing Club Montevideo	URU	8	0-2		1-0	2-1
Independiente Medellin	COL	6	1-1	0-0		1-0
Cerro Porteño	PAR	2	0-1	0-0	1-1	

Racing Club Montevideo URU 2 2
Atlético Junior * COL 2 0

Grupo 2		Pts	BRA	COL	MEX	PAR
São Paulo FC	BRA	13		1-0	2-0	3-0
Once Caldas	COL	11	2-1		1-1	1-0
Monterrey	MEX	6	0-0	2-1		2-1
Nacional Asuncion	PAR	3	0-2	0-2	2-0	

Grupo 3		Pts	ARG	PER	PER	BOL
Estudiantes La Plata	ARG	13		1-0	5-1	2-0
Alianza Lima	PER	12	4-1		2-0	1-0
Juan Aurich	PER	6	0-2	4-2		2-0
Bolivar	BOL	4	0-0	1-3	2-0	

Juan Aurich * PER 2 2
UAG Tecos MEX 0 1

Grupo 4		Pts	PAR	PER	ARG	BOL
Libertad	PAR	12		1-1	1-1	4-0
Universitario	PER	10	0-0		2-0	0-0
Lanús	ARG	8	0-2	0-0		1-0
Blooming	BOL	1	1-2	1-2	1-4	

Libertad PAR 0 3
Deportivo Táchira * VEN 1 1

Grupo 5		Pts	BRA	ECU	URU	ECU
Internacional	BRA	12		3-0	2-0	2-1
Deportivo Quito	ECU	10	1-1		2-1	1-0
Cerro	URU	8	0-0	2-0		0-0
Emelec	ECU	2	0-0	0-1	1-2	

Emelec ECU 0 2
Newell's Old Boys * ARG 0 1

Grupo 6		Pts	URU	ARG	MEX	ECU
Nacional Montevideo	URU	12		2-2	2-0	3-2
Banfield	ARG	11	0-2		2-1	4-1
Morelia	MEX	5	0-0	1-1		2-1
Deportivo Cuenca	ECU	4	0-0	1-4	2-0	

Grupo 7		Pts	ARG	BRA	CHI	VEN
Vélez Sarsfield	ARG	13		2-0	2-1	4-0
Cruzeiro	BRA	11	3-0		4-1	2-0
Colo Colo	CHI	8	1-1	1-1		1-0
Deportivo Italia	VEN	1	0-1	2-2	2-3	

Cruzeiro BRA 1 7
Real Potosi * BRA 1 0

Grupo 8		Pts	CHI	BRA	CHI	VEN
Universidad de Chile	CHI	12		2-1	0-0	1-0
Flamengo	BRA	10	2-2		2-0	3-2
Universidad Católica	CHI	7	2-2	2-0		1-1
Caracas FC	VEN	2	1-3	1-3	0-0	

Universidad Católica CHI 2 3 5p
Colón Santa Fe * ARG 3 2 3p

* Home team in the first leg

COPA SANTANDER LIBERTADORES 2010

Round of 16			Quarter-finals			Semi-finals			Final		
Internacional	1	2									
Banfield *	3	0									
			Internacional *	1	1						
			Estudiantes LP	0	2						
San Luis *	0	1									
Estudiantes LP	1	3									
						Internacional *	1	1			
						São Paulo FC	0	2			
Cruzeiro *	3	3									
Nacional Mont'deo	1	0									
			Cruzeiro *	0	0						
			São Paulo FC	2	2						
Universitario *	0 0 1p										
São Paulo FC	0 0 3p										
									Internacional	2	3
									Guadalajara *	1	2
Univ. de Chile	1	2									
Alianza Lima *	0	2									
			Univ. de Chile	3	1						
			Flamengo *	2	2						
Corinthians	0	2									
Flamengo *	1	1									
						Univ. de Chile	1	0			
						Guadalajara *	1	2			
Libertad	0	2									
Once Caldas *	0	1									
			Libertad	0	2						
			Guadalajara *	3	0						
Vélez Sarsfield	0	2									
Guadalajara *	3	0									

* Home team in the first leg • Guadalajara and San Luis received byes to the Round of 16 after their forced withdrawl in the 2009 tournament

Top scorers: **8** - Thiago Ribeiro BRA, Cruzeiro • **7** - Jose Fernandez PER, Alianza & Kleber BRA, Cruzeiro • **6** - Giuliano BRA, Inter & Luis Tejada PAN, Juan Aurich

PRELIMINARY ROUND

Metropolitano, Barranquilla
28-01-2010, 18:10, 18 026, Vera ECU

Atlético Junior   2

Acuna [12], Arzuaga [91+]

Adrian Berbia - Roman Torres, Cesar Fawcett (Jhon Valencia 80), Haider Palacio, Roger Cambindo••♦74 - Paulo Arango•, Alexander Jaramillo•, Jorge Casanova (Martin Arzuaga 62), Emerson Acuna (Victor Cortes 82) - Giovanni Hernandez, Carlos Bacca. Tr: Diego Umana

Racing Club Montevideo   2

Mirabajes [28], Pallas [67]

Jorge Contreras• - Ignacio Pallas, Hector Hernandez, Rodrigo Brasesco, Danny Tejera - Diego Scotti, Dario Flores• (Alejandro Reyes 78), Santiago Ostolaza, Mathias Mirabaje (Jean Pierre Barrientos 67) - Liber Quinones (Nestor Silva 62), Martin Cauteruccio••♦45. Tr: Juan Verzeri

Parque Central, Montevideo
4-02-2010, 21:10, 4768, Oliveira BRA

Racing Club Montevideo   2

Quinones 2 [14p 88]

Jorge Contreras• - Ignacio Pallas, Hector Hernandez, Rodrigo Brasesco, Danny Tejera - Dario Flores• (Gaston Machado 79), Santiago Ostolaza•, Mathias Mirabaje (Jean Pierre Barrientos 68), Federico Vega - Nestor Silva (Roman Marcelo 72), Liber Quinones. Tr: Juan Verzeri

Atlético Junior   0

Adrian Berbia• - Roman Torres, Cesar Fawcett•, Haider Palacio, Pedro Tavima - Alexander Jaramillo (Victor Cortes 52♦93+), Paulo Arango, Jorge Casanova•, Emerson Acuna (Fram Pacheco 77) - Giovanni Hernandez, Carlos Bacca (Martin Arzuaga• 46). Tr: Diego Umana

Elias Aguirre, Chiclayo
27-01-2010, 21:20, 10 312, Pozo CHI

Juan Aurich   2

Tejada 2 [11 60]

Diego Morales - Roberto Guizasola, Jesus Alvarez, Jorge Araujo, Willy Rivas - Juan Carlos La Rosa•, Gianfranco Espejo•, Reimond Manco - Luis Tejada• (Manuel Barreto 81), Ysrael Zuniga (Ricardo Ciciliano 57), Pedro Ascoy (Franco Mendoza 90). Tr: Luis Fernando Suarez

Estudiantes Tecos   0

Mario Rodriguez - Juan Carlos Leano, Diego Jimenez•, Marcelo Alatorre (Jorge Zamogilny 86), Joel Sanchez (Freddy Bareiro 66), Oswaldo Alanis - Rafael Medina•, Elgabry Rangel, Alberto Ramirez (Rubens Sambueza• 56) - Mauro Cejas, Rodrigo Ruiz. Tr: Miguel Herrera

Tres de Marzo, Zapopan
3-02-2010, 20:20, 3000, Soto VEN

Estudiantes Tecos   1

Bareiro [77]

Mario Rodriguez - Juan Carlos Leano, Diego Jimenez, Marcelo Alatorre (Samuel Ochoa 20), Daniel Alcantar (Roberto Gutierrez 46) - Rafael Medina (Mauro Cejas 46), Elgabry Rangel, Jorge Zamogilny, Rubens Sambueza - Rodrigo Ruiz•, Freddy Bareiro. Tr: Miguel Herrera

Juan Aurich   2

Tejada [41], Ciciliano [75]

Diego Morales• - Roberto Guizasola•, Jesus Alvarez•, Jorge Araujo, Willy Rivas•♦65 - Ricardo Ciciliano, Juan Carlos La Rosa, Gianfranco Espejo, Reimond Manco• (Cesar Sanchez 77) - Luis Tejada (Ysrael Zuniga 81), Pedro Ascoy (Jose Guevara 62). Tr: Luis Fernando Suarez

Pueblo Nuevo, San Cristóbal
26-01-2010, 21:00, 16 382, Buitrago COL

Deportivo Táchira   1

Maita [27]

Manuel Sanhouse - Daniel Benitez, Gerson Chacon•, Jose Granados, Jong Viafara - Pedro Fernandez••♦69, Nicolas Diez (Jorge Rojas 63), Edgar Perez (Jaison Ibarrola 76) - Jose Villafraz, Daniel Arismendi (Jose Mauricio Parra 71), Armando Maita. Tr: Carlos Maldonado

Libertad   0

Bernado Medina - Pedro Sarabia•, Jorge Caballero•, Miguel Samudio•, Ismael Benegas - Edgar Robles• (Jose Nunez 55), Victor Caceres, Victor Ayala, Sergio Aquino• - Roberto Gamarra (Javier Gonzalez 66), Pablo Velazquez• (Rodolfo Gamarra 66). Tr: Javier Torrente

Defensores del Chaco, Asunción
2-02-2010, 20:10, 1252, Baldassi ARG

Libertad   3

Rodolfo Gamarra [40], Velazquez 2 [67 81]

Bernado Medina - Pedro Sarabia, Miguel Samudio, Ismael Benegas (Jorge Caballero 72) - Sergio Aquino, Victor Caceres•, Gustavo Cristaldo (Javier Gonzalez 46), Jorge Moreira (Wilson Pittoni 55), Victor Ayala - Pablo Velazquez•, Rodolfo Gamarra. Tr: Javier Torrente

Deportivo Táchira   1

Boada [29]

Manuel Sanhouse - Pedro Boada, Daniel Benitez•, Gerson Chacon (David Solari 83), Jose Granados•, Jong Viafara - Jorge Rojas, Nicolas Diez - Jose Villafraz, Armando Maita• (Daniel Arismendi 79), Jaison Ibarrola (Edgar Perez 68). Tr: Carlos Maldonado

El Coloso, Rosario
27-01-2010, 18:30, 15 292, Silvera URU

Newell's Old Boys   0

Sebastian Peratta - Agustin Alayes, Rolando Schiavi, Nahuel Roselli (Diego Torres 46), Juan Insaurralde - Lucas Bernardi (Cristian Sanchez Prette 71), Leonel Vangioni•, Diego Mateo, Mauro Formica - Jorge Achucarro (Juan Quiroga 82), Joaquin Boghossian. Tr: Roberto Sensini

Emelec   0

Marcelo Elizaga - Julio Fleitas, Mariano Mina, Gabriel Achilier - Carlos Quinonez• (Enner Valencia 57), David Quiroz, Pablo Perez (Hernan Peirone 92+), Pedro Quinonez - Santiago Biglieri•, Joao Rojas•, Enner Valencia (Jose Quinonez 57). Tr: Jorge Luis Sampaoli

George Capwell, Guayaquil
10-02-2010, 21:10, 14 634, Ruiz COL

Emelec   2

Rojas [46], Jose Quinonez [65]

Marcelo Elizaga - Julio Fleitas, Mariano Mina, Gabriel Achilier - David Quiroz (Carlos Quinonez 80), Pablo Perez, Fernando Gimenez (Jose Quinonez 25), Pedro Quinonez• - Santiago Biglieri• (Eduardo Morante 92+), Joao Rojas, Jaime Ayovi. Tr: Jorge Luis Sampaoli

Newell's Old Boys   1

Barrientos [52]

Sebastian Peratta - Agustin Alayes, Rolando Schiavi♦84, Juan Insaurralde - Lucas Bernardi (Mauricio Sperdutti 79), Hugo Barrientos, Leonel Vangioni (Marcelo Estigarribia 70), Franco Dolci, Mauro Formica - Jorge Achucarro• (Cristian Nunez 87), Joaquin Boghossian. Tr: Roberto Sensini

Victor Ugarte, Potosi
27-01-2010, 19:50, 7064, Rivera PER

Real Potosi   0

Correa [88]

Mauro Machado - Edemir Rodriguez, Gerardo Yecerotte•, Ronald Eguino•, Alvaro Ricaldi• - Edgar Clavijo (Augusto Andaveris 46), Gonzalo Galindo, Eduardo Ortiz (Roberto Correa 28), Miguel Loayza•, Fernando Argaranaz - Christian Ruiz (Jorge Florentin 74). Tr: Sergio Apaza

Cruzeiro   1

Wellington Paulista [7]

Fabio - Leonardo Silva•, Diego Renan, Gil - Marquinhos Parana, Henrique, Elicarlos - Pedro Ken (Fabinho 75), Gilberto♦22, Wellington Paulista (Jonathan 52), Kleber (Thiago Ribeiro 68). Tr: Adilson Batista

Mineirão, Belo Horizonte
3-02-2010, 21:50, 36 574, Abal ARG

Cruzeiro   7

Wellington Paulista [29], Thiago Ribeiro [30], Kleber [39], Jonathan [45], Eliandro [87], Bernardo [88], Guerron [91+]

Fabio - Jonathan, Leonardo Silva, Diego Renan, Gil - Marquinhos Parana, Henrique•, Elicarlos (Joffre Guerron 48) - Wellington Paulista (Bernado 67), Kleber (Eliandro 73), Thiago Ribeiro. Tr: Adilson Batista

Real Potosi   0

Mauro Machado - Edemir Rodriguez, Alvaro Ricaldi, Gerardo Yecerotte•♦46, Ronald Eguino - Eduardo Ortiz, Gonzalo Galindo••♦74, Edgar Clavijo, Helmut Gutierrez•, Fernando Argaranaz (Miguel Loayza 64) - Augusto Andaveris (Pastor Torrez 88). Tr: Sergio Apaza

Estanislao Lopez, Santa Fe
26-01-2010, 20:10, 14 902, Larrionda URU

Colón Santa Fe   3

Nieto [5], Fuertes [56], Bertoglio [69]

Diego Pozo - Marcelo Goux, Salustiano Candia, German Rivarola, Ariel Garce• - Alejandro Capurro, Ivan Moreno y Fabianesi• (Eduardo Coudet• 54), Ricardo Gomez (Juan Lucero 46), Facundo Bertoglio - Federico Nieto, Esteban Fuertes (Cristian Pellerano 76). Tr: Antonio Mohamed

Universidad Católica   2

Morales 2 [35 81]

Paulo Garces - Ismael Fuentes•, Hans Martinez, David Henriquez - Damian Diaz, Rodrigo Toloza (Pablo Vranjican• 78), Jorge Ormeno•♦92+, Rodrigo Valenzuela, Francisco Silva• (Angel Carreno• 41), Milovan Mirosevic (Fernando Meneses 67) - Juan Jose Morales. Tr: Marco Antonio Figueroa

San Carlos, Santiago
9-02-2010, 19:20, 12 272, Torres PAR

Universidad Católica   3 5p

Henriquez [40], Toloza [74], Bertoglio [69]

Paulo Garces - Ismael Fuentes, Leonel Mena, Hans Martinez•, David Henriquez - Damian Diaz, Rodrigo Toloza•, Rodrigo Valenzuela (Rodrigo Mannara 77), Angel Carreno (Pablo Vranjican 57), Milovan Mirosevic - Juan Morales. Tr: Marco Antonio Figueroa

Colón Santa Fe   2 3p

Fabianesi [53], Fuertes [55p]

Diego Pozo• - Salustiano Candia••♦69, Marcello Goux, German Rivarola, Ariel Garce (Eduardo Coudet 45) - Alejandro Capurro•, Ivan Moreno y Fabianesi•, Nicolas Torres•, Facundo Bertoglio• (Josimar Mosquera 73) - Federico Nieto, Esteban Fuertes (Cristian Pellerano 60). Tr: Antonio Mohamed

GRUPO 1		Pl	W	D	L	F	A	Pts	BRA	URU	COL	PAR
Corinthians	BRA	6	5	1	0	9	3	16		2-1	1-0	2-1
Racing Club Montevideo	URU	6	2	2	2	4	5	8	0-2		1-0	2-1
Independiente Medellin	COL	6	1	3	2	3	4	6	1-1	0-0		1-0
Cerro Porteño	PAR	6	0	2	4	3	7	2	0-1	0-1	1-1	

Defensores del Chaco, Asunción
11-02-2010, 20:15, 15 219, Laverni ARG

Cerro Porteño   **1**
Ramirez [56]

Diego Barreto - Miguel Torren, Ivan Piris, David Mendoza (Julio Dos Santos 46), Diego Herner - Javier Villarreal, Alberto Martinez (Rodrigo Burgos• 70), Luis Caceres - Ivan Gonzalez (Carlos Recalde 46), Pablo Zeballos, Cesar Ramirez. Tr: Pedro Troglia

Independiente Medellin   **1**
Pardo [17]

Aldo Bobadilla - Anselmo De Almeida, Ricardo Calle, Juan Valencia, Leiton Jimenez - Juan Lopez•, Juan Ortiz, Luis Arias, Malher Moreno (Nelson Barahona 65) - Mario Gimenez (Cesar Valoyes 46), Edgar Pardo (Cesar Rivas 86). Tr: Leonel Alvarez

El Campin, Bogotá
10-03-2010, 19:50, 23 886, Pezzotta ARG

Independiente Medellin   **1**
Valoyes [75]

Aldo Bobadilla - Anselmo De Almeida, Ricardo Calle, Juan Valencia, Leiton Jimenez - Juan Ortiz•, Nelson Barahona (Cesar Valoyes 69), John Restrepo, Luis Arias - Mario Gimenez (Malher Moreno 56), Edgar Pardo (Cesar Rivas 87). Tr: Leonel Alvarez

Corinthians   **1**
Dentinho [84]

Felipe - Chicao, William, Roberto Carlos - Ralf, Marcelo Mattos• (Morais 84), Elias, Jucilei•, Danilo (Dentinho 59) - Ronaldo (Souza 74), Jorge Henrique•. Tr: Mano Menezes

Parque Central, Montevideo
25-03-2010, 21:15, 2492, Abal ARG

Racing Club Montevideo   **1**
Ostolaza [74]

Jorge Contreras - Ignacio Pallas, Hector Hernandez, Rodrigo Brasesco• , Danny Tejera - Santiago Ostolaza, Matias Mirabaje• (Mathias Abero 83), Jorge Cazulo (Jean Pierre Barrientos 62), Federico Vega• - Nestor Silva (Liber Quinones 73), Martin Cauteruccio. Tr: Juan Verzeri

Independiente Medellin   **0**

Aldo Bobadilla - Anselmo De Almeida, Ricardo Calle, Juan Valencia•, Leiton Jimenez - Juan Ortiz•, Hector Vasco (Nelson Barahona 78), John Restrepo•, Luis Arias - Mario Gimenez♦84, Edgar Pardo (Cesar Rivas 84). Tr: Leonel Alvarez

Parque Central, Montevideo
14-04-2010, 21:50, 2669, Baldassi ARG

Racing Club Montevideo   **0**

Jorge Contreras - Ignacio Pallas, Hector Hernandez (Alejandro Reyes 83), Rodrigo Brasesco, Danny Tejera• - Santiago Ostolaza, Matias Mirabaje, Jorge Cazulo (Jean Pierre Barrientos 64), Federico Vega (Nicolas Lopez 81) - Liber Quinones, Martin Cauteruccio. Tr: Juan Verzeri

Corinthians   **2**
Dentinho [33], Elias [87]

Julio Cesar - Chicao, William, Moacir•, Roberto Carlos - Ralf, Elias, Jucilei, Danilo (Paulo Andre 83) - Ronaldo (Jorge Henrique• 70), Dentinho (Iarley 72). Tr: Mano Menezes

Pacaembú, São Paulo
24-02-2010, 21:50, 31 035, Orosco BOL

Corinthians   **2**
Elias 2 [10] [70]

Felipe - Chicao, William, Alessandro (Jucilei 71), Roberto Carlos• - Ralf, Elias, Tcheco, Matias De Federico (Souza 45) - Ronaldo•, Jorge Henrique• (Dentinho 84). Tr: Mano Menezes

Racing Club Montevideo   **1**
Cauteruccio [1]

Jorge Contreras - Hector Hernandez, Dario Flores••♦57, Rodrigo Brasesco, Danny Tejera, Ignacio Pallas• - Santiago Ostolaza, Federico Vega•, Matias Mirabaje (Carlos Keosseian 65) - Martin Cauteruccio (Nicolas Lopez 83), Liber Quinones• (Jean Pierre Barrientos 72). Tr: Juan Verzeri

Defensores del Chaco, Asunción
17-03-2010, 21:50, 17 321, Pozo CHI

Cerro Porteño   **0**

Diego Barreto - Julio Irrazabal, Diego Herner, Miguel Torren•, Ivan Piris - Julio Dos Santos, Luis Caceres (Carlos Recalde 71), Jorge Britez♦82, Jorge Nunez• - Pablo Zeballos, Cesar Ramirez• (Sebastian Ereros 64). Tr: Pedro Troglia

Corinthians   **1**
Ronaldo [40]

Felipe - Chicao, William, Moacir•, Roberto Carlos - Ralf, Elias, Jucilei•, Danilo - Ronaldo (Souza 83), Dentinho• (Jorge Henrique 71). Tr: Mano Menezes

Pacaembú, São Paulo
1-04-2010, 19:15, 30 321, Carrillo PER

Corinthians   **2**
Ronaldo [36], Chicao [63]

Rafael Santos - Chicao, William, Moacir, Roberto Carlos - Ralf•, Elias, Jucilei, Danilo (Tcheco 90) - Ronaldo (Iarley 87), Dentinho (Jorge Henrique 81). Tr: Mano Menezes

Cerro Porteño   **1**
Dos Santos [79]

Diego Barreto - Ernesto Cristaldo, Ivan Piris, Diego Herner•, Luis Cardozo - Rodrigo Burgos• (Luis Caceres 74), Javier Villarreal, Jorge Nunez• (Julio Irrazabal 60), Julio Dos Santos - Pablo Zeballos, Roberto Nanni (Sebastian Ereros 70). Tr: Pedro Troglia

La Olla, Asunción
22-04-2010, 20:50, 2728, Rivera PER

Cerro Porteño   **0**

Ezequiel Medran - Miguel Torren•, Ivan Piris, Fidel Perez•, Julio Irrazabal - Javier Villarreal, Carlos Recalde, Alberto Martinez - Ivan Gonzalez (Ernesto Cristaldo 63), Roberto Nanni (Ramon Cardozo 82), Sebastian Ereros (Cesar Ramirez 68). Tr: Pedro Troglia

Racing Club Montevideo   **0**

Jorge Contreras - Danny Tejera, Ignacio Pallas•, Hector Hernandez (Jean Pierre Barrientos 54), Rodrigo Brasesco - Santiago Ostolaza•, Federico Vega•, Alejandro Reyes 79), Matias Mirabaje• - Jorge Cazulo•, Liber Quinones (Nestor Silva 71), Martin Cauteruccio•. Tr: Juan Verzeri

Centenario, Montevideo
9-03-2010, 20:00, 1435, Beligoy ARG

Racing Club Montevideo   **2**
Mirabaje [18], Cauteruccio [68]

Jorge Contreras - Hector Hernandez, Rodrigo Brasesco•, Danny Tejera, Ignacio Pallas - Santiago Ostolaza•, Federico Vega, Matias Mirabaje (Nestor Silva 86) - Martin Cauteruccio, Jean Pierre Barrientos (Gonzalo Aguilar• 74), Liber Quinones (Jorge Cazulo 59). Tr: Juan Verzeri

Cerro Porteño   **1**
Caceres [83]

Diego Barreto - Diego Herner•, Miguel Torren, Ivan Piris, Julio Irrazabal•, Luis Cardozo (Julio Dos Santos• 45) - Luis Caceres, Javier Villarreal♦78, Carlos Recalde•, (Ramon Cardozo 59) - Pablo Zeballos, Cesar Ramirez (Sebastian Ereros 74). Tr: Pedro Troglio

Palogrande, Manizales
18-03-2010, 21:45, 4651, Soto VEN

Independiente Medellin   **0**

Aldo Bobadilla - Anselmo De Almeida•, Ricardo Calle (Lewis Ochoa 72♦89), Juan Valencia, Leiton Jimenez - Juan Ortiz (Tressor Moreno 61), Nelson Barahona (Mario Gimenez 80), John Restrepo, Luis Arias - Cesar Valoyes••♦66, Edgar Pardo. Tr: Leonel Alvarez

Racing Club Montevideo   **0**

Jorge Contreras - Hector Hernandez, Rodrigo Brasesco, Danny Tejera, Ignacio Pallas - Santiago Ostolaza, Matias Mirabaje• (Alejandro Reyes 84), Jorge Cazulo (Jean Pierre Barrientos• 46), Federico Vega - Martin Cauteruccio, Liber Quinones (Nestor Silva 69). Tr: Juan Verzeri

Atanasio Girardot, Medellin
8-04-2010, 18:15, 8066, Buckley PER

Independiente Medellin   **1**
Arias [55]

Aldo Bobadilla - Anselmo De Almeida, Ricardo Calle, Juan Valencia, Leiton Jimenez - Juan Ortiz, John Restrepo, Luis Arias, Malher Moreno (Nelson Barahona• 46) - Cesar Valoyes (Cesar Rivas 90), Edgar Pardo (Hector Vasco 84). Tr: Leonel Alvarez

Cerro Porteño   **0**

Ezequiel Medran - Ivan Piris, Fidel Perez•, Luis Cardozo•, Ernesto Cristaldo - Carlos Recalde (Julio Dos Santos 78), Jorge Nunez, Alberto Martinez (Luis Caceres 59), Rodrigo Burgos♦67 - Roberto Nanni (Sebastian Ereros 78), Ramon Cardozo. Tr: Pedro Troglio

Pacaembú, São Paulo
22-04-2010, 21:50, 29 541, Beligoy ARG

Corinthians   **1**
Valencia OG [23]

Julio Cesar - Chicao, William, Moacir, Roberto Carlos - Ralf, Elias, Jucilei, Danilo (Edu 88) - Iarley (Souza 78), Dentinho (Jorge Henrique 65). Tr: Mano Menezes

Independiente Medellin   **0**

Aldo Bobadilla - Anselmo De Almeida, Ricardo Calle, Juan Valencia, Juan Ortiz•, Nelson Barahona (Hernan Pertuz 77), Hector Vasco (Malher Moreno 46), John Restrepo - Mario Gimenez (Cesar Valoyes 58), Edgar Pardo. Tr: Leonel Alvarez

GRUPO 2		Pl	W	D	L	F	A	Pts	BRA	COL	MEX	PAR
São Paulo FC	BRA	6	4	1	1	9	2	**13**		1-0	2-0	3-0
Once Caldas	COL	6	3	2	1	8	5	**11**	2-1		1-1	1-0
Monterrey	MEX	6	1	3	2	8	8	**6**	0-0	2-1		2-1
Nacional Asuncion	PAR	6	1	0	5	3	10	**3**	0-2	0-2	2-0

Defensores del Chaco, Asunción
9-02-2010, 19:20, 966, Beligoy ARG
Nacional Asuncion 0

German **Caffa** - Arturo **Aquino**•, Marcos **Miers**, Raul **Piris** (Celso **Gonzalez** 70), Ricardo **Mazacotte** - Marcos **Riveros**, Fabio **Ramos**, Marcos **Melgarejo** (Ramon **Caceres** 46), Aldo **Paniagua** (Fabian **Caballero** 46) - Guillermo **Beltran**•, Victor **Aquino**. Tr: Ever **Almeida**

Once Caldas 2
Castrillon 22, Santoya 64
Hector **Landazuri** - Oswaldo **Vizcarrondo**, Jose **Velez**, Luis **Nunez**, Alexis **Henriquez**, Diego **Amaya** - Jaime **Castrillon**, Diego **Arias** - Fernando **Cardenas** (Juan **Baena** 76), Fernando **Uribe** (Sebastian **Tagliabue** 82), Dany **Santoya** (John **Valencia** 67). Tr: Juan Carlos **Osorio**

Morumbi, São Paulo
10-02-2010, 21:50, 34 501, Pezzotta ARG
São Paulo FC 2
Washington 2 12 76
Rogerio **Ceni** - Miranda, Xandao, Richarlyson (Cicinho 74), Renato Silva - Jean (Leo Lima 90), Jorge Wagner, Cleber Santana, Hernanes• - Marcelinho (Marlos 82), Washington. Tr: Ricardo Gomes

Monterrey 0

Omar **Ortiz** - Eduardo **Guevara**, Diego **Cervantes**, Hector **Morales**, Sergio **Perez**• - Gerardo **Galindo** (Luis **Rodriguez**• 72), Juan **Medina**, Jesus **Arellano** (Osvaldo **Martinez** 61), Jesus **Zavala** - Abraham **Carreno**, Val **Baiano** (Sergio **Santana** 61). Tr: Victor Vucetich

---

Tecnolólico, Monterrey
24-02-2010, 21:10, 20 366, Rivera PER
Monterrey 2
Santana 60, Martinez 68
Omar **Ortiz** - Diego **Cervantes** (Val **Baliano** 62), Jose **Basanta**•, Hector **Morales**, Sergio **Perez** - Juan **Medina** (Neri **Cardozo** 61), Luis **Perez**•, Osvaldo **Martinez**, Walter **Ayovi**, Jesus **Arellano** (Gerardo **Galindo** 71) - Sergio **Santana**. Tr: Victor **Vucetich**

Nacional Asuncion 1
Miranda 67p
German **Caffa**• - Alfredo **Rojas**, Arturo **Aquino**•, Herminio **Miranda**, Ricardo **Mazacotte** - Orlando **Bordon**, Marcos **Riveros**•, Carlos **Ruiz**•, Ramon **Caceres**• (Marcos **Melgarejo** 67) - Fabian **Caballero**•, Ariel **Bogado** (Guillermo **Beltran**• 46). Tr: Ever **Almeida**

Palogrande, Manizales
25-02-2010, 19:10, 21 766, Pozo CHI
Once Caldas 2
Uribe 49, Moreno 71
Luis **Martinez** - Oswaldo **Vizcarrondo**, Jose **Velez**, Luis **Nunez**, Alexis **Henriquez**• - John **Valencia**, Jaime **Castrillon** (Fernando **Cardenas** 46), Diego **Arias** - Fernando **Uribe** (Diego **Amaya** 81), Dany **Santoya** (Juan **Baena** 70), Dayro **Moreno**•. Tr: Juan Carlos **Osorio**

São Paulo FC 1
Rogerio Ceni 32
Rogerio **Ceni** - Miranda, Xandao, Richarlyson, Cicinho - Jean, Jorge Wagner, Cleber Santana, Hernanes - Marcelinho (Rodrigo Souto 76), Washington. Tr: Ricardo Gomes

---

Palogrande, Manizales
10-03-2010, 17:30, 20 127, Antequera BOL
Once Caldas 1
Valencia 58
Luis **Martinez** - Oswaldo **Vizcarrondo**, Jose **Velez**, Luis **Nunez**, Alexis **Henriquez**• - John **Valencia**, Diego **Arias**, Jaime **Castrillon** (Diego **Amaya** 46) - Fernando **Uribe** (Juan **Baena** 77), Fernando **Cardenas** (Dany **Santoya** 56), Dayro **Moreno**•. Tr: Juan Carlos **Osorio**

Monterrey 1
Morales 33
Jonathan **Orozco**• - Duilio **Davino**•, Jose **Basanta**, Hector **Morales**•, Sergio **Perez** - Osvaldo **Martinez** (Severo **Meza** 77), Neri **Cardozo**, Walter **Ayovi**, William **Paredes**• (Gerardo **Galindo** 72•82) - Sergio **Santana** (Val **Baiano** 63), Jesus **Zavala**••56. Tr: Victor **Vucetich**

Tecnolólico, Monterrey
17-03-2010, 21:15, 26 725, Buckley PER
Monterrey 2
Martinez 18p, Cardozo 46
Jonathan **Orozco** - Severo **Meza** (Diego **Cervantes** 62), Duilio **Davino** (Aldo de **Nigris** 67), Hector **Morales**, Jose **Basanta**• - Osvaldo **Martinez**, Neri **Cardozo**, Walter **Ayovi**, William **Paredes** - Sergio **Santana** (Sergio **Perez** 62), Abraham **Carreno**. Tr: Victor **Vucetich**

Once Caldas 2
Moreno 1, Castrillon 66
Luis **Martinez** - Oswaldo **Vizcarrondo**, Jose **Velez**, Luis **Nunez**•, Alexis **Henriquez**•, Diego **Amaya** (Dayron **Perez** 56) - John **Valencia**, Diego **Arias** - Fernando **Uribe** (Jaime **Castrillon** 46), Dany **Santoya** (Fernando **Cardenas** 46), Dayro **Moreno**. Tr: Juan Carlos **Osorio**

Morumbi, São Paulo
18-03-2010, 21:30, 31 411, Ubriaco URU
São Paulo FC 3
Dagoberto 30, Leo Lima 33, Washington 55
Rogerio **Ceni** - Alex Silva, Miranda, Richarlyson (Rodrigo Souto• 80), Junior Cesar - Jean (Cicinho 75), Cleber Santana, Hernanes, Leo Lima - Washington (Fernandinho 72), Dagoberto. Tr: Ricardo Gomes

Nacional Asuncion 0

German **Caffa** - Alfredo **Rojas** (Arturo **Aquino** 46), Marcos **Miers**, Herminio **Miranda**, Raul **Piris**, Ricardo **Mazacotte** (Victor **Aquino** 46) - Blas **Irala**, Marcos **Riveros**•, Ramon **Caceres**, Aldo **Paniagua** - Guillermo **Beltran** (Orlando **Bordon** 65). Tr: Ever **Almeida**

Tecnolólico, Monterrey
31-03-2010, 18:50, 28 472, Laverni ARG
Monterrey 0

Jonathan **Orozco** - Jose **Basanta**, Hector **Morales**, Sergio **Perez** (Juan **Medina** 82) - Osvaldo **Martinez**, Neri **Cardozo**, Walter **Ayovi**•, Jesus **Zavala**, William **Paredes** - Sergio **Santana** (Jesus **Arellano** 59), Val **Baiano** (Abraham **Carreno** 59). Tr: Victor **Vucetich**

São Paulo FC 0

Rogerio **Ceni** - Alex Silva, Miranda•, Junior Cesar•, Cicinho (Jean 71), Jorge Wagner, Cleber Santana, Hernanes (Xandao 82), Rodrigo Souto, Washington, Dagoberto (Fernandinho 56). Tr: Ricardo Gomes

---

Palogrande, Manizales
1-04-2010, 21:45, 17 086, Gomez VEN
Once Caldas 1
Valencia 14
Hector **Landazuri** - Oswaldo **Vizcarrondo**, Jose **Velez**, Luis **Nunez**, Alexis **Henriquez** - John **Valencia**, Jaime **Castrillon** (Diego **Amaya** 75), Diego **Arias** - Fernando **Uribe** (Sebastian **Hernandez** 70), Dany **Santoya** (Fernando **Cardenas** 56), Dayro **Moreno**•. Tr: Juan Carlos **Osorio**

Nacional Asuncion 0

German **Caffa** - Marcos **Miers**•, Herminio **Miranda**, Raul **Piris**, Ricardo **Mazacotte** - Blas **Irala**, Orlando **Bordon**•, Fabio **Ramos**•, Marcos **Melgarejo** (Arturo **Aquino** 62), Ramon **Caceres** (Sergio **Gomez** 88) - Fabian **Caballero** (Victor **Aquino** 69). Tr: Ever **Almeida**

Defensores del Chaco, Asunción
21-04-2010, 20:50, 341, Orosco BOL
Nacional Asuncion 2
Paniagua 4, Beltran 67
German **Caffa** - Alfredo **Rojas**, Marcos **Miers**•, Herminio **Miranda**, Raul **Piris** (Gilberto **Velazquez** 46) - Blas **Irala**•, Orlando **Bordon**, Ramon **Caceres** - Aldo **Paniagua** - Fabian **Caballero** (Fabio **Ramos** 74), Victor **Aquino**• (Guillermo **Beltran** 61). Tr: Juan **Battaglia**

Monterrey 2

Jonathan **Orozco** - Eduardo **Guevara** (William **Paredes** 70), Diego **Cervantes**, Sergio **Perez**, Jose **Recio**• (Neri **Cardozo** 71) - Juan **Medina**, Luis **Rodriguez**, Jesus **Zavala**, Jesus **Arellano**• (Osvaldo **Martinez** 78) - Brayan **Martinez**, Val **Baiano**. Tr: Victor **Vucetich**

Morumbi, São Paulo
21-04-2010, 21:50, 50 461, Abal ARG
São Paulo FC 1
Fernandinho 40
Rogerio **Ceni** - Alex Silva, Miranda, Richarlyson•, Cicinho - Jorge Wagner• (Washington 66), Hernanes (Cleber Santana 86), Marlos, Rodrigo Souto - Fernandinho (Jean 60), Dagoberto. Tr: Ricardo Gomes

Once Caldas 0

Luis **Martinez** - Oswaldo **Vizcarrondo**, Jose **Velez**, Luis **Nunez**, Alexis **Henriquez** - Dayron **Perez** (Fernando **Cardenas** 46), Jaime **Castrillon** (Fernando **Uribe** 72), John **Valencia**, Diego **Arias** - Dany **Santoya** (Diego **Amaya** 72), Dayro **Moreno**•. Tr: Juan Carlos **Osorio**

GRUPO 3		Pl	W	D	L	F	A	Pts	ARG	PER	PER	BOL
Estudiantes La Plata	ARG	6	4	1	1	11	5	**13**		1-0	5-1	2-0
Alianza Lima	PER	6	4	0	2	12	7	**12**	4-1		2-0	1-0
Juan Aurich	PER	6	2	0	4	7	13	**6**	0-2	4-2		2-0
Bolivar	BOL	6	1	1	4	3	8	**4**	0-0	1-3	2-0	

Hernando Siles, La Paz
10-02-2010, 17:30, 16 852, Haro ECU
Bolivar **1**
Ferreira [89p]

Carlos **Arias** - Limbert **Mendez**, Ignacio **Ithurralde** (**Charles** 46), Ronald **Rivero** - Walter **Flores**, **Alex Da Rosa**•, Didi **Torrico**, Leonel **Reyes** (Enrique **Parada** 71), Abdon **Reyes** - William **Ferreira**, **Anderson** (Jose **Rios** 56). Tr: Santiago **Escobar**

Alianza Lima **3**
Fernandez 2 [73 74], Montano [91+]

Salomon **Libman** - Edgar **Villamarin**, Carlos **Solis**•, Hector **Sosa**, Amilton **Prado** - Joel **Sanchez**• (Alexander **Sanchez** 66), Henry **Quinteros** (Juan **Jayo**• 62), Jean **Tragodara**, Edgar **Gonzalez** - Wilmer **Aguirre**, Jose **Fernandez** (Johnnier **Montano** 79). Tr: Gustavo **Costas**

Centenario, Quilmes, Buenos Aires
11-02-2010, 15:30, 10 704, Fagundes BRA
Estudiantes La Plata **5**
Boselli 3 [6p 59 72], Re [43], Gonzalez [89]

Agustin **Orion** - Leandro **Desabato**, Christian **Cellay**•, German **Re** (Faustino **Rojo** 64), Clemente **Rodriguez** - Jose **Sosa** (Leandro **Gonzalez** 82), Enzo **Perez** (Maximiliano **Nunez** 77), Juan **Veron**, Rodrigo **Brana**•, Leandro **Benitez** - Mauro **Boselli**. Tr: Luis **Suarez**

Juan Aurich **1**
Tejada [34]

Diego **Morales** - Jerson **Vasquez**•, Jorge **Araujo**, Jesus **Alvarez**, Roberto **Guizasola**♦**44** - Reimond **Manco** (Jose **Guevara** 57), Luis **La Rosa** (Ysrael **Zuniga** 67), Gianfranco **Espejo**, Ricardo **Ciciliano** - Luis **Tejada**, Pedro **Ascoy** (Cesar **Sanchez** 46). Tr: Luis **Suarez**

Alejandro Villanueva, Lima
18-02-2010, 19:30, 16 310, Escalante VEN
Alianza Lima **4**
Aguirre 3 [18 34 74], Fernandez [84]

Salomon **Libman** - Edgar **Villamarin**, Carlos **Solis**, Hector **Sosa**, Amilton **Prado** - Joel **Sanchez**• (Alexander **Sanchez** 70), Henry **Quinteros** (Juan **Jayo** 76), Jean **Tragodara** (Oscar **Vilchez** 85), Edgar **Gonzalez** - Wilmer **Aguirre**, Jose **Fernandez**. Tr: Gustavo **Costas**

Estudiantes La Plata **1**
Sosa [1]

Agustin **Orion** - Leandro **Desabato**, Christian **Cellay**•, German **Re**, Clemente **Rodriguez** - Jose **Sosa** (Faustino **Rojo** 90), Enzo **Perez** (Maximiliano **Nunez** 46), Juan **Veron**, Rodrigo **Brana**, Leandro **Benitez** (Jeronimo **Morales** 62) - Mauro **Boselli**. Tr: Alejandro **Sabella**

Elias Aguirre, Chiclayo
24-02-2010, 17:30, 10 759, Polic CHI
Juan Aurich **2**
Ciciliano [11], Tejada [37]

Diego **Morales** - Willy **Rivas**, Jorge **Araujo**, Jesus **Alvarez** - Reimond **Manco** (Franco **Mendosa** 68), Juan **La Rosa**, Gianfranco **Espejo**, Ricardo **Ciciliano** (William **Chiroque** 45) - Jose **Guevara**, Luis **Tejada** (Ysrael **Zuniga** 83), Pedro **Ascoy**••♦**38**. Tr: Luis **Suarez**

Bolivar **0**

Carlos **Arias** - Luis **Torrico**, Ronald **Rivero**•, Limbert **Mendez**• (Enrique **Parada** 72), Ignacio **Ithurralde** - Abdon **Reyes**• (**Charles** 45), Walter **Flores**, **Alex Da Rosa** - William **Ferreira**, **Anderson** (Didi **Torrico** 62). Tr: Santiago **Escobar**

Hernando Siles, La Paz
9-03-2010, 18:00, 7887, Galeano PAR
Bolivar **0**

Carlos **Arias** - Ronald **Rivero**, Ignacio **Ithurralde** - Didi **Torrico** (Jose **Rios** 59), Enrique **Parada**, Leonel **Reyes**, Abdon **Reyes**, Walter **Flores**, **Alex Da Rosa** (**Anderson** 72), **Charles**• - William **Ferreira**. Tr: Santiago **Escobar**

Estudiantes La Plata **0**

Agustin **Orion**• - Leandro **Desabato**, Christian **Cellay**, Marcos **Angeleri**, German **Re**, Clemente **Rodriguez** - Jose **Sosa** (Maximiliano **Nunez** 75), Enzo **Perez** (Matias **Sanchez** 57), Juan **Veron**•, Rodrigo **Brana**• - Mauro **Boselli**• (Leandro **Gonzalez** 90). Tr: Alejandro **Sabella**

Alejandro Villanueva, Lima
10-03-2010, 19:50, 24 742, Rojas PER
Alianza Lima **2**
Fernandez [41], Tragodara [59]

Salomon **Libman** - Edgar **Villamarin**•, Carlos **Solis**, Hector **Sosa**•, Amilton **Prado** - Joel **Sanchez**, Henry **Quinteros** (Walter **Vilchez** 75), Jean **Tragodara** (Alexander **Sanchez** 74), Edgar **Gonzalez**• - Wilmer **Aguirre**, Jose **Fernandez** (Johnnier **Montano** 84). Tr: Gustavo **Costas**

Juan Aurich **0**

Diego **Morales** - Jorge **Araujo**, Jesus **Alvarez**, Willy **Rivas**, Roberto **Guizasola** - Ricardo **Ciciliano**, Miguel **Cevasco** (Franco **Mendoza**• 60), Juan **La Rosa**•, Gianfranco **Espejo** (Reimond **Manco** 46) - William **Chiroque**• (Ysrael **Zuniga** 66), Luis **Tejada**•. Tr: Luis **Suarez**

Elias Aguirre, Chiclayo
16-03-2010, 20:00, 13 253, Simon BRA
Juan Aurich **4**
Guizasola [25], Tejada [44], Manco [59], Ascoy [87]

Diego **Morales** - Willy **Rivas** (Jerson **Vasquez**• 49), Jorge **Araujo**, Jesus **Alvarez**, Roberto **Guizasola** - Reimond **Manco**• (William **Chiroque** 85), Juan **La Rosa**, Gianfranco **Espejo**, Ricardo **Ciciliano** (Ysrael **Zuniga** 72) - Luis **Tejada**•, Pedro **Ascoy**. Tr: Luis **Suarez**

Alianza Lima **2**
Sanchez [3], Ovelar [72]

Salomon **Libman**• - Edgar **Villamarin**, Carlos **Solis**, Hector **Sosa**, Amilton **Prado** - Joel **Sanchez**, Henry **Quinteros** (Johnnier **Montano** 69), Jean **Tragodara** (Walter **Vilchez** 81), Edgar **Gonzalez** - Wilmer **Aguirre**•, Jose **Fernandez** (Roberto **Ovelar** 62). Tr: Gustavo **Costas**

Centenario, Quilmes, Buenos Aires
23-03-2010, 19:30, 8907, Marcelo BRA
Estudiantes La Plata **2**
Sosa [51], Boselli [79]

Agustin **Orion** - Leandro **Desabato**, Christian **Cellay**, Marcos **Angeleri**, German **Re** - Jose **Sosa** (Jeronimo **Morales** 86), Enzo **Perez**• (Marcelo **Carrusca** 45), Juan **Veron**•, Rodrigo **Brana** - Mauro **Boselli**, Gaston **Fernandez** (Maximiliano **Nunez** 65). Tr: Alejandro **Sabella**

Bolivar **0**

Carlos **Arias** - Luis **Torrico**, Ronald **Rivero**•, Ignacio **Ithurralde** - Leonel **Reyes**•, Abdon **Reyes** (Enrique **Parada** 61), Mario **Ovando** (Rudy **Cardozo** 84), Walter **Flores**•, **Alex Da Rosa** (**Anderson** 61), **Charles** - William **Ferreira**. Tr: Santiago **Escobar**

Elias Aguirre, Chiclayo
30-03-2010, 20:30, 19 904, Amarilla PAR
Juan Aurich **0**

Diego **Morales** - Jerson **Vasquez**, Jorge **Araujo**•, Jesus **Alvarez**♦**87**, Roberto **Guizasola** - Reimond **Manco** (Victor **Balta** 88), Juan **La Rosa** (William **Chiroque** 61), Gianfranco **Espejo**•, Ricardo **Ciciliano** - Luis **Tejada**♦**90**, Pedro **Ascoy** (Ysrael **Zuniga** 84). Tr: Luis **Suarez**

Estudiantes La Plata **2**
Fernandez [52], Brana [68]

Agustin **Orion** - Leandro **Desabato**, Christian **Cellay**, Marcos **Angeleri**, German **Re**, Clemente **Rodriguez**• (Faustino **Rojo** 83) - Jose **Sosa** (Matias **Sanchez** 89), Juan **Veron**, Rodrigo **Brana**• - Mauro **Boselli**, Gaston **Fernandez** (Enzo **Perez** 64). Tr: Alejandro **Sabella**

Alejandro Villanueva, Lima
8-04-2010, 20:30, 11 285, Soto VEN
Alianza Lima **1**
Fernandez [6]

Salomon **Libman** - Edgar **Villamarin**••♦**86**, Walter **Vilchez**•, Hector **Sosa**, Amilton **Prado**• - Joel **Sanchez** (Alexander **Sanchez**• 64), Henry **Quinteros**, Jean **Tragodara** (Eduardo **Uribe** 83), Edgar **Gonzalez** - Wilmer **Aguirre**, Jose **Fernandez** (Roberto **Ovelar**• 64). Tr: Gustavo **Costas**

Bolivar **0**

Carlos **Arias** - Ronald **Rivero**, Ariel **Juarez**, Ignacio **Ithurralde** - Leonel **Reyes** (Didi **Torrico** 77), Abdon **Reyes** (Jose **Rios** 87), Walter **Flores**•, **Charles**, Rudy **Cardozo** - William **Ferreira**, **Anderson**• (**Alex Da Rosa** 77). Tr: Santiago **Escobar**

Hernando Siles, La Paz
20-04-2010, 20:15, 2484, Osorio CHI
Bolivar **1**
Flores [71], De Rosa [86]

Carlos **Arias** - Ronald **Rivero**, Ariel **Juarez** (Enrique **Parada** 88), Ignacio **Ithurralde**• - Leonel **Reyes**, Abdon **Reyes**, Walter **Flores**, **Charles**•, Rudy **Cardozo** (Jose **Rios** 58) - William **Ferreira**, **Anderson** (**Alex Da Rosa** 69). Tr: Luis **Suarez**

Juan Aurich **0**

Diego **Morales**• - Jerson **Vasquez**, Jorge **Araujo**, Jhonny **Lalopu** - Franco **Mendoza**, Juan **La Rosa**, Gianfranco **Espejo** (Miguel **Cevasco**• 76), Cesar **Sanchez**, William **Chiroque** (Fernando **Garcia** 80) - Ysrael **Zuniga**•, Manuel **Barreto** (Gary **Correa**• 64). Tr: Luis **Suarez**

Centenario, Quilmes, Buenos Aires
20-04-2010, 21:15, 14 982, Silvera URU
Estudiantes La Plata **1**
Veron [95+]

Agustin **Orion** - Leandro **Desabato**, Christian **Cellay**•, Marcos **Angeleri**, Clemente **Rodriguez**• (German **Re** 88) - Jose **Sosa**, Enzo **Perez**, Juan **Veron**•, Maximiliano **Nunez** (Leandro **Gonzalez** 82), Rodrigo **Brana**• - Mauro **Boselli**. Tr: Alejandro **Sabella**

Alianza Lima **0**

George **Forsyth**• - Walter **Vilchez**••♦**92+**, Carlos **Solis**, Hector **Sosa**•, Amilton **Prado**• - Joel **Sanchez**, Henry **Quinteros**• (Oscar **Vilchez** 81), Jean **Tragodara**• (Eduardo **Uribe** 87), Edgar **Gonzalez** - Wilmer **Aguirre**, Jose **Fernandez** (Johnnier **Montano** 73). Tr: Gustavo **Costas**

GRUPO 4		Pl	W	D	L	F	A	Pts	PAR	PER	ARG	BOL
Libertad	PAR	6	3	3	0	10	3	**12**		1-1	1-1	4-0
Universitario	PER	6	2	4	0	5	2	**10**	0-0		2-0	0-0
Lanús	ARG	6	2	2	2	6	6	**8**	0-2	0-0		1-0
Blooming	BOL	6	0	1	5	3	13	**1**	1-2	1-2	1-4	

La Fortaleza, Lanús, Buenos Aires
9-02-2010, 21:40, 4220, Seneme BRA
Lanús 0

Agustin **Marchesin** - Maximiliano **Velazquez**, Hernan **Grana** (Cristian Menendez 78), **Jadson**, Santiago **Hoyos** - Matias **Fritzler**, Agustin **Pelletieri**, Sebastian **Blanco**, Marcos **Aguirre** (Santiago **Salcedo** 68) - Diego **Lagos** (Eduardo **Ledesma** 68), Gonzalo **Castillejos**. Tr: Luis **Zubeldia**

Libertad 2
Rodolfo Gamarra [67], Velazquez [73]

Bernardo **Medina** - Ismael **Benegas**, Miguel **Samudio**•, Pedro **Sarabia**• - Victor **Ayala**, Sergio **Aquino**, Jorge **Moreira** (Wilson **Pittoni** 46), Victor **Caceres** - Pablo **Velazquez**, Javier **Gonzalez** (Gustavo **Mencia** 76), Rodolfo **Gamarra** (Omar **Pouso** 68). Tr: Javier **Torrente**

Tahuichi, Santa Cruz
11-02-2010, 21:30, 10 600, Quintana PAR
Blooming 1
Gomez [89]

Andres **Jemio** - Fabricio **Brandao**, Juan **Sanchez** (David **Villalba** 61), Andres **Imperiale**•, Wilder **Zabala** - Lorgio **Alvarez**, Jose **Chavez**•, Jesus **Gomez**•, Luiz Carlos **Vieira** (Julio **Hurtado** 57) - Jose **Castillo** (Roger **Suarez** 57), Damian **Akerman**. Tr: Carlos **Aragones**

Universitario 2
Orejuela [52], Espinoza [76]

Raul **Fernandez** - John **Galliquio**•, Carlos **Galvan**, Renzo **Revoredo**•, Jesus **Rabanal** - Antonio **Gonzales** (Luis **Hernandez**• 71), Rainer **Torres**• (Luis **Ramirez** 79), Jorge **Vasquez**, Rodolfo **Espinoza** - Carlos **Orejuela** (Gianfranco **Labarthe** 64), Piero **Alva**. Tr: Juan **Reynoso**

Defensores del Chaco, Asunción
16-02-2010, 21:25, 457, Silvera URU
Libertad 4
Caceres [45], Roldolfo Gamarra 2 [68] [91+], Ayala [90]

Bernardo **Medina** - Ismael **Benegas**, Miguel **Samudio**, Pedro **Sarabia** - Victor **Ayala**, Sergio **Aquino**• (Omar **Pouso** 69), Jorge **Moreira** (Wilson **Pittoni** 38), Victor **Caceres** - Pablo **Velazquez**, Javier **Gonzalez** (Rodrigo **Albornoz** 66), Rodolfo **Gamarra**. Tr: Javier **Torrente**

Blooming 0

Andres **Jemio** - Fabricio **Brandao**••♦[52], Juan **Sanchez**, Andres **Imperiale**••♦[49], Wilder **Zabala** - Lorgio **Alvarez**•, Jose **Chavez** (Julio **Hurtado** 67), Jorge **Andia** (Raul **Gonzalez** 80), Jesus **Gomez**, Luiz Carlos **Vieira** (Omar **Morales** 53) - Damian **Akerman**. Tr: Carlos **Aragones**

Monumental, Lima
17-02-2010, 21:30, 12 507, Soto VEN
Universitario 2
Alva [18], Labarthe [88]

Raul **Fernandez**• - John **Galliquio**, Carlos **Galvan**, Renzo **Revoredo**•, Jesus **Rabanal** - Antonio **Gonzales**, (Gianfranco **Labarthe** 59), Rainer **Torres**, Jorge **Vasquez** (Giancario **Carmona** 86), Rodolfo **Espinoza** - Carlos **Orejuela** (Luis **Ramirez** 69), Piero **Alva**•. Tr: Juan **Reynoso**

Lanús 0

Agustin **Marchesin** - Maximiliano **Velazquez**•, Hernan **Grana** (Cristian Menendez 84), **Jadson**, Rodrigo **Erramuspe** - Matias **Fritzler**, Sebastian **Blanco** (Diego **Lagos** 64), Eduardo **Ledesma**, Guido **Pizarro** (Marcos **Aguirre** 73) - Santiago **Salcedo**, Gonzalo **Castillejos**. Tr: Luis **Zubeldia**

Tahuichi, Santa Cruz
25-02-2010, 18:00, 3709, Roman BRA
Blooming 1
Vieira [9]

Andres **Jemio** - Juan **Sanchez**, Omar **Morales**, Wilder **Zabala** - Lorgio **Alvarez**, David **Villalba** (Jorge **Andia** 46), Jose **Chavez**, Jesus **Gomez**•, Luiz Carlos **Vieira** (Julio **Hurtado** 61) - Luis **Sillero** (Roger **Suarez** 55), Damian **Akerman**. Tr: Carlos **Aragones**

Lanús 4
Blanco [24], Salcedo [39], Lagos 2 [60] [76]

Agustin **Marchesin** - Maximiliano **Velazquez**• (Carlos **Arce** 46), Hernan **Grana**, **Jadson**, Santiago **Hoyos**, Rodrigo **Erramuspe** - Matias **Fritzler**, Agustin **Pelletieri**, Sebastian **Blanco**• (Javier **Carrasco** 83) - Santiago **Salcedo**, Gonzalo **Castillejos** (Diego **Lagos** 56). Tr: Luis **Zubeldia**

Monumental, Lima
25-02-2010, 21:20, 16 530, Ponce ECU
Universitario 0

Raul **Fernandez** - John **Galliquio**, Carlos **Galvan**, Renzo **Revoredo**, Jesus **Rabanal** - Antonio **Gonzales**• (Gianfranco **Labarthe** 60), Rainer **Torres**, Luis **Ramirez**, Rodolfo **Espinoza** - Victor **Piriz**, Piero **Alva**•. Tr: Juan **Reynoso**

Libertad 0

Bernardo **Medina** - Ismael **Benegas**, Miguel **Samudio**, Adalberto **Roman**, Pedro **Sarabia** - Victor **Ayala**, Sergio **Aquino**• (Omar **Pouso** 78), Victor **Caceres** - Pablo **Velazquez**, Javier **Gonzalez**• (Jorge **Moreira** 75), Rodolfo **Gamarra**• (Rodrigo **Albornoz** 63). Tr: Javier **Torrente**

Defensores del Chaco, Asunción
23-03-2010, 21:45, 270, Fagundes PAR
Libertad 1
Ayala [56]

Bernardo **Medina** - Adalberto **Roman**, Miguel **Samudio**, Pedro **Sarabia** - Victor **Ayala**, Sergio **Aquino**•, Victor **Caceres**, Edgar **Robles** (Jorge **Moreira** 79) - Pablo **Velazquez**, Javier **Gonzalez** (Wilson **Pittoni** 46), Rodolfo **Gamarra**. Tr: Javier **Torrente**

Universitario 1
Ramirez [87]

Raul **Fernandez** - John **Galliquio**•, Carlos **Galvan**•, Jesus **Rabanal** - Antonio **Gonzales** (Jorge **Vasquez** 72), Miguel **Torres**, Luis **Ramirez**•, Giancarlo **Carmona**, Rodolfo **Espinoza**• - Gianfranco **Labarthe** (Victor **Piriz** 66), Piero **Alva** (Carlos **Orejuela** 83). Tr: Juan **Reynoso**

La Fortaleza, Lanús, Buenos Aires
24-03-2010, 21:50, 4271, Polic CHI
Lanús 1
Salcedo [17p]

Agustin **Marchesin** - Maximiliano **Velazquez**, Hernan **Grana** (Marcos **Aguirre** 77), **Jadson**, Santiago **Hoyos**, Rodrigo **Erramuspe** - Agustin **Pelletieri**, Sebastian **Blanco**, Eduardo **Ledesma**• (Guido **Pizarro** 70) - Santiago **Salcedo**, Gonzalo **Castillejos**• (Diego **Lagos** 60). Tr: Luis **Zubeldia**

Blooming 0

Andres **Jemio** - Raul **Gonzalez**, Andres **Imperiale**•, Fabricio **Brandao** - Lorgio **Alvarez**, David **Villalba** (Wilder **Zabala** 57), Jose **Chavez** (Julio **Hurtado** 81), Jorge **Andia**, Jesus **Gomez**, Luiz Carlos **Vieira** - Jose **Castillo**. Tr: Carlos **Aragones**

Defensores del Chaco, Asunción
30-03-2010, 20:15, 902, Oliveira BRA
Libertad 1
Roman [4]

Bernardo **Medina** - Adalberto **Roman**, Miguel **Samudio** (Gustavo **Mencia** 66), Pedro **Sarabia**• - Victor **Ayala**, Wilson **Pittoni** (Rodrigo **Albornoz** 70), Sergio **Aquino**, Victor **Caceres** - Roberto **Gamarra**, Edgar **Robles**, Pablo **Velazquez** (Javier **Gonzalez**• 77). Tr: Javier **Torrente**

Lanús 1
Velazquez [84]

Agustin **Marchesin** - Maximiliano **Velazquez**, Hernan **Grana**, **Jadson**, Santiago **Hoyos**• (Matias **Fritzler**• 60), Rodrigo **Erramuspe** - Agustin **Pelletieri**• (Leandro **Diaz**• 60), Sebastian **Blanco**•, Eduardo **Ledesma** - Diego **Lagos** (Marcos **Aguirre** 60), Santiago **Salcedo**••♦[40]. Tr: Luis **Zubeldia**

Monumental, Lima
6-04-2010, 20:30, 18 884, Lopes BRA
Universitario 0

Raul **Fernandez** - John **Galliquio**, Carlos **Galvan**, Renzo **Revoredo**, Jesus **Rabanal**• - Antonio **Gonzales** (Giancarlo **Carmona** 46), Rainer **Torres**, Luis **Ramirez**, Rodolfo **Espinoza** - Gianfranco **Labarthe** (Carlos **Orejuela** 68), Piero **Alva**. Tr: Juan **Reynoso**

Blooming 0

Andres **Jemio** - Fabricio **Brandao**, Omar **Morales**, Andres **Imperiale**, Wilder **Zabala** - Lorgio **Alvarez**, David **Villalba**• (Jorge **Andia** 82), Jose **Chavez**, Jesus **Gomez**, Luiz Carlos **Vieira** (Julio **Hurtado** 90) - Jose **Castillo** (Luis **Sillero** 80). Tr: Carlos **Aragones**

Tahuichi, Santa Cruz
15-04-2010, 18:30, 804, Larrionda URU
Blooming 1
Hurtado [27]

Andres **Jemio** - Dustin **Maldonado**, Andres **Imperiale**, Omar **Morales**, Wilder **Zabala** - David **Villalba**, Julio **Hurtado**, Jorge **Andia**•, Jorge **Gonzalez** (Lorgio **Alvarez** 46) - Luis **Sillero** (Damian **Akerman** 46), Jose **Castillo** (Luiz Carlos **Vieira** 62). Tr: Carlos **Aragones**

Libertad 2
Roman [38], Rodolfo Gamarra [53]

Bernardo **Medina** - Ismael **Benegas**, Miguel **Samudio**, Adalberto **Roman**, Pedro **Sarabia**• - Victor **Ayala**•, Sergio **Aquino**, Victor **Caceres** - Pablo **Velazquez** (Roberto **Gamarra** 76), Javier **Gonzalez** (Gustavo **Cristaldo** 46), Rodolfo **Gamarra** (Edgar **Robles** 82). Tr: Goyo **Perez**

La Fortaleza, Lanús, Buenos Aires
15-04-2010, 19:30, 4198 Simon BRA
Lanús 0

Agustin **Marchesin** - Maximiliano **Velazquez**, **Jadson**, Santiago **Hoyos**, Rodrigo **Erramuspe** (Hernan **Grana** 46) - Agustin **Pelletieri**♦[95+], Sebastian **Blanco**, Guido **Pizarro**, Marcos **Aguirre**• (Javier **Carrasco** 76) - Gonzalo **Castillejos** (Cristian **Menendez** 77), Leandro **Diaz**♦[95+]. Tr: Luis **Zubeldia**

Universitario 2

Raul **Fernandez**♦[95+] - John **Galliquio**•♦[95+], Carlos **Galvan**, Renzo **Revoredo**, Jesus **Rabanal** - Antonio **Gonzales**• (Raul **Ruidiaz** 61), Rainer **Torres** (Jorge **Vasquez** 90), Giancarlo **Carmona**, Rodolfo **Espinoza** - Gianfranco **Labarthe** (Victor **Piriz** 68), Piero **Alva**•. Tr: Juan **Reynoso**

GRUPO 5		Pl	W	D	L	F	A	Pts	BRA	ECU	URU	ECU
Internacional	BRA	6	3	3	0	8	2	**12**		3-0	2-0	2-1
Deportivo Quito	ECU	6	3	1	2	5	7	**10**	1-1		2-1	1-0
Cerro	URU	6	2	2	2	5	5	**8**	0-0	2-0		0-0
Emelec	ECU	6	0	2	4	2	6	**2**	0-0	0-1	1-2	

Centenario, Montevideo
9-02-2010, 18:00, 6021, Osorio CHI

Cerro   **2**

Dadomo [19], Mora [62]

Damian **Frascarelli** - Pablo **Melo**, Daniel **Leites**, Danilo **Asconeguy**, Walter **Ibanez** - Richard **Pellejero**, Claudio **Dadomo** (Fabian **Trujillo** 90), Pablo **Caballero**, Sebastian **Suarez•** - Rodrigo **Mora** (Raul **Molina** 86), Alvaro **Mello**. Tr: Pablo **Repetto**

Deportivo Quito   **0**

Oswaldo **Ibarra** - Geovanny **Caicedo**, Luis **Checa**, Pedro **Esterilla** (Jose **Vizcaino** 73), Angel **Escobar**, Ivan **Hurtado** - Roberto **Castro•**, Michael **Arroyo•**, Luis **Saritama•** - Ivan **Borghello** (Franco **Niell** 39), Marcos **Pirchio**. Tr: Ruben **Insua**

Olimpico Atahualpa, Quito
11-03-2010, 21:30, 4088, Buitrago COL

Deportivo Quito   **1**

Minda [33]

Oswaldo **Ibarra** - Isaac **Mina•**, Luis **Checa**, Ivan **Hurtado•**, Jose **Aguirre♦44** - Michael **Arroyo** (Mauricio **Donoso** 62), Roberto **Castro**, Tilson **Minda•**, Luis **Saritama** - Marcos **Pirchio** (Ivan **Borghello** 62), Franco **Niell•**. Tr: Ruben **Insua**

Internacional   **1**

Giuliano [40]

Roberto **Abbondanzieri•** - **Juan**, Gonzalo **Sorondo**, **Indio**, Bruno **Silva•**, **Kleber** - **Sandro**, Pablo **Guinazu•**, **Giuliano•** (Wilson **Mathias** 80) - **Edu** (Andres **D'Alessandro•** 70), Alecsandro• (Taison 85). Tr: Jorge **Fossati**

Beira-Rio, Porto Alegre
31-03-2010, 21:50, 36 897, Torres PAR

Internacional   **1**

Ibanez OG [59], Alecsandro [72]

Roberto **Abbondanzieri** - **Nei**, **Indio**, **Bolivar**, **Kleber** - **Sandro**, Pablo **Guinazu•**, **Giuliano** (Wilson **Mathias** 88), Andres **D'Alessandro** (Andrezinho 75) - Alecsandro•, **Walter•** (Taison 83). Tr: Jorge **Fossati**

Cerro   **0**

Damian **Frascarelli** - Pablo **Melo•**, Daniel **Leites•**, Danilo **Asconeguy**, Walter **Ibanez** - Sebastian **Suarez** (Fabian **Trujillo** 82), Richard **Pellejero**, Claudio **Dadomo•** (Maximiliano **Lombardi•** 80), Pablo **Caballero** - Rodrigo **Mora** (Sergio **Suffo** 63), Alvaro **Mello**. Tr: Pablo **Repetto**

George Capwell, Guayaquil
14-04-2010, 17:30, 3774, Escalante VEN

Emelec   **0**

Javier **Klimowicz** - Luis **Zambrano**, Silvano **Estacio**, Mariano **Mina**, Julio **Fleitas** - Pedro **Quinonez•** (Polo **Wila** 67), Jose **Quinonez•**, Fernando **Gimenez** (Fernando **Gaibor** 71) - Enner **Valencia** (Angel **Mena** 77), Hernan **Peirone•**, Santiago **Biglieri**. Tr: Jorge **Sampaoli**

Internacional   **0**

Roberto **Abbondanzieri** - **Nei**, **Bolivar**, Gonzalo **Sorondo**, **Kleber** - **Sandro**, Pablo **Guinazu**, **Giuliano** (Andrezinho 70), Andres **D'Alessandro** (Edu 85) - Alecsandro, **Walter** (Taison 66). Tr: Jorge **Fossati**

Beira-Rio, Porto Alegre
23-02-2010, 21:50, 39 304, Abal ARG

Internacional   **2**

Nei [53], Alecsandro [87]

Roberto **Abbondanzieri** - **Nei** (Taison 64), Gonzalo **Sorondo•**, **Bolivar•**, **Danilo**, **Kleber** - **Sandro**, Pablo **Guinazu**, **Giuliano** (Andrezinho 81) - Alecsandro, **Edu** (Walter• 77). Tr: Jorge **Fossati**

Emelec   **1**

Quiroz [49]

Marcelo **Elizaga** - Eduardo **Morante•** (Jose **Quinonez** 75), Mariano **Mina•**, Julio **Fleitas**, Gabriel **Achilier** - David **Quiroz**, Pedro **Quinonez**, Pablo **Perez•** - Jaime **Ayovi** (Hernan **Peirone** 90), Enner **Valencia** (Santiago **Biglieri** 46), Joao **Rojas**. Tr: Jorge **Sampaoli**

Atilio Olivera, Rivera
18-03-2010, 19:15, 25 510, Laverni ARG

Cerro   **0**

Mathias **Rolero** - Pablo **Melo•**, Daniel **Leites•**, Danilo **Asconeguy**, Walter **Ibanez** - Sebastian **Suarez**, Richard **Pellejero**, Claudio **Dadomo•**, Pablo **Caballero** - Rodrigo **Mora** (Maximiliano **Lombardi** 79), Alvaro **Mello** (Raul **Molina** 87). Tr: Pablo **Repetto**

Internacional   **0**

Roberto **Abbondanzieri** - **Indio**, Gonzalo **Sorondo**, Bruno **Silva•** (Nei• 58), **Kleber** - **Sandro•**, Pablo **Guinazu**, **Giuliano•** (Taison 80), Andres **D'Alessandro** (Andrezinho 72) - **Edu•**, Alecsandro. Tr: Jorge **Fossati**

George Capwell, Guayaquil
1-04-2010, 18:30, 4217, Haro ECU

Emelec   **0**

Marcelo **Elizaga** - Luis **Zambrano**, Mariano **Mina•**, Julio **Fleitas**, Gabriel **Achilier••♦79** - David **Quiroz•**, Jose **Quinonez** - Jaime **Ayovi**, Joao **Rojas** (Enner **Valencia** 68), Hernan **Peirone** (Silvano **Estacio** 46), Santiago **Biglieri**. Tr: Jorge **Sampaoli**

Deportivo Quito   **1**

Hurtado [91+p]

Oswaldo **Ibarra** - Isaac **Mina**, Luis **Checa**, Angel **Escobar•**, Pedro **Esterilla** (Mauricio **Donoso** 60), Ivan **Hurtado** - Michael **Arroyo** (Juan Carlos **Paredes** 73), Tilson **Minda**, Luis **Saritama•** - Franco **Niell**, Ivan **Borghello** (Marcos **Pirchio•** 46). Tr: Ruben **Insua**

Beira-Rio, Porto Alegre
22-04-2010, 19:30, 31 360, Amarilla PAR

Internacional   **3**

Andrezinho [4], Bolivar [61], Giuliano [92+]

Roberto **Abbondanzieri** - **Nei**, Gonzalo **Sorondo**, **Bolivar**, **Kleber** (Fabiano **Eller** 79) - **Sandro•**, Pablo **Guinazu**, Andres **D'Alessandro•**, **Andrezinho•** (Giuliano 85) - Alecsandro, **Walter** (Edu 68♦89). Tr: Jorge **Fossati**

Deportivo Quito   **0**

Oswaldo **Ibarra** - Geovanny **Caicedo**, Isaac **Mina**, Luis **Checa**, Pedro **Esterilla•** (Roberto **Castro** 46), Ivan **Saritama•** (Franco **Niell** 75) - Marcos **Pirchio** (Mauricio **Donoso** 46), Ivan **Borghello•**. Tr: Ruben **Insua**

George Capwell, Guayaquil
11-03-2010, 19:15, 9793, Carrillo PER

Emelec   **1**

Perez [70]

Marcelo **Elizaga** - Mariano **Mina** (Angel **Mena** 82), Julio **Fleitas**, Gabriel **Achilier** - David **Quiroz**, Pedro **Quinonez**, Pablo **Perez•** - Jaime **Ayovi•**, Enner **Valencia** (Hernan **Peirone** 54), Joao **Rojas•**, Santiago **Biglieri•**. Tr: Jorge **Sampaoli**

Cerro   **2**

Caballero [52], Dadomo [57]

Mathias **Rolero** - Pablo **Melo•**, Daniel **Leites**, Danilo **Asconeguy**, Walter **Ibanez** - Sebastian **Suarez**, Richard **Pellejero**, Claudio **Dadomo•**, Pablo **Caballero** (Marcelo **Mansilla** 82) - Rodrigo **Mora** (Raul **Molina** 89), Alvaro **Mello** (Fabian **Trujillo** 79). Tr: Pablo **Repetto**

Olimpico Atahualpa, Quito
25-03-2010, 19:15, 5719, Espinel ECU

Deportivo Quito   **1**

Arroyo [64]

Oswaldo **Ibarra•** - Geovanny **Caicedo**, Luis **Checa**, Pedro **Esterilla**, Luis **Tenorio**, Angel **Escobar** - Michael **Arroyo** (Jose **Vizcaino** 88), Tilson **Minda**, Luis **Saritama•** - Franco **Niell** (Marcos **Pirchio** 84), Ivan **Borghello** (Roberto **Castro** 85). Tr: Ruben **Insua**

Emelec   **0**

Marcelo **Elizaga** - Luis **Zambrano**, Eduardo **Morante•**, Mariano **Mina•**, Gabriel **Achilier•** - David **Quiroz**, Pedro **Quinonez**, Jose **Quinonez** - Enner **Valencia** (Santiago **Biglieri** 46), Joao **Rojas** (Silvano **Estacio** 70), Hernan **Peirone** (Jaime **Ayovi** 63). Tr: Jorge **Sampaoli**

Olimpico Atahualpa, Quito
13-04-2010, 18:15, 6836, Ruiz COL

Deportivo Quito   **2**

Mina [20], Checa [87]

Oswaldo **Ibarra** - Isaac **Mina•**, Luis **Checa**, Angel **Escobar** (Mauricio **Donoso** 45), Ivan **Hurtado** - Michael **Arroyo**, Tilson **Minda•**, Luis **Saritama**, Juan Carlos **Paredes** (Roberto **Castro** 68) - Marcos **Pirchio** (Daniel **Solano** 77), Franco **Niell**. Tr: Ruben **Insua**

Cerro   **1**

Dadomo [26p]

Damian **Frascarelli** - Pablo **Melo**, Daniel **Leites**, Danilo **Asconeguy**, Walter **Ibanez** - Claudio **Dadomo** (Jonathan **Soto** 88), Pablo **Caballero** (Marcelo **Mansilla** 82), Sebastian **Suarez•**, Richard **Pellejero** - Alvaro **Mello•** (Fabian **Trujillo** 73), Rodrigo **Mora**. Tr: Pablo **Repetto**

Luis Troccoli, Montevideo
22-04-2010, 19:30, 2669, Gamboa BOL

Cerro   **0**

Damian **Frascarelli** - Daniel **Leites** (Jonathan **Soto** 64), Danilo **Asconeguy**, Walter **Ibanez**, Ignacio **Amarilla•** (Fernando **Alvez** 46) - Sebastian **Suarez♦75**, Richard **Pellejero•**, Claudio **Dadomo**, Pablo **Caballero** - Rodrigo **Mora•**, Alvaro **Mello•** (Ricardo **Queiro** 75). Tr: Pablo **Repetto**

Emelec   **0**

Marcelo **Elizaga•** - Silvano **Estacio•**, Eduardo **Morante**, Julio **Fleitas•**, Gabriel **Achilier•** - David **Quiroz••♦79**, Pedro **Quinonez**, Fernando **Gimenez** - Jaime **Ayovi** (Hernan **Peirone** 62), Joao **Rojas•** (Jose **Quinonez** 90), Santiago **Biglieri** (Enner **Valencia** 58). Tr: Jorge **Sampaoli**

GRUPO 6		Pl	W	D	L	F	A	Pts	URU	ARG	MEX	ECU
Nacional Montevideo	URU	6	3	3	0	9	4	**12**		2-2	2-0	3-2
Banfield	ARG	6	3	2	1	13	8	**11**	0-2		2-1	4-1
Morelia	MEX	6	1	2	3	4	8	**5**	0-0	1-1		2-1
Deportivo Cuenca	ECU	6	1	1	4	7	13	**4**	0-0	1-4	2-0	

Florencio Sola, Banfield, Buenos Aires
10-02-2010, 18:30, 5804, Arias PAR

Banfield   **2**
Rodriguez [55], Battion [79]

Cristian **Lucchetti** - Victor Lopez, Julio Barraza•, Marcelo **Bustamente**, Jonatan Maidana - Walter Erviti (Emmanuel Pio 83), Marcelo Quinteros (Julio Marchant 90), Roberto **Battion**, James Rodriguez - Sebastian Fernandez, Ruben Ramirez. Tr: Julio Falcioni

Morelia   **1**
Rey [90]

Moises **Munoz** - Fernando **Salazar**, Marvin **Cabrera**, Adrian Aldrete♦**52**, Mauricio **Romero•** - Hugo **Droguett**, Gabriel **Pereyra** (Elias Hernandez 69), Jorge **Hernandez** - Aldo Ramirez, Miguel Sabah (Luis Rey 80), Jared Borgetti (Jaime Duran 58).Tr: Tomas **Boy**

Estadio Morelos, Morelia
23-02-2010, 21:10, 21 493, Penuela COL

Morelia   **0**

Moises **Munoz** - Jaime Duran•, Fernando Salazar, Marvin **Cabrera**, Enrique Perez - Hugo Droguett, Jorge Hernandez (Gabriel Pereyra 59) - Aldo Ramirez (Luis Silva 74), Luis **Rey**, Jared **Borgetti•**, Elias Hernandez (Miguel Sabah 60♦**84**). Tr: Tomas **Boy**

Nacional Montevideo   **0**

Rodrigo **Munoz** - Christian Nunez, Alejandro Lembo•, Sebastian **Coates•**, Ernesto Goni - Alvaro Gonzalez, Raul Ferro (Sergio Blanco 78), Oscar Morales, Mauricio Pereyra (Maximiliano Calzada 68), Mario **Regueiro•** - Gustavo Varela (Sebastian Balsas• 60). Tr: Eduardo Acevedo

---

Florencio Sola, Banfield, Buenos Aires
16-03-2010, 19:30, 9507, Seneme BRA

Banfield   **0**

Cristian **Lucchetti** - Victor Lopez•, Julio Barraza• (Emmanuel Pio 83), Marcelo **Bustamente•** (Cristian Garcia 70), Jonatan Maidana - Walter Erviti, Marcelo Quinteros, Roberto Battion (Mathias Cardaccio 65), James Rodriguez• - Sebastian Fernandez, Ruben Ramirez. Tr: Julio Falcioni

Nacional Montevideo   **2**
Coates [34], Godoy [41]

Rodrigo **Munoz** - Alejandro Lembo (Gonzalo Godoy 22), Sebastian Coates, Ernesto Goni - Alvaro Gonzalez, Raul Ferro• (Sebastian Balsas 58), Maximiliano Calzada•, Angel Morales (Mauricio Pereyra 72), Oscar Morales, Mario Regueiro - Gustavo Varela. Tr: Eduardo Acevedo

---

Alejandro Aguilar, Cuenca
7-04-2010, 17:30, 4683, Pozo CHI

Deportivo Cuenca   **0**

Esteban **Dreer** - John Narvaez•, Diego Ianiero•, Juan Guerron, Arlin Ayovi• - Giancarlo Ramos (Jose Granda 86), Gabriel **Mendez**, Mauricio Hurtado (William Espana 55), Carlos Garces (Jefferson Najera 76), Jhon Garcia• - Luis Escalada•. Tr: Paul Velez

Nacional Montevideo   **0**

Rodrigo **Munoz•** - Gonzalo Godoy, Sebastian Coates•, Ernesto Goni• - Alvaro Gonzalez•, Raul Ferro, Maximiliano Calzada• (Gianni Guigou 77), Oscar Morales♦**91•**, Mario **Regueiro** - Sergio Blanco (Mauricio Pereyra 61), Gustavo Varela (Christian Nunez 90). Tr: Eduardo Acevedo

---

Parque Central, Montevideo
11-02-2010, 19:00, 11 299, Osses CHI

Nacional Montevideo   **3**
Regueiro 2 [46] [65], Morales [85p]

Rodrigo Munoz - Christian Nunez, Alejandro Lembo, Sebastian Coates - Alvaro Gonzalez (Sergio Blanco 69), Angel Morales, Oscar Morales, Mauricio Pereyra, Mario Regueiro• (Sebastian Balsas 79) - Gustavo Varela•, Santiago Garcia (Diego Vera 60). Tr: Eduardo Acevedo

Deportivo Cuenca   **2**
Granada [25], Escalada [67]

Esteban **Dreer** - Diego **Ianiero**, Juan Guerron, Jaime Chila, Arlin Ayovi - Jose Granda (Christian Cordero 75), Giancarlo Ramos, Gabriel Mendez•, Mauricio Hurtado• (William Espana 65), Jhon Garcia - Luis Escalada (Darwin Caicedo 81). Tr: Paul Velez

---

Alejandro Aguilar, Cuenca
9-03-2010, 21:30, 7700, Perluzzo VEN

Deportivo Cuenca   **2**
Mendez [59], Escalada [83]

Esteban **Dreer** - Marco Quinonez, John Narvaez, Diego Ianiero, Juan Guerron, Jaime Chila - Gabriel Mendez (Fernando Fajardo 88), Jose Granda (William Espana 46), Giancarlo Ramos♦**87**, Jhon Garcia - Luis Escalada (Jorge Ladines• 84). Tr: Paul Velez

Morelia   **0**

Moises **Munoz** - Jaime Duran•, Fernando Salazar, Marvin Cabrera, Mauricio Romero• - Hugo Droguett•, Ismael Pineda•, Jorge Hernandez (Pedro Beltran 67) - Luis Rey (Miguel Sansores 77), Jared Borgetti, Elias Hernandez• (Mario Moreno 79♦**86**). Tr: Tomas Boy

---

Estadio Morelos, Morelia
16-03-2010, 21:15, 14 066, Rivera PER

Morelia   **2**
Borgetti 2 [19] [27]

Moises **Munoz•** - Jaime Duran, Fernando Salazar•, Marvin Cabrera• (Enrique Perez 63), Mauricio Romero•, Christian Sanchez - Hugo Droguett, Pedro Beltran (Jorge Gastelum 69) - Luis Rey (Oscar Rojas 66), Jared Borgetti, Elias Hernandez. Tr: Tomas Boy

Deportivo Cuenca   **1**
Ladines [76]

Esteban **Dreer** - Marco Quinonez, John Narvaez, Diego Ianiero, Juan Guerron, William Espana• - Jaime Chila (Christian Cordero 60) - Gabriel Mendez•, Jose Granda• (Jefferson Najera 85), Jhon Garcia - Luis Escalada (Carlos Garces 73). Tr: Paul Velez

---

Parque Central, Montevideo
21-04-2010, 19:30, 12 780, Oliveira BRA

Nacional Montevideo   **2**
Regueiro [3], Pereyra [78]

Rodrigo Munoz - Alejandro Lembo, Sebastian Coates, Ernesto Goni - Alvaro Gonzalez (Christian Nunez 58), Raul Ferro•, Maximiliano Calzada, Matias Cabrera (Sergio Blanco 87), Angel Morales (Mauricio Pereyra 75), Mario Regueiro - Gustavo Varela. Tr: Eduardo Acevedo

Morelia   **0**

Miguel **Fraga** - Jaime Duran•, Luis Silva•, Marvin Cabrera•, Enrique Perez - Ismael Pineda (Elias Hernandez 72), Oscar Rojas, Pedro Beltran, Jorge Hernandez• - Mario Moreno (Miguel Sansores 64), Jared Borgetti. Tr: Tomas Boy

---

Alejandro Aguilar, Cuenca
17-02-2010, 19:15, 11 345, Roldan COL

Deportivo Cuenca   **1**
Mendez [86p]

Esteban **Dreer** - Diego Ianiero (Christian Cordero 74), Juan Guerron, Jaime Chila•, Arlin Ayovi• - Jose Granda•, Mauricio Hurtado (William Espana 46), Giancarlo Ramos, Gabriel Mendez•, Jhon Garcia• (Jorge Ladines 46) - Luis Escalada. Tr: Paul Velez

Banfield   **4**
Erviti [35], Fernandez 2 [38] [60], Rodriguez [71]

Cristian **Lucchetti** - Victor Lopez, Julio Barraza•, Marcelo Bustamente••♦**85**, Jonatan Maidana - Walter Erviti, (Emmanuel Pio 74), Marcelo Quinteros, Roberto Battion•, James Rodriguez - Sebastian Fernandez (Cristian Garcia 80), Ruben Ramirez (Jose Shaffer 86). Tr: Julio Falcioni

---

Centenario, Montevideo
10-03-2010, 22:30, 34 468, Lopes BRA

Nacional Montevideo   **2**
Varela [6], Regueiro [41]

Rodrigo Munoz - Christian Nunez• (Maximiliano Calzada 59), Alejandro Lembo•, Sebastian Coates•, Ernesto Goni (Leonardo Burian 84) - Alvaro Gonzalez, Raul Ferro (Santiago Garcia 70), Angel Morales, Oscar Morales•, Mario Regueiro - Gustavo Varela. Tr: Eduardo Acevedo

Banfield   **2**
Rodriguez 2 [18] [37p]

Cristian **Lucchetti** - Victor Lopez, Julio Barraza•, Jonatan Maidana, Jose Shaffer - Walter Erviti (Emmanuel Pio• 79), Marcelo Quinteros (Santiago Ladino 85), Roberto Battion, James Rodriguez• (Mathias Cardaccio 89) - Sebastian Fernandez, Ruben Ramirez•. Tr: Julio Falcioni

---

Estadio Morelos, Morelia
31-03-2010, 21:10, 16 516, Ruiz COL

Morelia   **1**
Borgetti [78]

Moises **Munoz** - Jaime Duran, Fernando Salazar (Hugo Droguett• 46), Mauricio Romero, Christian Sanchez, Enrique Perez - Jorge Gastelum••♦**74**, Gabriel Pereyra (Jorge Hernandez 79), Adrian Aldrete (Jared Borgetti 46) - Miguel Sabah, Elias Hernandez. Tr: Tomas Boy

Banfield   **1**
Laso [92+]

Cristian **Lucchetti** - Victor Lopez, Santiago Ladino, Mauro Dos Santos•, Jonatan Maidana - Walter Erviti, Marcelo Quinteros (Maximiliano Laso• 87), Roberto Battion♦**66**, James Rodriguez - Cristian Garcia (Luis Salmeron 61), Sebastian Fernandez• (Emmanuel Pio 68). Tr: Julio Falcioni

---

Florencio Sola, Banfield, Buenos Aires
21-04-2010, 19:30, 5486, Galeano PAR

Banfield   **4**
Ramirez 2 [48] [68], Erviti [87], Lucchetti [90p]

Cristian **Lucchetti** - Victor Lopez, Julio Barraza (Mathias Cardaccio• 46), Santiago Ladino, Jonatan Maidana - Walter Erviti, Federico Sardella, Marcelo Quinteros, James Rodriguez (Mauro Dos Santos 79) - Cristian Garcia (Sebastian Fernandez 53), Ruben Ramirez. Tr: Julio Falcioni

Deportivo Cuenca   **1**
Mendez [72]

Esteban **Dreer** - John Narvaez•, Diego Ianiero, Juan Guerron, Arlin Ayovi - Gabriel Mendez, Jose Granda•, (Pablo Arevalo 80), Fernando Fajardo, Michael Endara, Christian Cordero (Jose Valdiviezo 82) - Luis Escalada (Jefferson Najera 76). Tr: Paul Velez

GRUPO 7		Pl	W	D	L	F	A	Pts	ARG	BRA	CHI	VEN
Vélez Sarsfield	ARG	6	4	1	1	10	5	**13**		2-0	2-1	4-0
Cruzeiro	BRA	6	3	2	1	12	6	**11**	3-0		4-1	2-0
Colo Colo	CHI	6	2	2	2	8	10	**8**	1-1	1-1		1-0
Deportivo Italia	VEN	6	0	1	5	4	13	**1**	0-1	2-2	2-3	

José Amalfitani, Buenos Aires
10-02-2010, 20:50, 11 100, Vazquez URU

Vélez Sarsfield 2
Silva 5, Martinez 77
German Montoya - Sebastian Dominguez•, Pablo Lima• (Alejandro Cabral 63), Nicolas Otamendi•, Fabian Cubero• - Nicolas Cabrera (Juan Martinez 63), Maximiliano Moralez•, Victor Zapata, Leandro Somoza• - Hernan Lopez, Santiago Silva• (Rolando Zarate 83). Tr: Ricardo Gareca

Cruzeiro 0
Fabio - Jonathan, Gil••♦37, Leonardo Silva•, Diego Renan (Thiago Heleno 39) - Marquinhos Parana, Henrique, Elicarlos - Gilberto♦2, Thiago Ribeiro (Pedro Ken 51), Kleber (Wellington Paulista 67). Tr: Adilson Batista

Monumental, Santiago
16-02-2010, 19:00, 10 840, Carrillo PER

Colo Colo 1
Paredes 58
Francisco Prieto - Paulo Magalhaes• (Jose Fuenzalida 46), Sebastian Toro, Andres Cerececa - Macnelly Torres (Diego Olate 90), Rodrigo Millar, Charles Aranguiz•, Rodrigo Melendez - Esteban Paredes•, Cristian Bogado• (Claudio Graf 81). Tr: Hugo Tocalli

Deportivo Italia 0
Jose Fernandez - David McIntosh, Marcelo Maidana, Carlos Lopez, Rafael Lobo (Diomar Diaz 82) - Gabriel Urdaneta, Leopoldo Jimenez•, Evelio Hernandez, Gianfranco Di Julio (Felix Casseres 74) - Cristian Casseres•, Richard Blanco (Amir Buelvas 90). Tr: Eduardo Sarago

Olimpico, Caracas
23-02-2010, 18:00, 1351, Haro ECU

Deportivo Italia 0
Jose Fernandez - David McIntosh, Marcelo Maidana•, Carlos Lopez, Rafael Lobo - Gabriel Urdaneta, Leopoldo Jimenez•, Evelio Hernandez (Felix Casseres 62), Gianfranco Di Julio• (Diomar Diaz 80) - Emerson Panigutti (Richard Blanco 74), Cristian Casseres. Tr: Eduardo Sarago

Vélez Sarsfield 1
Lopez 54
German Montoya - Sebastian Dominguez, Pablo Lima•, Nicolas Otamendi, Fabian Cubero• - Nicolas Cabrera• (Gaston Diaz 80), Maximiliano Moralez (Alejandro Cabral 85), Victor Zapata, Leandro Somoza - Hernan Lopez, Santiago Silva (Juan Martinez 70). Tr: Ricardo Gareca

Mineirão, Belo Horizonte
24-02-2010, 19:30, 32 927, Ruiz COL

Cruzeiro 4
Thiago Ribeiro 7, Kleber 2 62p 72p, Pedro Ken 69
Fabio - Jonathan, Leonardo Silva, Thiago Heleno, Diego Renan - Marquinhos Parana•, Henrique•, (Bernado 82), Elicarlos (Pedro Ken 27), Roger (Wellington Paulista 54) - Thiago Ribeiro•, Kleber. Tr: Adilson Batista

Colo Colo 1
Paredes
Francisco Prieto - Diego Olate••♦57, Sebastian Toro, Andres Scotti•, Roberto Cerececa••♦67 - Macnelly Torres (Paulo Magalhaes• 59), Rodrigo Millar, Charles Aranguiz•, Rodrigo Melendez• - Esteban Paredes (Arturo Sanhueza• 72), Ezequiel Miralles. Tr: Hugo Tocalli

Olimpico, Caracas
11-03-2010, 19:45, 212, Vera ECU

Deportivo Italia 2
Blanco 11, McIntosh 65
Alan Liebeskind - David McIntosh•, Marcelo Maidana, Carlos Lopez, Daniel Diez (Rafael Lobo 87♦88) - Bladimir Morales•, Diomar Diaz (Felix Casseres 67), Gabriel Urdaneta - Emerson Panigutti (Cristian Casseres 77), Richard Blanco. Tr: Eduardo Sarago

Cruzeiro 2
Kleber 2 26 50
Fabio - Jonathan, Thiago Heleno, Leonardo Silva•, Diego Renan (Gil 64) - Marquinhos Parana, Henrique•, Pedro Ken, Roger (Eliandro 74) - Thiago Ribeiro• (Bernado 90), Kleber♦86. Tr: Adilson Batista

Monumental, Santiago
16-03-2010, 22:00, 11 204, Amarilla PAR

Colo Colo 1
Paredes 57
Francisco Prieto - Paulo Magalhaes, Miguel Riffo, Sebastian Toro, Andres Scotti• - Rodrigo Millar, Charles Aranguiz, Arturo Sanhueza (Macnelly Torres 45), Rodrigo Melendez (Jose Fuenzalida 81) - Esteban Paredes•, Ezequiel Miralles•. Tr: Hugo Tocalli

Vélez Sarsfield 1
Silva 92+
German Montoya - Gaston Diaz (Franco Razzotti 63), Sebastian Dominguez, Nicolas Otamendi, Papa, Fabian Cubero - Maximiliano Moralez (Rolando Zarate 84), Victor Zapata••♦59, Leandro Somoza - Hernan Lopez (Juan Martinez 68), Santiago Silva•. Tr: Ricardo Gareca

Mineirão, Belo Horizonte
24-03-2010, 21:50, 17 237, Arias PAR

Cruzeiro 2
Fabinho 6, Pedro Ken 69
Fabio - Jonathan, Thiago Heleno, Leonardo Silva, Diego Renan - Marquinhos Parana (Fabricio 86), Henrique•, Gilberto (Pedro Ken 67), Fabinho• - Wellington Paulista, Thiago Ribeiro• (Eliandro 87). Tr: Adilson Batista

Deportivo Italia 0
Jose Fernandez - David McIntosh, Marcelo Maidana, Carlos Lopez, Daniel Diez• (Evelio Hernandez 80) - Gabriel Urdaneta, Leopoldo Jimenez, Alain Giroletti•, Diomar Diaz (Cristian Casseres 73) - Emerson Panigutti (Felix Casseres 65), Richard Blanco. Tr: Eduardo Sarago

José Amalfitani, Buenos Aires
25-03-2010, 19:00, 9325, Silvera URU

Vélez Sarsfield 2
Lopez 14, Silva 30
German Montoya - Gaston Diaz, Sebastian Dominguez, Nicolas Otamendi, Emiliano Papa, Fabian Cubero• - Maximiliano Moralez (Juan Martinez 83), Leandro Somoza• (Franco Razzotti 75), Alejandro Cabral - Hernan Lopez (Nicolas Cabrera 90), Santiago Silva•. Tr: Ricardo Gareca

Colo Colo 1
Miralles 9
Francisco Prieto - Miguel Riffo•, Sebastian Toro (Claudio Graf• 80), Andres Scotti, Roberto Cerececa• - Macnelly Torres, Rodrigo Millar••♦87, Charles Aranguiz• (Jose Fuenzalida 61), Rodrigo Melendez• - Esteban Paredes, Ezequiel Miralles. Tr: Hugo Tocalli

Mineirão, Belo Horizonte
31-03-2010, 19:30, 43 374, Roldan COL

Cruzeiro 3
Thiago Ribeiro 32, Kleber 2 48 53
Fabio - Jonathan, Thiago Heleno (Gil 33), Leonardo Silva, Diego Renan - Marquinhos Parana, Henrique, Gilberto• (Fabricio 69), Fabinho - Thiago Ribeiro (Wellington Paulista 76), Kleber•. Tr: Adilson Batista

Vélez Sarsfield 0
German Montoya - Gaston Diaz (Pablo Lima• 51), Sebastian Dominguez, Nicolas Otamendi, Emiliano Papa, Fabian Cubero - Maximiliano Moralez (Nicolas Cabrera 75), Victor Zapata, Leandro Somoza••♦82 - Hernan Lopez (Juan Martinez 57), Santiago Silva•. Tr: Ricardo Gareca

Olimpico, Caracas
6-04-2010, 18:45, 207, Rodriguez.M MEX

Deportivo Italia 3
Panigutti 16, Blanco 87p
Jose Fernandez - David McIntosh, Marcelo Maidana, Carlos Lopez, Rafael Lobo (Richard Blanco 60) - Bladimir Morales (Diomar Diaz 67), Alain Giroletti•, Gabriel Urdaneta• - Emerson Panigutti, Felix Casseres, Cristian Casseres (Evelio Hernandez 81). Tr: Eduardo Sarago

Colo Colo 3
Bogado 27, Miralles 2 39 58
Francisco Prieto - Paulo Magalhaes, Sebastian Toro, Andres Scotti•, Roberto Cerececa - Macnelly Torres, Jose Fuenzalida (Miguel Riffo 84), Charles Aranguiz, Rodrigo Melendez• (Arturo Sanhueza 52) - Cristian Bogado, Ezequiel Miralles. Tr: Hugo Tocalli

Monumental, Santiago
15-04-2010, 20:50, 8402, Torres PAR

Colo Colo 1
Millar 61
Francisco Prieto - Paulo Magalhaes (Jose Fuenzalida 46), Sebastian Toro•, Andres Scotti♦80, Roberto Cerececa (Matias Quiroga 66) - Macnelly Torres, Rodrigo Millar, Charles Aranguiz (Claudio Graf 90), Rodrigo Melendez• - Cristian Bogado, Ezequiel Miralles•. Tr: Hugo Tocalli

Cruzeiro 1
Thiago Ribeiro 57
Fabio - Jonathan, Gil•, Leonardo Silva•, Diego Renan (Thiago Heleno 65) - Marquinhos Parana, Henrique, Gilberto, Fabinho (Fabricio 46) - Wellington Paulista (Roger 75), Thiago Ribeiro. Tr: Adilson Batista

José Amalfitani, Buenos Aires
15-04-2010, 21:50, 5408, Ubriaco URU

Vélez Sarsfield 3
Zapata 42, Lopez 2 48p 83, Papa 73
German Montoya - Gaston Diaz, Sebastian Dominguez (Fernando Tobio 63), Nicolas Otamendi•, Emiliano Papa, Fabian Cubero• - Maximiliano Moralez, Leandro Coronel (Alejandro Cabral 77), Victor Zapata - Juan Martinez, Hernan Lopez. Tr: Ricardo Gareca

Deportivo Italia 0
Alan Liebeskind - Norberto Riascos, Marcelo Maidana, Carlos Lopez, Daniel Diez• - Bladimir Morales, Evelio Hernandez (Felix Casseres 70), Diomar Diaz, Gianfranco Di Julio - Emerson Panigutti (Amir Buelvas 44), Cristian Casseres (Yhonny Salcedo 77). Tr: Eduardo Sarago

GRUPO 8		Pl	W	D	L	F	A	Pts	CHI	BRA	CHI	VEN
Universidad de Chile	CHI	6	3	3	0	10	6	12		2-1	0-0	1-0
Flamengo	BRA	6	3	1	2	11	9	10	2-2		2-0	3-2
Universidad Católica	CHI	6	1	4	1	5	5	7	2-2	2-0		1-1
Caracas FC	VEN	6	0	2	4	5	11	2	1-3	1-3	0-0	

Sausalito, Viña del Mar
18-02-2010, 19:15, 10 091, Buckley PER
Universidad de Chile 1
Olivera [2p]
Esteban **Conde** - Mauricio **Victorino•**, Matias **Rodriguez**, Rafael **Olarra**, Jose **Contreras** - Marco **Estrada•**, Walter **Montillo** (Diego **Rivarola** 55), Alvaro **Fernandez** (Marcelo **Diaz** 82), Felipe **Seymour** - Gabriel **Vargas** (Edson **Puch** 55), Juan **Olivera**. Tr: Gerardo **Pelusso**
Caracas FC 0

Renny **Vega** - Alejandro **Cichero•**, Jose **Rey**, Giovanny **Romero**, Gabriel **Cichero** - Franklin **Lucena** (Zamir **Valoyes** 71), Jesus **Gomez** (Rodrigo **Prieto** 60), Edgar **Jimenez**, Alejandro **Guerra•**, Dario **Figueroa** (Bremer **Pinango** 79) - Rafael **Castellin**. Tr: Noel **Sanvicente**

Olimpico, Caracas
10-03-2010, 20:20, 19 400, Roldan COL
Caracas FC 1
Castellin [65]
Renny **Vega** - Alejandro **Cichero•**, Giovanny **Romero•** (Rodrigo **Prieto** 56), Gabriel **Cichero**, Jaime **Bustamante** - Franklin **Lucena**, Jesus **Gomez** (Alexander **Gonzalez** 79), Edgar **Jimenez**, Alejandro **Guerra** - Rafael **Castellin•** (Fernando **Aristigueta** 77), Zamir **Valoyes•**. Tr: Andrade
Flamengo 3
Vagner Love 2 [36p 75], Rodrigo Alvim [92+]
Bruno• - Leo **Moura**, Juan, Alvaro, Fabricio - Dejan **Petkovic** (Ronaldo **Angelim** 59), Kleberson, Fernando (Rodrigo **Alvim** 53), **Toro••♦**53 - Vinicius **Pacheco** (Gonzalo **Fierro** 83), **Vagner Love**. Tr: Andrade

San Carlos, Santiago
24-03-2010, 19:30, 9103, Pitana ARG
Universidad Católica 1
Morales [82]
Paulo **Garces** - Ismael **Fuentes**, Waldo **Ponce•**, David **Henriquez•** - Francisco **Silva**, Rodrigo **Valenzuela** (Pablo **Vranjican** 68), Milovan **Mirosevic**, Rodrigo **Toloza** (Fernando **Meneses** 54), Damian **Diaz** (Hans **Martinez** 46) - Juan **Morales**, Matias **Rubio**. Tr: Marco **Figueroa**
Caracas FC 1
Bustamante [50]
Renny **Vega** - Alejandro **Cichero**, Pablo **Camacho**, Gabriel **Cichero**, Jaime **Bustamante** - Jesus **Gomez•**, Bremer **Pinango•**, Edgar **Jimenez**, Alejandro **Guerra•** (Cesar **Gonzalez** 74), Dario **Figueroa** (Zamir **Valoyes** 85) - Rafael **Castellin•** (Rodrigo **Prieto** 89). Tr: Noel **Sanvicente**

San Carlos, Santiago
14-04-2010, 20:50, 7709, Pezzota ARG
Universidad Católica 2
Diaz [2], Silva [45]
Paulo **Garces** - Ismael **Fuentes**, Waldo **Ponce•** (Diego **Rosende** 82), David **Henriquez**, Hans **Martinez** (Fernando **Meneses** 67) - Francisco **Silva**, Rodrigo **Valenzuela**, Jorge **Ormeno** (Matias **Rubio** 76), Milovan **Mirosevic**, Damian **Diaz** - Juan **Morales**. Tr: Marco **Figueroa**
Flamengo 0

Bruno - Leo **Moura**, Ronaldo **Angelim**, Juan, Alvaro (Fabricio 25) - **Willians** (Vinicius **Pacheco•** 46), Dejan **Petkovic** (Gonzalo **Fierro** 46), Claudio **Maldonado**, Toro - Vagner **Love**, Bruno **Mezenga**. Tr: Andrade

Maracanã, Rio de Janeiro
24-02-2010, 21:50, 30 930, Amarilla PAR
Flamengo 2
Leo Moura [11], Adriano [58]
Marcelo Lomba - Leo **Moura** (Everton **Silva** 75), Juan, Alvaro, Fabricio - **Willians♦**3, Kleberson, Toro - Vinicius **Pacheco** (Fernando 60), Vagner **Love•** (Dejan **Petkovic** 75), **Adriano**. Tr: **Andrade**
Universidad Católica 0

Paulo **Garces** - Ismael **Fuentes**, Waldo **Ponce•**, David **Henriquez** (Leonel **Mena•** 70), Hans **Martinez** - Francisco **Silva•**, Rodrigo **Valenzuela**, Milovan **Mirosevic♦**42, Rodrigo **Toloza** (Rodrigo **Mannara** 68), Damian **Diaz** - Juan **Morales** (Pablo **Vranjican** 54). Tr: Marco **Figueroa**

Olimpico, Caracas
17-03-2010, 18:00, 15 500, Morales MEX
Caracas FC 0

Renny **Vega** - Alejandro **Cichero•**, Giovanny **Romero** (Pablo **Camacho** 79), Gabriel **Cichero**, Jaime **Bustamante** - Franklin **Lucena**, Jesus **Gomez**, Edgar **Jimenez**, Dario **Figueroa** (Alejandro **Guerra** 56) - Rafael **Castellin•**, Rodrigo **Prieto** (Zamir **Valoyes** 56). Tr: Noel **Sanvicente**
Universidad Católica 0

Paulo **Garces** - Ismael **Fuentes** (Jorge **Ormeno** 46), Marcos **Gonzalez**, David **Henriquez**, Hans **Martinez**, Diego **Rosende** (Rodrigo **Valenzuela** 72) - Francisco **Silva**, Milovan **Mirosevic**, Rodrigo **Toloza**, Damian **Diaz** (Matias **Rubio** 46) - Pablo **Vranjican**. Tr: Marco **Figueroa**

Maracanã, Rio de Janeiro
8-04-2010, 16:00, 20 330, Silvera URU
Flamengo 2
Michael [67], Leo Moura [82]
Bruno• - Leo **Moura**, Ronaldo **Angelim**, Juan, Alvaro - **Willians•**, Kleberson (Bruno **Mezenga** 46), Michael (Claudio **Maldonado** 86), Toro - Vinicius **Pacheco•** (Dejan **Petkovic** 59), Vagner **Love•**. Tr: **Andrade**
Universidad de Chile 2
Montillo [43], Rodriguez [92+]
Esteban **Conde** - Mauricio **Victorino**, Matias **Rodriguez•**, Jose **Rojas•**, Rafael **Olarra**, Jose **Contreras** - Walter **Montillo** (Nelson **Pinto** 90), Manuel **Iturra•**, Felipe **Seymour**, Edson **Puch** - Juan **Olivera** (Diego **Rivarola** 78). Tr: Gerardo **Pelusso**

Monumental, Santiago
21-04-2010, 20:50, 9286, Pozo CHI
Universidad de Chile 0

Miguel **Pinto** - Juan **Gonzalez**, Juan **Abarca**, Mauricio **Arias** (Juan **Olivera** 90) - Manuel **Iturra•** (Felipe **Seymour•** 46), Marcelo **Diaz•**, Alvaro **Fernandez** 46) - Marcelo **Diaz•**, Alvaro **Fernandez** 76), Nelson **Pinto**, Jose Luis **Silva** (Walter **Montillo** 69) - Diego **Rivarola**, Gabriel **Vargas•**. Tr: Gerardo **Pelusso**
Universidad Católica 0

Paulo **Garces** - Ismael **Fuentes**, Leonel **Mena**, Hans **Martinez** (Diego **Rosende** 46) - Francisco **Silva**, Rodrigo **Valenzuela•**, Jorge **Ormeno•**, Milovan **Mirosevic**, Damian **Diaz♦**89, Fernando **Meneses•** (Pablo **Vranjican** 46) - Juan **Morales** (Angel **Carreno** 72). Tr: Marco **Figueroa**

Francisco Rumoroso, Coquimbo
9-03-2010, 21:15, 11 667, Puga CHI
Universidad Católica 2
Rubio [21], Silva [70]
Paulo **Garces** - Ismael **Fuentes•**, Waldo **Ponce**, David **Henriquez**, Hans **Martinez**, Diego **Rosende** - Francisco **Silva**, Rodrigo **Toloza•** (Adan **Vergara** 90), Damian **Diaz** - Pablo **Vranjican•** (Juan **Morales•** 73), Matias **Rubio** (Francisco **Pizarro** 83). Tr: Marco **Figueroa**
Universidad de Chile 2
Olivera [19], Puch [91+]
Esteban **Conde** - Mauricio **Victorino**, Matias **Rodriguez**, Rafael **Olarra**, Jose **Contreras•** - Marco **Estrada•** (Manuel **Iturra** 77), Walter **Montillo**, Edson **Puch•**, Felipe **Seymour** (Alvaro **Fernandez** 84) - Juan **Olivera**, Eduardo **Vargas** (Diego **Rivarola** 73). Tr: Gerardo **Pelusso**

Monumental, Santiago
17-03-2010, 21:50, 20 936, Larrionda URU
Universidad de Chile 2
Vargas [42], Seymour [54]
Esteban **Conde** - Mauricio **Victorino**, Matias **Rodriguez**, Rafael **Olarra**, Jose **Contreras** - Marco **Estrada** (Nelson **Pinto** 52), Walter **Montillo**, Edson **Puch**, Felipe **Seymour** - Juan **Olivera**, Eduardo **Vargas•**. Tr: Gerardo **Pelusso**
Flamengo 1
Rodrigo Alvim [50]
Bruno - Leo **Moura** (Everton **Silva** 78), Juan, Alvaro•, Fabricio - Rodrigo **Alvim**, Willians, Kleberson (Gonzalo **Fierro•** 60) - Vinicius **Pacheco** (Dejan **Petkovic** 67), Vagner **Love**, **Adriano**. Tr: Andrade

Olimpico, Caracas
13-04-2010, 21:00, 6353, Antequera BOL
Caracas FC 1
Gonzalez [76]
Renny **Vega** - Alejandro **Cichero•**, Pablo **Camacho**, Gabriel **Cichero•**, Jaime **Bustamante** - Jesus **Gomez•**, (Cesar **Gonzalez•** 72), Bremer **Pinango** (Franklin **Lucena•** 46), Edgar **Jimenez**, Alejandro **Guerra♦**67 - Rodrigo **Prieto** (Dario **Figueroa** 46), Zamir **Valoyes**. Tr: Noel **Sanvicente**
Universidad de Chile 3
Victorino [18], Olivera [32p], Rodriguez [35]
Miguel **Pinto** - Mauricio **Victorino**, Matias **Rodriguez**, Jose **Rojas**, Rafael **Olarra**, Jose **Contreras** - Walter **Montillo•** (Marco **Estrada** 88), Manuel **Iturra**, Edson **Puch** (Eduardo **Vargas•** 8) (Diego **Rivarola** 75), Felipe **Seymour** - Juan **Olivera•**, Tr: Gerardo **Pelusso**

Maracanã, Rio de Janeiro
21-04-2010, 21:50, 34 106, Larrionda URU
Flamengo 3
Ronaldo Angelim [17], Michael [19], David [75]
Bruno - Leo **Moura**, Ronaldo **Angelim**, Juan, David - Willians•, Claudio **Maldonado** (Kleberson 84), Michael• (Gonzalo **Fierro** 80) - Vinicius **Pacheco** (Dejan **Petkovic** 69), Vagner **Love**, **Adriano**. Tr: Andrade
Caracas FC 2
Castellin [14], Gomez [67]
Javier **Toyo** - Alejandro **Cichero•**, Giovanny **Romero•**, Leonardo **Bautista**, Jaime **Bustamante** - Franklin **Lucena**, Cesar **Gonzalez** (Jesus **Gomez** 40), Edgar **Jimenez**, Dario **Figueroa** - Rafael **Castellin** (Fernando **Aristiguieta** 74), Zamir **Valoyes** (Alexander **Gonzalez** 61). Tr: Noel **Sanvicente**

ROUND OF SIXTEEN

Florencia Sola, Buenos Aires
28-04-2010, 21:50, 6794, Larrionda URU

Banfield   **3**

Rodriguez [47], Battion [59], Fernandez [81]

Cristian **Lucchett** - Victor **Lopez**, Julio **Barraza••♦84**, Santiago **Ladino**, Jonatan **Maidana** - Walter **Erviti**, Marcelo **Quinteros**, Roberto **Battion**, James **Rodriguez** (Mauro **Dos Santos** 86) - Sebastian **Fernandez•** (Federico **Sardella** 90), Ruben **Ramirez**. Tr: Julio **Falcioni**

Internacional   **1**

Kleber [50]

Roberto **Abbondanzieri** - **Nei**, Gonzalo **Sorondo**, Fabiano **Eller•**, **Bolivar**, **Kleber♦58** - **Sandro**, Pablo **Guinazu•**, Andres **D'Alessandro** (Everton 89), **Andrezinho** (Taison 88) - **Alecsandro•** (**Walter** 85). Tr: Jorge **Fossati**

Beira-Rio, Porto Alegre
6-05-2010, 19:30, 34 643, Roldan COL

Internacional   **2**

Alecsandro [42], Walter [58]

Roberto **Abbondanzieri** - **Nei•**, Gonzalo **Sorondo**, **Bolivar•**, Fabiano **Eller•** - **Sandro**, Pablo **Guinazu•**, Andres **D'Alessandro•** (Glayson 90), **Andrezinho** (Giuliano 70) - **Alecsandro**, **Walter** (Everton 89). Tr: Jorge **Fossati**

Banfield   **0**

Cristian **Lucchetti** - Victor **Lopez**, Marcelo **Bustamente** (Maximiliano **Laso** 81), Santiago **Ladino** (Mauro **Dos Santos** 90), Jonatan **Maidana** - Walter **Erviti**, Marcelo **Quinteros** (Mathias **Cardaccio** 75), Roberto **Battion•**, James **Rodriguez••♦82** - Sebastian **Fernandez**, Ruben **Ramirez**. Tr: Julio **Falcioni**

Alfonso Lastras, San Luis Potosi
27-04-2010, 18:45, 5666, Soto VEN

San Luis   **0**

Carlos **Trejo** - Diego **Martinez•**, Pablo **Aguilar**, Oscar **Mascorro** - Noe **Maya** (Diego **de la Torre** 46), Ignacio **Torres•**, Juan Pablo **Rodriguez**, Braulio **Luna**, Guillermo **Rangel** (Rodolfo **Salinas** 72) - Alfredo **Moreno•**, Blas **Perez** (Victor **Lojero** 62). Tr: Marcos **Ambris**

Estudiantes La Plata   **1**

Gonzalez [25]

Agustin **Orion•** - Christian **Cellay**, Faustino **Rojo** (Raul **Iberbia** 76), Federico **Fernandez**, Clemente **Rodriguez••♦69** - Matias **Sanchez•**, Marcelo **Carrusca** (German **Re** 70), Maximiliano **Nunez**, Leandro **Benitez** - Gaston **Fernandez** (Enzo **Perez** 63), Leandro **Gonzalez•**. Tr: Alejandro **Sabella**

Centenario, Quilmes
5-05-2010, 19:30, 9359, Carrillo PER

Estudiantes La Plata   **3**

Gonzalez [4], Benitez 2 [50 55]

Agustin **Orion** - Leandro **Desabato**, Faustino **Rojo** (German **Re** 79), Marcos **Angeleri**, Federico **Fernandez** - Marcelo **Carrusca** (Jose **Sosa** 36), Juan **Veron** (Matias **Sanchez** 67), Maximiliano **Nunez**, Leandro **Benitez•** - Mauro **Boselli**, Leandro **Gonzalez**. Tr: Alejandro **Sabella**

San Luis   **1**

De la Torre [7]

Carlos **Trejo** - Pablo **Aguilar**, Gonzalo **Pineda**, Oscar **Mascorro**, Edwin **Hernandez•** - Cesar **Gonzalez**, Ignacio **Torres** (Blas **Perez** 64), Braulio **Luna**, Jesus **Palacios**, Diego **de la Torre•** (Juan Pablo **Rodriguez** 75) - Alfredo **Moreno**. Tr: Marcos **Ambris**

Mineirão, Belo Horizonte
29-04-2010, 19:00, 32 254, Baldassi ARG

Cruzeiro   **3**

Thiago Ribeiro 3 [7 22 42]

Fabio - **Jonathan**, **Gil**, Leonardo **Silva**, Diego **Renan** - **Fabricio** (Elicarlos 48), **Marquinhos Parana**, **Henrique** - **Gilberto** (Joffre **Guerron** 76), **Thiago Ribeiro**, **Kleber**. Tr: Adilson **Batista**

Nacional Montevideo   **1**

Regueiro [51]

Rodrigo **Munoz** - Christian **Nunez**, Alejandro **Lembo•**, Sebastian **Coates** - Alvaro **Gonzalez**, Raul **Ferro•**, Angel **Morales** (Gonzalo **Godoy•** 70), Oscar **Morales** (Mauricio **Pereyra** 81), Mario **Regueiro** - Gustavo **Varela** (Diego **Vera** 39). Tr: Eduardo **Acevedo**

Parque Central, Montevideo
5-05-2010, 21:50, 13 919, Beligoy ARG

Nacional Montevideo   **0**

Rodrigo **Munoz** - Christian **Nunez** (Mauricio **Pereyra•** 63), Alejandro **Lembo•**, Sebastian **Coates•**♦54 - Alvaro **Gonzalez** (Gonzalo **Godoy** 83), Raul **Ferro•**, Maximiliano **Calzada** (Diego **Vera** 46), Angel **Morales**, Oscar **Morales**, Mario **Regueiro** - Gustavo **Varela♦70**. Tr: Eduardo **Acevedo**

Cruzeiro   **3**

Thiago Ribeiro [29], Diego Renan [48], Gilberto [80]

Fabio - **Jonathan**, **Gil•**, Leonardo **Silva•53**, Diego **Renan** - **Fabricio** (Pedro **Ken** 71), **Marquinhos Parana**, **Henrique** - **Gilberto**, Thiago **Ribeiro** (Wellington **Paulista** 83), **Kleber** (Thiago **Heleno•** 57). Tr: Adilson **Batista**

Monumental, Lima
28-04-2010, 17:30, 37 034, Laverni ARG

Universitario   **0**

Luis **Llontop** - Carlos **Galvan**, Renzo **Revoredo**, Jesus **Rabanal•**, Antonio **Gonzales** (Luis **Hernandez** 46) - Rainer **Torres•**, Jorge **Vasquez** (Raul **Ruidiaz** 61), Giancarlo **Carmona** (Miguel **Torres** 83), Rodolfo **Espinoza•** - Victor **Piriz**, Piero **Alva•**. Tr: Juan **Reynoso**

São Paulo FC   **0**

Rogerio **Ceni•** - Alex **Silva**, **Richarlyson••♦65**, **Miranda**, **Cicinho** (**Jean•** 37) - Jorge **Wagner**, **Hernanes**, **Marlos** (Junior **Cesar** 68), Rodrigo **Souto** - **Washington** (Renato **Silva** 84), **Dagoberto**. Tr: Ricardo **Gomes**

Morumbi, São Paulo
4-05-2010, 19:30, 43 838, Torres PAR

São Paulo FC   **0 3p**

Rogerio **Ceni** - Alex **Silva**, **Miranda**, Junior **Cesar**, **Cicinho** (Jean 75) - Jorge **Wagner** (Washington 46), **Hernanes•**, **Marlos**, Rodrigo **Souto** - **Fernandinho** (Marcelinho 90), **Dagoberto**. Tr: Ricardo **Gomes**

Universitario   **0 1p**

Luis **Llontop•** - Carlos **Galvan**, Renzo **Revoredo**, Jesus **Rabanal** - Rainer **Torres** (Luis **Ramirez** 78), Jorge **Vasquez** (Miguel **Torres•** 74), Giancarlo **Carmona**, Luis **Hernandez**, Rodolfo **Espinoza** - Victor **Piriz•** (Gianfranco **Labarthe** 46), Piero **Alva•**. Tr: Juan **Reynoso**

Alejandro Villanueva, Lima
29-04-2010, 19:15, 29 247, Simon BRA

Alianza Lima   **0**

George **Forsyth** - Edgar **Villamarin•**, Carlos **Solis**, Hector **Sosa**, Amilton **Prado** - Joel **Sanchez** (Alexander **Sanchez** 73), Henry **Quinteros** (Johnnier **Montano** 59), Jean **Tragodara**, Edgar **Gonzalez** - Wilmer **Aguirre**, Jose **Fernandez** (Claudio **Velazquez** 60). Tr: Gustavo **Costas**

Universidad de Chile   **1**

Rivarola [86]

Miguel **Pinto** - Mauricio **Victorino**, Matias **Rodriguez**, Jose **Rojas**, Rafael **Olarra**, Jose **Contreras** (Alvaro **Fernandez** 68) - Walter **Montillo**, Manuel **Iturra**, Felipe **Seymour•** (Nelson **Pinto** 84) - Juan **Olivera** (Diego **Rivarola** 73), Eduardo **Vargas**. Tr: Gerardo **Pelusso**

Monumental, Santiago
6-05-2010, 21:00, 28 663, Vera ECU

Universidad de Chile   **2**

Vargas [63], Seymour [92+]

Miguel **Pinto** - Mauricio **Victorino•**, Matias **Rodriguez•**, Jose **Rojas**, Rafael **Olarra**, Jose **Contreras** (Edson **Puch** 46) - Walter **Montillo**, Manuel **Iturra**, Felipe **Seymour** - Juan **Olivera•** (Diego **Rivarola** 86), Eduardo **Vargas** (Alvaro **Fernandez** 77). Tr: Gerardo **Pelusso**

Alianza Lima   **2**

Fernandez 2 [24 87]

George **Forsyth•** - Edgar **Villamarin•** (Walter **Vilchez** 46), Carlos **Solis•**, Hector **Sosa**, Amilton **Prado•** - Joel **Sanchez•**, Henry **Quinteros** (Oscar **Vilchez•** 55), Jean **Tragodara** (Johnnier **Montano** 71), Edgar **Gonzalez•** - Wilmer **Aguirre**, Jose **Fernandez**. Tr: Gustavo **Costas**

Maracanã, Rio de Janeiro
28-04-2010, 21:50, 72 442, Amarilla PAR

Flamengo   **1**

Adriano [66p]

Bruno - Leo **Moura**, Ronaldo **Angelim**, **Juan**, **David** - **Romulo**, **Willians** (Gonzalo **Fierro•** 86), Claudio **Maldonado** (Toro 78), **Michael♦37** - Vagner **Love** (Vinicius **Pacheco** 82), **Adriano**. Tr: **Rogerio**

Corinthians   **0**

Julio **Cesar** - **Chicao**, **William**, Roberto **Carlos•**, **Ralf**, **Elias**, **Jucilei**, **Danilo** (Jorge **Henrique** 72), **Ronaldo** (Souza 63), **Moacir•**, **Dentinho** (**Iarley** 68). Tr: Mano **Menezes**

Pacaembú, São Paulo
5-05-2010, 21:50, 35 561, Silvera URU

Corinthians   **2**

David OG [28], Ronaldo [39]

Felipe - **Chicao•**, **William**, **Alessandro** (Paulinho 79), Roberto **Carlos**, **Ralf**, **Elias** (Jucilei 70), **Danilo**, **Ronaldo**, Jorge **Henrique** (Iarley• 67), **Dentinho**. Tr: Mano **Menezes**

Flamengo   **1**

Vagner Love [49]

Bruno• - Leo **Moura**, Ronaldo **Angelim**, **Juan•**, **David•** - **Romulo•**, **Willians•**, Claudio **Maldonado** (Toro 88) - Vinicius **Pacheco** (Kleberson 46), Vagner **Love** (Gonzalo **Fierro** 79), **Adriano**. Tr: **Rogerio**

Palogrande, Manizales
29-04-2010, 21:30, 10 981, Fagundes BRA

Once Caldas **0**

Luis **Martinez** - Oswaldo **Vizcarrondo**, Jose **Velez**, Luis **Nunez**, Alexis **Henriquez**, Diego **Amaya** (Sebastian **Hernandez** 67) - John **Valencia**, Jaime **Castrillon** (Dany **Santoya** 56), Diego **Arias** - Fernando **Uribe**, Dayro **Moreno**. Tr: Juan Carlos **Osorio**

Libertad **0**

Bernardo **Medina•** - Ismael **Benegas**, Adalberto **Roman•**, Arnaldo **Vera•**, Pedro **Sarabia** - Victor **Ayala** (Edgar **Robles** 74), Miguel **Samudio** (Omar **Pouso** 81), Sergio **Aquino•**, Victor **Caceres** - Pablo **Velazquez** (Roberto **Gamarra** 39), Rodolfo **Gamarra**. Tr: Goyo **Robles**

Defensores del Chaco, Asunción
6-05-2010, 21:00, 2000, Pezzotta ARG

Libertad **2**
Roberto Gamarra 2 73p 89

Bernardo **Medina** - Ismael **Benegas** (Aldo **Olmedo** 64), Adalberto **Roman**, Arnaldo **Vera**, Pedro **Sarabia** - Victor **Ayala•**, Miguel **Samudio** (Manuel **Maciel** 58), Sergio **Aquino**, Victor **Caceres** - Pablo **Velazquez** (Roberto **Gamarra•** 64), Rodolfo **Gamarra**. Tr: Goyo **Perez**

Once Caldas **1**
Moreno 55

Luis **Martinez** - Oswaldo **Vizcarrondo•**, Jose **Velez**, Luis **Nunez**, Alexis **Henriquez** - Diego **Arias**, John **Valencia** (Jaime **Castrillon** 65), Dayron **Perez** (Diego **Amaya** 61), Carlos **Johnson•** - Fernando **Uribe** (Dany **Santoya** 71), Dayro **Moreno**. Tr: Juan Carlos **Osorio**

Jalisco, Guadalajara
27-04-2010, 21:00, 8322, Ruiz COL

Guadalajara **3**
Bravo 2 25 79, Reynoso 92+p

Liborio **Sanchez** - Mario de **Luna**, Hector **Reynoso**, Miguel **Ponce•**, Omar **Esparza** - Edgar **Mejia•** (Patricio **Araujo** 66), Christian **Perez** (Xavier **Baez** 79), Edgar **Solis**, Marco **Fabian** (Ulises **Davila** 66) - Omar **Arellano**, Omar **Bravo**. Tr: Jose **Real**

Vélez Sarsfield **0**

German **Montoya♦90** - Gaston **Diaz**, Sebastian **Dominguez**, Nicolas **Otamendi**, Emiliano **Papa** (Marco **Torsiglieri** 46), Fabian **Cubero** (Ivan **Bella** 81) - Maximiliano **Moralez**, Victor **Zapata**, Leandro **Somoza** - Juan **Martinez**, Hernan **Lopez** (Rolando **Zarate** 80). Tr: Ricardo **Gareca**

José Amalfitani, Buenos Aires
4-05-2010, 21:50, 10 055, Seneme BRA

Vélez Sarsfield **2**
Silva 3, Zarate 88

Marcelo **Barovero** - Gaston **Diaz•** (Juan **Martinez** 56), Sebastian **Dominguez**, Nicolas **Otamendi•**, Emiliano **Papa**, Fabian **Cubero** - Maximiliano **Moralez** (Ricardo **Alvarez** 69), Victor **Zapata** (Rolando **Zarate** 79), Leandro **Somoza** - Hernan **Lopez**, Santiago **Silva**. Tr: Ricardo **Gareca**

Guadalajara **0**

Liborio **Sanchez•** - Mario de **Luna**, Hector **Reynoso•**, Omar **Esparza**, Christian **Perez**, Miguel **Ponce•** - Edgar **Solis•**, Edgar **Mejia**, Jorge **Enriquez** (Patricio **Araujo** 81) - Omar **Arellano** (Ulises **Davila•** 63), Omar **Bravo•** (Xavier **Baez** 76).Tr: Jose **Real**

QUARTER-FINALS

Beira-Rio, Porto Alegre
13-05-2010, 21:15, 40 115, Silvera URU

Internacional **1**
Sorondo 88

Roberto **Abbondanzieri** - **Nei•** (**Glaydson** 77), **Bolivar•**, Gonzalo **Sorondo**, **Kleber** - **Sandro•**, Pablo **Guinazu•**, Andres **D'Alessandro•** (**Giuliano** 77), **Andrezinho** - **Alecsandro**, **Walter** (**Taison** 64). Tr: Jorge **Fossati**

Estudiantes La Plata **0**

Agustin **Orion** - Leandro **Desabato**, Christian **Cellay**, German **Re**, Federico **Fernandez**, Clemente **Rodriguez•** - Matias **Sanchez•**, Jose **Sosa•** (Leandro **Benitez** 72), Enzo **Perez** (Dario **Stefanatto** 85), Juan **Veron** - Mauro **Boselli**. Tr: Alejandro **Sabella**

Centenario, Quilmes
20-05-2010, 19:45, 14 500, Ruiz COL

Estudiantes La Plata **2**
Gonzalez 19, Perez 21

Agustin **Orion** - Leandro **Desabato**, Christian **Cellay**, German **Re**, Clemente **Rodriguez** (Federico **Fernandez** 90) - Matias **Sanchez**, Jose **Sosa**, Enzo **Perez**, Juan **Veron•** - Mauro **Boselli•**, Leandro **Gonzalez** (Marcos **Angeleri** 46). Tr: Alejandro **Sabella**

Internacional **1**
Giuliano 88

Roberto **Abbondanzieri** - **Nei** (**Walter** 69), Gonzalo **Sorondo•**, **Fabiano Eller**, **Bolivar**, **Kleber** - **Sandro•** (**Edu** 86), Pablo **Guinazu•**, Andres **D'Alessandro•** (**Giuliano** 77), **Andrezinho** - **Alecsandro**. Tr: Jorge **Fossati**

Mineirão, Belo Horizonte
12-05-2010, 21:50, 48 602, Ruiz COL

Cruzeiro **0**

Fabio - **Jonathan•**, **Gil**, **Thiago Heleno**, Diego **Renan** (Joffre **Guerron** 55) - **Fabricio** (**Fabio Santos** 62), Marquinhos **Parana**, **Henrique** - **Gilberto** (**Roger•** 79), **Thiago Ribeiro**, **Kleber**. Tr: Adilson **Batista**

São Paulo FC **2**
Dagoberto 23, Hernanes 65

Rogerio **Ceni** - Alex **Silva•**, Junior **Cesar** (Jorge **Wagner** 80), **Xandao•**, **Cicinho** (**Jean** 81) - **Hernanes•**, **Marlos**, Rodrigo **Souto**, **Richarlyson•** - **Fernandao** (Washington 82), **Dagoberto•**. Tr: Ricardo **Gomes**

Morumbi, São Paulo
19-05-2010, 21:50, 52 196, Larrionda URU

São Paulo FC **2**
Hernanes 23, Dagoberto 53

Rogerio **Ceni** - Alex **Silva•**, **Miranda** (**Xandao** 86), Junior **Cesar**, **Cicinho**, **Marlos**, Rodrigo **Souto•**, **Richarlyson•** (**Jean** 83) - **Fernandao**, **Dagoberto•** (**Fernandinho** 77). Tr: Ricardo **Gomes**

Cruzeiro **0**

Fabio - **Jonathan** (**Thiago Heleno** 29), **Gil**, Leonardo **Silva**, Diego **Renan** (**Elicarlos** 59) - **Fabricio** (Wellington **Paulista** 46), Marquinhos **Parana•**, **Henrique** - **Gilberto**, **Thiago Ribeiro**, **Kleber♦2**. Tr: Adilson **Batista**

Maracanã, Rio de Janeiro
12-05-2010, 19:30, 72 442, Amarilla PAR

Flamengo 2
Adriano [39], Juan [88]

Bruno• - Leo Moura, Ronaldo Angelim, Juan•, David• - Romulo (Michael 21), Willians, Claudio Maldonado (Dejan Petkovic 46), Kleberson (Denis Marques 72) - Vagner Love, Adriano. Tr: Rogerio

Universidad de Chile 3
Victorino [4], Olarra [24], Fernandez [47]

Miguel Pinto - Mauricio Victorino, Matias Rodriguez, Jose Rojas, Rafael Olarra - Walter Montillo (Edson Puch 82), Manuel Iturra••♦45, Alvaro Fernandez, Felipe Seymour - Juan Olivera (Diego Rivarola 74), Eduardo Vargas• (Nelson Pinto 46). Tr: Gerardo Pelusso

Santa Laura, Santiago
20-05-2010, 21:15, 20 000, Silvera URU

Universidad de Chile 1
Montillo [73]

Miguel Pinto - Mauricio Victorino, Matias Rodriguez•, Jose Rojas, Rafael Olarra - Walter Montillo• (Jose Contreras 80), Alvaro Fernandez, Felipe Seymour, Nelson Pinto• - Juan Olivera (Diego Rivarola 85), Eduardo Vargas (Edson Puch 56). Tr: Gerardo Pelusso

Flamengo 2
Vagner Love [45], Adriano [78]

Bruno - Leo Moura, Ronaldo Angelim, Juan•, David - Willians••♦89, Kleberson (Bruno Mezenga 87), Toro (Vinicius Pacheco 80), Michael (Dejan Petkovic 46) - Vagner Love♦95+, Adriano. Tr: Rogerio

Jalisco, Guadalajara
11-05-2010, 20:15, 15 011, Pozo CHI

Guadalajara 3
Bravo 2 [7 80], Vazquez [29]

Liborio Sanchez - Mario de Luna, Hector Reynoso, Patricio Araujo, Christian Perez - Xavier Baez, Julio Nava (Edgar Solis 70), Abraham Coronada• (Omar Esparza 64), Marco Fabian• - Omar Arellano (Ricardo Vazquez 18), Omar Bravo•. Tr: Jose Real

Libertad 0

Bernardo Medina - Aldo Olmedo, Adalberto Roman, Arnaldo Vera•, Pedro Sarabia• - Victor Ayala (Jorge Moreira 46), Miguel Samudio (Manuel Maciel 72), Sergio Aquino, Victor Caceres - Roberto Gamarra (Pablo Velazquez 46), Rodolfo Gamarra. Tr: Goyo Perez

Defensores del Chaco, Asunción
18-05-2010, 21:15, 260, Baldassi ARG

Libertad 2
Roman [20], Maciel [68]

Bernardo Medina - Adalberto Roman, Arnaldo Vera•, Pedro Sarabia•, Miguel Samudio (Manuel Maciel 41) - Wilson Pittoni (Roberto Gamarra 59), Sergio Aquino, Jorge Moreira, Victor Caceres - Pablo Velazquez, Rodolfo Gamarra (Ariel Nunez 62). Tr: Goyo Perez

Guadalajara 0

Liborio Sanchez - Mario de Luna, Hector Reynoso, Patricio Araujo•, Omar Esparza• - Christian Perez, Edgar Solis (Miguel Ponce• 73), Xavier Baez•, Jorge Enriquez (Edgar Mejia• 68) - Omar Arellano (Ulises Davila 56), Omar Bravo•. Tr: Jose Real

SEMI-FINALS

Beira-Rio, Porto Alegre
28-07-2010, 20:15, 52 035, Soto VEN

Internacional 1
Giuliano [68]

Renan - Nei, Indio, Bolivar•, Kleber - Andres D'Alessandro, Andrezinho (Giuliano 65), Sandro, Pablo Guinazu - Alecsandro, Taison (Rafael Sobis 87). Tr: Celso Roth

São Paulo FC 0

Rogerio Ceni - Alex Silva, Miranda, Junior Cesar, Jean• - Hernanes, Marlos, Junior Cesar, Rodrigo Souto, Richarlyson• (Cleber Santana 71) - Fernandao, Dagoberto (Henrique 73). Tr: Ricardo Gomes

Morumbi, São Paulo
5-08-2010, 21:50, 62 129, Amarilla PAR

São Paulo FC 2
Alex Silva [30], Ricardo Oliveira [54]

Rogerio Ceni - Alex Silva, Miranda, Junior Cesar, Jean - Cleber Santana (Marlos 74), Hernanes, Rodrigo Souto (Marcelinho 87) - Fernandao•, Dagoberto (Fernandinho 83), Ricardo Oliveira. Tr: Ricardo Gomes

Internacional 1
Alecsandro [52]

Renan - Nei, Indio, Bolivar, Kleber• - Sandro, Pablo Guinazu, Andres D'Alessandro (Giuliano 81), Tinga••♦79 - Alecsandro, Taison (Wilson Mathias 89). Tr: Celso Roth

Azteca, Mexico City
27-07-2010, 20:15, 52 035, Soto VEN

Guadalajara 1
Arellano [52]

Luis Michel• - Hector Reynoso, Omar Esparza•, Miguel Ponce, Jose Magallon - Edgar Mejia•, Alberto Medina (Marco Fabian 70), Xavier Baez•, Adolfo Bautista - Omar Arellano, Omar Bravo. Tr: Jose Real

Universidad de Chile 1
Olarra [47]

Miguel Pinto - Mauricio Victorino, Matias Rodriguez, Jose Rojas•, Rafael Olarra, Jose Contreras (Angel Rojas 80) - Walter Montillo, Manuel Iturra, Felipe Seymour (Nelson Pinto 87) - Juan Olivera (Diego Rivarola 67), Edson Puch. Tr: Gerardo Pelusso

Estadio Nacional, Santiago
3-08-2010, 21:15, 40 060, Pezzotta ARG

Universidad de Chile 0

Miguel Pinto - Mauricio Victorino, Matias Rodriguez, Jose Rojas (Angel Rojas 63), Alvaro Fernandez (Gabriel Vargas 75), Jose Contreras (Diego Rivarola 46) - Walter Montillo, Manuel Iturra, Felipe Seymour - Juan Olivera•, Edson Puch. Tr: Gerardo Pelusso

Guadalajara 2
Baez [22], Magallon [55]

Luis Michel - Mario de Luna, Hector Reynoso, Miguel Ponce, Jose Magallon - Edgar Mejia•, Xavier Baez, Adolfo Bautista (Ulises Davila 83), Marco Fabian (Dionicio 86), Patricio Araujo• - Omar Bravo• (Ricardo Vazquez 90). Tr: Jose Real

Copa Libertadores Final 1st Leg	Estadio Omnilife Zapopan, Guadalajara	Wednesday 11-08-2010
Kick-off: 19:50		Attendance: 30 870

GUADALAJARA   1 2   INTERNACIONAL

Adolfo Bautista [45]   Giuliano [72], Bolívar [76]

GUADALAJARA
Red and white striped shirts, Navy blue shorts, White socks
Tr: Jose Luis Real

Luis Michel

Miguel Angel Ponce   Mario de Luna [92+]   Hector Reynoso (c)   Jonny Magallon

Edgar Mejia   Xavier Baez [86]
                     Ulises Dávila

Marco Fabian [75]   Omar Arellano [69]
[79] Dionicio Escalante   Adolfo Bautista   Patricio Araujo

Omar Bravo

Alecsandro [34]   Taison [86]
Everton [72]   Wilson Matias
Rafael Sobis

Andres D'Alessandro   Sandro [88]

Pablo Guinazu †   Giuliano

Kleber   Indio   Bolivar (c)   Nei

Renan

Tr: Celso Roth
White shirts, White shorts, Red socks
INTERNACIONAL

MATCH STATS
Guadalajara		Inter
4	Shots	13
1	Shots on Goal	5
12	Fouls Committed	10
0	Corner Kicks	3
0	Caught Offside	1

MATCH OFFICIALS
REFEREE
Hector Baldassi ARG
ASSISTANTS
Ricardo Casas ARG
Hernan Maidana ARG
4TH OFFICIAL
Saúl Laverni ARG

(C) Captain † Man of the Match

I think it's fair enough that people will say Inter are favourites, but you should only start celebrating after matches not before.

Adolfo Bautista

We need to stay focused for the second leg and try and enjoy ourselves. That'll be the key. That and winning the game of course.

Edgar Mejia

We've picked up an important win, but we mustn't think that the title's in the bag. We've got a lead but we have to play as if the tie's level at 0-0 and we still need a positive result. I want to win my tenth title with Inter.

Indio

Copa Libertadores Final 2nd Leg	Beira-Rio Porto Alegre	Wednesday 18-08-2010
Kick-off: 22:00		Attendance: 56 000

INTERNACIONAL 3 2 GUADALAJARA

Rafael Sobis [61], **Leandro Damiao** [75], **Giuliano** [89]   **Marco Fabian** [42], **Omar Bravo** [92+]

INTERNACIONAL
Red shirts, White shorts, White socks
Tr: Celso Roth

MATCH STATS

Inter		Guadalajara
20	Shots	9
8	Shots on Goal	3
10	Fouls Committed	19
4	Corner Kicks	1
2	Caught Offside	0

Renan

Nei   Bolivar (c) [65]   Indio   Kleber

Pablo Guinazu   Sandro

Andres D'Alessandro

Tinga [84]   Taison [73]
Wilson Mathias   Leandro Damiao

Rafael Sobis † [65]
Giuliano

MATCH OFFICIALS
REFEREE
Oscar Ruiz COL
ASSISTANTS
Abraham Gonzalez COL
Humberto Clavijo COL
4TH OFFICIAL
Jose Buitrago COL

(C) Captain † Man of the Match

Omar Bravo

Omar Arellano [87]
Adolfo Bautista

Marco Fabian [19]

Xavier Baez [82]
Michel Vazquez

Patricio Araujo

Jonny Magallon   Hector Reynoso (c)   Mario de Luna [10]   Miguel Angel Ponce [79]
Dionicio Escalante

Luis Michel

Tr: Jose Luis Real
White shirts, Navy blue shorts, Navy blue socks

GUADALAJARA

Tonight, we were down undeservedly. They were tough matches but now, it's time for celebration. I hope we can lift the World Cup trophy in Abu Dhabi. We won because we put our heart on the pitch.
Pablo Guinazu

This year's achievement has a different taste. In 2006, we had the pressure of having already lost a final in 1980. Tonight, it was calmer. Two titles with the team of my heart is just too much!
Rafael Sobis

(Of the fight between the two sets of players after the final whistle...) What happened is that a fan entered the field and hit our player. That's what caused the problem. It shouldn't have happened. I don't know why they let something like this happen. It seems it's OK to happen when it's here.
Jose Luis Real

COPA NISSAN SUDAMERICANA 2010

First Round

Olimpia	PAR	0	1
Defensor Sporting *	URU	2	1
Oriente Petrolero	BOL	2	1
Univ. de Chile *	CHI	2	0
Atlético Huila *	COL	4	1
Trujillanos	VEN	1	1
River Plate	URU	0	4
Guaraní *	PAR	2	2
Colo Colo	CHI	0	3
Univ'tario Sucre *	BOL	2	1
Indep'te Santa Fe *	COL	0	4
Deportivo Lara *	VEN	2	0
Univ. San Martín	PER	2	2
Deportivo Quito *	ECU	3	1
Un. Cesar Vallejo *	PER	1	1
Barcelona	ECU	2	3

Second Round

Independiente *	ARG	1	1
Argentinos Juniors	ARG	0	1
Sport Huancayo	PER	0	2
Defensor Sporting *	URU	9	0
Banfield	ARG	1	1
Velez Sarsfield *	ARG	0	1
Oriente Petrolero *	BOL	2	1
Deportes Tolima	COL	0	2
Newell's Old Boys *	ARG	1	1
Estudiantes LP	ARG	0	1
Atlético Huila *	COL	1	0
San José	BOL	1	4
Unión San Felipe	CHI	1 1 8p	
Guaraní *	PAR	1 1 7p	
LDU Quito	ECU	Bye	
Palmeiras	BRA	0	3
Vitória *	BRA	2	0
Cerro Porteño	PAR	0	2
Univ'tario Sucre *	BOL	1	2
Indep'te Santa Fe *	COL	1	0
Caracas FC	VEN	1	0
Grêmio Prudente *	BRA	0	0
Atlético Mineiro	BRA	0	1
Avai	BRA	3	0
Santos *	BRA	1	1
Univ. San Martín *	PER	2	0
Emelec	ECU	1	5
Peñarol	URU	1	2
Barcelona *	ECU	0	1
Grêmio	BRA	1	0
Goiás EC *	BRA	1	2

Round of 16

Independiente	0	4
Defensor Sporting *	1	2
Banfield *	2	0
Deportes Tolima	0	3
Newell's Old Boys *	6	0
San José	0	2
Unión San Felipe *	4	1
LDU Quito	2	6
Palmeiras	1	3
Univ'tario Sucre *	0	1
Indep'te Santa Fe	0	1
Atlético Mineiro *	2	0
Avai	1	3
Emelec *	2	1
Peñarol	0	3
Goiás EC *	1	2

Quarter-finals

Team		
Independiente	2	0
Deportes Tolima *	2	0
Newell's Old Boys *	0	0
LDU Quito	0	1
Palmeiras	1	2
Atlético Mineiro *	1	0
Avai	2	0
Goiás EC *	2	1

Semi-finals

Team		
Independiente	2	2
LDU Quito *	3	1
Palmeiras	1	1
Goiás EC *	0	2

Final

Team			
Independiente	0	3	5p
Goiás EC	2	1	3p

* Home team in the first leg

FINAL 1ST LEG

Serra Dourada, Goiânia

1-12-2010, 35 500, Carlos Torres PAR

Scorers - Rafael Moura 15, Otacilio Neto 21

Goiás - Harlei - Ernando, Rafael Toloi, Marcao, Douglas - Carlos Alberto●, Wellington Saci, Amaral - Otacilio Neto● (Everton Santos 70), Marcelo Costa (Felipe 87), Rafael Moura. Tr: Arthur Neto

Indep'te - Hilario Navarro - Eduardo Tuzzio, Julian Velazquez●, Leonel Galeano●, Fernando Godoy (Patricio Rodriguez 46) - Nicolas Cabrera (Carlos Matheu 80), Roberto Battion, Hernan Fredes (Maxi Velazquez 87), Lucas Mareque - Facundo Parra. Andres Silvera ♦58. Tr: Antonio Mohamed

FINAL 2ND LEG

Libertadores de America, Buenos Aires

8-12-2010, Oscar Ruiz COL

Scorers - Julian Velazquez 19 Facundo Parra 2 27 35 for Independiente; Rafael Moura 22 for Goiás

Indep'te - Hilario Navarro● - Eduardo Tuzzio, Carlos Matheu●, Julian Velazquez●, Nicolas Cabrera - Roberto Battion, Hernan Fredes (Maxi Velazquez 108), Lucas Mareque - Nicolas Martinez (Martin Gomez 66), Facundo Parra, Patricio Rodriguez (Leandro Gracian 71). Tr: Antonio Mohamed

Goiás - Harlei - Ernando, Rafael Toloi● Marcao, Douglas (Everton Santos 65) - Carlos Alberto, Wellington Saci, Amaral - Otacilio Neto● (Felipe 76), Marcelo Costa, Rafael Moura●. Tr: Arthur Neto

Top scorers: 8 - Rafael Moura BRA, Goiás ● 6 - Rodrigo Mora URU, Defensor

OFC

OCEANIA FOOTBALL CONFEDERATION

It's an extraordinary fact that the OFC was the only confederation at the 2010 FIFA World Cup in South Africa whose representatives did not lose a single match! That New Zealand remained undefeated should of course be tempered with the fact that they didn't win a match either and were knocked out after the first round but big defeats at the hands of Italy, Slovakia and Paraguay didn't materialise and they left with their heads held high. Of particular note was the 1-1 draw with defending champions Italy and the fact that the Kiwis finished above the Italians in the final standings. There was very little other international activity during 2010 with the exception of the participation of New Caledonia and Tahiti in the 2010 Coupe de l'Outre-Mer in Paris, France, a tournament that is likely to help drive up standards in the francophone countries of Oceania. New Caledonia will be the focus of international football in the region in 2011 with its capital Noumea hosting the

THE FIFA BIG COUNT OF 2006 FOR OCEANIA

	Male	Female		Total
Number of players	486 000	56 000	Referees and Assistant Referees	3 000
Professionals	n/a		Admin, Coaches, Technical, Medical	29 000
Amateurs 18+	59 000		Number of clubs	2 000
Youth under 18	175 000		Number of teams	13 000
Unregistered	301 000		Clubs with women's teams	n/a
Total Players	573 000		Players as % of population	4.68%

Pacific Games during which the football competition is likely to act as a qualifying tournament for the 2014 FIFA World Cup in Brazil. The OFC Champions League continues to go from strength to strength and in 2010 it produced a major surprise when Papua New Guinea's Hekari United beat Waitakere United of New Zealand in the final. It was a breakthrough that had been anticipated since the defection of Australia to the Asian Football Confederation but it came sooner than expected and from a surprising source, with Papua New Guinea having very little track record in club football. Whether Hekari's triumph represents a sea change for the island states of the Pacific remains to be seen but with the prospect of following in Hekari's footsteps to the FIFA Club World Cup, club football in Oceania should continue to grow - even if there is very little prospect of avoiding defeat once there, as Hekari were quick to find out after losing to Dubai's Al Wahda.

Oceania Football Confederation (OFC)

Ericsson Stadium, 12 Maurice Road, Penrose, PO Box 62 586, Auckland 6, New Zealand
Tel +64 9 5258161   Fax +64 9 5258164
info@ofcfoot.org.nz   www.oceaniafootball.com
President: David Chung PNG
General Secretary: Tai Nicholas COK
Vice-President: Fred de Jong NZL
OFC Formed: 1966

OFC EXECUTIVE COMMITTEE

President: David Chung PNG
Vice-President: Fred de Jong NZL

Martin Alufurai SOL   Lee Harmon COK
Lambert Matlock VAN   Toetu Petana SAM   Dr MS Sahu Khan FIJ

MAP OF OFC MEMBER NATIONS

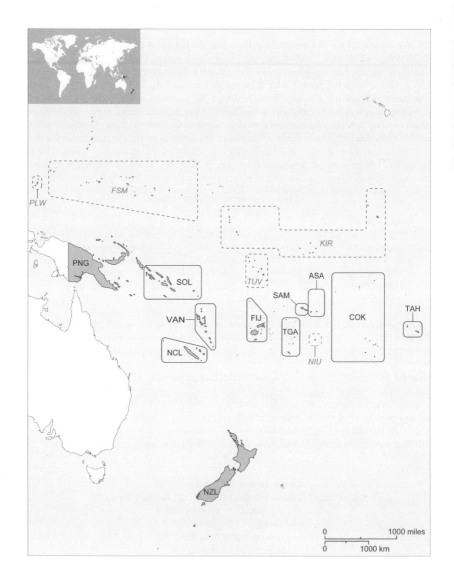

OFC MEMBER ASSOCIATIONS (11)
ASA - **American Samoa** • COK - **Cook Islands** • FIJ - **Fiji** • NCL - **New Caledonia** • NZL - **New Zealand**
PNG - **Papua New Guinea** • SAM - **Samoa** • SOL - **Solomon Islands** • TAH - **Tahiti** • TGA - **Tonga** • VAN - **Vanuatu**

ASSOCIATE OFC MEMBER ASSOCIATIONS (5)
KIR - **Kiribati** • FSM - **Micronesia** • NIU - **Niue** • PLW - **Palau** • TUV - **Tuvalu**
None of these five nations are affiliated to FIFA

OCEANIA NATIONAL TEAM TOURNAMENTS

OCEANIA NATIONS CUP

Year	Host Country	Winners	Score	Runners-up	Venue
1973	New Zealand	New Zealand	2-0	Tahiti	Auckland
1980	New Caledonia	Australia	4-2	Tahiti	Nouméa
1996	Home & away	Australia	6-0 5-0	Tahiti	Papeete & Canberra
1998	Australia	New Zealand	1-0	Australia	Brisbane
2000	Tahiti	Australia	2-0	New Zealand	Stade de Pater, Papeete
2002	New Zealand	New Zealand	1-0	Australia	Ericsson Stadium, Auckland
2004	Home & away	Australia	5-1 6-0	Solomon Islands	Honaria & Sydney
2008	Home & away	New Zealand	3-1 3-0	New Caledonia	League system

There was no final in 2008. The results listed were between the first and second placed teams in the FIFA World Cup qualifying group for Oceania. Semi-finals were not played in 1973, 1980, 2004 and 2008

OCEANIA NATIONS CUP MEDALS TABLE

	Country	G	S	B	F	SF
1	Australia	4	2		6	4
2	New Zealand	4	1	2	4	4
3	Tahiti		3	1	3	3
4	New Caledonia	1	2			
5	Solomon Islands		1	2	1	2
6	Fiji			2		1
7	Vanuatu					2
		8	8	9	14	16

This table represents the Gold (winners), Silver (runners-up) and Bronze (semi-finalists) placings in the OFC Nations Cup, along with the number of appearances in the final and semi-finals.

PACIFIC GAMES

Year	Host Country	Winners	Score	Runners-up	Venue
1963	Fiji	New Caledonia	8-2	Fiji	Suva
1966	New Caledonia	Tahiti	2-0	New Caledonia	Noumea
1969	Papua New Guinea	New Caledonia	2-1	Tahiti	Port Moresby
1971	Tahiti	New Caledonia	7-1	New Hebrides	Papeete
1975	Guam	Tahiti	2-1	New Caledonia	Guam
1979	Fiji	Tahiti	3-0	Fiji	Suva
1983	Western Samoa	Tahiti	1-0	Fiji	Apia
1987	New Caledonia	New Caledonia	1-0	Tahiti	Noumea
1991	Papua New Guinea	Fiji	1-1 ?-?p	Solomon Isl	Port Moresby
1995	Tahiti	Tahiti	2-0	Solomon Isl	Papeete
2003	Fiji	Fiji	2-0	New Caledonia	Suva
2007	Samoa	New Caledonia	1-0	Fiji	Apia

SOUTH PACIFIC MINI GAMES

Year	Host Country	Winners	Score	Runners-up	Venue
1981	Solomon Islands	Tahiti	1-0	New Caledonia	Honiara
1985	Cook Islands	Tahiti	2-0	Fiji	Rarotonga
1989	Tonga	Papua New Guinea	0-0 4-3p	Fiji	Nuku'alofa
1993	Vanuatu	Tahiti	3-0	Fiji	Port Vila

POLYNESIAN CUP

Year	Host Country	Winners	Score	Runners-up	Venue
1994	Western Samoa	Tahiti	1-0	Tonga	Apia
1996	Tonga	Tonga	1-0	Western Samoa	Nuku'alofa
1998	Cook Islands	Tahiti	5-0	Cook Islands	Rarotonga
2000	Tahiti	Tahiti	2-0	Cook Islands	Papete

Competitions have always been organised on a league basis. The result listed is the game between the top two in the league standings

MELANESIAN CUP

Year	Host Country	Winners	Score	Runners-up	Venue
1988	Solomon Islands	Fiji	3-1	Solomon Islands	Solomon Islands
1989	Fiji	Fiji	3-0	New Caledonia	Fiji
1990	Vanuatu	Vanuatu	1-0	New Caledonia	Vanuatu
1992	Vanuatu	Fiji	2-2	New Caledonia	Vanuatu
1994	Solomon Islands	Solomon Islands	1-0	Fiji	Solomon Islands
1996	Papua New Guinea	Papua New Guinea	1-1	Solomon Islands	Papua New Guinea
1998	Vanuatu	Fiji	2-1	Vanuatu	Vanuatu
2000	Fiji	Fiji	2-2	Solomon Islands	Fiji

A final was played only in the first competition in 1988. The results listed after then are between the first two teams in the league standings

OCEANIA CLUB TOURNAMENTS

OFC CHAMPIONS LEAGUE

Year	Winners	Country	Score	Country	Runners-up
1987	Adelaide City	AUS	1-1 4-1p	NZL	Mount Wellington
1999	South Melbourne	AUS	5-1	FIJ	Nadi
2001	Wollongong City Wolves	AUS	1-0	VAN	Tafea FC
2005	Sydney FC	AUS	2-0	NCL	AS Magenta
2006	Auckland City	NZL	3-1	TAH	AS Piraé
2007	Waitakere United	NZL	1-2 1-0	FIJ	Ba
2008	Waitakere United	NZL	1-3 5-0	SOL	Kossa
2009	Auckland City	NZL	7-2 2-2	SOL	Koloale
2010	Hekari United	PNG	3-0 1-2	NZL	Waitakere United

OCEANIA YOUTH TOURNAMENTS

OFC U–20 CHAMPIONSHIP

Year	Host Country	Winners	Score	Runners-up	Venue
1974	Tahiti	Tahiti	2-0	New Zealand	Papeete
1978	New Zealand	Australia	5-1 †	Fiji	Auckland
1980	Fiji	New Zealand	2-0	Australia	Suva
1982	Papua New Guinea	Australia	4-3	New Zealand	Port Moresby
1985	Australia	Australia	3-2 †	Israel	Sydney
1987	New Zealand	Australia	1-1 †	Israel	Auckland
1988	Fiji	Australia	1-0	New Zealand	Suva
1990	Fiji	Australia	6-0 †	New Zealand	Suva
1992	Tahiti	New Zealand	1-0 †	Tahiti	Papeete
1994	Fiji	Australia	1-0	New Zealand	Suva
1996	Tahiti	Australia	2-1	New Zealand	Papeete
1998	Samoa	Australia	2-0	Fiji	Apia
2001	New Cal/Cook Is	Australia	1-2 3-1	New Zealand	Auckland & Coffs Harbour
2003	Vanuatu/Fiji	Australia	11-0 4-0	Fiji	Melbourne & Ba
2005	Solomon Islands	Australia	3-0	Solomon Islands	Honiara
2007	New Zealand	New Zealand	3-2	Fiji	Waitakere
2009	Tahiti	Tahiti	0-0	New Caledonia	Papeete

The 1978, 1985, 1987, 1990, 1992, 2007 and 2009 tournaments were played as leagues • The results shown are those between the top two teams

OFC U–17 CHAMPIONSHIP

Year	Host Country	Winners	Score	Runners-up	Venue
1983	New Zealand	Australia	2-1	New Zealand	Mount Smart, Auckland
1986	Chinese Taipei	Australia	0-1	New Zealand	CKF Stadium, Kaohsiung
1989	Australia	Australia	5-1	New Zealand	
1991	New Zealand	Australia	1-1 1-0	New Zealand	Napier
1993	New Zealand	Australia	3-0	Soloman Islands	

OCEANIA U–17 CHAMPIONSHIP (CONT'D)

Year	Host Country	Winners	Score	Runners-up	Venue
1995	Vanuatu	Australia	1-0	New Zealand	
1997	New Zealand	New Zealand	1-0	Australia	
1999	Fiji	Australia	5-0	Fiji	Churchill Park, Lautoka
2001	Samoa/Cook Isl	Australia	3-0 6-0	New Zealand	Canberra & Auckland
2003	Home & away	Australia	3-1 4-0	New Caledonia	Nouméa
2005	New Caledonia	Australia	1-0	Vanuatu	Nouméa
2007	Tahiti	New Zealand	2-1	Tahiti	Papeete
2009	New Zealand	New Zealand	2-0	Tahiti	Auckland

From 1983 to 1991 and in 2007 and 2009 the tournaments were played as leagues • The results shown are those between the top two teams

OCEANIA WOMEN'S TOURNAMENTS

OCEANIA WOMEN'S CHAMPIONSHIP

Year	Host Country	Winners	Score	Runners-up	Venue
1983	New Caledonia	New Zealand	3-2	Australia	Nouméa
1986	New Zealand	Chinese Taipei	4-1	Australia	Christchurch
1989	Australia	Chinese Taipei	1-0	New Zealand	Brisbane
1991	Australia	New Zealand	1-0 0-1 †	Australia	Sydney
1995	Papua N. Guinea	Australia	1-2 1-0 †	New Zealand	Port Moresby
1998	New Zealand	Australia	3-1	New Zealand	Mount Smart, Auckland
2003	Australia	Australia	2-0 †	New Zealand	Belconnen, Canberra
2007	Papua N. Guinea	New Zealand	7-0	Papua New Guinea	Lae
2010	New Zealand	New Zealand	11-0	Papua New Guinea	Auckland

† The 1991, 1995, 2003 and 2007 tournaments were played as leagues • The results shown are those between the top two teams

OCEANIA WOMEN'S U-20 CHAMPIONSHIP

Year	Host Country	Winners	Score	Runners-up	Venue
2002	Tonga	Australia	6-0	New Zealand	Nuku'alofa
2004	Papua New Guinea	Australia	14-1	Papua New Guinea	Lloyd Robson Oval, Port Moresby
2006	Samoa	New Zealand	6-0	Tonga	JS Blatter Complex, Apia
2010	New Zealand	New Zealand	8-0	Cook Islands	North Harbour, Auckland

OCEANIA WOMEN'S U-19 CHAMPIONSHIP

Year	Host Country	Winners	Score	Runners-up	Venue
2010	New Zealand	New Zealand	10-0	Solomon Islands	North Harbour, Auckland

YOUTH TOURNAMENTS IN OCEANIA 2010

OFC U–20 WOMEN'S CHAMPIONSHIP NEW ZEALAND 2010

	Pl	W	D	L	F	A	Pts	COK	TGA	ASA
New Zealand	3	3	0	0	27	0	9	8-0	11-0	8-0
Cook Islands	3	1	1	1	5	9	4		1-1	4-0
Tonga	3	1	1	1	5	12	4			4-0
American Samoa	3	0	0	3	0	16	0			

New Zealand qualified for the FIFA U–20 Women's World Cup 2010 in Germany • Matches played at North Harbour, Auckland 21/01/2010 - 25/01/2010

OFC U–17 WOMEN'S CHAMPIONSHIP NEW ZEALAND 2010

	Pl	W	D	L	F	A	Pts	SOL	PNG	TGA
New Zealand	3	3	0	0	37	0	9	10-0	9-0	18-0
Solomon Islands	3	2	0	1	6	10	6		1-0	5-0
Papua New Guinea	3	1	0	2	4	10	3			4-0
Tonga	3	0	0	3	0	27	0			

New Zealand qualified for the FIFA U–17 Women's World Cup 2010 in Trinidad and Tobago • Matches played at North Harbour, Auckland, 12/04/2010 - 16/04/2010

WOMEN'S TOURNAMENTS IN OCEANIA 2010

OFC WOMEN'S CHAMPIONSHIP NEW ZEALAND 2010

First Round Group Stage

Group A	Pl	W	D	L	F	A	Pts	COK	TAH	VAN
New Zealand	3	3	0	0	31	0	9	10-0	7-0	14-0
Cook Islands	3	2	0	1	3	10	6		1-0	2-0
Tahiti	3	1	0	2	5	9	3			5-1
Vanuatu	3	0	0	3	1	21	0			

Group B	Pl	W	D	L	F	A	Pts	SOL	TGA	FIJ
Papua New Guinea	3	3	0	0	8	1	9	2-1	3-0	3-0
Solomon Islands	3	1	1	1	5	2	4		4-0	0-0
Tonga	3	1	0	2	2	8	3			2-1
Fiji	3	0	1	2	1	5	1			

Semi-finals

New Zealand	8	Cook Islands	0
Solomon Islands	0	Papua New Guinea	1

Final

New Zealand	11
Papua New Guinea	0

Third Place Play-off

Cook Islands	2
Solomon Islands	0

Held in New Zealand from 29-09-2010 to 8-10-2010

CLUB TOURNAMENTS IN OCEANIA 2009–10

OFC CHAMPIONS LEAGUE 2009-10

First Round Groups

Group A		Pl	W	D	L	F	A	Pts	NZL	NZL	NCL	TAH
Waitakere United	NZL	6	3	3	0	15	6	12		1-1	4-1	2-0
Auckland City	NZL	6	3	3	0	13	5	12	2-2		2-1	5-0
AS Magenta	NCL	6	1	3	2	13	10	6	1-1	1-1		8-1
AS Manu-Ura	TAH	6	0	1	5	3	23	1	1-5	0-2	1-1	

Group B		Pl	W	D	L	F	A	Pts	PNG	FIJ	VAN	SOL
Hekari United	PNG	6	4	1	1	15	7	13		1-2	4-0	2-1
Lautoka	FIJ	6	4	0	2	12	6	12	0-1		1-2	3-0
Tafea	VAN	6	2	2	2	8	11	8	3-3	1-3		0-0
Marist	SOL	6	0	1	5	3	14	1	1-4	1-3	0-2	

Final

Hekari United	3	1
Waitakere United	0	2

GROUP A		Pl	W	D	L	F	A	Pts	NZL	NZL	NCL	TAH
Waitakere United	NZL	6	3	3	0	15	6	12		1-1	4-1	2-0
Auckland City	NZL	6	3	3	0	13	5	12	2-2		2-1	5-0
AS Magenta	NCL	6	1	3	2	13	10	6	1-1	1-1		8-1
AS Manu-Ura	TAH	6	0	1	5	3	23	1	1-5	0-2	1-1	

Kiwitea Street, Auckland
17-10-2009, 15:00, 875, Parsons AUS

Auckland City — 5

Vicelich [18], Coombes [34], Koprivic 3 [69 79 90]

Jacob Spoonley - Ian Hogg, James Pritchett, Ivan Vicelich, Greg Uhlmann, Matt Williams, Lee Ki Hyung (Adam McGeorge 74), Chad Coombes (Adam Dickinson 72), Alex Feneridis, Daniel Koprivic, Keryn Jordan (Jason Hayne 62). Tr: Paul Posa

AS Manu-Ura — 0

Daniel Tapeta - Rex Faura●, Philippe Moreta●, Vetea Tepa◆74, Fraddy Tauihara, Henri Tapea, Tetahio Auraa, Jean-Francois Kabeu, Hiroana Poroiae, Auguste Washetine, Billy Mataitai. Tr: Patrick Pito

Numa-Daly Magenta, Nouméa
24-10-2009, 16:00, 1500, Hauata TAH

AS Magenta — 1

Scott OG [78]

Jean-Yann Dounezek - Benjamin Longue, Jeremie Dokunengo●, Andre Sinedo●, Joris Gorendiawe●, Noel Kaudre, Pierre Wajoka, Jules Wea, Lamo Xewe (Jedidja Saiko 89), Paul Poatinda, Ludovic Boit (Poulidor Toto 57). Tr: Alain Moizan

Waitakere United — 1

Fisher [37]

Danny Robinson - Jason Rowley●, Aaron Scott, Tim Myers, Neil Sykes, Martin Bullock (Allan Pearce 71), Jeremy Christie●, Jake Butler, Brent Fisher, Benjamin Totori (Ryan de Vries 79), Roy Krishna◆74. Tr: Neil Emblen

Fred Taylor Park, Waitakere
7-11-2009, 15:00, 850, Docherty AUS

Waitakere United — 2

Totori [55], Fisher [86p]

Danny Robinson - Jason Rowley, Aaron Scott, Tim Myers, Neil Sykes, Jeremy Christie, Jake Butler, Brent Fisher, Benjamin Totori (Jason Hicks 87), Allan Pearce (Dakota Lucas 73), Dimas da Silva (Martin Bullock 68). Tr: Neil Emlen

AS Manu-Ura — 0

Jonathan Torohia - Rex Faura, Fraddy Tauihara●, Henri Tapea●, Tetahio Auraa (Heitini Tupea 82), Jean-Francois Kabeu, Hiroana Poroiae, Stephane Tuairau (Philippe Moreta 70), Auguste Washetine●, Hiashi Kake, Billy Mataitai (Aldo Tauihara◆ 65). Tr: Patrick Pito

Kiwitea Street, Auckland

8-11-2009, 15:00, 1200, Varman FIJ

Auckland City 2

Williams [47], Koprivic [52]

Paul Gothard - Ian **Hogg**, James **Pritchett** (Chad **Coombes** 72), Ivan **Vicelich**, Greg **Uhlmann**, Matt **Williams**, Lee Ki Hyung, Alex **Feneridis** (Adam **McGeorge** 31), Jason **Hayne•**, Daniel **Koprivic**, Keryn **Jordan** (Adam **Dickinson** 46). Tr: Paul **Posa**

AS Magenta 1

Xewe [6]

Jean-Yann **Dounezek** - Benjamin **Longue**, Steeven **Longue**, Andre **Sinedo•**, Joris **Gorendiawe**, Noel **Kaudre**, Pierre **Wajoka•**, Jules **Wea**, Lamo **Xewe** (Jedidja 85), Paul **Poatinda•**, Ludovic **Boit** (Pjilippe **Kokone** 58). Tr: Alain **Moizan**

Fred Taylor Park, Waitakere

28-11-2009, 15:00, 1200, Cross NZL

Waitakere United 1

Fisher [42]

Danny **Robinson** - Jason **Rowley•**, Aaron **Scott**, Neil **Sykes** (Dimas da **Silva** 87), Martin **Bullock•** (Ryan de **Vries** 76), Jeremy **Christie**, Jake **Butler**, Brent **Fisher**, Benjamin **Totori**, Allan **Pearce** (Dakota **Lucas** 90), Neil **Emblem**. Tr: Neil **Emblem**

Auckland City 1

Coombes [30]

Jacob **Spoonley** - Ian **Hogg**, James **Pritchett**, Ivan **Vicelich•**, Greg **Uhlmann**, Matt **Williams•**, Lee Ki Hyung, Chad **Coombes**, Jason **Hayne** (Adam **Dickinson** 56♦81), Adam **McGeorge•**, Daniel **Koprivic** (Keryn **Jordan** 72). Tr: Paul **Posa**

Stade Paea, Papeete

27-11-2009, 17:00, 750, O'Leary NZL

AS Manu-Ura 1

Mataitai [68]

Daniel **Tapeta** - Rex **Faura♦85**, Fraddy **Tauihara**, Henri **Tapea**, Aldo **Tauihara** (Matahi **Hauata** 90), Tetahio **Auraa** (Billy **Mataitai** 61), Jean-Francois **Kabeu•**, Hiroana **Poroiae** (Heitini **Tupea** 72), Stephane **Tuairau•**, Auguste **Washetine**, Hiashi **Kake**. Tr: Partick **Pito**

AS Magenta 1

Kokone [46]

Jean-Yann **Dounezek** - Benjamin **Longue**, Jeremie **Dokunengo**, Steeven **Longue**, Joris **Gorendiawe**, Noel **Kaudre•**, Pierre **Wajoka**, Jules **Wea**, Lamo **Xewe**, Paul **Poatinda•**, Pjilippe **Kokone•** (Ludovic **Boit** 59). Tr: Alain **Moizan**

Stade Paea, Papeete

13-02-2010, 19:30, 750, Varman FIJ

AS Manu-Ura 0

Jonathan **Torohia** - Vetea **Tepa•**, Heitini **Tupea** (Aldo **Tauihara** 78), Henri **Tapea**, Tetahio **Auraa**, Jean-Francois **Kabeu**, Hiroana **Poroiae**, Stephane **Tuairau**, Auguste **Washetine**, Hiashi **Kake•**, Billy **Mataitai**. Tr: Patrick **Pito**

Auckland City 2

Hogg [64], Koprivic [89]

Jacob **Spoonley** - Ian **Hogg**, James **Pritchett**, Ivan **Vicelich•**, Greg **Uhlmann**, Matt **Williams** (Paul **Urlovic** 71), Lee Ki Hyung, Chad **Coombes** (Alex **Feneridis** 67), Jason **Hayne•**, Adam **McGeorge**, Daniel **Koprivic•** (Milos **Nikolic** 90). Tr: Paul **Posa**

Fred Taylor Park, Waitakere

20-02-2010, 15:00, 700, Jacques TAh

Waitakere United 4

Bullock [40], Totori [41], De Vries [79], Fisher [82]

Danny **Robinson** - Aaron **Scott•**, Tim **Myers**, Neil **Sykes**, Martin **Bullock**, Jake **Butler**, Brent **Fisher** (Dimas da **Silva** 83), Benjamin **Totori** (Jack **Pelter** 69), Allan **Pearce** (Ryan de **Vries** 78), Roy **Krishna**, Neil **Emblen•**. Tr: Neil **Emblem**

AS Magenta 1

Boit [32]

Jean-Yann **Dounezek** - Benjamin **Longue•**, Andre **Sinedo•**, Joris **Gorendiawe**, Marius **Bako**, Pierre **Wajoka**, Roy **Kayara**, Jules **Wea**, Lamo **Xewe** (Steeven **Longue** 89), Andre **Naxue**, Ludovic **Boit** (Jean-Phillipe **Saiko** 58). Tr: Alain **Moizan**

Numa-Daly Magenta, Noumeá

6-03-2010, 15:00, 1500, Hauata TAH

AS Magenta 1

Sinedo [53]

Michel **Hne** - Benjamin **Longue**, Steeven **Longue**, Andre **Sinedo**, Noel **Kaudre**, Pierre **Wajoka**, Jules **Wea** (Lamo **Xewe** 78), Andre **Naxue**, Paul **Poatinda** (Roy **Kayara** 65), Jean-Phillipe **Saiko** (Ludovic **Boit** 83). Tr: Alain **Moizan**

Auckland City 1

Koprivic [12]

Jacob **Spoonley** - Ian **Hogg**, Sam **Campbell**, James **Pritchett**, Greg **Uhlmann**, Matt **Williams** (Alex **Feneridis** 78), Lee Ki Hyung, Adam **McGeorge**, Paul **Urlovic** (Chad **Coombes** 55), Daniel **Koprivic**, Adam **Dickinson** (Grant **Young** 63). Tr: Paul **Posa**

Stade Paea, Papeete

19-03-2010, 19:30, 203, Assiene-Ambassa NCL

AS Manu-Ura 1

Poroiae [30]

Daniel **Tapeta** - Vetea **Tepa•**, Heitini **Tupea**, Fraddy **Tauihara**, Henri **Tapea**, Tetahio **Auraa**, Jean-Francois **Kabeu**, Hiroana **Poroiae**, Stephane **Tuairau** (Jean-Yves **Li Wa Ut** 66), Auguste **Washetine•**, Hiashi **Kake•**. Tr: Patrick **Pito**

Waitakere United 5

Rowley 2 [28 62], Krishna [42], Pearce 2 [49 64]

Danny **Robinson** - Jason **Rowley**, Tim **Myers•**, Neil **Sykes**, Martin **Bullock** (Zane **Sole** 88), Jake **Butler**, Brent **Fisher** (Dakota **Lucas** 88), Allan **Pearce**, Roy **Krishna**, Neil **Emblem**, Ryan de **Vries** (Jack **Pelter** 72). Tr: Neil **Emblem**

Numa-Daly Magenta, Noumeá

27-03-2010, 15:00,

AS Magenta 8

AS Manu-Ura 1

Kiwitea Street, Auckland

28-03-2010, 15:00, 2500, Hauata TAH

Auckland City 2

Koprivic [29], Uhlmann [71]

Jacob **Spoonley** - Ian **Hogg**, Ivan **Vicelich•**, Greg **Uhlmann•**, Matt **Williams** (Grant **Young** 66), Lee Ki Hyung, Chad **Coombes•**, Alex **Feneridis** (Paul **Urlovic** 83), Jason **Hayne•**, Daniel **Koprivic**, Adam **Dickinson**. Tr: Paul **Posa**

Waitakere United 2

Totori 2 [3 59]

Danny **Robinson** - Jason **Rowley** (Tim **Myers** 81), Aaron **Scott**, Neil **Sykes**, Martin **Bullock**, Jake **Butler••♦75**, Brent **Fisher**, Benjamin **Totori** (Jack **Pelter** 76), Allan **Pearce**, Roy **Krishna**, Neil **Emblem**. Tr: Neil **Emblem**

GROUP B		Pl	W	D	L	F	A	Pts	PNG	FIJ	VAN	SOL
Hekari United	PNG	6	4	1	1	15	7	13		1-2	4-0	2-1
Lautoka	FIJ	6	4	0	2	12	6	12	0-1		1-2	3-0
Tafea	VAN	6	2	2	2	8	11	8	3-3	1-3		0-0
Marist	SOL	6	0	1	5	3	14	1	1-4	1-3	0-2	

Korman, Port Vila

17-10-2009, 15:00, 4000, Cross NZL

Tafea 3

Namatak [1], Tom [34], Sakama [45]

Alfred **Malas** - Roger **Joe**, Fredy **Vava**, Geoffrey **Gete**, Robert **Tom**, Silas **Namatak•**, Moise **Poide** (Alphonse **Qorig** 84), Francois **Sakama**, Michael **Kaltack** (Richard **Iwai** 67), Jean Nako **Naprapol**, Etienne **Mermer** (Jonah **Turu** 46). Tr: Graham **Demas**

Hekari United 3

Jack [40], Manuca [42], Mela [50]

Gure **Gabina** - Lorima **Dau•**, Cyril **Muta•**, Charles **Paranda**, Koriak **Upaiga** (Brian **Tuhiana** 75), Benjamin **Mela**, David **Muta** (Abraham **Enoch** 63), Eric **Komeng** (Michael **Foster** 89), Pita **Bolatoga•**, Tuimasi **Manuca**, Kema **Jack**. Tr: Jerry **Allen**

Lawson Tama, Honiara

18-10-2009,, 15:00, 16 000, Kerr NZL

Marist 1

Iniga [82]

Fred **Hale** (Michael **Kouma** 46) - Christanto **Misiga**, Derol **Melo•**, David **Houpere•**, Joseph **Lani**, Abraham **Iniga•**, Michael **Misitana** (Tutizama **Tanito** 87), Clifford **Huta**, Gibson **Hosea**, Commins **Menapi**, Joe **Luwi•** (Michael **Patiti** 73). Tr: Patrick **Miniti**

Lautoka 3

Hassan [14], Kautoga [20], Arrarte [90]

James **Chronopoulos** - Samuela **Kautoga**, Samuela **Vula•**, Malakai **Waqa** (Semesa **Nakosia** 75), Ilatia **Tuilau•**, Keni **Doidoi**, Nahuel **Arrarte**, Marika **Robanakadavu•**, Kamal **Hassan**, Jone **Vono** (Samuela **Drudru** 88), Muni **Naidu** (Sailesh **Samy** 69). Tr: Imdad **Ali**

Lawson Tama, Honiara

7-11-2009, 15:00, 8000, Achari FIJ

Marist 0

Navusu **Kitu** - Christanto **Misiga** (David **Houpere** 70), Emmanuel **Poila**, Joseph **Lani**, Martin **Ruhasia**, John **Wayne•**, Abraham **Iniga**, Clifford **Huta**, Lenson **Bisili** (Commins **Menapi** 80), Michael **Patiti**, Johan **Firisi Doiwale** (Joe **Luwi** 76). Tr: Patrick **Miniti**

Tafea 2

Sakama [48], Mermer [51]

Alfred **Malas** - Jacques **Mafil Nawan**, Fredy **Vava**, Geoffrey **Gete**, Robert **Tom**, Silas **Namatak**, Richard **Iwai** (Michael **Kaltack** 54), Francois **Sakama**, Talom **Iarueli**, Jean Nako **Naprapol**, Etienne **Mermer** (Jonah **Turu** 87). Tr: Graham **Demas**

PMRL, Port Moresby
7-11-2009, 15:00, 10 000, Saohu SOL

Hekari United 1

Jack [28]

Gure **Gabina** - Lorima **Dau** (Tagaya **Lepani** 78), Cyril **Muta**, Brian **Tuhiana**, Charles **Paranda●**, Benjamin **Mela** (Kluivert **Dagi** 84), David **Muta●**, Pita **Bolatoga** (Eric **Komeng** 73), Tuimasi **Manuca**, Joachim **Waroi**, Kema **Jack**. Tr: Jerry **Allen**

Lautoka 2

Nawatu [57], Smith [69]

James **Chronopoulos** - Samuela **Kautoga**, Samuela **Vula**, Malakai **Waqa**, Ilatia **Tuilau**, Keni **Doidoi** (Muni **Naidu** 90), Nahuel **Arrarte**, Marika **Robanakadavu**, Salesh **Kumar**, Valerio **Nawatu●** (Apisai **Smith●** 67), Kamal **Hassan●** (Sailesh **Samy** 88). Tr: Imdad **Ali**

Churchill Park, Lautoka
29-11-2009, 15:00, 6000, Hauata TAH

Lautoka 1

Nawatu [45]

James **Chronopoulos** - Samuela **Kautoga**, Samuela **Vula**, Malakai **Waqa**, Ilatia **Tuilau♦**31, Keni **Doidoi●**, Nahuel **Arrarte●**, Marika **Robanakadavu** (Muni **Naidu** 88), Salesh **Kumar**, Valerio **Nawatu●** (Apisai **Smith** 80), Kamal **Hassan●**. Tr: Imdad **Ali**

Tafea 2

Naprapol [22], Sakama [77]

Alfred **Malas** - Jacques **Mafil Nawan**, Roger **Joe**, Fredy **Vava**, Geoffrey **Gete●** (Moise **Poide** 90), Robert **Tom**, Silas **Namatak**, Richard **Iwai** (Michael **Kaltack** 60), Francois **Sakama**, Jean Nako **Naprapol**, Etienne **Mermer** (Jonah **Turu** 71). Tr: Graham **Demas**

PMRL, Port Moresby
5-12-2009, 15:00, 2000, Beath AUS

Hekari United 2

Jack [48], Waroi [52]

Gure **Gabina** - Cyril **Muta**, Charles **Paranda**, Koriak **Upaiga**, Michael **Foster**, David **Muta**, Samuel **Kini**, Pita **Bolatoga●**, Tuimasi **Manuca** (Lorima **Dau** 88), Joachim **Waroi** (Eric **Komeng** 56), Kema **Jack●**. Tr: Jerry **Allen**

Marist 1

Menapi [82]

Navusu **Kitu** - Emmanuel **Poila**, Joseph **Lani**, Martin **Ruhasia**, Charlie **Taniro●**, Arnold **Keni**, John **Wayne** (Tutizama **Tanito** 63), Abraham **Iniga**, Clifford **Huta** (Michael **Patiti** 56), Tolei Ini **Kopuria** (Johan **Firisi** **Doiwale** 85), Commins **Menapi**. Tr: Patrick **Miniti**

PMRL, Port Moresby
13-02-2010, 15:00, 5000, O'Leary NZL

Hekari United 4

Manuca [14], Maemae 2 [20 28], Waroi [84]

Gure **Gabina** - Gideon **Omokirio**, Cyril **Muta**, Koriak **Upaiga**, David **Muta**, Andrew **Lepani** (Charles **Paranda** 63), Stanley **Waita** (Samuel **Kini** 78), Alick **Maemae●**, Henry **Fa'Arodo**, Tuimasi **Manuca**, Kema **Jack** (Joachim **Waroi** 66). Tr: Tommy **Mana**

Tafea 0

Alfred **Malas** - Samson **Obed●** (Jonah **Turu** 67), Jacques **Mafil Nawan**, Roger **Joe**, Fredy **Vava**, Silas **Namatak●**, Moise **Poide**, Francois **Sakama**, Frazer **Maebule** (Richard **Iwai** 46), Michael **Kaltack** (Robert **Tom** 81), Jean Nako **Naprapol**. Tr: Graham **Demas**

Churchill Park, Lautoka
14-02-2010, 15:00, 4000, Benischke GER

Lautoka 3

Vakatalesau [8], Avinesh [48], Vono [73]

Aliverti **Baleloa** - Samuela **Kautoga**, Samuela **Vula●**, Malakai **Waqa**, Alvin **Avinesh** (Leone **Vurukania** 83), Salesh **Kumar**, Apisai **Smith** (Sailesh **Samy** 52), Marika **Robanakadavu**, Osea **Vakatalesau** (Elvin **Prasad** 85), Jone **Vono**, Muni **Naidu**. Tr: Imdad **Ali**

Marist 0

Navusu **Kitu** - Jacob **Pekau**, Emmanuel **Poila**, Arnold **Keni**, Jerry **Sam** (Michael **Misitana** 52), Abraham **Iniga** (Derol **Melo** 60), George **Lui** (Michael **Sira** 83), Francis **Saemala**, Lenson **Bisili**, Joe **Luwi**, Commins **Menapi**. Tr: Patrick **Miniti**

Korman, Port Vila
6-03-2010, 15:00, 4000, Assiene-Ambassa NCL

Tafea 0

Alfred **Malas** - Samson **Obed**, Jacques **Mafil Nawan**, Roger **Joe** (Etienne **Mermer** 43), Fredy **Vava**, Geoffrey **Gete**, Robert **Tom**, Richard **Iwai**, Frazer **Maebule●** (Moise **Poide** 72), Michael **Kaltack**, Jean Nako **Naprapol** (Jonah **Turu** 67). Tr: Graham **Demas**

Marist 0

Navusu **Kitu** - Jacob **Pekau**, Emmanuel **Poila**, Arnold **Keni**, Simon **Tova**, Abraham **Iniga**, Lenson **Bisili●**, Gibson **Hosea**, Joe **Luwi** (Ben **Hibiscus** 82), Commins **Menapi**, Tutizama **Tanito●**. Tr: Patrick **Miniti**

Churchill Park, Lautoka
7-03-2010, 15:00, 5000, Kerr NZL

Lautoka 0

Aliverti **Baleloa** - Samuela **Kautoga●**, Malakai **Waqa**, Leone **Vurukania**, Alvin **Avinesh**, Salesh **Kumar●**, Marika **Robanakadavu●●♦**90, Valerio **Nawatu** (Apisai **Smith** 70), Kamal **Hassan**, Osea **Vakatalesau●**, Jone **Vono** (Muni **Naidu** 62). Tr: Imdad **Ali**

Hekari United 1

Fa'Arodo [54]

Gure **Gabina** - Gideon **Omokirio**, Cyril **Muta**, Koriak **Upaiga**, David **Muta**, Pita **Bolatoga●**, Stanley **Waita** (Eric **Komeng** 84), Alick **Maemae**, Henry **Fa'Arodo** (Andrew **Lepani** 90), Tuimasi **Manuca**, Joachim **Waroi** (Kema **Jack** 40). Tr: Tommy **Mana**

Lawson Tama, Honiara
27-03-2010, 15:00, 10 000, Kerr NZL

Marist 1

Menappi [78]

Navusu **Kitu** - Jacob **Pekau**, Emmanuel **Poila**, Arnold **Keni**, Simon **Tova** (Michael **Sira●** 34), Abraham **Iniga**, George **Lui**, Gibson **Hosea** (Michael **Misitana** 68), Michael **Patiti** (Lenson **Bisili** 51), Joe **Luwi**, Commins **Menapi**. Tr: Patrick **Miniti**

Hekari United 4

Maemae 2 [18 30], Fa'Arodo [20], Bolatoga [40]

Gure **Gabina** - Gideon **Omokirio**, Cyril **Muta**, Koriak **Upaiga**, David **Muta**, Pita **Bolatoga** (Eric **Komeng** 58), Stanley **Waita** (Samuel **Kini** 66), Alick **Maemae**, Henry **Fa'Arodo**, Tuimasi **Manuca** (Benjamin **Mela** 89), Kema **Jack**. Tr: Tommy **Mana**

Korman, Port Vila
27-03-2010, 15:00, 5000, Hester NZL

Tafea 1

Gete [57]

Lautoka 3

Vula [35], Vono [51], Samy [86]

FINAL

1st leg. PMRL Stadium, Port Moresby
17-04-2010, 15:00, 15 000, Parsons AUS

Hekari United 3

Jack 2 [27 73], Maemae [49]

Gure **Gabina** - Gideon **Omokirio**, Cyril **Muta**, Tuimasi **Manuca** (Eric **Komeng** 76), David **Muta** (c), (Benjamin **Mela** 87), Pita **Bolatonga**, Kema **Jack**, Koriak **Upaiga**, Stanley **Waita**, Alick **Maemae●**, Henry **Fa'arodo**. Tr: Jerry **Allen** SOL

Waitakere United 0

Danny **Robinson** - Jason **Rowley**, Aaron **Scott** (Allan **Pearce** 78), Tim **Myers●**, Martin **Bullock**, Brent **Fisher**, Benjamin **Totori** (Dakota **Lucas** 88), Neil **Sykes** (c), Roy **Krishna**, Neil **Emblen**, Jack **Pelter** (Paul **Seaman** 84). Tr: Neil **Emblen** ENG

2nd leg. Fred Taylor Park, Auckland
2-05-2010, 14:00, 3 000, Hauata TAH

Waitakere United 2

Emblen [3], Fisher [84p]

Danny **Robinson●** - Jason **Rowley**, Tim **Myers**, Martin **Bullock●**, Brent **Fisher**, Benjamin **Totoro** (Dakota **Lucas** 70), Allan **Pearce●**, Neil **Sykes** (Jack **Pelter** 61), Roy **Krishna** (Ryan **De Vries** 57), Neil **Emblen**, Jake **Butler** (c). Tr: Neil **Emblen** ENG

Hekari United 1

Jack [35p]

Gure **Gabina** - Gideon **Omokirio**, Cyril **Muta●**, Tuimasi **Manuca●** (Joachim **Waroi** 80), David **Muta** (c), Pita **Bolatonga●**, Kema **Jack**, Koriak **Upaiga**, Stanley **Waita**, Alick **Maemae**. Henry **Fa'arodo**. Tr: Jerry **Allen** SOL

UEFA

UNION DES ASSOCIATIONS EUROPEENNES DE FOOTBALL

It took 80 years but a European nation finally won the FIFA World Cup outside of Europe when Spain beat the Netherlands in the 2010 World Cup Final in South Africa. It crowned an extraordinary four years for the Spanish national team who became the eighth different winners of the trophy after their victory in Johannesburg and only the third nation to hold the world and European titles at the same time. Between February 2007 and July 2010, Spain played 55 matches of which they won 50 and drew three, losing just twice - a staggering record that no other national team in history can match. At the end of the year Dutch legend Johann Cruijff stated that the current Barcelona team was one of the three greatest teams in history alongside Real Madrid from the 1950s and Ajax in the early 1970s, teams that have changed the course of football. He could have been talking

THE FIFA BIG COUNT OF 2006 FOR EUROPE

	Male	Female		Total
Number of players	55 283 000	6 364 000	Referees and Assistant Referees	322 000
Professionals	60 000		Admin, Coaches, Technical, Medical	2 100 000
Amateurs 18+	11 101 000		Number of clubs	202 000
Youth under 18	9 386 000		Number of teams	872 000
Unregistered	40 622 000		Clubs with women's teams	13 000
Total Players	64 069 000		Players as % of population	7.59%

about Spain who used seven Barca players at the finals in South Africa alongside the best Real Madrid had to offer. Spain didn't have it all their own way, however, especially Barcelona who were beaten in the semi-final of the UEFA Champions League by a Jose Mourinho inspired Internazionale who went on to beat Bayern 2-0 in the final in Madrid, a brace from Argentine striker Diego Milito bringing the trophy back to the black and blue half of Milan after an absence of 45 years. It was a truly memorable year for Inter who won a fifth consecutive Serie A title as well as the Coppa Italia to become the first Italian team to win the fabled treble. 2010 also saw the first UEFA Europa League Final in which Atlético Madrid won their first European trophy since winning the Cup Winners Cup in 1962 after beating Fulham 2-1 in Hamburg, Uruguay's Diego Forlan scoring the second of his two goals just before the end of extra-time.

Union des associations européennes de football (UEFA)
Route de Genève 46, 1260 Nyon, Switzerland
Tel +41 22 9944444   Fax +41 22 9944488
info@uefa.com   www.uefa.com
President: Michel Platini FRA   Secretary General: Gianni Infantino ITA
UEFA Formed: 1954

UEFA EXECUTIVE COMMITTEE

President: Michel Platini FRA	1st Vice-President: Senes Erzik TUR	2nd Vice-President: Geoffrey Thompson ENG
3rd Vice-President: Angel María Villar Llona ESP	4th Vice-President: Marios Lefkaritis CYP	5th Vice-President: Joseph Mifsud MLT

ORDINARY MEMBERS OF THE EXECUTIVE COMMITTEE

Giancarlo Abete ITA	Frantisek Laurinec SVK	Dr Gilberto Madail POR
Grigory Surkis UKR	Liutauras Varanavicius LTU	Allan Hansen DEN
Avraham Luzon ISR	Mircea Sandu ROU	Michael van Praag NED
Dr Theo Zwanziger GER		Hon President: Lennart Johansson SWE
FIFA Exco member: Michel D'Hooghe BEL	Secretary General: Gianni Infantino ITA	FIFA Exco member: Franz Beckenbauer GER

MAP OF UEFA MEMBER NATIONS

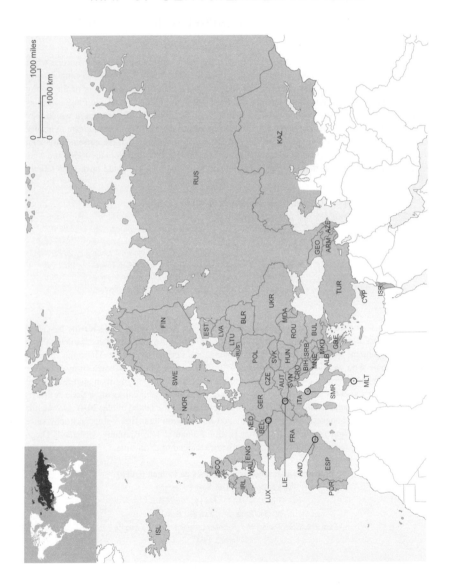

UEFA MEMBER ASSOCIATIONS (53)

ALB - Albania • AND - Andorra • ARM - Armenia • AUS - Austria • AZE - Azerbaijan • BLR - Belarus • BEL - Belgium
BIH - Bosnia-Herzegovina • BUL - Bulgaria • CRO - Croatia • CYP - Cyprus • CZE - Czech Republic • DEN - Denmark • ENG - England
EST - Estonia • FRO - Faroe Islands • FIN - Finland • FRA - France • GEO - Georgia • GER - Germany • GRE - Greece • HUN - Hungary
ISL - Iceland • IRL - Republic of Ireland • ISR - Israel • ITA - Italy • KAZ - Kazakhstan • LVA - Latvia • LIE - Liechtenstein • LTU - Lithuania
LUX - Luxembourg • MKD - Macedonia FYR • MLT - Malta • MDA - Moldova • MNE - Montenegro • NED - Netherlands • NIR - Northern Ireland
NOR - Norway • POL - Poland • POR - Portugal • ROU - Romania • RUS - Russia • SMR - San Marino • SCO - Scotland • SRB - Serbia
SVK - Slovakia • SVN - Slovenia • ESP - Spain • SWE - Sweden • SUI - Switzerland • TUR - Turkey • UKR - Ukraine • WAL - Wales

EUROPEAN NATIONAL TEAM TOURNAMENTS

UEFA EUROPEAN CHAMPIONSHIP

Year	Host Country	Winners	Score	Runners-up	Venue
1960	France	Soviet Union	2-1	Yugoslavia	Parc des Princes, Paris
1964	Spain	Spain	2-1	Soviet Union	Bernabeu, Madrid
1968	Italy	Italy	1-1 2-0	Yugoslavia	Stadio Olimpico, Roma
1972	Belgium	Germany FR	3-0	Soviet Union	Heysel, Brussels
1976	Yugoslavia	Czechoslovakia	2-2 5-4p	Germany FR	Crvena Zvezda, Belgrade
1980	Italy	Germany FR	2-1	Belgium	Stadio Olimpico, Rome
1984	France	France	2-0	Spain	Parc des Princes, Paris
1988	Germany FR	Netherlands	2-0	Soviet Union	Olympiastadion, Munich
1992	Sweden	Denmark	2-0	Germany	Nya Ullevi, Gothenburg
1996	England	Germany	2-1	Czech Republic	Wembley, London
2000	Belgium/Netherlands	France	2-1	Italy	Feijenoord Stadion, Rotterdam
2004	Portugal	Greece	1-0	Portugal	Estadio da Luz, Lisbon
2008	Austria/Switzerland	Spain	1-0	Germany	Ernst Happel, Vienna
2012	Poland/Ukraine				Olympic Stadium, Kyiv

UEFA EUROPEAN CHAMPIONSHIP MEDALS TABLE

	Country	G	S	B	F	SF
1	Germany	3	3	1	6	7
2	Spain	2	1		3	3
3	France	2		1	2	4
4	Soviet Union	1	3		4	5
5	Czechoslovakia	1	1	2	2	3
6	Italy	1	1	1	2	3
7	Netherlands	1		4	1	5
8	Denmark	1		1	1	3
9	Greece	1			1	1
10	Yugoslavia		2		2	3
11	Portugal		1	2	1	3
12	Belgium		1	1	1	2
13	England			2		2
14	Hungary			1		2
15	Czech Republic			1		1
	Sweden			1		1
	Russia			1		1
	Turkey			1		1
		13	13	20	26	50

This table represents the Gold (winners), Silver (runners-up) and
Bronze (semi-finalists) placings in the UEFA European
Championship, along with the number of appearances in the final
and semi-finals

EUROPEAN CLUB TOURNAMENTS

UEFA CHAMPIONS LEAGUE

Year	Winners	Country	Score	Country	Runners-up
1956	Real Madrid	ESP	4-3	FRA	Stade de Reims
1957	Real Madrid	ESP	2-0	ITA	Fiorentina
1958	Real Madrid	ESP	3-2	ITA	Milan
1959	Real Madrid	ESP	2-0	FRA	Stade de Reims
1960	Real Madrid	ESP	7-3	FRG	Eintracht Frankfurt

UEFA CHAMPIONS LEAGUE (CONT'D)

Year	Winners	Country	Score	Country	Runners-up
1961	Benfica	POR	3-2	ESP	Barcelona
1962	Benfica	POR	5-3	ESP	Real Madrid
1963	Milan	ITA	2-1	POR	Benfica
1964	Internazionale	ITA	3-1	ESP	Real Madrid
1965	Internazionale	ITA	1-0	POR	Benfica
1966	Real Madrid	ESP	2-1	YUG	Partizan Beograd
1967	Celtic	SCO	2-1	ITA	Internazionale
1968	Manchester United	ENG	4-1	POR	Benfica
1969	Milan	ITA	4-1	NED	Ajax
1970	Feyenoord	NED	2-1	SCO	Celtic
1971	Ajax	NED	2-0	GRE	Panathinaikos
1972	Ajax	NED	2-0	ITA	Internazionale
1973	Ajax	NED	1-0	ITA	Juventus
1974	Bayern München	FRG	1-1 4-0	ESP	Atlético Madrid
1975	Bayern München	FRG	2-0	ENG	Leeds United
1976	Bayern München	FRG	1-0	FRA	AS Saint-Étienne
1977	Liverpool	ENG	3-1	FRG	Borussia Mönchengladbach
1978	Liverpool	ENG	1-0	BEL	Club Brugge
1979	Nottingham Forest	ENG	1-0	SWE	Malmö FF
1980	Nottingham Forest	ENG	1-0	FRG	Hamburger SV
1981	Liverpool	ENG	1-0	ESP	Real Madrid
1982	Aston Villa	ENG	1-0	FRG	Bayern München
1983	Hamburger SV	FRG	1-0	ITA	Juventus
1984	Liverpool	ENG	1-1 4-2p	ITA	Roma
1985	Juventus	ITA	1-0	ENG	Liverpool
1986	Steaua Bucuresti	ROU	0-0 2-0p	ESP	Barcelona
1987	FC Porto	POR	2-1	FRG	Bayern München
1988	PSV Eindhoven	NED	0-0 6-5p	POR	Benfica
1989	Milan	ITA	4-0	ROU	Steaua Bucuresti
1990	Milan	ITA	1-0	POR	Benfica
1991	Crvena Zvezda Beograd	YUG	0-0 5-3p	FRA	Olympique Marseille
1992	Barcelona	ESP	1-0	ITA	Sampdoria
1993	Olympique Marseille	FRA	1-0	ITA	Milan
1994	Milan	ITA	4-0	ESP	Barcelona
1995	Ajax	NED	1-0	ITA	Milan
1996	Juventus	ITA	1-1 4-2p	NED	Ajax
1997	Borussia Dortmund	GER	3-1	ITA	Juventus
1998	Real Madrid	ESP	1-0	ITA	Juventus
1999	Manchester United	ENG	2-1	GER	Bayern München
2000	Real Madrid	ESP	3-0	ESP	Valencia
2001	Bayern München	GER	1-1 5-4p	ESP	Valencia
2002	Real Madrid	ESP	2-1	GER	Bayer Leverkusen
2003	Milan	ITA	0-0 3-2p	ITA	Juventus
2004	FC Porto	POR	3-0	FRA	Monaco
2005	Liverpool	ENG	3-3 3-2p	ITA	Milan
2006	Barcelona	ESP	2-1	ENG	Arsenal
2007	Milan	ITA	2-1	ENG	Liverpool
2008	Manchester United	ENG	1-1 6-5p	ENG	Chelsea
2009	Barcelona	ESP	2-0	ENG	Manchester United
2010	Internazionale	ITA	2-0	GER	Bayern München

UEFA CHAMPIONS LEAGUE MEDALS TABLE - NATIONS

	Country	G	S	B	F	SF
1	Italy	12	14	8	26	34
2	Spain	12	9	20	21	41
3	England	11	6	18	17	35
4	Germany	6	8	10	14	24
5	Netherlands	6	2	5	8	13
6	Portugal	4	5	2	9	11
7	France	1	5	8	6	14
8	Scotland	1	1	6	2	8
9	Romania	1	1	2	2	4
	Serbia	1	1	2	2	4
11	Belgium		1	3	1	4
12	Greece		1	2	1	3
13	Sweden		1	1	1	2
14	Hungary			3		3
	Switzerland			3		3
	Ukraine			3		3
17	Austria			2		2
	Bulgaria			2		2
	Poland			2		2
20	Czech Republic			1		1
	Russia			1		1
	Slovakia			1		1
	Turkey			1		1
		55	55	106	110	216

This table represents the Gold (winners), Silver (runners-up) and Bronze (semi-finalists) placings of clubs representing the above countries in the UEFA Champions League, along with the number of appearances in the final and semi-finals

UEFA CHAMPIONS LEAGUE MEDALS TABLE - CLUBS

	Club		G	S	B
	Crvena Zvezda Beograd	SER	1		2
	PSV Eindhoven	NED	1		2
20	Feyenoord	NED	1		1
21	Aston Villa	ENG	1		
22	Stade de Reims	FRA		2	
	Valencia	ESP		2	
24	Chelsea	ENG		1	4
25	Atlético Madrid	ESP		1	2
	Leeds United	ENG		1	2
	AS Monaco	FRA		1	2
	Panathinaikos	GRE		1	2
29	Arsenal	ENG		1	1
	Borussia Mönchengladbach	GER		1	1
	AS Saint-Étienne	FRA		1	1
32	Bayer Leverkusen	GER		1	
	Club Brugge	BEL		1	
	Eintracht Frankfurt	GER		1	
	Fiorentina	ITA		1	
	Malmö FF	SWE		1	
	Partizan Beograd	SRB		1	
	Roma	ITA		1	
	Sampdoria	ITA		1	
40	Dynamo Kyiv	UKR			3
41	RSC Anderlecht	BEL			2
	CSKA Sofia	BUL			2
	FC Zürich	SUI			2
44	FK Austria	AUT			1
	Girondins Bordeaux	FRA			1
	Deportivo La Coruna	ESP			1
	Derby County	ENG			1
	Dinamo Bucuresti	ROU			1
	Dukla Praha	CZE			1
	Dundee	SCO			1
	Dundee United	SCO			1
	Galatasaray	TUR			1
	IFK Göteborg	SWE			1
	Hibernian Edinburgh	SCO			1
	1.FC Köln	GER			1
	Legia Warszawa	POL			1
	FC Nantes	FRA			1
	Olympique Lyonnais	FRA			1
	Paris Saint-Germain	FRA			1
	Rába ETO Györ	HUN			1
	Glasgow Rangers	SCO			1
	SK Rapid Wien	AUT			1
	Real Sociedad	ESP			1
	Spartak Moskva	RUS			1
	Spartak Trnava	SVK			1
	Standard CL	BEL			1
	Tottenham Hotspur	ENG			1
	Ujpesti TE	HUN			1
	Vasas Budapest	HUN			1
	Villarreal	ESP			1
	Widzew Lódz	POL			1
	Young Boys Berne	SUI			1
			55	55	106

UEFA CHAMPIONS LEAGUE MEDALS TABLE - CLUBS

	Club		G	S	B
1	Real Madrid	ESP	9	3	9
2	Milan	ITA	7	4	2
3	Liverpool	ENG	5	2	3
4	Bayern München	GER	4	4	5
5	Ajax	NED	4	2	2
6	Barcelona	ESP	3	3	6
7	Internazionale	ITA	3	2	3
8	Manchester United	ENG	3	1	7
9	Juventus	ITA	2	5	3
10	Benfica	POR	2	5	1
11	FC Porto	POR	2		1
12	Nottingham Forest	ENG	2		
13	Glasgow Celtic	SCO	1	1	2
14	Hamburger SV	GER	1	1	1
	Olympique Marseille	FRA	1	1	1
	Steaua Bucuresti	ROU	1	1	1
17	Borussia Dortmund	GER	1		2

EUROPEAN CUP WINNERS' CUP

Year	Winners	Country	Score	Country	Runners-up
1961	Fiorentina	ITA	2-0 2-1	SCO	Rangers
1962	Atlético Madrid	ESP	1-1 3-0	ITA	Fiorentina
1963	Tottenham Hotspur	ENG	5-1	ESP	Atlético Madrid
1964	Sporting CP	POR	3-3 1-0	HUN	MTK Budapest
1965	West Ham United	ENG	2-0	FRG	TSV München 1860
1966	Borussia Dortmund	FRG	2-1	ENG	Liverpool
1967	Bayern München	FRG	1-0	SCO	Rangers
1968	Milan	ITA	2-0	FRG	Hamburger SV
1969	Slovan Bratislava	CZE	3-2	ESP	Barcelona
1970	Manchester City	ENG	2-1	POL	Gornik Zabrze
1971	Chelsea	ENG	1-1 2-1	ESP	Real Madrid
1972	Rangers	SCO	3-2	URS	Dynamo Moskva
1973	Milan	ITA	1-0	ENG	Leeds United
1974	1.FC Magdeburg	GDR	2-0	ITA	Milan
1975	Dynamo Kyiv	URS	3-0	HUN	Ferencváros
1976	RSC Anderlecht	BEL	4-2	ENG	West Ham United
1977	Hamburger SV	FRG	2-0	BEL	RSC Anderlecht
1978	RSC Anderlecht	BEL	4-0	AUT	FK Austria
1979	Barcelona	ESP	4-3	FRG	Fortuna Düsseldorf
1980	Valencia	ESP	0-0 5-4p	ENG	Arsenal
1981	Dynamo Tbilisi	URS	2-1	GDR	Carl Zeiss Jena
1982	Barcelona	ESP	2-1	BEL	Standard CL
1983	Aberdeen	SCO	2-1	ESP	Real Madrid
1984	Juventus	ITA	2-1	POR	FC Porto
1985	Everton	ENG	3-1	AUT	SK Rapid Wien
1986	Dynamo Kyiv	URS	3-0	ESP	Atlético Madrid
1987	Ajax	NED	1-0	GDR	Lokomotive Leipzig
1988	KV Mechelen	BEL	1-0	NED	Ajax
1989	Barcelona	ESP	2-0	ITA	Sampdoria
1990	Sampdoria	ITA	2-0	BEL	RSC Anderlecht
1991	Manchester United	ENG	2-1	ESP	Barcelona
1992	Werder Bremen	GER	2-0	FRA	Monaco
1993	Parma	ITA	3-1	BEL	Royal Antwerp FC
1994	Arsenal	ENG	1-0	ITA	Parma
1995	Real Zaragoza	ESP	2-1	ENG	Arsenal
1996	Paris Saint-Germain	FRA	1-0	AUT	SK Rapid Wien
1997	Barcelona	ESP	1-0	FRA	Paris Saint-Germain
1998	Chelsea	ENG	1-0	GER	VfB Stuttgart
1999	Lazio	ITA	2-1	ESP	Real Mallorca

CUP WINNERS' CUP MEDALS TABLE - NATIONS

	Country	G	S	B	F	SF
1	England	8	5	8	13	21
2	Spain	7	7	5	14	19
3	Italy	7	4	9	11	20
4	Germany	4	4	9	8	17
5	Belgium	3	4	5	7	12
6	Scotland	2	2	4	4	8
7	Ukraine	2	-	-	2	2
8	France	1	2	6	3	9
9	German DR	1	2	3	3	6
10	Netherlands	1	1	6	2	8
11	Portugal	1	1	3	2	5
12	Georgia	1		1	1	2
13	Czechoslovakia	1			1	1

CUP WINNERS' CUP MEDALS TABLE - NATIONS (CONT'D)

	Country	G	S	B	F	SF
14	Austria		3	1	3	4
15	Hungary		2	1	2	3
16	Russia		1	5	1	6
17	Poland		1	1	1	2
18	Czech Republic			3		3
19	Croatia			2		2
	Serbia			2		2
	Bulgaria			2		2
22	Romania			1		1
	Wales			1		1
		39	39	78	78	156

This table represents the Gold (winners), Silver (runners-up) and Bronze (semi-finalists) placings of clubs representing the above countries in the European Cup Winners' Cup, along with the number of appearances in the final and semi-finals

CUP WINNERS' CUP MEDALS TABLE - CLUBS

	Club		G	S	B
1	Barcelona	ESP	4	2	
2	RSC Anderlecht	BEL	2	2	
3	Milan	ITA	2	1	
4	Chelsea	ENG	2		2
5	Dynamo Kyiv	UKR	2		
6	Atlético Madrid	ESP	1	2	2
	Arsenal	ENG	1	2	
8	Glasgow Rangers	SCO	1	2	
9	Sampdoria	ITA	1	1	1
	West Ham United	ENG	1	1	1
	Fiorentina	ITA	1	1	1
	Paris Saint-Germain	FRA	1	1	1
13	Ajax	NED	1	1	
	Hamburger SV	GER	1	1	
	Parma	ITA	1	1	
16	Bayern München	GER	1		3
17	Juventus	ITA	1		2
	Real Zaragoza	ESP	1		2
19	Aberdeen	SCO	1		1
	Dinamo Tbilisi	GEO	1		1
	Manchester City	ENG	1		1
	Manchester United	ENG	1		1
	KV Mechelen	BEL	1		1
	Sporting CP	POR	1		1
	Tottenham Hotspur	ENG	1		1
26	Borussia Dortmund	GER	1		
	Everton	ENG	1		
	Lazio	ITA	1		
	1.FC Magdeburg	GDR	1		
	Slovan Bratislava	SVK	1		
	Valencia	ESP	1		
	Werder Bremen	GER	1		
33	Real Madrid	ESP		2	
	SK Rapid Wien	AUT		2	
35	Dinamo Moskva	RUS		1	2
36	FK Austria	AUT		1	1
	Carl Ziess Jena	GDR		1	1
	AS Monaco	FRA		1	1
	Standard CL	BEL		1	1
	Liverpool	ENG		1	1
41	Ferencváros	HUN		1	
	Fortuna Düsseldorf	GER		1	
	Górnik Zabrze	POL		1	
	Leeds United	ENG		1	
	VfB Leipzig	GDR		1	
	Real Mallorca	ESP		1	
	MTK-VM Budapest	HUN		1	

CUP WINNERS' CUP MEDALS TABLE - CLUBS (CONT'D)

	Club		G	S	B
	TSV München 1860	GER		1	
	FC Porto	POR		1	
	Royal Antwerp FC	BEL		1	
	VfB Stuttgart	GER		1	
52	Feyenoord	NED			3
53	Benfica	POR			2
	Glasgow Celtic	SCO			2
	Lokomotiv Moskva	RUS			2
	PSV Eindhoven	NED			2
57	Atalanta	ITA			1
	Baník Ostrava	CZE			1
	Bayer Uerdingen	GER			1
	SK Beveren	BEL			1
	Girondins Bordeaux	FRA			1
	Borussia Mönchengladbach	GER			1
	Cardiff City	WAL			1
	Club Brugge	BEL			1
	CSKA Sofia	BUL			1
	Deportivo La Coruña	ESP			1
	1.FC Köln	GER			1
	Dukla Praha	CZE			1
	Dunfermline Athletic	SCO			1
	Berliner FC	GDR			1
	Dinamo Bucuresti	ROU			1
	Dinamo Zagreb	CRO			1
	Eintracht Frankfurt	GER			1
	Hajduk Split	CRO			1
	Legia Warszawa	POL			1
	Olympique Lyonnais	FRA			1
	Olympique Marseille	FRA			1
	FC Nantes	FRA			1
	Napoli	ITA			1
	1.FC Nürnberg	GER			1
	OFK Beograd	SER			1
	Crvena Zvezda Beograd	SER			1
	Roma	ITA			1
	FSV Zwickau	GDR			1
	FC Schalke 04	GER			1
	Slavia Sofia	BUL			1
	Sparta Praha	CZE			1
	Spartak Moskva	RUS			1
	Torino	ITA			1
	FC Twente Enschede	NED			1
	Ujpesti TE	HUN			1
	Racing Club Genk	BEL			1
	Vicenza	ITA			1
	Wolverhampton Wanderers	ENG			1
			39	39	78

FAIRS CUP

Year	Winners	Country	Score	Country	Runners-up
1958	Barcelona	ESP	2-2 6-0	ENG	London Select XI
1960	Barcelona	ESP	0-0 4-1	ENG	Birmingham City
1961	Roma	ITA	2-2 2-0	ENG	Birmingham City
1962	Valencia	ESP	6-2 1-1	ESP	Barcelona
1963	Valencia	ESP	2-1 2-0	YUG	Dinamo Zagreb

FAIRS CUP (CONT'D)

Year	Winners	Country	Score	Country	Runners-up
1964	Real Zaragoza	ESP	2-1	ESP	Valencia
1965	Ferencváros	HUN	1-0	ITA	Juventus
1966	Barcelona	ESP	0-1 4-2	ESP	Real Zaragoza
1967	Dinamo Zagreb	YUG	2-0 0-0	ENG	Leeds United
1968	Leeds United	ENG	1-0 0-0	HUN	Ferencváros
1969	Newcastle United	ENG	3-0 3-2	HUN	Újpesti Dózsa
1970	Arsenal	ENG	1-3 3-0	BEL	RSC Anderlecht
1971	Leeds United	ENG	2-2 1-1	ITA	Juventus

FAIRS CUP MEDALS TABLE – NATIONS

	Country	G	S	B	F	SF
1	Spain	6	3	1	9	10
2	England	4	4	5	8	13
3	Italy	1	2	4	3	7
4	Hungary	1	2	2	3	5
5	Croatia	1	1		2	2
6	Belgium		1	2	1	3
7	Scotland			4		4
8	Germany			3		3
9	Serbia			2		2
10	Netherlands			1		1
11	Switzerland			1		1
12	Turkey			1		1
		13	13	26	26	52

This table represents the Gold (winners), Silver (runners-up) and Bronze (semi-finalists) placings of clubs representing the above countries in the Fairs Cup, along with the number of appearances in the final and semi-finals

FAIRS CUP MEDALS TABLE – CLUBS

	Club		G	S	B
1	Barcelona	ESP	3	1	
2	Leeds United	ENG	2	1	1
3	Valencia	ESP	2	1	
4	Ferencvaros	HUN	1	1	1
5	Dinamo Zagreb	CRO	1	1	
	Real Zaragoza	ESP	1	1	
7	Roma	ITA	1		1
8	Arsenal	ENG	1		
	Newcastle United	ENG	1		

FAIRS CUP MEDALS TABLE – CLUBS (CONT'D)

	Club		G	S	B
10	Birmingham City	ENG		2	1
11	Juventus	ITA		2	
12	RSC Anderlecht	BEL		1	
	London Select XI	ENG		1	
	Ujpesti TE	HUN		1	
15	Internazionale	ITA			2
	1.FC Köln	GER			2
17	Ajax	NED			1
	Atlético Madrid	ESP			1
	Belgrade Select XI	SRB			1
	Bologna	ITA			1
	Chelsea	ENG			1
	Crvena Zvezda	SRB			1
	Dundee	SCO			1
	Eintracht Frankfurt	GER			1
	Göztepe Izmir	TUR			1
	Hibernian	SCO			1
	Lausanne-Sports	SUI			1
	RFC Liège	BEL			1
	Liverpool	ENG			1
	Kilmarnock	SCO			1
	Manchester United	ENG			1
	MTK-VM Budapest	HUN			1
	Rangers	SCO			1
	Union St Gilloise	BEL			1
			13	13	26

UEFA CUP

Year	Winners	Country	Score	Country	Runners-up
1972	Tottenham Hotspur	ENG	2-1 1-1	ENG	Wolverhampton Wanderers
1973	Liverpool	ENG	3-0 0-2	FRG	Borussia Mönchengladbach
1974	Feyenoord	NED	2-2 2-0	ENG	Tottenham Hotspur
1975	Borussia Mönchengladbach	FRG	0-0 5-1	NED	FC Twente Enschede
1976	Liverpool	ENG	3-2 1-1	BEL	Club Brugge
1977	Juventus	ITA	1-0 1-2	ESP	Athletic Bilbao
1978	PSV Eindhoven	NED	0-0 3-0	FRA	SEC Bastia
1979	Borussia Mönchengladbach	FRG	1-1 1-0	YUG	Crvena Zvezda Beograd
1980	Eintracht Frankfurt	FRG	2-3 1-0	FRG	Borussia Mönchengladbach
1981	Ipswich Town	ENG	3-0 2-4	NED	AZ 67 Alkmaar
1982	IFK Göteborg	SWE	1-0 3-0	FRG	Hamburger SV
1983	RSC Anderlecht	BEL	1-0 1-1	POR	Benfica

UEFA CUP

Year	Winners	Country	Score	Country	Runners-up
1984	Tottenham Hotspur	ENG	1-1 1-1 4-3p	BEL	RSC Anderlecht
1985	Real Madrid	ESP	3-0 0-1	HUN	Videoton SC
1986	Real Madrid	ESP	5-1 0-2	FRG	1.FC Köln
1987	IFK Göteborg	SWE	1-0 1-1	SCO	Dundee United
1988	Bayer Leverkusen	FRG	0-3 3-0 3-2p	ESP	Español
1989	Napoli	ITA	2-1 3-3	FRG	VfB Stuttgart
1990	Juventus	ITA	3-1 0-0	ITA	Fiorentina
1991	Internazionale	ITA	2-0 0-1	ITA	Roma
1992	Ajax	NED	2-2 0-0	ITA	Torino
1993	Juventus	ITA	3-1 3-0	GER	Borussia Dortmund
1994	Internazionale	ITA	1-0 1-0	AUT	Austria Salzburg
1995	Parma	ITA	1-0 1-1	ITA	Juventus
1996	Bayern München	GER	2-0 3-1	FRA	Bordeaux
1997	Schalke 04	GER	1-0 0-1 4-1p	ITA	Internazionale
1998	Internazionale	ITA	3-0	ITA	Lazio
1999	Parma	ITA	3-0	FRA	Olympique Marseille
2000	Galatasaray	TUR	0-0 4-1p	ENG	Arsenal
2001	Liverpool	ENG	5-4	ESP	CD Alavés
2002	Feyenoord	NED	3-2	GER	Borussia Dortmund
2003	FC Porto	POR	3-2	SCO	Glasgow Celtic
2004	Valencia	ESP	2-0	FRA	Olympique Marseille
2005	CSKA Moskva	RUS	3-1	POR	Sporting CP
2006	Sevilla	ESP	4-0	ENG	Middlesbrough
2007	Sevilla	ESP	2-2 3-1p	ESP	Espanyol
2008	Zenit St Petersburg	RUS	2-0	SCO	Rangers
2009	Shakhtar Donetsk	UKR	2-1	GER	Werder Bremen

UEFA CUP MEDALS TABLE - NATIONS

	Country	G	S	B	F	SF
1	Italy	9	6	12	15	27
2	Germany	6	8	22	14	36
3	England	6	4	4	10	14
4	Spain	5	4	10	9	19
5	Netherlands	4	2	2	6	8
6	Russia	2		1	2	3
7	Sweden	2			2	2
8	Belgium	1	2	3	3	6
9	Portugal	1	2	2	3	5
10	Ukraine	1		1	1	2
11	Turkey	1			1	1
12	France		4	5	4	9
13	Scotland		3		3	3
14	Austria		1	1	1	2
	Hungary		1	1	1	2
	Serbia		1	1	1	2
17	Czech Republic			2		2
	German DR			2		2
	Romania			2		2
20	Bosnia-Herzegovina			1		1
	Croatia			1		1
	Denmark			1		1
	Greece			1		1
	Switzerland			1		1
		38	38	76	76	152

This table represents the Gold (winners), Silver (runners-up) and Bronze (semi-finalists) placings of clubs representing the above countries in the UEFA Cup, along with the number of appearances in the final and semi-finals

UEFA CUP MEDALS TABLE - CLUBS

	Club		G	S	B
1	Internazionale	ITA	3	1	3
2	Juventus	ITA	3	1	1
3	Liverpool	ENG	3		
4	Borussia Mönchengladbach	GER	2	2	1
5	Tottenham Hotspur	ENG	2	1	1
6	Parma	ITA	2		1
	Real Madrid	ESP	2		1
8	Feyenoord	NED	2		
	IFK Göteborg	SWE	2		
	Sevilla	ESP	2		
11	RSC Anderlecht	BEL	1	1	
12	Bayern München	GER	1		3
13	Bayer Leverkusen	GER	1		1
	FC Schalke 04	GER	1		1
15	Ajax	NED	1		
	CSKA Moskva	RUS	1		
	Eintracht Frankfurt	GER	1		
	Galatasaray	TUR	1		
	Ipswich Town	ENG	1		
	Napoli	ITA	1		
	FC Porto	POR	1		
	PSV Eindhoven	NED	1		
	Shakhtar Donetsk	UKR	1		
	Valencia	ESP	1		
	Zenit St Petersburg	RUS	1		
26	Borussia Dortmund	GER		2	1
27	RCD Espanyol	ESP		2	

UEFA CUP MEDALS TABLE - CLUBS (CONT'D)

	Club		G	S	B
	Olympique Marseille	FRA	2		
29	1.FC Köln	GER	1	3	
	Werder Bremen	GER	1	3	
31	Hamburger SV	GER	1	2	
	VfB Stuttgart	GER	1	2	
33	AZ Alkmaar	NED	1	1	
	Club Brugge	BEL	1	1	
	Fiorentina	ITA	1	1	
	Lazio	ITA	1	1	
	Sporting CP	POR	1	1	
	Twente Enschede	NED	1	1	
39	Arsenal	ENG	1		
	Austria Salzburg	AUT	1		
	CD Alavés	ESP	1		
	Athletic Bilbao	ESP	1		
	SEC Bastia	FRA	1		
	Benfica	POR	1		
	Girondins Bordeaux	FRA	1		
	Glasgow Celtic	SCO	1		
	Crvena Zvezda Beograd	SRB	1		
	Dundee United	SCO	1		
	Middlesbrough	ENG	1		
	Glasgow Rangers	SCO	1		
	Roma	ITA	1		
	Torino	ITA	1		
	Videoton SC	HUN	1		
	Wolverhampton Wanderers	ENG	1		
55	Barcelona	ESP			4
56	Atlético Madrid	ESP			2
	1.FC Kaiserslautern	GER			2
	Milan	ITA			2
59	AEK Athens	GRE			1
	AJ Auxerre	FRA			1
	Boavista	POR			1

UEFA CUP MEDALS TABLE - CLUBS (CONT'D)

Club		G	S	B
Bohemians Praha	CZE			1
Bologna	ITA			1
Brondbyernes IF	DEN			1
Cagliari	ITA			1
MSV Duisburg	GER			1
1.FC Dynamo Dresden	GDR			1
Dynamo Kyiv	UKR			1
Ferencváros	HUN			1
Genoa 1893	ITA			1
Grasshopper-Club	SUI			1
Hajduk Split	CRO			1
Hertha BSC Berlin	GER			1
Karlsruher SC	GER			1
Leeds United	ENG			1
VfB Leipzig	GDR			1
Racing Club Lens	FRA			1
AS Monaco	FRA			1
RWD Molenbeek	BEL			1
Newcastle United	ENG			1
Nottingham Forest	ENG			1
Osasuna	ESP			1
Paris Saint-Germain	FRA			1
Radnicki Nis	SRB			1
Slavia Praha	CZE			1
FC Sochaux	FRA			1
Spartak Moskva	RUS			1
Steaua Bucuresti	ROU			1
Tenerife	ESP			1
FC Tirol	AUT			1
Universitatea Craiova	ROU			1
Villarreal	ESP			1
KSV Waregem	BEL			1
Zeljeznicar Sarajevo	BIH			1
		38	38	76

UEFA EUROPA LEAGUE

Year	Winners	Country	Score	Country	Runners-up
2010	Atlético Madrid	ESP	2-1	ENG	Fulham

UEFA EUROPA LEAGUE MEDALS TABLE - NATIONS

	Country	G	S	B	F	SF
1	Spain	1			1	1
2	England		1	1	1	2
3	Germany			1		1

This table represents the Gold (winners), Silver (runners-up) and Bronze (semi-finalists) placings of clubs representing the above countries in the UEFA Cup, along with the number of appearances in the final and semi-finals

UEFA EUROPA LEAGUE MEDALS TABLE - CLUBS

	Club		G	S	B
1	Atlético Madrid	ESP	1		
2	Fulham	ENG		1	
3	Hamburger SV	GER			1
	Liverpool	ENG			1

EUROPEAN YOUTH TOURNAMENTS

UEFA EUROPEAN UNDER–21 CHAMPIONSHIP

Year	Host Country	Winners	Score	Runners-up	Venue
1978		Yugoslavia	1-0 4-1	German DR	Halle & Mostar
1980		Soviet Union	0-0 1-0	German DR	Rostock & Moscow
1982		England	3-1 2-3	Germany FR	Sheffield & Bremen
1984		England	1-0 2-0	Spain	Seville & Sheffield
1986		Spain	1-2 2-1 3-0p	Italy	Rome & Valladolid
1988		France	0-0 3-0	Greece	Athens & Besançon
1990		Soviet Union	4-2 3-1	Yugoslavia	Sarajevo & Simferopol
1992		Italy	2-0 0-1	Sweden	Ferrara & Växjö
1994	France	Italy	1-0	Portugal	Montpellier
1996	Spain	Italy	1-1 4-2p	Spain	Barcelona
1998	Romania	Spain	1-0	Greece	Bucharest
2000	Slovakia	Italy	2-1	Czech Republic	Bratislava
2002	Switzerland	Czech Republic	0-0 3-1p	France	St Jakob Park, Basel
2004	Germany	Italy	3-0	Serbia & Montenegro	Ruhrstadion, Bochum
2006	Portugal	Netherlands	3-0	Ukraine	Bessa, Oporto
2007	Netherlands	Netherlands	4-1	Serbia	Euroborg, Groningen
2009	Sweden	Germany	4-0	England	Swedbank Stadion, Malmö

UEFA EUROPEAN UNDER–19 CHAMPIONSHIP

Year	Host Country	Winners	Score	Runners-up	Venue
1981	West Germany	Germany FR	1-0	Poland	Düsseldorf
1982	Finland	Scotland	3-1	Czechoslovakia	Helsinki
1983	England	France	1-0	Czechoslovakia	White Hart Lane, London
1984	Soviet Union	Hungary	0-0 3-2p	Soviet Union	Zentralny, Moscow
1986	Yugoslavia	German DR	3-1	Italy	Subotica
1988	Czechoslovakia	Soviet Union	3-1	Portugal	Frydek-Mistek
1990	Hungary	Soviet Union	0-0 4-2p	Portugal	Bekescsaba
1992	Germany	Turkey	2-1	Portugal	Bayreuth
1993	England	England	1-0	Turkey	City Ground, Nottingham
1994	Spain	Portugal	1-1 4-1p	Germany	Merida
1995	Greece	Spain	4-1	Italy	Katerini
1996	France/Luxemb	France	1-0	Spain	Besançon
1997	Iceland	France	1-0	Portugal	Reykjavík
1998	Cyprus	Republic of Ireland	1-1 4-3p	Germany	Larnaca
1999	Sweden	Portugal	1-0	Italy	Norrköping
2000	Germany	France	1-0	Ukraine	Nürnberg
2001	Finland	Poland	3-1	Czech Republic	Helsinki
2002	Norway	Spain	1-0	Germany	Ullevaal, Oslo
2003	Liechtenstein	Italy	2-0	Portugal	Rheinpark Stadion, Vaduz
2004	Switzerland	Spain	1-0	Turkey	Colovray, Nyon
2005	Nth. Ireland	France	3-1	England	Windsor Park, Belfast
2006	Poland	Spain	2-1	Scotland	Miejski, Poznan
2007	Austria	Spain	1-0	Greece	Linzer, Linz
2008	Czech Republic	Germany	3-1	Italy	Strelnice, Jablonec nad Nisou
2009	Ukraine	Ukraine	2-0	England	Olympiyskiy, Donetsk
2010	France	France	2-1	Spain	Michel d'Ornano, Caen

Played as an U-18 tournament from 1981 to 2001

UEFA EUROPEAN UNDER–17 CHAMPIONSHIP

Year	Host Country	Winners	Score	Runners-up	Venue
1982	Italy	Italy	1-0	Germany FR	Falconara
1984	Germany FR	Germany FR	2-0	Soviet Union	Ulm
1985	Hungary	Soviet Union	4-0	Greece	Budapest

UEFA EUROPEAN UNDER–17 CHAMPIONSHIP

Year	Host Country	Winners	Score	Runners-up	Venue
1986	Greece	Spain	2-1	Italy	Athens
1987	France	Italy	1-0	Soviet Union	Paris
1988	Spain	Spain	0-0 4-2p	Portugal	Teresa Rivero, Madrid
1989	Denmark	Portugal	4-1	German DR	Vejle
1990	East Germany	Czechoslovakia	3-2	Yugoslavia	Erfurt
1991	Swtzerland	Spain	2-0	Germany	Wankdorf, Berne
1992	Cyprus	Germany	2-1	Spain	Ammokostos, Larnaca
1993	Turkey	Poland	1-0	Italy	Inönü, Istanbul
1994	Rep. Ireland	Turkey	1-0	Denmark	Tolka Park, Dublin
1995	Belgium	Portugal	2-0	Spain	Brussels
1996	Austria	Portugal	1-0	France	Wien
1997	Germany	Spain	0-0 5-4p	Austria	Celle
1998	Scotland	Republic of Ireland	2-1	Italy	McDiarmid Park, Perth
1999	Czech Republic	Spain	4-1	Poland	Olomouc
2000	Israel	Portugal	2-1	Czech Republic	Ramat Gan
2001	England	Spain	1-0	France	Stadium of Light, Sunderland
2002	Denmark	Switzerland	0-0 4-2p	France	Farum Park, Farum
2003	Portugal	Portugal	2-1	Spain	Fontelo Municipal, Viseu
2004	France	France	2-1	Spain	Gaston Petit, Chateauroux
2005	Italy	Turkey	2-0	Netherlands	E. Mannucci, Pontedera
2006	Luxembourg	Russia	2-2 5-3p	Czech Republic	Josy Barthel, Luxembourg
2007	Belgium	Spain	1-0	England	RFC Tournai, Tournai
2008	Turkey	Spain	4-0	France	Mardan Sports Complex, Antalya
2009	Germany	Germany	2-1	Netherlands	Magdeburg Stadium, Magdeburg
2010	Liechtenstein	England	2-1	Spain	Rheinpark, Vaduz

Played as an U-16 tournament prior to 2002

EUROPEAN WOMEN'S TOURNAMENTS

UEFA EUROPEAN WOMEN'S CHAMPIONSHIP

Year	Host Country	Winners	Score	Runners-up	Venue
1984		Sweden	1-0 0-1 4-3p	England	Gothenburg & Luton
1987	Norway	Norway	2-1	Sweden	Ullevål, Oslo
1989	Germany FR	Germany FR	4-1	Norway	Osnabrück
1991	Denmark	Germany	3-1	Norway	Aalborg Stadion
1993	Italy	Norway	1-0	Italy	Dino Manuzzi, Cesena
1995	Germany	Germany	3-2	Sweden	Fritz Walter Stadion, Kaiserslautern
1997	Norway/Sweden	Germany	2-0	Italy	Ullevål, Oslo
2001	Germany	Germany	1-0	Sweden	Donaustadion, Ulm
2005	England	Germany	3-1	Norway	Ewood Park, Blackburn
2009	Finland	Germany	6-2	England	Olympiastadion, Helsinki

UEFA WOMEN'S CHAMPIONS LEAGUE

Year	Winners	Country	Score	Country	Runners-up
2002	1.FFC Frankfurt	GER		SWE	Umeå IK
2003	Umeå IK	SWE	4-1 3-0	DEN	Fortuna Hjørring
2004	Umeå IK	SWE	3-0 5-0	GER	1.FFC Frankfurt
2005	1.FFC Turbine Potsdam	GER	2-0 3-1	SWE	Djurgården/Alvsjö
2006	1.FFC Frankfurt	GER	4-0 3-2	GER	1.FFC Turbine Potsdam
2007	Arsenal	ENG	1-0 0-0	SWE	Umeå IK
2008	1.FFC Frankfurt	GER	1-1 3-2	SWE	Umeå IK
2009	FCR 2001 Duisburg	GER	6-0 1-1	RUS	Zvezda-2005
2010	1.FFC Turbine Potsdam	GER	0-0 7-6p	FRA	Olympique Lyonnais

UEFA EUROPEAN WOMEN'S UNDER–19 CHAMPIONSHIP

Year	Host Country	Winners	Score	Runners-up	Venue
1998		Denmark	2-0 2-3	France	Aabenraa & Niederbronn-les-Bains
1999	Sweden	Sweden	1-0	Germany	Bromölla
2000	France	Germany	4-2	Spain	La Libération, Boulogne
2001	Norway	Germany	3-2	Norway	Aråsen, Lillestrom
2002	Sweden	Germany	3-1	France	Olympia, Helsingborg
2003	Germany	France	2-0	Norway	Alfred Kunze Sportpark, Leipzig
2004	Finland	Spain	2-1	Germany	Pohjola Stadion, Vantaa
2005	Hungary	Russia	2-2 6-5p	France	ZTE, Zalaegerszeg
2006	Switzerland	Germany	3-0	France	Neufeld, Berne
2007	Iceland	Germany	2-0	England	Laugardalsvöllur, Reykjavík
2008	France	Italy	1-0	Norway	Vallée du Cher, Tours
2009	Belarus	England	2-0	Sweden	Gorodskoi, Borisov
2010	Macedonia	France	2-1	England	Gradski, Skopje

The first three tournaments were played as U-18 championships

UEFA EUROPEAN WOMEN'S UNDER–17 CHAMPIONSHIP

Year	Host Country	Winners	Score	Runners-up	Venue
2008	Switzerland	Germany	3-0	France	Colovray, Nyon
2009	Switzerland	Germany	7-0	Spain	Colovray, Nyon
2010	Switzerland	Spain	0-0 4-1p	Republic of Ireland	Colovray, Nyon

UEFA CHAMPIONS LEAGUE 2009–10

Second Qualifying Round

RB Austria Salzburg	AUT	1	1
Bohemians	IRL	1	0
Pyunik Yerevan	ARM	0	0
Dinamo Zagreb	CRO	0	3
FH Hafnarfjördur	FRO	0	0
FK Aktobe	KAZ	4	2
Maccabi Haifa	ISR	6	4
Glentoran	NIR	0	0
FK Ventspils	LVA	3	3
F91 Dudelange	LUX	0	1
Makedonija Skopje	MKD	0	0
BATE Borisov	BLR	2	2
WIT Georgia	GEO	0	1
NK Maribor	SVN	0	3
FC Kobenhavn	DEN	6	6
Mogren Budva	MNE	0	0
KF Tiranë	ALB	1	0
Stabæk IF	NOR	1	4
EB/Streymur	ISL	0	0
APOEL Nicosia	CYP	2	3
Rhyl	WAL	0	0
Partisan Beograd	SRB	4	8
FK Baku	AZE	2	4
Ekranas Panevezys	LTU	2	2
Levski Sofia	BUL	4	5
Sant Julia	AND	0	0
Wisla Krakow	POL	1	0
Levadia Tallinn	EST	1	1
Debreceni VSC	HUN	2	1
Kalmar FF	SWE	0	3
Inter Turku	FIN	0	0
Sheriff Tiraspol	MDA	1	1
Zrinjski Mostar	BIH	1	0
Slovan Bratislava	SVK	0	4

Third Qualifying Round

RB Austria Salzburg	AUT	1	2
Dinamo Zagreb	CRO	1	1
FK Aktobe	KAZ	0	3
Maccabi Haifa	ISR	0	4
FK Ventspils	LVA	1	1
BATE Borisov	BLR	0	2
FC Zürich	SUI	2	3
NK Maribor	SVN	3	0
FC Kobenhavn	DEN	3	0
Stabæk IF	NOR	1	0
APOEL Nicosia	CYP	2	0
Partisan Beograd	SRB	0	1
Sparta Praha	CZE	3	0
Panathinaikos	GRE	1	3
Sporting CP	POR	0	1
FC Twente Enschede	NED	0	1
FK Baku	AZE	0	0
Levski Sofia	BUL	0	2
Levadia Tallinn	EST	0	0
Debreceni VSC	HUN	1	1
RSC Anderlecht	BEL	5	1
Sivasspor	TUR	0	3
Shakhtar Donetsk	UKR	2	0
FC Timisoara	ROU	2	0
Sheriff Tiraspol	MDA	0	1
Slavia Praha	CZE	0	1
Slovan Bratislava	SVK	0	0
Olympiacos	GRE	2	2
Celtic	SCO	0	2
Dinamo Moskva	RUS	1	0

Play-off Round

RB Austria Salzburg	AUT	1	0
Maccabi Haifa	ISR	2	3
FK Ventspils	LVA	0	1
FC Zürich	SUI	3	2
FC Kobenhavn	DEN	1	1
APOEL Nicosia	CYP	0	3
Panathinaikos	GRE	2	0
Atlético Madrid	ESP	3	2
Sporting CP	POR	2	1
Fiorentina	ITA	2	1
Levski Sofia	BUL	1	0
Debreceni VSC	HUN	2	2
Olympique Lyonnais	FRA	5	3
RSC Anderlecht	BEL	1	1
FC Timisoara	ROU	0	0
VfB Stuttgart	GER	2	0
Sheriff Tiraspol	MDA	0	0
Olympiacos	GRE	2	1
Celtic	SCO	0	1
Arsenal	ENG	2	3

Group Stage

Group A		Pts
Girondins Bordeaux	FRA	16
Bayern München	GER	10
Juventus	ITA	8
Maccabi Haifa	ISR	0

Group B		Pts
Manchester United	ENG	13
CSKA Moskva	RUS	10
VfL Wolfsburg	GER	7
Besiktas	TUR	4

Group C		Pts
Real Madrid	ESP	13
Milan	ITA	9
Olympique Marseille	FRA	7
FC Zürich	SUI	4

Group D		Pts
Chelsea	ENG	14
FC Porto	POR	12
Atlético Madrid	ESP	3
APOEL Nicosia	CYP	3

Group E		Pts
Fiorentina	ITA	15
Olympique Lyonnais	FRA	13
Liverpool	ENG	7
Debreceni VSC	HUN	0

Group F		Pts
Barcelona	ESP	11
Internazionale	ITA	9
Rubin Kazan	RUS	6
Dynamo Kyiv	UKR	5

Group G		Pts
Sevilla	ESP	13
VfB Stuttgart	GER	9
Unirea Urziceni	ROU	8
Rangers	SCO	2

Group H		Pts
Arsenal	ENG	13
Olympiacos	GRE	10
Standard CL	BEL	5
AZ Alkmaar	NED	4

Play-off round losers qualify for the Europa League group stage. Losers in the third qualifying round qualify for the play-off round in the Europa League

First qualifying round: Hibernians MLT 0-2 0-4 **Mogren Budva** MNE • Tre Fiori SMR 1-1 1-1 4-5p **Sant Julia** AND

CLUB TOURNAMENTS IN EUROPE 2009–10

UEFA CHAMPIONS LEAGUE 2009-10

Round of 16			Quarter-finals			Semi-finals			Final		
Internazionale *	2	1									
Chelsea	1	0									
			Internazionale *	1	1						
			CSKA Moskva	0	0						
Sevilla	1	1									
CSKA Moskva *	1	2									
						Internazionale *	3	0			
						Barcelona	1	1			
Arsenal	1	5									
FC Porto *	2	0									
			Arsenal *	2	1						
			Barcelona	2	4						
VfB Stuttgart *	1	0									
Barcelona	1	4									
									Internazionale	2	
									Bayern München	0	
Olympique Lyonnais *	1	1									
Real Madrid	0	1									
			Olympique Lyonnais *	3	0						
			Girondins Bordeaux	1	1						
Olympiacos *	0	1									
Girondins Bordeaux	1	2									
						Olympique Lyonnais	0	0			
						Bayern München *	1	3			
Manchester United	3	4									
Milan *	2	0									
			Manchester United	1	3						
			Bayern München *	2	2						
Fiorentina	1	3									
Bayern München *	2	2									

* Home team in the first leg •

Top scorers: **8** - Lionel Messi ARG, Barcelona • **7** - Cristiano Ronaldo POR, Real Madrid & Ivica Olic CRO, Bayern München • **6** - Diego Milito ARG, Internazionale • **5** - Nicklas Bendtner DEN, Arsenal; Wayne Rooney ENG, Manchester United & Marouane Chamakh MAR, Girondins Bordeaux • **4** - Michael Owen ENG, Manchester United; Stevan Jovetic MNE, Fiorentina; Edin Dzeko BIH, VfL Wolfsburg; Arjen Robben NED, Bayern München; Cesc Fabregas ESP, Arsenal & Radamel Falcao COL, FC Porto

See **Oliver's Almanack of World Football 2010** for details of matches played in the preliminary rounds and group stage

ROUND OF SIXTEEN

San Siro, Milan
24-02-2010, 20:45, 78 971, Mejuto ESP
Internazionale   2
Milito [3], Cambiasso [55]

Julio Cesar - Maicon, Lucio, Walter Samuel, Javier Zanetti - Esteban Cambiasso, Dejan Stankovic (Sulley Muntari 84), Thiago Motta• (Mario Balotelli 58) - Wesley Sneijder - Samuel Eto'o (Goran Pandev 68), Diego Milito•. Tr: Jose Mourinho

Chelsea   1
Kalou [51]

Petr Cech (Hilario 61) - Branislav Ivanovic, Ricardo Carvalho, John Terry, Frank Lampard - Michael Ballack, John Mikel, Florent Malouda - Nicolas Anelka, Didier Drogba, Salomon Kalou• (Daniel Sturridge 78). Tr: Carlo Ancelotti

---

Stamford Bridge, London
16-03-2010, 19:45, 38 112, Stark GER
Chelsea   0

Ross Turnbull - Branislav Ivanovic, Alex•, John Terry•, Yuriy Zhirkov (Salomon Kalou 73) - Michael Ballack (Joe Cole 63), John Mikel, Frank Lampard - Nicolas Anelka, Didier Drogba•◆87, Florent Malouda•. Tr: Carlo Ancelotti

Internazionale   1
Eto'o [78]

Julio Cesar• - Maicon, Lucio•, Walter Samuel, Javier Zanetti - Thiago Motta• (Marco Materazzi 90), Esteban Cambiasso - Wesley Sneijder (McDonald Mariga 84) - Samuel Eto'o•, Diego Milito, Goran Pandev (Dejan Stankovic 75). Tr: Jose Mourinho

---

Luzhniki, Moscow
24-02-2010, 20:30, 28 600, Brych GER
CSKA Moskva   1
González [66]

Igor Akinfeev - Aleksey Berezutskiy, Vasiliy Berezutskiy, Sergei Ignashevich, Georgiy Shchennikov - Evgeniy Aldonin•, Deividas Semberas - Milos Krasic, Keisuke Honda• (Pavel Mamayev 83), Mark Gonzalez• - Tomas Necid. Tr: Leonid Slutskiy

Sevilla   1
Negredo [25]

Andres Palop - Marius Stankevicius, Federico Fazio, Julien Escude, Fernando Navarro - Romaric, Didier Zokora - Jesus Navas, Renato (Lautaro Acosta 88), Adriano (Diego Perotti 59) - Alvaro Negredo (Frederic Kanoute 76). Tr: Manuel Jimenez

---

Sánchez-Pizjuán, Seville
16-03-2010, 20:45, 29 666, Kassai HUN
Sevilla   1
Perotti [41]

Andres Palop - Marius Stankevicius, Federico Fazio, Ivica Dragutinovic, Fernando Navarro (Adriano 75) - Renato (Alvaro Negredo 71), Didier Zokora - Jesus Navas, Diego Perotti, Diego Capel (Frederic Kanoute 46) - Luis Fabiano•. Tr: Manuel Jimenez

CSKA Moskva   2
Necid [39], Honda [55]

Igor Akinfeev - Aleksey Berezutskiy•, Vasiliy Berezutskiy, Sergei Ignashevich, Georgiy Shchennikov• - Evgeniy Aldonin, Deividas Semberas• - Milos Krasic (Chidi Odiah 72), Keisuke Honda (Elvir Rahimic 82), Mark Gonzalez• (Pavel Mamayev 88) - Tomas Necid. Tr: Leonid Slutskiy

---

Estádio do Dragão, Porto
17-02-2010, 19:45, 40 717, Hansson SWE
FC Porto   2
Varela [11], Falcao [51]

Helton - Jorge Fucile•, Rolando, Bruno Alves•, Alvaro Pereira• - Ruben Micael (Fernando Belluschi 85), Fernando•, Raul Meireles (Tomas Costa 68) - Varela, Radamel Falcao, Hulk (Mariano Gonzalez 81). Tr: Jesualdo Ferreira

Arsenal   1
Campbell [18]

Lukasz Fabianski - Bakari Sagna, Sol Campbell, Thomas Vermaelen, Gael Clichy - Abou Diaby•, Denilson, Cesc Fabregas - Tomas Rosicky (Theo Walcott 68), Nicklas Bendtner (Carlos Vela 83), Samir Nasri (Emmanuel Eboue 88). Tr: Arsene Wenger

---

Emirates, London
9-03-2010, 19:45, 59 661, De Bleeckere BEL
Arsenal   5
Bendtner 3 [10 25 91+p], Nasri [63], Eboué [66]

Manuel Almunia - Bakari Sagna, Sol Campbell, Thomas Vermaelen•, Gael Clichy - Alexandre Song - Tomas Rosicky (Emmanuel Eboue 57), Abou Diaby, Samir Nasri (Denilson 73), Andrey Arshavin (Theo Walcott 76) - Nicklas Bendtner•. Tr: Arsene Wenger

FC Porto   0

Helton - Jorge Fucile•, Rolando, Bruno Alves, Alvaro Pereira• - Ruben Micael (Freddy Guarin 76), Nuno Coelho (Cristian Rodriguez 46), Raul Meireles - Varela (Mariano Gonzalez 76), Radamel Falcao•, Hulk. Tr: Jesualdo Ferreira

---

Mercedes-Benz Arena, Stuttgart
23-02-2010, 20:45, 39 430, Kuipers NED
VfB Stuttgart   1
Cacau [25]

Jens Lehmann - Stefano Celozzi, Serdar Tasci, Matthieu Delpierre, Cristian Molinaro• - Timo Gebhart• (Sebastian Rudy 84), Christian Trasch (Zdravko Zuzmanovic 58), Sami Khedira•, Aleksandr Hleb - Cacau, Pavel Pogrebnyak (Ciprian Marica 64). Tr: Christian Gross

Barcelona   1
Ibrahimovic [52]

Victor Valdes - Carles Puyol, Rafael Marquez• (Gabriel Milito 59), Gerard Pique•, Maxwell - Xavi, Yaya Toure (Thierry Henry 53), Sergio Busquets, Andres Iniesta - Lionel Messi, Zlatan Ibrahimovic. Tr: Josep Guardiola

---

Camp Nou, Barcelona
17-03-2010, 20:45, 88 543, Hamer LUX
Barcelona   4
Messi 2 [13 60], Pedro [22], Bojan [89]

Victor Valdes - Dani Alves, Gerard Pique, Carles Puyol, Maxwell - Sergio Busquets (Zlatan Ibrahimovic 66), Yaya Toure - Pedro, Lionel Messi, Andres Iniesta (Bojan Krkic 88) - Thierry Henry (Gabriel Milito 78). Tr: Josep Guardiola

VfB Stuttgart   0

Jens Lehmann• - Stefano Celozzi (Timo Gebhart 46), Georg Niedermeier, Matthieu Delpierre, Cristian Molinaro - Christian Trasch, Zdravko Kuzmanovic•, Sami Khedira, Aleksandr Hleb - Cacau, Pavel Pogrebnyak• (Ciprian Marica 70). Tr: Christian Gross

---

Stade de Gerland, Lyon
16-02-2010, 20:45, 40 327, Atkinson ENG
Olympique Lyonnais   1
Makoun [47]

Hugo Lloris - Anthony Reveillere, Cris, Jean-Alain Boumsong (Aly Cissokho - Jeremy Toulalan - Sidney Govou•, Jean Makoun, Miralem Pjanic (Kim Kallstrom 78), Cesar Delgado (Michel Bastos 89) - Lisandro Lopez (Bafetimbi Gomis 81). Tr: Claude Puel

Real Madrid   0

Iker Casillas - Alvaro Arbeloa•, Sergio Ramos, Raul Albiol, Marcelo (Ezequiel Garay 46) - Xabi Alonso•, Mahamadou Diarra, Esteban Granero - Kaka - Cristiano Ronaldo, Gonzalo Higuain (Karim Benzema 64). Tr: Manuel Pellegrini

---

Bernabéu, Madrid
10-03-2010, 20:45, 71 569, Rizzoli ITA
Real Madrid   1
Ronaldo [6]

Iker Casillas - Sergio Ramos, Raul Albiol, Ezequiel Garay, Alvaro Arbeloa (Mahamadou Diarra 83) - Lassana Diarra, Guti - Esteban Granero• (Rafael van der Vaart• 62), Kaka (Raul 76), Cristiano Ronaldo - Gonzalo Higuain. Tr: Manuel Pellegrini

Olympique Lyonnais   1
Pjanic [75]

Hugo Lloris - Anthony Reveillere, Cris•, Jean-Alain Boumsong (Kim Kallstrom 46), Aly Cissokho - Jeremy Toulalan - Sidney Govou, Jean Makoun (Maxime Gonalons 46), Miralem Pjanic (Ederson 83), Cesar Delgado• - Lisandro Lopez. Tr: Claude Puel

---

Karaiskakis, Piraeus
23-02-2010, 21:45, 29 773, Webb ENG
Olympiacos   0

Antonios Nikopolidis - Vassilios Torosidis, Avraam Papadopoulos•, Olof Mellberg, Raul Bravo - Enzo Maresca, Cristian Ledesma (Jaouad Zairi• 64), Ieroklis Stoltidis - Lomana LuaLua, Konstantinos Mitroglou (Matt Derbyshire 77), Jesus Datolo. Tr: Bozidar Bandovic

Girondins Bordeaux   1
Ciani [45]

Cedric Carrasso - Matthieu Chalme, Marc Planus, Michael Ciani•, Benoit Tremoulinas - Fernando, Ludovic Sane• - Jaroslav Plasil (Yoan Gouffran 82), Yoann Gourcuff, Wendel (Jussie 83) - Marouane Chamakh. Tr: Laurent Blanc

---

Stade Chaban-Delmas, Bordeaux
17-03-2010, 20:45, 31 004, Benquerença POR
Girondins Bordeaux   2
Gourcuff [5], Chamakh [88]

Cedric Carrasso - Matthieu Chalme, Ludovic Sane, Michael Ciani, Benoit Tremoulinas - Fernando, Alou Diarra••◆68 - Jaroslav Plasil (Gregory Sertic 84), Yoann Gourcuff, Wendel (Jussie 90) - Marouane Chamakh. Tr: Laurent Blanc

Olympiacos   1
Mitroglu [65]

Antonios Nikopolidis - Vassilios Torosidis•, Avraam Papadopoulos•, Olof Mellberg••◆94+, Raul Bravo - Enzo Maresca, Ieroklis Stoltidis (Cristian Ledesma 80) - Jaouad Zairi (Konstantinos Mitroglou 63), Lomana LuaLua, Jesus Datolo - Matt Derbyshire••◆50. Tr: Bozidar Bandovic

San Siro, Milan
16-02-2010, 20:45, 78 587, Benquerença POR

Milan   **2**

Ronaldinho [3], Seedorf [85]

Dida - Daniele **Bonera**, Alessandro **Nesta**, Thiago Silva, Luca **Antonini** (Giuseppe **Favalli** 38) - David **Beckham** (Clarence **Seedorf** 72), Andrea Pirlo, Massimo **Ambrosini** - Alexandre **Pato**, Klaas-Jan **Huntelaar** (Filippo **Inzaghi** 77), **Ronaldinho•**. Tr: Leonardo

Manchester United   **3**

Scholes [36], Rooney 2 [66 74]

Edwin van der Sar - **Rafael** (Wes Brown 90), Rio **Ferdinand**, Jonny **Evans**, Patrice **Evra** - **Nani** (Luis **Valencia** 65), Darren **Fletcher**, Michael **Carrick••♦93+**, Paul **Scholes**, **Park** Ji Sung - Wayne **Rooney•**. Tr: Alex Ferguson

Old Trafford, Manchester
10-03-2010, 19:45, 74 595, Busacca SUI

Manchester United   **4**

Rooney 2 [13 46], Park [59], Fletcher [88]

Edwin **van der Sar** - Gary **Neville** (Dimitar Berbatov 66), Rio **Ferdinand**, Nemanja **Vidic**, Patrice **Evra** - Luis **Valencia**, Darren **Fletcher**, Paul **Scholes•** (Darron **Gibson** 73), **Park** Ji Sung, **Nani** - Wayne **Rooney** (**Rafael** 66). Tr: Alex Ferguson

Milan   **0**

Christian **Abbiati** - Ignazio **Abate** (David **Beckham** 64), Daniele **Bonera** (Clarence **Seedorf** 46), Thiago **Silva**, Marek **Jankulovski** - Mathieu **Flamini•**, Andrea **Pirlo**, Massimo **Ambrosini** - Klaas-Jan **Huntelaar**, Marco **Borriello** (Filippo **Inzaghi** 69), **Ronaldinho•**. Tr: Leonardo

Allianz Arena, Munich
17-02-2010, 20:45, 66 000, Ovrebø NOR

Bayern München   **2**

Robben [45p], Klose [89]

Hans Jorg **Butt** - Philipp **Lahm**, Daniel **Van Buyten** (Diego **Contento** 46), Martin **Demichelis**, Holger **Badstuber** - Mark van **Bommel•**, Bastian **Schweinsteiger** - Arjen **Robben**, Franck **Ribery** - Mario **Gomez** (Miroslav **Klose•** 66), Thomas **Muller** (Ivica **Olic** 66). Tr: Louis **van Gaal**

Fiorentina   **1**

Krøldrup [50]

Sebastien **Frey** - Lorenzo **De Silvestri**, Per **Kroldrup**, Cesare **Natali** (Manuel **Pasqual** 85), Massimo **Gobbi♦73** - Riccardo **Montolivo** (Marco **Donadel** 84), Mario **Bolatti** - Marco **Marchionni•**, Stevan **Jovetic** (**Felipe** 75), Juan **Vargas•** - Alberto **Gilardino**. Tr: Cesare **Prandelli**

Artemio Franchi, Florence
9-03-2010, 20:45, 42 762, Undiano ESP

Fiorentina   **3**

Vargas [28], Jovetic 2 [54 64]

Sebastien **Frey** - Lorenzo **De Silvestri**, Per **Kroldrup•**, Cesare **Natali**, **Felipe•** (Manuel **Pasqual** 80) - Riccardo **Montolivo**, Cristiano **Zanetti** - Marco **Marchionni**, Stevan **Jovetic**, Juan **Vargas** (**Keirrison** 82) - Alberto **Gilardino**. Tr: Cesare **Prandelli**

Bayern München   **2**

Van Bommel [60], Robben [65]

Hans Jorg **Butt** - Philipp **Lahm**, Daniel **Van Buyten**, Holger **Badstuber**, David **Alaba** - Arjen **Robben**, Mark van **Bommel•**, Bastian **Schweinsteiger•**, Franck **Ribery** (Danijel **Pranjic** 90) - Thomas **Muller**, Mario **Gomez** (Miroslav **Klose** 30). Tr: Louis **van Gaal**

QUARTER-FINALS

San Siro, Milan
31-03-2010, 20:45, 69 398, Webb ENG

Internazionale   **1**

Milito [65]

Julio **Cesar** - **Maicon**, Marco **Materazzi•**, Walter **Samuel**, Javier **Zanetti** - Esteban **Cambiasso**, Dejan **Stankovic** - Wesley **Sneijder** - Samuel **Eto'o**, Diego **Milito**, Goran **Pandev** (McDonald **Mariga** 90). Tr: Jose **Mourinho**

CSKA Moskva   **0**

Igor **Akinfeev** - Aleksey **Berezutskiy**, Vasiliy **Berezutskiy**, Sergei **Ignashevich**, Georgiy **Shchennikov** - Evgeniy **Aldonin•** (Elvir **Rahimic** 76), Deividas **Semberas** - Milos **Krasic•**, Keisuke **Honda** (Alan **Dzagoev** 70), Pavel **Mamayev** (Mark **Gonzalez** 73) - Tomas **Necid**. Tr: Leonid **Slutskiy**

Luzhniki, Moskva
6-04-2010, 20:30, 54 400, Lannoy FRA

CSKA Moskva   **0**

Igor **Akinfeev** - Aleksey **Berezutskiy**, Vasiliy **Berezutskiy** (Chidi **Odiah** 14**••♦**49), Sergei **Ignashevich**, Georgiy **Shchennikov** - Deividas **Semberas**, Keisuke **Honda** (Elvir **Rahimic** 77) - Pavel **Mamayev**, Alan **Dzagoev**, Mark **Gonzalez** - Tomas **Necid** (**Guilherme** 71). Tr: Leonid **Slutskiy**

Internazionale   **1**

Sneijder [6]

Julio **Cesar** - **Maicon**, **Lucio**, Walter **Samuel**, Javier **Zanetti** - Dejan **Stankovic•**, Esteban **Cambiasso** - Wesley **Sneijder** (Sulley **Muntari** 86) - Samuel **Eto'o**, Diego **Milito** (Mario **Balotelli** 74), Goran **Pandev** (Cristian **Chivu** 63). Tr: Jose **Mourinho**

Emirates, London
31-03-2010, 19:45, 59 572, Busacca SUI

Arsenal   **2**

Walcott [69], Fabregas [85p]

Manuel **Almunia** - Bakari **Sagna** (Theo **Walcott** 66), William **Gallas** (Denilson 45), Thomas **Vermaelen**, Gael **Clichy** - Cesc **Fabregas•**, Alexandre **Song•**, Abou **Diaby•** - Samir **Nasri**, Nicklas **Bendtner**, Andrei **Arshavin•** (Emmanuel **Eboue•** 27). Tr: Arsene Wenger

Barcelona   **2**

Ibrahimovic 2 [46 69]

Victor **Valdes** - Dani **Alves**, Gerard **Pique•**, Carles **Puyol♦84**, **Maxwell** - Sergio **Busquets**, **Xavi** - **Pedro**, Lionel **Messi** (Gabriel **Milito** 86), Seydou **Keita** - Zlatan **Ibrahimovic** (Thierry **Henry** 77). Tr: Josep Guardiloa

Camp Nou, Barcelona
6-04-2010, 20:45, 93 330, Stark GER

Barcelona   **4**

Messi 4 [21 37 42 88]

Victor **Valdes** - Dani **Alves**, Rafael **Marquez**, Gabriel **Milito**, Eric **Abidal** (**Maxwell** 53) - **Xavi**, Sergio **Busquets**, Seydou **Keita** - **Pedro** (Andres **Iniesta** 85), Lionel **Messi**, Bojan **Krkic** (Yaya **Toure** 56). Tr: Josep **Guardiola**

Arsenal   **1**

Bendtner [18]

Manuel **Almunia** - Bakari **Sagna**, Thomas **Vermaelen**, Mikael **Silvestre** (Emmanuel **Eboue•** 63), Gael **Clichy** - **Denilson•**, Abou **Diaby** - Theo **Walcott**, Samir **Nasri**, Tomas **Rosicky•** (**Eduardo** 73) - Nicklas **Bendtner**. Tr: Arsene Wenger

Stade de Gerland, Lyon
30-03-2010, 20:45, 37 859, Brych GER

Olympique Lyonnais	3
	Lisandro 2 [10 77p], Bastos [32]

Hugo **Lloris** - Anthony **Reveillere**, **Cris**, Mathieu **Bodmer**, Aly **Cissokho** - Jean **Makoun**, Jeremy **Toulalan** - Cesar **Delgado** (Maxime **Gonalons** 86), Miralem **Pjanic** (Sidney **Govou**• 66), **Michel Bastos** (Kim **Kallstrom** 66) - Lisandro **Lopez**•. Tr: Claude **Puel**

Girondins Bordeaux	1
	Chamakh [14]

Cedric **Carrasso** - Matthieu **Chalme** (Henrique 83), Ludovic **Sane**, Michael **Ciani**, Benoit **Tremoulinas** - Jaroslav **Plasil**, Fernando - Yoan **Gouffran** (David **Bellion** 84), Yoann **Gourcuff**, **Wendel** (Jussie 72) - Marouane **Chamakh**. Laurent **Blanc**

Stade Chaban-Delmas, Bordeaux
7-04-2010, 20:45, 31 962, Undiano ESP

Girondins Bordeaux	1
	Chamakh [45]

Cedric **Carrasso** - Ludovic **Sane**, Marc **Planus** (Fernando **Cavenaghi** 84), Michael **Ciani**, Benoit **Tremoulinas** - Jaroslav **Plasil**, Alou **Diarra** (Matthieu **Chalme** 70) - **Wendel**, Yoann **Gourcuff**, Jussie (Yoan **Gouffran** 77) - Marouane **Chamakh**. Tr: Laurent **Blanc**

Olympique Lyonnais	0

Hugo **Lloris** - Anthony **Reveillere**, **Cris**, Jean-Alain **Boumsong** (Mathieu **Bodmer** 77), Aly **Cissokho**• - Jeremy **Toulalan**•, Maxime **Gonalons**• - **Michel Bastos** (Ederson 88), Kim **Kallstrom**•, Cesar **Delgado**• - Bafetimbi **Gomis** (Miralem **Pjanic** 66). Tr: Claude **Puel**

Allianz Arena, Munich
30-03-2010, 20:45, 66 000, De Bleeckere BEL

Bayern München	2
	Ribéry [77], Olic [92+]

Hans Jorg **Butt** - Philipp **Lahm**, Daniel **Van Buyten**, Martin **Demichelis**, Holger **Badstuber**• - Mark **van Bommel**, Danijel **Pranjic** (Anatoliy **Tymoshchuk** 89) - **Hamit** Altintop (Miroslav **Klose** 86), Franck **Ribery** - Thomas **Muller** (Mario **Gomez** 73), Ivica **Olic**•. Tr: Louis **van Gaal**

Manchester United	1
	Rooney [2]

Edwin **van der Sar** - Gary **Neville**•, Rio **Ferdinand**, Nemanja **Vidic**, Patrice **Evra** - Nani (Ryan **Giggs** 82), Darren **Fletcher**, Michael **Carrick** (Dimitar **Berbatov** 70), Paul **Scholes**•, **Park** Ji Sung (Luis **Valencia** 70) - Wayne **Rooney**•. Tr: Alex **Ferguson**

Old Trafford, Manchester
7-04-2010, 19:45, 74 482, Rizzoli ITA

Manchester United	3
	Gibson [3], Nani 2 [7 41]

Edwin **van der Sar** - **Rafael**••◆50, Rio **Ferdinand**, Nemanja **Vidic**, Patrice **Evra** - Darren **Fletcher**, Michael **Carrick** (Dimitar **Berbatov** 80), Darron **Gibson** (Ryan **Giggs** 81) - Luis **Valencia**, Nani - Wayne **Rooney** (John **O'Shea** 55). Tr: Alex **Ferguson**

Bayern München	2
	Olic [42], Robben [74]

Hans Jorg **Butt** - Philipp **Lahm**, Daniel **Van Buyten**, Martin **Demichelis**, Holger **Badstuber**• - Mark **van Bommel**•, Bastian **Schweinsteiger** - Arjen **Robben** (Hamit Altintop 76), Franck **Ribery** - Thomas **Muller** (Mario **Gomez** 46), Ivica **Olic** (Danijel **Pranjic** 84). Tr: Louis **van Gaal**

SEMI-FINALS

San Siro, Milan
20-04-2010, 20:45, 79 000, Benquerença POR

Internazionale	3
	Sneijder [30], Maicon [48], Milito [61]

Julio **Cesar** - **Maicon** (Cristian Chivu 73), **Lucio**, Walter **Samuel**, Javier **Zanetti** - Esteban **Cambiasso**, Thiago **Motta** - Wesley **Sneijder** - Samuel **Eto'o**•, Diego **Milito** (Mario **Balotelli** 75), Goran **Pandev** (Dejan **Stankovic**• 56). Tr: Jose **Mourinho**

Barcelona	1
	Pedro [19]

Victor **Valdes** - Dani **Alves**•, Gerard **Pique**•, Carles **Puyol**•, **Maxwell** - **Xavi**, Sergio **Busquets**• - **Pedro**, Lionel **Messi**, Seydou **Keita**• - Zlatan **Ibrahimovic** (Eric **Abidal** 62). Tr: Josep **Guardiola**

Camp Nou, Barcelona
28-04-2010, 20:45, 96 214, De Bleeckere BEL

Barcelona	1
	Pique [84]

Victor **Valdes** - Dani **Alves**, Yaya **Toure**, Gerard **Pique**, Gabriel **Milito** (Maxwell 46) - **Xavi**, Sergio **Busquets** (Bojan **Krkic** 63), Seydou **Keita** - Lionel **Messi**, Zlatan **Ibrahimovic** (Jeffren 63), **Pedro**. Tr: Josep **Guardiola**

Internazionale	0

Julio **Cesar** - Javier **Zanetti**, **Lucio**, **Maicon**, Walter **Samuel** - Cristian **Chivu**, Thiago **Motta**, Wesley **Sneijder** (Sulley **Muntari** 66), Esteban **Cambiasso** - Samuel **Eto'o** (McDonald **Mariga** 86), Diego **Milito** (Ivan **Cordoba** 80). Tr: Jose **Mourinho**

Allianz Arena, Munich
21-04-2010, 20:45, 66 000, Rosetti ITA

Bayern München	1
	Robben [69]

Hans Jorg **Butt** - Philipp **Lahm**, Daniel **Van Buyten**, Martin **Demichelis**, Diego **Contento** - Bastian **Schweinsteiger**, Danijel **Pranjic**• (Mario **Gomez** 63) - Arjen **Robben** (Hamit Altintop 85), Franck **Ribery**◆37 - Thomas **Muller**, Ivica **Olic** (Anatoliy **Tymoshchuk** 46). Tr: Louis **van Gaal**

Olympque Lyonnais	0

Hugo **Lloris** - Anthony **Reveillere**, **Cris**, Jeremy **Toulalan**••54, Aly **Cissokho** - Maxime **Gonalons**, Kim **Kallstrom** - Ederson (Michel **Bastos**• 70), Miralem **Pjanic** (Jean **Makoun** 56), Cesar **Delgado** (Sidney **Govou** 79) - Lisandro **Lopez**. Tr: Claude **Puel**

Stade de Gerland, Lyon
27-04-2010, 20:45, 39 414, Busacca SUI

Olympique Lyonnais	0

Hugo **Lloris** - Anthony **Reveillere**, **Cris**••◆59, Jean-Alain **Boumsong**, Aly **Cissokho** (Bafetimbi **Gomis** 46) - Maxime **Gonalons**•, Jean **Makoun** - Sidney **Govou**, Cesar **Delgado** (Miralem **Pjanic** 67), **Michel Bastos** - Lisandro **Lopez** (Ederson 79). Tr: Claude **Puel**

Bayern München	3
	Olic 3 [26 67 78]

Hans Jorg **Butt** - Philipp **Lahm**, Daniel **Van Buyten** (Martin **Demichelis** 46), Holger **Badstuber**, Diego **Contento** - Bastian **Schweinsteiger** (David **Alaba** 78), Mark **van Bommel** - Arjen **Robben** (Miroslav **Klose** 76), Hamit Altintop• - Thomas **Muller**, Ivica **Olic**. Tr: Louis **van Gaal**

UEFA Champions League Final	Santiago Bernabeu Madrid	Saturday 22-05-2010
Kick-off: 20:45		Attendance: 80 100

INTERNAZIONALE 2 0 BAYERN MUNCHEN

Diego Milito 2 [35] [70]

INTERNAZIONALE
Black and blue striped shirts, Black shorts, White socks
Tr: Jose Mourinho (POR)

MATCH STATS

Int		Bay
9	Shots	13
7	Shots on Goal	6
13	Fouls Committed	16
2	Corner Kicks	6
0	Caught Offside	0
34%	Possession	66%

MATCH OFFICIALS

REFEREE
Howard Webb ENG

ASSISTANTS
Darren Cann ENG
Mike Mullarkey ENG

4TH OFFICIAL
Martin Atkinson ENG

(C) Captain † Man of the Match

12 Julio Cesar

13 Maicon   6 Lucio   25 Walter Samuel   [68] 26 Cristian Chivu [30]
5 Dejan Stankovic

4 Javier Zanetti (c)   19 Esteban Cambiasso

10 Wesley Sneijder

9 Samuel Eto'o   [92+] 22 Diego Milito †   [79] 27 Goran Pandev
23 Marco Materazzi   11 Sulley Muntari

[74] 11 Ivica Olic   25 Thomas Müller
33 Mario Gomez

[63] 8 Hamit Altintop   10 Arjen Robben
18 Miroslav Klose

31 Bastian Schweinsteiger   17 Mark van Bommel (c) [78]

28 Holger Badstubber 6 Martin Demichelis [26] 5 Daniel Van Buyten 21 Philipp Lahm

22 Hans-Jörg Butt

Tr: Luis van Gaal (NED)
Red and white striped shirts, Red shorts, Black socks

BAYERN MUNCHEN

It was a provocation in a football sense when Van Gaal said before the match Inter are a defensive team. We didn't lose our personality, we're a very compact team and we managed to play and win with counters. After the second goal the match was over. With Bayern attacking with so many players it was easier for us to control the middle of the pitch and from there we attacked. We played a beautiful final and we deserved to win.

Jose Mourinho

It was no surprise to me how the match went. The surprise is we lost. We knew they would be very well organised defensively. We knew Diego Milito and Wesley Sneijder could be decisive and that's how it went. We didn't create as many chances as usual. The Müller chance in the second half would have made it a different game. To attack is much more difficult than to defend and we had to attack in a reduced space.

Louis van Gaal

UEFA EUROPA LEAGUE 2009-10 KNOCKOUT STAGE

Round of 32	Round of 16	Quarter-Final	Semi-Final	Final

Round of 32

At'tico Madrid*† 1 2
Galatasaray 1 1

Everton * 2 0
Sporting CP 1 3

Werder Bremen 0 4
FC Twente * 1 1

Club Brugge * 1 0
Valencia 0 3

Benfica 1 4
Hertha BSC * 1 0

FC København * 1 1
Oly. Marseille † 3 3

Lille OSC * 2 1
Fenerbahçe 1 1

UnireaUrziceni† 0 1
Liverpool * † 1 3

Hamburger SV * 1 2
PSV Eindhoven 0 3

Athletic Bilbao * 1 0
RSC Anderlecht 1 4

Panathinaikos * 3 3
Roma 2 2

RB Salzburg 2 0
Standard CL * † 3 0

VfL Wolfsburg † 2 4
Villarreal * 2 1

Hapoel Tel Aviv 0 0
Rubin Kazan * † 3 0

Juventus † 2 0
Ajax * 1 0

Shakhtar D'tsk 1 1
Fulham * 2 1

Round of 16

Atlético Madrid * 0 2
Sporting CP 0 2

Werder Bremen 1 4
Valencia * 1 4

Benfica * 1 2
Oly. Marseille 1 1

Lille OSC * 1 0
Liverpool 0 3

Hamburger SV * 3 3
RSC Anderlecht 1 4

Panathinaikos * 1 0
Standard CL 3 1

VfL Wolfsburg 1 2
Rubin Kazan * 1 1

Juventus * 3 1
Fulham 1 4

Quarter-Final

Atlético Madrid 2 0
Valencia * 2 0

Benfica * 2 1
Liverpool 1 4

Hamburger SV * 2 3
Standard CL 1 1

VfL Wolfsburg 1 0
Fulham * 2 1

Semi-Final

Atlético Madrid * 1 1
Liverpool 0 2

Hamburger SV * 0 1
Fulham 0 2

Final

Atlético Madrid 2
Fulham 1

* Home team in the first leg • † Qualified as third placed team in the UEFA Champions League

UEFA Europa League Final	Nordbank Arena Hamburg	Wednesday 12-05-2010
Kick-off: 20:45		Attendance: 49 000

ATLETICO MADRID   2   1   FULHAM

Diego Forlan 2 32 116   **Simon Davies** 37

ATLETICO MADRID

Red and White striped shirts, Blue shorts, Red socks

Tr: Quique Flores

MATCH STATS		
AM		FUL
27	Shots	11
10	Shots on Goal	3
15	Fouls Committed	17
9	Corner Kicks	2
0	Caught Offside	9
54%	Possession	46%

43 David de Gea

17 Tomás Ujfalusi   21 Luis Perea   18 Alvaro Dominguez   3 Antonio López (c)

12 Paulo Assunção   8 Raúl Garcia 114

19 José Antonio Reyes
78
14 Eduardo Salvio 107

20 Simão Sabrosa
68
9 José Manuel Jurado

7 Diego Forlan † 117   10 Sergio Agüero
119
2 Juan Valera

MATCH OFFICIALS

REFEREE
Nicola Rizzoli ITA

ASSISTANTS
(TOUCHLINE)
Cristiano Copelli ITA
Luca Maggiani ITA

ASSISTANTS
(PENALTY AREA)
Paolo Tagliavento ITA
Andrea De Marco ITA

4TH OFFICIAL
Gianluca Rocchi ITA

(C) Captain † Man of the Match

25 Bobby Zamora
55
23 Clint Dempsey

11 Zoltán Gera

29 Simon Davies

16 Damian Duff
84
10 Erik Nevland

20 Dickson Etuhu

13 Danny Murphy (c)
118
27 Jonathan Greening

3 Paul Konchesky   5 Brede Hangeland 63   18 Aaron Hughes   6 Chris Baird

1 Mark Schwarzer

Tr: Roy Hodgson

Blue-grey shirts, White shorts, White socks

FULHAM

Fulham are a very well-organised side and they made it very difficult for us to find that second goal. It was like we played two matches against that defence of theirs. They were great opponents but I would say that overall we deserved the victory. Atlético are a big, big club and we have made thousands of people happy tonight. This is a massive occasion in the history of the club. We are thrilled to have won a very tough final and a very difficult competition.

Quique Flores

Obviously we are very disappointed. I thought we put on another very good show and the game was heading for penalties. In fact, despite the obvious fatigue, the players were looking good value – well-organised and disciplined – but unfortunately Diego Forlán popped up and there was no time to recover. All the same, it has been a magnificent achievement – everyone wants to finish first but to finish second is something we can be very proud of.

Roy Hodgson

UEFA CHAMPIONS LEAGUE 2010–11

Second Qualifying Round

Third Qualifying Round

BSC Young Boys	SUI	2	1
Fenerbahçe	TUR	2	0

Play-off Round

BSC Young Boys	SUI	3	0
Tottenham Hotspur	ENG	2	4

Group Stage

Group A		Pts
Tottenham Hotspur	ENG	11
Internazionale	ITA	10
FC Twente Enschede	NED	6
Werder Bremen	GER	6

Werder Bremen	GER	3	2
Sampdoria	ITA	1	3

Omonia Nicosia	CYP	3	2
Renova Cepciste	MKD	0	0
RB Austria Salzburg	AUT	5	0
HB Tórshavn	FRO	0	1
FK Aktobe	KAZ	2	1
Olimpi Rustavi	GEO	0	1
Hapoel Tel Aviv	ISR	5	1
Zeljeznicar Sarajevo	BIH	0	0
AIK Stockholm	SWE	1	0
Jeunesse d'Esch	LUX	0	0
Linfield	NIR	0	0
Rosenborg BK	NOR	0	2
BATE Borisov	BLR	5	1
FH Hafnarfjördur	ISL	1	0

Omonia Nicosia	CYP	1	0
RB Austria Salzburg	AUT	1	1

RB Austria Salzburg	AUT	2	1
Hapoel Tel Aviv	ISR	3	1

Group B		Pts
Schalke 04	GER	13
Olympique Lyonnais	FRA	10
Benfica	POR	6
Hapoel Tel Aviv		5

FK Aktobe	KAZ	1	1
Hapoel Tel Aviv	ISR	0	3

AIK Stockholm	SWE	0	0
Rosenborg BK	NOR	1	3

Rosenborg BK	NOR	2	0
FC København	DEN	1	1

Group C		Pts
Manchester United	ENG	14
Valencia	ESP	11
Rangers	SCO	6
Bursaspor	TUR	1

BATE Borisov	BLR	0	2
FC København	DEN	0	3

Levadia Tallinn	EST	1	2
Debreceni VSC	HUN	1	3

Debreceni VSC	HUN	0	1
FC Basel	SUI	2	3

FC Basel	SUI	1	3
Sheriff Tiraspol	MDA	0	0

Group D		Pts
Barcelona	ESP	14
FC København	DEN	10
Rubin Kazan	RUS	6
Panathinaikos	GRE	2

Sheriff Tiraspol	MDA	3	0
Dinamo Tiranë	ALB	1	1
Dinamo Zagreb	CRO	5	0
FC Koper	SVN	1	3
Liepajas Metalurgs	LVA	0	0
Sparta Praha	CZE	3	2
Inter Baku	AZE	0 1 8p
Lech Poznan	POL	1 0 9p
Litex Lovech	BUL	1	4
Rudar Pljevlja	MNE	0	0
Birkirkara	MLT	1	0
MSK Zilina	SVK	0	3

Sheriff Tiraspol	MDA	1 1 6p
Dinamo Zagreb	CRO	1 1 5p

Sparta Praha	CZE	1	1
Lech Poznan	POL	0	0

Sparta Praha	CZE	0	0
MSK Zilina	SVK	2	1

Group E		Pts
Bayern München	GER	15
Roma	ITA	10
FC Basel	SUI	6
CFR Cluj-Napoca	ROU	4

Litex Lovech	BUL	1	1
MSK Zilina	SVK	1	3

Dynamo Kyiv	UKR	3	3
KAA Gent	BEL	0	1

Dynamo Kyiv	UKR	1	1
Ajax	NED	1	2

Group F		Pts
Chelsea	ENG	15
Olympique Marseille	FRA	12
Spartak Moskva	RUS	9
MSK Zilina	SVK	0

Ajax	NED	1	3
POAK Thessaloniki	GRE	1	3

Unirea Urziceni	ROU	0	0
Zenit St Petersburg	RUS	0	1

Zenit St Petersburg	RUS	1	0
AJ Auxerre	FRA	0	2

Group G		Pts
Real Madrid	ESP	16
Milan	ITA	8
Ajax	NED	7
AJ Auxerre	FRA	3

Sporting Braga	POR	3	1
Celtic	SCO	0	2

Sporting Braga	POR	1	4
Sevilla	ESP	0	3

Group H		Pts
Shakhtar Donetsk	UKR	15
Arsenal	ENG	12
Sporting Braga	POR	9
Partizan Beograd	SRB	0

Partizan Beograd	SRB	3	1
Pyunik Yerevan	ARM	1	0
Ekranas Panevezys	LTU	1	0
HJK Helsinki	FIN	0	2
Bohemians	IRL	1	0
TNS Llansantffraid	WAL	0	4

Partizan Beograd	SRB	3	2
HJK Helsinki	FIN	0	1

Partizan Beograd	SRB	2 2 3p
RSC Anderlecht	BEL	2 2 2p

The home team in the first leg
of pre-group stage matches
is list above their opponents

TNS Llansantffraid	WAL	1	0
RSC Anderlecht	BEL	3	3

First qualifying round: Santa Coloma AND 0-3 3-4 **Birkirkara** MLT • Tre Fiori SMR 0-3 1-4 **Rudar Pljevlja** MNE

UEFA CHAMPIONS LEAGUE 2010-11

Round of 16	Quarter-finals	Semi-finals	Final

Milan *
Tottenham Hotspur

Valencia *
Schalke 04

Roma *
Shakhtar Donetsk

Arsenal *
Barcelona

FC Kobenhavn *
Chelsea

Olymp. Lyonnais *
Real Madrid

Olymp. Marseille *
Manchester United

Internazionale *
Bayern München

* Home team in the first leg

Europa League Qualifiers

Play-off round losers qualify for the
Europa League group stage. Losers
in the third qualifying round qualify
for the play-off round while the
third placed teams in the group
stage qualify for the first knockout
round

FIRST QUALIFYING ROUND

Comunal, Andorra La Vella
29-06-2010, 19:00, Buttimer IRL

Santa Coloma — 0

Match awarded to Birkirkara after the match was cancelled due to a poor pitch

Birkirkara — 3

Ta'Qali, Ta'Qali
6-07-2010, 18;00, 878, Madden SCO

Birkirkara — 4

Galea 2 [10][31], Cilia 2 [35][45]

Ezequiel **Lovizon** - Branko **Nisevic**, Nikolai **Vukanac**•, Joseph **Zerafa** (Carl **Pulo** 68), Thomas **Paris** - Paul **Fenech**, Trevor **Cilia** (Angus **Buhagiar** 82), Shaun **Bajada** (Alan **Tabone** 75), Rowen **Muscat** - Michael **Galea**(c), Andrew **De Cesare**•. Tr: Paul **Zammit**

Santa Coloma — 3

Urbani.N [21], Jimenez [44], Urbani.M [85]

Ricardo **Fernandez** - David **Ribolleda** (**Txema Garcia**• 46), Alfonso **Sanchez**•, Javier **Sanchez**, Xavier **Gil** - Josep **Ayala**(c), Oscar **Sonejee** (Gilbert **Sanchez** 77), Genis **Garcia** (Eric **Bodjo** 54), Manolo **Jimenez**, Mariano **Urbani** - Norberto **Urbani**•. Tr: Xavier Roura **Cuadros**

Olimpico, Serravalle
30-06-2010, 20:30, 681, Sant MLT

Tre Fiori — 0

Massimiliano **Micheletti** - Sandro **Macerata**, Giacomo **Benedettini**, Andrea **Martini**, Matteo **Andreini** - Ignacio **Nardone**, Nicola **Canarezza**•(c), Altin **Lisi**•, Fabio **Vannoni** (Cristian **Menin** 56), Paolo **Tarini** (Federico **Amici** 73) - Sossio **Aruta** (Simone **Grana** 89). Tr: Floriano **Sperindo**

Rudar Pljevlja — 3

Useni [31], Vlahovic [40], Jovanovic [95+]

Milos **Radanovic** - Blazo **Igumanovic**, Mijusko **Bojovic**, Veselin **Bojic** - Nikola **Sekulic**• (Dusan **Micic** 60), Bojan **Ivanovic**, Nermin **Useni**, Predrag **Brnovic** (Aleksandar **Minic**• 75), Danilo **Tomic**• (Ivica **Jovanovic** 68), Nedjeljko **Vlahovic** - Predrag **Randelovic**(c). Tr: Nebojsa **Vignjevic**

Gradski, Podgorica
7-07-2010, 18:00, 400, Sidenco MDA

Rudar Pljevlja — 4

Randjelovic 2 [7][67], Vlahovic [83], Jovanovic [85]

Milos **Radanovic** - Blazo **Igumanovic**, Mijusko **Bojovic**, Veselin **Bojic** - Nikola **Sekulic** (Dusan **Micic** 78), Bojan **Ivanovic**, Nermin **Useni** (Ivica **Jovanovic**• 61), Predrag **Brnovic**, Danilo **Tomic** (Miroje **Jovanovic** 46), Nedjeljko **Vlahovic** - Predrag **Randelovic**(c). Tr: Nebojsa Vignjevic

Tre Fiori — 1

Vannoni [29]

Massimiliano **Micheletti** - Ignacio **Nardone**, Sandro **Macerata**, Giacomo **Benedettini**•, Matteo **Andreini** - Nicola **Canarezza**•(c), Altin **Lisi**, Fabio **Vannoni**, Federico **Macina** (Jacopo **Manzari** 80), Paolo **Tarini**• (Daniele 87) - Cristian **Menin** (Federico **Amici** 53). Tr: Floriano **Sperindo**

SECOND QUALIFYING ROUND

GSP, Nicosia
13-07-2010, 20:00, 13 400, Kovarik CZE

Omonia Nicosia — 3

Konstantinou 2 [7p][62], Davidson [29]

Antonis **Georgallides** - Timo **Wenzel**, Hristos **Karipidis**, Yuval **Shpungin** (Giorgos **Efrem** 46), **Davidson**, Konstantinos **Makrides**, Dimitrios **Grammozis** (Giorgos **Panagi** 83), Noel **Kaseke**, Leandro, Michalis **Konstantinou**•, Efstathios **Aloneftis** (Victor 81). Tr: Takis **Lemonis**

Renova Cepciste — 0

Armend **Elezi** - Agron **Memedi**•, Metodija **Stepanovski**, Faruk **Statovci**•, Darko **Ignjatovski**♦6, Igorce **Stojanov**, Muharem **Bajrami** (Saimir **Fetai** 67), Vulnet **Emini** (Argjent **Gafuri** 81), Fisnik **Nuhiu**, Fisnik **Gashi**•, Iljber **Ali**• (Boban **Jancevski** 89). Tr: Nedzat **Sabani**

Filip II Arena, Skopje
29-07-2010, 16:30, 600, Pereira POR

Renova Cepciste — 0

Armend **Elezi** - Agron **Memedi**, Metodija **Stepanovski**, Faruk **Statovci** (Muharem **Bajrami** 61), Igorce **Stojanov**, Vulnet **Emini** (Saimir **Fetai** 82), Fisnik **Nuhiu**, Argjent **Gafuri**, Fisnik **Gashi** (Marjan **Mickov** 51), Iljber **Ali**, Boban **Jancevski**. Tr: Nedzat **Sabani**

Omonia Nicosia — 2

Aloneftis [15], Leandro [24]

Antonis **Georgallides** - Hristos **Karipidis**, Iago **Bouzon**, **Davidson**, Giorgos **Efrem**, Konstantinos **Makrides** (Hernan **Rengifo** 46), Noel **Kaseke**, Ilias **Charalambous**, Leandro, Michalis **Konstantinou** (Lomana **LuaLua** 63), Efstathios **Aloneftis** (Rueda 74). Tr: Takis **Lemonis**

Red Bull Arena, Salzburg
13-07-2010, 18:00, 9100, Satchi MDA

RB Austria Salzburg — 5

Zarate [21], Jantscher [43], Ulmer [46], Walner [64], Hierlander [82]

Gerhard **Tremmel** - Christian **Schwegler**, Franz **Schiemer**, Andreas **Ulmer**, Ibrahim **Sekagya**, David Mendes da Silva (Nikola **Pokrivac**• 60), Jakob **Jantscher**, Dusan **Svento** (Simon **Cziommer** 60), Christoph **Leitgeb**, Roman **Wallner** (Stefan **Hierlander** 75), Gonzalo **Zarate**. Tr: Huub Stevens

HB Tórshavn — 0

Marcin **Dawid** - Thordur **Hreidarsson**, Hans a **Lag** (Rogvi **Holm** 77), Hendrik **Rubeksen**, Milan **Kuljic** (Levi **Hanssen** 59), Pætur **Jorgensen**, Frodi **Benjaminsen**, Simun **Samuelsen**, Rogvi **Poulsen**, Vagnur **Mortensen**, Andrew av **Flotum** (Tor-Ingar **Akselsen** 57). Tr: Kristjan **Gudmundsson**

Gundadalur, Tórshavn
20-07-2010, 17:00, 250, Asumaa FIN

HB Tórshavn — 1

Samuelsen [73]

Tordur **Thomsen** - Thordur **Hreidarsson**, Rogvi **Holm**, Hendrik **Rubeksen**, Pætur **Jorgensen**, Frodi **Benjaminsen**, Simun **Samuelsen**•, Rogvi **Poulsen**, Vagnur **Mortensen**•, Andrew av **Flotum**• (Kristin **Mouritsen** 89), Levi **Hanssen**. Tr: Kristjan **Gudmundsson**

RB Austria Salzburg — 0

Alexander **Walke** - Milan **Dudic**, Franz **Schiemer**, Andreas **Ulmer**, Ibrahim **Sekagya**, David Mendes da Silva (Nikola **Pokrivac** 34), Jakob **Jantscher** (Louis **N'Gwat-Mahop** 71), Simon **Cziommer** (Dusan **Svento** 46), Stefan **Hierlander**, Christoph **Leitgeb**•, Gonzalo **Zarate**. Tr: Huub Stevens

---

Tcentralny, Aktobe
14-07-2010, 21:00, 11 500, Yildirim TUR

FK Aktobe — 2

Smakov 2 [40p][53]

Andrey **Sidelnikov** - Khalifa **Ba**, Petr **Badlo**, Samat **Smakov**, Alain Bono **Mboune**, Marat **Khayrullin**, Konstantin **Golovskoy** (Murat **Tleshev** 71), Andrey **Karpovich**, Evgeniy **Averchenko** (Aslan **Darabaev** 80), Titi **Essomba**, Ivan **Peric** (Nikita **Khokhlov** 87). Tr: Vladimir **Mukhanov**

Olimpi Rustavi — 0

Grigol **Bediashvili** - Lekso **Kvakhadze**, Giorgi **Rekhviashvili**, Giorgi **Gongadze**•, Revaz **Kemoklidze**, Luka **Razmadze**, Giorgi **Chelidze** (Grigol **Dolidze** 85), David **Bolkvadze** (Giorgi **Khidesheli** 74), Revaz **Getsadze**, Irakli **Modebadze**, Giorgi **Chedia** (Denis **Dobrovolski** 55). Tr: Teimurasz **Makharadze**

Poladi, Rustavi
21-07-2010, 16:00, 4200, Deaconu ROU

Olimpi Rustavi — 1

Rekhviashvili [30]

Grigol **Bediashvili** (Zurab **Batiashvili** 79), Lekso **Kvakhadze**, Giorgi **Rekhviashvili**, Temur **Gongadze**, Revaz **Kemoklidze**•, Luka **Razmadze**, Giorgi **Chelidze** (Grigol **Dolidze** 68), Denis **Dobrovolski**•, David **Bolkvadze**, Revaz **Getsadze** (Giorgi **Chedia** 53), Irakli **Modebadze**. Tr: Teimurasz **Makharadze**

FK Aktobe — 1

Tleshev [90]

Andrey **Sidelnikov** - Khalifa **Ba**•, Samat **Smakov**, Emil **Kenzhisariev**, Alain Bono **Mboune**• (Petr **Badlo** 90), Marat **Khayrullin**, Konstantin **Golovskoy**• (Nikita **Khokhlov** 86), Andrey **Karpovich**•, Evgeniy **Averchenko**, Titi **Essomba**, Ivan **Peric** (Murat **Tleshev**• 46). Tr: Vladimir **Mukhanov**

Bloomfield, Tel Aviv
13-07-2010, 20:00, 10 931, Clattenburg ENG

Hapoel Tel Aviv   **5**
Lala 3 [10 31 38], Shivhon [12], OG [28]

Galil Ben Shanan - Douglas (Bevan Fransman 65), Dedi Ben Dayan, Omri Kende, Avihay Yadin, Yossi Shivhon (Victor Merey 74), Walid Badir, Gil Vermouth, Itay Shechter, Eran Zahavy, Maharan Lala (Romain Rocchi 56). Tr: Eli Guttmann

Zeljeznicar Sarajevo   **0**

Ibrahim Sehic - Mirko Radovanovic, Jadranko Bogicevic•, Elvis Mesic, Srdjan Savic, Zajko Zeba (Goran Gancev• 46), Edin Visca, Milan Culum (Muamer Svraka 46), Mirsad Beslija, Lazar Popovic (Damir Rovcanin 88), Srdjan Stanic. Tr: Amar Osim

---

Kosevo, Sarajevo
21-07-2010, 20:15, 4500, Clos ESP

Zeljeznicar Sarajevo   **0**

Ibrahim Sehic - Mirko Radovanovic, Goran Gancev (Srdjan Stanic 46), Jadranko Bogicevic, Elvis Mesic, Srdjan Savic• (Milan Culum 76), Zajko Zeba•, Edin Visca, Mirsad Beslija (Barjo Spahic 77), Muamer Svraka, Damir Rovcanin•. Tr: Amar Osim

Hapoel Tel Aviv   **1**
Douglas [76]

Galil Ben Shanan - Douglas, Dedi Ben Dayan, Omri Kende, Avihay Yadin, Yossi Shivhon (Victor Merey 60), Walid Badir, Gil Vermouth, Itay Shechter, Eran Zahavy• (Gal Shish 71), Maharan Lala (Romain Rocchi 46). Tr: Eli Guttmann

---

Råsunda, Stockholm
13-07-2010, 19:00, 11 515, Siejewicz POL

AIK Stockholm   **1**
Engblom [57]

Ivan Turina - Per Karlsson, Nils-Eric Johansson, Walid Atta, Helgi Danielsson, Daniel Tjernstrom, Kenny Pavey, Dulee Johnson (Daniel Gustafsson 85), Goran Ljubojevic (Admir Catovic 54), Antonio Flavio, Pontus Engblom. Tr: Alex Miller

Jeunesse d'Esch   **0**

Marc Oberweis - Eric Hoffmann, Adrien Portier, Thomas Fullenwarth (Clayton De Sousa• 82), Charles Leweck, Gregory Servais, Rene Peters, Kevin Martin, Dan Collette, Stephane Piron (Sergio Pupovac 46), Roxan Valiente (Loic Cantonnet 87). Tr: Jacques Muller

---

Stade de la Frontière, Esch
21-07-2010, 17:00, 1568, Jones WAL

Jeunesse d'Esch   **0**

Marc Oberweis - Eric Hoffmann•, Adrien Portier, Thomas Fullenwarth (Loic Cantonnet• 21), Charles Leweck, Gregory Servais, Rene Peters, Kevin Martin, Dan Collette•, Roxan Valiente• (Keiven Goncalves 68), Sergio Pupovac (Stephane Piron 59). Tr: Jacques Muller

AIK Stockholm   **0**

Ivan Turina - Niklas Backman, Per Karlsson, Nils-Eric Johansson, Walid Atta, Helgi Danielsson, Daniel Tjernstrom, Kenny Pavey, Dulee Johnson, Antonio Flavio (Viktor Lundberg 77), Pontus Engblom (Goran Ljubojevic 69). Tr: Alex Miller

---

Windsor Park, Belfast
14-07-2010, 20:45, 1715, Ennjimi FRA

Linfield   **0**

Alan Blayney - Kris Lindsay, Noel Bailie, Billy Joe Burns (James Ervin 76), Aaron Burns, Damian Curran, Philip Lowry (Mark McAllister 70), Robert Garrett•, Jamie Mulgrew, Brian McCaul (Michael Carvill 61), Peter Thompson. Tr: David Jeffrey

Rosenborg BK   **0**

Daniel Orlund - Mikael Lustig, Mikael Dorsin•, Vadim Demidov, Kris Stadsgaard, Anthony Annan•, Fredrik Winsnes, Markus Henriksen, Abdou Razak Traore (Roar Strand 46), Morten Moldskred (Trond Olsen 87), Steffen Iversen. Tr: Nils Arne Eggen

---

Lerkendal, Trondheim
21-07-2010, 20:45, 6645, Schorgenhofer AUT

Rosenborg BK   **2**
Prica [32], Henriksen [87]

Daniel Orlund - Mikael Lustig, Mikael Dorsin, Vadim Demidov, Kris Stadsgaard, Anthony Annan, Per Skjelbred (Paul Munster 81), Markus Henriksen, Morten Moldskred (Trond Olsen 74), Steffen Iversen, Rade Prica (Fredrik Winsnes 74). Tr: Nils Arne Eggen

Linfield   **0**

Alan Blayney - Kris Lindsay, Noel Bailie, Billy Joe Burns, Aaron Burns (Paul Munster 81), Damian Curran•, Philip Lowry (Michael Carvill 68), Robert Garrett•, Jamie Mulgrew, Brian McCaul (Curtis Allen 63), Peter Thompson. Tr: David Jeffrey

---

Gradski, Borisov
14-07-2010, 18:00, 5200, Kakos GRE

BATE Borisov   **5**
Nekhaychik 3 [48 85 88], Bressan [58], Rodionov [90]

Sergey Veremko - Igor Shitov•, Aleksandr Yurevich, Artem Radkov•, Maksim Bordachev, Dmitry Likhtarovich (Edgar Olekhnovich 62), Renan Bressan (Aleksandr Volodko 68), Pavel Nekhaychik, Aleksandr Pavlov, Artem Kontsevoy• (Maksim Skavysh 78), Vitaliy Rodionov. Tr: Viktor Goncharenko

FH Hafnarfjördur   **0**
Bjornsson [89]

Gunnleifur Gunnleifsson• - Tommy Nielsen (Torger Motland 66), Petur Vioarsson, Gudmundur Sæversson, Bjorn Sverrisson, Hafthor Thrastarson (Freyr Bjarnason 59), Hjortur Valgardsson, Matthias Vilhjalmsson, Atli Gudnason, Atli Bjornsson, Olafur Snorrason. Tr: Heimir Gudjonsson

---

Kaplakriki, Hafnarfjordur
21-07-2010, 21:15, 522, Kaasik EST

FH Hafnarfjördur   **0**

Gunnleifur Gunnleifsson - Tommy Nielsen (Freyr Bjarnason 78), Petur Vidarsson•, Jon Jonsson•, Bjorn Sverrisson, Hafthor Thrastarson, Hjortur Valgardsson• (Bjarki Gunnlaugsson• 43), Torger Motland, Matthias Vilhjalmsson, Atli Bjornsson (Atli Gudnason 64), Olafur Snorrason. Tr: Heimir Gudjonsson

BATE Borisov   **1**
Rodionov [15]

Sergey Veremko• - Sergey Sosnovskiy, Igor Shitov, Maksim Bordachev, Dmitry Likhtarovich, Aleksandr Volodko (Aleksandr Yurevich 77), Renan Bressan, Edgar Olekhnovich (Aleksandr Pavlov 59), Dmitriy Baga, Maksim Skavysh (Aleh Patotskiy• 71). Tr: Viktor Goncharenko

---

Oláh Gábor utcai, Debrecen
21-07-2010, 19:00, 7500, Hagen NOR

Debreceni VSC   **3**
Coulibaly [24], Yannick [32], Szakaly [55]

Mindaugas Malinauskas - Adam Komlosi, Marcell Fodor, Mirsad Mijadinoski, Zoltan Nagy, Zoltan Kiss, Peter Szakaly (Joszef Varga 73), Peter Czvitkovics, Yannick Mbengono (Tibor Dombi 85), Adamo Coulibaly, Tamas Kulcsar (Laszlo Rezes• 46). Tr: Andras Herczeg

Levadia Tallinn   **2**
Nahk [3], Leitan [53]

Martin Kaalma - Andrei Kalimullin•, Igor Morozov•, Maksim Podholjuzin, Vitali Leitan, Konstantin Nahk•, Deniss Malov••♦74, Felipe Nunes (Igor Subbotin 80), Taijo Teniste, Vladislav Ivanov, Tarmo Neemelo. Tr: Igor Prins

---

Sheriff, Tiraspol
14-07-2010, 19:00, 6951, Stalhammar SWE

Sheriff Tiraspol   **3**
Volkov [9], Nikolic [62], Nadson [70]

Vladislav Stoyanov - Vladimir Volkov•, Vazha Tarkhnishvili, Ognjen Vranjes, Nadson, Vladimir Brankovic, Baco Nikolic• (Serhei Gheorghiev 75), Fred (Artiom Haciaturov 90), Vitalie Bulat (Alexandr Erokhin 46), Milos Adamovic, Franca. Tr: Andrey Sosnitskiy

Dinamo Tiranë   **1**
Malacarne [12]

Isli Hidi - Arjan Pisha, Erion Xhafa, Lucas Malacarne, Esteban Garcia• (Rafael Sosa 79), Emiljano Vila, Gjergj Muzaka (Igli Allmuca 72), Marko Putincanin•, Pape Diop•, Nestor Martinena, Elis Bakaj♦68. Tr: Luis Manuel Blanco

---

Qemal Stafa, Tirana
20-07-2010, 18:00, 3000, Trattou CYP

Dinamo Tiranë   **1**
Vila [18]

Isli Hidi - Arjan Pisha, Erion Xhafa (Roland Peqini 71), Renato Malota (Esteban Garcia 65), Lucas Malacarne, Emiljano Vila•, Gjergj Muzaka (Asion Daja 88), Marko Putincanin•, Rafael Sosa•, Nestor Martinena, Fatjon Sefa. Tr: Luis Manuel Blanco

Sheriff Tiraspol   **0**

Vladislav Stoyanov - Vladimir Volkov, Vazha Tarkhnishvili•, Ognjen Vranjes, Nadson, Vladimir Brankovic•, Baco Nikolic (Amath Diedhiou 46), Alexandr Erokhin, Vitalie Bulat (Fred• 57), Milos Adamovic (Miral Samardzic 80), Franca. Tr: Andrey Sosnitskiy

Maksimir, Zagreb
13-07-2010, 20:15, 7116, Kinhofer GER

Dinamo Zagreb   5
Mandzukic 2 [30 63], Slepicka [38], Sammir [77], Etto [80]

Tomislav **Butina** - Luis **Ibanez** (Tomislav 85), Leonard **Mesaric•**, **Etto, Sammir•**, Mathias **Chago**, Milan **Badelj** (Adrian Calello 76), Igor **Biscan**, Pedro **Morales** (Ilija Sivonjic• 60), Mario **Mandzukic•**, Miroslav **Slepicka**. Tr: Velimir **Zajec**

FC Koper   1
Bubanja [11]

Ermin **Hasic** - Kristijan **Polovanec**, Enes **Handanagic**, Andraz **Struna** (Aljaz Struna 56), Nebosja **Kovacevic**, Miran **Pavlin** (Ivica Guberac 85), Amir **Karic•**, Ivan **Sesar**, Danijel **Marceta•**, Mitja **Brulc** (Enej Jelenic 78), Davor **Bubanja**. Tr: Nedzad **Okcic**

Letna, Prague
21-07-2010, 20:00, 8025, Strahonja CRO

Sparta Praha   2
Matejovsky [12], Zeman [43]

Jaromir **Blazek** - Tomas **Repka**, Jiri **Kladrubsky**, Erich **Brabec**, Manuel **Pamic**, Marek **Matejovsky** (Igor Zofcak 56), Juraj **Kucka** (Niklas Hoheneder 46), Kamil **Vacek•**, Milos **Lacny** (Martin Zeman 41), Vaclav **Kadlec**, Jiri **Jeslinek**. Tr: Jozef **Chovanec**

Liepajas Metalurgs   0

Viktors **Spole** (Pavels Steinbors 46) - Oskars **Klava•**, Antons **Jemelins** (Igor **Alekseev•** 70), Jurica **Puljiz** (Intars Kirhners 64), Takafumi **Akahoshi**, Maksims **Rafalskis**, Tomas **Tamosauskas•**, Pavels **Surnins•**, Vitalijus **Kavaliauskas**, Deniss **Rakels**, Jurgis **Kalns**. Tr: Rudiger **Abramczik**

Lovech Stadion, Lovech
13-07-2010, 20:00, 6900, Olsiak SVK

Litex Lovech   1
Popov [8]

Rodrigo **Galatto** - Alexandre **Barthe**, Petar **Zanev**, Plamen **Nikolov**, Nikolaj **Bodurov**, **Wellington** (Florin Bratu 69), **Sandrinho**, Doka **Madureira** (Momchil Tsvetanov 78), Nebojsa **Jelenkovic**, Wilfried **Niflore**, Ivelin **Popov** (Hristo **Yanev** 61). Tr: Angel **Chervenkov**

Rudar Pljevlja   0

Milos **Radanovic** - Blazo **Igumanovic•**, Mijusko **Bojovic••♦85**, Veselin **Bojic**, Bojan **Ivanovic**, Dusan **Micic**, Nermin **Useni•** (Vladan Adzic 89), Predrag **Brnovic** (Nikola Sekulic 79), Miroje **Jovanovic** (Ivica Jovanovic 56), Nedjeljko **Vlahovic**, Predrag **Randelovic•**. Tr: Nebojsa **Vignjevic**

Pod Dubnom, Zilina
21-07-2010, 19:30, 5511, Szabo HUN

MSK Zilina   3
Piacek [21], Lietava [77], Oravec [92+]

Martin **Dubravka** - Stanislav **Angelovic•**, Jozef **Piacek**, Ondrej **Sourek**, Patrik **Mraz**, Robert **Jez**, Emil **Rilke** (Pavol Poliacek 71), Tomas **Majtan** (Stefan Zosak 59), Tomas **Oravec**, Bello **Babatounde** (Lubomir **Guldan** 90), Ivan **Lietava•**. Tr: Pavel **Hapal**

Birkirkara   0

Ezequiel **Lovizon** - Patrik **Borg**, Branko **Nisevic** (Ryan Scicluna 87), Nikolai **Vukanac**, Joseph **Zerafa**, Paul **Fenech•**, Shaun **Bajada**, Rowen **Muscat** (Thomas Paris 75), Michael **Galea•**, Alan **Tabone** (Carl Pulo 67), Angus **Buhagiar•**. Tr: Paul **Zammit**

Sportni Park, Nova Gorica
20-07-2010, 20:15, 720, Banti ITA

FC Koper   3
Handanagic [11], Guberac [54], Brulc [78p]

Ermin **Hasic** - Kristijan **Polovanec•**, Enes **Handanagic**, Aljaz **Struna**, Andraz **Struna**, Nebosja **Kovacevic** (Pedro Morales 46), Amir **Karic** (Milidrag **Maric•** 60), Ivan **Sesar•** (Sasa Bozicic• 68), Danijel **Marceta**, Mitja **Brulc**, Enej **Jelenic•**. Tr: Nedzad **Okcic**

Dinamo Zagreb   0

Tomislav **Butina** - Luis **Ibanez** (Leonard Mesaric 57), Tomislav **Barbaric**, Adrian **Calello**, **Etto, Sammir**, Mathias **Chago•**, Igor **Biscan♦77**, Miroslav **Slepicka** (Pedro Morales 46), **Dodo**, Ilija **Sivonjic** (Dario Simic 78). Tr: Velimir **Zajec**

Tofik Bakhramov, Baku
13-07-2010, 17:00, 7000, Kever SUI

Inter Baku   0

Georgi **Lomaia** - Zhivko **Zhelev**, Dmitriy **Kruglov•** (Elgiz **Karamli•** 52), Vladimir **Levin•**, Ilia **Kandelaki**, Kakha **Mzhavanadze**, Aleksandr **Chertoganov**, Bronislav **Cervenka**, Petar **Zlatinov**, David **Odikadze** (Arif **Dashdemirov** 81), Robertas **Poskus** (Girts Karlsons 83). Tr: Kakhaber **Tskhadadze**

Lech Poznan   1
Wichniarek [47]

Krzysztof **Kotorowski** - Seweryn **Gancarczyk•**, Bartosz **Bosacki**, Grzegorz **Wojtkowiak**, Marcin **Kikut•**, Tomasz **Bandrowski**, Sergey **Krivets**, Semir **Stilic** (Jacek Kielb 63), Slawomir **Peszko** (Jakub Wilk 90), Dimitrije **Injac** (Artur **Wichniarek** (Tomasz Mikolajczak 71). Tr: Jacek **Zielinski**

Pod Goricom, Podgorica
20-07-2010, 20:30, 2137, Sukhina RUS

Rudar Pljevlja   0

Milos **Radanovic** - Blazo **Igumanovic**, Vladan **Adzic•**, Veselin **Bojic**, Bojan **Ivanovic**, Dusan **Micic•**, (Nikola Sekulic 78), Nermin **Useni•**, Predrag **Brnovic** (Miroje **Jovanovic** 58), Nedjeljko **Vlahovic** (Ferid **Idrizovic** 46), Ivica **Jovanovic**, Predrag **Randelovic**. Tr: Nebojsa **Vignjevic**

Litex Lovech   4
Niflore [28], Jelenkovic [39], Bratu 2 [74 90]

Rodrigo **Galatto** - Alexandre **Barthe**, Petar **Zanev**, Ivaylo **Petkov**, Plamen **Nikolov**, Nikolaj **Bodurov•**, **Wellington•**, **Sandrinho** (Hristo Yanev 77), Nebojsa **Jelenkovic**, Wilfried **Niflore** (Florin Bratu 72), Ivelin **Popov** (Georgi Milanov 63). Tr: Angel **Chervenkov**

Partizan, Belgrade
14-07-2010, 20:45, 11 134, Skjerven NOR

Partizan Beograd   3
Tomic [29], Moreira [45], Cleo [59]

Radisa **Ilic** - Ivan **Stevanovic**, Marko **Jovanovic**, Aleksandar **Lazevski•**, Mladen **Krstajic**, Nemanja **Tomic**, Radosav **Petrovic** (Branislav Jovanovic 85), Almami **Moreira** (Aleksandar Davidov 75), Sasa **Ilic**, **Cleo**, Marko **Scepovic** (Milos Bogunovic 55). Tr: Aleksandar **Stanojevic**

Pyunik Yerevan   1
Yedigaryan [30]

Artur **Lesko** - Sargis **Hovsepyan**, Artur **Yuspashyan**, Vahagn **Minasyan•**, Artak **Yedigaryan** (Artur **Barseghyan** 90), Karlen **Mkrtchyan**, Gevorg **Ghazaryan**, David **Manoyan**, Yinka **Adedeji**, Pizelli, Hovhannes **Goharyan** (Mihran **Manasyan** 66). Tr: Vardan **Minasyan**

Daugava, Liepaja
13-07-2010, 19:00, 3330, Eisner AUT

Liepajas Metalurgs   0

Viktors **Spole** - Oskars **Klava•**, Jurica **Puljiz**, Maksims **Rafalskis•** (Jevgenijs Golovins 70), Tomas **Tamosauskas**, Pavels **Surnins**, Intars **Kirhners** (Igor Alekseev 54), Vitalijus **Kavaliauskas**, Deniss **Rakels**, Jurgis **Kalns**, Kristaps **Grebis**. Tr: Rudiger **Abramczik**

Sparta Praha   3
Kadlec [37], Wilfried 2 [51 58]

Jaromir **Blazek** - Tomas **Repka**, Niklas **Hoheneder**, Jiri **Kladrubsky**, Erich **Brabec**, Libor **Sionko**, Marek **Matejovsky**, Igor **Zofcak** (Kamil Vacek 65), Juraj **Kucka** (Jiri Jeslinek 78), Bony **Wilfried** (Milos Lacny 83), Vaclav **Kadlec**. Tr: Jozef **Chovanec**

Miejski, Poznan
21-07-2010, 20:00, 13 700, Mazic SRB

Lech Poznan   0 9p

Krzysztof **Kotorowski** - Seweryn **Gancarczyk**, Manuel **Arboleda**, Bartosz **Bosacki**, Grzegorz **Wojtkowiak**, Ivan **Durdevic** (Jakub Wilk 98), Sergey **Krivets**, Semir **Stilic•**, Slawomir **Peszko**, Dimitrije **Injac•**, Artur **Wichniarek** (Jacek Kielb 78). Tr: Jacek **Zielinski**

Inter Baku   0 8p

Georgi **Lomaia•** - **Accioly**, Vladimir **Levin•**, Ilia **Kandelaki**, Kakha **Mzhavanadze** (Arif Dashdemirov 71), Aleksandr **Chertoganov•**, Bronislav **Cervenka•**, Petar **Zlatinov•**, David **Odikadze**, Nizami **Hajiyev** (Dmitriy **Kruglov** 46), Robertas **Poskus** (Girts Karlsons• 84). Tr: Kakhaber **Tskhadadze**

Ta'Qali National, Ta'Qali
13-07-2010, 18:00, 688, Evans WAL

Birkirkara   0
Vukanac [1]

Ezequiel **Lovizon•** - Branko **Nisevic**, Nikolai **Vukanac** (Patrick Borg 72), Joseph **Zerafa•**, Paul **Fenech**, Carl **Pulo•** (Andrew Scicluna 81), Shaun **Bajada**, Michael **Galea**, Alan **Tabone**, Andrew **Decesare•** (Ryan Scicluna 85), Angus **Buhagiar•**. Tr: Paul **Zammit**

MSK Zilina   0

Martin **Dubravka** - Stanislav **Angelovic•**, Jozef **Piacek•**, Ondrej **Sourek•**, Patrik **Mraz•**, Robert **Jez**, Stefan **Zosak** (Vladimir Leitner 80), Emil **Rilke** (Pavol Poliacek 60), Tomas **Majtan** (Dominik Fotyik 68), Tomas **Oravec**, Bello **Babatounde**. Tr: Pavel **Hapal**

Hanrapetakan, Yerevan
21-07-2010, 17:00, 4500, Borski POL

Pyunik Yerevan   0

Artur **Lesko** - Varazdat **Haroyan•**, Sargis **Hovsepyan**, Artur **Yuspashyan•**, Artak **Yedigaryan** (Edgar **Manucharyan** 49), Karlen **Mkrtchyan**, Gevorg **Ghazaryan•**, David **Manoyan**, Yinka **Adedeji**, Pizelli, Hovhannes **Goharyan•** (Edgar Malakyan 61). Tr: Vardan **Minasyan**

Partizan Beograd   1
Cleo [45]

Radisa **Ilic** - Ivan **Stevanovic•**, Marko **Jovanovic**, Mladen **Krstajic** (Vojislav Stankovic 36), Joseph **Kizito•**, Nemanja **Tomic•**, Radosav **Petrovic** (Branislav Jovanovic 83), Almami **Moreira**, Sasa **Ilic**, **Cleo**, Marko **Scepovic** (Aleksandar Davidov 66). Tr: Aleksandar **Stanojevic**

Aukstaitija, Panevezys
14-07-2010, 18:00, 2500, Vollquartz DEN

Ekranas Panevezys   **1**

Radavicius [3]

Vytautas Cerniauskas - Dainius Glev020ckas•, Andrius Sidlauskas•, Dusan Matovic, Ramunas Radavicius•, Aurimas Kucys• (Zilvinas Banys• 85), Andrius Arlauskas, Giedrius Tomkevicius, Vits Rimkus, Stephen Ademolu (Tadas Markevicius 90), Serghei Pogreban (Egidijus Varnas 65). Tr: Valdas Urbonas

HJK Helsinki   **0**

Ville Wallen - Tuomas Kansikas, Peter Magnusson•, Juhani Ojala•, Medo, Rafinha, Sebastian Sorsa (Johannes Westo 83), Aki Riihilahti (Cheyne Fowler 76), Erfan Zeneli (Jarno Parikka 62), Dawda Bah, Danny Hoesen. Tr: Anntti Muurinen

---

Töölön, Helsinki
21-07-2010, 18:00, 6030, McDonald SCO

HJK Helsinki   **2**

Ojala [77], Sidlauskas OG [119]

Ville Wallen - Tuomas Kansikas, Pyry Karkkainen, Juhani Ojala, Medo, Rafinha, Sebastian Sorsa, Aki Riihilahti (Cheyne Fowler 100), Juho Makela (Erfan Zeneli 72), Jarno Parikka (Akseli Pelvas 63), Dawda Bah. Tr: Antti Muurinen

Ekranas Panevezys   **0**

Tadas Kauneckas - Dainius Gleveckas, Andrius Sidlauskas, Dusan Matovic, Ramunas Radavicius, Aurimas Kucys, Andrius Arlauskas (Marius Skinderis 90), Dominykas Galkevicius (Serghei Pogreban 58), Giedrius Tomkevicius, Vits Rimkus (Egidijus Varnas 68), Stephen Ademolu. Tr: Valdas Urbonas

---

Dalymount Park, Dublin
13-07-2010, 2314, Nihuis NED

Bohemians   **1**

Brennan [66]

Barry Murphy - Owen Heary, Connor Powell, Ken Oman, Brian Shelly•, Paul Keegan, Kilian Brennan, Ruaidhri Higgins, Raffael Cretaro• (Jason Byrne 75), Patrick Madden, Mark Quigley. Tr: Pat Fenlon

The New Saints   **0**

Paul Harrison - Danny Holmes, Christopher Marriott, Philip Baker, Steve Evans, Scott Ruscoe, Barry Hogan, Craig Jones•, Chris Sharp, Matthew Williams (Alex Darlington 83), Matthew Berkeley (Jamie Wood 77). Tr: Mike Davies

---

Park Hall, Oswestry
20-07-2010, 20:00, 1056, Vad HUN

The New Saints   **4**

Jones [6], Williams 2 [14 73], Sharp [20]

Paul Harrison - Danny Holmes, Christopher Marriott, Philip Baker, Steve Evans, Scott Ruscoe, Barry Hogan, Craig Jones, Chris Sharp• (Alex Darlington 90), Matthew Williams, Matthew Berkeley (Jamie Wood 89). Tr: Mike Davies

Bohemians   **0**

Barry Murphy - Owen Heary, Connor Powell• (Jason McGuinness• 46), Ken Oman, Brian Shelly, Paul Keegan•, Kilian Brennan, Ruaidhri Higgins (Glenn Cronin 46), Jason Byrne (Aaron Greene 67), Patrick Madden, Mark Quigley. Tr: Pat Fenlon

---

THIRD QUALIFYING ROUND

Stade de Suisse, Berne
28-07-20:15, 19 091, Moen NOR

BSC Young Boys   **2**

Dudar [18], Costanzo [89p]

Roman Burki - Emiliano Dudar, Scott Sutter, Christoph Spycher, Francois Affolter, Ammar Jemal, Thierry Doubai (Emmanuel Mayuka 83), Senad Lulic (Alberto Regazzoni 65), David Degen, Moreno Costanzo•, Henri Bienvenu (Marco Schneuwly 58). Tr: Vladimir Petkovic

Fenerbahçe   **2**

Emre [5], Stoch [42]

Volkan Demirel - Bekir Irtegun•, Onder Turaci•, Andre Santos, Fabio Bilica•, Emre Belozoglu• (Deivid 85), Colin Kazim-Richards••♦43, Alex• (Semih Senturk 80), Cristian, Miroslav Stoch, Gokhan Unal (Selcuk Sahin 72). Tr: Aykut Kocaman

---

Sükrü Saracoglu, Istanbul
4-08-2010, 20:15, 35 260, Braamhaar NED

Fenerbahçe   **0**

Volkan Demirel - Bekir Irtegun• (Gokhan Gonul 46), Ilhan Eker, Andre Santos, Fabio Bilica•, Emre Belozoglu•, Alex (Selcuk Sahin 46), Cristian, Miroslav Stoch••♦53, Gokhan Unal, Issiar Dia (Semih Senturk 81). Tr: Aykut Kocaman

BSC Young Boys   **1**

Bienvenu [40]

Marco Wolfli - Emiliano Dudar, Scott Sutter, Christoph Spycher, Francois Affolter•, Ammar Jemal•, Thierry Doubai (Mario Raimondi 70), Senad Lulic (Christian Schneuwly 78), David Degen•, Moreno Costanzo (Xavier Hochstrasser• 62), Henri Bienvenu. Tr: Vladimir Petkovic

---

GSP, Nicosia
27-07-2010, 18:00, 16 657, Vad HUN

Omonia Nicosia   **1**

LuaLua [91+]

Dragoslav Jevric - Hristos Karipidis, Iago Bouzon, Davidson, Giorgos Efrem, Konstantinos Makrides, Noel Kaseke• (Andreas Avraam 64), Ilias Charalambous, Michalis Konstantinou (Hernan Rengifo 82), Efstathios Aloneftis (Lomana LuaLua 46). Tr: Takis Lemonis

RB Austria Salzburg   **1**

Zarate [8]

Gerhard Tremmel - Rabiu Afolabi, Christian Schwegler•, Franz Schiemer• (Milan Dudic 86), Andreas Ulmer, Ibrahim Sekagya, David Mendes da Silva•, Dusan Svento (Jakob Jantscher 81), Christoph Leitgeb, Roman Wallner• (Somen Tchoyi 71), Gonzalo Zarate. Tr: Huub Stevens

---

Red Bull Arena, Salzburg
4-08-2010, 20:30, 14 400, Johannesson SWE

RB Austria Salzburg   **4**

Svento [21], Schiemer 2 [37 40], Boghossian [58]

Gerhard Tremmel - Rabiu Afolabi, Christian Schwegler, Franz Schiemer (Thomas Augustinussen 70), Ibrahim Sekagya, David Mendes da Silva• (Stefan Hierlander 82), Jakob Jantscher•, Dusan Svento, Christoph Leitgeb (Louis N'Gwat-Mahop 85), Gonzalo Zarate, Joaquin Boghossian•. Tr: Huub Stevens

Omonia Nicosia   **1**

Rengifo [91+]

Antonis Georgallides - Hristos Karipidis, Iago Bouzon, Davidson, Konstantinos Makrides, Noel Kaseke (Andreas Avraam• 67), Ilias Charalambous•, Leandro, Michalis Konstantinou (Hernan Rengifo 72), Lomana LuaLua (Giorgos Efrem 59), Efstathios Aloneftis. Tr: Takis Lemonis

---

Tcentralny, Aktobe
28-07-2010, 21:00, 12 100, Kever SUI

FK Aktobe   **1**

Smakov [67p]

Andrey Sidelnikov - Khalifa Ba, Petr Badlo, Samat Smakov, Emil Kenzhisariev, Alain Bono Mboune, Marat Khayrullin (Nikita Khokhlov 80), Andrey Karpovich•, Evgeniy Averchenko (Aslan Darabaev• 55), Titi Essomba, Ivan Peric• (Murat Tleshev 45). Tr: Vladimir Mukhanov

Hapoel Tel Aviv   **0**

Vincent Enyeama - Douglas•, Dedi Dayan, Omri Kende, Avihay Yadin, Walid Badir (Ben Sahar 57), Romain Rocchi (Yossi Shivhon• 68), Itay Shechter, Eran Zahavy, Maharan Lala• (Ben Sahar 57). Tr: Eli Guttmann

---

Bloomfield, Tel Aviv
3-08-2010, 20:00, 12 000, Schorgenhofer AUT

Hapoel Tel Aviv   **3**

Zahavi [16], Sahar [31], Ba OG [35]

Vincent Enyeama - Douglas, Omri Kende, Gal Shish•, Avihay Yadin, Yossi Shivhon (Romain Rocchi 64), Walid Badir•, Gil Vermouth, Itay Shechter, Ben Sahar (Maharan Lala 54), Eran Zahavy (Shay Abutbul 70). Tr: Eli Guttmann

FK Aktobe   **1**

Tleshev [90]

Andrey Sidelnikov - Khalifa Ba•, Petr Badlo•, Samat Smakov, Emil Kenzhisariev, Alain Bono Mboune•, Nikita Khokhlov (Anton Chichulin 56), Marat Khayrullin•, Evgeniy Averchenko (Murat Tleshev• 46), Titi Essomba, Ivan Peric•. Tr: Vladimir Mukhanov

Råsunda, Stockholm
28-07-2010, 20:45, 16 768, Kinhofer GER

AIK Stockholm 0

Ivan Turina• - Niklas Backman, Per Karlsson, Nils-Eric Johansson, Robert Ahman-Persson•, Helgi Danielsson (Viktor Lundberg 75), Daniel Tjernstrom, Kenny Pavey, Dulee Johnson, Goran Ljubojevic (Pontus Engblom 82), Mohamed Bangura•. Tr: Alex Miller

Rosenborg BK 1
Henriksen 33

Daniel Orlund - Mikael Lustig, Mikael Dorsin, Vadim Demidov, Kris Stadsgaard, Anthony Annan, Per Skjelbred, Markus Henriksen, Morten Moldskred (Trond Olsen 78), Steffen Iversen, Rade Prica (Fredrik Winsnes 72). Tr: Nils Arne Eggen

Lerkendal, Trondheim
4-08-2010, 20:45, 14 709, Iturralde ESP

Rosenborg BK 3
Prica 55, Demidov 64, Lustig 76

Daniel Orlund - Mikael Lustig, Mikael Dorsin, Vadim Demidov, Kris Stadsgaard, Anthony Annan, Per Skjelbred, Markus Henriksen, Morten Moldskred (Trond Olsen 55), Steffen Iversen (Roar Strand 74), Rade Prica (Mushaga Bakenga 82). Tr: Nils Arne Eggen

AIK Stockholm 0

Ivan Turina - Per Karlsson, Nils-Eric Johansson•, Walid Atta, Robert Ahman-Persson (Viktor Lundberg 69), Helgi Danielsson, Daniel Tjernstrom, Kenny Pavey, Dulee Johnson, Goran Ljubojevic (Antonio Flavio 59), Mohamed Bangura. Tr: Alex Miller

Gradski, Borisov
28-07-2010, 19:00, 5300, Tudor ROU

BATE Borisov 0

Sergey Veremko - Igor Shitov•, Aleksandr Yurevich, Artem Radkov, Maksim Bordachev, Dmitry Likhtarovich (Maksim Skavysh 77), Pavel Nekhaychik, Aleksandr Pavlov, Edgar Olekhnovich, Artem Kontsevoy (Renan Bressan 65), Vitaliy Rodionov (Dmitriy Baga 85). Tr: Viktor Goncharenko

FC København 0

Johan Wiland - Zdenek Pospech, Solvi Ottesen, William Kvist, Mikael Antonsson, Oscar Wendt, Hjalte Norregaard, Claudemir, Martin Vingaard, Cesar Santin (Jesper Gronkjaer 82), Dame N'Doye•. Tr: Stale Solbakken

Parken, Copenhagen
4-08-2010, 19:10, 15 533, Clattenburg ENG

FC København 3
Santin 2, Kvist 27, N'Doye 59

Johan Wiland - Zdenek Pospech, Solvi Ottesen•, William Kvist, Mikael Antonsson, Oscar Wendt, Hjalte Norregaard (Jesper Gronkjaer 54), Claudemir (Mathias Jorgensen 88), Martin Vingaard, Cesar Santin (Thomas Kristensen 80), Dame N'Doye. Tr: Stale Solbakken

BATE Borisov 2
Kontsevoy 40, Nyakhaychyk 44

Sergey Veremko - Sergey Sosnovskiy••♦92+, Aleksandr Yurevich, Artem Radkov, Maksim Bordachev (Dmitriy Baga 82), Dmitry Likhtarovich (Edgar Olekhnovich 61), Renan Bressan, Pavel Nekhaychik•, Aleksandr Pavlov• (Maksim Skavysh 69), Artem Kontsevoy, Vitaliy Rodionov. Tr: Viktor Goncharenko

Szusza Ferenc, Budapest
28-07-2010, 20:00, 5217, Muniz ESP

Debreceni VSC 0

Istvan Verpecz - Adam Komlosi, Marcell Fodor, Csaba Bernath, Mirsad Mijadinoski, Zoltan Kiss, Joszef Varga, Peter Czvitkovics, Laszlo Rezes (Balazs Farkas 54), Yannick Mbengono (Tibor Dombi 74), Adamo Coulibaly. Tr: Andras Herczeg

FC Basel 2
Stocker 34, Xhaka 92+

Franco Costanzo - Cagdas Atan, David Abraham, Behrang Safari, Samuel Inkoom, Benjamin Huggel, Valentin Stocker• (Granit Xhaka 88), Xherdan Shaqiri (Fwayo Tembo 62), Adilson Cabral•, Alexander Frei, Jacques Zoua (Federico Almerares 75). Tr: Thorsten Fink

St Jakob Park, Basel
4-08-2010, 19:45, 17 376, Bexborodov RUS

FC Basel 3
Cagdas Atan 26, Chipperfield 59, Shaqiri 64

Franco Costanzo - Cagdas Atan, David Abraham, Behrang Safari, Samuel Inkoom•, Benjamin Huggel (Granit Xhaka 87), Gilles Yapi-Yapo (Adilson Cabral 77), Scott Chipperfield (Federico Almerares 67), Xherdan Shaqiri, Fwayo Tembo, Jacques Zoua. Tr: Thorsten Fink

Debreceni VSC 1
Coulibaly 74

Istvan Verpecz - Adam Komlosi, Csaba Bernath, Mirsad Mijadinoski, Zoltan Kiss, Joszef Varga, Peter Czvitkovics (Balazs Farkas 81), Zsolt Laczko, Yannick Mbengono (Peter Kabat 67), Adamo Coulibaly, Tamas Kulcsar (Adam Bodi 67). Tr: Andras Herczeg

Sheriff, Tiraspol
28-07-2010, 20:00, 9150, Kakos GRE

Sheriff Tiraspol 1
Erokhin 35

Vladislav Stoyanov - Vladimir Volkov (Serhei Gheorghiev 88), Vazha Tarkhnishvili•, Ognjen Vranjes, Miral Samardzic, Nadson (Fred 32), Vladimir Brankovic, Alexandr Erokhin•, Milos Adamovic, Franca, Amath Diedhiou (Baco Nikolic 66). Tr: Andrey Sosnitskiy

Dinamo Zagreb 1
Sammir 3

Tomislav Butina - Luis Ibanez, Leonard Mesaric, Tomislav Barbaric••♦61, Leandro Cufre, Adrian Calello•, Etto, Sammir (Ilija Sivonjic 85), Mathias Chago, Milan Badelj (Dodo 69), Miroslav Slepicka (Dario Simic 63). Tr: Velimir Zajec

Maksimir, Zagreb
4-08-2010, 20:00, 7811, Braamhaar NED

Dinamo Zagreb 1 5p
Sammir 55p

Filip Loncaric - Leonard Mesaric (Luis Ibanez 46), Sime Vrsaljko, Leandro Cufre•, Arijan Ademi (Adrian Calello 76), Etto, Sammir, Milan Badelj•, Igor Biscan, Miroslav Slepicka, Ante Rukavina (Dodo 88). Tr: Velimir Zajec

Sheriff Tiraspol 1 6p
Volkov 16

Vladislav Stoyanov• - Vladimir Volkov, Ognjen Vranjes, Miral Samardzic•, Nadson (Alexandru Scripcenco 95), Vladimir Brankovic, Alexandr Erokhin, Fred• (Artiom Haciaturov 79), Milos Adamovic•, Franca, Amath Diedhiou (Baco Nikolic• 72). Tr: Andrey Sosnitskiy

Letna, Prague
27-07-2010, 20:30, 14 588, Tagliavento ITA

Sparta Praha 1
Brabec 75

Jaromir Blazek - Tomas Repka, Niklas Hoheneder, Jiri Kladrubsky, Erich Brabec, Manuel Pamic, Libor Sionko, Marek Matejovsky (Lukas Hejda 90), Juraj Kucka•, Bony Wilfried• (Lukas Tresnak 86), Vaclav Kadlec (Jiri Jeslinek 72). Tr: Jozef Chovanec

Lech Poznan 0

Krzysztof Kotorowski - Seweryn Gancarczyk, Manuel Arboleda, Bartosz Bosacki, Grzegorz Wojtkowiak•, Sergey Krivets (Tomasz Mikolajczak 84), Semir Stilic (Jakub Wilk 86), Kamil Drygas•, Slawomir Peszko•, Dimitrije Injac, Artur Wichniarek (Joel Tshibamba 77). Tr: Jacek Zielinski

Miejski, Poznan
4-08-2010, 20:00, 13 200, Fautrel FRA

Lech Poznan 0

Krzysztof Kotorowski - Seweryn Gancarczyk, Manuel Arboleda•, Bartosz Bosacki♦80, Grzegorz Wojtkowiak• (Jacek Kielb 86), Jakub Wilk (Joel Tshibamba 53), Sergey Krivets, Kamil Drygas (Semir Stilic 57), Slawomir Peszko, Dimitrije Injac, Artur Wichniarek. Tr: Jacek Zielinski

Sparta Praha 1
Kladrubsky 50p

Jaromir Blazek - Tomas Repka•, Niklas Hoheneder, Jiri Kladrubsky, Erich Brabec•, Manuel Pamic, Libor Sionko♦85, Marek Matejovsky♦80, Juraj Kucka (Lukas Hejda 75), Bony Wilfried• (Milos Lacny 90), Vaclav Kadlec (Igor Zofcak 67). Tr: Jozef Chovanec

Lovech Stadion, Lovech
27-07-2010, 19:00, 7000, Jakobsson ISL

Litex Lovech 1
Tom 79

Rodrigo Galatto - Alexandre Barthe•, Petar Zanev, Ivaylo Petkov, Plamen Nikolov•, Nikolaj Bodurov, Wellington (Iliya Milanov 89), Sandrinho (Florin Bratu 73), Nebojsa Jelenkovic (Hristo Yanev 85), Wilfried Niflore, Ivelin Popov. Tr: Angel Chervenkov

MSK Zilina 1
Majtan 65

Martin Dubravka - Lubomir Guldan, Vladimir Leitner, Jozef Piacek•, Ondrej Sourek, Robert Jez, Emil Rilke (Stefan Zosak 78), Tomas Majtan, Tomas Oravec• (Juraj Chupac 87), Momodou Ceesay (Ivan Lietava 89), Bello Babatounde. Tr: Pavel Hapal

Pod Dubnom, Zilina
4-08-2010, 19:30, 8123, Einwaller AUT

MSK Zilina 3
Rilke 52, Oravec 70, Ceesay 84

Martin Dubravka - Lubomir Guldan, Ondrej Sourek, Mario Pecalka, Patrik Mraz, Robert Jez, Emil Rilke (Pavol Poliacak 81), Tomas Majtan (Stefan Zosak 63), Tomas Oravec, Momodou Ceesay (Dominik Fotyik 90), Bello Babatounde. Tr: Pavel Hapal

Litex Lovech 1
Sandrinho 50

Rodrigo Galatto - Petar Zanev, Dzemal Berberovic•, Plamen Nikolov, Nikolaj Bodurov•, Hristo Yanev (Wellington 61), Sandrinho, Georgi Milanov, Nebojsa Jelenkovic•, Wilfried Niflore• (Florin Bratu 66), Ivelin Popov••♦53. Tr: Angel Chervenkov

Lobanovskiy, Dinamo, Kyiv
27-07-2010, 20:00, 14 503, Collum SCO

Dynamo Kyiv   **3**

Yarmolenko [19], Shevchenko [80], Zozulya [92+]

Denis **Boyko** - **Danilo Silva**, **Betao•**, Taras **Mikhalik**, Ognjen **Vukojevic**, Denys **Garmash**, Gerson **Magrao**, Roman **Eremenko** (Roman **Zozulya** 76), Andriy **Shevchenko**, Andriy **Yarmolenko**, Artem **Milevskiy** (Facundo **Bertoglio** 50). Tr: Valeriy **Gazzaev**

KAA Gent   **0**

Bojan **Jorgacevic** - Roy **Myrie** (Tim **Smolders** 73), Erlend **Hanstveit**, Stef **Wils**, Adriano **Duarte•**, Bernd **Thijs**, Christophe **Lepoint**, Christophe **Grondin**, Mbaye **Leye** (Shlomi **Arbeitman** 59), Yassine **El Ghanassi**, Stijn **De Smet•** (Elimane **Coulibaly** 83). Tr: Francky **Dury**

Jules Ottenstadion, Ghent
4-08-2010, 20:30, 6049, Cakir TUR

KAA Gent   **1**

Coulibaly [85]

Bojan **Jorgacevic** - Marko **Suler**, Roy **Myrie**, Kenny **Thompson•**, Adriano **Duarte•** (Shlomi **Arbeitman** 46), Bernd **Thijs**, Christophe **Lepoint** (Tim **Smolders** 69), Christophe **Grondin•**, Yassine **El Ghanassi**, Adnan **Custovic** (Zlatan **Ljubijankic** 46), Elimane **Coulibaly**. Tr: Francky **Dury**

Dynamo Kyiv   **3**

Harmash [32], Milevskiy [55], Husyev [90]

Denis **Boyko** - **Danilo Silva•**, **Betao**, Taras **Mikhalik**, Ognjen **Vukojevic**, Denys **Garmash**, Gerson **Magrao** (Badr **El Kaddouri•** 43), Roman **Eremenko** (Roman **Zozulya** 68), Andriy **Shevchenko**, Andriy **Yarmolenko** (Oleg **Gusev** 77), Artem **Milevskiy•**. Tr: Valeriy **Gazzaev**

Amsterdam ArenA, Amsterdam
28-07-2010, 20:45, 24 151, Chapron FRA

Ajax   **1**

Suarez [13]

Maarten **Stekelenburg** - Gregory **van der Wiel**, Toby **Alderweireld**, Jan **Vertonghen•**, Vurnon **Anita**, Eyong **Enoh•**, Siem de **Jong**, Urby **Emanuelson•** (Jeffrey **Sarpong** 79), Rasmus **Lindgren** (Demy **de Zeeuw** 62), Miralem **Sulejmani** (Christian **Eriksen** 67), Luis **Suarez•**. Tr: Martin **Jol**

PAOK Thessaloniki   **1**

Ivic [72]

Konstantinos **Chalkias** - Bruno **Cirillo**, Stilianos **Malezas**, Miroslaw **Sznaucner**, Anis **Boussaidi•**, Pablo **Garcia**, **Vitolo•**, Olivier **Sorlin**, Vladimir **Ivic** (Georgios **Fotakis** 75), Dimitrios **Salpingidis** (Thanasis **Papazoglou** 90), **Vieirinha**. Tr: Pavlos **Dermitzakis**

Toumba, Thessaloniki
4-08-2010, 21:45, 24 109, Velasco ESP

PAOK Thessaloniki   **3**

Vieirinha [16], Salpigidis [56], Ivic [91+]

Dario **Kresic** - Bruno **Cirillo•**, Pablo **Contreras**, Miroslaw **Sznaucner** (Lucio **Filomeno** 83), Anis **Boussaidi**, Pablo **Garcia**, **Vitolo** (Zlatan **Muslimovic** 63), Olivier **Sorlin**, Vladimir **Ivic•**, Dimitrios **Salpingidis**, **Vieirinha**. Tr: Pavlos **Dermitzakis**

Ajax   **3**

Suarez [48], De Jong [50], Lindgren [55]

Maarten **Stekelenburg** - Gregory **van der Wiel**, Toby **Alderweireld**, Jan **Vertonghen**, Vurnon **Anita•**, Siem **de Jong**, Urby **Emanuelson**, Rasmus **Lindgren**, Demy **de Zeeuw**, Miralem **Sulejmani** (Christian **Eriksen** 78), Luis **Suarez** (Oleguer 90). Tr: Martin **Jol**

Steaua, Bucharest
27-07-2010, 20:30, 12 000, Paixao POR

Unirea Urziceni   **0**

Giedrius **Arlauskis** - George **Galamaz•**, Valeriu **Bordeanu**, Vasile **Maftei**, Petre **Marin**, Sorin **Paraschiv•**, Razvan **Paduretu•**36, Laurentiu **Marinescu**, Sorin **Frunza** (Marius **Onofras** 72), Marius **Bilasco** (Maurice **Dale** 89), Adrian **Neaga** (Raul **Rusescu** 86). Tr: Roni **Levy**

Zenit St Petersburg   **3**

Vyacheslav **Malafeev** - Aleksandr **Anyukov**, Fernando **Meira**, Nicolas **Lombaerts**, Tomas **Hubocan**, Roman **Shirokov** (Viktor **Fayzulin** 70), Konstantin **Zyryanov** (Aleksandro **Rosina•** 59), Vladimir **Bystrov** (Maksim **Kannunikov** 80), **Danny**, Aleksandr **Kerzhakov**, Igor **Denisov•**. Tr: Luciano **Spalletti**

Petrovsky, Saint Petersburg
4-08-2010, 20:30, 21 100, Dean ENG

Zenit St Petersburg   **1**

Danny [33]

Vyacheslav **Malafeev•** - Aleksandr **Anyukov•**, Fernando **Meira**, Nicolas **Lombaerts**, Tomas **Hubocan•**, Roman **Shirokov•**, (Viktor **Fayzulin** 64), Konstantin **Zyryanov**, Vladimir **Bystrov** (Alessandro **Rosina** 46), **Danny**, Aleksandr **Kerzhakov** (Maksim **Kannunikov** 77), Igor **Denisov**. Tr: Luciano **Spalletti**

Unirea Urziceni   **0**

Giedrius **Arlauskis** - George **Galamaz**, Epaminonda **Nicu**, Pablo **Brandan**, Valeriu **Bordeanu**, Vasile **Maftei**, Laurentiu **Marinescu**, Sorin **Frunza** (Marius **Onofras** 88), Marius **Bilasco**, Raul **Rusescu** (Adrian **Neaga** 58), **Semedo** (Maurice **Dale** 53). Tr: Roni **Levy**

Municipal, Braga
28-07-2010, 20:00, 12 295, Gumienny BEL

Sporting Braga   **3**

Alan [26p], Echiejile [76], Matheus [88]

Mario **Felgueiras** - Alberto **Rodriguez**, **Moises**, Miguel **Garcia**, Uwa **Echiejile**, Andres **Madrid**, Leandro **Salino•**, **Vandinho**, Paulo **Cesar**, **Lima** (Matheus 66), **Alan** (Heldre **Barbosa** 90). Tr: **Domingos**

Celtic   **0**

Lukasz **Zaluska** - Jos **Hooiveld•**, **Cha** Du Ri, Charlie **Mulgrew•**, Glenn **Loovens•**, Efrain **Juarez** (James **Forrest** 79), Scott **Brown**, Shaun **Maloney** (Daryl **Murphy** 71), Joe **Ledley**, **Ki** Sung Yong•, Georgios **Samaras**. Tr: Neil **Lennon**

Parkhead, Glasgow
4-08-2010, 19:45, 53 592, Bebek CRO

Celtic   **2**

Hooper [52], Juarez [79]

Lukasz **Zaluska** - Jos **Hooiveld•**, **Cha** Du Ri, Charlie **Mulgrew** (Marc-Antoine **Fortune** 46), Glenn **Loovens**, Efrain **Juarez**, Scott **Brown•** (Pat **McCourt** 88), Shaun **Maloney** (Daryl **Murphy** 64), Joe **Ledley**, Gary **Hooper**, Georgios **Samaras**. Tr: Neil **Lennon**

Sporting Braga   **1**

Paulo Cesar [20]

Mario **Felgueiras** - Alberto **Rodriguez•**, **Moises**, Miguel **Garcia•**, Uwa **Echiejile•**, Andres **Madrid** (Paulao 86), Leandro **Salino** (Albert **Meyong** 90), **Vandinho**, Paulo **Cesar**, **Alan**, **Matheus•** (Lima 67). Tr: **Domingos**

Partizan, Belgrade
28-07-2010, 20:45, 14 350, Yefet ISR

Partizan Beograd   **3**

Iliev [8], Sasa Ilic [42], Costanzo [89p]

Radisa **Ilic** - Ivan **Stevanovic**, Marko **Jovanovic**, Aleksandar **Lazevski**, Mladen **Krstajic** (Vojislav 73), Nemanja **Tomic**, Radosav **Petrovic**, Almami **Moreira** (Aleksandar 46), Sasa **Ilic** (Branislav **Jovanovic•** 69), **Cleo**, Ivica **Iliev**. Tr: Aleksandar **Stanojevic**

HJK Helsinki   **0**

Ville **Wallen** - Tuomas **Kansikas**, Pyry **Karkkainen**, Juhani **Ojala**, **Medo•**, Cheyne **Fowler** (Jarno **Parikka** 46), **Rafinha**, Sebastian **Sorsa**, Aki **Riihilahti**, Erfan **Zeneli** (Johnnes **Westo** 27), Juho **Makela** (Akseli **Pelvas** 73). Tr: Antti **Muurinen**

Töölön, Helsinki
4-08-2010, 19:00, 4230, Kralovec CZE

HJK Helsinki   **1**

Kamara [39]

Ville **Wallen** - Tuomas **Kansikas**, Peter **Magnusson**, Juhani **Ojala**, **Medo•**, **Rafinha**, Sebastian **Sorsa**, Aki **Riihilahti** (Cheyne **Fowler** 33), Akseli **Pelvas** (Juho **Makela** 62), Jarno **Parikka** (Johannes **Westo** 75), Dawda **Bah**. Tr: Antti **Muurinen**

Partizan Beograd   **2**

Cleo 2 [9] [92+]

Radisa **Ilic** - Ivan **Stevanovic**, Marko **Jovanovic•**, Aleksandar **Lazevski**, Mladen **Krstajic** (Vojislav **Stankovic** 82), Nemanja **Tomic**, Radosav **Petrovic** (Branislav 70), Sasa **Ilic**, Milan **Smiljanic**, **Cleo**, Ivica **Iliev** (Aleksandar **Davidov** 62). Tr: Aleksandar **Stanojevic**

Racecourse Ground, Wrexham
27-07-2010, 19:45, 2486, Ceferin SVN

The New Saints   **1**

Jones [52]

Paul **Harrison** - Danny **Holmes**, Christopher **Marriott** (Tommy **Holmes** 21), Philip **Baker**, Steve **Evans**, Scott **Ruscoe**, Barry **Hogan**, Chris **Sharp** (Alex **Darlington** 84), Matthew **Williams**, Matthew **Berkeley** (Christian **Sergeant** 78). Tr: Mike **Davies**

RSC Anderlecht   **3**

Kljestan [7], Legear [18], Suarez [73]

Silvio **Proto** - Ondrej **Mazuch** (Jan **Lecjaks** 83), Olivier **Deschacht**, Roland **Juhasz**, Lucas **Biglia**, Moubarak **Boussoufa•**, Jonathan **Legear**, Cheikhou **Kouyate**, Sacha **Kljestan** (Kanu 87), Guillaume **Gillet**, Matias **Suarez** (Tom **De Sutter** 7). Tr: Ariel **Jacobs**

Constant Vanden Stock, Brussels
3-08-2010, 20:30, 19 338, Balaj ROU

RSC Anderlecht   **3**

De Sutter [17], Lukaku 2 [69] [74]

Silvio **Proto** - Roland **Juhasz**, Victor **Bernardez**, Nemanja **Rnic**, Jan **Lecjaks**, Thomas **Chatelle**, Lukas **Marecek**, Sacha **Kljestan** (Aeron **Edwards** 73), Matias **Suarez** (Christophe **Gillet** 46), Tom **De Sutter** (Romelu **Lukaku** 59), Pablo **Chavarria**. Tr: Ariel **Jacobs**

The New Saints   **0**

Paul **Harrison** - Danny **Holmes**, Philip **Baker**, Steve **Evans** (Aeron **Edwards** 73), Tommy **Holmes•**, Scott **Ruscoe**, Barry **Hogan**, Craig **Jones**, Chris **Sharp** (Alex **Darlington** 83), Matthew **Williams**, Jamie **Wood** (Christian **Sergeant** 87). Tr: Mike **Davies**

PLAY-OFF ROUND

Stade de Suisse, Berne
17-08-2010, 20:45 30 166, De Bleeckere BEL

BSC Young Boys   **3**
Lulic [4], Bienvenu [13], Hochstrasser [28]

Marco Wolfli - Scott Sutter, Francois Affolter, Ammar Jemal, Christoph Spycher - Thierry Doubai, Xavier Hochstrasser - David Degen (Mario Raimondi 89), Moreno Costanzo (Christian Schneuwly 65), Senad Lulic - Henri Bienvenu•. Tr: Vladimir Petkovic

Tottenham Hotspur   **2**
Bassong [42], Pavlyuchenko [83]

Heurelho Gomes - Vedran Corluka, Sebastien Bassong•, Michael Dawson, Benoit Assou-Ekotto• (Tom Huddlestone 35) - Giovani Dos Santos, Wilson Palacios, Luka Modric (Niko Kranjcar 46), Gareth Bale - Jermain Defoe (Robbie Keane 66), Roman Pavlyuchenko. Tr: Harry Redknapp

---

White Hart Lane, London
25-08-2010, 19:45, 34 709, Duhamel FRA

Tottenham Hotspur   **4**
Crouch [3 5 61 78p], Defoe [32]

Heurelho Gomes (Carlo Cudicini 46) - Vedran Corluka, Michael Dawson, Ledley King, Benoit Assou-Ekotto - Aaron Lennon, Tom Huddlestone, Wilson Palacios•, Gareth Bale (Niko Kranjcar 82) - Peter Crouch, Jermain Defoe (Roman Pavlyuchenko• 62). Tr: Harry Redknapp

BSC Young Boys   **0**

Marco Wolfli - Scott Sutter (Alberto Regazzoni 61), Ammar Jemal, Francois Affolter, Christoph Spycher - David Degen•, Xavier Hochstrasser, Thierry Doubai (Christian Schneuwly 82), Senad Lulic••◆77 - Moreno Costanzo (Marco Schneuwly 61) - Henri Bienvenu. Tr: Vladimir Petkovic

---

Weserstadion, Bremen
18-08-2010, 20:45 25 276, Lannoy FRA

Werder Bremen   **3**
Fritz [51], Frings [67p], Pizarro [69]

Tim Wiese - Petri Pasanen (Sebastian Boenisch 77), Per Mertesacker, Sebastian Prodl, Clemens Fritz• - Torsten Frings - Philipp Bargfrede, Aaron Hunt (Marko Marin 85), Tim Borowski - Claudio Pizarro, Hugo Almeida (Marko Arnautovic 88). Tr: Thomas Schaaf

Sampdoria   **1**
Pazzini [90]

Gianluca Curci - Massimo Volta•, Daniele Gastaldello, Stefano Lucchini••66, Reto Ziegler• - Franco Semioli (Marius Stankevicius 68), Angelo Palombo, Fernando Tissone (Andrea Poli 60), Daniele Mannini (Stefano Guberti 65) - Antonio Cassano•, Giampaolo Pazzini. Tr: Domenico Di Carlo

---

Luigi Ferraris, Genoa
24-08-2010, 20:45 25 574, Kassai HUN

Sampdoria   **3**
Pazzini 2 [8 13], Cassano [85]

Gianluca Curci - Marius Stankevicius, Massimo Volta, Daniele Gastaldello•, Reto Ziegler - Franco Semioli, Angelo Palombo•, Daniele Dessena•, Stefano Guberti (Fernando Tissone 66) - Giampaolo Pazzini, Antonio Cassano (Nicola Pozzi 90). Tr: Domenico Di Carlo

Werder Bremen   **2**
Rosenborg [93+], Pizarro [100]

Tim Wiese - Clemens Fritz, Per Mertesacker, Sebastian Prodl•, Petri Pasanen (Sebastian Boenisch 79) - Philipp Bargfrede, Torsten Frings - Tim Borowski (Marko Arnautovic• 63), Claudio Pizarro•, Marko Marin - Sandro Wagner (Markus Rosenberg 72). Tr: Thomas Schaaf

---

Red Bull Arena, Salzburg
18-08-2010, 20:45, 18 900, Proenca POR

RB Austria Salzburg   **2**
Pokrivac [28], Wallner [67p]

Gerhard Tremmel - Dusan Svento, Rabiu Afolabi, Ibrahim Sekagya, Christian Schwegler - Nikola Pokrivac, Franz Schiemer• (Alan 67) - Gonzalo Zarate (Joaquin N'Gwat-Mahop 78), Christoph Leitgeb, Jakob Jantscher• - Joaquin Boghossian (Roman Wallner 59). Tr: Huub Stevens

Hapoel Tel Aviv   **3**
Enyeama [3p], Sahar [44], Shechter [53]

Vincent Enyeama• - Omri Kende•, Douglas, Walid Badir, Dedi Ben Dayan - Eran Zahavy, Avihay Yadin, Yossi Shivhon• (Romain Rocchi 72), Gil Vermouth (Bevan Fransman 90) - Ben Sahar (Victor Merey 79), Itay Shechter•. Tr: Eli Guttmann

---

Bloomfield, Tel Aviv
24-08-2010, 21:45, 13 348, Vink NED

Hapoel Tel Aviv   **1**
Zahavi [92+]

Vincent Enyeama - Omri Kende•, Douglas, Walid Badir, Dedi Ben Dayan - Eran Zahavy, Avihay Yadin, Romain Rocchi (Shay Abutbul 74), Gil Vermouth - Ben Sahar (Gal Shish 90), Victor Merey (Bevan Fransman 65). Tr: Eli Guttmann

RB Austria Salzburg   **1**
Douglas OG [42]

Gerhard Tremmel - Dusan Svento, Rabiu Afolabi, Ibrahim Sekagya, Christian Schwegler - Nikola Pokrivac, David Mendes da Silva - Louis N'Gwat-Mahop• (Alan 65), Christoph Leitgeb, Gonzalo Zarate - Roman Wallner (Joaquin Boghossian 74). Tr: Huub Stevens

---

Lerkendal, Tronheim
17-08-2010, 20:45, 18 822, Rocchi ITA

Rosenborg BK   **2**
Iversen [23], Henriksen [57]

Daniel Orlund - Mikael Lustig, Kris Stadsgaard, Vadim Demidov, Mikael Dorsin - Anthony Annan• - Per Skjelbred, Steffen Iversen (Fredrik Winsnes 85), Markus Henriksen - Trond Olsen• (Mushaga Bakenga 65), Rade Prica. Tr: Nils Arne Eggen

FC København   **1**
Gronkjær [84]

Johan Wiland - Zdenek Pospech, Mathias Jorgensen, Mikael Antonsson, Oscar Wendt - William Kvist•, Claudemir, Thomas Kristensen (Hjalte Norregaard 67), Martin Vingaard• (Martin Bergvold 67) - Dame N'Doye, Jesper Gronkjær. Tr: Stale Solbakken

---

Parken, Copenhagen
25-08-2010, 20:45, 31 180, Brych GER

FC København   **1**
Ottesen [33]

Johan Wiland - Zdenek Pospech, Solvi Ottesen, Mikael Antonsson, Oscar Wendt - Claudemir, William Kvist, Martin Vingaard (Mathias Jorgensen 90), Jesper Gronkjær (Peter Larsson 90) - Dame N'Doye, Cesar Santin (Hjalte Norregaard 67). Tr: Stale Solbakken

Rosenborg BK   **0**

Daniel Orlund - Mikael Lustig, Kris Stadsgaard•, Simen Wangberg (Roar Strand 46), Mikael Dorsin - Vadim Demidov - Per Skjelbred (Fredrik Winsnes 63), Markus Henriksen• - Trond Olsen (Morten Moldskred 77), Steffen Iversen, Rade Prica. Tr: Nils Arne Eggen

---

St Jakob-Park, Basel
18-08-2010, 20:45, 13 460, Hauge NOR

FC Basel   **1**
Stocker [54]

Franco Costanzo - Cagdas Atan, David Abraham, Behrang Safari, Samuel Inkoom, Benjamin Huggel, Gilles Yapi-Yapo, Valentin Stocker, Xherdan Shaqiri (Fwayo Tembo 71), Alexander Frei (Scott Chipperfield 88), Jacques Zoua• (Federico Almerares 80). Tr: Thorsten Fink

Sheriff Tiraspol   **0**

Vladislav Stoyanov - Vladimir Volkov (Serhei Gheorghiev 90), Ognjen Vranjes•, Miral Samardzic•, Nadson, Vladimir Brankovic•, Alexandr Erokhin••86, Benjamin Balima, Florent Rouamba•, Milos Adamovic (Artiom Haciaturov 79), Amath Diedhiou (Marko Durovic 57). Tr: Andrey Sosnitskiy

---

Sheriff, Tiraspol
24-08-2010, 21:45, 12 300, Hansson SWE

Sheriff Tiraspol   **0**

Vladislav Stoyanov - Ognjen Vranjes•, Vazha Tarkhnishvili••◆76, Nadson, Vladimir Volkov• - Florent Rouamba - Milos Adamovic, Fred (Marko Durovic 76) - Benjamin Balima, Franca (Artiom Haciaturov 79), Amath Diedhiou (Baco Nikolic 66). Tr: Andrey Sosnitskiy

FC Basel   **3**
Streller [74], Frei 2 [80 87]

Franco Costanzo - Samuel Inkoom, David Abraham, Cagdas Atan•, Behrang Safari - Samuel Zoua, Benjamin Huggel, Gilles Yapi-Yapo (Beg Ferati 86), Valentin Stocker (Xherdan Shaqiri 85) - Alexander Frei•, Marco Streller (Scott Chipperfield 78). Tr: Thorsten Fink

---

Letna, Prague
17-08-2010, 20:45, 18 744, Atkinson ENG

Sparta Praha   **0**

Jaromir Blazek - Clovis Adiaba, Tomas Repka•, Erich Brabec•, Manuel Pamic - Niklas Hoheneder - Igor Zofcak (Martin Zeman 77), Juraj Kucka, Stepan Vachousek• (Jiri Jeslinek 90), Milos Lacny (Lukas Tresnak 68) - Leonard Kweuke. Tr: Jozef Chovanec

MSK Zilina   **2**
Cessay [51], Oravec [73]

Martin Dubravka - Lubomir Guldan, Jozef Piacek, Mario Pecalka, Patrik Mraz - Emil Rilke (Stefan Zosak 79), Bello Babatounde, Robert Jez, Tomas Majtan (Pavol Poliacek 88) - Momodou Ceesay• (Ondrej Sourek 90), Tomas Oravec. Tr: Pavel Hapal

---

Pod Dubnom, Zilina
25-08-2010, 20:45, 10 892, Benquerenca POR

MSK Zilina   **1**
Ceesay [18]

Martin Dubravka - Lubomir Guldan, Mario Pecalka•, Jozef Piacek, Patrik Mraz - Emil Rilke• (Stefan Zosak 90), Bello Babatounde, Robert Jez, Tomas Majtan (Pavol Poliacek 74) - Momodou Ceesay (Sergio Vittor 80), Tomas Oravec. Tr: Pavel Hapal

Sparta Praha   **0**

Jaromir Blazek - Clovis Adiaba (Leonard Kweuke 46), Niklas Hoheneder, Lukas Hejda, Manuel Pamic (Lukas Tresnak 86) - Jiri Kladruhskye - Libor Sionko (Pavel Kaderabek 61), Juraj Kucka•, Stepan Vachousek•, Ladislav Krejci - Bony Wilfried. Tr: Jozef Chovanec

Lobanovski Dynamo, Kyiv
17-08-2010, 21:45, 16 500, Busacca SUI
Dynamo Kyiv   **1**
Gusev [66]
Maksim **Koval** - Leandro Almeida, **Betao**, Taras
Mikhalik, Goran **Popov** - Roman **Eremenko**, Ognjen
Vukojevic• - Oleg **Gusev** (Danilo Silva 82), Denys
Garmash••♦56, Andriy **Yarmolenko** (Andre 70),
Andriy **Shevchenko** (Badr El Kaddouri 77). Tr: Valeriy
Gazzaev
Ajax   **1**
Vertonghen [57]
Maarten **Stekelenburg** - Gregory van der **Wiel**,
Oleguer, Jan **Vertonghen**, Vurnon **Anita•** (Miralem
Sulejmani 61) - Eyong **Enoh** (Christian **Eriksen** 69),
Siem de **Jong**, Demy de **Zeeuw** - Luis **Suarez**, Mounir
El Hamdaoui, Urby **Emanuelson**. Tr: Martin **Jol**

Amsterdam ArenA, Amsterdam
25-08-2010, 20:45, 50 249, Undiano ESP
Ajax   **2**
Suarez [43], El Hamdaoui [75]
Maarten **Stekelenburg** - Gregory van der **Wiel**, Toby
Alderweireld•, Jan **Vertonghen•**, Urby **Emanuelson** -
Eyong **Enoh**, Siem de **Jong**, Demy de **Zeeuw** - Luis
Suarez•, Mounir **El Hamdaoui** (Andre Ooijer 85),
Christian **Eriksen** (Miralem **Sulejmani** 73). Tr: Martin
Jol
Dynamo Kyiv   **1**
Shevchenko [84p]
Maksim **Koval** - Danilo **Silva•**, Taras **Mikhalik**, Evgen
Khacheridi, Goran **Popov** - Oleg **Gusev•** (Milos
Ninkovic 76), Roman **Eremenko•**, Ognjen
Vukojevic• (Andre 88), Andriy **Yarmolenko** - Andriy
Shevchenko•, Artem **Milevskiy** (Guilherme 86).
Tr: Valeriy **Gazzaev**

Petrovsky, Saint Petersburg
17-08-2010, 20:30, 21 405, Kuipers NED
Zenit St Petersburg   **1**
Kerzhakov [3]
Vyacheslav **Malafeev** - Aleksandr **Anyukov**, Bruno
Alves, Nicolas **Lombaerts**, Tomas **Hubocan** - Sergey
Semak (Konstantin **Zyryanov** 89), Igor **Denisov**,
Roman **Shirokov** - Danko **Lazovic** (Szabolcs **Huszti**
60), Aleksandr **Kerzhakov** (Aleksandr **Bukharov** 78),
Danny•. Tr: Luciano **Spalletti**
AJ Auxerre   **0**

Olivier **Sorin** - Cedric **Hengbart**, Adama **Coulibaly**,
Jean-Pascal **Mignot•**, Stephane **Grichting** - Benoit
Pedretti, Delvin **Ndinga** - Dennis **Oliech** (Julien
Quercia 90), Anthony **Le Tallec•**, Valter **Birsa** (Roy
Contout• 70) - Ireneusz **Jelen**. Tr: Jean **Fernandez**

Abbé-Deschamps, Auxerre
25-08-2010, 20:45, 15 277, Skomina SVN
AJ Auxerre   **2**
Hengbart [9], Jelen [53]
Olivier **Sorin** - Cedric **Hengbart•**, Adama **Coulibaly**,
Jean-Pascal **Mignot**, Stephane **Grichting** - Benoit
Pedretti, Delvin **Ndinga** - Dennis **Oliech** (Kamel
Chafni 86), Anthony **Le Tallec** (Valter **Birsa** 64), Roy
Contout• - Ireneusz **Jelen**. Tr: Jean **Fernandez**
Zenit St Petersburg   **0**

Vyacheslav **Malafeev♦**65 - Aleksandr **Anyukov•**,
Bruno **Alves•**, Fernando **Meira** (Aleksandr **Bukharov**
79), Tomas **Hubocan••♦**80 - Konstantin **Zyryanov**
(Danko **Lazovic** 55), Sergey **Semak•**, Roman
Shirokov - Vladimir **Bystrov•** (Yuriy **Zhevnov** 67),
Aleksandr **Kerzhakov**, **Danny**. Tr: Luciano **Spalletti**

Municipal, Braga
18-08-2010, 19:45, 16 646, Stark GER
Sporting Braga   **1**
Matheus [62]
Felipe - Miguel **Garcia•**, **Moises**, Alberto **Rodriguez**,
(**Silvio** 46), Uwa **Echiejile** - Leandro **Salino**,
Vandinho, Luis **Aguiar** (**Lima** 57) - **Alan**, **Matheus**
(**Elton** 75), Paulo **Cesar•**. Tr: Domingos **Paciencia**
Sevilla   **0**

Andres **Palop** - Mouhamadou **Dabo**, Federico **Fazio**,
Julien **Escude•**, Fernando **Navarro•** - Jesus **Navas**,
Didier **Zokora**, **Renato** (Luca **Cigarini** 83), Diego
Capel• (Diego **Perotti** 70) - Luis **Fabiano**, Frederic
Kanoute (Alvaro **Negredo** 80). Tr: Antonio **Alvarez**

Sanchez Pizjuan, Seville
24-08-2010, 20:45,
Sevilla   **3**
Luis Fabiano [60], Jesus Navas [84], Kaoute [91+]
Andres **Palop** - Abdoulay **Konko** (**Renato** 61),
Federico **Fazio**, Julien **Escude•**, Mouhamadou **Dabo**
(Alvaro **Negredo** 78) - Jesus **Navas**, Didier **Zokora•**,
Luca **Cigarini** (Jose **Carlos** 61), Diego **Perotti•** -
Frederic **Kanoute**, Luis **Fabiano**. Tr: Antonio **Alvarez**
Sporting Braga   **4**
Matheus [31], Lima 3 [58] [85] [90]
Felipe - **Silvio**, **Moises**, Alberto **Rodriguez**, Uwa
Echiejile• - **Alan**, Leandro **Salino•** (**Vandinho**, Luis
Aguiar• (**Lima** 55), Paulo **Cesar** (**Paulao** 68) -
Matheus (**Elton** 80). Tr: Domingos **Paciencia**

Partizan, Belgrade
18-08-2010, 20:45, 28 565, Larsen DEN
Partizan Beograd   **2**
Cleo [57], Lecjaks OG [64]
Radisa **Ilic** - Ivan **Stevanovic**, Marko **Jovanovic**,
Mladen **Krstajic**, Aleksandar **Lazevski** - Radosav
Petrovic, Almami **Moreira** (Milan **Smiljanic** 53) -
Nemanja **Tomic** (Aleksandar **Davidov** 74), Sasa **Ilic**,
Ivica **Iliev** (Milos **Bogunovic** 87) - **Cleo**.
Tr: Aleksandar **Stanojevic**
RSC Anderlecht   **2**
Gillet [54], Juhasz [66]
Silvio **Proto** - Ondrej **Mazuch**, Olivier **Deschacht**,
Roland **Juhasz**, Jan **Lecjaks** - Jan **Polak** (Ziguy
Badibanga 90), Cheikhou **Kouyate•**, Guillaume
Gillet• - Matias **Suarez**, Romelu **Lukaku** (Kanu 61),
Moubarak **Boussoufa** (Lukas **Marecek** 84). Tr: Ariel
Jacobs

Constant Vanden Stock, Brussels
24-08-2010, 20:45, 19 551, Thomson SCO
RSC Anderlecht   **2 2p**
Lukaku [64], Gillet [71]
Silvio **Proto** - Guillaume **Gillet**, Roland **Juhasz**, Ondrej
Mazuch, Olivier **Deschacht•** - Matias **Suarez**, Lucas
Biglia, Cheikhou **Kouyate•** (Jonathan **Legear** 60), Jan
Polak - Romelu **Lukaku•**, Moubarak **Boussoufa**.
Tr: Ariel **Jacobs**
Partizan Beograd   **2 3p**
Cleo 2 [15] [53]
Radisa **Ilic** - Ivan **Stevanovic•**, Marko **Jovanovic•**,
Mladen **Krstajic**, Aleksandar **Lazevski** - Nemanja
Tomic (Vojislav **Stankovic** 82), Radosav **Petrovic•**,
Milan **Smiljanic**, Sasa **Ilic** (Aleksandar **Davidov•** 19)
- **Cleo•**, Ivica **Iliev** (Milos **Bogunovic** 101).
Tr: Aleksandar **Stanojevic**

GROUP A		Pl	W	D	L	F	A	Pts	ENG	ITA	NED	GER
Tottenham Hotspur	ENG	6	3	2	1	18	11	**11**		3-1	4-1	3-0
Internazionale	ITA	6	3	1	2	12	11	**10**	4-3		1-0	4-0
FC Twente Enschede	NED	6	1	3	2	9	11	**6**		2-2		1-1
Werder Bremen	GER	6	1	2	3	6	12	**5**	2-2		0-2	

Die Grolsch Veste, Enschede
14-09-2010, 20:45, 23 800, Proenca POR

FC Twente Enschede   **2**
Janssen [20], Milito OG [30]

Nikolai Mihailov - Roberto Rosales, Douglas•, Peter Wisgerhof, Dwight Tiendalli - Wout Brama, Luuk de Jong, Theo Janssen - Bryan Ruiz, Marc Janko (Emir Bajrami 78), Nacer Chadli (Denny Landzaat 88). Tr: Michel Preud'homme

Internazionale   **2**
Sneijder [13], Eto'o [41]

Julio Cesar - Maicon•, Lucio, Walter Samuel, Javier Zanetti - Esteban Cambiasso, McDonald Mariga - Samuel Eto'o, Wesley Sneijder, Goran Pandev (Coutinho 61) - Diego Milito (Sulley Ali Muntari 87). Tr: Rafael Benitez

---

San Siro, Milan
29-09-2010, 20:45, 48 126, Undiano ESP

Internazionale   **4**
Eto'o 3 [21 27 81], Sneijder [34]

Julio Cesar (Luca Castellazzi 46) - Maicon, Ivan Cordoba, Lucio (Davide Santon 62), Cristian Chivu - Dejan Stankovic (Obi Chukwuma 80), Esteban Cambiasso - Coutinho, Wesley Sneijder, Jonathan Biabiany - Samuel Eto'o. Tr: Rafael Benitez

Werder Bremen   **0**

Tim Wiese - Wesley, Sebastian Prodl•, Per Mertesacker, Mikael Silvestre - Philipp Bargfrede, Daniel Jensen• - Marko Arnautovic, Tim Borowski (Petri Pasanen 46), Marko Marin (Aaron Hunt 63) - Hugo Almeida (Sandro Wagner 77). Tr: Thomas Schaaf

---

White Hart Lane, London
2-11-2010, 19:45, 34 103, Kassai HUN

Tottenham Hotspur   **3**
Van der Vaart [18], Crouch [61], Pavlyuchenko [89]

Carlo Cudicini - Alan Hutton•, William Gallas, Younes Kaboul, Benoit Assou-Ekotto - Aaron Lennon (Wilson Palacios 85), Tom Huddlestone, Luka Modric•, Gareth Bale - Rafael van der Vaart (Jermaine Jenas• 46) - Peter Crouch (Roman Pavlyuchenko 76). Tr: Harry Redknapp

Internazionale   **1**
Eto'o [80]

Luca Castellazzi - Maicon, Lucio•, Walter Samuel•, Cristian Chivu• - Sulley Ali Muntari (Obiora Nwankwo 53), Javier Zanetti - Jonathan Biabiany (Coutinho 64), Wesley Sneijder, Goran Pandev (Diego Milito 71) - Samuel Eto'o. Tr: Rafael Benitez

---

White Hart Lane, London
24-11-2010, 19:45, 33 546, Benquerenca POR

Tottenham Hotspur   **3**
Kaboul [6], Modric [45], Crouch [79]

Heurelho Gomes - Alan Hutton, William Gallas, Younes Kaboul, Benoit Assou-Ekotto - Aaron Lennon, Jermaine Jenas (Wilson Palacios 19), Luka Modric, Gareth Bale (Niko Kranjcar 81) - Roman Pavlyuchenko (Jermain Defoe 57), Peter Crouch. Tr: Harry Redknapp

Werder Bremen   **0**

Tim Wiese - Clemens Fritz•, Sebastian Prodl•, Per Mertesacker, Dominik Schmidt - Felix Kroos• (Onur Ayik 55), Daniel Jensen (Petri Pasanen 86), Philipp Bargfrede, Marko Marin - Aaron Hunt (Lennart Thy 79) - Sandro Wagner•. Tr: Thomas Schaaf

---

Weserstadion, Bremen
14-09-2010, 20:45, 30 344, Busacca SUI

Werder Bremen   **2**
Almeida [43], Marin [47]

Tim Wiese - Clemens Fritz, Petri Pasanen, Sebastian Prodl, Mikael Silvestre - Torsten Frings - Philipp Bargfrede (Aaron Hunt 37), Wesley (Tim Borowski• 67), Marko Marin - Marko Arnautovic, Hugo Almeida (Sandro Wagner 79). Tr: Thomas Schaaf

Tottenham Hotspur   **2**
Pasanen OG [12], Crouch [18]

Carlo Cudicini - Vedran Corluka, Younes Kaboul, Ledley King, Benoit Assou-Ekotto - Tom Huddlestone - Aaron Lennon (Wilson Palacios 75), Jermaine Jenas•, Gareth Bale - Rafael van der Vaart (Robbie Keane 49), Peter Crouch. Tr: Harry Redknapp

---

San Siro, Milan
20-10-2010, 20:45, 49 551, Skomina SVN

Internazionale   **4**
Zanetti [2], Eto'o 2 [11p 35], Stankovic [14]

Julio Cesar - Maicon, Lucio, Walter Samuel, Cristian Chivu• (Goran Pandev 61) - Javier Zanetti, Dejan Stankovic (Davide Santon 50) - Jonathan Biabiany (Ivan Cordoba 75), Wesley Sneijder, Coutinho - Samuel Eto'o. Tr: Rafael Benitez

Tottenham Hotspur   **3**
Bale 3 [52 90 91+]

Heurelho Gomes♦ [8] - Alan Hutton, William Gallas, Sebastian Bassong, Benoit Assou-Ekotto - Aaron Lennon, Jermaine Jenas, Tom Huddlestone (Wilson Palacios• 80), Gareth Bale - Luka Modric (Carlo Cudicino 10) - Peter Crouch (Robbie Keane 67). Tr: Harry Redknapp

---

Weserstadion, Bremen
2-11-2010, 20:45, 30 200, Hamer LUX

Werder Bremen   **0**

Sebastian Mielitz - Philipp Bargfrede (Marko Arnautovic 58),Per Mertesacker, Sebastian Prodl, Wesley - Torsten Frings♦75, Daniel Jensen - Aaron Hunt, Claudio Pizarro, Marko Marin - Hugo Almeida. Tr: Thomas Schaaf

FC Twente Enschede   **2**
Chadli [81], De Jong [84]

Nikolai Mihailov - Roberto Rosales, Peter Wisgerhof, Douglas•, Thilo Leugers• - Denny Landzaat, Luuk de Jong (Mitch Stockentree 90), Rasmus Bengtsson• (Michael Schimpelsberger 76) - Bryan Ruiz, Marc Janko, Nacer Chadli (Dario Vujicevic 86). Tr: Michel Preud'homme

---

Die Grolsch Veste, Enschede
7-12-2010, 20:45, 24 000, Velasco ESP

FC Twente Enschede   **3**
Landzaat [22p], Rosales [56], Chadli [64]

Sander Boschker - Roberto Rosales, Peter Wisgerhof, Douglas, Dwight Tiendalli - Wout Brama, Denny Landzaat, Theo Janssen - Luuk de Jong, Marc Janko (Dario Vujicevic 73), Nacer Chadli. Tr: Michel Preud'homme

Tottenham Hotspur   **3**
Wisgerhof OG [12], Defoe 2 [47 59]

Heurelho Gomes - Vedran Corluka, William Gallas, Sebastian Bassong, Benoit Assou-Ekotto - Niko Kranjcar (Peter Crouch 86), Jermaine Jenas• (Aaron Lennon 34), Wilson Palacios, Gareth Bale - Roman Pavlyuchenko (Robbie Keane 73), Jermain Defoe. Tr: Harry Redknapp

---

White Hart Lane, London
29-09-2010, 19:45, 32 318, Hauge NOR

Tottenham Hotspur   **4**
Van der Vaart [47], Pavlyuchenko [50p 64p], Bale [85]

Heurelho Gomes - Alan Hutton, Sebastien Bassong, Ledley King, Benoit Assou-Ekotto - Rafael van der Vaart••♦56, Tom Huddlestone, Luka Modric (Aaron Lennon 82), Gareth Bale - Peter Crouch (Jermaine Jenas 66), Roman Pavlyuchenko (Robbie Keane 89). Tr: Harry Redknapp

FC Twente Enschede   **1**
Chadli [56]

Nikolai Mihailov• - Roberto Rosales•, Douglas, Peter Wisgerhof, Nicky Kuiper• - Wout Brama, Theo Janssen - Bryan Ruiz, Denny Landzaat (Luuk de Jong 69), Emir Bajrami (Nacer Chadli 28) - Marc Janko. Tr: Michel Preud'homme

---

Die Grolsch Veste, Enschede
20-10-2010, 20:45, 23 248, Larsen DEN

FC Twente Enschede   **1**
Janssen [75]

Nikolai Mihailov - Roberto Rosales, Peter Wisgerhof (Rasmus Bengtsson 24), Douglas, Dwight Tiendalli• - Wout Brama•, Denny Landzaat (Luuk de Jong 86), Theo Janssen - Bryan Ruiz, Marc Janko, Nacer Chadli. Tr: Michel Preud'homme

Werder Bremen   **1**
Arnautovic [80]

Tim Wiese (Sebastian Mielitz 37) - Clemens Fritz•, Sebastian Prodl, Per Mertesacker, Petri Pasanen - Wesley, Torsten Frings, Philipp Bargfrede (Marko Marin 78) - Aaron Hunt - Claudio Pizarro, Hugo Almeida (Marko Arnautovic 60). Tr: Thomas Schaaf

---

San Siro, Milan
24-11-2010, 20:45, 29 466, Lannoy FRA

Internazionale   **1**
Cambiasso [55]

Luca Castellazzi - Ivan Cordoba•, Lucio•, Marco Materazzi, Javier Zanetti - Dejan Stankovic, Esteban Cambiasso - Jonathan Biabiany (Davide Santon 79), Wesley Sneijder (Obiora Nwankwo 86), Goran Pandev (Cristiano Biraghi 90) - Samuel Eto'o. Tr: Rafael Benitez

FC Twente Enschede   **0**

Nikolai Mihailov - Roberto Rosales, Peter Wisgerhof, Douglas, Thilo Leugers• (Bart Buysse 80) - Wout Brama, Theo Janssen - Luuk de Jong - Bryan Ruiz, Marc Janko (Denny Landzaat 70), Nacer Chadli. Tr: Michel Preud'homme

---

Weserstadion, Bremen
7-12-2010, 20:45, 30 400, Cakir TUR

Werder Bremen   **3**
Prodl [39], Arnautovic [49], Pizarro [88]

Tim Wiese - Dominik Schmidt, Per Mertesacker, Sebastian Prodl, Petri Pasanen• (Mikael Silvestre 83) - Clemens Fritz, Torsten Frings (Philipp Bargfrede 78) - Marko Marin, Aaron Hunt - Hugo Almeida (Claudio Pizarro 76), Marko Arnautovic. Tr: Thomas Schaaf

Internazionale   **0**

Paolo Orlandoni - Javier Zanetti (Felice Natalino 54), Ivan Cordoba - Esteban Cambiasso, Cristiano Biraghi - Obiora Nwankwo, Sulley Muntari - Davide Santon (Jonathan Biabiany 50), Thiago Motta (McDonald Mariga 76), Goran Pandev - Samuel Eto'o. Tr: Rafael Benitez

GROUP B		Pl	W	D	L	F	A	Pts	GER	FRA	POR	ISR
Schalke 04	GER	6	4	1	1	10	3	13		3-0	2-0	3-1
Olympique Lyonnais	FRA	6	3	1	2	11	10	10	1-0		2-0	2-2
Benfica	POR	6	2	0	4	7	12	6	1-2	4-3		2-0
Hapoel Tel Aviv	ISR	6	1	2	3	7	10	5	0-0	1-3	3-0	

Stade de Gerland, Lyon
14-09-2010, 20:45, 35 552, Bebek CRO

Olympique Lyonnais   **1**

Bastos 21

Hugo Lloris - Anthony Reveillere, Pape Diakhate, Dejan Lovren, Thimothee Kolodziejczak• - Miralem Pjanic, Jeremy Toulalan, Yoann Gourcuff (Jean Makoun 86) - Jimmy Briand (Kim Kallstrom 90), Lisandro Lopez, Michel Bastos• (Jeremy Pied 71). Tr: Claude Puel

Schalke 04   **0**

Manuel Neuer - Christoph Moritz, Benedikt Howedes♦38, Nicolas Plestan, Hans Sarpei (Lukas Schmitz 75) - Jermaine Jones (Peer Kluge 70) - Ivan Rakitic, Ciprian Deac (Joel Matip 45) - Jefferson Farfan, Klaas-Jan Huntelaar, Raul. Tr: Felix Magath

---

Estadio da Luz, Lisbon
14-09-2010, 20:45, 31 512, Nikolaev RUS

Benfica   **2**

Luisao 21, Oscar Cardozo 68

Roberto - Ruben Amorim, Luisao, David Luiz, Fabio Coentrao - Javier Garcia (Maxi Pereira 57) - Javier Saviola (Cesar Peixoto 87), Oscar Cardozo. Tr: Jorge Jesus

Hapoel Tel Aviv   **0**

Vincent Enyeama - Dani Bondarv, Douglas, Bevan Fransman (Walid Badir 74), Dedi Ben Dayan• - Romain Rocchi (Yossi Shivhon 61), Gil Vermouth, Avihay Yadin, Eran Zahavy - Ben Sahar (Toto Tamuz 57), Itay Shechter•. Tr: Eli Guttmann

---

Bloomfield, Tel Aviv
29-09-2010, 19:45, 12 226, Webb ENG

Hapoel Tel Aviv   **1**

Enyeama 79p

Vincent Enyeama - Dani Bondarv, Douglas, Walid Badir•, Dedi Ben Dayan• - Gil Vermouth, Romain Rocchi (Yossi Shivhon 59), Avihay Yadin, Eran Zahavy (Shay Abutbul - Ben Sahar (Toto Tamuz 76), Itay Shechter•. Tr: Eli Guttmann

Olympique Lyonnais   **3**

Bastos 2 7p 36, Pjanic 94+

Hugo Lloris - Pape Diakhate, Dejan Lovren•, Anthony Reveillere, Aly Cissokho, Kim Kallstrom, Michel Bastos (Maxime Gonalons 88), Jeremy Toulalan, Yoann Gourcuff (Miralem Pjanic 76), Jimmy Briand•, Bafetimbi Gomis (Jeremy Pied• 63). Tr: Claude Puel

---

Veltins-Arena, Gelsenkirchen
29-09-2010, 19:45, 50 436, Rocchi ITA

Schalke 04   **2**

Farfan 73, Huntelaar 85

Manuel Neuer - Atsuto Uchida• (Hans Sarpei 58), Kyriakos Papadopoulos, Christoph Metzelder, Lukas Schmitz - Jefferson Farfan•, Joel Matip, Ivan Rakitic (Jermaine Jones 66) - Klaas-Jan Huntelaar, Jurado (Peer Kluge 78), Raul. Tr: Felix Magath

Benfica   **0**

Roberto - Maxi Pereira, Luisao, David Luiz, Cesar Peixoto - Nicolas Gaitan• (Eduardo Salvio• 46), Javi Garcia•, Fabio Coentrao - Javier Saviola (Pablo Aimar 63), Carlos Martins, Oscar Cardozo (Alan Kardec 71). Tr: Jorge Jesus

---

Veltins-Arena, Gelsenkirchen
20-10-2010, 20:45, 50 900, Collum SCO

Schalke 04   **3**

Raul 2 3 58, Jurado 68

Manuel Neuer - Atsuto Uchida, Benedikt Howedes, Christoph Metzelder, Lukas Schmitz - Jefferson Farfan• (Junmin 67), Jermaine Jones (Joel Matip 75), Christoph Moritz (Ivan Rakitic 53) - Klaas-Jan Huntelaar, Jurado, Raul. Tr: Felix Magath

Hapoel Tel Aviv   **1**

Shechter 93+

Vincent Enyeama - Omri Kende, Douglas, Walid Badir, Gal Shish - Gil Vermouth•, Shay Abutbul (Salim Toama 58), Avihay Yadin (Bevan Fransman 73), Eran Zahavy - Toto Tamuz (Ben Sahar 58), Itay Shechter. Tr: Eli Guttmann

---

Stade de Gerland, Lyon
20-10-2010, 20:45, 36 816, Undiano ESP

Olympique Lyonnais   **2**

Briand 21, Lisandro 51

Hugo Lloris - Anthony Reveillere•, Cris, Pape Diakhate, Aly Cissokho - Yoann Gourcuff (Kim Kallstrom 71), Maxime Gonalons, Miralem Pjanic - Jimmy Briand, Lisandro Lopez (Bafetimbi Gomis 83), Michel Bastos (Jeremy Pied 65). Tr: Claude Puel

Benfica   **0**

Roberto - Maxi Pereira, Luisao, David Luiz, Fabio Coentrao - Nicolas Gaitan•♦43, Javi Garcia•, Carlos Martins• (Eduardo Salvio 77) - Javier Saviola (Cesar Peixoto 57), Pablo Aimar (Franco Jara 71), Alan Kardec. Tr: Jorge Jesus

---

Bloomfield, Tel Aviv
2-11-2010, 19:45, 13 094, De Bleeckere BEL

Hapoel Tel Aviv   **0**

Vincent Enyeama - Dani Bondarv, Douglas (Bevan Fransman 42), Walid Badir•, Dedi Ben Dayan - Gil Vermouth, Eran Zahavy•, Shay Abutbul, Salim Toama (Yossi Shivhon 61), Toto Tamuz, Ben Sahar (Victor Merey 70). Tr: Eli Guttmann

Schalke 04   **0**

Manuel Neuer - Atsuto Uchida, Benedikt Howedes•, Christoph Metzelder, Sergio Escudero - Peer Kluge (Christoph Moritz 46) - Jefferson Farfan (Ciprian Deac 80), Jurado, Ivan Rakitic• (Edu 74), Klaas-Jan Huntelaar•, Raul. Tr: Felix Magath

---

Estadio da Luz, Lisbon
2-11-2010, 19:45, 37 394, Thomson SCO

Benfica   **4**

Alan Kardec 20, Coentrao 2 32 67, Javi Garcia 42

Roberto - Maxi Pereira, Luisao•, David Luiz, Cesar Peixoto - Javi Garcia, Carlos Martins (Felipe Menezes 75), Fabio Coentrao - Javier Saviola• (Franco Jara 70), Eduardo Salvio, Alan Kardec (Weldon 71). Tr: Jorge Jesus

Olympique Lyonnais   **3**

Gourcuff 74, Gomis 85, Lovren 95+

Hugo Lloris - Anthony Reveillere, Cris, Pape Diakhate (Bafetimbi Gomis 63), Dejan Lovren• - Maxime Gonalons - Miralem Pjanic• (Jean Makoun 71), Yoann Gourcuff - Michel Bastos, Jimmy Briand, Jeremy Pied (Alexandre Lacazette 70). Tr: Claude Puel

---

Veltins-Arena, Gelsenkirchen
24-11-2010, 20:45, 51 132, Rizzoli ITA

Schalke 04   **3**

Farfan 13, Huntelaar 2 20 89

Manuel Neuer - Atsuto Uchida, Benedikt Howedes, Christoph Metzelder, Lukas Schmitz - Peer Kluge, Jermaine Jones• (Joel Matip 70) - Jefferson Farfan• (Edu 65), Jurado (Ciprian Deac 85) - Klaas-Jan Huntelaar, Raul. Tr: Felix Magath

Olympique Lyonnais   **0**

Hugo Lloris - Anthony Reveillere, Pape Diakhate, Dejan Lovren, Aly Cissokho (Bafetimbi Gomis 46) - Yoann Gourcuff (Miralem Pjanic 60), Jeremy Toulalan•, Kim Kallstrom - Michel Bastos•, Lisandro Lopez (Jeremy Pied 74), Jimmy Briand. Tr: Claude Puel

---

Bloomfield, Tel Aviv
24-11-2010, 20:45, 11 668, Hamer LUX

Hapoel Tel Aviv   **3**

Zahavi 2 24 92+, Douglas 74

Vincent Enyeama - Dani Bondarv, Douglas, Bevan Fransman•, Dedi Ben Dayan• - Gil Vermouth, Shay Abutbul (Walid Badir 78), Avihay Yadin•, Eran Zahavy - Itay Shechter (Yossi Shivhon 57) - Toto Tamuz (Ben Sahar• 84). Tr: Eli Guttmann

Benfica   **0**

Roberto - Maxi Pereira, Luisao, David Luiz, Fabio Coentrao - Eduardo Salvio (Carlos Martins 66), Javi Garcia (Franco Jara 79), Nicolas Gaitan - Javier Saviola• (Oscar Cardozo 46), Pablo Aimar, Alan Kardec. Tr: Jorge Jesus

---

Stade de Gerland, Lyon
7-12-2010, 20:45, 32 245, Moen NOR

Olympique Lyonnais   **2**

Lisandro 62, Lacazette 88

Hugo Lloris - Anthony Reveillere, Cris, Pape Diakhate, Aly Cissokho (Jeremy Pied 78) - Jean Makoun, Maxime Gonalons, Miralem Pjanic (Alexandre Lacazette 68) - Jimmy Briand, Bafetimbi Gomis (Michel Bastos 59), Lisandro Lopez. Tr: Claude Puel

Hapoel Tel Aviv   **2**

Sahar 63, Zahavi 69

Vincent Enyeama - Dani Bondarv, Bevan Fransman, Douglas, Gal Shish• - Gil Vermouth, Shay Abutbul (Walid Badir 82), Avihay Yadin, Eran Zahavy - Toto Tamuz (Salim Toama 62), Itay Shechter (Ben Sahar• 25). Tr: Eli Guttmann

---

Estadio da Luz, Lisbon
7-12-2010, 20:45, 23 348, Webb ENG

Benfica   **1**

Luisao 87

Roberto - Maxi Pereira (Pablo Aimar• 46), Luisao, David Luiz•, Fabio Coentrao - Ruben Amorim, Javi Garcia, Cesar Peixoto (Nicolas Gaitan 46) - Javier Saviola•, Carlos Martins (Eduardo Salvio 79), Oscar Cardozo. Tr: Jorge Jesus

Schalke 04   **2**

Jurado 19, Howedes 81

Manuel Neuer - Atsuto Uchida, Benedikt Howedes, Christoph Metzelder, Lukas Schmitz - Jurado (Erik Jendrisek 88), Peer Kluge (Joel Matip 82), Kyriakos Papadopoulos, Ivan Rakitic• - Raul, Klaas-Jan Huntelaar• (Edu 85). Tr: Felix Magath

GROUP C		Pl	W	D	L	F	A	Pts	ENG	ESP	SCO	TUR
Manchester United	ENG	6	4	2	0	7	1	**14**		1-1	0-0	1-0
Valencia	ESP	6	3	2	1	15	4	**11**	0-1		3-0	6-1
Rangers	SCO	6	1	3	2	3	6	**6**	0-1	1-1		1-0
Bursaspor	TUR	6	0	1	5	2	16	**1**	0-3	0-4	1-1	

Old Trafford, Manchester
14-09-2010, 20:45, 74 408, Benquerenca POR
Manchester United   **0**

Tomasz Kuszczak - Wes Brown, Rio Ferdinand, Chris Smalling, Fabio (Jonny Evans 75) - Luis Valencia (Ryan Giggs• 63), Darren Fletcher, Darron Gibson, Park Ji Sung (Michael Owen 75) - Wayne Rooney, Javier Hernandez. Tr: Alex Ferguson

Rangers   **0**

Allan McGregor - Kirk Broadfoot, David Weir, Madjid Bougherra, Sasa Papac - Lee McCulloch• - Steven Whittaker, Steven Davis, Maurice Edu, Steven Naismith - Kenny Miller (Kyle Lafferty 81). Tr: Walter Smith

Atatürk, Bursa
14-09-2010, 20:45, 25 000, Moen NOR
Bursaspor   **0**

Dimitar Ivankov - Omer Erdogan, Ali Tandogan, Milan Stepanov, Gokcek Vederson, Huseyin Cimsir (Turgay Bahadir 60), Federico Insua, Volkan Sen, Ozan Ipek, Ivan Ergic (Gustav Svensson 77), Leonel Nunez (Sercan Yildirim 60). Tr: Ertugrul Saglam

Valencia   **4**
Costa ¹⁶, Aduriz ⁴¹, Hernandez ⁶⁸, Soldado ⁷⁶

Cesar Sanchez - Bruno Saltor, David Navarro, Ricardo Costa, Jeremy Mathieu, Mehmet Topal, Joaquin, Pablo Hernandez, Tino Costa (Manuel Fernandes 81), Alejandro Dominguez (Juan Mata 77), Artiz Aduriz (Roberto Soldado 73). Tr: Juan Carlos Carcedo

Mestalla, Valencia
29-09-2010, 19:45, 34 946, Kassai HUN
Valencia   **0**

Cesar Sanchez - Miguel, David Navarro, Hedwiges Maduro, Jeremy Mathieu - Pablo Hernandez, David Albelda (Mehmet Topal 86), Tino Costa (Manuel Fernandes 74), Juan Mata - Alejandro Dominguez (Artiz Aduriz• 60) - Roberto Soldado. Tr: Unai Emery

Manchester United   **1**
Hernandez ⁸⁵

Edwin van der Sar - Rafael (John O'Shea 90), Rio Ferdinand, Nemanja Vidic, Patrice Evra - Michael Carrick - Darren Fletcher, Anderson (Javier Hernandez 76) - Nani, Dimitar Berbatov (Federico Macheda 85), Park Ji Sung. Tr: Alex Ferguson

Ibrox, Glasgow
29-09-2010, 19:45, 41 905, Gumienny BEL
Rangers   **1**
Naismith ¹⁸

Allan McGregor - Steven Whittaker, Madjid Bougherra, David Weir, Sasa Papac• - Kirk Broadfoot - Steven Davis, Lee McCulloch, Maurice Edu - Steven Naismith, Kenny Miller (Kyle Lafferty 87). Tr: Walter Smith

Bursaspor   **0**

Dimitar Ivankov - Ali Tandogan•, Omer Erdogan•, Milan Stepanov•, Gokcek Vederson - Gustav Svensson, Ivan Ergic (Federico Insua 39) - Volkan Sen, Pablo Batalla (Turgay Bahadir 72), Ozan Ipek - Sercan Yildirim (Leonel Nunez 72). Tr: Ertugrul Saglam

Ibrox, Glasgow
20-10-2010, 20:45, 45 153, Rizzoli ITA
Rangers   **1**
Edu ³⁴

Allan McGregor - Ricky Foster, Madjid Bougherra•, David Weir•, Sasa Papac, Steven Whittaker - Steven Naismith, Steven Davis, Maurice Edu•, Vladimir Weiss (Kyle Lafferty 88) - Kenny Miller. Tr: Walter Smith

Valencia   **1**
Edu OG ⁴⁶

Cesar Sanchez - Bruno Saltor, David Navarro, Ricardo Costa, Jeremy Mathieu - Mehmet Topal, Tino Costa (Manuel Fernandes 77) - Alejandro Dominguez (Roberto Soldado 46) - Pablo Hernandez, Artiz Aduriz•, Juan Mata• (Vicente 85). Tr: Unai Emery

Old Trafford, Manchester
20-10-2010, 20:45, 72 610, Rocchi ITA
Manchester United   **1**
Nani ⁷

Tomasz Kuszczak - Rafael, Chris Smalling, Nemanja Vidic, Patrice Evra - Darren Fletcher, Michael Carrick, Anderson (Javier Hernandez 77) - Nani•, Federico Macheda, Park Ji Sung (Gabriel Obertan 70). Tr: Alex Ferguson

Bursaspor   **0**

Dimitar Ivankov - Ali Tandogan• (Mustafa Keceli 70), Omer Erdogan, Milan Stepanov (Ibrahim Ozturk 46), Gokcek Vederson - Volkan Sen, Gustav Svensson, Ivan Ergic, Ozan Ipek• - Federico Insua - Sercan Yildirim (Turgay Bahadir 46). Tr: Ertugrul Saglam

Mestalla, Valencia
2-11-2010, 19:45, 26 821, Brych GER
Valencia   **3**
Soldado 2 ³³ ⁷¹, Tino Costa ⁹⁰

Cesar Sanchez - Miguel, David Navarro, Ricardo Costa, Jeremy Mathieu - Joaquin (Pablo Hernandez 85), Ever Banega (Tino Costa• 70), Juan Mata - Roberto Soldado (Manuel Fernandes 78), Artiz Aduriz. Tr: Unai Emery

Rangers   **0**

Allan McGregor - Kirk Broadfoot, David Weir, Madjid Bougherra, Sasa Papac - Lee McCulloch - Steven Whittaker, Steven Davis, Maurice Edu (Kyle Lafferty 84), Steven Naismith - Kenny Miller. Tr: Walter Smith

Atatürk, Bursa
2-11-2010, 19:45, 19 050, Stark GER
Bursaspor   **0**

Dimitar Ivankov - Ali Tandogan, Omer Erdogan, Ibrahim Ozturk, Gokcek Vederson - Turgay Bahadir, Gustav Svensson, Ivan Ergic, Volkan Sen (Ismail Odabasi 82) - Federico Insua (Ozan Ipek 74) - Sercan Yildirim (Leonel Nunez 74). Tr: Ertugrul Saglam

Manchester United   **3**
Fletcher ⁴⁸, Obertan ⁷³, Bebe ⁷⁷

Edwin van der Sar - Rafael, Chris Smalling, Nemanja Vidic, Patrice Evra (Fabio 81) - Paul Scholes, Michael Carrick - Nani (Park Ji Sung 29), Darren Fletcher (Bebe 63), Gabriel Obertan - Dimitar Berbatov. Tr: Alex Ferguson

Ibrox, Glasgow
24-11-2010, 20:45, 49 764, Busacca SUI
Rangers   **0**

Allan McGregor - Steven Davis, Steven Whittaker•, Kirk Broadfoot, David Weir, Ricky Foster - Lee McCulloch - Steven Naismith•, Kyle Hutton• (James Beattie 88), Vladimir Weiss (John Fleck 79) - Kenny Miller. Tr: Walter Smith

Manchester United   **1**
Rooney ⁸⁷ᵖ

Edwin van der Sar - John O'Shea, Jonny Evans, Chris Smalling, Fabio - Ryan Giggs, Michael Carrick, Paul Scholes (Anderson 67), Nani (Gabriel Obertan 77) - Dimitar Berbatov (Javier Hernandez 76), Wayne Rooney. Tr: Alex Ferguson

Mestalla, Valencia
24-11-2010, 20:45, 31 225, Paixao POR
Valencia   **6**
Mata ¹⁷ᵖ, Soldado 2 ²¹ ⁵⁵, Aduriz ³⁰, Joaquin ³⁷, Dominguez ⁷⁸

Miguel Angel Moya (Vicente Guaita 23) - Bruno Saltor, Ricardo Costa, Hedwiges Maduro, Jordi Alba• - Joaquin, Tino Costa, David Albelda•, Juan Mata - Artiz Aduriz (Alejandro Dominguez 61), Roberto Soldado (Isco 71). Tr: Unai Emery

Bursaspor   **1**
Batalla ⁶⁹

Dimitar Ivankov - Mustafa Keceli, Ibrahim Ozturk, Omer Erdogan•, Gokcek Vederson (Serdar Aziz• 46) - Federico Insua, Ivan Ergic (Pablo Batalla 59), Gustav Svensson, Volkan Sen - Sercan Yildirim (Ismail Odabasi 84), Turgay Bahadir. Tr: Ertugrul Saglam

Old Trafford, Manchester
7-12-2010, 20:45, 74 513, Proenca POR
Manchester United   **1**
Anderson ⁶²

Ben Amos - Rafael, Rio Ferdinand (Chris Smalling 50), Nemanja Vidic, Fabio - Nani (Ryan Giggs 81), Michael Carrick, Anderson• (Darren Fletcher 90), Park Ji Sung - Dimitar Berbatov, Wayne Rooney. Tr: Alex Ferguson

Valencia   **1**
Pablo Hernandez ³²

Guaita - Miguel, Ricardo Costa, Dealbert, Jeremy Mathieu - Pablo Hernandez (Sofiane Feghouli 81), Ever Banega, David Albelda, Jordi Alba (Juan Mata 68) - Alejandro Dominguez (Isco 54) - Artiz Aduriz. Tr: Unai Emery

Atatürk, Bursa
7-12-2010, 20:45, 9673, Chapron FRA
Bursaspor   **1**
Sercan Yildirim ⁷⁹

Yavuz Ozkan - Mustafa Keceli, Serdar Aziz (Omer Erogan 46), Milan Stepanov, Gokcek Vederson - Bekir Ozan Has•, Huseyin Cimsir (Pablo Batalla 46) - Sercan Yildirim, Federico Insua, Ozan Ipek • - Leonel Nunez (Turgay Bahadir 62). Tr: Ertugrul Saglam

Rangers   **1**
Miller ¹⁹

Allan McGregor - Darren Cole (Jordan McMillan 83), Steven Whittaker, David Weir, Madjid Bougherra, Ricky Foster - Steven Davis, Lee McCulloch, Kyle Hutton, Steven Naismith (Vladimir Weiss 71) - Kenny Miller (James Beattie• 83). Tr: Walter Smith

GROUP D		Pl	W	D	L	F	A	Pts	ESP	DEN	RUS	GRE
Barcelona	ESP	6	4	2	0	14	3	**14**		2-0	2-0	5-1
FC København	DEN	6	3	1	2	7	5	**10**	1-1		1-0	3-1
Rubin Kazan	RUS	6	1	3	2	2	4	**6**	1-1	1-0		0-0
Panathinaikos	GRE	6	0	2	4	2	13	**2**	0-3	0-2	0-0	

Camp Nou, Barcelona
14-09-2010, 20:45, 69 738, Rizzoli ITA
Barcelona   **5**
Messi 2 [22] [45], Villa [33], Pedro [78], Dani Alves [93+]

Victor Valdes - Dani Alves, Gerard Pique (Gabriel Milito 75), Carles Puyol, Eric Abidal - Xavi (Javier Mascherano 79), Sergio Busquets, Andres Iniesta - Lionel Messi, David Villa (Bojan Krkic 69), Pedro. Tr: Josep Guardiola

Panathinaikos   **1**
Govou [20]

Alexandros Tzorvas - Stergos Marinos, Jean-Alain Boumsong, Cedric Kante, Loukas Vyntra - Gilberto Silva, Simao - Sidney Govou (Luis Garcia 71), Kostas Katsouranis (Giorgios Karagounis• 64), Sebastian Leto (Sotirios Ninis 81) - Djibril Cisse. Tr: Nikos Nioplias

Parken, Copenhagen
14-09-2010, 20:45, 29 661, Einwaller AUT
FC København   **1**
N'Doye 87

Johan Wiland - Zdenek Pospech, Solvi Ottesen, Mikael Antonsson, Oscar Wendt - Martin Vingaard (Hjalte Norregaard 89), Claudemir (Mathias Jorgensen 89), William Kvist, Jesper Gronkjær - Dame N'Doye, Cesar Santin (Christian Bolanos 75). Tr: Stale Solbakken

Rubin Kazan   **0**

Sergey Ryzhikov - Lasha Salukvadze, Aleksandr Orekhov•, Salvatore Bocchetti (Oleg Zuzmin 66), Cristian Ansaldi - Vitaliy Kaleshin•, Rafal Murawski, Christian Noboa, Carlos Eduardo (Gokdeniz Karadeniz 77) - Obafemi Martins (Alan Kasaev 58), Sergey Kornilenko. Tr: Kurban Berdiyev

Centralni, Kazan
29-09-2010, 19:45, 23 950, Cakir TUR
Rubin Kazan   **1**
Noboa [30p]

Sergey Ryzhikov - Vitaliy Kaleshin, Lasha Salukvadze•, Cesar Navas, Salvatore Bocchetti, Cristian Ansaldi• - Aleksandr Ryazantsev, Rafal Murawski, Christian Noboa (Bebars Natcho 89), Gokdeniz Karadeniz (Obafemi Martins 64) - Sergey Kornilenko (Macbeth Sibaya• 62). Tr: Kurban Berdiyev

Barcelona   **1**
Villa [60p]

Victor Valdes - Dani Alves, Gerard Pique•, Carles Puyol•, Maxwell - Xavi, Javier Mascherano (Lionel Messi 61), Sergio Busquets - Pedro, Andres Iniesta, David Villa (Bojan Krkic 86). Tr: Josep Guardiola

Spiros Louis, Athens
29-09-2010, 19:45, 43 607, Collum SCO
Panathinaikos   **0**

Alexandros Tzorvas - Stergos Marinos, Josu Sarriegi, Gilberto Silva••48, Loukas Vyntra - Sotirios Ninis (Damien Plessis 58), Simao, Kostas Katsouranis (Giorgios Karagounis• 46), Sebastian Leto - Luis Garcia (Nikos Spyropoulos 46) - Djibril Cisse. Tr: Nikos Nioplias

FC København   **2**
N'Doye [28], Vingaard [37]

Johan Wiland - Zdenek Pospech, Mathias Jorgensen, Mikael Antonsson, Oscar Wendt - Christian Bolanos (Hjalte Norregaard 58), Martin Vingaard - Jesper Gronkjær - Dame N'Doye• (Cesar Santin 77). Tr: Stale Solbakken

Spiros Louis, Athens
20-10-2010, 20:45, 36 748, Grafe GER
Panathinaikos   **0**

Alexandros Tzorvas - Loukas Vyntra, Jean-Alain Boumsong, Josu Sarriegi, Nikos Spyropoulos - Kostas Katsouranis (Lazaros Christodoulopoulos 61), Simao - Stergos Marinos (Charis Mavrias 78), Giorgios Karagounis (Damien Plessis 61), Luis Garcia - Djibril Cisse. Tr: Nikos Nioplias

Rubin Kazan   **0**

Sergey Ryzhikov - Vitaliy Kaleshin, Salvatore Bocchetti, Cesar Navas, Cristian Ansaldi - Alan Kasaev (Petr Bystrov 86), Christian Noboa, Bebars Natcho, Aleksandr Ryazantsev - Gokdeniz Karadeniz (Obafemi Martins 65), Sergey Kornilenko (Macbeth Sibaya 90). Tr: Kurban Berdiyev

Camp Nou, Barcelona
20-10-2010, 20:45, 75 852, Lannoy FRA
Barcelona   **2**
Messi 2 [19] [92+]

Jose Pinto - Dani Alves, Gerard Pique, Carles Puyol, Eric Abidal - Javier Mascherano - Sergio Busquets, Maxwell (Xavi 73) - Lionel Messi, David Villa (Pedro 73), Andres Iniesta• (Seydou Keita 89). Tr: Josep Guardiola

FC København   **0**

Johan Wiland - Zdenek Pospech•, Mathias Jorgensen, Mikael Antonsson, Oscar Wendt (Peter Larsson 89) - Martin Vingaard (Christian Bolanos 62), William Kvist, Claudemir, Jesper Gronkjær - Dame N'Doye•, Cesar Santin (Kenneth Zohore 75). Tr: Stale Solbakken

Centralni, Kazan
2-11-2010, 19:45, 16 400, Chapron FRA
Rubin Kazan   **0**

Sergey Ryzhikov - Vitaliy Kaleshin, Cesar Navas, Salvatore Bocchetti, Cristian Ansaldi - Aleksandr Ryazantsev, Christian Noboa, Bebars Natcho, Alan Kasaev (Gokdeniz Karadeniz 72) - Carlos Eduardo (Obafemi Martins 73), Sergey Kornilenko (Aleksey Medvedev 85). Tr: Kurban Berdiyev

Panathinaikos   **0**

Alexandros Tzorvas - Loukas Vyntra•, Cedric Kante, Kostas Katsouranis, Jean-Alain Boumsong (Stergos Marinos• 58), Nikos Spyropoulos - Gilberto Silva, Simao - Luis Garcia (Sidney Govou 69), Djibril Cisse, Giorgios Karagounis• (Lazaros Christodoulopoulos 81). Tr: Nikos Nioplias

Parken, Copenhagen
2-11-2010, 19:45, 37 049, Balaj ROU
FC København   **1**
Claudemir [32]

Johan Wiland - Zdenek Pospech•, Mathias Jorgensen, Mikael Antonsson, Oscar Wendt - Christian Bolanos (Thomas Delaney 90), William Kvist, Claudemir, Martin Vingaard (Solvi Ottesen 90) - Dame N'Doye, Jesper Gronkjær. Tr: Stale Solbakken

Barcelona   **1**
Messi [31]

Victor Valdes• - Dani Alves, Gerard Pique, Carles Puyol, Eric Abidal - Sergio Busquets•, Xavi, Seydou Keita - David Villa (Pedro 80), Lionel Messi, Andres Iniesta. Tr: Josep Guardiola

Spiros Louis, Athens
24-11-2010, 20:45, 58 466, Rocchi ITA
Panathinaikos   **0**

Alexandros Tzorvas - Loukas Vyntra, Jean-Alain Boumsong, Cedric Kante, Nikos Spyropoulos - Kostas Katsouranis (Damien Plessis 67), Gilberto Silva - Stergos Marinos (Elin Dimoutsos• 46), Lazaros Christodoulopoulos (Antonis Petropoulos 63), Lazaros Christodoulopoulos - Djibril Cisse. Tr: Jesualdo Ferreira

Barcelona   **3**
Pedro 2 [27] [69], Messi [62]

Victor Valdes - Dani Alves, Gerard Pique• (Eric Abidal 70), Carles Puyol, Adriano (Maxwell 76) - Xavi (Seydou Keita 70), Javier Mascherano, Andres Iniesta - Pedro, Lionel Messi, David Villa. Tr: Josep Guardiola

Centralni, Kazan
24-11-2010, 20:45, 18 720, Atkinson ENG
Rubin Kazan   **1**
Noboa [45p]

Sergey Ryzhikov - Vitaliy Kaleshin• (Lasha Salukvadze 85), Cesar Navas, Salvatore Bocchetti, Cristian Ansaldi - Aleksandr Ryazantsev•, Christian Noboa, Bebars Natcho, Alan Kasaev (Petr Bystrov 69) - Gokdeniz Karadeniz, Sergey Kornilenko (Aleksey Medvedev 81). Tr: Kurban Berdiyev

FC København   **0**

Johan Wiland - Zdenek Pospech, Mathias Jorgensen, Mikael Antonsson, Oscar Wendt• - Christian Bolanos•, William Kvist, Claudemir, Martin Vingaard (Kenneth Zohore 73) - Dame N'Doye, Jesper Gronkjær. Tr: Stale Solbakken

Camp Nou, Barcelona
7-12-2010, 20:45, 50 436, Eriksson SWE
Barcelona   **2**
Fontas [51], Victor Vazquez [83]

Jose Pinto - Gerard Pique, Sergio Busquets, Andreu Fontas - Javier Mascherano - Jonathan dos Santos (Lionel Messi 63), Thiago Alcantara, Maxwell - Jeffren (Victor Vazquez 13), Bojan Krkic (Barta 35), Adriano. Tr: Josep Guardiola

Rubin Kazan   **0**

Sergey Ryzhikov• - Oleg Kuzmin, Cesar Navas, Salvatore Bocchetti, Cristian Ansaldi - Aleksandr Ryazantsev (Alan Kasaev 62), Vitaliy Kaleshin, Christian Noboa, Rafal Murawski - Gokdeniz Karadeniz (Petr Bystrov 75) - Obafemi Martins (Aleksey Medvedev 66). Tr: Kurban Berdiyev

Parken, Copenhagen
7-12-2010, 20:45, 36 797, Meyer GER
FC København   **3**
Vingaard [26], Gronkjær [50p], Cisse OG [73]

Johan Wiland - Zdenek Pospech, Mathias Jorgensen, Mikael Antonsson (Solvi Ottesen 77), Oscar Wendt - Christian Bolanos, William Kvist, Claudemir, Martin Vingaard - Dame N'Doye (Cesar Santin 80), Jesper Gronkjær• (Kenneth Zohore 87). Tr: Stale Solbakken

Panathinaikos   **0**
Kante [92+]

Alexandros Tzorvas - Loukas Vyntra, Jean-Alain Boumsong, Cedric Kante, Nikos Spyropoulos - Gilberto Silva (Sotirios Ninis 46), Simao• - Stergos Marinos•, Luis Garcia• (Antonis Petropoulos 74), Lazaros Christodoulopoulos (Sebastian Leto• 46) - Djibril Cisse. Tr: Jesualdo Ferreira

GROUP E		Pl	W	D	L	F	A	Pts	GER	ITA	SUI	ROU
Bayern München	GER	6	5	0	1	16	6	**15**		2-0	3-0	3-2
Roma	ITA	6	3	1	2	10	11	10	3-2		1-3	2-1
FC Basel	SUI	6	2	0	4	8	11	6	1-2	2-3		1-0
CFR Cluj-Napoca	ROU	6	1	1	4	6	12	4	0-4	1-1	2-1	

Allianz Arena, Munich
15-09-2010, 20:45, 66 000, Lannoy FRA

Bayern München   **2**

Muller [79], Klose [83]

Hans Jorg Butt - Philipp Lahm, Daniel Van Buyten, Holger Badstuber, Diego Contento - Mark van Bommel, Bastian Schweinsteiger - Ivica Olic (Mario Gomez• 67), Toni Kroos, Hamit Altintop (Miroslav Klose 67) - Thomas Muller (Danijel 82). Tr: Louis van Gaal

Roma   **0**

Julio Sergio - Aleandro Rosi, Nicolas Burdisso, Juan, Marco Cassetti - Matteo Brighi, David Pizarro, Daniele De Rossi, Simone Perrotta - Francesco Totti (Jeremy Menez 87), Marco Borriello. Tr: Claudio Ranieri

---

Constantin Radulescu, Cluj-Napoca
15-09-2010, 20:45, 9593, Kelly IRL

CFR 1907 Cluj   **2**

Rada [9], Traore [12]

Nuno Claro - Cristian Panin•, Cadu, Hugo Alcantara, Ionut Rada• - Emmanuel Culio, Ioan Hora (Emmanuel Kone 54), Gabriel Muresan, Emil Dica - Lacina Traore (Ferdinando Sforzini 79), Rafael Bastos (Roberto de Zerbi 53). Tr: Sorin Cartu

FC Basel   **1**

Stocker [45]

Franco Costanzo - Samuel Inkoom, David Abraham, Cagdas Atan, Behrang Safari (Scott Chipperfield 73) - Xherdan Shaqiri, Benjamin Huggel, Gilles Yapi-Yapo, Valentin Stocker (Fwayo Tembo 73) - Alexander Frei, Marco Streller•. Tr: Thorsten Fink

---

St Jakob-Park, Basel
28-09-2010, 20:45, 37 500, Thomson SCO

FC Basel   **1**

Frei [18]

Franco Costanzo - Samuel Inkoom, David Abraham, Beg Ferati, Behrang Safari - Xherdan Shaqiri (Scott Chipperfield 80), Gilles Yapi-Yapo (Federico Almerares 90), Benjamin Huggel (Adilson Cabral 87), Valentin Stocker - Alexander Frei, Marco Streller•. Tr: Thorsten Fink

Bayern München   **2**

Schweinsteiger 2 [56p] [89]

Hans Jorg Butt - Philipp Lahm, Daniel Van Buyten, Holger Badstuber•, Danijel Pranjic• - Mark van Bommel, Bastian Schweinsteiger• - Hamit Altintop (Mario Gomez 46), Thomas Muller, Toni Kroos• (Ivica Olic 57) - Miroslav Klose (Anatoliy Tymoshchuk 77). Tr: Louis van Gaal

---

Olimpico, Rome
28-09-2010, 20:45, 30 252, Eriksson SWE

Roma   **2**

Mexes [69], Borriello [71]

Bogdan Lobont - Cicinho (Marco Cassetti 64), Philippe Mexes, Nicolas Burdisso, Paolo Castellini - Jeremy Menez (Adriano 46), David Pizarro, Daniele De Rossi, Simone Perrotta - Francesco Totti, Mirko Vucinic (Marco Borriello 64). Tr: Claudio Ranieri

CFR 1907 Cluj   **1**

Rada [78]

Nuno Claro - Cristian Panin, Hugo Alcantara, Cadu, Ionut Rada - Emil Dica•, Dominique Kivuvu, Edimar (Emmanuel Kone 68), Emmanuel Culio - Ioan Hora (Roberto de Zerbi 76), Lacina Traore (Sasa Bjelanovic 82). Tr: Sorin Cartu

---

Olimpico, Rome
19-10-2010, 20:45, 22 365, Nikolaev RUS

Roma   **2**

Borriello [21]

Bogdan Lobont - Marco Cassetti•, Philippe Mexes, Nicolas Burdisso, John Arne Riise (Paolo Castellini 60) - Rodrigo Taddei, David Pizarro, Matteo Brighi, Simone Perrotta (Julio Baptista 74) - Francesco Totti, Marco Borriello. Tr: Claudio Ranieri

FC Basel   **3**

Frei [12], Inkoom [44], Cabral [93+]

Franco Costanzo - Samuel Inkoom•, David Abraham, Beg Ferati, Behrang Safari - Xherdan Shaqiri, Benjamin Huggel, Gilles Yapi-Yapo, Valentin Stocker (Scott Chipperfield• 70) - Alexander Frei (Federico Almerares 90), Marco Streller (Adilson Cabral 81). Tr: Thorsten Fink

---

Allianz Arena, Munich
19-10-2010, 20:45, 64 000, Atkinson ENG

Bayern München   **3**

Cado OG [32], Panin OG [37], Gomez [77]

Hans Jorg Butt - Philipp Lahm, Anatoliy Tymoshchuk, Holger Badstuber, Danijel Pranjic• - Andreas Ottl, Bastian Schweinsteiger• (Edson Braafheid 79) - Hamit Altintop, Toni Kroos, Thomas Muller - Mario Gomez. Tr: Louis van Gaal

CFR 1907 Cluj   **2**

Cadu [28], Culio [86]

Eduard Stancioiu - Ionut Rada, Felice Piccolo, Cadu, Cristian Panin• - Emmanuel Culio, Emil Dica•, Dominique Kivuvu, Rafael Bastos (Ioan Hora 56) - Lacina Traore (Sasa Bjelanovic 76), Roberto de Zerbi. Tr: Sorin Costa

---

St Jakob-Park, Basel
3-11-2010, 20:45, 36 375, Kuipers NED

FC Basel   **2**

Frei [69], Shaqiri [83]

Franco Costanzo - Samuel Inkoom, David Abraham, Beg Ferati (Scott Chipperfield 88), Behrang Safari - Xherdan Shaqiri, Benjamin Huggel, Gilles Yapi-Yapo, Valentin Stocker•• ♦91+ - Alexander Frei, Marco Streller•. Tr: Thorsten Fink

Roma   **3**

Menez [16], Totti [26p], Greco [76]

Julio Sergio - Marco Cassetti•, Juan, Nicolas Burdisso (Guillermo Burdisso 81), John Arne Riise - Jeremy Menez• (Leandro Greco 75), Daniele De Rossi, Fabio Simplicio, Simone Perrotta• - Francesco Totti, Mirko Vucinic (Marco Borriello 70). Tr: Claudio Ranieri

---

Constantin Radulescu, Cluj-Napoca
3-11-2010, 20:45, 14 097, Gumienny BEL

CFR 1907 Cluj   **0**

Eduard Stancioiu - Ionut Rada, Felice Piccolo, Cadu (Tony Da Silva 78), Cristian Panin - Emmanuel Culio, Rafael Bastos• (Ioan Hora 46), Emil Dica (Edimar 46), Tomas Costa - Roberto de Zerbi, Lacina Traore•. Tr: Sorin Cartu

Bayern München   **3**

Gomez 3 [12] [24] [71], Muller [90]

Hans Jorg Butt - Philipp Lahm, Daniel Van Buyten, Martin Demichelis, Danijel Pranjic - Anatoliy Tymoshchuk, Andreas Ottl• - Hamit Altintop, Bastian Schweinsteiger• (Thomas Muller 75), Toni Kroos - Mario Gomez. Tr: Louis van Gaal

---

Olimpico, Rome
23-11-2010, 20:45, 42 789, Undiano ESP

Roma   **3**

Borriello [49], De Rossi [81], Totti [84p]

Julio Sergio - Marco Cassetti, Philippe Mexes•, Nicolas Burdisso, John Arne Riise - Leandro Greco• (Fabio Simplicio 46), Daniele De Rossi•, Matteo Brighi (Francesco Totti 75) - Jeremy Menez• - Marco Borriello, Mirko Vucinic (David Pizarro 82). Tr: Claudio Ranieri

Bayern München   **2**

Gomez 2 [33] [39]

Thomas Kraft• - Philipp Lahm, Daniel Van Buyten, Martin Demichelis, Danijel Pranjic - Anatoliy Tymoshchuk, Andreas Ottl - Thomas Muller (Diego Contento 73), Toni Kroos•, Franck Ribery (Hamit Altintop 77) - Mario Gomez. Tr: Louis van Gaal

---

St Jakob-Park, Basel
23-11-2010, 20:45, 34 239, Duhamel FRA

FC Basel   **1**

Almerares [15]

Franco Costanzo - Samuel Inkoom, David Abraham, Beg Ferati, Behrang Safari - Fwayo Tembo (Cagdas 90), Gilles Yapi-Yapo, Adilson Cabral, Xherdan Shaqiri (Granit Xhaka 87) - Federico Almerares•, Alexander Frei (Reto Zanni 90). Tr: Thorsten Fink

CFR 1907 Cluj   **0**

Nuno Claro - Tony Da Silva, Cadu•, Felice Piccolo♦88, Ionut Rada - Emmanuel Culio (Ferdinando Sforzini 74), Tomas Costa• - Dominique Kivuvu, Leo Veloso (Emmanuel Kone 58) - Rafael Bastos, Lacina Traore (Sasa Bjelanovic 46). Tr: Sorin Cartu

---

Allianz Arena, Munich
8-12-2010, 20:45, 64 000, Hansson SWE

Bayern München   **3**

Ribery 2 [35] [50], Tymoshchuk [37]

Thomas Kraft - Philipp Lahm, Anatoliy Tymoshchuk, Breno, Diego Contento - Mark van Bommel, Toni Kroos (Hamit Altintop 68) - Thomas Muller, Bastian Schweinsteiger, Franck Ribery - Mario Gomez•. Tr: Louis van Gaal

FC Basel   **0**

Franco Costanzo - Samuel Inkoom, David Abraham, Beg Ferati, Behrang Safari - Xherdan Shaqiri (Fwayo Tembo 76), Gilles Yapi-Yapo, Valentin Stocker - Marco Streller (Granit Xhaka 46), Alexander Frei•. Tr: Thorsten Fink

---

Constantin Radulescu, Cluj-Napoca
8-12-2010, 20:45, 12 800, Collum SCO

CFR 1907 Cluj   **1**

Traore [88]

Eduard Stancioiu - Cristian Panin, Ionut Rada, Cadu, Edimar (Sasa Bjelanovic 63) - Emmanuel Kone, Emil Dica (Leo Veloso 46), Dominique Kivuvu, Emmanuel Culio• - Roberto de Zerbi (Rafael Bastos 78), Lacina Traore•. Tr: Alin Minteuan

Roma   **1**

Borriello [21]

Bogdan Lobont - Marco Cassetti (Cicinho 64), Philippe Mexes, Nicolas Burdisso, Paolo Castellini - Daniele De Rossi - Matteo Brighi, Fabio Simplicio - Marco Borriello, Jeremy Menez (Leandro Greco 46), Francesco Totti. Tr: Claudio Ranieri

GROUP F		Pl	W	D	L	F	A	Pts	ENG	FRA	RUS	SVK
Chelsea	ENG	6	5	0	1	14	4	15		2-0	4-1	2-1
Olympique Marseille	FRA	6	4	0	2	12	3	12	1-0		0-1	1-0
Spartak Moskva	RUS	6	3	0	3	7	10	9	0-2	0-3		3-0
MSK Zilina	SVK	6	0	0	6	3	19	0	1-4	0-7	1-2	

Vélodrome, Marseille
15-09-2010, 20:45, 45 729, Meyer GER
Olympique Marseille   **0**

Steve **Mandanda** - Cesar **Azpilicueta**, **Hilton**, Gabriel **Heinze**, Taye **Taiwo** - Edouard **Cisse** - Benoit **Cheyrou**, Matthieu **Valbuena**, Lucho **Gonzalez** (Jordan **Ayew** 83), Andre **Ayew** - **Brandao**• (Andre-Pierre **Gignac** 62). Tr: Didier **Deschamps**

Spartak Moskva   **1**
         Azpilicueta OG [81]

Andrey **Dykan** - Sergey **Parshivlyuk**, Nicolas **Pareja**, Marek **Suchy**, Evgeniy **Makeev** - Aleksandr **Sheshukov** (**Ari** 88) - Aiden **McGeady** (Renat **Sabitov** 83), **Alex**• (**Martin Stranzl** 90), **Ibson**, Dmitriy **Kombarov** - **Welliton**. Tr: Valeriy **Karpin**

Luzhniki, Moscow
28-09-2010, 20:45, 33 124, Hanson SWE
Spartak Moskva   **3**
         Ari 2 [34 61], Ibson [89]

Andrey **Dykan** - Sergey **Parshivlyuk**, Marek **Suchy**, Nicolas **Pareja**, Evgeniy **Makeev** - Aleksandr **Sheshukov** (Renat **Sabitov** 90), **Ari** - Aiden **McGeady**, **Alex**, Dmitriy **Kombarov** (Cristian **Maidana** 84) - **Welliton** (**Ibson** 67). Tr: Valeriy **Karpin**

MSK Zilina   **0**

Martin **Dubravka** - Lubomir **Guldan**•, Jozef **Piacek**, Ondrej **Sourek**, Patrik **Mraz** - Mario **Pecalka**• (Momodou **Ceesay** 46), Sergio **Vittor** - Emil **Rilke** (Admir **Vladavic** 65), Robert **Jez**, Tomas **Majtan** (Stanislav **Angelovic** 81) - Tomas **Oravec**. Tr: Pavel **Hapal**

Stamford Bridge, London
3-11-2010, 20:45, 40 477, Cakir TUR
Chelsea   **4**
   Anelka [49], Drogba [62p], Ivanovic 2 [66 92+]

Petr **Cech** - Paulo **Ferreira**, Branislav **Ivanovic**, **Alex**, Ashley **Cole** - John **Mikel**• (Joshua **McEachran** 69), **Ramires**, Yuriy **Zhirkov** - Salomon **Kalou**, Didier **Drogba** (Daniel **Sturridge** 76), Nicolas **Anelka** (Gael **Kakuta** 76). Tr: Carlo **Ancelotti**

Spartak Moskva   **1**
         Bazhenov [86]

Andrey **Dykan** - Andrey **Ivanov**•, Nicolas **Pareja**, Marek **Suchy**, Evgeniy **Makeev** - **Ibson**, Aleksandr **Sheshukov** (Nikola **Drincic** 67) - Aiden **McGeady** (Nikita **Bazhenov** 80), **Alex** (Alexandr **Kozlov** 68), Dmitriy **Kombarov**• - **Welliton**. Tr: Valeriy **Karpin**

Stamford Bridge, London
23-11-2010, 20:45, 40 266, Schorgenhofer AUT
Chelsea   **2**
         Sturridge [51], Malouda [86]

Ross **Turnbull** - Paulo **Ferreira**, Branislav **Ivanovic**, Jeffrey **Bruma**, Patrick **van Aanholt** - **Ramires**•, Joshua **McEachran** (Jacob **Mellis** 90), Florent **Malouda** - Daniel **Sturridge** (Nicolas **Anelka** 74), Didier **Drogba**, Gael **Kakuta** (Salomon **Kalou** 46). Tr: Carlo **Ancelotti**

MSK Zilina   **1**
         Bello [19]

Martin **Dubravka** - Stanislav **Angelovic**, Mario **Pecalka**, Jozef **Piacek**, Roman **Gergel** - Robert **Jez**, Lubomir **Guldan**, Bello **Babatounde**, Admir **Vladavic** (Emil **Rilke** 90) - Tomas **Oravec** (Momodou **Ceesay** 64), Tomas **Majtan** (Pavol **Poliacek** 85). Tr: Pavel **Hapal**

Pod Dubnom, Zilina
15-09-2010, 20:45, 10 829, Kuipers NED
MSK Zilina   **1**
         Oravec [55]

Martin **Dubravka** - Lubomir **Guldan** (Stanislav **Angelovic** 79), Jozef **Piacek**, Mario **Pecalka**, Patrik **Mraz** - Robert **Jez**, Bello **Babatounde** (Pavol **Poliacek** 57), Momodou **Ceesay** (Tomas **Majtan** 62), Admir **Vladavic** - Tomas **Oravec**. Tr: Pavel **Hapal**

Chelsea   **4**
   Essien [13], Anelka 2 [24 28], Sturridge [48]

Petr **Cech** - Branislav **Ivanovic**, John **Terry**, **Alex**, Yuriy **Zhirkov** - Michael **Essien**, John **Mikel**, Yossi **Benayoun** (Joshua **McEachran** 79) - Daniel **Sturridge** (Gael **Kakuta** 62), Nicolas **Anelka**, Florent **Malouda** (Patrick **van Aanholt** 88). Tr: Carlo **Ancelotti**

Luzhniki, Moscow
19-10-2010, 20:45, 70 012, Velasco ESP
Spartak Moskva   **0**

Andrey **Dykan** - Sergey **Parshivlyuk**, Nicolas **Pareja**, Marek **Suchy**, Evgeniy **Makeev** - **Ibson**, Aleksandr **Sheshukov** - Aiden **McGeady**, **Ari** (Zhano **Ananidze** 84), Dmitriy **Kombarov** - **Welliton**. Tr: Valeriy **Karpin**

Chelsea   **2**

Petr **Cech** - Paulo **Ferreira**, Branislav **Ivanovic**, John **Terry**, Ashley **Cole** (Patrick **van Aanholt** 87) - Michael **Essien**, John **Mikel**, Yuriy **Zhirkov**• - Salomon **Kalou** (Joshua **McEachran** 74), Nicolas **Anelka**, Florent **Malouda** (Gael **Kakuta** 82). Tr: Carlo **Ancelotti**

Pod Dubnom, Zilina
3-11-2010, 20:45, 9664, Johannesson SWE
MSK Zilina   **0**

Martin **Dubravka** - Stanislav **Angelovic**, Mario **Pecalka**•, Ondrej **Sourek**, Vladimir **Leitner** - Robert **Jez**, Sergio **Vittor** (Stefan **Zosak** 34) - Bello **Babatounde**, Admir **Vladavic** (Roman **Gergel** 60) - Momodou **Ceesay** (Tomas **Majtan** 78), Tomas **Oravec**. Tr: Pavel **Hapal**

Olympique Marseille   **3**
  Gignac 3 [12 21 54], Heinze [24], Remy [36], Gonzalez 2 [52 63]

Steve **Mandanda** - Cesar **Azpilicueta**, Souleymane **Diawara**, Stephane **Mbia**•, Gabriel **Heinze** (Taye **Taiwo** 62) - Lucho **Gonzalez**, Charles **Kabore**, Benoit **Cheyrou** - Matthieu **Valbuena** (Andre **Ayew** 62), Andre-Pierre **Gignac** (**Brandao** 72), Loic **Remy**. Tr: Didier **Deschamps**

Vélodrome, Marseille
8-12-2010, 20:45, 50 604, Bezborodov RUS
Olympique Marseille   **2**
         Brandao [81]

Steve **Mandanda** - Charles **Kabore**, Souleymane **Diawara**, Gabriel **Heinze**, Taye **Taiwo** - Fabrice **Abriel** (Lucho **Gonzalez** 63), Leyti **N'Diaye** (Jordan **Ayew** 86), Benoit **Cheyrou** - Matthieu **Valbuena** (Andre **Ayew**• 63), **Brandao**, Loic **Remy**. Tr: Didier **Deschamps**

Chelsea   **0**

Petr **Cech** - Jose **Bosingwa** (Patrick **van Aanholt** 80), Branislav **Ivanovic**, John **Terry** (Jeffrey **Bruma** 72), Paulo **Ferreira** - Michael **Essien**, Joshua **McEachran**, **Ramires** - Salomon **Kalou**, Didier **Drogba** (Daniel **Sturridge** 62), Florent **Malouda**. Tr: Carlo **Ancelotti**

Stamford Bridge, London
28-09-2010, 20:45, 40 675, De Bleeckere BEL
Chelsea   **2**
         Terry [7], Anelka [28p]

Petr **Cech** - Branislav **Ivanovic**, John **Terry**, **Alex**, Ashley **Cole** - Michael **Essien**, John **Mikel**• (Joshua **McEachran** 88), Yuriy **Zhirkov** (Daniel **Sturridge** 73) - Gael **Kakuta** (**Ramires** 61), Nicolas **Anelka**, Florent **Malouda**. Tr: Carlo **Ancelotti**

Olympique Marseille   **0**

Steve **Mandanda** - Charles **Kabore**, Souleymane **Diawara**, Stephane **Mbia**•, Gabriel **Heinze**• - Lucho **Gonzalez**, Edouard **Cisse**, Benoit **Cheyrou** (Matthieu **Valbuena** 59) - Loic **Remy**, Andre-Pierre **Gignac** (Andre **Ayew** 59), **Brandao**. Tr: Didier **Deschamps**

Vélodrome, Marseille
19-10-2010, 20:45, 49 250, Vad HUN
Olympique Marseille   **1**
         Diawara [48]

Steve **Mandanda** - Cesar **Azpilicueta**, Souleymane **Diawara**, Gabriel **Heinze**, Taye **Taiwo**• - Lucho **Gonzalez** (Fabrice **Abriel** 74), Stephane **Mbia**•, Andre **Ayew**•, Matthieu **Valbuena**•, Andre-Pierre **Gignac** (Edouard **Cisse** 83), **Brandao** (Loic **Remy** 66). Tr: Didier **Deschamps**

MSK Zilina   **0**

Martin **Dubravka** - Stanislav **Angelovic**, Jozef **Piacek**, Ondrej **Sourek**, Vladimir **Leitner** - Robert **Jez**, Lubomir **Guldan**•, Stefan **Zosak** (Admir **Vladavic** 79), Roman **Gergel** (Emil **Rilke** 63) - Tomas **Majtan** (Tomas **Oravec** 68), Momodou **Ceesay**. Tr: Pavel **Hapal**

Luzhniki, Moscow
23-11-2010, 20:45, 43 217, Stark GER
Spartak Moskva   **0**

Andrey **Dykan** - Evgeniy **Makeev**, Marek **Suchy**, Nicolas **Pareja**, Martin **Stranzl** - Aleksandr **Sheshukov** (Nikola **Drincic** 75), **Ibson**• (Zhano **Ananidze** 76) - Aiden **McGeady**, **Ari**, Dmitriy **Kombarov** - **Welliton**♦[56]. Tr: Valeriy **Karpin**

Olympique Marseille   **3**
   Valbuena [18], Remy [54], Brandao [68]

Steve **Mandanda** - Cesar **Azpilicueta**, Souleymane **Diawara**, Stephane **Mbia**•, Gabriel **Heinze** - Lucho **Gonzalez** (Edouard **Cisse** 82), Andre **Ayew** - Loic **Remy** (Charles **Kabore** 82), **Brandao**, Matthieu **Valbuena** (Benoit **Cheyrou** 69). Tr: Didier **Deschamps**

Pod Dubnom, Zilina
8-12-2010, 20:45, 7208, Blom NED
MSK Zilina   **1**
         Majtan [48]

Martin **Dubravka** - Stanislav **Angelovic**, Jozef **Piacek**•, Mario **Pecalka**•, Roman **Gergel** - Lubomir **Guldan**• - Pavol **Poliacek**• (Emil **Rilke** 46), Robert **Jez** (Momodou **Ceesay** 69), Bello **Babatounde**•, Tomas **Majtan** (Patrik **Mraz** 84) - Tomas **Oravec**. Tr: Pavel **Hapal**

Spartak Moskva   **2**
         Alex [54], Ibson [61]

Andrey **Dykan** - Evgeniy **Makeev** (Filip **Ozobic** 55), Marek **Suchy**, Martin **Stranzl**, Kirill **Kombarov** (Andrey **Ivanov** 82) - Aleksandr **Sheshukov**, **Ibson**♦[77] - Aiden **McGeady**, **Alex**, Dmitriy **Kombarov**• - Alexandr **Kozlov** (Nikola **Drincic** 46). Tr: Valeriy **Karpin**

GROUP G		Pl	W	D	L	F	A	Pts	ESP	ITA	NED	FRA
Real Madrid	ESP	6	5	1	0	15	2	**16**		2-0	2-0	4-0
Milan	ITA	6	2	2	2	7	7	**8**	2-2		0-2	2-0
Ajax	NED	6	2	1	3	6	10	**7**	0-4	1-1		2-1
AJ Auxerre	FRA	6	1	0	5	3	12	**3**	0-1	0-2	2-1	

Bernabeu, Madrid
15-09-2010, 20:45, 69 639, Skomina SVN
Real Madrid   **2**
Anita OG [31], Higuain [73]

Iker Casillas - Alvaro Arbeloa, Ricardo Carvalho, Pepe, Marcelo - Xabi Alonso• (Lassana Diarra 84), Sami Khedira - Angel Di Maria (Pedro Leon 80), Mesut Ozil (Sergio Canales 88), Cristiano Ronaldo - Gonzalo Higuain. Tr: Jose Mourinho

Ajax   **0**

Maarten Stekelenburg - Gregory van der Wiel, Toby Alderweireld, Andre Ooijer, Vurnon Anita - Demy de Zeeuw• (Teemu Tainio 69), Eyong Enoh, Urby Emanuelson - Mounir El Hamdaoui, Siem de Jong, Miralem Sulejmani (Christian Eriksen 85). Tr: Martin Jol

---

San Siro, Milan
15-09-2010, 20:45, 69 317, Balaj ROU
Milan   **2**
Ibrahimovic 2 [66 69]

Christian Abbiati - Gianluca Zambrotta•, Alessandro Nesta, Daniele Bonera, Luca Antonini (Ignazio Abate 70) - Massimo Ambrosini (Kevin Prince Boateng 15), Andrea Pirlo, Clarence Seedorf• - Alexandre Pato (Robinho 55), Zlatan Ibrahimovic, Ronaldinho. Tr: Massimiliano Allegri

AJ Auxerre   **0**

Olivier Sorin - Cedric Hengbart, Adama Coulibaly, Jean-Pascal Mignot, Stephane Grichting• - Dennis Oliech, Benoit Pedretti, Delvin Ndinga, Steven Langil (Kamel Chafni 80) - Valter Birsa (Anthony Le Tallec 73), Ireneusz Jelen. Tr: Jean Sammaritano

---

Abbé-Deschamps, Auxerre
28-09-2010, 20:45, 19 525, Larsen DEN
AJ Auxerre   **0**

Olivier Sorin - Cedric Hengbart, Adama Coulibaly, Stephane Grichting, Dariusz Dudka - Roy Contout (Ireneusz Jelen• 46), Benoit Pedretti, Delvin Ndinga, Steven Langil (Alain Traore• 77) - Dennis Oliech, Kamel Chafni (Julien Quercia 88). Tr: Jean Fernandez

Real Madrid   **1**
Di Maria [81]

Iker Casillas - Alvaro Arbeloa, Pepe, Sergio Ramos•, Marcelo - Sami Khedira, Lassana Diarra• (Angel Di Maria 73) - Gonzalo Higuain (Mahamadou Diarra 86), Xabi Alonso, Cristiano Ronaldo• - Karim Benzema (Mesut Ozil 58). Tr: Jose Mourinho

---

Amsterdam ArenA, Amsterdam
28-09-2010, 20:45, 51 276, Brych GER
Ajax   **1**
El Hamdaoui [23]

Maarten Stekelenburg - Gregory van der Wiel, Jan Vertonghen, Toby Alderweireld, Vurnon Anita (Miralem Sulejmani 39) - Eyong Enoh•, Siem de Jong, Demy de Zeeuw (Rasmus Lindgren 80) - Luis Suarez, Mounir El Hamdaoui, Urby Emanuelson. Tr: Martin Jol

Milan   **0**
Ibrahimovic [37]

Christian Abbiati - Gianluca Zambrotta•, Alessandro Nesta, Thiago Silva, Luca Antonini - Gennaro Gattuso•, Andrea Pirlo, Mathieu Flamini• (Kevin Prince Boateng 51), Clarence Seedorf (Ignazio Abate 86), Zlatan Ibrahimovic. Tr: Massimiliano Allegri

---

Amsterdam ArenA, Amsterdam
19-10-2010, 20:45, 51 383, Benquerenca POR
Ajax   **2**

Maarten Stekelenburg - Gregory van der Wiel, Andre Ooijer♦55, Jan Vertonghen, Urby Emanuelson - Eyong Enoh, Demy de Zeeuw, Rasmus Lindgren - Miralem Sulejmani (Oleguer 60), Mounir El Hamdaoui, Luis Suarez•. Tr: Martin Jol

AJ Auxerre   **1**

Olivier Sorin - Cedric Hengbart•, Adama Coulibaly, Stephane Grichting•, Dariusz Dudka - Roy Contout (Maxime Bourgeois 75), Benoit Pedretti, Delvin Ndinga, Valter Birsa - Kamel Chafni• (Julien Quercia 65) - Dennis Oliech••♦85. Tr: Jean Fernandez

---

Bernabeu, Madrid
19-10-2010, 20:45, 71 657, Proenca POR
Real Madrid   **2**
Ronaldo [13], Ozil [14]

Iker Casillas - Alvaro Arbeloa, Ricardo Carvalho, Pepe, Marcelo - Xabi Alonso, Sami Khedira - Angel Di Maria• (Esteban Granero 87), Mesut Ozil (Lassana Diarra 83), Cristiano Ronaldo - Gonzalo Higuain (Karim Benzema 89). Tr: Jose Mourinho

Milan   **0**

Marco Amelia - Gianluca Zambrotta, Alessandro Nesta, Daniele Bonera•, Luca Antonini• - Gennaro Gattuso (Kevin Prince Boateng• 59), Andrea Pirlo, Clarence Seedorf - Alexandre Pato (Filippo Inzaghi 78), Zlatan Ibrahimovic, Ronaldinho (Robinho 71). Tr: Massimiliano Allegri

---

Abbé-Deschamps, Auxerre
3-11-2010, 20:45, 18 727, Clattenburg ENG
AJ Auxerre   **2**
Sammaritano [9], Langil [84]

Olivier Sorin - Cedric Hengbart, Adama Coulibaly, Stephane Grichting, Dariusz Dudka - Roy Contout (Kamel Chafni 80), Benoit Pedretti, Delvin Ndinga, Valter Birsa - Frederic Sammaritano (Jeremy Berthod 85) - Julien Quercia (Steven Langil 62). Tr: Jean Fernandez

Ajax   **1**
Alderweireld [79]

Maarten Stekelenburg - Gregory van der Wiel•, Toby Alderweireld, Jan Vertonghen•, Vurnon Anita (Miralem Sulejmani 58) - Eyong Enoh (Siem de Jong 46), Demy de Zeeuw (Christian Eriksen 83), Rasmus Lindgren - Luis Suarez•, Mounir El Hamdaoui, Urby Emanuelson. Tr: Martin Jol

---

San Siro, Milan
3-11-2010, 20:45, 76 357, Webb ENG
Milan   **2**
Inzaghi 2 [68 78]

Christian Abbiati - Ignazio Abate•, Alessandro Nesta, Thiago Silva, Gianluca Zambrotta - Kevin Prince Boateng•, Andrea Pirlo, Gennaro Gattuso• (Clarence Seedorf 84) - Alexandre Pato (Massimo Ambrosini 72), Zlatan Ibrahimovic•, Ronaldinho (Filippo Inzaghi 60). Tr: Massimiliano Allegri

Real Madrid   **2**
Higuain [45], Pedro Leon [94+]

Iker Casillas - Sergio Ramos, Ricardo Carvalho•, Pepe• (Pedro Leon 30), Marcelo - Xabi Alonso, Sami Khedira - Cristiano Ronaldo, Mesut Ozil (Raul Albiol 90), Angel Di Maria - Gonzalo Higuain (Karim Benzema 74). Tr: Jose Mourinho

---

Amsterdam ArenA, Amsterdam
23-11-2010, 20:45, 48 491, Thomson SCO
Ajax   **0**

Maarten Stekelenburg - Gregory van der Wiel, Toby Alderweireld, Jan Vertonghen, Vurnon Anita - Eyong Enoh•, Siem de Jong (Rasmus Lindgren 77), Miralem Sulejmani (Christian Eriksen 88) - Luis Suarez, Mounir El Hamdaoui (Demy de Zeeuw• 46), Urby Emanuelson. Tr: Martin Jol

Real Madrid   **4**
Benzema [36], Arbeloa [44], Ronaldo 2 [70 81p]

Iker Casillas - Sergio Ramos••♦91+, Alvaro Arbeloa, Raul Albiol•, Marcelo - Xabi Alonso••♦87, Lassana Diarra (David Mateos 82) - Cristiano Ronaldo•, Mesut Ozil, Pedro Leon (Angel Di Maria 65) - Karim Benzema (Sergio Canales 82). Tr: Jose Mourinho

---

Abbé-Deschamps, Auxerre
23-11-2010, 20:45, 19 244, Skomina SVN
AJ Auxerre   **0**

Olivier Sorin - Cedric Hengbart (Kamel Chafni 59), Stephane Grichting, Adama Coulibaly, Dariusz Dudka - Dennis Oliech, Benoit Pedretti, Delvin Ndinga, Valter Birsa - Frederic Sammaritano (Julien Quercia 65) - Roy Contout (Alain Traore 82). Tr: Jean Fernandez

Milan   **2**
Ibrahimovic [64], Ronaldinho [91+]

Christian Abbiati - Ignazio Abate, Alessandro Nesta•, Thiago Silva, Gianluca Zambrotta - Gennaro Gattuso (Rodney Strasser• 90), Massimo Ambrosini•, Mathieu Flamini, Clarence Seedorf (Kevin Prince Boateng 76), Zlatan Ibrahimovic (Ronaldinho 85). Tr: Massimiliano Allegri

---

Bernanbeu, Madrid
8-12-2010, 20:45, 54 917, Gumienny BEL
Real Madrid   **4**
Benzema 3 [12 72 88], Ronaldo [49]

Jerzy Dudek (Adan 45) - Alvaro Arbeloa, Raul Albiol•, Ricardo Carvalho, Marcelo (Ezequiel Garay 76) - Esteban Granero, Lassana Diarra, Mahamadou Diarra• - Pedro Leon, Karim Benzema, Cristiano Ronaldo (Pablo Sarabia 73). Tr: Jose Mourinho

AJ Auxerre   **0**

Olivier Sorin - Dariusz Dudka, Adama Coulibaly, Jean-Pascal Mignot•, Stephane Grichting - Benoit Pedretti (Frederic Sammaritano 62), Kamel Chafni - Dennis Oliech, Alain Traore, Valter Birsa (Steven Langil 90) - Roy Contout (Julien Quercia 73). Tr: Jean Fernandez

---

San Siro, Milan
8-12-2010, 20:45, 72 960, Larsen DEN
Milan   **0**

Marco Amelia - Daniele Bonera, Thiago Silva, Mario Yepes, Luca Antonini - Mathieu Flamini (Kevin Prince Boateng 26), Andrea Pirlo, Massimo Ambrosini (Zlatan Ibrahimovic 63) - Robinho (Alexander Merkel 75), Clarence Seedorf, Ronaldinho. Tr: Massimiliano Allegri

Ajax   **2**
De Zeeuw [57], Alderweireld [66]

Maarten Stekelenburg - Gregory van der Wiel, Toby Alderweireld, Jan Vertonghen, Urby Emanuelson - Eyong Enoh, Christian Eriksen, Demy de Zeeuw (Rasmus Lindgren 82) - Luis Suarez• (Teemu Tainio 90), Siem de Jong (Mounir El Hamdaoui 84), Miralem Sulejmani•. Tr: Frank de Boer

GROUP H		Pl	W	D	L	F	A	Pts	UKR	ENG	POR	SRB
Shakhtar Donetsk	UKR	6	5	0	1	12	6	15		2-1	2-0	1-0
Arsenal	ENG	6	4	0	2	18	7	12	5-1		6-0	3-1
Sporting Braga	POR	6	3	0	3	5	11	9	0-3	2-0		2-0
Partizan Beograd	SRB	6	0	0	6	2	13	0	0-3	1-3	0-1	

Emirates, London
15-09-2010, 20:45, 59 333, Hamer LUX
Arsenal **6**
Fabregas 2 9p 53, Arshavin 30, Chamakh 34, Vela 2 69 84

Manuel Almunia - Bakari Sagna•, Laurent Koscielny, Sebastien Squillaci, Gael Clichy - Alexandre Song (Denilson 63), Jack Wilshere - Samir Nasri, Cesc Fabregas, Andrey Arshavin (Emmanuel Eboue 69) - Marouane Chamakh (Carlos Vela 63). Tr: Arsene Wenger

Sporting Braga **0**

Felipe• - Alberto Rodriguez•, Moises, Miguel Garcia, Silvio, Luis Aguiar, Hugo Viana (Marcio Mossoro 55), Vandinho, Paulo Cesar (Helder Barbosa 70), Alan, Matheus (Lima 60). Tr: Domingos Paciencia

Donbass Arena, Donetsk
15-09-2010, 20:45, 48 512, Velasco ESP
Shakhtar Donetsk **1**
Srna 71

Andriy Pyatov - Darijo Srna•, Oleksandr Kucher, Yaroslav Rakitskiy, Razvan Rat - Tomas Hubschman, Oleksiy Gai - Douglas Costa, Jadson (Alex Teixeira 58), Willian - Luiz Adriano (Vitaliy Vitsenets 83). Tr: Mircea Lucescu

Partizan Beograd **0**

Vladimir Stojkovic - Aleksandar Miljkovic, Stefan Savic, Mladen Krstajic (Vojislav Stankovic 90), Aleksandar Lazevski - Medo, Milan Smiljanic (Radosav Petrovic• 74), Sasa Ilic, Nemanja Tomic - Ivica Iliev (Pierre Boya• 58), Cleo. Tr: Aleksandar Stanojevic

Partizan, Belgrade
28-09-2010, 20:45, 29 348, Stark GER
Partizan Beograd **1**
Cleo 33p

Vladimir Stojkovic - Ivan Stevanovic, Marko Jovanovic•56, Mladen Krstajic, Aleksandar Lazevski - Nemanja Tomic (Stefan Savic 59), Medo, Radosav Petrovic (Milan Smiljanic 69), Sasa Ilic• - Pierre Boya (Ivica Iliev 83), Cleo. Tr: Aleksandar Stanojevic

Arsenal **3**
Arshavin 15, Chamakh 71, Squillaci 82

Lukasz Fabianski - Bakari Sagna, Johan Djourou, Sebastien Squillaci, Kieran Gibbs - Tomas Rosicky, Denilson, Alexandre Song, Andrey Arshavin (Gael Clichy 83) - Jack Wilshere (Samir Nasri 74) - Marouane Chamakh (Carlos Vela 74). Tr: Arsene Wenger

Municipal, Braga
28-09-2010, 20:45, 12 083, Blom NED
Sporting Braga **0**

Felipe - Miguel Garcia, Alberto Rodriguez (Paulao 36), Moises, Silvio - Vandinho (Marcio Mossoro 74), Leandro Salino (Lima 55) - Alan, Luis Aguiar, Paulo Cesar• - Matheus•. Tr: Domingos Paciencia

Shakhtar Donetsk **3**
Luiz Adriano 2 56 72, Douglas Costa 92+p

Andriy Pyatov - Darijo Srna, Oleksandr Kucher, Yaroslav Rakitskiy, Razvan Rat• - Tomas Hubschman• (Vitaliy Vitsenets 78), Oleksiy Gai (Jadson 66) - Douglas Costa•, Henrikh Mkhitaryan, Willian - Luiz Adriano (Eduardo 75). Tr: Mircea Lucescu

Municipal, Braga
19-10-2010, 20:45, 11 454, Duhamel FRA
Sporting Braga **2**
Lima 35, Matheus 90

Felipe - Silvio, Moises, Paulao, Uwa Echiejile - Alan, Vandinho, Andres Madrid• (Luis Aguiar• 73), Paulo Cesar (Leandro Salino 69) - Lima (Marcio Mossoro 87), Matheus. Tr: Domingos Paciencia

Partizan Beograd **0**

Vladimir Stojkovic - Aleksandar Miljkovic, Stefan Savic, Mladen Krstajic, Aleksandar Lazevski - Nemanja Tomic (Stefan Babovic 88), Almami Moreira• (Medo 46), Milan Smiljanic, Sasa Ilic - Marko Scepovic (Pierre Boya 55), Cleo. Tr: Aleksandar Stanojevic

Emirates, London
19-10-2010, 20:45, 60 016, Moen NOR
Arsenal **5**
Song 19, Nasri 42, Fabregas 60p, Wilshere 66, Chamakh 69

Lukasz Fabianski - Emmanuel Eboue, Sebastien Squillaci, Johan Djourou, Gael Clichy - Alexandre Song, Jack Wilshere - Tomas Rosicky, Cesc Fabregas (Denilson 63), Samir Nasri (Theo Walcott 72) - Marouane Chamakh (Andrey Arshavin 72). Tr: Arsene Wenger

Shakhtar Donetsk **1**
Eduardo 82

Andriy Pyatov - Darijo Srna, Oleksandr Kucher, Yaroslav Rakitskiy, Razvan Rat - Oleksiy Gai (Jadson 68), Tomas Hubschman• - Henrikh Mkhitaryan, Alex Teixeira, Willian (Douglas Costa 46) - Luiz Adriano• (Eduardo 64). Tr: Mircea Lucescu

Partizan, Belgrade
3-11-2010, 20:45, 28 295, Hansson SWE
Partizan Beograd **0**

Vladimir Stojkovic - Aleksandar Miljkovic, Marko Jovanovic, Mladen Krstajic, Aleksandar Lazevski - Radosav Petrovic•, Almami Moreira•, Ivica Iliev• (Marko Scepovic 78), Sasa Ilic - Pierre Boya (Stefan Babovic 59), Cleo. Tr: Aleksandar Stanojevic

Sporting Braga **1**
Moises 35

Felipe - Silvio, Moises•, Alberto Rodriguez, Uwa Echiejile - Vandinho, Luis Aguiar - Alan (Andres Madrid 68), Marcio Mossoro (Leandro Salino• 51), Paulo Cesar - Matheus (Lima 88). Tr: Domingos Paciencia

Donbass Arena, Donetsk
3-11-2010, 20:45, 51 153, Busacca SUI
Shakhtar Donetsk **2**
Chygrynskiy 28, Eduardo 45

Andriy Pyatov - Darijo Srna, Dmitro Chigrinskiy, Yaroslav Rakitskiy, Razvan Rat• - Oleksiy Gai• (Alex Teixeira 62), Tomas Hubschman• - Jadson (Douglas Costa 73), Eduardo, Willian - Luiz Adriano (Marcelo Moreno 88). Tr: Mircea Lucescu

Arsenal **1**
Walcott 10

Lukasz Fabianski - Emmanuel Eboue•, Sebastien Squillaci, Johan Djourou, Gael Clichy - Craig Eastmond (Carlos Vela 59), Jack Wilshere - Theo Walcott (Jay Emmanuel-Thomas 82), Tomas Rosicky, Samir Nasri - Nicklas Bendtner (Marouane Chamakh 73). Tr: Arsene Wenger

Municipal, Braga
23-11-2010, 20:45, 14 809, Kassai HUN
Sporting Braga **2**
Matheus 2 83 93+

Felipe - Miguel Garcia•, Moises, Alberto Rodriguez, Uwa Echiejile - Vandinho (Hugo Viana 90), Leandro Salino - Alan, Luis Aguiar• (Andres Madrid 80), Matheus - Lima (Elton 81). Tr: Domingos Paciencia

Arsenal **0**

Lukasz Fabianski - Emmanuel Eboue•, Sebastien Squillaci, Johan Djourou•, Kieran Gibbs - Theo Walcott (Carlos Vela• 77), Denilson•, Jack Wilshere, Tomas Rosicky• - Cesc Fabregas (Samir Nasri 69) - Nicklas Bendtner (Marouane Chamakh 73). Tr: Arsene Wenger

Partizan, Belgrade
23-11-2010, 20:45, 17 473, De Bleeckere BEL
Partizan Beograd **0**

Vladimir Stojkovic - Ivan Stevanovic, Marko Jovanovic, Mladen Krstajic, Aleksandar Lazevski - Radosav Petrovic (Medo 64), Milan Smiljanic• - Stefan Babovic•, Almami Moreira (Aleksandar Davidov 73), Sasa Ilic• (Ivica Iliev 84) - Cleo. Tr: Aleksandar Stanojevic

Shakhtar Donetsk **3**
Stepanenko 52, Jadson 59, Eduardo 68

Andriy Pyatov - Darijo Srna, Dmitro Chigrinskiy•, Yaroslav Rakitskiy, Razvan Rat - Oleksiy Gai• (Vitaliy Vitsenets 74), Taras Stepanenko• - Douglas Costa (Eduardo 62), Jadson (Alex Teixeira 75), Willian - Luiz Adriano. Tr: Mircea Lucescu

Emirates, London
8-12-2010, 20:45, 58 845, Tagliavento ITA
Arsenal **3**
Van Persie 30p, Walcott 73, Nasri 77

Lukasz Fabianski - Bakari Sagna♦85, Sebastien Squillaci, Laurent Koscielny, Kieran Gibbs (Emmanuel Eboue 24) - Samir Nasri, Alexandre Song, Denilson, Andrei Arshavin (Theo Walcott 67) - Robin van Persie, Marouane Chamakh (Nicklas Bendtner 76). Tr: Arsene Wenger

Partizan Beograd **1**
Cleo 52

Vladimir Stojkovic - Stefan Savic, Marko Jovanovic, Mladen Krstajic, Aleksandar Lazevski - Radosav Petrovic, Medo - Stefan Babovic (Aleksandar Davidov 81), Almami Moreira (Darko Brasanac 90), Sasa Ilic - Cleo. Tr: Aleksandar Stanojevic

Donbass Arena, Donetsk
8-12-2010, 20:45, 47 627, Brych GER
Shakhtar Donetsk **2**
Rat 78, Luiz Adriano 83

Andriy Pyatov - Darijo Srna, Dmitro Chigrinskiy, Yaroslav Rakitskiy, Razvan Rat - Oleksiy Gay (Vasiliy Kobin 84), Taras Stepanenko - Douglas Costa (Alex Teixeira 62), Jadson (Henrikh Mkhitaryan 73), Willian - Luiz Adriano. Tr: Mircea Lucescu

Sporting Braga **0**

Artur - Miguel Garcia, Anibal Capela, Alberto Rodriguez, Silvio - Vandinho, Leandro Salino (Helder Barbosa 81) - Alan (Lima 68), Luis Aguiar (Hugo Viana 72), Paulo Cesar - Matheus. Tr: Domingos Paciencia

UEFA EUROPA LEAGUE 2010–11
EARLY ROUNDS FOR TEAMS IN GROUPS A TO C

First Qualifying Round

Trans Narva	EST	0	0
MyPa-47	FIN	2	5
NSI Runavik	FRO	0	1
Gefle IF	SWE	2	2
Dinamo Tbilisi	GEO	2	0
Flora Tallinn	EST	1	0
Ulysses Yerevan	ARM	0	0
Bnei Yehuda	ISR	0	1
Shakhter Karagandy	KAZ	1	0
Ruch Chorzow	POL	2	1
Olimpia Ljubljana	SVN	0	0
Siroki Brijeg	BIH	2	3
Kalmar FF	SWE	1	3
EB/Streymur	FRO	0	0
Zeta Golubovci	MNE	1	0
Dacia Chisinau	MDA	1	0
CS Grevenmacher	LUX	3	1
Dundalk	IRL	3	2

Second Qualifying Round

MyPa-47	FIN	3	5
Sant Julia	AND	0	0
Differdange	LUX	3	0
Spartak Subotica	SRB	3	2
Gefle IF	SWE	1	1
Dinamo Tbilisi	GEO	2	2
Shamrock Rovers	IRL	1	1
Bnei Yehuda	ISR	1	0
Valletta	MLT	1	0
Ruch Chorzow	POL	1	0
FK Austria Wien	AUT	2	1
Siroki Brijeg	BIH	2	0
FK Baku	AZE	0	2
Buducnost P'gorica	MNE	3	1
Brøndby IF	DEN	3	0
FC Vaduz	LIE	0	0
Kalmar FF	SWE	0	2
Dacia Chisinau	MDA	0	0
Levski Sofia	BUL	6	2
Dundalk	IRL	0	0

Third Qualifying Round

MyPa-47	FIN	1	3
FC Timisoara	ROU	2	3
Spartak Subotica	SRB	2	0
Dnipro D'petrovsk	UKR	1	2
SK Sturm Graz	AUT	2	1
Dinamo Tbilisi	GEO	0	1
Shamrock Rovers	IRL	0	0
Juventus	ITA	2	1
Jagiellonia B'stok	POL	1	2
Aris Thessaloniki	GRE	2	2
Ruch Chorzow	POL	1	0
FK Austria Wien	AUT	3	3
Nordsjælland	DEN	0	1
Sporting CP	POR	1	2
Buducnost P'gorica	MNE	1	0
Brøndby IF	DEN	2	1
Kalmar FF	SWE	1	2
Levski Sofia	BUL	1	5

Play-off Round

FC Timisoara	ROU	0	0
Manchester City	ENG	1	2
Dnipro D'petrovsk	UKR	0	0
Lech Poznan †	POL	1	0
SK Sturm Graz	AUT	1	0
Juventus	ITA	2	1
RB Austria Salzburg	AUT	Bye	
Bayer Leverkusen	GER	3	3
Tavriya Simferopol	UKR	0	1
Aris Thessaloniki	GRE	1	1
FK Austria Wien	AUT	0	1
Atlético Madrid	ESP	Bye	
Rosenborg BK	NOR	Bye	
Sporting CP	POR	0	3
Brøndby IF	DEN	2	0
FC Vaslui	ROU	0	0
Lille OSC	FRA	0	2
Feyenoord	NED	1	0
KAA Gent †	BEL	0	2
AIK Stockholm †	SWE	0	1
Levski Sofia	BUL	0	2

† Champions League 3rd qualifying round loser • Champions League play-off round losers qualified directly for the Europa League group stage
The home teams in the first leg are listed above their opponents

UEFA EUROPA LEAGUE 2010–11
EARLY ROUNDS FOR TEAMS IN GROUPS D TO F

First Qualifying Round　　**Second Qualifying Round**　　**Third Qualifying Round**　　**Play-off Round**

First Qualifying Round

Team	Country	Leg 1	Leg 2
Laçi	ALB	1	1
Dnepr Mogilev	BLR	1	7
FC Nitra	SVK	2	1
Györi ETO	HUN	2	3
TPS Turku	FIN	3	4
Port Talbot Town	WAL	1	0
Anorthosis F'gusta	CYR	3	1
Banants Yerevan	ARM	0	0
Sibenik	CRO	0	3
Sliema Wanderers	MLT	0	0
Randers	DEN	6	1
F91 Dudelange	LUX	1	2

Second Qualifying Round

Team	Country	Leg 1	Leg 2
Stabæk Fotball	NOR	2	1
Dnepr Mogilev	BLR	2	1
WIT Georgia	GEO	0	0
Banik Ostrava	CZE	6	0
FK Atyrau	KAZ	0	0
Györi ETO	HUN	3	2
Dinamo Minsk	BLR	5	5
Kalev Sillamäe	EST	1	0
Maritimo	POR	3	3
Sporting Fingal	IRL	2	2
Honka Espoo	FIN	1	1
Bangor City	WAL	1	2
Cercle Brugge	BEL	0	2
TPS Turku	FIN	1	1
Anorthosis F'gusta	CYR	0	3
Sibenik	CRO	2	0
Videoton	HUN	1	0
NK Maribor	SVN	1	2
ND Gorica	SVN	0	1
Randers	DEN	3	1
Lausanne-Sport	SUI	1	1
Borac Banja Luka	BIH	0	1

Third Qualifying Round

Team	Country	Leg 1	Leg 2
Dnepr Mogilev	BLR	1	2
Banik Ostrava	CZE	0	1
Györi ETO	HUN	0	1 4p
Montpellier	FRA	1	0 3p
Maccabi Haifa	ISR	1	1
Dinamo Minsk	BLR	0	3
Maritimo	POR	8	2
Bangor City	WAL	2	1
AZ Alkmaar	NED	2	0
IFK Göteborg	SWE	0	1
Cercle Brugge	BEL	1	1
Anorthosis F'gusta	CYR	0	3
NK Maribor	SVN	3	3
Hibernian	SCO	0	2
Randers	DEN	2	1
Lausanne-Sport	SUI	3	1

Play-off Round

Team	Country	Leg 1	Leg 2
Villarreal	ESP	5	2
Dnepr Mogilev	BLR	0	1
PAOK Thessaloniki †	GRE	1	1
Fenerbahçe †	TUR	1	0
Györi ETO	HUN	0	1
Dinamo Zagreb †	CRO	2	2
Club Brugge	BEL	2	3
Dinamo Minsk	BLR	1	2
Dynamo Kyiv	UKR	Bye	
BATE Borisov †	BLR	3	2
Maritimo	POR	0	1
AZ Alkmaar	NED	2	1
FK Aktobe †	KAZ	0	2
Sheriff Tiraspol	MDA	Bye	
CSKA Moskva	RUS	4	2
Anorthosis F'gusta	CYR	0	1
Sparta Praha	CZE	Bye	
Città di Palermo	ITA	3	2
NK Maribor	SVN	0	3
Lausanne-Sport	SUI	1	1 4p
Lokomotiv Moskva	RUS	1	1 3p

† Champions League 3rd qualifying round loser • Champions League play-off round losers qualified directly for the Europa League group stage
The home teams in the first leg are listed above their opponents

UEFA EUROPA LEAGUE 2010–11
EARLY ROUNDS FOR TEAMS IN GROUPS G TO I

First Qualifying Round

Team			
Olimpia Balti	MDA	0	1
Khazar Lenkoran	AZE	0	1
Llanelli	WAL	2	2
Tauras Taurage	LTU	2	3
Tobol Kostanay	KAZ	1	1
Zrinjski Mostar	BIH	2	2

Second Qualifying Round

Team			
Olimpia Balti	MDA	0	1
Dinamo Bucuresti	ROU	2	5
Molde FK	NOR	1	1
FK Jelgava	LVA	0	2
Tauras Taurage	LTU	0	1
APOEL Nicosia	CYP	3	3
Zrinjski Mostar	BIH	4	9
Tre Penne	SMR	1	2
Motherwell	SCO	1	1
Breidablik	ISL	0	0

Third Qualifying Round

Team			
Dinamo Bucuresti	ROU	3	0
Hajduk Split	CRO	1	3
Crvena Zvezda	SRB	1	1
Slovan Bratislava	SVK	2	1
Molde FK	NOR	2	2
VfB Stuttgart	GER	3	2
APOEL Nicosia	CYP	1	3
FK Jablonec	CZE	0	1
Odense BK	DEN	5	0
Zrinjski Mostar	BIH	3	0
Aalesunds SK	NOR	1	0
Motherwell	SCO	1	3
SIBIR Novosibirsk	RUS	1	1
Apollon Limassol	CYP	0	2

Play-off Round

Team			
Zenit St Petersburg	RUS	Bye	
RSC Anderlecht	BEL	Bye	
Dundee United	SCO	0	1
AEK Athens	GRE	1	1
Hajduk Split	CRO	4	1
Unirea Urziceni †	ROU	1	1
Slovan Bratislava	SVK	0	2
VfB Stuttgart	GER	1	2
BSC Young Boys	SUI	Bye	
Getafe	ESP	1	1
APOEL Nicosia	CYP	0	1
Odense BK	DEN	2	1
Motherwell	SCO	1	0
SIBIR Novosibirsk	RUS	1	0
PSV Eindhoven	NED	0	5
Omonia Nicosia †	CYP	0	2
Metalist Kharkiv	UKR	1	2
Sampdoria	ITA	Bye	
Debreceni VSC †	HUN	2	2
Litex Lovech †	BUL	0	1

† Champions League 3rd qualifying round loser • Champions League play-off round losers qualified directly for the Europa League group stage
The home teams in the first leg are listed above their opponents

UEFA EUROPA LEAGUE 2010–11
EARLY ROUNDS FOR TEAMS IN GROUPS J TO L

First Qualifying Round

Team			
UE Santa Coloma	AND	0	0
Mogren Budva	MNE	3	2
Portadown	NIR	1	1
Skonto Riga	LVA	1	0
Karabakh Agdam	AZE	4	1
Metalurg Skopje	MKD	1	1
Torpedo Zhodino	BLR	3	3
Fylkir Reykjavik	ISL	0	1
KR Reykjavik	ISL	3	2
Glentoran	NIR	0	2
FC Zestafoni	GEO	5	0
Faetano	SMR	0	0
Rabotnicki Skopje	MKD	5	6
Lusitanos	AND	0	0
KF Tirana	ALB	0	1
Zalaegerszegi TE	HUN	0	0
Cliftonville	NIR	1	0
Cibalia Vinkovci	CRO	0	0

Second Qualifying Round

Team			
Besa Kavajë	ALB	0	1
Olympiacos	GRE	5	6
Maccabi Tel Aviv	ISR	2	1
Mogren Budva	MNE	0	2
Siauliai	LTU	0	0
Wisla Krakow	POL	2	5
Portadown	NIR	1	1
Karabakh Agdam	AZE	2	1
OFK Beograd	SRB	2	1
Torpedo Zhodino	BLR	2	0
KR Reykjavik	ISL	0	2
Karpaty Lviv	UKR	3	3
FC Zestafoni	GEO	3	0
Dukla B. Bystrica	SVK	0	1
Rabotnicki Skopje	MKD	1	0
Mika Ashtarak	ARM	0	0
Elfsborg IF	SWE	2	1
Iscra-Stali Ribnita	MDA	1	0
Ventspils	LVA	0	1
Teteks	MKD	0	3
FC Utrecht	NED	4	1
KF Tirana	ALB	0	1
Besiktas	TUR	3	4
Vikingur	FRO	0	0
Suduva Marijampole	LTU	0	2
SK Rapid Wien	AUT	2	4
Cliftonville	NIR	1	0
Cibalia Vinkovci	CRO	0	0

Third Qualifying Round

Team			
Olympiacos	GRE	2	0
Maccabi Tel Aviv	ISR	1	1
Wisla Krakow	POL	0	2
Karabakh Agdam	AZE	1	3
Galatasaray	TUR	2	5
OFK Beograd	SRB	2	1
Karpaty Lviv	UKR	1	1
FC Zestafoni	GEO	0	0
Rabotnicki Skopje	MKD	0	0
Liverpool	ENG	2	2
Elfsborg IF	SWE	5	2
Teteks	MKD	0	1
FC Utrecht	NED	1	3
FC Luzern	SUI	0	1
Inter Turku	FIN	1	2
KRC Genk	BEL	5	3
Viktoria Plzen	CZE	1	0
Besiktas	TUR	1	3
Beroe S. Zagora	BUL	1	0
SK Rapid Wien	AUT	1	3
CSKA Sofia	BUL	3	2
Cliftonville	NIR	0	1

Play-off Round

Team			
Paris St-Germain	FRA	2	3
Maccabi Tel Aviv	ISR	0	4
Sevilla	ESP	Bye	
Borussia Dortmund	GER	4	1
Karabakh Agdam	AZE	0	0
Galatasaray	TUR	2	1
Karpaty Lviv	UKR	2	1
Liverpool	ENG	1	2
Trabzonspor	TUR	0	1
Napoli	ITA	1	2
Elfsborg IF	SWE	0	0
Steaua Bucuresti	ROU	1 0	4p
Grasshopper-Club	SUI	0 1	3p
Celtic †	SCO	2	0
FC Utrecht	NED	0	4
KRC Genk	BEL	0	2
FC Porto	POR	3	4
Besiktas	TUR	2	4
HJK Helsinki †	FIN	0	0
SK Rapid Wien	AUT	1	3
Aston Villa	ENG	1	2
CSKA Sofia	BUL	3	2
The New Saints †	WAL	0	2

† Champions League 3rd qualifying round loser • Champions League play-off round losers qualified directly for the Europa League group stage
The home teams in the first leg are listed above their opponents

UEFA EUROPA LEAGUE 2010–11

Group Stage

Group A

		Pl	W	D	L	F	A	Pts	ENG	POL	ITA	AUT
Manchester City	ENG	6	3	2	1	11	6	11		3-1	1-1	3-0
Lech Poznan	POL	6	3	2	1	11	8	11	3-1		1-1	2-0
Juventus	ITA	6	0	6	0	7	7	6	1-1	3-3		0-0
RB Austria Salzburg	AUT	6	0	2	4	1	9	2	0-2	0-1	1-1	

Group B

		Pl	W	D	L	F	A	Pts	GER	GRE	ESP	NOR
Bayer 04 Leverkusen	GER	6	3	3	0	8	2	12		1-0	1-1	4-0
Aris Thessaloniki	GRE	6	3	1	2	7	5	10	0-0		1-0	2-0
Atlético Madrid	ESP	6	2	2	2	9	7	8	1-1	2-3		3-0
Rosenborg BK	NOR	6	1	0	5	3	13	3	0-1	2-1	1-2	

Group C

		Pl	W	D	L	F	A	Pts	POR	FRA	BEL	BUL
Sporting CP	POR	6	4	0	2	14	6	12		1-0	5-1	5-0
Lille OSC	FRA	6	2	2	2	8	6	8	1-2		3-0	1-0
KAA Gent	BEL	6	2	1	3	8	13	7	3-1	1-1		1-0
Levski Sofia	BUL	6	2	1	3	6	11	7	1-0	2-2	3-2	

Group D

		Pl	W	D	L	F	A	Pts	ESP	GRE	CRO	BEL
Villarreal	ESP	6	4	0	2	8	5	12		1-0	3-0	2-1
PAOK Thessaloniki	GRE	6	3	2	1	5	3	11	1-0		1-0	1-1
Dinamo Zagreb	CRO	6	2	1	3	4	5	7	2-0	0-1		0-0
Club Brugge	BEL	6	0	3	3	4	8	3	1-2	1-1	0-2	

Group E

		Pl	W	D	L	F	A	Pts	UKR	BLR	NED	MDA
Dynamo Kyiv	UKR	6	3	2	1	10	6	11		2-2	2-0	0-0
BATE Borisov	BLR	6	3	1	2	11	11	10	1-4		4-1	3-1
AZ Alkmaar	NED	6	2	1	3	8	10	7	1-2	3-0		2-1
Sheriff Tiraspol	MDA	6	1	2	3	5	7	5	2-0	0-1	1-1	

Group F

		Pl	W	D	L	F	A	Pts	RUS	CZE	ITA	SUI
CSKA Moskva	RUS	6	5	1	0	18	3	16		3-0	3-1	5-1
Sparta Praha	CZE	6	2	3	1	12	12	9	1-1		3-2	3-3
Città di Palermo	ITA	6	2	1	3	7	11	7	0-3	2-2		1-0
Lausanne-Sport	SUI	6	0	1	5	5	16	1	0-3	1-3	0-1	

Group G

		Pl	W	D	L	F	A	Pts	RUS	BEL	GRE	CRO
Zenit St Petersburg	RUS	6	6	0	0	18	6	18		3-1	4-2	2-0
RSC Anderlecht	BEL	6	2	1	3	8	8	7	1-3		3-0	2-0
AEK Athens	GRE	6	2	1	3	9	13	7	0-3	1-1		3-1
Hajduk Split	CRO	6	1	0	5	5	13	3	2-3	1-0	1-3	

Group H

		Pl	W	D	L	F	A	Pts	GER	SUI	ESP	DEN
VfB Stuttgart	GER	6	5	0	1	16	6	15		3-0	1-0	5-1
BSC Young Boys	SUI	6	3	0	3	10	10	9	4-2		2-0	4-2
Getafe	ESP	6	2	1	3	4	8	7	0-3	1-0		2-1
Odense BK	DEN	6	1	1	4	8	14	4	1-2	2-0	1-1	

Group I

		Pl	W	D	L	F	A	Pts	NED	UKR	ITA	HUN
PSV Eindhoven	NED	6	4	2	0	10	3	14		0-0	1-1	3-0
Metalist Kharkiv	UKR	6	3	2	1	9	4	11	0-2		2-1	2-1
Sampdoria	ITA	6	1	2	3	4	7	5	1-2	0-0		1-0
Debreceni VSC	HUN	6	1	0	5	4	13	3	1-2	0-5	2-0	

Group J

		Pl	W	D	L	F	A	Pts	FRA	ESP	GER	UKR
Paris Saint-Germain	FRA	6	3	3	0	9	4	12		4-2	0-0	2-0
Sevilla	ESP	6	3	1	2	10	7	10	0-1		2-2	4-0
Borussia Dortmund	GER	6	2	3	1	10	7	9	1-1	0-1		3-0
Karpaty Lviv	UKR	6	0	1	5	4	15	1	1-1	0-1	3-4	

Group K

		Pl	W	D	L	F	A	Pts	ENG	ITA	ROU	NED
Liverpool	ENG	6	2	4	0	8	3	10		3-1	4-1	0-0
Napoli	ITA	6	1	4	1	8	9	7	0-0		1-0	0-0
Steaua Bucuresti	ROU	6	1	3	2	9	11	6	1-1	3-3		3-1
FC Utrecht	NED	6	0	5	1	5	7	5	0-0	3-3	1-1	

Group L

		Pl	W	D	L	F	A	Pts	POR	TUR	AUT	BUL
FC Porto	POR	6	5	1	0	14	4	16		1-1	3-0	3-1
Besiktas	TUR	6	4	1	1	9	6	13	1-3		2-0	1-0
SK Rapid Wien	AUT	6	1	0	5	5	12	3	1-3	1-2		1-2
CSKA Sofia	BUL	6	1	0	5	4	10	3	0-1	1-2	0-2	

Round of 32

- Benfica †
- VfB Stuttgart
- BATE Borisov
- Paris Saint-Germain
- Besiktas
- Dynamo Kyiv
- Aris Thessaloniki
- Manchester City
- Rubin Kazan †
- FC Twente Enschede †
- BSC Young Boys
- Zenit St Petersburg
- PAOK Thessaloniki
- CSKA Moskva
- Sevilla
- FC Porto
- Lille OSC
- PSV Eindhoven
- Rangers †
- Sporting CP
- Metalist Kharkiv
- Bayer Leverkusen
- Napoli
- Villarreal
- RSC Anderlecht
- Ajax †
- FC Basel †
- Spartak Moskva †
- Sparta Praha
- Liverpool
- Lech Poznan
- Sporting Braga †

‡ Qualified as a Champions League play-off round loser • † Qualified as a third placed team from the Champions League group stage

YOUTH TOURNAMENTS IN EUROPE 2010

UEFA EUROPEAN U-17 CHAMPIONSHIP 2010

Qualifying Round Group 1

	Pl	W	D	L	F	A	Pts	SRB	AZE	KAZ
England	3	3	0	0	11	2	**9**	1-0	4-0	6-2
Serbia	3	1	1	1	1	1	**4**		0-0	1-0
Azerbaijan	3	1	1	1	3	5	4			3-1
Kazakhstan	3	0	0	3	3	10	**0**		Played in AZE	

Qualifying Round Group 2

	Pl	W	D	L	F	A	Pts	ROU	LTU	FRO
Spain	3	3	0	0	19	2	**9**	4-1	9-1	6-0
Romania	3	2	0	1	6	4	**6**		1-0	4-0
Lithuania	3	1	0	2	4	12	3			3-2
Faroe Islands	3	0	0	3	2	13	**0**		Played in ROU	

Qualifying Round Group 3

	Pl	W	D	L	F	A	Pts	BEL	DEN	MNE
Croatia	3	2	1	0	4	2	**7**	1-0	2-1	1-1
Belgium	3	1	1	1	4	3	**4**		3-1	1-1
Denmark	3	1	0	2	10	6	3			8-1
Montenegro	3	0	2	1	3	10	**2**		Played in MNE	

Qualifying Round Group 4

	Pl	W	D	L	F	A	Pts	POL	ISR	ARM
Austria	3	2	1	0	7	3	**7**	4-2	2-0	1-1
Poland	3	2	0	1	13	5	**6**		7-0	4-1
Israel	3	1	0	2	6	10	3			6-1
Armenia	3	0	1	2	3	11	**1**		Played in POL	

Qualifying Round Group 5

	Pl	W	D	L	F	A	Pts	GER	FIN	MKD
Turkey	3	2	0	1	5	3	**6**	1-2	2-0	2-1
Germany	3	2	0	1	4	2	**6**		0-1	2-0
Finland	3	2	0	1	6	4	6			5-2
Macedonia FYR	3	0	0	3	3	9	**0**		Played in MKD	

Qualifying Round Group 6

	Pl	W	D	L	F	A	Pts	SWE	BUL	LVA
Republic of Ireland	3	2	1	0	3	1	**7**	0-0	2-1	1-0
Sweden	3	1	2	0	2	0	**5**		0-0	2-0
Bulgaria	3	1	1	1	5	2	4			4-0
Latvia	3	0	0	3	0	7	**0**		Played in BUL	

Qualifying Round Group 7

	Pl	W	D	L	F	A	Pts	UKR	EST	SVN
France	3	2	1	0	7	3	**7**	1-1	3-1	3-1
Ukraine	3	1	2	0	2	1	**5**		0-0	1-0
Estonia	3	1	1	1	2	3	4			1-0
Slovenia	3	0	0	3	1	5	**0**		Played in EST	

Qualifying Round Group 8

	Pl	W	D	L	F	A	Pts	NIR	MLT	AND
Netherlands	3	2	0	1	6	2	**6**	1-0	1-2	4-0
Northern Ireland	3	2	0	1	4	1	**6**		2-0	2-0
Malta	3	1	1	1	2	3	4			0-0
Andorra	3	0	1	2	0	6	**1**		Played in AND	

Qualifying Round Group 9

	Pl	W	D	L	F	A	Pts	NOR	ITA	MDA
Greece	3	1	2	0	3	2	**5**	1-0	0-0	2-2
Norway	3	1	1	1	2	1	**4**		2-0	0-0
Italy	3	1	1	1	5	2	4			5-0
Moldova	3	0	2	1	2	7	**2**		Played in ITA	

Qualifying Round Group 10

	Pl	W	D	L	F	A	Pts	GEO	CYP	SCO
Portugal	3	2	1	0	6	3	**7**	2-0	2-1	2-2
Georgia	3	2	0	1	6	5	**6**		4-2	2-1
Cyprus	3	1	0	2	5	7	3			2-1
Scotland	3	0	1	2	4	6	**1**		Played in SCO	

Qualifying Round Group 11

	Pl	W	D	L	F	A	Pts	SVK	LUX	ALB
Hungary	3	2	1	0	7	1	**7**	1-0	1-1	5-0
Slovakia	3	2	0	1	5	1	**6**		2-0	3-0
Luxembourg	3	1	1	1	4	5	4			3-2
Albania	3	0	0	3	2	11	**0**		Played in HUN	

Qualifying Round Group 12

	Pl	W	D	L	F	A	Pts	BIH	ISL	RUS
Wales	3	2	1	0	7	5	**7**	2-2	3-2	2-1
Bosnia-Herzegovina	3	0	3	0	3	3	**3**		1-1	0-0
Iceland	3	0	2	1	4	5	2			1-1
Russia	3	0	2	1	2	3	**2**		Played in WAL	

Qualifying Round Group 13

	Pl	W	D	L	F	A	Pts	SUI	BLR	SMR
Czech Republic	3	3	0	0	9	0	**9**	4-0	1-0	4-0
Switzerland	3	2	0	1	12	4	**6**		2-0	10-0
Belarus	3	1	0	2	4	3	3			4-0
San Marino	3	0	0	3	0	18	**0**		Played in BLR	

Elite Round Group 1

	Pl	W	D	L	F	A	Pts	NED	GEO	UKR
Czech Republic	3	2	0	1	3	2	**6**	1-0	0-1	2-1
Netherlands	3	2	0	1	4	2	**6**		2-1	2-0
Georgia	3	1	1	1	4	4	4			2-2
Ukraine	3	0	1	2	3	6	**1**		Played in CZE	

Elite Round Group 2

	Pl	W	D	L	F	A	Pts	CRO	BIH	ROU
Portugal	3	2	1	0	7	2	**7**	2-0	1-1	4-1
Croatia	3	2	0	1	5	3	**6**		2-1	3-0
Bosnia-Herzegovina	3	0	2	1	5	6	2			3-3
Romania	3	0	1	2	4	10	**1**		Played in BIH	

Elite Round Group 3

	Pl	W	D	L	F	A	Pts	IRL	AUT	FIN
Greece	3	2	1	0	7	3	**7**	3-0	2-2	2-1
Republic of Ireland	3	2	0	1	4	3	**6**		3-0	1-0
Austria	3	0	2	1	5	8	2			3-3
Finland	3	0	1	2	4	6	**1**		Played in GRE	

Elite Round Group 4

	Pl	W	D	L	F	A	Pts	BEL	NIR	POL
Spain	3	2	0	1	6	1	**6**	0-1	4-0	1-0
Belgium	3	2	0	1	3	1	**6**		0-1	2-0
Northern Ireland	3	2	0	1	2	4	**6**			1-0
Poland	3	0	0	3	0	5	**0**		Played in NIR	

Elite Round Group 5	Pl	W	D	L	F	A	Pts	FRA	WAL	NOR
Turkey	3	2	1	0	4	1	7	1-0	1-1	2-0
France	3	2	0	1	5	1	6		4-0	1-0
Wales	3	0	2	1	1	5	2			0-0
Norway	3	0	1	2	0	3	1	Played in FRA		

Elite Round Group 6	Pl	W	D	L	F	A	Pts	GER	SRB	HUN
Switzerland	3	2	0	1	5	3	6	1-0	1-2	3-1
Germany	3	2	0	1	5	2	6		4-1	1-0
Serbia	3	1	1	1	3	5	4			0-0
Hungary	3	0	1	2	1	4	1	Played in SUI		

Elite Round Group 7	Pl	W	D	L	F	A	Pts	SWE	SVK	MLT
England	3	3	0	0	11	0	9	4-0	2-0	5-0
Sweden	3	2	0	1	7	4	6		2-0	5-0
Slovakia	3	1	0	2	2	4	3			2-0
Malta	3	0	0	3	0	12	0	Played in ENG		

UEFA EUROPEAN U-17 CHAMPIONSHIP LIECHTENSTEIN 2010

First Round Group Stage

Group A	Pl	W	D	L	F	A	Pts	FRA	POR	SUI
Spain	3	3	0	0	8	1	9	2-1	2-0	4-0
France	3	2	0	1	5	3	6		1-0	3-1
Portugal	3	1	0	2	3	3	3			3-0
Switzerland	3	0	0	3	1	10	0			

Group B	Pl	W	D	L	F	A	Pts	TUR	CZE	GRE
England	3	3	0	0	6	2	9	2-1	3-1	1-0
Turkey	3	1	1	1	5	4	4		1-1	3-1
Czech Republic	3	0	2	1	2	4	2			0-0
Greece	3	0	1	2	1	4	1	Finals held in Liechtenstein from 18-05-2010 to 30-05-2010		

Semi-finals

England	2
France	1

Turkey	1
Spain	3

Final

England	2
Spain	1

UEFA EUROPEAN U-19 CHAMPIONSHIP 2010

Qualifying Round Group 1	Pl	W	D	L	F	A	Pts	IRL	ALB	SMR
Italy	3	3	0	0	11	0	9	2-0	5-0	4-0
Republic of Ireland	3	2	0	1	7	2	6		2-0	5-0
Albania	3	1	0	2	4	8	3			4-1
San Marino	3	0	0	3	1	13	0	Played in SMR		

Qualifying Round Group 2	Pl	W	D	L	F	A	Pts	SVK	FIN	SVN
England	3	3	0	0	8	2	9	2-0	3-1	3-1
Slovakia	3	2	0	1	5	2	6		4-0	1-0
Finland	3	1	0	2	3	7	3			2-0
Slovenia	3	0	0	3	1	6	0	Played in SVN		

Qualifying Round Group 3	Pl	W	D	L	F	A	Pts	GER	MDA	LUX
Turkey	3	2	1	0	4	2	7	2-1	1-0	1-1
Germany	3	2	0	1	9	2	6		5-0	3-0
Moldova	3	1	0	2	2	7	3			2-1
Luxembourg	3	0	1	2	2	6	1	Played in LUX		

Qualifying Round Group 4	Pl	W	D	L	F	A	Pts	SUI	LTU	EST
Croatia	3	3	0	0	6	1	9	1-0	2-1	3-0
Switzerland	3	2	0	1	10	1	6		5-0	5-0
Lithuania	3	1	0	2	2	7	3			2-1
Estonia	3	0	0	3	1	10	0	Played in LTU		

Qualifying Round Group 5	Pl	W	D	L	F	A	Pts	GRE	FRO	BLR
Serbia	3	3	0	0	8	0	9	1-0	2-0	5-0
Greece	3	2	0	1	3	1	6		2-0	1-0
Faroe Islands	3	0	1	2	0	4	1			0-0
Belarus	3	0	1	2	0	6	1	Played in SRB		

Qualifying Round Group 6	Pl	W	D	L	F	A	Pts	ROU	AUT	ARM
Scotland	3	2	0	1	9	2	6	3-0	0-1	6-1
Romania	3	2	0	1	5	3	6		4-0	1-0
Austria	3	2	0	1	6	5	6			5-1
Armenia	3	0	0	3	2	12	0	Played in AUT		

Qualifying Round Group 7	Pl	W	D	L	F	A	Pts	NIR	ISL	BUL
Bosnia-Herzegovina	3	2	0	1	3	5	6	0-4	1-3	2-1
Northern Ireland	3	1	2	0	5	1	5		0-0	1-1
Iceland	3	1	1	1	3	3	4			3-2
Bulgaria	3	0	1	2	4	6	1	Played in BIH		

Qualifying Round Group 8	Pl	W	D	L	F	A	Pts	ESP	WAL	MKD
Portugal	3	3	0	0	7	0	9	1-0	3-0	3-0
Spain	3	2	0	1	6	2	6		1-0	5-1
Wales	3	1	0	2	3	5	3			
FYR Macedonia	3	0	0	3	2	11	0	Played in E		

Qualifying Round Group 9

	Pl	W	D	L	F	A	Pts	HUN	LVA	LIE
Russia	3	2	1	0	9	2	7	2-1	1-1	6-0
Hungary	3	2	0	1	10	3	6		5-1	4-0
Latvia	3	1	1	1	6	6	4			4-0
Liechtenstein	3	0	0	3	0	14	0	Played in HUN		

Qualifying Round Group 10

	Pl	W	D	L	F	A	Pts	CZE	MLT	CYP
Netherlands	3	3	0	0	7	1	9	1-0	1-0	5-1
Czech Republic	3	2	0	1	7	2	6		4-0	3-1
Malta	3	0	1	2	1	6	1			1-1
Cyprus	3	0	1	2	3	9	1	Played in MLT		

Qualifying Round Group 11

	Pl	W	D	L	F	A	Pts	BEL	KAZ	AND
Norway	3	3	0	0	11	2	9	4-2	2-0	5-0
Belgium	3	2	0	1	10	4	6		4-0	4-0
Kazakhstan	3	1	0	2	2	7	3			2-1
Andorra	3	0	0	3	1	11	0	Played in BEL		

Qualifying Round Group 12

	Pl	W	D	L	F	A	Pts	MNE	GEO	SWE
Ukraine	3	2	1	0	3	1	7	1-1	1-0	1-0
Montenegro	3	0	3	0	2	2	3		1-1	0-0
Georgia	3	0	2	1	1	2	2			0-0
Sweden	3	0	2	1	0	1	2	Played in SWE		

Qualifying Round Group 13

	Pl	W	D	L	F	A	Pts	AZE	POL	ISR
Denmark	3	2	0	1	5	2	6	3-0	1-2	1-0
Azerbaijan	3	2	0	1	5	4	6		2-1	3-0
Poland	3	1	1	1	4	4	4			1-1
Israel	3	0	1	2	1	5	1	Played in ISR		

Elite Round Group 1

	Pl	W	D	L	F	A	Pts	BEL	SCO	MNE
Croatia	3	3	0	0	6	1	9	2-1	1-0	3-0
Belgium	3	2	0	1	7	4	6		2-1	4-1
Scotland	3	1	0	2	5	3	3			4-0
Montenegro	3	0	0	3	1	11	0	Played in CRO		

Elite Round Group 2

	Pl	W	D	L	F	A	Pts	GRE	HUN	ROU
Portugal	3	2	1	0	7	4	7	1-1	3-2	3-1
Greece	3	2	1	0	4	1	7		1-0	2-0
Hungary	3	1	0	2	5	4	3			3-0
Romania	3	0	0	3	1	8	0	Played in HUN		

Elite Round Group 3

	Pl	W	D	L	F	A	Pts	IRL	UKR	BIH
England	3	2	1	0	6	1	7	1-0	1-1	4-0
Republic of Ireland	3	2	0	1	2	1	6		1-0	1-0
Ukraine	3	1	1	1	5	3	4			4-1
Bosnia-Herzegovina	3	0	0	3	1	9	0	Played in UKR		

Elite Round Group 4

	Pl	W	D	L	F	A	Pts	TUR	NOR	AZE
Spain	3	2	1	0	8	3	7	3-2	1-1	4-0
Turkey	3	2	0	1	6	4	6		2-1	2-0
Norway	3	0	2	1	3	4	2			1-1
Azerbaijan	3	0	1	2	1	7	1	Played in TUR		

Elite Round Group 5

	Pl	W	D	L	F	A	Pts	RUS	CZE	NIR
Italy	3	2	0	1	6	5	6	1-3	2-0	3-2
Russia	3	1	2	0	8	6	5		3-3	2-2
Czech Republic	3	1	1	1	6	6	4			3-1
Northern Ireland	3	0	1	2	5	8	1	Played in RUS		

Elite Round Group 6

	Pl	W	D	L	F	A	Pts	SVK	GER	POL
Netherlands	3	2	1	0	5	0	7	0-0	3-0	2-0
Slovakia	3	1	1	1	2	2	4		2-1	0-1
Germany	3	1	0	2	5	6	3			4-1
Poland	3	1	0	2	2	6	3	Played in NED		

Elite Round Group 7

	Pl	W	D	L	F	A	Pts	SRB	DEN	SUI
Austria	3	2	0	1	8	6	6	2-0	4-3	2-3
Serbia	3	2	0	1	7	6	6		3-2	4-2
Denmark	3	1	0	2	6	7	3			1-0
Switzerland	3	1	0	2	5	7	3	Played in AUT		

UEFA EUROPEAN U-19 CHAMPIONSHIP FRANCE 2010

First Round Group Stage

Group A	Pl	W	D	L	F	A	Pts	ENG	AUT	NED
France	3	2	1	0	10	2	7	1-1	5-0	4-1
England	3	1	1	1	4	4	4		3-2	0-1
Austria	3	1	0	2	3	8	3			1-0
Netherlands	3	1	0	2	2	5	3			

Group B	Pl	W	D	L	F	A	Pts	CRO	POR	ITA
Spain	3	3	0	0	7	2	9	2-1	2-1	3-0
Croatia	3	1	1	1	6	2	4		5-0	0-0
Portugal	3	1	0	2	3	7	3			2-0
Italy	3	0	1	2	0	5	1	Finals held in France from 18-07-2010 to 30-07-2010		

Semi-finals

France	2
Croatia	1

England	1
Spain	3

Final

France	2
Spain	1

WOMEN'S TOURNAMENTS IN EUROPE 2010

UEFA WOMEN'S U-17 CHAMPIONSHIP 2010

First Qualifying Round Group 1

	Pl	W	D	L	F	A	Pts	WAL	BLR	MKD
England	3	3	0	0	17	0	9	3-0	7-0	7-0
Wales	3	1	1	1	3	4	4		2-0	1-1
Belarus	3	1	0	2	1	9	3			1-0
FYR Macedonia	3	0	1	2	1	9	1	Played in MKD		

First Qualifying Round Group 2

	Pl	W	D	L	F	A	Pts	ITA	FRO	GEO
Switzerland	3	3	0	0	32	1	9	2-1	7-0	23-0
Italy	3	2	0	1	35	2	6		7-0	27-0
Faroe Islands	3	1	0	2	7	14	3			7-0
Georgia	3	0	0	3	0	57	0	Played in SUI		

First Qualifying Round Group 3

	Pl	W	D	L	F	A	Pts	HUN	CRO	GRE
Norway	3	3	0	0	14	1	9	5-1	4-0	5-0
Hungary	3	2	0	1	7	7	6		3-2	3-0
Croatia	3	1	0	2	4	7	3			2-0
Greece	3	0	0	3	0	10	0	Played in HUN		

First Qualifying Round Group 4

	Pl	W	D	L	F	A	Pts	DEN	TUR	SVN
Republic of Ireland	3	3	0	0	9	0	9	1-0	3-0	5-0
Denmark	3	2	0	1	5	1	6		3-0	2-0
Turkey	3	1	0	2	1	6	3			1-0
Slovenia	3	0	0	3	0	8	0	Played in SVN		

First Qualifying Round Group 5

	Pl	W	D	L	F	A	Pts	POL	ROU	BUL
Belgium	3	2	1	0	11	3	7	1-1	3-1	7-1
Poland	3	2	1	0	6	1	7		3-0	2-0
Romania	3	1	0	2	2	6	3			1-0
Bulgaria	3	0	0	3	1	10	0	Played in POL		

First Qualifying Round Group 6

	Pl	W	D	L	F	A	Pts	UKR	KAZ	MDA
Netherlands	3	3	0	0	13	1	9	2-1	2-0	9-0
Ukraine	3	2	0	1	12	3	6		6-1	5-0
Kazakhstan	3	1	0	2	3	9	3			2-1
Moldova	3	0	0	3	1	16	0	Played in MDA		

First Qualifying Round Group 7

	Pl	W	D	L	F	A	Pts	FRA	ISL	ISR
Germany	3	2	1	0	11	0	7	1-0	0-0	10-0
France	3	2	0	1	10	2	6		2-1	8-0
Iceland	3	1	1	1	8	2	4			7-0
Israel	3	0	0	3	0	25	0	Played in ISL		

First Qualifying Round Group 8

	Pl	W	D	L	F	A	Pts	FIN	LVA	EST
Sweden	3	3	0	0	26	1	9	4-1	8-0	14-0
Finland	3	2	0	1	13	4	6		5-0	7-0
Latvia	3	1	0	2	3	13	3			3-0
Estonia	3	0	0	3	0	24	0	Played in SWE		

First Qualifying Round Group 9

	Pl	W	D	L	F	A	Pts	CZE	SCO	LTU
Austria	3	3	0	0	21	3	9	5-1	3-1	13-1
Czech Republic	3	2	0	1	24	5	6		5-0	18-0
Scotland	3	1	0	2	14	8	3			13-0
Lithuania	3	0	0	3	1	44	0	Played in LTU		

First Qualifying Round Group 10

	Pl	W	D	L	F	A	Pts	SRB	RUS	ARM
Spain	3	2	1	0	26	2	7	2-2	3-0	21-0
Serbia	3	2	1	0	16	3	7		2-1	12-0
Russia	3	1	0	2	20	5	3			19-0
Armenia	3	0	0	3	0	52	0	Played in SRB		

UEFA EUROPEAN WOMEN'S U-17 CHAMPIONSHIP 2010

Second Qualifying Round

Group 1

	Pl	W	D	L	F	A	Pts	ITA	ENG	SRB
Netherlands	3	3	0	0	5	1	9	2-0	2-1	1-0
Italy	3	1	1	1	6	3	4		0-0	6-1
England	3	1	1	1	4	3	4			3-1
Serbia	3	0	0	3	2	10	0			

Group 2

	Pl	W	D	L	F	A	Pts	DEN	SUI	BEL
Spain	3	2	1	0	7	1	7	5-1	0-0	2-0
Denmark	3	2	0	1	4	5	6		2-0	1-0
Switzerland	3	0	2	1	0	2	2			0-0
Belgium	3	0	1	2	0	3	1			

Group 3

	Pl	W	D	L	F	A	Pts	SWE	POL	UKR
Rep. of Ireland	3	2	1	0	6	3	7	2-1	1-1	3-1
Sweden	3	2	0	1	11	3	6		4-1	6-0
Poland	3	0	2	1	4	7	2			2-2
Ukraine	3	0	1	2	3	11	1			

Group 4

	Pl	W	D	L	F	A	Pts	NOR	AUT	FIN
Germany	3	3	0	0	8	0	9	4-0	1-0	3-0
Norway	3	2	0	1	3	5	6		1-0	2-1
Austria	3	1	0	2	1	2	3			1-0
Finland	3	0	0	3	1	6	0			

Semi-finals

Spain	3
Netherlands	0

Germany	0
Rep. of Ireland	1

Final

Spain	0 4p
Rep. of Ireland	0 1p

Third Place Play-off

Germany	3
Netherlands	0

Finals in Nyon, Switzerland, 22-06-2010 to 26-06-2010
Group 1 in Italy; Group 2 in Spain; Group 3 in Ukraine; Group 4 in Austria

UEFA WOMEN'S U-19 CHAMPIONSHIP 2010

First Qualifying Round Group 1

	Pl	W	D	L	F	A	Pts	FIN	CRO	FRO
Republic of Ireland	3	3	0	0	13	2	9	3-2	3-0	7-0
Finland	3	2	0	1	5	4	6		2-1	1-0
Croatia	3	1	0	2	4	5	3			3-0
Faroe Islands	3	0	0	3	0	11	0	Played in CRO		

First Qualifying Round Group 2

	Pl	W	D	L	F	A	Pts	CZE	EST	SVN
Sweden	3	2	1	0	18	2	7	1-0	8-0	12-0
Czech Republic	3	2	0	1	5	3	6		3-1	2-1
Estonia	3	1	0	2	2	11	3			1-0
Slovenia	3	0	1	2	3	5	1	Played in EST		

First Qualifying Round Group 3

	Pl	W	D	L	F	A	Pts	BIH	WAL	MDA
Denmark	3	3	0	0	14	1	9	7-0	2-1	5-0
Bosnia-Herzegovina	3	2	0	1	9	9	6		6-2	3-0
Wales	3	1	0	2	8	8	3			5-0
Moldova	3	0	0	3	0	13	0	Played in DEN		

First Qualifying Round Group 4

	Pl	W	D	L	F	A	Pts	SCO	BUL	NIR
Italy	3	3	0	0	14	0	9	2-0	6-0	6-0
Scotland	3	2	0	1	7	3	6		5-1	2-0
Bulgaria	3	1	0	2	2	11	3			1-0
Northern Ireland	3	0	0	3	0	9	0	Played in BUL		

First Qualifying Round Group 5

	Pl	W	D	L	F	A	Pts	POL	ISR	LTU
Netherlands	3	2	1	0	17	2	7	1-1	9-1	7-0
Poland	3	2	1	0	10	1	7		6-0	3-0
Israel	3	1	0	2	4	16	3			3-1
Lithuania	3	0	0	3	1	13	0	Played in NED		

First Qualifying Round Group 6

	Pl	W	D	L	F	A	Pts	ENG	SVK	BLR
Norway	3	2	1	0	11	2	7	1-1	5-1	12-0
England	3	2	1	0	8	2	7		3-1	4-0
Slovakia	3	1	0	2	7	9	3			5-1
Belarus	3	0	0	3	1	21	0	Played in ENG		

First Qualifying Round Group 7

	Pl	W	D	L	F	A	Pts	TUR	SRB	GEO
France	3	3	0	0	17	1	9	5-1	5-0	7-0
Turkey	3	1	1	1	15	6	4		1-1	13-0
Serbia	3	1	1	1	4	6	4			3-0
Georgia	3	0	0	3	0	23	0	Played in TUR		

First Qualifying Round Group 8

	Pl	W	D	L	F	A	Pts	HUN	LVA	ARM
Belgium	3	2	1	0	14	2	7	0-0	4-2	10-0
Hungary	3	2	1	0	11	0	7		7-0	4-0
Latvia	3	1	0	2	8	13	3			6-2
Armenia	3	0	0	3	2	20	0	Played in HUN		

First Qualifying Round Group 9

	Pl	W	D	L	F	A	Pts	AUT	KAZ	GRE
Russia	3	3	0	0	9	1	9	1-0	3-0	5-1
Austria	3	2	0	1	4	2	6		2-1	2-0
Kazakhstan	3	1	0	2	3	6	3			2-1
Greece	3	0	0	3	2	9	0	Played in AUT		

First Qualifying Round Group 10

	Pl	W	D	L	F	A	Pts	UKR	CYP	AZE
Spain	3	3	0	0	11	1	9	4-0	4-1	3-0
Ukraine	3	2	0	1	5	4	6		2-0	3-0
Cyprus	3	1	0	2	4	6	3			3-0
Azerbaijan	3	0	0	3	0	9	0	Played in AZE		

Second Qualifying Round Group 1

	Pl	W	D	L	F	A	Pts	SWE	IRL	TUR
England	3	3	0	0	9	2	9	3-2	3-0	3-0
Sweden	3	2	0	1	9	3	6		4-0	3-0
Republic of Ireland	3	1	0	2	3	9	3			3-2
Turkey	3	0	0	3	2	9	0	Played in SWE		

Second Qualifying Round Group 2

	Pl	W	D	L	F	A	Pts	AUT	SUI	HUN
France	3	2	1	0	5	0	7	0-0	1-0	4-0
Austria	3	1	2	0	4	2	5		1-1	3-1
Switzerland	3	1	1	1	6	3	4			5-1
Hungary	3	0	0	3	2	12	0	Played in HUN		

Second Qualifying Round Group 3

	Pl	W	D	L	F	A	Pts	NOR	POL	SRB
Germany	3	3	0	0	18	0	9	3-0	7-0	8-0
Norway	3	2	0	1	10	4	6		6-1	4-0
Poland	3	0	1	2	2	14	1			1-1
Serbia	3	0	1	2	1	13	1	Played in SRB		

Second Qualifying Round Group 4

	Pl	W	D	L	F	A	Pts	RUS	CZE	ISL
Spain	3	2	0	1	8	3	6	1-0	5-0	2-3
Russia	3	2	0	1	7	1	6		6-0	1-0
Czech Republic	3	1	0	2	2	12	3			2-1
Iceland	3	1	0	2	4	5	3	Played in RUS		

Second Qualifying Round Group 5

	Pl	W	D	L	F	A	Pts	SCO	DEN	FIN
Netherlands	3	2	1	0	6	1	7	0-0	2-1	4-0
Scotland	3	2	1	0	5	2	7		2-1	3-1
Denmark	3	1	0	2	4	5	3			2-1
Finland	3	0	0	3	2	9	0	Played in NED		

Second Qualifying Round Group 6

	Pl	W	D	L	F	A	Pts	BEL	UKR	BIH
Italy	3	3	0	0	11	1	9	5-0	3-0	3-1
Belgium	3	2	0	1	4	6	6		2-1	2-0
Ukraine	3	1	0	2	7	5	3			6-0
Bosnia-Herzegovina	3	0	0	3	1	11	0	Played in BEL		

UEFA EUROPEAN WOMEN'S U-19 CHAMPIONSHIP FYR MACEDONIA 2010

First Round Group Stage

Group A	Pl	W	D	L	F	A	Pts	ENG	ITA	SCO
Germany	3	3	0	0	11	3	9	2-1	4-1	5-1
England	3	2	0	1	6	4	6		2-1	3-1
Italy	3	0	1	2	5	9	1			3-3
Scotland	3	0	1	2	5	11	1			

Group B	Pl	W	D	L	F	A	Pts	FRA	ESP	MKD
Netherlands	3	3	0	0	11	0	9	2-0	2-0	7-0
France	3	2	0	1	7	3	6		1-0	6-1
Spain	3	1	0	2	6	3	3			6-0
Macedonia FYR	3	0	0	3	1	19	0			

Semi-finals

France	1 5p
Germany	1 3p

Netherlands	0 4p
England	0 5p

Final

France	2
England	1

Finals held in Macedonia from 24-05-2009 to 5-06-2010

UEFA WOMEN'S CHAMPIONS LEAGUE 2010

First Qualifying Round

		Pl	W	D	L	F	A	Pts	SCO	LTU	GEO
Bayern München	GER	3	3	0	0	32	2	9	5-2	8-0	19-0
Glasgow City	SCO	3	2	0	1	13	5	6		2-0	9-0
Gintra Univer'tas	LTU	3	1	0	2	7	11	3			7-1
Norchi Dinamoeli	GEO	3	0	0	3	1	35	0			Played in LTU

		Pl	W	D	L	F	A	Pts	BUL	FRO	MKD
Montpellier HSC	FRA	3	3	0	0	12	1	9	3-0	2-0	7-1
NSA Sofia	BUL	3	2	0	1	7	4	6		2-1	5-0
KI Klaksvik	FRO	3	1	0	2	5	6	3			4-2
Tikvesanka	MKD	3	0	0	3	3	16	0			Played in MKD

		Pl	W	D	L	F	A	Pts	POR	WAL	MLT
Brøndby IF	DEN	3	3	0	0	12	0	9	1-0	5-0	6-0
1° Dezembro	POR	3	2	0	1	13	1	6		3-0	10-0
Cardiff City	WAL	3	1	0	2	10	9	3			10-1
Birkirkara	MLT	3	0	0	3	1	26	0			Played in DEN

		Pl	W	D	L	F	A	Pts	SVK	TUR	SVN
Torres	ITA	3	3	0	0	13	0	9	1-0	9-0	3-0
Slovan Duslo Sala	SVK	3	1	1	1	4	4	4		2-1	2-2
Trabzonspor	TUR	3	1	0	2	3	11	3			2-0
ZNK Krka	SVN	3	0	1	2	2	7	1			Played in SVN

		Pl	W	D	L	F	A	Pts	ROU	NIR	MDA
Linköpings FC	SWE	3	3	0	0	20	0	9	6-0	3-0	11-0
CFF Clujana	ROU	3	2	0	1	10	6	6		1-0	9-0
Glentoran	NIR	3	1	0	2	2	4	3			2-0
Roma Calfa	MDA	3	0	0	3	0	22	0			Played in SWE

		Pl	W	D	L	F	A	Pts	CYP	ISR	IRL
WFC Rossiyanka	RUS	3	3	0	0	19	0	9	1-0	7-0	11-0
Apollon Limassol	CYP	3	2	0	1	6	1	6		4-0	2-0
Maccabi Holon	ISR	3	1	0	2	2	11	3			2-0
St Francis	IRL	3	0	0	3	0	15	0			Played in CYP

		Pl	W	D	L	F	A	Pts	NOR	EST	CRO
Everton	ENG	3	3	0	0	11	1	9	1-0	7-0	3-1
Team Strømmen	NOR	3	2	0	1	14	1	6		5-0	9-0
Levadia Tallinn	EST	3	1	0	2	4	13	3			4-1
WFC Osijek	CRO	3	0	0	3	2	16	0			Played in CRO

Round of 32

Turbine Potsdam	GER	8	8
Honka Espoo *	FIN	1	0

AZ Alkmaar *	NED	1	1
Brøndby IF	DEN	2	1

Zvezda-2005	RUS	3	5
2000 Sarajevo *	BIH	0	0

Everton LFC	ENG	0	2
Røa IL *	NOR	3	0

Arsenal	ENG	9	9
PAOK *	GRE	0	0

Alma KTZH *	KAZ	1	0
Sparta Praha	CZE	0	2

Linköpings FC	SWE	2	3
FC Zürich *	SUI	0	0

Universit. Vitebsk *	BLR	1	3
FCR Duisburg	GER	5	6

Umeå IK	SWE	5	6
Zhilstroy Kharkiv *	UKR	0	0

Rayo Vallecano *	ESP	1	1
WFC Rossiyanka	RUS	3	2

Bayern München	GER	5	4
Vik. Szombathely *	HUN	0	2

Standard Liege *	BEL	0	1
Montpellier HSC	FRA	0	3

Torres *	ITA	4	2
Valur Reykjavík	ISL	1	1

Unia Raciborz *	POL	1	1
SV Neulengbach	AUT	3	0

Fortuna Hjørring *	DEN	4	1
Bardolino Verona	ITA	0	2

Masinac Nis *	SRB	0	0
Olymp. Lyonnais	FRA	3	5

Round of 16

Turbine Potsdam *	1	4
Brøndby IF	0	0

Zvezda-2005	0	1
Røa IL *	0	1

Arsenal	3	2
Sparta Praha *	0	0

Linköpings FC	1	0
FCR Duisburg *	1	2

Umeå IK	1	1
WFC Rossiyanka *	0	1

Bayern München	0	0
Montpellier HSC *	0	1

Torres	4	4
SV Neulengbach *	1	1

Fortuna Hjørring *	0	0
Olymp. Lyonnais	1	5

UEFA WOMEN'S CHAMPIONS LEAGUE 2010

Quarter-finals	Semi-finals	Final

1.FFC Turbine Potsdam *   5   5
Røa IL   0   0

1.FFC Turbine Potsdam   1 0 1p
FCR 2001 Duisburg *   0 1 3p

Arsenal   1   0
FCR 2001 Duisburg *   2   2

1.FFC Turbine Potsdam   0 7p
Olympique Lyonnais   0 6p

Umeå IK *   0   2
Montpellier HSC   0   2

Umeå IK   2   0
Olympique Lyonnais *   3   0

UEFA WOMEN'S CHAMPIONS LEAGUE FINAL 2010
Coliseum Alfonso Pérez, Getafe, 20-05-2010, 20:30, 10 372, Kirsi Heikkinen FIN

1.FFC Turbine Potsdam   0 7p
Olympique Lyonnais   0 6p

Potsdam - Anna Sarholz - Bianca Schmidt, Babett Peter, Josephine Henning - Jennifer Zietz (c),
Viola Odebrecht, Tabea Kemme• (Corina Schröder 106), Nadine Keßler (Isabel Kerschowski 66) -
Fatmire Bajramaj, Anja Mittag•, Jessica Wich (Yuki Nagasato 66). Tr: Bernd Schröder
Lyon - Sarah Bouhaddi - Corine Franco, Laura Georges (c)•, Wendie Renard•, Amelie Rybäck -
Shirley Cruz Traña• (Simone 105), Ingvild Stensland (Aurélie Kaci 70), Amandine Henry, Louisa
Necib (Isabell Herlovsen 90), Lara Dickenmann - Elodie Thomis. Tr: Farid Benstiti
Penalties: (Lyon first) Franco ✓; Zietz ✗; Dickenmann ✓; Peter ✓; Kaci ✓; Odebrecht ✓;
Henry ✗; Mittag ✗; Herlovsen ✗; Kerschowski ✓; Renard ✓; Nagasato ✓; Simone ✓;
Bajramaj ✓; Bouhaddi ✓; Sarholz ✓; Thomis ✗; Schmidt ✓

Torres   0   1
Olympique Lyonnais * 3   0

* Home team in the first leg

THE (VERY) UNOFFICIAL WORLD CHAMPIONSHIP

This unofficial world championship is based on the system that boxing uses to decide its world champions - if you beat the world champions then the mantle passes to you. The series starts in 1908 when the England amateur team won the first official Olympic title - then the world championship of football. In many cases the sequence leads naturally to the FIFA World Cup final, but where it doesn't the title is vacated and the final is used to restart the sequence.

THE (VERY) UNOFFICIAL WORLD CHAMPIONSHIP

Champions	Opponents	Score	Venue	Date
England	Denmark	2-0	London	24-10-1908
Denmark	England	2-1	Copenhagen	5-05-1910
England	Denmark	3-0	London	21-10-1911
Netherlands	England	2-1	The Hague	24-03-1913
England	Netherlands	2-1	Hull	15-11-1913
Denmark	England	3-0	Copenhagen	5-06-1914
Sweden	Denmark	4-0	Stockholm	8-10-1916
Denmark	Sweden	2-1	Stockholm	14-10-1917
Norway	Denmark	3-1	Oslo	16-06-1918
Denmark	Norway	4-0	Copenhagen	6-10-1918
Norway	Denmark	3-2	Oslo	21-09-1919
Sweden	Norway	3-0	Oslo	27-06-1920
Netherlands	Sweden	5-4	Antwerp	29-08-1920
Belgium	Netherlands	3-0	Antwerp	31-08-1920
Italy	Belgium	3-2	Antwerp	5-05-1921
Czechoslovakia	Italy	5-1	Prague	27-05-1923
Switzerland	Czechoslovakia	1-0	Paris	30-05-1924
Uruguay	Switzerland	3-0	Paris	9-06-1924
Argentina	Uruguay	3-2	Montevideo	31-08-1924
Uruguay	Argentina	1-0	Montevideo	16-11-1924
Argentina	Uruguay	1-0	Buenos Aires	5-01-1925
Uruguay	Argentina	2-0	Santiago	24-10-1926
Argentina	Uruguay	1-0	Montevideo	14-07-1927
Uruguay	Argentina	1-0	Buenos Aires	30-08-1927
Argentina	Uruguay	3-2	Lima	20-11-1927
Uruguay	Argentina	2-1	Amsterdam	13-06-1928
Paraguay	Uruguay	3-1	Asuncion	15-08-1928
Argentina	Paraguay	4-1	Buenos Aires	10-11-1929
Uruguay	Argentina	4-2	Montevideo	30-07-1930
Brazil	Uruguay	2-0	Rio de Janeiro	6-09-1931
Spain	Brazil	3-1	Genoa	27-05-1934
Italy	Spain	1-0	Florence	1-06-1934
England	Italy	3-2	London	14-11-1934
Scotland	England	2-0	Glasgow	6-04-1935
Wales	Scotland	2-1	Dundee	2-12-1936
England	Wales	2-1	Middlesbrough	17-11-1937
Scotland	England	1-0	London	9-04-1938
Vacated				
Italy	Hungary	4-2	Paris	19-06-1938
Switzerland	Italy	3-1	Zurich	12-11-1939
Hungary	Switzerland	3-0	Budapest	31-03-1940
Germany	Hungary	7-0	Cologne	6-04-1941
Switzerland	Germany	2-1	Berne	20-04-1941
Hungary	Switzerland	2-1	Zurich	16-11-1941
Germany	Hungary	5-3	Budapest	3-05-1942
Sweden	Germany	3-2	Berlin	20-09-1942
Switzerland	Sweden	3-1	Zurich	15-11-1942
Hungary	Switzerland	3-1	Geneva	16-05-1943
Sweden	Hungary	7-2	Budapest	7-11-1943
Switzerland	Sweden	3-0	Geneva	25-11-1945

THE (VERY) UNOFFICIAL WORLD CHAMPIONSHIP

Champions	Opponents	Score	Venue	Date
England	Switzerland	4-1	London	11-05-1946
France	England	2-1	Paris	19-05-1946
England	France	3-0	London	3-05-1947
Switzerland	England	1-0	Zurich	18-05-1947
France	Switzerland	2-1	Lausanne	8-06-1947
Italy	France	3-1	Paris	4-04-1948
England	Italy	4-0	Turin	16-05-1948
Scotland	England	3-1	London	9-04-1949
England	Scotland	1-0	Glasgow	15-04-1950
USA	England	1-0	Belo Horizonte	29-06-1950
Chile	USA	5-2	Recife	2-07-1950
Vacated				
Uruguay	Brazil	2-1	Rio de Janeiro	16-07-1950
Chile	Uruguay	2-0	Santiago	13-04-1952
Brazil	Chile	3-0	Santiago	20-04-1952
Peru	Brazil	1-0	Lima	19-03-1953
Uruguay	Peru	3-0	Lima	28-03-1953
Paraguay	Uruguay	4-1	Montevideo	10-04-1954
Vacated				
West Germany	Hungary	3-2	Berne	4-07-1954
Belgium	West Germany	2-0	Brussels	26-09-1954
Italy	Belgium	1-0	Bari	16-01-1955
Yugoslavia	Italy	4-0	Turin	29-05-1955
Austria	Yugoslavia	2-1	Vienna	30-10-1955
France	Austria	3-1	Paris	25-03-1956
Hungary	France	2-1	Paris	7-10-1956
Norway	Hungary	2-1	Oslo	12-06-1957
Denmark	Norway	2-0	Tammerfors	19-06-1957
Sweden	Denmark	2-1	Copenhagen	30-06-1957
West Germany	Sweden	1-0	Hamburg	20-11-1957
Czechoslovakia	West Germany	3-2	Prague	2-04-1958
Nth. Ireland	Czechoslovakia	1-0	Halmstad	8-06-1958
Argentina	Nth. Ireland	3-1	Halmstad	11-06-1958
Czechoslovakia	Argentina	6-1	Helsingborg	15-06-1958
Nth. Ireland	Czechoslovakia	2-1	Malmö	17-06-1958
France	Nth. Ireland	4-0	Norrkoping	19-06-1958
Brazil	France	5-2	Stockholm	24-06-1958
Uruguay	Brazil	3-0	Guayaquil	12-12-1959
Argentina	Uruguay	4-0	Buenos Aires	17-08-1960
Spain	Argentina	2-0	Seville	11-06-1961
Czechoslovakia	Spain	1-0	Viña del Mar	31-05-1962
Mexico	Czechoslovakia	3-1	Viña del Mar	7-06-1962
Vacated				
Brazil	Czechoslovakia	3-1	Santiago	17-06-1962
Paraguay	Brazil	2-0	La Paz	17-03-1963
Bolivia	Paraguay	2-0	Cochabamba	24-03-1963
Paraguay	Bolivia	2-0	Asuncion	25-07-1965
Argentina	Paraguay	3-0	Buenos Aires	1-08-1965
Italy	Argentina	3-0	Turin	22-06-1966
Soviet Union	Italy	1-0	Sunderland	16-07-1966

THE (VERY) UNOFFICIAL WORLD CHAMPIONSHIP

Champions	Opponents	Score	Venue	Date
West Germany	Soviet Union	2-1	Liverpool	25-07-1966
England	West Germany	4-2	London	30-07-1966
Scotland	England	3-2	London	15-04-1967
Soviet Union	Scotland	2-0	Glasgow	10-05-1967
Austria	Soviet Union	1-0	Vienna	15-10-1967
Soviet Union	Austria	3-1	Leningrad	16-06-1968
Sweden	Soviet Union	1-0	Moscow	6-08-1969
France	Sweden	3-0	Paris	1-11-1969
Switzerland	France	2-1	Basle	3-05-1970
Vacated				
Brazil	Italy	4-1	Mexico City	21-06-1970
Italy	Brazil	2-0	Rome	9-06-1973
Poland	Italy	2-1	Stuttgart	23-06-1974
West Germany	Poland	1-0	Frankfurt	3-07-1974
England	West Germany	2-0	London	12-03-1975
Czechoslovakia	England	2-1	Bratislava	30-10-1975
West Germany	Czechoslovakia	2-0	Hanover	17-11-1976
France	West Germany	1-0	Paris	23-02-1977
Rep. Ireland	France	1-0	Dublin	30-03-1977
Bulgaria	Rep. Ireland	2-0	Sofia	1-06-1977
France	Bulgaria	3-1	Paris	16-11-1977
Italy	France	2-1	Mar del Plata	2-06-1978
Netherlands	Italy	2-1	Buenos Aires	21-06-1978
Argentina	Netherlands	3-1	Buenos Aires	25-06-1978
Bolivia	Argentina	2-1	La Paz	18-07-1979
Paraguay	Bolivia	2-0	Asuncion	1-08-1979
Chile	Paraguay	1-0	Santiago	5-12-1979
Brazil	Chile	2-1	Belo Horizonte	24-06-1980
Uruguay	Brazil	2-1	Montevideo	10-01-1981
Peru	Uruguay	2-1	Montevideo	23-08-1981
Chile	Peru	2-1	Santiago	23-03-1982
Peru	Chile	1-0	Lima	30-03-1982
Poland	Peru	5-1	La Coruna	22-06-1982
Italy	Poland	2-0	Barcelona	8-07-1982
Switzerland	Italy	1-0	Rome	27-10-1982
Soviet Union	Switzerland	1-0	Lausanne	13-04-1983
Portugal	Soviet Union	1-0	Lisbon	13-11-1983
Yugoslavia	Portugal	3-2	Lisbon	2-06-1984
Belgium	Yugoslavia	2-0	Lens	13-06-1984
France	Belgium	5-0	Nantes	16-06-1984
Bulgaria	France	2-0	Sofia	2-05-1985
Netherlands	Bulgaria	1-0	Heerenveen	4-09-1985
Belgium	Netherlands	1-0	Brussels	16-10-1985
Netherlands	Belgium	2-1	Rotterdam	20-11-1985
West Germany	Netherlands	3-1	Dortmund	14-05-1986
Denmark	West Germany	2-0	Queretaro	13-06-1986
Spain	Denmark	5-1	Queretaro	18-06-1986
Belgium	Spain	1-1 5-4p	Puebla	22-06-1986
Argentina	Belgium	2-0	Mexico City	25-06-1986
Italy	Argentina	3-1	Zurich	10-06-1987
Wales	Italy	1-0	Brescia	4-06-1988
Netherlands	Wales	1-0	Amsterdam	14-09-1988
Italy	Netherlands	1-0	Rome	16-11-1988
Romania	Italy	1-0	Sibiu	29-03-1989
Poland	Romania	2-1	Warsaw	12-04-1989
England	Poland	3-0	London	3-06-1989
Uruguay	England	2-1	London	22-05-1990
Belgium	Uruguay	3-1	Verona	17-06-1990
Spain	Belgium	2-1	Verona	21-06-1990
Yugoslavia	Spain	2-1	Verona	26-06-1990
Argentina	Yugoslavia	0-0 3-2p	Florence	30-06-1990
West Germany	Argentina	1-0	Rome	8-07-1990
Wales	Germany	1-0	Cardiff	5-06-1991
Germany	Wales	4-1	Nuremberg	16-10-1991
Italy	Germany	1-0	Turin	25-03-1992
Switzerland	Italy	1-0	Berne	1-05-1993
Portugal	Switzerland	1-0	Oporto	13-10-1993
Italy	Portugal	1-0	Milan	17-11-1993
France	Italy	1-0	Naples	6-02-1994
Vacated				
Brazil	Italy	0-0 3-2p	Los Angeles	17-07-1994
Norway	Brazil	4-2	Oslo	30-05-1997
Italy	Norway	1-0	Marseille	27-06-1998
France	Italy	0-0 4-3p	Paris	3-07-1998
Russia	France	3-2	Paris	5-06-1999
Israel	Russia	4-1	Haifa	23-02-2000
Czech Republic	Israel	4-1	Prague	26-04-2000
Germany	Czech Republic	3-2	Nuremberg	3-06-2000
England	Germany	1-0	Charleroi	17-06-2000
Romania	England	3-2	Charleroi	20-06-2000
Italy	Romania	2-0	Brussels	24-06-2000
France	Italy	2-1	Rotterdam	2-07-2000
Spain	France	2-1	Valencia	28-03-2001
Netherlands	Spain	1-0	Rotterdam	27-03-2002
Vacated				
Brazil	Germany	2-0	Yokohama	30-06-2002
Paraguay	Brazil	1-0	Fortaleza	21-08-2002
Costa Rica	Paraguay	2-1	Alajuela	29-03-2003
Chile	Costa Rica	1-0	Santiago	30-04-2003
Costa Rica	Chile	1-0	San José	8-06-2003
Canada	Costa Rica	1-0	Foxboro	12-07-2003
Cuba	Canada	2-0	Foxboro	14-07-2003
Costa Rica	Cuba	3-0	Foxboro	16-07-2003
Mexico	Costa Rica	2-0	Mexico City	24-07-2003
Peru	Mexico	3-1	New Jersey	20-08-2003
Chile	Peru	2-1	Santiago	9-09-2003
Uruguay	Chile	2-1	Montevideo	15-11-2003
Jamaica	Uruguay	2-0	Kingston	18-02-2004
Nigeria	Jamaica	2-0	London	31-05-2004
Angola	Nigeria	1-0	Luanda	20-06-2004
Zimbabwe	Angola	2-0	Harare	27-03-2005
Nigeria	Zimbabwe	5-1	Abuja	8-10-2005
Romania	Nigeria	3-0	Bucharest	16-11-2005
Uruguay	Romania	2-0	Los Angeles	23-05-2006
Vacated				
Italy	France	1-1 5-3p	Berlin	9-07-2006
Croatia	Italy	2-0	Livorno	16-08-2006
Macedonia	Croatia	2-0	Skopje	17-11-2007
Israel	Macedonia	1-0	Tel Aviv	21-11-2007
Finland	Israel	2-0	Tampere	20-08-2008
Russia	Finland	3-0	Moscow	15-10-2008
Argentina	Russia	3-2	Moscow	12-08-2009
Brazil	Argentina	3-1	Rosario	5-09-2009
Bolivia	Brazil	2-1	La Paz	11-10-2009
Peru	Bolivia	1-0	Lima	14-10-2009
Vacated				
Spain	Netherlands	1-0	Johannesburg	11-07-2010
Argentina	Spain	4-1	Buenos Aires	7-09-2010
Japan	Argentina	1-0	Saitama	8-10-2010

CALENDAR OF EVENTS

FIFA AND WORLD FOOTBALL

Fixed dates for friendly internationals
9-02-2011, 10-08-2011, 29-02-2012, 15-08-2012, 14-11-2012,
6-02-2013, 14-08-2013, 5-03-2014, 13-08-2014, 19-11-2014

Fixed dates for official competitions
26/30-03-2011, 4/8-06-2011, 3/7-09-2011, 8/12-10-2011, 12/16-11-2011, 8/12-09-2012
13/17-10-2012, 23/27-03-2013, 8/12-06-2013, 7/11-09-2013, 12/16-10-2013
16/20-11-2013, 6/10-09-2014, 11/15-11-2014

FIFA U-17 World Cup Mexico 2011
18th June to 10th July 2011

FIFA U-20 World Cup Colombia 2011
29th July to 20th August 2011

FIFA Women's World Cup Germany 2011
26th June to 17th July 2011

FIFA Club World Cup Japan 2011
2011

Men's and Women's Olympic Football Tournaments London 2012
27th July to 12th August 2012 (football starts two days before the opening ceremony on 25th July)

FIFA Club World Cup Japan 2012
2012

FIFA Confederations Cup Brazil 2013
2013

2014 FIFA World Cup Brazil
13th June to 13th July 2014

2018 FIFA World Cup Russia
2018

2022 FIFA World Cup Qatar
2022

THE AFC AND ASIAN FOOTBALL

AFC Asian Cup Australia 2015
4th to 26th January 2015

CAF AND AFRICAN FOOTBALL

CAF Africa Cup of Nations Equatorial Guinea and Gabon 2012
21st January to 12th February 2012

CAF Africa Cup of Nations Libya 2014
2014

CAF Africa Cup of Nations South Africa 2016
2016

CONCACAF

CONCACAF Gold Cup USA 2011
5th to 25th June 2011

CONMEBOL AND SOUTH AMERICAN FOOTBALL

Copa America Argentina 2011
1st to 24th July 2011

Copa America Brazil 2015
2015

UEFA AND FOOTBALL IN EUROPE

Euro 2012 Poland/Ukraine
8th June to 1st July 2012

Euro 2016 France
2016